266-

CHILTON'S FORD REPAIR MANUAL 1980-1987

CHILTON BOOK COMPANY

*ONE OF THE **DIVERSIFIED PUBLISHING COMPANIES,***
*A PART OF **CAPITAL CITIES/ABC, INC.***

Manufactured in USA

Chilton Way, Radnor, PA 19089
ISBN 0-8019-7773-8
Library of Congress Catalog Card No. 86-47793
6789012345 1098765432

SAFETY NOTICE

Proper service and repair procedures are vital to the safe, reliable operation of all motor vehicles, as well as the personal safety of those performing repairs. This manual outlines procedures for servicing and repairing vehicles using safe effective methods. The procedures contain many NOTES, CAUTIONS and WARNINGS which should be followed along with standard safety procedures to eliminate the possibility of personal injury or improper service which could damage the vehicle or compromise its safety.

It is important to note that repair procedures and techniques, tools and parts for servicing motor vehicles, as well as the skill and experience of the individual performing the work vary widely. It is not possible to anticipate all of the conceivable ways or conditions under which vehicles may be serviced, or to provide cautions as to all of th epossible hazards that may result. Standard and accepted safety precautions and equipment should be used when handling toxic or flammable fluids, and safety goggles or other protection should be used during cutting, grinding chiseling, prying, or any other process that can cause material removal or projectiles.

Some procedures require the use of tools specially designed for a specific purpose. Before substituting another tool or procedure, you must be completely satisfied that neither your personal safety, nor the performance of the vehicle will be endangered.

PART NUMBERS

Part numbers listed in this reference are not recommendations by Chilton for any product by brand name. They are references that can be used with interchange manuals and aftermarket supplier catalogs to locate each brand supplier's discrete part number.

Although information in this manual is based on industry sources and is as complete as possible at the time of publication, the possibility exists that some car manufacturers made later changes which could not be included here. While striving for total accuracy, Chilton Book Company cannot assume responsibility for any errors, changes, or omissions that may occur in the compilation of this data.

Rear Wheel Drive

1

INDEX

1 REAR WHEEL DRIVE CARS

VEHICLE IDENTIFICATION CHART

It is important for servicing and ordering parts to be certain of the vehicle and engine identification. The VIN (vehicle identification number) is a 17 digit number visible through the windshield on the driver's side of the dash and contains the vehicle and engine identification codes. It can be interpreted as follows:

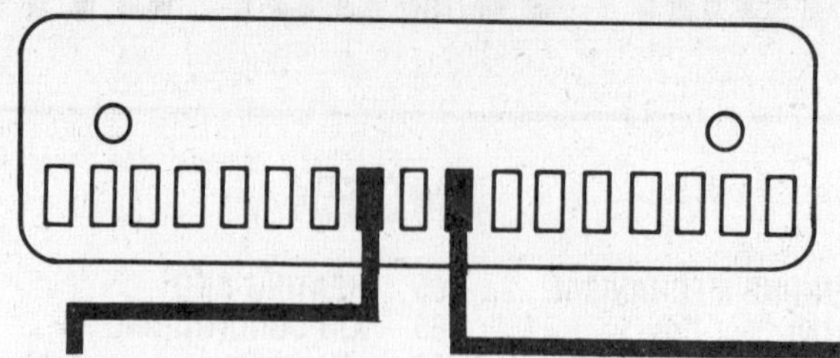

Engine Code

Code	Cu. In.	Liters	Cyl.	Fuel Sys.	Eng. Mfg.
A	140	2.3	4	2V	Ford
T	140	2.3	4 (Turbo)	EFI	Ford
W	140	2.3	4 (Turbo)	EFI	Ford
L	149	2.4	6	Diesel	BMW
B	200	3.3	6	1V	Ford
3	232	3.8	V6	2V	Ford
D	255	4.2	V8	2V	Ford
F	302	5.0	V8	VV	Ford
M	302 HO	5.0	V8	4V	Ford
G	351 HO	5.8	V8	4V	Ford

Model Year

Code	Year
B	1981
C	1982
D	1983
E	1984
F	1985
G	1986
H	1987
J	1988

The seventeen digit Vehicle Identification Number can be used to determine engine identification and model year. The tenth digit indicates model year, and the fourth digit indicates engine code.

GENERAL ENGINE SPECIFICATIONS

Year	VIN	No. Cylinder Displacement cu. in. (liter)	Fuel System Type	Net Horsepower @ rpm	Net Torque @ rpm (ft.lbs.)	Bore × Stroke (in.)	Compression Ratio	Oil Pressure @ 2000 rpm
1981	A	4-140 (2.3)	2 bbl	88 @ 4600	118 @ 2600	3.781 × 3.126	9.0:1	40-60
	B	6-200 (3.3)	1 bbl	88 @ 3800	154 @ 1400	3.680 × 3.130	8.6:1	30-50
	D	8-255 (4.2)	2 bbl	115 @ 3400	195 @ 2200	3.680 × 3.000	8.2:1	40-60
	D	8-255 (4.2)	VV	120 @ 3400	205 @ 2600	3.680 × 3.000	8.2:1	40-60
	F	8-302 (5.0)	2 bbl	130 @ 3400	235 @ 1600	4.000 × 3.000	8.4:1	40-60
	F	8-302 (5.0)	VV	130 @ 3400	235 @ 1800	4.000 × 3.000	8.4:1	40-60
	F	8-302 (5.0)	EFI	130 @ 3400	230 @ 2000	4.000 × 3.000	8.4:1	40-60
	G	8-351 (5.8)HO	VV	145 @ 3200	270 @ 1800	4.000 × 3.500	8.3:1	40-60
1982	A	4-140 (2.3)	2 bbl	86 @ 4600	117 @ 2600	3.781 × 3.126	9.0:1	40-60
	B	6-200 (3.3)	1 bbl	87 @ 3800	154 @ 1400	3.680 × 3.130	8.6:1	30-50
	3	6-232 (3.8)	2 bbl	112 @ 4000	175 @ 2600	3.810 × 3.390	8.8:1	54-59
	3	6-232 (3.8)	VV	118 @ 4000	186 @ 2600	3.810 × 3.390	8.8:1	54-59
	D	8-255 (4.2)	2 bbl	122 @ 3400	209 @ 2400	3.680 × 3.000	8.2:1	40-60
	D	8-255 (4.2)	VV	120 @ 3400	205 @ 2600	3.680 × 3.000	8.2:1	40-60
	F	8-302 (5.0)	VV	132 @ 3400	236 @ 1800	4.000 × 3.000	8.4:1	40-60
	F	8-302 (5.0)	EFI	143 @ 3400	232 @ 3200	4.000 × 3.000	8.4:1	40-60
	G	8-351 (5.8)HO	2 bbl	140 @ 3400	265 @ 2000	4.000 × 3.500	8.3:1	40-60

GENERAL ENGINE SPECIFICATIONS

Year	VIN	No. Cylinder Displacement cu. in. (liter)	Fuel System Type	Net Horsepower @ rpm	Net Torque @ rpm (ft.lbs.)	Bore × Stroke (in.)	Com-pression Ratio	Oil Pressure @ 2000 rpm
1983	A	4-140 (2.3)	2 bbl	88 @ 4800	118 @ 2800	3.781 × 3.126	9.0:1	40-60
	X	6-200 (3.3)	1 bbl①	88 @ 3800	154 @ 1400	3.680 × 3.130	8.6:1	30-50
	3	6-232 (3.8)	2 bbl	120 @ 3600	250 @ 1600	3.810 × 3.390	8.7:1	40-60
	F	8-302 (5.0)	EFI ②	130 @ 3200	240 @ 2000	4.000 × 3.000	8.4:1	40-60
	G	8-351 (5.8)HO⑧	2 bbl	140 @ 3400	265 @ 2000	4.000 × 3.500	8.3:1	40-60
1984	A	4-140 (2.3)	2 bbl	88 @ 4000	122 @ 2400	3.781 × 3.126	9.0:1	40-60
	T	4-140 (2.3)T③	EFI	175 @ 4400	210 @ 3000	3.781 × 3.126	8.0:1	40-60
	W	4-140 (2.3)T	EFI	145 @ 4600	180 @ 3600	3.781 × 3.126	8.0:1	40-60
	L	6-149 (2.4)	Diesel	114 @ 4800	150 @ 2400	3.150 × 3.189	23:1	57-85
	3	6-232 (3.8)	CFI ①	120 @ 3600	250 @ 1600	3.810 × 3.390	8.7:1	40-60
	F	8-302 (5.0)	CFI	140 @ 3200	250 @ 1600④	4.000 × 3.000	8.4:1	40-60
	M	8-302 (5.0)HO	4 bbl	205 @ 4400	265 @ 3200	4.000 × 3.000	8.3:1	40-60
	G	8-351 (5.8)HO⑧	VV	180 @ 3600	285 @ 2400	4.000 × 3.500	8.3:1	40-60
1985	A	4-140 (2.3)	2 bbl	88 @ 4000	124 @ 2800	3.781 × 3.126	9.0:1	40-60
	W	4-140 (2.3)T	EFI	145 @ 4600	180 @ 3600	3.781 × 3.126	8.0:1	40-60
	T	4-140 (2.3)T③	EFI	175 @ 4400	210 @ 3000	3.781 × 3.126	8.0:1	40-60
	L	6-149 (2.4)	Diesel	114 @ 4800	150 @ 2400	3.150 × 3.189	23:1	57-85
	3	6-232 (3.8)	2 bbl	120 @ 3600	250 @ 1600	3.810 × 3.390	8.7:1	40-60
	F	8-302 (5.0)	CFI	165 @ 3200	250 @ 1600	4.000 × 3.000	8.4:1	40-60
	M	8-302 (5.0)HO	4 bbl	210 @ 4400	265 @ 3200	4.000 × 3.000	8.3:1	40-60
	G	8-351 (5.8)⑧	2 bbl	180 @ 3600	285 @ 2400	4.000 × 3.500	8.3:1	40-60
1986	A	4-140 (2.3)	2 bbl	88 @ 4200	122 @ 2600	3.781 × 3.126	9.0:1	40-60
	T	4-140 (2.3)T⑥	EFI	145 @ 4400	180 @ 3000	3.781 × 3.126	8.0:1	40-60
	W	4-140 (2.3)T⑦	EFI	155 @ 4600	190 @ 2800	3.781 × 3.126	8.0:1	40-60
	3	6-232 (3.8)	CFI ①	120 @ 3600	205 @ 1600	3.810 × 3.390	8.7:1	40-60
	F	8-302 (5.0)	SEFI	150 @ 3200	270 @ 2000	4.000 × 3.000	8.9:1	40-60
	M	8-302 (5.0)HO	4 bbl	210 @ 4400	265 @ 3200	4.000 × 3.000	8.3:1	40-60
	G	8-351 (5.8)	2 bbl	180 @ 3600	285 @ 2400	4.000 × 3.500	8.3:1	40-60
1987-88	A	4-140 (2.3)OHC	EFI	88 @ 4200	122 @ 2600	3.781 × 3.126	9.0:1	40-60
	W	4-140 (2.3)T	EFI	155 @ 4600	190 @ 2800	3.781 × 3.126	8.0:1	40-60
	3	6-232 (3.8)	EFI	120 @ 3600	205 @ 1600	3.810 × 3.390	8.7:1	40-60
	F	8-302 (5.0)	SEFI	150 @ 3200	270 @ 2000	4.000 × 3.000	8.9:1	40-60
	M	8-302 (5.0)HO	EFI	210 @ 4400	265 @ 3200	4.000 × 3.000	8.3:1	40-60
	G	8-351 (5.8)HO⑧	4V	180 @ 3600	285 @ 2400	4.000 × 3.500	8.3:1	40-60

■Horsepower and torque are SAE net figures. They are measured at the rear of the transmission with all accessories installed and operating. Since the figures vary when a given engine is installed in different models, some are representative rather than exact.

T—Turbocharger
EFI—Electronic fuel injection
SEFI—Sequential electronic fuel injection
HO—High output
HSC—High Swirl Combustion
CFI—Central fuel injection
VV—Variable Venturi carburetor

① Canadian models are equipped with a 2-bbl carburetor
② Some Mustang/Capri models are equipped with a 4-bbl carburetor
③ SVO
④ On models equipped with dual exhaust the horsepower is 155 @ 3600 rpm and the torque is 265 @ 2000
⑤ Some models are equipped with EFI
⑥ Manual Transmission
⑦ Automatic Transmission
⑧ Canada and police only

GASOLINE ENGINE TUNE-UP SPECIFICATIONS

Year	VIN	No. Cylinder Displacement cu. in. (liter)	Spark Plugs Type	Spark Plugs Gap (in.)	Ignition Timing (deg.) MT	Ignition Timing (deg.) AT	Compression Pressure (psi)	Fuel Pump (psi)	Idle Speed (rpm) MT	Idle Speed (rpm) AT	Valve Clearance In.	Valve Clearance Ex.
1981	A	4-140 (2.3)	AWSF-42	.034	6B	6B	NA	5½-6½	700	700	Hyd.	Hyd.
	B	6-200 (3.3)	BSF-92	.050	10B	10B	NA	5½-6½	900	700①	Hyd.	Hyd.
	D	8-255 (4.2)	ASF-52	.050	10B	10B	NA	5½-6½	900	700①	Hyd.	Hyd.
	F	8-302 (5.0)	ASF-52	.050	8B	8B	NA	5½-6½	800	800	Hyd.	Hyd.
	G	8-351 (5.8)	ASF-52	.050	—	①④	NA	6½-8	—	600④	Hyd.	Hyd.
1982	A	4-140 (2.3)	AWSF-42	.034	①	①	NA	5½-6½	850	750	Hyd.	Hyd.
	B	6-200 (3.3)	BSF-92	.050	①	①	NA	6-8	700①	600 (700)①	Hyd.	Hyd.
	D	8-255 (4.2)	ASF-52	.050	10B	10B	NA	5½-6½	900	700①	Hyd.	Hyd.
	3	6-232 (3.8)	AGSP-52	.044	①	①	NA	6-8	①	①	Hyd.	Hyd.
	F	8-302 (5.0)	ASF-52	.050	—	①④	NA	6-8⑧	①④	①④	Hyd.	Hyd.
	G	8-351 (5.8)	ASF-52	.050	—	①④	NA	6½-8	—	600④	Hyd.	Hyd.
1983	A	4-140 (2.3)	AWSF-44	.044	①	①	NA	5½-6½	850	800	Hyd.	Hyd.
	X	6-200 (3.3)	BSF-92	.050	①	①	NA	6-8	600	600	Hyd.	Hyd.
	3	6-232 (3.8)	AWSF-52	.044	①	①	NA	39	550	550	Hyd.	Hyd.
	F	8-302 (5.0)	ASF-52②	.050	①	①	NA	6-8 ③	—	550	Hyd.	Hyd.
	G	8-351 (5.8)	ASF-42	.044	①	①	NA	6-8	—	700/ 600	Hyd.	Hyd.
1984	A	4-140 (2.3)	AWSF-44	.044	①	①	NA	5-7	850	750	Hyd.	Hyd.
	W	4-140 (2.3)T	AWSF-32	.034	①	①	NA	39	①④	①④	Hyd.	Hyd.
	T	4-140 (2.3)	AWSF-32	.034	①	①	NA	39	①④	①④	Hyd.	Hyd.
	3	8-232 (3.8)	AWSF-54	.044	①	①	NA	39	—	550	Hyd.	Hyd.
	F	8-302 (5.0)	ASF-52	.050	①	①	NA	39	550	550	Hyd.	Hyd.
	M	8-302 (5.0) HO	ASF-42	.044	①	①	NA	6-8	700	700	Hyd.	Hyd.
	G	8-351 (5.8)	ASF-42	.044	①	①	NA	6-8	—	600	Hyd.	Hyd.
1985	A	4-140 (2.3)	AWSF-44	.044	①	①	NA	6-8	850	750	Hyd.	Hyd.
	W	4-140 (2.3)T	AWSF-32	.034	①	①	NA	39	750	750	Hyd.	Hyd.
	T	4-140 (2.3)T	AWSF-32	.034	①	①	NA	39	①④	①④	Hyd.	Hyd.
	3	6-232 (3.8)	AGSP-52	.044	①	①	NA	6-8	600	600	Hyd.	Hyd.
	F	8-302 (5.0)	ASF-52	.050	①	①	NA	39	—	550	Hyd.	Hyd.
	M	8-302 (5.0) HO	ASF-42	.044	①	①	NA	6-8	700	700	Hyd.	Hyd.
	G	8-351 (5.8)	ASF-42	.044	①	①	NA	6-8	—	600 ⑥	Hyd.	Hyd.
1986	A	4-140 (2.3)	AWSF-44C	.044	①	①	NA	6-8	750	750	Hyd.	Hyd.
	T	4-140 (2.3)T	AWSF-32C	.034	①	①	NA	39	825/ 975	825/ 975	Hyd.	Hyd.
	W	4-140 (2.3)T	AWSF-32C	.034	①	①	NA	39	825/ 975	825/ 975	Hyd.	Hyd.
	3	6-232 (3.8)	AWSF-54	.044	①	①	NA	39	—	550	Hyd.	Hyd.
	F	8-302 (5.0)	ASF-32C	.044	①	①	NA	39	①④	①④		

GASOLINE ENGINE TUNE-UP SPECIFICATIONS

Year	VIN	No. Cylinder Displacement cu. in. (liter)	Spark Plugs Type	Spark Plugs Gap (in.)	Ignition Timing (deg.) MT	Ignition Timing (deg.) AT	Compression Pressure (psi)	Fuel Pump (psi)	Idle Speed (rpm) MT	Idle Speed (rpm) AT	Valve Clearance In.	Valve Clearance Ex.
1986	M	8-302 (5.0) HO	ASF-42	.044	①	①	NA	6-8	700	700	Hyd.	Hyd.
	G	8-351 (5.8)	ASF-32C	.044	①	①	NA	6-8	650	650	Hyd.	Hyd.
1987	A	4-140 (2.3)	AWSF-44C	.044	①	①	NA	35	750	750	Hyd.	Hyd.
	3	6-232 (3.8)	AWSF-54	.044	①	①	NA	35	—	550	Hyd.	Hyd.
	F	8-302 (5.0)	ASF-32C	.044	①	①	NA	35	①④	①④	Hyd.	Hyd.
	M	8-302 (5.0) HO	ASF42	.044	①	①	NA	35	700	700	Hyd.	Hyd.
	G	8-351 (5.8)	ASF-32C	.044	①	①	NA	6-8	650	650	Hyd.	Hyd.
1988	SEE UNDERHOOD SPECIFICATIONS STICKER											

NOTE: The underhood specifications sticker often reflects tune-up specifications changes made in production. Sticker figures must be used if they disagree with those in this chart.

T—Turbocharger
B—Before top dead center
HO—High output
— Not applicable
HSC—High Swirl Combustion

① Calibrations vary depending upon the model; refer to the underhood calibration sticker

② The carbureted models use spark plug ASF-42 (.044) and the idle speed is 700 rpm

③ On fuel injected models the pressure is 39 psi

④ Electronic engine control models. The ignition timing, idle speed and idle mixture are not adjustable

⑤ SVO Mustang

⑥ 700 rpm with the VOTM on

DIESEL ENGINE TUNE-UP SPECIFICATIONS

Year	VIN	No. Engine Displacement cu. in. (liter)	Valve Clearance Intake (in.)	Valve Clearance Exhaust (in.)	Intake Valve Opens (deg.)	Injection Pump Setting (deg.)	Injection Nozzle Pressure (psi) New	Injection Nozzle Pressure (psi) Used	Idle Speed (rpm)	Cranking Compression Pressure (psi)
1985	L	6-149 (2.4)	0.010	0.010	6	2.5	2133	NA	750 ±50	348
1986	L	6-149 (2.4)	0.010	0.010	6	2.5	2133	NA	750 ±50	348

CAPACITIES

Year	Model	No. Cylinder Displacement cu. in. (liter)	Engine Crankcase (qts.) with Filter	Engine Crankcase (qts.) without Filter	Transmission (pts.) 4-Spd	Transmission (pts.) 5-Spd	Transmission (pts.) Auto.	Drive Axle (pts.)	Fuel Tank (gal.)	Cooling System (qts.)
1981	Fairmont, Zephyr	4-140 (2.3)	5	4	2.8 ①	—	16 ②	③	14.7 ④	8.6
		6-200 (3.3)	5	4	2.8 ①	—	14.5 ②	③	16 ④	8.1
		8-255 (4.2)	5	4	—	—	19 ②	③	16 ④	13.5
		8-302 (5.0)	5	4	—	—	20.5 ②	③	16 ④	14.0
	Mustang, Capri	4-140 (2.3)	5	4	2.8	—	⑦ ②	③	12.5	9
		4-140 (2.3) T	5	4.5 ⑬	3.5	—	⑦ ②	③	11.5	9.2
		6-200 (3.3)	5	4	2.8	—	12 ⑦	③	12.5	8.1
		8-255 (4.2)	5	4	4.5	4.5	19	③	12.5	13.7
		8-302 (5.0)	5	4	4.5	4.5	19	③	12.5	14.2

1 REAR WHEEL DRIVE CARS

CAPACITIES

Year	Model	No. Cylinder Displacement cu. in. (liter)	Engine Crankcase (qts.) with Filter	Engine Crankcase (qts.) without Filter	Transmission (pts.) 4-Spd	Transmission (pts.) 5-Spd	Transmission (pts.) Auto.	Drive Axle (pts.)	Fuel Tank (gal.)	Cooling System (qts.)
1981	T-bird, XR7	6-200 (3.3)	5	4	—	—	16	3.5	17.5	13.2
		8-255 (4.2)	5	4	—	—	20	3.5	17.5	13.2
		8-302 (5.0)	5	4	—	—	20	3.5	17.5	12.8
	Cougar, Granada	4-140 (2.3)	5	4	2.8	—	16	3.5	14.7	8.6
		6-200 (3.3)	5	4	—	—	16	3.5	16.0	8.1
		8-255 (4.2)	5	4	—	-	19	3.5	16.0	13.5
	Ford, Mercury	8-255 (4.2)	5	4	—	—	24	③	20	15.2
		8-302 (5.0)	5	4	—	—	24	③	20	13.3
		8-351 (5.8)	5	4	—	—	24	③	20	14.0
	Town Car, Continental, Mark VI	8-255 (4.2)	5	4	—	—	24	③	20	15.2
		8-302 (5.0)	5	4	—	—	24	③	20	13.3
		8-351 (5.8)	5	4	—	—	24	③	20	14.0
1982	Fairmont, Zephyr	4-140 (2.3)	5	4	2.8 ①	—	16	③	14.7 ⑥	10.2
		6-200 (3.3)	5	4	2.8 ①	—	14.5	③	16	8.1
		8-255 (4.2)	5	4	—	—	19	③	16	13.5
		8-302 (5.0)	5	4	—	—	20.5	③	16	14.0
	Mustang, Capri	4-140 (2.3)	5	4	2.8	—		③	15.4	9
		4-140 (2.3)T	5	4.5 ⑬	3.5	—	⑦	③	15.4	10.2
		6-200 (3.3)	5	4	2.8	—	12	③	15.4	8.1
		8-255 (4.2)	5	4	4.5	4.5	19	③	15.4	15
		8-302 (5.0)	5	4	4.5	4.5	19	③	15.4	14.2
	T-bird. XR7	6-200 (3.3)	5	4	—	—	22	3.25	21	8.4
	Continental	3-232 (3.8)	5	4	—	—	24	3.25	21 ⑩	8.6
		8-255 (4.2)	5	4	—	—	24	3.25	21	15
		8-302 (5.0)	5	4	—	—	24	3.25	22.6	13.4
	Cougar, Granada	4-140 (2.3)	5	4	—	—	16	③	16.0 ⑥	10.2
		6-200 (3.3)	5	4	—	—	22	3.25	16.0 ⑥	8.4
		3-232 (3.8)	5	4	—	—	22	3.25	16.0 ⑥	8.3
	Ford, Mercury	8-255 (4.2)	5	4	—	—	24	③	20	15.2
		8-302 (5.0)	5	4	—	—	24	⑥	20	15
		8-351 (5.8)	5	4	—	—	24	⑥	20	16
	Town Car, Mark VI	8-255 (4.2)	5	4	—	—	24	⑥	20	15.2
		8-302 (5.0)	5	4	—	—	24	⑥	20	15
		8-351 (5.8)	5	4	—	—	24	⑥	20	16
1983	Fairmont, Zephyr	4-140 (2.3)	5	4	2.8	—	16	3.25 ⑪	16	10.2
		6-200 (3.3)	5	4	—	—	22	3.25 ⑪	16	8.4
	Mustang, Capri	4-140 (2.3)	5	4 ⑬	2.8	4.75	16	3.25 ⑪	15.4	9.4
		3-232 (3.8)	5	4	—	—	22	3.25 ⑪	15.4	8.4
		8-302 (5.0)	5	4	4.5	4.5	—	3.55	15.4	13.4

CAPACITIES

Year	Model	No. Cylinder Displacement cu. in. (liter)	Engine Crankcase (qts.) with Filter	without Filter	Transmission (pts.) 4-Spd	5-Spd	Auto.	Drive Axle (pts.)	Fuel Tank (gal.)	Cooling System (qts.)
1983	LTD, Marquis	4-140- (2.3)	5	4	2.8	—	16	3.25 ⑪	16	9.4
		6-200 (3.3)	5	4	—	—	22	3.25 ⑪	16	8.5
		6-232 (3.8)	5	4	—	—	22 ⑨	3.25 ⑪	16	10.8
	T-bird, Cougar	4-140 (2.3)	5	4.5 ⑫	4.75	4.75	—	3.25 ⑪	18	8.7
		3-232 (3.8)	5	4	—	—	22 ⑤	3.25 ⑪	21	10.7
	Continental	8-302 (5.0)	5	4	—	—	22 ⑮	3.25 ⑪	20.7 ⑭	13.4
	Ford, Mercury	8-302 (5.0)	5	4	—	—	24	③	20	15
		8-351 (5.8)	5	4	—	—	24	③	20	16
	Town Car, Mark VI	8-302 (5.0)	5	4	—	—	24	③	20	15
		8-351 (5.8)	5	4	—	—	24	③	20	16
1984	Mustang, Capri	4-140 (2.3)	5	4 ⑬	2.8	4.75	16	3.25 ⑪	15.4	9.4
		6-232 (3.8)	5	4	—	—	22	3.25 ⑪	15.4	8.4
		8-302 (5.0)	5	4	4.5	4.5	—	3.55	15.4	13.4
	LTD, Marquis	4-140 (2.3)	5	4	2.8	—	16	3.25	16	9.4
		6-200 (3.3)	5	4	—	—	22	3.25 ⑪	16	8.5
		6-232 (3.8)	5	4	—	—	22 ⑨	3.25 ⑪	16	10.8
	T-bird, Cougar	4-140 (2.3)	5	4 ⑫	4.75	4.75	—	3.25 ⑪	18	8.7
		6-232 (3.8)	5	4	—	—	22 ⑮	3.25 ⑪	21	10.7
		8-302 (5.0)	5	4	—	—	22 ⑮	3.25 ⑪	20.7 ⑭	13.4
	Mark VII, Continental	4-140 (2.30	5	4 ⑫	4.75	4.75	—	3.25 ⑪	18	8.7
		6-149 (2.4)	7.9	6.9	—	—	15	③	21	11.8
		6-232 (3.8)	5	4	—	—	22	3.25 ⑪	21	10.7
		8-302 (5.0)	5	4	—	—	22	3.25 ⑪	20.7 ⑭	13.4
	Ford, Mercury,	8-302 (5.0)	5	4	—	—	24	③	20	15
	Town Car	8-351 (5.8)	5	4	—	—	24	③	20	16
1985	Mustang, Capri	4-140 (2.3)	5	4 ⑬	2.8	4.75	16	3.25 ⑪	15.4	9.4
		6-232 (3.8)	5	4	—	—	22	3.25 ⑪	15.4	13.4
		8-302 (5.0)	5	4	4.5	4.5	—	3.25	15.4	13.4
	LTD, Marquis	4-140 (2.3)	5	4	2.8	—	16	3.25	16	9.4
		6-232 (3.8)	5	4	—	—	22	3.25 ⑪	16	10.8
	T-bird, Cougar	4-140 (2.3)	5	4.5	4.75	4.75	—	3.25 ⑪	18	8.7
		6-232 (3.8)	5	4	—	—	22 ⑮	3.25 ⑬	21	10.7
		8-302 (5.0)	5	4	—	—	22	3.25	20	13.4
	Mark VII, Continental	4-140 (2.3)	5	4.5 ⑬	4.75	4.75	—	3.25 ⑪	18	8.7
		6-149 (2.4)	7.9	6.9	—	—	15	③	21	11.8
		6-232 (3.8)	5	4	—	—	22	3.25 ⑪	21	10.7
		8-302 (5.0)	5	4	—	—	22	3.25 ⑪	20.7 ⑭	13.4
	Ford, Mercury	8-302 (5.0)	5	4	—	—	24	③	20	15
	Town Car	8-351 (5.8)	5	4	—	—	24	③	20	16

CAPACITIES

Year	Model	No. Cylinder Displacement cu. in. (liter)	Engine Crankcase (qts.) with Filter	Engine Crankcase (qts.) without Filter	Transmission (pts.) 4-Spd	Transmission (pts.) 5-Spd	Transmission (pts.) Auto.	Drive Axle (pts.)	Fuel Tank (gal.)	Cooling System (qts.)
1986	Mustang,	4-140 (2.3)	5	4 ⑬	2.8	4.75	16	3.25 ⑪	15.4	9.4
	Capri	6-232 (3.8)	5	4	—	—	22	3.25 ⑪	15.4	13.4
		8-302 (5.0)	5	4	4.5	4.5	—	3.25	15.4	13.4
	LTD,	4-140 (2.3)	5	4	2.8	—	16	3.25	16	9.4
	Marquis	6-232 (3.8)	5	4	—	—	22	3.25 ⑪	16	10.8
	T-bird,	4-140 (2.30	5	4.5 ⑬	4.75	4.75	—	3.25 ⑪	18	8.7
	Cougar	6-232 (3.8)	5	4	—	—	22 ⑮	3.25 ⑪	21	10.7
		8-302 (5.0)	5	4	—	—	22	3.25	20	13.4
	Mark VII,	4-140 (2.3)	5	4.5 ⑬	4.75	4.75	—	3.25 ⑪	18	8.7
	Continental	6-232 (3.8)	5	4	—	—	22	3.25 ⑪	21	10.7
		8-302 (5.0)	5	4	—	—	22	3.25 ⑪	20.7	13.4
	Ford, Mercury	8-302 (5.0)	5	4	—	—	24	③	20	15
	Town Car	8-351 (5.8)	5	4	—	—	24	③	20	10
1987-88	Mustang	4-140 (2.3)	5	4	3.7	3.7	22	4.5	15.4	10
		8-302 (5.0)	5	4	3.7	3.7	22	3.25	15.4	14.1
	T-bird,	4-140 (2.3)	5	4.5 ⑪	4.75	4.75	16	3.25 ⑪	18	10
	Cougar	6-232 (3.8)	5	4	—	—	22 ⑮	3.25 ⑪	21	11.8
		8-302 (5.0)	5	4	—	—	22 ⑮	3.25 ⑪	20.7	14.1
	Mark VII,	4-140 (2.3)	5	4.5 ⑬	4.75	4.75	16	3.25	18	10
	Continental	6-232 (3.8)	5	4	—	—	22	3.25	21	11.8
		8-302 (5.0)	5	4	—	—	22	3.25	20.7 ⑭	14.1
	Ford, Mercury	8-302 (5.0)	5	4	—	—	24	③	20	15
	Town Car	8-351 (5.8)	5	4	—	—	24	③	20	16

① 4-speed overdrive—4.5 pts.
② 81 w/c4; 3.25 pts.
③ 6.75 in. axle, 2.5 pts.
7.5 in. axle, 3.5 pts.
8.5 in axle, 4.0 pts.
④ Station Wagon—14 gals.
⑤ Lincoln—18 gals.
⑥ 20 gals. optional
⑦ C3, 16 pts,—C4, 14 pts.
⑧ C5, 22 pts.
⑨ AOD Trans.—24 pts.
⑩ Continental—20 gals STD.
22.6 gal. opt.
⑪ Traction-lok—3.55 pts.
⑫ 5-speed Trans.—4.75 pts.
⑬ Turbo 4.5, add .5 w/filter
⑭ Continental—22.3
⑮ Turbo models—10.5

CAMSHAFT SPECIFICATIONS

All measurements given in inches.

Year	VIN	No. Cylinder Displacement cu. in. (liter)	Journal Diameter 1	2	3	4	5	Lobe Lift In.	Ex.	Bearing Clearance	Camshaft End Play
1981	A	4-140 (2.3)	1.7713–1.7720	1.7713–1.7720	1.7713–1.7720	1.7713–1.7720	–	.2437	.2437	.001–.003	.001–.007
	B	6-200 (3.3)	1.8095–1.8105	1.8095–1.8105	1.8095–1.8105	1.8095–1.8105	–	.245	.245	.001–.003	.001–.007
	F	8-302 (5.0)	2.0805–2.0815	2.0655–2.0665	2.0505–2.0515	2.0355–2.0365	2.0205–2.0215	.2375	.2474	.001–.003	.001–.007
	G	8-351 (5.8)	2.0805–2.0815	2.0655–2.0665	2.0505–2.0515	2.0355–2.0365	2.0205–2.0215	.2780	.2830	.001–.003	.001–.007
	D	8-255 (4.2)	2.0805–2.0815	2.0655–2.0665	2.0505–2.0515	2.0355–2.0365	2.0205–2.0215	.2375	.2375	.001–.003	.001–.007
1982	A	4-140 (2.3)	1.7713–1.7720	1.7713–1.7720	1.7713–1.7720	1.7713–1.7720	–	.2437	.2437	.001–.003	.001–.007
	B	6-200 (3.3)	1.8095–1.8105	1.8095–1.8105	1.8095–1.8105	1.8095–1.8105	–	.245	.245	.001–.003	.001–.007
	3	6-232 (3.8)	2.0515–2.0505	2.0515–2.0505	2.0515–2.0505	2.0515–2.0505	–	.240	.241	.001–.003	①
	D	8-255 (4.2)	2.0805–2.0815	2.0655–2.0665	2.0505–2.0515	2.0355–2.0365	2.0205–2.0215	.2375	.2375	.001–.003	.001–.007
	F	8-302 (5.0)	2.0805–2.0815	2.0655–2.0665	2.0505–2.0515	2.0355–2.0365	2.0205–2.0215	.2375	.2474	.001–.003	.001–.007
	G	8-351 (5.8)	2.0805–2.0815	2.0655–2.0665	2.0505–2.0515	2.0355–2.0365	2.0205–2.0215	.2780	.2830	.001–.003	.001–.007
1983	A	4-140 (2.3)	1.7713–1.7720	1.7713–1.7720	1.7713–1.7720	1.7713–1.7720	–	.2437	.2437	.001–.003	.001–.007
	X	6-200 (3.3)	1.8095–1.8105	1.8095–1.8105	1.8095–1.8105	1.8095–1.8105	–	.245	.245	.001–.003	.001–.007
	3	6-232 (3.8)	2.0515–2.0505–	2.0515–2.0505–	2.0515–2.0505–	2.0515–2.0505–	–	.240	.241	.001–①.003	
	F	8-302 (5.0)	2.0805–2.0815	2.065–2.0665	2.0505–2.0515	2.0355–2.0365	2.0205–2.0215	.2375 ②	.2474 ②	.001–.003	.001–.007
	G	8-351 (5.8)	2.0805–2.0815	2.0655–2.0665	2.0505–2.0515	2.0355–2.0365	2.0205–2.0215	.2780	.2830	.001–.003	.001–.007
1984	A,T W	4-140 (2.3)	1.7713–1.7720	1.7713–1.7720	1.7713–1.7720	1.7713–1.7720	–	.2381	.2381	.001–.003	.001–.007
	L	6-149 (2.4)	1.2582–1.2589	1.2582–1.2589	1.2582–1.2589	1.2582–1.2589	1.2582–1.2589	.374	.376	.0039	–
	3	6-232 (3.8)	2.0515–2.0505	2.0515–2.0505	2.0515–2.0505	2.0515–2.0505	–	.240	.241	.001–.003	①

CAMSHAFT SPECIFICATIONS

All measurements given in inches.

Year	VIN	No. Cylinder Displacement cu. in. (liter)	Journal Diameter					Lobe Lift		Bearing Clearance	Camshaft End Play
			1	2	3	4	5	In.	Ex.		
1984	F, M	8-302 (5.0)	2.0805–2.0815	2.0655–2.0665	2.0505–2.0515	2.0355–2.0365	2.0205–2.0215	.2375 ②	.2474 ②	.001–.003	.001–.007
	G	8-351 (5.8)	2.0805–2.0815	2.0655–2.0665	2.0505–2.0515	2.0355–2.0365	2.0205–2.0215	.2780	.2830	.001–.003	.001–.007
1985	A, W	4-140 (2.3)	1.7713–1.7720	1.7713–1.7720	1.7713–1.7720	1.7713–1.7720	—	.400	.400	.001–.003	.001–.007
	L	6-149 (2.4)	1.2582–1.2589	1.2582–1.2589	1.2582–1.2589	1.2582–1.2589	1.2582–1.2589	.374	.376	.0039	—
	3	6-232 (3.8)	2.0515–2.0505	2.0515–2.0505	2.0515–2.0505	2.0515–2.0505	—	.240	.241	.001–.003	①
	F, M	8-302 (5.0)	2.0805–2.0815	2.0655–2.0665	2.0505–2.0515	2.0355–2.0365	2.0205–2.0215	.2375 ②	.2474 ②	.001–.003	.001–.007
	G	8-351 (5.8)	2.0805–2.0815	2.0655–2.0665	2.0505–2.0515	2.0355–2.0365	2.0505–2.0215	.2780	.2830	.001–.003	.001–.007
1986	A,T W	4-140 (2.3)	1.7713–1.7720	1.7713–1.7720	1.7713–1.7720	1.7713–1.7720	—	.400	.400	.001–.003	.001–.007
	3	6-232 (3.8)	2.0515–2.0505	2.0515–2.0505	2.0515–2.0505	2.0515 2.0505	—	.240	.241	.001–.003	①
	F, M	8-302 (5.0)	2.0805–2.0815	2.0655–2.0665	2.0505–2.0515	2.0355–2.0365	2.0205–2.0515	.2375 ②	.2474 ②	.001–.003	.001–.007
	G	8-351 (5.8)	2.0805–2.0815	2.0655–2.0665	2.0505–2.0515	2.0355–2.0365	2.0505–2.0515	.2780	.2830	.001–.003	.001–.007
1987	A, W	4-140 (2.3)	1.7713–1.7720	1.7713–1.7720	1.7713–1.7720	1.7713–1.7720	—	.400	.400	.001–.003	.001–.007
	3	6-232 (3.8)	2.0515–2.0505	2.0515–2.0505	2.0515–2.0505	2.0515–2.0505	—	.240	.241	.001–.003	①
	F, M	8-302 (5.0)	2.0805–2.0815	2.0655–2.0665	2.0505–2.0515	2.0355–2.0365	2.0205–2.0215	.2375 ②	.2474 ②	.001–.003	.001–.007
	G	8-351 (5.8)	2.0805–2.0815	2.0655–2.0665	2.0505–2.0515	2.0355–2.0365	2.0205–2.0215	.2780	.2830	.001–.003	.001–.007

① The end play is controlled by the button & spring on the camshaft end

② On the 83-85 H.O. engine, intake lobe lift is .2600, exhaust is .2780 On the 86-88 H.O. engine, intake lobe lift is .2780, exhaust is .2780

CRANKSHAFT AND CONNECTING ROD SPECIFICATIONS

All measurements are given in inches.

Year	VIN	No. Cylinder Displacemen Brg. cu. in. (liter)	Crankshaft Main Brg. Oil Journal Dia.	Shaft Clearance	Thrust End-play	Journal on No.	Connecting Rod Oil Diameter	Side Clearance	Clearance
1981	A	4-140 (2.3)	2.3990–2.3982	0.0008–0.0015	0.004–0.008	3	2.0464–2.0472	0.0008–0.0015	0.0035–0.0105
	B	6-200 (3.3)	2.2482–2.2490	0.0008–0.0015	0.004–0.008	5	2.1232–2.1240	0.0008–0.0015	0.0035–0.0105
	D	8-255 (4.2)	2.2482–2.2490	①	0.004–0.008	3	2.1228–2.1236	0.0008–0.0026	0.010–0.020
	F	8-302 (5.0)	2.2482–2.2490	①	0.004–0.008	3	2.1228–2.1236	0.0008–0.0015	0.010–0.020
	G	8-351 (5.8)	2.2994–3.0002	0.0008–0.0015④	0.004–0.008	3	2.3103–2.3111	0.0008–0.0015	0.010–0.020
1982	A	4-140 (2.3)	2.3990–2.3982	0.0008–0.0015	0.004–0.008	3	2.0464–2.0472	0.0008–0.0015	0.0035–0.0105
	B	6-200 (3.3)	2.2482–2.2490	0.0008–0.0015	0.004–0.008	5	2.1232–2.1240	0.0008–0.0015	0.0035–0.0105
	3	6-232 (3.8)	2.5190	0.0001–0.0010	0.004–0.008	3	2.3103–2.3111	0.0008–0.0026	0.0047–0.0114
	D	8-255 (4.2)	2.2482–2.2490	①	0.004–0.008	3	2.1228–2.1236	0.0008–0.0026	0.010–0.020
	F	8-302 (5.0)	2.2482–2.2490	①	0.004–0.008	3	2.1228–2.1236	0.0008–0.0015	0.010–0.020
	G	8-351 (5.8)	2.2994–3.0002	0.0008–0.0015④	0.004–0.008	3	2.3103–2.3111	0.0008–0.0015	0.010–0.020
1983	A	4-140 (2.3)	2.3990–2.3982	0.0008–0.0015	0.004–0.008	3	2.0464–2.0472	0.0008–0.0015	0.0035–0.0105
	X	6-200 (3.3)	2.2482–2.2490	0.0008–0.0015	0.004–0.008	5	2.1232–2.1240	0.0008–0.0015	0.0035–0.0105
	3	6-232 (3.8)	2.5190	0.0001–0.0010	0.004–0.008	3	2.3103–2.3111	0.0008–0.0026	0.0047–0.0114
	F	8-302 (5.0)	2.2482–2.2490	①	0.004–0.008	3	2.1228–2.1236	0.0008–0.0015	0.010–0.020
	G	8-351 (5.8)	2.2994–3.0002	0.0008–0.0015④	0.004–0.008	3	2.3103–2.3111	0.0008–0.0015	0.010–0.020
1984	A,T, W	4-140 (2.3)	2.3990–2.3982	0.0008–0.0015	0.004–0.008	3	2.0464–2.0472	0.0008–0.0015	0.0035–0.0105
	3	6-232 (3.8)	2.5190	0.0001–0.0010	0.004–0.008	3	2.3103–2.3111	0.0008–0.0026	0.0047–0.0114
	F,M	8-302 (5.0)	2.2482–2.2490	①	0.004–	3	2.1228–2.1236	0.0008–0.0015	0.010–0.020
	G	8-351 (5.8)	2.2994–3.0002	0.0008–0.0015④	0.004–0.008	3	2.3103–2.3111	0.0008–0.0015	0.010–0.020
	L	6-149 (2.4)	②	0.0008–0.0018	0.003–0.006	6	③	0.0008–0.0016	0.0016

CRANKSHAFT AND CONNECTING ROD SPECIFICATIONS

All measurements are given in inches.

Year	VIN	No. Cylinder Displacement cu. in. (liter)	Crankshaft: Main Brg. Journal Dia.	Crankshaft: Main Brg. Oil Clearance	Crankshaft: Shaft End-play	Crankshaft: Thrust on No.	Connecting Rod: Journal Diameter	Connecting Rod: Oil Clearance	Connecting Rod: Side Clearance
1985	A,T, W	4-140 (2.3)	2.3990–2.3982	0.0008–0.0015	0.004–0.008	3	2.0464–2.0472	0.0008–0.0015	0.0035–0.0105
	3	6-232 (3.8)	2.5190	0.0001–0.0010	0.004–0.008	3	2.3103–2.3111	0.0008–0.0026	0.0047–0.0114
	F,M	8-302 (5.0)	2.2482–2.2490	0.0004–0.0015 (1)	0.004–0.015	3	2.1228–2.1236	0.0008–0.0015	0.010–0.020
	G	8-351 (5.8)	2.2994–3.0002	0.0008–0.0015 (4)	0.004–0.008	3	2.3103–2.3111	0.0008–0.0015	0.010–0.020
	L	6-149 (2.4)	(2)	0.0008–0.0018	0.003–0.006	6	(3)	0.0008–0.006	0.0016
1986	A,T, W	4-140 (2.3)	2.3990–2.3982	0.0008–0.0015	0.004–0.008	3	2.0464–2.0472	0.0008–0.0015	0.0035–0.0105
	3	6-232 (3.8)	2.5190	0.0001–0.0010	0.004–0.008	3	2.3103–2.3111	0.0008–0.0026	0.0047–0.0114
	F,M	8-302 (5.0)	2.2482–2.2490	0.0004–0.0015	0.004–0.008	3	2.1228–2.1236	0.0008–0.0015	0.010–0.020
	G	8-351 (5.8)	2.2994–3.0002	0.0008–0.0015 (4)	0.004–0.008	3	2.3103–2.3111	0.0008–0.0015	0.010–0.020
1987-88	A,W	4-140 (2.3)	2.3990–2.3982	0.0008–0.0015	0.004–0.008	3	2.0464–2.0472	0.0008–0.0015	0.0035–0.0105
	3	6-232 (3.8)	2.5190	0.0001–0.0010	0.004–0.008	3	2.3103–2.3111	0.0008–0.0026	0.0047–0.0114
	F,M	8-302 (5.0)	2.2482–2.2490	0.0004–0.0015	0.004–0.008	3	2.1228–2.1236	0.0008–0.0015	0.010–0.020
	G	8-351 (5.8)	2.2994–3.0002	0.0008–0.0015 (4)	0.004–0.008	3	2.3103–2.3111	0.0008–0.0015	0.010–0.020

NA—Not available

(1) 1981 No. 1—0.0001–0.0015
No. 3-5—0.0004–0.0015
1982-84 No. 1—0.0004–0.0025
No. 3-5—0.0004–0.0015
1985-87 All bearings—0.0004–0.0015

(2) Yellow mark—2.3615–2.3618
Green mark—2.3613–2.3615
White mark—2.3610–2.3612

(3) Red mark—1.8885–1.8887
Blue mark—1.8888–1.8903

(4) No. 1—0.0001–0.0005

VALVE SPECIFICATIONS

Year	VIN	No. Cylinder Displacement cu. in. (liter)	Seat Angle (deg.)	Face Angle (deg.)	Spring Test Pressure (lbs. @ in.)	Spring Installed Height (in.)	Stem-to-Guide Clearance (in.): Intake	Stem-to-Guide Clearance (in.): Exhaust	Stem Diameter (in.): Intake	Stem Diameter (in.): Exhaust
1981	A	4-140 (2.3)	45	44	(1)	$1\frac{9}{16}$	0.0010–0.0027	0.0015–0000030	0.3420	0.3415
	B	6-200 (3.3)	45	44	51–57@1.59	$1\frac{19}{32}$	0.0008–0.0025	0.0010–0.0027	0.3104	0.3102
	D	8-255 (4.2)	45	44	(2)	(3)	0.0010–0.0027	0.0015–0.0032	0.3420	0.3415

VALVE SPECIFICATIONS

Year	VIN	No. Cylinder Displacement cu. in. (liter)	Seat Angle (deg.)	Face Angle (deg.)	Spring Test Pressure (lbs. @ in.)	Spring Installed Height (in.)	Stem-to-Guide Clearance (in.)		Stem Diameter (in.)	
							Intake	Exhaust	Intake	Exhaust
1981	F	8-302 (5.0)	45	44	②	③	0.0010–0.0027	0.0015–0.0032	0.3420	0.3415
	G	8-351 (5.8)	45	44	②	③	0.0010–0.0027	0.0015–0.0032	0.3420	0.3415
1982	A	4-140 (2.3)	45	44	167 @ 1.16	1 9/16	0.0010–0.0027	0.0015–0.0032	0.3420	0.3415
	B	6-200 (3.3)	45	44	55 @ 1.59	1 19/32	0.0008–0.0025	0.0010–0.0027	0.3104	0.3102
	D	8-255 (4.2)	⑤	⑥	⑦	–	0.0010–0.0027	0.0015–0.0032	0.3420	0.3420
	F	8-302 (5.0)	45	45	②	③	0.0010–0.0027	0.0015–0.0032	0.3420	0.3420
	G	8-351 (5.8)	45	45	204 @ 1.33 ⑧	1 49/64 ⑨	0.0010–0.0027	0.0015–0.0027	0.3416–0.3423	0.3411–0.3418
1983	A	4-140 (2.3)	45	44	149 @ 1.12	1 9/16	0.0010–0.0027	0.0015–0.0032	0.3420	0.3415
	X	6-200 (3.3)	45	44	55 @ 1.59	1 19/32	0.0008–0.0025	0.0010–0.0027	0.3104	0.3102
	F	8-302 (5.0)	45	45	②	③	0.0010–0.0027	0.0015–0.0032	0.3420	0.3420
	G	8-351 (5.8)	45	45	204 @ 1.33 ⑧	1 49/64 ⑨	0.0010–0.0027	0.0015–0.0027	0.3416–0.3423	0.3411–0.3418
1984	A,T, W	4-140 (2.3)	45	44	154 @ 1.12	1 9/16	0.0010–0.0027	0.0015–0.0032	0.3420	0.3415
	3	6-232 (3.8)	⑤	⑤	215 @ 1.79	1 3/4	0.0010–0.0027	0.0015–0.0032	0.3420	0.3415
	F, M	8-302 (5.0)	45	45	②	③	0.0010–0.0027	0.0015–0.0032	0.3420	0.3420
	L	6-149 (2.4)	45	45	⑩	–	0.0008–0.0010	0.0008–0.0010	–	–
	G	8-351 (5.8)	45	45	204 @ 1.33 ⑧	1 49/64 ⑨	0.0010–0.0027	0.0015–0.0027	0.3416–0.3423	0.3411–0.3418
1985	A,T, W	4-140 (2.3)	45	44	154 @ 1.12	1 9/16	0.0010–0.0027	0.0015–0.0032	0.3420	0.3415
	3	6-232 (3.8)	⑤	⑤	215 @ 1.79	1 3/4	0.0010–0.0027	0.0015–0.0032	0.3420	0.3415
	F, M	8-302 (5.0)	45	45	②	③	0.0010–0.0027	0.0015–0.0032	0.3420	0.3420
	L	6-149 (2.4)	45	45	⑩	–	0.0008–0.0010	0.0008–0.0010	–	–
	G	8-351 (5.8)	45	45	204 @ 1.33 ⑧	1 49/64 ⑨	0.0010–0.0027	0.0015–0.0027	0.3416–0.3423	0.3411–0.3418
1986	A,T, W	4-140 (2.3)	45	44	154 @ 1.12	1 9/16	0.0010–0.0027	0.0015–0.0032	0.3420	0.3415

VALVE SPECIFICATIONS

Year	VIN	No. Cylinder Displacement cu. in. (liter)	Seat Angle (deg.)	Face Angle (deg.)	Spring Test Pressure (lbs. @ in.)	Spring Installed Height (in.)	Stem-to-Guide Clearance (in.)		Stem Diameter (in.)	
							Intake	Exhaust	Intake	Exhaust
1986	3	6-232 (3.8)	⑤	⑤	215 @ 1.79	1¾	0.0010–0.0027	0.0015–0.0032	0.3420	0.3415
	F, M	8-302 (5.0)	45	45	②	③	0.0010–0.0027	0.0015–0.0032	0.3420	0.3420
	G	8-351 (5.8)	45	45	204 @ 1.33 ⑧	$1\frac{49}{64}$ ⑨	0.0010–0.0027	0.0015–0.0027	0.3416–0.3423	0.3411–0.3418
1987–88	A,T,	4-140 (2.3)	45	44	154 @ 1.12	$1\frac{9}{16}$	0.0010–0.0027	0.0015–0.0032	0.3420	0.3415
	3	6-232 (3.8)	⑤	⑤	215 @ 1.79	1¾	0.0010–0.0027	0.0015–0.0032	0.3420	0.3415
	F, M	8-302 (5.0)	45	45	②	③	0.0010–0.0027	0.0015–0.0032	0.3420	0.3420
	G	8-351 (5.8)	45	45	204 @ 1.33 ⑧	$1\frac{49}{64}$ ⑨	0.0010–0.0027	0.0015–0.0027	0.3416–0.3423	0.3411–0.3418

① Intake: 71-70 @ 1.56
Exhaust: 159-175 @ 1.16

② 1981-82
Intake: 205 @ 1.36
Exhaust 200 @ 1.20
1983-87
Intake: Std. 205 @ 1.36
Intake: HO 204 @ 1.33
Exhaust: 205 @ 1.05

③ Intake: $1\frac{11}{16}$
Exhaust: $1\frac{19}{32}$

⑤ Intake: $1\frac{11}{16}$
Exhaust: $1\frac{9}{32}$

⑥ Intake: 44° 30'–45°
Exhaust: 45 ° 30' – 45° 45'

⑦ Intake: 192 @ 1.40
Exhaust: 191 @ 1.23

⑧ Exhaust: 205 @ 1.15

⑨ Exhaust: $1\frac{37}{64}$

⑩ Install spring in tool No.6513-00. Apply torque until a click is heard and multiply the torque reading by two

PISTON AND RING SPECIFICATIONS

All measurments are given in inches.

Year	VIN	No. Cylinder Displacement cu. in. (liter)	Piston Clearance	Ring Gap			Ring Side Clearance		
				Top Compression	Bottom Compression	Oil Control	Top Compression	Bottom Compression	Oil Control
1981	A	4-140 (2.3)	①	0.010–0.020	0.010–0.020	0.015–0.055	0.002–0.004	0.002–0.004	Snug
	B	6-200 (3.3)	0.0013–0.0021	0.008–0.016	0.008–0.016	0.015–0.055	0.002–0.004	0.002–0.004	Snug
	D	8-255 (4.2)	0.0014–0.0026	0.010	0.010	0.015	0.002	0.002	Snug
	F	8-302 (5.0)	0.0018–0.0026	0.020	0.020	0.055	0.004	0.004	Snug
	G	8-351 (5.8)	0.0022–0.0030	0.020	0.020	0.055	0.004	0.004	Snug
1982	A	4-140 (2.3)	①	0.010–0.020	0.010–0.020	0.015–0.055	0.002–0.004	0.002–0.004	Snug
	3	6-232 (3.8)	③	0.010–0.022	0.010–0.022	0.015–0.055	0.002–0.004	0.002–0.004	Snug
	B	6-200 (3.3)	0.0013–0.0021	0.008–0.016	0.008–0.016	0.015–0.055	0.002–0.004	0.002–0.004	Snug

PISTON AND RING SPECIFICATIONS

All measurments are given in inches.

Year	VIN	No. Cylinder Displacement cu. in. (liter)	Piston Clearance	Ring Gap Top Compression	Ring Gap Bottom Compression	Ring Gap Oil Control	Ring Side Clearance Top Compression	Ring Side Clearance Bottom Compression	Ring Side Clearance Oil Control
1982	D	8-255 (4.2)	0.0014–0.0026	0.010	0.010	0.015	0.002	0.002	Snug
	F	8-302 (5.0)	0.0018–0.0026	0.020	0.020	0.055	0.004	0.004	Snug
	G	8-351 (5.8)	0.0022–0.0030	0.020	0.020	0.055	0.004	0.004	Snug
1983	A	4-140 (2.3)	①	0.010–0.020	0.010–0.020	0.015–0.055	0.002–0.004	0.002–0.004	Snug
	3	6-232 (3.8)	③	0.010–0.022	0.010–0.022	0.015–0.055	0.002–0.004	0.002–0.004	Snug
	X	6-200 (3.3)	0.0013–0.0021	0.008–0.016	0.008–0.016	0.015–0.055	0.002–0.004	0.002–0.004	Snug
	F	8-302 (5.0)	0.0018–0.0026	0.020	0.020	0.055	0.004	0.004	Snug
	G	8-351 (5.8)	0.0022–0.0030	0.020	0.020	0.055	0.004	0.004	Snug
1984	A	4-140 (2.3)	①	0.010–0.020	0.010–0.020	0.015–0.055	0.002–0.004	0.002–0.004	Snug
	T, W	4-140 (2.3)	0.0030–0.0038	0.010–0.020	0.010–0.020	0.015–0.055	0.002–0.004	0.002–0.004	Snug
	3	6-232 (3.8)	③	0.010–0.022	0.010–0.022	0.015–0.055	0.002–0.004	0.002–0.004	Snug
	F, M	8-302 (5.0)	0.0018–0.0026	0.020	0.020	0.055	0.004	0.004	Snug
	G	8-351 (5.8)	0.0022–0.0030–	0.020	0.020	0.055	0.004	0.004	Snug
	L	6-149 (2.4)	②	0.008–0.016	0.008–0.016	0.010–0.020	0.024–0.055	0.002–0.003	0.0012–0.0024
1985	A	4-140 (2.3)	①	0.010–0.020	0.010–0.020	0.015–0.055	0.002–0.004	0.002–0.004	Snug
	T, W	4-140 (2.3)	0.0030–0.0038	0.010–0.020	0.010–0.020	0.015–0.055	0.002–0.004	0.002–0.004	Snug
	3	6-232 (3.8)	③	0.010–0.022	0.010–0.022	0.015–0.055	0.002–0.004	0.002–0.004	Snug
	F, M	8-302 (5.0)	0.0018–0.0026	0.020	0.020	0.055	0.004	0.004	Snug
	G	8-351 (5.8)	0.0022–0.0030	0.020	0.020	0.055	0.004	0.004	Snug
	L	6-149 (2.4)	②	0.008–0.016	0.008–0.016	0.010–0.020	0.024–0.055	0.002–0.003	0.0012–0.0024
1986	A	4-140 (2.3)	①	0.010–0.020	0.010–0.020	0.015–0.055	0.002–0.004	0.002–0.004	Snug
	T, W	4-140 (2.3)	0.0030–0.0038	0.010–0.020	0.010–0.020	0.015–0.055	0.002–0.004	0.002–0.004	Snug

PISTON AND RING SPECIFICATIONS

All measurments are given in inches.

Year	VIN	No. Cylinder Displacement cu. in. (liter)	Piston Clearance	Ring Gap Top Compression	Ring Gap Bottom Compression	Ring Gap Oil Control	Ring Side Clearance Top Compression	Ring Side Clearance Bottom Compression	Ring Side Clearance Oil Control
1986	3	6-232 (3.8)	③	0.010–0.022	0.010–0.022	0.015–0.055	0.002–0.004	0.002–0.004	Snug
	F, M	8-302 (5.0)	0.0018–0.0026	0.020	0.020	0.055	0.004	0.004	Snug
	G	8-351 (5.8)	0.0022–0.0030	0.020	0.020	0.055	0.004	0.004	Snug
1987-88	A, W	4-140 (2.3)	①	0.010–0.020	0.010–0.020	0.015–0.055	0.002–0.004	0.002–0.004	Snug
	3	6-232 (3.8)	③	0.010–0.022	0.010–0.022	0.015–0.055	0.002–0.004	0.002–0.004	Snug
	F, M	8-302 (5.0)	0.0018–0.0026	0.020	0.020	0.055	0.004	0.004	Snug
	G	8-351 (5.8)	0.0022–0.0030	0.020	0.020	0.055	0.004	0.004	Snug

①1981-82 Non turbo: 0.0014–0.0022
1981-82 Turbo: 0.0034–0.0042
1983 0.0014–0.0022
1984-87: 0.0030–0.0038

②Alcan pistons: 0.0010–0.0021
KS pistons: 0.0016–0.0027
Mahle pistons: 0.0018–0.0029

③1982-83: 0.0014–0.0022
1984-87: 0.0014–0.0032

TORQUE SPECIFICATIONS

All readings in ft. lbs.

Year	VIN	No. Cylinder Displacement cu. in. (liter)	Cylinder Head Bolts	Main Bearing Bolts	Rod Bearing Bolts	Crankshaft Pulley Bolts	Flywheel Bolts	Manifold Intake	Manifold Exhaust	Spark Plugs
1981	A	4-140 (2.3)	80–90⑧	80–90	30–36	100–120	54–64	③	⑫	5-10
	B	6-200 (3.3)	70–75	60–70	21–26	85–100	75–85	–	18–24	10–15
	D	8-255 (4.2)	65–72	60–70	19–24	70–90	75–85	18–20①	18–24	10–15
	F	8-302 (5.0)	65–72	60–70	19–24	70–90	75–85	23–25①	18–24	10–15
	G	8-351 (5.8)	105–112	95–105	40–45	70–90	75–85	23–25①	18–24	10–15
1982	A	4-140 (2.3)	80–90⑧	80–90	30–36	100–120	54–64	③	⑫	5-10
	3	6-232 (3.8)	⑤	65-81	31-36	85–100	75–85	18	15–22	5–11
	B	6-200 (3.3)	70–75	60–70	21–26	85–100	75–85	–	18–24	10–15
	D	8-255 (4.2)	65–72	60–70	19–24	70–90	75–85	18–20①	18–24	10–15
	F	8-302 (5.0)	65–72	60–70	19–24	70–90	75–85	23–25①	18–24	10–15
	G	8-351 (5.8)	105–112	95–105	40–45	70–90	75–85	23–25①	18–24	10–15
1983	A	4-140 (2.3)	80–90⑧	80–90	30–36	100–120	54–64	③	⑫	5-10
	3	6-232 (3.8)	⑤	65-81	31-36	85–100	75–85	18	15–22	5–11
	B	6-200 (3.3)	70–75	60–70	21–26	85–100	75–85	–	18–24	10–15
	D	8-255 (4.2)	65–72	60–70	19–24	70–90	75–85	18–20①	18–24	10–15
	F	8-302 (5.0)	65–72	60–70	19–24	70–90	75–85	23–25①	18–24	10–15
	G	8-351 (5.8)	105–112	95–105	40–45	70–90	75–85	23–25①	18–24	10–15
1984	A,T	4-140 (2.3)	80–90⑧	80–90	30–36	100–120	54–64	③	⑫	5-10
	3	6-232 (3.8)	②	65-81	31-36	85–100	75–85	18	15–22	5–11

TORQUE SPECIFICATIONS

All readings in ft. lbs.

Year	VIN	No. Cylinder Displacement cu. in. (liter)	Cylinder Head Bolts	Main Bearing Bolts	Rod Bearing Bolts	Crankshaft Pulley Bolts	Flywheel Bolts	Manifold Intake	Manifold Exhaust	Spark Plugs
1984	F	8-302 (5.0)	65–72	60–70	19–24	70–90	75–85	23–25①	18–24	10–15
	G	8-351 (5.8)	105–112	95–105	40–45	70–90	75–85	23–25①	18–24	10–15
	L	6-149 (2.4)	⑩	43–48	⑪	16–17	71–81	14–17	14–17	14–22
1985	A,T	4-140 (2.3)	80–90⑧	80–90	30–36	100–120	54–64	③	⑫	5-10
	3	6-232 (3.8)	②	65-81	31-36	85–100	75–85	18	15–22	5–11
	F	8-302 (5.0)	65–72	60–70	19–24	70–90	75–85	23–25①	18–24	10–15
	G	8-351 (5.8)	105–112	95–105	40–45	70–90	75–85	23–25①	18–24	10–15
	L	6-149 (2.4)	⑩	43–48	⑪	16–17	71–81	14–17	14–17	14–22
1986	A,T	4-140 (2.3)	80–90⑧	80–90	30–36	100–120	54–64	③	⑫	5-10
	3	6-232 (3.8)	②	65-81	31-36	85–100	75–85	18	15–22	5–11
	F	8-302 (5.0)	65–72	60–70	19–24	70–90	75–85	23–25①	18–24	10–15
	G	8-351 (5.8)	105–112	95–105	40–45	70–90	75–85	23–25①	18–24	10–15
1987-88	A	4-140 (2.3)	80–90⑧	75–85	30–36	103–133	54–64	15–22	20-30	5-10
	3	6-232 (3.8)	②	65-81	31-36	20–28	54-64	⑨	15–22	5–11
	F	8-302 (5.0)	65–72	60–70	19–24	70–90	75–85	23–25①	18–24	10–15
	G	8-351 (5.8)	105–112	95–105	40–45	70–90	75–85	23–25①	18–24	10–15

① Retorque with engine hot

② a. Tighten in (4) steps:
37 ft. lbs. (50 Nm)
45 ft, lbs. (60 Nm)
52 ft. lbs. (70 Nm)
59 ft. lbs. (80 Nm)
b. Back-off all bolts 2–3 revolutions
c. Repeat Step a (above)

③ Turbo: 5–7 ft. lbs., then 14–21 ft. lbs.
Non-Turbo: 13–18 ft. lbs.

④ a. Tighten in (4) steps:
3–6 ft. lbs.
6–11 ft. lbs.
11–15 ft. lbs.
15–18 ft. lbs.
b. Retighten to 15–18 ft. lbs.
c. Retighten to 15–18 ft. lbs. with engine hot

⑤ Torque bolts in (4) steps:
1. 47 ft. lbs.
2. 55 ft. lbs.
3. 63 ft. lbs.
4. 74 ft. lbs.

⑧ Tighten in two steps: 50–60 ft. lbs. and then 80–90 ft. lbs.

⑨ Tighten in (3) steps:
7 ft. lbs. (10 Nm)
15 ft. lbs. (20 Nm)
24 ft. lbs. (32 Nm)

⑩ Tighten in (4) steps:
1. 22–29 ft. lbs.
2. 36-43 ft. lbs.
3. +73°
4. Run engine for 25 minutes then turn each bolt 90°

⑪ Tighten in (2) steps:
14 ft. lbs.
70 degrees

⑫ Tighten first to 60-84 in. lb.; then to 16-23 ft. lb.

BRAKE SPECIFICATIONS

All measurements in inches unless noted

Year	Model	Lug Nut Torque (ft. lbs.)	Master Cylinder Bore	Brake Disc Minimum Thickness	Brake Disc Maximum Runout	Standard Brake Drum Diameter	Minimum Lining Thickness Front	Minimum Lining Thickness Rear
1981	Fairmont Zephyr	80–105	7/8	0.810	0.003	9.00①	0.125	0.030
	Mustang Capri	80–105	7/8	0.810	0.003	9.00①	0.125	0.030
	Thunderbird XR-7	80–105	7/8	0.810	0.003	9.00①	0.125	0.030

BRAKE SPECIFICATIONS

All measurements in inches unless noted

Year	Model	Lug Nut Torque (ft. lbs.)	Master Cylinder Bore	Brake Disc Minimum Thickness	Brake Disc Maximum Runout	Standard Brake Drum Diameter	Minimum Lining Thickness Front	Minimum Lining Thickness Rear
1981	Cougar Granada	80–105	7/8	0.810	0.003	9.00①	0.125	0.030
	Ford Mercury	80–105	1	0.972	0.003	10.00②	0.125	0.030
	Town Car Mark VI	80–105	1	0.972	0.003	10.00②	0.125	0.030
	Continental	80–105	1	0.972	0.003	10.00②	0.125	0.030
1982	Fairmont Zephyr	80–105	7/8	0.810	0.003	9.00①	0.125	0.030
	Mustang Capri	80–105	7/8	0.810	0.003	9.00①	0.125	0.030
	Thunderbird XR-7	80–105	7/8	0.810	0.003	9.00①	0.125	0.030
	Cougar Granada	80–105	7/8	0.810	0.003	9.00①	0.125	0.030
	Ford Mercury	80–105	1	0.972	0.003	10.00②	0.125	0.030
	Town Car Mark VI	80–105	1	0.972	0.003	10.00②	0.125	0.030
	Continental	80–105	1	0.972	0.003	10.00②	0.125	0.030
1983	Fairmont Zephyr	80–105	7/8	0.810	0.003	9.00①	0.125	0.030
	Mustang Capri	80–105	7/8	0.810	0.003	9.00①	0.125	0.030
	Thunderbird Cougar	80–105	7/8	0.810	0.003	9.00①	0.125	0.030
	LTD Marquis	80–105	7/8	0.810	0.003	9.90①	0.125	0.030
	Ford Mercury	80–105	1	0.972	0.003	10.00②	0.125	0.030
	Town Car Mark VI	80–105	1	0.972	0.003	10.00②	0.125	0.030
	Continental	80–105	1 1/8	0.972③	0.003④	–	0.125	0.125
1984	Mustang Capri	80–105	7/8	0.810	0.003	9.00①	0.125	0.030
	Thunderbird Cougar	80–105	7/8	0.810	0.003	9.00①	0.125	0.030
	LTD Marquis	80–105	7/8	0.810	0.003	9.90①	0.125	0.030
	Ford Mercury	80–105	1	0.972	0.003	10.00②	0.125	0.030
	Town Car	80–105	1	0.972	0.003	10.00②	0.125	0.030
	Continental Mark VII	80–105	1 1/8	0.972③	0.003④	–	0.125	0.125

BRAKE SPECIFICATIONS

All measurements in inches unless noted

Year	Model	Lug Nut Torque (ft. lbs.)	Master Cylinder Bore	Brake Disc Minimum Thickness	Brake Disc Maximum Runout	Standard Brake Drum Diameter	Minimum Lining Thickness Front	Minimum Lining Thickness Rear
1985	Mustang Capri	80–105	7/8	0.810	0.003	9.00①	0.125	0.030
	Thunderbird Cougar	80–105	7/8	0.810	0.003	9.00①	0.125	0.030
	LTD Marquis	80–105	7/8	0.810	0.003	9.90①	0.125	0.030
	Ford Mercury	80–105	1	0.972	0.003	10.00②	0.125	0.030
	Town Car	80–105	1	0.972	0.003	10.00②	0.125	0.030
	Continental Mark VII	80–105	1 1/8	0.972③	0.003④	–	0.125	0.125
1986	Mustang Capri	80–105	7/8	0.810	0.003	9.00①	0.125	0.030
	Thunderbird Cougar	80–105	7/8	0.810	0.003	9.00①	0.125	0.030
	LTD Marquis	80–105	7/8	0.810	0.003	9.90①	0.125	0.030
	Ford Mercury	80–105	1	0.972	0.003	10.00②	0.125	0.030
	Town Car	80–105	1	0.972	0.003	10.00②	0.125	0.030
	Continental Mark VII	80–105	1 1/8	0.972③	0.003④	–	0.125	0.125
1987-88	Mustang	80–105	7/8	0.810	0.003	9.00①	0.125	0.030
	Mustang (5.0L)	80–105	7/8	0.972③	0.003	9.00	0.125	0.030⑤
	Thunderbird Cougar	80–105	7/8	0.810	0.003	9.00①	0.125	0.030
	Thunderbird (Turbo)	80–105	7/8	0.972③	0.003	9.00	0.125	0.030⑤
	Ford Mercury	80–105	1	0.972	0.003	10.00②	0.125	0.030
	Town Car	80–105	1	0.972	0.003	10.00②	0.125	0.030
	Continental Mark VII	80–105	1	0.972③	0.003④	–	0.125	0.125

① 10.00 optional
② 11.00 optional
③ 0.895 w/rear disc brake
④ 0.004 w/rear disc brake
⑤ 0.125 w/rear disc brake

WHEEL ALIGNMENT

Year	Model	Caster Range (deg.)	Caster Preferred Setting (deg.)	Camber Range (deg.)	Camber Preferred Setting (deg.)	Toe-in (in.)	Steering Axis Inclination (deg.)
1981	Fairmont/Zepher (Sedan)	1/8P–1 7/8P	1P	5/16N–1 3/16P	7/16P	1/16–5/16	15 1/4
	(Wagon)	1/8N–1 5/8P	3/4P	1/4N–1 1/4P	1/2P	1/16–5/16	15 1/4
	Mustang/Capri	1/4P–1 3/4P	1P	1/2N–1P	1/4P	1/16–5/16	15 1/4
	Thunderbird XR-7	1/8P–1 7/8P	1P	1/2N–1 1/4P	3/8P	1/16–5/16	15 1/3
	Cougar/Granada	1/8P–1 7/8P	1P	5/16N–1 3/16	7/16P	1/16–5/16	15 1/4
	Ford/Mercury	2 1/4P–3 3/4P	3P	1/4N–1 1/4P	1/2P	1/16–3/16	10 31/32
	Town Car Continental Mark VI	2 1/4P–3 3/4P	3P	1/4N–1 1/4P	1/2P	1/16–3/16	11
1982	Fairmont/Zepher	1/8P–1 7/8P	1P	5/16N–1 3/16P	7/16P	1/16–5/16	15 1/4
	Mustang/Capri	1/4P–1 3/4P	1P	1/2N–1P	1/4P	1/16–5/16	15 1/4
	Thunderbird XR-7	1/8P–1 7/8P	1P	1/2N–1 1/4P	3/8P	1/16–5/16	15 1/3
	Cougar/Granada	1/8P–1 7/8P	1P	5/16N–1 3/16	7/16P	1/16–5/16	15 1/4
	Ford/Mercury	2 1/4P–3 3/4P	3P	1/4N–1 1/4P	1/2P	1/16–3/16	10 31/32
	Town Car Mark VI	2 1/4P–3 3/4P	3P	1/4N–1 1/4P	1/2P	1/16–3/16	11
	Continental	1 3/8P–2 1/8P	1 1/4P	1/2N–1 1/4P	3/8P	0–1/4	—
1983	Fairmont/Zepher	1/8P–1 7/8P	1P	5/16N–1 3/16P	7/16P	1/16–5/16	15 1/4
	Mustang/Capri	1/2P–2P	1 1/4P	3/4N–3/4P	0	1/16–5/16	—
	Thunderbird Cougar	1/2P–2	1 1/4P	1/2N–1P	1/4P	1/16–5/16	—
	LTD/Marquis (Sedan)	1 1/8P–2 1/8P	1 5/8P	5/16N–1 3/16	7/16P	1/16–5/16	—
	(Wagon)	1/8N–1 7/8P	7/8P	1/4N–1 1/4P	1/2P	1/16–5/16	—
	Ford/Mercury	2 1/4P–3 3/4P	3P	1/4N–1 1/4P	1/2P	1/16–3/16	10 31/32
	Town Car Mark VI	2 1/4P–3 3/4P	3P	1/4N–1 1/4P	1/2P	1/16–3/16	11
	Continental	1 3/8P–2 1/8P	1 1/4P	1/2N–1 1/4P	3/8P	0–1/4	—
1984	Mustang/Capri	1/2P–2P	1 1/4P	3/4N–3/4P	0	1/16–5/16	—
	Thunderbird Cougar	1/2P–2	1 1/4P	1/2N–1P	1/4P	1/16–5/16	—
	LTD/Marquis (Sedan)	1 1/8P–2 1/8P	1 5/8P	5/16N–1 3/16	7/16P	1/16–5/16	—
	(Wagon)	1/8N–1 7/8P	7/8P	1/4N–1 1/4P	1/2P	1/16–5/16	—
	Ford/Mercury	2 1/4P–3 3/4P	3P	1/4N–1 1/4P	1/2P	1/16–3/16	10 31/32
	Town Car	2 3/8P–4 1/8P	3 1/8P	1/4N–1 1/4P	1/2P	1/16–3/16	11
	Continental Mark VII	7/8P–2 15/16P	1 3/4P	7/8N–7/8P	0	0–1/4	11

WHEEL ALIGNMENT

Year	Model	Caster Range (deg.)	Caster Preferred Setting (deg.)	Camber Range (deg.)	Camber Preferred Setting (deg.)	Toe-in (in.)	Steering Axis Inclination (deg.)
1985	Mustang/Capri	1/2P–2P	1 1/4P	3/4N–3/4P	0	1/16–5/16	—
	Thunderbird Cougar	1/2P–2	1 1/4P	1/2N–1P	1/4P	1/16–5/16	—
	LTD/Marquis (Sedan)	1 1/8P–2 1/8P	1 5/8P	5/16N–1 3/16	7/16P	1/16–5/16	—
	(Wagon)	1/8N–1 7/8P	7/8P	1/4N–1 1/4P	1/2P	1/16–5/16	—
	Ford/Mercury	2 1/4P–3 3/4P	3P	1/4N–1 1/4P	1/2P	1/16–3/16	10 31/32
	Town Car	2 1/4P–4P	3P	1/4N–1 1/4P	1/2P	1/16–3/16	11
	Continental Mark VII	5/8P–2 3/4P	1 1/2P	3/4N–3/4P	0	0–1/4	11
1986	Mustang/Capri	1/2P–2P	1 1/4P	3/4N–3/4P	0	1/16–5/16	—
	Thunderbird Mark VII	1/2P–2	1 1/4P	1/2N–1P	1/4P	1/16–5/16	—
	LTD/Marquis (Sedan)	1 1/8P–2 1/8P	1 5/8P	5/16N–1 3/16	7/16P	1/16–5/16	—
	(Wagon)	1/8N–1 7/8P	7/8P	1/4N–1 1/4P	1/2P	1/16–5/16	—
	Ford/Mercury	2 1/4P–3 3/4P	3P	1/4N–1 1/4P	1/2P	1/16–3/16	10 31/32
	Town Car	2 1/4P–4P	3P	1/4N–1 1/4P	1/2P	1/16–3/16	11
	Continental Mark VII	5/8P–2 3/4P	1 1/2P	3/4N–3/4P	0	0–1/4	11
1987-88	Mustang	1/2P–2P	1 1/4P	3/4N–3/4P	0	1/16–5/16	—
	Thunderbird Cougar	1/2P–2	1 1/4P	1/2N–1P	1/4P	1/16–5/16	—
	Ford/Mercury	2 1/4P–3 3/4P	3P	1/4N–1 1/4P	1/2P	1/16–3/16	10 31/32
	Town Car	2 1/4P–4P	3P	1/4N–1 1/4P	1/2P	1/16–3/16	11
	Continental Mark VII	5/8P–2 3/4P	1 1/2P	3/4N–3/4P	0	0–1/4	11
	Thunderbird Turbo	13/32P–1 29/32P	1 5/32P	9/16N–31/32P	1 5/32P	3/16	—

P Positive
N Negative

ROUTINE MAINTENANCE

Air Cleaner Element

All engines are equipped with a dry type, replaceable air filter element. The element should be replaced evry 10,000 miles or yearly. If your vehicle is operated under severely dusty conditions or severe operating conditions, more frequent changes are necessary. Inspect the element at least twice a year. Early spring and at the beginning of fall are good times for the inspection. Remove the element and check for holes in the filter. Check the cleaner housing for signs of dirt or dust that has leaked through the filter element. Place a light on the inside of the element and look through the filter at the light. If no glow of light can be seen through the element material, replace the filter. If holes in the filter are apparent or signs of dirt leakage through the filter are noticed, replace the filter.

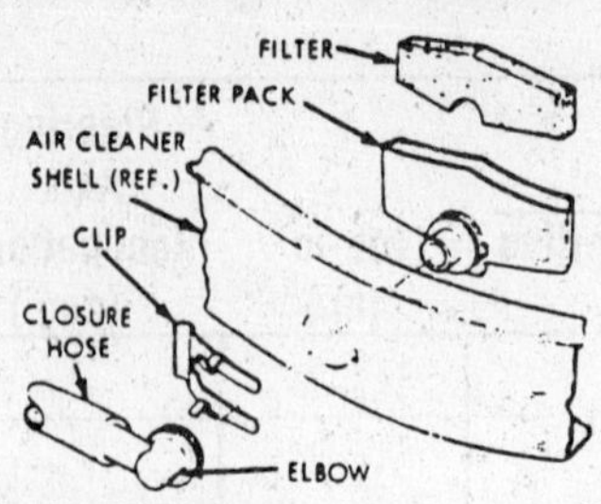

Crankcase ventilation hose and filter pack assembly

REMOVAL & INSTALLATION

Air Cleaner Assembly

1. Disconnect all hoses, ducts and vacuum tubes from the air cleaner assembly.
2. Remove the top cover wing nut and grommet (if equipped). Remove any side bracket mount retaining bolts (if equipped). Remove the air cleaner assembly from the top of the carburetor or intake assembly.

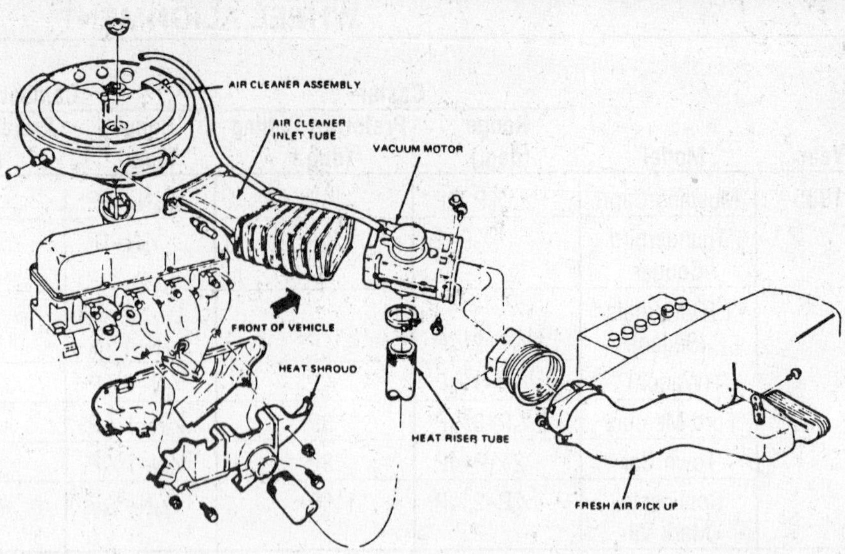

Air cleaner used on 1981-82 and 1984-86 non-Turbo 4-140 engines

3. Remove the cover and the element, wipe clean all inside surfaces of the air cleaner housing and cover. Check the condition of the mounting gasket (cleaner base to carburetor). Replace the mounting gasket if it is worn or broken.
4. Reposition the cleaner assembly, element and cover on the carburetor or intake assembly.
5. Reconnect all hoses, duct and vacuum hoses removed. Tighten the wing nut finger tight.

Element

The element can, in most cases, be replaced by removing the wing nut and cleaner assembly cover. If the inside of the housing is dirty; however, remove the assembly for cleaning to prevent dirt from entering the carburetor.

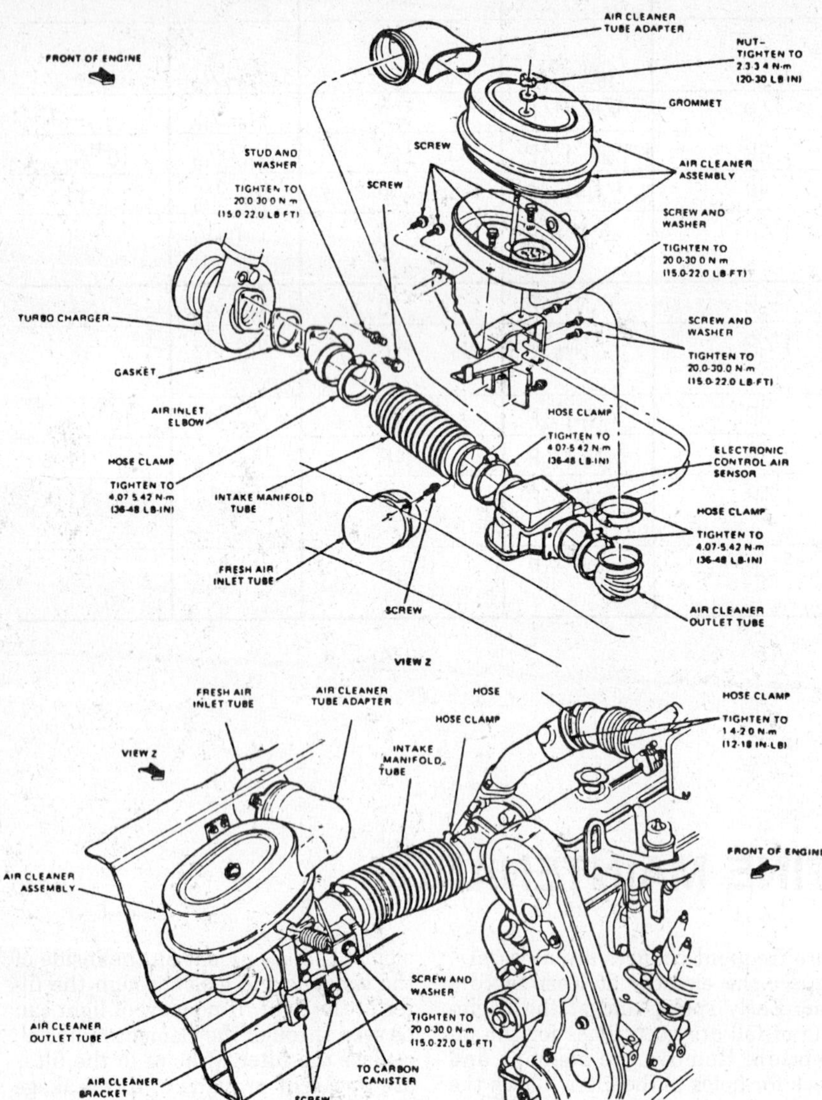

1984-86 4-140 Turbo air cleaner

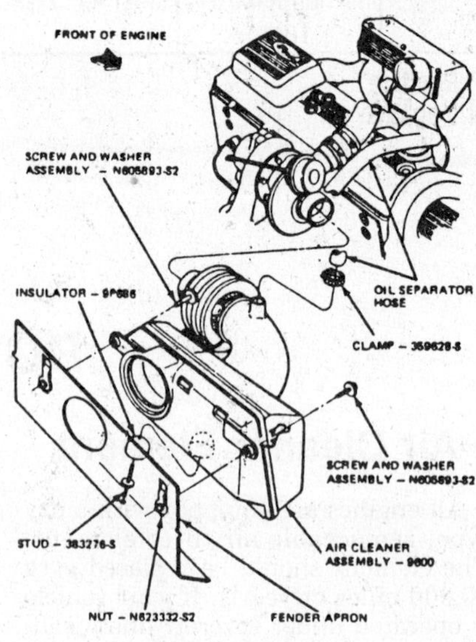

Diesel air cleaner

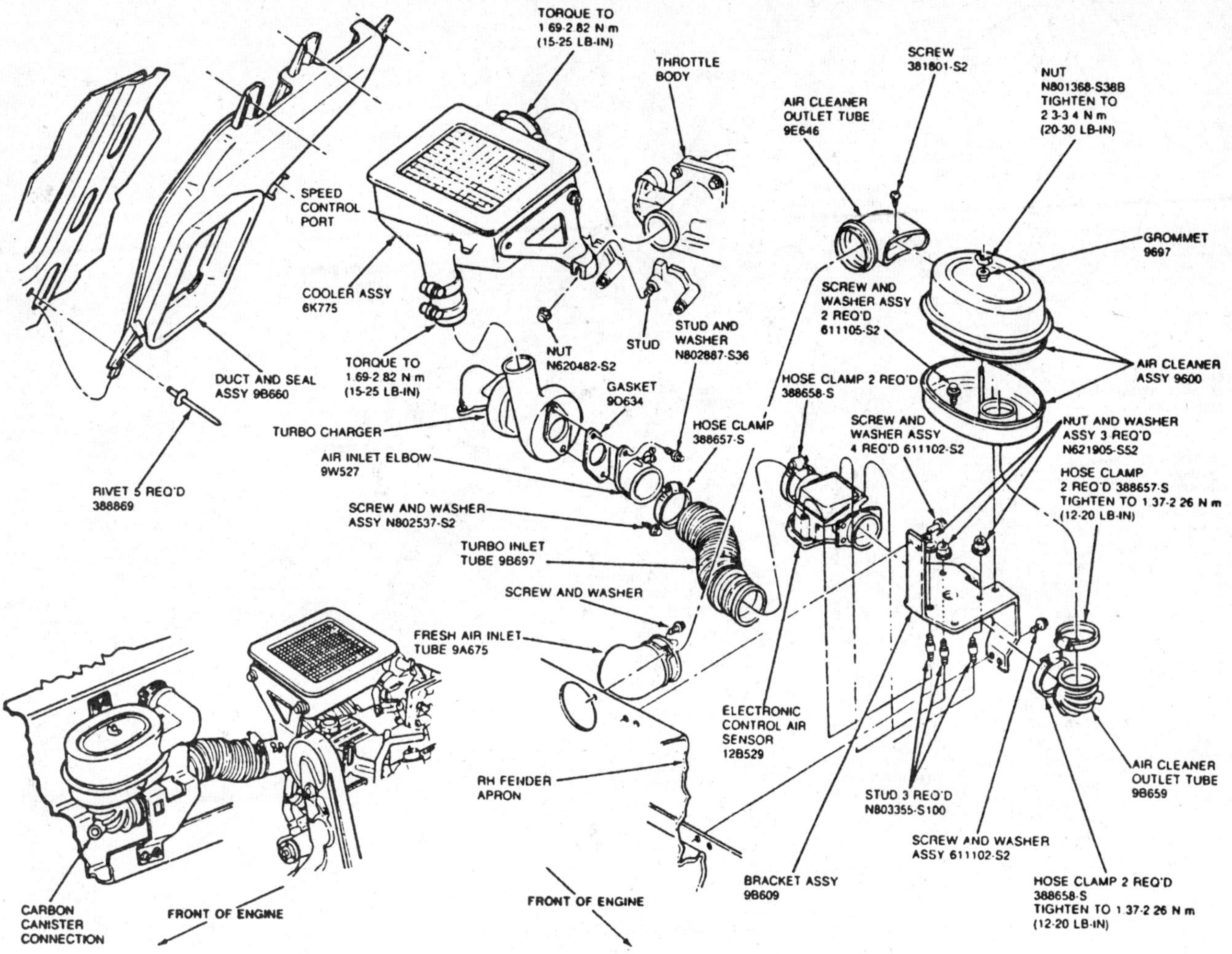

1987-4-140 Turbo air cleaner

Crankcase Ventilation Filter

Replace or inspect cleaner mounted crankcase ventilation filter (on models equipped) at the same time the air cleaner filter element is serviced. To replace the filter, simply remove the air cleaner top cover and pull the filter from its housing. Push a new filter into the housing and install the air cleaner cover. If the filter and plastic holder need replacement, remove the clip mounting the feed tube to the air cleaner housing (hose already removed) and remove the assembly from the air cleaner. Installation is the reverse of removal.

Fuel Filter

REPLACEMENT

CAUTION

NEVER SMOKE WHEN WORKING AROUND OR NEAR GASOLINE! MAKE SURE THAT THERE IS NO IGNITION SOURCE NEAR YOUR WORK AREA!

Carbureted Engines

6-200
6-232
8-255
8-302 w/Motorcraft 2150

8-351

A carburetor mounted gas filter is used. These filters screw into the float chamber. To replace one of these filters:

1. Wait until the engine is cold.

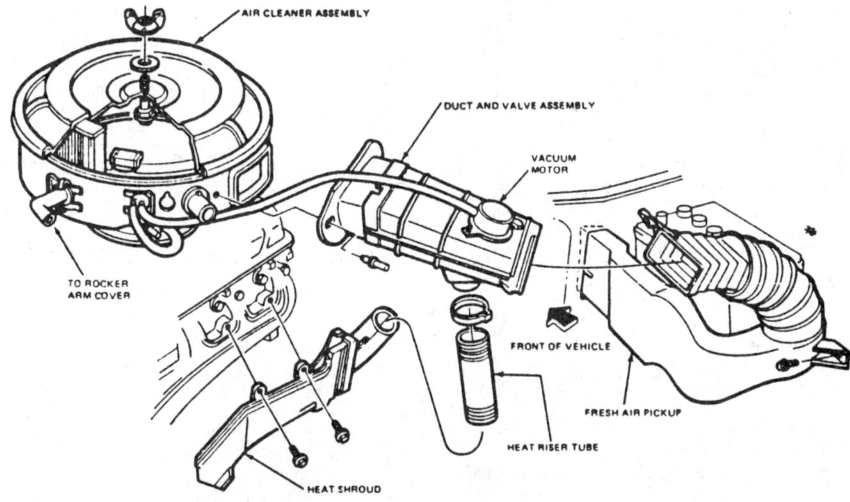

Typical 1980-83 V8 air cleaner

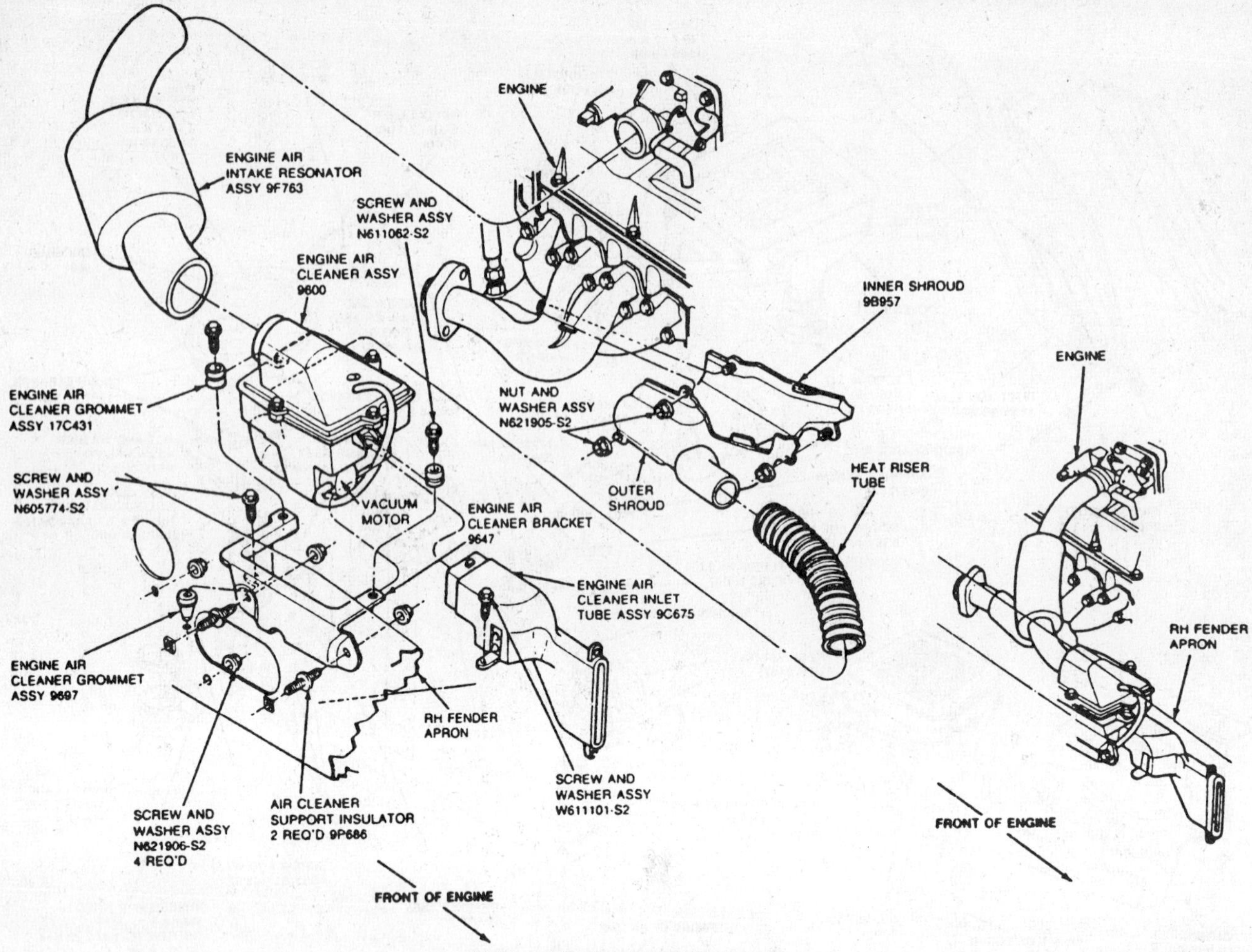

1987 non-Turbo 4-140 air cleaner

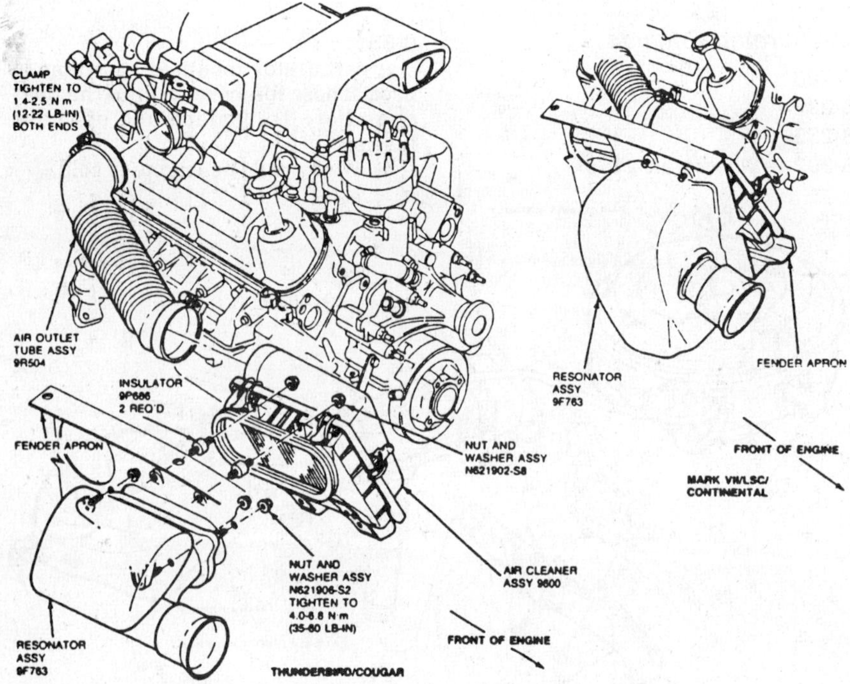

1986-87 8-302 air cleaner

2. Remove the air cleaner assembly.
3. Place some absorbant rags under the filter.
4. Remove the hose clamp and slide the rubber hose from the filter.

CAUTION

It is possible for gasoline to spray in all directions when removing the hose! This rarely happens, but it is possible, so protect your eyes!

5. Move the fuel line out of the way and unscrew the filter from the carburetor.
6. Coat the threads of the new filter

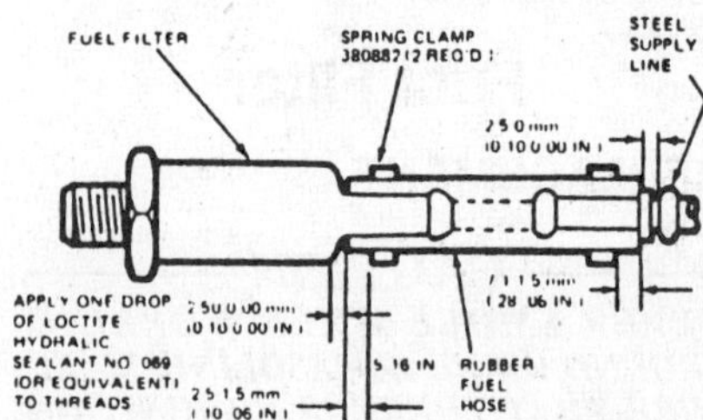

Screw-in type fuel filter with hose connection

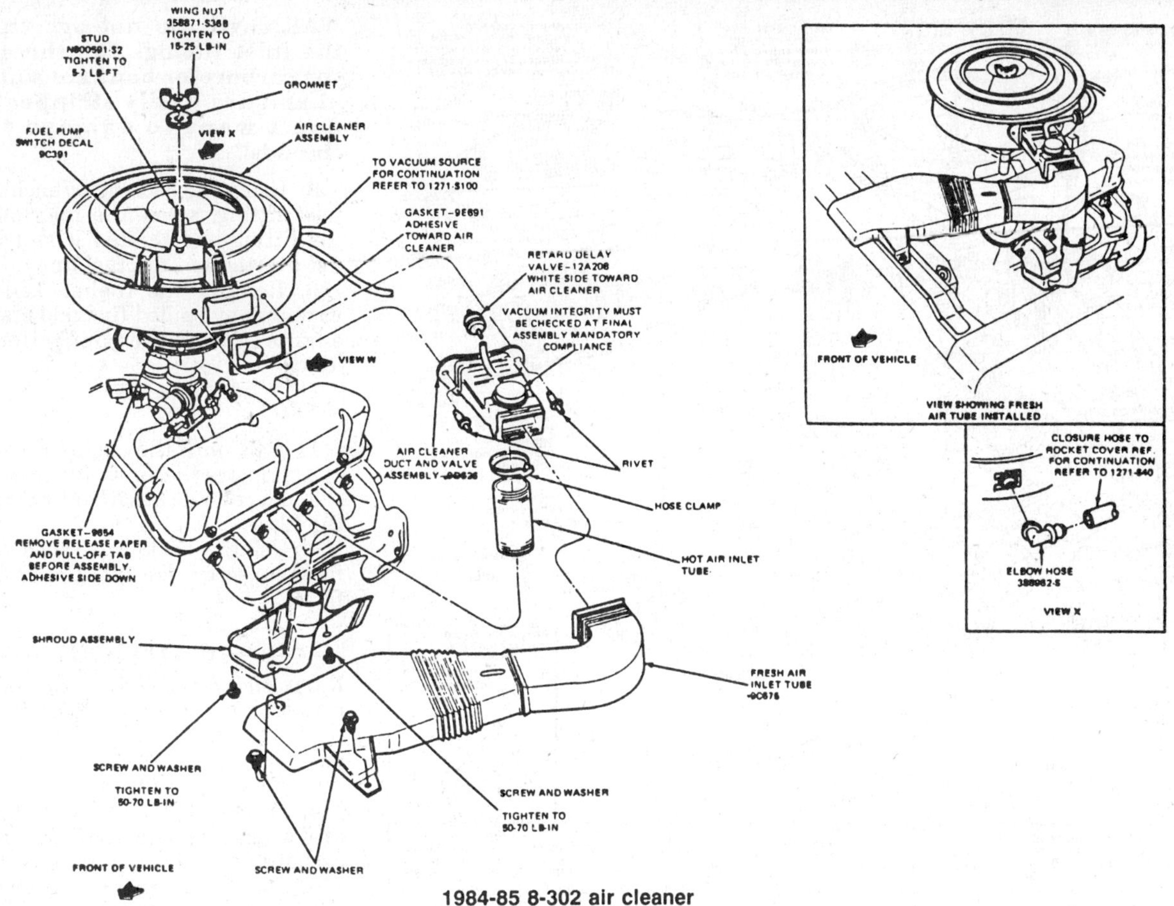

1984-85 8-302 air cleaner

with non-hardening, gasoline-proof sealer and screw it into place by hand. Tighten it snugly with the wrench.

WARNING: Do not overtighten the filter! The threads in the carburetor bowl are soft metal and are easily stripped! You don't want to damage these threads!!

7. Connect the hose to the new filter. Most replacement filters come with a new hose and clamps. Use them.

8. Remove the fuel-soaked rags, wipe up any spilled fuel and start the engine. Check the filter connections for leaks.

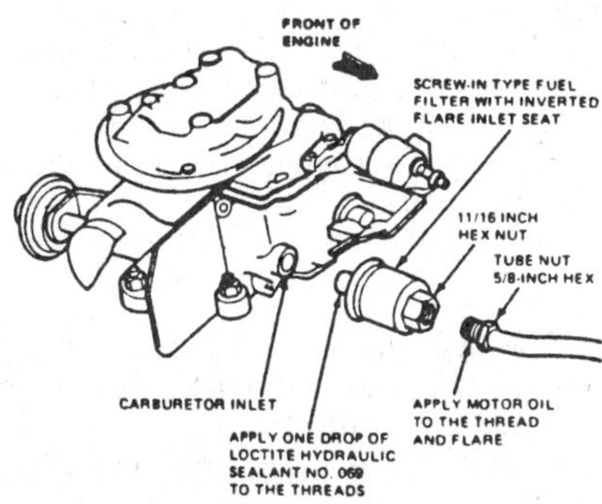

Screw-in type fuel filter with an inverted flare inlet seat

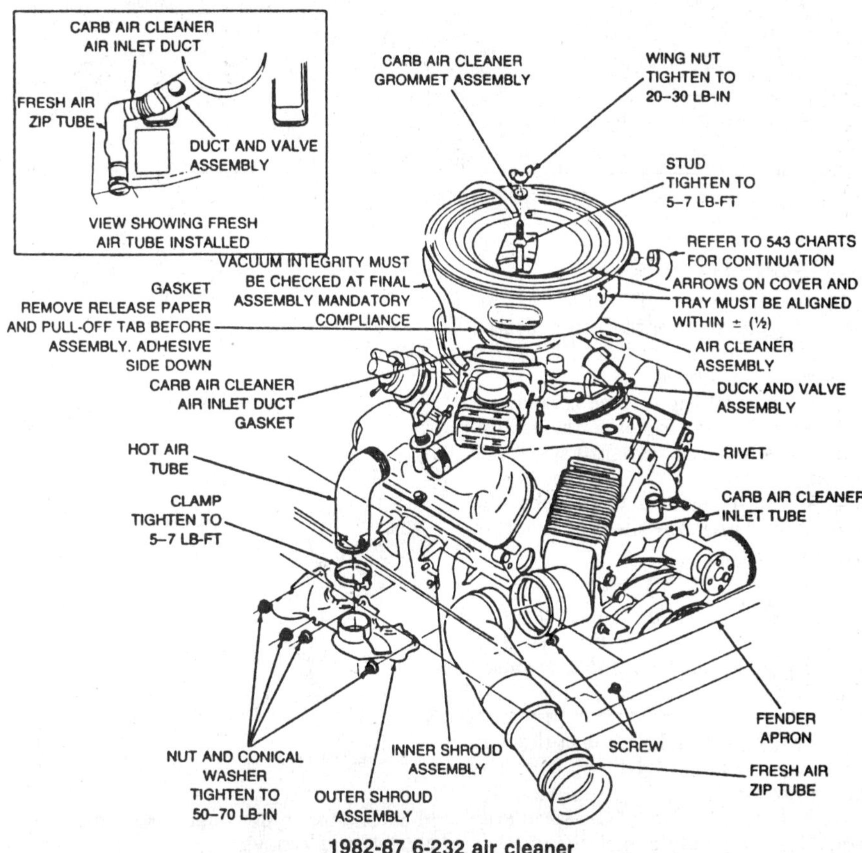

1982-87 6-232 air cleaner

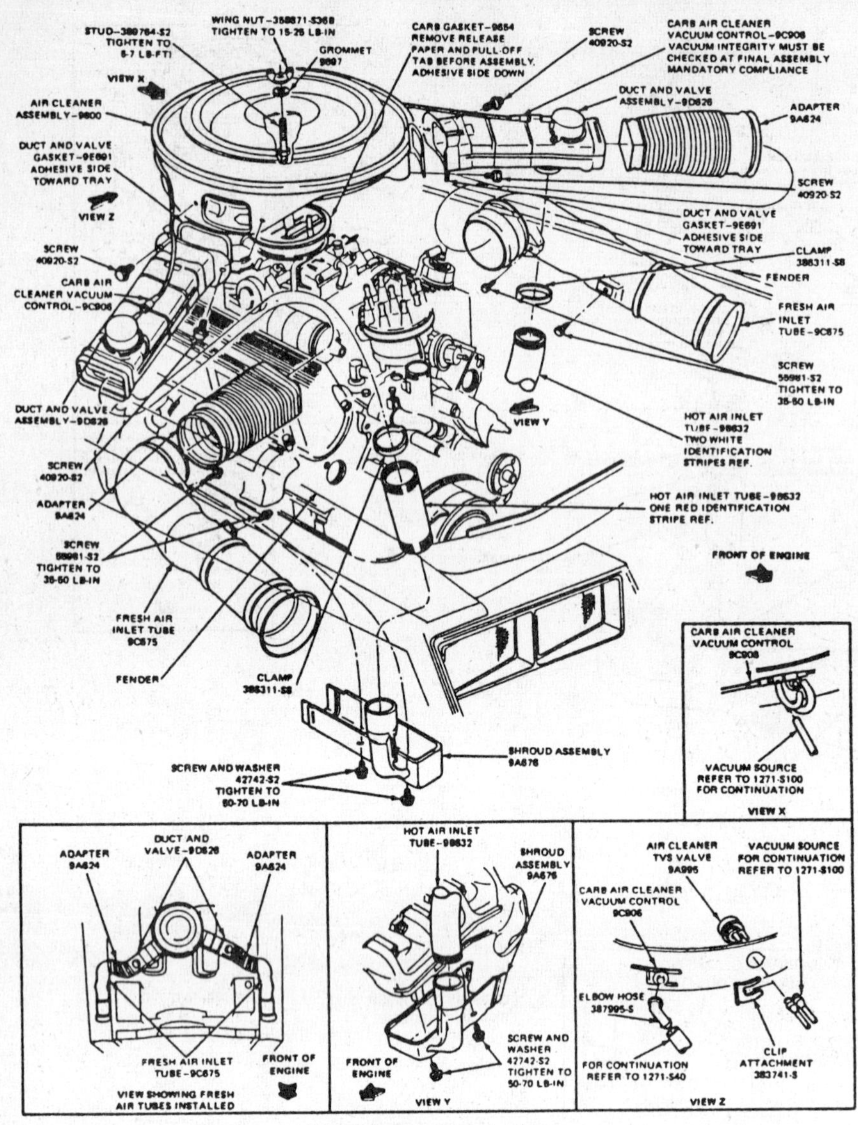

1983-85 8-302HO air cleaner

8-302 w/2700VV or 7200VV

Model 2700VV and 7200VV carburetors use a replaceable filter located behind the carburetor inlet fitting. To replace these filters:

1. Wait until the engine is cold.
2. Remove the air cleaner assembly.
3. Place some absorbant rags under the inlet fitting.
4. Using a back-up wrench on the inlet fitting, unscrew the fuel line from the inlet fitting.

CAUTION

It is possible for gasoline to spray in all directions when unscrewing the line! This rarely happens, but it is possible, so protect your eyes!

5. Move the fuel line out of the way and unscrew the inlet fiting from the carburetor.
6. Pull out the filter. The spring behind the filter may come with it.
7. Install the new filter. Some new filters come with a new spring. Use it.
8. Coat the threads of the inlet fitting with non-hardening, gasoline-proof sealer and screw it into place by hand. Tighten it snugly with the wrench.

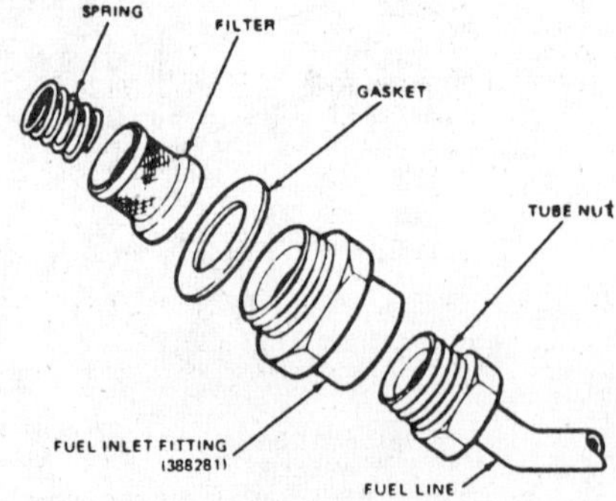

In-carburetor type filter used on the 2700VV and 7200VV

WARNING: Do not overtighten the inlet fitting! The threads in the carburetor bowl are soft metal and are easily stripped! You don't want to damage these threads!!

9. Using the back-up wrench on the inlet fitting, screw the fuel line into the fitting and tighten it snugly. Do not overtighten the fuel line!
10. Remove the fuel-soaked rags, wipe up any spilled fuel and start the engine. Check the connections for leaks.

4-140

1. Wait until the engine is cold.
2. Remove the air cleaner assembly.
3. Place some absorbant rags under the filter.
4. Using a back-up wrench on the filter, unscrew the fuel line from the filter.

CAUTION

It is possible for gasoline to spray in all directions when unscrewing the line! This rarely happens, but it is possible, so protect your eyes!

5. Move the fuel line out of the way and unscrew the filter from the carburetor.
6. Coat the threads of the new filter with non-hardening, gasoline-proof sealer and screw it into place by hand. Tighten it snugly with the wrench.

WARNING: Do not overtighten the filter! The threads in the carburetor bowl are soft metal and are easily stripped! You don't want to damage these threads!!

7. Using the back-up wrench on the filter, screw the fuel line into the filter and tighten it snugly. Do not overtighten the fuel line!
8. Remove the fuel-soaked rags, wipe up any spilled fuel and start the engine. Check the connections for leaks.

Fuel Injected Gasoline Engines

The inline filter is mounted on the same bracket as the fuel supply pump on the frame rail under the car, back by the fuel tank. To replace the filter:

1. Raise and support the rear end on jackstands.
2. With the engine off, depressurize the fuel system. See the Fuel System section.
3. Remove the quick-disconnect fittings at both ends of the filter. See the Fue System section.
4. Remove the filter and retainer from the bracket.
5. Remove the rubber insulator ring from the filter.

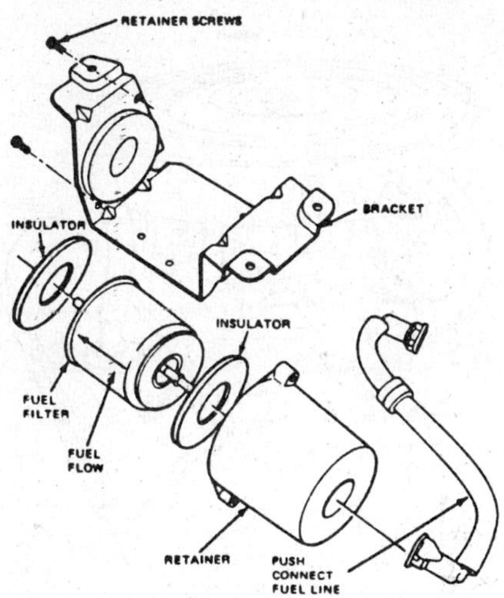

In-line fuel filter used on Thunderbird and Cougar with fuel injection

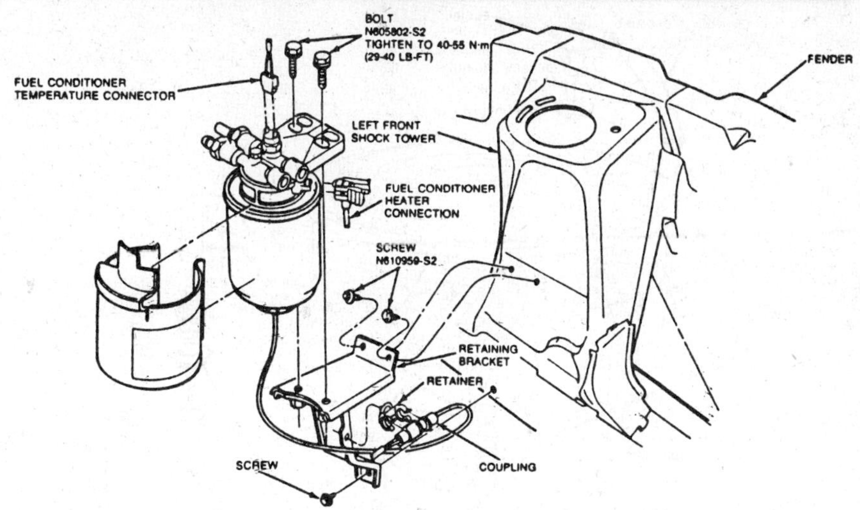

Diesel fuel filter

6. Remove the filter from the retainer.
7. Install the new filter into the retainer, noting the direction of the flow arrow.
8. Install a new rubber insulator ring.
9. Install the retainer and filter on the bracket and tighten the screws to 60 in.lb.
10. Install the fuel lines using new retainer clips.
11. Start the engine and check for leaks.

Diesel Engines

1. Drain the fuel from the fuel filter by opening the vent screw on the top of the filter and then depressing the drain valve on the bottom of the filter.
2. Disconnect the Water-in-Fuel sensor connector.
3. Remove the filter cartridge using a standard oil filter wrench, if necessary.
4. Remove the protective cover.
5. Remove the drain valve from the old filter and install it on the new filter.
6. Install the protective cover.
7. Coat the surface of the sealing gasket with engine oil and install the filter on the adapter. Turn the filter until the gasket contacts the sealing surface of the filter adapter.
8. Turn the filter an additional ½ turn.
9. Close the vent screw.
10. Start the engine, check for fuel leaks and tighten the filter further, if necessary.

PCV Valve

All models use a closed ventilation system with a sealed breather cap connected to the air cleaner by a rubber

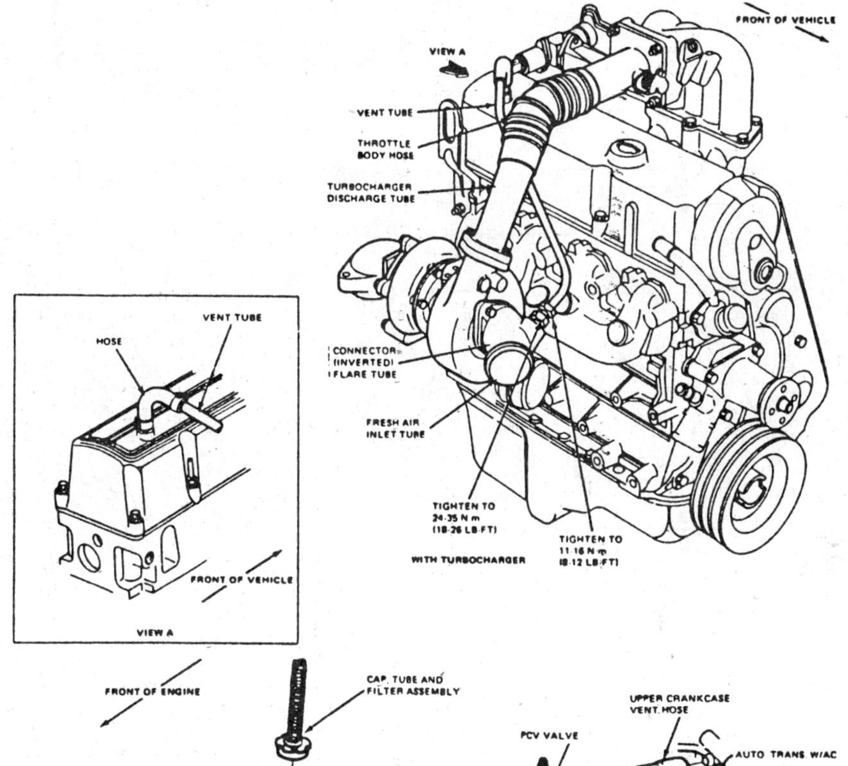

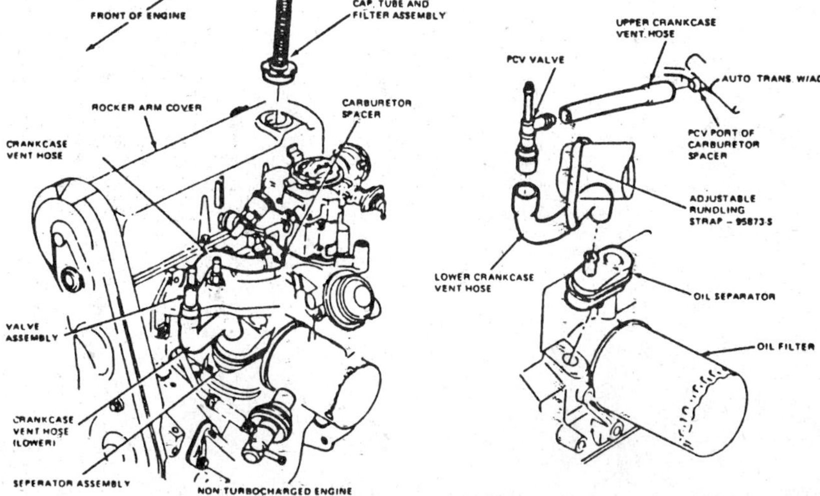

4-140 late model PCV system

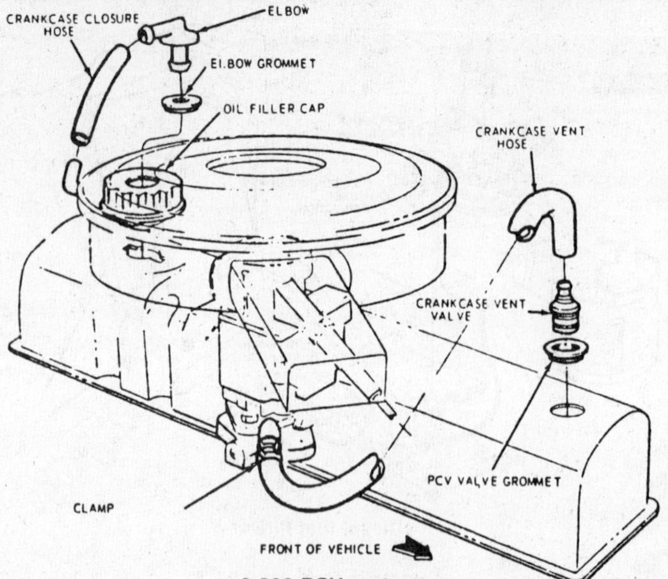

6-200 PCV system

WITH TURBOCHARGER

1984-87 4-140 PCV system

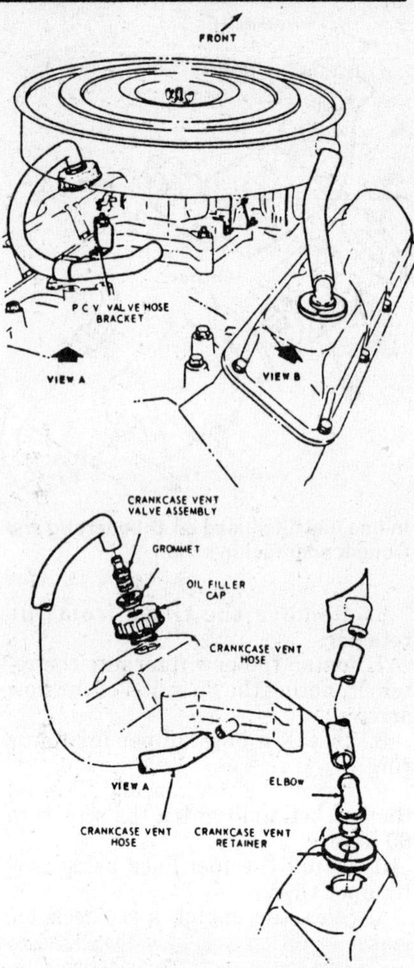

PCV valve installation – 302 V8

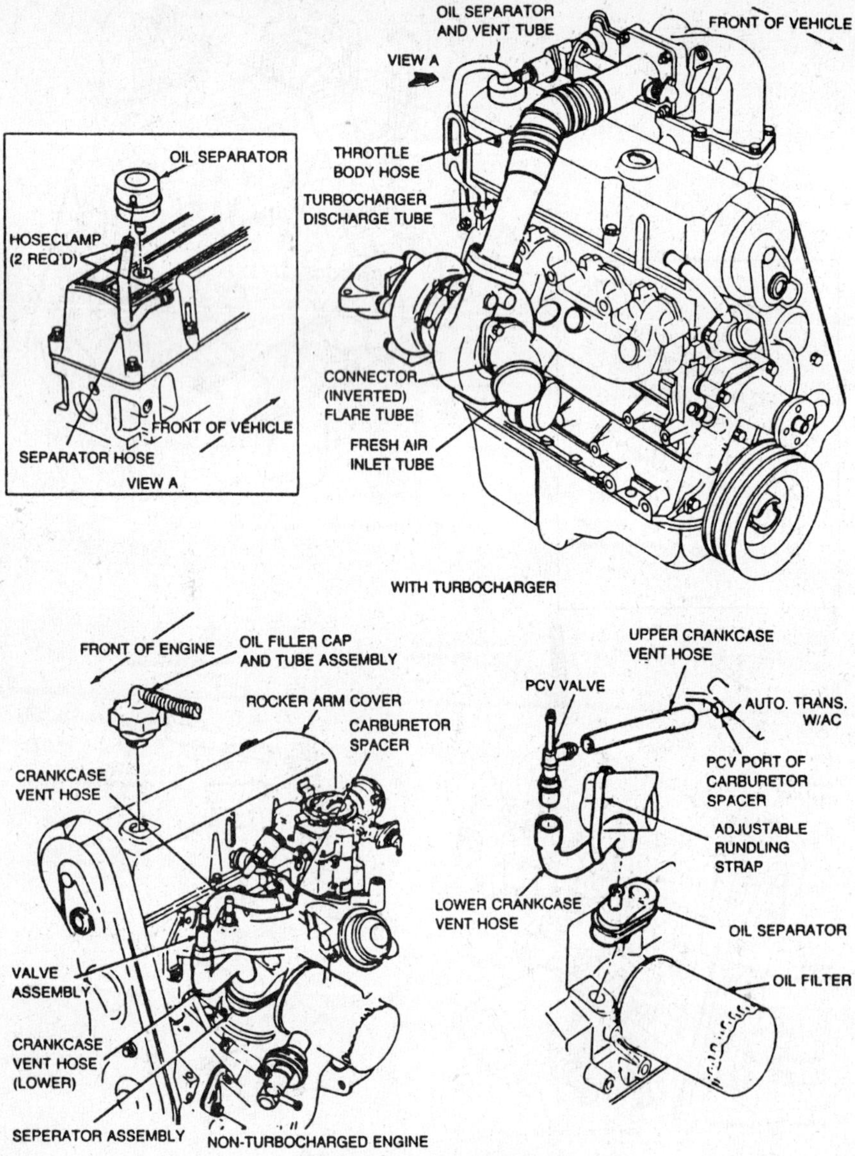

hose. The PCV valve is usually mounted in the valve cover and connected to the intake manifold by a rubber hose. Its task is to regulate the amount of crankcase (blow-by) gases which are recycled.

Since the PCV valve works under severe load it is very important that it be replaced at the interval specified in the maintenance chart. Replacement involves removing the valve from the grommet in the rocker arm cover disconnecting the hose(s) and installing a new valve. Do not attempt to clean a used valve.

Heat Riser

Some models are equipped with exhaust control (heat riser) valves located near the head pipe connection in the exhaust manifold. These valves aid initial warm-up in cold weather by restricting exhaust gas flow slightly. The heat generated by this restriction is transferred to the intake manifold where it results in improved fuel vaporization.

The operation of the exhaust control valve should be checked every 6 months or 6,000 miles. Make sure that the thermostatic spring is hooked on the stop pin and that the tension holds the valve shut. Rotate the counterweight by hand and make sure that it moves freely through about 90° of rotation. A valve which is operating properly will open when light finger pressure is applied (cold engine). Lubricate the shaft bushings with a mixture of penetrating oil and graphite. Operate the valve manually a few times to work in the lubricant.

Evaporative Emissions Canister

The canister functions to cycle the fuel vapor from the fuel tank and carburetor float chamber into the intake manifold and eventually into the cylinders for combustion. The activated charcoal element within the canister acts as a storage device for the fuel vapor at times when the engine operating condition will not permit fuel vapor to burn efficiently.

The only required service for the evaporative emissions canister is inspection at the interval specified in the maintenance chart. If the charcoal element is gummed up the entire canister should be replaced. Disconnect the canister purge hose(s), loosen the canister retaining bracket, lift out the canister. Installation is the reverse of removal.

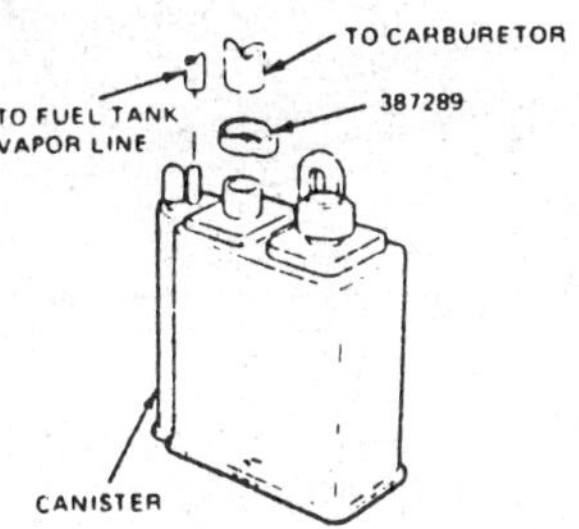

Typical carbon canister

Battery

FLUID LEVEL (EXCEPT MAINTENANCE FREE BATTERIES)

Check the battery electrolyte level at least once a month, or more often in hot weather or during periods of extended car operation. The level can be checked through the case on translucent polypropylene batteries; the cell caps must be removed on other models. The electrolyte level in each cell should be kept filled to the split ring inside, or the line marked on the outside of the case.

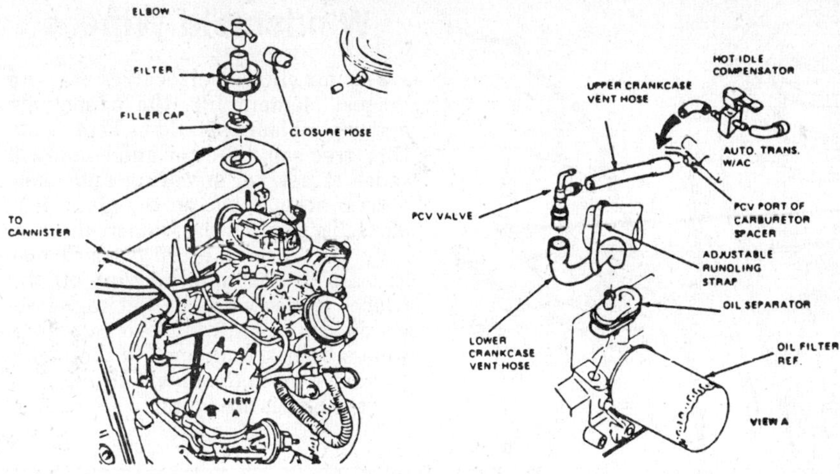

1982 4-140 PCV system

If the level is low, add only distilled water, or colorless, odorless drinking water, through the opening until the level is correct. Each cell is completely separate from the others, so each must be checked and filled individually.

If water is added in freezing weather, the car should be driven several miles to allow the water to mix with the electrolyte. Otherwise, the battery could freeze.

SPECIFIC GRAVITY (EXCEPT MAINTENANCE FREE BATTERIES)

At least once a year, check the specific gravity of the battery. It should be between 1.20 in.Hg and 1.26 in.Hg at room temperature.

The specific gravity can be check with the use of an hydrometer, an inexpensive instrument available from many sources, including auto parts

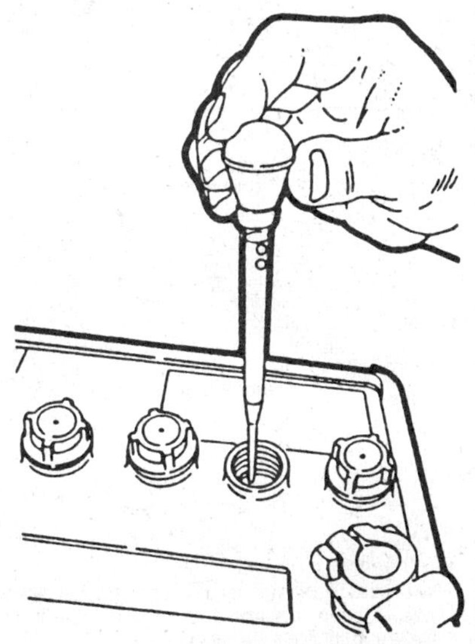

Checking the battery with a hydrometer

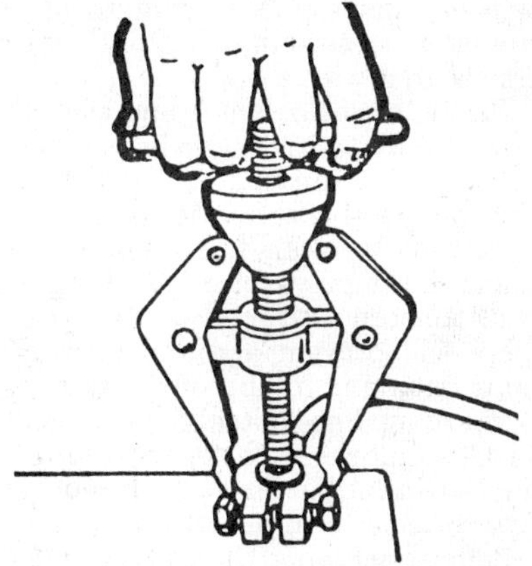

Use a puller to remove the battery cable

stores. The hydrometer has a squeeze bulb at one end and a nozzle at the other. Battery electrolyte is sucked into the hydrometer until the float is lifted from its seat. The specific gravity is then read by noting the position of the float. Generally, if after charging, the specific gravity between any two cells varies more than 50 points (0.50), the battery is bad and should be replaced.

It is not possible to check the specific gravity in this manner on sealed (maintenance free) batteries. Instead, the indicator built into the top of the case must be relied on to display any signs of battery deterioration. If the indicator is dark, the battery can be assumed to be OK. If the indicator is light, the specific gravity is low, and the battery should be charged or replaced.

CABLES AND CLAMPS

Once a year, the battery terminals and the cable clamps should be cleaned. Loosen the clamps and remove the cables, negative cable first. On batteries with posts on top, the use of a puller specially made for the pur-

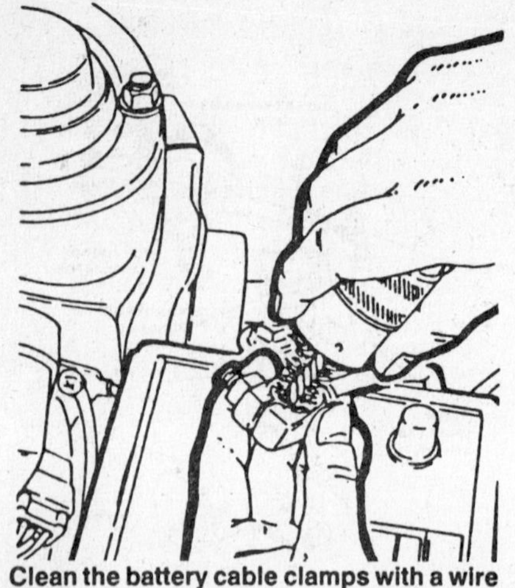

Clean the battery cable clamps with a wire brush

pose is recommended. These are inexpensive, and available in auto parts stores. Side terminal battery cables are secured with a bolt.

Clean the cable lamps and the battery terminal with a wire brush, until all corrosion, grease, etc., is removed and the metal is shiny. It is especially important to clean the inside of the clamp thoroughly, since a small deposit of foreign material or oxidation there will prevent a sound electrical connection and inhibit either starting or charging. Special tools are available for cleaning these parts, one type for conventional batteries and another type for side terminal batteries.

Before installing the cables, loosen the battery holddown clamp or strap, remove the battery and check the battery tray. Clear it of any debris, and check it for soundness. Rust should be wire brushed away, and the metal given a coat of anti-rust paint. Replace the battery and tighten the holddown clamp or strap securely, but be careful not to overtighten, which will crack the battery case.

After the clamps and terminals are clean, reinstall the cables, negative cable last; do not hammer on the clamps to install. Tighten the clamps securely, but do not distort them. Give the clamps and terminals a thin external coat of grease after installation, to retard corrosion.

Check the cables at the same time that the terminals are cleaned. If the cable insulation is cracked or broken, or if the ends are frayed, the cable should be replaced with a new cable of the same length and gauge.

CAUTION

Keep flame or sparks away from the battery; it gives off explosive hydrogen gas! Battery electrolyte contains sulphuric acid. If you should splash any on your skin or in your eyes, flush the affected area with plenty of clear water! If it lands in your eyes, get medical help immediately!

Windshield Wipers

For maximum effectiveness and longest element lift, the windshield and wiper blades should be kept clean. Dirt, tree sap, road tar and so on will cause streaking, smearing and blade deterioration if left on the glass. It is advisable to wash the windshield carefully with a commercial glass cleaner at least once a month. Wipe off the rubber blades with the wet rag afterwards. Do not attempt to move the wipers by hand; damage to the motor and drive mechanism will result.

If the blades are found to be cracked, broken or torn, they should be replaced immediately. Replacement intervals will vary with usage, although ozone deterioration usually limits blade lift to about one year. If the wiper pattern is smeared or streaked, or if the blade chatters across the glass, the elements should be replaced. It is easiest and most sensible to replace the elements in pairs.

There are basically three different types of refills, which differ in their method of replacement. One type has two release buttons, approximately ⅓ of the way up from the ends of the blade frame. Pushing the buttons

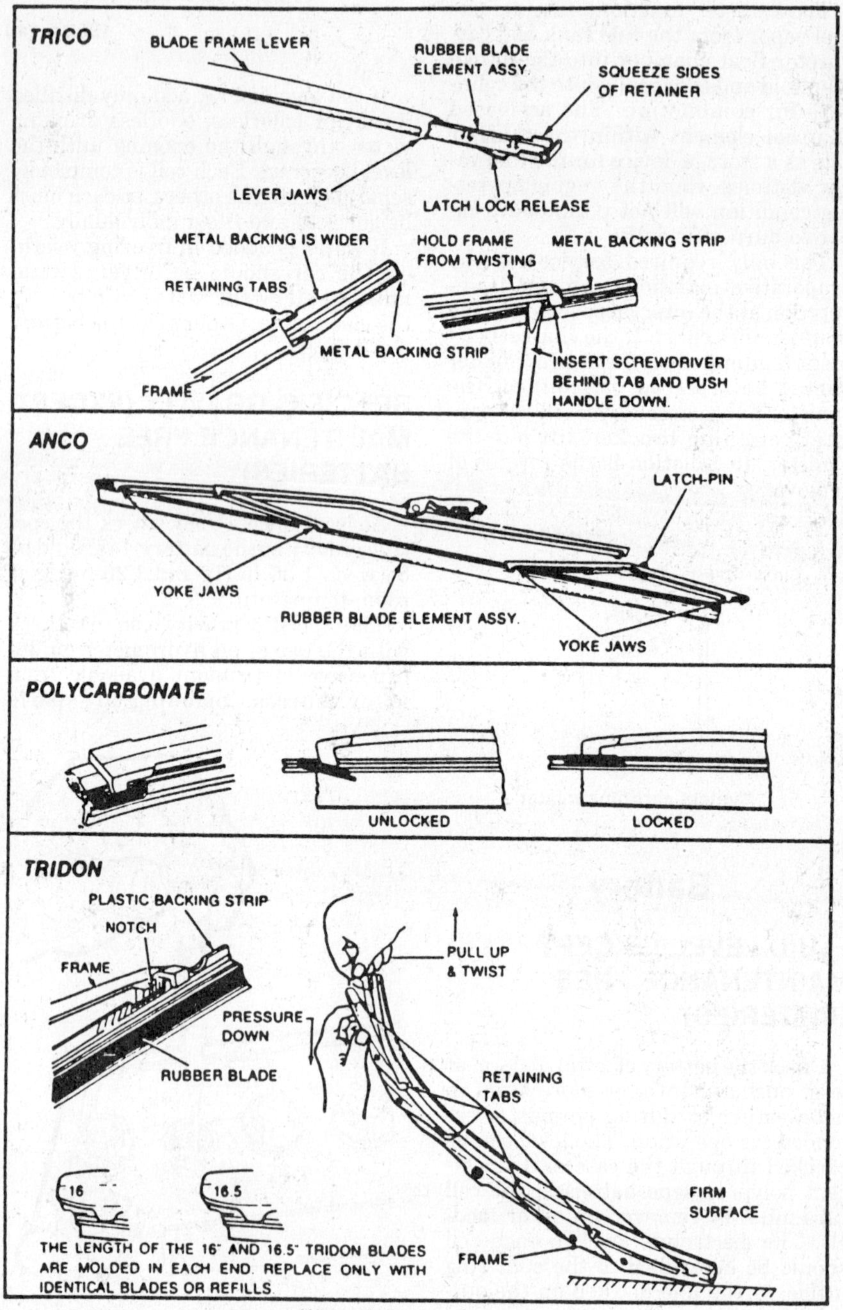

Wiper insert replacement

down releases a lock and allows the rubber filler to be removed from the frame. The new filler slides back into the frame and locks in place.

The second type of refill has two metal tabs which are unlocked by squeezing them together. The rubber filler can then be withdrawn from the frame jaws. A new refill is installed by inserting the refill into the front frame jaws and sliding it rear ward to engage the remaining frame jaws. There are usually four jaws. Be certain when installing that the refill is engaged in all of them. At the end of its travel, the tabs will lock into place on the front jaws of the wiper blade frame.

The third type is a refill made from polycarbonate. The refill has a simple locking device at one end which flexes downward out of the groove into which the jaws of the holder fit, allowing easy release. By sliding the new refill through all the jaws and pushing through the slight resistance when it reaches the end of its travel, the refill will lock into position.

Regardless of the type of refill used, make sure that all of the frame jaws are engaged as the refill is pushed into place and locked. The metal blade holder and frame will scratch the glass if allowed to touch it.

Belts

Once a year or at 12,000 mile intervals, the tension (and condition) of the alternator, power steering (if so equipped), air conditioning (if so equipped), and Thermactor air pump drive belts should be checked, and, if necessary, adjusted. Loose accessory drive belts can lead to poor engine cooling and diminish alternator, power steering pump, air conditioning compressor or Thermactor air pump output. A belt that is too tight places a severe strain on the water pump, alternator, power steering pump, compressor or air pump bearings.

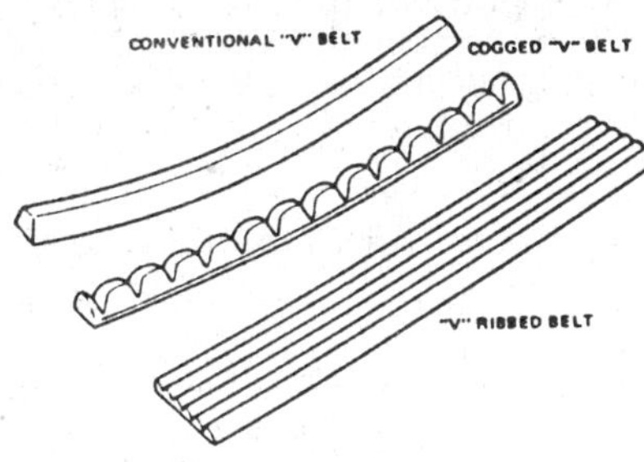

Drive belt types

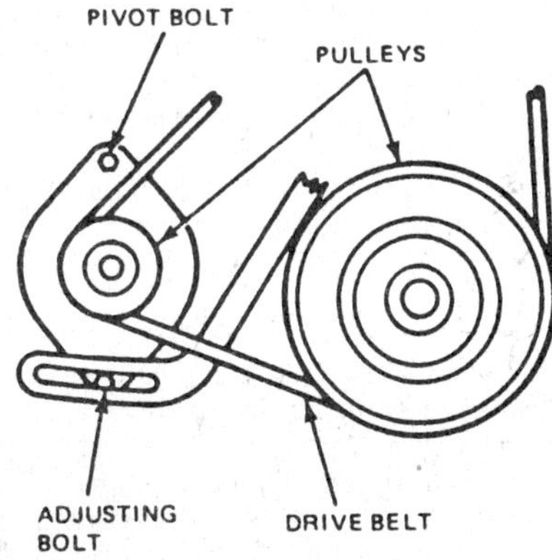

Alternator belt adjustment

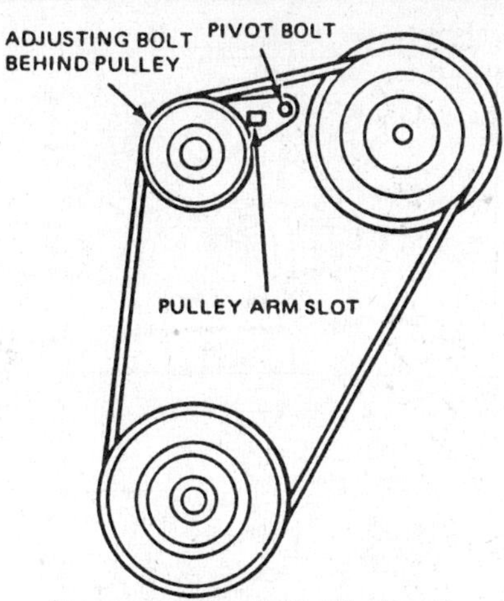

Air conditioning belt adjustment

Replace any belt that is so glazed, worn or stretched that it cannot be tightened sufficiently.

NOTE: The material used in late model drive belts is such that the belts do not show wear. Replace belts at least every three years.

On vehicles with matched belts, replace both belts. New ½", ⅜" and $^{15}/_{32}$" wide belts are to be adjusted to a tension of 140 lbs.; ¼" wide belts are adjusted to 80 lbs., measured on a belt tension gauge. Any belt that has been operating for a minimum of 10 minutes is considered a used belt. In the first 10 minutes, the belt should stretch to its maximum extent. After 10 minutes, stop the engine and recheck the belt tension. Belt tension for a used belt should be maintained at 110 lbs. (all except ¼" wide belts) or 60 lbs. (¼" wide belts). If a belt tension gauge is not available, the following procedures may be used.

ADJUSTMENTS FOR ALL EXCEPT THE SERPENTINE (SINGLE) BELT

CAUTION

On models equipped with an electric cooling fan, disconnect the negative battery cable or fan motor wiring harness connector before replacing or adjusting drive belts. The fan may come on, under certain circumstances, even though the ignition is off!

Alternator (Fan Drive) Belt

1. Position the ruler perpendicular to the drive belt at its longest straight run. Test the tightness of the belt by pressing it firmly with your thumb. The deflection should not exceed ¼".
2. If the deflection exceeds ¼", loosen the alternator mounting and adjusting arm bolts.
3. Place a 1" open-end or adjustable wrench on the adjusting ridge cast on the body, and pull on the wrench until the proper tension is achieved.

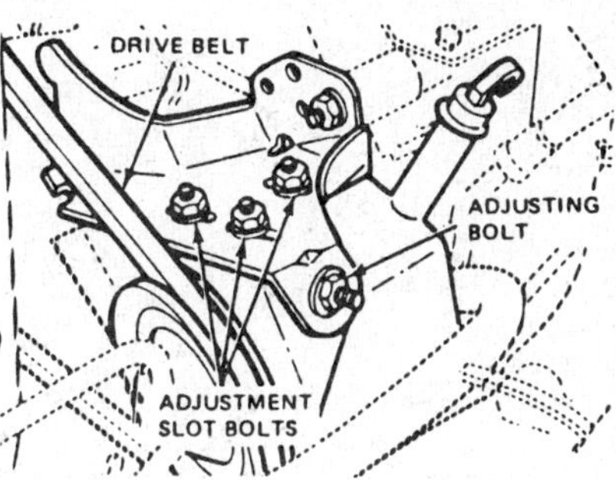

Power Steering belt adjustment (slider type)

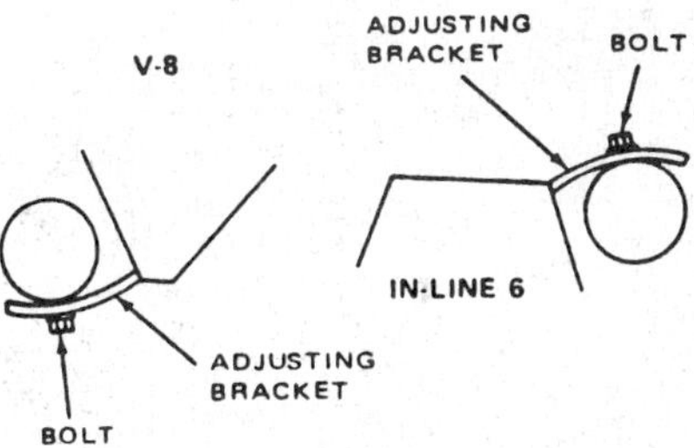

Air pump adjustment points

4. Holding the alternator in place to maintain tension, tighten the adjusting arm bolt. Recheck the belt tension. When the belt is properly tensioned, tighten the alternator mounting bolt.

Power Steering Drive Belt

4-140, 6-200

1. Hold a ruler perpendicular to the drive belt at its longest run, test the tightness of the belt by pressing it firmly with your thumb. The deflection should not exceed ¼".
2. To adjust the belt tension, loosen the adjusting and mounting bolts on the front face of the steering pump cover plate (hub side).
3. Using a pry bar or broom handle on the pump hub, move the power steering pump toward or away from the engine until the proper tension is reached. Do not pry against the reservoir as it is relatively soft and easily deformed.
4. Holding the pump in place, tighten the adjusting arm bolt and then recheck the belt tension. When the belt

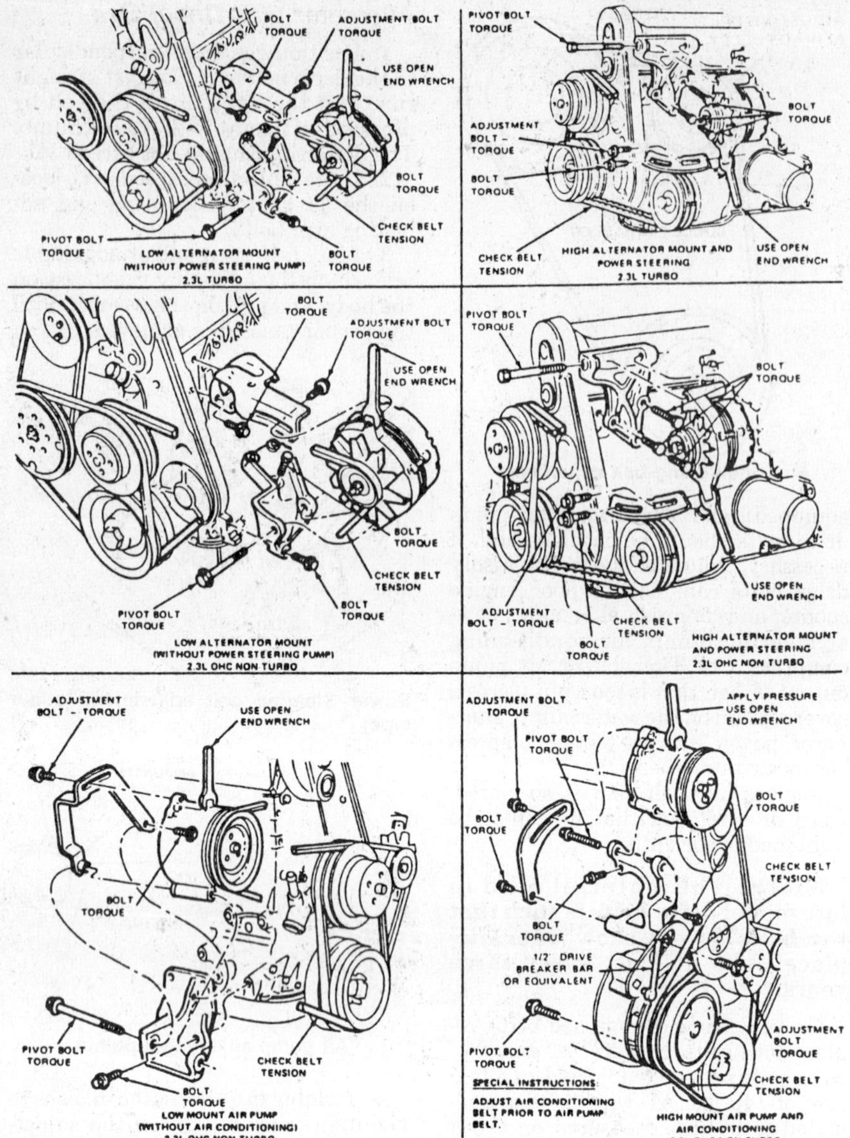

Belt installation late model 4-140 engines

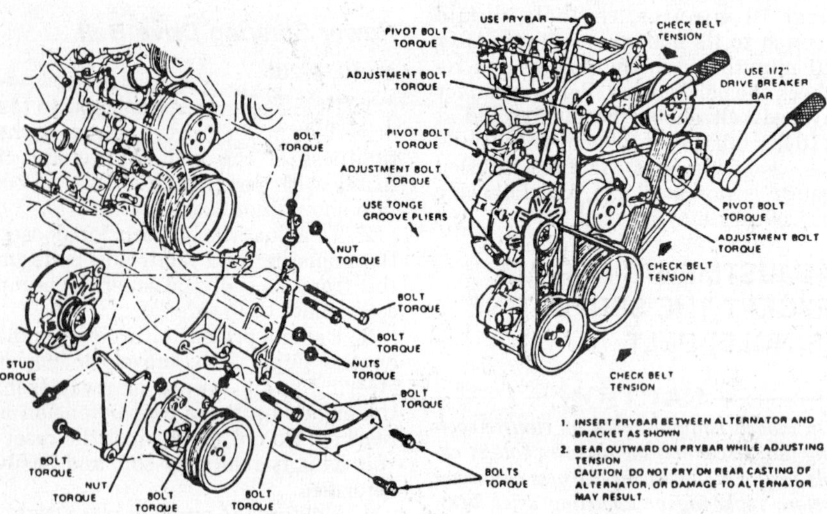

Belt installation late model V8 engines

is properly tensioned tighten the mounting bolts.

V8 MODELS

1. Position a ruler perpendicular to the drive belt at its longest run. Test the tightness of the belt by pressing it firmly with your thumb. The deflection should be about ¼".
2. To adjust the belt tension, loosen the three bolts in the three elongated adjusting slots at the power steering pump attaching bracket.
3. Turn the steering pump drive belt adjusting nut as required until the proper deflection is obtained. Turning the adjusting nut clockwise will increase tension and decrease deflection; counterclockwise will decrease tension and increase deflection.
4. Without disturbing the pump, tighten the three attaching bolts.

Air Conditioning Compressor Drive Belt

1. Position a ruler perpendicular to the drive belt at its longest run. Test the tightness of the belt by pressing it firmly with your thumb. The deflection should not exceed ¼".
2. If the engine is equipped with an idler pulley, loosen the idler pulley adjusting bolt, insert a pry bar between the pulley and the engine (or in the idler pulley adjusting slot), and adjust the tension accordingly. If the engine is not equipped with an idler pulley, the alternator must be moved to accomplish this adjustment, as outlined under Alternator (Fan Drive) Belt.
3. When the proper tension is reached, tighten the idler pulley adjusting bolt (if so equipped) or the alternator adjusting and mounting bolts.

Thermactor Air Pump Drive Belt

1. Position a ruler perpendicular to the drive belt at its longest run. Test the tightness of the belt by pressing it firmly with your thumb. The deflection should be about ¼".
2. To adjust the belt tension, loosen the adjusting arm bolt slightly. If necessary, also loosen the mounting belt slightly.
3. Using a pry bar or broom handle, pry against the pump rear cover to move the pump toward or away from the engine as necessary.

CAUTION

Do not pry against the pump housing itself, as damage to the housing may result.

4. Holding the pump in place, tighten the adjusting arm bolt and recheck the tension. When the belt is properly tensioned, tighten the mounting bolt.

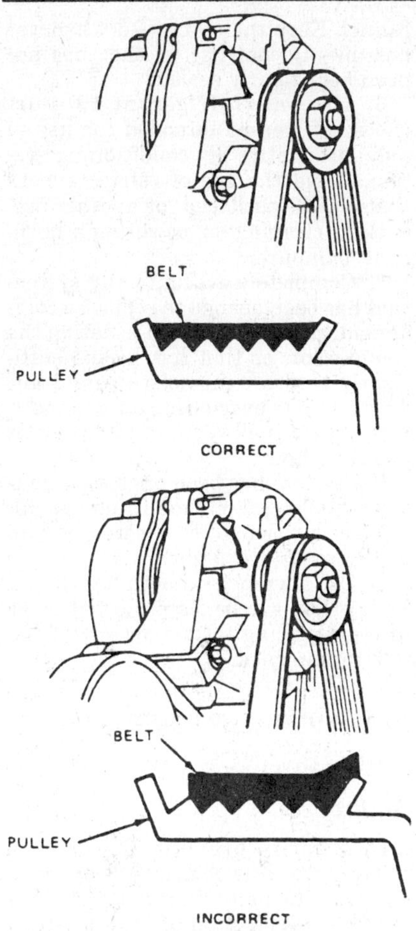

Ribbed belt installation

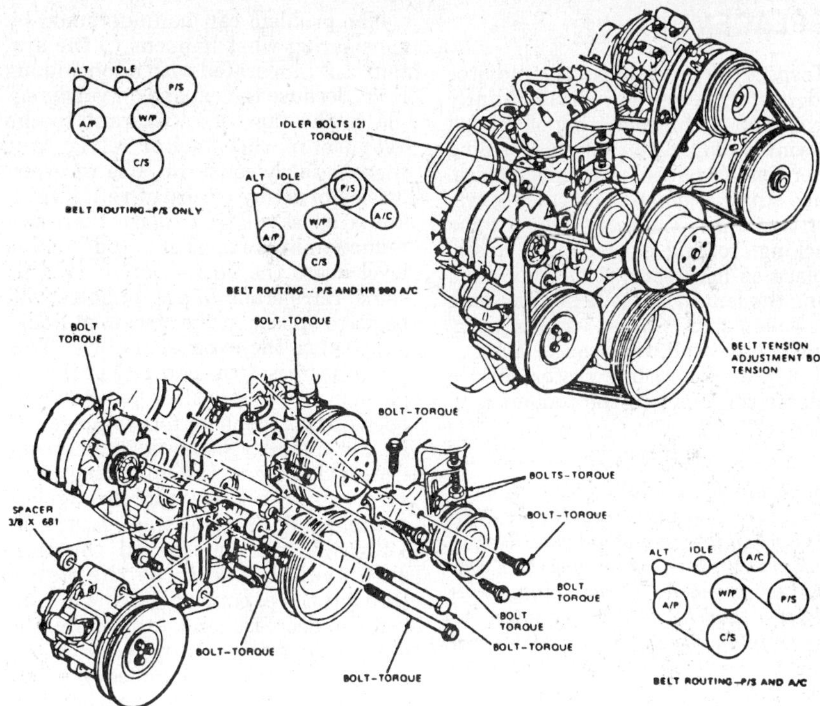

Belt installation late model V6 engines

SERPENTINE (SINGLE) DRIVE BELT MODELS

Most late models feature a single, wide, ribbed V-belt that drives the water pump, alternator, and (on some models) the air conditioner compressor. To install a new belt, loosen the bracket lock bolt, retract the belt tensioner with a pry bar and slide the old belt off of the pulleys. Slip on a new belt and release the tensioner and tighten the lock bolt. The spring powered tensioner eliminates the need for periodic adjustments.

WARNING: Check to make sure that the V-ribbed belt is located properly in all drive pulleys before applying tensioner pressure.

Hoses

CAUTION

On models equipped with an electric cooling fan, disconnect the negative battery cable, or fan motor wiring harness connector before replacing any radiator/heater hose. The fan may come on, under certain circumstances, even though the ignition is Off!

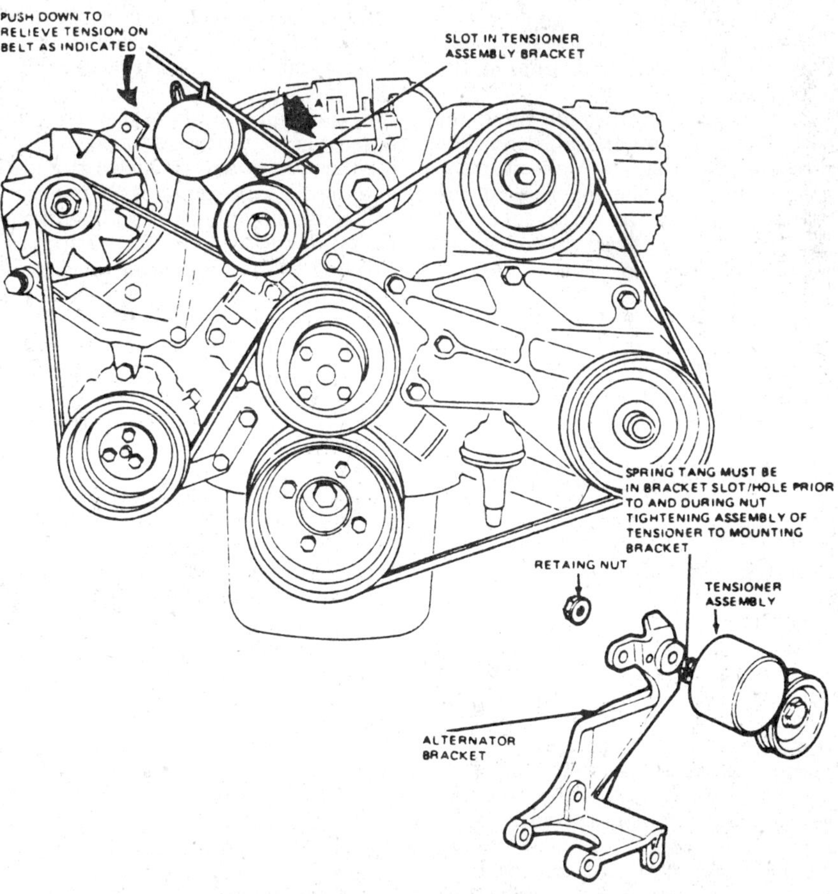

Serpentine belt adjustment

REPLACEMENT

Inspect the condition of the radiator and heater hoses periodically. Early spring and at the beginning of the fall or winter, when you are performing other maintenance, are good times. Make sure the engine and cooling system are cold. Visually inspect for cracking, rotting or collapsed hoses, replace as necessary. Run your hand along the length of the hose. If a weak or swollen spot is noted when squeezing the hose wall, replace the hose.

1. Drain the cooling system into a suitable container (if the coolant is to be reused).

CAUTION

When draining the coolant, keep in mind that cats and dogs are attracted by the ethylene glycol antifreeze, and are quite likely to drink any that is left in an uncovered container or in puddles on the ground. This will prove fatal in sufficient quantity. Always drain the coolant into a sealable container. Coolant should be reused unless it is contaminated or several years old.

2. Loosen the hose clamps at each end of the hose that requires replacement.
3. Twist, pull and slide the hose off the radiator, water pump, thermostat or heater connection.
4. Clean the hose mounting connections. Position the hose clamps on the new hose.
5. Coat the connection surfaces with a water resistant sealer and slide the hose into position. Make sure the hose clamps are located beyond the raised bead of the connector (if equipped) and centered in the clamping area of the connection.
6. Tighten the clamps to 20-30 in.lb. Do not overtighten.
7. Fill the cooling system.
8. Start the engine and allow it to reach normal operating temperature. Check for leaks.

Air Conditioning

GENERAL SERVICING PROCEDURES

The most important aspect of air conditioning service is the maintenance of pure and adequate charge of refrigerant in the system. A refrigeration system cannot function properly if a significant percentage of the charge is lost. Leaks are common because the severe vibration encountered in an automobile can easily cause a sufficient cracking or loosening of the air conditioning fittings. As a result, the extreme operating pressures of the system force refrigerant out.

The problem can be understood by considering what happens to the system as it is operated with a continuous leak. Because the expansion valve regulates the flow of refrigerant to the evaporator, the level of refrigerant there is fairly constant. The receiver-drier stores any excess of refrigerant, and so a loss will first appear there as a reduction in the level of liquid. As this level nears the bottom of the vessel, some refrigerant vapor bubbles will begin to appear in the stream of liquid supplied to the expansion valve. This vapor decreases the capacity of the expansion valve very little as the valve opens to compensate for its presence. As the quantity of liquid in the condenser decreases, the operating pressure will drop there and throughout the high side of the system. As the R-12 continues to be expelled, the pressure available to force the liquid through the expansion valve will continue to decrease, and, eventually, the valve's orifice will prove to be too much of a restriction for adequate flow even with the needle fully withdrawn.

At this point, low side pressure will start to drop, and severe reduction in cooling capacity, marked by freeze-up of the evaporator coil, will result. Eventually, the operating pressure of the evaporator will be lower than the pressure of the atmosphere surrounding it, and air will be drawn into the system wherever there are leaks in the low side.

Because all atmospheric air contains at least some moisture, water will enter the system and mix with the R-12 and the oil. Trace amounts of moisture will cause sludging of the oil, and corrosion of the system. Saturation and clogging of the filter-drier, and freezing of the expansion valve orifice will eventually result. As air fills the system to a greater and greater extend, it will interfere more and more with the normal flows of refrigerant and heat.

A list of general precautions that should be observed while doing this follows:

1. Keep all tools as clean and dry as possible.
2. Thoroughly purge the service gauges and hoses of air and moisture before connecting them to the system. Keep them capped when not in use.
3. Thoroughly clean any refrigerant fitting before disconnecting it, in order to minimize the entrance of dirt into the system.
4. Plan any operation that requires opening the system beforehand in order to minimize the length of time it will be exposed to open air. Cap or seal the open ends to minimize the entrance of foreign material.
5. When adding oil, pour it through an extremely clean and dry tube or funnel. Keep the oil capped whenever possible. Do not use oil that has not been kept tightly sealed.
6. Use only refrigerant 12. Purchase refrigerant intended for use in only automotive air conditioning system. Avoid the use of refrigerant 12 that may be packaged for another use, such as cleaning, or powering a horn, as it is impure.
7. Completely evacuate any system that has been opened to replace a component, other than when isolating the compressor, or that has leaked sufficiently to draw in moisture and air. This requires evacuating air and moisture with a good vacuum pump for at least one hour.

   If a system has been open for a considerable length of time it may be advisable to evacuate the system for up to 12 hours (overnight).
8. Use a wrench on both halves of a fitting that is to be disconnected, so as to avoid placing torque on any of the refrigerant lines.

ADDITIONAL PREVENTIVE MAINTENANCE CHECKS

Antifreeze

In order to prevent heater core freeze-up during A/C operation, it is necessary to maintain permanent type antifreeze protection of +15°F (-9°C) or lower. A reading of -15°F (-26°C) is ideal since this protection also supplies sufficient corrosion inhibitors for the protection of the engine cooling system.

WARNING: Do not use antifreeze longer than specified by the manufacturer.

Radiator Cap

For efficient operation of an air conditioned car's cooling system, the radiator cap should have a holding pressure which meets manufacturer's specifications. A cap which fails to hold these pressure should be replaced.

Condenser

Any obstruction of or damage to the condenser configuration will restrict the air flow which is essential to its efficient operation. It is therefore, a good rule to keep this unit clean and in proper physical shape.

NOTE: Bug screens are regarded as obstructions.

Condensation Drain Tube

This single molded drain tube expels the condensation, which accumulates on the bottom of the evaporator housing, into the engine compartment.

If this tube is obstructed, the air conditioning performance can be restricted and condensation buildup can spill over onto the vehicle's floor.

SAFETY PRECAUTIONS

Because of the importance of the necessary safety precautions that must be exercised when working with air conditioning systems and R-12 refrigerant, a recap of the safety precautions are outlined.

1. Avoid contact with a charged refrigeration system, even when working on another part of the air conditioning system or vehicle. If a heavy tool comes into contact with a section of copper tubing or a heat exchanger, it can easily cause the relatively soft material to rupture.
2. When it is necessary to apply force to a fitting which contains refrigerant, as when checking that all system couplings are securely tightened, use a wrench on both parts of the fitting involved, if possible. This will avoid putting torque on the refrigerant tubing. (It is advisable, when possible, to use tube or line wrenches when tightening these flare nut fittings.)
3. Do not attempt to discharge the system by merely loosening a fitting, or removing the service valve caps and cracking these valves. Precise control is possibly only when using the service gauges. Place a rag under the open end of the center charging hose while discharging the system to catch any drops of liquid that might escape. Wear protective gloves when connecting or disconnecting service gauge hoses.
4. Discharge the system only in a well ventilated area, as high concentrations of the gas can exclude oxygen and act as an anesthetic. When leak testing or soldering this is particularly important, as toxic gas is formed when R-12 contacts any flame.
5. Never start a system without first verifying that both service valves are backseated, if equipped, and that all fittings are throughout the system are snugly connected.
6. Avoid applying heat to any refrigerant line or storage vessel. Charging may be aided by using water heated to less than 125°F (52°C) to warm the refrigerant container. Never allow a refrigerant storage container to sit out in the sun, or near any other source of heat, such as a radiator.
7. Always wear goggles when working on a system to protect the eyes. If refrigerant contacts the eye, it is advisable in all cases to see a physician as soon as possible.
8. Frostbite from liquid refrigerant should be treated by first gradually warming the area with cool water, and then gently applying petroleum jelly. A physician should be consulted.
9. Always keep refrigerant can fittings capped when not in use. Avoid sudden shock to the can which might occur from dropping it, or from banging a heavy tool against it. Never carry a refrigerant can in the passenger compartment of a car.
10. Always completely discharge the system before painting the vehicle (if the paint is to be baked on), or before welding anywhere near the refrigerant lines.

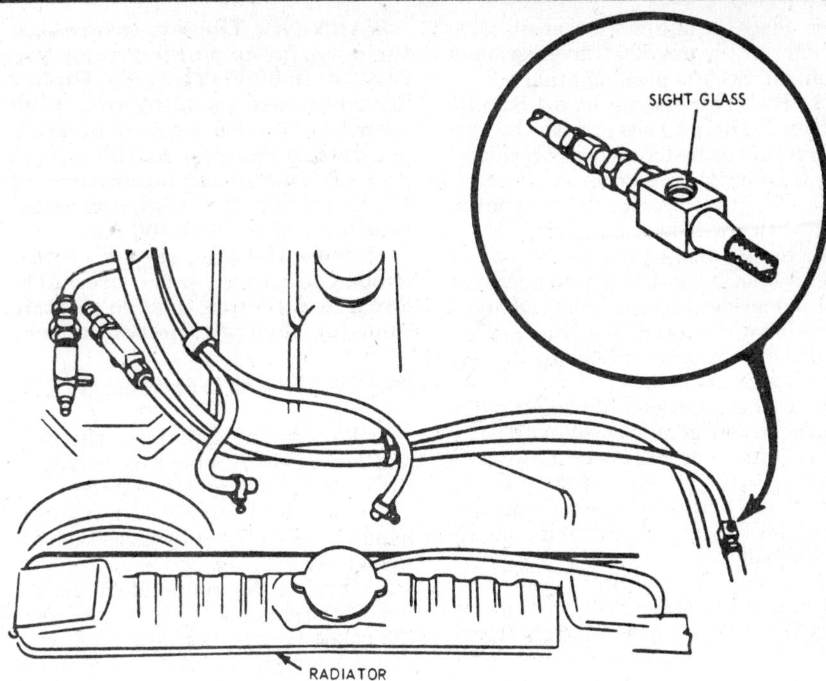

Typical air conditioning sight glass location

TEST GAUGES

Most of the service work performed in air conditioning requires the use of a set of two gauges, one for the high (head) pressure side of the system, the other for the low (suction) side.

The low side gauge records both pressure and vacuum. Vacuum readings are calibrated from 0 to 30 inches Hg and the pressure graduations read from 0 to no less than 60 psi.

The high side gauge measures pressure from 0 to at last 600 psi.

Both gauges are threaded into a manifold that contains two hand shut-off valves. Proper manipulation of these valves and the use of the attached test hoses allow the user to perform the following services:

1. Test high and low side pressures.
2. Remove air, moisture, and contaminated refrigerant.
3. Purge the system (of refrigerant).
4. Charge the system (with refrigerant).

The manifold valves are designed so that they have no direct effect on gauge readings, but serve only to provide for, or cut off, flow of refrigerant through the manifold. During all testing and hook-up operations, the valves are kept in a close position to avoid disturbing the refrigeration system. The valves are opened only to purge the system or refrigerant or to charge it.

INSPECTION

CAUTION

The compressed refrigerant used in the air conditioning system expands into the atmosphere at a temperature of –21.7°F (–30°C) or lower. This will freeze any surface, including your eyes, that it contacts. In addition, the refrigerant decomposes into a poisonous gas in the presence of a flame. Do not open or disconnect any part of the air conditioning system.

Sight Glass Check

You can safely make a few simple checks to determine if your air conditioning system needs service. The tests work best if the temperature is warm (about 70°F [21.1°C]).

NOTE: If your vehicle is equipped with an aftermarket air conditioner, the following system check may not apply. You should contact the manufacturer of the unit for instructions on systems checks.

1. Place the automatic transmission in Park or the manual transmission in Neutral. Set the parking brake.

2. Run the engine at a fast idle (about 1,500 rpm) either with the help of a friend or by temporarily readjusting the idle speed screw.

3. Set the controls for maximum cold with the blower on High.

4. Locate the sight glass in one of the system lines. Usually it is on the left alongside the top of the radiator.

5. If you see bubbles, the system must be recharged. Very likely there is a leak at some point.

6. If there are no bubbles, there is either no refrigerant at all or the system is fully charged. Feel the two hoses going to the belt-driven compressor. If they are both at the same temperature, the system is empty and must be recharged.

7. If one hose (high pressure) is warm and the other (low pressure) is cold, the system may be all right. However, you are probably making these tests because you think there is something wrong, so proceed to the next step.

8. Have an assistant in the car turn the fan control on and off to operate the compressor clutch. Watch the sight glass.

9. If bubbles appear when the clutch is disengaged and disappear when it is engaged, the system is properly charged.

10. If the refrigerant takes more than 45 seconds to bubble when the clutch is disengaged, the system is overcharged. This usually causes poor cooling at low speeds.

CAUTION

If it is determined that the system has a leak, it should be corrected as soon as possible. Leaks may allow moisture to enter and cause a very expensive rust problem.

NOTE: Exercise the air conditioner for a few minutes, every two weeks or so, during the cold months. This avoids the possibility of the compressor seals drying out from lack of lubrication.

TESTING THE SYSTEM

1. Connect a gauge set.

2. Close (clockwise) both gauge set valves.

4. Park the car in the shade, at least 5 feet from any walls. Start the engine, set the parking brake, place the transmission in NEUTRAL and establish an idle of 1,100-1,300 rpm.

5. Run the air conditioning system for full cooling, in the MAX or COLD mode.

6. The low pressure gauge should read 5-20 psi; the high pressure gauge should indicate 120-180 psi.

WARNING: These pressures are the norm for an ambient temperature of 70-80°F (21-27°F). Higher air temperatures along with high humidity will cause higher syustem pressures. At idle speed and an ambient temperature of 110°F (43°F), the high pressure reading can exceed 300 psi.

Under these extreme conditions, you can keep the pressures down by directing a large electric floor fan through the condenser.

DISCHARGING THE SYSTEM

1. Remove the caps from the high and low pressure charging valves in the high and low pressure lines.

2. Turn both manifold gauge set hand valves to the fully closed (clockwise) position.

3. Connect the manifold gauge set.

4. If the gauge set hoses do not have the gauge port actuating pins, install fitting adapters T71P-19703-S and R on the manifold gauge set hoses. If the car does not have a service access gauge port valve, connect the gauge set low pressure hose to the evaporator service access gauge port valve. A special adapter, T77L-19703-A, is required to attach the manifold gauge set to the high pressure service access gauge port valve.

5. Place the end of the center hose away from you and the car.

6. Open the low pressure gauge valve slightly and allow the system pressure to bleed off.

7. Whe the system is just about empty, open the high pressure valve very slowly to avoid losing an excessive amount of refrigerant oil. Allow any remaining refrigerant to escape.

EVACUATING THE SYSTEM

NOTE: This procedure requires the use of a vacuum pump.

1. Connect the manifold gauge set.

2. Discharge the system.

3. On 1983 and later models, make sure that the low pressure gauge set hose is connected to the low pressure service gauge port on the top center of the accumulator/drier assembly and the high pressure hose connected to the high pressure service gauge port on the compressor discharge line.

4. Connect the center service hose to the inlet fitting of the vacuum pump.

5. Turn both gauge set valves to the wide open position.

6. Start the pump and note the low side gauge reading.

7. Operate the pump until the low pressure gauge reads 25-30 in.Hg. Continue running the vacuum pump for 10 minutes more. If you've replaced some component in the system, run the pump for an additional 20-30 minutes.

8. Leak test the system. Close both gauge set valves. Turn off the pump. The needle should remain stationary at the point at which the pump was turned off. If the needle drops to zero rapidly, there is a leak in the system which must be repaired.

LEAK TESTING

Some leak tests can be performed with a soapy water solution. There must be at least a ½ lb. charge in the system for a leak to be detected. The most extensive leak tests are performed with either a Halide flame type leak tester or the more preferable electronic leak tester.

In either case, the equipment is expensive, and, the use of a Halide detector can be **extremely** hazardous!

CHARGING THE SYSTEM

CAUTION

NEVER OPEN THE HIGH PRESSURE SIDE WITH A CAN OF REFRIGERANT CONNECTED TO THE SYSTEM! OPENING THE HIGH PRESSURE SIDE WILL OVERPRESSURIZE THE CAN, CAUSING IT TO EXPLODE!

1980-82

1. Connect the gauge set.

2. Close (clockwise) both gauge set valves.

3. Connect the center hose to the refrigerant can opener valve.

CAUTION

KEEP THE CAN IN AN UPRIGHT POSITION!

4. Make sure the can opener valve is closed, that is, the needle is raised, and connect the valve to the can. Open the valve, puncturing the can with the needle.

5. Loosen the center hose fitting at the pressure gauge, allowing refrigerant to purge the hose of air.

6. Open the low side gauge set valve and the can valve.

7. Start the engine and turn the air conditioner to the maximum cooling mode. Run the engine at about 1,500 rpm. The compressor will operate and pull refrigerant gas into the system.

NOTE: To help speed the process, the can may be placed, upright, in a pan of warm water, not exceeding 125°F (52°C).

8. If more than one can of refrigerant is needed, close the can valve and

gauge set low side valve when the can is empty and connect a new can to the opener. Repeat the charging process until the sight glass indicates a full charge. The frost line on the outside of the can will indicate what portion of the can has been used.

CAUTION

NEVER ALLOW THE HIGH PRESSURE SIDE READING TO EXCEED 240 psi!

9. When the charging process has been completed, close the gauge set valve and can valve. Run the system for at least five minutes to allow it to normalize. Low pressure side reading should be 4-25 psi; high pressure reading should be 120-210 psi at an ambient temperature of 70-90°F (21-32°C).

10. Loosen both service hoses at the gauges to allow any refrigerant to escape. Remove the gauge set and install the dust caps on the service valves.

NOTE: Multi-can dispensers are available which allow a simultaneous hook-up of up to four 1 lb. cans of R-12.

CAUTION

Never exceed the recommended maximum charge for the system.

The maximum charge for systems is:
1980-81: 3½ lbs.
1982: 2½ lbs.

1983-87

1. Connect the gauge set.
2. Close (clockwise) both gauge set valves.
3. Connect the center hose to the refrigerant can opener valve.
4. Make sure the can opener valve is closed, that is, the needle is raised, and connect the valve to the can. Open the valve, puncturing the can with the needle.
5. Loosen the center hose fitting at the pressure gauge, allowing refrigerant to purge the hose of air. When the air is bled, tighten the fitting.

CAUTION

IF THE LOW PRESSURE GAUGE SET HOSE IS NOT CONNECTED TO THE ACCUMULATOR/DRIER, KEEP THE CAN IN AN UPRIGHT POSITION!

6. Disconnect the wire harness snap-lock connector from the clutch cycling pressure switch and install a jumper wire across the two terminals of the connector.
7. Open the low side gauge set valve and the can valve.
8. Allow refrigerant to be drawn into the system.
9. When no more refrigerant is drawn into the system, start the engine and run it at about 1,500 rpm. Turn on the system and operate it at the full high position. The compressor will operate and pull refrigerant gas into the system.

NOTE: To help speed the process, the can may be placed, upright, in a pan of warm water, not exceeding 125°F (52°C).

10. If more than one can of refrigerant is needed, close the can valve and gauge set low side valve when the can is empty and connect a new can to the opener. Repeat the charging process until the sight glass indicates a full charge. The frost line on the outside of the can will indicate what portion of the can has been used.

CAUTION

NEVER ALLOW THE HIGH PRESSURE SIDE READING TO EXCEED 240 psi!

11. When the charging process has been completed, close the gauge set valve and can valve. Remove the jumper wire and reconnect the cycling clutch wire. Run the system for at least five minutes to allow it to normalize. Low pressure side reading should be 4-25 psi; high pressure reading should be 120-210 psi at an ambient temperature of 70-90°F (21-32°C).

12. Loosen both service hoses at the gauges to allow any refrigerant to escape. Remove the gauge set and install the dust caps on the service valves.

NOTE: Multi-can dispensers are available which allow a simultaneous hook-up of up to four 1 lb. cans of R-12.

CAUTION

Never exceed the recommended maximum charge for the system!

The maximum charge for systems is 2½ lb.

Troubleshooting Basic Air Conditioning Problems

Problem	Cause	Solution
There's little or no air coming from the vents (and you're sure it's on)	• The A/C fuse is blown • Broken or loose wires or connections • The on/off switch is defective	• Check and/or replace fuse • Check and/or repair connections • Replace switch
The air coming from the vents is not cool enough	• Windows and air vent wings open • The compressor belt is slipping • Heater is on • Condenser is clogged with debris • Refrigerant has escaped through a leak in the system • Receiver/drier is plugged	• Close windows and vent wings • Tighten or replace compressor belt • Shut heater off • Clean the condenser • Check system • Service system
The air has an odor	• Vacuum system is disrupted • Odor producing substances on the evaporator case • Condensation has collected in the bottom of the evaporator housing	• Have the system checked/repaired • Clean the evaporator case • Clean the evaporator housing drains
System is noisy or vibrating	• Compressor belt or mountings loose • Air in the system	• Tighten or replace belt; tighten mounting bolts • Have the system serviced
Sight glass condition		
Constant bubbles, foam or oil streaks	• Undercharged system	• Charge the system
Clear sight glass, but no cold air	• No refrigerant at all	• Check and charge the system
Clear sight glass, but air is cold	• System is OK	
Clouded with milky fluid	• Receiver drier is leaking dessicant	• Have system checked
Large difference in temperature of lines	• System undercharged	• Charge and leak test the system
Compressor noise	• Broken valves • Overcharged • Incorrect oil level • Piston slap • Broken rings • Drive belt pulley bolts are loose	• Replace the valve plate • Discharge, evacuate and install the correct charge • Isolate the compressor and check the oil level. Correct as necessary. • Replace the compressor • Replace the compressor • Tighten with the correct torque specification
Excessive vibration	• Incorrect belt tension • Clutch loose • Overcharged • Pulley is misaligned	• Adjust the belt tension • Tighten the clutch • Discharge, evacuate and install the correct charge • Align the pulley
Condensation dripping in the passenger compartment	• Drain hose plugged or improperly positioned • Insulation removed or improperly installed	• Clean the drain hose and check for proper installation • Replace the insulation on the expansion valve and hoses
Frozen evaporator coil	• Faulty thermostat • Thermostat capillary tube improperly installed • Thermostat not adjusted properly	• Replace the thermostat • Install the capillary tube correctly • Adjust the thermostat

Troubleshooting Basic Air Conditioning Problems (cont.)

Problem	Cause	Solution
Low side low—high side low	• System refrigerant is low	• Evacuate, leak test and charge the system
	• Expansion valve is restricted	• Replace the expansion valve
Low side high—high side low	• Internal leak in the compressor—worn	• Remove the compressor cylinder head and inspect the compressor. Replace the valve plate assembly if necessary. If the compressor pistons, rings or cylinders are excessively worn or scored replace the compressor
	• Cylinder head gasket is leaking	• Install a replacement cylinder head gasket
	• Expansion valve is defective	• Replace the expansion valve
	• Drive belt slipping	• Adjust the belt tension
Low side high—high side high	• Condenser fins obstructed	• Clean the condenser fins
	• Air in the system	• Evacuate, leak test and charge the system
	• Expansion valve is defective	• Replace the expansion valve
	• Loose or worn fan belts	• Adjust or replace the belts as necessary
Low side low—high side high	• Expansion valve is defective	• Replace the expansion valve
	• Restriction in the refrigerant hose	• Check the hose for kinks—replace if necessary
	• Restriction in the receiver/drier	• Replace the receiver/drier
	• Restriction in the condenser	• Replace the condenser
Low side and high side normal (inadequate cooling)	• Air in the system	• Evacuate, leak test and charge the system
	• Moisture in the system	• Evacuate, leak test and charge the system

Front Wheel Bearings

ADJUSTMENT

The front wheels each rotate on a set of opposed, tapered roller bearings as shown in the accompanying illustration. The grease retainer at the inside of the hub prevents lubricant from leaking into the brake drum.

1. Raise and support the front end on jackstands.
2. Remove the grease cap and remove excess grease from the end of the spindle.
3. Remove the cotter pin and nut lock shown in the illustration.
4. Rotate the wheel, hub and drum assembly while tightening the adjusting nut to 17-25 ft.lb. in order to seat the bearings.
5. Back off the adjusting nut ½, then retighten the adjusting nut to 10-15 in.lb.
6. Locate the nut lock on the adjusting nut so that the castellations on the lock are lined up with the cotter pin hole in the spindle.
7. Install the new cotter pin, bending the ends of the cotter pin around the castellated flange of the nut lock.

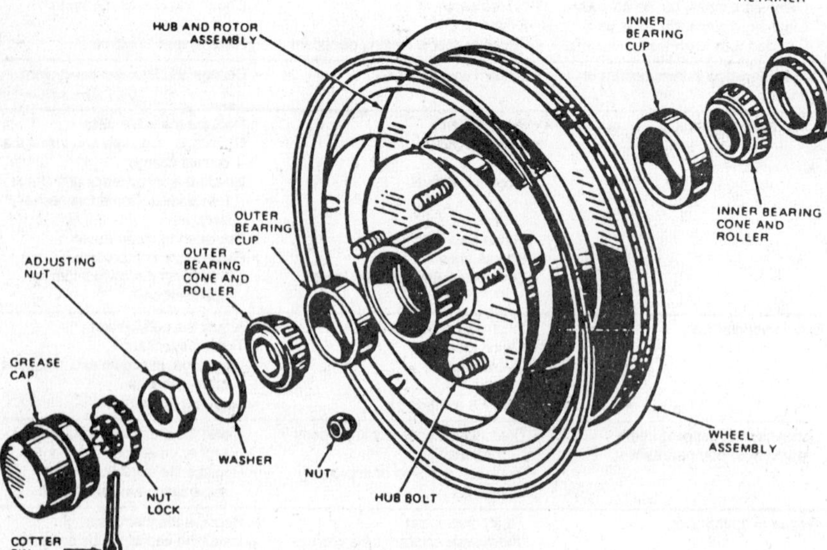

Front hub disassembled

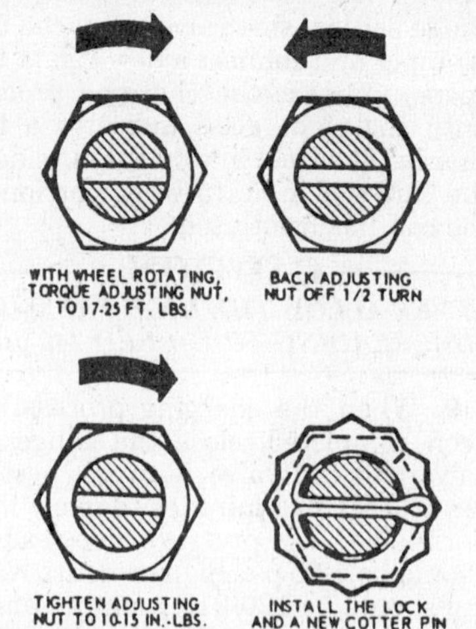

Front wheel bearing adjusting sequence

8. Check the wheel for proper rotation, then install the grease cap. If the wheel still does not rotate properly, inspect and clean or replace the wheel bearings and cups.

REMOVAL, REPACKING, AND INSTALLATION

Before handling the bearings, there are a few things that you should remember to do and not to do.

Remember to DO the following:

- Remove all outside dirt from the housing before exposing the bearing.
- Treat a used bearing as gently as you would a new one.
- Work with clean tools in clean surroundings.
- Use clean, dry canvas gloves, or at least clean, dry hands.
- Clean solvents and flushing fluids are a must.
- Use clean paper when laying out the bearings to dry.
- Protect disassembled bearings from rust and dirt. Cover them up.
- Use clean rags to wipe bearings.
- Keep the bearings in oil-proof paper when they are to be stored or are not in use.
- Clean the inside of the housing before replacing the bearing.

Do NOT do the following:

- Don't work in dirty surroundings.
- Don't use dirty, chipped or damaged tools.
- Try not to work on wooden work benches or use wooden mallets.
- Don't handle bearings with dirty or moist hands.
- Do not use gasoline for cleaning; use a safe solvent.
- Do not spin-dry bearings with compressed air. They will be damaged.
- Do not spin dirty bearings.
- Avoid using cotton waste or dirty cloths to wipe bearings.

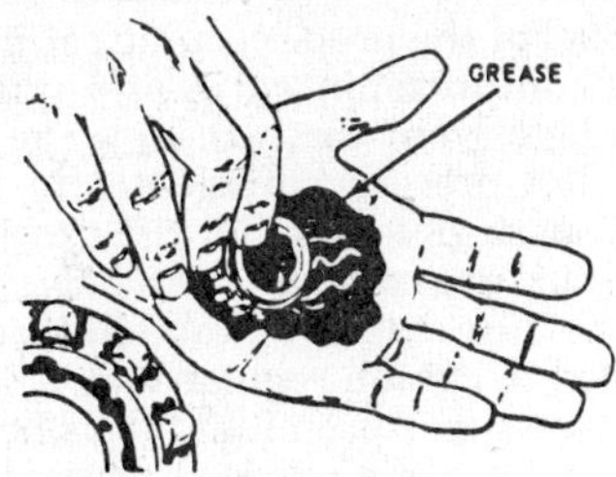

Packing bearings

• Try not to scratch or nick bearing surfaces.

• Do not allow the bearing to come in contact with dirt or rust at any time.

1. Raise and support the front end on jackstands.
2. Remove the wheel cover. Remove the wheel.
3. Remove the caliper from the disc and wire it to the underbody to prevent damage to the brake hose. For floating caliper brakes, see the brake section under Caliper Removal and Installation.
4. Remove the grease cap from the hub. Then, remove the cotter pin, nut lock, adjusting nut and flat washer from the spindle. Remove the outer bearing assembly from the hub.
5. Pull the hub and disc assembly off the wheel spindle.
6. Remove and discard the old grease retainer. Remove the inner bearing cone and roller assembly from the hub.
7. Clean all grease from the inner and outer bearing cups with solvent. Inspect the cups for pits, scratches, or excessive wear. If the cups are damaged, remove them with a drift.
8. Clean the inner and outer cone and roller assemblies with solvent and shake them dry. If the cone and roller assemblies show excessive wear or damage, replace them with the bearing cups as a unit.
9. Clean the spindle and the inside of the hub with solvent to thoroughly remove all old grease.
10. Covering the spindle with a clean cloth, brush all loose dirt and dust from the brake assembly. Remove the cloth carefully so as to not get dirt on the spindle.
11. If the inner and/or outer bearing cups were removed, install the replacement cups on the hub. Be sure that the cups seat properly in the hub.
12. It is imperative that all old grease be removed from the bearings and surrounding surfaces before repacking. The new lithium-based grease is not compatible with the sodium base grease used in the past.
13. Install the hub and disc on the wheel spindle. To prevent damage to the grease retainer and spindle threads, keep the hub centered on the spindle.
14. Install the outer bearing cone and roller assembly and the flat washer on the spindle. Install the adjusting nut.
15. Adjust the wheel bearings by torquing the adjusting nut to 17-25 ft.lb. with the wheel rotating to seat the bearing. Then back off the adjusting nut ½ turn. Retighten the adjusting nut to 10-15 in.lb. Install the locknut so that the castellations are aligned with the cotter pin hole. Install the cotter pin. Bend the ends of the cotter pin around the castellations of the locknut to prevent interference with the radio static collector in the grease cap. Install the grease cap.

WARNING: New bolts must be used when servicing floating caliper units. The upper bolt must be tightened first. For floating caliper units, see the brake section under Caliper Assembly Service. For sliding caliper units, see the brake section under Shoe and Lining Replacement.

11. Install the wheels.
12. Install the wheel cover.

Tires and Wheels

Inspect the tires regularly for wear and damage. Remove stones or other foreign particles which may be lodged in the tread. If tread wear is excessive or irregular it could be a sign of front end problems, or simply improper inflation.

The inflation should be checked at least once per month and adjusted if necessary. The tires must be cold (driven less than one mile) or an inaccurate reading will result. Do not forget to check the spare.

The correct inflation pressure for your vehicle can be found on a decal mounted to the car. Depending upon model and year, the decal can be located at the driver's door, the passenger's door or the glove box. If you cannot find the decal a local automobile tire dealer can furnish you with information.

Inspect tires for uneven wear that might indicate the need for front end alignment or tire rotation. Tires should be replaced when a tread wear indicator appears as a solid band across the tread.

When you buy new tires, give some thought to these points, especially if you are switching to larger tires or to another profile series (50, 60, 70, 78):

1. The wheels must be the correct width for the tire. Tire dealers have charts of tire and rim compatibility. A mismatch can cause sloppy handling and rapid tread wear. The old rule of thumb is that the tread width should match the rim width (inside bead to inside bead) within an inch. For radial tires, the rim width should be 80% or less of the tire (not tread) width.
2. The height (mounted diameter) of the new tires can greatly change speedometer accuracy, engine speed at a given road speed, fuel mileage, acceleration, and ground clearance. Tire makers furnish full measurement specifications. Speedometer drive gears are available from Ford dealers for correction.

NOTE: Dimensions of tires marked the same size may vary significantly, even among tires from the same maker.

3. The spare tire should be usable, at least for low speed operation, with the new tires.

Troubleshooting Basic Wheel Problems

Problem	Cause	Solution
The car's front end vibrates at high speed	• The wheels are out of balance • Wheels are out of alignment	• Have wheels balanced • Have wheel alignment checked/adjusted
Car pulls to either side	• Wheels are out of alignment • Unequal tire pressure • Different size tires or wheels	• Have wheel alignment checked/adjusted • Check/adjust tire pressure • Change tires or wheels to same size
The car's wheel(s) wobbles	• Loose wheel lug nuts • Wheels out of balance • Damaged wheel • Wheels are out of alignment • Worn or damaged ball joint • Excessive play in the steering linkage (usually due to worn parts) • Defective shock absorber	• Tighten wheel lug nuts • Have tires balanced • Raise car and spin the wheel. If the wheel is bent, it should be replaced • Have wheel alignment checked/adjusted • Check ball joints • Check steering linkage • Check shock absorbers
Tires wear unevenly or prematurely	• Incorrect wheel size • Wheels are out of balance • Wheels are out of alignment	• Check if wheel and tire size are compatible • Have wheels balanced • Have wheel alignment checked/adjusted

Tire Size Comparison Chart

"Letter" sizes			Inch Sizes	Metric-inch Sizes		
"60 Series"	"70 Series"	"78 Series"	1965–77	"60 Series"	"70 Series"	"80 Series"
			5.50-12, 5.60-12	165/60-12	165/70-12	155-12
		Y78-12	6.00-12			
		W78-13	5.20-13	165/60-13	145/70-13	135-13
		Y78-13	5.60-13	175/60-13	155/70-13	145-13
			6.15-13	185/60-13	165/70-13	155-13, P155/80-13
A60-13	A70-13	A78-13	6.40-13	195/60-13	175/70-13	165-13
B60-13	B70-13	B78-13	6.70-13	205/60-13	185/70-13	175-13
			6.90-13			
C60-13	C70-13	C78-13	7.00-13	215/60-13	195/70-13	185-13
D60-13	D70-13	D78-13	7.25-13			
E60-13	E70-13	E78-13	7.75-13			195-13
			5.20-14	165/60-14	145/70-14	135-14
			5.60-14	175/60-14	155/70-14	145-14
			5.90-14			
A60-14	A70-14	A78-14	6.15-14	185/60-14	165/70-14	155-14
	B70-14	B78-14	6.45-14	195/60-14	175/70-14	165-14
	C70-14	C78-14	6.95-14	205/60-14	185/70-14	175-14
D60-14	D70-14	D78-14				
E60-14	E70-14	E78-14	7.35-14	215/60-14	195/70-14	185-14
F60-14	F70-14	F78-14, F83-14	7.75-14	225/60-14	200/70-14	195-14
G60-14	G70-14	G77-14, G78-14	8.25-14	235/60-14	205/70-14	205-14
H60-14	H70-14	H78-14	8.55-14	245/60-14	215/70-14	215-14
J60-14	J70-14	J78-14	8.85-14	255/60-14	225/70-14	225-14
L60-14	L70-14		9.15-14	265/60-14	235/70-14	
	A70-15	A78-15	5.60-15	185/60-15	165/70-15	155-15
B60-15	B70-15	B78-15	6.35-15	195/60-15	175/70-15	165-15
C60-15	C70-15	C78-15	6.85-15	205/60-15	185/70-15	175-15
	D70-15	D78-15				
E60-15	E70-15	E78-15	7.35-15	215/60-15	195/70-15	185-15
F60-15	F70-15	F78-15	7.75-15	225/60-15	205/70-15	195-15
G60-15	G70-15	G78-15	8.15-15/8.25-15	235/60-15	215/70-15	205-15
H60-15	H70-15	H78-15	8.45-15/8.55-15	245/60-15	225/70-15	215-15
J60-15	J70-15	J78-15	8.85-15/8.90-15	255/60-15	235/70-15	225-15
	K70-15		9.00-15	265/60-15	245/70-15	230-15
L60-15	L70-15	L78-15, L84-15	9.15-15			235-15
	M70-15	M78-15				255-15
		N78-15				

Note: Every size tire is not listed and many size comparisons are approximate, based on load ratings. Wider tires than those supplied new with the vehicle, should always be checked for clearance.

4. There shouldn't be any body interference when loaded, on bumps, or in turning.

The only sure way to avoid problems with these points is to stick to tire and wheel sizes available as factory options.

TIRE ROTATION

Tires should be rotated periodically to get the maximum tread lift available. A good time to do this is when changing over from regular tires to snow tires, or about once per year. If front end problems are suspected have them corrected before rotating the tires. Torque the lug nuts to 70-115 ft.lb.

NOTE: Mark the wheel position or direction of rotation on radial, or studded snow tires before removing them.

CAUTION

Avoid overtightening the lug nuts to prevent damage to the brake disc or drum. Alloy wheels can also be cracked by overtightening. Use of a torque wrench is highly recommended. Tighten the lug nuts in a criss-cross sequence shown to 85 ft.lb.

FLUIDS AND LUBRICANTS

Fuel Recommendations

GASOLINE ENGINES

It is important to use fuel of the proper octane rating in your car. Octane rating is based on the quantity of anti-knock compounds added to the fuel and it determines the speed at which the gas will burn. The lower the octane rating, the faster it burns. The higher the octane, the slower the fuel will burn and a greater percentage of compounds in the fuel prevent spark ping (knock), detonation and preignition (dieseling).

As the temperature of the engine increases, the air/fuel mixture exhibits a tendency to ignite before the spark plug is fired. If fuel of an octane rating too low for the engine is used, this will allow combustion to occur before the piston has completed its compression stroke, thereby creating a very high pressure very rapidly.

Fuel of the proper octane rating, for the compression ratio and ignition timing of your car, will slow the combustion process sufficiently to allow the spark plug enough time to ignite the mixture completely and smoothly. Many non-catalyst models are designed to run on regular fuel. The use of some super-premium fuel is no substitution for a properly tuned and maintained engine. Chances are that if your engine exhibits any signs of spark ping, detonation or pre-ignition when using regular fuel, the ignition timing should be checked against specifications or the cylinder head should be removed for decarbonizing.

Vehicles equipped with catalytic converters must use UNLEADED GASOLINE ONLY. Use of unleaded fuel shortened the life of spark plugs, exhaust systems and EGR valves and can damage the catalytic converter. Most converter equipped models are designed to operate using unleaded gasoline with a minimum rating of 87 octane. Use of unleaded gas with octane ratings lower than 87 can cause persistent spark knock which could lead to engine damage.

Light spark knock may be noticed when accelerating or driving up hills. The slight knocking may be considered normal (with 87 octane) because the maximum fuel economy is obtained under condition of occasional light spark knock. Gasoline with an octane rating higher than 87 may be used, but it is not necessary (in most cases) for proper operation.

If spark knock is constant, when using 87 octane, at cruising speeds on level ground, ignition timing adjustment may be required.

DIESEL ENGINES

Automotive diesel fuel with a cetane rating of 40 is sufficient.

Engine

OIL RECOMMENDATION

Gasoline Engines

When adding the oil to the crankcase or changing the oil or filter, it is important that oil of an equal quality to original be used in your car. The use of inferior oils may void your warranty. Generally speaking, oil that has been rated **SF** by the American Petroleum Institute will prove satisfactory.

Oil of the SF variety performs a multitude of functions in addition to its basic job of reducing friction of the engine's moving parts. Through a balanced formula of polymeric dispersants and metallic detergents, the oil prevents high temperature and low temperature deposits and also keeps sludge and dirt particles in suspension. Acids, particularly sulphuric acid, as well as other products of combustion of sulphur fuels, are neutralized by the oil. These acids, if permitted to concentrate, may cause corrosion and rapid wear of the internal parts of the engine.

It is important to choose an oil of the proper viscosity for climatic and operational conditions. Viscosity in an index of the oil's thickness at different temperatures. A thicker oil (higher numerical rating) is needed for high temperature operation, whereas thinner oil (lower numerical rating) is required for cold weather operation. Due to the need for an oil that embodies both these characteristics in parts of the country where there is wide temperature variation within a small period of time, multigrade oils have been developed. Basically a multigrade oil is thinner at low temperatures and thicker at high temperatures. For example, a 10W-40 oil exhibits the characteristics of a 10 weight oil when the car is first started and the oil is cold. Its lighter weight allows it to travel to the lubricating surfaces quicker and offer less resistance to starter motor cranking then, let's say, a straight 30 weight oil. But after the engine reaches operating temperature, the 10W-40 oil begins acting like a straight 40 weight oil, its heavier weight providing greater lubricating protection and less susceptibility to foaming than a straight 30 weight oil. Whatever your driving needs, the oil viscosity/temperature chart should prove useful in selecting the proper grade. The SAE viscosity rating is printed or stamped on the top of every oil container.

Diesel Engines

Engine oil, meeting API specification **SF/CD** and Ford specification ESE-M2C153-C is recommended. You can use either SAE 30W or SAE 15W-40 weight oils.

OIL LEVEL CHECK

The engine oil level should be checked frequently. For instance, at each refueling stop. Be sure that the vehicle is parked on a level surface with the engine off. Also, allow a few minutes after turning off the engine for the oil to drain into the pan or an inaccurate reading will result.

1. Open the hood and remove the engine oil dipstick.
2. Wipe the dipstick with a clean, lint-free rag and reinsert it. Be sure to insert it all the way.
3. Pull out the dipstick and note the oil level. It should be between the SAFE (MAX) mark and the ADD (MIN) mark.
4. If the level is below the lower mark, replace the dipstick and add fresh oil to bring the level within the proper range. Do not overfill.
5. Recheck the oil level and close the hood.

NOTE: Use a multi-grade oil with API classification SF.

Oil Viscosity—Temperature Chart

When Outside Temperature is Consistently	Use SAE Viscosity Number
SINGLE GRADE OILS	
−10°F to 32°F	10W
10°F to 60°F	20W-20
32°F to 90°F	30
Above 60°F	40
MULTIGRADE OILS	
Below 32°F	5W-30*
−10°F to 90°F	10W-30
Above—10°F	10W-40
Above 10°F	20W-40
Above 20°F	20W-50

*When sustained high-speed operation is anticipated, use the next higher grade.

ADD 2 / ADD 1 → SAFE ← WARRANTY

ADD → SAFE ← WARRANTY

ADD ← SAFE → ←MAX. OVERFILL

(Note lubricant level should be within the safe range)

Typical engine oil dipstick

OIL CHANGE

NOTE: The engine oil and oil filter should be changed at the same time, at the recommended intervals on the maintenance schedule chart.

1. Run the engine to normal operating temperature.
2. After the engine has reached operating temperature, shut it off, firmly apply the parking brake, and block the wheels.
3. Raise and support the front end on jackstands.
4. Place a drip pan beneath the oil pan and remove the drain plug.

CAUTION

The oil could be very hot! Protect yourself by using rubber gloves if necessary.

5. Allow the engine to drain thoroughly.

WARNING: On some V8 engines a dual sump oil pan was used. When changing the oil, both drain plugs (front and side) must be removed. Failure to remove both plugs can lead to an incorrect oil level reading!

6. While the oil is draining, replace the filter as described below.
7. When the oil has completely drained, clean the threads of the plug and coat them with non-hardening sealer or Teflon® tape and install the plug. Tighten it snugly.

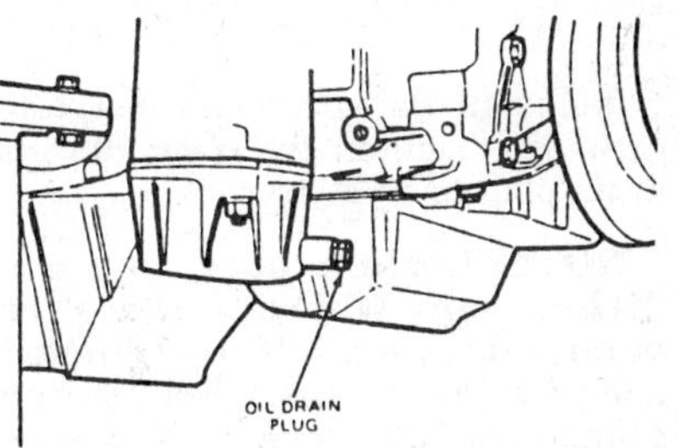

Diesel oil filter drain plug

WARNING: The threads in the oil pan are easily stripped! Don not overtighten the plug!

8. Fill the crankcase with the proper amount of oil shown in the Capacities Chart.
9. Start the engine and check for leaks.

REPLACING THE OIL FILTER

Gasoline Engines

1. Place the drip pan beneath the oil filter.
2. Using an oil filter wrench, turn the filter counterclockwise to remove it.

CAUTION

The oil could be very hot! Protect yourself by using rubber gloves if necessary.

3. Wipe the contact surface of the new filter clean and coat the rubber gasket with clean engine oil.
4. Clean the mating surface of the adapter on the block.
5. Screw the new filter into position on the block using hand pressure only. Do not use a strap wrench to install the filter! Then hand-turn the filter ½-¾ additional turn.

Diesel Engine

1. Place the drip pan beneath the oil filter.
2. Remove the drain plug from the filter housing.
3. Remove the 2 housing cover attaching nuts and remove the cover and filter cartridge.
4. Clean the cover in a safe solvent and dry it thoroughly.
5. Install a new gasket on the cover.

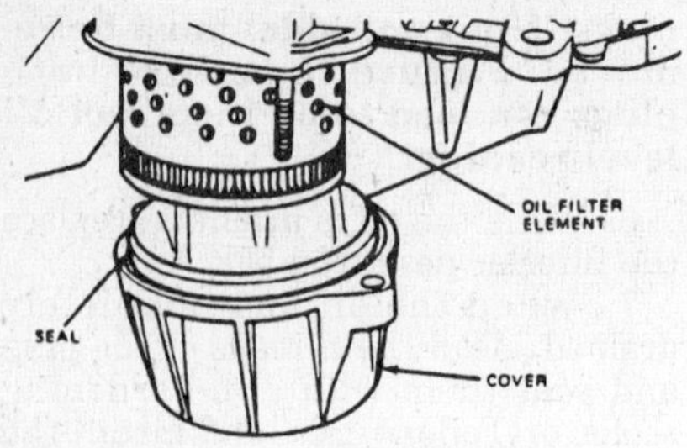

Diesel oil filter cover and element removal

6. Install the cover and new filter cartridge. Tighten the cover nut and drain plug to 15 ft.lb.

NOTE: Certain operating conditions may warrant more frequent oil changes. If the vehicle is used for short trips, where the engine does not have a chance to fully warm up before it is shut off, water condensation and low temperature deposits may make it necessary to change to oil sooner. If the vehicle is used mostly in stop-and-go traffic, corrosive acids and high temperature deposits may necessitate shorter oil changing intervals. The shorter intervals also apply to industrial or rural areas where high concentrations of dust and other airborne particulate matter contaminate the oil. Finally, if the car is used for towing trailers, a severe load is placed on the engine causing the oil to thin out sooner, making necessary the shorter oil changing intervals.

Transmission

FLUID RECOMMENDATIONS

Manual Transmissions:

- ET Series 4-sp – SAE 85W/90
- RAD – SAE 85W/90
- RUG – SAE 85W/90
- RAP – SAE 85W/90
- T50D 5-sp – Dexron®II ATF

85W/90 gear oil may be used in the T50D transmission in very warm climates or if gear/bearing noise is excessive. Conversely, Dexron®II may be used in the 82ET 4-sp in very cold climates, or if hard shifting is a continuing problem.

Automatic Transmissions:

- 1980 C3 – Type F
- 1981-86 C3 – Dexron®II
- C4 – Dexron®II
- C5 – Type H
- C6 – Dexron®II
- FMX – Type F
- AOD – Dexron®II
- ZF – Dexron®II
- A4LD – Dexron®II

LEVEL CHECK

Automatic Transmissions

It is very important to maintain the proper fluid level in an automatic transmission. If the level is either too high or too low, poor shifting operation and internal damage are likely to occur. For this reason a regular check of the fluid level is essential.

1. Drive the vehicle for 15-20 minutes to allow the transmission to reach operating temperature.

2. Park the car on a level surface, apply the parking brake and leave the engine idling. Shift the transmission and engage each gear, then place the gear selector in P (PARK).

3. Wipe away any dirt in the areas of the transmission dipstick to prevent it from falling into the filler tube. Withdraw the dipstick, wipe it with a clean, lint-free rag and reinsert it until it seats.

4. Withdraw the dipstick and note the fluid level. It should be between the upper (FULL) mark and the lower (ADD) mark.

5. If the level is below the lower mark, use a funnel and add fluid in small quantities through the dipstick filler neck. Keep the engine running while adding fluid and check the level after each small amount. Do not overfill.

Manual Transmission

The fluid level should be checked every 6 months/6,000 miles, whichever comes first.

1. Park the car on a level surface, turn off the engine, apply the parking brake and block the wheels.

2. Remove the filler plug from the side of the transmission case with a proper size wrench. The fluid level should be even with the bottom of the filler hole.

3. If additional fluid is necessary, add it through the filler hole using a siphon pump or squeeze bottle.

4. Replace the filler plug; do not overtighten.

DRAIN AND REFILL

Automatic Transmission

C3, C4, C5

1. Raise the vehicle, so that the transmission oil pan is readily accessible. Safely support on jackstands.

2. Disconnect the fluid filler tube from the pan and allow the fluid to drain into an appropriate container.

3. Remove the transmission oil pan attaching bolts, pan and gasket.

To install the transmission oil pan:

4. Clean the transmission oil pan and transmission mating surfaces.

5. Install the transmission oil pan in the reverse order of removal, torquing the attaching bolts to 10-16 ft.lb. and using a new gasket. Fill the transmission with 3 qts. of the correct type fluid.

6. Lower the vehicle. Start the engine and move the gear selector through shift pattern. Allow the engine to reach normal operating temperature.

7. Check the transmission fluid.

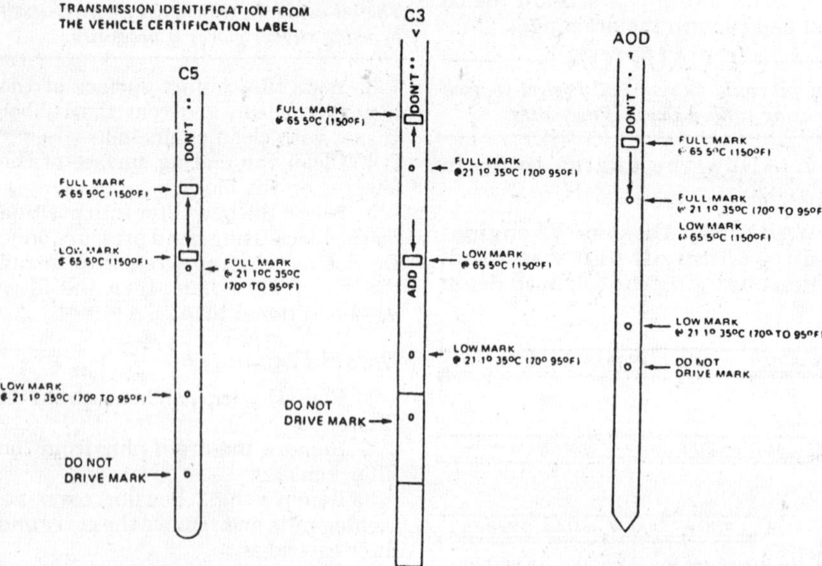

Automatic transmission dipstick markings for late models

Add fluid, if necessary, to maintain correct level.

C6, FMX, AOD, A4LD

1. Raise the car and support on jackstands.
2. Place a drain pan under the transmission.
3. Loosen the pan attaching bolts and drain the fluid from the transmission.
4. When the fluid has drained to the level of the pan flange, remove the remaining pan bolts working from the rear and both sides of the pan to allow it to drop and drain slowly.
5. When all of the fluid has drained, remove the pan and clean it thoroughly. Discard the pan gasket.
6. Place a new gasket on the pan, and install the pan on the transmission. Tighten the attaching bolts to 12-16 ft.lb.
7. Add three 3 quarts of fluid to the transmission through the filler tube.
8. Lower the vehicle. Start the engine and move the gear selector through shift pattern. Allow the engine to reach normal operating temperature.
9. Check the transmission fluid. Add fluid, if necessary, to maintain correct level.

ZF

1. Raise and support the vehicle safely.
2. Place a drain pan underneath the transmission oil pan.
3. Remove the drain plug and allow the fluid to drain.
4. After all of the fluid has drained, clean the drain plug and reinstall. Tighten the drain plug to 11 ft.lb.
5. Lower the vehicle. Add 3 quarts of fluid through the transmission filler tube.
6. Start the engine and check the fluid level after moving the selector through all positions. Add fluid, if necessary, to correct level.

Manual Transmission

1. Place a suitable drain pan under the transmission.
2. Remove the drain plug and allow the gear lube to drain out.
3. Replace the drain plug, remove the filler plug and fill the transmission to the proper level with the required fluid.
4. Reinstall the filler plug.

Rear Axle (Differential)

FLUID LEVEL CHECK

Like the manual transmission, the rear axle fluid should be checked every six months/6,000 miles. A filler plug is provided near the center of the rear cover or on the upper (driveshaft) side of the gear case. Remove the plug and check to ensure that the fluid level is even with the bottom of the filler hole. Add SAE 85W/90/95 gear lube as required. If the vehicle is equipped with a limited slip rear axle, add the required special fluid. Install the filler plug but do not overtighten.

DRAIN AND REFILL

Normal maintenance does not require changing the rear axle fluid. However, to do so, remove the rear drain plug (models equipped), the lower two cover bolts, or the cover. Catch the drained fluid in a suitable container. If the rear cover was removed, clean the mounting surfaces of the cover and rear housing. Install a new gasket (early models) or (on late models) apply a continuous bead of Silicone Rubber Sealant (D6AZ-19562-A/B or the equivalent) around the rear housing face inside the circle of bolt holes. Install the cover and tighten the bolts. Parts must be assembled within a half hour after the sealant is applied. If the fluid was drained by removing the two lower cover bolts, apply sealant to the bolts before reinstallation. Fill the rear axle through the filler hole with the proper lube. Add friction modifier to limited slip models if required.

Coolant

FLUID RECOMMENDATIONS

When additional coolant is required to maintain the proper level, always add a 50/50 mixture of antifreeze and water.

LEVEL CHECK

CAUTION

Exercise extreme care when removing the cap from a hot radiator! Wait a few minutes until the engine has time to cool somewhat, then wrap a thick towel around the radiator cap and slowly turn it counterclockwise to the first stop. Step back and allow the pressure to release from the cooling system. Then, when the steam has stopped venting, press down on the cap, turn it one more stop counterclockwise and remove the cap.

The coolant level in the radiator should be checked on a monthly basis, preferably when the engine is cold. On a cold engine, the coolant level should be maintained at one inch below the filler neck on vertical flow radiators, and 2½" below the filler neck at the **COLD FILL** mark on crossflow radiators. On cars equipped with the Coolant Recovery System, the level is maintained at the **COLD LEVEL** mark in the translucent plastic expansion bottle. Top up as necessary with a mixture of 50% water and 50% ethylene glycol antifreeze, to ensure proper rust, freezing and boiling protection. If you have to add coolant more often than once a month or if you have to add more than one quart at a time, check the cooling system for leads. Also check for water in the crankcase oil, indicating a blown cylinder head gasket.

DRAIN AND REFILL

CAUTION

When draining the coolant, keep in mind that cats and dogs are attracted by the ethylene glycol antifreeze, and are quite likely to drink any that is left in an uncovered container or in puddles on the ground. This will prove fatal in sufficient quantity! Always drain the coolant into a sealable container. Coolant should be reused unless it is contaminated or several years old.

Completely draining and refilling the cooling system every two years at least will remove accumulated rust, scale and other deposits.

NOTE: Use a good quality antifreeze with water pump lubricants, rust inhibitors and other corrosion inhibitors along with acid neutralizers. Use a permanent type coolant that meets specification ESE-M97B44A or the equivalent.

1. Drain the existing antifreeze and coolant. Open the radiator and engine drain petcocks (models equipped), or disconnect the bottom radiator hose, at the radiator outlet. Set the heater temperature controls to the full HOT position.

NOTE: Before opening the radiator petcock, spray it with some penetrating lubricant.

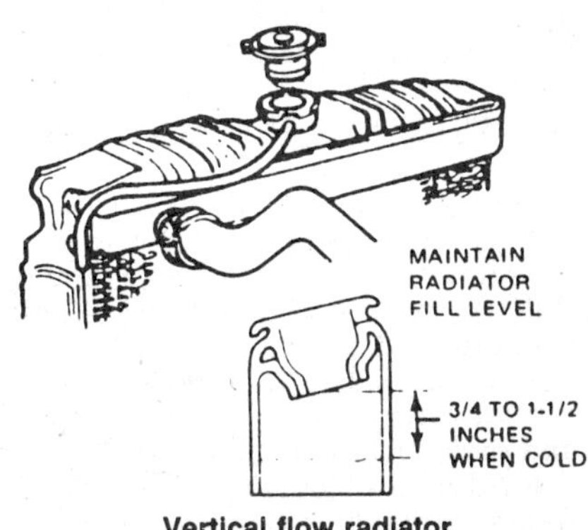

Vertical flow radiator

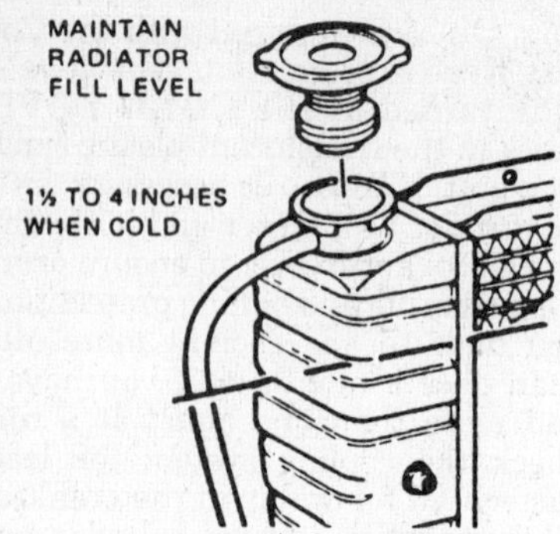

Crossflow radiator

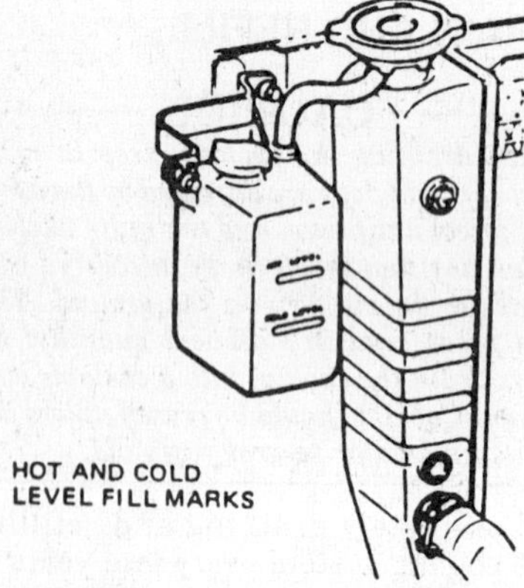

Coolant recovery system

2. Close the petcock or reconnect the lower hose and fill the system with water.
3. Add a can of quality radiator flush. If equipped with a V6 or diesel engine, be sure the flush is safe to use in engines having aluminum components.
4. Idle the engine until the upper radiator hose gets hot.
5. Drain the system again.
6. Repeat this process until the drained water is clear and free of scale.
7. Close all petcocks and connect all the hoses.
8. If equipped with a coolant recovery system, flush the reservoir with water and leave empty.
9. Determine the capacity of your cooling system (see capacities specifications). Add a 50/50 mix of quality antifreeze (ethylene glycol) and water to provide the desired protection.

SYSTEM INSPECTION

Most permanent antifreeze/coolant have a colored dye added which makes the solution an excellent leak detector. When servicing the cooling system, check for leakage at:

- All hoses and hose connections
- Radiator seams, radiator core, and radiator draincock
- All engine block and cylinder head freeze (core) plugs, and drain plugs
- Edges of all cooling system gaskets (head gaskets, thermostat gasket)
- Transmission fluid cooler
- Heating system components, water pump
- Check the engine oil dipstick for signs of coolant in the engine oil
- Check the coolant in the radiator for signs of oil in the coolant

Investigate and correct any indication of coolant leakage.

Check the Radiator Cap

While you are checking the coolant level, check the radiator cap for a worn or cracked gasket. If the cap doesn't seal properly, fluid will be lost and the engine will overheat.

A worn cap should be replaced with a new one.

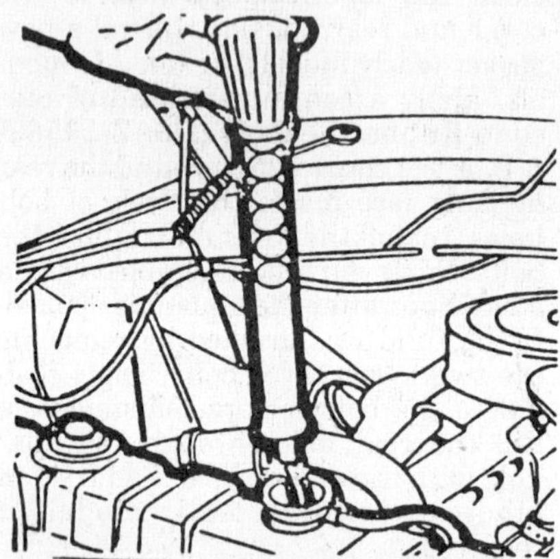
Testing coolant condition with a tester

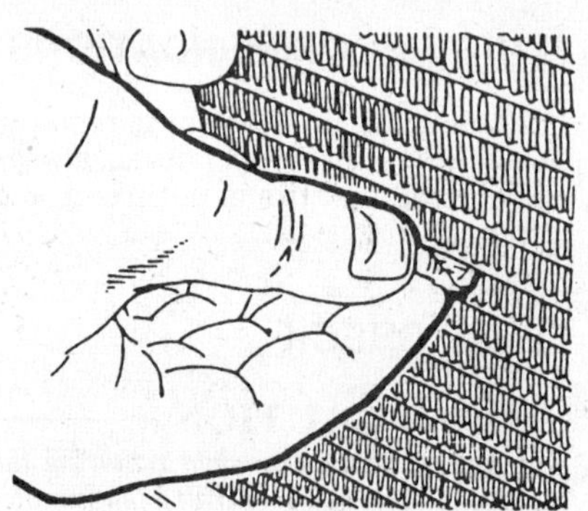
Clean debris from the radiator fins

Clean Radiator of Debris

Periodically clean any debris such as leaves, paper, insects, etc., from the radiator fins. Pick the large pieces off by hand. The smaller pieces can be washed away with water pressure from a hose.

Carefully straighten any bent radiator fins with a pair of needle nose pliers. Be careful, the fins are very soft. Don't wiggle the fins back and forth too much. Straighten them once and try not to move them again.

CHECKING SYSTEM PROTECTION

A 50/50 mix of coolant concentrate and water will usually provide protection to -35°F (-37°C). Freeze protection may be checked by using a cooling system hydrometer. Inexpensive hydrometers (floating ball types) may be obtained from a local department store (automotive section) or an auto supply store. Follow the directions packaged with the coolant hydrometer when checking protection.

Master Cylinder

LEVEL CHECK

The brake fluid in the master cylinder should be checked every 6 months/6,000 miles.

Cast Iron Reservoir

1. Park the vehicle on a level surface and open the hood.
2. Pry the retaining spring bar holding the cover onto the master cylinder to one side.
3. Clean any dirt from the sides and top of the cover before removal. Remove the master cylinder cover and gasket.
4. Add fluid, if necessary, to within 3/8" of the top of the reservoir, or to the full level indicator (on models equipped).
5. Push the gasket bellows back into the cover. Reinstall the gasket and cover and position the retainer spring bar.

Plastic Reservoir

Check the fluid level on the side of the reservoir. If fluid is required, remove the screw on the and remove the filler cap and gasket from the master cylinder. Fill the reservoir to the full line in the reservoir. Install the filler cap, making sure the gasket is properly seated in the cap.

FLUID RECOMMENDATION

Use only Heavy Duty Brake Fluid meeting DOT3 specifications.

Power Steering

LEVEL CHECK

Check the power steering fluid level every 6 months/6,000 miles.

1. Park the vehicle on a level surface. Run the engine until normal operating temperature is reached.
2. Turn the steering all the way to the left and then all the way to the

right several times. Center the steering wheel and shut off the engine.
3. Open the hood and check the power steering reservoir fluid level.
4. Remove the filler cap and wipe the dipstick attached clean.
5. Re-insert the dipstick and tighten the cap. Remove the dipstick and note the fluid level indicated on the dipstick.
6. The level should be at any point below the Full mark, but not below the Add mark.
7. Add fluid as necessary. Do not overfill.

FLUID RECOMMENDATION

Add power steering fluid; do not overfill the reservoir.

Steering Gear Lubricant

EXCEPT RACK AND PINION STEERING

If there is binding in the steering gear or if the wheels do not return to a straight-ahead position after a turn, the lubricant level of the steering gear should be checked. Remove the filler plug using a $^{11}/_{16}''$ open-end wrench and remove the lower cover bolt using a $^{9}/_{16}''$ wrench, to expose both holes. Slowly turn the steering wheel to the left until it stops. At this point, lubricant should be rising in the lower cover bolt hole. Then slowly turn the steering wheel to the right until it stops. At this point, lubricant should be rising in the filler plug hole. If the lubricant does not rise when the wheel is turned, add a small amount of SAE 90 steering gear lubricant until it does. Replace the cover bolt and the filler plug when finished.

Chassis Greasing

NOTE: Depending on the year and model, vehicles may have plugs or grease fittings in all steering/suspension linkage or pivot points. Follow the instructions under Ball Joints if equipped with these plugs. Newer models have sealed points and lubrication is not necessary.

BALL JOINTS

1. Park the vehicle on a level surface, set the parking brake, block the rear wheels, raise the front end and support it with jackstands.
2. Wipe away any dirt from the ball joint lubrication plugs.

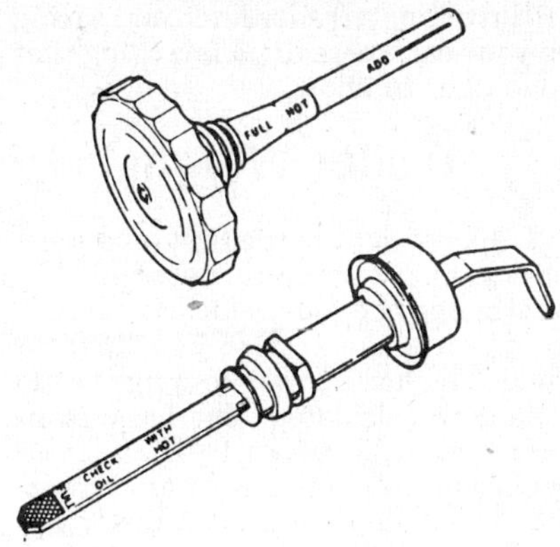

Typical power steering pump reservoir dipsticks

NOTE: The upper ball joint has a plug on the top; the lower ball joint has one on the bottom.

3. Pull out the plugs and install grease fittings.
4. Using a hand-operated grease gun containing multi-purpose grease, force lubricant into the joint until the joint boot swells.
5. Remove the grease fitting and push in the lubrication plug.
6. Lower the vehicle.

STEERING ARM STOPS

The steering arm stops are attached to the lower control arm. They are located between each steering arm and the upturned end of the front suspension strut.
1. Park the vehicle on a level surface, set the parking brake, block the rear wheels, raise the front end and support it with jackstands.
2. Clean the friction points and apply multi-purpose grease.
3. Lower the vehicle.

MANUAL TRANSMISSION AND CLUTCH LINKAGE

On models so equipped, apply a small amount of chassis grease to the pivot points of the transmission and clutch linkage as per the chassis lubrication diagram.

AUTOMATIC TRANSMISSION LINKAGE

On models so equipped, apply a small amount of 10W engine oil to the kickdown and shift linkage at the pivot points.

PARKING BRAKE LINKAGE

At yearly intervals or whenever binding is noticeable in the parking brake linkage, lubricate the cable guides, levers and linkage with a suitable chassis grease.

OUTSIDE VEHICLE MAINTENANCE

Lock Cylinders

Apply graphite lubricant sparingly through the key slot. Insert the key and operate the lock several times to be sure that the lubricant is worked into the lock cylinder.

Door Hinges and Hinge Checks

Spray a silicone lubricant on the hinge pivot points to eliminate any binding conditions. Open and close the door several times to be sure that the lubricant is evenly and thoroughly distributed.

Trunk Lid

Spray a silicone lubricant on all of the pivot and friction surfaces to eliminate any squeaks or binds. Work the trunk lid to distribute the lubricant

Body Drain Holes

Be sure that the drain holes in the doors and rocker panels are cleared of obstruction. A small screwdriver can be used to clear them of any debris.

PUSHING AND TOWING

WARNING: Push-starting is not recommended for cars equipped with a catalytic converter. Raw gas collecting in the converter may cause damage. Jump starting is recommended.

To push-start your manual transmission equipped car (automatic transmission models cannot be push started), make sure of bumper alignment. If the bumper of the car pushing does not match with your car's bumper, it would be wise to tie an old tire either on the back of your car, or on the front of the pushing car. Switch the ignition to **ON** and depress the clutch pedal. Shift the transmission to third gear and hold the accelerator pedal about halfway down. signal the push car to proceed, when the car speed reaches about 10 mph, gradually release the clutch pedal. The car engine should start, if not have the car towed.

If the transmission and rear axle are in proper working order, the car can be towed with the rear wheels on the ground for distances under 15 miles at speeds no greater then 30 mph. If the transmission or rear is known to be damaged or if the car has to be towed over 15 miles or over 30 mph the car must be dollied or towed with the rear wheels raised and the steering wheel secured so that the front wheels remain in the straight-ahead position. The steering wheel must be clamped with a special clamping device designed for towing service. If the key controlled lock is used damage to the lock and steering column may occur.

JACKING

Your car is equipped with either a scissors type jack, or a bumper jack. The scissor-type jack is placed under the side of the car so that it fits into the notch in the vertical rocker panel flange nearest the wheel to be changed. These jacking notches are located approximately 8 inches from the wheel opening on the rocker panel flanges. Bumper jack slots or flats are provided on the front and rear bumper. Be sure the jack is inserted firmly and is straight before raising the vehicle.

When raising the car with a scissors or bumper jack follow these precautions: Park the car on level spot, put the selector in P (PARK) with an automatic transmission or in reverse if your car has a manual transmission, apply the parking brake and block the front and the back of the wheel that is diagonally opposite the wheel being changed. These jacks are fine for changing a tire, but never crawl under the car when it is supported only by the scissors or bumper jack.

CAUTION

If you're going to work beneath the vehicle, always support it on jackstands!

TRAILER TOWING

Factory trailer towing packages are available on most cars. However, if you are installing a trailer hitch and wiring on your car, there are a few thing that you ought to know.

Trailer Weight

Trailer weight is the first, and most important, factor in determining whether or not your vehicle is suitable for towing the trailer you have in mind. The horsepower-to-weight ratio should be calculated. The basic standard is a ratio of 35:1. That is, 35 pounds of GVW for every horsepower.

To calculate this ratio, multiply you engine's rated horsepower by 35, then subtract the weight of the vehicle, including passengers and luggage. The resulting figure is the ideal maximum trailer weight that you can tow. One point to consider: a numerically higher axle ratio can offset what appears to be a low trailer weight. If the weight of the trailer that you have in mind is somewhat higher than the weight you just calculated, you might consider changing your rear axle ratio to compensate.

Hitch Weight

There are three kinds of hitches: bumper mounted, frame mounted, and load equalizing.

Bumper mounted hitches are those which attach solely to the vehicle's bumper. Many states prohibit towing with this type of hitch, when it attaches to the vehicle's stock bumper, since it subjects the bumper to stresses for which it was not designed. Aftermarket rear step bumpers, designed for trailer towing, are acceptable for use with bumper mounted hitches.

Frame mounted hitches can be of the type which bolts to two or more points on the frame, plus the bumper, or just to several points on the frame. Frame mounted hitches can also be of the tongue type, for Class I towing, or, of the receiver type, for classes II and III.

Load equalizing hitches are usually used for large trailers. Most equalizing hitches are welded in place and use equalizing bars and chains to level the vehicle after the trailer is hooked up.

The bolt-on hitches are the most common, since they are relatively easy to install.

Check the gross weight rating of your trailer. Tongue weight is usually figured as 10% of gross trailer weight. Therefore, a trailer with a maximum gross weight of 2,000 lb. will have a maximum tongue weight of 200 lb. Class I tarilers fall into this category. Class II trailers are those with a gross weight rating of 2,000-3,500 lb., while Class III trailers fall into the 3,500-6,000 lb. category. Class IV trailers are those over 6,000 lb. and are for use with fifth wheel trucks, only.

When you've determined the hitch that you'll need, follow the manufacturer's installation instructions, exactly, especially when it comes to fastener torques. The hitch will subjected to a lot of stress and good hitches come with hardened bolts. Never substitute an inferior bolt for a hardened bolt.

Wiring

Wiring the car for towing is fairly easy. There are a number of good wiring kits available and these should be used, rather than trying to design your own. All trailers will need brake lights and turn signals as well as tail lights and side marker lights. Most states require extra marker lights for overly wide trailers. Also, most states have recently required back-up lights for trailers, and most trailer manufacturers have been building trailers with back-up lights for several years.

Additionally, some Class I, most Class II and just about all Class III trailers will have electric brakes.

Add to this number an accessories wire, to operate trailer internal equipment or to charge the trailer's battery, and you can have as many as seven wires in the harness.

Determine the equipment on your trailer and buy the wiring kit necessary. The kit will contain all the wires needed, plus a plug adapter set which included the female plug, mounted on the bumper or hitch, and the male plug, wired into, or plugged into the trailer harness.

When installing the kit, follow the manufacturer's instructions. The color coding of the wires is standard throughout the industry.

One point to note, some domestic vehicles, and most imported vehicles, have separate turn signals. On most domestic vehicles, the brake lights and rear turn signals operate with the same bulb. For those vehicles with separate turn signals, you can purchase an isolation unit so that the brake lights won't blink whenever the turn signals are operated, or, you can go to your local electronics supply house and buy four diodes to wire in series with the brake and turn signal bulbs. Diodes will isolate the brake and turn signals. The choice is yours. The isolation units are simple and quick to install, but far more expensive than the diodes. The diodes, however, require more work to install properly, since they require the cutting of each bulb's wire and soldering in place of the diode.

One final point, the best kits are

those with a spring loaded cover on the vehicle mounted socket. This cover prevents dirt and moisture from corroding the terminals. Never let the vehicle socket hang loosely. Always mount it securely to the bumper or hitch.

Cooling

ENGINE

One of the most common, if not THE most common, problem associated with trailer towing is engine overheating.

With factory installed trailer towing packages, a heavy duty cooling system is usually included. Heavy duty cooling systems are available as optional equipment on most cars, with or without a trailer package. If you have one of these extra-capacity systems, you shouldn't have any overheating problems.

If you have a standard cooling system, without an expansion tank, you'll definitely need to get an aftermarket expansion tank kit, preferably one with at least a 2 quart capacity. These kits are easily installed on the radiator's overflow hose, and come with a pressure cap designed for expansion tanks.

Another helpful accessory is a Flex Fan. These fan are large diameter units are designed to provide more airflow at low speeds, with blades that have deeply cupped surfaces. The blades then flex, or flatten out, at high speed, when less cooling air is needed. These fans are far lighter in weight than stock fans, requiring less horsepower to drive them. Also, they are far quieter than stock fans.

If you do decide to replace your stock fan with a flex fan, note that if your car has a fan clutch, a spacer between the flex fan and water pump hub will be needed.

Aftermarket engine oil coolers are helpful for prolonging engine oil life and reducing overall engine temperatures. Both of these factors increase engine life.

While not absolutely necessary in towing Class I and some Class II trailers, they are recommended for heavier Class II and all Class III towing.

Engine oil cooler systems consist of an adapter, screwed on in place of the oil filter, a remote filter mounting and a multi-tube, finned heat exchanger, which is mounted in front of the radiator or air conditioning condenser.

TRANSMISSION

An automatic transmission is usually recommended for trailer towing.

Maintenance Interval Chart

Operation	Thousand Miles 1980–82	Thousand Miles 1983–87
ENGINE		
Air cleaner replacement—exc. V8	30	30
Air cleaner replacement—V8	30	30
Air intake temperature control system check	22.5	22.5
Carburetor idle speed and mixture, fast idle, throttle solenoid adj	30	30
Cooling system check	12	12
Coolant replacement; system draining and flushing	52.5	52.5
Crankcase breather cap cleaning	52.5	52.5
Crankcase breather filter replacement (in air cleaner)	52.5	52.5
Distributor breaker points inspection	—	—
Distributor breaker points replacement	—	—
Distributor cap and rotor inspection	22.5	22.5
Drive belts adjustment	30	30
Evaporative control system check; inspect carbon canister	52.5	52.5
Exhaust control valve (heat riser) lubricatin and inspection	15	15
Exhaust gas recirculation system (EGR) check	15	15
Fuel filter replacement	12	12
Ignition timing adjustment	②	②
Intake manifold bold torque check (V8 only)	15	15
Oil change (Turbo—every 5,000 miles)	7.5	7.5
Oil filter replacement (Turbo—each oil change)	15	15
PCV system valve replacement, system cleaning	52.5	52.5
Spark plug replacement; plug wire check	30	30
Thermactor air injection system check	22.5	22.5
Automatic transmission band adjustment	①	①
Automatic transmission fluid level check	15	15
Brake system inspection, lining replacement	30	30
Brake master cylinder reservoir fluid level check	30	30
Clutch pedal free-play adjustment	—	—
Front suspension ball joints and steering linkage lubrication	30	30
Front wheel bearings cleaning, adjustment and repacking	30	30
Manual transmission fluid level check	15	15
Power steering pump reservoir fluid level check	15	15
Rear axle fluid level check	15	15
Steering arm stop lubrication; steering linkage inspection	15	15

① Normal service—12,000 mi. only; severe (fleet) service—6,000/18,000/30,000 mi. intervals
② Periodic adjustment unnecessary

Modern automatics have proven reliable and, of course, easy to operate, in trailer towing.

The increased load of a trailer, however, causes an increase in the temperature of the automatic transmission fluid. Heat is the worst enemy of an automatic transmission. As the temperature of the fluid increases, the life of the fluid decreases.

It is essential, therefore, that you install an automatic transmission cooler.

The cooler, which consists of a multi-tube, finned heat exchanger, is usually installed in front of the radiator or air conditioning compressor, and hooked inline with the transmission cooler tank inlet line. Follow the cooler manufacturer's installation instructions.

Select a cooler of at least adequate capacity, based upon the combined gross weights of the car and trailer.

Cooler manufacturers recommend that you use an aftermarket cooler in addition to, and not instead of, the present cooling tank in your car radiator. If you do want to use it in place of the radiator cooling tank, get a cooler at least two sizes larger than normally necessary.

NOTE: A transmission cooler can, sometimes, cause slow or harsh shifting in the transmission during cold weather, until the fluid has a chance to come up to normal operating temperature. Some coolers can be purchased with or retrofitted with a temperature bypass valve which will allow fluid flow through the cooler only when the fluid has reached operating temperature, or above.

TUNE-UP PROCEDURES

In order to extract the full measure of performance and economy from your engine it is essential that it be properly tuned at regular intervals. A regular tune-up will keep your vehicle's engine running smoothly and will prevent the annoying minor breakdowns and poor performance associated with an untuned engine.

A complete tune-up should be performed every 12,000 miles or twelve months, whichever comes first. This interval should be halved if the vehicle is operated under severe conditions, such as trailer towing, prolonged idling, continual stop and start driving, or if starting or running problems are noticed. It is assumed that routine maintenance has been kept up, as this will have a decided effect on the results of a tune-up. All of the applicable steps of a tune-up should be followed in order, as the result is a cumulative one.

If the specifications on the tune-up sticker in the engine compartment disagree with the Tune-Up Specifications chart in this section, the figures on the sticker must be used. The sticker often reflects changes made during the production run.

Spark Plugs

A typical spark plug consists of a metal shell surrounding a ceramic insulator. A metal electrode extends downward through the center of the insulator and protrudes a small distance. Located at the end of the plug and attached to the side of the outer metal shell is the side electrode. The side electrode bends in at a 90° angle so that its tip is even with, and parallel to, the tip of the center electrode. The distance between these two electrodes (measured in thousandths of an inch) is called the spark plug gap. The spark plug in no way produces a spark but merely provides a gap across which the current can arc. The coil produces anywhere from 20,000 to 40,000 volts or more, which travels to the distributor where it is distributed through the spark plug wires to the spark plugs. The current passes along the center electrode and jumps the gap to the side electrode, and, in so doing, ignites the air/fuel mixture in the combustion chamber.

SPARK PLUG HEAT RANGE

Spark plug heat range is the ability of the plug to dissipate heat. The longer the insulator (or the farther it extends into the engine), the hotter the plug will operate; the shorter the insulator the cooler it will operate. A plug that absorbs little heat and remains too cool will quickly accumulate deposits of oil and carbon since it is not hot enough to burn them off. This leads to plug fouling and consequently to misfiring. A plug that absorbs too much heat will have to deposits, but, due to the excessive heat, the electrodes will burn away quickly and in some instances, pre-ignition may result. Preignition takes place when plug tips get so hot that they glow sufficiently to ignite the fuel/air mixture before the actual spark occurs. This early ignition will usually cause a pinging during low speeds and heavy loads.

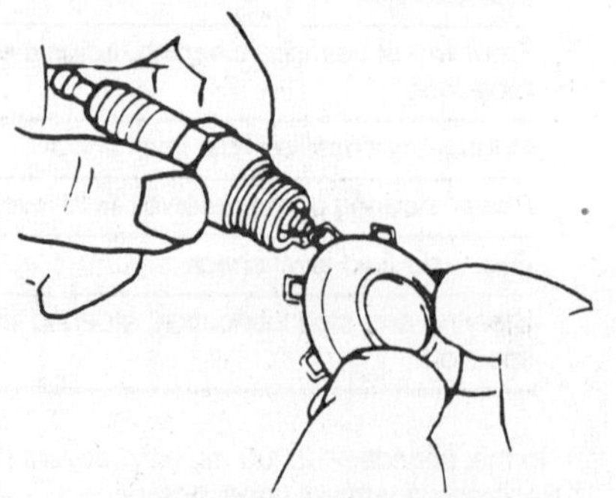

Checking spark plug gap

The general rule of thumb for choosing the correct heat range when picking a spark plug is: if most of your driving is long distance, high speed travel, use a colder plug; if most of your driving is stop and go, use a hotter plug. Original equipment plugs are compromise plugs, but most people never have occasion to change their plugs from the factory recommended heat range.

REPLACING SPARK PLUGS

A set of spark plugs usually requires replacement after about 10,000 miles on cars with conventional ignition systems and after about 20,000 to 30,000 miles on cars with electronic ignition, depending on your style of driving. In normal operation, plug gap increases about 0.001" (0.0254mm) for every 1,000-2,500 miles. As the gap increases, the plug's voltage requirement also increases. It requires a greater voltage to jump the wider gap and about two to three times as much voltage to fire a plug at high speeds than at idle.

When you're removing spark plugs, you should work on one at a time. Don't start by removing the plug wires all at once, because unless you number them, they may become mixed up. Take a minute before you begin and number the wires with tape. The best location for numbering is near where the wires come out of the cap.

NOTE: Apply a small amount of silicone dielectric compound (D7AZ-19A331-A or the equivalent) to the inside of the terminal boots whenever an ignition wire is disconnected from the plug, or coil/distributor cap connection.

1. Twist the spark plug boot and remove the boot and wire from the plug. Do not pull on the wire itself as this will ruin the wire.

2. If possible, use a brush or rag to clean the area around the spark plug. Make sure that all the dirt is removed so that none will enter the cylinder after the plug is removed.

3. Remove the spark plug using the proper size socket. Either a 5/8" or 13/16" size socket depending on the engine. Turn the socket counterclockwise to remove the plug. Be sure to hold the socket straight on the plug to avoid breaking the plug, or rounding off the hex on the plug.

4. Once the plug is out, check it to determine engine condition. This is crucial since plug readings are vital signs of engine condition.

5. Use a round wire feeler gauge to check the plug gap. The correct size gauge should pass through the electrode gap with a slight drag. If you're in doubt, try one size smaller and one larger. The smaller gauge should go through easily while the larger one shouldn't go through at all. If the gap is incorrect, use the electrode bending tool on the end of the gauge to adjust the gap. When adjusting the gap, always bend the side electrode. The center electrode is non-adjustable.

6. Squirt a drop of penetrating oil on the threads of the new plug and install it. Don't oil the threads too heavily. Turn the plug in clockwise by hand until it is snug.

7. When the plug is finger tight, tighten it with a wrench. Take care not to overtighten. Torque to 15 ft.lb.

8. Install the plug boot firmly over the plug. Proceed to the next plug.

CHECKING AND REPLACING SPARK PLUG CABLES

Visually inspect the spark plug cables for burns, cuts, or breaks in the insulation. Check the spark plug boots and the nipples on the distributor cap and coil. Replace any damaged wiring. If no physical damage is obvious, the wires can be checked with an ohmmeter for excessive resistance. About 5,000Ω per foot is normal.

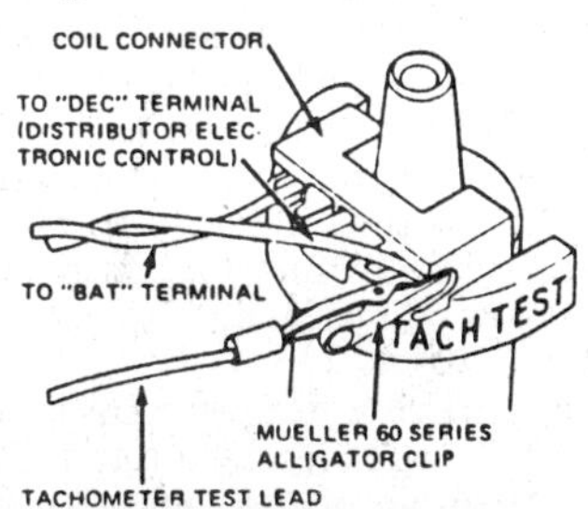

Attaching dwell/tachometer lead to coil connector (electronic ignition)

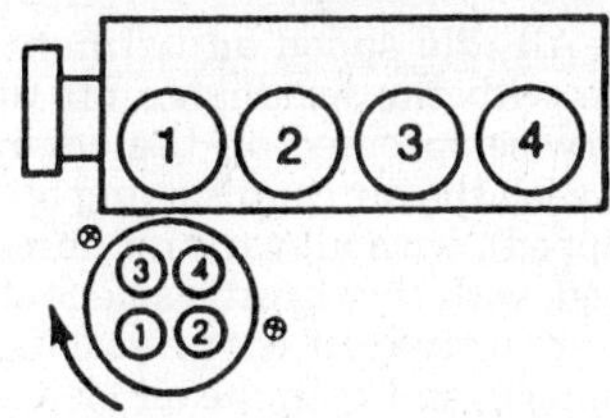

Ford Motor Co. 4-140 (2300 cc)
Engine firing order: 1-3-4-2
Distributor rotation: clockwise

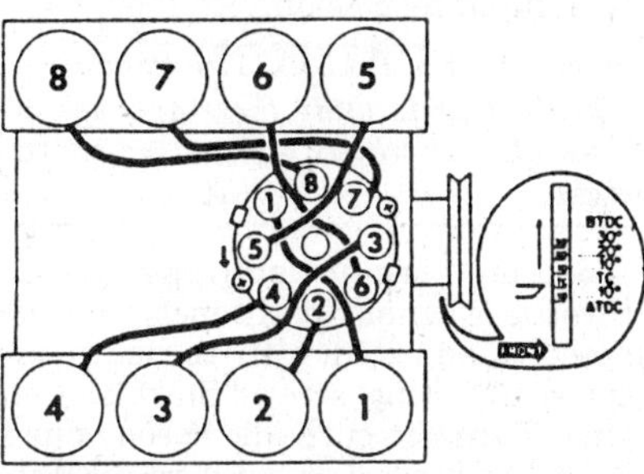

Ford Motor Co. 255,302 (Exc.H.O.)
Engine firing order:1-5-4-2-6-3-7-8
Distribution rotation: counterclockwise

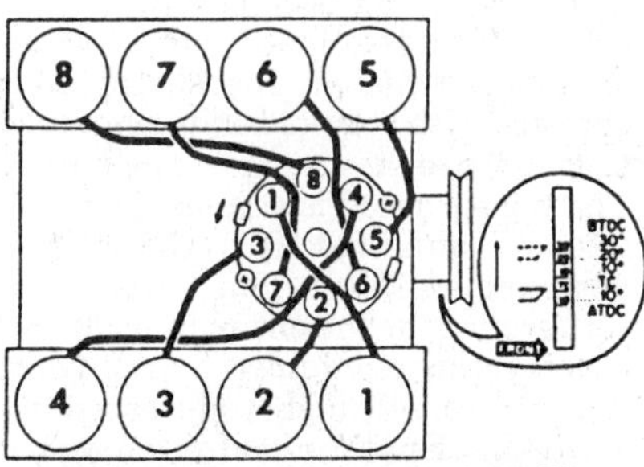

Ford Motor Co. H.O. 302, 351, 65 V8
Engine firing order: 1-3-7-2-6-5-4-8
Distributor rotation: counterclockwise

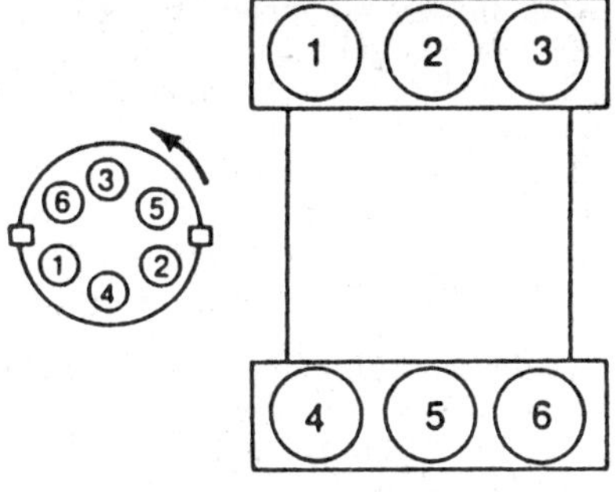

Ford Motor Co. 232 V6
Firing order: 1-4-2-5-3-6

NOTE: Apply a small amount of silicone dielectric compound (D7AZ-19A331-A or the equivalent) to the inside of the terminal boots whenever an ignition wire is disconnected from the plug. or coil/distributor cap connection.

When installing a new set of spark plug cables, replace the cables one at a time so there will be no mixup. Start by replacing the longest cable first. Install the boot firmly over the spark plug. Route the wire exactly the same as the original. Insert the nipple firmly into the tower on the distributor cap. Repeat the process for each cable.

Idle Speed and Mixture Adjustments Carbureted Engines

NOTE: Since the design of the 2700VV and 7200VV carburetor is different from all other Motorcraft carburetors in many respects, the adjusting procedures are necessarily different as well. Although the idle speed adjustment alone is identical, there is further information you will need to know in order to adjust the 2700VV and 7200VV properly. Refer to the Fuel System Section for an explanation.

In order to limit exhaust emissions, plastic caps have been installed on the idle fuel mixture screw(s), which prevent the carburetor from being adjusted on an overly rich idle fuel mixture. Under no circumstances should these limiters be modified or removed. A satisfactory idle should be obtained within the range of the limiter(s).

Refer to the procedures following this one for models equipped with fuel injection or for models equipped with an Automatic Overdrive Transmission (AOD).

ADJUSTMENT

1. Start the engine and run it at idle until it reaches operating temperature (about 10-20 minutes, depending on

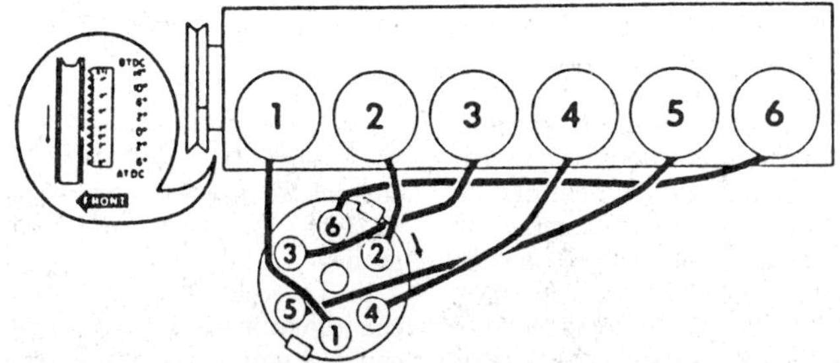

Ford Motor Co. 200 Engine Firing order: 1-5-3-6-2-4 Distributor rotation: clockwise

outside temperatures). Stop the engine.

2. Check the ignition timing.

3. Remove the air cleaner, taking note of the hose locations, and check that the choke plate is in the open position (plate in vertical position). Check the accompanying illustrations to see where the carburetor adjustment locations are. If you cannot reach them with the air cleaner installed, leave it off temporarily. Otherwise, reinstall the air cleaner assembly including all the hose connections.

NOTE: Leaving the air cleaner removed will affect the idle speed, therefore, adjust the curb idle speed to a setting 50-100 rpm higher than specified, if the air cleaner is off. When the air cleaner is reinstalled the idle speed should be to specifications.

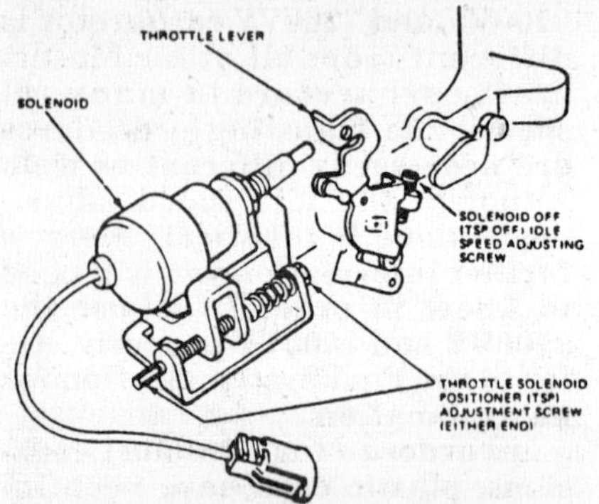

Location of idle speed adjustment—Motorcraft 2100, 2150, 4300, 4350 (all with TSP)

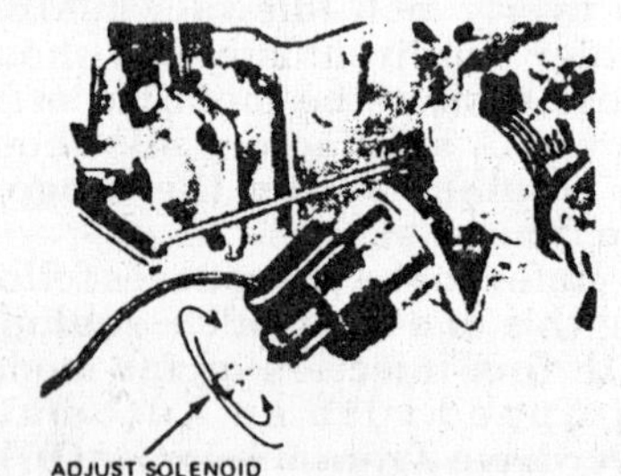

Location of idle speed adjustment—Motorcraft 2150 with solenoid dashpot TSP

4. Attach a tachometer to the engine, with the positive wire connected to the distributor side of the ignition coil, and the negative wire connected to a good ground, such as an engine mount. In order to attach an alligator clip to the distributor side (terminal) of the coil (primary connection), it will be necessary to lift off the connector and slide a female loop type connector (commercially available) sown the rubber connector over the loop connector and connect the alligator clip of your tachometer. On late models a tach connector is provided.

5. All idle speed adjustments are made with the headlights off (unless otherwise specified on the engine decal), with the air conditioning off (if so equipped), with all vacuum hoses connected, with the throttle solenoid positioner activated (connected, if so equipped), and with the air cleaner on. (See Note after Step 3.) Finally, all idle speed adjustments are made in Neutral on cars with manual transmission, and in Drive on cars equipped with automatic transmission.

CAUTION

Whenever performing these adjustments, block all four wheels and set the parking brake.

6a. On cars not equipped with a throttle solenoid positioner, the idle speed is adjusted with the curb idle speed adjusting screw. Start the engine. Turn the curb idle speed adjusting screw inward or outward until the correct idle speed (see Tune-Up Specifications chart) is reached, remembering to make the 50-100 rpm allowance if the air cleaner is removed.

6b. On cars equipped with a throttle solenoid positioner, the idle speed is adjusted with solenoid adjusting screw (nut), in two stages. Start the engine. The higher speed is adjusted with the solenoid connected. Turn the solenoid adjusting screw (nut) on 1 or 4 barrel carburetors, or the entire bracket on 2 barrel carburetors inward or outward until the correct higher idle speed (see Tune-Up Specifications chart) is reached, remembering to make the 50-100 rpm allowance if the air cleaner is removed. After making this adjustment on cars equipped with 2-barrel carburetors, tighten the solenoid adjusting locknut. The lower idle speed is adjusted with the solenoid lead wire disconnected near the harness (not at the carburetor). Place automatic transmission equipped cars in Neutral for this adjustment. Using the curb idle speed adjusting screw on the carburetor, turn the idle speed adjusting screw inward or outward until the correct lower idle speed (see Tune-Up Specifications chart) is reached, remembering again to make the 50-100 rpm allowance if the air cleaner is removed. Finally, reconnect the solenoid, slightly depress the throttle lever and allow the solenoid plunger to fully extend.

7. If removed, install the air cleaner. Recheck the idle speed. If it is not correct, Step 6 will have to be repeated and the approximate corrections made.

8. To adjust the idle mixture, turn the idle mixture screw(s) inward to obtain the smoothest idle possible within the range of the limiter(s).

9. Turn off the engine and disconnect the tachometer.

NOTE: If any doubt exists as to the proper idle mixture setting for your car, have the exhaust emission level checked at a diagnostic center or garage with an exhaust (HC/CO) analyzer or an air/fuel ratio meter.

Fuel Injected Engines

NOTE: Prior to adjusting the curb idle speed, set the parking brake and block all four wheels. Make all adjustments with the engine at normal operating temperature. Have all accessories turned off. If the underhood Emissions Sticker gives different specs and procedures than those following, always follow the sticker as it will reflect production changes and calibration differences.

Vehicles equipped with EEC-IV, curb idle speed (RPM) is controlled by the EEC-IV processor and the idle speed control device. If the control system is operating properly, these speeds are self compensating and cannot be changed by traditional adjustment techniques.

ADJUSTMENT

6-232 Central Fuel Injection (CFI)

NOTE: The EEC-IV system and an idle speed motor control the curb idle speed on models equipped with the V6 engine. The idle speed is not adjustable except for minimum and maximum throttle stop adjustment screw clearance. Too little clearance will prevent the throttle from closing as required thus causing a faster than normal idle speed. Any other problems with the system must be checked by EEC-IV system diagnosis.

The exact sequence must be followed when checking the adjustment.

1. Adjustment is checked with the idle speed motor plunger fully retracted. Run the engine until normal operating temperature is reached, shut the engine off. Remove the air cleaner.

2. Locate the self test connector and self test input connector. Both are under the hood by the driver's side strut tower.

3. Connect a jumper wire between the single input connector and the signal return pin of the self test connector. The signal return pin is on the upper right of the plug when the plug is

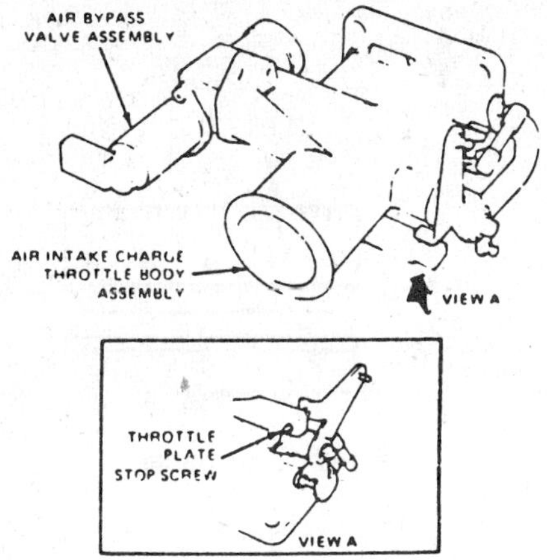

EFI adjustment

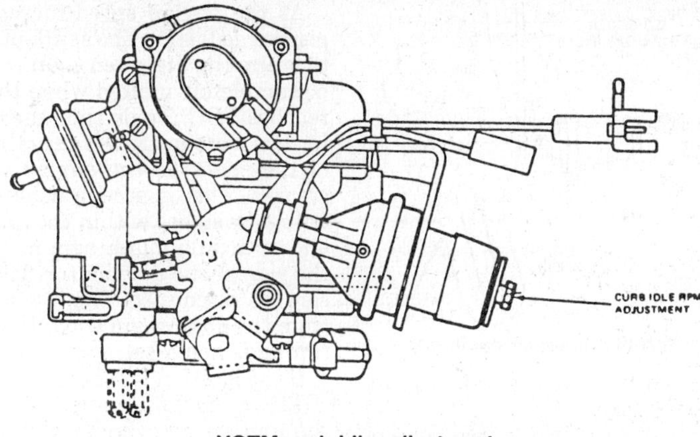

VOTM curb idle adjustment

held straight on with the four prongs on the bottom facing you.

4. The motor plunger should retract when the jumper wire is connected and the ignition key turned to the Run position. If not, the EEC-IV system requires testing and service.

5. Wait about ten seconds until the plunger is fully retracted. Turn the key Off and remove the jumper.

6. If the idle speed was too high, remove the throttle stop adjusting screw and install a new one. With the throttle plates completely closed, turn the throttle stop adjusting screw in until a gap of 0.005" (0.127mm) is present between the screw tip and the throttle lever contact surface. Turn the screw in an additional 1½ turns to complete the adjustment.

7. If the speed was too low, remove the dust cover from the motor tip. Push the tip back toward the motor to remove any play. Measure the clearance between the motor tip and throttle lever by passing a $^9/_{32}$" (7mm) drill bit between the tip and lever. A slight drag should be felt.

8. If adjustment is required, turn the motor bracket adjusting screw until proper clearance is obtained. Tighten the lock and install the dust cover.

V8 through 1985 w/Central Fuel Injection (CFI)

1. Connect a tachometer, start the engine and allow it to reach normal operating temperature.

2. Shut the engine Off and restart it. Run the engine at about 2,000 rpm for a minute. Allow the engine to return to idle and stabilize for about 30 seconds. Place the gear selector in Reverse. (Parking brake ON and all four wheels blocked).

3. Adjust the curb idle as required using the saddle bracket adjusting screw.

4. If the rpm figure is too low, turn off the engine and turn the adjusting screw one full turn. If the speed is too high, turn off the engine and turn the screw counterclockwise.

5. Repeat Steps 2 and 4 until correct idle speed is obtained.

1986-88 V8 with Sequential Electronic Fuel Injection

1. Apply the parking brake, block the drive wheels and place the vehicle in neutral.

2. Start the engine and let it run until it reaches normal operating temperature, then turn the engine off. Connect a suitable tachometer.

3. Turn off all accessories and place the transmission in park or neutral. Check the throttle linkage for freedom of movement and correct as necessary.

4. Check for vacuum leaks. Place the transmission in neutral and operate the engine at 1,800 rpm for at least 30 seconds. Place the transmission in drive (AT) or leave in neutral for (MT) and allow the engine to stabilize.

5. Check the idle speed and if the curb idle speed falls into specification, do not adjust. If the curb idle speed does not meet specifications, turn the engine off and disconnect the positive terminal of the battery for five minutes and ten reconnect it. Repeat STEPS 4 and 5.

6. If the curb idle speed is still out of specifications, the problem could be with the EEC-IV system and the diagnostic check of the system should be made.

7. If the curb idle speed is still out specifications, back out the throttle screw until the idle speed reaches 575 ± 20 rpm (base 8-302 AT) 625 ± 20 rpm (8-302 H.O. AT) 700 ± 20 rpm (8-302 H.O. MT) then back out the throttle plate stop screw ½ additional turn to bring the throttle plate linkage into the normal operating range of the ISC system.

8. Shut off the engine and remove all test equipment.

4-140 EFI Turbo

NOTE: Idle speed is controlled by the EEC-IV system and a air bypass valve. If the following procedure does not correct idle rpm, EEC-IV system diagnosis is required.

1. Run the engine until normal operating temperature is reached. Turn off all accessories.

2. Turn Off the engine. Disconnect the power lead to the idle speed bypass control valve. Connect a tachometer to the engine.

3. Start the engine and run at 2,000 rpm for two minutes. If the electric cooling fan comes on, disconnect the wiring harness connector.

4. Let the engine return to normal idling rpm and check speed on the tachometer.

5. Adjust the rpm if necessary with the throttle plate stop screw.

6. Turn the engine Off and reconnect the by-pass valve lead and cooling fan harness.

7. Restart the engine and check the idle speed.

Diesel Engine

ADJUSTMENT

1. Connect a diesel engine tachometer to the engine. Start the engine and allow normal operating temperature to be reached. Check the idle speed

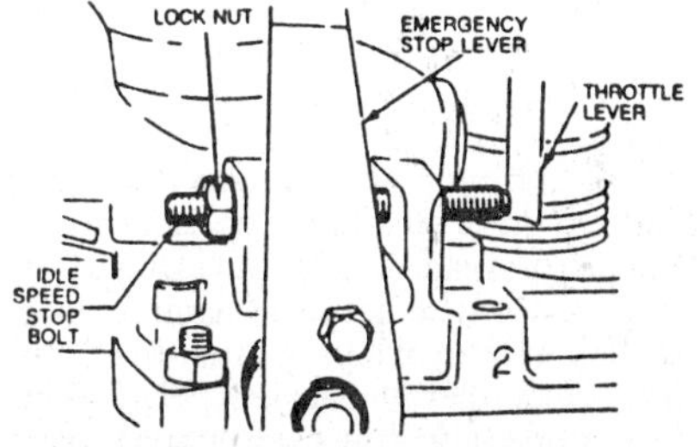

Diesel idle speed adjustment points

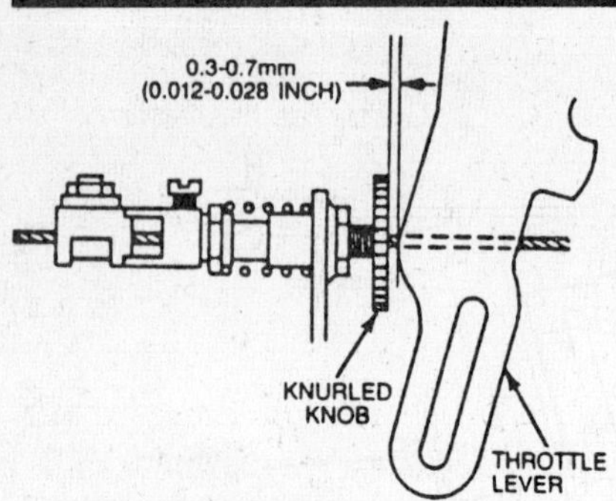

Diesel throttle advance cable gap

against what is specified on the underhood sticker.

2. If adjustment is required, loosen the locknut on the idle speed screw. Turn the screw clockwise to increase the speed or counterclockwise to decrease the speed. Tighten the locknut.

3. Check the gap between the knurled knob on the throttle advance cable and the throttle lever. Turn the knurled nut until a gap of 0.3-0.7mm is obtained.

IGNITION TIMING

Ignition timing is the measurement, in degrees of crankshaft rotation, of the point at which the spark plugs fire in each of the cylinders. It is measured in degrees before or after Top Dead Center (TDC) of the compression stroke. Ignition timing is controlled by turning the distributor body in the engine.

Ideally, the air/fuel mixture in the cylinder will be ignited by the spark plug just as the piston passes TDC of the compression stroke. If this happens, the piston will be beginning the power stroke just as the compressed and ignited air/fuel mixture starts to expand. The expansion of the air/fuel mixture starts to expand. The expansion of the air/fuel mixture then forces the piston down on the power stroke and turns the crankshaft.

Because it takes a fraction of a second for the spark plug to ignite the mixture in the cylinder, the spark plug must fire a little before the piston reaches TDC. Otherwise, the mixture will not be completely ignited as the piston passes TDC and the full power of the explosion will not be used by the engine.

The timing measurement is given in degrees of crankshaft rotation before the piston reaches TDC (BTDC). If the setting for the ignition timing is 5° BTDC, each spark plug must fire 5° before each piston reaches TDC. This only holds true, however, when the engine is at idle speed.

As the engine speed increases, the pistons go faster. The spark plugs have to ignite the fuel even sooner if it is to be completely ignited when the piston reaches TDC. To do this, the distributor has a means to advance the timing of the spark as the engine speed increases. This is accomplished by centrifugal weights within the distributor and a vacuum diaphragm mounted on the side of the distributor. It is necessary to disconnect the vacuum lines from the diaphragm when the ignition timing is being set.

If the ignition is set too far advanced (BTDC), the ignition and expansion of the fuel in the cylinder will occur too soon and tend to force the piston down while it is still traveling up. This causes engine ping. If the ignition spark is set tool far retarded after TDC (ATDC), the piston will have already passed TDC and started on its way down when the fuel is ignited. This will cause the piston to be forced down for only a portion of its travel. This will result in poor engine performance and lack of power.

The timing is best checked with a timing light. This device is usually connected in series with the No. 1 spark plug. The current that fires the spark plug also causes the timing light to flash.

There is a notch on the crankshaft pulley on 6-200 engines. A scale of degrees of crankshaft rotation is attached to the engine block in such a position that the notch will pass close by the scale. On the V6 and V8 engines, the scale is located on the crankshaft pulley and a pointer is attached to the engine block so that the scale will pass close by. When the engine is running, the timing light is aimed at the mark on the crankshaft pulley and the scale.

ADJUSTMENT

NOTE: Some engines have monolithic timing set at the factory. The monolithic system uses a timing receptacle on the front of the engine which can be connected to digital readout equipment, which electronically determines timing. Timing can also be adjusted in the conventional way. Many 1980 and later models are equipped with EEC engine controls. All ignition timing is controlled by the EEC module. Initial ignition timing is not adjustable and no attempt at adjustment should be made on EEC-III models, or models equipped with an indexed distributor base. For a description of EEC systems, refer to the Unit Repair sections on

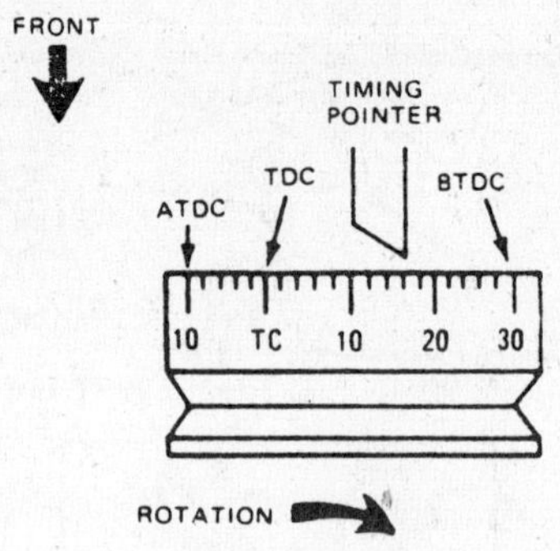

4-140 timing marks

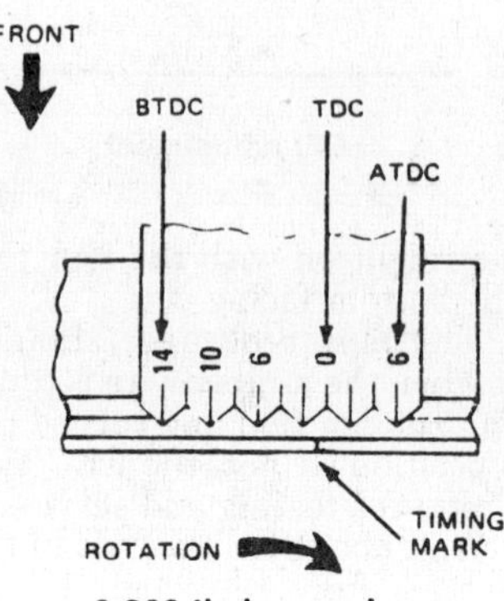

6-200 timing marks

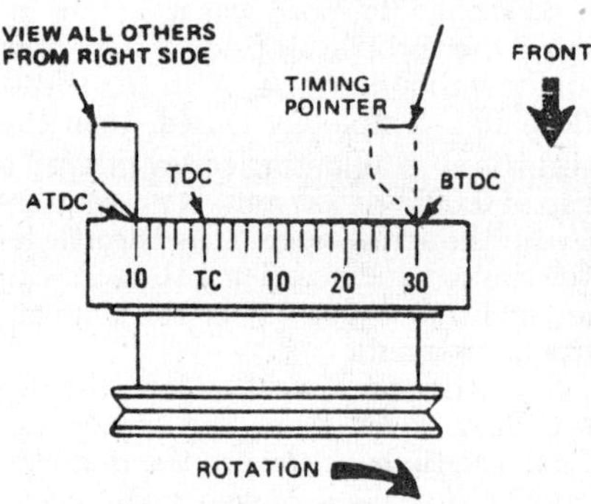

V6 and V8 timing marks

Electronic Ignition Systems and on Engine Controls. Requirements vary from model to model. Always refer to the Emissions Specification Sticker for exact timing procedures.

1. Locate the timing marks and pointer on the lower engine pulley and engine's front cover.

2. Clean the marks and apply chalk or brightly colored paint to the pointer.

3. On 1981 and later models, if the ignition module has (-12A224-) as a basic part number, disconnect the two wire connector (yellow and black wires). On engines equipped with the EEC-IV system, disconnect the single white (Black on some models) wire connector near the distributor.

4. Attach a timing light and tachometer according to manufacturer's specifications.

5. Disconnect and plug all vacuum lines leading to the distributor.

6. Start the engine, allow it to warm to normal operating temperature, then set the idle to the specifications given on the underhood sticker (for timing).

7. On 1981 and later models equipped with the module mentioned in Step 3, jumper the pins in the module connector for the yellow and black wires.

8. Aim the timing light at the timing mark and pointer on the front of the engine. If the marks align when the timing light flashes, remove the timing light, set the idle to its proper specification, and connect the vacuum lines at the distributor. If the marks do not align when the light flashes, turn the engine off and loosen the distributor holddown clamp slightly.

9. Start the engine again, and observe the alignment of the timing marks. To advance the timing, turn the distributor counterclockwise on 6-200 engines, and clockwise, for the 6-232 and V8 engines. When altering the timing, it is wise to tap the distributor lightly with a wooden hammer handle to move it in the desired direction. Grasping the distributor with your hand may result in a painful electric shock. When the timing marks are aligned, turn the engine off and tighten the distributor holddown clamp. Remove the test equipment, reconnect the vacuum hoses and white (black) single wire connector (EEC-IV).

10. On 1981 and later models equipped with the module mentioned in Step 3, remove the jumper connected in Step 7 and reconnect the two wire connector. Test the module operation as follows:

  a. Disconnect and plug the vacuum source hose to the ignition timing vacuum switch.

  b. Using an external vacuum source, apply vacuum greater than 12 in. Hg to the switch, and compare the ignition timing with the requirements below.

- 4-cylinder: per specifications less 32-40°
- 6-cylinder: per specifications less 21-27°
- 8-cylinder: per specifications less 16-20°

TACHOMETER CONNECTION

The coil connector used with DuraSpark is provided with a cavity for connection of a tachometer, so that the connector doesn't have to be removed to check engine rpm.

Install the tach lead with an alligator clip on its end into the cavity marked TACH TEST and connect the other lead to a good ground.

If the coil connector must be removed, pull it out horizontally until it is disengaged from the coil terminal.

VALVE CLEARANCE ADJUSTMENT

Diesel Engine

WARNING: The adjustment procedure is for a cold engine only!

1. Remove the valve cover.

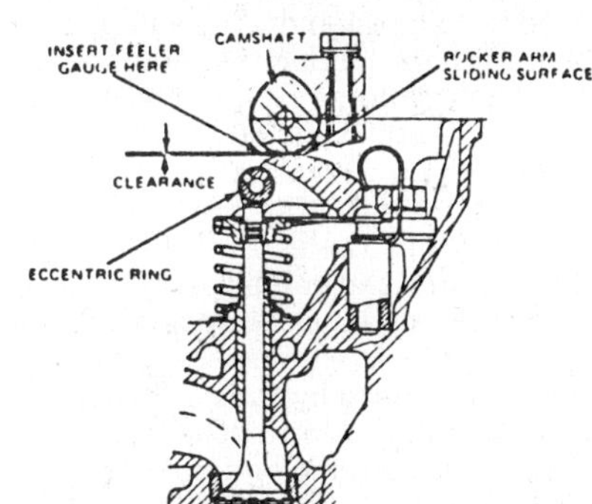

Valve train crossview-2.4L diesel engine

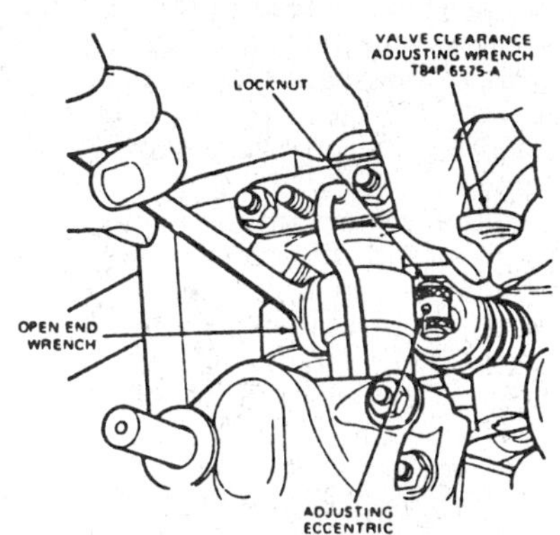

Eccentric adjustment-2.4L diesel engine

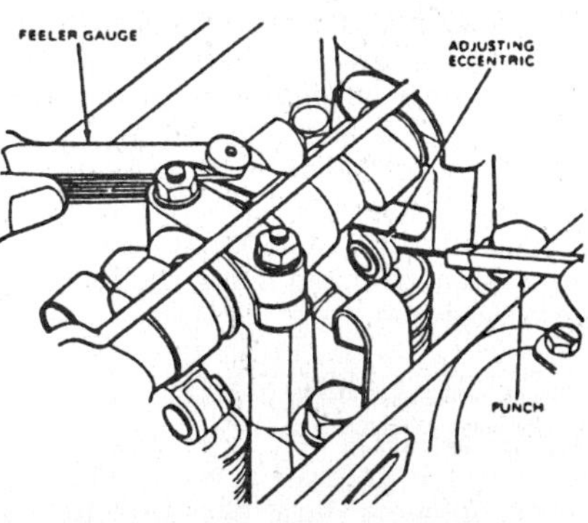

Valve clearance-2.4L diesel engine

2. Position the camshaft so that base circle of the lobe of the valve to be adjusted is facing the rocker arm.

3. Loosen the adjusting eccentric locknut using a valve clearance adjusting Wrench, Tool T84P-6575-A, or equivalent and a 12mm open end wrench.

4. Rotate the eccentric using a small punch until the valve clearance is adjusted to specification: Intake: 0.012" (0.30mm); Exhaust: 0.016" (0.40mm). Tighten the eccentric locknut.

5. Repeat Steps 2, 3 and 4 for each valve.

6. Install the valve cover.

7. Start the engine and check for oil leaks.

ELECTRONIC IGNITION SYSTEMS

DuraSpark Ignition

Basically, four electronic ignition systems have been used in Ford Motor Company vehicles from 1977-87:

1. DuraSpark I
2. DuraSpark II
3. DuraSpark III
4. Universal Distributor-TFI (EEC-IV)

In 1977, the DuraSpark systems, were introduced. DuraSpark I and DuraSpark II systems are nearly identical in operation, and virtually identical in appearance. The DuraSpark I uses a special control module which senses current flow through the ignition coil and adjust the dwell, or coil on-time for maximum spark intensity. If the DuraSpark I module senses that the ignition is ON, but the distributor shaft is not turning, the current to the coil is turned OFF by the module. The DuraSpark II system does not have this feature. The coil is energized for the full amount of time that the ignition switch is ON. Keep this in mind when servicing the DuraSpark II system, as the ignition system could inadvertently fire while performing ignition system services (such as distributor cap removal) while the ignition is ON. All DuraSpark II systems are easily identified by having a two-piece, flat topped distributor cap.

In 1980, the new DuraSpark III system was introduced. This version is based on the previous systems, but the input signal is controlled by the EEC system, rather than as function of engine timing and distributor armature position. The distributor, rotor, cap, and control module are unique to this system; the spark plugs and plug wires are the same as those used with the DuraSpark II system. Although the DuraSpark II and III control modules are similar in appearance, they cannot be interchanged between systems.

Some engines use a special DuraSpark Dual Mode ignition control module. The module is equipped with an altitude sensor, an economy modulator, or pressure switches (turbocharged engines only). This module, when combined with the additional switches and sensor, varies the base engine timing according to altitude and engine load conditions. DuraSpark Dual Mode ignition control modules have three wiring harness from the module.

1981 49-state and 1982 Canadian 4-140 engines with automatic transmissions have Dual Mode Crank Retard ignition module, which has the same function as the DuraSpark II module plug an ignition timing retard function which is operational during engine cranking. The spark timing retard feature eases engine starting, but allows normal timing advance as soon as the engine is running. This module can be identified by the presence of a white connector shell on the four-pin connector at the module.

Some 1981 and later DuraSpark II systems used with some 8-255 and 8-302 cu. in. engines are quipped with a Universal Ignition Module (UIM) which includes a run-retard function. The operation of the module is basically the same as the DuraSpark Dual Mode module.

The Universal Distributor (EEC-IV) has a diecast base which incorporates an externally mounted TFI-IV ignition module, and contains a Hall Effect vane switch stator assembly and provision for fixed octane adjustment. No distributor calibration is required and initial timing adjustment is normally not required. The primary function of the EEC-IV Universal Distributor system is to direct high secondary voltage to the spark plugs. In addition, the distributor supplies crankshaft position and frequency information to a computer using a profile Ignition Pickup. The Hall Effect switch in the distributor consists of a Hall Effect device on one side and a magnet on the other side. A rotary cup which has windows and tabs rotates and passes through the space between the device and the magnet. When a window is between the sides of the switch the magnetic path is not completed and the switch is Off, sending no signal. When a tab passes between the switch the magnetic path is completed and the Hall Effect Device is turned On and a signal is sent. The voltage pulse (signal) is used by is EEC-IV system for sensing crankshaft position and computing the desired spark advance based on engine demand and calibration.

DURASPARK OPERATION

With the ignition switch **ON**, the primary circuit is on and the ignition coil is energized. When the armature spokes approach the magnetic pickup coil assembly, they induce the voltage which tells the amplifier to turn the coil primary current off. A timing circuit in the amplifier module will turn the current on again after the coil field has collapsed. When the current is on, it flows from the battery through the ignition switch, the primary windings of the ignition coil, and through the amplifier module circuits to ground. When the current is off, the magnetic field built up in the ignition coil is allowed to collapse, inducing a high voltage into the secondary windings of the coil. High voltage is produced each time the field is thus built up and collapsed. When DuraSpark is used in conjunction with the EEC, the EEC computer tells the DuraSpark module when to turn the coil primary current off or on. In this case, the armature position is only a reference signal of engine timing, used by the EEC computer in combination with other reference signals to determine optimum ignition spark timing.

The high voltage flows through the coil high tension lead to the distributor cap where the rotor distributes it to one of the spark plug terminals in the distributor cap. This process is repeated for every power stroke of the engine.

Ignition system troubles are caused by a failure in the primary and/or the secondary circuit; incorrect ignition timing; or incorrect distributor advance. Circuit failures may be caused by shorts, corroded or dirty terminals, loose connections, defective wire insulation, cracked distributor cap or rotor, defective pick-up coil assembly or amplifier module, defective distributor points or fouled spark plugs.

If an engine starting or operating trouble is attributed to the ignition system, start the engine and verify the complaint. On engines that will not start, be sure that there is gasoline in the fuel tank and the fuel is reaching the carburetor. Then locate the ignition system problem using the following procedures.

TROUBLESHOOTING DURASPARK I

The following DuraSpark II troubleshooting procedures may be used on DuraSpark I systems with a few variations. The DuraSpark I module has internal connections which shut off the primary circuit in the run mode when the engine stalls. To perform the above troubleshooting procedures, it is necessary to by-pass these connections. However, with these connections by-passed, the current flow in the primary becomes so great that it will damage both the ignition coil and module unless a ballast resistor is installed in series with the primary circuit at the BAT terminal of the ignition coil. Such a resistor is available from Ford (Motorcraft part number DY-36). A 1.3Ω, 100 watt wire-wound power resistor can also be used.

To install the resistor, proceed as follows.

WARNING: The resistor will become very hot during testing.

1. Release the BAT terminal lead from the coil by inserting a paper cup through the hole in the rear of the horseshoe coil connector and manipulating it against the locking tab in the connector until the lead comes free.
2. Insert a paper clip in the BAT terminal of the connector of the coil. Using jumper leads, connect the ballast resistor as shown.
3. Using a straight pin, pierce both the red and white leads of the module to short these two together. This will by-pass the internal connections of the module which turn off the ignition circuit when the engine is not running.

CAUTION

Pierce the wires only AFTER the ballast resistor is in place or you could damage the ignition coil and module.

4. With the ballast resistor and by-pass in place, proceed with the DuraSpark II troubleshooting procedures.

TROUBLESHOOTING DURASPARK II

The following procedures can be used to determine whether the ignition system is working or not. If these procedures fail to correct the problem, a full troubleshooting procedure should be performed.

Preliminary Checks

1. Check the battery's state of charge and connections.
2. Inspect all wires and connections for breaks, cuts, abrasions, or burn spots. Repair as necessary.
3. Unplug all connectors one at a time and inspect for corroded or burned contacts. Repair and plug connectors back together. DO NOT re-

move the dielectric compound in the connectors.

4. Check for loose or damaged spark plug or coil wires. A wire resistance check is given at the end of this section. If the boots or nipples are removed on 8mm ignition wires, reline the inside of each with new silicone dielectric compound (Motorcraft WA-10).

Special Tools

To perform the following tests, two special tools are needed; the ignition test jumper shown in the illustration and a modified spark plug. Use the illustration to assembly the ignition test jumper. The test jumper must be used when performing the following tests. The modified spark plug is basically a spark plug with the side electrode removed. Ford makes a special tool called a Spark Tester for this purpose, which besides not having a side electrode is equipped with a spring clip so that it can be grounded to engine metal. It is recommended that the Spark Tester be used as there is less change of being shocked.

Run Mode Spark Test

NOTE: The wire colors given here are the main colors of the wires, not the dots or hashmarks.

STEP 1

1. Remove the distributor cap and rotor from the distributor.

2. With the ignition off, turn the engine over by hand until one of the teeth on the distributor armature aligns with the magnet in the pickup coil.

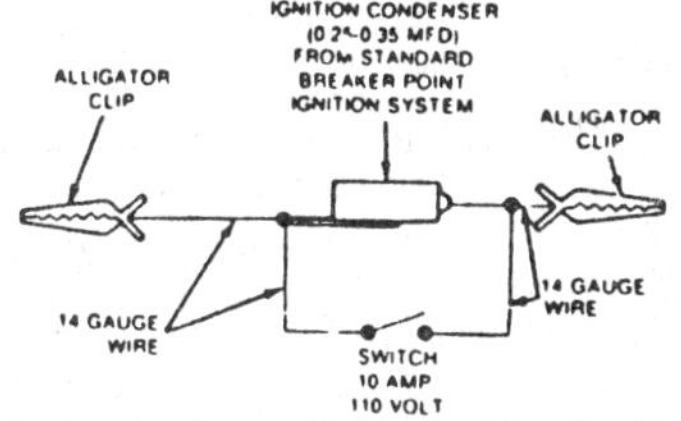

Test jumper wire switch used for testing Dura Spark ignition systems

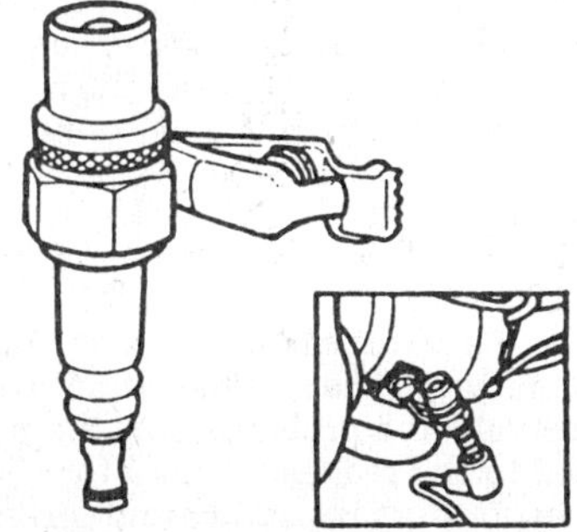

Spark plug tester; actually a modified spark plug (side electrode removed) with a spring for ground

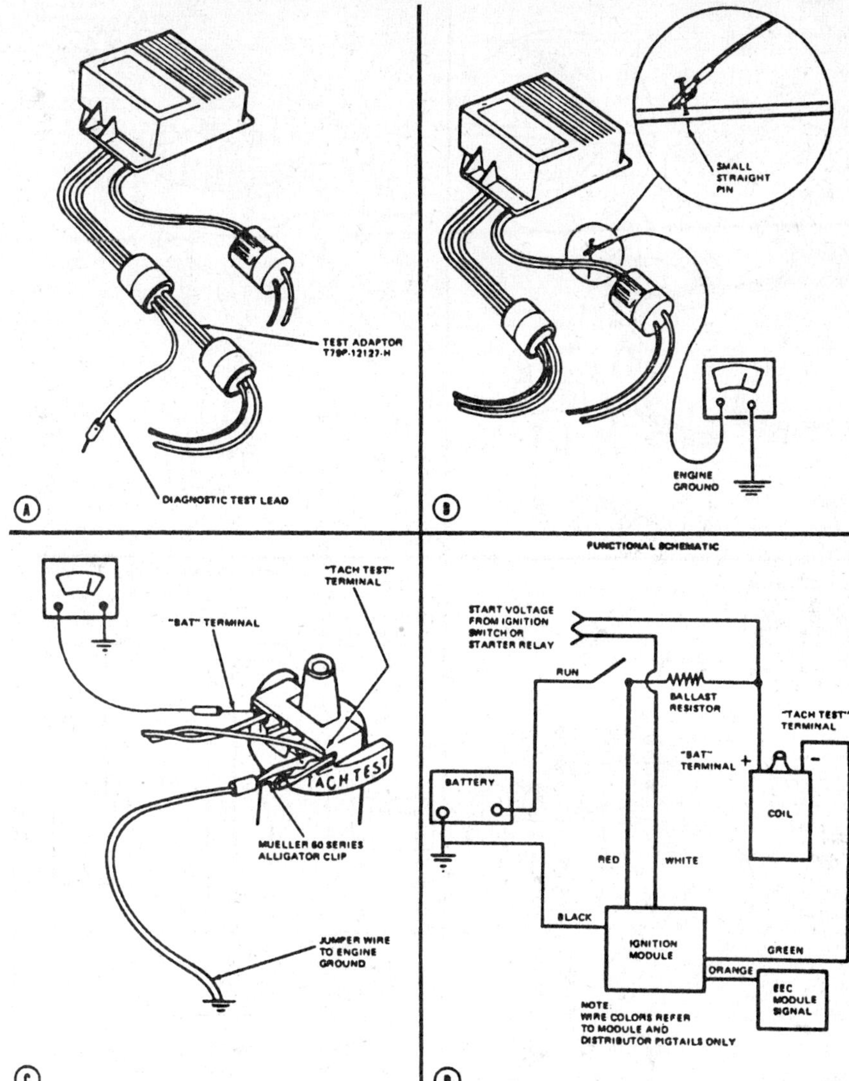

Testing the Dura Spark ignition on models with EEC

3. Remove the coil wire from the distributor cap. Install the modified spark plug (see Special Tools, above) in the coil wire terminal and using heavy gloves and insulated pliers, hold the spark plug shell against the engine block.

4. Turn the ignition to RUN (not START) and tap the distributor body with a screwdriver handle. There should be a spark at the modified spark plug or at the coil wire terminal.

5. If a good spark is evident, the primary circuit is OK: perform the Start Mode Spark Test. If there is no spark, proceed to STEP 2.

STEP 2

1. Unplug the module connector(s) which contain(s) the green and black module leads.

2. In the harness side of the connector(s), connect the special test jumper (see Special Tools, above) between the leads which connect to the green and black leads of the module pig tails. Use paper clips on connector socket holes to make contact. Do not allow clips to ground.

3. Turn the ignition switch to RUN (not START) and close the test jumper switch. Leave closed for about 1 second, then open. Repeat several times. There should be a spark each time the switch is opened. On DuraSpark I systems, close the test switch for 10 seconds is adequate.

4. If there is no spark, the problem is probably in the primary circuit through the ignition switch, the coil, the green lead or the black lead, or the ground connection in the distributor; Perform STEP 3. If there is a spark, the primary circuit wiring and coil are probably OK. The problem is probably in the distributor pick-up, the module red wire, or the module: perform STEP 6.

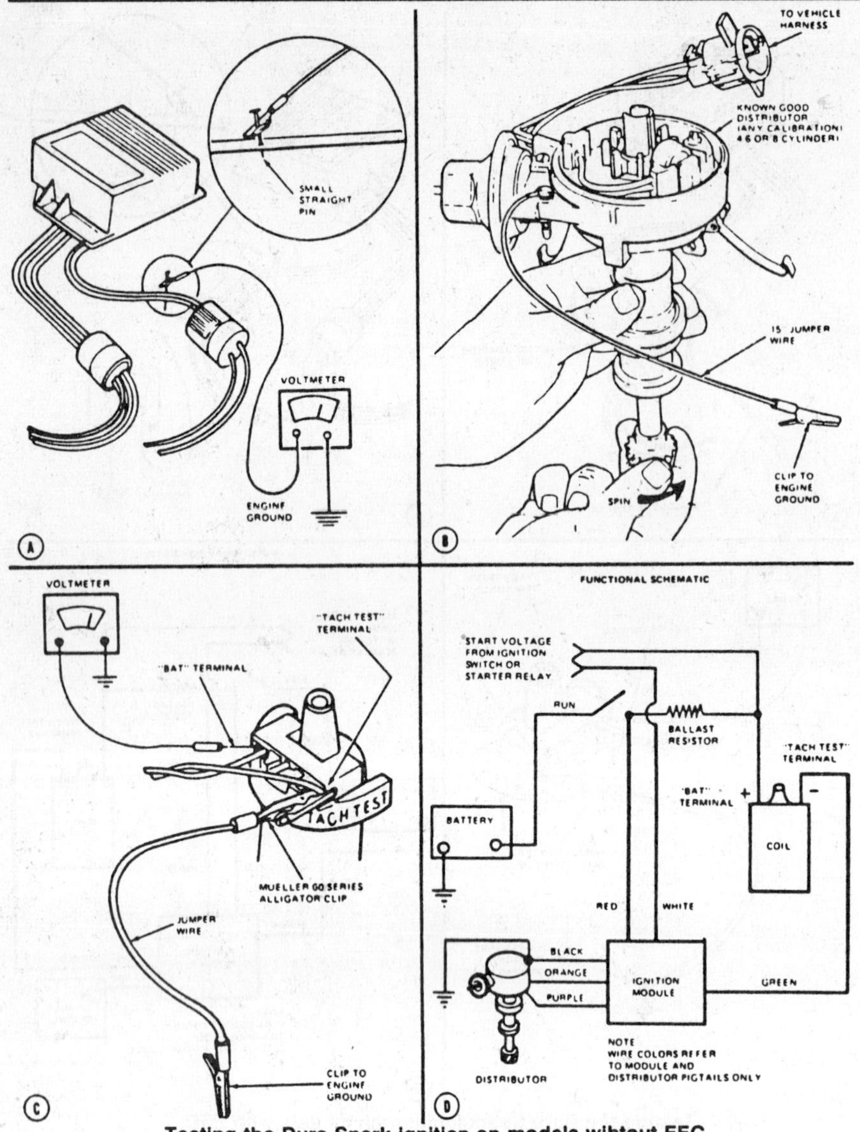

Testing the Dura Spark Ignition on models wihtout EEC

STEP 3

1. Disconnect the test jumper lead from the black lead and connect it to a good ground. Turn the test jumper switch on and off several times as in STEP 2.

2. If there is no spark, the problem is probably in the green lead, the coil, or the coil feed circuit: perform STEP 5.

3. If there is spark, the problem is probably in the black lead or the distributor ground connection: perform STEP 4.

STEP 4

1. Connect an ohmmeter between the black lead and ground. With the meter on its lowest scale, there should be no measurable resistance in the circuit. If there is resistance, check the distributor ground connection and the black lead from the module. Repair as necessary, remove the ohmmeter, plug in all connections and repeat STEP 1.

2. If there is no resistance, the primary ground wiring is OK: perform STEP 6.

STEP 5

1. Disconnect the test jumper from the green lead and ground and connect it between the TACH-TEST terminal of the coil and a good ground to the engine.

2. With the ignition switch in the RUN position, turn the jumper switch on. Hold it on for about 1 second then turn it off as in Step 2. Repeat several times. There should be a spark each time the switch in turned off. If there is no spark, the problem is probably in the primary circuit running through the ignition switch to the coil BAT terminal, or in the coil itself. Check coil resistance (test given later in this section), and check the coil for internal shorts or opens. Check the coil feed circuit for opens, shorts, or high resistance. Repair as necessary, reconnect all connectors and repeat STEP 1. If there is spark, the coil and its feed circuit are OK. The problem could be in the green lead between the coil and the module. Check for an open or short, repair as necessary, reconnect all connectors and repeat STEP 1.

STEP 6

To perform this step, a voltmeter which is not combined with a dwell meter is needed. The slight needle oscillations (½v) you'll be looking for may not be detectable on the combined voltmeter/dwell meter unit.

1. Connect a voltmeter between the orange and purple leads on the harness side of the module connectors.

CAUTION

On catalytic converter equipped cars, disconnect the air supply line between the Thermactor by-pass valve and the manifold before cranking the engine with the ignition off. This will prevent damage to the catalytic converter. After testing, run the engine for at least 3 minutes before reconnecting the by-pass valve, to clear excess fuel from the exhaust system.

2. Set the voltmeter on its lowest scale and crank the engine. The meter needle should oscillate slightly (about ½v). If the meter does not oscillate, check the circuit through the magnetic pick-up in the distributor for open, shorts, shorts to ground and resistance. Resistance between the orange and purple leads should be 400-1,000Ω, and between each lead and ground should be more than 70,000Ω. Repair as necessary, reconnect all connectors and repeat STEP 1.

If the meter oscillates, the problem is probably in the power feed to the module (red wire) or in the module itself: proceed to STEP 7.

STEP 7

1. Remove all meters and jumpers and plug in all connectors.

2. Turn the ignition switch to the RUN position and measure voltage between the battery positive terminal and engine ground. It should be 12 volts.

3. Next, measure voltage between the red lead of the module and engine ground. To mark this measurement, it will be necessary to pierce the red wire with a straight pin and connect the voltmeter to the straight pin and to ground. DO NOT ALLOW THE STRAIGHT PIN TO GROUND ITSELF!

4. The two readings should be within one volt of each other. If not within one volt, the problem is in the power feed to the red lead. Check for shorts, open, or high resistance and correct as necessary. After repairs, repeat Step 1.

If the readings are within one volt, the problem is probably in the module.

Replace it with a good module and repeat STEP 1. If this corrects the problem, reconnect the old module and repeat STEP 1. If the problem returns, permanently install the new module.

Start Mode Spark Test

NOTE: The wire colors given here are the main colors of the wires, not the dots or hashmarks.

1. Remove the coil wire from the distributor cap. Install the modified spark plug mentioned under Special Tools, above, in the coil wire and ground it to engine metal either by its spring clip (Spark Tester) or by holding the spark plug shell against the engine block with insulated pliers.

NOTE: See CAUTION under STEP 6 of Run Mode Spark Test, above.

2. Have an assistant crank the engine using the ignition switch and check for spark. If there is good spark, the problem is probably in distributor cap, rotor, ignition cables or spark plugs. If there is no spark, proceed to Step 3.
3. Measure the battery voltage. Next, measure the voltage at the white wire of the module while cranking the engine. To mark this measurement, it will be necessary to pierce the white wire with a straight pin and connect the voltmeter to the straight pin and to ground. DO NOT ALLOW THE STRAIGHT PIN TO GROUND ITSELF. The battery voltage and the voltage at the white wire should be within 1 volt of each other. If the readings are not within 1 volt of each other, check and repair the feed through the ignition switch to the white wire. Recheck for spark (Step 1). If the readings are within 1 volt of each other, or if there is still no spark after the power feed to white wire is repaired, proceed to Step 4.
4. Measure the coil BAT terminal voltage while cranking the engine. The reading should be within 1 volt of battery voltage. If the readings are not within 1 volt of each other, check and repair the feed through the ignition switch to the coil. If the readings are within 1 volt of each other, the problem is probably in the ignition module. Substitute another module and repeat the test for spark (Step 1).

TFI SYSTEM TESTING

NOTE: If the engine operates but has no power, the problem could be in the EEC system. Check the initial timing, if the engine is operating at a fixed 10° BTDC the system is in fail-safe mode. Have the EEC system check with necessary diagnostic equipment.

After performing any test which requires piercing a wire with a straight pin, remove the straight pin and seal the holes in the wire with silicone sealer.

Ignition Coil Secondary Voltage

1. Disconnect the secondary (high voltage) coil wire from the distributor cap and install a spark tester (see Special Tools, located with the DuraSpark Troubleshooting) between the coil wire and ground.
2. Crank the engine. A good, strong spark should be noted at the spark tester. If spark is noted, but the engine will not start, check the spark plugs, spark plug wiring, and fuel system. If there is no spark at the tester:
   a. Check the ignition coil secondary wire resistance; it should be no more than 5,000Ω per inch.
   b. Inspect the ignition coil for damage and/or carbon tracking.
   c. With the distributor cap removed, verify that the distributor shaft turns with the engine; if it does not, repair the engine as required.
   d. If the fault was not found in a, b, or c, proceed to the next test.

Ignition Coil Primary Circuit Switching

1. Insert a small straight pin in the wire which runs from the coil negative (−) terminal to the TFI module, about 1″ (25.4mm) from the module.

CAUTION

The pin must not touch ground.

2. Connect a 12VDC test lamp between the straight pin and an engine ground.
3. Crank the engine, noting the operation of the test lamp. If the test lamp flashes, proceed to the next test. If the test lamp lights but does not flash, proceed to the Wiring Harness test. If the test lamp does not light at all, proceed to the Primary Circuit Continuity test.

Ignition Coil Resistance

Replace the ignition coil if the resistance is out of the specification range.

Wiring Harness

1. Disconnect the wiring harness connector from the TFI module; the connector tabs must be PUSHED to disengage the connector. Inspect the connector form damage, dirt, and corrosion.
2. Attach the negative lead of a voltmeter to the base of the distributor. Attach the other voltmeter lead to a small straight pin.
   a. With the ignition switch in the RUN position, insert the straight pin onto the NO.1 terminal of the TFI module connector. Note the voltage reading and proceed to b.
   b. With the ignition switch in the RUN position, move the straight pin to the No. 2 connector terminal. Again, note the voltage reading, then proceed to c.
   c. Move the straight pin to the No. 3 connector terminal, then turn the ignition switch to the START position. Note the voltage reading then turn the Ignition OFF.
3. The voltage readings from a, b, and c should all be at least 90% of the available battery voltage. If the readings are okay, proceed to the Stator Assembly and Module test. If any reading is less than 90% of the battery voltage, inspect the wiring, connectors, and/or ignition switch for defects. If the voltage is low only at the No. 1 terminal, proceed to the ignition coil primary voltage test.

Stator Assembly and Module

1. Remove the distributor from the engine.
2. Remove the TFI module from the distributor.
3. Inspect the distributor terminals, ground screw, and stator wiring for damage. Repair as necessary.
4. Measure the resistance of the stator assembly, using an ohmmeter. If the ohmmeter reading is 800-975Ω, the stator is okay, but the TFI module must be replaced. If the ohmmeter reading is less than 800Ω or more than 975Ω; the TFI module is okay, but the stator assembly must be replaced.
5. Reinstall the TFI module and the distributor.

Primary Circuit Continuity

This test is performed in the same manner as the previous Wiring Harness test, but only the NO. 1 terminal conductor is tested (ignition switch in RUN position). If the voltage is less than 90% of the available battery voltage, proceed to the next test.

Ignition Coil Primary Voltage

1. Attach the negative lead of a voltmeter to the distributor base.
2. Turn the ignition switch ON and connect the positive voltmeter lead to the negative (−) ignition coil terminal. Note the voltage reading and turn the ignition OFF. If the voltmeter reading is less than 90% of the available battery voltage, inspect the wiring between the ignition module and the negative (−) coil terminal, then proceed to the last test, which follows.

Ignition Coil Supply Voltage

1. Attach the negative lead of a voltmeter to the distributor base.
2. Turn the ignition switch ON and connect the positive voltmeter lead to the positive (+) ignition coil terminal.

NOTE: Note the voltage reading then turn the ignition OFF.

If the voltage reading is at least 90% of the battery voltage, yet the engine will still not run: check the ignition coil connector and terminals for corrosion, dirt, and/or damage. Replace the ignition switch if the connectors and terminals are okay.

3. Connect any remaining wiring.

GENERAL TESTING – ALL SYSTEMS

Ignition Coil Test

The ignition coil must be diagnosed separately from the rest of the ignition system.

1. Primary resistance is measured between the two primary (low voltage) coil terminals, with the coil connector disconnected and the ignition switch off. Primary resistance must be 0.71-0.77Ω for DuraSpark I. For DuraSpark II, it must be 1.13-1.23Ω. For TFI systems, the primary resistance should be 0.3-1.0Ω.
2. On DuraSpark ignitions, the secondary resistance is measured between the BATT and high voltage (secondary) terminals of the ignition coil with the ignition off, and wiring from the coil disconnected. Secondary resistance must be 7,350-8,250Ω on DuraSpark I systems. DuraSpark II figure is 7,700-9,300Ω. For TFI systems, the primary resistance should be 8,000-11,500Ω.
3. If resistance tests are all right, but the coil is still suspected, test the coil on a coil tester by following the test equipment manufacturer's instructions for a standard coil. If the reading differs from the original test, check for a defective harness.

Resistance Wire Test

Replace the resistance wire if it doesn't show a resistance of 1.05-1.15Ω for DuraSpark II. The resistance wire isn't used on DuraSpark I or TFI systems.

Spark Plug Wire Resistance

Resistance on these wires must not exceed 5,000Ω per inch. To properly measure this, remove the wires from the plugs, and remove the distributor cap. Measure the resistance through the distributor cap at that end. Do not pierce any ignition wire for any reason. Measure only from the two ends.

NOTE: Silicone grease must be re-applied to the spark plug wires whenever they are removed.

When removing the wires from the spark plugs, a special tool such as the one pictured should be used. Do not pull on the wires. Grasp and twist the boot to remove the wire.

Whenever the high tension wires are removed from the plugs, coil, or distributor, silicone grease must be applied to the boot before reconnection. Use a clean small screwdriver blade to coat the entire interior surface with Ford silicone grease D7AZ-19A331-A, Dow Corning #111, or General Electric G-627.

Adjustments.

The air gap between the armature and magnetic pick-up coil in the distributor is not adjustable, nor are there any adjustments for the amplifier module. Inoperative components are simply replaced. Any attempt to connect components outside the vehicle may result in component failure.

ENGINE ELECTRICAL

Ignition Coil

REMOVAL & INSTALLATION

1. Disconnect the battery ground.
2. Disconnect the two small and one large wire from the coil.
3. Disconnect the condenser connector from the coil, if equipped.
4. Unbolt and remove the coil.
5. Installation is the reverse of removal.

Ignition Module

REMOVAL & INSTALLATION

Removing the module, on all models, is a matter of simply removing the fasteners that attach it to the fender or firewall and pulling apart the connectors. When unplugging the connectors, pull them apart with a firm, straight pull. NEVER PRY THEM APART! To pry them will cause damage. When reconnecting them, coat the mating ends with silicone dielectric grease to waterproof the connection. Press the connectors together firmly to overcome any vacuum lock caused by the grease.

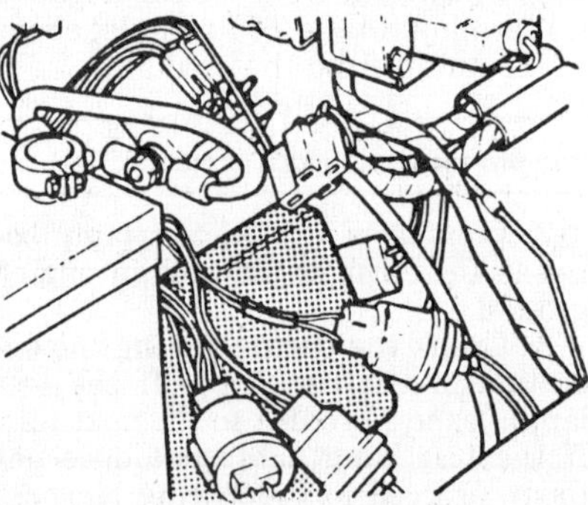

Typical control module

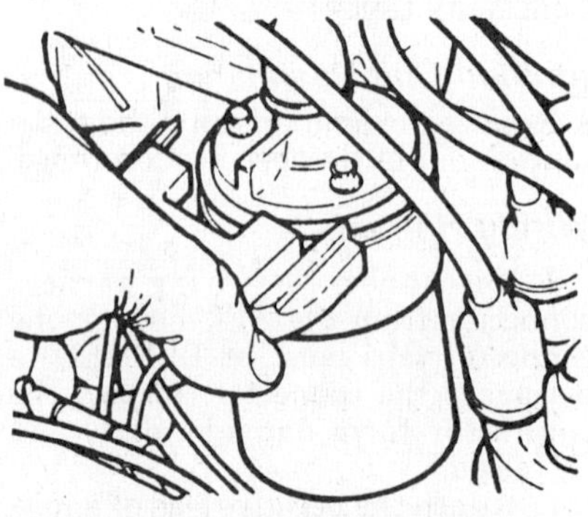

Typical coil connector removal

NOTE: If the locking tabs weaken or break, don't replace the unit. Just secure the connection with electrical tape or tie straps.

Distributor

REMOVAL & INSTALLATION

1. Remove the air cleaner on V6 and V8 engines. On 4- and 6-cylinder inline engines, removal of a Thermactor® (air) pump mounting bolt and drive belt will allow the pump to be moved to the side and permit access to the distributor. If necessary, disconnect the Thermactor® air filter and lines as well.
2. Remove the distributor cap and position the cap and ignition wires to the side.
3. Disconnect the wire harness plug from the distributor connector. Disconnect and plug the vacuum hoses from the vacuum diaphragm assembly. (DuraSpark®III systems are not equipped with a vacuum diaphragm).
4. Rotate the engine (in normal direction of rotation) until No. 1 piston is on TDC (Top Dead Center) of the compression stroke. The TDC mark on

the crankshaft pulley and the pointer should align. Rotor tip pointing at No. 1 position on distributor cap.

5. On DuraSpark®I or II, turn the engine a slight bit more (if required) to align the stator (pick-up coil) assembly pole with an (closest) armature pole. On DuraSpark®III, the distributor sleeve groove (when looking down from the top) and the cap adaptor alignment slot should align. On models equipped with EEC-IV (1984 and later), remove the rotor (2 screws) and note the position of the polarizing square and shaft plate for reinstallation reference.

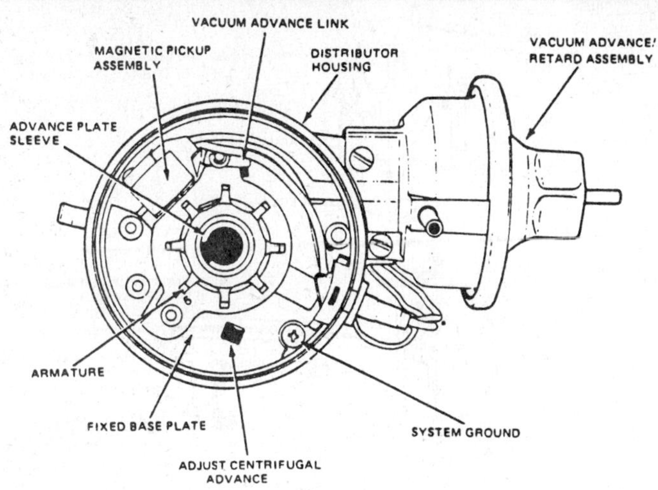

Breakerless V8 distributor (cap and rotor removed)

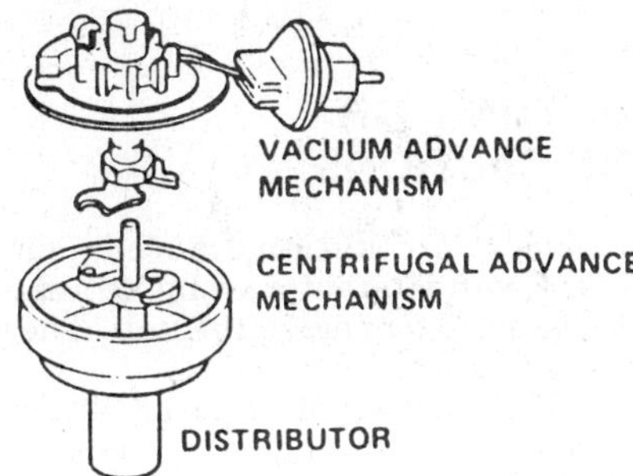

Dual advance distributor (typical)

6. Scribe a mark on the distributor body and engine black to indicate the position of the rotor tip and position of the distributor in the engine. DuraSpark®III and some EEC-IV system distributors are equipped with a notched base and will only locate at one position on the engine.

7. Remove the holddown bolt and clamp located at the base of the distributor. (Some DuraSpark®III and EEC-IV system distributors are equipped with a special holddown bolt that requires a Torx® Head Wrench for removal). Remove the distributor from the engine. Pay attention to the direction the rotor tip points when the drive gear disengages. For reinstallation purposes, the rotor should be at this position to insure proper gear mesh and timing.

8. Avoid turning the engine, if possible, while the distributor is removed. If the engine is turned from TDC position, TDC timing marks will have to be reset before the distributor is installed; Steps 4 and 5.

9. Position the distributor in the engine with the rotor aligned to the marks made on the distributor, or to the place the rotor pointed when the distributor was removed. The stator and armature or polarizing square and shaft plate should also be aligned. Engage the oil pump intermediate shaft and insert the distributor until fully seated on the engine, if the distributor does not fully seat, turn the engine slightly to fully engage the intermediate shaft.

10. Follow the above procedures on models equipped with an indexed distributor base. Make sure when positioning the distributor that the slot in the distributor base will engage the block tab and the sleeve/adaptor slots are aligned.

11. After the distributor has been fully seated on the block install the holddown bracket and bolt. On models equipped with an indexed base, tighten the mounting bolt. On other models, snug the mounting bolt so the distributor can be turned for ignition timing purposes.

12. The rest of the installation is in the reverse order of removal. Check and reset the ignition timing on applicable models.

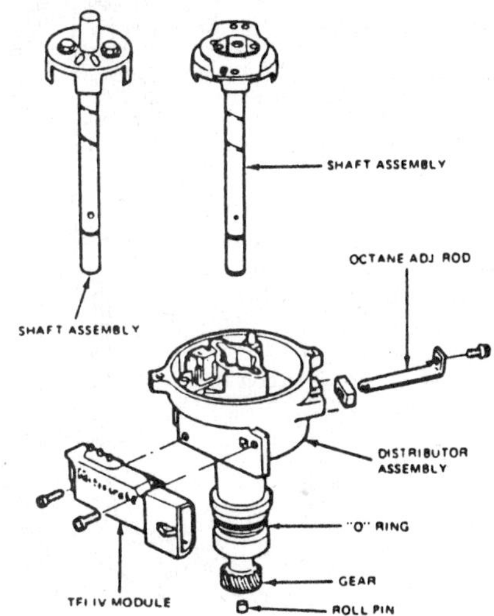

Universal TFI distributor

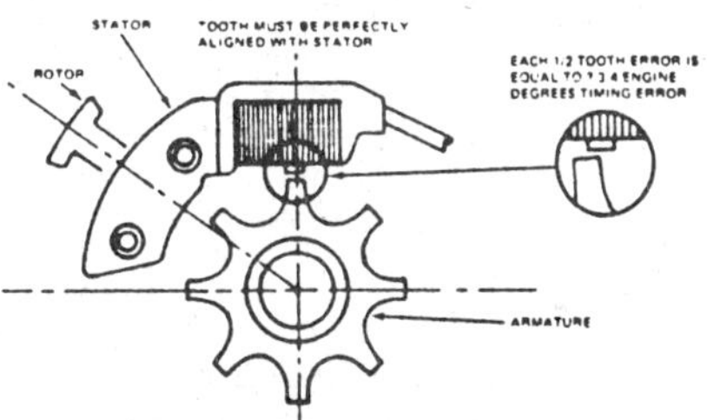

Breakerless distributor static timing position

NOTE: A silicone compound is used on rotor tips, distributor cap contacts and on the inside of the connectors on the spark plugs cable and module couplers. Always apply silicone dielectric compound after servicing any component of the ignition system. Various models use a multi-point rotor which do not require the application of dielectric compound.

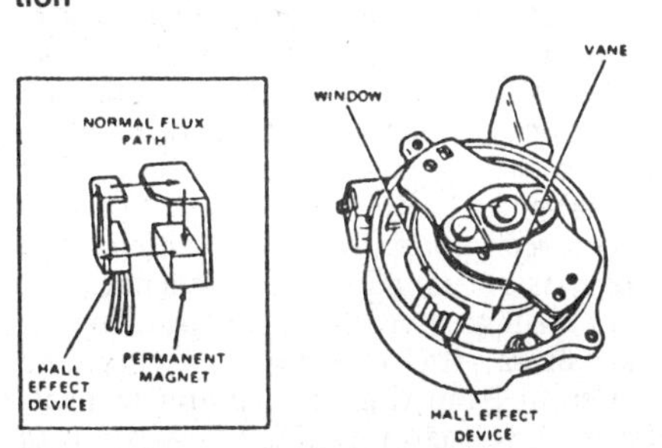

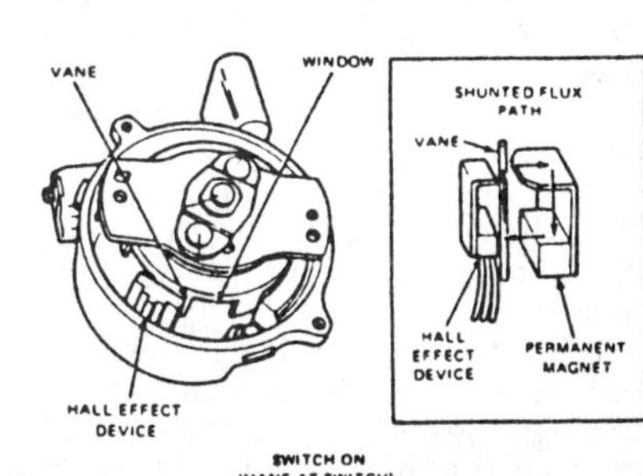

Hall Effect-On/Off switching

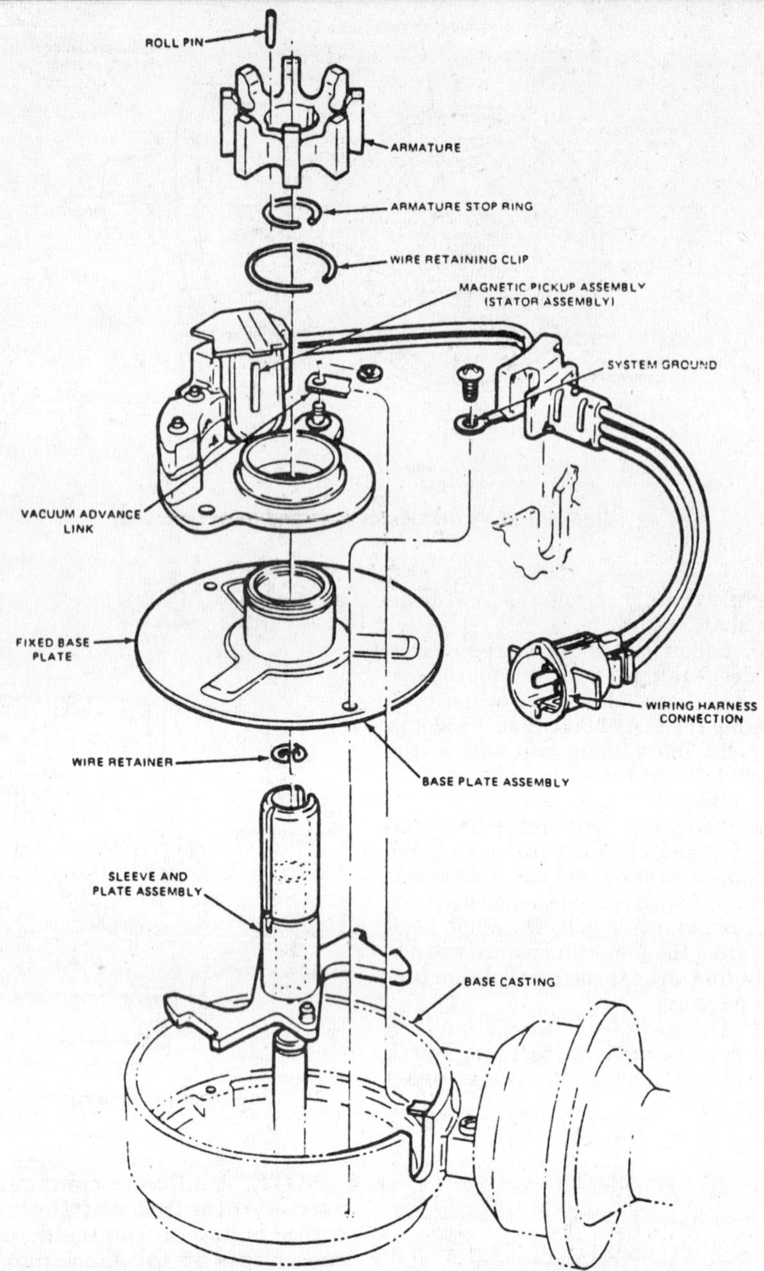

Exploded view of breakerless V8 distributor

Alternator

The alternator charging system consists of the alternator, voltage regulator, warning light, battery, and fuse link wire.

A failure of any component of the charging system can cause the entire system to stop functioning. Because of this, the charging system can be very difficult to troubleshoot when problems occur.

When the ignition key is turned on, current flows from the battery, through the charging system indicator light on the instrument panel, to the voltage regulator, and to the alternator. Since the alternator is not producing any current, the alternator warning light comes on. When the engine is started, the alternator begins to produce current and turns the alternator light off. As the alternator turns and produces current, the current is divided in two ways: part to the battery to charge the battery and power the electrical components of the vehicle, and part is returned to the alternator to enable it to increase its output. In this situation, the alternator is receiving current from the battery and from itself. A voltage regulator is wired into the current supply to the alternator to prevent it from receiving too much current which would cause it to put out too much current. Conversely, if the voltage regulator does not allow the alternator to receive enough current, the battery will not be fully charged and will eventually go dead.

The battery is connected to the alternator at all times, whether the ignition key is turned on or not. If the battery were shorted to ground, the alternator would also be shorted. This would damage the alternator. To prevent this, a fuse link is installed in the wiring between the battery and the alternator. If the battery is shorted, the fuse link is melted, protecting the alternator.

ALTERNATOR PRECAUTIONS

Several precautions must be observed with alternator equipped vehicles to avoid damaging the unit. They are as follows:

1. If the battery is removed for any reason, make sure that it is reconnected with the correct polarity. Reversing the battery connections may result in damage to the one-way rectifiers.
2. When utilizing a booster battery as a starting aid, always connect it as follows: positive to positive, and negative (booster battery) to a good ground on the engine of the car being started.
3. Never use a fast charger as a booster to start cars with alternating current (AC) circuits.
4. When servicing the battery with a fast charger, always disconnect the car battery cables.
5. Never attempt to polarize an alternator.
6. Avoid long soldering times when replacing diodes or transistors. Prolonged heat is damaging to alternators.
7. Do not use test lamps of more than 12 volts (V) for checking diode continuity.
8. Do not short across or ground any of the terminals on the alternator.
9. The polarity of the battery, alternator, and regulator must be matched and considered before making any electrical connections within the system.
10. Never separate the alternator on an open circuit. Make sure that all connections within the circuit are clean and tight.
11. Disconnect the battery terminals when performing any service on the electrical system. This will eliminate the possibility of accidental reversal of polarity.
12. Disconnect the battery ground cable if arc welding is to be done on any part of the car.

CHARGING SYSTEM TROUBLESHOOTING

There are many possible ways in which the charging system can malfunction. Often the source of a problem is difficult to diagnose, requiring special equipment and a good deal of experience. This is usually not the case, however, where the charging system fails completely and causes the dash board warning light to come on or the battery to become dead. To troubleshoot a complete system failure only two pieces of equipment are needed: a test light, to determine that current is reaching a certain point; and a current indicator (ammeter), to determine the direction of the current flow and its measurement in amps.

This test works under three assumptions:

1. The battery is known to be good and fully charged.
2. The alternator belt is in good condition and adjusted to the proper tension.
3. All connections in the system are clean and tight.

NOTE: In order for the current indicator to give a valid reading, the car must be equipped with battery cables which are of the same gauge size and quality as original equipment battery cables.

1. Turn off all electrical components on the car. Make sure the doors of the car are closed. If the car is equipped with a clock, disconnect the clock by removing the lead wire from the rear of the clock. Disconnect the positive battery cable from the battery and connect the ground wire on a test light to the disconnected positive battery cable. Touch the probe end of the test light to the positive battery post. The test light should not light. If the test light does light, there is a short or open circuit on the car.
2. Disconnect the voltage regulator wiring harness connector at the voltage regulator. Turn on the ignition key. Connect the wire on a test light to a good ground (engine bolt). Touch the probe end of a test light to the ignition wire connector into the voltage regulator wiring connector. This wire corresponds to the **I** terminal on the regulator. If the test light goes on, the charging system warning light circuit is complete. If the test light does not come on and the warning light on the instrument panel is on, either the resistor wire, which is parallel with the warning light, or the wiring to the voltage regulator, is defective. If the test light does not come on and the warning light is not on, either the bulb is defective or the power supply wire form the battery through the ignition switch to the bulb has an open circuit. Connect the wiring harness to the regulator.
3. Examine the fuse link wire in the wiring harness from the starter relay to the alternator. If the insulation on the wire is cracked or split, the fuse link may be melted. Connect a test light to the fuse link by attaching the ground wire on the test light to an engine bolt and touching the probe end of the light to the bottom of the fuse link wire where it splices into the alternator output wire. If the bulb in the test light does not light, the fuse link is melted.
4. Start the engine and place a current indicator on the positive battery cable. Turn off all electrical accessories and make sure the doors are closed. If the charging system is working properly, the gauge will show a draw of less than 5 amps. If the system is not working properly, the gauge will show a draw of more than 5 amps. A charge moves the needle toward the battery, a draw moves the needle away from the battery. Turn the engine off.
5. Disconnect the wiring harness from the voltage regulator at the regulator at the regulator connector. Connect a male spade terminal (solderless connector) to each end of a jumper wire. Insert one end of the wire into the wiring harness connector which corresponds to the **A** terminal on the regulator. Insert the other end of the wire into the wiring harness connector which corresponds to the **F** terminal on the regulator. Position the connector with the jumper wire installed so that it cannot contact any metal surface under the hood. Position a current indicator gauge on the positive battery cable. Have an assistant start the engine. Observe the reading on the current indicator. Have your assistant slowly raise the speed of the engine to about 2,000 rpm or until the current indicator needle stops moving, whichever comes first. Do not run the engine for more than a short period of time in this condition. If the wiring harness connector or jumper wire becomes excessively hot during this test, turn off the engine and check for a grounded wire in the regulator wiring harness. If the current indicator shows a charge of about three amps less than the output of the alternator, the alternator is working properly. If the previous tests showed a draw, the voltage regulator is defective. If the gauge does not show the proper charging rate, the alternator is defective.

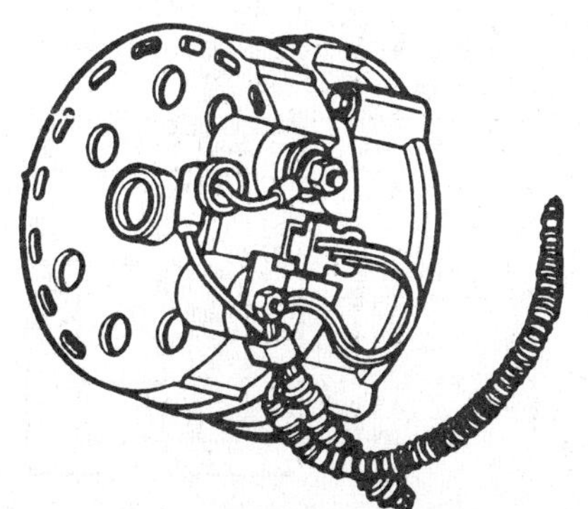

Side terminal alternator

REMOVAL & INSTALLATION

1. Disconnect the negative battery cable from the battery.
2. Disconnect the wires from the alternator.
3. Loosen the alternator mounting bolts and remove the drive belt.

NOTE: Some 1981 and later cars are equipped with a ribbed, K-section belt and automatic tensioner. A special tool must be made to remove the tension from the tensioner arm. Loosen the idler pulley pivot and adjuster bolts before using the tool. See the accompanying illustration for tool details.

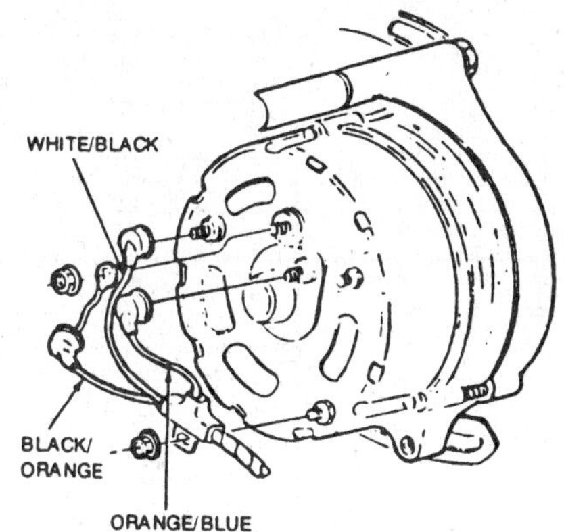

Rear terminal alternator

4. Remove the alternator mounting bolts and spacer (if equipped), and remove the alternator.
5. To install, position the alternator on its brackets and install the attaching bolts and spacer (if so equipped).
6. Connect the wires to the alternator.
7. Position the drive belt on the alternator pulley. Adjust the belt tension as outlined under ROUTINE MAINTENANCE.
8. Connect the negative battery cable.

Starter

There are two different types of starters are used on these cars. All gas-

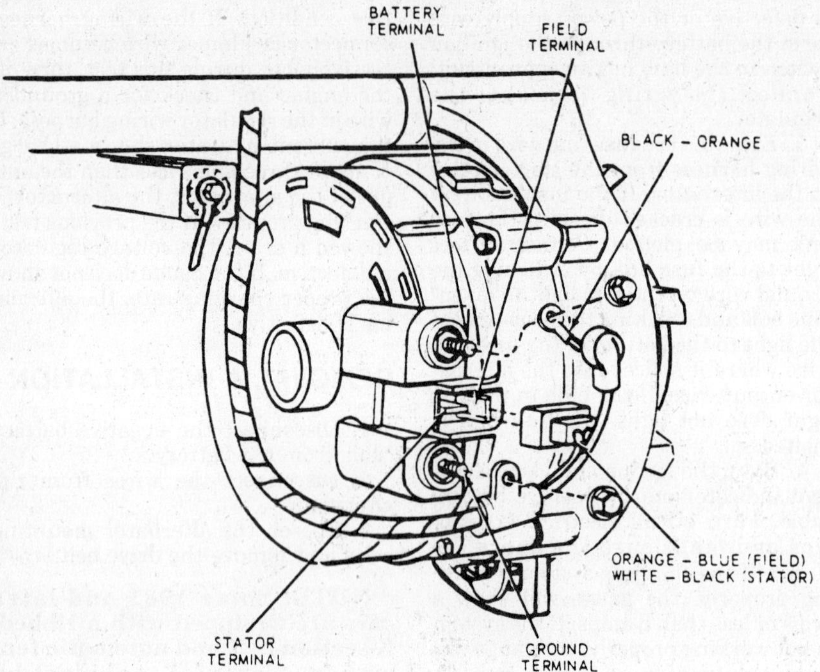

Alternator terminal locations-side terminal type

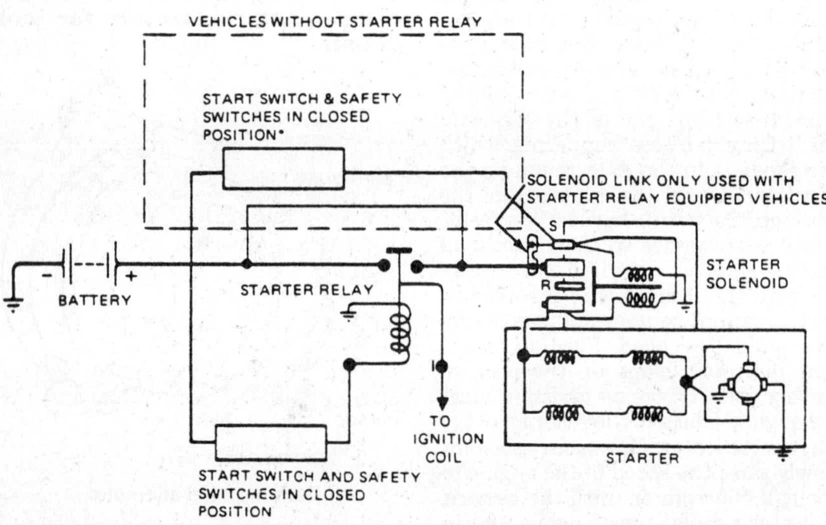

Solenoid actuated starter circuit

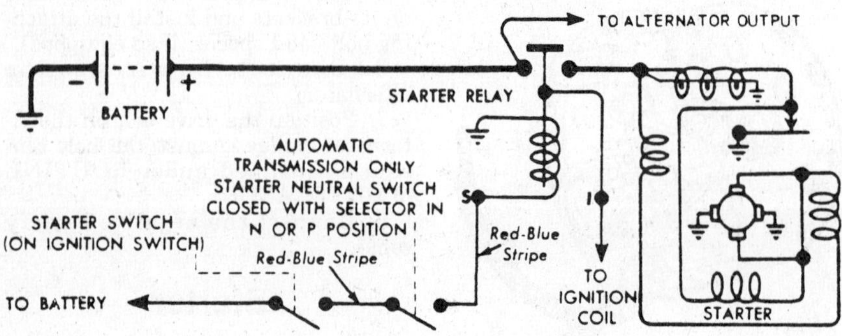

Positive engagement starter circuit

oline engines use a positive engagement starter. A solenoid actuated starter is used on the diesel. Since a greater amount of starting power is required by the diesel, the solenoid actuated starter is constructed with more coil and armature windings to deliver the necessary current. The presence of a solenoid mechanism is incidental and does not affect starting power.

The positive engagement starter system employs a starter relay, usually mounted inside the engine compartment on a fender wall, to transfer battery current to the starter. The relay is activated by the ignition switch and, when engaged, it creates a direct current from the battery to the starter windings. Simultaneously, the armature begins to turn the starter drive is pushed out to engage the flywheel.

In the solenoid actuated starter system, battery current is first directed to a solenoid assembly which is mounted on the starter case. The current closes the solenoid contacts, which engages the drive pinion and directs current to the coil windings, causing the armature to rotate. While this system does not need a starter relay, some models were nevertheless equipped with one in order to simplify assembly procedures. These vehicles also have a connector link attached to the solenoid, which provides a hook up for the relay wire.

REMOVAL & INSTALLATION

Except Diesel

1. Disconnect the negative battery cable.
2. Raise the front of the car and install jackstands beneath the frame. Firmly apply the parking brake and place blocks in back of the rear wheels.
3. Tag and disconnect the wiring at the starter.
4. Turn the front wheels fully to the right. On some later models it will be necessary to remove the frame brace. On many models, it will be necessary to remove the two bolts retaining the

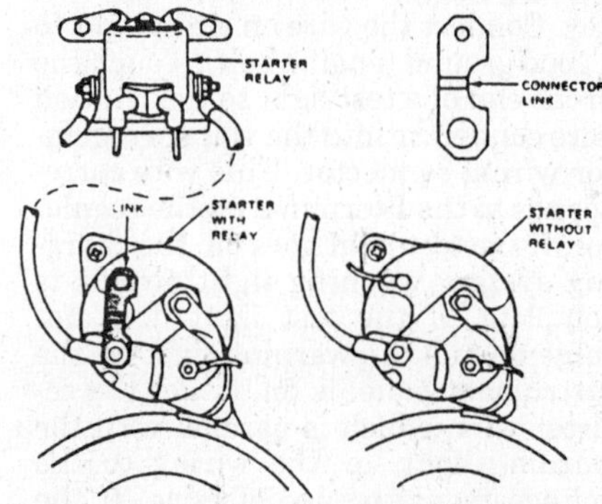

Solenoid connector link for use with starter relay

steering idler arm to the frame to gain access to the starter.

5. Remove the starter mounting bolts and remove the starter.

6. Reverse the above procedure to install. Torque the mounting bolts to 12-15 ft.lb. on starters with 3 mounting bolts and 15-20 ft.lb. on starters with 2 mounting bolts. Torque the idler arm retaining bolts to 28-35 ft.lb. (if removed). Make sure that the nut securing the heavy cable to the starter is snugged down tightly.

2,443cc Diesel Engine

1. Disconnect the battery ground (negative) cable.
2. Remove the bolt holding the dipstick tube to the intake manifold.
3. Remove the wires from the starter solenoid. Remove the front starter support bracket.
4. Remove the two starter to torque converter housing mounting bolts.
5. Pull the dipstick tube outward slightly allowing clearance for starter motor removal. Remove the starter motor.
6. Position the starter to torque converter housing and install the two bolts. Tighten to 30-40 ft.lb.
7. Install the starter support bracket and tighten the attaching bolts to 14-20 ft.lb.
8. Connect the cables to the starter solenoid. Tighten the red wire to 80-120 in.lb. Tighten the black wire to 25 in.lb.
9. Reposition the dipstick to the intake manifold, install the bolt and tighten to 6-7 ft.lb.
10. Install the battery ground cable.

OVERHAUL – EXCEPT DIESEL

Brush Replacement

1. Remove the starter from the engine as previously outlined.
2. Remove the starter drive plunger lever cover and gasket.
3. Loosen and remove the brush cover band and remove the brushes from their holder.
4. Remove the two through-bolts from the starter frame.
5. Separate the drive-end housing, starter frame and brush end plate assemblies.
6. Remove the starter drive plunger lever and pivot pin, and remove the armature.
7. Remove the ground brush retaining screws from the frame and remove the brushes.
8. Cut the insulated brush leads from the field coils, as close to the field connection point as possible.
9. Clean and inspect the starter motor.

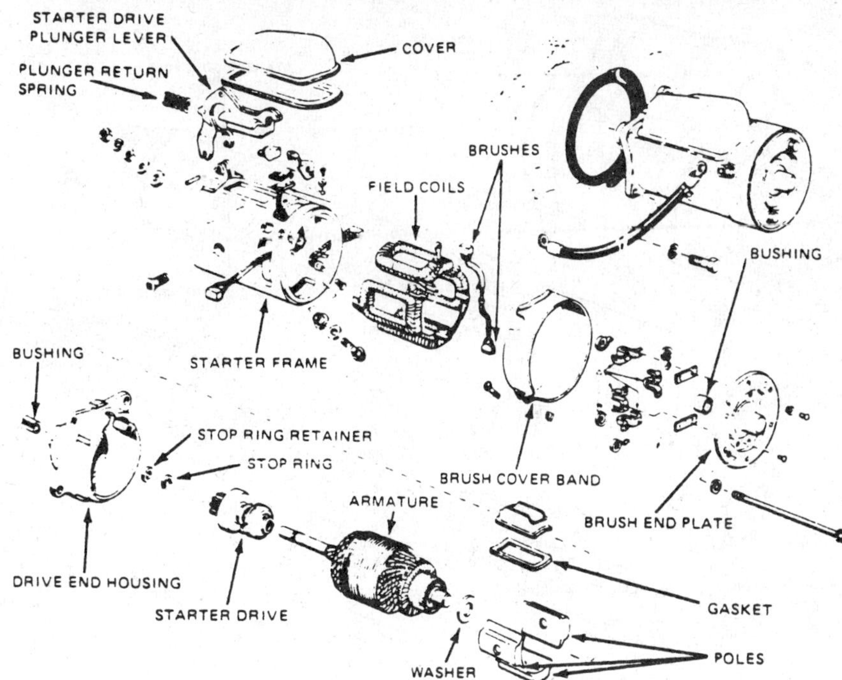

Exploded view of positive engagement starter

10. Replace the brush end plate if the insulator between the field brush holder and the end plate is cracked or broken.
11. Position the new insulated field brushes lead on the field coil connection. Position and crimp the clip provided with the brushes to hold the brush lead to the connection. Solder the lead, clip, and connection together using resin core solder. Use a 300 watt soldering iron.
12. Install the ground brush leads to the frame with the retaining screws.
13. Install the starter drive plunger lever and pivot pin, and install the armature.
14. Assemble the drive-end housing, starter frame and brush end plate assemblies.
15. Install the two through-bolts in the starter frame. Torque the through-bolts to 55-75 in.lb.
16. Install the brushes in their holders and install the brush cover band.
17. Install the starter drive plunger lever cover and gasket.
22. Install the starter on the engine as previously outlined.

Drive Replacement

1. Remove the starter as outlined previously.
2. Remove the starter drive plunger lever and gasket and the brush cover band.
3. Remove the two through-bolts from the starter frame.
4. Separate the drive end housing from the starter frame.
5. The starter drive plunger lever return spring may fall out after detaching the drive end housing. If not, remove it.
6. Remove the pivot pin which attaches the starter drive plunger lever to the starter frame and remove the lever.
7. Remove the stop ring retainer and stop ring from the armature shaft.
8. Slide the starter drive off the armature shaft.
9. Examine the wear pattern on the starter drive teeth. There should be evidence of full contact between the starter drive teeth and the flywheel ring gear teeth. If there is evidence of irregular wear, examine the flywheel ring gear for damage and replace if necessary.
10. Apply a thin coat of white grease to the armature shaft before installing the drive gear. Place a small amount of grease in the drive end housing bearing. Slide the starter drive on the armature shaft.
11. Install the stop ring retainer and stop ring on the armature shaft.
12. Install the starter drive plunger lever on the starter frame and install the pin.
13. Assemble the drive end housing on the starter frame.
14. install the two through-bolts in the starter frame. Tighten the starter through bolts to 55-75 in.lb.
15. Install the starter drive plunger lever and gasket and the brush cover band.
16. Install the starter as outlined previously.

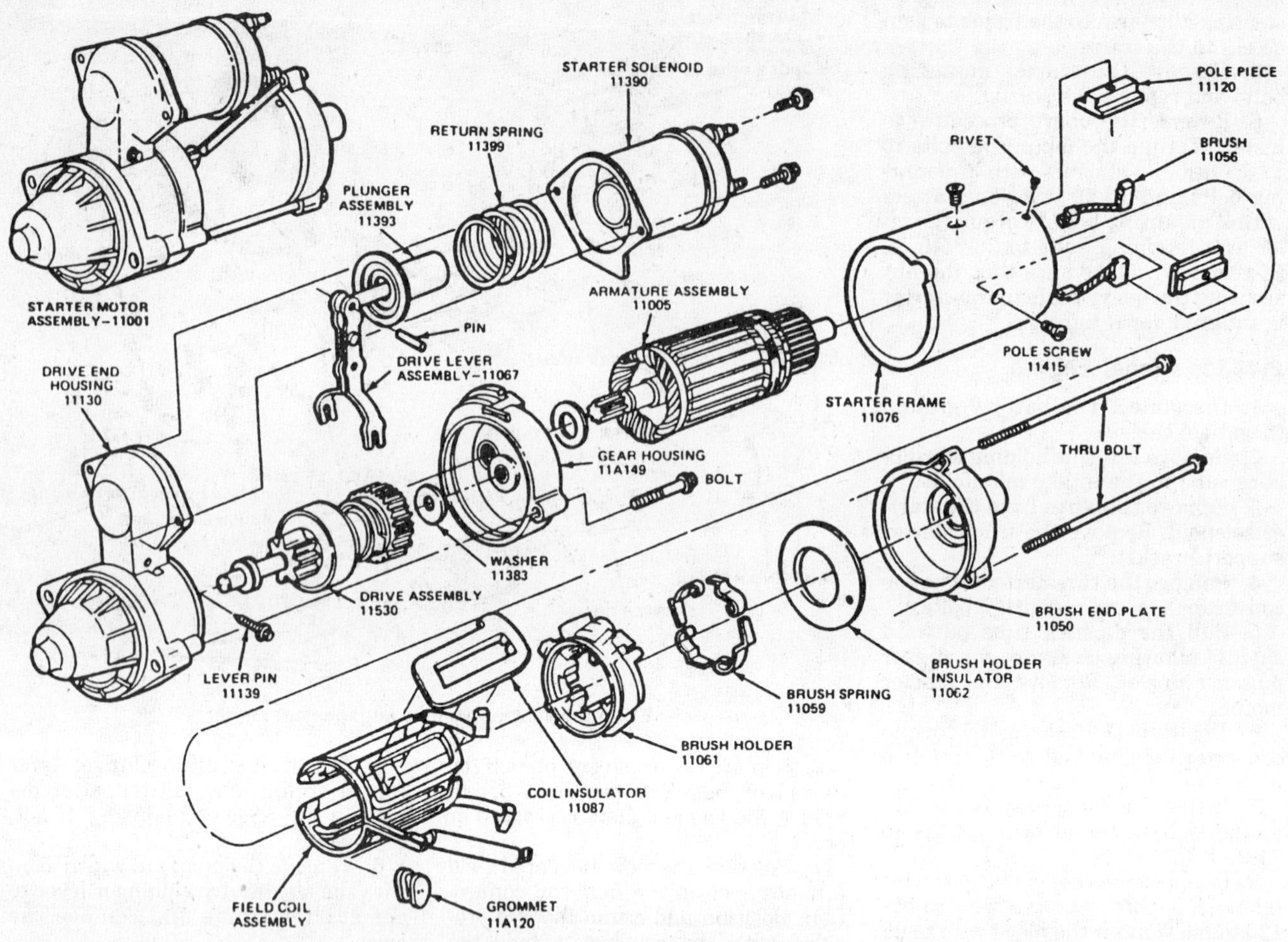

An exploded view of the diesel engine starter

OVERHAUL – DIESEL

1. Disconnect the field coil connection from the solenoid motor terminal.
2. Remove the solenoid attaching screws, solenoid and plunger return spring. Rotate the solenoid 90° to remove it.
3. Remove the through-bolts and brush end plate.
4. Rempove the brush springs and brushes from the plastic brush holder and remove the brush holder. Keep track of the location of the brush holder with regard to the brush terminals.
5. Remove the frame assembly.
6. Remove the armature assembly.
7. Remove the screw from the gear housing and remove the gear housing.
8. Remove the plunger and lever pivot screw and remove the plunger and lever.
9. Remove the gear, output shaft and drive assembly.
10. Remove the thrust washer, retainer, drive stop ring and slide the drive assembly off of the output shaft.

WARNING: Don't wash the drive because the solvent will wash out the lubricant, causing the drive to slip. Use a brush or compressed air to clean the drive, field coils, armature, gear and housing.

11. Inspect the armature windings for broken or burned insulation, and open connections at the commutator. Check for any signs of grounding.
12. Check the commutator for excessive runout. If the commutator is rough or more than 0.127mm out-of-round, replace it or correct the problem as necessary.
13. Check the plastic brush holder for cracks or broken pads. Replace the brushes if worn to a length less than ¼" (6mm) in length. Inspect the field coils and plastic bobbins for burned or damaged areas. Check the continuity of the coil and brush connections. A brush replacement kit is available. Any other worn or damaged parts should be replaced.
14. Apply a thin coating of Lubriplate 777®, or equivalent on the output shaft splines. Slide the drive assembly onto the shaft and install a new stopring, retainer and thrust washer. Install the shaft and drive assembly into the drive end housing.
15. Install the plunger and lever assembly making sure that the lever notches engage the flange ears of the starter drive. Attach the lever pin screw and tighten it to 10 ft.lb.
16. Lubricate the gear and washer. Install the gear and washer on the end of the output shaft.
17. Install the gear housing and tighten the mounting screw to 84 in.lb.
18. After lubricating the pinion, install the armature and washer on the end of the shaft.
19. Position the grommet around the field lead and press it into the starter frame notch. Install the frame assembly on the gear housing, making sure that the grommet is positioned in the notch in the housing.
20. Install the brush holder on the end of the frame, lining up the notches in the brush holder with the ground brush terminals. The brush holder is symmetrical and can be installed with either notch and brush terminal.
21. Install the brush springs and brushes. The positive brush leads must be placed in their respective slots to prevent grounding.
22. Install the brush endplate, mak-

ing sure that the insulator is properly positioned. Install and tighten the through-bolts to 84 in.lb.

NOTE: The brush endplate has a threaded hole in the protruding ear which must be oriented properly so the starter-to-vacuum pump support bracket can be installed.

23. Install the return spring on the solenoid plunger and install the solenoid. Attach the 2 solenoid attaching screws and tighten them to 84 in.lb. Apply a sealing compound to the junction of the solenoid case flange, gear and drive end housings.
24. Attach the motor field terminal to the **M** terminal of the solenoid, and tighten the fasteners to 30 in.lb.
25. Check the starter no-load current draw. Maximum draw should be 190 amps.

Battery

REMOVAL AND INSTALLATION

1. Remove the holddown screws from the battery box. Loosen the nuts that secure the cable ends to the battery terminals. Lift the battery cables from the terminals with a twisting motion.
2. If there is a battery cable puller available, make use of it. Lift the battery from the vehicle.
3. Before installing the battery in the vehicle, make sure that the battery terminals are clean and free from corrosion. Use a battery terminal cleaner on the terminals and on the inside of the battery cable ends. If a cleaner is not available, use a heavy sandpaper to remove the corrosion. A mixture of baking soda and water will neutralize any acid. Place the battery in the vehicle. Install the cables on the terminals. Tighten the nuts on the cable ends. Smear a light coating of grease on the cable ends and the tops of the terminals. This will prevent buildup of oxidized acid on the terminals and the cable ends. Install and tighten the nuts of the battery box.

ENGINE MECHANICAL

Engine Overhaul Tips

Most engine overhaul procedures are fairly standard. In addition to specific parts replacement procedures and complete specifications for your individual engine, this section also is a guide to accept rebuilding procedures. Examples of standard rebuilding practice are shown and should be used along with specific details concerning your particular engine.

Competent and accurate machine shop services will ensure maximum performance, reliability and engine life.

In most instances it is more profitable for the do-it-yourself mechanic to remove, clean and inspect the component, buy the necessary parts and deliver these to a shop for actual machine work.

On the other hand, much of the rebuilding work (crankshaft, block, bearings, piston rods, and other components) is well within the scope of the do-it-yourself mechanic.

TOOLS

The tools required for an engine overhaul or parts replacement will depend on the depth of your involvement. With a few exceptions, they will be the tools found in a mechanic's tool kit. More in-depth work will require any or all of the following:

- a dial indicator (reading in thousandths) mounted on a universal base
- micrometers and telescope gauges
- jaw and screw-type pullers
- scraper
- valve spring compressor
- ring groove cleaner
- piston ring expander and compressor
- ridge reamer
- cylinder hone or glaze breaker
- Plastigage®
- engine stand

The use of most of these tools is illustrated in this section. Many can be rented for a one-time use from a local parts jobber or tool supply house specializing in automotive work.

Occasionally, the use of special tools is called for. See the information on Special Tools and Safety Notice in the front of this book before substituting another tool.

INSPECTION TECHNIQUES

Procedures and specifications are given in this section for inspecting, cleaning and assessing the wear limits of most major components. Other procedures such as Magnaflux® and Zyglo® can be used to locate material flaws and stress cracks. Magnaflux® is a magnetic process applicable only to ferrous materials. The Zyglo® process coats the material with a fluorescent dye penetrant and can be used on any

material Check for suspected surface cracks can be more readily made using spot check dye. The dye is sprayed onto the suspected area, wiped off and the area sprayed with a developer. Cracks will show up brightly.

OVERHAUL TIPS

Aluminum has become extremely popular for use in engines, due to its low weight. Observe the following precautions when handling aluminum parts:

- Never hot tank aluminum parts (the caustic hot tank solution will eat the aluminum.
- Remove all aluminum parts (identification tag, etc.) from engine parts prior to the tanking.
- Always coat threads lightly with engine oil or anti-seize compounds before installation, to prevent seizure.
- Never overtorque bolts or spark plugs especially in aluminum threads.

Stripped threads in any component can be repaired using any of several commercial repair kits (Heli-Coil®, Microdot®, Keenserts®, etc.).

When assembling the engine, any parts that will be frictional contact must be prelubed to provide lubrication at initial start-up. Any product specifically formulated for this purpose can be used, but engine oil is not recommended as a prelube.

When semi-permanent (locked, but removable) installation of bolts or nuts is desired, threads should be cleaned and coated with Loctite® or other similar, commercial non-hardening sealant.

REPAIRING DAMAGED THREADS

Several methods of repairing damaged threads are available. Heli-Coil® (shown here), Keenserts® and Microdot® are among the most widely used. All involve basically the same principle – drilling out stripped threads, tapping the hole and installing a prewound insert – making welding, plugging and oversize fasteners unnecessary.

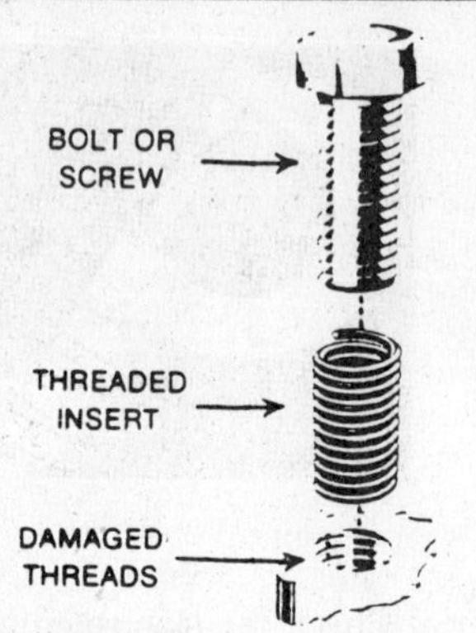

Damaged bolt holes can be repaired with thread repair inserts

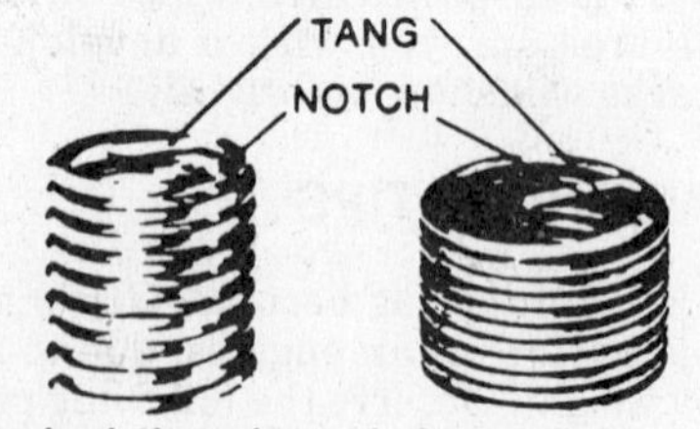

Standard thread repair insert (left) and spark plug thread insert (right)

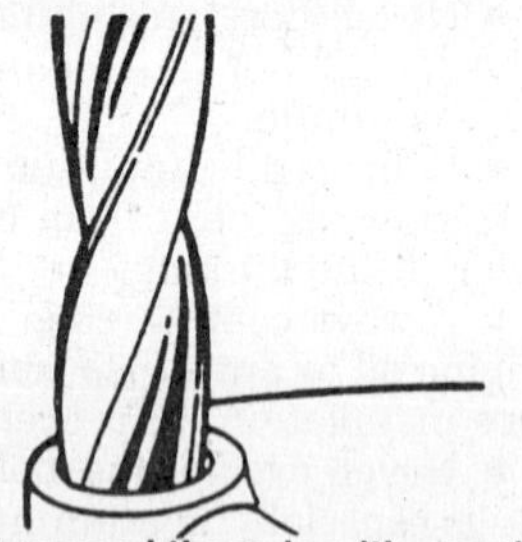

Drill out the damaged threads with specified drill. Drill completely through the hole or to the bottom of a blind hole

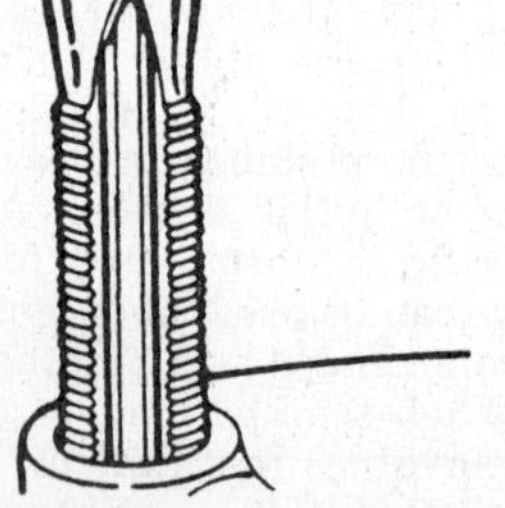

With the tap supplied, tap the hole to receive the thread insert. Keep the tap well oiled and back it out frequently to avoid clogging the threads

Two types of thread repair inserts are usually supplied: a standard type for most Inch Coarse, Inch Fine, Metric Course and Metric Fine thread sizes and a spark lug type to fit most spark plug port sizes. Consult the individual manufacturer's catalog to determine exact applications. Typical thread repair kits will contain a selection of prewound threaded inserts, a tap (corresponding to the outside diameter threads of the insert) and an installation tool. Spark plug inserts

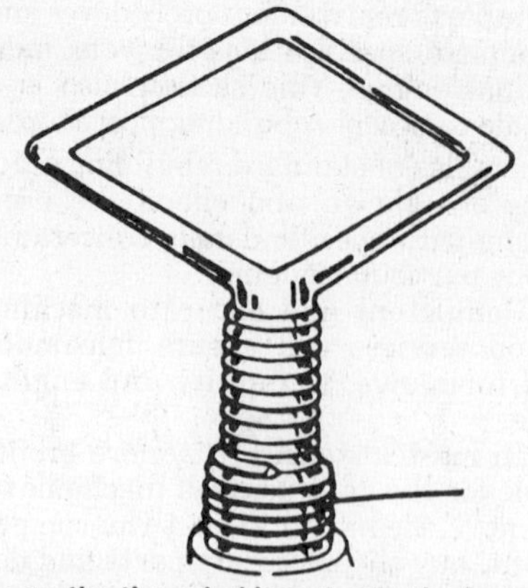

Screw the threaded insert onto the installation tool until the tang engages the slot. Screw the insert into the tapped hole until it is ¼-½ turn below the top surface. After installation break off the tang with a hammer and punch

usually differ because they require a tap equipped with pilot threads and a combined reamer/tap section. Most manufacturers also supply blister-packed thread repair inserts separately in addition to a master kit containing a variety of taps and inserts plus installation tools.

Before effecting a repair to a threaded hole, remove any snapped, broken or damaged bolts or studs. Penetrating oil can be used to free frozen threads. The offending item can be removed with locking pliers or with a screw or stud extractor. After the hole is clear, the thread can be repaired, as shown in the series of accompanying illustrations.

Checking Engine Compression

A noticeable lack of engine power, excessive oil consumption and/or poor fuel mileage measured over an extended period are all indicators of internal engine war. Worn piston rings, scored or worn cylinder bores, blown head gaskets, sticking or burnt valves and worn valve seats are all possible culprits here. A check of each cylinder's compression will help you locate the problems.

As mentioned earlier, a screw-in type compression gauge is more accurate that the type you simply hold against the spark plug hole, although it takes slightly longer to use. It's worth it to obtain a more accurate reading. Follow the procedures below.

Gasoline Engines

1. Warm up the engine to normal operating temperature.
2. Remove all the spark plugs.
3. Disconnect the high tension lead from the ignition coil.
4. On fully open the throttle either by operating the carburetor throttle linkage by hand or by having an assistant floor the accelerator pedal.
5. Screw the compression gauge into the no.1 spark plug hole until the fitting is snug.

WARNING: Be careful not to crossthread the plug hole. On aluminum cylinder heads use extra care, as the threads in these heads are easily ruined.

6. Ask an assistant to depress the accelerator pedal fully on both carbureted and fuel injected vehicles. Then, while you read the compression gauge, ask the assistant to crank the engine two or three times in short bursts using the ignition switch.
7. Read the compression gauge at the end of each series of cranks, and record the highest of these readings. Repeat this procedure for each of the engine's cylinders. Compare the highest reading of each cylinder to the compression pressure specification in the Tune-Up Specifications chart. The specs in this chart are maximum values.

A cylinder's compression pressure is usually acceptable if it is not less than 80% of maximum. The difference between any two cylinders should be no more than 12–14 pounds.

8. If a cylinder is unusually low, pour a tablespoon of clean engine oil into the cylinder through the spark plug hole and repeat the compression test. If the compression comes up after adding the oil, it appears that the cylinder's piston rings or bore are damaged or worn. If the pressure remains low, the valves may not be seating properly (a valve job is needed), or the head gasket may be blown near that cylinder. If compression in any two adjacent cylinders is low, and if the addition of oil doesn't help the compression, there is leakage past the head gasket. Oil and coolant water in the combustion chamber can result from this problem. There may be evidence of water droplets on the engine dipstick when a head gasket has blown.

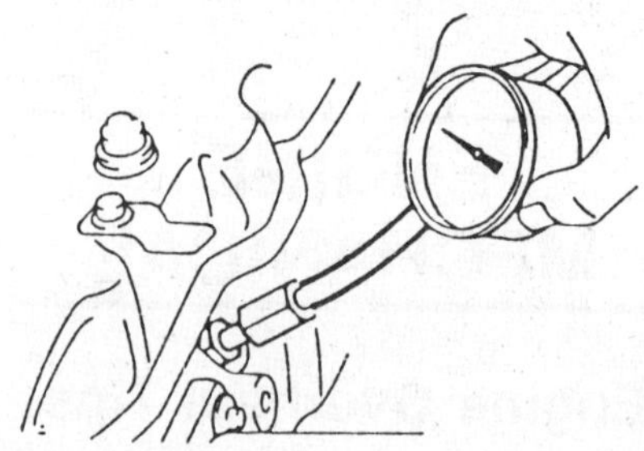

The screw-in type compression gauge is more accurate

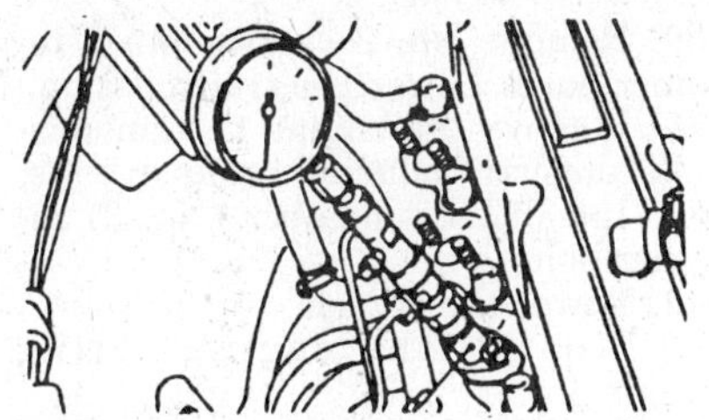

Diesel engines require a special compression gauge adaptor

Diesel Engines

Checking cylinder compression on diesel engines is basically the same procedure as on gasoline engines except for the following:

1. A special compression gauge adaptor suitable for diesel engines (because these engines have much greater compression pressures) must be used.
2. Remove the injector tubes and remove the injectors from each cylinder.

WARNING: Don't forget to remove the washer underneath each injector. Otherwise, it may get lost when the engine is cranked.

3. When fitting the compression gauge adaptor to the cylinder head, make sure the bleeder of the gauge (if equipped) is closed.
4. When reinstalling the injector assemblies, install new washers underneath each injector.

Engine

REMOVAL & INSTALLATION

WARNING: Disconnect the negative battery cable before beginning any work. Always label all disconnected hoses, vacuum lines and wires, to prevent incorrect reassembly. Do not disconnect any air conditioning lines unless you are thoroughly familiar with A/C systems and the hazards involved; escaping refrigerant (Freon®) will freeze any surface it contacts, including skin and eyes. Have the system discharged professionally before required repairs are started.

Gasoline Engine

1. Scribe the hood hinge outline on the underhood, disconnect the hood and remove.
2. Drain the entire cooling system and crankcase.

CAUTION

When draining the coolant, keep in mind that cats and dogs are attracted by the ethylene glycol antifreeze, and are quite likely to drink any that is left in an uncovered container or in puddles on the ground. This will prove fatal in sufficient quantity. Always drain the coolant into a sealable container. Coolant should be reused unless it is contaminated or several years old.

3. Remove the air cleaner, disconnect the battery at the cylinder head. On automatic transmission equipped cars, disconnect the fluid cooler lines at the radiator. On the 4-140, remove the exhaust manifold shroud.
4. Remove the upper and lower radiator hoses and remove the radiator. If equipped with air conditioning, unbolt the compressor and position compressor out of way with refrigerant lines intact. Unbolt and lay the refrigerant condenser forward without disconnecting the refrigerant lines.

NOTE: If there is not enough slack in the refrigerant lines to position the compressor out of the way, the refrigerant in the system must be evacuated (using proper safety precautions) before the lines can be disconnected from the compressor.

5. Remove the fan, fan belt and upper pulley. On models equipped with an electric cooling fan, disconnect the power lead and remove the fan and shroud as an assembly.
6. Disconnect the heater hoses from the engine. On the 4-140, disconnect the heater hose from the water pump and choke fittings.
7. Disconnect the alternator wires at the alternator, the starter cable at the starter, the accelerator rod at the carburetor.
8. Disconnect and plug the fuel tank line at the fuel pump on models equipped with fuel injection, depressurize the fuel system.
9. Disconnect the coil primary wire at the coil. Disconnect the wires at the oil pressure and water temperature sending units. Disconnect the brake booster vacuum line, if so equipped.
10. Remove the starter and dust seal.
11. On cars with manual transmission, remove the clutch retracting spring. Disconnect the clutch equalizer shaft and arm bracket at the underbody rail and remove the arm bracket and equalizer shaft.
12. Raise the car and safely support on jackstands. Remove the flywheel or converter housing upper retaining bolts.
13. Disconnect the exhaust pipe or pipes at the exhaust manifold. Disconnect the right and left motor mount at the underbody bracket. Remove the flywheel or converter housing cover. On models so equipped, disconnect the engine roll damper on the left front of the engine from the frame.
14. On cars with manual transmission, remove the lower wheel housing bolts.
15. On models with automatic transmission, disconnect the throttle valve vacuum line at the intake manifold and disconnect the converter from the flywheel. Remove the converter housing lower retaining bolts. On models with power steering, disconnect the power steering pump from the cylinder head. Remove the drive belt and wire steering pump out of the way. Do not disconnect the hoses.
16. Lower the car. Support the transmission and flywheel or converter housing with a jack.
17. Attach an engine lifting hook. Lift the engine up and out of the compartment and onto a workstand.
18. Place a new gasket on the exhaust pipe flange.
19. Attach an engine sling and lifting device. Lift the engine from the workstand.
20. Lower the engine into the engine compartment. Be sure the exhaust manifold(s) is in proper alignment with the muffler inlet pipe(s), and the dowels in the block engage the holes in the flywheel housing.

On cars with automatic transmission, start the converter pilot into the crankshaft, making sure that the converter studs align with the flexplate holes.

On cars with manual transmission, start the transmission main drive gear into the clutch disc. If the engine hangs up after the shaft enters, rotate the crankshaft slowly (with transmission in gear) until the shaft and clutch disc splines mesh. Rotate 4-140 engines clockwise only, when viewed from the front.

21. Install the flywheel or converter housing upper bolts.
22. Install the engine support insulator to bracket retaining nuts. Disconnect the engine lifting sling and remove the lifting brackets.
23. Raise the front of the car. Connect the exhaust line(s) and tighten the attachments.
24. Install the starter.
25. On cars with manual transmission, install the remaining flywheel housing-to-engine bolts. Connect the clutch release rod. Position the clutch equalizer bar and bracket, and install the retaining bolts. Install the clutch pedal retracting spring.
26. On cars with automatic transmission, remove the retainer holding the converter in the housing. Attach the converter to the flywheel. Install the converter housing inspection cover and the remaining converter housing retaining bolts.
27. Remove the support from the transmission and lower the car.

28. Connect the engine ground strap and coil primary wire.
29. Connect the water temperature gauge wire and the heater hose at the coolant outlet housing. Connect the accelerator rod at the bellcrank.
30. On cars with automatic transmission, connect the transmission filler tube bracket. Connect the throttle valve vacuum line.
31. On cars with power steering, install the drive belt and power steering pump bracket. Install the bracket retaining bolts. Adjust the drive belt to proper tension.
32. Remove the plug from the fuel tank line. Connect the flexible fuel line and the oil pressure sending unit wire.
33. Install the pulley, belt, spacer, and fan. Adjust the belt tension.
34. Tighten the alternator adjusting bolts. Connect the wires and the battery ground cable. On the 4-140, install the exhaust manifold shroud.
35. Install the radiator. Connect the radiator hoses. On air conditioned cars, install the compressor and condenser.
36. On cars with automatic transmission, connect the fluid cooler lines. On cars with power brakes, connect the brake booster line.
37. Install the oil filter. Connect the heater hose at the water pump and carburetor choke (4-140).
38. Bring the crankcase to the full level with the correct grade of oil. Run the engine at fast idle and check for leaks. Install the air cleaner and make the final engine adjustments.
39. Install and adjust the hood.

2,443cc Diesel Engine

1. Disconnect the negative battery cable.
2. Disconnect the wiring assembly for the engine underhood light.
3. Scribe the hinge mark locations and remove the hood.
4. Drain the the cooling system. Drain the engine oil.

CAUTION

When draining the coolant, keep in mind that cats and dogs are attracted by the ethylene glycol antifreeze, and are quite likely to drink any that is left in an uncovered container or in puddles on the ground. This will prove fatal in sufficient quantity. Always drain the coolant into a sealable container. Coolant should be reused unless it is contaminated or several years old.

5. Remove the air cleaner assembly.
6. Remove the fan shroud attaching bolts and remove the fan shroud. Remove the engine cooling fan assembly.
7. Remove the upper and lower radiator hoses.
8. Disconnect the transmission oil cooler tubes from the radiator fittings.
9. Remove the radiator assembly.
10. Disconnect the muffler inlet pipe.
11. Label and disconnect the vacuum hoses and wiring harnesses.
12. Disconnect the engine oil cooler hoses.
13. Disconnect the accelerator cable at the fuel injection pump.
14. Disconnect the fuel line from the tank to fuel injection pump.
15. Disconnect the transmission gear shift linkage.
16. Disconnect the battery ground cable at engine.
17. Remove the coolant expansion bottle and position it out of the way.
18. Disconnect the heater hoses at the dash panel (firewall).
19. Disconnect the wire to A/C compressor clutch.
20. Disconnect the power steering pump hose(s).
21. Disconnect the fuel lines at the injectors.
22. Disconnect the wiring harness to instrument panel. Disconnect the engine ground leads.
23. Install engine support Tool D79F-6000-A or equivalent (bar and J-hook or chain).
24. Raise the vehicle and safely support on jackstands.
25. Remove the muffler inlet pipe.
26. Remove the lower engine oil cooler bracket and brace.
27. Remove the stabilizer bar, bracket retaining bolts and position it forward.
28. Remove the left hand front fender splash shield.
29. Disconnect the steering gear input shaft-to-steering column shaft coupling.
30. Remove the retainer nuts to the engine insulator supports.
31. Position a jack under the engine. Raise the engine assembly. Position the steering gear out of the way.
32. Lower the engine assembly.
33. Remove the converter housing access cover.
34. Remove the converter assembly retainer nuts.
35. Insert a pair of locking pliers in the converter housing to hold the converter in place during engine removal.

NOTE: Make sure that the upper jaw of the locking pliers contacts the converter while clamped to the converter housing. This will apply adequate pressure on the converter to prevent separation during engine movements and removal.

36. Remove No. 3 crossmember retainer nuts.
37. Remove the transmission gear shift lever bellcrank.
38. Raise the transmission.
39. Remove No. 3 crossmember retainer bolts. Lower the transmission.
40. Remove the engine to transmission converter housing retainer bolts.
41. Install crossmember (No. 3) retainer bolts.
42. Lower the vehicle.
43. Install the engine lifting equipment.
44. Remove the engine support Tool D79T-6000-A or equivalent.
45. Remove the engine assembly.
46. Position the engine on engine work stand and service as necessary.
47. Install the engine lifting equipment. Raise the engine and install it in the vehicle.
48. Install the engine support Tool D79T-6000-A or equivalent.
49. Remove the engine lifting equipment. Raise the vehicle and safely support it on jackstands.
50. The remainder of installation is the reverse of removal.

Valve Rocker Arm Cover

REMOVAL & INSTALLATION

4-140
6-200

1. Remove the air cleaner assembly and mounting brackets.
2. Label for identification and remove all wires and vacuum hoses interfering with valve cover removal. Remove the PCV valve with hose. Re-

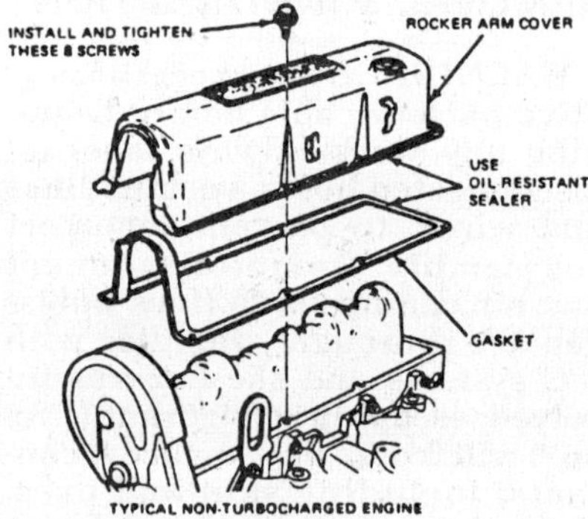

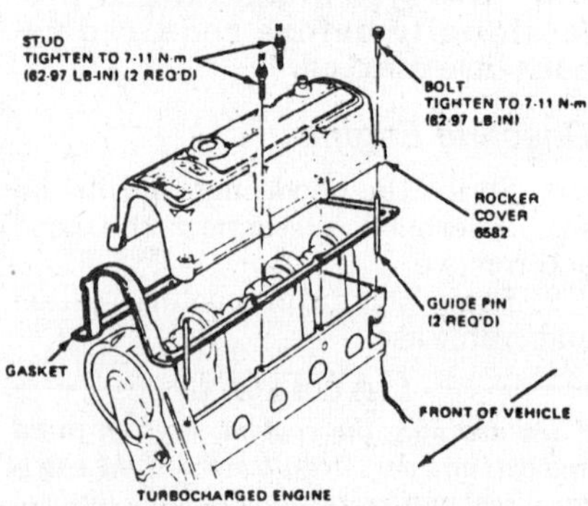

4-140 rocker arm cover installation

move the accelerator control cable bracket if necessary.

NOTE: 4-140 Turbocharged models require removal of the air intake tube and air throttle body. Refer to the Fuel SYSTEM SECTION 4 for procedures.

3. Remove the valve cover retaining bolts. On 4-140 models, the front bolts equipped with rubber sealing washers must be installed in the same location to prevent oil leakage.
4. Remove the valve cover. Clean all old gasket material from the valve cover and cylinder head gasket surfaces.
5. Installation is the reverse of removal. Use oil resistant sealing compound and a new valve cover gasket. When installing the valve cover gasket, make sure all the gasket locating tangs are engaged into the cover notches provided.

V6 and V8 Engines

NOTE: When disconnecting wires and vacuum lines, label them for reinstallation identification.

1. Remove the air cleaner assembly.
2. On the right side:
   a. Disconnect the automatic choke heat chamber hose from the inlet tube near the right valve cover if equipped.
   b. Remove the automatic choke heat tube if equipped and remove the PCV valve and hose from the valve cover. Disconnect the EGR valve hoses.
   c. Remove the Thermactor® bypass valve and air supply hoses as necessary to gain clearance.
   d. Disconnect the spark plug wires from the plugs with a twisting pulling motion; twist and pull on the boots only, never on the wire; position the wires and mounting bracket out of the way.
   e. Remove the valve cover mounting bolts; remove the valve cover.
3. On the left side:
   a. Remove the spark plug wires and bracket.
   b. Remove the wiring harness and any vacuum hose from the bracket.
   c. Remove the valve cover mounting bolts and valve cover.
4. Clean all old gasket material from the valve cover and cylinder head mounting surfaces.

NOTE: Some 6-232 engines were not equipped with valve cover gaskets in production. Rather, RTV silicone gasket material was originally used. Scrape away the old RTV sealant and clean the cover. Spread an even bead $^{3}/_{16}''$ (4mm) wide of RTV sealant on the valve covers and reinstall, or install with gaskets.

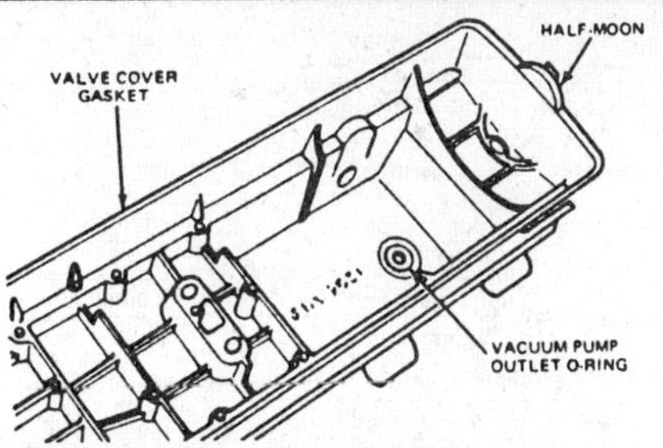

Diesel valve cover gasket and vacuum pump O-ring installation

5. Installation is the reverse of removal. Use oil resistant sealing compound and a new valve cover gasket. When installing the valve cover gasket, make sure all the gasket tangs are engaged into the cover notches provided.

2,443cc Diesel Engine

1. Loosen the turbocharger crossover pipe boot clamps and remove the crossover pipe.
2. Disconnect the vacuum pump hose. Disconnect the breather hose.
3. Remove the oil trap. Remove the threaded sleeves that attach the rocker cover to the cylinder head. Remove the cover.
4. Inspect the cover gasket and vacuum pump mounting O-ring. Install a new gasket and O-ring if necessary. Clean all gasket mounting surfaces.
5. Install gasket and O-ring in position. Install cover after making sure the half-moon seal is fully seated in the cylinder head.
6. Tighten retainers to 10-12 ft.lb.
7. Connect the oil trap, breather hose, vacuum hose and turbocharger crossover pipe.
8. Run the engine and check for oil and intake air leaks.

Rocker Arm (Cam Follower) and Hydraulic Lash Adjuster

REMOVAL & INSTALLATION

4-140 Engine

NOTE: A special tool is required to compress the lash adjuster.

1. Remove the valve cover and associated parts as required.
2. Rotate the camshaft so that the base circle of the cam is against the cam follower you intend to remove.
3. Remove the retaining spring from the cam follower, if so equipped.
4. Using special tool T74P-6565-B or a valve spring compressor tool, collapse the lash adjuster and/or depress the valve spring, as necessary, and slide the cam follower over the lash adjuster and out from under the camshaft.
5. Install the cam follower in the reverse order of removal. Make sure that the lash adjuster is collapsed and released before rotating the camshaft.

Rocker Arm Shaft/Rocker Arms

REMOVAL & INSTALLATION

6-200

1. Remove the rocker arm (valve) cover (see previous section).
2. Remove the rocker arm shaft mounting bolts, two turns at a time for each bolt. Start at the end of the rocker shaft and work toward the middle.
3. Lift the rocker arm shaft assembly from the engine. Remove the pin and washer from each end of the shaft. Slide the rocker arms, spring and sup-

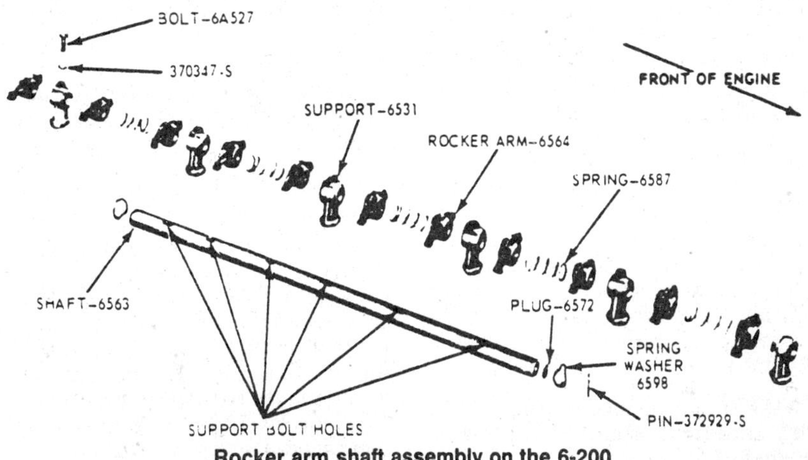

Rocker arm shaft assembly on the 6-200

ports off the shaft. Keep all parts in order or label them for position.

4. Clean and inspect all parts, replace as necessary.

5. Assemble the rocker shaft parts in reverse order of removal. Be sure the oil holes in the shaft are pointed downward. Reinstall the rocker shaft assembly on the engine.

NOTE: Lubricate all parts with motor oil before installation.

V6 and V8 Engines

1. On the right side, remove:

a. Disconnect the automatic choke heat chamber air inlet hose.

b. Remove the air cleaner and duct.

c. Remove the automatic choke heat tube (6-232, 8-302).

d. Remove the PCV fresh air tube from the rocker cover, and disconnect the EGR vacuum amplifier hoses.

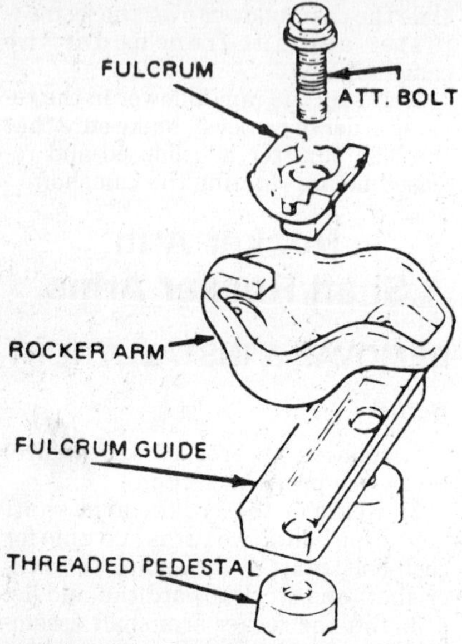

1980-82 255, 302, 351W rocker arm assembly

2. Remove the Thermactor® bypass valve and air supply hoses.

3. Disconnect the spark plug wires.

4. On the left side, remove:

a. Remove the wiring harness from the clips.

b. Remove the rocker arm cover.

5. Remove the rocker arm stud nut or bolt, fulcrum seat and rocker arm.

6. Lubricate all parts with heavy SF oil before installation. When installing, rotate the crankshaft until the lifter is on the base of the cam circle (all the way down) and assemble the rocker arm. Torque the nut or bolt to 17-23 ft.lb.

NOTE: Some later engines use RTV sealant instead of valve cover gaskets.

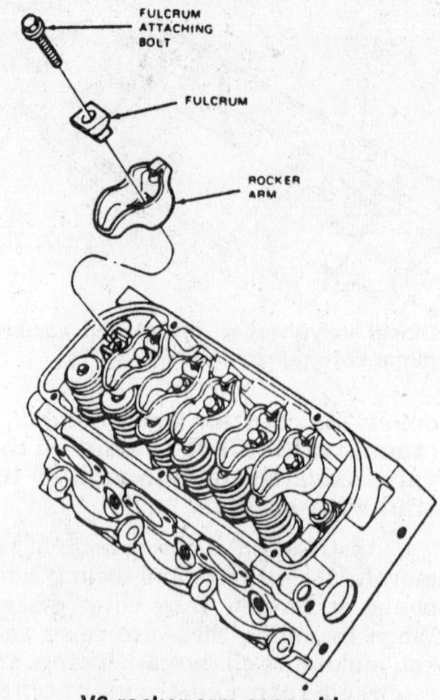

V6 rocker arm assembly

2,443cc Diesel Engine

1. Disconnect the negative battery cable. Remove the valve cover and vacuum pump.

2. Rotate the engine until the base circle (heel) of the cam lobe for the rocker arm being removed is facing the rocker arm.

3. Remove the spring clip retaining the rocker arm. Compress the valve spring slightly using tool T84P-6513-C or the equivalent and remove the rocker arm.

CAUTION

Be sure that the valve keys remain in position when slightly compressing the valve spring.

4. Install the rocker arm in the reverse order of removal.

Intake Manifold

REMOVAL & INSTALLATION

4-140 Engine

NOTE: For engines with fuel injection, refer to the illustration provided.

1. Drain the cooling system.

CAUTION

When draining the coolant, keep in mind that cats and dogs are attracted by the ethylene glycol antifreeze, and are quite likely to drink any that is left in an uncovered container or in puddles on the ground. This will prove fatal in sufficient quantity. Always drain the coolant into a sealable container. Coolant should be reused unless it is contaminated or several years old.

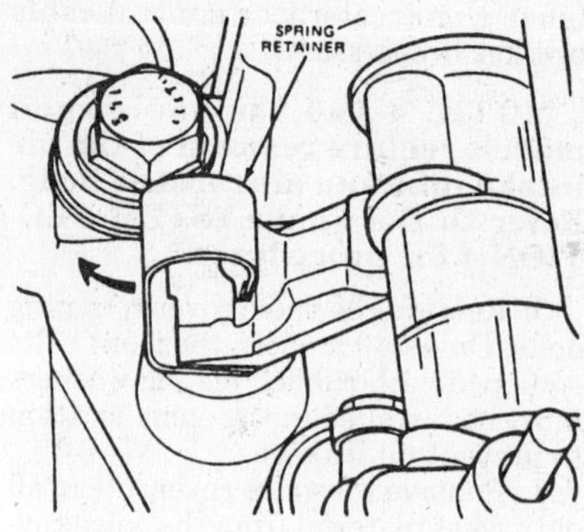

Diesel rocker arm retaining clip

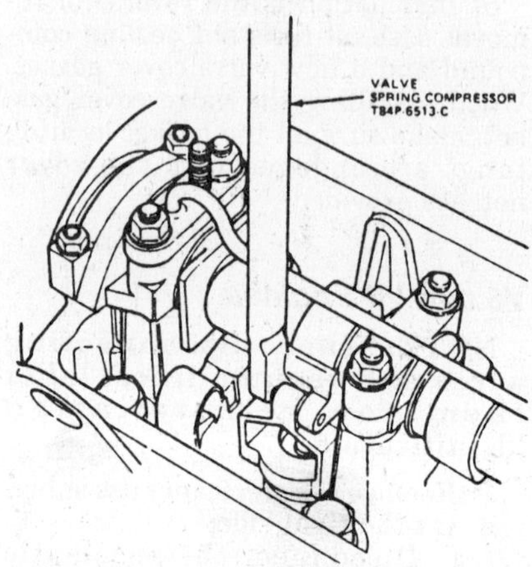

Diesel valve spring compressor installation

2. Remove the air cleaner and disconnect the throttle linkage from the carburetor.

3. Disconnect the fuel and vacuum lines from the carburetor.

4. Disconnect the carburetor solenoid wire at the quick-disconnect.

5. Remove the choke water housing and thermostatic spring from the carburetor.

6. Disconnect the water outlet and crankcase ventilation hoses from the intake manifold.

7. Disconnect the deceleration valve-to-carburetor hose (if equipped) at the carburetor.

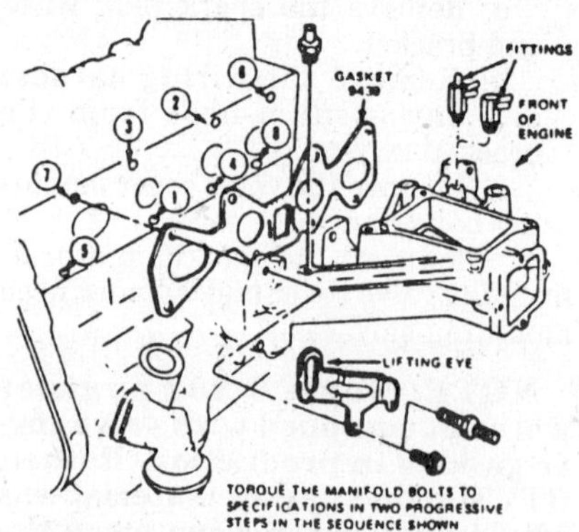

4-140 intake manifold installation

8. Starting from each end and working towards the middle, remove the intake manifold attaching bolts and remove the manifold.
9. Clean all old gasket material from the manifold and cylinder head.
10. Apply water-resistant sealer to the intake manifold gasket and position it on the cylinder head.
11. Install the intake manifold attaching nuts. Follow the sequence given in the illustrations.
12. Connect the water and crankcase ventilation hoses to the intake manifold.
13. Connect the deceleration valve-to-carburetor hose to the carburetor.
14. Position the choke water housing and thermostatic spring on the carburetor and engage the end of the spring coil in the slot and the choke adjusting lever. Align the tab on the spring housing. Tighten the choke water housing attaching screws.
15. Connect the carburetor solenoid wire.
16. Connect the fuel and vacuum lines to the carburetor.
17. Connect the throttle linkage to the carburetor.
18. Install the air cleaner and fill the cooling system.

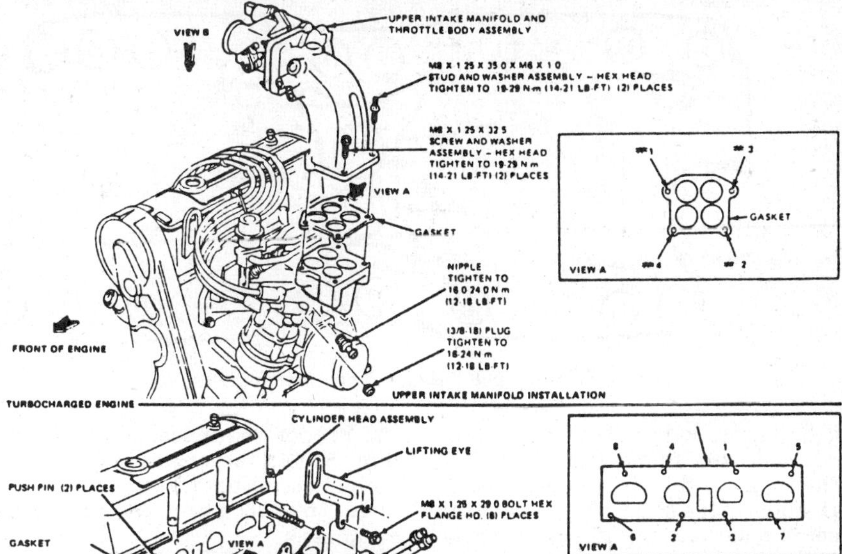

Intake manifold installation—4-140 turbo engine

6-200

On 6-cylinder in-line engines, the intake manifold is integral with the cylinder head and cannot be removed.

V6 and V8 Engines

1. Drain the cooling system and disconnect the negative battery cable. Remove the air cleaner assembly.

CAUTION

When draining the coolant, keep in mind that cats and dogs are attracted by the ethylene glycol antifreeze, and are quite likely to drink any that is left in an uncovered container or in puddles on the ground. This will prove fatal in sufficient quantity. Always drain the coolant into a sealable container. Coolant should be reused unless it is contaminated or several years old.

2. Disconnect the upper radiator hose and water pump by-pass hose from the thermostat housing and/or intake manifold. Disconnect the temperature sending unit wire connector. Remove the heater hose from the choke housing bracket and disconnect the hose from the intake manifold.
3. Disconnect the automatic choke heat chamber air inlet tube and electric wiring connector from the carburetor. Remove the crankcase ventilation hose, vacuum hoses and EGR hose and coolant lines (if equipped). Label the various hoses and wiring for reinstallation identification.
4. Disconnect the Thermactor® air supply hose at the check valve. Loosen the hose clamp at the check valve bracket and remove the air by-pass valve from the bracket and position to one side.

CAUTION

On CFI (fuel injected) engines. System pressure must be released before disconnecting the fuel lines. See the FUEL SYSTEM Section 4 for pressure release and fuel line procedures.

5. Remove all carburetor and automatic transmission linkage attached to the carburetor or intake manifold. Remove the speed control servo and bracket, if equipped. Disconnect the fuel line and any remaining vacuum hoses or wiring from the carburetor, CFI unit, solenoids, sensors, or intake manifold.
6. On V8 engines, disconnect the distributor vacuum hoses from the

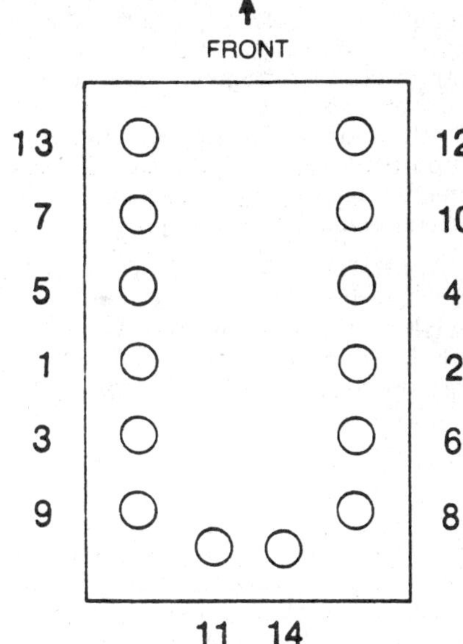

V6 intake manifold torque sequence

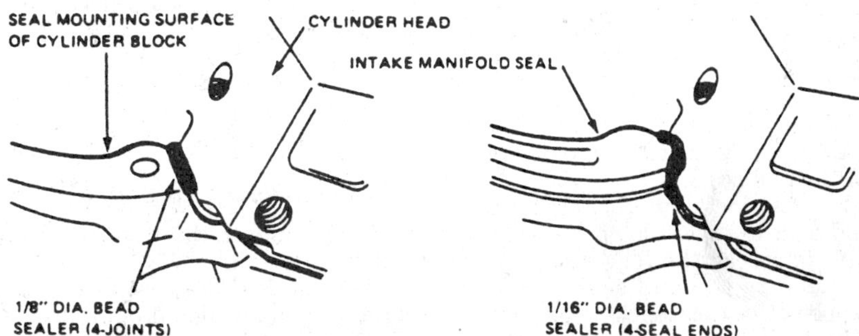

Sealer application area for intake manifold installation on all V8s

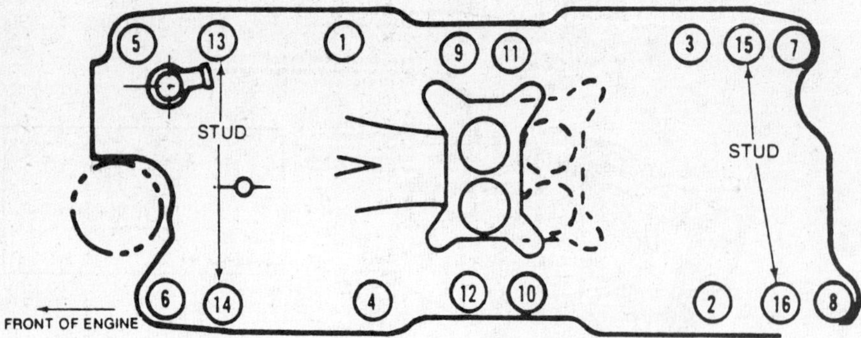

Intake manifold bolt tightening sequence—351W V8

distributor. Remove the distributor cap and mark the relative position of the rotor on the distributor housing. Disconnect the spark plug wires at the spark plugs and the wiring connector at the distributor. Remove the distributor holddown bolt and remove the distributor. (See Distributor Removal and Installation).

NOTE: Distributor removal is not necessary on 6-232 engines.

7. If your car is equipped with air conditioning and the compressor or mounting brackets interfere with manifold removal, remove the brackets and compressor and position them out of the way. Do not disconnect any compressor lines.
8. Remove the intake manifold mounting bolts. Lift off the intake manifold and carburetor, or CFI unit, as an assembly.

WARNING: The manifold on 6-232 engines is sealed at each end with an RTV type sealer. If prying at the front of the manifold is necessary to break the seal, take care not to damage the machined surfaces.

9. Clean all gasket mounting surfaces. 6-232 engines have aluminum cylinder heads and intake manifold; exercise care when cleaning the old gasket material or RTV sealant from the machined surfaces.
10. End seals are not used on 6-232 engines. Apply a ⅛" (3mm) bead of RTV sealant at each end of the engine where the intake manifold seats. Install the intake gaskets and the manifold.
11. On V8 engines, make sure the intake gaskets interlock with the end seals. Use silicone rubber sealer (RTV) on the end seals.
12. After installing the intake manifold, run a finger along the manifold ends to spread the RTV sealer and to make sure the end seals have not slipped out of place.
13. Torque the manifold mounting bolts to the required specifications in the proper sequence. Recheck the torque after the engine has reached normal operating temperature.
14. Install the brackets and compressor.
15. On V8 engines, connect the distributor vacuum hoses to the distributor.
16. Install the distributor cap.
17. Connect the spark plug wires at the spark plugs and the wiring connectors at the distributor.
18. Install the distributor. (See Distributor Removal and Installation).
19. install all carburetor and automatic transmission linkage attached to the carburetor or intake manifold.
20. Install the speed control servo and bracket, if equipped.
21. Connect the fuel line and any remaining vacuum hoses or wiring at the carburetor, CFI unit, solenoids, sensors, or intake manifold.
22. Connect the Thermactor® air supply hose at the check valve.
23. Install the air by-pass valve on its bracket.
24. Connect the automatic choke heat chamber air inlet tube and electric wiring connector at the carburetor.
25. Install the crankcase ventilation hose, vacuum hoses and EGR hose and coolant lines (if equipped).
26. Connect the upper radiator hose and water pump by-pass hose at the thermostat housing and/or intake manifold.
27. Connect the temperature sending unit wire connector.
28. Install the heater hose on the choke housing bracket and connect the hose at the intake manifold.
29. Fill the cooling system and connect the negative battery cable.
30. Install the air cleaner assembly.

2,443cc Diesel Engine

1. Disconnect the negative battery cable.
2. Remove the diagnostic plug bracket and position it out of the way. Disconnect the turbocharger boost pressure indicator connector.
3. Disconnect the engine oil dipstick tube clamp from the intake manifold and position the dipstick out of the way. Disconnect and label the hoses, lines and cables interfering with manifold removal. Disconnect the turbocharger air crossover pipe boot clamps.
4. Remove the intake manifold-to-cylinder head attaching bolts and the intake manifold.
5. Clean the head and intake manifold gasket surfaces. Reinstall the intake manifold with a new mounting gasket in the reverse order of removal. Tighten the mounting bolts to 14-17 ft.lb.

Exhaust Manifold

NOTE: Although, in most cases, the engine does not have exhaust manifold gasket installed by the factory, aftermarket gaskets are available from parts stores.

REMOVAL & INSTALLATION

4-140 Engine

1. Remove the air cleaner.
2. Remove the heat shroud from the exhaust manifold. On turbocharged models, remove the turbocharger.
3. Place a block of wood under the exhaust pipe and disconnect the exhaust pipe from the exhaust manifold.

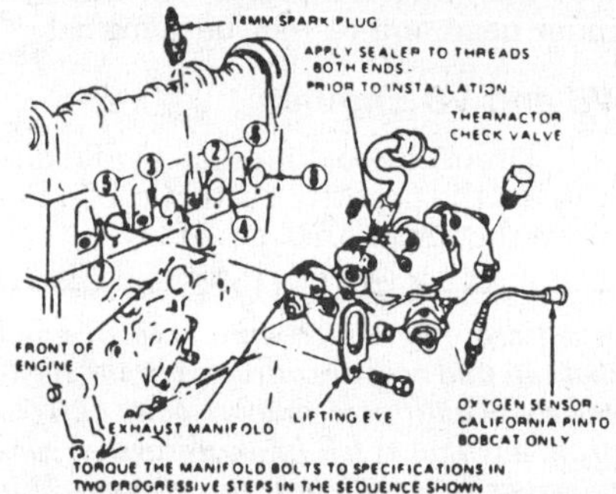

4-140 exhaust manifold torque sequence

4. Remove the exhaust manifold attaching nuts and remove the manifold.
5. Install a light coat of graphite grease on the exhaust manifold mating surface and position the manifold on the cylinder head.
6. Install the exhaust manifold attaching nuts and tighten them in the sequence shown in the illustration to 12-15 ft.lb.
7. Connect the exhaust pipe to the exhaust manifold and remove the wood support from under the pipe.
8. Install the air cleaner.

6-200

1. Remove the air cleaner and heat duct body.

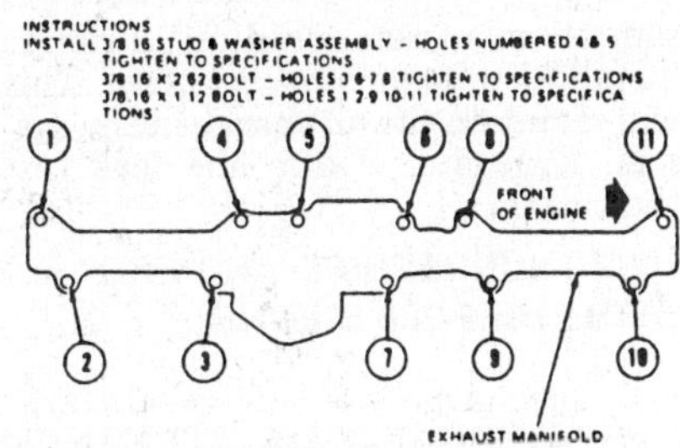

6-200 exhaust manifold torque sequence

2. Disconnect the muffler inlet pipe and remove the choke hot air tube from the manifold.
3. Remove the EGR tube and any other emission components which will interfere with manifold removal.
4. Bend the exhaust manifold attaching bolt lock tabs back, remove the bolts and the manifold.
5. Clean all manifold mating surfaces and place a new gasket on the muffler inlet pipe.
6. Re-install the manifold by reversing the removal procedure. Torque the attaching bolts in the sequence shown. After installation, warm the engine to operating temperature and re-torque the bolts to specifications.

V6, V8 Engines

1. If removing the right side exhaust manifold, remove the air cleaner and related parts and the heat stove, if so equipped.
2. On 8-351M engines: if the left exhaust manifold is being removed, first drain the engine oil and remove the oil filter. On 6-232, 8-255, 8-302 and 8-351W engines, dipstick and tube removal may be required. Remove any speed control brackets that interfere.
3. Disconnect the exhaust manifold(s) from the muffler (or converter) inlet pipe(s).

NOTE: On certain vehicles with automatic transmission and column shift it may be necessary to disconnect the selector lever cross-shaft for clearance.

4. Disconnect the spark plug wires and remove the spark plugs and heat shields. Disconnect the EGR sensor (models so equipped), and heat control valve vacuum line (models so equipped).

NOTE: On some engines the spark plug wire heat shields are removed with the manifold. Transmission dipstick tube and Thermactor® air tube removal may be required on certain models. Air tube removal is possible by cutting the tube clamp at the converter.

5. Remove the exhaust manifold attaching bolts and washers, and remove the manifold(s).
6. Inspect the manifold(s) for damaged gasket surfaces, cracks, or other defects.
7. Clean the mating surfaces of the manifold(s), cylinder head and muffler inlet pipe(s).
8. Install the manifold(s) in reverse order of removal. Torque the mounting bolts to the value listed in the Torque Specifications chart. Start with the centermost bolt and work outward in both directions.

WARNING: Slight warpage may occur on 6-232 manifolds. Elongate the holes in the manifold as necessary. Do not, however, elongate the lower front No. 5 cylinder hole on the left side, nor the lower rear No. 2 cylinder hole on the right side. These holes are used as alignment pilots.

2,443cc Diesel Engine

1. Disconnect the battery ground cable.
2. Disconnect the muffler inlet pipe at the turbo outlet and cap turbo outlet.
3. Disconnect the EGR valve vacuum line.
4. Disconnect the inlet duct at turbo and cap turbo inlet.
5. Loosen the clamp at the turbo crossover pipe boot.
6. Remove the clamp attaching the turbo oil feed tube to the oil return tube.
7. Remove the bolts attaching the oil feed tube to the turbo.

CAUTION

Cap the oil feed tube and oil feed inlet port on the turbo, to prevent contamination of the turbo oiling system.

8. Disconnect the oil return line from the turbo oil drain port.

CAUTION

Cap the oil return line and the oil return port on the turbo, to prevent contamination of the turbo oiling system.

9. Remove the bolts attaching the exhaust manifold to the cylinder head and remove the exhaust manifold and turbo as an assembly. Cap the turbo outlet-to-crossover pipe.
10. Clean the exhaust manifold and cylinder head gasket mating surfaces.
11. Install the exhaust manifold, with a new gasket, making sure the turbo outlet is installed in crossover pipe boot. Tighten bolts to 14-17 ft.lb., and tighten the crossover pipe boot clamp.
12. Remove the caps and install the oil feed line, with a new gasket, on the turbo oil inlet port. Tighten bolts to 14-17 ft.lb.
13. Remove the caps and connect the oil return line to the turbo oil return port. Tighten fitting 29-36 ft.lb.
14. Install the oil feed tube to the exhaust manifold clamp and tighten to 6.5-7 ft.lb.
15. Remove the cap and connect the inlet duct to the turbo inlet.
16. Remove the cap and connect the muffler inlet pipe to the turbo exhaust outlet. Tighten bolts to 31-35 ft.lb.
17. Connect the EGR valve vacuum line.
18. Connect the battery ground cable.
19. Run the engine and check for intake, exhaust and oil leaks.

Air Conditioning Compressor

REMOVAL & INSTALLATION

2-Cylinder York or Tecumseh Compressor

1980-83

1. Discharge the system and disconnect the two hoses from the compressor. Cap the openings immediately!
2. Energize the clutch and remove the clutch mounting bolt.
3. Install a 5/8–11 bolt in the clutch driveshaft hole. With the cltuch still energized, tighten the bolt to remove the clutch from the shaft.
4. Disconnect the clutch wire at the connector.
5. Loosen the idler pulley or alternator and remove the drive belt and clutch, then remove the mounting bolts and compressor.
6. Installation is the reverse of re-

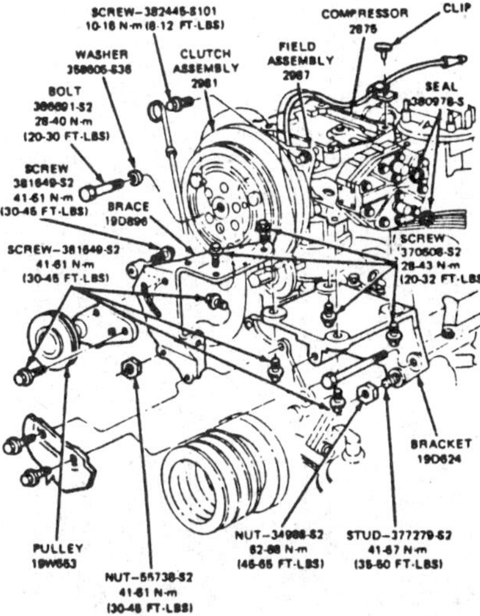

Air conditioning compressor installation on 1980-83 V8 with automatic transmission

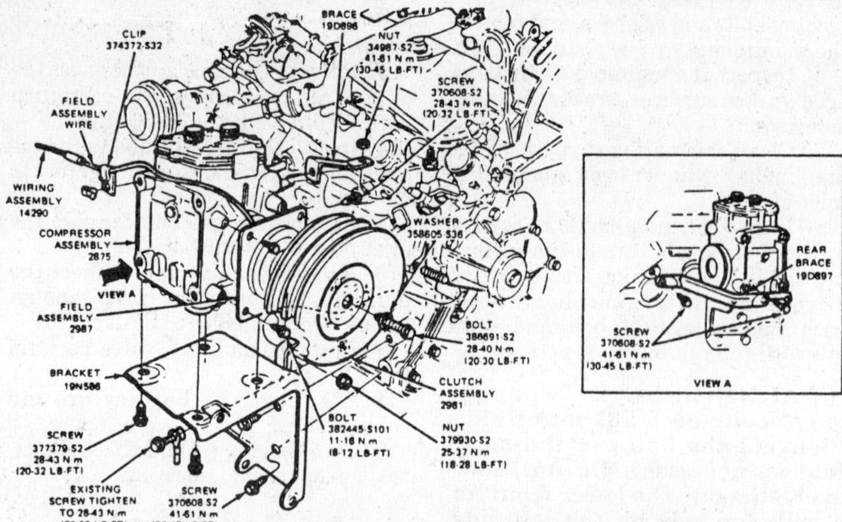

Air conditioning compressor installation on the 1981 6-200

moval. Prior to installation, if a new compressor is being installed, drain the oil from the old compressor into a calibrated container, then drain the oil from the new compressor into a clean container and refill the new compressor with the same amount of oil that was in the old one. Install the clutch and bolt finger-tight, install the compressor on the mounting bracket and install those bolts finger-tight. Connect the clutch wire and energize the clutch. Tighten the clutch bolt to 23 ft.lb. Tighten the compressor mounting bolts to 30 ft.lb. Make all other connections and evacuate, charge and leak test the system. See ROUTINE MAINTENANCE.

FS-6 6-Cylinder Axial Compressor

1982-83 THUNDERBIRD AND XR-7 WITH THE 6-232 ENGINE

1. Discharge the refrigerant system. See ROUTINE MAINTENANCE for the proper procedures.
2. Disconnect the two refrigerant lines from the compressor. Cap the openings immediately!
3. Remove tension from the drive belt. Remove the belt
4. Disconnect the clutch wire at the connector.
5. Remove the bolt attaching the support brace to the front brace and the nut attaching the support brace to the intake manifold. Remove the support brace.
6. Remove the two bolts attaching the rear support to the bracket.
7. Remove the bolt attaching the compressor tab to the front brace and the two bolts attaching the compressor front legs to the bracket.
8. Remove the compressor.
9. Installation is the reverse of removal. Use new O-rings coated with clean refrigerant oil at all fittings. New, replacement compressors contain 10 oz. of refrigerant oil. Prior to installation, pour off 4 oz. of oil. This will maintain the oil charge in the system. Evacuate, charge and leak test the system.

1982 THUNDERBIRD AND XR-7 WITH THE 6-200 ENGINE

1. Discharge the refrigerant system. See ROUTINE MAINTENANCE for the proper procedures.
2. Disconnect the two refrigerant lines from the compressor. Cap the openings immediately!
3. Remove tension from the drive belt. Remove the belt
4. Disconnect the clutch wire at the connector.
5. Remove the bolt attaching the support brace to the compressor upper mounting lug.
6. Remove the two bolts attaching the bracket to the compressor lower front mounting lugs.
7. Remove the compressor from the engine.
8. Installation is the reverse of removal. Use new O-rings coated with clean refrigerant oil at all fittings. New, replacement compressors contain 10 oz. of refrigerant oil. Prior to installation, pour off 4 oz. of oil. This will maintain the oil charge in the system. Evacuate, charge and leak test the system.

1982 THUNDERBIRD AND XR-7 WITH THE 8-255 ENGINE
1982-85 CONTINENTAL WITH THE 8-302 ENGINE
1984-85 THUNDERBIRD, COUGAR AND MARK VII WITH THE 8-302 ENGINE
1986-87 MODELS WITH MANUAL AIR CONDITIONING AND THE 8-302 ENGINE

1. Discharge the refrigerant system. See ROUTINE MAINTENANCE for the proper procedures.
2. Disconnect the two refrigerant lines from the compressor. Cap the openings immediately!
3. Remove tension from the drive belt. Remove the belt
4. Disconnect the clutch wire at the connector.
5. Remove the two nuts from the rear support bracket. Remove the three bolts from the front bosses on the bracket. On 1985-86 models, remove one bolt from the front of the tubular brace and remove the tubular brace.
6. Rotate the compressor towards the left side of the engine compartment until the compressor upper boss clears the support.
7. Remove the compressor and rear support as an assembly.

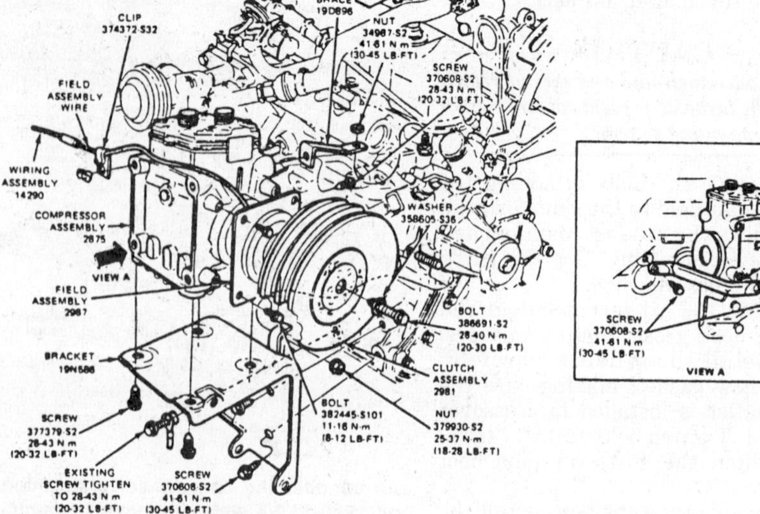

Air conditioning compressor installation on the 1982 6-200

8. Installation is the reverse of removal. Use new O-rings coated with clean refrigerant oil at all fittings. New, replacement compressors contain 10 oz. of refrigerant oil. Prior to installation, pour off 4 oz. of oil. This will maintain the oil charge in the system. Evacuate, charge and leak test the system.

1986-87 MODELS WITH AUTOMATIC TEMPERATURE CONTROL AND THE 8-302 ENGINE

1. Discharge the refrigerant system. See ROUTINE MAINTENANCE for the proper procedures.
2. Disconnect the two refrigerant lines from the compressor. Cap the openings immediately!
3. Remove tension from the drive belt. Remove the belt
4. Disconnect the clutch wire at the connector.
5. Remove the two bolts attaching the rear compressor brace to the power steering pump support. Remove the three bolts attaching the front bosses of the compressor to the power steering pump and the compressor brace.
6. Remove the compressor and rear support as an assembly.
7. Installation is the reverse of removal. Install all bolts finger-tight before tightening any of them. Use new O-rings coated with clean refrigerant oil at all fittings. New, replacement compressors contain 10 oz. of refrigerant oil. Prior to installation, pour off 4 oz. of oil. This will maintain the oil charge in the system. Evacuate, charge and leak test the system.

HR-980 Radial Compressor

1983-87 THUNDERBIRD AND COUGAR WITH 4-140 and 6-232 ENGINES AND MANUAL AIR CONDITIONING

1. Discharge the refrigerant system. See ROUTINE MAINTENANCE for the proper procedures.
2. Disconnect the two refrigerant lines from the compressor. Cap the openings immediately!
3. Remove the bolt and washer from the adjusting bracket and remove the drive belts.
4. Remove the bolt attaching the compressor bracket to the compressor lower mounting lug.
5. Remove the compressor.
6. Installation is the reverse of removal. If a new compressor is being installed, it contains 8 fl.oz. of refrigerant oil. Prior to installing the compressor, drain 4 oz. of the oil from the compressor. This will maintain the oil charge in the system. Evacuate, charge and leak test the system.

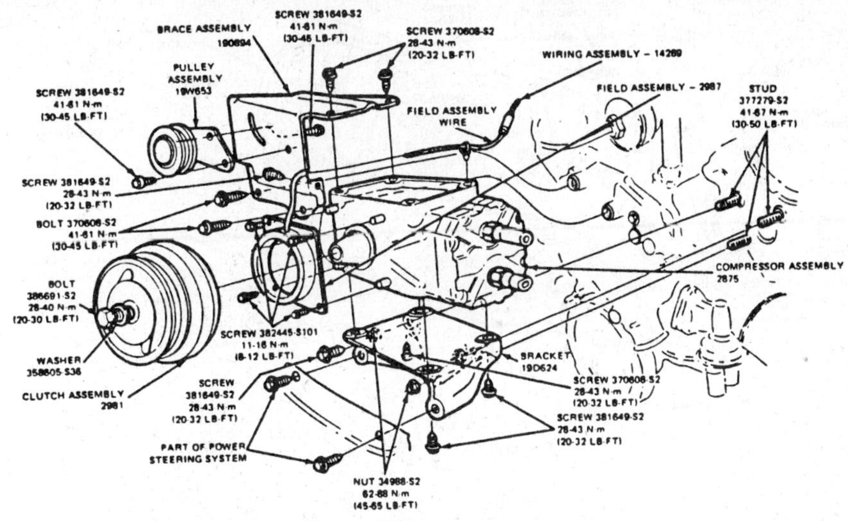

Air conditioning compressor installation on the 8-255

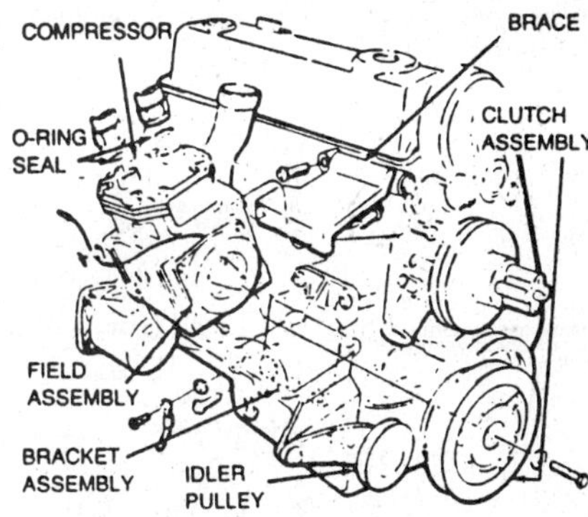

Air conditioning compressor installation on the 1981-82 4-140 for use in 49 states and Canada with manual transmission

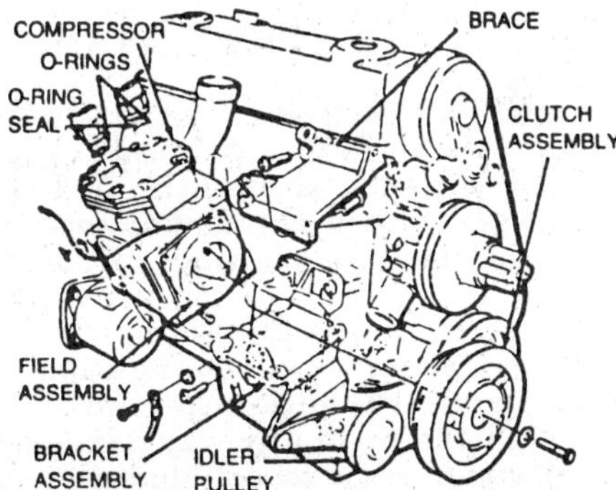

Air conditioning compressor installation on the 1981-82 4-140 for use in 49 states with manual transmission and in California with both manual and automatic transmissions

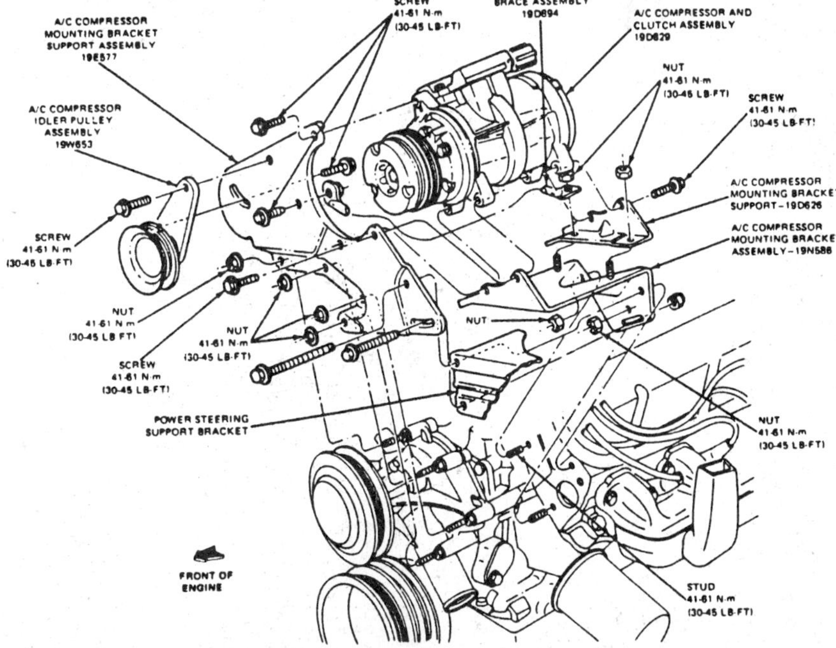

Air conditioning installation on 1984-87 cars with the 8-302 and manual air conditioning

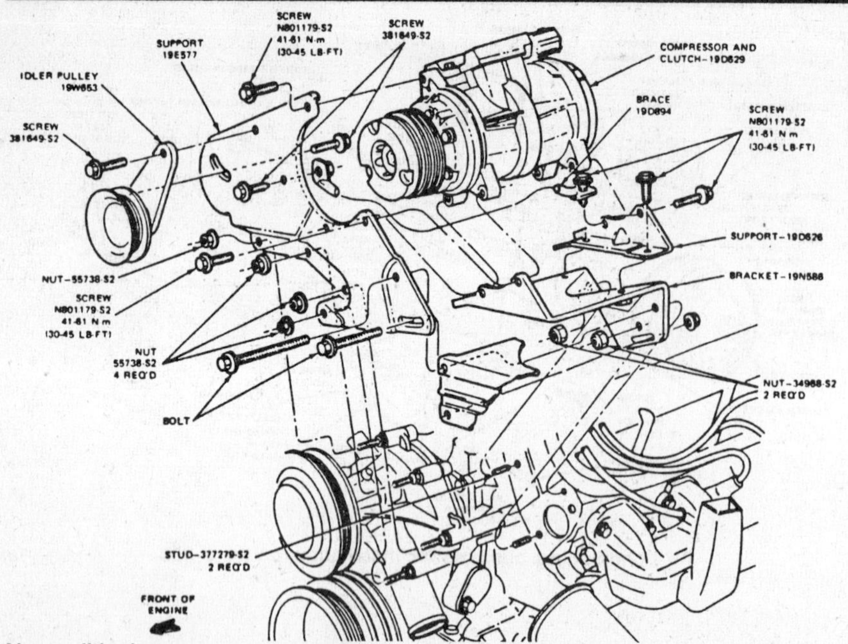

Air conditioning compressor installation 1985-87 cars with the 8-302 and automatic temperature control

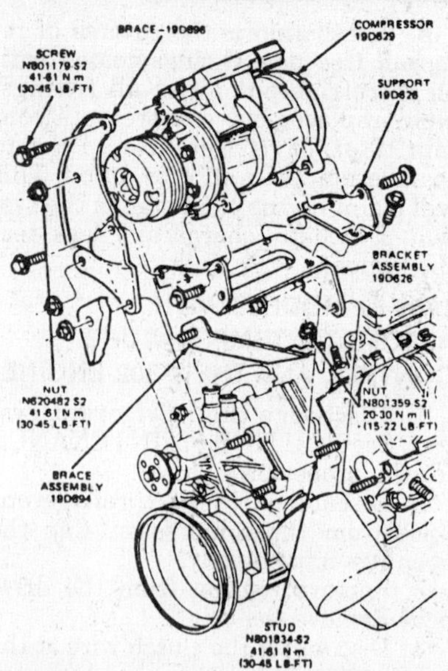

Air conditioning compressor installation on the 6-232 with the FS-6 6-cylinder compressor

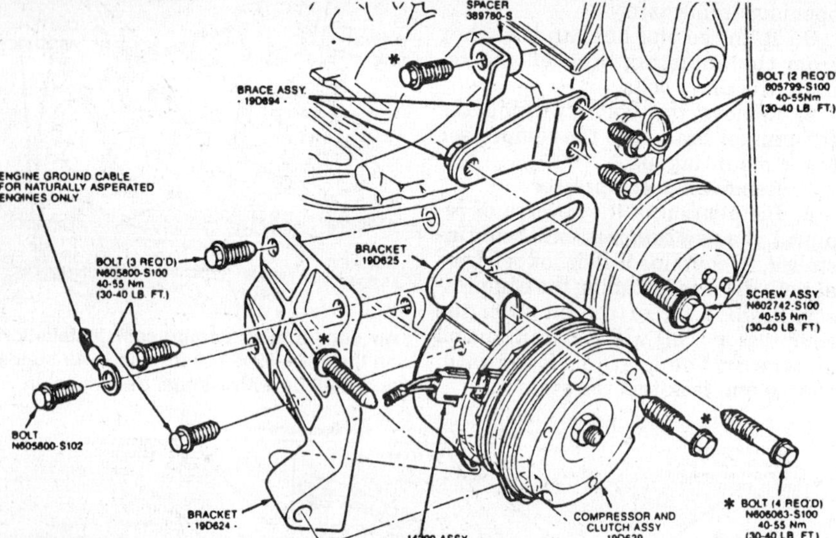

Air conditioning compressor installation on 1984-87 4-140 non-Turbo engines without a Thermacto® air pump

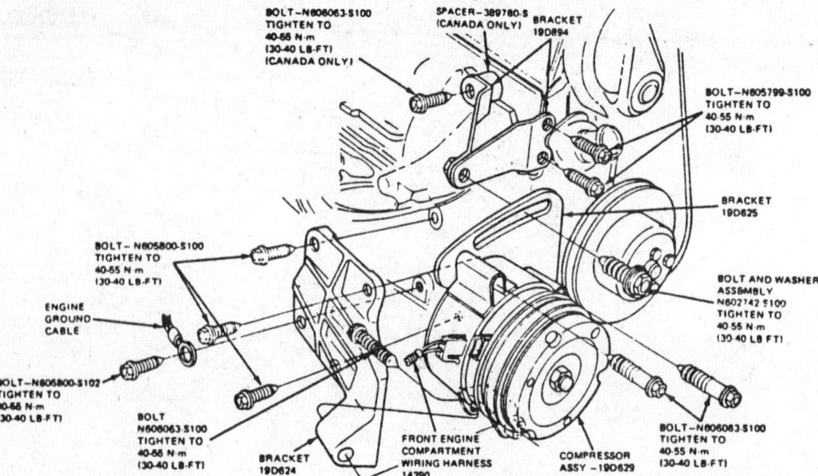

Air conditioning compressor installation on 1984-87 4-140 Turbo engines

6P148 3-Cylinder Axial Compressor

1986-87 Thunderbird and Cougar with the 6-232

1. Discharge the refrigerant system. See ROUTINE MAINTENANCE for the proper procedures.
2. Disconnect the two refrigerant lines from the compressor. Cap the openings immediately!
3. Remove tension from the drive belt. Remove the belt
4. Disconnect the clutch wire at the connector.
5. Unbolt and remove the compressor.
6. Installation is the reverse of removal. Evacuate, charge and leak test the system.

Turbocharger

NOTE: The turbocharger is serviced by replacement only.

REMOVAL & INSTALLATION

NOTE: Before starting removal/service procedures, clean the area around the turbocharger with a non-caustic solution. Cover the openings of component connections to prevent the entry of dirt and foreign materials. Exercise care when handling the turbocharger not to nick, bend or in any way damage the compressor wheel blades.

Except Diesel Engine

1. Disconnect the negative battery cable.

2. Drain the cooling system.

CAUTION

When draining the coolant, keep in mind that cats and dogs are attracted by the ethylene glycol antifreeze, and are quite likely to drink any that is left in an uncovered container or in puddles on the ground. This will prove fatal in sufficient quantity. Always drain the coolant into a sealable container. Coolant should be reused unless it is contaminated or several years old.

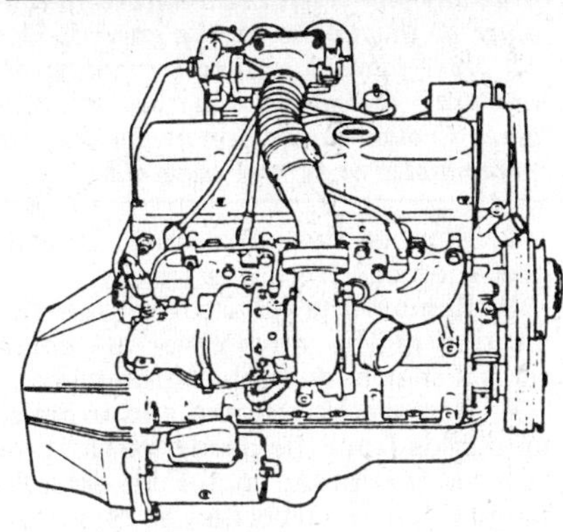

4-140 turbocharger installation

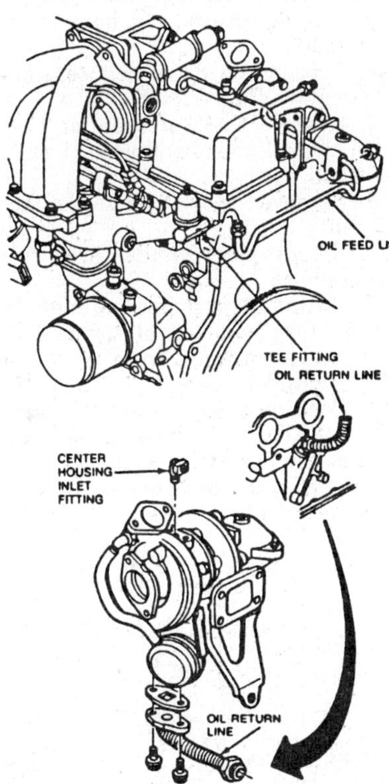

Turbo oil supply and return lines—4-140 engine

3. Loosen the upper clamp on the turbocharger inlet hose. Remove the two bolts mounting the throttle body discharge tube to the turbo.

4. Label for identification and location all vacuum hoses and tubes to the turbo and disconnect them.

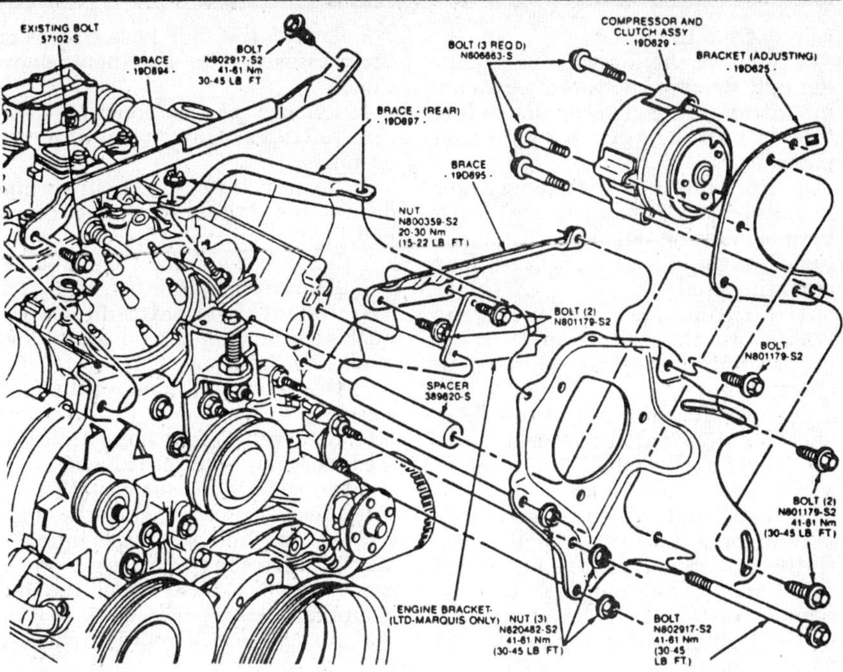

Air conditioning compressor installation on the 1982-87 6-232 with the HR-980 radial compressor

5. Disconnect the PCV tube from the turbo air inlet elbow. Remove the throttle busy discharge tube and hose as an assembly.

6. Disconnect the ground wire from the air inlet elbow. Remove (disconnect) the water outlet connection (and fitting if a new turbo unit is to be installed) from the turbo center housing.

7. Remove the turbo oil supply feed line. Disconnect the oxygen sensor connector at the turbocharger.

8. Raise and support the front of the vehicle on jackstands. Disconnect the exhaust pipe from the turbocharger.

9. Disconnect the oil return line from the bottom of the turbocharger. Take care not to damage or kink the line.

10. Disconnect the water inlet tube at the turbo center housing.

11. Remove the lower turbo mounting bracket-to-engine bolt. Lower the

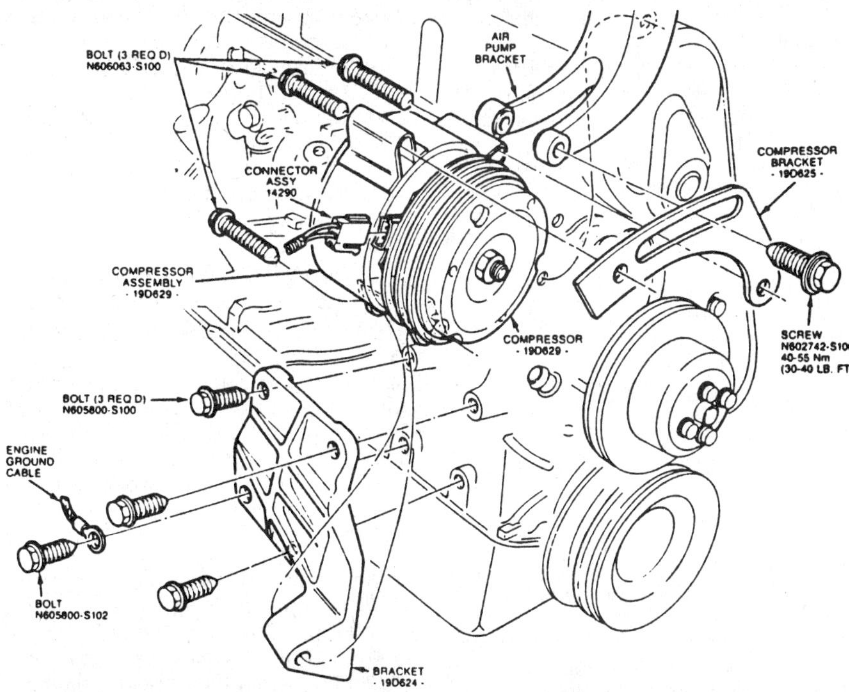

Air conditioning compressor installation on 1984 4-140 non-Turbo engines with a Thermactor® air pump

vehicle from the stands.

12. Remove the lower front mounting nut. Remove the three remaining mounting nuts evenly while sliding the turbocharger away from mounting.

13. Position a new turbocharger mounting gasket in position with the bead side facing outward. Install the turbocharger in position over the four mounting studs.

14. Position the lower mounting bracket over the two bottom studs. Using new nuts, start the two lower then the two upper mountings. Do not tighten them completely at this time; allow for slight turbo movement.

15. Raise and support the front of the vehicle on jackstands.

16. Install and tighten the lower gasket and connect the return line. Tighten the mounting bolts to 14-21 ft.lb.

18. Connect the water inlet tube assembly. Install the exhaust pipe on turbo. Tighten the mounting nuts to 25-35 ft.lb.

19. Lower the vehicle. Tighten the turbo mounting nut to 28-40 ft.lb.

20. Connect the water outlet assembly to the turbocharger, tighten the fasteners to 11-14 ft.lb. Hold the fitting with a wrench when tightening the line.

21. Install the air inlet tube to the turbo inlet elbow (15-22 ft.lb.). Tighten the clamp.

22. Connect the PCV tube and all vacuum lines.

23. Connect the oxygen sensor and other wiring and lines.

24. Connect the oil supply line. Connect the intake tube. Fill the cooling system.

25. Connect the negative battery cable. Start the engine and check for coolant leaks. Check vehicle operation.

WARNING: When installing the turbocharger, or after an oil and filter change, disconnect the distributor feed harness and crank the engine with the starter motor until the oil pressure light on the dash goes out. Oil pressure must be up before starting the engine.

2,443cc Diesel Engine

CAUTION

Do not accelerate the engine before engine oil pressure has been built up. Also do not switch off the engine while it is running at high speed (the turbocharger will continue to spring for a long time without oil pressure). These conditions can damage the engine and/or turbocharger.

1. Remove the two bolts attaching the exhaust pipe to the turbocharger.

2. Remove the EGR tube and clamps.

3. Loosen the four hose clamps on the crossover tube and then remove tube.

4. Remove the air cleaner assembly and bellows. Cap turbocharger openings.

5. Remove the two oil supply line bolts on top of the turbocharger center housing.

6. Remove the clamp from oil lines.

7. Remove the oil return line.

8. Remove the bolt and sealing washers attaching the oil supply line to oil filter housing.

9. Disconnect and remove the EGR valve.

10. Remove the four bolts attaching the turbocharger to the exhaust manifold and remove the turbocharger.

11. Clean the mating surfaces of the turbocharger and exhaust manifold.

12. Position the turbocharger on the exhaust manifold and install the four mounting bolts. Tighten to 17-20 ft.lb.

13. Install the EGR valve. Tighten to 18 ft.lb.

14. Install the oil supply line using new seals. Tighten the bolt to 26-33 ft.lb.

CAUTION

Do not overtighten bolt. Oil leaks may occur if overtightened.

15. Install the clamp retaining the oil lines.

16. Install the oil supply line bolts to the turbocharger housing and tighten to 15-18 ft.lb.

17. Remove the protective caps from the turbocharger and install the air cleaner assembly and bellows.

18. Install the crossover tube. Tighten the hose clamps snugly.

19. Install the EGR tube clamp.

20. Install the two bolts attaching the exhaust pipe to the turbocharger and tighten them to 17-20 ft.lb.

21. Run the engine and check for oil and air leaks.

Cylinder Head

REMOVAL & INSTALLATION

NOTE: On cars with air conditioning, remove the mounting bolts and the drive belt, and position the compressor out of the way. Remove the compressor upper mounting bracket from the cylinder head.

CAUTION

If the compressor refrigerant lines do not have enough slack to permit repositioning of the compressor without first disconnecting the refrigerant lines, the air conditioning system will have to be evacuated. See ROUTINE MAINTENANCE.

4-140 Engine

NOTE: Set the engine at TDC position for No. 1 piston, if possible prior to head removal.

1. Drain the cooling system.

CAUTION

When draining the coolant, keep in mind that cats and dogs are attracted by the ethylene glycol antifreeze, and are quite likely to drink any that is left in an uncovered container or in puddles on the ground. This will prove fatal in sufficient quantity. Always drain the coolant into a sealable container. Coolant should be reused unless it is contaminated or several years old.

2. Remove the air cleaner. Disconnect the negative battery cable.

3. Remove the valve cover. Note the location of the valve cover attaching screws that have rubber grommets.

4. Remove the intake and exhaust manifolds from the head. See the procedures for intake manifold, exhaust manifold, and turbocharger removal.

5. Remove the camshaft drive belt cover. Note the location of the belt cover attaching screws that have rubber grommets.

6. Loosen the drive belt tensioner and remove the belt.

7. Remove the water outlet elbow from the cylinder head with the hose attached.

8. Remove the cylinder head attaching bolts.

9. Remove the cylinder head from the engine.

10. Clean all gaskets material and carbon from the top of the cylinder block and pistons and from the bottom of the cylinder head.

11. Position a new cylinder head gasket on the engine. Rotate the camshaft so that the hear locating pin is at the five o'clock position to avoid damage to the valves and pistons.

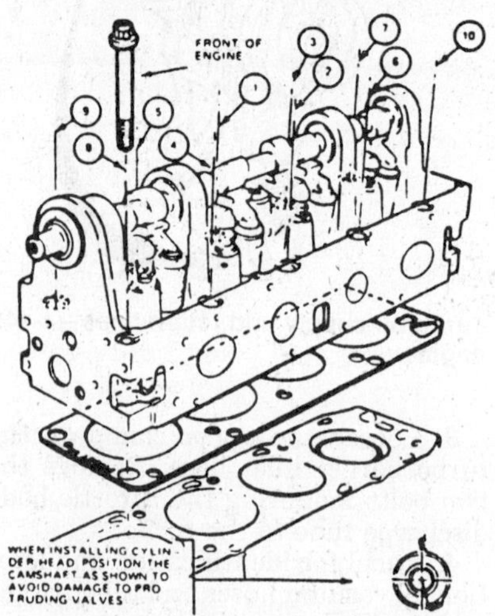

4-140 cylinder head installation

NOTE: If you encounter difficulty in positioning the cylinder head on the engine block, it may be necessary to install guide studs in the block to correctly align the head and the block. To fabricate guide studs, obtain two new cylinder head bolts and cut their heads off with a hack saw. Install the bolts in the holes in the engine block which correspond with cylinder head bolt holes Nos. 3 and 4, as identified in the cylinder head bolt tightening sequence illustration. Then, install the head gasket and head over the bolts. Install the cylinder head attaching bolts, replacing the studs with the original head bolts.

12. Using a torque wrench, tighten the head bolts in the sequence shown in the illustration.
13. Install the camshaft drive belt. See Camshaft Drive Belt Installation.
14. Install the camshaft drive belt cover and its attaching bolts. Make sure the rubber grommets are installed on the bolts. Tighten the bolts to 6-13 ft.lb.
15. Install the water outlet elbow and a new gasket on the engine and tighten the attaching bolts to 12-15 ft.lb.
16. Install the intake and exhaust manifolds. See the procedures for intake and exhaust manifold installation.
17. Install the air cleaner and the valve cover.
18. Fill the cooling system.

6-200

CAUTION

When draining the coolant, keep in mind that cats and dogs are attracted by the ethylene glycol antifreeze, and are quite likely to drink any that is left in an uncovered container or in puddles on the ground. This will prove fatal in sufficient quantity. Always drain the coolant into a sealable container. Coolant should be reused unless it is contaminated or several years old.

1. Drain the cooling system, remove the air cleaner and disconnect the negative battery cable.

WARNING: On cars with air conditioning, remove the mounting bolts and the drive belt, and position the compressor out of the way of the left cylinder head. Remove the compressor upper mounting bracket from the cylinder head.

If the compressor refrigerant lines do not have enough slack to permit repositioning of the compressor without first disconnecting the refrigerant lines, the air conditioning system will have to be evacuated. See ROUTINE MAINTENANCE.

2. Disconnect the exhaust pipe at the manifold end, swing the exhaust pipe down and remove the flange gasket.
3. Disconnect the fuel and vacuum lines from the carburetor. Disconnect the intake manifold line at the intake manifold.
4. Disconnect the accelerator and retracting spring at the carburetor. Disconnect the transmission kickdown linkage, if equipped.
5. Disconnect the carburetor spacer outlet line at the spacer. Disconnect the radiator upper hose and the heater hose at the water outlet elbow. Disconnect the radiator lower hose and the heater hose at the water pump.
6. Disconnect the distributor vacuum control line at the distributor. Disconnect the gas filter line on the inlet side of the filter.
7. Disconnect and label the spark plug wires and remove the plugs. Disconnect the temperature sending unit wire.
8. Remove the rocker arm cover.
9. Remove the rocker arm shaft attaching bolts and the rocker arm and shaft assembly. Remove the valve pushrods, keep them in order for installation in their original positions.
10. Remove the remaining cylinder head bolts and lift off the cylinder head. Do not pry under the cylinder head as damage to the mating surfaces can easily occur.

To help in installation of the cylinder head, two 6" x $^7/_{16}$–14 bolts with their heads cut off and the head end slightly tapered and slotted, for installation and removal with a screwdriver, will reduce the possibility of damage during head replacement.

11. Clean the cylinder head and block surfaces. Be sure of flatness and no surface damage.
12. Apply cylinder head gasket sealer to both sides of the new gasket and slide the gasket down over the two guide studs in the cylinder block.

WARNING: Apply gasket sealer only to steel shim head gaskets. Steel/asbestos composite head gaskets are to be installed without any sealer.

13. Carefully lower the cylinder head over the guide studs. Place the exhaust pipe flange on the manifold studs (new gasket).
14. Coat the threads of the end bolts for the right side of the cylinder head with a small amount of water-resistant sealer. Install, but do not tighten, two head bolts at opposite ends to hold the head gasket in place. Remove the guide studs and install the remaining bolts.

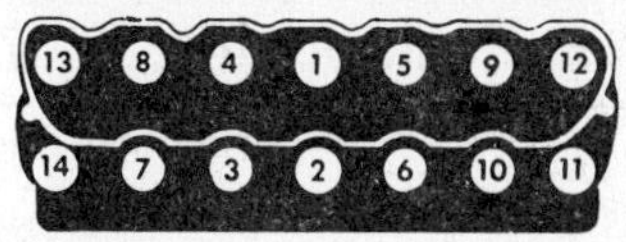

Cylinder head bolt tightening sequence—200, 250 cyl.

15. Cylinder head torquing should proceed in three steps and in the prescribed order. Tighten them first to 55 ft.lb., then give them a second tightening to 65 ft.lb. The final step is to 75 ft.lb., at which they should remain undisturbed.
16. Lubricate both ends of the pushrods and install them in their original locations.
17. Apply lubricant to the rocker arm pads and the valve stem tips and position the rocker arm shaft assembly on the head. Be sure the oil holes in the shaft are in a down position.
18. Tighten all the rocker shaft retaining bolts to 30-35 ft.lb. and do a preliminary valve adjustment (make sure there are no tight valve adjustments).
19. Hook up the exhaust pipe.
20. Reconnect the heater and radiator hoses.
21. Reposition the distributor vacuum line, the carburetor gas line and the intake manifold vacuum line on the engine. Hook them up to their respective connections and reconnect the battery cable to the cylinder head.
22. Connect the accelerator rod and retracting spring. Connect the choke control cable and adjust the choke. Connect the transmission kickdown linkage.
23. Reconnect the vacuum line at the distributor. Connect the fuel inlet line at the fuel filter and the intake manifold vacuum line at the vacuum pump.
24. Lightly lubricate the spark plug threads and install them. Connect spark plug wires and be sure the wires are all the way down in their sockets. Connect the temperature sending unit wire.
25. Fill the cooling system. Run the engine to stabilize all engine part temperatures.
26. Adjust engine idle speed and idle fuel air adjustment.
27. Coat one side of a new rocker cover gasket with oil-resistant sealer. Lay the treated side of the gasket on the cover and install the cover. Be sure the gasket seals evenly all around the cylinder head.

6-232

1. Drain the cooling system.

CAUTION

When draining the coolant, keep in mind that cats and dogs are attracted by the ethyl-

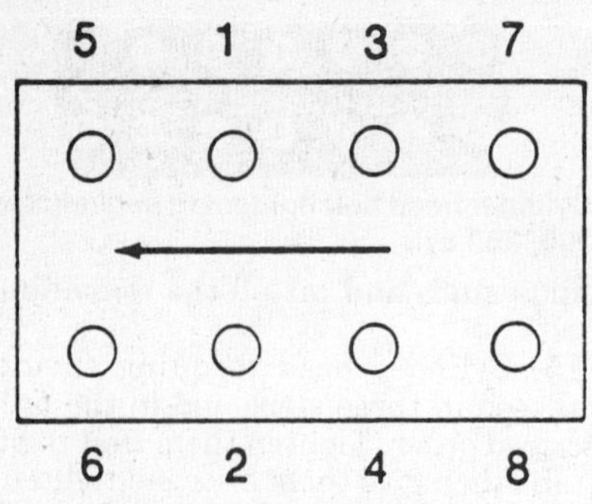

V6 cylinder head torque sequence

ene glycol antifreeze, and are quite likely to drink any that is left in an uncovered container or in puddles on the ground. This will prove fatal in sufficient quantity. Always drain the coolant into a sealable container. Coolant should be reused unless it is contaminated or several years old.

2. Disconnect the cable from the battery negative terminal.
3. Remove the air cleaner assembly including air intake duct and heat tube.
4. Loosen the accessory drive belt idler. Remove the drive belt.
5. If the left cylinder head is being removed:
   a. If equipped with power steering, remove the pump mounting brackets' attaching bolts, leaving the hoses connected, place the pump/bracket assembly aside in a position to prevent the fluid from leaking out.
   b. If equipped with air conditioning, remove the mounting brackets' attaching bolts, leaving the hoses connected, and position the compressor aside.
6. If the right cylinder head is being removed:
   a. Disconnect the Thermactor® diverter valve and hose assembly at the by-pass valve and downstream air tube.
   b. Remove the assembly.
   c. Remove the accessory drive idler.
   d. Remove the alternator.
   e. Remove the Thermactor® pump pulley. Remove the Thermactor® pump.
   f. Remove the alternator bracket.
   g. Remove the PCV valve.
7. Remove the intake manifold.
8. Remove the valve rocker arm cover attaching screws. Loosen the silicone rubber gasketing material by inserting a putty knife under the cover flange. Work the cover loosen and remove. The plastic rocker arm covers will break if excessive prying is applied.
9. Remove the exhaust manifold(s).
10. Loosen the rocker arm fulcrum attaching bolts enough to allow the rocker arm to be lifted off the pushrod and rotated to one side.
11. Remove the pushrods. Label the pushrods since they should be installed in the original position during assembly.
12. Remove the cylinder head attaching bolts. Remove the cylinder head(s).
13. Remove and discard the old cylinder head gasket(s). Discard the cylinder head bolts.
14. Lightly oil all bolt and stud bolt threads before installation except those specifying special sealant.
15. Clean the cylinder head, intake manifold, valve rocker arm cover and cylinder head gasket surfaces. If the cylinder head was removed for a cylinder head gasket replacement, check the flatness of the cylinder head and block gasket surfaces.
16. Position new head gasket(s) on the cylinder block using the dowels for alignment.
17. Position the cylinder heads to the block.
18. Apply a thin coating of pipe sealant or equivalent to the threads of the short cylinder head bolts (nearest to the exhaust manifold). Do not apply sealant to the long bolts. Lightly oil the cylinder head bolt flat washers. Install the flat washers and cylinder head bolts (Eight each side).

CAUTION

Always use new cylinder head bolts to assure a leak tight assembly. Torque retention with used bolts can vary, which may result in coolant or compression leakage at the cylinder head mating surface area.

19. Tighten the attaching bolts in sequence. Back off the attaching bolts 2-3 turns. Repeat tightening sequence.

NOTE: When the cylinder head attaching bolts have been tightened using the above sequential procedure, it is not necessary to retighten the bolts after extended engine operation. However, the bolts can be checked for tightness if desired.

20. Dip each pushrod end in heavy engine oil. Install the push rods in their original position. For each valve rotate the crankshaft until the tappet rests on the heel (base circle) of the camshaft lobe.
21. Position the rocker arms over the pushrods, install the fulcrums, and tighten the fulcrum attaching bolts to 61-132 in.lb.

WARNING: Fulcrums must be fully seated in cylinder head and pushrods must be seated in rocker arm sockets prior to final tightening.

22. Lubricate all rocker arm assemblies with heavy engine oil. Finally tighten the fulcrum bolts to 19-25 ft.lb. For final tightening, the camshaft may be in any position.

NOTE: If the original valve train components are being installed, a valve clearance check is not required. If a component has been replaced, perform a valve clearance check.

23. Install the exhaust manifold(s).
24. Apply a $\frac{1}{8}$-$\frac{3}{16}$" (3-4mm) bead of RTV silicone sealant to the rocker arm cover flange. make sure the sealer fills the channel in the cover flange. The rocker arm cover must be installed within 15 minutes after the silicone sealer application. After this time, the sealer may start to set-up, and its sealing effectiveness may be reduced.
25. Position the cover on the cylinder head and install the attaching bolts. Note the location of the wiring harness routing clips and spark plug wire routing clip stud bolts. Tighten the attaching bolts to 36-60 in.lb. torque.
26. Install the intake manifold.
27. Install the spark plugs, if necessary.
28. Connect the secondary wires to the spark plugs.
29. Install the oil fill cap. If equipped with air conditioning, install the compressor mounting and support brackets.
30. On the right cylinder head:
   a. Install the PCV valve.
   b. Install the alternator bracket. Tighten attaching nuts to 30-40 ft.lb.
   c. Install the Thermactor® pump and pump pulley.
   d. Install the alternator.
   e. Install the accessory drive idler.
   f. Install the Thermactor® diverter valve and hose assembly. Tighten the clamps securely.
31. Install the accessory drive belt and tighten to the specified tension.
32. Connect the cable to the battery negative terminal.
33. Fill the cooling system with the specified coolant.

WARNING: This engine has an aluminum cylinder head and requires a compatible coolant formulation to avoid radiator damage.

34. Start the engine and check for coolant, fuel, and oil leaks.
35. Check and, if necessary, adjust the curb idle speed.
36. Install the air cleaner assembly including the air intake duct and heat tube.

V8 Engines

1. Drain the cooling system.

CAUTION

When draining the coolant, keep in mind that cats and dogs are attracted by the ethylene glycol antifreeze, and are quite likely to drink any that is left in an uncovered container or in puddles on the ground. This will prove fatal in sufficient quantity. Always drain the coolant into a sealable container. Coolant should be reused unless it is contaminated or several years old.

2. Remove the intake manifold and the carburetor or CFI unit as an assembly.
3. Disconnect the spark plug wires, marking them as to placement. Position them out of the way of the cylinder head. Remove the spark plugs.
4. Disconnect the exhaust pipes at the manifolds.
5. Remove the rocker arm covers.
6. On cars with air conditioning, remove the mounting bolts and the drive belt, and position the compressor out of the way of the left cylinder head. Remove the compressor upper mounting bracket from the cylinder head.

NOTE: If the compressor refrigerant lines do not have enough slack to permit repositioning of the compressor without first disconnecting the refrigerant lines, the air conditioning system will have to be evacuated by a trained air conditioning serviceman. Under no circumstances should an untrained person attempt to disconnect the air conditioning refrigerant lines.

7. In order to remove the left cylinder head, on cars equipped with power steering, it may be necessary to remove the steering pump and bracket, remove the drive belt, and wire or tie the pump out of the way, but in such a way as to prevent the loss of its fluid.
8. In order to remove the right head it may be necessary to remove the alternator mounting bracket bolt and spacer, the ignition coil, and the air cleaner inlet duct from the right cylinder head.
9. In order to remove the left cylinder head on a car equipped with a Thermactor® air pump system, disconnect the hose from the air manifold on the left cylinder head.

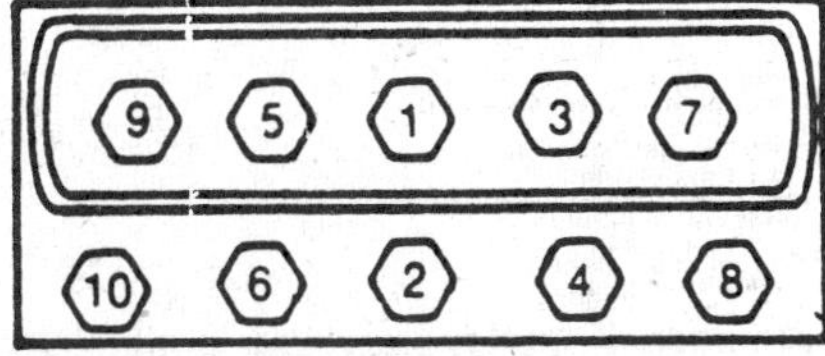

V8 cylinder head torque sequence

10. If the right cylinder head is to be removed on a car equipped with a Thermactor® system, remove the Thermactor® air pump and its mounting bracket. Disconnect the hose from the air manifold on the right cylinder head.
11. Loosen the rocker arm stud nuts enough to rotate the rocker arms to the side, in order to facilitate the removal of the pushrods. Remove the pushrods in sequence, so that they may be installed in their original positions. Remove the exhaust valve stem caps, if equipped.
12. Remove the cylinder head attaching bolts, noting their positions, Lift the cylinder head off the block. Remove and discard the old cylinder head gasket. Clean all mounting surfaces.
13. Position the new cylinder head gasket over the dowels on the block. Position new gaskets on the muffler inlet pipes at the exhaust manifold flange.
14. Position the cylinder head on the block, and install the head bolts, each in its original position. On engines on which the exhaust manifold has been removed from the head to facilitate removal, it is necessary to properly guide the exhaust manifold studs into the muffler inlet pipe flange when installing the head.
15. Step-torque the cylinder head retaining bolts first to 50 ft.lb. then to 60 ft.lb., and finally to the torque specification listed in the Torque Specifications chart. Tighten the exhaust manifold-to-cylinder head attaching bolts to specifications.
16. Tighten the nuts on the exhaust manifold studs at the muffler inlet flanges to 18 ft.lb.
17. Clean and inspect the pushrods one at a time. Clean the oil passage within each pushrod with solvent and blow the passage out with compressed air. Check the ends of the pushrods for nicks, grooves, roughness, or excessive wear. Visually inspect the pushrods for straightness, and replace any bent ones. Do not attempt to straighten pushrods.
18. Install the pushrods in their original positions. Apply Lubriplate® or a similar product to the valve stem tips and to the pushrod guides in the cylinder head. Install the exhaust valve stem caps.
19. Apply Lubriplate® or a similar product to the fulcrum seats and sockets. Turn the rocker arms to their proper position and tighten the stud nuts enough to hold the rocker arms in position. Make sure that the lower ends of the pushrods have remained properly seated in the valve lifters. Tighten the stud nuts 17-23 ft.lb. in order given under the preliminary valve adjustment.
20. Install the valve covers.
21. Install the intake manifold and carburetor, following the procedure under Intake Manifold Installation.
22. Reinstall all other items removed.

Diesel Engine

1. Disconnect the battery ground cable.
2. Drain the cooling system. Disconnect the heater hose(s).

CAUTION

When draining the coolant, keep in mind that cats and dogs are attracted by the ethylene glycol antifreeze, and are quite likely to drink any that is left in an uncovered container or in puddles on the ground. This will prove fatal in sufficient quantity. Always drain the coolant into a sealable container. Coolant should be reused unless it is contaminated or several years old.

3. Loosen and remove the accessory drive belts.
4. Remove the valve cover.
5. Disconnect the diagnostic connectors.
6. Disconnect the coolant temperature switch and glow plug connector.
7. Disconnect the breather hose and bracket.
8. Remove the clamp attaching the oil dipstick tube to the intake manifold and position out of the way.
9. Disconnect the boost pressure switch connector.
10. Disconnect the radiator hose from the cylinder head.
11. Disconnect the temperature controlled idle boost coolant hose.
12. Remove the vacuum pump from cylinder head.

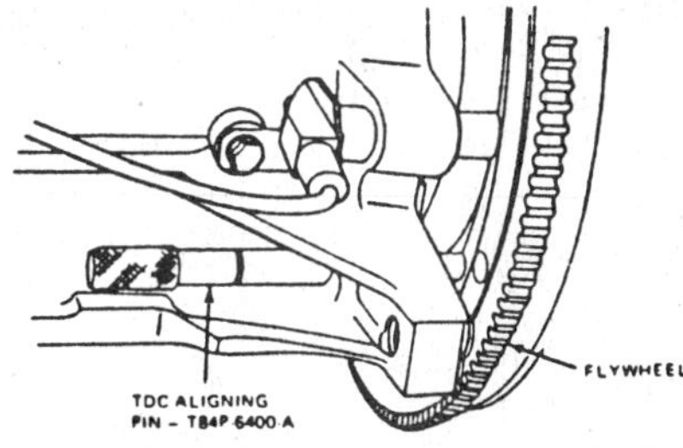

TDC alignment pin installation—2.4L diesel engine

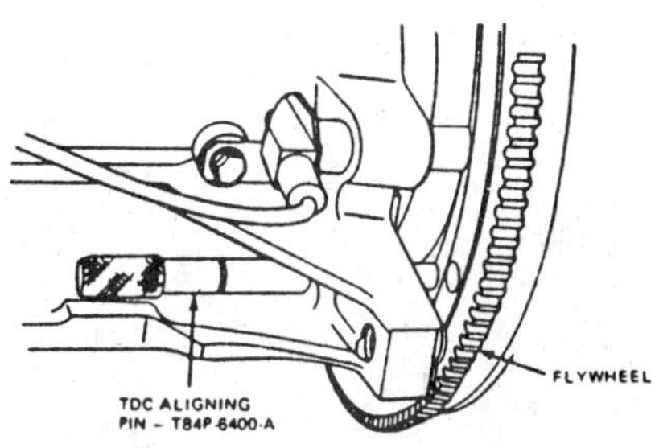

Diesel engine TDC aligning pin

13. Disconnect No. 1 nozzle to the injection pump leak hose.
14. Disconnect the injection lines from the nozzles and injection pump.

WARNING: Cap the nozzles and lines.

15. Disconnect the turbocharger oil lines.
16. Rotate the crankshaft until No. 1 cylinder is at TDC of compression stroke (intake and exhaust valves on base circle). Install TDC Aligning Pin, T84P-6400-A or equivalent.
17. Loosen the camshaft drive sprocket retaining bolt.
18. Loosen the camshaft drive belt tensioning roller nut and bolt, and remove the drive belt.
19. Loosen the cylinder head bolts in sequence, and remove the cylinder head.
20. Clean the gasket sealing surfaces on the cylinder head and crankcase. Check for warpage.

WARNING: Use care when cleaning the gasket surfaces. Slight scoring of these surfaces can cause leakage due to high compression pressures.

21. Clean the top of each piston.
22. Using a dial indicator D82L-4201-A and Piston Height Gauge D84P-6100-A or equivalent, measure the amount the piston top extends above crankcase gasket surface as follows:
    a. Mount the dial indicator and bracket with the dial indicator tip on the piston.
    b. Rotate the crankshaft to position the piston at TDC, using dial indicator.
    c. Zero the dial indicator with the tip on the crankcase.
    d. Move the tip to the front of the piston. Record the measurement.
    e. Move the tip to the rear of the piston. Record the measurement.
    f. Repeat this procedure for each cylinder.
    g. Average the two readings for each cylinder.

Mounting the dial indicator

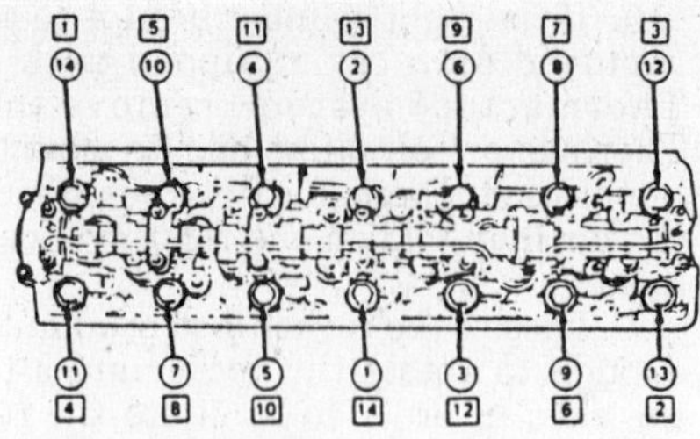

2.4L diesel engine—head bolt removal and installation sequence

    h. Using the measurement of the highest piston, refer to the chart provided and select the correct cylinder head gasket.
23. Clean carbon and oil deposits from the cylinder head bolts.

WARNING: Keep oil and/or antifreeze from entering cylinder head bolt holes. If either enters the bolt holes, carefully blow them out with compressed air. The presence of oil and/or antifreeze in the bolt holes could result in insufficient cylinder head bolt tightening, or a cracked crankcase.

24. Position the correct cylinder head gasket on the crankcase.
25. Carefully lower the cylinder head onto the crankcase, using care not to damage the gasket.
26. Install and tighten the cylinder head bolts, in sequence, to 36-43 ft.lb. Wait 15 minutes and tighten the bolts, in sequence, an additional 90°.
27. Install and adjust the drive belt.
28. Connect the turbocharger oil lines and tighten them to 14-18 ft.lb.
29. Connect the nozzle high pressure lines to the nozzles and injection pump. Tighten them to 14-18 ft.lb., using a fuel line wrench.
30. Connect the No. 1 nozzle to the injection pump leak hose.
31. Install the vacuum pump on the cylinder head and tighten to 6-7 ft.lb.
32. Connect the temperature controlled, idle boost coolant hose.
33. Connect the radiator hoses to the cylinder head.
34. Connect the oil pressure switch connector.
35. Install the oil dipstick tube.
36. Install the breather hose and bracket.
37. Connect the coolant temperature switch and glow plug connectors.
38. Connect the diagnostic connectors.
39. Install the valve cover loosely.
40. Install and adjust accessory drive belts.
41. Connect the heater hose(s).
42. Fill and bleed the cooling system. Connect the battery ground cable.
43. Start and run engine for 15-20 minutes. Shut off the engine, remove the valve cover and tighten the cylinder head bolts an additional 90°.
44. Install valve cover.

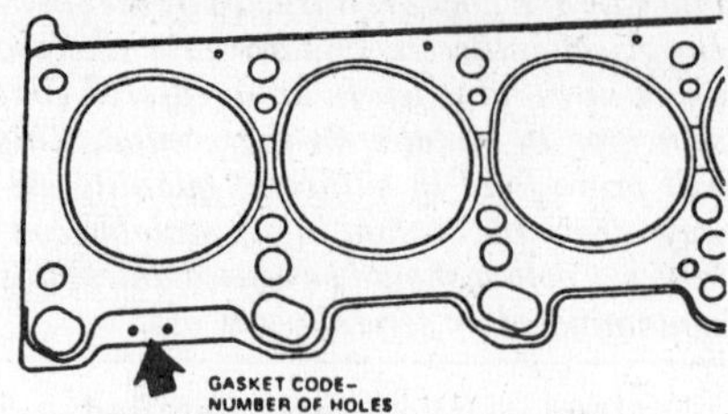

HIGHEST PISTON PROTRUSION OF ALL 6 PISTONS mm	CYL. HEAD GASKET CODE NO. OF HOLES	THICKNESS OF CYL. HEAD GASKET mm
0.60 – 0.70	1	1.4
0.70 – 0.85	2	1.5
0.85 – 1.00	3	1.6

2.4L diesel engine—cylinder head gasket identification

PRELIMINARY VALVE ADJUSTMENT

V6 and V8 Engine Only

This adjustment is actually part of the installation procedure for the individually mounted rocker arms found on the V-type engine, and is necessary to achieve an accurate torque value for each rocker arm nut.

By its nature, an hydraulic valve lifter will expand when it is not under load. Thus, when the rocker arms are removed and the pressure via the pushrod is taken off the lifter, the lifter expands to its maximum. If the lifter happens to be at the top of the camshaft lobe when the rocker arm is being reinstalled, a large amount of torque would be necessary when tighten the rocker arm nut just to overcome the pressure of the expanded lifter. This makes it very difficult to get an

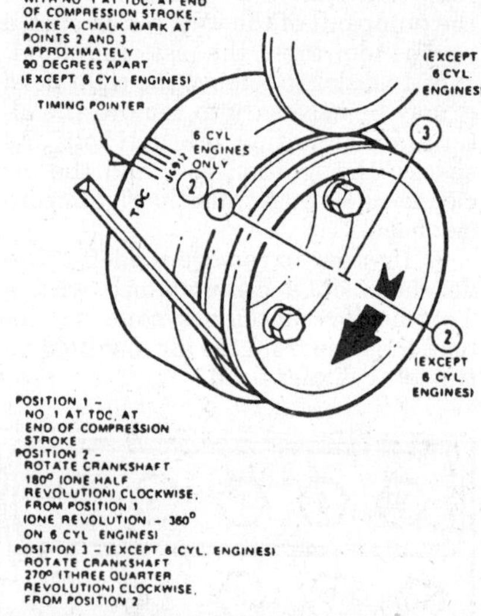

Crankshaft pulley marking preliminary valve adjustment

accurate torque setting with individually mounted rocker arms. For this reason, the rocker arms are installed in a certain sequence which corresponds to the low points of the camshaft lobes.

1. Turn the engine until the No. 1 cylinder is at TDC of the compression stroke and the timing pointer is aligned with the mark on the crankshaft damper.

2. Scribe a mark on the damper at this point.

3. Scribe two additional marks on the damper of a V8; a single line on a V6. (see the illustration).

4. With the timing pointer aligned with Mark 1 on the damper, tighten the following valves to the specified torque:

- 6-232: No. 1 intake and exhaust; No. 3 intake and exhaust; No. 4 exhaust and No. 6 intake.
- 8-255, 8-302 (Exc. HO): No. 1, 7 and 8 Intake; No. 1, 5, and 4 Exhaust.
- 8-302HO, 8-351: No. 1, 4 and 8 Intake; No. 1, 3 and 7 Exhaust.

5. Rotate the crankshaft 180° to point 2 and tighten the following valves:

- 6-232: No. 2 intake; No. 3 exhaust; No. 4 intake; No. 5 intake and exhaust; No. 6 exhaust.
- 8-255, 8-302 (Exc. HO): No. 5 and 4 Intake; No. 2 and 6 Exhaust
- 8-302HO, 8-351: No. 3 and 7 Intake; No. 2 and 6 Exhaust

6. Rotate the crankshaft 270° to point 3 and tighten the following valves:

- 8-302 (Exc. HO): No. 2, 3, and 6 Intake; No. 7, 3 and 8 Exhaust
- 8-302HO, 8-351: No. 2, 5 and 6 Intake; No. 4, 5 and 8 Exhaust

7. Rocker arm tighten specifications are:

- 6-232, 8-255, 8-302 and 8-351W: Tighten nut until it contacts the rocker shoulder, then torque to 18-20 ft.lb.
- 8-351C, 8-351M: Tighten bolt to 18-25 ft.lb.

CYLINDER HEAD OVERHAUL

1. Remove the cylinder head(s) from the car engine (see Cylinder Head Removal and Installation). Place the head(s) on a workbench and remove any manifolds that are still connected. Remove all rocker arm retaining parts and the rocker arms, if still installed. On the 4-140, remove the camshaft (see Camshaft Removal).

2. Turn the cylinder head over so that the mounting surface is facing up and support it evenly on wood blocks.

CAUTION

6-232 engines use aluminum cylinder heads; exercise care when cleaning.

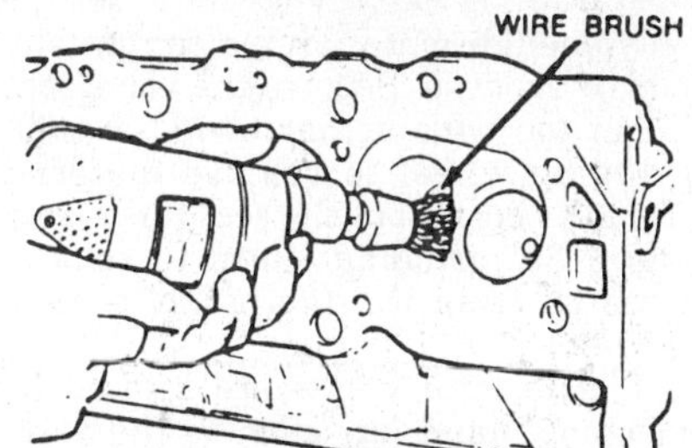

Remove the carbon from the cylinder head with a wire brush and electric drill

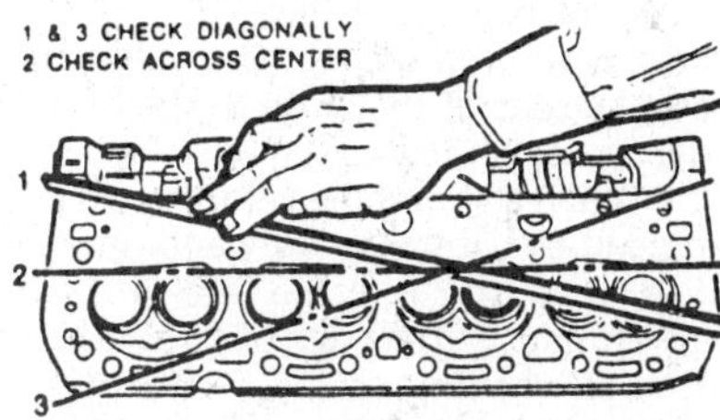

Check the cylinder head for warpage

3. Use a scraper and remove all of the gasket material stuck to the head mounting surface. Mount a wire carbon removal brush in an electric drill and clean away the carbon on the valves and head combustion chambers.

CAUTION

When scraping or decarbonizing the cylinder head, take care not to damage or nick the gasket mounting surface!

4. Number the valve heads with a permanent felt-tip marker for cylinder location.

Resurfacing

If the cylinder head is warped resurfacing by a machine shop is required. Place a straightedge across the gasket surface of the head. Using feeler gauges, determine the clearance at the center and along the length between the head and straightedge. Measure clearance at the center and along the length between the head and straightedge. Measure clearance at the center and along the lengths of both diagonals. If warpage exceeds 0.003" (0.08mm) in a 6" (152mm) span, or 0.006" (0.15mm) over the total length the cylinder head must be resurfaced.

Valves and Springs

REMOVAL & INSTALLATION

1. Block the head on its side, or install a pair of head-holding brackets made especially for valve removal.

2. Use a socket slightly larger than the valve stem and keepers, place the socket over the valve stem and gently hit the socket with a plastic hammer to break loose any varnish buildup.

3. Remove the valve keepers, retainer, spring shield and valve spring using a valve spring compressor (the locking C-clamp type is the easiest kind to use).

4. Put the parts in a separate container numbered for the cylinder being worked on; do not mix them with other parts removed.

5. Remove and discard the valve stem oil seals. A new seal will be used at assembly time.

6. Remove the valves from the cylinder head and place them, in order, through numbered holes punched in a stiff piece of cardboard or wood valve holding stick.

NOTE: The exhaust valve stems, on some engines, are equipped with small metal caps. Take care not to lose the caps. Make sure to reinstall them at assembly time. Replace any caps that are worn.

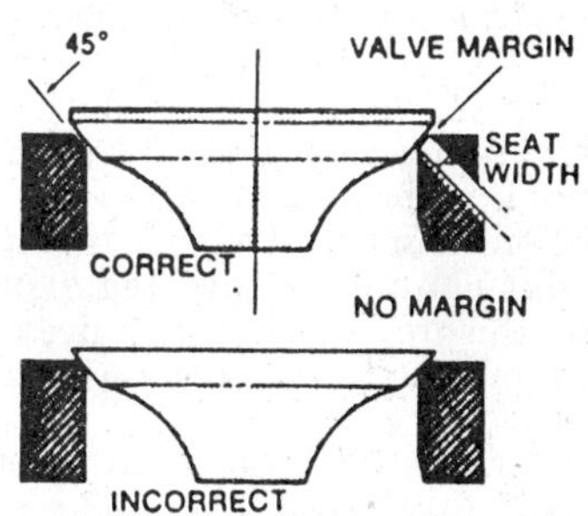

Valve seat width and centering

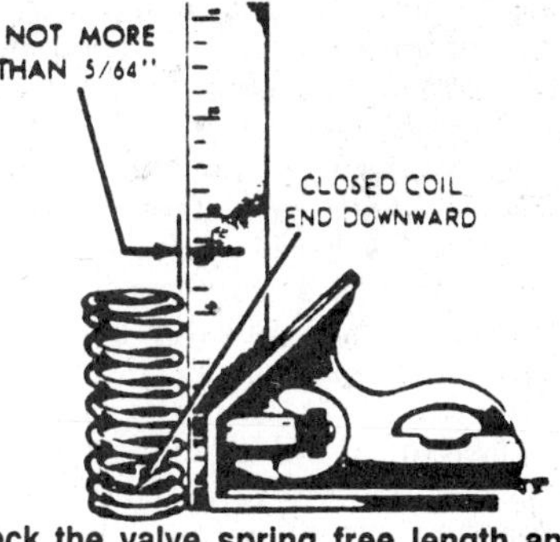

Check the valve spring free length and squareness

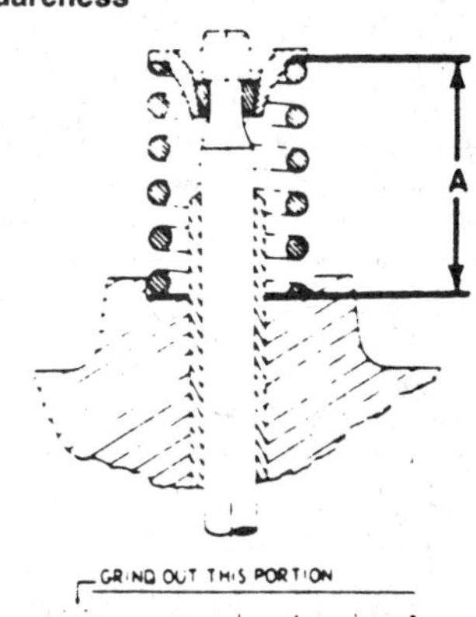

Measure the valve spring installed height (A) with a modified steel rule

7. Use an electric drill and rotary wire brush to clean the intake and exhaust valve ports, combustion chamber and valve seats. In some cases, the carbon will need to be chipped away. Use a blunt pointed drift for carbon chipping. Be careful around the valve seat areas.

8. Use a wire valve guide cleaning brush and safe solvent to clean the valve guides.

9. Clean the valves with a revolving wires brush. Heavy carbon deposits may be removed with the blunt drift.

NOTE: When using a wire brush to clean carbon on the valve ports, valves etc., be sure that the deposits are actually removed, rather than burnished.

10. Wash and clean all valve springs, keepers, retaining caps etc., in safe solvent.

11. Clean the head with a brush and some safe solvent and wipe dry.

12. Check the head for cracks. Cracks in the cylinder head usually start around an exhaust valve seat because it is the hottest part of the combustion chamber. If a crack is suspected but cannot be detected visually have the area checked with dye penetrant or other method by the machine shop.

13. After all cylinder head parts are reasonably clean, check the valve stem-to-guide clearance. If a dial indicator is not on hand, a visual inspection can give you a fairly good idea if the guide, valve stem or both are worn.

14. Insert the valve into the guide until slight away from the valve seat. Wiggle the valve sideways. A small amount of wobble is normal, excessive wobble means a worn guide or valve stem. If a dial indicator is on hand, mount the indicator so that the stem of the valve is at 90° to the valve stem, as close to the valve guide as possible. Move the valve off the seat, and measure the valve guide-to-stem clearance by rocking the stem back and forth to actuate the dial indicator. Measure the valve stem using a micrometer and compare to specifications to determine whether stem or guide wear is causing excessive clearance.

15. The valve guide, if worn, must be repaired before the valve seats can be resurfaced. Ford supplies valves with oversize stems to fit valve guides that are reamed to oversize for repair. The machine shop will be able to handle the guide reaming for you. In some cases, if the guide is not too badly worn, knurling may be all that is required.

16. Reface, or have the valves and valve seats refaced. The valve seats should be a true 45° angle. Remove only enough material to clean up any pits or grooves. Be sure the valve seat is not too wide or narrow. Use a 60° grinding wheel to remove material from the bottom of the seat for raising and a 30° grinding wheel to remove material from the top of the seat to narrow.

17. After the valves are refaced by machine, hand lap them to the valve seat. Clean the grinding compound off and check the position of face-to-seat contact. Contact should be close to the center of the valve face. If contact is close to the top edge of the valve, narrow the seat; if too close to the bottom edge, raise the seat.

18. Valves should be refaced to a true angle of 44°. Remove only enough metal to clean up the valve face or to correct runout. If the edge of a valve head, after machining, is $^{1}/_{32}$" (0.8mm) or less replace the valve. The tip of the valve stem should also be dressed on the valve grinding machine, however, do not remove more than 0.010" (0.254mm).

19. After all valve and valve seats have been machined, check the remaining valve train parts (springs, retainers, keepers, etc.) for wear. Check the valve springs for straightness and tension.

20. Install the valves in the cylinder head and metal caps.

21. Install new valve stem oil seals.

22. Install the valve keepers, retainer, spring shield and valve spring using a valve spring compressor (the locking C-clamp type is the easiest kind to use).

23. Check the valve spring installed height, shim or replace as necessary.

CHECKING VALVE SPRINGS

Place the valve spring on a flat surface next to a carpenter's square. Measure the height of the spring, and rotate the spring against the edge of the square to measure distortion. If the spring height varies (by comparison) by more than $^{1}/_{16}$" (1.6mm) or if the distortion exceeds $^{1}/_{16}$" (1.6mm), replace the spring.

Have the valve springs tested for spring pressure at the installed and compressed (installed height minus valve lift) height using a valve spring tester. Springs should be within one pound, plus or minus each other. Replace springs as necessary.

VALVE SPRING INSTALLED HEIGHT

After installing the valve spring, measure the distance between the spring mounting pad and the lower edge of the spring retainer. Compare the measurement to specifications. If the installed height is incorrect, add shim washers between the spring mounting pad and the spring. Use only washers designed for valve springs, available at most parts houses.

VALVE STEM OIL SEALS

Umbrella type oil seals fitting on the valve stem over the top of the valve guide are used on the 6-200. The 4-140 and 6-232 use a positive valve stem seal using a Teflon® insert. Teflon® seals are available for other engines but usually require valve guide machining. Consult your automotive machine shop for advice on having positive valve stem oil seals installed.

When installing valve stem oil seals, ensure that a small amount of oil is able to pass the seal to lubricate the valve stems and guide walls, otherwise, excessive wear will occur.

VALVE SEATS

If the valve seat is damaged or burnt and cannot be serviced by refacing, it may be possible to have the seat machined and an insert installed. Consult an automotive machine shop for their advice.

NOTE: The aluminum heads on 6-232 engines are equipped with inserts.

VALVE GUIDES

Worn valve guides can, in most cases, be reamed to accept a valve with an oversized stem. Valve guides that are not excessively worn or distorted may, in some cases, be knurled rather than reamed. However, if the valve stem is worn reaming for an oversized valve stem is the answer since a new valve would be required.

Knurling is a process in which metal is displaced and raised, thereby reducing clearance. Knurling also produces excellent oil control. The possibility of knurling instead of reaming the valve guides should be discussed with a machinist.

HYDRAULIC VALVE CLEARANCE

Hydraulic valve lifters operate with zero clearance in the valve train, and because of this the rocker arms are nonadjustable. The only means by which valve system clearances can be altered is by installing over or undersize pushrods; but, because of the hydraulic lifter's natural ability to compensate for slack in the valve train, all components of all the valve system should be checked for wear if there is excessive play in the system.

When a valve in the engine is in the closed position, the valve lifter is resting on the base circle of the camshaft lobe and the pushrod is in its lowest position. To remove this additional clearance from the valve train, the valve lifter expands to maintain zero clearance in the valve system. When a rocker arm is loosened or removed from the engine, the lifter expands to it fullest travel. When the rocker arm is reinstalled on the engine, the proper valve setting is obtained by tightening the rocker arm to a specified limit. But with the lifter fully expanded, if the camshaft lobe is on a high point it will require excessive torque to compress the lifter and obtain the proper setting. Because of this, when any component of the valve system has been removed, a preliminary valve adjustment procedure must be followed to ensure that when the rocker arm is reinstalled on the engine and tightened, the camshaft lobe for that cylinder is in the low position.

To determine whether a shorter or loner push rod is necessary, make the following check:

Mark the crankshaft pulley as described under Preliminary Valve Adjustment procedure. Follow each step in the procedure. As each valve is positioned, mount a suitable hydraulic lifter compressor tool on the rocker arm. Slowly apply pressure to bleed down the lifter until the plunger is completely bottomed. Take care to avoid excessive pressure that might bend the

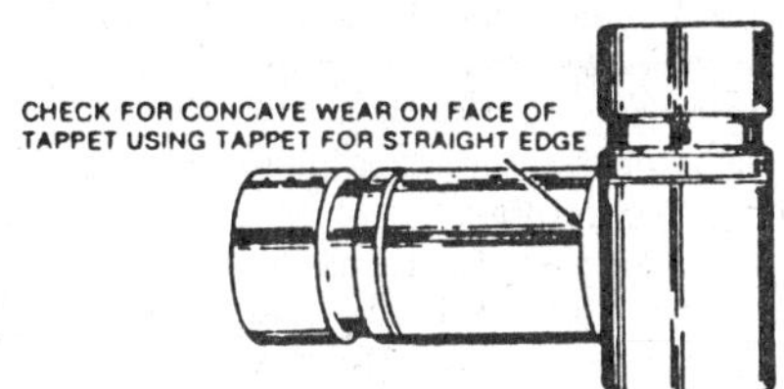

Check the filter face for squareness

pushrod. Hold the lifter in bottom position and check the available clearance between the rocker arm and the valve stem tip with a feeler gauge. If the clearance is less than specified, install an undersized pushrod. If the clearance is greater than specified, install an oversized pushrod. When compressing the valve spring to remove the pushrods, be sure the piston in the individual cylinder is below TDC to avoid contact between the valve and the piston. To replace a pushrod, it will be necessary to remove the valve rocker arm shaft assembly on in-line engines. Upon replacement of a valve pushrod, valve rocker arm shaft assembly or hydraulic valve lifter, the engine should not be cranked or rotated until the hydraulic lifters have had an opportunity to leak down to their normal operation position. The leak down rate can be accelerated by using the tool shown on the valve rocker arm and applying pressure in a direction to collapse the lifter.

Collapsed tappet gap

4-140
6-200

- Allowable: 0.085-0.209″ (2.159-5.309mm)
- Desired: 0.110-0.184″ (2.794-4.673mm)

6-232

- Allowable: 0.088-0.189″ (2.235-4.800mm)

V8 Engines

- 8-255 cu in.
  Allowable: 0.098-0.198″ (2.489-5.029mm)
  Desired: 0.123-0.173″ (3.124-4.394mm)
- 8-302 and 8-351
  Allowable: 0.089-0.193″ (2.260-4.902mm)
  Desired: 0.096-0.163″ (2.438-4.140mm)

VALVE CLEARANCE W/ HYDRAULIC VALVE LASH ADJUSTERS

4-140 Engine

Hydraulic valve lash adjusters are used in the valve train. These units are placed at the fulcrum point of the cam followers (or rocker arms). Their action is similar to the hydraulic tappets used in push rod engines.

1. Position the camshaft so that the base circle of the lobe is facing the cam follower of the valve to be checked.
2. Using the tool shown in the illustration, slowly apply pressure to the cam follower until the lash adjuster is completely collapsed. Hold the follower in this position and insert a 0.045″ (1.14mm) feeler gauge between the base circle of the cam and the follower.

NOTE: The minimum gap is 0.035″ (0.89mm) and the maximum is 0.055″ (1.39mm). The desired gap is between 0.040-0.050″ (1.02-1.27mm).

3. If the clearance is excessive, remove the cam follower and inspect it for damage.
4. If the cam follower seems OK, measure the valve spring assembled height to be sure the valve is not sticking. See the Valve Specifications chart.
5. If the valve spring assembled height is OK, check the dimensions of the camshaft.
6. If the camshaft dimensions are OK, the lash adjuster should be cleaned and tested.
7. Replace any worn parts as necessary.

NOTE: For any repair that includes removal of the camshaft follower (rocker arm), each affected hydraulic lash adjuster must be collapsed after installation of the camshaft follower, and then released. This step must be taken prior to any rotation of the camshaft.

HYDRAULIC VALVE LIFTER INSPECTION

Remove the lifters from their bores and remove any gum and varnish with safe solvent. Check the lifters for concave wear. If the bottom of the lifter is worn concave or flat, replace the lifter. Lifters are built with a convex bottom, flatness indicates wear. If a worn lifter is detected, carefully check the camshaft for wear.

NOTE: Mark lifters for cylinder and position location. Lifters must be reinstalled in the same bore from which they were removed.

To test lifter leak down, submerge the lifter in a container of kerosene. Chuck a used pushrod or its equivalent into a drill press. Position the container of kerosene so the pushrod acts on the lifter plunger. Pump the lifter with the drill press until resistance increases. Pump several more times to bleed any air from the lifter. Apply very firm, constant pressure to the lifter and observe the rate which fluid bleeds out of the lifter. If the lifter bleeds down very quickly (less than 15 seconds), the lifter should be replaced. If the time exceeds 60 seconds, the lifter is sticking and should be cleaned or replaced. If the lifter is operating properly (leak down time 15-60 seconds) and not worn, lubricate and reinstall it in the engine.

Crankshaft Pulley (Vibration Damper)

REMOVAL & INSTALLATION

Gasoline Engines

1. Remove the fan shroud, as required. If necessary, drain the cooling system and remove the radiator. Remove drive belts from pulley.

CAUTION

When draining the coolant, keep in mind that cats and dogs are attracted by the ethylene glycol antifreeze, and are quite likely to drink any that is left in an uncovered container or in puddles on the ground. This will prove fatal in sufficient quantity. Always drain the coolant into a sealable container. Coolant should be reused unless it is contaminated or several years old.

2. On those engines with a separate pulley, remove the retaining bolts and separate the pulley from the vibration damper.
3. Remove the vibration damper/pulley retaining bolt from the crankshaft end.
4. Using a puller, remove the damper/pulley from the crankshaft.
5. Upon installation, align the key slot of the pulley hub to the crankshaft key. Complete the assembly in the reverse order of removal. Torque the retaining bolts to specifications.

Diesel Engine

1. Remove the fan and clutch.
2. Remove all the drive belts.
3. Remove the 6 bolts securing the pulley and damper to the flange and remove the pulley and damper.
4. Using holding fixture T84P-6316-A, or equivalent, remove the flange retaining bolt.
5. Remove the flange using a puller.
6. Installation is the reverse of removal. When installing the vibration damper, make sure to align the guide pin with the hole in the flange. Torque the flange bolt to 287-317 ft.lb. Torque the pulley/damper bolts to 15-20 ft.lb.

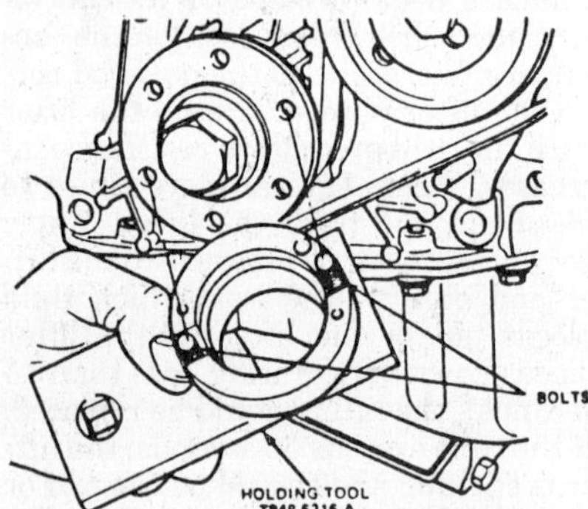

Aligning the bolts during diesel crankshaft vibration damper installation

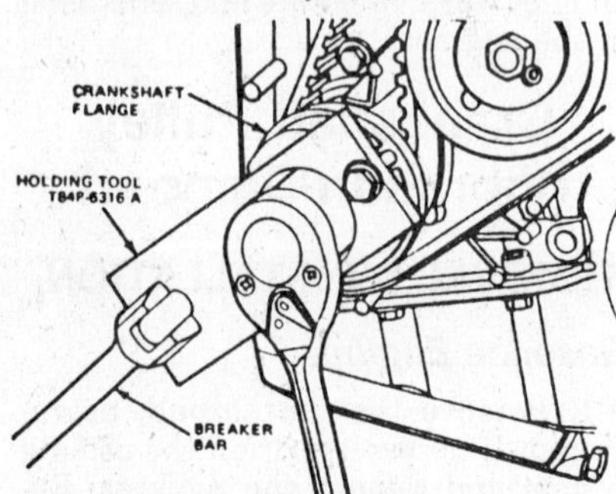

Diesel crankshaft flange removal

Timing Cover and Chain

REMOVAL & INSTALLATION

6-200

1. Drain the cooling system and crankcase.

CAUTION

When draining the coolant, keep in mind that cats and dogs are attracted by the ethylene glycol antifreeze, and are quite likely to drink any that is left in an uncovered container or in puddles on the ground. This will prove fatal in sufficient quantity. Always drain the coolant into a sealable container. Coolant should be reused unless it is contaminated or several years old.

2. Disconnect the upper radiator hose from the intake manifold and the lower hose from the water pump. On cars with automatic transmission, disconnect the cooler lines from the radiator.
3. Remove the radiator, fan and pulley, and engine drive belts. On models with air conditioning, remove the condenser retaining bolts and position the condenser forward. Do not disconnect the refrigerant lines.
4. Remove the cylinder front cover retaining bolts and front oil pan bolts and gently pry the cover away from the block.
5. Remove the crankshaft pulley bolt and use a puller to remove the vibration damper.
6. With a socket wrench of the proper size on the crankshaft pulley bolt, gently rotate the crankshaft in a clockwise direction until all slack is removed from the lift side of the timing chain. Scribe a mark on the engine block parallel to the present position on the left side of the chain. Next, turn the crankshaft in a counterclockwise direction to remove all the slack from the right side of the chain. Force the left side of the chain outward with your fingers and measure the distance between the reference point and the present position of the chain. If the distance exceeds ½" (12.7mm), replace the chain and sprockets.
7. Crank the engine until the timing marks are aligned as shown in the illustration. Remove the bolt, slide the sprocket and chain forward and remove them as an assembly.
8. Position the sprockets and chain on the engine, making sure that the timing marks are aligned, dot-to-dot.
9. Reinstall the front cover, applying oil resistant sealer to the new gasket. Trim away the exposed portion of the old oil pan gasket flush with front of the engine block. Cut and position the required portion of a new gasket to the oil pan, applying sealer to both sides of it.
10. Install the fan, pulley and belts. Adjust the belt tension.
11. Install the radiator, connect the radiator hoses and transmission cooling lines. If equipped with air conditioning, install the condenser.
12. Fill the crankcase and cooling system. Start the engine and check for leaks.

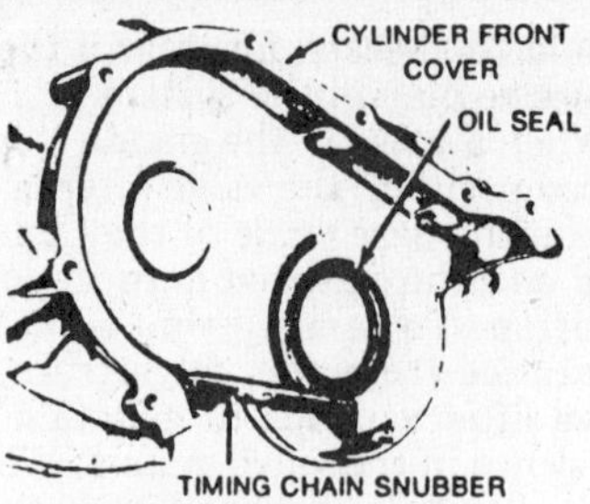

6-200 timing gear cover

6-232

1. Disconnect the negative battery cable from the battery. Drain the cooling system.

CAUTION

When draining the coolant, keep in mind that cats and dogs are attracted by the ethylene glycol antifreeze, and are quite likely to drink any that is left in an uncovered container or in puddles on the ground. This will prove fatal in sufficient quantity. Always drain the coolant into a sealable container. Coolant should be reused unless it is contaminated or several years old.

2. Remove the air cleaner and air duct assemblies.
3. Remove the radiator fan shroud and position it back over the water pump. Remove the fan clutch assembly and shroud.
4. Remove all drive belts. If equipped with power steering, remove the pump with the hoses attached and position it out of the way. Be sure to keep the pump upright to prevent fluid leakage.
5. If your car is equipped with air conditioning, remove the front compressor mounting bracket. It is not necessary to remove the compressor.
6. Disconnect the coolant by-pass hose and the heater hose at the water pump.
7. Disconnect the upper radiator hose at the thermostat housing. Remove the distributor.
8. If your car is equipped with a tripminder, remove the flow meter support bracket and allow the meter to be supported by the hoses.

9. Raise the front of the car and support on jackstands.
10. Remove the crankshaft pulley using a suitable puller. Remove the fuel pump shield.
11. Disconnect the fuel line from the carburetor at the fuel pump. Remove the mounting bolts and the fuel pump. Position pump out of the way with tank line still attached.
12. Drain the engine oil and remove the oil filter.
13. Disconnect the lower radiator hose at the water pump.
14. Remove the oil pan mounting bolts and lower the oil pan.

NOTE: The front cover cannot be removed unless the oil pan is lowered.

15. Lower the car from the jackstands.
16. Remove the front cover mounting bolts.

NOTE: Water pump removal is not necessary. A front cover mounting bolt is located behind the oil filter adapter. If the bolt is not removed and the cover is pried upon breakage will occur.

17. Remove the timing indicator. Remove the front cover and water pump assembly.
18. Remove the camshaft thrust button and spring from the end of the camshaft. Remove the camshaft sprocket attaching bolts.
19. Remove the camshaft sprocket, crankshaft sprocket and timing chain by pulling forward evenly on both sprockets. If the crankshaft sprocket is difficult to remove, position two small prybars, one on each side, behind the sprocket and pry forward.
20. Clean all gasket surfaces on the front cover, cylinder block, fuel pump and oil pan.
21. Install a new front cover oil seal. If a new front cover is to be installed:
   a. Install the oil pump, oil filter adapter and intermediate shaft from the old cover.
   b. Remove the water pump from the old cover.
   c. Clean the mounting surface, install a new mounting gasket and the pump on the new front cover. Pump attaching bolt torque is 13-22 ft.lb.
22. Rotate the crankshaft, if necessary, to bring No. 1 piston to TDC with the crankshaft keyway at the 12 o'clock position.
23. Lubricate the timing chain with motor oil. Install the chain over the two gears making sure the marks on both gears are positioned across from each other. Install the gears and chain on the cam and crankshaft. Install the camshaft mounting bolts. Tighten the bolts to 15-22 ft.lb.
24. Install the camshaft thrust button and spring. Lubricate the thrust button with polyethylene grease before installation.

WARNING: The thrust button and spring must be bottomed in the camshaft seat and must not be allowed to fall out during front cover installation.

25. Position a new cover gasket on the front of the engine and install the cover and water pump assemblies. Install the timing indicator. Torque the front cover bolts to 15-22 ft.lb.
26. Install the oil pan.
27. Connect the lower radiator hose at the water pump.
28. Install the oil filter.
29. Fill the crankcase.
30. Install the fuel pump.
31. Connect the fuel line at the carburetor and at the fuel pump.

WARNING: When installing the fuel pump, turn the crankshaft 180° to position the fuel pump drive eccentric away from the fuel pump arm. Failure to turn the drive eccentric away from the pump arm can cause stress on the pump mounting threads and strip them out when installing the pump.

32. Install the crankshaft pulley.
33. Install the fuel pump shield.
34. Lower the front of the car.
35. If your car is equipped with a tripminder, install the flow meter support bracket.
36. Connect the upper radiator hose at the thermostat housing.
37. Install the distributor.
38. Connect the coolant by-pass hose and the heater hose at the water pump.
39. If your car is equipped with air conditioning, install the front compressor mounting bracket.
40. If equipped with power steering, install the pump. Be sure to keep the pump upright to prevent fluid leakage.

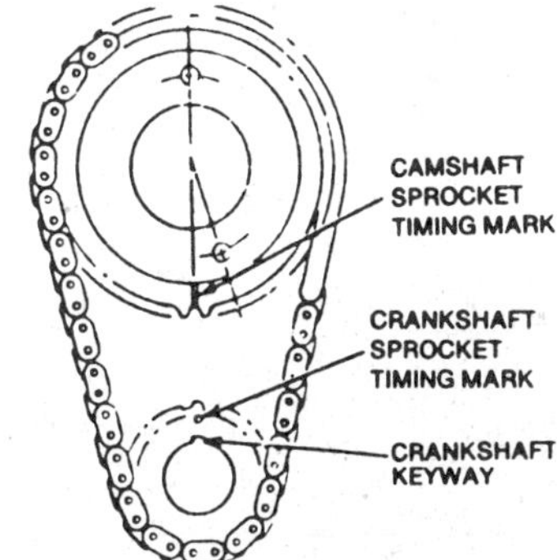

V6 engine timing mark alignment

41. Install all drive belts.
42. Install the fan clutch assembly.
43. Install the radiator fan shroud.
44. Install the air cleaner and air duct assemblies.
45. Connect the negative battery cable at the battery.
46. Fill the cooling system.

V8 Engines

1. Drain the cooling system, remove the air cleaner and disconnect the battery.

CAUTION

When draining the coolant, keep in mind that cats and dogs are attracted by the ethylene glycol antifreeze, and are quite likely to drink any that is left in an uncovered container or in puddles on the ground. This will prove fatal in sufficient quantity. Always drain the coolant into a sealable container. Coolant should be reused unless it is contaminated or several years old.

2. Disconnect the transmission cooler lines and radiator hoses and remove the radiator.
3. Disconnect the heater hose at water pump. Slide the water pump bypass hose clamp toward the pump.
4. Loosen the alternator mounting bolts at the alternator. Remove the alternator support bolt at the water pump. Remove the Thermactor® pump on all engines so equipped. If equipped with power steering or air conditioning, unbolt the component, remove the belt, and lay the pump or compressor aside with the lines attached.
5. Remove the fan, spacer, pulley, and drive belt.
6. Drain the crankcase.
7. Remove the pulley from the crankshaft pulley adapter. Remove the capscrew and washer from the front end of the crankshaft. Remove the crankshaft pulley adapter with a puller.
8. Disconnect the fuel pump outlet line at the pump. Remove the fuel pump retaining bolts and lay the pump to the side. Remove the engine oil dipstick.
9. Remove the front cover attaching bolts.
10. Remove the crankshaft oil slinger if so equipped.
11. Check timing chain deflection, using the procedure outlined in Step 6 of the 6-200 Cylinder Cover and Chain Removal.
12. Rotate the engine until the sprocket timing marks are aligned as shown in the valve timing illustration.
13. Remove the crankshaft sprocket capscrew, washers, and fuel pump eccentric. Slide both sprockets and chain forward and off as an assembly.
14. Position the sprockets and chain

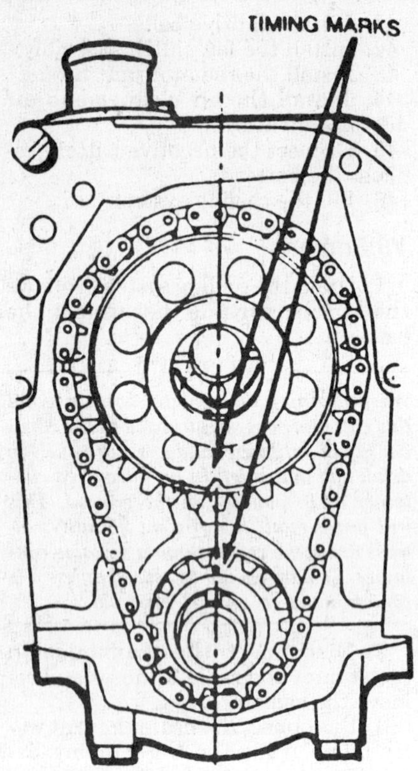

V8 engines timing mark alignment

on the camshaft and crankshaft with both timing marks dot-to-dot on a centerline. Install the fuel pump eccentric, washers and sprocket attaching bolt. Torque the sprocket attaching bolt to 40-45 ft.lb.

15. Install the crankshaft front oil slinger.
16. Clean the front cover and mating surfaces of old gasket material. Install a new oil seal in the cover. Use a seal driver tool, if available.
17. Coat a new cover gasket with sealer and position it on the block.

NOTE: Trim away the exposed portion of the oil pan gasket flush with the cylinder block. Cut and position the required portion of a new gasket to the oil pan, applying sealer to both sides of it.

18. Install the front cover, using a crankshaft-to-cover alignment tool. Coat the threads of the attaching bolts with sealer. Torque the attaching bolt to 12-15 ft.lb.
19. Install the fuel pump and connect the fuel pump outlet tube.
20. Install the crankshaft pulley adapter and torque the attaching bolt. Install the crankshaft pulley.
21. Install the water pump pulley, drive belt, spacer and fan.
22. Install the alternator support bolt at the water pump. Tighten the alternator mounting bolts. Adjust the drive belt tension. Install the Thermactor® pump if so equipped.
23. Install the radiator and connect all coolant and heater hoses. Connect the battery cables.
24. Refill the cooling system and the crankcase. Install the dipstick.
25. Start the engine and operate it at fast idle.
26. Check for leaks, install the air cleaner. Adjust the ignition timing and make all final adjustments.

Front Cover Oil Seal

REMOVAL & INSTALLATION

Except 4-140

It is recommended to replace the cover seal any time the front cover is removed.

NOTE: On 6-232 engines, the seal may be removed, after the crank pulley is off without removing the cover.

1. With the cover removed from the car, drive the old seal from the rear of cover with a pinpunch. Clean out the recess in the cover.
2. Coat the new seal with grease and drive it into the cover until it is fully seated. Check the seal after installation to be sure the spring is properly positioned in the seal.

4-140 Camshaft Drive Belt and Cover

The correct installation and adjustment of the camshaft drive belt is mandatory if the engine is to run properly. The camshaft controls the opening of the camshaft and the crankshaft. When any given piston is on the intake stroke the corresponding intake valve must be open to admit air/fuel mixture into the cylinder. When the same piston is on the compression and power strokes, both valves in that cylinder must be closed. When the piston is on the exhaust stroke, the exhaust valve for that cylinder must be open. If the opening and closing of the valves is not coordinated with the movements of the pistons, the engine will run very poorly, if at all.

The camshaft drive belt also turns the engine auxiliary shaft. The distributor is driven by the engine auxiliary shaft. Since the distributor controls ignition timing, the auxiliary shaft must be coordinated with the camshaft and crankshaft, since both valves in any given cylinder must be closed and the piston in that cylinder near the top of the compression stroke when the spark plug fires.

Due to this complex interrelationship between the camshaft, the crankshaft and the auxiliary shaft, the cogged pulleys on each component must be aligned when the camshaft drive belt is installed.

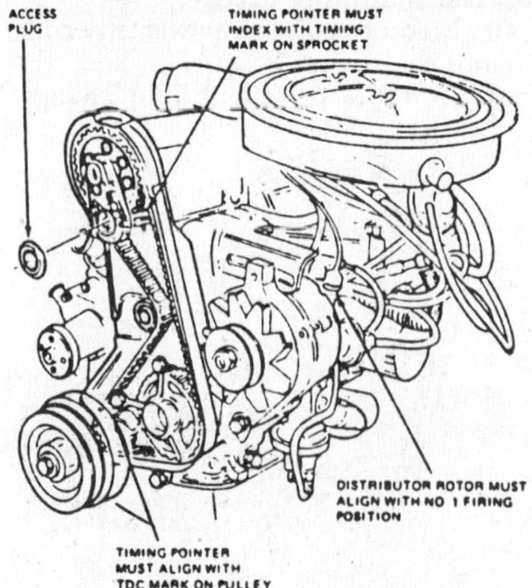

4-140 camshaft drive train installation

TROUBLESHOOTING

Should the camshaft drive belt jump timing by a tooth or two, the engine could still run; but very poorly. To visually check for correct timing of the crankshaft, auxiliary shaft, and the camshaft follow this procedure:

NOTE: There is an access plug provided in the cam drive belt cover so that the camshaft timing can be checked without moving the drive belt cover.

1. Remove the access plug.
2. Turn the crankshaft until the timing marks on the crankshaft indicate TDC.
3. Make sure that the timing mark on the camshaft drive sprocket is aligned with the pointer on the inner belt cover. Also, the rotor of the distributor must align with the No. 1 cylinder firing position.

WARNING: Never turn the crankshaft of any of the overhead cam engines in the opposite direction of normal rotation. Backward rotation of the crankshaft may cause the timing belt to slip and alter the timing.

REMOVAL & INSTALLATION

1. Set the engine to TDC as described in the troubleshooting section. The crankshaft and camshaft timing marks should align with their respective pointers and the distributor rotor should point to the No. 1 plug tower.
2. Loosen the adjustment bolts on the alternator and accessories and remove the drive belts. To provide clear-

ance for removing the camshaft belt, remove the fan and pulley.

3. Remove the belt outer cover.
4. Remove the distributor cap from the distributor and position it out of the way.
5. Loosen the belt tensioner adjustment and pivot bolts. Lever the tensioner away from the belt and retighten the adjustment bolt to hold it away.
6. Remove the crankshaft bolt and pulley. Remove the belt guide behind the pulley.
7. Remove the camshaft drive belt.
8. Install the new belt over the crankshaft pulley first, then counterclockwise over the auxiliary shaft sprocket and the camshaft sprocket. Adjust the belt fore and aft so that it is centered on the sprockets.
9. Loosen the tensioner adjustment bolt, allowing it to spring back against the belt.
10. Rotate the crankshaft two complete turns in the normal rotation direction to remove any belt slack. Turn the crankshaft until the timing check marks are lined up. If the timing has slipped, remove the belt and repeat the procedure.
11. Tighten the tensioner adjustment bolt to 14-21 ft.lb., and the pivot bolt to 28-40 ft.lb.
12. Replace the belt guide and crankshaft pulley, distributor cap, belt outer cover, fan and pulley, drive belts and accessories. Adjust the accessory drive belt tension. Start the engine and check the ignition timing.

Camshaft Drive Belt

REMOVAL & INSTALLATION

2,443cc Diesel Engine

1. Disconnect the negative battery cable. Drain the cooling system. Remove the upper radiator hose. Remove the fan shroud.

CAUTION

When draining the coolant, keep in mind that cats and dogs are attracted by the ethylene glycol antifreeze, and are quite likely to drink any that is left in an uncovered container or in puddles on the ground. This will prove fatal in sufficient quantity. Always drain the coolant into a sealable container. Coolant should be reused unless it is contaminated or several years old.

2. Remove all drive belts (alternator, air, etc.). Remove the fan and clutch and water pump pulley.
3. Remove the crankshaft damper and pulley.
4. Disconnect the heater hose from the thermostat housing.
5. Remove the four bolts attaching

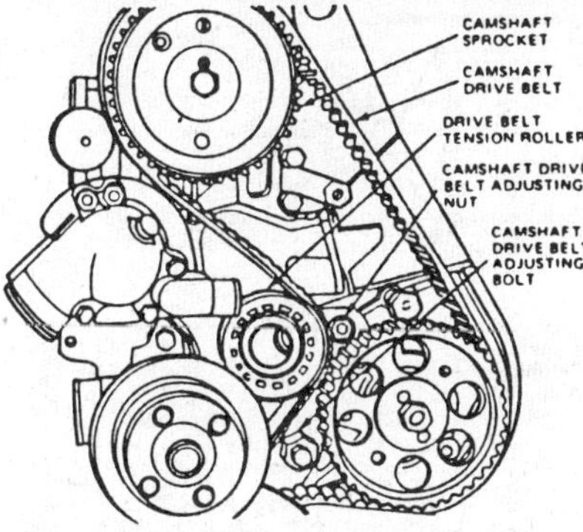

2.4L diesel engine-camshaft drive belt installation

the camshaft drive belt cover to the crankcase and remove the cover.

6. Remove the valve cover. Turn the engine until No. 1 cylinder is at TDC on the compression stroke with the intake and exhaust valves on base circle (heel) of the cam. Install TDC Aligning Pin Tool T84P6400A or the equivalent between the lower engine block and the flywheel.
7. Install Cam Positioning Tool T84P6256A or the equivalent. Loosen the camshaft sprocket bolt.
8. Mark the belt, with a piece of chalk, for direction of rotation, if the belt is to be reused.
9. Loosen the bolts on the belt tensioner, relieve pressure and remove the belt.
10. If you're installing a new belt or one with less than 10,000 miles on it, insert a feeler gauge 0.098" (2.489mm) between the Cam Positioning Tool T84P6256A (or equivalent) and the right front gasket mating surface of the cylinder head.
11. Install an Injection Pump Aligning Pin Tool T84P9000A (or equivalent) through the injection pump sprocket to hold it in position.
12. Rotate the cam sprocket clockwise against the pin. Install the camshaft drive belt.
13. Start the belt at the crankshaft, route the belt around the intermediate shaft sprocket, injection pump sprocket camshaft sprocket and finally the tension roller. Keep belt slack to a minimum during installation.

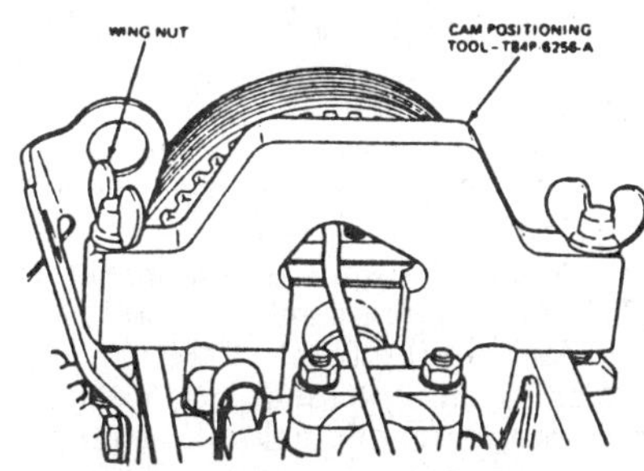

2.4L diesel engine – cam positioning tool installation

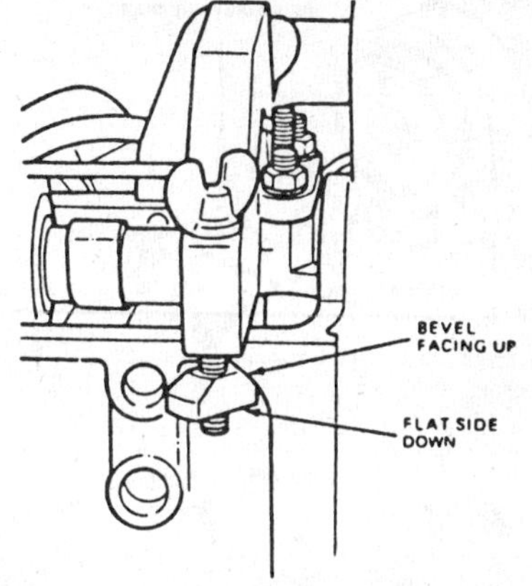

2.4L engine-cam positioning tool nut position

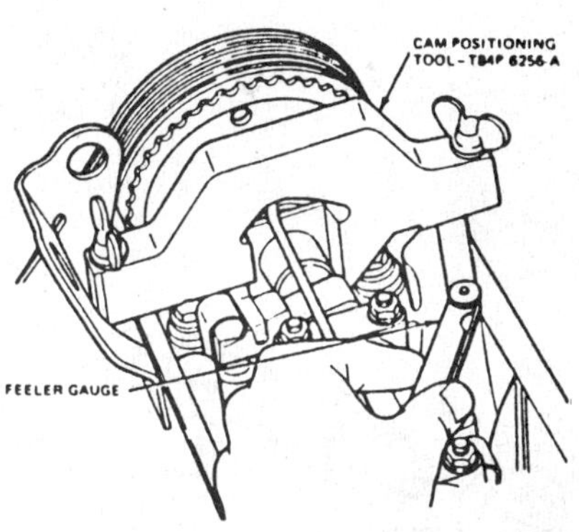

2.4L diesel engine cam positioning with feeler gauge

2.4L diesel engine – injector pump alignment pin installation

14. Hand tighten the belt tensioner until all slack is removed.
15. Remove the Injection Pump Aligning Pin. Adjust the belt tension by applying 34-36 ft.lb. using a dial type torque wrench. If the old drive belt (more than 10,000 miles) is reinstalled apply 23-25 ft.lb. Tighten the two tensioner holding bolts to 15-18 ft.lb.
16. Tighten the camshaft sprocket bolt to 41-47 ft.lb. Check and adjust (if necessary) the injection pump timing.
17. Remove the Camshaft Positioning Tool and the TDC Alignment Tool.
18. Install the belt cover and tighten the mounting bolts to 6-7 ft.lb.

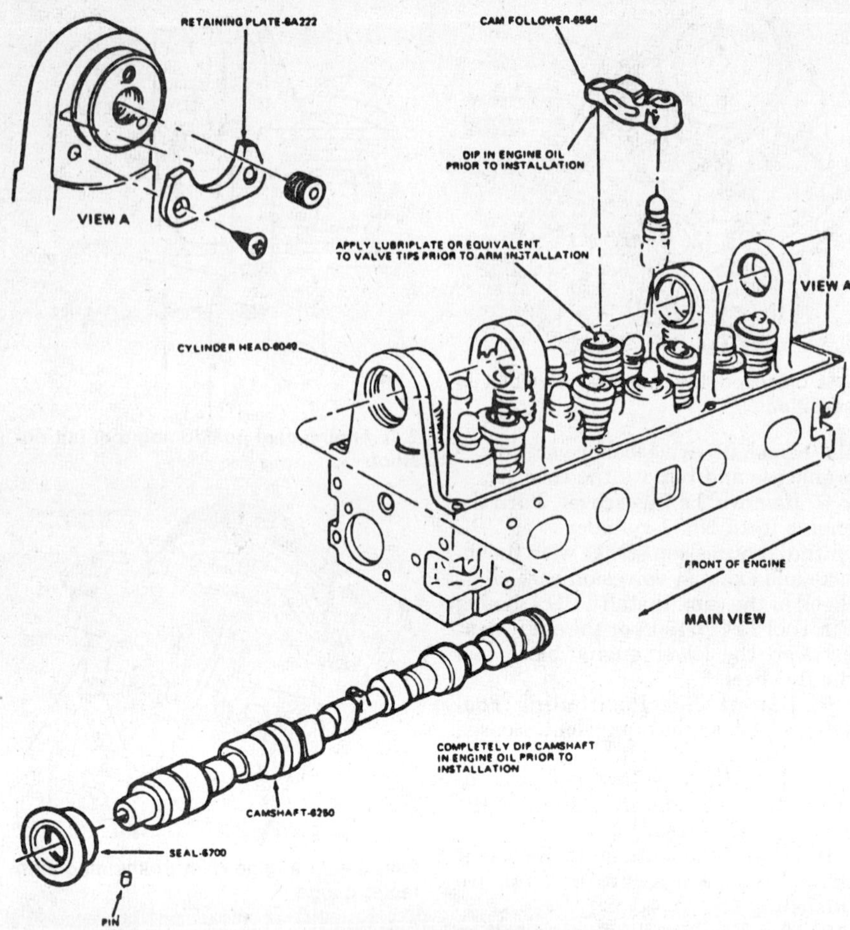

4-140 camshaft installation

19. Connect the heater hose at the thermostat housing.
20. Install the crankshaft damper and pulley.
21. Install the fan and clutch and water pump pulley.
22. Install all drive belts (alternator, air, etc.).
23. Install the fan shroud.
24. Install the upper radiator hose.
25. Fill the cooling system.
26. Connect the negative battery cable.

Camshaft

REMOVAL & INSTALLATION

4-140 Engine

NOTE: The following procedure covers camshaft removal and installation with the cylinder head on or off the engine. If the cylinder head has been removed start at Step 9.

1. Drain the cooling system. Remove the air cleaner assembly and disconnect the negative battery cable.

CAUTION

When draining the coolant, keep in mind that cats and dogs are attracted by the ethylene glycol antifreeze, and are quite likely to drink any that is left in an uncovered container or in puddles on the ground. This will prove fatal in sufficient quantity. Always drain the coolant into a sealable container. Coolant should be reused unless it is contaminated or several years old.

2. Remove the spark plug wires from the plugs, disconnect the retainer from the valve cover and position the wires out of the way. Disconnect the rubber vacuum lines as necessary.
3. Remove all drive belts. Remove the alternator mounting bracket-to-cylinder head mounting bolts, position the bracket and alternator out of the way.
4. Disconnect and remove the upper radiator hose. Disconnect the radiator shroud.
5. Remove the fan blades and water pump pulley and fan shroud. Remove the cam belt and valve covers.
6. Align the engine timing marks at TDC. Remove the cam drive belt.
7. Jack up the front of the car and support it on jackstands. Remove the front motor mount bolts. Disconnect the lower radiator hose from the radiator. Disconnect and plug the automatic transmission cooler lines.
8. Position a piece of wood on a floor jack and raise the engine carefully as far as it will go. Place blocks of wood between the engine mounts and crossmember pedestals.
9. Remove the rocker arms as described earlier.
10. Remove the camshaft drive gear and belt guide using a suitable puller. Remove the front oil seal with a sheet metal screw and slide hammer.
11. Remove the camshaft retainer located on the rear mounting stand, by unbolting the two bolts.
12. Remove the camshaft by carefully withdrawing it toward the front of the engine. Caution should be used to prevent damage to the cam bearings, lobes and journals.
13. Check the camshaft journals and lobes for wear. Inspect the cam bearings. If they are worn, the cylinder head must be removed for new bearings to be installed by a machine shop.
12. Install the camshaft. Caution should be used to prevent damage to the cam bearings, lobes and journals. Coat the camshaft with heavy SF oil before sliding it into the cylinder head.
13. Install the camshaft retainer located on the rear mounting stand.
14. Install a new front oil seal.
15. Install the camshaft drive gear and belt guide. Apply a coat of sealer or Teflon® tape to the cam drive gear bolt before installation.
16. Install the rocker arms as described earlier.
17. Remove the blocks of wood between the engine mounts and crossmember pedestals and lower the engine onto the mounts.
18. Lower the front of the car.
19. Install the front motor mount bolts.
20. Connect the lower radiator hose at the radiator.
21. Connect the automatic transmission cooler lines.
22. Align the engine timing marks at TDC.
23. Install the cam drive belt.
24. Install the cam belt and valve covers.
25. Install the fan blades and water pump pulley and fan shroud.
26. Connect and install the upper radiator hose.
27. Install the alternator and mounting bracket on the cylinder head.
28. Install all drive belts.
29. Install the spark plug wires on the plugs.
30. Connect the plug wires to the retainer on the valve cover.
31. Connect the rubber vacuum lines as necessary.
32. Fill the cooling system.
33. Install the air cleaner assembly.
34. Connect the negative battery cable.

WARNING: After any procedure requiring removal of the rocker arms, each lash adjuster must be fully collapsed after assembly, then released. This must be done before the camshaft is turned. See Valve Clearance – Hydraulic Valve Lash Adjusters.

6-200

1. Remove the cylinder head.
2. Remove the cylinder front cover, timing chain and sprockets as outlined in the preceding section.
3. Disconnect and remove the radiator, condenser and grille. Remove the gravel deflector.
4. Using a magnet, remove the valve lifters and keep them in order so that they can be installed in their original positions.
5. Remove the camshaft thrust plate and remove the camshaft by pulling it from the front of the engine. Use care not to damage the camshaft lobes or journals while removing the cam from the engine.
6. Before installing the camshaft, coat the lobes with engine assembly lubricant and the journals and all valve parts with heavy oil. Clean the oil passage at the rear of the cylinder block with compressed air.

V6 and V8 Engines

1. Remove or reposition the radiator, A/C condenser and grille components as necessary to provide clearance to remove the camshaft.
2. Remove the cylinder front cover and timing chain as previously described.
3. Remove the intake manifold and related parts described earlier.
4. Remove the crankcase ventilation valve and tubes from the valve rocker covers. Remove the EGR cooler, if so equipped.
5. Remove the rocker arm covers and loosen the valve rocker arm fulcrum bolts and rotate the rocker arms to the side.
6. Remove the valve pushrods and identify them so that they can be installed in their original positions.
7. Remove the valve lifters and place them in a rack so that they can be installed in their original bores.
8. Remove the camshaft thrust plate or button and spring and carefully remove the camshaft by pulling toward the front of the engine. Be careful not to damage the camshaft bearings.
9. Before installing, oil the camshaft journals with heavy engine oil SF and apply Lubriplate® or equivalent to the lobes. Carefully slide the camshaft through the bearings.
10. Install the camshaft thrust plate with the groove towards the cylinder block.
11. Lubricate the lifters with heavy SF engine oil and install in their original bores.
12. Apply Lubriplate® or equivalent to the valve stem tips and each end of the pushrods. Install the pushrods in their original position.
13. Lubricate the rocker arms and fulcrum seats with heavy SF engine oil and position the rocker arms over the push rods.
14. Install all other parts previously removed.
15. Fill the crankcase and cooling system and adjust the timing.

2,443cc Diesel Engine

1. Disconnect the negative battery cable.
2. Remove the valve cover and vacuum pump. Remove the fan and clutch assembly and all accessory drive belts.
3. Remove the camshaft drive belt cover. Remove all rocker arms.
4. Turn the engine until the No. 1 piston is at TDC on the compression stroke. Install the TDC Alignment Pin (refer to cam belt section).
5. Loosen the camshaft sprocket bolt. Loosen the drive belt tensioner. Remove the drive belt and camshaft sprocket.
6. Mark the camshaft bearing caps for position and installation direction. Remove the bearing caps and the camshaft.
7. Install the camshaft and the bearing caps. Bearing caps are torqued to 6-7 ft.lb. for the 6mm nuts and 14-17 ft.lb. for the 8mm nuts.
8. Install the drive belt and camshaft sprocket. Adjust the drive belt tension.
9. Remove the TDC Alignment Pin (refer to cam belt section).
10. Install all rocker arms.
11. Install the camshaft drive belt cover.
12. Install the fan and clutch assembly and all accessory drive belts.
13. Install the valve cover and vacuum pump.
14. Connect the negative battery cable.

CHECKING THE CAMSHAFT

Degrease the camshaft using safe solvent, clean all oil grooves. Visually inspect the cam lobes and bearing journals for excessive wear. If a lobe is questionable, check all lobes and journals with a micrometer.

Measure the lobes from nose to base and again at 90°. The lift is determined by subtracting the second measurement from the first. If all exhaust lobes and all intake lobes are not identical, the camshaft must be reground or replaced. Measure the bearing journals and compare to specifications. If a journal is worn there is a good chance that the cam bearings are worn too, requiring replacement.

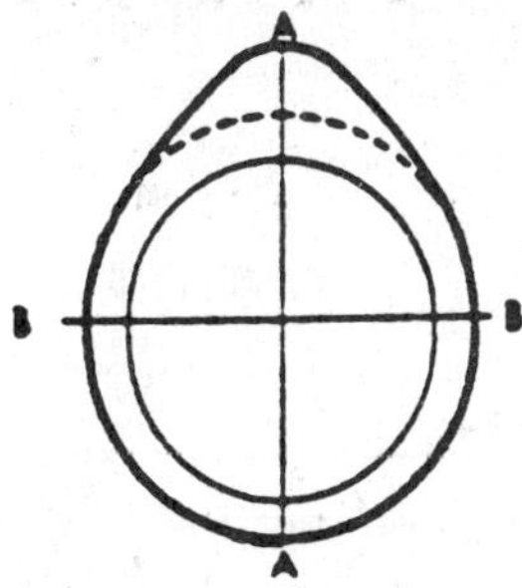

Camshaft lobe measurement

If the lobes and journals appear intact, place the front and rear cam journals in V-blocks and rest a dial indicator on the center journal. Rotate the camshaft to check for straightness, if deviation exceeds 0.001" (0.025mm), replace the camshaft.

Auxiliary Shaft

REMOVAL & INSTALLATION

4-140 Engine

1. Remove the camshaft drive belt cover.
2. Remove the drive belt. Remove the auxiliary shaft sprocket. A puller may be necessary to remove the sprocket.
3. Remove the distributor and fuel pump.
4. Remove the auxiliary shaft cover and thrust plate.
5. Withdraw the auxiliary shaft from the block.

WARNING: The distributor drive gear and the fuel pump eccentric on the auxiliary shaft must not be allowed to touch the auxiliary shaft bearings during removal and installation. Completely coat the shaft with oil before sliding it into place.

6. Slide the auxiliary shaft into the housing and insert the thrust plate to hold the shaft.
7. Install a new gasket and auxiliary shaft cover.

NOTE: The auxiliary shaft cover and cylinder front cover share a gasket. Cut off the old gasket around the cylinder cover and use half of the new gasket on the auxiliary shaft cover.

8. Fit a new gasket into the fuel pump and install the pump.

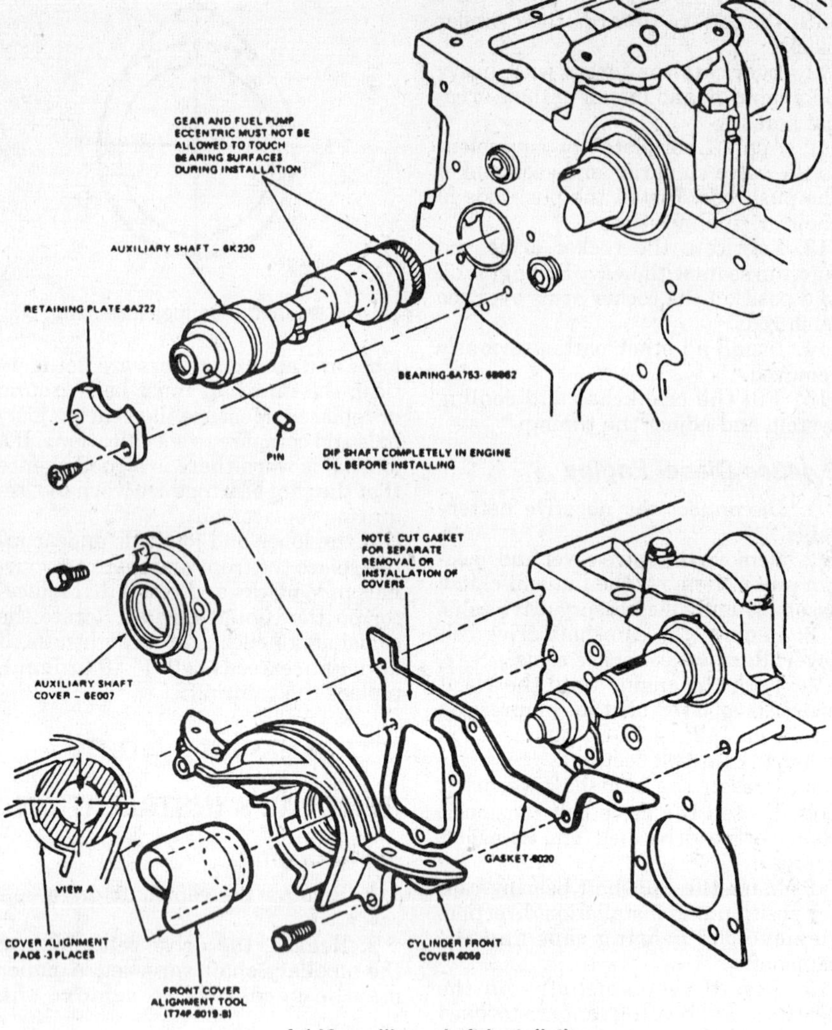

4-140 auxiliary shaft installation

9. Insert the distributor and install the auxiliary shaft sprocket.
10. Align the timing marks and install the drive belt.
11. Install the drive belt cover.
12. Check the ignition timing.

Engine Front Cover/Sprockets

REMOVAL & INSTALLATION

Diesel Engine

1. Disconnect the battery ground cable.
2. Drain the cooling system.

CAUTION

When draining the coolant, keep in mind that cats and dogs are attracted by the ethylene glycol antifreeze, and are quite likely to drink any that is left in an uncovered container or in puddles on the ground. This will prove fatal in sufficient quantity. Always drain the coolant into a sealable container. Coolant should be reused unless it is contaminated or several years old.

3. Loosen and remove the accessory drive belts.
4. Remove the engine cooling fan.
5. Remove the vibration damper.
6. Disconnect the heater hose from thermostat housing.
7. Remove the four bolts attaching the camshaft drive belt cover to the crankcase and remove the cover.
8. Remove the camshaft drive belt.
9. Remove the bolts attaching the intermediate shaft sprocket using Holding Tool T84P-6316-A or equivalent.

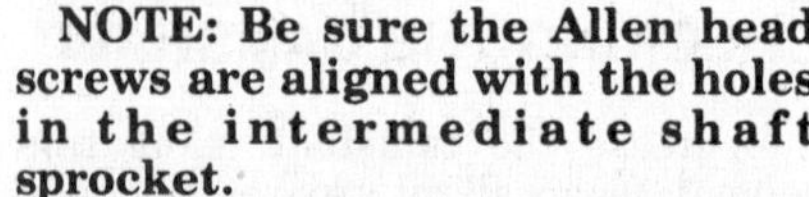

NOTE: Be sure the Allen head screws are aligned with the holes in the intermediate shaft sprocket.

10. Remove the vibration damper flange and sprocket retaining bolt and remove the flange and sprocket using puller, T67L-3600-A or equivalent.
11. Remove the three oil pan-to-front cover attaching bolts. Loosen, but DO NOT REMOVE, the remaining oil pan bolts.

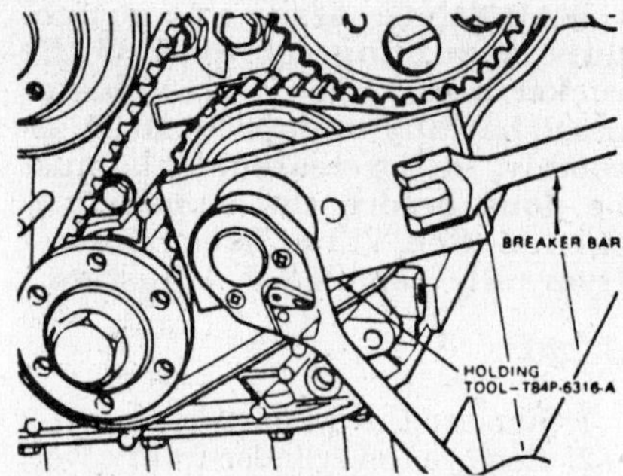

Diesel engine intermediate shaft sprocket removal

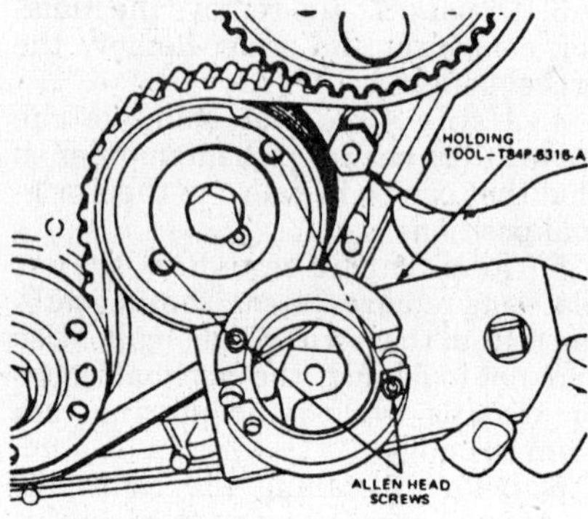

Diesel inttermediate shaft allen head screws

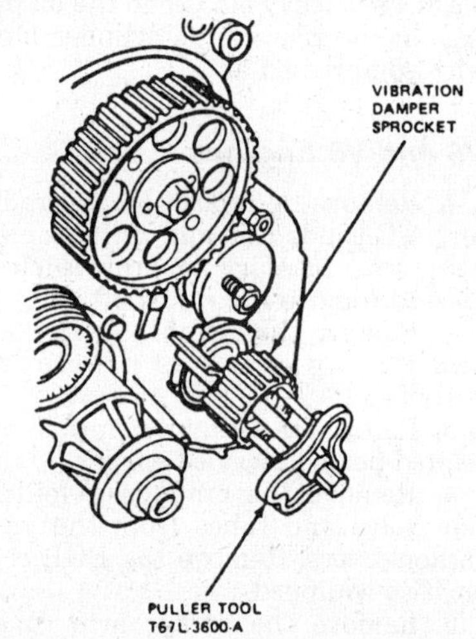

Diesel vibration damper sprocket removal

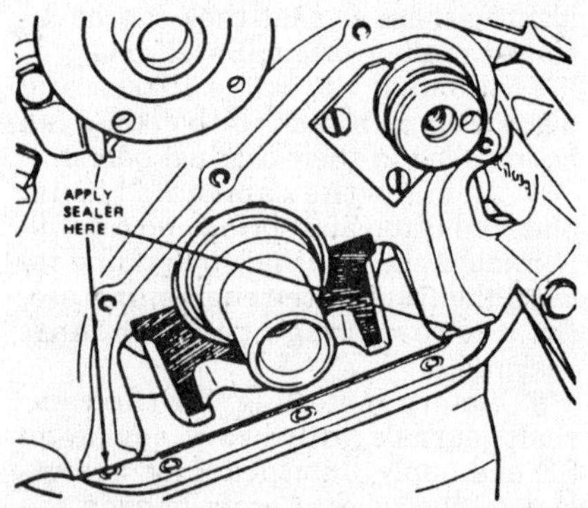

Diesel front cover gasket sealing areas

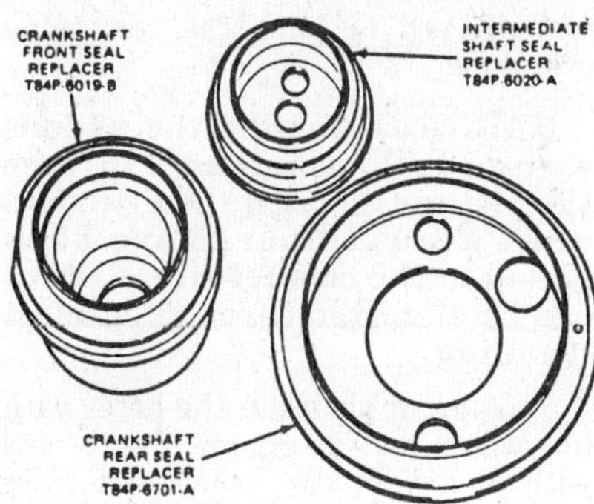

Diesel front, rear and intermediate shaft seals installation tools

12. Remove the six bolts attaching the front cover to the crankcase, and remove cover.
13. Clean the front cover and crankcase gasket mating surfaces.
14. Inspect and replace the crankshaft and intermediate shaft oil seals, if necessary.
15. If the oil pan gasket is damaged, install a new pan gasket.
16. Install the new front cover gasket.

NOTE: Coat the areas where front cover gasket meets oil pan gasket with a 1/4" (6mm) RTV Sealant, D6AZ-19562-A or equivalent sealer. RTV Sealant should be applied immediately prior to front cover installation. When applying RTV Sealant always use the bead size specified and join the components within 15 minutes of application. After this amount of time the sealant begins to set-up and its sealing effectiveness may be reduced.

17. Position the front engine cover on the crankcase, and tighten the 6mm bolts to 6-7 ft.lb. and the 8mm bolts to 14-17 ft.lb.
18. Install the three oil pan-to-front cover attaching bolts. Tighten the oil pan bolts to 6.5-7 ft.lb.
19. Position the vibration damper flange and sprocket on the crankshaft, with the shoulder toward front of vehicle.
20. Position the intermediate shaft sprocket on the intermediate shaft, guiding the locating pin into the bore.
21. Install Holding Tool T84P-6316-A or equivalent.

NOTE: Align the Allen head screws in the tool with the holes in the intermediate shaft.

22. Install and tighten the vibration damper flange and sprocket bolt to 282-311 ft.lb.
23. Install and tighten the intermediate shaft sprocket bolt to 40-47 ft.lb. Remove Tool T84P-6316-A or equivalent.
24. Install and adjust the camshaft drive belt.
25. Install the camshaft drive belt cover and tighten the bolts to 6-7 ft.lb.
26. Connect the heater hose to the thermostat housing.
27. Install the vibration damper and pulley. Tighten to 16-17 ft.lb.
28. Install the fan assembly.
29. Install and adjust the accessory drive belts.
30. Connect the battery ground cable.
31. Start the engine. Check for oil leaks.

Crankshaft and Intermediate Shaft Front Oil Seal

REMOVAL & INSTALLATION

1. Remove the engine front cover.
2. Using an arbor press, press the old seal(s) out of the front cover.
3. Position the new seals on the front cover and install, using T84P-6019-B for crankshaft seal, or T84P-6020-A or equivalent for the intermediate shaft seal.
4. Lubricate the seal lips with engine oil.
5. Install the engine front cover.

Pistons and Connection Rods

REMOVAL & INSTALLATION

NOTE: Although, in most cases, the pistons and connecting rods can be removed from the engine (after the cylinder head and oil pan are removed) while the engine is still in the car, it is far easier to remove the engine from the car. If removing pistons with the engine still installed, disconnect the radiator hoses, automatic transmission cooler lines and radiator shroud. Unbolt front mounts before jacking up the engine. Block the engine in position with wooden blocks between the mounts.

1. Remove the engine from the car. Remove the cylinder head(s), oil pan and front cover (if necessary).
2. Because the top piston ring does not travel to the very top of the cylinder bore, a ridge is built up between the end of the travel and the top of the cylinder. Pushing the piston and connecting rod assembly past the ridge is difficult and may cause damage to the piston. If new rings are installed and the ridge has not been removed, ring breakage and piston damage can occur when the ridge is encountered at engine speed.
3. Turn the crankshaft to position the piston at the bottom of the cylinder bore. Cover the top of the piston with a rag. Install a ridge reamer in the bore and follow the manufacturer's instructions to remove the ridge. Use caution; avoid cutting too deeply or into the ring travel area. Remove the rag and cuttings from the top of the piston. Remove the ridge from all cylinders.
4. Check the edges of the connecting rod and bearing cap for numbers or matchmarks, if none are present mark the rod and cap numerically and in sequence from front to back of engine. The numbers or marks not only tell from which cylinder the piston cam from but also ensures that the rod caps are installed in the correct matching position.
5. Turn the crankshaft until the connecting rod is at the bottom of travel. Remove the two attaching nuts and the bearing cap. Take two pieces of rubber tubing and cover the rod bolts to prevent crank or cylinder scoring. Use a wooden hammer handle to help push the piston and rod up and out of the cylinder. Reinstall the rod cap in proper position. Remove all pistons and connecting rods. Inspect cylinder walls and deglaze or hone as necessary.
6. Installation is in the reverse order of removal. Lubricate each piston, rod bearing and cylinder wall. Install a ring compressor over the piston, position the piston with the mark toward the front of engine and carefully install. Position the connecting rod with the bearing insert installed over the crank journal. Install the rod cap with the bearing in its proper position. Secure with rod nuts and torque to the proper specifications. Install all rod and piston assemblies.

CLEANING AND INSPECTION

1. Use a piston ring expander and remove the rings from the piston.
2. Clean the ring grooves using an appropriate cleaning tool, exercising care to avoid cutting too deeply.
3. Clean all varnish and carbon from the piston with a safe solvent. Do not use a wire brush or caustic solution on the pistons.
4. Inspect the pistons for scuffing, scoring, cracks, pitting or excessive ring groove wear. If wear is evident, the piston must be replaced.
5. Have the piston and connecting rod assembly checked by a machine shop for correct alignment, piston pin wear and piston diameter. If the piston

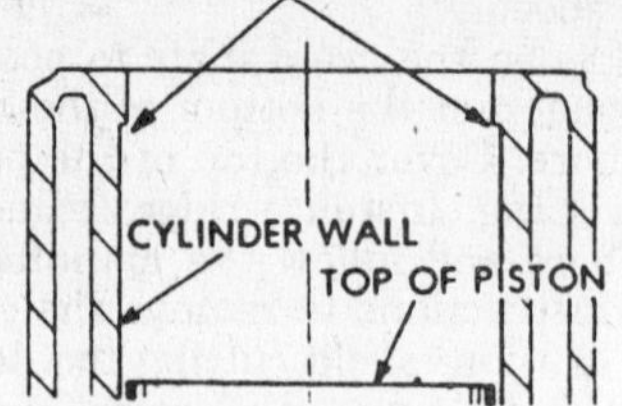

Cylinder bore ridge

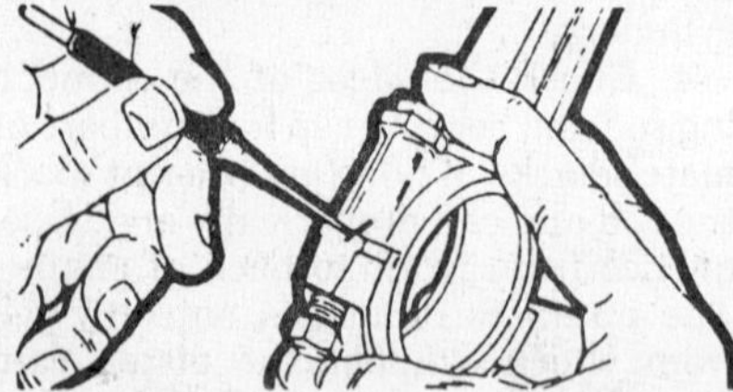

Match the connecting rod and cap with scribe marks

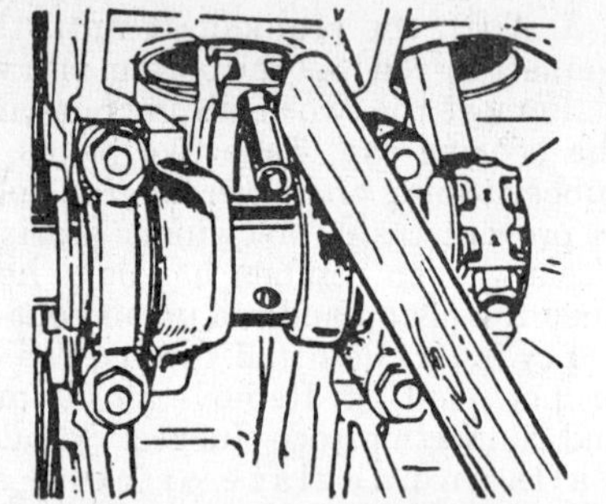

Push the piston out with a hammer handle

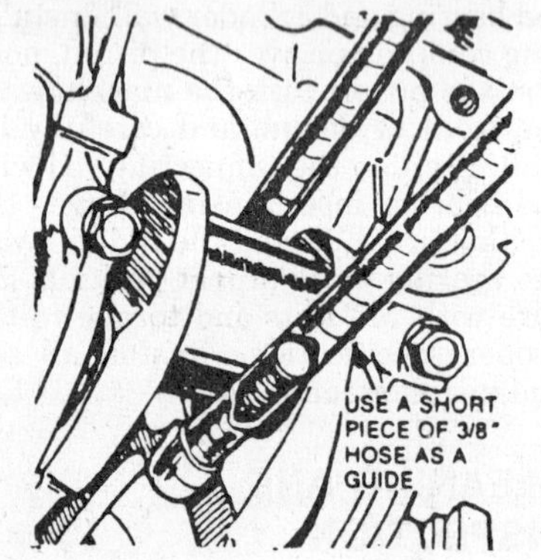

Use lengths of vacuum hose or rubber tubing to protect the crankshaft journals and cylinder walls during installation

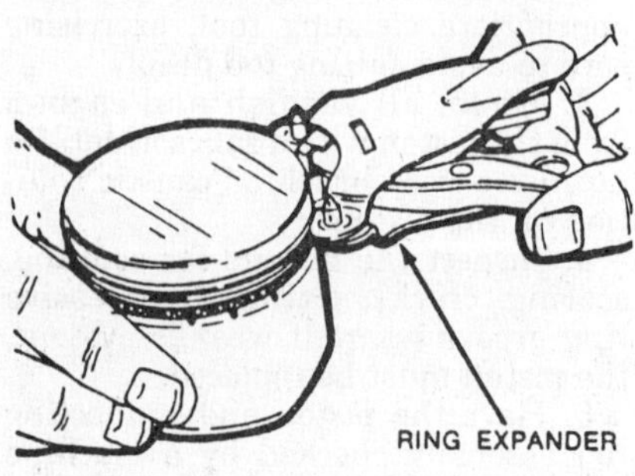

Remove piston rings

has collapsed it will have to be replaced or knurled to restore original diameter. Connecting rod bushing replacement, piston pin fitting and piston changing can be handled by the machine shop.

MEASURING THE OLD PISTONS

Check used piston-to-cylinder bore clearance as follows:

1. Measure the cylinder bore diameter with a telescope gauge.
2. Measure the piston diameter. When measuring the pistons for size or taper, measurements must be made with the piston pin removed.
3. Subtract the piston diameter from the cylinder bore diameter to determine piston-to-bore clearance.
4. Compare the piston-to-bore clearances obtained with those clearances recommended. Determine if the piston-to-bore clearance is in the acceptable range.
5. When measuring taper, the largest reading must be at the bottom of the skirt.

SELECTING NEW PISTONS

1. If the used piston is not acceptable, check the service piston size and determine if a new piston can be selected. (Service pistons are available in standard, high limit and standard oversize.
2. If the cylinder bore must be reconditioned, measure the new piston diameter, then hone the cylinder bore to obtain the preferred clearance.
3. Select a new piston and mark the piston to identify the cylinder for which it was fitted. (On some vehicles, oversize pistons may be found. These pistons will be 0.254mm [0.010"] oversize).

CYLINDER HONING

1. When cylinders are being honed, follow the manufacturer's recommendations for the use of the hone.
2. Occasionally, during the honing operation, the cylinder bore should be thoroughly cleaned and the selected piston checked for correct fit.
3. When finish-honing a cylinder bore, the hone should be moved up and down at a sufficient speed to obtain a very fine uniform surface finish in a cross-hatch pattern of approximately 45–65° included angle. The finish marks should be clean but not sharp, free from imbedded particles and torn or folded metal.
4. Permanently mark the piston for the cylinder to which it has been fitted and proceed to hone the remaining cylinders.

WARNING: Handle the pistons with care. Do not attempt to force the pistons through the cylinders until the cylinders have been honed to the correct size. Pistons can be distorted through careless handling.

5. Thoroughly clean the bores with hot water and detergent. Scrub well with a stiff bristle brush and rinse thoroughly with hot water. It is extremely essential that a good cleaning operation be performed. If any of the abrasive material is allowed to remain in the cylinder bores, it will rapidly wear the new rings and cylinder bores. The bores should be swabbed several times with light engine oil and a clean cloth and then wiped with a clean dry cloth. CYLINDERS SHOULD NOT BE CLEANED WITH KEROSENE OR GASOLINE! Clean the remainder of the cylinder block to remove the excess material spread during the honing operation.

PISTON PIN REMOVAL & INSTALLATION

Use care at all times when handling and servicing connecting rods and pistons. To prevent possible damage to

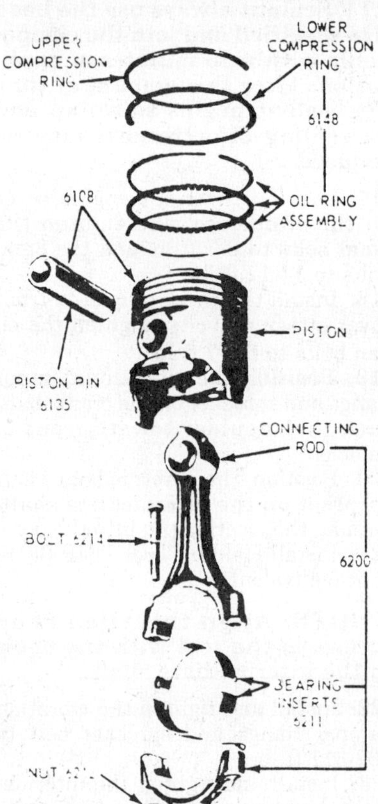

Typical piston and connecting rod assembly

these units, do not clamp the rod or piston in a vise since they may become distorted. Do not allow the pistons to strike against one another, against hard objects or bench surfaces, since distortion of the piston contour or nicks in the soft aluminum material may result.

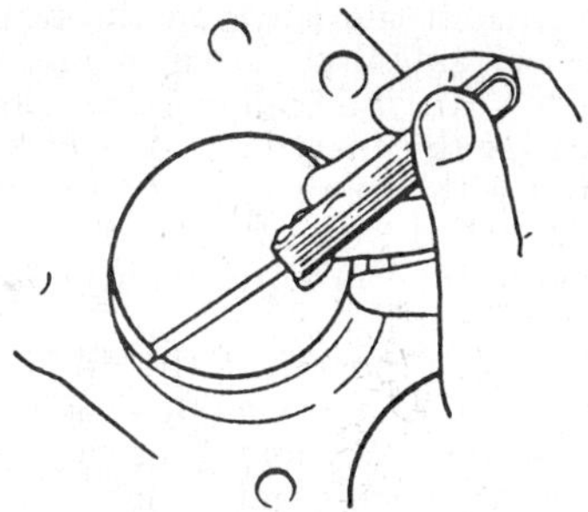
Check the piston ring end gap

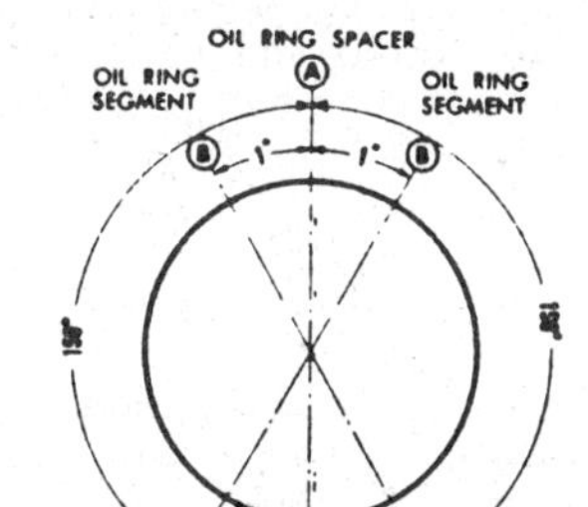

Piston ring spacing (all engines)

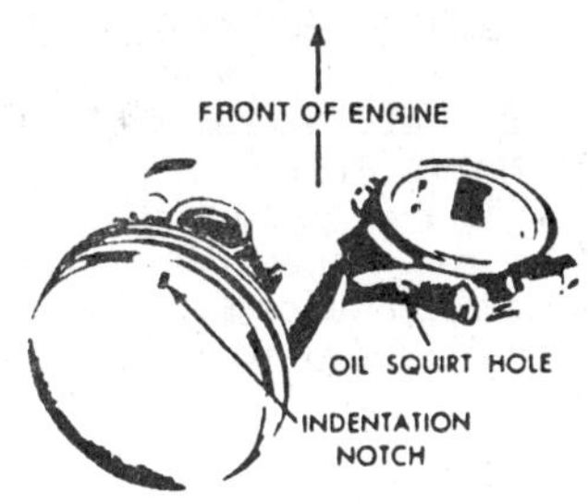

Piston and rod positioning on the 6-200

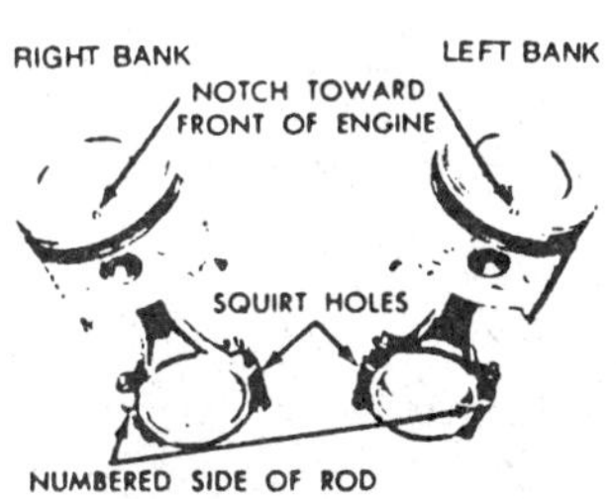

Piston and rod positioning on the V6-232, V8-255, 302, 351W

1. Remove the piston rings using a suitable piston ring remover.
2. Remove the piston pin lockring, if used. Install the guide bushing of the piston pin removing and installing tool.
3. Install the piston and connecting rod assembly on a support, and place

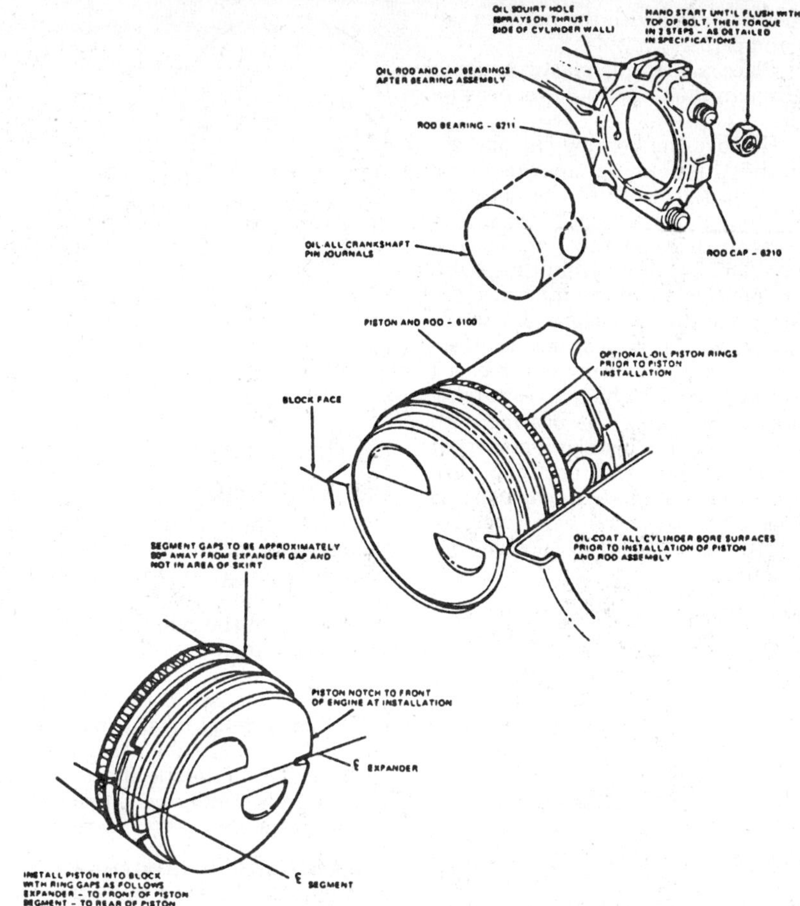

4-140 piston rings and connecting rods

the assembly in an arbor press. Press the pin out of the connecting rod, using the appropriate piston pin tool.

4. Assembly is the reverse of disassembly. Use new lockrings where needed.

Connecting Rods and Bearings

Wash connecting rods in cleaning solvent and dry with compressed air. Check for twisted or bent rods and inspect for nicks or cracks. Replace connecting rods that are damaged.

Inspect journals for roughness and wear. Slight roughness may be removed with a fine grit polishing cloth saturated with engine oil. Burrs may be removed with a fine oil stone by moving the stone on the journal circumference. Do not move the stone back and forth across the journal. If the journals are scored or ridged, the crankshaft must be replaced.

The connecting rod journals should be checked for out-of-round and correct size with a micrometer.

NOTE: Crankshaft rod journals will normally be standard size. If any undersized bearings are used, the size will be stamped on a counterweight.

If plastic gauging material is to be used:

1. Clean oil from the journal bearing cap, connecting rod and outer and inner surfaces of the bearing inserts. Position the insert so that the tang is

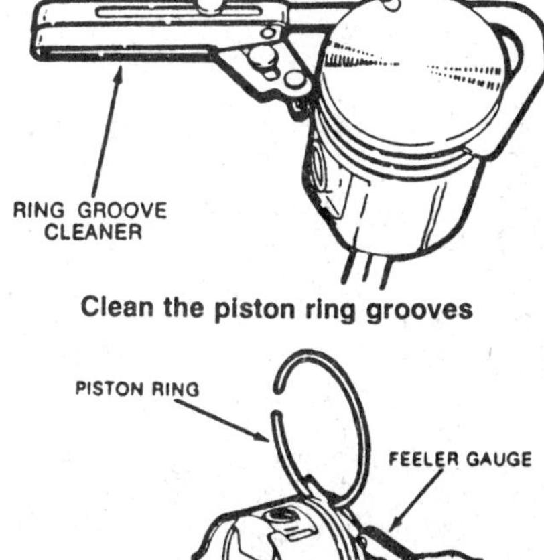

Clean the piston ring grooves

Check the piston ring side clearance

properly aligned with the notch in the rod and cap.

2. Place a piece of plastic gauging material in the center of lower bearing shell.

3. Remove the bearing cap and determine the bearing clearances by comparing the width of the flattened plastic gauging material at its widest point with the graduation on the container. The number within the graduation on the envelope indicates the clearance in thousandths of an inch or millimeters. If this clearance is excessive, replace the bearing and recheck the clearance with the plastic gauging material. Lubricate the bearing with engine oil before installation. Repeat the procedure on the remaining connecting rod bearings. All rods must be connected to their journals when rotating the crankshaft, to prevent engine damage.

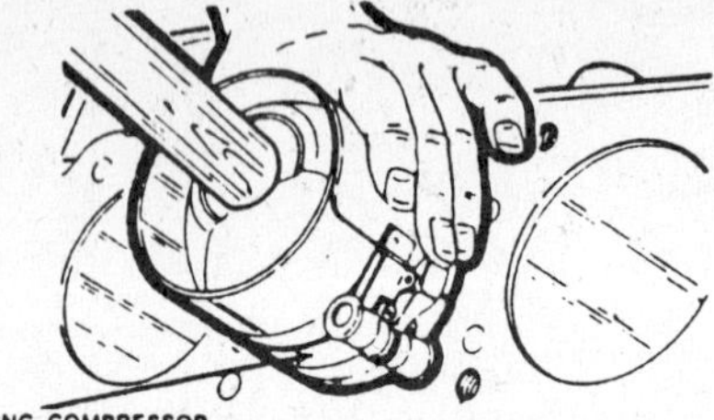

Install the piston using a ring compressor

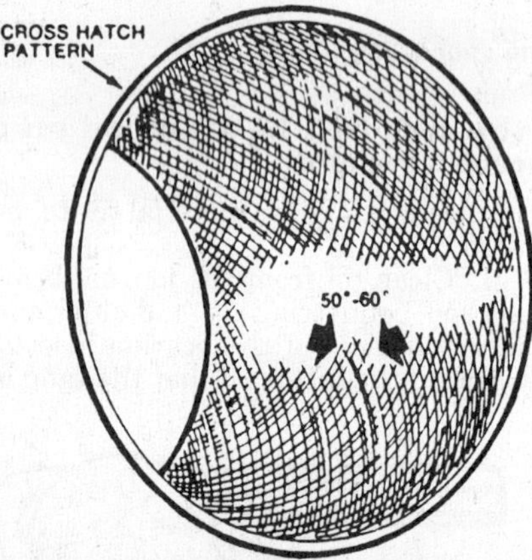

Cylinder bore after honing

CYLINDER BORE

Check the cylinder bore for wear using a telescope gauge and a micrometer, measure the cylinder bore diameter perpendicular to the piston pin at the point 2½" (63.5mm) below the top of the engine block. Measure the piston skirt perpendicular to the piston pin. The difference between the two measurement is the piston clearance. If the clearance is within specifications, finish honing or glaze breaking is all that is required. If clearance is excessive a slightly oversized piston may be required. If greatly oversize, the engine will have to be bored and 0.010" (0.254mm) or larger oversized pistons installed.

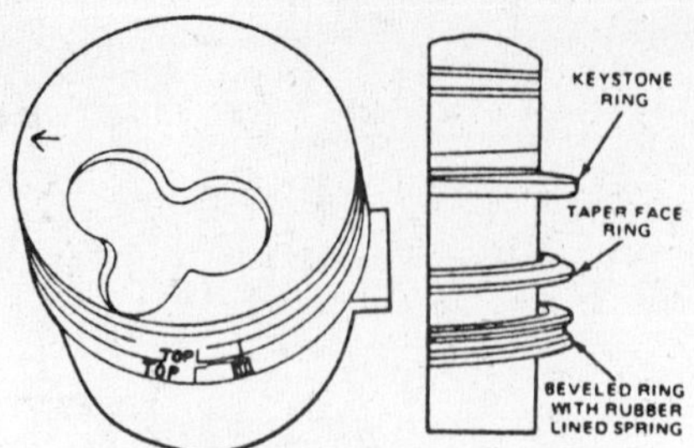

Diesel engine piston ring spacing

FITTING AND POSITIONING PISTON RINGS

1. Take the new piston rings and compress them, one at a time into the cylinder that they will be used in. Press the ring about 1" (25.4mm) below the top of the cylinder block using an inverted piston.

2. Use a feeler gauge and measure the distance between the ends of the ring; this is called measuring the ring end-gap. Compare the reading to the one called for in the specification table. File the ends of the ring with a fine file to obtain the necessary clearance.

WARNING: If inadequate ring end-gap exists, ring breakage will result.

3. Inspect the ring grooves on the piston for excessive wear or taper. If necessary, have the grooves recut for use with a standard ring and spacer. The machine shop can handle the job for you.

4. Check the ring grooves by rolling the new piston ring around the groove to check for burrs or carbon deposits. If any are found, remove them with a fine file. Hold the ring in the groove and measure side clearance with a feeler gauge. If clearance is excessive, spacer(s) will have to be added.

NOTE: Always add the spacer above the piston ring.

5. Install the rings on the piston, lower oil ring first. Use a ring installing tool on the compression rings. Consult the instruction sheet that comes with the rings to be sure they are installed with the correct side up. A mark on the ring usually faces upward.

6. When installing the oil rings, first install the expanding ring in the groove. Hold the ends of the ring butted together (they must not overlap) and install the bottom rail (scraper) with the end about 1" (25.4mm) away from the butted end of the control ring. Install the top rail about 1" (25.4mm) away from the butted end of the control but on the opposite side from the lower rail.

7. Install the two compression rings.

8. Consult the illustration for ring positioning, arrange the rings as shown, install a ring compressor and insert the piston and rod assembly into the engine.

Rear Main Oil Seal

REMOVAL & INSTALLATION

NOTE: Refer to the build dates listed below to determine if the engine is equipped with a split-type or one piece rear main oil seal. Engines after the dates indicated have a one-piece oil seal.

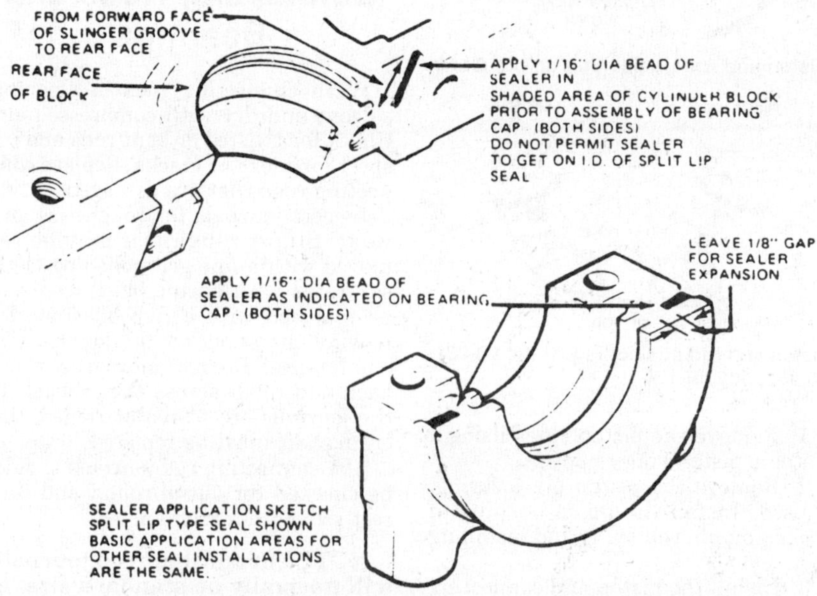

Rear main oil seal installation on all except 4-140

4-140 OHC after 9/28/81
6-232 after 4/1/83
8-302 after 12/1/82
Engines prior to the date indicated are equipped with a split type seal.

Split-Type Seal on Gasoline Engines

NOTE: The rear oil seal installed in these engines is a rubber type (split-lip) seal.

1. Remove the oil pan, and, if required, the oil pump.
2. Loosen all the main bearing caps allowing the crankshaft to lower slightly.

WARNING: The crankshaft should not be allowed to drop more than 1/32" (0.8mm).

3. Remove the rear main bearing cap and remove the seal from the cap and block. Be very careful not to scratch the sealing surface. Remove the old seal retaining pin from the cap, if equipped. It is not used with the replacement seal.
4. Carefully clean the seal grooves in the cap and block with solvent.
5. Soak the new seal halves in clean engine oil.
6. Install the upper half of the seal in the block with the undercut side of the seal toward the front of the engine. Slide the seal around the crankshaft journal until 3/8" (9.5mm) protrudes beyond the base of the block.
7. Tighten all the main bearing caps (except the rear main bearing) to specifications.
8. Install the lower seal into the rear cap, with the undercut side facing the front of the engine. Allow 3/8" (9.5mm) of the seal to protrude above the surface, at the opposite end from the block seal.
9. Squeeze a 1/16" (1.6mm) bead of silicone sealant onto the areas shown.
10. Install the rear cap and torque to specifications.
11. Install the oil pump and pan. Fill the crankcase with oil, start the engine, and check for leaks.

One-Piece Seal on Gasoline Engines

1. Remove the transmission, clutch and flywheel or driveplate after referring to the appropriate section for instructions.
2. Punch two holes in the crankshaft rear oil seal on opposite sides of the crankshaft just above the bearing cap to the cylinder block split line. Install a sheet metal screw in each of the holes or use a small slide hammer, and pry the crankshaft rear main oil seal from the block.

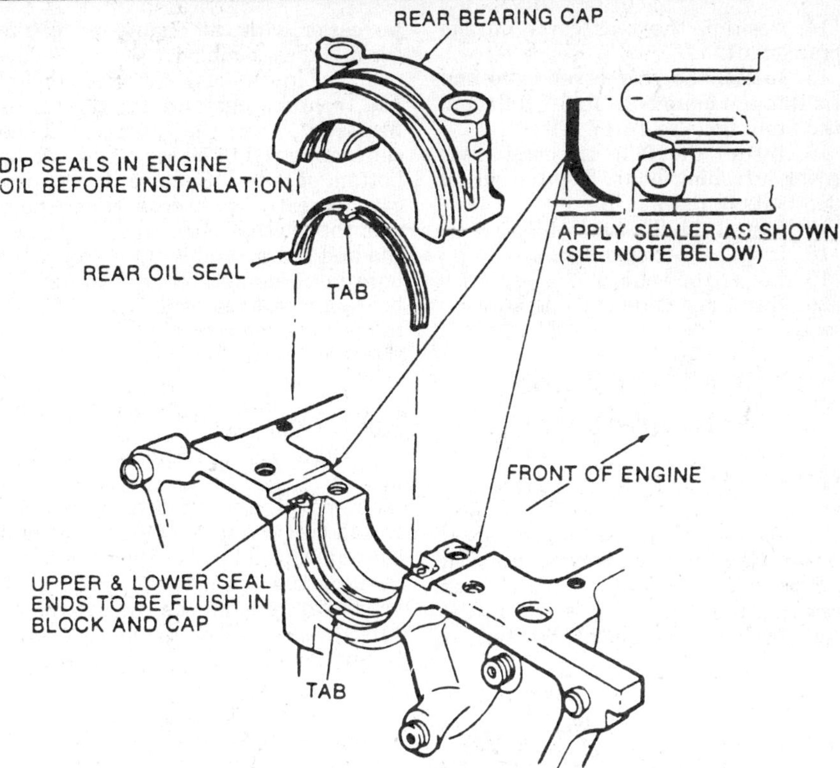

4-140 rear main oil seal replacement

WARNING: Use extreme caution not to scratch the crankshaft oil seal surface.

3. Clean the oil seal recess in the cylinder block and main bearing cap.
4. Coat the seal and all of the seal mounting surfaces with oil and install the seal in the recess, driving it into place with an oil seal installation tool or a large socket.
5. Install the driveplate or flywheel and clutch, and transmission in the reverse order of removal.

2,443cc Diesel Engine

1. Raise the vehicle and safely support on jackstands.
2. Remove the transmission.
3. Remove the flywheel driveplate.
4. Remove the four oil pan to rear engine cover attaching bolts.
5. Loosen, but DO NOT REMOVE the remaining oil pan bolts.
6. Remove the six engine rear cover bolts and remove the cover.
7. Clean the crankcase and the engine rear cover gasket mating surfaces.
8. Replace the oil pan gasket, if damaged.
9. Using an arbor press, press the old seal out of the cover.
10. Position a new seal on the cover and press in using Crankshaft Rear Seal Replacer T84P-6701-A, or equivalent.
11. Lubricate the sealing lips on the seal with engine oil.
12. Position a new rear cover gasket on the crankcase.
13. Apply gasket sealer at the points where the rear cover gasket meets the oil pan gasket.

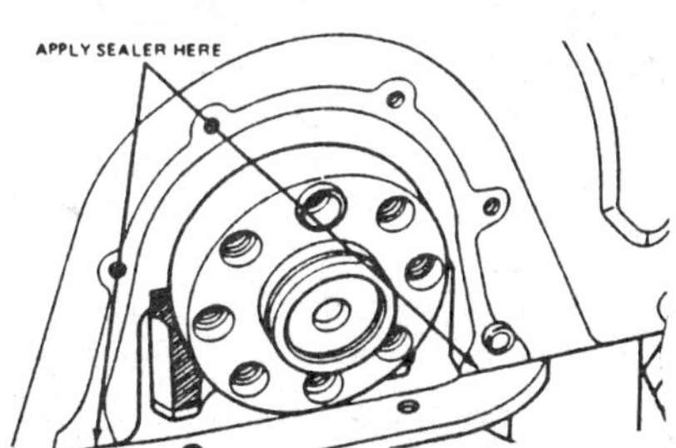

Diesel engine rear cover gasket-to-oil pan sealing points

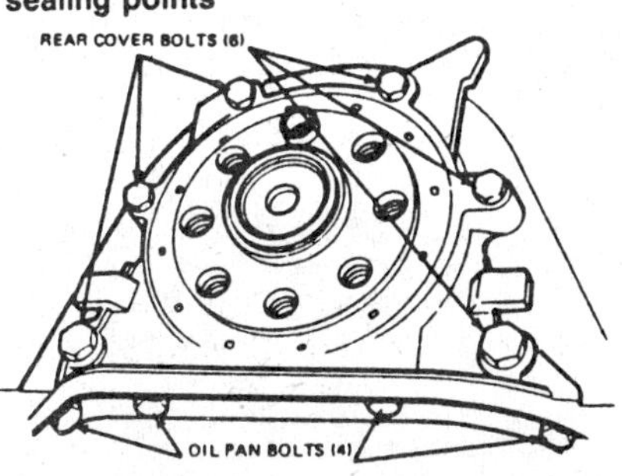

Diesel engine rear cover bolts

14. Position the rear cover on the crankshaft.
15. Install the rear cover bolts and tighten the 6mm bolts to 6-7 ft.lb. and the 8mm bolts to 14-17 ft.lb.
16. Install the four oil pan-to-rear cover attaching bolts. Tighten all oil pan bolts to 6.5-7 ft.lb.
17. Install the flywheel.
18. Install the transmission.
19. Lower the vehicle.
20. Run the engine and check for oil leaks.

Crankshaft and Bearings

REMOVAL & INSTALLATION

1. Rod bearings can be installed when the pistons have been removed for servicing (rings etc.) or, in most cases, while the engine is still in the car. Bearing replacement, however, is far easier with the engine out of the car and disassembled.

2. For in car service, remove the oil pan, spark plugs and front cover is necessary. Turn the engine until the connecting rod to be serviced is at the bottom of travel. Remove the bearing cap, place two pieces of rubber hose over the rod cap bolts and push the piston and rod assembly up the cylinder bore until enough room is gained for bearing insert removal. Take care not to push the rod assembly up too far or the top ring will engage the cylinder ridge or come out of the cylinder and require head removal for reinstallation.

3. Clean the rod journal, the connecting rod end and the bearing cap after removing the old bearing inserts. Install the new inserts in the rod and bearing cap, lubricate them with oil. Position the rod over the crankshaft journal and install the rod cap. Make sure the cap and rod numbers match, torque the rod nuts to specifications.

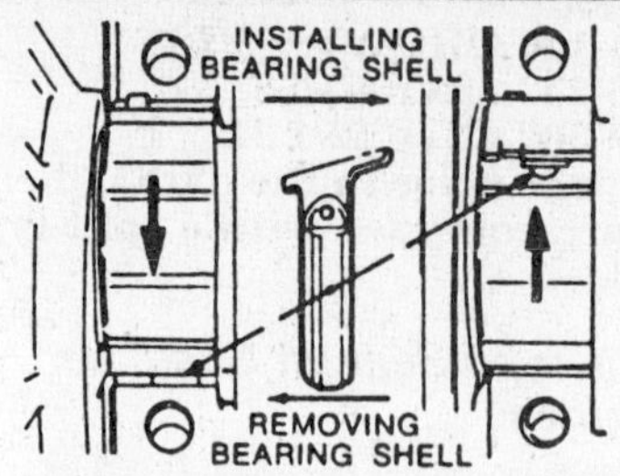

Remove or install the upper bearing insert using a roll-out pin

4. Main bearings may be replaced while the engine is still in the car by rolling them out and in.

5. Special roll out pins are available from automotive parts houses or can be fabricated from a cotter pin. The roll out pin fits in the oil hole of the main bearing journal. When the crankshaft is rotated opposite the direction of the bearing lock tab, the pin engages the end of the bearing and rolls out the insert.

6. Remove the main bearing cap and roll out the upper bearing insert. Remove the insert from the main bearing cap. Clean the inside of the bearing cap and crankshaft journal.

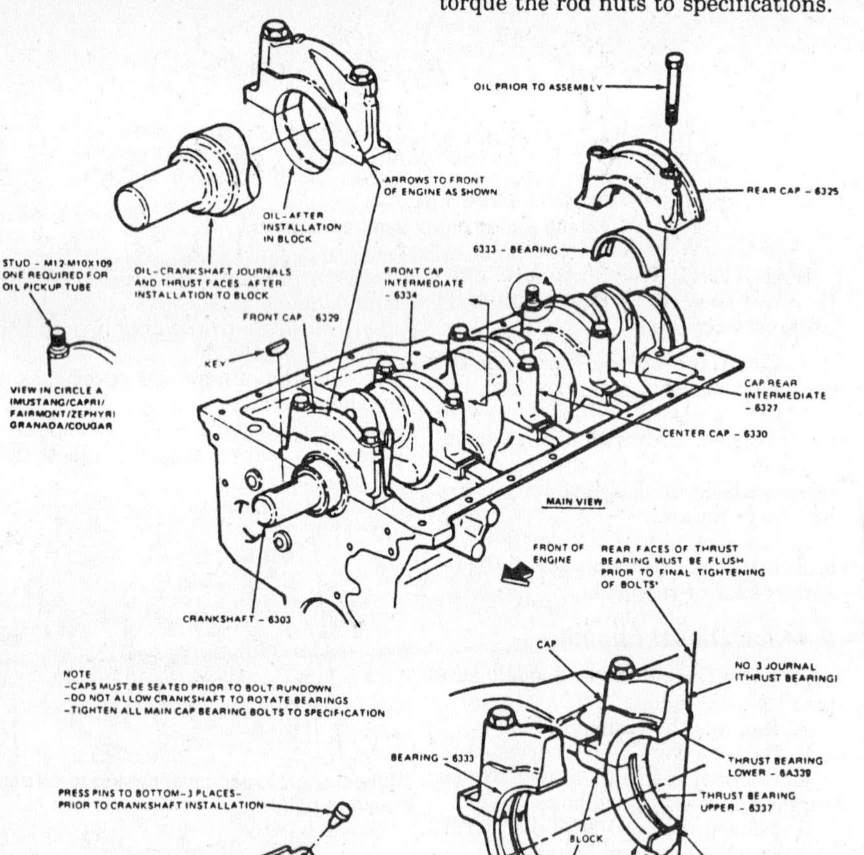

4-140 crankshaft and main bearing installation

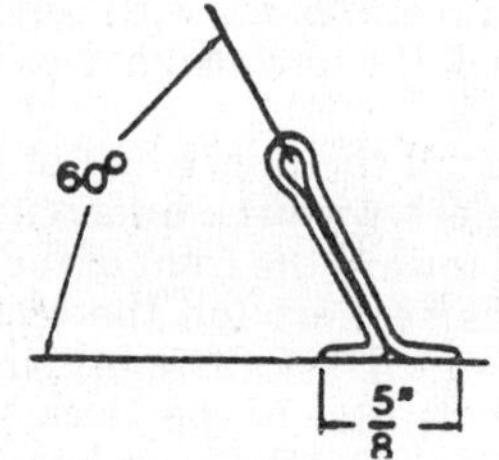

Home-made bearing roll-out pin

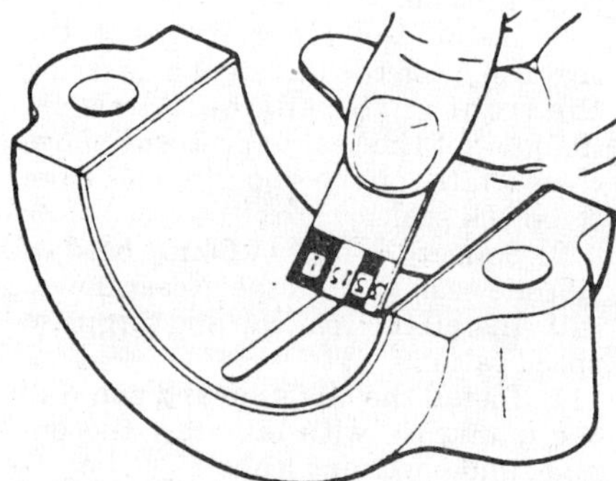

Measure Plastigage® to determine bearing clearance

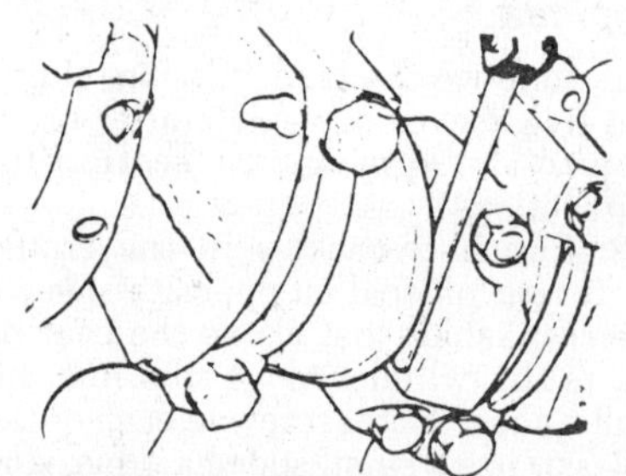

Check the connecting rod side clearance with a feeler gauge

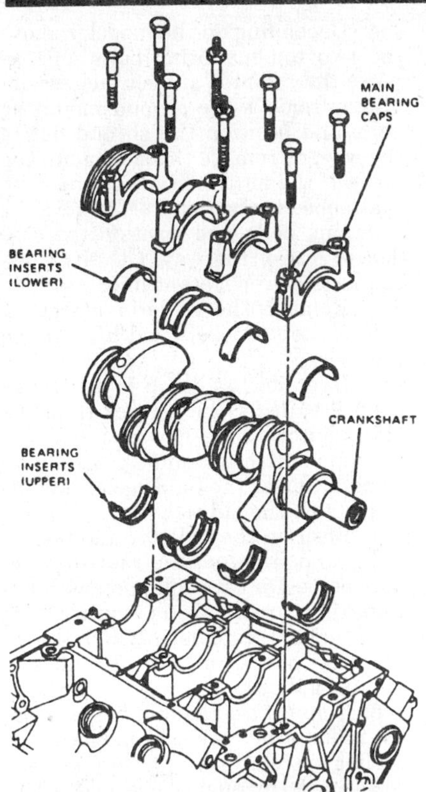

V6 crankshaft and main bearing installation

7. Lubricate and roll the upper insert into position, making sure the lock tab is anchored and the insert is not cocked. Install the lower bearing insert into the cap, lubricate it and install it on the engine. Make sure the main bearing cap is installed facing in the correct direction and torque it to specifications.

8. With the engine out of the car. Remove the intake manifold, cylinder heads, front cover, timing gears and/or chain, oil pan, oil pump and flywheel.

9. Remove the piston and rod assemblies. Remove the main bearing caps after marking them for position and direction.

10. Remove the crankshaft, bearing inserts and rear main oil seal. Clean the engine block and cap bearing saddles. Clean the crankshaft and inspect it for wear. Check the bearing journals with a micrometer for out-of-round condition and to determine what size rod and main bearing inserts to install.

11. Install the main bearing upper inserts and rear main oil seal half into the engine block.

12. Lubricate the bearing inserts and the crankshaft journals. Slowly and carefully lower the crankshaft into position.

13. Install the bearing inserts and rear main seal into the bearing caps. Install the caps working from the middle out. Torque the cap bolts to specifications in stages, rotating the crankshaft after each torque stage. Note the illustration for thrust bearing alignment.

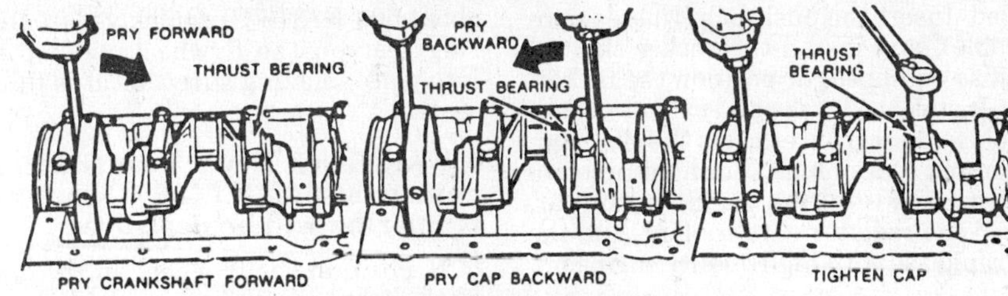

Aligning the thrust bearing

14. Remove the bearing caps, one at a time, and check the oil clearance with Plastigage®. Reinstall if clearance is within specifications. Check the crankshaft end-play. If it is within specifications, install the connecting rod and piston assemblies with new rod bearing inserts. Check the connecting rod bearing oil clearance and side play. If they are correct assemble the rest of the engine.

BEARING OIL CLEARANCE

Remove the cap from the bearing to be checked. Using a clean, dry rag, thoroughly clean all oil from the crankshaft journal and bearing insert.

NOTE: Plastigage® is soluble in oil, therefore, oil on the journal or bearing could result in erroneous readings.

Place a piece of Plastigage® along the full width of the bearing insert, reinstall cap, and torque to specification.

NOTE: Specifications are given in the Engine Specifications Chart.

Remove the bearing cap, and determine the bearing clearance by comparing the width of the Plastigage® to the scale on the Plastigage® envelope. Journal taper is determined by comparing the width of the bearing insert. Install the cap, and torque it to specifications.

NOTE: Do not rotate the crankshaft with the Plastigage® installed. If the bearing insert and journal appear intact, and are within tolerances, no further main bearing service is required. If the bearing or journal appear defective, the cause of failure should be determined before replacement.

CRANKSHAFT END-PLAY/CONNECTING ROD SIDE PLAY

Place a pry bar between a main bearing cap and crankshaft casting taking care not to damage any journals. Pry backward and forward, measuring the distance between the thrust bearing and crankshaft with a feeler gauge. Compare the reading with specifications. If too great a clearance is determined, a main bearing with a larger thrust surface or crank machining may be required. Check with an automotive machine shop for their advice.

Connecting rod clearance between the rod and crankthrow casting can be checked with a feeler gauge. Pry the rod carefully to one side as far as possible and measure the distance on the other side of the rod.

CRANKSHAFT REPAIRS

If a journal is damaged on the crankshaft, repair is possible by having the crankshaft machined to a standard undersize.

In most cases, however, since the engine must be removed from the car and disassembled, some thought should be given to replacing the damaged crankshaft with a reground shaft kit. A reground crankshaft kit contains the necessary main and rod bearings for installation. The shaft has been ground and polished to undersize specifications and will usually hold up well if installed correctly.

COMPLETING THE REBUILDING PROCESS

Fill the oil pump with oil, to prevent cavitating (sucking air) on initial engine start up. Install the oil pump and the pickup tube on the engine. Coat the oil pan gasket as necessary, and install the gasket and the oil pan. Mount the flywheel and the crankshaft vibration damper or pulley on the crankshaft.

NOTE: Always use new bolts when installing the flywheel. Inspect the clutch shaft pilot bushing in the crankshaft. If the bushing is excessively worn, remove it with an expanding puller and a slide hammer, and tap a new bushing into place.

Position the engine, cylinder head side up. Lubricate the lifters, and install them into their bores. Install the cylinder head, and torque it as specified. Insert the pushrods (where applicable), and install the rocker shaft(s) (if so equipped) or position the rocker.

Install the intake and exhaust manifolds, the carburetor(s), the distributor and spark plugs. Mount all accessories and install the engine in the car. Fill the radiator with coolant, and the crankcase with high quality engine oil.

BREAK-IN PROCEDURE

Start the engine, and allow it to run at low speed for a few minutes, while checking for leaks. Stop the engine, check the oil level, and fill as necessary. Restart the engine, and fill the cooling system to capacity. Check and adjust the ignition timing. Run the engine at low to medium speed (800-2,500 rpm) for approximately ½ hour, and retorque the cylinder head bolts. Road test the car, and check again for leaks.

NOTE: Some gasket manufacturers recommend not retorquing the cylinder head(s) due to the composition of the head gasket. Follow the directions in the gasket set.

Flywheel/Flex Plate and Ring Gear

NOTE: Flex plate is the term for a flywheel mated with an automatic transmission.

REMOVAL & INSTALLATION

All Engines

NOTE: The ring gear is replaceable only on engines mated with a manual transmission. Engines with automatic transmissions have ring gears which are welded to the flex plate.

1. Remove the transmission and transfer case.
2. Remove the clutch, if equipped, or torque converter from the flywheel. The flywheel bolts should be loosened a little at a time in a cross pattern to avoid warping the flywheel. On cars with manual transmissions, replace the pilot bearing in the end of the crankshaft if removing the flywheel.
3. The flywheel should be checked for cracks and glazing. It can be resurfaced by a machine shop.
4. If the ring gear is to be replaced, drill a hole in the gear between two teeth, being careful not to contact the flywheel surface. Using a cold chisel at this point, crack the ring gear and remove it.
6. Polish the inner surface of the new ring gear and heat it in an oven to about 600°F (316°C). Quickly place the ring gear on the flywheel and tap it into place, making sure that it is fully seated.

WARNING: Never heat the ring gear past 800°F (426°C), or the tempering will be destroyed.

7. Position the flywheel on the end of the crankshaft. Torque the bolts a little at a time, in a cross pattern, to the torque figure shown in the Torque Specifications Chart.
8. Install the clutch or torque converter.
9. Install the transmission and transfer case.

ENGINE COOLING

Radiator

REMOVAL & INSTALLATION

1. Drain the cooling system.

CAUTION

When draining the coolant, keep in mind that cats and dogs are attracted by the ethylene glycol antifreeze, and are quite likely to drink any that is left in an uncovered container or in puddles on the ground. This will prove fatal in sufficient quantity. Always drain the coolant into a sealable container. Coolant should be reused unless it is contaminated or several years old.

2. Disconnect the upper, lower and overflow hoses at the radiator.
3. On automatic transmission equipped cars, disconnect the fluid cooler lines at the radiator.

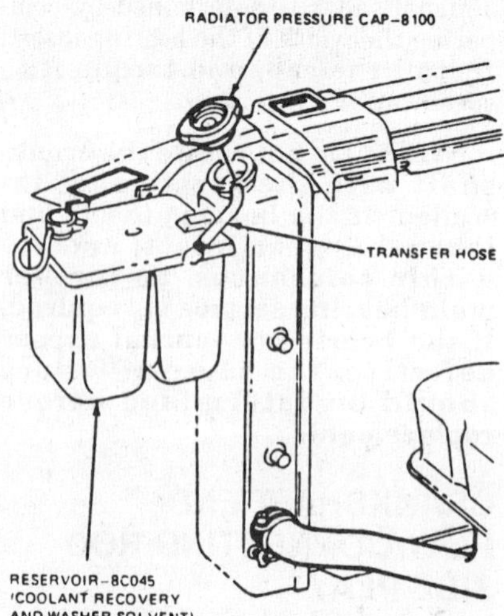

Coolant Recovery System—Typical

4. Depending on the model, remove the two top mounting bolts and remove the radiator and shroud assembly, or remove the shroud mounting bolts and position the shroud out of the way, or remove the side mounting bolts. If the air conditioner condenser is attached to the radiator, remove the retaining bolts and position the condenser out of the way. DO NOT disconnect the refrigerant lines.
5. Remove the radiator attaching bolts or top brackets and lift out the radiator.
6. If a new radiator is to be installed, transfer the petcock from the old radiator to the new one. On cars equipped with automatic transmissions, transfer the fluid cooler line fittings from the old radiator.
7. Position the radiator and install, but do not tighten, the radiator support bolts. On cars equipped with automatic transmissions, connect the fluid cooler lines. Then, tighten the radiator support bolts or shroud and mounting bolts.
8. Connect the radiator hoses. Close the radiator petcock. Fill and bleed the cooling system.
9. Start the engine and bring it to operating temperature. Check for leaks.
10. On cars equipped with automatic transmissions, check the cooler lines for leaks and interference. Check the transmission fluid level.

Electro-Drive Cooling Fan

REMOVAL & INSTALLATION

Various models, are equipped with a bracket-mounted electric cooling fan that replaces the conventional water pump mounted fan.

Operation of the fan motor is dependent on engine coolant temperature and air conditioner compressor clutch engagement. The fan will run only when the coolant temperature is approximately 180° or higher, or when the compressor clutch is engaged. The fan, motor and mount can be removed as an assembly after disconnecting the wiring harnesses and mounting bolts.

CAUTION

The cooling fan is automatic and may come on at any time without warning even if the ignition is switched OFF. To avoid possible injury, always disconnect the negative battery cable when working near the electric cooling fan.

Gasoline Engines

1. Disconnect the battery ground.
2. Remove the fan wiring harness from the clip.

3. Unplug the harness at the fan motor connector.
4. Remove the 4 mounting bracket attaching screws and remove the fan assembly from the car.
5. Remove the retaining clip from the end of the motor shaft and remove the fan.
6. Installation is the reverse of removal.

Diesel Engine

1. Disconnect the battery ground cable.
2. Raise the vehicle and support on jackstands.
3. Remove the bolts and nuts attaching the mounting brackets to the radiator support.
4. Disconnect the electrical connector to the fan.
5. Remove the bolts securing the hood latch to the radiator support and position the latch out of the way.
6. Remove the bolts and nuts attaching the mounting brackets to fan and motor assembly.
7. Remove the fan and motor assembly from the vehicle.
8. Position the fan and motor assembly in the vehicle.
9. Position the mounting brackets on the fan and motor assembly. Tighten the nut to 4-5 ft.lb.
10. Install the hood latch.
11. Connect the electrical connector to the fan and motor assembly.
12. Position the mounting brackets in the vehicle. Tighten the mounting bolts to 6-8 ft.lb. Tighten the mounting nuts to 4-5 ft.lb.
13. Lower the vehicle.
14. Connect the battery ground cable.

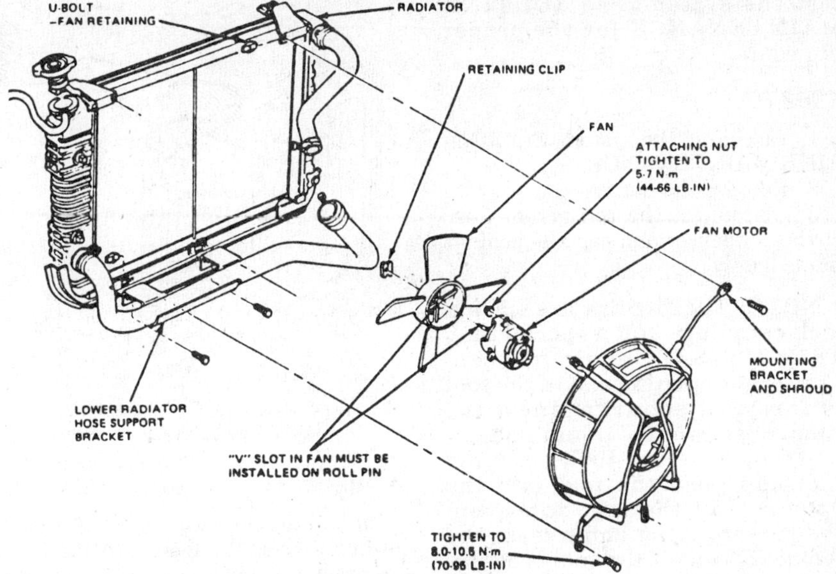

Gasoline engine electric cooling fan

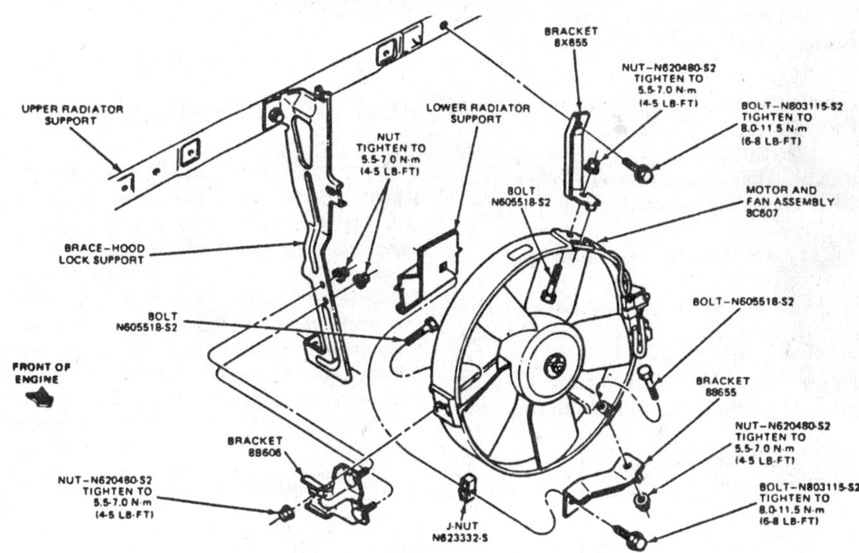

Diesel engine electric cooling fan

Air Conditioning Condenser

REMOVAL & INSTALLATION

1980-81

1. Discharge the system. See ROUTINE MAINTENANCE.
2. Remove the 6 attaching screws and remove the grille.
3. Move the ambient cutoff switch away from the front of the radiator and condenser.
4. Remove the battery.
5. Disconnect the refrigerant lines at the condenser and cap all openings immediately!
6. Remove the 4 bolts securing the condenser to the supports and remove the condenser.
7. Installation is the reverse of removal. Always use new O-rings coated with clean refrigerant oil at the pipe fittings. Evacuate, charge and leak

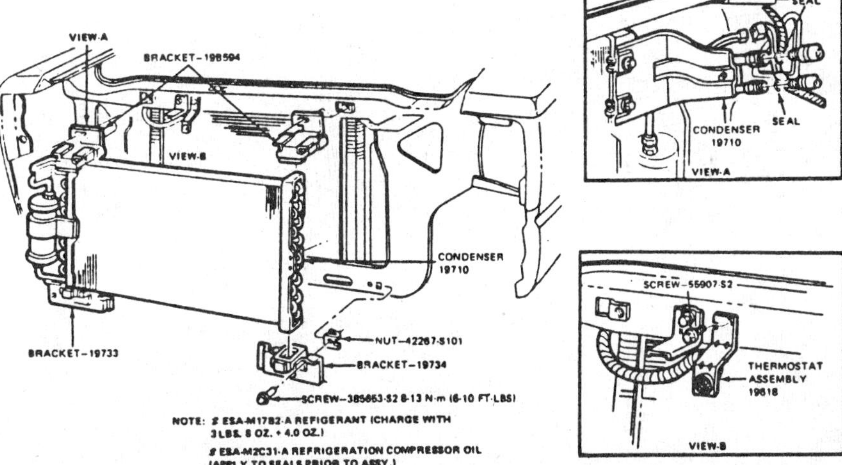

1980-81 Thunderbird and XR-7 air conditioning condenser installation

test the system. See ROUTINE MAINTENANCE for the proper procedure.

1982-87

1. Discharge the system. See ROUTINE MAINTENANCE.
2. Remove the battery.
3. Disconnect the refrigerant lines at the condenser and cap all openings immediately!

NOTE: The fittings are spring-lock couplings and a special tool, T81P-19623-G, should be used. The larger opening end of the tool is for ½" discharge lines; the smaller end for ⅜" liquid lines.

To operate the tool, close the tool and push the tool into the open side of the cage to expand the garter spring and release the female fitting. If the tool is not inserted straight, the garter spring will cock and not release.

After the garter spring is released, pull the fittings apart.

4. Remove the 4 bolts securing the condenser to the supports and remove the condenser.
5. Installation is the reverse of removal. Always use new O-rings coated with clean refrigerant oil at the pipe fittings.

To connect the couplings, check to ensure that the garter spring is in the cage of the male fitting, make sure the fittings are clean, install new O-rings made for this purpose, lubricate the O-rings with clean refrigerant oil and push the male and female fittings together until the garter springs snaps into place over the female fitting.

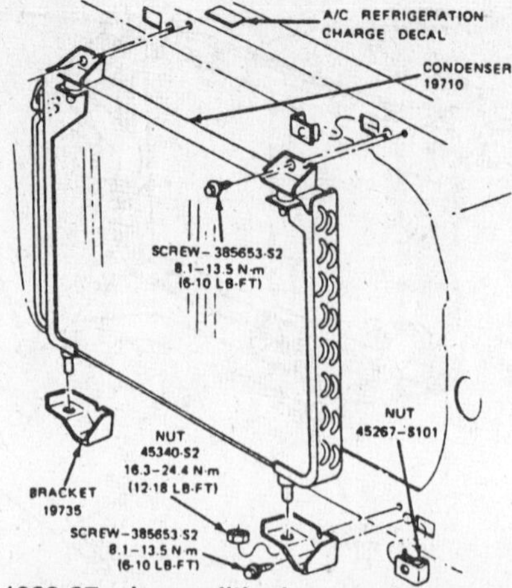

1982-87 air conditioning condenser installation

Evacuate, charge and leak test the system. See ROUTINE MAINTENANCE.

Thermostat

REMOVAL & INSTALLATION

CAUTION

When draining the coolant, keep in mind that cats and dogs are attracted by the ethylene glycol antifreeze, and are quite likely to drink any that is left in an uncovered container or in puddles on the ground. This will prove fatal in sufficient quantity. Always drain the coolant into a sealable container. Coolant should be reused unless it is contaminated or several years old.

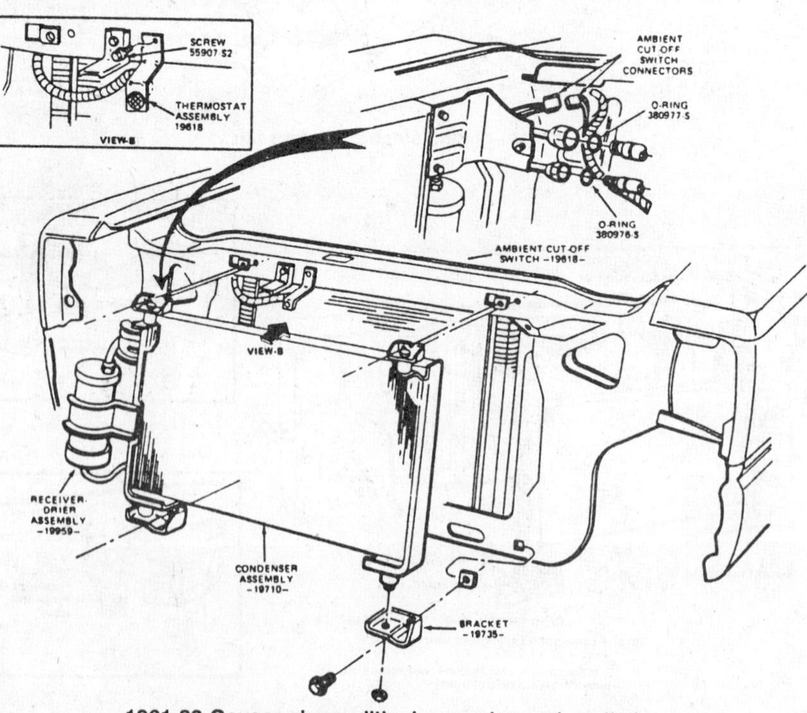

1981-82 Cougar air conditioning condenser installation

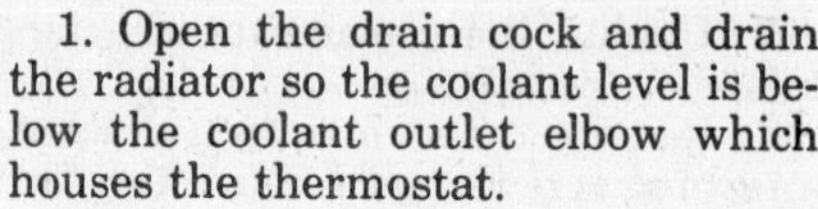

1. Open the drain cock and drain the radiator so the coolant level is below the coolant outlet elbow which houses the thermostat.

NOTE: On some models it will be necessary to remove the distributor cap, rotor and vacuum diaphragm in order to gain access to the thermostat housing mounting bolts.

2. Remove the outlet elbow retaining bolts and position the elbow sufficiently clear of the intake manifold or cylinder head to provide access to the thermostat.
3. Remove the thermostat and the gasket.

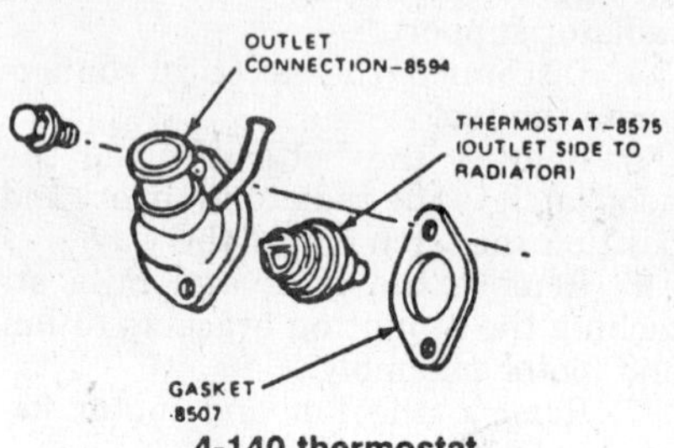

4-140 thermostat

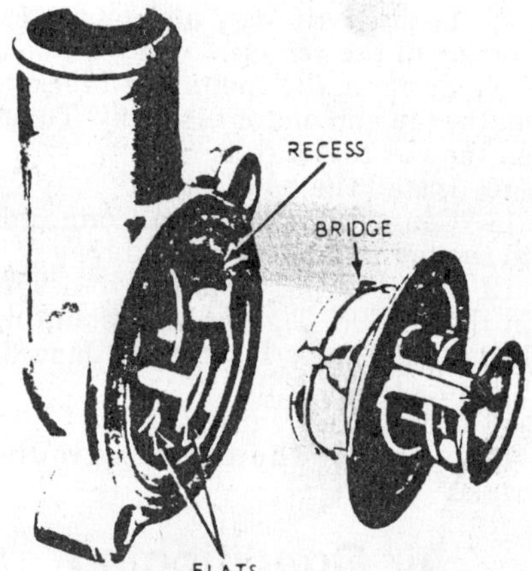

Installing thermostat—typical

4. Clean the mating surfaces of the outlet elbow and the engine to remove all old gasket material and sealer. Coat the new gasket with water-resistant sealer. Install the thermostat in the block on 8-351W, then install the gasket. On all other engines, position the gasket on the engine, and install the thermostat in the coolant elbow. The thermostat must be rotated clockwise to lock it in position on all 8-255, 8-302 and 8-351W engines. On the 4-140, be sure the full width of the heater outlet tube is visible within the thermostat port.
5. Install the outlet elbow and retaining bolts on the engine. Torque the bolts to 12-15 ft.lb.
6. Refill the radiator. Run the engine at operating temperature and check for leaks. Recheck the coolant level.

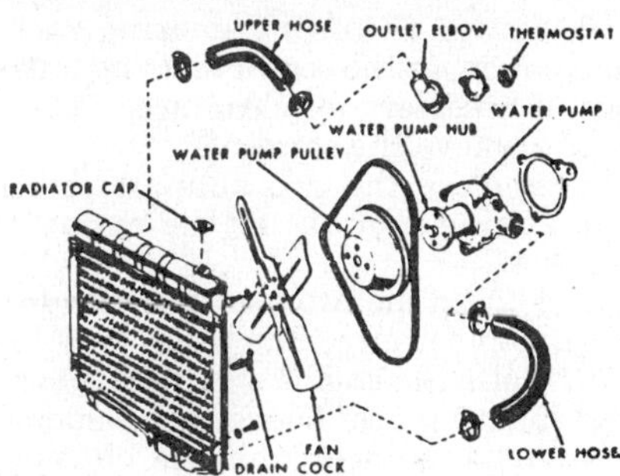

Typical cooling system and related parts—V8 with downflow radiator shown

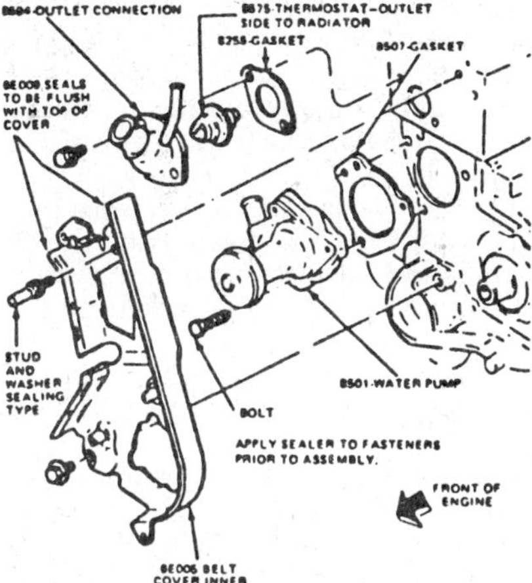

4-140 water pump, thermostat and inner timing bolt installation

Water Pump

REMOVAL & INSTALLATION

Gasoline Engines

1. Drain the cooling system.

CAUTION

When draining the coolant, keep in mind that cats and dogs are attracted by the ethylene glycol antifreeze, and are quite likely to drink any that is left in an uncovered container or in puddles on the ground. This will prove fatal in sufficient quantity. Always drain the coolant into a sealable container. Coolant should be reused unless it is contaminated or several years old.

2. Disconnect the negative battery cable.
3. On cars with power steering, remove the drive belt.
4. If the vehicle is equipped with air conditioning, remove the idler pulley bracket and air conditioner drive belt.
5. On engines with a Thermactor®, remove the belt.
6. Disconnect the lower radiator hose and heater hose from the water pump.
7. On cars equipped with a fan shroud, remove the retaining screws and position the shroud rearward.
8. Remove the fan, fan clutch and spacer from the engine, and if the car is equipped with an electric motor driven fan, remove the fan as an assembly for working clearance.
9. On the 4-140, remove the cam belt outer cover.
10. On cars equipped with a water pump mounted alternator, loosen the alternator mounting bolts, remove the alternator belt and remove the alternator adjusting arm bracket from the water pump. If interference is encountered, remove the air pump pulley and pivot bolts. Remove the air pump adjusting bracket. Swing the upper bracket aside. Detach the air conditioner compressor and lay it aside. Do not disconnect any of the A/C lines. Remove any accessory mounting brackets from the water pump.
11. Loosen the by-pass hose at the water pump, if so equipped.
12. Remove the water pump retaining screws and remove the pump from the engine.
13. Clean any gasket material from the pump mounting surface. On engines equipped with a water pump backing plate, remove the plate, clean the gasket surfaces, install a new gasket and plate on the water pump.
14. Remove the heater hose fitting from the old pump and install it on the new pump.
15. Coat both sides of the new gasket with a water-resistant sealer, then install the pump reversing the procedure.

2,443cc Diesel Engine

1. Drain the cooling system.

CAUTION

When draining the coolant, keep in mind that cats and dogs are attracted by the ethylene glycol antifreeze, and are quite likely to drink any that is left in an uncovered container or in puddles on the ground. This will prove fatal in sufficient quantity. Always drain the coolant into a sealable container. Coolant should be reused unless it is contaminated or several years old.

2. Loosen and remove the accessory drive belts.
3. Remove the fan and motor assembly.
4. Remove the water pump pulley.
5. Disconnect the heater hose from the thermostat housing.
6. Remove the camshaft drive belt cover.
7. Remove the three bolts attaching the water pump to the crankcase and remove the water pump.

NOTE: Do not loosen cam belt.

8. Clean the gasket mating surfaces of the water pump and crankcase.
9. Install the water pump with a new gasket, on the crankcase and tighten the bolts to 14-17 ft.lb.
10. Install the camshaft drive belt cover and tighten the bolts to 6-7 ft.lb.
11. Connect the heater hose to the thermostat housing.
12. Install the water pump pulley and the tighten bolts to 6-7 ft.lb.
13. Install the fan and motor assembly.
14. Install and adjust the accessory drive belts.

ENGINE LUBRICATION

Oil Pan

REMOVAL & INSTALLATION

NOTE: Always raise and safely support the vehicle safely on jackstands. When raising the engine, place a piece of wood between the jack and jacking point, make sure the hood is opened and the fan blades do not touch the radiator or that radiator hoses or transmission lines are not stretched.

4-140 Engine

1. Disconnect the negative battery cable.
2. Drain the crankcase and cooling system.

CAUTION

When draining the coolant, keep in mind that cats and dogs are attracted by the ethylene glycol antifreeze, and are quite likely to drink any that is left in an uncovered container or in puddles on the ground. This will prove fatal in sufficient quantity. Always drain the coolant into a sealable container. Coolant should be reused unless it is contaminated or several years old.

3. Remove the right and left engine support bolts and nuts or throughbolts. Disconnect the hydraulic damper if so equipped. Disconnect the hydraulic damper if so equipped. Disconnect the upper and lower radiator hoses.
4. Using a jack, raise the engine as far as it will go. Place blocks of wood between the mounts and the chassis brackets. Remove the jack.
5. Remove the steering gear retaining nuts and bolts. Remove the bolt retaining the steering flex coupling to the steering gear. Position the steering gear forward and down.
6. Remove the shake brace and starter.

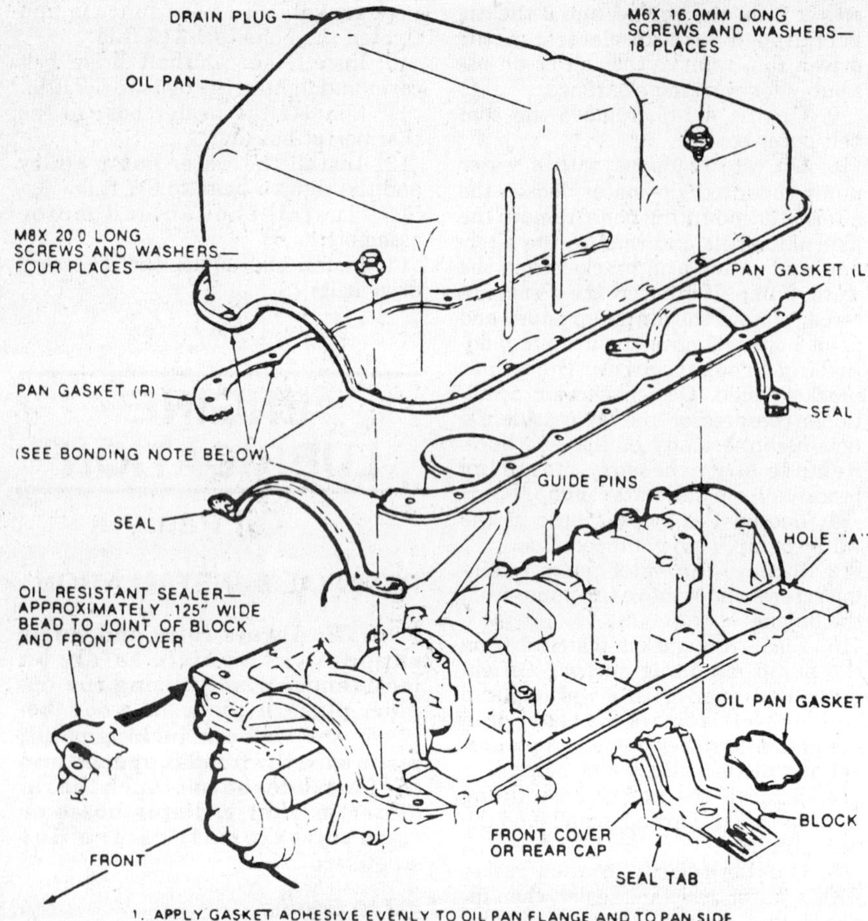

4-140 oil pan bolt installation

7. Remove the engine rear support-to-crossmember nuts.
8. Position a jack under the transmission and take up its weight.
9. Remove the oil pan retaining bolts. Remove the oil pan. It may be necessary to turn the crankshaft when removing the pan to avoid interference.
10. Position the new oil pan gasket and end seal on the cylinder block with gasket cement.
11. Position the oil pan on the cylinder block and install its retaining bolts.
12. Lower the jack under the transmission and install the crossmember nuts.
13. Replace the oil filter.
14. Position the flex coupling on the steering gear and install the retaining bolt.
15. Install the steering gear.
16. Install the shake brace. Install the starter.
17. Raise the engine enough to remove the wood blocks. Lower the engine and remove the jack. Install the engine support bolts and nuts. Connect the radiator hoses.
18. Lower the vehicle and fill the crankcase with oil and the cooling system with coolant.
19. Connect the battery.
20. Start the engine and check for leaks.

6-200

1. Disconnect the two oil cooler lines at the radiator.
2. Remove the two radiator top support bolts. Remove or position the fan shroud back over the fan.
3. Remove the oil level dipstick. Drain the crankcase.
4. Remove the four bolts and nuts attaching the sway bar to the chassis and allow the sway bar to hang down.
5. Remove the K-brace.
6. Lower the front steering rack and pinion, or the center link and linkage, if necessary for clearance.
7. Remove the starter.
8. Remove the two nuts attaching the engine mounts to the support brackets.
9. Loosen the two rear insulator-to-crossmember attaching bolts.
10. Raise the engine and place a 1¼" (3.175mm) spacer between the engine support insulator and the chassis brackets.
11. Position a jack under the transmission and raise it slightly.
12. Remove the oil pan attaching bolts and lower pan to the crossmember. Position the transmission cooler lines out of the way and remove the oil pan, rotating the crankshaft if required.
13. The oil pan has a two piece gasket. Coat the block surface and the oil pan gasket surfaces with oil resistant sealer, and position the gaskets on the cylinder block.
14. Position the oil pan seals in the cylinder front cover and rear bearing cap.
15. Insert the gasket tabs under the front and rear seals.
16. Position the oil pan on the cylinder block and install the attaching bolts.
17. Connect the transmission cooler lines.
18. Lower the jack from under transmission.
19. Raise the engine to remove the spacers and lower the engine on the chassis.
20. Tighten the two nuts attaching the rear support insulator to the crossmember.
21. Install the two engine support-to-chassis through-bolts and nuts.
22. Install the starter motor and the sway bar.
23. Install the K-brace, and fill the crankcase with oil.
24. Connect the oil cooler lines to the radiator and install the upper radiator support.
25. Lower the vehicle, start the engine and check for leaks.

6-232 Engine

1. Remove the air cleaner assembly including the air intake duct. Drain the cooling system.

CAUTION

When draining the coolant, keep in mind that cats and dogs are attracted by the ethylene glycol antifreeze, and are quite likely to drink any that is left in an uncovered container or in puddles on the ground. This will prove fatal in sufficient quantity. Always drain the coolant into a sealable container. Coolant should be reused unless it is contaminated or several years old.

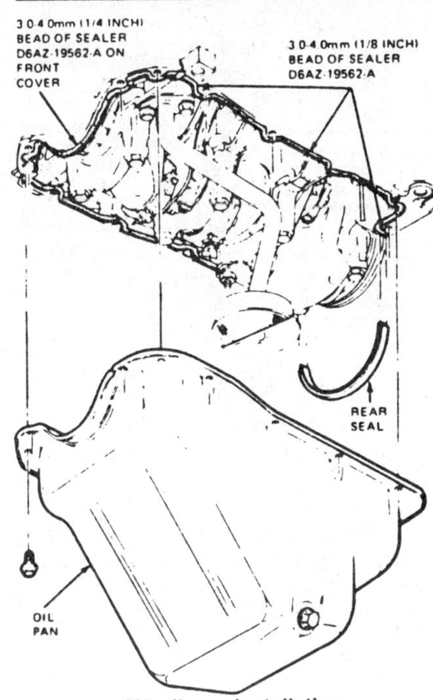

V6 oil pan installation

2. Remove the fan shroud attaching bolts and position the shroud back over the fan.
3. Remove the oil level dipstick.
4. Remove the screws attaching the vacuum solenoids to the dash panel. Lay the solenoids on the engine without disconnecting the vacuum hoses or electrical connectors.
5. Remove the exhaust manifold to exhaust pipe attaching nuts. Disconnect the radiator hoses from the radiator.
6. Drain the crankcase.
7. Remove the oil filter.
8. Remove the bolts attaching the shift linkage bracket to the transmission bell housing. Remove the starter motor for more clearance if necessary.
9. Disconnect the transmission cooler lines at the radiator. Remove power steering hose retaining clamp from frame.
10. Remove the converter cover.
11. On models equipped with rack and pinion steering, proceed with the following steps.
   a. Remove the engine damper-to-No. 2 crossmember bracket attaching bolt. The damper must be disconnected from the crossmember.
   b. Disconnect the steering flex coupling. Remove the two bolts attaching the steering gear to the main crossmember and let the steering gear rest on the frame away from the oil pan.
12. Remove the nut and washer assembly attaching the front engine insulator to the chassis.
13. Raise the engine 2-3" (51-76mm) or higher on some models and insert wood blocks between the engine mounts and the vehicle frame.

NOTE: Watch the clearance between the transmission dipstick tube and the Thermactor® downstream air tube. If the tubes contact before adequate pan-to-crossmember clearance is provided, lower the engine and remove the transmission dipstick tube and the downstream air tube.

14. Remove the oil pan attaching bolts. Work the oil pan loose and remove it.
15. On models with limited clearance, lower the oil pan onto the crossmember. Remove the oil pickup tube attaching nut. Lower the pickup tube/screen assembly into the pan and remove the oil pan through the front of the vehicle.
16. Remove the oil pan seal from the main bearing cap.
17. Clean the gasket surfaces on the cylinder block, oil pan and oil pick-up tube.
18. Apply an 8mm bead of RTV sealer to all matching surfaces of the oil pan and the engine front cover.
19. Install the oil pan.

NOTE: On models with limited clearance place the oil pick-up tube/screen assembly in the oil pan.

20. Remove the wood blocks between the engine mounts and the vehicle frame and lower the engine onto the mounts.
21. Install the nut and washer assembly attaching the front engine insulator to the chassis.
22. On models equipped with rack and pinion steering, proceed with the following steps.
   a. Connect the steering flex coupling.
   b. Install the two bolts attaching the steering gear to the main crossmember.
   c. Install the engine damper-to-No. 2 crossmember bracket attaching bolt. The damper must be connected to the crossmember.
23. Install the converter cover.
24. Connect the transmission cooler lines at the radiator.
25. Install the power steering hose retaining clamp to the frame.
26. Install the starter motor for more clearance if necessary.
27. Install the bolts attaching the shift linkage bracket to the transmission bell housing.
28. Install the oil filter.
29. Fill the crankcase.
30. Install the exhaust manifold to exhaust pipe attaching nuts.

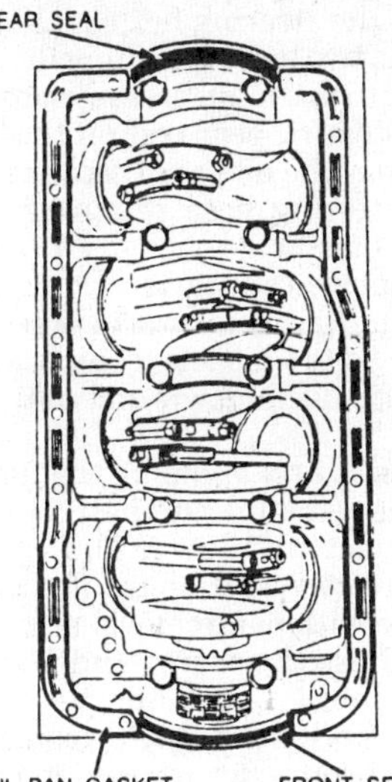

Typical oil pan gasket and seal installation

31. Connect the radiator hoses at the radiator.
32. Install the vacuum solenoids to the dash panel.
33. Install the oil level dipstick.
34. Install the fan shroud.
35. Install the air cleaner assembly including the air intake duct.
36. Fill the cooling system.
37. Start the engine and check the fluid levels in the transmission.
38. Check for engine oil, and transmission fluid leaks.

V8 Engines

WARNING: On vehicles equipped with a dual sump oil pan, both drain plugs must be removed to thoroughly drain the crankcase.

When raising the engine for oil pan removal clearance, drain the cooling system, disconnect the hoses, check the fan-to-radiator clearance when jacking. Remove the radiator if clearance is inadequate.

CAUTION

When draining the coolant, keep in mind that cats and dogs are attracted by the ethylene glycol antifreeze, and are quite likely to drink any that is left in an uncovered container or in puddles on the ground. This will prove fatal in sufficient quantity. Always drain the coolant into a sealable container. Coolant should be reused unless it is contaminated or several years old.

1. Remove the fan shroud attaching bolts, positioning the fan shroud back over the fan. Remove the dipstick and tube assembly. Disconnect the negative battery cable.
2. Drain the crankcase.
3. On rack and pinion models dis-

connect the steering flex coupling. Remove the two bolts attaching the steering gear to the main crossmember and let the steering gear rest on the frame away from the oil pan. Disconnect the power steering hose retaining clamp from the frame.

4. Remove the starter motor.

5. Remove the idler arm bracket retaining bolts (models equipped) and pull the linkage down and out of the way.

6. Disconnect and plug the fuel line from the gas tank at the fuel pump. Disconnect and lower the exhaust pipe/converter assemblies if they will interfere with pan removal and installation. Raise the engine and place two wood blocks between the engine mounts and the vehicle frame. Remove the converter inspection cover.

WARNING: On fuel injected models, depressurize the system prior to line disconnection.

7. Remove the rear K-brace (four bolts).

8. Remove the oil pan attaching bolts and lower the oil pan on the frame.

9. Remove the oil pump attaching bolts and the inset tube attaching nut from the No.3 main bearing cap stud and lower the oil pump into the oil pan.

10. Remove the oil pan, rotating the crankshaft as necessary to clear the counterweights.

11. Clean the gasket mounting surfaces thoroughly. Coat the surfaces on the block and pan with sealer. Position the pan side gaskets on the engine block. Install the front cover oil seal on the cover, with the tabs over the pan side gaskets. Install the rear main cap seal with the tabs over the pan side gaskets.

12. Position the oil pump and inlet tube into the oil pan. Slide the oil pan into position under the engine. With the oil pump intermediate shaft in position in the oil pump, position the oil pump on the cylinder block, and the inlet tube on the stud on the No. 3 main bearing cap attaching bolt. Install the attaching bolts and nut and tighten to specification.

Position the oil pan on the engine and install the attaching bolts. Tighten the bolts (working from the center toward the ends) 9-11 ft.lb. for $^5/_{16}''$ bolts and 7-9 ft.lb. for $^1/_4''$ bolts.

13. Position the steering gear on the main crossmember. Install the two attaching bolts and tighten them to specification. Connect the steering flex coupling.

14. Position the rear K-braces and install the four attaching bolts.

15. Raise the engine and remove the wood blocks.

16. Lower the engine and install the engine mount attaching bolts. Tighten them to specification. Install the converter inspection cover.

17. Install the oil dipstick and tube assembly, and fill crankcase with the specified engine oil. Install the idler arm.

18. Connect the transmission oil cooler lines. Connect the battery cable.

19. Position the shroud on the radiator and install the two attaching bolts. Start the engine and check for leaks.

Diesel Engine

Believe it or not, the engine must be removed from the car and mounted on a work stand for oil pan removal. Once this is done, the oil pan simply unbolts from the crankcase.

When installing the pan, use a 6mm bead of RTV gasket material on the split lines between the front and rear covers and the crankcase. Install the pan within 15 minutes of applying the bead.

Position a new oil pan gasket in the crankcase and torque the oil pan bolts to 72-84 in.lb.

Oil Pump

REMOVAL & INSTALLATION

Except 6-232 and Diesel Engines

1. Remove the oil pan.
2. Remove the oil pump inlet tube and screen assembly.
3. Remove the oil pump attaching bolts and remove the oil pump gasket and the intermediate shaft.
4. Prime the oil pump by filling the inlet and outlet ports with engine oil and rotating the shaft of pump to distribute it.
5. Position the intermediate driveshaft into the distributor socket.

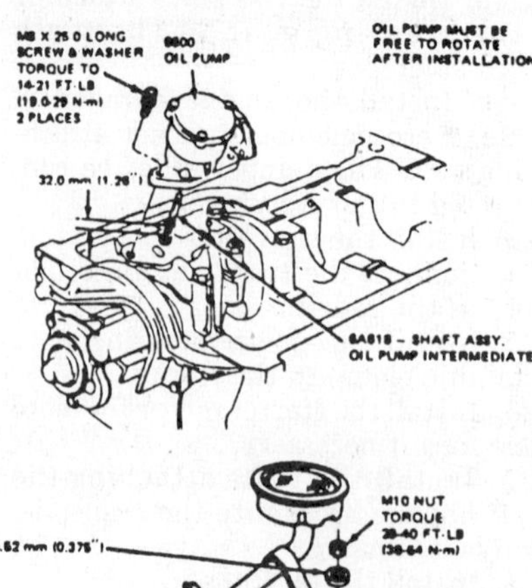

4-140 oil pump installation

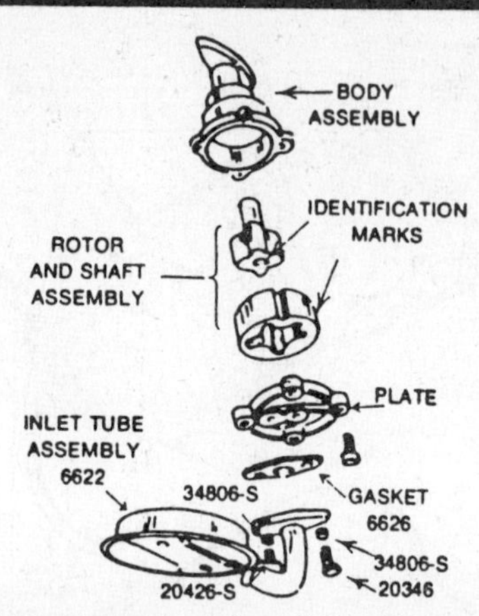

Oil pump used on 6 and 8 cylinder engines

6. Position a new gasket on the pump body and insert the intermediate driveshaft into the pump body.

7. Install the pump and intermediate shaft as an assembly.

WARNING: Do not force the pump if it does not seat readily. The driveshaft may be misaligned with the distributor shaft. To align, rotate the intermediate driveshaft into a new position.

8. Install and torque the oil pump attaching screws to:
- 4-140, 6-200 – 12-15 ft.lb.;
- 8-302 and 8-351W – 22-32 ft.lb.;
- 8-351C, 8-351M – 25-35 ft.lb.

9. Install the oil pan.

6-232 Engines

NOTE: The oil pump is mounted in the front cover assembly. Oil pan removal is necessary for pick-up tube/screen replacement or service.

1. Raise and safely support the vehicle on jackstands.
2. Remove the oil filter.
3. Remove the cover/filter mount assembly.
4. Lift the two pump gears from their mounting pocket in the front cover.
5. Clean all gasket mounting surfaces.
6. Inspect the mounting pocket for wear. If excessive wear is present, complete timing cover assembly replacement is necessary.
7. Inspect the cover/filter mounting gasket-to-timing cover surface for flatness. Place a straightedge across the flat and check the clearance with a feeler gauge. If the measured clearance exceeds 0.004" (0.102mm), replace the cover/filter mount.
8. Replace the pump gears if wear is excessive.
9. Remove the plug from the end of the pressure relief valve passage using

a small drill and slide hammer. Use caution when drilling.

10. Remove the spring and valve from the bore. Clean all dirt, gum and metal chips from the bore and valve. Inspect all parts for wear. Replace as necessary.

11. Install the valve and spring after lubricating them with engine oil. Install a new plug flush with the machined surfaces.

12. Install the pump gears and fill the pocket with petroleum jelly. Install the cover/filter mount using a new mounting gasket. Tighten the mounting bolts to 18-22 ft.lb. Install the oil filter, add necessary oil for correct level.

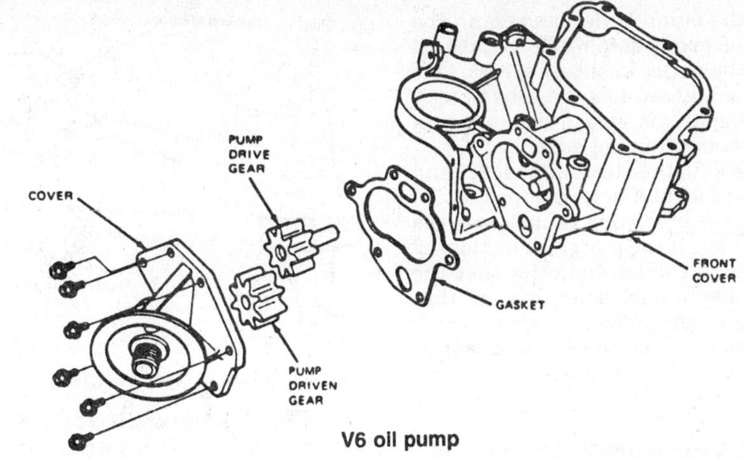

V6 oil pump

Diesel Engine

1. With the engine removed from vehicle and placed on an engine stand, remove the bolts attaching the oil pan to the crankcase.

2. Remove the two bolts attaching the oil pump pickup to the crankcase.

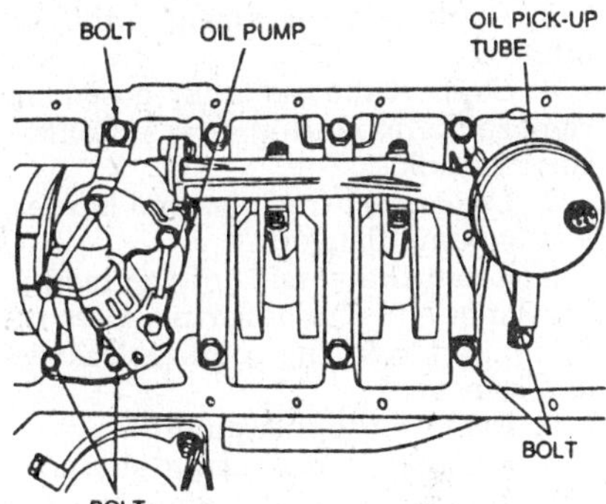

Diesel oil pump installation

3. Remove the three bolts attaching the oil pump to the crankcase, and remove the oil pump.

4. Remove the oil pump driveshaft, if necessary.

5. Install the oil pump driveshaft, if removed, making sure it is fully engaged with the intermediate shaft.

6. Install the oil pump on the crankcase, making sure the driveshaft is fully engaged in the oil pump. Tighten the oil pump and oil pick-up bolts to 16–17 ft.lb..

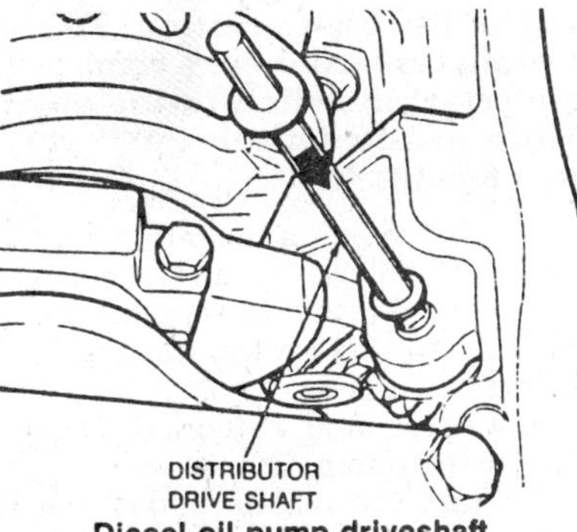

Diesel oil pump driveshaft

Oil Cooler

REMOVAL & INSTALLATION

Diesel Engine

1. Drain the oil from the crankcase.

2. Diconnect the oil lines at the cooler and cap the openings.

3. Remove the three bolts attaching the cooler to the mounting bracket.

4. Remove the cooler-to-radiator side support bolt.

5. Installation is the reverse of removal. The hoses and cooler tubes are color coded. Tighten the hose connections, using a back-up wrench, to 40 ft.lb.

6. Fill the crankcase with the proper amount of oil, run the engine and check for leaks.

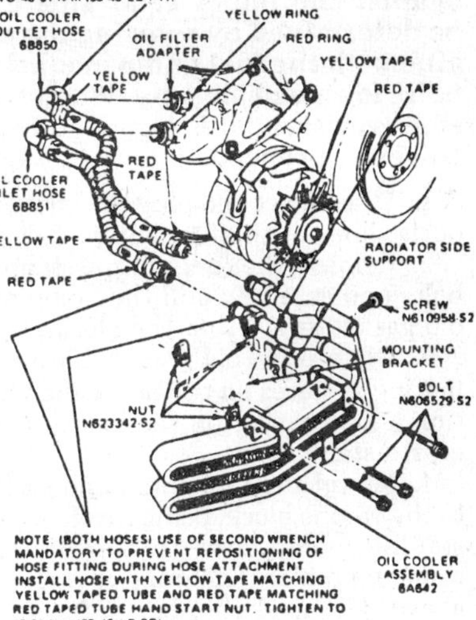

Diesel oil cooler installation

GASOLINE ENGINE FUEL SYSTEM

Mechanical Fuel Pump

A single-action, diaphragm-type, mechanical fuel pump, driven by the camshaft is found on all carbureted models.

The mechanical fuel pump is located at the lower left side of the engine block on the 6-200, at the lower left side of the cylinder front cover on V8 models and the right side front on the 6-232.

TESTING

No adjustments may be made to the fuel pump. Before removing and replacing the old fuel pump, the following test may be made while the pump is still installed on the engine.

1. If a fuel pressure gauge is available, connect the gauge to the engine and operate the engine until the pressure stops rising. Stop the engine and take the reading. If the reading is within the specifications given in the Tune-Up Specifications chart, the malfunctions is not in the fuel pump. Also check the pressure drop after the engine is stopped. A large pressure drop below the minimum specification indicates leaky valves. If the pump proves to be satisfactory, check the tank and inlet line.

2. If a fuel pressure gauge is not available, disconnect the fuel line at the pump outlet, place a vessel be-

neath the pump outlet, and crank the engine. A good pump will force the fuel out of the outlet in steady spurts. One pint in 25-30 seconds is a good flow. A worn diaphragm spring may not provide proper pumping action.

3. As a further test, disconnect and plug the fuel line from the tank at the pump, and hold your thumb over the pump inlet. If the pump is functioning properly, a suction indicates that the pump diaphragm is leaking, or that the diaphragm linkage is worn.

4. Check the crankcase for gasoline. A ruptured diaphragm may leak fuel into the engine.

REMOVAL & INSTALLATION

NOTE: Before removing the pump, rotate the engine so that the low point of the cam lobe is against the pump arm. This can be determined by rotating the engine with the fuel pump mounting bolts loosened slightly. When tension (resistance) is removed from the arm, proceed.

1. Disconnect and plug the inlet and outlet lines at the fuel pump.
2. Remove the fuel pump retaining bolts and carefully pull the pump and old gasket away from the block.
3. Discard the old gasket. Clean the mating surfaces on the block and position a new gasket on the block, using oil-resistant sealer.
4. Mount the fuel pump and gasket to the engine block, being careful to insert the pump lever (rocker arm) in the engine block, aligning it correctly above the camshaft lobe.

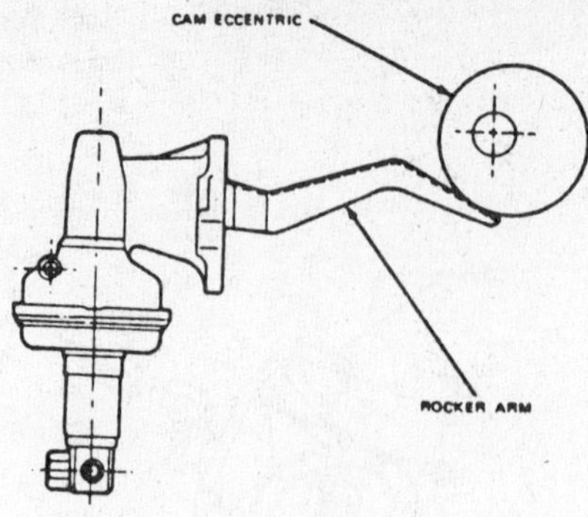

Typical mechanical fuel pump installation

NOTE: If resistance is felt while positioning the fuel pump on the block, the camshaft bole is probably on the high position. To ease installation, connect a remote engine starter switch to the engine and tap the switch until resistance fades.

5. While holding the pump securely against the block, install the retaining bolts. On 6-cylinder engines, torque the bolts to 12-15 ft.lb., and on V8, 20-24 ft.lb.
6. Unplug and reconnect the fuel line at the pump.
7. Start the engine and check for fuel leaks. Also check for oil leaks where the fuel pump attaches to the block.

Electric Fuel Pump

REMOVAL & INSTALLATION

All 1984 models equipped with a high output injected or turbocharged injected engine are equipped with two electric pumps. A low pressure pump is mounted in the tank and a high pressure pump is externally mounted.

All 1985-87 models are equipped with a single, in-tank, high pressure fuel pump.

CAUTION

Before servicing any part of the fuel injection it is necessary to depressurize the system. A special tool is available for testing and bleeding the system.

1984 Low Pressure In-Tank Pump

1. Disconnect the negative battery cable.
2. Depressurize the system and drain as much gas from the tank by pumping out through the filler neck.
3. Raise and support the rear end on jackstands.
4. Disconnect the fuel supply, return and vent lines at the right and left side of the frame.
5. Disconnect the wiring to the fuel pump.
6. Support the gas tank, loosen and remove the mounting straps. Remove the gas tank.
7. Disconnect the lines and harness at the pump flange.
8. Clean the outside of the mounting flange and retaining ring. Turn the fuel pump lock ring counterclockwise and remove.
9. Remove the fuel pump.
10. Clean the mounting surfaces. Put a light coat of grease on the mounting surfaces and on the new sealing ring. Install the new fuel pump.
11. Installation is in the reverse order of removal. If you have a single high pressure pump system, fill the tank with at least 10 gals. of gas. Turn the ignition key ON for three seconds. Repeat 6 or 7 times until the fuel system is pressurized. Check for any fitting leaks. Start the engine and check for leaks.

Fuel pump pressure and capacity test equipment

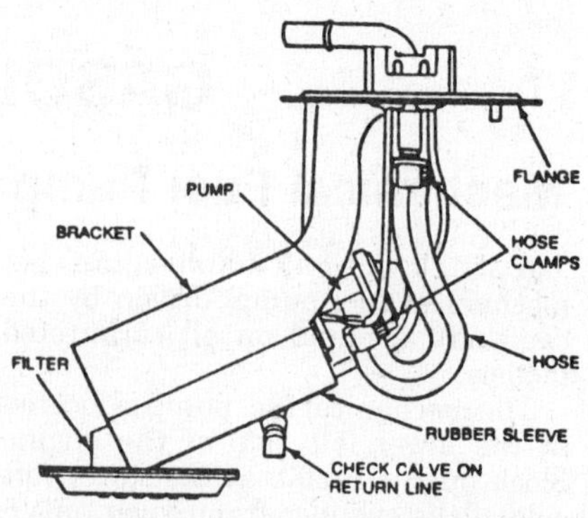

Low pressure in-tank electric fuel pump used with the 6-232 and 8-302 engines

1984 High Pressure External Pump

1. Disconnect the negative battery cable.
2. Depressurize the fuel system.
3. Raise and support the rear of the vehicle on jackstands.
4. Disconnect the inlet and outlet fuel lines.
5. Disconnect the electrical harness connection.

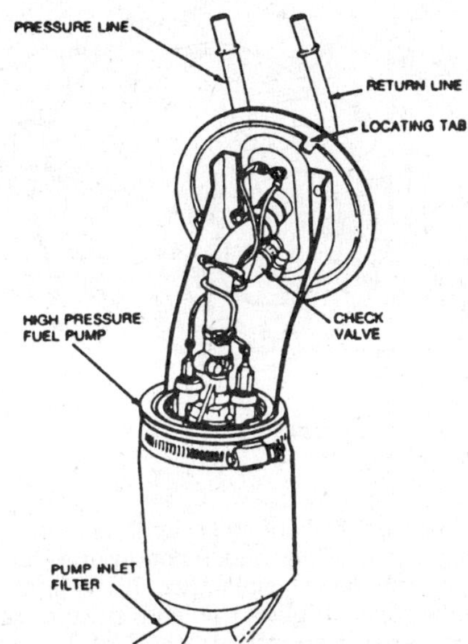

High pressure in-tank electric fuel pump

6. Bend down the retaining tab and remove the pump from the mounting bracket ring.
7. Install in reverse order, make sure the pump is indexed correctly in the mounting bracket insulator.

1985-87 High Pressure In-Tank Pump

1. Depressurize the system.
2. Disconnect the negative battery cable.
3. Drain as much gas from the tank by pumping out through the filler neck.
4. Raise and support the rear end on jackstands.
5. Disconnect the filler hose, fuel supply, return and vent lines at the right and left side of the frame.
6. Disconnect the wiring to the fuel pump.
7. Support the gas tank, loosen and remove the mounting straps. Remove the gas tank.
8. Disconnect the lines and harness at the pump flange.
9. Clean the outside of the mounting flange and retaining ring. Turn the fuel pump lock ring counterclockwise and remove.
10. Remove the fuel pump.
11. Clean the mounting surfaces. Put a light coat of grease on the mounting surfaces and on the new sealing ring. Install the new fuel pump.
12. Installation is in the reverse order of removal. If you have a single high pressure pump system, fill the tank with at least 10 gals. of gas. Turn the ignition key ON for three seconds. Repeat 6 or 7 times until the fuel system is pressurized. Check for any fitting leaks. Start the engine and check for leaks.

Quick-Connect Fuel Line Fittings

REMOVAL & INSTALLATION

NOTE: Quick-Connect (push) type fuel fittings are used on most models equipped with a pressurized fuel system. The fittings must be disconnected using proper procedures or the fitting may be damaged. Two types of retainers are used on the push connect fittings. Line sizes of 3/8" and 5/16" use a hairpin clip retainer, 1/4" line connectors use a duck bill clip retainer.

Hairpin Clip

1. Clean all dirt and/or grease from the fitting. Spread the two clip legs about 1/8" (3mm) each to disengage from the fitting and pull the clip outward from the fitting. Use finger pressure sure only, do not use any tools.
2. Grasp the fitting and hose assembly and pull away from the steel line. Twist the fitting and hose assembly slightly while pulling, if necessary, when a sticking condition exists.
3. Inspect the hairpin clip for damage, replace the clip if necessary. Reinstall the clip in position on the fitting.
4. Inspect the fitting and inside of

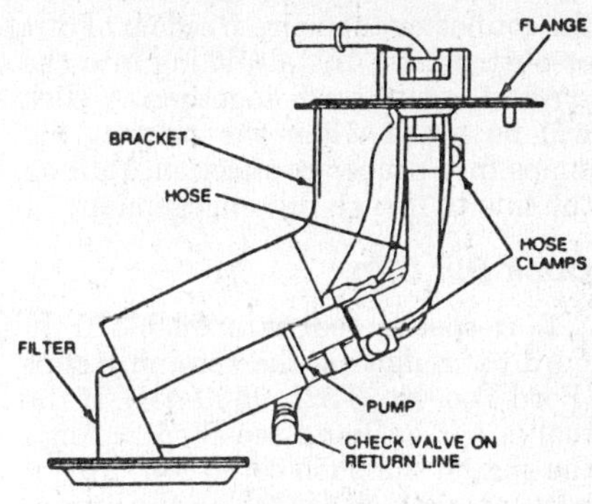

Low pressure in-tank electric fuel pump used with the 4-140 Turbo

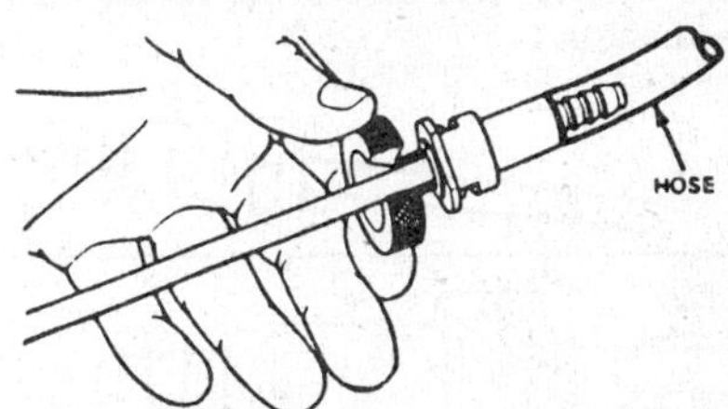

Connector removal using a push-connect disconnection tool

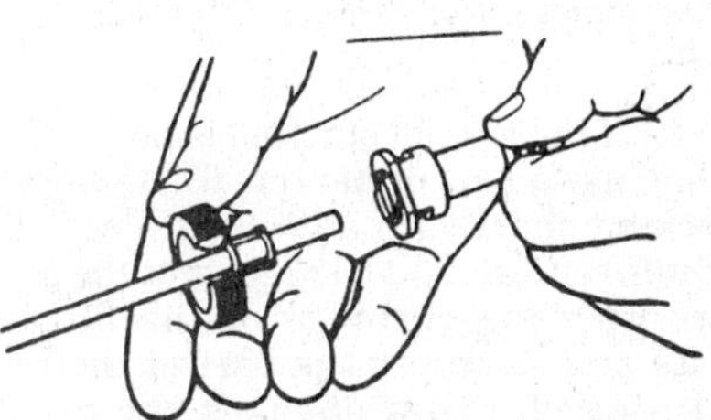

Pulling off the push-connect fitting

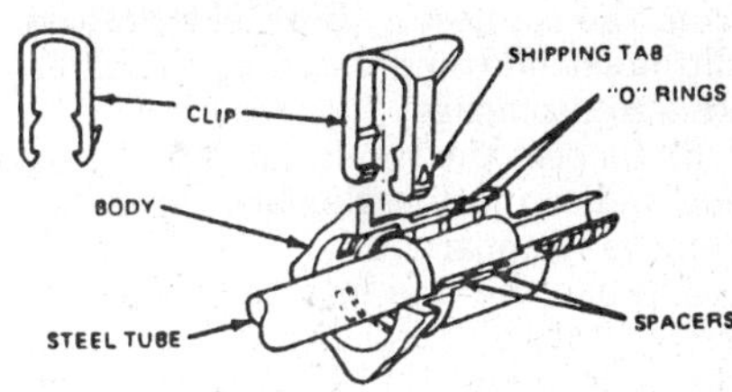

Pushconnect type fitting with hairpin clip

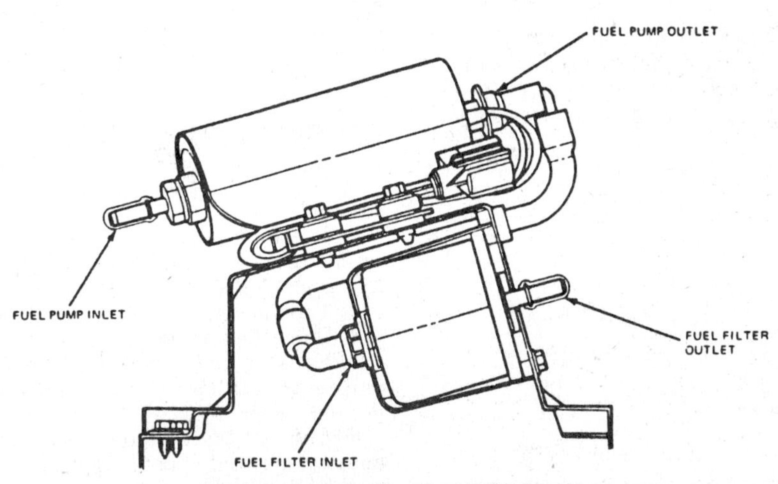

High pressure in-line electric fuel pump

the connector to insure freedom of dirt or obstruction. Install fitting into the connector and push together. A click will be heard when the hairpin clip snaps into proper connection. Pull on the line to insure full engagement.

Duck Bill Clip

1. A special tool is available from Ford for removing the retaining clips (Ford Tool No. T82L-9500-AH). If the tool is not on hand see Step 2. Align the slot on the push connector disconnect tool with either tab on the retaining clip. Insert the tool to disengage the clip. Pull the line from the connector.

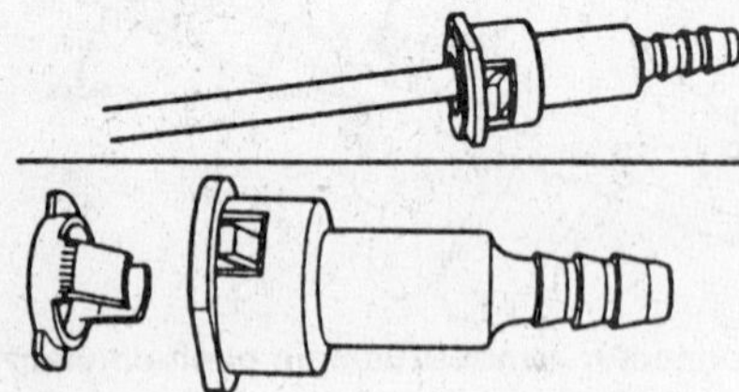

Push-connect type fitting with a duck-bill clip

2. If the special clip tool is not available, use a pair of narrow 6″ (152mm) locking pliers with a jaw width of 0.2″ (5mm) or less. Align the jaws of the pliers with the openings of the fitting case and compress the part of the retaining clip that engages the case. Compressing the retaining clip will release the fitting which may be pulled from the connector. Both sides of the clip must be compressed at the same time to disengage.

3. Inspect the retaining clip, fitting end and connector. Replace clip if any damage is apparent.

4. Push the line into the steel connector until a click is heard, indicating clip is in place. Pull on line to check engagement.

Electric Choke

All carbureted models use an electrically assisted choke to reduce exhaust emissions of carbon monoxide during warm-up. The system consists of a choke cap, a thermostatic spring, a bimetal sensing disc (switch) and a ceramic positive temperature coefficient (PTC) heater.

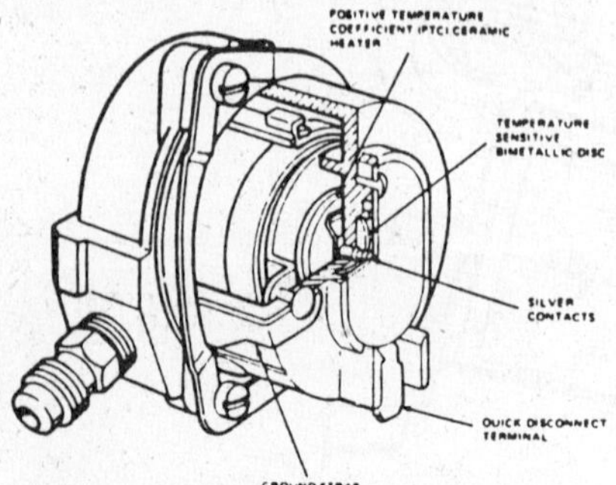

Electric choke components

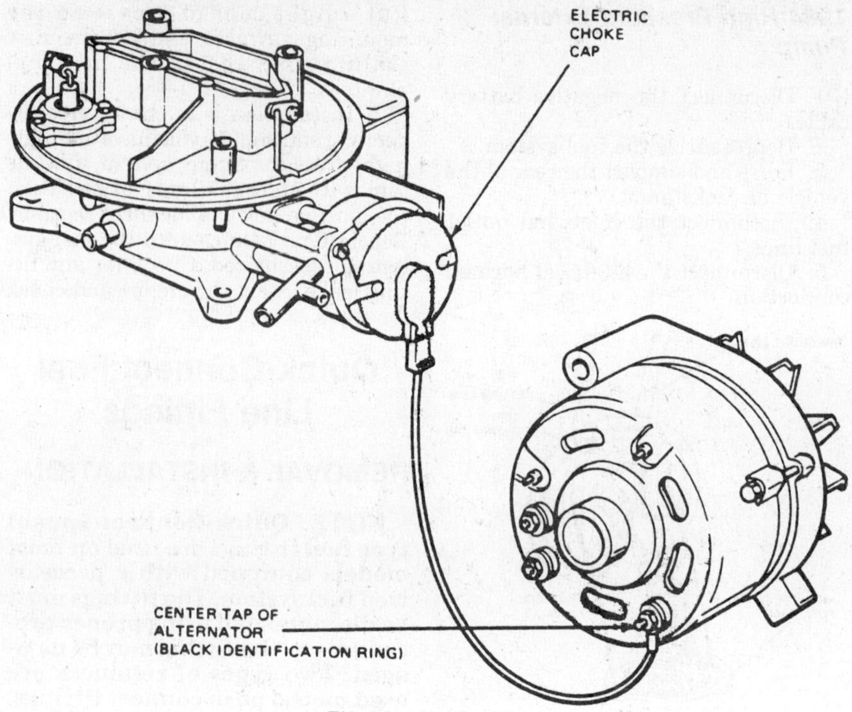

Electric choke wiring

The choke is powered from the center tap of the alternator, so that current is constantly applied to the temperature sensing disc. The system is grounded through the carburetor body. At temperatures below approximately 60°F (16°C), the switch is open and no current is supplied to the ceramic heater, thereby resulting in normal unassisted thermostatic spring choke action. When the temperature rises above 60°F (16°C), the temperature sensing disc closes and current is supplied to the heater, which in turn, acts on the thermostatic spring. Once the heater starts, it causes the thermostatic spring to pull the choke plate(s) open within 1½ minutes, which is sooner than it would open if non-assisted.

OPERATIONAL TEST

1. Detach the electrical lead from the choke cap.

2. Use a jumper lead to connect the terminal on the choke cap and the wire terminal, so that the electrical circuit is still completed.

3. Start the engine.

4. Hook up a test light between the connector on the choke lead and ground.

5. The test light should glow. If it does not, current is not being supplied to the electrically assisted choke.

6. Connect the test light between the terminal on the alternator and the terminal on the choke cap. If the light now glows, replace the lead, since it is not passing current to the choke assist.

CAUTION

Do not ground the terminal on the alternator while performing Step 6.

7. If the light still does not glow, the fault lies somewhere in the electrical system. Check the system out.

If the electrically assisted choke receives power but still does not appear to be functioning properly, reconnect

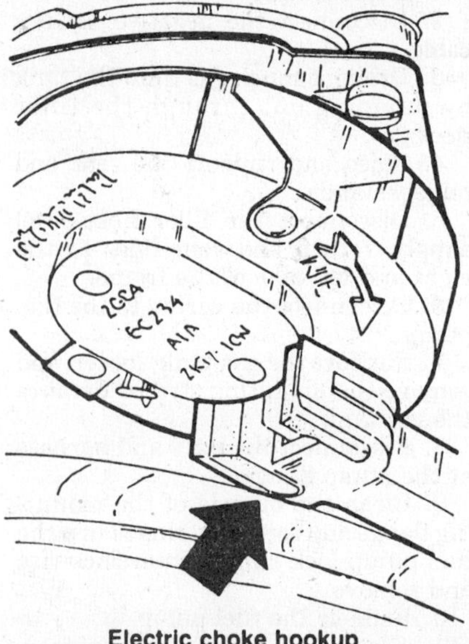

Electric choke hookup

the choke lead and proceed with the rest of the test.

8. Tape the bulb end of the thermometer to the metallic portion of the choke housing.

9. If the electrically assisted choke operates below 55°F (13°C), it is defective and must be replaced.

10. Allow the engine to warm up to 80-100°F (27-38°C); at these temperatures the choke should operate for about 1½ minutes.

11. If it does not operate for this length of time, check the bimetallic spring to see if it is connected to the tang on the choke lever.

12. If the spring is connected and the choke is not operating properly, replace the cap assembly.

Carburetors

THROTTLE SOLENOID (ANTI-DIESELING SOLENOID) TEST

1. Turn the ignition key on and open the throttle. The solenoid plunger should extend (solenoid energize).

2. Turn the ignition off. The plunger should retract, allowing the throttle to close.

WARNING: With the anti-dieseling de-energized, the carburetor idle speed adjusting screw must make contact with the throttle shaft to prevent the throttle plates from jamming in the throttle bore when the engine is turned off.

3. If the solenoid is functioning properly and the engine is still dieseling, check for one of the following:

a. High idle or engine shut off speed.

b. Engine timing not set to specification.

c. Binding throttle linkage.

d. Too low an octane fuel being used.

Correct any of these problems as necessary.

4. If the solenoid fails to function as outlined in Steps 1-2, disconnect the solenoid leads; the solenoid should de-energize. If it does not, it is jammed and must be replaced.

5. Connect the solenoid to a 12 V power source and to ground. Open the throttle so that the plunger can extend. If it does not, the solenoid is defective.

6. If the solenoid is functioning correctly and no other source of trouble can be found, the fault probably lies in the wiring between the solenoid and the ignition switch or in the ignition switch itself. Remember to reconnect the solenoid when finished testing.

CARBURETOR REMOVAL & INSTALLATION

1. Remove the air cleaner.

2. Disconnect the throttle cable or rod at the throttle lever. Disconnect the distributor vacuum line, exhaust gas recirculation line (1973 and later models), inline fuel filter, choke heat tube and the positive crankcase ventilation hose at the carburetor.

3. Disconnect the throttle solenoid (if so equipped) and electric choke assist at their connectors.

4. Remove the carburetor retaining nuts. Lift off the carburetor carefully, taking care not to spill any fuel. Remove the carburetor mounting gasket and discard it. Remove the carburetor mounting spacer, if so equipped, from the intake manifold.

5. Prior to installation, clean the gasket mounting surfaces of the intake manifold, spacer (if so equipped), and carburetor. When using a spacer, use two new gaskets, sandwiching the spacer between the gaskets. If a spacer is not used, only one new carburetor mounting gasket is required.

6. Place the new gasket(s) and spacer (if so equipped) on the carburetor mounting studs. Position the carburetor on top of the gasket and hand tighten the retaining nuts. Then tighten the nuts in a crisscross pattern to 10-15 ft.lb.

7. Connect the throttle linkage, the distributor vacuum line, exhaust gas recirculation line, inline fuel filter, choke heat tube, positive crankcase ventilation hose, throttle solenoid (if so equipped) and electric choke assist.

8. Perform the preliminary adjustments of idle speed and mixture settings.

OVERHAUL

All Types Except 2700 VV and 7200 VV

WARNING: The 2700 VV and 7200 VV are part of the extremely

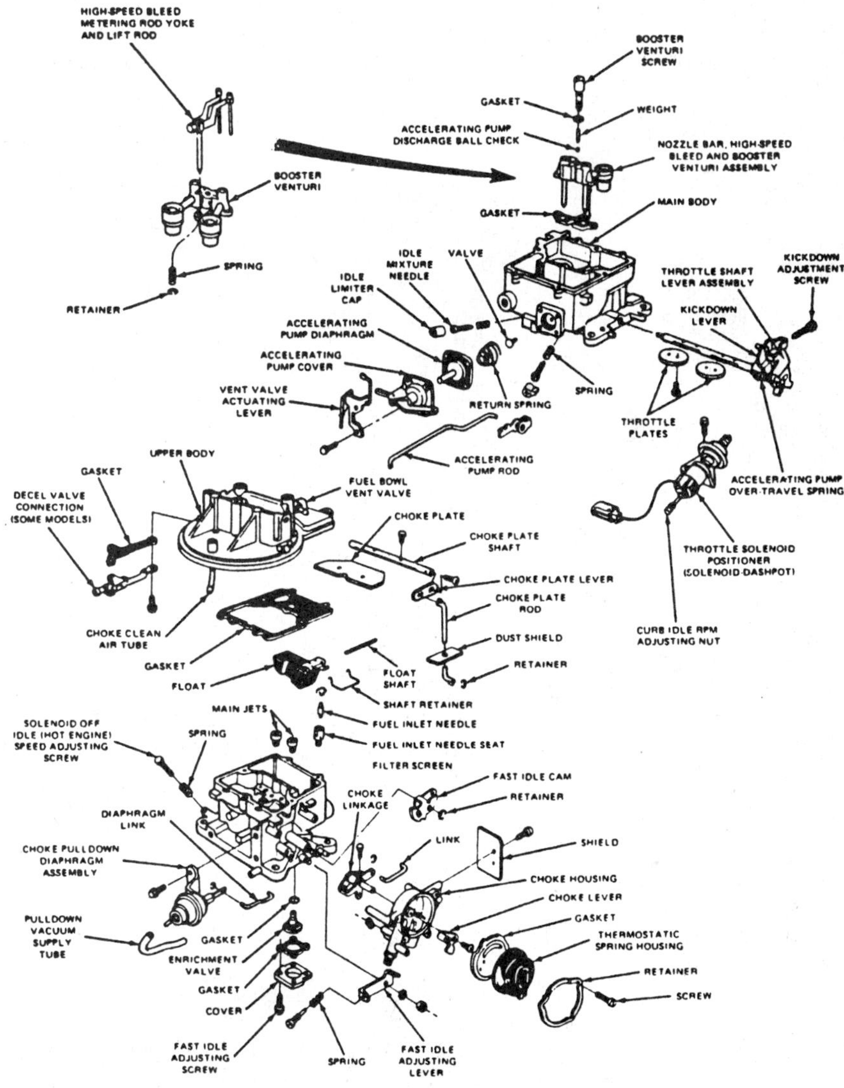

Exploded view—Motorcraft 2150-2V

sophisticated EEC system. Do not attempt to overhaul these units.

Efficient carburetion depends greatly on careful cleaning and inspection during overhaul, since dirt, gum, water, or varnish in or on the carburetor parts are often responsible for poor performance.

Overhaul your carburetor in a clean, dust free area. Carefully disassemble the carburetor, referring often to the exploded views. Keep all similar and look-alike parts segregated during the disassembly and cleaning to avoid accidental interchange during assembly. Make a note of all jet sizes.

When the carburetor is disassembled, wash all parts (except diaphragms, electric choke units, pump plunger, and any other plastic, leather, fiber, or rubber parts) in clean carburetor solvent. Do not leave parts in the solvent any longer than is necessary to sufficiently loosen the deposits. Excessive cleaning may remove the special finish from the float bowl and choke valve bodies, leaving these parts unfit for service. Rinse all parts in clean solvent and blow them dry with compressed air or allow them to air dry. Wipe clean all cork, plastic, leather, and fiber parts with a clean, lint-free cloth.

Blow out all passages and jets with compressed air and be sure that there are no restrictions or blockages. never use wire of similar tools to clean jets, fuel passages, or air bleeds. Clean all jets and valves separately to avoid accidental interchange.

Check all parts for wear or damage. If wear or damage is found, replace the defective parts. Especially check the following:

1. Check the float needle and seat for wear. If wear is found, replace the complete assembly.
2. Check the float hinge pin for wear and the float(s) for dents or distortion. Replace the float if fuel has leaked into it.
3. Check the throttle and choke shaft bores for wear or an out-of-round condition. Damage or wear to the throttle arm, shaft, or shaft bore will often require replacement of the throttle body. These parts require a close tolerance of fit; wear may allow air linkage, which could affect starting and idling.

NOTE: Throttle shafts and bushings are not included in overhaul kits. They can be purchased separately.

4. Inspect the idle mixture adjusting needles for burrs for grooves. Any such condition requires replacement of the needle, since you will not be able to obtain a satisfactory idle.
5. Test the accelerator pump check valves. They should pass air one way but on the other. Test for proper seating by blowing and sucking on the valve. Replace the valve is necessary. If the valve is satisfactory, wash the valve again to remove breath moisture.
6. Check the bowl cover for warped surfaces with a straightedge.
7. Closely inspect the valves and seats for wear and damage, replacing, as necessary.
8. After the carburetor is assembled, check the choke valve for freedom of operation.

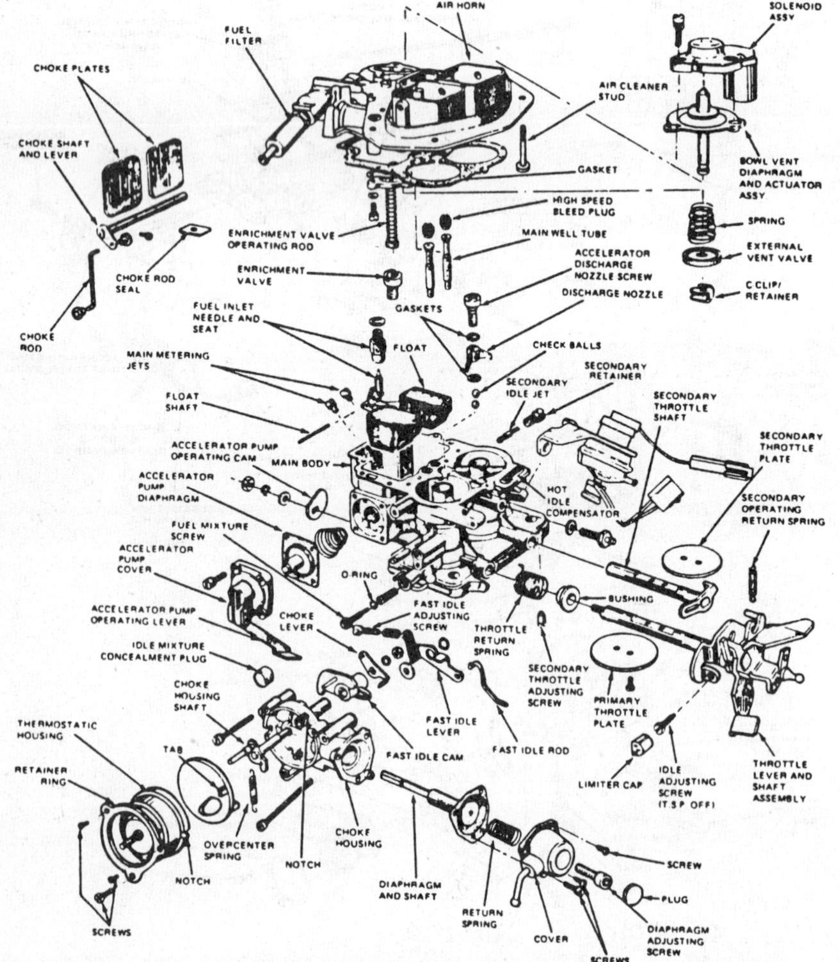

Motorcraft 5200 carburetor

Carburetor overhaul kits are recommended for each overhaul. These kits contain all gaskets and new parts to replace those which deteriorate most rapidly. Failure to replace all parts supplied with the kit (especially gaskets) can result in poor performance later.

Some carburetor manufacturers supply overhaul kits of three basic types: minor repair; major repair; and gasket kits. Basically, they contain the following:

Minor Repair Kits:
- All gasket
- Float needle valve
- Volume control screw
- All diaphragms
- Spring for the pump diaphragm

Major Repair Kits:
- All jets and gaskets
- All diaphragms
- Float needle valve
- Volume control screw
- Pump ball valve
- Float
- Complete intermediate rod
- Intermediate pump lever
- Some cover holddown screws and washers

Gasket Kits:
- All gaskets

After cleaning and checking all components, reassemble the carburetor, using new parts and referring to he exploded view. When reassembling, make sure that all screws and jets are tight in their seats, but do not overtighten as the tops will be distorted. Tighten all screws gradually, in rotation. Do not tighten needle valves into their seats; uneven jetting will result. Always use new gaskets. Be sure to adjust the float level when reassembling.

CARBURETOR ADJUSTMENTS

NOTE: Adjustments for the 2700VV and 7200VV, are covered following adjustments for all other carburetors.

AUTOMATIC CHOKE HOUSING ADJUSTMENT

All carburetors

By rotating the spring housing of the automatic choke, the reaction of the choke to engine temperature can be controlled. To adjust, remove the air cleaner assembly, loosen the thermostatic spring housing retaining screws and set the spring housing to the specified index mark. The marks are shown in the accompanying illustration. After adjusting the setting, tighten the retaining screws and replace the air cleaner assembly to the carburetor.

CHOKE PLATE PULLDOWN CLEARANCE ADJUSTMENT

Motorcraft 2150

1. Remove the air cleaner assembly.
2. Set the throttle on the stop step of the fast idle cam.
3. Noting the position of the choke housing cap, loosen the retaining screws and rotate the cap 90° in the rich (closing) direction.
4. Activate the pulldown motor by manually forcing the pulldown control diaphragm link in the direction of applied vacuum or by applying vacuum to the external vacuum tube.
5. Using a drill gauge of the specified diameter, measure the clearance between the choke plate and the center of the air horn wall nearest the fuel bowl.
6. To adjust, reset the diaphragm stop on the end of the choke pulldown diaphragm.
7. After adjusting, reset the choke housing cap to the specified notch. Check and reset fast idle speed, if necessary. Install the air cleaner.

Holley 1946

NOTE: On these carburetors, this adjustment is preset at the factory and protected by a tamper-proof plug.

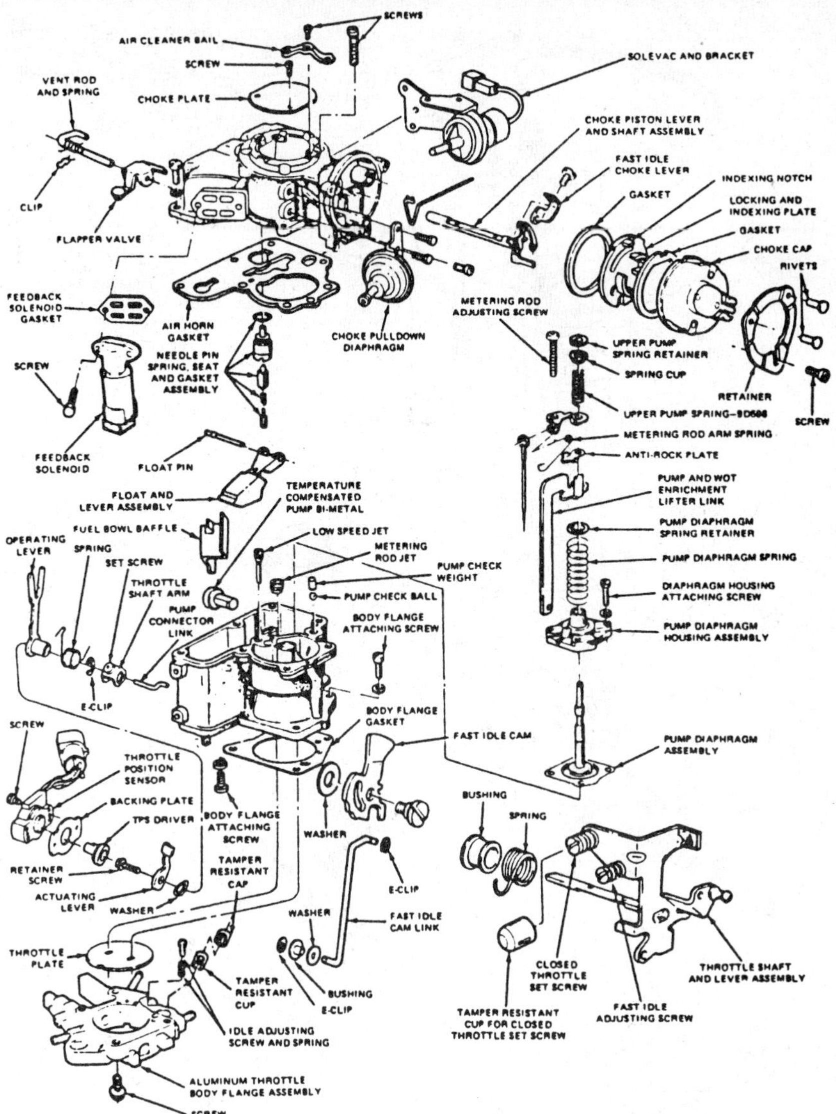

YFA feedback carburetor

Motorcraft 5200

1. Remove the choke thermostatic spring cover.
2. Pull the coolant cover and the thermostatic spring cover assembly, or electric assist assembly out of the way.
3. Set the fast idle cam on the second step.
4. Push the diaphragm stem against its top and insert the specified gauge between the wall and the lower edge of the choke plate.
5. Apply sufficient pressure against the upper edge of the choke plate to take up any slack in the linkage.
6. Turn the adjusting screw in or out of get the proper clearance.

Carter YFA

PISTON TYPE CHOKE

NOTE: This adjustment requires that the thermostatic spring housing and gasket (choke cap) are removed. Refer to the Choke Cap removal procedure below.

1. Remove the air cleaner assembly, then the choke cap.
2. Bend a 0.026" (0.66mm) diameter

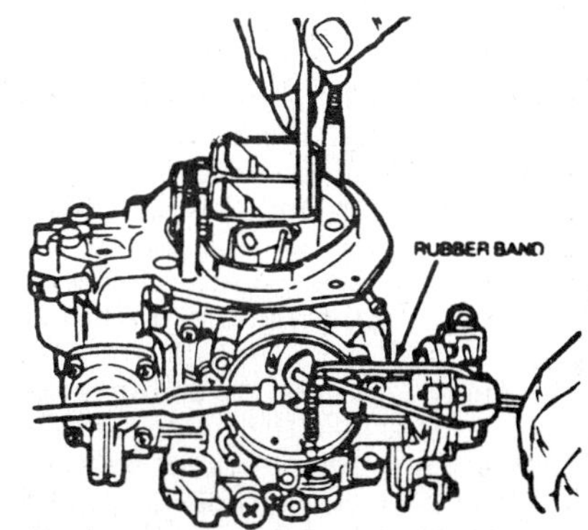

Motorcraft 5200 choke plate pulldown adjustment

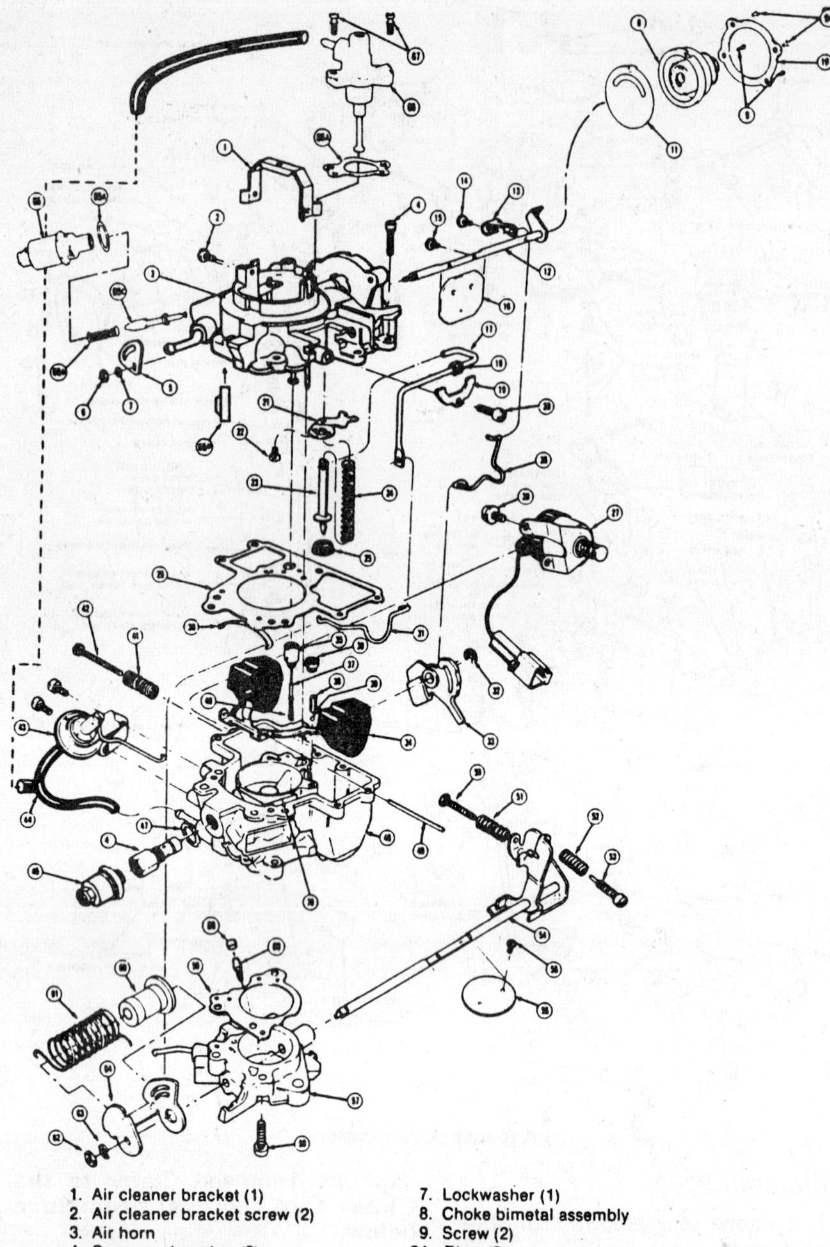

1. Air cleaner bracket (1)
2. Air cleaner bracket screw (2)
3. Air horn
4. Screw and washer (8)
5. Choke pulldown lever
6. Choke shaft nut
7. Lockwasher (1)
8. Choke bimetal assembly
9. Screw (2)
9A. Rivet (2)
10. Choke cover retainer
11. Choke thermostatic housing locating disc
12. Choke shaft and lever assembly
13. Choke control lever
14. Screw (1)
15. Screw (1)
16. Choke plate
17. Accelerator pump operating rod
18. Accelerator pump rod grommet
19. Rod retaining clamp
20. Screw (1)
21. Accelerator pump spring retaining plate
22. Screw (1)
23. Accelerator pump piston stem
24. Accelerator pump spring
25. Accelerator pump piston cup
26. Fast idle cam link
27. Anti-diesel solenoid
28. Screw (2)
29. Air horn gasket
30. Float-hinge retainer
31. Accelerator pump operating link
32. Retaining clip (fast idle cam)
33. Fast idle cam
34. Float assembly
35. Power valve body
36. Main metering jet
37. Power valve pin
38. Accelerator pump weight
39. Accelerator pump check ball
40. Power valve spring
41. Spring
42. Low idle (solenoid off) adjusting screw
43. Choke pulldown diaphragm assembly
44. Choke diaphragm vacuum hose
45. Fuel filter
46. Fuel inlet needle & seat assembly
47. Gasket
48. Main body assembly
49. Float hinge pin
50. Curb idle adjusting screw
51. Spring
52. Spring
53. Fast idle adjusting screw
54. Throttle shaft & Lever assembly
55. Screw (2)
56. Throttle plate
57. Throttle body assembly
58. Throttle body screw (3)
59. Throttle body gasket
60. Throttle return spring bushing
61. Throttle return spring
62. Nut
63. Lock washer
64. Throttle return spring bracket
65. Bowl vent solenoid
65A. Washer
65B. Spring
65C. Pintle
65D. Seal
66. Power valve piston assembly
66A. Gasket
67. Screw (2)
68. Idle mixture
69. Concealment plug idle mixture needle
70. Fuel bowl filler

Holley 1946 carburetor

wire gauge at a 90° angle approximately 1/8" (3mm) from one end. Insert the bent end of the gauge between the choke piston slot and the right hand slot in the choke housing. Rotate the choke piston lever counterclockwise until the gauge is shut in the piston slot.

3. Apply light pressure on the choke piston lever to hold the gauge in place. Then measure the clearance between the lower edge of the choke plate and the carburetor bore using a drill with the diameter equal to the specified pulldown clearance.

4. Bend the choke piston lever to obtain the proper clearance.

5. Install the choke cap.

DIAPHRAGM TYPE CHOKE

1. Activate the pulldown motor by applying an external vacuum source.

2. Close the choke plate as far as possible without forcing it.

3. Using a drill of the specified size, measure the clearance between the lower edge of the choke plate and the air horn wall.

4. If adjustment is necessary, bend the choke diaphragm link as required.

CHOKE CAP REMOVAL

NOTE: The automatic choke has two rivets and a screw, retaining the choke cap in place. There is a locking and indexing plate to prevent misadjustment.

1. Remove the air cleaner assembly from the carburetor.

2. Check the choke cap retaining ring rivets to determine if the mandrel is well below the rivet head. If the mandrel appears to be at or within the rivet head thickness, drive it down or out with an 1/16" (1.6mm) diameter punch.

3. Use a 1/8" diameter of No. 32 drill. for drilling the rivet heads. Drill into the rivet head until the rivet head comes loose from the rivet body.

4. After the rivet head is removed, drive the remaining portion of the rivet out of the hole with an 1/8" diameter punch.

NOTE: This procedure must be followed to retain the hole size.

5. Repeat Steps 1-4 for the remaining rivet.

6. Remove the screw in the conventional manner.

CHOKE CAP INSTALLATION

1. Install the choke cap gasket.
2. Install the locking and indexing plate.
3. Install the notched gasket.
4. Install the choke cap, making certain that the bimetal loop is positioned around the choke lever tang.
5. While holding the cap in place, actuate the choke plate to make certain the bimetal loop is properly engaged with the lever tang. Set the retaining clamp over the choke cap and orient the clamp to match the holes in the casting (the holes are not equally spaced). Make sure the retaining clamp is not upside down.
6. Place a rivet in the rivet gun and trigger it lightly to retain the rivet (1/8" diameter x 1/2" long x 1/4" diameter head).
7. Press the rivet fully into the casting after passing through the retaining clamp and pop the rivet (mandrel breaks off).
8. Repeat this step for the remaining rivet.
9. Install the screw in the conventional manner. Tighten to 17-20 in.lb.

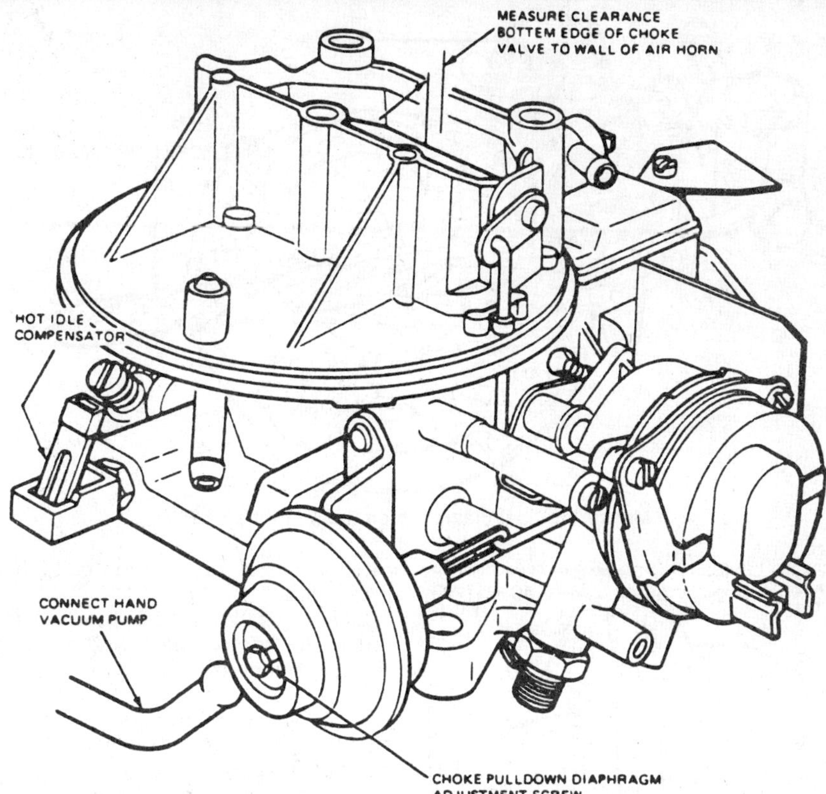

Adjusting the choke plate pulldown on the Motorcraft 2150

FLOAT LEVEL ADJUSTMENT

Autolite (Motorcraft) 2150

DRY ADJUSTMENT

This preliminary setting of the float level adjustment must be done with the carburetor removed from the engine.

1. Remove the air horn and see that the float is raised and the fuel inlet needle is seated. Check the distance between the top surface of the main body (with the gasket removed) and the top surface of the float. Depress the float tab to seat the fuel inlet needle. Take a measurement near the center of the float, at a point 1/8" (3mm) from the free end. If you are using a prefabricated float gauge, place the gauge in the corner of the enlarged end section of the fuel bowl. The gauge should touch the float near the end, but not on the end radius.

2. If necessary, bend the tab on the end of the float to bring the setting within the specified limits.

WET ADJUSTMENT

1. Bring the engine to its normal operating temperature, park the car on as nearly level a surface as possible, and stop the engine.
2. Remove the air cleaner assembly from the carburetor.
3. Remove the air horn retaining screws and the carburetor identification tag. Leave the air horn and gasket in position on the carburetor main body. Start the engine, let it idle for several minutes, rotate the air horn out of the way, and remove the gasket to provide access to the float assembly.
4. With the engine idling, use a standard depth scale to measure the vertical distance from the top machined surface of the carburetor main body to the level of the fuel in the fuel bowl. This measurement must be made at least 1/4" (6mm) away from any vertical surface in order to assure an accurate reading.
5. Stop the engine before making any adjustment to the float level. Adjustment is accomplished by bending the float tab (with contacts the fuel inlet valve) up or down as required to raise or lower the fuel level. After making an adjustment, start the engine, and allow it to idle for several minutes before repeating the fuel level check. Repeat as necessary until the proper fuel level is attained.
6. Reinstall the air horn with a new gasket and secure it with the screw. Include the installation of the identification tag in its proper location.
7. Check the idle speed, fuel mixture, and dashpot adjustments. Install the air cleaner assembly.

Motorcraft 5200

1. Remove the float bowl cover and hold it upside down.
2. With the float tang resting lightly on the spring loaded fuel inlet needle,

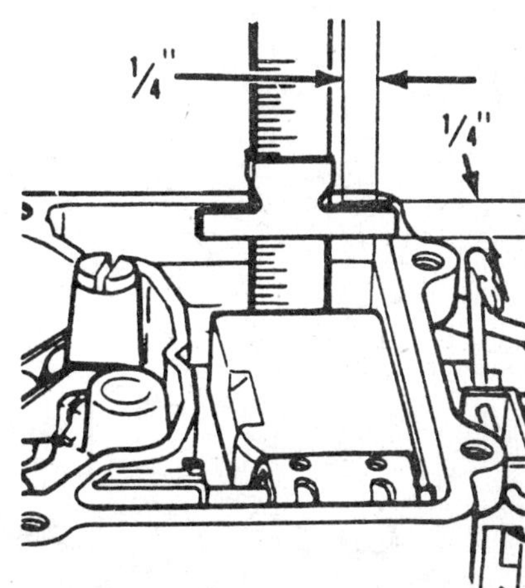

Motorcraft 2100, 2150 wet fuel level adjustment

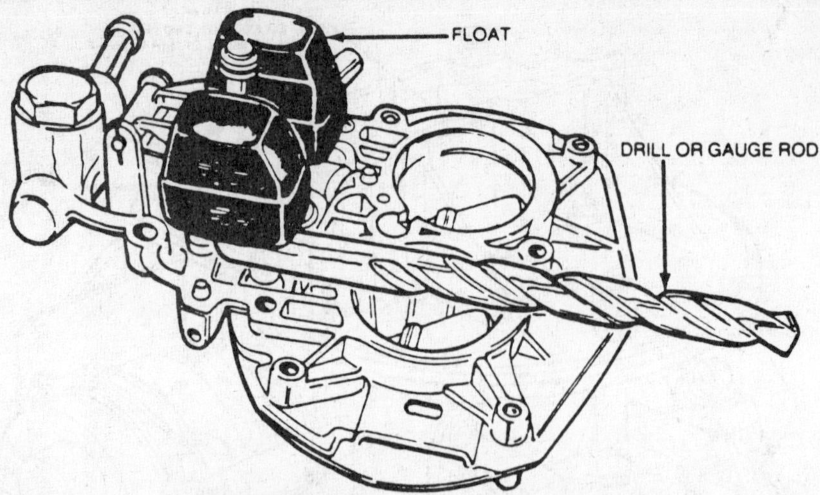

Measuring float clearance on the Motorcraft 5200

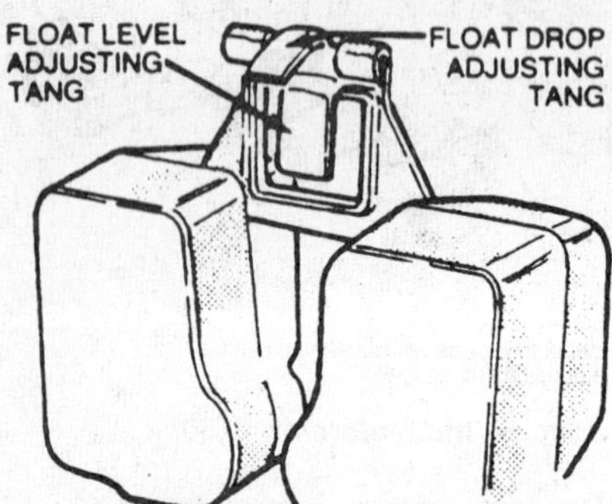

Motorcraft 5200 float adjustment

measure the clearance between the edge of the float and the bowl cover.

3. To adjust the float, bend the float tang. Make sure that both floats are adjusted equally.

Holley 1946

1. Remove the air horn and place a finger over the hinge pin retainer and catch the accelerator pump ball when it falls out.

2. Lay a ruler across the housing under the floats. The lowest point of the floats should be just touching the ruler for all except California models. For California models, the ruler should just contact the heel (raised step) of the float.

3. Bend the tang of the float to adjust.

Carter YFA

1. Invert the air horn assembly and check the clearance from the top of the float to the surface of the air horn with a T-scale. The air horn should be held at eye level when gauging and the float arm should be resting on the needle pin.

2. Do not exert pressure on the needle valve when measuring or adjusting the float. Bend the float arm as necessary to adjust the float level.

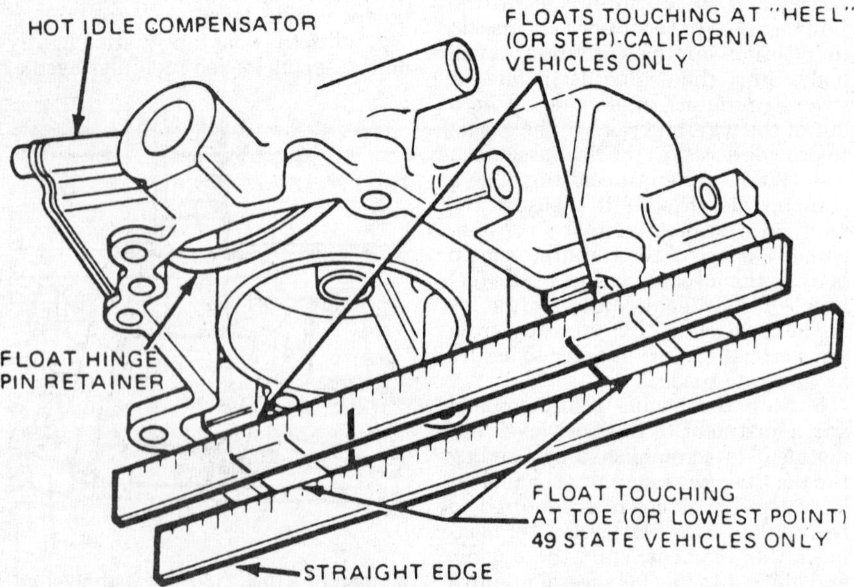

Holley 1946 float clearance adjustment

YFA float level adjustment

CAUTION

Do not bend the tab at the end of the float arm as it prevents the float from striking the bottom of the fuel bowl when empty and keeps the needle in place.

DECHOKE CLEARANCE ADJUSTMENT

Holley 1946

1. With the engine off, hold the throttle in the wide open position.

2. Insert the specified gauge between the upper edge of the choke plate and the air horn wall.

3. With a slight pressure against the choke shaft, a slight drag should be felt when the gauge is withdrawn.

4. To adjust, bend the unloader tab on the throttle lever.

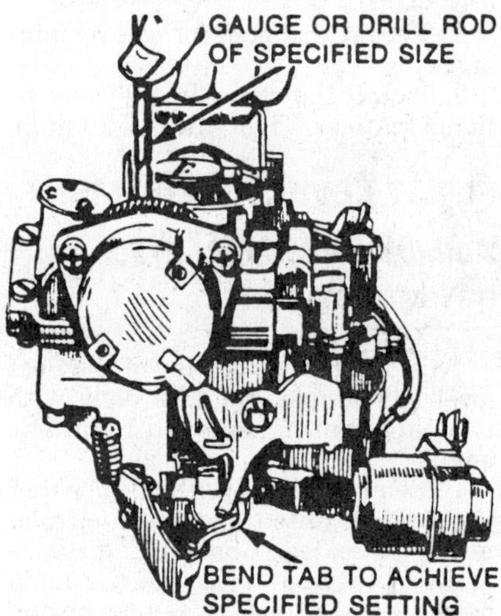

Holley 1946 dechoke adjustment

Motorcraft 5200

1. Hold the throttle wide open. Remove all slack from the choke linkage by applying pressure to the upper edge of the choke plate.

2. Measure the distance between

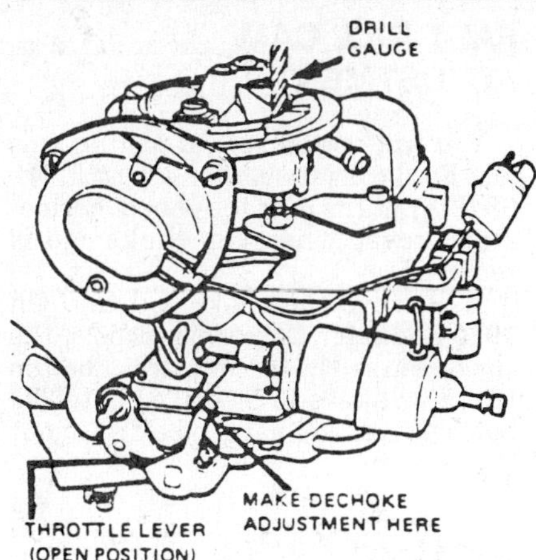

YFA dechoke adjustment

the lower edge of the choke plate and the air horn wall.

3. Adjust by bending the tab on the fast idle lever where it touches the cam.

Carter YFA

1. Remove the air cleaner assembly.
2. Hold the throttle plate fully open and close the choke plate as far as possible without forcing it. Use a drill of the proper diameter to check the clearance between the choke plate and air horn.
3. If the clearance is not within specification, adjust by bending the arm on the choke lever of the throttle lever. Bending the arm downward will decrease the clearance, and bending it upward will increase the clearance. Always recheck the clearance after making any adjustment.

ACCELERATOR PUMP STROKE ADJUSTMENT

Autolite (Motorcraft) 2150

In order to keep the exhaust emission level of the engine within the specified limits, the accelerating pump stroke has been preset at the factory. The additional holes are provided for differing engine-transmission-body applications only. The primary throttle shaft lever (overtravel lever) has four holes to control the pump stroke. The accelerating pump operating rod should be in the overtravel lever hole number listed in the Carburetor Specifications chart, and in the inboard hole (hole closest to the pump plunger) in the accelerating pump link. If the pump stroke has been changed from the specified settings, use the following procedure to correct the stroke.

1. Release the operating rod from the retaining clip by pressing the tab end of the clip toward the rod while pressing the rod away from the clip until it disengages.
2. Position the clip over the specified hole (see Carburetor Specifications chart) in the overtravel lever. Press the ends of the clip together and insert the operating rod through the clip and the overtravel lever. Release the clip to engage the rod.

ANTI-STALL DASHPOT ADJUSTMENT

All Carburetors

Having made sure that the engine idle speed and mixture are correct and that the engine is at normal operating temperature, loosen the anti-stall dashpot locking nut (see accompanying illustration). With the throttle held closed, depress the plunger with a screwdriver blade and measure the clearance between the throttle lever and the plunger tip. If the clearance is not as specified in the Carburetor Specifications chart, turn the dashpot until the proper clearance is obtained between the throttle lever and the plunger tip. After tightening the locking nut, recheck the adjustment.

FAST IDLE CAM INDEX SETTING

Motorcraft 5200

1. Insert a $^5\!/_{32}''$ drill between the lower edge of the choke plate and the air horn wall.
2. With the fast idle screw held on the second step of the fast idle cam, measure the clearance between the tang of the choke lever and the arm of the cam.
3. Bend the choke lever tang for adjustment.

Holley 1946

1. Position the fast idle adjusting screw on the second step of the fast idle cam.

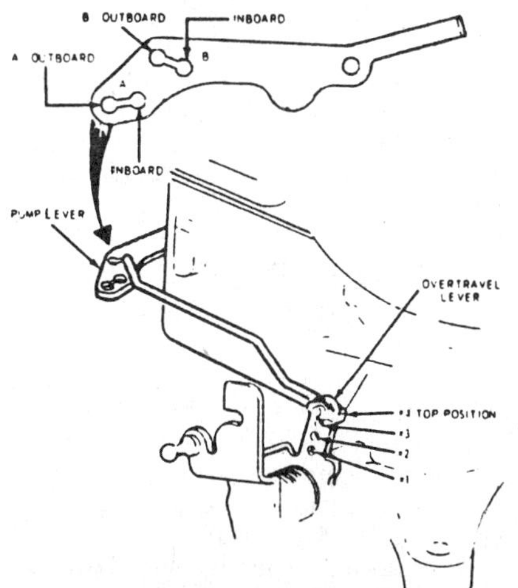

Accelerator pump stroke adjustment—Autolite (Motorcraft) 2100, 2150

2. Lightly move the choke plate towards the closed position.
3. Check the fast idle cam setting by placing the specified gauge between the upper edge of the choke plate and the air horn wall.
4. Bend the fast idle cam link to adjust.

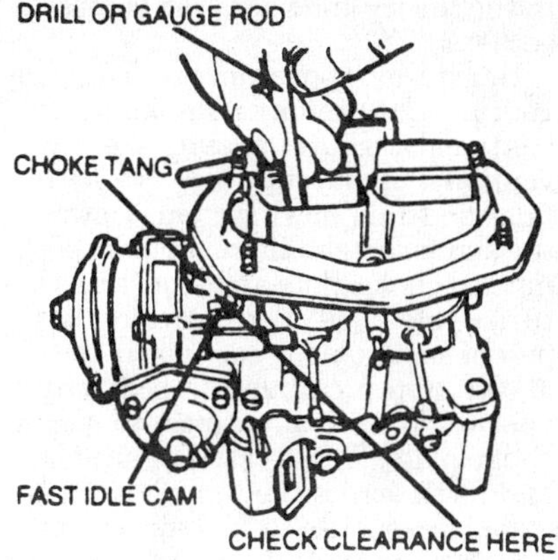

Motorcraft 5200 fast idle cam adjustment

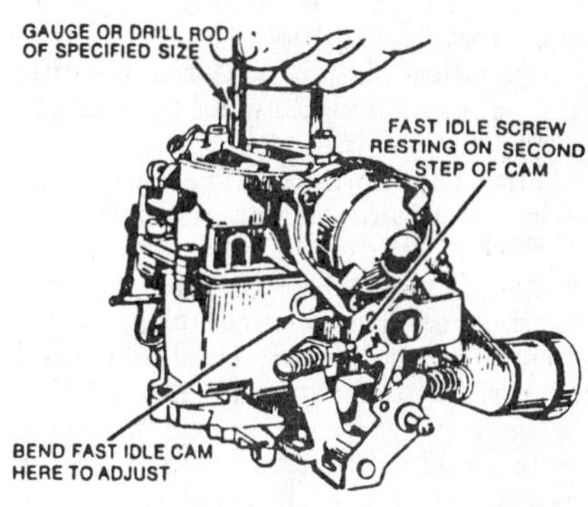

Holley 1946 fast idle cam position adjustment

Carter YFA

1. Put the fast idle screw on the second highest step of the fast idle cam against the shoulder of the high step.
2. Adjust by bending the choke plate connecting rod to obtain the specified clearance between the lower edge of the choke plate and the air horn wall.

THROTTLE AND DOWNSHIFT LINKAGE ADJUSTMENT

With Manual Transmission

Throttle linkage adjustments are not normally required, unless the carburetor or linkage have been removed from the car or otherwise disturbed. In all cases, the car is first brought to operating temperature, with the choke open the off the fast idle cam. The idle speed is then set to specifications.

Motorcraft 2700VV and 7200VV

DESIGN

Since the design of the 2700VV (variable venturi) carburetor differs considerably from the other carburetors in the Ford lineup, an explanation in the theory and operation is presented here.

In exterior appearance, the variable venturi carburetor is similar to conventional carburetor and, like a conventional carburetor, it uses a normal float and fuel bowl system. However, the similarity end there. In place of the normal choke plate and fixed area venturis, the 2700VV carburetor has a pair of small oblong castings in the top of the upper carburetor body where you would normally expect to see the choke plate. These castings slide back and forth across the top of the carburetor in response to fuel-air demands. Their movement is controlled by a spring-loaded diaphragm valve regulated by a vacuum signal taken below the venturis in the throttle bores. As the throttle is opened, the strength of the vacuum signal increases, opening the venturis and allowing more air to enter the carburetor.

Fuel is admitted into the venturi area by means of tapered metering rods that fit into the main jets. These rods are attached to the venturis, and, as the venturis open or close in response to air demand, the fuel needed to maintain the proper mixture increase or decreases as the metering rods slide in the jets. In comparison to a conventional carburetor with fixed venturis and a variable air supply, this system provides much more precise control of the fuel-air supply during all modes of operation. Because of the variable venturi principle, there are fewer fuel metering systems and fuel passages. The only auxiliary fuel metering systems required are an idle trim, accelerator pump (similar to a conventional carburetor), starting enrichment, and cold running enrichment.

NOTE: Adjustment, assembly and disassembly of this carburetor require special tools for some of the operations. These tools are available (see the Tools and Equipment Section). Do not attempt any operations on this carburetor without first checking to see if you need the special tools for that particular operation. The adjustment and repair procedures given here mention when and if you will need the special tools.

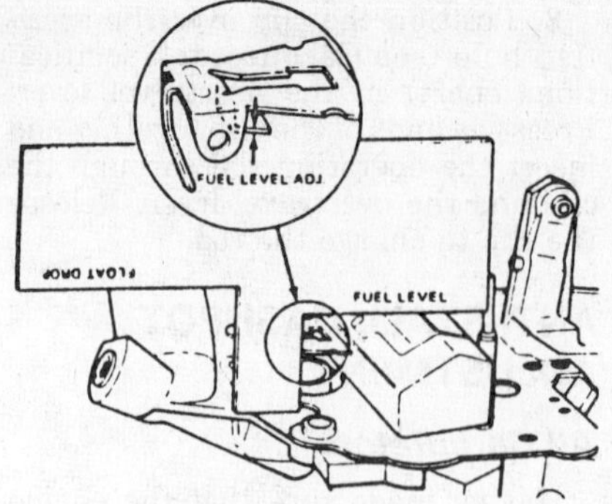

2700VV float adjustment

The Motorcraft model 7200 variable venturi (VV) carburetor shares most of its design features with the model 2700VV. The major difference between the two is that the 7200VV is designed to work with Ford's EEC (electronic engine control) feedback system. The feedback system precisely controls the air/fuel ration by varying signals to the feedback control monitor located on the carburetor, which opens or closes the metering valve in response. This expands or reduces the amount of control vacuum above the fuel bowl, leaning or richening the mixture accordingly.

FLOAT LEVEL ADJUSTMENT

1. Remove and invert the upper part of the carburetor, with the gasket in place.
2. Measure the vertical distance between the carburetor body, outside the gasket, and the bottom of the float.
3. To adjust, bend the float operating lever that contacts the needle valve. Make sure that the float remains parallel to the gasket surface.

FLOAT DROP ADJUSTMENT

1. Remove and hold upright the upper part of the carburetor.
2. Measure the vertical distance between the carburetor body, outside the gasket, and the bottom of the float.
3. Adjust by bending the stop tab on the float lever that contacts the hinge pin.

FAST IDLE SPEED ADJUSTMENT

1. With the engine warmed up and idling, place the fast idle lever on the step of the fast idle cam specified on the engine compartment sticker or in the specifications chart. Disconnect and plug the EGR vacuum line.
2. Make sure the high speed cam positioner lever is disengaged.
3. Turn the fast idle speed screw to adjust to the specified speed.

FAST IDLE CAM ADJUSTMENT

You will need a special tool for this job: Ford calls it a stator cap (#T77L-9848-A). It fits over the choke thermostatic lever when the choke cap is removed.

1. Remove the choke coil cap. On 1980 and later California models, the choke cap is riveted in place. The top rivets will have to be drilled out. The bottom rivet will have to be driven out from the rear. New rivets must be used upon installation.

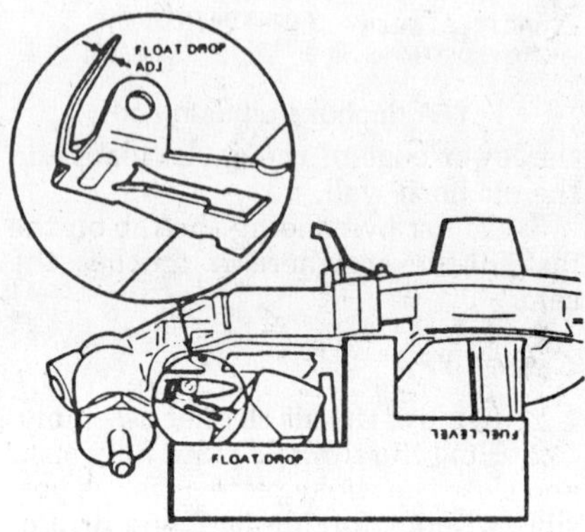

2700 VV float drop adjustment

2. Place the fast idle lever in the corner of the specified step of the fast idle cam (the highest step is first) with the high speed cam positioner retracted.
3. If the adjustment is being made with the carburetor removed, hold the throttle lightly close with a rubber band.
4. Turn the stator cap clockwise until the lever contacts the fast idle cam adjusting screw.
5. Turn the fast idle cam adjusting screw until the index mark on the cap lines up with the specified mark on the casting.
6. Remove the stator cap. Install the choke coil cap and set it to the specified housing mark.

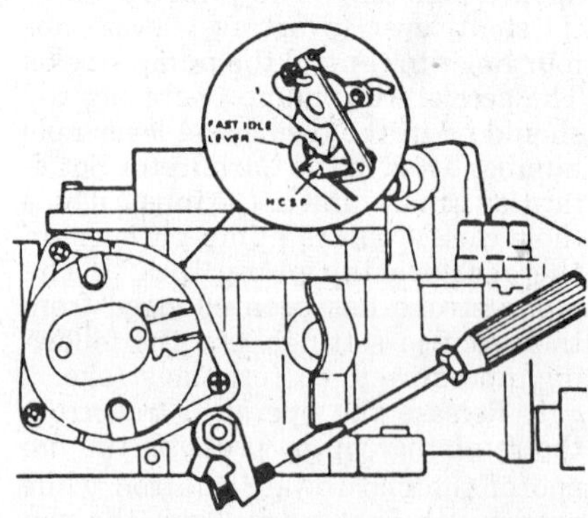

2700 VV fast idle speed adjustment

COLD ENRICHMENT METERING ROD ADJUSTMENT

A dial indicator and the stator cap are required for this adjustment.

1. Remove the choke coil cap. See Step 1 of the Fast idle Cam Adjustment.
2. Attach a weight to the choke coil mechanism to seat the cold enrichment rod.

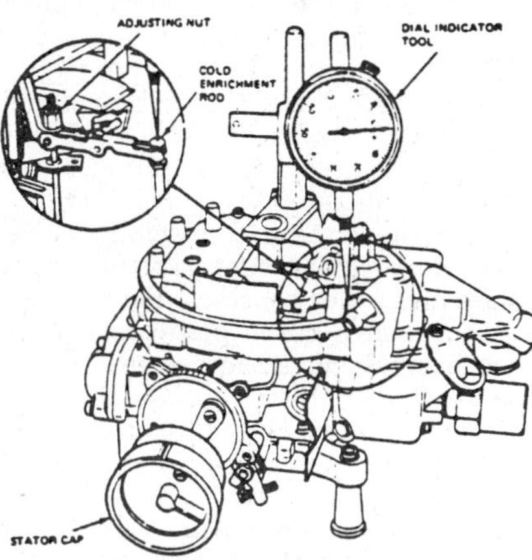

2700 VV cold enrichment metering rod adjustment

3. Install and zero a dial indicator with the tip of top of the enrichment rod. Raise and release the weight to verify zero on the dial indicator.
4. With the stator cap at the index position, the dial indicator should read the specified dimension. Turn the adjusting nut to correct it.
5. Install the choke cap at the correct setting.

CONTROL VACUUM ADJUSTMENT

1980-82

This adjustment is necessary only on non-feedback systems.

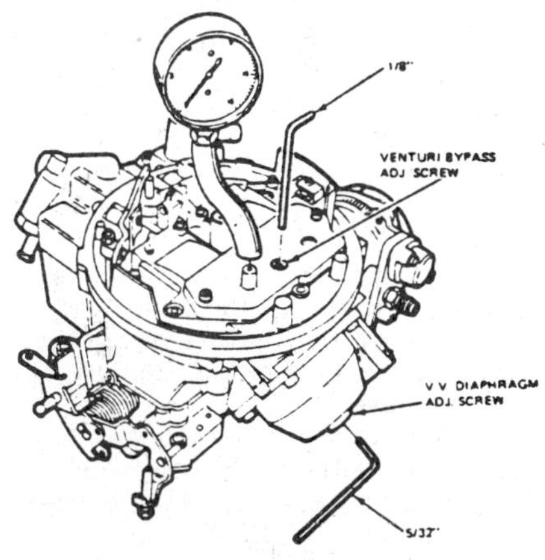

2700 VV control vacuum ajustment

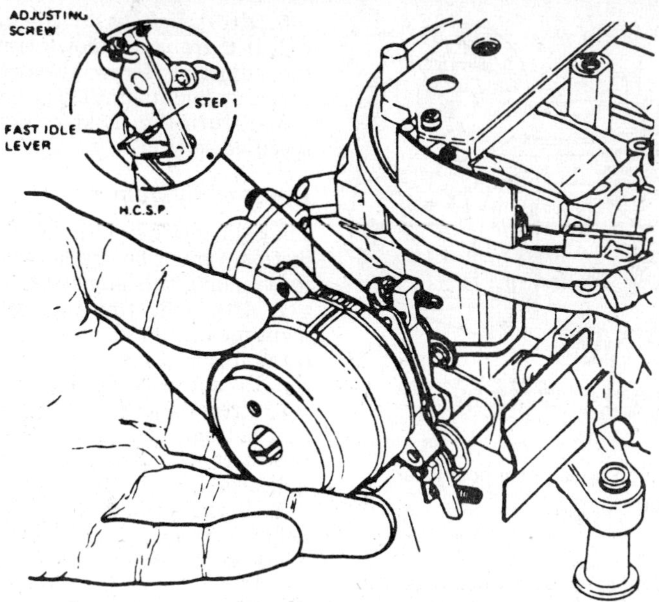

2700 VV fast idle cam adjustment

1. Remove the carburetor. Remove the venturi valve diaphragm plug with a center-punch.
2. If the carburetor has a venturi valve by-pass, remove it be removing the two cover retaining screw; invert and remove the by-pass screw plug from the cover with a drift. Install the cover.
3. Install the carburetor. Start the engine and allow it to reach normal operating temperature. Connect a vacuum gauge to the venturi valve cover. Set the idle speed to 500 rpm with the transmission in Drive.
4. Push and hold the venturi valve closed. Adjust the bypass screw to obtain a reading of 8 in. H_2O on the vacuum gauge. Make sure the idle speed remains constant. Open and close the throttle and check the idle speed.
5. With the engine idling, adjust the venturi valve diaphragm screw to obtain a reading of 6 in. H_2O. Set the curb idle to specification. Install new venturi valve bypass and diaphragm plugs.

INTERNAL VENT ADJUSTMENT

VENTURI VALVE LIMITER ADJUSTMENT

1. Remove the carburetor. Take off the venturi valve cover and the two rollers.
2. Use a center punch to loosen the expansion plug at the rear of the carburetor main body on the throttle side. Remove it.
3. Use an Allen wrench to remove the venturi valve wide open stop screw.
4. Hold the throttle wide open.
5. Apply a light closing pressure on the venturi valve and check the gap between the valve and the air horn wall. To adjust, move the venturi valve to the wide open position and insert an Allen wrench into the stop screw hole. Turn clockwise to increase the gap. Remove the wrench and check the gap again.
6. Replace the wide open stop screw and turn it clockwise until it contact the valve.
7. Push the venturi valve wide open and check the gap. Turn the stop screw to bring the gap to specifications.
8. Reassemble the carburetor with a new expansion plug.

CONTROL VACUUM REGULATOR ADJUSTMENT

There are two systems used. The earlier system's C.V.R. rod threads directly through the arm. The revised

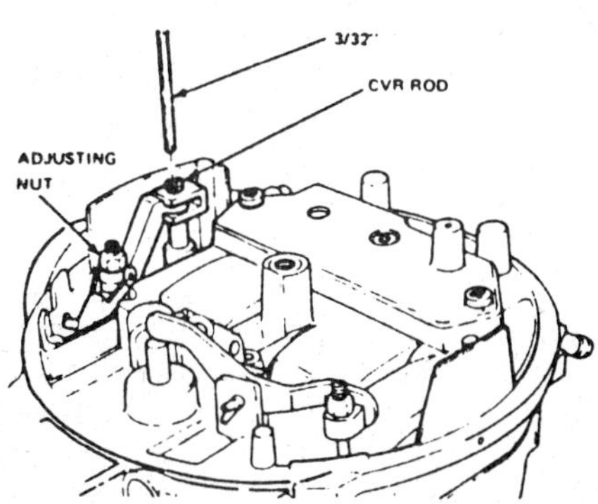

2700 VV control vacuum regulator adjustment

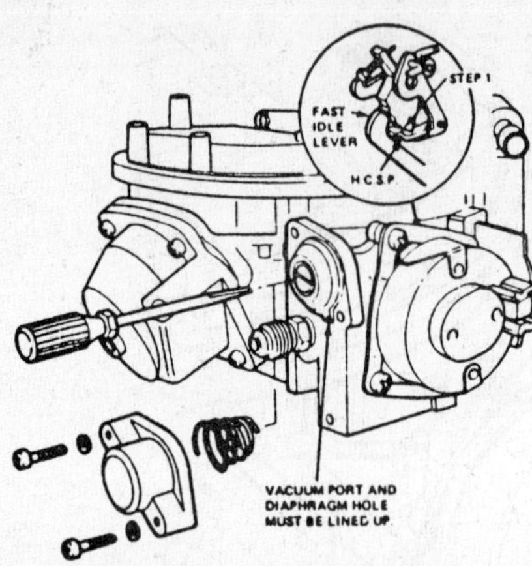

2700 VV high speed cam positioner adjustment

system, has a 3/8" nylon hex adjusting nut on the C.V.R. rod and a flange on the rod.

Early System

1. Make sure that the cold enrichment metering rod adjustment is correct.
2. Rotate the choke coil cap half a turn clockwise from the index mark. Work the throttle to set the fast idle cam.
3. Press down lightly on the regulator rod. If there is no down travel, turn the adjusting screw counterclockwise until some travel is felt.
4. Turn the regulator rod clockwise with an Allen wrench until the adjusting nut just begins to rise.
5. Press lightly on the regulator rod. If there is any down travel, turn the adjusting screw clockwise in 1/4 turn increments until it is eliminated.
6. Return the choke coil cap to the specified setting.

Revised System

The cold enrichment metering rod adjustment must be checked and set before making this adjustment.

1. After adjusting the cold enrichment metering rod, leave the dial indicator in place but remove the stator cap. Do not re-zero the dial indicator.
2. Press down on the C.V.R. rod until it bottoms on its seat. Measure this amount of travel with the dial indicator.
3. If the adjustment is incorrect, hold the 3/8" C.V.R. adjusting nut with a box wrench to prevent it from turning. Use a 3/32" Allen wrench to turn the C.V.R. rod; turning counterclockwise will increase the travel, and vice-versa.

DISASSEMBLY

WARNING: Special tools are required. If you have any doubts about your ability to successfully complete this procedure, leave it to a professional service person.

Upper Body

1. Remove the fuel inlet fitting, fuel filter, gasket and spring.
2. Remove the screws retaining the upper body assembly and remove the upper body.
3. Remove the float hinge pin and float assembly.
4. Remove the fuel inlet valve, seat and gasket.
5. Remove the accelerator pump rod and the choke control rod.
6. Remove the accelerator pump link retaining pin and the link.
7. Remove the accelerator pump swivel and the retaining nut.
8. Remove the E-ring on the choke hinge pin and slide the pin out of the casting.
9. Remove the cold enrichment rod adjusting nut, lever and swivel; remove the control vacuum nut and regulator as an assembly.
10. Remove the cold enrichment rod.
11. Remove the venturi valve cover plate and roller bearings. Remove the venturi valve cover plate and roller bearings. Remove the venturi air bypass screw.
12. Using special tool T77P-9928-A, press the tapered plugs out of the venturi valve pivot pins.
13. Remove the venturi valve pivot pins, bushings and the venturi valve.
14. Remove the metering rod pivot pins, springs and metering rods. Be sure to mark the rods so that you know on which side they belong. Also, keep the venturi valve blocked open when working on the jets.
15. Using tool T77L-9533-B, remove the cup plugs.
16. Using tool T77L-9533-A, turn each main metering jet clockwise, counting the number of turns until they bottom in the casting. You will need to know the number of turns when you reassemble the carburetor. Remove the jets and mark them so that you know on which side they belong. Don't lose the O-rings.
17. Remove the accelerator pump plunger assembly.
18. Remove the idle trim screws. Remove the venturi valve limiter adjusting screw.
19. Assembly is the reverse of disassembly.

Main Body

1. Remove the cranking enrichment solenoid and the O-ring seal.
2. Remove the venturi valve cover, spring guide, and spring. Remove the venturi valve.
3. Remove the throttle body.
4. Remove the choke heat shield.
5. Assembly is in the reverse order.

3/32"

2700 VV idle mixture adjustment

1. Fuel inlet fitting
2. Fuel inlet fitting gasket
3. Fuel filter
4. Fuel filter spring
5. Retaining E-ring
6. Accelerator pump rod
7. Choke control rod
8. Screw
8A. Screw
9. Upper body
10. Float hinge pin
11. Float assembly
12. Float bowl gasket
13. Fuel inlet valve
14. Fuel inlet seat
15. Fuel inlet seat gasket
16. Dust seal
17. Pin
18. Accelerator pump link
19. Accelerator pump swivel
20. Nut
21. Choke hinge pin
22. Cold enrichment rod lever
23. Cold enrichment rod swivel
24. Control vacuum regulator adjusting nut
25. Control vacuum regulator
26. Cold enrichment rod
27. Screw
28. Venturi valve cover plate
29. Roller bearing
30. Venturi air bypass screw
31. Venturi valve pivot plug
32. Venturi valve pivot pin
33. Venturi valve
34. Venturi valve pivot pin bushing
35. Metering rod pivot pin
36. Metering rod
37. Metering rod spring
38. Cup plug
39. Main metering jet assembly
40. O-ring
41. Accelerator pump return spring
42. Accelerator pump cup
43. Accelerator pump plunger
44. Internal vent valve
45. Retaining E-ring
46. Idle trim screw
47. Venturi valve limiter adjusting screw
48. Pipe plug

2700 VV upper body

1. Cranking enrichment solenoid
2. O-ring seal
3. Screw
4. Venturi valve diaphragm cover
5. Venturi valve diaphragm spring guide
6. Venturi valve diaphragm spring
7. Venturi valve diaphragm assembly
8. Main body
9. Venturi valve adjusting screw
10. Wide open stop screw
11. Plug expansion
12. Cranking fuel control assembly
13. Accelerator pump check ball
14. Accelerator pump check ball weight
15. Throttle body gasket
16. Screw
17. Choke heat shield

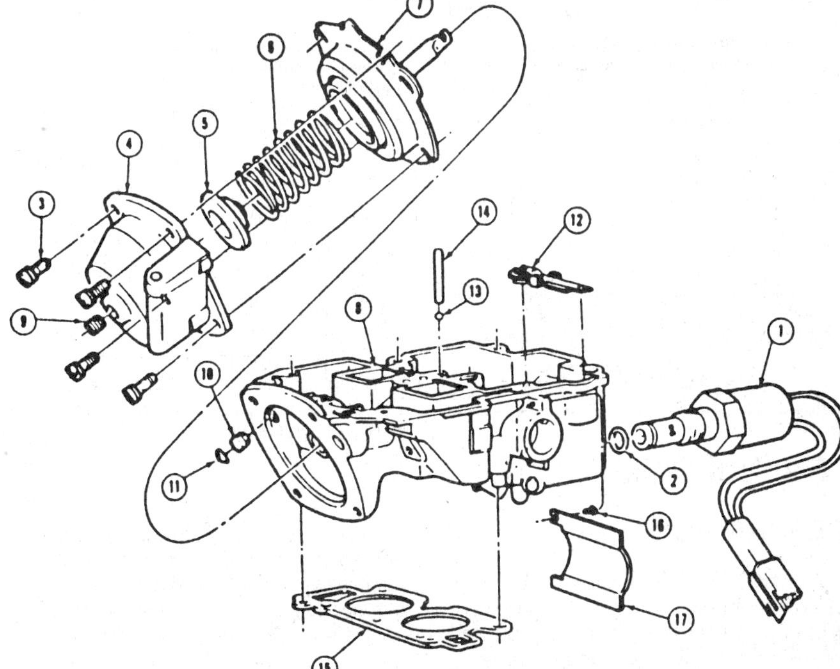

2700 VV main body

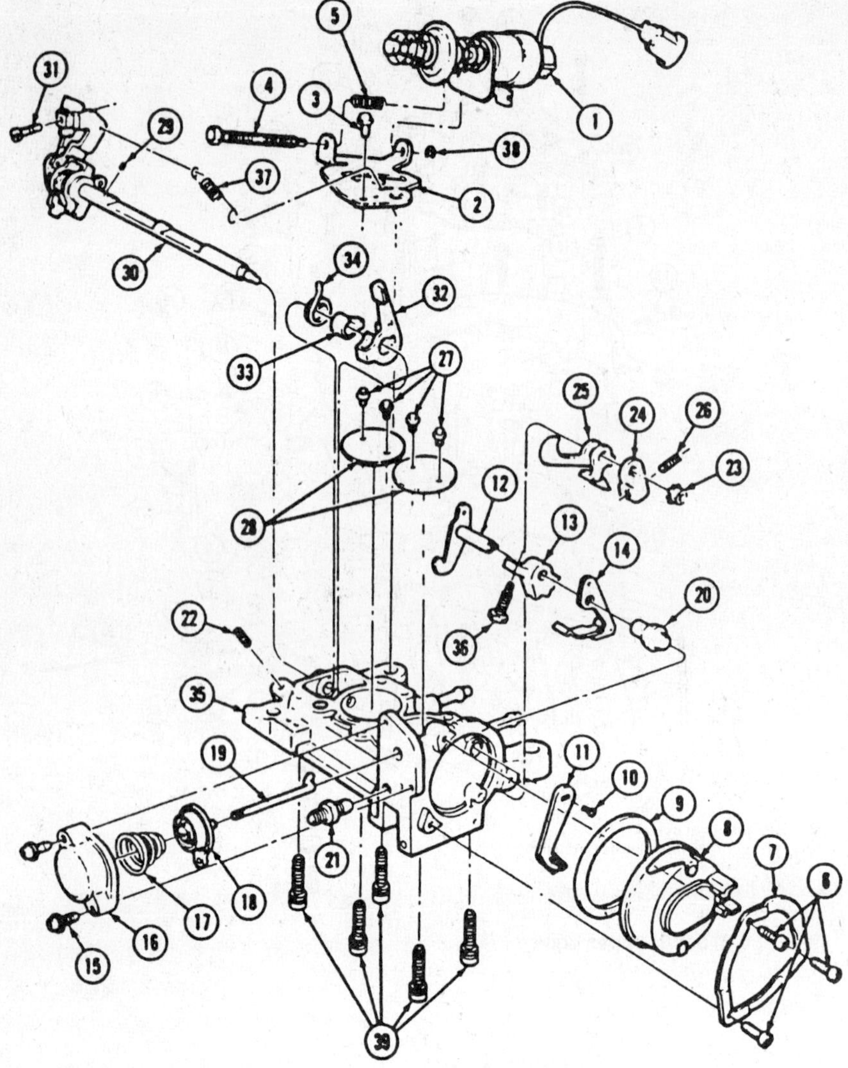

1. Throttle return control device
2. Throttle return control device bracket
3. Mounting screw
4. Adjusting screw
5. Adjusting screw spring
6. Screw
7. Choke thermostatic housing retainer
8. Choke thermostatic housing
9. Choke thermostatic housing gasket
10. Screw
11. Choke thermostatic lever
12. Choke lever and shaft assembly
13. Fast idle cam
14. High cam speed positioner assembly
15. Screw
16. High cam speed positioner diaphragm cover
17. High cam speed positioner diaphragm spring
18. High cam speed positioner diaphragm assembly
19. High cam speed positioner rod
20. Choke housing bushing

2700 VV throttle body

GASOLINE FUEL INJECTION

Central Fuel Injection

DESCRIPTION

Central Fuel Injection (CFI) is a throttle body injection system in which two fuel injectors are mounted in a common throttle body, spraying fuel down through the throttle valves at the bottom of the body and into the intake manifold.

OPERATION

Fuel is supplied from the fuel tank by a high pressure, in-tank fuel pump. The fuel passes through a filter and is sent to the throttle body where a regulator keeps the fuel delivery pressure at a constant 39 psi. The two fuel injectors are mounted vertically above the throttle plates and are connected in line with the fuel pressure regulator. Excess fuel supplied by the pump, but not needed by the engine, is returned to the fuel tank by a steel fuel return line.

The fuel injection system is linked with and controlled by the Electronic Engine Control (EEC) system.

Air and Fuel Control

The throttle body assembly is comprised of six individual components which perform the job of mixing the air and fuel to the ideal ratio for controlling exhaust emissions and providing performance and economy. The six components are: air control, fuel injector nozzles, fuel pressure regulator, fuel pressure diagnostic valve, cold engine speed control, and throttle position sensor.

Air Control

Air flow to the engine is controlled by two butterfly valves mounted in a two piece, die-cast aluminum housing called the throttle body. The butterfly valves, or throttle valves, are identical in design to the throttle plates of a conventional carburetor and are actuated by a similar linkage and pedal cable arrangement.

Fuel Injector Nozzles

The fuel injector nozzles are mounted in the throttle body and are electromechanical devices which meter and atomize the fuel delivered to the engine. The injector valve bodies consist of a solenoid actuated pintle and needle valve assembly. An electrical control signal from the EED electronic processor activates the solenoid causing the pintle to move inward off its seat and allowing fuel to flow. the fuel flow through the injector is controlled by the amount of time the injector solenoid holds the pintle off its seat.

Fuel Pressure Regulator

The fuel pressure regulator is mounted on the throttle body. The regulator smooths out fuel pressure drops from the fuel pump. It is not sensitive to back pressure in the return line to the tank.

A second function of the pressure regulator is to maintain fuel supply pressure upon engine and fuel pump shut down. The regulator acts as a check valve and traps fuel between itself and the fuel pump. This promotes rapid start ups and helps prevent fuel vapor formation in the lines, or vapor lock. The regulator makes sure that the pressure of the fuel at the injector nozzles stays at a constant 39 psi.

Fuel Pressure Diagnostic Valve

A Schrader-type diagnostic pressure valve is located at the top of the throttle body. This valve can be used by service personnel to monitor fuel pressure, bleed down the system pressure prior to maintenance and to bleed out air which may have been introduced during assembly or filter servicing. A special Ford Tool (T80L-9974-A) is used to accomplish these procedures.

CAUTION

Under no circumstances should compressed air be forced into the fuel system using the diagnostic valve.

Cold Engine Speed Control

The cold engine speed control serves the same purpose as the fast idle speed device on a carbureted engine, which is to raise engine speed during cold engine idle. A throttle stop cam positioner is used. the cam is positioned by a bimetal spring and an electric heating element. The cold engine speed control is attached to the throttle body. As the engine heats up, the fast idle cam on the cold engine speed control is gradually repositioned by the bimetal spring, heating element and EEC computer until normal idle speed is reached. The EEC computer automatically kicks down the fast idle cam to a lower step (lower engine speed) by supplying vacuum to the automatic kickdown motor which physically moves the high speed cam a predetermined time after the engine starts.

Throttle Position Sensor

This sensor is attached to the throttle body and is used to monitor changes in throttle plate position. the throttle position sensor sends this information to the computer, which uses it to select proper air/fuel mixture, spark timing and EGR control under different engine operating conditions.

Fuel System Inertia Switch

In the event of a collision, the electrical contacts in the inertia switch open and the fuel pump automatically shuts off. The fuel pump will shut off even if the engine does not stop running. The engine, however, will stop a few seconds after the fuel pump stops. It is not possible to restart the engine until the inertia switch is manually reset. The switch is located in the luggage compartment on the left hinge support on all models. To reset, depress both buttons on the switch at the same time.

CAUTION

Do not reset the inertia switch until the complete fuel system has been inspected for leaks.

FUEL CHARGING ASSEMBLY REMOVAL & INSTALLATION

1. Remove the air cleaner.
2. Release the pressure from the fuel system at the diagnostic valve using Tool T80L-9974-A or its equivalent.
3. Disconnect the throttle cable and transmission throttle valve lever.
4. Disconnect the fuel, vacuum and electrical connections. Use care to prevent combustion of spilled fuel.
5. Remove the fuel charging assembly retaining nuts then remove the fuel charging assembly.
6. Remove the mounting gasket from the intake manifold.
7. Installation is the reverse of removal. Tighten the fuel charging assembly nuts to 120 in.lb.

THROTTLE BODY DISASSEMBLY AND ASSEMBLY

1. Remove the air cleaner mounting stud in order to separate the upper body from the throttle body.
2. Turn the fuel charging assembly (throttle body) over and remove the four screws from the bottom of the throttle body.
3. Separate the throttle body (lower half) from the main body (upper half).
4. Remove the old gasket. If it is stuck and scraping is necessary, use only a plastic or wood scraper. Take care not to damage the gasket surfaces.
5. Remove the three pressure regulator mounting screws. Remove the pressure regulator.
6. Disconnect the electrical connectors at each injector by pulling outward on the connector and not on the wire. Loosen but do not remove the wiring harness retaining screw. Push in on the harness tabs to remove it from the upper body.
7. Remove the fuel injector retaining screw. Remove the injection retainer.
8. Pull the injectors, one at a time, from the upper body. Mark the injectors for identification, they must be reinstalled in the same position (choke or throttle side). Each injector is equipped with a small O-ring. If the O-ring does not come out with the injector, carefully pick out of body.
9. Remove the fuel diagnostic valve assembly.
10. Remove the choke cover by drilling the retaining rivets. A 1/8" or No. 30 drill is required. A choke mounting kit for installation is available from Ford.
11. Remove the choke cap retaining ring, choke cap and gasket. Remove the thermostat lever screw and lever. Remove the fast idle cam assembly and control rod positioner.
12. Hold the control diaphragm cover in position and remove the two mounting screws. Carefully remove the cover, spring and pull down diaphragm.
13. Remove the fast idle retaining nut, fast idle cam adjuster lever, fast idle lever and E-clip.
14. Remove the potentiometer (sensor) connector bracket retaining screw. Mark the throttle body and throttle position sensor for correct installation position. Remove the throttle sensor retaining screws and slide the sensor off of the throttle shaft. Remove the throttle positioner retaining screw and remove the throttle positioner.
15. Perform any necessary cleaning or repair.
16. Assemble the upper body by first installing the fuel diagnostic fuel pressure valve assembly.
17. Lubricate the new injector O-rings with a light grade oil. Install the O-rings on each injector. Install the injectors in their appropriate choke or throttle side position. Use a light, twisting, pushing motion to install the injectors.
18. Install the injector retainer and tighten the retaining screw to 30-60 in.lb.
19. Install the injector wiring harness and snap into position. Tighten the harness retaining screw to 8-10 in.lb.
20. Snap the electrical connectors into position on the injectors. Lubricate the fuel pressure regulator O-ring with light oil. Install the O-ring and new gasket on the regulator, install the regulator and tighten retaining screws to 27-40 in.lb.
21. Install the throttle positioner onto the throttle body. Tighten the retaining screw to 32-44 in.lb.
22. hold the throttle sensor (potentiometer) with the location identification mark (see step 14) in the 12 o'clock position. The two rotary tangs should be at 3 o'clock and 9 o'clock positions.
23. Slide the sensor onto the throttle shaft with the identification mark still in the 12 o'clock position. Hold the sensor firmly against the throttle body.
24. Rotate the sensor until the identification marks on the sensor and body are aligned. Install the retaining screws and tighten to 13-18 in.lb.
25. Install the sensor wiring harness bracket retaining screw, tighten to 18-22 in.lb. Install the E-clip, fast idle lever, fast idle adjustment lever and fast idle retaining nut. Tighten the retaining nut to 16-20 in.lb.
26. Install the pull down diaphragm, spring and cover. Hold the cover in position and tighten the retaining screws to 13-19 in.lb.
27. Install the fast idle control rod positioner, fast idle cam and the thermostat lever. Tighten the retaining screw to 13-19 in.lb.

28. Install the choke cap gasket, bimetal spring, cap and retaining ring. Install new rivets and snug them with the rivet gun. do not break rivets, loosely install so choke cover can rotate. Index choke and break rivets to tighten.
29. Install the gasket between the main body and the throttle body. Place the throttle body in position. Install the four retaining screws loosely. Install the air cleaner stud and tighten to 70-95 in.lb. Tighten the four retaining screws.
30. The rest of the assembly is in the reverse order of disassembly.

ELECTRONIC CONTROL SYSTEM

Electronic Control Assembly (ECA)

The Electronic Control Assembly (ECA) is a solid-state micro-computer consisting of a processor assembly and a calibration assembly. It is located under the instrument panel or passenger's seat and is usually covered by a kick panel. 1981-82 models use an EEC-III engine control system, while 1983 and later models use the EEC-IV. Although the two systems are similar in appearance and operation, the ECA units are not interchangeable. A multipin connector links the ECA with all system components. The processor assembly is housed in an aluminum case. It contains circuits designed to continuously sample input signals from the engine sensors. It then calculates and sends out proper control signals to adjust air/fuel ratio, spark timing and emission system operation. The processor also provides a continuous reference voltage to the B/MAP, EVP, and TPS sensors. EEC-III reference voltage is 8-10 volts, while EEC-IV systems use a 5 volt reference signal. The calibration assembly is contained in a black plastic housing which plugs into the top of the processor assembly. It contains the memory and programming information used by the processor to determine optimum operating conditions. different calibration information is used in different vehicle applications, such as California or Federal models. For this reason, careful identification of the engine, year, model and type of electronic control system is essential to insure correct component replacement.

ENGINE SENSORS

Air Charge Temperature Sensor (ACT)

The ACT is threaded into the intake manifold air runner. It is located behind the distributor on V6 engines and directly below the accelerator linkage on V8 engines. The ACT monitors air/fuel charge temperature and sends an appropriate signal to the ECA. This information is used to correct fuel enrichment for variations in intake air density due to temperature changes.

Barometric & Manifold Absolute Pressure Sensors (B/MAP)

The B/MAP sensor on V8 engines is located on the right fender panel in the engine compartment. The MAP sensor used on V6 engines is separate from the barometric sensor and is located on the left fender panel in the engine compartment. The barometric sensor signals the ECA of changes in atmospheric pressure and density to regulate calculated air flow into the engine. The MAP sensor monitors and signals the ECA of changes in intake manifold pressure which result from engine load, speed and atmospheric pressure changes.

Crankshaft Position (CP) Sensor

The purpose of the CP sensor is to provide the ECA with an accurate ignition timing reference (when the piston reaches 10°BTDC) and injector operation information (twice each crankshaft revolution). The crankshaft vibration damper is fitted with a 4 lobe pulse ring. As the crankshaft rotates, the pulse ring lobes interrupt the magnetic field at the tip of the CP sensor.

EGR Valve Position Sensor (EVP)

This sensor, mounted on EGR valve, signals the computer of EGR opening so that it may subtract EGR flow from total air flow into the manifold. In this way, EGR flow is excluded from air flow information used to determine mixture requirements.

Engine Coolant Temperature Sensor (ECT)

The ECT is threaded into the intake manifold water jacket directly above the water pump by-pass hose. The ECT monitors coolant temperature and signals the ECA, which then uses these signals for mixture enrichment (during cool operation), ignition timing and EGR operation. The resistance value of the ECT increases with temperature, causing a voltage signal drop as the engine warms up.

Exhaust Gas Oxygen Sensor (EGO)

The EGO is mounted in the right side exhaust manifold on V8 engines, in the left and right side exhaust manifolds on V6 models. The EGO monitors oxygen content of exhaust gases and sends a constantly changing voltage signal to the ECA. The ECA analyzes this signal and adjusts the air/fuel mixture to obtain the optimum (stoichiometric) ratio.

Knock Sensor (KS)

This sensor is used on various models equipped with the 6-232 engine. It is attached to the intake manifold in front of the ACT sensor. The KS detects engine vibrations caused by preignition or detonation and provides information to the ECA, which then retards the timing to eliminate detonation.

Thick Film Integrated Module Sensor (TFI)

The TFI module sensor plugs into the distributor just below the distributor cap and replaces the CP sensor on some engines. Its function is to provide the ECA with ignition timing information, similar to what the CP sensor provides.

Throttle Position Sensor (TPS)

The TPS is mounted on the right side of the throttle body, directly connected to the throttle shaft. The TPS senses the throttle movement and position and transmits an appropriate electrical signal to the ECA. These signals are used by the ECA to adjust the air/fuel mixture, spark timing and EGR operation according to engine load at idle, part throttle, or full throttle. The TPS is nonadjustable.

ON-CAR SERVICE

NOTE: Diagnostic and test procedures on the EEC-III and EEC-IV electronic control system require special test equipment. Have the testing done by a professional.

Fuel Pressure Tests

The diagnostic pressure valve (Schrader type) is located at the top of the Fuel charging main body. This valve provides a convenient point for service personnel to monitor fuel pressure, bleed down the system pressure prior to maintenance, and to bleed out air which may become trapped in the system during filter replacement. A pressure gauge with a adapter is required to perform pressure tests.

CAUTION

Under no circumstances should compressed air be forced into the fuel system using the diagnostic valve. Depressing the pin in the diagnostic valve will relieve system pressure by expelling fuel into the throttle body.

System Pressure Test

Testing fuel pressure requires the use of a special pressure gauge (T80L-9974-A or equivalent) that attaches to the diagnostic pressure tap on the fuel charging assembly. Depressurize the fuel system before disconnecting any lines.

1. Disconnect the fuel return line at the throttle body (in-tank high pressure pump) and connect the hose to a 1 quart calibrated container. Connect a pressure gauge.
2. Disconnect the electrical connector at the fuel pump. The connector is located ahead of fuel tank (in-tank high pressure pump) or just forward of pump outlet (in-line high pressure pump). Connect an auxiliary wiring harness to the connector of the fuel pump. Energize the pump for 10 seconds by applying 12 volts to the auxiliary harness connector, allowing the fuel to drain into the calibrated container. Note the fuel volume and pressure gauge reading.
3. Correct fuel pressure should be 35-45 psi (241-310 kPa). Fuel volume should be 10 oz. in 10 seconds (minimum) and fuel pressure should maintain a minimum of 30 psi (206 kPa) immediately after pump cut-off.

If the pressure condition is met, but the fuel flow is not, check for blocked filter(s) and fuel supply lines. After correcting the problem, repeat the test procedure. If the fuel flow is still inadequate, replace the high pressure pump. If the flow specification is met but the pressure is not, check for a worn or damaged pressure regulator valve on the throttle body. If both the pressure and fuel flow specifications are met, but the pressure drops excessively after de-energizing, check for a leaking injector valve(s) and/or pressure regulator valve. If the injector valves and pressure regulator valve are okay, replace the high pressure pump. If no pressure or flow is seen in the fuel system, check for blocked filters and fuel lines. If no trouble is found, replace the in-line fuel pump, in-tank fuel pump and the fuel filter inside the tank.

Fuel Injector Pressure Test

1. Connect pressure gauge T80L-9974-A, or equivalent, to the fuel pressure test fitting. Disconnect the coil connector from the coil. Disconnect the electrical lead from one injector and pressurize the fuel system. Disable the fuel pump by disconnecting the inertia switch or the fuel pump relay and observe the pressure gauge reading.
2. Crank the engine for 2 seconds. Turn the ignition OFF and wait 5 seconds, then observe the pressure drop. If the pressure drop is 2-16 psi (14-110 kPa), the injector is operating properly. Reconnect the injector, activate the fuel pump, then repeat the procedure for other injector.
3. If the pressure drop is less than 2 psi (14 kPa) or more than 16 psi (110 kPa), switch the electrical connectors on injectors and repeat the test. If the pressure drop is still incorrect, replace the disconnected injector with one of the same color code, then reconnect both injectors properly and repeat the test.
4. Disconnect and plug the vacuum hose at EGR valve. It may be necessary to disconnect the idle speed control (6-232) or the throttle kicker solenoid (8-302) and use the throttle body stop screw to set the engine speed. Start and run the engine at 1,800 rpm (2,000 rpm on 1984 and later models). Disconnect the left injector electrical connector. Note the rpm after the engine stabilizes (around 1,200 rpm). Reconnect the injector and allow the engine to return to high idle.
5. Perform the same procedure for the right injector. Note the difference between the rpm readings of the left and right injectors. If the difference is 100 rpm or less, check the oxygen sensor. If the difference is more than 100 rpm, replace both injectors.

CFI COMPONENT TESTS

NOTE: Complete CFT system diagnosis requires the use of special test equipment. Have the system tested professionally.

Before beginning any component testing, always check the following:

- Check the ignition and fuel systems to ensure there is fuel and spark.
- Remove the air cleaner assembly and inspect all vacuum and pressure hoses for proper connection to fittings. Check for damaged or pinched hoses.
- Inspect all sub-system wiring harnesses for proper connections to the EGR solenoid valves, injectors, sensors, etc.
- Check for loose or detached connectors and broken or detached wires. Check that all terminals are seated firmly and are not corroded. Look for partially broken or frayed wires or any shorting between the wires.
- Inspect the sensors for physical damage. Inspect the vehicle electrical system. Check the battery for full charge and cable connections for tightness.
- Inspect the relay connector and make sure the ECA power relay is securely attached and making a good ground connection.

High Pressure In-Tank Pump

Disconnect the electrical connector just forward of the fuel tank. Connect a voltmeter to the body wiring harness connector. Turn the key ON while watching the voltmeter. Voltage should rise to battery voltage, then return to zero after about 1 second. Momentarily turn the key to the **START** position. Voltage should rise to about 8 volts while cranking. If voltage is not specified, check electrical system.

High Pressure In-Line & Low Pressure In-Tank Pumps

Disconnect the electrical connector at the fuel pumps. Connect a voltmeter to the body wiring harness connector. Turn the key **ON** while watching the voltmeter. The voltage should rise to battery voltage, then return to zero after about 1 second. If the voltage is not as specified, check the inertia switch and the electrical system. Connect an ohmmeter to the in-line pump wiring harness connector. If no continuity is present, check the continuity directly at the in-line pump terminals. If no continuity at the in-line pump terminals, replace the in-line pump. If continuity is present, service or replace the wiring harness.

Connect an ohmmeter across the body wiring harness connector. If continuity is present (about 5 ohms), the low pressure pump circuit is OK. If no continuity is present, remove the fuel tank and check for continuity at the in-tank pump flange terminals on top of the tank. If continuity is absent at the in-tank pump flange terminals, replace the assembly. If continuity is present at the in-tank pump but not in the harness connector, service or replace the wiring harness at the in-tank pump.

Solenoid and Sensor Resistance Tests

All CFI components must be disconnected from the circuit before testing the resistance with a suitable ohmmeter. Replace any component whose measured resistance does not agree with the specifications chart. Shorting the wiring harness across a solenoid valve can burn out the circuitry in the ECA that control the solenoid valve actuator. Exercise caution when testing the solenoid valves to avoid accidental damage to ECA.

Electronic Multi-Point Injection (EFI)

DESCRIPTION

The Electronic Fuel Injector System (EFI) is classified as a multi-point, pulse time, mass air flow fuel injection system. Fuel is metered into the intake air stream in accordance with engine demand through four injectors mounted on a tuned intake manifold. A blow-through turbocharger system is utilized to reduce fuel delivery time and increase power.

An on board vehicle electronic engine control (EEC) computer accepts inputs from various engine sensors to compute the required fuel flow rate necessary to maintain a prescribed air/fuel ration throughout the entire engine operational range. The computer then outputs a command to the fuel injectors to meter the approximate quantity of fuel.

OPERATION

The fuel delivery sub-system consists of a high pressure, chassis mounted, electric fuel pump delivering fuel from the fuel tank through a 20 micron fuel filter to a fuel charging manifold assembly.

The fuel charging manifold assembly incorporates electrically actuated fuel injectors directly above each of the engine's four intake ports. The injectors, when energized, spray a metered quantity of fuel into the intake air stream.

A constant fuel pressure drop is maintained across the injector nozzles by a pressure regulator. The regulator is connected in series with the fuel injectors and positioned down stream from them. Excess fuel supplied by the pump, but not required by the engine, passes through the regulator and returns to the fuel tank through a fuel return line.

All injectors are energized simultaneously, once every crankshaft revolution. The period of time that the injectors are energized (injector on-time or the pulse width) is controlled by the vehicles' Engine Electronic Control (EEC) computer. Air entering the engine is measured by a vane air flow meter located between the air cleaner and the fuel charging manifold assembly. This air flow information and input from various other engine sensors is used to compute the required fuel flow rate necessary to maintain a prescribed air/fuel ratio for the given engine operation. The computer determines the needed injector pulse width and outputs a commend to the injector to meter the exact quantity of fuel.

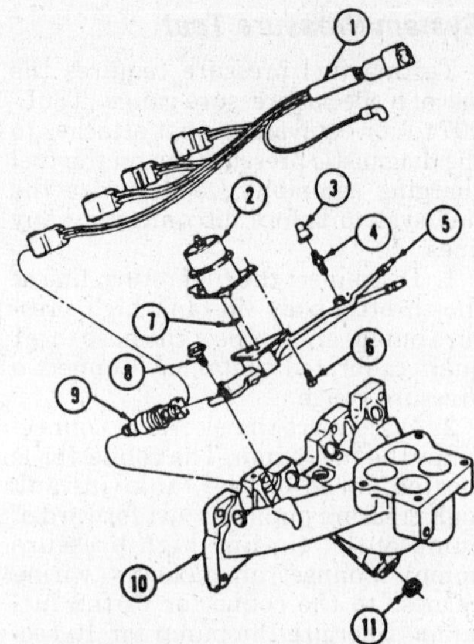

1. Wiring harness—fuel charging
2. Regulator assembly—fuel pressure
3. Cap—fuel pressure relief
4. Valve assembly—fuel pressure relief
5. Manifold assembly—fuel injection fuel supply
6. Screw—M5 × 0.8 × 10 socket head (3 req'd)
7. Seal—$\frac{5}{16}$ × .070 O-ring
8. Bolt (2 req'd)
9. Injector assembly—fuel (4 req'd)
10. Manifold—intake lower
11. Plug

4-140 engine – EFI components

COMPONENT DESCRIPTION

Fuel Injectors

The four fuel injector nozzles are electro-mechanical devices which both meter and atomize fuel delivered to the engine. The injectors are mounted in the lower intake manifold and are positioned so that their tips are directing fuel just ahead of the engine intake valves. The injector bodies consist of a solenoid actuated pintle and needle valve assembly. An electrical control signal from the Electronic Engine Control unit activates the injector solenoid causing the pintle to move inward off the seat, allowing fuel to flow. Since the injector flow orifice is fixed and the fuel pressure drop across the injector tip is constant, fuel flow to the engine is regulated by how long the solenoid is energized. Atomization is obtained by contouring the pintle at the point where the fuel separates.

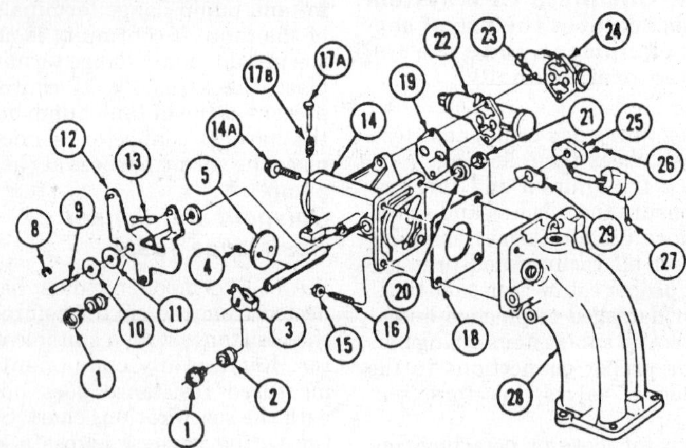

1. Spring—carburetor throttle return
2. Bushing—accelerator pump overtravel spring (2)
3. Lever—engine throttle
4. Screw—M4 × .7 × 8
5. Plate—air intake charge throttle
6. Shaft—air intake charge throttle
7. Spring—secondary throttle return
8. E-ring
9. Hub—throttle control
10. Spacer
11. Washer—nylon (2)
12. Lever—throttle control
13. Rod—engine secondary throttle control
14. Body—air intake charge throttle
14A. Bolt M8 × 1.25 × 30 hex flange head (2 req'd)
15. Nut—M8 (2 req'd)
16. Stud—M8 × 42.5 (2 req'd)
17A. Screw throttle stop
17B. Spring—throttle return control
18. Gasket—air charge control to intake manifold
19. Gasket—air bypass valve
20. Seal—throttle control shaft
21. Bushing—carburetor throttle shaft
22. Valve assembly—throttle air bypass
23. Bolt—M6 × 1.0 × 20 hex head flange
24. Valve assembly—throttle air bypass (alt.)
25. Potentiometer throttle position
26. Screw and washer assembly M4 × 22
27. Screw—M4 × 0.7 × 14.0 hex. washer tap
28. Manifold—intake upper
29. Gasket T.P.S.

4-140 engine – EFI components

Fuel Pressure Regulator

The fuel pressure regulator is attached to the fuel supply manifold assembly downstream of the fuel injectors. It regulates the fuel pressure supplied to the injectors. The regulator is a diaphragm operated relief valve in which one side of the diaphragm senses fuel pressure and the other side is subjected to intake manifold pressure. The nominal fuel pressure is established by a spring preload applied to the diaphragm. Balancing one side of the diaphragm with manifold pressure maintains a constant fuel pressure drop across the injectors. Fuel, in excess of that used by the engine, is bypassed through the regulator and returns to the fuel tank.

Air Vane Meter Assembly

The air vane meter assembly is located between the air cleaner and the throttle body and is mounted on a bracket near the left shock tower. The vane air meter contains two sensors which furnish input to the Electronic Control Assembly: a vane airflow sensor and a vane air temperature. The air vane meter measures the mass of air flow to the engine. Air flow through the body moves a vane mounted on a pivot pin. This vane is connected to a variable resistor (potentiometer) which in turn is connected to a 5 volt reference voltage. The output of this potentiometer varies depending on the volume of air flowing through the sensor. The temperature sensor in the air vane meter measures the incoming air temperature. These two inputs, air volume and temperature, are used by the Electronic Control Assembly to compute the mass air flow. This valve is then used to compute the fuel flow necessary for the optimum air/fuel ratio which is fed to the injectors.

Air Throttle Body Assembly

The throttle body assembly controls air flow to the engine through a single butterfly-type valve. The throttle position is controlled by conventional cable/cam throttle linkage. The body is a single piece die casting made of aluminum. It has a single bore with an air bypass channel around the throttle plate. This by-pass channel controls both cold and warm engine idle air flow control as regulated by an air bypass valve assembly mounted directly to the throttle body. The valve assembly is an electromechanical device controlled by the EEC computer. It incorporates a linear actuator which positions a variable area metering valve.

Other features of the air throttle body assembly include:

- An adjustment screw to set the throttle plate at a minimum idle airflow position.
- A preset stop to locate the WOT position.
- A throttle body mounted throttle position sensor.
- A PCV fresh air source located upstream of the throttle plate.
- Individual ported vacuum taps (as required) for PCV and EVAP control signals.

Fuel Supply Manifold Assembly

The fuel supply manifold assembly is the component that delivers high pressure fuel from the vehicle fuel supply line to the four fuel injectors. The assembly consists of a single preformed tube or stamping with four injector connector, a mounting flange for the fuel pressure regulator, a pressure relief valve for diagnostic testing or field service fuel system pressure bleed down and mounting attachments which locate the fuel manifold assembly and provide fuel injector retention.

Air Intake Manifold

The air intake manifold is a two piece (upper and lower intake manifold) aluminum casting. Runner lengths are turned to optimize engine torque and power output. The manifold provides mounting flanges for the air throttle body assembly, fuel supply manifold and accelerator control bracket and the EGR valve and supply tube. Vacuum taps are provided to support various engine accessories. Pockets for the fuel injectors are machined to prevent both air and fuel leakage. The pockets, in which the injectors are mounted, are placed to direct the injector fuel spray immediately in front of each engine intake valve.

COMPONENT REMOVAL & INSTALLATION

Fuel Charging Assembly

WARNING: If any of the sub-assemblies are to be serviced and/or removed, with the fuel charging assembly mounted to the engine, the following steps must be taken.

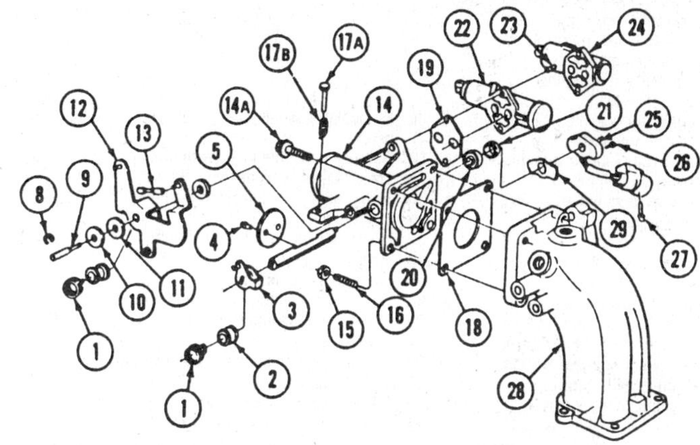

1. Spring—carburetor throttle return
2. Bushing—accelerator pump overtravel spring (2)
3. Lever—engine throttle
4. Screw—m4 × .7 × 8
5. Plate—air intake charge throttle
6. Shaft—air intake charge throttle
7. Spring—secondary throttle return
8. E-ring
9. Hub—throttle control
10. Spacer
11. Washer—nylon (2)
12. Lever—throttle control
13. Rod—engine secondary throttle control
14. Body—air intake charge throttle
14A. Bolt m8 × 1.25 × 30 hex flange head 2 req'd
15. Nut—m8 2 req'd
16. Stud—m8 × 42.5 2 req'd
17A. Screw throttle stop
17B. Spring—throttle return control
18. Gasket—air charge control to intake manifold
19. Gasket—air bypass valve
20. Seal—throttle control shaft
21. Bushing—carburetor throttle shaft
22. Valve assy—throttle air bypass
23. Bolt—m6 × 1.0 × 20 hex head flange
24. Valve assy—throttle air bypass (alt.)
25. Potentiometer throttle position
26. Screw and washer assy m4 × 22
27. Screw—m4 × 0.7 × 14.0 hex. washer tap
28. Manifold—intake upper
29. Gasket tps

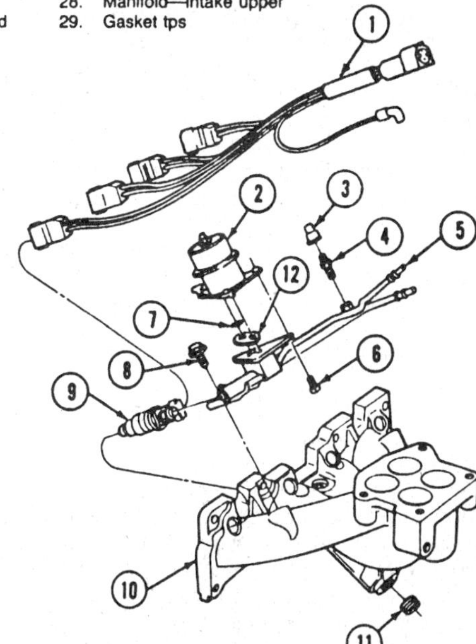

1. Wiring harness—fuel charging
2. Regulator assy—fuel pressure
3. Cap—fuel pressure relief
4. Valve assy—fuel pressure relief
5. Manifold assy—fuel injection fueld supply
6. Screw—m5 × 0.8 × 10 socket head 3 req'd
7. Seal—$^{9}/_{16}$ × .070 O-ring
8. Bolt (2 req'd)
9. Injector assy—fuel 4 req'd
10. Manifold—intake lower
11. Plug
12. Gasket—fuel pressure regulator

EFI components used on the 1985-86 4-140

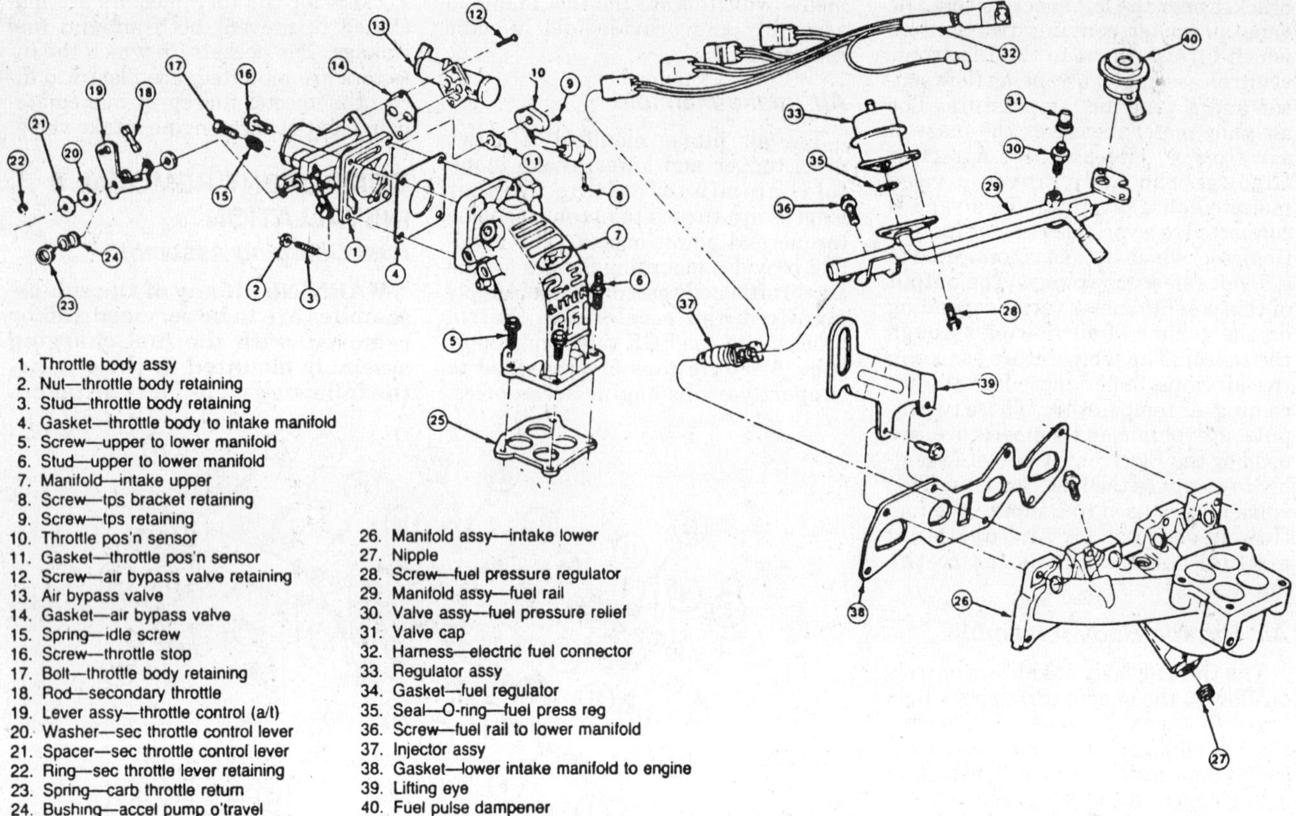

EFI components used on the 1987 4-140 Turbo

1. Make sure the ignition key is in the off position.
2. Drain the coolant from the radiator.

CAUTION

When draining the coolant, keep in mind that cats and dogs are attracted by the ethylene glycol antifreeze, and are quite likely to drink any that is left in an uncovered container or in puddles on the ground. This will prove fatal in sufficient quantity. Always drain the coolant into a sealable container. Coolant should be reused unless it is contaminated or several years old.

3. Disconnect the negative battery cable.
4. Remove the fuel cap to relieve fuel tank pressure.
5. Relieve the pressure from the fuel system at the pressure relief valve. Special tool T80L-9974-A or its equal is needed for this procedure.
6. Disconnect the fuel supply line.
7. Identify and disconnect the fuel return lines and vacuum connections.
8. Disconnect the injector wiring harness by disconnecting the ECT sensor in the heater supply tube, under the lower intake manifold.
9. Disconnect the air by-pass connector from EEC harness.

NOTE: Not all assemblies may be serviceable while on the engine. In some cases, removal of the fuel charging assembly may facilitate service of the various sub-assemblies. To remove the entire fuel charging assembly, the following should be observed.

10. Remove the engine air cleaner outlet tube between the vane air meter and air throttle body by loosening two the clamps.
11. Disconnect and remove the accelerator and speed control cables (if so equipped) from the accelerator mounting bracket and throttle lever.
12. Disconnect the top manifold vacuum fitting connections by disconnecting:
    a. Rear vacuum line at the dash panel vacuum tree.
    b. Front vacuum line at the air cleaner and fuel pressure regulator.
13. Disconnect the PCV system by removing the following:
    a. Two large forward facing connectors on the throttle body and intake manifold.
    b. Throttle body port hose at the straight plastic connector.
    c. Canister purge line at the straight plastic connector.
    d. PCV hose at the valve cover.
    e. Unbolt the PCV separator support bracket from the cylinder head and remove the PCV system.
14. Disconnect the EGR tube from the upper intake manifold by removing the two flange nuts.
15. Disconnect the EGR tube from the upper intake manifold by removing the two flange nuts.
16. Remove the dipstick and its tube.
17. Remove the fuel return line.
18. Remove the six manifold mounting nuts.
19. Remove the manifold with the wiring harness and gasket.
20. Installation is the reverse of removal. Tighten the manifold bolt 12-15 ft.lb.

Fuel Pressure Regulator

WARNING: Before attempting this procedure depressurize the fuel system.

1. Remove the vacuum line at the pressure regulator.
2. Remove the three Allen retaining screws from the regulator housing.
3. Remove the pressure regulator, gasket and O-ring. Discard the gasket and inspect the O-ring for deterioration.

WARNING: If scraping is necessary be careful not to damage the gasket surface.

4. Installation is the reverse of removal. Lubricate the O-ring with light

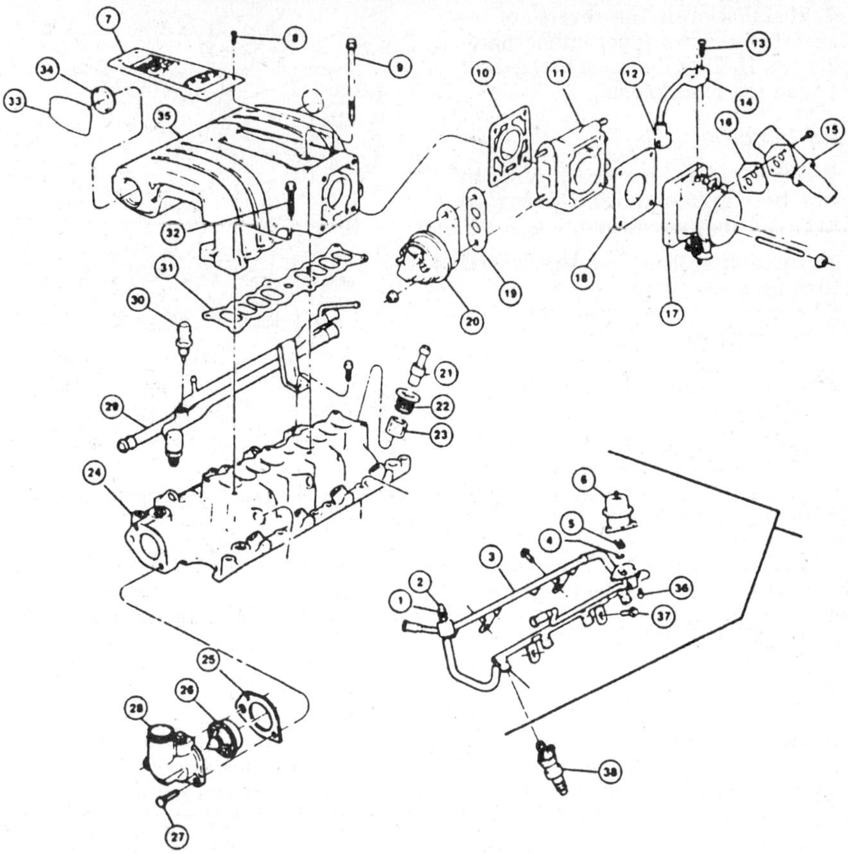

oil prior to installation. Tighten the three screws 27-40 in.lb.

Fuel Injector Manifold Assembly

1. Remove the fuel tank cap. Release the pressure from the fuel system.
2. Disconnect the fuel supply and return lines.
3. Disconnect the wiring harness from the injectors.
4. Disconnect the vacuum line from the fuel pressure regulator valve.
5. Remove the two fuel injector manifold retaining bolts.
6. Carefully disengage the manifold from the fuel injectors. Remove the manifold.
7. Installation is the reverse of removal. Torque the fuel manifold bolts 15-22 ft.lb.

Pressure Relief Valve

1. If the fuel charging assembly is mounted on the engine, the fuel system must be depressurized.
2. Using an open end wrench or suitable deep well socket, remove the pressure relief valve from the injection manifold.
3. Installation is the reverse of removal. Torque the valve 48-84 in.lb.

Throttle Position Sensor

1. Disconnect the throttle position sensor from the wiring harness.
2. Remove the two retaining screws.
3. Remove the throttle position sensor.
4. Installation is the reverse of removal. Torque the sensor screws 11-16 in.lb.

NOTE: This throttle position sensor is not adjustable.

Air By-pass Valve Assembly

1. Disconnect the air bypass valve assembly connector from the wiring harness.
2. Remove the two air bypass valve retaining screws.
3. Remove the air bypass valve and gasket.

WARNING: If necessary to remove the gasket by scraping, be careful not to damage the gasket surface.

4. Installation is the reverse of removal. Torque the air bypass valve assembly 71-102 in.lb.

Air Intake Throttle Body

1. Remove the four throttle body nuts. Make sure that the throttle position sensor connector and the air bypass valve connector have been disconnected from the harness. Disconnect the air cleaner outlet tube.
2. Identify and disconnect the vacuum hoses.
3. Remove the throttle bracket.
4. Carefully separate the throttle body from the upper intake manifold.
5. Remove and discard the gasket between the throttle body and the upper intake manifold.

WARNING: If scraping is necessary, be careful not to damage the gasket surfaces, or allow any material to drop into the manifold.

6. Installation is the reverse of removal. Tighten the throttle body-to-upper intake manifold nuts 12-15 ft.lb.

Upper Intake Manifold

1. Disconnect the air cleaner outlet tube from the air intake throttle body.
2. Unplug the throttle position sensor from the wiring harness.
3. Unplug the air by-pass valve connector.
4. Remove the three upper manifold retaining bolts.
5. Remove the upper manifold assembly.
6. Remove and discard the gasket from the lower manifold assembly.

WARNING: If scraping is necessary, be careful not to damage gasket surfaces, or allow any material to drop into the lower manifold.

1. Schrader valve
2. Cap-Schrader valve
3. Fuel rail assy
4. Seal O-ring 5/16-18 × 6.07 inch
5. Gasket, fuel pressure regulator
6. Fuel pressure regulator
7. Cover, upper manifold
8. Screw
9. Bolt 5/16-18 × 6.07 inch
10. Gasket, EGR spacer
11. EGR spacer
12. Connector, tp sensor (pia tps)
13. Screw
14. Sensor, throttle position
15. Throttle air bypass valve
16. Gasket, throttle air bypass valve
17. Throttle body assy
18. Gasket, throttle body
19. Gasket, EGR valve
20. EGR valve assy
21. PCV valve assy
22. PCV grommet
23. Element, crankcase vent
24. Lower intake manifold
25. Gasket, thermostat housing
26. Thermostat
27. Bolt 5/16-18 × 3.50 inch
28. Connector assy, engine coolant outlet
29. Tube, heater water supply and return
30. Sensor, EEC coolant temperature
31. Gasket, upper to lower manifold
32. Bolt 5/16-18 × 1.62 inch
33. Cover, decorative end
34. Plug—cap 1.75 inch dia.
35. Upper intake manifold
36. Screw—socket head 5.0 × 0.8 × 1.0
37. Botl, att rail assy to lower manifold
38. Fuel injector

Fuel injection components used on the 1987 8-302

7. Installation is the reverse of removal. Tighten the upper intake manifold bolts 15-22 ft.lb. Use a new gasket between the manifolds.

Fuel Injector

WARNING: The fuel system must be depressurized prior to starting this procedure.

1. Disconnect the fuel supply and return lines.
2. Remove the vacuum line from the fuel pressure regulator.
3. Disconnect the wiring harness.
4. Remove the fuel injector manifold assembly.
5. Carefully remove the connectors from the individual injectors.
6. Grasping the injectors body, pull up while gently rocking the injector from side to side.
7. Inspect the injector O-rings (two per injector) for signs of deterioration. Replace as needed.
8. Inspect the injector plastic hat (covering the injector pintle) and washer for signs of deterioration. Replace as needed. If a hat is missing, look for it in the intake manifold.
9. Installation is the reverse of removal. Lubricate all O-rings with a light oil. Carefully seat the fuel injector manifold assembly on the four injectors and secure the manifold with the attaching bolts. Torque the bolts 15-22 ft.lb.

Vane Air Meter

1. Loosen the hose clamp which secures engine air cleaner outlet hose to the vane meter assembly.
2. Remove air intake and outlet tube from the air cleaner.
3. Disengage four spring clamps and remove air cleaner front cover and air cleaner filter panel.
4. Remove the two screw and washer assemblies which secure the air meter to its bracket. Remove the vane air meter assembly.
5. Installation is the reverse of removal.

DIESEL FUEL SYSTEM

Injection Pump

REMOVAL & INSTALLATION

1. Disconnect the battery ground cable. Drain the cooling system.

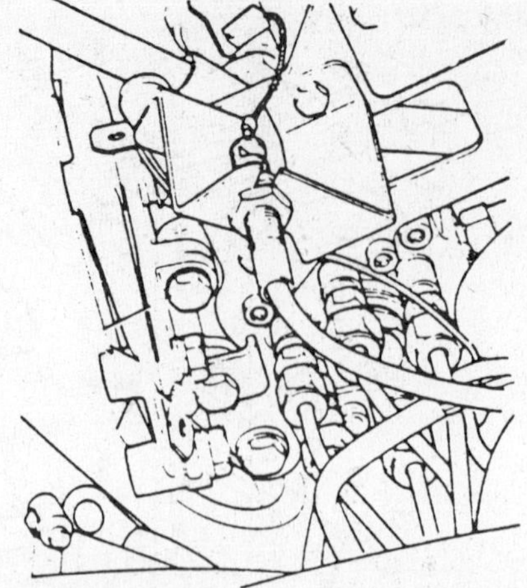

Injection pump rear mounting bolts – 2.4L diesel engine

CAUTION

When draining the coolant, keep in mind that cats and dogs are attracted by the ethylene glycol antifreeze, and are quite likely to drink any that is left in an uncovered container or in puddles on the ground. This will prove fatal in sufficient quantity. Always drain the coolant into a sealable container. Coolant should be reused unless it is contaminated or several years old.

2. Remove the accessory drive belts.
3. Remove the fan and clutch assembly or electric motor and fan assembly.
4. Remove the camshaft drive belt.
5. Install Injection Pump Sprocket Aligning Pin T84P-9000-A or equivalent and remove nut and washer attaching sprocket to the injection pump.
6. Install puller T67L-3600-A or equivalent and remove the sprocket. Remove the woodruff key from pump shaft.
7. Disconnect the clamp attaching the oil dipstick tube to the intake manifold, and position out of the way.
8. Disconnect the turbo pressure indicator switch connector. Remove the diagnostic plug bracket and position out of the way.
9. Loosen the clamp attaching the turbo crossover pipe boot to the intake manifold.
10. Remove the nuts attaching the intake manifold to cylinder head, and remove the intake manifold.

WARNING: To prevent fuel system contamination, cap all fuel lines and fittings.

11. Disconnect and cap the nozzle fuel lines at nozzles.
12. Remove the injection nozzle lines from injection pump using Fuel Line Nut Wrench T84P-9396-A or equivalent. Install caps on each end of each fuel line and pump fitting as it is removed and identify each fuel line accordingly.
13. Disconnect the coolant hoses from the idle speed boost housing.
14. Disconnect the electrical connector to the fuel shut-off and cold start accelerator valves, micro-switch and fuel pressure switch.
15. Disconnect the nozzle return line at the injection pump.
16. Disconnect the fuel return hose from the fuel return line on the left fender apron.
17. Disconnect the fuel inlet hose from the fuel inlet line on the left fender apron.
18. Disconnect the vacuum hoses at the altitude compensation valve. Note position of hoses, so they may be returned to the original position.
19. Disconnect the throttle cable and speed control cable, if equipped, from the injection pump.
20. Remove the three nuts attaching the injection pump to mounting bracket.
21. Remove the two nuts attaching the injection pump to the engine front cover, and remove the injection pump.
22. Install the injection pump in position. Line up the mark on the front cover with the mark on the injection pump mounting boss. Install the attaching nuts and bolts. Tighten to 14-17 ft.lb.
23. Connect the throttle cable, and speed control cable, if so equipped.
24. Remove the protective caps and install the fuel inlet hose to the fuel inlet line on left fender apron. Connect the fuel return hose to the fuel return line on the left fender apron.
25. Connect the vacuum hoses to the altitude compensation valve. Refer to the underhood sticker.
26. Connect the nozzle return line to the injection pump.
27. Connect the electrical connectors to the fuel pressure sensor, microswitch, cold start accelerator valve and fuel shut-off valve.
28. Connect the coolant hoses to the idle speed boost housing.

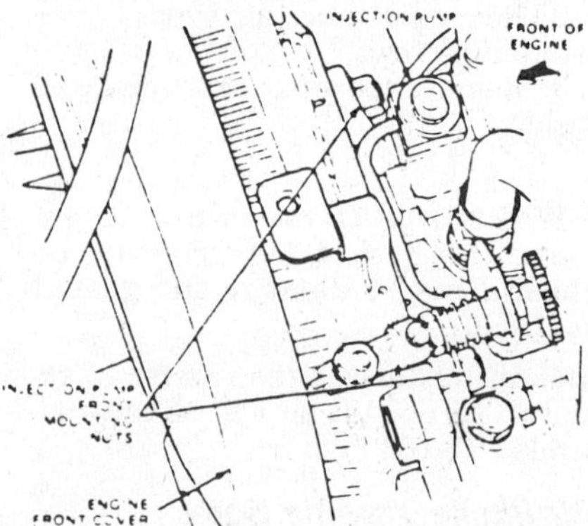

Injection pump front mounting bolts – 2.4L diesel engine

29. Install the fuel lines on injection pump, using Tool T84P-9396-A or equivalent, and tighten to 14-17 ft.lb.
30. Connect the fuel lines to the nozzles and tighten to 14-17 ft.lb.
31. Clean the intake manifold and cylinder head gasket mating surfaces. Position a new intake manifold gasket on the cylinder head, and install the intake manifold. Be sure the intake manifold inlet port is inserted into the turbo crossover pipe boot. Tighten attaching bolts to 14-17 ft.lb. Tighten the clamp at the cross-over pipe boot.
32. Install the diagnostic plug bracket on the cylinder head, and tighten to it 14-17 ft.lb.
33. Connect the turbo pressure indicator switch connector.
34. Position the oil dipstick tube to the intake manifold and install clamp.
35. Install the woodruff key in injection pump shaft.
36. Install the sprocket on injection pump. Install injection Pump Aligning Pin T84P-9000-A or equivalent, in sprocket. Install the sprocket attaching washer and nut and tighten to 33-36 ft.lb.

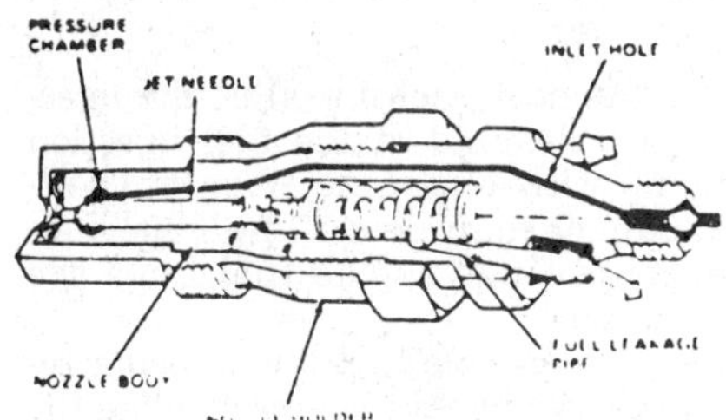
Injector nozzle

Injector pump aligning tool—2.4L diesel engine

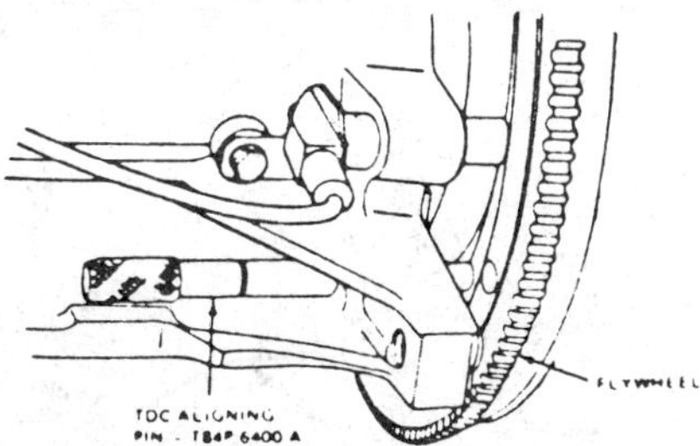
TDC aligning tool installation—24.L diesel engine

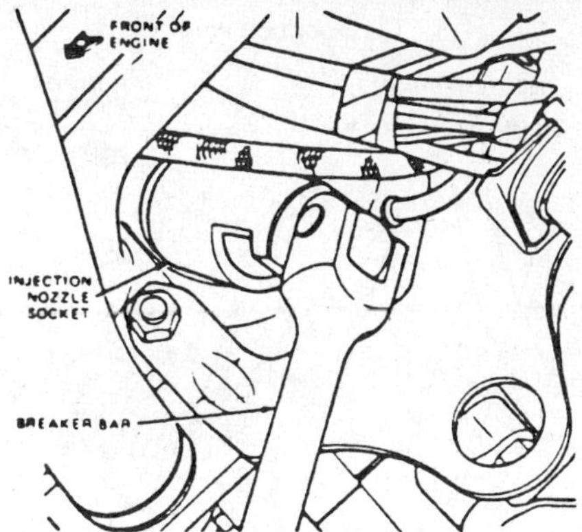

Injector nozzle removal and installation

37. Install and adjust the camshaft drive belt.
38. Install the camshaft drive belt cover and tighten it to 6-7 ft.lb.
39. Install the fan and clutch assembly or the electric motor and fan assembly.
40. Install and adjust the accessory drive belts.
41. Fill and bleed the cooling system.
42. Air bleed the fuel system.
43. Adjust the injection pump timing.
44. Connect the battery ground cable.
45. Start the engine and check for fuel, coolant and oil leaks.
46. Adjust the curb idle, fast idle and injection pump timing.

INJECTION TIMING

NOTE: Dynamic Timing Meter, Rotunda 078-00116, or equivalent, as well as other special tools, is necessary for this procedure.

1. Place the transmission in PARK.
2. Start the engine and run it to normal operating temperature.
3. Make sure that the throttle lever is against the stop screw.
4. Open the diagnostic connector and connect it to the adapter from the special tool.
5. Check the meter for rpm and injection timing.
6. Check the underhood decal for the rpm specification. If the rpm is not as specified, adjust it as outlined.
7. The proper injection timing is 5° ± 1½° at 1,500 rpm. If the timing is not as specified, proceed with the following steps.
8. Stop the engine.
9. Rotate the engine until #1 cylinder is at TDC on the compression stroke.
10. Remove the injection pump distributor head plug bolt and sealing washer.
11. Install adapter D84P-9000-D, Rotunda 014-00420, or equivalent into the injection pump. The plunger portion of the adapter must project into the pump so that it contacts the fuel injection pump plunger.
12. Mount the dial indicator, D84L-4201-A, or equivalent, into the adapter making sure that there is at least 0.25mm preload on the dial indicator.
13. Rotate the crankshaft clockwise until the dial indicator displays the lowest value. Set the dial indicator to 0.
14. Continue rotating the crankshaft clockwise until the #1 piston is again at TDC on the compression stroke.
15. Install the crankshaft holding tool T84P-6400-A, or equivalent, to hold the crankshaft in place.
16. Check the dial indicator.

If the timing belt has fewer than 10,000 miles of use the reading should be 0.65mm ± 0.04mm.

If the timing belt as more than 10,000 miles of use the reading should be 0.63mm ± 0.04mm.

17. If the timing is out of specification, install timing adapter T84P-9000-B, or equivalent, on the injection pump.
18. Loosen the injection pump mounting bolts and rotate the tool clockwise to increase the reading, or counterclockwise to decrease it.
19. Tighten the injection pump mounting bolts to 15 ft.lb., first tightening the rear bolts, then the front bolts.

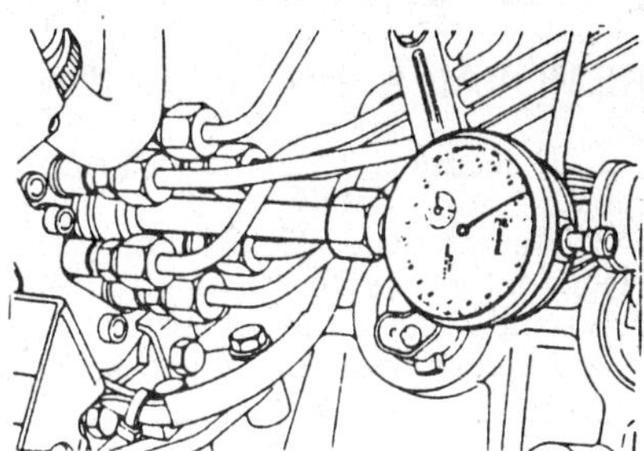
Diesel injection pump adaptor and dial indicator installation

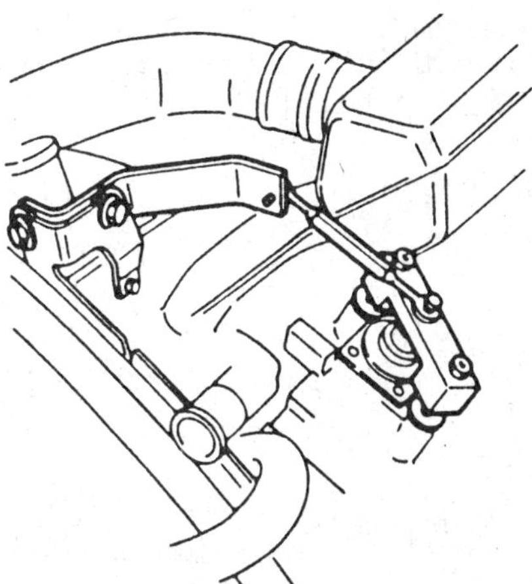
Diesel injector pump timing adapter

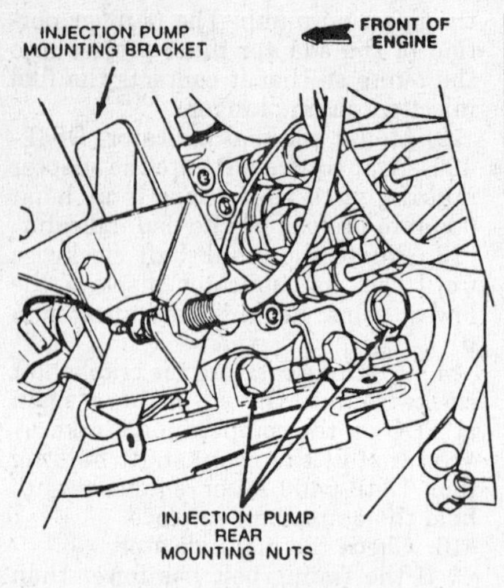

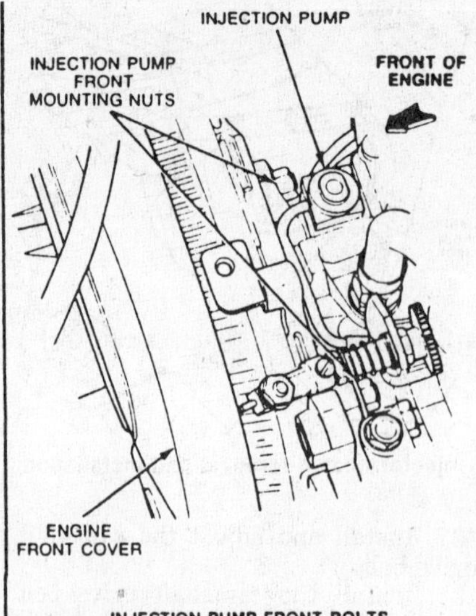

Diesel injection pump bolt tightening sequence

20. Remove the injection pump timing adapter and flywheel holding tool.
21. Rotate the engine 2 complete revolutions until the #1 cylinder is again at TDC compression. Check the dial indicator reading. If the reading is correct, remove the dial indicator and adapter and install the distributor head plug and sealing washer. Tighten the bolt to 84 in.lb. If the reading is still incorrect, repeat the timing procedure.

Fuel Shut-Off Valve

REMOVAL & INSTALLATION

1. Disconnect the battery ground cable.
2. Remove the nut attaching the electrical connector to the shut-off valve and remove the connector.
3. Remove the shut-off valve.

CAUTION

The piston and spring may fall out when removing the valve.

4. Replace the O-ring and valve, and install the valve on the injection pump. tighten to 11-18 ft.lb.

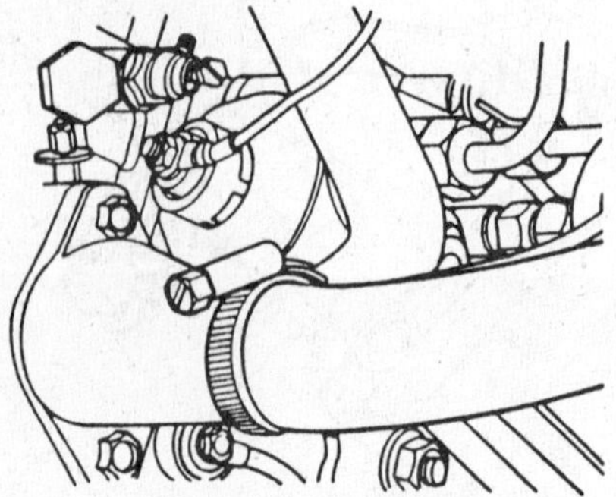

Diesel fuel shut-off valve

CAUTION

The piston and spring may fall out when installing valve.

5. Install the connector on the shutoff valve. Tighten the nut to 3-3.5 ft.lb.
6. Connect the battery ground cable. Run the engine and check for fuel leaks.

Injection Nozzles

REMOVAL & INSTALLATION

1. Pull off the leak-back lines from the injector nozzles.

NOTE: Make sure the area around the injector is clean.

2. Remove the fuel lines at the injectors and at the fuel injection pump with Fuel Line Wrench T84P-9395-A or equivalent. Cap all fuel lines and openings as the fuel lines are removed.
3. Unscrew the fuel injectors with Injector Nozzle Socket T84P-9527-A or equivalent. Note the injector order for installation.

NOTE: On injectors with sensors, disconnect the sensor plug wires and guide the sensor wires through Injector Nozzle Socket T84P-9527-A or equivalent, while installing the tool on the injector.

4. Plug the cylinder block injector nozzle opening.
5. Clean the injector nozzle opening in the cylinder block.
6. Install new heat shields into the injection nozzle openings.
7. Apply a copper based, anti-seize compound on the injector nozzle threads. Remove the protective plug in the cylinder block and install the injector nozzles in their original positions with Injector Nozzle Socket T84P-9527-A or equivalent. Tighten to 30-33 ft.lb.

NOTE: On injectors with sensors, guide the sensor plug wire through the socket before installing the injector nozzle. Reconnect the sensor wire after nozzle installation.

8. Remove the protective caps from the fuel lines, injector pump and injector nozzles and install the fuel lines using Fuel Line Wrench T84P-9396-A or equivalent. Tighten them to 15-18 ft.lb.

Injection Nozzle Fuel Lines

REMOVAL & INSTALLATION

1. If all the fuel lines are being removed, remove the intake manifold, and then remove all the fuel lines as an assembly.

NOTE: Do not remove the two clamps holding the fuel lines together.

2. Remove fuel line(s) at the injector nozzles and at the fuel injection pump with Fuel Line Wrench T84P-9395-A or equivalent. Cap all fuel lines and openings as the fuel lines are removed.
3. If only one fuel line is being removed, remove the clamps holding the fuel lines together and remove the fuel line.
4. If the fuel lines are being installed as an assembly, remove the protective caps and install the fuel lines (with clamps installed) on the injector nozzles and injection pump using Fuel Line Wrench T84P-9395-A or equivalent.
5. If only one fuel line is being installed, remove the protective caps and position the fuel line on the injector nozzle, and the injection line using

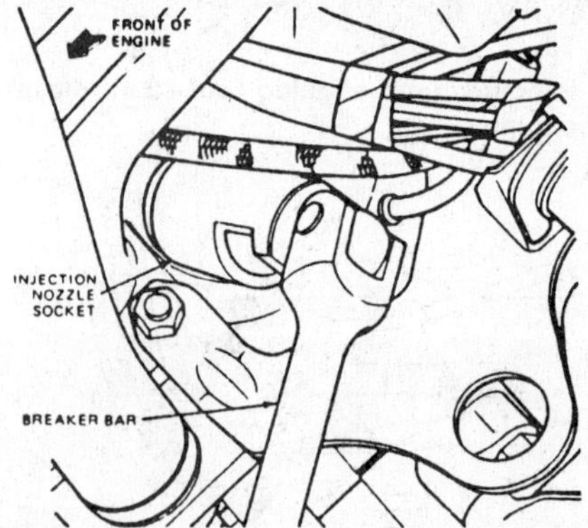

Diesel injection nozzle removal installation

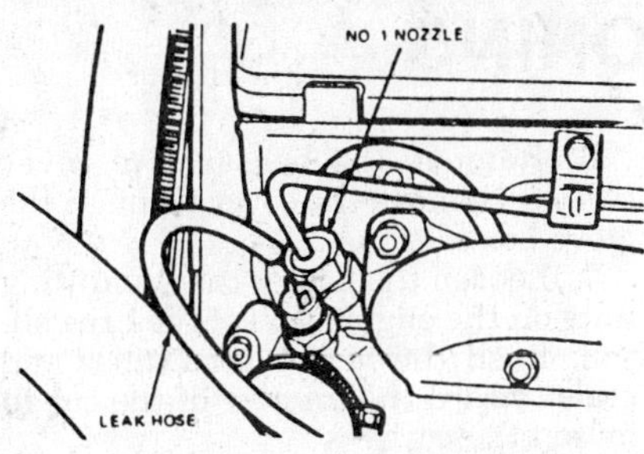

Diesel injection pump leak hose

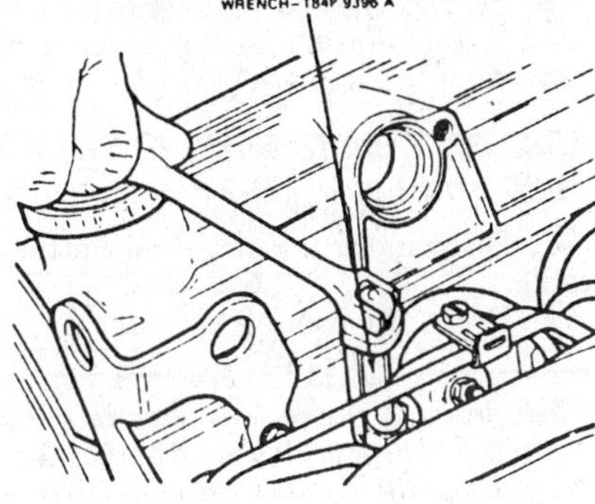

Diesel injection pump nozzle high pressure line removal

Fuel Line Wrench T84P-9395-A or equivalent. Install the clamps holding the fuel lines together.

6. Install the intake manifold if it was previously removed.

Glow Plugs

REMOVAL & INSTALLATION

1. Disconnect the battery ground cable.
2. Unscrew the glow plug electrical connection and remove the wire.
3. Remove the flow plug using a 12mm deepwell socket.
4. Coat the glow plug threads with a copper based, anti-seize compound.
5. Install the glow plug into the engine block using a 12mm deepwell socket.
6. Tighten the flow plug to 15-22 ft.lb.
7. Connect the electrical wire to the glow plug with the nut and tighten to 3-4 ft.lb.
8. Connect the battery ground cable.

Fuel Heater

REMOVAL & INSTALLATION

1. Disconnect the water-in-fuel sensor connector, fuel temperature sensor and fuel heater connector.
2. Drain the fuel from the fuel filter by opening the vent screw on the top of the filter and depressing the drain valve on the bottom of the filter.
3. Remove the filter cartridge using a standard oil filter wrench, if necessary.
4. Remove the fuel lines from the fuel filter adapter.
5. Remove the two bolts retaining the fuel heater/filter adapter to the bracket, and remove the vehicle.
6. Unscrew the fuel heater assembly from the fuel filter adapter.
7. Coat the seal with engine oil and install the fuel heater on the fuel filter adapter.
8. Position the fuel filter adapter (with fuel heater attached) to the bracket and install with two bolts. Tighten to 29-40 ft.lb.
9. Coat the surface of the sealing gasket with engine oil and install the filter on the adapter. Turn the filter until the gasket contacts the sealing surface of the filter adapter. Turn the filter an additional half turn.
10. Connect the Fuel-in-Water sensor, temperature sensor and fuel heater connectors.
11. Reconnect the fuel lines to the fuel filter and tighten the vent screw.
12. Start the engine and check for fuel leaks, tightening the filter further, if necessary.

Electric Fuel Pump

REMOVAL & INSTALLATION

1. Disconnect the electric fuel pump electrical connector.

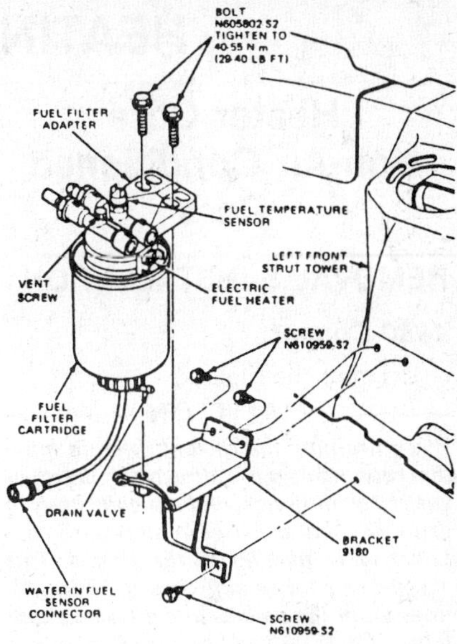

Diesel fuel heater

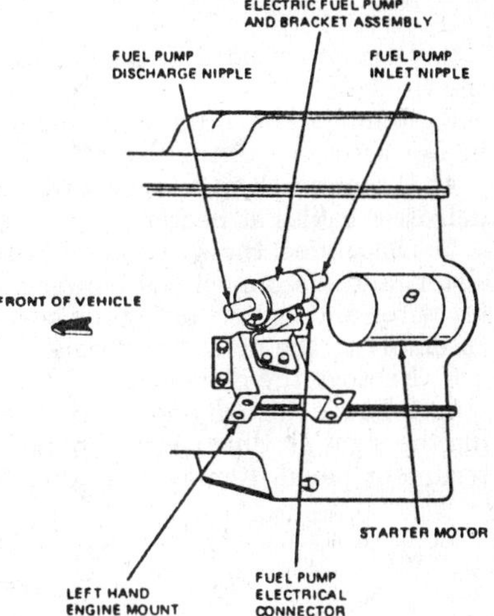

Diesel engine electric fuel pump

2. Remove the hose clamp on the inlet and outlet lines and remove the hoses from the fuel pump.
3. Remove the two fuel pump retaining screw and remove the fuel pump.
4. To install, reverse the removal steps. Tighten attaching screws to 9-11 ft.lb.

HEATING AND AIR CONDITIONING

Heater Core Non-Air Conditioned Cars

REMOVAL & INSTALLATION

1980 Cougar

1. Drain the coolant.

CAUTION

When draining the coolant, keep in mind that cats and dogs are attracted by the ethylene glycol antifreeze, and are quite likely to drink any that is left in an uncovered container or in puddles on the ground. This will prove fatal in sufficient quantity. Always drain the coolant into a sealable container. Coolant should be reused unless it is contaminated or several years old.

2. Disconnect both heater hoses at the firewall.
3. Remove the nuts retaining the heater assembly to the firewall.
4. Disconnect the temperature and defroster cables at heater.
5. Disconnect the wires from the resistor, and disconnect the blower motor wires and clip retaining the heater assembly to the defroster nozzle.
6. Remove the glove box.
7. Remove the bolt and nut connecting the right air duct control to the instrument panel. Remove the nuts retaining the right air duct and remove the duct assembly.
8. Remove the heater assembly from the bench.
9. Open the case and remove the core.
10. Installation is the reverse of removal.

1981-82 Cougar

It is not necessary to remove the heater case for access to the heater core.

1. Drain enough coolant from the radiator to drain the heater core.

CAUTION

When draining the coolant, keep in mind that cats and dogs are attracted by the ethylene glycol antifreeze, and are quite likely to drink any that is left in an uncovered container or in puddles on the ground. This will prove fatal in sufficient quantity. Always drain the coolant into a sealable container. Coolant should be reused unless it is contaminated or several years old.

2. Loosen the heater hose clamps on the engine side of the firewall and disconnect the heater hoses. Cap the heater core tubes.
3. Remove the glove box lines.
4. Remove the instrument panel-to-cowl brace retaining screws and remove the brace.
5. Move the temperature lever to **WARM**.
6. Remove the heater core cover screws. Remove the cover through the glove box.
7. Loosen the heater case mounting nuts on the engine side of the firewall.
8. Push the heater core tubes and seals toward the interior of the car to loosen the core.
9. Remove the heater core through the glove box opening.
10. Service these components as necessary, installation is the reverse of removal.

1980-87 Thunderbird 1980 and Later XR-7

1. Disconnect the negative battery cable.
2. Drain the cooling system.

CAUTION

When draining the coolant, keep in mind that cats and dogs are attracted by the ethylene glycol antifreeze, and are quite likely to drink any that is left in an uncovered container or in puddles on the ground. This will prove fatal in sufficient quantity. Always drain the coolant into a sealable container. Coolant should be reused unless it is contaminated or several years old.

3. Remove the instrument panel (see instrument panel removal and installation).
4. Disconnect the heater hoses from the heater core tubes. Plug the heater hoses and core tubes to prevent coolant spillage during removal.
5. Working under the hood at the firewall, remove the two nuts retaining the evaporator (heater) case to the dash.
6. From under the dash, remove the screws attaching the heater assembly support bracket and air inlet duct support bracket to the top cowl panel.

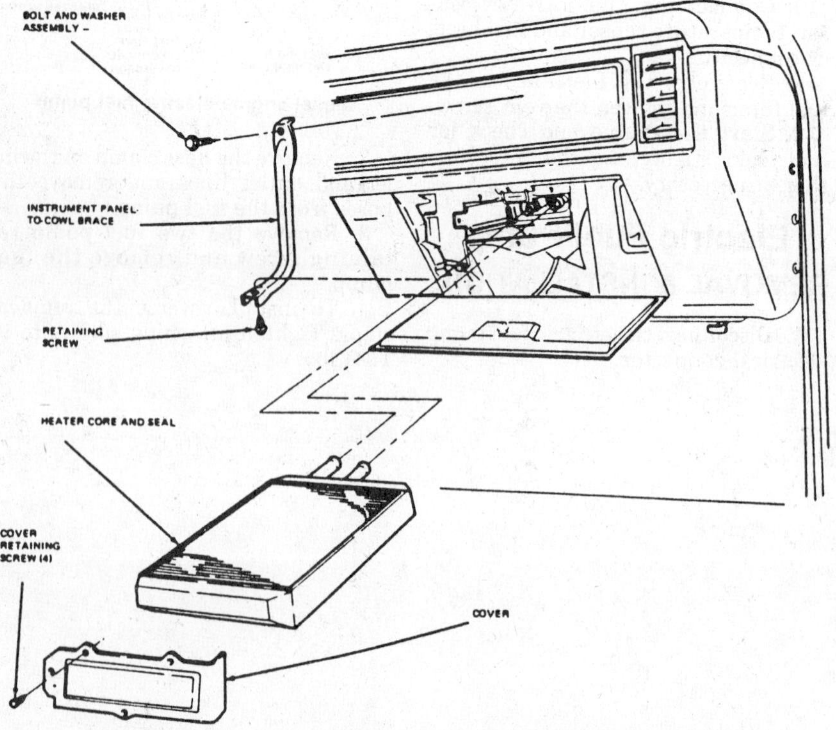

1981-82 Cougar heater core removal on cars without air conditioning

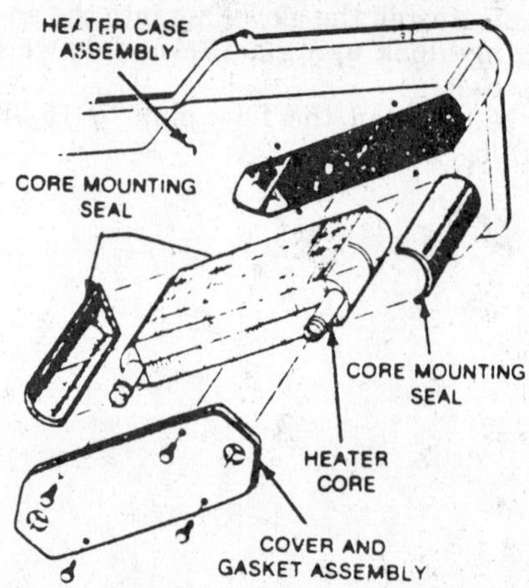

Typical heater core removal on all non-air conditioned cars, except 1981-82 Cougar

7. Remove the nut retaining the bracket at the left end of the heater assembly to the dash panel, and the nut retaining the bracket below the case to the dash panel.

8. Carefully pull the heater assembly away from the dash panel to gain access to the screws that retain the heater core access cover to the evaporator (heater) case.

9. Remove the cover retaining screws and the cover.

10. Lift the heater core and seals from the case. Remove the seals from the core tubes.

11. Install the heater core in the reverse order of removal. Fill the system with the correct coolant mix.

Mustang/Capri LTD/MARQUIS

1. Drain radiator coolant.

CAUTION

When draining the coolant, keep in mind that cats and dogs are attracted by the ethylene glycol antifreeze, and are quite likely to drink any that is left in an uncovered container or in puddles on the ground. This will prove fatal in sufficient quantity. Always drain the coolant into a sealable container. Coolant should be reused unless it is contaminated or several years old.

2. Disconnect heater hoses at core connections.
3. Remove glove box.
4. Remove instrument panel-to-cowl brace retaining screws and brace.
5. Move temperature control lever to warm position.
6. Remove four heater core cover retaining screws.
7. Remove heater core cover through glove box opening.

8. In engine compartment, loosen heater case assembly mounting stud nuts. (3).
9. Push heater core tubes and seal toward passenger compartment to loosen heater core assembly from heater case assembly.
10. Remove heater core from heater case assembly through the glove box opening.
11. Reverse procedure for installation.

Blower Motor Non-Air Conditioned Models

REMOVAL & INSTALLATION

The blower motor on all models except the 1980-82 Cougar XR-7, Thunderbird and 1982 Lincoln Continental is located inside the heater assembly. To replace the blower motor on all models except the 1980 and later Cougar XR-7 and Thunderbird, and 1981-82 Cougar, remove the heater assembly from the car. Once the heater assembly is removed, it is a simple operation to remove the motor attaching bolts and remove the motor. On all models except as noted, the motor and cage are removed as an assembly.

1981-82 Cougar

The right side ventilator assembly must be removed for access to the blower motor and wheel.

1. Remove the retaining screw from the right register duct mounting bracket.
2. Remove the screws holding the control cable lever assembly to the instrument panel.
3. Remove the glove box liner.
4. Remove the plastic rivets securing the grille to the floor outlet, and remove the grille.
5. Remove the right register duct and register assembly:
   a. Remove the register duct bracket retaining screw on the lower edge of the instrument panel, and disengage the duct from the opening and remove them through the glove box opening.
   b. Insert a thin blade under the retaining tab and pry the tab toward the louvers until retaining tab pivot clears the hole in the register opening. Pull the register assembly end out from the housing only enough to prevent the pivot from going back into the pivot hole. Pry the other retaining tab loose and remove the register assembly from the opening.
6. Remove the retaining screws securing the ventilator assembly to the blower housing. The upper right screw can be reached with a long extension through the register opening; the upper left screw can be reached through the glove box opening. The other two screws are on the bottom of the assembly.
7. Slide the assembly to the right, then down and out from under the instrument panel.
8. Remove the motor lead wire connector from the register and push it back through the hole in the case. Remove the right side cowl trim panel for access, and remove the ground terminal lug retaining screw.
9. Remove the hub clamp spring from the motor shaft and remove the blower wheel.
10. Remove the blower motor bolts from the housing and remove the motor.

1980 and Later Thunderbird and XR-7

1. Disconnect the negative battery cable.

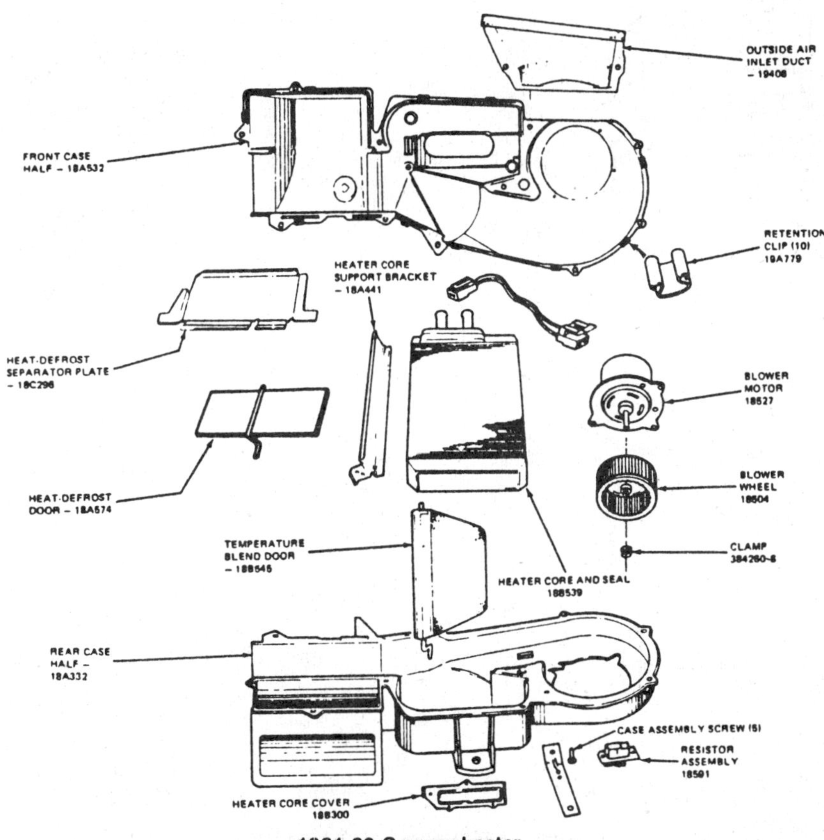

1981-82 Cougar heater

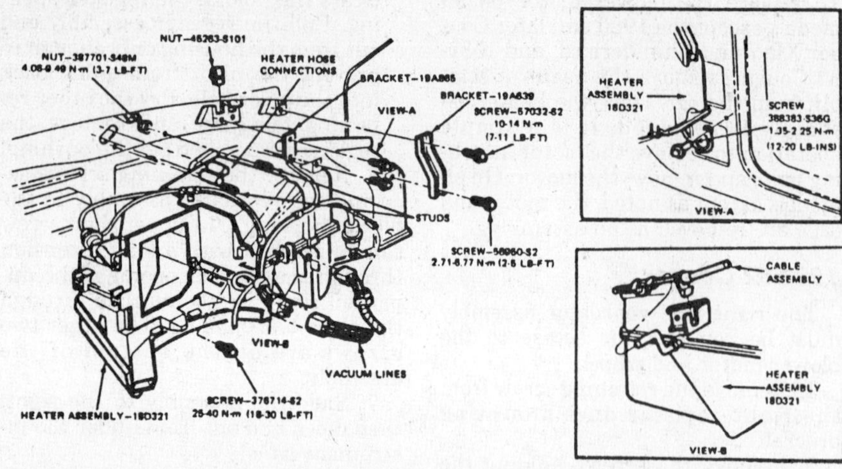

Heater used in all non-air conditioned 1980-87 models, except the 1981-82 Cougar

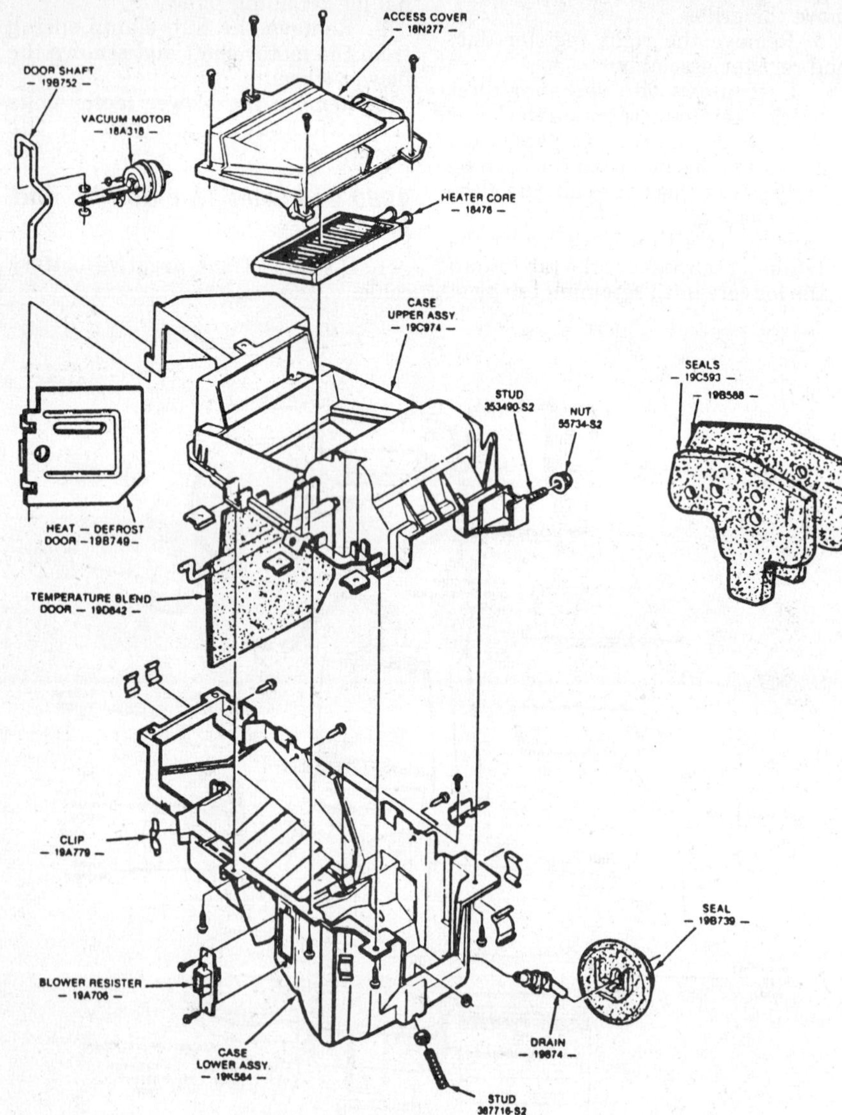

1983-84 heater disassembled

2. Remove the glove compartment and disconnect the hose from the outside-recirc. door vacuum motor.

3. Remove the lower instrument panel right side to cowl attaching bolt.

4. Remove the screw attaching the support brace to the top of the air inlet duct.

5. Disconnect the blower motor power lead at the wire connector.

6. Remove the nut retaining the blower housing lower support bracket to the evaporator (heater) case.

7. Remove the screw attaching the top of the air inlet duct to the heater assembly.

8. Move the air duct and blower housing assembly down and away from the heater case.

9. Remove the air inlet duct and blower housing assembly from the vehicle.

10. Remove the blower motor mounting plate screws and remove the blower motor and wheel assembly from the housing.

11. Service as necessary. Installation is the reverse of removal.

Heater Core Air Conditioned Models

REMOVAL & INSTALLATION

WARNING: Removal of the heater/air conditioner (evaporator) housing, if necessary, requires evacuation of the air conditioner refrigerant. This operation requires special tools and and a thorough familiarity with automotive refrigerant systems. Failure to follow proper safety precautions may cause personal injury. If you are not familiar with these systems, it is recommended that discharging and charging of the A/C system be performed by an experienced professional mechanic. For discharging, evacuating and charging procedures, see the ROUTINE MAINTENANCE section.

1980-87 Ford/Mercury, and Lincoln Town Car

1. Disconnect the negative battery cable.

2. Remove the heater hoses from the core tubes and plug the ends to prevent coolant loss.

3. Plug the heater core tubes to prevent coolant loss during plenum and core removal.

4. In the engine compartment, remove the bolt located under the windshield wiper motor. Remove the nut at

the upper left corner (engine side) of the evaporator case.

5. Disconnect the control system vacuum supply hose from the vacuum source and push the grommet and vacuum supply hose in the passenger compartment.

6. Remove the glove box assembly.

7. Loosen the right door sill plate and remove the right side cowl trim panel.

8. Remove the lower right instrument panel to side cowl bolt.

9. Remove the instrument panel.

NOTE: The following procedures apply to models without automatic temperature control systems.

10. Remove the bracket from the temperature control cable housing at the top of the plenum assembly. Disconnect the temperature control cable from the blend door crank arm.

11. Remove the push clip attaching the center register duct bracket to the plenum and rotate the bracket up to the right.

12. Disconnect the vacuum jumper harness at the multiple vacuum connector near the floor air distribution duct.

13. Disconnect the white vacuum hose from the outside recirculating door vacuum motor.

NOTE: The following procedures apply to models with automatic temperature control systems.

14. Disconnect the temperature control cable from the ATC sensor.

15. Disconnect the vacuum harness connector from the ATC sensor.

16. Disconnect the ATC sensor tube from the sensor and evaporator case connector. Also, disconnect the wire connector from the top end of the electric-vacuum relay, located on the right side of the plenum case.

17. Remove the two (2) attaching screws from the floor air distribution duct, at the seat side of the air distribution duct.

18. Remove the plastic push fastener, holding the air distribution duct to the left of the plenum and remove the air distribution duct.

19. Remove the final two (2) retaining nuts from the lower flange of the plenum assembly.

20. Move the plenum assembly toward the seat to allow the heater core tubes to clear the holes in the dash panel. Rotate the plenum assembly down and out from under the dash panel.

21. Installation is the reverse of removal. Refill the cooling system and check the heater operation.

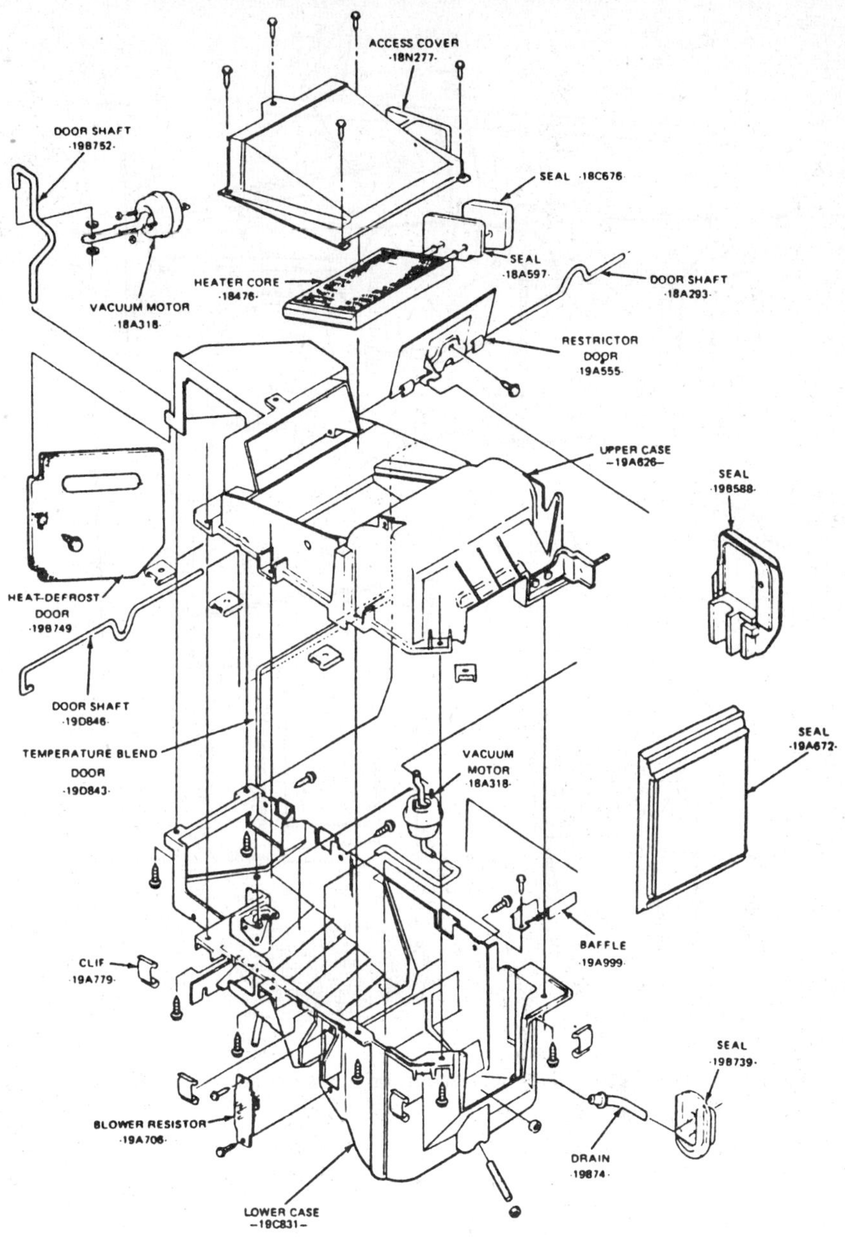

Exploded view of the heater used on 1980-81 Thunderbird and XR-7

MUSTANG/CAPRI

1. Remove the instrument panel and lay it on the front seat.

2. Drain the coolant from the cooling system. Disconnect the heater hoses from the core tubes and plug the tubes to prevent spillage.

CAUTION

When draining the coolant, keep in mind that cats and dogs are attracted by the ethylene glycol antifreeze, and are quite likely to drink any that is left in an uncovered container or in puddles on the ground. This will prove fatal in sufficient quantity. Always drain the coolant into a sealable container. Coolant should be reused unless it is contaminated or several years old.

3. From the engine compartment side remove the two (2) nuts attaching the evaporator case to the dash panel.

4. Under the dash area remove the screws attaching the evaporator case support bracket and the air inlet duct support bracket to the cowl top panel.

5. Remove the retaining nut from the bracket at the left end of the evaporator case and the nut attaching the heater core access cover to the evaporator case.

6. Carefully pull the evaporator case assembly away from the dash panel to gain access to the screws retaining the heater core access cover to the evaporator case.

7. Remove the heater core cover attaching screws and remove the cover.

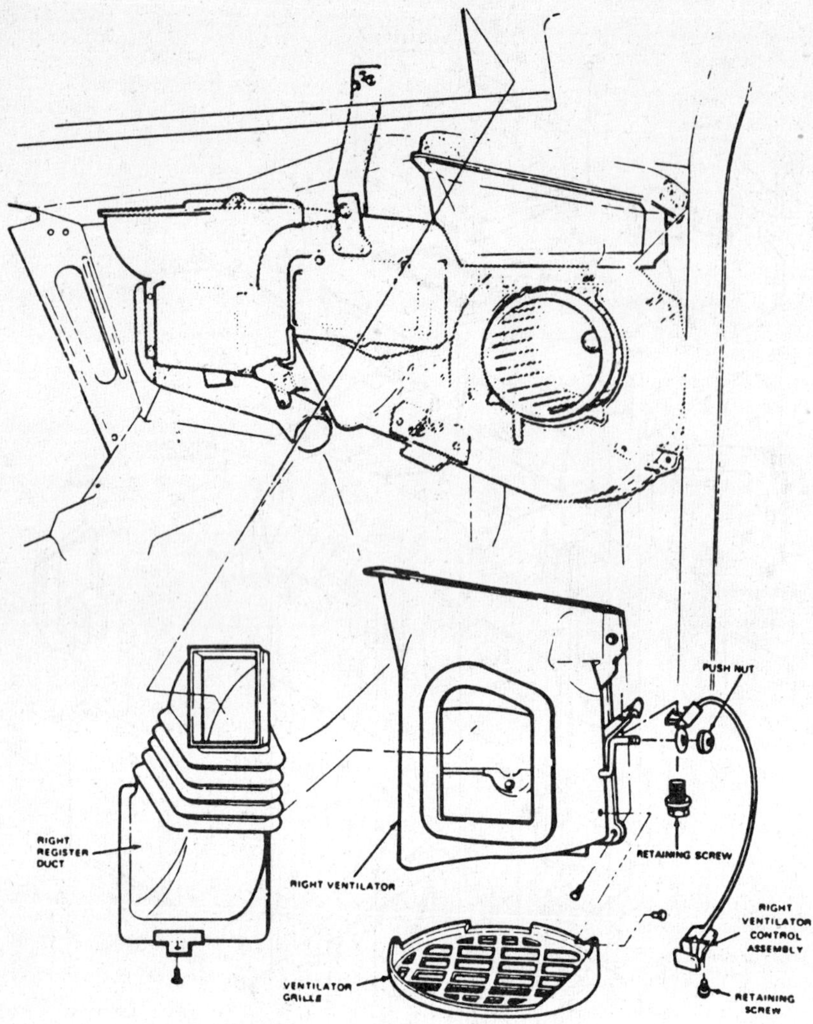

Right ventilator and register duct removal on non-air conditioned 1981-82 Cougar

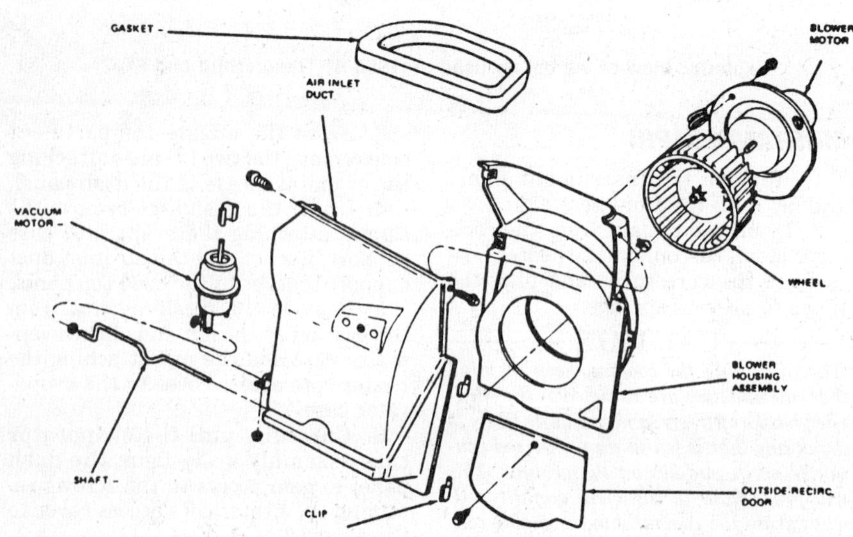

Air inlet duct and blower housing on air conditioned 1981-82 Cougar

8. Lift the heater core and seals from the evaporator case. Remove the two (2) seals from the core tubes.
9. Installation is the reverse of removal. Refill the cooling system and check heater operation.

1980-82 XR-7
1980-82 Thunderbird
1982 Continental

Heater core removal and installation for air conditioned models is the same as the procedure given earlier for non-air conditioned models. It is not necessary to discharge the A/C system; simply pull the evaporator case far enough away from the firewall to reach the heater core cover screws.

1981-82 Cougar

The instrument panel must be removed for access to the heater core.

1. Disconnect the battery ground cable.
2. Remove the instrument panel pad:
   a. Remove the screws attaching the instrument cluster trim panel to the pad.
   b. Remove the screw attaching the pad to the panel at each defroster opening.
   c. Remove the screws attaching the edge of the pad to the panel.
3. Remove the steering column opening cover.
4. Remove the nuts and bracket retaining the steering column to the instrument panel and lay the column against the seat.
5. Remove the instrument panel to brake pedal support screw at the column opening.
6. Remove the screws attaching the lower brace to the panel below the radio, and below the glove box.
7. Disconnect the temperature cable from the door and case bracket.
8. Unplug the 7-port vacuum hose connectors at the evaporator case.
9. Disconnect the resistor wire connector and the blower feed wire.
10. Remove the screws attaching the top of the panel to the cowl. Support the panel while doing this.
11. Remove the one screw at each end attaching the panel to the cowl side panels.
12. Move the panel rearward and disconnect the speedometer cable and any wires preventing the panel from lying flat on the seat.
13. Drain the coolant and disconnect the heater hoses from the heater core. Plug the core tubes.

CAUTION

When draining the coolant, keep in mind that cats and dogs are attracted by the ethylene glycol antifreeze, and are quite likely to

drink any that is left in an uncovered container or in puddles on the ground. This will prove fatal in sufficient quantity. Always drain the coolant into a sealable container. Coolant should be reused unless it is contaminated or several years old.

14. Remove the nuts retaining the evaporator case to the firewall in the engine compartment.
15. Remove the case support bracket screws and air inlet duct support bracket.
16. Remove the nut retaining the bracket to the dash panel at the left side of the evaporator case, and the nut retaining the bracket below the case to the dash panel.

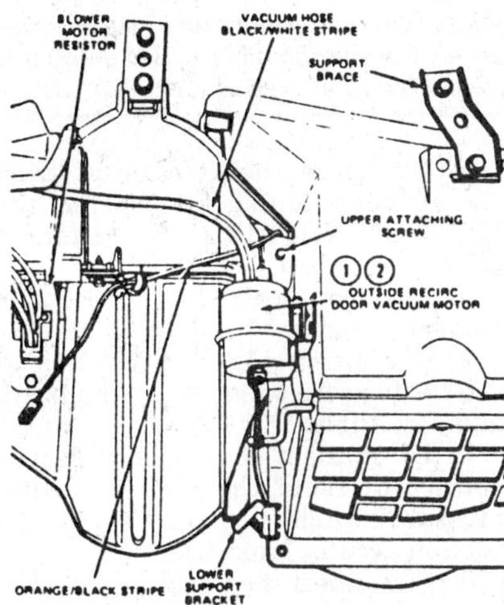

Air inlet and blower system assembled on 1981-82 Cougar

17. Pull the case assembly away from the panel to get to the screws retaining the heater core cover to the case.
18. Remove the cover screws and the cover.
19. Lift the heater core and seals from the evaporator case.
20. Service as required. Reinstall in the reverse order of removal.

1983 and Later Thunderbird and XR-7

WITH MANUAL AIR CONDITIONING

NOTE: Heater core removal requires instrument panel and heater/evaporator case assembly removal.

1. Disconnect the negative battery cable.
2. Remove the instrument panel (See Instrument Panel Removal and Installation).
3. Discharge the air conditioning system at the service access gauge port locate on the suction line. See the CAUTION NOTICE at the beginning of this procedure.
4. Once the air conditioning system has been discharged, remove the high and low pressure hoses. Use a second wrench to hold the fittings when loosening the lines. Plug the hose openings to prevent dirt and moisture from entering.
5. Drain the cooling system and remove the heater hoses from the heater core tubes. Plug the hoses and the heater core tubes.

CAUTION

When draining the coolant, keep in mind that cats and dogs are attracted by the ethylene glycol antifreeze, and are quite likely to drink any that is left in an uncovered container or in puddles on the ground. This will prove fatal in sufficient quantity. Always drain the coolant into a sealable container. Coolant should be reused unless it is contaminated or several years old.

6. Remove the screw that attaches the air inlet duct and blower housing support brace to the cowl top panel under the dash.
7. Disconnect the vacuum supply hose from the in-line vacuum check valve in the engine compartment.
8. Disconnect the blower motor wiring connector.
9. From under the hood, remove the two nuts retaining the evaporator case to the firewall.
10. From under the dash, remove the screw attaching the evaporator case support bracket to the cowl top panel.
11. Remove the nut that retains the bracket below the evaporator case to the dash panel.
12. Carefully pull the evaporator case away from the dash panel and remove the case from the vehicle.
13. Remove the heater core access cover from the evaporator case.
14. Remove the heater core and seals from the case. Remove the seals from the core fitting tubes.
15. Service as required. Install in the reverse order of removal. Fill the cooling system with the correct coolant mix. Have the air conditioning system charged. See the CAUTION NOTICE at the beginning of this procedure.

1983 Continental, Thunderbird and XR-7

With Automatic Temperature Control

NOTE: Core removal requires instrument panel and evaporator case assembly removal.

1. Disconnect the negative battery cable.
2. Remove the instrument panel. (See Instrument Panel Removal and Installation).
3. Discharge the air conditioning system at the service access gauge port located on the suction line. See the CAUTION NOTICE at the beginning of this procedure.
4. Once the air conditioning system has been discharged, remove the high and low pressure hoses. Use a second wrench to hold the receiver fittings when loosening the lines. Plug the hose openings to prevent dirt and moisture from entering.
5. Drain the cooling system and remove the heater hoses from the heater core tubes. Plug the hoses and heater core tubes.

CAUTION

When draining the coolant, keep in mind that cats and dogs are attracted by the ethylene glycol antifreeze, and are quite likely to drink any that is left in an uncovered container or in puddles on the ground. This will prove fatal in sufficient quantity. Always drain the coolant into a sealable container. Coolant should be reused unless it is contaminated or several years old.

6. Remove the screw attaching the air inlet duct and blower housing assembly support brace to the top cowl panel under the dash.
7. Disconnect the vacuum supply hose from the in-line vacuum check valve and the vacuum hose from the TBL (Thermal Blower Lockout Switch) in the engine compartment.
8. Disconnect the blower motor wiring connector.
9. From under the hood, remove the two nuts retaining the evaporator case to the firewall.
10. From under the dash, remove the screw attaching the evaporator case support bracket to the cowl top panel.
11. Remove the screw retaining the bracket below the evaporator case and dash panel.
12. Carefully pull the evaporator case assembly away from the dash panel and remove the assembly from the vehicle.
13. Remove the heater core access cover screws and the cover.
14. Lift the heater core and seals from the case assembly.
15. Remove the seals from the core.
16. Service as required. Install in the reverse order of removal. Fill the cooling system with the correct mixture of coolant. Have the air conditioning system recharged. See CAUTION NOTICE at the beginning of this procedure.

1984 and Later Mark VII

NOTE: Heater core removal requires instrument panel and heater/evaporator case assembly removal.

1. Disconnect the negative battery cable and drain the cooling system.

CAUTION

When draining the coolant, keep in mind that cats and dogs are attracted by the ethylene glycol antifreeze, and are quite likely to drink any that is left in an uncovered container or in puddles on the ground. This will prove fatal in sufficient quantity. Always drain the coolant into a sealable container. Coolant should be reused unless it is contaminated or several years old.

2. Discharge the refrigerant from the air conditioning system. See the CAUTION NOTICE at the beginning of this procedure.
3. Remove the air cleaner assembly from the engine.
4. Disconnect the heater hoses from the heater core tubes at the firewall. Plug the heater hoses and core tubes.
5. Disconnect the wire harness connector from the clutch cycling switch located at the top of the suction accumulator/drier.
6. Disconnect the liquid line and the accumulator/drier inlet tube from the evaporator core tubes. New O-rings will be required for re-installation. Hold the line connection fittings with a second wrench to prevent damage. Plug all lines after disconnecting.
7. Remove the two nuts retaining the accumulator/drier bracket to the firewall.
8. Position the drier and the liquid line aside and remove the two evaporator retaining nuts.
9. From inside the vehicle, remove the steering column opening cover from the instrument panel.
10. Remove the instrument panel left and right sound insulators.
11. Remove the right and left cowl trim panels.
12. Remove the right side finish panel from the instrument panel. Disconnect and position the console assembly out of the way.
13. Carefully pry the defroster opening grille from the instrument panel.
14. Remove the screw attaching the lower center of the instrument panel to the floor brace.
15. Remove the shroud from the steering column.
16. Remove the steering column reinforcement.
17. Disconnect the transmission gear indicator cable from the steering column.
18. Remove the steering column to bracket pedal support retaining nuts and lay the steering column down against the front seat.
19. Remove the nut attaching the instrument panel to the bracket pedal and steering column support.
20. Remove the instrument panel attaching screws. Pull the panel forward and disconnect wire connectors etc. and place the panel on the front seat.
21. Disconnect the wiring harness connectors from the blower motor and blower motor speed controller. Disconnect the automatic temperature control (ATC) sensor hose and elbow from the evaporator case. Disconnect the ATC harness at the control assembly.
22. Disconnect the antenna cable from the radio and the strap retaining the cable to the evaporator case.
23. Disconnect the rear seat duct adaptor from the floor duct.
24. Remove the bolts attaching the evaporator case to the panel and remove the evaporator assembly from the vehicle.
25. Remove the screws attaching the heater core access cover from the evaporator case. Remove the cover. Lift the heater core and seals from the evaporator case. Remove the seals from the core tubes. Service as required.
26. Position the evaporator assembly in position and install the three mounting bolts but do not tighten at this time. Be sure that the evaporator drain tube is through the dash opening and is not pinched or kinked.
27. Install the two evaporator case mounting nuts at the firewall under the hood. Tighten the three mounting bolts inside the vehicle that were previously installed.
28. Position the instrument panel near the dash panel (firewall) and connect the radio antenna, ATC harness, blower motor and controller harnesses, and the ATC sensor hose and elbow and all other instrument harness connectors that were removed.
29. Position the instrument panel and secure, be sure that the A/C plenum, attached to the instrument panel, is aligned and sealed at the evaporator case opening.
30. Install the nut retaining the instrument panel to the bracket pedal and steering column support. Position the steering column to the bracket pedal and column support bracket and install the retaining nuts.
31. Connect the transmission gear selector indicator cable and adjust if necessary.
32. Install the steering column opening reinforcement. Install the steering column shroud. Install the screw that attaches the lower center of the instrument panel to the floor brace.
33. Install the defroster grille. Install the right and left side cowl trim panels. Install the right and left side instrument panel sound insulators.
34. Install the rear seat heater duct assembly. Install the console assembly. Install the instrument panel right side finish panel and the steering column opening cover.
35. Install the remaining components in the reverse order of removal. have the A/C system recharged (see the CAUTION NOTICE at the beginning of this procedure) and check system operation.

1984 and Later Continental

NOTE: Heater core removal requires instrument panel and heater/evaporator case assembly removal.

1. Disconnect the negative battery cable and drain the cooling system.

CAUTION

When draining the coolant, keep in mind that cats and dogs are attracted by the ethylene glycol antifreeze, and are quite likely to drink any that is left in an uncovered container or in puddles on the ground. This will prove fatal in sufficient quantity. Always drain the coolant into a sealable container. Coolant should be reused unless it is contaminated or several years old.

2. Discharge the refrigerant from the air conditioning system. See the CAUTION NOTICE at the beginning of this procedure.
3. Remove the air cleaner assembly from the engine.
4. Disconnect the heater hoses at the heater core tubes. Plug the hoses and core tubes.
5. Disconnect the wiring harness connector from the clutch cycling pressure switch located on top of the suction accumulator/drier.
6. Disconnect the liquid line and the accumulator/drier inlet tube from the evaporator core tubes. New O-rings will be required for re-installation. Hold the connector fitting with a second wrench to prevent damage while disconnecting the lines. Cap the lines.
7. Remove the two nuts retaining the drier bracket to the firewall. Position the drier and lines of the the way. Remove the two nuts that mount the evaporator of the firewall.
8. From inside the vehicle, remove the steering column opening cover from the instrument panel.
9. Remove the instrument panel right and left sound insulators.
10. Remove the right and left side cowl trim panels.
11. Remove the ash tray receptacle from the instrument panel. Remove the two screws attaching the lower center of the instrument panel to the floor brace.
12. Remove the shroud from the steering column and disconnect the transmission gear indicator cable from the steering column.
13. Remove the instrument panel pad. Remove the steering column to brake pedal support retaining nuts and lower the steering column to the front seat.
14. Remove the nut attaching the in-

strument panel to the brake pedal and steering column support.

15. Remove the instrument panel attaching screws and lay the panel on the front seat after disconnecting the necessary wire harness connectors.

16. Disconnect the wiring harness connectors from the blower motor wires and the blower motor speed controller.

17. Disconnect the automatic temperature control (ATC) sensor hose and elbow from the evaporator case.

18. Disconnect the ATC harness at the control assembly.

19. Disconnect the radio antenna cable from the radio and from the retaining strap.

20. Use a sharp knife and carefully slit the carpet on the top of the transmission tunnel. Fold back the carpet to expose the rear seat heater duct.

21. Use a saw or hot knife to cut the top and side of the duct. Remove the top of the duct.

22. Remove the three evaporator case mounting bolts and remove the evaporator assembly.

23. Remove the screws that retain the heater core access cover. Remove the cover. Lift the heater core and tube seals from the evaporator case. Service the assembly as required.

24. Position the evaporator assembly to the dash (firewall) panel and install the three mounting bolts but do not tighten them at this time.

25. Make sure that the evaporator drain tube is through the opening in the dash and is not pinched or kinked. Install and tighten the two evaporator case mounting nuts on the firewall in the engine compartment.

26. Tighten the three case mounting bolts inside the vehicle.

27. Place the top piece that was cut from the rear seat heat duct into position and secure with duct tape. Be sure to cover all seams to prevent air leakage. Position the carpet back over the duct.

28. Position the instrument panel near the dash (firewall) and connect the radio antenna, ATC harness, blower motor and controller harnesses, ATC sensor hose and elbow and all other harness connectors removed from the instrument panel.

29. Position the instrument panel and secure with the mounting screws. Be sure that the A/C plenum, attached to the instrument panel, is properly aligned and sealed at the evaporator outlet opening.

30. Install the nut that attaches the instrument panel to the bracket pedal and steering column support.

31. Position the steering column to the brake pedal and column support and install the retaining nuts.

32. Connect the transmission gear selector indicator cable and adjust if necessary.

33. Install the steering column opening reinforcement. Install the steering column shroud.

34. Install the two screws to attach the lower center of the instrument panel to the floor brace. Install the right and left side cowl trim panels.

35. Install the right and left side instrument panel sound insulators. Install the instrument panel pad. Install the steering column opening cover.

36. Install the remaining components in the reverse order of removal. Have the A/C system recharged (see the CAUTION NOTICE at the beginning of this procedure) and check system operation.

Blower Motor Air Conditioned Models

REMOVAL & INSTALLATION

1980-87 Ford, Mercury, and Lincoln Town Car

1. Disconnect the ground cable from the battery.

2. Disconnect the blower motor lead connector from the wiring harness connector.

3. Remove the blower motor cooling tube from the blower motor.

4. Remove the four (4) retaining screws.

5. Turn the motor and wheel assembly slightly to the right so that the bottom edge of the mounting plate follows the contour of the wheel well splash panel. Lift up on the blower and remove it from the blower housing.

6. Installation is the reverse or removal.

1980-82 XR-7
1980-82 Thunderbird
1981-82 Cougar
1982 Continental
LTD
Marquis
1984-86 Mustang and Capri

NOTE: The air inlet duct and blower housing assembly must be remove for access to the blower motor.

1. Remove the glove box liner and disconnect the hose from the vacuum motor.

2. Remove the instrument panel lower right side to cowl attaching bolt.

3. Remove the screw attaching the brace to the top of the air inlet duct.

4. Disconnect the motor wire.

5. Remove the housing lower support bracket to case nut.

6. Remove the side cowl trim panel and remove the ground wire screw.

7. Remove the attaching screw at the top of the air inlet duct.

8. Remove the air inlet duct and housing assembly down an away from the evaporator case.

9. Remove the four blower motor mounting plate screws and remove the blower motor and wheel as an assembly from the housing. Do not remove the mounting plate from the motor.

1987 Mustang

1. Loosen glove compartment assembly by squeezing the sides together to disengage the retainer tabs.

2. Let the glove compartment and door hang down in front of instrument panel, and remove blower motor cooling hose.

3. Disconnect electrical wiring harness. Remove four screws attaching motor to housing. Pull motor and wheel out of housing.

1983 and Later Thunderbird and XR-7

WITH MANUAL AIR CONDITIONING

NOTE: Follow the previous procedure for 1980-82 models.

1983 and Later Continental
1983 and Later Thunderbird
1983 and Later XR-7
1984 and Later Mark VII

WITH AUTOMATIC AIR CONDITIONING

1. Remove the glove compartment (and shield on Continental models) and disconnect the hose from the outside/recirc. door vacuum motor.

2. Remove the instrument panel lower right side to side cowl attaching bolt.

3. Remove the screw attaching the support bracket to the top of the air duct.

4. Disconnect the power lead for the blower motor at the wire connector.

5. Remove the nut retaining the blower motor housing lower support bracket to the evaporator case.

6. Remove the side cowl trim panel. On Continental models; open the ash tray and remove the receptacle and remove the tow screws attaching the instrument panel to the transmission tunnel at the ashtray opening.

7. Remove the screw attaching the top of the air inlet duct to the evaporator case.

8. Move the air inlet duct and blower housing assembly down and away from the evaporator case. Remove the assembly.

9. Remove the blower plate mounting screws and remove the blower motor and wheel assembly.

10. Service as required. Install in the reverse order of removal.

Evaporator

REMOVAL & INSTALLATION

1980-81

1. Discharge the system at the service access port on the underside of the combination valve. See the ROUTINE MAINTENANCE section.

2. Remove the instrument panel and lay it on the front seat.

3. Drain the cooling system and disconnect the heater hoses at the core tubes.

CAUTION

When draining the coolant, keep in mind that cats and dogs are attracted by the ethylene glycol antifreeze, and are quite likely to drink any that is left in an uncovered container or in puddles on the ground. This will prove fatal in sufficient quantity. Always drain the coolant into a sealable container. Coolant should be reused unless it is contaminated or several years old.

4. Disconnect the refrigerant lines at the combination valve. Use a back-up wrench on the suction throttling valve manifold. Cap all openings immediately!.

5. Disconnect the wiring at the blower resistor. Remove the screw attaching the air inlet duct and blower housing assembly support brace to the cowl top panel.

6. Disconnect the black vacuum supply hose at the check valve, in the engine compartment.

7. In the engine compartment, remove the 2 nuts retaining the evaporator case to the firewall.

8. In the passenger compartment, remove the screw attaching the evaporator case support bracket to the cowl top panel.

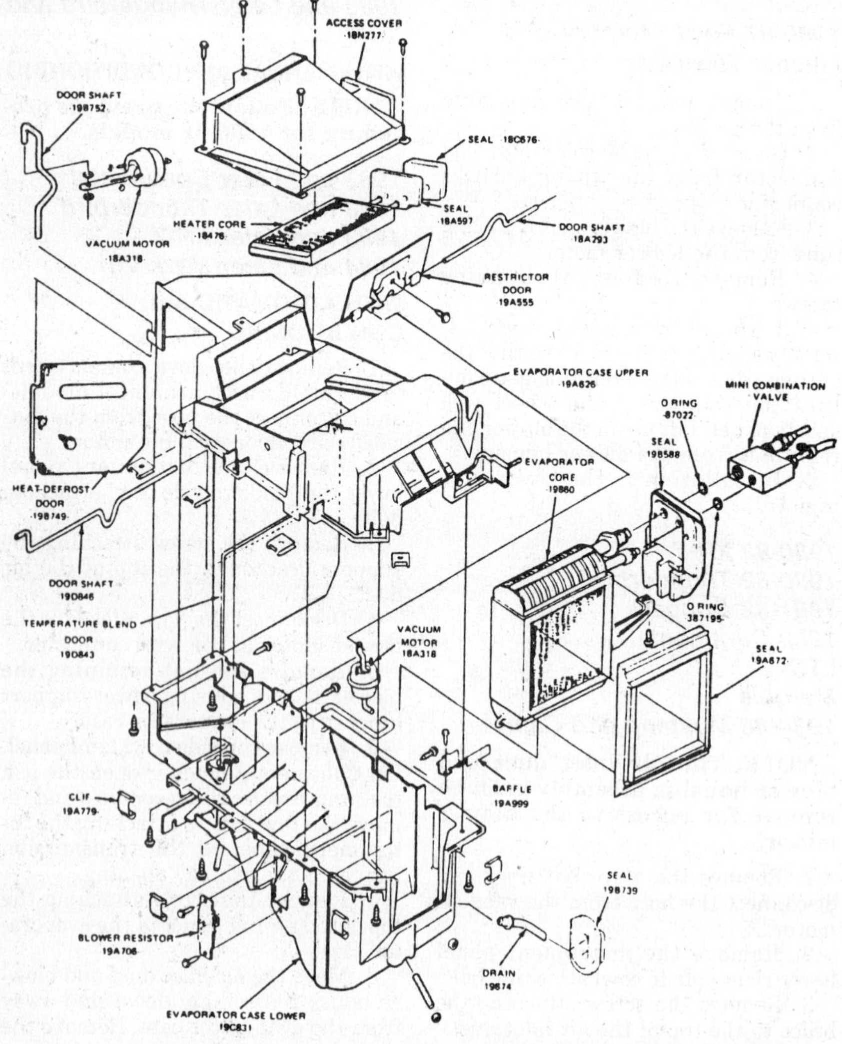

Evaporator case components for all 1980-81 models

9. Remove the nut retaining the left end of the evaporator case to the firewall and the nut retaining the bracket below the evaporator case, to the dash panel.

10. Carefully pull the case away from the firewall and remove the case from the car.

11. Remove the air inlet duct and blower housing from the case.

12. Remove the 5 screws retaining the access cover to the case and lift off the cover.

13. Remove the heater core from the case.

14. Remove the 2 nuts retaining the restrictor door vacuum motor to the mounting bracket.

15. Disengage the vacuum motor arm from the restrictor door.

16. Remove the 11 screws and 6 snap-clips securing the halves of the case and separate the case halves.

17. Lift out the evaporator core, seal and combination valve from the lower case half.

18. Assembly and installation is the reverse of removal and disassembly.

- Always use new O-rings coated with clean refrigerant oil.
- Be sure that the restrictor is installed in the evaporator inlet line.
- Make sure that the core seal fits over the case lower half edge.
- Make sure that the temperature blend door and heat/defrost door are properly positioned.
- Always use new sealer between the case halves.
- Make sure that the drain hose is not kinked.
- When everything is back together, turn on the blower and check for air leaks around the case.
- Evacuate, charge and leak test the system. See the ROUTINE MAINTENANCE section.

1982-84

1. Discharge the system at the service access port located on the suction line. See the ROUTINE MAINTENANCE section.

2. Remove the instrument panel and lay it on the front seat.

3. Drain the cooling system and disconnect the heater hoses at the core tubes.

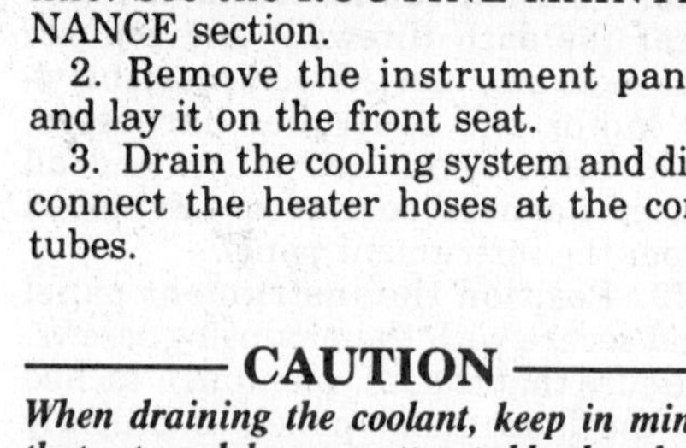

CAUTION

When draining the coolant, keep in mind that cats and dogs are attracted by the ethylene glycol antifreeze, and are quite likely to drink any that is left in an uncovered container or in puddles on the ground. This will prove fatal in sufficient quantity. Always drain the coolant into a sealable container. Coolant should be reused unless it is contaminated or several years old.

4. Disconnect the refrigerant lines using back-up wrenches at each fitting. Cap all openings immediately!.

5. Disconnect the wiring at the blower, and the ATC wiring on cars with electronic automatic temperature control. Remove the screw attaching the air inlet duct and blower housing assembly support brace to the cowl top panel.

6. Disconnect the black vacuum supply hose at the check valve, in the engine compartment, and, on cars with automatic temperature control, the vacuum hoses at the TBL switch, also in the engine compartment.

7. In the engine compartment, remove the 2 nuts retaining the evaporator case to the firewall.

8. In the passenger compartment, remove the screw attaching the evaporator case support bracket to the cowl top panel.

9. Remove the screw retaining the bracket below the case, to the firewall.

10. Carefully pull the case away from the firewall and remove the case from the car.

11. Remove the air inlet duct and blower housing from the case.

12. Remove the screws and snap-clips securing the halves of the case and separate the case halves.

13. Lift out the evaporator core and seal from the lower case half.

14. Assembly and installation is the reverse of removal and disassembly.

- Always use new O-rings coated with clean refrigerant oil.
- Make sure that the sore seal fits over the case lower half edge.
- Make sure that the temperature blend door and heat/defrost door are properly positioned.
- Always use new sealer between the case halves.
- Make sure that the drain hose is not kinked.
- When everything is back together, turn on the blower and check for air leaks around the case.
- Evacuate, charge and leak test the system. See the ROUTINE MAINTENANCE section.

1985 Thunderbird and Cougar 1986-87 All Models with Manual Air Conditioning

1. Discharge the system at the service access port located on the suction line. See the ROUTINE MAINTENANCE section.

2. Remove the instrument panel and lay it on the front seat.

3. Drain the cooling system and disconnect the heater hoses at the core tubes.

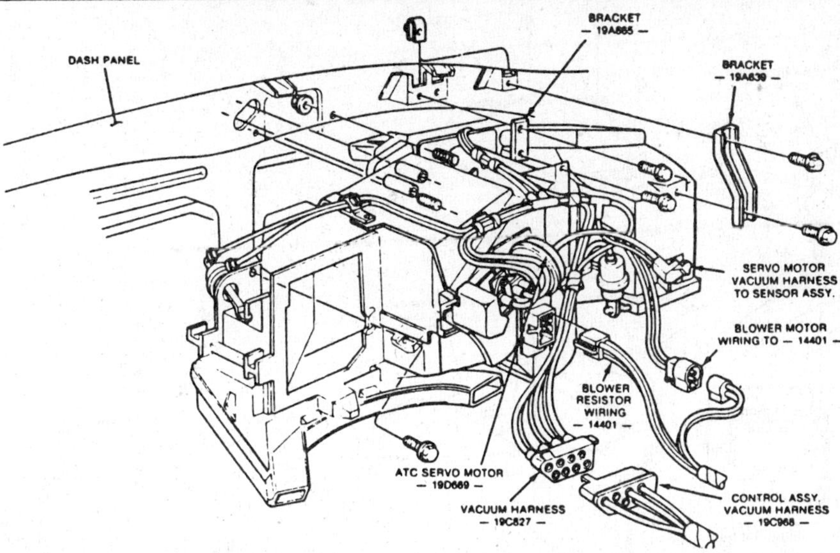

Evaporator installation for all 1982-84 models with automatic temperature control

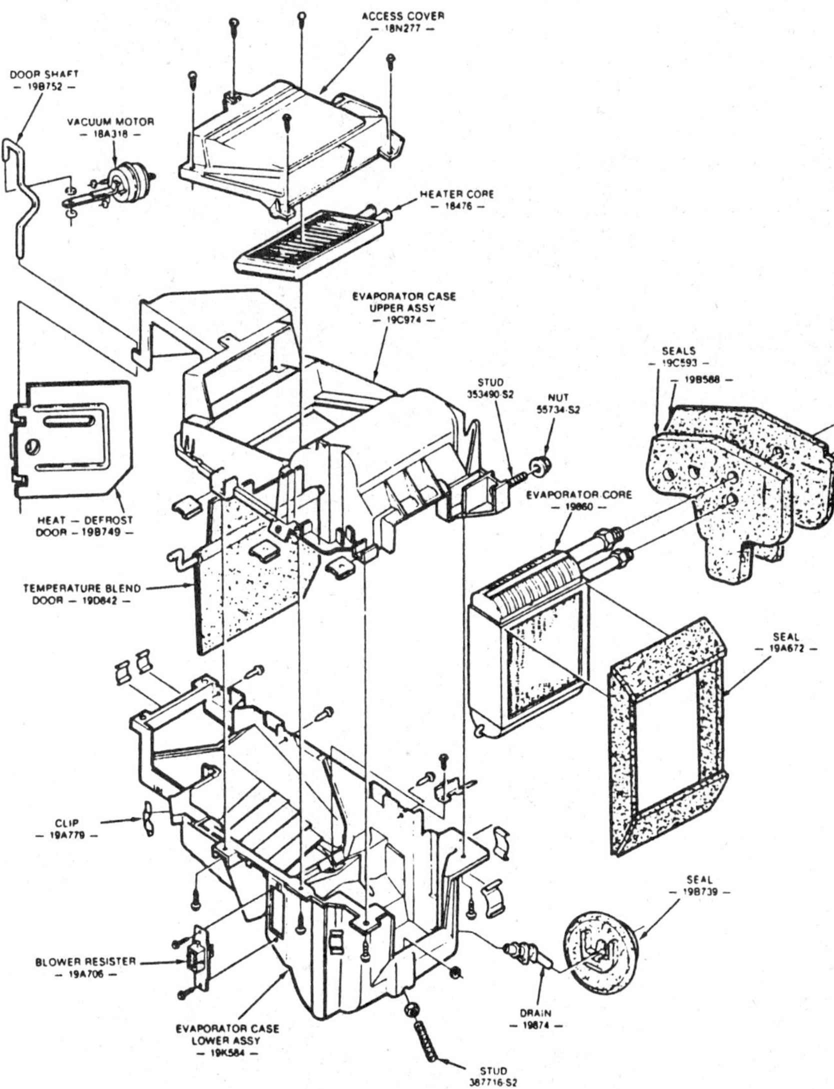

Evaporator case components for all 1982-84 models, except automatic temperature control

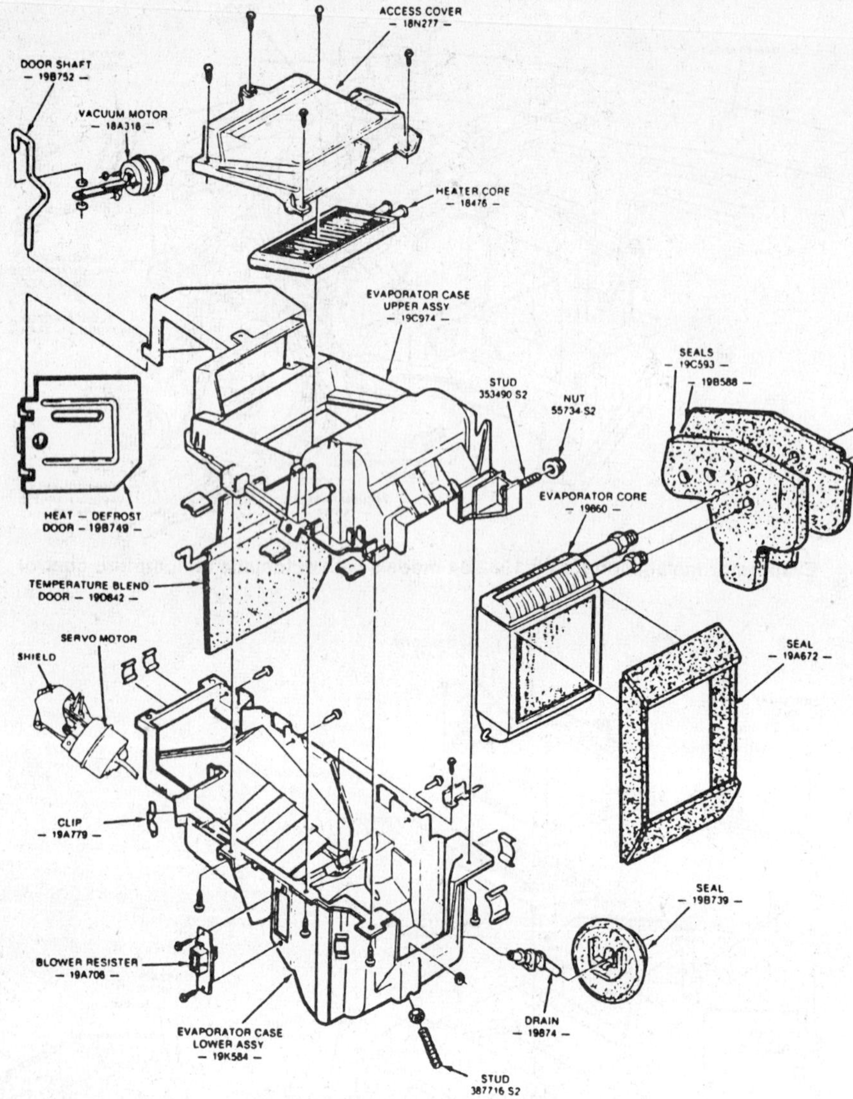

Evaporator case components for all 1984 models with automatic temperature control

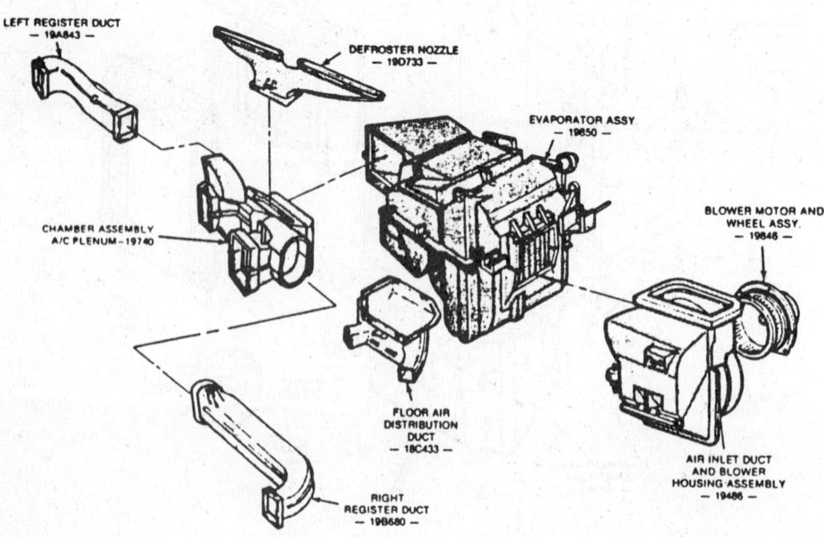

Evaporator used on all 1985-87 models, except automatic temperature control

CAUTION

When draining the coolant, keep in mind that cats and dogs are attracted by the ethylene glycol antifreeze, and are quite likely to drink any that is left in an uncovered container or in puddles on the ground. This will prove fatal in sufficient quantity. Always drain the coolant into a sealable container. Coolant should be reused unless it is contaminated or several years old.

4. Disconnect the refrigerant lines using back-up wrenches at each fitting. Cap all openings immediately!.
5. Disconnect the liquid line and accumulator/drier inlet tube from the evaporator core at the firewall. Cap all openings immediately.
6. Disconnect the wiring at the blower, and the ATC wiring on cars with electronic automatic temperature control.
7. Remove the screw attaching the air inlet duct and blower housing assembly support brace to the cowl top panel.
8. Disconnect the black vacuum supply hose at the check valve, in the engine compartment, and, on cars with automatic temperature control, the vacuum hoses at the TBL switch, also in the engine compartment.
9. In the engine compartment, remove the 2 nuts retaining the evaporator case to the firewall.
10. In the passenger compartment, remove the screw attaching the evaporator case support bracket to the cowl top panel.
11. Remove the screw retaining the bracket below the case, to the firewall.
12. Carefully pull the case away from the firewall and remove the case from the car.
13. Remove the air inlet duct from the case.
14. Remove the foam seal from the core tubes.
15. Drill a $^3/_{16}$" hole in both upright tabs on top of the evaporator case.
16. Using a small saw blade, cut the top of the case, between the raised outlines.
17. Remove the blower motor resistor from the case.
18. Fold the cut-out flap back from the opening and lift the core from the case.
19. Transfer the foam seals to the new core.
20. Position the core in the case and fold back the cut-out portion.
21. Install a spring nut on each of the two upright tabs. Be sure that the hole in the spring nut is aligned with the $^3/_{16}$" hole drilled in the tab flange.
22. Install a screw in each spring nut through the hole in the tab or flange to secure the cut-out cover in the closed position. Tighten the screws.

23. Seal the cut-out edges with caulk.
24. Assembly and installation is the reverse of removal and disassembly.

- Always use new O-rings coated with clean refrigerant oil.
- Make sure that the core seal fits over the case lower half edge.
- Make sure that the drain hose is not kinked.
- When everything is back together, turn on the blower and check for air leaks.
- Evacuate, charge and leak test the system. See the ROUTINE MAINTENANCE section.

1985 Continental and Mark VII

1. Discharge the system at the service access port located on the suction line. See ROUTINE MAINTENANCE.
2. Remove the instrument panel and lay it on the front seat.
3. Drain the cooling system and disconnect the heater hoses at the core tubes.

CAUTION

When draining the coolant, keep in mind that cats and dogs are attracted by the ethylene glycol antifreeze, and are quite likely to drink any that is left in an uncovered container or in puddles on the ground. This will prove fatal in sufficient quantity. Always drain the coolant into a sealable container. Coolant should be reused unless it is contaminated or several years old.

4. Disconnect the refrigerant lines using back-up wrenches at each fitting. Cap all openings immediately!.
5. Disconnect the ATC wiring.
6. Remove the screw attaching the air inlet duct and blower housing assembly support brace to the cowl top panel.
7. Disconnect all vacuum supply hoses in the engine compartment.
8. In the engine compartment, remove the 2 nuts retaining the evaporator case to the firewall.
9. In the passenger compartment, remove the screw attaching the evaporator case support bracket to the cowl top panel.
10. Remove the screw retaining the bracket below the case, to the firewall.
11. Carefully pull the case away from the firewall and remove the case from the car.
12. Remove the air inlet duct and blower housing from the case.
13. Remove the screws and snap-clips securing the halves of the case and separate the case halves.
14. Lift out the evaporator core and seal from the lower case half.
15. Assembly and installation is the reverse of removal and disassembly.

- Always use new O-rings coated with clean refrigerant oil.
- Make sure that the core seal fits over the case lower half edge.
- Always use new sealer between the case halves.
- Make sure that the drain hose is not kinked.
- When everything is back together, turn on the blower and check for air leaks around the case.
- Evacuate, charge and leak test the system. See the ROUTINE MAINTENANCE section.

1986-87 Mark VII

1. Discharge the system at the service access port located on the suction line. See ROUTINE MAINTENANCE.
2. Disconnect the battery ground cable.
3. Remove the air cleaner.
4. Drain the cooling system and disconnect the heater hoses at the core tubes.

CAUTION

When draining the coolant, keep in mind that cats and dogs are attracted by the ethylene glycol antifreeze, and are quite likely to drink any that is left in an uncovered container or in puddles on the ground. This will prove fatal in sufficient quantity. Always drain the coolant into a sealable container. Coolant should be reused unless it is contaminated or several years old.

5. Disconnect the wiring harness at the clutch cycling pressure switch, located on top of the suction accumulator/drier.
6. Disconnect the liquid line and accumulator/drier inlet tube from the evaporator core tubes, using back-up wrenches at each fitting. Cap all openings immediately!.
7. Working under the hood, remove the 2 nuts retaining the accumulator/drier bracket to the dash panel.
8. Position the accumulator/drier and liquid line aside and remove the 2 evaporator assembly retaining nuts.
9. In the passenger compartment, remove the steering column opening cover from the instrument panel.
10. Remove the right and left sound insulators from the instrument panel.
11. Remove the right and left cowl trim panels.
12. Remove the right side finish panel from the instrument panel.
13. Remove the console.
14. Carefully pry the defroster opening grille from the instrument panel.
15. Remove the screw attaching the lower center of the instrument panel to the floor brace.
16. Remove the steering column shroud.
17. Remove the steering column opening reinforcement.
18. Disconnect the transmission indicator cable from the steering column.
19. Remove the steering column-to-brake pedal support retaining nuts and lay the steering column down against the front seat.
20. Remove the nut attaching the instrument panel to the brake pedal support and steering column support.

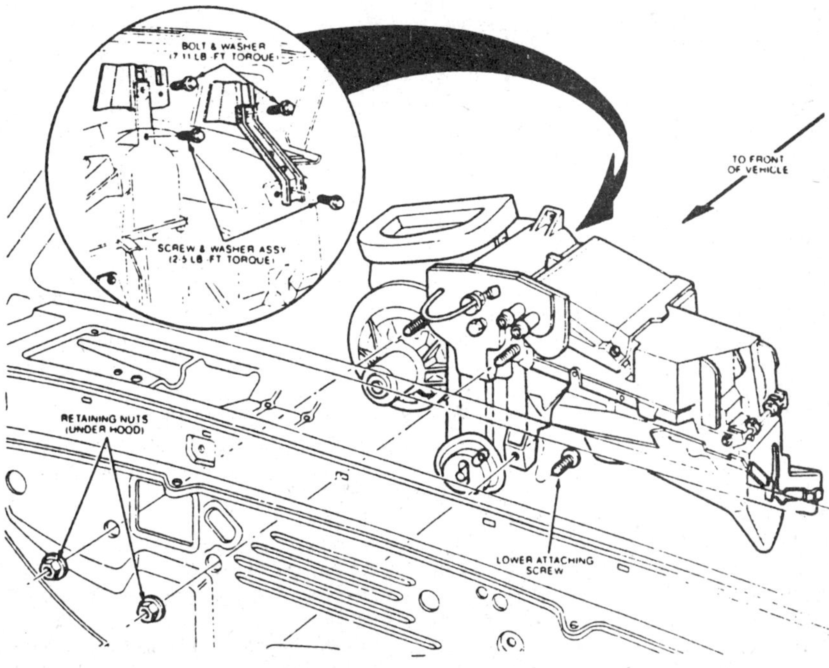

Evaporator case used on all 1987 models with electronic automatic temperature control

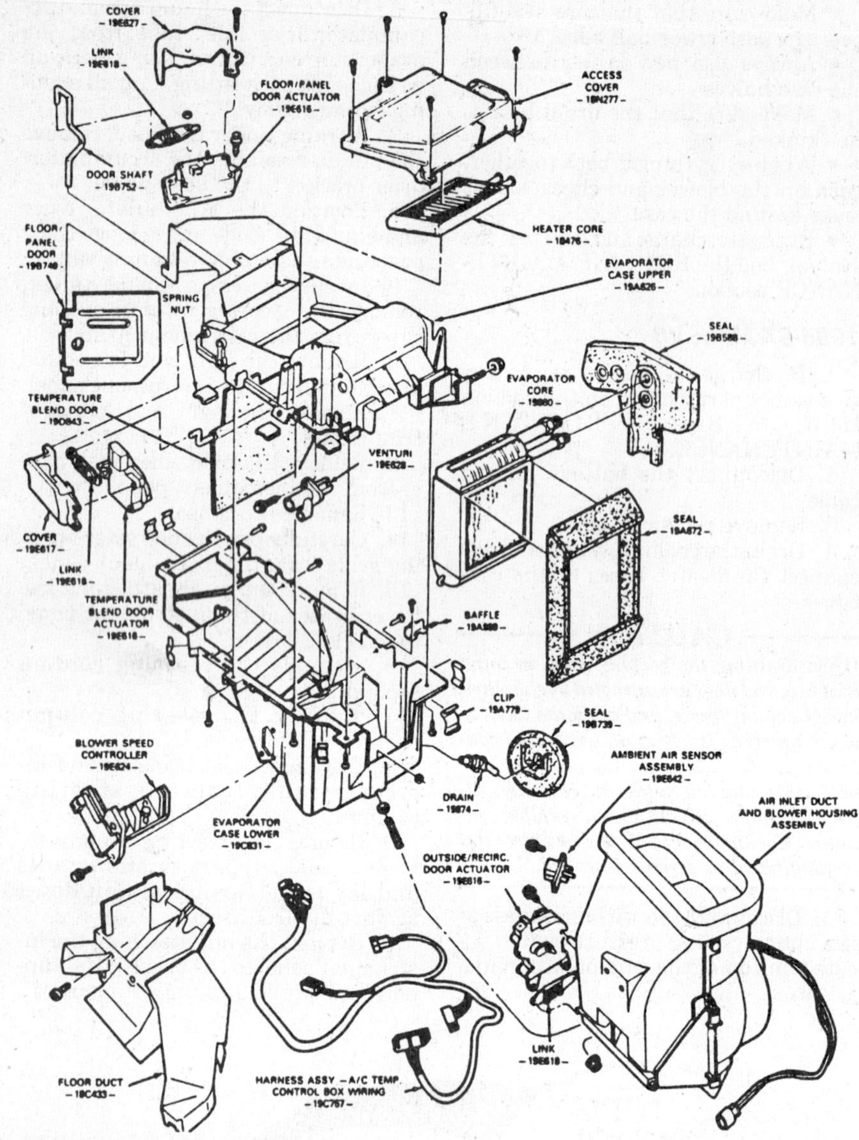

Exploded view of the evaporator case used in the 1987 Mark VII and Continental models with electronic automatic temperature control

21. Remove the instrument panel attaching screws and lay the panel on the front seat.
22. Disconnect the blower motor and blower motor speed control harnesses.
23. Disconnect the automatic temperature control sensor hose and elbow at the evaporator case.
24. Disconnect the automatic temperature control harness at the control assembly.
25. Disconnect the antenna cable from the radio and from the strap retaining cable at the case.
26. Disconnect the rear seat duct adapter at the floor duct.
27. Remove the 3 evaporator attaching screws and lift the evaporator assembly from the car.
28. Remove the air inlet duct and blower housing from the case.
29. Remove the screws and snap-clips securing the halves of the case and separate the case halves.
30. Lift out the evaporator core and seal from the lower case half.
31. Assembly and installation is the reverse of removal and disassembly.

- Position the evaporator assembly on the firewall and install the 3 attaching screws in the passenger compartment. DO NOT TIGHTEN THESE SCREWS AT THIS TIME!
- Install the 2 nuts that retain the evaporator to the firewall in the engine compartment.
- Now tighten all the attaching fasteners.
- Make sure the drain hose is not kinked.
- Always use new O-rings coated with clean refrigerant oil.
- Make sure that the core seal fits over the case lower half edge.
- Always use new sealer between the case halves.
- When everything is back together, turn on the blower and check for air leaks around the case.
- Evacuate, charge and leak test the system. See the ROUTINE MAINTENANCE section.

1986-87 All Models with Automatic Temperature Control

1. Discharge the system at the service access port located on the suction line. See ROUTINE MAINTENANCE.
2. Disconnect the battery ground cable.
3. Remove the air cleaner.
4. Drain the cooling system and disconnect the heater hoses at the core tubes. It may be necessary to blow the coolant from the core with compressed air.

CAUTION

When draining the coolant, keep in mind that cats and dogs are attracted by the ethylene glycol antifreeze, and are quite likely to drink any that is left in an uncovered container or in puddles on the ground. This will prove fatal in sufficient quantity. Always drain the coolant into a sealable container. Coolant should be reused unless it is contaminated or several years old.

5. Disconnect the wiring harness at the clutch cycling pressure switch, located on top of the suction accumulator/drier.
6. Disconnect the liquid line and accumulator/drier inlet tube from the evaporator core tubes, using back-up wrenches at each fitting. Cap all openings immediately!
7. Working under the hood, remove the 2 nuts retaining the accumulator/drier bracket to the dash panel.
8. Position the accumulator/drier and liquid line aside and remove the 2 evaporator assembly retaining nuts.
9. In the passenger compartment, remove the steering column opening cover from the instrument panel.
10. Remove the right and left sound insulators from the instrument panel.
11. Remove the right and left cowl trim panels.
12. Remove the ashtray from the instrument panel.
13. Remove the 2 screws attaching the lower center of the instrument panel to the floor brace.
14. Remove the steering column shroud.
15. Disconnect the transmission indicator cable from the steering column.
16. Remove the instrument panel pad.

17. Remove the steering column-to-brake pedal support retaining nuts and lay the steering column down against the front seat.
18. Remove the nut attaching the instrument panel to the brake pedal support and steering column support.
19. Remove the instrument panel attaching screws and lay the panel on the front seat.
20. Disconnect the blower motor and blower motor speed control harnesses.
21. Disconnect the automatic temperature control sensor hose and elbow at the evaporator case.
22. Disconnect the automatic temperature control harness at the control assembly.
23. Disconnect the antenna cable from the radio and from the strap retaining cable at the case.
24. Using a sharp knife, carefully slit the carpet on top of the transmission tunnel from the firewall straight back to the instrument panel support bracket.
25. Fold the carpet back to expose the rear seat duct.
26. Using a hot-knife, cut the top and side from the rear seat heat duct and remove the top from the floor duct.
27. Remove the 3 evaporator attaching screws and lift the evaporator assembly from the car.
28. Remove the air inlet duct and blower housing from the case.
29. Remove the screws and snap-clips securing the halves of the case and separate the case halves.
30. Lift out the evaporator core and seal from the lower case half.
31. Assembly and installation is the reverse of removal and disassembly.

- Position the evaporator assembly on the firewall and install the 3 attaching screws in the passenger compartment. DO NOT TIGHTEN THESE SCREWS AT THIS TIME!
- Install the 2 nuts that retain the evaportaor to the firewall in the engine compartment.
- Now tighten all the attaching fasteners.
- Make sure that the drain hose is not kinked.
- Always use new O-rings coated with clean refrigerant oil.
- When connecting the refrigerant lines, make ALL connections loosely BEFORE tightening any of them.
- Make sure that the core seal fits over the case lower half edge.
- Always use new sealer between the case halves.
- When everything is back together, turn on the blower and check for air leaks around the case.
- Evacuate, charge and leak test the system. See the ROUTINE MAINTENANCE section.

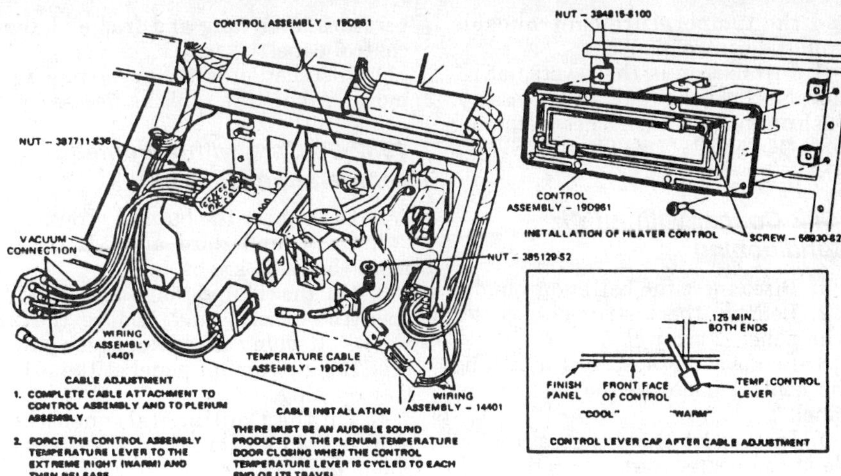

Heater control unit used on 1980-87 models

Control Panel

REMOVAL & INSTALLATION

1980-81 with or without Air Conditioning, except 1981 Cougar with Air Conditioning

1. Disconnect the battery ground.
2. Remove the 4 control assembly-to-instrument panel screws.
3. Pull the control panel towards you.
4. Disconnect the wiring from the panel connectors.
5. Disconnect the vacuum harness and the temperature control cable from the control panel.
6. Installation is the reverse of removal. Adjust the cables as necessary. Push on the vacuum harness retaining nut, DO NOT TRY TO SCREW IT ON!

1981-82 Cougar with Air Conditioning

1. Disconnect the battery ground.
2. Remove the instrument cluster trim panel (3 screws).
3. Disconnect the temperature cable at the evaporator case.
4. Remove the 4 screws attaching the control panel to the instrument panel.
5. Pull the control panel from the instrument panel.
6. Remove the pushnut retaining the cable to the control arm and disconnect the cable.
7. Disconnect the wire connectors from the control panel.
8. Remove the pushnuts retaining the vacuum harness to the control panel and pull off the vacuum harness.
9. Installation is the reverse of removal. Adjust the cable as necessary.

1982-83 with or without Manual Air Conditioning, except 1982 Cougar

1. Disconnect the battery ground.
2. Remove the 4 control assembly-to-instrument panel screws.
3. Pull the control panel towards you.
4. Disconnect the wiring from the panel connectors.
5. Disconnect the vacuum harness

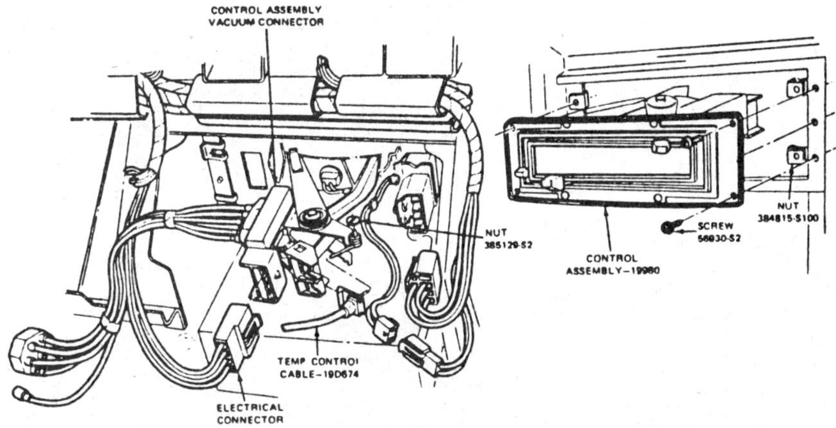

Heater/air conditioning control unit used on all 1980-87 models

and the temperature control cable from the control panel.

6. Installation is the reverse of removal. Adjust the cables as necessary. Push on the vacuum harness retaining nut, DO NOT TRY TO SCREW IT ON!

1982 Cougar without Air Conditioning

1. Disconnect the battery ground.
2. Remove the instrument cluster trim panel (3 screws).
3. Remove the 4 screws attaching the control panel to the instrument panel.
4. Disconnect the temperature cable at the heater case.
5. Pull the control panel from the instrument panel.
6. Remove the pushnut retaining the cable to the control arm, depress the white locking tang on the end of the cable and disconnect the cable.
7. Remove the pushnut retaining the temperature control cable end loop or the temperature lever.
8. Disconnect the wire connectors from the control panel.
9. Remove the pushnuts retaining the vacuum harness to the control panel and pull off the vacuum harness.
10. Depress the black locking tab on the end of the temperature control cable housing and disengage the function cable and housing from the temperature lever tang and frame of the control panel.
11. Installation is the reverse of removal. Adjust the cable as necessary.

1982-83 Cars with Automatic Temperature Control

1. Disconnect the battery ground.
2. On Thunderbird and XR-7, remove the radio knobs.
3. On the Thunderbird and XR-7, open the ashtray and remove the 2 screws attaching the center finish panel to the instrument panel at the ashtray opening.
4. On the Continental, open the ashtray and remove the ashtray receptacle.
5. On the Continental, remove the 4 screws attaching the center finish panel to the instrument panel at the ashtray opening and at the upper edge of the finish panel.
6. Pull the lower edge of the center finish panel away from the instrument panel and disengage the upper tabs of the finish panel from the instrument panel.
7. Remove the 4 screws attaching the control panel to the instrument panel.
8. Pull the control panel towards you about ½". Insert a screwdriver and remove the control panel harness connector locator from the hole in the instrument panel.
9. Pull the control panel from the instrument panel and disconnect the wire connectors from the control panel.
10. Disconnect the vacuum harness and temperature control cable from the control panel. Discard the pushnuts.
11. Installation is the reverse of removal. If the lamp wires become disconnected during the panel removal, put the clips back on the controls before installing the panel.

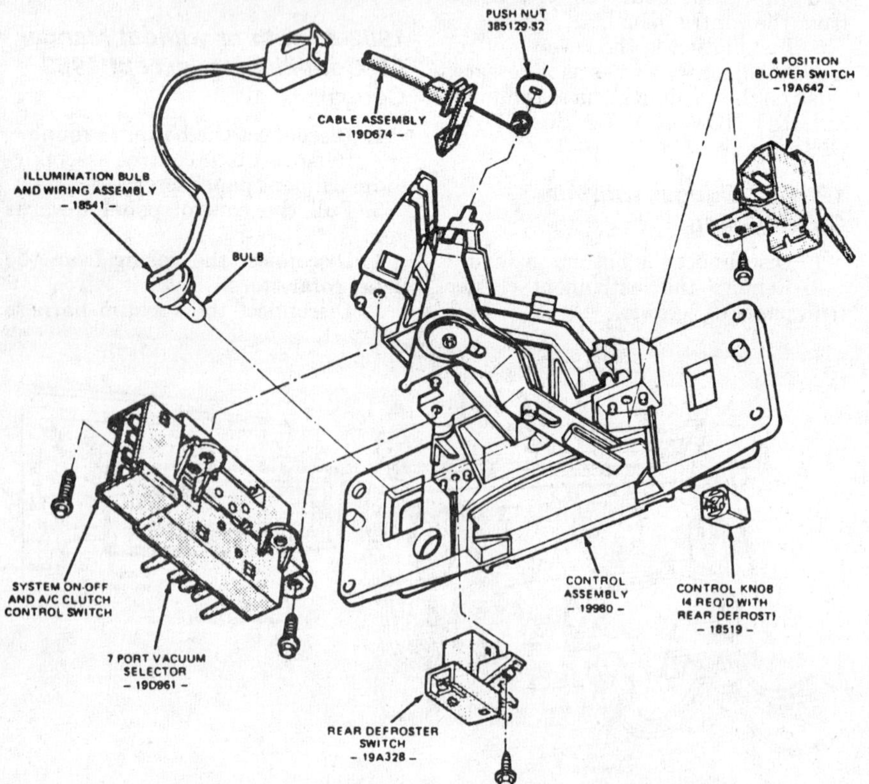

Automatic Temperature Control unit used on 1982-83 models

1984 without Air Conditioning

1. Disconnect the battery ground.
2. Remove the instrument cluster opening finish panel.
3. Remove the 4 screws attaching the control panel to the instrument panel.
4. Pull the control panel out and disconnect the wiring from the control panel.
5. Disconnect the vacuum harness and the temperature control cable from the control panel.
6. Installation is the reverse of removal. Remember that the vacuum harness nut is a pushnut. It does not screw on.

1984 Manual Air Conditioning

1. Disconnect the battery ground.
2. Remove the 4 screws attaching the control panel to the instrument panel.
3. Pull the control panel out and disconnect the wiring from the control panel.
4. Disconnect the vacuum harness and the temperature control cable from the control panel.
5. Installation is the reverse of removal. Remember that the vacuum harness nut is a pushnut. It does not screw on.

1984 with Automatic Temperature Control

1. Disconnect the battery ground.
2. Remove the radio knobs.
3. Open the ashtray and remove the 2 screws attaching the center finish panel to the instrument panel at the ashtray opening.
4. Pull the lower edge of the center finish panel away from the instrument panel and disengage the upper tabs of the finish panel from the instrument panel.
5. Remove the 4 screws attaching the control panel to the instrument panel.
6. Pull the control panel towards you about ½". Insert a screwdriver and remove the control panel harness connector locator from the hole in the instrument panel.

7. Pull the control panel from the instrument panel and disconnect the wire connectors from the control panel.
8. Disconnect the vacuum harness and temperature control cable from the control panel. Discard the pushnuts.
9. Installation is the reverse of removal. If the lamp wires become disconnected during the panel removal, put the clips back on the controls before installing the panel.

1984-87 Town Car, Continental and Mark VII

1. Disconnect the battery ground.
2. On the Continental, open the ashtray and remove the ashtray receptacle.
3. On the Continental, remove the 4 screws attaching the center finish panel to the instrument panel at the ashtray opening and at the upper edge of the finish panel.
4. On the Mark VII, remove the finish panel right side insert attaching screws.
5. Pull the lower edge of the center finish panel (Continental) or finish panel right insert (Mark VII) away from the instrument panel and disengage the upper tabs of the finish panel or insert from the instrument panel.
6. Remove the 4 screws attaching the control panel to the instrument panel.
7. Pull the control panel from the instrument panel and disconnect the wire connectors from the control panel.
8. Disconnect the vacuum harness and temperature control cable from the control panel.
9. Installation is the reverse of removal.

1985-87 without Air Conditioning

1. Disconnect the battery ground.
2. Remove the temperature control knob from the lever shaft.
3. Remove the instrument cluster opening finish panel.
4. Remove the 4 screws attaching the control panel to the instrument panel.
5. Pull the control panel out and disconnect the wiring from the control panel.
6. Disconnect the vacuum harness and the temperature control cable from the control panel.
7. Installation is the reverse of removal. Remember that the vacuum harness nut is a pushnut. It does not screw on.

1985-87 with Manual Air Conditioning

1. Disconnect the battery ground.
2. Remove the temperature control knob from the lever shaft.
3. Remove the center finish panel.
4. Remove the 4 screws attaching the control panel to the instrument panel.
5. Pull the control panel out and disconnect the wiring from the control panel.
6. Disconnect the vacuum harness and the temperature control cable from the control panel.
7. Installation is the reverse of removal. Remember that the vacuum harness nut is a pushnut. It does not screw on.

1985-86 Thunderbird and Cougar with Automatic Temperature Control

1. Disconnect the battery ground.
2. Remove the radio knobs.
3. Open the ashtray and remove the 2 screws attaching the center finish panel to the instrument panel at the ashtray opening.
4. Pull the lower edge of the center finish panel away from the instrument panel and disengage the upper tabs of the finish panel from the instrument panel.
5. Remove the 4 screws attaching the control panel to the instrument panel.
6. Pull the control panel towards you about ½″. Insert a screwdriver and remove the control panel harness connector locator from the hole in the instrument panel.
7. Pull the control panel from the instrument panel and disconnect the wire connectors from the control panel.
8. Disconnect the vacuum harness and temperature control cable from the control panel. Discard the pushnuts.
9. Installation is the reverse of removal. If the lamp wires become disconnected during the panel removal, put the clips back on the controls before installing the panel.

1987 Thunderbird and Cougar with Automatic Temperature Control

1. Disconnect the battery ground.
3. Remove the 4 screws attaching the center finish panel to the instrument panel.
4. Remove the 4 screws attaching the control panel to the instrument panel.
5. Pull the control panel towards you and remove the control panel harness connectors by disengaging the latches on the bottom of the control unit.
6. Disengage the rear window defroster switch connector.
7. Pull the control panel from the instrument panel and disconnect the wire connectors from the control panel.
8. Disconnect the vacuum harness and temperature control cable from the control panel. Discard the pushnuts.
9. Installation is the reverse of removal. If the lamp wires become disconnected during the panel removal, put the clips back on the controls before installing the panel.

WINDSHIELD WIPERS

Motor

REMOVAL & INSTALLATION

Ford, Mercury, Mark VI, 1982–87 Lincoln Town Car

1. Disconnect the battery ground cable.
2. 1982–87 models, remove the hood seal.
3. Disconnect the right washer nozzle hose and remove the right wiper arm and blade assembly from the pivot shaft.
4. Remove the windshield wiper motor and linkage cover by removing the two attaching screws.
5. Disconnect the linkage drive arm from the motor output arm crankpin by removing the retaining clip.
6. Disconnect the two push-on wire connectors from the motor.
7. Remove the three bolts that retain the motor to the dash panel extension and remove the motor.
8. To install, be sure the output arm is in the park position and reverse the removal procedure.

Fairmont, Zephyr, Mustang, Capri, Granada

1. Disconnect the battery ground cable.
2. Remove the right wiper and blade assembly.

NOTE: On Fairmont, Zephyr, and Granada models, also remove the left wiper arm and blade.

3. Remove the grille on the top of the cowl.
4. Disconnect the linkage drive arm

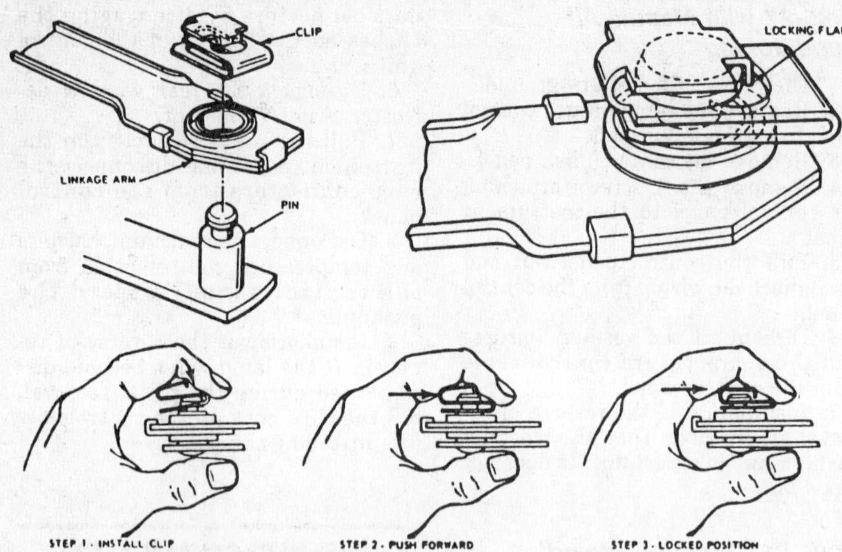

Removing or installing wiper arms connecting clips

from the motor crankpin after removing the clip.

5. Disconnect the wiper motor electrical connector and remove the three attaching screws from the motor. Pull the motor from the opening.

6. Be sure the motor crank arm is in the park position and reverse the removal procedure to install.

1980-83 Thunderbird and XR-7
1981-82 Cougar
1982-83 Continental

1. Disconnect the ground cable.
2. Remove the right hand wiper arm (on LTD and Marquis models remove the left side assembly also) from the pivot shaft and lay it on the top grille.
3. Remove the cowl top grille screws.
4. Reach under the left front corner of the grille to disconnect the linkage drive arm from the motor crank by removing the retaining clip.
5. Disconnect the electrical connector. Remove the motor mounting bolts and remove the motor.
6. Install in reverse order.

1984 and Later Mark VII, Thunderbird and Cougar

1. Turn the ignition switch to the On position. Turn the wiper switch on, when the blades are straight up on the windshield, turn the key switch Off.
2. disconnect the negative battery cable. Remove the arm and blade assemblies.
3. Remove the left side leaf guard screen. Disconnect the linkage drive arm from the wiper motor after removing the retaining clip.
4. Disconnect the electrical wiring harness connector from the wiper motor. Remove the wiper motor mounting bolts and the motor.
5. Install in the reverse order of removal. Before installing the arm and blade assemblies, turn on the key and allow the motor to cycle. Turn the wiper control switch Off so that the drives and motor will stop in the park position. Install the arm and blades assemblies.

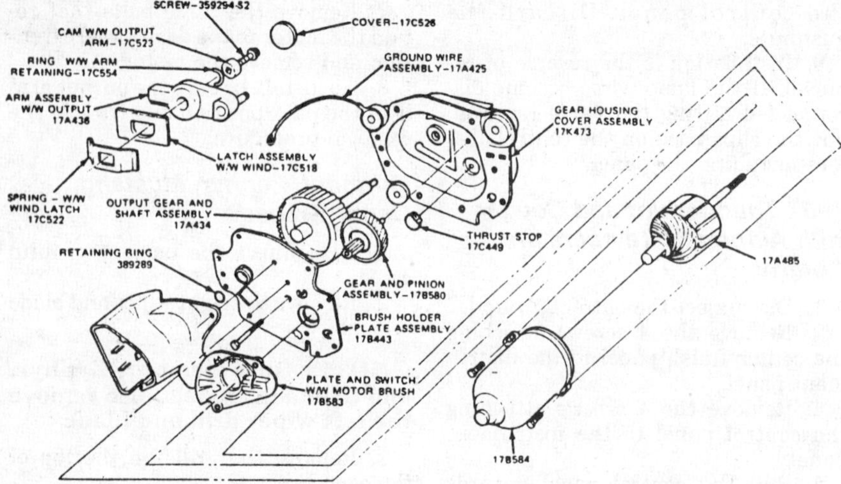

Windshield wiper motor used on 1983-87 models

Linkage

REMOVAL & INSTALLATION

1980

1. Disconnect the battery ground.
2. Remove the wiper arms from the pivot shafts.
3. Remove the cowl top grille attaching screw and lift off the grille.
4. Disconnect the linkage drive arm from the motor crankpin after removing the clip.
5. Remove the 2 bolts retaining the right pivot shaft to the cowl and remove the large nut, washer and spacer from the left pivot shaft.
6. Installation is the reverse of removal. Torque the pivot shaft retaining bolts to 84 in.lb. and the large nut to 110 in.lb.

1981-82

1. Disconnect the battery ground.
2. Remove the right wiper arm from the pivot shaft. On the Cougar, also remove the left wiper arm.
3. Remove the cowl top grille attaching screw and lift off the grille.
4. Disconnect the linkage drive arm from the motor crankpin after removing the clip.
5. On the Cougar, remove the 4 screws retaining the right and left pivot shafts.
   - On the Thunderbird and XR-7 and 1982 Continental, remove the 2 bolts retaining the right pivot shaft to the cowl and remove the large nut, washer and spacer from the left pivot shaft.
6. Installation is the reverse of removal. Torque the pivot shaft retaining bolts to 84 in.lb. and the large nut to 110 in.lb.

1983 All Models
1984-87 Continental

1. Disconnect the battery ground.
2. Remove the right wiper arm from the pivot shaft.
3. Remove the cowl top grille attaching screw and lift off the grille.
4. Disconnect the linkage drive arm from the motor crankpin after removing the clip.
5. Remove the 2 bolts retaining the right pivot shaft to the cowl and remove the large nut, washer and spacer from the left pivot shaft.
6. Installation is the reverse of removal. Torque the pivot shaft retaining bolts to 84 in.lb. and the large nut to 110 in.lb.

1984-87 Mark VII, Thunderbird and Cougar

1. Turn the wipers ON and, when the blades are in the straight up position, turn the ignition switch OFF.
2. Remove the wiper arms from the pivot shafts.
3. Disconnect the battery ground.
4. Remove the left and right cowl top grilles.
5. Disconnect the linkage drive arm from the motor crankpin after removing the clip.
6. Remove the pivot shafts attaching screws.
7. Installation is the reverse of removal. Torque the pivot fasteners to 110 in.lb.

Rear Wiper Motor and Linkage

REMOVAL & INSTALLATION

1982 Cougar Station Wagon

1. Turn the ignition switch OFF.
2. Pull the wiper arm from the pivot shaft.
3. Remove the pivot shaft nut and spacers.
4. Open the tailgate and remove the inner trim panel.
5. Remove the license plate housing.
6. Disconnect the license plate light wiring.
7. Disconnect the wiper motor wiring.
8. Remove the linkage arm locking clip, pry off the arm and remove the linkage.
9. Remove the motor and bracket attaching screws and remove the motor.
10. Installation is the reverse of removal.

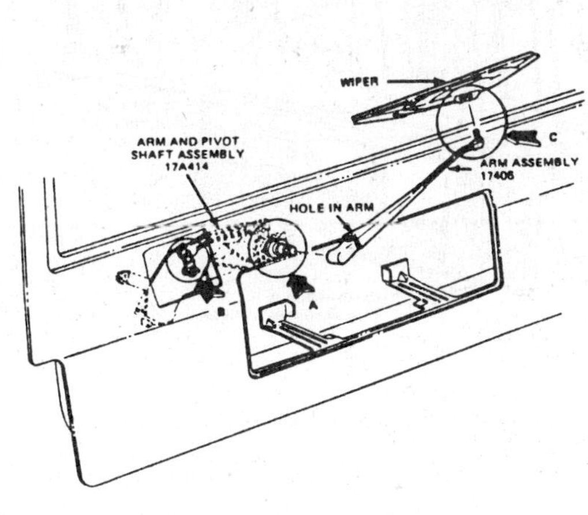

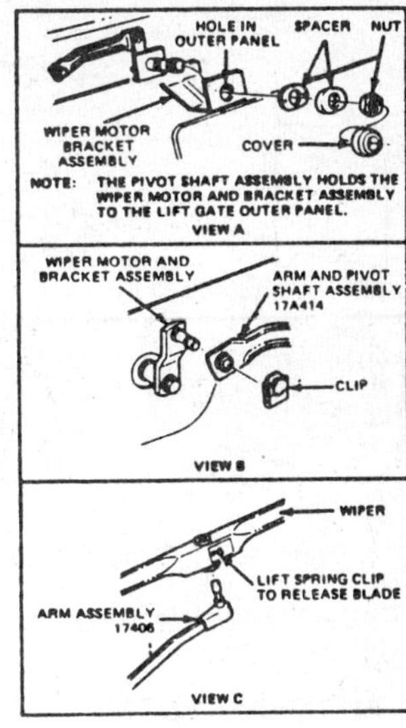

Rear wiper and pivot installation on the 1981-82 Cougar station wagon

INSTRUMENTS AND SWITCHES

Instrument Cluster

REMOVAL & INSTALLATION

WARNING: Extreme care must be exercised during the removal and installation of the instrument cluster and dash components to avoid damage or breakage. Wooden paddles should be used to separate dash components, if required. Tape or cover dash areas that may be damaged by the removal and installation of the dash components.

During the removal and installation procedures, slight variations may be required from the general outline, to facilitate the removal and installation of the instrument panel and cluster components, due to slight changes from model year to model year.

All Full-Size Models (Except Below)

1. Disconnect the battery ground cable.
2. Remove the lower steering column cover.
3. Remove the instrument cluster trim cover and the bottom half of the steering column shroud.
4. Reach behind the cluster and disconnect the cluster electrical feed plug and the speedometer cable.
5. Unsnap and remove the steering column shroud cover, if not previously done. Disconnect the transmission indictor cable from the tab in the shroud retainer.
6. Remove the attaching screw for the transmission indicator cable bracket to steering column. Disconnect the cable loop from the pin on the steering column.
7. Remove the cluster retaining screws and remove the cluster assembly.
8. The installation is the reverse of the removal procedure.

Lincoln Town Car

1. Disconnect the battery ground cable.
2. Remove the lower steering column cover.
3. Remove the instrument cluster trim cover. Remove the bottom half of the steering column shroud.
4. Reach behind the cluster and disconnect the cluster electrical feed plug and the speedometer cable.
5. Unsnap and remove the steering column shroud cover, if not previously done. Disconnect the transmission indictor cable from the tab in the shroud retainer.
6. Remove the attaching screw for the transmission indicator cable bracket to steering column. Disconnect the cable loop from the pin on the steering column.
7. Remove the cluster retaining screws and remove the cluster assembly.
8. The installation is the reverse of the removal procedure.

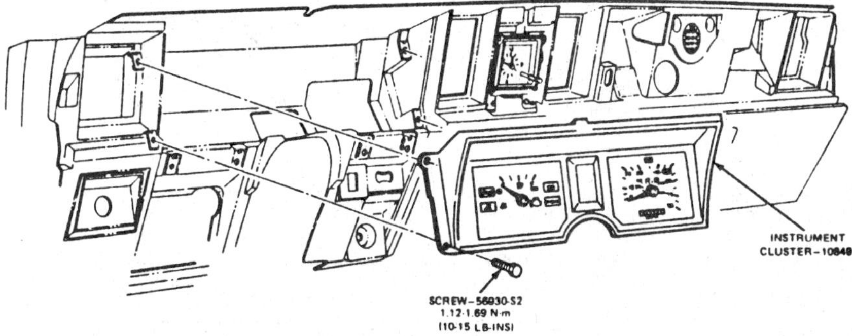

Standard instrument cluster found in the 1980-83 Thunderbird and XR-7

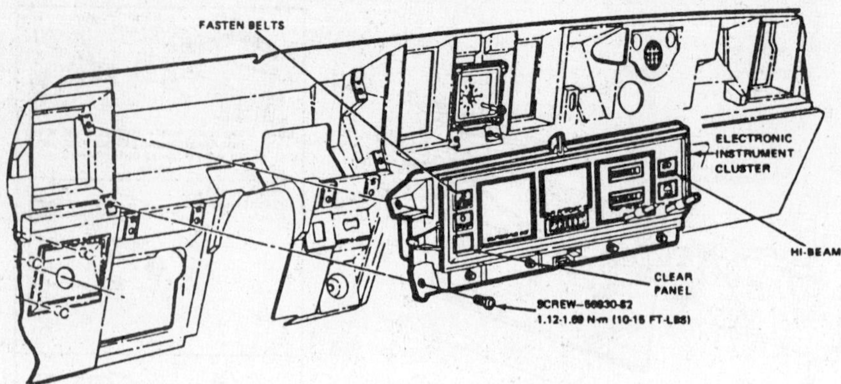

Electronic instrument cluster found in the 1980-83 Thunderbird and XR-7

1980-83 Thunderbird
1981-83 XR-7

STANDARD CLUSTER

1. Disconnect the negative battery cable.
2. Disconnect the speedometer cable.
3. Remove the instrument panel trim cover and steering column lower shroud.
4. Remove the attaching screw from the transmission indicator quadrant cable bracket to the steering column. Disconnect the cable loop from the pin on the steering column.
5. Remove the cluster retaining screws.
6. Remove the cluster from the instrument panel.
7. Reverse the removal procedure to install.

ELECTRONIC CLUSTER

1. Disconnect the negative battery cable.
2. Remove the instrument panel trim cover and steering column lower shroud.
3. Remove the cluster retaining screws.
4. Remove the attaching screw from the transmission indicator quadrant cable bracket to the steering column. Disconnect the cable loop from the pin on the steering column.
5. Pull the cluster away from the instrument panel and disconnect the speedometer cable.
6. Disconnect the electrical connections from the cluster. Disconnect the ground wire.
7. Remove the cluster from the instrument panel.
8. Reverse the removal procedure to install.

1981-82 Cougar

NOTE: Certain special ordered cluster assemblies have two printed circuits.

1. Disconnect the battery negative cable.
2. Remove the steering column shroud and the cluster trim cover.
3. Remove one screw from the shift quadrant control cable bracket to steering column and disconnect the cable loop from the pin on the shaft cane lever. Remove the plastic clamp from around the steering column.
4. Remove the retaining screws holding the cluster to the instrument panel.
5. Pull the cluster away from the instrument panel and disconnect the speedometer cable. Disconnect the electrical connectors and remove the cluster from the dash.
6. To install the cluster, reverse the removal procedure.

1982-83 Continental

1. Disconnect the battery ground.
2. Remove the steering column shroud.
3. Snap off the instrument panel mouldings.
4. Remove the 17 screws retaining the instrument panel trim assembly and lift it off.
5. Disconnect the shift selector cable at the steering column.
6. Remove the 4 cluster-to-instrument panel screws.
7. Pull the cluster out and disconnect the speedometer cable.
8. Disconnect the wiring harness connector at the back of the cluster.
9. Installation is the reverse of removal.

1984 Thunderbird and Cougar

STANDARD CLUSTER

1. Diconnect the battery ground.
2. Remove the steering column shroud.
3. Remove the 4 cluster trim retaining screws and lift off the trim.
4. Remove the 6 cluster-to-instrument panel screws.
5. Pull the cluster out and disconnect the speedometer cable.
6. Disconnect the electrical connectors and remove the cluster.
7. Installation is the reverse of removal.

ELECTRONIC CLUSTER

1. Disconnect the negative battery cable.
2. Remove the 4 lower instrument panel trim cover screws.
3. Remove the steering column cover.

Electronic instrument cluster found in the 1982-83 Continental

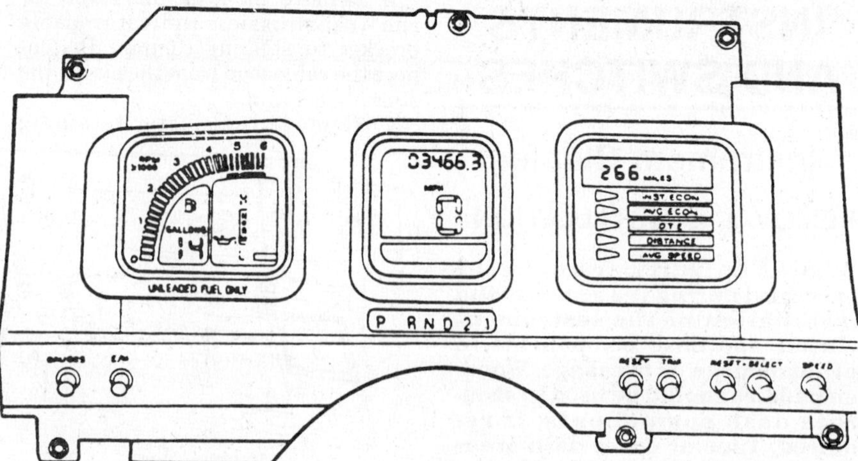

Electronic instrument cluster found in all 1980-87 models, except XR-7 and Thunderbird Turbo

4. Remove the 6 cluster trim panel retaining screws.
5. Remove the 4 cluster-to-instrument panel attaching screws.
6. Remove the attaching screw from the transmission selector cable bracket. Disconnect the cable loop from the pin on the steering column.
7. Pull the cluster away from the instrument panel and disconnect the speedometer cable.
8. Disconnect the electrical connections from the cluster. Disconnect the ground wire.
9. Remove the cluster from the instrument panel.
10. Reverse the removal procedure to install.

1984-87 Continental

1. Remove the steering column shroud.
2. Snap out the left and right instrument panel mouldings.
3. Remove the 2 center moulding retaining screws and remove the moulding above the climate control head.
4. Remove the ash tray receptacle.
5. Remove the 2 remaining center moulding screws.
6. Remove the 17 cluster trim panel screws and lift off the trim panel.
7. Disconnect the shift selector cable at the steering column.
8. Remove the 4 cluster-to-instrument panel screws.
9. Pull the cluster out and disconnect the electrical connectors.
10. Installation is the reverse of removal.

1984-85 Mark VII
1986-87 Mark VII, Except LSC

1. Remove the 4 instrument panel finish retaining screws and rotate the top of the panel toward the steering wheel and remove it.
2. Remove the 6 screws retaining the instrument panel pad and rotate the pad toward the steering wheel and remove it.
3. Remove the 4 screws retaining the instrument cluster to the instrument panel and remove the cluster.
4. Pull the cluster out and unplug the electrical connectors.
5. Installation is the reverse of removal.

1985-87 Thunderbird and Cougar

STANDARD CLUSTER

1. Disconnect the battery ground.
2. Remove the 2 lower trim covers.
3. Remove the steering column cover.
4. Disconnect the shift selector bracket and cable assembly from the column.
5. Move the shift lever and remove the cluster trim panel.
6. Remove the 4 cluster mounting screws.
7. Pull the bottom of the cluster toward the steering wheel.
8. Reach behind the cluster and unplug the 2 connectors.
9. Swing the bottom of the cluster out and remove the cluster.

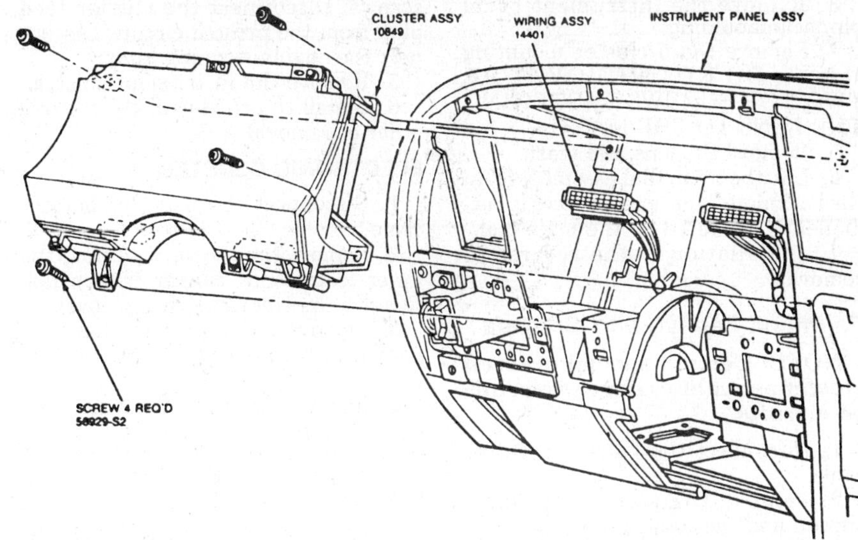

Removing the standard instrument cluster from the 1984-87 Thunderbird and Cougar

TURBO COUPE CLUSTER

1. Disconnect the battery ground.
2. Remove the steering column shroud.
3. Remove the 10 cluster trim screws and lift off the trim.
4. Remove the 4 cluster-to-instrument panel screws and pull the cluster out slightly.
5. Disconnect the cluster connectors.
6. Pull the boost gauge rubber tube off of the gauge nipple.
7. Remove the cluster.
8. Installation is the reverse of removal.

ELECTRONIC CLUSTER

1. Disconnect the negative battery cable.
2. Remove the 2 lower instrument panel trim covers.
3. Remove the steering column cover.
4. Disconnect the shift selector bracket and cable at the column.
5. Move the shift lever and remove the cluster trim panel.
6. Remove the 4 cluster-to-instrument panel attaching screws.
7. Pull the bottom of the cluster toward the steering wheel.
8. Reach behind the cluster and disconnect the electrical connections.
9. Swing the bottom of the cluster out and away from the instrument panel.
10. Installation is the reverse of removal.

1986-87 Mark VII LSC

1. Disconnect the battery ground.
2. Remove the cluster trim panel, disconnecting the warning lamp module connectors.

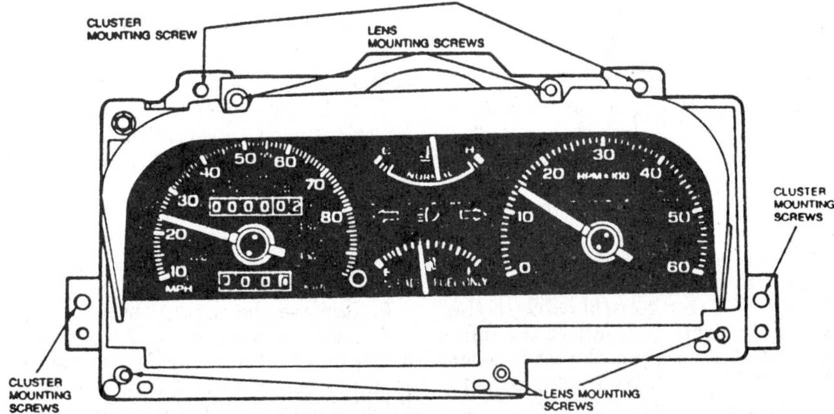

Conventional instrument cluster used on the 1984-87 Mark VII LSC

3. Remove the instrument panel pinnacle moulding.

4. Remove the 5 cluster mounting screws. DO NOT REMOVE THE TWO TOP SCREWS FASTENING THE LENS TO THE MASK!

5. Remove the lens and mask.

6. Lift the main dial assembly from the backplate. The speedometer is permanently mounted on the main dial.

7. Installation is the reverse of removal.

Fairmont, Zephyr, and Granada

NOTE: Certain special ordered cluster assemblies have two printed circuits.

1. Disconnect the battery negative cable.

2. remove the steering column shroud and the cluster trim cover.

3. Remove one screw from the shift quadrant control cable bracket to steering column and disconnect the cable loop from the pin n the shift cane lever. Remove the plastic clamp from around the steering column.

4. Remove the retaining screws holding the cluster to the instrument panel.

5. Pull the cluster away from the instrument panel and disconnect the speedometer cable. disconnect the electrical connectors and remove the cluster from the dash.

6. To install the cluster, reverse the removal procedure.

Mustang, Capri

1. Disconnect the battery ground cable.

2. Remove the instrument trim cover.

3. From under the dash, reach up and disconnect the speedometer cable.

4. Remove the cluster retaining screws and pull the cluster away from the dash. Disconnect the tachometer and wiring connectors. Remove the cluster assembly.

5. The installation is the reverse of the removal procedure.

1983–87 LTD, Marquis

STANDARD CLUSTER

1. Disconnect the negative battery cable.

2. Disconnect the speedometer cable. Remove the screws retaining the cluster trim panel and remove the panel.

3. Remove the steering wheel shroud. Remove the screw retaining the shift indictor control cable to the steering column. Disconnect the indicator cable loop from the shift lever pin. Remove the plastic clamp from the steering column.

4. Remove the cluster retaining screws. Disconnect the cluster feed plug from the printed circuit. Disconnect the engine warning lamp.

5. Remove the instrument cluster.

6. Install the cluster in the reverse order of removal.

ELECTRONIC CLUSTER

1. Disconnect the negative battery cable.

2. Remove the screws retaining the lower instrument cluster trim panel. Remove the steering column cover.

3. Remove the screws retaining the instrument cluster to the instrument panel.

4. Remove the screw attaching the transmission indictor cable bracket to the steering column. Disconnect the cable loop from the pin on the steering column.

5. Carefully pull the instrument cluster away from the panel and disconnect the speedometer cable. Disconnect the cluster feed plug and ground receptacle from the cluster back plate.

6. Remove the cluster assembly.

7. Install the cluster in the reverse order of removal.

Windshield Wiper Switch

REMOVAL & INSTALLATION

Thunderbird, Cougar, Mark VII, Continental

1. Disconnect the negative battery cable.

2. Remove the split steering column cover retaining screws.

3. Separate the two halves and remove the wiper switch retaining screws.

4. Disconnect the wire connector and remove the wiper switch.

5. The installation of the wiper switch is the reverse of the removal procedure.

Granada and Monarch

1. Disconnect the negative battery cable.

2. Separate the wiring connector after releasing the locking tabs.

3. Remove the two lower instrument panel screws and remove the lower instrument panel shield.

4. Remove the two steering column cover screws and separate the steering column cover halves.

5. Remove the wiring shield.

6. Using a number T-20 internal driver bit or its equivalent, remove the retaining screw and remove the windshield wiper/washer-turn signal arm assembly.

NOTE: The wiper/washer switch is an integral part of the turn signal switch arm and cannot be repaired separately.

Ford, Mercury, Fairmont, Zephyr, Mustang, Capri, Lincoln Town Car

1. Disconnect the negative battery cable.

2. Remove the split steering column cover retaining screws.

3. Separate the two halves and remove the wiper switch retaining screws.

4. Disconnect the wire connector and remove the wiper switch.

5. The installation of the wiper switch is the reverse of the removal procedure.

Rear Window Wiper Switch

REMOVAL & INSTALLATION

1982 Cougar Station Wagon

1. With the ignition switch OFF, remove the wiper switch knob.

2. Remove the two bezel retaining screws.

3. Pull the switch retainer away from the instrument panel.

4. Remove the washer switch retainer nut.

5. Separate the switch from the retainer.

6. Disconnect the electrical connector from the switch.

7. Installation is the reverse of removal.

Headlight Switch

REMOVAL & INSTALLATION

Ford/Mercury, LTD/Marquis, Mustang/Capri

1. Disconnect the negative battery cable.

2. Underneath the instrument panel, depress the shaft retaining knob and pull the knob straight out.

3. Unscrew the trim bezel and remove the locknut.

4. Underneath the instrument panel, move the switch toward the front of the car while tilting it downward.

5. Disconnect the wiring from the switch and remove the switch from the car.

6. Installation is the reverse of removal.

Lincoln Town Car

1. Disconnect the ground cable from the battery.

2. Remove the headlamp switch knob.
3. Remove the auto dimmer bezel and the autolamp delay bezel, if so equipped.
4. Remove the steering column lower shroud.
5. Remove lower LH instrument panel trim bezel.
6. Remove the five screws that retain the headlamp switch mounting bracket to the instrument panel.
7. Carefully pull the switch and bracket from the instrument panel and disconnect the wiring connector(s) from the headlamp switch.
8. Remove the locknut and one screw that retain the headlamp switch to the switch bracket.
9. Installation is the reverse order of the removal procedure.

1980-84 Thunderbird, Cougar, XR-7

1. Disconnect the battery ground.
2. Pull the switch to the full ON position.
3. Reach up under the instrument panel and, while depressing the release button, pull the knob out of the switch.
4. Unscrew the switch bezel and pull the switch from the instrument panel.
5. Unplug the wiring.
6. Tag and disconnect the vacuum lines on the Thunderbird with headlamp doors.
7. Installation is the reverse of removal.

1982-83 Continental

1. Disconnect the battery ground.
2. Remove the steering column shroud.
3. Unsap the finish moulding from the bottom edge of the cluster. Remove the 5 screws now exposed.
4. Remove the 4 lower instrument panel pad screws and carefully tilt the pad out from under the cluster lens.
5. Discinnect the headlamp switch wiring.
6. Remove the headlamp switch knobs.
7. Remove the headlamp switch retaining nut and the headlamp switch lens.
8. Remove the nut and screw that retains the switch to the lower left pad.
9. Installation is the reverse of removal.

1984-87 Continental and Mark VII
1985-87 Thunderbird and Cougar

1. Remove the headlamp switch lens screws and lift off the lens.
2. On cars equipped with Auto Lamp/Auto Dimmer, remove the control.
3. Remove the switch attaching screws and pull the switch from the instrument panel.
4. Disconnect the wiring and remove the switch.
5. Installation is the reverse of removal.

Speedometer Cable

REMOVAL & INSTALLATION

NOTE: Depending on year and model, some dash panels or the instrument cluster may require removal to gain access to the rear of the speedometer.

1. Reach up behind the speedometer and depress the flat, quick-disconnect tab, while pulling back on the cable.
2. If the inner cable is broken, raise and support the car and remove the cable-to-transmission clamp and pull the cable from the transmission.
3. Pull the core from the cable.
4. Installation is the reverse of removal. Lubricate the core with speedometer cable lubricant prior to installation.

Radio

REMOVAL & INSTALLATION

Lincoln Town Car

1. Disconnect the negative battery cable.
2. Remove the four radio plate-to-panel screws. Pull the radio with the front plate attached rearward until the rear bracket is clear.

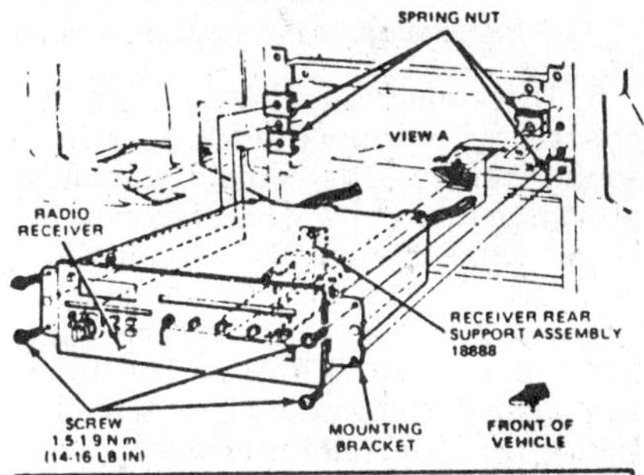

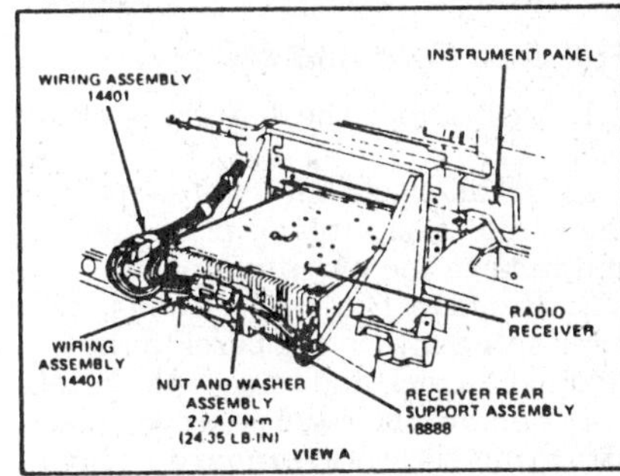

Installation of the stereo radio/tape player in the 1983-85 Continental and 1984-85 Mark VII

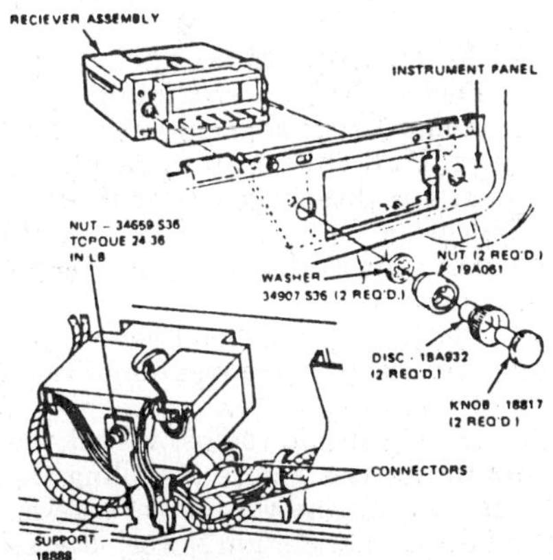

1980 radio installation

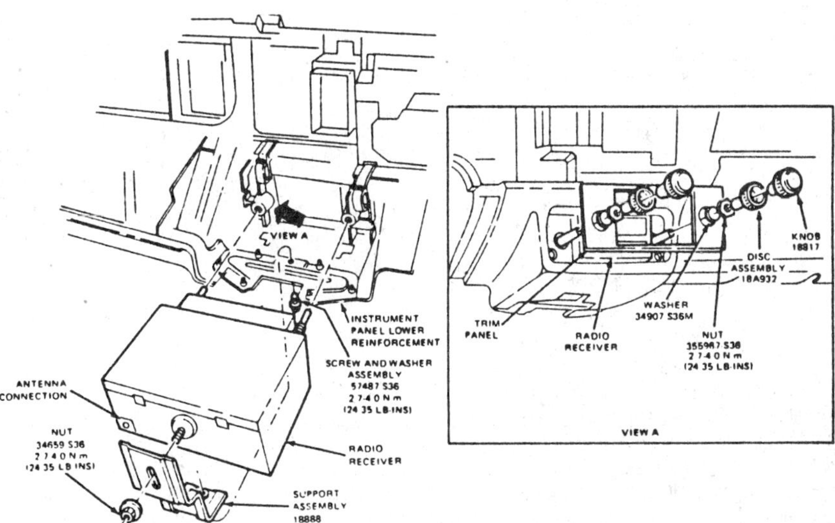

Radio installation in the 1981-82 Cougar

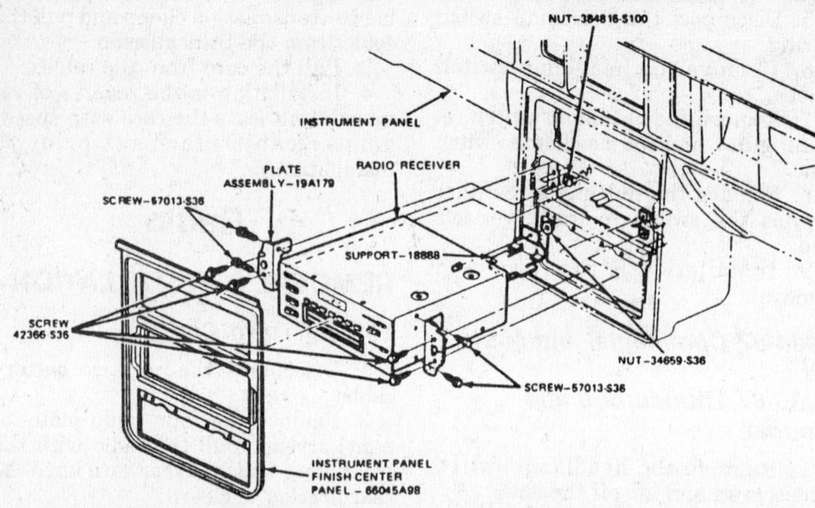

Installation of the electronic radio in the 1980-83 Thunderbird and XR-7

3. Disconnect the wires from the chassis. If equipped with premium sound, remove the control assembly attaching nut and washer, remove the switch, and remove the illumination lamp socket from the front bracket.

4. Remove the radio with the front plate attached. Remove the four screws and remove the plate. Installation is the reverse of removal.

Full Size Ford and Mercury

1. Disconnect the battery ground cable.

2. On all-electronic radios, remove the radio-to-mounting plate screws and remove the mounting plate.

3. Remove the radio knobs, the screws that attach the bezel to the instrument panel, and remove the bezel.

4. Remove the radio mounting plate attaching screws (standard radios), and disengage the radio by pulling it from the lower rear support bracket.

5. Disconnect all the leads from the radio.

6. Remove the radio mounting plate and the rear upper support; remove the radio from the instrument panel.

7. Reverse the procedure to install.

Granada and Monarch,

1. Disconnect the negative battery cable.

2. Remove the headlight switch from the instrument panel. Remove the heater, air conditioner, windshield wiper/washer knobs, and radio knobs and discs.

3. Remove the six screws which attach the applique to the instrument panel and remove the applique. Disconnect the antenna lead-in cable from the radio.

4. Remove the four screws which attach the radio bezel to the instrument panel. Slide the radio and bezel out of the lower rear support bracket and instrument panel opening toward the interior far enough to disconnect the electrical connections, and remove the radio.

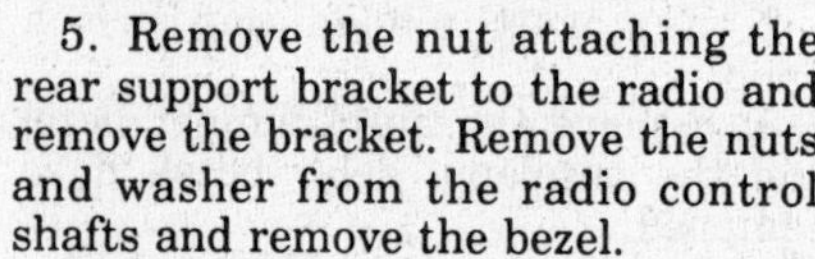

5. Remove the nut attaching the rear support bracket to the radio and remove the bracket. Remove the nuts and washer from the radio control shafts and remove the bezel.

6. To install, attach the rear support bracket to the radio. Install the bezel, washers and nuts.

7. Insert the radio with rear support bracket and bezel through the instrument panel opening far enough to connect the electrical leads and antenna lead-in cable. Install the radio upper rear support bracket into the lower rear support bracket.

8. Center the radio and bezel in the opening and install the four bezel attaching screws.

9. Install the instrument panel applique with its six attaching screws. Install all knobs removed from the instrument panel and radio. Install the headlight switch. Connect the negative battery cable.

Fairmont, Zephyr, Mustang, Capri, Granada and Futura

1. Disconnect the negative battery cable.

2. Disconnect the electrical, speaker, and antenna leads from the radio.

3. Remove the knobs, discs, and control shaft nuts and washers from the radio shafts.

4. Remove the ash tray receptacle and bracket.

5. Remove the rear support nut from the radio.

6. Remove the instrument panel lower reinforcement and the heater or air conditioning floor ducts.

7. Remove the radio from the rear support, and drop the radio down and out from behind the instrument panel.

8. To install, reverse the removal procedure.

LTD and Marquis

1. Disconnect the negative battery cable.

2. Remove the radio knobs (pull off). Remove the center trim panel.

3. Remove the radio mounting plate screws. Pull the radio towards the front seat to disengage it from the lower bracket.

4. Disconnect the radio and antenna connections.

5. Remove the radio. Remove the nuts and washers (conventional radios) as necessary.

6. On electronic radios, install the mounting plates before installing the retaining nuts and washers or screws. The rest of installation is the reverse of removal.

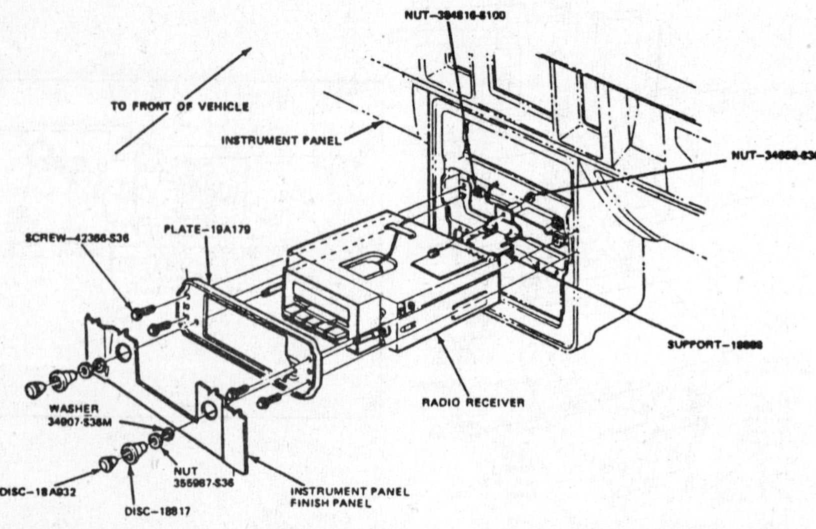

Installation of the stereo radio/tape player in the 1981-83 Thunderbird and XR-7

1981-82 Cougar

1. Disconnect the negative battery cable.
2. Disconnect the electrical, speaker, and antenna leads from the radio.
3. Remove the knobs, discs, and control shaft nuts and washers from the radio shafts.
4. Remove the ash tray receptacle and bracket.
5. Remove the rear support nut from the radio.
6. Remove the instrument panel lower reinforcement and the heater or air conditioning floor ducts.
7. Remove the radio fro the rear support, and drop the radio down and out from behind the instrument panel.
8. To install, reverse the removal procedure.

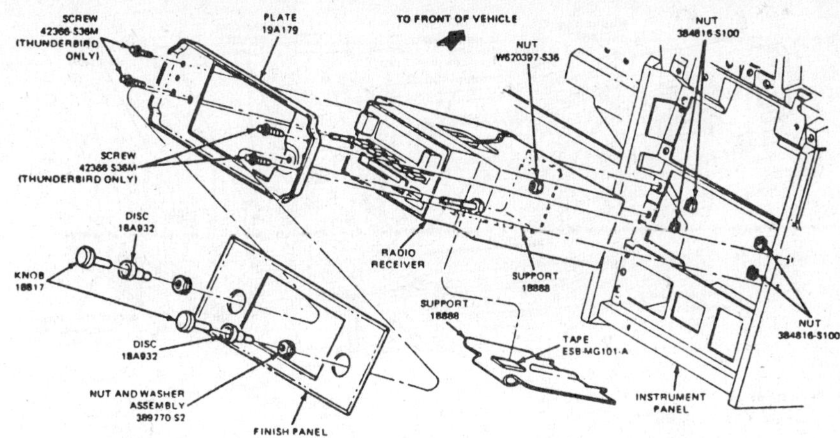

Radio installation in the 1984-86 Thunderbird and Cougar

1980-82 Thunderbird and XR-7
1983 Thunderbird and XR-7, exc. Electronic Radio
1984-85 Thunderbird and Cougar, exc. Electronic Radio

1. Disconnect the negative battery cable.
2. Remove the radio knobs (pull off). Remove the center trim panel.
3. Remove the radio mounting plate screws. Pull the radio towards the front seat to disengage it from the lower bracket.
4. Disconnect the radio and antenna connections.
5. Remove the radio. Remove the nuts and washers (conventional radios) or mounting plate screws (electronic radios) as necessary.
6. On electronic radios, install the mounting plates before installing the retaining nuts and washers or screws.

The rest of installation is the reverse of removal.

1982-87 Continental
1983 Thunderbird and XR-7 with Electronic Radio
1984-87 Thunderbird and Cougar with Electronic Radio
1984-87 Mark VII

1. Disconnect the battery ground.
2. Remove the center instrument trim panel.
3. Remove the 4 screws retaining the radio and mounting bracket to the instrument panel.
4. Push the radio forward and raise the back end slightly to clear the clip in the panel. Pull the radio out slowly.
5. Disconnect the antenna and wiring.
6. Installation is the reverse of removal.

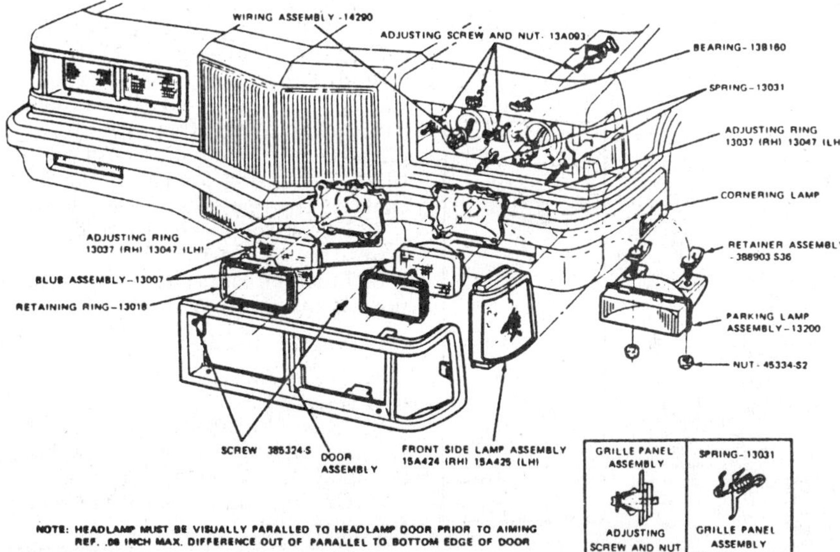

Headlight removal on the 1980-82 XR-7s

LIGHTING

Headlights

REMOVAL & INSTALLATION

All Except 1984 and Later Aerodynamic Headlamps

1. If the car is equipped with moveable headlamp covers, close the bypass valve to raise the headlamp covers. The valve is located in the vacuum lines near the reservoir and left fender.
2. On cars without moveable headlamp doors, remove the headlamp door retaining screws and remove the doors.
3. Remove the headlamp trim mounting screws and remove the trim.
4. Remove the retaining ring screws and remove the retaining ring from the headlamp. Pull the headlamp out and unplug it.
4. Installation is the reverse of removal.

Aerodynamic Headlamps

BULB ASSEMBLY

CAUTION

The halogen bulb contains pressurized gas. If the bulb is dropped or scratched it will shatter. Also, avoid touching the bulb glass with your bare fingers. Grasp the bulb only by its plastic base. Oil from bare skin will cause hot spots on the glass surface and lead to premature burnout. If you do touch the glass, clean it prior to installation.

1. Make sure that the headlamp switch is OFF.
2. Raise the hood. The bulb protrudes from the rear of the headlamp assembly.

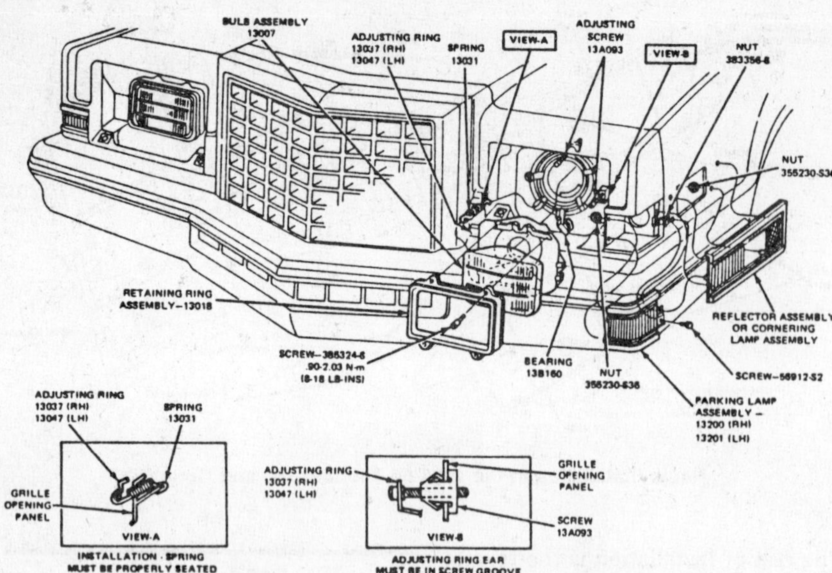

Headlight removal on the 1980-83 Thunderbirds

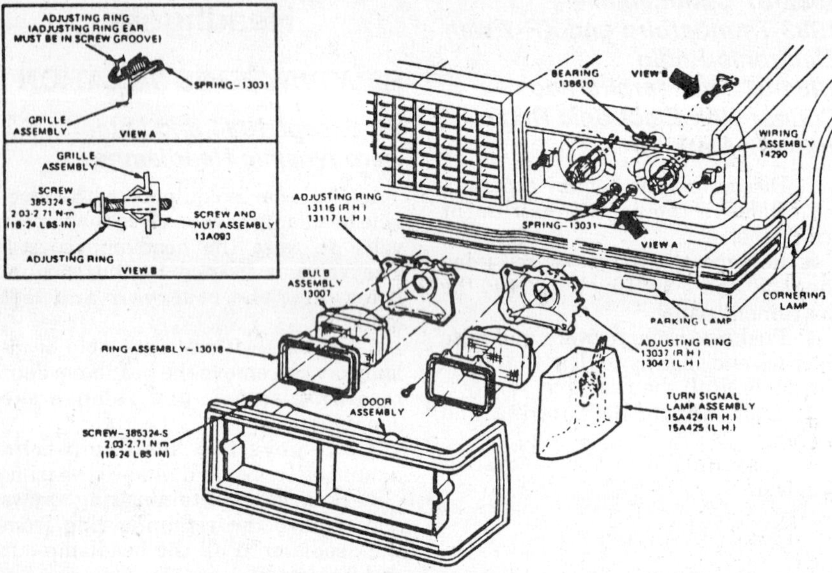

Headlight removal on the 1981-82 Cougars

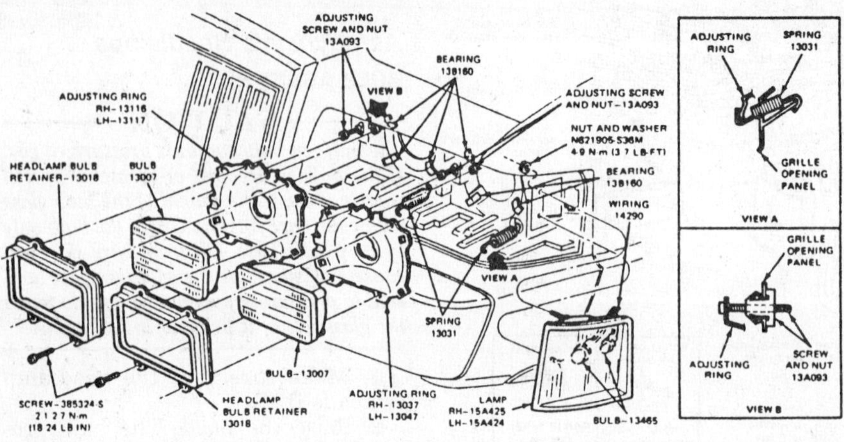

Headlight removal on the 1984 Mark VII with sealed beams

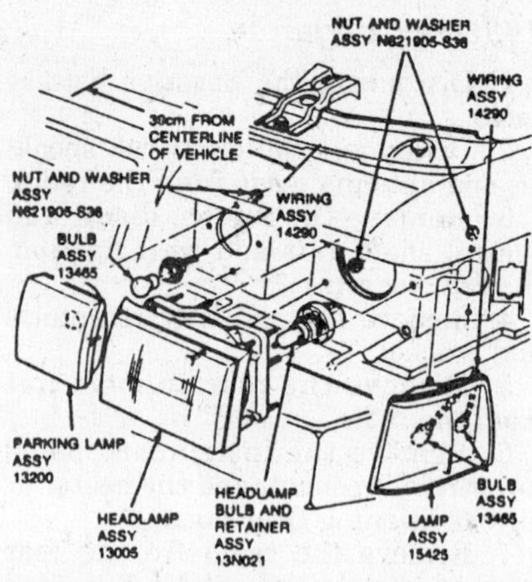

Headlamp unit removal on 1984-87 Mark VII with aerodynamic headlamps

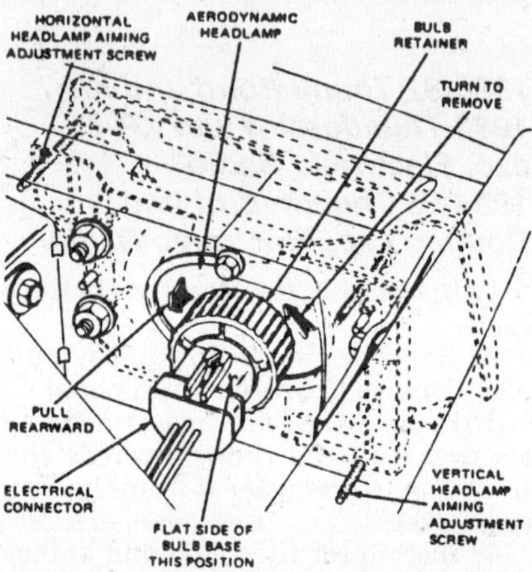

Headlamp unit disassembly on 1984-87 Mark VII with aerodynamic headlamps

3. Unplug the electrical connector from the bulb.
4. Rotate the bulb retaining ring 1/8 turn counterclockwise and remove it.
5. Pull the bulb straight back out of its socket. Don't rotate it.
6. When installing the bulb, push it into position, turning it slightly right or left to align the grooves in the forward part of the base with the tabs in the socket. When they are aligned, push the bulb firmly into position until the mounting flange on the base contacts the rear face of the socket.
7. Install the locking ring, turning it until a stop is felt.
8. Push the connector onto the bulb until it snaps into position.

HEADLAMP ASSEMBLY

1. Make sure that the headlamp switch is OFF.
2. Raise the hood. The bulb protrudes from the rear of the headlamp assembly.
3. Unplug the electrical connector from the bulb.
4. Remove the 3 nuts and washers from the rear of the headlamp.

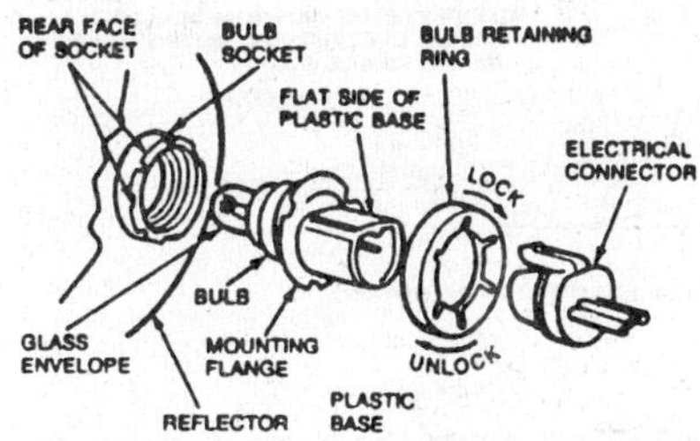

Headlamp bulb replacement on 1984-87 Mark VII with aerodynamic headlamps

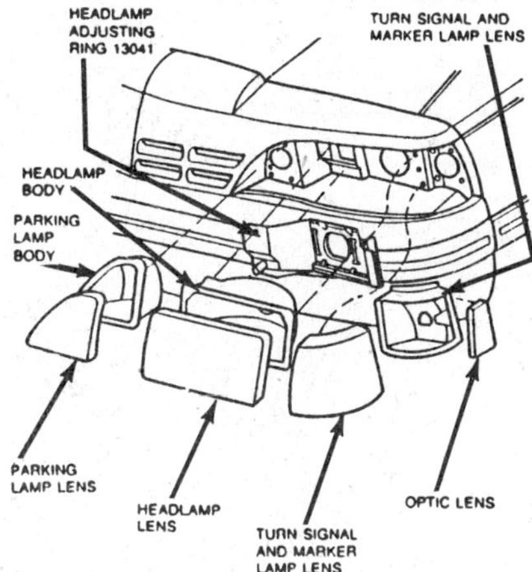

Headlight removal on 1987 Thunderbird and Cougars

5. Push forward on the headlamp at the bulb socket. It may be necessary to loosen the parking lamp and cornering lamp fasteners.
6. Remove the 3 clips which attach the headlamp to the black ring by prying them out from the base with a flat-bladed screwdriver.
7. Installation is the reverse of removal. Make sure that the black rubber shield is securely crimped on the headlamp.

CIRCUIT PROTECTION

Fuses, Fusible Links and Circuit Breakers

LOCATION

A fuse link is a short length of insulated wire, integral with the engine compartment wiring harness. It is several wire gauges smaller than the circuit it protects and is located in-line directly from the positive terminal of the battery.

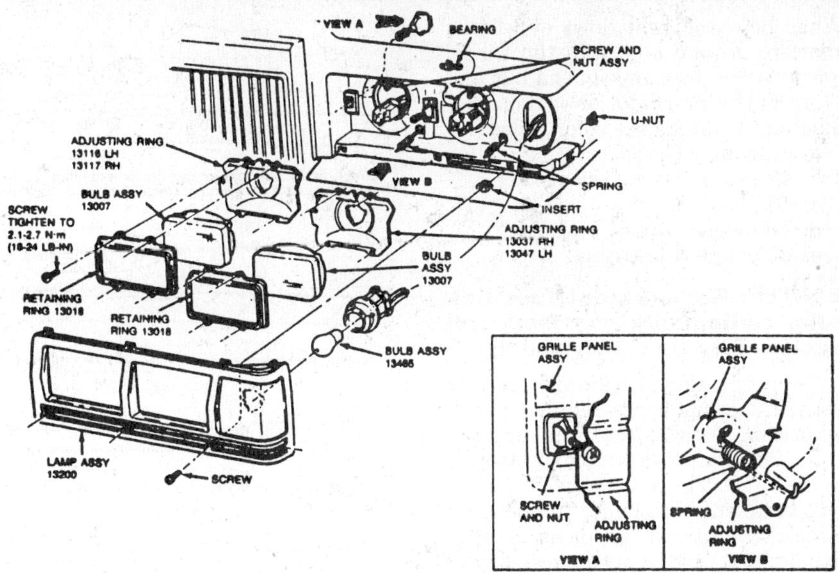

Headlight removal on the 1982-86 Continental

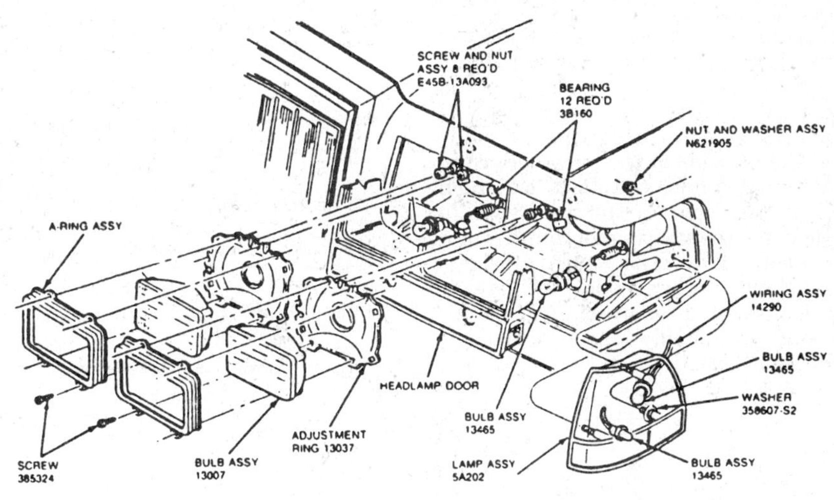

Headlight removal on the 1987 Continentals

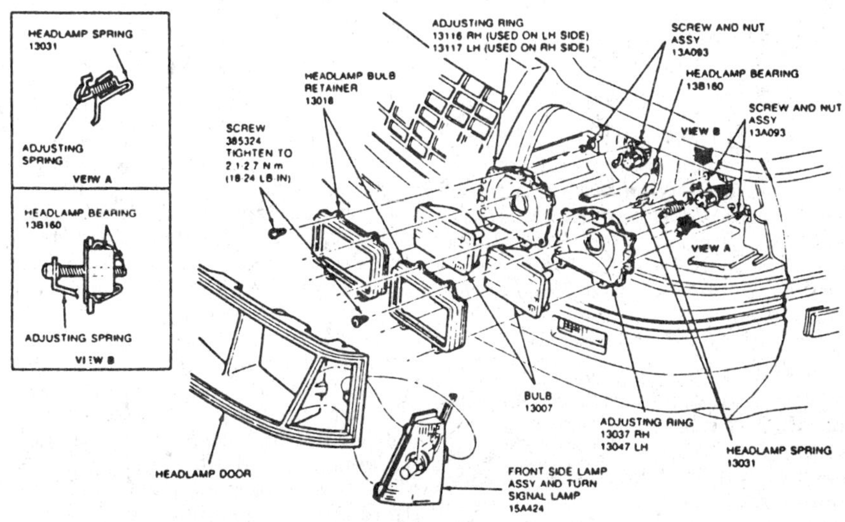

Headlight removal on 1984-86 Thunderbirds and Cougars

When heavy current flows or when a short to ground occurs in the wiring harness, the fuse link burns out and protects the alternator or wiring. Production fuse links are color coded:

a. 12 gauge: Grey.
b. 14 gauge: Dark Green.
c. 16 gauge: Black.
d. 18 gauge: Brown.
e. 20 gauge: Dark Blue.

NOTE: Replacement fuse link color coding may vary from production fuse link color coding.

Circuit breakers are used on certain electrical components requiring high amperage, such as the headlamp circuit, electrical seats and/or windows to name a few. The advantage of the circuit breaker is its ability to open and close the electrical circuit as the lead demands, rather than the necessity of a part replacement, should the circuit be opened with another protective device in line.

A fuse panel is used to house the numerous fuses protecting the various branches of the electrical system and is normally the most accessible. the mounting of the fuse panel is usually on the left side of the passenger compartment, under the dash, either on the side kick panel or on the firewall to the left of the steering column. Certain models will have the fuse panel exposed while other models will have it covered with a removable trim cover.

Fuses are simply snapped in and out for replacement.

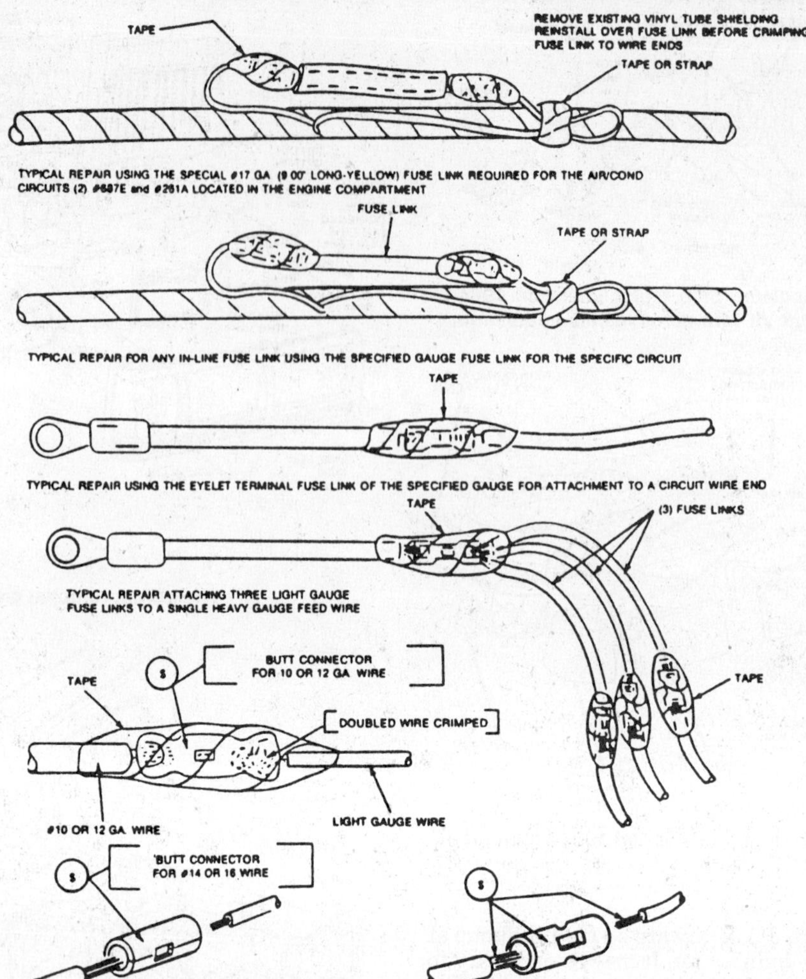

General fuse link repair procedure

MANUAL TRANSMISSION

Transmission

REMOVAL & INSTALLATION

CAUTION

The clutch driven disc contains asbestos, which has been determined to be a cancer causing agent. Never clean clutch surfaces with compressed air! Avoid inhaling any dust from any clutch surface! When cleaning clutch surfaces, use a commercially available brake cleaning fluid.

NOTE: This is a general removal & installation outline. Certain model vehicles may require the steps in a different sequence and may or may not have the components as listed.

1. Disconnect and remove starter and dust ring, if the clutch is to be removed. On floor shift models, remove the boot retainer and shifter lever.
2. On models with the 83ET, 84ET, and 85ET four speed transmission: working under the hood, remove the upper clutch housing-to-engine bolts.
3. Raise the car.
4. Matchmark the driveshaft and axle flange for reassembly. Disconnect the driveshaft at the rear universal joint and remove the driveshaft. Plug the extension housing.
5. Disconnect the speedometer cable at the transmission extension. Disconnect the seat belt sensor wires and the back-up lamp switch wires. Remove the clutch lever boot and cable on Mustang, and Capri if so equipped.
6. Disconnect the gear shift rods from the transmission shift levers. If the car is equipped with four speed, remove bolts that secure shift control bracket to extension housing. Support the engine with a jack.
7. Remove the bolt holding the extension housing to the rear support, and remove the muffler inlet pipe bracket to housing bolt.
8. Remove the two rear support bracket insulator nuts from the underside of the crossmember. Remove the crossmember.
9. Place a jack (equipped with a protective piece of wood) under the rear of the engine oil pan. Raise or lower the engine slightly as necessary to provide access to the bolts.
10. Remove transmission-to-flywheel housing bolts.
11. Slide the transmission back and out of the car. It may be necessary to slide the catalytic converter bracket forward to provide clearance on some models.

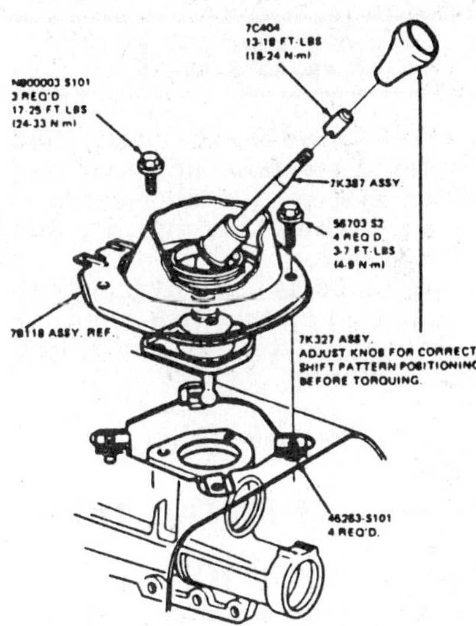

Shift lever installation on model 82ET 4-speed

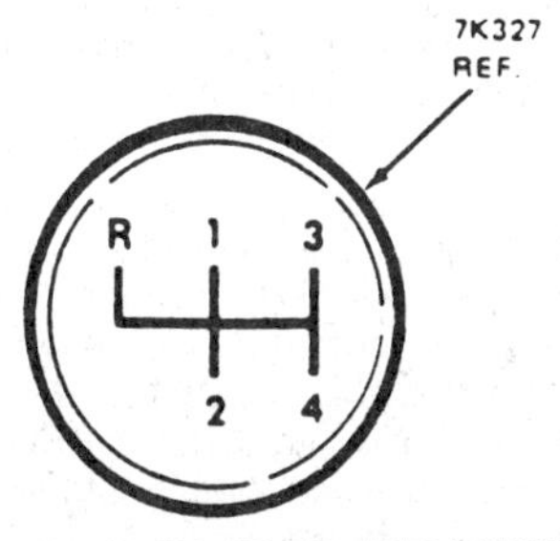

WITH LEVER IN NEUTRAL POSITION, INSTALL LOCKING NUT 7C404 UNTIL HAND TIGHT. THEN INSTALL KNOB 7K327 UNTIL HAND TIGHT BACK KNOB OFF UNTIL SHIFT PATTERN ALIGNS WITH THE OF DRIVE LINE. TIGHTEN LOCKING NUT 13 18 FT LBS (18-24 N·m) NO THREADS SHALL BE VISIBLE AFTER NUT HAS BEEN TIGHTENED. SHIFT PATTERN ALIGNMENT MUST BE WITHIN ± 15° OF ℄ OF DRIVE LINE.

Shift knob installation on model 82ET 4-speed

12. To remove the clutch, remove release lever retracting spring. Disconnect pedal at the equalizer bar, of the clutch cable from the housing, as applicable.
13. Remove bolts that secure engine rear plate to front lower part of bellhousing.
14. Remove bolts that attach bellhousing to cylinder block and remove housing and release lever as a unit. Remove the clutch release lever by pulling it through the window in the housing until the retainer spring disengages from the pivot.
15. Loosen six pressure plate cover attaching bolts evenly to release spring pressure. Mark cover and flywheel to facilitate reassembly in same position.
16. Remove six attaching bolts while holding pressure plate cover. Remove pressure plate and clutch disc.

CAUTION

Do not depress the clutch pedal while the transmission is removed.

17. Before installing the clutch, clean the flywheel surface. Inspect the flywheel and pressure plate for wear, scoring, or burn marks (blue color). Light scoring and wear may be cleaned up with emery paper; heavy wear may require refacing of the flywheel or replacement of the damaged parts.
18. Attach the clutch disc and pressure plate assembly to the flywheel. The three dowel pins on the flywheel, if so equipped, must be properly aligned. Damaged pins must be replaced. Avoid touching the clutch plate surface. Tighten the bolts finger tight.
19. Align the clutch disc with the pilot bushing. Torque cover bolts to 12-24 ft.lb. with the four cylinder, 12-20 ft.lb. for all others.
20. Lightly lubricate the release lever in the flywheel housing and install the dust shield.
21. Apply very little lubricant on the release bearing retainer journal. Fill the groove in the release bearing hub with grease. Clean all excess grease from the inside bore of the hub to prevent clutch disc contamination. Attach the release bearing and hub on the release lever.
22. Make sure the flywheel housing and engine block are clean. Any missing damaged mounting dowels must be replaced. Install the flywheel housing and torque the attaching bolts to 38-61 ft.lb. on all V8s, 38-55 ft.lb. on 6-200, and 28-38 ft.lb. on 4-140 and 6-170. Install the dust cover and torque the bolts to 17-20 ft.lb.
23. Connect the release rod or cable and the retracting spring. Connect the pedal-to-equalizer rod at the equalizer bar.
24. Install starter and dust ring.
25. After moving the transmission back just far enough for the pilot shaft to clear the clutch housing, move it upward and into position on the flywheel housing. It may be necessary to put the transmission in gear and rotate the output shaft to align the input shaft and clutch splines.
26. Move the transmission forward and into place against the flywheel housing, and install the transmission attaching bolts finger-tight.
27. Tighten the transmission bolts to 37-42 ft.lb. on all cars.
28. Install the crossmember and torque the mounting bolts to 20-30 ft.lb. Slowly lower the engine onto the crossmember.
29. Torque the rear mount to 30-50 ft.lb.
30. Connect gear shift rods and the speedometer cable.
31. Remove the plug from the extension housing and install the driveshaft, aligning the marks made previously.
32. Refill transmission to proper level. On floorshift models, install the boot retainer and shift lever.

LINKAGE ADJUSTMENT

Column Shift

NOTE: With the transmission in Neutral, the shift lever should be in a horizontal plane the parallel to the instrument panel line. Corrective adjustments should be made at the gear shift rods.

1. Place shift lever in Neutral.
2. Loosen two gear shift rod adjustment nuts.
3. Insert $^3/_{16}''$ diameter alignment pin through first and reverse gear shift lever and second and third gear shift lever. Align levers to insert pin.
4. Tighten gear shift rod adjustment nuts, and remove pin.
5. Check gear level for smooth crossover.

Floor Shift

1. Loosen three shift linkage adjustment nuts.
2. Install a ¼" diameter alignment pin through control bracket and levers.
3. Tighten three shift linkage adjustment nuts and remove alignment pin.
4. Check gear lever for smooth crossover.

Back-Up Light Switch

REMOVAL & INSTALLATION

1. Place the shift lever in neutral.

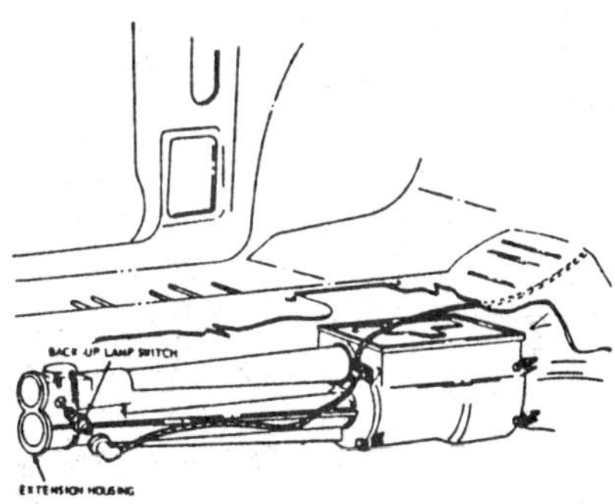

82ET back-up lamp switch

2. Raise and support the car on jackstands.
3. Unplug the electrical connector at the switch.
4. Unscrew the switch from the transmission extension housing.
5. Screw the new switch into place and tighten it to 60 in.lb.
6. Connect the wiring.

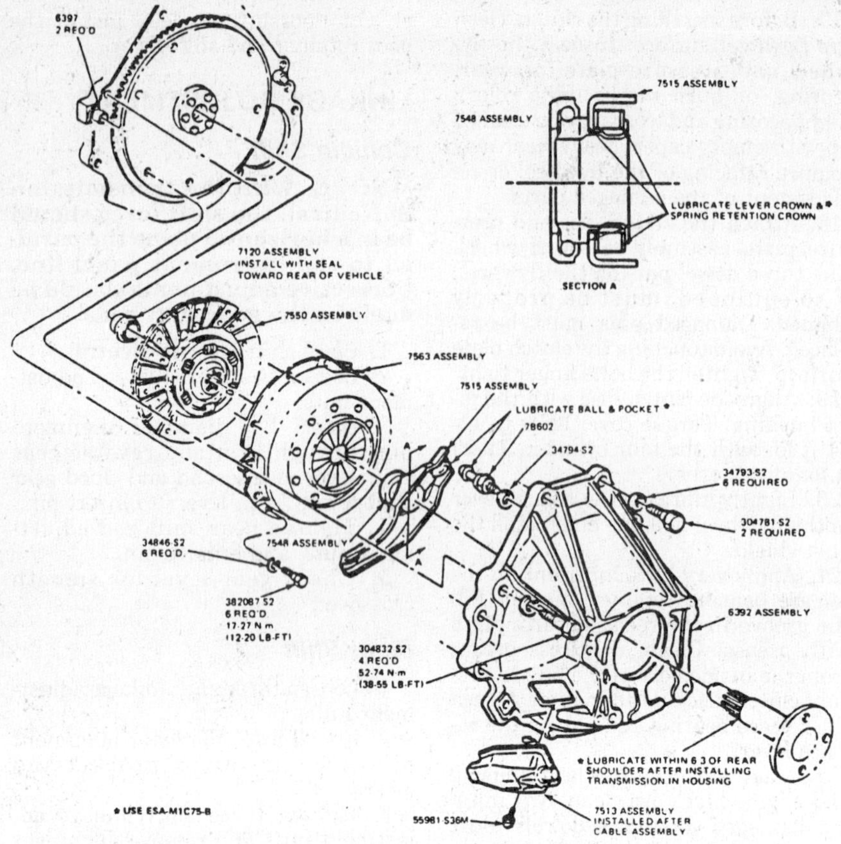

Clutch installation on the 1984 Thunderbird and Cougar with the 8-302

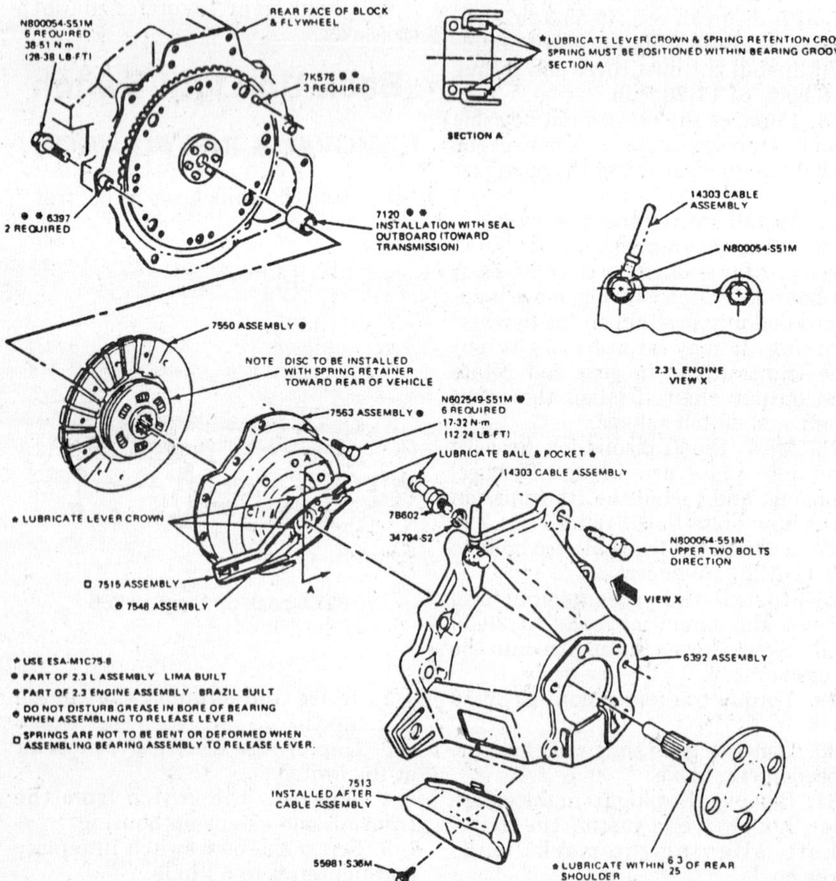

Clutch installation on 1981-82 and 1984 4-140 engines

CLUTCH

NOTE: Models through 1986 employ a mechanically actuated clutch system. Clutch release is accomplished through a cable linkage system.

1987 models use a hydraulically actuated clutch with a master cylinder, plastic reservoir, and slave cylinder

Clutch Disc

REMOVAL & INSTALLATION

CAUTION

The clutch driven disc contains asbestos, which has been determined to be a cancer causing agent. Never clean clutch surfaces with compressed air! Avoid inhaling any dust from any clutch surface! When cleaning clutch surfaces, use a commercially available brake cleaning fluid.

1. Disconnect and remove starter and dust ring, if the clutch is to be removed. On floorshift models, remove the boot retainer and shift lever.
2. On models with ET 4-speed transmission: working under the hood, remove the upper clutch housing-to-engine bolts.
3. Raise the car.
4. Matchmark the drive shaft and axle flange for reassembly. Disconnect the driveshaft at the rear universal joint and remove the driveshaft. Plug the extension housing.
5. Disconnect the speedometer cable at the transmission extension. Disconnect the seat belt sensor wires. Remove the clutch lever boot and cable on models so equipped.
6. Disconnect the gear shift rods from the transmission shift levers. If car is equipped with 4-speed, except SROD models, remove bolts that secure shift control bracket to extension housing. Support the engine with a jack.
7. Remove the bolt holding the extension housing to the rear support, and remove the muffler inlet pipe bracket to housing bolt.
8. Remove the two rear support bracket insulator nuts from the underside of the crossmember. Remove crossmember.
9. Place a jack (equipped with a protective piece of wood) under the rear of the engine oil pan. Raise or lower the engine slightly as necessary to provide access to the bolts.
10. Remove transmission-to-flywheel housing bolts.
11. Slide the transmission back and out of the car. It may be necessary to

slide the catalytic converter bracket forward to provide clearance on some models.

12. To remove the clutch, remove release lever retracting spring. Disconnect pedal at the equalizer bar, or the clutch cable from the housing, as applicable.

13. Remove bolts that secure engine rear plate to front lower part of bellhousing.

14. Remove bolts that attach bell housing to cylinder block and remove housing and release lever as a unit. Remove the clutch release lever by pulling it through the window in the housing until the retainer spring disengages from the pivot.

15. Loosen six pressure plate cover attaching bolts evenly to release spring pressure. Mark cover and flywheel to facilitate reassembly in same position.

16. Remove six attaching bolts while holding pressure plate cover. Remove pressure plate and clutch disc.

CAUTION

Do not depress the clutch pedal while the transmission is removed.

17. Before installing the clutch, clean the flywheel surface. Inspect the flywheel and pressure plate for wear, scoring, or burn marks (blue color). Light scoring and wear may require refacing of the flywheel or replacement of the damaged parts.

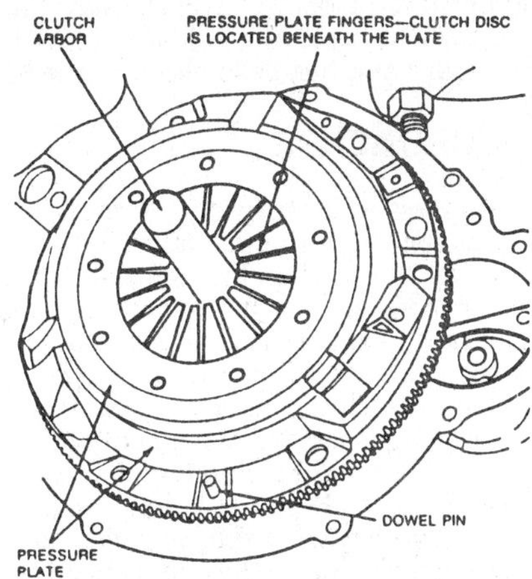

Typical clutch disc alignment

18. Attach the clutch disc and pressure plate assembly to the flywheel. The three dowl pins on the flywheel. The three dowel pins on the flywheel, if so equipped, must be properly aligned. Damaged pins must be replaced. Avoid touching the clutch plate surface. Tighten the bolts finger tight.

19. Align the clutch disc with the pilot bushing. Torque cover bolts to 12-24 ft.lb. with the four cylinder, 12-20 ft.lb. for all others.

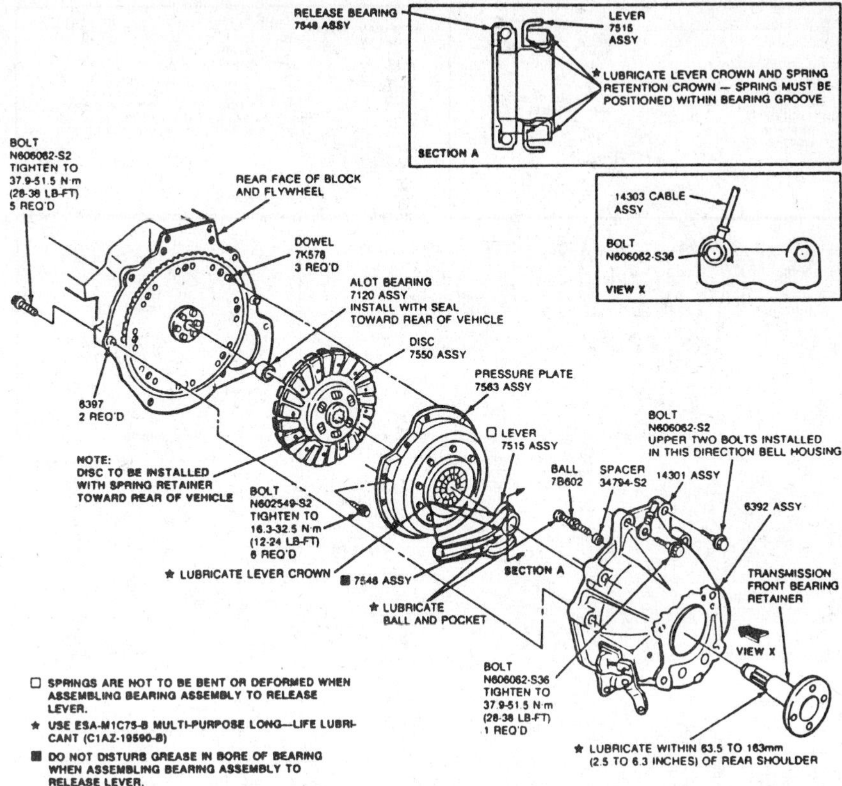

Clutch installation on the 1985-86 Thunderbird and Cougar with the 4-140

20. Lightly lubricate the release lever fulcrum ends. Install the release lever in the flywheel housing and install the dust shield.

21. Apply very little lubricant on the release bearing retainer journal. Fill the groove in the release bearing hub with grease. Clean all excess grease from the inside bore of the hub to prevent clutch disc contamination. Attach the release bearing and hub on the release lever.

22. Make sure the flywheel housing and engine block are clean. Any missing or damaged mounting dowels must be replaced. Install the flywheel housing and torque the attaching bolts to 38-61 ft.lb. on all V8s and 6-250, and 28-38 ft.lb. on 4-140. Install the dust cover and torque the bolts to 17-20 ft.lb.

23. Connect the release rod or cable and the retracting spring. Connect the pedal-to-equalizer rod at the equalizer bar.

24. Install starter and dust ring.

25. After moving the transmission back just far enough for the pilot shaft to clear the clutch housing, move it upward and into position on the flywheel housing. It may be necessary to put the transmission in gear and rotate the output shaft to align the input shaft and clutch splines.

26. Move the transmission forward and into place against the flywheel housing, and install the transmission attaching bolts finger-tight.

27. Tighten the transmission bolts to 37-42 ft.lb. on all cars.

28. Install the crossmember and torque the mounting bolts to 20-30 ft.lb. Slowly lower the engine onto the crossmember.

29. Torque the rear mount to 30-50 ft.lb.

30. Connect gear shift rods and the speedometer cable.

31. Remove the plug from the extension housing and install the driveshaft, aligning the marks made previously.

32. Refill the transmission to proper level. On floorshift models, install the boot retainer and shift lever.

NOTE: All models have self-adjusting clutches. No adjustments are necessary.

ADJUSTMENTS

All models, through 1986, have self-adjusting clutches. No adjustments are necessary.

Self-Adjusting Clutch

The free play in the clutch is adjusted by a built in mechanism that allows the clutch controls to be self-adjusted during normal operation.

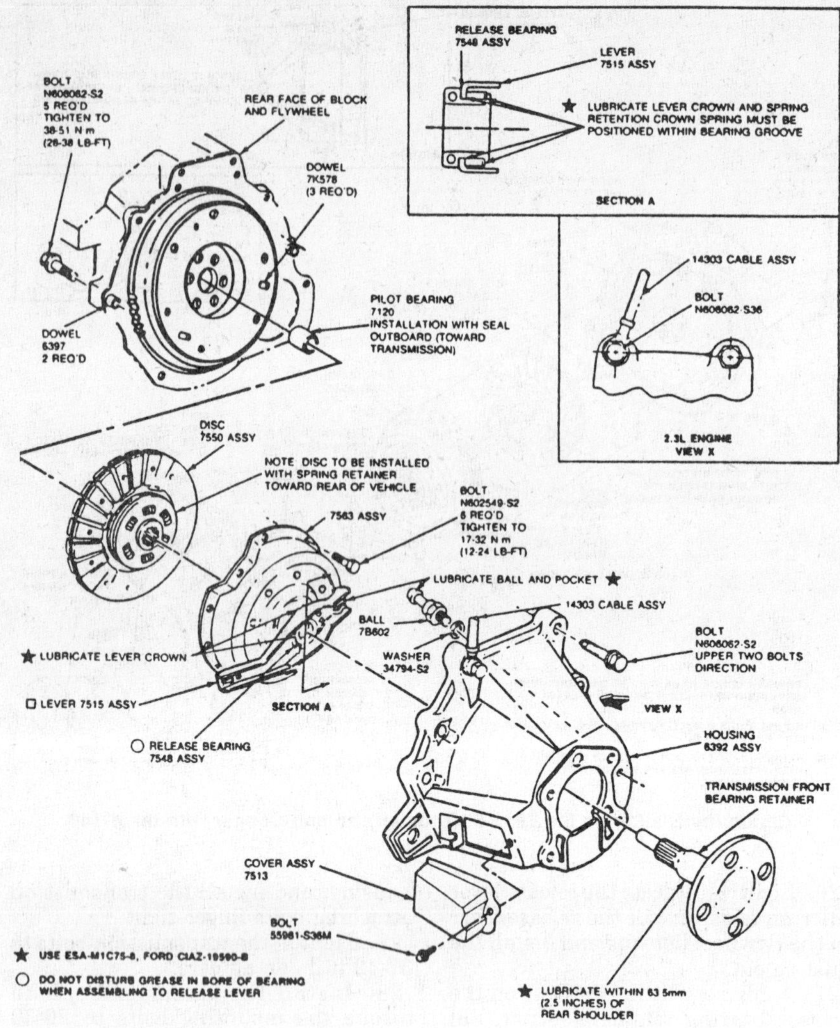

Clutch installation on the 1987 Thunderbird and Cougar with the 4-140

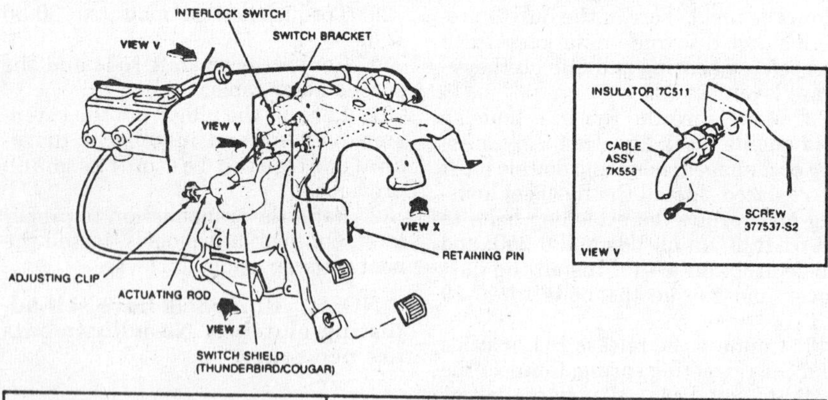

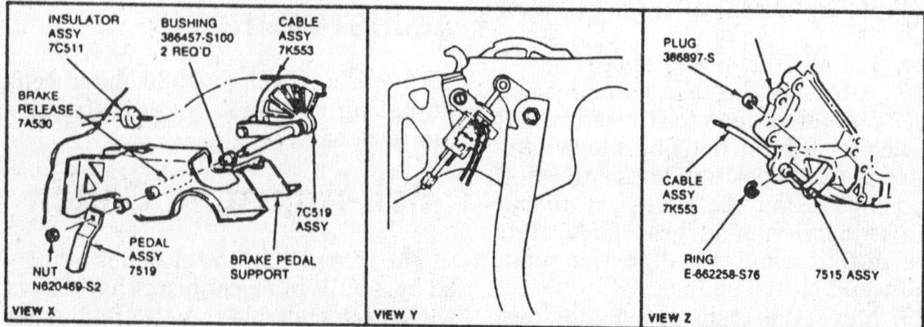

Self-adjusting clutch components

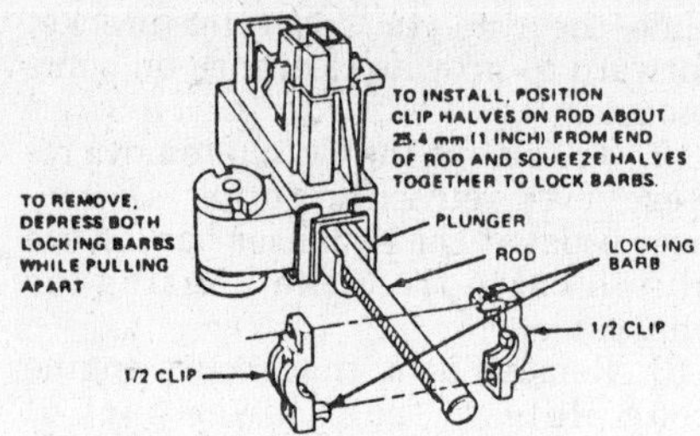

Starter/clutch interlock switch self-adjuster clip installation

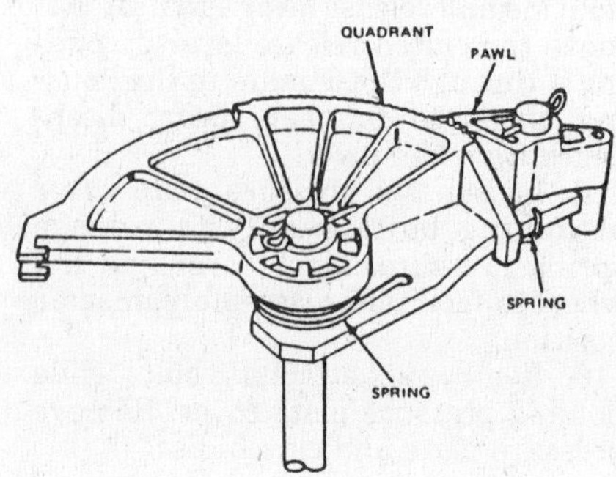

Self-adjusting clutch mechanism

The self-adjusting feature should be checked every 5,000 miles. This is accomplished by insuring that the clutch pedal travels to the top of its upward position. Grasp the clutch pedal with your hand or put your foot under the clutch pedal, pull up on the pedal until it stops. Very little effort is required (about 10 lbs.) During the application of upward pressure, a click may be heard which means an adjustment was necessary and has been accomplished.

COMPONENTS

The self-adjusting clutch control mechanism is automatically adjusted by a device on the clutch pedal. The system consists of a spring loaded gear quadrant, a spring loaded pawl, and a clutch cable which is spring loaded to preload the clutch release lever bearing to compensate for movement of the release lever, as the clutch disc wears. The spring loaded pawl located at the top of the clutch pedal, engages the gear quadrant when the clutch pedal is depressed and pulls the cable through its continuously adjusted stroke. Clutch cable adjustments are not required because of this feature.

STARTER/CLUTCH INTERLOCK SWITCH

The starter/clutch switch is designed to prevent starting the engine unless the clutch pedal is fully depressed. The switch is connected between the ignition switch and the starter motor relay coil and maintains an open circuit with the clutch pedal up (clutch engaged).

The switch is designed to self-adjust automatically the first time the clutch pedal is pressed to the floor. The self-adjuster consists of a two-piece clip snapped together over a serrated rod. When the plunger or rod is extended, the clip bottoms out on the switch body and allows the rod to ratchet over the serrations to a position determined by the clutch pedal travel limit. In this way, the switch is set to close the starter circuit when the clutch is pressed all the way to the floor (clutch disengaged).

Testing Continuity

1. Disconnect inline wiring connector at jumper harness.
2. Using a test lamp or continuity tester, check that switch is open with clutch pedal up (clutch engaged), and closed at approximately 1" (25.4mm) from the clutch pedal full down position (clutch disengaged).
3. If switch does not operate, check to see if the self-adjusting clip is out of position on the rod. It should be near the end of the rod.
4. If the self-adjusting clip is out of position, remove and reposition the clip to about 1" (25.4mm) from the end of the rod.
5. Reset the switch by pressing the clutch pedal to the floor.
6. Repeat Step 2. If switch is damaged, replace it.

REMOVAL &INSTALLATION

Starter/Clutch Interlock Switch

1. Disconnect the wiring connector.
2. Remove the retaining pin from the clutch pedal.
3. Remove the switch bracket attaching screw.
4. Lift the switch and bracket assembly upward to disengage tab from pedal support.
5. Move the switch outward to disengage actuating rod eyelet from clutch pedal pin and remove switch from vehicle.

WARNING: Always install the switch with the self-adjusting clip about 1" (25.4mm) from the end of the rod. The clutch pedal must be fully up (clutch engaged). Otherwise, the switch may be misadjusted.

6. Place the eyelet end of the rod onto the pivot pin.
7. Swing the switch assembly around to line up hole in the mounting boss with the hole in the bracket.
8. Install the attaching screw.
9. Replace the retaining pin in the pivot pin.
10. Connect the wiring connector.

Clutch Pedal Assembly

1. Remove the starter/clutch interlock switch.
2. Remove the clutch pedal attaching nut.
3. Pull the clutch pedal off the clutch pedal shaft.
4. Align the square hole of the clutch pedal with the clutch pedal shaft and push the clutch pedal on.
5. Install the clutch pedal attaching nut and tighten to 32-50 ft.lb.
6. Install the starter/clutch interlock switch.

Self-Adjusting Assembly

1. Disconnect the battery cable from the negative terminal of the battery.
2. Remove the steering wheel using a steering wheel puller Tool T67L-3600-A or equivalent.
3. Remove the lower dash panel section to the left of the steering column.
4. Remove the shrouds from the steering column.
5. Disconnect the brake lamp switch and the master cylinder pushrod from the brake pedal.
6. Rotate the clutch quadrant forward and unhook the clutch cable from the quadrant. Allow the quadrant to slowly swing rearward.
7. Remove the bolt holding the brake pedal support bracket lateral brace to the left side of the vehicle.
8. Disconnect all electrical connectors to the steering column.
9. Remove the 4 nuts that hold the steering column to the brake pedal support bracket and lower the steering column to the floor.
10. Remove the 4 booster nuts that hold the brake pedal support bracket to the dash panel.
11. Remove the bolt that holds the brake pedal support bracket to the underside of the instrument panel, and remove the brake pedal support bracket assembly from the vehicle.
12. Remove the clutch pedal shaft nut and the clutch pedal as outlined.
13. Slide the self-adjusting mechanism out of the brake pedal support bracket.
14. Remove the self-adjusting mechanism shaft bushings from either side of the brake pedal support bracket and replace if worn.
15. Lubricate the self-adjusting mechanism shaft with motor oil and install the mechanism into the brake pedal support bracket.
16. Position the quadrant towards the top of the vehicle. Align the flats on the shaft with the flats in the clutch pedal assembly, and install the retaining nuts. Tighten to 32-50 ft.lb.
17. Position the brake pedal support bracket assembly beneath the instrument panel aligning the four holes with the studs in the dash panel. Install the four nuts loosely. Install the bolt through the support bracket into the instrument panel and tighten to 13-25 ft.lb.
18. Tighten the four booster nuts that hold the brake pedal support bracket to the dash panel to 13-25 ft.lb.
19. Connect the brake lamp switch and the master cylinder pushrod to the brake pedal.
20. Attach the clutch cable to the quadrant.
21. Position the steering column onto the four studs in the support bracket and start the four nuts.
22. Connect the steering column electrical connectors.
23. Install the steering column shrouds.
24. Install the brake pedal support lateral brace.
25. Tighten the steering column attaching nuts to 20-37 ft.lb.
26. Install the lower dash panel section.
27. Install the steering wheel.
28. Connect the battery cable to the negative terminal on the battery.
29. Check the steering column for proper operation.
30. Depress the clutch pedal several times to adjust cable.

Quadrant Pawl, Self-Adjusting

1. Remove the self-adjusting mechanism.
2. Remove the two hairpin clips that hold the pawl and quadrant on the shaft assembly.
3. Remove the quadrant and quadrant spring.
4. Remove the pawl spring.
5. Remove the pawl.
6. Lubricate the pawl and quadrant pivot shafts with M1C75B or equivalent grease.
7. Install pawl. Position the teeth of the pawl toward the long shaft, and the spring hole at the end of the arm. Do not position the spring hole beneath the arm.
8. Insert the straight portion of the spring into the hole, with the coil up.
9. Keeping the straight portion in the hole rotate the spring 180 degrees to the left and slide the coiled portion of the spring over the boss.
10. Hook the bend portion of the spring under the arm.
11. Install the retainer clip on opposite side of spring.
12. Place the quadrant spring on the shaft with the bent portion of the spring in the hole in the arm.

13. Place the lubricated quadrant on the shaft aligning the projection at the bottom of the quadrant to a position beneath the arm of the shaft assembly. Push the pawl up so the bottom tooth of the pawl meshes with bottom tooth of quadrant.

14. Install the quadrant retainer pin.

15. Grasp the straight end of the quadrant spring with pliers and position behind the ear of the quadrant.

16. Install the self-adjusting mechanism.

17. Install the clutch pedal assembly.

Clutch Cable Assembly

1. Lift the clutch pedal to its upward most position to disengage the pawl and quadrant. Push the quadrant forward, unhook the cable from the quadrant and allow to slowly swing rearward.

2. Open the hood and remove the screw that holds the cable assembly isolator to the dash panel.

3. Pull the cable through the dash panel and into the engine compartment. On 4-140 EFI turbocharged and 8-302 engines, remove cable bracket screw from fender apron.

4. Raise the vehicle and safely support on jackstands.

5. Remove the dust cover from the bell housing.

6. Remove the clip retainer holding the cable assembly to the bell housing.

7. Slide the ball on the end of the cable assembly through the hole in the clutch release lever and remove the cable.

8. Remove the dash panel isolator from the cable.

9. Install the dash panel isolator on the cable assembly.

10. Insert the cable through the hole in the bell housing and through the hole in the clutch release lever. Slide the ball on the end of the cable assembly away from the hole in the clutch release lever.

11. Install the clip retainer that holds the cable assembly to the bell housing.

12. Install the dust shield on the bell housing.

13. Push the cable assembly into the engine compartment and lower the vehicle. On 4-140 EFI turbocharged and 8-302 engines, install cable bracket screw in fender apron.

14. Push the cable assembly into the hole in the dash panel and secure the isolater with a screw.

15. Install the cable assembly by lifting the clutch pedal to disengage the pawl and quadrant, the, pushing the quadrant forward, hook the end of the cable over the rear of the quadrant.

16. Depress clutch pedal several times to adjust cable.

Hydraulic Clutch

MASTER CYLINDER REMOVAL & INSTALLATION

1. Remove the slave cylinder as outlined below.

2. Unbolt and remove the reservoir.

3. Turn the master cylinder 45° clockwise and slowly pull it out.

4. Installation is the reverse of removal.

SLAVE CYLINDER REMOVAL & INSTALLATION

1. Raise and support the front end on jackstands.

2. Unbolt and remove the dust cover.

3. Unlatch the slave cylinder from the transmission housing bracket.

4. Place a drip pan under the cylinder and disconnect the fluid line. Cap the line.

5. Installation is the reverse of removal.

CLUTCH INTERLOCK SWITCH REMOVAL & INSTALLATION

1. Remove the switch mounting bracket nuts.

2. Disconnect the wiring.

3. Remove the switch and bracket.

4. Installation is the reverse of removal.

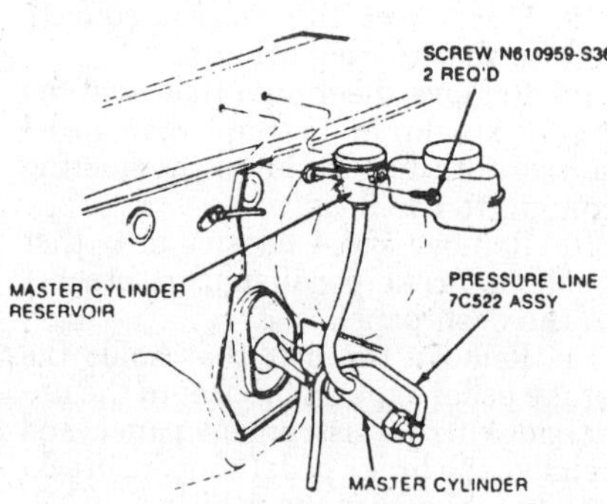

Hydraulic clutch master and slave cylinders

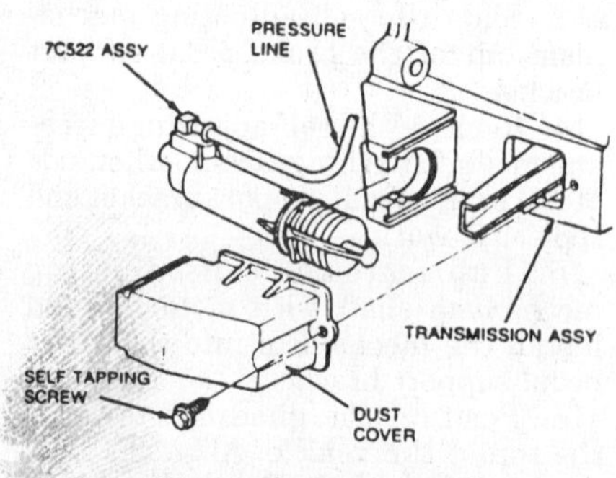

Slave cylinder removal

AUTOMATIC TRANSMISSION

Pan REMOVAL & Filter Change

NOTE: Refer to ROUTINE MAINTENANCE for current fluid requirements.

C3, C4, C5

1. Raise the vehicle, so that the transmission oil pan is readily accessible. Safely support on jackstands.

2. Disconnect the fluid filler tube from the pan and allow the fluid to drain into an appropriate container.

3. Remove the transmission oil pan attaching bolts, pan and gasket.

4. Clean the transmission oil pan and transmission mating surfaces.

5. Install the transmission oil pan in the reverse order of removal, torquing the attaching bolts to 12-16 ft.lb. and using a new gasket. Fill the transmission with 3 qts. of the correct type fluid.

6. Lower the vehicle. Start the engine and move the gear selector through shift pattern. Allow the engine to reach normal operating temperature.

7. Check the transmission fluid. Add fluid, if necessary, to maintain correct level.

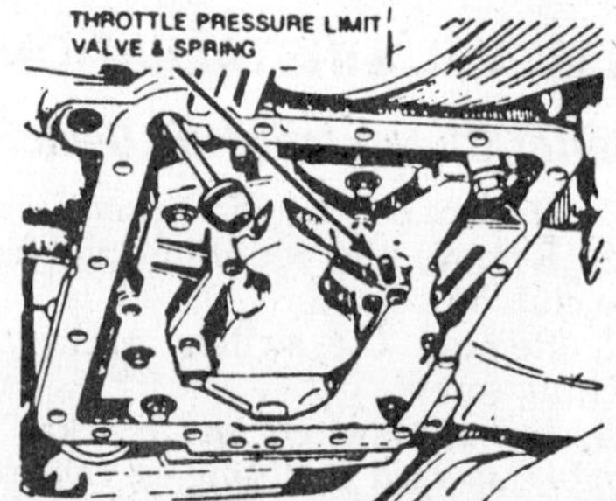

C4 throttle limit valve and spring. They are held in place by the transmission filter. The valve is installed with the large end towards the valve body, the spring fits over the valve stem

C6, FMX, and AOD

1. Raise the car and support on jackstands.

2. Place a drain pan under the transmission.

3. Loosen the pan attaching bolts and drain the fluid from the transmission.

4. When the fluid has drained to the level of the pan flange, remove the remaining pan bolts working from the rear and both sides of the pan to allow it to drop and drain slowly.

5. When all of the fluid has drained, remove the pan and clean it thoroughly. discard the pan gasket.
6. Place a new gasket on the pan, and install the pan on the transmission. Tighten the attaching bolts to 12-16 ft.lb.
7. Add three quarts of fluid to the transmission through the filler tube.
8. Lower the vehicle. Start the engine and move the gear selector through shift pattern. Allow the engine to reach normal operating temperature.
9. Check the transmission fluid. Add fluid, if necessary, to maintain correct level.

ZF Transmission

NOTE: Fluid change is required every 30,000 miles. Required fluid is Dexron®II or equivalent.

1. Raise and support the vehicle safely.
2. Place a drain pan underneath the transmission oil pan.
3. Remove the drain plug and allow the fluid to drain.
4. After all of the fluid has drained, clean the drain plug and reinstall. Tighten the drain plug to 11 ft.lb.
5. Lower the vehicle. Add three quarts of fluid through the transmission filler tube.
6. Start the engine and check the fluid level after moving the selector through all positions. Add fluid, if necessary, to correct level.

JATCO

1. Raise the car and support on jackstands.
2. Place a drain pan under the transmission.
3. Loosen the pan attaching bolts from the rear forward, leaving just the 2 front bolts in place and drain the fluid from the transmission.
4. When the fluid has drained, remove the pan.
5. Clean it thoroughly and discard the pan gasket.
6. Place a new gasket on the pan, and install the pan on the transmission. Tighten the attaching bolts to 48-60 in.lb.
7. Add three quarts of DEXRON®II fluid to the transmission through the filler tube.
8. Lower the vehicle. Start the engine and move the gear selector through shift pattern. Allow the engine to reach normal operating temperature, then, increase the engine speed to 1,200 rpm.
9. Check the transmission fluid. Add fluid, if necessary, to maintain correct level.

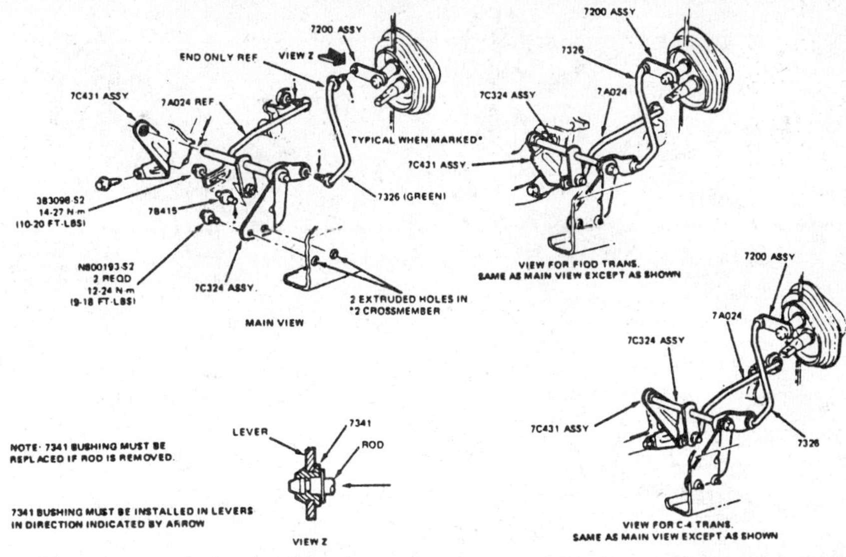

Manual linkage on column shift 1980-81 Thunderbird and Cougar models with either the AOD, or C4 transmission

Adjustments

SHIFT LINKAGE ADJUSTMENT

Column Shift

EXCEPT JATCO

1. With the engine off, place the gear selector in the D (Drive) position, or D (overdrive) position (AOD). Either hang a weight on the shifter or have an assistant sit in the car and hold the selector against the stop.
2. Loosen the adjusting nut or clamp at the shift lever so that the shift rod if free to slide. On models with a shift cable, remove the nut from the transmission lever and disconnect the cable from the transmission.
3. Place the manual shift lever on the transmission in the D (Drive) or D (Overdrive) position. This is the second detent position from the full counterclockwise position.
4. Tighten the adjusting bolt. On cars with a cable, position the cable end on the transmission lever stud, aligning the flats. Tighten the adjusting nut.
5. Check the pointer alignment and transmission operation for all selector positions. If not correct, adjust linkage.

JATCO

1. Place the selector in **N**.

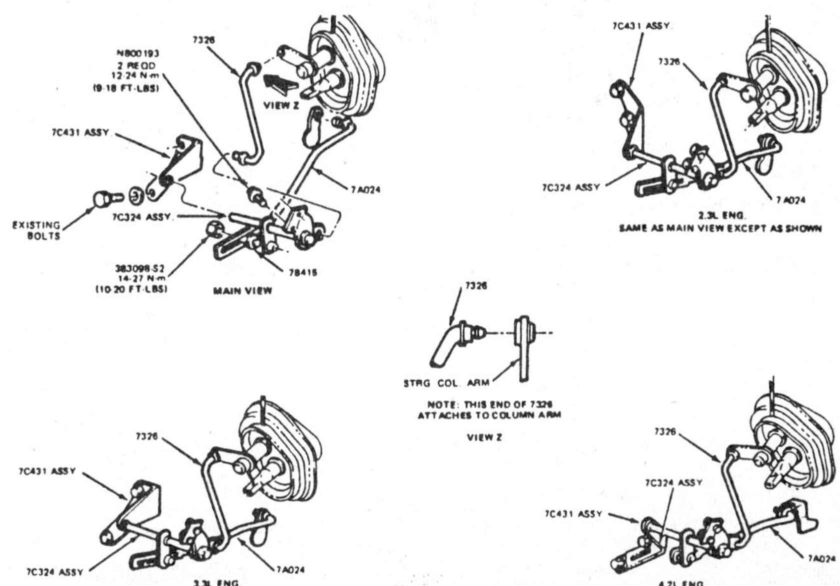

Manual linkage on column shift 1981 Cougar models with 4-140, 6-200 or 8-255 engines

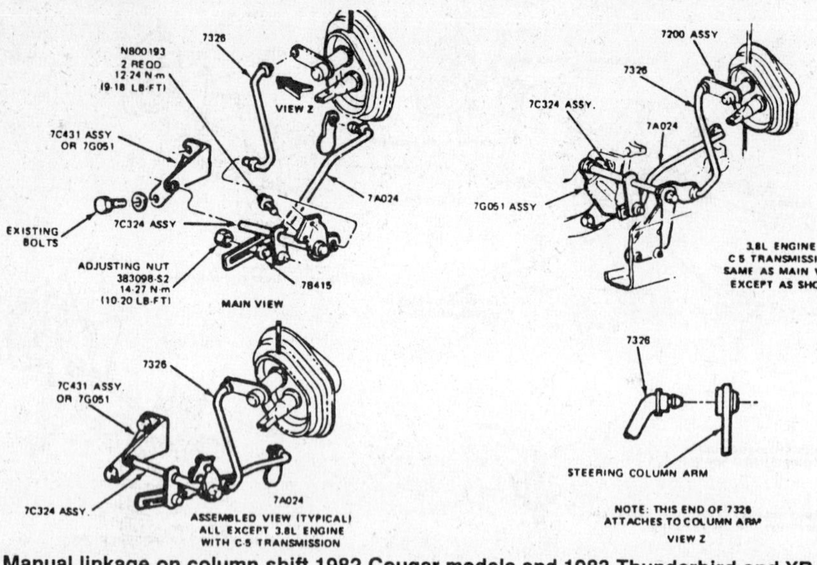

Manual linkage on column shift 1982 Cougar models and 1983 Thunderbird and XR-7 models, except AOD transmission

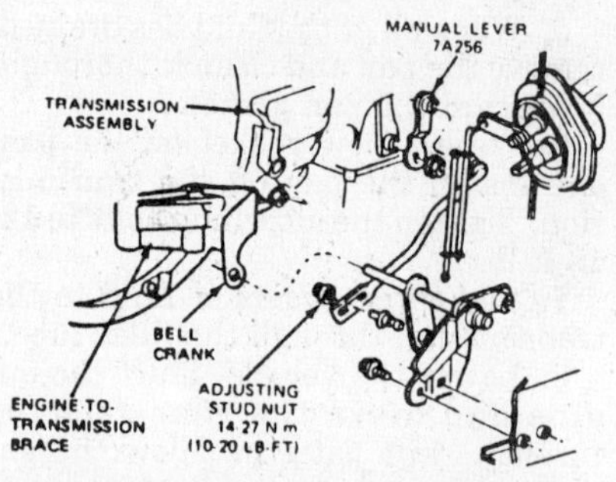

Manual linkage on column shift Continental models with the diesel engine

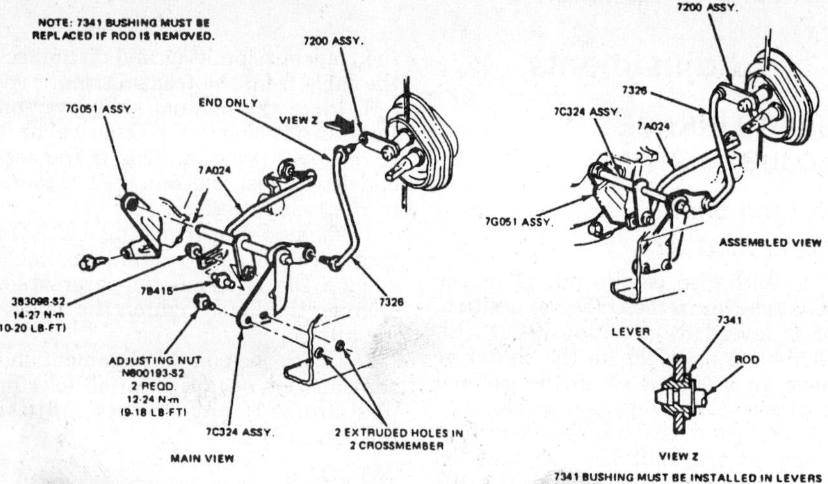

Manual linkage on column shift 1982-83 models with the AOD transmission

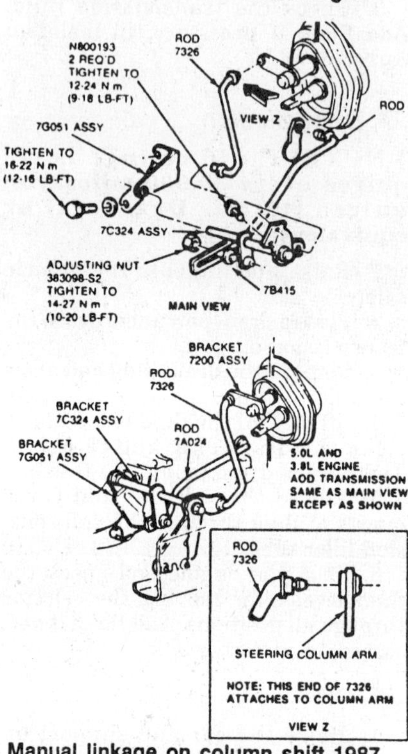

Manual linkage on column shift 1987 Continental, Thunderbird and Cougar models with the AOD transmission

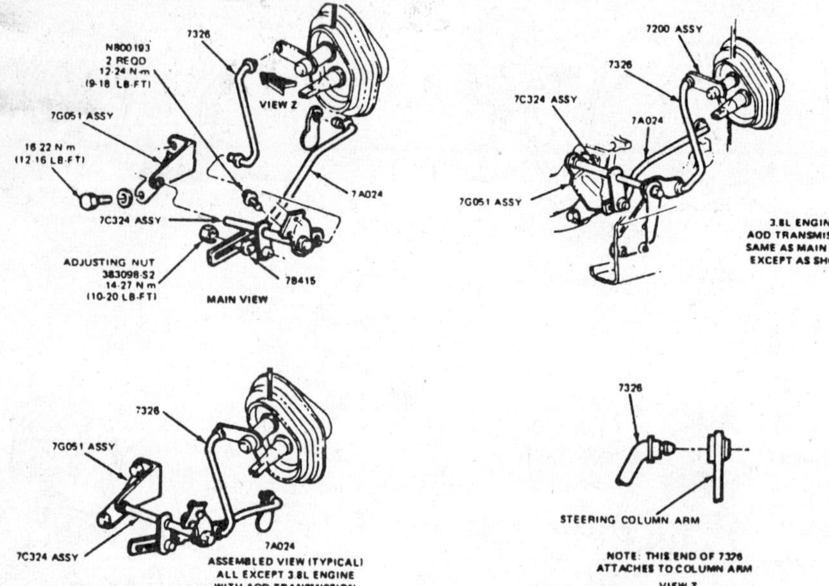

Manual linkage on column shift 1984-86 Thunderbird and Cougar models

2. Raise and support the front end on jackstands.

3. Disconnect the clevis from the lower end of the selector lever operating arm.

4. Move the transmission lever to the neutral position, third detent from the rear.

5. Loosen the two clevis retaining nuts and adjust the clevis so that it freely enters the selector lever operating arm hole. Tighten the clevis retaining nuts to secure the adjustment.

6. Connect the clevis and lever and secure it with the spring washer, flat washer and retaining clip.

7. Lower the vehicle and check the operation of the transmission in each selector lever position.

Floor or Console Shift

1. Place the transmission shift lever in D.

2. Raise the vehicle and loosen the manual lever shift rod retaining nut. Move the transmission lever to D1 or D position. D is the fourth detent from the rear.

3. With the transmission shift lever and transmission manual lever in position, tighten the nut at point A to 10-20 ft.lb.

4. Check transmission operation for all selector lever detent positions.

BACK-UP LIGHT SWITCH

NOTE: Vehicles with a floor mounted shifter incorporate the back-up light switch into the neutral start switch. For those vehicles, see the Neutral Start Switch section, below.

REMOVAL, INSTALLATION AND ADJUSTMENT

Column Mounted Shifters

1. Working under the instrument panel, disconnect the wiring at the switch.

2. On cars so equipped, disconnect the 2 parking brake release vacuum hoses.

3. Remove the 2 screws securing the switch to the steering column and remove the switch.

4. On all cars, check the column to make sure that the metal switch actuator is secured to the shift tube and that it is seated as far as possible forward against the shift tube bearing. Also check for a broken or damaged actuator.

5. When installing the new switch, align the hole in the switch with the hole in the bracket and insert a No. 43 drill through the holes.

6. Place the shift lever in the DRIVE position and hold it against the detent. Install and tighten the switch mounting screws.

7. Remove the drill bit.

8. Connect the wires.

NEUTRAL START SWITCH REMOVAL, INSTALLATION AND ADJUSTMENT

NOTE: The neutral safety switch on C3, AOD, A4LD and ZF transmission is non-adjustable.

1980-84 Floor Mounted Shifter

1. Raise and support the front end on jackstands.

2. Remove the downshift linkage rod from the transmission downshift lever.

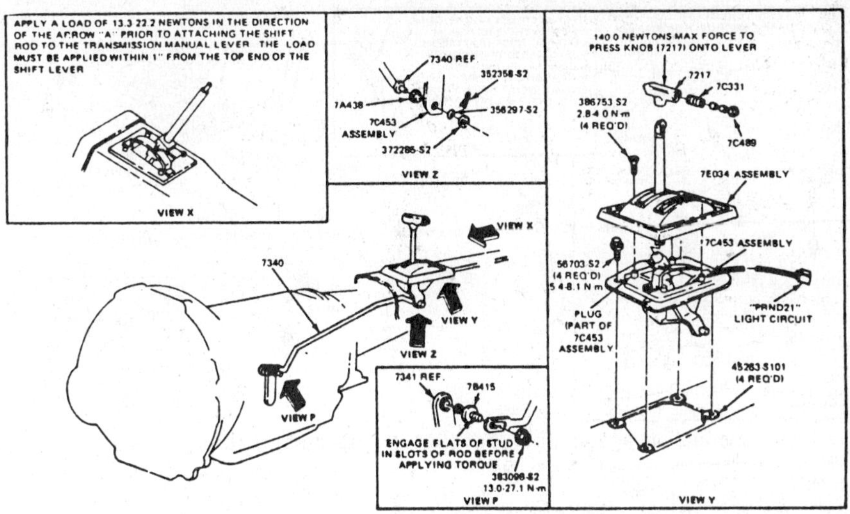

Manual linkage on column shift 4—and 6-cylinder floor shift 1981 Cougar models

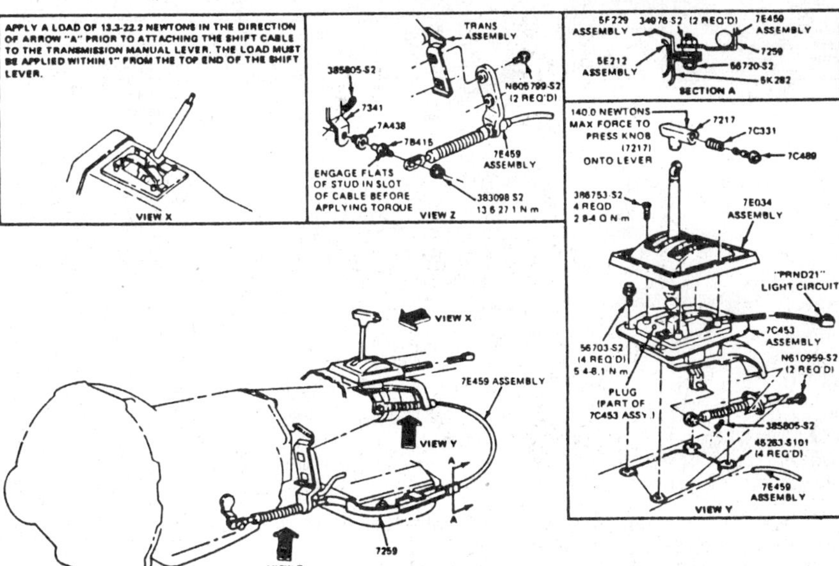

Manual linkage on floor shift 1981 Cougar models with the 8-255 engine

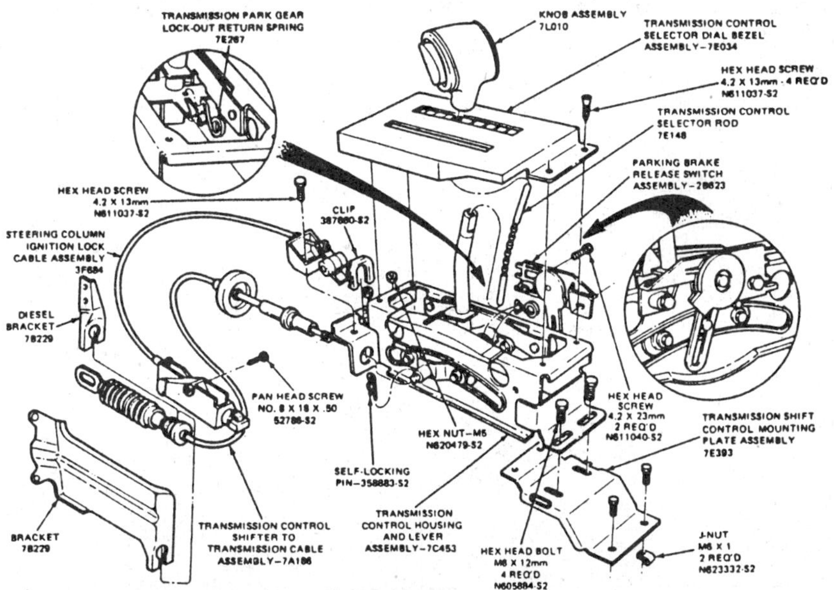

Manual linkage on floor shift 1984-85 Mark VII models with the diesel engine

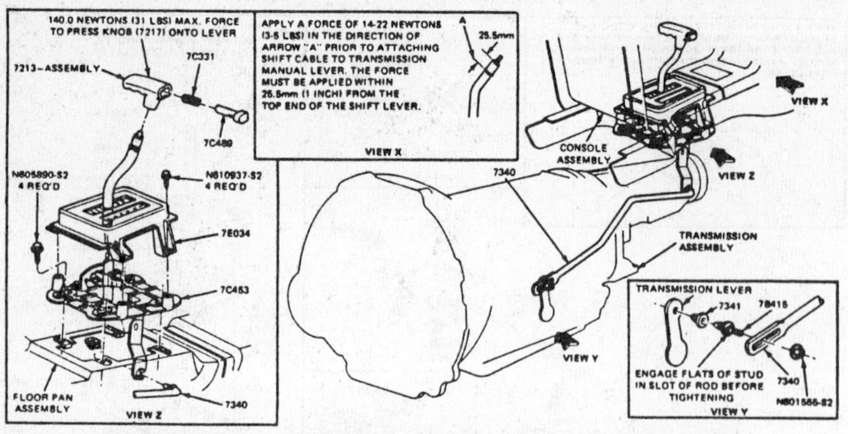

Manual linkage on floor shift 1984-86 Thunderbird Turbo models

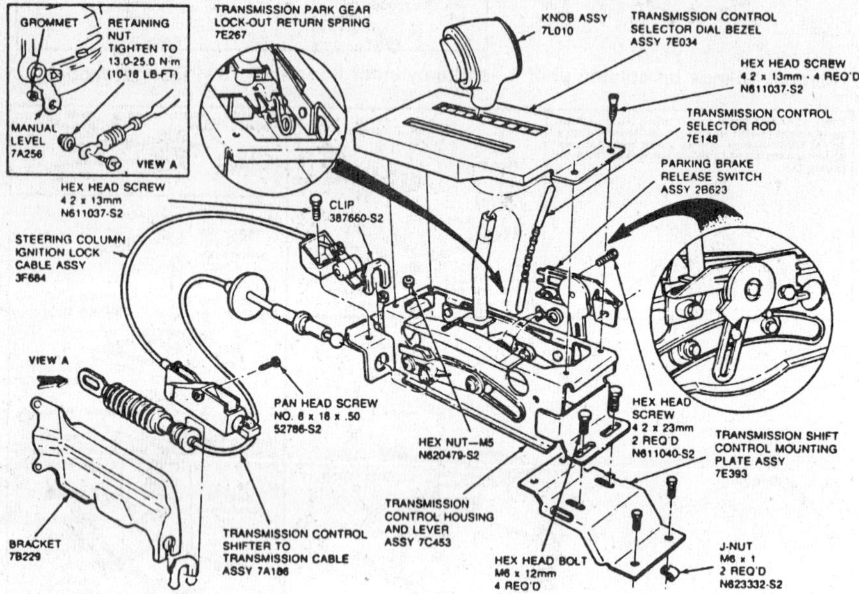

Manual linkage on floor shift 1986-87 Mark VII models

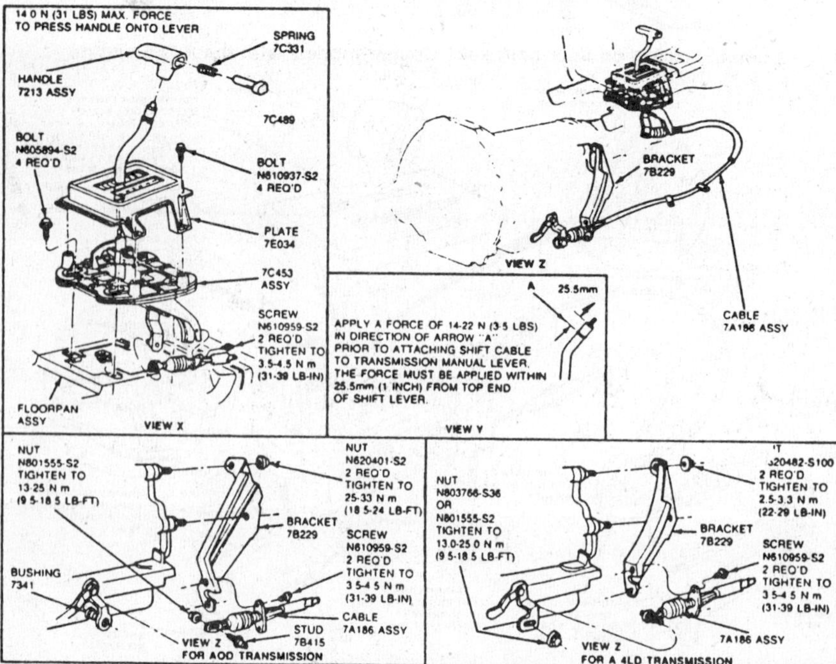

Manual linkage on floor shift 1987 Thunderbird Turbo models

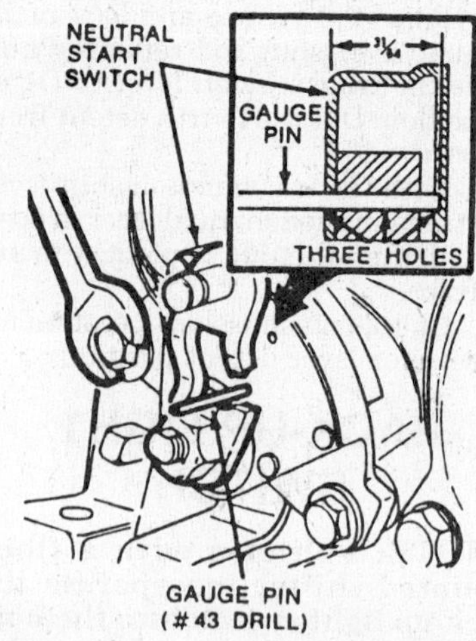

C4 neutral start switch adjustment

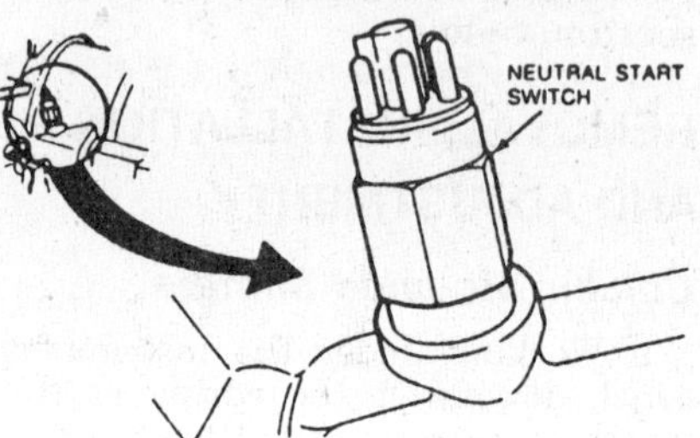

Neutral start switch used on the C3, AOD and A4LD

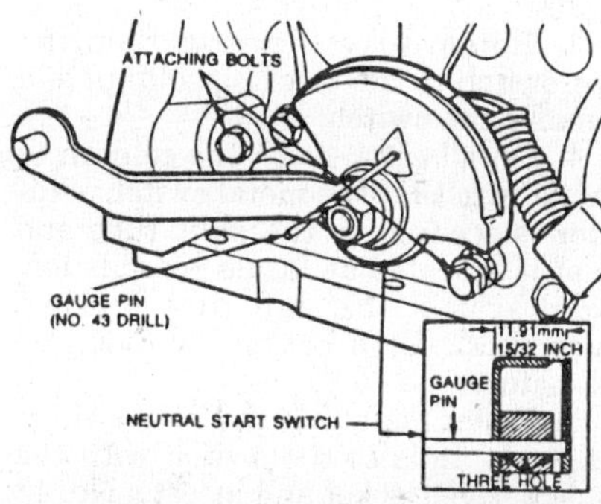

Neutral start switch adjustment on the C5

3. Apply penetrating oil to the downshift lever shaft and nut. Remove the transmission downshift outer lever retaining nut and lever.

4. Remove the 2 switch attaching screws.

5. Unplug the connector and remove the switch.

6. Position the new switch on the transmission and install the bolts loosely.

7. Place the transmission lever in NEUTRAL, rotate the switch until the hole in the switch aligns with the depression in the case and insert a No. 43 drill bit through the hole and into the depression. Make sure the drill bit is fully inserted. Tighten the switch bolts to 60 in.lb. Remove the gauge pin.

8. The remainder of installation is the reverse of removal. Torque the shaft nut to 20 ft.lb.

1985-87 C5 w/Floor Shift

1. Raise and support the front end on jackstands.
2. Remove the downshift linkage rod from the transmission downshift lever.
3. Apply penetrating oil to the downshift lever shaft and nut. Remove the transmission downshift outer lever retaining nut and lever.
4. Remove the 2 switch attaching screws.
5. Unplug the connector and remove the switch.
6. Position the new switch on the transmission and install the bolts loosely.
7. Place the transmission lever in NEUTRAL, rotate the switch until the hole in the switch aligns with the depression in the case and insert a No. 43 drill bit through the hole and into the depression. Make sure the drill bit is fully inserted. Tighten the switch bolts to 60 in.lb. Remove the gauge pin.
8. The remainder of installation is the reverse of removal. Torque the shaft nut to 20 ft.lb.

1985-87 AOD w/Floor Shift

1. Place the selector lever in the MANUAL LOW position.
2. Diasconnect the battery ground.
3. Raise and support the car on jackstands.
4. Disconnect the switch harness by pushing the harness straight up off the switch with a long screwdriver underneath the rubber plug section.
5. Using special tool socket T74P-77247-A, or equivalent, on a ratchet extension at least 9½" (241mm) long, unscrew the switch. Once the tool is on the switch, reach around the rear of the transmission over the extension housing.
6. Installation is the reverse of removal. Use a new O-ring. Torque the switch to 11 ft.lb.

1984-85 ZF w/Floor Switch

1. Raise and support the car on jackstands.
2. Unplug the switch connector.
3. Remove the switch retaining bolt and pull out the switch.
4. Installation is the reverse of removal. Tighten the bolt to 10 ft.lb.

DOWNSHIFT (THROTTLE) LINKAGE ADJUSTMENT

All Models Except AOD, A4LD, JATCO and ZF Transmissions

1. With the engine off, disconnect the throttle and downshift return springs, if equipped.
2. Hold the carburetor throttle lever in the wide open position against the stop.

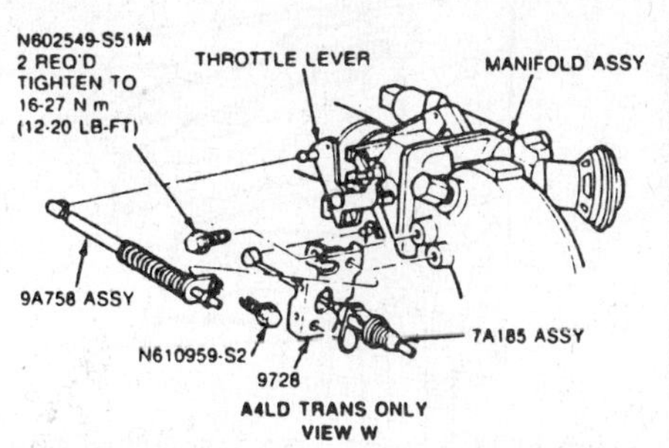

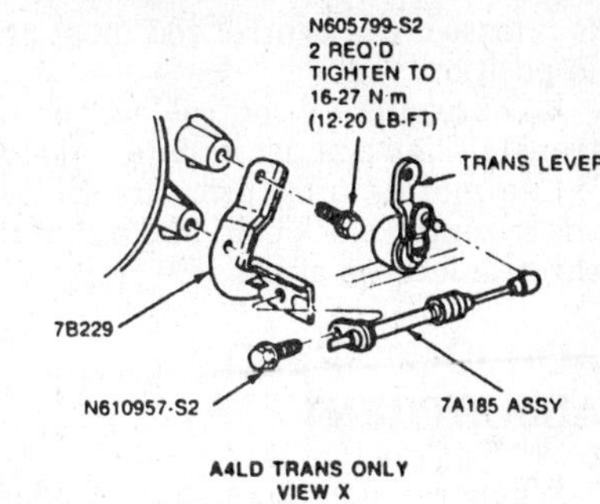

A4LD downshift linkage

3. Hold the transmission downshift linkage in the full downshift position against the internal stop.
4. Turn the adjustment screw on the carburetor downshift lever to obtain 0.010-0.080" (0.254-2.032mm) clearance between the screw tip and the throttle shaft lever tab.
5. Release the transmission and carburetor to their normal free positions. Install the throttle and downshift return springs, if removed.

JATCO

1. Move the ignition switch to the **ON** position.
2. Loosen the kickdown swithc to engage when the accelerator pedal is between $^7/_{16}$-$^{15}/_{16}$" of full travel. The downshift solenoid will click when the switch engages.
3. Tighten the attaching nut and check for proper operation.

A4LD

1. Make sure that the cable is connected at the transmission kickdown lever.
2. Disconnect the cable at the throttle lever.
3. Rotate the throttle lever to the wide open position.
4. While holding the throttle lever in the wide open position, attach the cable, install the clip and push the locking lever into place.

AOD

1. With the engine off, remove the air cleaner and make sure the fast idle cam is released; the throttle lever must be at the idle stop.
2. Turn the linkage lever adjusting screw counterclockwise until the end of the screw is flush with the face of the lever.
3. Turn the linkage adjustment screw in until there is a maximum clearance of 0.005" (0.127mm) between the throttle lever and the end of the adjustment screw.
4. Turn the linkage lever adjusting screw clockwise three full turns. A

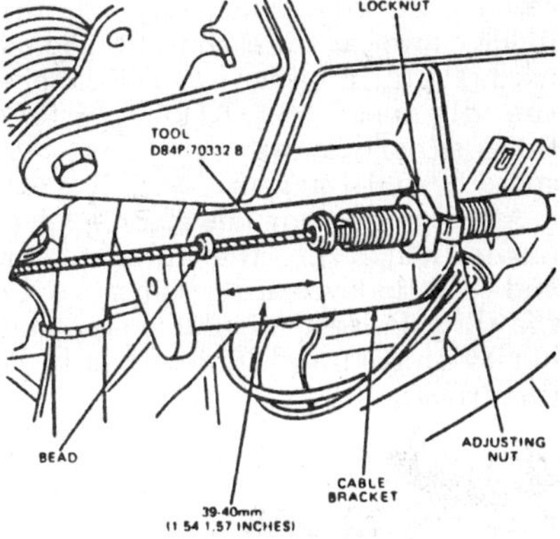

ZF transmission kickdown cable adjustment

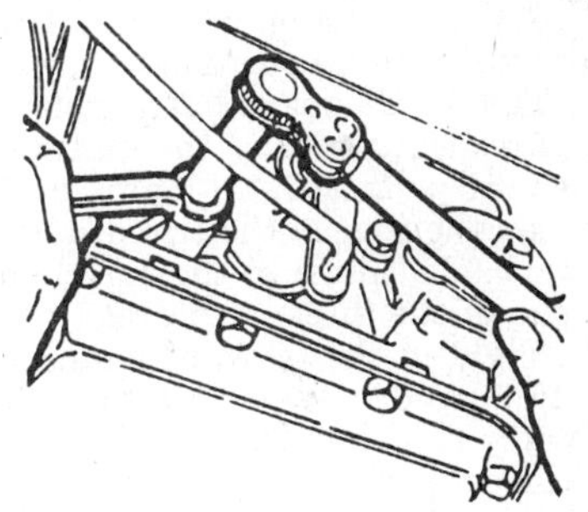

C4 and C5 intermediate band adjustment

minimum of one turn is permissible if the screw travel is limited.

5. If it is not possible to turn the adjusting screw at least one full turn or if the initial gap of 0.005" (0.127mm) could not be obtained, perform the linkage adjustment at the transmission.

AOD Alternate Method

If you are unable to adjust the throttle valve control linkage at the carburetor, as described above, proceed as follows.

1. At the transmission, loosen the 8 mm bolt on the throttle (TV) control rod sliding trunnion block. Make sure the trunnion block slides freely on the control rod.
2. Push up on the lower end of the TV control rod to insure that the carburetor linkage lever is held against the throttle lever. When the pressure

is released, the control rod must stay in position.

3. Force the TV control lever on the transmission against its internal stop. While maintaining pressure tighten the trunnion block bolt. Make sure the throttle lever is at the idle stop.

AOD IDLE SPEED ADJUSTMENT

Whenever it is necessary to adjust the idle speed by more than 50 rpm either above or below the factory specifications, the adjustment screw on the linkage lever at the carburetor should used. 1½ turns either way will change the idle speed by 50-100 rpm; 2½ turns either way will change the idle speed by 100-150 rpm.

After making any idle speed adjustments, make sure the linkage lever and throttle lever are in contact with the throttle lever at its idle stop and verify that the shift lever is in N (neutral).

ZF TRANSMISSION KICKDOWN CABLE ADJUSTMENT

1. Set the injection pump top lever to the full throttle position.
2. Tighten the rear adjusting nut on the threaded barrel of the adjusting cable until a gap of 1½" (38mm) exists between the edge of the crimped bead on the cable closest to the barrel and the end of the threaded barrel.
3. Tighten the forward adjusting nut to 80-106 in.lb. to lock the cable assembly to the bracket maintaining the correct position.
4. Recheck the gap, readjust if necessary.

BAND ADJUSTMENTS

NOTE: No external adjustments are possible on AOD and ZF transmissions.

C3 Front Band

1. Wipe clean the area around the adjusting screw on the side of the transmission, near the left front corner of the transmission.
2. Remove the adjusting screw locknut and discard it.
3. Install a new locknut on the adjusting screw but do not tighten it.
4. Tighten the adjusting screw to exactly 10 ft.lb.
5. Back off the adjusting screw exactly 2 turns.
6. Hold the adjusting screw so that it does not turn and tighten the adjusting screw locknut to 35-45 ft.lb.

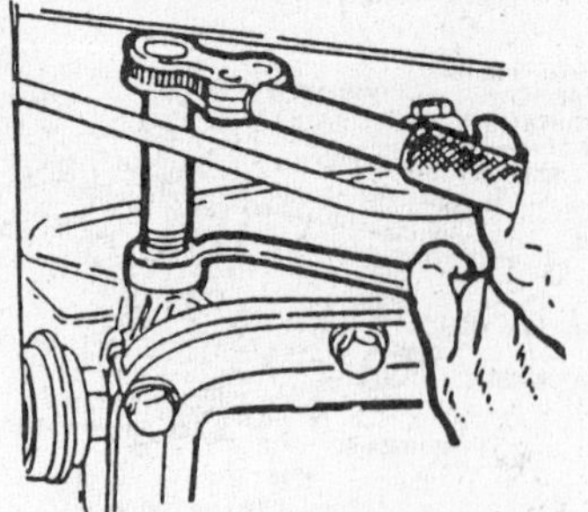

C4, and C5 low-reverse band adjustment

C4 and C5 Intermediate Band

1. Clean all the dirt from the adjusting screw and remove and discard the locknut.
2. Install a new locknut on the adjusting screw using a torque wrench, tighten the adjusting screw to 10 ft.lb.
3. Back off the adjusting screw exactly 1¾ turns for the C4 and 4¼ turns for the C5.
4. Hold the adjusting screw steady and tighten the locknut to 35 ft.lb.

C4, and C5 Low-Reverse Band

1. Clean all dirt from around the band adjusting screw, and remove and discard the locknut.
2. Install a new locknut of the adjusting screw. Using a torque wrench, tighten the adjusting screw to 10 ft.lb.
3. Back off the adjusting screw exactly three full turns.
4. Hold the adjusting screw steady and tighten the locknut to 35 ft.lb.

C6 Intermediate Band Adjustment

1. Raise the car on a hoist or place it on jackstands.
2. Clean the threads of the intermediate band adjusting screw.
3. Loosen the adjustment screw locknut.
4. Tighten the adjusting screw to 10 ft.lb. and back the screw off exactly 1½ turns. Tighten the adjusting screw locknut to 35 ft.lb.

FMX Front Band Adjustment

1. Drain the transmission fluid and remove the oil pan, fluid filter screen, and clip.
2. Clean the pan and filter screen and remove the old gasket.
3. Loosen the front servo adjusting screw locknut.
4. Pull back the actuating rod and insert a ¼" (6mm) spacer bar between the adjusting screw and the servo piston stem. Tighten the adjusting screw to 10 in.lb. torque. Remove the spacer bar and tighten the adjusting screw an additional ¾ turn. Hold the adjusting screw fast and tighten the locknut securely (20-25 ft.lb.).
5. Install the transmission fluid filter screen and clip. Install pan with a new pan gasket.
6. Refill the transmission to the mark on the dipstick. Start the engine, run for a few minutes, shift the selector lever through all positions, and place it in Park. Recheck the fluid level and add fluid if necessary.

FMX Rear Band Adjustments

On certain cars with a console floor shift, the entire console shift lever and linkage will have to be removed to gain access to the rear band external adjusting screw.

1. Locate the external rear band adjusting screw on the transmission case, clean all dirt from the threads, and coat the threads with light oil.

NOTE: The adjusting screw is located on the upper right side of the transmission case. Access if often through a hole in the front floor to the right of center under the carpet.

2. Loosen the locknut on the rear band external adjusting screw.
3. Using torque wrench tighten the adjusting screw to 10 ft.lb. torque. If the adjusting screw is tighten than 10 ft.lb. torque, loosen the adjustng screw and retighten to the proper torque.
4. Back off the adjusting screw exactly 1½ turns. Hold the adjusting screw steady while tightening the locknut to the proper torque (35-40 ft.lb.).

JATCO Band Servo

1. Raise and support the front end on jackstands.
2. Remove the servo cover attching bolts and take off the cover.
3. Loosen the band adjusting screw locknut and tighten the adjusting screw to 9-11 ft.lb.
4. Back off the adjusting screw 2 turns. Hold the adjusting screw stationary and tighten the locknut to 22-29 ft.lb.
5. Lower the vehicle.

Transmission

REMOVAL & INSTALLATION

C3

1. Raise and safely support the vehicle.
2. Place a drain pan under the transmission fluid pan. Starting at the rear of the pan and working toward the front, loosen the attaching bolts and allow the fluid to drain. Then remove all of the pan attaching bolts except two at the front, to allow the fluid to further drain. After all the fluid has drained, install two bolts on the rear

side of the pan to temporarily hold it in place.

3. Remove the converter drain plug access cover and adapter plate bolts from the lower end of the converter housing.

4. Remove the four flywheel to converter attaching nuts. Crank the engine to turn the converter to gain access to the nuts, using a wrench on the crankshaft pulley attaching bolt. On belt driven overheat camshaft engines, never turn the engine backwards.

5. Crank the engine until the converter drain plug is accessible and remove the plug. Place a drain pan under the converter to catch the fluid. After all the fluid has been drained from the converter, reinstall the plug and tighten to specification.

6. Remove the driveshaft and install the extension housing seal replacer tool in the extension housing.

7. Remove the speedometer cable from the extension housing.

8. Disconnect the shift rod at the transmission manual lever. Disconnect the downshift rod at the transmission downshift lever.

9. Remove the starter-to-converter housing attaching bolts and position the starter out of the way.

10. Disconnect the neutral start switch wires from the switch.

11. Remove the vacuum line from the transmission vacuum unit.

12. Position a transmission jack under the transmission and raise it slightly.

13. Remove the engine rear support-to-crossmember nut.

14. Remove the crossmember-to-frame side support attaching bolts and remove the crossmember.

15. Remove the inlet pipe steady rest from the inlet pipe and rear engine support; then disconnect the muffler inlet pipe at the exhaust manifold and secure it.

16. Lower the jack under the transmission and allow the transmission to hang.

17. Position a jack to the front of the engine and raise the engine to gain access to the two upper converter housing-to-engine attaching bolts.

18. Disconnect the oil cooler lines at the transmission. Plug all openings to keep out dirt.

19. Remove the lower converter housing-to-engine attaching bolts.

20. Remove the transmission filter tube.

21. Secure the transmission to the jack with a safety chain.

22. Remove the two upper converter housing-to-engine attaching bolts. Move the transmission to the rear and down to remove it from under the vehicle.

23. Tighten the converter drain plug to 20-30 ft.lb. if not previously done.

24. Position the converter to the transmission making sure the converter hub is fully engaged in the pump gear. The dimension given in the illustration is for guidance only. It does not indicate engagement.

25. With the converter properly installed, place the transmission on the jack and secure with safety chain.

26. Rotate the converter so the drive studs and drain plug are in alignment with their holes in the flywheel.

27. With the transmission mounted on a transmission jack, move the converter and transmission assembly forward into position being careful not to damage the flywheel and the converter pilot.

During this move, to avoid damage, do not allow the transmission to get into a nosed down position as this will cause the converter to move forward and disengage from the pump gear. The converter must rest squarely against the flywheel. This indicates that the converter pilot is not binding in the engine crankshaft.

28. Install the two upper converter housing-to-engine attaching bolts and tighten to 28-38 ft.lb.

29. Remove the safety chain from the transmission.

30. Insert the filler tube in the stub tube and secure it to the cylinder block with the attaching bolt. Tighten the bolt to 28-38 ft.lb. If the stub tube is loosened or dislodged, it should be replaced.

31. Install the oil cooler lines in the retaining clip at the cylinder block. Connect the lines to the transmission case.

32. Remove the jack supporting the front of the engine.

33. Position the muffler inlet pipe support bracket to the converter housing and install the four lower converter housing-to-engine attaching bolts. Tighten the bolts to 28-38 ft.lb.

34. Raise the transmission. Position the crossmember to the frame side supports and install the attaching bolts. Tighten the bolts to 30-40 ft.lb.

35. Lower the transmission and install the rear engine support-to-crossmember nut. Tighten the nut to 30-40 ft.lb.

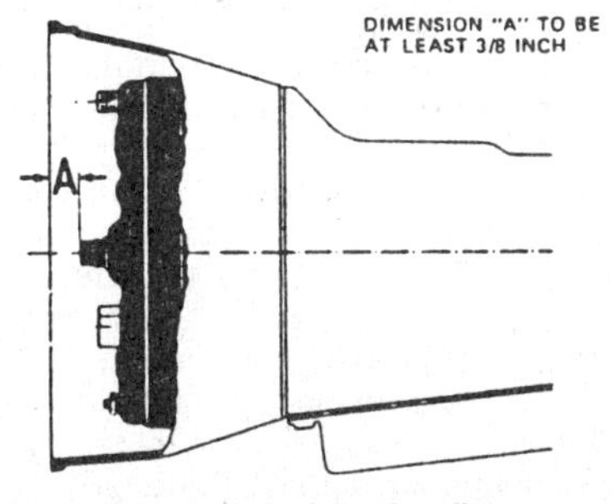

C3 converter hub-to-housing flange position

36. Remove the transmission jack.

37. Install the vacuum hose on the transmission vacuum unit. Install the vacuum line into the retaining clip.

38. Connect the neutral start switch plug to the switch.

39. Install the starter and tighten the attaching bolts.

40. Install the four flywheel-to-converter attaching nuts.

41. Install the converter drain plug access cover and adaptor plate bolts. Tighten the bolts to 15-20 ft.lb.

42. Connect the muffler inlet pipe to the exhaust manifold.

43. Connect the transmission shift rod to the manual lever.

44. Connect the downshift rod to the downshift lever.

45. Connect the speedometer cable to the extension housing.

46. Install the driveshaft. Tighten the companion flange U-bolt attaching nuts to 30 ft.lb.

47. Adjust the manual and downshift linkage as required.

48. Lower the vehicle. Fill the transmission to the proper level with Dexron®II. Pour in 5 quarts of fluid; then run the engine and add fluid as required.

49. Check the transmission, converter assembly and oil cooler lines for leaks.

C4

1. Raise and safely support the vehicle.

2. place the drain pan under the transmission fluid pan. Remove the fluid filler tube from the pan and drain the transmission fluid. On some models it may be necessary to loosen the pan attaching bolts and allow the fluid to drain. Start loosening the bolts at the rear of the pan and work toward the front. Finally remove all of the pan attaching bolts except two at the front, to allow the fluid to further drain. After the fluid has drained, install two bolts on the rear side of the pan to temporarily hold it in place.

3. Remove the converter drain plug access cover from the lower end of the converter housing.

4. Remove the converter-to-flywheel attaching nuts. Place a wrench on the crankshaft pulley attaching bolt to turn the converter to gain access to the nuts.

5. With the wrench on the crankshaft pulley attaching bolt, turn the converter to gain access to the converter drain plug. Then, remove the plug. Place a drain pan under the converter to catch the fluid. After the fluid has drained from the converter, reinstall the plug.

6. Remove the driveshaft and install the extension housing seal replacer tool in the extension housing.
7. Remove the vacuum line hose from the transmission vacuum unit. Disconnect the vacuum line from the retaining clip. Disconnect the transmission regulated spark (T.R.S.) switch wire at the transmission, if so equipped.
8. Remove the engine support to crossmember bolts or nuts.
9. Remove the speedometer cable from the extension housing.
10. Disconnect the oil cooler lines from the transmission case.
11. Disconnect the selector rod or cable at the transmission manual lever. Disconnect the downshift rod at the transmission downshift lever.
12. On console and floor shift vehicles, disconnect the column lock rod at the transmission, if so equipped.
13. Disconnect the starter cable. Remove the starter attaching bolts and remove the starter from the converter housing.
14. Remove the bolt that secures the transmission fluid filler tube to the cylinder head and lift the fluid fitter tube from the case.
15. Position the transmission jack to support the transmission and secure the transmission to the jack with a safety chain.
16. Remove the crossmember attaching bolts and lower the crossmember.
17. Remove the five converter housing-to-engine attaching bolts. Lower the transmission and remove it from under the vehicle.
18. Torque the converter drain plug to 20-30 ft.lb.
19. Position the converter to the transmission making sure the converter drive flats are fully engaged in the pump gear.
20. With the converter properly installed, place the transmission on the jack. Secure the transmission to the jack with a safety chain.
21. Rotate the converter so that the studs and drain plug are in alignment with their holes in the flywheel.
22. With the transmission mounted on a transmission jack, move the converter and transmission assembly forward into position, using care not to damage the flywheel and the converter pilot. The converter must rest squarely against the flywheel. This indicates that the converter pilot is not binding in the engine crankshaft.
23. Install the five converter housing-to-engine attaching bolts. Torque the bolts to 23-28 ft.lb. Remove the safety chain from the transmission.
24. Position the crossmember and install the attaching bolts. Torque the bolts to 40-50 ft.lb.
25. Lower the transmission and install the engine support to crossmember bolts or nuts. Torque the bolts or nuts to 30-40 ft.lb.
26. Install the flywheel to the converter attaching nuts. Torque the nuts to 23-28 ft.lb.
27. Remove the transmission jack. Install the fluid filler tube in the transmission case or pan. Secure the tube to the cylinder head with the attaching bolt. Install the vacuum hose on the transmission vacuum unit. Install the vacuum line retaining clip. Connect the transmission regulated spark (T.R.S.) switch wires to the switch, if so equipped.
28. Connect the fluid cooling lines to the transmission case.
29. Connect the downshift rod to the downshift lever.
30. Connect the selector rod or cable to the transmission manual lever. Connect the column lock rod on console and floor shift vehicles, if so equipped.
31. Connect the speedometer cable to the extension housing.
32. Install the converter housing cover and torque the attaching bolts to 12-16 ft.lb.
33. Install the starter and torque the attaching bolts to 25-30 ft.lb. Connect the starter cable.
34. Install the driveshaft. Torque the companion flange U-bolts attaching nuts to 25-30 ft.lb.
35. Lower the vehicle. Fill the transmission to the proper level with fluid. Adjust the manual and downshift linkage as required.

C5

1. Open the hood and install protective covers on the fenders.
2. Disconnect the battery negative cable.
3. On Cougar models equipped with a 6-232 engine, remove the air cleaner assembly.
4. Remove the fan shroud attaching bolts and position the shroud back over the fan.
5. On Cougar models equipped with a 6-232 engine, loosen the clamp and disconnect the Thermactor® air injection hose at the catalytic converter check valve. The check valve is located on the right side of the engine compartment near the dash panel.
6. On Cougar models equipped with a 6-232 engine, remove the two transmission-to-engine attaching bolts located at the top of the transmission bell housing. These bolts are accessible from the engine compartment.
7. Raise and safely support the vehicle.
8. Remove the driveshaft.
9. Disconnect the muffler inlet pipe from the catalytic converter outlet pipe. Support the muffler/pipe assembly by wiring it to a convenient underbody bracket.
10. Remove the nuts attaching the exhaust pipe(s) to the exhaust manifold(s).
11. Pull back on the catalytic coverts to release the converter hangers from the mounting bracket.
12. Remove the speedometer clamps bolt and pull the speedometer out of the extension housing.
13. Separate the neutral start switch harness connector.
14. Disconnect the kick down rod at the transmission lever.
15. Disconnect the shift linkage at the linkage bellcrank. On vehicles equipped with floor mounted shift, remove the shift cable routing bracket attaching bolts and disconnect the cable at the transmission lever.
16. Remove the converter dust shield.
17. Remove the torque converter to drive plate attaching nuts. To gain access to the converter nuts, turn the crankshaft and drive plate using a ratchet handle and socket on the crankshaft pulley attaching bolt.
18. Remove the starter attaching bolts.
19. Loosen the nuts attaching the rear support to the No. 3 crossmember.
20. Position a transmission jack under the transmission oil pan. Secure the transmission to the jack with a safety chain.
21. Remove the through bolts attaching the No. 3 crossmember to the body brackets.
22. Lower the transmission enough to allow access to the cooler line fittings. Disconnect the cooler lines.
23. On Cougar models, remove the (4) remaining transmission-to-engine attaching bolts (2 each side). On all models, remove the (6) transmission-to-engine attaching bolts.
24. Pull the transmission back to disengage the converter studs from the drive plate. Lower the transmission out of the vehicle.
25. Raise the transmission into the vehicle. As the transmission is being slowly raised into position, rotate the torque converter until the studs and drain plug are aligned with the holes in the drive plate.
26. Move the converter/transmission assembly forward against the back of the engine. Make sure the converter studs engage the drive plate and that the transmission dowels on the back of the engine engage the bolts holes in the bellhousing.
27. On Cougar models equipped with a 6-232 engine, install four transmission-to-engine attaching bolts (2 each side). On all other models, install the

(6) transmission-to-engine attaching bolts. Tighten the attaching bolts to 40-50 ft.lb.

28. Connect the cooler lines.

29. Raise the transmission and install the No. 3 crossmember through bolts. Tighten the attaching nuts to 20-30 ft.lb.

30. Remove the safety chain and transmission jack.

31. Tighten the rear support attaching nuts to 30-50 ft.lb.

32. Position the starter and install the attaching bolts.

33. Install the torque converter to drive plate attaching nuts. Tighten the attaching nuts to 20-30 ft.lb.

34. Position the dust shield and on vehicles with column mounted shift, position the linkage bellcrank bracket. Install the attaching bolts and tighten to 12-16 ft.lb.

35. Connect the shift linkage to the linkage bellcrank. On vehicles equipped with floor mounted shift, connect the cable to the shift lever and install the routing bracket attaching bolt.

36. Connect the kick down rod to the transmission lever.

37. Connect the neutral start switch harness.

38. Install the speedometer and the clamp bolt. Tighten the clamp bolt to 35-54 in.lb.

39. Install the catalytic converts using new seal(s) at the pipe(s) to exhaust manifold connection(s).

40. Install the pipe(s) to exhaust manifold attaching nuts. Do not tighten the attaching nuts.

41. Remove the wire supporting the muffler/pipe assembly and connect the pipe to the converter outlet. Do not tighten the attaching nuts.

42. Align the exhaust system and tighten the manifold and converter outlet attaching nuts.

43. Install the driveshaft.

44. Check and if necessary, adjust the shift linkage.

45. Lower the vehicle.

46. On Cougar models equipped with a 6-232 engine, install the two transmission-to-engine attaching bolts located at the top of the transmission bellhousing.

47. On Cougar models equipped with a 6-232 engine, connect the Thermactor® air injection hose to the converter check valve.

48. Position the fan shroud and install the attaching bolts.

49. On Cougar models equipped with a 6-232 engine, install the air cleaner assembly.

50. Connect the battery negative cable.

51. Start the engine. Make sure the engine cranks only when the selector lever is positioned in the neutral (N) or Park (P) detent.

52. Fill the transmission with type H fluid.

53. Raise the vehicle and inspect for fluid leaks.

C6

1. Working from the engine compartment, remove the two bolts retaining the fan shroud to the radiator.

2. Raise and safely support the vehicle.

3. Place the drain pan under the transmission fluid pan. Starting at the rear of the pan and working toward the front, loosen the attaching bolts and allow the fluid to drain. Finally remove all of the pan attaching bolts except two at the front, to allow the fluid to further drain. After the fluid has drained, install two bolts on the rear side of the pan to temporarily hold it in place.

4. Remove the converter drain plug access cover and adapter plate bolts from the lower end of the converter housing.

5. Remove the converter-to-flywheel attaching nuts.

6. Disconnect the driveshaft from the rear axle and slide the shaft rearward from the transmission. Install the seal installation tool in the extension housing to prevent fluid leakage.

7. Disconnect the speedometer cable from the extension housing.

8. Disconnect the downshift rod from the transmission downshift lever.

9. Disconnect the shift cable form the manual lever at the transmission.

10. Remove the two bolts that secure the shift cable bracket to the converter housing and position the cable and bracket out of the way.

11. Remove the starter motor attaching bolts and position the starter out of the way.

12. Disconnect the rubber hose from the vacuum diaphragm at the rear of the transmission. Remove the vacuum tube from the retaining clip at the transmission. Disconnect the transmission regulated spark (T.R.S.) switch wire at the transmission, if so equipped.

13. Disconnect the muffler inlet pipe at the exhaust manifolds and allow the pipe to hang.

14. Remove the crossmember to frame side support bolts and nuts. Remove the nuts securing the rear engine supports to the crossmember. Position a jack under the transmission and raise it slightly. Remove the bolts securing the rear engine support to the extension housing and remove the crossmember and rear supports from the vehicle.

15. Loosen the parking brake adjusting nut at the equalizer and remove the cable from the idler hook attaching to the floor pan.

16. Lower the transmission, then disconnect the oil cooler lines from the transmission case.

17. Secure the transmission to the jack with a chain.

18. Remove the six bolts that attach the converter housing to the cylinder block.

19. Remove the bolt that secures the transmission filler tube to the cylinder block. Lift the filler tube and dipstick from the transmission.

20. Move the transmission away from the cylinder block.

21. Carefully lower the transmission and remove it from under the vehicle.

22. Remove the converter and mount the transmission in a holding fixture.

23. Torque the converter drain plug to 14-28 ft.lb.

24. Position the converter to the transmission making sure the converter drive flats are fully engaged in the pump gear.

25. With the converter properly installed, place the transmission on the jack. Secure the transmission to the jack with the safety chain.

26. Rotate the converter so that the studs and drain plug are in alignment with their holes in the flywheel.

27. With the transmission mounted on a transmission jack, move the converter and transmission assembly forward into position using care not to damage the flywheel and converter pilot. The converter must rest squarely against the flywheel. This indicates that the converter pilot is not binding in the engine crankshaft.

28. Install a new O-ring on the lower end of the transmission filler tube. Insert the tube in the transmission case and secure the tube to the engine with the attaching bolts.

29. Install the converter housing-to-engine attaching bolts. Torque the bolts to 40-50 ft.lb. Remove the safety chain from the transmission.

30. Connect the oil cooler lines to the transmission case.

31. Raise the transmission.

32. Position the parking brake cable in the idler hook and tighten the adjusting nut at the equalizer.

33. Place the rear engine supports on the crossmember and position the crossmember on the frame side supports.

34. Secure the engine rear supports to the extension housing with the attaching bolts. Torque the bolts and nuts to 35-40 ft.lb.

35. Remove the transmission jack from under the vehicle and install the crossmember-to-frame side support bolts and nuts. Torque the bolts to 35-40 ft.lb.

36. Install and torque the engine rear support-to-crossmember attaching nuts.
37. Connect the muffler inlet pipe to the exhaust manifolds.
38. Connect the vacuum line to the vacuum diaphragm making sure that the metal tube is secured in the retaining clip. Connect the transmission regulated spark (T.R.S.) switch wire to the switch, if so equipped.
39. Position the starter motor to the converter housing and secure it with the attaching bolts.
40. Install the torque converter-to-flywheel attaching nuts and torque them to 20-30 ft.lb.
41. Position the shift cable bracket to the converter housing and install the two attaching bolts.
42. Connect the shift cable to the manual lever at the transmission.
43. Connect the downshift rod to the lever on the transmission.
44. Connect the speedometer cable to the extension housing.
45. Install the driveshaft.
46. Install the converter drain plug access cover and adapter plate bolts. Torque the bolts to 12-16 ft.lb.
47. Adjust the manual and downshift linkage as required.
48. Lower the vehicle.
49. Working from the engine compartment, position the fan shroud to the radiator and secure with the two attaching bolts.
50. Fill the transmission to the proper level with Dexron®II ATF.
51. Check the transmission, converter assembly and oil cooler lines for leaks.

FMX

1. Position the vehicle in the work area, but do not raise at this time.
2. Remove the two upper bolts and lockwashers which attach the converter housing to the engine.
3. Raise and safely support the vehicle.
4. Place the drain pan under the transmission fluid pan. Starting at the rear of the pan and working toward the front, loosen the attaching bolts and allow the fluid to drain. Finally remove all of the pan attaching bolts except two at the front, to allow the fluid to further drain. With fluid drained, install two bolts on the rear side of the pan to temporarily hold it in place.
5. Remove the converter drain plug access cover from the lower end of the converter housing.
6. Remove the converter-to-flywheel attaching nuts. Place a wrench on the crankshaft pulley attaching bolt to turn the converter to gain access to the nuts.
7. With the wrench on the crankshaft pulley attaching bolt, turn the converter to gain access to the converter drain plug, and remove the plug. Place a drain pan under the converter to catch the fluid. After the fluid has been drained, reinstall the plug.
8. Disconnect the driveshaft from the rear companion flange (marking it to assure correct assembly). Slide the shaft rearward from the transmission. Position a seal installation tool in the extension housing to prevent fluid leakage.
9. Disconnect the vacuum hoses from the vacuum diaphragm unit and the tube from the extension housing clip.
10. Install the converter housing front plate to hold the converter in place when the transmission is removed. Under no conditions should the converter be left attached to the engine when the transmission is removed. This could damage the input shaft, converter and pump.
11. Disconnect the starter cables from the starter and remove the starter.
12. Disconnect the oil cooler lines from the transmission.
13. Disconnect the downshift linkage from the transmission.
14. Disconnect the selector rod or cable from the transmission manual lever.
15. Disconnect the speedometer cable from the extension housing. Disconnect the exhaust inlet pipes at the exhaust manifolds.
16. Support the transmission on a transmission jack. Secure the transmission to the jack with safety chain. Remove the two engine rear support to transmission bolts. Remove the two crossmember to frame side rail attaching bolts and nuts. Raise the transmission slightly to take the weight off the crossmember. Remove the rear support to crossmember bolt and nut and remove the crossmember.
17. Lower the transmission slightly and disconnect the fluid filter tube.
18. Remove the remaining converter housing to engine attaching bolts. Move the transmission and converter assembly to the rear and down to remove it.
19. Torque the converter drain plug to 15-28 ft.lb.
20. If the converter has been removed from the converter housing, carefully position the converter to the transmission making sure the converter drive flats are fully engaged in the pump gear.
21. With the converter properly installed, place the transmission on the jack. Secure the transmission to the jack with safety chain.
22. Rotate the converter until the studs and drain plug are in alignment with their holes in the flywheel.
23. With the transmission mounted on a transmission jack, move the converter and transmission assembly forward into position, using care not to damage the flywheel and converter pilot. The converter must rest squarely against the flywheel. This indicates that the converter pilot is not binding in the engine crankshaft.
24. Install the lower converter housing-to-engine bolts. Torque bolts to 40-50 ft.lb. Remove the safety chain from the transmission.
25. Connect the fluid filler tube.
26. Install the crossmember.
27. Lower the transmission until the extension housing rests on the crossmember, and then install the rear support-to-crossmember bolts. Connect the exhaust inlet pipes at the exhaust manifolds.
28. Install the converter attaching nuts. Install the access plates.
29. Connect the oil cooler inlet and outlet lines to the transmission case.
30. Coat the front universal joint yoke seal and spline with C1AZ-19590-B lubricant (or equivalent), and install the driveshaft. Be sure that the driveshaft markings match those of the companion flange for correct balance.
31. Connect the speedometer cable at the transmission.
32. Connect the manual selector rod or cable to the transmission manual lever.
33. Connect the downshift linkage at the transmission downshift lever.
34. Install the starter motor and connect the starter cables.
35. Connect the vacuum hoes to the vacuum diaphragm unit and the tube to its clip.
36. Lower the transmission and install the upper two converter housing-to-engine bolts. Torque bolts to 40-50 ft.lb.
37. Lower the vehicle and fill the transmission with type F fluid.
38. Check the transmission, converter assembly, and fluid cooler lines for fluid leaks. Adjust the manual and downshift linkages.

Automatic Overdrive (AOD)

1. Raise and safely support the vehicle.
2. Place the drain pan under the transmission fluid pan. Starting at the rear of the pan and working toward the front, loosen the attaching bolts and allow the fluid to drain. Finally removal all of the pan attaching bolts except two at the front, to allow the fluid to further drain. With fluid drained, install two bolts on the rear side of the pan to temporarily hold it in place.
3. Remove the converter drain plug access cover from the lower end of the converter housing.

4. Remove the converter-to-flywheel attaching nuts. place a wrench on the crankshaft pulley attaching bolt to turn the converter to gain access to the nuts.
5. Place a drain pan under the converter to catch the fluid. With the wrench on the crankshaft pulley attaching bolts, turn the converter to gain access to the converter drain plug and remove the plug. After the fluid has been drained, reinstall the plug.
6. Disconnect the driveshaft from the rear axle and slide shaft rearward from the transmission. Install a seal installation tool in the extension housing to prevent fluid leakage.
7. Disconnect the cable from the terminal on the starter motor. Remove the three attaching bolts and remove the starter motor. Disconnect the neutral start switch wires at the plug connector.
8. Remove the rear mount-to-crossmember attaching bolts and the two crossmember-to-frame attaching bolts.
9. Remove the two engine rear support-to-extension housing attaching bolts.
10. Disconnect the TV linkage rod from the transmission TV lever. Disconnect the manual rod from the transmission manual lever at the transmission.
11. Remove the two bolts securing the bellcrank bracket to the converter housing.
12. Raise the transmission with a transmission jack to provide clearance to remove the crossmember. Remove the rear mount from the crossmember and remove the crossmember from the side supports.
13. Lower the transmission to gain access to the oil cooler lines.
14. Disconnect each oil line from the fittings on the transmission.
15. Disconnect the speedometer cable from the extension housing.
16. Remove the bolt that secures the transmission fluid filler tube to the cylinder block. Lift the filler tube and the dipstick from the transmission.
17. Secure the transmission to the jack with the chain.
18. Remove the converter housing-to-cylinder block attaching bolts.
19. Carefully move the transmission and converter assembly away from the engine and, at the same time, lower the jack to clear the underside of the vehicle.
20. Remove the converter and mount the transmission in a holding fixture.
21. Tighten the converter drain plug to 20-28 ft.lb.
22. Position the converter on the transmission, making sure the converter drive flats are fully engaged in the pump gear by rotating the converter.
23. With the converter properly installed, place the transmission on the jack. Secure the transmission to the jack with a chain.
24. Rotate the converter until the studs and drain plug are in alignment with the holes in the flywheel.

WARNING: Lube the pilot bushing.

25. Align the yellow balancing marks on converter and flywheel for Continental.
26. move the converter and transmission assembly forward into position, using care not to damage the flywheel and the converter pilot. The converter must rest squarely against the flywheel. This indicates that the converter pilot is not binding in the engine crankshaft.
27. Install and tighten the converter housing-to-engine attaching bolts to 40-50 ft.lb. make sure that the vacuum tube retaining clips are properly positioned.
28. Remove the safety chain from around the transmission.
29. Install a new O-ring on the lower end of the transmission filler tube. Insert the tube in the transmission case and secure the tube to the engine with the attaching bolts.
30. Connect the speedometer cable to the extension housing.
31. Connect the oil cooler lines to the right side of the transmission case.
32. Position the crossmember on the side supports. Position the rear mount on the crossmember and install the attaching bolt and nut.
33. Secure the engine rear support to the extension housing and tighten the bolts to 35-40 ft.lb.
34. Lower the transmission and remove the jack.
35. Secure the crossmember to the side supports with the attaching bolts and tighten them to 35-40 ft.lb.
36. Position the bellcrank to the converter housing and install the two attaching bolts.
37. Connect the TV linkage rod to the transmission TV lever. Connect the manual linkage rod to the manual lever at the transmission.
38. Secure the converter-to-flywheel attaching nuts and tighten them to 20-30 ft.lb.
39. Install the converter housing access cover and secure it with the attaching bolts.
40. Secure the starter motor in place with the attaching bolts. Connect the cable to the terminal on the starter. Connect the neutral start switch wires at the plug connector.
41. Connect the driveshaft to the rear axle.
42. Adjust the shift linkage as required.
43. Adjust throttle linkage.
44. Lower the vehicle.
45. Fill the transmission to the correct level with Dexron®II. Start the engine and shift the transmission to all ranges, then recheck the fluid level.

ZF

1. Remove the kickdown cable and insert from the injection pump side lever and cable bracket located in the engine compartment.
2. Place the transmission gear selector in the Neutral position.
3. Raise and safely support the vehicle.
4. Remove the outer manual lever and nut from the transmission manual shift lever shaft.
5. Remove the position sensor from the converter housing.
6. Remove the engine to transmission brace from the lower end of the converter housing and engine block. On models with column shift, remove the two bolts that secure the bellcrank bracket to the brace.
7. Place a suitable wrench on the crankshaft pulley center bolt and turn the engine to gain access to the converter to drive plate mounting bolts. Remove the fastening nuts, turning the engine as necessary.
8. Drain the fluid from the transmission. Remove the driveshaft after marking the rear driveshaft yoke and companion flange for reinstallation reference.
9. Disconnect the neutral safety switch electrical connector. Remove the vibration damper from the transmission extension housing.
10. Position a suitable transmission type floor jack under the transmission for support.
11. Remove the rear transmission support to crossmember attaching nuts and the two crossmember to side support attaching bolts.
12. Remove the transmission to exhaust system support brackets.

NOTE: Exhaust system hardware may have to be removed in order to gain enough clearance for crossmember removal.

13. Disconnect the transmission cooler lines from the transmission fittings. See Quick Disconnect Fitting instructions in the FUEL SYSTEM Section.
14. Disconnect the speedometer wiring harness from the transmission extension housing.
15. Remove the starter motor mounting bolts and the starter motor.
16. Secure the transmission to the floor jack, and lower the jack slightly.

17. Remove the four converter housing to engine attaching bolts.
18. Remove the transmission filler tube and dipstick.
19. Carefully move the transmission back and away from the engine. Be sure the converter is mounted fully on the transmission. Lower the transmission and remove from the car.
20. Remove the transmission from the jack and service as required.
21. Secure the transmission on the jack. Insure that the converter is positioned fully back on the transmission shaft and that the mounting studs are in approximate alignment with the crankshaft mounted flexplate hole positions.
22. Move the transmission assembly into position and raise. Align the mounting studs to flexplate indicating that the converter pilot if not binding on the engine crankshaft.
23. Install the transmission fluid filler tube and install the four converter housing to engine mounting bolts. Tighten the mounting bolts to 38-48 ft.lb.
24. Connect the transmission cooler lines to the transmission. Connect the speedometer wiring harness to its connector. Install the extension housing vibration damper. Tighten the mounting bolts to 18-25 ft.lb.
25. Install the rear exhaust system support.
26. Install the crossmember on the side supports and secure the mounting bolts and nuts. Secure the rear engine support to the extension housing and crossmember. Install any removed exhaust system hardware.
27. Install and tighten the converter to flexplate mounting nuts to 20-34 ft.lb.
28. Install the engine to transmission brace on the lower end of the converter housing. Tighten the bolts to 15-18 ft.lb.
29. On models equipped with a column mounted shift, install the bellcrank on the transmission brace. Tighten the bolts to 10-20 ft.lb.
30. Remove the transmission jack.
31. Guide the kickdown cable up into the engine compartment.
32. Install the manual control lever onto the transmission lever shaft. Tighten the mounting nut to 10-20 ft.lb.
33. Connect the neutral safety switch harness. Install the position sensor to the converter housing.
34. Install the driveshaft after aligning the flange reference marks.
35. Lower the vehicle and adjust the shift linkage and kickdown cable as required.
36. Add an initial amount of transmission fluid, start the engine and move the transmission control lever through all positions. Recheck the fluid and add if necessary.

DRIVELINE

Driveshaft and U-Joints

The driveshaft is the means by which the power from the engine and transmission (in the front of the car) is transferred to the differential and rear axles, and finally to the rear wheels.

The driveshaft assembly incorporates two universal joints, one at each end, and a slip yoke at the front end of the assembly, which fits into the back of the transmission.

All driveshafts are balanced when installed in a car. It is therefore imperative that before applying undercoating to the chassis, the driveshaft and universal joint assembly be completely covered to prevent the accidental application of undercoating to the surfaces, and the subsequent loss of balance.

DRIVESHAFT REMOVAL

The procedure for removing the driveshaft assembly, complete with universal joint and slip yoke, is as follows:

1. Mark the relationship of the rear dirveshaft yoke and the drive pinion flange of the axle. If the original yellow alignment marks are visible, there is not need for new marks. The purpose of this marking is to facilitate installation of the assembly in its exact original position, thereby maintaining proper balance.
2. Remove the four bolts or U-clamps which hold the rear universal joint to the pinion flange. Wrap tape around the loose bearing caps in order to prevent them from falling off the spider.
3. Pull the driveshaft toward the rear of the vehicle until the slip yoke clears the transmission housing and the seal. Plug the hole at the rear of the transmission housing or place a container under the opening to catch any fluid which might leak.

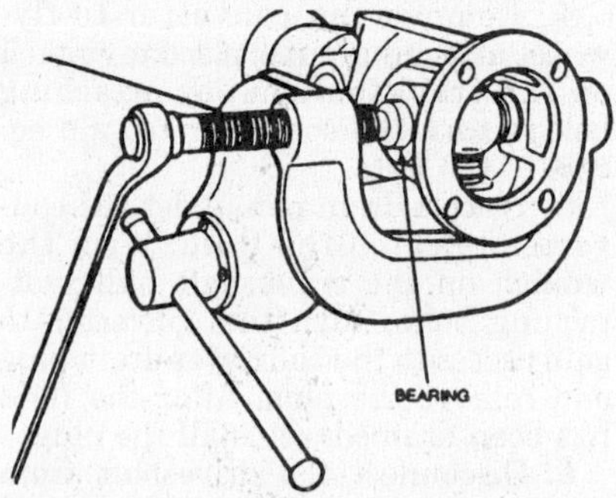

Pressing the bearing from the double cardan center yoke

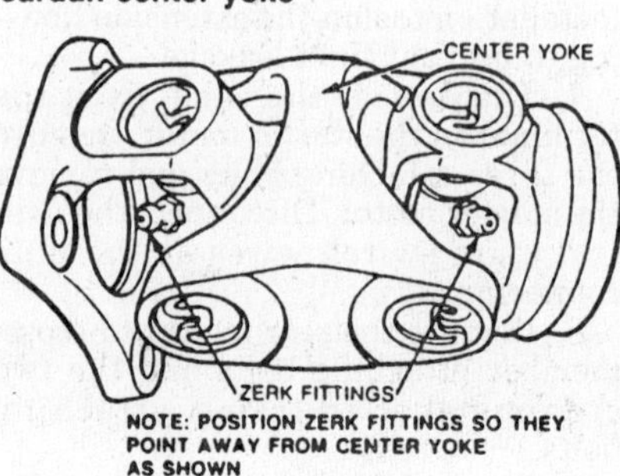

Grease fitting locations on the double cardan joint

UNIVERSAL JOINT OVERHAUL

1. Position the driveshaft assembly in a sturdy vise.
2. Remove the snaprings which retain the bearings in the slip yoke (front only) and in the driveshaft (front and rear).
3. Using a large vise or an arbor press and a socket smaller than the

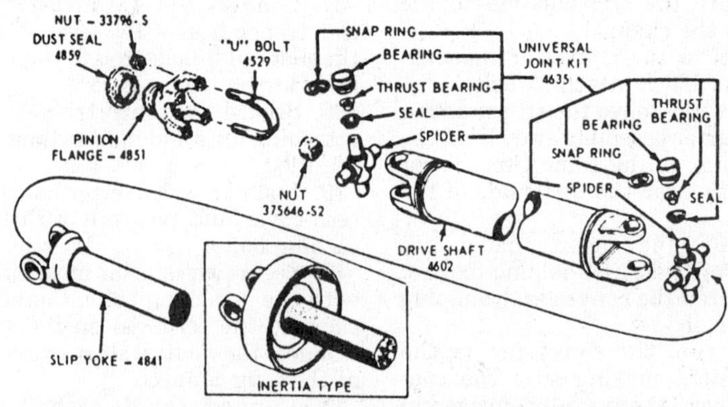

Single cardan driveshaft and U-joints

bearing cap on one side and a socket larger than the bearing cap on the other side, drive one of the bearings in toward the center of the universal joint, which will force the opposite bearing out.

4. As each bearing is forced far enough out of the universal joint assembly that it is accessible, grip it with a pair of pliers, and pull it from the driveshaft yoke. Drive the spider in the opposite direction in order to make the opposite bearing accessible, and pull it free with a pair of pliers. Use this procedure to remove all bearings from both universal joints.

5. After removing the bearings, lift the spider from the yoke.

6. Thoroughly clean all dirt and foreign matter from the yokes on both ends of the driveshaft.

WARNING: When installing new bearings in the yokes, it is advisable to use an arbor press. However, if this tool is not available, the bearings should be driven into position with extreme car, as a heavy jolt on the needle bearings can easily damage or misalign them, greatly shortening their lift and hampering their efficiency.

7. Start a new bearing into the yoke at the rear of the driveshaft.

8. Position a new spider in the rear yoke and press the new bearing ¼" (6mm) below the outer surface of the yoke.

9. With the bearing in position, install a new snapring.

10. Start a new bearing into the opposite side of the yoke.

11. Press the bearing until the opposite bearing, which you have just installed, contacts the inner surface of the snapring.

12. Install a new snapring on the second bearing. It may be necessary to grind the surface of this second snapring.

13. Reposition the driveshaft in the vise, so that the front universal joint is accessible.

14. Install the new bearings, new spider, and new snaprings in the same manner as you did for the rear universal joint.

15. Position the slip yoke on the spider. Install new bearings, nylon thrust bearings, and snaprings.

16. Check both reassembled joints for freedom of movement. If misalignment of any part is causing a bind, a sharp rap on the side of the yoke with a brass hammer should seat the bearing needle and provide the desired freedom of movement. Care should be exercised to firmly support the shaft end during this operation, as well as to prevent blows to the bearings themselves.

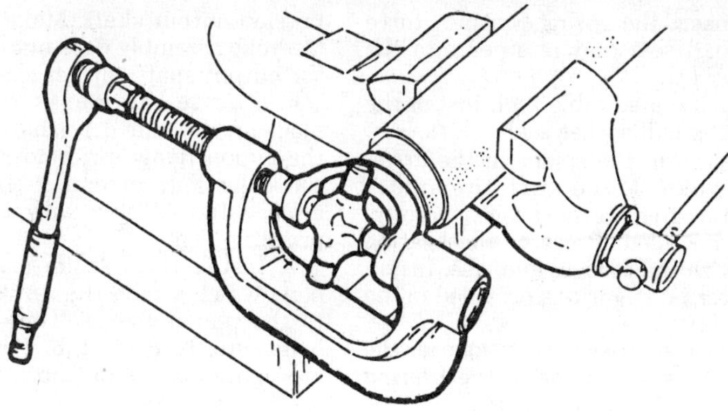

Installing universal joint bearing

Under no circumstances should the driveshaft be installed in a car if there is any binding in the universal joints.

DOUBLE CARDAN JOINT REPLACEMENT (REAR)

1. Working at the rear axle end of the shaft, mark the position of the spiders, the center yoke, and the centering socket yoke as related to the companion flange. The spiders must be assembled with the bosses in their original position to provide proper clearances.

2. Using a large vise or an arbor press and a socket smaller than the bearing cap on one side and a socket larger than the bearing cap on the other side, drive one of the bearings in toward the center of the universal joint, which will force the opposite bearing out.

3. Remove the driveshaft from the vise.

4. Tighten the bearing in the vise and tap on the yoke to free the bearing from the center yoke. Do not tap on the driveshaft tube.

5. Reposition the sockets on the yoke and force the opposite bearing outward and remove it.

6. Position the sockets on one of the remaining bearings and force it outward approximately ⅜" (9.5mm).

7. Grip the bearing in the vise and tap on the weld yoke to free the bearing from the center yoke. Do not tap on the driveshaft tube.

8. Reposition the sockets on the yoke to press out the remaining bearing.

9. Remove the spider from the center yoke.

10. Remove the bearings from the driveshaft yoke as outlined above and remove the spider from the yoke.

11. Insert a suitable tool into the centering ball socket located in the companion flange and pry out the rubber seal. Remove the retainer, three piece ball seat, washer and spring from the ball socket.

12. Inspect the centering ball socket assembly for worn or damaged parts. If any damage is evident replace the entire assembly.

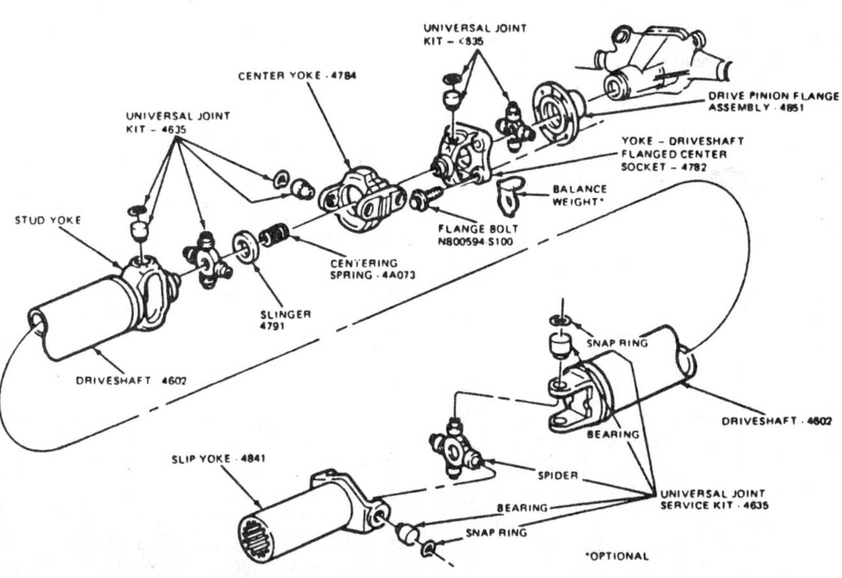

Exploded view of the driveshaft and U-joints with a double cardan U-joint

13. Insert the spring, washer, three piece ball seat and retainer into the ball socket.
14. Using a suitable tool, install the centering ball socket seal.
15. Position the spider in the driveshaft yoke. Make sure the spider bosses are in the same position as originally installed. Press in the bearing cups with the sockets and vise. Install the internal snaprings provided in the repair kit.
16. Position the center yoke over the spider ends and press in the bearing cups. Install the snaprings.
17. Install the spider in the companion flange yoke. Make sure the spider bosses are in the position as originally installed. Press on the bearing cups and install the snaprings.
18. Position the center yoke over the spider ends and press on the bearing cups. Install the snaprings.

DRIVESHAFT INSTALLATION

1. Carefully inspect the rubber seal on the output shaft and the seal in end of the transmission extension housing. Replace them if they are damaged.
2. Examine the lugs on the axle pinion flange and replace the flange if the lugs are shaved or distorted.
3. Coat the yoke spline with special-purpose lubricant. The Ford part number for this lubricant if B8A-19589-A.
4. Remove the plug from the rear of the transmission housing.
5. Insert the yoke into the transmission housing and onto the transmission output shaft. Make sure that the yoke assembly does not bottom on the output shaft with excessive force.
6. Locate the marks which you made on the rear driveshaft yoke and the pinion flange prior to removal of the driveshaft assembly. Install the driveshaft assembly with the marks properly aligned.
7. Install the U-bolts and nuts or bolts which attach the universal joint to the pinion flange. Torque the U-bolts nuts to 8-15 ft.lb. Flange bolts are tighten to 70-95 ft.lb.

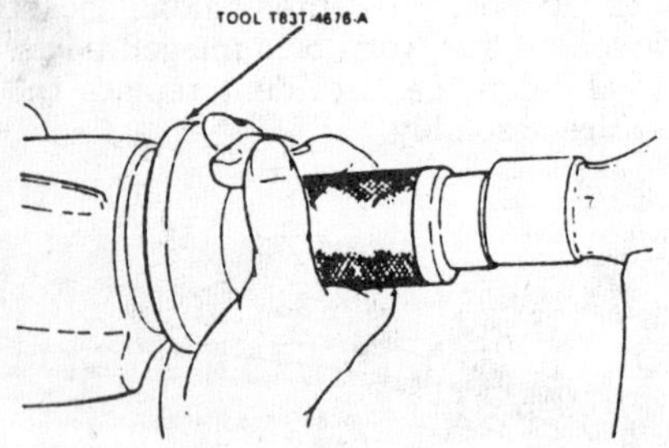

Pinion seal installation

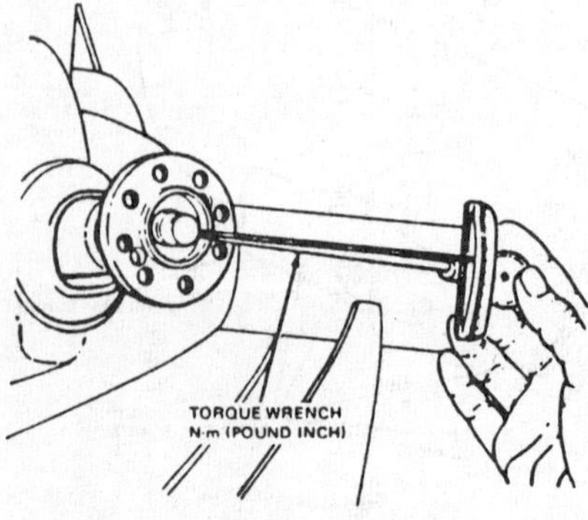

Measuring pinion bearing preload

REAR AXLE

Pinion Oil Seal

REMOVAL & INSTALLATION

NOTE: Special tools are needed for this job.

1. Raise and support the vehicle and remove the rear wheels and brake drums, or calipers.
2. Mark the driveshaft and yoke for reassembly and disconnect the driveshaft from the rear yoke.
3. With a socket on the pinion nut and an inch lb. torque wrench, rotate the drive pinion several revolutions. Check and record the torque required to turn the drive pinion.
4. Remove the pinion nut. Use a flange holding tool to hold the flange while removing the pinion nut. Discard the pinion nut.
5. Mark the yoke and the drive pinion shaft for reassembly reference.
6. Remove the rear yoke with a puller.
7. Inspect the seal surface of the yoke and replace it with a new one if the seal surface is pitted, grooved, or otherwise damaged.
8. Remove the pinion oil seal using tools 1175-AC and T50T-100A.
9. Before installing the new seal, coat the lip of the seal with rear axle lubricant.
10. Install the seal, driving it into place with a seal driver.
11. Install the yoke on the pinion shaft. Align the marks made on the pinion shaft and yoke during disassembly.
12. Install a new pinion nut. Tighten the nut until endplay is removed from the pinion bearing. Do not overtighten.
13. Check the torque required to turn the drive pinion. The pinion must be turned several revolutions to obtain an accurate reading.
14. Tighten the pinion nut to obtain the torque reading observed during disassembly (Step 3) plus 5 in.lb. Tighten the nut minutely each time, to avoid overtightening. Do not loosen and then retighten the nut. Pinion preload should be 8-14 in.lb.

NOTE: If the desired torque is exceeded a new collapsible pinion spacer sleeve must be installed and the pinion gear preload reset.

15. Install the driveshaft, aligning the index marks made during disassembly. Install the rear brake drums, or calipers, and wheels.

Axle Shaft and Bearing

NOTE: Both integral and removable carrier type axles are used. The axle type and ratio are stamped on a plate attached to a rear housing cover bolt. Axle types also indicate whether the axle shafts are retained by C-locks. To properly identify a C-lock axle, drain the lubricant, remove the rear cover and look for the C-lock on the end of the axle shaft in the differential side gear bore. If the axle has no cover (solid housing) it is not a C-lock. If the second letter of the axle model code is F, it is a Traction-Lok axle. Always refer to the axle tag code and ratio when ordering parts.

REMOVAL & INSTALLATION

NOTE: Bearings must be pressed on and off the shaft with an arbor press. Unless you have access to one, it is inadvisable to attempt any repair work on the axle shaft bearing assemblies.

Flange Type

1. Remove the wheel, tire, and brake drum. With the disc brakes, remove the caliper, retainer, nuts and rotor. New anchor plate bolts will be needed for reassembly.
2. Remove the nuts holding the retainer plate in the backing plate, or axle shaft retainer bolts from the housing. Disconnect the brake line with drum brakes.
3. Remove the retainer and install nuts, finger-tight, to prevent the brake backing plate from being dislodged.
4. Pull out the axle shaft and bearing assembly, using a slide hammer.

On models with a tapered roller bearing, the tapered cup will normally remain in the axle housing when the shaft is removed. The cup must be removed from the housing to prevent seal damage when the shaft is reinstalled. The cup can be removed with a

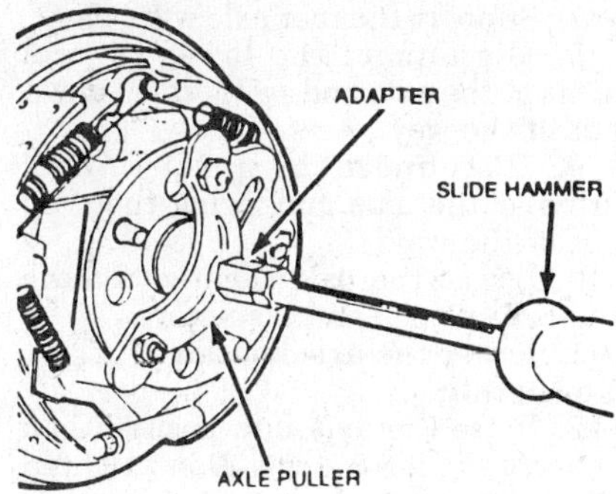

Typical axle shaft removal

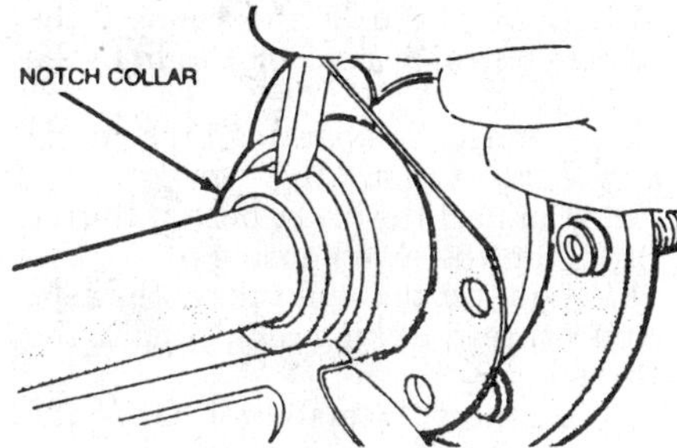

Loosening the bearing retaining ring on the 6¾ inch rear axle

slide hammer and an expanding puller.

WARNING: If end-play is found to be excessive, the bearing should be replaced. Shimming the bearing is not recommended as this ignores end-play of the bearing itself and could result in improper bearing seating.

5. Using a chisel, nick the bearing retainer in 3 or 4 places. The retainer does not have to be cut, but merely collapsed sufficiently to allow the bearing retainer to be slid from the shaft.
6. Press off the bearing and install the new one by pressing it into position. With tapered bearings, place the lubricated seal and bearing on the axle shaft (cup rib ring facing the flange). make sure that the seal is the correct length. Disc brake seal rims are black, drum brake seal rims are grey. Press the bearing and seal onto the shaft.
7. Press on the new retainer.

NOTE: Do not attempt to press the bearing and the retainer on at the same time.

8. On ball bearing models, to replace the seal: remove the seal from the housing with an expanding cone type puller and a slide hammer. the seal must be replaced whenever the shaft is removed. Wipe a small amount of sealer onto the outer edge of the new seal before installation; do not put sealer on the sealing lip. Press the seal into the housing with a seal installation tool.
9. Assemble the shaft and bearing in the housing, being sure that the bearing is seated properly in the housing. On ball bearing models, be careful not to damage the seal with the shaft. With tapered bearings, first install the tapered cup on the bearing, and lubricate the outer diameter of the cup and the seal with axle lube. Then install the shaft and bearing assembly into the housing.
10. Install the retainer, drum or rotor and caliper, wheel and tire. Bleed the brakes.

C-Lock Type

1. Jack up and support the rear of the car.
2. Remove the wheels and tires from the brake drums.
3. Place a drain pan under the housing and drain the lubricant by loosening the housing cover.
4. Remove the locks securing the brake drums to the axle shaft flanges and remove the drums.
5. Remove the housing cover and gasket, if used.
6. Position jackstands under the rear frame member and lower the axle housing. This is done to give easy access to the inside of the differential.
7. Working through the opening in the differential case, remove the side gear pinion shaft lockbolt and the side gear pinion shaft.
8. Push the axle shafts inward and remove the C-locks from the inner end of the axle shafts. Temporarily replace the shaft and lockbolt to retain the differential gears in position.
9. Remove the axle shafts with a slide hammer. Be sure the seal is not damaged by the splines on the axle shaft.
10. Remove the bearing and oil seal from the housing. Both the seal and bearing can be removed with a slide hammer. Two types of bearings are used on some axles, one requiring a press fit and the other a loose fit. A loose fitting bearing does not necessarily indicate excessive wear.
11. Inspect the axle shaft housing and axle shafts for burrs or other irregularities. Replace any worn or damaged parts. A light yellow color on the bearing journal of the axle shaft is normal, and does not require replacement of the axle shaft. Slight pitting and wear is also normal.
12. Lightly coat the wheel bearing rollers with axle lubricant. Install the bearings in the axle housing until the bearing seats firmly against the shoulder.
13. Wipe all lubricant from the oil seal bore, before installing the seal.
14. Inspect the original seals for wear. If necessary, these may be replace with new seals, which are prepacked with lubricant and do not require soaking.
15. Install the oil seal.

CAUTION

Installation of the seal without the proper tool can cause distortion and seal leakage. Seals may be colored coded for side identification. Do not interchange seals form side to side, if they are coded.

16. Remove the lockbolt and pinion shaft. Carefully slide the axle shafts into place. Be careful that you do not damage the seal with the splined end of the axle shaft. Engage the splined end of the shaft with the differential side gears.

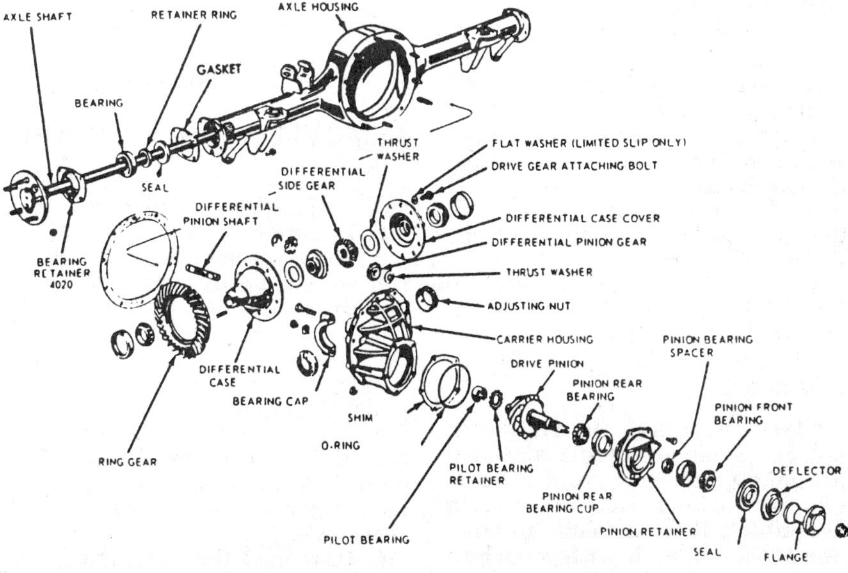

Removeable carrier axle carrier assembly

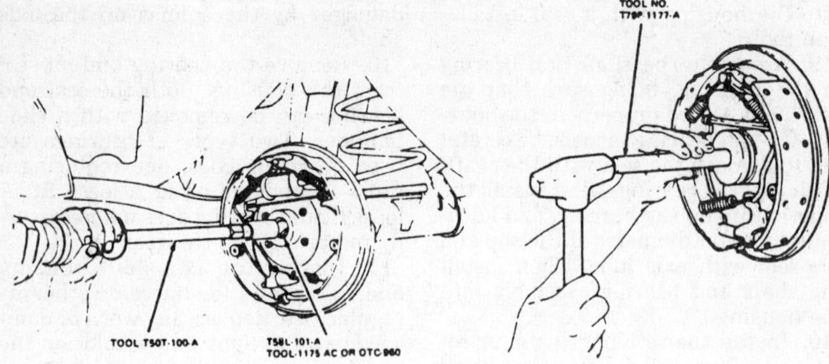

Typical axle seal replacement

17. Install the axle shaft C-locks on the inner end of the axle shafts and seat the C-locks in the counterbore of the differential side gears.
18. Rotate the differential pinion gears until the differential pinion shaft can be installed. Install the differential pinion shaft lockbolt. Tighten to 15-22 ft.lb.
19. Install the brake drum on the axle shaft flange.
20. Install the wheel and tire on the brake drum and tighten the attaching nuts.
21. Clean the gasket surface of the rear housing and install a new cover gasket and the housing cover. Some models do not use a paper gasket. On these models, apply a bead of silicone sealer on the gasket surface. The bead should run inside the bolt holes.
22. Raise the rear axle so that it is in the running position. Add the amount of specified lubricant to bring the lubricant level to ½" (12.7mm) below the filler hole.

AXLE SHAFT SEAL REPLACEMENT

1. Remove the axle shaft from the rear axle assembly, following the procedures previously discussed.
2. Using a two-fingered seal puller (slide hammer), remove the seal from the axle housing.
3. Thoroughly clean the recess in the rear axle housing from which the seal was removed.
4. Position a new seal on the housing and drive it into place with a seal installation tool. If this tool is not available, a wood block may be substituted.

NOTE: Although the right and left end seals are identical, there are many different types of seals which have been used on rear axle assembles. It is advisable to have one of the old seals with you when you are purchasing new ones.

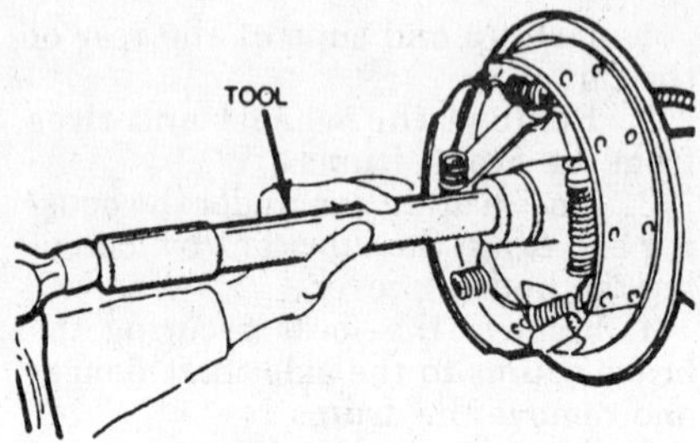

Installing rear axle oil seal

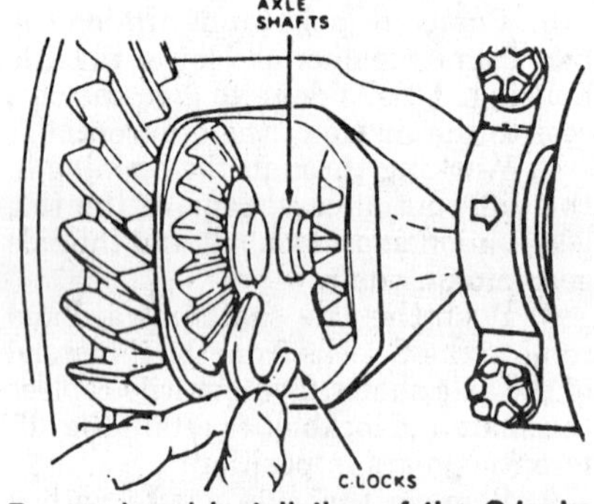

Removal and installation of the C-locks on a 7½ inch rear axle

5. When the seal is properly installed, install the axle shaft.

Axle Housing

REMOVAL & INSTALLATION

1. Raise the vehicle and support it on jackstands placed under the frame.
2. Remove the rear wheels.
3. Place an indexing mark on the rear yoke and driveshaft, and disconnect the shaft.
4. Disconnect the shock absorbers from the axle tubes. Disconnect the stabilizer bar at the axle bracket, on vehicles so equipped.
5. Disconnect the brake hose from the tee fitting on the axle housing. Disconnect the brake lines at the clips on the housing. Disconnect the vent tube at the axle.
6. Disconnect the parking brake cable at the frame mounting.
7. Support the rear axle with a jack.
8. Disconnect the lower control arms at the axle and swing them down out of the way.
9. Disconnect the upper control arms at the axle and swing them up out of the way.
10. Lower the axle slightly, remove the coil springs and insulators.
11. Lower the axle housing.

To install:

12. Raise the axle into position and connect the lower arms. Don't tighten the bolts yet.
13. Lower the axle slightly and install the coil springs and insulators.
14. Raise the axle and connect the upper control arms. Don't tighten the bolts yet.
15. Connect the parking brake cable at the frame mounting.
16. Connect the brake hose at the tee fitting on the axle housing.
17. Connect the vent tube at the axle. Apply thread locking compound to the threads.
18. Connect the stabilizer bar at the axle bracket, on vehicles so equipped.
19. Connect the shock absorbers from the axle tubes.
20. Connect the driveshaft.
21. Install the rear wheels.
22. Lower the vehicle.
23. Once the car is back on its wheels, observe the following torques:

Removeable carrier axles:

- Lower control arm bolts – 90 ft.lb.
- Lower shock absorber nuts – 85 ft.lb.
- Upper control arm bolts – 120 ft.lb.

Integral carrier axles:

- Lower arm bolts – 100 ft.lb.
- Lower shock absorber nuts – 55 ft.lb.
- Upper arm bolts – 100 ft.lb.

WARNING: Bleed and adjust the brakes accordingly.

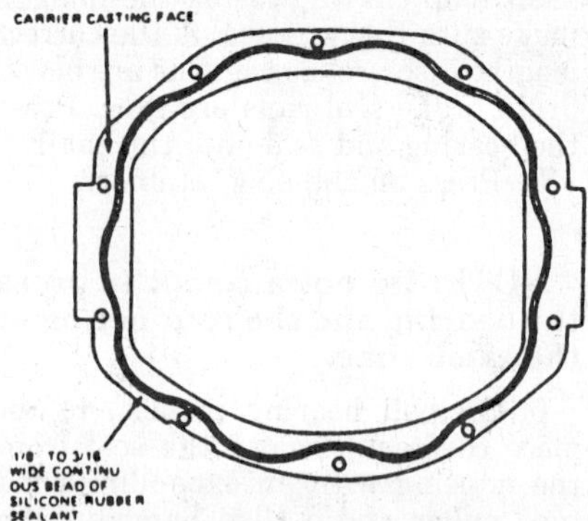

Installing sealer on rear axle housing cover

FRONT SUSPENSION

Each front wheel rotates on a spindle. The spindle's upper and lower ends attach to the upper and lower ball joints which mount to an upper and lower arm respectively. The upper arm pivots on a bushing and shaft assembly bolted to the frame. The lower arm pivots on the No. 2 crossmember bolt. The coil spring is seated between the lower arm and the top of the spring housing on the underside of the upper arm. A shock absorber is bolted to the lower arm at the bottom and the top of the spring housing.

Coil Spring and Lower Control Arm

REMOVAL & INSTALLATION

1. Raise the car and support it with stands placed in back of the lower arms.
2. Remove the wheel from the hub. Remove the two bolts and washers that hold the caliper and brake hose bracket to the spindle. Remove the caliper from the rotor and wire it back out of the way. Remove the hub and rotor from the spindle.
3. Disconnect the lower end of the shock absorber and push it up to the retracted position.
4. Disconnect the stabilizer bar link from the lower arm.
5. Remove the cotter pins from the upper and lower ball joint stud nuts.
6. Remove the two bolts and nuts holding the strut to the lower arm.
7. Loosen the lower ball joint stud nut two turns. Do not remove this nut.
8. Install spreader tool T57P-3006-A between the upper and lower ball joint studs.
9. Expand the tool until the tool exerts considerable pressure on the studs. Tap the spindle near the lower stud with a hammer to loosen the stud with tool pressure only.
10. Position the floor jack under the lower arm and remove the lower ball joint stud nut.
11. Lower the floor jack and remove the spring and insulator.
12. Remove the A-arm-to-crossmember attaching parts and remove the arm from the car.
13. Reverse the above procedure to install. If the lower control arm was replaced because of damage, check front end alignment. Torque lower arm-to-no. 2 crossmember nut to 60-90 ft.lb. Torque the strut-to-lower arm bolts to 80-115 ft.lb. The caliper-to-spindle bolts are torqued to 90-120 ft.lb. Torque the ball joint-to-spindle attaching nut to 60-90 ft.lb.

Shock Absorber

REMOVAL & INSTALLATION

1. Remove the nut, washer, and bushing from the upper end of the shock absorber.
2. Raise the vehicle on a hoist and install jackstands under the frame rails.
3. Remove the two bolts securing the shock absorber to the lower arm and remove the shock absorber.
4. Inspect the shock absorber for leaks. Extend and compress the unit several times to check the damping action and remove any trapped air. Replace in paris if necessary.
5. Install a new bushing and washer on the top of the shock absorber and position the unit inside the front spring. Install the two lower attaching bolts and torque them to 8-15 ft.lb.
6. Remove the safety stands and lower the vehicle.
7. Place a new bushing and washer on the shock absorber top stud and install the attaching nut. Torque to 22-30 ft.lb.

Upper Control Arm

REMOVAL & INSTALLATION

1. Perform Steps 1-11 of the previous Coil Spring and Lower Control Arm Removal and Installation procedure.
2. Remove the upper arm inner shaft attaching bolts and remove the arm and shaft from the chassis as an assembly.
3. Reverse above procedure to install. Torque the ball joint-to-spindle attaching nut to 60-90 ft.lb.
4. Adjust front end alignment.

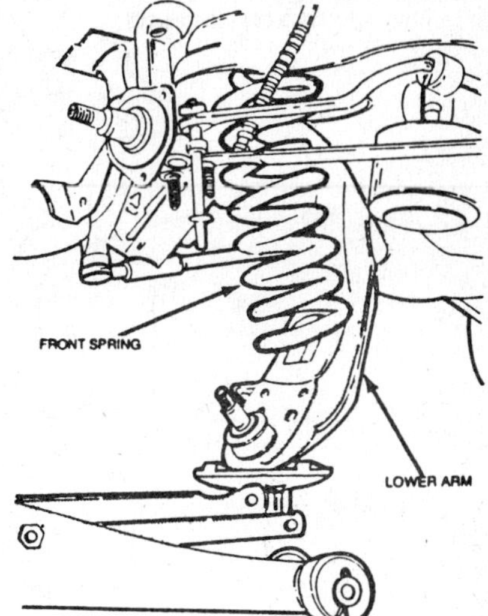

Removing front spring

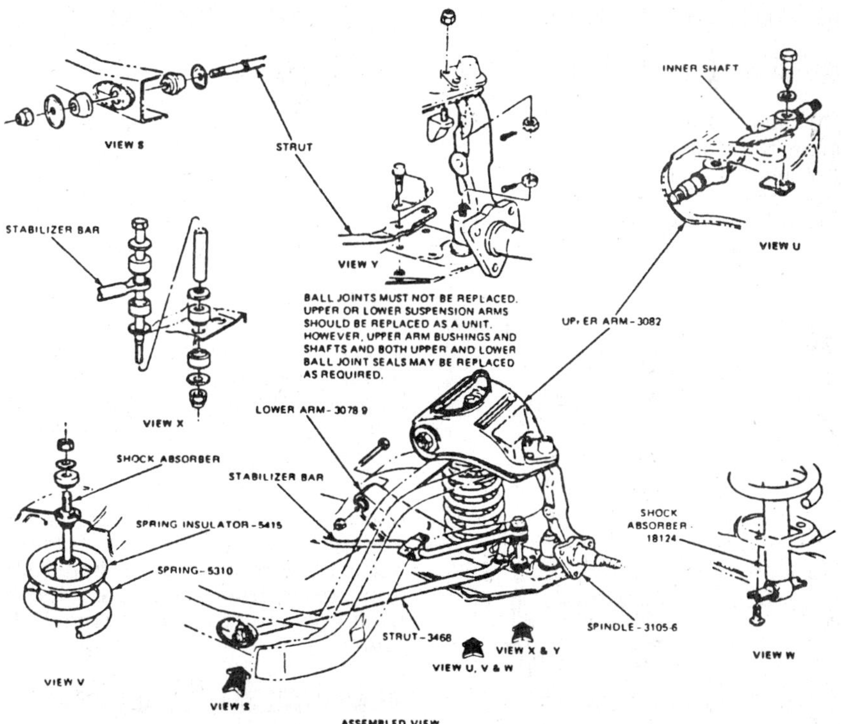

Coil spring front suspension

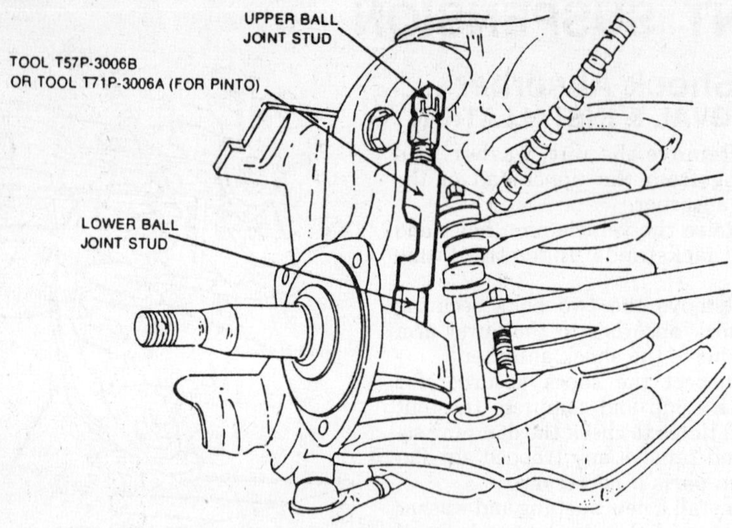

Loosening lower ball joint stud

Lower Ball Joint

INSPECTION

1. Raise the vehicle by placing a floor jack under the lower arm or, raise the vehicle on a hoist and place a jackstand under the lower arm and lower the vehicle onto it to remove the preload from the lower ball joint.
2. Have an assistant grasp the top and bottom of the wheel and apply alternate in and out pressure to the top and bottom of the wheel.
3. Radial play of ¼″ (6mm) is acceptable measured at the inside of the wheel adjacent to the lower arm.

REMOVAL & INSTALLATION

1. Raise the vehicle on a hoist and allow the front wheels to fall to their full down position.
2. Drill a ⅛″ (3mm) hole completely through each ball joint attaching rivet.
3. Use a ⅜″ (9.5mm) drill in the pilot hole to drill off the head of the rivet.
4. Drive the rivets from the lower arm.
5. Place a jack under the lower arm and lower the vehicle about 6″ (152mm).
6. Remove the lower ball joint stud cotter pin and attaching nut.
7. Using a suitable tool, loosen the ball joint from the spindle and remove the ball joint from the lower arm.
8. Clean all metal burrs from the lower arm and install the new ball joint, using the service part nuts and bolts to attach the ball joint to the lower arm. Do not attempt to rivet the ball joint again once it has been removed.
9. Check front end alignment.

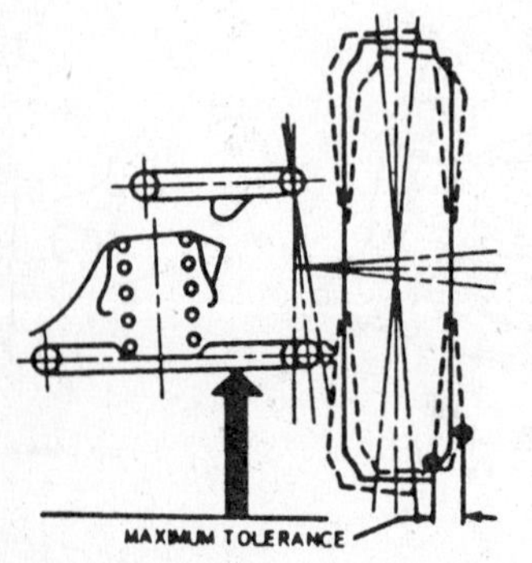

Measuring lower ball joint radial play

Upper Ball Joint

INSPECTION

1. Raise the vehicle by placing a floor jack under the lower arm. Do not allow the lower arm to hang freely with the vehicle on a hoist or bumper jack.
2. Have an assistant grasp the top and bottom of the tire and move the wheel in and out.
3. As the wheel is being moved, observe the upper control arm where the spindle attaches to it. Any movement between the upper part of the spindle and the upper ball joint indicates a bad ball joint which must be replaced.

NOTE: During this check, the lower ball joint will be unloaded and may move; this is normal and not an indication of a bad ball joint. Also, do not mistake a loose wheel bearing for a defective ball joint.

REMOVAL & INSTALLATION

1. Raise the vehicle and support on jackstands allowing the front wheels to fall to their full down position.
2. Drill a ⅛″ (3mm) hole completely through each ball joint attaching rivet.
3. Using a large chisel, cut off the head of each rivet and drive them from the upper arm.
4. Place a jack under the lower arm and lower the vehicle about 6″ (152mm).
5. Remove the cotter pin and attaching nut from the ball joint stud.
6. Using a suitable tool, loosen the ball joint stud from the spindle and remove the ball joint from the upper arm.
7. Clean all metal burrs from the upper arm and install the new ball joint, using the service part nuts and bolts to attach the ball joint to the upper arm. Do not attempt to rivet the ball joint again once it has been removed.
8. Check front end alignment.

Sway (Stabilizer) Bar

REMOVAL & INSTALLATION

1. Raise the front end and place support under both front wheels. A pair of drive-on ramps is ideal for this purpose.
2. Disconnect the stabilizer bar from each link, or disconnect the links at the control arms.
3. Remove the stabilizer bar brackets and remove the bar.
4. Installation is the reverse of removal. Torque the link-to-control arm nuts and/or link-to-bar nuts to 18 ft.lb. and the bar bracket screws to 20 ft.lb.

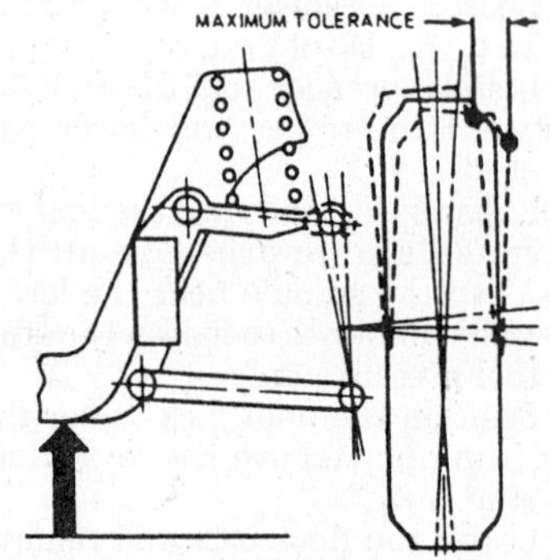

Measuring upper ball joint radial play

Spindle

REMOVAL & INSTALLATION

1. Raise and support the front end on jackstands.
2. Remove the front wheels.
3. Remove the caliper-to-anchor plate bolts and wire the caliper and anchor plate up away from the rotor and spindle.

4. Remove the front hub and rotor assembly.

5. Unbolt and remove the caliper shield.

6. Using a ball joint separator, disconnect the spindle connecting rod link from the spindle.

7. Remove the cotter pins and loosen both ball joint stud nuts a few turns each, but don't remove them yet.

8. Position a ball joint remover between the upper and lower ball joint studs. The tool must seat firmly against the ends of both studs; not against the stud nuts.

9. Turn the tool with a wrench until the tool places the studs under considerable tension, and, with a hammer, sharply hit the spindle near the studs to break them loose in the spindle. DON'T LOOSEN THE STUDS IN THE SPINDLE WITH TOOL PRESSURE ALONE! DON'T HIT THE BOOT SEAL WITH THE HAMMER!

10. Position a floor jack under the lower arm and install a safety chain through the spring and around the lower arm.

11. Remove the upper and lower ball stud nuts, lower the jack and remove the spindle.

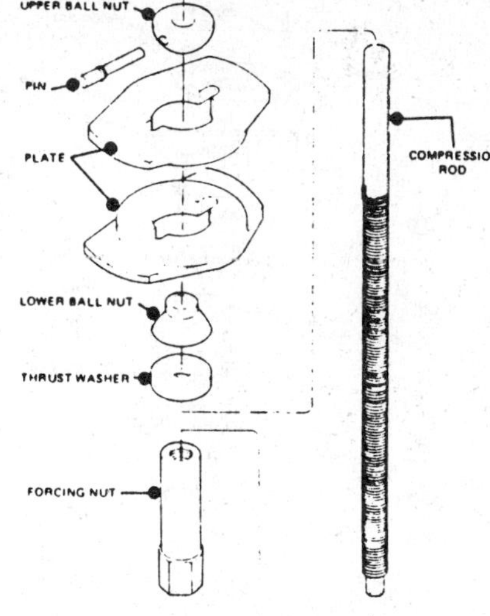

Exploded view of a MacPherson strut

12. Position the spindle on the lower ball stud and install the nut. Torque the nut to 75-90 ft.lb. and install a new cotter pin.

13. Raise the lower arm and guide the upper ball stud into the spindle. Install the stud nut and torque it to 105-120 ft.lb. Install a new cotter pin.

14. Remove the floor jack.

15. Connect the spindle connecting rod to the spindle and install a new nut. Torque the nut to 43-47 ft.lb. and install a new cotter pin.

16. Install the caliper splash shield and torque the fasteners to 15 ft.lb.

17. Install the hub and rotor.

18. Install the caliper anchor plate on the spindle. Torque the bolts to 90-120 ft.lb.

19. Install the wheels.

FRONT SUSPENSION MACPHERSON STRUT TYPE

The design utilizes stock struts with coil springs mounted between the lower arm and a spring pocket in the No. 2 crossmember. The shock struts are non-repairable, and must be replaced as a unit. The ball joints lower suspension arm bushings are not separately

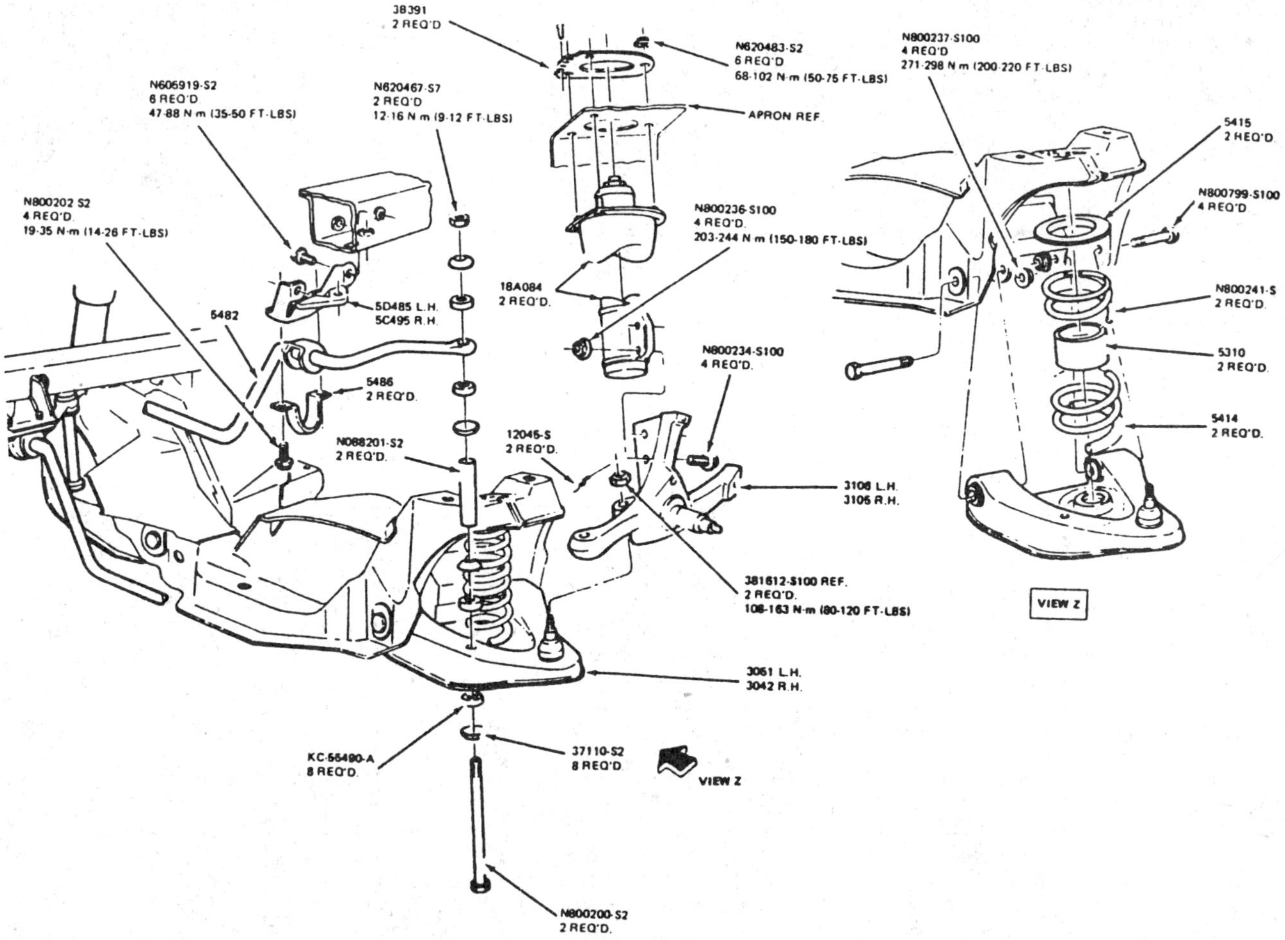

1980 front suspension

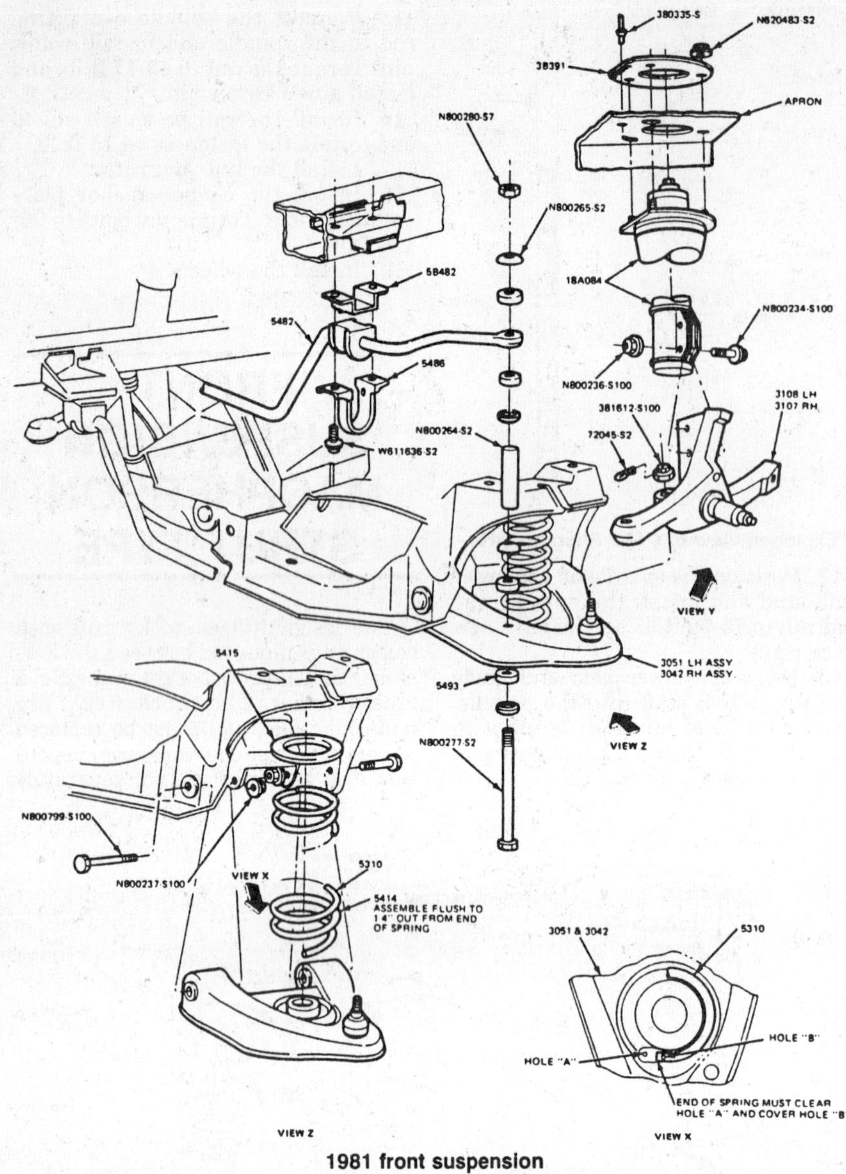

1981 front suspension

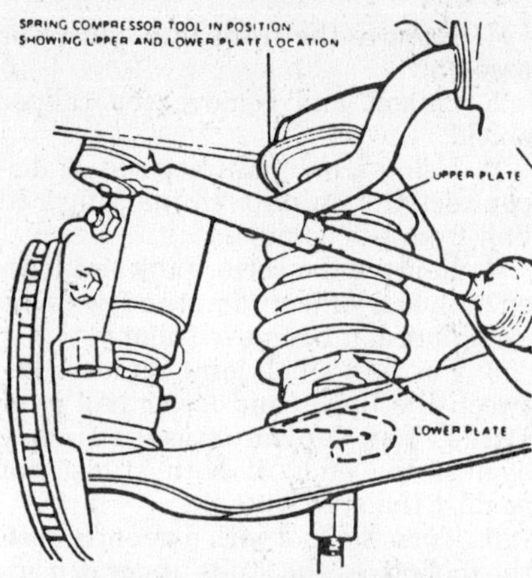

Spring compressor in position

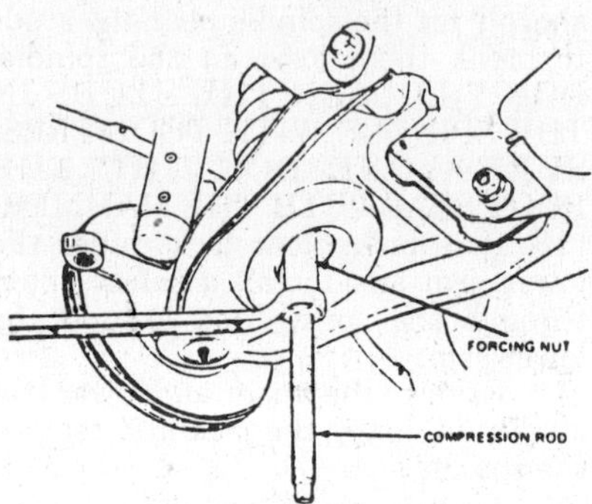

Spring compressed for removal

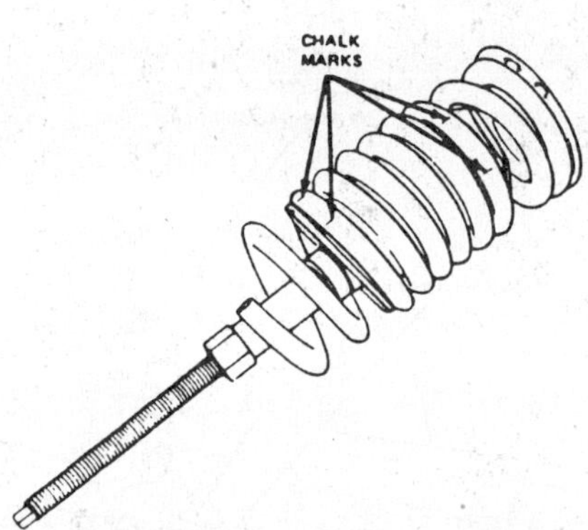

Spring removed from car

serviced, and they also must be replaced by replacing the suspension arm assembly. The ball joint seal can be replaced separately.

Springs

WARNING: Always use extreme caution when working with coil springs. make sure the vehicle is supported sufficiently.

REMOVAL

1. Raise the front of the vehicle and place safety stands under both sides of the jack pads just back of the lower arms.
2. Remove the wheel and tire assembly.
3. Disconnect the stabilizer bar link from the lower arm.
4. Remove the steering gear bolts, and move the steering gear out of the way.
5. Disconnect the tie rod from the steering spindle.
6. Using a spring compressor, install one plate with the pivot ball seat down into the coils of the spring. Rotate the plate, so that it is fully seated into the lower suspension arm spring seat.
7. Install the other plate with the pivot ball seat up into the coils of the spring. Insert the ball nut through the coils of the spring. Insert the ball nut through the coils of the spring, so it rests in the upper plate.
8. Insert the compression rod into the opening in the lower arm through the lower and upper plate. Install the upper ball nut on the rod, and return the securing pin.

NOTE: This pin can only be inserted one way into the upper ball nut because of a stepped hole design.

9. With the upper ball nut secured turn the upper plate, so it walks up the coil until it contacts the upper spring seat.
10. Install the lower ball nut, thrust bearing and forcing nut on the compression rod.
11. Rotate the nut until the spring is compressed enough so that it is free in its seat.
12. Remove the two lower control arm pivot bolts and nuts, and disengage the lower arm from the frame crossmember and remove the spring assembly.

13. If a new spring is to be installed, mark the position of the upper and lower plates on the spring with chalk. Measure the compressed length of the spring as well as the amount of the spring curvature to assist in the compressing and installation of a new spring.

14. Loosen the nut to relieve spring tension, and remove the tools from the spring.

INSTALLATION

1. Assemble the spring compressor tool, and locate it in the same position as indicted in Step 13 of the removal procedure.

WARNING: Before compressing the coil spring, be sure the upper ball nut securing pin is inserted properly.

2. Compress the coil spring until the spring height reaches the dimension in Step 13.
3. Position the coil spring assembly into the lower arm.

WARNING: Make sure that the lower end of the spring is properly positioned between the two holes in the lower arm spring pocket depression.

4. To finish installing the coil spring reverse the removal procedure.

Ball Joints

Ball joints are not replaceable. If the ball joints are found to be defective the lower control arm assembly must be replaced.

INSPECTION

1. Support the vehicle in normal driving position with both ball joints loaded.
2. Wipe the grease fitting and checking surface, so they are free of dirt and grease. The checking surface is the round boss into which the grease fitting is threaded.
3. The checking surface should project outside the cover. If the checking surface is inside the cover, replace the lower arm assembly.

Shock Strut

REMOVAL

1. Place the ignition key in the unlock position to permit free movement of the front wheels.
2. Working from the engine compartment remove the nut that attaches the strut to the upper mount. A screwdriver in the slot will hold the rod stationary while removing the nut.

WARNING: The vehicle should not be driven while the nut is removed so make sure the car is in position for hoisting purposes.

3. Raise the front of the vehicle by the lower control arms, and place safety stands under the frame jacking pads, rearward of the wheels.
4. Remove the tire and wheel assembly.
5. Remove the brake caliper, rotor assembly, and dust shield.
6. Remove the two lower nuts and bolts attaching the strut to the spindle.
7. Lift the strut up from the spindle to compress the rod, then pull down and remove the strut.

INSTALLATION

1. With the rod half extended, place the rod through the upper mount and hand start the mount as soon as possible.
2. Extend the strut and position into the spindle.
3. Install the two lower mounting bolts and hand start the nuts.
4. Tighten the nut that attaches the strut to the upper body mount to 60-75 ft.lb. This can be done from inside the engine compartment.

NOTE: Position a suitable tool in the slot to hold the rod stationary while the nut is being tightened.

5. Remove the suspension load from the lower control arms by lower-

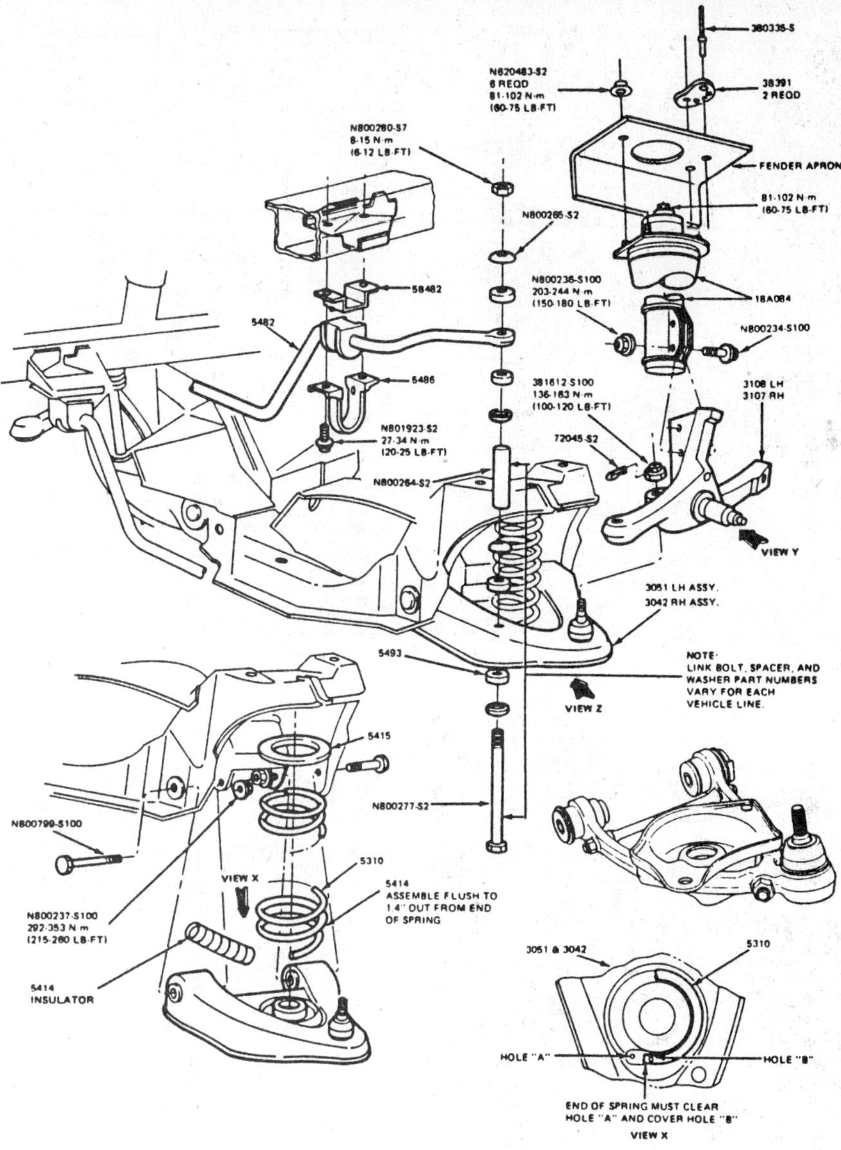

1982 front suspension

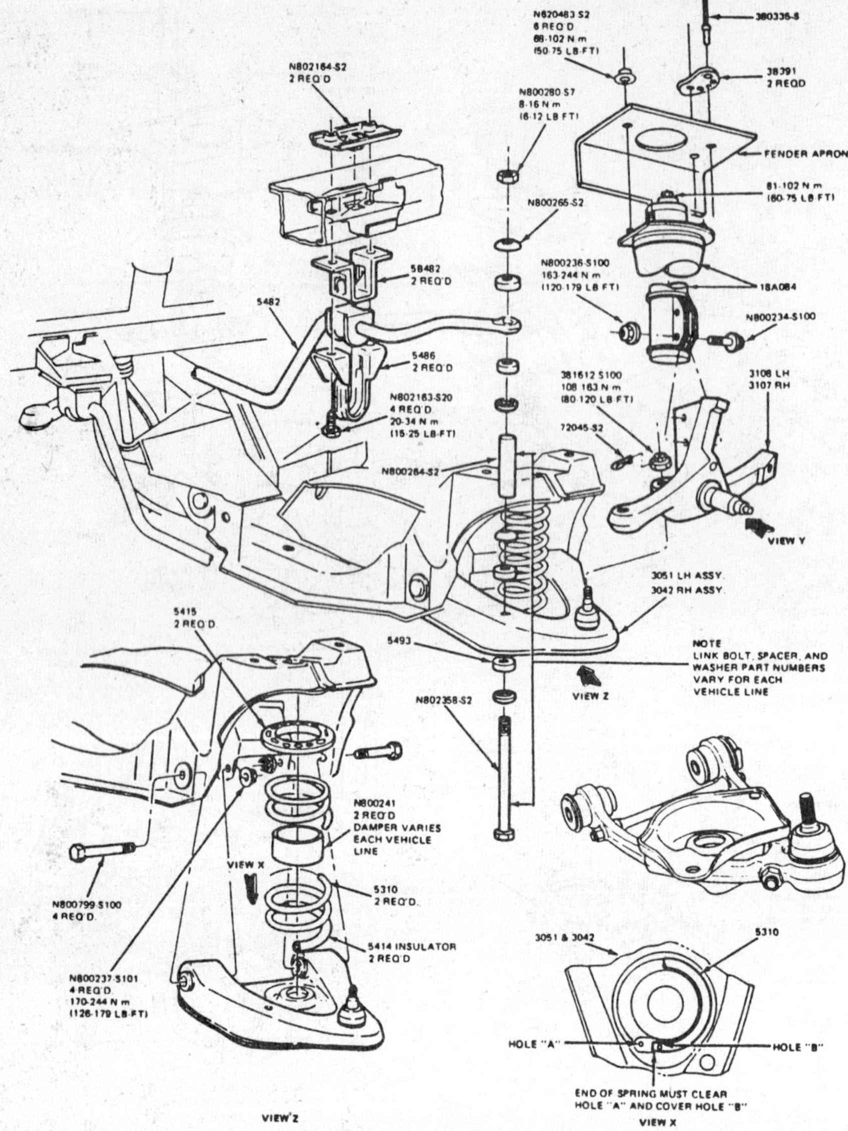

1983-86 front suspension

ing the hoist and tighten the lower mounting nuts to 150 ft.lb.

6. Raise the suspension control arms and install the brake caliper, rotor assembly and dust shield.

7. Install the tire and wheel assembly.

8. Remove the safety stands and lower the vehicle.

Lower Control Arm

REMOVAL

1. Raise the front of the vehicle and position safety stands under both sides of the jack pads, just to the rear of the lower arms.

2. Remove the wheel and tire assembly.

3. Disconnect the stabilizer bar link from the lower arm.

4. Remove the disc brake caliper, rotor and dust shield.

5. Remove the steering gear bolts and position out of the way.

6. Remove the cotter pin from the ball joint stud nut, and loosen the ball joint nut one or two turns.

7. Tap the spindle sharply to relieve the stud pressure.

8. Remove the tie rod end from the spindle. Place a floor jack under the lower arm, supporting the arm at both bushings. Remove both lower arm bolts, lower the jack and remove the coil spring as outlined earlier in the section.

9. Remove the ball nut and remove the arm assembly.

INSTALLATION

1. Place the new arm assembly into the spindle and tighten the ball joint nut to 100 ft.lb. Install the cotter pin.

2. Position the coil spring in the upper spring pocket. Make sure the insulator is on top of the spring and the lower end is properly positioned between the two holes in the depression of the lower arm.

3. Carefully raise the lower arm with the floor jack until the bushings are properly positioned in the crossmember.

4. Install the lower arm bolts and nuts, finger tight only.

5. Install and tighten the steering gear bolts.

6. Connect the tie rod end and tighten the nut to 35-47 ft.lb.

7. Connect the stabilizer link bolt and nut and tighten to 10 ft.lb.

8. Install the brake dust shield, rotor and caliper.

9. Install the wheel and tire assembly.

10. Remove the safety stands and lower the vehicle. After the vehicle has been lowered to the floor and at curb height, tighten the lower arm nuts to 210 ft.lb.

Sway Bar

REMOVAL & INSTALLATION

1980-84
1985-87 Thunderbird and Cougar

1. Raise and support the front end on jackstands.

2. Disconnect the stabilizer bar from the links, or the links from the lower arm.

3. Disconnect the bar from the retaining clamps.

4. Installation is the reverse of removal. Torque the bar fasteners to 25 ft.lb.; the link-to-arm fasteners to 12 ft.lb.

Spindle

REMOVAL & INSTALLATION

1980-84
1985-87 Thunderbird and Cougar

1. Raise and support the front end on jackstands under the frame.

2. Remove the wheels.

3. Remove the calipers and suspend them out of the way.

4. Remove the hub and rotor assemblies.

5. Remove the rotor dust shields.

6. Unbolt the stabilizer links from the control arms.

7. Using a separator, disconnect the tie rod ends from the spindle.

8. Remove the cotter pin and loosen the ball joint stud nut a few turns. Don't remove it at this time!
9. Using a hammer, tap the spindle boss sharply to relieve stud pressure.
10. Support the lower control arm with a floor jack, compress the coil spring and remove the stud nut.
11. Remove the two bolts and nuts attaching the spindle to the shock strut. Compress the shock strut until working clearance is obtained.
12. Remove the spindle.

To install:

13. Place the spindle on the ball joint stud, and install the stud nut, but don't tighten it yet.
14. Lower the shock strut until the attaching holes are aligned with the holes in the spindle. Install two new bolts and nuts.
15. Tighten the ball stud nut to 80-120 ft.lb. and install the cotter pin.
16. Torque the shock strut-to-spindle attaching nuts to 80-120 ft.lb. for 1980-81 cars; 150-180 ft.lb. for 1982-85 cars; 140-200 ft.lb. for 1986-87 cars.
17. Lower the floor jack.
18. Install the stabilizer links. Torque the nuts to 12 ft.lb.
19. Attach the tie rod ends and torque the nuts to 45 ft.lb.
20. The remainder of installation is the reverse of removal.

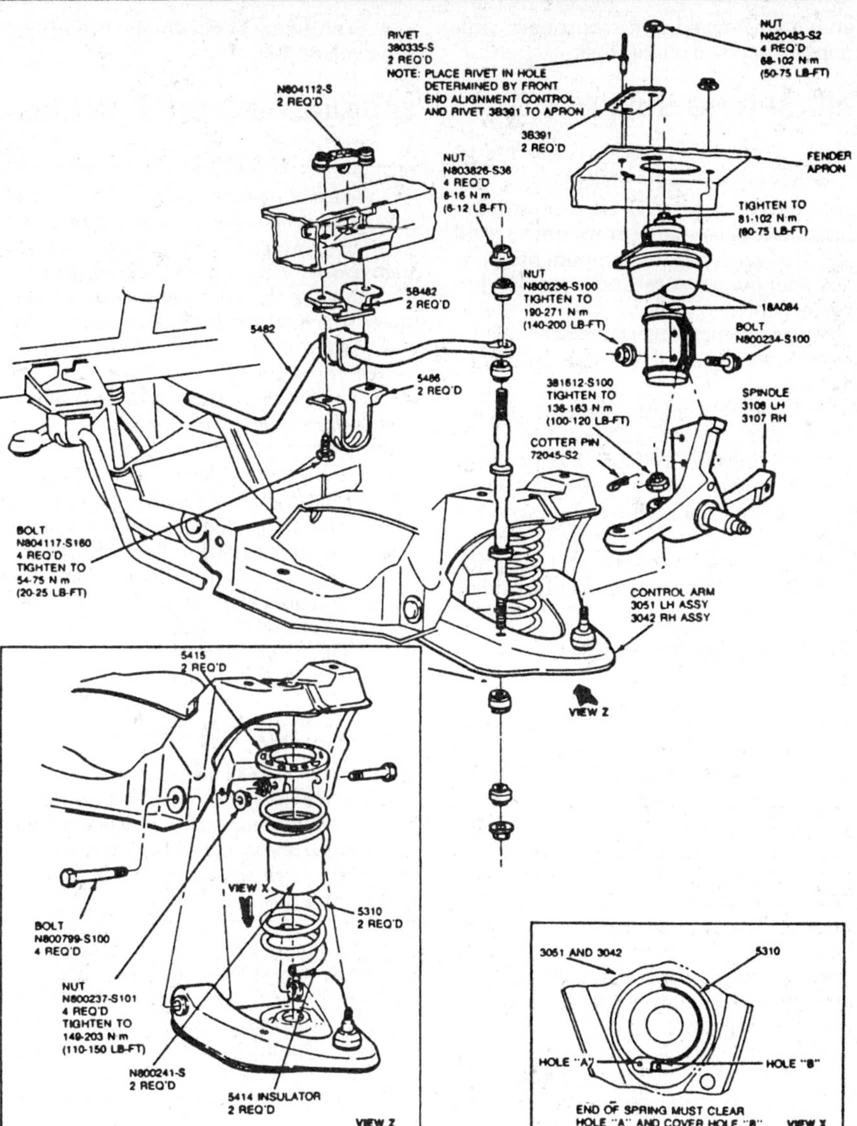

1987 front suspension

AIR SUSPENSION

CAUTION

Do not remove an air spring under any circumstances when there is pressure in the air spring. Do not remove any components supporting an air spring without either exhausting the air or providing support for the air spring.

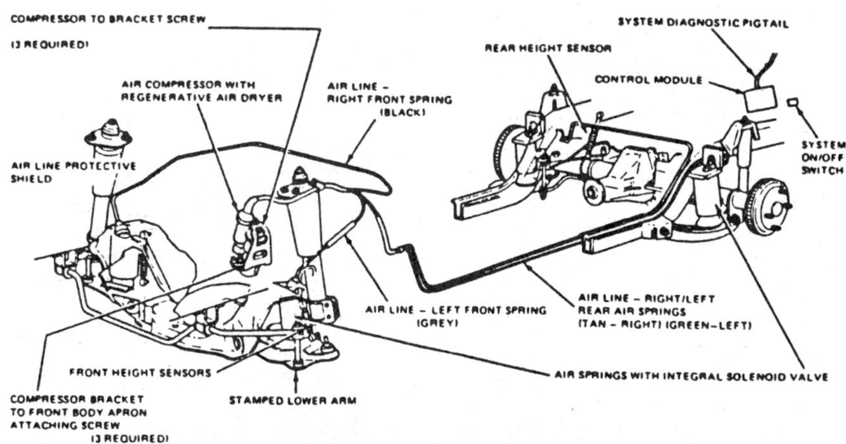

Air suspension system

Components

SUSPENSION FASTENERS

Suspension fasteners are important attaching parts in that they could affect performance of vital components and systems and/or could result in major service expense. They must be replaced with fasteners of the same part number, or with an equivalent part, if replacement becomes necessary. Do not use a replacement part of less quality or substitute design. Torque values must be used, as specified, during assembly to assure proper retention of parts. New fasteners must be used whenever old fasteners are loosened or removed and when new component parts are installed.

AIR SPRING SUSPENSION

• Air compressor (less dryer), regenerative dryer, O-ring mounting bracket and the isolator mounts are all serviced as separate components.

• Height sensors and modules are replaceable.

• Air springs are replaceable as assemblies (including the solenoid valve).

• Air spring solenoid valves and external O-rings are replaceable.

• Air lines are replaceable, however quick connect unions and bulk tubing are available to mend a damaged air line.

• Collet and O-rings of the quick connect type fittings are replaceable.

FRONT SUSPENSION

• Gas filled shock absorber struts must be replaced as assemblies. They are not servicable. Replace only the damaged shock absorber strut. It is not necessary to replace in matched pairs.

• Strut upper mounts may be replaced individually.

• Air springs are replaced as assemblies. It is not necessary to replace in pairs.

• The lower control arm is replaceable as an assembly with the ball joint and bushings included.

• The spindle is replaceable.

• The stabilizer bar is replaceable with stabilizer bar-to-body insulators included.

• The stabilizer bar-to-body bushing is replaceable.

REAR SUSPENSION

The following rear suspension components may be replaced individually:

• Gas filled shock absorbers must be replaced as assemblies. They are not serviceable. Replace only the damaged shock absorber. It is not necessary to replace in matched pairs.

• Air springs are replaced as assemblies. It is not necessary to replace in pairs.

• Lower control arms, including both end bushings, are replaceable as assemblies. (Must be replaced in pairs).

• Upper control arms, including body end bushing, are replaceable as assemblies. (Must be replaced in pairs).

• Stabilizer bar is replaceable with stabilizer bar-to-axle insulator included.

• Stabilizer bar-to-body bushings are replaceable.

JACKING AND SUPPORTING

CAUTION

The electrical power supply to the air suspension system must be shut off prior to hoisting, jacking or towing an air suspension vehicle. This can be accomplished by disconnecting the battery or turning off the power switch located in the trunk on the LH side. Failure to do so may result in unexpected inflation or deflation of the air springs which may result in shifting of the vehicle during these operations.

Raise the front of the vehicle at the No. 2 crossmember until the tires are above the floor. Support the vehicle body with jackstands at each front corner and then lower the floor jack so that the front suspension is in full rebound. Repeat this procedure for the rear suspension, except raise the body at the rear jacking location.

Air Spring System

CAUTION

Power to the air system must be shut-off by turning the air suspension switch (in luggage compartment) Off or by disconnecting the battery when servicing any air suspension components.

• Do not attempt to install or inflate any air spring that has become unfolded.

• Any spring which has unfolded must be refolded, prior to being installed in a vehicle.

• Do not attempt to inflate any air spring which has been collapsed while uninflated from the rebound hanging position to the jounce stop.

• After inflating an air spring in hanging position, it must be inspected for proper shape.

• Failure to follow the above procedures may result in a sudden failure of the air spring or suspension system.

Air Spring Solenoid

The air spring solenoid valve has a two stage solenoid pressure relief fitting similar to a radiator cap. A clip is first removed, and rotation of the solenoid out of the spring will release air from the assembly before the solenoid can be removed.

1. Turn the air suspension switch Off.
2. Raise the vehicle. Remove wheel and tire assembly.
3. Disconnect the electrical connector and then disconnect the air line.
4. Remove the solenoid clip. Rotate the solenoid counterclockwise to the first stop.

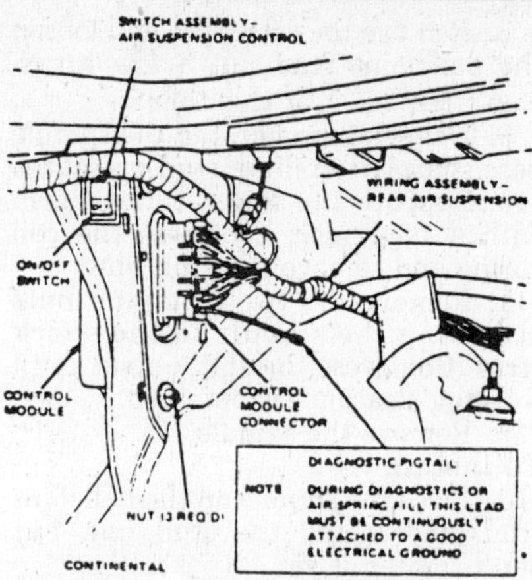

Air suspension cut-off switch – Continental

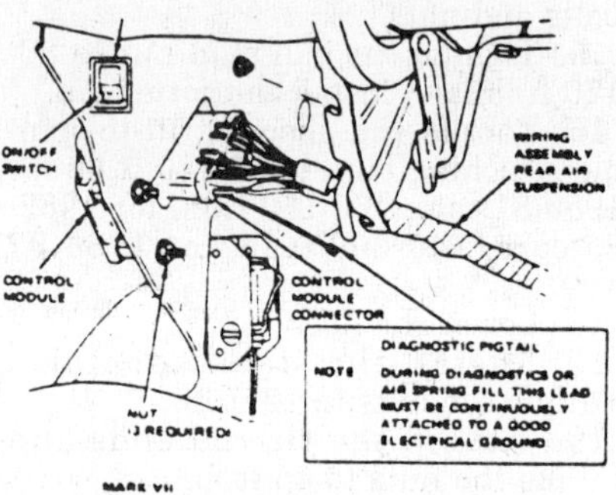

Air suspension cut-off switch – Mark VII

5. Pull the solenoid straight out slowly to the second stop to bleed air from the system.

CAUTION

Do not fully release solenoid until air is completely bled from the air spring.

6. After the air is fully bled from the system, rotate the solenoid counterclockwise to the third stop, and remove the solenoid from the air spring assembly.
7. Check the solenoid O-ring for abrasion or cuts. Replace O-ring as required. Lightly grease the O-ring area of solenoid with silicone dielectric compound WA-10, D7AZ-19A331-A or equivalent.
8. Insert the solenoid into the air spring end cap and rotate clockwise to the third stop, push into the second stop, then rotate clockwise to the first stop.
9. Install solenoid clip. Connect the air line and the electrical connector.
10. Refill the air spring(s). Install the wheel and tire assembly.

Air Spring Fill

1. Turn On the air suspension switch. Diagnostic pigtail is to be ungrounded.
2. Connect a battery charger to reduce battery drain.

3. Cycle the ignition from the Off to Run position, hold in the Run position for a minimum of five seconds, then return to the Off position. Driver's door is open with all other doors shut.

4. Change the diagnostic pigtail from an ungrounded state to a grounded state by attaching a lead from the diagnostic pigtail to vehicle ground. The pigtail must remain grounded during the spring fill sequence.

5. While applying the brakes, turn the ignition switch to the Run position. (The door must be open. Do not start the vehicle). The warning lamps will blink continuously once every two seconds to indicate the spring pump sequence has been entered.

6. To fill a rear spring(s), close and open the door twice. After a 6 second delay, the front spring will be filled for 60 seconds.

7. To fill a front spring(s), close and open the door twice. After a 6 second delay, the front spring will be filled for 60 seconds.

8. To fill rear and front spring, fill the rear spring first (step 6). When the rear fill has finished, close and open the door once to initiate the front spring fill.

9. Terminate the air spring fill by turning the ignition switch to Off, actuating the brake, or ungrounding the diagnostic pigtail. The diagnostic pigtail must be ungrounded at the end of the spring fill.

10. Lower vehicle and start engine. Allow the vehicle to level with doors closed.

Air Spring – Front or Rear

1. Turn the air suspension switch Off.

2. Raise and support the vehicle. Suspension must be at full rebound.

3. Remove tire and wheel assembly.

4. Remove the air spring solenoid.

5. Remove the spring to lower arm fasteners. Remove the clip for front spring and/or remove bolts for rear spring.

6. Push down on the spring clip on the collar of the air spring and rotate collar counterclockwise to release the spring from the body spring seat. Remove the air spring.

7. Install the air spring solenoid. Correctly position the solenoid. For LH installation (front or rear spring), the notch on the collar is to be in line with the centerline of the solenoid. For RH installation (front or rear), the flat on the collar is to be in line with the centerline of the solenoid.

8. Install the air spring into the body spring seat, taking care to keep the solenoid air and electrical connections clean and free of damage. Rotate the air spring collar until the spring clip snaps into place. Be sure that the air spring collar is retained by the three rolled tabs on the body spring seat.

9. Attach and secure the lower arm to spring attachment with suspension at full rebound and supported by the shock absorbers.

CAUTION

The air springs may be damaged is suspension is allowed to compress before spring is inflated.

10. Replace the tire and wheel assembly.

11. Lower the vehicle until the tire and wheel assembly are 1-3" (25-

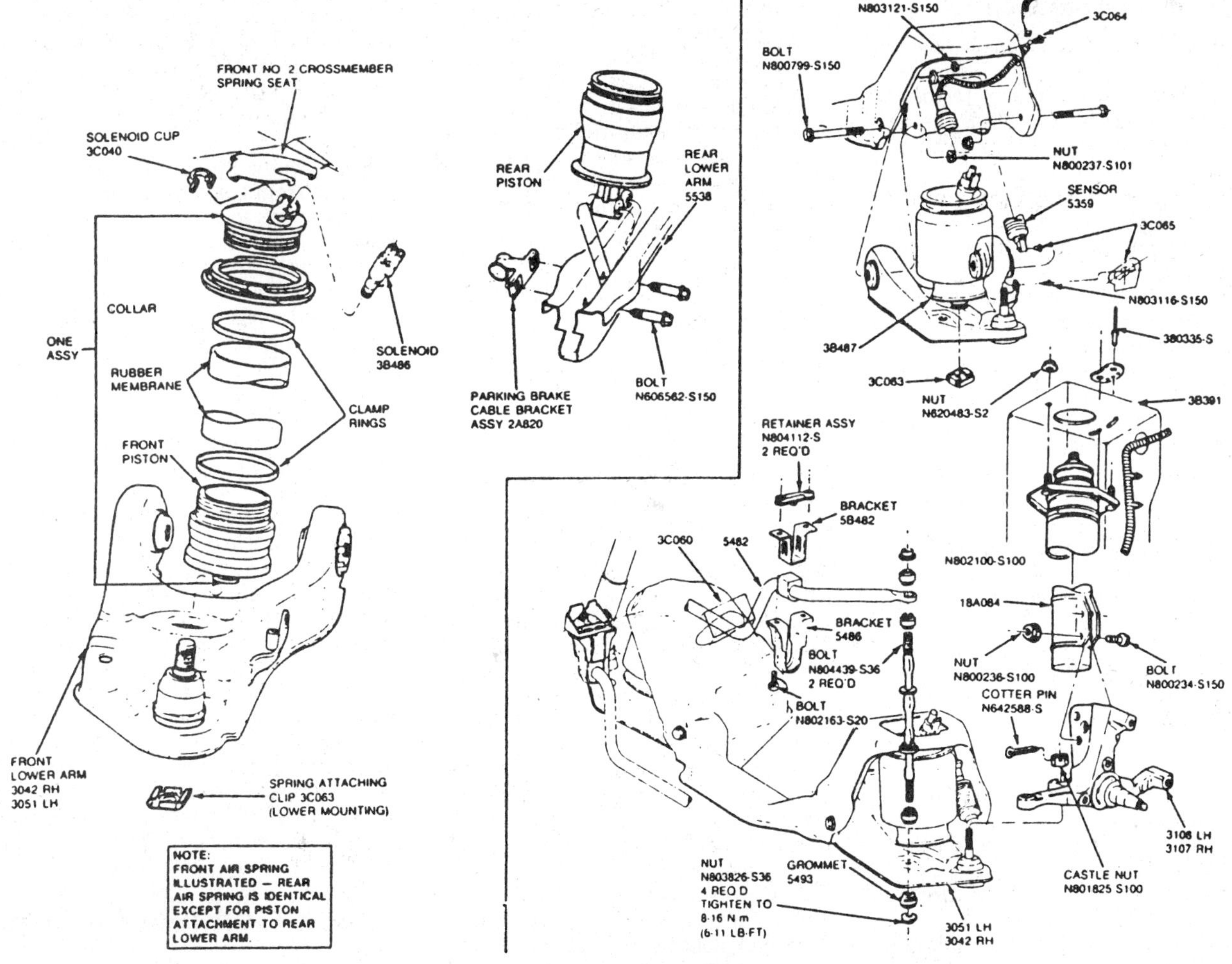

Air spring front suspension

75mm) above floor. Refill the air spring(s).

Air Compressor and Dryer Assembly

1. Turn the air suspension switch Off.
2. Disconnect the electrical connector located on the compressor.
3. Remove the air line protector cap form the dryer by releasing the two latching pins located on the bottom of the cap 180° apart.
4. Disconnect the four air lines from dryer.
5. Remove the three screws retaining the air compressor to mounting bracket.
6. Position the air compressor and dryer assembly to the mounting bracket and install the three mounting screws.
7. Connect the four air lines into the dryer.
8. Connect the electrical connection. Install the air line protector cap onto the dryer.
9. Turn the air suspension switch On.

Dryer, Air compression

1. Turn the air suspension switch Off.
2. Remove the air line protector cap from the dryer by releasing the two latching pins located on the bottom of the cap 180° apart.
3. Disconnect the four air lines from the dryer.
4. Remove the dryer retainer clip and screw.
5. Remove from the head assembly.
6. Check to ensure the old O-ring is not in the head assembly.
7. Check the dryer end to ensure new O-ring is in proper position.
8. Insert the dryer into the head assembly and install the retainer clip and screw.
9. Connect the four air liens into the dryer.
10. Install the air line protector cap onto the dryer.
11. Turn the air suspension switch On.

Mounting Bracket, Air Compressor

1. Turn the air suspension switch Off.
2. Remove the air compressor and dryer assembly.
3. Raise and support the vehicle on jackstands.
4. Remove the left front tire and wheel assembly.
5. Remove the left front inner fender liner.
6. Remove the three bolts attaching the mounting bracket to body side apron.
7. Position the mounting bracket to the body side apron with the two locating tabs.
8. Secure the three bolts attaching the bracket to the body side apron.
9. Install the left front inner fender liner.
10. Install the tire and wheel assembly.
11. Lower the vehicle.
12. Install compressor and dryer assembly. Turn the air suspension switch On.

Front Height Sensors

1. Turn the air suspension switch Off.
2. Disconnect the sensor electrical connector. The front sensor connectors are located in the engine compartment behind the shock towers.
3. Push the front sensor connector through the access hole in the rear of the shock tower.
4. Raise and support the vehicle on jackstands. Suspension must be at full rebound.
5. Disconnect the bottom and then the top end of the sensor from the attaching studs.
6. Disconnect the sensor wire harness from the plastic clips on the shock tower and remove sensor.
7. Connect the top and then the bottom end of the sensor to the attaching studs. Route the sensor electrical connector as required to connect to the vehicle wire harness.
8. Lower the vehicle. Connect the sensor connector. Turn the air suspension switch On.

Rear Height Sensor

1. Turn the air suspension switch Off.
2. Disconnect the electrical connector located in the luggage compartment in front of the forward trim panel. Also pull the luggage compartment carpet back for access to the sensor sealing grommet located on the floor pan.
3. Raise and support the vehicle on jackstands. Suspension must be at full rebound.
4. Disconnect the bottom and then the top end of the sensor from the attaching studs.
5. Push upwards on the sealing grommet to unseat and then push sensor through the floor pan hole into the luggage compartment.
6. Lower the vehicle.
7. Connect the sensor connector and then push sensor through the floor pan hole being sure to seat the sealing grommet. Replace the luggage compartment carpet.
8. Raise and support the vehicle on jackstands.
9. Connect the top and then the bottom end of the sensor. Lower the vehicle.
10. Turn the air suspension switch On.

Control Module

1. Turn the air suspension switch Off. Ignition switch is also to be Off.
2. Remove the left luggage compartment trim panel.
3. Disconnect the wire harness from the module.
4. Remove the three attaching nuts.
5. Remove the module.
6. Position the module and secure it with the three attaching nuts.
7. Connect the wire harness to the module.
8. Attach the left luggage compartment trim panel. Turn the air suspension switch On.

Nylon Air Line

If a leak is detected in an air line, it can be serviced by carefully cutting the line with a sharp knife to ensure a good, clean, straight cut. Then, install a service fitting. If more tube is required, it can be obtained in bulk. The four air lines are color coded to show which spring they are connecting, but do not require orientation at the air compressor dryer. A protective plastic cap and convoluted tube protect the air lines from the dryer rearward over the left shock tower in the engine compartment. Routing of the lines after exiting the protective tube follows:

- Left Front/Grey: Down and through the rear wall of the left shock tower to the air spring solenoid.
- Right Front/Black: To cowl and along cowl on the right side of the vehicle, forward and down through the rear wall of the right shock tower to the air spring solenoid.
- Left Rear/Green, Right Rear/Tan: Through the left side apron into the fender well, through the left upper dash panel (sealing grommet) into the passenger compartment, down the dash panel to the left rocker, along the rocker to the left rear fender well, over the fender well into the luggage compartment. The left air line goes down through the floor pan (sealing grommet) in front of the left rear shock tower. The right air line goes across the rear seat support and then down through the floor pan (sealing grommet) in front of the right rear shock tower.

Quick Connect Fittings

If a leak is detected in any of the eight quick connect fittings, it can be

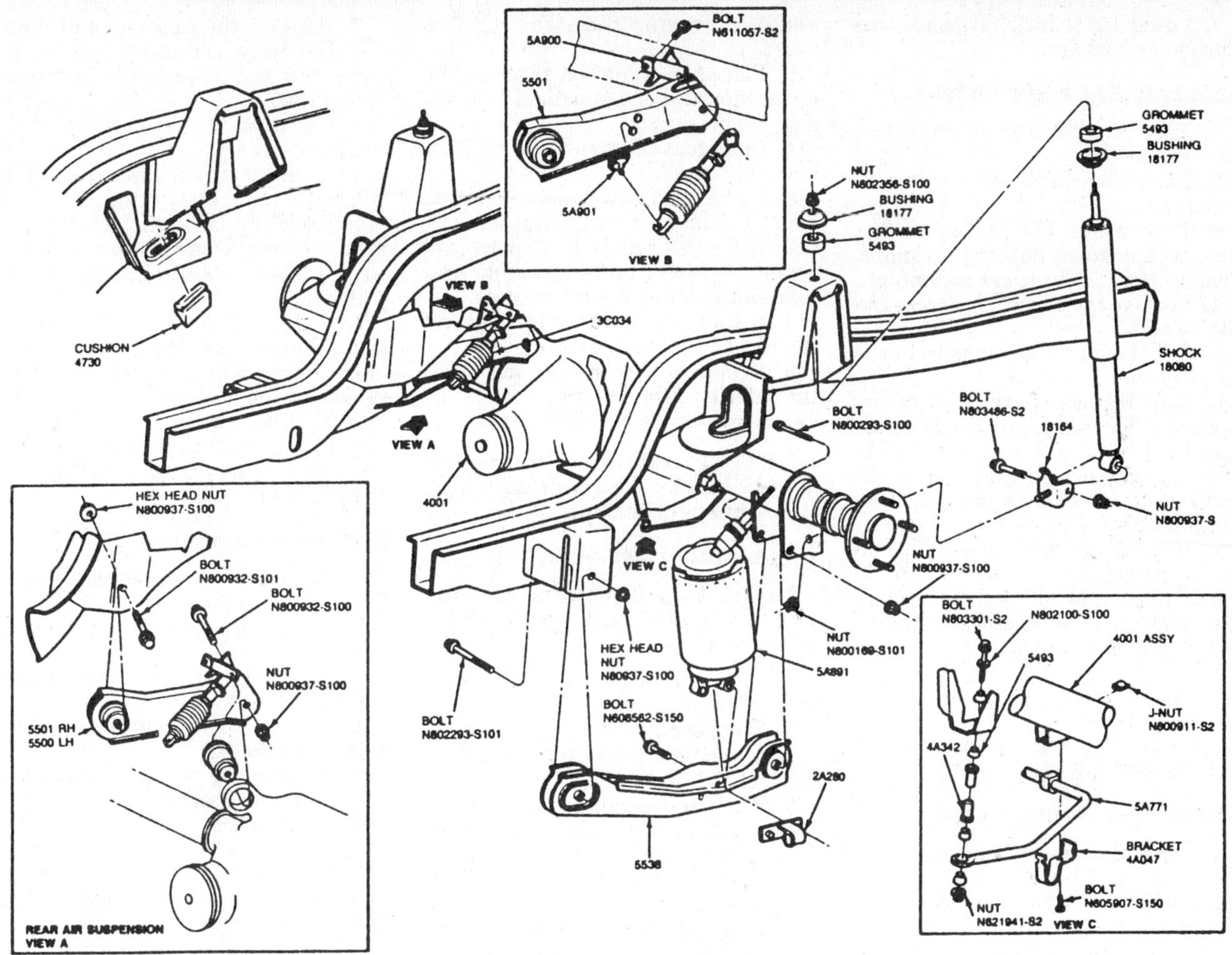

Air spring rear suspension

serviced using a repair kit containing a new O-ring, collet, release ring, and O-ring removal tool. The outer housing of the fitting cannot be serviced.

To remove the collet and O-ring, insert a scrap piece of air line, grasp the air line firmly (do not use pliers) and pull straight out (DO NOT use the release button). A force of 30-50 lbs. is required to remove the collet. After the retainer is removed, use the repair tool to remove the old O-ring.

To service, insert the new O-ring and seat it in the bottom of the fitting housing. The, insert the new collet, being sure the end with four prongs is inserted. Press the collet into position with finger pressure. Install the new release button.

O-ring Seals

The areas that have O-ring seals that can be serviced are:

- air compressor head to dryer: One O-ring.
- Air spring solenoid to end cap: Two O-rings each solenoid.
- Quick connect fitting: Four O-rings at the dryer, one O-ring at each spring.

If air leaks are detected in these areas, the components can be removed, following the procedures outlined in this Section, and new O-rings can be installed.

Air Suspension Switch

1. Disconnect the electrical connector.
2. Depress the retaining clips that retain the switch to the brace, and remove switch.
3. Push the switch into position in the brace, making sure retaining clips are fully seated.
4. Connect the electrical connector.

Compressor Relay

1. Disconnect the electrical connector.
2. Remove the screw retaining the relay to the left front shock tower and remove the relay.
3. Position the relay on the shock tower and install the retaining screw.
4. Connect the electrical connector.

FRONT SUSPENSION COMPONENTS

CAUTION

Power to the air system must be shut-off by turning the air suspension switch (in luggage compartment) Off or by disconnecting the battery when servicing any suspension components.

Stabilizer Bar Link Insulators

To replace the link insulator on each stabilizer link, use the following procedure:

1. Turn the air suspension switch Off.
2. Raise the vehicle and support on jackstands.
3. Remove the nut, washer, and insulator from the end of the stabilizer bar link attaching bolt.
4. Remove the bolt and the remaining washers, insulator and spacer.
5. Install the stabilizer bar link insulators by reversing the removal procedure.
6. Tighten the attaching nut.

7. Lower the vehicle. Turn air suspension system On.

Stabilizer Bar and/or Bushing

1. Turn the air suspension switch Off.
2. Raise the vehicle and support on jackstands.
3. Disconnect the stabilizer bar from each link and bushing U-clamps. Remove the stabilizer bar assembly.
4. Remove the adapter brackets and U-clamps.
5. Cut the worn bushings from the stabilizer bar.
6. Coat the necessary parts of the stabilizer bar with Ford Rubber Suspension Insulator Lubricant. E25Y-19553-A or equivalent, and slide bushings onto the stabilizer bar. Reinstall the U-clamps.
7. Reinstall the adapter brackets on the U-clamps.
8. Using a new nut and bolt, secure each end of the stabilizer bar to the lower suspension arm.
9. Using new bolts, clamp the stabilizer bar to the attaching brackets on the side rail.
10. Lower the vehicle. Turn air suspension switch On.

Shock Strut Replacement

1. Turn the air suspension switch Off.
2. Turn the ignition key to the unlocked position to allow free movement of the front wheels.
3. From the engine compartment, loosen but do not remove the one 16mm strut-to-upper mount attaching nut. A suitable tapered tool inserted in the slot will hold the rod stationary while loosening the nut. The vehicle should be raised and must not be driven with the nut loosened or removed.
4. Raise and support the vehicle. Position safety stands under the lower control arms as far outboard as possible being sure that the lower sensor mounting bracket is clear. Lower until vehicle weight is supported by the lower arms.
5. Remove tire and wheel assembly.
6. Remove the brake caliper and wire out of the way.
7. Remove the strut-to-upper mount attaching nut and then the two lower nuts and bolts attaching the strut to the spindle.

WARNING: The strut should be held firmly during the removal of the last bolt since the gas pressure will cause the strut to fully extend when removed.

8. Lift the strut up from the spindle to compress the rod and then remove the strut.
9. Prime the new strut by extending and compressing the strut rod five times.
10. Place the strut rod through the upper mount, hand start and secure a new 16mm nut.
11. Compress the strut, and position onto the spindle.
12. Install two new lower mounting bolts, and hand start the nuts.
13. Raise the vehicle to remove load from the lower control arms, and tighten the lower mounting nuts.
14. Install the brake caliper, install the tire and wheel assembly.
15. Remove safety stands and lower the vehicle to the ground.
16. Turn air suspension switch On.

NOTE: Front wheel alignment should be checked and adjusted, if out of specification.

Upper Mount Assembly

NOTE: Upper mounts are one piece units and cannot be disassembled.

1. Turn the air suspension system Off.
2. Turn the ignition key to the unlocked position to allow free movement of the front wheels.
3. From the engine compartment, loosen but do not remove the three 12mm upper mount retaining nuts. Vehicle should be in place over a hoist and must not be driven with these nuts removed. Do not remove the pop rivet holding the camber plate in position.
4. Loosen 16mm strut rod nut at this time.
5. Raise the vehicle and position safety stands under the lower control arms as far outboard as possible being sure that the lower sensor mounting bracket is clear. Lower until the vehicle weight is supported by the lower arms.
6. Remove the tire and wheel assembly.
7. Remove brake caliper and rotate out of position and wire securely out of the way.
8. Remove the upper mount retaining nuts and the two lower nuts and bolts that attach the strut to the spindle.

WARNING: The strut should be held firmly during the removal of the last bolt since the gas pressure will cause the strut to fully extend when removed.

9. Lift the strut up from the spindle to compress the rod, and then remove the strut.
10. Remove the upper mount from the strut.
11. Install a new upper mount on the strut and hand start a new 16mm nut.
12. Position the upper mount studs into the body and start and secure three new nuts. Secure the strut rod 16mm nut.
13. Compress the strut and position onto the spindle.
14. Install two new lower mounting bolts, and hand start nuts.
15. Raise the vehicle to remove load from the lower control arms and tighten the lower mounting nuts to 126-179 ft.lb.
16. Install the brake caliper. Install the tire and wheel assembly.
17. Remove safety stands and lower vehicle to the ground.
18. Turn air suspension switch On.
19. Front wheel alignment should be checked and adjusted if out of specification.

Spindle Assembly

1. Turn the air suspension switch Off.
2. Raise and support the vehicle on jackstands.
3. Remove the wheel and tire assembly.
4. Remove the brake caliper, rotor and dust shield.
5. Remove the stabilizer link from the lower arm assembly.
6. Remove the tie rod end from the spindle.
7. Remove the cotter pin from the ball joint stud nut, and loosen the nut one or two turns.

CAUTION

DO NOT remove the nut from the ball joint stud at this time.

8. Tap the spindle boss smartly to relieve stud pressure.
9. Place a floor jack under the lower arm, compress the air spring and remove the stud nut.
10. Remove the two bolts and nuts attaching the spindle to the shock strut. Compress the shock strut until working clearance is obtained.
11. Remove the spindle assembly.
12. Place the spindle on the ball joint stud, and install the new stud nut. DO NOT tighten at this time.
13. Lower the shock strut until the attaching holes are in line with the holes in the spindle. Install two new bolts and nuts.
14. Tighten ball joint stud nut and install cotter pin.
15. Lower the floor jack from under the suspension arm, and remove jack.
16. Tighten the shock strut to spindle attaching nuts.
17. Install stabilizer bar link and tighten attaching nut.
18. Attach the tie rod end, and tighten the retaining nut.
18. Attach the tie rod end, and tighten the retaining nut.

19. Install the disc brake dust shield, rotor, and caliper.
20. Install the wheel and tire assembly.
21. Remove the safety stands, and lower the vehicle.
22. Turn air suspension switch On.
23. Front wheel alignment should be checked and adjusted if out of specification.

Suspension Control Arm

1. Turn the air suspension switch Off.
2. Raise the vehicle and support on jackstands, so the control arms hang free (full rebound).
3. Remove the wheel and tire assembly.
4. Disconnect the tie rod assembly from the steering spindle.
5. Remove the steering gear bolts, if necessary, and position the gear so that the suspension arm bolt may be removed.
6. Disconnect the stabilizer bar link from the lower arm.
7. Disconnect the lower end of the height sensor from the lower control arm sensor mounting stud. Remove the sensor mounting stud and unscrew from lower arm, noting the position of stud on the lower arm bracket.
8. Remove the cotter pin from the ball joint stud nut, and loosen the ball joint nut one or two turns. DO NOT remove the nut at this time. Tap the spindle boss smartly to relieve stud pressure.
9. Vent the air spring(s) to atmospheric pressure. Then, reinstall the solenoid.
10. Remove the air spring to lower arm fastener clip.
11. Remove the ball joint nut, and raise the entire strut and spindle assembly (strut, rotor, caliper and spindle). Wire it out of the way to obtain working room.
12. Remove the suspension arm to crossmember nuts and bolts. and remove the arm from the spindle.
13. Position the arm into the crossmember and install new arm to crossmember bolts and nuts. DO NOT tighten at this time.
14. Remove the wire from the strut and spindle assembly and attach to the ball joint stud. Install a new ball joint stud nut. DO NOT tighten at this time.
15. Position the air spring in the arm and install a new fastener.
16. Attach the sensor mounting stud and screw to lower arm in the same position as original arm location. Connect the lower end of sensor to the lower arm mounting stud.
17. With a suitable jack, raise the suspension arm to curb height.
18. With the jack still in place, tighten the lower arm to crossmember attaching nut to 150-180 ft.lb.
19. Tighten ball joint stud nut to 100-120 ft.lb., and install a new cotter pin. Remove jack.
20. Install the steering gear to crossmember bolts and nuts (if removed). Hold the bolts, and tighten nuts to 90-100 ft.lb.
21. Position the tie rod assembly into the steering spindle, and install the retaining nut. Tighten the nut to 35 ft.lb., and continue tightening the nut to align the next castellation with cotter pin hole in the stud. Install a new cotter pin.
22. Connect the stabilizer bar link to the lower suspension arm, and tighten the attaching nut to 9-12 ft.lb.
23. Install the wheel and tire assembly, and lower the vehicle but DO NOT allow tires to touch the ground.
24. Turn the air suspension switch On.
25. Refill the air spring(s).
26. Front wheel alignment should be checked and adjusted if out of specification.

REAR SUSPENSION

Shock Absorber

CAUTION

Power to the air system must be shut-off by turning the air suspension switch (in luggage compartment) Off or by disconnecting the battery when servicing any suspension components.

1. Turn the air suspension switch Off.
2. Open the luggage compartment and remove inside trim panels to gain access to the upper shock stud.
3. Loosen but do not remove the shock rod attaching nut.
4. Raise the vehicle and position two safety stands under the rear axle. Lower the vehicle until weight is supported by the rear axle.
5. Remove the upper attaching nut, washer and insulator and then remove the lower shock protective cover (right shock only) and lower shock absorber cross bolt and nut from the lower shock brackets.
6. From under the vehicle, compress the shock absorber to clear it from the hold in the upper shock tower.

CAUTION

Shock absorbers will extend unassisted. Do not apply heat or flame to the shock absorber tube during removal.

7. Remove the shock absorber.
8. Prime the new shock absorber by extending and compressing shock absorber five times.
9. Place the inner washer and insulator on the upper attaching stud. Position stud through shock tower mounting hole and position an insulator, washer on stud from the luggage compartment. Hand start the attaching nut and then secure.
10. Place the shock absorber's lower mounting eye between the ears of the lower shock mounting bracket, compressing shock as required. Insert the bolt, (bolt head must seat on the inboard side of the shock bracket), through the shock bracket and the shock absorber mounting eye. Hand start and then secure the original attaching nut.
11. Install the protective cover, to the right shock absorber. This is done by inserting the bolt point and nut into the cover's open end, sliding the cover over the shock bracket, and snapping the closed end of the cover over the bolt head. Properly installed, the cover will completely conceal the bolt point, nut, and bolt head. The rounded or closed end of the cover should be pointing inboard.
12. Raise the vehicle and remove safety stands from under axle, then lower the vehicle.
13. Reinstall the inside trim panels.
14. Turn air suspension switch On.

Lower Control Arm

NOTE: If one arm requires replacement, replace the other arm also.

1. Turn the air suspension switch Off.
2. Raise and support the vehicle so that the suspension will be at full rebound.
3. Remove tire and wheel assembly.
4. Vent air spring(s) to atmospheric pressure. Then, reinstall the solenoid.
5. Remove the two air spring-to-lower arm bolts and remove the air spring from the lower arm.
6. Remove the frame-to-arm and the axle-to-arm bolts and remove the arm from the vehicle.
7. Position the lower arm assembly into the front arm brackets, and insert a new, arm-to-frame pivot bolt and nut with nut facing outwards. DO NOT tighten at this time.
8. Position the rear bushing in the axle bracket and install a new arm-to-axle pivot bolt and nut with nut facing outwards. DO NOT tighten at this time.
9. Install two new air spring-to-arm bolts. DO NOT tighten at this time.
10. Using a suitable jack, raise the axle to curb height. Tighten the lower arm front bolt, the rear pivot bolt, and the air spring-to-arm bolt being sure

that the air spring piston is flat on the lower arm. Remove the jack.

11. Replace tire and wheel assembly.
12. Lower the vehicle.
13. Turn the air suspension switch On.
14. Refill the air spring(s).

Upper Control Arm and Axle Bushing

NOTE: If one arm requires replacement, replace the other arm also.

1. Turn the air suspension switch Off.
2. Raise and support the vehicle so that the suspension will be at full rebound.
3. On the right side detach rear height sensor from side arm. Note position of the sensor adjustment bracket on the upper arm.
4. Remove the upper arm-to-axle pivot bolt and nut.
5. Remove the upper arm-to-frame pivot bolt and nut. Remove upper arm from vehicle.

If upper arm axle bushing is to be replaced, use Tool T78P-5638-A or equivalent and the following procedure:

6. Place the upper arm axle bushing remover tool in position and remove the bushing assembly.
7. Using the installer tool, install the bushing assembly into the bushing ear of the rear axle.
8. Place the upper arm into the bracket of body side rail. Insert a new upper arm-to-frame pivot bolt and nut (nut facing outboard). DO NOT tighten at this time.
9. Align the upper arm-to-axle pivot hole with the hole in the axle bushing. If required, raise the axle using a suitable jack to align. Install a new pivot bolt and nut (nut inboard). DO NOT tighten at this time.
10. On the right side, attach rear height sensor to the arm. Set the adjustment bracket to the same position as on the replaced arm and tighten nut.
11. Using a suitable jack, raise the axle to curb height, and tighten the front upper arm bolt, and the rear upper arm bolt.
12. Remove the jackstands supporting the axle.
13. Lower the vehicle.
14. Turn the air suspension switch On.

Stabilizer Bar Link Insulators

1. Turn the air suspension switch Off.
2. Raise and support the vehicle on jackstands.
3. Remove the nut, washer and insulator from the end of the stabilizer bar link attaching bolt.
4. Remove the bolt and the remaining spacer, washer and insulators.
5. Install the stabilizer bar link insulators by reversing the removal procedure. A new bolt and nut must be used.
6. Tighten the attaching nut.
7. Lower the vehicle.
8. Turn the air suspension switch On.

Stabilizer Bar Bushings

1. Turn the air suspension switch Off.
2. Raise and support the vehicle on jackstands.
3. Disconnect the stabilizer bar from each link and bushing U-clamp. Remove the stabilizer bar assembly.
4. Remove the U-clamps.
5. Cut the worn bushings from the stabilizer bar.
6. Coat the necessary parts of the stabilizer bar with Ford Rubber Suspension Insulator Lubricant E25Y-19553-A or equivalent and slide new bushings onto the stabilizer bar. Reinstall U-clamps.
7. Using new bolts and nuts, attach stabilizer bar to the axle. Do not tighten bolts at this time.
8. Using new bolts and nuts, attach the link end of the stabilizer bar to the body. Tighten the link attaching nut and then the axle attaching bolts.
9. Lower the vehicle.
10. Turn the air suspension switch On.

WHEEL ALIGNMENT

Except MacPherson Strut

NOTE: The procedure for checking and adjusting front wheel alignment requires specialized equipment and professional skills. The following descriptions and adjustment procedures are for general reference only.

Front wheel alignment is the position of the front wheels relative to each other and to the vehicle. It is determined, and must be maintained to provide safe, accurate steering with minimum tire wear. Many factors are involved in wheel alignment and adjustments are provided to return those that might change due to normal wear to their original value. The factors which determine wheel alignment are dependent on one another; therefore, when one of the factors is adjusted, the others must be adjusted to compensate.

Descriptions of these factors and their affects on the car are provided below.

NOTE: Do not attempt to check and adjust the front wheel alignment without first making a thorough inspection of the front suspension components.

CAMBER

Camber angle is the number of degrees that the centerline of the wheel inclined from the vertical. Camber reduces loading of the outer wheel bearing and improves the tire contact patch while cornering.

CASTER

Caster angle is the number of degrees that a line drawn through the steering knuckle pivots is inclined from the vertical, toward the front or rear of the car (when viewed from the side of the car). Caster improves the directional stability and decreases susceptibility to crosswinds or road surface deviations.

TOE-IN

Toe-in is the difference of the distance between the centers of the front and rear of the front wheels. It is most commonly measured in inche[illegible] but is occasionally referred to as an [illegible]le between the wheels. Toe-in is necessary to compensate for the tendency of the wheels to deflect rearward while in motion. Due to this tendency, the wheels of a vehicle, with properly adjusted toe-in, are traveling straight forward when the vehicle itself is traveling straight forward, resulting in directional stability and minimum tire wear.

Steering wheel spoke misalignment is often an indication of incorrect front end alignment. Care should be exercised when aligning the front end to maintain steering wheel spoke position. When adjusting the tie rod ends, adjust each an equal amount (in the opposite direction) to increase or decrease toe-in. If, following toe-in adjustment, further adjustments are necessary to center the steering wheel spokes, adjust the tie rod ends an equal amount in the same direction.

ADJUSTMENT PROCEDURES

Install Ford Tool T65P-3000-D, or its equivalent, on the frame rail, position the hooks around the upper control arm pivot shaft, and tighten the adjusting nuts slightly. Loosen the pivot shaft retaining bolts to permit adjustment.

To adjust caster, loosen or tighten either the front or rear adjusting nut. After adjusting caster, adjust the camber by loosening or tightening both nuts an equal amount. Tighten the shaft retaining bolts to specifications, remove the tool, and recheck the adjustments.

Adjust toe-in by loosening the clamp bolts, and turning the adjuster sleeves at the outer ends of the tie rod. Turn the sleeves an equal amount in the opposite direction, to maintain steering wheel spoke alignment.

MacPherson Strut

The caster and camber are set at the factory and cannot be changed. Only the toe is adjustable.

TOE ADJUSTMENT

Toe is the difference in width (distance), between the front and rear inside edges of the front tires.

1. Turn the steering wheel, from left to right, several times and center.

NOTE: If car has power steering, start the engine before centering the steering wheel.

2. Secure the centered steering wheel with a steering wheel holder, or any device that will keep it centered.
3. Release the tie rod end bellows clamps so the bellows will not twist while adjustment is made. Loosen the jam nuts on the tie rod ends. Adjust the left and right connector sleeves until each wheel has one-half of the desired toe setting.

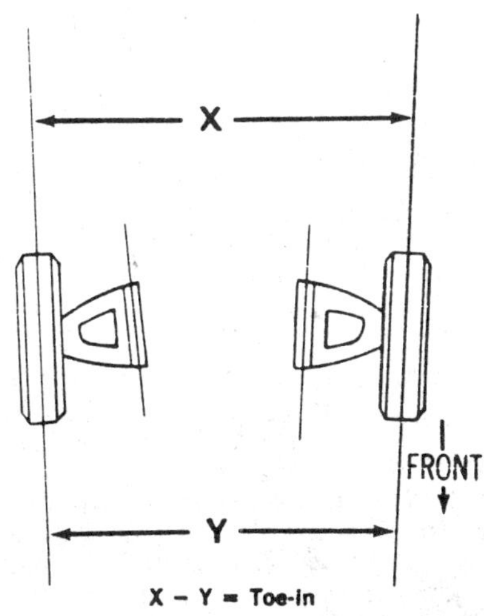

Toe-in

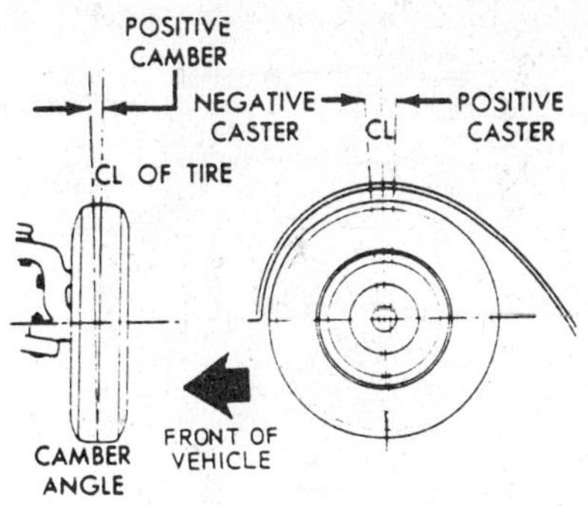

Caster and camber angles

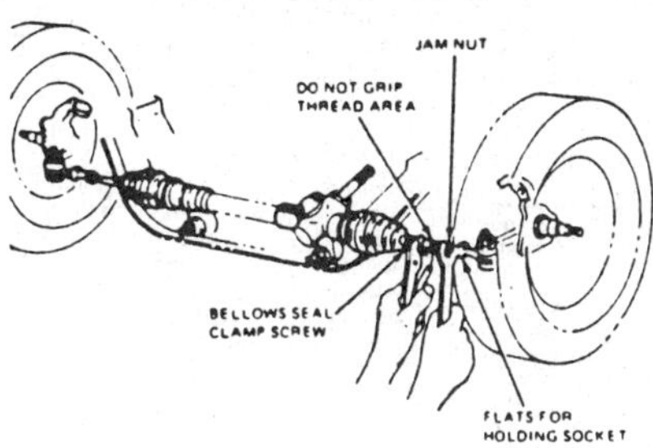

Toe adjustment on MacPherson strut front ends

4. After the adjustment has been made, tighten the jam nuts and secure the bellows clamps. Release the steering wheel lock and check for steering wheel center. Readjust, if necessary until steering wheel is centered and toe is within specs.

REAR SUSPENSION

NOTE: Refer to previous Air Suspension section for procedures on models so equipped.

Coil Spring

REMOVAL & INSTALLATION

Spring Between Axle Housing and Frame

1. Place a jack under the rear axle housing. Raise the vehicle and place jackstands under the frame side rails.
2. Disconnect the lower studs of the shock absorbers from the mounting brackets on the axle housing.
3. Lower the axle housing until the springs are fully seated.
4. Remove the springs and insulators from the vehicle.
5. Place the insulators in each upper seat and position the springs between the upper and lower seats.
6. With the springs in position, raise the axle housing until the lower studs of the rear shock absorbers reach the mounting brackets on the axle housing. Connect the lower studs and install the attaching nuts.
7. Remove the jackstands and lower the vehicle.

Spring Between Lower Control Arm and Frame

NOTE: If one spring must be replaced, the other should be replaced also. If the car has a stabilizer bar, the bar must be removed first.

1. Raise and support the car at the rear crossmember, while supporting the axle with a jack.
2. Lower the axle until the shocks are fully extended.
3. Place a jack under the lower arm pivot bolt. Remove the pivot bolt and nut. Carefully and slowly lower the arm until the spring load is relieved.
4. Remove the spring and insulators.
5. To install, tape the insulator in place in the frame, and place the lower insulator in place on the arm. Install the internal damper in the spring.
6. Position the spring in place and slowly raise the jack under the lower arm. Install the pivot bolt and nut, with the nut facing outwards. Do not tighten the nut.
7. Raise the axle to curb height, and tighten the lower pivot bolt to 70-100 ft.lb.
8. Install the stabilizer bar, if removed. The proper torque is 20-27 ft.lb. Remove the crossmember stands and lower the car.

TURN DOWNWARD TO INCREASE ROD LENGTH

TURN UPWARD TO DECREASE ROD LENGTH

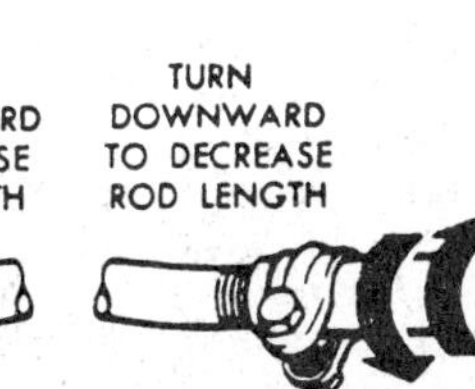

TURN UPWARD TO INCREASE ROD LENGTH

LEFT-HAND SLEEVE

RIGHT-HAND SLEEVE

Tie-rod (toe-in) adjustments

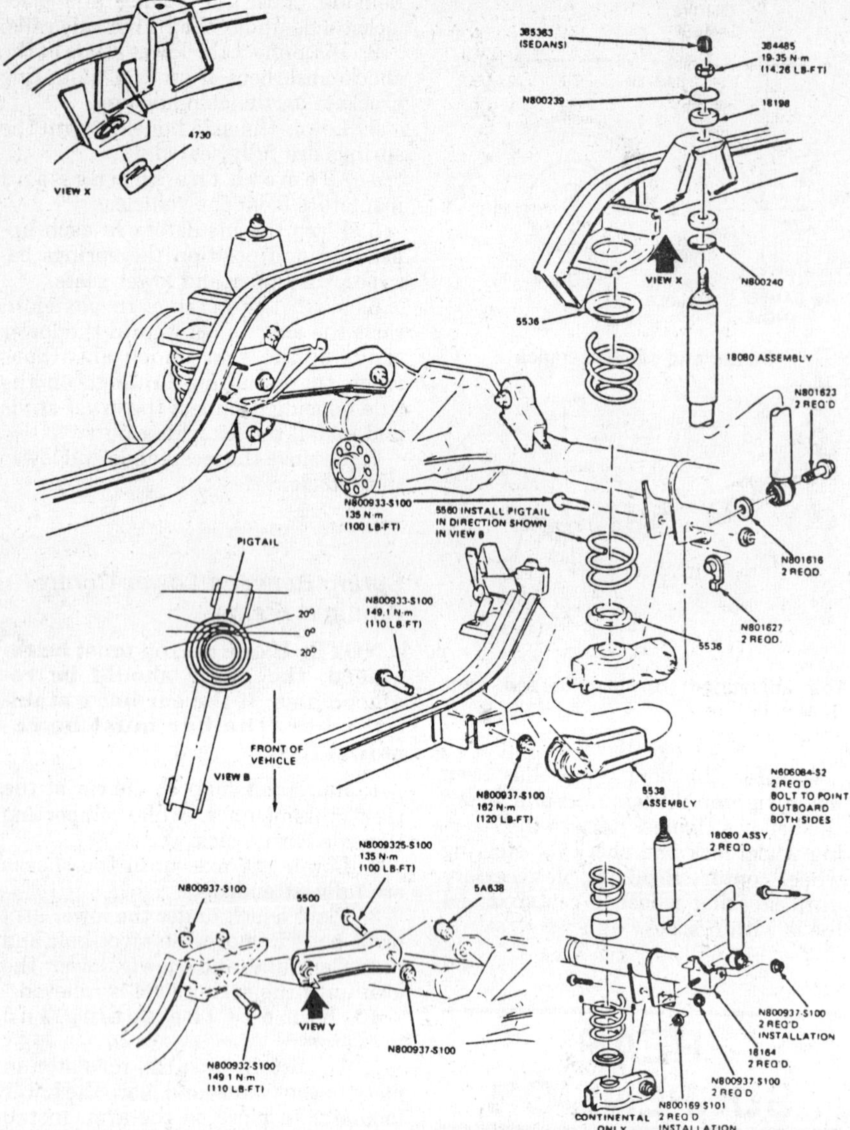

Rear suspension used on the 1980-85 Continental and Mark VII and 1980-86 Thunderbird and Cougar

Leaf Springs

REMOVAL & INSTALLATION

1. Raise the vehicle and place supports beneath the underbody and axle.
2. Disconnect the lower end of the shock absorber and position it out of the way. Remove the supports from under the axle.
3. Remove the spring plate nuts from the U-bolt and remove the spring plate. With a jack, raise the rear axle just enough to remove the weight of the housing from the spring.
4. Remove the two rear shackle attaching nuts, the shackle bar, and the two inner bushings.
5. Remove the rear shackle assembly and the two outer bushings.
6. Remove the nut from the spring mounting bolt and tap the bolt out of the bushing at the front hanger. Lift out the spring assembly.

NOTE: All used attaching components (nuts, bolts, etc.) must be discarded and replaced with new ones prior to assembly. Bushings may be lubricated with soap and water to ease bolt installation; do not use grease or oil.

7. Position the leaf spring under the axle housing and insert the shackle assembly into the rear hanger bracket and the rear eye of the spring.
8. Install the shackle inner bushings, the shackle plate, and the locknuts. Hand tighten the locknuts.
9. Position the spring eye in the front hanger, slip the washer on the front hanger bolt, and, from the inboard side, insert the bolt through the hanger and eye. Install the locknut on the hanger bolt finger-tight.
10. Lower the rear axle housing so that it rests on the spring. Place the spring plate on the U-bolt and tighten the nuts.
11. Attach the lower end of the shock absorber to the spring plate using a new nut.
12. Place jackstands under the rear axle. Lower the vehicle until the spring is in the approximate curb load position, and tighten the front hanger locknut.
13. Tighten the rear shackle locknuts.
14. Remove the jackstands and lower the vehicle.

Shock Absorber

REMOVAL & INSTALLATION

NOTE: Purge a new shock of air by repeatedly extending it in its normal position and compressing it while inverted.

Spring Between Axle Housing and Frame

1. Raise the vehicle and install jackstands.
2. Remove the shock absorber outer attaching nut, washer and insulator from the stud at the top side of the spring upper seat. Compress the shock sufficiently to clear the spring seat hole, and remove the inner insulator and washer from the upper attaching stud.
3. Remove the locknut and disconnect the shock absorber lower stud at the mounting bracket on the axle housing. Remove the shock absorber.
4. Position a new inner washer and insulator on the upper attaching stud. Place the upper stud in the hole in the upper spring seat. While maintaining the shock in this position, install a new outer insulator, washer, and nut on the stud from the top side of the spring upper seat.
5. Extend the shock absorber. Locate the lower stud in the mounting bracket hole on the axle housing and install the locknut.

Spring Between Lower Control Arm and Frame

1. Remove the upper attaching nut, washer, and insulator. Access is through the trunk on sedans or side panel trim covers on station wagons and hatchbacks. Sedan studs have rubber caps.
2. Raise the car. Compress the

shock to clear the upper tower. Remove the lower nut and washer; remove the shock.

3. Purge the shock of air and compress. Place the lower mounting eye over the lower stud and install the washer and a new locking nut. do not tighten the nut yet.

4. Place the insulator and washer on the upper stud. Extend the shock, install the stud through the upper mounting hole.

5. Torque the lower mounting nut to 40-55 ft.lb.

6. Lower the car. Install the outer insulator and washer on the upper stud, and install a new nut. Tighten to 14-26 ft.lb. Install the trim panel on station wagons and hatchbacks or the rubber cap on sedans.

With Leaf Springs

1. Remove the lower end of the shock absorber from the spring plate.

2. Remove the nut retaining the upper end of the shock absorber to the mounting bracket underneath the car.

3. Compress and remove the shock absorber. Discard the nuts.

4. Transfer the washers and bushings to the new shock absorber. Insert the upper stud through the mounting bracket, and install a new attaching nut finger-tight.

5. Compress and install the shock absorber to the spring plate. Install the washer, bushings, and attaching nuts.

6. Tighten the upper and lower attaching nuts.

Sway (Stabilizer) Bar

REMOVAL & INSTALLATION

1. Raise and support the rear end on jackstands.

2. Remove the 4 stabilizer bar-to-lower arm bolts.

3. Remove the stabilizer bar.

4. Installation is the reverse of removal. Torque the new bolts to 20 ft.lb. on 1980-81 cars; 45-50 ft.lb. on 1982-87 cars.

Rear Control Arms

REMOVAL & INSTALLATION

1. Raise and support the vehicle on jackstands positioned on the rear frame pads.

2. Position a floor jack under the rear axle and raise slightly. Position jackstands at both ends of the axle to support the axle weight.

3. Position a jack under the lower arm pivot bolt and raise to support. Remove the pivot bolt and nut.

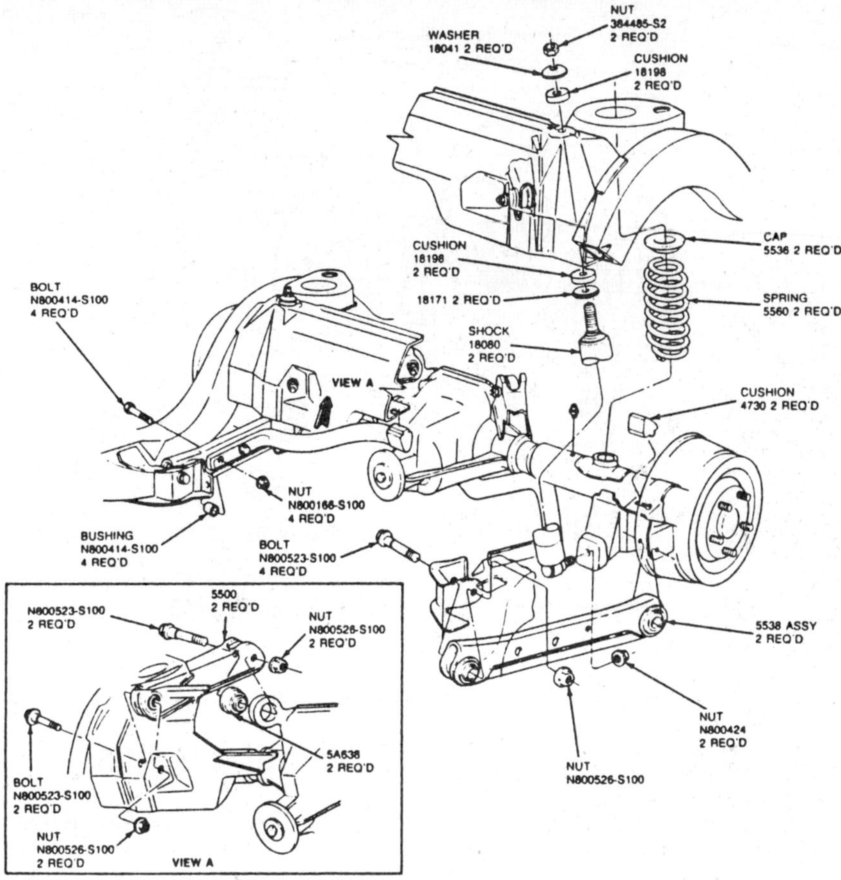

Rear suspension used on the 1986-87 Continental and Mark VII and 1987 Thunderbird and Cougar

4. Lower the jack slowly and remove the coil spring. Remove the control arm.

5. Install the control arm in the reverse order of removal.

STEERING COLUMN SERVICE

Steering Wheel

REMOVAL & INSTALLATION

1. Open the hood and disconnect the negative cable from the battery.

2. On models with safety crash pads, remove the crash pad attaching screws from the underside of the steering wheel spoke and remove the pad. On all models equipped with a horn button, remove the horn button or ring by pressing down evenly and turning it counterclockwise approximately 20° and then lifting it from the steering wheel. On 1981 and later models, pull straight out on the hub cover. Disconnect the horn wires from the crash pad on models so equipped.

3. Remove and discard the nut from the end of the shaft. Install a steering wheel puller on the end of the shaft and remove the wheel.

CAUTION

The use of a knock-off type steering wheel puller or the use of a hammer on the steering shaft will damage the collapsible column.

4. Lubricate the upper surface of the steering shaft upper bushing with white grease. Transfer all serviceable parts to the new steering wheel.

5. Position the steering wheel on the shaft so that the alignment marks line up. Install a locknut and torque it to 30-40 ft.lb. Connect the horn wires.

6. Install the horn button or ring by turning it clockwise or install the crash pad.

Turn Signal Switch

REPLACEMENT

1. Remove the four screws retaining the steering column shroud.

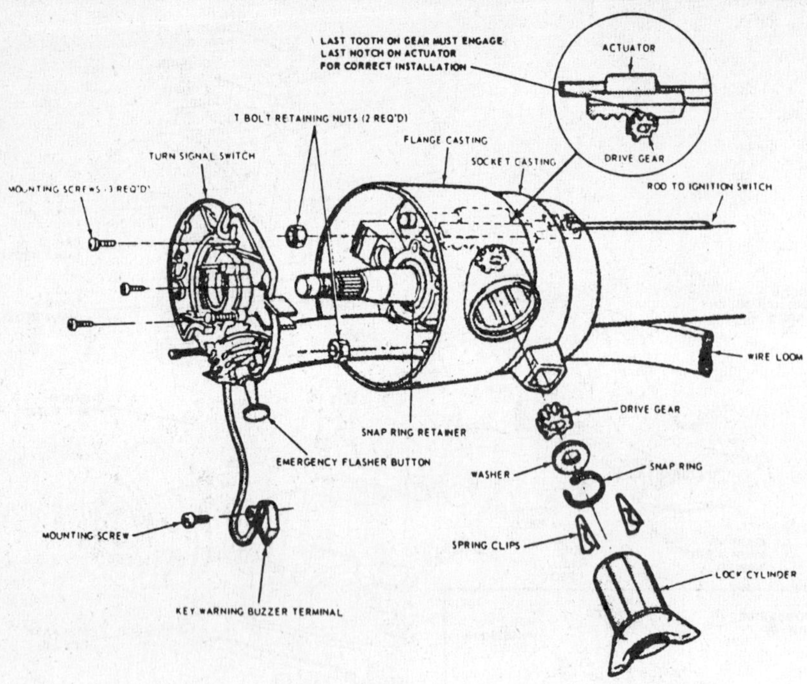

Turn signal switch and lock cylinder on fixed columns

2. Remove the turn signal lever by pulling and twisting straight out.
3. Peel back the foam shield. Disconnect the two electrical connectors.
4. Remove the two attaching screws and disengage the switch from the housing.
5. To install, position the switch to the housing and install the screws. Stick the foam to the switch.
6. Install the lever by aligning the key and pushing the lever fully home.
7. Install the two electrical connectors, test the switch, and install the shroud.

Ignition Switch

REMOVAL & INSTALLATION

1980-81

1. Disconnect the battery ground.
2. On tilt columns, remove the upper extension shroud by unsnapping the shroud from the retaining clip at the 9 o'clock position.
3. Remove the trim shroud halves.
4. Disconnect the switch wiring.
5. Drill out the break-off head bolts attaching the switch to the lock cylinder with a ⅛" drill bit.
6. Remove the remainder of the bolts with a screw extractor.
7. Disengage the switch from the actuator pin.

To install:

8. Slide the switch carrier to the switch lock position. Insert a $^{7}/_{16}$" drill bit shank through the switch housing and into the carrier, thereby, preventing any movement. New replacement switch already have a pin installed for this purpose.
9. Turn the key to the LOCK position and remove the key.
10. Position the switch on the actuator pin.
11. Install new break-off bolts and hand tighten them.
12. Push the switch towards the steering wheel, parallel with the column, to remove any slack between the bolts and the switch slots.
13. While holding the switch in this position, tighten the bolts until the heads break off.
14. Remove the drill bit or packaging pin.
15. Connect the wiring.
16. The remainder of installation is the reverse of removal.

1982-87

1. Disconnect the battery ground.
2. On tilt columns, remove the upper extension shroud by unsnapping the shroud from the retaining clip at the 9 o'clock position.
3. Remove the trim shroud halves.
4. Disconnect the switch wiring.
5. On 1982-85 cars, drill out the break-off head bolts attaching the switch to the lock cylinder with a ⅛" drill bit. Remove the remainder of the bolts with a screw extractor.
6. On 1986-87 cars, remove the bolts securing the switch to the lock cylinder housing.
7. Disengage the switch from the actuator pin.

To install:

8. Slide the switch carrier to the ON RUN position. New replacement switches will be in this position.
9. Turn the key to the ON RUN position.
10. Position the switch on the actuator pin.
11. On 1982-85 cars, install new break-off bolts and hand tighten them.

    On 1986-87 cars, install the bolts and tighten them to 50-60 in.lb.
12. Push the switch towards the steering wheel, parallel with the column, to remove any slack between the bolts and the switch slots.
13. While holding the switch in this position, tighten the bolts until the heads break off.

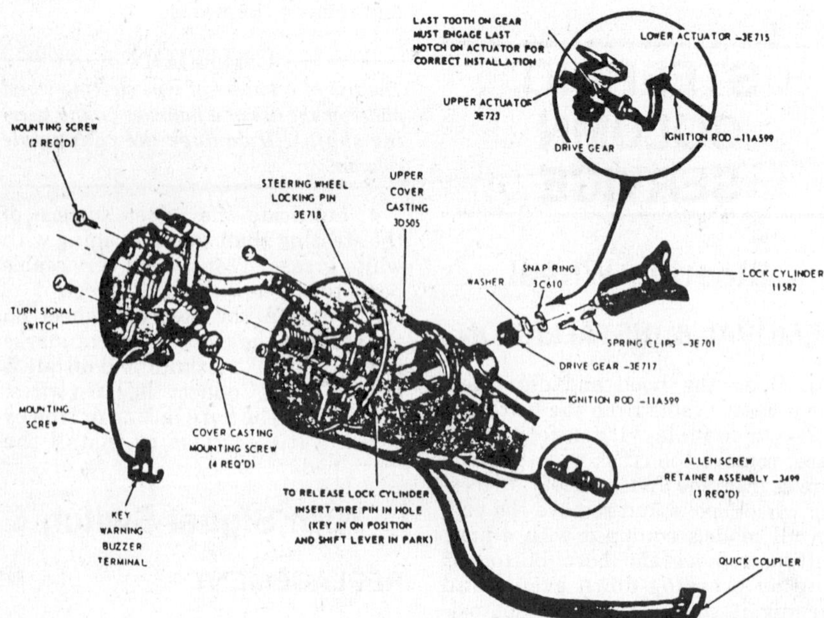

Turn signal switch and lock cylinder on tilt columns

14. Remove the drill bit or packaging pin.
15. Connect the wiring.
16. The remainder of installation is the reverse of removal.

Ignition Lock Cylinder

REMOVAL & INSTALLATION FUNCTIONAL LOCK CYLINDER

1. Disconnect the battery ground.
2. On tilt columns, remove the upper extension shroud by unsnapping the shroud from the retaining clip at the 9 o'clock position.
3. Remove the trim shroud halves.
4. Unplug the wire connector at the key warning switch.
5. Place the shift lever in PARK and turn the key to RUN.
6. Place a ⅛" wire pin in the hole in the casting surrounding the lock cylinder and depress the retaining pin while pulling out on the cylinder.
7. When installing the cylinder, turn the lock cylinder to the RUN position and depress the retaining pin, then insert the lock cylinder into its housing in the flange casting. Assure that the cylinder is fully seated and aligned in the interlocking washer before turning the key to the OFF position. This will allow the cylinder retaining pin to extend into the cylinder cast housing hole.
8. The remainder of installation is the reverse of removal.

REMOVAL & INSTALLATION NON-FUNCTIONING LOCK CYLINDER

1. Disconnect the battery ground.
2. Remove the steering wheel.
3. On tilt columns, remove the upper extension shroud by unsnapping the shroud from the retaining clip at the 9 o'clock position.
4. Remove the steering column trim shrouds.
5. Disconnect the wiring at the key warning switch.
6. Using a ⅛" drill bit, mounted in a right angle drive drill adapter, drill out the retaining pin, going no deeper than ½" (12.7mm).
7. Tilt the column to the full down position. Place a chisel at the base of the ignition lock cylinder cap and using a hammer break away the cap from the lock cylinder.
8. Using a ⅜" drill bit, drill down the center of the ignition lock cylinder key slot about 1¾" (44mm), until the lock cylinder breaks loose from the steering column cover casting.

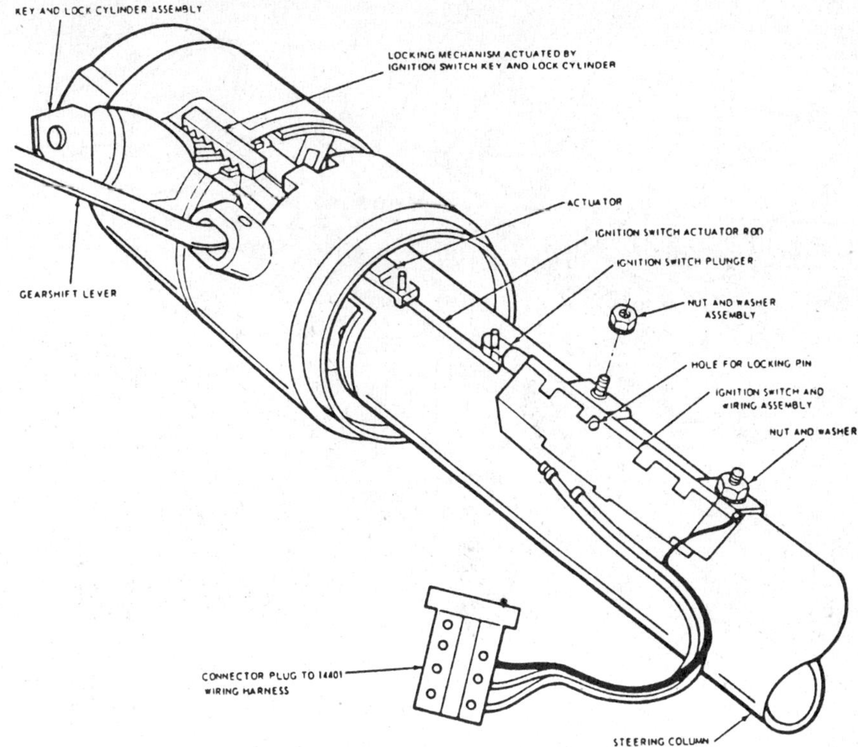

Ignition switch assembly

9. Remove the lock cylinder and the drill shavings from the housing.
10. Remove the upper bearing snapring washer and steering column lock gear.
11. Carefully inspect the steering column housing for signs of damage from the previous operation. If any damage is apparent, the components should be replaced.
12. Installation is the reverse of removal.

Steering Column

REMOVAL & INSTALLATION

1. Disconnect the battery ground.

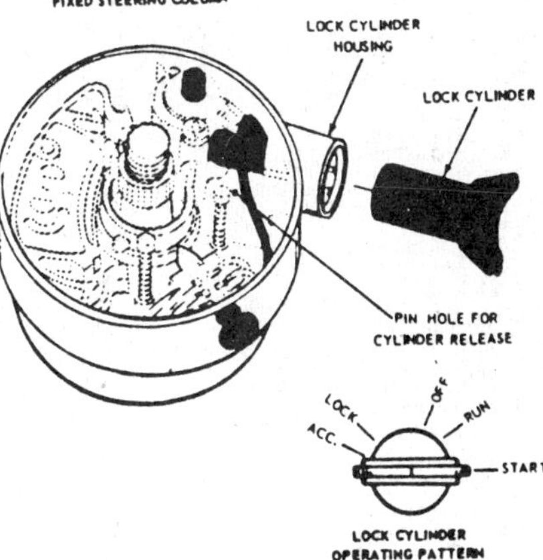

Lock cylinder replacement

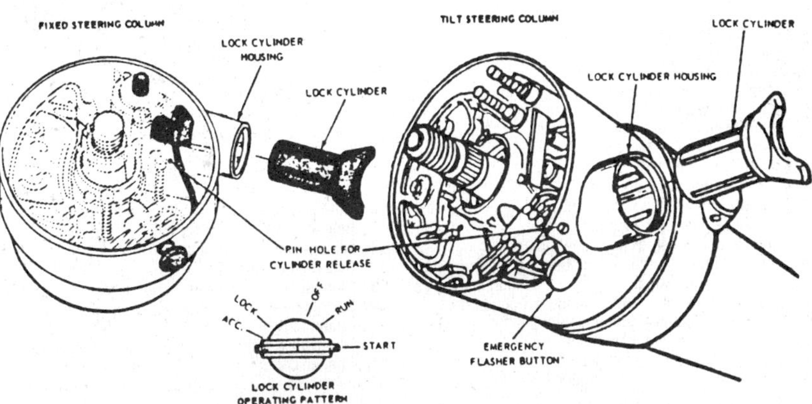

Lock cylinder replacement on locking type column

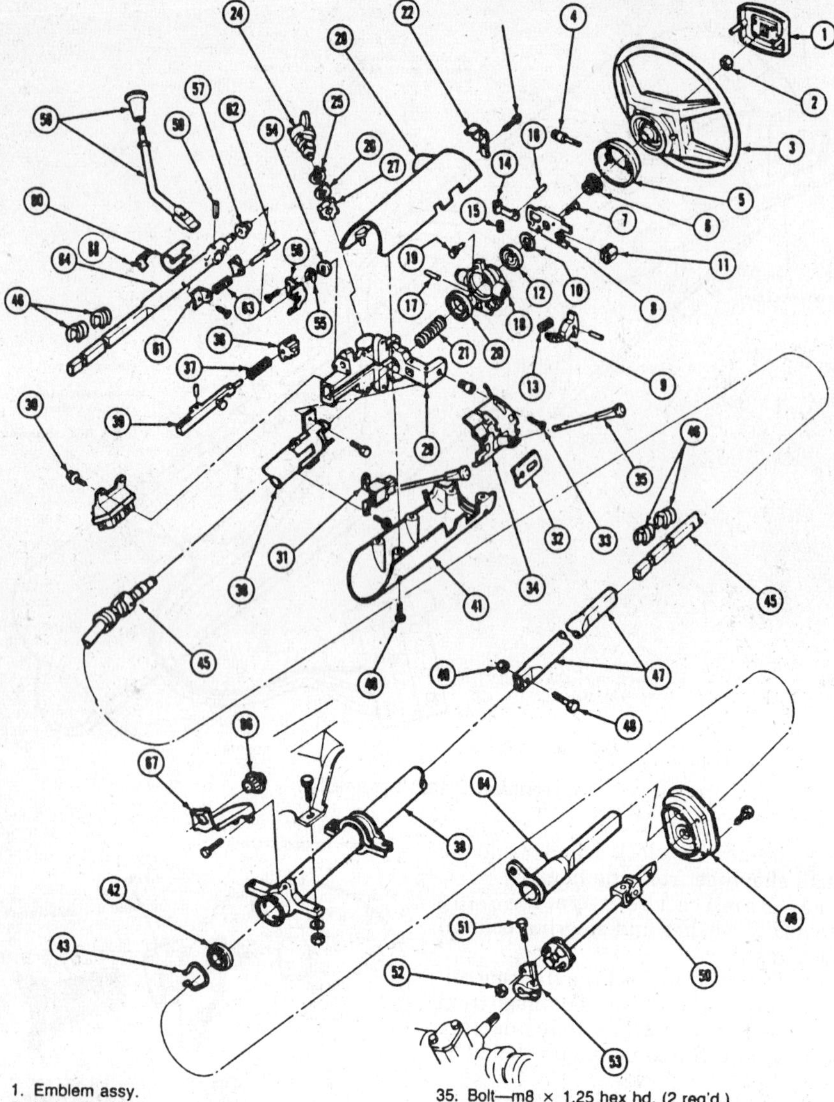

1. Emblem assy.
2. Nut—3/8-18 hex
3. Wheel assy.—stng.
4. Lock cyl.—(body)
5. Key—(body)
6. Ring
7. Bearing
8. Gear—stng. col. lock
9. Shroud—upper
10. Bolt (break off head) (2 req'd.)
11. Switch assy.—ignition
12. Nut—7/16-14 hex lock
13. Shaft assy.—stng. col. lower
14. Bolt—3/8-24 × 1.22
15. Flange—stng. shaft lower
16. Nut—3/8-16 hex lock
17. Cam—turn sig. turn off
18. Lock—stng. col. position
19. Shaft—stng. gear upper
20. Anti-rattle clips (4 req'd.)
21. Shaft—stng. gear lower
22. Bolt—7/16-14 × 1.50 hex
23. Pawl—stng. col. lock
24. Spring—stng. col. lock
25. Actuator assy.—stng. col. lock
26. Housing—stng. col. lock cyl.
27. Bearing assy.—stng. gear shaft lower
28. Ring—stng. gear shaft lower bearing retainer
29. Boot assy.—stng. col.
30. Screw—no. 8-18 × .62 pan hd. tap (2 req'd.)
31. Retainer—stng. col. upper bearing
32. Retainer—stng. col. upper bearing
33. Sleeve—stng. col. upper bearing
34. Bearing assy.—stng. col. upper
35. Bolt—m8 × 1.25 hex hd. (2 req'd.)
36. Tube assy.—col. outer
37. Wash/wipe switch & screws (body)
38. Bracket & cable assy.—trans. cont. selector (body)
39. Screw—no. 8-18 × .62 pan hd. tap (2 req'd.)
40. Handle & shank assy.—turn sig. switch
41. Shroud—stng. col. lower
42. Screw—no. 8-18 × 1.50 pan hd. tap (4 req'd.)
43. Pin—5mm spring coiled
44. Lever assy.—trans. cont. selector
45. Cover—trans. cont. sel. lever opening
46. Tube assy.—trans. cont. selector
47. Bracket—trans. gear shift support
48. Bushing—trans. gear shift shaft
49. Arm—trans. cont. selector
50. Insulator—stng. gear shaft
51. Seal—stng. gear shaft
52. Ring—5/16 retainer (external)
53. Washer—8.23 flat
54. Insert—trans. control selector position
55. Bearing—trans. gear shift lever socket
56. Screw—m5—0.8 × 12.5 flat head (3 req'd.)
57. Retainer—stng. col. lever (2 req'd.)
58. Screw 4mm—0.7 × 12.7 type "D" oval (2 req'd.)
59. Nut—5/16-18 hex prevail torque (2 req'd.)
60. Bolt—5/16-18 × 1.50 flg. pilot (2 req'd.)
61. Lever—trans. gear shift selector
62. Screw—no. 8—32 × .50 hex wshr. hd.
63. Plunger—trans. control selector lever
64. Spring—trans. control selector lever return
65. Foam cover
66. Screw (4 req'd.)
67. Spacer clip
68. Switch assy.—turn signal

1980-81 column shift steering column with tilt wheel

2. Unbolt the flexible coupling from the steering input shaft.
3. Disengage the safety strap and bolt from the flexible coupling.
4. Disconnect the transmission shift rod from the control selector lever.

NOTE: Column-type automatic transmission linkage use oil impregnated plastic grommets to connect the rods and levers. Whenever a grommet-type connection is changed, the grommets should be replaced.

5. Remove the steering wheel.
6. Remove the steering column trim shrouds.
7. Remove the steering column cover.
8. Remove the hood release lever.
9. Disconnect all electrical and vacuum connections at the column.
10. Loosen the 4 nuts securing the column to the brake pedal support bracket, allowing the column to be lowered enough to access the selector lever cable and cable. Don't lower the column too far or damage to the lever and/or cable will occur!
11. Reach between the column and instrument panel and gently lift off the selector cable from the pin on the lever.
12. Remove the cable clamp from the steering column tube.
13. Remove the 4 dust boot-to-dash panel screws.
14. Remove the 4 nuts attaching the column to the brake pedal support.
15. Lower the column to clear the 4 mounting bolts and pull the column out.

To install:

16. Position the column in the car.
17. Install the column collar-to-brake pedal support nuts loosely.
18. Install the selector cable clamp loosely.
19. Attach the cable to the lever pin.
20. Tighten the 4 column-to-brake pedal support nuts to 35 ft.lb.
21. Move the shift selector to the DRIVE position, against the drive stop. Rotate the selector bracket clockwise or counterclockwise until the selector pointer in the cluster centers on the letter **D**. Tighten the bracket nut.
22. Connect the electrical and vacuum connectors.
23. Install the safety strap and bolt on the flange on the steering input flange.
24. Install the 2 nuts connecting the steering shaft to the flexible coupling. Tighten the nuts to 35 ft.lb. The safety strap must be properly positioned to avoid metal-to-metal contact. The flexible coupling must not be distorted when the nuts are tightened. Pry the

shaft up or down to allow a ± ⅛" (3mm) insulator flatness.

25. Connect the shift rod to the shift lever on the lower end of the steering column. Make sure the grommet is replaced.

26. The remainder of installation is the reverse of removal. Adjust the shift linkage.

RECIRCULATING BALL STEERING LINKAGE

Pitman Arm

REMOVAL & INSTALLATION

1. Raise and support the front end on jackstands.
2. Remove the cotter pin and nut securing the center link to the Pitman arm.
3. Using a tie rod end separator, disconnect the center link from the Pitman arm.
4. Matchmark the Pitman arm and steering gear.
5. Remove the nut securing the Pitman arm to the steering gear shaft.
6. Using a puller, remove the Pitman arm from the gear shaft.
7. Position the wheels in the straight ahead position.
8. Align the matchmarks on the Pitman arm and gear. Some cars will have blind teeth on both the gear shaft and Pitman arm for alignment. Position the Pitman arm on the gear shaft and install the lockwasher and nut. Torque the nut to 236-250 ft.lb.
9. Connect the center link and Pitman arm. Torque the nut to 45 ft.lb. and install a new cotter pin. Always tighten the nut to align the cotter pin hole.

Idler Arm

REMOVAL & INSTALLATION

1. Raise and support the front end on jackstands.
2. Remove the cotter pin, nut and washer attaching the center link to the idler arm.
3. Unbolt the idler arm and bracket from the frame.
4. Installation is the reverse of removal. Install all fasteners loosely until all fasteners are installed. Torque the idler arm bracket-to-frame bolts to 50 ft.lb.; the idler arm-to-center link nut to 70 ft.lb.

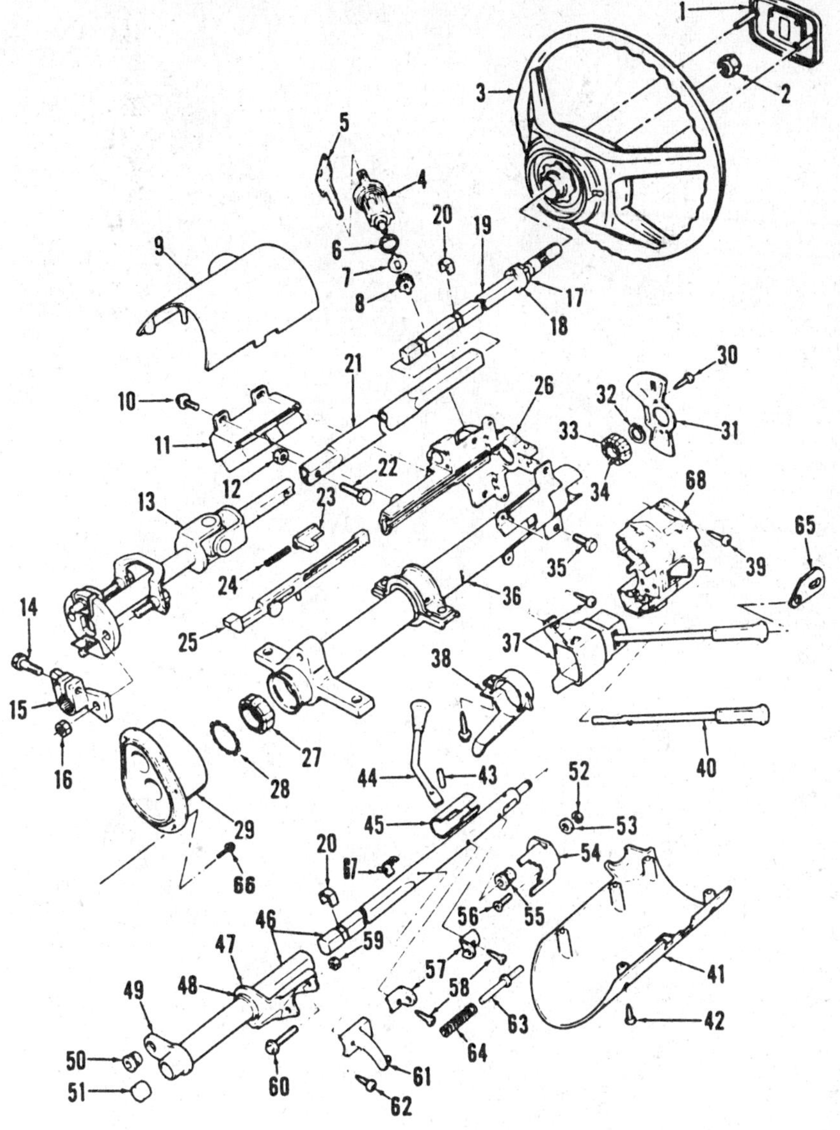

1. Emblem assy.
2. Bolt
3. Wheel assy.—strng.
4. Handle & shank assy. tilt strng. wheel lever
5. Extension—strng. col. shroud
6. Spring—strng. col. upper bearing
7. Screw
8. Plate strng. col. clip retainer
9. Lever strng. col. link
10. Ring ¾ retaining type
11. Clip—strng. col. shroud
12. Bearing assy.—strng. col. upper
13. Pin 4mm × 25.6 straight round end
14. Release lever
15. Spring—strng. col. release lever
16. Pin—4mm × 5.75
17. Pivot pin
18. Flange casting
19. Bumpers
20. Bearing assy.—strng. col. upper
21. Position spring
22. Cover—strng. col. lock actuator
23. Screw no. 8-18 × .62 pan head tapping
24. Lock cyl. (body)
25. Ring 24 × 1.07 retainer type
26. Bearing
27. Gear—strng. col. lock
28. Shroud—upper
29. Housing—strng. col. lock cyl.
30. Bolt (break off head) (2 req'd.)
31. Wash/wipe switch & screws (body)
32. Foam cover—turn signal & w/w switch
33. Screw no. 8-18 × .62 pan head tap (2 req'd.)
34. Turn signal switch
35. Handle & shank assy.—turn sig. switch
36. Pawl—strng. col. lock
37. Spring—strng. col. lock
38. Tube assy. col. outer
39. Actuator assy.—strng. col. lock
40. Screw no. 8-18 × 1.50 pan head tap (5 req'd.)
41. Shroud—strng. col. lower
42. Bearing assy.—strng. gear shaft lower
43. Ring—strng. gear shaft lower bearing retainer
44. Boot assy.—strng. col.
45. Shaft assy.—strng. col. upper
46. Anti-rattle clips (2 req'd.)
47. Shaft—strng. gear lower
48. Bolt 7/16-14 × 1.50 hex
49. Nut 7/16-14 hex lock
50. Shaft assy.—strng. col. lower
51. Bolt—⅜-24 × 1.22
52. Nut ⅜-16 hex lock
53. Flange—strng. shaft lower
54. Lever—strng. col. lock actuator
55. Spring—strng. col. lock
56. Knob—strng. col. lock actuator
57. Screw—strng. wheel

1981-84 non-tilt column shift used on Thunderbird, Cougar and XR-7

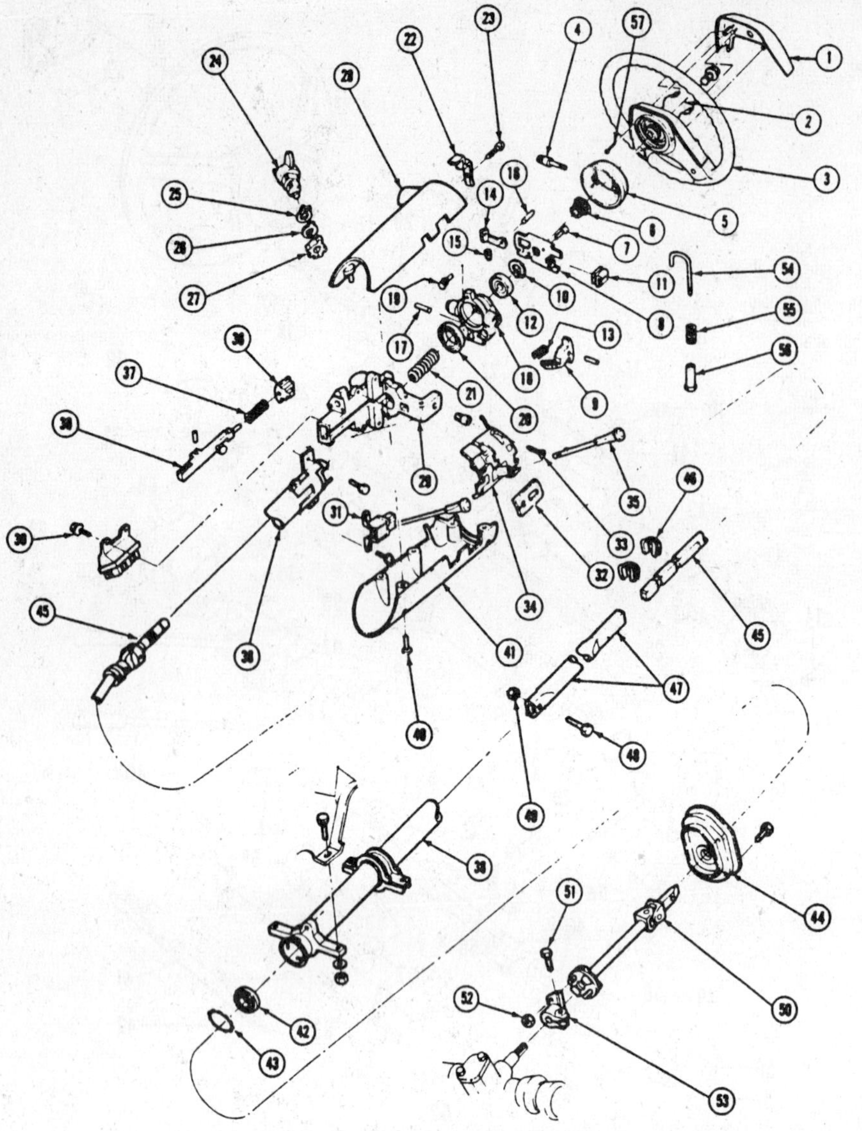

1. Emblem assy.
2. Nut 5/8-18 hex.
3. Wheel assy.—strng.
4. Handle & shank assy. tilt strng. wheel lever
5. Extension—strng. col. shroud
6. Spring—strng. col. upper bearing
7. Screw
8. Plate strng. col. clip retainer
9. Lever strng. col. link
10. Ring 3/4 retaining type
11. Clip—strng. col. shroud
12. Bearing assy.—strng. col. upper
13. Pin 4mm × 25.6 straight round end
14. Release lever
15. Spring—strng. col. release lever
16. Pin—4mm × 5.75
17. Pivot pin
18. Flange casting
19. Bumpers
20. Bearing assy.—strng. col. upper
21. Position spring
22. Cover—strng. col. lock actuator
23. Screw no. 8-18 × .62 pan head tapping
24. Lock cyl. (body)
25. Ring 24 × 1.07 retainer type
26. Bearing
27. Gear—strng. col. lock
28. Shroud—upper
29. Housing—strng. col. lock cyl.
30. Bolt (break off head) (2 req'd.)
31. Wash/wipe switch & screws (body)
32. Foam cover—turn signal & w/w switch
33. Screw no. 8-18 × .62 pan head tap (2 req'd.)
34. Turn signal switch
35. Handle & shank assy.—turn sig. switch
36. Pawl—strng. col. lock
37. Spring—strng. col. lock
38. Tube assy. col. outer
39. Actuator assy.—strng. col. lock
40. Screw no. 8-18 × 1.50 pan head tap (5 req'd.)
41. Shroud—strng. col. lower
42. Bearing assy.—strng. gear shaft lower
43. Ring—strng. gear shaft lower bearing retainer
44. Boot assy.—strng. col.
45. Shaft assy.—strng. col. upper
46. Anti-rattle clips (2 req'd)
47. Shaft—strng. gear lower
48. Bolt 7/16-14 × 1.50 hex
49. Nut 7/16-14 hex lock
50. Shaft assy.—strng. col. lower
51. Bolt—3/8-24 × 1.22
52. Nut 3/8-16 hex lock
53. Flange—strng. shaft lower
54. Lever—strng. col. lock actuator
55. Spring—strng. col. lock
56. Knob—strng. col. lock actuator

Tilt steering column with floor shift for 1985-86 Thunderbird, Cougar and Mark VII

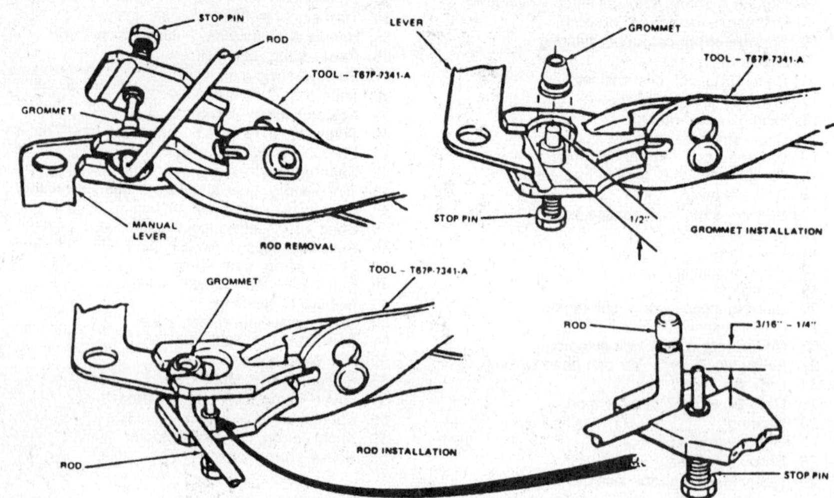

Replacing a shift lever grommet

Center Link

REMOVAL & INSTALLATION

1. Raise and support the front end on jackstands.
2. Remove the cotter pins and nuts attaching the inner connecting rod ends to the center link.
3. Using a tie rod end separator, disconnect the inner rod ends from the center link.
4. Remove the cotter pin and nut attaching the idler arm to the center link.
5. Remove the cotter pin and nut attaching the Pitman arm to the center link.
6. Installation is the reverse of removal. Install all fasteners loosely until all fasteners are installed. Torque

the connecting rod ends to 45 ft.lb.; idler arm to 70 ft.lb.; Pitman arm to 45 ft.lb.

Tie Rod Ends

REMOVAL & INSTALLATION

1. Raise and support the front end.
2. Remove the cotter pin and nut from the rod end ball stud.
3. Loosen the sleeve and clamp bolts and remove the rod end from the spindle arm center link using a ball joint separator.
4. Remove the rod end from the sleeve, counting the exact number of turns required.
5. Install the new end using the exact number of turns it took to remove the old one.
6. Install all parts. Torque the stud to 40-43 ft.lb. and the clamp to 20-22 ft.lb.
7. Check the toe-in.

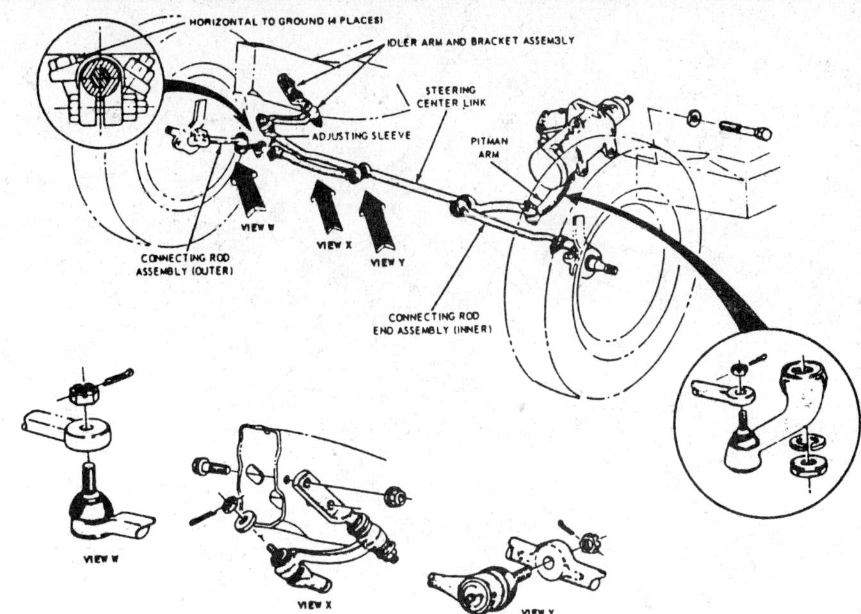

Recirculating ball power steering linkage

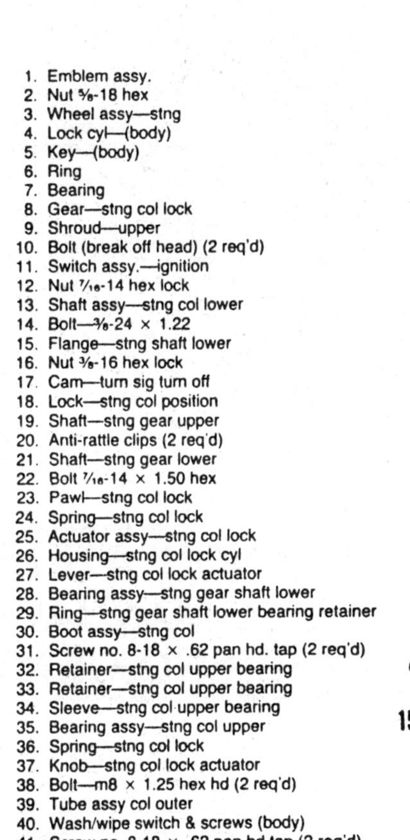

1. Emblem assy.
2. Nut ⅝-18 hex
3. Wheel assy—stng
4. Lock cyl—(body)
5. Key—(body)
6. Ring
7. Bearing
8. Gear—stng col lock
9. Shroud—upper
10. Bolt (break off head) (2 req'd)
11. Switch assy.—ignition
12. Nut 7/16-14 hex lock
13. Shaft assy—stng col lower
14. Bolt—⅜-24 × 1.22
15. Flange—stng shaft lower
16. Nut ⅜-16 hex lock
17. Cam—turn sig turn off
18. Lock—stng col position
19. Shaft—stng gear upper
20. Anti-rattle clips (2 req'd)
21. Shaft—stng gear lower
22. Bolt 7/16-14 × 1.50 hex
23. Pawl—stng col lock
24. Spring—stng col lock
25. Actuator assy—stng col lock
26. Housing—stng col lock cyl
27. Lever—stng col lock actuator
28. Bearing assy—stng gear shaft lower
29. Ring—stng gear shaft lower bearing retainer
30. Boot assy—stng col
31. Screw no. 8-18 × .62 pan hd. tap (2 req'd)
32. Retainer—stng col upper bearing
33. Retainer—stng col upper bearing
34. Sleeve—stng col upper bearing
35. Bearing assy—stng col upper
36. Spring—stng col lock
37. Knob—stng col lock actuator
38. Bolt—m8 × 1.25 hex hd (2 req'd)
39. Tube assy col outer
40. Wash/wipe switch & screws (body)
41. Screw no. 8-18 × .62 pan hd tap (2 req'd)
42. Handle & shank assy—turn sig switch
43. Shroud—stng col lower
44. Screw no. 8-18 × 1.50 pan hd tap (5 req'd)
45. Foam cover
46. Screw (4 req'd)

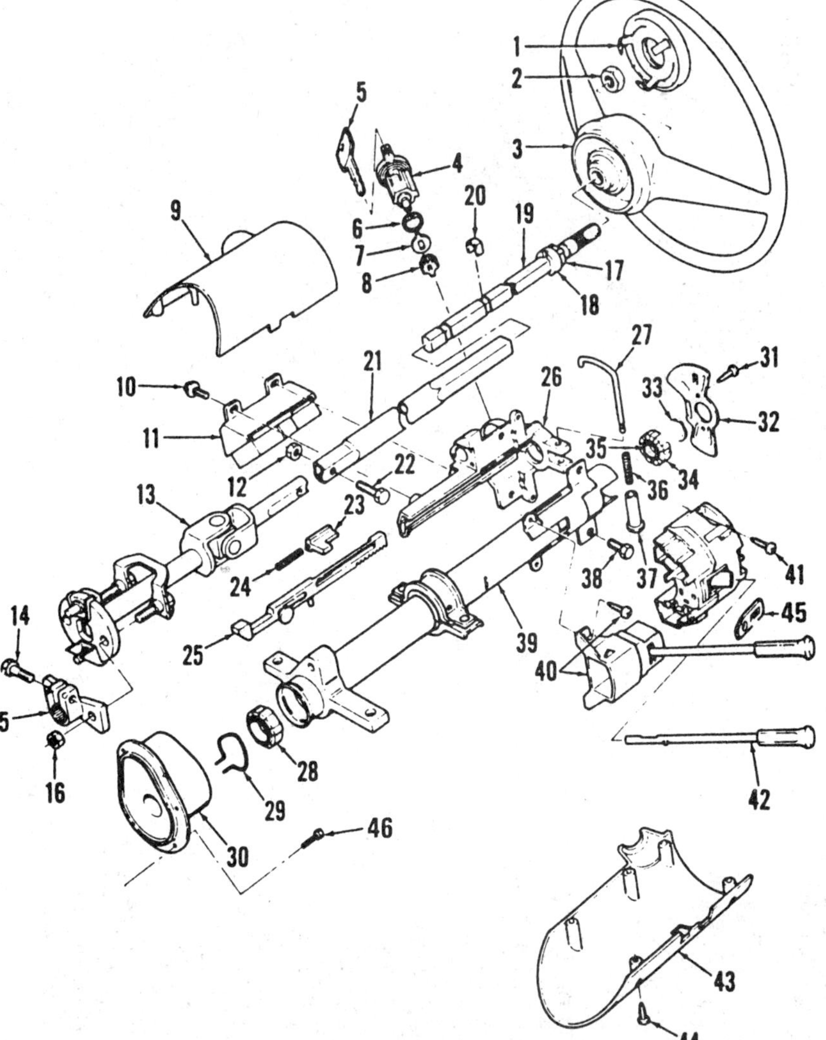

Extruded absorber type column for 1981-82 Cougar with floor shift

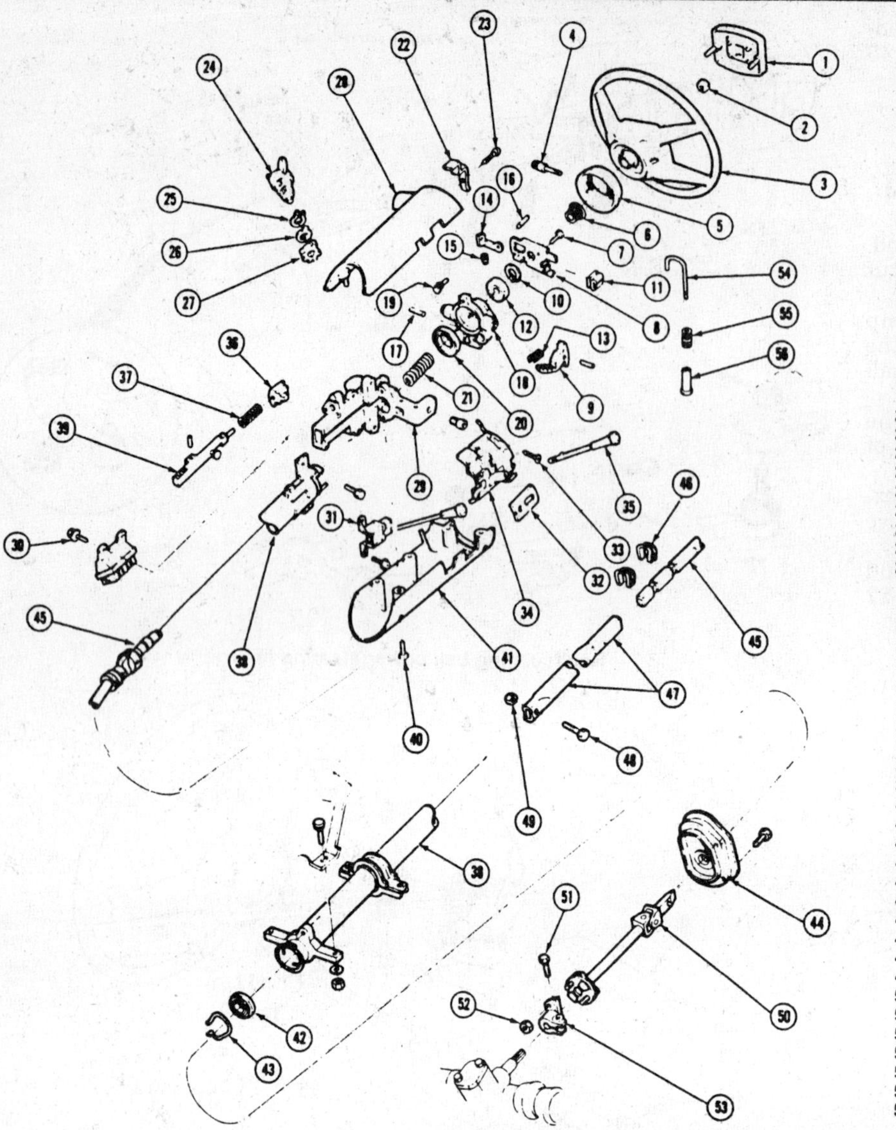

1. Emblem assy.
2. Nut 3/8-18 hex.
3. Wheel assy.—strng.
4. Handle & shank assy. tilt strng. wheel lever
5. Extension—strng. col. shroud
6. Spring—strng. col. upper bearing
7. Screw
8. Plate strng. col. clip retainer
9. Lever strng. col. link
10. Ring 3/4 retaining type
11. Clip—strng. col. shroud
12. Bearing assy.—strng. col. upper
13. Pin 4mm × 25.6 straight round end
14. Release lever
15. Spring—strng. col. release lever
16. Pin—4mm × 5.75
17. Pivot pin
18. Flange casting
19. Bumpers
20. Bearing assy.—strng. col. upper
21. Position spring
22. Cover—strng. col. lock actuator
23. Screw no. 8-18 × .62 pan head tapping
24. Lock cyl. (body)
25. Ring 24 × 1.07 retainer type
26. Bearing
27. Gear—strng. col. lock
28. Shroud—upper
29. Housing—strng. col. lock cyl.
30. Bolt (break off head) (2 req'd.)
31. Wash/wipe switch & screws (body)
32. Foam cover—turn signal & w/w switch
33. Screw no. 8-18 × .62 pan head tap (2 req'd.)
34. Turn signal switch
35. Handle & shank assy.—turn sig. switch
36. Pawl—strng. col. lock
37. Spring—strng. col. lock
38. Tube assy. col. outer
39. Actuator assy.—strng. col. lock
40. Screw no. 8-18 × 1.50 pan head tap (5 req'd.)
41. Shroud—strng. col. lower
42. Bearing assy.—strng. gear shaft lower
43. Ring—strng. gear shaft lower bearing retainer
44. Boot assy.—strng. col.
45. Shaft assy.—strng. col. upper
46. Anti-rattle clips (2 req'd)
47. Shaft—strng. gear lower
48. Bolt 7/16-14 × 1.50 hex
49. Nut 7/16-14 hex lock
50. Shaft assy.—strng. col. lower
51. Bolt—3/8-24 × 1.22
52. Nut 3/8-16 hex lock
53. Flange—strng. shaft lower
54. Lever—strng. col. lock actuator
55. Spring—strng. col. lock
56. Knob—strng. col. lock actuator

Tilt steering column with floor shift for 1982 Cougar

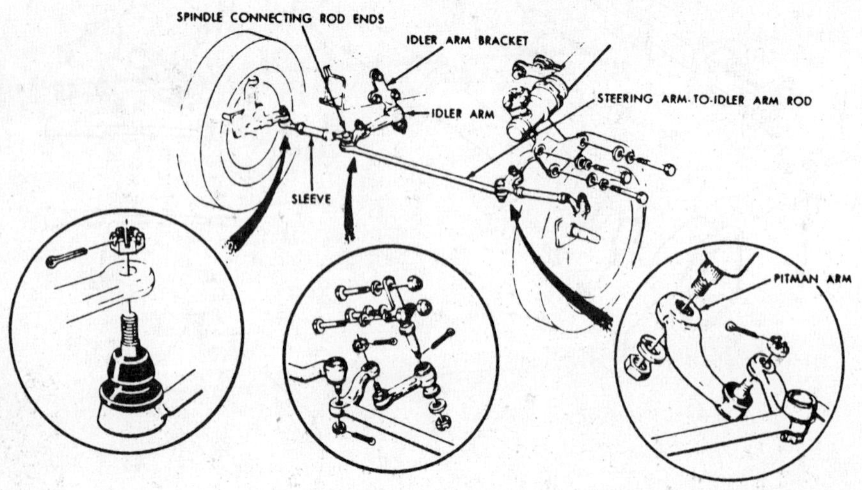

Typical manual steering linkage

RECIRCULATING BALL MANUAL STEERING GEAR

Steering Gear

INSPECTION

Before any steering gear adjustments are made, it is recommended that the front end of the car be raised and a thorough inspection be made for stiffness or lost motion in the steering gear, steering linkage, and front suspension. Worn or damaged parts should be replaced, since a satisfactory adjustment of the steering gear cannot be obtained if bent or badly worn parts exist.

It is also very important that the steering gear be properly aligned in the car. Misalignment of the gear places a stress on the steering worm shaft, therefore a proper adjustment is impossible. To align the steering gear, loosen the mounting bolts to permit the gear to align itself. Check the steering gear mounting seat and if there is a gap at any of the mounting bolts, proper alignment may be obtained by placing shims where excessive gap appears. Tighten the steering gear bolts. Alignment of the gear in the car is very important and should be done carefully so that a satisfactory, trouble-free gear adjustment may be obtained.

STEERING WORM AND SECTOR GEAR ADJUSTMENT

The ball nut assembly and the sector gear must be adjusted properly to maintain a minimum amount of steering shaft end-play and a minimum amount of backlash between the sector gear and the ball nut. There are only two adjustments that may be done on this steering gear and they should be done as given below:

1. Disconnect the pitman arm from the steering pitman-to-idler arm rod.
2. Loosen the locknut on the sector shaft adjustment screw and turn the adjusting screw counterclockwise.
3. Measure the worm bearing preload by attaching an inch-pound torque wrench to the steering wheel nut. With the steering wheel off center, note the reading required to rotate the input shaft about 1½ turns to either side of center. If the torque reading is not about 4-5 in.lb., adjust the gear as given in the next step.
4. Loosen the steering shaft bearing adjustment locknut and tighten or back off the bearing adjusting screw until the preload is within the specified limits.
5. Tighten the steering shaft bearing adjuster locknut and recheck the preload torque.
6. Turn the steering wheel slowly to either stop. Turn gently against the stop to avoid possible damage to the ball return guides. Then rotate the wheel 2¾ turns to center the ball nut.
7. Turn the sector adjusting screw clockwise until the proper torque (9-10 in.lb.) is obtained that is necessary to rotate the worm gear past its center (high spot).
8. While holding the sector adjusting screw, tighten the sector screw adjusting locknut to 32-40 ft.lb. and recheck the backlash adjustment.

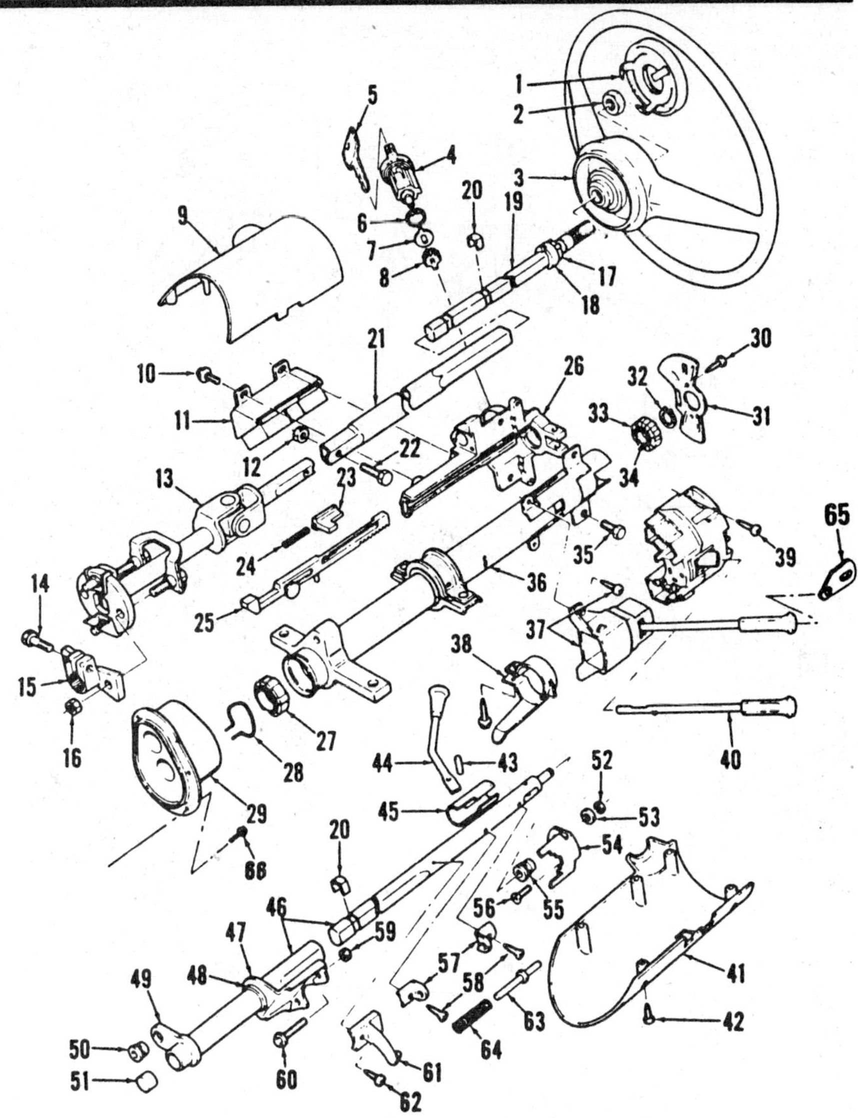

1. Emblem assy.
2. Nut ⅝-18 hex
3. Wheel assy—stng
4. Lock cyl—(body)
5. Key—(body)
6. Ring
7. Bearing
8. Gear—stng col lock
9. Shroud—upper
10. Bolt (break off head) (2 req'd)
11. Switch assy.—ignition
12. Nut ⅜-16 hex lock
13. Shaft assy—stng col lower
14. Bolt—⅜-24 × 1.22
15. Flange—stng shaft lower
16. Nut ⅜-16 hex lock
17. Cam—turn sig turn off
18. Lock—stng col position
19. Shaft—stng gear upper
20. Anti-rattle clips (4 req'd)
21. Shaft—stng gear lower
22. Bolt ⅜-16 × 1⅜ hex
23. Pawl—stng col lock
24. Spring—stng col lock
25. Actuator assy—stng col lock
26. Housing—stng col lock cyl
27. Bearing assy—stng gear shaft lower
28. Ring—stng gear shaft lower bearing retainer
29. Boot assy—stng col
30. Screw no. 8-18 × .62 pan hd. tap (2 req'd)
31. Retainer—stng col upper bearing
32. Retainer—stng col upper bearing
33. Sleeve—stng col upper bearing
34. Bearing assy—stng col upper
35. Bolt—m8 × 1.25 hex hd (2 req'd)
36. Tube assy col outer
37. Wash/wipe switch & screws (body)
38. Bracket & cable assy—trans cont sel (body)
39. Screw no. 8-18 × .62 pan hd tap (2 req'd)
40. Handle & shank assy—turn sig switch
41. Shroud—stng col lower
42. Screw no. 8-18 × 1.50 pan hd tap (4 req'd)
43. Pin 5 mm spring coiled
44. Lever assy—trans cont selector
45. Cover—trans cont sel lever opening
46. Tube assy—trans cont selector
47. Bracket—trans gear shift support
48. Bushing—trans gear shift shaft
49. Arm—trans cont selector
50. Insulator—stng gear shaft
51. Seal—stng gear shaft
52. Ring—5⁄16 retainer (external)
53. Washer—8.23 flat
54. Insert—trans control selector position
55. Bearing—trans gear shift lever socket
56. Screw—m5-0.8 × 12.5 flat head (3 req'd)
57. Retainer—stng col lever (2 req'd)
58. Screw 4 mm—0.7 × 12.7 type "D" oval (2 req'd)
59. Nut 5⁄16-18 hex prevail torque (2 req'd)
60. Bolt 5⁄16-18 × 1.50 flg pilot (2 req'd)
61. Lever—trans gear shift selector
62. Screw no. 8—32 × .50 hx wshr hd
63. Plunger—trans control selector lever
64. Spring—trans control selector lever return
65. Foam cover
66. Screw (4 req'd)

Modular column with automatic transmission for the 1980 Thunderbird and XR-7

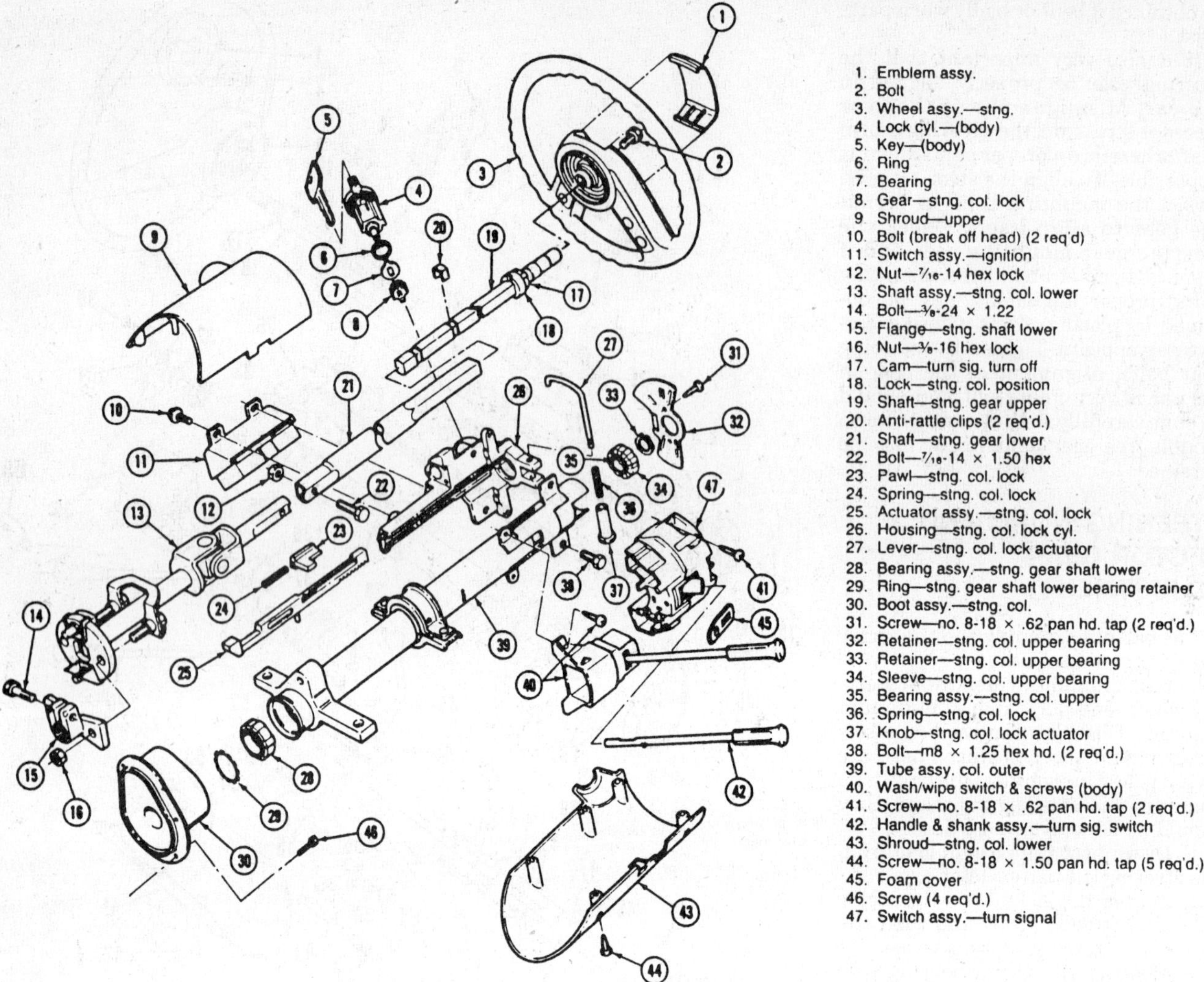

Non-tilt steering column with floor shift for 1985-86 Thunderbird and Cougar

9. Connect the pitman arm to the steering arm-to-idler.

REMOVAL & INSTALLATION

1. Remove the bolt(s) that retains the flex coupling to the steering shaft.
2. Remove the nut and lock washer that secures the Pitman arm to the sector shaft. Using a puller, remove the Pitman arm from the sector shaft. Do not hammer on the end of the puller as this can damage the steering gear.
3. On vehicles with standard transmissions it may be necessary to disconnect the clutch linkage to obtain clearance. On 8-cylinder models, it may be necessary to lower the exhaust system.
4. Remove the bolts that attach the steering gear to the side rail. Remove the gear.
5. Position the steering gear and flex coupling on the steering shaft. Install steering gear-to-side rail bolts and torque to 50-65 ft.lb.
6. Install the clutch linkage if disconnected. Reposition the exhaust system if it was lowered.
7. Place the Pitman arm on the sector shaft and install the attaching nut and lock washer. Torque the nut to 150-225 ft.lb.
8. Install the flex coupling attaching nut(s) and torque to 18-23 ft.lb.

1981-82 COUGAR MANUAL RACK AND PINION STEERING

ADJUSTMENTS

The rack and pinion gear provides two means of service adjustment. The gear must be removed from the vehicle to perform both adjustments.

Support Yoke to Rack

1. Clean the exterior of the steering gear thoroughly and mount the gear by installing two long bolts and washers through the mounting boss bushings and attaching to Bench Mounted Holding Fixture, Tool T57L-500-B or equivalent.
2. Remove the yoke cover, gasket, shims, and yoke spring.
3. Clean the cover and housing flange areas thoroughly.
4. Reinstall the yoke and cover, omitting the gasket, shims, and the spring.
5. Tighten the cover bolts lightly until the cover just touches the yoke.
6. Measure the gap between the cover and the housing flange. With the gasket, add selected shims to give a combined pack thickness 0.13-0.15mm greater than the measured gap.

7. Remove the cover.
8. Assemble the gasket next to the housing flange, then the selected shims, spring, and cover.
9. Install cover bolts, sealing the threads with ESW-M46-132A or equivalent, and tighten.
10. Check to see that the gear operates smoothly without binding or slackness.

Pinion Bearing Preload

1. Clean the exterior of the steering gear thoroughly and place the gear in the bench mounted holding fixture as outlined under Support Yoke to Back Adjustment.
2. Loosen the bolts of the yoke cover to relieve spring pressure on the rack.
3. Remove the pinion cover and gasket. Clean the cover flange area thoroughly.
4. Remove the spacer and shims.
5. Install a new gasket, and fit shims between the upper bearing and the spacer until the top of the spacer is flush with the gasket. Check with a straightedge, using light pressure.
6. Add one shim, 0.0025-0.0050" (0.0635-0.1270mm) to the pack in order to preload the bearings. The spacer must be assembled next to the pinion cover.
7. Install the cover and bolts.

Tie Rod Articulation Effort

1. Install the hook end of a pull scale through the hole in the tie rod end stud. The effort to move the tie rod should be 1-5 lb. (0.45-2.27 kg). Do not damage the tie rod end.
2. Replace the ball joint/tie rod assembly if the effort falls outside this range. Save the tie rod end for use on the new tie rod assembly.

REMOVAL & INSTALLATION

1. Disconnect the negative battery cable from the battery.
2. Remove the one bolt retaining the flexible coupling to the input shaft.
3. Leave the ignition key in the ON position, and raise the vehicle on a hoist.
4. Remove the two tie rod end retaining cotter pins and nuts. Separate the studs from the spindle arms, using the ball joint separator tool. Do not use a hammer or similar tool as this may damage spindle arms or rod studs.
5. Support the steering gear, and remove the two nuts, insulator washers, and bolts retaining the steering gear to the No. 2 crossmember.
6. Remove the steering gear assembly from the vehicle.
7. Insert the input shaft into the flexible coupling aligning the flats and

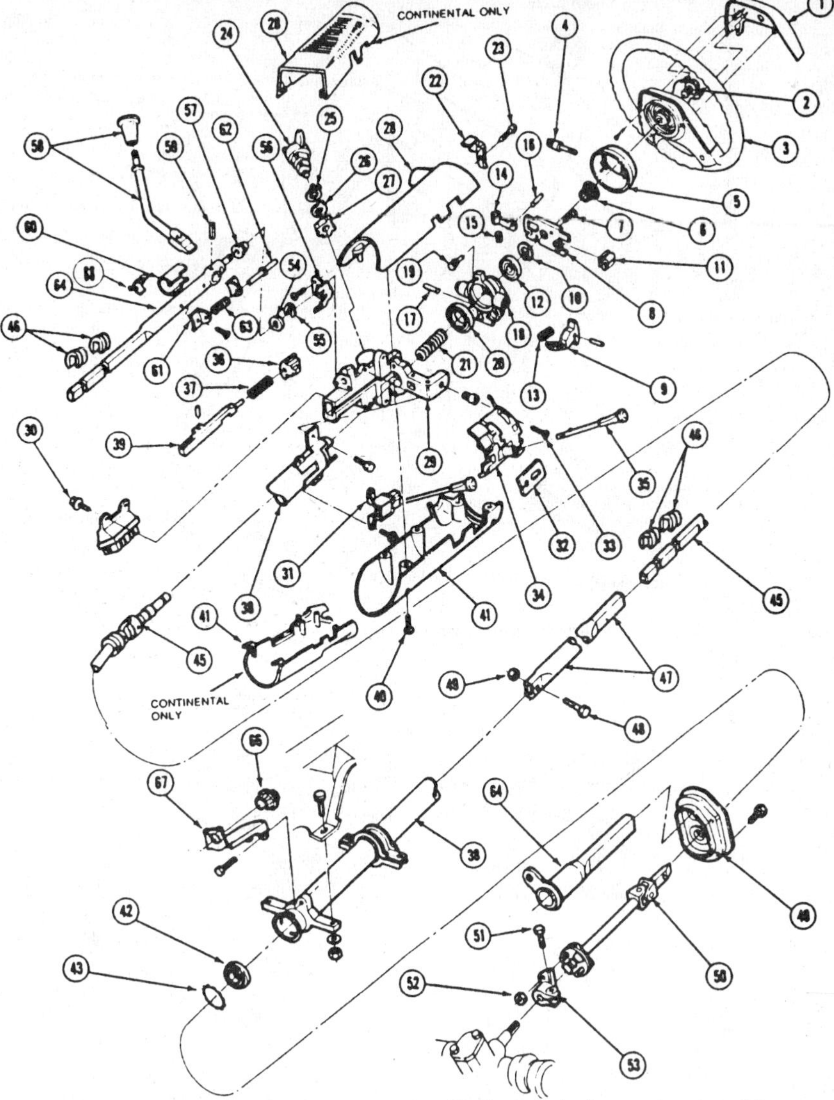

1. Emblem assy.
2. Bolt
3. Wheel assy.—strng.
4. Handle & shank assy. tilt strng. wheel lever
5. Extension—strng. col. shroud
6. Spring—strng. col. upper bearing
7. Screw
8. Plate strng. col. clip retainer
9. Lever strng. col. link
10. Ring 3/4 retaining type
11. Clip—strng. col. shroud
12. Bearing assy.—strng. col. upper
13. Pin 4mm × 25.6 straight round end
14. Release lever
15. Spring—strng. col. release lever
16. Pin—4mm × 5.75
17. Pivot pin
18. Flange casting
19. Bumpers
20. Bearing assy.—strng. col. upper
21. Position spring
22. Cover—strng. col. lock actuator
23. Screw no. 8-18 × .62 pan head tapping
24. Lock cyl. (body)
25. Ring 24 × 1.07 retainer type
26. Bearing
27. Gear—strng. col. lock
28. Shroud—upper
29. Housing—strng. col. lock cyl.
30. Bolt (2 req'd.)
31. Wash/wipe switch & screws (body)
32. Foam cover—turn signal & w/w switch
33. Screw no. 8-18 × .62 pan head tap (2 req'd.)
34. Turn signal switch
35. Handle & shank assy.—turn sig. switch
36. Pawl—strng. col. lock
37. Spring—strng. col. lock
38. Tube assy. col. outer
39. Actuator assy.—strng. col. lock
40. Screw no. 8-18 × 1.50 pan head tap (5 req'd.)
41. Shroud—strng. col. lower
42. Bearing assy.—strng. gear shaft lower
43. Ring—strng. gear shaft lower bearing retainer
44. Boot assy.—strng. col.
45. Shaft assy.—strng. col. upper
46. Anti-rattle clips
47. Shaft—strng. gear lower
48. Bolt 7/16-14 × 1.50 hex
49. Nut 7/16-14 hex lock
50. Shaft assy.—strng. col. lower
51. Bolt—3/8-24 × 1.22
52. Nut 3/8-16 hex lock
53. Flange—strng. shaft lower
54. Ring—5/16 retainer
55. Washer—8.23 flat
56. Insert—trans. control selector position
57. Bearing—trans. gear shift lever socket
58. Lever assy.—trans. control selector
59. Pin 5mm spring coiled
60. Cover—trans. control selector lever opening
61. Screw 4mm—0.7 × 12.7 type "D" oval (2 req'd.)
62. Plunger—trans. control selector lever
63. Spring—trans. control selector lever return
64. Tube assy.—trans. control selector
66. Bushing—trans. gear shift shaft
67. Brkt.—trans. gear shift support
68. Spacer clip

Tilt column with column shift for 1981-87 Thunderbird, Cougar, XR-7 and Continental

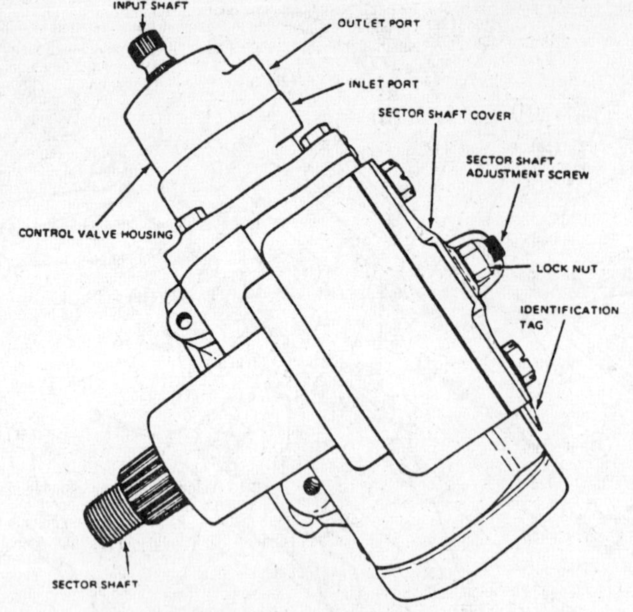

Ford integral power steering gear

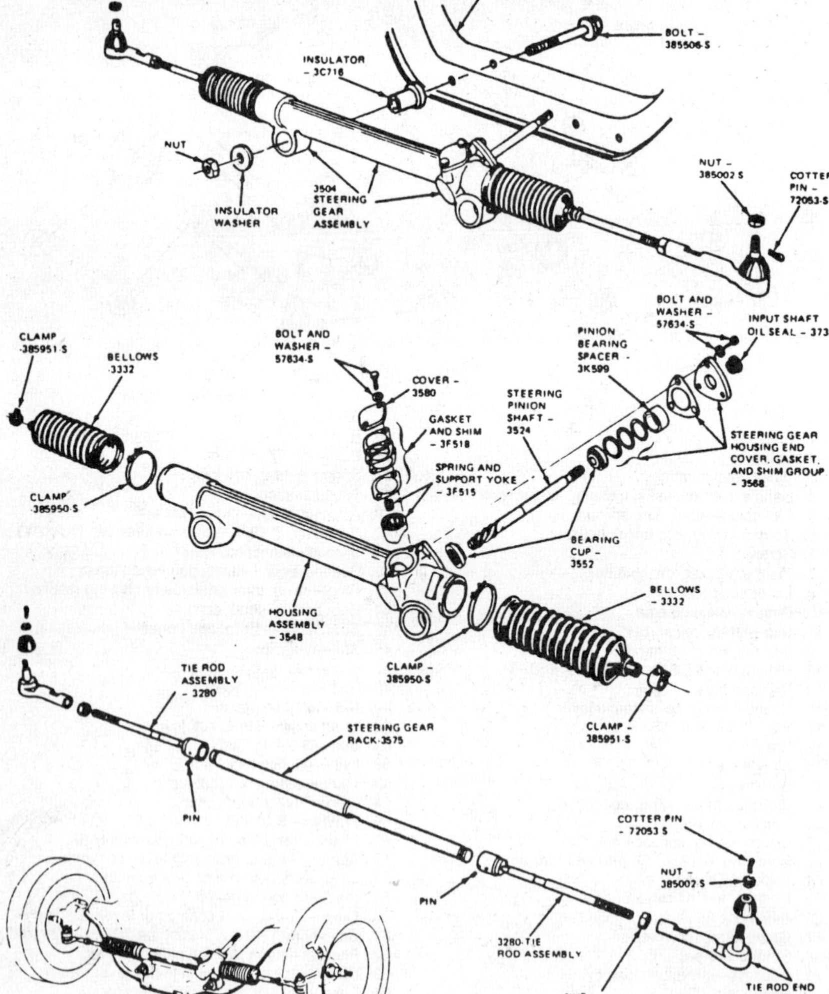

Manual rack and pinion steering gear

position the steering gear to the No. 2 crossmember. Install the two bolts.

8. Connect the tie rod ends to the spindle arms, and install the two retaining nuts. Tighten the nuts to specifications, and install the two cotter pins.

9. Lower the vehicle, and install the one bolt retaining the flexible coupling to the input shaft. Tighten the bolt to specifications.

10. Turn the ignition key to the OFF position.

11. Connect the negative battery cable to the battery.

12. Check the toe, and reset if necessary.

Tie Rod Ends

REMOVAL & INSTALLATION

1. Remove the cotter pin and nut at the spindle. Separate the tie rod end stud from the spindle with a puller.

2. Matchmark the position of the locknut with paint on the tie rod. Unscrew the locknut. Unscrew the tie rod end, counting the number of turns required to remove.

3. Install the new end the same number of turns. Attach the tie rod end stud to the spindle. Install the nut and torque to 35 ft.lb., then continue to tighten until the cotter pin holes align. Install a new cotter pin. Check the toe and adjust if necessary, then torque the tie rod end locknut to 35 ft.lb.

Power Steering

Two different power steering systems have been used:

- Ford Integral System
- Ford Integral Rack and Pinion System

ADJUSTMENTS

Ford Integral System

MESH LOAD

During the vehicle breaking-in period, some factory adjustments may change. These changes will not necessarily affect operation of the steering gear assembly, and need not be adjusted unless there is excessive lash or other malfunctioning. Adjust the total overcenter position load to eliminate excessive lash between the sector and rack teeth as follows:

1. Disconnect the Pitman arm from the sector shaft.

2. Disconnect the fluid return line

at the reservoir and cap the reservoir return line pipe.

3. Place the end of the return line in a clean container and turn the steering wheel from left to right to discharge the fluid from the gear.

4. Turn the steering wheel to 45° from the left stop.

5. Using an in.lb. torque wrench on the steering wheel nut, determine the torque required to rotate the shaft slowly approximately ⅛ turn from the 45° position.

6. Turn the steering wheel back to center, and determine the torque required to rotate the shaft back and forth across the center position. Loosen the nut, and turn the adjuster screw until the reading is 11 to 12 in.lb. greater than the torque measured at 45° from the stop. Tighten the nut while holding the screw in place.

7. Recheck the readings and replace the Pitman arm and steering wheel hub cover.

8. Connect the fluid return line to the reservoir and fill the reservoir. Do not pry against the reservoir to obtain proper belt load. Pressure may deform the reservoir causing it to leak.

9. Recheck belt tension and adjust, if necessary. Torque the bolts and nut to 30-40 ft.lb.

VALVE SPOOL CENTERING CHECK

1. Install a 0-2,000 psi (0-13,790 kpa) pressure gauge in the pressure line between the power steering pump outlet port and the integral steering gear inlet port. Be sure the valve on the gauge is fully open.

2. Check the fluid level and add fluid, if necessary.

3. Start the engine and turn the steering wheel from stop-to-stop to bring the steering lubricant to normal operating temperature. Turn off the engine and recheck fluid level. Add fluid, if necessary.

4. With the engine running at approximately 1,000 rpm and the steering wheel centered, attach an in.lb. torque wrench to the steering wheel nut. Apply sufficient torque in each direction to get a gauge reading of 250 psi (1,723.75 kpa).

5. The reading should be the same in both directions at 250 psi (1,723.75 kpa). If the difference between the readings exceeds 4 in.lb., remove the steering gear and install a thicker or thinner valve centering shim in the housing. Use as many shims as necessary, but do not allow thickness of the shim pack to exceed 0.030" (0.762mm). The piston must be able to bottom on the valve housing face. No clearance is allowed in this area.

6. Test for clearance between the piston end and valve housing face as follows:

a. Hold the valve assembly so the piston is up and try to turn the input shaft to the right.

b. If there is no clearance, the input shaft will not turn. If there is clearance, the piston and worm will rotate together.

c. If two or more shims must be used to center the spool valve, and a restriction or interference condition is experienced when turning the piston to its stop on the valve housing, replace the shaft and control assembly. If steering effort is heavy to the left, increase shim thickness. If steering effort is light to the left, decrease shim thickness.

7. When performing the valve spool centering check outside the vehicle, use the procedures described above except take torque and pressure readings at the right and left stops instead of at either side of center.

Ford Integral Rack and Pinion System

The power rack and pinion steering gear provides for only one service adjustment. The gear must be removed from the vehicle to perform this adjustment.

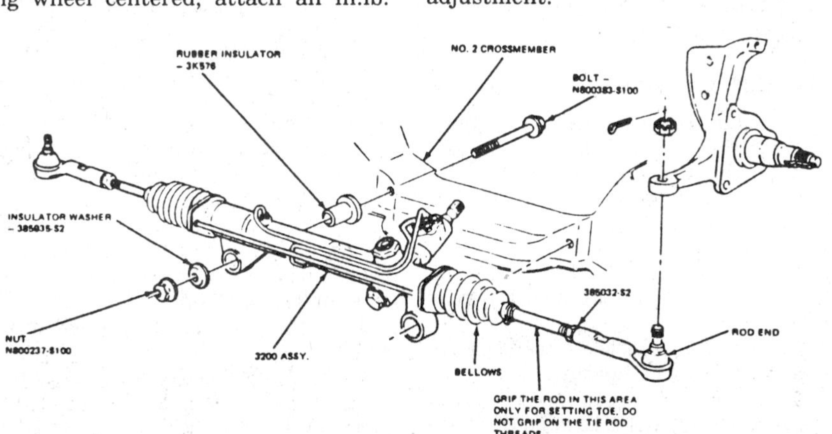

Power rack and pinion steering gear

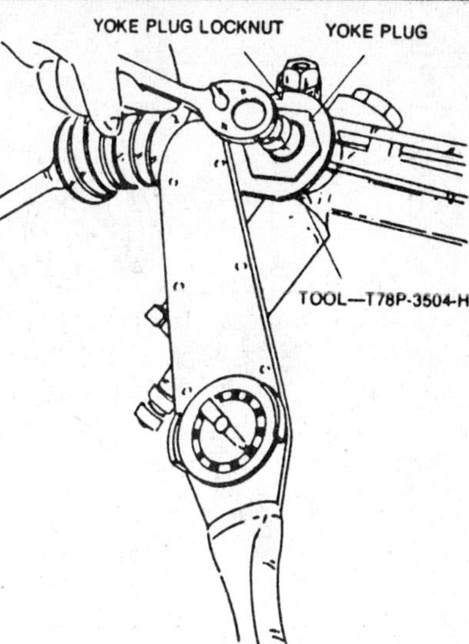

Tightening yoke plug locknut

RACK YOKE PLUG PRELOAD

1. Clean the exterior of the steering gear thoroughly.

2. Install two long bolts and washers through the bushing, and attach to the bench mounted holding fixture, Tool T57L-500-B or equivalent.

3. Do not remove the external pressure lines, unless they are leaking or damaged. If these lines are removed, they must be replaced with new lines.

4. Drain the power steering fluid by rotating the input shaft lock-to-lock twice using Tool T74P-3505-R or equivalent. Cover ports on valve housing with shop cloth while draining gear.

5. Insert an inch-pound torque wrench with maximum capacity of 30-60 in.lb. into the input shaft torque adapter, Tool T74P-3504-R or equivalent. Position the adapter and wrench on the input shaft splines.

6. Loosen the yoke plug locknut with wrench, Tool T78P-3504-H or equivalent.

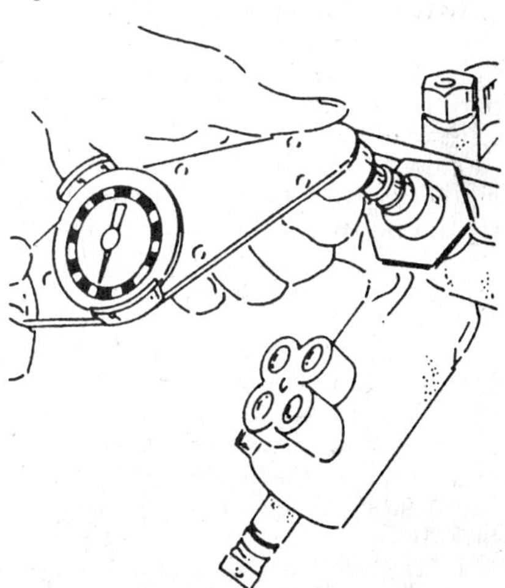

Adjusting yoke bearing preload

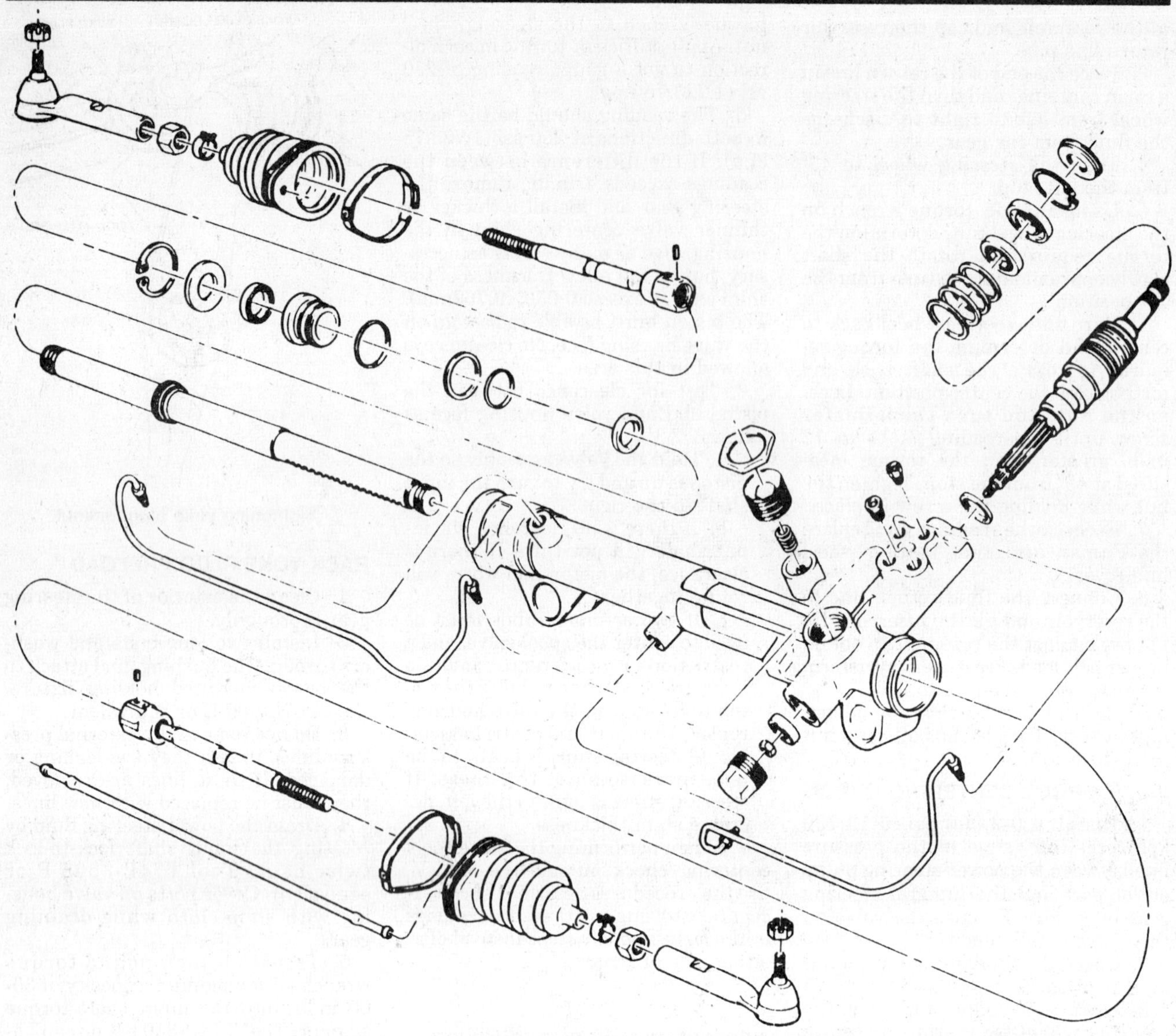

Power rack and pinion steering linkage used on all 1980-87 models

7. Loosen yoke plug with a 3/4" socket wrench.

8. With the rack at the center of travel, tighten the yoke plug to 45-50 in.lb. Clean the threads of the yoke plug prior to tightening to prevent a false reading.

9. Back off the yoke plug approximately 1/8 turn (44° minimum to 54° maximum) until the torque required to initiate and sustain rotation of the input shaft is 7-18 in.lb.

10. Place Tool T78P-3504-H or equivalent on the yoke plug locknut. While holding the yoke plug, tighten the locknut to 44-66 ft.lb. Do not allow the yoke plug to move while tightening or the preload will be affected. Recheck input shaft torque after tightening locknut.

11. If the external pressure lines were removed, they must be replaced with new service line. Remove the copper seals from the housing ports prior to installation of new lines.

STEERING GEAR REMOVAL & INSTALLATION

Ford Integral System

1. Tag the pressure and return lines for future identification.

2. Disconnect the pressure and return lines from the steering gear. Plug the lines and ports in the gear to prevent entry of dirt.

3. Remove the bolts that secure the flexible coupling to the steering gear and column.

4. Raise the vehicle and remove the sector shaft attaching nut.

5. Remove the Pitman arm from the sector shaft with Tool T64P-3590-F. Remove the tool from the Pitman arm. Do not damage the seals.

6. On vehicles with standard transmissions, remove the clutch release lever retracting spring to provide clearance for removing the steering gear.

7. Support the steering gear. Remove the steering gear attaching bolts.

8. Remove the clamp bolt that holds the flexible coupling to the steering gear. Work the gear free of the flex coupling and remove.

9. If the flex coupling did not come off with the gear, lift it off the shaft.

10. Slide the flex coupling into place on the steering shaft assembly. Turn the steering wheel so the spokes are in the normal position.

11. Center the steering gear input shaft.

12. Slide the steering gear input shaft into the flex coupling and into place on the frame side rail. Install the attaching bolts and torque to 35-40 ft.lb.

13. Be sure the wheels are in the straight ahead position. Then install the Pitman arm on the sector shaft. Install and tighten the sector shaft and attaching bolts. Torque the bolts to 55-70 ft.lb.
14. Move the flex coupling into place on the input and steering column shaft. Install the attaching bolts and torque to 18-22 ft.lb.
15. Connect the pressure and the return lines to the steering gear. Tighten lines.
16. Disconnect the coil wire.
17. Fill the reservoir. Turn on the ignition and turn the steering wheel from stop-to-stop to distribute the fluid.
18. Recheck the fluid level and add fluid, if necessary.
19. Install the coil wire. Start the engine and turn the steering wheel from left to right. Inspect for fluid leaks.

Ford Integral Rack and Pinion System

1. Disconnect the negative battery cable from the battery.
2. Remove the one bolt retaining the flexible coupling to the input shaft.
3. Leave the ignition key in the On position, and raise the vehicle on a hoist.
4. Remove the two tie rod end retaining cotter pins and nuts. Separate the studs from the spindle arms, using the ball joint separator tool.
5. Support the steering gear, and remove the two nuts, insulator, washers, and bolts retaining the steering gear to the No. 2 crossmember. Lower the gear slightly to permit access to the pressure and return line fittings.
6. Disconnect the pressure and return lines from the steering gear valve housing. Plug the lines and parts in the valve housing to prevent entry of dirt.
7. Remove the steering gear assembly from the vehicle.
8. Support and position the steering gear, so that the pressure and return line fittings can be connected to the valve housing. Tighten the fittings to 15-20 ft.lb. The design allows the hoses to swivel when tightened properly. do not attempt to eliminate looseness by overtightening, since this can cause damage to the fittings.

NOTE: The rubber insulators must be pushed completely inside the gear housing before the installation of the gear housing on the No. 2 crossmember.

9. No gap is allowed between the insulator and the face of the gear boss. A rubber lubricant should be used to facilitate proper installation of the insulators in the gear housing. Insert

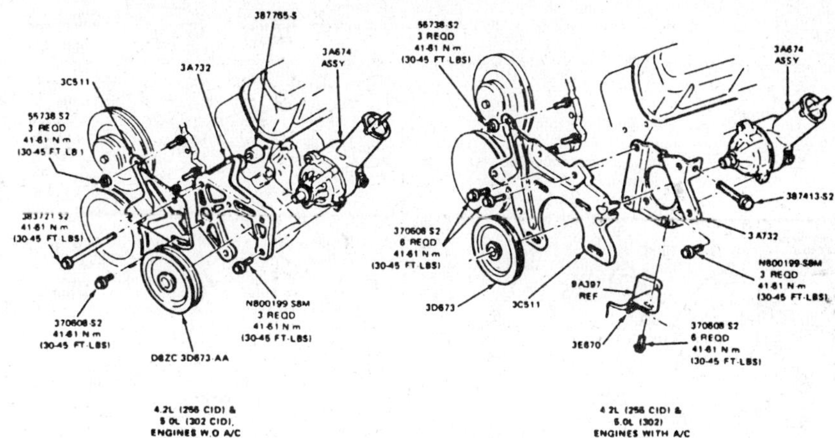

Power steering pump installation on 1980-81 models

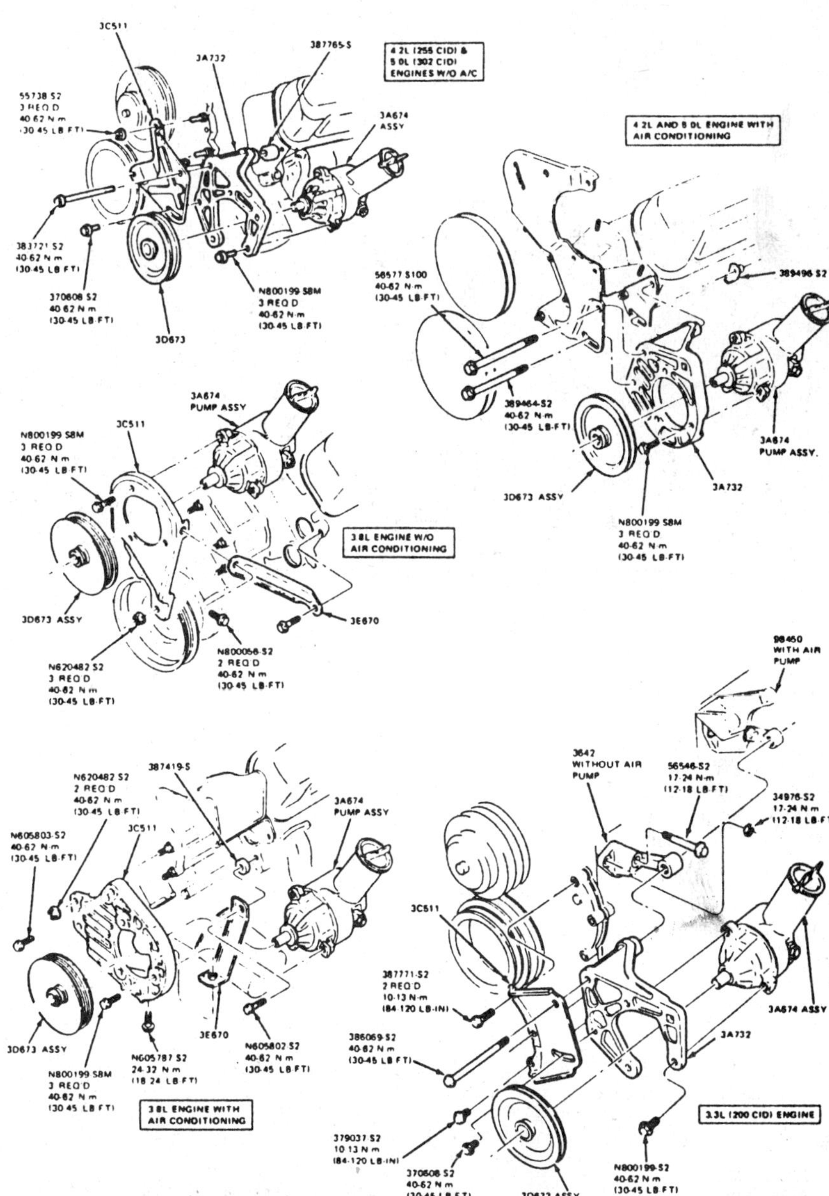

Power steering pump installation on 1982 Thunderbird, XR-7 and Continental

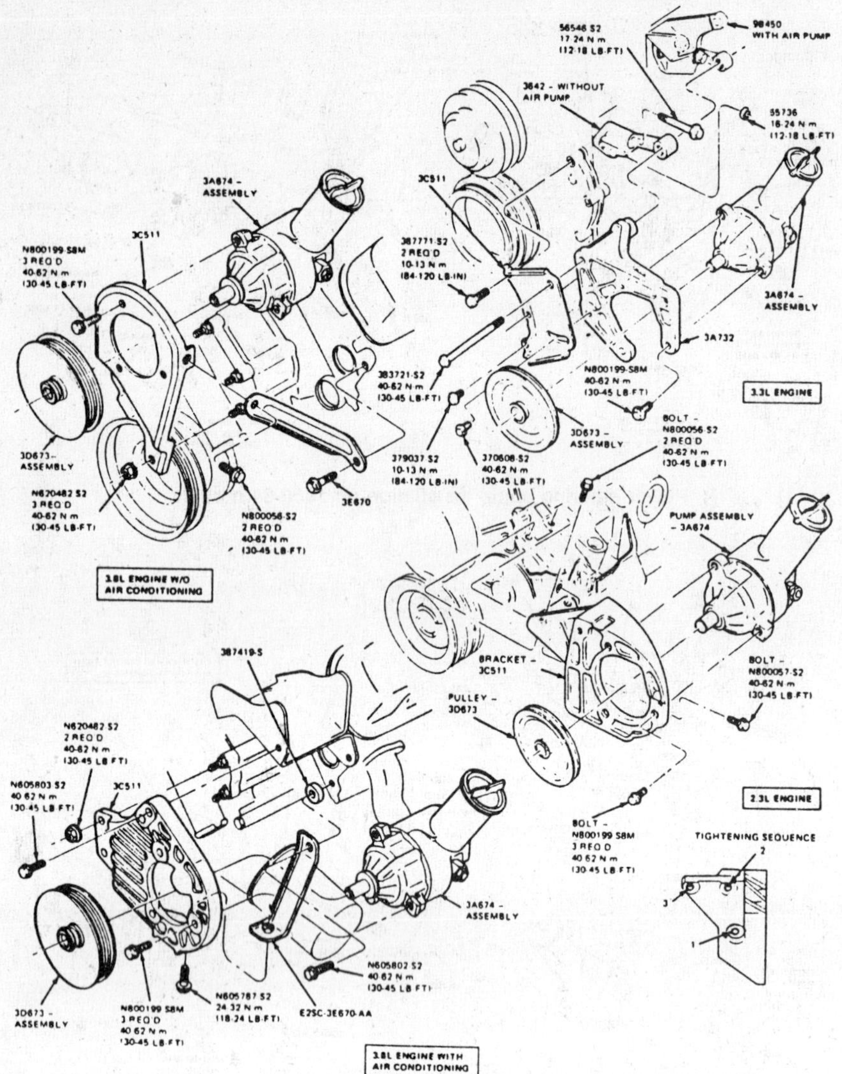

Power steering pump installation on 1982 Cougar

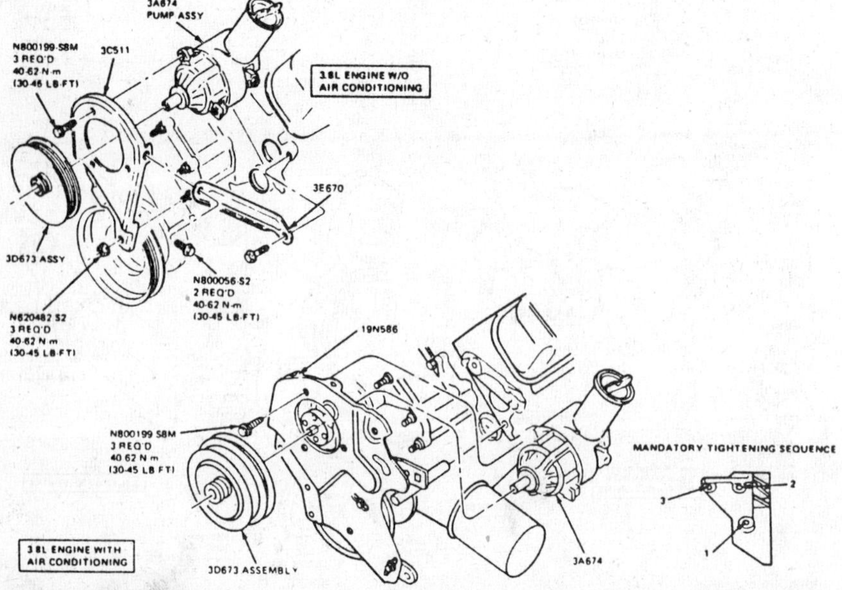

Power steering pump installation on 1985-87 Thunderbird and XR-7 with the 6-232

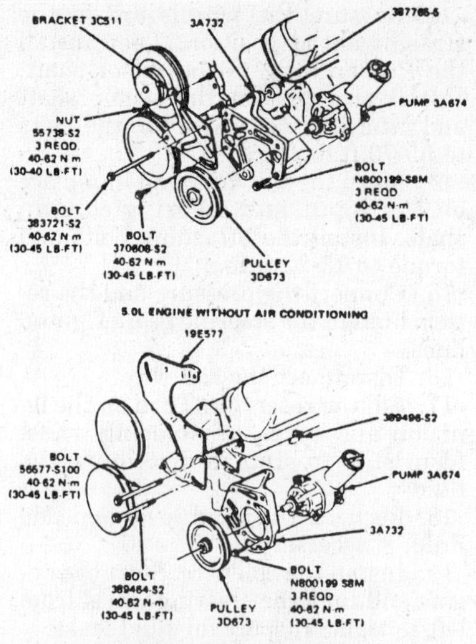

Power steering pump installation on 1983-84 Thunderbird and XR-7 with the 8-302

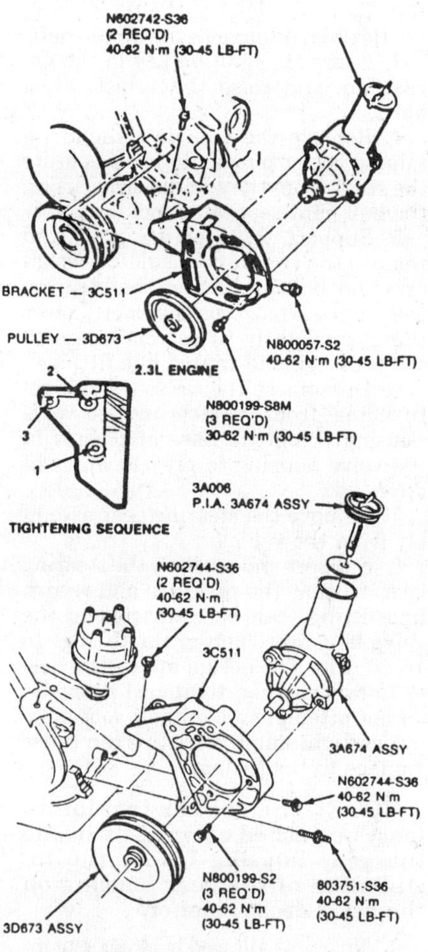

Power steering pump installation on the 1985-87 Thunderbird and Cougar with the 4- 140

the input shaft into the flexible coupling, and position the steering gear to the No. 2 crossmember. Install the two bolts, insulator washers, and nuts. Tighten the two nuts to 80-100 ft.lb.

10. Connect the tie rod ends to the spindle arms, and install the two retaining nuts. Tighten the nuts to 35-45 ft.lb., then, after tightening to specification, tighten the nuts to their nearest cotter pin castellation, and install two new cotter pins.

11. Lower the vehicle, and install the one bolt retaining the flexible coupling to the input shaft. Tighten the bolt to 18-23 ft.lb.

12. Turn the ignition key to the Off position.

13. Connect the negative battery cable to the battery.

14. Remove the coil wire.

15. Fill the power steering pump reservoir.

16. Engage the starter, and cycle the steering wheel to distribute the fluid. Check the fluid level and add as required.

17. Install the coil wire, start the engine, and cycle the steering wheel. Check for fluid leaks.

18. If the tie rod ends were loosened, check the wheel alignment.

Power Steering Pump

REMOVAL & INSTALLATION

1. Drain the fluid from the pump reservoir by disconnecting the fluid return hose at the pump. Disconnect the pressure hose from the pump.

2. Remove the mounting bolts from the front of the pump. After removal, move the pump inward to loosen the belt tension and remove the belt from the pulley. Remove the pump from the car.

3. To install the pump, position on mounting bracket and loosely install the mounting bolts and nuts. Put the drive belt over the pulley and move the pump outward against the belt until the proper belt tension is obtained. Do not pry against the pump body. Measure the belt tension with a belt tension gauge for the proper adjustment. Only in cases where a belt tension gauge is not available should the belt deflection method be used.

4. Tighten the mounting bolts and nuts.

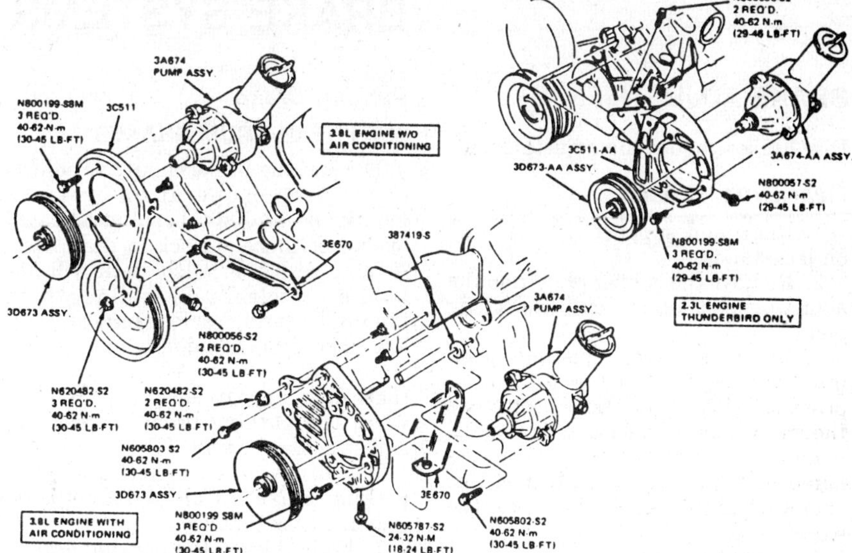

Power steering pump installation on the 1983-84 Thunderbird and XR-7 with the 4-140 and 6-232

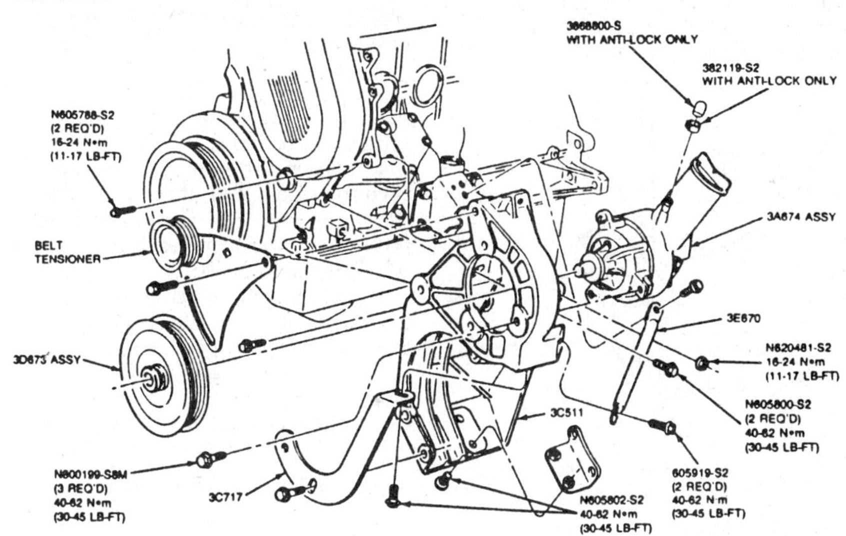

Power steering pump installation on the 1984-85 Continental with the diesel engine

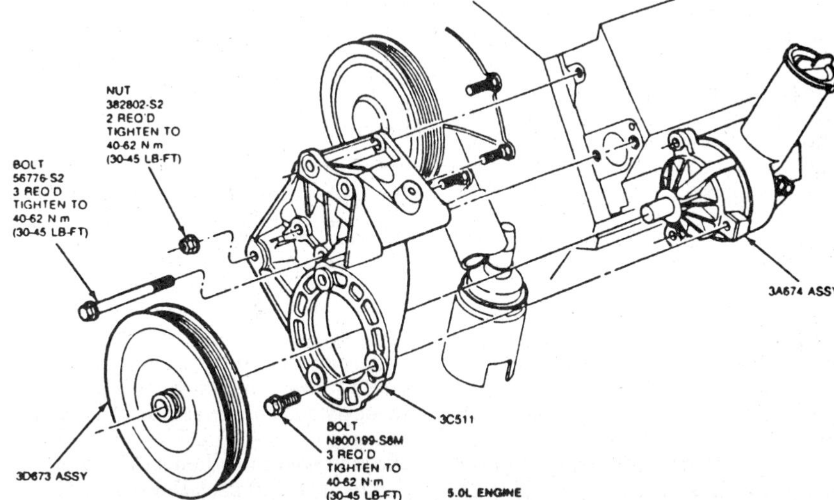

Power steering pump installation on 1985-87 Thunderbird, Cougar, Mark VII nd Continental with the 8-302

BRAKE SYSTEMS

BRAKE ADJUSTMENTS

Disc brakes require no adjustments

Rear Drum Brakes

1. Raise and support the rear end on jackstands.
2. Remove the rubber plug from the adjusting slot in the brake backing plate.
3. Insert a brake adjusting spoon into the slot and engage the lowest possible tooth on the star wheel. Move the end of the brake spoon downward to move the star wheel upward and expand the adjusting screw. Repeat this operation until the brakes lock the wheel.
4. Insert a small screwdriver or piece of firm wire (coat-hanger wire) into the adjusting slot and push the automatic adjuster lever out and free of the star wheel on the adjusting screw.

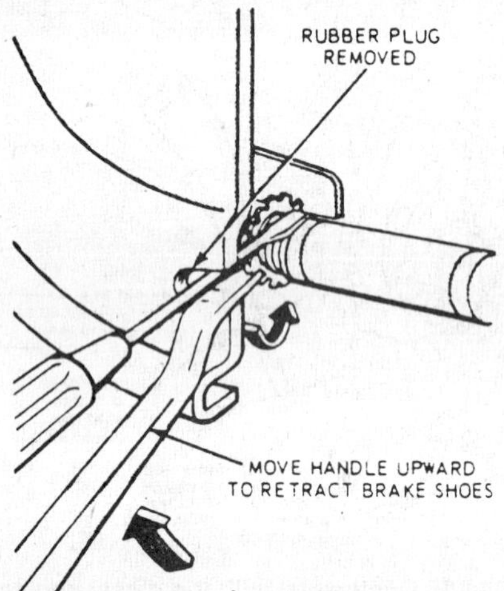

Backing off brake adjusting starwheel

5. Holding the adjusting lever out of the way, engage the topmost tooth possible on the star wheel with a brake adjusting spoon. Move the end of the adjusting spoon upward to move the adjusting screw star wheel downward and contract the adjusting screw. Back off the adjusting screw star wheel until the wheel springs freely with a minimum of drag. Keep track of the number of turns the star wheel is backed off.
6. Repeat this operation for the other side. When backing off the brakes on the other side, the adjusting lever must be backed off the same number of turns to prevent side-to-side brake pull.
7. When both sides are adjusted, make several stops, while backing the car, to equalize both of the wheels.
8. Road test the car.

Parking Brake

WITH REAR DRUM BRAKES

The parking brake should be adjusted for proper operation every 12 months or 12,000 miles and adjusted whenever there is slack in the cables. A cable with too much slack will not hold a vehicle on an incline which presents a serious safety hazard. Usually, a rear brake adjustment will restore parking brake efficiency, but if the cables appear loose or stretched when the parking brake is released, adjust as necessary.

The procedure for adjusting the parking brake on all pedal actuated systems is as follows:

1. Fully release the parking brake.
2. Depress the parking brake pedal one notch from its normal released position. On vacuum release brakes, the first notch is approximately 2" (51mm) of travel.
3. Taking proper safety precautions, raise the car and place the transmission in Neutral.
4. Loosen the equalizer locknut and turn the adjusting nut forward against the equalizer until moderate drag is felt when turning the rear wheels. Tighten the locknut.
5. Release the parking brake, making sure that the brake shoes return to the fully released position.
6. Lower the car and apply the parking brake. Under normal conditions, the third notch will hold the car if the brake is adjusted properly.

WITH REAR DISC BRAKES

1. Fully release the parking brake.
2. Place the transmission in Neutral. If it is necessary to raise the car to reach the adjusting nut and observe the parking brake levers, use an axle hoist or a floor jack positioned beneath the differential. This is necessary so that the rear axle remains at the curb attitude, not stretching the parking brake cables.

CAUTION

If you are raising the rear of the car only, block the front wheels.

3. Locate the adjusting nut beneath the car on the driver's side. While observing the parking brake actuating levers on the rear calipers, tighten the adjusting nut until the levers just begin to move. Then, loosen the nut sufficiently for the levers to fully return to the stop position. The levers are in the stop position when a 1/4" (6mm) pin can be inserted past the side of the lever into the holes in the cast iron housing.
4. Check the operation of the parking brake. Make sure the actuating levers return to the stop position by attempting to pull them rear ward. If the lever moves rearward, the cable adjustment is too tight, which will cause a dragging rear brake and consequent brake overheating and fade.

Brake Light Switch

REMOVAL & INSTALLATION

1. Raise the locking tab and unplug the wiring harness at the switch.
2. Remove the hairpin clip from the stud and slide the switch up and down, remove the switch and washers off of the pedal.

NOTE: It is not necessary to remove the pushrod from the stud.

3. Installation is the reverse of removal. Position the U-shaped side nearest the pedal and directly over/under the pin. Slide the switch up and down trapping the pushrod and bushing between the switch sideplates.

HYDRAULIC SYSTEM

Master Cylinder

REMOVAL & INSTALLATION

Except 4 Wheel Anti-Lock

1. Disconnect the brake lines from the master cylinder.
2. Remove the two nuts and lockwashers that attach the master cylinder to the brake booster.
3. Remove the master cylinder from the booster.
4. Reverse the above procedure to install. Torque the master cylinder attaching nuts to 13-25 ft.lb.
5. Fill the master cylinder and bleed the entire brake system.
6. Refill the master cylinder.

OVERHAUL

Except 4 Wheel Anti-Lock

1. Remove the cylinder from the car and drain the brake fluid.
2. Mount the cylinder in a vise so that the outlets are up then remove the seal from the hub.

3. Remove the stopscrew from the bottom of the front reservoir.
4. Remove the snapring from the front of the bore and remove the rear piston assembly.
5. Remove the front piston assembly using compressed air. Cover the bore opening with a cloth to prevent damage to the piston.
6. Clean metal parts in brake fluid and discard the rubber parts.
7. Inspect the bore for damage or wear, and check the pistons for damage and proper clearance in the bore.

CAUTION

Late models are equipped with aluminum master cylinders. DO NOT HONE! If the bore is pitted or scored deeply, the master cylinder assembly must be replaced.

8. If the bore is only slightly scored or pitted it may be honed. Always use hones that are in good condition and completely clean the cylinder with brake fluid when the honing is completed. If any evidence of contamination exist in the master cylinder, the entire hydraulic system should be flushed and refilled with clean brake fluid. Blow out the passages with compressed air.

NOTE: The rebuilding kit may contain secondary and primary piston assemblies instead of just rubber seals. In this case, seal installation is not required.

9. Install new secondary seals in the two grooves in the flat end of the front piston. The lips of the seals will be facing away from each other.
10. Install a new primary seal and the seal protector on the opposite end of the front piston with the lips of the seal facing outward.
11. Coat the seals with brake fluid. Install the spring on the front piston with the spring retainer in the primary seal.
12. Insert the piston assembly, spring end first, into the bore and use a wooden rod to seat it.
13. Coat the rear piston seals with brake fluid and install them into the piston grooves with the lips facing the spring end.
14. Assemble the spring onto the piston and install the assembly into the bore spring first. Install the snapring.
15. Hold the piston train at the bottom of the bore and install the stopscrew. Install a new seal on the hub. Bench-bleed the cylinder or install and bleed the cylinder on the car.

Pressure Differential Warning Valve

Since the introduction of dual mas-

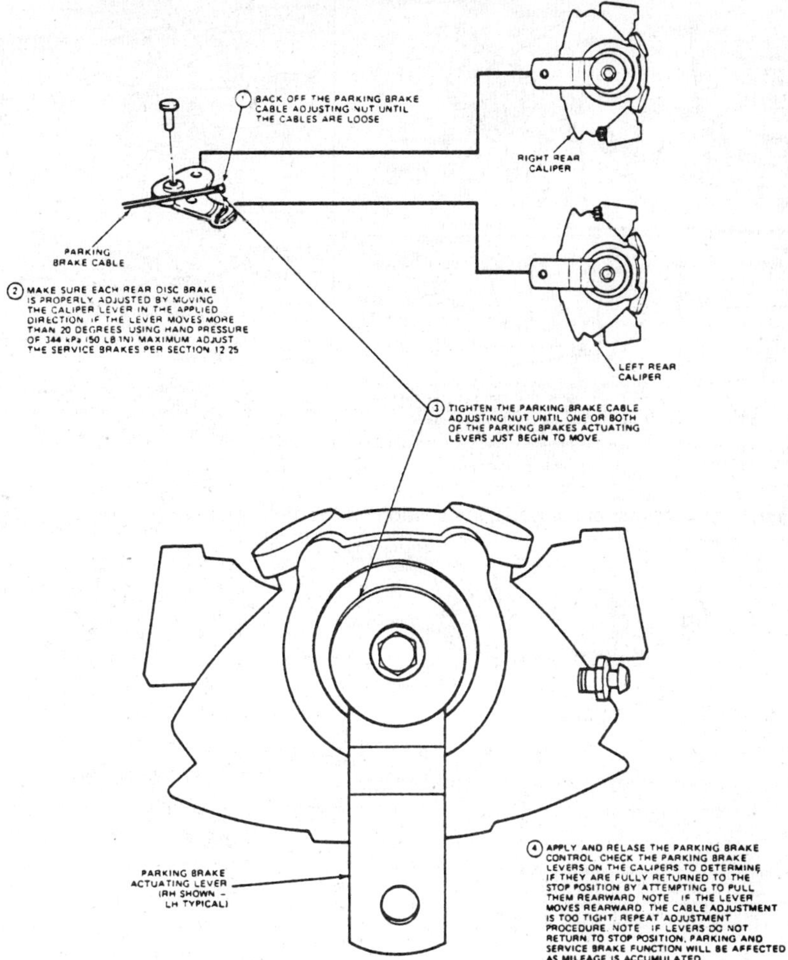

Parking brake adjustment on models with rear disc brakes

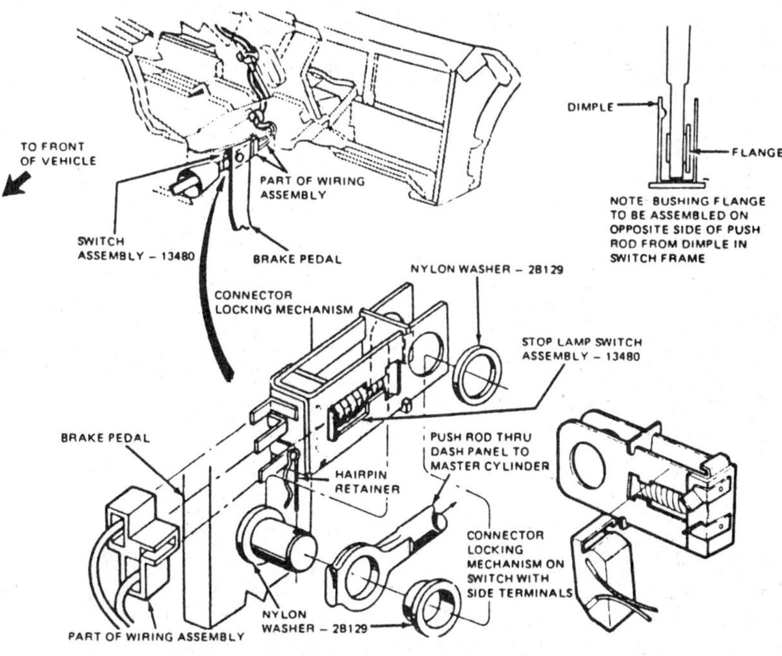

Typical brake light switch installation

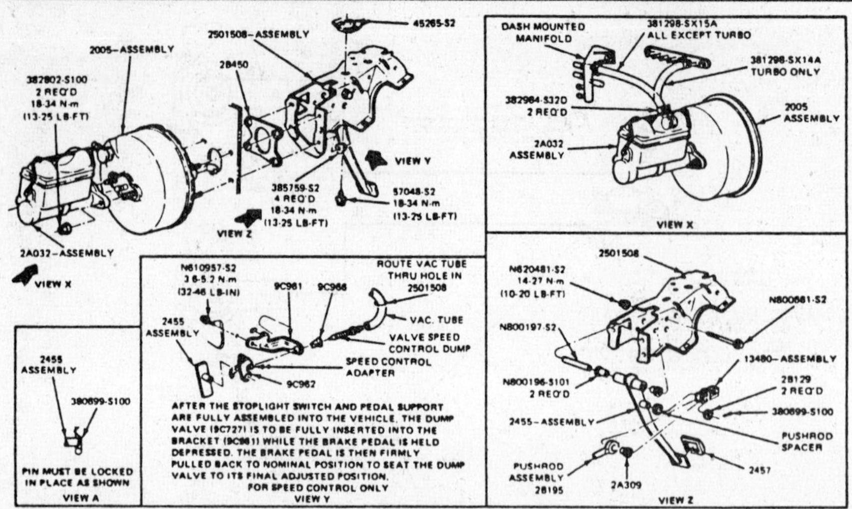

Master cylinder and brake pedal installation on the 1984-87 Thunderbird and Cougar

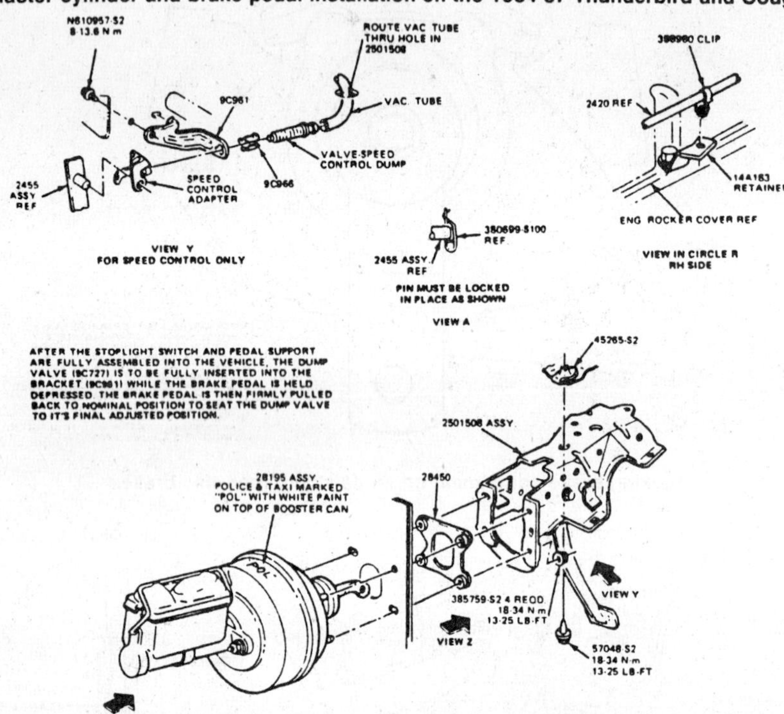

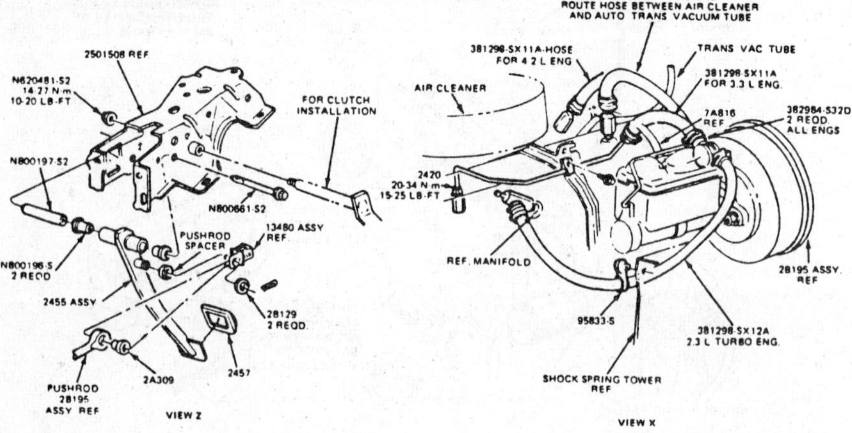

Master cylinder and brake pedal installation on the 1980-81 models

ter cylinders to the hydraulic brake system, a pressure differential warning signal has been added. This signal consists of a warning light on the dashboard activated by a differential pressure switch located below the master cylinder. The signal indicates a hydraulic pressure differential between the front and rear brakes of 80-150 psi, and should warn the driver that a hydraulic failure has occurred.

After repairing and bleeding any part of the hydraulic system the warning light may remain on due to the pressure differential valve remaining in the off-center position. To centralize the valve a pressure difference must be created in the opposite branch of the hydraulic system that was repaired or bled last.

NOTE: Front wheel balancing of cars equipped with disc brakes may also cause a pressure differential in the front branch of the system.

VALVE CENTERING PROCEDURE

1. Turn the ignition to either the **ACC** or **ON** position.
2. Check the fluid level in the mas-

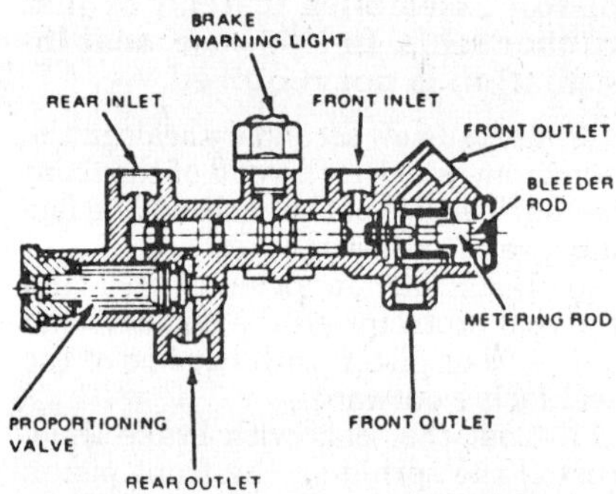

1980-82 3-way aluminum control valve assembly (contains metering, pressure differential and proportioning valves)

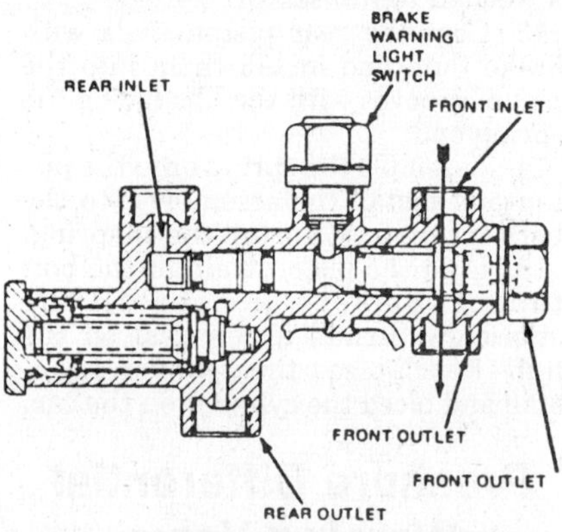

1980-87 2-way aluminum control valve assembly (contains the pressure differential and proportioning valves)

ter cylinder reservoirs. Fill to within ¼" (6mm) of the top if necessary.

3. Depress the brake pedal firmly. The valve will centralize itself causing the brake warning light to go out.

4. Turn the ignition off.

5. Prior to driving the vehicle, check the operation of the brakes and obtain a firm pedal.

Proportioning Valve

On vehicles equipped with front disc and rear drum brakes, a proportioning valve is an important part of the system. It is installed in the hydraulic line to the rear brakes. Its function is to maintain the correct proportion between line pressures to the front and rear brakes. No attempt at adjustment of this valve should be made, as adjustment is preset and tampering will result in uneven braking action.

To assure correct installation when replacing the valve, the outlet to the rear brakes is stamped with the letter **R**.

Metering Valve

On vehicles through 1980 equipped with front disc brakes, a metering valve is used. This valve is installed in the hydraulic line to the front brakes, and functions to delay pressure build-up to the front brakes on application. Its purpose is to reduce front brake pressure until rear brake pressure builds up adequately to overcome the rear brake shoe return springs. In this way disc brake pad lift is extended because it prevents the front disc brakes from carrying all or most of the braking load at low operating line pressures.

The metering valve can be checked very simply. With the car stopped, gently apply the brakes. At about 1" (25mm) of travel, a very small change in pedal effort (like a small bump) will be felt if the valve is operating properly. Metering valves are not serviceable and must be replaced if defective.

Brake Hoses and Lines

HYDRAULIC BRAKE LINE CHECK

The hydraulic brake lines and brake linings are to be inspected at the recommended intervals in the maintenance schedule. Follow the steel tubing from the master cylinder to the flexible hose fitting at each wheel. If a section of the tubing is found to be damaged, replace the entire section with tubing of the same type (steel, not

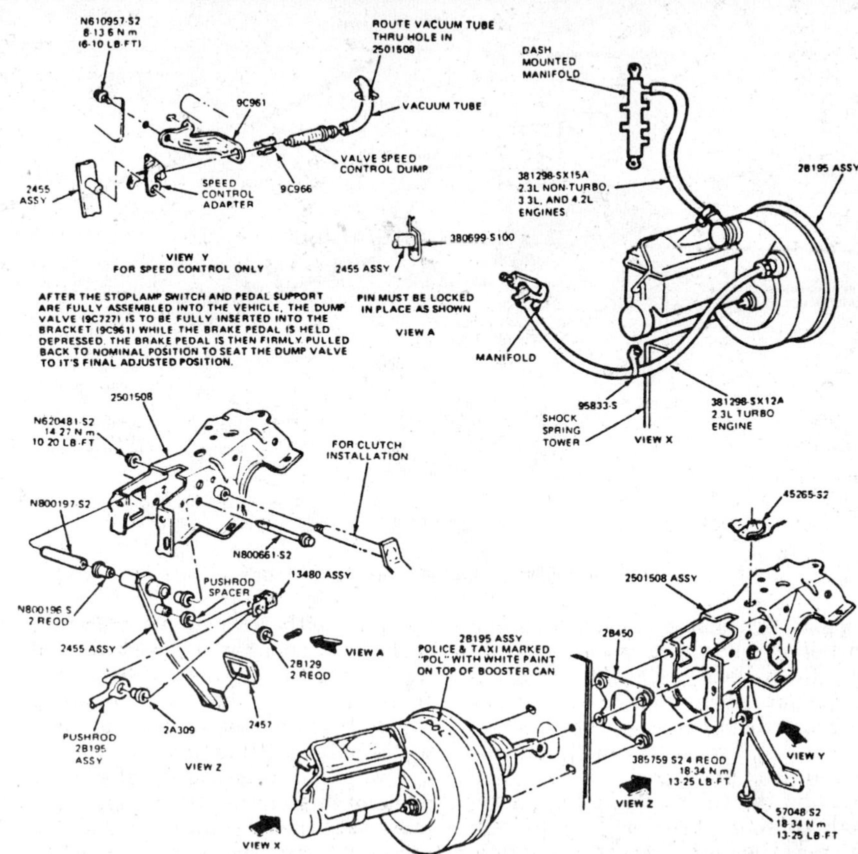

Master cylinder and brake pedal installation on the 1982-83 Thunderbird, Cougar and XR-7 models

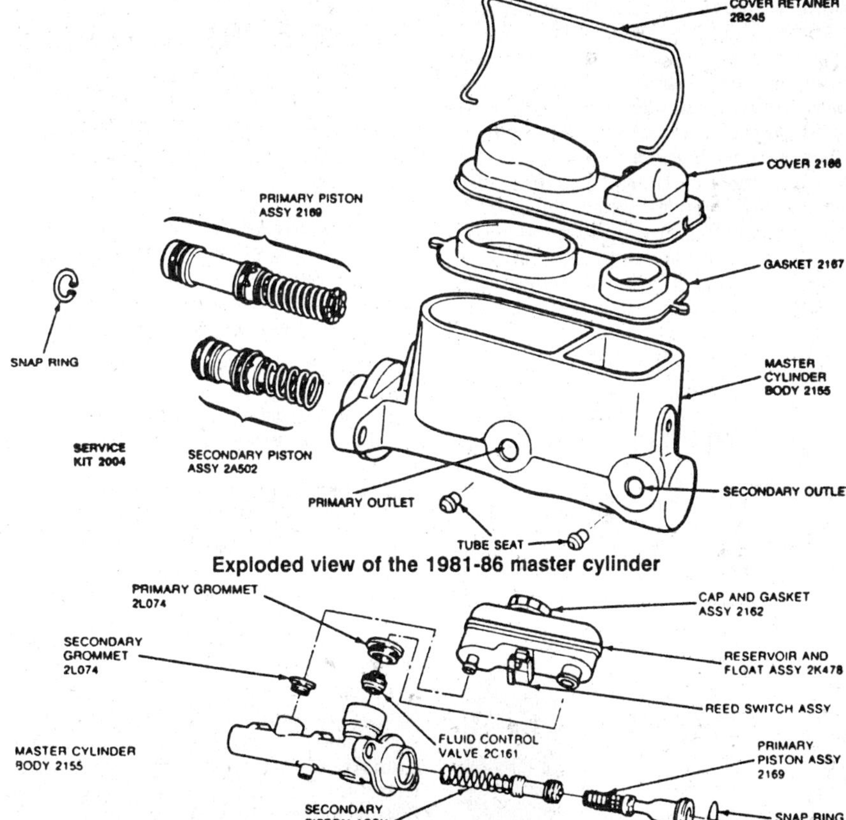

Exploded view of the 1981-86 master cylinder

Exploded business view of the 1987 master cylinder

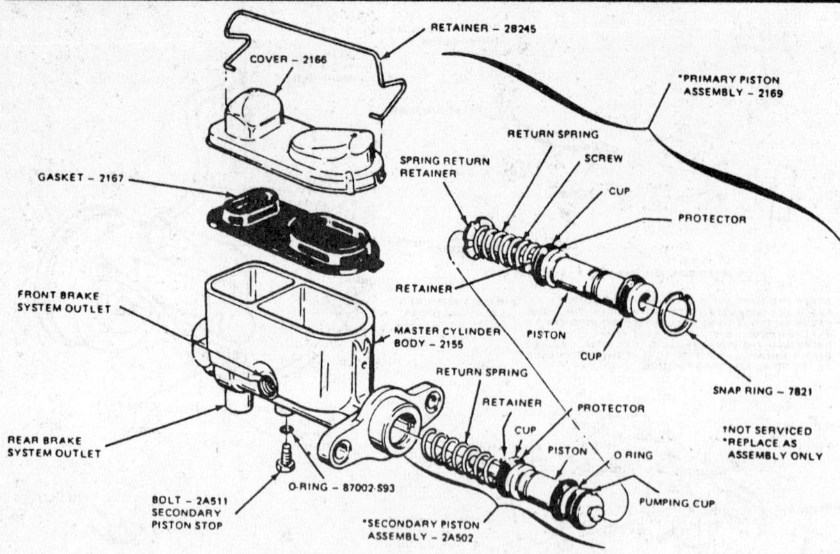

Exploded view of the 1980 master cylinder

copper), size, shape, and length. When installing a new section of brake tubing, flush clean brake fluid or denatured alcohol through to remove any dirt or foreign material from the line. Be sure to flare both ends to provide sound, leak-proof connections. When bending the tubing to fit the underbody contours, be careful not to kink or crack the line. Torque all hydraulic connections to 10-15 lbs.

Check the flexible brake hoses that connect the steel tubing to each wheel cylinder. Replace the hose if it shows any signs of softening, cracking, or other damage. When installing a new front brake hose, position the hose to avoid contact with other chassis parts. Place a new copper gasket over the hose fitting and thread the hose assembly into the front wheel cylinder. A new rear brake hose must be positioned clear of the exhaust pipe or shock absorber. Thread the hose into the rear brake tube connector. When installing either a new front or rear brake hose, engage the opposite end of the hose to the bracket on the frame. Install the horseshoe type retaining clip and connect the tube to the hose with the tube fitting nut.

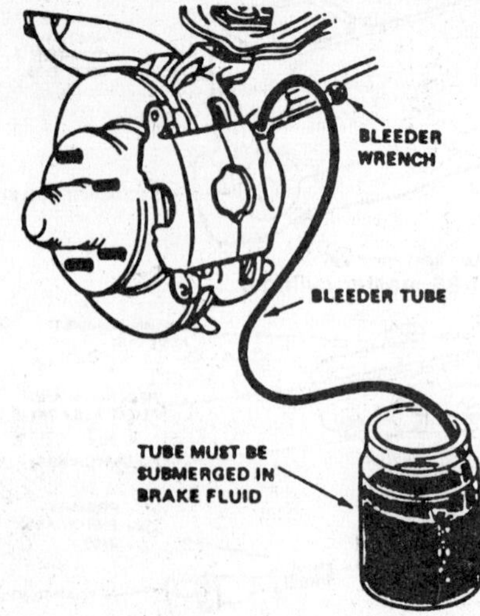

Brake bleeding equipment

Always bleed the system after hose or line replacement. Before bleeding, make sure that the master cylinder is topped up with high temperature, extra heavy duty fluid of at least SAE 70R3 quality.

Bleeding the Hydraulic System

See the **4 Wheel Anti-Lock Section** if your vehicle is equipped with that system.

NOTE: Since the front and rear hydraulic systems are independent of each other, if it is known that only one system has air in it, only that system has to be bled.

1. Fill the master cylinder with brake fluid.
2. Install a 3/8" box-end wrench to the bleeder screw on the right rear wheel.
3. Push a piece of small diameter rubber tubing over the bleeder screw until it is flush against the wrench. Submerge the other end of the rubber tubing in a glass jar partially filled with clean brake fluid. Make sure the rubber tube fits on the bleeder screw snugly.
4. Have a friend apply pressure to the brake pedal. Open the bleeder screw and observe the bottle of brake fluid. If bubbles appear in the glass jar; there is air in the system. When your friend has pushed the pedal to the floor, immediately close the bleed screw before he release the pedal.

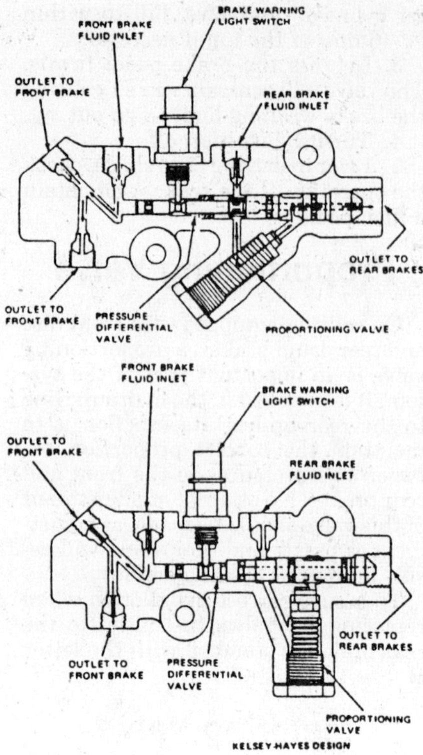

Control valve assembly on models with 4-wheel disc brakes

5. Repeat this procedure until no bubbles appear in the jar. Refill the master cylinder right front and left front wheels, in that order. Periodically refill the master cylinder so it does not run dry.
6. Center the pressure differential warning valve as outlined in the Pressure Differential Warning Valve section.

POWER ASSIST SYSTEMS

Vacuum Booster

REMOVAL & INSTALLATION

1. Working inside the car below the instrument panel, disconnect the booster valve operating rod from the brake pedal assembly.
2. Open the hood and disconnect the wires from the stop light switch at the brake master cylinder.
3. Disconnect the brake line at the master cylinder outlet fitting.
4. Disconnect the manifold vacuum hose from the booster unit.
5. Remove the four bracket-to-dash panel attaching bolts.
6. Remove the booster and bracket

assembly from the dash panel, sliding the valve operating rod out from the engine side of the dash panel.

7. Mount the booster and bracket assembly to the dash panel by sliding the valve operating rod in through the hole in the dash panel, and installing the attaching bolts.

8. Connect the manifold vacuum hose to the booster.

9. Connect the brake line to the master cylinder outlet fitting.

10. Connect the stop light switch wires.

11. Working inside the car below the instrument panel, install the rubber boot on the valve operating rod at the passenger side of the dash panel.

12. Connect the valve operating rod to the brake pedal with the bushings, eccentric shoulder bolt, and nut.

Hydro-Boost Hydraulic Booster

REMOVAL & INSTALLATION

A hydraulically powered brake booster is used on Continental, Mark VII and Thunderbird Turbo models. The power steering pump provides the fluid pressure to operate both the brake booster and the power steering gear.

The hydro-boost assembly contains a valve which controls pump pressure while braking, a lever to control the position of the valve and a boost piston to provide the force to operate a conventional master cylinder attached to the front of the booster. The hydro-boost also has a reserve system, designed to store sufficient pressurized fluid to provide at least 2 brake applications in the event of insufficient fluid flow from the power steering pump. The brakes can also be applied unassisted if the reserve system is depleted.

Before removing the hydro-boost, discharge the accumulator by making several brake applications until a hard pedal is felt.

1. Working from inside the vehicle, below the instrument panel, disconnect the pushrod from the brake pedal. Disconnect the stoplight switch wires at the connector. Remove the hairpin retainer. Slide the stoplight switch off the brake pedal far enough for the switch outer hole to clear the pin. Remove the switch from the pin. Slide the pushrod, nylon washers and bushing off the brake pedal pin.

2. Open the hood and remove the nuts attaching the master cylinder to the hydro-boost. Remove the master cylinder. Secure it to one side without disturbing the hydraulic lines.

3. Disconnect the pressure, steering gear and return lines from the booster. Plug the lines to prevent the entry of dirt.

4. Remove the nuts attaching the hydro-boost. Remove the booster from the firewall, sliding the pushrod link out of the engine side of the firewall.

5. Install the hydro-boost on the firewall and install the attaching nuts.

6. Install the master cylinder on the booster.

7. Connect the pressure, steering gear and return lines to the booster.

8. Working below the instrument panel, install the nylon washer, booster pushrod and bushing on the brake pedal pin. Install the switch so that it straddles the pushrod with the switch slot on the pedal pin and the switch outer hole just clearing the pin. Slide the switch completely onto the pin and install the nylon washer. Attach these parts with the hairpin retainer. Connect the stoplight switch wires and install the wires in the retaining clip.

9. Remove the coil wire so that the engine will not start. Fill the power steering pump and engage the starter. Apply the brakes with a pumping action. Do not turn the steering wheel until air has been bled from the booster.

10. Check the fluid level and add as required. Start the engine and apply the brakes, checking for leaks. Cycle the steering wheel.

11. If a whine type noise is heard, suspect fluid aeration.

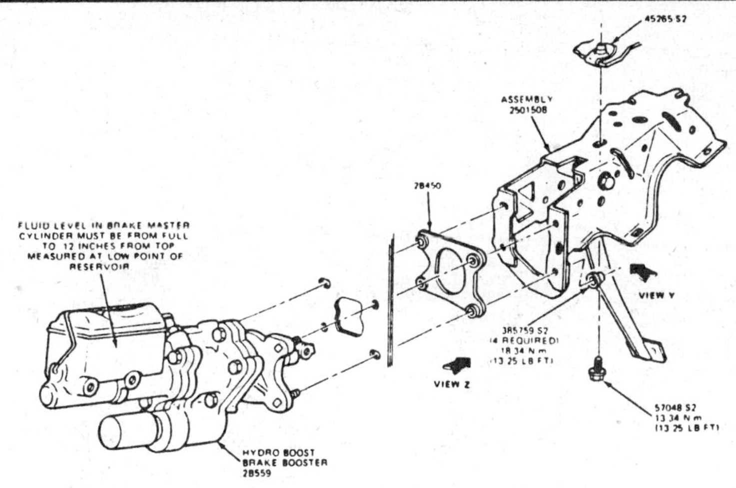

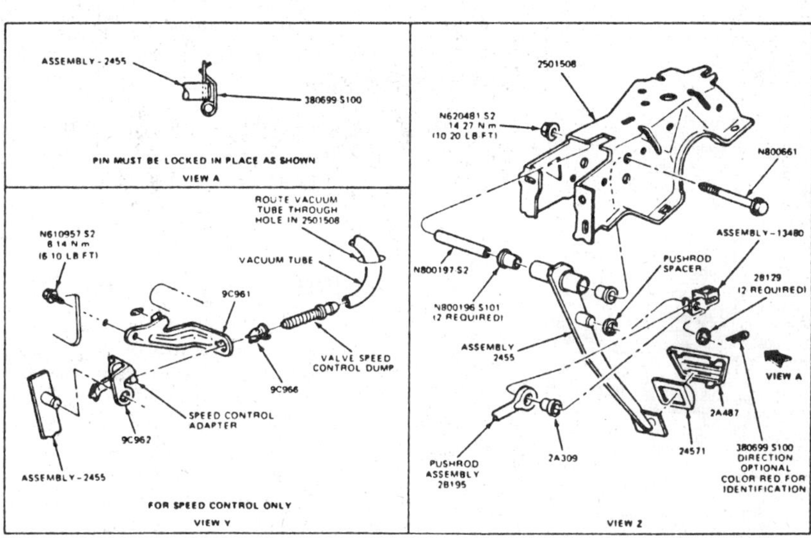

Hydro-Boost power brake system

4-WHEEL ANTI-LOCK BRAKE SYSTEM

The 4 Wheel Anti-Lock brake system is a compact integral power brake system that uses brake fluid for both brake function and hydraulic boost. The system is used on 1982-87 Continentals, 1984-87 Mark VIIs and 1987 Thunderbird Turbo Coupe.

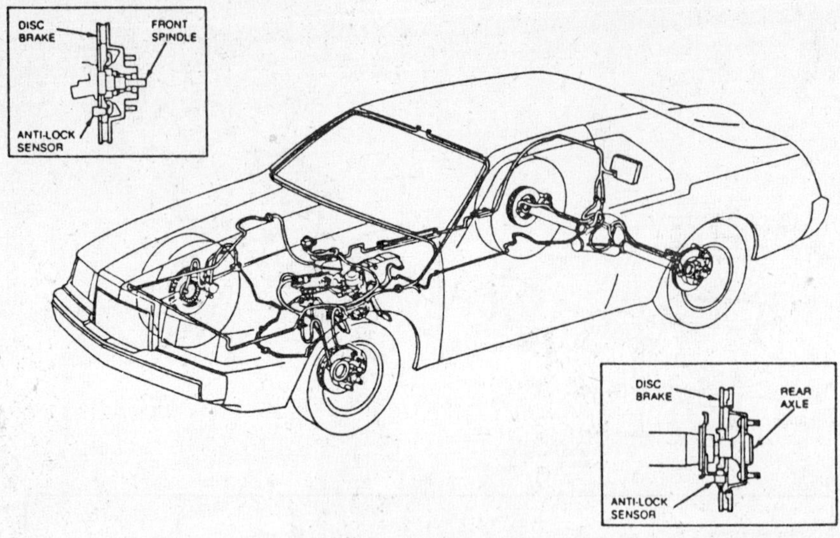

Anti-skid brake system

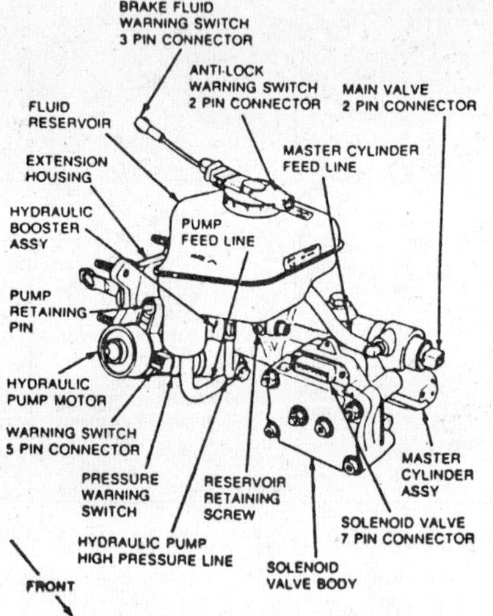

Anti-skid hydraulic cylinder/booster unit

Individual front wheel brake circuits and a combined rear wheel brake circuit are used. Major components of the system are:

Master Cylinder and Hydraulic Booster

The master cylinder and brake booster are mounted in the conventional manner. The booster control valve is located in a parallel bore above the master cylinder centerline and is operated by a lever mechanism connected to the brake pedal pushrod.

Electric Pump and Accumulator

A high pressure electric pump runs for short periods at frequent intervals to charge the hydraulic accumulator. The accumulator is a gas filled pressure chamber that is part of the pump and motor assembly. The pump, motor and accumulator are mounted to the master cylinder/booster assembly.

Valve Body Assembly

The valve body contains three pairs of solenoid valves, one pair for each front wheel and the third pair for both the rear wheels combined. The paired solenoid valves are inlet/outlet valves with the inlet valve normally open and the outlet valve normally closed. The valve body is bolted to the inboard side of the master cylinder/booster assembly.

Reservoir and Fluid Level Warning Switches

A translucent plastic reservoir having two main chambers is connected to the pump assembly and master cylinder by two low pressure hoses. Integral fluid level switches are part of the reservoir cap assembly. The reservoir is mounted to the hydraulic unit with a screw and bracket and a push-in tube outlet that seats in a grommet mounted in the brake booster housing.

Wheel Sensors

Four variable reluctance electronic sensor assemblies are used, each is provided with a 104 tooth ring. Each sensor is connected to an electric controller through a wiring harness. The front sensors are bolted to front spindle mounted brackets. The front toothed sensor rings are pressed into the inside of the front disc rotors. The rear sensors are bolted to the rear brake axle adapters. The toothed rear sensor rings are pressed on the axle shafts, inboard of the axle shaft flange.

Electronic Controller

The electronic controller is a non-repairable unit consisting of two microprocessors and the necessary circuitry for operation. The controller monitors system operation during normal driving as well as during anti-lock (panic) braking. Under wheel locking conditions signals are triggered from the controller that open and close solenoid valves resulting in moderate pulsations in the brake pedal and equal anti-locking control to all four wheels.

System Operation

The hydraulic pump maintains between 2,030 to 2,610 psi pressure in the accumulator which is connected by a high pressure hose to the booster chamber and control valve. When the brakes are applied, a scissor/lever mechanism activates the control valve and pressure, proportional to brake pedal travel, enters the booster chamber. The pressure is transmitted through the normally open solenoid valve through the proportioning valve to the rear brakes. The same pressure moves the booster piston against the master cylinder piston, shutting off the central valves in the master cylinder. This applies pressure to the front wheels through the two normally open solenoid valves. The electronic controller monitor the elctro-mechanical components of the system. Malfunction of the anti-lock system will cause the electronic controller to shut off or inhibit the anti-lock system. Normal power assisted braking remains if the anti-lock system shuts off. Malfunctions are indicated by one or two warning lamps inside the vehicle.

The 4-wheel anti-lock system is self-monitoring. When the ignition switch is placed in the Run position, the electronic controller will preform a preliminary self check on the anti-lock electrical system as indicated by a three to four second illumination of the amber Check Anti-Lock Brakes lamp in the overhead console. During vehicle operation, including normal and anti-lock braking operation is continually monitored. Should a problem occur, either the Check Anti-Lock Brakes or the Brake Warning Lamp(s) will be illuminated. Inspection of the system and any necessary repairs should be done before any further vehicle operation.

Brake System Bleeding

CAUTION

The 4-Wheel Anti-Lock brake system is under high accumulator hydraulic pressure most of the time. Before servicing any component which contains high pressure, it is mandatory that the high pressure in the system be discharged.

SYSTEM DISCHARGING (DEPRESSURIZING)

Turn the ignition to the Off position. Pump the brake pedal a minimum of twenty times until an increase in pedal force is clearly felt.

FRONT BRAKE BLEEDING

The front brakes can be bled in the conventional manner, with or without the accumulator being charged. Refer to the previous brake bleeding section at the beginning of this section for instructions.

REAR BRAKE BLEEDING

A fully charged accumulator is required for successful rear brake system bleeding. Once accumulator pressure is applied to the system, the rear brakes can be bled by opening the rear caliper bleeder screw while holding the brake pedal in the applied position with the ignition switch in the Run position. Repeat the procedure until an air free flow of brake fluid comes from the bleeder screw. Close the bleeder screw. Close the bleeder screw. Add fluid to the master cylinder reservoir until required level is reached.

CAUTION

Care must be used when opening the bleeder screws. The fluid is under high pressure and could cause injury if splashed into eyes, etc.

Hydraulic Reservoir

CHECKING FLUID LEVEL AND REFILLING

1. With the ignition switch On, pump the brake pedal until the hydraulic pump motor starts.
2. Wait until the pump shuts off and check the brake fluid level in the reservoir. If the level is below the MAX fill line, add fluid until the line is reached.

WARNING: Do not overfill! The level may be over the MAX line depending upon the accumulator charge. Perform the above procedure before adding or removing brake fluid.

Component Removal and Installation

HYDRAULIC CYLINDER/BOOSTER UNIT ASSEMBLY

CAUTION

Depressurize the system before working on the system. To depressurize the system, turn the ignition OFF and pump the brake pedal at least 20 times, until an obvious increase in pedal pressure is felt.

1. Disconnect the negative battery cable.
2. Disconnect the electrical connectors from the fluid reservoir cap, main valve, solenoid valve body, pressure warning switch, hydraulic pump motor and the ground connector from the master cylinder. Label them for installation identification.
3. Disconnect the brake lines from the solenoid valve body and plug them to prevent fluid loss.
4. Disconnect the booster pushrod from the brake pedal by first disconnecting the spotlight switch wires at the connector on the brake pedal. Then, remove the hairpin connector at the stoplight switch and slide the switch off the pedal pin until the large end of the switch (outer hole) is off of the pin. Remove the switch using a twisting motion. Remove the unit's four retaining nuts at the firewall.
5. Remove the booster from the engine compartment.
6. Install in the reverse order. Bleed the brake system.

HYDRAULIC ACCUMULATOR

CAUTION

Depressurize the system before working on the system.

1. Disconnect the negative battery cable. Disconnect the electrical connector at the hydraulic pump motor.
2. Use a 8mm hex wrench, loosen and unscrew the accumulator. Do not allow any dirt to enter the open port.
3. Loosen and remove the accumulator mounting block, if necessary.
4. Install in the reverse order using new O-ring seals.
5. Turn the ignition switch to the On position. Check that the Check Anti-Lock Brakes lamp goes out after a maximum of one minute. Fill the reservoir as necessary.

HYDRAULIC PUMP MOTOR

CAUTION

Depressurize the system before working on the system.

1. Disconnect the negative battery cable.
2. Disconnect the electrical connections at the hydraulic pump motor and pressure warning switch.
3. Use a 8mm hex wrench and remove the accumulator, make sure not dirt falls into the open port.
4. Remove the suction line between the reservoir and the pump at the reservoir by twisting the hose and pulling. Plug the hose to prevent fluid loss. Install a plugged piece of large vacuum hose on the reservoir nipple to prevent fluid loss.
5. Remove the banjo bolt (hollow hex headed bolt) connecting the high pressure hose to the booster housing, at the housing. Be sure to catch and save the sealing O-rings, one on each side of the banjo bolt head.
6. Remove the allen headed bolt attaching the pump and motor assembly to the extension housing which is located directly under the accumulator. A long extension and universal swivel socket will help reach the bolt.
7. Move the pump assembly toward the engine and remove the retainer pin on the inboard side of the extension housing. Remove the pump and motor assembly.
8. Installation is in the reverse order of removal. Tighten the allen head bolt to 60-84 in.lb. Tighten the banjo bolt to 12-15 ft.lb. after installing new O-rings (if necessary). Install a new O-ring on the accumulator and tighten to 30-40 ft.lb.
9. Turn the ignition switch to On. Check that the Check Anti-Lock Brakes lamp goes out after a maximum of one minute. Check the brake level in the reservoir, add fluid if necessary.

RESERVOIR ASSEMBLY

CAUTION

Depressurize the system before working on the system.

1. Disconnect the negative battery cable.
2. Remove the electrical connectors from the reservoir cap. Unlock and remove the cap.
3. Empty the reservoir of as much fluid as possible using a large rubber syringe or suction gun.
4. Remove the line between the pump and reservoir, from the reservoir by twisting and pulling the hose from the reservoir fitting.

5. Remove the return line between the reservoir and master cylinder at the reservoir in the same manner as Step 4.
6. Remove the allen head reservoir mounting screw.
7. Pry the reservoir from the booster housing carefully. Be sure the short sleeve and O-ring are removed from the booster housing.
8. Install the reservoir mounting bracket in its guide on the bottom of the reservoir. Check to be sure that the short sleeve and O-ring are in position at the bottom of the reservoir. Wet the mounting grommet with brake fluid.
9. Insert the reservoir into the grommet as far as it will go on the booster housing, make sure the short sleeve and O-ring are in place. The reservoir should be held vertical to the booster during installation.
10. The rest of the installation is in the reverse order of removal.
11. Fill the reservoir to the correct level with a charged accumulator.

ELECTRONIC CONTROLLER

The controller is located in the luggage compartment in front of the forward trim panel.

1. Disconnect the 35 pin connector from the controller.
2. Remove the three retaining screws holding the controller to the seat back brace and remove the controller.
3. Install in the reverse order.

PRESSURE SWITCH

CAUTION

Depressurize the system before working on the system.

1. Disconnect the negative battery cable.
2. Disconnect the valve body seven pin connector. Failure to disconnect the connector can result in damage to the connector if struck by removal tool.
3. Remove the pressure switch with special socket T85P-20215-B or equivalent.
4. Inspect the mounting O-ring, replace if necessary. Install the switch in the reverse order of removal. Tighten to 15-25 ft.lb.

FRONT WHEEL SENSOR

1. Disconnect the harness connector on the inside of the engine compartment for either the right or left sensor.
2. Raise and support the front side of the vehicle to be worked on. Remove wheel, caliper and disc rotor assemblies.
3. Disengage the wire grommet at the shock tower and draw the sensor cable carefully through the grommet mounting hole. Remove the harness from the mounting brackets.
4. Loosen the 5mm set screw that hold the sensor to the mounting bracket. Remove the sensor through the hole in the disc brake splash shield.
5. Clean the sensor face, if reusing the original sensor. Install in the reverse order of removal. Install a new paper spacer on the sensor mounting flange before installation.

REAR WHEEL SENSOR

1. Disconnect the sensor connector for the side requiring service. The connector is located on the inside of the luggage compartment behind the forward trim panel.
2. Lift the carpet and push the sensor wire mounting grommet through the mounting hole.
3. Raise and support the rear of the vehicle. Remove the wire harness from the retaining brackets and C-clip. Pull rearward on the clip to disengage.
4. Remove the wheel, caliper and rotor assemblies.
5. Remove the sensor mounting bolt. Slip the grommet out of the splash shield and pull the sensor wire through the hole.
6. Install in the reverse order. If the original sensor is to be used clean the sensor face. Install a new paper spacer on the sensor mounting flange before installation.

FRONT WHEEL SENSOR RING

NOTE: Toothed sensor ring replacement requires the use of an arbor press. An automotive machine shop or well equipped garage should be able to handle the job.

1. Remove the rotor assembly.
2. Position the rotor face up on the arbor press bed.
3. Using the proper adapters, press each stud down until they contact the sensor ring.
4. Position an approximate adapter on the top of all five studs and press the studs and sensor ring from the rotor.
5. Install the studs into the rotor using the press. Install the sensor ring with the press until the ring bottoms in position.
6. Install the rotor in the reverse order of removal.

REAR WHEEL SENSOR RING

1. Remove the rear axle shaft. Install the necessary adapter between the axle shaft flange and sensor ring.
2. Position the axle in an arbor press and remove the sensor ring.
3. Press the sensor ring into position until a gap of 47mm between the sensor ring and face of the axle flange is obtained.
4. Reinstall the axle shaft and removed components.

REAR DRUM BRAKES

Duo-Servo Self-Adjusting Drum Brakes

Drum brakes on all Ford cars employ single anchor, internally expanding, and self-adjusting brake assemblies. The automatic adjusting continuously maintains correct operating clearance between the linings and the drums by adjusting the brake in small increments in direct proportion to lining wear. When applying the brakes while backing up, the linings tend to follow the rotating drum counterclockwise, thus forcing the upper end of the primary shoe against the anchor pin. Simultaneously, the wheel cylinder pushes the upper end of the secondary shoe and cable guide outward, away from the anchor pin. This movement of the secondary shoe causes the cable to pull the adjusting lever upward and against the end of the tooth on the adjusting screw star wheel. As lining wear increases, the upward travel of the adjusting lever also increases. When the linings have worn sufficiently to allow the lever to move upward far enough, it passes over the end of the tooth and engages it. Upon release of the brakes, the adjusting spring pulls the adjuster level downward, turning the star wheel and expanding the brakes.

INSPECTION

CAUTION

Brake shoes contain asbestos, which has been determined to be a cancer causing agent. Never clean the brake surfaces with compressed air! Avoid inhaling any dust from any brake surface! When cleaning brake surfaces, use a commercially available brake cleaning fluid.

1. Raise the rear of the car and support the car with safety stands. Make sure the parking brake is not on.

2. Remove the lug nuts that attach the wheels to the axle shaft and remove the tires and wheels from the car. Using a pair of pliers, remove the Tinnerman nuts from the wheel studs. Pull the brake drum of the axle shaft. If the brakes are adjusted too tightly to remove the drum, see Step 3. If you can remove the drum, see Step 4.

3. If the brakes are too tight to remove the drum, get under the car (make sure you have safety stands under the car to support it) and remove the rubber plug from the bottom of the brake backing plate. Shine a flashlight into the slot in the plate. You will see the top of the adjusting screw star wheel and the adjusting lever for the automatic brake adjusting mechanism. To back off on the adjusting screw, you must first inert a small, thin screwdriver or a piece of firm wire (coat hanger wire) into the adjusting slot and push the adjusting lever away from the adjusting screw. Then, insert a brake adjusting spoon into the slot and engage the top of the star wheel. Lift up on the bottom of the adjusting spoon to force the adjusting screw star wheel downward. Repeat this operation until the brake drum is free of the brake shoes and can be pulled off.

4. Clean the brake shoes and the inside of the brake drum. There must be at least $^1/_{16}$" (1.6mm) of brake lining above the heads of the brake shoe attaching rivets. The lining should not be cracked or contaminated with grease or brake fluid. If there is grease or brake fluid on the lining it must be replaced and the source of the leak must be found and corrected. Brake fluid on the lining means leaking wheel cylinders. Grease on the brake lining means a leaking grease retainer (front wheels) or axle seal (rear brakes). If the lining is slightly glazed but otherwise in good condition, it can be cleaned up with medium sandpaper. Lift up the bottom of the wheel cylinder boots and inspect the ends of the wheel cylinders. A small amount of fluid in the end of the cylinder should be considered normal. If fluid runs out of the cylinder when the boots are lifted, however, the wheel cylinder must be rebuilt or replaced. Examine the inside of the brake drum; it should have a smooth, dull finish. If excessive brake shoe wear caused grooves to wear in the drum it must be machined or replaced. If the inside of the drum is slightly glazed, but otherwise good, it can be cleaned up with medium sandpaper.

5. If no repairs are required, install the drum and wheel. If the brake adjustment was changed to remove the drum, adjust the brakes until the drum will just fit over the brakes. After the wheel is installed it will be necessary to complete the adjustment. See Brake Adjustment in this section.

Brake Shoes

REMOVAL

CAUTION

Brake shoes contain asbestos, which has been determined to be a cancer causing agent. Never clean the brake surfaces with compressed air! Avoid inhaling any dust from any brake surface! When cleaning brake surfaces, use a commercially available brake cleaning fluid.

WARNING: If you are not thoroughly familiar with the procedures involved in brake replacement, only disassembly and assemble one side at a time, leaving the other wheel intact as a reference.

1. Remove the brake drum. See the inspection procedure.

2. Place the hollow end of the brake spring service tool (available at auto parts stores) on the brake shoe anchor pin and twist it to disengage one of the brake retracting springs. Repeat this operation to remove the other spring.

CAUTION

Be careful that the springs do not slip off the tool during removal, as they could cause personal injury.

3. Reach behind the brake backing plate and place a finger on the end of one of the brake holddown spring mounting pins. Using a pair of pliers, grasp the washer on the top of the holddown spring that corresponds to the pin that you are holding. Push down on the pliers and turn them 90 degrees to align the slot in the washer with the head on the spring mounting pin. Remove the spring and washer and repeat this operation on the holddown spring on the other brake shoe.

4. Place the tip of a screwdriver on the top of the brake adjusting screw and move the screwdriver upward to lift up on the brake adjusting lever. When there is enough slack in the automatic adjuster cable, disconnect the loop on the top of the cable from the anchor. Grasp the top of each brake shoe and move it outward to disengage it from the wheel cylinder (and parking brake link on rear wheels). When the brake shoes are clear, lift them from the backing plate. Twist the shoes slightly and the automatic adjuster assembly will disassemble itself.

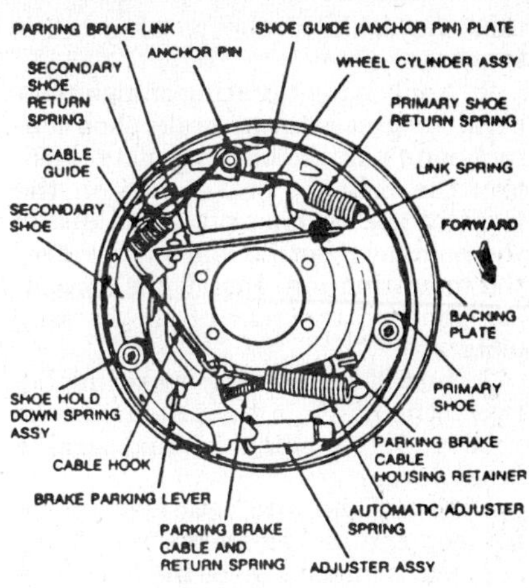

9 inch drum brake

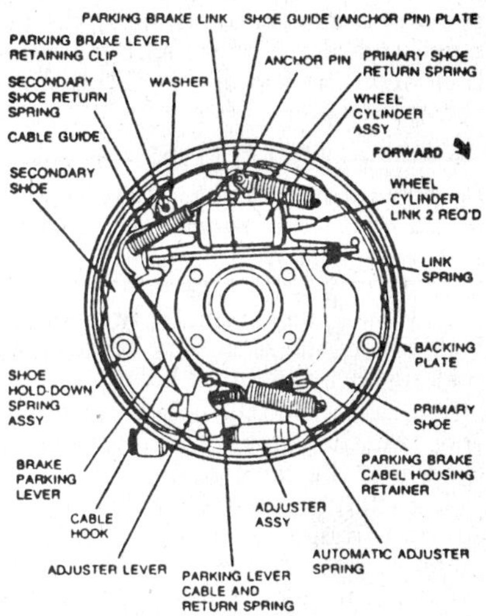

10 inch drum brake

5. Grasp the end of the brake cable spring with a pair of pliers and, using the brake lever as a fulcrum, pull the end of the spring away from the lever. Disengage the cable from the brake lever.

INSTALLATION

1. The brake cable must be connected to the secondary brake shoe before the shoe is installed on the backing plate. To do this, first transfer the parking brake lever from the old secondary shoe to the new one. This is accomplished by spreading the bottom of the horseshoe clip and disengaging the lever. Position the lever on the new secondary shoe and install the spring washer and the horseshoe clip. Close the bottom of the clip after installing it. Grasp the metal tip of the parking brake cable with a pair of pliers. Position a pair of side cutter pliers on the end of the cable coil spring, and using the plier as a fulcrum, pull the coil spring back with the side cutters. Posi-

tion the cable in the parking brake lever.

2. Apply a light coating of high temperature grease to the brake shoe contact points on the backing plate. Position the primary brake shoe on the front of the backing plate and install the holddown spring and washer over the mounting pin. Install the secondary shoe on the rear of the backing plate.

3. Install the parking brake link between the notch in the primary brake shoe and the notch in the parking brake lever.

4. Install the automatic adjuster cable loop end on the anchor pin. Make sure the crimped side of the loop faces the backing plate.

5. Install the return spring in the primary brake shoe and, using the tapered end of the brake spring service tool, slide the top of the spring onto the anchor pin.

CAUTION

Be careful to make sure that the spring does not slip off the tool during installation, as it could cause injury.

6. Install the automatic adjuster cable guide in the secondary brake shoe, making sure the flared hole in the cable guide is inside the hole in the brake shoe. Fit the cable into the groove in the top of the cable guide.

7. Install the secondary shoe return spring through the hole in the cable guide and the brake shoe. Using the brake spring tool, slide the top of the spring onto the anchor pin.

8. Clean the threads on the adjusting screw and apply a light coating of high temperature grease to the threads. Screw the adjuster closed, then open it ½ turn.

9. Install the adjusting screw between the brake shoes with the star wheel nearest to the secondary shoe. Make sure the star wheel is in a position that is accessible from the adjusting slot in the backing plate.

10. Install the short hooked end of the automatic adjuster spring in the proper hole in the primary brake shoe.

11. Connect the hooked end of the automatic adjuster cable and the free end of the automatic adjuster spring in the slot in the top of the automatic adjuster lever.

12. Pull the automatic adjuster lever (the lever will pull the cable and spring with it) downward and to the left and engage the pivot hook of the lever in the hole in the secondary brake shoe.

13. Check the entire brake assembly to make sure that everything is installed properly. Make sure that the shoes engage the wheel cylinder properly and are flush on the anchor pin. Make sure that the automatic adjuster cable is flush on the anchor pin and in the slot on the back of the cable guide. Make sure that the adjusting lever rests on the adjusting screw star wheel. Pull upward on the adjusting cable until the adjusting lever is free of the star wheel, then release the cable. The adjusting lever should snap back into place on the adjusting screw star wheel and turn the wheel one tooth.

14. Expand the brake adjusting screw until the brake drum will just fit over the brake shoes.

15. Install the wheel and drum and adjust the brakes.

Wheel Cylinders

REPLACEMENT

1. Remove the brake shoes.

2. On rear brakes, loosen the brake line on the rear of the cylinder but do not pull the line away from the cylinder or it may bend.

3. On front brakes, disconnect the metal brake line from the rubber brake hose where they join in the wheel well. Pull off the horseshoe clip that attaches the rubber brake hose to the underbody of the car. Loosen the hose at the cylinder, then turn the whole brake hose to remove it from the wheel cylinder.

4. Remove the bolts and lockwashers that attach the wheel cylinder to the backing plate and remove the cylinder.

5. Position the new wheel cylinder on the backing plate and install the cylinder attaching bolts and lockwashers.

6. Attach the metal brake line or rubber hose by reversing the procedure given in Steps 2 or 3.

7. Install the brakes.

OVERHAUL

Since the travel of the pistons in the wheel cylinder changes when new brakes shoes are installed, it is possible for previously good wheel cylinders to start leaking after new brakes are installed, Therefore, to save yourself the expense of having to replace new brakes that become saturated with brake fluid and the aggravation of having to take everything apart again, it is strongly recommended that wheel cylinders be rebuilt every time new brake shoes are installed. This is especially true on high mileage cars.

1. Remove the brakes.

CAUTION

Brake shoes contain asbestos, which has been determined to be a cancer causing agent. Never clean the brake surfaces with compressed air! Avoid inhaling any dust from any brake surface! When cleaning brake surfaces, use a commercially available brake cleaning fluid.

2. Place a bucket or old newspapers under the brake backing plate to catch the brake fluid that will run out of the wheel cylinder.

3. Remove the boots from the ends of the wheel cylinders.

4. Push one piston toward the center of the cylinder to force the opposite piston and cup out of the other end of the cylinder. Reach in the open end of the cylinder and push the spring cup, and piston out of the cylinder.

5. Remove the bleeder screw from the rear of the cylinder, on the back of the backing plate.

6. Inspect the inside of the wheel cylinder. If it is scored in any way, the cylinder must be honed with a wheel cylinder hone or fine emery paper, and finished with crocus cloth if emery paper is used. If the inside of the cylinder is excessively worn, the cylinder will have to be replaced, as only 0.003" (0.0762mm) of material can be removed from the cylinder walls. When honing or cleaning the wheel cylinders, keep a small amount of brake fluid in the cylinder to serve as a lubricant.

7. Clean any foreign matter from the pistons. The sides of the pistons must be smooth for the wheel cylinders to operate properly.

8. Clean the cylinder bore with alcohol and a lint-free rag. Pull the rag through the bore several times to remove all foreign matter and dry the cylinder.

9. Install the bleeder screw and the return spring in the cylinder.

10. Coat new cylinder cups with new brake fluid and install them in the cylinder. Make sure that they are square in the bore or they will leak.

11. Install the pistons in the cylinder after coating them with new brake fluid.

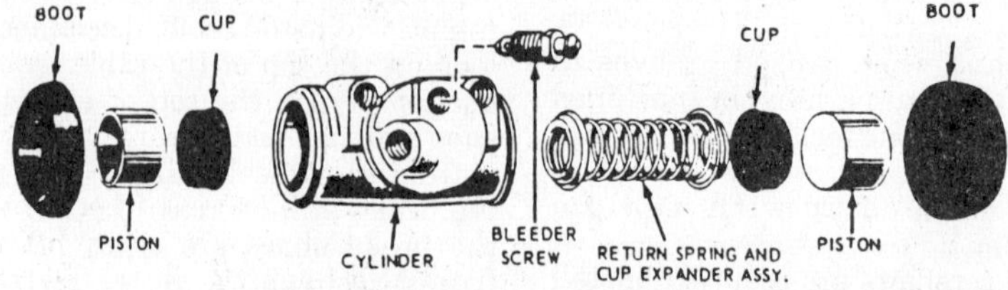

Wheel cylinder disassembled

12. Coat the insides of the boots with new brake fluid and install them on the cylinder. Install the brakes.

FRONT DISC BRAKES

Inspection

1. Raise the vehicle until the wheel and tire clear the floor. Place safety stands under the vehicle.
2. Remove the wheel cover. Remove the wheel and tire from the hub and disc.

CAUTION

Brake shoes contain asbestos, which has been determined to be a cancer causing agent. Never clean the brake surfaces with compressed air! Avoid inhaling any dust from any brake surface! When cleaning brake surfaces, use a commercially available brake cleaning fluid.

3. Visually inspect the shoe and lining assemblies. If the lining material has worn to a thickness of 0.030" (0.762mm) or less, or if the lining is contaminated with brake fluid, replace all pad assemblies on both front wheels. Make all thickness measurements across the thinnest section of the pad assembly. A slight taper on a used lining should be considered normal.
4. To check disc runout, tighten the wheel bearing adjusting nut to eliminate end-play. Check to make sure the disc can still be rotated.
5. Hand spin the disc and visually check for runout. If the disc appears to be out of round or if it wobbles, it needs to be machined or replaced. When the runout check is finished, loosen the wheel bearing adjusting nut and retighten to specifications, in order to prevent bearing damage.
6. Visually check the disc for scoring. Minor scores can be removed with fine emery cloth. If it is excessively scored, it must be machined or replaced.
7. The caliper should be visually checked. If excess leakage is evident, the caliper should be replaced.
8. Install the wheel and hub assembly.

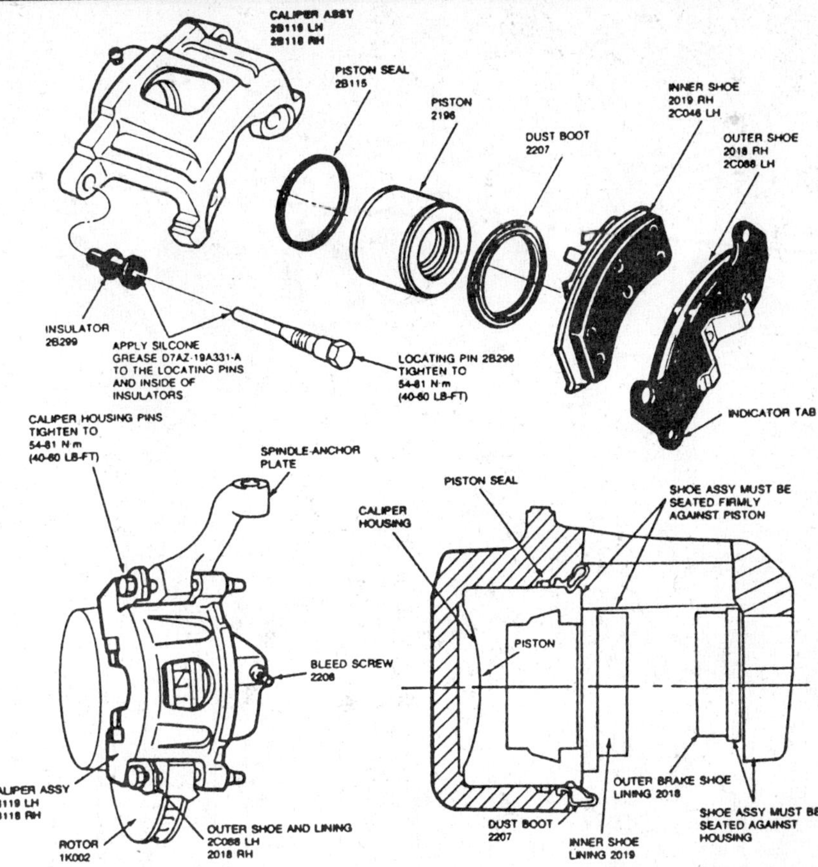

Exploded view of the caliper used on the 1986-87 Thunderbird Turbo, Mark VII and Continental

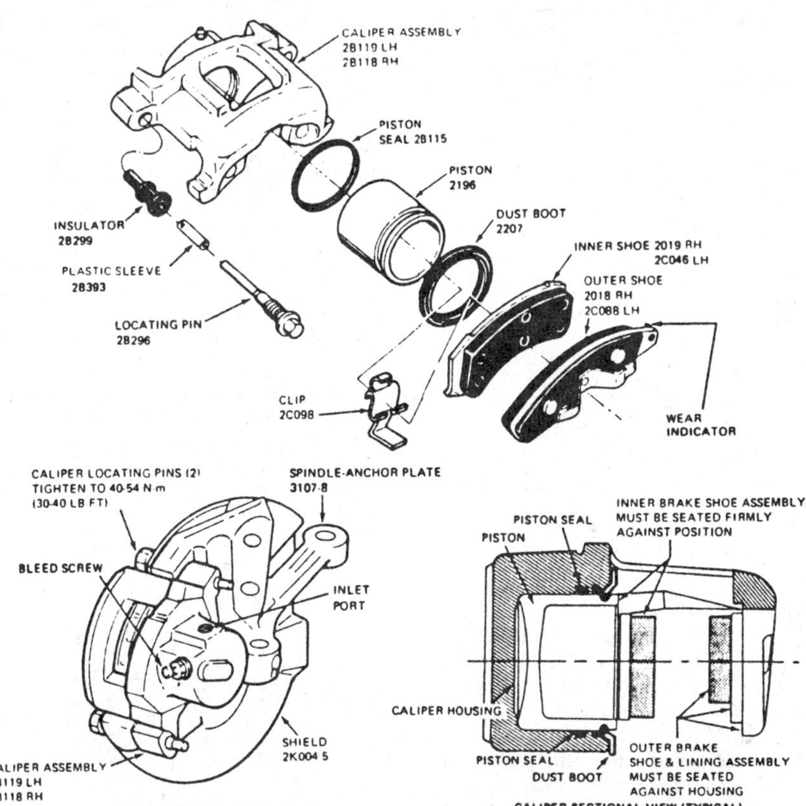

Front disc brake components for the 1980-82 Thunderbird, Cougar and XR-7

Brake Pads

REPLACEMENT

Ford Single Piston Sliding Caliper Disc Brakes

1. Remove the master cylinder cap, and check the fluid level in the prima-

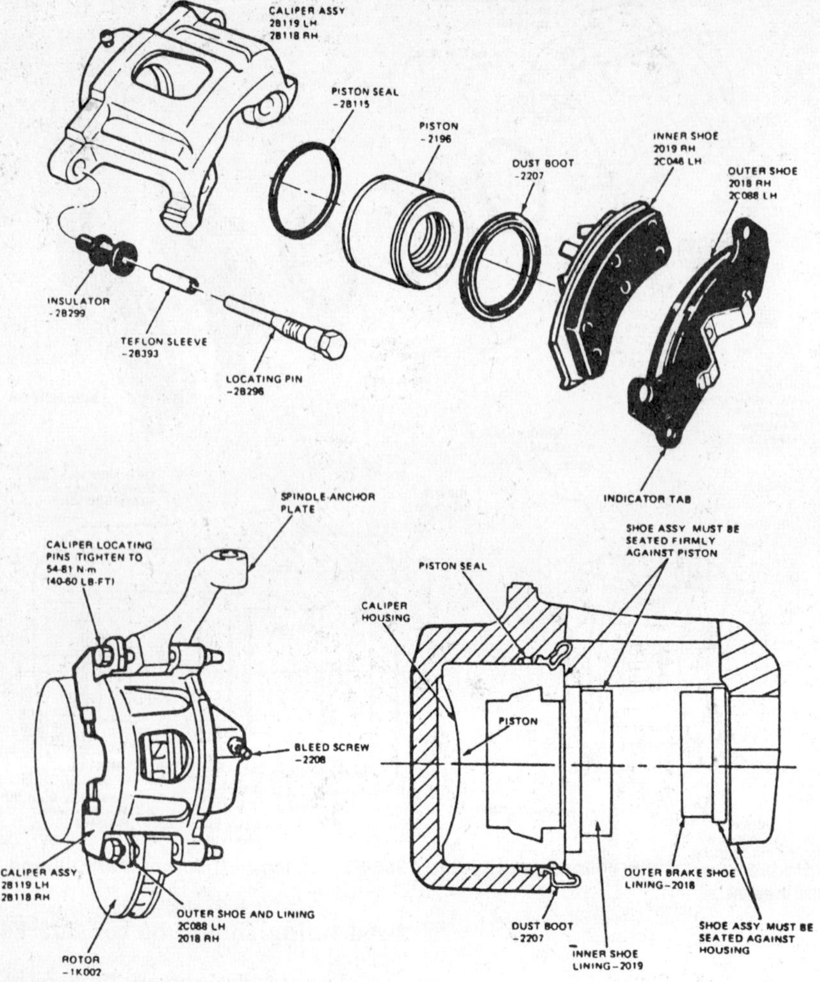

Front disc brake components for the 1982-85 Continental and 1984-85 Mark VII, except those models with anti-skid brakes

ry (large) reservoir. Remove brake fluid until the reservoir is half full. Discard this fluid.

2. Raise and safely support the vehicle. Remove the wheel and tire assembly from the hub. Be careful to avoid damage to or interference with the caliper splash shield or bleeder screw fitting.

CAUTION

Brake shoes contain asbestos, which has been determined to be a cancer causing agent. Never clean the brake surfaces with compressed air! Avoid inhaling any dust from any brake surface! When cleaning brake surfaces, use a commercially available brake cleaning fluid.

3. Remove the caliper locating pins.

4. Lift the caliper assembly from the integral spindle/anchor plate and rotor. Remove the outer shoe from the caliper assembly on Continental and Mark VII models slip shoe down the caliper leg until clip is disengaged.

5. Remove the inner shoe and lining assembly. On Continental and Mark VII models, pull shoe straight out of piston. This could require a force as high as 20-30 lbs. Inspect both rotor braking surfaces. Minor scoring or building of lining material does not require machining or replacement of the rotor.

6. Suspend the caliper inside the fender housing with a wire hooked through the outer leg hole of the caliper. Be careful not to damage the caliper or stretch the brake hose.

7. Remove and discard the plastic sleeves that are located inside the caliper locating pin insulators. These parts must not be reused.

8. Remove and discard the caliper locating insulator. These parts must not be reused.

9. Use a 4" (101mm) C-clamp and a block of wood 2¾" x 1" and approximately ¾" thick (70mm x 25mm x 19mm) to seat the caliper hydraulic piston in its bore. This must be done to provide clearance for the caliper assembly to fit over the rotor when installed. Remove the C-clamp from the caliper (the caliper piston will remain seated in its bore).

CAUTION

On Continental and Mark VII models, the piston is made of phenolic material and must not be seated in bore by applying C-clamp directly to the piston.

10. Install new locating pin insulators and plastic sleeves in the caliper housing. Do not use a sharp edge tool to insert the insulators in the caliper housing. Check to see if both insulator flanges straddle the housing holes and if the plastic sleeves are bottomed in the insulators as well as slipped under the upper lip.

11. Install the correct inner shoe and lining assembly in the caliper piston. All vehicles, except the Continental and Mark VII have a separate anti-rattle clip and insulator that must be installed to the inner shoe and lining prior to their assembly to the caliper. The inner shoes are marked LH or RH and must be installed in the proper caliper. Also, care should be taken not to bend the anti-rattle clips too far in the piston or distortion and rattles can result.

Inner shoe installation on Continental and Mark VII models is accomplished by holding each end of the shoe, making sure it is square with the piston, and pushing the shoe in firmly until the clip snaps in position. do not allow shoe or clip tangs to cock during installation to avoid bending clip.

12. Install the correct outer brake shoe and lining assembly (RH/LH), making sure that the clip and/or buttons located on the shoe are properly seated. The outer shoe can be identified as right hand or left hand by the war indicator which must always be installed toward the front of the vehicle or by a LH or RH mark. Refill the master cylinder.

WARNING: Make certain that the two round torque buttons on all vehicles, except the Continental and Mark VII models, are seated solidly in the two holes of the outer caliper leg and that the shoe is held tightly against the housing by the spring clip. If the buttons are not seated, a temporary loss of brakes may occur!

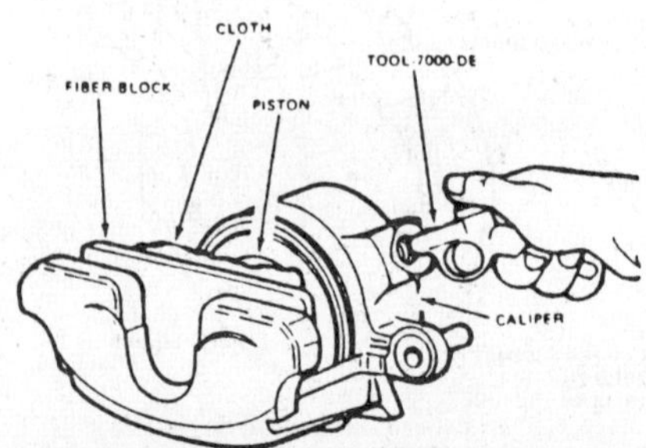

Removing the piston from the caliper with compressed air

13. Install the wheel and tire assembly, and tighten the wheel attaching nuts to 80-105 ft.lb.
14. Pump the brake pedal prior to moving the vehicle to position the brake linings.
15. Road test the vehicle.

CALIPER SERVICE

Ford Single Piston Sliding Caliper Disc Brakes

CAUTION

Brake shoes contain asbestos, which has been determined to be a cancer causing agent. Never clean the brake surfaces with compressed air! Avoid inhaling any dust from any brake surface! When cleaning brake surfaces, use a commercially available brake cleaning fluid.

1. Remove the caliper assembly from the vehicle as outlined in Pad Replacement. Disconnect the brake hose. Place a cloth over the piston before applying air pressure to prevent damage to the piston.
2. Apply air pressure to the fluid port in the caliper with a rubber tipped nozzle to remove the piston. On Continental and Mark VII models, use layers of shop towels to cushion possible impact of the phenolic piston against the caliper iron when piston comes out of the piston bore. Do not use a screwdriver or similar tool to pry piston out of the bore, damage to the phenolic piston may result. If the piston is seized and cannot be forced from the caliper, tap lightly around the piston while applying air pressure. Use care because the piston can develop considerable force from pressure buildup.
3. Remove the dust boot from the caliper assembly.
4. Remove the rubber piston seal from the cylinder, and discard it.
5. Clean all metal parts and phenolic piston with isopropyl alcohol. Then, clean out and dry the grooves and passageways with compressed air. Make suer the caliper bore and component parts are thoroughly clean.
6. Check the cylinder bore and piston for damage or excessive wear. Replace the piston if it is pitted, scored, corroded, or the plating is worn off. Do not replace phenolic piston cosmetic surface irregularities or small chips between the piston boot groove and shoe face.
7. Apply a film of clean brake fluid to the new caliper piston seal, and install it in the cylinder bore. Be sure the seal does not become twisted but is firmly seated in the groove.
8. Install a new dust boot by seating the flange squarely in the outer groove of the caliper bore.
9. Coat the piston with brake fluid, and install the piston in the cylinder bore. Be sure to use a wood block or other flat stock when installing the piston back into the piston bore. Never apply C-clamp directly to a phenolic piston, and be sure pistons are not cocked. Spread the dust boot over the piston as it is installed. Seat the dust boot in the piston groove.
10. Install the caliper over the rotor as outlined.

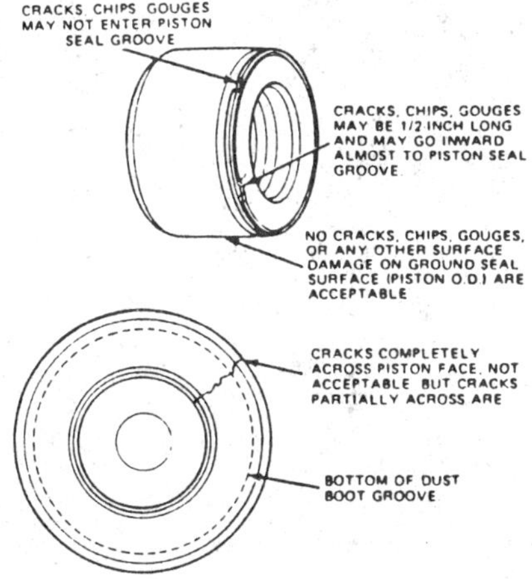

Checking piston surface for irregularities

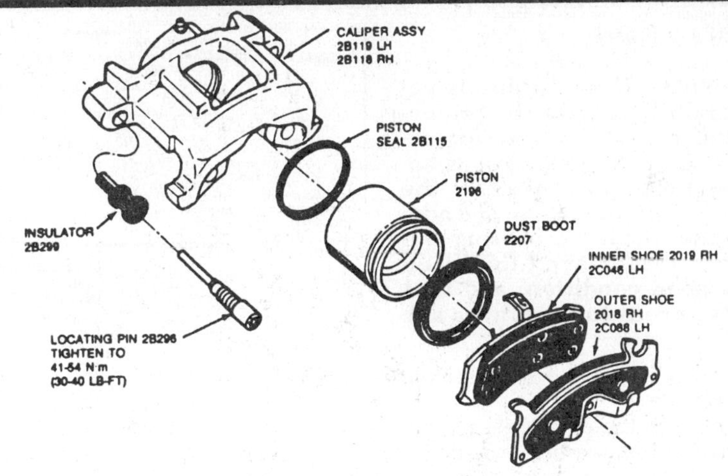

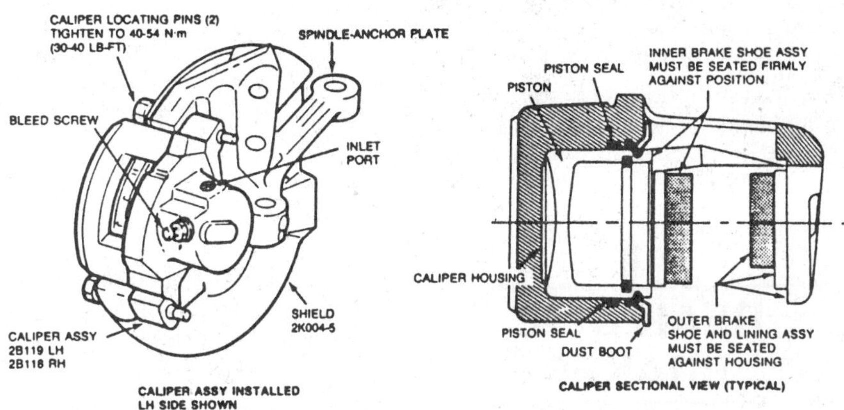

Front brake components for all 1983-87 models except the 1986-87 Thunderbird Turbo, Mark VII and Continental

Hub and Disc

REMOVAL

1. Raise and safely support the vehicle. Remove the wheel.

CAUTION

Brake shoes contain asbestos, which has been determined to be a cancer causing agent. Never clean the brake surfaces with compressed air! Avoid inhaling any dust from any brake surface! When cleaning brake surfaces, use a commercially available brake cleaning fluid.

2. Remove the caliper. Slide the caliper assembly away from the disc and suspend it with a wire loop. It is not necessary to disconnect the brake line.
3. Remove the grease cap from the hub. Remove the cotter pin, nut lock, adjusting nut, and flat washer from the spindle.
4. Remove the outer wheel bearing cone and roller assembly from the hub.
5. Remove the hut and disc assembly from the spindle.

INSTALLATION

WARNING: If a new disc is being installed, remove the protective coating with carburetor degreaser. If the original disc is being installed, make sure that the grease in the hub is clean and adequate, that the inner bearing and grease retainer are lubricated and in good condition, and that the disc breaking surfaces are clean.

1. Install the hub and disc assembly on the spindle.
2. Lubricate the outer bearing and install the thrust washer and adjusting nut.
3. Adjust the wheel bearing as outlined in the Wheel Bearing Adjustment section.
4. Install the nut lock, cotter pin, and grease cap.
5. Install the caliper assembly.
6. Install the wheel and tire assembly and torque the nuts to 75-110 ft.lb.
7. Lower the vehicle and road test it.

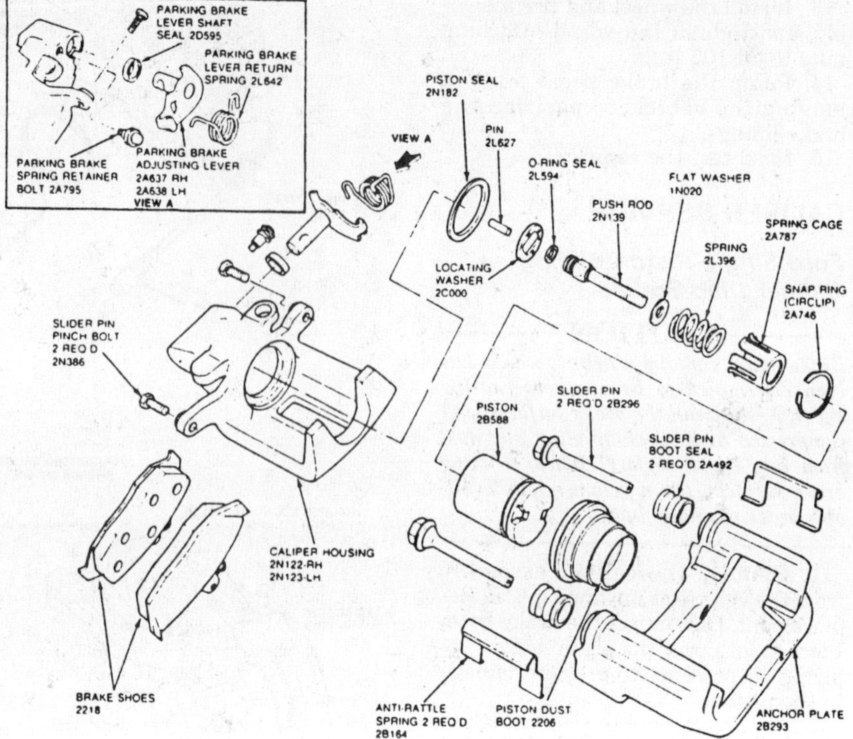

Rear disc brake caliper used on the Thunderbird Turbo

REAR DISC BRAKES

Disc Brake Pads

REMOVAL & INSTALLATION

1. Remove the caliper as outlined earlier. In this case, however, it is not necessary to disconnect the brake line. Simply wire the caliper to the frame to prevent the brake line from breaking.

CAUTION

Brake shoes contain asbestos, which has been determined to be a cancer causing agent. Never clean the brake surfaces with compressed air! Avoid inhaling any dust from any brake surface! When cleaning brake surfaces, use a commercially available brake cleaning fluid.

2. Remove the pads and inspect them. If they are worn to within 1/8" (3mm) of the shoe surface, they must be replace. Do not replace pads on just one side of the car. Uneven braking will result.
3. To install new pads, remove the disc and install the caliper without the pads. Use only the key to retain the caliper.
4. Seat the special tool firmly against the piston by holding the shaft and rotating the tool handle.
5. Loosen the handle 1/4 turn. Hold the handle and rotate the tool shaft clockwise until the caliper piston bottoms in the bore. It will continue to turn after it bottoms.
6. Rotate the handle until the piston is firmly seated.
7. Remove the caliper and install the disc.
8. Place the new inner brake pad on the anchor plate. Place the new outer pad in the caliper.
9. Reinstall the caliper according to the directions given earlier.

Caliper

REMOVAL & INSTALLATION

Continental and Mark VII

1. Raise the vehicle, and install safety stands. Block both front wheels if a jack is used.
2. Remove the wheel and tire assembly from the axle. Use care to avoid damage or interference with the splash shield.
3. Disconnect the parking brake cable from the lever. Use care to avoid kinking or cutting the cable or return spring.

CAUTION

Brake shoes contain asbestos, which has been determined to be a cancer causing agent. Never clean the brake surfaces with compressed air! Avoid inhaling any dust from any brake surface! When cleaning brake surfaces, use a commercially available brake cleaning fluid.

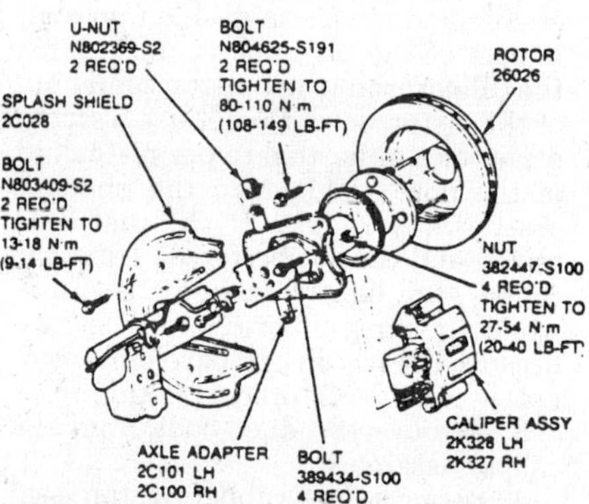

Rear disc brake component mounting on the Thunderbird Turbo

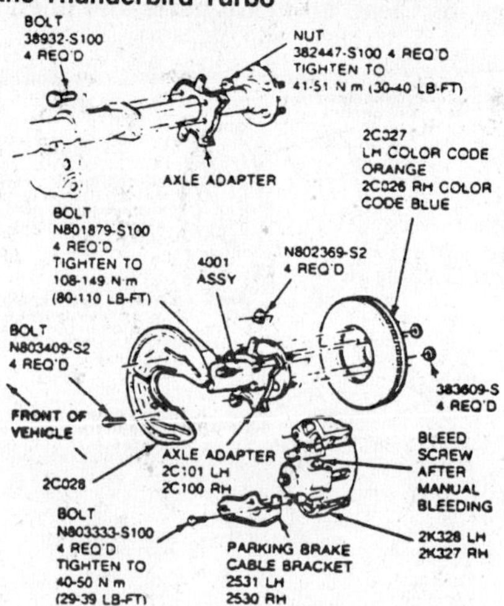

Rear disc brake component mounting on the Mark VII and Continental

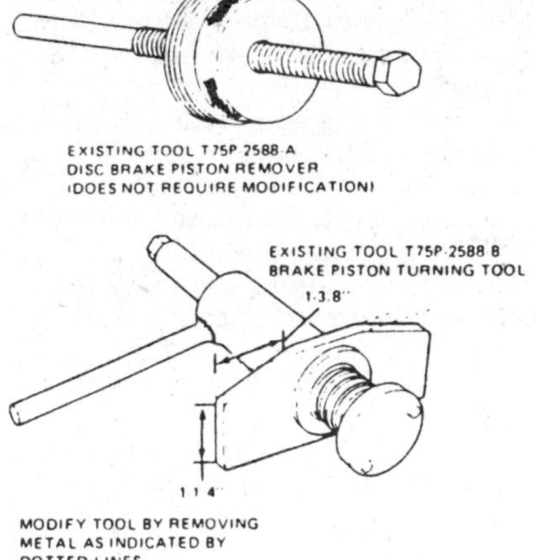

Special tools needed for servicing the rear disc brake caliper

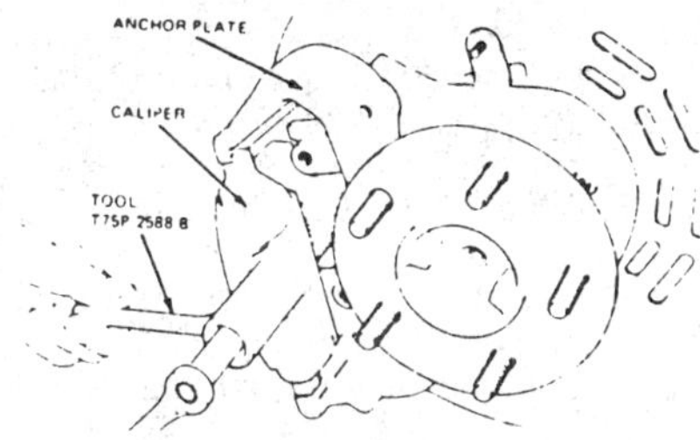

Adjusting the piston depth

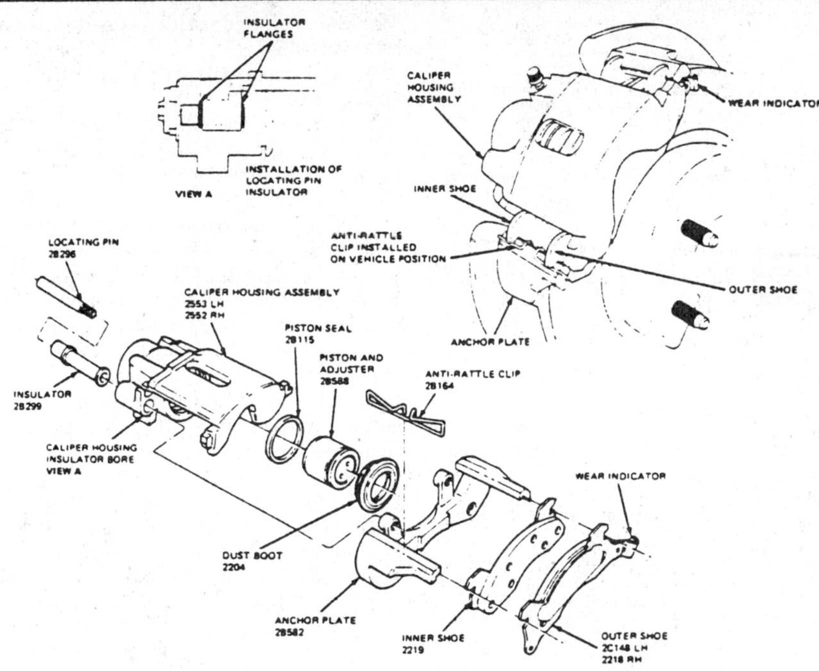

Continental rear disc brakes

4. Remove the caliper locating pins.

5. Lift the caliper assembly away from the anchor plate by pushing the caliper upward toward the anchor plate, and then rotate the lower end of the anchor plate.

6. If insufficient clearance between the caliper and shoe and lining assemblies prevents removal of the caliper, it is necessary to loosen the caliper end retainer ½ turn, maximum, to allow the piston to be forced back into its bore. To loosen the end retainer, remove the parking brake lever, then mark or scribe the end retainer and caliper housing to be sure that the end retainer is not loosened more than ½ turn. Force the piston back in its bore, then remove the caliper.

CAUTION

If the retainer must be loosened more than ½ turn, the seal between the thrust screw and the housing may be broken, and brake fluid may leak into the parking brake mechanism chamber. In this case, the end retainer must be removed, and the internal parts cleaned and lubricated; refer to Caliper Overhaul.

7. Remove the outer shoe and lining assembly from the anchor plate. mark shoe for identification if it is to be reinstalled.

8. Remove the two rotor retainer nuts and the rotor from the axle shaft.

9. Remove the inner brake shoe and lining assembly from the anchor plate.

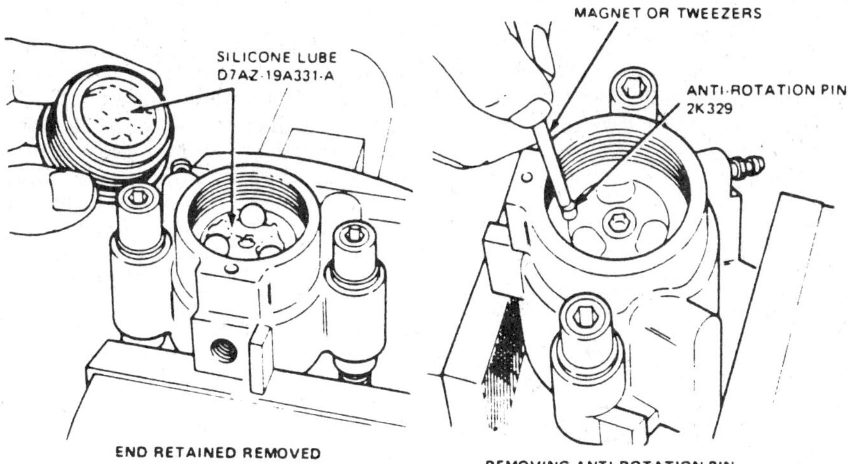

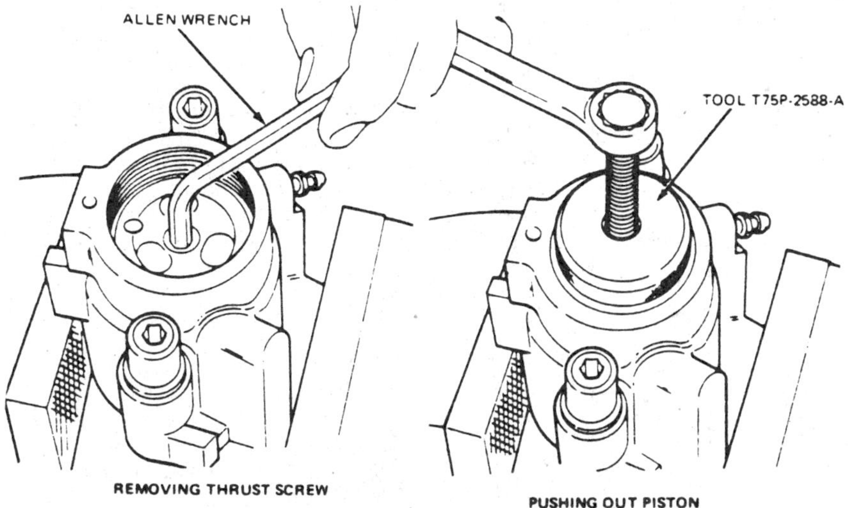

Servicing the caliper assembly

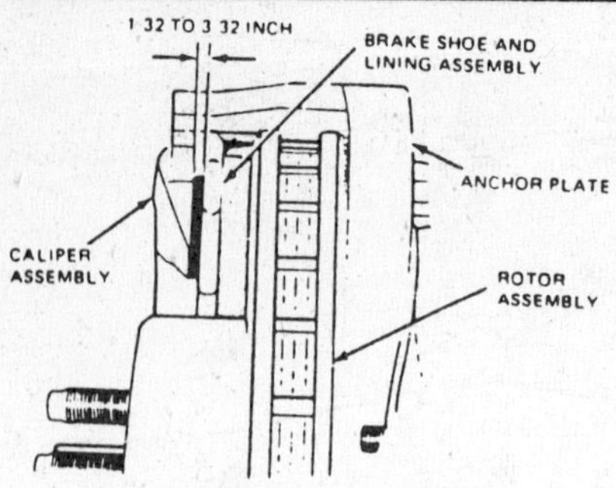

Checking lining clearance

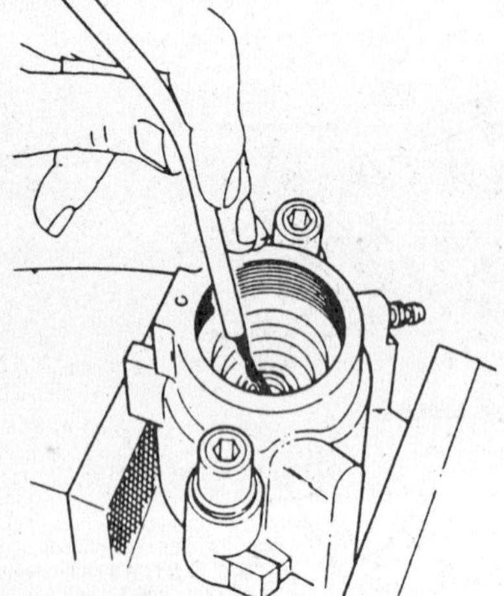

Filling the piston/adjuster assembly with clean fluid

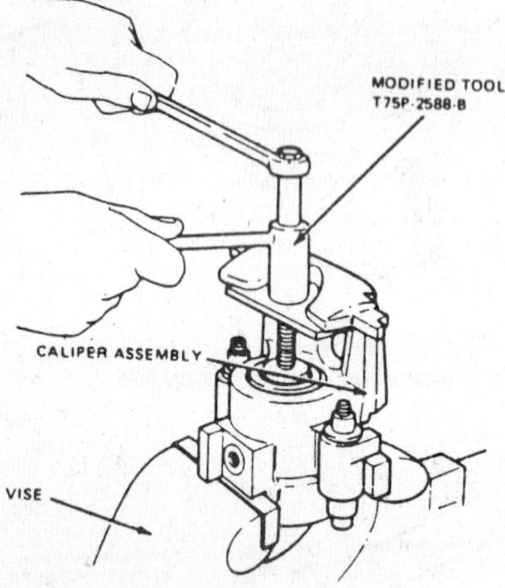

Bottoming the piston in the caliper

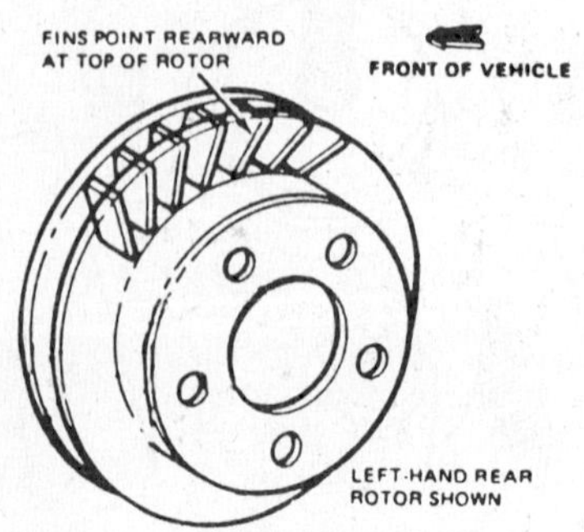

1982 Continental rear rotor

Mark shoe for identification if it is to be reinstalled.

10. Remove anti-rattle clip from anchor plate.

11. Remove the flexible hose from the caliper by removing the hollow retaining bolt that connects the hose fitting to the caliper.

12. Clean the caliper, anchor plate, and rotor assemblies and inspect for signs of brake fluid leakage, excessive wear, or damage. The caliper must be inspected for leakage both in the piston boot area and at the operating shaft seal area. Lightly sand or wire brush any rust or corrosion from the caliper and anchor plate sliding surfaces as well as the outer and inner brake shoe abutment surfaces. Inspect the brake shoes for wear. If either lining is worn to within 1/8" (3mm) of the shoe surface, both shoe and lining assemblies must be replaced using the shoe and lining removal procedures.

13. If the end retainer has been loosened only 1/2 turn, reinstall the caliper in the anchor plate without shoe and lining assemblies. Tighten the end retainer to 75-96 ft.lb. Install the parking brake lever on its keyed spline. The lever arm must point down and rearward. The parking brake cable will then pass freely under the axle. Tighten the retainer screw to 16-22 ft.lb. The parking brake lever must rotate freely after tightening the retainer screw. Remove the caliper from the anchor plate.

14. If new shoe and lining assemblies are to be installed, the piston must be screwed back into the caliper bore, using Tool T75P-2588-B or equivalent to provide installation clearance. This tool requires a slight modification for use on Continental rear disc brakes. This modification will not prevent using the tool on prior year applications. New tools purchased from the Special Service Tool catalog under the T75P-2588-B number will already be modified. Remove the rotor, and install the caliper, less shoe and lining assemblies, in the anchor plate. While holding the shaft, rotate the tool handle counterclockwise until the tool is seated firmly against the piston. Now, loosen the handle about 1/4 turn. While holding the handle, rotate the tool shaft clockwise until the piston is fully bottomed in its bore; the piston will continue to turn even after it becomes bottomed. When there is not further inward movement of the piston and the tool handle is rotated until there is a firm seating force, the piston is bottomed. Remove the tool and the caliper from the anchor plate.

15. Lubricate anchor plate sliding ways with lithium or silicone grease. Use only specified grease because a lower temperature type of lubricant may melt and contaminate the brake pads. Use care to prevent any lubricant from getting on the braking surface.

16. Install the anti-rattle clip on the lower rail of the anchor plate.

17. Install inner brake shoe and lining assembly on the anchor plate with the lining toward the rotor.

18. Be sure shoes are installed in their original positions as marked for identification before removal.

19. Install rotor and two retainer nuts.

20. Install the correct hand outer brake shoe and lining assembly on the anchor plate with the lining toward the rotor and wear indicator toward the upper portion of the brake.

21. Install the flexible hose by placing a new washer on each side of the fitting outlet and inserting the attaching bolt through the washers and fitting. Tighten to 20-30 ft.lb.

22. Position the upper tab of the caliper housing on the anchor plate upper abutment surface.

23. Rotate the caliper housing until it is completely over the rotor. Use care so that the piston dust boot is not damaged.

24. Piston Position Adjustment: Pull the caliper outboard until the inner shoe and lining is firmly seated against the rotor, and measure the clearance between the outer shoe and caliper. The clearance must be 1/32-3/32" (0.8-2.4mm). If it is not, remove the caliper, then readjust the piston to obtain required gap. Follow the procedure given in Step 13, and rotate the shaft counterclockwise to narrow gap and clockwise to widen gap (1/4 turn of the piston move it approximately 1/16" [1.6mm]). **WARNING: A clearance greater than 3/32" (2.4mm) may allow the adjuster to be pulled out of the piston when the service brake is applied. This will cause the parking brake mechanism to fail to adjust. It is then necessary to replace the piston/adjuster assembly following the procedures under Overhaul.**

25. Lubricate locating pins and inside of insulator with silicone grease.

26. Add one drop of Loctite® E0AC-19554-A or equivalent to locating pin threads.

27. Install the locating pins through caliper insulators and into the anchor plate; the pins must be hand inserted and hand started. Tighten to 29-37 ft.lb.

28. Connect the parking brake cable to the lever on the caliper.

29. Bleed the brake system. Replace rubber bleed screw cap after bleeding.

30. Fill the master cylinder as required to within 1/8" (3mm) of the top of the reservoir.

31. Caliper Adjustment: With the engine running, pump the service brake lightly (approximately 14 lbs. pedal effort) about 40 times. Allow at least one second between pedal applications. As an alternative, with the engine Off, pump the service brake lightly (approximately 87 lbs. pedal effort) about 30 times. Now check the parking brake for excessive travel or very light effort. In either case, repeat pumping the service brake, or if necessary, check the parking brake cable for proper tension. The caliper levers must return to the Off position when the parking brake is released.

32. Install the wheel and tire assembly. Tighten the wheel lug nuts. Install the wheel cover. Remove the safety stands, and lower the vehicle.

33. Be sure a firm brake pedal application is obtained, and then road test for proper brake operation, including parking brakes.

CALIPER OVERHAUL

All Models

1. Remove the caliper assembly from the vehicle as outlined.

CAUTION

Brake shoes contain asbestos, which has been determined to be a cancer causing agent. Never clean the brake surfaces with compressed air! Avoid inhaling any dust from any brake surface! When cleaning brake surfaces, use a commercially available brake cleaning fluid.

2. Remove the caliper and retainer.

3. Lift out the operating shaft, thrust bearing, and balls.

4. Remove the thrust screw anti-rotation pin with a magnet or tweezers.

NOTE: Some anti-rotation pins may be difficult to remove with a magnet or tweezers. In that case, use the following procedure.

a. Adjust the piston out from the caliper bore using the modified piston adjusting tool. The piston should protrude from the housing at least 1" (25mm).

b. Push the piston back into the caliper housing with the adjusting tool. With the tool in position on the caliper, hold the tool shaft in place, and rotate the handle counterclockwise until the thrust screw clears the anti-rotation pin. Remove the thrust screw and the anti-rotation pin.

5. Remove the thrust screw by rotating it counterclockwise with a ¼" allen wrench.

6. Remove the piston adjuster assembly by installing Tool T75P-2588-A or equivalent through the back of the caliper housing and pushing the piston out.

WARNING: Use care not to damage the polished surface in the thrust screw bore, and do not press or attempt to move the adjuster can. It is a press fit in the piston!

7. Remove and discard the piston seal, boot, thrust screw C-ring seal, end retainer O-ring seal, end retainer lip seal, and pin insulators.

8. Clean all metal parts with isopropyl alcohol. use clean, dry, compressed air to clean out and dry the grooves and passages. Be sure the caliper bore and component parts are completely free of any foreign material.

9. Inspect the caliper bores for damage or excessive wear. The thrust screw bore must be smooth and free of pits. If the piston is pitted, scored, or the chrome plating is worn off, replace the piston/adjuster assembly.

10. The adjuster can must be bottomed in the piston to be properly seated and provide consistent brake function. If the adjuster can is loose in the piston, appears high in the piston, or is damaged, or if brake adjustment is regularly too tight, too loose, or nonfunctioning, replace the piston/adjuster assembly.

WARNING: Do not attempt to service the adjuster at any time. When service is necessary replace the piston/adjuster assembly.

11. Check adjuster operation by first assembling the thrust screw into the piston/adjuster assembly, pulling the two pieces apart by hand approximately ¼" (6mm), and then releasing them. When pulling on the two pieces, the brass drive ring must remain stationary, causing the nut to rotate. When releasing the two parts, the nut must remain stationary, and the drive ring must rotate. If the action of the components does not follow this pattern, replace the piston/adjuster assembly.

12. Inspect ball pockets, threads, grooves, and bearing surfaces of the thrust screw and operating shaft for wear, pitting, or brinelling. Inspect balls and anti-rotation pin for wear, brinelling, or pitting. Replace operating shaft, balls, thrust screw, and anti-rotation pin if any of these parts are worn or damaged. A polished appearance on the ball paths is acceptable if there is no sign of wear into the surface.

13. Inspect the thrust bearing for corrosion, pitting, or wear. Replace if necessary.

14. Inspect the bearing surface of the end plug for wear or brinnelling. Replace if necessary. A polished appearance on the bearing surface is acceptable if there is no sign of wear into the surface.

15. Inspect the lever for damage. Replace if necessary.

16. Lightly sand or wire brush any rust or corrosion from the caliper housing insulator bores.

17. Apply a coat of clean brake fluid to the new caliper piston seal, and install it in the cylinder bore. Be sure that the seal is not twisted and that it is seated fully in the groove.

18. Install a new dust boot by seating the flange squarely in the outer groove of the caliper bore.

19. Coat the piston/adjuster assembly with clean brake fluid, and install it in the cylinder bore. Spread the dust boot over the piston, like it is installed. Seat the dust boot in the piston groove.

20. Install the caliper in a vise and fill the piston/adjuster assembly with clean brake fluid to the bottom edge of the thrust screw bore.

21. Coat a new thrust screw O-ring seal with clean brake fluid, and install it in the groove in the thrust screw.

22. Install the thrust screw by turning it into the piston/adjuster assembly with a ¼" allen wrench until the top surface of the thrust screw is flush with the bottom of the threaded bore. Use care to avoid cutting the O-ring seal. Index the thrust screw, so that the notches on the thrust screw and caliper housing are aligned. Then install the anti-rotation pin.

WARNING: The thrust screw and operating shaft are not interchangeable from side to side because of the ramp direction in the ball pockets. The pocket surface of the operating shaft and the thrust screw are stamped with the proper letter (R or L), indicating part usage.

23. Place a ball in each of the three pockets of the thrust screw, and apply a liberal amount of silicone grease on all components in the parking brake mechanism.

24. Install the operating shaft on the balls.

25. Coat the thrust bearing with silicone grease and install it on the operating shaft.

26. Install a new lip seal and O-ring on the end retainer.

27. Coat the O-ring seal and lip seal with a light film of silicone grease, and install the end retainer in the caliper. Hold the operating shaft firmly seated against the internal mechanism while installing the end retainer to prevent mislocation of the balls. If the lip seal is pushed out of position, reset the seal. Tighten the end retainer to 75-95 ft.lb.

28. Install the parking brake lever on its keyed spline. The lever arm must point down and rearward. The parking brake cable will then pass freely under the axle. Tighten the lever retaining screw to 16-22 ft.lb. The parking brake lever must rotate freely after tightening.

29. Arrange the caliper in a vise and bottom the piston with modified Tool T75P-2588-B.

30. Install new pin insulators in the caliper housing. Check to see if both insulator flanges straddle the housing holes.

31. Install the caliper on the vehicle.

Brake Discs

REMOVAL & INSTALLATION

1. Raise the car and support it. Remove the wheels.

CAUTION

Brake shoes contain asbestos, which has been determined to be a cancer causing agent. Never clean the brake surfaces with compressed air! Avoid inhaling any dust from any brake surface! When cleaning brake surfaces, use a commercially available brake cleaning fluid.

2. Remove the caliper, as outlined earlier.

3. Remove the retaining bolts and remove the disc from the axle.

4. Inspect the disc for excessive rust, scoring or pitting. A certain amount of rust on the edge of the disc is normal. Refer to the specifications chart and measure the thickness of the disc, using a micrometer. If the disc is below specifications, replace it.

5. Reinstall the discs, keeping in mind that the two sides are not interchangeable. The words **left** and **right** are cast into the inner surface of the raised section of the disc. Proper reinstallation of the discs is important, since the cooling vanes cast into the disc must face opposite forward rotation.

6. Reinstall the caliper.

7. Install the wheels and lower the car.

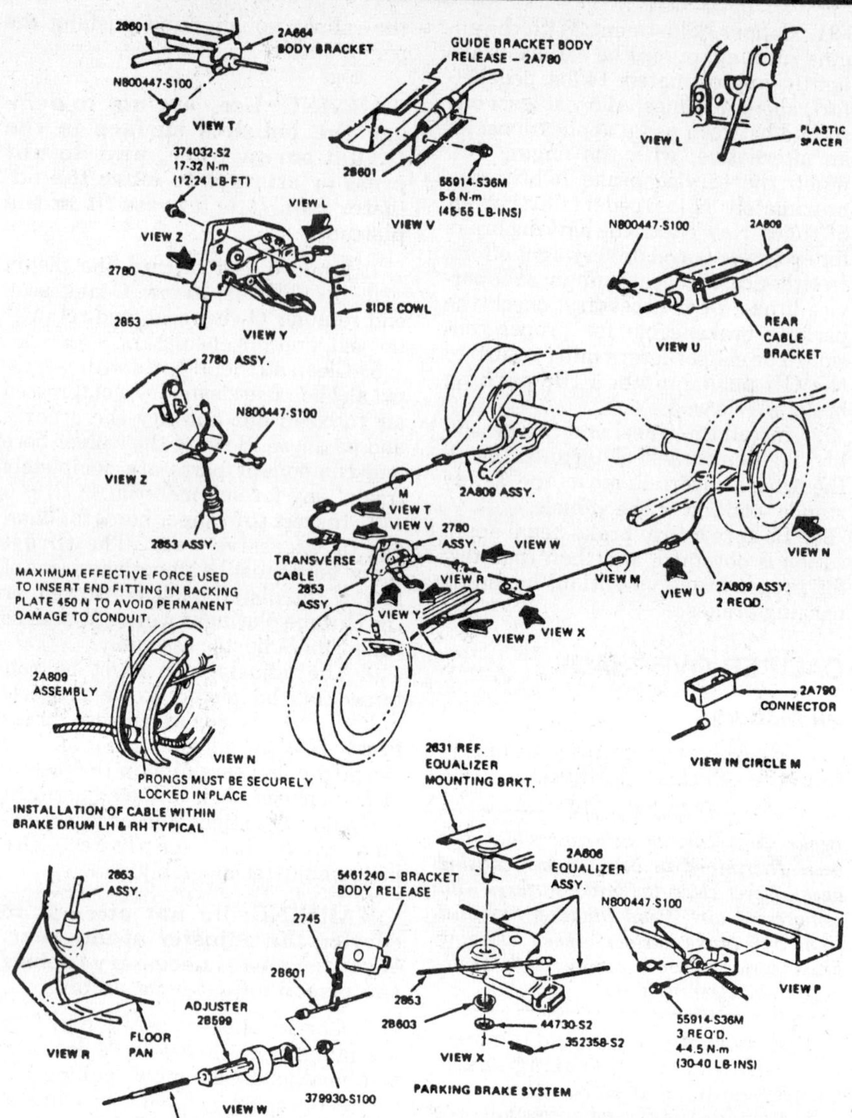

Parking brake components used on the 1981-82 Cougar

PARKING BRAKE

CAUTION

Brake shoes contain asbestos, which has been determined to be a cancer causing agent. Never clean the brake surfaces with compressed air! Avoid inhaling any dust from any brake surface! When cleaning brake surfaces, use a commercially available brake cleaning fluid.

Front Cables

REMOVAL & INSTALLATION

Ford, Mercury and Lincoln Town Car

1. Raise vehicle and loosen adjusting nut at adjuster.

2. Disconnect cable from intermediate cable connector located along LH frame side rail.

3. Remove conduit retainer from frame. Remove screw holding the plastic inner fender apron to the frame, at the rear of the fender panel.

4. Pull back the fender apron and remove the spring clip retainer that holds the parking brake cable to the frame.

5. Pull the cable through the frame and let it hang in wheel housing. Lower the vehicle.

6. Inside the passenger compartment, remove the sound deadener cover from the cable at the dash panel.

7. Remove the spring retainer and cable end from the clevis at the parking brake control.

8. Remove conduit from the cable assembly. Push the cable down through the dash panel, and remove cable from inside the wheel housing.

9. Installation is the reverse of the removal procedure. Adjust the parking brake.

All Other Models Except Thunderbird Turbo

1. Raise and support the rear end on jackstands.

2. Remove the adjusting nut at the equalizer and remove the equalizer from the cable.

3. Remove the clip that holds the cable to the frame or body bracket.

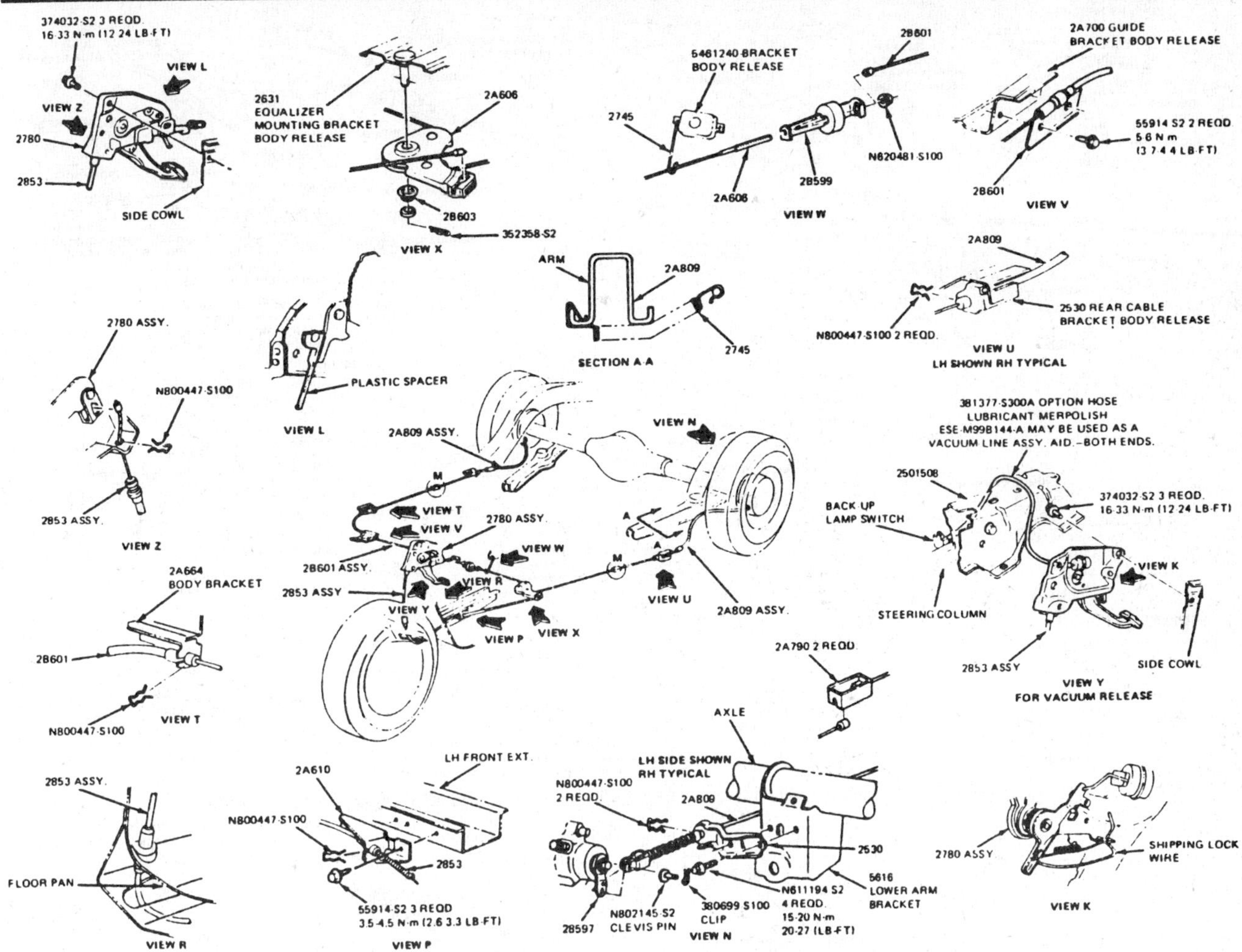

1982 Continental parking brake components

4. Remove the clip that retains the cable to the parking brake control, inside the car.
5. Disconnect the cable from the control assembly.

NOTE: Some cars have cables with snap-in fittings. On these cables, compress the tangs and remove them from the mounting surface.

8. Pull the cable up through the opening in the dash panel.
9. Installation is the reverse of removal. Adjust the parking brake.

Thunderbird Turbo

1. Raise and support the rear end on jackstands.
2. Remove the adjusting nut at the equalizer and remove the equalizer from the cable.
3. Remove the clip that holds the cable to the frame or body bracket.
4. Remove the clip that retains the cable to the parking brake control, inside the car.
5. Disconnect the cable from the control assembly.

NOTE: Some cars have cables with snap-in fittings. On these cables, compress the tangs and remove them from the mounting surface.

8. Pull the cable up through the opening in the dash panel.
9. Installation is the reverse of removal. Adjust the parking brake.

Intermediate Cables

REMOVAL & INSTALLATION

Ford, Mercury and Lincoln Town Car

1. Raise vehicle and loosen the cable adjusting nut.
2. Disconnect parking brake release spring at frame.
3. Disconnect the cable from the cable connectors, and remove it from the vehicle.
4. Installation is the reverse of the removal procedure. Adjust the parking brake.

All Other Models

1. Raise and support the rear end on jackstands.
2. Remove the cable adjusting nut.
3. Disconnect the intermediate cable ends from the left rear and the transverse cables.
4. Remove the cotter pin, washer and spring from the pin protruding from the equalizer assembly, and remove the lever.

NOTE: The intermediate cable cannot be separated from the lever.

5. Installation is the reverse of removal. Adjust the parking brake.

Transverse Cable

REMOVAL & INSTALLATION

All Models Except Ford, Mercury and Lincoln Town Car

1. Raise and support the rear end on jackstands.

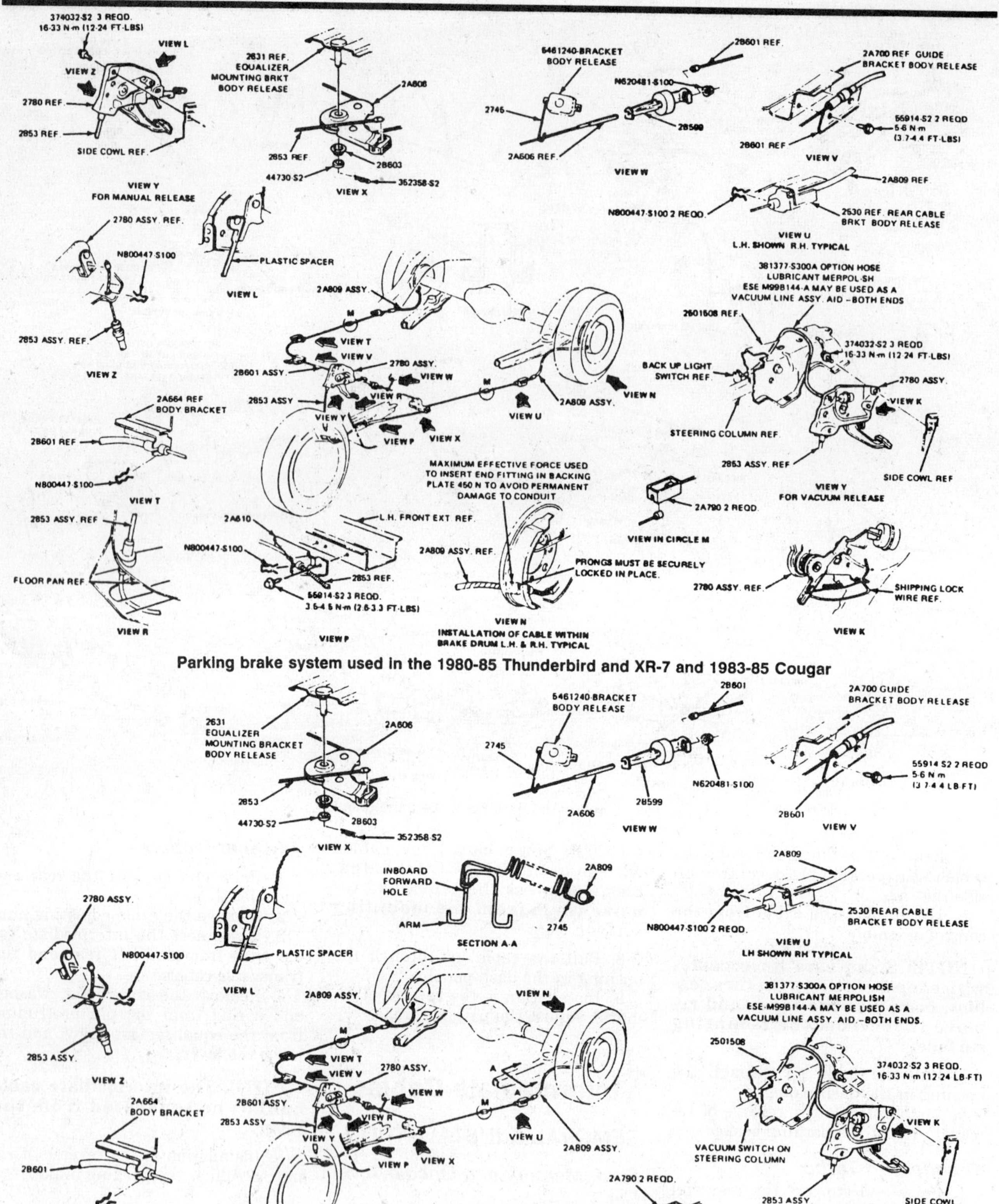

Parking brake system used in the 1980-85 Thunderbird and XR-7 and 1983-85 Cougar

Parking brake system used in the 1983-85 Continental and 1984-85 Mark VII

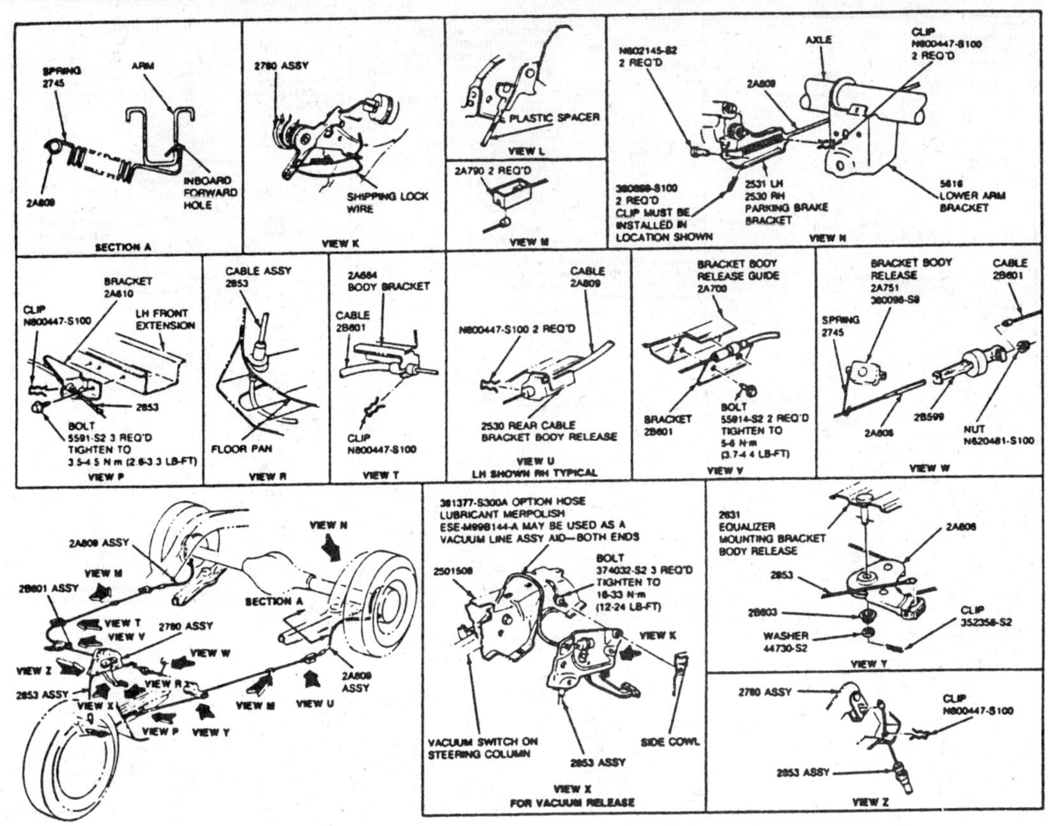

Parking brake system used in the 1986 Continental and Mark VII

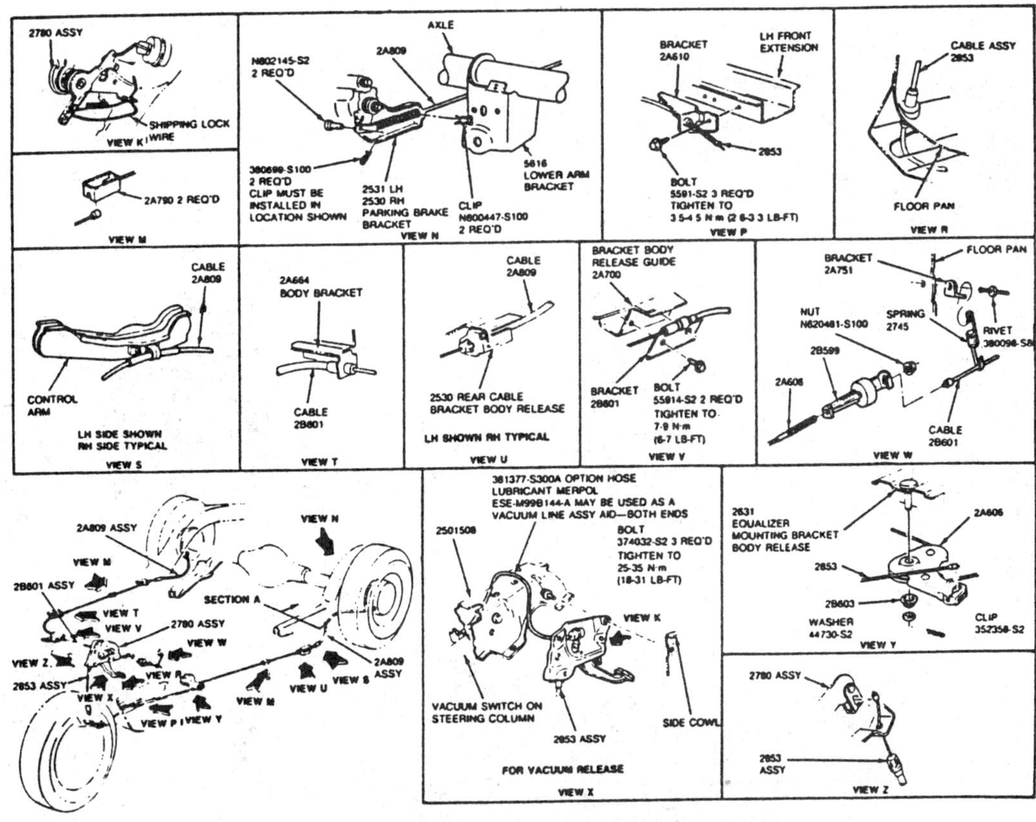

Parking brake system used in the 1987 Continental and Mark VII

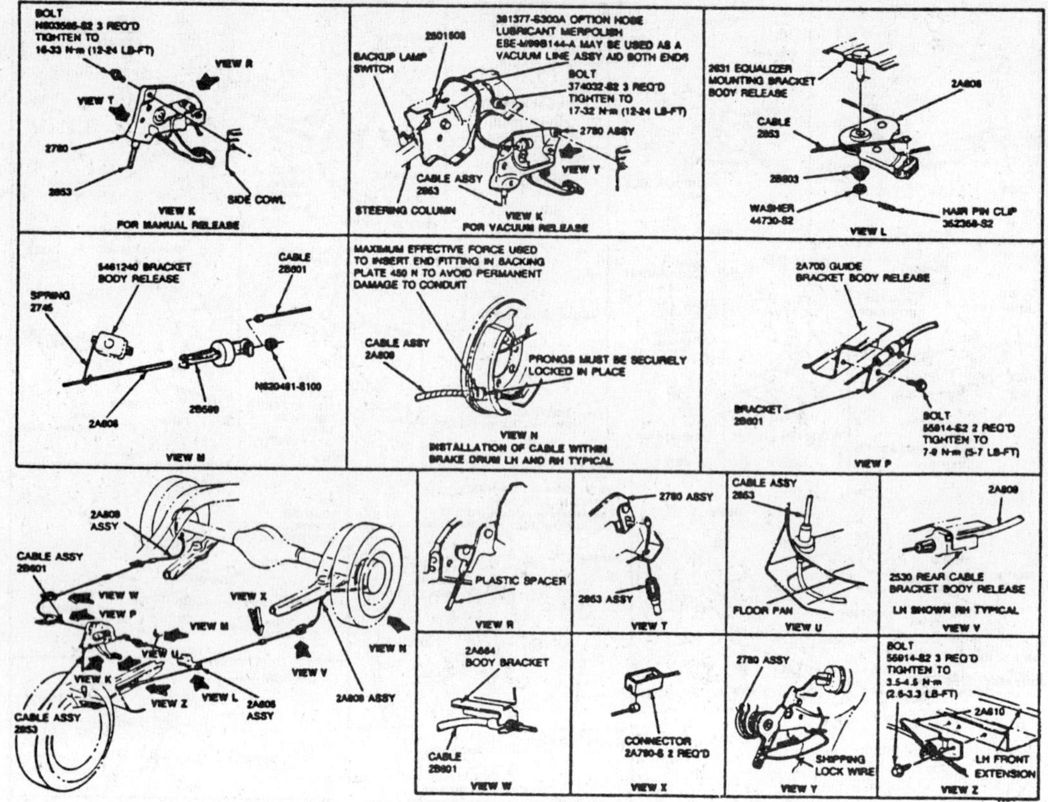

Parking brake system used in the 1986-87 Thunderbird and Cougar, except the Turbo Coupe

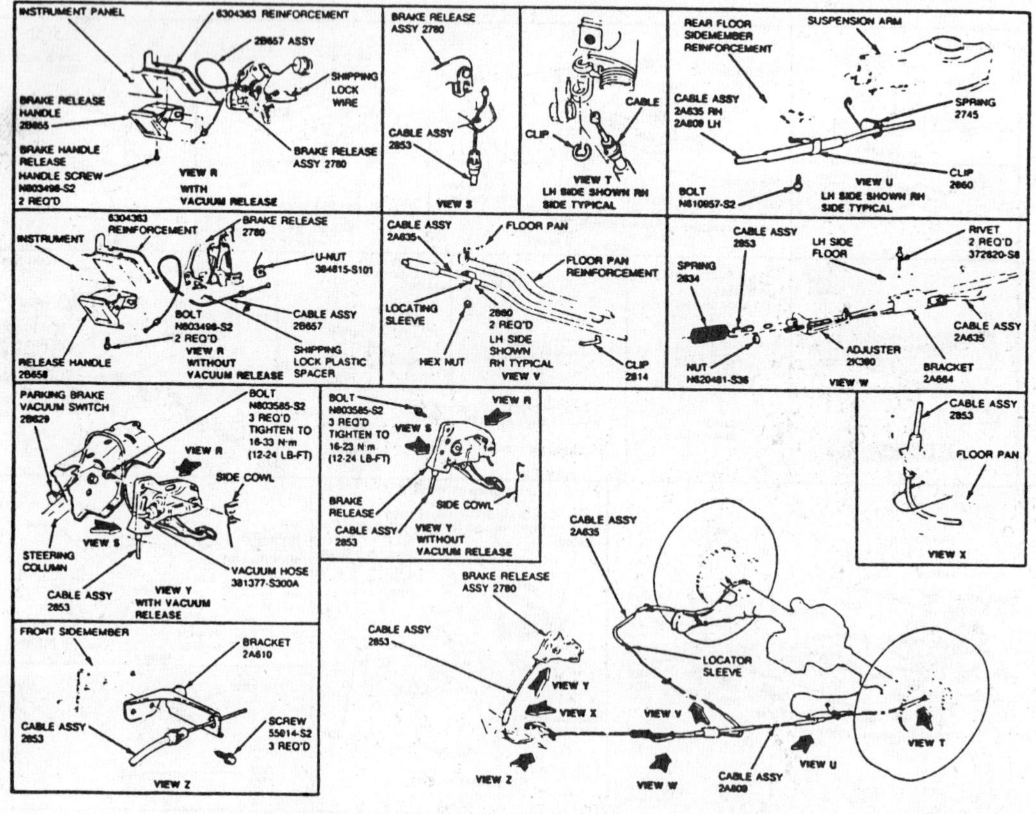

Parking brake system used in the Thunderbird Turbo Coupe

2. Remove the adjusting nut.
3. Remove the transverse cable ends from the right rear and intermediate cables.
4. Remove the hairpin clips or conduit brackets and remove the cable.
5. Installation is the reverse of removal. Adjust the parking brake.

Rear Cables

REMOVAL & INSTALLATION

All Models Except Thunderbird Turbo

1. Raise and support the rear end on jackstands.
2. Remove the equalizer adjusting nut and remove the equalizer.
3. Disconnect the rear cables from the right and left rear cable connectors.
4. Remove the cable from the retainer hooks.
5. Remove the hairpin clip retaining the cable housing to the side rail bracket.
6. On cars with rear drum brakes:
   a. Remove the brake drums.
   b. Remove the brake shoes and disconnect the cable end from the self-adjusting lever.
   c. Compress the pronged retainers and remove the cable assembly from the backing plate.
7. On cars with rear disc brakes, remove the clevis pin securing the cable to the caliper actuating arm.
8. Installation is the reverse of removal. Adjust the parking brake.

Thunderbird Turbo

1. Raise and support the rear end on jackstands.
2. Remove the adjuster nut.
3. Disconnect the parking brake release spring from the right cable at the equalizer.
4. Disconnect the right cable from the adjuster and the side rail bracket.
5. Remove all cable retaining brackets.
6. Disconnect the left cable from the equalizer and body side rail bracket.
7. Remove the clips retaining the cables to the calipers and remove the cable ends from the parking brake lever arm.
8. Installation is the reverse of removal.

ET SERIES TRANSMISSIONS

Transmission Case

DISASSEMBLY

1. Using a 10mm wrench, remove the ten cover bolts and lift off the cover.
2. Drain the lubricant.
3. Using a pencil size magnet, remove the shift rail detent plug, the spring and the plunger from the upper left side of the case.
4. Working through the shift turret opening in the extension housing, remove the access plug from the rear of the housing.
5. After shifting into Reverse gear, remove the roll pin from the gear shift shaft offset lever, then slide the offset lever and bushing off the shaft.
6. Remove the 5th speed interlock pilot bolt from the front top of the extension housing.
7. Remove the 6 extension housing bolts, then slide the housing and the gasket off the output shaft.
8. Remove the snapring, the speedometer drive gear and the drive ball from the output shaft.
9. Remove the 5th gear synchronizer snapring from the output shaft, then slide the retaining spacer off the output shaft.
10. Shift the transmission into 1st gear. Using a hammer and a punch, drive out the roll pin located inside the case, which secures the 1st, 2nd, 3rd, 4th and Reverse selector pin, then remove the selector pin.
11. Slide the shifter shaft, the 5th speed shift fork and the synchronizer from the output shaft as an assembly.
12. Remove the interlock sleeve bolt from the right side of the case.

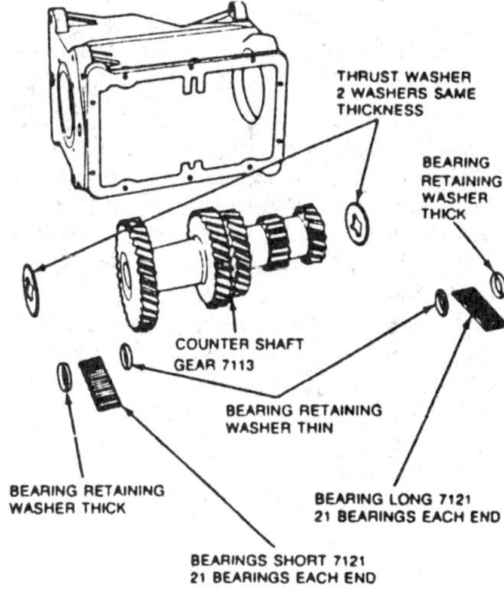

82ET countershaft disassembled

13. Remove the interlock sleeve, the 3rd-4th speed shift fork and the 1st-2nd speed shift fork from the case.
14. Working inside the case, remove the C-clip from the Reverse gear selector fork pivot pin. Remove the pivot pin, then lift the Reverse gear selector fork relay lever, the spring and the Reverse gearshift fork from the case.

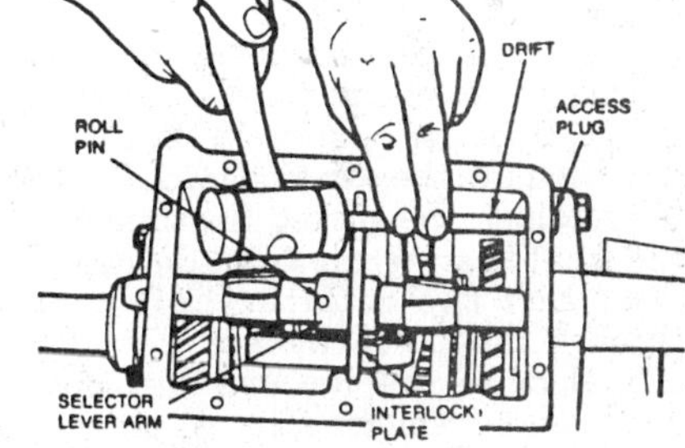

82ET interlock plate access plug

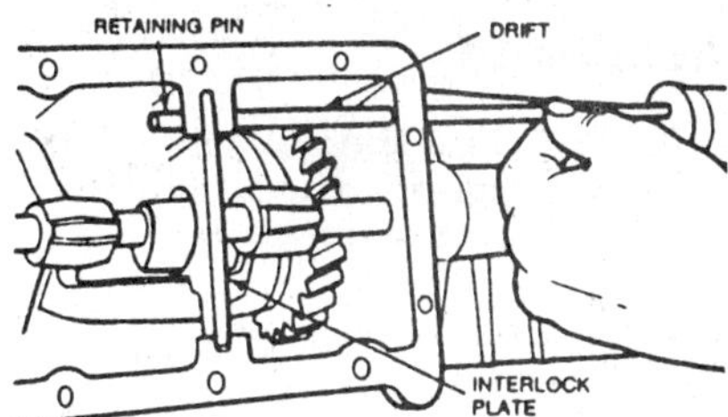

82ET interlock plate retaining pin removal

15. Slide the 5th speed main drive gear off the output shaft.
16. Remove the snapring located at the rear of the 5th speed cluster gear.
17. Using a puller, remove the 5th speed cluster gear.

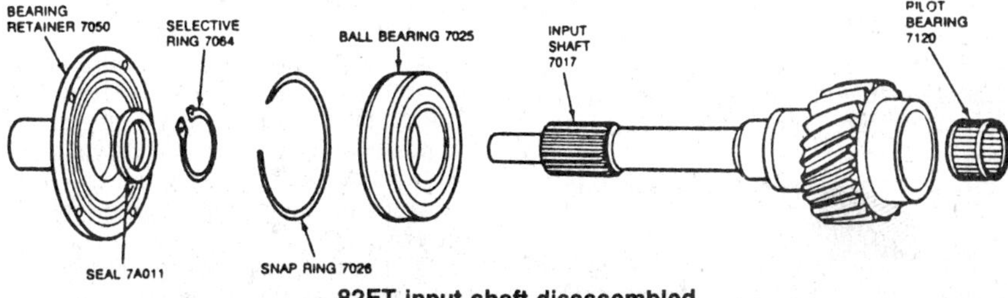

82ET input shaft disassembled

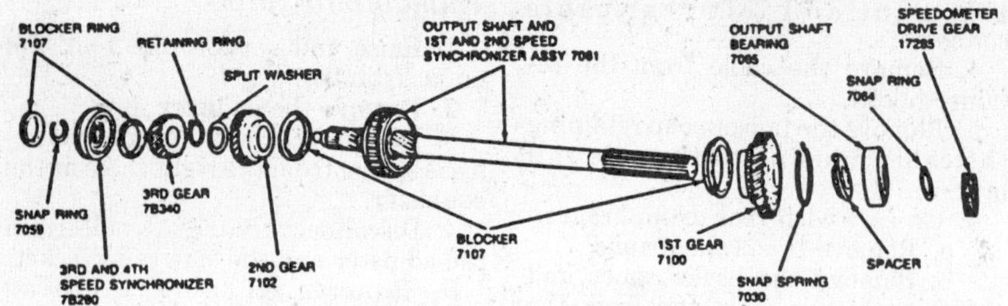

82ET output shaft disassembled

18. Remove the output shaft rear bearing snapring and the bearing cup.

19. Remove the 4 input shaft bearing retainer bolts, the bearing retainer, the seal, the shim and the O-ring from the case.

20. Without loosing the roller bearings, the thrust washers and the thrust bearing, rotate the input shaft so that the teeth recess face the countershaft gear, then lift the input gear from the case.

21. Remove the output shaft assembly through the top of the transmission case.

22. Remove the snapring from the rear of the case and the countershaft gear rear bearing cup from the case.

23. Remove the three bolts, the bearing retainer, the gasket, the shim and the front bearing cup from the case.

24. Lift the countershaft gear through the top of the case.

25. Remove the Reverse idler gear and shaft by removing the roll pin that secures the shaft to the case.

ASSEMBLY

NOTE: Coat the bolts and plugs used throughout the case with a thread sealant to prevent leakage.

1. Hold the Reverse idler gear into position with the long end of the hub facing to the rear of the case. Slide the idler gear shaft through the case and gear and align the roll pin holes, then secure the shaft with the roll pin.

2. Lower the countershaft and bearings into place and install the rear bearing cup, then secure with the snapring.

3. Position the front bearing cup, the shim, a new gasket and the bearing retainer to the front of the case. Install the bearing retainer cap bolts and torque to 7-10 ft.lb. (while rotating the gear). If the gear rotating effort increases while torquing the bearing retainer, replace the shim with a thinner one.

4. The correct end play is 0.001-0.005".

NOTE: Decrease the shim thickness to increase the end play and increase the shim thickness to reduce end play.

5. Lower the main shaft into the case through the case cover opening.

6. Apply a coat of polyethylene grease to the thrust washers and the thrust bearing. Place the thrust washer on the 3rd-4th speed synchronization thrust surface. Place the thrust bearing and the remaining thrust washer on the 3rd-4th speed synchronizer.

7. Without disturbing the roller bearings, carefully install the input shaft assembly in the case with the blank portion of the teeth facing the countershaft gear.

8. Coat a new input shaft O-ring with polyethylene grease and position it in the bearing retainer groove.

9. Install the output shaft bearing cup and the snapring into the rear of the case.

10. Position the shim and bearing retainer into the case. Install the bearing retainer bolts and torque to 8-10 ft.lb. (while rotating the input shaft).

NOTE: If the input shaft turning effort increases when torquing the bearing retainer bolts, replace the shim with a thicker one.

11. Install a dial indicator on the case. Pry the output shaft toward the dial indicator and zero the indicator. Pry the output shaft in the opposite direction. The end play should be between 0.001-0.005". Increase shim thickness to decrease end play or decrease shim thickness to increase end play. Remove the dial indicator.

12. Install the spring and the Reverse fork on the relay lever. Position the relay lever assembly in the case, then install the pivot pin in the case and lever assembly. Secure the lever with a C-clip.

13. Install the 5th speed cluster gear and secure with a snapring.

14. Slide the 5th speed main drive gear onto the output shaft. Coat the blocking ring with polyethylene grease and position it on the main drive gear.

15. Position the 1st-2nd and the 3rd-4th shift forks onto the main shaft assembly.

16. Place the interlock gear selector sleeve between the 2 shifter forks and install the interlock pilot bolt in the right side of the case.

17. With the synchronizer thrust surface facing the rear of the output shaft, install the shifter shaft, the 5th speed shift fork and the 5th speed synchronizer as an assembly.

18. Working through the cover opening in the case, install the gearshift selector pin in the shifter shaft and secure with a roll pin.

19. Slide the 5th speed synchronizer retaining plate onto the output shaft and secure with a snapring.

20. Secure the speedometer drive gear ball to the output shaft with polyethylene grease then slide the speedometer drive gear onto the shaft over the ball and secure with a snapring.

21. Using a new gasket, position the extension housing on the case. Install the two pilot bolts, one in the upper left side of the housing and the other in the lower right corner. Install the four remaining bolts and torque to 40-60 ft.lb.

22. Install the 5th gear pilot bolt in the top of the extension housing.

23. Shift the into Reverse gear. Install the offset lever on the rear of the shifter shaft and secure with a roll pin.

24. Install the detent plunger, the spring and the plug in the upper right side of the case, then torque the plug to 12-14 ft.lb.

25. Install the access plug in the rear of the extension housing.

26. Using a new gasket place the cover on the case and torque the bolts to 8-10 ft.lb.

Output Shaft

DISASSEMBLY

1. Slide the 3rd-4th speed synchronizer off the front end of the output shaft.

2. Slide the 3rd speed gear off the front of the output shaft.

3. Remove the snapring and the 2nd speed gear thrust washer from the output shaft. Slide the 2nd speed gear and the synchronizer blocking ring off the output shaft.

4. Remove the 1st-2nd speed synchronizer snapring from the output shaft, then press the synchronizer off the output shaft.

5. Remove the snapring from the rear of the output shaft. Place the output shaft in a press, then remove the 1st speed gear, the thrust washer and the output shaft rear bearing.

ASSEMBLY

1. Position the 1st gear thrust washer and the bearing on the rear of the output shaft. Apply pressure on

the bearing inner race until the bearing is bottomed on the spacer and shaft.

2. Select a snapring that will not allow any clearance between the bearing race and the ring groove. Then press the 1st-2nd gear synchronizer and the Reverse sliding gear into place, then secure with the snapring.

3. Slide the 2nd gear and the thrust washer into position, then secure with the snapring.

4. Slide the 3rd gear and the 3rd-4th synchronizer into place. Make sure the thrust surface of the synchronizer hub is facing forward.

Input Shaft

DISASSEMBLY

1. If not previously removed, remove the roller bearings from the input shaft.

2. Place the input gear in a press and press the input gear from the bearing.

ASSEMBLY

1. With the taper toward the front of the gear, apply pressure on the inner race and press the bearing onto the input gear until it is bottomed.

2. Apply a heavy coat of polyethylene on the inner bearing surface of the gear. Insert the 15 roller bearings into the gear.

Countershaft Gear

DISASSEMBLY

1. Place the countershaft gear in a press and remove the rear bearing.

2. Place the countershaft in a vise protected with wood blocks and pry the front bearing from the countershaft.

ASSEMBLY

1. With the taper facing outward, exert pressure on the inner race of the front bearing and press the bearing until it is bottomed on the gear.

2. Install the rear bearing in the same manner.

Input Shaft Gear Bearing Retainer

DISASSEMBLY

1. Place the bearing retainer in a vise.

2. Using a slide impact type puller, remove the seal from the bearing retainer.

ASSEMBLY

Install the seal in the retainer with the lip facing forward. Make sure the seal is bottomed in the retainer.

Extension Housing

DISASSEMBLY

1. Carefully remove the seal from the extension housing.

2. Using a suitable driver, remove the bushing.

ASSEMBLY

Install the bushing and the seal using a suitable driver.

RAD TRANSMISSION

Transmission Case

DISASSEMBLY

1. Remove the side cover assembly and the shift forks.

2. Remove the clutch gear bearing retainer.

3. Remove the clutch gear bearing-to-gear stem snapring. Pull the clutch gear outward until a screwdriver can be inserted between the bearing and the case. Remove the clutch gear bearing.

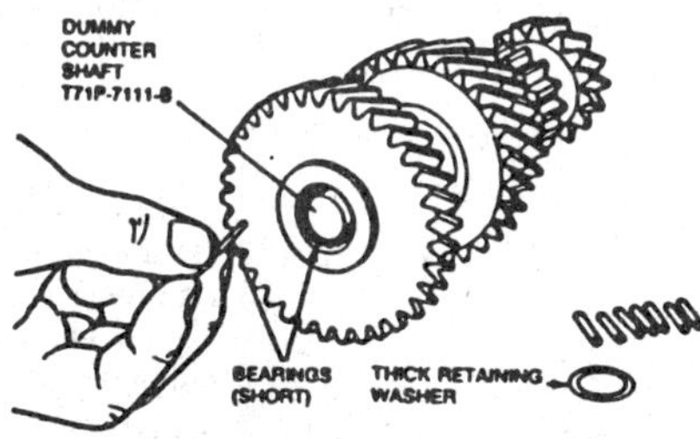

82ET countershaft gear assembly

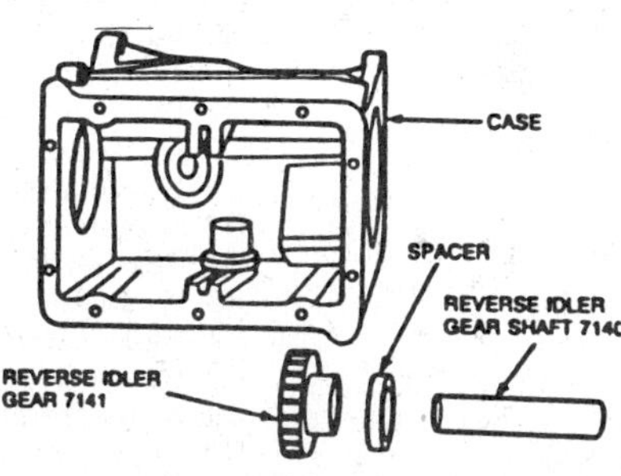

82ET reverse idle gear disassembled

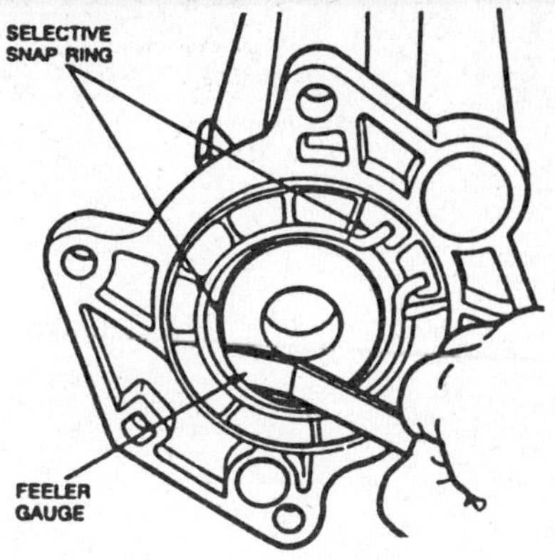

Measuring output shaft bearing snap-ring thickness on the 82ET

Part Number	Thickness (Inches)	Identification
D1FZ-7030-A	0.0679	Color Coded — Copper
D1FZ-7030-B	0.0689	Letter — W
D1FZ-7030-C	0.0699	Letter — V
D1FZ-7030-D	0.0709	Letter — U
D1FZ-7030-E	0.0719	None
D1FZ-7030-F	0.0728	Color Coded — Blue
D1FZ-7030-G	0.0738	Color Coded — Black
D1FZ-7030-H	0.0748	Color Coded — Brown

82ET output shaft bearing snap-ring thickness determination chart

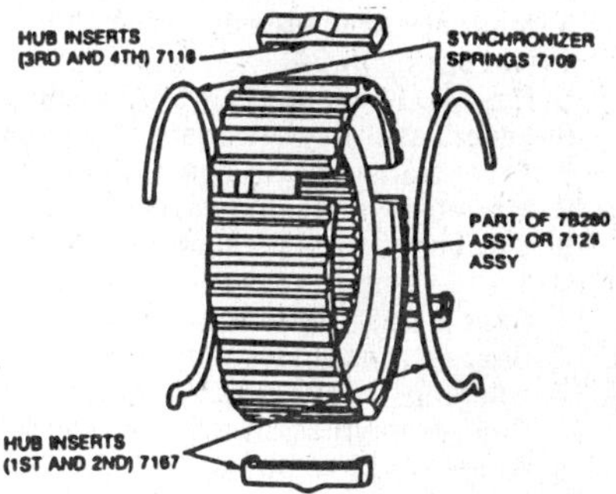

82ET synchronizer spring installation

4. Remove the speedometer driven gear and the extension bolts.

5. Remove the Reverse idler shaft snapring.

6. Remove the mainshaft and the extension assembly through the rear of the case.

7. Remove the clutch gear and the 3rd speed blocking ring from inside the case. Remove the 14 roller bearings from the clutch gear.

8. Expand the snapring which retains the mainshaft rear bearing and remove the extension.

9. Using a dummy shaft, drive the countershaft and the key out through the rear of the case. Remove the gear, the two tanged thrust washers and the dummy shaft. Remove the bearing washer and the 27 roller bearings from each end of the countergear.

10. Using a long drift, drive the Reverse idler shaft and key through the rear of the case.

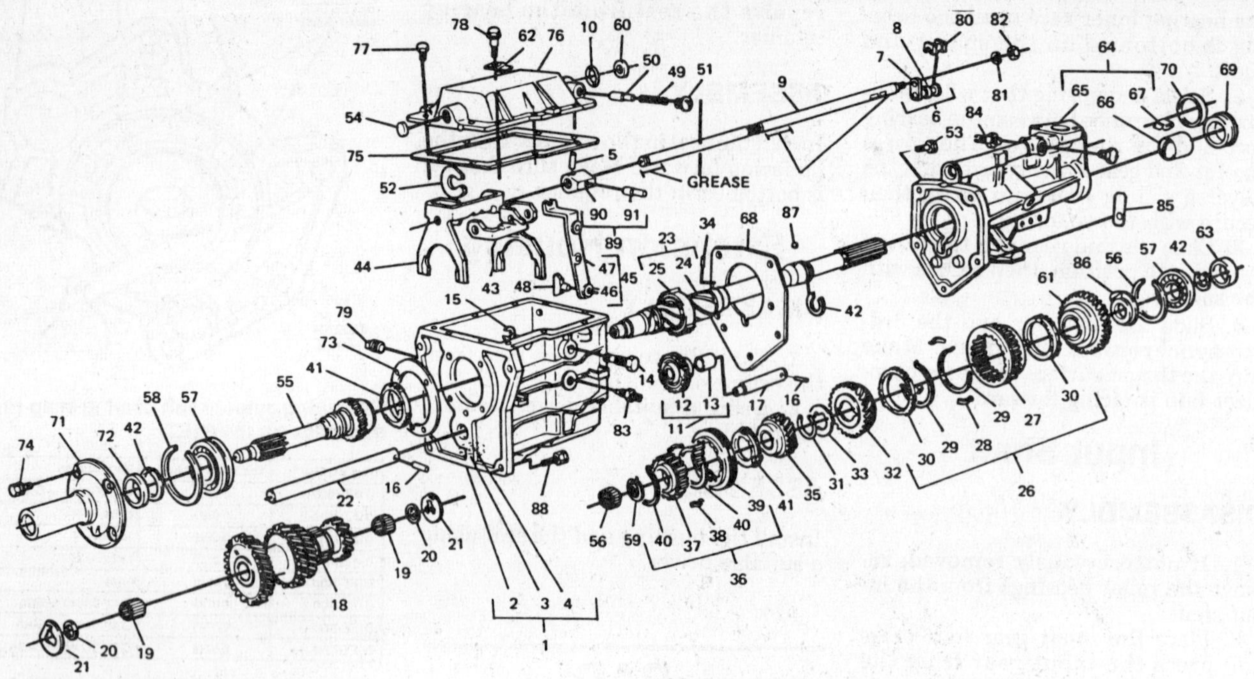

1 Case assembly—transmission
2 Case—transmission
3 Magnet—transmission case chip
4 Nut spring 9/64
5 Pin—3/16 diameter x 13/16 rolled spring
6 Lever assembly—transmission gearshift shaft offset
7 Lever transmission gearshift shaft offset
8 Pin—transmission gearshift shaft offset lever
9 Shaft—transmission shifter
10 Seal—O-ring
11 Gear & bush assembly—transmission reverse idler sliding
12 Gear—transmission reverse idler sliding
13 Bushing—transmission reverse idler gear
14 Pin—transmission reverse gear selector fork pivot
15 Ring—7/16 retaining
16 Pin—¼ x 1 spring
17 Shaft—transmission reverse idler gear
18 Gear—transmission countershaft
19 Roller—transmission countershaft bearing
20 Washer—208/.918 flat
21 Washer—transmission countershaft gear thrust
22 Countershaft—transmission
23 Shaft assembly—transmission output
24 Shaft—transmission output
25 Hub—transmission synchronizer 1st & 2nd gear cluster
26 Shaft and gear assembly—transmission output
27 Gear—transmission reverse sliding
28 Insert—transmission synchronizer hub
29 Spring—transmission synchronizer retaining
30 Ring—transmission synchronizer blocking
31 Ring—transmission 2nd speed gear retaining snap
32 Gear—transmission 2nd speed
33 Washer—transmission 2nd speed gear thrust
34 Pin—⅛ x ¼ rolled spring
35 Gear—transmission 3rd speed
36 Synchronizer assembly—3rd & 4th speed
37 Hub—transmission synchronizer
38 Insert—transmission synchronizer hub
39 Sleeve—transmission 3rd & 4th gear clutch hub
40 Spring—transmission synchronizer retaining
41 Ring—transmission synchronizer blocking
42 Ring—transmission m/d gear bearing shaft snap
43 Fork—transmission 1st & 2nd gear shift
44 Fork—transmission 3rd & 4th gear shift
45 Lever assembly—transmission reverse gear shaft relay
46 Retaining—transmission reverse gear shaft relay lever
47 Lever—transmission reverse gear shaft relay
48 Fork—transmission reverse gear shift
49 Spring—transmission shifter interlock
50 Plunger—transmission meshlock
51 Screw—m12 x 10 round head flat
52 Plate—transmission gear selector interlock
53 Screw & washer assembly—m10 x 30 hex head
54 Plug—¾ diameter welch type
55 Shaft—transmission input
56 Roller—transmission mainshaft bearing
57 Bearing assembly—transmission m/d gear ball
58 Ring—m/d gear bearing retaining snap
59 Ring—1.00 retaining
60 Seal—transmission shift shaft
61 Gear—transmission 1st speed
62 Clip—spark control switch wire retaining
63 Gear—speedometer drive
64 Extension assembly—transmission
65 Extension—transmission
66 Bushing—transmission extension
67 Stop—transmission gear shift lever reverse
68 Gasket—transmission extension
69 Seal assembly—transmission extension oil
70 Plug—transmission extension
71 Retainer—transmission input shaft gear bearing
72 Seal assembly—transmission input shaft oil
73 Gasket—transmission input shaft bearing retainer
74 Bolt—M8 x 20 hex head-lock
75 Gasket—transmission case cover
76 Cover—transmission case
77 Screw—m6 x 20 hex head
78 Bolt—m6 x 32 hex washer HD shoulder
79 Plug—½-14 pipe (filler)
80 Bushing—transmission gear shift damper
81 Washer—spring lock
82 Nut—hexagon
83 Switch assembly—back-up lamp
84 Switch assembly—transmission seat belt warning sensor
85 Tag—transmission service identification
86 Washer—transmission 1st gear thrust
87 Ball—.25 diameter
88 Screw & lockwasher assembly—m12 x 40
89 Arm assembly—transmission control selector
90 Arm—transmission control selector
91 Pin—transmission gear shift

Exploded view of the Ford RAD

11. Remove the Reverse idler gear and the tanged steel thrust washer.

ASSEMBLY

1. Using a dummy shaft, grease and load a row of 27 roller bearings and a thrust washer at each end of countergear.
2. Place the countergear assembly into the case from the rear. Place a tanged thrust washer (tang away from the gear) at each end. Install the countershaft and the key, making sure that the tangs align with the notches in the case.
3. Install the Reverse idler gear thrust washer, the gear and the shaft with a key from the rear of the case.

NOTE: Be sure the thrust washer is between the gear and the rear of the case with the tang toward the notch in the case.

4. Expand the snapring in the extension housing. Assemble the extension over the rear of the mainshaft and onto the rear bearing. Seat the snapring in the rear bearing groove.
5. Install the 14 mainshaft pilot bearings into the clutch gear cavity. Assemble the 3rd speed blocking ring onto the clutch gear clutching surface with the teeth toward the gear.
6. Place the clutch gear, the pilot bearings and the 3rd speed blocking ring assembly over the front of the mainshaft assembly; be sure the blocking rings align with the keys in the 2nd-3rd synchronizer assembly.
7. Stick the extension gasket to the case with grease. Install the clutch gear, the mainshaft and the extension together; be sure the clutch gear engages the teeth of the countergear anti lash plate. Torque the extension bolts to 45 ft.lb.
8. Place the bearing over the stem of the clutch gear and into the front case bore. Install the front bearing to the clutch gear snapring.
9. Install the clutch gear bearing retainer and the gasket. The retainer oil return hole must be at the bottom. Torque the retainer bolts to 10 ft.lb.
10. Install the Reverse idler gear shaft E-ring.
11. Shift the synchronizer sleeves to the Neutral positions. Install the cover, the gasket and the forks; aligning the forks with the synchronizer sleeve grooves. Torque the side cover bolts to 10 ft.lb.
12. Install the speedometer driven gear.

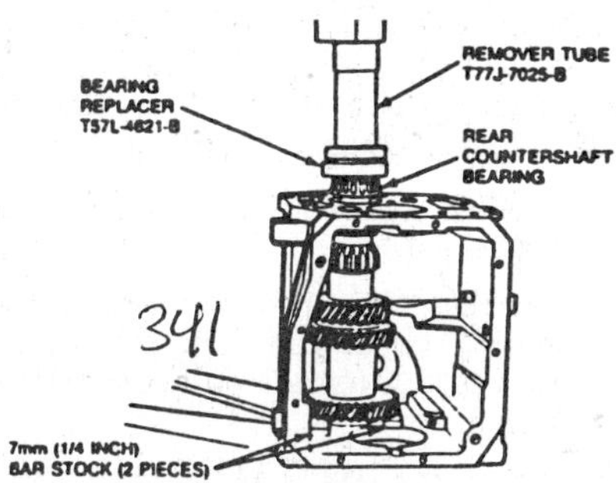

Installing the countershaft rear bearing on the T50D

Mainshaft

DISASSEMBLY

1. Remove the 2nd-3rd speed sliding clutch hub snapring from the mainshaft. Remove the clutch assembly, the 2nd speed blocking ring and the 2nd gear from front of the mainshaft.
2. Depress the speedometer drive gear retaining clip and remove the gear. Some units have a metal speedometer driver gear which must be pulled off.
3. Remove the rear bearing snapring.
4. Support the Reverse gear and press on the rear of the mainshaft. Remove the Reverse gear, the thrust washer, the spring washer, the rear bearing and the snapring.

NOTE: When pressing off the rear bearing, be careful not to cock the bearing on the shaft.

5. Remove the 1st and Reverse sliding clutch hub snapring. Remove the clutch assembly, 1st speed blocking ring and the 1st gear; sometimes the synchronizer hub and gear must be pressed off.

ASSEMBLY

1. Turn the front of the mainshaft up.

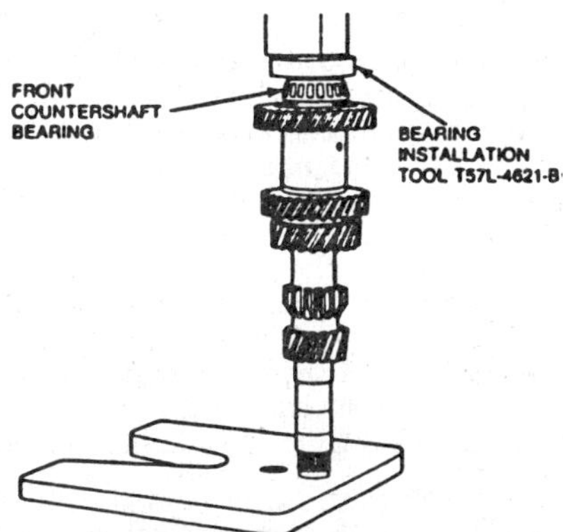

Installing the front countershaft bearing on the T50D

2. Install the 2nd gear with the clutching teeth up; the rear face of the gear butts against the flange on the mainshaft.
3. Install a blocking ring with the clutching teeth down. The three blocking rings are the same.
4. Install the 2nd-3rd speed synchronizer assembly with the fork slot down; press it onto the mainshaft splines.

NOTE: Both synchronizer assemblies are the same. Be sure that the blocking ring notches align with the synchronizer assembly keys.

5. Install the synchronizer snapring; both synchronizer snaprings are the same.
6. Turn the rear of the shaft up, then install the 1st gear with the clutching teeth up; the front face of the gear butts against the flange on the mainshaft.
7. Install a blocking ring with the clutching teeth down.
8. Install the 1st-Reverse synchronizer assembly with the fork slot down, then press it onto the mainshaft splines; be sure the blocking ring notches align with the synchronizer assembly keys.
9. Install the snapring.
10. Install the Reverse gear with the clutching teeth down.
11. Install the steel Reverse gear thrust washer and the spring washer.
12. Press the rear ball bearing onto the shaft with the snapring slot down.
13. Install the snapring.
14. Install the speedometer drive gear and the retaining clip; press on the metal speedometer drive gear.

Clutch Keys and Springs

REPLACEMENT

The keys and the springs may be replaced if worn or broken, but the hubs and sleeves are matched pairs, they must be kept together.

1. Mark the hub and sleeve for reassembly.
2. Push the hub from the sleeve, then remove the keys and the springs.
3. Place the three keys and the two springs (one on each side of hub) in position, so the three keys are engaged by both springs; the tanged ends of the springs should not be installed into the same key.
4. Slide the sleeve onto the hub by aligning the marks.

NOTE: A groove around the outside of the synchronizer hub marks the end that must be oppo-

site the fork slot in the sleeve when assembled.

Extension Oil Seal and Bushing

REPLACEMENT

1. Remove the seal.
2. Using the bushing removal and installation tool, drive the bushing into the extension housing.
3. Drive the new bushing in from the rear. Lubricate the inside of the bushing and the seal. Install a new oil seal with the extension seal installation tool or other suitable tool.

Clutch Bearing Retainer Oil Seal

REPLACEMENT

1. Pry the old seal out.
2. Install the new seal using the seal installer. Seat the seal in the bore.

T50D TRANSMISSION

Transmission Case

DISASSEMBLY

1. Drain the lubricant. Remove the side cover and the shift forks.
2. Remove the clutch gear bearing retainer. Remove the bearing-to-gear stem snapring and pull out on the clutch gear until a small pry bar can be inserted between the bearing, the large snapring and case to pry the bearing off.

NOTE: The clutch gear bearing is a slip fit on the gear and in the case. Removal of the bearing will provide clearance for the clutch gear and the mainshaft removal.

3. Remove the extension housing bolts, then remove the clutch gear, the mainshaft and the extension as an assembly.
4. Spread the snapring which holds the mainshaft rear bearing and remove the extension case.
5. Using a dummy shaft, drive the countershaft and its woodruff key out through the rear of the case. Remove the countergear assembly and the bearings.
6. Using a long drift, drive the Reverse idler shaft and the woodruff key through the rear of the case.

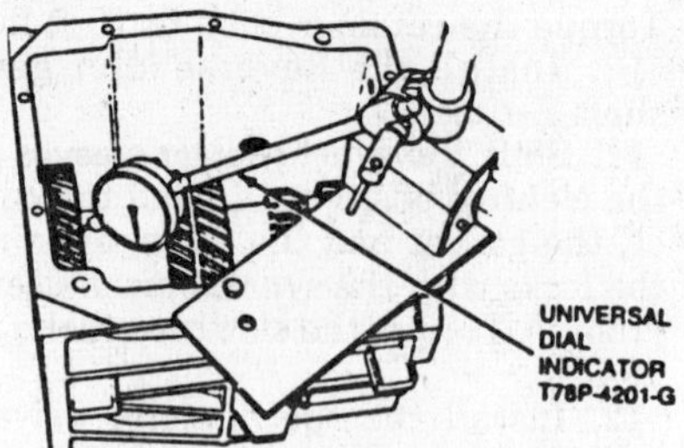

Dial indicator positioning

7. Expand and remove the 3rd-4th speed sliding clutch hub snapring from the mainshaft. Remove the clutch assembly, the 3rd gear blocking ring and the 3rd speed gear from the front of the mainshaft.
8. Press in the speedometer gear retaining clip and slide the gear off the mainshaft. Remove the rear bearing snapring from the mainshaft.
9. Using an arbor press, support the 1st gear on press plates, then press the 1st gear, the thrust washer, the spring washer, the rear bearing and snapring from the rear of the mainshaft.

CAUTION

Be sure to center the gear, the washers, the bearings and the snapring when pressing the rear bearing.

10. Expand and remove the 1st-2nd sliding clutch hub snapring from the mainshaft, then remove the clutch assembly, the 2nd speed blocking ring and the 2nd speed gear from the rear of the mainshaft.

NOTE: After thoroughly cleaning the parts and the transmission case, inspect and replace the damaged or worn parts. When checking the bearings, do not spin them at high speeds. Clean and rotate the bearings by hand to detect the roughness or unevenness. Spinning can damage the balls and the races.

ASSEMBLY

1. Grease both inside ends of the countergear. Install a dummy shaft into the countergear, then load a row of roller bearings (27) and thrust washers at each end of the countergear.
2. Position the countergear assembly into the case through the rear opening. Place a tanged thrust washer at each end of the countergear.
3. Install the countergear shaft and woodruff key from the rear of the case.

NOTE: Make sure that the shaft engages both thrust washers and that the tangs align with their notches in the case.

4. Install the Reverse idler gear, the shaft and the woodruff key. Install the extension-to-rear bearing snapring. Assemble the extension housing over the rear of the mainshaft and onto the rear bearing.
5. Install the 14 mainshaft pilot bearings into the clutch opening and the 4th speed blocking ring onto the clutching surface of the clutch gear (with the clutching teeth facing the gear).
6. Assemble the clutch gear, the pilot bearings and the 4th speed blocking ring unit over the front of the mainshaft. Do not assemble the bearing to the gear at this point.

CAUTION

Be sure that the blocking ring notches align with the 3rd-4th synchronizer assembly keys.

7. Install the extension-to-case gasket and secure it with grease. Install the clutch gear, the mainshaft and the extension housing as an assembly. Install the extension-to-case bolts (apply sealer to the bottom bolt) and torque to 45 ft.lb.
8. Install the outer snapring on the front bearing and place the bearing over the stem of the clutch gear and into the case bore.
9. Install the snapring to the clutch gear stem. Install the clutch gear bearing retainer and the gasket, with the retainer oil return hole at the bottom.
10. Place the synchronizer sleeves into the Neutral positions and install the cover, the gasket and the fork assemblies to the case; be sure the forks align with the synchronizer sleeve grooves. Torque the cover bolts to 22 ft.lb.

Mainshaft

ASSEMBLY

Install the following parts with the front of the mainshaft facing up:

1. Install the 3rd speed gear with the clutching teeth up; the rear face of the gear will abut with the mainshaft flange.
2. Install a blocking ring (with the clutching teeth down) over the 3rd speed gear synchronizing surface.

NOTE: The four blocking rings are the same.

3. Press the 3rd-4th synchronizer assembly (with the fork slot down) onto the mainshaft splines until it bottoms.

CAUTION

The blocking ring notches must align with the synchronizer assembly keys.

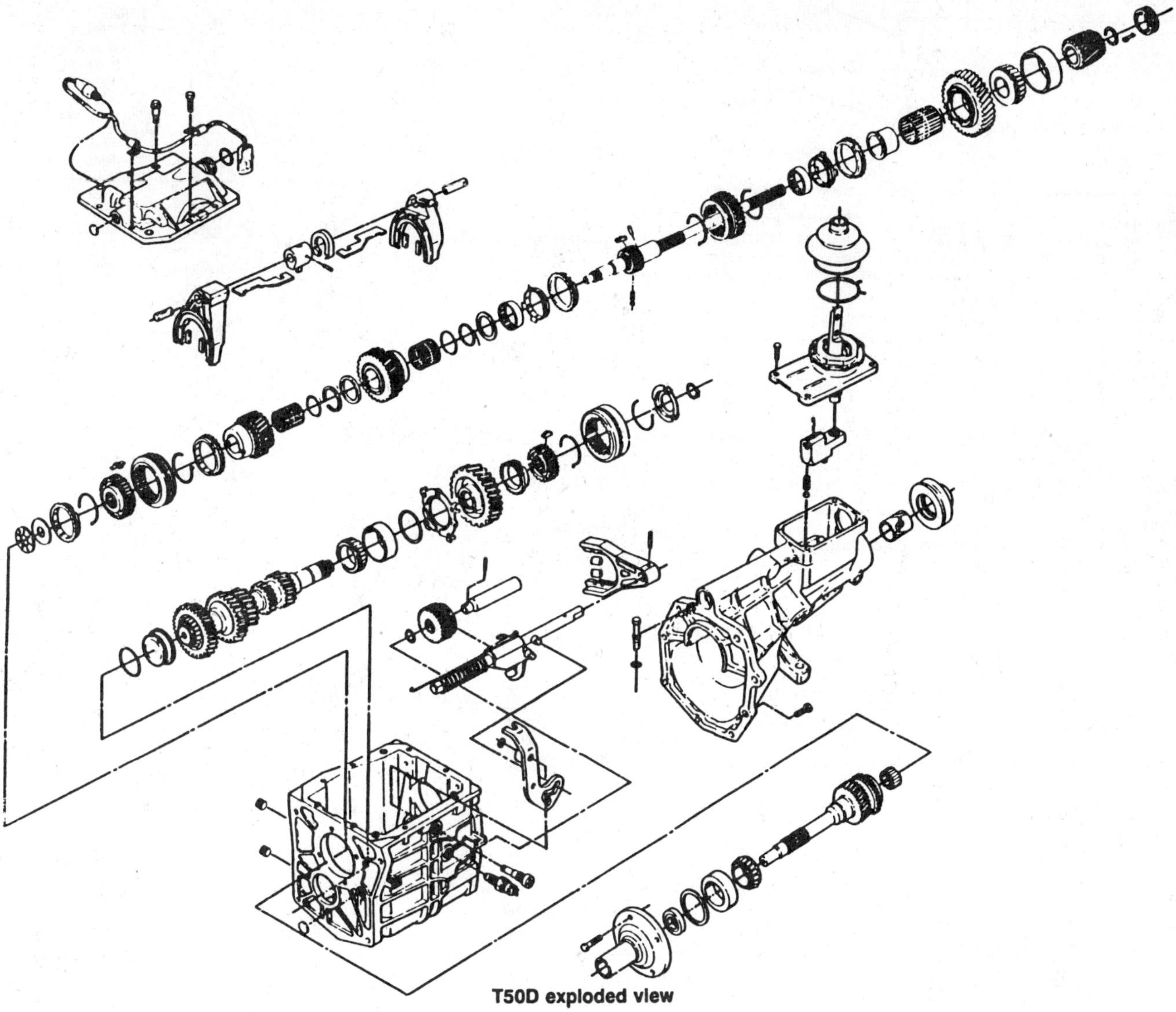

T50D exploded view

4. Install the synchronizer hub-to-mainshaft snapring; both synchronizer snaprings are the same.

Install the following parts with the rear of the mainshaft facing up:

5. Install the 2nd speed gear with the clutching teeth up; the front face of the gear will abut with the flange on the mainshaft.

6. Install a blocking ring (with the clutching teeth down) over the 2nd speed gear synchronizing surface.

7. Press the 1st-2nd synchronizer assembly (with the fork slot down) onto the mainshaft.

CAUTION

The blocking ring notches must align with the synchronizer assembly keys.

8. Install the synchronizer hub-to-mainshaft snapring.

9. Install a blocking ring with the notches down so they align with the 1st-2nd synchronizer assembly keys.

10. Install the 1st gear with the clutching teeth down. Install the 1st gear thrust washer and the spring washer.

11. Press the rear ball bearing (with the slot down) onto the mainshaft. Install the snapring. Install the speedometer gear and clip.

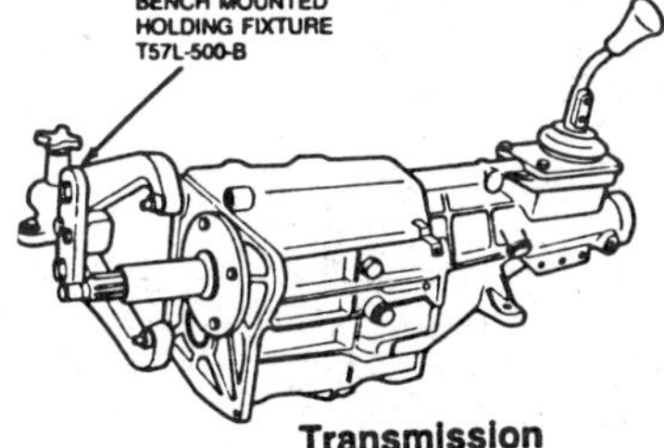

Transmission

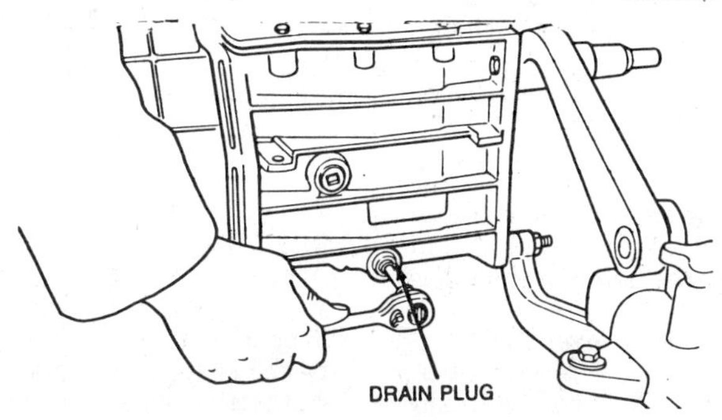

Removing the drain plug

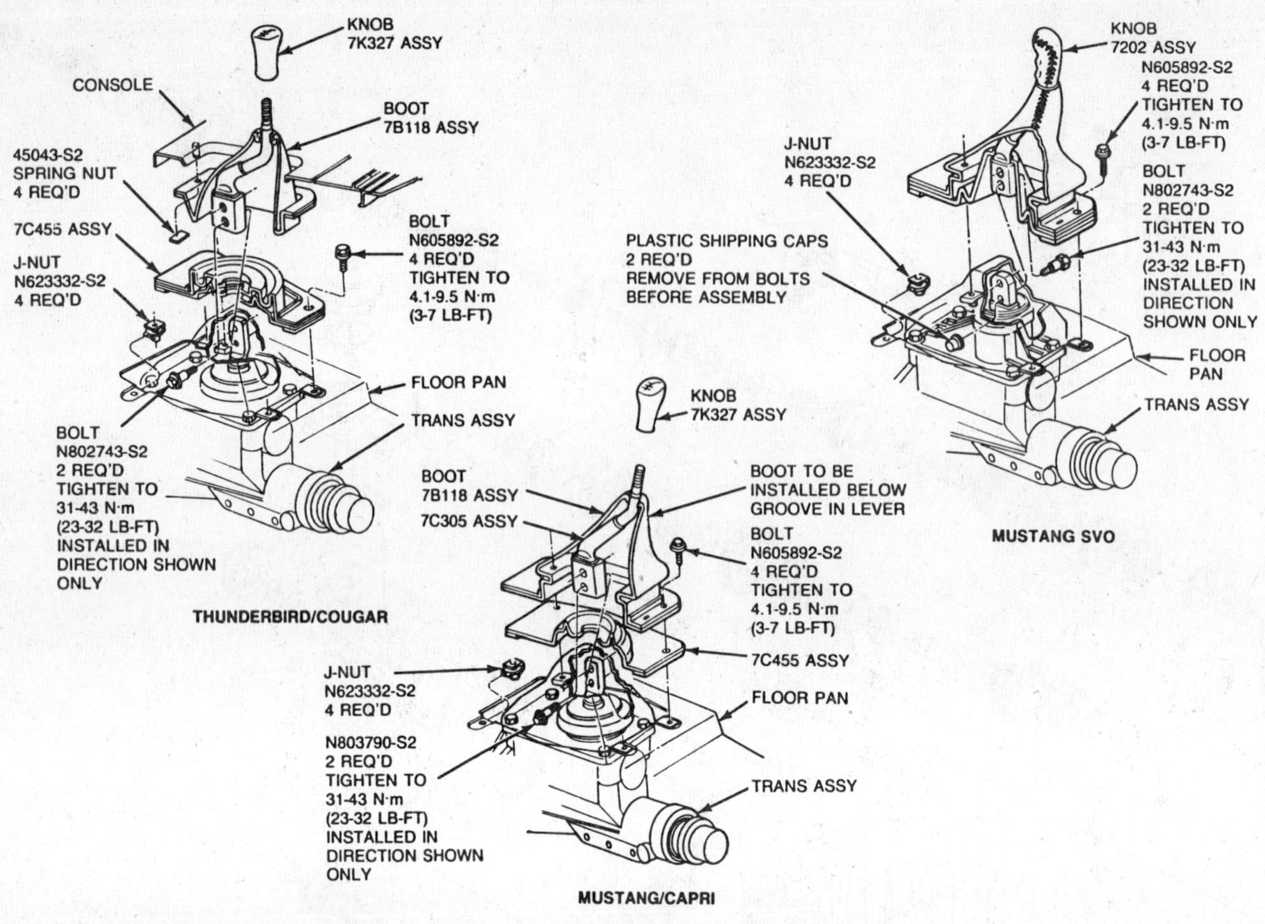

Shifters

RUG TRANSMISSION

Transmission Case

DISASSEMBLY

1. Place the transmission so that it is resting on the bell housing.
2. Drive the spring pin from the shifter shaft arm assembly and the shifter shaft, then remove the shifter shaft arm assembly.
3. Remove the five extension housing-to-case bolts and the extension housing.
4. Press down on the speedometer gear retainer, then remove the gear and the retainer from the mainshaft.
5. Remove the snaprings from the shifter shaft, then the Reverse shifter shaft cover, the shifter shaft detent cap, the spring, the ball and the interlock lock pin.
6. Pull the Reverse lever shaft outward to disengage the Reverse idler, then remove the idler shaft with the gear attached.
7. Remove the Reverse gear snapring, the Reverse countershaft gear and the gears.
8. Turn the case on its side and remove the clutch gear bearing retainer bolts, the retainer and the gasket.
9. Remove the clutch gear ball bearing-to-bell housing snapring, then the bell housing-to-case bolts.
10. Turn the case so that it rests on the bell housing, then expand the mainshaft bearing snapring and remove the case by lifting it off the mainshaft.

NOTE: Make sure that the mainshaft assembly, the countergear and shifter shaft assembly stay with the bell housing.

11. Lift the entire mainshaft assembly complete with shifter forks and countergear from the bell housing.

ASSEMBLY

1. Using a press, install the shielded ball bearing to the clutch gear shaft with the snapring groove up.
2. Install the snapring on the clutch gear shaft. Place the pilot bearings into the clutch gear cavity, using heavy grease to hold them in place.
3. Assemble the clutch gear to the mainshaft and the detent lever to the shift shaft with the roll pin.
4. Position the 1st-2nd gear shifter so that it engages the detent lever.
5. Assemble the 3rd-4th gear shifter fork to the detent bushing and slide the assembly on the shift shaft to place it below the 1st-2nd shifter fork arm.
6. Install the shifter assembly to the synchronizer sleeve grooves on the mainshaft.
5. With the front of the bell housing resting on wooden blocks, place a thrust washer over the hole for the countergear shaft. The thrust washer must be placed in the holes in the bellhousing.
6. Mesh the countershaft gears to the mainshaft gears and install this assembly into the bellhousing.
7. Turn the bellhousing on its side, then install the snapring to the ball bearing on the clutch gear and the bearing retainer to the bell housing. Use sealant on the four retaining bolts.
8. Turn the bell housing (so that it is resting on the blocks) and install the Reverse lever to the case using grease

to hold it in place. When installing the Reverse lever, the screwdriver slot should be parallel to the front of the case.

9. Install the Reverse lever snapring and the roller bearing-to-countergear opening with the snapring groove inside of the case.

10. Using rubber cement, install the gasket on the bell housing. Before installing the case, make sure the synchronizers are in the Neutral position, the detent bushing slot is facing outward and the Reverse lever is flush with the inside wall of the case.

11. Expand the snapring in the mainshaft case opening and let it slide over the bearing.

12. Install the interlock lock pin with locking compound to hold the shifter shaft in place and the idler shaft so it engages with the Reverse lever inside the shaft.

13. Install the cover over the screwdriver arm to hold the Reverse lever in place.

14. Install the detent ball, the spring and the cap in the case, then the Reverse gear (with the chamfer on the gear teeth facing up). Push the Reverse gear onto the splines and secure with a snapring.

15. Install the smaller Reverse gear on the countergear shaft (with the shoulder resting against the countergear bearing) and secure with a snapring.

16. Install the snapring, the thrust washer and the Reverse idler gear (with the gear teeth chamfer facing down) to the idler shaft, then secure with the thrust washer and the snapring.

17. Install the shifter shaft snaprings and engage the speedometer gear retainer in the hole in the mainshaft (with the retainer loop toward the front), then slide the speedometer gear over the mainshaft and into position.

NOTE: Before installation, heat the gear to 175°F (80°C); use an oven or heat lamp, not a torch.

18. Place the extension housing and the gasket on the case, then loosely install the two pilot bolts (one in the top right hand corner and the other in the bottom left hand corner) and the other three bolts. The pilot bolts must be installed in the right holes to prevent splitting the case.

19. Assemble the shifter shaft arm over the shifter shaft, align with the drilled hole near the end of the shaft, then drive the spring pin into the shifter shaft arm and shaft.

20. Turn the case on its side and loosely install the two pilot bolts through the bell housing and then the four retaining bolts.

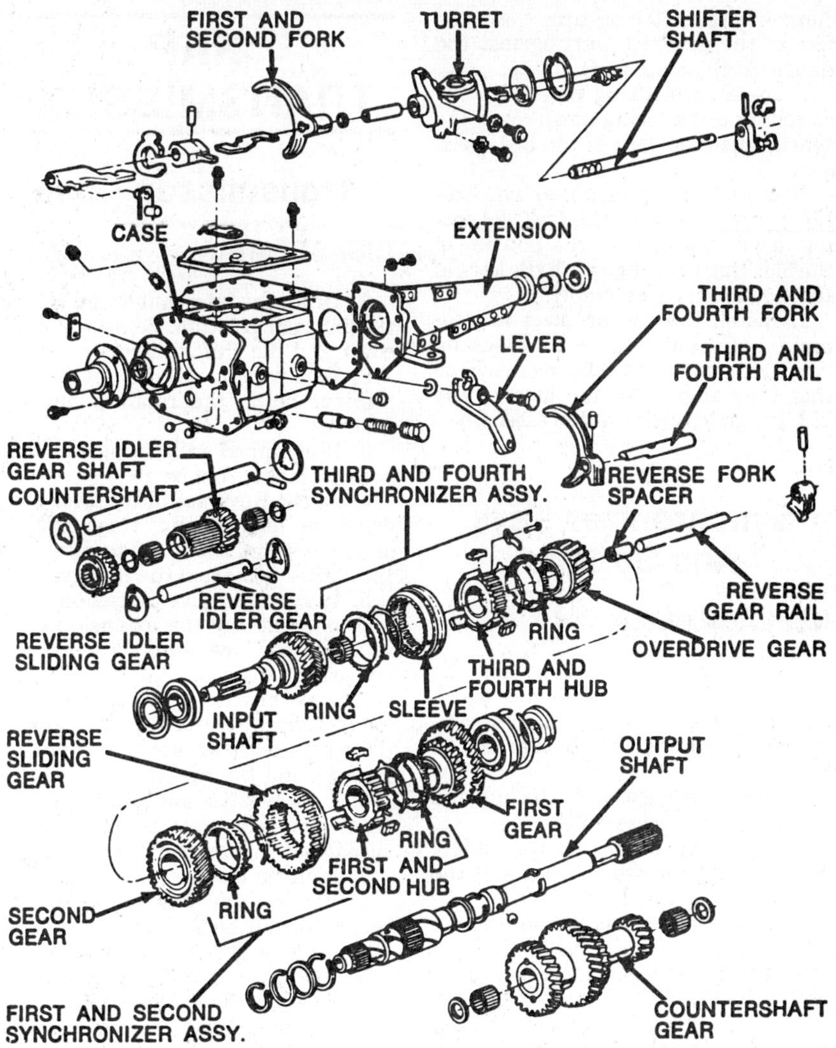

Exploded view of the Ford single rail 4-speed overdrive

Mainshaft

DISASSEMBLY

1. Separate the shift shaft assembly and countergear from the mainshaft.

2. Remove the clutch gear and the blocking ring from the mainshaft; make sure you don't lose any of the clutch gear roller bearings.

3. Remove the 3rd-4th gear synchronizer hub snapring and the hub, using an arbor press (if necessary).

4. Remove the blocking ring and the 3rd speed gear. Using an arbor press and press plates, remove the ball bearing from the rear of the mainshaft. Remove the remaining parts from the mainshaft keeping them in order for later reassembly.

ASSEMBLY

1. With the rear of the mainshaft turned up, install the 2nd speed gear with the clutching teeth facing upward; the rear face of the gear will butt against the flange of the mainshaft.

2. Install a blocking ring (with the clutching teeth down) over the 2nd speed gear.

3. Install the 1st-2nd synchronizer assembly (with the fork slot down), then press it onto the splines on the mainshaft until it bottoms.

NOTE: Make sure the notches of the blocking ring align with the keys of the synchronizer assembly.

4. Install the synchronizer hub-to-mainshaft snapring, then install a blocking ring (with the notches facing down) so they align with the keys of the 1st-2nd gear synchronizer assembly.

5. Install the 1st speed gear (with the clutching teeth down), then the rear ball bearing (with the snapring groove down) and press it into place on the mainshaft.

6. Turn the mainshaft up and install the 3rd speed gear (with the

clutching teeth facing up); the front face of the gear will butt against the flange on the mainshaft.

7. Install a blocking ring (with the clutching teeth facing down) over the synchronizer surface of the 3rd speed gear.

8. Install the 3rd-4th gear synchronizer assembly (with the fork slot facing down); make sure the notches of the blocking ring align with the keys of the synchronizer assembly.

9. Install the synchronizer hub-to-mainshaft snapring and a blocking ring (with the notches facing down) so that they align with the keys of the 3rd-4th gear synchronizer assembly.

Synchronizer Keys And Springs

REPLACEMENT

1. The synchronizer hubs and the sliding sleeves are an assembly which should be kept together as an assembly; the keys and the springs can be replaced.

2. Mark the position of the hub and the sleeve for reassembly.

3. Push the hub from the sliding sleeve; the keys will fall out and the springs can be easily removed.

4. Place the new springs in position (with one on each side of the hub) so that the three keys are engaged by both springs.

5. Place and hold the keys in position, then slide the sleeve into the hub aligning the marks made during disassembly.

Extension Oil Seal

REPLACEMENT

1. Pry the oil seal and drive the bushing from rear of the extension housing.

2. Coat the inside diameter of the seal and bushing with transmission fluid and install them.

Drive Gear Bearing Oil Seal

REPLACEMENT

Pry out the old seal and install a new one making sure that it bottoms properly in its bore.

RAP TRANSMISSION

Transmisson Case

DISASSEMBLY

1. Drain the lubricant and shift into the 2nd gear position. Remove the side cover and the shift controls.

2. Remove the four front bearing retainer bolts, the retainer and the gasket.

3. If equipped with an output companion flange, remove it.

4. At the Reverse shifter lever boss, drive the lock pin up, then pull the shift shaft out about ⅛" to disengage the shifter fork from the Reverse gear.

5. Remove the five extension housing bolts and tap the extension (with soft hammer) rearward. When the idler gear shaft is out (as far as it will go), move the extension housing to the left so that the Reverse fork clears the Reverse gear, then remove extension housing and the gasket.

6. Remove the speedometer gear outer snapring, then tap or slide the speedometer from the mainshaft.

7. Remove the 2nd snapring.

8. Remove the Reverse gear from the mainshaft and the rear part of the Reverse idler gear from the case.

9. Remove the front bearing snapring and the spacer washer.

10. Pull the front bearing from the case.

11. Remove the rear retainer lock bolt.

12. Shift the 1st-2nd and the 3rd-4th clutch sliding sleeves forward for clearance.

13. Remove the mainshaft and the rear bearing retainer assembly from the case.

14. Remove the front Reverse idler gear and the thrust washer from the case (the gear teeth must face forward).

15. Using a dummy shaft, drive the countergear shaft out through the rear of the case. Remove the countergear and the tanged thrust washers.

ASSEMBLY

1. Place the case on its side and install the countergear tanged washers with the tangs in the thrust face notches, secure them with grease.

2. Install the countergear (with a dummy shaft) in the case. Drive the countergear shaft through the rear of the case, forcing the dummy shaft out through the front. Install the shaft key and tap the shaft in until it is flush with the rear face of the case.

3. Install the front Reverse idler gear with the teeth forward, using grease to secure the thrust washer in place.

4. Use heavy grease to secure the 16 roller bearings and the washer in the main drive gear, mate the main drive gear with the mainshaft. Hold them together by moving the 3rd-4th clutch sliding sleeve forward.

5. Place a new gasket on the rear of the case. Install the mainshaft and drive gear assembly into the case.

6. Align the rear bearing retainer with the case, then install the locating pin and the locking bolt.

7. Install the bearing snapring on the front main bearing. Tap the bearing into the case, then install the spacer washer and the thickest snapring that can be fitted.

8. Install the front bearing retainer and the gasket, using sealer on the bolts.

9. Install the rear Reverse idler gear, engaging the splines with the portion of the gear in the case.

10. Slide the Reverse gear onto the shaft. Install the speedometer gear and the two thickest snaprings that can be fitted.

11. Install the idler shaft into the extension housing until the hole in the shaft aligns with the lockpin hole, then drive the lockpin and a sealant coated plug into place.

12. Place the Reverse shifter shaft and the detent into the extension housing, using grease to hold the Reverse shift fork in position. Install the shaft O-ring, after the shaft is in place.

13. Put the tanged thrust washer on the Reverse idler shaft; the tang must be in the notch of the extension housing thrust face.

14. Place the 1st-2nd and the 3rd-4th clutch sliding sleeves in the Neutral positions. Pull the Reverse shift shaft part way out and push the Reverse shift fork in as far as possible. Start the extension housing onto the mainshaft and push in on the shifter shaft to engage the shift fork with the Reverse gear collar. When the fork engages, turn the shifter shaft to let the Reverse gear go to the rear and the extension housing to fit in place.

15. Install the Reverse shift shaft lockpin.

16. Install the extension housing bolts.

NOTE: Use sealant on the upper left side bolt.

17. Position the 1st-2nd clutch sliding sleeve into 2nd gear and the 3rd-4th clutch sliding sleeve into Neutral positions. Position the forward shift forks into the sliding sleeves.

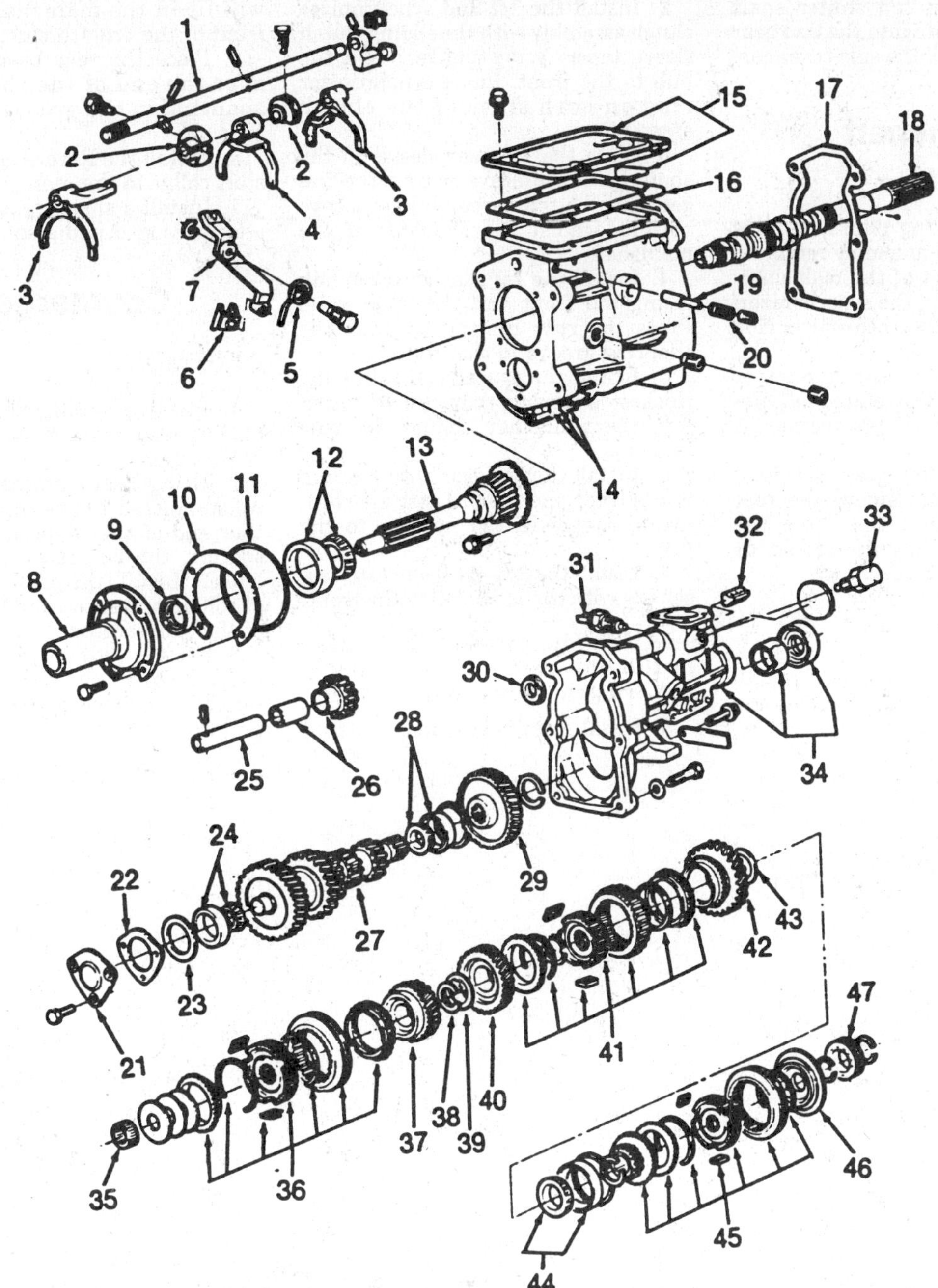

1. Shifter shaft
2. Gear selector interlock
3. 3rd/4th shifter fork
4. 1st/2nd shifter fork
5. Shift lever return spring
6. Reverse shifter fork
7. Reverse shift lever
8. Bearing retainer
9. Input shaft oil seal
10. Input shaft front bearing shim
11. Bearing retainer seal
12. Input shaft bearing assembly
13. Input shaft
14. Case assy.
15. Cover assy.
16. Cover gasket
17. Extension gasket
18. Output shaft
19. Meshlock plunger
20. Interlock shifter spring
21. Countershaft gear front retainer
22. Retainer gasket
23. Front bearing shim
24. Front bearing assy.
25. Reverse idler gear shaft
26. Reverse idler gear and bushing
27. Countershaft cluster gear
28. Rear bearing assy.
29. 5th speed cluster gear
30. Shifter shaft seal
31. Back-up switch
32. Lever reverse stop
33. 5th speed inhibitor plunger
34. Extension housing assy.
35. Mainshaft roller bearing
36. 3rd/4th synchronizer assy.
37. 3rd speed gear
38. Snap ring
39. Thrust washer
40. 2nd speed gear
41. 1st/2nd synchronizer assy.
42. 1st speed gear
43. Thrust washer
44. Output shaft bearing assy.
45. 5th speed synchronizer assy.
46. Retaining spacer
47. Speedometer drive gear

Ford Rap five speed overdrive

18. Place the 1st-2nd shifter shaft and the detent plate into the 2nd gear position and install the side cover gasket, with sealant.

Mainshaft

DISASSEMBLY

1. Using snapring pliers, remove the 3rd-4th clutch assembly retaining ring from the front of the mainshaft. Remove the washer, the syncrhonizer/clutch assembly, the synchronizer ring and the 3rd gear.
2. Spread the rear bearing retainer snapring and slide the retainer off. Remove the rear bearing-to-mainshaft snapring.
3. Support the 2nd gear and press the mainshaft out; remove the rear bearing, the 1st gear, the sleeve, the 1st-2nd clutch/synchronizer assembly and the 2nd gear.

ASSEMBLY

1. At the rear of the shaft, install the 2nd gear with the hub facing the rear.
2. Install the 1st-2nd synchronizer clutch assembly with the sliding clutch sleeve taper facing the rear and the hub to the front. Put a synchronizer ring on both sides of the clutch assemblies.
3. Place the 1st gear sleeve on the shaft. Press the sleeve on until the 2nd gear, the clutch assembly and sleeve bottom against the shoulder of the mainshaft.
4. Install the 1st gear with the hub facing the front and the inner race. Press the rear bearing on with the snapring groove to the front.
5. Install the spacer and select the thickest snapring that can be fitted into the mainshaft behind the rear bearing.
6. Install the 3rd gear with the hub to the front and the 3rd gear synchronizing ring with the notches to the front.
7. Install the 3rd-4th gear clutch assembly with the taper facing the front.

NOTE: Make sure that the keys in the hub match the notches in the 3rd gear synchronizing ring.

8. Install the thickest snapring that will fit in the mainshaft groove in front of the 3rd-4th clutch assembly.
9. Place the rear bearing retainer over the end of the shaft and the snapring in the groove of the rear bearing.
10. Install the Reverse gear with the shift collar to the rear.
11. Install a snapring, the speedometer drive gear and a snapring.

Countergear

ASSEMBLY

1. Install a dummy shaft and a tubular roller bearing spacer into the countergear.
2. Using heavy grease to hold the rollers, install 20 bearing rollers in either end of the countergear, the two spacers, the 20 more rollers, then a spacer. Install the same combination of rollers and spacers in the other end of the countergear.
3. Set the countergear assembly in the bottom of the case, be sure the tanged thrust washers are in their proper position.

Front Wheel Drive 2

INDEX

2 FRONT WHEEL DRIVE CARS

VEHICLE IDENTIFICATION CHART

It is important for servicing and ordering parts to be certain of the vehicle and engine identification. The VIN (vehicle identification number) is a 17 digit number visible through the windshield on the driver's side of the dash and contains the vehicle and engine identification codes. It can be interpreted as follows:

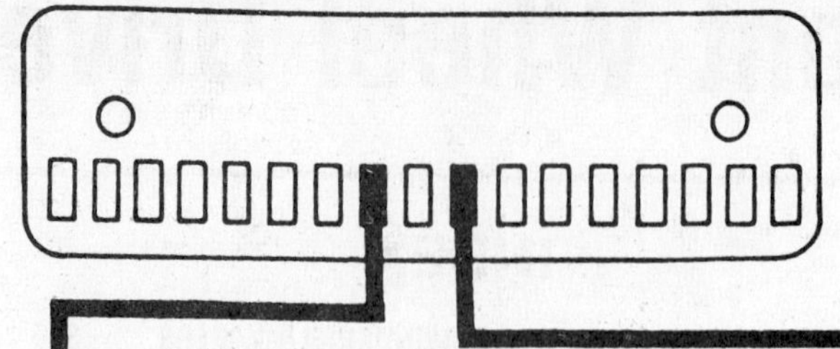

Engine Code					
Code	Cu. In.	Liters	Cyl.	Fuel Sys.	Eng. Mfg.
1	79	1.3	4	2 bbl	Ford
2	98	1.6	4	2 bbl	Ford
5	98	1.6	4	E.F.I.	Ford
4	98	1.6 HO	4	2 bbl	Ford
7	98	1.6 MHO	4	2 bbl	Ford
8	98	1.6 Turbo	4	E.F.I.	Ford
J	98	1.6	4	E.F.I.	Ford
9	116	1.9	4	2 bbl	Ford
J	116	1.9 HO	4	E.F.I.	Ford
H	122	2.0	4	Diesel	Toyo Kogyo
R	140	2.3 HSC	4	1/E.F.I.	Ford
X	140	2.3	4	C.F.I.	Ford
S	140	2.3 HO	4	C.F.I.	Ford
D	154	2.5	4	CFI	Ford
U	182	3.0	6	EFI	Ford

Model Year	
Code	Year
B	1981
C	1982
D	1983
E	1984
F	1985
G	1986
H	1987
J	1988

The seventeen digit Vehicle Identification Number can be used to determine engine identification and model year. The tenth digit indicates model year, and the fourth digit indicates engine code.

GENERAL ENGINE SPECIFICATIONS

Year	VIN	No. Cylinder Displacement cu. in. (liter)	Fuel System Type	Net Horsepower @ rpm	Net Torque @ rpm (ft.lbs.)	Bore × Stroke (in.)	Com-pression Ratio	Oil Pressure @ rpm
1981	1	4-79 (1.3)	2 bbl	NA	NA	3.15 × 2.54	8.0:1	35-45 @ 2000
	2	4-98 (1.6)	2 bbl	65 @ 5200	85 @ 3000	3.15 × 3.13	8.8:1	35-45 @ 2000
1982	2	4-98 (1.6)	2 bbl	70 @ 4600	89 @ 3000	3.15 × 3.13	8.8:1	35-65 @ 2000
1983	2	4-98 (1.6)	2 bbl	70 @ 4600	89 @ 3000	3.15 × 3.13	8.8:1	35-65 @ 2000
1984	2	4-98 (1.6)	2 bbl	70 @ 4600	88 @ 2600	3.15 × 3.13	9.0:1	35-65 @ 2000
	4	4-98 (1.6 HO)	2 bbl	80 @ 5400	88 @ 3000	3.15 × 3.13	9.0:1	35-65 @ 2000
	5	4-98 (1.6)	E.F.I.	120 @ 5200	120 @ 3400	3.15 × 3.13	8.0:1	35-65 @ 2000
	H	4-122 (2.0)	Diesel	52 @ 4000	82 @ 2400	3.39 × 3.39	22.7:1	55-60 @ 2000
	R	4-140 (2.3 HSC)	1/EFI	84 @ 4600	118 @ 2600	3.70 × 3.30	9.0:1	55-70 @ 2000
1985	2	4-98 (1.6)	2 bbl	70 @ 4600	88 @ 2600	3.15 × 3.13	9.0:1	35-65 @ 2000
	4	4-98 (1.6 HO)	2 bbl	80 @ 5400	88 @ 3000	3.15 × 3.13	9.0:1	35-65 @ 2000
	5	4-98 (1.6)	E.F.I.	120 @ 5200	120 @ 3400	3.15 × 3.13	8.0:1	35-65 @ 2000
	8	4-98 (1.6 Turbo)	E.F.I.	84 @ 5200	90 @ 2800	3.15 × 3.13	9.0:1	35-65 @ 2000

GENERAL ENGINE SPECIFICATIONS

Year	VIN	No. Cylinder Displacement cu. in. (liter)	Fuel System Type	Net Horsepower @ rpm	Net Torque @ rpm (ft.lbs.)	Bore × Stroke (in.)	Com-pression Ratio	Oil Pressure @ rpm
1985	7	4-98 (1.6 MHO)	2 bbl	80 @ 5400	88 @ 3000	3.15 × 3.13	9.0:1	35-65 @ 2000
	H	4-122 (2.0)	Diesel	52 @ 4000	82 @ 2400	3.39 × 3.39	22.7:1	55-60 @ 2000
	R	4-140 (2.3 HSC)	1 bbl	84 @ 4600	118 @ 2600	3.70 × 3.30	9.0:1	55-70 @ 2000
	X	4-140 (2.3)	C.F.I.	100 @ 4600	125 @ 3200	3.70 × 3.30	9.0:1	55-70 @ 2000
	S	4-140 (2.3 HSC)	C.F.I.	100 @ 4600	125 @ 3200	3.70 × 3.30	9.0:1	55-70 @ 2000
1986	9	4-116 (1.9)	2 bbl	86 @ 4800	100 @ 3000	3.23 × 3.46	9.0:1	35-65 @ 2000
	J	4-116 (1.9 HO)	E.F.I.	108 @ 5200	114 @ 4000	3.23 × 3.46	9.0:1	35-65 @ 2000
	H	4-122 (2.0)	Diesel	52 @ 4000	82 @ 2400	3.39 × 3.39	22.7:1	55-60 @ 2000
	R	4-140 (2.3 HSC)	1 bbl	84 @ 4600	118 @ 2600	3.70 × 3.30	9.0:1	35-65 @ 2000
	X	4-140 (2.3)	C.F.I.	100 @ 4600	125 @ 3200	3.70 × 3.30	9.0:1	55-10 @ 2000
	D	4-154 (2.5)	CFI	88 @ 4600	130 @ 2800	3.68 × 3.62	9.7:1	40-60 @ 2000
	U	6-182 (3.0)	EFI	140 @ 4800	160 @ 3000	3.50 × 3.15	9.3:1	55-70 @ 2000
1987-88	9	4-116 (1.9)	2 bbl	86 @ 4800	100 @ 3000	3.23 × 3.46	9.0:1	35-65 @ 2000
	J	4-116 (1.9 HO)	E.F.I.	108 @ 5200	114 @ 4000	3.23 × 3.46	9.0:1	35-65 @ 2000
	H	4-122 (2.0)	Diesel	52 @ 4000	82 @ 2400	3.39 × 3.39	22.7:1	55-60 @ 2000
	R	4-140 (2.3 HSC)	1 bbl	84 @ 4600	118 @ 2600	3.70 × 3.30	9.0:1	35-65 @ 2000
	X	4-140 (2.3)	C.F.I.	100 @ 4600	125 @ 3200	3.70 × 3.30	9.0:1	55-70 @ 2000
	D	4-154 (2.5)	CFI	88 @ 4600	130 @ 2800	3.68 × 3.62	9.7:1	55-70 @ 2000
	U	6-182 (3.0)	EFI	140 @ 4800	160 @ 3000	3.50 × 3.15	9.3:1	40-60 @ 2000

HO—High Output
HSC—High Swirl Combustion
MHO—Methanol Fuel Injection
EFI—Electronic Fuel Injection
CFI—Central Fuel Injection

GASOLINE ENGINE TUNE-UP SPECIFICATIONS

Year	VIN	No. Cylinder Displacement cu. in. (liter)	Spark Plugs Type	Spark Plugs Gap (in.)	Ignition Timing (deg.) MT	Ignition Timing (deg.) AT	Com-pression Pressure (psi)	Fuel Pump (psi)	Idle Speed (rpm) MT	Idle Speed (rpm) AT	Valve Clearance In.	Valve Clearance Ex.
1981	1	4-79 (1.3)	①④	.044	10B	10B	—	4-6	①	①	Hyd.	Hyd.
	2	4-98 (1.6)	AGSP-32④	.044	10B	10B	—	4-6	800	800	Hyd.	Hyd.
1982	2	4-98 (1.6)	AGSP-32④	.044	10B	10B	—	4-6	800	800	Hyd.	Hyd.
1983	2	4-98 (1.6)	AWSF-34	.044	8B②	10B	—	③	800	750	Hyd.	Hyd.
1984	2	4-98 (1.6)	AWSF-34	.044	8B	8B	—	4-6	700	700	Hyd.	Hyd.
	4	4-98 (1.6 HO)	AWSF-34	.044	12B	14B	—	4-6	800	800	Hyd.	Hyd.
	5	4-98 (1.6 EFI)	AWSF-22	.034	10B	10B	—	35-45	800	750	Hyd.	Hyd.
	R	4-140(2.3 HSC)	AWSF-52	.044	15B	15B ⑤	—	4-6	800	700	Hyd.	Hyd.
1985	2	4-98 (1.6)	AWSF-34	.044	8B	8B	—	4-6	700	700	Hyd.	Hyd.
	4	4-98 (1.6 HO)	AWSF-34	.044	12B	14B	—	4-6	800	800	Hyd.	Hyd.
	5	4-98 (1.6 EFI)	AWSF-24	.044	10B	10B	—	35-45	800	750	Hyd.	Hyd.
	8	4-98 (1.6 Turbo)	AWSF-22C	.044	8B	8B	—	35-45	800	750	Hyd.	Hyd.
	7	4-98 (1.6 MHO)	AWSF-34	.044	12B	14B	—	4-6	800	800	Hyd.	Hyd.
	R	4-140 (2.3 HSC)	AWSF-52C	.044	10B	10B	—	4-6	800	750	Hyd.	Hyd.

GASOLINE ENGINE TUNE-UP SPECIFICATIONS

Year	VIN	No. Cylinder Displacement cu. in. (liter)	Spark Plugs Type	Spark Plugs Gap (in.)	Ignition Timing (deg.) MT	Ignition Timing (deg.) AT	Compression Pressure (psi)	Fuel Pump (psi)	Idle Speed (rpm) MT	Idle Speed (rpm) AT	Valve Clearance In.	Valve Clearance Ex.
1985	X	4-140 (2.3 CFI)	AWSF-52C	.044	10B	10B	—	35-45	725	570	Hyd.	Hyd.
	S	4-140 (2.3 HSC/CFI)	AWSF-52C	.044	10B	10B	—	35-45	725	570	Hyd.	Hyd.
1986	9	4-116 (1.9)	AWSF-34C	.044	10B	10B	—	4-6	750	750	Hyd.	Hyd.
	J	4-116 (1.9 HO/EFI)	AWSF-24C	.044	10B	10B	—	35-45	900	800	Hyd.	Hyd.
	R	4-140 (2.3 HSC)	AWSF-44C	.044	10B	10B	—	4-6	800	750	Hyd.	Hyd.
	X	4-140 (2.3 CFI)	AWSF-52	.044	10B	10B	—	35-46	750	650	Hyd.	Hyd.
	D	4-154 (2.5)	AWSF–32C	.044	10B	10B	—	35-45	725	650	Hyd.	Hyd.
	U	6-182 (3.0)	AWSF–32C	.044	—	10B	—	35-45	—	625	Hyd.	Hyd.
1987	9	4-116 (1.9)	AWSF-34C	.044	10B	10B	—	4-6	750	750	Hyd.	Hyd.
	J	4-116 (1.9 HO/EFI)	AWSF-24C	.044	10B	10B	—	35-45	800	750	Hyd.	Hyd.
	R	4-140 (2.3 HSC)	AWSF-44C	.044	10B	10B	—	4-6	800	750	Hyd.	Hyd.
	X	4-140 (2.3 EFI)	AWSF-52	.044	10B	10B	—	35-45	750	650	Hyd.	Hyd.
	D	4-154 (2.5)	AWSF–32C	.044	10B	10B	—	35-45	725	650	Hyd.	Hyd.
	U	6-182 (3.0)	AWSF–32C	.044	—	10B	—	35-45	—	625	Hyd.	Hyd.
1988	SEE UNDERHOOD SPECIFICATIONS STICKER											

① The Calibration levels may vary from model to model. Always refer to the underhood sticker for your car requirements.

② EFI models—10B

③ Carbureted models 4-6 psi. Fuel injected models 35-45 psi.

④ There are two different plug designs used on the 1.6L engine. All 1981 Escort/Lynx models and 1982 EXP/LN7 models built before 9/4/81 use gasket equipped plugs. All 1982 and later Escort/Lynx and EXP/LN7 models built after 9/4/81 are equipped with tappered seat plugs. Do not interchange types.

⑤ 1 bbl models—10B

HO—High Output
HSC—High Swirl Combustion
MHO—Methanol High Output
EFI—Electronic Fuel Injection
CFI—Central Fuel Injection
B—Before Top Dead Center

DIESEL ENGINE TUNE-UP SPECIFICATIONS

Year	VIN	No. Engine Displacement cu. in. (liter)	Valve Clearance Intake (in.)	Valve Clearance Exhaust (in.)	Intake Valve Opens (deg.)	Injection Pump Setting (deg.)	Injection Nozzle Pressure (psi) New	Injection Nozzle Pressure (psi) Used	Idle Speed (rpm)	Cranking Compression Pressure (psi)
1984	H	4-122 (2.0)	.010	.014 ①	13	TDC Hot	1990–2105	1849–1990	725±50	390-435 @ 2000
1985	H	4-122 (2.0)	.010	.014	13	TDC Hot	1990–2105	1849–1990	725±50	390-435 @ 2000
1986	H	4-122 (2.0)	.010	.014	13	TDC Hot	1990–2105	1849–2105	725±50	390-435 @ 2000
1987	H	4-122 (2.0)	.010	.014	13	TDC Hot	1990–2105	1849–2105	725±50	390-435 @ 2000
1988	SEE UNDERHOOD SPECIFICATION STICKER									

Note: See the Diesel Injection Timing Procedure text in this section.

① The valve clearance specifications are set Cold.

TDC—Top Dead Center

CAPACITIES

Year	VIN	No. Cylinder Displacement cu. in.000024r)	Engine Crankcase (qts.) with Filter	Engine Crankcase (qts.) without Filter	Transmission (pts.) MT	Transmission (pts.) AT	Drive Axle (pts.)	Fuel Tank (gals.)	Cooling System (qts.)
1981	1	4-79 (1.3)	4.0	3.5	5.0	①	②	10.0	6.3
	2	4-98 (1.6)	4.0	3.5	5.0	①	②	10.0	6.4
1982	2	4-98 (1.6)	4.0	3.5	5.0	①	②	10.0	6.4
1983	2	4-98 (1.6)	4.0	3.5	5.0/6.1⑦	①	②	③	6.4
1984	2	4-98 (1.6)	4.0	3.5	5.0/6.1⑦	①	②	③	8.1
	4	4-98 (1.6HO)	4.0	3.5	5.0/6.1⑦	①	②	③	8.1
	5	4-98 (1.6/EFI)	4.0	3.5	5.0/6.1⑦	①	②	③	8.1
	H	4-122 (2.0 Diesel)	7.2	7.0	6.1	①	②	④	8.1
	R	4-140 (2.3 HSC)	4.5	4.0	6.1	①	②	④	8.1
1985	2	4-98 (1.6)	4.0	3.5	5.0/6.1⑦	①	②	③	8.1
	4	4-98 (1.6 HO)	4.0	3.5	5.0/6.1⑦	①	②	③	8.1
	5	4-98 (1.6 EFI)	4.0	3.5	5.0/6.1⑦	①	②	③	8.1
	8	4-98 (1.6 Turbo)	4.0	3.5	5.0/6.1⑦	①	②	③	8.1
	7	4-98 (1.6 MHO)	4.0	3.5	5.0/6.1⑦	①	②	③	8.1
	H	4-122 (2.0 Diesel)	7.2	7.0	6.1	①	②	④	8.1
	R	4-140 (2.3 HSC)	4.5	4.0	6.1	①	②	④	8.1
	X	4-140 (2.3 CFI)	4.5	4.0	5.0/6.1⑦	①	②	④	8.1
	S	4-140 (2.3 HSC/CFI)	4.5	4.0	5.0/6.1⑦	①	②	④	8.1
1986	9	4-116 (1.9)	5.0	4.5	5.0/6.1⑦	⑤	②	⑥	8.3
	J	4-116 (1.9 HO/EFI)	5.0	4.5	5.0/6.1⑦	⑤	②	⑥	8.3
	H	4-122 (2.0 Diesel)	7.2	7.0	6.1	①	②	③	8.1
	R	4-140 (2.3 HSC)	4.5	4.0	6.1	①	②	④	8.1
	X	4-140 (2.3 CFI)	4.5	4.0	5.0/6.1⑦	①	②	④	8.1
	D	4-154 (2.5)	5.0	4.5	④	①	②	③	8.3
	U	6-182 (3.0)	4.5	4.0	–	①	②	③	11.0
1987-88	9	4-116 (1.9)	5.0	4.5	5.0/6.1⑦	⑤	②	⑥	8.3
	J	4-116 (1.9 HO/EFI)	5.0	4.5	5.0/6.1⑦	⑤	②	⑥	8.3
	H	4-122 (2.0 Diesel)	7.2	7.0	6.1	①	②	③	8.1
	R	4-140 (2.3 HSC)	4.5	4.0	6.1	①	②	④	8.1
	X	4-140 (2.3 CFI)	4.5	4.0	5.0/6.1⑦	①	②	④	8.1
	D	4-154 (2.5)	5.0	4.5	6.1	①	②	③	8.3
	U	6-182 (3.0)	4.5	4.0	–	①	②	③	11.0

① Total dry capacity—converter, cooler and sump drained.
1981-82: 19.6 pints
1983-87: 16.6 pints

② Included in transmission capacity.

③ 1983-87: 10 gallons-—FE models
13 gallons—Standard models
13 gallons—EXP/LN7 models

④ 1984-85: 14 gallons
1986-87: 15.2 gallons

⑤ All automatic transaxle models except the all wheel drive models are 8.3 pts. The all wheel drive models are 10.0 pts.

⑥ Standard fuel tank is 15.4 gallons. All wheel drive model fuel tank is 13.2 gallons.

⑦ 4 speed—5.0 pts
5 speed—6.1 pts.

CAMSHAFT SPECIFICATIONS

All measurements given in inches.

Year	VIN	No. Cylinder Displacement cu. in. (liter)	Journal Diameter 1	2	3	4	5	Lobe Lift	Bearing Clearance	Camshaft End Play
1981	1	4-79 (1.3)	1.761–1.762	1.771–1.772	1.781–1.782	1.791–1.792	1.801–1.802	.229	.0008–.0028	.0018–.0060
	2	4-98 (1.6)	1.761–1.762	1.771–1.772	1.781–1.782	1.791–1.792	1.801–1.802	.229	.0008–.0028	.0018–.0060
1982	2	4-98 (1.6)	1.761–1.762	1.771–1.772	1.781–1.782	1.791–1.792	1.801–1.802	.229	.0008–.0028	.0018–.0060
1983	2	4-98 (1.6)	1.761–1.762	1.771–1.772	1.781–1.782	1.791–1.792	1.801–1.802	.229	.0008–.0028–	.0018–.0060–
1984	2	4-98 (1.6)	1.761–1.762	1.771–1.772	1.781–1.782	1.791–1.792	1.801–1.802	.229	.0008–.0028	.0018–.0060
	4	4-98 (1.6 HO)	1.761–1.762	1.771–1.772	1.781–1.782	1.791–1.792	1.801–1.802	.240	.0008–.0028	.0018–.0060
	5	4-98 (1.6 EFI)	1.761–1.762	1.771–1.772	1.781–1.782	1.791–1.792	1.801–1.802	.240	.0008–.0028	.0018–.0060
	H	4-122 (2.0 Diesel)	1.2582–1.2589	1.2582–1.2589	1.2582–1.2589	1.2582–1.2589	1.2582–1.2589	NA	.001–.0026	.008–.0059
	R	4-140 (2.3 HSC)	2.006–2.008	2.006–2.008	2.006–2.008	2.006–2.008	2.006–2.008	①	.001–.003	.009–.003
1985	2	4-98 (1.6)	1.761–1.762	1.771–1.772	1.781–1.782	1.791–1.792	1.801–1.802	.229	.0008–.0028	.0018–.0060
	4	4-98 (1.6 HO)	1.761–1.762	1.771–1.772	1.781–1.782	1.791–1.792	1.801–1.802	.240	.0008–.0028	.0018–.0060
	5	4-98 (1.6 EFI)	1.761–1.762	1.771–1.772	1.781–1.782	1.791–1.792	1.801–1.802	.240	.0008–.0028	.0018–.0060
	8	4-98 (1.6 Turbo)	1.761–1.762	1.771–1.772	1.781–1.782	1.791–1.792	1.801–1.801	.240	.0008–.0028	.0018–.0060
	7	4-98 (1.6 MHO)	1.761–1.762	1.771–1.772	1.781–1.782	1.791–1.792	1.801–1.802	.240	.0008–.0028	.0018–.0060
	H	4-122 (2.0 Diesel)	1.2582–1.2589	1.2582–1.2589	1.2582–1.2589	1.2582–1.2589	1.2582–1.2589	NA	.001–.0026	.008–.0059
	R	4-140 (2.3 HSC)	2.006–2.008	2.006–2.008	2.006–2.008	2.006–2.008	2.006–2.008	①	.001–.003	.009–.003
	X	4-140 (2.3 CFI)	2.006–2.008	2.006–2.008	2.006–2.008	2.006–2.008	2.006–2.008	①	.001–.003	.009–.003
	S	4-140 (2.3 HSC/CFI)	2.006–2.008	2.006–2.008	2.006–2.008	2.006–2.008	2.006–2.008	①	.001–.003	.009
1986	9	4-116 (1.9)	1.8017–1.8007	1.8017–1.8007	1.8017–1.8007	1.8017–1.8007	1.8017–1.8007	.240	.0013–.0033	.006–.0018
	J	4-116 (1.9 HO/EFI)	1.8017–1.8007	1.8017–1.8007	1.8017–1.8007	1.8017–1.8007	1.8017–1.8007	.240	.0013–.0033	.006–.0018
	H	4-122 (2.0 Diesel)	1.2582–1.2589	1.2852–1.2589	1.2582–1.2589	1.2582–1.2589	1.2582–1.2589	NA	.001–.0026	.008–.0059
	R	4-140 (2.3 HSC)	2.006–2.008	2.006–2.008	2.006–2.008	2.006–2.008	2.006–2.008	①	.001–003	.009

CAMSHAFT SPECIFICATIONS

All measurements given in inches.

Year	VIN	No. Cylinder Displacement cu. in. (liter)	Journal Diameter 1	2	3	4	5	Lobe Lift	Bearing Clearance	Camshaft End Play
1986	X	4-140 (2.3 CFI)	2.006–2.008	2.006–2.008	2.006–2.008	2.006–2.008	2.006–2.008	①②	.001–.003	.009
	D	4-154 (2.5)	2.006–2.008	2.006–2.008	2.006–2.008	2.006–2.008	2.006–2.008	①	.001–.003	.009–
	U	6-182 (3.0)	2.0074–2.0084	2.0074–2.0084	2.0074–2.0084	2.0074–2.0084	2.0074–2.0084	.260	.001–.003	①
1987-88	9	4-116 (1.9)	1.8017–1.8007	1.8017–1.8007	1.8017–1.8007	1.8017–1.8007	1.8017–1.8007	.240	.0013–.0033	.006–.0018
	J	4-116 (1.9 HO/EFI)	1.8017–1.8007	1.8017–1.8007	1.8017–1.8007	1.8017–1.8007	1.8017–1.8007	.240 .240	.0013–.0013	.006–.0018
	H	4-122 (2.0 Diesel)	1.2582–1.2589	1.2582–1.2589	1.2582–1.2589	1.2582–1.2589	1.2582–1.2589	NA	.001–.0026	.008–.0059
	R	4-140 (2.3 HSC)	2.006–2.008	2.006–2.008	2.006–2.008	2.006–2.008	2.006–2.008	① ①	.001–.003	.009
	X	4-140 (2.3 CFI)	2.006–2.008	2.006–2.008	2.006–2.008	2.006–2.008	2.006–2.008	①② ①②	.001–.003	.009
	D	4-154 (2.5)	2.203–2.204	2.186–2.187	2.186–2.187	2.203–2.204	—	③	.001–.003	.009
	U	6-182 (3.0)	2.0074–2.0084	2.0074–2.0084	2.0074–2.0084	2.0074–2.0084	—	.260	.001–.003	0.005

NA—Not available at time of publication
① Intake—.249 in.
Exhaust—.239 in.
② 2.3L HO engine .2625 in.
③ Intake: 0.392
Exhaust: 0.377

CRANKSHAFT AND CONNECTING ROD SPECIFICATIONS

All measurements are given in inches.

Year	VIN	No. Cylinder Displacement cu. in. (liter)	Crankshaft Main Brg. Journal Dia.	Main Brg. Oil Clearance	Shaft End-play	Thrust on No.	Connecting Rod Journal Diameter	Oil Clearance	Side Clearance
1981	1	4-79 (1.3)	2.2826–2.2834	0.0008–0.0015	0.004–0.008	3	1.885–1.886	0.0002–0.0003	0.004–0.011
	2	4-98 (1.6)	2.2826–2.2834	0.0008–0.0015	0.004–0.008	3	1.885–1.886	0.0002–0.0003	0.004–0.011
1982	2	4-98 (1.6)	2.2826–2.2834	0.0008–0.0015	0.004–0.008	3	1.885–1.886	0.0002–0.0003	0.004–0.011
1983	2	4-98 (1.6)	2.2826–2.2834	0.0008–0.0015	0.004–0.008	3	1.885–1.886	0.0002–0.0003	0.004–0.011
1984	2	4-98 (1.6)	2.2826–2.2834	0.0008–0.0015	0.004–0.008	3	1.885–1.886	0.0002–0.0003	0.004–0.011
	4	4-98 (1.6 HO)	2.2826–2.2834	0.0008–0.0015	0.004–0.008	3	1.885–1.886	0.0002–0.0003	0.004–0.011
	5	4-98 (1.6 EFI)	2.2826–2.2834	0.0008–0.0015	0.004–0.008	3	1.885–1.886	0.0002–0.0003	0.004–0.011

CRANKSHAFT AND CONNECTING ROD SPECIFICATIONS

All measurements are given in inches.

Year	VIN	No. Cylinder Displacement cu. in. (liter)	Crankshaft Main Brg. Journal Dia.	Crankshaft Main Brg. Oil Clearance	Crankshaft Shaft End-play	Crankshaft Thrust on No.	Connecting Rod Journal Diameter	Connecting Rod Oil Clearance	Connecting Rod Side Clearance
	H	4-122 (2.0 Diesel)	2.3598–2.3605	0.0012–0.0020	0.0016–0.0011	3	2.0055–2.0061	0.0010–0.0022	0.0043–0.0103
	R	4-140 (2.3 HSC)	2.2489–2.2490	0.0008–0.0015	0.004–0.008	3	2.1232–2.1240	0.0008–0.0015	0.0035–0.0105
1985	2	4-98 (1.6)	2.2826–2.2834	0.0008–0.0015	0.004–0.008	3	1.885–1.886	0.0002–0.0003	0.004–0.011
	4	4-98 (1.6 HO)	2.2826–2.2834	0.0008–0.0015	0.004–0.008	3	1.885–1.886	0.0002–0.0003	0.004–0.011
	5	4-98 (1.6 EFI)	2.2826–2.2834	0.0008–0.0015	0.004–0.008	3	1.885–1.886	0.0002–0.0003	0.004–0.011
	7	4-98 (1.6 MHO)	2.2826–2.2834	0.0008–0.0015	0.004–0.008	3	1.885–1.886	0.0002–0.0003	0.004–0.011
	8	4-98 (1.6 Turbo)	2.2826–2.2834	0.0008–0.0015	0.004–0.008	3	1.885–1.886	0.0002–0.0003	0.004–0.011
	H	4-122 (2.0 Diesel)	2.3598–2.3605	0.0012–0.0020	0.0016–0.0011	3	2.0055–2.0061	0.0010–0.0020	0.0043–0.0103
	R	4-140 (2.3 HSC)	2.2489–2.2490	0.0008–0.0015	0.004–0.008	3	2.1232–2.1240	0.0008–0.0015	0.0035–0.0105
	S	4-140 (2.3 HSC/CFI)	2.2489–2.2490	0.0008–0.0015	0.004–0.008	3	2.1232–2.1240	0.0008–0.0015	0.0055–0.0105
1986	9	4-116 (1.9)	2.2827–2.2835	0.0008–0.0015	0.004–0.008	3	1.8854–1.8862	0.0008–0.0015	0.004–0.011
	J	4-116 (1.9 HO/EFI)	2.2827–2.2835	0.0008–0.0015	0.004–0.008	3	1.8854–1.8862	0.0008–0.0015	0.004–0.011
	H	4-122 (2.0 Diesel)	2.3598–2.3605	0.0012–0.0020	0.0016–0.0011	3	2.0055–2.0061	0.0010–0.0020	0.0043–0.0103
	R	4-140 (2.3 HSC)	2.2489–2.2490	0.0008–0.0015	0.004–0.008	3	2.1232–2.1240	0.0008–0.0015	0.0035–0.0105
	X	4-140 (2.3 CFI)	2.2489–2.2490	0.0008–0.0015	0.004–0.008	3	2.1232–2.1240	0.0008–0.0015	0.0035–0.0105
	D	4-154 (2.5)	2.2489–2.2490	0.0008–0.0015–	0.004–0.008–	3	2.1232–2.1240	0.0008–0.0015–	0.0035–0.0105
	U	6-182 (3.0)	2.5190–2.5198	0.001–0.0014	0.004–0.008	3	2.1253–2.1261	0.001–0.0014	0.006–0.014
1987-88	9	4-116 (1.9)	2.2821–2.2835	0.0008–0.0015	0.004–0.008	3	1.8854–1.8862	0.0008–0.0015	0.004–0.011
	J	4-116 (1.9 HO/EFI)	2.2827–2.2835	0.0008–0.0015	0.004–0.008	3	1.8854–1.8862	0.0008–0.0015	0.004–0.011
	H	4-122 (2.0 Diesel)	2.3598–2.3605	0.0012–0.0020	0.0016–0.0011	3	2.0055–2.0061	0.0010–0.0020	0.0043–0.0103
	R	4-140 (2.3 HSC)	2.2489–2.2490	0.0008–0.0015	0.004–0.008	3	2.1232–2.1240	0.0008–0.0015	0.0035–0.0105
	X	4-140 (2.3 CFI)	2.2489–2.2490	0.0008–0.0015	0.004–0.008	3	2.1232–2.1240	0.0008–0.0015	0.0035–0.0105

CRANKSHAFT AND CONNECTING ROD SPECIFICATIONS

All measurements are given in inches.

Year	VIN	No. Cylinder Displacement cu. in. (liter)	Crankshaft Main Brg. Journal Dia.	Crankshaft Main Brg. Oil Clearance	Crankshaft Shaft End-play	Crankshaft Thrust on No.	Connecting Rod Journal Diameter	Connecting Rod Oil Clearance	Connecting Rod Side Clearance
1987-88	D	4-154 (2.5)	2.2489–2.2490	0.0008–0.0015–	0.004–0.008–	3	2.1232–2.1240	0.0008–0.0015–	0.0035–0.0105
	U	6-182 (3.0)	2.5190–2.5198	0.001–0.0014	0.004–0.008	3	2.1253–2.1261	0.001–0.0014	0.006–0.014

VALVE SPECIFICATIONS

Year	VIN	No. Cylinder Displacement cu. in. (liter)	Seat Angle (deg.)	Face Angle (deg.)	Spring Test Pressure (lbs. @ in.)	Spring Installed Height (in.)	Stem-to-Guide Clearance (in.) Intake	Stem-to-Guide Clearance (in.) Exhaust	Stem Diameter (in.) Intake	Stem Diameter (in.) Exhaust
1981	1	4-79 (1.3)	45	45.5	200 @ 1.09	1.480	0.0008–0.0027	0.0018–0.0037	0.316	0.315
	2	4-98 (1.6)	45	45.5	200 @ 1.09	1.480	0.0008–0.0027	0.0018–0.0037	0.316	0.315
1982	2	4-98 (1.6)	45	45.5	200 @ 1.09	1.480	0.0008–0.0027	0.0018–0.0037	0.316	0.315
1983	2	4-98 (1.6)	45	45.5	200 @ 1.09	1.480	0.0008–0.0027	0.0008–0.0037	0.316	0.315
1984	2	4-98 (1.6)	45	45.5	200 @ 1.09	1.480	0.0008–0.0027	0.0008–0.0037	0.316	0.315
	4	4-98 (1.6 HO)	45	45.5	216 @ 1.016	1.450–1.480	0.0008–0.0027	0.0008–0.0037	0.316	0.315
	5	4-98 (1.6 EFI)	45	45.5	216 @ 1.016	1.450–1.480	0.0008–0.0027	0.0008–0.0037	0.316	0.315
	H	4-122 (2.0 Diesel)	45	45.5	NA	1.7760	0.0016–0.0029	0.0018–0.0031	0.3138	0.3138
	R	4-140 (2.3 HSC)	45	45.5	182 @ 1.10	1.490	0.0018	0.0023	0.3415	0.3411
1985	2	4-98 (1.6)	45	45.5	200 @ 1.09	1.480	0.0008–0.0027	0.0018–0.0037	0.316	0.315
	4	4-98 (1.6 HO)	45	45.5	216 @ 1.016	1.450–1.480	0.0008–0.0027	0.0008–0.0037	0.316	0.315
	5	4-98 (1.6 EFI)	45	45.5	216 @ 1.016	1.450–1.480	0.0008–0.0027	0.0008–0.0037	0.316	0.315
	7	4-98 (1.6 MHO)	45	45.5	200 @ 1.09	1.480	0.0008–0.0027	0.0008–0.0037	0.316	0.315
	8	4-98 (1.6 Turbo)	45	45.5	216 @ 1.016	1.450–1.480	0.0008–0.0027	0.0008–0.0037	0.316	0.315
	H	4-122 (2.0 Diesel)	45	45	NA	1.7760	0.0016–0.0029	0.0018–0.0031	0.3138	0.3138
	R	4-140 (2.3 HSC)	45	45.5	182 @ 1.10	1.490	0.0018	0.0023	0.3415	0.3411

VALVE SPECIFICATIONS

Year	VIN	No. Cylinder Displacement cu. in. (liter)	Seat Angle (deg.)	Face Angle (deg.)	Spring Test Pressure (lbs. @ in.)	Spring Installed Height (in.)	Stem-to-Guide Clearance (in.) Intake	Exhaust	Stem Diameter (in.) Intake	Exhaust
1985	X	4-140 (2.3 CFI)	45	45.5	182 @ 1.10	1.490	0.0018	0.0023	0.3415	0.3411
	S	4-140 (2.3 HSC/CFI)	45	45.5	182 @ 1.10	1.490	0.0018	0.0023	0.3415	0.3411
1986	9	4-116 (1.9)	45	45	200 @ 1.09	1.440–1.480	0.0008–0.0027	0.0018–0.0037	0.316	0.315
	J	4-116 (1.9 HO/EFI)	45	45	216 @ 1.016	1.440–1.480	0.0008–0.0027	0.0018–0.0037	0.316	0.315
	H	4-122 (2.0 Diesel)	45	45	NA	1.7760	0.0016–0.0029	0.0018–0.0031	0.3138	0.3138
	R	4-140 (2.3 HSC)	45	45.5	182 @ 1.10	1.40	0.0018	0.0023	0.316	0.315
	X	4-140 (2.3 CFI)	45	45.5	182 @ 1.10	1.40	0.018	0.0023	0.316	0.315
	D	4-154 (2.5)	45	45	182 @ 1.03	1.49	0.0018	0.0023	0.3415–0.3422–	0.3411–0.3418–
	U	6-182 (3.0)	45	44	185 @ 1.11	1.58	0.0010–0.0028	0.0015–0.0033	0.3126–0.3134	0.3121–0.3129
1987–88	9	4-116 (1.9)	45	45	200 @ 1.09	1.48–1.44	0.0008–0.0027	0.0018–0.0037	0.316	0.315
	J	4-116 (1.9 HO/EFI)	45	45	216 @ 1.016	1.48–1.44	0.0008–0.0027	0.0018–0.0037	0.316	0.315
	H	4-122 (2.0 Diesel)	45	45	NA	1.7760	0.0016–0.0029	0.0018–0.0031	0.3138	0.3138
	R	4-140 (2.3 HSC)	45	45.5	182 @ 1.10	1.49	0.0018	0.0023	0.316	0.315
	X	4-140 (2.3 CFI)	45	45.5	182 @ 1.10	1.49	0.0018	0.0023	0.316	0.315
	D	4-154 (2.5)	45	45	182 @ 1.03	1.49	0.0018	0.0023	0.3415–0.3422–	0.3411–0.3418–
	U	6-182 (3.0)	45	44	185 @ 1.11	1.58	0.0010–0.0028	0.0015–0.0033	0.3126–0.3134	0.3121–0.3129

PISTON AND RING SPECIFICATIONS

All measurments are given in inches.

Year	VIN	No. Cylinder Displacement cu. in. (liter)	Piston Clearance	Ring Gap Top Compression	Ring Gap Bottom Compression	Ring Gap Oil Control	Ring Side Clearance Top Compression	Ring Side Clearance Bottom Compression	Ring Side Clearance Oil Control
1981	1	4-79 (1.3)	0.0008–0.0016	0.012–0.020	0.012–0.020	0.016–0.055	0.001–0.003	0.002–0.003	Snug
	2	4-98 (1.6)	0.0008–.0016	0.012–0.020	0.012–0.020	0.016–0.055	0.001–0.003	0.002–0.003	Snug
1982	2	4-98 (1.6)	0.0012–.0020	0.012–0.020	0.021–0.020	0.016–0.055	0.001–0.003	0.002–0.003	Snug

PISTON AND RING SPECIFICATIONS

All measurments are given in inches.

Year	VIN	No. Cylinder Displacement cu. in. (liter)	Piston Clearance	Ring Gap Top Compression	Ring Gap Bottom Compression	Ring Gap Oil Control	Ring Side Clearance Top Compression	Ring Side Clearance Bottom Compression	Ring Side Clearance Oil Control
1983	2	4-98 (1.6)	0.0018–0.0026	0.012–0.020	0.021–0.020	0.016–0.055	0.001–0.003	0.002–0.003	Snug
1984	2	4-98 (1.6)	0.0018–0.0026	0.012–0.020	0.012–0.020	0.016–0.055	0.001–0.003	0.002–0.003	Snug
	4	4-98 (1.6 HO)	0.0018–0.0026	0.012–0.020	0.012–0.020	0.016–0.055	0.001–0.003	0.002–0.003	Snug
	5	4-98 (1.6 EFI)	0.0018–0.0026	0.012–0.020	0.012–0.020	0.016–0.055	0.001–0.003	0.002–0.003	Snug
	H	4-122 (2.0 Diesel)	0.0013–0.0020	0.0079–0.0157	0.0079–0.0157	0.0079–0.0157	0.0020–0.0035	0.0016–0.0031	Snug
	R	4-140 (2.3 HSC)	0.0013–0.0021	0.008–0.016	0.008–0.016	0.015–0.055	0.002–0.004	0.002–0.004	Snug
1985	2	4-98 (1.6)	0.0018–0.0026	0.012–0.020	0.012–0.020	0.016–0.055	0.001–0.003	0.002–0.003	Snug
	4	4-98 (1.6 HO)	0.0018–0.0026	0.012–0.020	0.012–0.020	0.016–0.055	0.001–0.003	0.002–0.003	Snug
	5	4-98 (1.6 EFI)	0.0018–0.0026	0.012–0.020	0.012–0.020	0.016–0.055	0.001–0.003	0.002–0.003	Snug
	7	4-98 (1.6 MHO)	0.0018–0.0026	0.012–0.020	0.012–0.020	0.016–0.055	0.001–0.003	0.002–0.003	Snug
	8	4-98 (1.6 Turbo)	0.0018–0.0026	0.012–0.020	0.012–0.020	0.016–0.055	0.001–0.003	0.002–0.003	Snug
	H	4-122 (2.0 Diesel)	0.0013–0.0020	0.0079–0.0157	0.0079–0.0157	0.0079–0.0157	0.0020–0.0035	0.0016–0.0031	Snug
	R	4-140 (2.3 HSC)	0.0013–0.0021	0.008–0.016	0.008–0.016	0.015–0.055	0.002–0.004	0.002–0.004	Snug
	X	4-140 (2.3 CFI)	0.0013–0.0021	0.008–0.016	0.008–0.016	0.015–0.055	0.002–0.004	0.002–0.004	Snug
	S	4-140 (2.3 HSC/CFI)	0.0013–0.0021	0.008–0.016	0.008–0.016	0.015–0.055	0.002–0.004	0.002–0.004	Snug
1986	9	4-116 (1.9)	0.0016–.0024	0.010–0.020	0.010–0.020	0.016–0.055	0.0015–0.0032	0.0015–0.0035	Snug
	J	4-116 (1.9 HO/EFI)	0.0016–0.0024	0.010–0.020	0.010–0.020	0.016–0.055	0.0015–0.0032	0.0015–0.0035	Snug
	H	4-122 (2.0 Diesel)	0.0012–0.0020	0.0079–0.0157	0.0079–0.0157	0.0079–0.0157	0.0020–0.0035	0.0016–0.0031	Snug
	R	4-140 (2.3 HSC)	0.0013–0.0021	0.008–0.016	0.008–0.016	0.0015–0.055	0.002–0.004	0.002–0.004	Snug
	X	4-140 (2.3 CFI)	0.0013–0.0021	0.008–0.016	0.008–0.016	0.015–0.055	0.002–0.004	0.002–0.004	Snug
	D	4-154 (2.5)	0.0012–0.0022	0.008–0.016	0.008–0.016	0.015–0.055	0.002–0.004	0.002–0.004	Snug
	U	6-182 (3.0)	0.0014–0.0022	0.010–0.020	0.010–0.020	0.010–0.049	0.0012–0.0031	0.0012–0.0031	Snug

PISTON AND RING SPECIFICATIONS

All measurments are given in inches.

Year	VIN	No. Cylinder Displacement cu. in. (liter)	Piston Clearance	Ring Gap Top Compression	Ring Gap Bottom Compression	Ring Gap Oil Control	Ring Side Clearance Top Compression	Ring Side Clearance Bottom Compression	Ring Side Clearance Oil Control
1987-88	9	4-116 (1.9)	0.0016–.0024	0.010–0.020	0.010–0.020	0.016–0.055	0.0015–0.0032	0.0015–0.0035	Snug
	J	4-116 (1.9 HO/EFI)	0.0016–0.0024	0.010–0.020	0.010–0.020	0.016–0.055	0.0015–0.0032	0.0015–0.0035	Snug
	H	4-122 (2.0 Diesel)	0.0013–0.0020	0.0079–0.0157	0.0079–0.0157	0.0079–0.0157	0.0020–0.0035	0.0016–0.0031	Snug
	R	4-140 (2.3 HSC)	0.0013–0.0021	0.008–0.016	0.008–0.016	0.015–0.055	0.002–0.004	0.002–0.004	Snug
	X	4-140 (2.3 CFI)	0.0013–0.0021	0.008–0.016	0.008–0.016	0.015–0.055	0.002–0.004	0.002–0.004	Snug
	D	4-154 (2.5)	0.0012–0.0022	0.008–0.016	0.008–0.016	0.015–0.055	0.002–0.004	0.002–0.004	Snug
	U	6-182 (3.0)	0.0014–0.0022	0.010–0.020	0.010–0.020	0.010–0.049	0.0012–0.0031	0.0012–0.0031	Snug

TORQUE SPECIFICATIONS

All readings in ft. lbs.

Year	VIN	No. Cylinder Displacement cu. in. (liter)	Cylinder Head Bolts	Main Bearing Bolts	Rod Bearing Bolts	Crankshaft Pulley Bolts	Flywheel Bolts	Manifold Intake	Manifold Exhaust	Spark Plugs
1981	1	4-79 (1.3)	①	67-80	19-25	74-90	59-69	12-15 ②	15-20	17-22
	2	4-98 (1.6)	①	67-80	19-25	74-90	59-69	12-15 ②	15-20	17-22
1982	2	4-98 (1.6)	①	67-80	19-25	74-90	59-69	12-15 ②	15-20	17-22
1983	2	4-98 (1.6)	①	67-80	19-25	74-90	59-69	12-15 ②	15-20	8-15
1984	2	4-98 (1.6)	①	67-80	19-25	74-90	59-69	12-15 ②	15-20	8-15
	4	4-98 (1.6 HO)	①	67-80	19-25	74-90	59-69	12-15 ②	15-20	8-15
	5	4-98 (1.6 EFI)	①	67-80	19-25	74-90	59-69	12-15 ②	15-20	8-15
	H	4-122 (2.0 Diesel)	①	61-65	51-54	115-123	130-137	12-16	16-19 ③	–
	R	4-140 (2.3 HSC)	④	51-66	21-26	140-170	54-64	15-23	20-30 ③	5-10
1985	2	4-98 (1.6)	①	67-80	19-25	74-90	59-69	12-15 ②	15-20	8-15
	4	4-98 (1.6 HO)	①	67-80	19-25	74-90	59-69	12-15 ②	15-20	8-15
	5	4-98 (1.6 EFI)	①	67-80	19-25	74-90	59-69	12-15 ②	15-20	8-15
	8	4-98 (1.6 Turbo)	①	67-80	19-25	74-90	59-69	12-15 ②	15-20	8-15
	7	4-98 (1.6 MHO)	①	67-80	19-25	74-90	59-69	12-15 ②	15-20	8-15
	H	4-122 (2.0 Diesel)	①	61-65	51-54	115-123	130-137	12-16	16-19 ③	
	R	4-140 (2.3 HSC)	④	51-66	21-26	140-170	54-64	15-23	20-30 ③	5-10

TORQUE SPECIFICATIONS

All readings in ft. lbs.

Year	VIN	No. Cylinder Displacement cu. in. (liter)	Cylinder Head Bolts	Main Bearing Bolts	Rod Bearing Bolts	Crankshaft Pulley Bolts	Flywheel Bolts	Manifold Intake	Manifold Exhaust	Spark Plugs
1985	X	4-140 (2.3 CFI)	④	51-66	21-26	140-170	54-64	15-23	20-30 ③	5-10
	S	4-140 (2.3 HSC/CFI)	④ ④	51-66	21-26	140-170	54-64	15-23	20-30 ③	5-10
1986	9	4-116 (1.9)	①	67-80	19-25	74-90	59-69	12-15	15-20	8-15
	J	4-116 (1.9 HO/EFI)	①	67-80	19-25	74-90	59-69	12-15	15-20	8-15
	H	4-122 (2.0 Diesel)	①	61-65	51-54	115-123	130-137	12-16	16-19 ③	5-10
	R	4-140 (2.3 HSC)	④	51-56	21-26	140-170	54-64	15-23	20-30 ③	5-10
	X	4-140 (2.3 CFI)	④	51-66	21-26	140-170	54-64	15-23	20-30 ③	5-10
	D	4-154 (2.5)	70-76	51-66	21-26	140-170	54-64	15-23	20-30	5-10
	U	6-182 (3.0)	63-80	65-81	⑤	141-169	54-64	⑤	20-30	5-10
1987-88	9	4-116 (1.9)	①	67-80	19-25	74-90	59-69	12-15	15-20	8-15
	J	4-116 (1.9 HO/EFI)	①	67-80	19-25	74-90	59-69	12-15	15-20	8-15
	H	4-122 (2.0 Diesel)	①	61-65	51-54	115-123	130-137	12-16	16-19 ③	5-10
	R	4-140 (2.3 HSC)	④	51-66	21-26	140-170	54-64	15-23	20-30 ③	5-10
	X	4-140 (2.3 CFI)	④	51-66	21-26	140-170	54-64	15-23	20-30 ③	5-10
	D	4-154 (2.5)	70-76	51-66	21-26	140-170	54-64	15-23	20-30	5-10
	U	6-182 (3.0)	63-80	65-81	⑤	141-169	54-64	⑥	20-30	5-10

CAUTION: Verify the correct original equipment engine is in the vehicle by referring to the VIN engine code before torquing any bolts.

① Please refer to "Cylinder Head" procedure in text for instructions

② Manifold stud nuts: 12-13 ft. lbs.

③ Tighten in two stages.

④ Tighten in two steps: 52-59 ft. lbs. and then the final torque of 70-76 ft. lbs.

⑤ Step 1: Torque to 20-28 ft. lb.
Step 2: Back off at least 2 full turns
Step 3: Torque to 20-26 ft. lb.

⑥ Step 1: 11 ft. lb.
Step 2: 18 ft. lb.
Step 3: 24 ft. lb.

WHEEL ALIGNMENT

Year	Model	Caster Range (deg.)	Caster Preferred Setting (deg.)	Camber Range (deg.)	Camber Preferred Setting (deg.)	Toe-in (in.)	Wheel Turning Angle (deg.)
1981	Escort, Lynx	9/10P-2 2/5P	1 21/32P①	②	③	1/50N-11/50P	Left 19.97 Right 17.04
1982-83	Escort, Lynx, EXP, LN7	35/64P-2 1/20P	1 1/3①	④	⑤	1/50N-11/50P	Left 20.0 Right 17.0
1984	Escort, Lynx, EXP	21/32P-2 5/32P	1 2/5①	④	⑤	1/64N-7/32P	Left 20.0 Right 18.2
	Tempo, Topaz EXP	35/64P-2 1/20P	1 1/3①	⑥	⑦	1/32N-7/32P	Left 20.0 Right 18.2
1985-86	Escort, Lynx, EXP	1 11/16P-3 3/16P	2 7/16①	⑧	⑨	7/32N-1/64P	Left 20.0 Right 18.2
	Tempo/Topaz Sport Coupe	1 5/8P-3 1/8P	2 3/8①	⑩	⑪	7/32N-1/64P	Left 20.0 Right 18.2
	Tempo/Topaz exc. Sport Coupe	1 11/16P-3 3/16P	2 7/16①	⑫	⑬	7/32N-1/64P	Left 20.0 Right 18.4
	Taurus Sedan	3P-6P	4P	1 1/10N-1/10P	1/2N	7/32N-1/32P	18.25
	Sable Sedan	2 7/8P-5 7/8P	3 7/8P	1 1/10N-1/10P	1/2N	7/32N-1/32P	18.25
	Taurus/Sable Station Wagon	2 13/16P-5 13/16P	3 13/16P	1 1/32N-5/32P	7/16N	7/32N-1/32P	Left 18.25
1987-88	Escort, Lynx, EXP	1 5/8P-3 1/8P	2 3/8①	⑭	⑮	0-1/4P	Left 20.0 Right 18.2
	Tempo, Topaz Sport Coupe	1 11/16P-3 3/16P	2 7/16①	⑯	⑰	0-1/4P	Left 20.0 Right 18.2
	Taurus Sedan	3P-6P	4P	1 1/10N-1/10P	1/2N	7/32N-1/32P	18.25
	Sable Sedan	2 7/8P-5 7/8P	3 7/8P	1 1/10N-1/10P	1/2N	7/32N-1/32P	18.25
	Taurus/Sable Station Wagon	2 13/16P-5 13/16P	3 13/16P	1 1/32N-5/32P	7/16N	7/32N-1/32P	18.25

① Caster and camber are not adjustable. Measurements must be made by turning the wheel left and right through their respective sweep angles.
② Left: 1P-2 1/2P
Right: 35/64P-2P
③ Left: 1 3/4P
Right: 1 1/3P
④ Left: 1 2/5P-2 9/10P
Right: 61/64P-2 29/64P
⑤ Left: 2 5/32P
Right: 1 11/16P
⑥ Left: 1 1/8P-2 5/8P
Right: 11/16P-2 1/5
⑦ Left: 1 29/32P
Right: 1 1/2P
⑧ Left: 5/8P-2 1/8P
Right: 3/16P-1 11/16P
⑨ Left: 1 3/8P
Right: 15/16P
⑩ Left: 7/16P-1 15/16P
Right: 0-1 1/2P
⑪ Left: 1 3/16P
Right: 3/4P
⑫ Left: 13/32P-1 29/32P
Right: 1/32N-1 15/32P
⑬ Left: 1 5/32P
Right: 23/32P
⑭ Left: 5/16P-1 13/16P
Right: 0-1 1/2P
⑮ Left: 1 1/16P
Right: 3/4P
⑯ Left: 21/32P-2 5/32P
Right: 7/32P-1 23/32P
⑰ Left: 1 13/32P
Right: 31/32P

ROUTINE MAINTENANCE

Air Cleaner

The air cleaner element should be replaced every 30 months or 30,000 miles. More frequent changes are necessary if the car is operated in dust and sand.

REMOVAL & INSTALLATION

1.6L Base and HO Engines

NOTE: The crankcase emission filter should be changed each time you replace the air cleaner element.

1. Remove the wing nut that retains the air cleaner assembly to the carburetor. Remove any support bracket bolts (engine to air cleaner). Disconnect the air duct tubing, vacuum lines and heat tubes connected to the air

cleaner.

2. Remove the air cleaner assembly from the car.

NOTE: Removing the air cleaner as an assembly helps prevent dirt from falling into the carburetor.

3. Remove the spring clips that hold the top of the air cleaner to the body. Remove the cover.

4. Remove the air cleaner element. Disconnect the spring clip that retains the emission filter to the air cleaner body, and remove the filter.

5. Clean the inside of the air cleaner body by wiping with a rag. Check the mounting gasket (gaskets, if the car is equipped with a spacer), replace any gasket(s) that show wear.

6. Install a new emission filter and a new air cleaner element.

7. Install the air cleaner element. Reconnect the spring clip that retains the emission filter to the air cleaner body, and install the filter.

8. Install the spring clips that hold the top of the air cleaner to the body. install the cover.

9. Install the air cleaner assembly from the car.

10. Install the wing nut that retains the air cleaner assembly to the carburetor. install any support bracket bolts (engine to air cleaner). reconnect the air duct tubing, vacuum lines and heat tubes connected to the air cleaner.

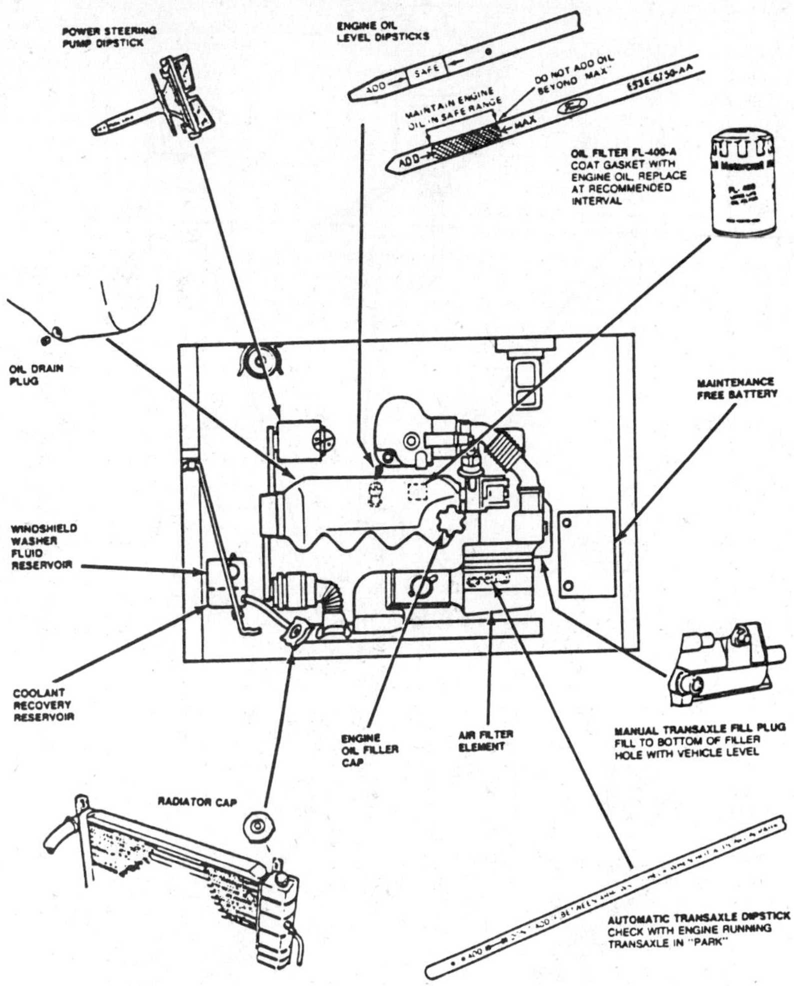

Lubrication and service points—1.6L and 1.9L EFI engines

1.6L and 1.9L EFI Engines

1. Unclip the air intake tube and remove the tube from the air cleaner tray.

2. Unclip the air cleaner tray from the air cleaner assembly.

3. Pull the cleaner tray out to expose the air cleaner element.

4. Pull the air cleaner element from the tray. Visually inspect the air cleaner tray and cover for signs of dust or leaking holes in the filter or past the seals.

5. Assemble the air cleaner element to the tray making sure the element is installed in its original position. Check to see that the seal is fully seated into the groove in the tray.

6. Clip the air intake tube to the air cleaner tray.

2.3 HSC Engine

1. Loosen the air cleaner outlet tube clamp and disconnect the tube.

2. Disconnect the hot air tube, PCV inlet tube and the zip tube.

3. Disconnect the cold weather modulator vacuum hose at the temperature sensor.

4. Disconnect the vent hoses from the air cleaner cover.

5. Remove the air cleaner and cover retaining screws and the air cleaner assembly.

6. Inspect the inside surfaces of the cover for traces of dirt leakage past the cleaner element as a result of damaged seals, incorrect element or inadequate tightness of the cover retaining screws.

7. Remove the air cleaner element and clean the inside surfaces of the cleaner tray and cover.

8. Install a new air cleaner element, install the cover and assembly. Tighten the retaining screws to 22-32 in.lb.

9. Reconnect all vacuum and air duct hoses and lines.

PCV Valve

No PCV (positive crankcase ventilation) valve is used. Instead, an internal baffle and an orifice control the flow of crankcase gases.

Fuel Filter

The fuel filter should be replaced, immediately, upon evidence of dirt in the fuel system. Regular replacement of the fuel filter should be every 30,000 miles. If the engine seems to be suffering from fuel starvation, remove the filter and blow through it to see if it is clogged. If air won't pass through the filter easily, or if dirt is visible in the inlet passage, replace the filter.

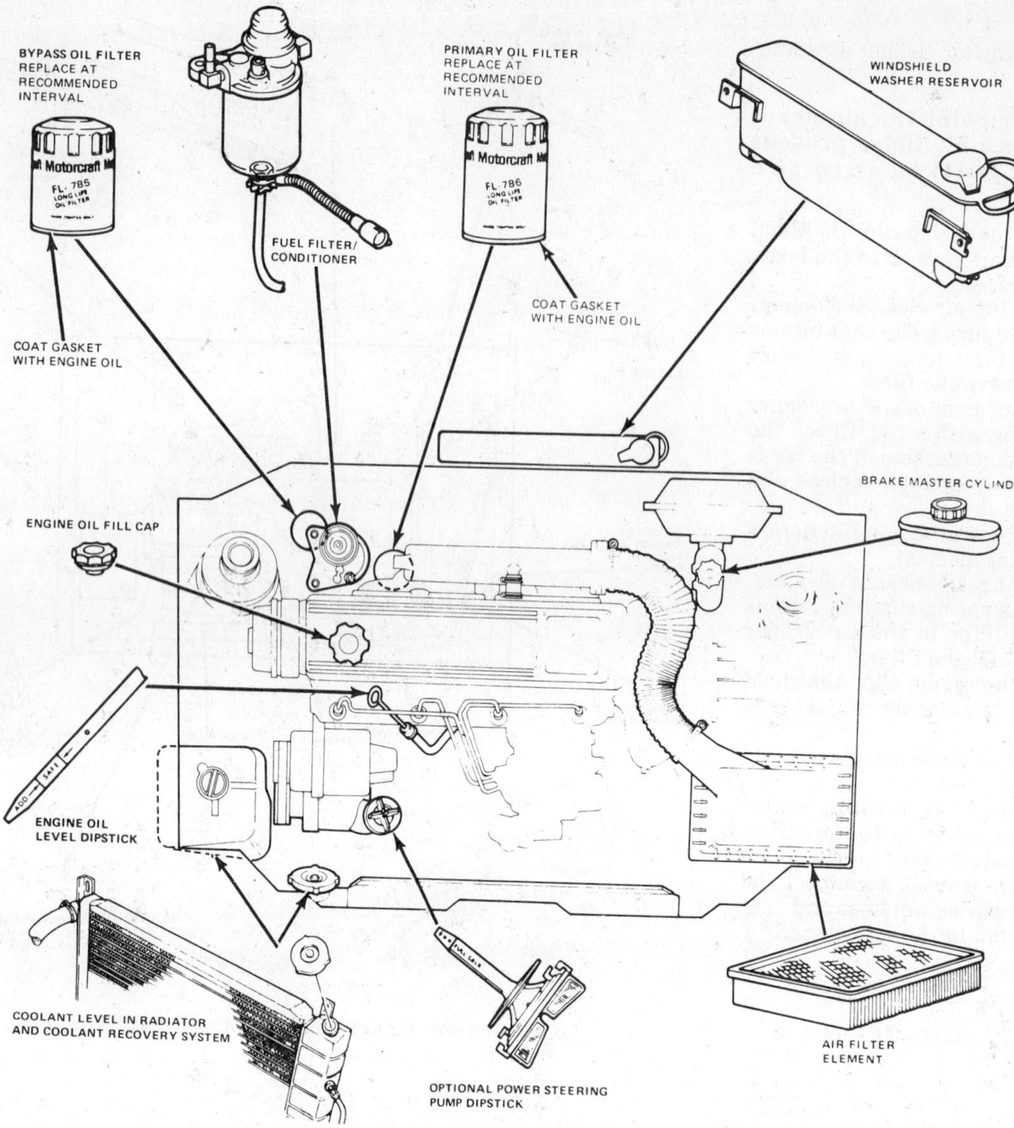

Lubrication and service points – 2.0L diesel engine

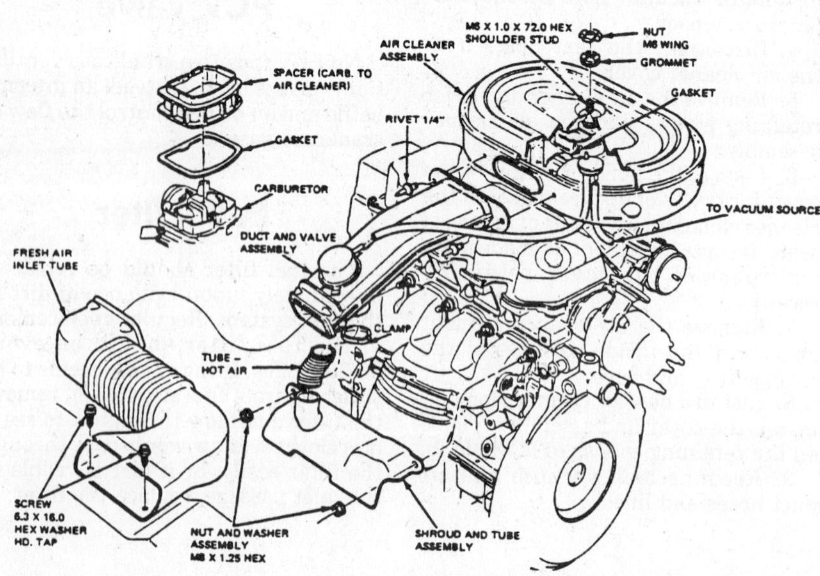

Air intake and cleaner system – 1.3L, 1.6L and 1.9L base engine

NOTE: A backup wrench is an open end wrench of the proper size used to hold a fuel filter or fitting in position while a fuel line is removed. A flared wrench is a special hex wrench with a narrow open end allowing the fuel line nut to be gripped tightly. A regular open end wrench may be substituted if used carefully so the fitting is not rounded.

The fuel filter on the non-EFI models contains a screen to minimize the amount of contaminants entering the carburetor via the fuel system. The fuel filter on the non-EFI models is located in the carburetor.

The EFI model fuel filter provides extremely fine filtration to protect the small metering orifices of the injector nozzles. The filter is a one-piece construction which cannot be cleaned. If the filter becomes clogged or restrict-

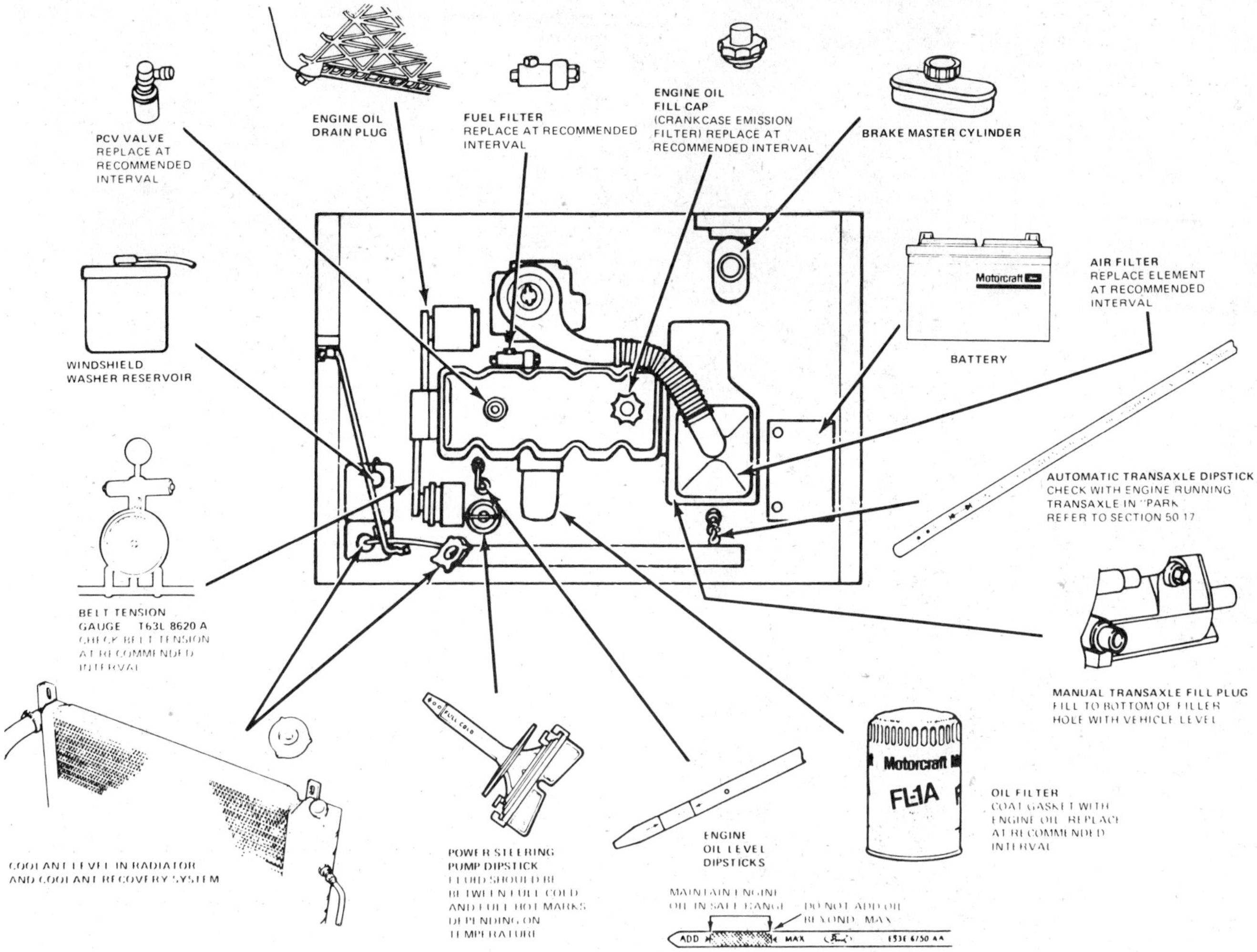

PCV VALVE
REPLACE AT
RECOMMENDED
INTERVAL
ENGINE OIL
DRAIN PLUG
FUEL FILTER
REPLACE AT RECOMMENDED
INTERVAL
ENGINE OIL
FILL CAP
(CRANKCASE EMISSION
FILTER) REPLACE AT
RECOMMENDED INTERVAL
BRAKE MASTER CYLINDER
AIR FILTER
REPLACE ELEMENT
AT RECOMMENDED
INTERVAL
BATTERY
WINDSHIELD
WASHER RESERVOIR
AUTOMATIC TRANSAXLE DIPSTICK
CHECK WITH ENGINE RUNNING
TRANSAXLE IN "PARK"
REFER TO SECTION 50 17
BELT TENSION
GAUGE T63L 8620 A
MANUAL TRANSAXLE FILL PLUG
FILL TO BOTTOM OF FILLER
HOLE WITH VEHICLE LEVEL
OIL FILTER
ENGINE
OIL LEVEL
DIPSTICKS
POWER STEERING
PUMP DIPSTICK

Lubrication and service points—2.3L FSC engine

ed, it should be replaced with a new filter. The filter is located downstream of the electric pump, mounted on the dash panel extension in the right rear corner of the engine compartment on the Escort/Lynx. And on the Tempo/Topaz the filter is mounted on the right fender apron.

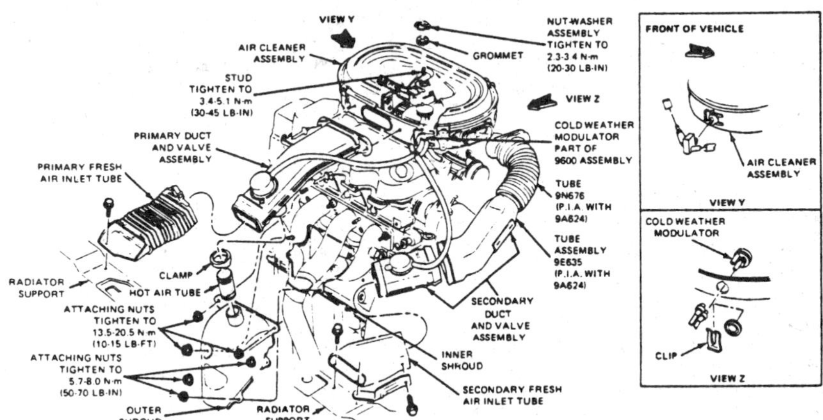

1.6L HO air intake system

REMOVAL & INSTALLATION

Gasoline Engines

ESCORT/LYNX/EXP WITH CARBURETOR

1. Remove the air cleaner assembly.
2. Use a backup wrench on the fuel filter (located in the carburetor inlet) inlet hex nut. Loosen the fuel line nut with a flare wrench. Remove the fuel line from the filter.
3. Unscrew the filter from the carburetor.

To Install:

4. Apply a drop of Loctite® Hydraulic Sealant No. 069 to the external threads of the fuel filter.
5. Hand start the new filter into the carburetor, then use a wrench to tighten the fuel filter to 6.5-8 ft.lb.
6. Apply a drop of engine oil to the fuel supply tube nut and flare, and hand start the nut into the filter inlet approximately two threads.
7. Use a backup wrench on the fuel filter to prevent the filter from rotating while tightening. Tighten the nut to 15-18 ft.lb.
8. Start the engine and check for fuel leaks.
9. Install the air cleaner assembly.

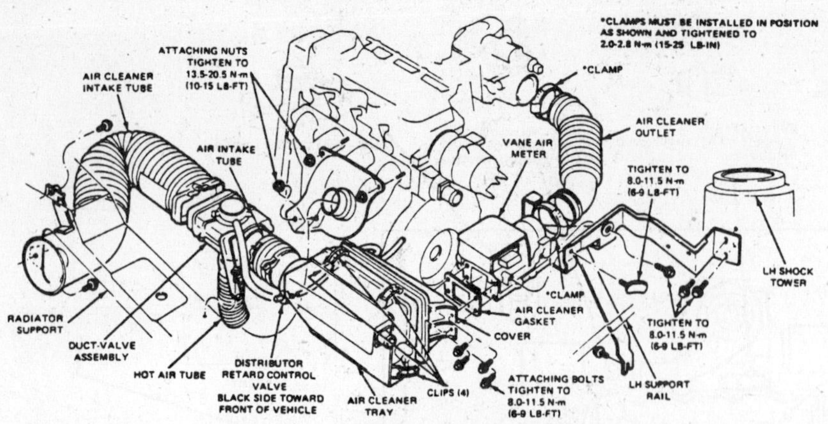

1.6L EFI air intake system

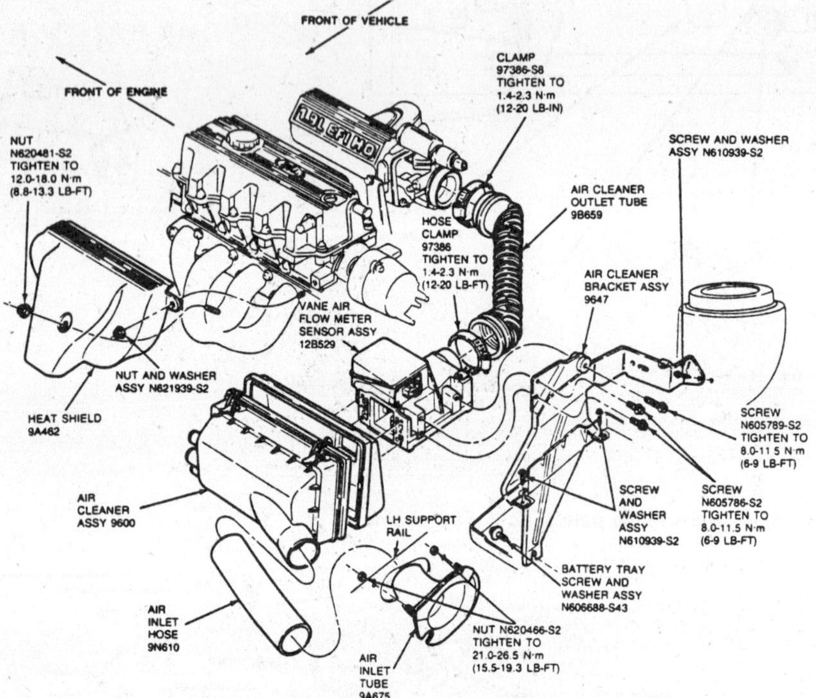

1.9L EFI air intake system

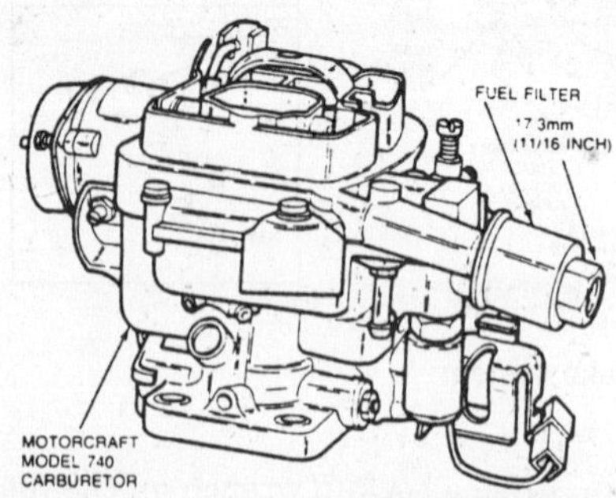

Fuel filter mounting Escort/Lynx/EXP with carburetor

ESCORT/LYNX/EXP WITH FUEL INJECTION

1. With the engine turned OFF,

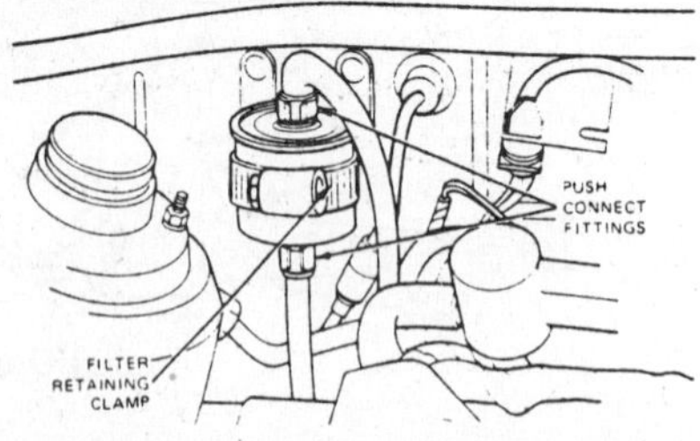

Fuel filter mounting Escort/Lynx/EXP—EFI engines

depressurize the fuel system on the EFI engines using special tool T80L-9974-A Fuel Pressure Gauge, or equivalent.

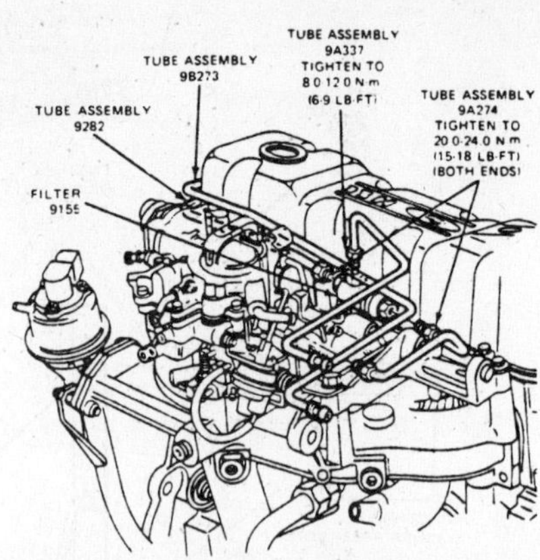

Fuel filter mounting Tempo/Topaz—Canada only

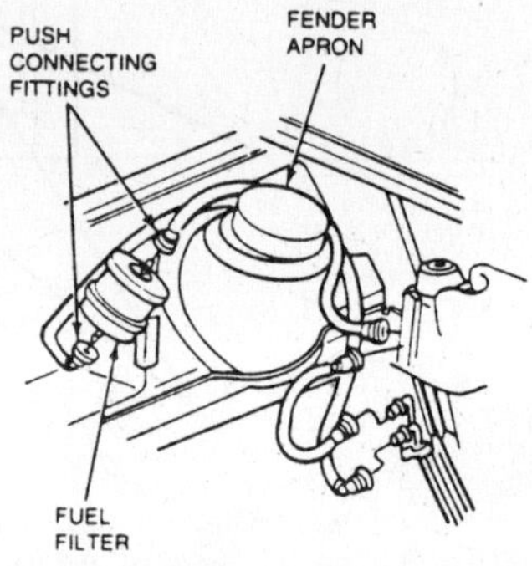

Fuel filter mounting Tempo/Topaz—CFI engines

2. Remove the push connect fittings from both side of the fuel filter.

NOTE: The fuel filter is located downstream of the electric fuel pump on the right rear corner of the engine compartment. Push connect fitting disconnection procedures are covered in FUEL SYSTEM.

3. Remove the filter from the mounting bracket by loosening the retaining clamp enough to allow the filter to pass through.
4. Install the fuel filter in the bracket, ensuring proper direction of the flow as noted earlier. Tighten the clamp to 15-25 in.lb.
5. Install the push connect fittings at both ends of the filter.
6. Start the engine and check for fuel leaks.

CANADIAN TEMPO/TOPAZ WITH CARBURETOR

1. Remove the air cleaner bonnet assembly if necessary.
2. Using a backup wrench on the return line fitting on the top of the fuel filter, remove the fuel line with a flare nut wrench.
3. Using a backup wrench on the fuel filter inlet fitting, remove the fuel

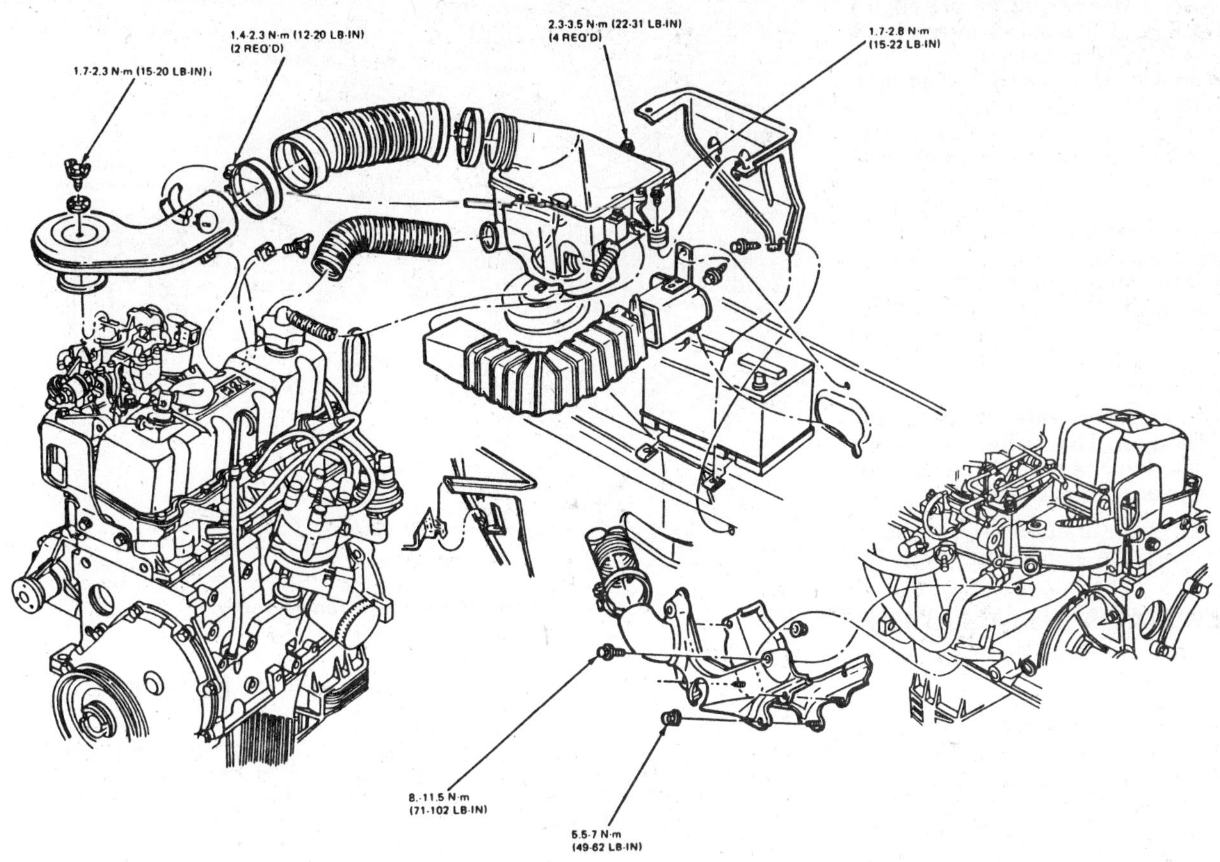

2.3L HSC air intake system

line from the fuel filter with a flare nut wrench.

4. Using a backup wrench on the fuel filter outlet fitting, loosen the fuel lin and remove the fuel filter from the engine with a flare nut wrench.

To Install:

5. Apply engine oil the fuel line nuts and flared ends.
6. Position the fuel filter with flow arrow on the filter directed towards the fuel line to the carburetor.
7. Finger-tighten the fitting at the fuel filter outlet.
8. Finger-tighten the return line fitting into the top of the filter.
9. Finger-tighten the fitting at the fuel filter inlet.
10. Using a backup wrench on the fuel filter fittings, tighten the fuel lines in the following sequence:
    a. Tighten the return line nut to 6-9 ft.lb.
    b. Tighten the nut on the fuel line at the filter outlet to 15-18 ft.lb.
    c. Tighten the nut on the fuel line from the fuel pump to the fuel filter to 15-18 ft.lb.
11. Inspect the fuel line routings and install the fuel line clips if loosened or removed during disassembly. Adjust the fuel lines if they are interfering with the carburetor, air pump, or fuel filter housing.
12. Start the engine and check for fuel leaks at all the fuel line connections, fuel pump, fuel filter and the carburetor while the engine is idling for two minutes. Retighten if necessary.
13. If removed, install the air filter bonnet assembly to the carburetor.

TEMPO/TOPAZ WITH FUEL INJECTION

1. Remove the air cleaner bonnet assembly for clearance if necessary.
2. Use a backup wrench on the return line fitting on the top of the fuel filter. Remove the fuel line using a flare wrench.
3. Use a backup wrench on the fuel filter inlet fitting. Remove the fuel line using a flare wrench.
4. Use a backup wrench on the fuel filter outlet fitting. Remove the fuel line using a flare wrench. Remove the fuel filter.
5. Position the fuel filter with the arrow on the filter pointing towards the fuel line to the carburetor.
6. Hand start all the fuel lines in their respective fittings.
7. Use a backup wrench and flare wrench to tighten all fuel lines. Tighten the return line first, the outlet line second and the inlet line last. Do not overtighten. Install the remaining parts in the reverse order of removal.

Taurus and Sable

The fuel filter is mounted under the vehicle, next to the right front corner of the fuel tank.

1. Refer to "Bleeding Fuel System" procedures in this section and reduce the pressure in the fuel system.
2. At the fuel filter bracket, loosen the worm gear clamp.
3. Using a pair of vise-grips, clamp the fuel line to prevent fuel from siphoning from the fuel tank.
4. Remove the clamps and the fuel lines from the fuel filter.
5. Slide the fuel filter from the bracket retaining clamp.
6. To install, use a new filter (position it with the arrow facing the fuel flow direction) and reverse the removal procedures. Torque the fuel filter clamp to 15-25 in.lb. (1.7-2.8 Nm).

Diesel Engine

The fuel filter/conditioner must be

serviced (water purged) at each engine oil change (7500 miles) interval. To purge water from the system:

1. Make sure the engine and ignition switch are off.
2. Place a suitable container under the fuel filter/conditioner water drain tube under the car.
3. Open the water drain valve at the bottom of the filter/conditioner element 2½-3 turns.
4. Pump the prime pump at the top of the filter from 10 to 15 strokes, or until all of the water is purged from the filter, and clear diesel fuel is apparent.

NOTE: If the water/fuel will not drain from the tube, open the drain valve one more turn or until the water/fuel starts to flow.

5. Close the drain valve and tighten.
6. Start the engine and check for leaks.

REMOVAL & INSTALLATION

1. Make sure that the engine and ignition are off.
2. Disconnect the module connector from the water level sensor located at the bottom of the filter element.
3. Use an appropriate filter strap wrench and turn the filter element counterclockwise to loosen from the top mounting bracket. Remove the element from the mount adapter.
4. Remove the water drain valve/sensor probe from the bottom of the element. Wipe the probe with a clean dry cloth.
5. Unsnap the sensor probe pigtail from the bottom of the filter element and wipe with a clean dry rag.
6. Snap the probe onto the new filter element.
7. Lubricate the two O-rings on the water sensor probe with a light film of oil. Screw the probe into the bottom of the new filter element and tighten.
8. Clean the gasket mounting surface of the adapter mount.
9. Lubricate the sealing gasket of the filter element with oil. Screw the filter element onto the mount adapter. Hand tighten the element, then back off the filter to a point where the gasket is just touching the adapter. Retighten by hand and then an additional ½-⅝ turn.
10. Reconnect the water level sensor module connector.
11. Prime the fuel system by pumping the primer handle until pressure is felt when pumping.
12. Start the engine and check for fuel leaks.

Evaporative Emission Canister

To prevent gasoline vapors from being vented into the atmosphere, an evaporative emission system captures the vapors and stores them in a charcoal filled canister.

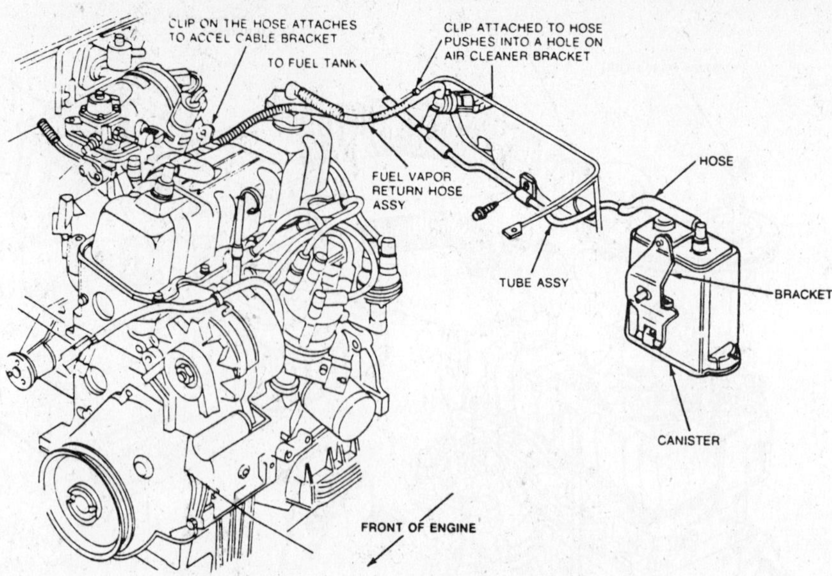

Evaporative canister—Tempo/Topaz

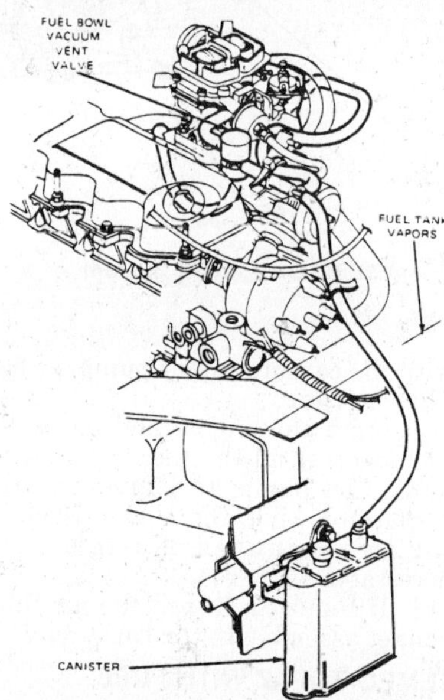

Evaporative canister—Escort/Lynx

SERVICING THE EMISSION CANISTER

Since the canister is purged of fumes when the engine is operating, no real maintenance is required. However, the canister should be visually inspected for cracks, loose connections, etc. Replacement is simply a matter of disconnecting the hoses, loosening the mount and replacing the canister.

Battery

Your car is equipped with a maintenance free battery which eliminates the need for periodic checking and adding fluid.

NOTE: If you replace your battery with a non-maintenance free battery see the following section.

FLUID LEVEL (EXCEPT MAINTENANCE FREE BATTERIES)

Check the battery electrolyte level at least once a month, or more often in hot weather or during periods of extended car operation. The level can be checked through the case on translucent polypropylene battery cases; the cell caps must be removed on other models. The electrolyte level in each cell should be kept filled to the split ring inside, or the line marked on the outside of the case.

If the level is low, add only distilled water, or colorless, odorless drinking water, through the opening until the level is correct. Each cell is completely separate from the others, so each must be checked and filled individually.

If water is added in freezing weather, the car should be driven several miles to allow the water to mix with the electrolyte. Otherwise, the battery could freeze.

SPECIFIC GRAVITY

At least once a year, check the specific gravity of the battery. It should be

Adjusting the battery fluid level

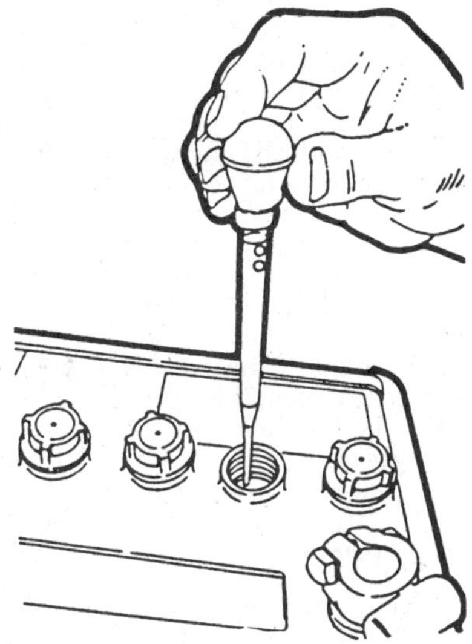

Checking the battery with a battery hydrometer

between 1.20 and 1.26 in.Hg at room temperature.

The specific gravity can be checked with the use of an hydrometer, an inexpensive instrument available from many sources, including auto parts stores. The hydrometer has a squeeze bulb at one end and a nozzle at the other. Battery electrolyte is sucked into the hydrometer until the float is lifted from its seat. The specific gravity is then read by noting the position of the float. Generally, if after charging, the specific gravity between any two cells varies more than 50 points (0.050), the battery is bad and should be replaced.

It is not possible to check the specific gravity in this manner on sealed maintenance free batteries. Instead, the indicator built into the top of the case (on some batteries) must be relied on to display any signs of battery deterioration. If the indicator is dark, the battery can be assumed to be OK. If the indicator is light the specific gravity is low, and the battery should be charged or replaced.

CABLES AND CLAMPS

Once a year, the battery terminals and the cable clamps should be cleaned. Loosen the clamps and remove the cables, negative cable first. On batteries with posts on top, the use of a puller specially made for the purpose is recommended. These are inexpensive, and available in auto parts stores. Side terminal battery cables are secured with a bolt.

Clean the cable clamps and the battery terminal with a wire brush, until all corrosion, grease, etc. is removed and metal is shiny. It is especially important to clean the inside of the clamp thoroughly, since a small deposit of foreign material or oxidation there will prevent a sound electrical connection and inhibit either starting or charging. Special tools are available for cleaning these parts, one type of conventional batteries and another type for side terminal batteries.

Before installing the cable, loosen the battery holddown clamp or strap, remove the battery and check the battery tray. Clear it of any debris, and check it for soundness. Rust should be wire brushed away, and the metal given a coat of anti-rust paint. Replace the battery and tighten the holddown clamp or strap securely, but be careful not to overtighten, which will crack the battery case.

After the clamps and terminals are clean, reinstall the cables, negative cable last; do not hammer on the clamps to install. Tighten the clamps securely, but do not distort them. Give the clamps and terminals a thin external coat of grease after installation, to retard corrosion.

Check the cables at the same time that the terminals are cleaned. If the cable insulation is cracked or broken, or if the ends are frayed, the cable should be replace with a new cable of the same length and gauge.

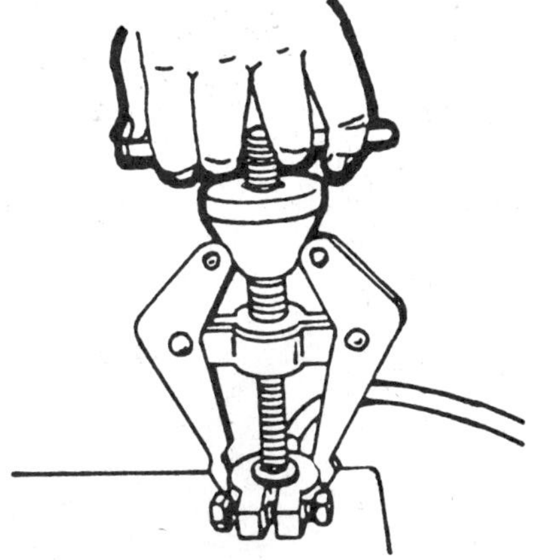

Use a puller to remove the battery cable

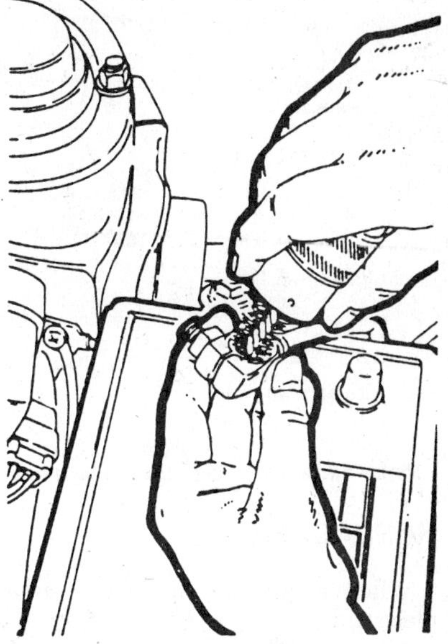

Clean the battery clamps with a wire brush

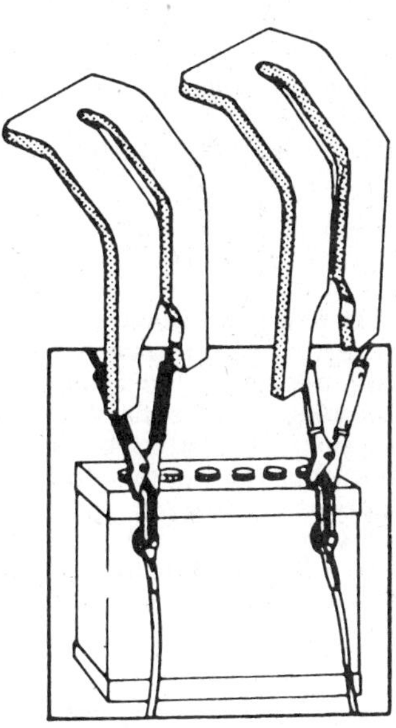

Side terminal batteries occasionally pose a problem when connecting jumper cables. There frequently isn't enough room to clamp the cables without touching sheet metal. Side terminal adaptors are available to alleviate this problem and should be removed after use

NOTE: Keep flame or sparks away from the battery; it gives off explosive hydrogen gas. Battery electrolyte contains sulphuric acid. If you should splash any on your skin or in your eyes, flush the affected areas with plenty of clear water; if it lands in your eyes, get medical help immediately.

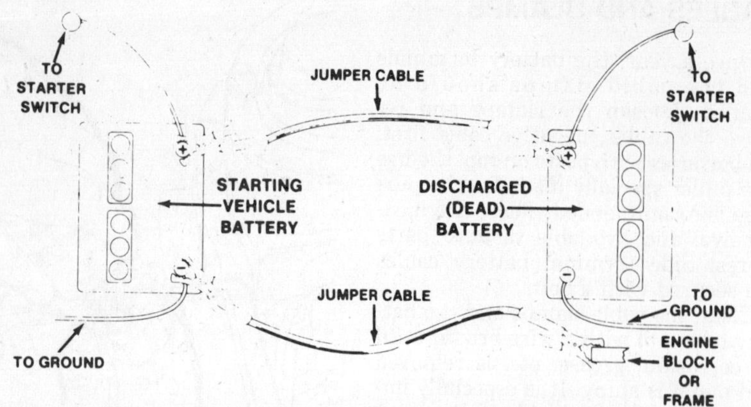

Make certain vehicles do not touch. This hook-up for negative ground cars only

REPLACEMENT

When it becomes necessary to replace the battery, select a battery with a rating equal to or greater than the battery originally installed. Deterioration, embrittlement and just plain aging of the battery cables, starter motor, and associated wires makes the battery's job harder in successive years. The slow increase in electrical resistance over time makes it prudent to install a new battery with a greater capacity then the old.

Belts

NOTE: Due to the compactness of the engine compartment, it may be necessary to disconnect some spark plug leads when adjusting or replacing drive belts. If a spark plug lead is disconnected it is necessary to coat the terminal of the lead with silicone grease (Part number D7AZ-19A331-A or the equivalent).

Your car may be equipped with 4 rib, 5 rib, or a conventional ¼″ (6mm) V-belt depending on accessories.

NOTE: On models equipped with power steering, the air pump belt tension cannot be adjusted until the power steering belt has been replaced and adjusted (or just adjusted if an old belt).

INSPECTION

Inspect all drive belts for excessive wear, cracks, glazed condition and frayed or broken cords. Replace any drive belt showing the above condition(s).

NOTE: If a drive belt continually gets cut, the crankshaft pulley might have a sharp projection on it. Have the pulley replaced if this condition exists.

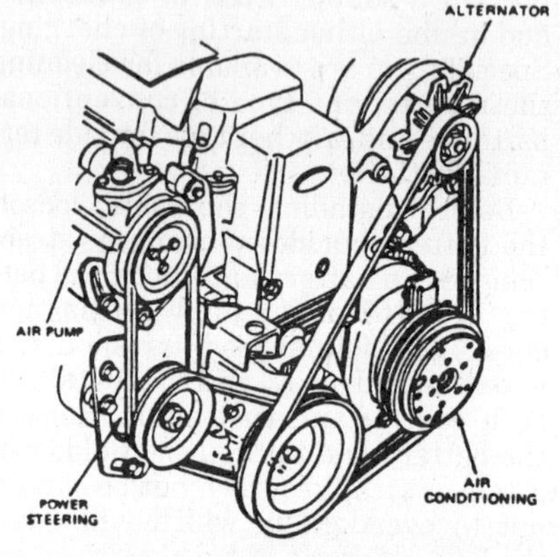

Drive belts, engine with air conditioning

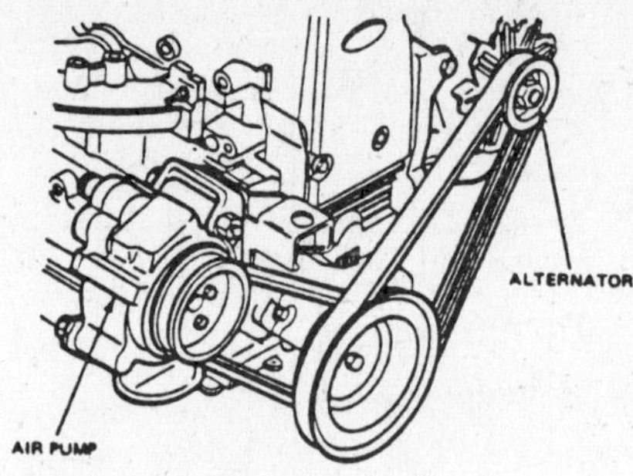

Drive belts, engine without air conditioning

REPLACEMENT

1. Loosen the pivot bolt and/or the adjustment bolt.
2. Move the driven unit (power steering pump, air pump, etc.) toward or away from the engine to loosen the belt. Remove the belt.
3. Install the new bolt on the driven unit and either move toward or away from the engine to put tension on the belt.
4. Snug up the mounting and/or adjusting bolt to hold the driven unit, but do not completely tighten.
5. See the following procedure for the deflection method of belt adjustment.

ADJUSTMENT

NOTE: Proper adjustment re-

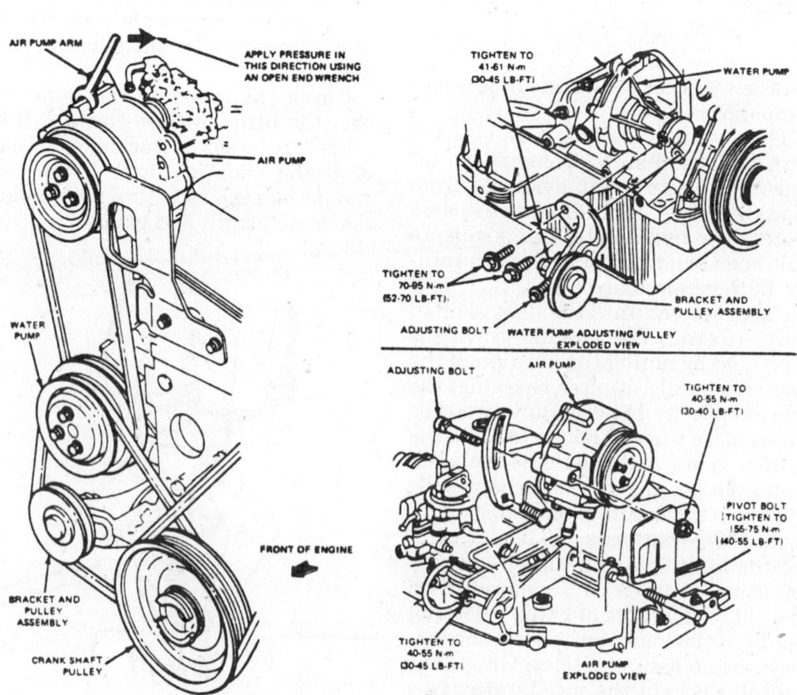

Belt tension adjustment—Air pump, Water pump

quires the use of the tension gauge. Since most people don't have the necessary gauge, a deflection method of adjustment is given.

1. Locate a point on the belt midway between the two pulleys driven.
2. The deflection of the belt should be:
   - For all belts with a distance of 12" (305) between pulley: 1/8-1/4" (3-6mm).
   - For all belts with a distance greater than 12" (305mm) between pulleys: 1/8-3/8" (3-6mm).
3. Correctly adjust the bolt deflection and tighten all mounting bolts. Start the engine and allow it to reach the normal operating temperature. Shut the engine OFF and recheck belt deflection. Readjust if necessary.

BELT TENSION ADJUSTMENT

2.5L Engine

The drive belt tension is maintained by an automatic tensioner which does not require adjustment.

3.0L Engine

1. Loosen the alternator adjusting arm bolt.
2. Adjust the drive belt tension using one of the following methods:
   a. Using the Belt Tension Gauge tool No. 021-00028, install it onto the drive belt, on the longest belt span between the pulleys and adjust the drive belt tension to 100-140 lbs. (new) or 80-100 lbs. (used).
   b. Apply thumb pressure on the longest belt span between the pulleys so that there is approximately 1/4-1/2" of deflection.
3. Torque the adjusting arm bolt 22-32 ft.lb. and recheck the belt tension.

ALTERNATOR BELT ADJUSTMENT

Modified Bracket

Some later models are equipped with a modified alternator bracket (high mount alternator). The bracket incorporates a slot that will accommodate a tapered pry bar, such as a lug wrench, to give a place to apply leverage.

Insert the tire lug wrench into the slot opening. Pry on the alternator until the correct belt tension is reached.

While maintaining belt tension, first tighten the 3/8" adjusting bolt (24-30 ft.lb.), then tighten the pivot bolt (45-65 ft.lb.).

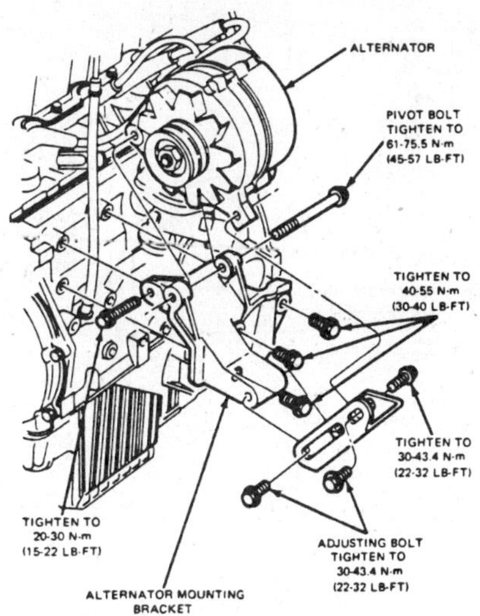

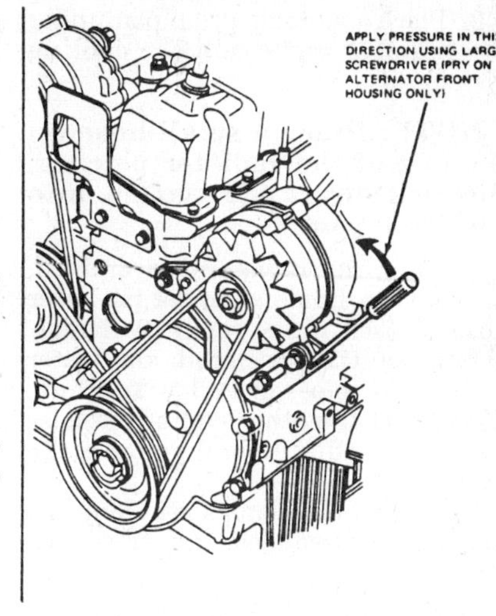

Belt tension adjustment—Alternator, etc.

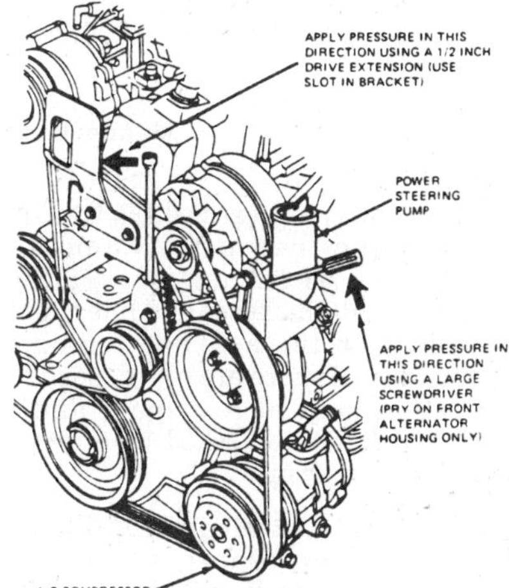

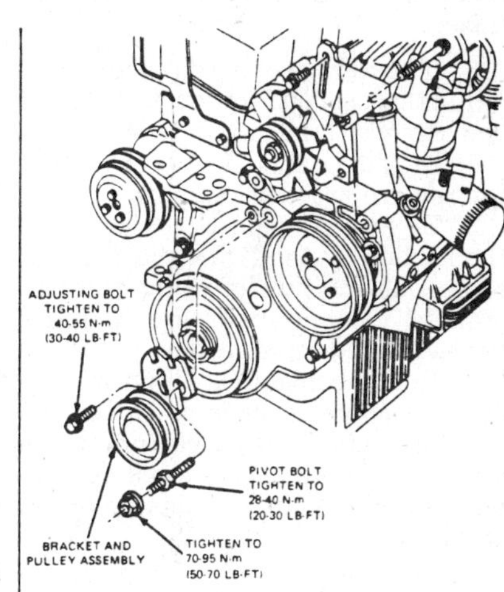

Belt tension adjustment—Power steering, etc.

Hoses

CAUTION

The cooling fan motor is controlled by a temperature switch. The fan may come on when the engine is off! It will continue to run until the correct temperature is reached. Before working on or around the fan, disconnect the negative battery cable or the fan wiring connector.

HOSE REPLACEMENT

1. Open the hood and cover the fenders to protect them from scratches.
2. Disconnect the negative (ground) battery cable at the battery.

CAUTION

When draining the coolant, keep in mind that cats and dogs are attracted by the ethylene glycol antifreeze, and are quite likely to drink any that is left in an uncovered container or in puddles on the ground. This will prove fatal in sufficient quantity. Always drain the coolant into a sealable container. Coolant should be reused unless it is contaminated or several years old.

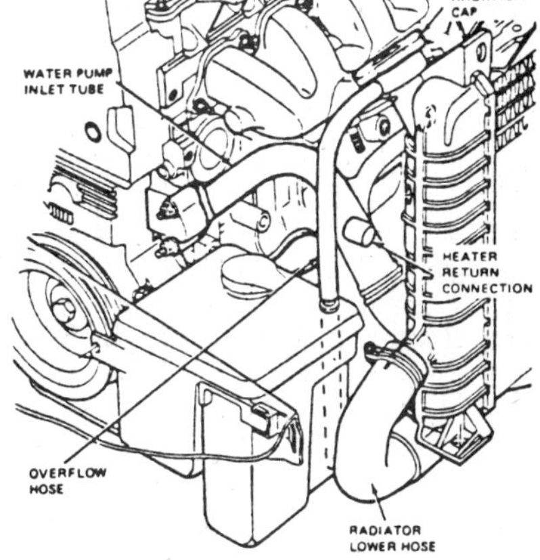

Hose locations

3. Place a suitable drain pan under the radiator and drain the cooling system.

NOTE: Place a small hose on the end of the radiator petcock, this will direct the coolant into the drain pan.

4. After the radiator has drained, position the drain pan under the lower hose. Loosen the lower hose clamps, disconnect the hose from the water pump inlet pipe and allow to drain. Disconnect the other end of the hose from the radiator and remove the hose.

5. Loosen the clamps retaining the upper hose, disconnect and remove the hose.

NOTE: If only the upper hose is to be replaced, drain off enough coolant so the level is below the hose.

6. If heater hoses need replacement, drain the coolant, loosen the clamps and remove the hose(s).

7. Installation of new hose(s) is in the reverse order of removal.

8. Be sure the petcock is closed. Fill the cooling system with the required protection mixture of water and permanent coolant/antifreeze. Connect the negative battery cable.

9. Run the engine until normal operating temperature is reached. Shut off the engine and check for coolant leaks. When the engine cools, recheck the coolant level in the radiator, or reservoir container.

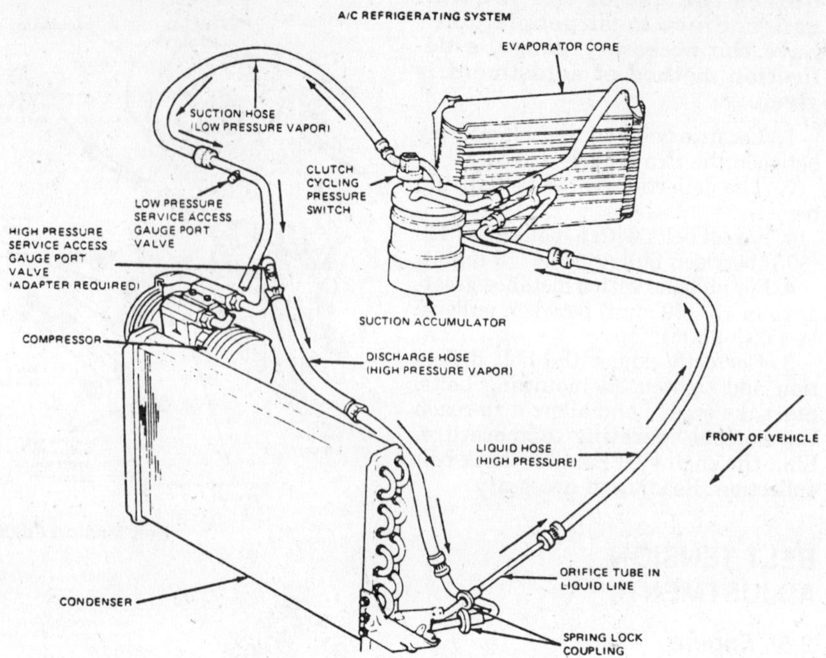

Air conditioning component layout

Air Conditioning System

SAFETY PRECAUTIONS

There are two particular hazards associated with air conditioning systems and they both relate to the refrigerant gas.

First, the refrigerant gas is an extremely cold substance. When exposed to air, it will instantly freeze any surface it comes in contact with, including you eyes. The other hazard relates to fire. Although normally nontoxic, refrigerant gas becomes highly poisonous in the presence of an open flame. One good whiff of the vapor formed by burning refrigerant can be fatal. Keep all forms of fire (including cigarettes) well clear of the air conditioning system.

CHECKING FOR OIL LEAKS

Refrigerant leaks show up as oily areas on the various components because the compressor oil is transported around the entire system along with the refrigerant. Look for only spots on all the hoses and lines, and especially on the hose and tubing connections. If there are oily deposits, the system may have a leak, and you should have it checked by a qualified repairman.

NOTE: A small area of oil on the front of the compressor is normal and no cause for alarm.

KEEP THE CONDENSER CLEAR

Periodically inspect the front of the condenser for bent fins or foreign material (dirt, bugs, leaves, etc.). If any cooling fins are bent, straighten them carefully with needlenosed pliers. You can remove any debris with a stiff bristle brush or hose.

OPERATE THE A/C SYSTEM PERIODICALLY

A lot of A/C problems can be avoided by simply running the air conditioner at least once a week, regardless of the season. Let the system run for at least 5 minutes a week (even in the winter), and you'll keep the internal parts lubricated as well as preventing the hoses from hardening.

REFRIGERANT LEVEL CHECK

The only way to accurately check the refrigerant level to measure the system evaporator pressures with a manifold gauge set, although rapid on/off cycling of the compressor clutch indicates that the A/C system is low on refrigerant. The normal refrigerant capacity is 41 oz. ± 1 oz.

MANIFOLD TEST GAUGES

Most of the service work performed in air conditioning requires the use of a set of two gauges, one for the high (head) pressure side of the system, the other for the low (suction) side.

The low side gauge records both pressure and vacuum. Vacuum readings are calibrated from 0 to 30 in.Hg and the pressure graduations read from 0 to no less than 60 psi. The high side gauge measures pressure from 0 to at last 600 psi.

Both gauges are threaded into a manifold that contains two hand shut-off valves. Proper manipulation of these valves and the use of the attached test hoses allow the user to perform the following services:

1. Test high and low side pressures.
2. Remove air, moisture, and contaminated refrigerant.
3. Purge the system (of refrigerant).
4. Charge the system (with refrigerant).

The manifold valves are designed so that they have no direct effect on gauge readings, but serve only to provide for, or cut off, flow of refrigerant through the manifold. During all test-

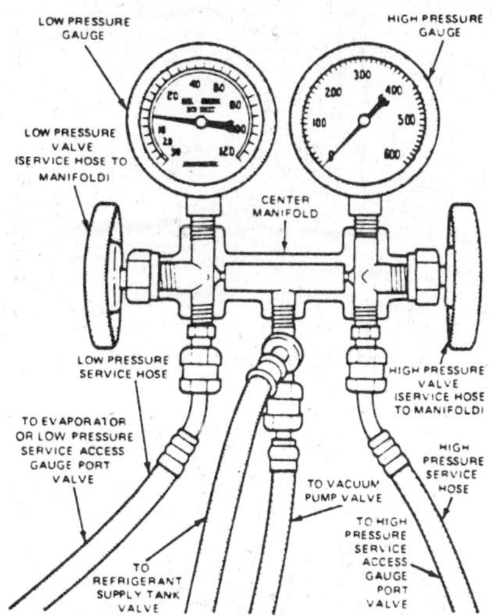

Air conditioning manifold gauge set

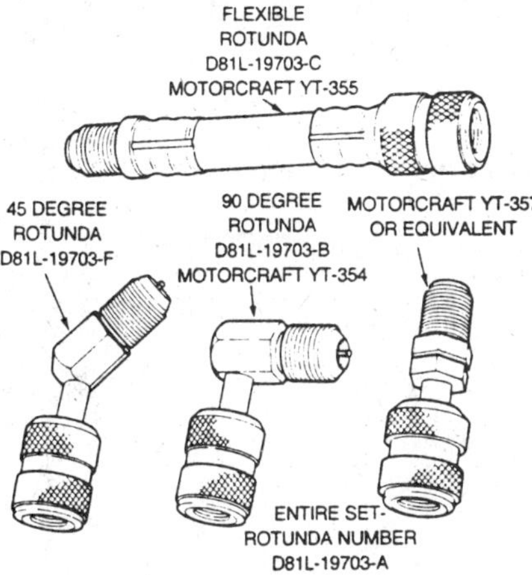

High pressure gauge port valve adapters

ing and hook-up operations, the valves are kept in a close position to avoid disturbing the refrigeration system. The valves are opened only to purge the system or refrigerant or to charge it.

MANIFOLD GAUGE SET ATTACHMENT

The following procedure is for the attachment of a manifold gauge set to the service gauge port valves. If charge station type of equipment is used, follow the equipment manufacturers instructions.

1. Turn both manifold gauge set valves fully clockwise to close the high and low pressure hoses at the gauge set refrigerant center outlet.

NOTE: Rotunda high side adapter set D81L-19703-A or Motorcraft Tool YT-354 or 355 or equivalent is required to connect the manifold gauge set or a charging station to the high pressure service access gauge port valve.

2. Remove the caps from the high and low pressure service gauge port valves.
3. If the manifold gauge set hoses do not have the valve depressing pins in them, install fitting adapters T71P-19703-S and R containing the pins on the manifold gauge hoses.
4. Connect the high and low pressure refrigerant hoses to their respective service ports, making sure they are hooked up correctly and fully seated. Tighten the fittings by hand and make sure they are not cross-threaded. Remember that an adapter is necessary to connect the manifold gauge hose to the high pressure fitting.

CHARGING THE SYSTEM

If the system has been completely purged of refrigerant, it must be evacuated before charging. A vacuum pump should be connected to the center hose of the manifold gauge set, both valves should be opened, and the vacuum pump operated until the low pressure gauge reads as close to 30 in.Hg as possible. If a part in the system has been replaced or excessive moisture is suspected, continue the vacuum pump operation for about 30 minutes.

Close the manifold gauge valves to the center hose, then disconnect the vacuum pump and connect the center hose to a charging cylinder, refrigerant drum or a small can refrigerant dispensing valve. Disconnect the wire harness from the clutch cycling pressure switch and install a jumper wire across the two terminals of the connector. Open the manifold gauge LOW side valve to allow refrigerant to enter the system, keeping the can(s) in an upright position to prevent liquid from entering the system.

When no more refrigerant is being drawn into the system, start the engine and move the function selector lever to the NORM A/C position and the blower switch to HI to draw the remaining refrigerant in. Continue to add refrigerant until the specified 3½ lbs. is reached. Close the manifold gauge low pressure valve and the refrigerant supply valve. Remove the jumper wire from the clutch cycling pressure switch connector and reconnect the pressure switch. Disconnect the manifold gauge set and install the service port caps.

Charging From Small Containers

When using a single can A/C charging kit, such as is available at local retailers, make the connection at the low pressure service port, located on the accumulator/drier. This is very important as connecting the small can to the high pressure port will cause the can to explode. Once the can is connected, charge the system as described above. If a manifold gauge set is being used, the low pressure valve must be closed whenever another can is being connected to the center hose. Hold the cans upright to prevent liquid refrigerant from entering the system and possibly damaging the compressor.

Windshield Wipers

BLADE AND ARM REPLACEMENT

1. Cycle the wiper arm and blade assembly and stop at a position on the windshield where removal can be accomplished without difficulty.
2. To remove the blade: Pull the wiper arm out and away from the windshield. Grasp the wiper blade assembly and pull away from the mounting pin of the wiper arm (Trico® type). Or pull back on the spring lock, where the arm is connected to the blade, and pull the wiper blade assembly from the wiper arm (Tridon® type).
3. To remove the wiper arm: Pull the bade and arm assembly away from the windshield. Move the slide latch (located at base of wiper arm) away from the arm mounting pivot shaft. The arm is now unlocked. Lift the arm up and away from the pivot shaft.
4. Installation is in the reverse order of removal.

Tires

INFLATION PRESSURE

Tire inflation is the most ignored item of auto maintenance. Gasoline mileage can drop as much as 0.8% for every 1 pound per square inch (psi) of under inflation.

Two items should be a permanent fixture in every glove compartment: a tire pressure gauge and a tread depth gauge. Check the tire air pressure (including the spare) regularly with a pocket type gauge. Kicking the tires won't tell you a thing, and the gauge on the service station air hose is notoriously inaccurate.

The tire pressures recommended for you car are usually found on a label attached to the door pillar or on the glove box inner cover or in the owner's manual. Ideally, inflation pressure should be checked when the tires are cool. When the air becomes heated it expands and the pressure increases. Every 10° rise (or drop) in temperature means a difference of 1 psi, which also explains why the tire appears to

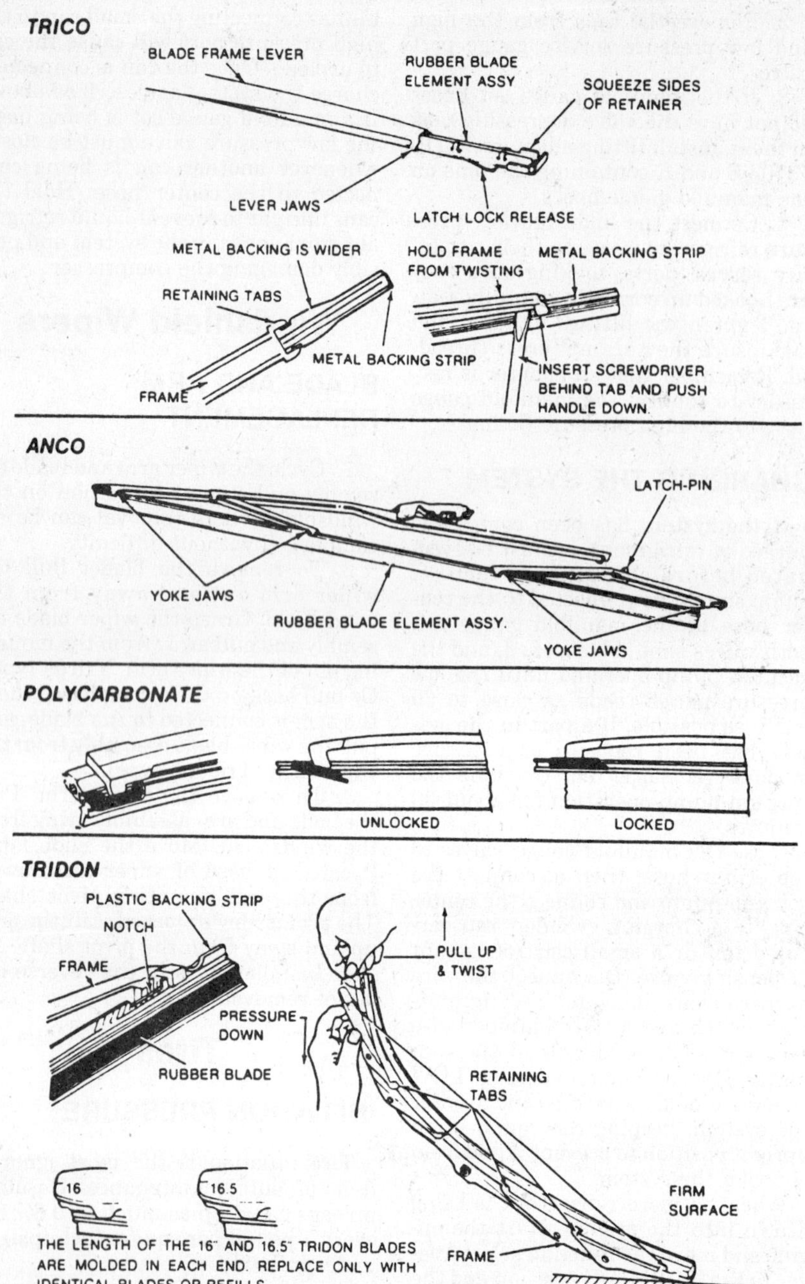

Wiper insert replacement

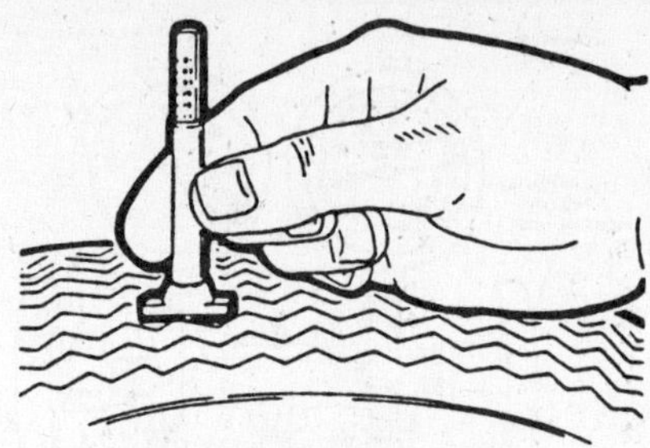

Tire thread depth gauge

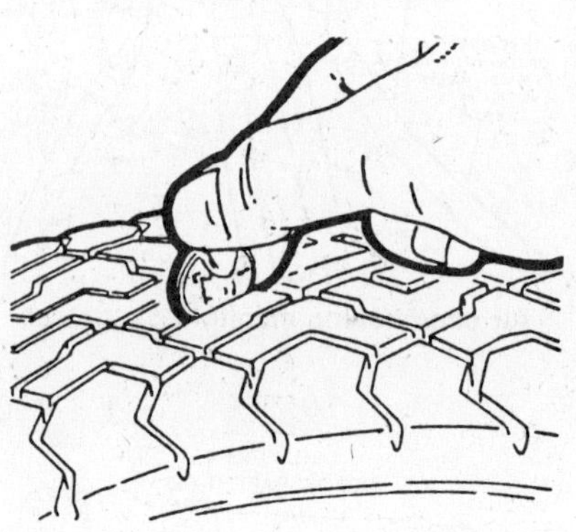

A penny used to determine tread depth

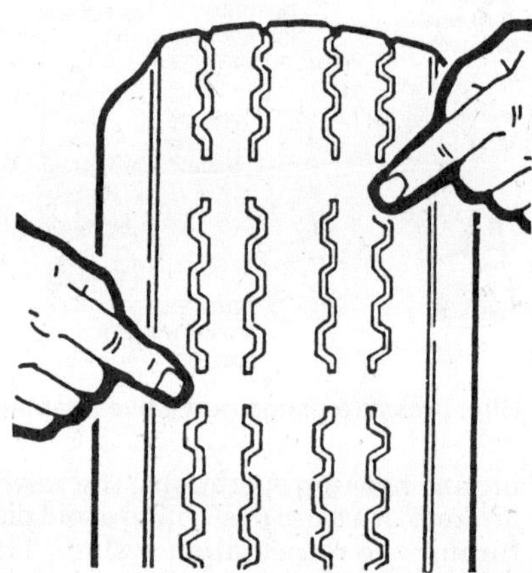

Replace a tire that shows the built-in "bump strip"

lose air on a very cold night. When it is impossible to check the ties cold, allow for pressure build-up due to heat. If the hot pressure exceeds the cold pressure by more than 15 psi, reduce you speed, lead or both. Otherwise internal heat is created in the tire. When the heat approaches the temperature at which the tire was cured, during manufacture, the tread can separate from the body.

CAUTION

Never counteract excessive pressure build-up by bleeding off air pressure (letting some air out). This will only further raise the tire operating temperature.

Before starting a long trip with lots of luggage, you can add about 2-4 psi to the tires to make them run cooler, but never exceed the maximum inflation pressure on the side of the tire.

TREAD DEPTH

All tires made since 1968 have 8 built-in tread wear indicator bars that show up as ½" (12.7mm) wide smooth bands across the tire when $^1/_{16}$" (1.5mm) of tread remains. The appearance of tread wear indicators means that the tires should be replaced. In fact, many states have laws prohibiting the use of tires with less than $^1/_{16}$" (1.5mm) of tread remains. The appearance of tread wear indicators means that the tires should be replace. In fact, many states have laws prohibiting the use of tires with less than $^1/_{16}$" (1.5mm) tread.

You can check you own tread depth with an inexpensive gauge or by using a Lincoln head penny. Slip the Lincoln penny into several tread grooves. If you can see the top of Lincoln's head in 2 adjacent grooves, the tires have less than $^1/_{16}$" (1.5mm) tread left and should be replaced. You can measure snow ties in the same manner by using the tails side of the Lincoln penny. If

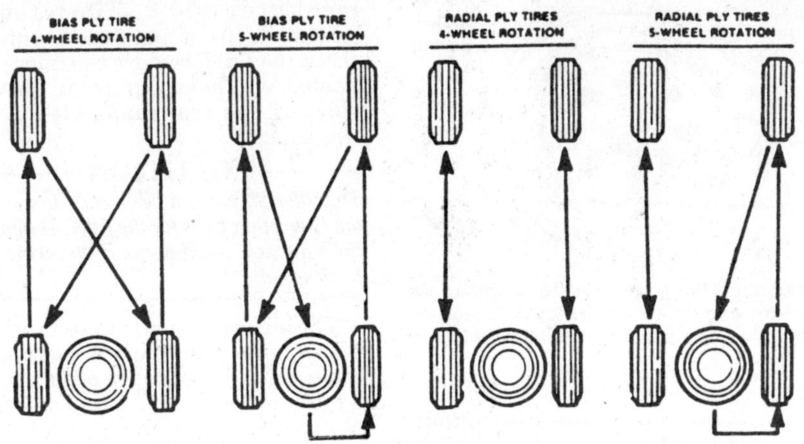

Tire rotation patterns

you see the top of the Lincoln memorial, it's time to replace the snow tires.

TIRE ROTATION

NOTE: Ford does not recommend tire rotation. They suggest that tires be replaced in pairs as needed without rotation.

Tire wear can be equalized by switching the position of the tires about every 6,000 miles. Including a conventional spare in the rotation pattern can give up to 20% more tire life.

CAUTION

Do not include the new SpaceSaver® of temporary spare tires in the rotation pattern.

There are certain exceptions to tire rotation, however. Studded snow tires should not be rotated, and radials should be kept on the same side of the car (maintain the same direction of rotation). The belts on radial tires get set in a pattern. If the direction of rotation is reversed, it can cause rough ride and vibration.

NOTE: When radials or studded snows are taken off the car, mark them, so you can maintain the same direction of rotation.

TIRE STORAGE

Store the tires at proper inflation pressures if they are mounted on wheels. All tires should be kept in a cool, dry place. If they are stored in the garage or basement, do not let them stand on a concrete floor; set them on strips of wood.

FLUIDS AND LUBRICANTS

Engine

FUEL RECOMMENDATIONS

Gasoline Engine

Unleaded gasoline having a Research Octane Number (RON) of 91, or an Antiknock Index of 87 is recommended for your car. Leaded gasoline will quickly interfere with the operation of the catalytic converter and just a few tankfuls of leaded gasoline will render the converter useless. This will cause the emission of much greater amounts of hydrocarbons and carbon monoxide from the exhaust system, void you warranty and cost a considerable amount of money for converter replacement.

Diesel Engine

The diesel engine is designed to use number 2-D diesel fuel. Use of number 1-D diesel fuel in temperatures +20°F is acceptable, but not necessary.

Do not use number 1-D diesel fuel in temperatures above +20°F as damage to the engine may result. Also fuel economy will be reduced with the use of number 1-D diesel fuel.

The 2.0L diesel engines are equipped with an electric fuel heater to prevent cold fuel problems. For best results in cold weather use winterized number 2-D diesel fuel which is blended to minimize cold weather operation problems.

CAUTION

DO NOT add gasoline, gasohol, alcohol or cetane improvers to the diesel fuel. Also, DO NOT use fluids such as either in the diesel air intake system. The use of these liquids or fluids will cause damage to the engine and/or fuel system.

OIL RECOMMENDATIONS

Oil meeting API classification SF or SF/CC or SF/CD is recommended for use in your vehicle. Viscosity grades 10W-30 or 10W-40 are recommended on models before 1984 and 5W-30 on models 1984 and later. See the viscosity-to-temperature chart in this section.

OIL LEVEL CHECK

It is a good idea to check the engine oil each time or at least every other time you fill your gas tank.

1. Be sure your car is on level ground. Shut off the engine and wait for a few minutes to allow the oil to drain back into the oil pan.

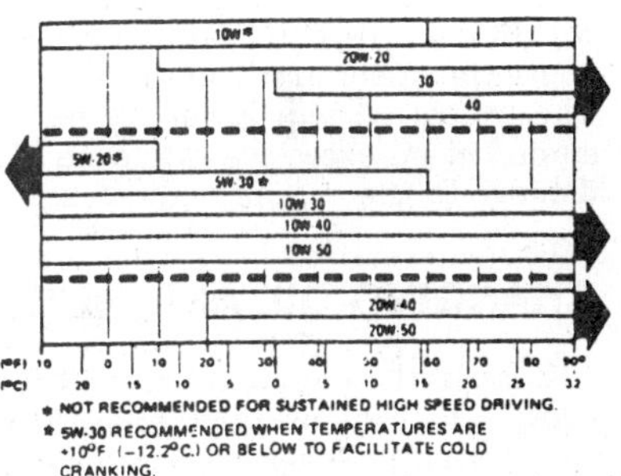

Engine oil viscosity recommendations—1981-83

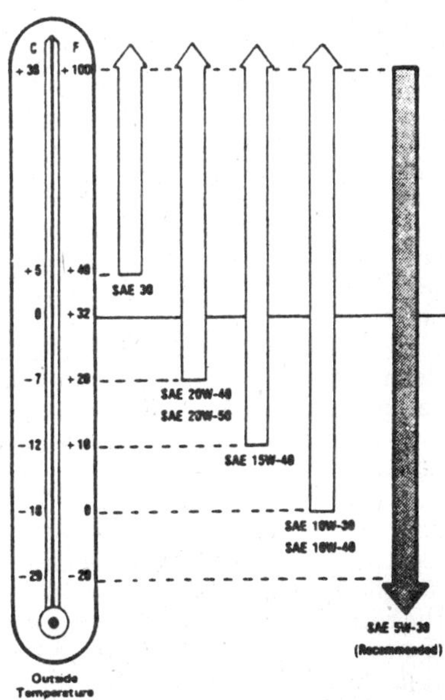

Engine oil viscosity recommendations—1984 and later

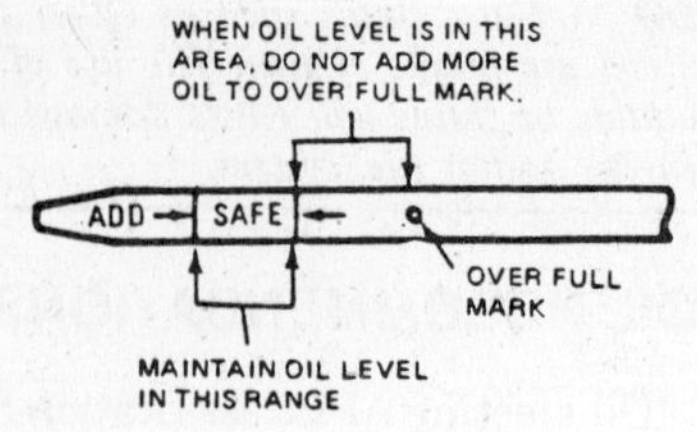

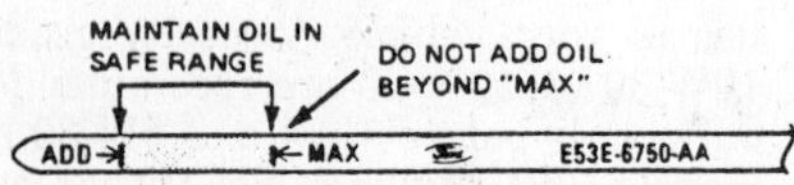

Engine oil level check recommendations

2. Remove the engine oil dipstick and wipe clean with a rag.
3. Reinsert the dipstick and push it down until it is fully seated in the tube.
4. Remove the stick and check the oil level shown. If the oil level is below the lower mark, add one quart.
5. If you wish, you may carefully fill the oil pan to the upper mark on the dipstick with less than a full quart. Do not, however, add a full quart when it would overfill the crankcase (level above the upper mark on the dipstick). The excess oil will generally be consumed at an excessive rate even if no damage to the engine seals occurs.

CHANGING OIL AND FILTER

Change the engine oil and oil filter every 7 months or 7,500 miles. If the car is used in severe service or dusty conditions, change the engine oil and oil filter every 3 months or 3,000 miles. Following these recommended intervals will help keep you car engine in good condition.

1. Make sure the engine is at normal operating temperature (this promotes complete draining of the old oil).
2. Apply the parking brake and block the wheels or raise and support the car evenly on jackstands.
3. Place a drain pan of about a gallon and a half capacity under the engine oil pan drain plug. Use the proper size wrench, loosen and remove the plug. Allow all the old oil to drain. Wipe the pan and the drain plug with a clean rag. Inspect the drain plug gasket, replace if necessary.
4. Reinstall and tighten the drain plug. DO NOT OVERTIGHTEN.
5. Move the drain pan under the engine oil filter. Use a strap wrench and loosen the oil filter (do not remove), allow the oil to drain. Unscrew the filter the rest of the way by hand. Use a rag, if necessary, to keep from burning your fingers. When the filter comes loose from the engine, turn the mounting base upward to avoid spilling the remaining oil.

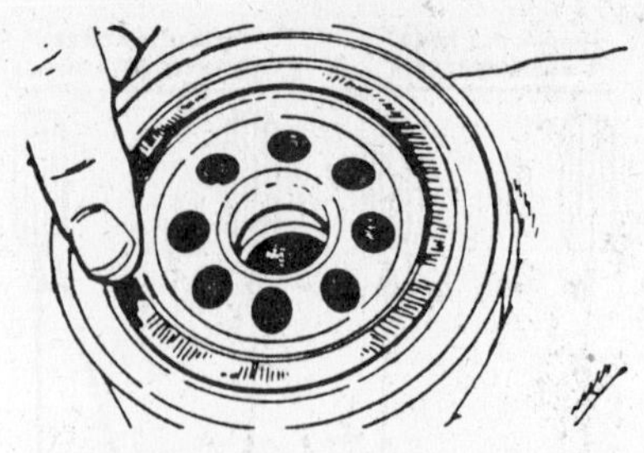

Lubricate the gasket on the new filter with clean engine oil. A dry gasket may not nake a good seal and will allow a filter to leak

6. Wipe the engine filter mount clean with a rag. Coat the rubber gasket on the new oil filter with clean engine oil, applying it with a finger. Carefully start the filter onto the threaded engine mount. Turn the filter until it touches the engine mounting surface. Tighten the filter, by hand, ½ turn more or as recommended by the filter manufacturer.
7. Lower the vehicle to the ground. Refill the crankcase with four quarts of engine oil. Replace the filler cap and start the engine. Allow the engine to idle and check for oil leaks. Shut off the engine, wait for several minutes, then check the oil level with the dipstick. Add oil if necessary.

Transaxle

SERVICE

Changing the fluid in either the automatic or manual transaxle is not necessary under normal operating conditions. However, the fluid levels should by checked at normal intervals as described previously in this section.

If your car is equipped with an automatic transaxle and the region in which you live has severe cold weather, a multi-viscosity automatic transaxle fluid should be used. Ask your dealer about the use of the MV Automatic Transaxle Fluid.

If you operate you car in very dusty conditions, tow a trailer, have extended idling or low speed operation, it may be necessary to change the ATX fluid at regular intervals (20 months, 20,000 miles or more often). Ask your dealer for his recommendations. A description of the fluid change procedure may be found in AUTOMATIC TRANSAXLE.

FLUID LEVELS

Manual Transaxle

Each time the engine oil is changed, the fluid level of the transaxle should be checked. The car must be resting on level ground or supported on jackstands (front and back) evenly. To check the fluid, remove the filler plug, located on the upper front (driver's side) of the transaxle with a 9/16" wrench.

CAUTION

The filler plug has a hex-head, do not mistake any other bolts for the filler. Damage to the transaxle could occur if the wring plug is removed.

The oil level should be even with the edge of the filler hole or within ¼" (6mm) of the hole. If the oil is low, add Type F or Dexron®II automatic fluid. Manual transmission type GL is NOT to be used.

NOTE: A rubber bulb syringe will be helpful in adding the Type F or Dexron®II fluid to the manual transaxle.

Automatic Transaxle

A dipstick is provided in the engine compartment to check the level of the automatic transaxle. Be sure the car is on level ground and that the car's engine and transmission have reached normal operating temperatures. Start the engine, put the parking brake on the transmission selector lever in the PARK position. Move the selector lever through all the positions and return to the PARK position. DO NOT TURN OFF THE ENGINE DURING THE FLUID LEVEL CHECK. Clean all dirt from the dipstick cap before removing the dipstick. Remove the dipstick and wipe clean. Reinsert the dipstick making sure it is fully seated. Pull the dipstick out of the tube and check the fluid level. The fluid level should be between the FULL and ADD marks.

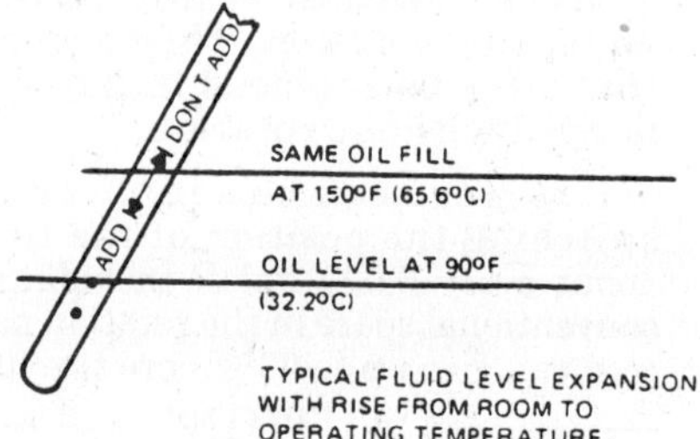

Dipstick markings showing typical fluid expansion from "room" to normal operating temperatures

If necessary, add enough fluid through the dipstick tube/filler to bring the level to the FULL mark on the dipstick. Use only Dexron®II fluid.

CAUTION

Do not overfill. Make sure the dipstick is fully seated.

Differential

The differential is incorporated with the transmission, hence transaxle. The transmission fluid lubricates the differential so any checks or fluid changes can be done by following the procedures above.

Cooling System

LEVEL CHECK

The cooling system of your car contains, among other items, a radiator and an expansion tank. When the engine is running heat is generated. The rise in temperature causes the coolant, in the radiator, to expand and builds up internal pressure. When a certain pressure is reached, a pressure relief valve in the radiator filler cap (pressure cap) is lifted from its seat and allows coolant to flow through the radiator filler neck, down a hose, and into the expansion reservoir.

When the system temperature and pressure are reduced in the radiator, the water in the expansion reservoir is syphoned back into the radiator.

Check the level in the coolant recovery reservoir at least one month. With the cold engine the level must be maintained at or above the ADD mark. At normal operating temperatures, the coolant level should be at the FULL HOT mark. If the level is below the recommended level a 50/50 mixture of coolant (antifreeze) and water should be added to the reservoir. If the reservoir is empty, add the coolant to the radiator and then fill the reservoir to the required level.

CAUTION

The cooling fan motor is controlled by a temperature switch. The fan may come on and run when the engine is off. It will continue to run until the correct temperature is reached. Take care not to get your fingers, etc. caught in the fan blades.

Never remove the radiator cap under any circumstances when the engine is operating. Before removing the cap, switch off the engine and wait until it has cooled. Even then, use extreme care when removing the cap from a hot radiator. Wrap a thick cloth around the cap and turn it slowly to the first stop. Step back while the pressure is released from the cooling system. When you are sure all the pressure has been released, press down on the cap – still with a cloth – turn and remove it.

SERVICING

Check the freezing protection rating of the coolant at least once a year, just before winter. Maintain a protection rating of at least 20°F (-29°C) to prevent engine damage as a result of freezing and to assure proper engine operating temperature. Rust and corrosion inhibitors tend to deteriorate with time, changing the coolant every 3 years or 30,000 miles is recommended for proper protection of the cooling system.

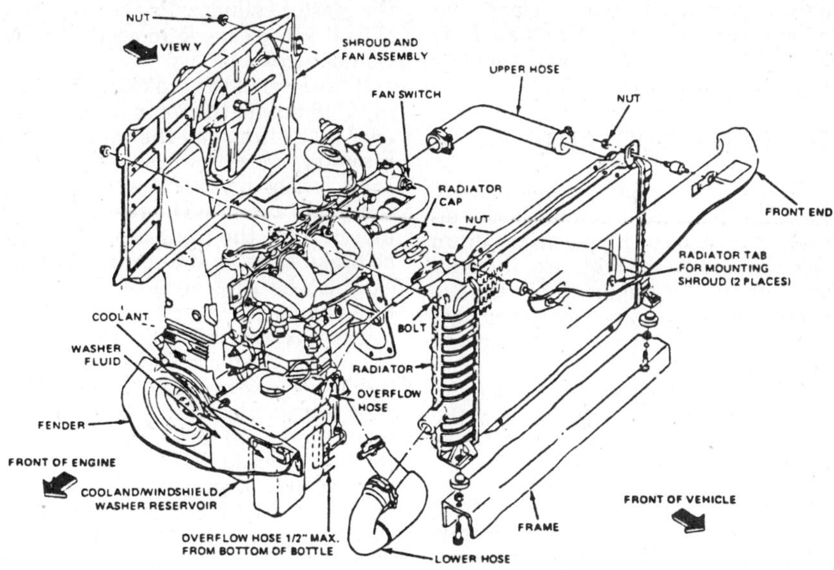

Cooling system

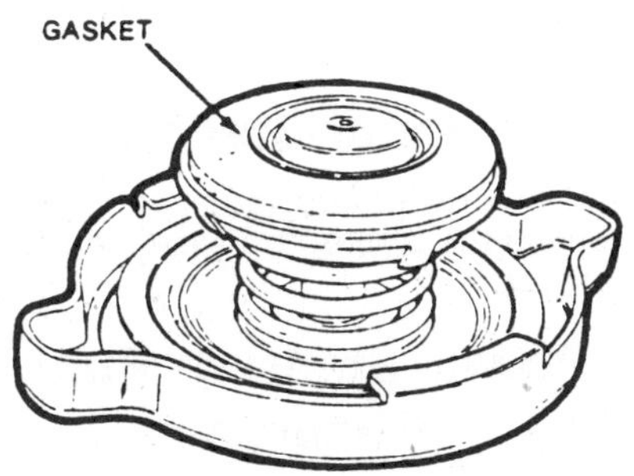

Check the radiator cap gasket for cuts or cracks

Check the coolant level in the radiator at least once a month, only when the engine is cool. Whenever coolant checks are made, check the condition of the radiator cap rubber seal. Make sure it is clean and free of any dirt particles. Rinse off with water if necessary. When replacing cap on radiator, also make sure that the radiator filler neck seat is clean. Check that overflow hose in the reservoir is not kinked and is inserted to within ½" (13mm) of bottom of the bottle.

ADDING COOLANT

Anytime you add coolant to the radiator, use a 50/50 mixture of coolant and water. If you have to add coolant more than once a month, or if you have to add more than one quart at a time, have the cooling system checked for leaks.

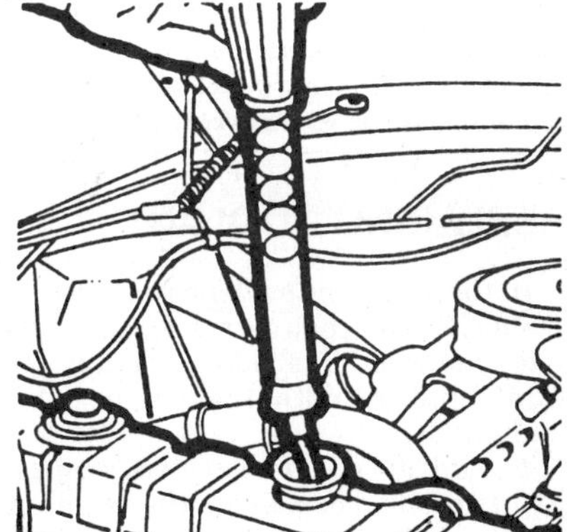

Testing coolant protection with an anti-freeze tester

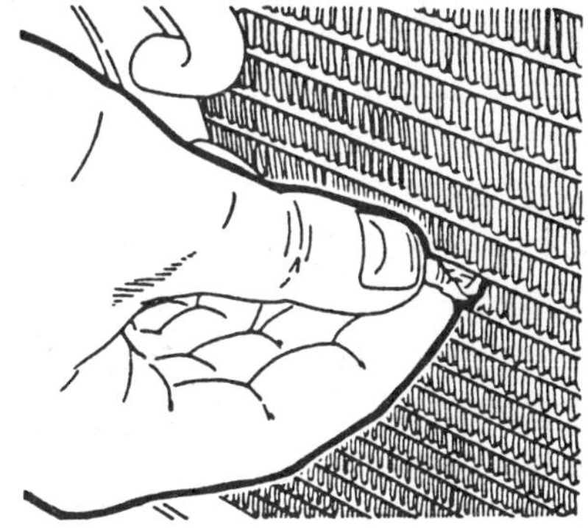

Clean the radiator fins of debris

COOLANT SPECIFICATION

This engine has an aluminum cylinder head and requires a special unique corrosion inhibited coolant formulation to avoid radiator damage. Use only a permanent type coolant that meets Ford Specifications such as Ford Cooling System Fluid, Prestone® II or other approved coolants.

DRAINING COOLANT

To drain the coolant, connect an 18" (457mm) long, 3/8" (9.5mm) inside diameter hose to the nipple on the drain valve located on the bottom of the radiator. With the engine cool, set the heater control to the maximum heat position, remove the radiator cap and open the drain valve or remove allen head plug (3/16") allowing the coolant to drain into a container. When all of the coolant is drained, remove the 3/8" hose and close the drain valve.

CAUTION

When draining the coolant, keep in mind that cats and dogs are attracted by the ethylene glycol antifreeze, and are quite likely to drink any that is left in an uncovered container or in puddles on the ground. This will prove fatal in sufficient quantity. Always drain the coolant into a sealable container. Coolant should be reused unless it is contaminated or several years old.

REPLACING COOLANT

If there is any evidence of rust or scaling in the cooling system the system should be flushed thoroughly before refilling. With the engine OFF and COOL:

1. Add 50 percent of system's capacity of specified coolant to the radiator. Then add water until the radiator is full.
2. Reinstall the radiator cap to the pressure relief position by installing the cap to the fully installed position and then backing off to the first stop.
3. Start and idle the engine until the upper radiator hose is warm.
4. Immediately shut off engine. Cautiously remove radiator cap and add water until the radiator is full. Reinstall radiator cap securely.
5. Add coolant to the ADD mark on the reservoir, then fill to the FULL HOT mark with water.
6. Check system for leaks and return the heater temperature control to normal position.

Brake Master Cylinder

LEVEL CHECK

The brake master cylinder is located under the hood, on the left side firewall. Before removing the master cylinder reservoir cap, make sure the vehicle is resting on level ground and clean all the dirt away from the top of the master cylinder. Pry the retaining clip off to the side. Remove the master cylinder cover.

If the level of the brake fluid is within 1/4" (6mm) of the top it is OK. If the level is less than half the volume of the reservoir, check the brake system for leaks. Leaks in the brake system most commonly occur at the rear wheel cylinders. or at the front calipers. Leaks at brake lines or the master cylinder can also be the cause of the loss of brake fluid.

There is a rubber diaphragm at the top of the master cylinder cap. As the fluid level lowers due to normal brake shoe wear or leakage, the diaphragm takes up the space. This is to prevent the loss of brake fluid out the vented cap and to help stop contamination by dirt. After filling the master cylinder to the proper level with brake fluid (Type DOT 3), but before replacing the cap, fold the rubber diaphragm up into the cap, then replace the cap on the reservoir and snap the retaining clip back in place.

Manual Steering

No periodic lubrication is required unless the system is disassembled for service.

Power Steering Pump Reservoir

LEVEL CHECK

Run the engine until it reaches normal operating temperature. While the engine is idling, turn the steering wheel all the way to the right and then left several times. Shut OFF the engine. Open the hood and remove the power steering pump dipstick. Wipe the dipstick clean and reinstall into the pump reservoir. Withdraw the dipstick and note the fluid level shown. The level must show between the cold full mark and the hot full mark. Add fluid if necessary, buy do not overfill. Remove any excess fluid with a suction bulb or gun.

Windshield Washer Reservoir

LEVEL CHECK

You can fill the water tank with plain water in the summer time, but the pre-mixed solvents available help dissolve grime and dirt better and provide protection against freezing in the winter. Add fluid through the filler cover when the level drops below the line on the side of the reservoir case.

JACKING

Contact points for jacking with either the jack supplied with the car, or with a floor jack are located on the side rocker flanges. When using a floor jack, the front of the car may be raised by positioning the jack under the front body rail behind the suspension arm-to-body bracket. The rear of the car may be raised by positioning the jack forward of the rear suspension rod on the bracket.

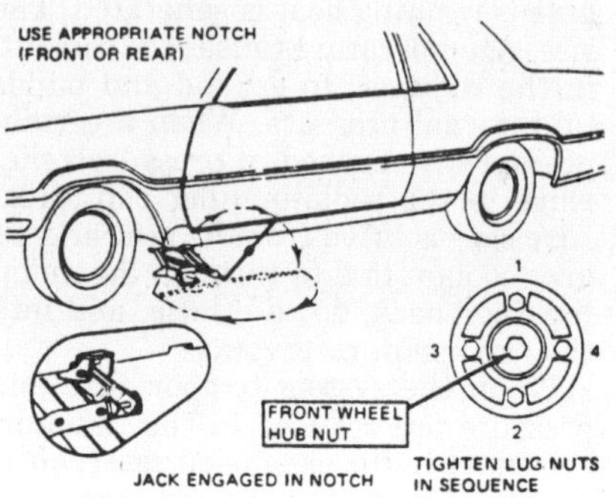

Jack locations, using the jack equipped with your car

TOWING

Whenever you are towing another vehicle, or being towed, make sure the chain or strap is sufficiently long and strong. Attach the chain securely at a point on the frame, shipping tie-down slots are provided on the front and rear of you car and should be used. Never attach a chain or strap to any steering or suspension part. Never try to start the vehicle when being towed, it might run into the back of the tow car. Do not allow too much slack in the tow line, the towed car could run over the line and damage to both cars could occur. If you car is being towed by a tow truck, the towing speed should be limited to 50 mph with the driving wheels off the ground. If it is necessary to tow the car with the drive wheels on the ground, speed should be limited to no more then 35 mph and the towing distance should not be greater than 50 miles. If towing distance is more than 50 miles the front of the car should be put on dollies.

NOTE: If the car is being towed with the front (drive) wheels on the ground, never allow the steering lock to keep the wheels straight, damage to the steering could occur.

PUSHING

Push starting is not recommended on wheels with a catalytic converter. Gas accumulation in the converter will cause damage to the system.

TRAILER TOWING

Factory trailer towing packages are available on most cars. However, if you are installing a trailer hitch and wiring on your car, there are a few thing that you ought to know.

Trailer Weight

Trailer weight is the first, and most important, factor in determining whether or not your vehicle is suitable for towing the trailer you have in mind. The horsepower-to-weight ratio should be calculated. The basic standard is a ratio of 35:1. That is, 35 pounds of GVW for every horsepower.

To calculate this ratio, multiply you engine's rated horsepower by 35, then subtract the weight of the vehicle, including passengers and luggage. The resulting figure is the ideal maximum trailer weight that you can tow. One point to consider: a numerically higher axle ratio can offset what appears to be a low trailer weight. If the weight of the trailer that you have in mind is somewhat higher than the weight you just calculated, you might consider changing your rear axle ratio to compensate.

Hitch Weight

There are three kinds of hitches: bumper mounted, frame mounted, and load equalizing.

Bumper mounted hitches are those which attach solely to the vehicle's bumper. Many states prohibit towing with this type of hitch, when it attaches to the vehicle's stock bumper, since it subjects the bumper to stresses for which it was not designed. Aftermarket rear step bumpers, designed for trailer towing, are acceptable for use with bumper mounted hitches.

Frame mounted hitches can be of the type which bolts to two or more points on the frame, plus the bumper, or just to several points on the frame. Frame mounted hitches can also be of the tongue type, for Class I towing, or, of the receiver type, for classes II and III.

Load equalizing hitches are usually used for large trailers. Most equalizing hitches are welded in place and use equalizing bars and chains to level the vehicle after the trailer is hooked up.

The bolt-on hitches are the most common, since they are relatively easy to install.

Check the gross weight rating of your trailer. Tongue weight is usually figured as 10% of gross trailer weight. Therefore, a trailer with a maximum gross weight of 2,000 lb. will have a maximum tongue weight of 200 lb. Class I tarilers fall into this category. Class II trailers are those with a gross weight rating of 2,000-3,500 lb., while Class III trailers fall into the 3,500-6,000 lb. category. Class IV trailers are those over 6,000 lb. and are for use with fifth wheel trucks, only.

When you've determined the hitch that you'll need, follow the manufacturer's installation instructions, exactly, especially when it comes to fastener torques. The hitch will subjected to a lot of stress and good hitches come with hardened bolts. Never substitute an inferior bolt for a hardened bolt.

Wiring

Wiring the car for towing is fairly easy. There are a number of good wiring kits available and these should be used, rather than trying to design your own. All trailers will need brake lights and turn signals as well as tail lights and side marker lights. Most states require extra marker lights for overly wide trailers. Also, most states have recently required back-up lights for trailers, and most trailer manufacturers have been building trailers with back-up lights for several years.

Additionally, some Class I, most Class II and just about all Class III trailers will have electric brakes.

Add to this number an accessories wire, to operate trailer internal equipment or to charge the trailer's battery, and you can have as many as seven wires in the harness.

Determine the equipment on your trailer and buy the wiring kit necessary. The kit will contain all the wires needed, plus a plug adapter set which included the female plug, mounted on the bumper or hitch, and the male plug, wired into, or plugged into the trailer harness.

When installing the kit, follow the manufacturer's instructions. The color coding of the wires is standard throughout the industry.

One point to note, some domestic vehicles, and most imported vehicles, have separate turn signals. On most domestic vehicles, the brake lights and rear turn signals operate with the same bulb. For those vehicles with separate turn signals, you can purchase an isolation unit so that the brake lights won't blink whenever the turn signals are operated, or, you can go to your local electronics supply house and buy four diodes to wire in series with the brake and turn signal bulbs. Diodes will isolate the brake and turn signals. The choice is yours. The isolation units are simple and quick to install, but far more expensive than the diodes. The diodes, however, require more work to install properly, since they require the cutting of each bulb's wire and soldering in place of the diode.

One final point, the best kits are those with a spring loaded cover on the vehicle mounted socket. This cover prevents dirt and moisture from corroding the terminals. Never let the vehicle socket hang loosely. Always mount it securely to the bumper or hitch.

Cooling

ENGINE

One of the most common, if not THE most common, problem associated with trailer towing is engine overheating.

With factory installed trailer towing packages, a heavy duty cooling system is usually included. Heavy duty cooling systems are available as optional equipment on most cars, with or without a trailer package. If you have one of these extra-capacity systems, you shouldn't have any overheating problems.

If you have a standard cooling system, without an expansion tank, you'll definitely need to get an aftermarket expansion tank kit, preferably one with at least a 2 quart capacity. These kits are easily installed on the radiator's overflow hose, and come with a pressure cap designed for expansion tanks.

Another helpful accessory is a Flex Fan. These fan are large diameter units are designed to provide more airflow at low speeds, with blades that have deeply cupped surfaces. The blades then flex, or flatten out, at high speed, when less cooling air is needed. These fans are far lighter in weight than stock fans, requiring less horsepower to drive them. Also, they are far quieter than stock fans.

If you do decide to replace your stock fan with a flex fan, note that if your car has a fan clutch, a spacer between the flex fan and water pump hub will be needed.

Aftermarket engine oil coolers are helpful for prolonging engine oil life and reducing overall engine temperatures. Both of these factors increase engine life.

While not absolutely necessary in towing Class I and some Class II trailers, they are recommended for heavier Class II and all Class III towing.

Engine oil cooler systems consist of an adapter, screwed on in place of the oil filter, a remote filter mounting and a multi-tube, finned heat exchanger, which is mounted in front of the radiator or air conditioning condenser.

TRANSMISSION

An automatic transmission is usually recommended for trailer towing. Modern automatics have proven reliable and, of course, easy to operate, in trailer towing.

The increased load of a trailer, however, causes an increase in the temperature of the automatic transmission fluid. Heat is the worst enemy of an automatic transmission. As the temperature of the fluid increases, the life of the fluid decreases.

It is essential, therefore, that you install an automatic transmission cooler.

The cooler, which consists of a multi-tube, finned heat exchanger, is usually installed in front of the radiator or air conditioning compressor, and hooked inline with the transmission cooler tank inlet line. Follow the cooler manufacturer's installation instructions.

Select a cooler of at least adequate capacity, based upon the combined gross weights of the car and trailer.

Cooler manufacturers recommend that you use an aftermarket cooler in addition to, and not instead of, the present cooling tank in your car radiator. If you do want to use it in place of the radiator cooling tank, get a cooler at least two sizes larger than normally necessary.

NOTE: A transmission cooler can, sometimes, cause slow or harsh shifting in the transmission during cold weather, until the fluid has a chance to come up to normal operating temperature. Some coolers can be purchased with or retrofitted with a temperature bypass valve which will allow fluid flow through the cooler only when the fluid has reached operating temperature, or above.

TUNE-UP PROCEDURES

Spark Plugs

Spark plugs ignite the air and fuel mixture in the cylinder as the piston reaches the top of the compression stroke. The controlled explosion that results forces the piston down, turning the crankshaft and the rest of the drive train.

Ford recommends that spark plugs be changed every 30,000 miles (60,000 Calif.). Under severe driving conditions, those intervals should be halved. Severe driving conditions are:

1. Extended periods of idling or low speed operation, such as off-road or door-to-door delivery.
2. Driving short distances (less than 10 miles) when the average temperature is below 10°F (-12°C) for 60 days or more.
3. Excessive dust or blowing dirt conditions.

When you remove the spark plugs, check their condition. They are in good indicator of the condition of the engine. It is a good idea to remove the spark plugs at regular intervals, such as every 6,000 or so miles, just so you can keep an eye on the mechanical state of the engine.

A small deposit of light tan or gray material on a spark plug that has been used for any period of time is considered normal. Any other color, or abnormal amounts of deposit, indicate that there is something amiss in the engine.

The gap between the center electrode and the side or ground electrode can be expected to increase not more than 0.001" (0.025mm) every 1,000 miles under normal conditions. When, and if, a plug fouls and begins to misfire, you will have to investigate, correct the cause of the fouling and either clean or replace the plug.

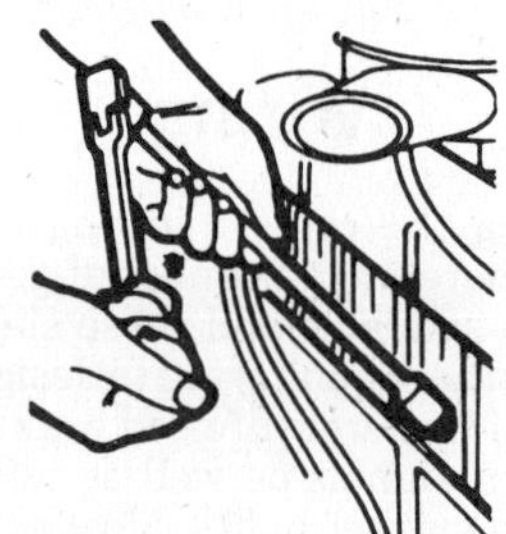

Remove the spark plugs with a ratchet and long extension

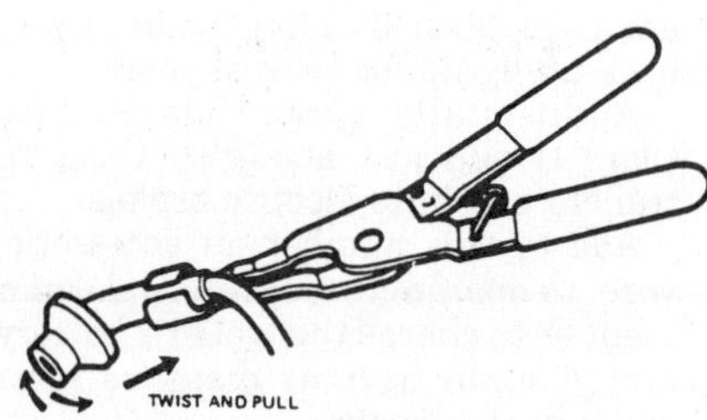

Special pliers used to remove the boots and wire from the spark plug

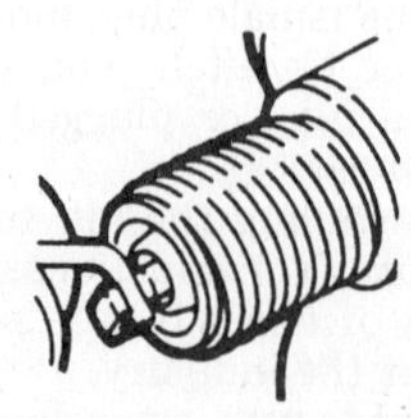

Check the spark plug gap with a wire feeler gauge

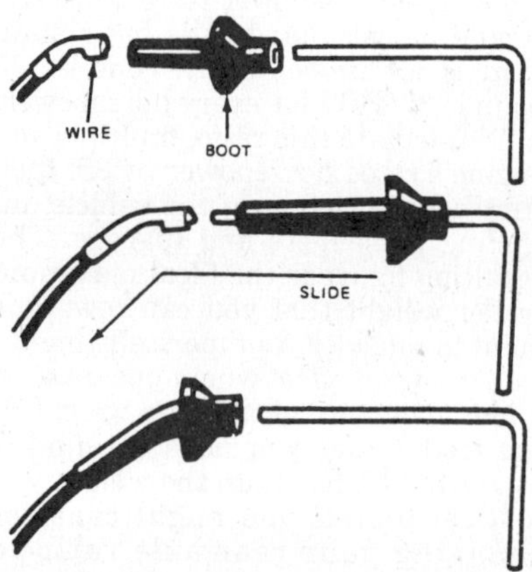

Use a bent "tool" to install new plug boots

SPARK PLUG HEAT RANGE

Spark plug heat range is the ability of the plug to dissipate heat. The longer the insulator (or the farther it extends into the engine), the hotter the plug will operate; the shorter the insulator the cooler it will operate. A plug that absorbs little heat and remains too cool will quickly accumulate deposits of oil and carbon since it is not hot enough to burn them off. This leads to plug fouling and consequently to misfiring. A plug that absorbs too much heat will have no deposits, but, due to the excessive heat, the electrodes will burn away quickly and in some instances, preignition may result. Preignition takes place when plug tips get so hot that they glow sufficiently to ignite the fuel/air mixture before the actual spark occurs. This early ignition will usually cause a pinging during low speeds and heavy loads.

The general rule of thumb of choosing the correct heat range when picking a spark plug is: if most of your driving is long distance, high speed travel, use a cooler plug; if most of your driving is stop and go, use a hotter plug. Original equipment plugs are compromise plugs, but most people never have occasion to change their plugs from the factory recommended heat range.

REPLACING SPARK PLUGS

WARNING: Two different plug designs are used on early 1.6L engines. The designs are: gasket equipped and tapered seat (no gasket). All 1981 Escort/Lynx models, and 1982 EXP/LN7 models built before 9/4/81 use gasket equipped plugs. All 1982 and later Escort/Lynx and EXP/LN7 models built after 9/4/81 are equipped with tapered seat plugs. DO NOT INTERCHANGE TYPES! Tighten gasket equipped plugs to 17-22 ft.lb. Tapered plugs are tightened to 10-15 ft.lb. DO NOT OVERTIGHTEN!

A Set of spark plugs usually requires replacement every 30,000 miles, depending on your style of driving. In normal operation, plug gap increases about 0.001" (0.025mm) for every 1,000-2,500 miles. As the gap increases, the plug's voltage requirement also increases. It requires greater voltage to jump the wider gap and about two to three times as much voltage to fire a plug at higher speeds than at idle.

The spark plugs used in your car require a deep spark plug socket for removal and installation. A special designed pair of plug wire removal pliers is also a good tool to have. The special pliers have cupped jaws that grip the plug wire boot and make the job of twisting and pulling the wire from the plug easier.

REMOVAL & INSTALLATION

NOTE: The original spark plug wires are marked for cylinder location. If replacement wires have been installed, be sure to tag them for proper location. It is a good idea to remove the wires one at a time, service the spark plug, reinstall the wire and move onto the next cylinder.

For easy access for servicing the spark plugs, remove the air cleaner assembly and air intake tube.

1. Twist the spark plug boot and gently pull it and the wire from the spark plug. This is where the special plug wire pliers come in handy.

CAUTION

Never pull on the wire itself, damage to the inside conductor could occur.

2. The plug wire boot has a cover which shields the plug cavity (in the head) against dirt. After removing the wire, blow out the cavity with air or clean it out with a small brush so dirt will not fall into the engine when the spark plug is removed.
3. Remove the spark plug with a plug socket. Turn the socket counterclockwise to remove the plug. Be sure to hold the socket straight on the plug to avoid breaking the insulator (a deep socket designed for spark plugs has a rubber cushion built-in to help prevent plug breakage).
4. Once the plug is out, compare it with the spark plug illustrations to determine the engine condition. This is crucial since spark plug readings are vital signs of engine condition and pending problems.
5. If the old plugs are to be reused, clean and regap them. If new spark plugs are to be installed, always check the gap. Use a round wire feeler gauge to check plug gap. The correct size gauge should pass through the electrode gap with a slight drag. If you're in doubt, try the next smaller and one size larger. The smaller gauge should go through easily and the larger should not go through at all. If adjustment is necessary use the bending tool on the end of the gauge. When adjusting the gap, always bend the side electrode. The center electrode is non-adjustable.
6. Squirt a drop of penetrating oil on the threads of the spark plug and install it. Don't oil the threads heavily. Turn the plug in clockwise by hand until it is snug.
7. When the plug is finger tight, tighten it to the proper torque 17-22 ft.lb. DO NOT OVERTIGHTEN.
8. Install the plug wire and boot firmly over the spark plug after coating the inside of the boot and terminal with a thin coat of dielectric compound (Motorcraft D7AZ-19A331-A or the equivalent).
9. Proceed to the next spark plug.

CHECKING AND REPLACING SPARK PLUG CABLES

Your car is equipped with a electronic ignition system which utilizes 8mm wires to conduct the hotter spark produced. The boots on these wires are designed to cover the spark plug cavities on the cylinder head.

Inspect the wires without removing them from the spark plugs, distributor cap or coil. Look for visible damage such as cuts, pinches, cracks or torn boots. Replace any wires that show damage. If the boot is damaged, it may be replaced by itself. It is not necessary to replace the complete wire just for the boot.

If no physical damage is obvious, remove the distributor cap with the wires attached and use an ohmmeter to check the resistance. Normal resistance should be less than 7,000Ω per foot of wire length. If resistance exceeds 7,000Ω per foot, replace the wire.

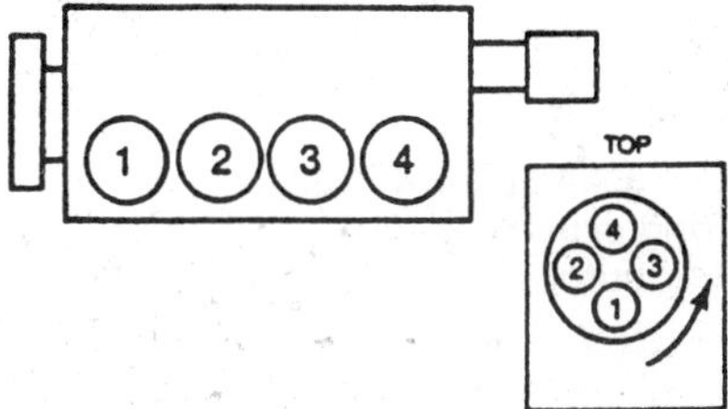

Escort/Lynx 1.3L, 1.6L, 1.9L engines
Firing order: 1-3-4-2
Distributor rotation: counterclockwise

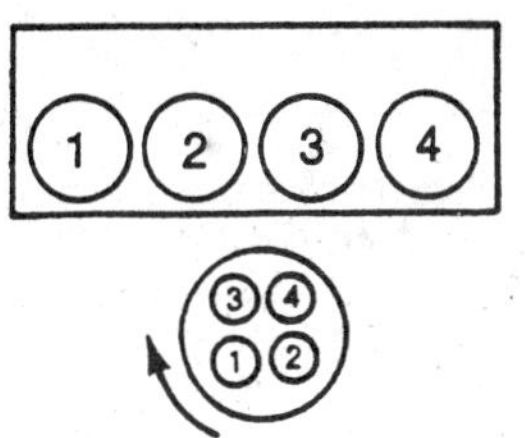

Tempo, Topaz 2.3L engine
Firing order; 1-3-4-2
Distributor rotation: clockwise

CAUTION

Do not, under any circumstances, puncture a spark plug wire with a sharp probe when checking resistance.

To replace the wire, grasp and twist the boot back and forth while pulling away from the spark plug. Use a special pliers if available.

NOTE: Always coat the terminals of any wire removed or replaced with a thin layer of dielectric compound.

When installing a wire be sure it is firmly mounted over or on the plug, distributor cap connector or coil terminal.

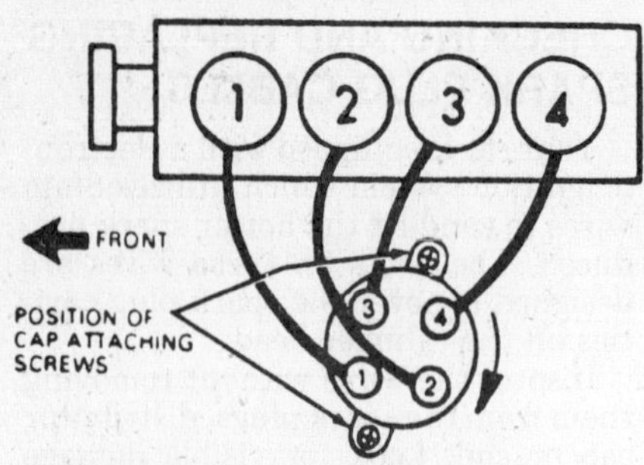

Ford 2500 cc 4 cyl (2.5L)
Firing order: 1–3–4–2
Distributor rotation: clockwise

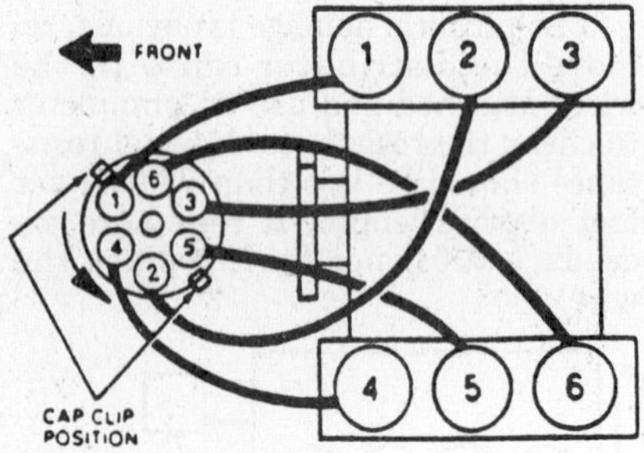

Ford 3000 cc 6 cyl (3.0L)
Firing order: 1–4–2–5–3–6
Distributor rotation: counterclockwise

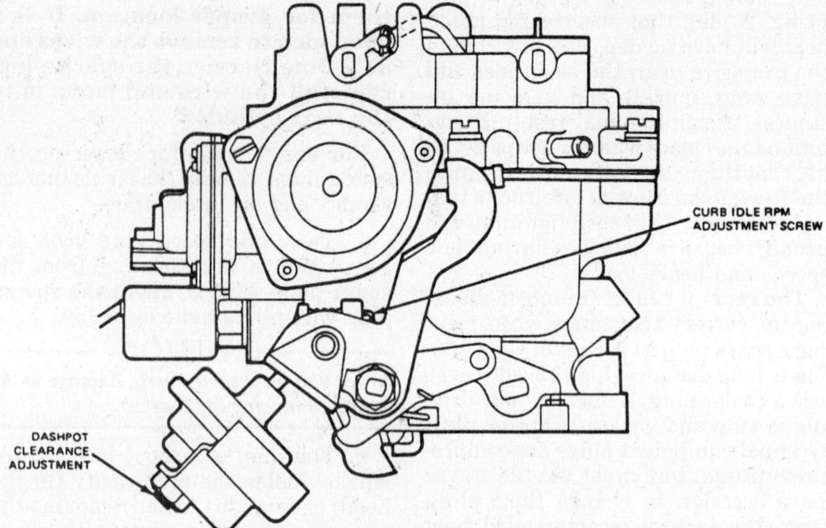

Location of curb idle adjusting screw

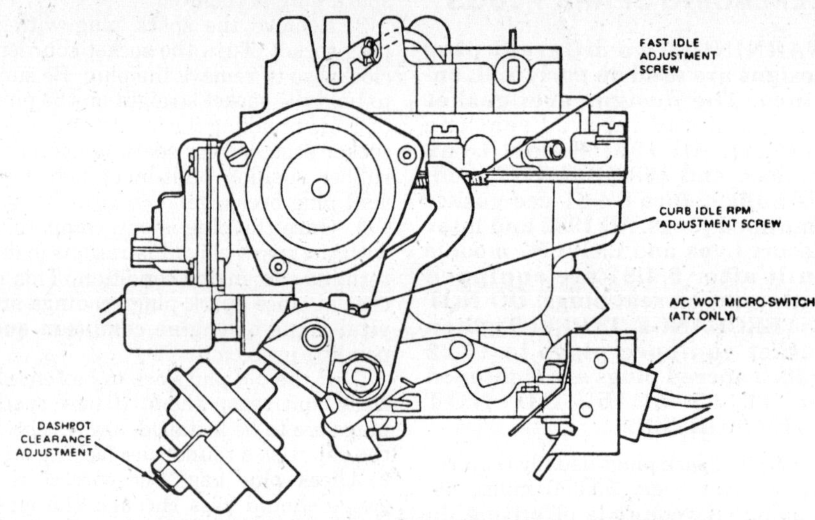

740 carburetor—fast idle and curb idle rpm adjustments

IDLE SPEED AND MIXTURE

NOTE: A tachometer must be used while making any idle rpm adjustments. Refer to the preceding section for tach hook up instructions.

Refer to emissions decal for idle speed and specific instructions. If the decal instructions differ from the following procedures, use the decal procedures. They reflect current production changes.

CURB IDLE

1.6L Engine w/740 Carb w/o Idle Speed Control

1. Place the transmission in Neutral or Park, set the parking brake and block the wheels. Connect tachometer.
2. Bring the engine to normal operating temperature.
3. Disconnect and plug the vacuum hose at the thermactor air control valve bypass sections.
4. Place the fast idle adjustment screw on the second highest step of the fast idle cam. Run engine until cooling fan comes on.
5. Slightly depress the throttle to allow the fast idle cam to rotate. Place the transmission in specified gear, and check/adjust the curb idle rpm to specification.

NOTE: Engine cooling fan must be running when checking curb idle rpm. (Use a jumper wire is necessary).

6. Place the transmission in Neutral or Park. Rev the engine momentarily. Place transmission in specified position and recheck curb idle rpm. Readjust if requires.
7. If the vehicle is equipped with a dashpot, check/adjust clearance to specification.
8. Remove the plug from the hose at the thermactor air control valve bypass sections and reconnect.
9. If the vehicle is equipped with an automatic transmission and curb idle adjustment is more than 50 rpm, an automatic transmission linkage adjustment may be necessary.

1.6L, 1.9L Engines w/740 & 5740 Carb – Mechanical Vacuum Idle Speed Control (ISC)

1. Place the transmission in Neutral or Park, set the parking brake and block the wheels. Connect tachometer.
2. Bring the engine to normal operating temperature.
3. Disconnect and plug the vacuum hose at the thermactor air control valve bypass section.
4. Place the fast idle adjustment

screw on the second highest step of the fast idle cam. Run the engine until cooling fan comes on.

5. Slightly depress the throttle to allow fast idle cam to rotate. Place the transmission in Drive (fan on) and check curb idle rpm to specification.

NOTE: Engine cooling fan must be running when checking curb idle rpm.

6. If adjustment is required:

a. Place the transmission in Park, deactivate the ISC by removing the vacuum hose at the ISC and plugging the hose.

b. Turn ISC adjusting screw until ISC plunger is clear of the throttle lever.

c. Place the transmission in Drive position, if rpm is not at the ISC retracted speed (fan on), adjust rpm by turning the throttle stop adjusting screw.

d. Place the transmission in Park, remove plug from the ISC vacuum line and reconnect the ISC.

e. Place transmission in Drive if rpm is not at the curb idle speed (fan on), adjust by turning the ISC adjustment screw.

7. Place transmission in Neutral or Park. Rev the engine momentarily. Place the transmission in specified position and recheck curb idle rpm. Readjust if required.

8. Remove the plug from the thermactor air control valve bypass section hose and reconnect.

9. If the vehicle is equipped with an automatic transmission and curb idle adjustment is more than 50 rpm, an automatic transmission linkage adjustment may be necessary.

1.6L, 1.9L Engines w/740 & 5740 Carb – Vacuum Operated Throttle Modulator (VOTM)

1. Place the transmission in Neutral or Park, set the parking brake and block the wheels. Connect the tachometer.

2. Bring the engine to normal operating temperature.

3. To check/adjust VOTM rpm:

• Place A/C heat selector in Heat position, blower switch on High.

• Disconnect the vacuum hose from VOTM and plug, install a slave vacuum hose from the intake manifold vacuum to the VOTM.

4. Disconnect and plug the vacuum hose at the Thermactor air control valve bypass section.

5. Run the engine until the engine cooling fan comes on.

6. Place the transmission in specified gear, and check/adjust VOTM rpm to specification.

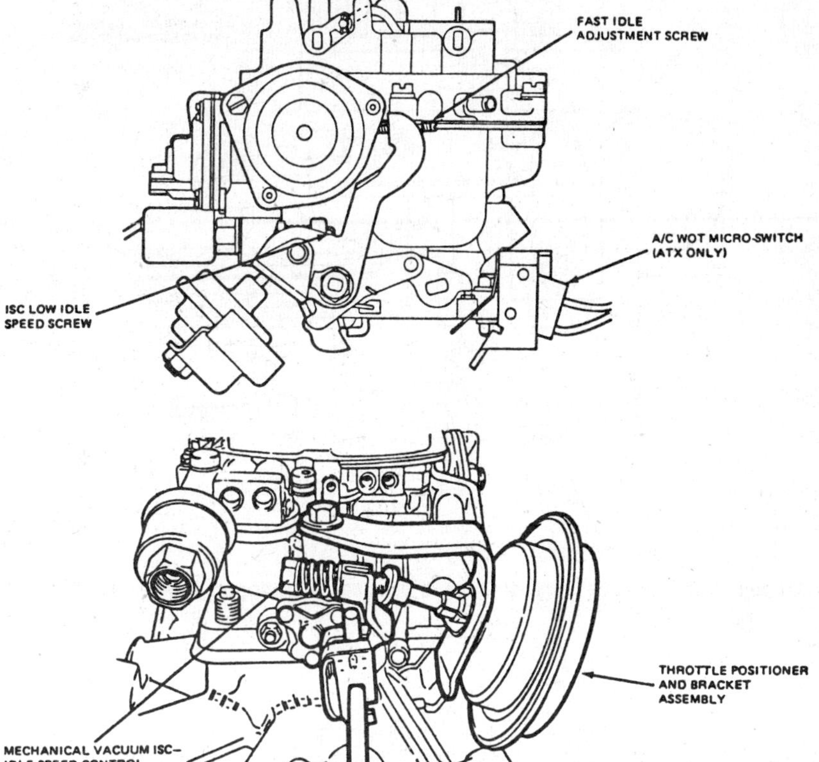

740 carburetor–mechanical idle speed control–curb idle

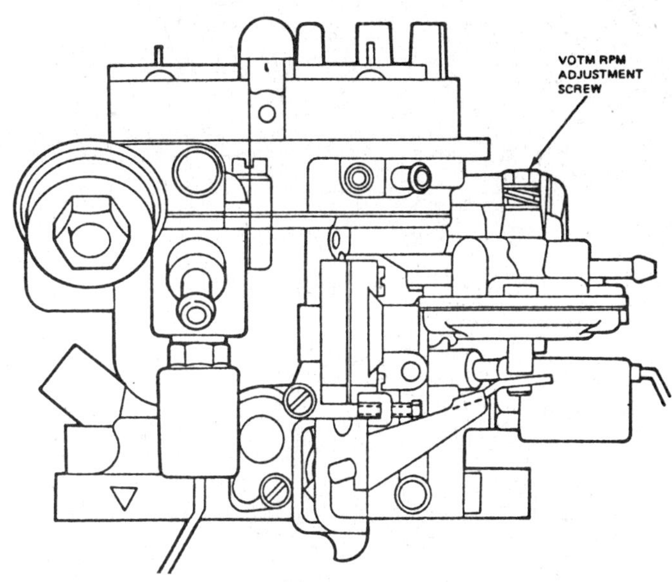

740 carburetor–VOTM adjustment

NOTE: Engine cooling fan must be running when checking VOTM rpm. Adjust rpm by turning screw on VOTM.

7. Remove the slave vacuum hose. Remove the plug from the VOTM vacuum hose and reconnect the hose to the VOTM.

8. Return the intake manifold vacuum supply source to original location.

9. Remove the plug from the vacuum hose at the Thermactor air control valve bypass section and reconnect.

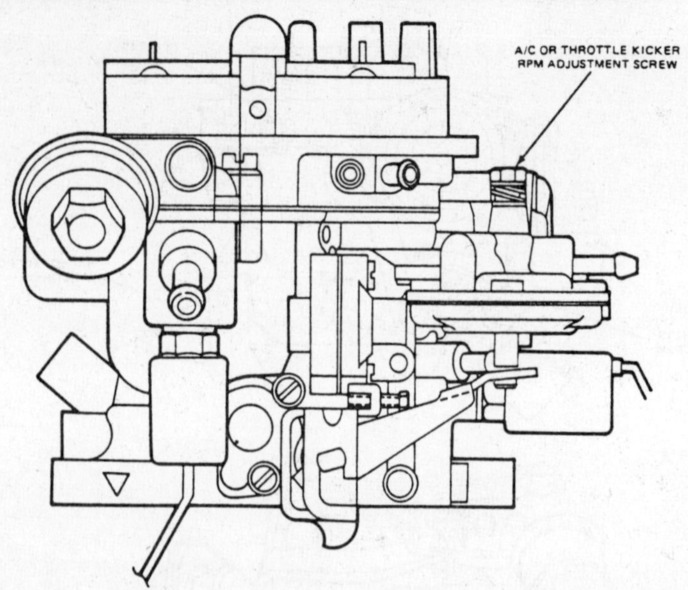

An adjustment is necessary, at times, if your car is equipped with air conditioning

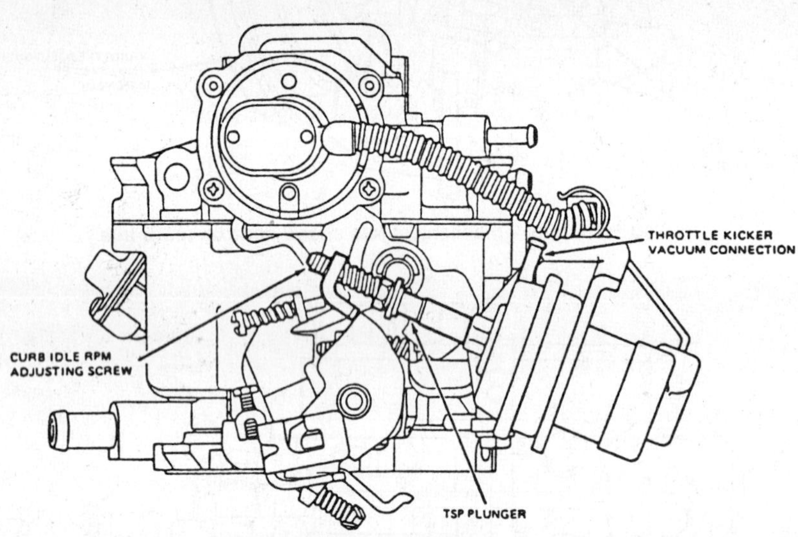

1949/6149FB – Curb idle adjustment

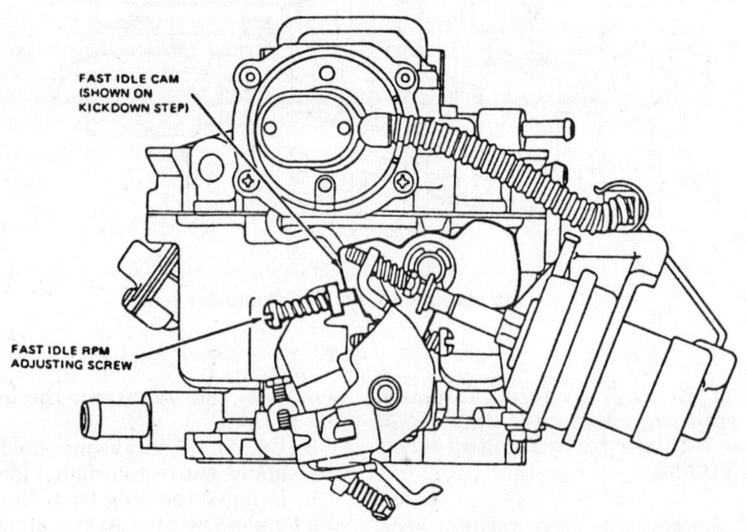

1949/6149FB – Fast isle adjustment

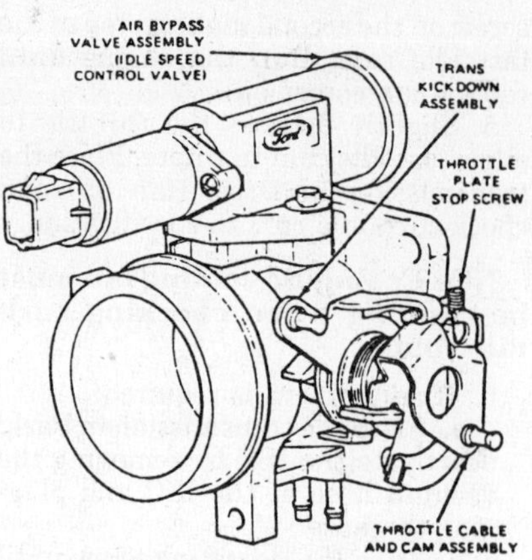

EFI – air intake throttle body assembly

Dashpot Clearance Adjustment 1.6, 1.9L Engines

NOTE: If the carburetor is equipped with a dashpot, it must be adjusted if the curb ilde speed is adjusted.

1. With the engine OFF, push the dashpot plunger in as far as possible and check the clearance between the plunger and the throttle lever pad.

NOTE: Refer to the emissions decal for proper dashpot clearance. If not available, set clearance to 0.138″ ± 0.020″ (3.5mm ± 0.5mm).

2. Adjust the dashpot clearance by loosening the mounting locknut and rotating the dashpot.

CAUTION

If the locknut is very tight, remove the mounting bracket, hold it in a suitable device, so that it will not bend, and loosen the locknut. Reinstall bracket and dashpot.

3. After gaining the required clearance, tighten the locknut and recheck adjustment.

Fast Idle RPM – 1.6L, 1.9L Engines

1. Place the transmission in Neutral or Park, set the parking brake and block the wheels. Connect tachometer.
2. Bring the engine to normal operating temperature.
3. Disconnect the vacuum hose at the EGR and plug.
4. Place the fast idle adjustment screw on the second highest step of the fast idle cam. Run engine until cooling fan comes on.
5. Check/adjust fast idle rpm to specification. If adjustment is required, loosen locknut, adjust and retighten.

NOTE: Engine cooling fan must be running when checking fast idle rpm. (Use a jumper wire is necessary).

6. Remove the plug from the EGR hose and reconnect.

Air Conditioning/Throttle Kicker Adjustment – 1.6L, 1.9L Engine

1. Place the transmission in Neutral or Park.
2. Bring engine to normal operating temperature.
3. Identify vacuum source to air bypass section of air supply control valve. If vacuum hose is connected to carburetor, disconnect and plug hose at air supply control valve. Install slave vacuum hose between intake manifold and air bypass connection on air supply control valve.
4. To check/adjust A/C or throttle kicker rpm:
   - If vehicle is equipped with A/C, place selector to maximum cooling, blower switch on High. Disconnect A/C compressor clutch wire.
   - If vehicle is equipped with kicker and no A/C, disconnect vacuum hose from kicker and plug, install slave vacuum hose from intake manifold vacuum to kicker.
5. Run engine until engine cooling fan comes on.
6. Place transmission in specified gear and check/adjust A/C or throttle kicker rpm to specification.

NOTE: Engine cooling fan must be running when checking A/C or throttle kicker rpm. Adjust rpm by turning screw on kicker.

7. If slave vacuum hose was installed to check/adjust kicker rpm, remove slave vacuum hose. Remove plug from kicker vacuum hose and reconnect hose to kicker.
8. Remove slave vacuum hose. Return intake manifold supply source to original condition. Remove plug from carburetor vacuum hose and reconnect to air bypass valve.

1.6L, 1.9L Engine w/Electronic Fuel Injection (EFI) – Initial Engine RPM Adjustment (ISC Disconnected)

NOTE: Curb idle RPM is controlled by the EEC IV processor and the Idle Speed Control (ISC) device (part of the fuel charging assembly). The purpose of this procedure is to provide a means of verifying the initial engine RPM setting with the ISC disconnected. If engine idle RPM is not within specification after performing this procedure, it will be necessary to have 1.6L, 1.9L EFI EEC IV diagnostics performed.

1. Place the transmission Neutral or Park, set the parking brake and block the wheels. Connect tachometer.
2. Bring the engine to the normal operating temperature and shut engine off.
3. Disconnect vacuum connector at the EGR solenoids and plug both lines.
4. Disconnect the idle speed control (ISC) power lead.
5. Electric cooling fan must be on during the idle speed setting procedure.
6. Start the engine and operate at 2,000 RPM for 60 seconds.
7. Place transmission in Neutral for MT and Drive for AT, check/adjust initial engine RPM within 120 seconds by adjusting throttle plate screw.
8. If idle adjustment is not completed within 120 second time limit, shut engine Off, restart and repeat Steps 6 and 7.
9. If the vehicle is equipped with an automatic transmission and initial engine RPM adjustment increases or decreases by more than 50 RPM, an automatic transmission linkage adjustment may be necessary.
10. Turn the engine Off and remove the plugs from the EGR vacuum lines at the EGR solenoid and reconnect.
11. Reconnect the idle speed control (ISC) power lead.

2.3L HSC Engine w/1949 and 6149 FB Curb Idle

NOTE: A/C-On RPM is non-adjustable. TSP-Off RPM is not required. Verify that TSP plunger extends with ignition key On.

1. Place the transaxle in Neutral or Park, set the parking brake and block the wheels. Connect tachometer.
2. Disconnect the throttle kicker vacuum line and plug.
3. Bring the engine to normal operating temperature. (Cooling fan should cycle).
4. Place the A/C selector in the Off position.
5. Place gear selector in specified position.
6. Activate the cooling fan by grounding the control wire with a jumper wire.
7. Check/adjust curb idle rpm. If adjustment is required, turn curb idle adjusting screw.
8. Place the transaxle in Neutral or Park. Rev the engine momentarily. Place the transaxle in specified position and recheck curb idle rpm. Readjust if required.
9. Reconnect the cooling fan wiring.
10. Turn the ignition key to the Off position.
11. Reconnect the vacuum line to the throttle kicker.
12. If the vehicle is equipped with an automatic transaxle and curb idle adjustment exceeds 50 rpm, an automatic transaxle linkage adjustment may be necessary.
13. Remove all test equipment and reinstall the air cleaner assembly.

2.3L HSC Engine w/1949 and 6149 FB TSP Off RPM

NOTE: This adjustment is not required as part of a normal engine idle RPM check/adjustment. Use if engine continues to run after ignition key is turned to OFF position.

1. Place the transaxle in Neutral or Park, set the parking brake and block the wheels. Connect tachometer.
2. Bring the engine to normal operating temperature.
3. Disconnect the throttle kicker vacuum line and plug.
4. Place the A/C selector to Off position.
5. Disconnect the electrical lead to the TSP and verify that plunger collapses. Check/adjust engine RPM to specification (600 RPM).
6. Adjust the TSP Off RPM to specification.
7. Shut the engine off, reconnect TSP electrical lead and throttle kicker vacuum line.

2.3L HSC Engine w/1949 and 6149 FB Fast Idle RPM

1. Place the transaxle in Neutral or Park, set the parking brake and block the wheels.
2. Bring the engine to normal operating temperature with the carburetor set on second step of fast idle cam.
3. Return the throttle to normal idle position.
4. Place the A/C selector in the Off position.
5. Disconnect the vacuum hose at the EGR valve and plug.
6. Place the fast idle adjusting screw on the specific step of the fast idle cam.
7. Check/adjust the fast idle rpm to specification.
8. Rev the engine momentarily, allowing engine to return to idle and turn ignition key to Off position.
9. Remove the plug from the EGR vacuum hose and reconnect.

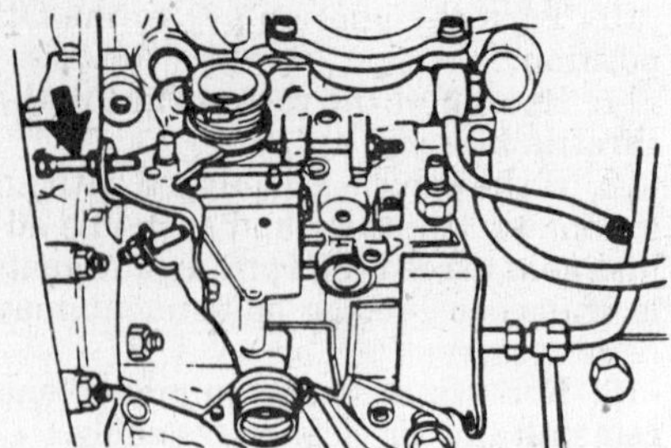

Diesel engine idle speed adjustment location

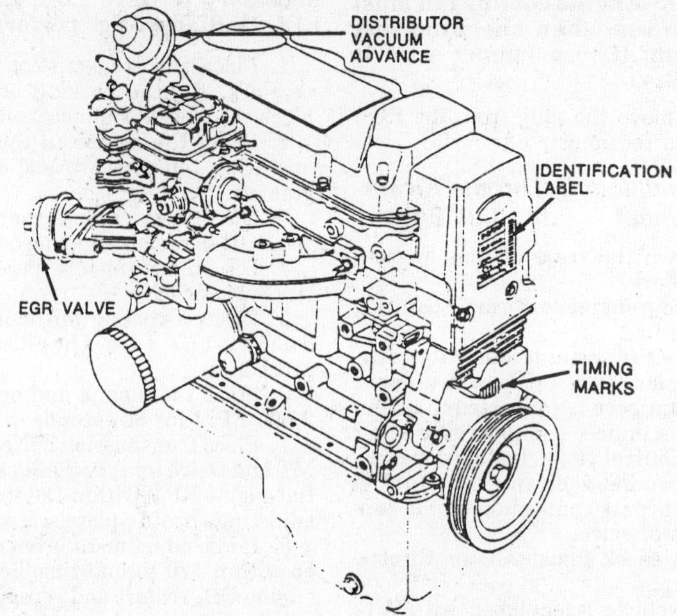

1.6L, 1.9L timing marks on the front cover

Diesel Engine

CURB IDLE

NOTE: A special diesel engine tachometer is required for this procedure.

1. Place the transmission in Neutral.
2. Bring the engine up to normal operating temperature. Stop engine.
3. Remove the timing hole cover. Clean the flywheel surface and install reflective tape.
4. Idle speed is measured with manual transmission in Neutral.
5. Check curb idle speed, using Rotunda 99-0001 or equivalent. Curb idle speed is specified on the vehicle Emissions Control Information decal (VECI). Adjust to specification by loosening the locknut on the idle speed bolt. Turn the idle speed adjusting bolt clockwise to increase, or counterclockwise to decrease engine idle speed. Tighten the locknut.
6. Place transmission in Neutral. Rev engine momentarily and recheck the curb idle RPM. Readjust if necessary.
7. Turn A/C On. Check the idle speed. Adjust to specification by loosening the nut on the A/C throttle kicker and rotating the screw.

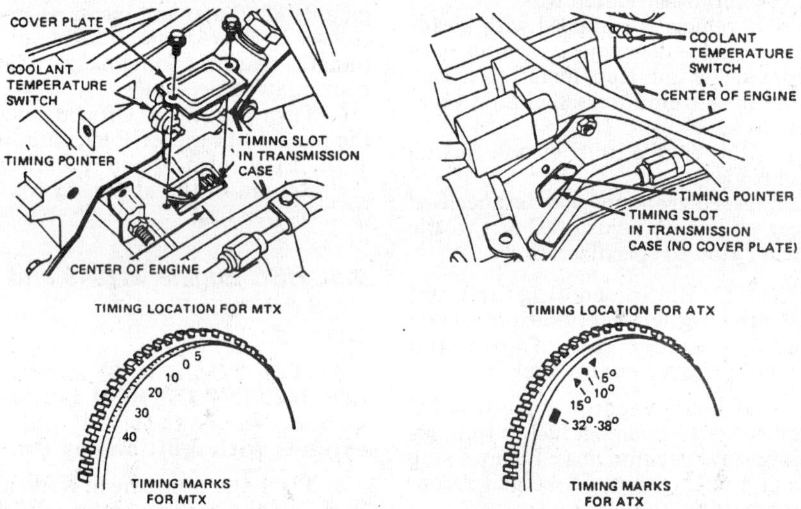

Timing marks and indentification—2.3L HSC engine

IGNITION TIMING

1. Timing marks on 1.3L, 1.6L, and 1.9L engines consist of a notch on the crankshaft pulley and a graduated scale molded into the camshaft drive belt cover. The number of degrees before or after TDC (top dead center) represented by each mark can be interpreted according to the decal affixed to the top of the belt cover (emissions decal).
2. Timing marks on 2.3 HSC engines are located on the flywheel edge (manual transaxle or flywheel face (automatic transaxle) and are visible through a slot in the transaxle case at the back of the engine. A cover plate retained by two screws must be removed to view the timing marks on manual cars. Each mark (small graduation) equals 2°. Early automatic cars have timing marks punched on the flywheel, the marks are 5° apart. The required degree mark should align with the timing slot pointer. Unless the emission decal specifies otherwise, timing for manual transaxle models is 10° BTDC and 15° BTDC for automatic transaxle models.
3. Turn the engine until No. 1 piston is at TDC on the compression stroke. Apply white paint or chalk to the rotating timing mark (notch on pulley or flywheel) after cleaning the metal surface.
4. Refer to the emissions decal for timing, engine rpm and vacuum hose (if equipped) status information. Disconnect and plug the distributor vacuum line(s) if equipped and required. On models equipped with the EEC IV system engine, disconnect the ignition spout wire (circuit 36-yellow/light green dots or black) from the distributor connector. On 1.6/1.9L engines equipped with a 2-bbl carburetor, disconnect the barometric pressure switch and connect a jumper wire across the ignition module black and yellow wire connector pins.
5. Attach a timing light and tachometer to the engine. Start the engine and allow to idle until normal operating temperature is reached.

Hook up to test on coil "Bat" terminal

"E" coil tachometer connection

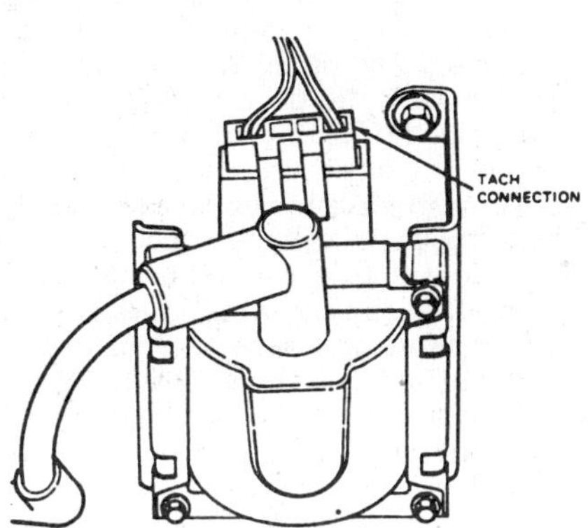

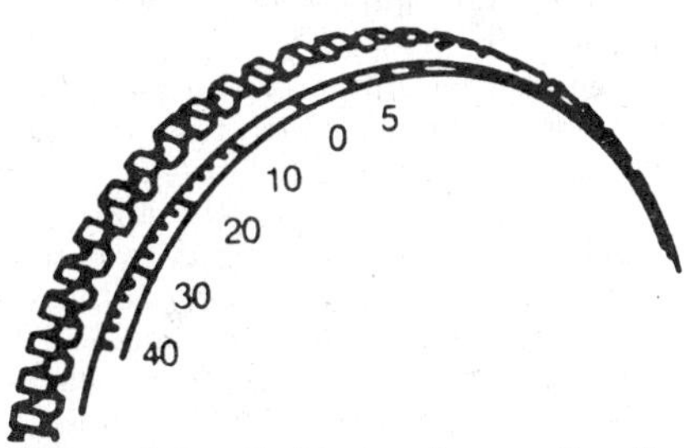

View of the timing marks on the flywheel—2.5L engine with M/T

View of the timing marks on the flywheel—2.5L engine with A/T

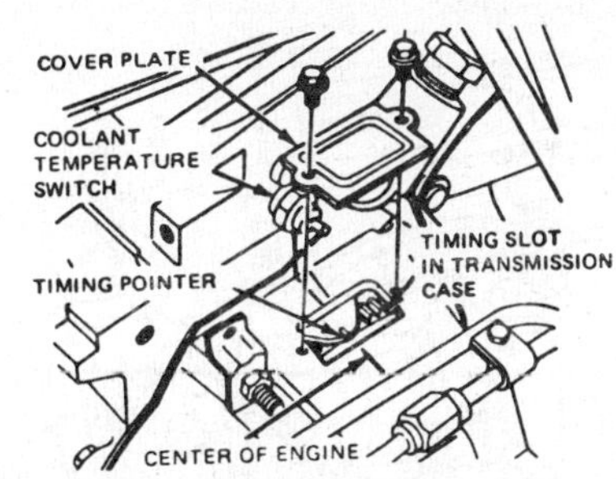

Location of the timing marks—2.5L engine with M/T

Location of the timing marks—2.5L engine with A/T

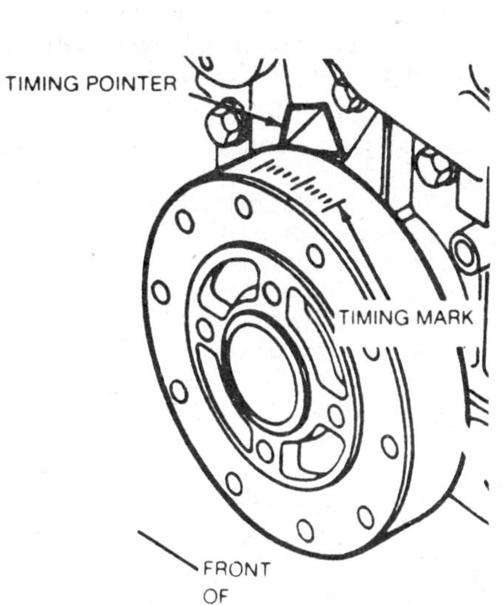

View of the timing marks on the 3.0L engine

TACHOMETER HOOKUP

Models equipped with a conventional type coil have an adapter on the top of the coil that provides a clip marked Tach Test. On models (TFI) equipped with an **E** type coil, the tach connection is made at the back of the wire harness connector. A cutout is provided and the tachometer lead wire alligator clip can be connected to the dark green/yellow dotted wire of the electrical harness plug.

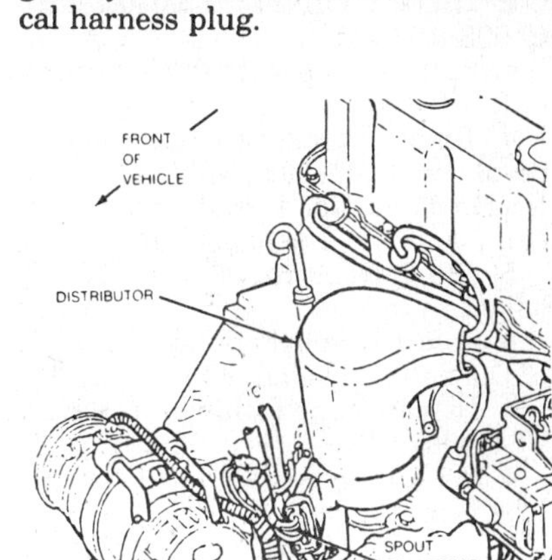

View of the in-line spout connector

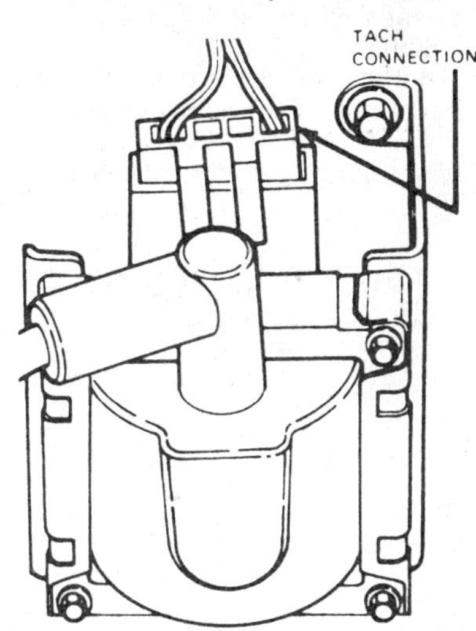

View of the tachometer connecting point of the "E" coil

6. Be sure the parking brake is applied and wheels blocked. Place the transmission in gear specified on emissions decal. Check idle rpm and adjust if necessary.

7. Aim the flashing timing light at the timing marks. If the proper marks are not aligned, loosen the distributor holddown bolt/nut slightly and rotate the distributor body until the marks are aligned. Tighten the holddown.

8. Recheck the ignition timing, readjust if necessary. Shut off the engine and reconnect vacuum hoses or spout connector. Start engine and readjust idle rpm is necessary.

VALVE LASH

VALVE LASH ADJUSTMENT

Gasoline Engines

The intake and exhaust valves are driven by the camshaft, working through hydraulic lash adjusters and stamped steel rocker arms. The lash adjusters eliminate the need for periodic valve lash adjustments.

Diesel Engine

1. Disconnect breather hose from the intake manifold and remove camshaft cover.
2. Rotate crankshaft until No. 1 piston is at TDC on the compression stroke.
3. Using a Go-No-Go feeler gauge, check the valve shim to cam lobe clearance for No. 1 and No. 2 intake valves, and No. 1 and No.3 exhaust valves.
   - Intake Valves: 0.20-0.30mm (0.008-0.011").
   - Exhaust Valves: 0.30-0.40mm (0.011-0.015").
4. Rotate crankshaft one complete revolution. Measure valve clearance for No.3 and No. 4 intake valves, and No. 2 and No. 4 exhaust valves.
5. If a valve is out of specifications, adjust as follows:
   - Rotate crankshaft until the lobe of the valve to be adjusted is down.
   - Install cam follower retainer, T84P-6513-B.
   - Rotate crankshaft until the cam lobe is on the base circle.
   - Using O-ring pick tool T71P-19703-C or equivalent, pry the valve adjusting shim out of the cam follower.
   - Valve shims are available in thicknesses ranging from 3.40mm to 4.60mm.
   - If the valve was too tight, install a new shim, of the appropriate size.
   - If the valve was too loose, install a new shim of the appropriate size.

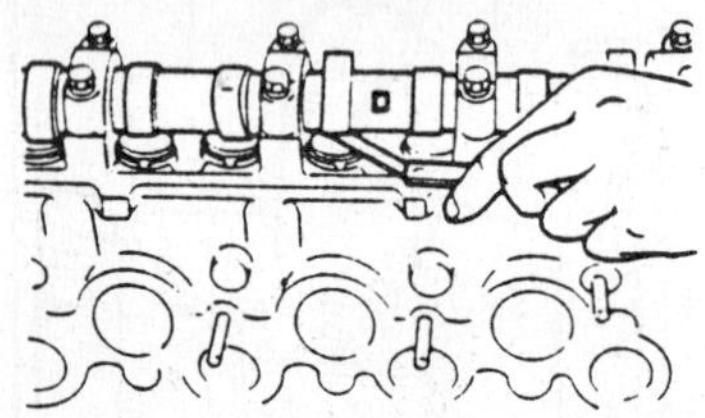

Checking the diesel engine valve clearance

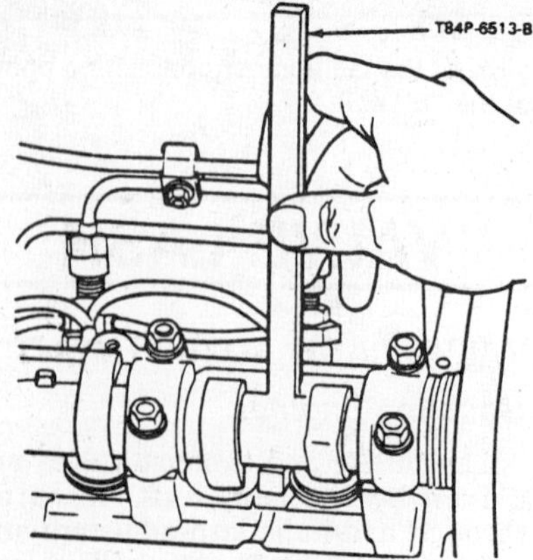

Cam follower retainer

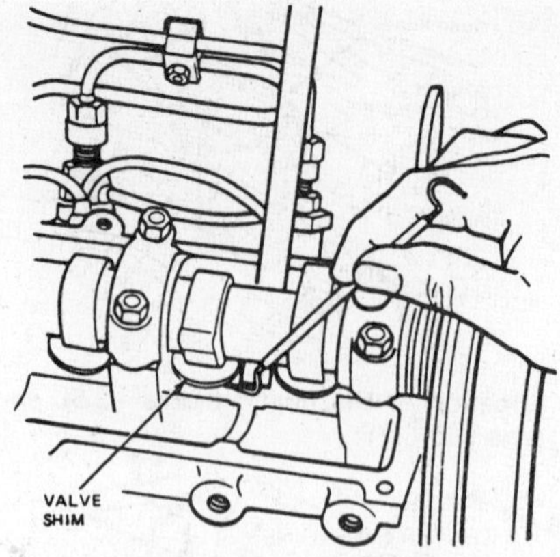

Shim removal adjustment

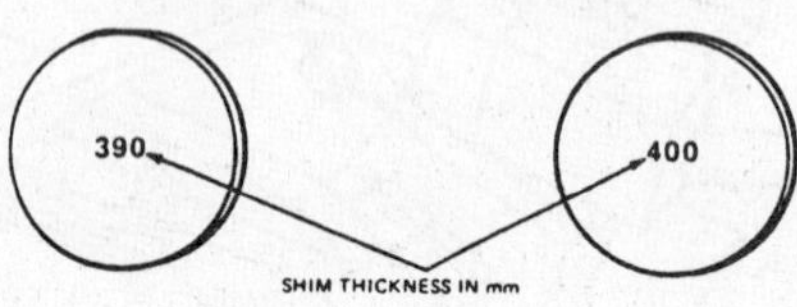

Valve shims

NOTE: Shim thickness is stamped on valve shim. Install new shim with numbers down, to avoid wearing the numbers off the shim. If numbers have been worn off, use a micrometer to measure shim thickness.

6. Rotate crankshaft until cam lobe is down and remove cam follower retainer.
7. Recheck valve clearance.
8. Repeat Steps 4, 5 and 6 for each valve to be adjusted.
9. Make sure the camshaft cover gasket is fully seated in the camshaft cover and install valve cover. Tighten bolts to 5-7 ft.lb.
10. Connect breather hose.

Electronic Ignition System

NOTE: This book contains simple testing procedures for your Ford's electronic ignition. More comprehensive testing on this system and other electronic control systems on your Ford can be found in CHILTON'S GUIDE TO ELECTRONIC ENGINE CONTROLS, book part number 7535, available at your local retailer.

Your car uses an electronic ignition system. The purpose of using an electronic ignition system is: To eliminate the deterioration of spark quality which occur in the breaker point ignition system as the breaker points wore. To extend maintenance intervals. To provide a more intense and reliable spark at every firing impulse in order to ignite the leaner gas mixtures necessary to control emissions.

The breaker points, point actuating cam and the condenser have been eliminated in the solid state distributor. They are replaced by an ignition module and a magnetic pulse-signal generator (pick-up).

The Dura Spark II is a pulse triggered, transistor controlled breakerless ignition system. With the ignition switch **ON**, the primary circuit is on and the ignition coil is energized. When the armature spokes approach the magnetic pick-up coil assembly, they induce a voltage which tells the amplifier to turn the coil primary current off. A timing circuit in the amplifier module will turn the current on again after the coil field has collapsed. When the current is on, it flows from the battery through the ignition switch, the primary windings of the ignition coil, and through the amplifier module circuits to ground. When the current is off, the magnetic field built up in the ignition coil is allowed to collapse, inducing a high voltage into the secondary windings of the coil. High voltage is produced each time the field is thus built up and collapsed.

A Universal Distributor equipped with either a TFI-I or TFI-IV system is used on some models, depending on year, engine option, and model. TFI stands for Thick Film Integrated which incorporates a molded thermoplastic module mounted on the distributor base. Models equipped with TFI also use an **E** coil which replaces the oil filled design used with Dura-Spark.

The Universal Distributor equipped with TFI-IV uses a vane switch stator assembly which replace the coil stator. The IV system incorporates provision for fixed octane adjustment and has no centrifugal or vacuum advance mechanisms. All necessary timing requirements are handled by the EEC-IV electronic engine control system.

TACHOMETER HOOKUP

Models equipped with a conventional type coil have an adapter on the top of the coil that provides a clip marked Tach Test. On models (TFI) equipped with an **E** type coil, the tach connection is made at the back of the wire harness connector. A cutout is provided and the tachometer lead wire alligator clip can be connected to the dark green/yellow dotted wire of the electrical harness plug.

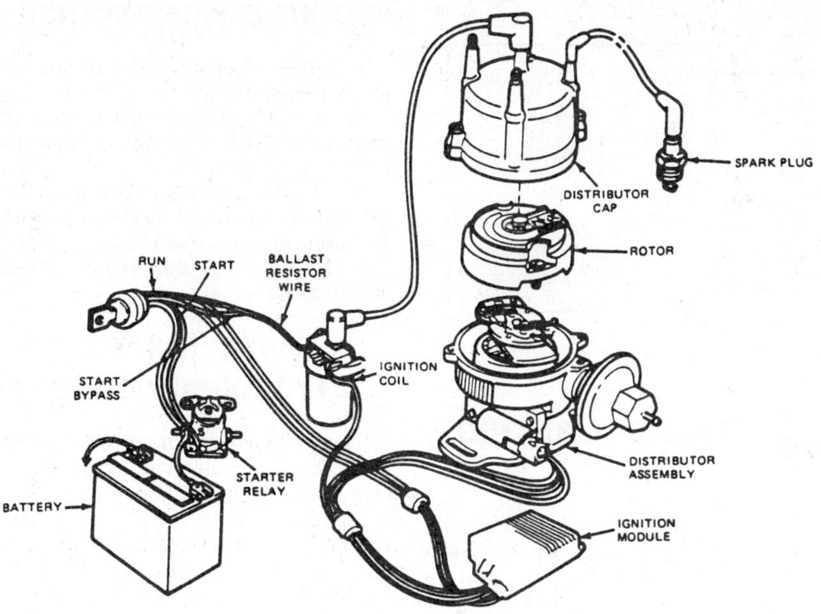

The Dura Spark ignition system

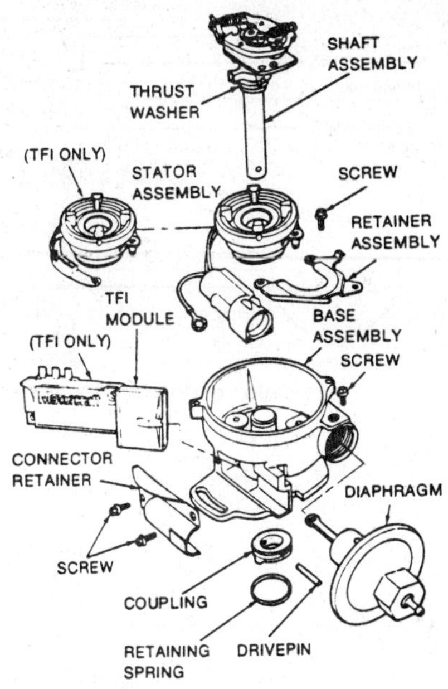

Semi-exploded view of the 1.6L, 1.9L non-EFI distributor

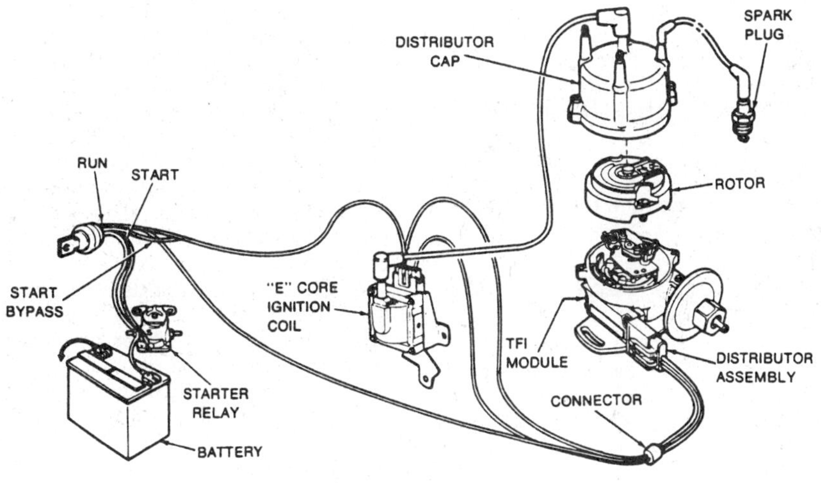

The TFI ignition system

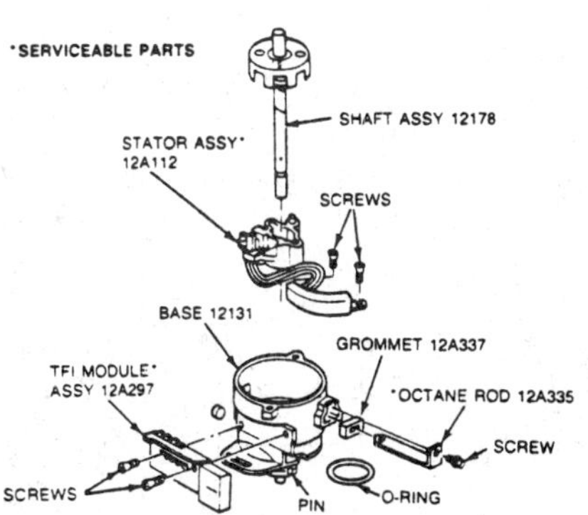

Semi-exploded view of the 1.6L, 1.9L EFI distributor

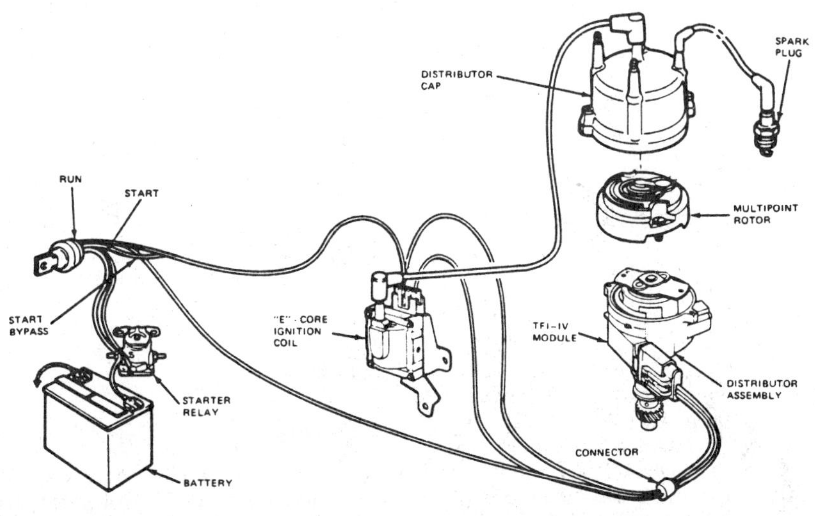

2.3L HSC TFI-IV on the Tempo/Topaz

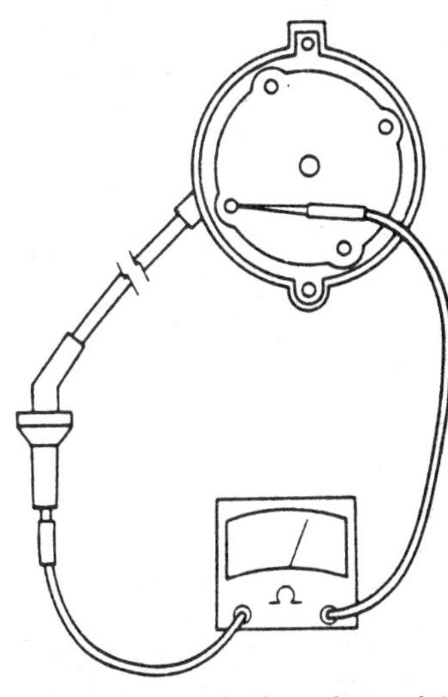

To check the spark plug wire resistance, measure from the cap terminal to the plug end of the wire with an ohmmeter. Resistance should be less than 5000 ohms per inch of plug wire length

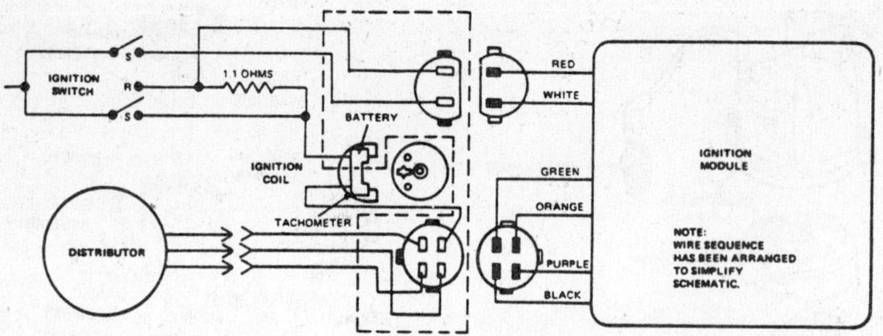

Color codes for the Dura Spark module and harness

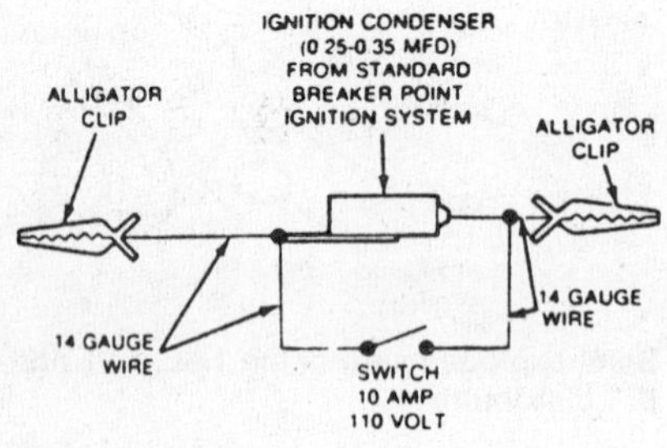

Test jumper switch used for trooubleshooting the Ford electronic ignition system

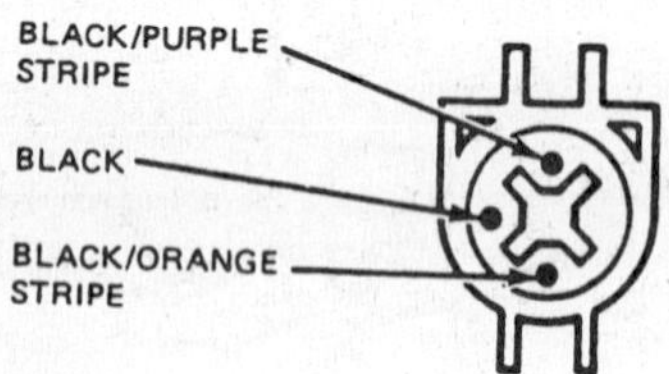

Dura Spark distributor connector color codes

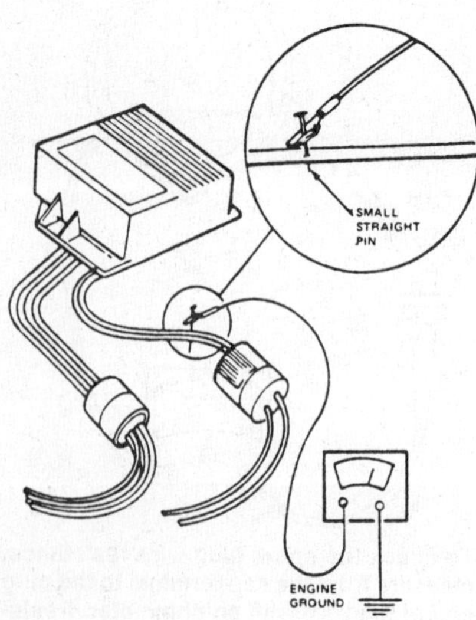

Inserting straight pint to test a circuit

Distributor Cap and Rotor

1. The distributor cap is held on by two cap screws. Release them with a screwdriver and lift the cap straight up and off, with the wires attached. Inspect the cap for cracks, carbon tracks, or a worn center contact. Replace it if necessary, transferring the wires one at a time from the old cap to the new.
2. Remove the screw retaining the ignition rotor and remove the rotor. Replace it if its contacts are worn, burned, or pitted. Do not file the contact.

NOTE: Always coat the cap and rotor contacts with dielectric compound.

CONTINUITY TEST – PLUG WIRES

1. Remove the distributor cap with plug wires attached.
2. Connect one end of an ohmmeter to the spark plug terminal end of the wire, the other to the inside corresponding terminal of the distributor cap.
3. Measure the resistance. If the reading is more than 5,000Ω per inch of cable, replace the wire.

Ignition Coil

PRIMARY RESISTANCE

1. Verify that the ignition switch is in the OFF position.
2. Remove the coil connector, clean and inspect for dirt or corrosion.
3. Measure the resistance between the positive and negative terminals of the coil with an ohmmeter. On TFI models, resistance should measure 0.3–1.0Ω. On Dura-Spark models, the resistance should measure 0.8–1.6Ω.
4. Replace the coil if resistance is not within specifications.

SECONDARY RESISTANCE

1. Follow Steps 1 and 2 of the Primary Resistance Test.
2. Measure resistance between the negative (BATT) and high tension lead terminal of the coil.
3. Resistance for Dura-Spark should be between 7,700–10,500Ω. TFI should be between 8000–11,500Ω.
4. Replace the coil if not within specifications.

Dura Spark II Troubleshooting

The following procedures can be used to determine whether the ignition system is working or not. If these procedures fail to locate and correct the problem, full troubleshooting procedures should be performed by a qualified service department.

PRELIMINARY CHECKS

1. Check the battery's state of charge and connections.
2. Inspect all wires and connections for breaks, cuts, abrasions, or burn spots. Repair as necessary.
3. Unplug all connectors one at a time and inspect for corroded or burned contacts. Repair and plug connectors back together. DO NOT remove the dielectric compound in the connectors.
4. Check for loose or damaged spark plug or coil wires. Check for excessive resistance. If the boots or nipples are removed on 8mm ignition wires, reline the inside of each with silicone dielectric compound (Motorcraft WA 10).

Special Tools

To perform the following tests, two special tools are needed: the ignition test jumper shown in the illustration and a modified spark plug. Use the illustration to assemble the ignition test jumper. The test jumper must be used when performing the following tests. The modified spark plug is basically a spark plug with the side electrode removed. Ford makes a special tool called a Spark Tester for this purpose, which besides not having a side electrode is equipped with a spring clip so that it can be grounded to engine metal. It is recommended that the Spark Tester be used as there is less chance of being shocked.

Run Mode Spark Test

NOTE: The wire colors given here are the main color of the wires, not the dots or stripe marks.

STEP 1

1. Remove the distributor cap and rotor from the distributor.

2. With the ignition off, turn the engine over by hand until one of the teeth on the distributor armature aligns with the magnet in the pick-up coil.

3. Remove the coil wire from the distributor cap. Install the modified spark plug (see Special Tools) in the coil wire terminal and using insulated pliers, hold the spark plug base against the engine block.

4. Turn the ignition to RUN (not START) and tap the distributor body with a screwdriver handle. There should be a spark at the modified spark plug or at the coil wire terminal.

5. If a good spark is evident, the primary circuit is OK, perform Start Mode Spark Test. If there is no spark, proceed to Step 2.

STEP 2

1. Unplug the module connector(s) which contain(s) the green and black module leads.

2. In the harness side of the connector(s), connect the special test jumper (see special tools) between the leads which connect the green and black leads of the module pig tails. Use paper clips on connector socket holes to make contact. Do not allow clips to ground.

3. Turn the ignition switch to RUN (not START) and close the test jumper switch. Leave closed for about one second, then open. Repeat several times. There should be a spark each time the switch is opened.

4. If there is NO spark, the problem is probably in the primary circuit through the ignition switch, the coil, the green lead or the black lead, or the ground connection in the distributor. Perform Step 3. If there IS a spark, the primary circuit wiring and coil are probably OK. The problem is probably in the distributor pick-up, the module red wire, or the module. Perform Step 6.

STEP 3

1. Disconnect the test jumper lead from the black lead and connect it to a good ground. Turn the test jumper switch on and off several times as in Step 2.

2. If there is NO spark, the problem is probably in the green lead, the coil, or the coil feed circuit. Perform Step 5.

3. If there IS spark, the problem is probably in the black lead or the distributor ground connections. Perform Step 4.

STEP 4

1. Connect an ohmmeter between the black lead and ground. With the meter on its lowest scale, there should be NO measurable resistance in the circuit. If there is resistance, check the distributor ground connections and the black lead from the module. Repair as necessary, remove the ohmmeter, plug in all connections and repeat Step 1.

2. If there is NO resistance, the primary ground wiring is OK. Perform Step 6.

STEP 5

1. Disconnect the test jumper from the green lead and ground and connect it between the TACH-TEST terminal of the coil and a good ground on the engine.

2. With the ignition switch in the RUN position, turn the jumper switch on. Hold it on for about one second then turn it off as in Step 2. Repeat several times. There should be a spark each time the switch is turned off. If there is NO spark, the problem is probably in the primary circuit running through the ignition switch to the coil BAT terminal, or in the coil itself. Check coil resistance (test given later in this section), and check the coil for internal shorts or opens. Check the coil feed circuit for opens, shorts or high resistance. Repair as necessary, reconnect all connectors and repeat Step 1. If there IS spark, the coil and its feed circuit are OK. The problem could be in the green lead between the coil and the module. Check for open or short, repair as necessary, reconnect all connectors and repeat Step 1.

STEP 6

To perform this step, a voltmeter which is not combined with a dwell meter is needed. The slight needle oscillations (0.5V) you'll be looking for may not be detectable on the combined voltmeter/dwell meter unit.

1. Connect a voltmeter between the orange and purple leads on the harness side of the module connectors.

CAUTION

On catalytic converter equipped cars, disconnect the air supply line between the Thermactor by-pass valve and the manifold before cranking the engine with the ignition off. This will prevent damage to the catalytic converter. After testing, run the engine for at least 3 minutes before reconnecting the by-pass valve, to clear excess fuel from the exhaust system.

2. Set the voltmeter on its lowest scale and crank the engine. The meter needle should oscillate slightly (about 0.5V). If the meter does not oscillate, check the circuit through the magnetic pick-up in the distributor for open shorts, shorts to ground and resistance. Resistance between the orange and purple leads should be 400–1,000Ω, and between each lead and ground should be more than 70,000Ω. Repair as necessary, reconnect all connectors and repeat Step 1.

3. If the meter oscillates, the problem is probably in the power feed to the module (red wire) or in the module itself. Proceed to Step 7.

STEP 7

1. Remove all meters and jumpers and plug in all connectors.

2. Turn the ignition switch to the RUN position and measure voltage between the battery positive terminal and engine ground. It should be 12 volts.

3. Next, measure voltage between the red lead of the module and engine ground. To make this measurement, it will be necessary to pierce the red wire with a straight pin and connect the voltmeter to the straight pin and to ground. DO NOT ALLOW THE STRAIGHT PIN TO GROUND ITSELF!

4. The two readings should be within one volts of each other. If not within one volt, the problem is in the power feed to the red lead. Check for shorts, open, or high resistance and correct as necessary. After repairs, repeat Step 1.

If the readings are within one volt, the problem is probably in the module. Replace with a good module and repeat Step 1. If this corrects the problem reconnect the old module and repeat Step 1. If the problem returns, replace the module.

Start Mode Spark Test

NOTE: The wire colors given here are the main color of the wires, not the dots and stripe marks.

1. Remove the coil wire from the distributor cap. Install the modified spark plug mentioned under Special Tools, above, in the coil wire and ground it to engine metal either by its spring clip (Spark Tester) or by holding the spark plug shell against the engine block with insulated pliers.

CAUTION

See the Caution under Step 6 of Run Mode Spark Test.

2. Have an assistant crank the engine using the ignition switch and check for spark. If there IS a good spark, the problem is most probably in the distributor cap, rotor, ignition cables or spark plugs. If there is NO spark, proceed to Step 3.

3. Measure the battery voltage. Next, measure the voltage at the white wire of the module while cranking the

engine. To make this measurement, it will be necessary to pierce the white wire with a straight pin and connect the voltmeter to the straight pin and to ground.

NOTE: DO NOT ALLOW THE STRAIGHT PIN TO GROUND ITSELF. The battery voltage and the voltage at the white wire should be within one volt of each other. If the readings are not within one volt of each other, check and repair the feed through the ignition switch to the white wire. Recheck for spark (Step 1). If the readings are within one volt of each other, or if there is still NO spark after power feed to white wire is repaired, proceed to Step 4.

4. Measure the coil **BAT** terminal voltage while cranking the engine. The reading should be within one volt of battery voltage. If the readings are not within one volt of each other, check and repair the feed through the ignition switch to the coil. If the readings are within one volt of each other, the problem is probably in the ignition module. Substitute another module and repeat test for spark (Step 1).

BALLAST RESISTOR

The ballast resistor wire is usually red with light green stripes. To check it you must disconnect it at the coil **BAT** connections and at the connector at the end of the wiring harness. The connector at the end of the wiring harness is a rectangular connector with eight terminals. Connect an ohmmeter to each end of the wire and set it to the **High** scale. The resistance of the wire should be between 1.05Ω and 1.15Ω. Any other reading merits replacement of the resistor wire with one of the correct service resistor wires.

TFI Troubleshooting

NOTE: Refer to the comments, preliminary checks and special tool paragraphs of the proceeding Dura-Spark Troubleshooting section. In addition to preliminary checks mentioned, check to be sure the TFI module is securely attached to the distributor.

VOLTAGE TEST

1. Disconnect the TFI module wire harness connector at the module. Check for battery voltage between each pin of the connector and ground. Use a straight pin the connector socket hole to make contact. Test as follows:
2. With the ignition switch in the Off position, check of 0 volts at each terminal. If voltage is present, check the ignition switch for problems.
3. Set the ignition switch to the RUN position. Check for battery voltage at the color/coded W/LBH and DG/YD wires. Check for 0 volts at the R/LB wire. If not as required, check the continuity of the ignition switch, coil and wires.
4. Disconnect the R/LB wire lug at the starter relay. Set the ignition switch to START. Check for battery voltage at all three wires. If voltage is not present, check the continuity of the ignition switch and R/LB wire. Reconnect the wire lug to the starter relay.

RUN MODE TEST

1. Remove the coil wire from the distributor cap. Install the modified spark plug (see special tools in previous section) in the coil wire terminal.
2. Unplug the wire connector at the TFI module. In the harness side of the connector, connect the special jumper (see special tools in previous section) between the ground and the color coded DG/YD lead. Use a straight pin in the socket to make the connection.

CAUTION

Do not leave the special jumper switch closed for more than a second at a time.

3. Place the ignition switch in the RUN position. Quickly close (no more than one second) and open the jumper switch. Repeat the closing and opening several times. Spark should occur each time the jumper switch is opened.
4. If there is no spark the problem is in the primary circuit. Check the coil for internal shorts or opens, check primary and secondary resistance. Replace the coil if necessary.
5. If there is spark when the jumper switch is opened, the problem is in the distributor or TFI module.

ENGINE ELECTRICAL

Distributor

REMOVAL & INSTALLATION

1.6L, 1.9L Engines

The camshaft driven distributor is located at the top left end of the cylinder head. It is retained by two holddown bolts at the base of the distributor shaft housing.

1. Turn engine to No. 1 piston at TDC of the compression stroke. Disconnect negative battery cable. Disconnect the vacuum hose(s) from the advance unit. Disconnect the wiring harness at the distributor.
2. Remove the capscrews and remove the distributor cap.
3. Scribe a mark on the distributor

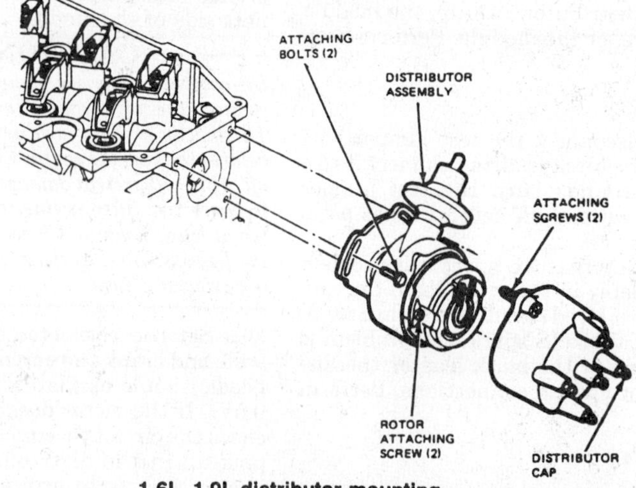

1.6L, 1.9L distributor mounting

body, showing the position of the ignition rotor. Scribe another mark on the distributor body and cylinder head, showing the position of the body in relation to the head. These marks can be used for reference when installing the distributor, as long as the engine remains undisturbed.

4. Remove the two distributor holddown bolts. Pull the distributor out of the head.

5. To install the distributor with the engine undisturbed, place the distributor in the cylinder head, seating the offset tang of the drive coupling into the groove on the end of the camshaft. Install the two distributor holddown screws and tighten them so that the distributor can just barely be moved. Install the rotor (if removed), the distributor cap and all wiring, then set the ignition timing.

6. If the crankshaft was rotated while the distributor was removed, the engine must be brought to TDC (Top Dead Center) on the compression stroke of the No. 1 cylinder. Remove the No. 1 spark plug. Place your finger over the hole and rotate the crankshaft slowly (use a wrench on the crankshaft pulley bolt) in the direction of normal engine rotation, until engine compression is felt.

WARNING: Turn the engine only in the direction of normal rotation. Backward rotation will cause the cam belt to slip or lose teeth, altering engine timing.

When engine compression is felt at the spark plug hole, indicating that the piston is approaching TDC, continue to turn the crankshaft until the timing mark on the pulley is aligned with the **0** mark (timing mark) on the engine front cover. Turn the distributor shaft until the ignition rotor is at the No. 1 firing position. Install the distributor into the cylinder head, as outlined in Step 5 of this procedure.

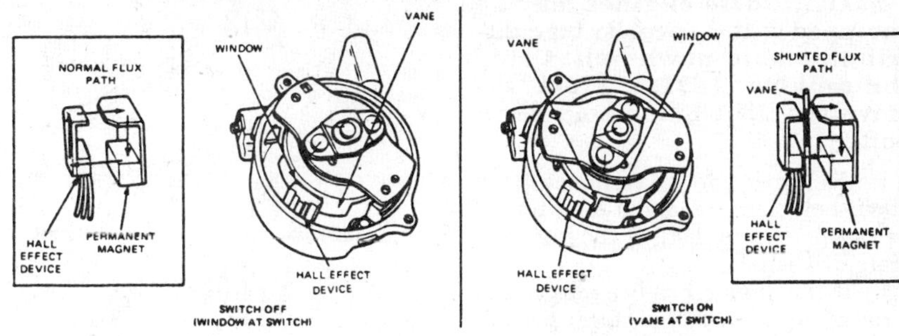

2.3L HSC—Hall effect distributor operation

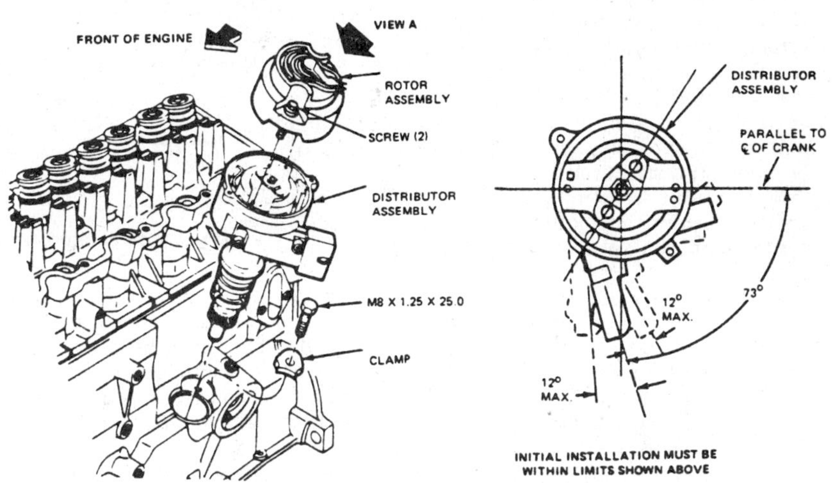

Distrbutor installation, 2.3L HSC engine

2.3L HSC Engine

The TFI-IV distributor is mounted on the side of the engine block. Some engines may be equipped with a security type distributor hold down bolt which requires a special wrench for removal. The TFI-IV distributor incorporates a Hall Effect advance switch stator assembly and an integrally mounted thick-film module. When the Hall Effect device is turned on and a pulse is produced, the EEC-IV electronics computes crankshaft position and engine demand to calibrate spark advance. Initial ignition timing adjustment/checking is necessary when the distributor has been removed. Repairs to the distributor are accomplished by distributor replacement.

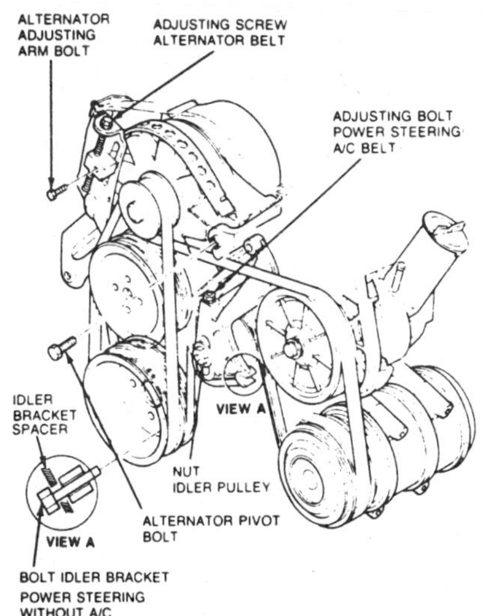

View of the drive belts—3.0L engine

1. Turn engine to No. 1 piston at TDC of the compression stroke. Disconnect the negative battery cable.

2. Disconnect the wiring harness at the distributor. Mark No. 1 spark plug wire cap terminal location on the distributor base. Remove the coil wire from the cap.

3. Remove he distributor cap with plug wires attached and position out of the way. Remove the rotor.

4. Remove the distributor base hold down bolt and clamp. Slowly remove the distributor from the engine. Be careful not to disturb the intermediate driveshaft.

5. Install in reverse order after aligning the center blade of the rotor with the reference mark made on the distributor base for No. 1 plug wire terminal location.

6. If the engine was disturbed (turned) while the distributor was out, the engine will have to reset at TDC before installation.

2.5L and 3.0L

1. Disconnect the primary wiring connector from distributor.

NOTE: Before removing the distributor cap, mark the relationship of the No. 1 wire tower on the distributor base.

2. Using a screwdriver, remove distributor cap (with the wires attached) and position it aside.

3. Turn the crankshaft to align the rotor with the No. 1 tower position, then remove the rotor.

4. Remove the TFI-IV harness connector.

NOTE: Some engines may be equipped with a security type distributor hold down bolt. Using the tool No. T82L-12270-A, remove the distributor hold down bolt.

5. Remove the distributor hold down bolt/clamp and the distributor; be careful not to disturb the intermediate driveshaft.

6. If the engine has been disturbed (crankshaft rotated), perform the following procedures:

a. Remove the No. 1 spark plug.

b. Rotate the crankshaft until the No. 1 piston is on the compression stroke. Align timing marks for correct initial timing.

c. Position the distributor shaft so that the center of the rotor is pointing toward the mark previously made on distributor base.

d. Continue rotating slightly so that the leading edge of the rotor is centered in the vane switch stator assembly.

e. Rotate distributor in the block to align the leading edge and the vane switch stator assembly, then verify that the rotor is pointing to the No. 1 cap terminal.

f. Install the distributor hold down bolt and clamp; DO NOT tighten it at this time.

NOTE: If the rotor and vane switch stator cannot be aligned by rotating the distributor in the block, pull the distributor out of block (enough) to disengage the distributor gear and rotate the distributor shaft to engage a different distributor gear tooth. Repeat Step 1 as necessary.

7. Reinstall the electrical harness connector to the distributor.

8. Install the distributor cap/ignition wire assembly. Check that the ignition wires are securely connected to the distributor cap and spark plugs. Torque the distributor cap screws to 18-23 in.lb. (2.0-2.6 Nm).

9. Using a timing light, set the initial timing by referring to the Vehicle Emission Control Information Decal.

10. Torque the distributor hold down bolt to 17-25 ft.lb. (23-34 Nm).

11. Check and/or adjust the initial timing (if necessary).

Alternator

ALTERNATOR PRECAUTIONS

To prevent damage to the alternator and regulator, the following precautionary measures must be taken when working with the electrical system.

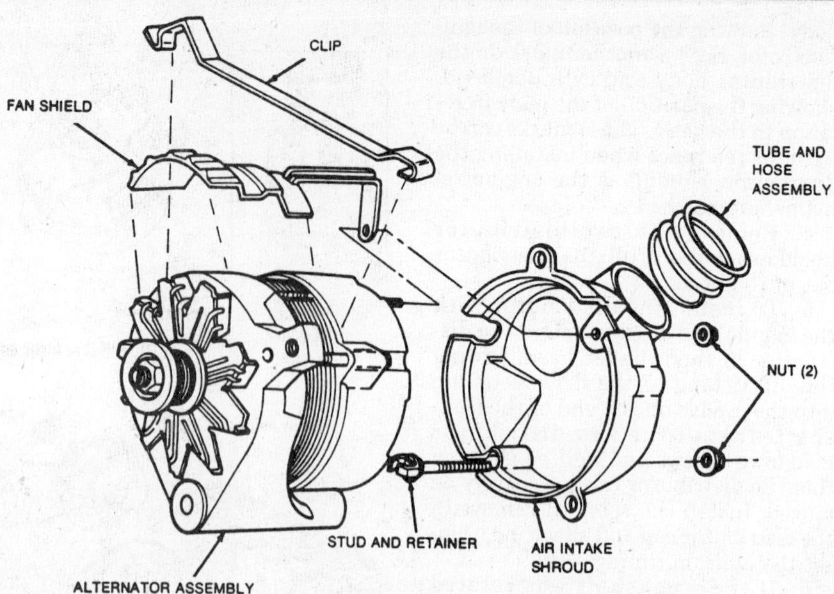

On air-conditioned cars, cool air shrouding is added

1. Never reverse battery connections. Always check the battery polarity visually. This is to be done before any connections are made to ensure that all of the connections correspond to the battery ground polarity of the car.

2. Booster batteries must be connected properly. Make sure the positive cable of the booster battery is connected to the positive terminal of the battery which is getting the boost. Engines must be shut off before cables are connected.

3. Disconnect the battery cables before using a fast charger; the charger has a tendency to force current through the diodes in the opposite directions for which they were designed.

4. Never use a fast charger as a booster for starting the car.

5. Never disconnect the voltage regulator while the engine is running, unless as noted for testing purposes.

6. Do not ground the alternator output terminal.

7. Do not operate the alternator on an open circuit with the field energized.

8. Do not attempt to polarize the alternator.

9. Disconnect the battery cables and remove the alternator before using an electric arc welder on the car.

10. Protect the alternator from excessive moisture. If the engine is to be steam cleaned, cover or remove the alternator.

REMOVAL & INSTALLATION

Except Taurus and Sable

1. Disconnect the negative battery cable.

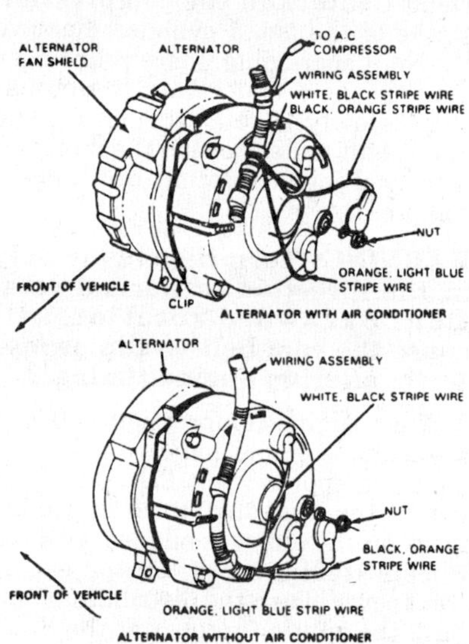

Harness connections for alternators

2. If equipped with a pulley cover shield, remove the shield at this time.

3. Loosen the alternator pivot bolt. Remove the adjustment bracket to alternator bolt (and nut, if equipped). Pivot the alternator to gain slack in the drive belt and remove the belt.

4. Disconnect and label (for correct installation) the alternator wiring.

NOTE: Some models use a push-on wiring connector on the field and stator connections. Pull or push straight when removing or installing, or damage to the connectors may occur.

5. Remove the pivot bolt and the alternator.

6. Install in the reverse order of removal. Adjust the drive belt tension so

that there is approx. 1/4-1/2" (6-13mm) deflection on the longest span between the pulleys. Reinstall the pulley shield, if equipped and connect the negative battery cable.

Taurus and Sable

The engines are equipped with V-ribbed belts. To increase the belt life, make sure that the V-grooves make proper contact on the pulleys.

2.5L Engine

1. Place a 1/2" flex handle in the square hole of the belt tensioner or an 18mm socket on the tensioner pulley nut.
2. Turn the tensioner counterclockwise and remove the drive belt.
3. At the back of the alternator, label and disconnect the electrical connectors.

NOTE: The alternator uses a push-on wiring connector on the field and stator connections. Depress the locking tab when removing the electrical connector from the alternator.

4. Remove the mounting bolts and the alternator from the vehicle.
5. To install, reverse the removal procedures. Torque the alternator-to-engine bolts to 45-57 ft.lb.
6. To install the drive belt, place it on the pulleys (except the alternator), turn the tensioner counterclockwise and position the belt on the alternator pulley so that the V-grooves are aligned correctly.

3.0L Engine

1. Disconnect the negative battery cable.
2. Remove the alternator adjusting arm bolt and the drive belt.
3. At the back of the alternator, label and disconnect the electrical connectors.

NOTE: The alternator uses a push-on wiring connector on the field and stator connections. Depress the locking tab when removing the electrical connector from the alternator.

4. Remove the pivot bolt and the alternator from the vehicle.
5. To install, reverse the removal procedures. Adjust the drive belt tension. Torque the pivot bolt to 45-57 ft.lb. and the adjusting arm bolt to 22-32 ft.lb.

Regulator

NOTE: Three different types of regulators are used, depending on models, engine, alternator output and type of dash mounted charging indicator used (light or ammeter). The regulators are 100% solid state and are calibrated and preset by the manufacturer. No readjustment is required or possible on these regulators.

SERVICE

Whenever system components are being replaced the following precautions should be followed so that the charging system will work properly and the components will not be damaged.

1. Always use the proper alternator.
2. The electronic regulators are color coded for identification. Never install a different coded regulator for the one being replaced. General coding identification follows, if the regulator removed does not have the color mentioned, identify the output of the alternator and method of charging indication, then consult a parts department to obtain the correct regulator. A black coded regulator is used in systems which use a signal lamp for charing indication. Gray coded regulators are used with an ammeter gauge. Neutral coded regulators are used on models equipped with a diesel engine. The special regulator must be used on vehicles equipped with a diesel engine to prevent glow plug failure.
3. Models using a charging lamp indicator are equipped with a 500Ω resistor on the back of the instrument panel.

REMOVAL & INSTALLATION

1. Disconnect the negative battery cable.
2. Unplug the wiring harness from the regulator.
3. Remove the regulator mounting bolts.
4. Install in the reverse order.

CHARGING SYSTEM TROUBLESHOOTING

There are many possible ways in which the charging system can malfunction. Often the source of a problem is difficult to diagnose, requiring special equipment and a good deal of experience. This is usually not the case, however, where the charging system fails completely and causes the dash board warning light to come on or the battery to become dead. To troubleshoot a complete system failure only two pieces of equipment are needed: a test light, to determine that current is reaching a certain point; and a current indicator (ammeter), to determine the direction of the current flow and its measurement in amps.

This test works under three assumptions:

1. The battery is known to be good and fully charged.
2. The alternator belt is in good condition and adjusted to the proper tension.
3. All connections in the system are clean and tight.

NOTE: In order for the current indicator to give a valid reading, the car must be equipped with battery cables which are of the same gauge size and quality as original equipment battery cables.

1. Turn off all electrical components on the car. Make sure the doors of the car are closed. If the car is equipped with a clock, disconnect the clock by removing the lead wire from the rear of the clock. Disconnect the positive battery cable from the battery and connect the ground wire on a test light to the disconnected positive battery cable. Touch the probe end of the test light to the positive battery post. The test light should not light. If the test light does light, there is a short or open circuit on the car.
2. Disconnect the voltage regulator wiring harness connector at the voltage regulator. Turn on the ignition key. Connect the wire on a test light to a good ground (engine bolt). Touch the probe end of a test light to the ignition wire connector into the voltage regulator wiring connector. This wire corresponds to the **I** terminal on the regulator. If the test light goes on, the charging system warning light circuit is complete. If the test light does not come on and the warning light on the instrument panel is on, either the resistor wire, which is parallel with the warning light, or the wiring to the voltage regulator, is defective. If the test light does not come on and the warning light is not on, either the bulb is defective or the power supply wire form the battery through the ignition switch to the bulb has an open circuit. Connect the wiring harness to the regulator.
3. Examine the fuse link wire in the wiring harness from the starter relay to the alternator. If the insulation on the wire is cracked or split, the fuse link may be melted. Connect a test light to the fuse link by attaching the ground wire on the test light to an engine bolt and touching the probe end of the light to the bottom of the fuse link wire where it splices into the alternator output wire. If the bulb in the test light does not light, the fuse link is melted.
4. Start the engine and place a current indicator on the positive battery

cable. Turn off all electrical accessories and make sure the doors are closed. If the charging system is working properly, the gauge will show a draw of less than 5 amps. If the system is not working properly, the gauge will show a draw of more than 5 amps. A charge moves the needle toward the battery, a draw moves the needle away from the battery. Turn the engine off.

5. Disconnect the wiring harness from the voltage regulator at the regulator at the regulator connector. Connect a male spade terminal (solderless connector) to each end of a jumper wire. Insert one end of the wire into the wiring harness connector which corresponds to the **A** terminal on the regulator. Insert the other end of the wire into the wiring harness connector which corresponds to the **F** terminal on the regulator. Position the connector with the jumper wire installed so that it cannot contact any metal surface under the hood. Position a current indicator gauge on the positive battery cable. Have an assistant start the engine. Observe the reading on the current indicator. Have your assistant slowly raise the speed of the engine to about 2,000 rpm or until the current indicator needle stops moving, whichever comes first. Do not run the engine for more than a short period of time in this condition. If the wiring harness connector or jumper wire becomes excessively hot during this test, turn off the engine and check for a grounded wire in the regulator wiring harness. If the current indicator shows a charge of about three amps less than the output of the alternator, the alternator is working properly. If the previous tests showed a draw, the voltage regulator is defective. If the gauge does not show the proper charging rate, the alternator is defective.

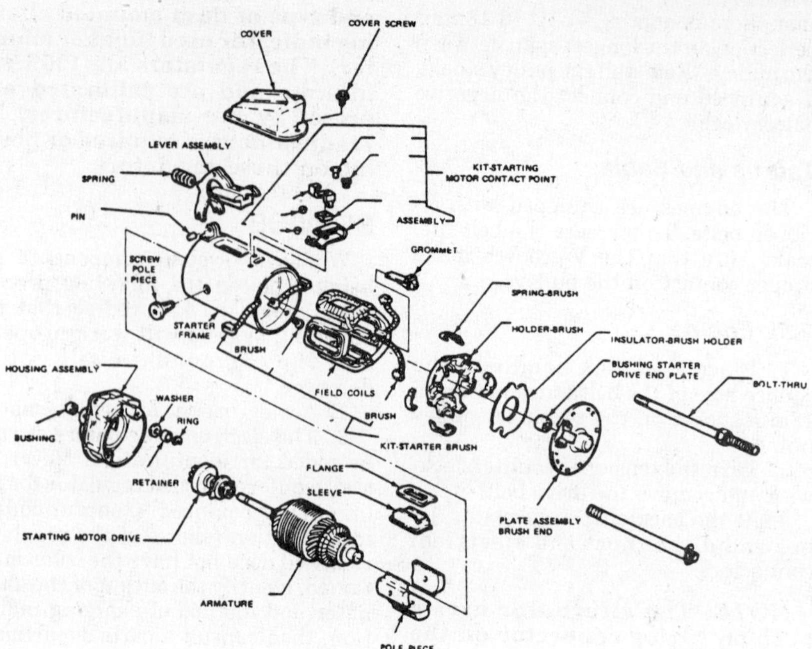

Exploded view of a starter motor

Starter

REMOVAL & INSTALLATION

1. Disconnect the negative battery cable.
2. Raise and safely support the front of the vehicle on jackstands. Disconnect the starter cable from the starter motor.
3. On models that are equipped with a manual transaxle, remove the three nuts that attach the roll restrictor brace to the starter mounting studs at the transaxle. Remove the brace.

   On models that are equipped with an automatic transaxle, remove the nose bracket mounted on the starter studs.
4. Remove the two bolts attaching the rear starter support bracket, remove the retaining nut from the rear of the starter motor and remove the support bracket.
5. On models equipped with a manual transaxle, remove the three starter mounting studs and the starter motor.

   On models equipped with a automatic transaxle, remove the two starter mounting studs and the starter motor.
6. Position the starter motor on the transaxle housing and install in the reverse order of removal. Tighten the mounting bolts or studs to 30-40 ft.lb.

OVERHAUL

Brush Replacement

1. Remove the top cover by taking out the retaining screw. Loosen and remove the two through bolts. Remove the starter drive end housing and the starter drive plunger lever return spring.
2. Remove the starter drive plunger lever pivot pin and lever, and remove the armature.
3. Remove the brush end plate.
4. Remove the ground brush retaining screws from the frame and remove the brushes.
5. Cut the insulated brush leads from the field coils, as close to the field connection point as possible.
6. Clean and inspect the starter motor.
7. Replace the brash end plate if the insulator between the field brush holder and the end plate is cracked or broken.
8. Position the new insulated field brushes lead on the field coil connections. Position and crimp the clip provided with the brushes to hold the brush lead to the connection. Solder the lead, clip, and connection together using rosin core solder. Use a 300W soldering iron.
9. Install the ground brush leads to the frame with the retaining screws.
10. Clean the commutator with special commutator paper.
11. Position the brush end plate to the starter frame, with the end plate boss in the frame slot.
12. Install the armature in the starter frame.
13. Install the starter drive gear plunger lever to the frame and starter drive assembly, and install the pivot pin.
14. Partially fill the drive end housing bearing bore with grease (approximately 1/4 full). Position the return spring on the plunger lever, and the drive end housing to the starter frame. Install the through-bolts and tighten to specified torque (55 to 75 in.lb.). Be sure that the stop ring retainer is seated properly in the drive end housing.
15. Install the commutator brushes in the brush holders. Center the brush springs on the brushes.
16. Position the plunger lever cover and brush cover band, with its gasket, on the starter. Tighten the band retaining screw.
17. Connect the starter to a battery to check its operation.

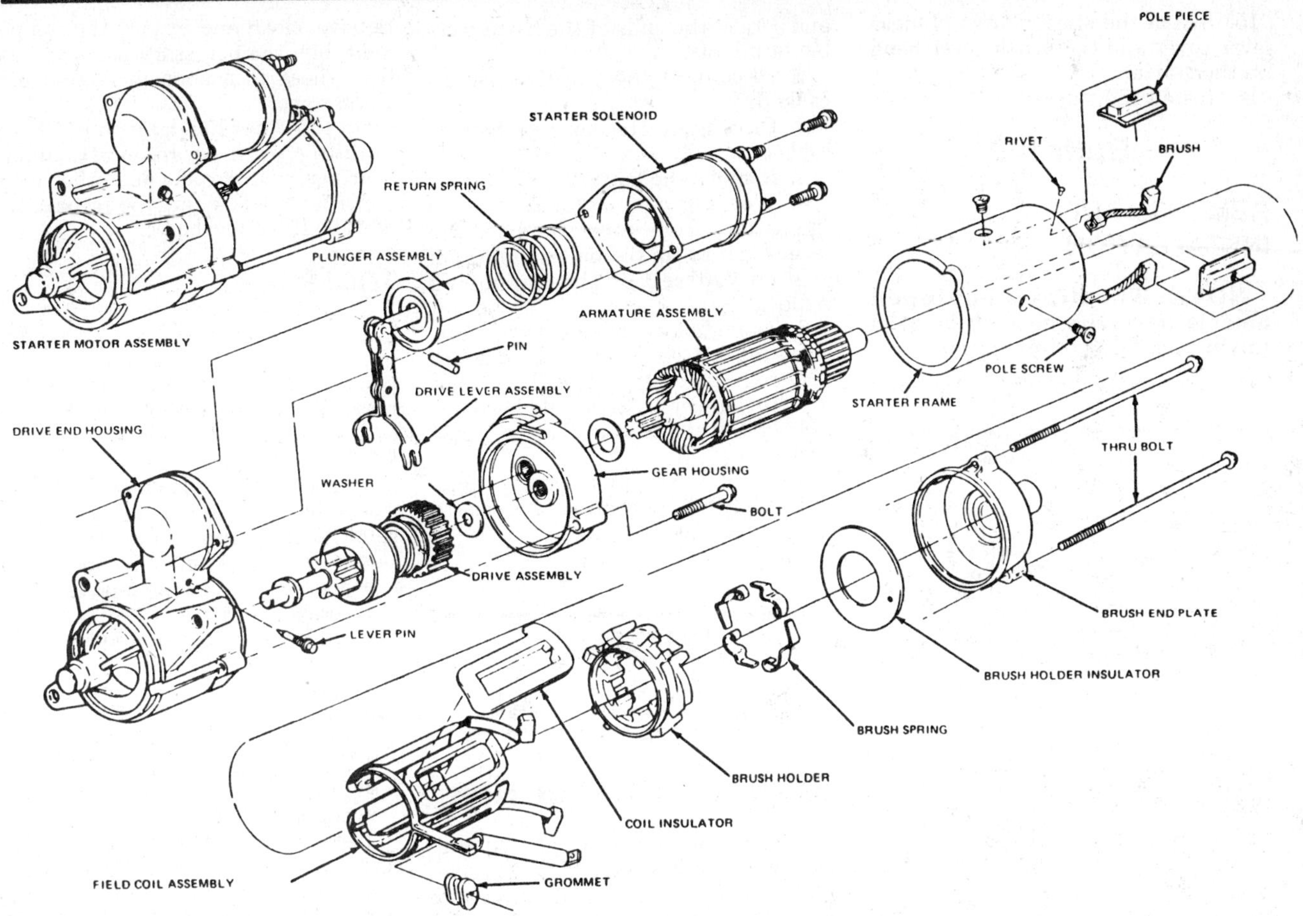

Exploded view of the diesel engine starter motor

STARTER DRIVE REPLACEMENT

1. Remove the starter from the engine.
2. Remove the starter drive plunger lever cover.
3. Loosen the through-bolts just enough to allow removal of the drive end housing and the starter drive plunger lever return spring.
4. Remove the pivot pin which attaches the starter drive plunger lever to the starter frame and remove the lever.
5. Remove the stop ring retainer and stop ring from the armature shaft.
6. Remove the starter drive from the armature shaft.
7. Inspect the teeth on the starter drive. If they are excessively worn, inspect the teeth on the ring gear of the flywheel. If the teeth on the flywheel are excessively worn, the flywheel ring gear should be replaced.
8. Apply a thin coat of white grease to the armature shaft, in the area in which the starter drive operates.
9. Install the starter drive on the armature shaft and install a new stopring.

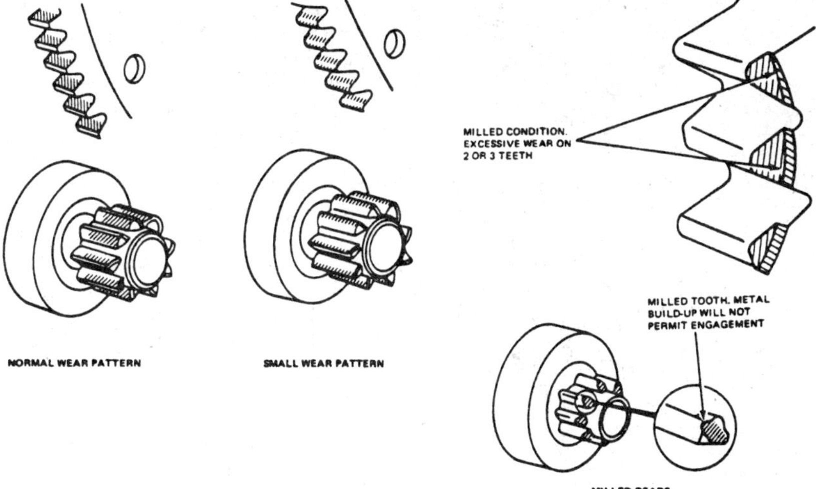

Starter drive gear wear patterns

10. Position the starter drive plunger lever on the starter frame and install the pivot pin. Make sure the plunger lever is properly engaged with the starter drive.
11. Install a new stop ring retainer on the armature shaft.
12. Fill the drive end housing bearing fore ¼ full with grease.
13. Position the starter drive plunger lever return spring and the drive end housing to the starter frame.
14. Tighten the starter through-bolts to 55–75 in.lb.

15. Install the starter drive plunger lever cover and the brush cover band on the starter.
16. Install the starter.

Battery

REMOVAL AND INSTALLATION

NOTE: The diesel equipped models have the battery located in the luggage compartment.

1. Loosen the battery cable bolts and spread the ends of the battery cable terminals.
2. Disconnect the negative battery cable first.
3. Disconnect the positive battery cable.
4. Remove the battery holddown.
5. Wearing heavy gloves, remove the battery from under the hood. Be careful not to tip the battery and spill acid on yourself or the car during removal.
6. To install, wearing heavy gloves, place the battery in its holder under the hood. Use care not to spill the acid.
7. Install the battery holddown.
8. Install the positive battery cable first.
9. Install the negative battery cable.
10. Apply a light coating of grease to the cable ends.

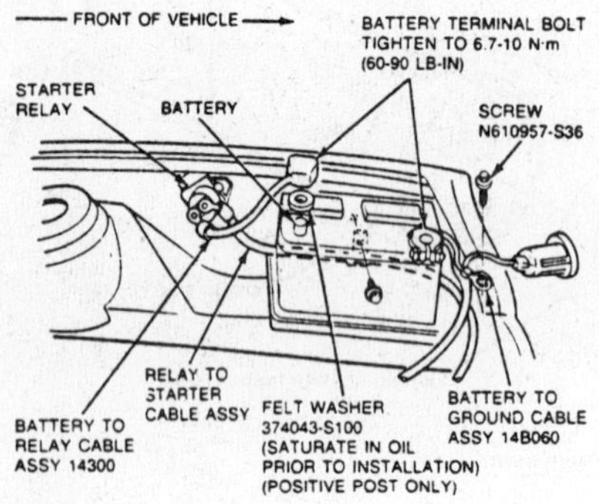

Battery mounting location – 1.6L and 1.9L engines

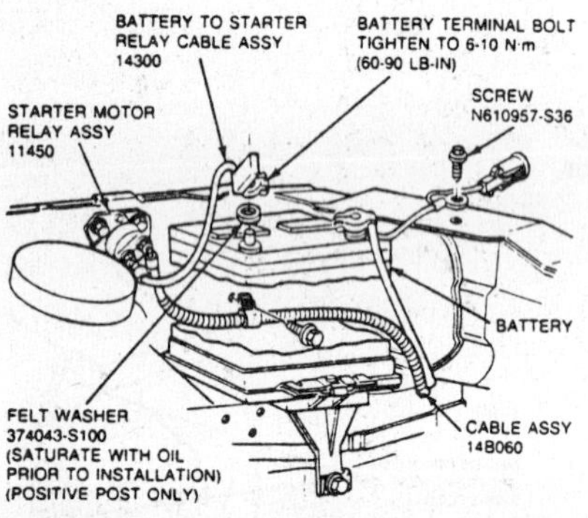

Battery mounting location – 2.3L HSC engine

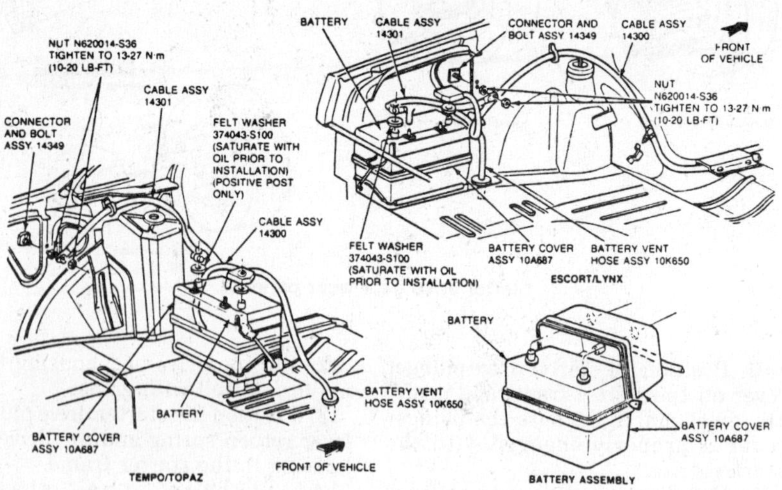

Battery mounting location – 2.0L diesel engine

ENGINE MECHANICAL

Engine Overhaul Tips

Most engine overhaul procedures are fairly standard. In addition to specific parts replacement procedures and complete specifications for your individual engine, this section also is a guide to accept rebuilding procedures. Examples of standard rebuilding practice are shown and should be used along with specific details concerning your particular engine.

Competent and accurate machine shop services will ensure maximum performance, reliability and engine life.

In most instances it is more profitable for the do-it-yourself mechanic to remove, clean and inspect the component, buy the necessary parts and deliver these to a shop for actual machine work.

On the other hand, much of the rebuilding work (crankshaft, block, bearings, piston rods, and other components) is well within the scope of the do-it-yourself mechanic.

TOOLS

The tools required for an engine overhaul or parts replacement will depend on the depth of your involvement. With a few exceptions, they will be the tools found in a mechanic's tool kit. More in-depth work will require any or all of the following:

- a dial indicator (reading in thousandths) mounted on a universal base
- micrometers and telescope gauges
- jaw and screw-type pullers
- scraper
- valve spring compressor
- ring groove cleaner
- piston ring expander and compressor
- ridge reamer
- cylinder hone or glaze breaker
- Plastigage®
- engine stand

The use of most of these tools is illustrated in this section. Many can be rented for a one-time use from a local parts jobber or tool supply house specializing in automotive work.

Occasionally, the use of special tools is called for. See the information on Special Tools and Safety Notice in the front of this book before substituting another tool.

INSPECTION TECHNIQUES

Procedures and specifications are given in this section for inspecting, cleaning and assessing the wear limits of most major components. Other procedures such as Magnaflux® and Zyglo® can be used to locate material flaws and stress cracks. Magnaflux® is a magnetic process applicable only to ferrous materials. The Zyglo® process coats the material with a fluorescent dye penetrant and can be used on any material Check for suspected surface cracks can be more readily made using spot check dye. The dye is sprayed onto the suspected area, wiped off and the area sprayed with a developer. Cracks will show up brightly.

OVERHAUL TIPS

Aluminum has become extremely popular for use in engines, due to its low weight. Observe the following precautions when handling aluminum parts:

• Never hot tank aluminum parts (the caustic hot tank solution will eat the aluminum.

• Remove all aluminum parts (identification tag, etc.) from engine parts prior to the tanking.

• Always coat threads lightly with engine oil or anti-seize compounds before installation, to prevent seizure.

• Never overtorque bolts or spark plugs especially in aluminum threads.

Stripped threads in any component can be repaired using any of several commercial repair kits (Heli-Coil®, Microdot®, Keenserts®, etc.).

When assembling the engine, any parts that will be frictional contact must be prelubed to provide lubrication at initial start-up. Any product specifically formulated for this purpose can be used, but engine oil is not recommended as a prelube.

When semi-permanent (locked, but removable) installation of bolts or nuts is desired, threads should be cleaned and coated with Loctite® or other similar, commercial non-hardening sealant.

REPAIRING DAMAGED THREADS

Several methods of repairing damaged threads are available. Heli-Coil® (shown here), Keenserts® and Microdot® are among the most widely used. All involve basically the same principle—drilling out stripped threads, tapping the hole and installing a prewound insert—making welding, plugging and oversize fasteners unnecessary.

Two types of thread repair inserts are usually supplied: a standard type for most Inch Coarse, Inch Fine, Metric Course and Metric Fine thread sizes and a spark lug type to fit most spark plug port sizes. Consult the individual manufacturer's catalog to determine exact applications. Typical thread repair kits will contain a selection of prewound threaded inserts, a tap (corresponding to the outside diameter threads of the insert) and an installation tool. Spark plug inserts usually differ because they require a tap equipped with pilot threads and a combined reamer/tap section. Most manufacturers also supply blister-packed thread repair inserts separately in addition to a master kit containing a variety of taps and inserts plus installation tools.

Before effecting a repair to a threaded hole, remove any snapped, broken or damaged bolts or studs. Penetrating oil can be used to free frozen threads. The offending item can be removed with locking pliers or with a screw or stud extractor. After the hole is clear, the thread can be repaired, as shown in the series of accompanying illustrations.

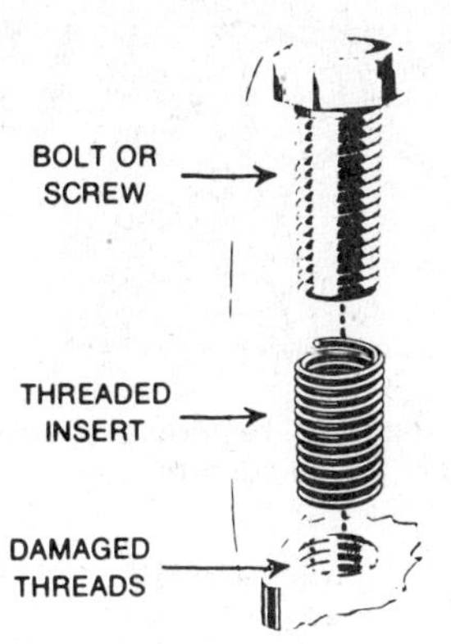

Damaged bolt holes can be repaired with thread repair inserts

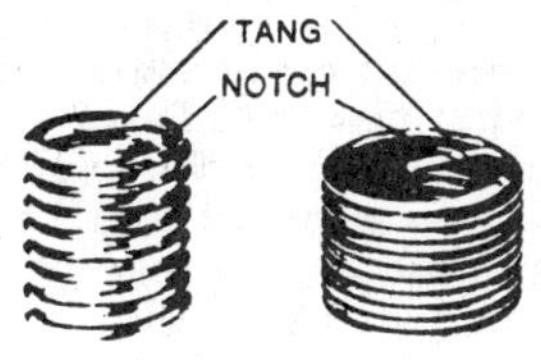

Standard thread repair insert (left) and spark plug thread insert (right)

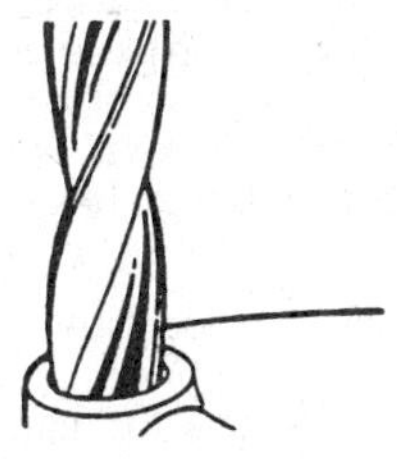

Drill out the damaged threads with specified drill. Drill completely through the hole or to the bottom of a blind hole

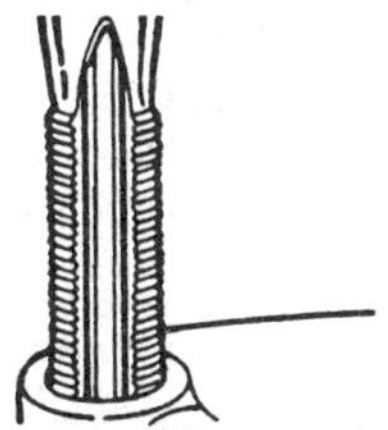

With the tap supplied, tap the hole to receive the thread insert. Keep the tap well oiled and back it out frequently to avoid clogging the threads

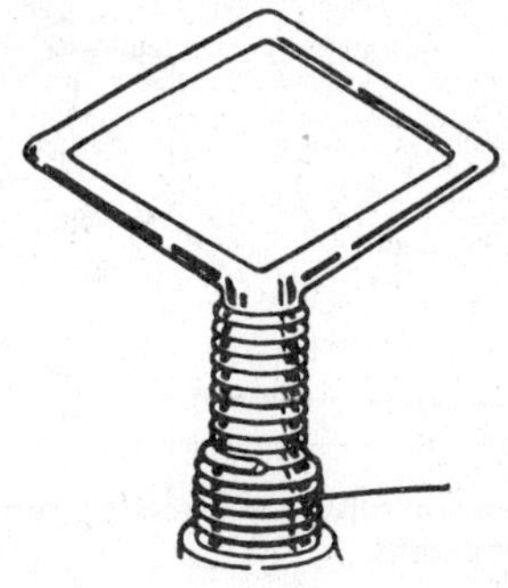

Screw the threaded insert onto the installation tool until the tang engages the slot. Screw the insert into the tapped hole until it is ¼-½ turn below the top surface. After installation break off the tang with a hammer and punch

Checking Engine Compression

A noticeable lack of engine power, excessive oil consumption and/or poor fuel mileage measured over an extended period are all indicators of internal engine war. Worn piston rings, scored or worn cylinder bores, blown head gaskets, sticking or burnt valves and worn valve seats are all possible culprits here. A check of each cylinder's compression will help you locate the problems.

As mentioned earlier, a screw-in type compression gauge is more accurate that the type you simply hold against the spark plug hole, although it takes slightly longer to use. It's worth it to obtain a more accurate reading. Follow the procedures below.

Gasoline Engines

1. Warm up the engine to normal operating temperature.
2. Remove all the spark plugs.
3. Disconnect the high tension lead from the ignition coil.
4. On fully open the throttle either by operating the carburetor throttle linkage by hand or by having an assistant floor the accelerator pedal.
5. Screw the compression gauge into the no.1 spark plug hole until the fitting is snug.

WARNING: Be careful not to crossthread the plug hole. On aluminum cylinder heads use extra care, as the threads in these heads are easily ruined.

6. Ask an assistant to depress the accelerator pedal fully on both carbureted and fuel injected vehicles. Then, while you read the compression gauge, ask the assistant to crank the engine two or three times in short bursts using the ignition switch.
7. Read the compression gauge at the end of each series of cranks, and record the highest of these readings. Repeat this procedure for each of the engine's cylinders. Compare the high-

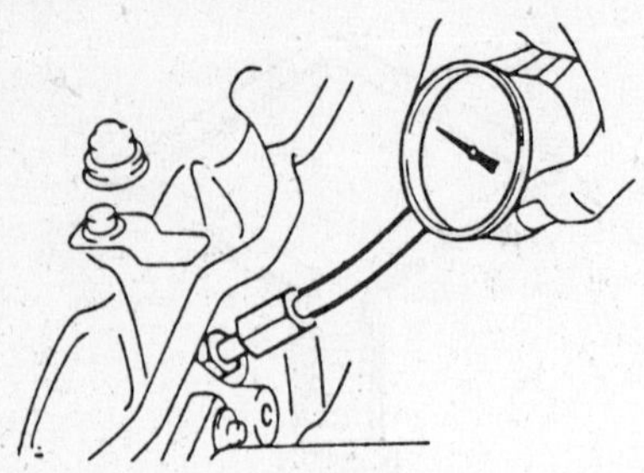

The screw-in type compression gauge is more accurate

est reading of each cylinder to the compression pressure specification in the Tune-Up Specifications chart. The specs in this chart are maximum values.

A cylinder's compression pressure is usually acceptable if it is not less than 80% of maximum. The difference between any two cylinders should be no more than 12–14 pounds.

8. If a cylinder is unusually low, pour a tablespoon of clean engine oil into the cylinder through the spark plug hole and repeat the compression test. If the compression comes up after adding the oil, it appears that the cylinder's piston rings or bore are damaged or worn. If the pressure remains low, the valves may not be seating properly (a valve job is needed), or the head gasket may be blown near that cylinder. If compression in any two adjacent cylinders is low, and if the addition of oil doesn't help the compression, there is leakage past the head gasket. Oil and coolant water in the combustion chamber can result from this problem. There may be evidence of water droplets on the engine dipstick when a head gasket has blown.

Diesel Engines

Checking cylinder compression on diesel engines is basically the same procedure as on gasoline engines except for the following:

1. A special compression gauge adaptor suitable for diesel engines (because these engines have much greater compression pressures) must be used.
2. Remove the injector tubes and remove the injectors from each cylinder.

WARNING: Don't forget to remove the washer underneath each injector. Otherwise, it may get lost when the engine is cranked.

3. When fitting the compression gauge adaptor to the cylinder head, make sure the bleeder of the gauge (if equipped) is closed.
4. When reinstalling the injector assemblies, install new washers underneath each injector.

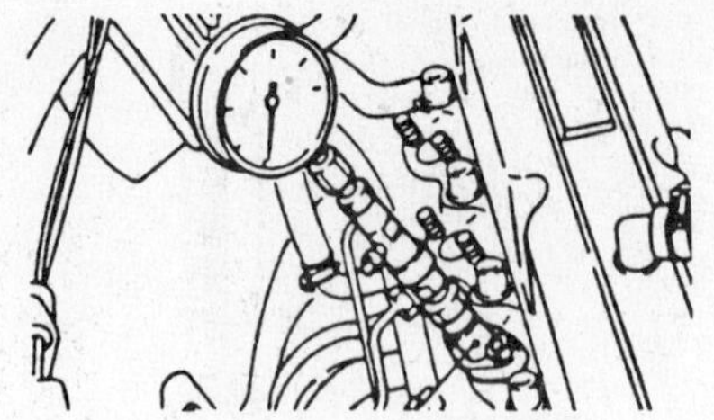

Diesel engines require a special compression gauge adaptor

Engine

REMOVAL & INSTALLATION

NOTE: A special engine support bar is necessary. The bar is used to support the engine/transaxle while disconnecting the various engine mounts Ford Part No. T81P6000A. A suitable support can be made using angle iron, a heavy J-hook and some strong chain.

1.6L, 1.9L Engine Engine w/Transaxle

NOTE: The following procedure is for engine and transaxle removal and installation as an assembly. Procedure for removing the engine only is in following section.

1. Mark the location of the hinges and remove the hood.
2. Remove the air cleaner, hot air tube and alternator fresh air intake tube.
3. Disconnect the battery cables, remove the battery and tray.
4. Drain the radiator, engine oil and transaxle fluid.

CAUTION

When draining the coolant, keep in mind that cats and dogs are attracted by the ethylene glycol antifreeze, and are quite likely to drink any that is left in an uncovered container or in puddles on the ground. This will prove fatal in sufficient quantity. Always drain the coolant into a sealable container. Coolant should be reused unless it is contaminated or several years old.

5. Remove the coil the mounting bracket and the coil wire harness.
6. If the vehicle is equipped with air conditioning, remove the compressor from the engine with the refrigerant hoses still attached. Position compressor to the side.

CAUTION

Never loosen air conditioning refrigerant lines, as the escaping refrigerant is a deadly poison and can freeze exposed skin instantly.

7. Disconnect the upper and lower radiator hose.
8. Disconnect the heater hoses from the engine.
9. If equipped with an automatic transaxle disconnect and plug the cooler lines at the rubber coupler.
10. Disconnect the electric fan.
11. Remove the fan motor, shroud assembly and the radiator.
12. If equipped with power steering, remove the filler tube.
13. Disconnect the following electrical connections:
    a. Main wiring harness
    b. Neutral safety switch (automatic only)
    c. Choke cap wire
    d. Starter cable
    e. Alternator wiring
14. Disconnect the fuel supply and return lines. Relieve fuel pressure on injected models before disconnecting fuel lines.
15. Disconnect the (3) altitude compensator lines if so equipped. Mark each line as you remove it. for easy installation.
16. Disconnect the vacuum lines from the "tree" on the firewall.
17. Disconnect the power brake booster vacuum line.
18. Disconnect the cruise control is so equipped.
19. Disconnect all carburetor linkage.
20. Disconnect all engine vacuum lines. Mark each line as you remove it, for easy installation.
21. Disconnect the clutch cable if so equipped.
22. Remove the thermactor pump bracket bolt.
23. Install engine support T81P-6000-A or equivalent. Using a short piece of chain, attach it to the engine using the 10 mm bolt holes at the transaxle, the exhaust manifold side of the head, and the thermactor bracket hole. Tighten the J-bolt. Place a piece of tape around the J-bolt threads where the bolt passes through the bottom of the support bar. This will act as a reference later.
24. Jack up the vehicle and support it with jackstands.
25. Remove the splash shields.
26. If equipped with a manual transaxle, remove the roll restrictor at the engine and body.
27. Remove the stabilizer bar.
28. Remove the lower control arm through-bolts at the body brackets.
29. Disconnect the left tie rod at the steering knuckle.
30. Disconnect the secondary air tube (catalyst) at the check valve.
31. Disconnect the exhaust system at the exhaust manifold and tail pipe.
32. Remove the right halfshaft from

the transaxle. Some fluid will leak out when the shaft is removed.

33. Remove the left side halfshaft.

34. Install shipping plugs T81P-1177-B or equivalent in the differential seals.

35. Disconnect the speedometer cable.

36. If equipped with an automatic transaxle, disconnect the shift selector cable. On manual transaxles, disconnect the shift control rod.

NOTE: Mark the position of the shift control before disconnecting it.

37. If equipped with power steering, disconnect the pump return line at the pump, and the pressure line at the intermediate fitting.

38. Remove the left front motor mount attaching bracket and remove the mount with its through-bolt. Remove the left rear motor mount stud nut. Carefully reach into the engine compartment and loosen the engine support bar J-bolt until the left rear motor mount stud clears the mounting bracket. Remove the left rear mount to transaxle attaching bracket.

39. Lower the vehicle, then tighten the support bar J-bolt until the piece of tape installed earlier contacts the bottom of the support bar. Attach a lifting sling to the engine, disconnect the right engine mount and lift the engine from the vehicle.

To Install:

40. Attach a lowering sling to the engine, Reconnect the right engine mount and lower the engine into the vehicle.

41. Install the left front motor mount attaching bracket and install the mount with its through-bolt. Install the left rear motor mount stud nut. Reach into the engine compartment and tighten the engine support bar J-bolt until the left rear motor mount stud clears the mounting bracket. Install the left rear mount to transaxle attaching bracket.

42. If equipped with power steering, reconnect the pump return line at the pump, and the pressure line at the intermediate fitting.

43. If equipped with an automatic transaxle, reconnect the shift selector cable. On manual transaxles, reconnect the shift control rod.

44. Reconnect the speedometer cable.

45. Remove the shipping plugs T81P-1177-B or equivalent in the differential seals.

46. Install the left side halfshaft.

47. Install the right halfshaft to the transaxle.

48. Reconnect the exhaust system at the exhaust manifold and tail pipe.

49. Reconnect the secondary air tube (catalyst) at the check valve.

50. Reconnect the left tie rod at the steering knuckle.

51. Install the lower control arm through-bolts at the body brackets.

52. Install the stabilizer bar.

53. If equipped with a manual transaxle, install the roll restrictor at the engine and body.

54. Install the splash shields.

55. Jack up the vehicle and support it with jackstands.

56. Remove the engine support T81P-6000-A or equivalent.

57. Install the thermactor pump bracket bolt.

58. Reconnect the clutch cable if so equipped.

59. Reconnect all engine vacuum lines. Mark each line as you Install it, for easy installation.

60. Reconnect all carburetor linkage.

61. Reconnect the cruise control is so equipped.

62. Reconnect the power brake booster vacuum line.

63. Reconnect the vacuum lines to the "tree" on the firewall.

64. Reconnect the (3) altitude compensator lines if so equipped. Mark each line as you Install it. for easy installation.

65. Reconnect the fuel supply and return lines. Relieve fuel pressure on injected models before reconnecting fuel lines.

66. Reconnect the following electrical connections:

a. Main wiring harness
b. Neutral safety switch (automatic only)
c. Choke cap wire
d. Starter cable
e. Alternator wiring

67. If equipped with power steering, install the filler tube.

68. Install the fan motor, shroud assembly and the radiator.

69. Reconnect the electric fan.

70. If equipped with an automatic transaxle reconnect and plug the cooler lines at the rubber coupler.

71. Reconnect the heater hoses to the engine.

72. Reconnect the upper and lower radiator hose.

73. If the vehicle is equipped with air conditioning, install the compressor to the engine.

74. Install the coil the mounting bracket and the coil wire harness.

75. Refill the radiator, engine oil and transaxle fluid.

76. Reconnect the battery cables, install the battery and tray.

77. Install the air cleaner, hot air tube and alternator fresh air intake tube.

78. Install the hood.

1.6L, 1.9L Engine
Engine Alone

NOTE: The following procedure is for engine only removal and installation.

1. Mark the position of the hinges on the hood underside and remove the hood.

2. Remove the air cleaner assembly. Remove the air feed duct and the heat tube. Remove the air duct to the alternator.

3. Disconnect the battery cables from the battery. Remove the battery. If equipped with air conditioning, remove compressor with line still connected and position out of the way.

CAUTION

Never loosen refrigerant lines, as the escaping refrigerant is a deadly poison and can freeze exposed skin instantly.

4. Drain the cooling system. Remove the drive belts from the alternator and thermactor pump. Disconnect the thermactor air supply hose. Disconnect the wiring harness at the alternator. Remove alternator and thermactor.

CAUTION

When draining the coolant, keep in mind that cats and dogs are attracted by the ethylene glycol antifreeze, and are quite likely to drink any that is left in an uncovered container or in puddles on the ground. This will prove fatal in sufficient quantity. Always drain the coolant into a sealable container. Coolant should be reused unless it is contaminated or several years old.

5. Disconnect and remove the upper and lower radiator hoses. If equipped with an automatic transaxle, disconnect and plug the fluid cooler lines at the radiator.

6. Disconnect the heater hoses from the engine. Unplug the electric cooling fan wiring harness. Remove the fan and radiator shroud as an assembly.

7. Remove the radiator. Label and disconnect all vacuum lines, including power brake booster, from the engine. Label and disconnect all linkage, including kickdown linkage if automatic, and wiring harness connectors from the engine.

8. If equipped with fuel injection, discharge the system pressure. Remove supply and return fuel lines to the fuel pump. Plug the line from the gas tank.

9. Raise and safely support the car on jackstands. Remove the clamp from the heater supply and return tubes. remove the tubes.

10. Disconnect the battery cable from the starter motor. Remove the

brace or bracket from the back of the starter and remove the starter.

11. Disconnect the exhaust system from the exhaust manifold. Drain the engine oil.

12. Remove the brace in front of the bell housing (flywheel or converter) inspection cover. Remove the inspection cover.

13. Remove the crankshaft pulley. If equipped with a manual transaxle, remove the timing belt cover lower attaching bolts.

14. If equipped with an automatic transaxle, remove the torque converter to flywheel mounting nuts.

15. Remove the lower engine to transaxle attaching bolts.

16. Loosen the hose clamps on the bypass hose and remove the hose from the intake manifold.

17. Remove the bolt and nut attaching the right front mount insulator to the engine bracket.

18. Lower the car from the jackstands.

19. Attach an engine lifting sling to the engine. Connect a chain hoist to the lifting sling and remove all slack. Remove the through bolt from the right front engine mount and remove the insulator.

20. If the car is equipped with a manual transaxle, remove the timing belt cover upper mounting bolts and remove the cover.

21. Remove the right front insulator attaching bracket from the engine.

22. Position a floor jack under the transaxle. Raise the jack just enough to take the weight of the transaxle.

23. Remove the upper bolts connecting the engine and transaxle.

24. Slowly raise the engine and separate from the transaxle. Be sure the torque converter stays on the transxaxle. Remove the engine from the car. On models equipped with manual transaxles, the engine must be separated from the input shaft of the transaxle before raising.

To install:

25. Slowly lower the engine and connect it to the transaxle.

26. Install the upper bolts connecting the engine and transaxle.

27. Lower the jack under the transaxle.

28. Install the right front insulator attaching bracket to the engine.

29. If the car is equipped with a manual transaxle, install the timing belt cover upper mounting bolts and install the cover.

30. Remove the engine sling from the engine. Install the through bolt to the right front engine mount and install the insulator.

31. Raise the car and support on jackstands.

32. Install the bolt and nut attaching the right front mount insulator to the engine bracket.

33. Install the bypass hose to the intake manifold and tighten the clamps.

34. Install the lower engine to transaxle attaching bolts.

35. If equipped with an automatic transaxle, install the torque converter to the flywheel.

36. Install the crankshaft pulley. If equipped with a manual transaxle, install the timing belt cover lower attaching bolts.

37. Install the brace in front of the bell housing (flywheel or converter) inspection cover. Install the inspection cover.

38. Reconnect the exhaust system to the exhaust manifold. Refill the engine oil.

39. Reconnect the battery cable to the starter motor. Install the brace or bracket to the back of the starter and install the starter.

40. Lower the car from the jackstands. Install the clamp to the heater supply and return tubes.

41. If equipped with fuel injection, install the supply and return fuel lines to the fuel pump.

42. Install the radiator. Reconnect all vacuum lines, including power brake booster, to the engine. Reconnect all linkage, including kickdown linkage if automatic, and wiring harness connectors to the engine.

43. Reconnect the heater hoses to the engine. Unplug the electric cooling fan wiring harness. Install the fan and radiator shroud as an assembly.

44. Reconnect the upper and lower radiator hoses. If equipped with an automatic transaxle, reconnect the fluid cooler lines at the radiator.

45. Refill the cooling system. Install alternator and thermactor. Install the drive belts to the alternator and thermactor pump. Reconnect the thermactor air supply hose. Reconnect the wiring harness at the alternator.

46. Install the battery. Reconnect the battery cables to the battery. If equipped with air conditioning, install the compressor.

47. Install the air cleaner assembly. Install the air feed duct and the heat tube. Install the air duct to the alternator.

48. Install the hood.

2.0L Diesel Engine

NOTE: Suitable jackstands or hoisting equipment are necessary to remove the engine and transaxle assembly. The assembly is removed from underneath the vehicle.

CAUTION

The air conditioning system contains refrigerant (R-12) under high pressure. Use extreme care when discharging the system. If the tools and know-how are not on hand, have the system discharged prior to the start of engine removal.

These procedures cover the removal and installation of the 2.0L Diesel engine and transaxle as an assembly.

1. Mark the position of the hood hinges and remove the hood.

2. Remove the negative ground cable from the battery that is located in luggage compartment.

3. Remove the air cleaner assembly.

4. Position a drain pan under the lower radiator hose. Remove the hose and drain the engine coolant.

CAUTION

When draining the coolant, keep in mind that cats and dogs are attracted by the ethylene glycol antifreeze, and are quite likely to drink any that is left in an uncovered container or in puddles on the ground. This will prove fatal in sufficient quantity. Always drain the coolant into a sealable container. Coolant should be reused unless it is contaminated or several years old.

5. Remove the upper radiator hose from the engine.

6. Disconnect the cooling fan at the electrical connector.

7. Remove the radiator shroud and cooling fan as an assembly. Remove the radiator.

8. Remove the starter cable from the starter.

9. Discharge air conditioning system (see opening CAUTION) if so equipped. Remove the pressure and suction lines from the air conditioning compressor.

10. Identify and disconnect all vacuum lines as necessary.

11. Disconnect the engine harness connectors (two) at the dash panel. Disconnect the glow plug relay connectors at the dash panel.

NOTE: Connectors are located under the plastic shield on the dash panel. Remove and save plastic retainer pins. Disconnect the alternator wiring connector on RH fender apron.

12. Disconnect the clutch cable from the shift lever on transaxle.

13. Disconnect the injection pump throttle linkage.

14. Disconnect the fuel supply and return hoses on the engine.

15. Disconnect the power steering pressure and return lines at the power steering pump, if so equipped. Remove the power steering lines bracket at the cylinder head.

16. Install Engine Support Tool

D79P-8000-A or equivalent to existing engine lifting eye.

17. Raise vehicle and safely support on jackstands.

18. Remove the bolt attaching the exhaust pipe bracket to the oil pan.

19. Remove the two exhaust pipes to exhaust manifold attaching nuts.

20. Pull the exhaust system out of rubber insulating grommets and set aside.

21. Remove the speedometer cable from the transaxle.

22. position an drain pan under the heater hoses. Remove one heater hose form the water pump inlet tube. Remove the other heater hose from the oil cooler.

23. Remove the bolts attaching the control arms to the body. Remove the stabilizer bar bracket retaining bolts and remove the brackets.

24. Halfshaft assemblies must be removed from the transaxle at this time.

25. On MT models, remove the shift stabilizer bar-to-transaxle attaching bolts. Remove the shift mechanism to shift shaft attaching nut and bolt at the transaxle.

26. Remove the LH rear insulator mount bracket from body bracket by removing the two nuts.

27. Remove the LH front insulator to transaxle mounting bolts.

28. Lower vehicle (see CAUTION below). Install lifting equipment to the two existing lifting eyes on engine.

CAUTION

Do not allow front wheels to touch floor.

29. Remove Engine Support Tool D79L-8000-A or equivalent.

30. Remove RH insulator intermediate bracket to engine bracket bolts, intermediate bracket to insulator attaching nuts and the nut on the bottom of the double ended stud attaching the intermediate bracket to engine bracket. Remove the bracket.

31. Carefully lower the engine and the transaxle assembly to the floor.

32. Raise the vehicle and safely support.

33. Position the engine and transaxle assembly directly below the engine compartment.

34. Slowly lower the vehicle over the engine and transaxle assembly.

CAUTION

Do not allow the front wheels to touch the floor.

35. Install the lifting equipment to both existing engine lifting eyes on engine.

36. Raise the engine and transaxle assembly up through engine compartment and position accordingly.

37. Install RH insulator intermediate attaching nuts and intermediate bracket to engine bracket bolts. Install nut on bottom of double ended stud attaching intermediate bracket to engine bracket. Tighten to 75-100 ft.lb.

38. Install Engine Support Tool D79L-8000-A or equivalent to the engine lifting eye.

39. Remove the lifting equipment.

40. Raise vehicle.

41. Position a suitable floor or transaxle jack under engine. Raise the engine and transaxle assembly into mounted position.

42. Install insulator to bracket nut and tighten to 75-100 ft.lb.

43. Tighen the LH rear insulator bracket to body bracket nuts to 75-100 ft.lb.

44. Install the lower radiator hose and install retaining bracket and bolt.

45. Install the shift stabilizer bar to transaxle attaching bolt. Tighten to 23-35 ft.lb.

46. Install the shift mechanism to input shift shaft (on transaxle) bolt and nut. Tighen to 7-10 ft.lb.

47. Install the lower radiator hose to the radiator.

48. Install the speedometer cable to the transaxle.

49. Connect the heater hoses to the water pump and oil cooler.

50. Position the exhaust system up and into insulating rubber grommets located at the rear of the vehicle.

51. Install the exhaust pipe to exhaust manifold bolts.

52. Install the exhaust pipe bracket to the oil pan bolt.

53. Place the stabilizer bar and control arm assembly into position. Install control arm to body attaching bolts. Install the stabilizer bar brackets and tighten all fasteners.

54. Halfshaft assemblies must be installed at this time.

55. Lower the vehicle.

56. Remove the Engine Support Tool D79L-6000-A or equivalent.

57. Connect the alternator wiring at RH fender apron.

58. Connect the engine harness to main harness and glow plug relays at dash panel.

NOTE: Reinstall plastic shield.

59. Connect the vacuum lines.

60. Install the air conditioning discharge and suction lines to A/C compressor, if so equipped. Do not charge system at this time.

61. Connect the fuel supply and return lines to the injection pump.

62. Connect the injection pump throttle cable.

63. Install the power steering pressure and return lines. Install bracket.

64. Connect the clutch cable to shift lever on transaxle.

65. Connect the battery cable to starter.

66. Install the radiator shroud and coolant fan assembly. Tighten attaching bolts.

67. Connect the coolant fan electrical connector.

68. Install the upper radiator hose to engine.

69. Fill and bleed the cooling system.

70. Install the negative ground battery cable to battery.

71. Install the air cleaner assembly.

72. Install the hood.

73. Charge air conditioning system, if so equipped. System can be charged at a later time if outside source is used.

74. Check and refill all fluid levels, (power steering, engine, MT).

75. Start the vehicle. Check for leaks.

2.3L HSC Engine

NOTE: The following procedure is for engine and transaxle removal and installation as an assembly.

CAUTION

The engine and transaxle assembly are removed together as a unit from underneath the car. Provision must be made to safely raise and support the car for power train removal and installation.

The air conditioning system (if equipped) must be discharged prior to engine removal. The refrigerant is contained under high pressure and is very dangerous when released. The system should be discharged by a knowledgeable person using the proper equipment.

1. Mark the position of the lines on the underside of the hood and remove the hood.

2. Disconnect the battery cables from the battery, negative cable first. Remove the air cleaner assembly.

3. Remove the radiator cap and disconnect the lower radiator hose from the radiator to drain the cooling system.

CAUTION

When draining the coolant, keep in mind that cats and dogs are attracted by the ethylene glycol antifreeze, and are quite likely to drink any that is left in an uncovered container or in puddles on the ground. This will prove fatal in sufficient quantity. Always drain the coolant into a sealable container. Coolant should be reused unless it is contaminated or several years old.

4. Remove the upper and lower radiator hoses. On models equipped with an automatic transaxle, disconnect and plug the oil cooler lines from the rubber connectors at the radiator.

5. Disconnect and remove the coil from the cylinder head. Disconnect the

cooling fan wiring harness. Remove the radiator shroud and electric fan as an assembly.

6. Be sure the air conditioning system is properly and safely discharged. Remove the hoses from the compressor. Label and disconnect all electrical harness connections, linkage and vacuum lines from the engine.

7. On automatic transaxle models disconnect the TV (throttle valve) linkage at the transaxle. On manual transaxle models disconnect the clutch cable from the lever at the transaxle.

8. Disconnect the fuel supply and return lines. Plug the fuel line from the gas tank. Disconnect the thermactor pump discharge hose at the pump.

9. Disconnect the power steering lines at the pump. Remove the hose support bracket from the cylinder head.

10. Install an engine support sling (Ford Tool T79L6000A, or equivalent), see the 1.6L removal and installating engine/transaxle assembly section for details.

11. Raise and safely support the car on jackstands.

12. Remove the starter cable from the starter motor terminal. Drain the engine oil and the transaxle lubricant.

13. Disconnect the hose from the catalytic converter. Remove the bolts retaining the exhaust pipe bracket to the oil pan.

14. Remove the exhaust pipe to exhaust manifold mounting nuts. Remove the pipes from the mounting bracket insulators and position out of the way.

15. Disconnect the speedometer cable from the transaxle. Remove the heater hoses from the water pump inlet and intake manifold connector.

16. Remove the water intake tube bracket from the engine block. Remove the two clamp attaching bolts from the bottom of the oil pan. Remove the water pump inlet tube.

17. Remove the bolts attaching the control arms to the body. Remove the stabilizer bar bracket retaining bolts and remove the brackets.

18. Remove the half shafts (drive axles) from the transaxle. Plug transaxle with shipping plugs or equivalent.

19. On models equipped with a manual transaxle, remove the roll restrictor nuts from the transaxle and pull the roll restrictor from mounting bracket.

20. On models equipped with a manual transaxle, remove the shift stabilizer bar to transaxle attaching bolts. Remove the shift mechanism to shift shaft attaching nut and bolt at the transaxle.

21. On models equipped with an automatic transaxle, disconnect the shift cable clip from the transaxle lever. Remove the manual shift linkage bracket bolts from the transaxle and remove the bracket.

22. Remove the left rear No. 4 insulator mount bracket from the body by removing the retaining nuts.

23. Remove the left front No. 1 insulator to transaxle mounting bolts.

24. Lower the car and support with stands so that the front wheels are just above the ground. Do not allow the wheels to touch the ground.

25. Connect an engine sling to the lifting brackets provided. Connect a hoist to the sling and apply slight tension. Remove and support sling (Step 10).

26. Remove the right hand insulator intermediate bracket to engine bracket bolts, intermediate bracket to insulator attaching nuts and the nut on the bottom of the double ended stud which attaches the intermediate bracket and engine bracket. Remove the bracket.

27. Lower the engine and transaxle assembly to the ground.

28. Raise and support the car at a height suitable from assembly to be removed.

To Install:

29. Raise the engine and transaxle assembly and lower it into the vehicle.

30. Install the right hand insulator intermediate bracket to engine bracket bolts, intermediate bracket to insulator attaching nuts and the nut on the bottom of the double ended stud which attaches the intermediate bracket and engine bracket. Install the bracket.

31. Connect an engine sling to the Lowering brackets provided. Connect a hoist to the sling and apply slight tension. Install and support sling.

32. Raise the car and support with stands so that the front wheels are just above the ground. Do not allow the wheels to touch the ground.

33. Install the left front No. 1 insulator to transaxle mounting bolts.

34. Install the left rear No. 4 insulator mount bracket to the body by removing the retaining nuts.

35. On models equipped with an automatic transaxle, reconnect the shift cable clip to the transaxle lever. Install the manual shift linkage bracket bolts to the transaxle and install the bracket.

36. On models equipped with a manual transaxle, install the shift stabilizer bar to transaxle attaching bolts. Install the shift mechanism to shift shaft attaching nut and bolt at the transaxle.

37. On models equipped with a manual transaxle, install the roll restrictor nuts to the transaxle and pull the roll restrictor to mounting bracket.

38. Remove the shipping plugs and install the half shafts (drive axles) to the transaxle.

39. Install the bolts attaching the control arms to the body. Install the stabilizer bar bracket retaining bolts and install the brackets.

40. Install the water intake tube bracket to the engine block. Install the two clamp attaching bolts to the bottom of the oil pan. Install the water pump inlet tube.

41. Reconnect the speedometer cable to the transaxle. Install the heater hoses to the water pump inlet and intake manifold connector.

42. Install the exhaust pipe to exhaust manifold mounting nuts. Install the pipes to the mounting bracket insulators.

43. Reconnect the hose to the catalytic converter. Install the bolts retaining the exhaust pipe bracket to the oil pan.

44. Install the starter cable to the starter motor terminal. Refill the engine oil and the transaxle lubricant.

45. Lower the car from the jackstands.

46. Remove the engine support sling.

47. Reconnect the power steering lines at the pump. Install the hose support bracket to the cylinder head.

48. Reconnect the fuel supply and return lines. Reconnect the thermactor pump discharge hose at the pump.

49. On automatic transaxle models reconnect the TV (throttle valve) linkage at the transaxle. On manual transaxle models reconnect the clutch cable to the lever at the transaxle.

50. Install the hoses to the compressor. Reconnect all electrical harness connections, linkage and vacuum lines to the engine. Be sure the air conditioning system is properly and safely recharged.

51. Reconnect and install the coil to the cylinder head. Reconnect the cooling fan wiring harness. Install the radiator shroud and electric fan as an assembly.

52. Install the upper and lower radiator hoses. On models equipped with an automatic transaxle, reconnect and plug the oil cooler lines to the rubber connectors at the radiator.

53. Reconnect the lower radiator hose to the radiator. Refill the cooling system.

54. Reconnect the battery cables to the battery. Install the air cleaner assembly.

55. Install the hood.

2.5L Engine

1. Using a scribing tool, mark the position of the hood hinges and remove hood.

2. Remove the negative battery ca-

ble. Remove the air cleaner and the air duct.

3. Place a drain pan under the radiator, open the draincock and drain the cooling system. Remove upper/lower radiator-to-engine cooling hoses.

CAUTION

When draining the coolant, keep in mind that cats and dogs are attracted by the ethylene glycol antifreeze, and are quite likely to drink any that is left in an uncovered container or in puddles on the ground. This will prove fatal in sufficient quantity. Always drain the coolant into a sealable container. Coolant should be reused unless it is contaminated or several years old.

4. If equipped with an ATX, use the Cooler Line Disconnect tool No. T82L-9500-AH to disconnect the oil cooling lines from the radiator and the transaxle. Be sure to plug the cooling lines to prevent fluid draining from the transaxle.

5. Remove the ignition coil and disconnect the electrical harness connector from the coolant fan.

6. Remove the radiator shroud, the cooling fan and the radiator.

7. If equipped with with A/C, remove the compressor and move it aside, DO NOT disconnect the refrigerant lines.

8. Label and disconnect all of the electrical connectors and vacuum lines, as necessary.

9. If equipped with a MTX, disconnect the TV linkage or clutch cable from the transaxle.

10. Disconnect the accelerator linkage and the fuel lines.

CAUTION

Before disconnecting the fuel lines, relieve the pressure in the fuel system.

11. Disconnect the thermactor pump discharge hose from the pump.

12. If equipped with power steering, disconnect lines from the pump.

13. Install an engine support tool to the engine lifting eye.

14. Raise and support the front of the vehicle on jackstands.

15. Remove the electrical connectors from the starter and the hose from the catalytic converter.

16. Remove the exhaust pipe bracket-to-oil pan bolt and the exhaust pipe-to-exhaust manifold nuts.

17. Remove the exhaust system from the rubber insulating grommets and set it aside.

18. Remove the speedometer cable from the transaxle.

19. Remove the heater hoses from the water pump inlet tube and the intake manifold.

20. Remove the water pump inlet tube clamp bolt from the engine and the clamp bolts from the underside of oil pan, then the inlet tube.

21. Remove the control arm-to-body bolts. Remove the stabilizer bar bracket bolts and the brackets.

22. Remove the halfshaft assemblies from the transaxle.

23. If equipped with a MTX, perform the following procedures:

a. Remove the roll restrictor-to-transaxle nuts.

b. Pull the roll restrictor from the mounting bracket.

c. Remove the shift stabilizer bar-to-transaxle bolts.

d. Remove the shift mechanism-to-shift shaft nut/bolt.

24. If equipped with an ATX, disconnect the shift cable-to-lever clip from the transaxle, the shift linkage bracket-to-transaxle bolts and the bracket.

25. Remove the left-hand rear insulator mount bracket-to-body nuts and the bracket.

26. Remove the left-hand front insulator-to-transaxle bolts.

27. Lower the vehicle but DO NOT allow front wheels to touch floor. Install a vertical hoist to the engine lifting eyes.

28. Remove the Engine Support tool.

29. Remove the right-hand No. 3A insulator intermediate bracket-to-engine bracket bolts, the intermediate bracket-to-insulator nuts, the intermediate bracket-to-engine bracket double ended stud bottom nut and the bracket.

30. Carefully lower the engine/transaxle assembly to the floor.

31. Remove the engine-to-transaxle bolts and separate the engine from the transaxle.

32. To install, reverse the removal procedures. Refill the cooling system. Check and/or refill the engine oil and the transaxle fluid. Start the engine and check for leaks.

3.0L Engine

1. Disconnect the battery cables from the battery. Place a drain pan under the radiator and drain the cooling system. Using a scribing tool, mark the hood hinge location and remove the hood.

CAUTION

When draining the coolant, keep in mind that cats and dogs are attracted by the ethylene glycol antifreeze, and are quite likely to drink any that is left in an uncovered container or in puddles on the ground. This will prove fatal in sufficient quantity. Always drain the coolant into a sealable container. Coolant should be reused unless it is contaminated or several years old.

2. If equipped with A/C, remove the compressor and move it aside; DO NOT discharge the A/C system.

3. Remove the air cleaner assembly, the battery and the battery tray.

4. Remove the integrated relay controller, the cooling fan and the radiator with fan shroud. Remove the engine bounce damper bracket from the shock tower.

5. Remove the evaporative emission line, the upper/lower radiator hose and the starter brace.

6. Remove the exhaust pipes from both exhaust manifolds. Remove and plug the power steering pump lines.

7. Bleed the pressure from the fuel system and remove the fuel lines. Remove and tag all of the necessary vacuum lines.

8. Disconnect the ground strap, the heater hoses, the accelerator cable linkage, the throttle valve linkage and the speed control cable (if equipped).

9. Disconnect the electrical cable connectors from the following items: the alternator, the A/C clutch, the oxygen sensor, the ignition coil, the radio frequency suppressor, the cooling fan voltage resistor, the engine coolant temperature sensor, the thick film ignition module, the fuel injectors, the ISC motor wire, the throttle position sensor, the oil pressure sending switch, the ground wire, the block heater (if equipped), the knock sensor, the EGR sensor and the oil level sensor.

10. Remove the engine mounting bolts and engine mounts. Remove the transaxle-to-engine mounting bolts and the transaxle brace assembly.

11. Connect an engine lifting plate and a vertical hoist to the engine, then remove the engine from the vehicle. Remove the main wire harness from the engine.

12. To install, reverse the removal procedures. Torque the transaxle brace assembly bolts to 40-55 ft.lb., the engine mount nuts to 55-75 ft.lb. and the engine mount bolts to 40-55 ft.lb. Refill the cooling system. Check and/or refill the crankcase and the transaxle. Start the engine and check for leaks.

NOTE: On the engine mount assembly 6F063 and 6F065 torque the engine mount nuts and engine mount bolts to 70-96 ft.lb.

Rocker Arms

REMOVAL & INSTALLATION

Gasoline Engines Except Taurus and Sable

1. Disconnect the negative battery cable. Remove the air cleaner and air inlet duct. Disconnect and label all hoses and wires connected to or crossing the valve cover. Remove the cover.

2. On 1.6 & 1.9L engines, remove the rocker arm nuts and discard. On 2.3L HSC engines, remove the rocker bolts and fulcrums. Remove the rocker arms. Keep all parts in order; they must be returned to their original positions.

3. Before installation, coat the valve tips and the rocker arm contact areas with Lubriplate® or the equivalent.

4. Rotate the engine until the lifter is on the base circle of the cam (valve closed).

CAUTION

On 1.6 & 1.9L engines, turn the engine only in the direction of normal rotation. Backward rotation will cause the camshaft belt to slip or lose teeth, altering valve timing and causing serious engine damage.

5. Install the rocker arm and new hex flange nuts or fulcrum and bolt. Be sure the lifter is on the base circle of the cam for each rocker arm as it is installed.

6. Clean the valve cover mating surfaces. Apply a bead of sealer to the cover flange and install the cover. Install all disconnected hoses and wires.

TAPPET CLEARANCE

NOTE: For 2.3L HSC engine refer to the illustration provided for that procedure. Tappet gap should be 0.072-0.174″.

The 1.6 & 1.9L engine is a cam in head engine with hydraulic tappets.

Valve stem to valve rocker arm clearance should be within specifications with the tappet completely collapsed. Repeated valve reconditioning operations (valve and/or valve seat refacing) will decrease the clearance to the point that if not compensated for, the tappet will cease to function and the valve will be held open.

To determine the rocker arm-to-tappet clearance, make the following check:

1. Connect an auxiliary starter switch in the starting circuit. Crank the engine with the ignition switch Off until No. 1 piston is on TDC after the compression stroke.

2. With the crankshaft in the position designated in Steps 3 and 4, position the hydraulic lifter compressor tool on the rocker arm. Slowly apply pressure to bleed down the tappet until it is completely bottomed. Hold the tappet in this position and check the available clearance between the rocker arm and the valve stem tip with a feeler gauge. The feeler gauge width must not exceed ⅜″ (9.5mm), in order to fit between the rails on the rocker arm. If the clearance is less than specifications, check the following for wear:

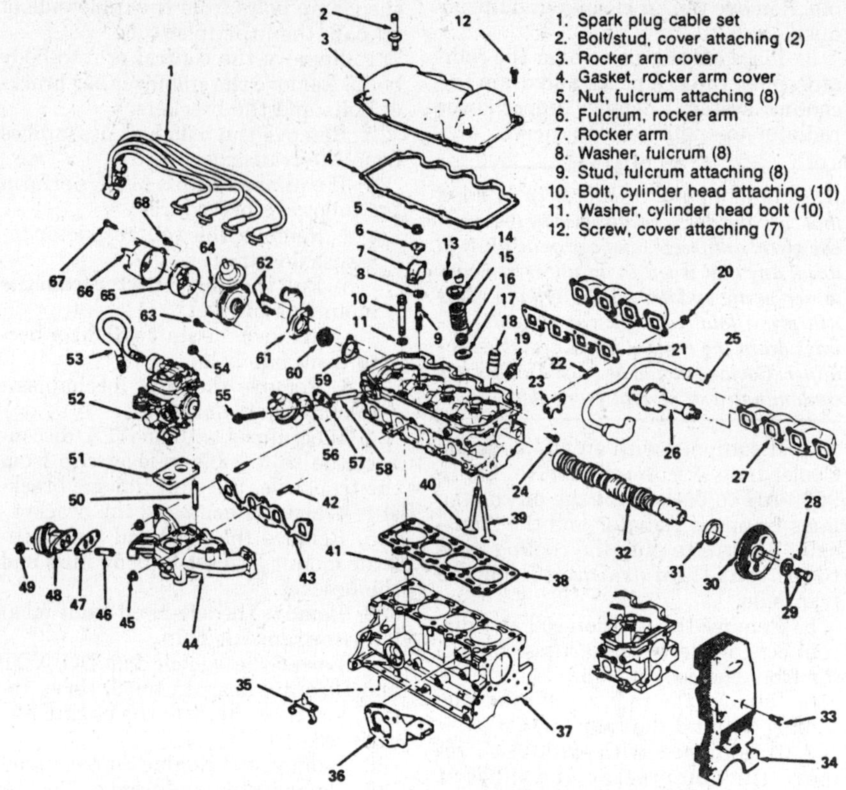

13. Keepers, valve springs
14. Retainer, valve spring
15. Valve spring
16. Seal, valve stem
17. Washer, valve spring
18. Valve lifter
19. Spark plug
20. Nut, manifold attaching (8)
21. Gasket, exhaust manifold
22. Stud, manifold attaching (8)
23. Plate, camshaft thrust
24. Bolt, thrust plate attaching (2)
25. EGR tube
26. Check valve, air injection
27. Exhaust manifold
28. Shaft key, cam sprocket
29. Bolt/washer sprocket attaching (1)
30. Camshaft sprocket
31. Seal, camshaft
32. Camshaft
33. Bolts (2) & nuts (2), cover attaching (2)
34. Timing belt cover
35. Crankcase ventilation baffle
36. Engine mount
37. Cylinder block
38. Gasket, cylinder head
39. Exhaust valve
40. Intake valve
41. Dowel, cylinder head alignment (2)
42. Stud, manifold attaching (6)
43. Gasket, intake manifold
44. Intake manifold
45. Nut, manifold attaching (6)
46. Stud, valve attaching (2)
47. Gasket, EGR valve
48. EGR valve
49. Nut, valve attaching (2)
50. Stud, carburetor attaching (4)
51. Gasket, carburetor mounting
52. Carburetor
53. Fuel line
54. Nut, carburetor attaching (4)
55. Bolt, pump attaching (2)
56. Fuel pump
57. Gasket, fuel pump
58. Push rod, fuel pump
59. Gasket, housing
60. Thermostat
61. Thermostat housing
62. Bolt, housing attaching (2)
63. Bolt, distributor attaching (3)
64. Distributor
65. Rotor
66. Distributor cap
67. Screwn cap attaching (2).
68. Screw, rotor attaching (2)

Exploded view of upper part of the 1.6L, 1.9L engines

- Fulcrum.
- Tappet.
- Cam lobe.
- Valve tip.

3. With the No. 1 piston on TDC at the end of the compression stroke (Position No. 1), check the following valves:

- No. 1 Intake No. 1 Exhaust.
- No. 2 Intake.

4. Rotate the crankshaft to Position No. 2 and check the following valves:

- No. 3 Intake No. 3 Exhaust.

5. Rotate the crankshaft another 180° from Position No. 2 back to TDC and check the following valves:

- No. 4 Intake No. 4 Exhaust.
- No. 2 Exhaust.

Collapsed tappet clearance should be 1.50-4.93mm (0.59-0.194″).

Rocker Arms/Shafts

REMOVAL & INSTALLATION

2.5L Engine

1. Raise the hood and place protective aprons on the fenders.

2. Remove the oil filler cap. Disconnect the PCV hose, the throttle linkage and the speed control cable from the top of the rocker arm cover (if equipped).

3. Remove the rocker arm cover-to-cylinder head bolts and the cover.

4. Remove the rocker arm fulcrum bolts, the fulcrums and the rocker arms. If necessary, remove the pushrods.

NOTE: When removing the rocker arm assemblies, be sure to keep all of the parts in order for installation purposes.

5. Using a putty knife, clean the gasket mounting surfaces. Inspect and/or replace any damaged parts.

NOTE: The following procedure may require the removal of the front timing cover.

6. To install the rocker arm components, perform the following procedures:

a. Position the pushrods in the hydraulic lifter.

b. Install the rocker arms, the fulcrums and the bolts onto the valves.

c. Position the crankshaft so that the timing marks, on the crankshaft and the camshaft sprockets, are facing each other (on the center line). Torque the rocker arm fulcrum bolts of the intake valves of cylinders No. 1 and 2 and the exhaust valves of cylinders No. 1 and 3 to 4.5-7.5 ft.lb. (6-10 Nm).

d. Turn the crankshaft one complete revolution so that the timing marks, on the crankshaft and the camshaft sprockets, are facing opposite each other (on the center line). Torque the rocker arm fulcrum bolts of the intake valves of cylinders No. 3 and 4 and the exhaust valves of cylinders No. 2 and 4 to 4.5-7.5 ft.lb. (6-10 Nm).

e. Apply SAE 50 oil to all of the fulcrums, the rocker arms and the pushrods. Torque all of the fulcrum bolts to 19.5-26.5 ft.lb. (26-38 Nm).

NOTE: Before torquing the rocker arm fulcrum bolts, be sure that the fulcrums are seated on the cylinder head slots and the pushrods are seated in the rocker arms/tappets.

7. To check the collapsed lifter gap, perform the following procedures:

a. Position the crankshaft so that the timing marks, on the crankshaft and the camshaft sprockets, are facing each other (on the center line). Using a feeler gauge, check the tappet gap of the intake valves of cylinders No. 1 and 2 and the exhaust valves of cylinders No. 1 and 3; the tappet gap should be 0.072-0.174" (1.80-4.34mm).

b. Turn the crankshaft one complete revolution so that the timing marks, on the crankshaft and the camshaft sprockets, are facing opposite each other (on the center line). Using a feeler gauge, check the tappet gap of the intake valves of cylinders No. 3 and 4 and the exhaust valves of cylinders No. 2 and 4; the tappet gap should be 0.072-0.174" (1.80-4.34mm).

8. To complete the installation, use a new gasket and reverse the removal procedures. Start the engine and check for leaks.

1. Dowell, pressure plate alignment
2. Flywheel
3. Seal, crankshaft rear
4. Bolt, retainer attaching (6)
5. Seal retainer
6. Gasket, retainer
7. Cylinder block
8. Engine lifting eye
9. Plug and gasket, monolithic timing
10. Plug, coolant drain
11. Gasket, pump (oil)
12. Oil pump
13. Gasket, pump (water)
14. Water pump
15. Bolt, pump (water) attaching (4)
16. Timing belt—installed view
17. Spring, tensioner
18. Bracket and idler, tensioner
19. Bolt, tensioner attaching (2)
20. Timing belt cover
21. Crankshaft pulley
22. Washer, pulley bolt (1)
23. Bolt, Pulley attaching (1)
24. Bolt, cover attaching (4)
25. Oil pump
26. Gasket, pick up tube
27. Pick up and tube assembly
28. Bolt, pick up attaching (2)
29. Gear, crankshaft
30. Guide, timing belt
31. Seal, crankshaft front
32. Bolt, pump (oil) attaching (6)
33. Bolt, brace attaching (1)
34. Seal, pan front
35. Gasket, pan side
36. Oil pan
37. Seal, drain plug
38. Plug, oil pan drain
39. Bolt, Pan attaching (18)
40. Gasket, Pan side
41. Seal, pan rear
42. Bolt, cap attaching (10)
43. Main bearing caps
44. Main bearing inserts, lower
45. Crankshaft
46. Main bearing inserts, upper
47. Oil pressure sending unit
48. Dowel, transmission alignment
49. Adapter, oil filter
50. Oil filter
51. Piston
52. Piston pin
53. Connecting rod
54. Connecting rod bearings
55. Connecting rod cap
56. Nut, cap attaching
57. Bolt, cap attaching

Exploded view of lower part of the 1.6L, 1.9L engines

3.0L Engine

1. Label and disconnect the ignition wires from the spark plugs.

2. Remove the ignition wire separators from the rocker arm cover mounting bolt studs.

3. To remove the left side rocker arm cover, remove the oil filler cap then disconnect the closure system hose.

4. To remove the right side rocker

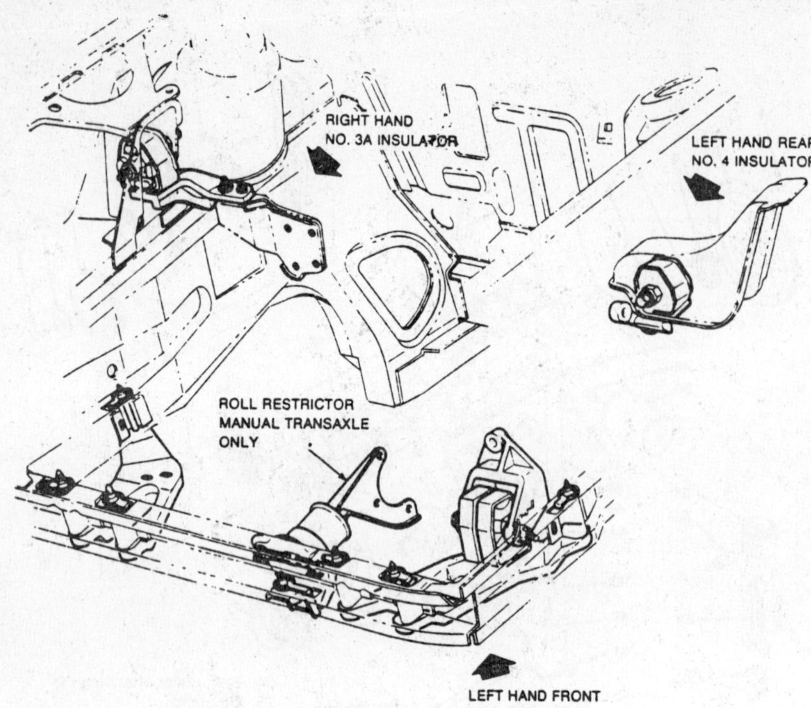

Typical 1.6L, 1.9L engine and transaxle mounting

arm cover, remove the PCV valve, disconnect the EGR tube, then disconnect the heater hoses.

5. Remove the rocker arm covers-to-cylinder head screws and the covers.

6. Remove the rocker arm fulcrum bolts, the fulcrums and the rocker arms. If necessary, remove the pushrods.

NOTE: When removing the rocker arm assemblies, be sure to keep all of the parts in order for installation purposes.

7. Using a putty knife, clean the gasket mounting surfaces. Inspect and/or replace any damaged parts.

8. To install the rocker arm components, first position the pushrods on the tappets. Install the rocker arms, the fulcrums and the bolts onto the valves, but DO NOT tighten the bolts. Using SAE 50 oil, apply it to all of the fulcrums, the rocker arms and the pushrods.

NOTE: Before torquing the rocker arm fulcrum bolts, be sure that the fulcrums are seated in the cylinder head slots and the pushrods are seated in the rocker arms/tappets.

9. For each valve, rotate the crankshaft until the tappet rests on the heel (base circle) of the camshaft lobe. Torque the rocker arm fulcrum bolts to 19-25 ft.lb. (25-35 Nm).

NOTE: If the original valve components are being installed, a valve clearance check is not required. Valve Clearance: 0.088-0.189″ (2.23-4.77mm).

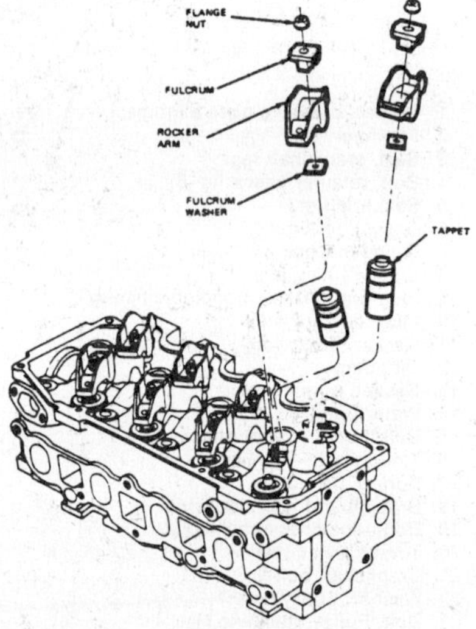

Exploded view of the upper valve train—1.6L, 1.9L engines

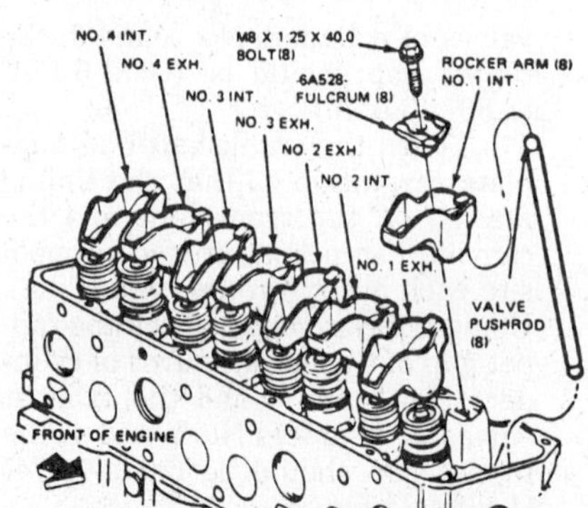

Valve train components—2.3L HSC

10. Rotate the crankshaft to place the No. 1 cylinder on TDC of the compression stroke, then allow the lifters to bleed down.

11. Using a feeler gauge, check that the valve clearances of cylinders No. 1, 3 & 6 (intake) and No. 1, 2 & 4 (exhaust) are 0.088-0.189″ (2.23-4.77mm).

12. Rotate the crankshaft one complete revolution, positioning the No. 2 cylinder on TDC of the compression stroke, then allow the lifters to bleed down.

13. Using a feeler gauge, check that the valve clearances of cylinders No. 2, 4 & 5 (intake) and No. 3, 5 & 6 (exhaust) are 0.088-0.189″ (2.23-4.77mm).

14. To complete the installation, use a new gasket and reverse the removal procedures. Start the engine and check for leaks.

Exhaust Manifold

REMOVAL & INSTALLATION

1.6L and 1.9L

1. Disconnect the negative battery cable.

2. Remove the air cleaner duct for access to the manifold.

3. Disconnect the Thermactor (air pump) line from the manifold. Disconnect the EGR tube. Remove heat shield. Disconnect sensor wire if equipped. Unbolt the exhaust pipe from the manifold flange. Remove the turbocharger, if equipped.

4. Unbolt and remove the exhaust manifold.

5. Clean the manifold and cylinder head mating surfaces. Place a new gasket on the exhaust pipe-to-manifold flange.

6. Install the manifold. Tighten the bolts in a circular pattern, working from the center to the ends, in three progressive steps.

2.5L Engine

1. Refer to the Intake Manifold Removal & Installation procedures in this section and remove the intake manifold.

2. Disconnect the exhaust pipe-to-exhaust manifold nuts.

3. Remove the heat shield from the exhaust manifold.

4. Disconnect the electrical connector from the EGO sensor.

5. Disconnect the thermactor check valve hose from the tube assembly. Remove the bracket-to-EGR valve nuts.

6. Remove the exhaust manifold-to-engine bolts and the manifold from the vehicle.
7. Using a putty knife, clean the gasket mounting surfaces.

NOTE: When installing the exhaust manifold, use the Alignment Stud tools No. T84P-6065-B to align the manifold with the block.

8. To install, use new gaskets and reverse the removal procedures. Torque the exhaust manifold-to-engine bolts (in two steps) to 20-30 ft.lb. (27-41 Nm), the exhaust manifold-to-exhaust pipe nuts to 25-34 ft.lb. (34-47 Nm) and the intake manifold-to-engine bolts to 15-23 ft.lb. (20-30 Nm). Refill the cooling system. Start engine and check for leaks.

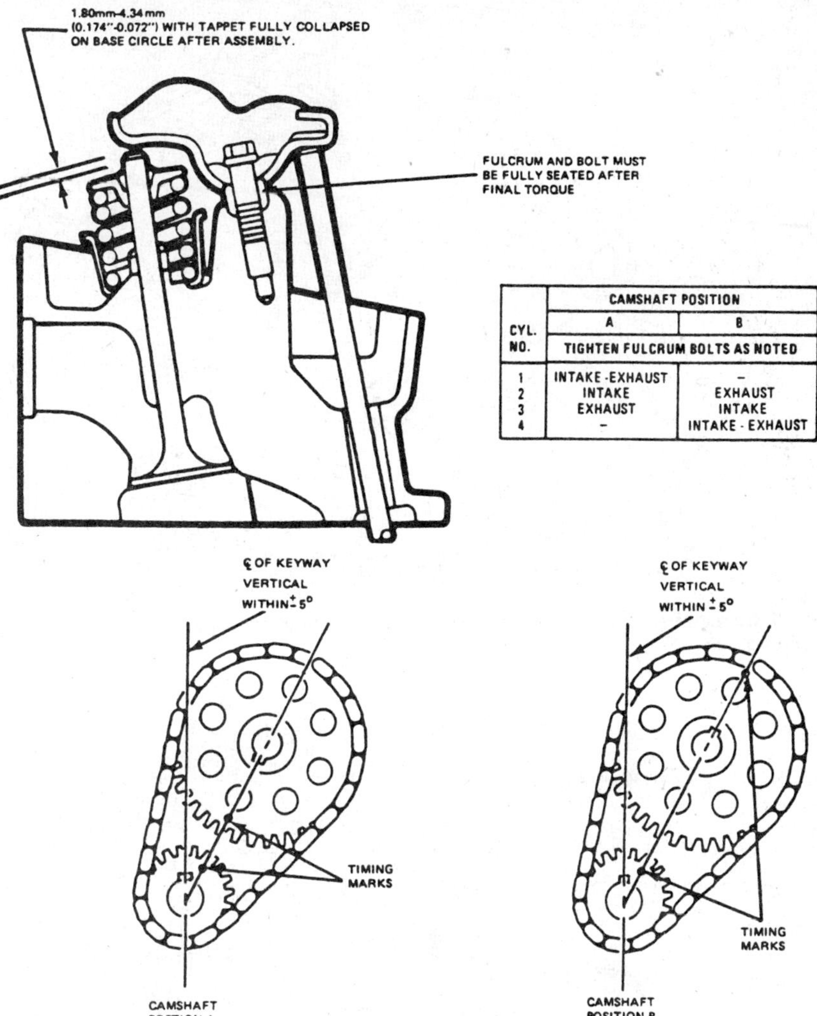

CYL. NO.	CAMSHAFT POSITION A	CAMSHAFT POSITION B
	TIGHTEN FULCRUM BOLTS AS NOTED	
1	INTAKE -EXHAUST	–
2	INTAKE	EXHAUST
3	EXHAUST	INTAKE
4	–	INTAKE - EXHAUST

Checking the collapsed tappet gap on 2.3L HSC engine

3.0L Engine

LEFT SIDE

1. Disconnect the negative battery cable. Remove the oil level indicator support bracket.
2. Disconnect and plug the power steering hoses at the power steering pump.
3. Remove the exhaust manifold-to-exhaust pipe nuts and separate the exhaust pipe from the exhaust manifold.
4. Remove the exhaust manifold-to-cylinder head bolts and the exhaust manifold from the engine.
5. Using a putty knife, clean gasket mounting surfaces. Lightly oil all of the bolt/stud threads prior to installation.
6. To install, use new gaskets and reverse the removal procedures. Torque the exhaust manifold-to-engine bolts to 15-22 fft.lb. (20-30 Nm) and the exhaust manifold-to-exhaust pipe nuts to 16-24 ft.lb. (21-32 Nm). Refill and bleed the power steering system.

3.0L Engine

RIGHT SIDE

1. Disconnect the negative battery cable. Remove the heater hose support bracket.
2. Disconnect and plug the heater hoses. Remove the EGR tube from the exhaust manifold; use a back-up wrench on the lower adapter.
3. Remove the exhaust manifold-to-exhaust pipe nuts and separate the pipe from the manifold.
4. Remove the exhaust manifold-to-engine bolts and the exhaust manifold from the engine.
5. Using a putty knife, clean the gasket mounting surfaces.

NOTE: Lightly oil all of the bolt and stud threads prior to installation.

6. To install, use new gaskets and reverse the removal procedures. Torque the exhaust manifold-to-engine bolts to 15-22 fft.lb. (20-30 Nm), the exhaust pipe-to-exhaust manifold nuts to 16-24 ft.lb. (21-32 Nm) and the EGR tube-to-exhaust manifold to 25-36 ft.lb. (35-50 Nm).

Diesel Engine

1. Remove the nuts attaching the muffler inlet pipe to the exhaust manifold.
2. Remove the bolts attaching the heat shield to the exhaust manifold.
3. Remove the nuts attaching the exhaust manifold to cylinder head and remove the exhaust manifold.
4. Install the exhaust manifold, using new gaskets, and tighten nuts to 16-20 ft.lb.
5. Install the exhaust shield and tighten bolts to 12-16 ft.lb.
6. Connect the muffler inlet pipe to the exhaust manifold and tighten the nuts to 25-35 ft.lb.
7. Run the engine and check for exhaust leaks.

Intake Manifold

REMOVAL & INSTALLATION

Carbureted Engines

1. Disconnect the negative battery terminal.
2. Remove the air cleaner housing.
3. Partially drain the cooling system and disconnect the heater hose from under the intake manifold.

CAUTION

When draining the coolant, keep in mind that cats and dogs are attracted by the ethylene glycol antifreeze, and are quite likely to

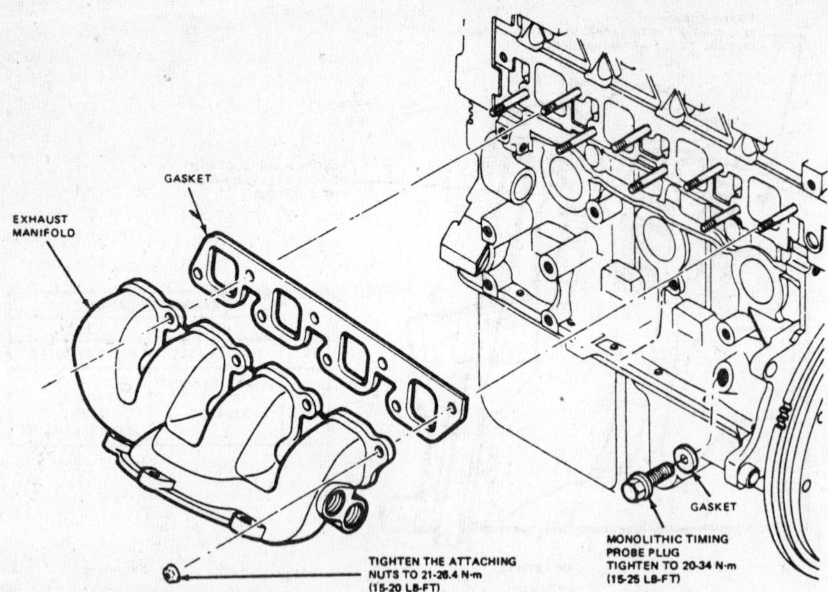

Install the exhaust manifold and tighten retaining bolts in the sequence shown—1.6L, 1.9L engines

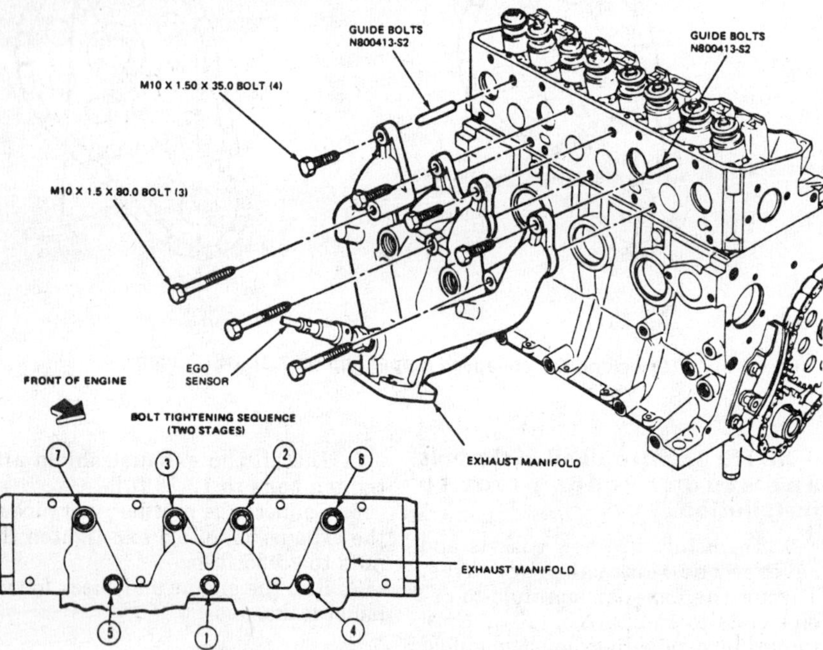

Exhuast manifold installation—2.3L HSC engine

drink any that is left in an uncovered container or in puddles on the ground. This will prove fatal in sufficient quantity. Always drain the coolant into a sealable container. Coolant should be reused unless it is contaminated or several years old.

---

4. Disconnect and label all vacuum and electrical connections.
5. Disconnect the fuel line and carburetor linkage.
6. Disconnect the EGR vacuum hose and supply tube.
7. On Escort & Lynx models, jack up the vehicle and support it with jackstands.
8. On Escort & Lynx models, remove the bottom (3) intake manifold nuts.
9. On Escort & Lynx models, remove the vehicle from the jackstands.
10. If equipped with automatic transmission disconnect the throttle valve linkage at the carburetor and remove the cable bracket attaching bolts.
11. If equipped with power steering (Escort/Lynx), remove the thermactor pump drive belt, the pump, the mounting bracket, and the by-pass hose.
12. Remove the fuel pump (Escort/Lynx). See the fuel pump removal procedure.
13. Remove the intake bolts, the manifold, and gasket.

NOTE: Do not lay the intake manifold flat as the gasket surfaces may be damaged.

To install:

14. Install the intake manifold, and gasket.
15. Install the fuel pump (Escort/Lynx).
16. If equipped with power steering (Escort/Lynx), install the thermactor pump drive belt, the pump, the mounting bracket, and the by-pass hose.
17. If equipped with automatic transmission reconnect the throttle valve linkage at the carburetor and install the cable bracket attaching bolts.
18. On Escort & Lynx models, jack up the vehicle and support it with jackstands.
19. On Escort & Lynx models, install the bottom (3) intake manifold nuts.
20. On Escort & Lynx models, remove the vehicle from the jackstands.
21. Reconnect the EGR vacuum hose and supply tube.
22. Reconnect the fuel line and carburetor linkage.
23. Reconnect all vacuum and electrical connections.
24. Reconnect the heater hose to under the intake manifold and refill the cooling system.
25. Install the air cleaner housing.
26. Reconnect the negative battery terminal.

2.5L Engine

1. Raise and secure the hood. Disconnect the negative battery cable.
2. Place a drain pan under the radiator, remove the radiator cap, open the draincock and drain the cooling system.

CAUTION

When draining the coolant, keep in mind that cats and dogs are attracted by the ethylene glycol antifreeze, and are quite likely to drink any that is left in an uncovered container or in puddles on the ground. This will prove fatal in sufficient quantity. Always drain the coolant into a sealable container. Coolant should be reused unless it is contaminated or several years old.

---

3. Remove the accelerator cable, the air cleaner assembly and the heat stove tube from the heat shield.
4. Label and remove the necessary vacuum lines.
5. Remove the thermactor belt, the

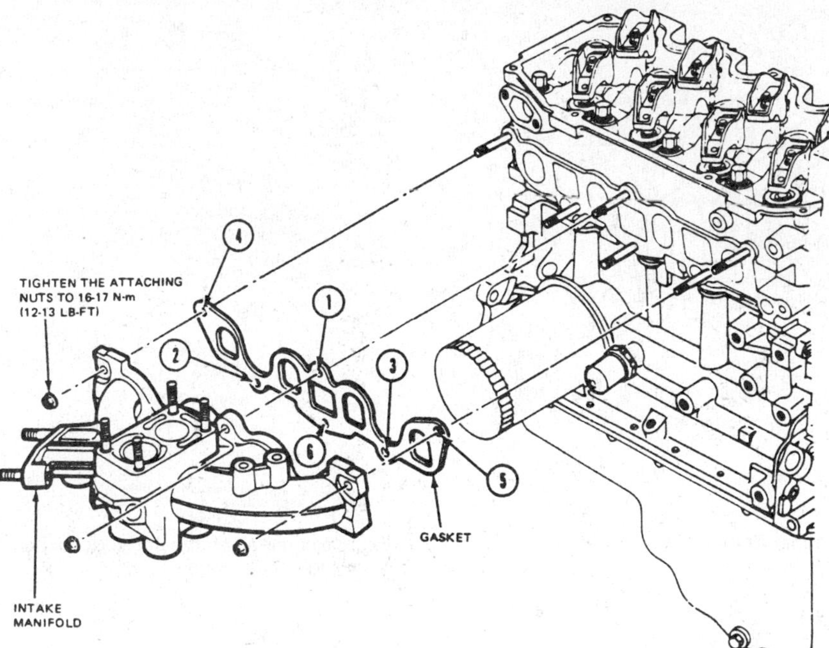

Install the intake manifold and tighten the retaining bolts in the sequence shown—1.6L, 1.9L carbureted engines

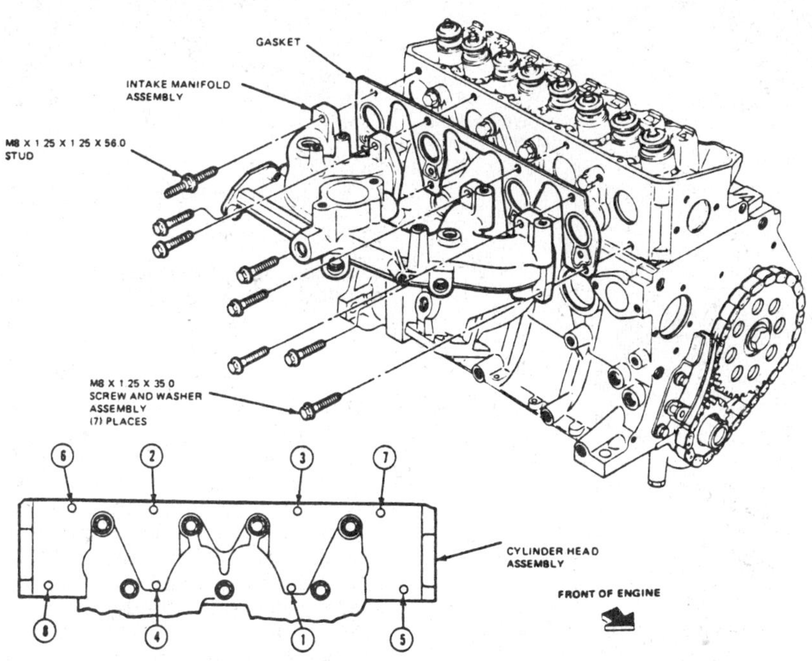

Intake manifold installation—2.3L HSC engine

hose below thermactor pump and the thermactor pump.

6. Remove the heat shield from the exhaust manifold.

7. Disconnect the thermactor check valve hose from the tube assembly. Remove the bracket-to-EGR valve nuts.

8. Disconnect the water inlet tube from the intake manifold.

9. Disconnect the EGR tube from the EGR valve.

10. Remove the intake manifold-to-engine bolts and the manifold.

11. Using a putty knife, clean the gasket mounting surfaces.

12. To install, use a new gasket and reverse the removal procedures. Torque the intake manifold-to-engine bolts to 15-23 fft.lb. (20-30 Nm). Refill the cooling system. Start engine and check for leaks.

3.0L Engine

1. Disconnect the negative battery cable. Drain the cooling system to a level below the intake manifold.

CAUTION

When draining the coolant, keep in mind that cats and dogs are attracted by the ethylene glycol antifreeze, and are quite likely to drink any that is left in an uncovered container or in puddles on the ground. This will prove fatal in sufficient quantity. Always drain the coolant into a sealable container. Coolant should be reused unless it is contaminated or several years old.

2. Refer to the "Throttle Body Removal & Installation" procedures in the FUEL SYSTEM section and remove the throttle body from the engine.

3. Reduce the pressure in the fuel system and disconnect the fuel lines.

4. Disconnect and remove the fuel injector electrical harness from the engine.

5. Label and disconnect the spark plug wires (for easy installation). Mark and remove the distributor from the engine.

6. Disconnect the upper radiator hose, the water outlet heater hose and the thermostat housing from the engine.

7. Remove the intake manifold-to-engine bolts/studs, the intake manifold; discard the side gaskets and end seals.

NOTE: The intake manifold assembly can be removed with the fuel rails and injectors in place.

8. Using a putty knife, clean the gasket/seal mounting surfaces.

9. To install, use new gaskets, sealant and reverse the removal procedures. Torque the intake manifold-to-engine bolts (in 2 steps) to 18 ft.lb. (24 Nm), the throttle body-to-engine bolts to 15-22 ft.lb. (20-30 Nm) and the thermostat housing-to-engine bolts to 6-8 ft.lb. Refill the cooling system. Start the engine and check for leaks. Check and/or adjust the idle speed, the transmission throttle linkage and the speed control.

NOTE: Lightly oil all of the bolts/stud threads before installation. When using a silicone rubber sealer, assembly must occur within 15 minutes after the sealer has been applied. After this time, the sealer may start to set-up and its sealing quality may be reduced. In high temperature/humidity conditions the sealant will start to set up in approximately 5 minutes.

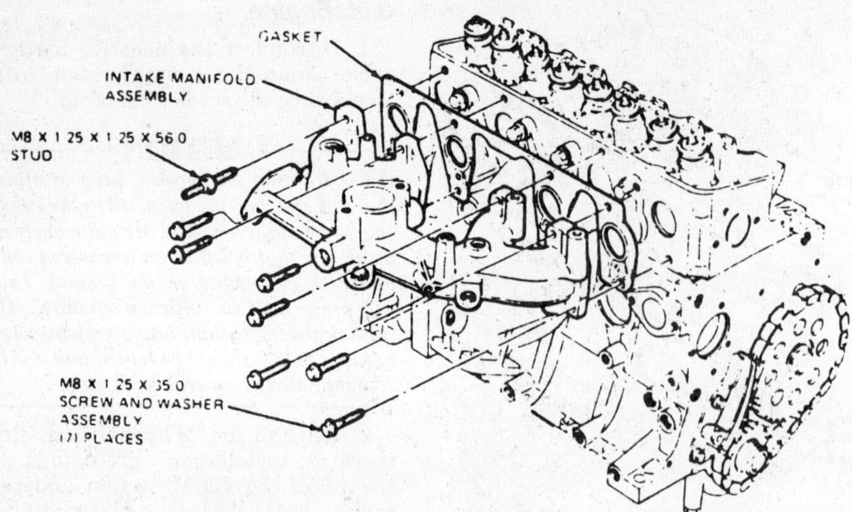

Exploded view of the intake manifold—2.5L engine

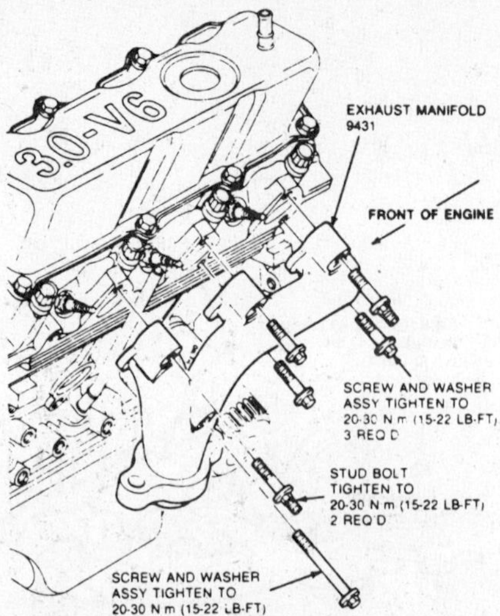

Exploded view of the left-side exhaust manifold—3.0L engine

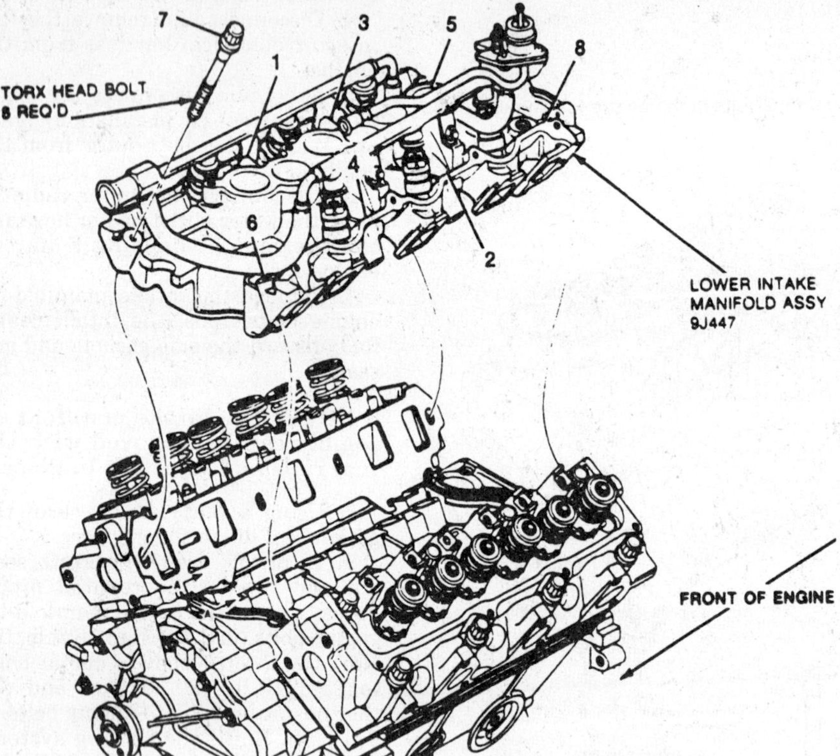

Exploded view and torque sequence of the intake manifold—3.0L engine

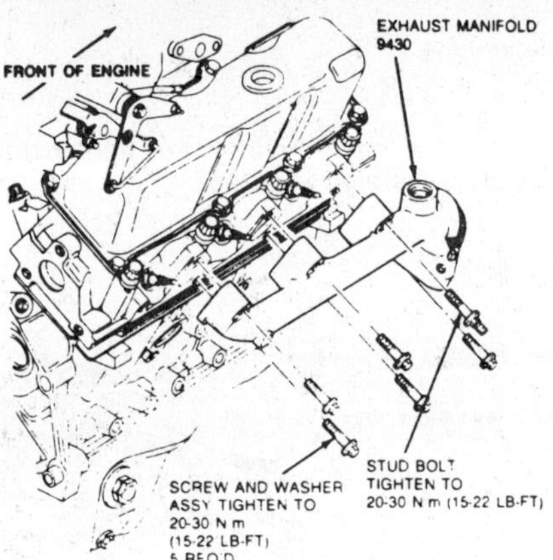

Exploded view of the right-side exhaust manifold—3.0L engine

Diesel Engine

1. Disconnect the air inlet duct from the intake manifold and install the protective cap in the intake manifold (part or Protective Cap Set T84P-9395-A or equivalent).
2. Disconnect the glow plug resistor electrical connector.
3. Disconnect the breather hose.
4. Drain the cooling system.

CAUTION

When draining the coolant, keep in mind that cats and dogs are attracted by the ethylene glycol antifreeze, and are quite likely to drink any that is left in an uncovered container or in puddles on the ground. This will prove fatal in sufficient quantity. Always drain the coolant into a sealable container. Coolant should be reused unless it is contaminated or several years old.

5. Disconnect the upper radiator hose at the thermostat housing.
6. Disconnect the tow coolant hoses at the thermostat housing.
7. Disconnect the connectors to the temperature sensors in the thermostat housing.
8. Remove the bolts attaching the intake manifold to the cylinder head and remove the intake manifold.
9. Clean the intake manifold and cylinder head gasket mating surfaces.
10. Install the intake manifold, using a new gasket, and tighten the bolts to 12-16 ft.lb.
11. Connect the temperature sensor connectors.
12. Connect the lower coolant hose to the thermostat housing and tighten the hose clamp.
13. Connect the upper coolant tube, using a new gasket and tighten bolts to 5-7 ft.lb.
14. Connect the upper radiator hose to the thermostat housing.
15. Connect the breather hose.
16. Connect the glow plug resistor electrical connector.
17. Remove the protective cap and install the air inlet duct.

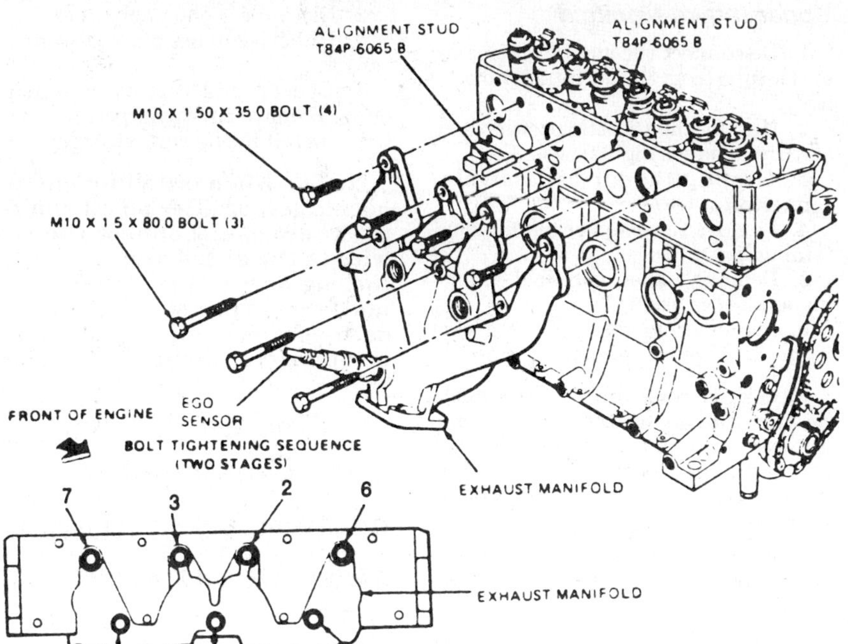

Exploded view and torque sequence of the exhaust manifold—2.5L engine

18. Fill and bleed the cooling system.
19. Run the engine and check for intake air leaks and coolant leaks.

Fuel Delivery Manifold

The air intake manifold is a two piece (upper and lower intake manifold) aluminum casting. Runner lengths are tuned to optimize engine torque and power output. The manifold provides mounting flanges for the air throttle body assembly, fuel supply manifold and accelerator control bracket and the EGR valve and supply tube. Vacuum taps are provided to support various engine accessories. Pockets for the fuel injectors are machined to prevent both air and fuel leakage. The pockets, in which the injectors are mounted, are placed to direct the injector fuel spray immediately in front of each engine intake valve.

Fuel Charging Assembly

NOTE: If sub-assemblies are to be serviced and/or removed, with the fuel charging assembly mounted to the engine, the following steps must be taken:

1. Open hood and install protective covers.
2. Make sure that ignition key is in Off position.
3. Drain coolant from radiator.

CAUTION

When draining the coolant, keep in mind that cats and dogs are attracted by the ethylene glycol antifreeze, and are quite likely to drink any that is left in an uncovered container or in puddles on the ground. This will prove fatal in sufficient quantity. Always drain the coolant into a sealable container. Coolant should be reused unless it is contaminated or several years old.

4. Disconnect the negative battery lead and secure it out of the way.
5. Remove fuel cap to relieve fuel tank pressure.
6. Release pressure from the fuel system at the fuel pressure relief valve on the fuel injection manifold assembly. Use tool T80L-9974-A or equivalent. To gain access to the fuel pressure relief valve, the valve cap must first be removed.
7. Disconnect the push connect fuel supply line. Using a small bladed screwdriver inserted under the hairpin clip tab, pop the clip free from the push connect tube fitting and disconnect the tube. Save the hairpin clip for use in reassembly.
8. Identify and disconnect the fuel return lines and vacuum connections.

NOTE: Care must be taken to avoid combustion from fuel spillage.

9. Disconnect the injector wiring harness by disconnecting the ECT sensor in the heater supply tube under lower intake manifold and the electronic engine control harness.
10. Disconnect air bypass connector from EEC harness.

NOTE: Not all assemblies may be serviceable while on the engine. In some cases, removal of the fuel charging assembly may facilitate service of the various sub-assemblies. To remove the entire fuel charging assembly, the following procedure should be followed:

REMOVAL & INSTALLATION

1. Remove the engine air cleaner outlet tube between the vane air meter and air throttle body by loosening two clamps.
2. Disconnect and remove the accelerator and speed control cables (if so eqiupped) from the accelerator mounting bracket and throttle lever.
3. Disconnect the top manifold vacuum fitting connections by disconnecting:
   a. Rear vacuum line to the dash panel vacuum tree.
   b. Front vacuum line to the air cleaner and fuel pressure regulator.
4. Disconnect the PCV system by disconnecting the hoses from:
   a. Two large forward facing connectors on the throttle body and intake manifold.
   b. Throttle body port hose at the straight plastic connector.
   c. Canister purge line at the straight plastic connector.
   d. PCV hose at rocker cover.
   e. Unbolt PCV separator support bracket from cylinder head and remove PCV system.
5. Disconnect the EGR vacuum line at the EGR valve.
6. Disconnect the EGR tube from the upper intake manifold by removing the two flange nuts.
7. Withdraw the dipstick and remove the dipstick tube by removing the tube bracket mounting nut and working the tube out of the block hole.
8. Remove the fuel return line.
9. Remove six manifold mounting nuts.
10. Remove the manifold with wiring harness and gasket.
11. Clean and inspect the mounting faces of the fuel charging manifold assembly and the cylinder head. Both surfaces must be clean and flat.
12. Clean and oil manifold stud threads.
13. Install a new gasket.
14. Install manifold assembly to head and secure with top middle nut (tighten nut finger tight only at this time).
15. Install fuel return line to the fitting in the fuel supply manifold. In-

stall two manifold mounting nuts, fingertight.

16. Install dipstick in block and secure with bracket nut fingertight.

17. Install remaining three manifold mounting nuts and tighten all six nuts to 12-15 ft.lb. observing specified tightening sequence.

18. Install EGR tube with two oil coated flange nuts tightened to 6-8.5 ft.lb.

19. Reinstall PCV system.

a. Mount separator bracket to head.

b. Install hose on rocker cover, tighten clamps.

c. Connect vacuum line to canister purge.

d. Connect vacuum line to throttle body port.

e. Connect large PCV vacuum line to throttle body.

f. Connect large PCV vacuum line to upper manifold.

20. Connect manifold vacuum connections:

a. Rear connection to vacuum tree.

b. Front connection to fuel pressure regulator and air cleaner.

21. Connect accelerator and speed control cables (if so equipped).

22. Install air supply tube and tighten clamps to 25 in.lb.

23. Connect the wiring harness at:

a. ECT sensor in heater supply tube.

b. Electronic Engine Control harness.

24. Connect the fuel supply hose from the fuel filter to the fuel rail.

25. Connect the fuel return line.

26. Connect negative battery cable.

27. Install engine coolant using prescribed fill procedure.

28. Start engine and allow to run at idle until engine temperature is stabilized. Check for coolant leaks.

29. If necessary, reset idle speed.

REMOVAL & INSTALLATION OF SUB-ASSEMBLIES

NOTE: To prevent damage to fuel chargine assembly, the unit should be placed on a work bench during disassembly and assembly procedures. The following is a step by step sequence of operations for servicing the assemblies of the fuel charging manifold. Some components may be serviced without a complete disassembly of the fuel charging manifold. To replace individual components, follow only the applicable steps.

These procedures are based on the fuel charging manifold having been removed from the vehicle.

Upper Intake Manifold

1. Disconnect the engine air cleaner outlet tube from the air intake throttle body.

2. Unplug the throttle position sensor from the wiring harness.

3. Unplug the air bypass valve connector.

4. Remove three upper manifold retaining bolts.

5. Remove upper manifold assembly and set it aside.

6. Remove and discard the gasket from the lower manifold assembly.

NOTE: If scraping is necessary, be careful not to damage the gasket surfaces of the upper and lower manifold assemblies, or allow material to drop into lower manifold.

7. Ensure that the gasket surfaces of the upper and lower intake manifolds are clean.

8. Place a new service gasket on the lower manifold assembly and mount the upper intake manifold to the lower, securing it with three retaining bolts. Tighten bolts to 15-22 ft.lb.

9. Ensure the wiring harness is properly installed.

10. Connect electrical connectors t air bypass valve and throttle position sensor and the vacuum hose to the fuel pressure regulator.

11. Connect the engine air cleaner outlet tube to the throttle body intake securing it with a hose clamp. Tighten to 15-25 in.lb.

Turbocharger

REMOVAL & INSTALLATION

1. Allow engine to cool. Disconnect intake hose between turbocharger and injector unit.

2. Disconnect oil supply lines.

3. Unbolt exhaust pipe. Disconnect sensors.

4. Loosen and remove mounting bolts. Remove turbocharger.

5. Install in the reverse order.

NOTE: When installing the turbocharger, or after an oil and filter change, disconnect the coil wire to the distributor and crank the engine with the starter motor until the oil pressure light on the dash goes out. Oil pressure must be up before starting the engine.

Air Conditioning Compressor

REMOVAL & INSTALLATION

Escort/EXP and Lynx/LN7

1981-83

1. Discharge the system following the recommended service procedures in ROUTINE MAINTENANCE. Observe all safety precautions.

2. Disconnect the alternator wire at the multiple connector.

3. Remove the carburetor air cleaner and the air intake and tube assembly from the radiator support.

4. Disconnect the alternator air tube from the air inlet on the radiator support.

5. Remove the alternator from the engine.

6. Disconnect the compressor clutch wires at the field coil connector on the compressor.

7. Disconnect the discharge hose and the suction hose from the compressor manifolds. Cap the refrigerant lines and compressor manifolds to prevent the entrance of dirt and moisture.

8. Raise the vehicle and remove two

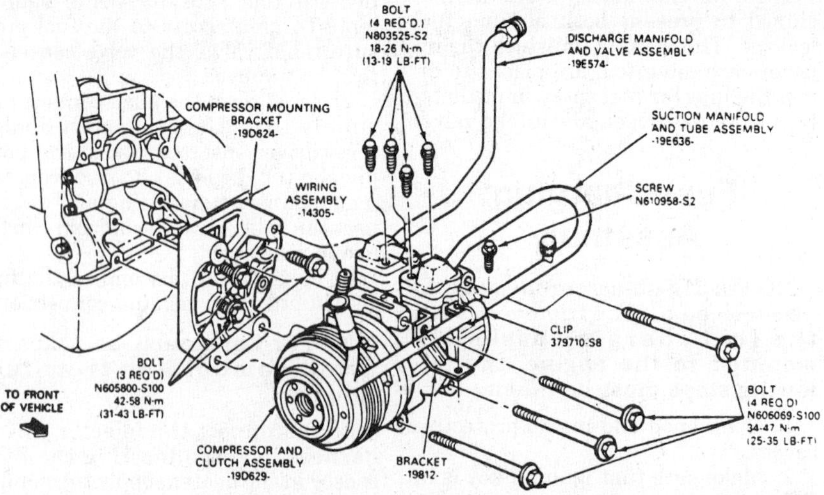

Escort/Lynx compressor mounting—typical

bolts attaching the front legs of the compressor to the mounting bracket.

9. Remove two screws attaching the heater water return tube to the underside of the engine supports.

10. Remove two bolts attaching the compressor bracket assembly to the compressor bracket.

11. Lower the vehicle and remove one bolt attaching the top of the compressor to the mounting bracket.

12. Tilt the top of the compressor toward the radiator to disengage the top mounting tab from the compressor bracket. Then, lift the compressor from the engine compartment, rear head first.

13. If the compressor is to be replaced, remove the clutch and field coil assembly and the compressor bracket assembly from the compressor.

14. Installation is the reverse of the removal procedure.

1984-87

1. Disconnect the alternator wires at the multiple connector and remove the alternator from the engine.

2. Discharge the A/C system and disconnect the compressor clutch wires at the field coil connector on the compressor.

3. On the 1.6L EFI and HO engines, remove the discharge and suction hoses at the compressor manifolds.

4. On the 1.6L Turbo and 2.0L Diesel engines, remove the discharge hose from the manifold tube with a ½" lock coupling tool (#T81P-19623-G2 or equivalent). Use a ⅝" spring lock coupling tool (#T83P-19632-C or equivalent) to remove the suction hose.

5. Remove the four retaining bolts attaching the compressor to the compressor bracket and remove the compressor from the engine compartment.

6. Installation is the reverse of the removal procedure.

Tempo/Topaz

1. Discharge the system following the recommended service procedures in ROUTINE MAINTENANCE. Observe all safety precautions.

2. Disconnect the compressor clutch wires at the field coil connector on the compressor.

3. Disconnect the discharge hose and the suction hose from the compressor manifolds. Cap the refrigerant lines and compressor manifolds to prevent the entrance of dirt and moisture.

4. Separate the discharge refrigerant line at the spring lock coupling above the compressor with Tool T81P-19623-G or equivalent and remove the lower end of the discharge line.

5. Loosen the two idler attaching screws and release the compressor belt tension.

6. Raise the vehicle and remove the four bolts attaching the front legs of the compressor to the mounting bracket.

7. Remove two screws attaching the heater water return tube to the underside of the engine supports.

8. Move the compressor to the left and remove the compressor from the underside of the vehicle.

9. If the compressor is to be replaced, remove the clutch and field coil assembly from the compressor.

10. Installation is the reverse of the removal procedure. If the compressor is to be replaced, drain the oil from the removed compressor into a calibrated measuring container. Record the amount of oil (fluid ounces) drained from the old compressor, discard the oil. Check the system for proper operation.

Cylinder Head

REMOVAL & INSTALLATION

1.6 & 1.9L Engine

NOTE: The engine must be overnight cold before removing the cylinder head, to reduce the possibility of warpage or distortion.

CAUTION

Always use new head bolts when reinstalling the cylinder head.

1. Disconnect the negative battery cable.

2. Drain the cooling system, disconnect the heater hose under the intake manifold, and disconnect the radiator upper hose at the cylinder head.

CAUTION

When draining the coolant, keep in mind that cats and dogs are attracted by the ethylene glycol antifreeze, and are quite likely to drink any that is left in an uncovered container or in puddles on the ground. This will prove fatal in sufficient quantity. Always drain the coolant into a sealable container. Coolant should be reused unless it is contaminated or several years old.

3. Disconnect the wiring from the cooling fan switch, remove the air cleaner assembly, remove the PCV hose, and disconnect all interfering vacuum hoses after marking them for reassembly.

4. Remove the valve cover and disconnect all accessory drive belts. Remove the crankshaft pulley. Remove the timing belt cover.

5. Set the No.1 cylinder to top dead center compression stroke. See distributor removal & installation procedure for details.

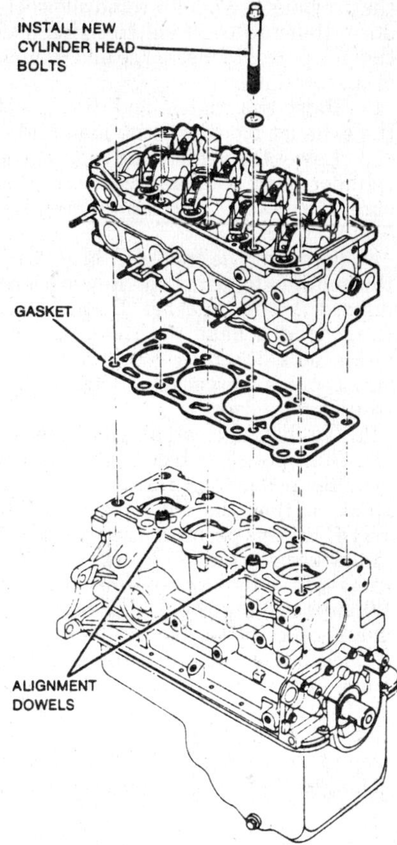

1.6L and 1.9L cylinder head installation

6. Remove the distributor cap and spark plug wires as an assembly.

7. Loosen both belt tensioner attaching bolts using special Ford tool T81P-6254-A or the equivalent. Secure the belt tensioner as far left as possible. Remove the timing belt and discard.

NOTE: Once the tension on the timing belt has been released, the belt cannot be used again.

8. Disconnect the tube at the EGR valve, then remove the PVS hose connectors using tool T81P-8564-A or equivalent. Label the connectors and set aside.

9. Disconnect the choke wire, the fuel supply and return lines, the accelerator cable and speed control cable (if equipped). Disconnect the altitude compensator, if equipped, from the dash panel and place on the heater/AC air intake.

NOTE: Use caution not to damage the compensator.

10. Disconnect and remove the alternator.

11. If equipped with power steering, remove the thermactor pump drive belt, the pump and its bracket. If equipped with a turbocharger, refer to

the previous section for removal procedure. Refer to the Fuel Injection section for pressure discharge and removal instructions.

12. Raise the vehicle and disconnect the exhaust pipe from the manifold.

13. Lower the vehicle and remove the cylinder head bolts and washers. Discard the bolts, they cannot be used again.

14. Remove the cylinder head with the manifolds attached. Remove and discard the head gasket. Do not place the cylinder head with combustion chambers down or damage to the spark plugs or gasket surfaces may result.

15. To install, clean all gasket material from both the block face and the cylinder head, then rotate the crankshaft so that the No.1 piston is 90° BTDC. In this position, the crankshaft pulley keyway is at 9 o'clock. Turn the camshaft so its keyway is at 6 o'clock. When installing the timing belt, turn the crankshaft keyway back to 12 o'clock but do not turn the camshaft from its 6 o'clock position. The crankshaft is turned 90° BTDC to prevent the valves from hitting the pistons when the cylinder head is installed.

16. Position the cylinder head gasket on the block and install the cylinder head using new bolts and washers. Tighten the bolts to 44 ft.lb. in the sequence shown, then back off 2 turns and retighten to 44 ft.lb. After tightening, turn the bolts an additional 90° in the same sequence. Complete the bolt tightening by turning an additional 90° in the same sequence.

17. Remaining installation is the reverse of removal. See Timing Belt Removal and Installation for timing belt installation procedures. Fill the cooling system only with Ford Cooling System Fluid, Prestone® II or the equivalent. Using the wrong type of coolant can damage the engine.

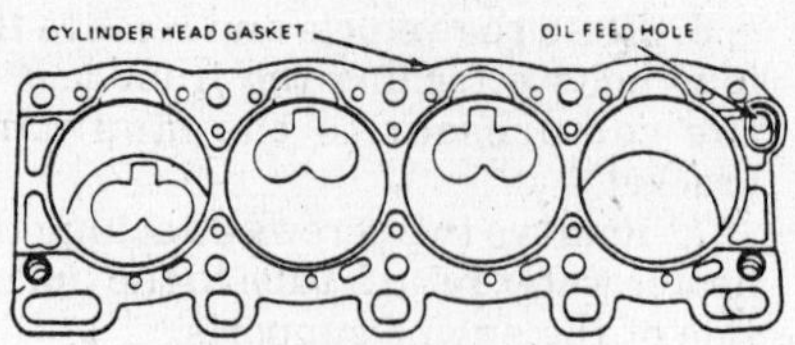

Head gasket installation

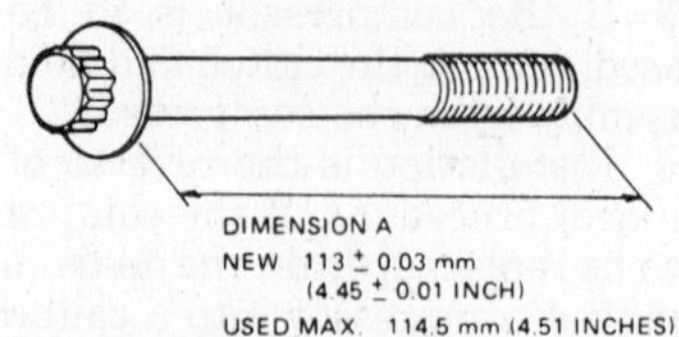

Head bolt dimension

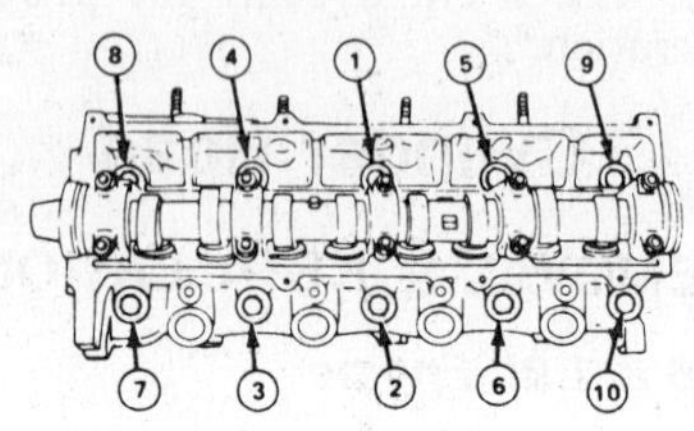

Torque sequence, cylinder head installation

2.3L HSC Engine

1. Disconnect the negative battery cable. Drain the cooling system by disconnecting the lower radiator hose.

CAUTION

When draining the coolant, keep in mind that cats and dogs are attracted by the ethylene glycol antifreeze, and are quite likely to drink any that is left in an uncovered container or in puddles on the ground. This will prove fatal in sufficient quantity. Always drain the coolant into a sealable container. Coolant should be reused unless it is contaminated or several years old.

2. Disconnect the heater hose at the fitting under the intake manifold. Disconnect the upper radiator hose at the cylinder head connector.

3. Disconnect the electric cooling fan switch at the plastic connector. Remove the air cleaner assembly. Label and disconnect any vacuum lines that will interfere with cylinder head removal.

4. Disconnect all drive belts. Remove rocker arm cover. Remove the distributor cap and spark plug wires as an assembly.

5. Disconnect the EGR tube at EGR valve. Disconnect the choke wire from the choke.

6. Disconnect the fuel supply and return lines at the rubber connector. Disconnect the accelerator cable and speed control cable, if equipped. Loosen the bolts retaining the thermactor pump pulley.

7. Raise and safely support the front of the car. Disconnect the exhaust pipe from the exhaust manifold. Lower car.

8. Loosen the rocker arm bolts until the arms can pivot for pushrod removal. Remove the pushrods. Keep the pushrods in order for installation in original position.

9. Remove the cylinder head bolts. Remove the cylinder head, gasket, thermactor pump, intake and exhaust manifolds as an assembly. Do not lay

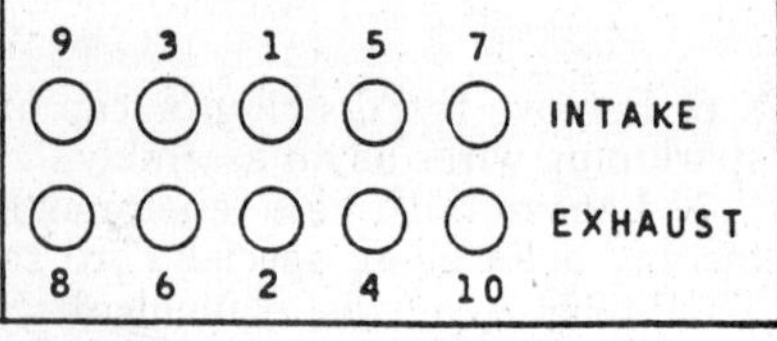

Tightening sequence for the 1.6L, 1.9L cylinder head

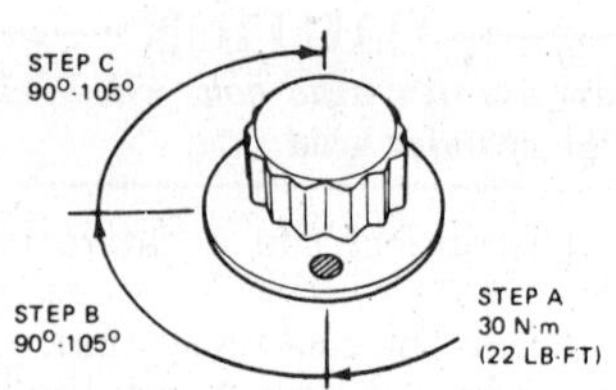

Head bolt tightening steps

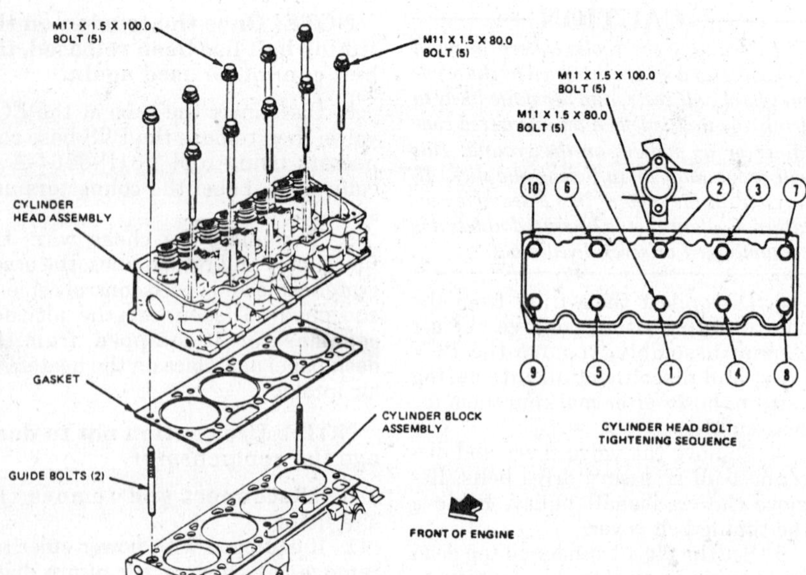

Torque sequence, cylinder head installation—2.3L HSC

the cylinder head down flat before removing the spark plugs. Take care not to damage the gasket surface.

10. Clean all gasket material from the head and block surfaces.

11. Position a new head gasket on the block surface. Do not use a sealer, unless directions with gasket specify.

12. To help with head installation alignment, purchase two head bolts and cut off the heads. Install the modified bolts at opposite corners of the block to act as guides.

13. Position the cylinder head over the guide bolts and lower onto the engine block.

14. Install head bolts, remove the guides and replace with regular bolts.

15. Tighten the heads bolts to 53-59 ft.lb. in two stages in the sequence shown.

16. The rest of the cylinder head installation is in the reverse order of removal.

2.5L Engine

1. Disconnect the negative battery cable. Remove the air cleaner assembly.

2. Place a drain pan under the radiator and drain the cooling system.

CAUTION

When draining the coolant, keep in mind that cats and dogs are attracted by the ethylene glycol antifreeze, and are quite likely to drink any that is left in an uncovered container or in puddles on the ground. This will prove fatal in sufficient quantity. Always drain the coolant into a sealable container. Coolant should be reused unless it is contaminated or several years old.

3. Disconnect the heater hose from under the intake manifold and the upper radiator hose from the cylinder head.

4. Disconnect the electrical harness connector from the cooling fan.

5. Label and disconnect the necessary vacuum hoses.

6. Remove the rocker arm cover, the rocker arms and the pushrods.

7. Loosen and remove the accessory drive belts.

8. Label and disconnect the spark plug wires, then remove the distributor from the engine.

9. Disconnect the EGR tube from the EGR valve, the choke cap wire from the throttle body, the accelerator cable and the speed control cable (if equipped).

10. Reduce the pressure in the fuel system and remove the fuel lines.

11. Loosen the Thermactor pump belt pulley, then raise and support the front of the vehicle on jackstands.

12. Disconnect the exhaust pipe from the exhaust manifold and the hose from the tube. Lower the vehicle.

NOTE: DO NOT remove the intake and/or exhaust manifolds from the cylinder head unless absolutely necessary.

13. Remove the cylinder head-to-engine bolts, the cylinder head (with the intake/exhaust manifolds and the Thermactor pump attached) and the gasket (discard it).

NOTE: If removing the cylinder head with the components attached, be sure not to lay the cylinder head flat, for physical damage may occur to the gasket surface or spark plugs.

14. Using a putty knife, clean the gasket mounting surfaces.

15. To install, use new gaskets, sealant (to hold the head gasket onto the engine block) and reverse the removal procedures. Torque the cylinder head-to-engine bolts in two steps to: 52-59 ft.lb. (70-80 Nm) on the first step, then 70-76 ft.lb. (95-103 Nm) on the second step. Refill the cooling system. Start the engine and check for leaks.

NOTE: When installing the cylinder head, use two Alignment Stud tools No. T84P-6065-A to guide the head into place.

3.0L Engine

1. Refer to the "Intake Manifold Removal & Installation" procedures in this section and remove the intake mainfold.

2. Loosen the accessory drive belt idler pulley and remove the drive belt.

3. On the left cylinder head, remove the alternator adjusting arm, the coil bracket and dipstick tube.

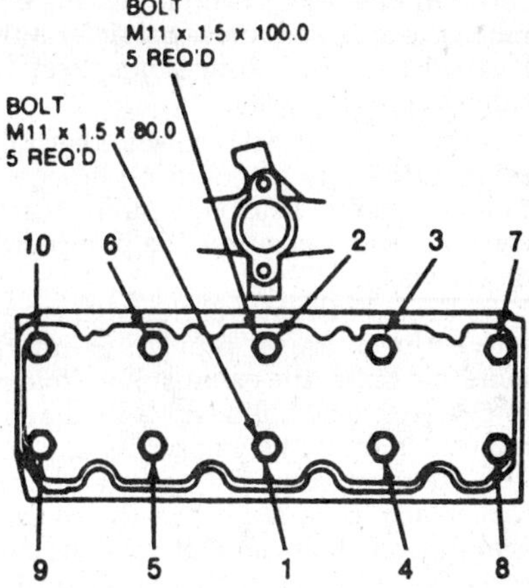

Cylinder head bolt torquing sequence—2.5L engine

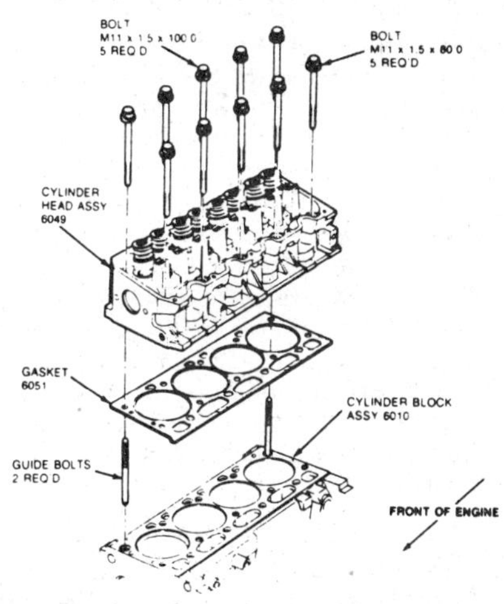

Installing the cylinder head—2.5L engine

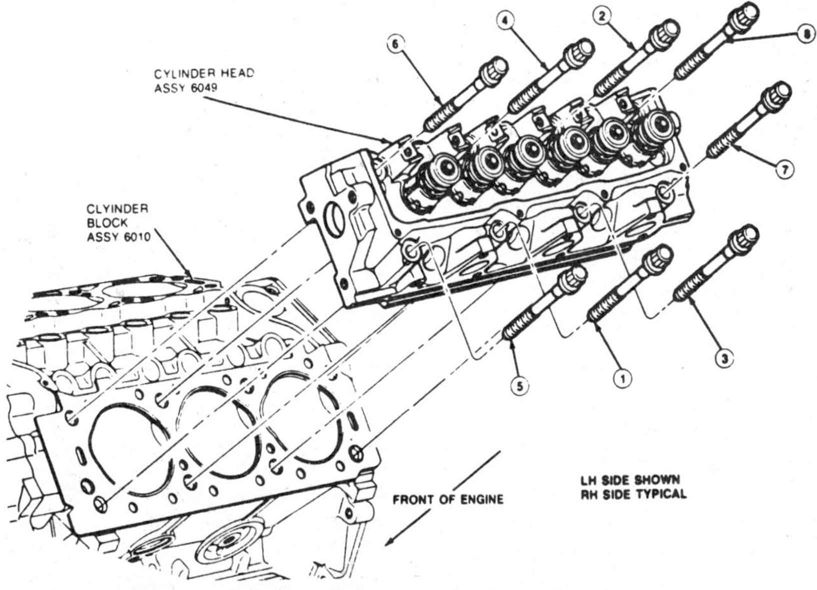

Cylinder head bolt torquing sequence— 3.0L engine

4. On the right cylinder head, remove the accessory drive belt idler pulley and the grounding strap throttle cable support bracket.

5. If equipped with power steering, remove the pump mounting bracket-to-engine bolts. Leave the pump hoses connected and position the pump out of the way.

6. From both sides of the engine, remove the exhaust pipe-to-exhaust manifold bolts, the exhaust manifolds-to-cylinder head bolts and the exhaust manifolds from the engine.

7. Remove the PCV valve and the rocker arm covers. Loosen the rocker arm fulcrum bolts enough to allow the rocker arm to be lifted from the pushrod and rotated to one side.

8. Remove the pushrods, keeping them in order for installation purposes.

9. Remove the cylinder head-to-engine bolts and the cylinder heads from the engine. Discard the cylinder head gaskets.

10. Using a putty knife, clean and inspect the gasket mounting surfaces.

11. To install, use new gaskets and reverse the removal procedures. Torque the cylinder head-to-engine bolts (in two steps) to 48-54 ft.lb. (1st step) and to 63-80 fft.lb. (2nd step), the rocker arm fulcrum bolts to 19-29 ft.lb. Start the engine and check for coolant, fuel, oil and exhaust leaks. Check and/or adjust the transmission throttle linkage and the speed control.

NOTE: Before installation, lightly oil the bolt and stud threads except for those specifying that a special sealant be applied. If the flat surface of the cylinder head is warp, do not plane or grind off more than 0.010" (0.254mm). If the head is machined past the resurface limit, it will have to be replaced with a new one.

Diesel Engine

1. Disconnect the battery ground cable from the battery, which is located in the luggage compartment.

2. Drain the cooling system.

CAUTION

When draining the coolant, keep in mind that cats and dogs are attracted by the ethylene glycol antifreeze, and are quite likely to drink any that is left in an uncovered container or in puddles on the ground. This will prove fatal in sufficient quantity. Always drain the coolant into a sealable container. Coolant should be reused unless it is contaminated or several years old.

3. Remove the camshaft cover, front and rear timing bolt covers, and front and rear timing belts.

4. Raise the vehicle and safely support on jackstands.

5. Disconnect the muffler inlet pipe at the exhaust manifold. Lower the vehicle.

6. Disconnect the air inlet duct at the air cleaner and intake manifold. Install a protective cover.

7. Disconnect the electrical connectors and vacuum hoses to the temperature sensors located in the thermostat housing.

8. Disconnect the upper and lower coolant hoses, and the upper radiator hose at the thermostat housing.

9. Disconnect and remove the injection lines at the injection pump and nozzles. Cap all lines and fittings with Cap Protective Set T84P-9395-A or equivalent.

10. Disconnect the glow plug harness from the main engine harness.

11. Remove the cylinder head bolts in the sequence shown. Remove the cylinder head.

12. Remove the glow plugs. Then, remove prechamber cups from the cylinder head using a brass drift.

13. Clean the prechamber cups, prechambers in the cylinder head and the cylinder head and crankcase gasket mating surfaces.

14. Install the prechambers in the cylinder heads, making sure the locating pins are aligned with the slots provided.

15. Install the glow plugs and tighten to 11-15 ft.lb. Connect glow plug harness to the glow plugs. Tighten the nuts to 5-7 ft.lb.

WARNING: Carefully blow out the head bolt threads in the crankcase with compressed air. Failure to thoroughly clean the thread bores can result in incorrect cylinder head torque or possible cracking of the crankcase.

16. Position a new cylinder head gasket on the crankcase making sure the cylinder head oil feed hold is not blocked.

17. Measure each cylinder head bolt dimension A. If the measurement is more than 114.5mm (4.51"), replace the head bolt.

WARNING: Rotate the camshaft in the cylinder head until the cam lobes for No. 1 cylinder are at the base circle (both valves closed). Then, rotate the crankshaft clockwise until No. 1 piston is halfway up in the cylinder bore toward TDC. This is to prevent contact between the pistons and valves.

18. Install the cylinder head on the crankcase.

NOTE: Before installing the cylinder head bolts, paint a white reference dot on each one, and apply a light coat of engine oil on the bolt threads.

19. Tighten cylinder head bolts as follows:

   a. Tighten bolts to 22 ft.lb. in the sequence shown.

   b. Using the painted reference marks, tighten each bolt in sequence, another 90°-105°.

   c. Repeat Step b turning the bolts another 90°-105°.

20. Connect the glow plug harness to main engine harness.

21. Remove the protective caps and install injection lines to the injection pump and nozzles. Tighten capnuts to 18-22 ft.lb.

22. Air bleed the system.

23. Connect the upper (with a new gasket) and lower coolant hoses, and the upper radiator hose to the thermostat housing. Tighten upper coolant hose bolts to 5-7 ft.lb.

24. Connect the electrical connectors and the vacuum hoses to the temperature sensors in the thermostat housing.

25. Remove the protective cover and install the air inlet duct to the intake manifold and air cleaner.

26. Raise vehicle and support on jackstands. Connect the muffler inlet pipe to the exhaust manifold. Tighten nuts to 25-35 ft.lb.

27. Lower the vehicle.

28. Install and adjust the front timing belt.

29. Install and adjust the rear timing belt.

30. Install the front upper timing belt cover and rear timing belt cover. Tighten the bolts to 5-7 ft.lb.

31. Check and adjust the valves as outlined. Install the valve cover and tighten the bolts to 5-7 ft.lb.

32. Fill and bleed the cooling system.

33. Check and adjust the injection pump timing.

34. Connect battery ground cable to battery. Run engine and check for oil, fuel and coolant leaks.

OVERHAUL

1. Remove the cylinder head form the car engine (see Cylinder Head Removal and Installation). Place the head on a workbench and remove any manifolds that are still connnected. Remove all rocker arm retaining parts and the rocker arms, if still installed or the camshaft (see Camshaft Removal).

2. Turn the cylinder head over so that the mounting surface is facing up and support evenly on wooden blocks.

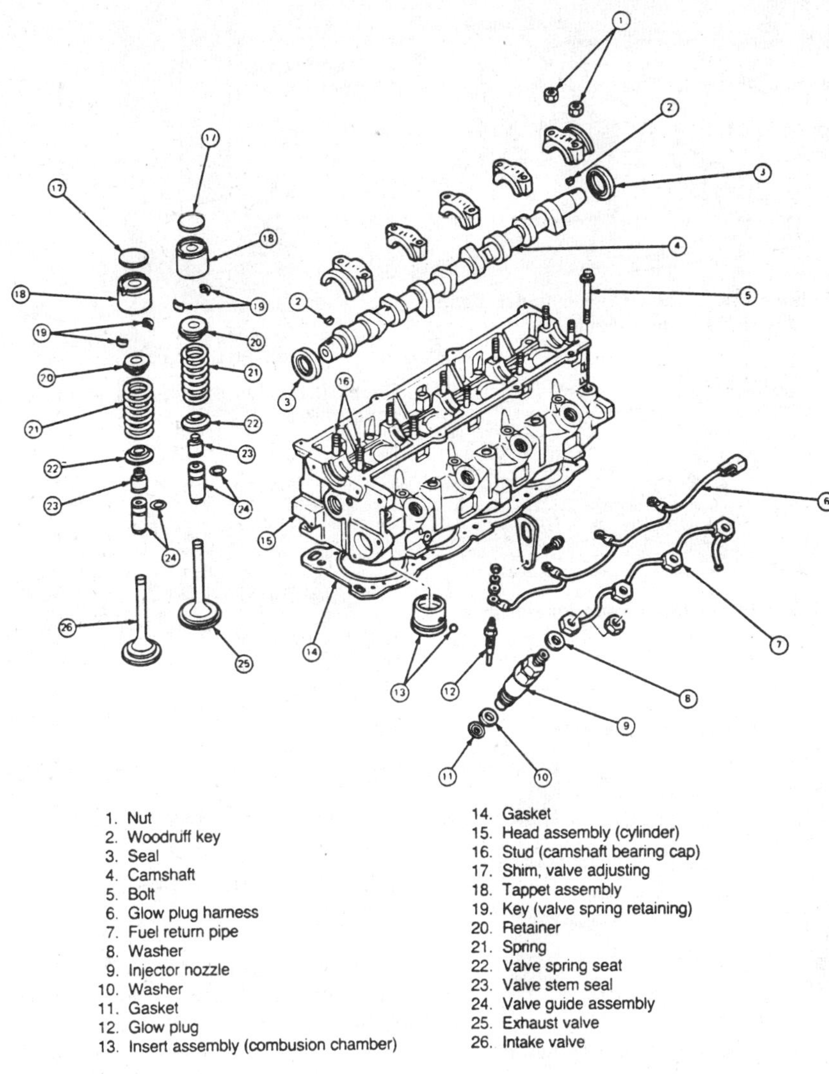

1. Nut
2. Woodruff key
3. Seal
4. Camshaft
5. Bolt
6. Glow plug harness
7. Fuel return pipe
8. Washer
9. Injector nozzle
10. Washer
11. Gasket
12. Glow plug
13. Insert assembly (combusion chamber)
14. Gasket
15. Head assembly (cylinder)
16. Stud (camshaft bearing cap)
17. Shim, valve adjusting
18. Tappet assembly
19. Key (valve spring retaining)
20. Retainer
21. Spring
22. Valve spring seat
23. Valve stem seal
24. Valve guide assembly
25. Exhaust valve
26. Intake valve

Diesel engine, cylinder head components

CAUTION

If the engine has an aluminum cylinder head, exercise care when cleaning.

3. Use a scraper and remove all of the gasket material stuck to the head mounting surface. Mount a wire carbon removal brush in an electric drill and clean away the carbon on the valves and head combustion chambers.

WARNING: When scraping or decarbonizing the cylinder head take care not to damage or nick the gasket mounting surface.

4. Number the valve heads with a permanent felt-tip marker for cylinder location.

RESURFACING

If the cylinder head is warped resurfacing by a machine shop is required. Place a straightedge across the gasket surface of the head. Using feeler gauges, determine the clearance at the center and along the length between the head and straightedge. Measure clearance at the center and along the lengths of both diagonals. If warpage exceeds 0.003″ (0.076mm) in a 6″ (152mm) span, or 0.006″ (0.15mm) over the total length the cylinder head must be resurfaced.

Valves and Springs

REMOVAL & INSTALLATION

1. Block the head on its side, or install a pair of head-holding brackets made especially for valve removal.
2. Use a socket slightly larger than the valve stem and keepers, place the socket over the valve stem and gently hit the socket with a plastic hammer to break loose any varnish buildup.
3. Remove the valve keepers, retainer, spring shield and valve spring using a valve spring compressor (the locking C-clamp type is the easiest kind to use).
4. Put the parts in a separate container numbered for the cylinder being worked on. Do not mix them with other parts removed.
5. Remove and discard the valve stem oil seal, a new seal will be used at assembly time.
6. Remove the valve from the cylinder head and place, in order, through numbered holes punched in a stiff piece of cardboard or wooden valve holding stick.

NOTE: The exhaust valve stems, on some engines, are equipped with small metal caps. Take care not to lose the caps. Make sure to reinstall them at assembly time. Replace any caps that are worn.

7. Use an electric drill and rotary wire brush to clean the intake and exhaust valve ports, combustion chamber and valve seats. In some cases, the carbon will need to be chipped away. Use a blunt pointed drift for carbon chipping, be careful around the valve seat areas.
8. Use a wire valve guide cleaning brush and safe solvent to clean the valve guides.
9. Clean the valves with a revolving wire brush. Heavy carbon deposits may be removed with the blunt drift.

NOTE: When using a wire brush to clean carbon on the valve ports, valves etc., be sure that the deposits are actually removed, rather than burnished.

10. Wash and clean all valve spring, keepers, retaining caps etc., in safe solvent.
11. Clean the head with a brush and some safe solvent and wipe dry.
12. Check the head for cracks. Cracks in the cylinder head usually start around an exhaust valve seat because it is the hottest part of the combustion chamber. If a crack is suspected buy cannot be detected visually have the area checked with dye penetrant or other method by the machine shop.
13. After all cylinder head parts are reasonably clean check the valve stem-to-guide clearance. If a dial indicator is not on hand, a visual inspection can give you a fairly good idea if the guide, valve stem or both are worn.
14. Insert the valve into the guide until slightly away from the valve seat. Wiggle the valve sideways. A small amount of wobble is normal, excessive wobble means a worn guide or valve stem. If a dial indicator is on hand, mount the indicator so that the stem

of the valve is at 90° to the valve stem, as close to the valve guide as possible. Move the valve off the seat, and measure the valve guide-to-stem clearance by rocking the stem back and forth to actuate the dial indicator. Measure the valve stem using a micrometer and compare to specifications to determine whether stem or guide wear is causing excessive clearance.

15. The valve guide, if worn, must be repaired before the valve seats can be resurfaced. Ford supplies valves with oversize stems to fit valve guides that are reamed to oversize for repair. The machine shop will be able to handle the guide reaming for you. In some cases, if the guide is not too badly worn, knurling may be all that is required.

16. Reface, or have the valves and valve seats refaced. The valve seats should be a true 45° angle. Remove only enough material to clean up any pits or grooves. Be sure the valve seat is not too wide or narrow. Use a 60° grinding wheel to remove material from the bottom of the seat for raising and a 30° grinding wheel to remove material from the top of the seat to narrow.

17. After the valves are refaced by machine, hand lap them to the valve seat. Clean the grinding compound off and check the position of face-to-seat contact. Contact should be close to the center of the valve face. If contact is close to the top edge of the valve narrow the seat; if too close to the bottom edge, raise the seat.

18. Valves should be refaced to a true angle of 44°. Remove only enough metal to clean up the valve face or to correct runout. If the edge of the valve head, after machining, is $\frac{1}{32}$" (0.8mm) or less replace the valve. The tip of the valve stem should also be dressed on the valve grinding machine, however, do not remove more than 0.010" (0.25mm).

19. After all valve and valve seats have been machined, check the remaining valve train parts (springs, retainers, keepers, etc.) for wear. Check the valve springs for straightness and tension.

20. Reassemble the head in the reverse order of disassembly using new valve guide seals and lubricating the valve stems. Check the valve spring installed height, shim or replace as necessary.

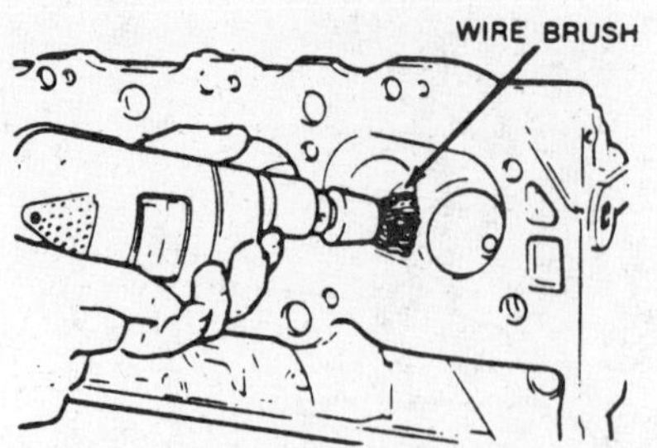

Remove the carbon from cylinder head witha wire brush and electric drill

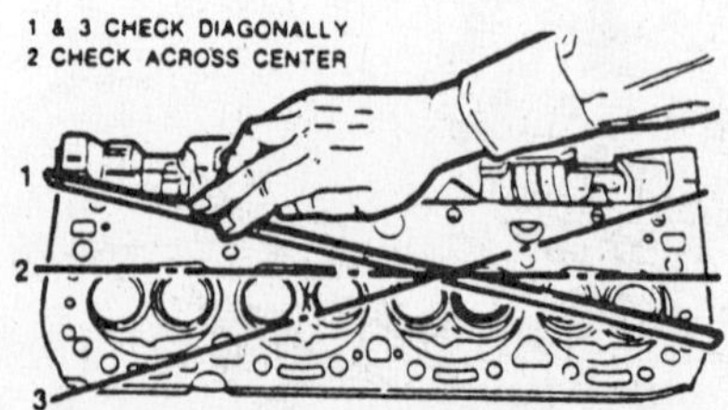

Check the cylinder head for warpage

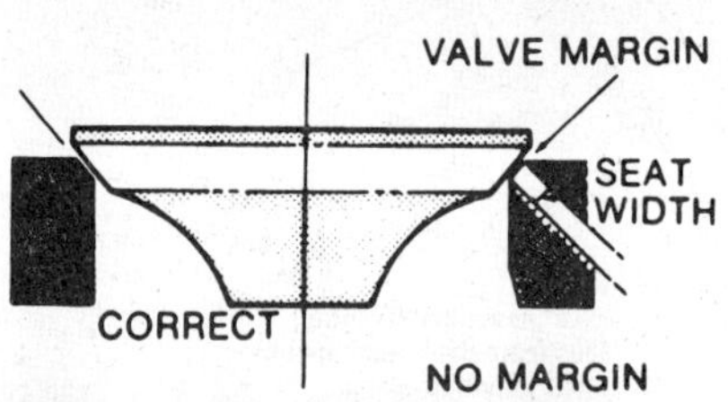

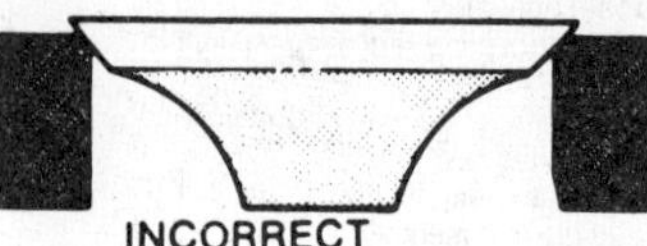

Valve seat width and centering

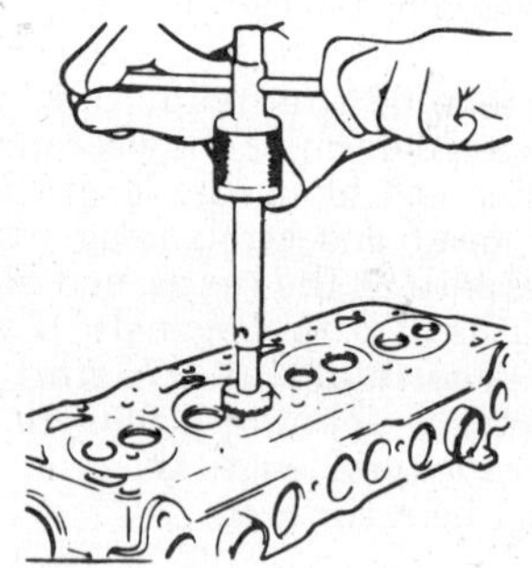

Reaming the valve seat with a hand reamer

CHECKING VALVE SPRINGS

Place the valve spring on a flat surface next to a carpenters square. Measure the height of the spring, and rotate the spring against the edge of the square to measure distortion. If the spring height varies (by comparison) by more than $\frac{1}{16}$" (1.6mm) or if the distortion exceeds $\frac{1}{16}$" (1.6mm), replace the spring.

Have the valve springs tested for spring pressure at the installed and compressed (installed height minus valve lift) height using a valve spring tester. Springs should be within one pound, plus or minus each other. Replace spring as necessary.

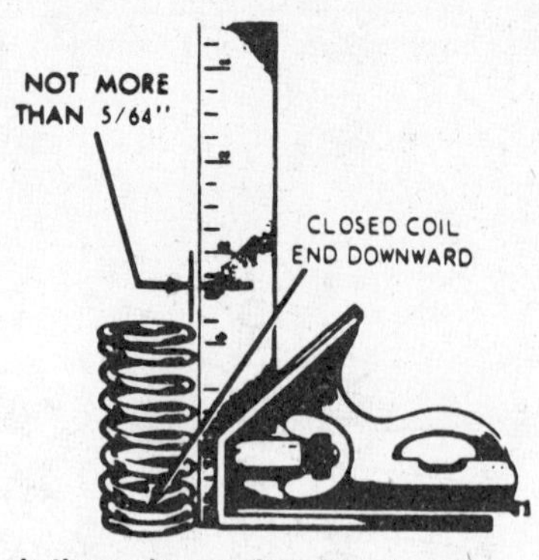

Check the valve spring free length and squareness

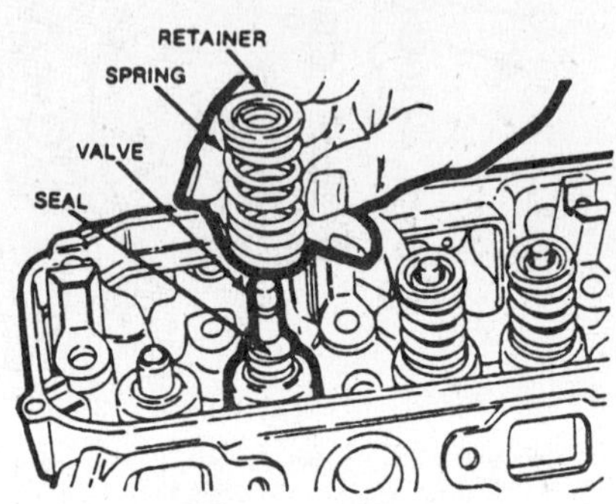

Install valve stem oil seals

VALVE SPRING INSTALLED HEIGHT

After installing the valve spring, measure the distance between the spring mounting pad and the lower edge of the spring retainer. Compare the measurement to specifications. If the installed height is incorrect, add shim washers between the spring mounting pad and the spring. Use only washers designed for valve springs, available at most parts houses.

VALVE STEM OIL SEALS

Most engines are equipped with a positive valve stem seal using a Teflon® insert. Teflon® seals are available for other engines buy usually require valve guide machining, consult your automotive machine shop for advice on having positive valve stem oil seals installed.

When installing valve stem oil seals, ensure that a small amount of oil is able to pass the seal to lubricate the valve stems and guide walls; otherwise, excessive wear will occur.

VALVE SEATS

If a valve seat is damaged or burnt and cannot be serviced by refacing, it may be possible to have the seat machined and an insert installed. Consult the automotive machine shop for their advice.

NOTE: The aluminum heads on V6 engines are equipped with inserts.

VALVE GUIDES

Worn valve guides can, in most cases, be reamed to accept a valve with an oversized stem. Valve guides that are not excessively worn or distorted may, in some cases, be knurled rather than reamed. However, if the valve stem is worn reaming for an oversized valve stem is the answer since a new valve would be required.

Knurling is a process in which metal is displaced and raised, thereby reducing clearance. Knurling also produces excellent oil control. The possibility of knurling instead of reaming the valve guides should be discussed with a machinist.

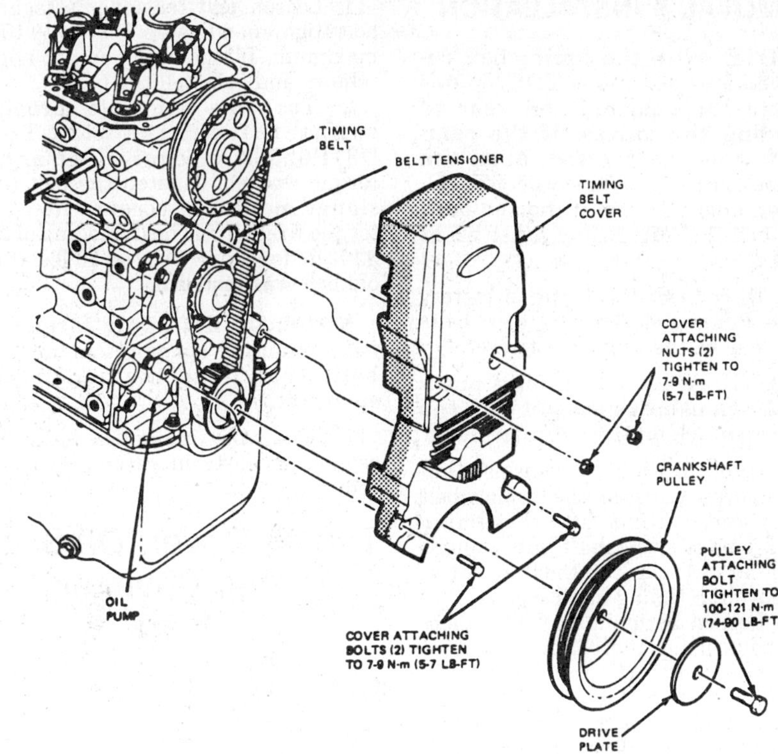

Timing cover and parts—1.6L and 1.9L engines

Timing Belt

CHECKING ENGINE TIMING

1.6 & 1.9L Engine

Should the camshaft drive belt jump timing by a tooth or two, the engine could still run, although very poorly. To visually check for correct timing, remove the No.1 spark plug and place your thumb over the hole. Use a wrench on the crankshaft pulley bolt to rotate the engine to TDC of the compression stroke for No. 1 cylinder.

WARNING: Turn the crankshaft only in the direction of normal rotation. Backward rotation will cause the belt to slip or lose teeth, altering engine timing.

As the No. 1 piston rises on the compression stroke, your thumb will be pushed out by compression pressure. At the same time, the timing notch on the crankshaft pulley will be approaching the **0**, or **TDC**, mark on the timing degree scale molded into the camshaft belt cover. Continue to turn the crankshaft until the pulley mark and **0** mark are aligned, indicating that No. 1 cylinder is at TDC.

Remove the alternator drive belt, and the power steering pump and air conditioning compressor drive belts, if so equipped. Remove the camshaft belt cover.

The camshaft sprocket has a mark next to one of the holes. The cylinder head is similarly marked. These marks should be aligned, dot-to-dot, indicating that camshaft timing is correct.

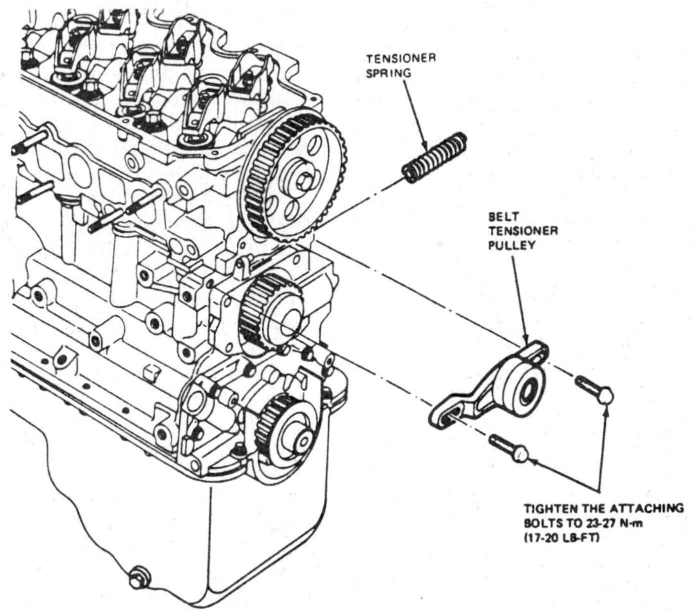

Tensioner and spring installation—1.6L and 1.9L engines

NOTE: As a further check, the distributor cap can be removed. The ignition rotor should be pointing toward the No. 1 spark plug tower in the cap.

If the marks are aligned, the engine timing is correct. If not, the belt must be removed from the cam sprocket and the camshaft turned until its marks are aligned (crankshaft still at TDC).

WARNING: Never attempt to rotate the engine by means of the camshaft sprocket. The 2:1 ratio between the camshaft and crankshaft sprockets will place a severe strain on the belt, stretching or tearing it.

REMOVAL & INSTALLATION

NOTE: With the timing belt removed and pistons at TDC, do not rotate the camshaft for fear of bending the valves. If the camshaft must be rotated, align the crankshaft pulley 90° BTDC. When actually installing the belt, the crankshaft pulley must be at TDC.

1. Disconnect the negative battery cable. Remove all accessory drive belts and remove the timing belt cover.

NOTE: Align the timing mark on the camshaft sprocket with the timing mark on the cylinder head.

2. After aligning the camshaft timing marks, reinstall the timing belt cover and confirm that the timing mark on the crankshaft pulley aligns with the TDC mark on the front cover. Remove the timing belt cover.
3. Loosen both timing belt attaching bolts using tool T81P-6254-A or equivalent. Pry the tensioner away from the belt as far as possible and hold it in that position by tightening one of the tensioner attaching bolts.

NOTE: Due to limited working space, special tools are required to remove the crankshaft pulley. Crankshaft wrench (Ford) tool number YA826 (to hold the pulley stationary) and crankshaft pulley wrench (Ford) T81P6312A or equivalents will make the job easier.

4. Remove the crankshaft pulley and remove and discard the timing belt.
5. To install new belt, fit the timing belt over the gears in a counterclockwise direction starting at the crankshaft. Ensure that belt span between crankshaft and camshaft is kept tight as belt is installed over remaining gears.
6. Loosen belt tensioner attaching bolts and allow tensioner to extend against the belt.
7. Tighten one tensioner attaching bolt using special tool mentioned earlier or its equivalent.
8. Install the crankshaft pulley, drive plate and pulley attaching bolt.
9. Hold the crankshaft pulley stationary using tool YA-826 or equivalent and torque pulley bolt to 74-90 ft.lb.
10. Disconnect the distributor wire harness. Crank the engine for 30 seconds after reconnecting the negative battery cable. Disconnect cable and realign timing marks. Check that the camshaft sprocket pointer is aligned with the TDC mark, and that the crankshaft is in the TDC position.
11. Loosen belt tensioner attaching bolt (tightened in step 7) 1/4 to 1/2 turn maximum. If the marks do not align, remove and reinstall the belt.
12. Turn the camshaft sprocket counterclockwise with Tool D81P6256A or equivalent and a torque wrench. Tighten the belt tensioner mounting screw when the torque wrench reaches a reading of 27-32 ft.lb. for a new belt, or 10 lbs. if an old belt was installed.

NOTE: Do not apply torque to the camshaft sprocket attaching bolt. Apply it to the hex on the sprocket.

13. Install the timing belt cover and remaining parts in reverse order of removal.

Timing Cover, Oil Seal, Timing Chain and Gears

REMOVAL & INSTALLATION

2.3L HSC Engine

NOTE: The engine must be removed from the car for the following procedure.

1. The front seal can be replaced after the drive pulley has been removed. Remove the bolt and washer retaining the pulley. Use a suitable puller and remove the crankshaft pulley. Install a front seal remover tool (Ford No. T74P6700A or equivalent) and remove the seal. Coat a new seal with grease and install with suitable tool (Ford No. T83T4676A or the equivalent). Drive the seal in until fully seated. Check the seal after installation to make sure the spring is in proper position around the seal. Install the crankshaft pulley, washer and bolt.
2. To remove the front cover, remove the crankshaft pulley as described above. Remove the front cover retaining bolts, pry the top of the cover away from the engine block and remove the cover.
3. Clean all gasket mounting surfaces. Check the play in the timing chain, replace chain if play is excessive. Check the timing chain tensioner blade for wear, if excessive replace the blade.
4. Turn the engine until the timing marks on the crank and cam gears align.
5. Remove the camshaft gear attaching bolt and washer. Slide the tow gears and chain forward and remove as an assembly.
6. Install in the reverse order. Make sure the timing marks on the camshaft and crank gears are in alignment.

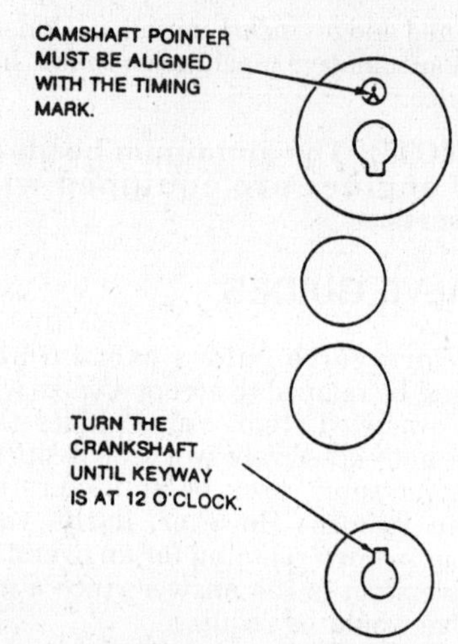

Camshaft and crankshaft alignment—1.6L and 1.9L engines

Check the timing chain damper, located in the front cover, for wear and replace damper if necessary. Lubricate gears, chain, tensioner blade and front cover oil seal before cover installation. Apply an oil resistant sealer to both sides of the front cover gasket.

2.0L Diesel Engine

IN CAR SERVICE

NOTE: This procedure is for Removal and Installation of the front timing belt for in-vehicle service of the water pump, camshaft, or cylinder head. The timing belt cannot be replaced with the engine installed in the vehicle.

1. Remove the front timing belt upper cover and the flywheel timing mark cover.
2. Rotate engine clockwise until the timing marks on the flywheel and the front camshaft sprocket are aligned with their pointers.
3. Loosen tensioner pulley lockbolt and slide the timing belt off the water pump and camshaft sprockets.
4. The water pump and/or camshaft can now be serviced.

FRONT BELT ADJUSTMENTS

1. Remove the flywheel timing mark cover.
2. Remove the front timing belt upper cover.
3. Remove the belt tension spring from the storage pocket in the front cover.
4. Install the tensioner spring in the belt tensioner lever and over the stud mounted on the front of the crankcase.
5. Loosen the tensioner pulley lockbolt.
6. Rotate the crankshaft pulley two revolutions clockwise until the fly-

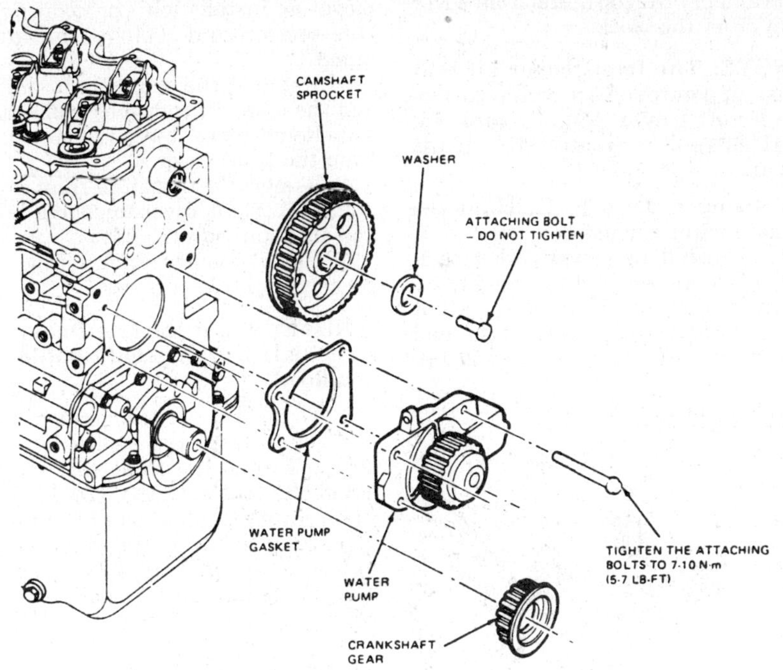

Timing components installation – 1.6L and 1.9L engines

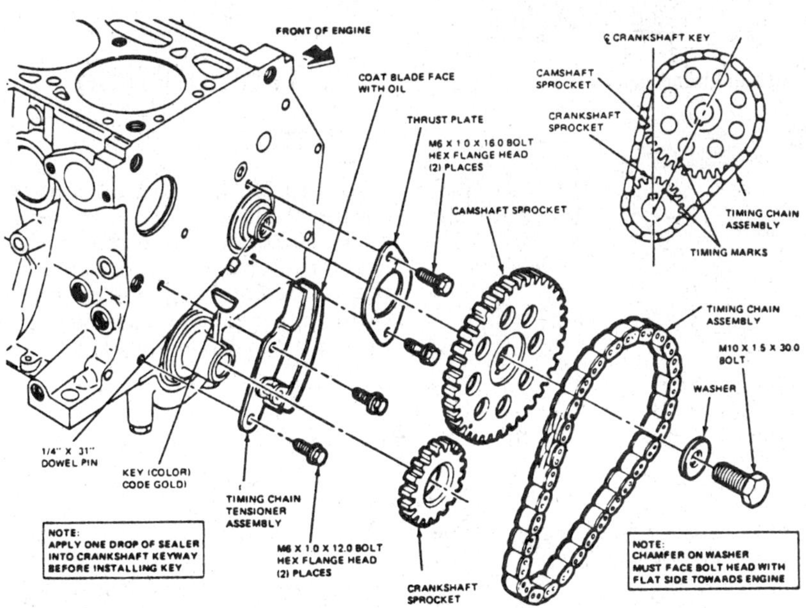

Timing gear components and alignment, 2.3L engine

wheel TDC timing mark aligns with the pointer on the rear cover plate.

7. Check the front camshaft sprocket to see that it is aligned with its timing mark.

8. Tighten the tensioner lockbolt to 23-34 ft.lb.

9. Check the belt tension using Rotunda Belt Tension Gauge model 21-0028 or equivalent. Belt tension should be 33-44 lbs.

10. Remove the tensioner spring and install it in the storage pocket in the front cover.

11. Install the front cover and tighten the attaching bolts to 5-7 ft.lb.

12. Install the flywheel timing mark cover.

REAR BELT ADJUSTMENTS

1. Remove the flywheel timing mark cover.

2. Remove the rear timing belt cover.

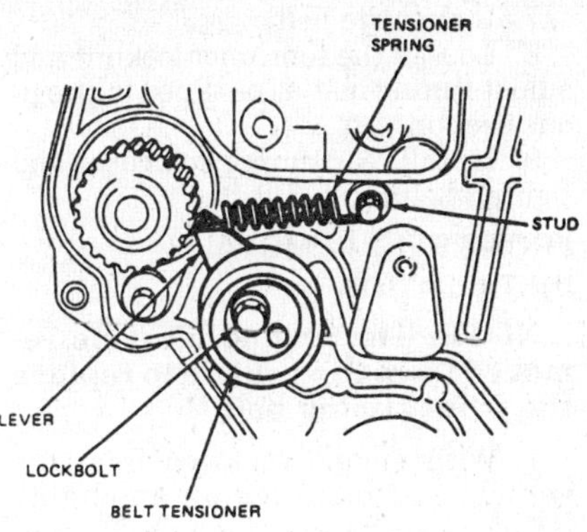

Front timing belt tensioner – diesel engine

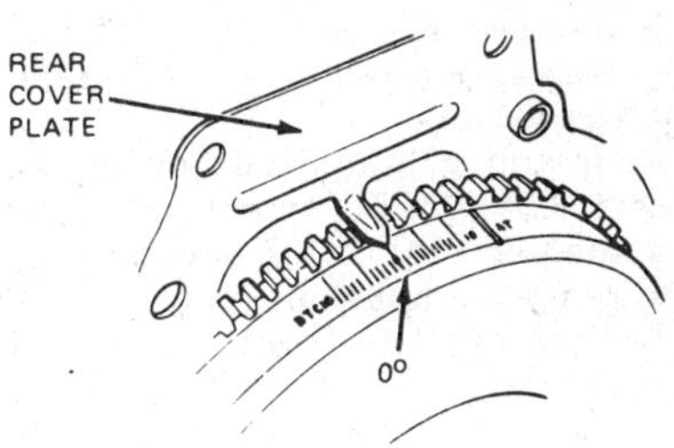

Flywheel timing marks – diesel engine

3. Loosen the tensioner pulley locknut.

4. Rotate the crankshaft two revolutions until the flywheel TDC timing mark aligns with the pointer on the rear cover plate.

5. Check that the camshaft sprocket and injection pump sprocket are aligned with their timing marks.

6. Tighten tensioner locknut to 15-20 ft.lb.

7. Check belt tension using Rotunda Belt Tension Gauge model 21-0028 or equivalent. Belt tension should be 22-33 lbs.

8. Install the rear timing belt cover. Tighten the 6mm bolts to 5-7 ft.lb. and the 8mm bolt to 12-16 ft.lb.

9. Install the flywheel timing mark cover.

REAR BELT REMOVAL & INSTALLATION

1. Remove the rear timing belt cover.

2. Remove the flywheel timing mark cover from clutch housing.

3. Rotate the crankshaft until the flywheel timing mark is at TDC on No. 1 cylinder.

4. Check that the injection pump and camshaft sprocket timing marks are aligned.

5. Loosen the tensioner locknut. With a screwdriver, or equivalent tool, inserted in the slot provided, rotate the tensioner clockwise to relieve belt tension. Tighten locknut snug.

6. Remove the timing belt.

7. Install the belt.
8. Loosen the tensioner locknut and adjust timing belt as outlined in previous section.
9. Install rear timing belt cover and tighten belts to 5-7 ft.lb.

FRONT BELT REMOVAL & INSTALLATION

NOTE: The engine must be removed from the vehicle to replace the front timing belt.

1. With engine removed from the vehicle and installed on an engine stand, remove front timing belt upper cover.
2. Install a Flywheel Holding Tool T84P6375A or equivalent.
3. Remove the six bolts attaching the crankshaft pulley to the crankshaft sprocket.
4. Install a crankshaft pulley Remover T58P6316D or equivalent using Adapter T74P6700B or equivalent, and remove crankshaft pulley.
5. Remove the front timing belt lower cover.
6. Loosen the tensioning pulley and remove timing belt.
7. Align the camshaft sprocket with the timing mark.

NOTE: Check the crankshaft sprocket to see that the timing marks are aligned.

8. Remove the tensioner spring from the pocket in the front timing belt upper cover and install it in the slot in the tensioner lever and over the stud in the crankcase.
9. Push the tensioner lever toward the water pump as far as it will travel and tighten lockbolt snug.
10. Install timing belt.
11. Adjust the timing belt tension as outlined in previous section.
12. Install the front timing belt lower cover and tighten bolts to 5-7 ft.lb.
13. Install the crankshaft pulley and tighten bolts to 17-24 ft.lb.
14. Install the front timing belt upper cover and tighten bolts to 5-7 ft.lb.

Front Cover

REMOVAL & INSTALLATION

2.5L Engine

1. Refer to the "Engine Removal & Installation" procedures in this section and remove the engine and the transmission from the vehicle as an assembly.
2. Remove the dipstick and the accessory drive pulley (if equipped). Remove the crankshaft pulley-to-crankshaft bolt, the washer and the pulley.
3. Remove front cover-to-engine bolts and pry the top of the front cover away from the block.

NOTE: The front cover oil seal must be removed in order to use the Front Cover Aligner tool No. T84P-6019-C to install the front cover.

4. Using a putty knife, clean the gasket mounting surfaces.
5. To install, use a new gasket, sealant, a new oil seal and reverse the removal procedures. Torque the front cover-to-engine bolts to 6-9 ft.lb. and the crankshaft pulley bolt to 140-170 ft.lb.

3.0L Engine

1. Refer to the "Water Pump Removal & Installation" procedures in this section and remove the water pump.
2. Remove the crankshaft pulley and the damper from the crankshaft.
3. Remove the lower radiator hose from the front cover.
4. Remove the oil pan-to-front cover bolts, the front cover-to-engine bolts and the front cover.
5. Using a putty knife, clean the gasket mounting surfaces.

NOTE: When the front cover is removed, the oil seal should be replaced.

6. To install, use new gaskets, sealant and reverse the removal procedures. Torque the front cover-to-engine bolts to 15-22 ft.lb. (20-30 Nm), the front cover-to-oil pan bolts to 80-106 in.lb. (9-12 Nm), the water pump-to-front cover bolts to 6-8 ft.lb. (8-12 Nm), the crankshaft damper-to-crankshaft bolt to 141-169 ft.lb. (190-230 Nm), the crankshaft pulley-to-crankshaft damper bolts to 20-28 ft.lb. (26-38 Nm), the water pump pulley-to-water pump bolts to 15-22 ft.lb. (20-30 Nm).

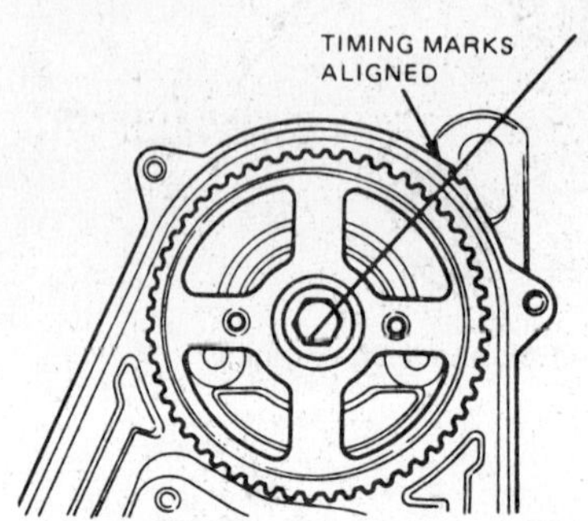

Camshaft timing mark—diesel engine

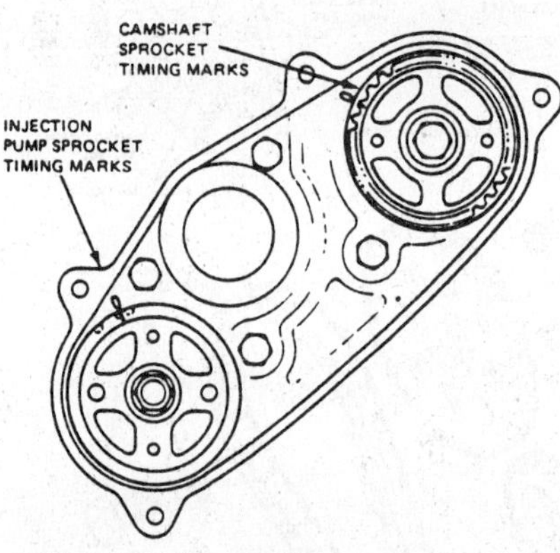

Camshaft and injector pump timing marks—diesel engine

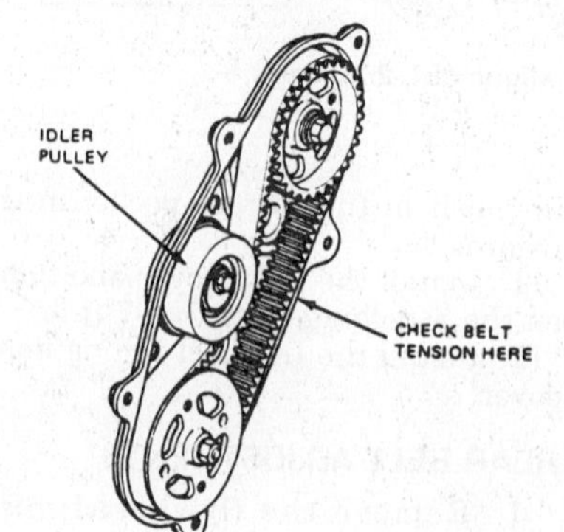

Timing belt tensioner, rear—diesel engine

Timing Chain

ADJUSTMENT

NOTE: No adjustments of the timing chain are necessary or possible. The ONLY check to be make is the deflection measurement. If the deflection is beyond specifications, replace the timing chain, the sprockets and/or the tensioners.

2.5L Engine

1. To check the timing chain deflection, first rotate the crankshaft in the counterclockwise direction (view from the front) to take up the slack.
2. Mark a reference point on the block, then measure the mid-section distance to the timing chain on the left side.
3. Rotate the crankshaft clockwise to take up the slack on the right side of the chain.
4. If the deflection exceeds ½", replace the timing chain and/or the sprockets.

NOTE: The deflection measurement is the difference between the two measurements.

5. Check the timing chain tensioner blade for wear depth. If the wear depth exceeds specification, replace the tensioner.

3.0L Engine

1. Refer to the "Rocker Arm Removal & Installation" procedures in this section and remove the left side valve cover.
2. Loosen the exhaust valve fulcrum bolt of the No. 5 cylinder and rotate the rocker to one side.
3. Using a dial indicator, install it onto the pushrod.
4. Rotate the crankshaft until the No. 1 cylinder is at the TDC of the compression stroke.

NOTE: The damper pulley timing mark should be on the TDC of the timing plate. This operation will take the slack from the right side of the timing chain.

5. Using the dial indicator, set the dial on zero.
6. Slowly turn the crankshaft counterclockwise until the slightest movement on the dial indicator is observed, then inspect the position of the damper pulley with the timing plate.
7. If the reading on the timing plate exceeds 6°, replace the timing chain and the sprockets.

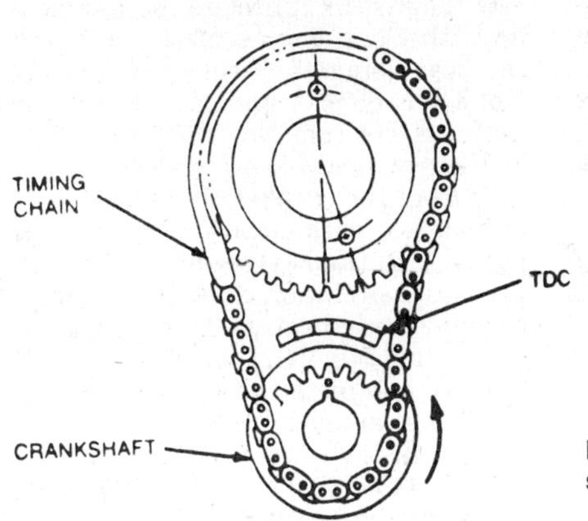

Checking the slack of the timing chain

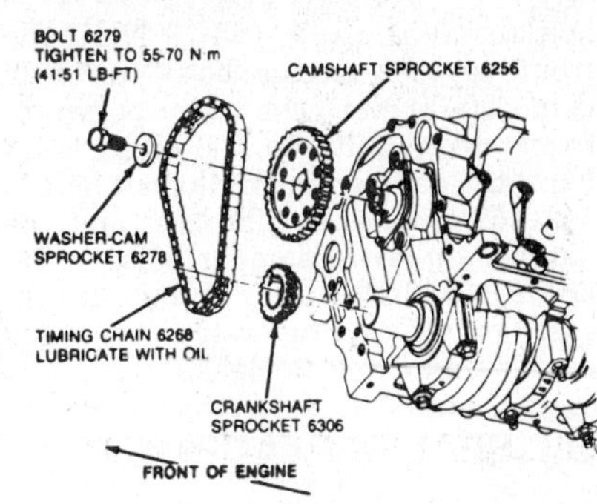

Exploded view of the timing chain and sprockets—3.0L engine

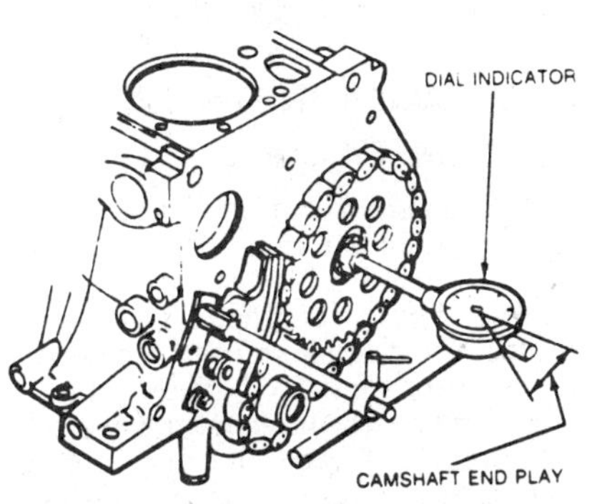

Using a dial micrometer to check the camshaft end play

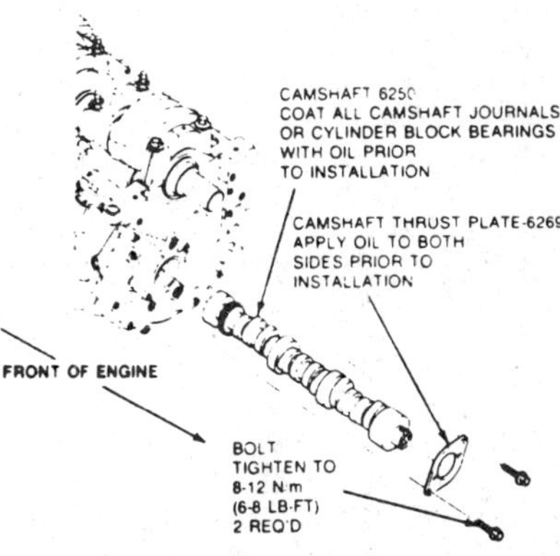

Exploded view of the camshaft—3.0L engine

REMOVAL & INSTALLATION

2.5L Engine

1. Refer to the "Engine Removal & Installation" procedures in this section and remove the engine and secure it to a workstand.
2. Refer to the "Front Cover Removal & Installation" procedures in this section and remove the front cover.
3. Rotate the crankshaft until the timing marks of the crankshaft and the camshaft sprockets are aligned.
4. Remove the camshaft sprocket bolt and washer, then slide the camshaft sprocket, the timing chain and the crankshaft sprocket off as an assembly.
5. Inspect and/or replace the parts as necessary.
6. To install, slide the sprocket/timing chain assembly onto the camshaft and crankshaft with timing marks aligned. Oil the timing chain, the sprockets and the tensioner after installation.
7. Apply oil resistant sealer to a new front cover gasket and position gasket onto the front cover.
8. Using the Front Cover Aligner tool No. T84P-6019-C, position it onto the end of the crankshaft, ensuring that the crank key is aligned with the keyway in the tool. Bolt the front cover to the engine. Tighten all the attaching bolts to specification. Remove the front cover aligner tool.
9. Lubricate the hub of the crankshaft pulley with Polyethylene Grease to prevent damage to the seal during installation and initial engine start. Install crankshaft pulley.
10. To complete the installation, reverse the removal procedures. Torque the camshaft sprocket-to-camshaft bolt to 41-56 fft.lb. (55-75 Nm), the front cover-to-engine bolts to 6-9 ft.lb. (8-12 Nm), the crankshaft pulley bolt to 140-170 ft.lb. (190-230 Nm). Refill the cooling system. Start the engine and check for leaks.

3.0L Engine

1. Refer to the "Engine Removal & Installation" procedures in this section and remove the engine and secure it to a workstand.
2. Refer to the "Front Cover Removal & Installation" procedures in this section and remove the front cover.
3. Rotate the crankshaft until the No. 1 piston is at the TDC of it's compression stroke and the timing marks are aligned.
4. Remove the camshaft sprocket-to-camshaft bolt and washer, then slide the sprockets and timing chain forward to remove them as an assembly.
5. Inspect the timing chain and sprockets for excessive wear; replace them, if necessary.
6. Using a putty knife, clean the gasket mounting surfaces.
7. Apply oil to the timing chain and sprockets after installation.

NOTE: The camshaft bolt has a drilled oil passage in it for timing chain lubrication. If the bolt is damaged do not replace it with a standard bolt.

8. Apply a bead of RTV sealant on the gap at the cylinder block.
9. Apply an oil resistant sealer No. B5A-19554-A, or equivalent, to a new front gasket and position the gasket onto the front cover.
10. Position the front cover on the engine taking care not to damage the front seal. Make sure the cover is installed over the alignment dowels.

NOTE: When installing the front cover onto the engine, make sure that the oil pan seal is not dislodged.

11. If necessary, replace the front cover seal using the Seal Installation tool No. T70P-6B070-A.
12. To complete the installation, reverse the removal procedures. Torque the camshaft sprocket-to-camshaft

bolt to 40-51 fft.lb. (55-70 Nm), the front cover-to-engine bolts to 15-22 ft.lb. (20-30 Nm), the water pump-to-front cover bolts to 6-8 ft.lb. (8-12 Nm), the damper-to-crankshaft bolt to 141-169 ft.lb. (190-230 Nm) and the damper pulley-to-damper bolts to 20-28 fft.lb. (26-38 Nm). Refill the crankcase and the cooling system. Start the engine and check for leaks.

OIL SEAL REPLACEMENT

2.5L Engine

1. Refer to the "Engine Removal & Installation" procedures in this section, then remove the engine from the vehicle and place it on a workstand.
2. Remove the drive belt(s), the crankshaft pulley bolt/washer and the crankshaft pulley.
3. Using the Damper Removal tool No. T77F-4220-B1, remove the crankshaft pulley.
4. Using the Front Seal Removal tool No. T74P-6700-A, remove the front cover oil seal.
5. Coat the new seal with grease. Using the Front Seal Replacer tool No. T83T-4676-A, install the seal into the cover; drive the seal in until it is fully seated. Check the seal after installation to ensure that the seal spring is properly positioned.
6. To complete the installation, reverse the removal procedures. Torque the crankshaft pulley-to-crankshaft bolt to 140-230 fft.lb. (190-230 Nm).

3.0L Engine

1. Disconnect the negative battery cable and loosen the accessory drive belts.
2. Raise and support the front of the vehicle on jackstands, then remove the right side front wheel.
3. Remove the crankshaft pulley-to-damper bolts. Disengage the accessory drive belts and remove the crankshaft pulley.
4. Using the Crankshaft Damper Removal tool No. T58P-6316-D and the Vibration Damper Removal Adapter tool No. T82L-6316-B, remove the crankshaft damper from the crankshaft.
5. Using a small pry bar, pry the oil seal from the front cover; be careful not to damage the front cover and the crankshaft.

NOTE: Before installation; inspect the front cover and shaft seal surface of the crankshaft damper for damage, nicks, burrs or other roughness which may cause the new seal to fail. Service or replace the components as necessary.

6. To install, lubricate the new seal lip with clean engine oil, then install the seal using the seal installer tool No. T82L-6316-A and the front cover seal replacer tool No. T70P-6B070-A, or their compatible equivalents.
7. Coat the crankshaft damper sealing surface with clean engine oil. Apply RTV to the keyway of the damper prior to installation. Install the damper using the vibration damper seal installer tool No. T82L-6316-A.
8. To complete the installation, reverse the removal procedures. Torque the crankshaft damper-to-crankshaft bolt to 141-169 ft.lb. (190-230 Nm), the crankshaft pulley-to-damper bolts to 20-28 ft.lb. (26-38 Nm).

Camshaft

REMOVAL & INSTALLATION

1.6 & 1.9L Engine

The camshaft can be removed with the engine in the car.

1. Remove the fuel pump and plunger. Set the engine to TDC on the compression stroke of No. 1 cylinder. Remove the negative battery cable.
2. Remove the alternator drive belt. Remove the power steering and air conditioning compressor drive belts, if equipped.
3. Remove the camshaft belt cover.
4. Remove the distributor.
5. Remove the rocker arms.
6. Remove the hydraulic valve lash adjusters. Keep the parts in order, as they must be returned to their original positions.
7. Remove and discard the timing belt.
8. Remove the camshaft sprocket and key.
9. Remove the camshaft thrust plate.
10. Remove the ignition coil and coil bracket.
11. Remove the camshaft through the back of the head towards the transaxle.
12. Before installing the camshaft, coat the bearing journals, cam lobe surfaces, seal and thrust plate groove with engine oil. Install the camshaft through the rear of the cylinder head. Rotate the camshaft during installation.
13. Install the camshaft thrust plate and tighten the two attaching bolts to 7-11 ft.lb.
14. Install the cam sprocket and key.
15. Install a new timing belt. See timing belt removal and installation procedure.
16. Install remaining parts in the reverse order of removal. When installing rocker arms, use new hex flange nuts.

2.3L HSC Engine

NOTE: The engine must be removed from the car to perform the following procedure.

1. Remove the oil dipstick, all drive belts and pulleys and remove the cylinder head.
2. Use a magnet or suitable tools to remove the hydraulic lifters from the engine. Keep the lifters in order if reusable.
3. Remove the crankshaft pulley and timing case cover.
4. Check camshaft end play, if excessive replace the thrust plate.
5. Remove the fuel pump and pushrod. Remove the timing chain, sprockets and tensioner.
6. Remove the camshaft thrust plate retaining bolts and the plate.
7. Carefully remove the camshaft from the engine. Use caution to avoid damage to the bearings, journals and lobes.
8. Install in reverse order. Apply lubricant to the camshaft lobes and journals and to the bottom of the lifters. Lubricate all assemblies with oil. Remove to gear and chain replacement section for alignment procedures.

2.5L Engine

1. Refer to the "Engine Removal & Installation" procedures in this section, then remove the engine and place it on a workstand.
2. Refer to the "Timing Chain Removal & Installation" procedures in this section and remove the timing chain with the camshaft sprocket.
3. Remove the cylinder head.
4. Using a magnet, remove the hydraulic tappets and keep them in order so that they can be installed in their original positions. If the tappets are stuck in the bores by excessive varnish, etc., use a Hydraulic Tappet Puller to remove the tappets.
6. Remove the oil pan.
7. To check the camshaft end play, install the camshaft sprocket to the camshaft and perform the following procedures:
   a. Push the camshaft toward the rear of the engine and install a dial indicator tool No. 4201-C, so that the indicator point is on the camshaft sprocket mounting bolt.
   b. Zero the dial indicator. Position a large screwdriver between the camshaft sprocket and the block.
   c. Pull the camshaft forward and release it. Compare the dial indicator reading with the camshaft end play specification of 0.009" (0.229mm).
   d. If the camshaft end play is over the amount specified, replace the thrust plate.

8. Remove the camshaft sprocket and the camshaft thrust plate.
9. Carefully remove the camshaft by pulling it toward the front of the engine. Use caution to avoid damaging the bearings, journals and lobes.
10. Using a putty knife, clean the gasket mounting surfaces.
11. Clean the oil pump inlet tube screen, the oil pan and the cylinder block gasket surfaces. Prime the oil pump by filling the inlet opening with oil and rotate the pump shaft until oil emerges from the outlet tube. Install the oil pump, the oil pump inlet tube screen and the oil pan.
12. To install, use new gaskets, sealant, lubricate the internal parts with SAE 50 weight oil and reverse the removal procedures. Torque the camshaft thrust plate bolts to 6-9 ft.lb. (8-12 Nm), the camshaft sprocket-to-camshaft bolt to 41-56 ft.lb. (55-75 Nm), the front cover-to-engine bolts to 6-9 ft.lb. (8-12 Nm), the damper pulley-to-crankshaft bolt to 140-170 ft.lb. (190-230 Nm), the cylinder head bolts-to-engine bolts (in 2 steps) to 70-76 ft.lb. (95-103 Nm) and the oil pan-to-engine bolts to 15-23 ft.lb. (20-30 Nm). Adjust the valves. Refill the cooling system and the crankcase. Start the engine and check for leaks. Check and/or adjust the ignition timing and the engine idle speed.

3.0L Engine

1. Refer to the "Engine Removal & Installation" procedures in this section, then remove the engine and place it on a workstand.
2. Ensure the cooling system, the fuel system and the crankcase have been drained.

CAUTION

When draining the coolant, keep in mind that cats and dogs are attracted by the ethylene glycol antifreeze, and are quite likely to drink any that is left in an uncovered container or in puddles on the ground. This will prove fatal in sufficient quantity. Always drain the coolant into a sealable container. Coolant should be reused unless it is contaminated or several years old.

3. Remove the idler pulley and bracket assembly. Remove the drive and accessory belts. Remove the water pump.
4. Remove the crankshaft pulley and damper. Remove the lower radiator hose. Remove the oil pan-to-front cover bolts, the front cover-to-engine bolts and the front cover from the engine.
5. Label and remove the spark plug wires and the rocker arm covers. Loosen the rocker arm fulcrum nuts and turn them to the side to expose the pushrods. Remove the pushrods and keep them in their original position.
6. Using a magnet, remove the hydraulic tappets and keep them in order so that they can be installed in their original positions. If the tappets are stuck in the bores by excessive varnish, use the Hydraulic Tappet Puller tool No. T70L-6500-A, to remove the tappets.
7. To check the camshaft end play, perform the following procedures:
   a. Push the camshaft toward the rear of the engine and install a Dial Indicator tool No. 4201-C, so that the indicator point is on the camshaft sprocket bolt. Zero the dial indicator.
   b. Using a medium pry bar, position it between the camshaft sprocket and the block.

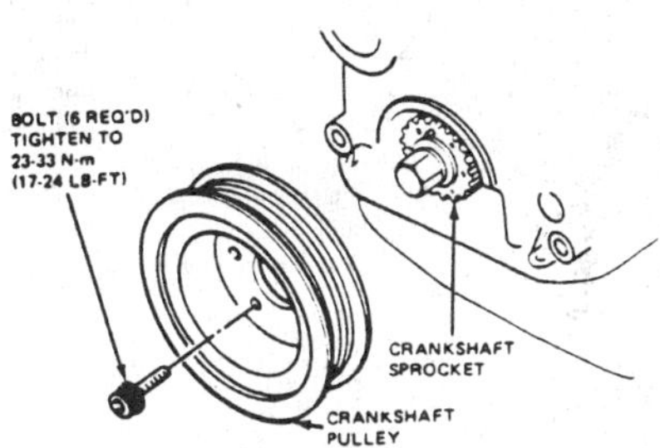

Crankshaft sprocket and pulley removal—diesel engine

NOTE: When applying pressure to the camshaft sprocket, be careful not to break the powdered metal camshaft sprocket.

   c. Pry the camshaft forward and release it. Compare the dial indicator reading with the camshaft end play specification of 0.009".
   d. If the camshaft end play is over the amount specified, replace the thrust plate.
8. Remove the timing chain and sprockets.
9. Remove the camshaft thrust plate. Carefully remove the camshaft by pulling it toward the front of the engine. Remove it slowly to avoid damaging the bearings, journals and lobes.
10. Using a putty knife, clean the gasket mounting surfaces.
11. To install, use new gaskets, sealant, lubricate the internal parts with SAE 50 weight oil and reverse the removal procedures. Torque the camshaft thrust plate-to-engine bolts to 6-8 ft.lb. (8-12 Nm), the front cover-to-engine bolts to 15-22 ft.lb. (20-30 Nm), the water pump-to-front cover bolts to 6-8 ft.lb. (8-12 Nm), the crankshaft

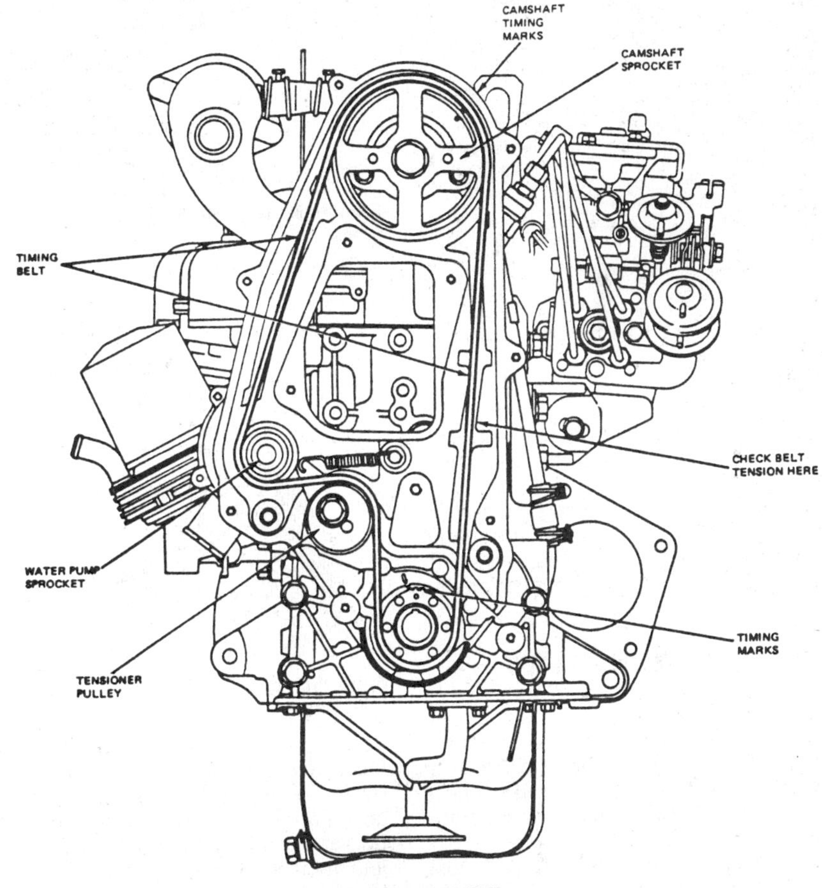

Front timing belt installation, diesel engine

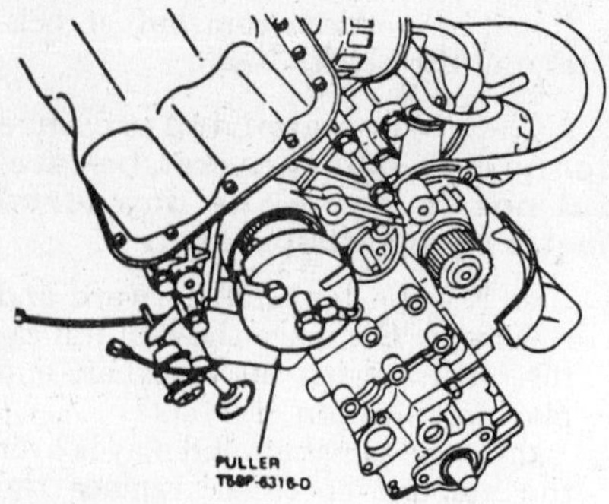

Crankshaft pulley removal—diesel engine

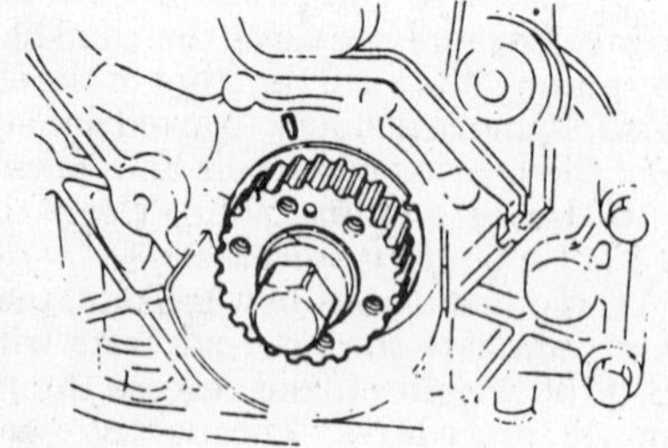

Loosening tensioner pulley—diesel engine

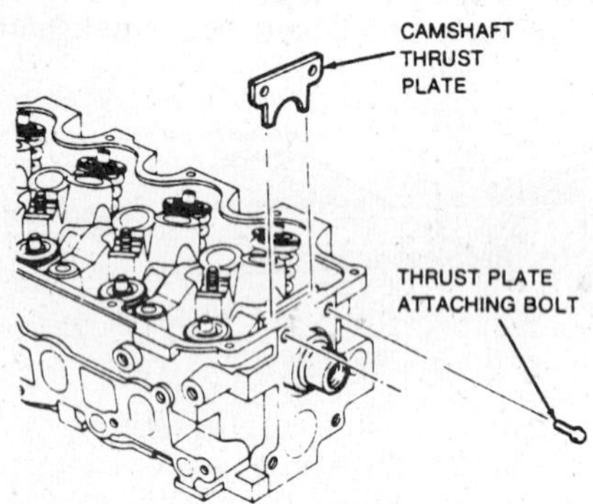

Camshaft thrust plate removal—1.6L and 1.9L engines

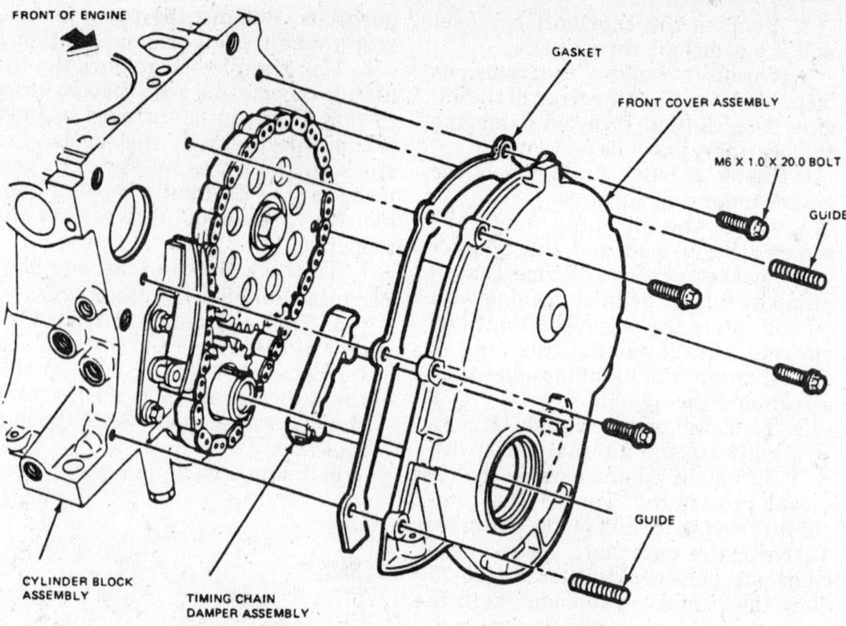

2.3 HSC Engine timing cover components

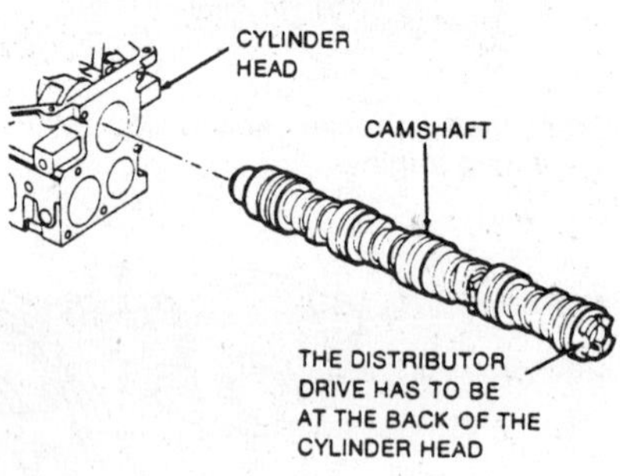

Camshaft installation—1.6L and 1.9L engines

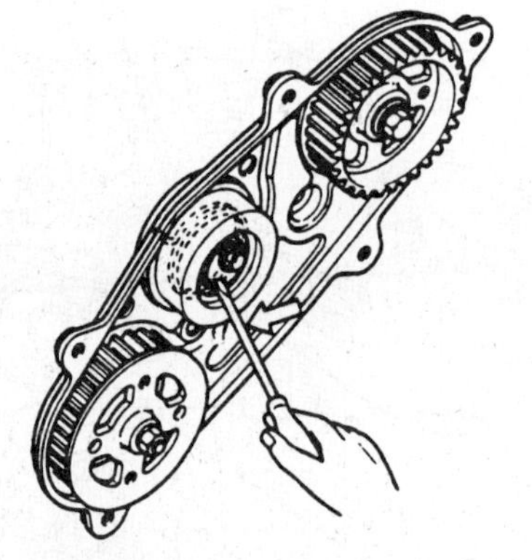

Front timing case cover installation—23. HSC engine

damper-to-crankshaft bolt to 141-169 ft.lb. (190-230 Nm) and the crankshaft pulley-to-damper bolts to 20-28 ft.lb. (26-38 Nm). Refill the cooling system and the crankcase. Start the engine and check for leaks. Check and/or adjust the ignition timing and the engine idle speed.

CHECKING CAMSHAFT

Degrease the camshaft using safe solvent, clean all oil grooves. Visually inspect the cam lobes and bearing journals for excessive wear. If a lobe is questionable, check all lobes and journals with a micrometer.

Measure the lobes from nose to base and again at 90°. The lift is determined by subtracting the second measurement from the first. If all exhaust lobes and all intake lobes are not identical, the camshaft must be reground or replaced. Measure the bearing journals and compare to specifications. If a journal is worn there is a good chance that the cam bearings are worn too, requiring replacement.

If the lobes and journals appear intact, place the front and rear cam journals in V-blocks and rest a dial indicator on the center journal. Rotate the camshaft to check for straightness, if deviation exceeds 0.001" (0.025mm), replace the camshaft.

Pistons and Connection Rods

REMOVAL & INSTALLATION

NOTE: Although, in most cases, the pistons and connecting rods can be removed from the engine (after the cylinder head and oil pan are removed) while the engine is still in the car, it is far easier to remove the engine from the car. If removing pistons with the engine still installed, disconnect the radiator hoses, automatic transmission cooler lines and radiator shroud. Unbolt front mounts before jacking up the engine. Block the engine in position with wood blocks between the mounts.

1. Remove the engine from the car. Remove cylinder head(s), oil pan and front cover (if necessary).

2. Because the top piston ring does not travel to the very top of the cylinder bore, a ridge is built up between the end of the travel and the top of the cylinder. Pushing the piston and connecting rod assembly past the ridge is difficult and may cause damage to the piston. If new rings are installed and the ridge has not been removed, ring breakage and piston damage can occur

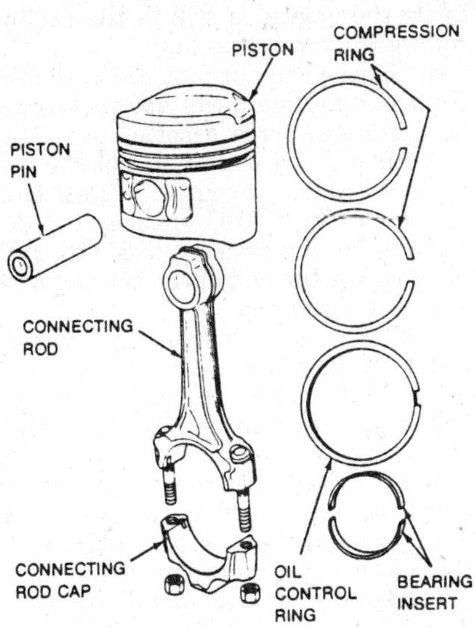

Piston and connecting rod assembly

when the ridge is encountered at engine speed.

3. Turn the crankshaft to position the piston at the bottom of the cylinder bore. Cover the top of the piston with a rag. Install a ridge reamer in the bore and follow the manufacturer's instructions to remove the ridge. Use caution. Avoid cutting too deeply or into the ring travel area. Remove the rag and cuttings from the top of the piston. Remove the ridge from all cylinders.

4. Check the edges of the connecting rod and bearing cap for numbers or matchmarks, if none are present mark the rod and cap numerically and in sequence from front to back of engine. The numbers or marks not only tell from which cylinder the piston came from buy also ensures that the rod caps are installed in the correct matching position.

5. Turn the crankshaft until the connecting rod is at the bottom of travel. Remove the two attaching nuts and the bearing cap. Take two pieces of rubber tubing and cover the rod bolts to prevent crank or cylinder scoring. Use a wooden hammer handle to help push the piston and rod up and out of the cylinder. Reinstall the rod cap in proper position. Remove all pistons and connecting rods. Inspect cylinder walls and deglaze or hone as necessary.

6. Installation is the reverse order of removal. Lubricate each piston, rod bearing and cylinder wall. Install a ring compressor over the piston, position piston with mark toward front of engine and carefully install. Position connecting rod with bearing insert installed over the crank journal. Install the rod cap with bearing in proper position. Secure with rod nuts and torque to proper specifications. Install all rod and piston assemblies.

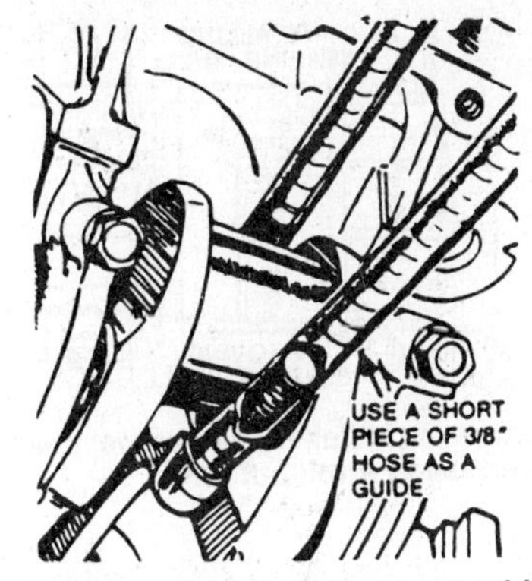

Use lengths of vacuum hose or rubber tubing to protect the crankshaft journals and cylinder walls during installation

Install the piston using a ring compressor

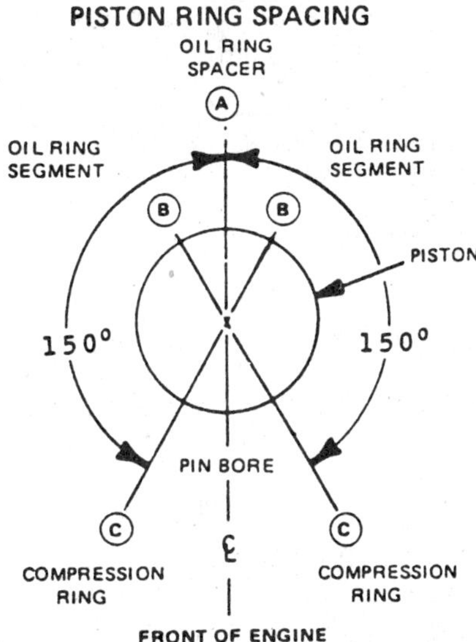

Recommended piston ring spacing. Refer to the ring manufacturer's instruction sheet before installing new piston rings

CLEANING AND INSPECTION

1. Use a piston ring expander and remove the rings from the piston.

2. Clean the ring grooves using an appropriate cleaning tool, exercise care to avoid cutting too deeply.

3. Clean all varnish and carbon from the piston with a safe solvent. Do not use a wire brush or caustic solution on the pistons.

4. Inspect the pistons for scuffing, scoring, cracks, pitting or excessive ring groove wear. If wear is evident, the piston must be replaced.

5. Have the piston and connecting rod assembly checked by a machine shop for correct alignment, piston pin wear and piston diameter. If the piston has collapsed it will have to be replace or knurled to restore original diameter. Connecting rod bushing replacement, piston pin fitting and piston changing can be handled by the machine shop.

CYLINDER BORE

Check the cylinder bore for wear using a telescope gauge and a micrometer, measure the cylinder bore diameter perpendicular to the piston pin at a point 2½" (63.5mm) below the top of the engine block. Measure the piston skirt perpendicular to the piston pin. The difference between the two measurements is the piston clearance. If the clearance is within specifications, finish honing or glaze breaking is all that is required. If clearance is excessive a slightly oversize piston may be required. If greatly oversize, the engine will have to be bored and 0.010" (0.25mm) or larger oversized pistons installed.

FITTING AND POSITIONING PISTON RINGS

1. Take the new piston rings and compress them, one at a time into the cylinder that they will be used in. Press the ring about 1" (25mm) below the top of the cylinder block using an inverted piston.

2. Use a feeler gauge and measure the distance between the ends of the ring. This is called measuring the ring end gap. Compare the reading to the one called for in the specifications table. File the ends of the ring with a fine file to obtain necessary clearance.

NOTE: If inadequate ring end gap is utilized, ring breakage will result.

3. Inspect the ring grooves on the piston for excessive wear or taper. If necessary have the grooves recut for use with a standard ring and spacer. The machine shop can handle the job for you.

4. Check the ring grooves by rolling the new piston ring around the groove to check for burrs or carbon deposits. If any are found, remove with a fine file. Hold the ring in the groove and

measure side clearance with a feeler gauge. If clearance is excessive, spacer(s) will have to be added.

NOTE: Always add spacers above the piston ring.

5. Install the ring on the piston, lower oil ring first. Use a ring installing tool on the compression rings. Consult the instruction sheet that comes with the rings to be sure they are installed with the correct side up. A mark on the ring usually faces upward.

6. When installing oil rings, first, install the expanding ring in the groove. Hold the ends of the ring butted together (they must not overlap) and install the bottom rail (scraper) with the end about 1" (25mm) away from the butted end of the control ring. Install the top rail about 1" (25mm) away from the butted end of the control but on the opposite side from the lower rail.

7. Install the two compression rings.

8. Consult the illustration for ring positioning, arrange the rings as shown, install a ring compressor and insert the piston and rod assembly into the engine.

Crankshaft and Bearings

REMOVAL & INSTALLATION

1. Rod bearings can be installed when the pistons have been removed for servicing (rings etc.) or, in most cases, while the engine is still in the car. Bearing replacement, however, is far easier with the engine out of the car and disassembled.

2. For in car service, remove the oil pan, spark plugs and front cover if necessary. Turn the engine until the connecting rod to be serviced is at the bottom of travel. Remove the bearing cap, place two pieces of rubber hose over the rod cap bolts and push the piston and rod assembly up the cylinder bore until enough room is gained for bearing insert removal. Take care not to push the rod assembly up too far or the top ring will engage the cylinder ridge or come out of the cylinder and require head removal for installation.

3. Clean the rod journal, the connecting rod end and the bearing cap after removing the old bearing inserts. Install the new inserts in the rod and bearing cap, lubricate them with oil. Position the rod over the crankshaft journal and install the rod cap. Make sure the cap and rod numbers match, torque the rod nuts to specifications.

4. Main bearings may be replaced while the engine is still in the car by rolling them out and in.

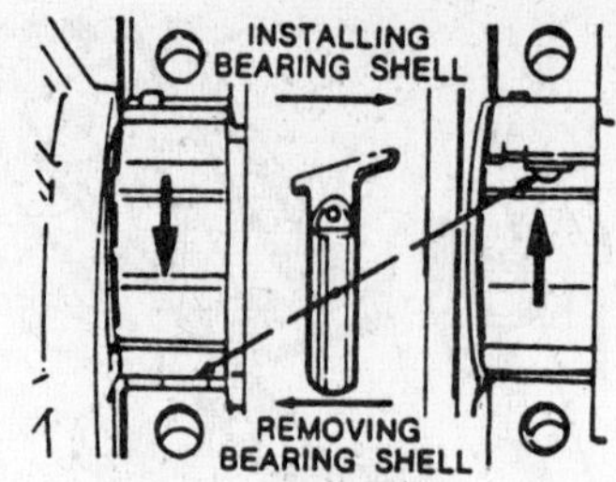

Remove or install the upper main bearing insert using a roll-out pin

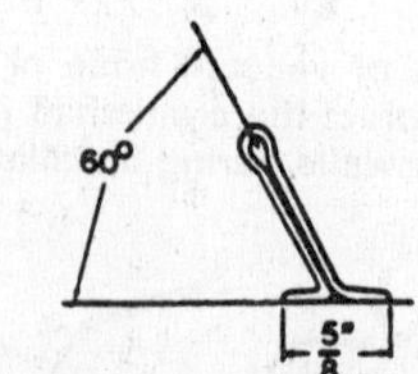

Home made roll-out pin

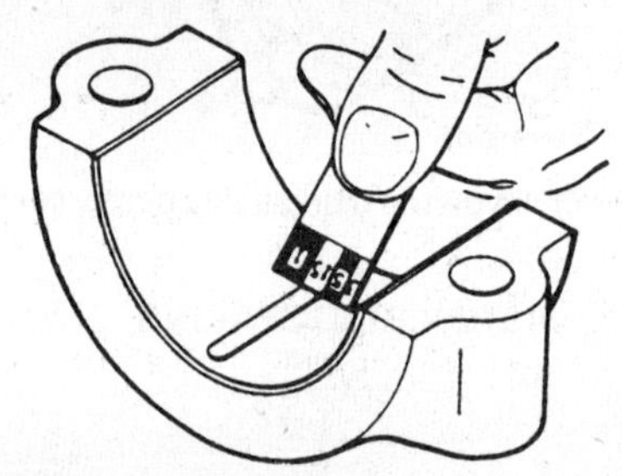

Measure the Plastigage® to determine bearing clearance

5. Special roll out pins are available from automotive parts houses or can be fabricated from a cotter pin. The roll out pin fits in the oil hole of the main bearing journal. When the crankshaft is rotated opposite the directions of the bearing lock tab, the pin engages the end of the bearing and rolls out the insert.

6. Remove main bearing cap and roll out upper bearing insert. Remove insert from main bearing cap. Clean the inside of the bearing cap and crankshaft journal.

7. Lubricate and roll upper insert into position, make sure the lock tab is anchored and the insert is not cocked. Install the lower bearing insert into the cap, lubricate and install on the engine. Make sure the main bearing cap is installed facing in the correct direction and torque to specifications.

8. With the engine out of the car, remove the intake manifold, cylinder heads, front cover, timing gears and/or chain, oil pan , oil pump and flywheel.

9. Remove the piston and rod assemblies. Remove the main bearing caps after marking them for position and direction.

10. Remove the crankshaft, bearing inserts and rear main oil seal. Clean the engine block and cap bearing saddles. Clean the crankshaft and inspect for wear. Check the bearing journals with a micrometer for out-of-round condition and to determine wheat size rod and main bearing inserts to install.

11. Install the main bearing upper inserts and rear main oil seal half into the engine block.

12. Lubricate the bearing inserts and

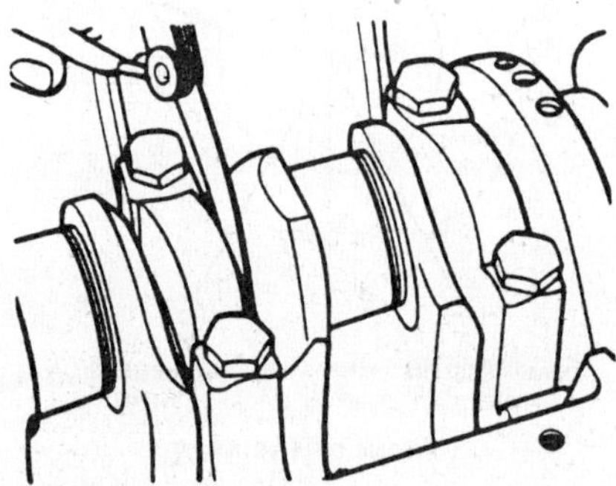

Check the crankshaft end-play with a feeler gauge

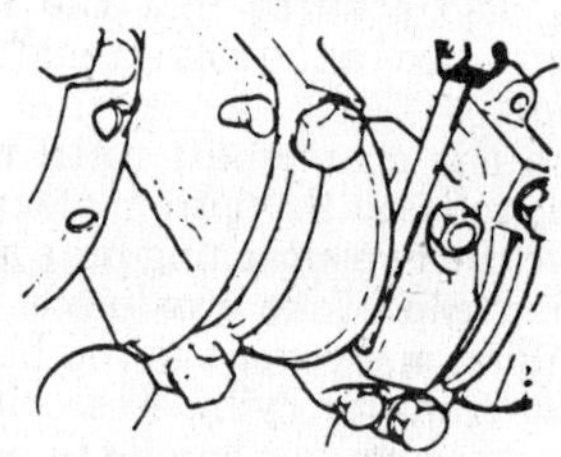

Check the connecting rod side clearance with a feeler gauge

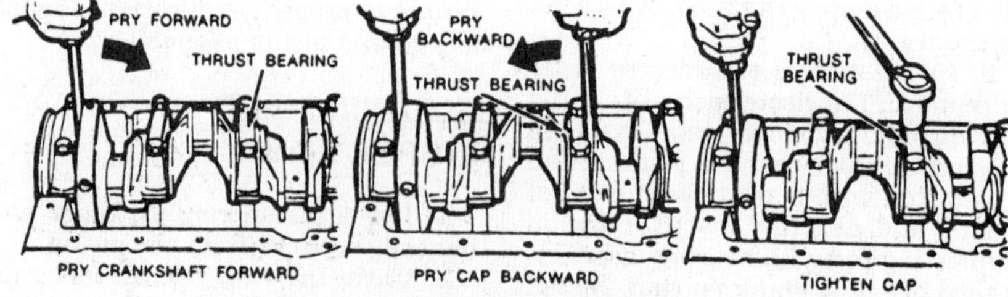

Aligning the thrust bearing

the crankshaft journals. Slowly and carefully lower the crankshaft into position.

13. Install the bearing inserts and rear main seal into the bearing caps, install the caps working from the middle out. Torque cap bolts to specifications in stages, rotate the crankshaft after each torque state. Note the illustration for thrust bearing alignment.

14. Remove bearing caps, one at a time and check the oil clearance with Plastigage®. Reinstall if clearance is within specifications. Check the crankshaft endplay, if within specifications install connecting rod and piston assemblies with new rod bearing inserts. Check connecting rod bearing oil clearance and side play, if correct assemble the rest of the engine.

BEARING OIL CLEARANCE

Remove cap from the bearing to be checked. Using a clean, dry rag, thoroughly clean all oil from crankshaft journal and bearing insert.

NOTE: Plastigage® is soluble in oil, therefore, oil on the journal or bearing could result in erroneous readings.

Place a pieced of Plastigage® along the full width of the bearing insert, reinstall cap, and torque to specifications.

NOTE: Specifications are given in the Engine Specifications Chart.

Remove bearing cap, and determine bearing clearance by comparing width of Plastigage® to the scale on Plastigage® envelope. Journal taper is determined by comparing width of the bearing insert, reinstall cap, and torque to specifications.

NOTE: Do not rotate crankshaft with Plastigage® installed. If bearing insert and journal appear intact, and are within tolerances, no further main bearing service is required. If bearing or journal appear defective, cause of failure should be determined before replacement.

CRANKSHAFT ENDPLAY/CONNECTING ROD SIDE PLAY

Place a pry bar between a main bearing cap and crankshaft casting taking care not to damage any journals. Pry backward and forward, measure the distance between the thrust bearing and crankshaft with a feeler gauge. Compare reading with specifications. If too great a clearance is determined, a main bearing with a larger thrust surface or crank machining may be required. Check with an automotive machine shop for their advice.

Connecting rod clearance between the rod and crankthrow casting can be checked with a feeler gauge. Pry the rod carefully on one side as far as possible and measure the distance on the other side of the rod.

CRANKSHAFT REPAIRS

If a journal is damaged on the crankshaft, repair is possible by having the crankshaft machined to a standard undersize.

In most cases, however, since the engine must be removed from the car and disassembled, some thought should be given to replacing the damaged crankshaft with a reground shaft kit. A reground crankshaft kit contains the necessary main and rod bearings for installation. The shaft has been ground and polished to undersize specifications and will usually hold up well if installed correctly.

Rear Main Bearing Oil Seal

REMOVAL & INSTALLATION

Gasoline Engines

1. Remove the transaxle.
2. Remove the rear cover plate, and flywheel.
3. Using a suitable tool, punch two holes in the metal surface of the seal between the lip and block.
4. Screw in the threaded end of a small slide hammer and remove the seal.
5. Clean the seal mounting surfaces. Coat the crankshaft and seal with engine oil.
6. Install the oil seal using a seal installing tool.
7. Reassembly the remaining parts in the reverse order of removal.

Completing the Rebuilding Process

1. Fill the oil pump with oil, to prevent cavitating (sucking air) on initial engine start up. Install the oil pump and the pickup tube on the engine. Coat the oil pan gasket as necessary, and install the gasket and the oil pan. Mount the flywheel and the crankshaft vibration damper or pulley on the crankshaft.

NOTE: Always use new bolts when install the flywheel. Inspect the clutch shaft pilot bushing in the crankshaft. If the bushing is excessively worn, remove it with an expanding puller and a slide hammer, and tap a new bushing into place.

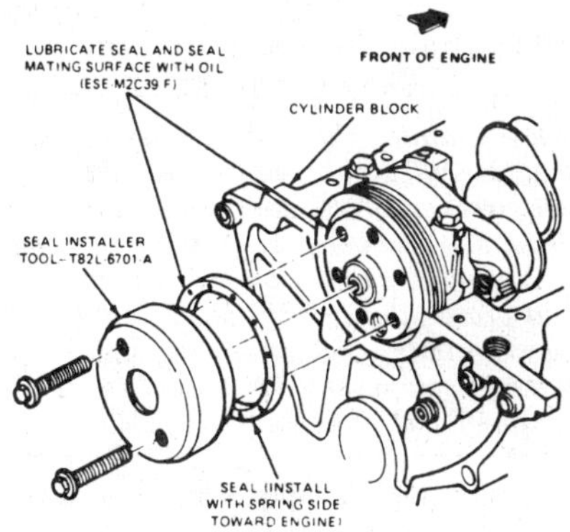

Installing the rear main oil seal—typical

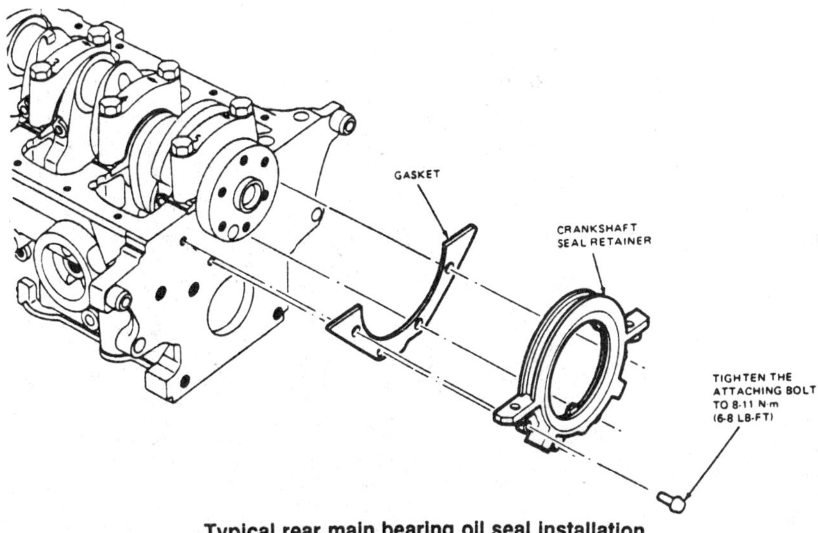

Typical rear main bearing oil seal installation

2. Position the engine, cylinder head side up. Lubricate the lifters, and install them into their bores. Install the cylinder head, and torque it as specified. Insert the pushrods (where applicable), and install the rocker shaft(s) (if so equipped) or position the rocker.

3. Install the intake and exhaust manifolds, the carburetor(s), the distributor and spark plugs. Mount all accessories and install the engine in the car. Fill the radiator with coolant, and the crankcase with high quality engine oil.

ENGINE COOLING

Radiator

REMOVAL & INSTALLATION

Except Taurus and Sable

1. Disconnect the negative battery cable. Drain the cooling system.

CAUTION

When draining the coolant, keep in mind that cats and dogs are attracted by the ethylene glycol antifreeze, and are quite likely to drink any that is left in an uncovered container or in puddles on the ground. This will prove fatal in sufficient quantity. Always drain the coolant into a sealable container. Coolant should be reused unless it is contaminated or several years old.

2. On models equipped, remove the carburetor air intake tube and alternator air tube from the radiator support.

3. Remove the upper shroud mountings, disconnect the wire harness to the electric fan motor and remove the shroud and fan as an assembly.

4. Remove the upper and lower radiator hoses. Disconnect the coolant recovery reservoir.

5. On models equipped with an automatic transaxle, disconnect and plug the cooler lines.

6. Remove radiator mountings, tilt radiator toward engine and lift from engine compartment.

7. Install the radiator in the reverse order. Be sure the lower radiator mounts are positioned correctly on the radiator support.

Taurus and Sable

1. Place a fluid catch pan under the radiator. Open the radiator draincock and remove the radiator cap, then drain the cooling system.

CAUTION

When draining the coolant, keep in mind that cats and dogs are attracted by the ethylene glycol antifreeze, and are quite likely to drink any that is left in an uncovered container or in puddles on the ground. This will prove fatal in sufficient quantity. Always drain the coolant into a sealable container. Coolant should be reused unless it is contaminated or several years old.

2. Remove the overflow hose from the radiator and the coolant tank.

3. Remove the upper shroud screws, lift the shroud from the lower retaining clips and position it over the fan.

4. Loosen the upper/lower radiator hose clamps, then using a twisting motion, remove the hoses from the radiator.

5. If equipped with an ATX, use the Cooler Line Disconnect tool No. T82L-9500-AH to disconnect the oil cooling lines from the radiator. Be sure to plug the cooling lines to prevent fluid draining from the transaxle.

6. Remove the upper radiator-to-vehicle screws, then tilt the radiator rearward (approx. 1"), lift it upward (clearing the support and the fan).

7. To install, reverse the removal procedures. Torque the upper radiator-to-support bolts to 13-20 ft.lb. (17-27 Nm), the upper shroud-to-radiator screws to 4-6 ft.lb. (5.5-8 Nm) and the hose clamps to 20-30 in.lb. (2.25-3.38 Nm).

NOTE: When installing the radiator, position the molded pins (at the bottom of nylon end tanks) in the slotted holes of the lower support rubber pads.

8. Install the cooling fluid (to a level of 1½" below the radiator filler neck), start the engine, operate it for 15 minutes and check for leaks.

NOTE: If installing new cooling fluid, use a 50/50 mixture of water and anti-freeze. Be sure to add 2 Cooling System Protector Pellets No. D9AZ-19558-A to the radiator.

Water Pump

REMOVAL & INSTALLATION

1.6 & 1.9L Engine

1. Disconnect the negative battery cable. Drain the cooling system.

CAUTION

When draining the coolant, keep in mind that cats and dogs are attracted by the ethylene glycol antifreeze, and are quite likely to drink any that is left in an uncovered container or in puddles on the ground. This will prove fatal in sufficient quantity. Always drain the coolant into a sealable container. Coolant should be reused unless it is contaminated or several years old.

2. Remove the alternator drive belt. If equipped with air conditioning or power steering, remove the drive belts.

3. Use a wrench on the crankshaft pulley to rotate the engine so No. 1 piston is on TDC of the compression stroke.

WARNING: Turn the engine only in the direction of normal rotation. Backward rotation will cause the camshaft belt to slip or lose teeth.

4. Remove the cam belt cover.

5. Loosen the bolt tensioner attaching bolts, then secure the tensioner over as far as possible.

6. Pull the bolt from the camshaft, tensioner, and water pump sprocket.

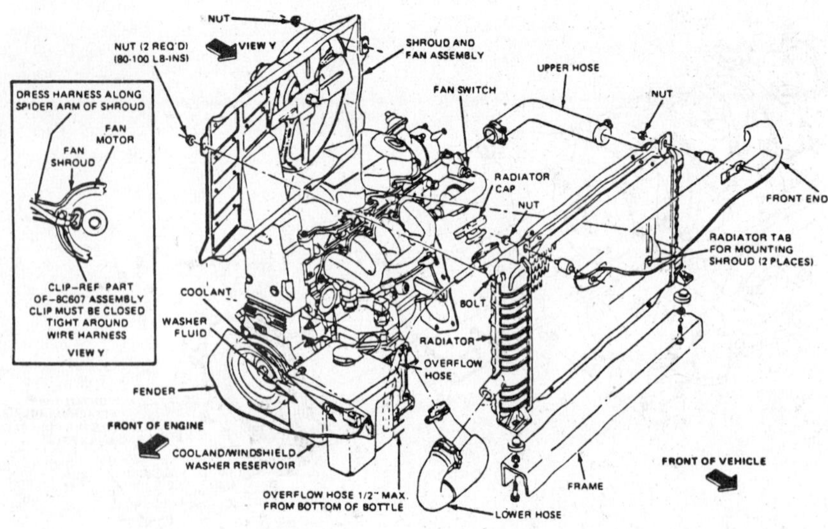

Typical engine cooling system components

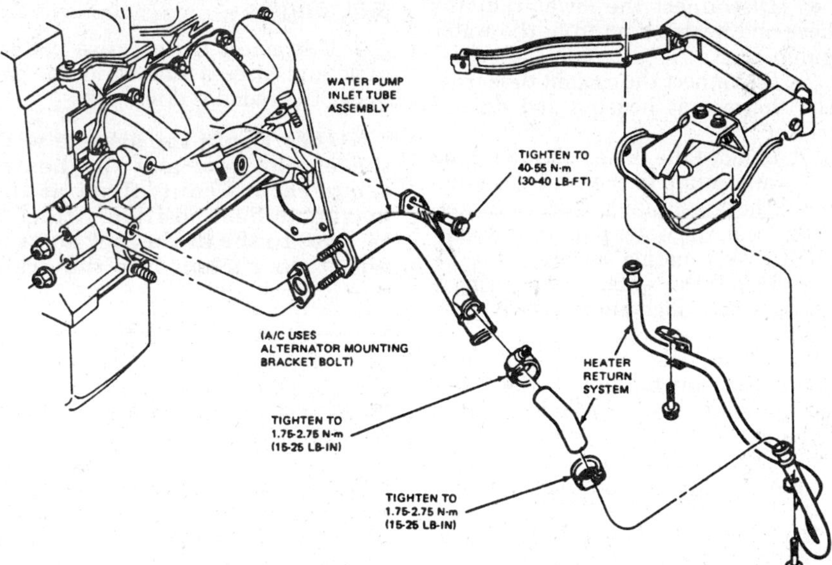

Typical water inlet system, car shown non air conditioned

TAB AND SLOT ORIENTATION
TOOL T82L-9500-AH

Using tool to remove and replace the transaxle oil cooler lines at the radiator

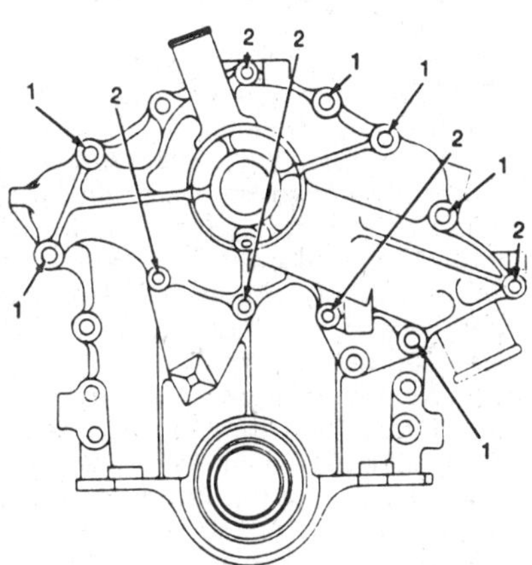

Position of the water pump bolts on the 3.0L engine – one M8 and two M6

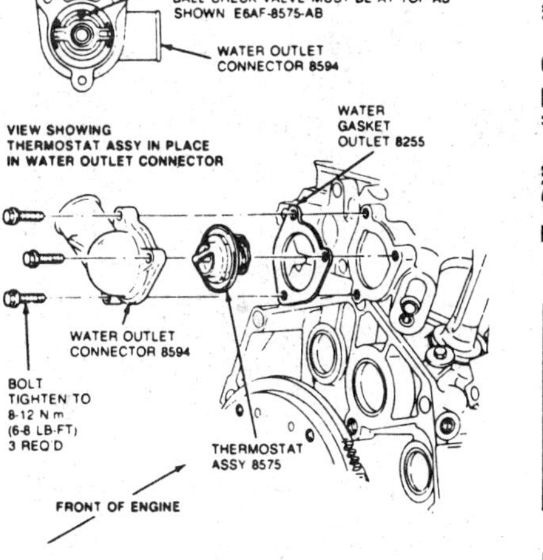

Exploded view of the thermostat and housing—3.0L engine

CYLINDER HEAD ASSY 6049
THERMOSTAT ASSY TO BE INSTALLED AS SHOWN 8575
M8 x 1.25 x M6 x 1.0 x 44.1 STUD AND WASHER TIGHTEN TO 16-24 N·m (12-18 LB-FT)
GASKET 8255
VENT PLUG 8A574
VIEW A
WATER OUTELT CONNECTION 8594
M8 x 1.25 x 30.0 BOLT HEX FLG. HD TIGHTEN TO 16-24 N·m (12-18 LB-FT)
(3/8-18) PIPE PLUG TIGHTEN TO 16-24 N·m (12-18 LB-FT)
THERMOSTAT ASSY 8575
ROTATE THE THERMOSTAT INTO CONNECTION IN CLOCKWISE DIRECTION, ENGAGING LOCKING FEATURES INTO WATER OUTLET CONNECTION
WATER OUTLET CONNECTION 8594
TAB
VIEW A

Exploded view of the thermostat and housing—2.5L engine

Do not remove it from, or allow it to change its position on, the crankshaft sprocket.

NOTE: Do not rotate the engine with the camshaft belt removed.

7. Remove the camshaft sprocket.
8. Remove the rear timing cover stud. Remove the heater return tube hose connection at the water pump inlet tube.
9. Remove the water pump inlet tube fasteners and the inlet tube and gasket.
10. Remove the water pump to the cylinder block bolts and remove the water pump and its gasket.
11. To install, make sure the mating surfaces on the pump and the block are clean.
12. Using a new gasket and sealer, install the water pump and tighten the bolts to 5-7 ft.lb. on models through 1982.

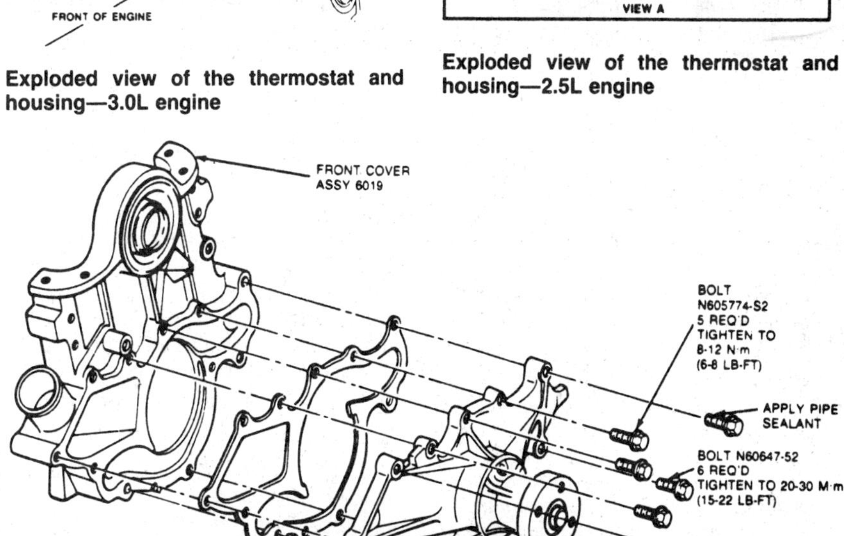

Exploded view of the water pump assembly—3.0L engine

1983 and later models – 30-40 ft.lb. Make sure the pump impeller turns freely.

13. Install remaining parts in the reverse order of removal. Use new gaskets and sealer. Install the camshaft sprocket over the cam key. See below the procedure. Install new timing belt and adjust tension. See Timing Belt Removal and Installation for procedure.

2.3L HSC Engine

1. Disconnect the negative battery cable. Drain the cooling system.

CAUTION

When draining the coolant, keep in mind that cats and dogs are attracted by the ethylene glycol antifreeze, and are quite likely to drink any that is left in an uncovered container or in puddles on the ground. This will prove fatal in sufficient quantity. Always drain the coolant into a sealable container. Coolant should be reused unless it is contaminated or several years old.

2. Loosen the thermactor pump mounting and remove the drive belt. Disconnect and remove the hose clamp below the pump. Remove the thermactor pump bracket mounting bolts and remove the thermactor and bracket as an assembly.
3. Loosen the water pump drive belt idler pulley and remove the drive belt.
4. Disconnect the heater hose from the water pump.
5. Remove the water pump mounting bolts and the pump.
6. Clean the engine mounting surface. Apply gasket cement to both sides of the mounting gasket and position the gasket on the engine.
7. Install the pump in reverse order of removal. Torque the mounting bolts to 15-22 ft.lb.
8. Add the proper coolant mixture, start the engine and check for leaks.

2.0L Diesel Engine

1. Remove the front timing belt upper cover.
2. Loosen and remove the front timing belt, refer to timing belt in-vehicle services. .
3. Drain the cooling system.

CAUTION

When draining the coolant, keep in mind that cats and dogs are attracted by the ethylene glycol antifreeze, and are quite likely to drink any that is left in an uncovered container or in puddles on the ground. This will prove fatal in sufficient quantity. Always drain the coolant into a sealable container. Coolant should be reused unless it is contaminated or several years old.

4. Raise the vehicle and support safely on jackstands.
5. Disconnect the lower radiator hose and heater hose from the water pump.
6. Disconnect the coolant tube from the thermostat housing and discard gasket.
7. Remove the three bolts attaching the water pump to the crankcase. Remove the water pump. Discard gasket.
8. Clean the water pump and crankshaft gasket mating surfaces.
9. Install the water pump, using a new gasket. Tighten bolts to 23-34 ft.lb.
10. Connect the coolant tube from the thermostat housing to the water pump using a new gasket. Tighten bolts to 5-7 ft.lb.
11. Connect the heater hose and lower radiator hose to the water pump.
12. Lower vehicle.
13. Fill and bleed the cooling system.
14. Install and adjust the front timing belt.
15. Run the engine and check for coolant leaks.
16. Install the front timing belt upper cover.

2.5L ENGINE

1. Open the hood, place protection aprons on the fenders and disconnect the negative battery cable.
2. Remove the radiator cap and position a drain pan under the radiator.

CAUTION

When draining the coolant, keep in mind that cats and dogs are attracted by the ethylene glycol antifreeze, and are quite likely to drink any that is left in an uncovered container or in puddles on the ground. This will prove fatal in sufficient quantity. Always drain the coolant into a sealable container. Coolant should be reused unless it is contaminated or several years old.

3. Raise and support the front of the vehicle on jackstands. Remove the lower radiator hose from the radiator and drain the coolant into the drain pan.
4. Remove the water pump inlet tube. Loosen the belt tensioner by inserting a ½" flex handle in the square hole of the tensioner, then rotate the tensioner counterclockwise and remove the drive belt from the vehicle.
5. Disconnect the heater hose from the water pump. Remove the three water pump-to-engine block bolts and the pump from the engine.
6. Using a putty knife, clean the gasket mounting surfaces.
7. To install, use a new gasket, sealant and reverse the removal procedures. Torque the water pump-to-engine bolts to 15-22 ft.lb. (20-30 Nm). Check and/or adjust the drive belt tension. Refill the cooling system, start the engine and check for leaks.

3.0L Engine

1. Disconnect the negative battery cable and place a suitable drain pan under the radiator draincock.

NOTE: Drain the system with the engine cool and the heater temperature control set at the maximum heat position. Attach a ⅜" hose to the drain cock so as to direct the coolant into the drain pan.

CAUTION

When draining the coolant, keep in mind that cats and dogs are attracted by the ethylene glycol antifreeze, and are quite likely to drink any that is left in an uncovered container or in puddles on the ground. This will prove fatal in sufficient quantity. Always drain the coolant into a sealable container. Coolant should be reüsed unless it is contaminated or several years old.

2. Remove the radiator cap, open the drain cock on the radiator and drain the cooling system.
3. Loosen the accessory drive belt idler pulley and remove the drive belts.
4. Remove the idler pulley bracket-to-engine nuts/bolt. Disconnect the heater hose from the water pump.
5. Remove the pulley-to-pump hub bolts. The pulley will remain loose on the hub due to the insufficient clearance between the inner fender and the water pump.
6. Remove the water pump-to-engine bolts, then lift the water pump and pulley out of the vehicle.
7. Using a putty knife, clean the gasket mounting surfaces.
8. To install, use a new gasket, sealant and reverse the removal procedures. Torque the water pump-to-engine bolts to 15-22 ft.lb. (20-30 Nm) for 8mm and to 6-8 ft.lb. (8-12 Nm) for 6mm and the water pump pulley-to-water pump bolts to 15-22 ft.lb. (20-30 Nm); be sure to apply a suitable thread sealer to the bolts before installing them. Check and/or adjust the drive belt tension. Refill the cooling system, start the engine and check for leaks.

Thermostat

REMOVAL & INSTALLATION

Except the 2.5L and 3.0L Engines

1. Disconnect the negative battery cable. Drain the radiator until the coolant level is below the thermostat.

CAUTION

When draining the coolant, keep in mind that cats and dogs are attracted by the ethylene glycol antifreeze, and are quite likely to

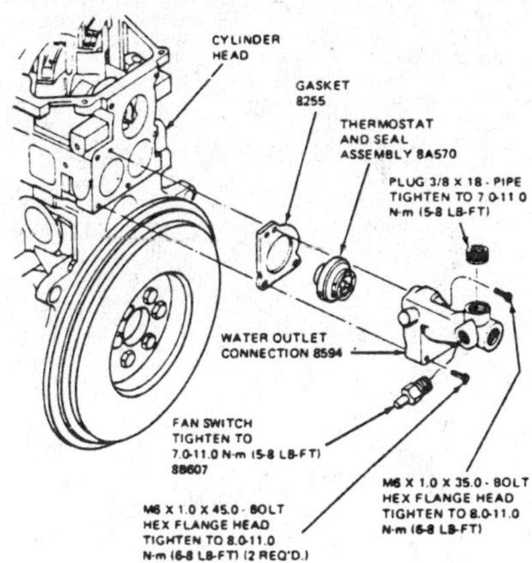

Typical thermostat installation

drink any that is left in an uncovered container or in puddles on the ground. This will prove fatal in sufficient quantity. Always drain the coolant into a sealable container. Coolant should be reused unless it is contaminated or several years old.

2. Disconnect the wire connector at the thermostat housing thermoswitch.
3. Loosen the top radiator hose clamp. Remove the thermostat housing mounting bolts and lift up the housing.
4. Remove the thermostat by turning counterclockwise.
5. Clean the thermostat housing and engine gasket mounting surfaces. Install new mounting gasket and fully insert the thermostat to compress the mounting gasket. Turn the thermostat clockwise to secure in housing.
6. Position the housing onto the engine. Install the mounting bolts and torque to 6-8 ft.lb. on 1.6 & 1.9L engines and 12-18 ft.lb. on 2.3L HSC engines.
7. The rest of the installation is in the reverse order of removal.

2.5L and 3.0L Engines

1. Raise the hood and place protective aprons on the fenders.
2. Disconnect the negative battery cable.
3. Position a drain pan under the radiator, remove the radiator cap, open the draincock and drain the coolant into the drain pan.

NOTE: Drain the cooling system to a level below the water outlet housing.

CAUTION

When draining the coolant, keep in mind that cats and dogs are attracted by the ethylene glycol antifreeze, and are quite likely to drink any that is left in an uncovered container or in puddles on the ground. This will prove fatal in sufficient quantity. Always drain the coolant into a sealable container. Coolant should be reused unless it is contaminated or several years old.

4. On the 2.5L engine, remove the vent plug from the water outlet housing.
5. Loosen the upper hose clamp at the radiator. Remove the water outlet housing-to-engine bolts, lift the outlet clear of the engine and remove the thermostat from the housing.
6. Using a putty knife, clean the gasket mounting surfaces.
7. To install, use a new gasket, sealant, thermostat and reverse the removal procedures. Torque the water outlet housing-to-engine bolts to 12-18 ft.lb. (16-24 Nm) for 2.5L engine and 6-8 ft.lb. (8-12 Nm) for 3.0L engine.

NOTE: When installing the thermostat, rotate it clockwise into the water outlet housing. On the 3.0L engine, position the thermostat ball check valve at the top.

Electric Fan

OPERATION

The electric cooling fan is mounted in the shroud behind the radiator.

A thermal switch mounted in the thermostat housing activates the fan when the coolant reaches a specified temperature. When the temperature is approximately 221°F (105°C) the thermal switch closes thus starting the fan.

The electric fan also operates when the air conditioner (if equipped) is turned on. When the temperature drops to between 185-193°F (85-90°C) the thermal switch opens and the fan shuts off.

CAUTION

Since the fan is governed by temperature the engine does not have to be on for the fan to operate. If any underhood operations must be performed on a warm engine, disconnect the wiring harness to the fan.

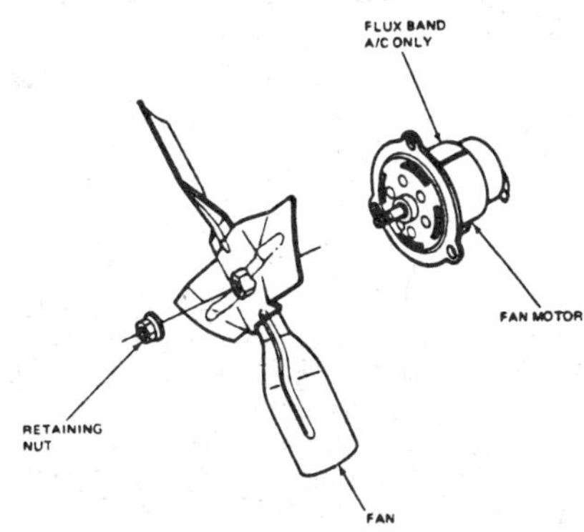

Cooling fan and electric motor

ENGINE LUBRICATION

Oil Pan

REMOVAL & INSTALLATION

1.6L, 1.9L and 2.3L Engines

The oil pan can be removed with the engine in the car. No suspension or chassis components need be removed. However, on Tempo/Topaz model, the transaxle case must be mounted to the engine.

1. Disconnect the negative battery terminal.
2. Jack up the vehicle and support it with stands.
3. Drain the oil. On Tempo/Topaz, drain cooling system and remove coolant tube (lower hose). Disconnect exhaust pipe. Move A/C line out of the way.

CAUTION

When draining the coolant, keep in mind that cats and dogs are attracted by the ethylene glycol antifreeze, and are quite likely to drink any that is left in an uncovered container or in puddles on the ground. This will prove fatal in sufficient quantity. Always drain the coolant into a sealable container. Coolant should be reused unless it is contaminated or several years old.

4. Disconnect the starter wires.
5. Remove the knee brace and roll restrictor.
6. Remove the starter bolts and the starter.
7. Remove the knee braces at the transaxle on Escort/Lynx models.
8. Remove the oil pan bolts and the pan.
9. Remove the front and rear oil pan seal, and the pan gasket.
10. Installation is the reverse or removal.
    a. When installing the pan on Escort/Lynx, apply a thin coating of sealer to the front and rear seals and also to the pan before installing the gasket. Tighten the pan bolts 6-8 ft.lb.
    b. When installing the pan on Tempo/Topaz bolt transaxle case to rear face of cylinder block to align oil pan.
    c. Apply a continuous $^{3}/_{16}$" (4.8mm) wide bead of Ford Silcone Gasket Sealer E3AZ-19562-A or equivalent, to the groove in the oil pan flange.
    d. Apply an extra beard of sealer to the cylinder block on each side of the front cover.

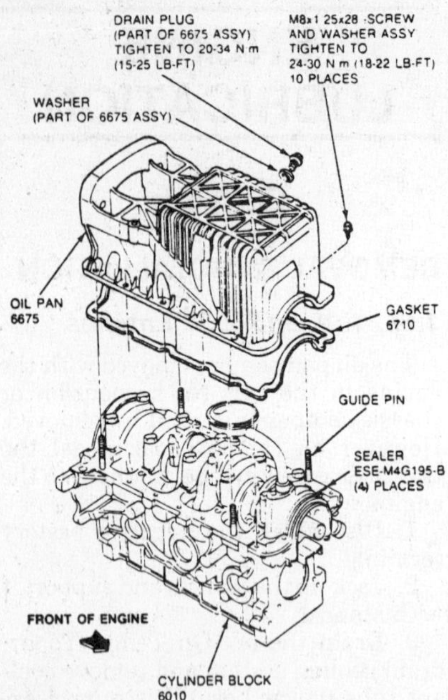

Oil pan installation–1.6L and 1.9L engines

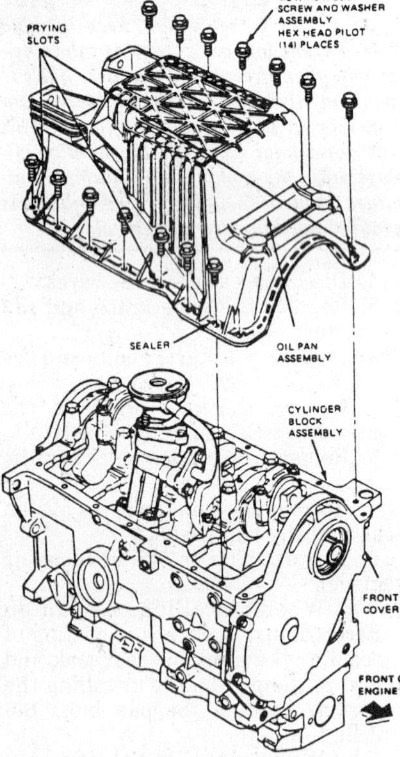

Oil pan installation–23.L HSC engine

e. Immediately place the oil pan against the cylinder block and install four corner bolts. Tighten bolts snug enough to allow horizontal movement of pan. Install and tighten oil pan to transaxle bolts, then back off bolts. Install the oil pan attaching bolts and tighten to 6-9 ft.lb.

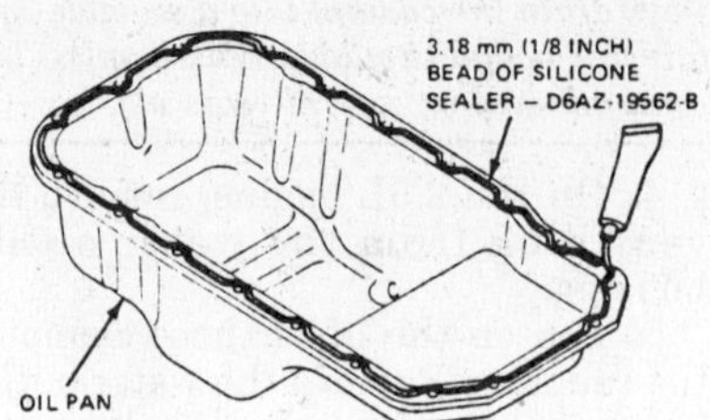

Applying sealant to the oil pan–2.0L diesel engine

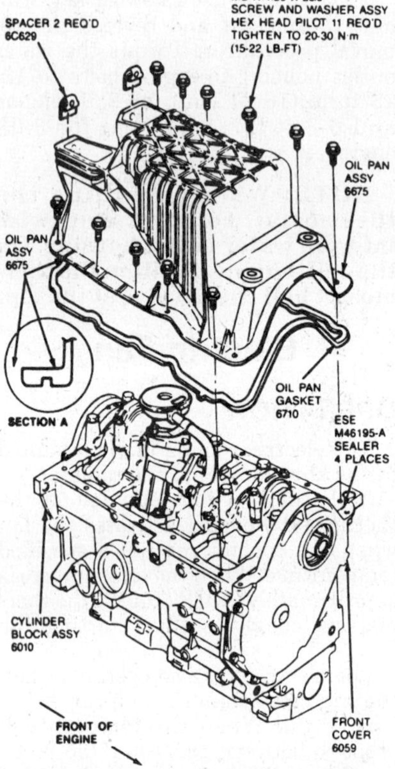

Exploded view of the oil pan assembly—2.5L engine

2.5L Engine

1. Disconnect negative ground cable at battery.
2. Raise and support the front of the vehicle of jackstands.
3. Remove the crankcase oil plug and drain the fluid. Remove the lower radiator hose and drain the cooling system.

CAUTION

When draining the coolant, keep in mind that cats and dogs are attracted by the ethylene glycol antifreeze, and are quite likely to drink any that is left in an uncovered container or in puddles on the ground. This will prove fatal in sufficient quantity. Always drain the coolant into a sealable container. Coolant should be reused unless it is contaminated or several years old.

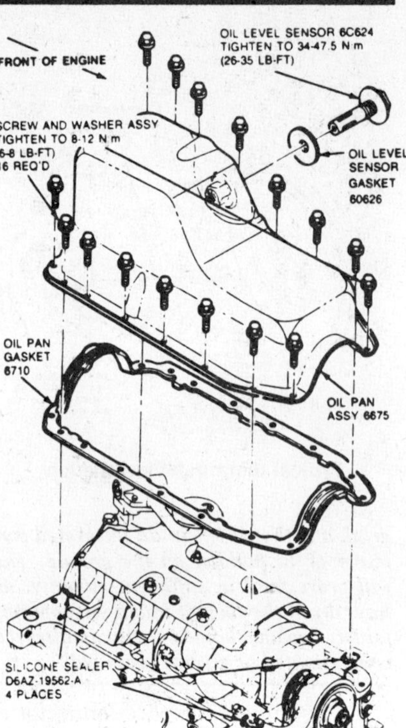

Exploded view of the oil pan assembly—3.0L engine

4. If equipped with a manual transaxle, remove the roll restrictor.
5. Disconnect the starter electrical connectors and the starter.
6. Disconnect the exhaust pipe from the oil pan.
7. Remove the engine coolant tube located near the lower radiator hose, the water pump and the oil pan tabs.
8. If equipped with A/C, position the air conditioner line off to the side.
9. Remove the oil pan-to-engine bolts and the pan.
10. Using a putty knife, clean the gasket mounting surfaces. Remove and clean oil pump pickup tube and screen assembly. After cleaning, install tube and screen assembly.

NOTE: Before proceeding, a trial installation of the pan to cylinder block must be performed to insure smooth pan installation, thus preventing smearing of the sealant. Check again for any residual oil that may have leaked down (particularly the rear of the engine) and clean as necessary.

11. To install, use new gaskets, sealant and reverse the removal procedures. Torque the oil pan-to-engine bolts to 15-23 ft.lb. (20-30 Nm). Refill the cooling system and the crankcase. Start the engine and check for leaks.

3.0L Engine

1. Disconnect the negative battery cable and remove the oil level dipstick.

2. Raise and support the front of the vehicle on jackstands. If equipped with a low oil level sensor, remove the retainer clip and the electrical connector from the sensor.
3. Drain the engine oil into an oil catch pan.
4. Disconnect the electrical connectors from the starter and remove the starter.
5. In the exhaust manifold, disconnect the electrical connector from the oxygen sensor.
6. Remove the catalytic converter and the exhaust pipe assembly.
7. From the torque converter housing, remove the lower engine/flywheel dust cover.
8. Remove the oil pan-to-engine mounting bolts and the pan from the engine.
9. Using a putty knife, clean the gasket mounting surfaces.
10. To install, use new gaskets, sealant and reverse the removal procedures. Torque the oil pan-to-engine bolts to 6-8 fft.lb. (8-12 Nm). Refill the cooling system and the crankcase. Start the engine and check for leaks.

Diesel Engine

1. Disconnect the negative battery cable.
2. Raise and safely support the vehicle on jackstands. Drain the engine oil.
3. Remove the bolts that attach the oil pan to the engine and remove the oil pan.
4. Clean all gasket mounting surfaces.
5. Apply a 1/8" (3mm) bead of Silicone Sealer on the oil pan mounting surface.
6. Install the oil pan and tighten the bolts to 5-7 ft.lb.

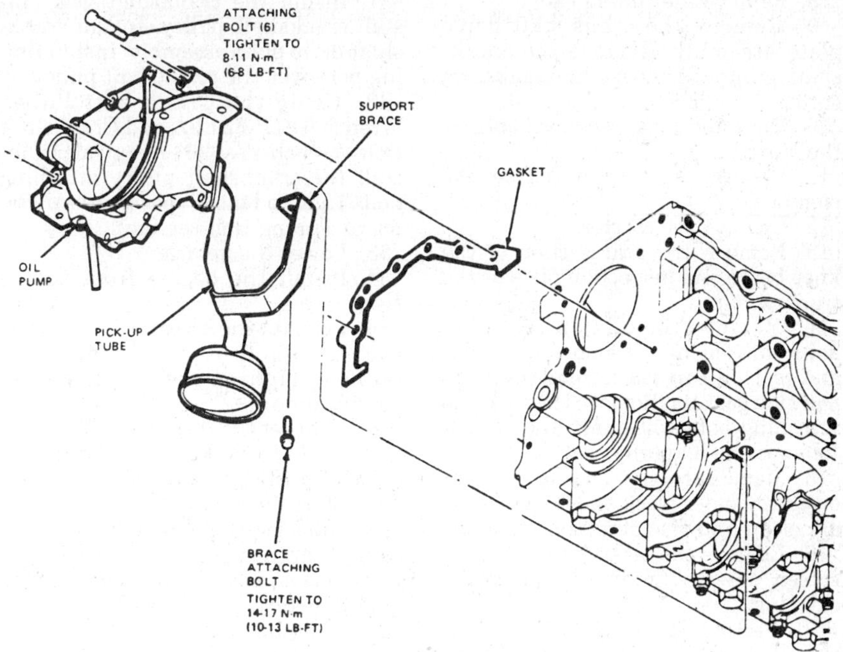

Oil pump installation – 1.6L and 1.9L engines

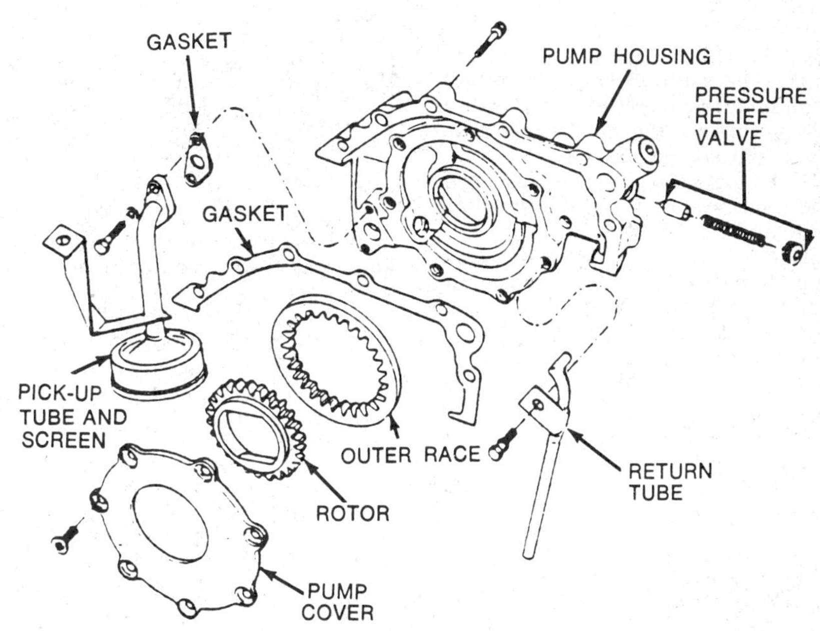

Exploded view of the oil pump – 1.6L and 1.9L engines

Oil Pump

REMOVAL & INSTALLATION

1.6 & 1.9L Engine

1. Disconnect the negative cable at the battery.
2. Loosen the alternator bolt on the alternator adjusting arm. Lower the alternator to remove the accessory drivebelt from the crankshaft pulley.
3. Remove the timing belt cover.

NOTE: Set No. 1 cylinder at TDC prior to timing belt removal.

4. Loosen both belt tensioner attaching bolts using Tool T8AP-6254-A or equivalent on the left bolt. Using a pry bar or other suitable tool pry the tensioner away from the belt. While holding the tensioner away from the belt, tighten one of the tensioner attaching bolts.
5. Disengage the timing belt from the camshaft sprocket, water pump sprocket and crankshaft sprocket.
6. Raise the vehicle and safely support on jackstands. Drain the crankcase.
7. Using a crankshaft Pulley Wrench T81P6312A and Crankshaft Bolt Wrench YA-826 or equivalent, remove the crankshaft pulley attaching bolt.

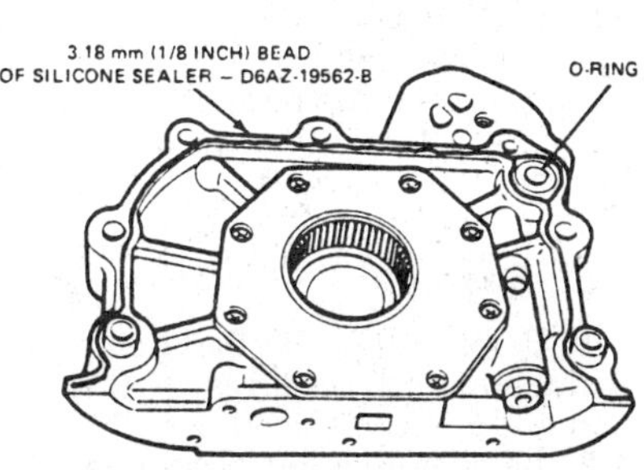

Oil pump assembly – 2.0L diesel engine

8. Remove the timing belt.
9. Remove the crankshaft drive plate assembly. Remove the crankshaft pulley. Remove the crankshaft sprocket.
10. Disconnect the starter cable at the starter.
11. Remove the knee brace from the engine.
12. Remove the starter.
13. Remove the rear section of the knee brace and inspection plate at the transmission.
14. Remove the oil pan retaining bolts and oil pan. Remove the front and rear oil pan seals. Remove the oil pan side gaskets. Remove the oil pump attaching bolts, oil pump and gasket. Remove the oil pump seal.
15. Make sure the mating surfaces on the cylinder block and the oil pump are clean and free of gasket material.
16. Remove the oil pick-up tube and screen assembly from the pump for cleaning.
17. Lubricate the outside diameter of the oil pump seal with engine oil.
18. Install the oil pump seal using Seal Installer T81P-6700-A or equivalent.
19. Install the pick-up tube and screen assembly on the oil pump. Tighten attaching bolts to 6-9 ft.lb.
20. Lubricate the oil pump seal lip with light engine oil.
21. Position the oil pump gasket over the locating dowels. Install attaching bolts and tighten to 5-7 ft.lb.
22. Apply a bead of Silicone Sealer approximately 3.0mm wide at the corner of the front and rear oil pan seals, and at the seating point of the oil pump to the block retainer joint.
23. Install the front oil pan seal by pressing firmly into the slot cut into the bottom of the pump.
24. Install the rear oil seal by pressing firmly into the slot cut into rear retainer assembly.

NOTE: Install the seal before the sealer has cured (within 10 minutes of application).

25. Apply adhesive sealer evenly to oil pan flange and to the oil pan side of the gasket. Allow the adhesive to dry past the wet stage and then install the gaskets on the oil pan. Position the oil pan on the cylinder block.
26. Install oil pan attaching bolts. Tighten bolts in the proper sequence to 6-8 ft.lb.
27. Position the transmission inspection plate and the rear section of the knee brace on the transmission. Install the two attaching bolts and tighten to specification.
28. Install the starter.
29. Install the knee brace.
30. Connect the starter cable.
31. Install the crankshaft gear. Install crankshaft pulley. Install crankshaft drive plate assembly. Install timing belt over the crankshaft pulley.
32. Using the Crankshaft Pulley Wrench T81P-6312-A and Crankshaft Bolt Wrench YA-826 or equivalent, install the crankshaft pulley attaching bolt. Tighten bolt to specification. (Refer to Timing Belt section).
33. Lower the vehicle.
34. Install the engine front timing cover.
35. Position the accessory drive belts over the alternator and crankshaft pulleys. Tighten the drive belts to specification.
36. Connect the negative cable at the battery. Fill crankcase to the proper level with the specified oil.
37. Start the engine and check for oil leaks. Make sure the oil pressure indicator lamp has gone out. If the lamp remains On, immediately shut off the engine, determine the case and correct the condition.

2.3L HSC Engine

1. Remove the oil pan.
2. Remove the oil pump attaching bolts an remove the oil pump and intermediate driveshaft.
3. Prime the oil pump by filling inlet port with engine oil. Rotate the pump shaft until oil flows from outlet port.
4. If the screen and cover assembly have been removed, replace the gasket. Clean the screen and reinstall the screen and cover assembly.
5. Position the intermediate driveshaft into the distributor socket.
6. Insert the intermediate driveshaft into the oil pump. Install the pump and shaft as an assembly.

WARNING: Do not attempt to force the pump into position if it will not seat. The shaft hex may be misaligned with the distributor shaft. To align, remove the oil pump and rotate the intermediate driveshaft into a new position.

7. Tighten the two attaching bolts to specification.
8. Install the oil pan and all related parts, refer to Oil Pan Installation.
9. Fill the crankcase to the proper level. Start the engine and check for oil pressure. Operate engine at fast idle and check for oil leaks.

2.5L Engine

1. Refer to the "Oil Pan Removal & Installation" procedures in this section and remove the oil pan.
2. Remove oil pump-to-engine bolts, the oil pump and the intermediate driveshaft.
3. Using a putty knife, clean the gasket mounting surfaces.
4. Prime the oil pump by filling the inlet port with engine oil. Rotate the pump shaft until oil flows from the outlet port.
5. If the screen and cover assembly have been removed, replace the gasket. Clean the screen, then reinstall the screen and cover assembly.
6. Position the intermediate driveshaft into the distributor socket.
7. Insert the intermediate driveshaft into the oil pump. Install the oil pump and the shaft as an assembly.

CAUTION

DO NOT attempt to force the pump into position if it will not seat. The shaft hex may be misaligned with the distributor shaft. To align, remove the oil pump and rotate the intermediate driveshaft into a new position.

8. Torque the oil pump-to-engine and the oil pan-to-engine bolts to 15-23 ft.lb. (20-30 Nm).
9. To complete the installation, use new gaskets, sealant and reverse the removal procedures. Refill the crankcase. Start engine and check the oil pressure. Operate the engine at fast idle and check for oil leaks.

3.0L Engine

1. Refer to the "Oil Pan Removal & Installation" procedures in this section and remove the oil pan.
2. Remove the oil pump-to-engine bolts, then lift the pump from the engine and withdraw the oil pump driveshaft.
3. Using a putty knife, clean the gasket mounting surfaces.
4. Prime the oil pump by filling either the inlet or the outlet port with engine oil. Rotate the pump shaft to distribute the oil within the oil pump body.
5. Insert the oil pump driveshaft into the pump with the retainer end facing inward. Place the oil pump in the proper position with a new gasket and install the mounting bolts.
6. Torque the oil pump-to-engine bolts to 30-40 ft.lb. (40-55 Nm). Clean and install the oil pump inlet tube and screen assembly with a new gasket.
7. To complete the installation, use new gaskets, sealant and reverse the removal procedures. Torque the oil pan-to-engine bolts to 6-8 ft.lb. (8-12 Nm). Refill the crankcase to the proper level with recommended engine oil. Start the engine and check the oil pressure. Operate the engine at fast idle and check for oil leaks.

Diesel Engine

NOTE: The engine must be removed from the car.

1. Disconnect the battery ground cable from the battery, which is located in the luggage compartment.
2. Remove the engine from the vehicle.
3. Remove accessory drive belts.
4. Drain the engine oil.
5. Remove the oil pan.
6. Remove the crankshaft pulley, front timing belt, front timing belt tensioner, and crankshaft sprocket as outlined.
7. Remove the bolts attaching the oil pump to the crankcase and remove the pump. Remove the crankshaft front oil seal.
8. Clean the oil pump and the crankcase gasket mating surfaces.
9. Apply a 1/8" (3mm) bead of Silicone Sealer on the oil pump-to-crankcase mating surface.
10. Install a new O-ring.
11. Install the oil pump, making sure the oil pump inner gear engages with the splines on the crankshaft. Tighten the 10mm bolts to 23-34 ft.lb. and the 8mm bolts to 12-16 ft.lb.
12. Install a new crankshaft front oil seal.
13. Clean the oil pan-to-crankcase mating surfaces.
14. Apply a 3/8" (3.8mm) bead of RTV silicone sealer on the oil pan-to-crankcase mating surface.
15. Install the oil pan and tighten the bolts to 5-7 ft.lb.
16. Install and adjust as necessary the crankshaft sprocket, front timing belt tensioner and front timing belt.
17. Install and adjust the accessory drive belts.
18. Install engine in the vehicle.
19. Fill and bleed the cooling system.
20. Fill the crankcase with the specified quantity and quality of oil.
21. Run the engine and check for oil, fuel and coolant leaks.

FUEL SYSTEM

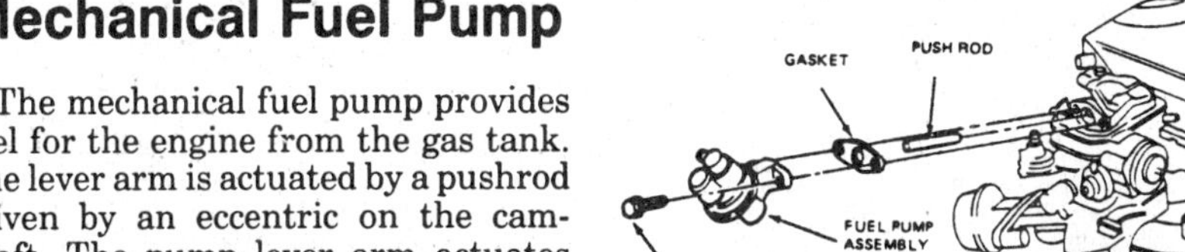

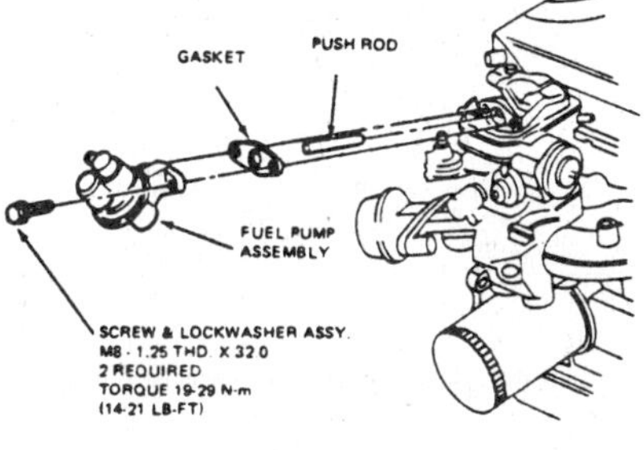

Typical fuel pump pushrod installation

Mechanical Fuel Pump

The mechanical fuel pump provides fuel for the engine from the gas tank. The lever arm is actuated by a pushrod driven by an eccentric on the camshaft. The pump lever arm actuates the internal diaphragm and provides fuel on demand to the carburetor when the engine is running.

REMOVAL & INSTALLATION

Except 2.5L Engine

1. Loosen the fuel outlet line using two flare wrenches. Loosen the fuel pump mounting bolts two turns.
2. Turn the engine until the fuel pump moves with just a little resistance on the mounting. The cam eccentric and pump lever are now in the low position.
3. Remove the rubber hose and clamp from the inlet side of the fuel pump.
4. Remove the outlet fuel line from the pump. Remove the mounting bolts and the fuel pump.
5. Installation is in the reverse order of removal. Mounting bolt torque is 14-21 ft.lb. Use a new mounting gasket, be sure the cam eccentric is in the lower position before installing the fuel pump.

NOTE: The fuel pump pushrod may come out when the fuel pump is removed. Be sure to install the pushrod before installing the fuel pump.

6. After installing the pump, start the engine and check for fuel leaks.

2.5L Engine

1. Loosen the threaded fuel lines at the fuel pump slightly. Have a rag handy to absorb any gasoline spillage.
2. Loosen the fuel pump mounting bolts two turns and free the fuel pump from the engine.
3. Bump the engine around (with the starter) until the fuel pressure (hold the pump against the engine) is reduced. The fuel pump drive lobe and pushrod are now at their low point.
4. Remove the fuel lines and vapor hose (if equipped). Remove the fuel pump mounting bolts and the fuel pump.
5. Remove the fuel pump mounting gasket and clean the engine mounting surface.
6. Remove and check the pushrod; replace it, if wear is apparent.
7. To install, use a new gasket and reverse the removal procedures. Torque the fuel pump-to-engine bolts to 11-19 ft.lb. The pushrod length should be 2.43".

FUEL PUMP CAPACITY CHECK

The fuel pump can fail in two ways: it can fail to provide a sufficient volume of gasoline under the proper pressure to the carburetor, or it can develop an internal or external leak. An external leak will be evident; not so with an internal leak. A quick check for an internal leak is to remove the oil dipstick and examine the oil on it. A fuel pump with an internal leak will leak fuel into the oil pan. If the oil on the dipstick is very thin and smells of gas, a defective fuel pump could be the cause.

To check the volume of gasoline from the fuel pump, disconnect the fuel pump line at the fuel filter. Connect a suitable rubber hose and clamp it to the fuel line. Insert it into a quart container. Start the engine. The fuel pump should provide one pint of gasoline in thirty seconds.

Electric Fuel Pump

REMOVAL & INSTALLATION

1.6L and 1.9L Engines

1.6 & 1.9L fuel injected models are equipped with an externally mounted electric fuel pump. The pump is located at the right rear, under the car, near the fuel tank. The pump is controlled by the EEC system, via a pump relay, which provides power to the pump under various operating conditions.

NOTE: Fuel pressure must be relieved before servicing the fuel system. A valve is provided on the fuel rail assembly for this purpose. Remove the air cleaner and attach a special pressure gauge tool (Rotunda T80L9974A or equivalent) to the valve and relieve the pressure.

1. Raise and support the rear of the car on jackstands.

2. Remove the pump mounting assembly by loosening the upper mounting bolt until the pump can be lowered. Remove the parking brake cable from mounting clip to provide necessary working room.

3. Disconnect the electrical connector and disconnect the fuel pump outlet fitting.

4. Disconnect the fuel pump inlet line from the pump.

CAUTION

Either drain the tank or raise the end of the line above the tank level to prevent draining.

5. Install the fuel pump in the reverse order of removal.

6. Install the pressure gauge on the fuel rail. Turn the ignition ON for 2 seconds. Turn the switch OFF. Repeat procedure several times, until the pressure gauge shows 35 psi. Remove the gauge. Start the engine and check for leaks.

3.0L Engine

The electric fuel pump is located in the fuel tank and is a part of the fuel gauge sending unit.

1. Position the vehicle on a level surface.

2. Refer to "Bleeding Fuel System" procedures in this section and reduce the pressure in the fuel system.

3. Remove the fuel from the fuel tank by pumping it out through the filler neck. Take precautions to avoid the risk of fire when handling gasoline.

4. Raise and support the rear of the vehicle on jackstands. Remove the fuel filler tube (neck).

5. Support the fuel tank and remove the fuel tank straps. Lower the fuel tank slightly, then remove the fuel lines, the electrical connectors and the vent lines.

6. Remove the fuel tank and place it on a workbench. Clean any dirt from around the fuel pump attaching flange.

7. Using a brass drift and a hammer, turn the fuel pump locking ring counterclockwise and remove it.

8. Remove the fuel pump assembly from the fuel tank and discard the flange gasket.

9. To install, perform the following procedures:

a. Using Multipurpose Long Life Lubricant C1AZ-19590 or equivalent, coat the new O-ring and install it in the fuel ring groove.

b. Refill the fuel tank.

c. Install a fuel pressure gauge and turn the ignition switch ON and OFF, 5-10 times, for three second intervals, until the pressure gauge reads 13 psi (CFI) or 30 psi (EFI).

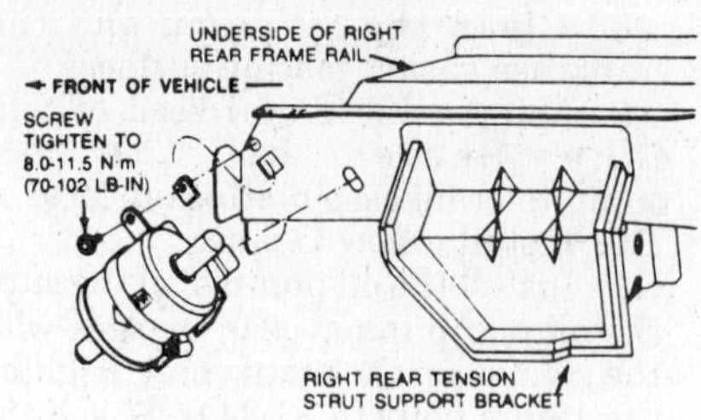

Exploded view of the fuel filter

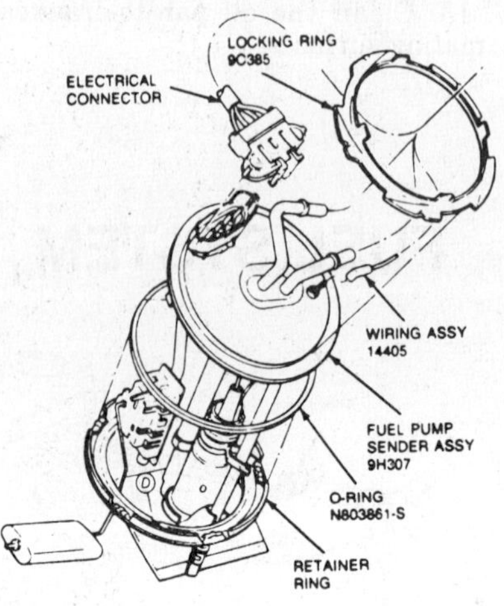

Exploded view of the fuel sender assembly

d. Remove the pressure gauge, start the engine and check for fuel leaks.

INERTIA SWITCH

A safety inertia switch is installed to shut off the electric fuel pump in case of collision. The switch is located on the left hand side of the car, behind the rearmost seat side trim panel, or inside the rear quarter shock tower access door. If the pump shuts off, or if the vehicle has been hit and will not start, check for leaks fist then reset the switch. The switch is reset by pushing down on the button provided.

Push Connect Fittings

Push connect fittings are designed with two different retaining clips. The fittings used with $^5/_{16}$" (8mm) diameter tubing use a hairpin clip. The fittings used with ¼" (6mm) and ½" (12.7mm) diameter tubing use a "duck bill" clip. Each type of fitting requires different procedures for service.

Push connect fitting disassembly must be accomplished prior to fuel component removal (filter, pump, etc.) except for the fuel tank where removal is necessary for access to the push connects.

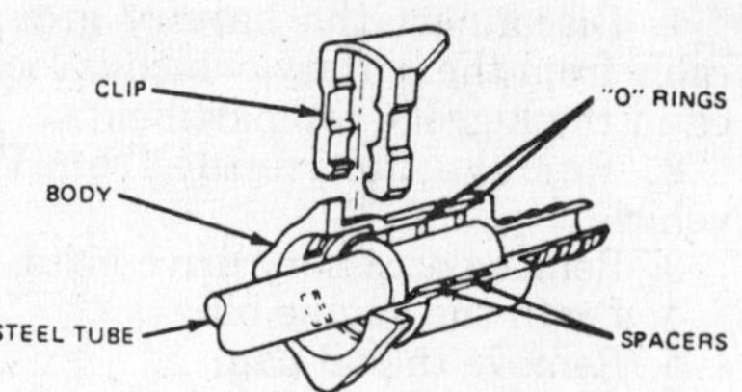

Push connect fittings with hairpin clip

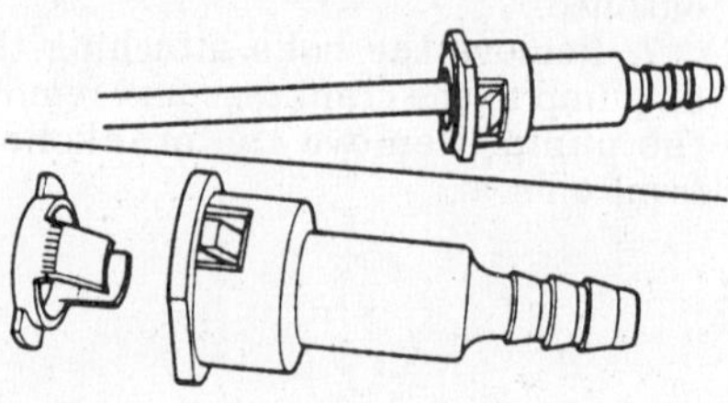

Push connect fittings with duck bill clip

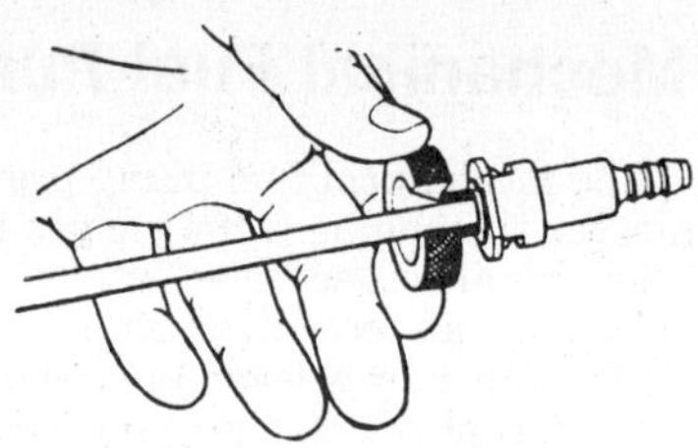

Removing push connect with tool

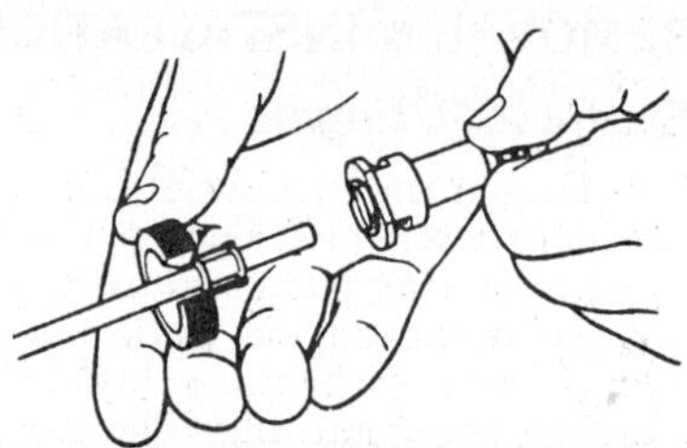

Pulling off push connect fitting

REMOVAL & INSTALLATION

$^5/_{16}$" Fittings (Hairpin Clip)

1. Inspect internal portion of fitting for dirt accumulation. If more than a light coating of dust is present, clean the fitting before disassembly.

2. Remove hairpin type clip from fitting. This is done (using hands only) by spreading the two clip legs about ⅛" (3mm) each to disengage the body and pushing the legs into the fitting. Complete removal is accomplished by lightly pulling from the triangular end of the clip and working it clear of the tube and fitting.

NOTE: Do not use any tools.

3. Grasp the fitting and hose assembly and pull in an axial direction to re-

move the fitting from the steel tube. Adhesion between sealing surfaces may occur. A slight twist of the fitting may be required to break this adhesion and permit effortless removal.

4. When fitting is removed from the tube end, inspect clip t ensure it has not been damaged. If damaged, replace the clip. If undamaged, immediately reinstall clip, insert clip into any two adjacent openings with the triangular portion pointing away from the fitting opening. Install clip to fully engage the body (legs of hairpin clip locked on outside of body). Piloting with an index finger is necessary.

5. Before installing fitting on the tube, wipe tube end with a clean cloth. Inspect the inside of the fitting to ensure it is free of dirt and/or obstructions.

6. To reinstall the fitting onto the tube, align the fitting and tube axially and push the fitting onto the tube end. When the fitting is engaged, a definite click will be heard. Pull on fitting to ensure it is fully engaged.

½" and ¼" Fittings (Duck Bill Clip)

The fitting consists of a body, spacers, O-rings and a duck bill retaining clip. The clip maintains the fitting to steel tube juncture. When disassembly is required for service, one of the two following methods are to be followed:

¼" FITTINGS

To disengage the tube from the fitting, align the slot on push connect disassembly Tool T82L-9500-AH or equivalent with either tab on the clip (90° from slots on side of fitting) and insert the tool. This disengages the duck bill from the tube. Holding the tool and the tube with one hand, pull fitting away from the tube.

NOTE: Only moderate effort is required if the tube has been properly disengaged. Use hands only. After disassembly, inspect and clean the tube sealing surface. Also inspect the inside of the fitting for damage to the retaining clip. If the retaining clip appears to be damaged, replace it.

Some fuel tubes have a secondary bead which aligns with the outer surface of the clip. These beads can make tool insertion difficult. If there is extreme difficulty, use the disassembly method following.

½" FITTING AND ALTERNATE METHOD FOR ¼" FITTING

This method of disassembly disengages the retaining clip from the fitting body.

Use a pair of narrow pliers, (6" [153mm] locking pliers are ideal). The pliers must have a jaw width of 0.2" (5mm) or less.

Align the jaws of the pliers with the openings in the side of the fitting case and compress the portion of the retaining clip that engages the fitting case. This disengages the retaining clip from the case (often one side of the clip will disengage before the other. It is necessary to disengage the clip from both openings). Pull the fitting off the tube.

NOTE: Only moderate effort is required if the retaining clip has been properly disengaged. Use hands only.

The retaining clip will remain on the tube. Disengage the clip from the tube bead and remove. Replace the retaining clip if it appears to be damaged.

NOTE: Slight ovality of the ring of the clip will usually occur. If there are no visible cracks and the ring will pinch back to its circular configuration, it is not damaged. If there is any doubt, replace the clip.

Install the clip into the body by inserting one of the retaining clip serrated edges on the duck bill portion into one of the window openings. Push on the other side until the clip snaps into place. Slide fuel line back into the clip.

BLEEDING FUEL SYSTEM

Central Fuel Injection (CFI) 2.5L Engine

1. On the left side of the luggage compartment, disconnect the electrical connector from the inertia switch.
2. Using the ignition switch, crank the engine for 15 seconds to reduce the pressure in the fuel system.
3. To pressurize the fuel system, perform the following procedures:
   a. Reconnect the electrical connector to the inertia switch.
   b. Start the engine and check for leaks.

Electronic Fuel Injection (EFI) 3.0L Engine

1. Remove the fuel tank cap and the air filter.
2. Disconnect the negative battery cable.
3. Using the Fuel Pressure Gauge tool No. T80L-9974-A, connect it to the pressure relief valve (remove the valve cap) on the fuel injection manifold.
4. Open the pressure relief valve and reduce the fuel pressure.
5. To pressurize the fuel system, perform the following:
   a. Tighten the pressure relief valve and remove the pressure gauge.
   b. Reinstall the negative battery cable.
   c. Start the engine and check for leaks.

Carburetor

Your car uses, depending on year and model, a staged two barrel unit (the second barrel is opened under heavy throttle situations), or a single barrel carburetor. Carburetors may be of the feed back or non-feedback type.

The staged carburetor usually has five basic metering system. They are: the choke system, idle system, main metering system, acceleration system and the power enrichment system.

The choke system is used for cold starting. It incorporates a bimetal spring and an electric heater for faster cold weather starts and improved driveability during warm-up.

The idle system is a separate and adjustable system for the correct air/fuel mixture at both idle and low speed operation.

The main metering system provides the necessary air/fuel mixture for normal driving speeds. A main metering system is provided for both primary and secondary stages of operation.

The accelerating system is operated from the primary stage throttle linkage. The system provides fuel to the primary stage during acceleration. Fuel is provided by a diaphragm pump located on the carburetor.

The power enrichment system consists of a vacuum operated power valve and airflow regulated pullover system for the secondary carburetor barrel. The system is used in conjunction with the main metering system to provide acceptable performance during mid and heavy acceleration.

REMOVAL & INSTALLATION

1. Remove the air cleaner assembly. Disconnect the throttle control cable and speed control (if equipped). Disconnect the fuel line at the filter.
2. Label and disconnect all vacuum hoses, wires and linkage attached to the carburetor. If your car is equipped with an automatic transaxle, disconnect the TV linkage.
3. Remove the four mounting bolts that attach the carburetor to the intake manifold, remove the carburetor.
4. Installation is in the reverse order of removal. If you car is equipped with an automatic transaxle, a TV linkage adjustment may be required.

OVERHAUL NOTES

NOTE: All major and minor repair kits contain detailed instructions and illustrations. Refer to them for complete rebuilding instructions.

To prevent damage to the throttle plates, make a stand using four bolts, eight flat washers and eight nuts. Place a washer and nut on the bolt, install through the carburetor base and secure with a nut.

Generally, when a carburetor requires major service, rebuilt one is purchased on an exchange basis, or a kit may be bought for overhauling the carburetor.

The kit contains the necessary parts (see below) and some form of instructions for carburetor rebuilding. The instructions may vary between a simple exploded view and detailed step-by-step rebuilding instructions. Unless you are familiar with carburetor overhaul, the latter should be used.

There are some general overhaul procedures which should always be observed:

Efficient carburetion depends greatly on careful cleaning and inspection during overhaul since dirt, gum, water, or varnish in or on the carburetor parts are often responsible for poor performance.

Overhaul you carburetor in a clean, dust free area. Carefully disassembly the carburetor, referring often to the exploded views. Keep all similar and lookalike parts segregated during disassembly and cleaning to avoid accidental interchange during assembly. Make a note of all jet sizes.

When the carburetor is disassembled, wash all parts (except diaphragms, electric choke units. pump plunger, and any other plastic, leather, fiber, or rubber parts) in clean carburetor solvent. Do not leave parts in the solvent any longer than is necessary to sufficiently loosen the deposits. Excessive cleaning may remove the special finish from the float bowl and choke valve bodies, leaving these parts unfit for service. Rinse all parts in clean solvent and blow them dry with compressed air or allow them to air dry. Wipe clean all cork, plastic, leather, and fiber parts with a clean, lint free cloth.

Blow out all passages and jets with compressed air and be sure that there are no restrictions or blockages. Never use wire or similar tools to clean jets, fuel passages, or air bleeds. Clean all jets and valves separately to avoid accidental interchange.

Check all parts for wear or damage. If wear or damage is found, replace the defective parts. Especially check the following:

1. Check the float needle and seat for wear. If wear is found, replace the complete assembly.
2. Check the float hinge pin for wear and the float(s) for dents or distortion. Replace the float if fuel has leaked into it.
3. Check the throttle and choke shaft bores for wear or an out-of-round condition. Damage or wear to the throttle arm, shaft, shaft bore will often require replacement of the throttle body. These parts require a close tolerance; wear may allow air leakage, which could affect starting and idling.

NOTE: Throttle shafts and bushings are usually not included in overhaul kits. They can be purchased separately.

4. Inspect the idle mixture adjusting needles for burrs or grooves. Any such condition requires replacement of the needle, since you will not be able to obtain a satisfactory idle.
5. Test the accelerator pump check valves. They should pass air one way but not the other. Test for proper seating by blowing and sucking on the valve. Replace the valve if necessary. If the valve is satisfactory, wash the valve again to remove breath moisture.
6. Check the bowl cover for warped surfaces with a straightedge.
7. Closely inspect the valves and seats for wear and damage, replacing as necessary.
8. After the carburetor is assembled, check the choke valve for freedom of operation.

Carburetor overhaul kits are recommended for each overhaul. These kits contain all gaskets and new parts to replace those that deteriorate most rapidly. Failure to replace all parts supplied with the kit (especially gaskets) can result in poor performance later.

Some carburetor manufacturers supply overhaul kits of three basic types: minor repair, major repair, and gasket kits. Basically, they contain the following:

Minor Repair Kits:

- All gaskets
- Float needle valve
- Volume control screw
- All diaphragms
- Spring for the pump diaphragm

Major Repair Kits:

- All jets and gaskets
- All diaphragms
- Float needle valve
- Volume control screw
- Pump ball valve
- Main jet carrier
- Float
- Other necessary items
- Some cover holddown screws and washers

Gasket Kits:

- All gaskets

After cleaning and checking all components, reassemble the carburetor, using new parts and referring to the exploded view. When reassembling, make sure that all screw and jets are tight in their seats, buy do not overtighten, as the tips will be distorted. Tighten all screws gradually, in rotation. Do not tighten needle valves into their seat; uneven jetting will result. Always use new gaskets. Be sure to adjust the float level when reassembling.

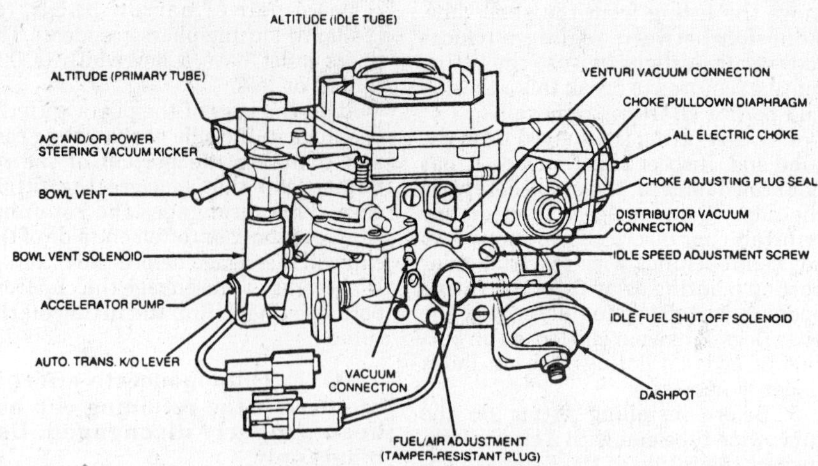

Motorcraft 740/5740 carburetor

Motorcraft 740/5740 Carburetor

ADJUSTMENTS

Fast Idle Cam

1. Set the fast idle screw on the kickdown step of the cam against the shoulder of the top step.
2. Manually close the primary choke plate, and measure the distance between the downstream side of the choke plate and the air horn wall.
3. Adjust the right fork of the choke bimetal shaft, which engages the fast idle cam, by bending the fork up and down to obtain the required clearance.

Fast Idle

1. Place the transmission in neutral or park.
2. Bring the engine to normal operating temperature.
3. Disconnect and plug the vacuum hose at the EGR and purge valves.
4. Identify the vacuum source to the air bypass section of the air supply control valve. If a vacuum hose is connected to the carburetor, disconnect the hose and plug the hose at the air supply control valve.
5. Place the fast idle adjustment on the second step of the fast idle cam. Run the engine until the cooling fan comes on.
6. While the cooling fan is on, check the fast idle rpm. If adjustment is necessary, loosen the locknut and adjust to specification on underhood decal.
7. Remove all plugs and reconnect hoses to their original position.

Dashpot

With the throttle set at the curb idle position, fully depress the dashpot stem and measure the distance between the stem and the throttle lever. Adjust by loosening the locknut and turning the dashpot.

Choke Plate Pulldown

NOTE: The following procedure requires the removal of the carburetor and also the choke cap which is retained by two rivets.

1. Remove the carburetor from the engine.
2. Remove the choke cap as follows:
   a. Check the rivets to determine if mandrel is well below the rivet head. If mandrel is within the rivet head thickness, drive it down or out with a $^1/_{16}$" (1.6mm) diameter tip punch.
   b. With a ⅛" (3mm) diameter drill, drill into the rivet head until the rivet head comes loose from the

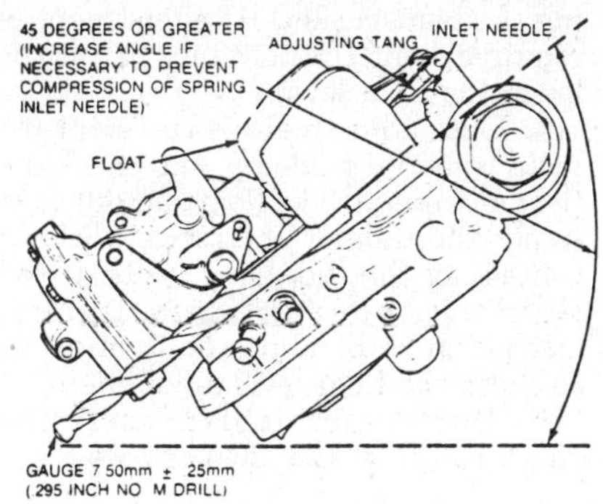

Float level adjustment—Motorcraft 740/5740 carburetor

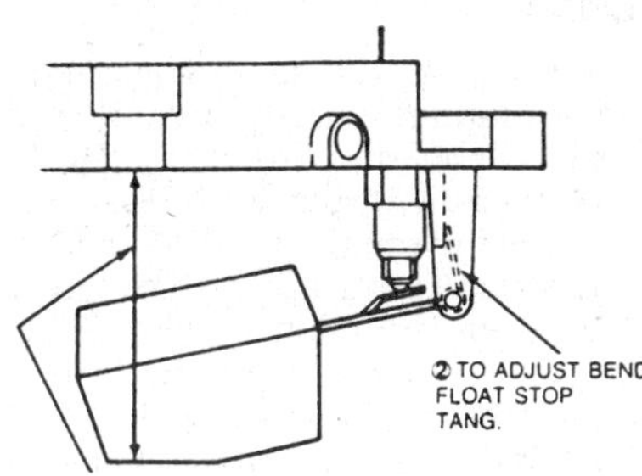

Float drop adjustment—Motorcraft 740/5740 carburetor

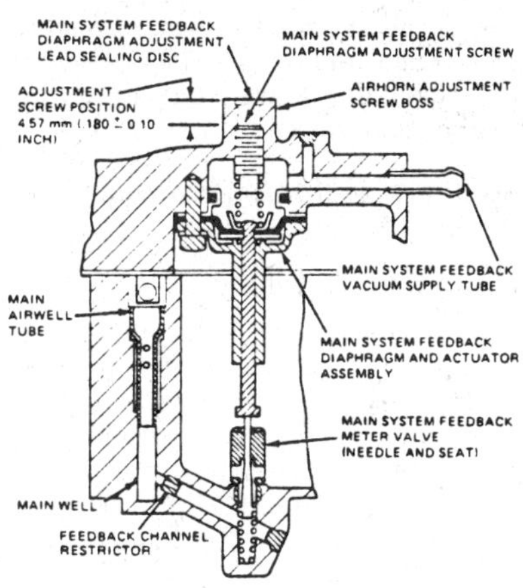

Diaphragm adjustment—6149 carb

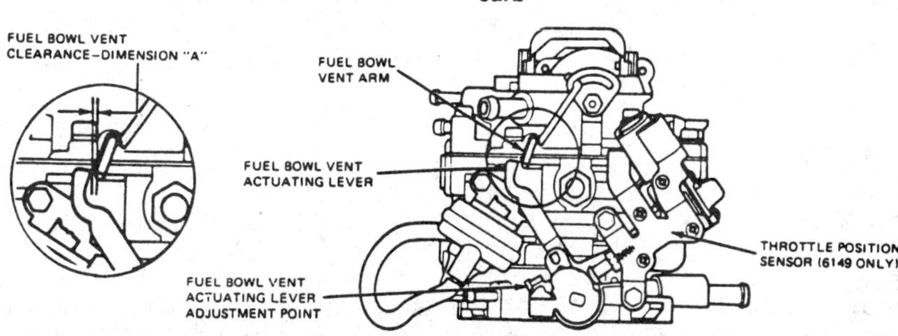

Lever clearance adjustment—6149 carb

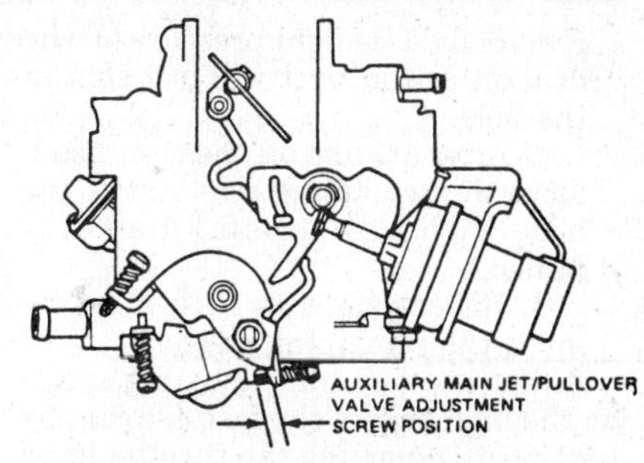

Timing adjustment—6149 carb

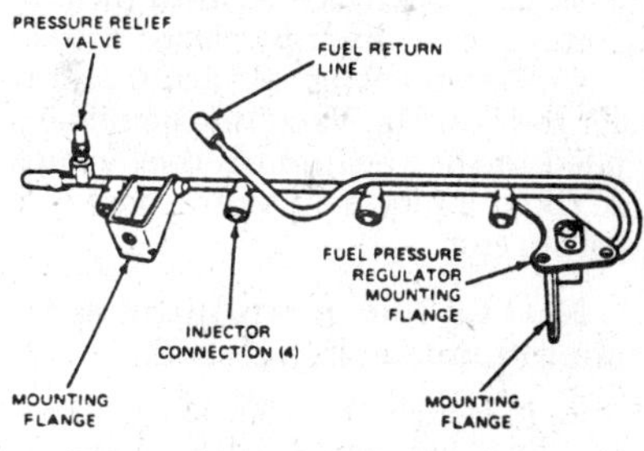

Vent adjustment—6149 carb

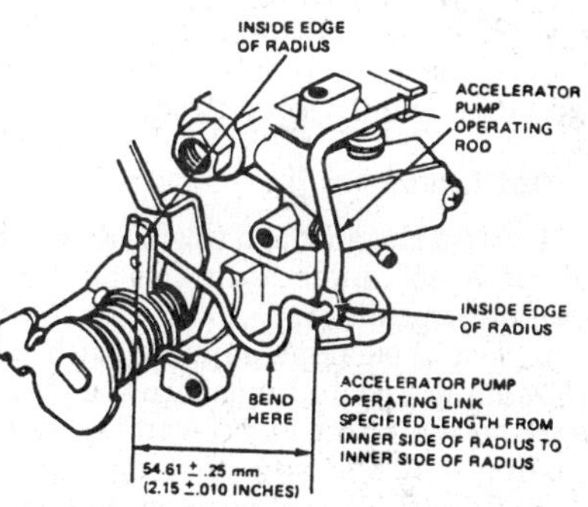

Accelerator pump stroke adjustment—6149 carb

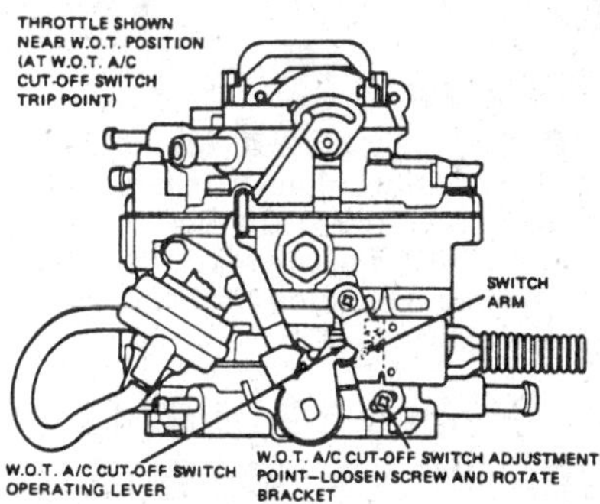

WOT/AC cut-off switch asjustment—6149 carb

rivet body. Use light pressure on the drill bit or the rivet will just spin in the hole.

c. After drilling off the rivet head, drive the remaining rivet out of the hole with a 1/8" (3mm) diameter punch.

d. Repeat steps (a thru c) to remove the remaining rivet.

3. Set the fast idle adjusting screw on the high step of the fast idle cam by temporarily opening the throttle lever and rotating the choke bimetal shaft lever counterclockwise until the choke plates are in the fully closed position.

4. With an external vacuum source, set to 17 in.Hg. Vacuum should be applied to the vacuum channel adjacent to the primary bore on the base of the carburetor.

NOTE: The modulator spring should not be depressed.

5. Measure the clearance between the downstream side of the choke plate and the air horn wall.

6. If an adjustment is necessary, turn the vacuum diaphragm adjusting screw in or out as required.

Float Level

1. Hold the air horn upside down, at about a 45° angle with the air horn gasket in position.

2. Use the gauge (supplied with the rebuilding kit) and measure the clearance between the float toe and air horn casting.

3. Adjust, if necessary, by removing the float and bending the adjusting tang. Use care when handling the float.

Float Drop

Hold the air horn in its normal installed position. Measure the clearance from the gasket to the bottom of the float. Adjust, if necessary, by removing the float and bending the float drop adjusting tab.

Holley 1949/6149 (Feedback) Carburetor

ADJUSTMENTS

Float Level

1. Remove the carburetor air horn.

2. With the air horn assembly removed, place a finger over float hinge pin retainer, and invert the main body. Catch the accelerator pump check ball and weight.

3. Using a straight edge, check the position of the floats. The correct dry float setting is that both pontoons at the extreme outboard edge be flush with the surface of the main body casting (without gasket). If adjustment is required, bend the float tabs to raise or lower the float level.

4. Once adjustment is correct, turn main body right side up, and check the float alignment. The float should move freely throughout its range without contacting the fuel bowl walls. If the float pontoons are misaligned, straighten by bending the float arms. Recheck the float level adjustment.

5. During assembly, insert the check ball first and then the weight.

Feedback Controlled Main System Diaphragm Adjustment (6149 Only)

1. Remove the main system feedback diaphragm adjustment screw lead sealing disc from the air horn screw boss, by drilling a 2.38mm diameter hole through the disc. Then, insert a small punch to pry the disc out.

2. Turn the main system feedback adjustment screw as required to position the top of the screw 4.57mm ± 0.25mm below the top of the air horn adjustment screw boss.

NOTE: For carburetors stamped with as S on the top of the air horn adjustment screw boss, adjust screw position to 6.35mm ± 0.25mm.

3. Install a new lead sealing disc and stake with a 1/4" (6mm) flat ended punch.

4. Apply an external vacuum source (hand vacuum pump – 10 in.Hg max.) and check for leaks. The diaphragm should hold vacuum.

Auxiliary Main Jet/Pullover Valve

Timing Adjustment

The length of the auxiliary main jet/pullover valve adjustment screw which protrudes through the back side (side opposite the adjustment screw head) of the throttle pick-up lever must be 8.76mm ± 0.25mm. To adjust turn screw in or out as required.

Mechanical Fuel Bowl Vent Adjustment Lever Clearance

OFF VEHICLE ADJUSTMENT

NOTE: There are two methods for adjusting lever clearance.

1. Secure the choke plate in the wide open position.

2. Set the throttle at the TSP Off position.

3. Turn the TSP Off idle adjustment screw counterclockwise until the throttle plate is closed in the throttle bore.

4. Fuel bowl vent clearance, Dimension **A**, should be 3.05mm ± 0.25mm.

5. If out of specification, bend the bowl vent actuator lever at the adjustment point to obtain the required clearance.

CAUTION

Do not bend fuel bowl vent arm and/or adjacent portion of the actuator lever.

NOTE: TSP Off rpm must be set after carburetor installation.

ON VEHICLE ADJUSTMENT

NOTE: This adjustment must be performed after curb idle speed has been set to specification.

1. Secure the choke plate in the wide open position.

2. Turn ignition key to the ON position to activate the TSP (engine not running). Open throttle so that the TSP plunger extends.

3. Verify that the throttle is in the idle set position (contacting the TSP plunger). Measure the clearance of the fuel bowl vent arm to the bowl vent actuating lever.

4. Fuel bowl vent clearance, Dimension **A**, should be 0.76mm.

NOTE: There is a difference in the on-vehicle and off-vehicle specification.

5. If out of specification, bend the bowl vent actuator lever at the adjustment point to obtain the required clearance.

WARNING: Do not bend fuel bowl vent arm and/or adjacent portion of the actuating lever.

Accelerator Pump Stroke Adjustment

1. Check the length of the accelerator pump operating link from its inside edge at the accelerator pump operating rod to its inside edge at the throttle lever hole. The dimension should be 54.61 ± 0.25mm.

2. Adjust to proper length by bending loop in operating link.

WOT A/C Cut-Off Switch Adjustment (1949 Only)

The WOT A/C cutoff switch is a normally closed switch (allowing current to flow at any throttle position other than wide open throttle).

1. Disconnect the wiring harness at the switch connector.

2. Connect a 12 volt DC power supply and test lamp. With the throttle at curb idle, TSP Off idle or fast idle position, the test light must be On. If the test lamp does not light, replace the switch assembly.

3. Rotate the throttle to the wide open position. The test lamp must go Off, indicating an open circuit.

4. If the lamp remains On, insert a 4.19mm drill or gauge between the throttle lever WOT stop and the WOT stop boss on the carburetor main body casting. Hold the throttle open as far as possible against the gauge. Loosen the two switch mounting screws sufficiently to allow the switch to pivot. Rotate the switch assembly so the test lamp just goes out with the throttle held in the above referenced position. If the lamp does not go Off within the allowable adjustment rotation, replace the switch. If the light goes out, tighten the two switch bracket-to-carburetor screws to 45 in.lb. and remove drill or gauge and repeat Step 3.

ELECTRONIC FUEL INJECTION

NOTE: This book contains simple testing and service procedures for for your car's fuel injection system. More comprehensive testing and diagnosis procedures, which cannot be included here, may be found in CHILTON'S GUIDE TO FUEL INJECTION AND FEEDBACK CARBURETORS, book part number 7488, available at your local retailer.

The Electronic Fuel Injection System (EFI) is a multi-point, pulse time, mass air flow fuel injection system. Fuel is metered into the air intake stream in accordance with engine demand through four injectors mounted on a tuned intake manifold. An onboard (EEC) computer receives input from various sensors to compute the required fuel flow rate necessary to maintain the necessary air/fuel ratio throughout the entire engine operational range.

The EFI system can be separated into four categories: Fuel Delivery, Air Induction, Sensors, and the Electronic Control Circuit.

NOTE: A brief testing section is included at the end of the EFI section: Special tools and skills are required. If the tools or knowledge is not on hand, have the system serviced by a qualified mechanic.

Fuel Injectors

The four fuel injector nozzles are electro-mechanical devices which both meter and atomize fuel delivered to the engine. The injectors are mounted in the lower intake manifold and are positioned so that their tips are directing fuel just ahead of the engine intake valves. The injector bodies consist of a solenoid actuated pintle and needle valve assembly. An electrical control signal from the Electronic Engine Control unit activates the injector solenoid causing the pintle to move inward off the seat, allowing fuel to flow. Since the injector flow orifice if fixed and the fuel pressure drop across the injector tip is constant, fuel flow to the engine is regulated by how long the solenoid is energized. Atomization is obtained by contouring the pintle at the point where the fuel separates.

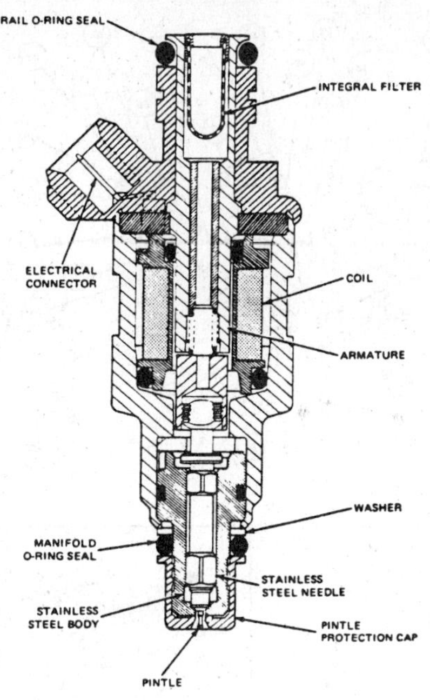

Fuel Injector

Fuel Pressure Regulator

The fuel pressure regulator is attached to the fuel supply manifold assembly downstream of the fuel injectors. It regulates the fuel pressure supplied to the injectors. The regulator is a diaphragm operated relief valve in which one side of the diaphragm senses fuel pressure and the other side is subjected to intake manifold pressure. The nominal fuel pressure is established by a spring preload applied to the diaphragm. Balancing one side of the diaphragm with manifold pressure maintains a constant fuel pressure drop across the injectors. Fuel, in excess of that used by the varies depending on the volume of air flowing through the sensor. The temperature sensor in the air vane meter measures the incoming air temperature. These two inputs, air volume and temperature, are used by the Electronic Control Assembly to compute the mass air flow. This value is then used to compute the fuel flow necessary for the optimum air/fuel ration which is fed to the injectors.

Air Throttle Body Assembly

The throttle body assembly controls air flow to the engine through a sing butterfly type valve. The throttle position is controlled by conventional cable/cam throttle linkage. The body is a single piece die casting made of aluminum. It has a single bore with an air bypass channel around the throttle plate. This bypass channel controls both cold and warm engine idle airflow control as regulated by an air bypass valve assembly mounted directly to the throttle body.

The valve assembly is an electro-mechanical device controlled by the EEC computer. It incorporates a linear actuator which positions a variable area metering valve.

Other features of the air throttle body assembly include:

1. An adjustment screw to set the throttle plate a a minimum idle airflow position.
2. A preset stop to locate the WOT position.
3. A throttle body mounted throttle position sensor.
4. A PCV fresh air source located upstream of the throttle plate.
5. Individual ported vacuum taps (as required) for PCV and EVAP control signals.

Fuel Supply Manifold Assembly

The fuel supply manifold assembly is the component that delivers high pressure fuel from the vehicle fuel supply line to the four fuel injectors. The assembly consists of a single preformed tube or stamping with four injector connectors, a mounting flange for the fuel pressure regulator, a pressure relief valve for diagnostic testing or field service fuel system pressure bleed down and mounting attachments which locate the fuel manifold assembly and provide fuel injector retention.

Air Intake Manifold

The air intake manifold is a two

piece (upper and lower intake manifold) aluminum casting. Runner lengths are tuned to optimize engine torque and power output. The manifold provides mounting flanges for the air throttle body assembly, fuel supply manifold and accelerator control bracket and the EGR valve and supply tube. Vacuum taps are provided to support various engine accessories. Pockets for the fuel injectors are machined to prevent both air and fuel leakage. The pockets, in which the injectors are mounted, are placed to direct the injector fuel spray immediately in front of each engine intake valve.

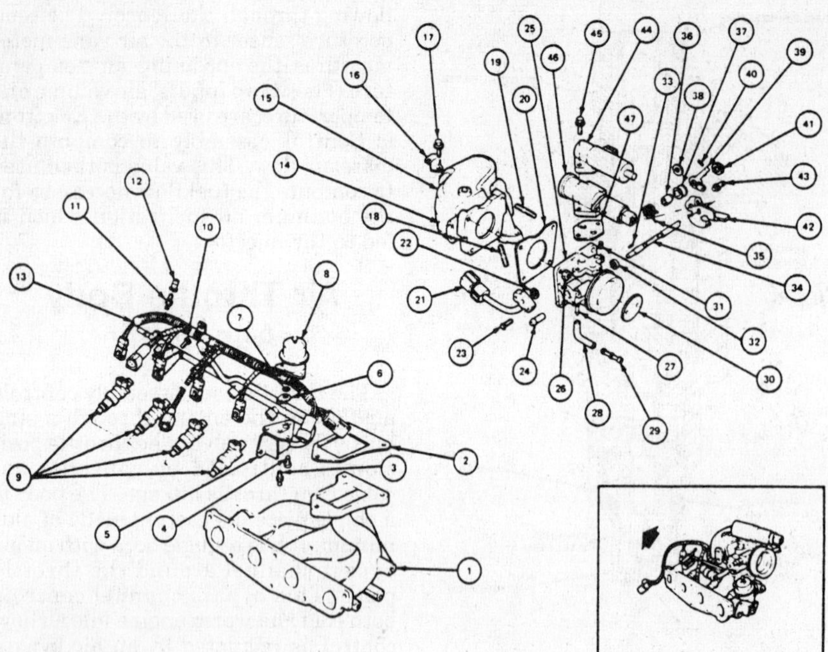

1. Manifold—intake lower
2. Gasket—intake manifold upper
3. Connector—¼ flareless x ⅛ external pipe
4. Screw—M5 x .8 x 10 socket head
5. Manifold assembly—fuel injection fuel supply
6. Gasket—fuel pressure regulator
7. Seal—$^{5}/_{16}$ x .070 "O" ring
8. Regulator assembly—fuel pressure
9. Injector assembly—fuel
10. Bolt—M8 x 1.25 x 20 hex flange head
11. Valve assembly—fuel pressure relief
12. Cap—fuel pressure relief
13. Wiring harness—fuel charging
14. Decal—carburetor identification
15. Manifold—intake upper
16. Retainer—wiring harness
17. Bolt—M8 x 1.25 x 30 hex flange head
18. Stud—M6 x 1.0 x 1.0 x 40
19. Stud—M8 x 1.25 x 1.25 x 47.5
20. Gasket—air intake charge to intake manifold
21. Potentiometer—throttle position
22. Bushing—carburetor throttle shaft
23. Screw and washer assembly M4 x 22
24. Tube—emission inlet
25. Body—air intake charge throttle
26. Nut—M8 x 1.25
27. Tube
28. Hose—vacuum
29. Connector
30. Plate—air intake charge throttle
31. Screw—M4 x .7 x 8
32. Seal—throttle control shaft
33. Pin—spring coiled $^{1}/_{16}$ x .42
34. Shaft
35. Spring—throttle return
36. Bushing—accelerator pump overtravel spring
37. Bearing—throttle control linkage
38. Spacer—throttle control torsion spring (MTX only)
39. Lever—carburetor transmission linkage
40. Screw—M5 x .8 x 16.25 slot head
41. Spacer—carburetor throttle shaft
42. Lever—carburetor throttle
43. Ball—carburetor throttle lever
44. Valve assembly—throttle air bypass (alt)
45. Bolt—M6 x 1.0 x 20 hex flange head
46. Valve assembly—throttle air bypass
47. Gasket—air bypass valve

EFI components

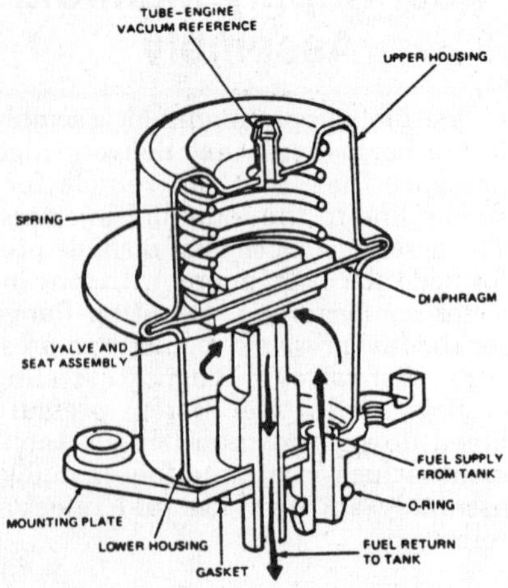

Fuel pressure regulator – EFI

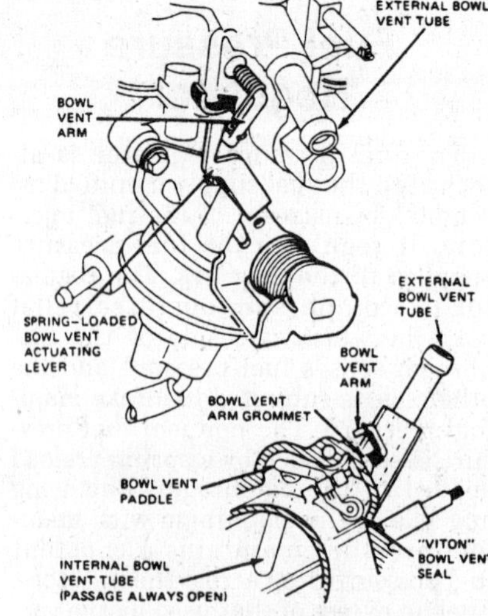

Fuel supply manifold – EFI

Fuel Charging Assembly

DISASSEMBLY

NOTE: If sub-assemblies are to be serviced and/or removed, with the fuel charging assembly mounted to the engine, the following steps must be taken:

1. Open hood and install protective covers.
2. Make sure that ignition key is in Off position.
3. Drain coolant from radiator.
4. Disconnect the negative battery lead and secure it out of the way.
5. Remove fuel cap to relieve fuel tank pressure.
6. Release pressure from the fuel system at the fuel pressure relief valve on the fuel injection manifold assembly. Use tool T80L-9974-A or equivalent. To gain access to the fuel pressure relief valve, the valve cap must first be removed.
7. Disconnect the push connect fuel supply line. Using a small bladed screwdriver inserted under the hairpin clip tab, pop the clip free from the push connect tube fitting and disconnect the tube. Save the hairpin clip for use in reassembly.
8. Identify and disconnect the fuel return lines and vacuum connections.

NOTE: Care must be taken to avoid combustion from fuel spillage.

9. Disconnect the injector wiring harness by disconnecting the ECT sensor in the heater supply tube under lower intake manifold and the electronic engine control harness.
10. Disconnect air bypass connector from EEC harness.

NOTE: Not all assemblies may be serviceable while on the engine. In some cases, removal of the fuel charging assembly may facilitate service of the various

sub-assemblies. To remove the entire fuel charging assembly, the following procedure should be followed:

REMOVAL & INSTALLATION

1. Remove the engine air cleaner outlet tube between the vane air meter and air throttle body by loosening two clamps.
2. Disconnect and remove the accelerator and speed control cables (if so eqiupped) from the accelerator mounting bracket and throttle lever.
3. Disconnect the top manifold vacuum fitting connections by disconnecting:
   a. Rear vacuum line to the dash panel vacuum tree.
   b. Front vacuum line to the air cleaner and fuel pressure regulator.
4. Disconnect the PCV system by disconnecting the hoses from:
   a. Two large forward facing connectors on the throttle body and intake manifold.
   b. Throttle body port hose at the straight plastic connector.
   c. Canister purge line at the straight plastic connector.
   d. PCV hose at rocker cover.
   e. Unbolt PCV separator support bracket from cylinder head and remove PCV system.
5. Disconnect the EGR vacuum line at the EGR valve.
6. Disconnect the EGR tube from the upper intake manifold by removing the two flange nuts.
7. Withdraw the dipstick and remove the dipstick tube by removing the tube bracket mounting nut and working the tube out of the block hole.
8. Remove the fuel return line.
9. Remove six manifold mounting nuts.
10. Remove the manifold with wiring harness and gasket.
11. Clean and inspect the mounting faces of the fuel charging manifold assembly and the cylinder head. Both surfaces must be clean and flat.
12. Clean and oil manifold stud threads.
13. Install a new gasket.
14. Install manifold assembly to head and secure with top middle nut (tighten nut finger tight only at this time).
15. Install fuel return line to the fitting in the fuel supply manifold. Install two manifold mounting nuts, fingertight.
16. Install dipstick in block and secure with bracket nut fingertight.
17. Install remaining three manifold mounting nuts and tighten all six nuts to 12-15 ft.lb. observing specified tightening sequence.

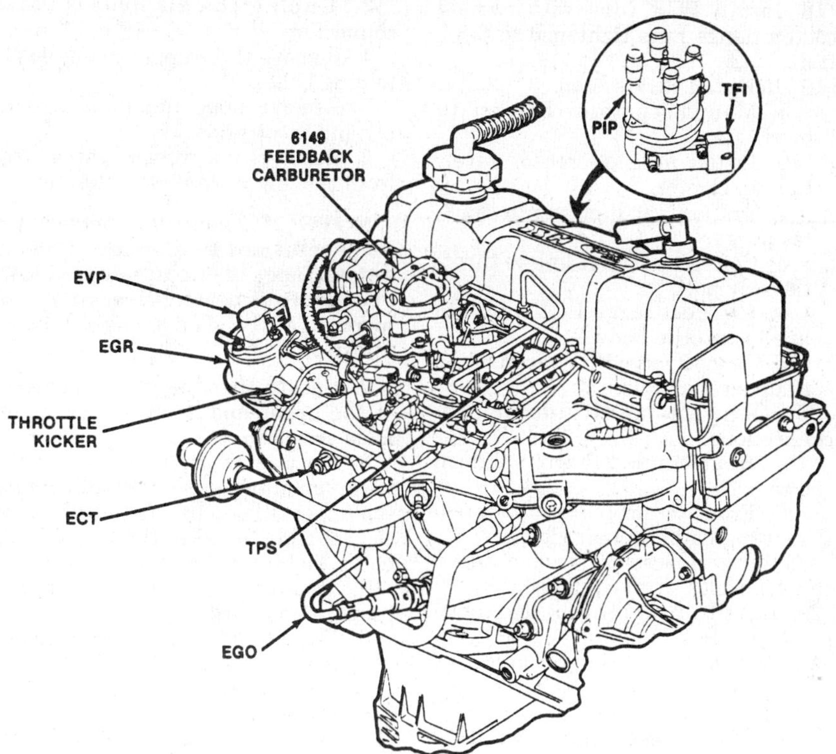

EEC-IV system—2.3L HSC engine

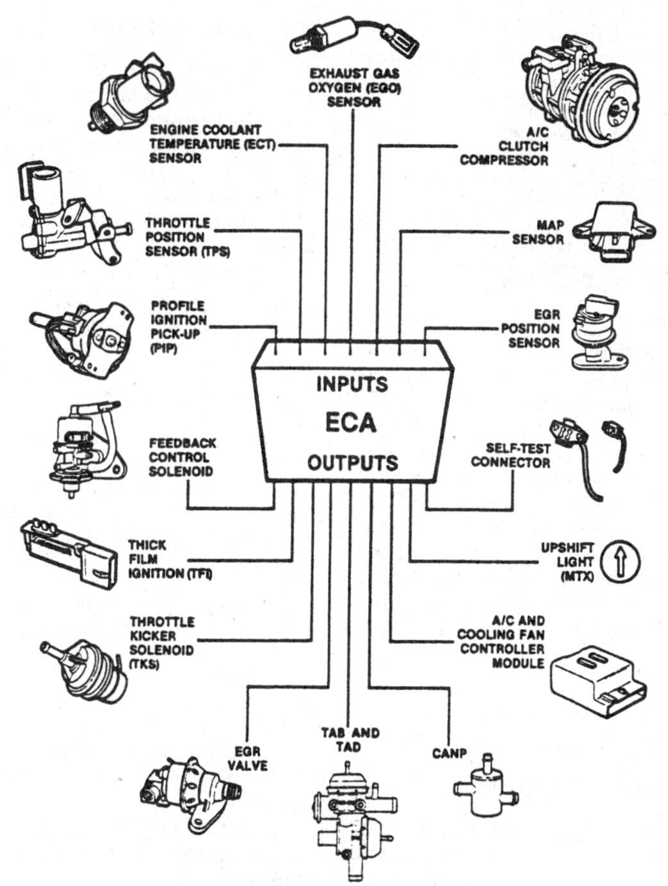

EEC-IV system inputs

18. Install EGR tube with two oil coated flange nuts tightened to 6-8.5 ft.lb.
19. Reinstall PCV system.
    a. Mount separator bracket to head.
    b. Install hose on rocker cover, tighten clamps.
    c. Connect vacuum line to canister purge.
    d. Connect vacuum line to throttle body port.
    e. Connect large PCV vacuum line to throttle body.
    f. Connect large PCV vacuum line to upper manifold.
20. Connect manifold vacuum connections:
    a. Rear connection to vacuum tree.
    b. Front connection to fuel pressure regulator and air cleaner.
21. Connect accelerator and speed control cables (if so equipped).
22. Install air supply tube and tighten clamps to 25 in.lb.
23. Connect the wiring harness at:
    a. ECT sensor in heater supply tube.
    b. Electronic Engine Control harness.
24. Connect the fuel supply hose from the fuel filter to the fuel rail.
25. Connect the fuel return line.
26. Connect negative battery cable.
27. Install engine coolant using prescribed fill procedure.
28. Start engine and allow to run at idle until engine temperature is stabilized. Check for coolant leaks.
29. If necessary, reset idle speed.

REMOVAL & INSTALLATION OF SUB-ASSEMBLIES

NOTE: To prevent damage to fuel chargine assembly, the unit should be placed on a work bench during disassembly and assembly procedures. The following is a step by step sequence of operations for servicing the assemblies of the fuel charging manifold. Some components may be serviced without a complete disassembly of the fuel charging manifold. To replace individual components, follow only the applicable steps.

These procedures are based on the fuel charging manifold having been removed from the vehicle.

Upper Intake Manifold

1. Disconnect the engine air cleaner outlet tube from the air intake throttle body.
2. Unplug the throttle position sensor from the wiring harness.
3. Unplug the air bypass valve connector.
4. Remove three upper manifold retaining bolts.
5. Remove upper manifold assembly and set it aside.
6. Remove and discard the gasket from the lower manifold assembly.

NOTE: If scraping is necessary, be careful not to damage the gasket surfaces of the upper and lower manifold assemblies, or allow material to drop into lower manifold.

7. Ensure that the gasket surfaces of the upper and lower intake manifolds are clean.
8. Place a new service gasket on the lower manifold assembly and mount the upper intake manifold to the lower, securing it with three retaining bolts. Tighten bolts to 15-22 ft.lb.
9. Ensure the wiring harness is properly installed.
10. Connect electrical connectors t air bypass valve and throttle position sensor and the vacuum hose to the fuel pressure regulator.
11. Connect the engine air cleaner outlet tube to the throttle body intake securing it with a hose clamp. Tighten to 15-25 in.lb.

Air Intake Throttle Body

1. Remove four throttle body nuts. Ensure that the throttle position sensor connector and air bypass valve connector have been disconnected from the harness. Disconnect air cleaner outlet tube.
2. Identify and disconnect vacuum hoses.
3. Remove throttle bracket.
4. Carefully separate the throttle body from the upper intake manifold.
5. Remove and discard the gasket between the throttle body and the upper intake manifold.

NOTE: If scraping is necessary, be careful not to damage the gasket surfaces of the throttle body and upper manifold assemblies, or allow material to drop into manifold.

6. Ensure that both throttle body and upper intake manifold gasket surfaces are clean.
7. Install the upper/throttle body gasket on the four studs of the upper intake manifold.
8. Secure the throttle bracket and secure with two nuts. Tighten to 12-15 ft.lb.
9. Install throttle bracket and secure with two nuts. Tighten to 12-15 ft.lb.
10. Connect the air bypass valve and throttle position sensor electrical connectors and appropriate vacuum lines.
11. If the fuel charging assembly is still mounted to the engine, connect the engine air cleaner outlet tube to the throttle body intake securing it with a hose clamp. Tighten the clamp to 15-25 in.lb.

Air Bypass Valve Assembly

1. Disconnect the air bypass valve assembly connector from the wiring harness.
2. Remove the two air bypass valve retaining screws.
3. Remove the air bypass valve and gasket.

NOTE: If scraping is necessary, be careful not to damage the air bypass valve or throttle body gasket surfaces, or drop material into throttle body.

4. Ensure that both the throttle body and air bypass valve gasket surfaces are clean.
5. Install gasket on throttle body surface and mount the air bypass valve assembly securing it with two retaining screws. Tighten to 71-102 in.lb.
6. Connect the electircal connector for the air bypass valve.

Throttle Position Sensor

1. Disconnect the throttle position sensor from the wiring harness.
2. Remove two throttle position sensor retaining screws.
3. Remove the throttle position sensor.
4. Install the throttle position sensor. Make sure that the rotary tangs on the sensor are in the proper alignment and the wires are pointing down.
5. Secure the sensor to the throttle body assembly with two retaining screws. Tighten to 11-16 in.lb.

NOTE: This throttle position sensor is not adjustable.

6. Connect the electrical connector to the harness.

Pressure Relief Valve

1. If the fuel charging assembly is mounted to the engine, remove fuel tank cap then release pressure from the system at the pressure relief valve on the fuel injection manifold using Tool T80L-9974-A or equivalent. Note the cap on the relief valve must be removed.
2. Using an open end wrench or suitable deep well socket, remove pressure relief valve for fuel injection manifold.
3. Install pressure relief valve and cap. Tighten valve to 48-84 in.lb. and the cap to 4-6 in.lb.

Fuel Injector Manifold Assembly

1. Remove fuel tank cap and release pressure from the fuel system at the fuel pressure relief valve using Tool T80L-9974-A or equivalent.
2. Disconnect the fuel supply and fuel return lines.
3. Disconnect the wiring harness from the injectors.
4. Disconnect vacuum line from fuel pressure regulator valve.
5. Remove two fuel injector manifolds retaining bolts.
6. Carefully disengage manifold from the fuel injectors and remove manifold.
7. Make sure the injector caps are clean and free of contamination.
8. Place fuel injector manifold over the four injectors making sure the injectors are well seated in the fuel manifold assembly.
9. Secure the fuel manifold assembly to the charging assembly using two retaining bolts.
10. Connect fuel supply and fuel return lines.
11. Connect fuel injector wiring harness.
12. Connect vacuum line to fuel pressure regulator.

Fuel Pressure Regulator

1. Be sure that the assembly is depressurized by removing fuel tank cap and releasing pressure from the fuel system at the pressure relief valve on the fuel injection manifold using Tool T80L-9974-A or equivalent.
2. Remove the vacuum line at the pressure regulator.
3. Remove three Allen retaining screws from regulator housing.
4. Remove pressure regulator assembly, gasket and O-ring. Discard gasket and inspect O-ring for signs of cracks or deterioration.

NOTE: If scraping is necessary, be careful not to damage the fuel pressure regulator or fuel supply line gasket surfaces.

5. Lubricate fuel pressure regulator O-ring with light oil ESF-M6C2-A or equivalent.
6. Make sure gasket surfaces of fuel pressure regulator and fuel injection manifold are clean.
7. Install O-ring and new gasket on regulator.
8. Install the fuel pressure regulator on the injector manifold. Tighten the three retaining screws to 27-40 in.lb.

Fuel Injector

1. Remove fuel tank cap and release pressure from the fuel system at the fuel pressure relief valve using Tool T80L-9974-A or equivalent.
2. Disconnect fuel supply and return lines.
3. Remove vacuum line from fuel pressure regulator.
4. Disconnect the fuel injector wiring harness.
5. Remove fuel injector manifold assembly.
6. Carefully remove connectors from individual injector(s) as required.
7. Grasping the injector's body, pull up while gently rocking the injector from side-to-side.
8. Inspect the injector O-rings (two per injector) for signs of deterioration. Replace as requried.
9. Inspect the injector plastic cover (covering the injector pintle) and washer for signs of deterioration. Replace as required. If hat is missing, look for it in intake manifold.
10. Lubricate new O-rings and install two on each injector (use a light grade oil ESF-M6C2-A or equivalent).
11. Install the injector(s). Use a light, twisting, pushing motion to install the injector(s).
12. Carefully seat the fuel injector manifold assembly on the four injectors and secure the manifold with two attaching bolts. Tighten to 15-22 ft.lb.
13. Connect the vacuum line to the fuel pressure regulator.
14. Connect fuel injector wiring harness.
15. Connect fuel supply and fuel return lines. Tighten fuel return line to 15-18 ft.lb.
16. Check entire assembly for proper alignment and seating.

Fuel Injector Wiring Harness

NOTE: Be sure the ignition if Off and the fuel system is depressurized.

1. Disconnect the electrical connectors from the four fuel injectors.
2. Disconnect the connectors from the main wiring harness and the throttle position sensor.
3. Remove wiring assembly.
4. Position wiring harness alongside the fuel injectors.
5. Snap the electrical connectors into position on the four injectors.
6. Connect the throttle position sensor, ECT sensor and main harness connectors.
7. Verify that all electrical connectors are firmly seated.

Vane Air Meter

1. Loosen the hose clamp which secures engine air cleaner outlet hose to the vane air meter assembly and position outlet hose out of the way.
2. Remove air intake and air outlet tube from the air cleaner.
3. Disengage four spring clamps and remove air cleaner front cover and air cleaner filter panel.
4. Remove four screws and washers from the flange of the air cleaner where it is attached to the vane air meter assembly. Pull the air cleaner base away from the vane air meter and remove the air cleaner gasket. If the gasket shoes signs of deterioration, replace it.

NOTE: If scraping is necessary, be careful not to damage the air cleaner outlet and vane air meter gasket surfaces.

5. Remove the electrical connector from the vane air meter assembly.
6. Remove the two screw and washer assemblies which secure the vane air meter assembly to the vane air meter bracket and remove the vane air meter assembly.
7. Clean mounting surfaces of air cleaner outlet flange and the vane air meter housing.
8. Place four retaining screws through the four holes in the air cleaner outlet flange and place a new gasket over the screws.
9. Mount the vane air meter assembly to the vane air meter bracket using two screw and washer assemblies. Note that these screws are not the physical size and care must be taken to ensure that the proper screw is in the proper hole. Tighten screws to 6-9 ft.lb.
10. Secure the air cleaner outlet to the vane air meter with the four screws mentioned in Step 2. Tighten to 6-9 ft.lb. Make sure the gasket is properly sealed and aligned.
11. Secure the engine air cleaner outlet tube to the vane air meter assembly with the hose clamp. Tighten to 15-25 in.lb.
12. Install the engine air cleaner cover and snap spring clips into position.
13. Secure the air intake duct to air cleaner.
14. Connect all hoses to air cleaner.

EFI EEC-IV FUEL SYSTEM

Components and Operation

The fuel subsystem included a high pressure electric fuel pump, fuel charging manifold, pressure regulator, fuel filter and both solid and flexible fuel lines. The fuel charging manifold includes four electronically controlled fuel injectors, each mounted directly above an intake port in the lower intake manifold. All injectors are energized simultaneously and spray once every crankshaft revolution, delivering a predetermined quantity of fuel into the intake airstream.

The fuel pressure regulator maintains a constant pressure drop across the injector nozzles. The regulator is referenced to intake manifold vacuum and is connected parallel to the fuel injectors and positioned on the far end of the fuel rail. Any excess fuel supplied by the pump passes through the regulator and is returned to the fuel tank via a return line.

NOTE: The pressure regulator reduces fuel pressure to 39-40 psi under normal operating conditions. At idle or high manifold vacuum condition, fuel pressure is reduced to about 30 psi.

The fuel pressure regulator is a diaphragm operated relief valve in which one side of the diaphragm senses fuel pressure and the other side senses manifold vacuum. Normal fuel pressure is established by a spring preload applied to the diaphgram. Control of the fuel system is maintained through the EEC power relay and the EEC-IV control unit, although electrical power is routed through the fuel pump relay and an inertia switch. The fuel pump relay is normally located on a bracket somewhere above the Electronic Control Assembly (ECA) and the Inertia Switch is located in the left rear kick panel. The fuel pump is usually mounted on a bracket at the fuel tank.

The inertia switch opens the power circuit to the fuel pump in the event of a collision. Once tripped, the switch must be reset manually by pushing the reset button on the assembly. Check that the inertia switch is reset before diagnosing power supply problems.

On-Car Service EEC-IV

The EFI-EEC IV system has a self-diagnostic capability to aid the technician in locating faults and troubleshooting components. Before removing any fuel lines or fuel system components, first relieve the fuel system pressure by using the same Schraeder adapter and fitting that is used to check fuel pressure at the fuel rail.

CAUTION

Exercise care to avoid the chance of fire whenever removing or installing fuel system components.

As in any service procedure, a routine inspection of the system for loose connections, broken wires or obvious damage is the best way to start. Perform the system Quick Test outlined below before going any further. Check all vacuum connections and secondary ignition wiring before assuming that the problem lies with the EEC-IV system. A self-diagnosis capability is built in to the EEC-IV system to aid in troubleshooting. The primary tool necessary to read the trouble codes stored in the system is an analog voltmeter or special Self Test Automatic Readout (STAR) tester (Motorcraft No. 007-0M004, or equivalent). While the self-test is not conclusive by itself, when activated it checks the EEC-IV system by testing its memory integrity and processing capability. The self-test also verifies that all sensors and actuators are connected and working properly.

When a service code is displayed on an analog voltmeter, each code number is represented by pulses or sweeps of the meter needle. A code 3, for example, will be read as three needle pulses followed by a 6 second delay. If a two digit code is stored, there will be a two second delay between the pulses for each digit of the number. Code 23, for example, will be displayed as two needle pulses, a two second pause, then three more pulses followed by a four second pause. All testing is complete when the codes have been repeated once. The pulse format is ½ second on-time for each digit, 2 seconds off-time between digits, 4 seconds off-time between codes and 6 seconds off-time before and after the ½ second separator pulse.

NOTE: If using the STAR tester, or equivalent, consult the manufacturers instructions included with the unit for correct hookup and trouble code interpretation.

In addition to the service codes, two other types of coded information are outputted during the self-test: engine identification and fast codes. Engine ID codes are one digit numbers equal to ½ the number of engine cylinders (e.g. 4 cylinder is code 2, 8 cylinder is code 4, etc.) Fast codes are simply the service codes transmitted at 100 times the normal rate in a short burst of information. Some meters may detect these codes and register a slight meter deflection just before the trouble codes are flashed. Both the ID and fast codes serve no purpose in the field and this meter deflection should be ignored.

ACTIVATING SELF-TEST MODE ON EEC-IV

Turn the ignition key OFF. On the 1.6 & 1.9L engine, connect a jumper wire from pin 5 self-test input to pin 2 (signal return) on the self-test connector. Set the analog voltmeter on a DC voltage range to read from 0-15 volts, then connect the voltmeter from the battery positive (+) terminal to pin 4 self-test output in the self-test connector. Turn the ignition switch ON (engine off) and read the trouble codes on the meter needle as previously described. A code 11 means that the EEC-IV system is operating properly and no faults are detected by the computer.

NOTE: This test will only detect "hard" failures that are present when the self-test is activated. For intermittent problems, remove the voltmeter clip from the self-test trigger terminal and wiggle the wiring harness. With the voltmeter still attached to the self-test output, watch for a needle deflection that signals an intermittent condition has occurred. The meter will deflect each time the fault is induced and a trouble code will be stored. Reconnect the self-test trigger terminal to the voltmeter to retrieve the code.

EEC-IV SYSTEM QUICK TEST

Correct test results for the quick test are dependent on the correct operation of related non-EEC components, such as ignition wires, battery, etc. It may be necessary to correct defects in these areas before the EEC-IV system will pass the quick test. Before connecting any test equipment to check the EEC system, make the following checks:

1. Check the air cleaner and intake ducts for leaks or restrictions. Replace the air cleaner if excessive amount of dust or dirt are found.
2. Check all engine vacuum hoses for proper routing according to the vacuum schematic on the underhood sticker.

Check for proper connections and repair any broken, cracked or pinched hoses or fittings.

3. Check the EEC system wiring harness connectors for tight fit, loose or detached terminals, corrosion, broken or frayed wires, short circuits to metal in the engine compartment or melted insulation exposing bare wire.

NOTE: It may be necessary to disconnect or disassembly the connector to check for terminal damage or corrosion and perform some of the inspections. Note the location of each pin the connector before disassembly. When doing continuity checks to make sure there are no breaks in the wire, shake or wiggle the harness and connector during testing to check for looseness or intermittent contact.

4. Check the control module, sensors and actuators for obvious physical damage.
5. Turn off all electrical loads then testing and make sure the doors are closed whenever reading are made. DO NOT disconnect any electrical connector with the key ON. Turn the key off to disconnect or reconnect the wiring harness to any sensor or the control unit.
6. Make sure he engine coolant and oil are at the proper level.
7. Check for leaks around the exhaust manifold, oxygen sensor and vacuum hoses connections with the engine idling at normal operating temperature.
8. Only after all the above checks have been performed should the voltmeter be connected to read the trouble codes. If not, the self-diagnosis system may indicate a failed component when all that is wring is a loose or broken connection.

EEC-IV System 2.3L HSC

The center of the EEC-IV system is a micro-processor called the electronic control assembly (ECA). The ECA receives data from a number of sensors and other electronic components (switches, relay, etc.). The ECA contains a specific calibration for optimizing emissions, fuel economy, and driveability. Based on information received and programmed into its memory, the ECA generates output signals to control various relay, solenoid, and other actuators.

The ECA is mounted in the passenger compartment inside the dash on the steering column lateral shake brace.

The 2.3L HSC-EEC-IV system features electronic control of:

- Engine enrichment (feedback carburetor)
- Engine spark advance
- Exhaust gas recirculation (EGR)
- Curb idle speed
- Evaporative emissions purge (on/off)
- Engine diagnostic (self-test)
- A/C cutout for W.O.T. power
- Thermactor air
- Upshift light (MTX)

The 2.3L HSC-EEC-IV system can be divided into three subsystem:

- Fuel
- Air
- Electronic engine control

FUEL SUBSYSTEM

The fuel subsystem consists of a mechanical fuel pump to deliver fuel from the fuel tank, a fuel filter to remove contaminants from the fuel, a 6149 feedback carburetor, and a feedback solenoid.

AIR SUBSYSTEM

The air subsystem consists of an air cleaner, an air cleaner valve assembly, and the associated air tubes.

Air cleaner and air valve operation is similar to the operation on previous models.

This system uses a 90°F (32°C) bimetal with a new stainless valve that replaces the old style brass valve. This system uses a blue 55°F (13°C) cold weather modulator (CWM).

ELECTRONIC ENGINE CONTROL (EEC) SUBSYSTEM

The electronic engine control subsystem consists of the ECA and various sensors and actuators. The ECA reads inputs from various sensors to compute the required fuel flow necessary to achieve the desired air/fuel ratio. This is performed by the ECA contolling outputs to the duty cycle solenoid on the cowl. The duty cycle on-time determines the amount of fuel delivered to the engine by leaning the mixture with more air or by controlling the power valve circuit in the 6149 Holley feedback carburetor.

The components which make up the 2.3L HSC-EEC-IV subsystem can be divided into three categories:

- Electronic control assembly (ECA)
- System inputs (sensors)
- System outputs (actuators)

SYSTEM INPUTS

In order for the ECA to control engine operation properly, it must first receive specific information on various operating conditions. These include:

- Crankshaft position and speed
- Throttle plate position
- Engine coolant temperature
- Exhaust gas oxygen level
- A/C (on/off)
- Intake manifold pressure
- EGR valve position
- MT/AT load or no-load

These conditions are monitored by inputs to the system provided by the following:

- Profile ignition pick-up (PIP) (replaces the crank position sensor)
- Throttle position sensor (TPS) (plunger style)
- Engine coolant temperature sensor (ECT)
- Exhaust gas oxygen sensor (EGO)
- A/C clutch compressor signal (ACC)
- Manifold absolute pressure sensor (MAP)
- EGR valve position sensor (EVP)
- Self-test input (STI)

SYSTEM OUTPUTS

When the ECA receives an input signal that indicates a change in one or more of the operating conditions, the change(s) must be evaluated to determine whether or not an output signal should be provided to control one of the following:

- Air/fuel ratio
- Spark timing
- Engine idle speed
- EGR
- Thermactor air/canister purge control
- A/C compressor on/off
- Engine cooling fan on/off
- MT gear selection (operator advised to shift to next highest gear)
- Self-test

These are controlled by system outputs applied to the following:

- Feedback control solenoid (FCS)
- TFI-IV ignition module
- Throttle kicker solenoid
- EGR solenoid (EGRV and EGRC)
- TAB and TAD (CANP vacuum teed to TAD)
- A/C and fan controller module
- Upshift light (MTX)
- Self-test output (STO)

ENGINE OPERATING MODES

In order to effectively operate the various engine functions, three control modes have been programmed into the ECA. These are:

- Normal engine operation
- Cold-or-hot engine operation
- Limited operating strategy (LOS)

In addition, fuel control operates in either an open loop mode (disregarding EGO sensor feedback) or a closed loop mode (using EGO sensor feedback).

Fuel control is in open loop mode

when the engine is cold, during W.O.T. operation, or during LOS operation.

Fuel control enters closed loop operation within 80 seconds after start-up for most temperatures. The system remains in closed loop operation for part throttle and idle situations.

Normal engine operation conditions are divided into five separate modes:

- Crank mode
- Underspeed mode
- Closed throttle mode
- Part throttle mode
- Wide open throttle mode (W.O.T.)

Normal engine operation provides an optimum calibration for each of these modes. A mode evaluation circuit in the ECA determines which mode is present at any given time of engine operation and adjusts the calibration, if required.

Crank mode

The crank mode is entered after initial engine power-up or after engine stall when the key is in START. A special operation program is used in the crank mode to aid engine starting. After engine start, one of the run modes is entered and normal engine operation is performed. If the engine stumbles during a run mode, the underspeed mode is entered to help it recover from the stumble, and to prevent it from stalling. A unique strategy is used in the underspeed mode in place of the normal engine run operation.

When the engine is cranked, fuel control is open loop operation the ECA sets engine timing at 10°-15° BTDC. The EGR solenoids are not energized, so the EGR valve is off. The canister purge solenoid is teed with the Thermactor air divert (TAD) solenoid, so, when the Thermactor air is upstream, the canister purge is off.

If the engine coolant is cold, the ECT sensor signal from the ECA causes the ECA to enrich the fuel to the engine through the feedback solenoid. In this operation, the ECT sensor is assisting the choke system to improve the cold start reaction and to provide good cold driveaway characteristics. At start-up, the TPS keeps the ECA informed on the position of the throttle plate.

Underspeed Mode

Operation in the underspeed mode (under 600 rpm) is similar to that previously described for the crank mode. The system switches from the underspeed mode to the normal run mode at about 600 rpm. The underspeed mode is used to provide additional fuel enrichment and increased airflow to the engine to help it recover from a stumble.

Closed Throttle Mode (Idle or Deceleration)

In the closed throttle mode, the air/fuel ratio is trimmed (by varying the duty cycle of the feedback solenoid to the carburetor) to obtain the desired mixture. To calculate what this output signal should be, the ECA evaluates signal inputs from the ECT sensor, MAP, EVP, PIP, TPS, and the EGO sensor. These sensors inform the ECA of the various conditions that must be evaluated in order for the ECA to determine the correct air/fuel ratio for the closed throttle condition present. Therefore, with the input from the EGO sensor fails to switch rich/lean, the ECA programming assumes the EGO sensor has cooled off, and the system goes to open loop fuel control. Ignition timing is also determined by the ECA, using these same inputs. The ECA has a series of tables programmed into the assembly at the factory. These tables provide the ECA with a reference of desired ignition timing for various operating conditions reflected by the sensor inputs.

The throttle kicker solenoid on/off is determined by the ECA as a function of rpm, ECT, A/C on or off, throttle mode, and time since start-up inputs. The EGR valve and the canister purge are off during a closed throttle condition. The signal from the TPS to the ECA indicates that the throttle plate is closed. The ECA then remove the energizing signal (if present) from the EGR solenoid.

Part Throttle Mode (Cruise)

The air/fuel ratio and ignition timing are calculated in the same manner as previously described for the closed throttle mode. The fuel control system remains in closed loop during part throttle operation, as long as the EGO sensor keeps switching from rich to lean.

In part throttle operation, the throttle kicker is positioned to provide a dashpot function in the event that the throttle is close. Again, as in the closed throttle mode, the ECA makes this determination based on the inputs from the applicable sensors.

The TPS provides the throttle plate position signal to the ECA. With the throttle plate being in the partially open position, the ECA energizes the EGR control and vent solenoids.

When the EGR solenoids are energized, the EGR flow rate is controlled by the EGR solenoids (EGRC and EGRV) by trapping, increasing, or venting vacuum to the EGR valve.

Wide Open Throttle Mode (W.O.T.)

Control of the air/fuel ratio in the W.O.T. mode is the same as in part, or closed throttle situations, except that the fuel control switches to the open loop, and the feedback solenoid vacuum signal decreases to provide additional fuel enrichment. This vacuum decrease is applied as a result of the W.O.T. signal from the TPS to the ECA. This signal from the TPS also causes the ECA to remove the energizing signal from the EGR solenoids (if present).

Some spark advance is added in W.O.T. for improved performance. In addition, the A/C clutch and cooling fan are turned off to aid performance.

Cold or Hot Engine Operation

This modified operation changes the normal engine operation output signals, as required, to adjust for uncommon operating conditions. These include a cold or an excessively hot engine.

Limited Operation Strategy (LOS)

In this operation, the ECA assumes a passive condition, so the TFI and feedback solenoid allow the vehicle to "limp home" when an electronic malfunction occurs. The EGR is off, the Thermactor is bypassing, CANP is shut off, timing is locked at 10° BTDC, and the fuel control is maximum rich (no vacuum or air bleed). On this system, the vehicle will run with the ECA disconnected because the TFI module will fire at 10° MT, or 15° AT, BTDC and the carburetor will supply fuel to the engine.

ENGINE OPERATION

Cold Start-Up

OPERATION AT FAST IDLE

The driver turns the key to the ON position.

The crank timing is in synchronization with the PIP signal from the distributor.

The ECA outputs a signal to the throttle kicker, which provides an airflow path through the throttle plates, and produces an increased idle speed. The amount of rpm increase over base provided is dependent on the temperature of the choke at start. As the driver goes from closed throttle to part throttle (kickdown) and back, the choke will decrease rpm (airflow) to a level still above base. As the engine warms up, the idle speed will continue to step down until the base rpm is reached.

The amount of fuel delivered to the engine is controlled by the ECA. The amount of enrichment provided is dependent on engine coolant temperature and engine load. As the engine warms up, the amount of fuel enrichment is decreased.

EGR and canister purge are off until the vehicle is warm and in closed loop (40 seconds on a hot start).

Spark timing is controlled by the ECA, which outputs a signal to the TFI ignition module. The spark advance varies with rpm, engine load, coolant temperature, and EGR.

The bimetal sensor in the air cleaner is cold. Vacuum is applied to the air door motor. The motor has pulled the fresh air door close and opened the air cleaner to heated air from the exhaust manifold heat stove.

Cold Driveaway

LIGHT THROTTLE (PART THROTTLE)

As engine coolant temperature increases and time since start increases, fuel enrichment provided by the ECA decreases.

The amount of extra airflow provided to overcome cold engine friction and to produce a high cam is decreased as engine temperature increases.

EGR and canister purge are off. The purge is not allowed on until approximately two minutes after engine coolant temperature reaches 130°F (55°C).

Spark advance is controlled by the ECA, which outputs a signal to the TFI ignition module.

The MT upshift light is enabled.

The bimetal in the air cleaner is still cold and vacuum is still applied to the air door motor. The fresh air door is closed and the air cleaner is opened to heated air.

Warm-up Driveaway

PARTLY WARM ENGINE
LIGHT THROTTLE ACCELERATION
ACCELERATION FROM A STOP
ABOUT ONE MINUTE AFTER COLD DRIVEAWAY FROM 0°F (-18°C)

Extra enrichment is provided as the vehicle is accelerated from a stop. The amount of fuel provided is controlled by the ECA and is based on engine coolant temperature and engine load.

The bimetal in the air cleaner has reached 90°F (32°C) and is starting to bleed vacuum off, causing the door to switch to fresh air. If ambient air is colder than 90°F (32°C), the door may modulate between positions.

EGR and canister purge are off. The canister purge is still commanded off by the ECA.

Spark advance is controlled by the ECA, which outputs a 12 volt signal to the TFI ignition module on the distributor. The MT upshift light is enabled.

Warm-Up Driveaway

PARTLY WARM ENGINE
LIGHT THROTTLE ACCELERATION
ACCELERATION FROM A STOP
ABOUT ONE MINUTE AFTER COLD DRIVEAWAY AT 30-40°F (-1 to +5°C)

The engine coolant temperature has reached approximately 100°F (38°C) and conditions are such that the ECA starts to control the amount of fuel delivery based on the output of the EGO sensor. The engine is now operating in closed loop mode with the EGO sensor providing the required feedback information.

The EGR is on along with the canister purge. The amount of EGR is controlled by the sonic EGR valve. Canister purge is controlled by a purge shutoff valve teed to the Thermactor air divert (TAD) solenoid.

The upshift light for the MT is now working in first, second, third and fourth gear, and is locked out in fifth gear. Conditions needed to activate the light are approximately 2,000 engine rpm and 4 in.Hg manifold vacuum.

The bimetal in the air cleaner has reached 90°F (32°C) and is starting to bleed vacuum off, causing the door to switch to fresh air. If ambient air is colder than 90°F (32°C), the door may modulate between positions.

Spark advance is controlled by the ECA, which outputs a 12 volt signal to the TFI ignition module on the distributor.

Acceleration at W.O.T.

ENGINE HOT

W.O.T. condition is determined by the throttle position sensor.

Extra fuel enrichment is provided by the ECA, and the system goes to open loop fuel control out of feedback control.

Canister purge and EGR are off. Thermactor air is bypassed.
Extra spark advance is added with the amount being controlled by the ECA. The ECA outputs a 12 volt reference signal to the TFI ignition module to command the correct amount of advance.

If the A/C is on during acceleration, the ECA turns off the A/C compressor. This feature is called, W.O.T. A/C Shutoff. The A/C remains off for approximately three seconds after returning to part throttle, and will shut off again when a part throttle to W.O.T. transition occurs.

The upshift light for the MT will not operate until approximately 3,600 rpm is satisfied.

The bimetal sensor is warm and has bled vacuum from the air door motor. The motor has released the fresh air door to the OPEN position. Since no vacuum is available during W.O.T., the door will go to the fresh air mode after the delay valve bleeds trapped vacuum.

Hot Curb Idle

CLOSED THROTTLE

Fuel delivery is controlled by the ECA, which is operating in closed loop (feedback) mode. Feedback information is provided by the EGO sensor. Closed throttle for 300 seconds will cause re-entry to open loop enrichment.

The air inlet door on the bemetal sensor opens to fresh air, buy cannot maintain the 90°F (32°C) temperature, due to underhood temperatures. Spark advance is controlled by the ECA.

If the A/C is on, the ECA commands the throttle kicker open for increased airflow to compensate for the extra load of the A/C compressor.

EGR and canister purge are off.

Hot Engine Shutdown

IGNITION OFF

The ECA is inoperative.
All ECA controlled outputs are off:

- Canister purge
- EGR
- Spark
- Fuel
- Throttle kicker
- Upshift light
- Thermactor air

Hot Cruise

ENGINE HOT LIGHT THROTTLE (PART THROTTLE)

Fuel delivery is controlled by the ECA, which is operating in closed loop (feedback) mode. Feedback information is provided by the EGO sensor.

Spark advance is controlled by the ECA through the TFI ignition module on the distributor.

EGR and canister purge are on. The amount of EGR is controlled by the sonic EGR valve.

The Thermactor system is operating and is in the downstream mode.
The bimetal sensor is warm and is modulating vacuum to the air inlet door to maintain a 90°F (32°C) temperature.

Deceleration

COASTING DOWN AT CLOSED THROTTLE–ENGINE HOT

EGR and canister purge are off.

Bimetal sensor in the air cleaner is hot. Vacuum to the air motor has been bled off, releasing the fresh air door to the OPEN position.

The ECA calculates a duty cycle for the fuel solenoid based on EGO input.

Spark advance is controlled by the ECA, which outputs a signal to the TFI ignition module on the distributor.

Airflow provided by the throttle kicker is also controlled by an output from the ECA.

Thermactor air goes upstream on a MT on deceleration.

TESTING

NOTE: Testing the EEC-IV system requires special equipment and an expert knowledge of the system. Troubleshooting and servicing should be performed by a qualified personnel only.

CENTRAL FUEL INJECTION TEMPO AND TOPAZ

In the CFI system, the throttle body assembly meters fuel/air into the induction system of the 2.3L HSC engine.

The new low pressure CFI fuel system has only five major parts:

FUEL PUMP (Mounted in tank)

FUEL FILTER (R.F. Inner Fender Panel)

THROTTLE BODY ASSEMBLY (Mounts to Intake Manifold)

INJECTOR (Single Solenoid)

PRESSURE REGULATOR (Regulates fuel pressure at 14.5 psi)

There is no choke system and only one throttle valve is needed. So that a fast idle can be obtained during cold engine start-up and to provide normal (lower RPM) curb idle when the engine is at operating temperature, engineers added an Idle Speed Control (ISC) to do that important job. A small shaft extends or retracts on command from signals sent to it from the EEC-IV computer. An Idle Tracking Switch (ITS) is part of the ISC assembly. It is needed to signal the computer wherever the throttle lever has contacted the plunger thereby signaling the need for control of engine idle RPM.

Throttle Position Sensor (TPS)

This non-adjustable sensor mounted to the throttle body and is interconnected to the throttle shaft. It sends an input signal to the EEC-IV computer in proportion to the amount of throttle plate opening (closed throttle, part throttle, and wide open throttle).

Air Control

A single butterfly valve controls the flow of air into the intake manifold. It looks and operates similar to the throttle valve(s) used with carburetors.

Located just above the throttle plate is the electromechanical fuel injector which meters and also atomizes the fuel delivered to the engine.

An electrical control signal sent to the fuel injector from the EEC-IV computer causes the solenoid actuated fuel metering ball to move off its seat and allows fuel to flow as required by engine demands.

Injector flow opening is fixed. As a result, fuel flow to the engine is controlled by how long (the amount of time) the solenoid is energized (remains on) with the fuel metering ball off its seat.

Fuel Pressure Regulator

Its location and design is such that supply line pressure drops are eliminated. Also, a second function of the pressure regulator is to maintain fuel supply pressure whenever the engine is not running (ignition key off). It acts as a downstream check valve and traps the fuel between itself and the fuel pump. By maintaining fuel pressure upon engine shutdown, fuel line vapor (vapor lock) does not develop.

Fuel Charging Assembly

Two major components make up the fuel charging assembly. They are the Throttle Body and Main body. Fuel is sent through internal passages to the injector tip. Any excess fuel is returned to the pressure regulator and from there it is returned to the fuel tank at a reduced pressure of somewhere between 3 and 6 psi.

Low Pressure Fuel Injector

Fuel flow into the air stream entering the cylinders is determined by the length of on-time the solenoid is energized. The longer on-time of the injector, the more fuel is permitted to flow into the intake system.

When the ball valve moves off its seat the small metering orifices are uncovered and a calibrated amount of fuel enters the intake manifold.

NOTE: The injector air gap is not adjustable and the injector is only serviced as an assembly.

CHECKING FUEL PRESSURE

To check the fuel pressure, disconnect the Inertia Switch which is located at the right side of the trunk area. Now, crank the engine for 15 seconds to reduce system pressure before you remove the clips at each end of the fuel line between the fuel filter and the fuel inlet at the charging assembly.

NOTE: Use extreme care to prevent combustion from fuel spillage.

Install an accurate fuel pressure gauge between the fuel filter line and the throttle body assembly fuel inlet. You'll need a T-fitting to accomplish this fuel pressure gauge connection.

Reconnect the inertia switch, start the engine and check fuel pressure at idle. Throughout acceleration, you should have a stable pressure of 13.0 to 16.0 psi without any excessively high or low readings. To remove the pressure gauge, again disconnect the inertia switch, crank the engine for 15 seconds, then remove the gauge. Reinstall the original fuel line securely. Reconnect the inertia switch and start the engine. Check carefully for any fuel leakage.

TESTING AND SERVICING

NOTE: The CFI system is controlled by the EEC-IV system. Testing the system requires special equipment and an expert knowledge of the system. Troubleshooting and servicing should be performed by qualified personnel only.

DIESEL FUEL SYSTEM

Glow Plugs

REMOVAL & INSTALLATION

1. Disconnect battery ground cable from the battery, located in the luggage compartment.

2. Disconnect glow plug harness from the glow plugs.
3. Using a 12mm deep well socket, remove the glow plugs.
4. Install glow plugs, using a 12mm deep well socket. Tighten the glow plugs to 11-15 ft.lb.
5. Connect glow plug harness to the glow plugs. Tighten the nuts to 5-7 ft.lb.
6. Connect battery ground cable to the battery located in the luggage compartment.
7. Check the glow plug system operation.

Injection Nozzles

REMOVAL & INSTALLATION

1. Disconnect and remove injection lines from injection pump and nozzles. Cap all lines and fittings using Protective Cap Set T84P-9395-A or equivalent.
2. Remove nuts attaching the fuel return line to the nozzles, and remove return line and seals.
3. Remove nozzles using a 27mm deep well socket.
3. Remove nozzles gaskets and washers from nozzle seat, using O-ring Pick Tool T71P-19703-C or equivalent.
5. Clean the outside of the nozzle assemblies using Nozzle Cleaning Kit, Rotunda model 14-0301 or equivalent, and a suitable solvent. Dry thoroughly.
6. Position new sealing gaskets in the nozzle seats.

NOTE: Install gasket with red painted surface facing up.

7. Position new copper washers in the nozzles bores.
8. Install nozzles and tighten to 44-51 ft.lb.
9. Position fuel return line on the nozzles, using new seals.
10. Install fuel return line retaining nuts and tighten to 10 ft.lb.
11. Install fuel lines on the injection pump and nozzles. Tighten capnuts to 18-22 ft.lb.
12. Air bleed fuel system.
13. Run engine and check for fuel leaks.

NOTE: Other servicing of the diesel fuel system requires special tool and equipment. Servicing should be done by a mechanic experienced with diesels.

Fuel Cutoff Solenoid

REMOVAL & INSTALLATION

1. Disconnect battery ground cable from the battery, located in the luggage compartment.
2. Remove connector from the fuel cutoff solenoid.
3. Remove fuel cutoff solenoid and discard the O-ring.
4. Install fuel cutoff solenoid using a new O-ring. Tighten to 30-33 ft.lb.
5. Connect electrical connector.
6. Connect battery ground cable.
7. Run engine and check for fuel leaks.

Injection Pump

REMOVAL & INSTALLATION

1. Disconnect battery ground cable from the battery. located in the luggage compartment.
2. Disconnect air inlet duct from the air cleaner and intake manifold. Install protective cap in intake manifold.

NOTE: Cap is part of Protective Cap Set, T84P-9395-A.

3. Remove rear timing belt cover and flywheel timing mark cover.
4. Remove rear timing belt.
5. Disconnect throttle cable and speed control cable, if so equipped.
6. Disconnect vacuum hoses at the altitude compensator and cold start diaphragm.
7. Disconnect fuel cutoff solenoid connector.
8. Disconnect fuel supply and fuel return hoses at injection pump.
9. Remove injection lines at the injection pump and nozzles. Cap all lines and fittings using Protective Cap Set T84P-9395-A or equivalent.
10. Rotate injection pump sprocket until timing marks are aligned. Install two M8 x 1.25 bolts in holes to hold the injection pump sprocket. Remove sprocket retaining nut.
11. Remove injection pump sprocket using Gear Puller T77F-4220-B1 and Adapter D80L-625-4 or equivalent, using two M8 x 1.25 bolts installed in the threaded holes in the sprocket.
12. Remove bolt attaching the injection pump to the pump front bracket.
13. Remove two nuts attaching the injection pump to the pump rear bracket and remove the pump.
14. Install injection pump in position on the pump bracket.
15. Install two nuts attaching the pump to the rear bracket and tighten to 23-34 ft.lb.
16. Install bolt attaching the pump to the front bracket and tighten to 12-16 ft.lb.
17. Install injection pump sprocket. Hold the sprocket in place using the procedure described in Step 10, Removal. Install the sprocket retaining nut and tighten to 51-58 ft.lb.
18. Remove protective caps and install the fuel lines at the injection pump and nozzles. Tighten the fuel line capnuts to 18-22 ft.lb.
19. Connect fuel supply and fuel return hoses at the injection pump.
20. Connect fuel cutoff solenoid connector.
21. Connect vacuum lines to the cold start diaphragm and altitude compensator.
22. Connect throttle cable and speed control cable, if so equipped.
23. Install and adjust the rear timing belt.
24. Remove protective cap and install the air inlet duct to the intake manifold and air cleaner.
25. Connect battery ground cable to battery.
26. Air bleed fuel system as outlined.
27. Check and adjust the injection pump timing.
28. Run engine and check for fuel leaks.
29. Check and adjust engine idle.

Injection Timing

ADJUSTMENT

NOTE: Engine coolant temperature must be above 80°C (176°F) before the injection timing can be checked and/or adjusted.

1. Disconnect the battery ground cable from the battery located in luggage compartment.
2. Remove the injection pump distributor head plug bolt and sealing washer.
3. Install Static Timing Gauge Adapter, Rotunda 14-0303 or equivalent with Metric Dial Indicator, so that indicator pointer is in contact with injection pump plunger.
4. Remove timing mark cover from transmission housing. Align timing mark (TDC) with pointer on the rear engine cover plate.
5. Rotate the crankshaft pulley slowly, counterclockwise until the dial indicator pointer stops moving (approximately 30-50° BTDC).
6. Adjust dial indicator to Zero.

NOTE: Confirm that dial indicator pointer does not move from Zero by slightly rotating crankshaft left and right.

7. Turn crankshaft clockwise until crankshaft timing mark aligns with indicator pin. Dial indicator should read 1.0mm ± 0.02mm. If reading is not within specification, adjust as follows:
   a. Loosen injection pump attaching bolt and nuts.

b. Rotate the injection pump toward the engine to advance timing and away from the engine to retard timing. Rotate the injection pump until the dial indicator reads 1.0mm ± 0.02mm.

c. Tighten the injection pump attaching nuts and bolt to 13-22 ft.lb.

d. Repeat Steps 5,6, and 7 to check that timing is adjusted correctly.

8. Remove the dial indicator and adapter and install the injection pump distributor head plug and tighten to 10-14.5 ft.lb.

9. Connect the battery ground cable to the battery.

10. Run the engine, check and adjust idle rpm, if necessary. Check for fuel leaks.

IDLE SPEED ADJUSTMENT

1. Place the transmission in Neutral.
2. Bring the engine up to normal operating temperature. Stop engine.
3. Remove the timing hole cover. Clean the flywheel surface and install reflective tape.
4. Idle speed is measured with manual transmission in Neutral.
5. Check curb idle speed, using Rotunda 99-0001 or equivalent. Curb idle speed is specified on the Vehicle Emissions Control Information decal (VECI). Adjust to specification by loosening the locknut on the idle speed bolt. Turn the idle speed adjusting bolt clockwise to increase, or counterclockwise to decrease engine idle speed. Tighten the locknut.
6. Place transmission in Neutral. Rev engine momentarily and recheck the curb idle RPM. Readjust if necessary.
7. Turn A/C On. Check the idle speed. Adjust to specification by loosening nut on the A/C throttle kicker and rotating screw.

HEATER

Heater Core

REMOVAL & INSTALLATION

NOTE: In some cases removal of the instrument panel may be necessary.

Without A/C

1. Disconnect the negative battery cable.
2. Drain the coolant.

CAUTION

When draining the coolant, keep in mind that cats and dogs are attracted by the ethylene glycol antifreeze, and are quite likely to drink any that is left in an uncovered container or in puddles on the ground. This will prove fatal in sufficient quantity. Always drain the coolant into a sealable container. Coolant should be reused unless it is contaminated or several years old.

3. Disconnect the heater hoses from the core tubes at the firewall, inside the engine compartment. Plug the core tubes to prevent coolant spillage when the core is removed.
4. Open the glove compartment. Remove the glove compartment. Remove the glove compartment liner.
5. Remove the core access plate screws and remove the access plate.
6. Working under the hood, remove the two nuts attaching the heater assembly case to the dash panel.
7. Remove the core through the glove compartment opening.
8. Install the core through the glove compartment opening.
9. Working under the hood, install the two nuts attaching the heater assembly case to the dash panel.

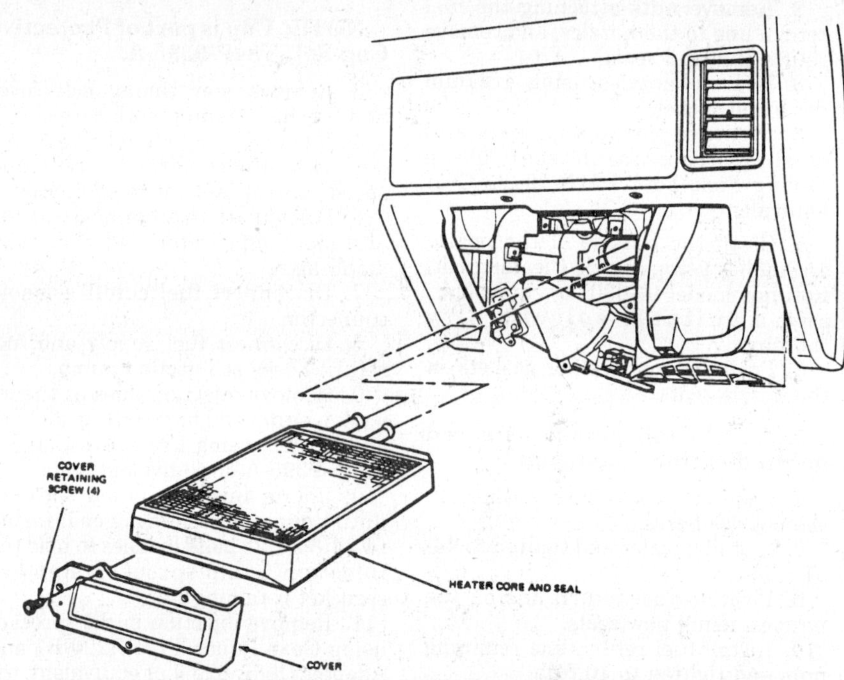

Heater core removal; without air conditioning

10. Install the core access plate screws and install the access plate.
11. Install the glove compartment. Install the glove compartment liner.
12. Reconnect the heater hoses to the core tubes at the firewall, inside the engine compartment.
13. Refill the cooling system with coolant.
14. Reconnect the negative battery cable.

With A/C

1. Disconnect the negative battery cable and drain the cooling system.

CAUTION

When draining the coolant, keep in mind that cats and dogs are attracted by the ethylene glycol antifreeze, and are quite likely to drink any that is left in an uncovered container or in puddles on the ground. This will prove fatal in sufficient quantity. Always drain the coolant into a sealable container. Coolant should be reused unless it is contaminated or several years old.

2. Disconnect the heater hoses from the heater core.
3. Working inside the vehicle, re-

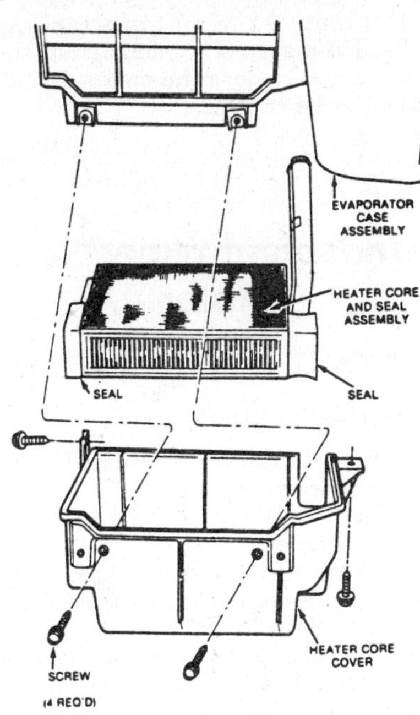

Heater core removal; with air conditioning

move the floor duct from the plenum (2 screws).

4. Remove the four screws attaching the heater core cover to the plenum, remove the cover and remove the heater core.
5. To install: Install the heater core and install the cover. Install the four screws attaching the heater core cover to the plenum.
6. Working inside the vehicle, Install the floor duct to the plenum (2 screws).
7. Reconnect the heater hoses to the heater core.
8. Reconnect the negative battery cable and refill the cooling system.

Blower Motor

REMOVAL & INSTALLATION

Without A/C

1. Disconnect the negative battery cable.
2. Remove the glove compartment and lower instrument panel reinforcing rail.
3. Disconnect the blower electrical connectors.
4. Remove the blower motor-to-case attaching screws. Remove the blower and fan as an assembly.
5. Installation is the reverse.

With A/C

1. Locate and remove two screws at each side of the glove compartment

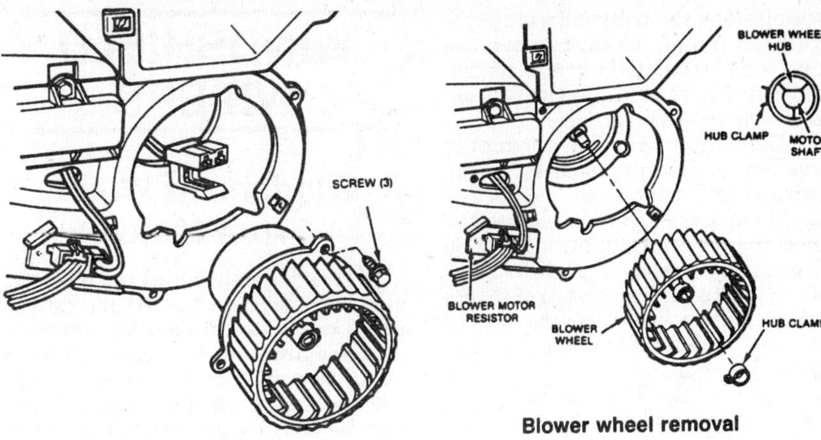

Blower motor and wheel removal

Blower wheel removal

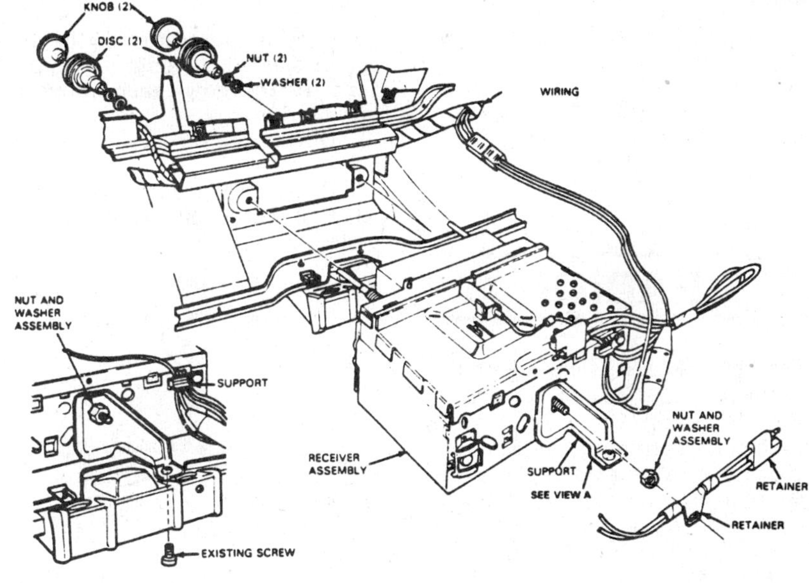

Radio installation

opening along the lower edge of the instrument panel. Then, remove the glove compartment door and instrument panel lower reinforcement from the instrument panel.

2. Disconnect the blower motor wires from the wire harness at the hardshell connector.

3. Remove the screws attaching the blower motor and mounting plate to the evaporator case.

4. Rotate the motor until the mounting plate flats clear the edge of the glove compartment opening and remove the motor.

5. Remove the hub clamp spring from the blower wheel hub. Then, remove the blower wheel from the motor shaft.

6. Installation is the reverse of removal.

RADIO

For best FM reception, adjust the antenna to 31" (787mm) in height. Fading or weak AM reception may be adjusted by means of the antenna trimmer control. located either on the right rear of front side of the radio chassis. See the owner's manual for position. To adjust the trimmer:

1. Extend the antenna to maximum height.

2. Tune the radio to a weak station around 1600 KC. Adjust the volume so that the sound is barely audible.

3. Adjust the trimmer to obtain maximum volume.

REMOVAL & INSTALLATION

1. Disconnect the negative battery cable.

NOTE: Remove the A/C floor duct if so equipped.

2. Remove the ash tray and bracket.

3. Pull the knobs from the shafts.

4. Working under the instrument panel, remove the support bracket nut from the radio chassis.

5. Remove the shaft nuts and washers.

6. Drop the radio down from behind the instrument panel. Disconnect the power lead, antenna, and speaker wires. Remove the radio.

7. Installation is the reverse.

WINDSHIELD WIPERS

Windshield Wiper Front Motor

NOTE: The internal permanent magnets used in the wiper motor are a ceramic (glass-like) material. Care must be exercised in handling the motor to avoid damaging the magnets. The motor must not be struck or tapped with a hammer or other object.

REMOVAL & INSTALLATION

The motor is located in the right rear corner of the engine compartment, in the cowl area above the firewall.

1. Disconnect the negative battery cable.

2. Remove the plastic cowl cover.

3. Disconnect the motor electrical connector.

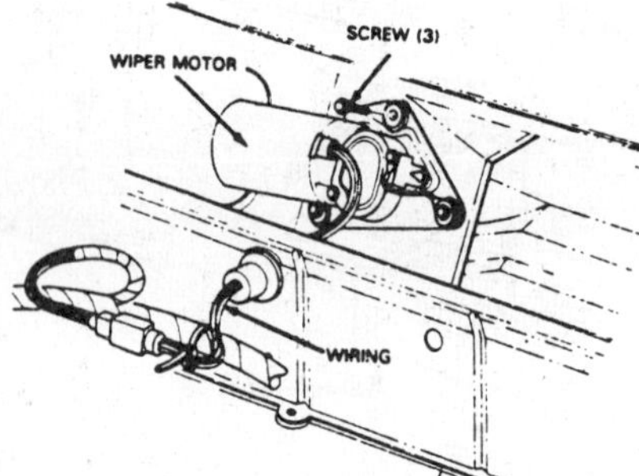

Wiper motor installation

4. Remove the motor attaching bolts. Disengage the motor from the linkage and remove the motor. Installation is the reverse.

Windshield Wiper Rear Motor

REMOVAL & INSTALLATION

Hatchback Models

1. Remove the wiper arm and blade from the wiper motor.

2. Remove the pivot shaft attaching nut and spacers.

3. Remove the liftgate inner trim panel. Disconnect the electrical connector to the wiper motor.

4. Remove the three screws holding the bracket to the inner door skin and remove the motor assembly, bracket and linkage assembly.

5. Installation is the reverse order of the removal procedure.

Station Wagon Models

1. Remove the wiper arm and blade from the wiper motor.

2. Remove the pivot shaft attaching nut and spacers.

3. Remove the screws attaching the license plate housing. Disconnect the license plate light and remove the housing. Remove the wiper motor and bracket assembly retaining screws, disconnect the electrical connector to the wiper motor and remove the motor.

4. Installation is the reverse order of the removal procedure.

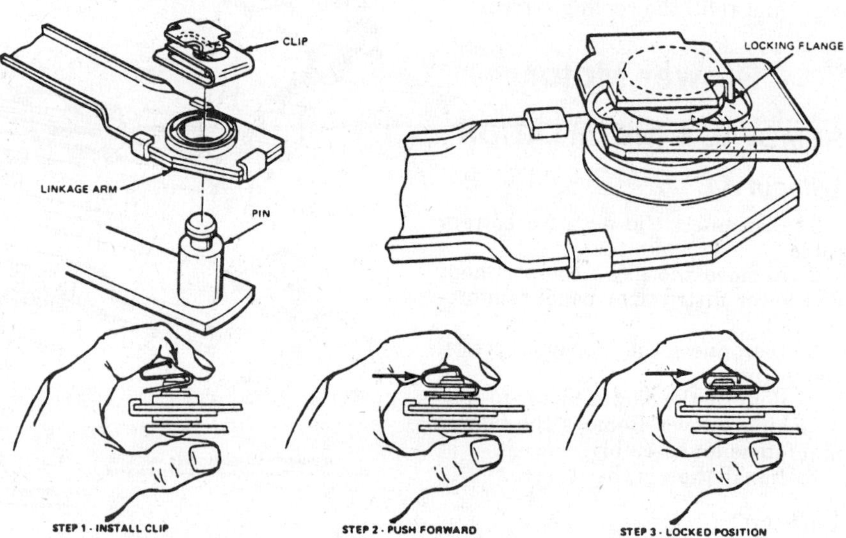

Removing and installing wiper linkage retaining clips

Wiper Linkage

REMOVAL & INSTALLATION

The wiper linkage is mounted below the cowl top panel and can be reached by raising the hood.

1. Remove the wiper arm and blade assembly from the pivot shaft. Pry the latch (on the arm) away from the shaft to unlock the arm from the pivot shaft.
2. Raise the hood and disconnect the negative battery cable.
3. Remove the clip and disconnect the linkage drive arm from the motor crank pin.
4. On Tempo/Topaz remove the screws retaining the pivot assemblies to the cowl.
6. On Escort/Lynx, EXP/LN-7 remove the large pivot retainer nuts from each pivot shaft.
7. Remove the linkage and pivot assembly from the cowl chamber.
8. Installation is the reverse of removal.

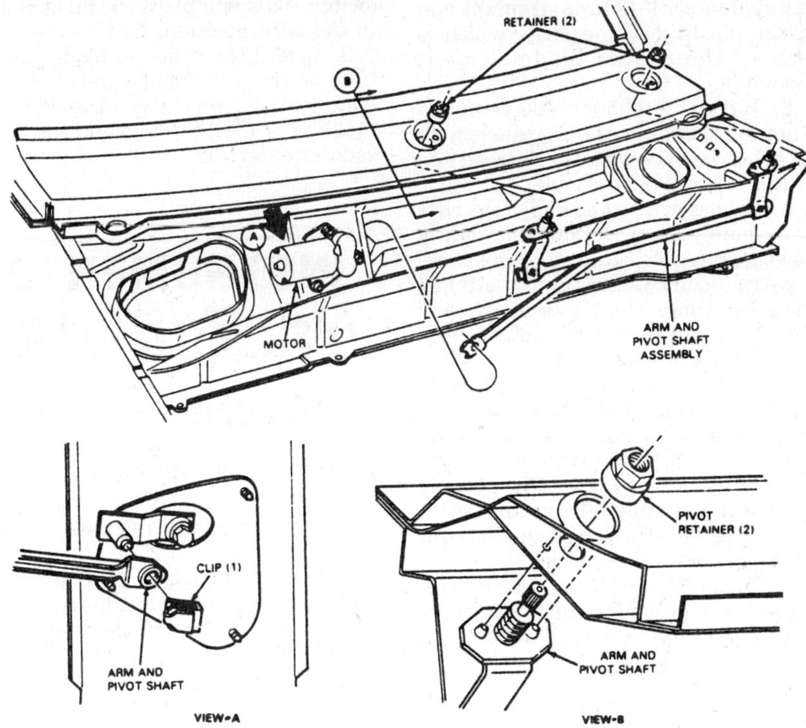

Wiper linkage

Wiper Arm Assembly

REMOVAL & INSTALLATION

1. Raise the blade end of the arm off the windshield and move the slide latch away from the pivot shaft.
2. The wiper arm should not be unlocked and can now be pulled off of the pivot shaft.
3. To install, position the auxiliary arm (if so equipped) over the pivot pin, hold it down and push the main arm head over the pivot shaft. Make sure the pivot shaft is in the park position.
4. Hold the main arm head on the pivot shaft while raising the blade end of the wiper arm and push the slide latch into the lock under the pivot shaft. Lower the blade to the windshield.

NOTE: If the blade does not touch the windshield, the slide latch is not completely in place.

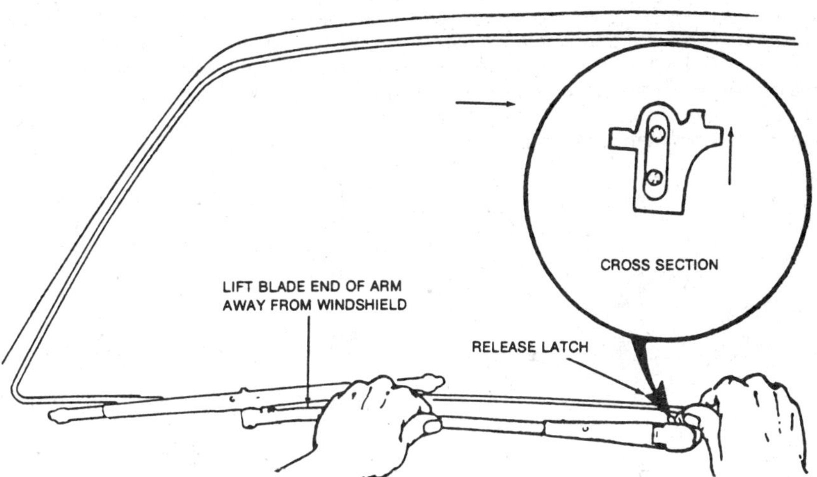

Removing the wiper arm and blade assembly

Wiper Blade (Tridon® Type)

REPLACEMENT

1. Pull up on the spring lock and pull the blade assembly from the pin.
2. To install, push the blade assembly onto the pin, so that the spring lock engages the pin.

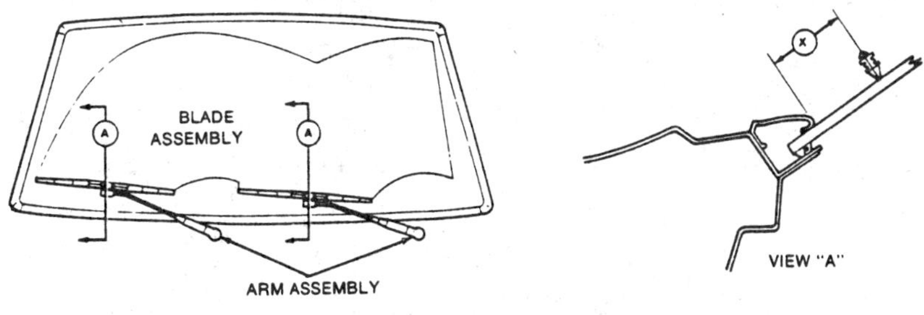

Vehicle	Dimension x (inches)	
	Driver's Side	Passenger Side
ESCORT AND LYNX FRONT 40-75 mm (1 5/8 – 3 in)		
THREE DOOR REAR 30-75 mm (1 1/8 – 3 in)		
FOUR DOOR REAR 20-60 mm (3/8 — 2 3/8 in)		

Wiper arm adjustment

Wiper Element (Tridon®)

REPLACEMENT

1. Locate a $\frac{7}{16}''$ (11mm) long notch

approximately 1″ (25mm) from the end of the plastic backing strip, which is part of the rubber blade element assembly.

2. With the wiper blade removed from the arm place the blade assembly on a firm surface with the notched end of the backing strip visible.

3. Push down on one end of the wiper assembly until the blade is tightly bowed than grasp the tip of the backing strip firmly, pulling and twisting at the same time. The backing strip will then snap out of the retaining tab on the end of the wiper frame.

4. Lift the wiper blade assembly from the surface and slide the backing strip down the frame until the notch lines up with the next retaining tab then twist slightly and the backing strip will snap out. Follow this same procedure with the remaining tabs until the element is removed.

5. To install the blade element reverse the above procedure and make sure all six tabs are locked to the backing strip.

Arm and Blade

ADJUSTMENT

1. With the arm and blade assemblies removed from the pivot shafts turn on the wiper switch and allow the motor to move the pivot shaft three or four cycles, and then turn off the wiper switch. This will place the pivot shafts in the park position.

2. Install the arm and blade assemblies on the pivot shafts to the correct distance between the windshield lower molding or weatherstrip and the blade saddle centerline.

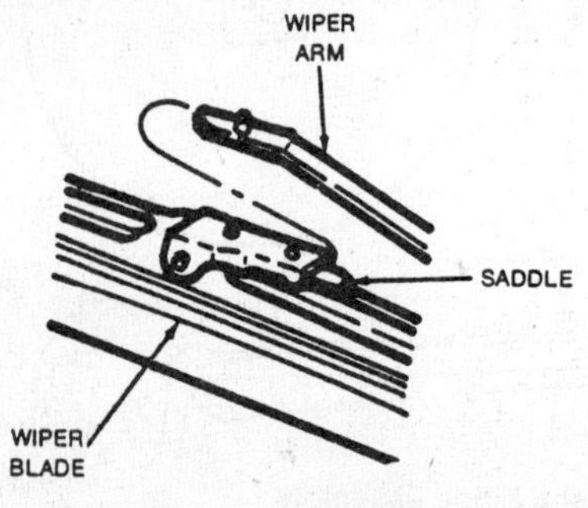

Rear window wiper blade removal

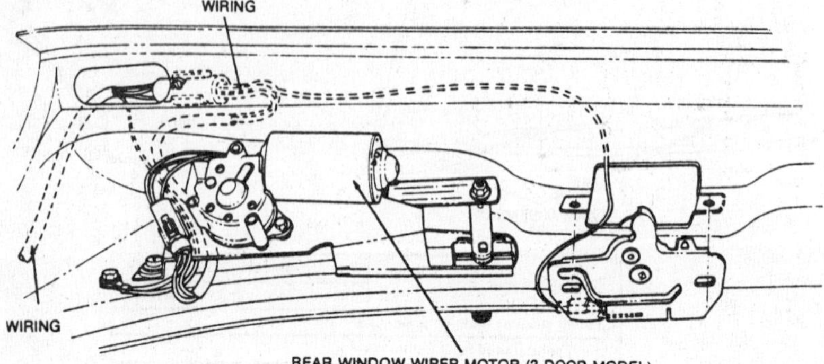

Rear window wiper motor installation

INSTRUMENTS AND SWITCHES

Headlight Switch

REMOVAL & INSTALLATION

1. Disconnect the negative battery terminal.

2. Remove the left hand air vent control cable, and drop the cable and bracket down out of the way (cars without air conditioning only).

3. Remove the fuse panel bracket retaining screws and move the fuse panel assembly out of the way.

4. Pull the headlight knob out, to the on position.

5. Reach behind the dashboard and depress the release button on the switch holding, while at the same time pulling the knob and shaft from the switch.

6. Remove the retaining nut from the dashboard.

7. Pull the switch from the dash and remove the electrical connections.

8. Installation is the reverse of removal.

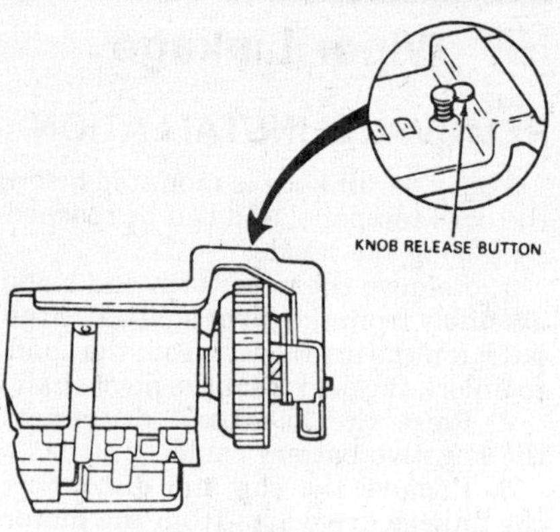

Headlight switch assembly

Instrument Cluster

REMOVAL & INSTALLATION

1. Disconnect the negative battery terminal.

2. Remove the bottom steering column cover.

3. Remove the steering column opening cover reinforcement screws.

NOTE: On cars equipped with speed control disconnect the wires from the amplified assembly.

4. Remove the steering column retaining screws from the steering column support bracket and lower the column.

5. Remove the column trim shrouds.

6. Disconnect all electrical connections from the column.

7. Remove the finish panel screws and the panel.

8. Remove the speedometer cable.

9. Remove the four cluster screws and remove the cluster.

10. Installation is the reverse of removal.

Wiper Switch

NOTE: The switch handle is an integral part of the switch and can not be removed separately. If there is any need for repairs to the wiper switch the multi-function switch must be replaced as a assembly.

REMOVAL

1. Disconnect the negative (ground) battery cable from the battery terminal.

2. Loosen the steering column attaching nuts enough to remove the upper trim shroud.

3. Remove the trim shrouds.

4. Disconnect the quick connect electrical connector.

5. Peel back the foam sight shield. Remove the two hex head screws holding the switch and remove the wash/wipe switch.

INSTALLATION

1. Position the switch on the col-

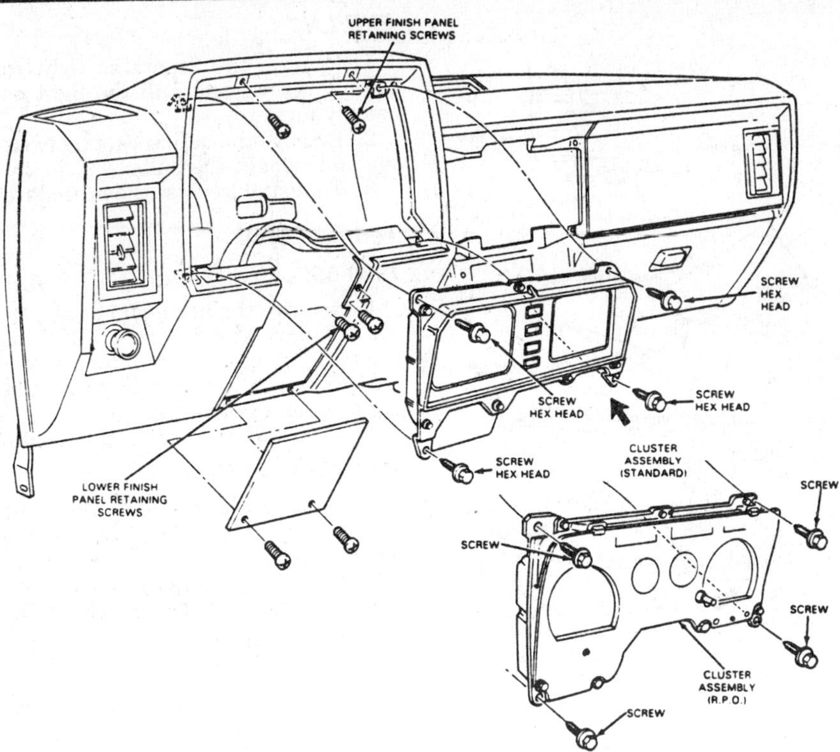

Typical instrument cluster installation

umn and install the two hex head screws. Replace the foam sight shield over the switch.

2. Connect the quick connect electrical connector.
3. Install the upper and lower trim shrouds.
4. Tighten the steering column attaching nuts to 17-25 ft.lb. (23-33 Nm).
5. Connect the negative (ground) battery cable to the battery terminal.
6. Check the steering column for proper operation.

Rear Wiper Switch

REMOVAL

1. Remove the two or four cluster opening finish panel retaining screws and remove the finish panel by rocking the upper edge toward the driver.
2. Disconnect the wiring connector from the rear washer switch.
3. Remove the washer switch from the instrument panel. On the Sable models, the switch is attached to the instrument panel with two retaining screws.

INSTALLATION

1. Install the cluster opening finish panel and the two or four retaining screws.
2. Connect the wiring connector.
3. Push the rear washer switch into the cluster finish panel until it snaps into place (on the Sable models, install the two retaining screws).

Speedometer Cable

REMOVAL & INSTALLATION

1. Remove the instrument cluster.
2. Pull the speedometer cable from the casing. If the cable is broken, disconnect the casing from the transaxle and remove the broken piece from the transaxle end.
3. Lubricate the new cable with graphite lubricant. Feed the cable into the casing from the instrument panel end.
4. Attach the cable to the speedometer. Install the cluster.

LIGHTING

Headlights

Two rectangular dual sealed beam headlamps are used on all models up to 1985½. A dash mounted switch controls them and the steering column dimmer switch controls the high and low beams.

All models 1985½ and later are equipped with flush mount headlights. On these models the bulb may be replaced without removing the lens and body assembly.

REMOVAL & INSTALLATION

Sealed Beam Type 1981-85

1. Remove the headlamp door by removing the retaining screws. After the screws are removed, pull the door slightly forward (certain models have upper locking tabs which disengage by lifting out on the lower edge and pulling downward) and disconnect the parking light (if equipped). Remove the headlight door.
2. Remove the lamp retaining ring screws, pull the headlamp from the connector.
3. Installation is in the reverse order of removal.

Aerodynamic Type 1985½ and later

CAUTION

The replaceable Halogen headlamp bulb contains gas under pressure. The bulb may shatter if the glass envelope is scratched or the bulb is dropped. Handle the bulb carefully. Grasp the bulb ONLY by its plastic base. Avoid touching the glass envelope. Keep the bulb out of the reach of children.

1. Check to see that the headlight switch is in the OFF position.
2. Raise the hood and locate the bulb installed in the rear of the headlight body.
3. Remove the electrical connector from the bulb by grasping the wires firmly and snapping the connector rearward.
4. Remove the bulb retaining ring by rotating it counterclockwise (when viewed from the rear) about ⅛ of a turn, then slide the ring off the plastic base.

NOTE: Keep the bulb retaining ring, it will be reused with the new bulb.

5. Carefully remove the headlight bulb from its socket in the reflector by gently pulling it straight backward out of the socket. DO NOT rotate the bulb during removal.

To install:

6. With the flat side of the plastic base of the bulb facing upward, insert the glass envelope of the bulb into the socket. Turn the base slightly to the left or right, if necessary to align the grooves in the forward part of the plastic base with the corresponding locating tabs inside the socket. When the

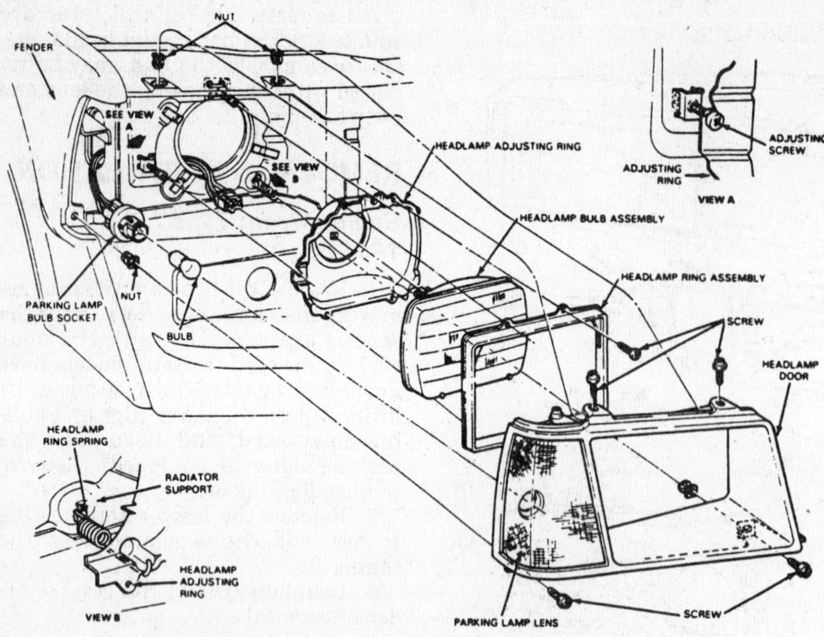

Headlight replacement—sealed beam type headlights

grooves are aligned, push the bulb firmly into the socket until the mounting flange on the base contacts the rear face of the socket.

7. Slip the bulb retaining ring over the rear of the plastic base against the mounting flange. Lock the ring into the socket by rotating the ring counterclockwise. A stop will be felt when the retaining ring is fully engaged.

8. Push the electrical connector into the rear of the plastic until it snaps and locks into position.

9. Turn the headlights on and check for proper operation.

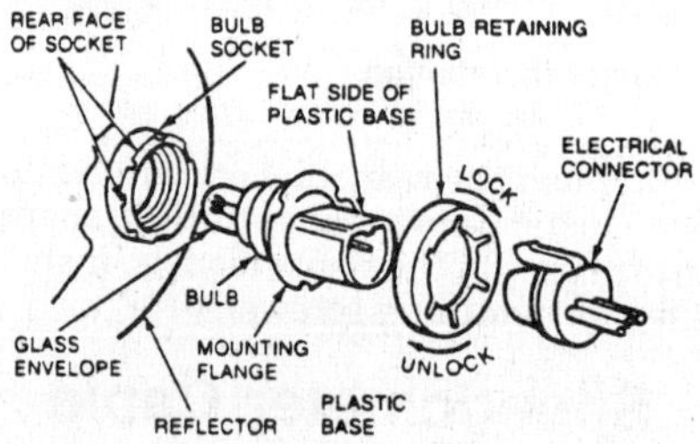

Halogen bulb replacement—aerodynamic type headlights

Front Turn Signal and Parking Lights

REMOVAL & INSTALLATION

Escort/Lynx

1981-85

1. Remove the screws that retain the headlamp door (bezel).
2. Pull the headlight door (bezel) forward and remove the parking light bulb socket from the light assembly.
3. To install, reverse the procedure.

1985½ AND LATER

1. Remove the 3 screws attaching the parking light to the headlight housing.
2. Hold the parking light with both hands and pull forward to release the hidden attachment.
3. From the side, remove the bulb socket and replace the bulb.
4. To install, reverse the procedure.

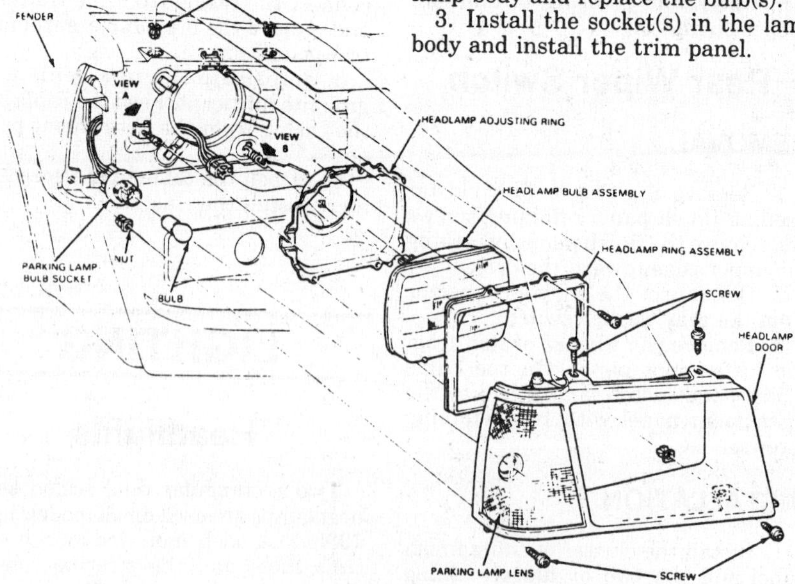

Front turn signal and parking light—1981-85 Escort/Lynx

EXP/LN7

1. Remove the 2 parking light retaining screws and pull the light assembly forward.
2. Remove the bulb socket by twisting and remove the bulb.
3. To install, reverse the procedure.

Tempo/Topaz

1984-85

1. Remove the headlamp door.
2. Remove the 3 screws attaching the parking light and pull forward.
3. Remove the bulb socket by twisting and remove the bulb.
4. To install, reverse the procedure.

1986 AND LATER

1. Remove the 2 screws retaining the parking light to the grille opening panel.
2. Hold the parking light with both hands and pull forward to release the hidden attachment.
3. Remove the bulb socket by twisting and replace the bulb.
4. To install, reverse the procedure.

Rear Turn Signal, Brake and Parking Lights

REMOVAL & INSTALLATION

All Models except Escort/Lynx 4-Door Liftgate

1. Bulbs can be serviced from the inside of the luggage compartment by removing the luggage compartment rear trim panel, if so equipped.
2. Remove the socket(s) from the lamp body and replace the bulb(s).
3. Install the socket(s) in the lamp body and install the trim panel.

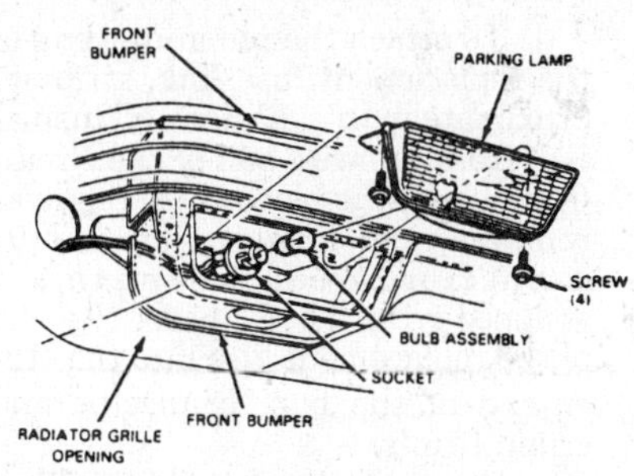

Front turn signal and parking light—EXP/LN7

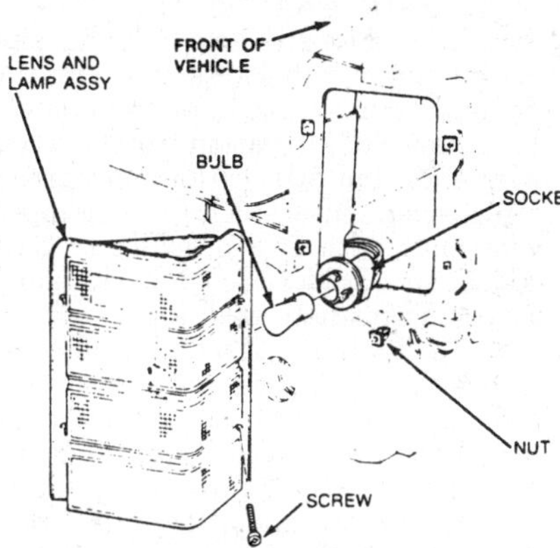

Rear turn signal and parking light—Escort/Lynx 4-door liftgate

Escort/Lynx 4-Door Liftgate

1. The bulbs may be serviced by removing the 4 screws retaining the light assembly to the rear quarter opening.
2. Pull the light assembly out of the opening and remove the light socket to replace the bulb.
3. To install, reverse the procedure.

TRAILER WIRING

Wiring the car for towing is fairly easy. There are a number of good wiring kits available and these should be used, rather than trying to design your own. All trailers will need brake lights and turn signals as well as tail lights and side marker lights. Most states require extra marker lights for overly wide trailers. Also, most states have recently required back-up lights for trailers, and most trailer manufacturers have been building trailers with back-up lights for several years.

Additionally, some Class I, most Class II and just about all Class III trailers will have electric brakes.

Add to this number an accessories wire, to operate trailer internal equipment or to charge the trailer's battery, and you can have as many as seven wires in the harness.

Determine the equipment on your trailer and buy the wiring kit necessary. The kit will contain all the wires needed, plus a plug adapter set which included the female plug, mounted on the bumper or hitch, and the male plug, wired into, or plugged into the trailer harness.

When installing the kit, follow the manufacturer's instructions. The color coding of the wires is standard throughout the industry.

One point to note: some domestic vehicles, and most imported vehicles, have separate turn signals. On most domestic vehicles, the brake lights and rear turn signals operate with the same bulb. For those vehicles with separate turn signals, you can purchase an isolation unit so that the brake lights won't blink whenever the turn signals are operated, or, you can go to your local electronics supply house and buy four diodes to wire in series with the brake and turn signal bulbs. Diodes will isolate the brake and turn signals. The choice is yours. The isolation units are simple and quick to install, but far more expensive than the diodes. The diodes, however, require more work to install properly, since they require the cutting of each bulb's wire and soldering in place of the diode.

One final point, the best kits are those with a spring loaded cover on the vehicle mounted socket. This cover prevents dirt and moisture from corroding the terminals. Never let the vehicle socket hang loosely; always mount it securely to the bumper or hitch.

CIRCUIT PROTECTION

Circuit breakers

Circuit breakers operate when a circuit overload exceeds its rated amperage. Once operated, they automatically reset after a certain period of time.

There are two kinds of circuit breaker, as previously mentioned, one type will reset itself. The second will not reset itself until the problem in the circuit has been repaired.

Turn Signal and Hazard Flasher

The turn signal flasher is located on the front side of the fuse panel. The hazard warning flasher is located on the rear side of the fuse panel.

Fuse Panel

The fuse panel is located below and to the left of the steering column.

Fuses are a one-time circuit protection. If a circuit is overloaded or shorts, the fuse will blow thus protecting the circuit. A fuse will continue to blow until the circuit is repaired.

Fuse Link

The fuse link is a short length of special, Hypalon (high temperature) insulated wire, integral with the engine compartment wiring harness and should not be confused with standard wire. It is several wire gauges smaller than the circuit which it protects. Under no circumstances should a fuse link replacement repair be made using a length of standard wire cut from bulk stock or from another wiring harness.

To repair any blown fuse link use the following procedure:

1. Determine which circuit is damaged, its location and the cause of the open fuse link. If the damaged fuse link is one of three fed by a common No. 10 or 12 gauge feed wire, determine the specific affected circuit.
2. Disconnect the negative battery cable.
3. Cut the damaged fuse link from the wiring harness and discard it. If the fuse link is one of three circuits fed by a single feed wire, cut it out of the harness at each splice end and discard it.
4. Identify and procure the proper fuse link and butt connectors for attaching the fuse link to the harness.
5. To repair any fuse link in a 3-link group with one feed:
   a. After cutting the open link out of the harness, cut each of the remaining undamaged fuse links close to the feed wire weld.
   b. Strip approximately ½" (13mm) of insulation from the detached ends of the two good fuse links, Then insert two wire ends into one end of a butt connector and carefully push one stripped end of the replacement fuse link into the same end of the butt connector and crimp all three firmly together.

NOTE: Care must be taken when fitting the three fuse links into the butt connector as the internal diameter is a snug fit for three wires. Make sure to use a proper crimping tool. Pliers, side cutter, etc. will not apply the

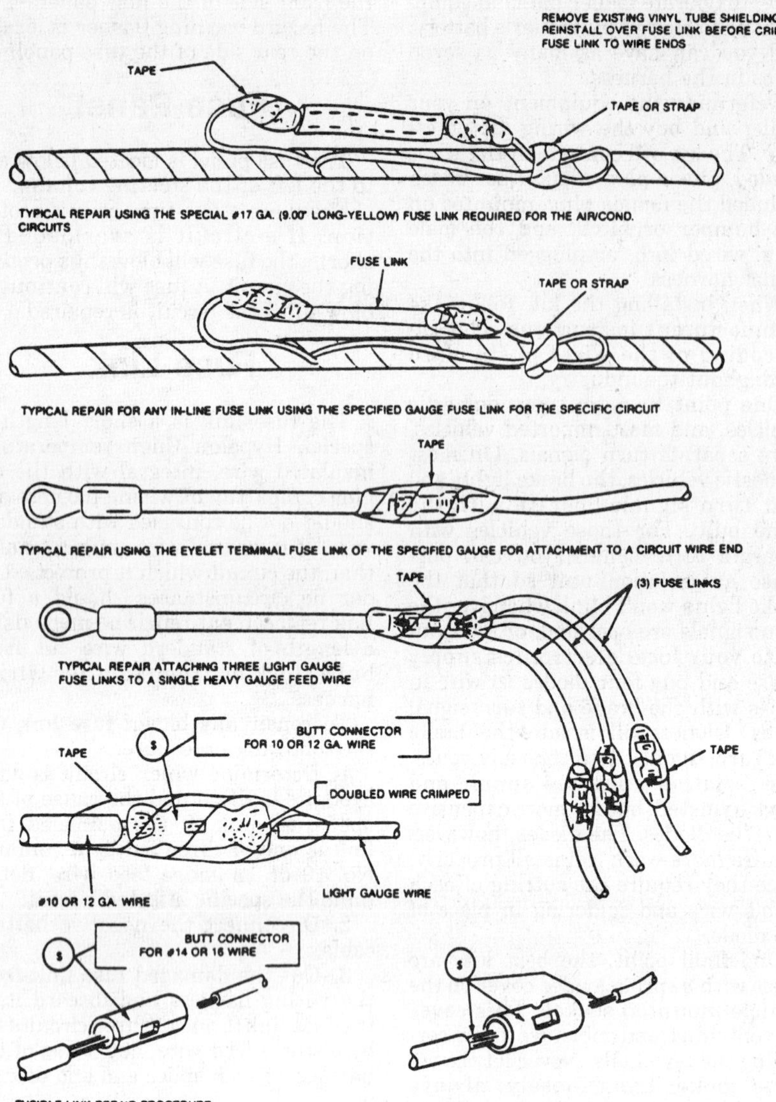

General fuse link repair procedures

proper crimp to retain the wires and withstand a pull test.

c. After crimping the butt connector to the three fuse links, cut the weld portion from the feed wire and strip approximately ½" (13mm) of insulation from the cut end. Insert the stripped end into the open end of the butt connector and crimp very firmly.

d. To attach the remaining end of the replacement fuse link, strip approximately ½" (13mm) of insulation from the wire end of the circuit from which the blown fuse link was removed, and firmly crimp a butt connector or equivalent to the stripped wire. Then, insert the end of the replacement link into the other end of the butt connector and crimp firmly.

e. Using rosin core solder with a consistency of 60 percent tin and 40 percent lead, solder the connectors and the wires at the repairs and insulate with electrical tape.

6. To replace any fuse link on a single circuit in a harness, cut out the damaged portion, strip approximately ½" (13mm) of insulation from the two wire ends and attach the appropriate replacement fuse link to the stripped wire ends with two proper size butt connectors. Solder the connectors and wires and insulate with tape.

7. To repair any fuse link which has an eyelet terminal on one end such as the charging circuit, cut off the open fuse link behind the weld, strip approximately ½" (13mm) of insulation from the cut end and attach the appropriate new eyelet fuse link to the cut stripped wire with an appropriate size butt connector. Solder the connectors and wires at the repair and insulate with tape.

8. Connect the negative battery cable to the battery and test the system for proper operation.

NOTE: Do not mistake a resistor wire for a fuse link. The resistor wire is generally longer and has print stating, "Resistor-don't cut or splice".

When attaching a single No. 16, 17, 18 or 20 gauge fuse link to a heavy gauge wire, always double the stripped wire end of the fuse link before inserting and crimping it into the butt connector for positive wire retention.

TRANSAXLE

Halfshafts

The front wheel drive halfshafts are a one piece design. Constant velocity joint (CV) are used at each end. The left hand (driver's side) halfshaft is solid steel and is shorter than the right side halfshaft. The right hand (passenger's side) halfshaft is depending on year and model, constructed of tubular steel or solid construction. The automatic and manual transaxles use similar halfshafts.

The halfshafts can be replaced individually. The CV joint or boots can be cleaned or replaced. Individual parts of the CV joints are not available. The inboard and outboard joints differ in size. CV joint parts are fitted and should never be mixed or substituted with a part from another joint. Inspect the boots periodically for cuts or splits. If a cut or split is found, inspect the joint, repack it with grease and install a new boot.

REMOVAL & INSTALLATION

Escort, Lynx, EXP, LN7, Tempo, Topaz

NOTE: Special tools are required for removing, installing and servicing halfshafts. They are listed by descriptive name (Ford part number). Front Hub Installer Adapter (T81P1104A), Wheel Bolt Adapters (T81P1104B or T83P1104BH), CV Joint Separator (T81P3514A), Front Hub Installer/Remover (T81P1104C), Shipping Plug Tool (T81P1177B), Dust Deflector Installer CV Joint (T83P3425AH), Differential Rotator (T81P4026A).

It is necessary to have on hand new hub nuts and new lower control arm to steering knuckle attaching nuts and bolts. Once removed, these parts must not be reused. The torque holding ability is destroyed during removal.

1. Loosen the front hub nut and the wheel lugs.
2. Jack up the front of the car and safely support it on jackstands.
3. Remove the tire and wheel assembly. Remove and discard the front hub nut. Save the washers.

NOTE: Halfshaft removal and installation are the same for Manual and Automatic transaxles EXCEPT: The configuration of the AT (automatic transaxle) differential case requires that the right hand halfshaft assembly be removed first. The differential service tool T81P4026 (Differential Rotator) is then inserted to drive the left hand halfshaft from the transaxle. If only the left hand halfshaft is to be serviced, removed the right hand halfshaft from the transaxle side and support it with a length of wire. Drive the left hand halfshaft assembly from the transaxle.

4. Remove the bolt that retains the brake hose to the strut.
5. Remove the nut and bolt securing the lower ball joint and separate the joint from the steering knuckle by inserting a pry bar between the stabilizer and frame and pulling downward. Take care not to damage the ball joint boot.

NOTE: The lower control arm ball joint fits into a pocket formed in a plastic disc rotor shield, on some models. The shield must be carefully bent back away from the ball joint while prying the ball joint out of the steering knuckle. Do not contact or pry on the lower control arm.

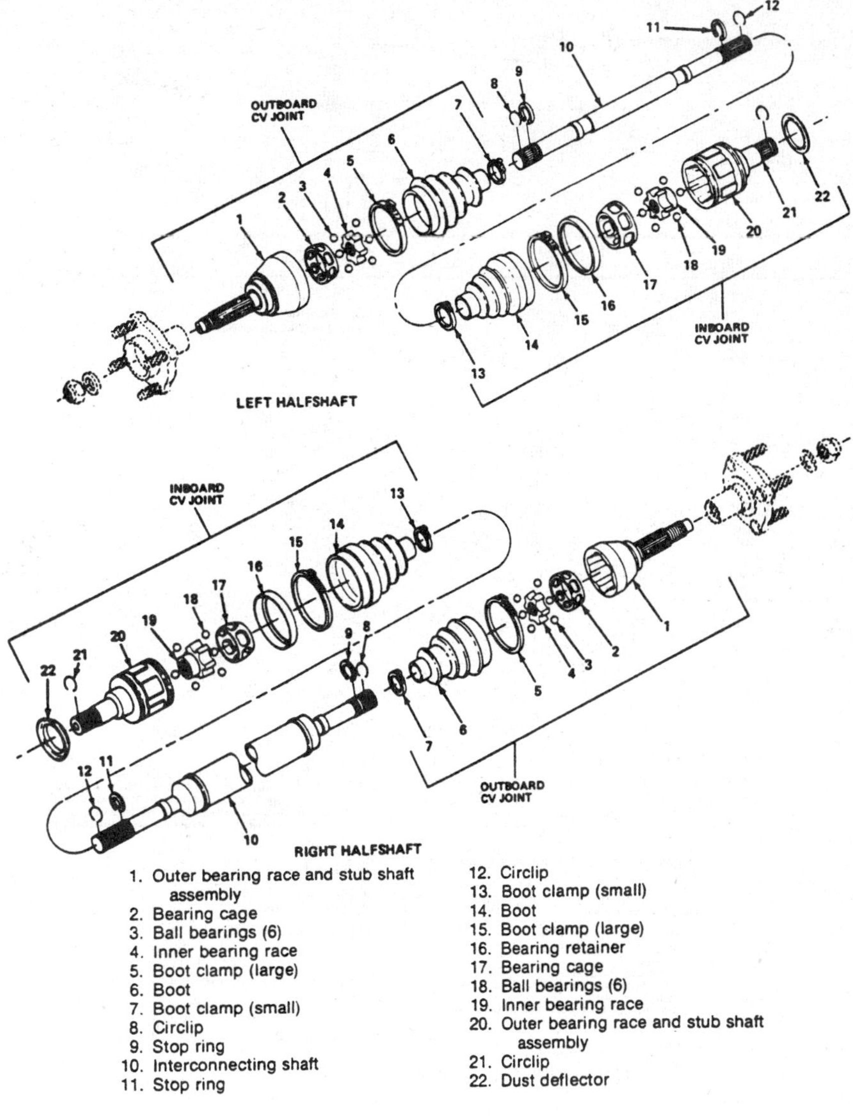

Halfshafts exploded view—1981-85

6. Remove the halfshaft from the differential housing, using a pry bar. Position the pry bar between the case and the shaft and pry the joint away from the case. Do not damage the oil seal, the CV joint boot or the CV dust deflector. Install tool number T81P1177B (Shipping plug) to prevent fluid loss and differential side gear misalignment.
7. Support the end of the shaft with a piece of wire, suspending it from a chassis member.
8. Separate the shaft from the front hub using the special remover/installer tool and adapters. Instructions for the use of the tool may be found in the Front Wheel Bearing section.

WARNING: Never use a hammer to force the shaft from the wheel hub. Damage to the internal parts of the CV joint may occur.

9. Install a new circlip on the inboard CV joint stub shaft. Align the splines of the inboard CV joint stub shaft with the splines in the differential. Push the CV joint into the differential until the circlip seats on the side gear. Some force may be necessary to seat.
10. Carefully align the splines of the outboard CV joint stub shaft with the splines in the front wheel hub. Push the shaft into the hub as far as possible. Install the remover/installer tool and pull the CV stub shaft through the hub.
11. Connect the control arm to the steering knuckle and install a new mounting bolt and nut. Torque to 37-44 ft.lb.

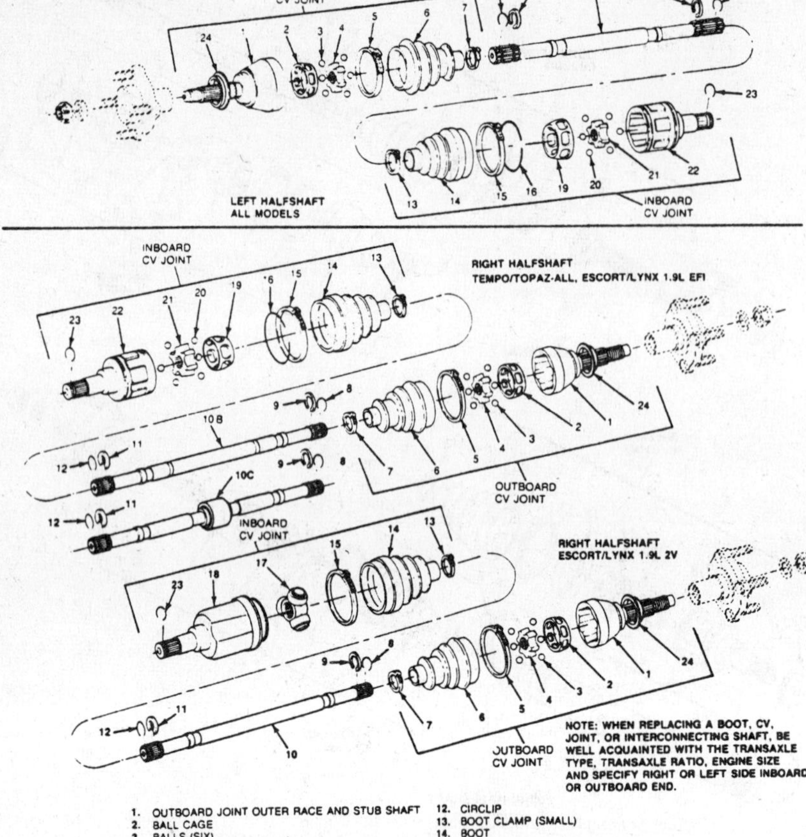

Halfshafts exploded view—1986 and later

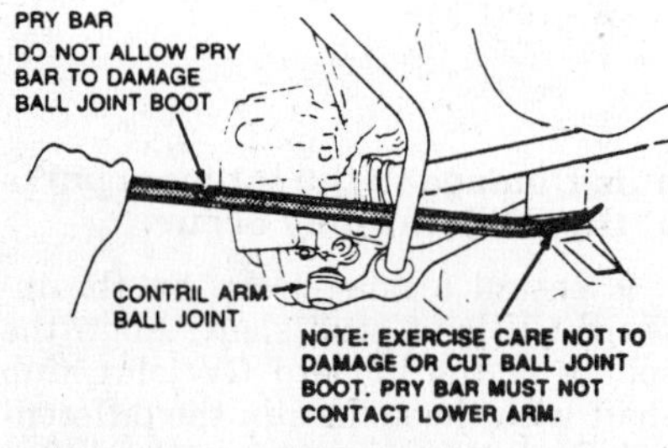

Separating the ball joint from the steering knuckle

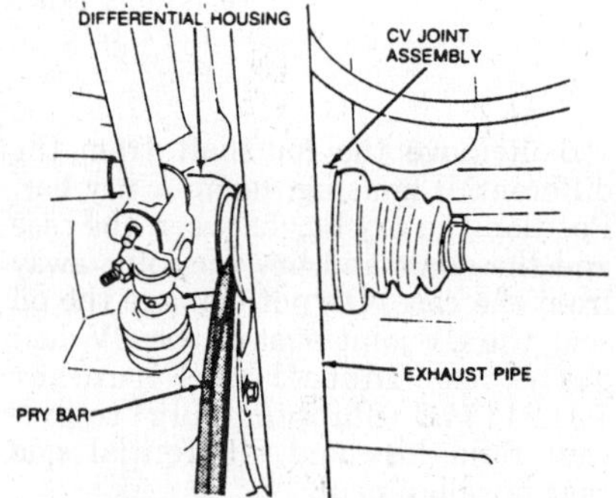

Separating the CV joint from the differential with a prybar

12. Connect the brake line to the strut.
13. Install the front hub washer and new hub nut. Install the tire and wheel assembly.
14. Lower the car to the ground. Tighten the center hub nut to 180-200 ft.lb. Stake the nut using a blunt chisel.

Taurus and Sable

When removing both the left and right halfshafts, shipping plug tools No. T81P-1177-B must be installed. Failure to use these tools can result in dislocation of the differential side gears. Should the gears become misaligned, the differential will have to be removed from the transaxle to realign the side gears.

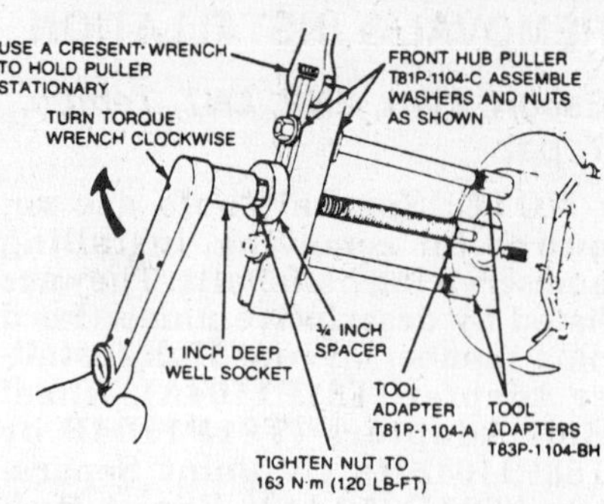

Installing the CV joint shaft with the special tool

CAUTION

***DO NOT** start this procedure unless the following parts are to known to be available: A new hub nut assembly, a new lower control arm-to-steering knuckle nut/bolt and a new inboard CV-joint stub shaft circlip. Once these parts are removed, they must not be reused during assembly; their torque holding ability or retension capability is destroyed during removal.*

REMOVAL & INSTALLATION

1. Remove the wheel cover/hub cover and loosen the wheel nuts. Remove the hub retainer and washer; the nut must be discarded after removal.
2. Raise and support the vehicle on jackstands, then remove the wheel/tire assembly.
3. Remove the ball joint-to-steering knuckle nut. Using a punch and a hammer, drive the bolt from the steering knuckle; discard the bolt/nut.
4. Using a medium pry bar, separate the ball joint from the steering knuckle.

NOTE: Position the end of the pry bar outside of the bushing pocket to avoid damaging the bushing. Use care to prevent damage to the ball joint boot.

5. Remove the stabilizer bar link from the stabilizer bar.
6. If removing the right side halfshaft/link shaft from the ATX or the MTX, perform the following procedures:
   a. Remove the bearing support-to-bracket bolts, then slide the shaft out of the transaxle. Using a piece of wire, support the end of the shaft from a convenient underbody component.

NOTE: DO NOT allow the shaft to hang unsupported, for damage to the outboard CV-joint may occur.

   b. Separate the outboard CV-

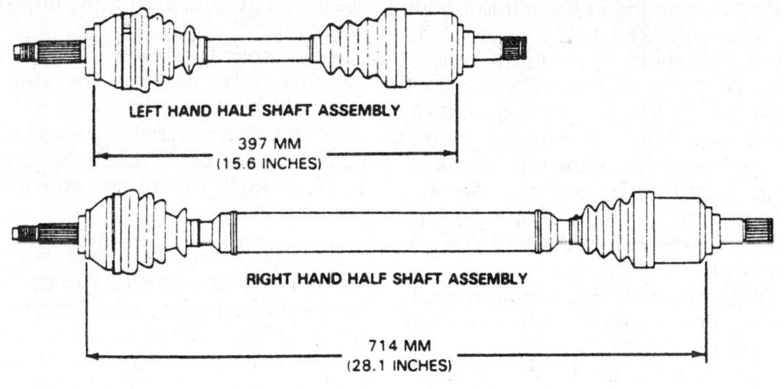

Halfshaft lengths—through 1983

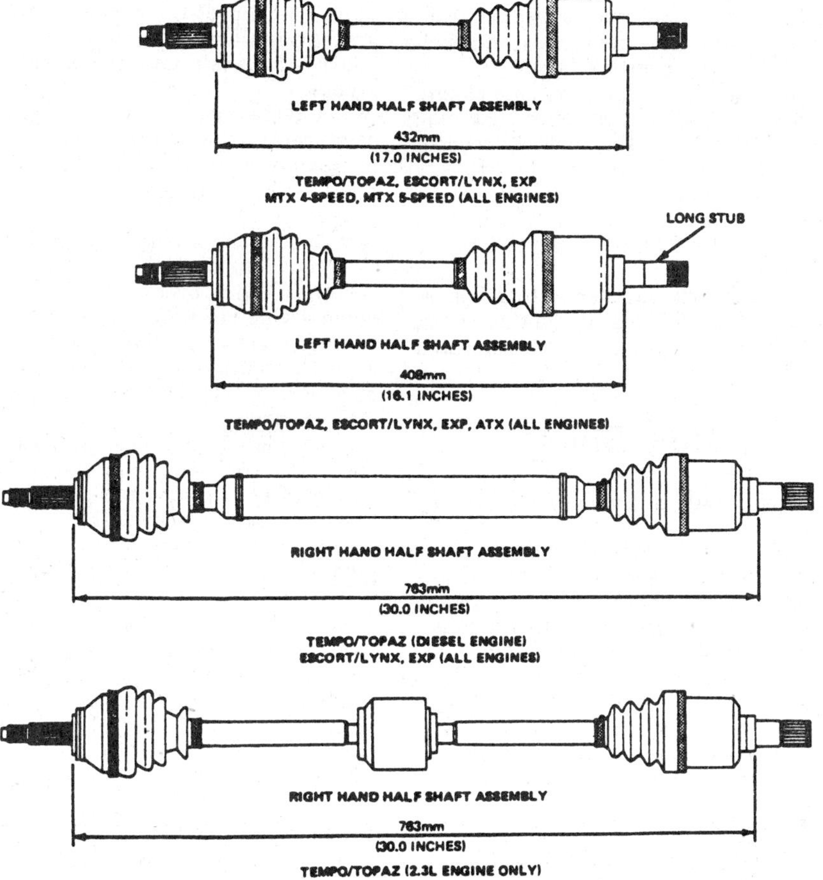

Halfshaft lengths—1984 and later

joint from the hub using the front hub remover tool No. T81P-1104-C, the meteric adapters tools No. T83-P-1104-BH, T86P-1104-Al and T81P-1104-A.

NOTE: NEVER use a hammer to separate the outboard CV-joint stub shaft from the hub; damage to the CV-joint threads and internal components may result. The right side link shaft and halfshaft assembly is removed as a complete unit.

7. If removing the right side halfshaft from the AXOD (overdrive) or the left side halfshaft from the MTX, perform the following procedures:

a. Position the CV-joint puller tool No. T86P-3514-A1 between the CV-joint and transaxle case. Turn the steering hub and/or wire the strut assembly out of the way.

b. Assemble the screw extension tool No. T86P-3514-A2 into the CV-Joint puller and hand tighten. Assemble the screw impact slide hammer tool No. D79-100-A onto the extension and remove the CV-joint.

c. Support the end of the shaft by suspending it from a convenient underbody component with a piece of wire. DO NOT allow the shaft to hang unsupported, damage to the outboard CV-joint may occur.

d. Separate the outboard CV-joint from the hub using the front hub remover tool No. T81P-1104-C, the meteric adapters tools No. T83-P-1104-BH, T86P-1104-Al and T81P-1104-A.

NOTE: Never use a hammer to separate the outboard CV-joint stub shaft from the hub. Damage to the CV-joint threads and internal components may result.

e. Remove the halfshaft assembly from the vehicle.

8. To remove the left side halfshaft from an ATX, perform the following procedures:

NOTE: Due to the ATX case configuration, the right side halfshaft assembly MUST BE removed first.

a. Remove the right hand halfshaft assembly (from the transaxle) and support it on a wire.

b. Insert the differential rotator tool No. T81P-4026-A into the transaxle and drive the left side inboard CV-joint assembly from the transaxle.

c. Support the end of the shaft by suspending it from a convenient underbody component with a piece of wire. DO NOT allow the shaft to hang unsupported, for damage to the outboard CV-joint may occur.

d. Using the front hub removal tool No. T81P-1104-C, the meteric adapter tools No. T83-P-1104-BH, T86P-1104-Al and T81P-1104-A, separate the outboard CV-joint from the hub.

NOTE: Never use a hammer to separate the outboard CV-joint halfshaft from the hub. Damage to the CV-joint threads and internal components may result.

e. Remove the halfshaft assembly from the vehicle.

9. To install, use a new circlip (on the inboard CV-joint), oil seal and reverse the removal procedures. Torque the control arm-to-steering knuckle

nut/bolt to 40-55 ft.lb.; the stabilizer bar-to-stabilizer link nut to 35-50 ft.lb.; the wheel lug nuts to 80-105 ft.lb. and the hub nut to 180-200 ft.lb. Refill the transaxle to the proper level with the specified fluid.

CV Joint and Boot

REMOVAL & INSTALLATION

Except Inboard on 5-Speed MT

1. Clamp the halfshaft in a vise that is equipped with soft jaw covers. Do not allow the vise jaws to contact the boot or boot clamp.
2. Cut the large boot clamp with a pair of side cutters and peel the clamp away from the boot. Roll the boot back over the shaft after the clamp has been removed.
3. Check the grease for contamination by rubbing some between two fingers. If the grease feels gritty, it is contaminated and the joint will have to be disassembled, cleaned and inspected. If the grease is not contaminated and the CV joints were operating satisfactorily, repack them with grease and install a new boot, or reinstall the old boot with a new clamp.
4. If disassembly is required, clamp the interconnecting shaft in a soft jawed vise with the CV joint pointing downward so that the inner bearing race is exposed.
5. Use a brass drift and hammer, give a sharp tap to the inner bearing race to dislodge the internal snapring and separate the CV joint from the interconnecting shaft. Take care to secure the CV joint so that it does not drop on the ground after separation. Remove the clamp and boot from the shaft.
6. Remove and discard the snapring at the end of the interconnecting shaft. The stop ring, located just below the snapring should be removed and replaced only if damaged or worn.
7. Clean the interconnecting shaft splines and install a new snapring, and stop ring if removed. To install the snapring correctly, start one end in the groove and work the snapring over the shaft end and into the groove.
8. Interconnecting shafts are different, depending on year and model application. The outboard end of the shaft is about ¼" (6mm) longer from the end of the boot groove to the shaft end than the inboard end. Take measurement to insure correct installation.
9. If removed, install a new boot. Make sure the boot is seated in the mounting groove and secure it in position with a new clamp.
10. Pack the CV joint and boot with the grease supplied in the joint or boot kit. The inboard joint should be packed with about 90 grams of grease; the boot with about 45 grams of grease. The outboard joint should be packed with about 45 grams of grease, and the boot with about 45 grams of grease. If grease from a replacement kit is not on hand, use only grease Ford Number E2FZ19590A or equivalent.
11. With the boot peeled back, position the CV joint on the shaft and tap into position using a plastic tipped hammer. The CV joint is fully seated when the snapring locks into the groove cut into the CV joint inner bearing race. Check for seating by attempting to pull the joint away from the shaft.
12. Remove all excess grease from the CV joint external surface and position the boot over the joint.
13. Before installing the boot clamp, make sure all air pressure that may have built up in the boot is removed. Pry up on the boot lip to allow the air to escape. Refer to the halfshaft length specifications and adjust the shaft to specs before tightening the boots clamps.
14. The large end clamp should be installed after making sure of the correct shaft length and that the boot is seated in its groove.

Dust Shield

REMOVAL & INSTALLATION

The dust shield on the outside end of the CV joint is removed by using a light hammer and drift and tapping lightly around the seal until it becomes free. Install the dust shield with the flange facing outboard. Special Tools T83T3132A1 and T83P3425AH or equivalent (Spindle/Axle Tool and Dust Seal Installer) are necessary to drive the seal into position.

Inboard CV-Joint 5-Speed

REMOVAL & INSTALLATION

1. Remove the large clamp and roll the boot back over the shaft. Remove the wire ring bearing retainer.
2. Remove the outer race. Pull the inner race and bearing assembly out until it rests against the snapring. Use a pair of snapring pliers and spread the stop ring and slide it back down the shaft.
3. Slide the inner bearing and race assembly down the shaft to allow access to the snapring. Remove the snapring.
4. Remove the inner race and bearing assembly. Remove the stop ring and boot if necessary.
5. Install a new boot and end clamp, fold the boot back, after cleaning the shaft splines. Install the stop ring in position.

NOTE: The LH interconnecting shaft is the same end for end. The outboard or inboard CV joint may be installed at either end. The RH interconnecting shaft is different end for end. The tapered faces of the center balance faces outboard.

6. Install a new snapring in the groove nearest the end of the shaft. Start one end of the snapring in the groove and word the snapring over the end of the shaft into the mounting groove.
7. Fill the boot with about 45 grams of grease and the outer race with about 90 grams of grease. Push the inner race and bearing assembly into the outer race by hand.
8. Install the wire ball retainer into the groove inside the outer race. Position the CV joint over the shaft and tap down with a plastic hammer until the snapring locks into the groove. Make sure the splines are aligned before hammering the joint into position.
9. Remove all excess grease from the outside of the CV joint. Position the boot and secure in retaining groove after removing trapped air and checking for proper length.

SERVICE

NOTE: Disassembly of the CV joints is necessary when the grease is contaminated. Contamination of the lubricant can damage the parts of the joint, an inspection is necessary to determine if replacement is required.

Outboard Joint (Wheel Hub Side)

DISASSEMBLY

NOTE: Two different bearing cage designs are used. One design uses four equal sized bearing cutouts and two elongated ones, the second design uses six equal sized cutouts. The step by step instructions will indicate the procedures necessary for the different designs.

1. After the stub shaft has been removed from the axle, clamp in a soft jawed vise with the bearings facing up.

2. Press down on the inner race until it tiles enough to allow the removal of a ball bearing. If the bearing is tight, it might be necessary to tap the inner race with a plastic faced hammer. Tap on the race, do not hit the cage.

3. When the cage is tilted, remove a ball. Repeat until all six balls have been removed. If the balls are tight, take a blunt edged pry bar and pry the balls from the cage. Be careful not to scratch or damage the inner race or cage.

4. Pivot the bearing cage and inner race 90° (straight up and down) to the center line of the outer race. Align the cage windows with the lands (grooves) in the outer race. When the windows are in alignment with the lands, lift the assembly from the outer race.

5. Separate the inner race from the cage.

- Six equal window type: rotate the inner race up and out of the cage.
- Two elongated window type: Pivot the inner race until it is straight up and down in the cage. Align one of the inner race bands with one of the elongated windows. Put the land through the elongated window and rotate the inner race up and lift out of the cage.

6. Wash all of the parts in safe solvent. Inspect the parts for wear. If the components of the CV joint are worn, a complete kit must be installed. Do not replace a joint merely because the parts appear polished. Shiny areas in the ball races and on the curves of the cage are normal. A CV joint should be replaced only if a component is cracked, broken, severely pitted or otherwise unserviceable.

ASSEMBLY

1. Apply a light coating of grease on the inner and outer races. Install the inner race in the bearing cage by turning the inner race 'in the bearing cage by turning the inner race 90°. Position the land through the cage window and rotate into position.

2. Install the inner race and cage assembly into the outer race. Install the assembly in the vertical position and pivot into position. The counterbores in the inner race must be facing upwards.

3. Align the bearing cage and inner race with the outer race. Tilt the inner race and cage and install a ball bearing. Repeat until all six bearings are installed.

4. Pack the CV joint with ⅓ of the packet of grease. Use only the specified grease, Ford Part Number E2FZ-19590-A or the equivalent. Pack the grease into the joint by forcing it through the splined hole in the inner race.

Inboard Joint (Transaxle Side)

DISASSEMBLY

1. Remove the circlip from the end of the CV joint stub shaft. Inspect the dust deflector. If it is cracked or damaged it must be replaced. Refer to the section that appears later in this section.

2. Use a pair of side cutters to cut the ball retainer and discard it. The retainer is not required for assembly of the CV joint.

3. Gently tap the CV joint on the bench until the bearing assembly comes loose and can be removed by hand.

4. Remove the balls from the cage by prying them out. Take care not to scratch or damage the inner ball race or cage.

5. Rotate the inner race until the cage windows are aligned with the lands. Lift from the cage through the wider side.

6. Clean all of the component parts in safe solvent and inspect for wear. If the components of the CV joint are worn, a complete kit must be installed. Do not replace a joint merely because the parts appear polished. Shiny areas in the ball races and on the curves of the cage are normal. A CV joint should be replaced only is a component is cracked, broken, severely pitted or otherwise unserviceable.

ASSEMBLY

1. Install a new circlip on the stub shaft. Do not over expand or twist the clip.

2. If the dust deflector needs replacing, do so now. See the next section for instructions.

3. Install the inner bearing race into the bearing cage. Install the race through the larger end of the cage with the inner race hub facing the large end of the cage.

4. Align the bearing cage and inner race. Install the ball bearings. Press the bearings into position with the heel of your hand.

5. Pack the outer race with grease. Use only the specified grease, Ford Part Number D8RZ-1950-A or the equivalent.

6. Position the inner race and bearing assembly into the outer race. The assembly should be installed with the inner hub facing the outer race.

7. Push the inner race and bearing assembly into the outer race.

DUST DEFLECTOR REPLACEMENT

NOTE: The dust deflector should be replaced only if inspection determines it to be cracked, broken or deteriorated.

Remove the old deflector. Soak the new dust deflector in a container of hot water and let it soak for five to ten minutes. Position the dust deflector over the sleeve with the ribbed side facing the CV joint. Tap the deflector into position with the Dust Deflector Installer (T81P3425A) and a hammer.

Front Axle Hub And Bearings Taurus and Sable

Front wheel bearings are located in the front knuckle, not the rotor. The bearings are protected by inner and outer grease seals and an additional inner grease shield immediately inboard of the inner grease seal. The wheel hub is installed with an interference fit to the constant velocity universal joint outer race shaft. The hub nut and washer are installed and tightened to 180-200 ft.lb. (240-270 Nm). The rotor fits loosely on the hub assembly and is secured when the wheel and wheel nuts are installed.

The front wheel bearings have a set-right design that requires no scheduled maintenance. The bearing design relies on component stack-up and deformation/torque at assembly to determine bearing setting. Therefore, bearings cannot be adjusted. In addition to maintaining bearing adjustment, the hub nut torque of 180-200 ft.lb. (240-270 Nm) restricts bearing/hub relative movement and maintains axial position of the hub. Due to the importance of the hub nut torque/tension relationship, certain precautions must be taken during service.

REMOVAL & INSTALLATION

1. Remove the wheelcover/hub cover from the wheel and tire assembly and loosen the lug nuts.

2. Remove the hub retaining nut and washer by applying sufficient torque to the nut to overcome the prevailing torque feature of the crimp in the nut collar. Do not use an impact type tool to remove the hub nut. The hub nut must be discarded after removal.

3. Loosen the three strut top mount to apron nuts.

4. Raise and support the vehicle safely. Remove the wheel and tire assembly.

5. Remove the brake caliper by removing the caliper locating pins and rotating the caliper off of the rotor, starting from the lower end of the caliper and lifting upward. Lift the caliper off the rotor and hang it free of the rotor. Do not allow the caliper assembly to hang from the brake hose. Support the caliper assembly with a length of wire.

6. Remove the rotor from the hub by pulling it off the hub bolts. If the rotor is difficult to remove from the hub, strike the rotor sharply between the studs with a rubber or plastic hammer.

NOTE: If the rotor will not pull off, apply a suitable penetrating fluid to the inboard and outboard rotor hub mating surfaces. Install a 3 jaw puller and remove the rotor by pulling on the rotor outside diameter and pushing on the hub center. If excessive force is required, check the rotor for lateral runout prior to installation.

7. The lateral runout must be checked with the nuts clamping the stamped section of the rotor. Remove the rotor splash shield.

8. Disconnect the lower control arm and tie rod from the steering knuckle. Loosen the strut pinch bolt, but do not remove the strut.

9. Install hub remover/installer T81P-1104-A with T81P-1104-C and hub knuckle adapters T83P-1104-BH1 and T86P-1104-A1 or equivalent.

10. Remove the hub, bearing and knuckle assembly by pushing out the constant velocity joint outer shaft until it is free of assembly. Wire the halfshaft to the body to maintain a level position.

11. Remove the strut bolt and slide the hub/bearings/knuckle assembly off the strut using spindle carrier lever T85M-3206-A or equivalent. Carefully remove the support wire and carry the hub/bearing /knuckle assembly to a suitable workbench.

12. On the bench, install front hub puller D80L-1002-L and shaft protector D80L-625-1 or equivalent, with the jaws of the puller on the knuckle bosses and remove the hub.

NOTE: Be sure the shaft protector is centered, clears the bearing ID and rests on the end face of the hub journal.

13. Remove the snapring, which retains the bearing in the knuckle assembly, with the snapring pliers and discard.

14. Using a suitable hydraulic press, place the front bearing spacer T86P-1104-A2 or equivalent step side up on the press plate and position the knuckle (outboard side up) on the spacer.

15. Install bearing remover T83P-1104-AH2 or equivalent centered on the bearing inner race and press the bearing out of the knuckle. Discard the old bearing.

16. Remove the halfshaft and place it in a suitable vise.

17. Remove the bearing dust seal by equally tapping on the outer edge with a light duty hammer and a suitable tool. Discard the dust seal.

18. Remove all foreign material from the knuckle bearing bore and hub bearing journal to ensure the correct seating of a new bearing.

NOTE: If the hub bearing journal is scored or damaged, replace the hub. Do not attempt to service a bad hub. The front wheel bearings are of a cartridge design and are pre-greased, sealed and require no schedule maintenance. The bearings are preset and cannot be adjusted. If a bearing is disassembled for any reason, it must be replaced as a unit. No individual service seals, roller or races are available.

19. Place the front bearing spacer T86P-1104-A or equivalent step side down on a press plate and position the knuckle (outboard side down) on a spacer. Position a new bearing in the inboard side of the knuckle.

20. Install the bearing installer T86P-1104-A3 or equivalent (undercut side facing the bearing) on the bearing outer race and press bearing into the knuckle.

21. Check that the bearing seats completely against the shoulder of the knuckle bore. The bearing installer must be installed as indicated above to prevent bearing damage during installation.

22. Install a new snapring in the knuckle groove with a suitable pair of snapring pliers. Place the front bearing spacer T86P-1104-A2 or equivalent on the arbor press plate and position the hub on the tool with the lugs facing downward. Position the knuckle assembly (outboard side down) on the hub barrel.

23. Place bearing remover T83P-1104-AH2 or equivalent flat side down, centered on the inner race of the bearing and press down on the tool until the bearing is fully seated onto the hub. Check that the hub rotates freely in the knuckle after installation.

24. Prior to the hub/bearing/knuckle installation, replace the bearing dust seal on the outboard CV-joint with a new seal from the bearing kit.

25. Install the dust seal, ensuring the seal flange faces outboard toward the bearing. Use drive tube T83P-3132-A1 and front bearing dust seal installer T86P-1104-A4 or equivalent.

26. Suspend the hub/bearing/knuckle assembly on the vehicle with a wire and attach the strut loosely to the knuckle. Lubricate the CV-joint stub shaft splines with a SAE 30 weight motor oil and insert the shaft onto the hub splines as far as possible using hand pressure only. Check that the splines are properly engaged.

27. Temporarily fasten the rotor to hub with washers and two wheel lugnuts. Insert a steel rod into the rotor diameter and rotate it clockwise to contact the knuckle.

28. Install the hub nut washer and new hub nut. Rotate the nut clockwise to seat the CV-joint. Tighten the nut to 180-200 ft.lb. do not use power or impact tools to install the hub nut. Remove the steel rod, washers and lug nuts.

29. Install the disc brake caliper over the rotor. Be sure the outer brake shoe spring hook is seated under the upper arm of the knuckle.

30. Complete installation of the front suspension components. Install the wheel and tire assembly, tighten the lug nuts finger tight. Lower the vehicle and block the wheels to prevent the vehicle from moving. Tighten the lug nuts to 80-105 ft.lb.

NOTE: Replacement lug nuts or studs must be of the same type and size as those being replaced.

31. Tighten the hub nut to 180-200 ft.lb. Install the wheel cover or hub cover. Lower the vehicle completely to the ground and remove wheel blocks. Road test the vehicle and check to see if the vehicle is operating properly.

Front Wheel Bearings Escort, Lynx, EXP, LN7, Tempo and Topaz

The bearing design relies on component stack up and deformation/torque at assembly to determine bearing setting. The bearings, therefore, cannot be adjusted after assembly.

The front bearings are located in the front suspension knuckle, not in the rotor or wheel hub. Two inner and one outer seal protect the bearings (the seal closer to the CV-joint is a shield) on models through 1983-1984 and later models use bearings of a cartridge design and are pregreased and sealed, and require no scheduled maintenance. The wheel hub is installed with a close slip fit through the wheel bearings and an interference fit over the splines of the halfshaft's constant velocity stub shaft. A flat washer and a staked hub nut maintain the correct endplay and prevent the wheel bearing inner races from spinning on the wheel hub.

REMOVAL

NOTE: The wheel hub and knuckle must be removed for bearing replacement or servicing. A special puller is required to remove and install the hub. (Ford Part Number T81P-1104-A, T81P-1104-C and adapters T81P-1104-B or T83P-1104-AH). The adaptors screw over the lugs and attach to the puller, which uses a long screw attached to the end of the stub shaft to pull off or install the hub.

1. Remove wheel cover and slightly loosen the lugs.
2. Remove the hub retaining nut and washer. The nut is crimped staked to the shaft. Use a socket and sufficient torque to overcome the locking force of the crimp.
3. Raise the front of the car and support safely with jackstands. Remove the tire and wheel assembly.
4. Remove the brake caliper and disc rotor. Refer to the BRAKE SYSTEM section for the necessary procedures.
5. Disconnect the lower control arm and tie rod from the steering knuckle. Loosen tow top strut mounting nuts, but do not remove them. Install the hub remover/installer tool and remove the hub. If the outer bearing is seized on the hub remove it with a puller.
6. Remove the front suspension knuckle.
7. On models through 1983, after the front knuckle is removed, pull out the inner grease shield, the inner seal and bearing.
8. Remove the outer grease seal and bearing.
9. If you hope to reuse the bearings, clean them in a safe solvent. After cleaning the bearings and races, carefully inspect them for damage, pitting, heat coloring etc. If damage etc. has occurred, replace all components (bearings, cups and seals). Always replace the seals with new ones. Always use a new hub nut whenever the old one has been removed.
10. If new bearings are to be used, remove the inner and outer races from the knuckle. A three jawed puller on a slide hammer will do the job.
11. Clean the interior bore of the knuckle.
12. On 1984 and later models, remove the snapring that retains the bearing in the steering knuckle.
13. Position the knuckle, outboard side up under a hydraulic press with appropriate adapters in place, and press the bearing from the knuckle.
14. Clean the interior bore of the knuckle.

INSTALLATION

1. On models through 1983, install the new bearing cups using a suitable driver. Be sure the cups are fully seated in the knuckle bore.
2. Pack the wheel bearings with multi-purpose lubricant (Ford part number C1AZ-19590-B or the equivalent). If a bearing packer is not available, place a large portion of grease into the palm of your hand and slide the edge of the roller cage through the grease with your other hand. Work as much grease as you can between the bearing rollers.
3. Put a sufficient amount of grease between the bearing cups in the center of the knuckle. Apply a thin film of grease on the bearing cups.
4. Place the outer bearing and new grease seal into the knuckle. Place a thin film of grease on all three lips of the new outer seal.
5. Turn the knuckle over and install the inner bearing and seal. Once again, apply a thin film of grease to the three lips of the seal.
6. Install the inner grease shield. A small block of wood may be used to tap the seal into the knuckle bore.
7. Keep the knuckle in the vertical position or the inner bearing will fall out. Start the wheel hub into the outer knuckle bore and push the hub as far as possible through the outer and inner bearings by hand.

NOTE: Prior to installing the hub, make sure it is clean and free from burrs. Use crocus cloth to polish the hub is necessary. It is important to use only hand pressure when installing the hub, make sure the hub is through both the outer and inner bearings.

8. With the hub as fully seated as possible through the bearings, position the hub and knuckle to the front strut. Refer to SUSPENSION AND STEERING for instructions on attaching the strut and knuckle.
9. On 1984 and later models, position the knuckle. outboard side down on the appropriate adapter and press in the new bearing. Be sure the bearing is fully seated. Install a new retainer snapring.
10. Install the hub using tool T83T-1104-AH3 and press. Check that the hub rotates freely.
11. Lubricate the stub shaft splines with a thin film of SAE 20 motor oil. Use hand pressure only and insert the splines into the knuckle and hub as far as possible.

NOTE: Do not allow the hub to back out of the bearings while installing the stub shaft, otherwise it will be necessary to start all over from Step 7.

12. Complete the installation of the suspension parts as described in SUSPENSION AND STEERING.
13. Install the hub remover/installer tool and tighten the center adapter to 120 foot pounds, this ensures the hub is fully seated.
14. Remove the installer tool and install the hub washer and nut. Tighten the hub nut finger tight.
15. Install the disc rotor, caliper etc. in reverse order of removal. Refer to the BRAKE SYSTEM section, if necessary, for procedures.
16. Install the tire and wheel assembly and snug the wheel lugs.
17. Lower the car to the ground, set the parking brake and block the wheels.
18. Tighten the wheel lugs to 80-105 ft.lb.
19. Tighten the center hub nut to 180-200 ft.lb. DO NOT USE A POWER WRENCH TO TIGHTEN THE HUB NUT.
20. Stake the hub nut using a rounded, dull chisel. DO NOT USE A SHARP CHISEL.

MANUAL TRANSAXLE

REMOVAL & INSTALLATION

Escort/Lynx/EXP

1. Disconnect the negative battery terminal.
2. Remove the two transaxle to engine top mounting bolts.
3. Remove the clutch cable from the clutch release lever, after wedging a wooden block about 7" (178mm) long under the clutch pedal to hold it slightly beyond its normal position.
4. Raise the vehicle and support it on jackstands.
5. Remove the brake line routing clamps from the front wheels.
6. Remove the bolt that secures the lower control arm ball joint to the steering knuckle assembly, and pry the lower control arm away from the knuckle. When installing, a new nut and bolt must be used.

NOTE: The plastic shield installed behind the rotor contains a molded pocket for the lower control arm ball joint. When removing the control arm from the knuckle, bend the shield toward the rotor to provide clearance.

7. Pry the right inboard CV-joint from the transaxle, then remove the CV joint and halfshaft by pulling outward on the steering knuckle. Wire the CV-joint/halfshaft assembly in a level position to prevent it from expanding.

NOTE: When the CV-joint is pulled out of the transaxle fluid will leak out. Install shipping plugs T81P-1177-B or the equivalent to prevent the dislocation of the of the differential side gears.

8. Repeat the procedures and remove the left hand CV-joint/halfshaft from the transaxle.
9. Remove the stabilizer bar.
10. Disconnect the speedometer cable and back-up light.
11. Remove the (3) nuts from the starter mounting studs which hold the engine roll restrictor bracket.
12. Remove the roll restrictor and the starter stud bolts.
13. Remove the stiffener brace.
14. Remove the shift mechanism crossover spring.
15. Remove the shift mechanism stabilizer bar.
16. Remove the shift mechanism.
17. Place a transmission jack under the transaxle.
18. Remove the rear transmission mounts.
19. Remove the front transmission mounts.
20. Lower the transaxle support jack until it clears the rear mount and support the engine with a jack, under the oil pan.
21. Remove the four remaining engine to transaxle bolts.
22. Remove the transaxle.

NOTE: The case may have sharp edges. Wear protective gloves when handling the transaxle.

23. Installation is the reverse of removal.

NOTE: When installing the CV-joint/halfshaft assemblies into the transaxle, install new circlips on the inner stub shaft, carefully install the assemblies into the transaxle to prevent damaging the oil seals, and insure that both joints are fully seated in the transaxle by lightly prying outward to confirm they are seated. If the circlips are not seated, the joints will move out of the transaxle.

Tempo/Topaz

1. Wedge a wood block approximately 7″ (178mm) long under the clutch pedal to hold the pedal up slightly beyond its normal position. Grasp the clutch cable and pull forward, disconnecting it from the clutch release shaft assembly. Remove the clutch casing from the rib on the top surface of the transaxle case.
2. Using a 13mm socket, remove the two top transaxle-to-engine mounting bolts. Using a 10mm socket, remove the air cleaner.
3. Raise and safely support the car. Remove the front stabilizer bar to control arm attaching nut and washer (driver's side). Discard the attaching nut. Remove the two front stabilizer bar mounting brackets. Discard the bolts.
4. Using a 15mm socket, remove the nut and bolt that secures the lower control arm ball joint to the steering knuckle assembly. Discard the nut and bolt. Repeat this procedure on the opposite side.
5. Using a large pry bar, pry the lower control arm away from the knuckle.

CAUTION

Exercise care not to damage or cut the ball joint boot. Pry bar must not contact the lower arm. Repeat this procedure on the opposite side.

6. Using a large pry bar, pry the left inboard CV-joint assembly from the transaxle.

NOTE: Lubricate will drain from the seal at this time. Install shipping plugs (T81P-1177-B or equivalent). Two plugs are required (one for each seal). Remove the inboard CV joint from the transaxle by grasping the left hand steering knuckle and swinging the knuckle and halfshaft outward from the transaxle.

CAUTION

Exercise care when using a pry bar to remove the CV joint assembly. If you're not careful, damage to the differential oil seal may result.

7. If the CV-joint assembly cannot be pried from the transaxle, insert Differential Rotator Tool (T81P-4026-A or equivalent), through the left side and tap the joint out. Tool can be used from either side of transaxle.
8. Wire the halfshaft assembly in a near level position to prevent damage to the assembly during the remaining operations. Repeat this procedure on the opposite side.
9. Using a small prybar, remove the backup lamp switch connector from the transaxle back-up lamp switch.
10. Using a 15mm socket, remove the three nuts from the starter mounting studs which hold the engine roll restrictor bracket. Remove the engine roll restrictor.
11. Using a 13mm deep will socket, remove the three starter stud bolts.
12. Using a 10mm socket, remove the shift mechanism to shift shaft attaching nut and bolt and control selector indicator switch arm. Remove the shift shaft.
13. Using a 15mm socket, remove the shift mechanism stabilizer bar to transaxle attaching bolt. Remove the $^{7}/_{32}$″ sheet metal screw and the control selector indicator switch and bracket assembly.
14. Using a 22mm (⅞″) crows foot wrench, remove the speedometer cable from the transaxle.
15. Using a 13mm universal socket, remove the two stiffener brace attaching bolts from the oil pan to clutch housing.
16. Position a suitable jack under the transaxle. Using an 18mm socket, remove the two nuts that secure the left hand rear No. 4 insulator to the body bracket.
17. Using a 13mm socket, remove the bolts that secure the left hand front No. 1 insulator to the body bracket. Lower the transaxle jack until the transaxle clears the rear insulator. Support the engine with a screw jackstand under the oil pan. Use a 2 x 4 piece of wood on top of the screw jack.
18. Using a 13mm socket, remove the four engine to transaxle attaching bolts. One of these bolts holding the ground strap and wiring loom stand off bracket.
19. Remove the transaxle from the rear face of the engine and lower transaxle from the vehicle.
20. Install in reverse order.

WARNING: The transaxle case casting may have sharp edges. Wear protective gloves when handling the transaxle assembly!

Taurus and Sable

1. Using a wood block approximately 7″ long, wedge it under the clutch pedal to hold the pedal up slightly beyond its normal position. Grasp the clutch cable and pull it forward, disconnecting it from the clutch release bearing assembly. Remove the clutch casing from the rib on the top surface of the transaxle case.
2. Using a 13mm socket, remove the two top transaxle-to-engine bolts.
3. Raise and support the front of the vehicle on jackstands.
4. If equipped, remove the front stabilizer bar-to-control arm nut and washer (driver's side); discard the nut. Remove the front stabilizer bar-to-chassis brackets; discard the bolts.
5. Using a 15mm socket, remove the lower control arm ball joint-to-steering knuckle nut and bolt; discard

the nut and bolt. Repeat this procedure on the opposite side.

6. Using a large pry bar, separate the lower control arm from the steering knuckle.

CAUTION

Exercise care not to damage or cut the ball joint boot. The pry bar must not contact the lower arm. Repeat this procedure on the opposite side.

7. Using a large pry bar, pry the left inboard CV-joint assembly from the transaxle.

NOTE: With the halfshaft removed from the transaxle, the lubricant will drain from the seal. To prevent fluid loss, install the shipping plugs No. T81P-1177-B; two plugs are required (one for each seal).

8. To remove the inboard CV-joint from the transaxle, grasp the left-hand steering knuckle, then swing the knuckle and halfshaft outward from the transaxle.

CAUTION

Exercise care when using a pry bar to remove the CV-joint assembly, or damage may occur to the differential oil seal.

9. If the CV-joint assembly cannot be pried from the transaxle, insert the differential rotator tool No. T81P-4026-A, or equivalent, through the left side and tap the joint out; the tool can be used from either side of transaxle.

10. Using a wire, support the halfshaft assembly in a rear level position to prevent damage to the assembly during the remaining operations; repeat this procedure on the opposite side.

11. Using a small pry bar, remove the backup lamp switch connector from the transaxle backup lamp switch.

12. Using a 13mm deep well socket, remove the starter-to-engine stud bolts.

13. Remove the shift mechanism-to-shift shaft nut/bolt, the control selector indicator switch arm and the shift shaft.

14. Using a 22mm (7/8") crows foot wrench, remove the speedometer cable from the transaxle.

15. Using a 13mm socket, remove the stiffener brace-to-clutch housing bolts.

16. Position a transaxle jack under the transaxle.

17. Using a 13mm wrench, remove the lower engine-to-transaxle bolts. Lower the transaxle jack until the transaxle clears the rear insulator. Support the engine with a screw jack stand under the oil pan; use a 2" x 4" piece of wood on top of the screw jack.

18. Remove the transaxle from the rear face of the engine and lower it from the vehicle.

19. To install, reverse the removal procedures. Torque the transaxle-to-engine bolts to 28-31 ft.lb. (38-42 Nm), the shift cable/bracket-to-transaxle bolts to 16-22 ft.lb. (22-30 Nm) for 10mm or 22-35 ft.lb. (31-47 Nm) for 12mm; the shift mechanism-to-shift shaft bolt to 7-10 ft.lb. (9-13 Nm); the stiffener brace-to-clutch housing bolts to 15-21 ft.lb. (21-28 Nm); the starter-to-engine stud bolts to 30-40 ft.lb. (41-54 Nm); the lower ball joint-to-steering knuckle nut/bolt to 37-44 ft.lb. (50-60 Nm) and the top transaxle-to-engine bolts to 28-31 ft.lb. (38-42 Nm). Check the transaxle fluid level; if adding fluid, use Dexron® II automatic transmission fluid. Set the hand brake, pump the clutch pedal several times to adjust the clutch.

CAUTION

The transaxle case casting may have sharp edges. Wear protective gloves when handling the transaxle assembly!

WARNING: NEVER attempt to start the engine with the CV-joints disconnected from the transaxle or side gear dislocation may occur!

CLUTCH

FREE PLAY ADJUSTMENT

The free play in the clutch is adjusted by a built in mechanism that allows the clutch controls to be self-adjusted during normal operation.

The self-adjusting feature should be checked every 5000 miles. This is accomplished by insuring that the clutch pedal travels to the top of its upward position. Grasp the clutch pedal with your hand or put your foot under the clutch pedal. pull up on the pedal until it stops. Very little effort is required (about 10 lbs.). During the application of upward pressure, a click may be heard which means an adjustment was necessary and has been accomplished.

Clutch Cable

REMOVAL & INSTALLATION

Escort, Lynx, EXP, LN7, Tempo, Topaz

1. From under the hood, use a pair of pliers and grasp the extended tip of the clutch cable (on top of transaxle). Unhook the clutch cable from the clutch throwout bearing release lever.

2. From inside the car, remove the fresh air duct next to the clutch pedal (non-air conditioned cars). Remove the shield from the brake pedal support bracket. On Tempo/Topaz models remove the panel above the clutch pedal.

3. Lift up on the clutch pedal to release the adjusting pawl. Rotate the adjustment gear quadrant forward. Unhook the clutch cable from the gear quadrant. Swing the quadrant to the rear.

4. Pull the clutch cable out from between the clutch pedal and the gear quadrant and from the isolator on the gear quadrant.

5. From under the hood, pull the clutch cable through the firewall and remove it from the car.

6. From under the hood, insert the clutch cable through the firewall into the drivers compartment.

7. Push the clutch cable through the isolator on the pedal stop bracket and through the recess between the clutch pedal and the adjusting gear quadrant.

8. Lift the clutch pedal to release the pawl and rotate the gear quadrant forward. Hook the clutch cable to the gear quadrant.

9. Install the fresh air duct. Install the shield on the brake pedal support.

10. Secure the clutch pedal in the up position. Use a piece of wire, tape, etc.

11. From under the hood, hook the cable to the clutch throwout bearing release lever.

12. Unfasten the clutch pedal and adjust the clutch by operating the clutch pedal several times. Pull up on the pedal to make sure it is reaching the maximum upward position.

Taurus and Sable

1. Using a support, prop Up the clutch pedal to release the pawl from the gear quadrant.

2. To gain access to the transaxle end of the clutch cable, remove the air cleaner.

3. Using a pair of pliers, grasp the clutch cable extended end and disconnect it from the clutch cable release bearing fork.

NOTE: When releasing the clutch cable from the release bearing fork, DO NOT grasp the wire strand portion of the inner cable, for you may cut it.

4. At the transaxle rib, disconnect the clutch cable from the insulator.

5. From above the clutch pedal pad, disconnect the panel.

6. At the brake pedal support brack-

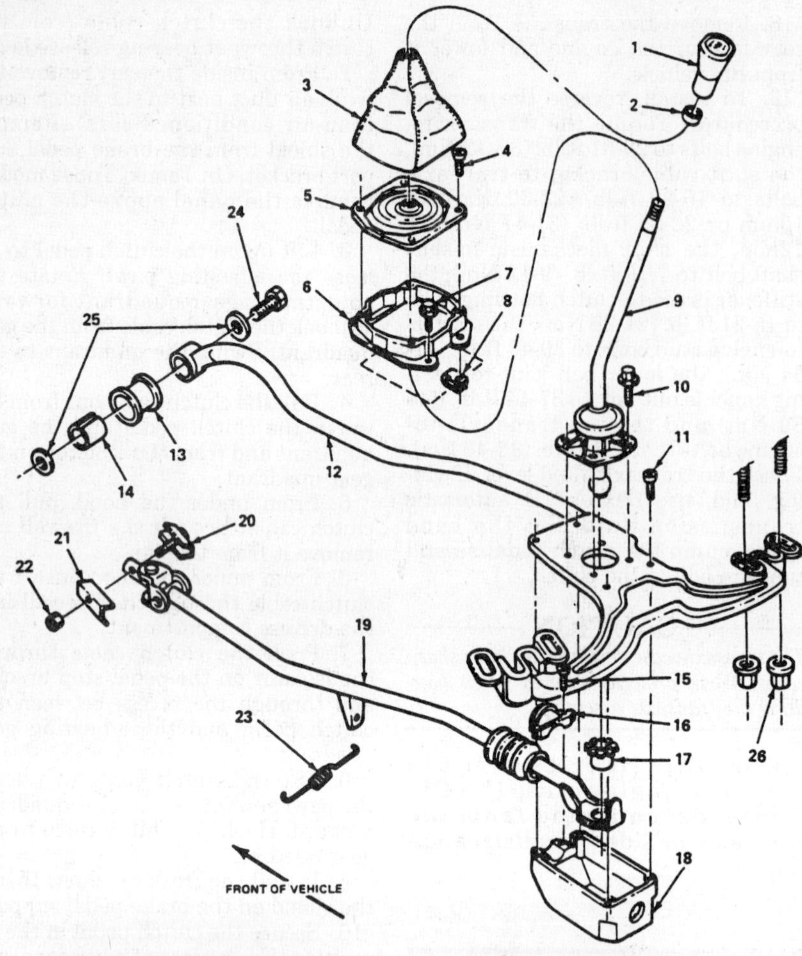

1. Knob—gear shift lever
2. Nut—shift knob locking
3. Upper boot assembly—gear shift lever
4. Screw—tapping (4 required)
5. Lower boot assembly—gear shift lever
6. Boot retainer assembly—gear shift lever
7. Bolt—boot retainer (4 required)
8. Nut—spring (4 required)
9. Lever assembly—gearshift
10. Bolt—tapping (4 required)
11. Screw—tapping (4 required)
12. Support assembly (shift stabilizer bar)
13. Bushing—gear shift stabilizer bar
14. Sleeve—gear shift rod
15. Screw—tapping (2 required)
16. Cover—control selector
17. Bushing—anti tizz
18. Housing—control selector
19. Assembly—shift rod and clevis
20. Assembly—clamp
21. Clamp—gear shift lever (2 required)
22. Nut—clamp assembly
23. Retaining spring—gear shift tube
24. Bolt—stabilizer bar attaching
25. Washer—flat (2 required)
26. Assembly—nut/washer (4 required)

Components of a typical manual shift linkage

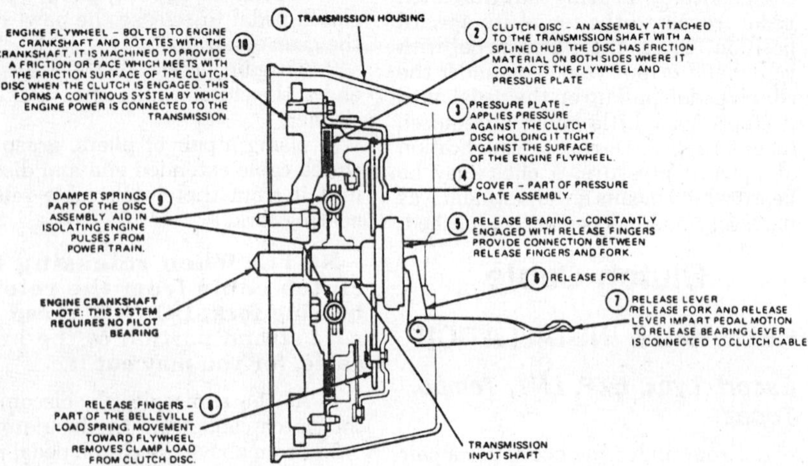

Operation of the clutch components

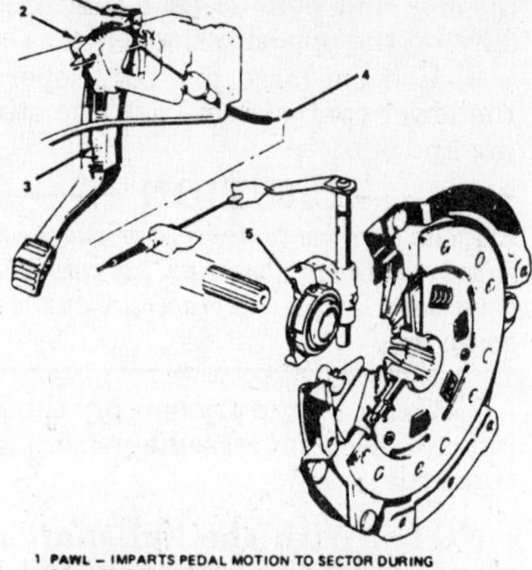

1 PAWL – IMPARTS PEDAL MOTION TO SECTOR DURING DOWNSTROKE. PAWL ENGAGES QUADRANT AT BEGINNING OF DOWNSTROKE.

2 QUADRANT–ACTUATES CABLE DURING PEDAL DOWNSTROKE FOLLOWING CABLE CORE AS CORE IS MOVED DURING DISC FACING WEAR.

3 ADJUSTER SPRING – KEEPS SECTOR IN FIRM CONTACT WITH CABLE. KEEPS RELEASE BEARING IN CONTACT WITH CLUTCH RELEASE FINGERS THROUGH CABLE LINKAGE WITH PEDAL IN UP POSITION.

4 CABLE

5 RELEASE BEARING

Indentification of the clutch parts

et, remove the rear screw (located nearest the instrument panel) and position the clutch shield away. Loosen the front screw and rotate the shield out of the way, then secure the front screw.

7. With the pawl in the released position, rotate the gear quadrant forward and disconnect the clutch cable from the gear quadrant. DO NOT allow the gear quadrant to swing rearward or snap back.

8. Pull the cable through the recess between the clutch pedal and the gear quadrant, then from the pedal assembly insulator.

9. Remove the cable through the engine compartment.

10. To install, reverse the removal procedures. Adjust the clutch by depressing the clutch pedal several times.

NOTE: When installing the clutch cable, make sure that it is routed under the brake lines and it is not trapped at the spring tower near the brake lines.

Pressure Plate and Clutch Disc

REMOVAL & INSTALLATION

Escort, Lynx, EXP, LN7, Tempo, Topaz

1. Remove the transaxle (refer to the previous Transaxle Removal and Installation sections).

2. Mark the pressure plate assembly and the flywheel so that they may

be assembled in the same position if the original pressure plate is to be reused.

3. Loosen the attaching bolts one turn at a time, in sequence, until spring pressure is relieved.

4. Support the pressure plate and clutch disc and remove the bolts. Remove the pressure plate and disc.

5. Inspect the flywheel, clutch disc, pressure plate, throwout bearing and the clutch fork for wear. If the flywheel shows any sign of overheating (blue discoloration), or if it is badly scored or grooved, it should be refaced or replaced. Replace any other parts that are worn.

6. Clean the pressure plate (if it is to be reused) and the flywheel surfaces thoroughly. Position the clutch disc and pressure plate into the installed position.

NOTE: The clutch disc must be assembled so that the flatter side is toward the flywheel.

Align the match marks on the pressure plate and flywheel (when reusing the original pressure plate). Support the clutch disc and pressure plate with a dummy shaft or clutch aligning tool.

7. Install the pressure plate to flywheel bolts. Tighten them gradually in a criss-cross pattern. Remove the aligning tool. Mounting bolt torque is 12-24 ft.lb.

8. Lubricate the release bearing and install it on the throwout fork.

9. Install the transaxle.

Taurus and Sable

1. Refer to the Transaxle Removal & Installation procedures in this section and remove the transaxle.

2. Make alignment marks on the pressure plate assembly and the flywheel for reassembly purposes.

3. Loosen the pressure plate-to-flywheel bolts one turn at a time, in sequence, until spring tension is relieved.

4. Support the pressure plate/clutch disc assembly and remove the bolts. Remove the pressure plate and the clutch disc.

5. Inspect the flywheel, the clutch disc, the pressure plate, the throwout bearing and the clutch fork for wear; replace the parts as necessary. If the flywheel shows signs of overheating (blue discoloration) or is badly grooved/scored, it should be refaced or replaced.

6. Clean the pressure plate and flywheel surfaces thoroughly. Position the clutch disc and pressure plate into the assembled position, aligning the match-marks. Support the assembly with the clutch arbor tool No. T81P-7550-A, or equivalent.

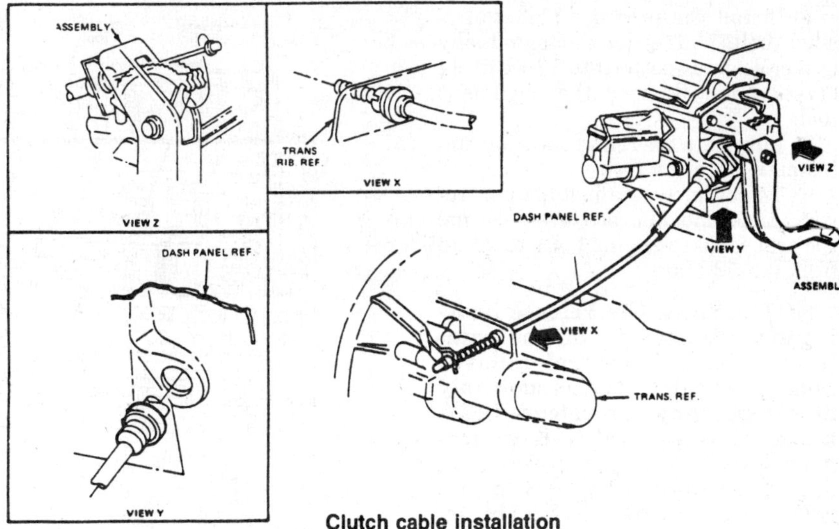

Clutch cable installation

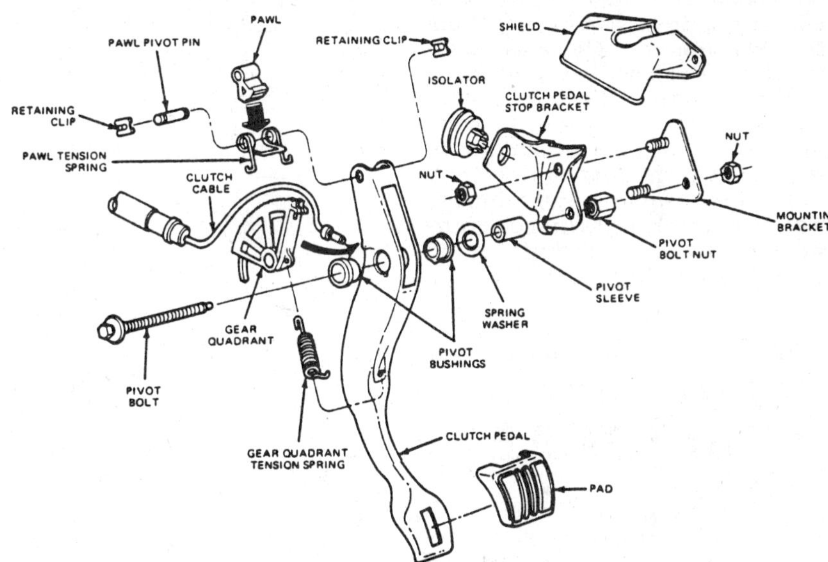

Self-adjusting clutch pedal components

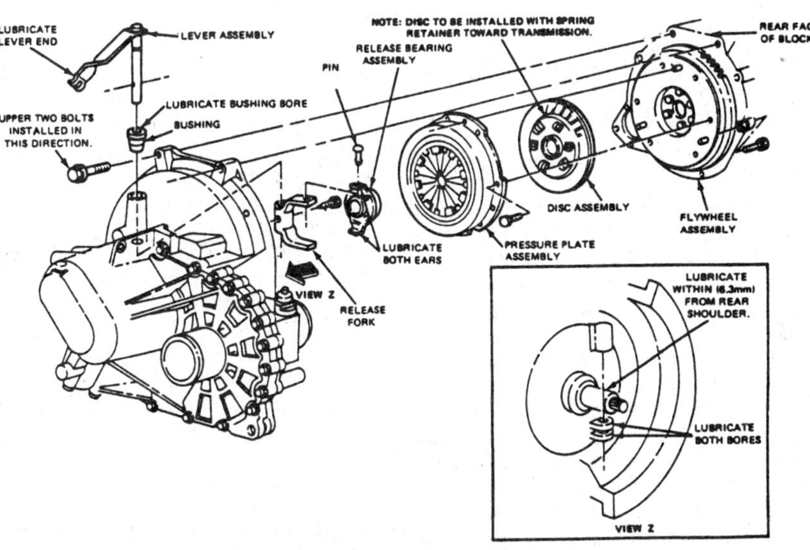

Clutch installation (exploded view)

7. Install the pressure plate-to-flywheel bolts and torque them gradually in a criss-cross pattern to 12-24 fft.lb. (17-32 Nm). Remove the alignment tool.

8. Lubricate the release bearing and install it onto the fork.

9. To complete the installation, reverse the removal procedures. Torque the transaxle-to-engine bolts to 28-38 ft.lb. (38-52 Nm).

NOTE: Since the release bearing in this system is constant-running, transaxle Neutral rollover noise can be detected as such only by disengaging the release bearing from the clutch release fingers. This is best accomplished by disconnecting the cable from the release lever and moving the lever away from the cable. If Neutral noise is evident under this condition, it is emanating from the transmission. Noise associated with the release bearing/clutch system will be evident during all or some portion of the pedal travel. During engagement and disengagement of the pawl and sector a "clicking" noise may be heard. This is normal and is in fact assurance that the adjusting mechanism is operating normally.

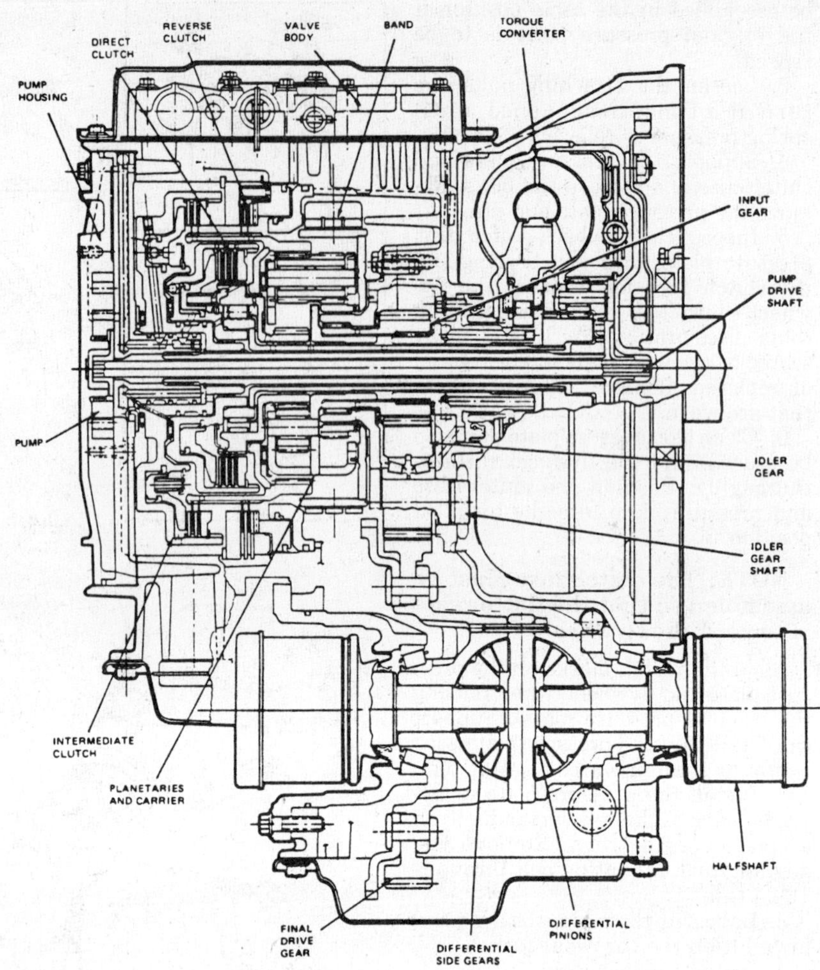

Automatic transaxle

AUTOMATIC TRANSAXLE

NOTE: On Tempo/Topaz models the 2.3L HSC engine and automatic transaxle must be removed together as a unit. Refer to the Engine Removal and Installation Section.

REMOVAL & INSTALLATION

Escort/Lynx/EXP/LN7

1. Disconnect the negative battery cable from the battery.

2. From under the hood, remove the bolts that attach the air manage valve to the AT (automatic transaxle) valve body cover. Disconnect the wiring harness connector from the neutral safety switch.

3. Disconnect the throttle valve linkage and the manual control lever cable. Remove the two transaxle to engine upper attaching bolts. The bolts are located below and on either side of the distributor.

4. Loosen the front wheel lugs slightly. Jack up the front of the car and safely support it on jackstands. Remove the tire and wheel assemblies.

5. Drain the transmission fluid. Disconnect the brake hoses from the strut brackets on both sides. Remove the pinch bolts that secure the lower control arms to the steering knuckles. Separate the ball joint from the steering knuckle. Remove the stabilizer bar attaching bracket. Remove the nuts that retain the stabilizer to the control arms. Remove the stabilizer bar. When removing the control arms from the steering knuckles, it will be necessary to bend the plastic shield slightly to gain ball joint clearance for removal.

6. Remove the tie rod ends from the steering knuckles. Use a special tie rod removing tool. Pry the right side halfshaft from the transaxle (see halfshaft removal section).

7. Remove the left side halfshaft from the transaxle. Support both right and left side halfshaft out of the way with wire.

8. Install sealing plugs or the equivalent into the transaxle halfshaft mounting holes.

9. Remove the starter support bracket. Disconnect the starter cable. Remove the starter mounting studs and the starter motor. Remove the transaxle support bracket.

10. Remove the lower cover from the transaxle. Turn the converter for access to the converter mounting nuts. Remove the nuts.

11. Remove the nuts that attach the left front insulator to the body bracket. Remove the bracket to body bolts and remove the bracket.

12. Remove the left rear insulator bracket attaching nut.

13. Disconnect the transmission cooler lines. Remove the bolts that attach the manual lever bracket to the transaxle case.

14. Position a floor jack with a wide saddle under the transaxle and remove the four remaining transaxle to engine attaching bolts.

15. The torque converter mounting studs must be clear of the engine flywheel before the transaxle can be lowered from the car. Take a small pry bar and place it between the flywheel and

the convertor. Carefully move the transaxle away from the engine. When the convertor mounting studs are clear lower the AT about 3" (76mm). Disconnect the speedometer cable from the AT. Lower the transaxle to the ground.

NOTE: When moving the transaxle away from the engine watch the mount insulator. If it interferes with the transaxle before the converter mounting studs clear the flywheel, remove the insulator.

16. Installation is in the reverse order of removal. Be sure to install new circlips on the halfshaft before reinstalling. Always use new pinch bolts when connecting the lower control arms to the steering knuckles.

Taurus and Sable

1. Disconnect the battery negative cable. Remove the air cleaner, the hoses and the tubes.
2. Using a screwdriver, place it in the shift cable/bracket assembly slot, to keep the assembly from moving, then remove the assembly-to-transaxle bolt and the assembly from the transaxle.
3. Disconnect the electrical connector from the neutral safety switch and the electrical bulkhead connector from the rear of the transaxle.
4. Disconnect the throttle valve cable from the throttle body lever and the throttle valve-to-transaxle bolt. Pull the throttle valve cable Up and disconnect it from the TV link.

NOTE: Pulling too hard on the throttle valve cable may bend the internal TV bracket.

5. On the left side, remove the engine support-to-strut nut/bolt. Remove the top torque converter housing-to-engine bolts.
6. Attach the engine support (3-bar system) hooks to the engine lifting points, tighten the hooks to slowly lift the engine.
7. Raise and support the front of the vehicle on jackstands. Remove the front wheel/tire assemblies.
8. Remove the tie rod-to-steering knuckle cotter pin and castle nut, then separate the tie rod end from the steering knuckle.
9. Remove the lower control arm ball joint-to-steering knuckle cotter pin and castle nut, then separate the ball joint from the steering knuckle.
10. Remove the stabilizer bar-to-control arm nuts.
11. Remove the rack/pinion-to-subframe nuts/bolts and the engine mount-to-subframe nuts. Using a piece of wire, support the steering gear from the tie rod end to the coil spring to hold the steering gear in position.
12. Disconnect the electrical connector from the oxygen sensor.
13. Remove the exhaust pipe-to-exhaust manifold nuts and the rear portion of the convertor pipe-to-exhaust pipe.
14. Using an assistant, lower the adjustable jacks and allow the subframe to lower. Rotate the front of the subframe down and pick up the rear of the subframe off the exhaust pipe. Work the subframe rearward until it can be lowered past the exhaust pipe.
15. Remove the subframe-to-chassis bolts. Remove the left side engine support mount-to-subframe nuts/bolts and lower the subframe.
16. Position a transmission jack under the transaxle oil pan. Remove the vehicle speed sensor from the transaxle.

NOTE: Vehicles equipped with electronic instrument clusters do not use a speedometer cable.

17. On the left side, remove the engine support-to-transaxle bolts. Remove the engine support-to-chassis bolts and the support.
18. Remove the separator plate-to-transaxle bolt and the starter-to-transaxle bolts, then position the starter out of the way. Remove the separator plate.
19. Using a ½" drive ratchet and a ⅞" deep socket on the crankshaft pulley bolt, rotate the crankshaft to align the torque converter bolts with the starter drive hole. As the torque converter-to-flywheel nuts are exposed, remove them.
20. Disconnect and plug the oil cooler lines from the transaxle.
21. To remove the halfshafts on the AXOD (Automatic Overdrive Transaxle), perform the following procedures:
    a. Screw the extension tool No. T86P-3514-A2, or equivalent, into the CV-Joint puller tool No. T86P-3514-A1 and install the slide hammer tool No. D79P-100-A onto the extension.
    b. Position the puller behind the inboard CV-joint and pull the CV-

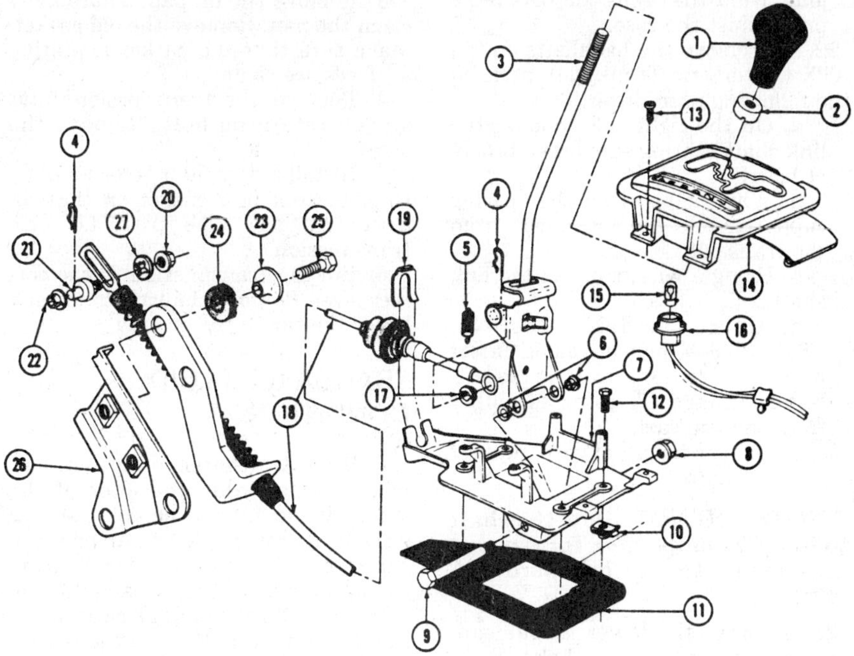

1. Knob assy., trans. gr. shift lever
2. Nut, trans. gr. shift lever ball lock
3. Lever & adaptor assy., trans. control selector
4. Pin, retaining
5. Spring, trans. park gear lockout rtn.
6. Bushing, trans. gear shift lever shaft
7. Housing, trans. control selector
8. Nut, M8-1.25 hex flg.
9. Bolt, M8 x 1.25 x 82.0 hex flg. pilot
10. Nut, M6-1.00 "U"
11. Seal, trans. control selector housing
12. Bolt, M6-1.00 x 25.0 hex flg. hd.
13. Screw, 4.2 x 13.0 hex wa. hd. tap.
14. Bezel assy., trans. control sel. dial
15. Bulb
16. Indicator bulb harness
17. Bushing, trans. gear shift lever cable
18. Cable & bracket assy.
19. Clip, hand brake cable spring lock
20. Nut & washer assy.
21. Stud, trans. gr. shift connecting rod adjusting
22. Bushing, trans. control shift rod clevis
23. Spacer, trans. control cable bracket
24. Insulator, trans. control cable bracket
25. Bolt, M10-1.5 x 20.0 hex flg. hd.
26. Retainer assy., trans. control cable bracket
27. Nut, 5/16-18 round push on

Shift lever components, automatic transaxle

joint from the transaxle; DO NOT pry against the case.

22. To remove the halfshafts on the ATX (Automatic Transaxle), perform the following procedures:

a. On the right side, remove the link shaft bearing support-to-bracket bolts.

b. While supporting the bearing support, slide the link shaft from the transaxle.

c. Using a wire, support the link shaft.

d. Using the driver tool No. T81P-4026-A, or equivalent, insert it into the transaxle to drive the left-hand inboard CV-joint assembly from the transaxle.

e. Using a length of wire, support the halfshaft.

NOTE: DO NOT allow the shaft to hang unsupported, for damage may result to the outboard CV-joint.

23. Remove the lower torque converter housing-to-engine bolts. Separate the transmission from the engine and carefully lower it out of the vehicle.

24. To install, reverse the removal procedures. Torque the transaxle-to-engine bolts to 41-50 ft.lb. (55-68 Nm); the control arm ball joint-to-steering knuckle nut to 36-44 ft.lb. (50-60 Nm); the tie rod end-to-steering knuckle nut to 23-35 ft.lb. (31-47 Nm); the starter-to-transaxle bolts to 30-40 ft.lb. (41-54 Nm); the engine support-to-transaxle bolts to 25-33 ft.lb. (34-45 Nm); the engine mount-to-subframe bolts to 55-70 fft.lb. (75-90 Nm); the subframe-to-chassis bolts to 40-50 ft.lb. (55-70 Nm); the stabilizer bar-to-control arm nuts to 98-125 ft.lb. (133-169 Nm) and the stabilizer U-clamp-to-chassis bolts to 60-70 ft.lb. (81-95 Nm). Check and add fluid to the transaxle.

TRANSMISSION FLUID AND FILTER

Drain and Refill

In normal service it should not be necessary nor it it required to drain and refill the AT fluid. However, under severe operation or dusty conditions the fluid should be changed every 20 months or 20,000 miles.

1. Raise the car and safely support it on jackstands.

2. Place a suitable drain pan underneath the transaxle oil pan. Loosen the oil pan mounting bolts and allow the fluid to drain until it reaches the level of the pan flange. Remove the attaching bolts, leaving one end attached so that the pan will tip and the rest of the fluid will drain.

3. Remove the oil pan. Thoroughly clean the pan. Remove the old gasket. Make sure that the gasket mounting surfaces are clean.

4. Remove the transmission filter screen retaining bolt. Remove the screen.

5. Install a new filter screen and O-ring. Place a new gasket on the pan and install the pan to the transmission.

6. Fill the transmission to the correct level. Remove the jackstands and lower the car to the ground.

TRANSAXLE FLUID CONDITION

Pull the transmission dipstick out. Observe the color and odor of the transmission fluid. The color should be red not brown or black. An odor can sometimes indicate an overheating condition, clutch disc or band failure.

Wipe the dipstick with a clean white rag. Examine the stain on the rag for specks of solids (metal or dirt) and for signs of contaminates (antifreeze, gum or varnish condition).

If examination shows evidence of metal specks or antifreeze contamination transaxle removal and inspection may be necessary.

THROTTLE VALVE CONTROL LINKAGE

The Throttle Valve (TV) Control Linkage System consists of a lever on the carburetor or throttle body of the injection unit, linkage shaft assembly, mounting bracket assembly, control rod assembly, a control lever on the transaxle and a lever return spring.

The coupling lever follows the movement of throttle lever and has an adjustment screw that is used for setting TV linkage adjustment when a line pressure gauge is used. If a pressure gauge is not available, a manual adjustment can be made.

A number of shift troubles can occur if the throttle valve linkage is not in adjustment. Some are:

1. **Symptom:** Excessively early and/or soft upshift with or without slip-bump feel. No forced downshaft (kickdown) function at appropriate speeds.

Cause: TV control linkage is set too short.

Remedy: Adjust linkage.

2. **Symptom:** Extremely delayed or harsh upshafts and harsh idle engagement.

Cause: TV control linkage is set too long.

Remedy: Adjust linkage.

3. **Symptom:** Harsh idle engagement after the engine is warmed up. Shift clunk when throttle is backed off after full or heavy throttle acceleration. Harsh coasting downshifts (automatic 3-2, 2-1 shift in D range). Delayed upshift at light acceleration.

Cause: Interference due to hoses, wires, etc. prevents return of TV control rod or TV linkage shaft. Excessive friction caused by binding grommets prevents the TV control linkage to return to its proper location.

Remedy: Correct the interference area, check for bent or twisted rods, levers. or damaged grommets. Repair or replace whatever is necessary. Check and adjust linkage is necessary.

4. **Symptom:** Eratic/delayed upshifts, possibly no kickdown, harsh engagement.

Cause: Clamping bolt on trun-

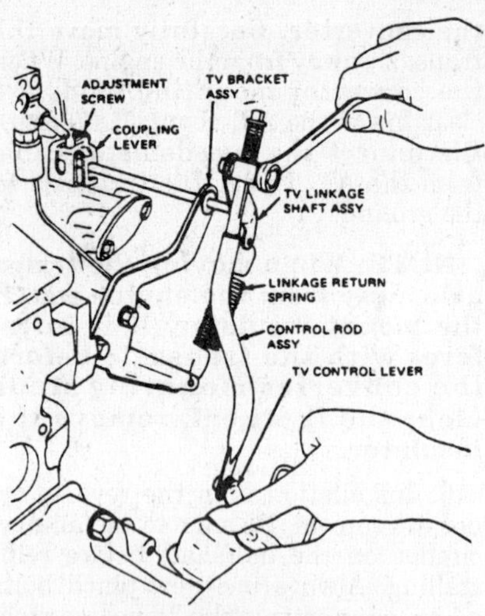

TV rod adjustment

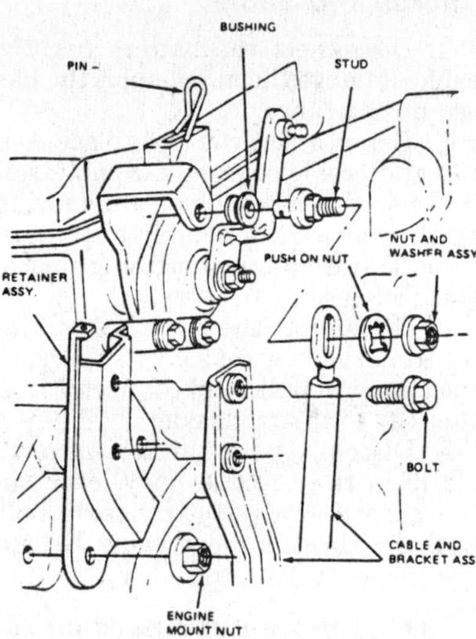

Exploded view of the installation of the shift cable and bracket

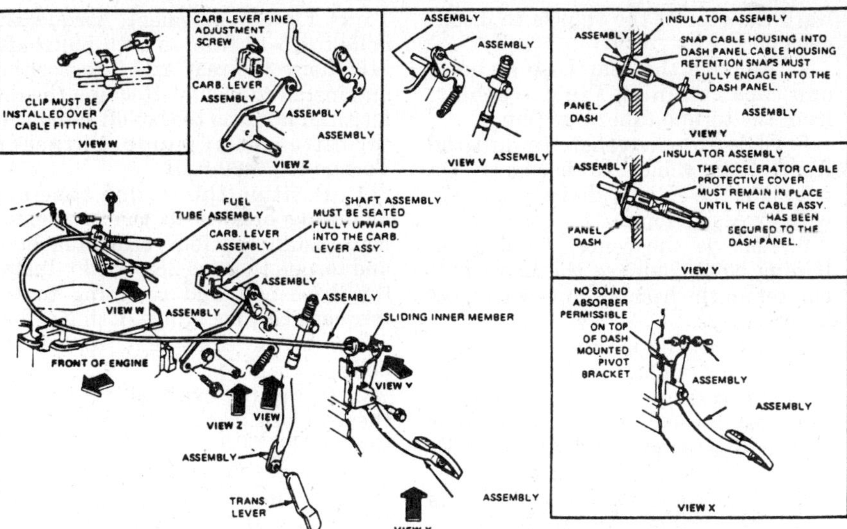

Throttle linkage cable and components; automatic transaxle

nion at the upper end of the TV control rod is loose.

Remedy: Reset TV control linkage.

5. **Symptom:** No upshift and harsh engagements.

Cause: TV control rod is disconnected or the linkage return spring is broken or disconnected.

Remedy: Reconnect TV control rod, check and replace the connecting grommet if necessary, reconnect or replace the TV return spring.

LINKAGE ADJUSTMENT

The TV control linkage is adjusted at the sliding trunnion block.

1. Adjust the curb idle speed to specification as shown on the under hood decal.
2. After the curb idle speed has been set, shut off the engine. Make sure the choke is completely opened. Check the carburetor throttle lever to make sure it is against the hot engine curb idle stop.
3. Set the coupling lever adjustment screw at its approximate midrange. Make sure the TV linkage shaft assembly is fully seated upward into the coupling lever.

CAUTION

If adjustment of the linkage is necessary, allow the EGR valve to cool so you won't get burned.

4. To adjust, loosen the bolt on the sliding block on the TV control rod a minimum of one turn. Clean any dirt or corrosion from the control rod, free-up the trunnion block so that it will slide freely on the control rod.
5. Rotate the transaxle TV control lever up using a finger and light force, to insure that the TV control lever is against its internal stop. With reducing the pressure on the control lever, tighten the bolt on the trunnion block.
6. Check the carburetor throttle lever to be sure it is still against the hot idle stop. If not, repeat the adjustment steps.

TRANSMISSION CONTROL LEVER ADJUSTMENT

1. Position the selector lever in Drive against the rear stop.
2. Raise the car and support it safely on jackstands. Loosen the manual lever to control lever nut.
3. Move the transmission lever to the Drive position, second detent from the rearmost position. Tighten the attaching nut. Check the operation of the transmission in each selector position. Readjust if necessary. Lower the car.

SHIFT LEVER CABLE REMOVAL & INSTALLATION

1. Remove the shift knob, locknut, console, bezel assembly, control cable clip and cable retaining pin.
2. Disengage the rubber grommet from the floor pan by pushing it into the engine compartment. Raise the car and safely support it on jackstands.
3. Remove the retaining nut and control cable assembly from the transmission lever. Remove the control cable bracket bolts. Pull the cable through the floor.
4. To install the cable, feed the round end through the floor board. Press the rubber grommet into its mounting hole.
5. Position the control cable assembly in the selector lever housing and install the spring clip. Install the bushing and control cable assembly on the selector lever and housing assembly shaft and secure it with the retaining pin.

   Install the bezel assembly, console, locknut and shift knob. Position the selector lever in the Drive position. The selector lever must be held in this position while attaching the other end of the control cable.
6. Position the control cable bracket on the retainer bracket and secure the tow mounting bolts.
7. Shift the control lever into the second detent from full rearward (Drive position).
8. Place the cable end on the transmission lever stud. Align the flats on the stud with the slot in the cable. Make sure the transmission selector lever has not moved from the second detent position and tighten the retaining nut.
9. Lower the car to the ground. Check the operation of the transmission selector in all positions. Make sure the neutral safety switch is operating properly. (The engine should start only in Park or Neutral position).

SELECTOR INDICATOR BULB REPLACEMENT

Remove the console and the four screws that mount the bezel. Lift the bezel assembly and disconnect the indicator bulb harness. Remove the indicator bulb. Install a new bulb and reverse the removal procedure.

Neutral Safety Switch

REMOVAL AND INSTALLATION

1. Disconnect the negative battery cable from the battery.
2. Remove the two hoses from the rear of the manage air valve. Remove all the vacuum hoses from the valve, label them for position before removal.
3. Remove the manage air valve supply hose band to intermediate shift control bracket attaching screw. Remove the air cleaner assembly.
4. Disconnect the neutral safety switch connector. Remove the two neutral safety switch retaining bolts and the neutral safety switch.
5. Installation is in the reverse order of removal.

Adjustment

When positioning the neutral safety switch a Number 43 drill (0.089") is used to align the hole in the switch and mount before the mounting bolts are tightened.

Transfer Case

REMOVAL & INSTALLATION

Tempo/Topaz All Wheel Drive Models Only

1. Drain the oil by removing the drive housing lower left hand retaining bolt.
2. Remove the vacuum line retaining bracket bolt. Remove the driveshaft front retaining bolts and caps. Disengage the front driveshaft from the drive yoke.
3. If the transfer case is to be disassembled, check the backlash before removal in order to reset to existing backlash at installation. The backlash should be 0.012-0.024" on a 3" radius.
4. Remove the three bolts retaining the vacuum motor shield and remove the shield.
5. Remove the vacuum lines from the vacuum servo. Remove the 13 bolts retaining the transfer case to the transaxle. Note the length and locations of the bolts.
6. Remove the the transfer case from the vehicle.
7. Position the transfer case to the transaxle.
8. Install the transfer case bolts in the proper positions. Torque them down to 23-38 ft.lb.
9. Install the vacuum motor supply hose connector. Position the vacuum motor shield and install the three retaining bolts. Torque the bolts to 7-12 ft.lb.
10. Position the driveshaft to the drive yoke. Install the retaining bolts and torque the bolts to 15-17 ft.lb. Install the vacuum line retaining bracket and bolt and torque it to 7-12 ft.lb.
11. Fill the transaxle and lower the vehicle. Road test the vehicle and check the performance of the transfer case.

Driveshaft

REMOVAL & INSTALLATION

Tempo/Topaz All Wheel Drive Models

1. Raise and support the vehicle safely. Be sure to support the driveshaft using a suitable jack or hoist under the center bearing during removal and installation.
2. To maintain the driveshaft balance, mark the U-joints so they may be installed in their original position.
3. Remove the U-joint retaining bolts and caps. Slide the driveshaft toward the rear of the vehicle to disengage it.
4. Remove the rear U-joint bolts and caps retaining the driveshaft, from the torque tube yoke flange.
5. Slide the driveshaft toward the front of the vehicle to disengage. Do not allow the splined shafts to contact with excessive force.
6. Remove the center bearing retaining bolts. Remove the driveshaft and retain the bearing cups with tape, if necessary.
7. Inspect the U-joint assemblies for wear and or damage, replace the U-joint if necessary.
8. Install the driveshaft at the rear torque yoke flange. Ensure that the U-joint is in its original position.
9. Install the U-joint retaining bolts and caps. Torque them to 15-17 ft.lb. Position the front U-joint. Install the U-joint retaining caps and bolts. Torque them to 15-17 ft.lb.
10. Install the center bearing and retaining bolts. Torque them to 23-30 fft.lb. Do not drop the assemble driveshafts as the impact may cause damage to the U-joint bearing cups.

Rear Axle Shafts

REMOVAL & INSTALLATION

Tempo/Topaz All Wheel Drive Models

1. Raise the vehicle on a hoist and support it safely. Position a hoist or a suitable transmission jack under the rear axle housing.
2. Remove the muffler and exhaust system from the catalytic converter back.
3. Remove the rear U-joint bolts and caps retaining the driveshaft, from the torque tube yoke flange. Lower the and support the driveshaft.
4. Remove the four retaining bolts from the torque tube support bracket. Remove the axle retaining bolt from the left hand differential support bracket.
5. Remove the axle retaining bolt from the center differential support bracket.
6. Lower the axle assembly and remove the inboard U-joint retaining bolts and caps from each of the halfshaft. Remove and wire the halfshaft assemblies out of the way.
7. Lower the jack and remove the rear axle from the vehicle.
8. Position the rear axle assembly under the vehicle. Raise the rear axle far enough for the U-joint and halfshaft assembies to be installed.
9. Position each inboard U-joint to the rear axle. Install the U-joint caps and retaining bolts. Using a T-30 Torx® bit or equivalent, torque the bolts to 15-17 ft.lb. to each halfshaft.
10. Raise the rear axle into position and install the bolts attaching the differential housing to the left hand center differential support bracket. Torque to 70-80 ft.lb.
11. Position the torque tube and mounting bracket to the crossmember. Install the four attaching bolts and torque them to 28-35 ft.lb. Install the driveshaft and retaining to the torque tube yoke flange. Using a T-30 Torx® bit or equivalent, torque the bolts to 15-17 ft.lb.
12. Install the exhaust system from the catalytic converter back. Install the muffler.
13. Check the lubricant level in the rear axle and add if necessary. Lower the vehicle and roadtest to check the rear axle for proper operation.

Rear Axle Shaft Bearing

REMOVAL & INSTALLATION

All Wheel Drive Models

1. Raise and support the vehicle safely. Remove the tire and wheel assembly.
2. Remove the brake drum. Remove the parking brake cable from the brake backing plate.
3. Remove the brake line from the wheel cylinder. Remove the outboard U-joint reatining bolts. Remove the outboard end of the halfshaft from the wheel stub shaft yoke and wire it to the control arm.
4. Remove and discard the control arm to spindle bolt, washer and nut. Remove the tie rod nut, bushing and washer and discard the nut.
5. Remove and discard the two bolts retaining the spindle to the strut. Remove the spindle from the vehicle. Mount the spindle and backing plate assembly in a suiatble vise.
6. Remove the cooter pin and nut attaching the stub shaft yoke to the stub shaft. Discard the cotter pin.
7. Remove the spindle and backing plate assembly from the vise. Remove the stub shaft yoke using a 2 jaw puller T77F-4220-B and shaft protector D80L625-S or equivalent.
8. Move the spindle and backing plate assembly into a vise and remove the wheel stub shaft.
9. Remove the snapring retaining the bearing. Remove the four bolts retaining the spindle to the backing plate and remove the backing plate.
10. Remove the spindle from the vise and mountit into a suiatble press. With the spindle side facing upward,

carefully press out the bearing from the spindle, using driver handle T80T-4000-W and bearing cup driver T87P-7120-B or equivalent. Discard the bearing after removal.

11. Mount the spindle in a press, spindle side facing down. Position a new bearing in the outboard side of the spindle and carefully press in the new bearing using driver handle T80T-4000-W and bearing installer D80L-630-8 or equivalent.

12. Remove the spindle from the press and mount it in a vise. Install the snapring retaining the bearing. Position the backing plate to the spindle and install the four retaining bolts.

13. Install the wheel stub shaft. Install the stub shaft yoke and attaching nut. Torque the nut to 120-150 ft.lb. install a new cotter pin.

14. Remove the spindle and backing plate assembly from the vise. Position the spindle onto the tie rod and then into the strut lower bracket. Insert two new strut to spindle bolts, but do not tighten them at this time.

15. Install the tie rod bushing washer and new nut. Install the new control arm to spindle bolt, washers and nut. Do not tighten them at this time.

16. Install a jack stand to support the suspension at the normal curcb height before tightening the fasteners.

17. Torque the spindle to strut bolts to 70-96 ft.lb. Torque the tie rod nut to 52-74 ft.lb. Torque the control arm to spindle nut to 60-86 ft.lb.

18. Position the outboard end of the halfshaft to the wheel stub shaft yoke. Install the retaining caps and bolts and torque them to 15-17 ft.lb.

19. Install the brake line to wheel cylinder. Install the parking brake cable and brake drum. Install the tire and wheel assembly, torque the lugs nuts to 80-105 ft.lb.

20. Lower the vehicle and bleed the brake system. Check and adjust the toe, if necessary.

FRONT SUSPENSION

MacPherson Strut and Coil Spring

REMOVAL & INSTALLATION

Escort, Lynx, EXP, LN7, Tempo, Topaz

NOTE: A coil spring compressor Ford Tool number T81P5310A for Escort/Lynx and EXP/LN-7 vehicles. DO NOT USE ON TEMPO/TOPAZ. Tempo/Topaz models require Rotunda 14-0259 or 86-0016 to compress the strut coil spring.

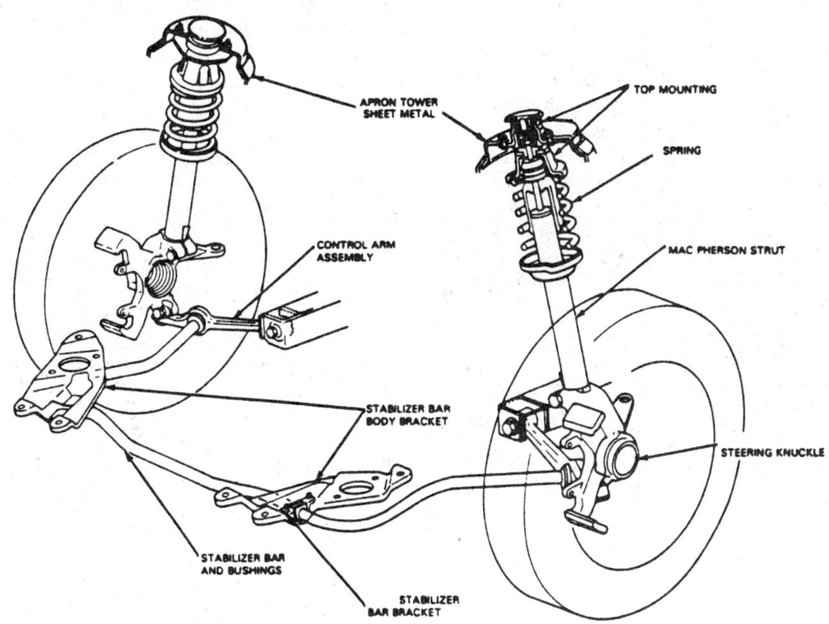

Front suspension components

1. Loosen the wheel lugs, raise the front of the car and safely support it on jackstands. Locate the jackstands under the frame jack pads, slightly behind the front wheels.
2. Remove the wheel assembly.
3. Remove the brake line from the strut mounting bracket.
4. Place a floor jack or small hydraulic jack under the lower control arm. Raise the lower arm and strut as far as possible without raising the car.
5. Install the coil spring compressors. On Escort/Lynx/EXP/LN-7 models, place the top jaw of the compressors on the second coil from the top of the spring. Install the bottom jaw so that five coils will be gripped. Compress the spring evenly, from side to side, until there is about 1/8" (3mm) between any two spring coils. On Tempo/Topaz models, place the top jaw of the compressor on the fifth or sixth coil from the bottom. After the tool is installed, take a measurement from the bottom of the plate. Using the measurement as a reference, compress the spring a minimum of 3½" (89mm). The coil spring must be compressed evenly. Always oil the compressor tool threads.
6. A pinch bolt retains the strut to the steering knuckle. Remove the pinch bolt.
7. Loosen, but do not remove, the two top mount to strut tower nuts. Lower the jack supporting the lower control arm.
8. Use a pry bar and slightly spread the pinch bolt joint (knuckle to strut connection).
9. Place a piece of 2" x 4" wood, 7½" long, against the shoulder on the steering knuckle. Use a short pry bar between the wooden block and the lower spring seat to separate the strut from the knuckle.
10. Remove the two strut upper mounting nuts.
11. Remove the MacPherson strut, spring and top mount assembly from the car.
12. Install the assembled strut, spring and upper mount into the car. If you have installed a new coil spring, be sure it has been compressed enough.
13. Position the two top mounting studs through the holes in the tower and install two new mounting nuts. Do not tighten the nuts completely.

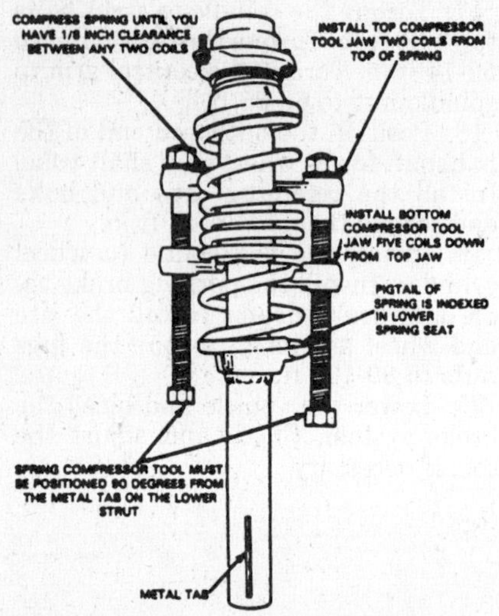

Typical coil spring compressor mounting

14. Install the bottom of the strut fully into the steering knuckle pinch joint.
15. Install a new pinch bolt and tighten it to 68-81 ft.lb. Tighten the tow upper mount nuts to 25-30 ft.lb.
16. Remove the coil spring compressor. Make sure the spring is fitting properly between the upper and lower seats.
17. Install the brake line to the strut bracket. Install the front tire and wheel assembly. Lower the car and tighten the lugs.

Taurus and Sable

1. Place the ignition switch to the OFF position and the steering column in the unlocked position.
2. Remove the hub nut. Loosen the strut-to-fender apron nuts; DO NOT remove the nuts.
3. Raise and support the front of the vehicle on jackstands. Remove the wheel assembly.

NOTE: When raising the vehicle, DO NOT lift it by using the lower control arms.

4. Remove the brake caliper (support it on a wire) and the rotor.
5. At the tie rod end, remove the cotter pin and the castle nut.
6. Using the tie rod end remover tool No. 3290-C and the tie rod remover adapter tool No. T81P-3504-C, separate the tie rod from the steering knuckle.
7. Remove the stabilizer bar link nut and the link from the strut.
8. Remove the lower arm-to-steering knuckle pinch bolt and nut; it may be necessary to use a drift punch to remove the bolt. Using a screwdriver, spread the knuckle-to-lower arm pinch joint and remove the lower arm from the steering knuckle.
9. Remove the halfshaft from the hub and support it on a wire.

NOTE: When removing the halfshaft, DO NOT allow it to move outward for the tripod CV-joint could separate from the internal parts, causing failure of the joint.

10. Remove the strut-to-steering knuckle pinch bolt. Using a small pry bar, spread the pinch bolt joint and separate the strut from the steering knuckle. Remove the steering knuckle/hub assembly from the strut tower.
11. Remove the strut-to-fender apron nuts and the strut assembly from the vehicle.
12. To install, reverse the removal procedures. Torque the strut-to-fender apron nuts to 22-32 ft.lb. (30-40 Nm); the strut-to-steering knuckle bolt to 70-95 ft.lb. (95-129 Nm); the control arm-to-steering knuckle bolt to 40-55 ft.lb. (54-74 Nm); the stabilizer bar-to-link assembly nut to 35-48 ft.lb. (47-65 Nm); the tie rod end-to-steering knuckle nut to 23-25 ft.lb. (31-47 Nm) and the hub nut to 180-200 ft.lb. (244-271 Nm). Check the front end alignment.

STRUT OVERHAUL

1. Place an 18mm deep socket that has an external hex drive top (Ford tool number D81P18045A1) over the strut shaft center nut. Insert a 6mm allen wrench into the shaft end. With the edge of the strut mount clamped in a vise, remove the top shaft mounting nut from the shaft while holding the allen wrench. Use vise grips, if necessary or a suitable extension to hold the allen wrench.

NOTE: Make a wooden holding device the will clamp the strut barrel into the bench vise. (See illustration). Do not clamp directly onto the strut barrel, damage may occur.

2. Clamp the strut into a bench vise. Remove the strut upper mount and the coil spring. If only the strut is to be serviced, do not remove the coil spring compressor from the spring.
3. If the coil spring is to be replaced, remove the compressor from the old spring and install it on the new.
4. Mount the strut (if removed) in the vise using the wooden fixture. Position the coil spring in the lower spring seat. Be sure that the pigtail of the spring is indexed in the seat. That is, follows the groove in the seat and fits flush. Be sure that the spring compressors are positioned 90° from the metal tab on the lower part of the strut.

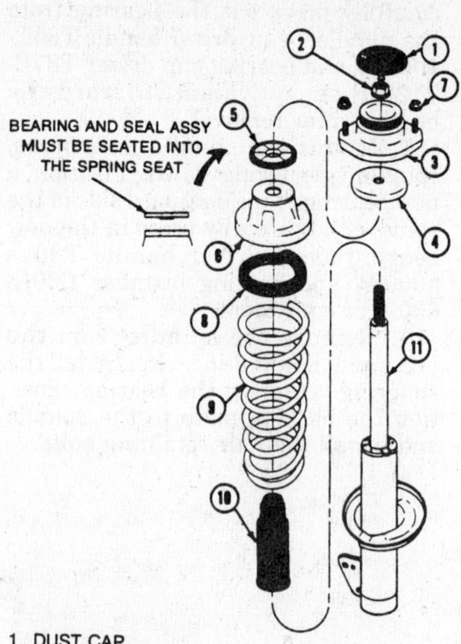

Typical strut upper mounting

5. Use a new nut and assembly the top mount to the strut. Tighten the shaft nut to 48-62 ft.lb.

Tension Struts

REMOVAL & INSTALLATION

1. Refer to the "Front Control Arm Removal & Installation" procedures in this section and remove the control arm from the vehicle.
2. Remove the tension strut-to-subframe nut, washer and insulator, then pull the tension strut rearward to remove it from the vehicle.
3. Remove the insulator from the tension strut.

NOTE: When installing the tension strut, use a new insulator, washer and nut.

4. To install, reverse the removal procedures. Torque the tension strut-to-subframe nut to 70-95 ft.lb. (95-129 Nm); the control arm-to-frame nut/bolt to 70-95 ft.lb. (95-129 Nm); the control arm-to-steering knuckle nut/bolt to 40-55 ft.lb. (54-74 Nm); the tension strut-to-control arm nut to 70-95 ft.lb. (95-129 Nm) and the wheel lug nuts to 80-105 ft.lb. (109-142 Nm). Check and, if necessary, adjust the front wheel alignment.

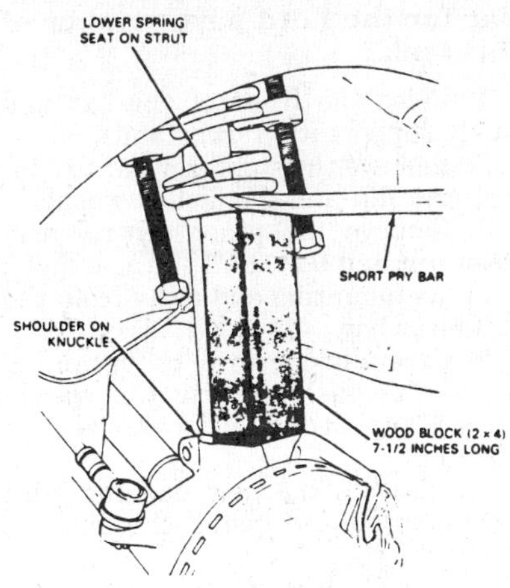

Block positioning

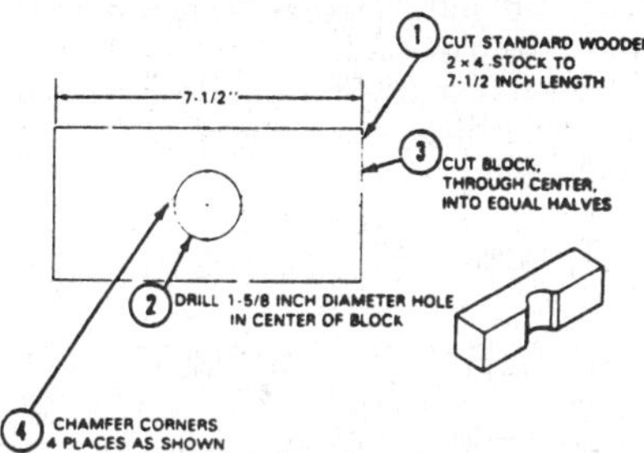

Strut holder construction

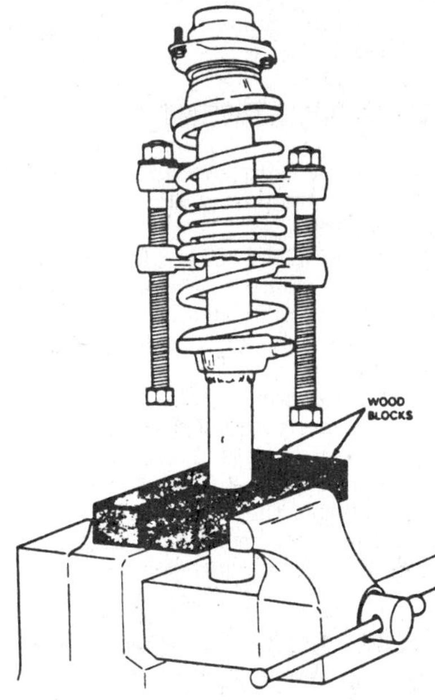

Mounting the strut in a bench vise

Steering Knuckle

REMOVAL & INSTALLATION

1. Loosen the wheel lugs, raise the front of the car and support safely on jackstand: Remove the tire and wheel assembly.
2. Remove the cotter pin from the tie rod end stud nut and remove the nut. Use a suitable removing tool and separate the tie rod end from the steering knuckle.
3. Remove the disc brake caliper, rotor and center hub. Loosen, but do not remove the two top strut mounting nut.
4. Remove the lower control arm to steering knuckle pinch bolt, slightly spread the connection after the bolt has been removed.
5. Remove the strut to steering knuckle pinch bolt, slightly spread the connection after the bolt has been removed. Remove the driveaxle from the knuckle hub.
6. Remove the steering knuckle from the strut.
7. Remove the wheel bearings and rotor splash shield.
8. Install the rotor splash shield and wheel bearings.
9. Install the steering knuckle onto the strut. Install a new pinch bolt and tighten to 66-81 ft.lb.
10. Install the center hub onto the stub driveshaft.
11. Install the lower control arm to the knuckle. Make sure the ball joint groove is aligned so the pinch bolt can slide through. Install a new pinch bolt and tighten to 37-44 ft.lb.
12. Install the rotor and disc brake caliper. Position the tie rod end into the steering knuckle, install a new nut and tighten to 23-35 ft.lb. Align the cotter pin slot and install a new cotter pin.
13. Install the tire and wheel assembly. Lower the car and tighten the wheel lugs.

Lower Control Arm and Ball Joint

REMOVAL & INSTALLATION

Escort, Lynx, EXP, LN7, Tempo, Topaz

1. Jack up the front of the car and safely support it on jackstands.
2. Remove the nut connecting the stabilizer bar to the control arm. Pull off the large dished washer located behind the nut.
3. Remove the lower control arm inner pivot (frame mount) bolt and nut. Remove the pinch bolt from the ball joint to steering knuckle. It may be necessary to use a drift pin to drive out the pinch bolt. Spread the connection slightly after the bolt has been removed. Remove the lower control arm.

NOTE: Be sure the steering wheel is in the unlocked position. DO NOT use a hammer to separate the ball joint from the steering knuckle.

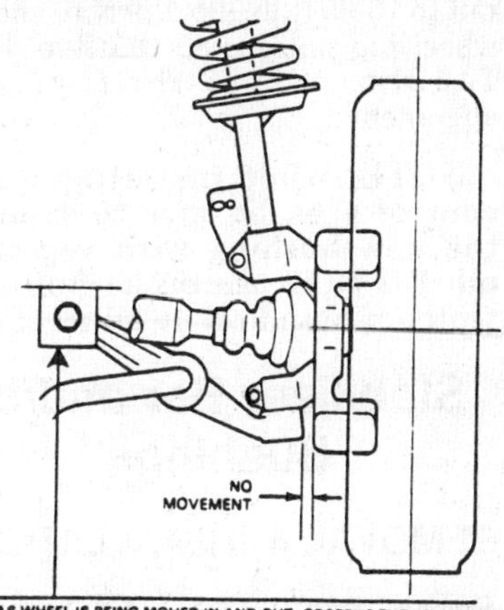

Checking the ball joint for excessive play

4. Installation is the reverse order of removal. When installing the ball joint into the steering knuckle, make sure the stud grooved is aligned so the pinch bolt to 37-44 ft.lb. When tightening the inner control arm mounting bolt/nut the torque should be 50-60 ft.lb. The stabilizer mounting nut is tightened to 75-80 ft.lb.

Taurus and Sable

1. Raise and support the front of the vehicle on jackstands. Remove the tire assembly. Position the steering column in the unlocked position.
2. Remove the tension strut-to-control arm nut and the dished washer.
3. Remove and discard the control arm-to-steering knuckle pinch bolt. Using a small pry bar, spread the pinch joint and separate the control arm from the steering knuckle.

NOTE: When separating the control arm from the steering knuckle, DO NOT use a hammer. Be careful not to damage the bolt seal.

4. Remove the control arm-to-frame nut/bolt, then the control arm from the frame and the tension strut.

NOTE: DO NOT allow the halfshaft to move outward or the tripod CV-joint could separate from the internal parts, causing failure of the joint.

5. To install, use a new pinch nut/bolt and reverse the removal procedures. Torque the control arm-to-frame nut/bolt to 70-95 ft.lb. (95-129 Nm); the control arm-to-steering knuckle nut/bolt to 40-55 ft.lb. (54-74 Nm); the tension strut-to-control arm

nut to 70-95 ft.lb. (95-129 Nm) and the wheel lug nuts to 80-105 ft.lb. (109-142 Nm). Check the front end alignment.

NOTE: When installing a new control arm, be sure to saturate the new bushing with vegetable oil; DO NOT use brake fluid, petroleum-based oil or mineral oil.

Stabilizer Bar and/or Bushings

REMOVAL & INSTALLATION

Escort, Lynx, EXP, LN7, Tempo, Topaz

1. Raise the front of the car and safely support it on jackstands. The tire and wheel assembly may be removed for convenience.
2. Remove the stabilizer bar insulator mounting bracket bolts, end nuts and washers. Remove the bar assembly.
3. Carefully cut the center mounting insulators from the stabilizers.

NOTE: A C-clamp type remover/installer tool is necessary to replace the control arm to stabilizer mounting bushings. The Ford part number of this tool is T81P5493A with T74P3044A1.

4. Remove the control arm inner pivot nut and bolt. Pull the arm down from the inner mounting and away from the stabilizer bar (if still mounted on car).
5. Remove the old bar to control arm insulator bushing with the clamp type tool.
6. Use vegetable oil and saturate the new control arm bushing. Install the bushing with the clamp type tool. Coat the center stabilizer bar bushings with Ruglyde® or an equivalent lubricant. Slide the bushings into place. Install the inner control arm mounting. Tighten to 60-75 ft.lb.
7. Install the stabilizer bar using new insulator mounting bracket bolts. Tighten to 50-60 ft.lb. Install new end nuts with the old dished washers. Tighten to 75-80 ft.lb.
8. Install tire and wheel assembly if removed. Lower the car.

Taurus and Sable

1. Raise and support the front of the vehicle on jackstands.

NOTE: DO NOT raise or support the vehicle on the front control arms.

2. Remove the stabilizer bar link-to-stabilizer bar nut, the stabilizer bar

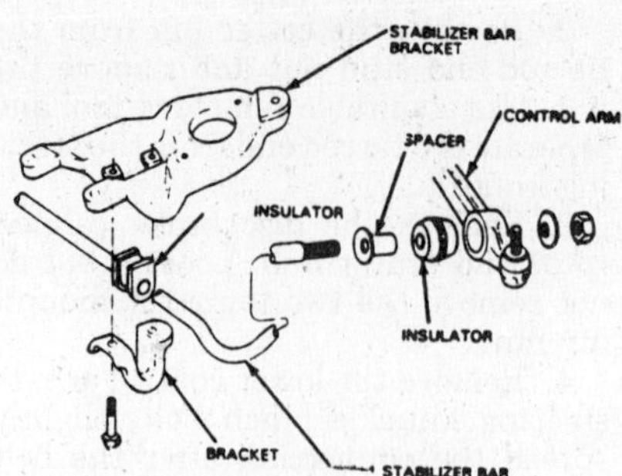

Stabilizer and related part mountings

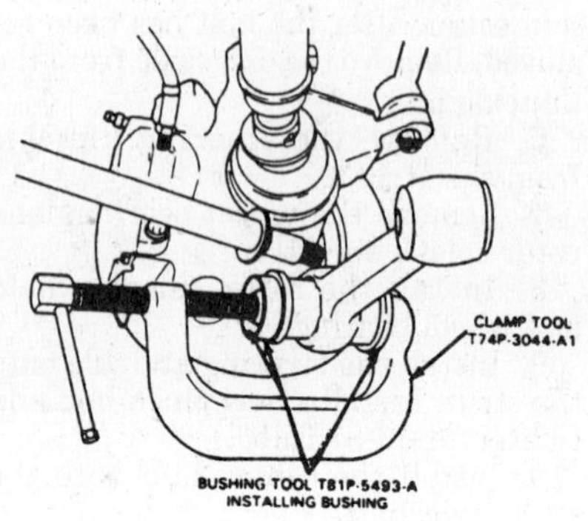

Using a "C"-clamp bushing tool

link-to-strut nut and the link from the vehicle.

3. Remove the steering gear-to-subframe nuts and the gear from the subframe.
4. Position a set of jackstands under the subframe and remove the rear subframe-to-frame bolts. Lower the subframe rear to obtain access to the stabilizer bar brackets.
5. Remove the stabilizer bar U-bracket bolts and the stabilizer bar from the vehicle.

NOTE: When removing the stabilizer bar, replace the insulators and the U-bracket bolts with new ones.

6. To install, reverse the removal procedures. Torque the U-bracket-to-subframe bolts to 21-32 ft.lb. (28-43 Nm); the subframe-to-steering gear bolts to 85-100 ft.lb. (115-135 Nm); the stabilizer bar-to-stabilizer bar link nut to 35-48 ft.lb. (47-65 Nm) and the stabilizer bar-to-strut nut to 35-48 ft.lb.

Lower Control Arm Inner Pivot Bushing

REMOVAL & INSTALLATION

NOTE: A special C-Clamp type removal/installation tool is required. See note under Stabilizer Bar for the Ford part number of this tool.

1. Raise the front of the car and safely support it on jackstands.
2. Remove the stabilizer bar to control arm nut and the dished washer.
3. Remove the inner control arm pivot nut and bolt. Pull the arm down from its mounting and away from the stabilizer bar.
4. Carefully cut away the retaining lip of the bushing. Use the special clamp type tool and remove the bushing.
5. Saturate the new bushing with vegetable oil and install the bushing using the special tool.
6. Position the lower control arm over the stabilizer bar and install into the inner body mounting using a new bolt and nut. Tighten the inner nut and bolt to 44-53 ft.lb. Tighten the stabilizer nut to 60-70 ft.lb. Be sure to install the dished washer ahead of the nut.

Front End Alignment

CASTER AND CAMBER

Caster and camber angles on your car are preset at the factory and cannot be adjusted in the field. Improper caster and camber can be corrected only through replacement of worn or bent parts.

TOE ADJUSTMENT

Toe is the difference in distance between the front and the rear of the front wheels.

1. Loosen the slide off the small outer boot clamp so the boot will not twist during adjustment.
2. Loosen the locknuts on the outer tie rod ends.
3. Rotate both (right and left) tie rods in exactly equal amounts during adjustment. This will keep the steering wheel centered.
4. Tighten the locknuts when the adjustment has been made. Install and tighten the boot clamps.

FRONT SUSPENSION TIPS AND INSPECTION

- Maintain the correct tire pressures.
- Raise the front of the car and support on jackstands. Grasp the upper and lower edges of the tire. Apply up and downward movement to the tire and wheel. Check for looseness in the front ball joints. See previous ball joint inspection illustration. Inspect the various mounting bushings for wear.

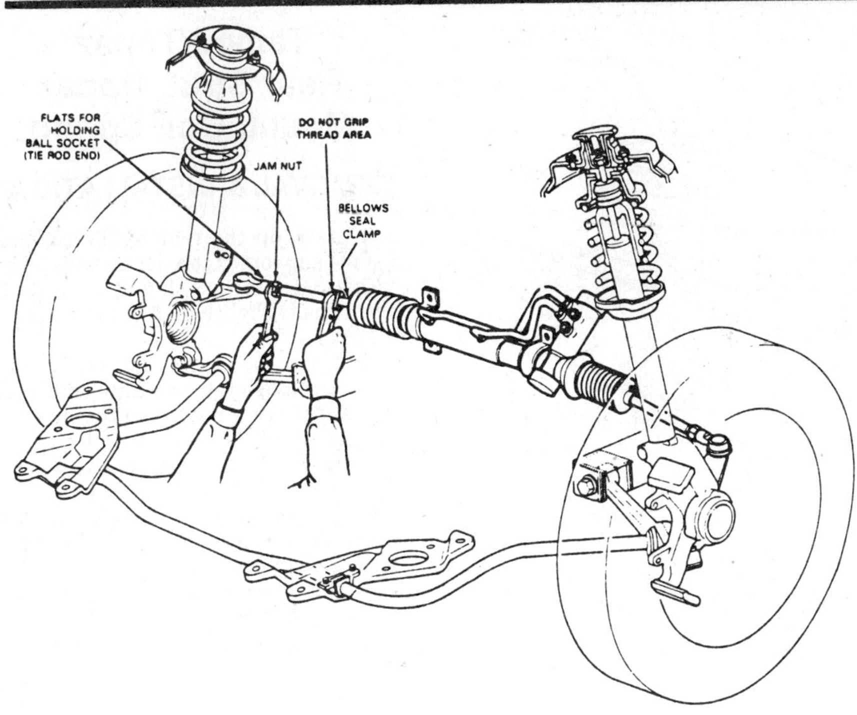

Adjusting front end toe

Tighten all loose nuts and bolts to specifications.

- Replace all worn parts found as soon as possible.
- Check the steering gear and assembly for looseness at its mountings. Check the tie rod ends for looseness.
- Check the shock absorbers. If any dampness from fluid leakage is observed, the shock should be replaced. Check the damping action of the shock by pushing up and down on each corner. If the damping effect is not uniform and smooth the shock should be suspect.

REAR SUSPENSION

Escort/Lynx/EXP/LN-7 Rear Coil Spring

REMOVAL & INSTALLATION

1. Jack up the rear of the car and safely support it on jackstands. The jackstand location should be on the frame pads slightly in front of the rear wheels.
2. Place a floor jack or small hydraulic jack under the rear control arm. Raise the control arm to its normal height with the jack, do not lift the car frame from the jackstands.
3. Remove the tire and wheel assembly. Remove the nut, bolt and washer that mounts the lower control arm to the wheel spindle.
4. Slowly lower the jack under the control arm. The coil spring will relax as the control arm is lowered. Lower the control arm until the spring can be removed.
5. Install a new upper spring insulator onto the top of the coil spring. Install the new spring on the control arm and slowly jack unto position. Be sure the spring is properly seated (indexed) in place on the control arm.
6. Jack up the control arm and position the top of the spring (insulator attached) into the body pocket.
7. Use a new attaching bolt, washers and nut to attach the control arm to the spindle. Tighten the nut and bolt to 90-100 ft.lb.
8. Install the tire and wheel assembly. Remove the car from the jackstands and lower to the ground.

Excort/Lynx/EXP/LN-7 Rear Shock Absorber Strut

REMOVAL & INSTALLATION

1. From inside the car, remove the rear compartment access panels (over the upper strut mount). On four door models remove the quarter trim panels.
2. Loosen, but do not remove the upper shock mounting nut.

NOTE: A special 18mm deep socket is required, the socket should have a hex drive outer head so that it can be turned with an open-end wrench, as well as a ratchet. A 6mm Allen wrench is also required.

To loosen the upper nut, place the socket over the nut, insert the Allen wrench through the center of the socket and into the upper strut rod. Hold the Allen wrench and loosen the nut by turning the socket with an open-end wrench. Use an extension to hold the Allen wrench, if necessary.

3. Jack up the rear of the car and support it safely on jackstands. Remove the rear tire and wheel assembly.
4. Remove the clip that holds the rear brake line to the shock. Locate the brake hose out of the way.
5. Loosen the two nuts and bolts that hold the shock to the wheel spin-

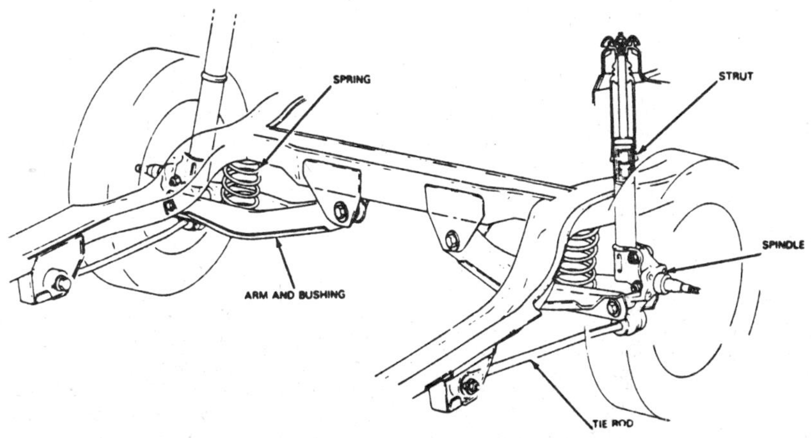

Rear suspension—Escort/Lynx/EXP

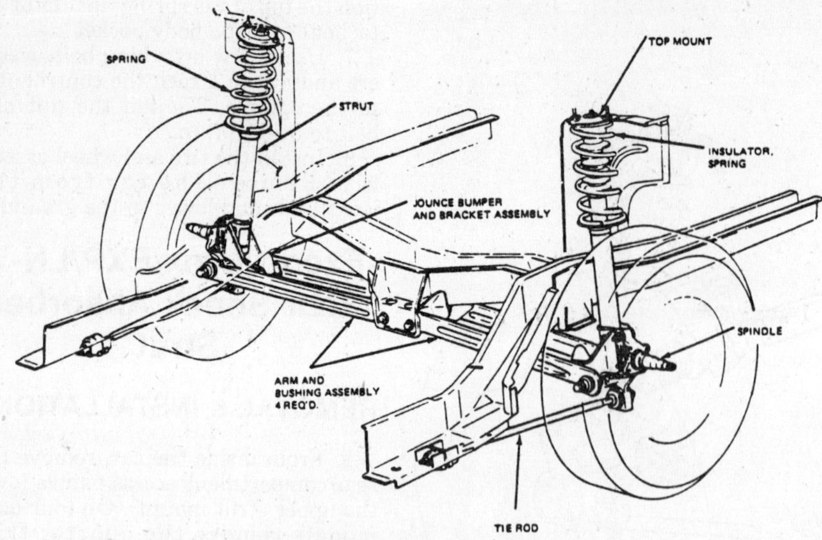

Tempo/Topaz, rear suspension

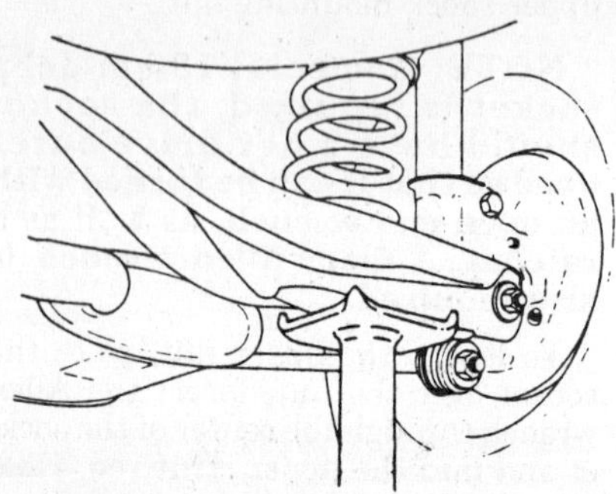

Supporting the rear suspension on Escort/Lynx/EXP

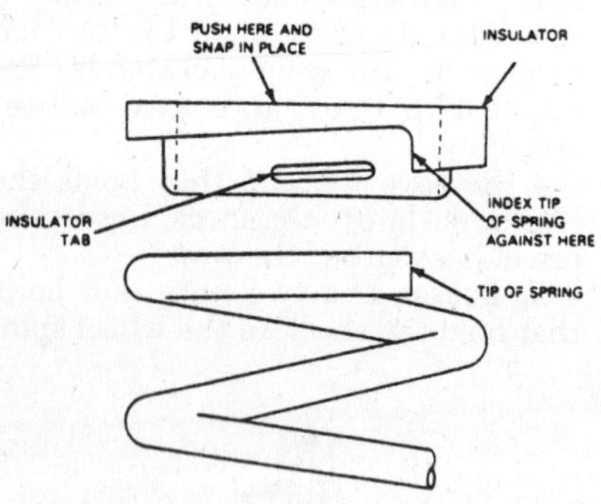

Rear spring installation on the Escort/Lynx/EXP

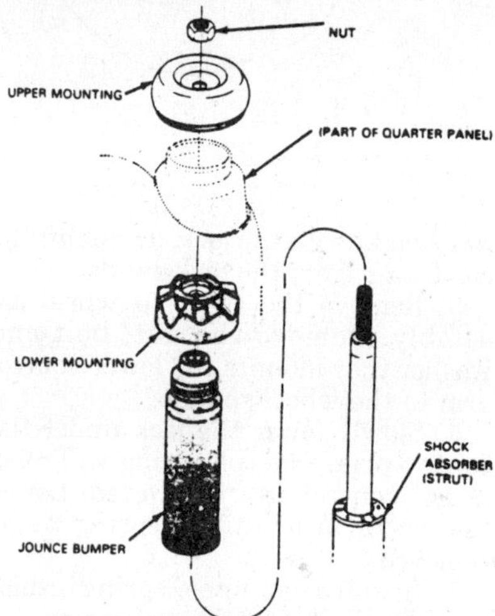

Rear strut mounting on the Escort/Lynx/EXP

dle. DO NOT REMOVE THEM at this time.

6. Remove the upper mounting nut, washer and rubber insulator.

7. Remove the two lower nuts and bolts and remove the shock strut assembly from the car.

8. Extend the shock to its maximum length. Install the new (upper mount) lower washer and insulator assembly. Lubricate the insulator with a tire lubricant. Position the upper part of the shock shaft through the upper mount.

9. Slowly push upwards on the shock until the lower mounting holes align with the mounting holes in the spindle. Install new lower mounting bolts and nuts, buy do not completely tighten at this time. The heads of the mounting bolts must face the rear of the car.

10. Install the new top rubber insulator and washer. Tighten the mounting nuts to 60-70 ft.lb.

11. Tighten the two lower mounting nuts and bolts to 90-100 ft.lb.

12. Install the brake hose with the retaining clip. Put the tire and wheel assembly back on. Remove the jackstands and lower the car.

13. Reinstall the access or trim panels.

Tempo/Topaz Rear Strut, Upper Mount, Coil Spring

REMOVAL & INSTALLATION

1. Jack up the rear of the car and safely support it on jackstands. The jackstand location should be on the frame pads slightly in front of the rear wheels.

2. Open the trunk and loosen, but do not remove the two nuts retaining the upper strut mount to the body.

3. Remove the wheel and tire assembly. Raise the control arm slightly with a floor jack and support the arm on a jackstand. Do not jack the arm more than necessary. Just relieve the suspended position.

4. Remove the bolt that retains the brake hose to the strut. Position the hose out of the way of the strut removal.

5. Remove the jounce bumper retaining bolts and remove the bumper from the strut.

6. Disconnect the lower strut mounting from the spindle. Remove the two top mounting nuts. Remove the strut assembly from the car.

7. Refer to the Front Strut/Coil Spring service procedure preceding

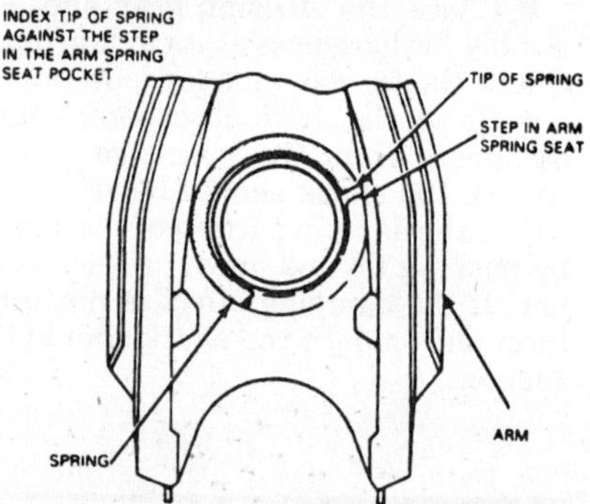

Indexing the rear coil spring on the Escort/Lynx/EXP

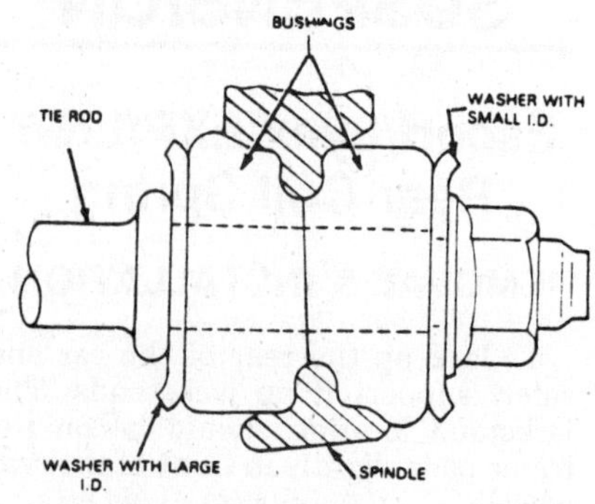

Typical tie rod installation

this section for instructions on coil spring removal & replacement.

8. Install the strut assembly in the reverse order of removal. The lower mounting bolts are tightened to 70-96 ft.lb. The upper to 25-30 ft.lb. Tighten the upper mounting nuts after the car is resting on the ground.

Taurus and Sable Rear Strut

REMOVAL & INSTALLATION

1. Raise and support the rear of the vehicle on jackstands. Remove the rear tires.

NOTE: DO NOT raise or support the vehicle using the tension struts.

2. Raise the rear lid and loosen (do not remove) the upper strut-to-body nuts.
3. Remove the brake differential control valve-to-control arm bolt. Using a wire, secure the control arm to the body to ensure proper support leaving 6" clearance to aid in the strut removal.
4. Remove the brake hose-to-strut bracket clip and move the hose out of the way.
5. If equipped, remove the stabilizer bar U-bracket from the vehicle.
6. If equipped, remove the stabilizer bar-to-stabilizer link nut, washer and insulator, then separate the stabilizer bar from the link.

NOTE: When removing the strut, be sure that the rear brake flex hose is not stretched or the steel brake tube is not bent.

7. Remove the tension strut-to-spindle nut, washer and insulator. Move the spindle rearward to separate it from the tension strut.
8. Remove the shock strut-to-spindle pinch bolt. If necessary, use a medium pry bar, spread the strut-to-spindle pinch joint to remove the strut.
9. Lower the jackstand and separate the shock strut from the spindle.
10. Support the shock strut, then remove the top strut-to-body nuts and the strut from the vehicle.
11. To install, reverse the removal procedures. Torque the shock strut-to-body nuts to 19-26 ft.lb. (26-35 Nm); the shock strut-to-spindle bolt to 55-81 ft.lb. (75-110 Nm); the control arm-to-spindle bolt to 52-74 ft.lb. (70-100 Nm); the control arm-to-body bolt to 52-74 ft.lb. (70-100 Nm); the tension strut-to-spindle nut to 52-74 ft.lb. (70-100 Nm); the stabilizer bar link-to-stabilizer bar nut to 6-12 ft.lb. (8-16 Nm) and the stabilizer U-bracket-to-body bolts to 15-25 ft.lb. (20-34 Nm).

Lower Control Arm

REMOVAL & INSTALLATION

Escort/Lynx/EXP/LN-7

1. Perform Steps 1-4 of the Coil Spring Removal Section.
2. After the spring and insulator have been removed. Take out the inner mounting bolt and nut. Remove the control arm.
3. Installation is in the reverse order of removal. Be sure that the coil is properly indexed (seated) when jacking into position.

Tempo/Topaz

1. Raise and support the car on jackstands positioned ahead of the rear wheels on the body pads.
2. Remove the wheel and tire assembly.
3. Remove the control arm to spindle bolt and nut.
4. Remove the center mounting bolt and nut.
5. Remove the control arm.
6. Install in the reverse order.

Taurus and Sable

1. Raise and support the rear of the vehicle on jackstands. Remove the rear tires.

NOTE: DO NOT raise or support the vehicle using the tension struts.

2. From the left side of the front control arm, disconnect the brake proportioning valve.
3. From the front of the control arms, disconnect the parking brake cable.
4. Remove the control arm-to-spindle bolt, washer and nut.
5. Remove the control arm-to-body nut/bolt and the arm from the vehicle.

NOTE: When installing new control arms, be sure that the offset is facing upwards; the arms are stamped with "Bottom" on the lower edge. The flange edge of the right side rear arm stamping MUST face the front of the vehicle; the other three MUST face the rear of the vehicle.

6. To install, position the arm (cam where required) at the center of the vehicle (insert the bolts but do not tighten) and reverse the removal procedures. Torque the control arm-to-spindle bolts to 52-74 ft.lb. (70-100 Nm) and the control arm-to-body nuts to 52-74 ft.lb. (70-100 Nm). Check the rear wheel alignment.

Tie Rod End

REMOVAL & INSTALLATION

Escort/Lynx/EXP/LN-7

1. Jack up the rear of the car and safely support it on jackstands. Remove the tire and wheel assembly.
2. At the front mounting bracket of the tie rod, take a sharp tool and scribe a vertical mark at the mounting bolt head center. This is so the tie rod can be mounted in the same position.
3. Remove the nut, washer and insulator that mount the rear of the tie rod to the wheel spindle.
4. Remove the front mounting nut and bolt that attach the tie rod to the front bracket. Remove the tie rod.

NOTE: It may be necessary to separate the front body bracket slightly apart with a pry bar to remove the tie rod.

5. Install new mounting bushings on the spindle end of the tie rod (reverse the removal order). Install the tie rod through the spindle and install the bushings, washer and nut. Tighten the nut to 65-75 ft.lb.
6. Use a floor jack or a small hydraulic jack and slowly raise the rear control arm to its curb height.
7. Line up the new front mounting bolt with the mark you scribed on the mounting bracket. Install the bolt and nut (bolt head facing inward). Tighten the nut and bolt to 90-100 ft.lb.

Tempo/Topaz

1. Raise and support the car on jackstands positioned ahead of the rear wheels on the body pads.
2. Loosen the two top strut mounting nuts, but do not remove them.
3. Position a jack under the rear suspension to relieve the suspended position.
4. Remove the wheel and tire assembly.
5. Remove the two upper mounting stud nuts.
6. Remove the nut that retains the tie rod to the rear spindle.
7. Remove the nut that retains the tie rod to the body.
8. Lower the rear suspension slightly until the upper strut mounting studs clear the body mounting holes.
9. Move the spindle rearward until the tie rod can be removed.
10. Install in the reverse order. The upper strut mounting nuts are tightened to 20-30 ft.lb. The tie rod mounting nuts are tightened to 52-74 ft.lb. The suspension should be at normal ride height before the tie rod mounting nuts are tightened.

Stabilizer Bar/Link

REMOVAL & INSTALLATION

Taurus and Sable

1. Raise and support the rear of the vehicle on jackstands. Remove the rear tires.

NOTE: DO NOT raise or support the vehicle using the tension struts.

2. Remove the stabilizer bar-to-link (both sides) nuts, washers and insulators.
3. Remove the stabilizer bar U-bracket-to-body bolts and the stabilizer bar from the vehicle.
4. Remove the stabilizer link-to-shock strut bracket nut, washer and insulator; inspect the condition of the insulators and replace them if necessary.
5. To install, reverse the removal procedures. Torque the stabilizer link-to-shock strut bracket nut to 6-12 ft.lb. (8-16 Nm); the stabilizer bar U-bracket-to-body bolts to 15-25 ft.lb. (20-34 Nm) and the stabilizer bar-to-link nuts to 6-12 ft.lb. (8-16 Nm).

Rear Tension Strut

REMOVAL & INSTALLATION

Taurus and Sable

1. Raise and support the rear of the vehicle on jackstands. Remove the rear tires.

NOTE: DO NOT raise or support the vehicle using the tension struts.

2. Loosen but DO NOT remove the shock strut-to-body nuts.
3. Remove the tension strut-to-spindle nut and the tension strut-to-body nut.
4. Move the spindle rearward and remove the tension strut from the vehicle.

NOTE: The tension strut bushings at the front and the rear are different; the rear bushings have indentations in them.

5. To install, use new tension strut washers/bushings and reverse the removal procedures. Torque the tension strut-to-spindle nut to 52-74 ft.lb. (70-100 Nm) and the tension strut-to-body bracket nut 52-74 ft.lb. (70-100 Nm). Check the rear wheel alignment.

Rear Wheel Spindle

REMOVAL & INSTALLATION

1. Raise the rear of the car and safely support it on jackstands. Remove the tire and wheel assembly.
2. Disconnect the rear brake hose bracket from the strut mounting. Remove the rear brake drum, shoe assembly and brake backing plate. The backing plate is retained by four bolts, loosen and remove the bolts, and the backing plate.
3. Remove the tie rod to spindle retaining nut, washer and insulator. Remove the shock (strut) lower mounting nuts and bolts. Remove the nut and bolt retaining the lower control arm to the spindle. Remove the spindle.
4. Installation is in the reverse order of removal. Torque the mounting bolts and nuts.

Escort/Lynx/EXP/LN-7

- Shock mount: 90-100 ft.lb.
- Control arm: 90-100 ft.lb.
- Tie rod: 65-75 ft.lb.

Tempo/Topaz/Taurus/Sable

- Spindle-to-Strut bolts: 70-96 ft.lb.
- Tie rod nut: 52-74 ft.lb.
- Control arm-to-Spindle nut: 60-86 ft.lb.

Taurus and Sable Rear Wheel Bearings

ADJUSTMENT

The following procedure should be performed whenever the wheel is excessively loose on the spindle or it does not rotate freely.

NOTE: The rear wheel uses a tapered roller bearing which may feel loose when properly adjusted; this feel should be considered normal.

1. Raise and support the rear of the vehicle on jackstands.
2. Remove the wheelcover or the ornament and nut covers. Remove the hub grease cap.

NOTE: If the vehicle is equipped with styled steel or aluminum wheels, the wheel assembly must be removed to remove the dust cover.

3. Remove the cotter pin and the nut retainer.
4. Back off the hub nut one full turn.
5. While rotating the hub/drum assembly, tighten the adjusting nut to 17-25 ft.lb. (23-24 Nm). Back off the adjusting nut ½ turn, then retighten it to 10-15 in.lb. (1.1-1.7 Nm).
6. Position the nut retainer over the adjusting nut so that the slots are in line with cotter pin hole (without rotating the adjusting nut).
7. Install the cotter pin and bend the ends around the retainer flange.
8. To complete the installation, reverse the removal procedures.

REMOVAL & INSTALLATION

1. Raise the vehicle and support it safely. Remove the wheel from the hub and drum.
2. Remove the grease cap from the hub, making sure not to damage the cap. Remove the cotter pin, nut retainer, adjusting nut and keyed flat washer from the spindle. Discard the cotter pin.
3. Pull the hub and drum assembly off the spindle being careful not to drop the outer bearing asembly. Remove the outer bearing assembly.
4. Using a suitable seal remover, remove and discard the grease seal. Remove the inner bearing assembly from the hub.
5. Installation is the reverse order of the removal procedure. Be sure to use a new grease seal and new cotter pin at the installation.

Escort and Lynx EXP and LN7 Tempo and Topaz Rear Wheel Bearings

REMOVAL & INSTALLATION

All Models Except All Wheel Drive

The rear wheel bearings are located in the brake drum hub. The inner wheel bearing is protected by a grease seal. A washer and spindle nut retain the hub/drum assembly and control the bearing end play.

NOTE: For rear axle shaft bearing remove and installation, refer to the rear axle removal and installation procedure in this section.

1. Raise and support the rear of the vehicle. Remove wheel, dust cover, cotter pin nut retainer, adjusting nut and keyed flatwasher from the spindle.
2. Pull the hub and drum assembly off the spindle being careful not to drop the outer bearing assembly.

3. Remove the outer bearing assembly. Using seal remover tool 1175-AC or equivalent, remove the grease seal. Remove the inner bearing assembly from the hub.

4. Wipe all lubricant from the spindle and the inside of the hub. Cover the spindle with a clean cloth and vacuum all the loose dust and dirt from the brake assembly. Carefully remove the cloth to prevent dirt from falling onto the spindle.

5. Clean both bearing assemblies and cups using a suitable solvent. Inspect the bearing assemblies and cups for excessive wear, scratches, pits or other damage. Replace all worn and damaged parts as necessary.

NOTE: Be sure to let the solvent dry before repacking the bearings. Do not spin dry the bearings with air pressure.

6. If the cups are to be replaced, remove them with a slide hammer D79P-100-A and bearing cup puller T77F, 1102-A or equivalent.

7. Pack the bearings with a multipurpose grease.

8. Coat the cups with a thin film of grease. Install the inner bearings and a new grease seal.

9. Coat the bearing surfaces of the spindle with a thin film of grease. Slowly and carefully slide the drum and hub over the spindle and brake shoes. Install the outer bearing over the spindle and into the hub.

10. Install the keyed flat washer and adjusting nut on the spindle.

11. Tighten the adjusting nut to between 17-25 ft.lb.

12. Back-off the adjusting nut ½ turn. Then retighten it to between 10-15 ft.lb.

13. Position the nut retainer on the nut and install the cotter pin. Do not tighten the nut to install the cotter pin.

14. Spread the ends of the cotter pin and bend then around the nut retainer. Install the center grease cap.

15. Install the tire and wheel assembly. Lower the car and tighten the wheel lugs to 80-105 ft.lb.

Rear End Alignment

Rear toe is adjustable but requires special equipment and procedures. If you suspect an alignment problem have it checked by a qualified repair shop. The alignment chart in this section is for factory setting reference.

STEERING

Steering Wheel

REMOVAL & INSTALLATION

Escort, Lynx, EXP, LN7, Tempo, Topaz

1. Disconnect the negative (ground) battery cable from the battery.

2. Remove the steering wheel center hub cover (See illustration). Lift up on the outer edges, do not use a sharp tool or remove the screws from behind the steering wheel cross spoke. Loosen and remove the center mounting nut.

3. Remove the steering wheel with a crowfoot steering wheel puller. DO NOT USE a knock-off type puller it will cause damage to the collapsible steering column.

4. To reinstall the steering wheel, align the marks on the steering shaft and steering wheel. Place the wheel onto the shaft. Install a new center mounting nut. Tighten the nut to 30-40 ft.lb.

5. Install the center cover on the steering wheel. Connect the negative battery cable.

Taurus and Sable

1. Disconnect the negative battery cable. Position the steering wheel so that the wheels are in the straight-forward position.

2. From the rear of the steering wheel, remove the steering wheel-to-horn pad screws.

3. Disconnect the horn pad electrical connectors. If equipped with cruise control, disconnect the electrical connector from the slip ring terminal.

4. Remove and discard the steering wheel-to-steering column nut.

5. Firmly grasp the steering wheel and pull it from the steering column; DO NOT use a wheel puller.

6. To install, reverse the removal procedures. Torque the steering wheel-to-steering column nut to 50-62 ft.lb. (68-84 Nm).

Turn Signal (Combination Switch)

REMOVAL & INSTALLATION

Escort, Lynx, EXP, LN7, Tempo, Topaz

The turn signals, emergency (hazard) warning, horn, flash-to-pass and the headlight dimmer are all together on a combination switch.

1. Disconnect the negative (ground) cable from the battery.

2. Remove the steering column shroud by taking out the five mounting screws. Remove both halves of the shroud.

3. Remove the switch lever by using a twisting motion while pulling the lever straight out from the switch.

4. Peel back the foam cover to expose the switch.

5. Disconnect the two electrical connectors. Remove the two self-tapping screws that attach the switch to the lock cylinder housing. Disengage the switch from the housing.

6. Transfer the ground brush located in the turn signal switch canceling

Typical manual rack and pinion steering

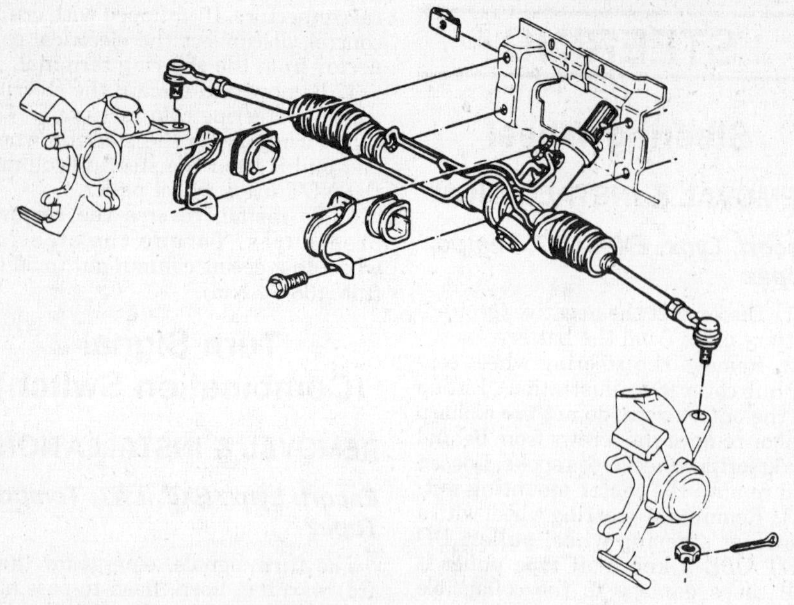

Typical power rack and pinion

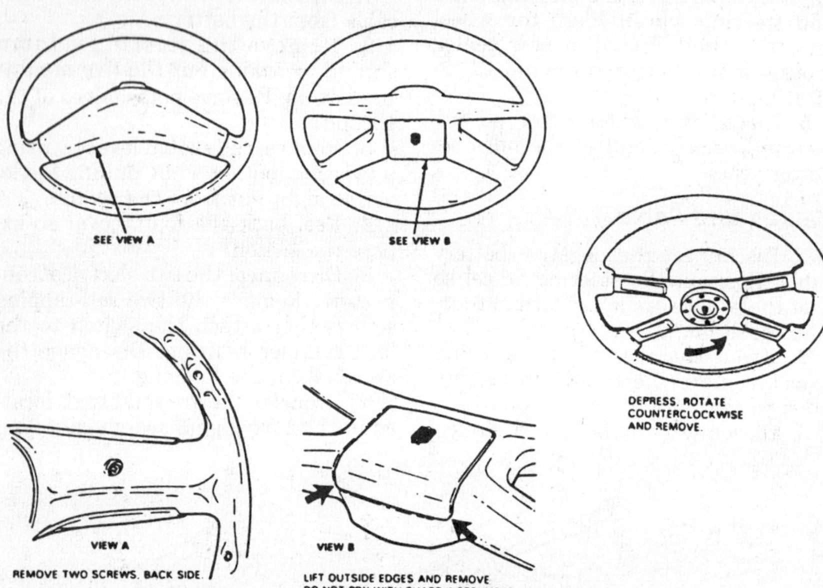

Typical wheel horn pad removal and installation

cam to the new switch, if your car is equipped with speed control.

7. To install the new switch, align the switch with the holes in the lock cylinder housing. Install the two self-tapping screws.

8. Install the foam covering the switch. Install the handle by aligning the key on the lever with the keyway in the switch. Push the lever into the switch until it is fully engaged.

9. Reconnect the two electrical connectors. Install the upper and lower steering column shrouds.

10. Connect the negative battery cable. Test the switch operation.

Taurus and Sable

The combination switch is mounted on the steering column and consists of the following switches: turn signal, cornering lights, hazard warning, headlight dimmer, headlight flash-to-pass, windshield washer and windshield wiper.

1. Refer to the "Steering Wheel Removal & Installation" procedures in this section and remove the steering wheel.

2. If equipped with a tilt-steering column, position the steering wheel in the lowest position and remove the tilt lever.

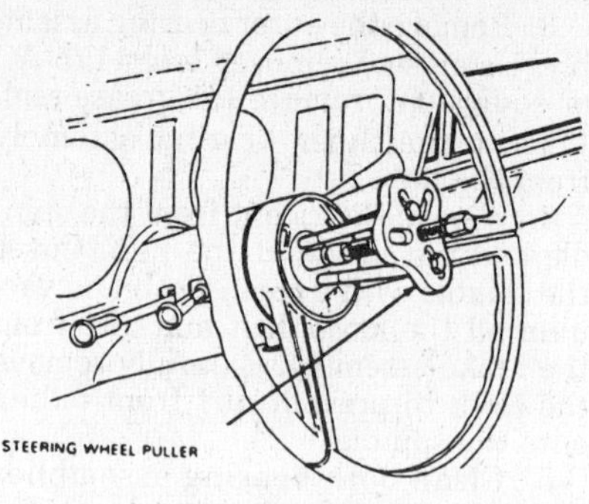

Removing the steering wheel

3. Remove the ignition lock cylinder from the steering column.

4. Remove the upper/lower shroud-to-steering column screws and the shrouds from the steering column.

5. Remove the electrical harness-to-steering column retainer and disconnect the electrical connectors from the steering column.

6. Remove the combination switch-to-steering column screws and the switch from the steering column.

7. To install, reverse the removal procedures. Torque the combination switch-to-steering column screws to 18-27 in.lb. (2-3 Nm), the shroud-to-steering column screws to 6-10 in.lb. (0.7-1.0 Nm), the steering wheel-to-steering column nut to 50-62 ft.lb. (68-84 Nm) and the tilt lever-to-steering column screw to 6-8.5 in.lb. (0.7-1.0 Nm).

Ignition Switch

REMOVAL & INSTALLATION

Escort, Lynx, EXP, LN7, Tempo, Topaz

1. Disconnect the negative (ground) battery cable from the battery.

2. Remove the upper and lower steering column shrouds by taking out the five retaining screws.

3. Disconnect the electrical harness at the ignition switch.

4. Remove the nuts and bolts retaining the steering column mounting brackets and lower the steering wheel and column to the front seat.

5. Use an ⅛" (3mm) drill bit and drill out the break-off head bolts mounting the ignition switch.

6. Take a small screw extractor (Easy Out) and remove the bolts.

7. Remove the ignition switch by disconnecting it from the actuator pin.

NOTE: If reinstalling the old switch, it must be adjusted to the Lock or Run (depending on year and model) position. Slide the

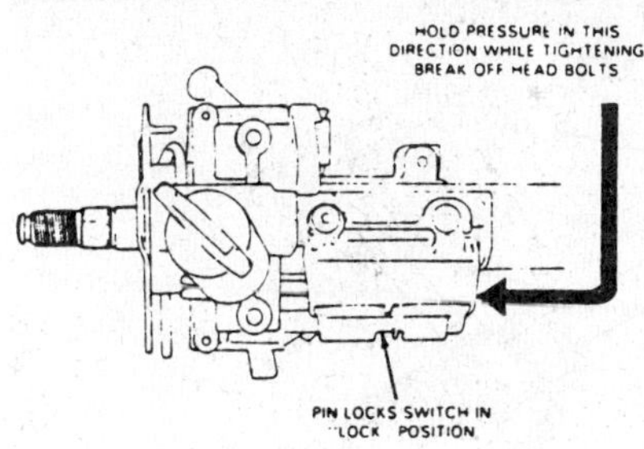

Typical ignition switch installation

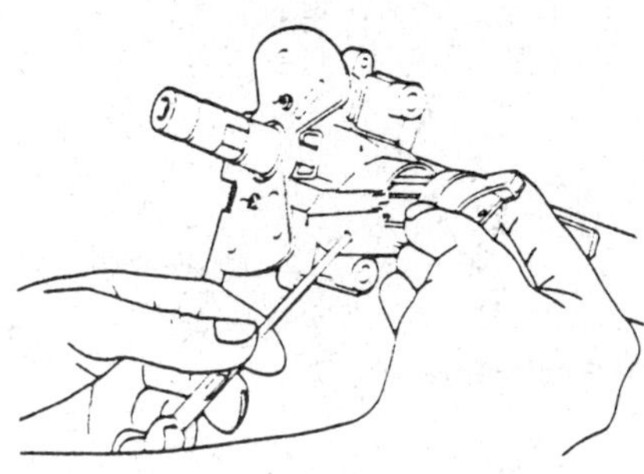

Ignition lock assembly replacement

carrier of the switch to the required position and insert a 1/16" (1.5mm) drill bit or pin through the switch housing into the carrier. This keeps the carrier from moving when the switch is connected to the actuator. It may be necessary to wiggle the carrier back and forth to line up the holes when installing the drill or pin. New switches come with a pin in place.

8. When installing the ignition switch, rotate the key lock cylinder to the required position.
9. Install the ignition switch by connecting it to the actuator and loosely installing the two new mounting screws.
10. Move the switch up the steering column until it reaches the end of its elongated screw slots. Hold the switch in position, tighten the mounting screws until the heads bread off (special break-off bolts), or tighten to 15-25 ft.lb. if non-break off head bolts are used.
11. Remove the pin or drill bit that is locking the actuator carrier in position.
12. Raise the steering column and secure the mounting brackets.
13. Connect the wiring harness to the ignition switch. Install the upper and lower steering column shrouds.
14. Connect the negative battery cable.
15. Check the ignition for operation. Make sure the car will start in Neutral and Park, if equipped with automatic transaxle, but be sure it will not start in Drive or reverse. Make sure the steering (wheel) locks when the key switch is in the LOCK position.

Ignition Lock Cylinder Assembly

REMOVAL & INSTALLATION

Escort, Lynx, EXP, LN7, Tempo, Topaz

1. Disconnect the negative (ground) battery cable from the battery.
2. Remove the steering column lower shroud on Escort/Lynx/EXP/LN-7. On Tempo/Topaz models, remove the two trim halves by removing the five attaching screws. On models with tilt wheel, remove the upper extension shroud by unsnapping from a retaining clip that is located at the nine o'clock position.
3. Disconnect the warning buzzer electrical connector. Turn the key cylinder to the Run position.
4. Take a 1/8" (3mm) diameter pin or small punch and push on the cylinder retaining pin. The pin is visible through a hole in the mounting surrounding the key cylinder. As you push on the pin pull out on the lock cylinder.
5. To reinstall the switch, make sure it is in the **RUN** position. Push in on the retaining pin and insert the cylinder into the casting. Be sure it is fully seated and aligned with the interlocking washer. Turn the key cylinder to the **OFF** position. When the lock cylinder is turned to the **OFF** position, the retaining pin locks the cylinder into the casting.
6. Rotate the lock cylinder through the different positions to make sure it is working freely.
7. Connect the wire to the buzzer, mount the shrouds and/or trim panels, connect the battery cable and test the operation of the lock cylinder.

Ignition Lock/Switch

REMOVAL & INSTALLATION

Taurus and Sable

1. Disconnect the negative battery cable.
2. Turn the ignition lock cylinder to the Run position.
3. Using a 1/8" diameter punch, insert it through the access hole in the bottom of the lower steering column shroud, depress the retaining pin and remove the ignition lock cylinder.
4. If equipped with a tilt steering column, remove the tilt lever-to-steering column screw and the tilt lever.
5. Remove the lower instrument panel cover screws and the cover.
6. Using a Phillips head screw driver, remove the upper/lower steering column shrouds.
7. Remove the steering column-to-support bracket nuts/bolts and lower the steering column.
8. Disconnect the electrical harness connector from the ignition switch.
9. Using the Torx Driver tool No. D83L-2100-A, remove the ignition lock actuator cover plate Torx® head bolt and the cover plate.
10. Using the driver tool No. D83L-2100-A, or equivalent, remove the ignition switch-to-actuator assembly Torx® head bolts and the cover assembly from the actuator assembly, then slide the lock actuator from the actuator assembly.
11. To install the ignition switch-to-actuator assembly, perform the following procedures:
    a. Position the ignition switch in the RUN position.

NOTE: To position the ignition switch in the RUN position, turn the switch drive shaft fully clockwise to the START position and release it.

    b. Using a small ruler, insert the lock actuator into the actuator assembly to a depth of 0.46-0.54" (11.75-13.25mm).
    c. While holding the lock actuator at the proper depth, install the ignition switch.
    d. Using new tamper-resistant Torx® head bolts, torque the ignition switch-to-actuator assembly bolts to 30-48 in.lb. (3.4-5.4 Nm).
12. To install the lock cylinder, perform the following procedures:
    a. While measuring the lock actuator, turn the ignition switch to the Lock position and install it, the depth should be 0.92-1.0" (23.5-25.5mm); if this specification is not met, repeat the lock actuator installation.
    b. Using a new tamper-resistant Torx® head bolt, torque the cover-to-lock actuator assembly bolt to 30-48 in.lb. (3.4-5.4 Nm).
13. Check the operation of the ignition lock cylinder; if the operation is OK, remove the ignition lock cylinder.
14. To complete the installation, reverse the removal procedures and reinstall the ignition lock cylinder. Torque the steering column support bracket-to-instrument panel nuts/bolts to 15-25 ft.lb. (20-34 Nm), the shroud-to-steering column screws to 6-10 in.lb. (0.7-1.1 Nm) and the tilt release lever-to-steering column screw to 6.5-8.5 ft.lb. (9-11 Nm).

Manual Rack and Pinion Steering

If your car is equipped with manual steering, it is of the rack and pinion type. The gear input shaft is connected to the steering shaft by a double U-joint. A pinion gear, machined on the input shaft, engages the rack. The rotation of the input shaft pinion causes the rack to move laterally. The rack has tow tie rods whose ends are connected to the front wheels. When the rack moves so do the front wheel knuckles. Toe adjustment is made by turning the outer tie rod ends in or out equally as required.

REMOVAL & INSTALLATION

1. Disconnect the negative battery cable from the battery. Jack up the front of the car and support it safely on jackstands.
2. Turn the ignition switch to the **On/Run** position. Remove the lower access (kick) panel from below the steering wheel.
3. Remove the intermediate shaft bolts at the gear input shaft and at the steering column shaft.
4. Spread the slots of the clamp to loosen the intermediate shaft at both ends. The next steps must be performed before the intermediate shaft and gear input shaft can be separated.
5. Turn the steering wheel full left so the tie rod will clear the shift linkage. Separate the outer tie rod ends from the steering knuckle by using a tie rod end remover.
6. Remove the left tie rod end from the tie rod (wheel must be at full left position). Disconnect the speedometer cable from the transmission if the car is equipped with an automatic transaxle. Disconnect the secondary air tube at the check valve. Disconnect the exhaust pipe from the exhaust manifold and wire it out of the way to allow enough room to remove the steering gear.
7. Remove the exhaust hanger bracket from below the steering gear. Remove the steering gear mounting brackets and rubber mounting insulators.
8. Have someone help by holding the gear from the inside of the car. Separate the intermediate shaft from the input shaft.
9. Make sure the gear is still in the full left turn position. Rotate the gear forward and down to clear the input shaft through the opening. Move the gear to the right to clear the splash panel and other linkage that interferes with the removal. Lower the gear and remove from under the car.

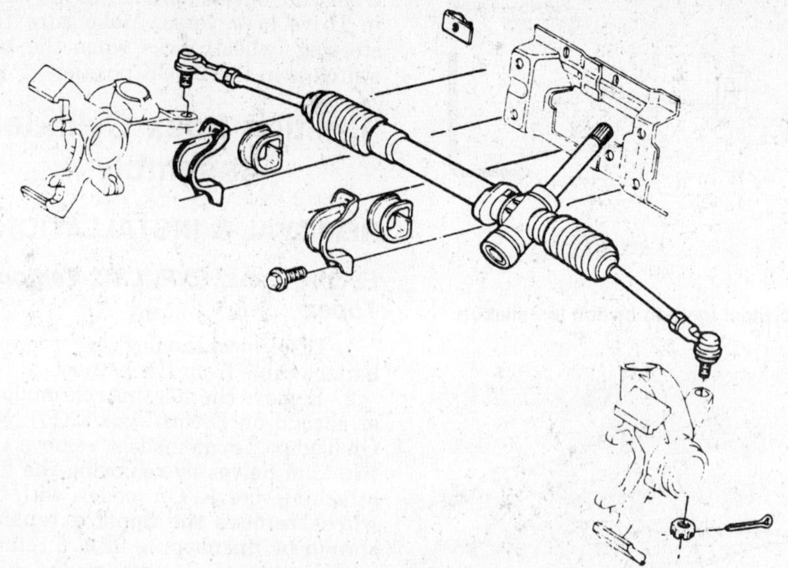

Manual steering gear replacement

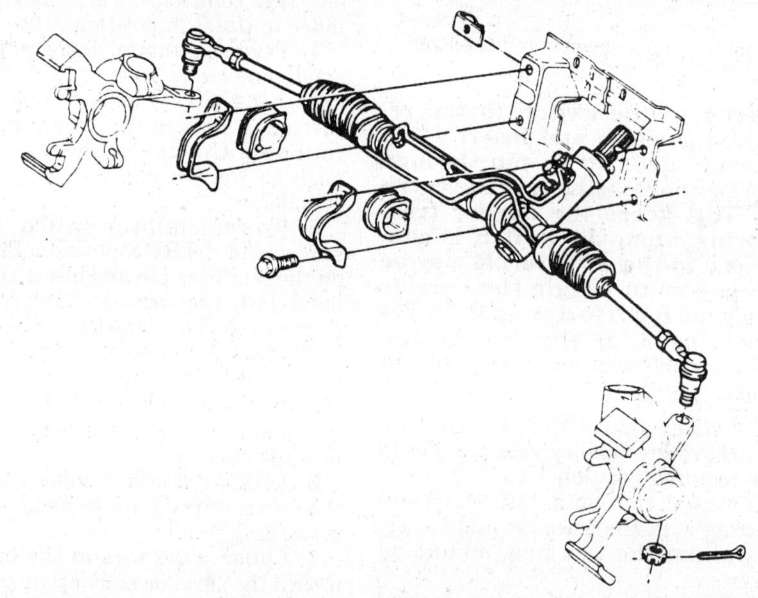

Power steering gear replacement

10. Installation is in the reverse order of removal. Have the toe adjustment checked after installing a new rack and pinion assembly.

Integral Power Rack and Pinion Steering

A rotary design control valve uses relative rotational motion of the input shaft and valve sleeve to direct fluid flow. When the steering wheel is turned, resistance of the wheels and the weight of the car cause a torsion bar to twist. The twisting causes the valve to move in the sleeve and aligns fluid passages for right, left and straight ahead position. The pressure forces on the valve and helps move the rack to assist in the turning effort. The piston is attached directly to the rack. The housing tube functions as the power cylinder. The hydraulic areas of the gear assembly are always filled with fluid. The mechanical gears are filled with grease making periodic lubrication unnecessary. The fluid and grease act as a cushion to absorb road shock.

REMOVAL & INSTALLATION

Escort, Lynx, EXP, LN7, Tempo, Topaz

Removal and installation is basically

the same as the manual rack and pinion steering. However, the pressure and return lines must be disconnected at the intermediate connectors and drained of fluid. It is necessary to remove the pressure switch from the pressure line.

Taurus and Sable

1. From inside the vehicle, remove the steering shaft weather boot-to-dash panel nuts.
2. Remove the intermediate shaft-to-steering column shaft bolts and set the weather boot aside. Remove the steering gear input shaft pinch bolt and the intermediate shaft.
3. Raise and support the front of the vehicle on jackstands.
4. Remove the left front wheel and the heat shield, then cut the bundling strap lines from the steering gear.
5. Remove the tie rod ends from the steering knuckles.
6. Position a drain pan under the vehicle, then disconnect the pressure and return hoses from the steering gear and drain the fluid.

NOTE: The pressure and return hoses are located on the front of the valve housing.

7. Remove the steering gear-to-chassis nuts.

NOTE: The steering gear bolts are pressed into the housing; no attempt should be made to remove them.

8. While pushing the weather boot into the vehicle, lift the steering gear from the mounting holes, rotate the gear (so that the input shaft will pass between the brake booster and the floorpan) and work it through the left fender apron opening.

NOTE: If the steering gear appears to be stuck, check the right side tie rod to ensure that it is not caught on anything.

9. To install, use new plastic seals on the hydraulic line fittings and reverse the removal procedures. Torque the steering gear-to-chassis nuts to 85-100 ft.lb. (115-135 Nm); the ttie rod end-to-steering knuckle nuts to 35-50 ft.lb. (48-68 Nm); the intermediate shaft-to-steering gear bolt to 30-38 ft.lb. (41-51 Nm). Refill the power steering pump reservoir and bleed the system.

ADJUSTMENT

The power steering gear preload adjustment must be performed with the steering gear removed from the vehicle.

1. Refer to the "Power Steering Gear Removal & Installation" procedures in this section and remove the power steering gear from the vehicle.
2. Mount the steering gear in a holding fixture (tool No. T57L-500-B, or equivalent).

NOTE: If the steering gear mounting holes in the holding fixture are too small, drill the holes larger using a $^{9}/_{16}$" drill bit.

3. DO NOT remove the external pressure lines from the steering gear unless they are leaking or damaged. If they are removed, they must be replaced with new ones.
4. Using the pinion shaft torque adjuster tool No. T86P-3504-K, or equivalent, position it on the input shaft and rotate the shaft (twice), from lock-to-lock, to drain the power steering fluid.
5. Using the pinion housing yoke locknut wrench (tool No. T86P-3504-E, or equivalent), loosen the yoke plug locknut and the yoke plug.
6. Position the steering gear in the center of it's travel and torque the yoke plug to 45-50 in.lb. (5-5.6 Nm); be sure to clean the yoke plug threads before torquing.
7. Mark the position of the 0 mark on the steering gear housing. Using the disc-yoke preload adjuster tool (No. T86P-3504-H), back off the adjuster to align the 48° mark with the 0 mark.
8. Using the pinion housing yoke locknut wrench to hold the yoke plug, torque the yoke plug locknut to 40-50 ft.lb. (54-68 Nm).

NOTE: When torquing the yoke plug locknut, DO NOT allow the yoke plug to move.

9. To install the steering gear, reverse the removal procedures. Refill the power steering reservoir, bleed the system and check for leaks.

Tie Rod Ends

REMOVAL & INSTALLATION

Escort, Lynx, EXP, LN7, Tempo, Topaz

1. Remove and discard the cotter pin and nut from the worn tie rod end stud.
2. Disconnect the tie rod end from the steering knuckle with an appropriate puller.
3. Hold the end with a wrench and loosen the jam nut.
4. Measure the depth of the tie rod end and count the number of turns as you unscrew it.
5. Clean the tie rod threads. Screw in the new end the same number of turns as the one removed. Check depth measurement. Complete installation in the reverse order of removal. Have the toe setting checked and adjusted.

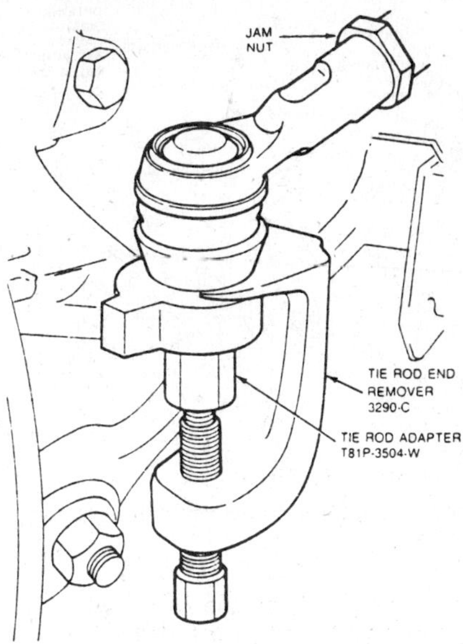

Tie rod end replacement

Taurus and Sable

1. Raise and support the front of the vehicle on jackstands.
2. Remove the discard the cotter pin and the nut from the tie rod end ball stud.
3. Using the tie rod remover tool No. TOOL-3290-C, or equivalent, separate the tie rod end from the steering knuckle.
4. While holding the tie rod end, loosen the tie rod jam nut.
5. Note the depth of the tie rod end-to-tie rod, then remove the tie rod end from the tie rod.
6. To install, reverse the removal procedures. Torque the tie rod-to-steering knuckle nut to 36 ft.lb. (48 Nm) and the tie rod end-to-tie rod nut to 35-50 ft.lb. (47-68 Nm). Check and, if necessary, adjust the toe-in.

Power Steering Pump

REMOVAL & INSTALLATION

Escort/Lynx/EXP/LN-7

1. Remove the air cleaner, air pump and belt. Remove the reservoir extension and plug the hole with a clean rag.

NOTE: On 1986 and later vehicles equipped with a remote reservoir, remove the reservoir supply hose at the pump, drain the fluid, and plug the cap opening at the pump to prevent dirt from entering.

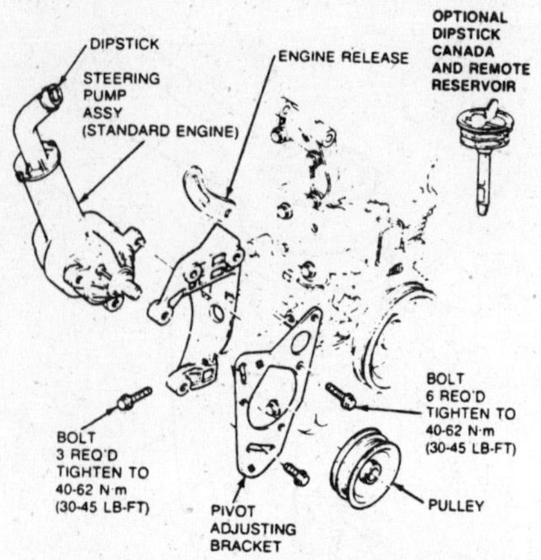

Power steering pump mounting—typical

2. From under the car, loosen the pump adjusting bolt. Remove the pump to bracket mounting bolt and disconnect the fluid return line. Be prepared to catch any spilled fluid in a suitable container.
3. From above, loosen the adjusting bolt and remove the drive belt. Remove the two remaining mounting bolts. Remove the adjusting bolts.
4. Remove the pump by passing the pulley end through the adjusting bracket opening.
5. Remove the pressure hose from the pump.
6. Installation is in the reverse order. Fill the pump with fluid and check for proper operation.

Tempo/Topaz

1. Loosen the alternator and remove the drive belt. Pivot the alternator to its most upright position.
2. Remove the radiator overflow bottle. Loosen and remove the power steering pump drive belt. Mark the pulley and pump drive hub with paint or grease pencil for location reference.
3. Remove the pulley retaining bolts and the two pulleys from the pump shaft.
4. Remove the return line from the pump. Be prepared to catch any spilled fluid in a suitable container.
5. Back off the pressure line attaching nut completely. The line will separate from the pump connection when the pump is removed.
6. Remove the three pump mounting bolts and remove the pump.
7. Place the pump in position and connect the pressure line loosely, Install the pump in the reverse order.

Diesel Engine Models

1. Remove the drive belts.
2. On air conditioned models, remove the alternator.
3. Remove both braces from the support bracket on air conditioned models.
4. Disconnect the power steering fluid lines and drain the fluid into a suitable container.
5. Remove the four bracket mounting bolts and remove the pump and bracket assembly.
6. The pulley must be remove before the pump can be separated from the mounting bracket. Tool T65P3A733C or equivalent is required to remove and install the drive pulley.
7. Install the pump and mounting bracket in the reverse order of removal.

Taurus and Sable

2.5L ENGINE

1. Disconnect the negative battery cable.
2. Using a ½" drive ratchet, insert it into the square hole of the drive belt tensioner pulley, rotate the pulley clockwise and remove the drive belt.
3. Position a drain pan under the vehicle, disconnect the power steering pump fluid lines and drain the fluid into the pan.
4. Using the hub puller tool No. T69L-10300-B, or equivalent, remove the pulley from the power steering pump.
5. Remove the pump-to-bracket bolts and the pump from the vehicle.
6. To install, reverse the removal procedures.
7. Using the steering pump pulley replacer tool No. T65P-3A733-C, or equivalent, press the pump pulley onto the shaft so that the pulley is flush with the pump shaft ± 0.10" (± 0.25mm).

NOTE: When installing the pump pulley, the small diameter tool threads must be fully engaged in the pump shaft.

8. Fill the pump reservoir with power steering fluid, bleed the system and check for leaks.

3.0L ENGINE

1. Disconnect the negative battery cable.
2. Loosen the idler pulley and remove the power steering belt.
3. Remove the pulley from the pump hub and the return line from the pump.
4. Back off the pressure line nut until the line separates from the pump.
5. Remove the pump-to-bracket bolts and the pump from the vehicle.
6. To install, reverse the removal procedures. Torque the pump-to-bracket bolts to 30-45 ft.lb. (40-62 Nm). Refill the power steering pump reservoir, bleed the system and check for leaks.

SYSTEM BLEEDING

1. Using power steering pump fluid, fill the power steering reservoir to the maximum fill line.
2. Run the engine until it reaches normal operating temperature.
3. Turn the steering wheel from the left-to-right (all the way) several times.

NOTE: When turning the steering wheel, do not hold it in the far left or right positions too long.

4. Check and, if necessary, refill the power steering system.
5. If air remains in the system, it must be purged by performing the following procedures:
   a. Remove the power steering pump dipstick cap assembly.
   b. Using type F automatic transmission fluid, fill the reservoir to the COLD FULL mark on the pump dipstick.
   c. Disconnect the ignition coil wire. Raise and support the front of the vehicle on jackstands.
   d. Using the starter motor, crank the engine, then check the fluid level; do not turn the steering wheel at this time.
   e. Check and, if necessary, refill the pump reservoir. Using the starter motor, crank the engine and cycle the steering wheel from lock-to-lock, then recheck the fluid level.
   f. Using the vacuum tester tool No. 021-00014, or equivalent, press the rubber stopper into the pump reservoir. Install the coil wire and start the engine.
   g. Apply 15 in.Hg to the pump reservoir for at least three minutes (engine idling).

NOTE: As the air is being purged from the system, the vacuum will fall off; be sure to maintain adequate vacuum with the vacuum source.

   h. Release and remove the vacuum source. Check and, if necessary, refill the power steering pump reservoir to the Cold Full mark.
   i. With the engine idling, connect 15 in.Hg to the pump reservoir. Every 30 seconds for approx. 5 min., turn the steering wheel from lock-to-lock; DO NOT hold the steering wheel in the lock position.

NOTE: When bleeding the power steering system, be sure to maintain adequate vacuum.

   j. Release the vacuum, remove the vacuum equipment and add fluid, if necessary.
   k. Start the engine, cycle the steering wheel and check for oil leaks.

BRAKE SYSTEM

Brake Adjustment

FRONT DISC BRAKES

Front disc brakes require no adjustment. Hydraulic pressure maintains the proper pad-to-disc contact at all times.

REAR DRUM BRAKES

The rear drum brakes, on your car, are self-adjusting. The only adjustment necessary should be an initial one after new brake shoes have been installed or some type of service work has been done on the rear brake system.

NOTE: After any brake service, obtain a firm brake pedal before moving the car. Adjusted brakes must not drag. The wheel must turn freely. Be sure the parking brake cables are not too tightly adjusted.

A special brake shoe gauge is necessary, if your car is equipped with 8″ (203mm) brakes, for making an accurate adjustment after installing new brake shoes. The special gauge measures both the drum diameter and the brake shoe setting.

Since no adjustment is necessary except when service work is done on the rear brakes, we will assume that the car is jacked up and safely supported by jackstands, and that the rear drums have been removed. (If not, refer to the appropriate sections of this section for the procedures necessary).

Cars Equipped with 7″ (178mm) Brakes

Pivot the adjuster quadrant (see illustration) until the third or fourth notch from the outer end of the quadrant meshes with the knurled pin on the adjuster strut. Install the hub and drum.

Cars Equipped with 8″ (203mm) Brakes

Measure and set the special brake gauge to the inside diameter of the brake drum. Lift the adjuster lever from the starwheel teeth. Turn the starwheel until the brake shoes are adjusted out to the shoe setting fingers of the brake gauge. Install the hub and drum.

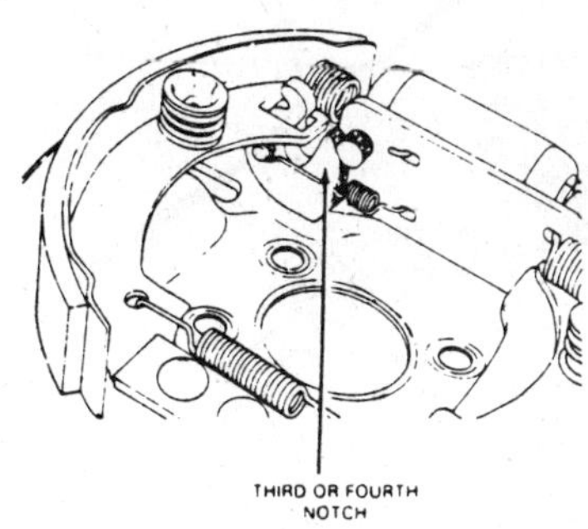

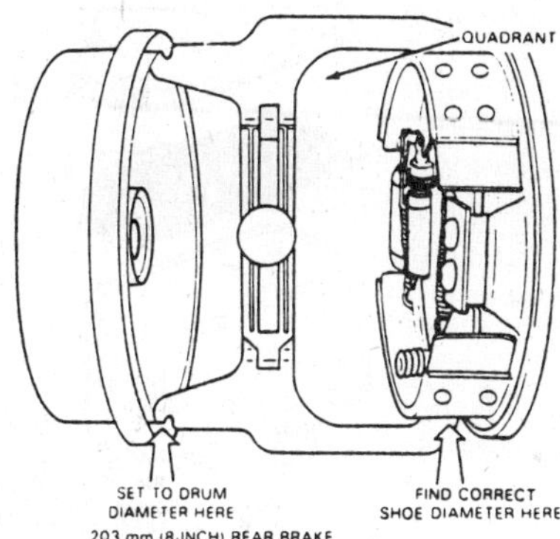

Rear brake shoe adjustment

NOTE: Complete the adjustment (7″ or 8″ brakes) by applying the brakes several times. After the brakes have been properly adjusted, check their operation by making several stops from varying forward speeds.

Adjustment for Brake Drum Removal

If the brake drum will not come off for brake servicing, pry the rubber plug from the backing plate inspection hole and use the following procedure:

On 7″ (178mm) brakes: Insert a thin blade screwdriver through the hole until it contacts the adjuster assembly pivot. Apply side pressure to the pivot point allowing the adjuster quadrant to ratchet and back off the brake adjustment.

On 8″ (203mm) brakes: Remove the brake line to axle retention bracket. This will allow sufficient room for the use of a thin screwdriver and brake adjusting tool. Push the adjuster lever away from the adjuster wheel with the screwdriver and release adjustment with the brake tool.

Master Cylinder

The fluid reservoir of the master cylinder has a large and small compartment. The larger serves the right front and left rear brakes, while the smaller serves the left front and right rear brakes.

Always be sure that the fluid level of the reservoirs is within 1/4″ (6mm) of the top. Use only DOT 3 approved brake fluid.

REMOVAL & INSTALLATION

Models without Power Brakes

1. Disconnect the negative (ground) battery cable from the battery.
2. From under the dash panel, disconnect the wires to the stoplight switch. Remove the spring clip that retains the stoplight switch and the master cylinder pushrod to the brake pedal.
3. Slide the stoplight switch off the brake pedal pin. Remove the switch.
4. From under the hood, loosen the two retaining nuts mounting the master cylinder to the firewall. Disconnect the brake lines from the master cylinder.
5. Slide the master cylinder pushrod, washers and bushings from the brake pedal pin.

NOTE: Models with speed control have an adapter instead of a washer on the brake pedal mounting pin.

6. Remove the cylinder mounting nuts. Lift the cylinder out and away from the firewall.

CAUTION

Take care not to spill any brake fluid on the painted surfaces of your car. If you spill any on you car, flush off with water as soon as possible. Brake fluid will act like a paint remover.

To install:

1. Insert the master cylinder pushrod through the opening in the firewall. Place the cylinder mounting flange over the studs on the firewall and loosely install the mounting nuts.
2. Coat the nylon pushrod mounting bushing with oil. Install the wash-

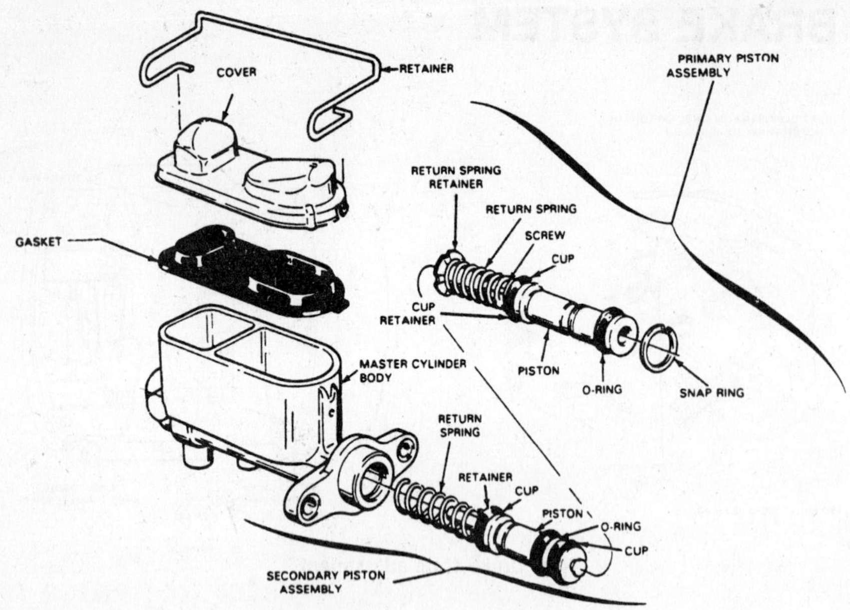

Exploded view of the master cylinder

er, pushrod and bushing on the brake pedal shaft. (Speed control models use a snap-on adapter instead of a washer).

3. Position the stoplight switch on the brake pedal pin. Install the nylon bushing and washer and secure with the spring pin.

4. Connect the wires to the stoplight switch.

5. Connect the brake lines to the master cylinder, but do not tighten them completely.

6. Secure the cylinder mounting nuts. Fill the master cylinder to within ¼" (6mm) of the top. Slowly pump the brake pedal to help evacuate the air in the master cylinder.

NOTE: Cover the brake line connections (at the master cylinder) with a rag to prevent brake fluid spray.

7. Tighten the brake lines at the master cylinder. Add brake fluid if necessary.

8. Connect the negative battery cable. Bleed the entire brake system. Centralize the pressure differential valve (refer to the following sections).

9. Check for hydraulic leads. Road test the car.

Escort and Lynx EXP and LN7 Tempo and Topaz With Power Brake

1. Disconnect the brake lines from the master cylinder.

2. Remove the two nuts that mount the master cylinder to the brake booster.

3. Pull the master cylinder forward and away from the booster.

CAUTION

Brake fluid acts like a paint remover. If you spill any on the finish of your car, flush it off with water.

To install:

1. Slip the master cylinder base over the pushrod at the poser brake booster. Align the mounting flange and place over the mounting studs on the booster. Loosely secure with the two mounting nuts.

2. Connect the brake lines to the master cylinder. Tighten the mounting nuts. Tighten the brake lines.

3. Fill the master cylinder to within ¼" (6mm) of the top. Bleed the brake system. Centralize the pressure differential valve (refer to the following sections). Check for system leaks. Road test the car.

Taurus and Sable

1. Disconnect and plug the brake lines from the master cylinder.

2. Disconnect the electrical connector (brake warning lamp) from the master cylinder.

3. Remove the master cylinder-to-power booster nuts and the master cylinder from the vehicle.

4. To install, reverse the removal procedures. Torque the master cylinder-to-power booster nuts to 13-25 ft.lb. (18-33 Nm). Bleed the brake system.

MASTER CYLINDER OVERHAUL

Referring to the exploded view of the dual master cylinder components, disassemble the unit as follows: Clean the exterior of the cylinder and remove the filler cover and diaphragm. Any brake fluid remaining in the cylinder should be poured out and discarded. Remove the secondary piston stop bolt from the bottom of the cylinder and remove the bleed screw, if required. With the primary piston depressed, remove the snapring from its retaining groove at the rear of the cylinder bore. Withdraw the pushrod and the primary piston assembly from the bore.

Remove the secondary piston assembly. If the piston does not come out easily, apply air pressure carefully through the secondary outlet port to assist in piston removal.

NOTE: Do not remove the outlet tube seats, outlet check valves and outlet check valve springs from the cylinder body unless they are damaged.

All components should be cleaned in clean isopropyl alcohol or clean brake fluid and inspected for chipping, excessive wear and damage. Check to ensure that all recesses, openings and passageways are clear and free of foreign matter. Dirt and cleaning solvent may be removed by using compressed air. After cleaning, keep all parts on a clean surface. Inspect the cylinder bore for etching, pitting, scoring or rusting. Since honing is not recommended for aluminum master cylinders, deep scratches or pitting will require master cylinder replacement.

During the assembly operation, be sure to use all parts supplied with the master cylinder repair kit. With the exception of the master cylinder body, submerge all parts in extra heavy duty brake fluid. Carefully insert the complete secondary piston and return spring assembly into the cylinder bore and install the primary piston assembly into the bore. With the primary piston depressed, install the snapring into its groove in the cylinder bore. Install the pushrod, boot and retainer (if equipped), then install the pushrod assembly into the primary piston. Be sure that the retainer is properly seated and is holding the pushrod securely. Position the inner end of the pushrod boot (if equipped) in the master cylinder body retaining groove. Install the secondary piston stop bolt and O-ring at the bottom of the master cylinder body. Install the bleed screw (if equipped) and position the gasket on the master cylinder filler cover. Be sure that the gasket is securely seated.

Reinstall the master cylinder and fill the brake fluid. Install the cover and secure with the retainer. Bleed the brake system and road test the car.

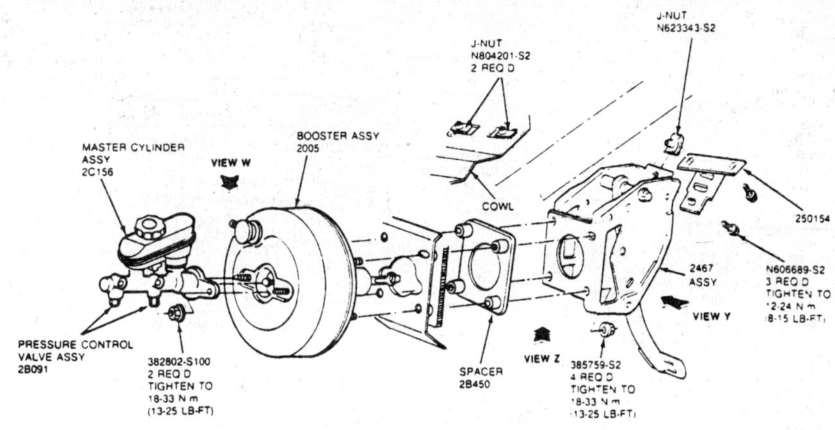

Power booster and master cylinder assembly

Vacuum Booster

REMOVAL & INSTALLATION

Escort, Lynx, EXP, LN7, Tempo and Topaz

1. Working from inside the car, beneath the instrument panel, remove the booster pushrod from the brake pedal.
2. Disconnect the stop light switch wires and remove the switch from the brake pedal. Use care not to damage the switch during removal.
3. Raise the hood and remove the master cylinder from the booster.
4. Remove the manifold vacuum hose from the booster.
5. Remove the booster to firewall attaching bolts and remove the booster from the car.
6. Reverse above procedure to reinstall.

Taurus and Sable

1. Refer to the "Master Cylinder Removal & Installation" procedures in this section and remove the master cylinder from the power brake booster; it is not necessary to remove the brake tubes from the master cylinder.
2. Remove the vacuum hose from the power brake booster.
3. From under the instrument panel, remove the pushrod retainer and outer nylon washer from the brake pin.
4. Remove the power brake booster-to-pedal support nuts. Slide the booster pushrod and pushrod bushing off of the brake pedal pin.
5. Move the booster forward until the studs clear the dash panel and remove the it from the vehicle.
6. To install, reverse the removal procedures. Torque the power brake booster-to-brake assembly bracket nuts to 12-22 ft.lb. (16-30 Nm) and the master cylinder-to-power brake booster nuts to 13-25 ft.lb. (18-34 Nm). If the brake tubes were disconnected, bleed the brake system.

TESTING THE POWER BRAKE BOOSTER

The power brake booster depends on vacuum produced by the engine for proper operation.

If you suspect problems in the power brake system, check the following:

1. Inspect all hoses and hose connections. All unused vacuum connectors should be sealed. Hoses and connections should be tightly secured and in good condition. The hoses should be pliable with no holes or cracks and no collapsed areas.
2. Inspect the check valve which is located in line between the intake manifold and booster. Disconnect the hose on the intake manifold side of the valve. Attempt to blow through the valve. If air passes through the valve, it is defective and must be replaced.
3. Check the level of brake fluid in the master cylinder. If the level is low, check the system for fluid leaks.
4. Idle the engine briefly and then shut it off. Pump the brake pedal several times to exhaust all of the vacuum stored in the booster. Keep the brake pedal depressed and start the engine. The brake pedal should drop slightly, if vacuum is present after the engine is started less pressure should be necessary on the brake pedal. If no drop, or action is felt the power brake booster should be suspect.
5. With the parking brake applied and the wheels blocked, start the engine and allow to idle in Neutral (Park if automatic). Disconnect the vacuum line to the check valve on the intake manifold side. If vacuum is felt, connect the hose and repeat Step 4. Once again, if no action is felt on the brake pedal, suspect the booster.
6. Operate the engine at a fast idle for about ten seconds, shut off the engine. Allow the car to sit for about ten minutes. Depress the brake pedal with moderate force (about 20 pounds). The pedal should feel about the same as when the engine was running. If the brake pedal feels hard (no power assist) suspect the power booster.

Brake Control Valve

REPLACEMENT

Escort, Lynx, EXP, LN7, Tempo and Topaz

The brake control valve is located to the left and below the master cylinder and mounted to the shock (strut) tower by a removable bracket. Use the proper size flare wrench and disconnect the brake lines to the valve. Disconnect the warning switch wire. Remove the bolt(s) retaining the valve to the mount and remove the valve. Installation is in the reverse order of removal. Bleed the brake system after installing the new valve.

Taurus and Sable Sedans

The control valve is mounted to the floorpan near the left-rear wheel. It utilizes a mechanical linkage to the lower suspension arm to vary the valve performance based on the rear weight of the vehicle.

1. Raise and support the rear of the vehicle on jackstands.

NOTE: DO NOT raise or support the vehicle using the tension struts.

2. Label and disconnect the brake tubes from the control valve assembly.
3. Remove the valve bracket-to-underbody screws and the control valve assembly from the vehicle.

NOTE: The service replacement control valve will have a red plastic gauge clip on it, which MUST NOT BE removed until installation.

4. To install, make sure that the rear suspension is in the Full rebound position and the control valve operating screw is loose, then reverse the re-

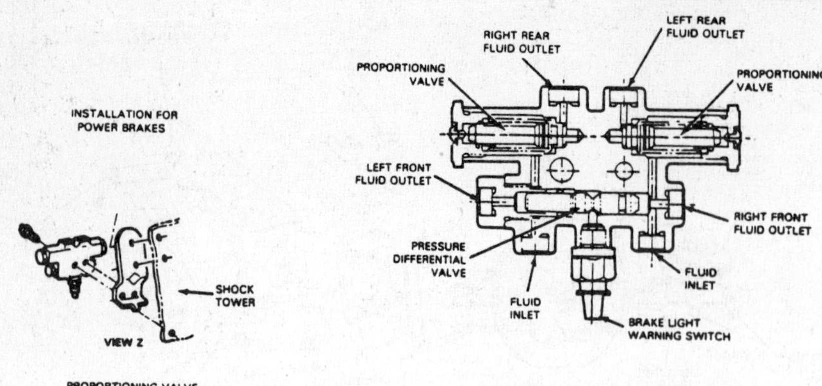

Combination brake valve

moval procedures. Torque the control valve-to-underbody screws to 8-10 ft.lb. (11-13 Nm). Perform the control valve assembly adjustment procedures. Bleed the rear brake system.

Taurus and Sable Station Wagon

The control valves are screwed into the bottom of the master cylinder. They control the braking pressure to the rear wheels to minimize rear wheel skidding during hard braking.

1. Disconnect and plug the primary and/or secondary brake tube from the master cylinder.
2. Remove the pressure control valve(s) from the master cylinder.
3. To install, reverse the removal procedures. Torque the control valve-to-master cylinder to 10-18 ft.lb. (13-24 Nm). Bleed the brake system.

ADJUSTMENT

Taurus and Sable Sedan

1. Place the vehicle on a hoist or an alignment machine, so that the vehicle is at the curb load level and the wheels are on a flat surface.
2. At the control valve, loosen the adjuster screw.
3. Using a piece of rubber or plastic tubing 5/8-21/64" (16-16.5mm), 3/8" OD x 1/4" ID, slice it lengthwise (on one edge), then install it on the operating rod.
4. Make sure that the adjuster is resting on the lower mounting bracket; tighten the set screw.

NOTE: DO NOT change the position of the upper nut on the valve operating rod; the dimension will position the valve for normal operation.

5. To decrease the rear brake pressure, perform the following procedures:
   a. Make sure that the vehicle is at curb height.
   b. Loosen the control valve set screw.
   c. Move the piston Down the operating rod 1mm for each 60 psi pressure decrease.
   d. Tighten the set screw in the desired position.
6. To increase the rear brake pressure, perform the following procedures:
   a. Make sure that the vehicle is at curb height.
   b. Loosen the control valve set screw.
   c. Move the piston Up the operating rod 1mm for each 60 psi pressure increase.
   d. Tighten the set screw in the desired position.

Pressure Differential Valve

If a loss of brake fluid occurs on either side of the diagonally split system when the brakes are applied, a piston mounted in the valve moves off center allowing the brakes on the non-leaking side of the split system to operate. When the piston moves off center a brake warning switch, located in the center of the valve body, will turn on a dash mounted warning light indicating brake problems.

After repairs are made on the brake system and the system bled, the warning switch will reset itself when you pump the brake pedal and the dash light will turn off.

Proportioning Valve

The dual proportioning valve, located between the rear brake system inlet and outlet port, controls the rear brake system hydraulic pressure. When the brakes are applied, the dual proportioning valve reduces pressure to the rear wheels and provides balanced braking.

TROUBLESHOOTING THE PROPORTIONING VALVE

If the rear brakes lock-up during light brake application or do not lock-up under heavy braking the problem could be with the dual proportioning valve.

1. Check tires and tire pressures.
2. Check the brake linings for thickness, and for contamination by fluid, grease etc.
3. Check the brake system hoses, steel lines, calipers and wheel cylinders for leaks.
4. If none of the proceeding checks have uncovered any problems, suspect the proportioning valve.

NOTE: Take the car to a qualified service center and ask them to do a pressure test on the valve. If a pressure test is not possible, replace the control valve.

Bleeding the Brake System

It is necessary to bleed the brake system of air whenever a hydraulic component, of the system, has been rebuilt or replaced, or if the brakes feel spongy during application.

Your car has a diagonally split brake system. Each side of this system must be bled as an individual system. **Bleed the right rear brake, left front brake, left rear brake and right front brake. Always start with the longest line from the master cylinder first.**

CAUTION

When bleeding the system(s) never allow the master cylinder to run completely out of brake fluid. Always use DOT 3 heavy duty brake fluid or the equivalent. Never reuse brake fluid that has been drained from the system or that has been allowed to stand in an opened container for an extended period of time. If your car is equipped with power brakes, remove the reserve vacuum stored in the booster by pumping the brake pedal several times before bleeding the brakes.

1. Clean all of the dirt away from the master cylinder filler cap.
2. Raise and support the car on jackstands. Make sure your car is safely supported and it is raised evenly front and back.
3. Starting with the right rear wheel cylinder. Remove the dust cover from the bleeder screw. Place the proper size box wrench over the bleeder fitting and attach a piece of rubber

tubing (about three feet long and snug fitting) over the end of the fitting.

4. Submerge the free end of the rubber tube into a container half filled with clean brake fluid.

5. Have a friend pump up the brake pedal and then push down to apply the brakes while you loosen the bleeder screw. When the pedal reaches the bottom of its travel close the bleeder fitting before your friend release the brake pedal.

6. Repeat Step 5 until air bubbles cease to appear in the container in which the tubing is submerged. Tighten the fitting, remove the rubber tubing and replace the dust cover.

7. Repeat Steps 3 through 6 to the left front wheel, then to the left rear and right front.

NOTE: Refill the master cylinder after each wheel cylinder or caliper is bled. Be sure the master cylinder top gasket is mounted correctly and the brake fluid level is within 1/4" (6mm) of the top.

8. After bleeding the brakes, pump the brake pedal several times, this ensures proper seating of the rear linings and the front caliper pistons.

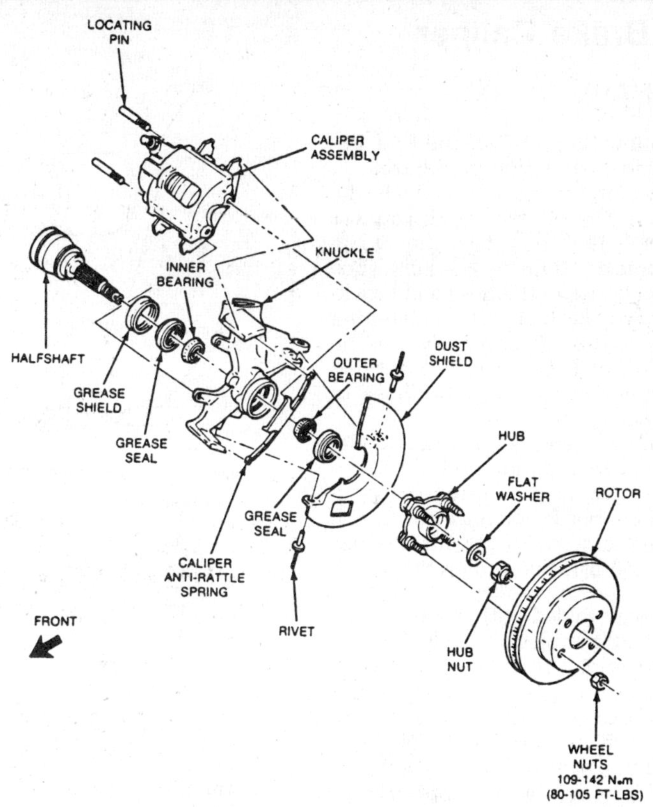

Disc brake components

FRONT DISC BRAKES

CAUTION

Some brake pads contain asbestos, which has been determined to be a cancer causing agent. Never clean the brake surfaces with compressed air! Avoid inhaling any dust from any brake surface! When cleaning brake surfaces, use a commercially available brake cleaning fluid.

Disc Brake Pads

INSPECTION

1. Loosen the front wheel lugs slightly, then raise the front of the car and safely support it on jackstands.

2. Remove the front wheel and tire assemblies.

3. The cut out in the top of the front brake caliper allows visual inspection of the disc brake pad. If the lining is worn to within 1/8" (3mm) of the metal disc shoe (check local inspection requirements) replace all four pads (both sides).

4. While you are inspecting the brake pads, visually inspect the caliper for hydraulic fluid leaks. If a leak is visible the caliper will have to be rebuilt or replaced.

PAD REMOVAL & INSTALLATION

1. Loosen the front wheel lugs slightly, then raise the front of the car and safely support it on jackstands.

2. Remove the front wheel and tire assemblies.

3. Remove the master cylinder cap. Siphon off some fluid from each reservoir until they are half full. Replace the cap.

4. Remove the anti-rattle spring from the bottom of the caliper by pushing up on the center until the tabs are free of the mounting holes.

5. Back out the Torx® headed caliper locating pins. DO NOT REMOVE THEM ALL THE WAY. If removed, the pins are difficult to install and require new guide bushings.

6. Lift the caliper assembly from the knuckle, anchor plate and rotor.

7. Remove the outer and inner disc brake pads. The outer pad has two clips that fit into the bosses on the outer edge of the caliper. The inner pad uses a three point clip that fits inside the caliper piston.

8. Suspend the caliper, with wire, inside the fender housing.

CAUTION

Do not suspend in such a way to put stress on the brake hose.

9. Use a 4" (102mm) C-clamp and a block of 2$\frac{3}{4}$"x 1" (70mm x 25mm) piece of wood to seat the caliper piston back in its bore. Place the wood against the face of the piston, attach the clamp and slowly close it pushing the piston into the caliper. Extra care must be taken during this procedure to prevent damage to the aluminum piston.

NOTE: The piston must be fully seated in its bore to provide clearance for the caliper with the new pads to fit over the disc rotor.

10. Install the inner brake pad with the mounting clips onto the caliper piston. Install the outer pad, make sure the slips are properly seated on the caliper bosses.

11. Unwire the caliper from the fender well. Mount the caliper over the rotor and fasten the Torx® headed pins. Reinstall the anti-rattle spring making sure it is firmly located in the mounting holes.

12. Refill the master cylinder to correct levels.

13. Pump the brakes several times to position the new pads.

14. Install the wheels and tighten the lugs snugly.

15. Lower the car from the jackstands. Tighten the lug nuts to 80-105 ft.lb.

16. Road test the car.

Brake Caliper

OVERHAUL

1. Follow Steps 1-3 of the Pad Removal and Installation procedure.
2. Disconnect the hydraulic brake hose from the caliper. To disconnect the hose, loosen the tube fitting at the frame bracket. Remove the horseshoe clip from between the hose and bracket. Remove the hollow bolt fastening the hose to the caliper and remove the hose. Do not loosen the two gaskets used in mounting the brake hose to the caliper.
3. Follow Steps 4-7 of the Pad Removal and Installation procedures.
4. The next step requires a controllable air source. If you have one fine, if not take the caliper(s) to your local gas station and ask them to do Step 5 for you.
5. Place a folded cloth, shop rag, etc. over the caliper piston. Apply air pressure through the brake line fitting hole with a rubber tipped air blow gun. The air pressure will force the caliper piston from its bore. If the piston is seized, tap lightly on the caliper with a plastic hammer while applying air pressure.

CAUTION

Apply air pressure slowly. Pressure can built up inside the caliper and the piston may come out with considerable force.

6. Remove the dust boot and piston seal from the caliper. Clean all parts with alcohol or clean brake fluid. Blow out the passage ways in the caliper. Check the condition of the caliper bore and piston. If they are pitted or scored or show excessive wear, replacement will be necessary. Slight scoring in the caliper bore may be cleaned up by light honing. Replace the piston if it is scored.
7. Apply a coating of brake fluid to the new caliper piston seal and caliper bore. Some rebuilding kits provide a lubricant for this purpose. Install the seal in the caliper bore, make sure it is not twisted and is firmly seated in the groove.
8. Install the new dust seal in the caliper mounting groove, be sure it is mounted firmly.
9. Coat the piston with clean brake fluid or the special lubricant and install it in the caliper bore, make sure it is firmly seated in the bottom of the caliper bore. Spread the dust boot over the piston and seat in the piston groove.
10. Install the brake pads as outlined in the previous section.
11. Install the caliper over the rotor. Mount the caliper as described in the previous section.

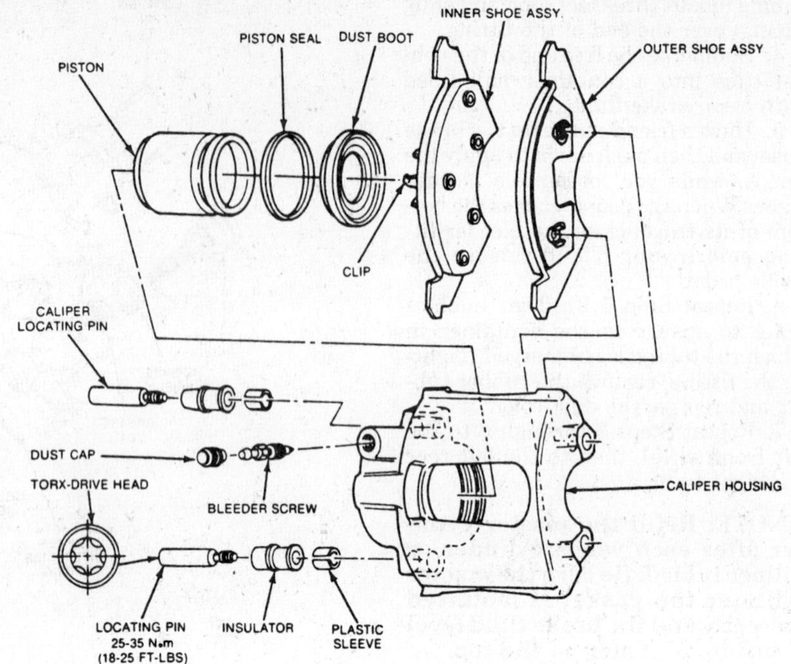

Caliper, exploded view

12. Install the bake hose to the caliper. Be sure to use a new gasket on each side of the hose fitting. Position and install the upper end of the hose, remember to put the horseshoe clip in place, take care not to twist the hose.
13. Bleed the brake system and centralize the brake warning switch.
14. Fill the master cylinder to the correct level. Refer to Steps 12-15 of the Pad Removal and Installation for the remaining procedures.

Front Brake Disc (Rotor)

REMOVAL & INSTALLATION

1. Follow Steps 1-6 of the Pad Removal and Installation omitting Step 3 (it is not necessary to siphon off any brake fluid).
2. Suspend the caliper with a piece of wire from the fender support, do not put any stress on the brake hose.
3. Pull the rotor outward from the wheel hub.
4. Installation is in the reverse order of removal.

Front Wheel Bearings Taurus and Sable

The bearing design relies on component stack up and deformation/torque at assembly to determine bearing setting. The bearings, therefore, cannot be adjusted after assembly.

The front bearings are located in the front suspension knuckle, not in the rotor or wheel hub. Two inner and one outer seal protect the bearings (the seal closer to the CV-joint is a shield) on models through 1983-1984 and later models use bearings of a cartridge design and are pregreased and sealed, and require no scheduled maintenance. The wheel hub is installed with a close slip fit through the wheel bearings and an interference fit over the splines of the halfshaft's constant velocity stub shaft. A flat washer and a staked hub nut maintain the correct endplay and prevent the wheel bearing inner races from spinning on the wheel hub.

REMOVAL

NOTE: The wheel hub and knuckle must be removed for bearing replacement or servicing. A special puller is required to remove and install the hub. (Ford Part Number T81P-1104-A, T81P-1104-C and adapters T81P-1104-B or T83P-1104-AH). The adaptors screw over the lugs and attach to the puller, which uses a long screw attached to the end of the stub shaft to pull off or install the hub.

1. Remove wheel cover and slightly loosen the lugs.
2. Remove the hub retaining nut and washer. The nut is crimped staked to the shaft. Use a socket and suffi-

cient torque to overcome the locking force of the crimp.

3. Raise the front of the car and support safely with jackstands. Remove the tire and wheel assembly.

4. Remove the brake caliper and disc rotor. Refer to the appropriate sections for the necessary procedures.

5. Disconnect the lower control arm and tie rod from the steering knuckle. Loosen tow top strut mounting nuts, but do not remove them. Install the hub remover/installer tool and remove the hub. If the outer bearing is seized on the hub remove it with a puller.

6. Remove the front suspension knuckle.

7. On models through 1983, after the front knuckle is removed, pull out the inner grease shield, the inner seal and bearing.

8. Remove the outer grease seal and bearing.

9. If you hope to reuse the bearings, clean them in a safe solvent. After cleaning the bearings and races, carefully inspect them for damage, pitting, heat coloring etc. If damage etc. has occurred, replace all components (bearings, cups and seals). Always replace the seals with new ones. Always use a new hub nut whenever the old one has been removed.

10. If new bearings are to be used, remove the inner and outer races from the knuckle. A three jawed puller on a slide hammer will do the job.

11. Clean the interior bore of the knuckle.

12. On 1984 and later models, remove the snapring that retains the bearing in the steering knuckle.

13. Position the knuckle, outboard side up under a hydraulic press with appropriate adapters in place, and press the bearing from the knuckle.

14. Clean the interior bore of the knuckle.

INSTALLATION

1. On models through 1983, install the new bearing cups using a suitable driver. Be sure the cups are fully seated in the knuckle bore.

2. Pack the wheel bearings with multi-purpose lubricant (Ford part number C1AZ-19590-B or the equivalent). If a bearing packer is not available, place a large portion of grease into the palm of your hand and slide the edge of the roller cage through the grease with your other hand. Work as much grease as you can between the bearing rollers.

3. Put a sufficient amount of grease between the bearing cups in the center of the knuckle. Apply a thin film of grease on the bearing cups.

4. Place the outer bearing and new grease seal into the knuckle. Place a thin film of grease on all three lips of the new outer seal.

5. Turn the knuckle over and install the inner bearing and seal. Once again, apply a thin film of grease to the three lips of the seal.

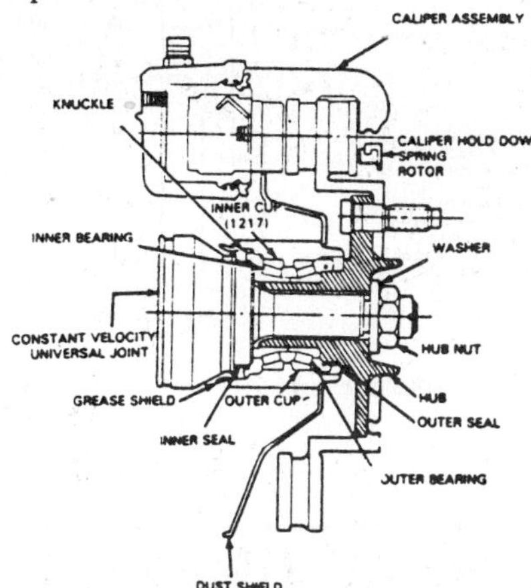

Cross section of the front wheel bearings —through 1982

6. Install the inner grease shield. A small block of wood may be used to tap the seal into the knuckle bore.

7. Keep the knuckle in the vertical position or the inner bearing will fall out. Start the wheel hub into the outer knuckle bore and push the hub as far as possible through the outer and inner bearings by hand.

NOTE: Prior to installing the hub, make sure it is clean and free from burrs. Use crocus cloth to polish the hub is necessary. It is important to use only hand pressure when installing the hub, make sure the hub is through both the outer and inner bearings.

8. With the hub as fully seated as possible through the bearings, position the hub and knuckle to the front strut. Refer to STEERING AND SUSPENSION for instructions on attaching the strut and knuckle.

9. On 1984 and later models, position the knuckle. outboard side down

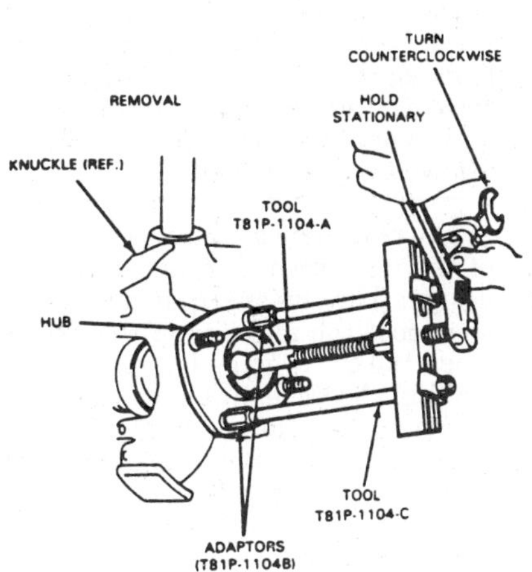

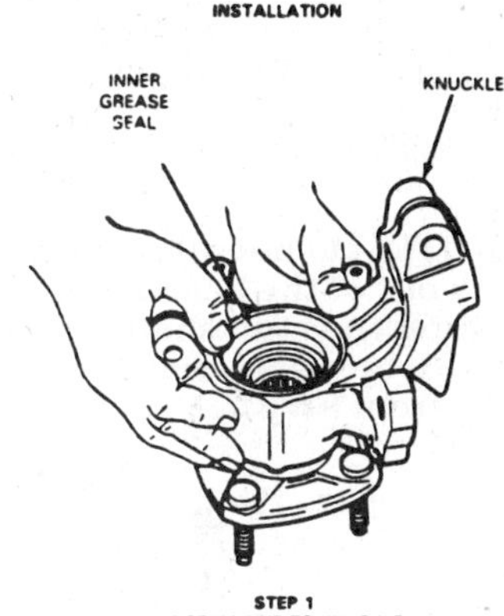

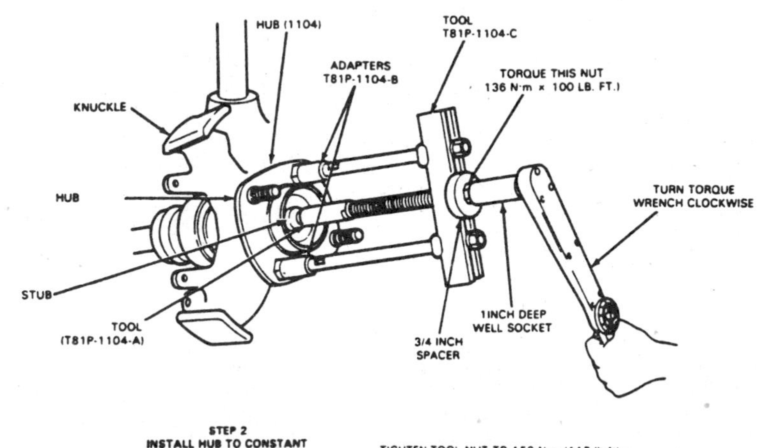

Using the front stub shaft remover/installer tool

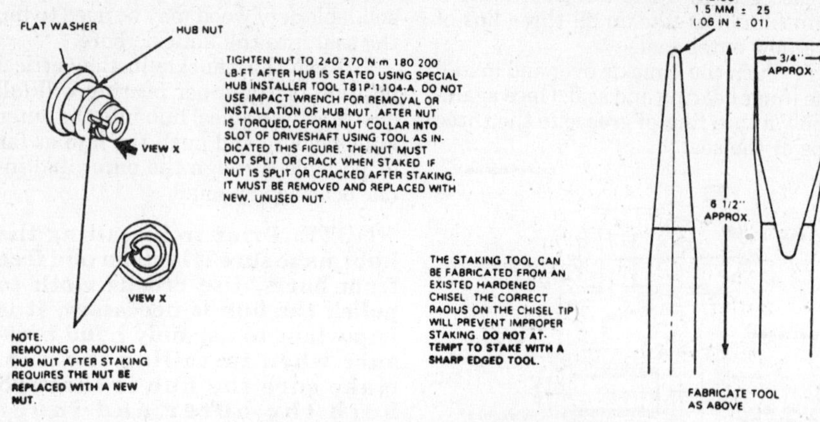

How to stake the front wheel retainer nut

on the appropriate adapter and press in the new bearing. Be sure the bearing is fully seated. Install a new retainer snapring.

10. Install the hub using tool T83T-1104-AH3 and press. Check that the hub rotates freely.

11. Lubricate the stub shaft splines with a thin film of SAE 20 motor oil. Use hand pressure only and insert the splines into the knuckle and hub as far as possible.

NOTE: Do not allow the hub to back out of the bearings while installing the stub shaft, otherwise it will be necessary to start all over from Step 7.

12. Complete the installation of the suspension parts as described in STEERING AND SUSPENSION.

13. Install the hub remover/installer tool and tighten the center adapter to 120 foot pounds, this ensures the hub is fully seated.

14. Remove the installer tool and install the hub washer and nut. Tighten the hub nut finger tight.

15. Install the disc rotor, caliper etc. in reverse order of removal. Refer to the proceeding sections, if necessary, for procedures.

16. Install the tire and wheel assembly and snug the wheel lugs.

17. Lower the car to the ground, set the parking brake and block the wheels.

18. Tighten the wheel lugs to 80-105 ft.lb.

19. Tighten the center hub nut to 180-200 ft.lb. DO NOT USE A POWER WRENCH TO TIGHTEN THE HUB NUT.

20. Stake the hub nut using a rounded, dull chisel. DO NOT USE A SHARP CHISEL.

REAR BRAKES

CAUTION

Some brake pads contain asbestos, which has been determined to be a cancer causing agent. Never clean the brake surfaces with compressed air! Avoid inhaling any dust from any brake surface! When cleaning brake surfaces, use a commercially available brake cleaning fluid.

The rear brakes used on your car are of the non-servo leading/trailing shoe design. This means that the leading shoe does the majority of the braking when the car is going forward and the trailing shoe does the majority of the braking when the car is backing up.

The brakes are self-adjusting. The only time any adjustment should be necessary is during servicing of brake shoe replacement. Depending on the model of your car, either 7" (178mm) or 8" (203mm) brakes are used.

BRAKE SHOE INSPECTION

Two access holes, covered by a rubber plug, are provided in the brake backing plate. By removing the plugs the brake lining thickness and condition can be inspected.

Rear Brake Drum

REMOVAL & INSTALLATION

All Models

1. Remove the wheel cover, loosen the lugs, jack up the rear end of your car and safely support it on jackstands.

2. Remove the wheel lugs and the tire and wheel assembly.

3. Remove the center grease car from the brake drum hub. Remove the cotter pin, nut retainer, spindle nut, and keyed flat washer.

4. Make sure the parking brake is completely released. Slide the brake drum off of the spindle. Be careful not to drop the outer bearing. Make sure that you keep the drum straight and not drag the inner grease seal across the spindle threads.

NOTE: If the hub and drum assembly will not slide off of the spindle, the brake shoe adjustment will have to be backed off.

On 7" (178mm) brakes: Insert a thin blade screwdriver in to the inspection slot until it contacts the adjuster assembly pivot. Apply side pressure on the pivot point to allow the adjuster quadrant to ratchet and release the brake adjustment.

On 8" (203mm) brakes: Remove the brake line to axle bracket to gain enough room so a thin bladed screwdriver and brake adjusting tool may be inserted in the inspection slot. Push the adjusting lever away from the adjuster screw wheel. Back off the starwheel with the adjusting tool.

5. Inspect the brake drum for scoring, etc. Have the drum turned if necessary. Perform any necessary brake work. Pack the wheel bearings if required. Reinstall the brake drum in the reverse order of removal. Consult the next section on rear wheel bearing service for proper bearing adjustment when reinstalling the brake drum.

Rear Wheel Bearings

REMOVAL, PACKING, INSTALLATION AND ADJUSTMENT

The rear wheel bearings are located in the brake drum hub. The inner wheel bearing is protected by a grease seal. A washer and spindle nut retain the hub/drum assembly and control the bearing endplay.

1. Complete Steps 1-4 in the proceeding Drum Removal section.

2. The outer bearing will be loose when the drum is removed and may be lifted out by hand. The inner bearing is retained by a grease seal. To remove the inner bearing, insert a wooden dowel or soft drift through the hub from the outer bearing side and carefully drive out the inner bearing and grease seal.

3. Clean the bearings, cups and hubs with a suitable solvent. Inspect the bearings and cups for damage or heat discoloring. Replace as a set if necessary. Always install a new grease seal.

4. If new bearings are to be used,

SPINDLE
GASKET WHITE FOAM
BOLT 40-64 N·m 29-47 LB-FT
INNER BEARING
WASHER
ADJUSTING NUT
NUT RETAINER
I.D. SAME AS SPINDLE HUB
DRUM BRAKE
INNER GREASE SEAL
HUB AND DRUM
OUTER BEARING
DUST COVER
COTTER PIN
ADJUSTER NUT A
NUT RETAINER B
SPREAD ENDS AND BEND AROUND NUT RETAINER
COTTER PIN C

BEARING ADJUSTMENT: TIGHTEN ADJUSTING NUT "A" TO 23-34 N·m (17-25 LB-FT) WHILE ROTATING HUB AND DRUM ASSEMBLY. BACK OFF ADJUSTING NUT APPROXIMATELY 100 DEGREES. POSITION NUT RETAINER "B" OVER ADJUSTING NUT SO SLOTS ARE IN LINE WITH COTTER PIN HOLE WITHOUT ROTATING ADJUSTING NUT. INSTALL COTTER PIN.

NOTE: THE SPINDLE HAS A PREVAILING TORQUE FEATURE THAT PREVENTS ADJUSTING THE NUT BY HAND.

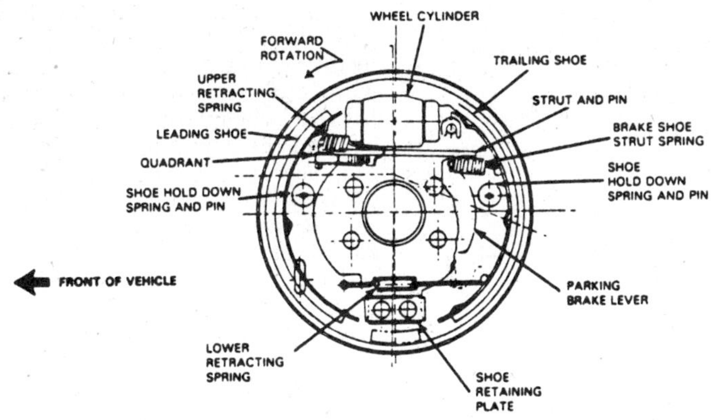

7 inch rear brakes

use a three jawed slidehammer puller to remove the cups from the drum hub. Install the new bearing cups using a suitable driver. Make sure they are fully seated in the hub.

5. Pack the bearings with a multi-purpose grease. (See the front wheel bearing section for packing instructions).

6. Coat the cups with a thin film of grease. Install the inner bearing and grease seal.

7. Coat the bearing surfaces of the spindle with a thin film of grease. Slowly and carefully slide the drum and hub over the spindle and brake shoes. Install the outer bearing over the spindle and into the hub.

8. Install the keyed flat washer and adjusting nut on the spindle.

9. Tighten the adjusting nut to between 17-25 ft.lb.

10. Back off the adjusting nut ½ turn. Then retighten it to between 10-15 in.lb.

11. Position the nut retainer on the nut and install the cotter pin. Do not tighten the nut to install the cotter pin.

12. Spread the ends of the cotter pin and bend then around the nut retainer. Install the center grease cap.

13. Install the tire and wheel assembly. Lower the car and tighten the wheel lugs.

Rear Brake Shoes Tips

After any brake service work, obtain a firm brake pedal before moving the car. Adjusted brakes must not put a drag on the wheel, the wheel must turn freely.

The rear brakes are self-adjusting and require adjustment only after new shoes have been installed or service work has been done which required the disassembly of the brake shoes.

When adjusting the rear brake shoes, make sure the parking brakes cables are not adjusted too tightly. After the brakes have been installed and adjusted, check the operation of the brakes by making several stops from varying speeds. Readjust if necessary.

REMOVAL & INSTALLATION

7" (178mm) Rear Brakes

1. Perform Steps 1-4 of the Brake Drum Removal section.

2. Remove the holddown pins and springs by pushing down on and rotating the outer washer 90°. It may be necessary to hold the back of the pin (behind the backing plate) while pressing down and turning the washer.

3. After the holddown pins and spring have been removed from both brake shoes, remove both shoes and the adjuster assembly by lifting up and away from the bottom anchor plate and shoe guide. Take care not to damage the wheel cylinder boots when removing the shoes from the wheel cylinder.

4. Remove the parking brake cable from the brake lever to allow the removal of the shoes and adjuster assembly.

5. Remove the lower shoe to shoe spring by rotating the leading brake shoe to release the spring tension. Do not pry the spring from the shoe.

6. Remove the adjuster strut from the trailing shoe by pulling the strut away from the shoe and twisting it downward toward yourself until the spring tension is released. Remove the spring from the slot.

7. Remove the parking brake lever from the trailing shoe by disconnecting the horseshoe clip and spring washer and pulling the lever from the shoe.

8. If for any reason the adjuster assembly must be taken apart, do the following: pull the adjuster quadrant (U-shaped lever) away from the knurled pin on the adjuster strut by rotating the quadrant in either direction until the teeth are no longer engaged with the pin. Remove the spring and slide the quadrant out of the slot

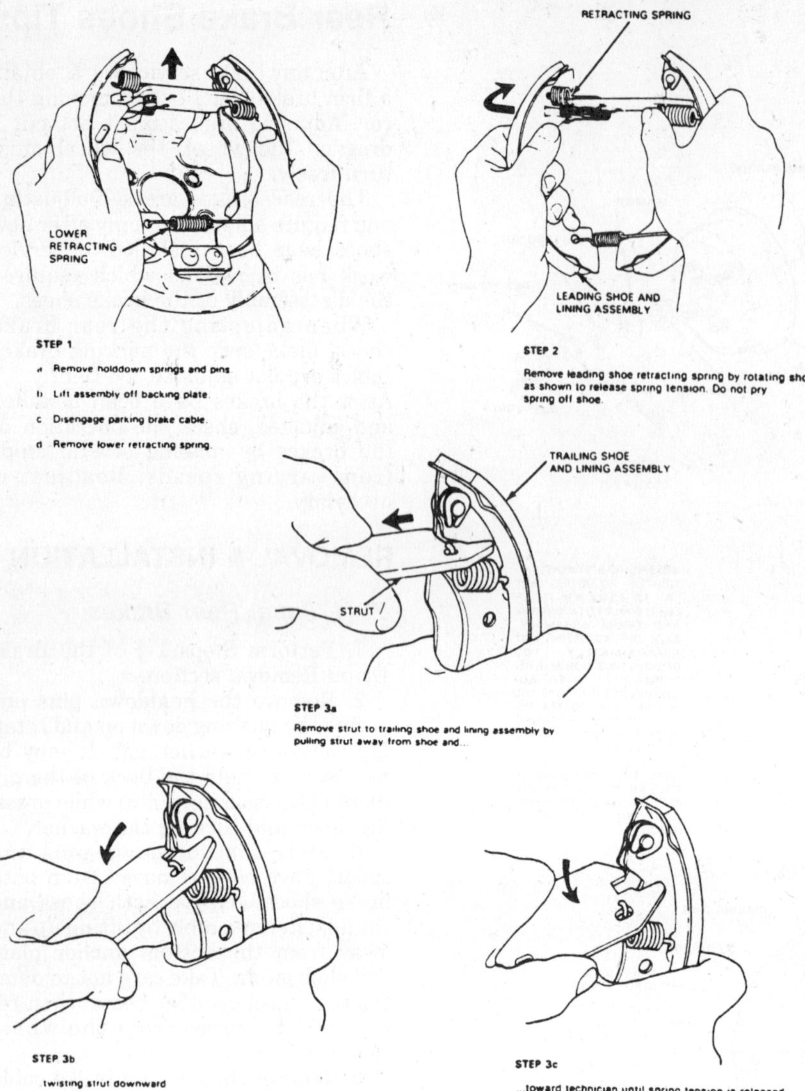

Removing the 7 inch rear brake shoes

on the end of the adjuster strut. Do not put too much stress on the spring during disassembly.

To install:

1. Clean the brake backing (mounting) plate with a soft paint brush or vacuum cleaner.

CAUTION

Never inhale the dust from the brake linings. Asbestos dust when inhaled can be injurious to your health. Use a vacuum cleaner. Do not blow off the dust with air pressure.

2. Apply a thin film of high temperature grease at the points on the backing plate where the brake shoes make contact.
3. Apply a thin film of multi-purpose grease to the adjuster strut at the point between the quadrant and strut.
4. If the adjuster has been disassembled, install the quadrant mounting pin into the slot on the adjuster strut and install the adjuster spring.
5. Assemble the parking brake lever to the trailing shoe. Install the spring washer and a new horseshoe clip, squeeze the clip with pliers until the lever is secured on the shoe.
6. Install the adjuster strut attaching spring on to the trailing shoe. Attach the adjusting strut by fastening the spring in the slot and pivoting the strut into position. This will tension the spring. Make sure the end of the spring where the hook is parallel to the center line of the spring coils is hooked into the web of the brake shoe. The installed spring should be flat against the web and parallel to the adjuster strut.
7. Install the shoe to shoe spring with the longest hook attached to the trailing shoe.
8. Install the leading shoe to adjuster strut spring by installing the spring to both parts and pivoting the leading shoe over the quadrant and into position, this will tension the spring.
9. Place the shoes and adjuster assembly onto the backing plate. Spread the shoes slightly and position them into the wheel cylinder piston inserts and anchor plate. Take care not to damage the wheel cylinder boots.
10. Attach the parking brake cable to the parking brake lever.
11. Install the holddown pins, springs, and washers.
12. Adjust the brakes as described in the proceeding brake adjustment section.
13. Install the rear drums and adjust the bearings as described in the previous section.

8" (203mm) Rear Brakes

1. Perform Steps 1-4 of the Brake Drum Removal section.
2. Remove the holddown pins and springs by pushing down on and rotating the outer washer 90°. It may be necessary to hold the back of the pin (behind the backing plate) while pressing down and turning the washer.
3. After the holddown pins and springs have been removed, remove both shoes and the adjuster assembly by lifting up and away from the anchor plate and wheel cylinder. Take care not to damage the wheel cylinder boots or bend the adjusting lever.
4. Disconnect the parking brake cable from the parking brake lever.
5. Remove the lower shoe to shoe spring and the upper spring attaching the adjusting lever to the brake shoe. This will separate the brake shoes and disengage the adjuster.
6. Spread the horseshoe clip and remove the parking brake lever from the trailing shoe.

To install:

1. Clean the brake backing (mounting) plate with a soft paint brush or vacuum cleaner.

CAUTION

Never inhale the dust from the brake linings. Asbestos dust when inhaled can be injurious to your health. Use a vacuum cleaner. Do not blow off the dust with air pressure.

2. Apply a thin film of high temperature grease at the points on the backing plate where the brake shoes make contact.
3. Apply a thin film of multi-purpose grease to the threads of the adjuster screw and to the socket end of the adjuster. Turn the adjuster screw

REMOVAL PROCEDURE

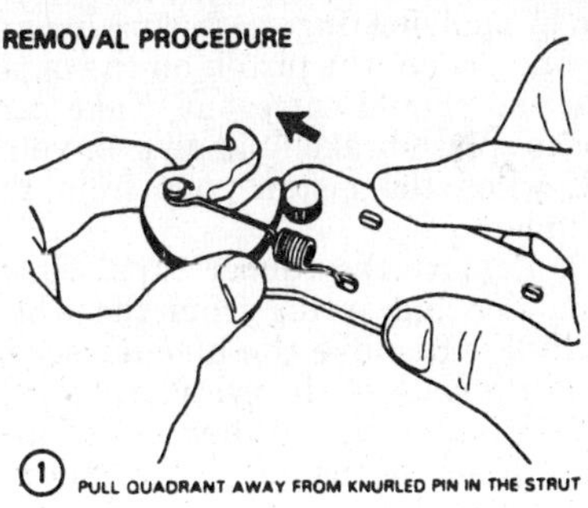

① PULL QUADRANT AWAY FROM KNURLED PIN IN THE STRUT

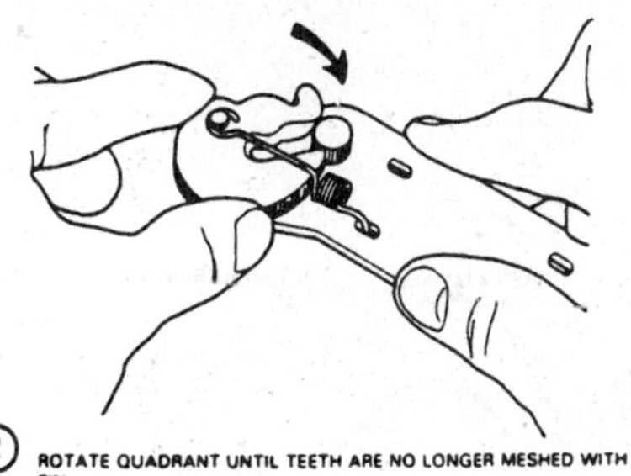

② ROTATE QUADRANT UNTIL TEETH ARE NO LONGER MESHED WITH PIN.

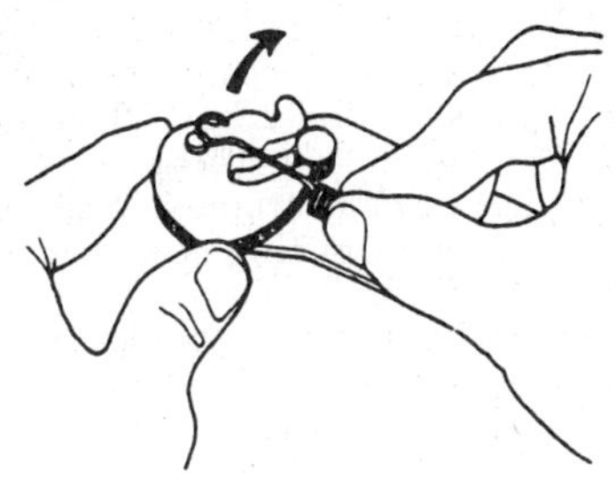

③ REMOVE THE SPRING AND SLIDE QUADRANT OUT OF STRUT — BE CAREFUL NOT TO OVERSTRESS SPRING.

INSTALLATION PROCEDURE

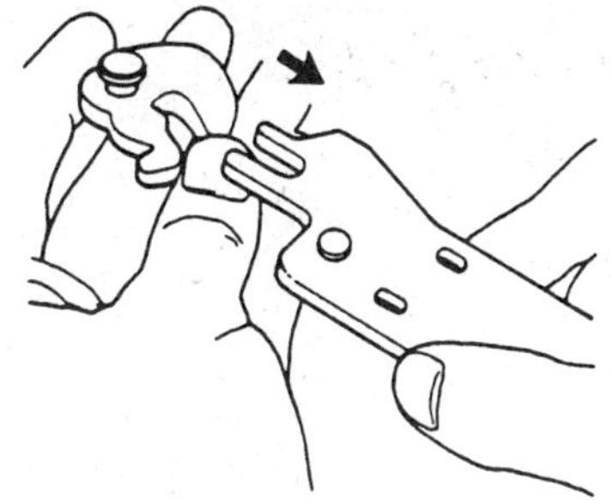

INSTALL ADJUSTER QUADRANT PIN INTO SLOT IN STRUT TURN ASSEMBLY OVER AND INSTALL SPRING

7 inch brakes; quadrant removal and installation

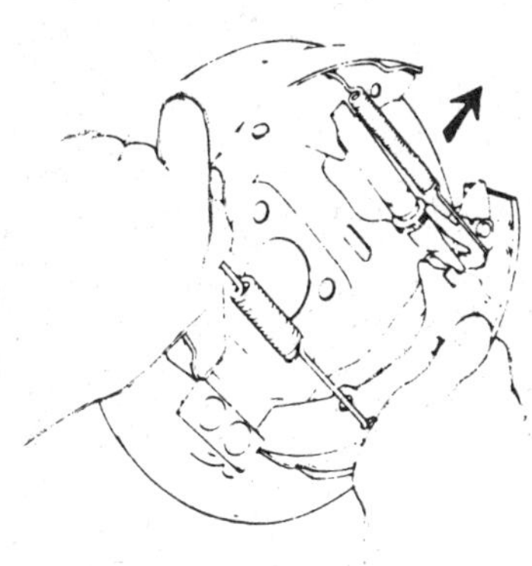

8 inch brakes; removal

into the socket and then back off from bottom a number of threads.

4. Install the parking brake lever on the trailing shoe. Use a new horseshoe clip. Be sure to pull the spring washer in position. Connect the parking brake cable to the parking brake lever.

5. Attach the lower retracting spring between the two brake shoes and install the shoes on the backing plate. It will be necessary to spread the shoes apart to mount them on the anchor plate and wheel cylinder.

6. Install the adjuster screw assembly between the slot in the leading shoe and the slots in the trailing shoe and parking brake lever. Lengthen the screw if necessary. The adjuster socket blades are marked **L** for left side or **R** for right side and fit onto the trailing shoe and the parking brake lever (slots provided). The letter must face up toward the wheel cylinder when the blade is installed. This permits the deeper of the two slots to fit onto the parking brake lever.

7. Install the adjusting lever, also marked **L** or **R**, by sliding the groove over the parking brake lever pin slot and into a groove on the starwheel.

8. Attach the upper retracting spring to the leading shoe anchor hole. Use a pair of brake spring pliers, stretch the spring and attach the other end onto the adjuster lever notch.

NOTE: If the adjuster lever does not contact the starwheel after installing the spring, make sure that the adjuster socket is installed correctly. (see Step 6).

9. Install the holdown pins, spring and washers.

10. Adjust the brakes, using a brake adjusting tool as described in the brake adjustment section. Do not adjust with shoe drag on the drum. The wheel must turn freely.

11. Install the brake drum and adjust the wheel bearings.

12. Lower the car and road test.

Rear Wheel Cylinder

REMOVAL & INSTALLATION

Escort, Lynx, EXP, LN7, Tempo and Topaz

1. Remove the rear wheel, brake drum and brake shoes as described in the proceeding sections.

2. Disconnect the rear brake line from the back of the wheel cylinder.

3. Remove the bolts that attach the wheel cylinder to the brake backing (mounting) plate.

4. Remove the wheel cylinder.

5. Installation is in the reverse order of removal.

Taurus and Sable

1. Raise and support the rear of the vehicle on jackstands.

NOTE: DO NOT raise or support the vehicle using the tension struts.

2. Remove the wheelcover or the ornament and nut covers. Remove the hub grease cap.

NOTE: If the vehicle is equipped with styled steel or aluminum wheels, the wheel/tire assembly must be removed to remove the dust cover.

3. Remove the cotter pin and the nut retainer.

4. Remove the hub nut, the thrust washer, the outer bearing and the brake drum assembly.

5. Remove the brake shoes, the retainers and the springs from the backing plate.

6. Disconnect and plug the brake tube at the rear-side of the wheel cylinder.

7. Remove the wheel cylinder-to-backing plate bolts and the wheel cylinder from the vehicle.

8. To install, reverse the removal procedures. Torque the wheel cylinder-to-backing plate bolts to 7.5 ft.lb. (10-14 Nm). Adjust the rear wheel bearing. Bleed the rear brake system.

OVERHAULING THE WHEEL CYLINDER

Wheel cylinders need not be rebuilt unless they are leaking. To check the wheel cylinder for leakage, carefully pull the lower edge of the rubber end boot away from the cylinder. Excessive brake fluid in the boot or running out of the boot, when the edges are pulled away from the cylinder, denotes leakage. A certain (slight) amount of fluid in the boot is normal.

1. It is not necessary to remove the cylinder from the brake backing (mounting) plate to rebuild the cylinder, however removal makes the job easier.

2. Disengage and remove the rubber boots from both ends of the wheel cylinder. The piston should come out with the boot. If not, remove the pis-

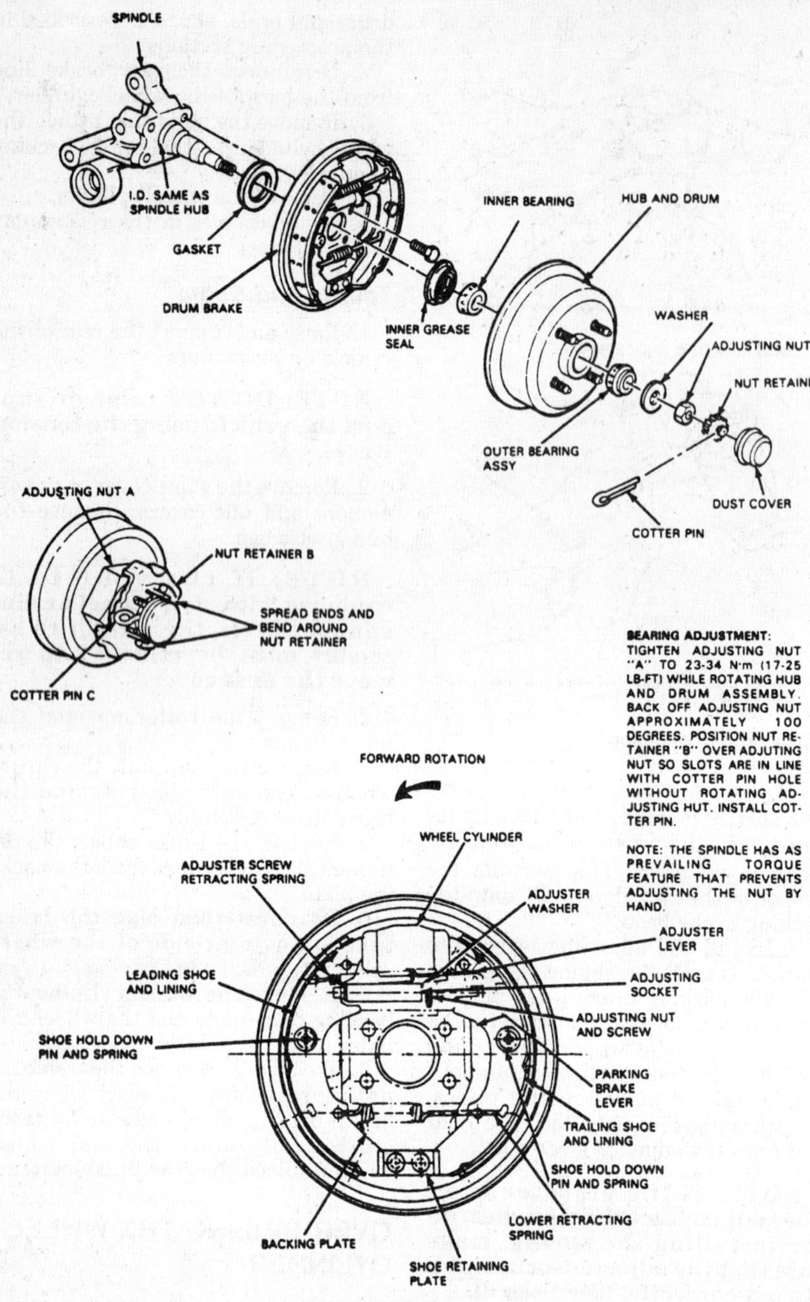

8 inch rear brakes

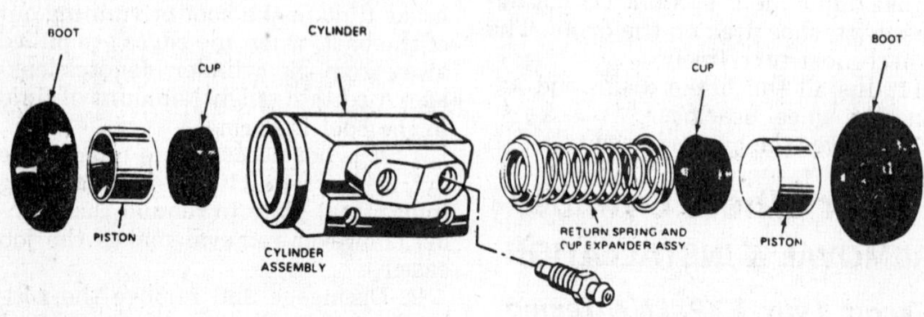

Exploded view of a rear wheel brake cylinder

ton by applying finger pressure inward on one piston, the piston on the opposite end should come out. Take care not to splash brake fluid all over yourself when the piston pops from the cylinder.

3. Remove the rubber cups, center expander and spring from the wheel cylinder. Remove the bleeder screw from the back of the cylinder.

4. Discard all rubber boots and cups. Wash the pistons and cylinder in denatured alcohol or clean brake fluid.

5. Inspect the pistons for scratches, scoring or other visible damage. Inspect the cylinder bore for score marks or rust. The cylinder may be honed (with a brake cylinder hone) if necessary. Do not hone more than 0.003" (0.076mm) beyond original diameter. If the scoring or pitting is deeper, replace the cylinder.

6. After honing the cylinder, wash again with alcohol or clean brake fluid. Check the bleeder screw hole to make sure it is opened. Wipe the cylinder bore with a clean cloth. Install the bleeder screw.

7. Never reuse the old rubber parts. Always use all of the parts supplied in the rebuilding kit.

8. Apply a light coat of brake fluid, or the special lubricant if supplied with the rebuilding kit, on the pistons, rubber cups and cylinder bore.

9. Insert the spring and expander assembly into the cylinder bore. Put the cups, facing in, and the pistons into the cylinder. Install the boots and fit the outer lips into the retaining grooves on the outer edges of the wheel cylinder.

10. Install the wheel cylinder onto the backing plate. Be sure that the inlet port (where the brake hose connects) is toward the rear of the car. Install the brake shoes, drum and wheel assembly. Adjust and bleed the brake system. Road test the car.

PARKING BRAKE

The parking brake control is hand operated and mounted on the floor between the front seats. When the control lever is pulled up (from the floor) an attached cable applies the rear brakes.

Cable

REMOVAL & INSTALLATION

1. Pull up slowly on the control lever and stop at the seventh notch position, count the clicks as you pull up on

the handle. The adjusting nut is now accessible. Remove the adjusting nut. Completely release the control handle (push the release button and lower to the floor.

2. Raise the car and safely support on jackstands.
3. Disconnect the rear parking brake cables from the front equalizer and rod assembly.
4. If the front equalizer and rod assembly is to be replaced, drill out the rivets that hold the cable guide to the floor pan. Remove the equalizer and rod assembly from the parking brake control lever and withdraw it through the floor pan.
5. To install the front equalizer and rod assembly, feed the adjusting rod end of the assembly through the floor pan and into the parking control lever clevis. Attach the cable guide to the floor pan using new pop rivets. Borrow a pop rivet gun from a friend.
6. If the rear parking brake cable is to be replaced, first disconnect from the front equalizer and rod assembly. Remove the hairpin clip that holds the cable to the floor pan tunnel bracket.
7. Remove the wire retainer that hold the cable to the fuel tank mounting bracket. Remove the cable from the retaining clip.
8. Remove the rear tire and wheel assemblies and the brake drums.
9. Disconnect the parking brake cable from the trailing shoe parking brake levers. Depress the cable prongs that hold the cable in the backing plate hole. Remove the cable through the holes.
10. Installation is in the reverse order of removal.

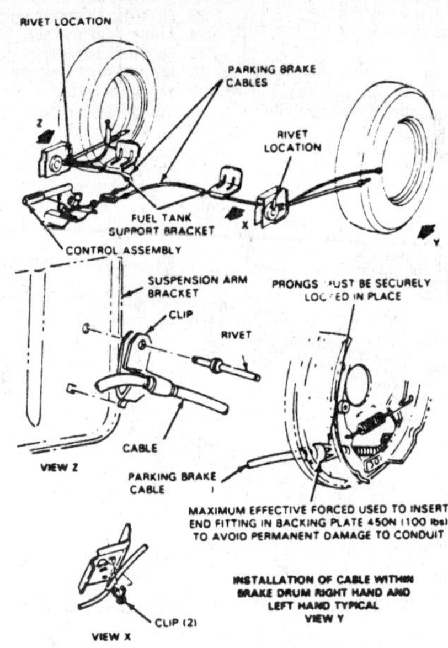

Parking brake cable installation

11. Adjust the parking brake cable as per instructions in the next section.

CABLE ADJUSTMENT

Escort, Lynx, EXP, LN7, Tempo and Topaz

1. If a new cable has been installed, the parking brake lever control should be in the seventh notch and the adjusting nut run down to the approximate position it was removed from. Release the hand brake and pump the brake pedal several times. If you car has power brakes, start the engine and allow it to idle when pumping the brakes. Shut off the engine.
2. Place the control lever in the twelfth notch, two notches before complete application. Tighten the adjusting nut until the rear brakes have a slight drag when the parking brake control lever is completely released. Repeat the parts of this step as necessary.
3. Loosen the adjusting nut until there is no rear brake drag when the control lever is completely released.
4. Lower the car and test the parking brake application.

Taurus and Sable

1. Raise and support the rear of the vehicle on jackstands.

NOTE: DO NOT raise or support the vehicle using the tension struts.

2. Make sure that the parking brake is fully released and the transmission is in Neutral.
3. At the parking brake cable equalizer, turn the adjusting nut until drag is felt at the rear wheel.
4. Loosen the adjusting nut until no brake drag is felt.

NOTE: If the parking brake cables have been replaced, in a foot-operated control assembly, set the parking brake lever with approx. 100 lbs. of pressure, then release the control and repeat the procedure.

5. Lower the vehicle and check the operation of the parking brake.

MANUAL TRANSAXLE OVERHAUL

Transaxle Case

DISASSEMBLY

4-Speed

1. Insert a drift into the input shift shaft hole and shift the transaxle into Neutral by either pushing or pulling the shaft into the center detent position.
2. Place the transaxle on a bench with the clutch housing face down and drain the transaxle fluid.
3. Remove the Reverse idler shaft retaining bolt.
4. Remove the detent plunger retaining screw. Using a magnet, remove the detent spring and the plunger.

NOTE: Label these parts for they appear similar to the input shift shaft plunger and spring contained in the clutch case.

5. Using a 19mm socket, remove the shift fork interlock sleeve retaining pin.
6. Using a 10mm socket, remove the clutch housing-to-transaxle case.
7. Tap the transaxle case with a plastic tipped hammer to break the seal between the case halves.

CAUTION

While separating the case halves, be careful that the tapered roller bearing cups or shims do not drop out. DO NOT insert pry bars between the case halves.

8. Remove the case magnet. Remove the Reverse idler shaft and gear by lifting the shaft straight upward.
9. Using a 4mm Allen wrench, remove the set screw from the shift lever assembly.
10. Using a pair of pliers, rotate the shift lever shaft 90° to disengage the Reverse inhibitor plunger from the detent notch in the shift lever shaft. Slide the shaft toward the differential (away from the expansion plug in the clutch housing) and remove the shift lever assembly.

NOTE: If equipped with a 4.05:1 final drive ratio, it may be necessary to tilt the differential assembly slightly, to remove the shift lever assembly.

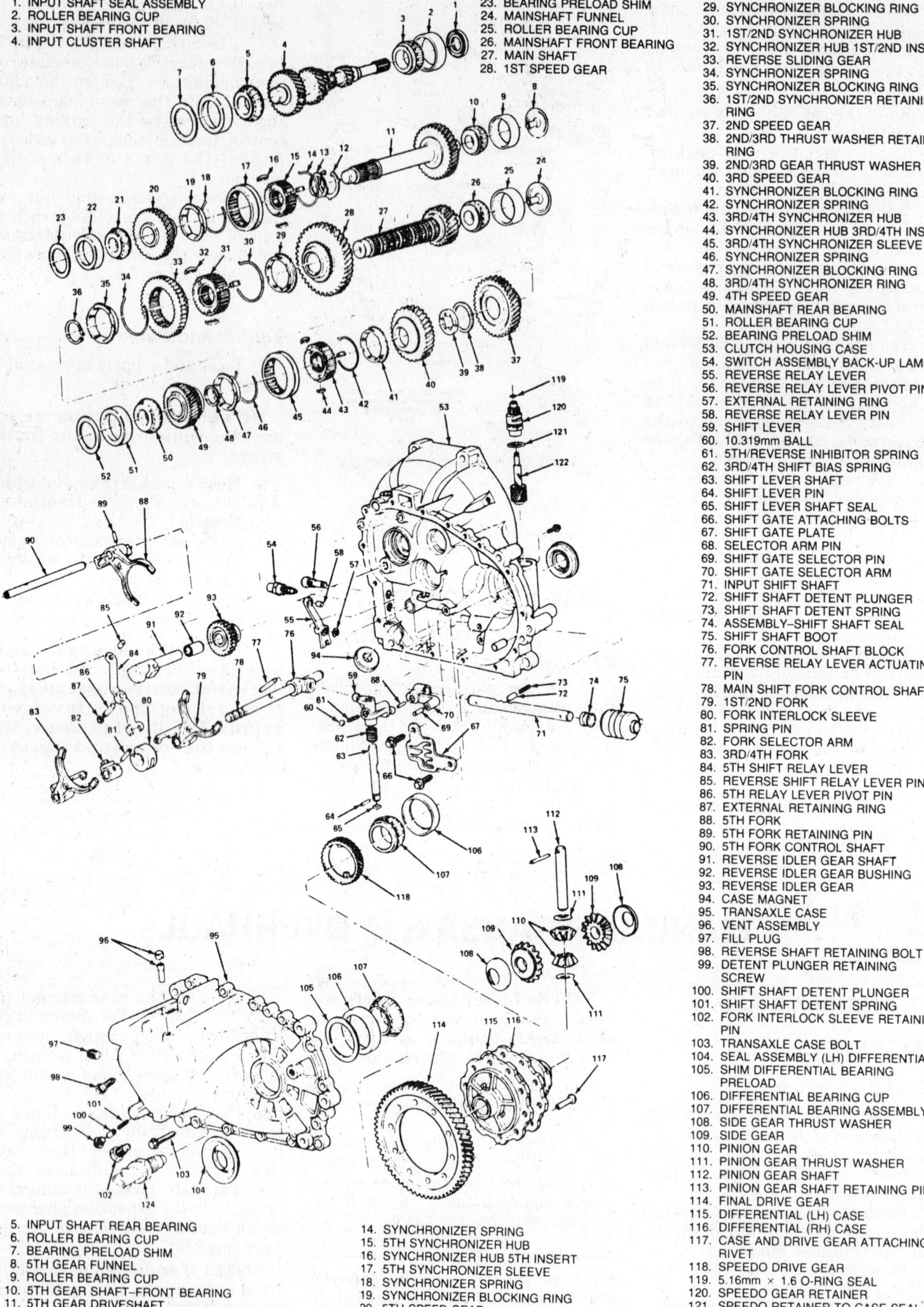

MTX 4 speed transaxle—exploded view

11. Remove the main shaft assembly, the input cluster shaft assembly and the main shift control shaft assembly as one unit.
12. Lift the differential and final drive gear assembly from the clutch housing case.

5-Speed

NOTE: The following procedures are used in conjunction with the 4-speed procedures.

1. Remove the C-clip retaining ring from the 5th gear shift relay lever.
2. Remove the 5th gear shift relay lever.
3. Using a punch, drive the roll spring pin from the shift lever shaft.
4. Gently pry the shift shaft lever to remove it from the case.
5. To disengage the inhibitor, insert a punch into the shift shaft lever hole and rotate the shaft 90°.
6. To prevent the ball and inhibitor spring from shooting out, hold a rag over the hole in the lever.
7. Remove the shift shaft, then the ball and spring from the inhibitor.
8. Remove the shift lever and the 3rd-4th bias spring as an assembly.
9. Remove the 5th gear shaft and gear fork assembly from the case.

ASSEMBLY

1. Place the differential and the final drive gear assembly into the clutch housing case.
2. Position the main shift control shaft assembly, so that the shift forks engage their respective slots in the synchronizer sleeves, on the main shaft assembly.
3. Mesh the main shaft assembly with the input cluster shaft assembly. Hold the input cluster shaft assembly, the main shaft and the main shift control shaft in their respective working positions, lower them into their bores in the clutch housing case as a unit.
4. Position the shift lever assembly in its working position, with one shift lever pin located in the socket of the input shift shaft selector plate arm assembly and the other in the socket of the main shift control shaft block. Slide the shift lever shaft through the shift lever and into its clutch housing bore. Rotate the shift lever shaft so the Reverse inhibitor notch faces the Reverse inhibitor plunger.
5. Position the shift lever shaft so the set screw hole on the shaft aligns with the hole in the shift lever.
6. Make sure the selector pin is in the Neutral gate of the control selector plate, then position the fork selector arm finger so that it is partially engaged with the 1st-2nd fork and the 3rd-4th fork.

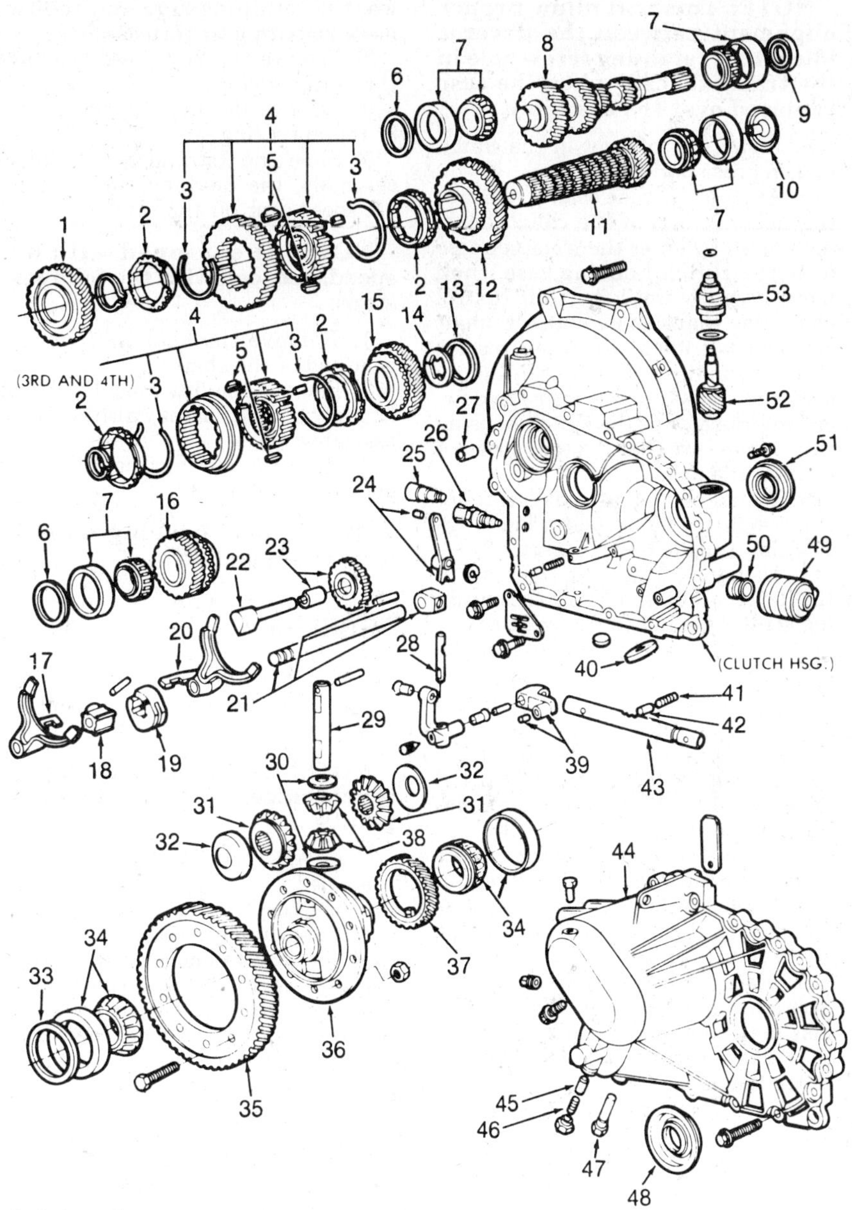

1. 2nd speed gear
2. Synchronizer blocking ring
3. Synchronizer spring
4. 1st and 2nd synchronizer assy.
5. Synchronizer hub 1st/2nd insert
6. Input shaft seal
7. Input shaft bearing and cup-front and rear
8. Input cluster shaft
9. Input shaft seal
10. Mainshaft funnel
11. Main shaft
12. 1st speed gear
13. 2nd/3rd gear thrust washer retaining ring
14. 2nd/3rd gear thrust washer
15. 3rd speed gear
16. 4th speed gear
17. 3rd/4th fork
18. Fork selector arm
19. Fork interlock sleeve
20. 1st/2nd fork
21. Main shift shaft
22. Reverse idler shaft
23. Reverse idler gear
24. Reverse relay lever
25. Reverse relay lever pivot pin
26. Back-up lamp switch
27. Dowel
28. Shift lever shaft
29. Pinion shaft
30. Pinion thrust washer
31. Side gear kit
32. Side gear thrust washer
33. Shim
34. Differential bearing assembly
35. Final drive output gear
36. Transaxle case assy
37. Speedometer drive gear
38. Differential pinion gear
39. Input shift shaft selector plate arm
40. Case magnet
41. Input detent shift shaft spring
42. Input shift shaft detent plunger
43. Input shift shaft
44. Transaxle case
45. Main shift shaft detent plunger
46. Main shift shaft detent spring
47. Fork interlock sleeve retaining spring
48. Differential seal assembly

Exploded view of the MTX 5 speed

7. Engage the Reverse idler gear groove with the pin at the end of the Reverse relay lever, then slide the shaft through the gear and into its bore. Align the retaining screw hole in the case.

NOTE: This will allow proper alignment between the Reverse idler shaft retaining screw hole in the transaxle case when the case is placed over the assembly.

8. Install the magnet in the clutch housing case pocket.
9. Apply a $^1/_{16}$" wide bead of sealer to the clean surface of the clutch housing. Carefully lower the transaxle case over the clutch housing case, then move it gently until the shift control shaft, the main shaft and the input cluster shaft align with their respective bores in the transaxle case. Gently slide the transaxle case over the dowels and flush onto the clutch housing case. Make sure that the case does not bind on the magnet.
10. Install the 14 transaxle case-to-clutch housing bolts and torque to 13-17 ft.lb. using a 10mm socket.
11. Using a drift, align the bore in the Reverse idler shaft with the retaining screw hole in the transaxle case.
12. Install the Reverse idler shaft retaining bolt and torque to 16-20 ft.lb.
13. Apply Teflon pipe sealant to the threads of the interlock sleeve retaining pin. Using a drift, align the interlock sleeve slot with the hole in the transaxle case, then install the retaining pin and torque to 12-15 ft.lb.
14. Apply Teflon® pipe sealant to the threads of the detent plunger retaining screw. Install the detent plunger and spring, then torque the retaining screw to 9-12 ft.lb.
15. Place the transaxle in an upright position. Insert a drift through the hole in the input shift shaft, then shift the transaxle in and out of the gears to check the assembly.

Mainshaft

DISASSEMBLY

1. Using a puller and an arbor press, remove the tapered roller bearing from the pinion end of the main shaft, then label the bearing for proper installation.

NOTE: The bearing does not have to be removed to disassemble the main shaft, only to replace it (if damaged).

2. Remove and label the bearing on the 4th gear end of the shaft.
3. Remove the 4th gear and synchronizer blocking ring.
4. Remove the 3rd-4th synchronizer retaining ring.
5. Slide the 3rd-4th gear synchronizer assembly, the blocking ring and the 3rd speed gear from the shaft.
6. Remove the 2nd-3rd thrust washer retaining ring and the two piece 2nd-3rd gear thrust washer.
7. Remove the 2nd speed gear and the blocking ring.
8. Remove the 1st-2nd synchronizer retaining ring.
9. Slide the 1st-2nd synchronizer assembly, the blocking ring and the 1st speed gear off the shaft.

NOTE: If equipped with a 5-speed, proceed with the following steps:

1. Remove the bearing from the gear end of the shaft.
2. Remove the 5th gear, the blocking ring and the synchronizer assembly.
3. Press the bearing from the pinion end of the shaft.

NOTE: This bearing must be pressed on and off.

ASSEMBLY

1. Clean, inspect and lightly oil the parts with the appropriate transaxle fluid.

NOTE: Before assembling the synchronizers note the following points:

a. All index marks must be aligned.
b. Place the tab of the synchronizer spring into the groove on one of the inserts and snap the spring into place. Place the tab of the other spring into the same insert on the other side of the synchronizer assembly, then rotate the spring in the opposite direction and snap it into place.
c. The sleeve and the hub have an extremely close fit and must be held square to prevent jamming. Do not force the sleeve onto the hub.

2. Slide the blocking ring and the 1st speed gear onto the main shaft. Slide the 1st-2nd synchronizer assembly into place, making sure that the shift fork groove on the reversing slide gear faces the 1st speed gear. Install the synchronizer retaining ring.

NOTE: When installing the synchronizer, align the 3 grooves in the 1st gear blocking ring with the synchronizer inserts.

3. Install the 2nd speed blocking ring and speed gear.
4. Install the thrust washer halves and the retaining ring.
5. Slide the 3rd speed gear onto the shaft followed by the 3rd speed gear synchronizer blocking ring and the 3rd-4th gear synchronizer assembly, then the synchronizer retaining ring.
6. Install the 4th gear blocking ring and gear.
7. Using a $1^1/_{16}$" socket and an arbor press, install the bearing on the 4th gear end of the shaft. Install the bearing on the pinion end of the shaft in the same manner.

NOTE: Make sure the bearings are placed on the same end as labeled during the disassembly and that they are seated against the shoulder of the main shaft.

Internal Shift Linkage

DISASSEMBLY

1. Cover the Reverse inhibitor plunger bore, then slide the shift lever shaft from its bore.

CAUTION

To avoid possible eye injury, make sure that the inhibitor bore area is covered so that the plunger does not spring from the case when removing the shift lever shaft.

2. Using a 30mm deep socket, remove the back up lamp switch.
3. Remove the C-clip and the Reverse relay lever.

NOTE: It is not necessary to remove the pivot pin.

4. Using a 10mm socket, remove the 2 control selector plate bolts and the plate from the case.
5. With the input shift shaft in the center detent position, drive the spring pin through the selector plate arm assembly and the input shift shaft into the recess of the clutch housing.
6. Remove the shift shaft boot. Using a drift, rotate the input shift shaft 90°. Without damaging the seal, pull the input shift shaft out. Remove the input shift shaft selector plate arm assembly and the spring pin.
7. Using a pencil magnet, remove the input shift shaft detent plunger and spring, then label them for proper installation. Using a seal remover/installer tool No. T77F-7288-A and a Slide Hammer tool No. T50T-100-A, remove the transaxle input shift shaft oil seal assembly.

ASSEMBLY

1. Grease the lip of the new oil seal and install it, using the tools described in the disassembly procedure.
2. Using a small drift, force the detent spring and plunger down into the bore while sliding the input shift shaft into its bore and over the plunger.

NOTE: Be careful not to damage the shift shaft oil seal.

3. Install the selector plate arm in its working position and slide the shaft through the selector plate arm. Align the hole in the selector plate arm with the hole in the shaft and install the roll pin, then install the boot.

NOTE: When properly installed the pin on the selector arm will be facing up. make sure the notches in the shift shaft face the detent plunger.

4. Install the selector plate and torque the attaching bolts to 6-8 fft.lb.

NOTE: The pin in the selector arm must ride in the cut out of the gate in the selector plate.

5. If removed, apply Teflon® type sealant to the threads of the Reverse relay lever pivot pin. Install the Reverse relay lever and the retaining clip.

NOTE: Make sure the pin at the end of the lever faces outward.

6. Apply Teflon® type sealant to the threads of the back up lamp switch and install the switch.
7. Using a small drift, depress the Reverse inhibitor plunger and slide the shift lever shaft (with the oil relief flat first) through the case pedestal. Install the shaft so that the main shaft assembly or the differential will not interfere with the shift lever shaft.

Main Shift Control Shaft

DISASSEMBLY

1. Rotate the 3rd-4th shift fork on the shaft until the notch in the fork is located over the interlock sleeve. Rotate the 1st-2nd shift fork on the shaft until the notch in the fork is located over the selector arm finger. With the forks in position, slide the 3rd-4th fork and interlock sleeve off the shaft.
2. Using a 5mm punch, remove the selector arm retaining pin.
3. Remove the selector arm and the 1st-2nd shift fork from the shaft.
4. If equipped with a 5 speed, remove the roll pin (using a drift punch), then slide the fork from the shaft.

ASSEMBLY

1. Clean and lightly oil the parts with the appropriate transaxle fluid.
2. Install the 1st-2nd shift fork and the selector arm on the shaft.
3. Align the hole in the selector arm with the hole in the shaft. Make sure the selector arm finger is aligned with the oil relief flats on the detent end of the shift shaft, then install the retaining pin.
4. Position the slot in the 1st-2nd fork over the fork selector arm finger. Position the slot in the 3rd-4th fork over the interlock sleeve. Slide the 3rd-4th fork and interlock sleeve onto the main shift control shaft, then align the interlock sleeve spines on the fork selector arm and slide into position.
5. If equipped with a 5 speed, hold the shaft with the hole on the left, then install the fork (the protruding spline must point toward the long end of the shaft) and the roll pin.

Input Cluster Shaft Seal

REMOVAL & INSTALLATION

1. Working from the outside of the case, remove the input shaft seal using a seal remover tool No. T77F-7050-A and a hammer. Position the remover tool against the seal by placing it in the slot cut in the case.
2. To install, lightly oil the input shaft seal and tap into place with a 1¼" socket and a hammer.

Input Cluster Shaft Bearings

REMOVAL

1. Using a Bearing Puller/Installer No. D79L-4621-A and an arbor press, remove the bearing cone and the roller assemblies.
2. Label the bearings for correct installation.

INSTALLATION

1. Thoroughly clean and lightly oil the bearings.
2. Using the tools used during removal, press the bearings on the proper end.

Bearing Cups

The input cluster shaft and the main shaft are supported at each end by tapered roller bearings. The cups, which support the bearings, are located in the transaxle case and the clutch housing case; they can be removed and installed by hand. The shims, used to preload the tapered roller bearings, are located behind the bearing cups in the transaxle case. It is important to keep the preload shim with its matching cup during disassembly. Also, label the bearing cups if they are removed from the case. Prior to installation, lightly grease the bearing cups.

TRANSFER CASE OVERHAUL

All Wheel Drive

REBUILDING

1. Remove the transfer case.
2. Remove the 4 side cover bolts, remove the cover and discard the gasket.
3. Remove the 4 gear housing bolts and remove the gear housing subassembly.
4. Remove the O-ring and shims from the gear housing. Wire the shim pack together for reuse and discard the O-ring.
5. Place the gear housing in a soft-jawed vise, clamped on the drive flange.
6. Using a plastic mallet, drive the drive gear from the housing. Remove and discard the collapsible spacer.
7. Remove the inner bearing cone from the drive gear using a press and bearing remover D79L-4621-A, or equivalent. When using the press, install anut on the end of the shaft.
8. Clean the drive gear in a safe solvent and install a new inner bearing cone using the press and bearing installer T62F-4621-A and seal plate T75L-1165-B, or equivalents.
9. Mount the drive gear housing in a soft-jawed vise.
10. Remove the drive gear housing oil seal using a suitable prybar.
11. Remove the inner and outer drive gear bearing using a brass drift and hammer.
12. Remove the gear housing from the vise. Install new inner and outer drive bearing races using T87P-4676-A and handle T-80T-4000-W, or equivalent.
13. Lubricate and install a new outer drive bearing cone. Install a new oil seal using seal installer T87P-7065-B and handle T80T-4000-W, or equivalent. Grease the seal lip.
14. Install a new collapsible spacer on the drive gear stem.
15. Install the drive gear into the gear housing.
16. Install the end yoke, washer and nut.
17. Tighten the pinion nut, in small increments, until the rotational torque is 15-32 in.lb. with new bearings.

WARNING: Do not exceed this torque value or a new spacer will have to be used!

18. Remove the snaprings from the vacuum servo shaft and shift fork. Re-

move the shift motor assembly. Remove the shift fork and clips.

CAUTION

Always wear protective goggles when removing or installing snaprings.

19. Remove the transfer case bearing cap retaining bolts and the bearing cap.
20. Rotate the bearing and remove the 2-piece snapring from the bearing.
21. Using a screwdriver, remove the inner snapring which positions the input gear on the ball bearing. Slide the bearing towards the input gear and remove the outer snapring.
22. Slide the input gear towards the ball bearing until the input gear and bearing can be lifted out of the transfer case.
23. Remove the ball bearing from the input gear.
24. Remove the shift collar from the clutch shaft.
25. Remove the pinion nut and washer from the clutch shaft. Use a breaker bar and clutch shaft wrench T87P-7120-A, or equivalent. Tap the clutch shaft from the transfer case with a soft drift.
26. Remove the pinion gear, outer bearing and shims from the transfer case. Wire the shims together for reuse. Remove the clutch shaft collapsible spacer and discard it.
27. Remove the clutch shaft inner bearing using a press and bearing remover D84L-1123-A, or equivalent.
28. Mount the clutch shaft in a vise. Remove the clutch needle bearing which centers the input gear, using bearing remover T87P-7120-C and slide hammer T50T-100-A, or their equivalents. Discard the bearing.
29. Install a new clutch shaft needle bearing using a hammer and bearing installer T87P-7120-C, or equivalent. Pack the bearing with grease to maintain proper needle position.
30. Install the clutch shaft inner bearing cone using a press and bearing installer D84L-1123-A, or equivalent.
31. Mount the transfer case in holding fixture T57L-500-B, or equivalent. Install the clutch shaft inner bearing cup remover T87P-7120-D, or equivalent, and tighten it.

    Install slide hammer T50T-100-A, or equivalent, into the cup remover and remove the inner bearing cup. Remove the outer bearing using the same procedure.
32. Wipe the bearing bores clean. Install the inner and outer bearing cups using installer T87P-7120-B and handle T80T-4000-W, or their equivalents.
33. Install a new collapsible spacer on the clutch shaft.
34. Install the clutch shaft in the transfer case. Assemble the original shim stack and pinion gear.
35. Assemble the washer and pinion nut. Tighten the nut using a breaker bar and clutch shaft wrench T87P-7120-A, or equivalent, in small increment while checking the shaft rotational effort. The effort should be 10-15 in.lb. with new bearings. Do not exceed this figure or a new spacer will have to be used!
36. Position the original shim pack and a new O-ring onto the gear housing. Lubricate the O-ring.
37. Install the gear housing sub-assembly on the case. Tighten the bolts to 8-12 ft.lb.
38. Check the backlash between the drive gear and pinion gear using dial indicator 4201-C, or equivalent. Backlash should be 0.004-0.006″.

    Check the gear tooth contact pattern using a white marking compound. The contact pattern should be within the primary area of the drive gear tooth surface. If the pattern isn't correct, with a backlash of 0.004-0.006″, adjust the drive pinion gear shim pack. Increasing the shim pack will move the contact pattern towards the toe end and vice-versa.
39. Install the shift collar onto the clutch shaft.
40. Slide the ball bearing onto the input gear.
41. Install the input gear into the transfer case. Slide the small end of the input gear into the clutch shaft.
42. Install the snapring onto the end of the shaft. Slide the bearing outboard and install the snapring onto the inner end of the input shaft. Make sure that the snaprings are completely seated in their grooves.
43. Install the 2-piece snapring into the groove for the ball bearing and transfer case.
44. Install the bearing cap and 2 retaining bolts. Torque the bolts to 18-24 ft.lb.
45. Inspect the shift fork clips and replace them if damaged. Install the shift fork onto the clutch collar.
46. Install a new O-ring onto the vacuum servo shaft. Lubricate the O-ring with clean ATF.
47. Install the vacuum servo assembly into the transfer case. Make sure the snapring is fully seated.
48. Install the shift fork snaprings.
49. Install the side cover using RTV silicone gasket material. Torque the bolts to 7-12 ft.lb. The bead must be continuous inside the bolt holes.
50. Install the transfer case and a new gasket, onto the transaxle. Perform a backlash check.

TRANSFER CASE BACKLASH CHECK

1. Drain the fluid, if any.
2. Loosen the 2 rear engine mounting bolts just far enough to gain access to the transfer case cup plug. DO NOT REMOVE THE BOLTS!
3. Remove the cup plug using a hammer and chisel.
4. Install backlash checking tool T87P-4020-B, or equivalent, through the cup plug hole, into the input gear. Tighten the tool's wing nut.
5. Mount dial indicator tool 4201-C, or equivalent, on the lower control arm. Position the stylus on the end of the backlash tool.
6. Push down on the backlash tool and note the reading. The reading should be 0.012-0.024″ on a 3″ radius. If the reading is okay, remove the tool and install the plug, tighten the bolts and refill the unit. If not, proceed:
7. Remove the dial indicator and backlash tool.
8. Remove the transfer case.
9. Discard the gasket and position a new Maximum Thickness Gasket, 7A191-AA, on the transfer case.
10. Install the transfer case and tighten the bolts to 23-28 ft.lb.
11. Reassemble the backlash too and dial indicator. Recheck the backlash. If the measurement still isn't correct, select a new mounting gasket based on the following, readings = gasket number, information:
    - 0.012-0.020″ = 7A191-HA
    - 0.021-0.024″ = 7A191-GA
    - 0.025-0.030″ = 7A191-FA
    - 0.031-0.035″ = 7A191-EA
    - 0.036-0.042″ = 7A191-DA
    - 0.043-0.048″ = 7A191-CA
    - 0.049-0.054″ = 7A191-BA
    - 0.055-0.064″ = 7A191-AA

11. Install the new gasket and recheck the backlash.
12. Remove the tools, replace the plug, tighten the bolts and refill the unit.

Ranger/Bronco II 3

INDEX

GENERAL ENGINE SPECIFICATIONS

Year	No. Cylinder Displacement cu. in. (liter)	Fuel System Type	Net Horsepower @ rpm	Net Torque @ rpm (ft. lbs.)	Bore × Stroke (in.)	Compression Ratio	Oil Pressure @ rpm
1983-87	4-122 (2.0)	1-bbl	73 @ 4000	107 @ 2400	3.52 × 3.13	9.0:1	40-60
	4-134 (2.2)	Diesel	59 @ 4000	90 @ 2500	3.50 × 3.50	22.0:1	40-60
	4-140 (2.3)	1-bbl	79 @ 3800	124 @ 2200	3.78 × 3.13	9.0:1	40-60
	6-173 (2.8)	2-bbl	115 @ 4600	150 @ 2600	3.66 × 2.70	8.7:1	40-60

GASOLINE ENGINE TUNE-UP SPECIFICATIONS

Year	No. Cylinder Displacement cu. in. (liter)	Spark Plugs Type	Spark Plugs Gap (in.)	Ignition Timing (deg.) MT	Ignition Timing (deg.) AT	Fuel Pump (psi)	Idle Speed (rpm) MT	Idle Speed (rpm) AT	Valve Clearance In.	Valve Clearance Ex.
1983-87	4-122 (2.0)	AWSF52	0.044	6B	6B	5-7	825	725	Hyd	Hyd
	4-140 (2.3)	AWSF44	0.044	10B	10B	5-7	900	800	Hyd	Hyd
	6-173 (2.8)	AWSF32	0.044	10B	10B	5-7	900	800	0.014	0.016

DIESEL ENGINE TUNE-UP SPECIFICATIONS

Year	No. Engine Displacement cu. in. (liter)	Valve Clearance Intake (in.)	Valve Clearance Exhaust (in.)	Injection Pump Timing (deg.)	Injection Nozzle Pressure (psi) New	Idle Speed (rpm)	Cranking Compression Pressure (psi)
1983-87	4-134 (2.2)	0.012	0.012	2°B	1957	700	427

CAPACITIES

Year	No. Cylinder Displacement cu. in. (liter)	Crankcase Incl. Filter (qts.)	Transmission (pts.) 4-Spd	Transmission (pts.) 5-Spd	Transmission (pts.) Auto.	Transfer Case (pts.)	Drive Axle (pts.) Front	Drive Axle (pts.) Rear	Fuel Tank (gal.)	Cooling System (qts.)
1983-87	4-122 (2.0)	5.0	3.0	3.0	15.0	3.0	1.0	①	②	③
	4-140 (2.3)	6.0	3.0	3.0	15.0	3.0	1.0	①	②	③
	4-134 (2.2)	7.0	3.0	3.6	16.0	2.0	1.0	5.0	13.0	10.0
	6-173 (2.8)	5.0	3.0	3.6	16.0	2.0	1.0	5.0	②	③
	6-179 (2.9)	5.0	3.0	3.6	16.0	3.0	1.0	5.0	②	③

① 6¾″ RG: 3.0
7½″ RG: 4.0
② Ranger: 13.0
Bronco II: 17.0
③ Ranger W/Air: 7.2
Ranger WO/Air: 6.5
Bronco II W/Air: 7.8
Bronco II WO/Air: 7.2

CAMSHAFT SPECIFICATIONS

(All measurements in inches)

Engine	Journal Diameter				Bearing Clearance	Lobe Lift		Camshaft End Play
	1	2	3	4		Intake	Exhaust	
4-122(2000)	All 1.7713–1.7720				0.0010–0.0030	0.2381	0.2381	0.0010–0.0070
4-140(2300)	All 1.7713–1.7720				0.0010–0.0030	0.2381	0.2381	0.0010–0.0070
6-173(2800)	1.7285–1.7293	1.7135–1.7143	1.6985–1.6992	1.6835–1.6842	0.0010–0.0030–	0.2555	0.2555	0.0008–0.0040
4-134(2200) Diesel	2.0472	2.0374	2.0177	—	0.0024–0.0047	0.2570	0.2570	0.0008–0.0071

CRANKSHAFT AND CONNECTING ROD SPECIFICATIONS

All measurements are given in inches.

Year	No. Cylinder Displacement cu. in. (liter)	Crankshaft				Connecting Rod		
		Main Brg. Journal Dia.	Main Brg. Oil Clearance	Shaft End-play	Thrust on No.	Journal Diameter	Oil Clearance	Side Clearance
1983-87	4-122 (2.0)	2.399–2.398	0.0008–0.0015	0.004–0.008	3	2.0462–2.0472	0.0008–0.0015	0.0035–0.0105
	4-134 (2.2)	2.5590–2.5592	0.0016–0.0036	0.0055–0.0154	3	2.0865–2.0867	0.0014–0.0030	0.0094–0.0134
	4-140 (2.3)	2.399–2.398	0.0008–0.0015	0.004–0.008	3	2.0462–2.0472	0.0008–0.0015	0.0035–0.0105
	6-173 (2.8)	2.2433–2.2441	0.0008–0.0015	0.004–0.008	3	2.1252–2.1260	0.0006–0.0016	0.004–0.011

VALVE SPECIFICATIONS

Year	No. Cylinder Displacement cu. in. (liter)	Seat Angle (deg.)	Face Angle (deg.)	Spring Test Pressure (lbs. @ in.)	Spring Installed Height (in.)	Stem-to-Guide Clearance (in.)		Stem Diameter (in.)	
						Intake	Exhaust	Intake	Exhaust
1983-87	4-122 (2.0)	45	44	149 @ 1.12	1.49–1.55	0.0010–0.0027	0.0015–0.0032	0.3416–0.3423	0.3411–0.3418
	4-134 (2.2)	①	①	②	③	0.0015–0.0046	0.0020–0.0051	0.3148–0.3152	0.3148–0.3152
	4-140 (2.3)	45	44	149 @ 1.12	1.53–1.59	0.0010–0.0027	0.0015–0.0032	0.3416–0.3423	0.3411–0.3418
	6-173 (2.8)	45	44	143 @ 1.22	1.58–1.61	0.0008–0.0025	0.0018–0.0035	0.3159–0.3167	0.3149–0.3156

① Intake: 45
Exhaust: 30
② Outer: 40 @ 1.59
Inner: 28 @ 1.49
③ Outer: 1.587
Inner: 1.488

PISTON AND RING SPECIFICATIONS

Year	No. Cylinder Displacement cu. in. (liter)	Piston Clearance	Ring Gap Top Compression	Ring Gap Bottom Compression	Ring Gap Oil Control	Ring Side Clearance Top Compression	Ring Side Clearance Bottom Compression	Ring Side Clearance Oil Control
1983–87	4-122 (2.0)	0.0014–0.0022	0.0100–0.0200	0.0100–0.0200	0.0150–0.0550	0.0020–0.0040	0.0020–0.0040	SNUG
	4-134 (2.2)	0.0021–0.0031	0.0157–0.0217	0.0118–0.0157	0.0138–0.0217	0.0020–0.0035	0.0016–0.0031	0.0012–0.0028
	4-140 (2.3)	0.0014–0.0022	0.0100–0.0200	0.0100–0.0200	0.0150–0.0550	0.0020–0.0040	0.0020–0.0040	SNUG
	6-173 (2.8)	0.0011–0.0019	0.0150–0.0230	0.0150–0.0230	0.0150–0.0550	0.0020–0.0033	0.0020–0.0033	SNUG

TORQUE SPECIFICATIONS

All readings in ft. lbs.

Year	No. Cylinder Displacement cu. in. (liter)	Cylinder Head Bolts	Main Bearing Bolts	Rod Bearing Bolts	Crankshaft Pulley Bolt	Flywheel Bolts	Manifold Intake	Manifold Exhaust
1983–87	4-122 (2.0)	80–90	80–90	30–36	100–120	56–64	14–21	16–23
	4-134 (2.2)	80–85	80–85	50–54	253–289	95–137	12–17	17–20
	4-140 (2.3)	80–90	80–90	30–36	100–120	56–64	14–21	16–23
	6-173 (2.8)	70–85	65–75	19–24	85–96	47–52	15–18	20–30

ROUTINE MAINTENANCE

Air Cleaner Element

All engines are equipped with a dry type, replaceable air filter element. The element should be replaced every 10,000 miles or yearly. If your vehicle is operated under severely dusty conditions or regularly in stop-and-go traffic, more frequent changes are necessary. Inspect the element at least twice a year; early spring and fall are good times of the year for inspection. Remove the element and check for holes in the filter, then check the element housing for signs of dirt or dust that has leaked through the filter element. Place a light on the inside of the element and look through the filter at the light. If no glow can be seen through the element material, replace the element. If holes in the filter are apparent or signs of dirt leakage through the filter are noticed, replace the element.

REMOVAL & INSTALLATION

2.0 & 2.3L EFI Engine

1. Disconnect the inlet tube and idle bypass tube from the air cleaner cover.
2. Disconnect the electrical connector to the throttle air bypass valve.
3. Remove the air cleaner cover by loosening the knurl nuts holding the air cleaner case together.
4. Lift the paper element out of the air cleaner case and wipe the case clean with a clean rag.
5. Install a new air cleaner element into the case, making sure it is seated properly, then install the case cover and tighten the knurl nuts until they are finger tight.
6. Reconnect the electrical connector to the throttle air bypass valve.
7. Reconnect the inlet tube and idle

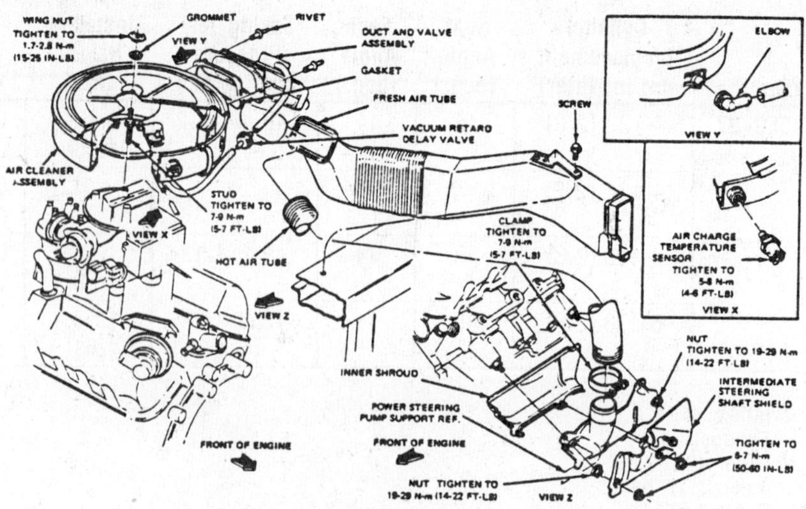

Air cleaner assembly—6-173 engine

air bypass tube to the air cleaner cover.

2.8L V6 Engine

The air cleaner element can be replaced by removing the center wing nut and air cleaner cover and then lifting out the old element. If the inside of the housing is dirty, the entire air cleaner assembly should be removed from the engine and wiped clean to prevent any dirt from entering the carburetor. To remove the air cleaner assembly, disconnect the air ducts and any vacuum lines attached to the air cleaner housing. Disconnect any mounting brackets (if equipped) and lift the air cleaner housing off of the engine. Replace the cleaner mounting gasket if it is worn or broken. When installing, reconnect all brackets, ducts and vacuum hoses and tighten the wing nut finger tight.

Fuel Filter

The fuel filters for mechanical fuel pumps are located on the carburetor where the fuel inlet line is attached. Fuel injected engines with electric fuel pumps have three filters: one inside the inline reservoir, one at the electric fuel pump mounted on the chassis and a third on the low pressure electric fuel pump mounted inside the fuel

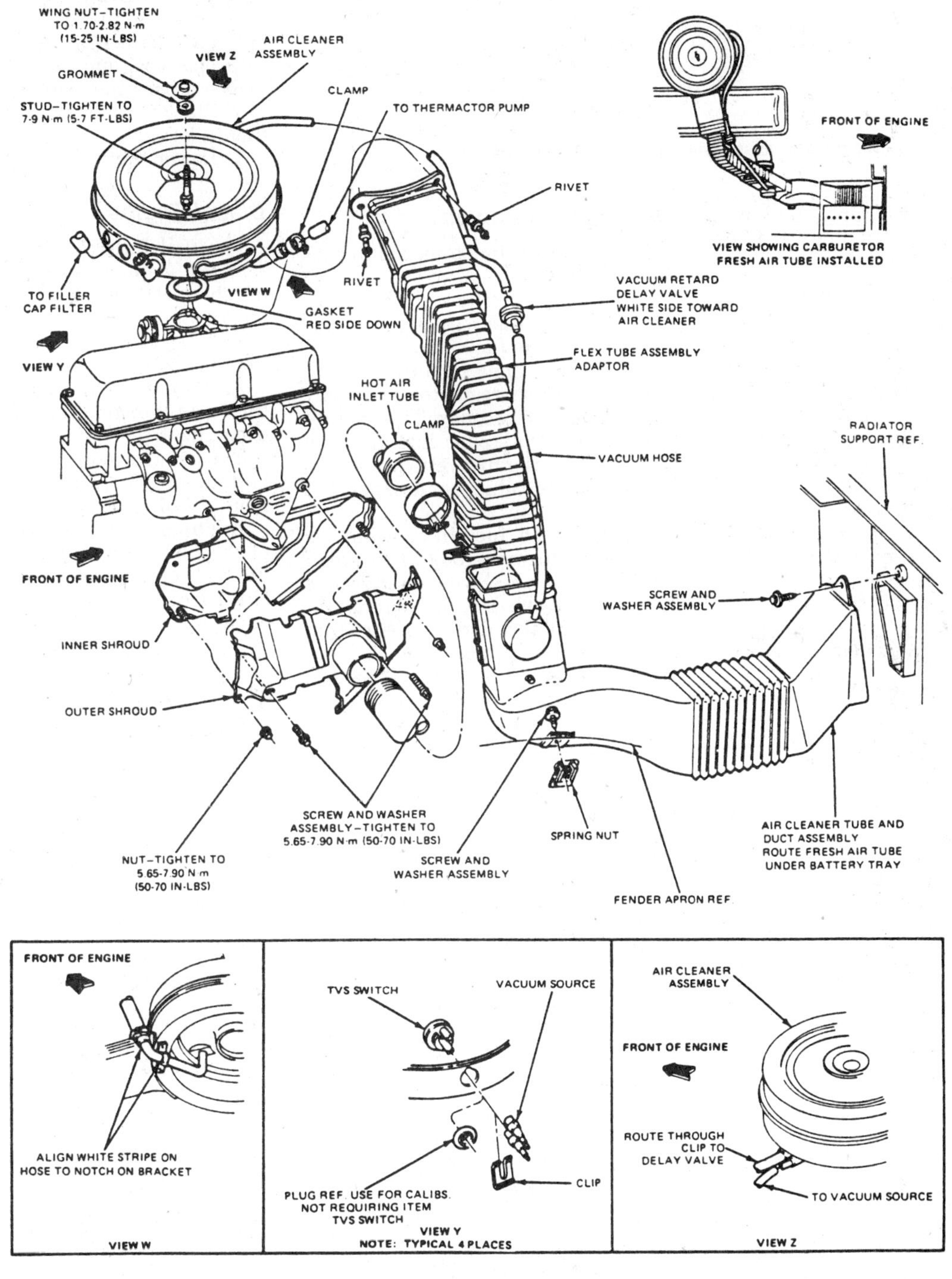

Air cleaner assembly—4-122, 140 engines

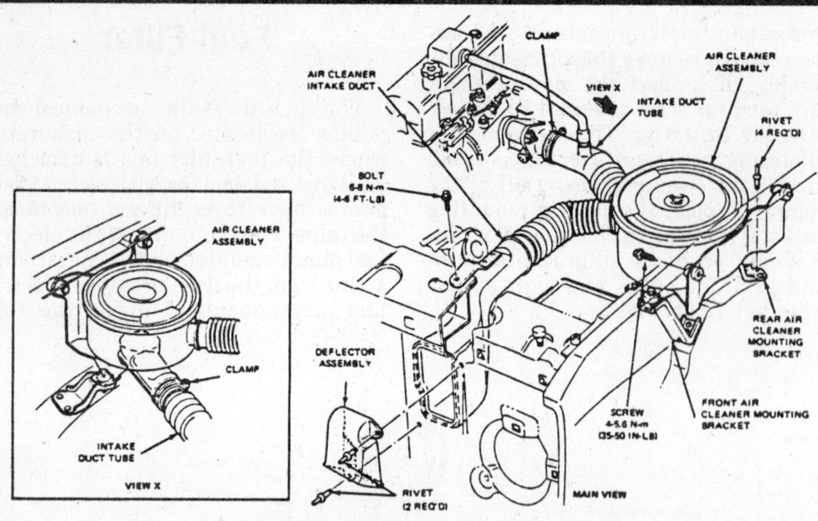

Air cleaner assembly – 4-134 diesel engine

tank itself. Normally, only the filters at the chassis mounted pump and fuel reservoir are replaced as part of normal maintenance. A high speed surge problem is indicative of a clogged fuel filter.

CAUTION

On fuel injected engines, the fuel system is under constant pressure, even when the engine is turned off. Follow the instructions for relieving fuel system pressure before attempting any service to the fuel system. Whenever working on or around any open fuel system, take precautions to avoid the risk of fire and use clean rags to catch any fuel spray while disconnecting fuel lines.

REMOVAL & INSTALLATION

Carbureted Engine

1. Remove the air cleaner assembly.
2. Using two wrenches, one on the fuel line and one holding the filter, loosen and disconnect the fuel inlet line from the carburetor fuel inlet at the filter. Use a clean rag under the fitting to catch any fuel.
3. Unscrew the fuel filter from the carburetor fuel inlet.
4. Apply one drop of Loctite® (or equivalent) hydraulic sealant to the external threads of the new fuel filter, then thread the filter into the carburetor inlet port.
5. Tighten the fuel filter to 6-8 ft.lb. (9-11Nm). Do not overtighten.
6. Thread the fuel supply line into the filter and, using two wrenches as before, tighten the fuel supply line nut to 15-18 ft.lb. (20-24Nm).
7. Start the engine and check for fuel leaks.
8. Install the air cleaner assembly. Dispose of any gasoline soaked rags properly.

Fuel Injected Engine

1. Remove the fuel tank cap to vent tank pressure.
2. Disconnect the vacuum hose from the fuel pressure regulator located on the engine fuel rail.
3. Connect a hand vacuum pump to the fuel pressure regulator and apply 25 in.Hg for ten seconds. This will release the fuel pressure into the fuel tank through the fuel return line.
4. Raise the vehicle and support it safely.
5. Locate the fuel filter which is mounted on the underbody, forward of the right rear wheel well, on the same bracket as the electric fuel pump.
6. Clean all dirt and/or grease from the fuel filter fittings. "Quick Connect" fittings are used on all models equipped with a pressurized fuel system. These fittings must be disconnected using the proper procedure or the fittings may be damaged. The fuel filter uses a "hairpin" clip retainer.
7. Spread the two hairpin clip legs about 1/8" (3mm) each to disengage it from the fitting, then pull the clip outward. Use finger pressure only; do not use any tools. Disconnect both fittings from the fuel filter.
8. Remove the fuel filter and retainer from the metal mounting bracket.
9. Remove the rubber insulator ring from the filter and the filter from the retainer. Note that the direction of fuel flow (arrow on the filter) points to the open end of the retainer.
10. Place the new filter into the retainer with the flow arrow pointing toward the open end.
11. Install the insulator ring. Replace the insulator(s) if the filter moves freely after installation of the retainer. Install the retainer on the metal bracket and tighten the mounting bolts to 51-60 in.lb. (5-7Nm).
12. Push the quick connect fittings onto the filter ends. Ford recommends that the retaining clips be replaced whenever removed. A click will be heard when the hairpin clip snaps into its proper position. Pull on the lines to insure proper connection.
13. Start the engine and check for fuel leaks.
14. Lower the vehicle.

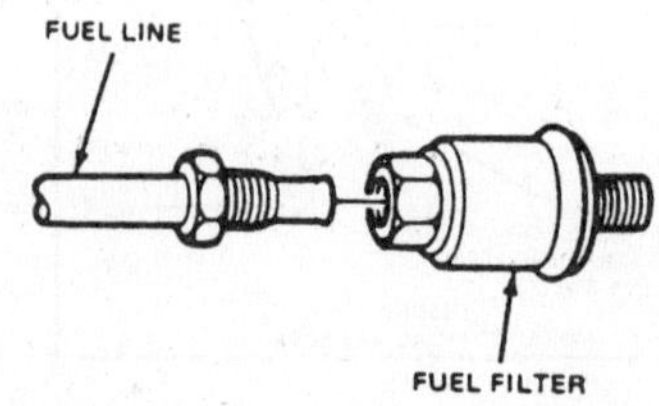

Gasoline fuel filter – Screw-in type

Diesel Engine

The fuel filter/conditioner must be serviced (water purged) at each engine oil change (7500 miles) interval. To purge water from the system:

1. Make sure the engine and ignition switch are off.
2. Place a suitable container under the fuel filter/conditioner water drain tube under the car.
3. Open the water drain valve at the bottom of the filter/conditioner element 2½-3 turns.
4. Pump the prime pump at the top of the filter from 10 to 15 strokes, or until all of the water is purged from the filter, and clear diesel fuel is apparent.

NOTE: If the water/fuel will not drain from the tube, open the drain valve one more turn or until the water/fuel starts to flow.

5. Close the drain valve and tighten.
6. Start the engine and check for leaks.

REMOVAL & INSTALLAION

1. Make sure that the engine and ignition are off.
2. Disconnect the module connector from the water level sensor located at the bottom of the filter element.
3. Use an appropriate filter strap wrench and turn the filter element counterclockwise to loosen from the top mounting bracket. Remove the element from the mount adapter.
4. Remove the water drain valve/sensor probe from the bottom of the element. Wipe the probe with a clean dry cloth.
5. Unsnap the sensor probe pigtail from the bottom of the filter element and wipe with a clean dry rag.
6. Snap the probe onto the new filter element.

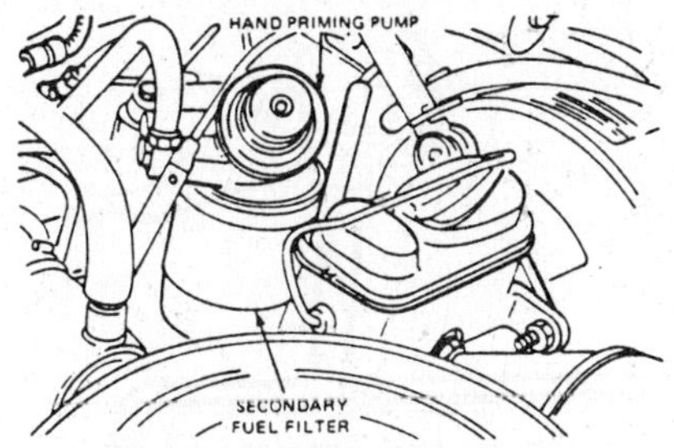

Priming the pump and fuel filter assembly—diesel engine

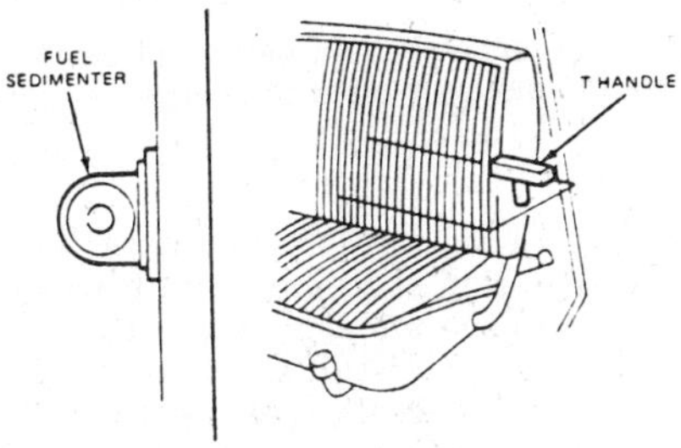

Diesel fuel sedimenter draining

7. Lubricate the two O-rings on the water sensor probe with a light film of oil. Screw the probe into the bottom of the new filter element and tighten.
8. Clean the gasket mounting surface of the adapter mount.
9. Lubricate the sealing gasket of the filter element with oil. Screw the filter element onto the mount adapter. Hand tighten the element, then back off the filter to a point where the gasket is just touching the adapter. Retighten by hand and then an additional ½-⅝ turn.
10. Reconnect the water level sensor module connector.
11. Prime the fuel system by pumping the primer handle until pressure is felt when pumping.
12. Start the engine and check for fuel leaks.

PCV Valve

All models use a closed crankcase ventilation system with a sealed breather cap connected to the air cleaner by a rubber hose. The PCV valve is usually mounted in the valve cover and connected to the intake manifold by a rubber hose. The system is used to regulate the amount of crankcase (blow-by) gases which are recycled into the combustion chambers for burning with the normal fuel charge.

The only maintenance required on the PCV system is to replace the PCV valve and/or air filter element in the air cleaner at the intervals specified in the maintenance chart. Replacement involves removing the valve from the grommet in the valve cover and installing a new valve. No attempt should be made to clean an old PCV valve; it should be replaced.

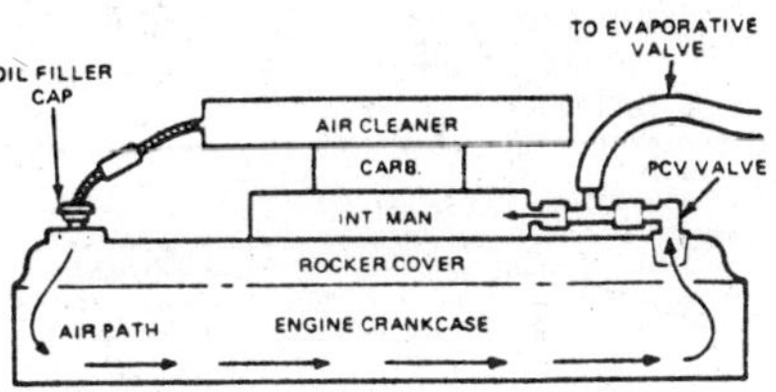

Typical PCV system

Evaporative Emissions Canister

The canister functions to cycle the fuel vapor from the fuel tank and carburetor float chamber into the intake manifold and eventually into the cylinders for combustion with the normal fuel charge. The activated charcoal within the canister acts as a storage device for the fuel vapor at times when the engine is not operating or when the engine operating condition will not permit fuel vapor to burn efficiently.

The only required service for for the evaporative canister is inspection at the interval specified in the maintenance chart. If the charcoal element is saturated with fuel, the entire canister should be replaced. Disconnect the canister purge hose(s), loosen the canister retaining bracket and lift out the canister. Installation is the reverse of removal.

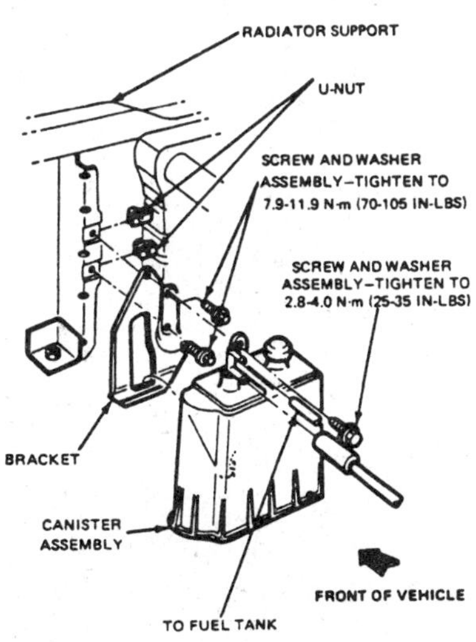

Evaporative Canister

Battery

All trucks use a maintenance free battery as standard equipment, eliminating the need for periodic fluid level checks and the possibility of specific gravity tests. Nevertheless, the battery does require some attention. An indicator is built into the top of the maintenance free battery to show the condition and state of charge. If the indicator is dark, the battery can be assumed to be OK. If the indicator is light, the specific gravity is low and the battery should either be recharged or replaced.

NOTE: Never disconnect the battery with the ignition ON or the engine running or serious onboard computer damage could occur.

Once a year, the battery terminals and cable clamps should be cleaned. Loosen the terminal mounting bolt (if equipped) and remove the cable and clamp with a suitable terminal removal tool. Clean the cable clamps and terminal posts with a suitable wire brush until all corrosion is removed and the clamps and posts are shiny. Special wire brush terminal cleaning tools are available from aftermarket sources to make this job quick and easy. It is especially important to clean the inside of the clamp (or contact side of the side terminal) thoroughly, since a small de-

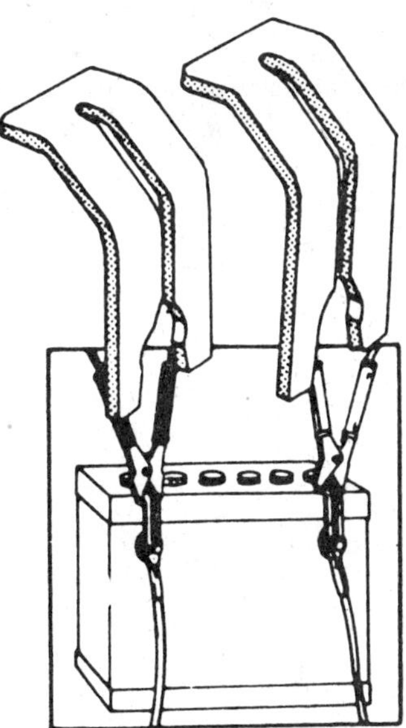

Side terminal batteries occasionally pose a problem when connecting jumper cables. There frequently isn't enough room to clamp the cables without touching sheet metal. Side terminal adaptors are available to alleviate this problem and should be removed after use

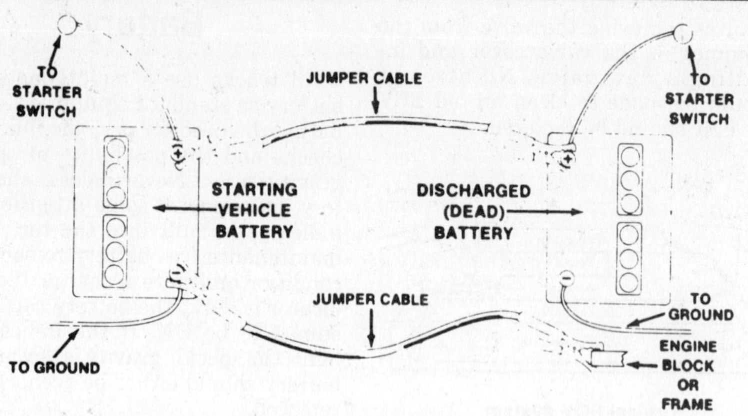

Make certain vehicles do not touch. This hook-up for negative ground cars only

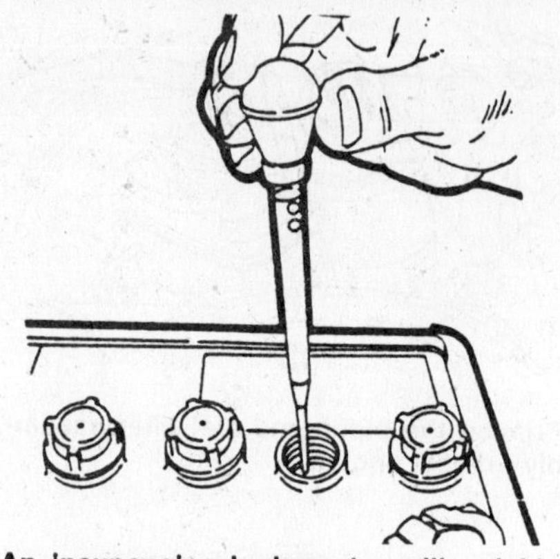

An inexpensive hydrometer will quickly test the battery's state of charge

posit of foreign material or oxidation will prevent a sound electrical connection and could inhibit charging or starting ability.

Before installing the cables, loosen the battery holddown clamp, lift out the battery and check the battery tray. Clear any debris such as leaves or dirt and check the tray for soundness. Rust and corrosion should be wire brushed away and the metal coated with anti-rust paint. Reinstall the battery and tighten the holddown clamp securely, but be careful not to overtighten and crack the battery case.

After the clamps and terminals are clean, install the terminals (positive cable first), then apply a thin external coat of grease to retard corrosion. Check the cables while cleaning the clamps, looking for frayed or broken insulation. If the cable has frayed ends or excessive corrosion is present, the cable should be replaced with a new cable of the same length and gauge.

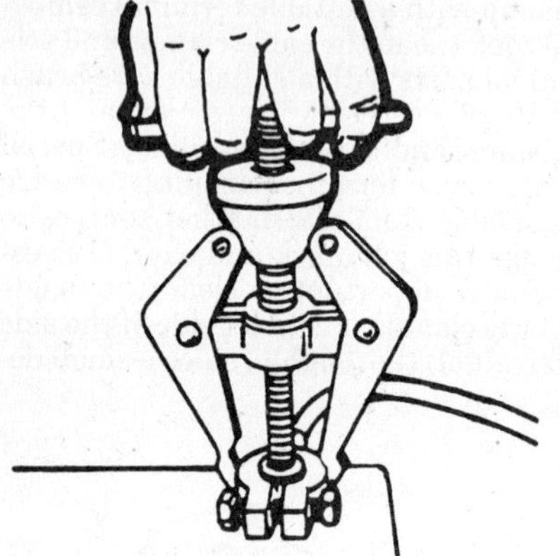

Top terminal battery cable can be removed with this inexpensive tool

Clean the cable ends with a stiff wire cleaning tool

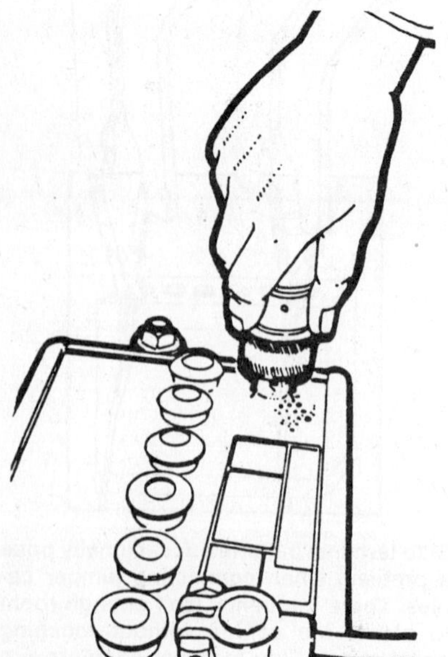

Clean the battery posts with a wire terminal cleaner

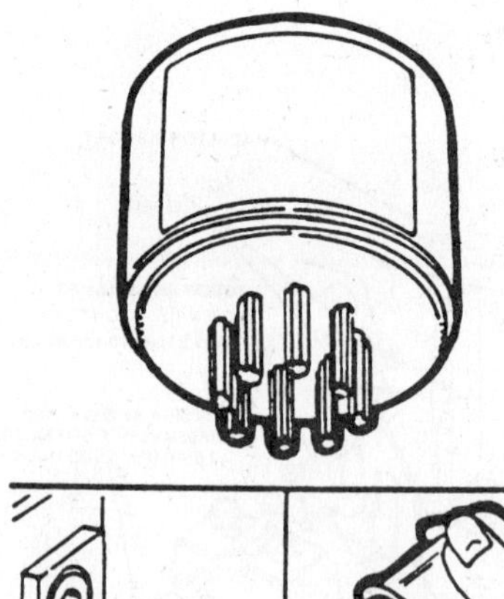

Side terminal batteries require a special wire brush for cleaning

CAUTION

Keep flame or sparks away from the battery as it gives off explosive hydrogen gas. Battery electrolyte contains sulfuric acid. If you should get any on your skin or in your eyes, flush the affected area with plenty of clear water immediately. In the case of eye contact, seek medical help immediately. It's also a good idea to wear some sort of filter when wire brushing excessive corrosion to avoid inhaling dust particles.

Belts

INSPECTION

The belts which drive the engine accessories such as the alternator or generator, the air pump, power steering pump, air conditioning compressor and water pump are of either the V-belt design or flat, serpentine design. Older belts show wear and damage readily, since their basic design was a belt with a rubber casing. As the casing wore, cracks and fibers were readily apparent. Newer design, caseless belts do not show wear as readily, and many untrained people cannot distinguish between a good, serviceable belt and one that is worn to the point of failure. It is a good idea, therefore, to visually inspect the belts regularly and replace them, routinely, every two to three years.

ADJUSTING

Belts are normally adjusted by loosening the bolts of the accessory being driven and moving that accessory on its pivot points until the proper tension is applied to the belt. The accessory is held in this position while the bolts are tightened. To determine proper belt tension, you can purchase a belt tension gauge or simply use the deflection method. To determine deflection, press inward on the belt at the mid-point of its longest straight run. The belt should deflect (move inward) 3/8-1/2" (10–13mm). Some long V-belts and most serpentine belts have idler pulleys which are used for adjusting purposes. Just loosen the idler pulley and move it to take up tension on the belt.

REMOVAL & INSTALLATION

To remove a drive belt, simply loosen the accessory being driven and move it on its pivot point to free the belt. Then, remove the belt. If an idler pulley is used, it is often necessary, only, to loosen the idler pulley to provide enough slack the remove the belt.

It is important to note, however, that on engines with many driven accessories, several or all of the belts may have to be removed to get at the one to be replaced.

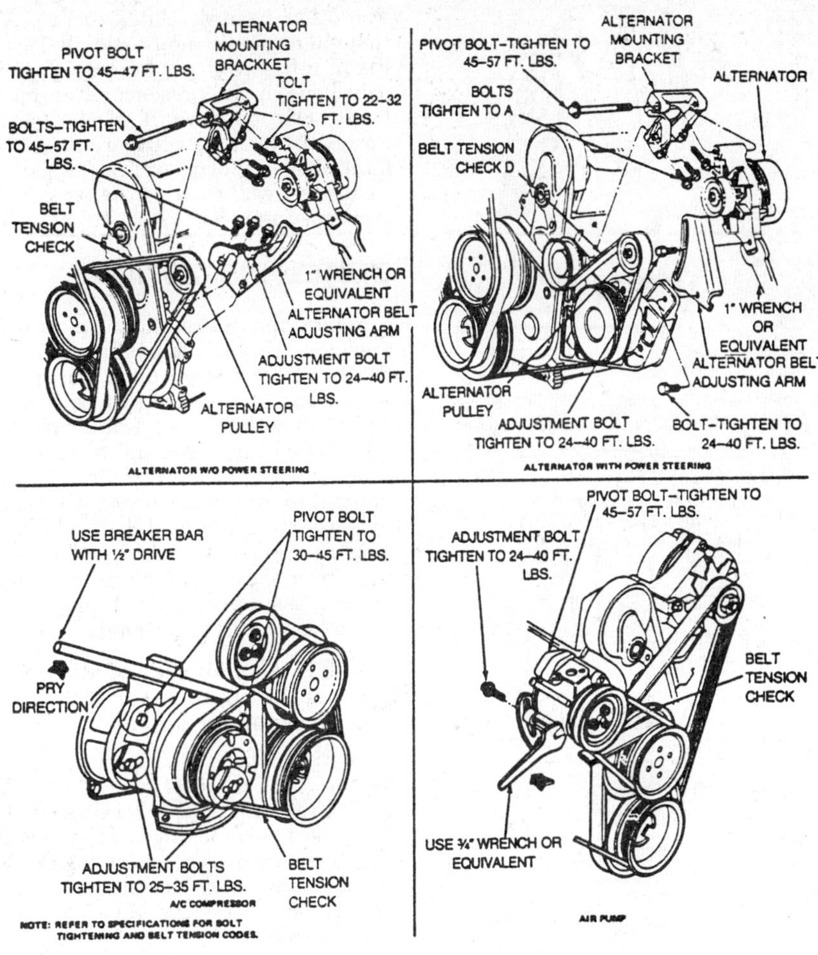

Belt tension adjustment—4-122, 140 engines

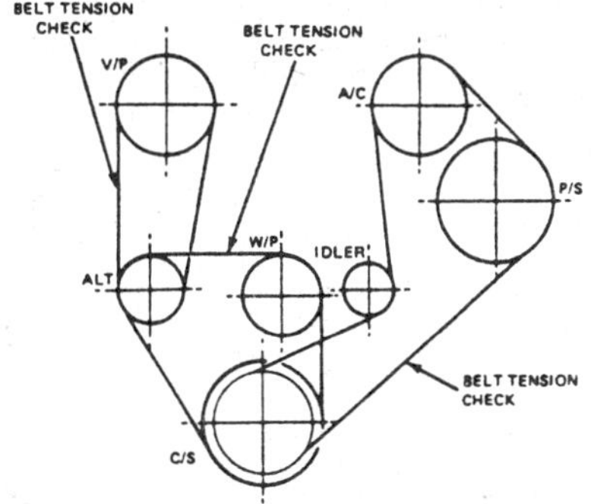

Belt tension adjustment—4-134 diesel engine

Hoses

REMOVAL & INSTALLATION

Radiator hoses are generally of two constructions, the preformed (molded) type, which is custom made for a particular application, and the spring loaded type, which is made to fit sever-

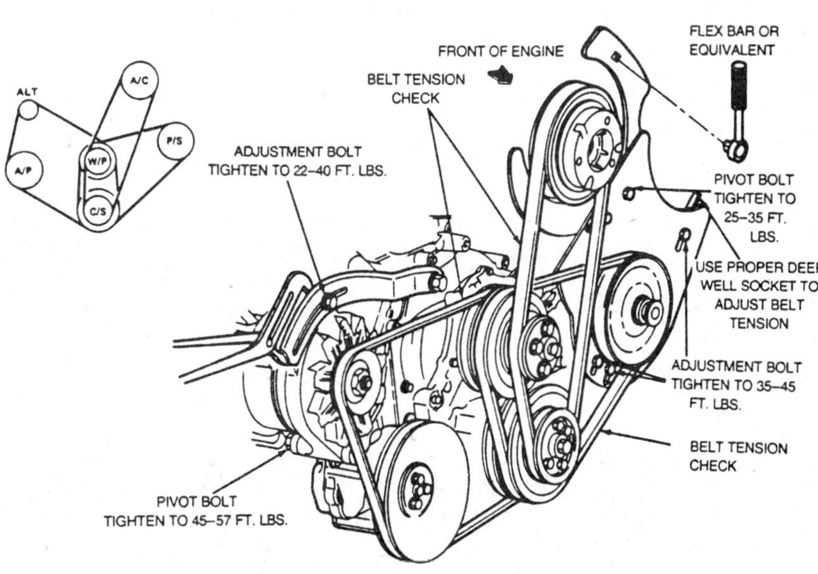

Belt tension adjustments—6-173 engine

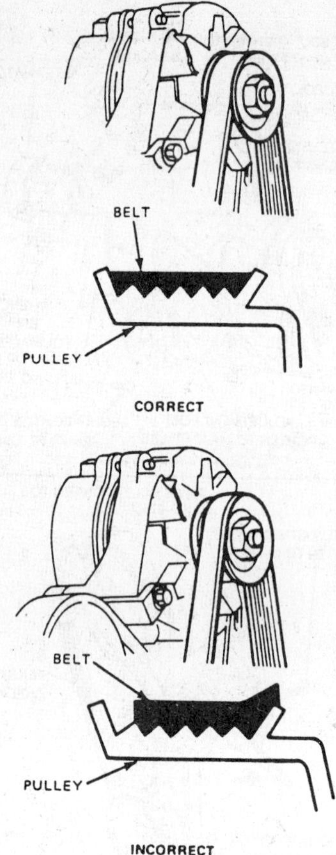

Checking ribbed belt alignment

al different applications. Heater hoses are all of the same general construction.

Hoses are retained by clamps. To replace a hose, loosen the clamp and slide it down the hose, away from the attaching point. Twist the hose from side to side until it is free, then pull it off. Before installing the new hose, make sure that the outlet fitting is as clean as possible. Coat the fitting with non-hardening sealer and slip the hose into place. Install the clamp and tighten it.

Air Conditioning System

PRECAUTIONS

There are two particular hazards associated with air conditioning systems and they both relate to the refrigerant gas. First, the refrigerant gas is an extremely cold substance. When exposed to the air it will instantly freeze any surface it comes in contact with, including skin and eyes. Always wear safety goggles when performing any service on the air conditioning system.

The other hazard relates to fire. Although normally non-toxic, R-12 or Freon refrigerant gas becomes highly poisonous in the presence of an open flame. One good whiff of the vapor formed by burning refrigerant can be fatal. Keep all forms of fire (including cigarettes) well clear of the air conditioning system.

SYSTEM INSPECTION

Refrigerant leaks show up as oily areas on the various components because the compressor oil is transported around the entire system along with the refrigerant. Look for oily spots on all the hoses and lines, especially on the hose and tubing connections. If there are oily deposits visible, the system may have a leak. The oily residue soon picks up dust or dirt particles from the surrounding air and appears greasy, eventually building up into a heavy, dirt impregnated grease.

NOTE: A small area of oil on the front of the compressor is normal and no cause for alarm.

Another type of leak may appear at the internal Schraeder type A/C charging valve core in the service access gauge port valve fittings. If tightening the valve core does not stop the leak, it should be replaced. Missing service access gauge port valve caps can also cause a refrigerant leak by allowing dirt to contaminate the valve during charging.

Periodically inspect the front of the condenser for bent fins or foreign material (dirt, bugs, leaves, etc.), and clean the condenser thoroughly. Straighten any bent fins carefully with needlenosed pliers. Debris may be removed with a stiff bristle brush or water pressure from a garden hose.

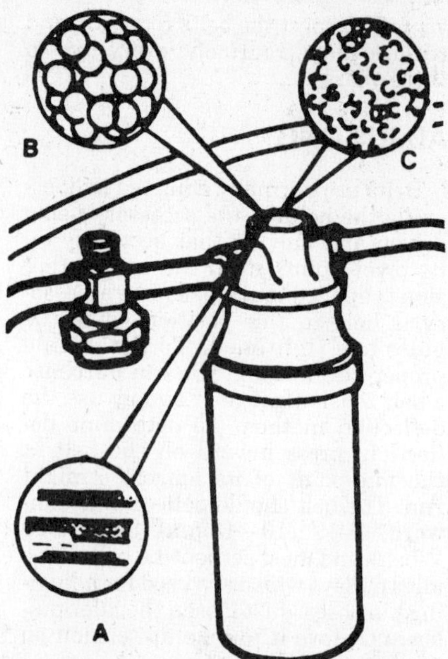

Oil streaks (A), constant bubbles (B) or foam (C) indicate there is not enough refrigerant in the system. Occasional bubbles during initial operation is normal. A clear sight glass indicates a proper charge of refrigerant or no refrigerant at all, which can be determined by the presence of cold air at the outlets in the car. If the glass is clouded with a milky white substance, have the receiver/drier checked professionally

A lot of air conditioner problems can be avoided by simply running the system at least once a week, regardless of the season. Let the A/C run for at least five minutes (even in the winter) and you'll keep the internal parts lubricated and prevent the hoses from hardening.

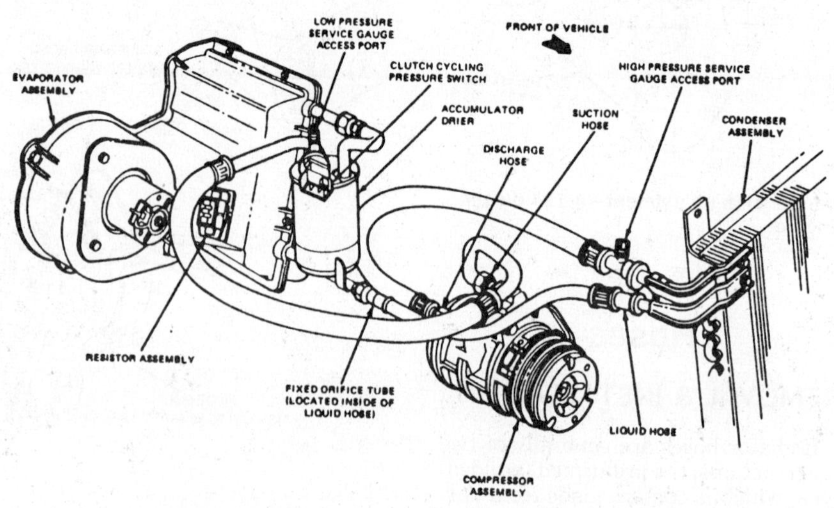

Typical air conditioning system, showing all components

REFRIGERANT LEVEL CHECK

The only way to check the refrigerant level on the truck is to measure the system evaporator pressures with a manifold gauge set, although rapid on/off cycling of the compressor clutch indicates that the A/C system is low on refrigerant. The normal refrigerant capacity is 3½ lbs.

TEST GAUGES

Most of the service work performed in air conditioning requires the use of a set of two gauges, one for the high (head) pressure side of the system, the other for the low (suction) side.

The low side gauge records both pressure and vacuum. Vacuum readings are calibrated from 0 to 30 inches and the pressure graduations read from 0 to no less than 60 psi. The high side gauge measures pressure from 0 to at least 600 psi.

Both gauges are threaded into a manifold that contains two hand shut-off valves. Proper manipulation of these valves and the use of the attached test hoses allow the user to perform the following services:

1. Test high and low side pressures.
2. Remove air, moisture, and contaminated refrigerant.
3. Purge the system (of refrigerant).
4. Charge the system (with refrigerant).

The manifold valves are designed so that they have no direct effect on gauge readings, but serve only to provide for, or cut off, flow of refrigerant through the manifold. During all testing and hook-up operations, the valves are kept in a close position to avoid disturbing the refrigeration system. The valves are opened only to purge the system or refrigerant or to charge it.

DISCHARGING THE SYSTEM

Service access gauge port valves are used in the refrigerant system. These are Schraeder type valves, similar to a tire valve with a depressing pin in the center of the valve body. The high pressure (discharge) valve is located in the compressor discharge manifold, just before the accumulator/drier. This valve requires an adapter (YT-354 or 355) to connect a manifold gauge set to it. The other service access port valve is located on the side of the accumulator and is the low pressure (suction) connection. It is extremely important that these two valves not be confused, since connecting a can of Freon to the high pressure side of the A/C system will cause the can to explode.

To connect a manifold gauge set to the service gauge port valves, proceed as follows:

1. Turn both manifold gauge set valves fully clockwise to close the high and low pressure hoses.
2. Remove the caps from the high and low pressure service gauge port valves.
3. If the manifold gauge set hoses do not have the valve depressing pins in them, install fitting adapters (T71P-19703-S and R) containing the pins on the manifold gauge hoses. Remember that an adapter is necessary to connect the manifold gauge hose to the high pressure fitting.
4. Connect the high and low pressure refrigerant hoses to their respective service ports, making sure they are hooked up correctly and fully seated. Tighten the fittings by hand and make sure they are not cross-threaded.
5. Place the open end of the center hose on the manifold gauge set away from your body, then slowly open the LOW pressure valve on the manifold set a slight amount to allow the refrigerant to flow out the center hose and slowly depressurize the A/C system.
6. After the system is nearly discharged, open the high pressure valve very slowly to avoid losing any refrigerant oil and allow any remaining Freon in the compressor and high pressure line to discharge.

CAUTION

Do not attempt this procedure in a closed garage. The refrigerant will displace the oxygen in the air and could result in suffocation in a very short time. Allowing the refrigerant to vent quickly will carry away the refrigerant oil; open the valves slowly and only slightly. Remember that escaping refrigerant will freeze any surface it touches, including skin and eyes. Wear safety glasses at all times.

CHARGING THE SYSTEM

If the system has been completely purged of refrigerant, it must be evacuated before charging. A vacuum pump should be connected to the center hose of the manifold gauge set, both valves should be opened, and the vacuum pump operated until the low pressure gauge reads as close to 30 in.Hg as possible. If a part in the system has been replaced or excessive moisture is suspected, continue the vacuum pump operation for about 30 minutes.

Close the manifold gauge valves to the center hose, then disconnect the vacuum pump and connect the center hose to a charging cylinder, refrigerant drum or a small can refrigerant dispensing valve. Disconnect the wire harness from the clutch cycling pressure switch and install a jumper wire across the two terminals of the connector. Open the manifold gauge LOW side valve to allow refrigerant to enter the system, keeping the can(s) in an upright position to prevent liquid from entering the system.

When no more refrigerant is being drawn into the system, start the engine and move the function selector lever to the NORM A/C position and the blower switch to HI to draw the remaining refrigerant in. Continue to add refrigerant until the specified 3½ lbs. is reached. Close the manifold gauge low pressure valve and the refrigerant supply valve. Remove the jumper wire from the clutch cycling pressure switch connector and reconnect the pressure switch. Disconnect the manifold gauge set and install the service port caps.

Charging From Small Containers

When using a single can A/C charging kit, such as is available at local retailers, make the connection at the low pressure service port, located on the accumulator/drier. This is very important as connecting the small can to the high pressure port will cause the can to explode. Once the can is connected, charge the system as described above. If a manifold gauge set is being used, the low pressure valve must be closed whenever another can is being connected to the center hose. Hold the cans upright to prevent liquid refrigerant from entering the system and possibly damaging the compressor.

Windshield Wipers

For maximum effectiveness and longest element life, the windshield and wiper blades should be kept clean. Dirt, tree sap, road tar and so on will cause streaking, smearing and blade deterioration if left on the windshield. It is advisable to wash the windshield carefully with a commercial glass cleaner at least once a month. Wipe off the rubber blades with a wet rag afterwards. Do not attempt to move the wipers back and forth by hand; damage to the motor and drive mechanism will result.

If the blades are found to be cracked, broken or torn they should be replaced immediately. Replacement intervals will vary with usage, although ozone deterioration usually limits blade lift to about one year. If the wiper pattern is smeared or streaked, or if the blade chatters across the glass, the blades should be replaced. It is easiest and most sensible to replace them in pairs.

There are basically three different types of wiper blade refills, which differ in their method of replacement. One type has two release buttons, approximately 1/3 of the way up from the ends of the blade frame. Pushing the buttons down releases a lock and allows the rubber blade to be removed from the frame. The new blade slides back into the frame and locks in place.

The second type of refill has two metal tabs which are unlocked by squeezing them together. The rubber blade can then be withdrawn from the frame jaws. A new one is installed by inserting it into the front frame jaws and sliding it rearward to engage the remaining frame jaws. There are usually four jaws; be certain when installing that the refill is engaged in all of them. At the end of its travel, the tabs will lock into place on the front jaws of the wiper blade frame.

The third type is a refill made from polycarbonate. The refill has a simple locking device at one end which flexes downward out of the groove into which the jaws of the holder fit, allowing easy release. By sliding the new refill through all the jaws and pushing through the slight resistance when it reaches the end of its travel, the refill will lock into position.

Regardless of the type of refill used, make sure that all of the frame jaws are engaged as the refill is pushed into place and locked. The metal blade holder and frame will scratch the glass if allowed to touch it.

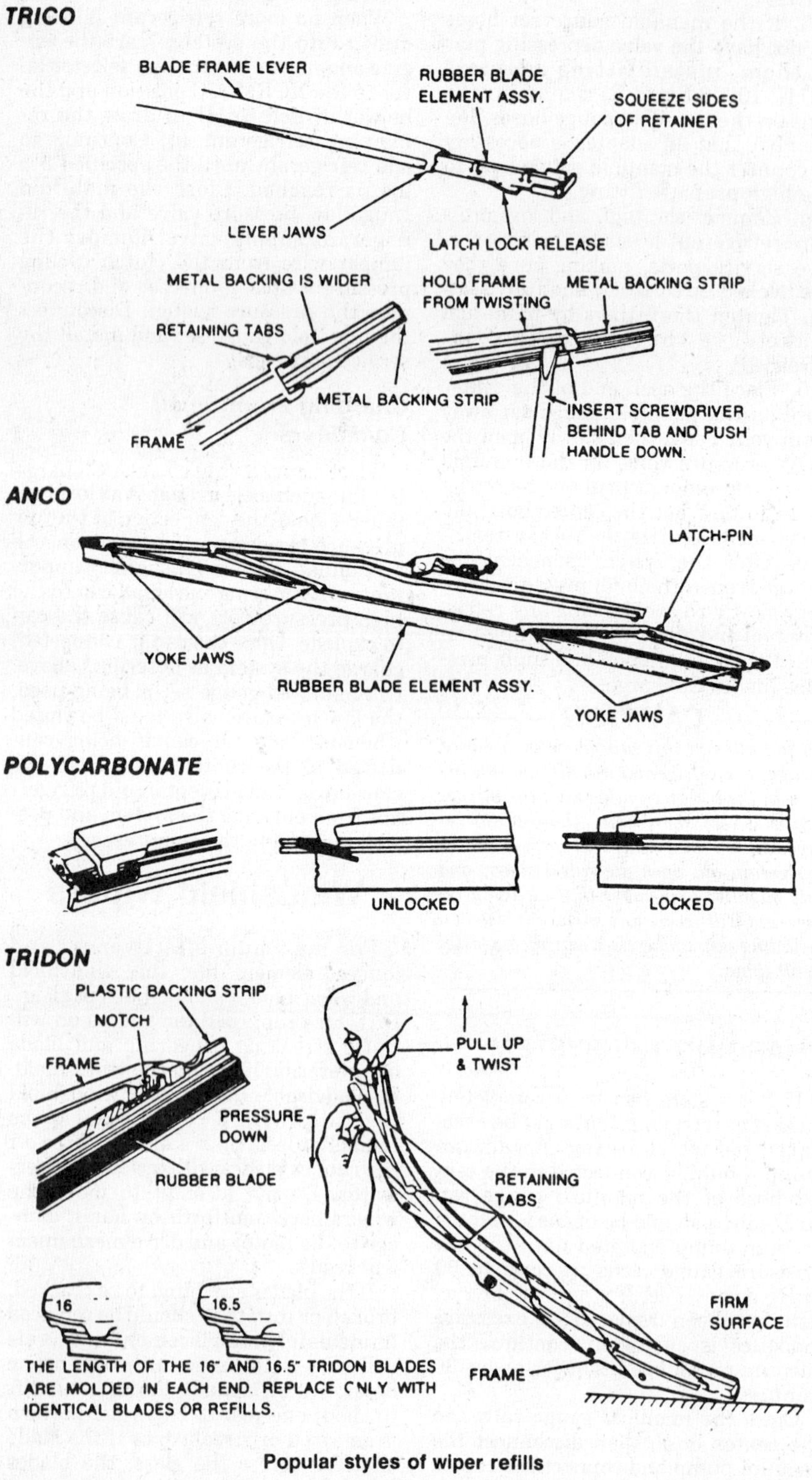

Popular styles of wiper refills

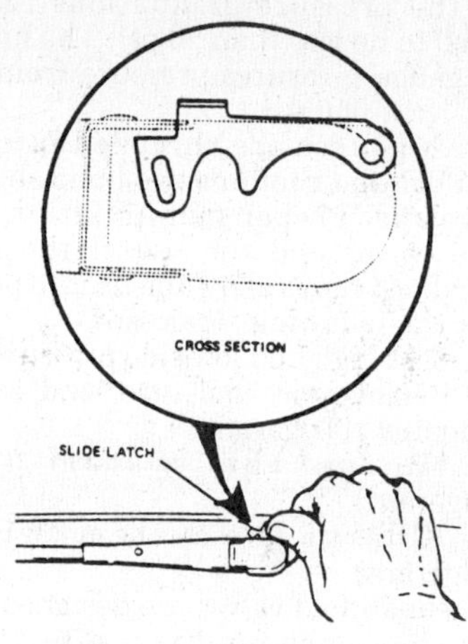

Wiper arm replacement

Tires and Wheels

Inspect the tire treads for cuts, bruises and other damage. Check the air valves to be sure that they are tight. Replace any missing valve caps. The tires should be checked frequently for proper air pressure. A chart in the glove compartment or on the driver's door pillar gives the recommended inflation pressure. Pressures can increase as much as 6 psi due to heat buildup. It is a good idea to have your own accurate gauge, and to check pressures weekly. Not all gauges on service station air pumps can be trusted.

Inspect tires for uneven wear that might indicate the need for front end alignment or tire rotation. Tires should be replaced when a tread wear indicator appears as a solid band across the tread. When buying new tires, give some thought to the following points, especially if you are switching to larger tires or a different profile series (50, 60, 70, 78):

1. All four tires should be of the same construction type. Radial, bias, or bias/belted tires should not be mixed.

2. The wheels must be the correct width for the tire. Tire dealers have charts of tire and rim compatibility. A mismatch can cause sloppy handling and rapid tire wear. The tread width should match the rim width (inside bead to inside bead) within an inch. For radial tires, the rim width should be 80% or less of the tire (not tread) width.

3. The height (mounted diameter) of the new tires can greatly change speedometer accuracy, engine speed at a given road speed, fuel mileage, acceleration, and ground clearance. Tire manufacturers furnish full measurement specifications.

NOTE: Dimensions of tires marked the same size may vary significantly, even among tires from the same manufacturer.

4. The spare tire should be usable, at least for low speed operation, with the new tires.

5. There shouldn't be any body interference when loaded, on bumps, or in turning.

TIRE ROTATION

Tire rotation is recommended every 6,000 miles or so, to obtain maximum tire wear. The pattern you use depends on whether or not you have a usable spare. Radial tires should not be cross-switched (from one side of the truck to the other); they last longer if their direction of rotation is not changed. They will wear very rapidly if their direction of rotation is reversed.

NOTE: Mark the wheel position or direction of rotation on radial tires or studded snow tires before removing them.

CAUTION

Avoid overtightening the lug nuts to prevent damage to the brake disc or drum. Alloy wheels can also be cracked by overtightening. Use of a torque wrench is highly recommended. Lug nuts should be tightened in sequence to 85-115 ft.lb.

TEMPORARY SPARE TIRE

The temporary spare tire is lighter in weight and easier to handle than a conventional tire, but it is limited to emergency use only. The temporary spare tire pressure should be checked periodically and inflated to the pressure marked on the sidewall. When the temporary spare tire is in use, vehicle speed should be kept below 50 mph and the flat conventional tire should be repaired or replaced as soon as possible. The temporary spare is stored underneath the cargo bed in the rear of the vehicle. To remove the temporary spare from storage:

1. Insert the lugwrench into the actuator hole at the rear of the truck and rotate it counterclockwise.

2. Slide the spare rearward and separate it from the retainer.

3. To stow the cable/retainer without the temporary spare, insert the cable fitting into the tire carrier rear wall slot. Position the wheel retainer against the carrier and rotate the lugwrench clockwise until all slack is removed. Do not overtighten.

4. To install the temporary spare tire into its holder, first insert the lugwrench into the actuator and rotate it counterclockwise while pulling on the cable until adequate cable is available.

5. Install the retainer through the wheel center with the valve stem facing downward and rearward to allow the tire pressure to be checked.

6. Rotate the lugwrench clockwise until the tire is secured; the raising mechanism will slip. Check for proper seating against the underbody brackets and retighten if necessary.

CAUTION

Do not overtighten the retaining bolt with the lugwrench as damage to the spare may occur by compressing the sidewalls against the supports. Improper installation of the spare tire may result in damage to the rear axle, tire or brake lines.

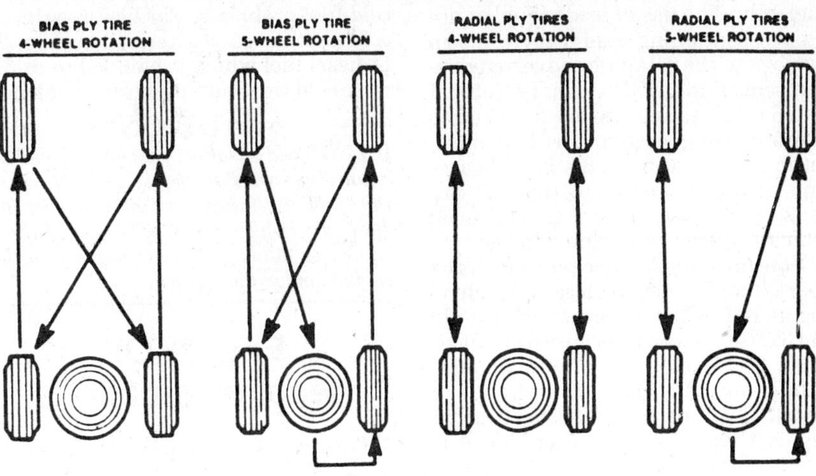

Tire rotation pattern

Tread wear indicators are built into tires

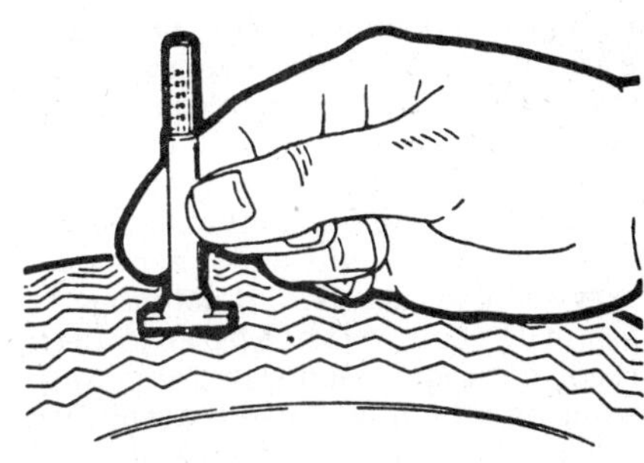

Checking tread depth with an inexpensive depth tester

FLUIDS AND LUBRICANTS

Fuel Recommendations

Gasoline Engines

The truck is equipped with a catalytic converter and must use unleaded fuel only. The use of leaded fuel or additives containing lead will result in damage to the catalytic converter, oxygen sensor and EGR valve. Both the 4 and 6 cylinder engines are designed to operate using gasoline with a minimum octane rating of 87. Use of gasoline with a rating lower than 87 can cause persistent, heavy spark knock which can lead to engine damage.

You may notice occasional, light spark knock when accelerating or driving up hills. This is normal and should not cause concern because the maximum fuel economy is obtained under conditions of occasional light spark knock. Gasoline with an octane rating higher than 87 may be used, but it is not necessary for proper operation.

Gasohol, a mixture of gasoline and ethanol (grain alcohol) is available in some areas. Your truck should operate satisfactorily on gasohol blends containing no more than 10% ethanol by volume and having an octane rating of 87 or higher. In some cases, methanol (wood alcohol) or other alcohols may be added to gasoline. Again, your truck should operate satisfactorily on blends containing up to 5% methanol by volume when cosolvents and other necessary additives are used. If not properly formulated with appropriate cosolvents and corrosion inhibitors, such blends may cause driveability problems or damage emission and fuel system materials. If you are uncertain as to the presence of alcohols in the gasoline you are purchasing, check the label on the pump or ask the attendant.

NOTE: Discontinue use of any gasohol or alcohol/gasoline blend if driveability or fuel system problems occur. Do not use such fuels unless they are unleaded.

Some models are equipped with a remote fuel filler door release, located between the driver seat and the door. If the filler door cannot be opened by pulling the release lever, there is a manual override cord located on the left side of the jack stowage compartment. The manual release is a cord attached to a handle marked "Fuel Filler Door Manual Release."

Diesel Engine

The diesel engine is designed to use number 2-D diesel fuel. Use of number 1-D diesel fuel in temperatures +20°F is acceptable, but not necessary.

Do not use number 1-D diesel fuel in temperatures above +20°F as damage to the engine may result. Also fuel economy will be reduced with the use of number 1-D diesel fuel.

The diesel engines are equipped with an electric fuel heater to prevent cold fuel problems. For best results in cold weather use winterized number 2-D diesel fuel which is blended to minimize cold weather operation problems.

CAUTION

DO NOT add gasoline, gasohol, alcohol or cetane improvers to the diesel fuel. Also, DO NOT use fluids such as either in the diesel air intake system. The use of these liquids or fluids will cause damage to the engine and/or fuel system.

Engine Oil Recommendations

To insure proper engine performance and durability, the proper quality engine oil is essential. Using the proper grade of oil for your engine will not only prolong its life, it will improve fuel economy. Ford recommends that you use Motorcraft® oil or an equivalent that meets Ford Specification ESE-M2C153-C and API (American Petroleum Institute) Categories SF, SF/CC or SF/CD.

Engine oils with improved fuel economy properties are currently available. They offer the potential for small improvements in fuel economy by reducing the amount of fuel burned by the engine to overcome friction. These improvements are often difficult to measure in everyday driving, but over the course of a year can offer significant savings. These oils are recommended to be used in conjunction with the recommended API Category.

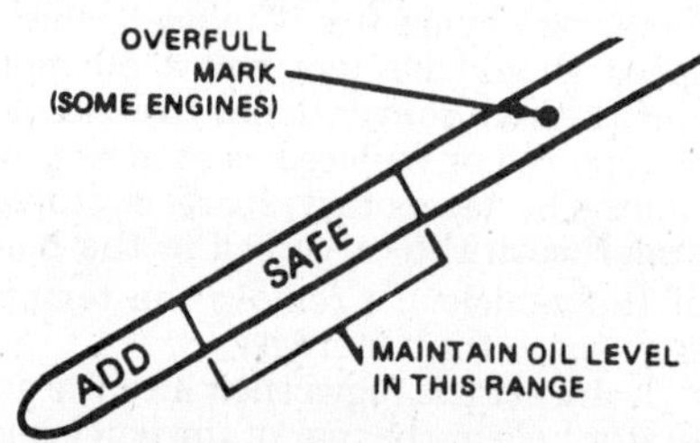

Checking engine oil level

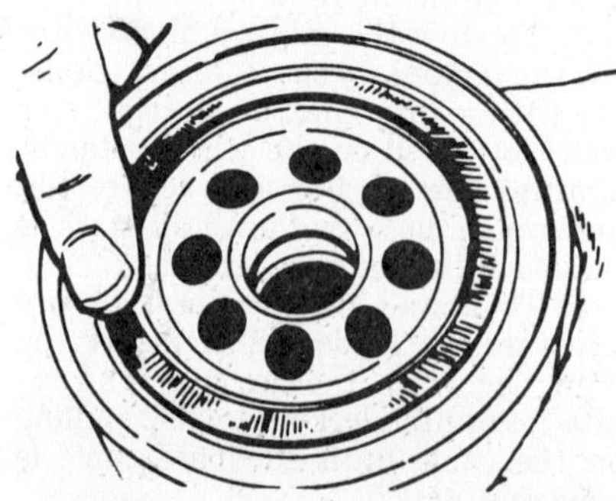

Lubricate the gasket on the new filter with clean engine oil. A dry gasket may not make a good seal and will allow the filter to leak

A symbol has been developed by the API to help consumers select the proper grade of engine oil. It should be printed on top of the oil container to show oil performance by the API designation. This symbol should match the manufacturer recommendation. The center section will show the SAE (Society of Automotive Engineers) rating, while the top outer ring contains the API rating. The bottom outer ring will have the words "Energy Conserving" only if the oil has proven fuel saving capabilities.

CHECKING ENGINE OIL LEVEL

It is normal to add some oil between oil changes. The engine oil level should be checked every 500 miles.

1. Park the truck on a level surface and turn the engine off. Open the hood.
2. Wait a few minutes to allow the oil to drain back into the crankcase.
3. While protecting yourself from engine heat, pull the dipstick out and wipe it clean with a suitable paper towel or clean rag.
4. Reinsert the dipstick and make sure it is pushed all the way down and seated on the tube, then remove the dipstick again and look at the oil level scale on the end of the dipstick. The oil level should fall within the safe range on the dipstick scale.
5. If necessary, add oil to the engine to bring the level up. Be careful not to overfill the crankcase and wipe the dipstick off before checking the oil level again.

OIL AND FILTER CHANGE

The engine oil and filter should be changed at the recommended intervals on the maintenance schedule chart. The oil filter protects the engine by removing harmful, abrasive or sludgy particles from the system without blocking the flow of oil to vital engine parts. It is recommended that the filter be changed along with the oil at the specified intervals.

NOTE: Changing the oil requires the use of an oil filter wrench to remove the filter. It's also a good idea to have some oil dry (or kitty litter) handy to absorb any oil that misses the drain pan.

1. Start the engine and allow it to reach normal operating temperature. Park the truck on a level surface and shut the engine off.
2. Set the parking brake firmly and block the drive wheels.

3. Place a drip pan of at least 5 quart capacity beneath the oil pan.

4. Loosen the oil pan drain plug with a suitable wrench, then finish threading it out by hand while pressing in slightly until it is free. Be careful, the oil will be hot.

5. Allow the oil to drain completely before replacing the drain plug. Tighten the plug securely, but do not overtighten.

6. Position the drain pan under the oil filter, then use an oil filter band wrench to loosen the filter. Once the filter is loose, finish removing it by hand. Again, be careful, the oil and filter will be hot.

7. Clean the filter mounting base on the engine block and lightly coat the gasket of the new filter with a thin film of oil. Install the new filter by hand and tighten it another ½-¾ turn after the gasket contacts the filter base. Tighten the filter by hand, do not use the filter wrench.

8. Fill the crankcase with the recommended oil and start the engine to check for leaks. It is normal for the oil warning light to remain on for a few seconds after startup until the oil filter fills up. Once the oil light goes out, check for leaks from the filter mounting and drain plug. If no leaks are noticed, stop the engine and check the oil level on the dipstick. Top up if necessary.

Manual Transmission

FLUID LEVEL CHECK

The 5-speed manual transmission uses standard transmission lubricant, Ford part number D8DZ-19C547-A or equivalent. The fluid level is checked by removing the filler plug on the side of the transmission case. Clean the plug and remove it. The fluid should be up to the bottom of the filler plug hole.

If additional fluid is required, add it through the filler plug hole to bring the level up. Use only fluid meeting Ford specification ESP-M2C83-C. Install the filler plug when the fluid level is correct, making sure it is fully seated.

DRAINING MANUAL TRANSMISSION

The fluid can be drained from the manual transmission simply by removing the drain plug on the transmission bottom pan. Use a suitable container to catch the old fluid, then replace the plug and remove the filler plug on the side of the transmission to add new fluid. Add fluid until the level is at the base of the filler plug hole.

Hydraulic Clutch

FLUID LEVEL CHECK

The clutch system in the truck does not have free play. It is automatically self-adjusting and should not require any routine service throughout the life of the vehicle. The fluid level in the clutch reservoir will slowly increase as the clutch wears. As long as the fluid is visible at or above the step in the translucent reservoir body, top-off is not recommended and should be avoided. This will help prevent overflow and possible contamination of the fluid while the diaphragm and cap are removed. If it becomes necessary to remove the reservoir cap, thoroughly clean the reservoir cap before removing it to prevent dirt or water from entering the reservoir.

Automatic Transmission

FLUID LEVEL CHECK

Correct automatic transmission fluid level is important for proper operation. Low fluid level causes transmission slippage, while overfilling can cause foaming, loss of fluid or malfunction. Since transmission fluid expands as temperature rises, it is advisable to check the fluid level at operating temperature (after about 20 miles of driving), however, the fluid level can be checked at room temperature.

To check the fluid level, park the vehicle on a level surface and apply the parking brake. Start the engine and hold the foot brake while moving the transmission shift lever through all the gear positions, allowing sufficient time for each gear to engage. Return the shifter to the PARK position and leave the engine running.

Secure all loose clothing and remove any jewelry, then open the hood. While protecting yourself against engine heat, wipe the dipstick cap clean, then remove the dipstick. Wipe the dipstick clean then reinsert it into the tube, making sure it is fully seated. Remove the dipstick again and read the fluid level on the dipstick scale. At normal operating temperature, the level on the dipstick should be within the crosshatched area or between the arrows. At room temperature, the level should be between the middle and top hole on the dipstick.

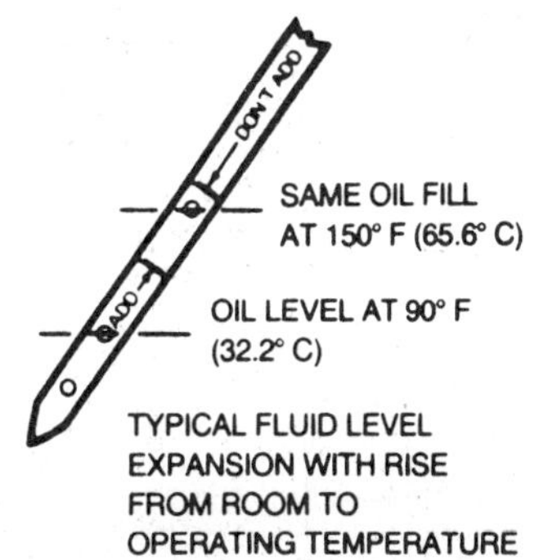

Checking automatic transmission fluid level

If fluid has to be added, use a small necked funnel to add the necessary amount of Dexron®II through the dipstick tube to bring the level up to normal. Do not bring the level above the crosshatched area on the dipstick. If overfilled, the excess transmission fluid must be removed. Once the fluid level is correct, reinsert the dipstick and make sure it is fully seated.

PAN AND FILTER SCREEN SERVICE

Normal maintenance and lubrication requirements do not include periodic automatic transmission fluid changes. However, if the transmission is used under continuous or severe conditions, the transmission and torque converter should be drained and refilled with Dexron®II. The following procedure is for a partial draining of the transmission, in order to remove the pan to replace the pan gasket or clean the filter screen.

1. Park the truck on a level surface and place a drip pan under the transmission to catch the fluid.

2. Slowly loosen the pan attaching bolts. When all the bolts are loose, gradually remove the bolts from one end to allow the pan to tilt down and the fluid to drain out.

3. When all of the fluid has drained from the transmission oil pan, remove the remaining mounting bolts and lower the pan.

4. Thoroughly clean the pan and screen in solvent or kerosene and remove any old gasket material from the pan or transmission housing. Clean all gasket mating surfaces thoroughly, but be careful not to scratch any aluminum surfaces. Do not attempt to reuse an old pan gasket.

5. Place a new gasket on the pan, then install the pan on the transmission.

6. Add three quarts of fluid to the transmission through the filler tube, then check the transmission fluid level as described above.

Drive Axle

FLUID LEVEL CHECK

The ability of any axle to deliver qui-

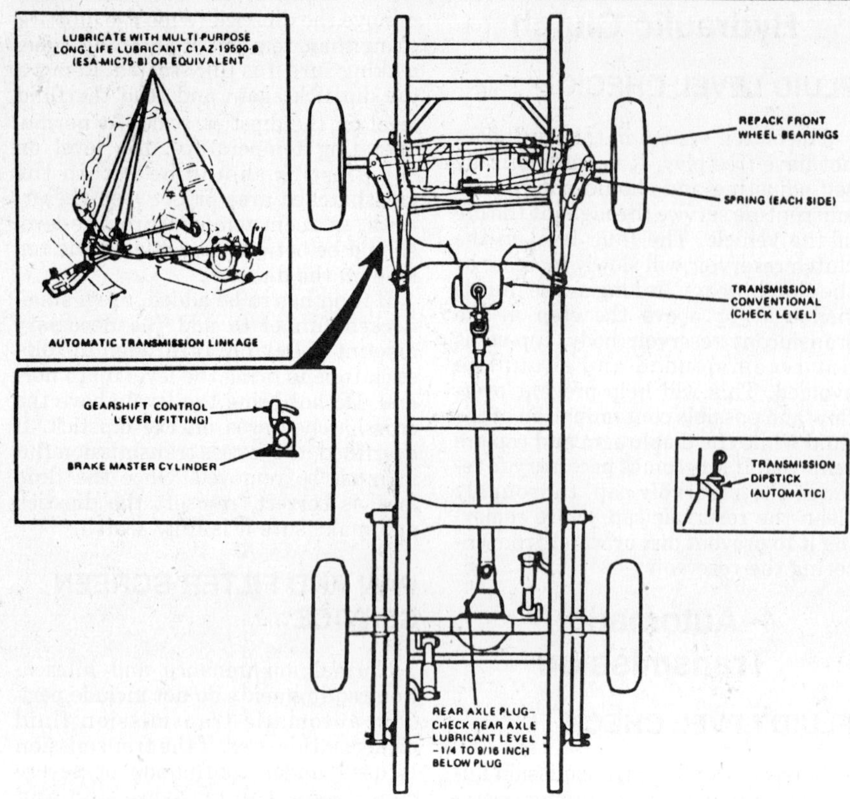

Lubrication chart—2WD models

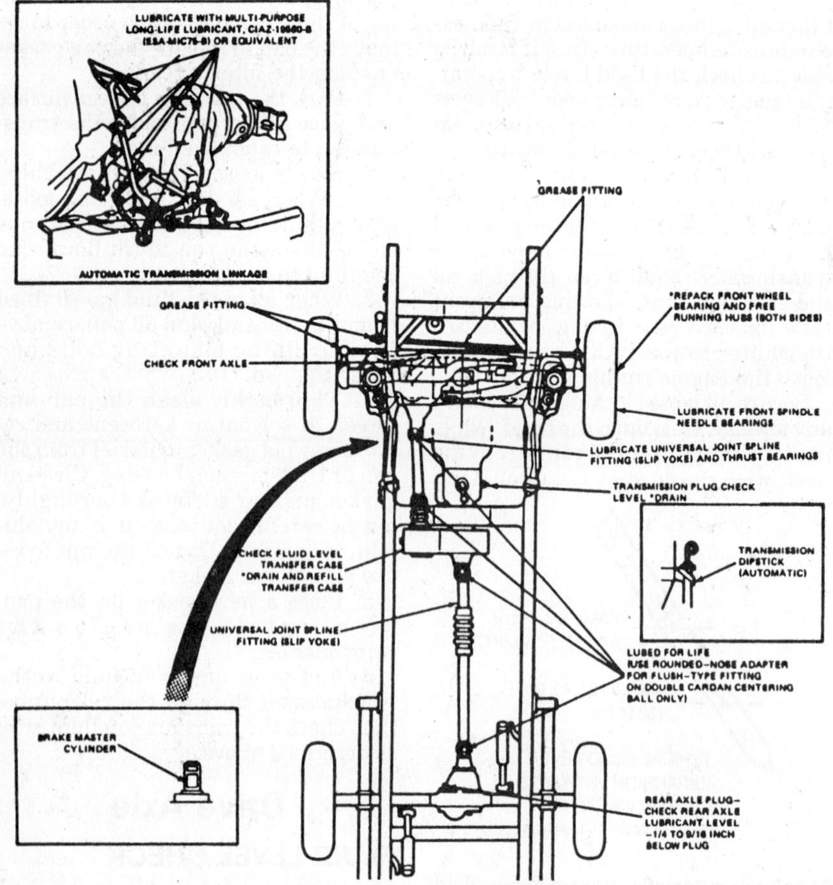

Lubrication chart—4WD models

et, trouble free operation over a period of years is largely dependent upon the use of a good quality gear lubricant. Ford recommends the use of hypoid gear lubricant part number E0AZ-19580-A or any equivalent lubricant meeting Ford specification ESP-M2C154-A in their conventional or Traction-Lok® axles. Trucks equipped with Dana axles should use hypoid gear lubricant part number C6AZ-19580-E or any equivalent lubricant meeting Ford specification ESW-M2C105-A.

To check the fluid level in the rear axle, remove the filler plug located on the side of the axle housing and make sure the axle fluid is within ¼" (6mm) below the bottom of the filler hole. If not, top up by adding lubricant through the filler hole. Do not overfill.

NOTE: If any water is noted in the axle when checking the fluid level, the axle lubricant should be drained and replaced. Change the axle lubricant if the axle is submerged in water, especially if the water covers the vent hole.

DRAINING REAR AXLE LUBRICANT

1. Drive the truck for 10-15 miles at highway speeds to warm the axle lubricant to operating temperature and minimum viscosity.
2. Raise the truck and support it safely with jackstands. Place a drain pan under the axle.
3. Clean the filler plug area of the axle housing to prevent the entry of rust or dirt into the axle assembly.
4. Remove the filler plug and use a suitable suction type utility pump (manual or powered) to drain the axle lubricant by inserting the pump suction hose through the axle filler hole down into the lowest portion of the axle carrier housing. Make sure all the lubricant is removed.
5. Fill the axle housing with 3.5 pints of the specified hypoid gear lubricant (3.6 pints on Dana axles), then check the fluid level as described above. Top off if necessary, but do not overfill.
6. Install the filler plug and torque it to 15-30 ft.lb. (20-40 Nm).

Cooling System

The truck is equipped with a coolant recovery system with a one piece, molded reservoir. Coolant in the system expands with heat and overflows into the coolant expansion reservoir. When the system cools down, coolant is drawn back into the radiator. Be careful not to confuse the windshield washer reservoir with the coolant recovery reservoir.

The coolant level should be checked in both the radiator and recovery reservoir at least once a month and then only when the engine is cool. Never, under any circumstances, attempt to check the coolant level in the radiator when the engine is hot or operating. On a full system, it is normal to have coolant in the expansion reservoir when the engine is hot.

Whenever coolant level checks of the radiator are made, check the condition of the radiator cap rubber seal. Make sure it is clean and free of any dirt particles. Rinse with water, if necessary, and make sure the radiator filler neck seat is clean. Check that the overflow hose is not kinked and is attached to the reservoir. If you have to add coolant more than once a month, or if you have to add more than one quart at a time, check the cooling system for leaks.

COOLANT CHECK AND CHANGE

CAUTION

Never attempt to check the radiator coolant level while the engine is hot. Use extreme care when removing the radiator cap. Wrap a thick towel around the cap and turn it slowly to the first stop. Step back while the pressure is released from the cooling system. When all pressure has vented, press down on the cap (still wrapped in the towel) and remove it. Failure to follow this procedure may result in serious personal injury from hot coolant or steam blowout and/or damage to the cooling system.

On systems with a coolant recovery tank, maintain the coolant level at the level marks on the recovery bottle. The coolant should be at the base of the filler neck in the radiator. The truck uses an aluminum radiator and requires coolant with corrosion inhibitors to prevent radiator damage. Use only a permanent type coolant that meets

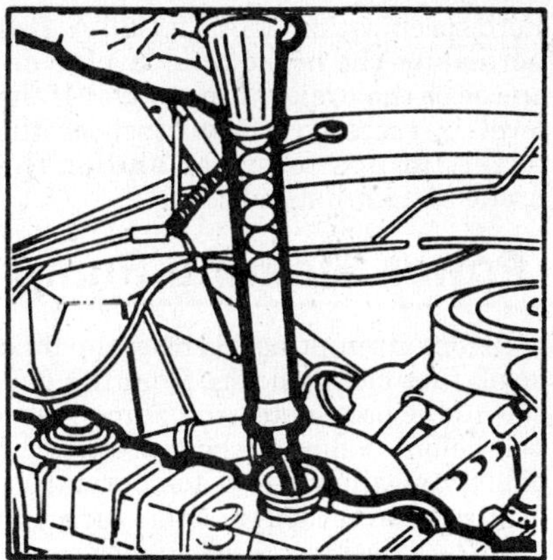

Checking anti-freeze protection with an inexpensive tester

MAINTAIN FLUID LEVEL BETWEEN FILLER NECK SEAT AND 38mm (1.5 INCHES) BELOW FILLER NECK SEAT. ADD COOLANT ONLY WHEN FLUID LEVEL IS MORE THAN 38mm (1.5 INCHES) BELOW FILLER NECK SEAT.

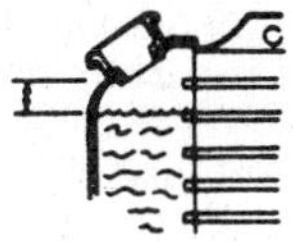

Checking the engine coolant level

Ford specification ESE-M97B44-A. Do not use alcohol or methanol antifreeze.

For best protection against freezing and overheating, maintain an approximate 50% water and 50% ethylene glycol antifreeze mixture in the cooling system. Do not mix different brands of antifreeze to avoid possible chemical damage to the cooling system. Avoid using water that is known to have a high alkaline content or is very hard, except in emergency situations. Drain and flush the cooling system as soon as possible after using such water.

NOTE: Never add cold water to an overheated engine while the engine is not running.

After filling the radiator, run the engine until it reaches normal operating temperature, to make sure that the thermostat has opened and all the air is bled from the system.

DRAINING, FLUSHING AND REFILLING

CAUTION

When draining the coolant, keep in mind that cats and dogs are attracted by the ethylene glycol antifreeze, and are quite likely to drink any that is left in an uncovered container or in puddles on the ground. This will prove fatal in sufficient quantity. Always drain the coolant into a sealable container. Coolant should be reused unless it is contaminated or several years old.

To drain the cooling system, allow the engine to cool down **BEFORE ATTEMPTING TO REMOVE THE RADIATOR CAP**. Then turn the cap until it hisses. Wait until all pressure is off the cap before removing it completely. To avoid burns and scalding, always handle a warm radiator cap with a heavy rag.

1. At the dash, set the heater TEMP control lever to the fully HOT position.
2. With the radiator cap removed, drain the radiator by loosening the petcock at the bottom of the radiator. Flush the radiator with water until the fluid runs clear. Disconnect the lower radiator hose from the radiator and drain any remaining coolant from the engine block.
3. Close the petcock and reconnect the lower radiator hose, then refill the system with a 50/50 mix of ethylene glycol antifreeze and water. Fill the system to the bottom of the radiator filler neck, then reinstall the radiator cap after allowing several minutes for trapped air to bubble out. Back the radiator cap off to the first stop (pressure relief position).

NOTE: Fill the fluid reservoir tank up to the MAX COLD level.

4. Operate the engine at 2,000 rpm for a few minutes with the heater control lever in the MAX HEAT position.
5. Turn the engine off, then wrap a rag around the radiator cap and remove it. Be careful, the coolant will be hot. Top off the radiator coolant level, if necessary, then reinstall the radiator cap to its down and locked position.
6. Start the engine and allow it to reach normal operating temperature, then check the system for leaks.

RADIATOR CAP INSPECTION

Allow the engine to cool sufficiently before attempting to remove the radiator cap. Use a rag to cover the cap,

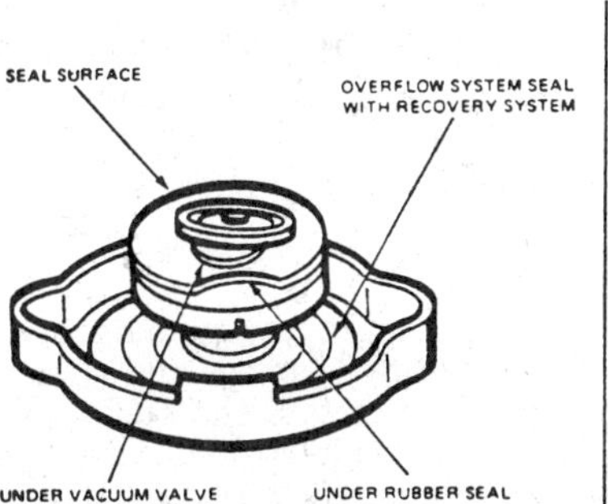

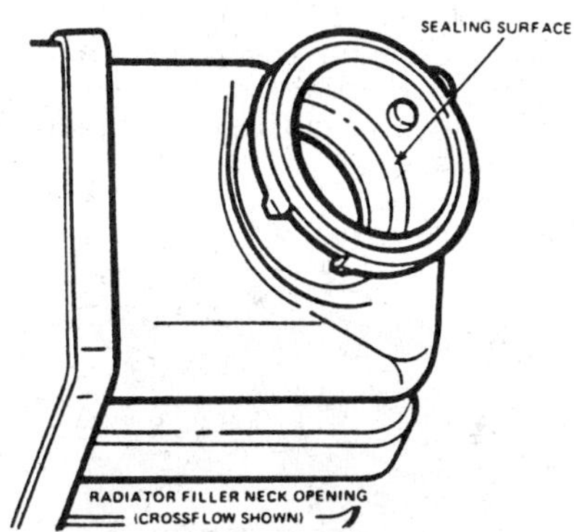

Cleaning and inspecting the radiator cap, and the filler neck opening

then remove by pressing down and turning counterclockwise to the first stop. If any hissing is noted (indicating the release of pressure), wait until the hissing stops completely, then press down again and turn counterclockwise until the cap can be removed.

CAUTION

DO NOT attempt to remove the radiator cap while the engine is hot. Severe personal injury from steam burns can result.

Check the condition of the radiator cap gasket and seal inside of the cap. The radiator cap is designed to seal the cooling system under normal operating conditions which allows the build up of a certain amount of pressure (this pressure rating is stamped or printed on the cap). The pressure in the system raises the boiling point of the coolant to help prevent overheating. If the radiator cap does not seal, the boiling point of the coolant is lowered and overheating will occur. If the cap must be replaced, purchase the new cap according to the pressure rating which is specified for your vehicle.

Prior to installing the radiator cap, inspect and clean the filler neck. If you are reusing the old cap, clean it thoroughly with clear water. After turning the cap on, make sure the arrows align with the overflow hose.

Brake Master Cylinder

To check the brake fluid level, visually inspect the translucent master cylinder reservoir. The fluid level should be at the maximum level line of the reservoir. If the level is low, top it off using DOT 3 brake fluid meeting Ford specification ESA-M6C25-A. It is normal for the brake fluid level to decrease as the brake linings wear. If the level is excessively low, inspect the brake linings for wear and/or the brake system for leaks.

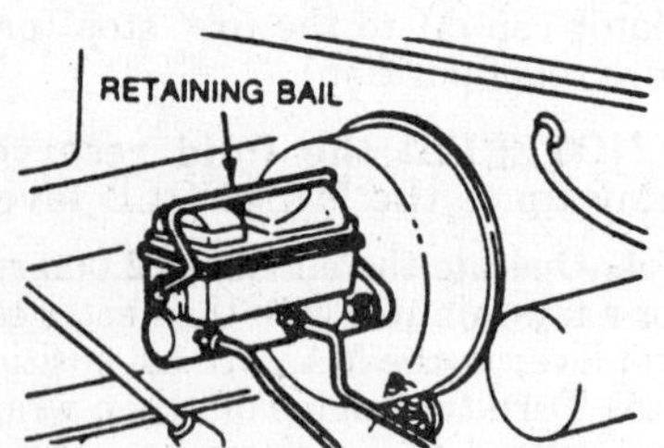

Brake master cylinder assembly

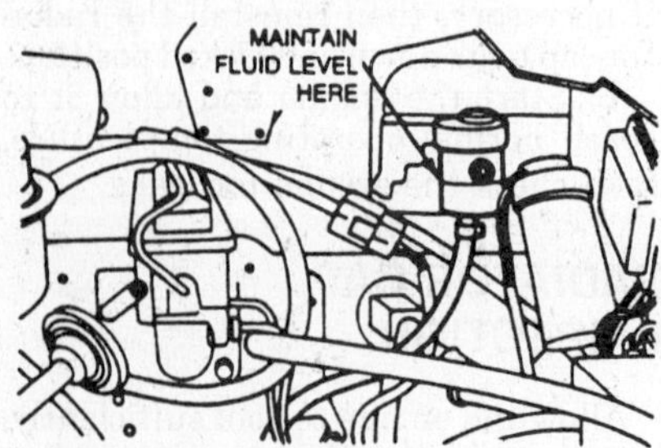

Clutch master cylinder reservoir

Power Steering Pump

Before attempting to check the fluid level, first clean all dirt from the outside of the power steering pump reservoir before removing the cap. Start the engine and allow it to reach normal operating temperature, then turn the steering wheel from lock-to-lock several times to bleed any air out of the system. Turn the engine off and check the fluid level on the power steering pump dipstick. The level should be within the FULL HOT scale on the dipstick. If necessary, top the reservoir up with fluid that meets Ford specification ESW-M2C33-F, such as Motorcraft Automatic Transmission and Power Steering Fluid Type F. Do not overfill.

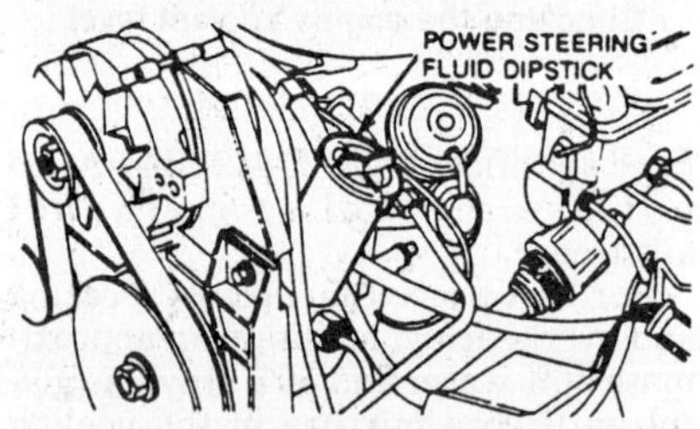

Power steering pump reservoir

Chassis Greasing

The front ball joints should be lubricated at 30,000 mile intervals. Locate the ball joint grease fittings, wipe them clean, then use a suitable grease gun to lubricate the ball joints. Inspect the ball joints for any obvious wear or damage and replace parts as necessary. Although there are no lubrication requirements, all suspension bushings should be inspected at this time for wear or damage and replaced as required. If equipped with grease fittings, the universal joints should be greased at this time also. U-joints without grease fittings require no lubrication.

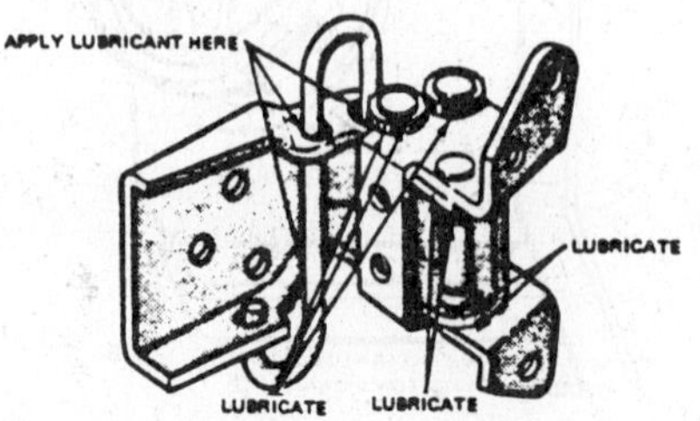

Door hinge lubrication points

WHEEL BEARINGS

The front wheel bearings should be inspected and repacked with grease every 30,000 miles. A good quality, high temperature wheel bearing grease should be used. The procedure involves removing the front brake rotors. Refer to the Brake Section for removal and repacking information.

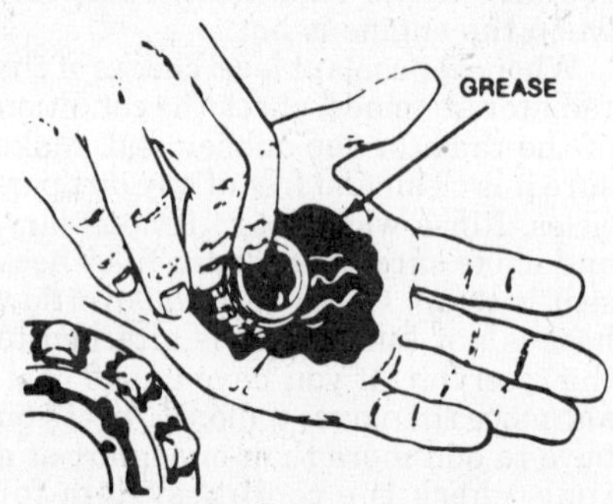

Packing the wheel bearings with grease

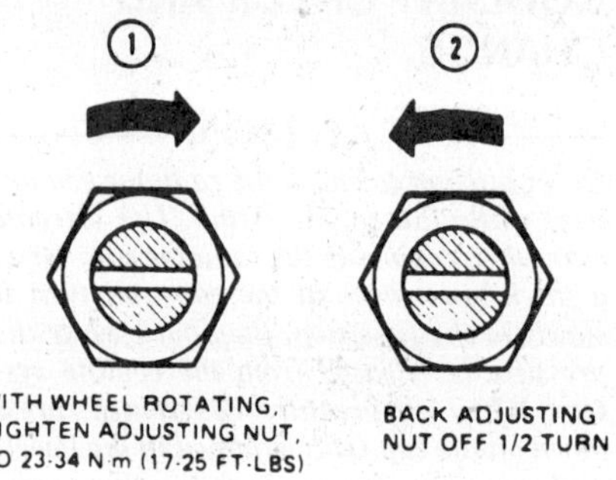

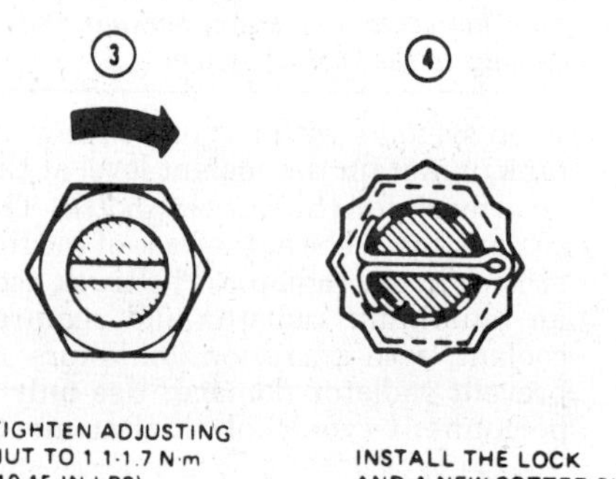

Front wheel bearing adjustment procedure

THROTTLE AND TRANSMISSION LINKAGE

Inspect the transmission linkage for signs of wear or damage and service as required. Lubricate the shift linkage at the points illustrated with multi-purpose lubricant such as Ford part number C1AZ-19590-B or equivalent.

Disconnect the throttle cable from the ball stud on the throttle lever and lubricate the stud with multi-purpose

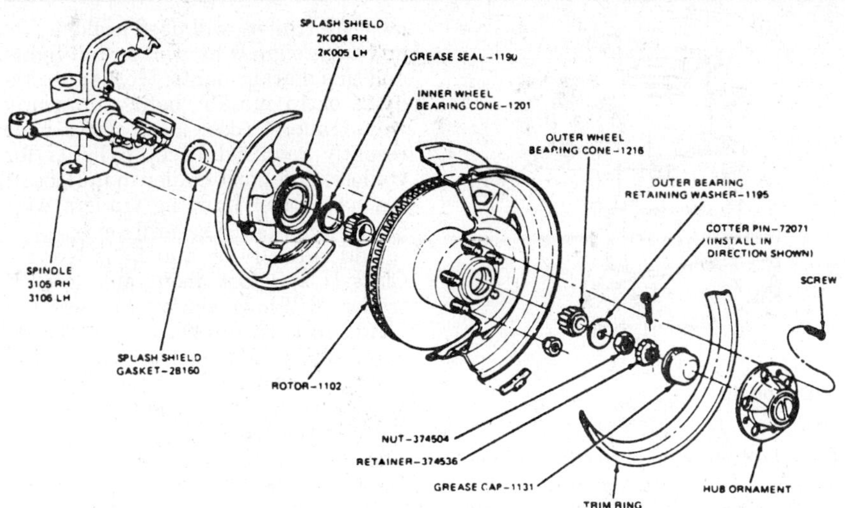

Exploded view of the wheel bearings, grease seal and front hub

lubricant, then reconnect the ball stud and cable.

PARKING BRAKE LINKAGE

Once a year, or whenever binding is noticed in the parking brake mechanism, lubricate the cable guides, levers and linkages with multi-purpose grease.

LOCK CYLINDERS AND LATCH ASSEMBLIES

Apply graphite lubricant sparingly thought the key slot. Insert the key and operate the lock several times to be sure that the lubricant is worked into the lock cylinder.

Lubricate the hood, rear liftgate and door latches with polyethylene grease, then operate the mechanism several times to be sure the lubricant is worked into the latch assembly.

DOOR HINGES AND HINGE CHECKS

Spray a silicone lubricant on the hinge pivot points to eliminate any binding conditions. Open and close the door several times to be sure that the lubricant is evenly and thoroughly distributed.

REAR LIFTGATE

Spray a silicone lubricant on all of the pivot and friction surfaces to eliminate any squeaks or binds. Work the tailgate to distribute the lubricant.

BODY DRAIN HOLES

Be sure that the drain holes in the doors and rocker panels are cleared of obstruction. A small screwdriver can be used to clear them of any debris.

PUSHING AND TOWING

Vehicles with catalytic converters should never be push started due to the possibility of serious converter damage. If the vehicle won't start, follow the instructions for the use of jumper cables.

Improper towing of the truck could result in transmission damage. Always unload the vehicle before towing it. Tow chain attachments must be make to the structural members of the vehicle, with the chains routed under a 4″ x 4″ x 48″ wood crossbeam placed under the bottom edge of the front bumper against the air spoiler or under the metal rear bumper supports against the wrecker towing tabs, in such a manner that they do not come into contact with suspension, steering, brake, cooling system, exhaust system, bumper or air spoiler components. Make sure the parking brake is released and the transmission gearshift lever is in Neutral. To move a vehicle with an inoperative rear axle, the rear wheels must be raised. If the transmission is inoperative, the rear wheels must be raised or the driveshaft disconnected.

CAUTION

Never tow your truck by using a tow bar that attaches to the bumper only. This will damage the bumper and result in property damage or personal injury. Do not attempt to use the steering column lock to hold the front wheels in a straight ahead position when towing from the rear.

JACKING AND HOISTING

Scissors jacks or hydraulic jacks are recommended for all vehicles. To change a front tire, place the jack in position from the side of the vehicle under the horizontal portion of the underbody member behind the wheel. To change a rear tire, place the jack in position from the side of the vehicle under the horizontal portion of the underbody member ahead of the wheel.

Make sure that you are on level ground, that the transmission is in Reverse or, with automatic transmissions, Park. The parking brake is set, and the tire diagonally opposite to the one to be changed is blocked so that it will not roll. Loosen the lug nuts before you jack the wheel to be changed completely free of the ground.

CAUTION

Never crawl under any vehicle when it is supported only by a jack. The jack is meant to raise the vehicle only. If any service is to

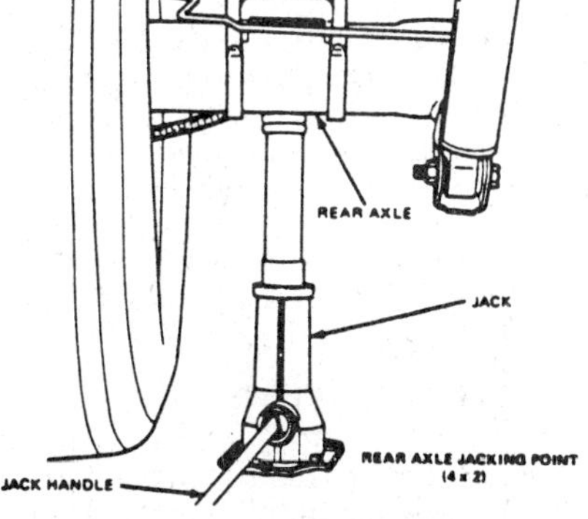

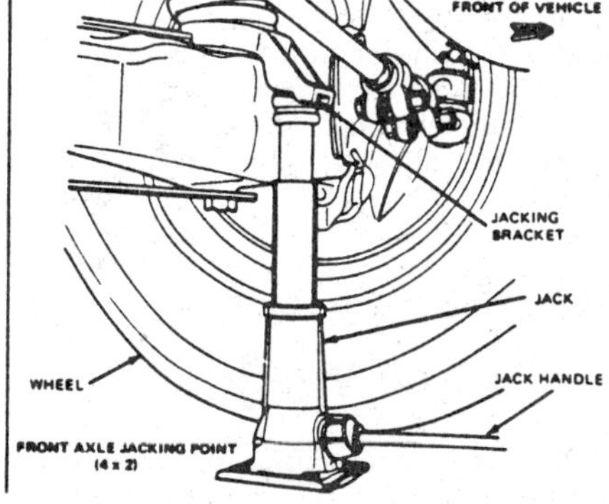

Jack positioning – 2WD models

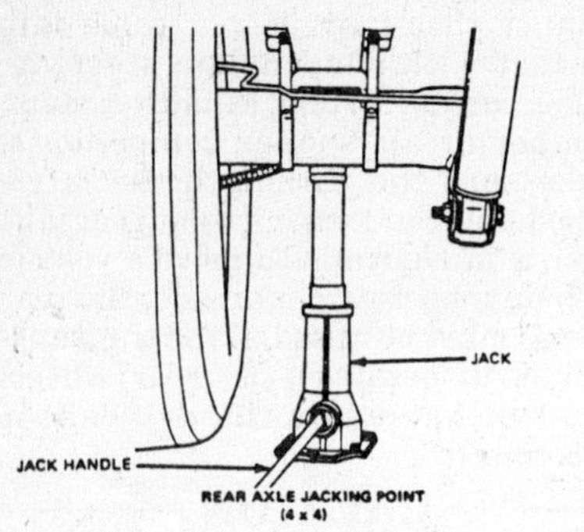

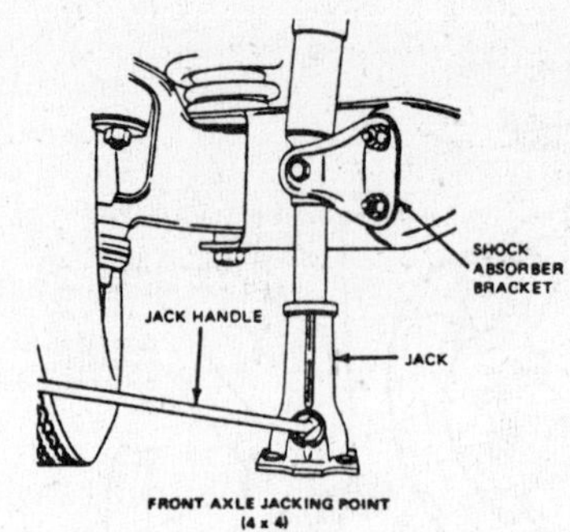

Jack positioning – 4WD models

be performed under the truck, use jackstands to support the weight and make sure they are secure before placing any portion of your body under the truck. Never start the engine while the truck is supported only by a jack.

TRAILER TOWING

Factory trailer towing packages are available on most cars. However, if you are installing a trailer hitch and wiring on your car, there are a few thing that you ought to know.

Trailer Weight

Trailer weight is the first, and most important, factor in determining whether or not your vehicle is suitable for towing the trailer you have in mind. The horsepower-to-weight ratio should be calculated. The basic standard is a ratio of 35:1. That is, 35 pounds of GVW for every horsepower.

To calculate this ratio, multiply you engine's rated horsepower by 35, then subtract the weight of the vehicle, including passengers and luggage. The resulting figure is the ideal maximum trailer weight that you can tow. One point to consider: a numerically higher axle ratio can offset what appears to be a low trailer weight. If the weight of the trailer that you have in mind is somewhat higher than the weight you just calculated, you might consider changing your rear axle ratio to compensate.

Hitch Weight

There are three kinds of hitches: bumper mounted, frame mounted, and load equalizing.

Bumper mounted hitches are those which attach solely to the vehicle's bumper. Many states prohibit towing with this type of hitch, when it attaches to the vehicle's stock bumper, since it subjects the bumper to stresses for which it was not designed. Aftermarket rear step bumpers, designed for trailer towing, are acceptable for use with bumper mounted hitches.

Frame mounted hitches can be of the type which bolts to two or more points on the frame, plus the bumper, or just to several points on the frame. Frame mounted hitches can also be of the tongue type, for Class I towing, or, of the receiver type, for classes II and III.

Load equalizing hitches are usually used for large trailers. Most equalizing hitches are welded in place and use equalizing bars and chains to level the vehicle after the trailer is hooked up.

The bolt-on hitches are the most common, since they are relatively easy to install.

Check the gross weight rating of your trailer. Tongue weight is usually figured as 10% of gross trailer weight. Therefore, a trailer with a maximum gross weight of 2,000 lb. will have a maximum tongue weight of 200 lb. Class I tarilers fall into this category. Class II trailers are those with a gross weight rating of 2,000-3,500 lb., while Class III trailers fall into the 3,500-6,000 lb. category. Class IV trailers are those over 6,000 lb. and are for use with fifth wheel trucks, only.

When you've determined the hitch that you'll need, follow the manufacturer's installation instructions, exactly, especially when it comes to fastener torques. The hitch will subjected to a lot of stress and good hitches come with hardened bolts. Never substitute an inferior bolt for a hardened bolt.

Wiring

Wiring the car for towing is fairly easy. There are a number of good wiring kits available and these should be used, rather than trying to design your own. All trailers will need brake lights and turn signals as well as tail lights and side marker lights. Most states require extra marker lights for overly wide trailers. Also, most states have recently required back-up lights for trailers, and most trailer manufacturers have been building trailers with back-up lights for several years.

Additionally, some Class I, most Class II and just about all Class III trailers will have electric brakes.

Add to this number an accessories wire, to operate trailer internal equipment or to charge the trailer's battery, and you can have as many as seven wires in the harness.

Determine the equipment on your trailer and buy the wiring kit necessary. The kit will contain all the wires needed, plus a plug adapter set which included the female plug, mounted on the bumper or hitch, and the male plug, wired into, or plugged into the trailer harness.

When installing the kit, follow the manufacturer's instructions. The color coding of the wires is standard throughout the industry.

One point to note, some domestic vehicles, and most imported vehicles, have separate turn signals. On most domestic vehicles, the brake lights and rear turn signals operate with the same bulb. For those vehicles with separate turn signals, you can purchase an isolation unit so that the brake lights won't blink whenever the turn signals are operated, or, you can go to your local electronics supply house and buy four diodes to wire in series with the brake and turn signal bulbs. Diodes will isolate the brake and turn signals. The choice is yours. The isolation units are simple and quick to install, but far more expensive than the diodes. The diodes, however, require more work to install properly, since they require the cutting of each bulb's wire and soldering in place of the diode.

One final point, the best kits are those with a spring loaded cover on the vehicle mounted socket. This cover prevents dirt and moisture from corroding the terminals. Never let the vehicle socket hang loosely. Always mount it securely to the bumper or hitch.

Cooling

ENGINE

One of the most common, if not THE most common, problem associated with trailer towing is engine overheating.

With factory installed trailer towing packages, a heavy duty cooling system is usually included. Heavy duty cooling systems are available as optional equipment on most cars, with or without a trailer package. If you have one of these extra-capacity systems, you shouldn't have any overheating problems.

If you have a standard cooling system, without an expansion tank, you'll definitely need to get an aftermarket expansion tank kit, preferably one with at least a 2 quart capacity. These kits are easily installed on the radiator's overflow hose, and come with a pressure cap designed for expansion tanks.

Another helpful accessory is a Flex Fan. These fan are large diameter units are designed to provide more airflow at low speeds, with blades that have deeply cupped surfaces. The blades then flex, or flatten out, at high speed, when less cooling air is needed. These fans are far lighter in weight than stock fans, requiring less horsepower to drive them. Also, they are far quieter than stock fans.

If you do decide to replace your stock fan with a flex fan, note that if your car has a fan clutch, a spacer between the flex fan and water pump hub will be needed.

Aftermarket engine oil coolers are helpful for prolonging engine oil life and reducing overall engine temperatures. Both of these factors increase engine life.

While not absolutely necessary in towing Class I and some Class II trailers, they are recommended for heavier Class II and all Class III towing.

Engine oil cooler systems consist of an adapter, screwed on in place of the oil filter, a remote filter mounting and a multi-tube, finned heat exchanger, which is mounted in front of the radiator or air conditioning condenser.

TRANSMISSION

An automatic transmission is usually recommended for trailer towing. Modern automatics have proven reliable and, of course, easy to operate, in trailer towing.

The increased load of a trailer, however, causes an increase in the temperature of the automatic transmission fluid. Heat is the worst enemy of an automatic transmission. As the temperature of the fluid increases, the life of the fluid decreases.

It is essential, therefore, that you install an automatic transmission cooler.

The cooler, which consists of a multi-tube, finned heat exchanger, is usually installed in front of the radiator or air conditioning compressor, and hooked inline with the transmission cooler tank inlet line. Follow the cooler manufacturer's installation instructions.

Select a cooler of at least adequate capacity, based upon the combined gross weights of the car and trailer.

Cooler manufacturers recommend that you use an aftermarket cooler in addition to, and not instead of, the present cooling tank in your car radiator. If you do want to use it in place of the radiator cooling tank, get a cooler at least two sizes larger than normally necessary.

NOTE: A transmission cooler can, sometimes, cause slow or harsh shifting in the transmission during cold weather, until the fluid has a chance to come up to normal operating temperature. Some coolers can be purchased with or retrofitted with a temperature bypass valve which will allow fluid flow through the cooler only when the fluid has reached operating temperature, or above.

TUNE-UP PROCEDURES

The engine tune-up is a routine service designed to restore the maximum capability of power, performance, reliability and economy to the engine. It is essential for efficient and economical operation and becomes increasingly more important each year to insure that pollutant levels are in compliance with federal emission standards.

The interval between tune-ups is a variable factor which depends on the year and engine in your van and the way it is driven in average use. The extent of the tune-up is usually determined by the length of time since the previous service. It is advisable to follow a definite and thorough tune-up procedure consisting of three steps: Analysis, the process of determining whether normal wear is responsible for performance loss and the inspection of various parts such as spark plugs; Parts Replacement or Service; and Adjustment, where engine adjustments are returned to the original factory specifications.

The replaceable parts normally involved in a major tune-up include the spark plugs, air filter, fuel filter, distributor cap, rotor and spark plug wires. In addition to these parts and the adjustments involved in properly adapting them to your engine, the normal tune-up should include a check of the ignition timing and idle speed, although with modern electronic engine controls, these items are usually not adjustable. Refer to the underhood emission control sticker for specific instructions on checking the timing, as well as specifications for spark plug gap and idle speed. In addition to the above, the valve adjustment should be checked with the engine cold. The 2.0L and 2.3L 4-cylinder engines have hydraulic lash adjusters that do not require periodic service, however, the 2.8L V6 and the 2.2L diesel engine have valves that are adjustable and clearances should be checked and adjusted, if necessary, at every tune-up.

CAUTION

When working on or around a running engine, make sure there is adequate ventilation. Make sure the transmission is in Neutral or Park with the parking brake firmly applied and always keep hands, clothing and tools well clear of the hot exhaust manifold(s) and radiator. Remove any jewelry, do not wear loose clothing and tuck long hair up under a cap. Use EXTREME caution when working around spinning fan blades or belts. When the engine is running, do not grasp the ignition wires, distributor cap or coil wire, as the high energy ignition system can deliver a potentially fatal shock of 20,000 volts. Whenever working around the distributor, even if the engine is not running, make sure the ignition is switched OFF.

This section gives specific procedures on how to tune-up your van and is intended to be as complete and basic as possible. It is advisable to read the entire section before beginning a tune-up.

Spark Plugs

The function of a spark plug is to ignite the air/fuel mixture in the cylinder as the piston reaches the top of its compression stroke. The expansion of the ignited mixture forces the piston down, which turns the crankshaft and supplies power to the drivetrain.

A typical spark plug consists of a metal shell surrounded by a ceramic insulator. A metal electrode extends downward through the center of the insulator and protrudes a small distance. Located at the end of the plug and attached to the side of the outer metal shell is the side electrode. The side electrode bends in at a 90° angle so that its tip is even with, and parallel to, the tip of the center electrode. The distance between these two electrodes (measured in thousandths of an inch) is called the spark plug gap.

The spark plug in no way produces a spark, but merely provides a gap across which the current from the ignition coil can arc. The ignition coil produces from 20,000 to 40,000 volts which travels to the distributor where it is distributed through the spark plug wires to the spark plugs. This current passes along the center electrode and jumps the gap to the side electrode and, in doing so, ignites the air/fuel mixture.

The average life of a spark plug is about 25,000 miles, depending on the type of driving and vehicle use. If the van is driven at high speeds more often, the plugs will probably not need as much attention as those used for constant stop-and-go driving. The electrode end of the spark plug is a good indicator of the internal condition of your engine. If a spark plug is fouled and causing the engine to misfire, the problem will have to be found and corrected. It is a good idea to remove the plugs once in a while to check their condition and see just how the engine is performing. A small amount of light tan colored deposits on the electrode end of the spark plug is normal and the plugs do not require replacement unless extremely worn.

SPARK PLUG HEAT RANGE

Spark plug heat range is the ability of the plug to dissipate heat. The longer the insulator (or the farther it extends into the engine), the hotter the plug will operate. Conversely, the shorter the insulator, the cooler the plug will operate. A plug that absorbs little heat and remains too cool will quickly accumulate deposits of oil and carbon since it is not hot enough to burn them off. This can lead to plug fouling and misfiring. A plug that absorbs too much heat will have no deposits but, due to the excess heat, the electrodes will burn away quickly and in some instances preignition may result. Preignition takes place when the plug tips get so hot that they glow sufficiently to ignite the fuel/air mixture before the actual spark occurs. This condition is usually described as a spark knock or "ping" during low speeds and under heavy load.

The general rule of thumb for choosing the correct heat range when picking a spark plug is to use a colder plug for long distance, high speed operation and a hotter plug for stop-and-go, heavy traffic operation. Original equipment plugs are usually a compromise, but most owners never have occasion to change from the factory recommended heat range.

REPLACING SPARK PLUGS

A set of spark plugs usually requires replacement after about 20,000 to 30,000 miles on engines with electronic ignition, depending on your style of driving. In normal operation, the spark plug gap will increase about 0.001" for every 1,000-2,500 miles. As the gap increases, the plug's voltage requirement also increases. It requires a greater voltage to jump the wider gap and about two to three times as much voltage to fire a plug at high speeds than at idle.

When removing the spark plugs, you should work on one at a time. Don't start by removing all the plug wires at once or they may become mixed up. Take a minute and number all the plug wires with tape before removing them from the plugs. The best location for numbering is near where the plug wires come out of the cap.

1. Twist the spark plug boot and remove the boot and wire from the plug. Do not pull on the wire itself or you will ruin it.
2. If possible, use a brush or rag to clean the area around the spark plug. Make sure that all the dirt is removed so that none will enter the cylinder after the plug is removed.
3. Remove the spark plug from the cylinder head using the proper size socket (5/8" for AWSF and ASF plugs) and ratchet. A universal joint and short extension may make this job easier. Turn the socket counterclockwise to remove the plug, but make sure the socket is firmly seated and straight on the plug or you will crack the insulator or round off the hex.
4. Once the plug is removed, check its condition against the plugs shown in the color insert to determine engine condition. This is crucial since plugs readings are vital signs of engine operating condition.
5. Use a round wire feeler gauge to check the plug gap. The correct size gauge should pass through the electrode gap with a slight drag. If in doubt, try one size smaller and one size larger. The smaller should pass through easily, while the larger shouldn't go through at all. If the gap is incorrect, use the electrode bending tool on the end of the gauge to adjust the gap. When adjusting the gap, always bend the side electrode; the center electrode is non-adjustable.
6. Squirt a drop of penetrating oil on the threads of the spark plug and install it. Don't oil the plug too heavily. Turn the plug in clockwise by hand until it is snug. Be careful not to cross-thread the plug when installing.
7. When the plug is finger tight, tighten it with a torque wrench to 10-15 ft.lb.
8. Install the spark plug boot firmly over the plug and proceed to the next one.

NOTE: Coat the inside of each spark plug boot with silicone grease (Motorcraft WA-10-D7AZ-19A331A, Dow Corning No. 111 or General Electric G627 are acceptable). Failure to do so could result in a misfired plug.

CHECKING AND REPLACING SPARK PLUG WIRES

Visually inspect the spark plug wires for burns, cuts or breaks in the insulation. Check the spark plug boots and the nipples on the distributor cap and coil. Replace any damaged wiring. If no physical damage is obvious, remove the distributor cap with the wires attached and use an ohmmeter to check the resistance. Normal resistance should be less than 7,000Ω per foot of wire length. If resistance exceeds 7,000Ω per foot, replace the wire.

WARNING: Do not, under any circumstances, puncture a spark plug wire with a sharp probe when checking resistance!

When installing a new set of spark plug wires, replace them one at a time so there is no mixup. Start by replacing the longest wire first and make

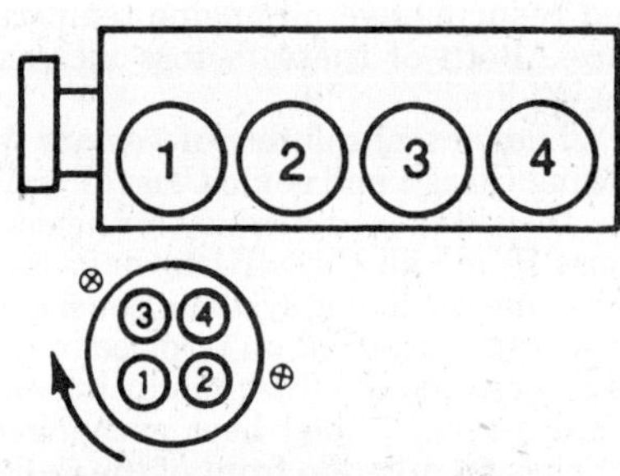

4-122, 140 engine
Firing order: 1-3-4-2
Distributor rotation: clockwise

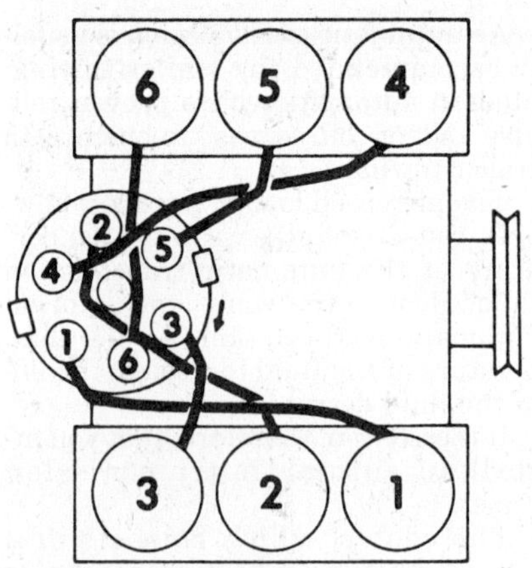

6-173 cu. in. engine
Firing order: 1-4-2-5-3-6
Distributor rotation: clockwise

sure the boot is installed firmly over the spark plug and distributor cap tower. Route the wire exactly the same way as the original and make sure the wire loom clips are fastened securely when done.

IDLE SPEED AND MIXTURE

Idle Mixture Adjustment

CARBURETORS

NOTE: For this procedure, Ford recommends a propane enrichment procedure. This requires special equipment not available to the general public. In lieu of this equipment the following procedure may be followed to obtain a satisfactory idle mixture.

1. Block the wheels, set the parking brake and run the engine to bring it to normal operating temperature.
2. Disconnect the hose between the emission canister and the air cleaner.
3. On engines equipped with the Thermactor air injection system, the routing of the vacuum lines connected to the dump valve will have to be temporarily changed. Mark them for reconnection before switching them.
4. For valves with one or two vacuum lines at the side, disconnect and plug the lines.
5. For valves with one vacuum line at the top, check the line to see if it is connected to the intake manifold or an intake manifold source such as the carburetor or distributor vacuum line. If not, remove and plug the line at the dump valve and connect a temporary length of vacuum hose from the dump valve fitting to a source of intake manifold vacuum.
6. Remove the limiter caps from the mixture screws by CAREFULLY cutting them with a sharp knife.
7. Place the transmission in neutral and run the engine at 2500 rpm for 15 seconds.
8. Place the automatic transmission in Drive; the manual in neutral.
9. Adjust the idle speed to the higher of the two figures given on the underhood sticker.
10. Turn the idle mixture screw(s) to obtain the highest possible rpm, leaving the screw(s) in the leanest position that will maintain this rpm.
11. Repeat Steps 7 thru 10 until further adjustment of the mixture screw(s) does not increase the rpm.
12. Turn the screw(s) in until the lower of the two idle speed figures is reached. Turn the screw(s) in 1/4 turn increments each to insure a balance.
13. Turn the engine off and remove the tachometer. Reinstall all equipment.

NOTE: Rough idle, that cannot be corrected by normal service procedures may be caused by leakage between the EGR valve body and diaphragm. To determine if this is the cause: Tighten the EGR bolts to 15 ft.lb. Connect a vacuum gauge to the intake manifold. Lift to exert a sideways pressure on the diaphragm housing. If the idle changes or the

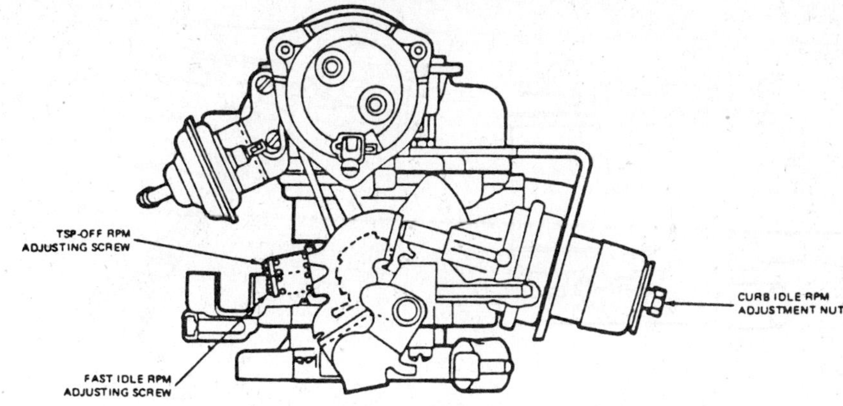

Carter YFA-1V & YFA-1V Feedback carburetor – idle speed adjustment

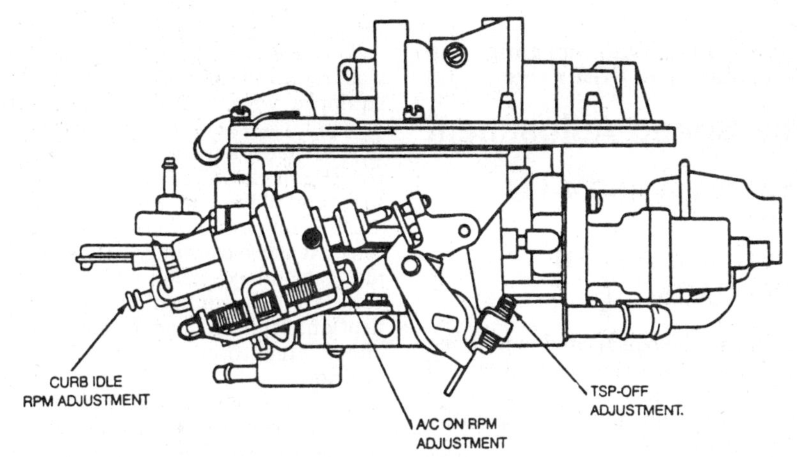

Motorcraft 2150A-2V carburetor – idle speed adjustments w/AC

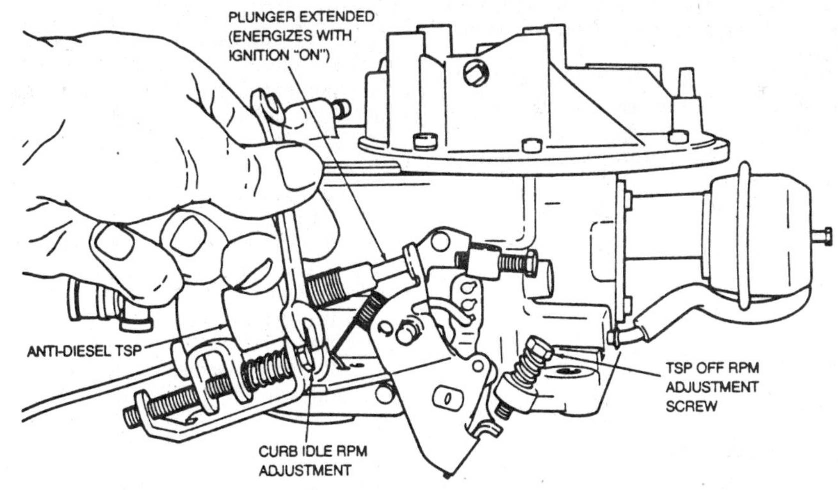

Motorcraft 2150A-2V carburetor – idle speed adjustments wo/AC

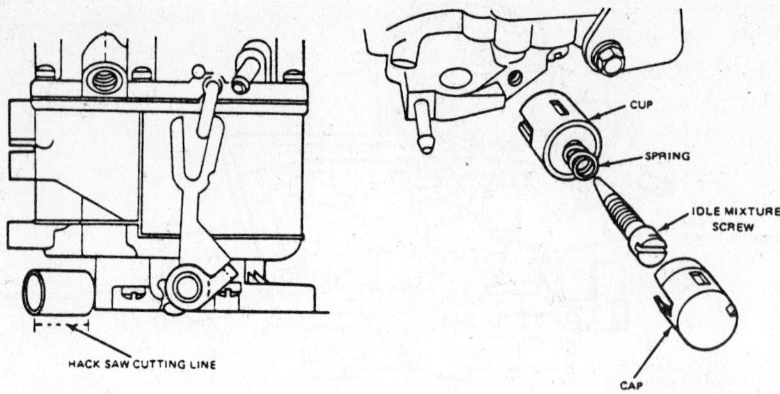

Mixture screw locking caps—Carter YFA-1V & YFA-1V Feedback carburetor

reading on the vacuum gauge varies, replace the EGR valve.

Idle Speed Adjustment

4-122 (2.0L) AND 4-140 (2.3L) YFA-IV & YFA IV-FB (FEEDBACK)

1. Block the wheels and apply parking brake. Place the transmission in Neutral or Park.
2. Bring engine to normal operating temperature.
3. Place A/C selector in the Off position.
4. Place transmission in specified position as referred to on emissions decal.
5. Check/adjust curb idle RPM. If adjustment is required, turn the hex head adjustment at the rear of the TSP (throttle solenoid positioner) housing.
6. Place the transmission in Neutral or Park. Rev the engine momentarily. Place transmission in specified position and recheck curb idle RPM. Readjust if required.
7. Turn the ignition key to the Off position.
8. If a curb idle RPM adjustment was required and the carburetor is equipped with a dashpot, adjust the dashpot clearance to specification as follows: Turn key to On position. Open throttle to allow TSP solenoid plunger to extend to the curb idle position. Collapse dashpot plunger to maximum extent. Measure clearance between tip of plunger and extension pad on throttle vent lever. If required, adjust to specification. Tighten dashpot locknut. Recheck clearance. Turn key to Off position.
9. If curb idle adjustment was required, check/adjust the bowl vent setting as follows: Turn ignition key to the On position to activate the TSP (engine not running). Open throttle to allow the TSP solenoid plunger to extend to the curb idle position. Secure the choke plate in the wide open position. Open throttle so that the throttle vent lever does not touch the bowl vent rod. Close the throttle to the idle set position and measure the travel of the fuel bowl vent rod from the open throttle position. Travel of the bowl vent rod should be within specification (0.100-0.150"). If out of specification, bend the throttle vent lever at notch to obtain required travel.
10. Remove all test equipment and reinstall air cleaner assembly. Tighten the holddown bolt to specification.

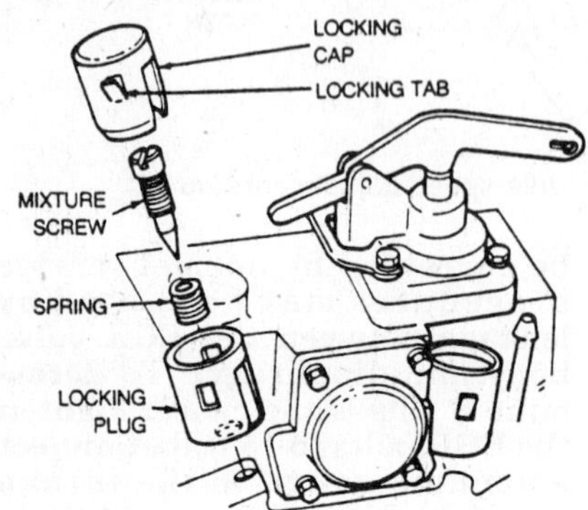

Mixture screw locking caps—Motorcraft 2150A-2V

6-173 (2.8L), 6-232 (3.8L) & 8-302 (5.0L) 2150-2V FB (FEEDBACK)

1. Set parking brake and block wheels.
2. Place the transmission in Park.
3. Bring the engine to normal operating temperature.
4. Disconnect the electric connector on the EVAP purge solenoid.
5. Disconnect and plug the vacuum hose to the VOTM kicker.
6. Place the transmission in Drive position.
7. Check/adjust curb idle rpm, if adjustment is required: Adjust with the the curb idle speed screw or the saddle bracket adjusting screw, depending on how equipped.
8. Place the transmission in Neutral or Park. Rev the engine momentarily. Place the transmission in Drive position and recheck curb idle rpm. Readjust if required.
9. Remove the plug from the vacuum hose to the VOTM kicker and reconnect.
10. Reconnect the electrical connector on the EVAP purge solenoid.

4-134 (2.2L) DIESEL

NOTE: A special tachometer is required to check engine RPM on a diesel engine.

1. Block the wheels and apply the parking brake.
2. Start and run engine until the normal operating temperature is reached. Shut off engine.
3. Connect diesel engine tachometer.
4. Start engine and check RPM. Refer to emissions decal for latest specifications. RPM is usually adjusted in Neutral for manual transmissions and Drive for automatic models.
5. The adjustment bolt is located on the bell crank at the top of the injector pump. The upper bolt is for curb idle, the lower for max speed.
6. Loosen the locknut. Turn the adjustment screw clockwise to increase RPM, counter-clockwise to lower the RPM.
7. Tighten the locknut. Increase engine speed several times and recheck idle. Readjust if necessary.

Ignition Timing

TACHOMETER HOOKUP

Models equipped with a "conven-

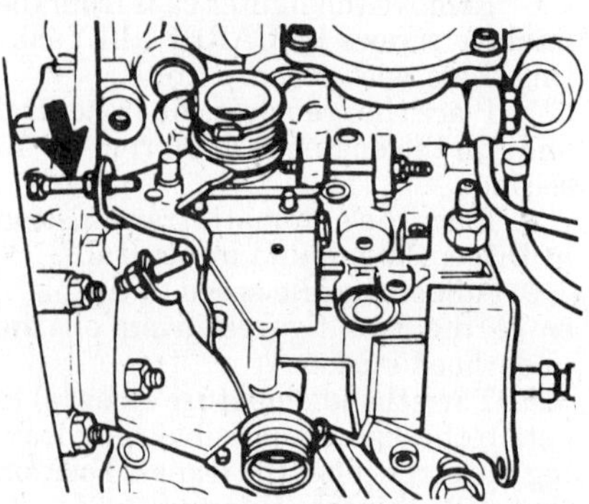

Diesel engine idle speed adjusting location

tional" type coil have an adapter on the top of the coil that provides a clip marked "Tach Test". On models (TFI) equipped with an "E" type coil, the tach connection is made at the back of the wire harness connector. A cut-out is provided and the tachometer lead wire alligator clip can be connected to the dark green/yellow dotted wire of the electrical harness plug.

ADJUSTMENT

NOTE: On models equipped with EEC III, all ignition timing is controlled by the EEC III module. Initial ignition timing is not adjustable and no attempt at adjustment should be made. Models equipped with the TFI-IV ignition system do not require ignition timing as routine maintenance, since the system adjusts itself. An initial check can be made. Refer to the following two procedure paragraphs.

1. Locate the timing marks on the crankshaft pulley and the front of the engine.
2. Clean the timing marks so that you can see them.
3. Mark the timing marks with a piece of chalk or with paint. Color the mark on the scale that will indicate the correct timing when it is aligned with the mark on the pulley or the pointer. It is also helpful to mark the notch in the pulley or the tip of the pointer with a small dab of color.
4. Attach a tachometer to the engine. (See tachometer hook-up instructions).
5. Attach a timing light according to the manufacturer's instructions. If the timing light has three wires, one is attached to the No. 1 spark plug with an adapter. The other wires are connected to the battery. The red wire goes to the positive side of the battery and the black wire is connected to the negative terminal of the battery.

NOTE: Refer to emissions decal in the engine compartment to determine if the vacuum line(s) should be disconnected.

6. Disconnect the vacuum line to the distributor at the distributor and plug the vacuum line. A golf tee does a fine job.
7. Check to make sure that all of the wires clear the fan and then start the engine.
8. Adjust the idle to the correct setting.
9. Aim the timing light at the timing marks. If the marks that you put on the flywheel or pulley and the engine are aligned when the light flashes, the timing is correct. Turn off the engine and remove the tachometer and the timing light. If the marks are not in alignment, proceed with the following steps.
10. Turn off the engine.
11. Loosen the distributor lockbolt just enough so that the distributor can be turned with a little effort.
12. Start the engine. Keep the wires of the timing light clear of the fan.
13. With the timing light aimed at the pulley and the marks on the engine, turn the distributor in the direction of rotor rotation to retard the spark, and in the opposite direction of rotor rotation to advance the spark. Align the marks on the pulley and the engine with the flashes of the timing light.
14. When the marks are aligned, tighten the distributor lockbolt and recheck the timing with the timing light to make sure that the distributor did not move when you tightened the lockbolt.
15. Turn off the engine and remove the timing light.

MODELS EQUIPPED WITH EEC-IV AND TFI

The connection between the EEC-IV microprocessor and the Thick Film Integrated (TFI) ignition module is called the SPOUT circuit. SPOUT simply means "spark out" since a signal carried to the TFI shuts off the coil and produces a spark for firing the spark plugs. A description of the system operation to control spark and advance follows:

1. The TFI-IV module sends a voltage signal to the PIP (Profile Ignition Pickup) sensor, part of the Hall Effect assembly inside the distributor.
2. The PIP sensor then provides crankshaft position information and sends this signal back to the TFI module.
3. The TFI module sends the information to the EEC-IV module and the required spark timing need is calculated.
4. The required timing information goes back to the TFI module through electrical circuitry (the SPOUT) and the coil turns off the primary circuit to fire the spark plugs at the precise time.
5. The TFI module also determines dwell and limits primary circuit to a safe value. If there is an open in the SPOUT signal wire, the TFI module will use the PIP sensor to provide spark; but the engine will only run at basic timing setting.
6. To check basic timing the SPOUT wire must be disconnected. An inline connector is provided on the "yellow with green dot" or "black" single SPOUT wire. The wire is located between the distributor and engine harness. With the wire disconnected the TFI module is locked into no advance and basic timing may be checked and adjusted if necessary. See preceding paragraph.

VALVE ADJUSTMENT

GASOLINE ENGINES

All gasoline engines used, except the 2.8L V6, are equipped with hydraulic valve lifters or lash adjusters. Hydraulic valve lifters or lash adjusters operate with zero clearance in the valve train, and because of this the rocker arms are non-adjustable. The only means by which valve system clearances can be altered is by installing over or undersize pushrods except on OHC (overhead cam) models; but, because of the hydraulic lifter's natural ability to compensate for slack in the valve train, all components of all the valve system should be checked for wear if there is excessive play in the system. Refer to Rocker Arm section.

2.8L V6 Engine

This procedure applies to the 2.8L V6 engine only. The engine should be cold for valve adjustment.

1. Remove the air cleaner assembly, then remove the rocker arm covers. This may involve removing some thermactor components to gain working clearance.
2. Place a finger on the adjusting screw of the intake valve rocker arm for cylinder No. 5 to detect the slightest motion.
3. Using a remote starter button, or

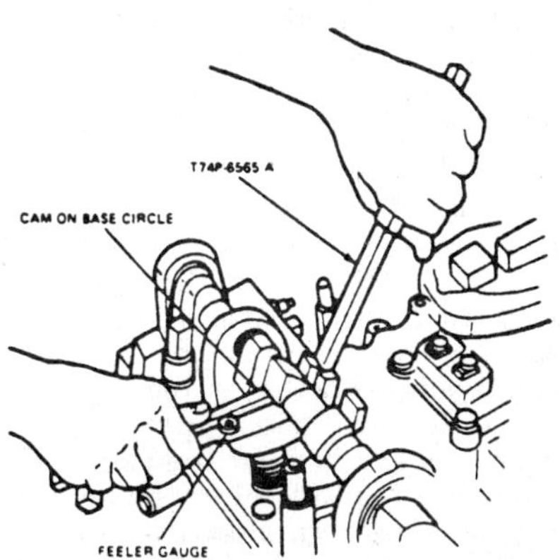

Checking the valve lash—4-122, 140 engines

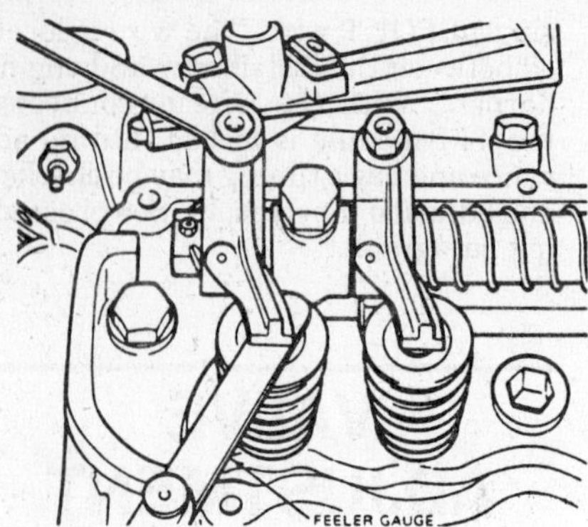

Adjusting the valve lash – 6-173 engine

To adjust both valves for cylinder number	1	4	2	5	3	6
The intake valve must be opening for cylinder number	5	3	6	1	4	2

Valve adjusting arrangement – 6-173 engine

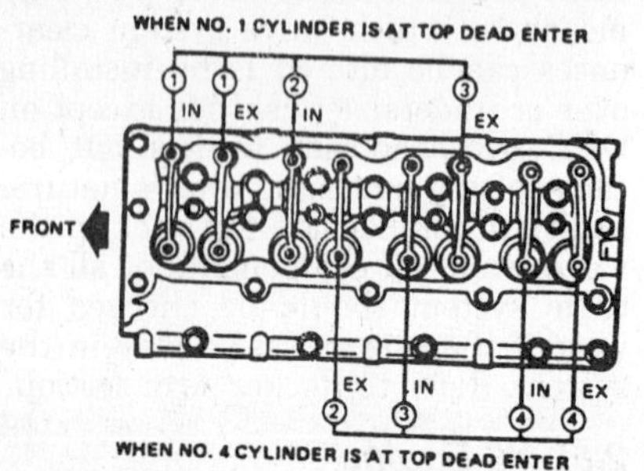

Diesel engine valve adjusting sequence

an assistant turning the ignition key on and off, "bump" the engine over in small increments until the intake valve for No. 5 cylinder just begining to open. This will place the camshaft in the correct position to adjust the valves on No. 1 cylinder.

4. Adjust the No. 1 intake valve so that a 0.014" (0.35mm) feeler gauge has a light to moderate drag and a 0.015" (0.36mm) feeler gauge is very tight. Turn the adjusting screw clockwise to decrease lash and counterclockwise to increase lash. The adjusting screws are self-locking and will stay in a set position.

NOTE: Do not use a step-type go/no-go feeler gauge. Use a blade-type set. When checking lash, insert the feeler between the rocker arm and valve tip at the front (or rear) edge of the valve tip and move toward the opposite edge with a rearward (or forward) motion that is parallel to the centerline of the crankshaft. Do not insert the feeler at the outboard edge and move inward toward the carburetor perpendicular to the crankshaft centerline or this will result in an erroneous "feel" that will lead to excessively tight valves.

5. Using the same method, adjust the No. 1 exhaust valve lash so that a 0.016" (0.40mm) feeler gauge has a slight to moderate drag and a 0.017" (0.41mm) is very tight.

6. Adjust the remaining valves in firing order 1-4-2-5-3-6 by positioning the camshaft according to the following chart:

7. Clean the rocker arm gasket mounting surfaces. Using new gaskets or a suitable RTV sealant, install the rocker arm covers. Install any thermactor components that were removed.

8. Reinstall the air cleaner assembly. Start the engine and check for oil and vacuum leaks.

Diesel Engine

1. Warm the engine until normal operating temperature is reached.

2. Remove the valve cover. Check the head bolt torque in sequence.

3. Turn the engine to bring the No. 1 piston to TDC (top dead center) of the compression stroke.

4. Adjust the following valves: No. 1 Intake and Exhaust. No. 2 Intake. No. 3 Exhaust.

5. Rotate the crankshaft 360° and bring No. 4 piston to TDC of the compression stroke.

6. Adjust the following valves: No. 2 Exhaust. No. 3 Intake. No. 4 Intake and Exhaust.

7. To adjust the valves, loosen the locknut on the rocker arm. Rotate the adjusting screw clockwise to reduce clearance, counter-clockwise to increase clearance. Clearance is checked with a flat feeler gauge that is passed between the rocker arm and valve stem.

8. After adjustments are made, be sure the locknuts are tight. Be sure mounting surfaces are clean. Install the valve cover and new valve cover gasket.

Electronic Ignition System

NOTE: This book contains simple testing procedures for your Ford's electronic ignition. More comprehensive testing on this system and other electronic control systems on your Ford can be found in CHILTON'S GUIDE TO ELECTRONIC ENGINE CONTROLS, book part number 7535, available at your local retailer.

Your car uses an electronic ignition system. The purpose of using an electronic ignition system is: To eliminate the deterioration of spark quality which occur in the breaker point ignition system as the breaker points

The Dura Spark II is a pulse triggered, transistor controlled breakerless ignition system. With the ignition switch **ON**, the primary circuit is on and the ignition coil is energized. When the armature spokes approach the magnetic pick-up coil assembly, they induce a voltage which tells the amplifier to turn the coil primary current off. A timing circuit in the amplifier module will turn the current on again after the coil field has collapsed. When the current is on, it flows from the battery through the ignition switch, the primary windings of the ignition coil, and through the amplifier module circuits to ground. When the current is off, the magnetic field built up in the ignition coil is allowed to collapse, inducing a high voltage into the secondary windings of the coil. High voltage is produced each time the field is thus built up and collapsed.

A Universal Distributor equipped with either a TFI-I or TFI-IV system is used on some models, depending on year, engine option, and model. TFI stands for Thick Film Integrated which incorporates a molded thermoplastic module mounted on the distributor base. Models equipped with TFI also use an **E** coil which replaces the oil filled design used with Dura-Spark.

The Universal Distributor equipped with TFI-IV uses a vane switch stator assembly which replace the coil stator. The IV system incorporates provision for fixed octane adjustment and has no centrifugal or vacuum advance mechanisms. All necessary timing requirements are handled by the EEC-IV electronic engine control system.

TACHOMETER HOOKUP

Models equipped with a conventional type coil have an adapter on the top of the coil that provides a clip marked Tach Test. On models (TFI) equipped with an **E** type coil, the tach connection is made at the back of the wire harness connector. A cutout is provided and the tachometer lead wire alligator clip can be connected to the dark green/yellow dotted wire of the electrical harness plug.

Distributor Cap and Rotor

1. The distributor cap is held on by two cap screws. Release them with a screwdriver and lift the cap straight up and off, with the wires attached. Inspect the cap for cracks, carbon tracks, or a worn center contact. Replace it if necessary, transferring the wires one at a time from the old cap to the new.
2. Remove the screw retaining the ignition rotor and remove the rotor. Replace it if its contacts are worn, burned, or pitted. Do not file the contact.

NOTE: Always coat the cap and rotor contacts with dielectric compound.

CONTINUITY TEST – PLUG WIRES

1. Remove the distributor cap with plug wires attached.
2. Connect one end of an ohmmeter to the spark plug terminal end of the wire, the other to the inside corresponding terminal of the distributor cap.
3. Measure the resistance. If the reading is more than 5,000Ω per inch of cable, replace the wire.

Ignition Coil

PRIMARY RESISTANCE

1. Verify that the ignition switch is in the OFF position.
2. Remove the coil connector, clean and inspect for dirt or corrosion.
3. Measure the resistance between the positive and negative terminals of the coil with an ohmmeter. On TFI models, resistance should measure 0.3–1.0Ω. On Dura-Spark models, the resistance should measure 0.8–1.6Ω.
4. Replace the coil if resistance is not within specifications.

SECONDARY RESISTANCE

1. Follow Steps 1 and 2 of the Primary Resistance Test.
2. Measure resistance between the

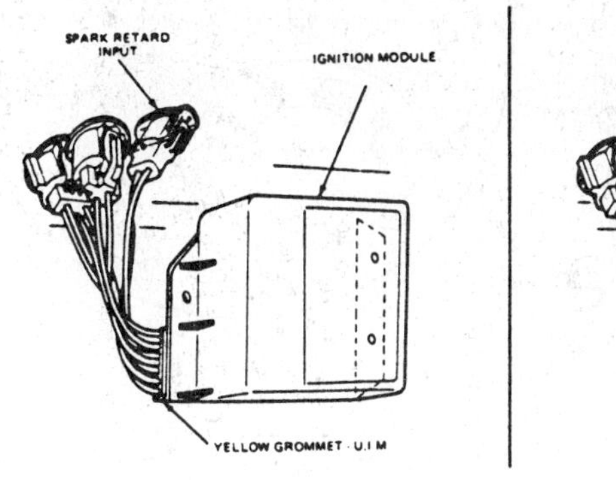

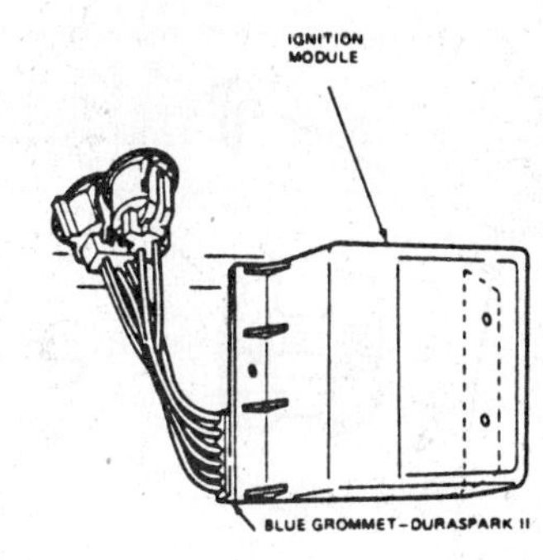

Two types of Dura Spark II ignition modules

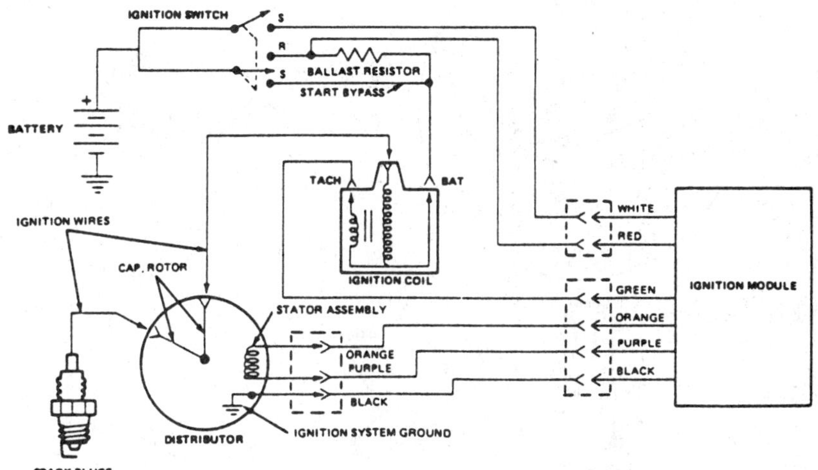

Dura Spark II circuit operation

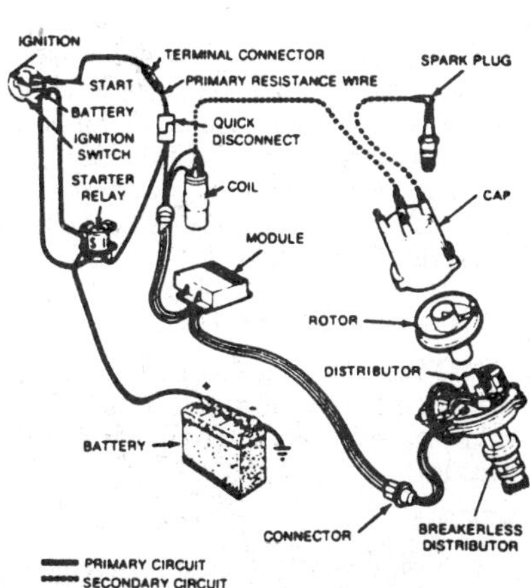

The Dura Spark II ignition system

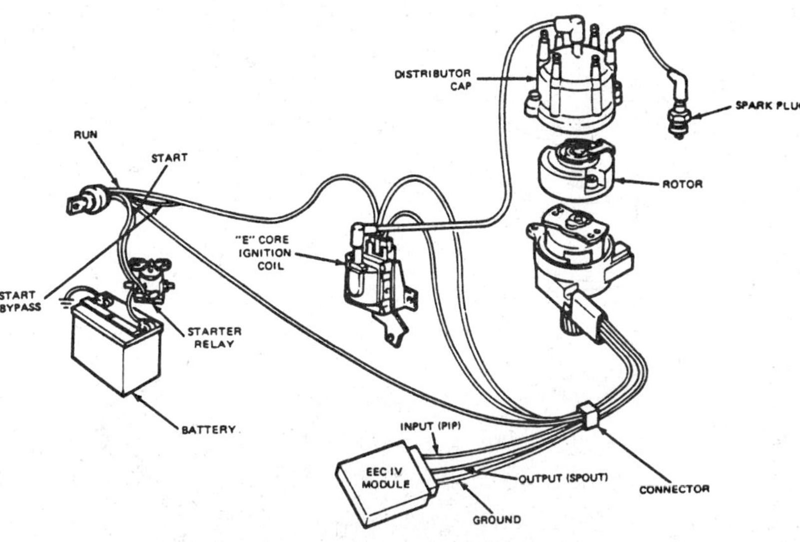

The EEC-IV Thick Film Integrated (TFI) ignition system

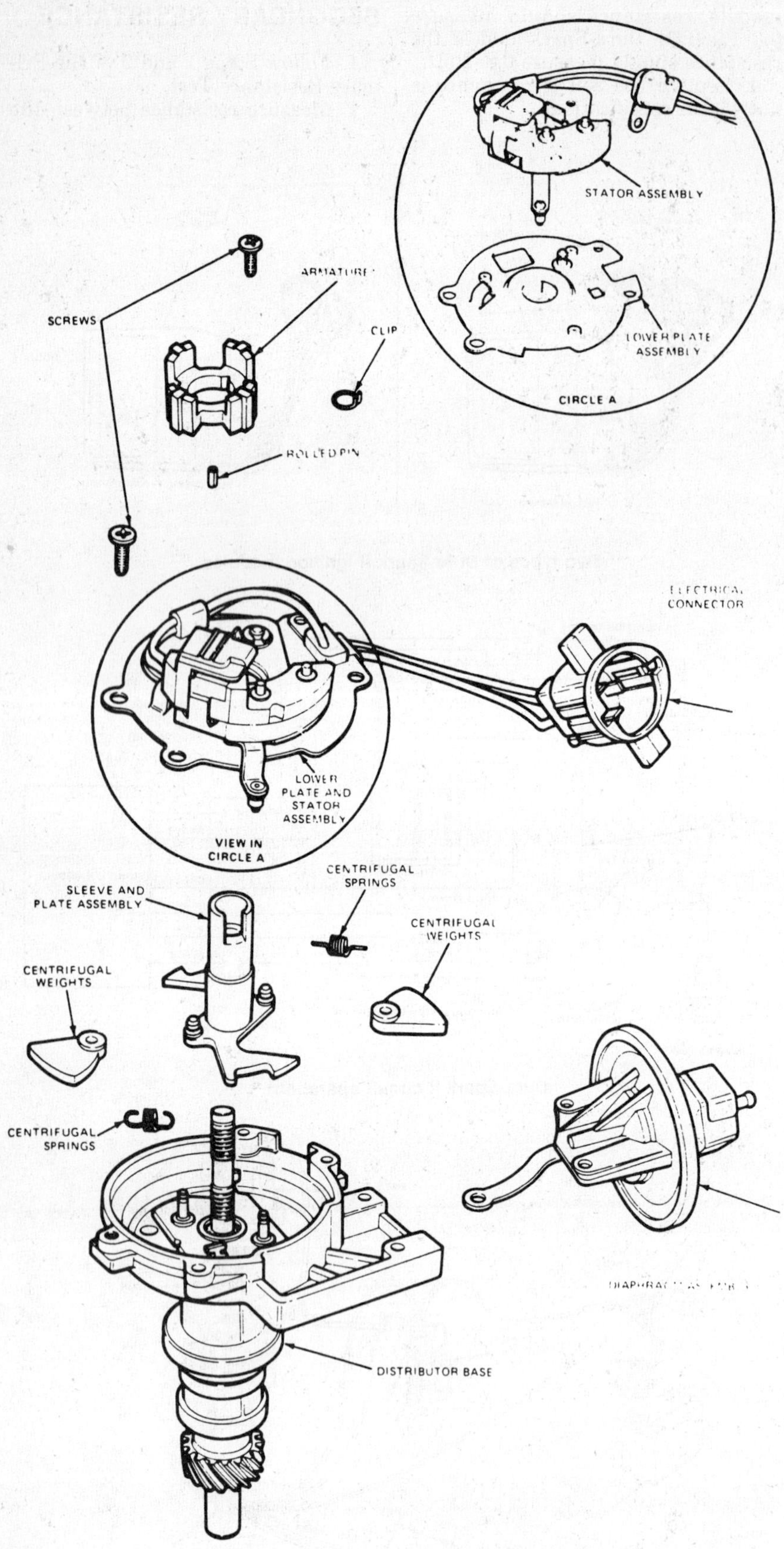

Dura Spark II distributor assembly—4-122, 140 engines

negative (BATT) and high tension lead terminal of the coil.

3. Resistance for Dura-Spark should be between 7,700–10,500Ω. TFI should be between 8000–11,500Ω.

4. Replace the coil if not within specifications.

Dura Spark II Troubleshooting

The following procedures can be used to determine whether the ignition system is working or not. If these procedures fail to locate and correct the problem, full troubleshooting procedures should be performed by a qualified service department.

PRELIMINARY CHECKS

1. Check the battery's state of charge and connections.
2. Inspect all wires and connections for breaks, cuts, abrasions, or burn spots. Repair as necessary.
3. Unplug all connectors one at a time and inspect for corroded or burned contacts. Repair and plug connectors back together. DO NOT remove the dielectric compound in the connectors.
4. Check for loose or damaged spark plug or coil wires. Check for excessive resistance. If the boots or nipples are removed on 8mm ignition wires, reline the inside of each with silicone dielectric compound (Motorcraft WA 10).

Special Tools

To perform the following tests, two special tools are needed: the ignition test jumper shown in the illustration and a modified spark plug. Use the illustration to assemble the ignition test jumper. The test jumper must be used when performing the following tests. The modified spark plug is basically a spark plug with the side electrode removed. Ford makes a special tool called a Spark Tester for this purpose, which besides not having a side electrode is equipped with a spring clip so that it can be grounded to engine metal. It is recommended that the Spark Tester be used as there is less chance of being shocked.

Run Mode Spark Test

NOTE: The wire colors given here are the main color of the wires, not the dots or stripe marks.

STEP 1

1. Remove the distributor cap and rotor from the distributor.
2. With the ignition off, turn the engine over by hand until one of the

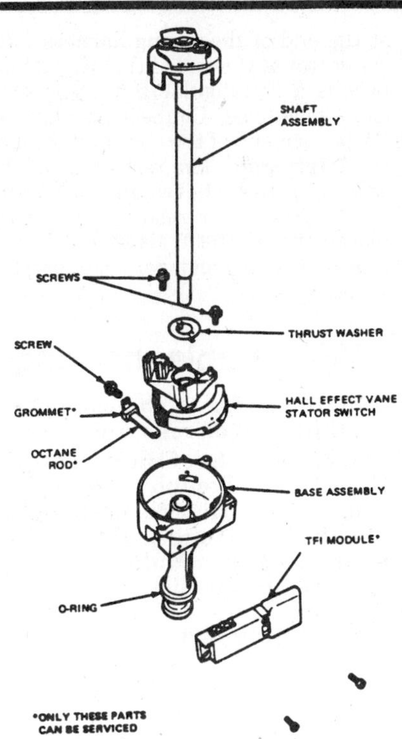

Exploded view of the EEC-IV distributor

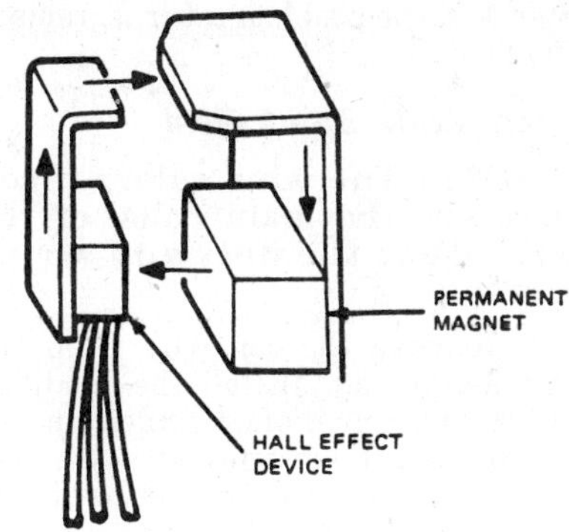

Magnetic Flux Field

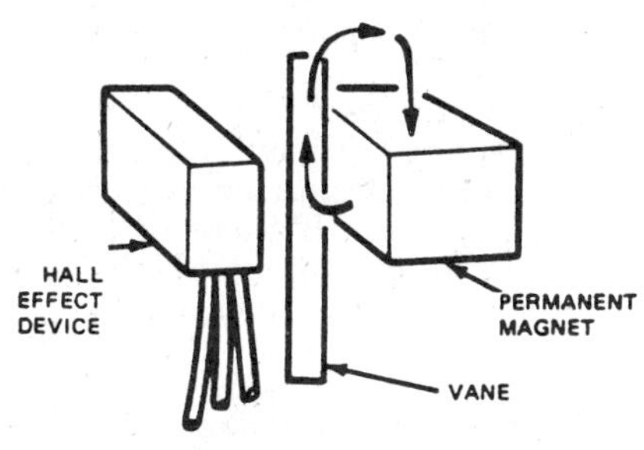

Activating the Hall Effect Device

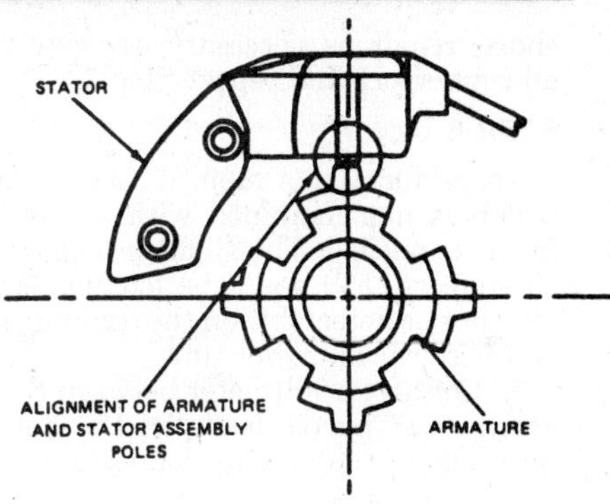

Dura Spark II armature-stator assembly alignment

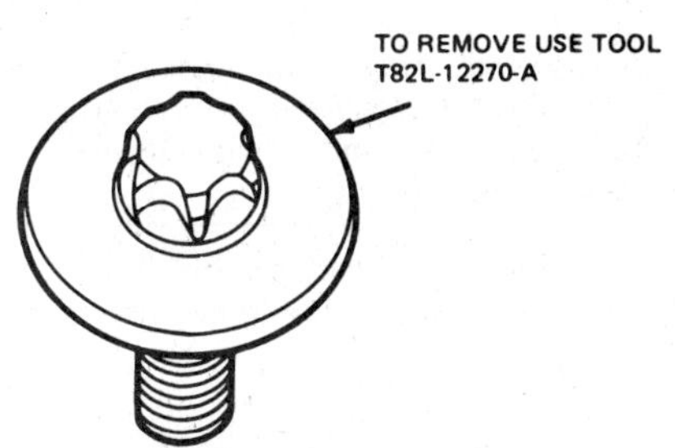

Security-type hold-down bolt

teeth on the distributor armature aligns with the magnet in the pick-up coil.

3. Remove the coil wire from the distributor cap. Install the modified spark plug (see Special Tools) in the coil wire terminal and using insulated pliers, hold the spark plug base against the engine block.

4. Turn the ignition to RUN (not START) and tap the distributor body with a screwdriver handle. There should be a spark at the modified spark plug or at the coil wire terminal.

5. If a good spark is evident, the primary circuit is OK, perform Start Mode Spark Test. If there is no spark, proceed to Step 2.

STEP 2

1. Unplug the module connector(s) which contain(s) the green and black module leads.

2. In the harness side of the connector(s), connect the special test jumper (see special tools) between the leads which connect the green and black leads of the module pig tails. Use paper clips on connector socket holes to make contact. Do not allow clips to ground.

3. Turn the ignition switch to RUN (not START) and close the test jumper switch. Leave closed for about one second, then open. Repeat several times. There should be a spark each time the switch is opened.

4. If there is NO spark, the problem is probably in the primary circuit through the ignition switch, the coil, the green lead or the black lead, or the ground connection in the distributor. Perform Step 3. If there IS a spark, the primary circuit wiring and coil are probably OK. The problem is probably in the distributor pick-up, the module red wire, or the module. Perform Step 6.

STEP 3

1. Disconnect the test jumper lead from the black lead and connect it to a good ground. Turn the test jumper switch on and off several times as in Step 2.

2. If there is NO spark, the problem is probably in the green lead, the coil, or the coil feed circuit. Perform Step 5.

3. If there IS spark, the problem is probably in the black lead or the distributor ground connections. Perform Step 4.

STEP 4

1. Connect an ohmmeter between the black lead and ground. With the meter on its lowest scale, there should be NO measurable resistance in the circuit. If there is resistance, check the distributor ground connections and the black lead from the module. Repair as necessary, remove the ohmmeter, plug in all connections and repeat Step 1.

2. If there is NO resistance, the primary ground wiring is OK. Perform Step 6.

STEP 5

1. Disconnect the test jumper from the green lead and ground and connect it between the TACH-TEST terminal of the coil and a good ground on the engine.

2. With the ignition switch in the RUN position, turn the jumper switch on. Hold it on for about one second then turn it off as in Step 2. Repeat several times. There should be a spark each time the switch is turned off. If there is NO spark, the problem is probably in the primary circuit running through the ignition switch to the coil BAT terminal, or in the coil itself. Check coil resistance (test given later in this section), and check the coil for internal shorts or opens. Check the coil feed circuit for opens, shorts or high resistance. Repair as necessary, reconnect all connectors and repeat Step 1. If there IS spark, the coil and its feed circuit are OK. The problem could be in the green lead between the coil and the module. Check for open or

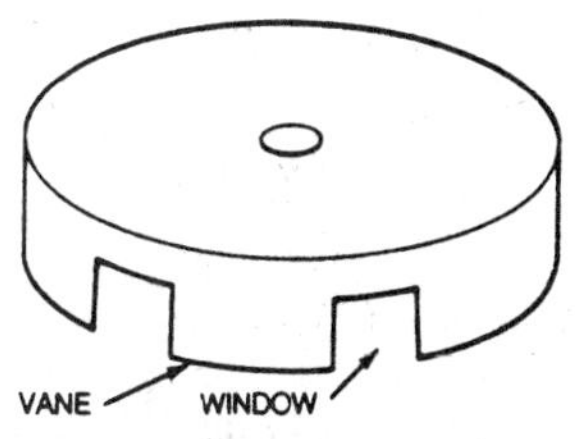

Rotary Vane Cap

short, repair as necessary, reconnect all connectors and repeat Step 1.

STEP 6

To perform this step, a voltmeter which is not combined with a dwell meter is needed. The slight needle oscillations (0.5V) you'll be looking for may not be detectable on the combined voltmeter/dwell meter unit.

1. Connect a voltmeter between the orange and purple leads on the harness side of the module connectors.

CAUTION

On catalytic converter equipped cars, disconnect the air supply line between the Thermactor by-pass valve and the manifold before cranking the engine with the ignition off. This will prevent damage to the catalytic converter. After testing, run the engine for at least 3 minutes before reconnecting the by-pass valve, to clear excess fuel from the exhaust system.

2. Set the voltmeter on its lowest scale and crank the engine. The meter needle should oscillate slightly (about 0.5V). If the meter does not oscillate, check the circuit through the magnetic pick-up in the distributor for open shorts, shorts to ground and resistance. Resistance between the orange and purple leads should be 400–1,000Ω, and between each lead and ground should be more than 70,000Ω. Repair as necessary, reconnect all connectors and repeat Step 1.

3. If the meter oscillates, the problem is probably in the power feed to the module (red wire) or in the module itself. Proceed to Step 7.

STEP 7

1. Remove all meters and jumpers and plug in all connectors.

2. Turn the ignition switch to the RUN position and measure voltage between the battery positive terminal and engine ground. It should be 12 volts.

3. Next, measure voltage between the red lead of the module and engine ground. To make this measurement, it will be necessary to pierce the red wire with a straight pin and connect the voltmeter to the straight pin and to ground. DO NOT ALLOW THE STRAIGHT PIN TO GROUND ITSELF!

4. The two readings should be within one volts of each other. If not within one volt, the problem is in the power feed to the red lead. Check for shorts, open, or high resistance and correct as necessary. After repairs, repeat Step 1.

If the readings are within one volt, the problem is probably in the module. Replace with a good module and repeat Step 1. If this corrects the problem reconnect the old module and repeat Step 1. If the problem returns, replace the module.

Start Mode Spark Test

NOTE: The wire colors given here are the main color of the wires, not the dots and stripe marks.

1. Remove the coil wire from the distributor cap. Install the modified spark plug mentioned under Special Tools, above, in the coil wire and ground it to engine metal either by its spring clip (Spark Tester) or by holding the spark plug shell against the engine block with insulated pliers.

CAUTION

See the Caution under Step 6 of Run Mode Spark Test.

2. Have an assistant crank the engine using the ignition switch and check for spark. If there IS a good spark, the problem is most probably in the distributor cap, rotor, ignition cables or spark plugs. If there is NO spark, proceed to Step 3.

3. Measure the battery voltage. Next, measure the voltage at the white wire of the module while cranking the engine. To make this measurement, it will be necessary to pierce the white wire with a straight pin and connect the voltmeter to the straight pin and to ground.

NOTE: DO NOT ALLOW THE STRAIGHT PIN TO GROUND ITSELF. The battery voltage and the voltage at the white wire should be within one volt of each other. If the readings are not within one volt of each other, check and repair the feed through the ignition switch to the white wire. Recheck for spark (Step 1). If the readings are within one volt of each other, or if there is still NO spark after power feed to white wire is repaired, proceed to Step 4.

4. Measure the coil **BAT** terminal voltage while cranking the engine. The reading should be within one volt of battery voltage. If the readings are not within one volt of each other, check and repair the feed through the ignition switch to the coil. If the readings are within one volt of each other, the problem is probably in the ignition module. Substitute another module and repeat test for spark (Step 1).

BALLAST RESISTOR

The ballast resistor wire is usually red with light green stripes. To check it you must disconnect it at the coil **BAT** connections and at the connector at the end of the wiring harness. The connector at the end of the wiring harness is a rectangular connector with eight terminals. Connect an ohmmeter to each end of the wire and set it to the **High** scale. The resistance of the wire should be between 1.05Ω and 1.15Ω. Any other reading merits replacement of the resistor wire with one of the correct service resistor wires.

TFI Troubleshooting

NOTE: Refer to the comments, preliminary checks and special tool paragraphs of the proceeding Dura-Spark Troubleshooting section. In addition to preliminary checks mentioned, check to be sure the TFI module is securely attached to the distributor.

VOLTAGE TEST

1. Disconnect the TFI module wire harness connector at the module. Check for battery voltage between each pin of the connector and ground. Use a straight pin the connector socket hole to make contact. Test as follows:

2. With the ignition switch in the Off position, check of 0 volts at each terminal. If voltage is present, check the ignition switch for problems.

3. Set the ignition switch to the RUN position. Check for battery voltage at the color/coded W/LBH and DG/YD wires. Check for 0 volts at the R/LB wire. If not as required, check the continuity of the ignition switch, coil and wires.

4. Disconnect the R/LB wire lug at the starter relay. Set the ignition switch to START. Check for battery voltage at all three wires. If voltage is not present, check the continuity of the ignition switch and R/LB wire. Reconnect the wire lug to the starter relay.

RUN MODE TEST

1. Remove the coil wire from the distributor cap. Install the modified spark plug (see special tools in previous section) in the coil wire terminal.

2. Unplug the wire connector at the TFI module. In the harness side of the connector, connect the special jumper (see special tools in previous section) between the ground and the color coded DG/YD lead. Use a straight pin in the socket to make the connection.

CAUTION

Do not leave the special jumper switch closed for more than a second at a time.

3. Place the ignition switch in the RUN position. Quickly close (no more than one second) and open the jumper switch. Repeat the closing and opening several times. Spark should occur each time the jumper switch is opened.

4. If there is no spark the problem is in the primary circuit. Check the coil for internal shorts or opens, check primary and secondary resistance. Replace the coil if necessary.

5. If there is spark when the jumper switch is opened, the problem is in the distributor or TFI module.

ENGINE ELECTRICAL

Ignition Coil

REMOVAL & INSTALLATION

1. Disconnect the battery ground.
2. Disconnect the two small and one large wire from the coil.
3. Disconnect the condenser connector from the coil, if equipped.
4. Unbolt and remove the coil.
5. Installation is the reverse of removal.

Ignition Module

REMOVAL & INSTALLATION

Removing the module, on all models, is a matter of simply removing the fasteners that attach it to the fender or firewall and pulling apart the connectors. When unplugging the connectors, pull them apart with a firm, straight pull. NEVER PRY THEM APART! To pry them will cause damage. When reconnecting them, coat the mating ends with silicone dielectric grease to waterproof the connection. Press the connectors together firmly to overcome any vacuum lock caused by the grease.

NOTE: If the locking tabs weaken or break, don't replace the unit. Just secure the connection with electrical tape or tie straps.

Alternator

PRECAUTIONS

To prevent damage to the alternator and regulator, the following precautions should be taken when working with the electrical system.

1. Never reverse the battery connections.
2. Booster batteries for starting must be connected properly: positive-to-positive and negative cable from jumper to a ground point on the dead battery vehicle.
3. Disconnect the battery cables before using a fast charger; the charger has a tendency to force current through the diodes in the opposite direction for which they were designed. This burns out the diodes.
4. Never use a fast charger as a booster for starting the vehicle.
5. Never disconnect the voltage regulator while the engine is running.
6. Avoid long soldering times when replacing diodes or transistors. Prolonged heat is damaging to AC generators.
7. Do not use test lamps of more than 12 volts (V) for checking diode continuity.
8. Do not short across or ground any of the terminals on the AC generator.
9. The polarity of the battery, generator, and regulator must be matched and considered before making any electrical connections within the system.
10. Never operate the alternator on an open circuit. Make sure that all connections within the circuit are clean and tight.
11. Disconnect the battery terminals when performing any service on the electrical system. This will eliminate the possibility of accidental reversal of polarity.
12. Disconnect the battery ground cable if arc welding is to be done on any part of the car.

CHARGING SYSTEM TROUBLESHOOTING

There are many possible ways in which the charging system can malfunction. Often the source of a problem is difficult to diagnose, requiring special equipment and a good deal of experience. This is usually not the case, however, where the charging system fails completely and causes the dash board warning light to come on or the battery to become dead. To troubleshoot a complete system failure only two pieces of equipment are needed: a test light, to determine that current is reaching a certain point; and a current indicator (ammeter), to determine the direction of the current flow and its measurement in amps.
This test works under three assumptions:

1. The battery is known to be good and fully charged.
2. The alternator belt is in good condition and adjusted to the proper tension.
3. All connections in the system are clean and tight.

NOTE: In order for the current indicator to give a valid reading, the car must be equipped with battery cables which are of the same gauge size and quality as original equipment battery cables.

1. Turn off all electrical components on the car. Make sure the doors of the car are closed. If the car is equipped with a clock, disconnect the clock by removing the lead wire from the rear of the clock. Disconnect the positive battery cable from the battery and connect the ground wire on a test light to the disconnected positive battery cable. Touch the probe end of the test light to the positive battery post. The test light should not light. If the test light does light, there is a short or open circuit on the car.
2. Disconnect the voltage regulator wiring harness connector at the voltage regulator. Turn on the ignition key. Connect the wire on a test light to a good ground (engine bolt). Touch the probe end of a test light to the ignition wire connector into the voltage regulator wiring connector. This wire corresponds to the **I** terminal on the regulator. If the test light goes on, the charging system warning light circuit is complete. If the test light does not come on and the warning light on the instrument panel is on, either the resistor wire, which is parallel with the warning light, or the wiring to the voltage regulator, is defective. If the test light does not come on and the warning light is not on, either the bulb is defective or the power supply wire form the battery through the ignition switch to the bulb has an open circuit. Connect the wiring harness to the regulator.
3. Examine the fuse link wire in the wiring harness from the starter relay to the alternator. If the insulation on the wire is cracked or split, the fuse link may be melted. Connect a test light to the fuse link by attaching the ground wire on the test light to an engine bolt and touching the probe end of the light to the bottom of the fuse link wire where it splices into the alternator output wire. If the bulb in the test light does not light, the fuse link is melted.
4. Start the engine and place a current indicator on the positive battery cable. Turn off all electrical accessories and make sure the doors are closed. If the charging system is working properly, the gauge will show a draw of less than 5 amps. If the system

is not working properly, the gauge will show a draw of more than 5 amps. A charge moves the needle toward the battery, a draw moves the needle away from the battery. Turn the engine off.

5. Disconnect the wiring harness from the voltage regulator at the regulator at the regulator connector. Connect a male spade terminal (solderless connector) to each end of a jumper wire. Insert one end of the wire into the wiring harness connector which corresponds to the **A** terminal on the regulator. Insert the other end of the wire into the wiring harness connector which corresponds to the **F** terminal on the regulator. Position the connector with the jumper wire installed so that it cannot contact any metal surface under the hood. Position a current indicator gauge on the positive battery cable. Have an assistant start the engine. Observe the reading on the current indicator. Have your assistant slowly raise the speed of the engine to about 2,000 rpm or until the current indicator needle stops moving, whichever comes first. Do not run the engine for more than a short period of time in this condition. If the wiring harness connector or jumper wire becomes excessively hot during this test, turn off the engine and check for a grounded wire in the regulator wiring harness. If the current indicator shows a charge of about three amps less than the output of the alternator, the alternator is working properly. If the previous tests showed a draw, the voltage regulator is defective. If the gauge does not show the proper charging rate, the alternator is defective.

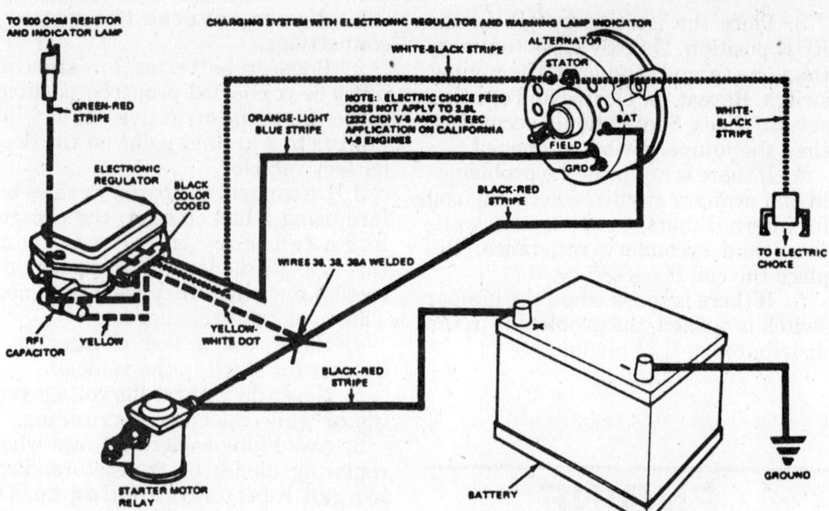

Electronic regulator with warning lamp charging system

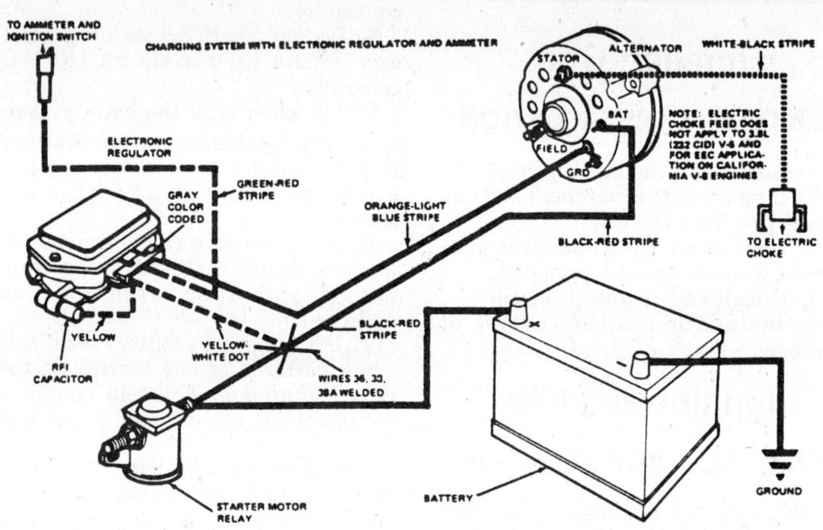

Electronic regulator with ammeter charging system

REMOVAL & INSTALLATION

1. Open the hood and disconnect the battery ground cable.
2. Remove the adjusting arm bolt.
3. Remove the alternator through-bolt. Remove the drive belt from the alternator pulley and lower the alternator.

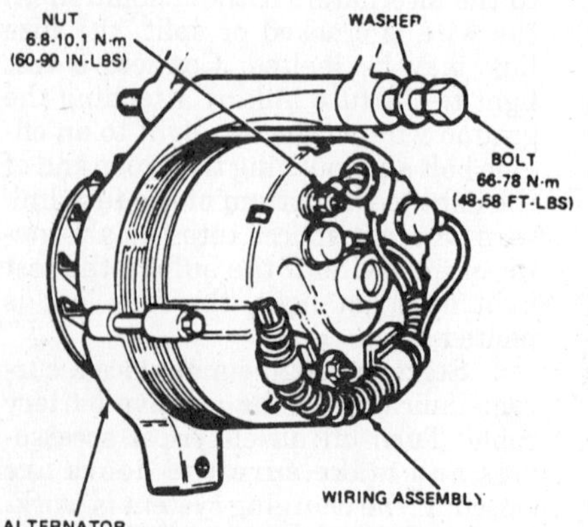

Rear terminal alternator contact locations

4. Label all of the leads to the alternator so that you can install them correctly and disconnect the leads from the alternator.
5. Remove the alternator from the vehicle.
6. To install, reverse the above procedure.

Belt Tension Adjustment

The fan belt drives the alternator and water pump. If the belt is too loose, it will slip and the alternator will not be able to produce its rated current. Also, the water pump will not operate efficiently and the engine could overheat. Check the tension of the belt by pushing your thumb down on the longest span of the belt, midway between the pulleys. Belt deflection should be approximately ½". To adjust belt tension, proceed as follows:

1. Loosen the alternator mounting bolt and the adjusting arm bolts.
2. Apply pressure on the alternator front housing only, moving the alternator away from the engine to tighten the belt. Do not apply pressure to the rear of the cast aluminum housing of an alternator; damage to the housing could result.
3. Tighten the alternator mounting bolt and the adjusting arm bolts when the correct tension is reached.

Regulator

The alternator regular has been designed to control the charging system's rate of charge. The electromechanical regulator is calibrated at the factory and is not adjustable.

REMOVAL & INSTALLATION

1. Disconnect the negative terminal

of the battery. On some models it may be necessary to move the battery.

2. Disconnect all of the electrical leads (harness connectors) at the regulator.

3. Remove all of the hold-down screws, then remove the unit from the vehicle.

4. Install the new voltage regulator using the hold-down screws from the old one, or new ones if they are provided with the replacement regulator. Tighten the hold-down screws.

5. Connect all the harness connectors to the new regulator.

Starter Motor

REMOVAL & INSTALLATION

Positive Engagement Type

1. Disconnect the positive battery terminal.
2. Raise the vehicle and disconnect the starter cable at the starter terminal.
3. Remove all of the starter attaching bolts that attach the starter to the bellhousing.
4. Remove the starter from the engine.
5. Install the starter in the reverse order of removal.

Solenoid Actuated Type

1. Disconnect the battery ground cable.
2. Raise the vehicle and disconnect the cables and wires at the starter solenoid.
3. Turn the front wheels to the right and remove the two bolts attaching the steering idler arm to the frame.
4. Remove the starter mounting bolts and remove the starter.
5. Install in the reverse order of removal

STARTER RELAY

REPLACEMENT

Gasoline Engine

The starter relay is mounted on the inside of the right wheel well. To replace it, disconnect the negative battery cable from the battery, disconnect all of the electrical leads from the relay and remove the relay from the fender wall. Replace in the reverse order of removal.

STARTER DRIVE REPLACEMENT

Gasoline Engine

1. Remove the starter as described above.

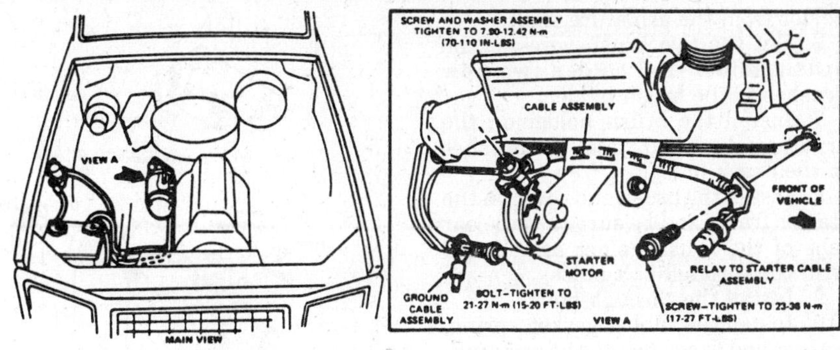

Stater, exploded view—gasoline engines

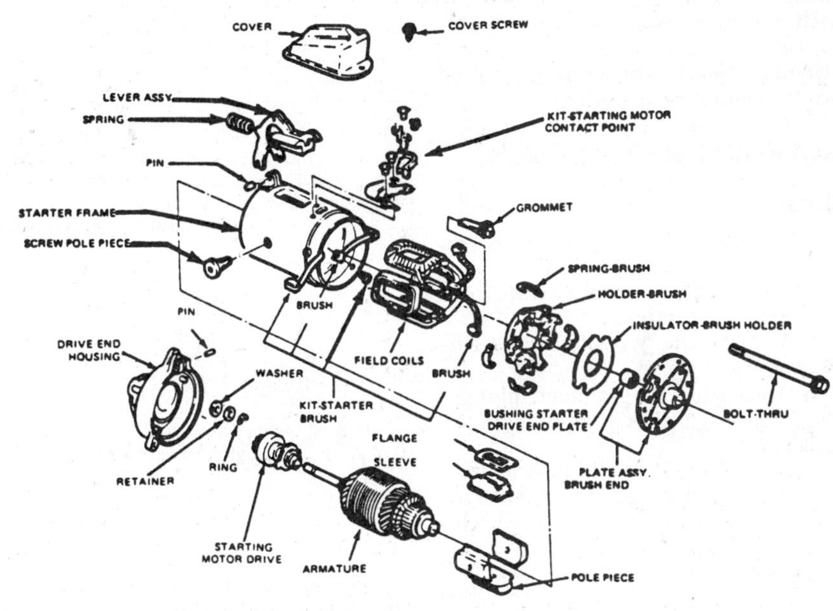

Starter, exploded view

2. Remove the starter drive plunger cover.
3. Remove the pivot pin retaining the starter drive plunger lever.
4. Loosen the through bolts enough to allow removal of the drive end housing, starter drive plunger lever and return spring.
5. Remove the drive gear stop ring retainer and stop ring from the end of the armature shaft and remove the drive gear assembly.
6. Apply a thin coating of Lubriplate® 777 or equivalent on the armature shaft splines. Install the drive gear assembly on the armature shaft and install a new stop ring.
7. Position the starter gear plunger lever on the starter frame. Make sure the plunger lever properly engages the starter drive assembly.
8. Install a new stop ring retainer. Partially fill the drive end housing bearing bore with grease (approximately ¼ full), then position the starter drive plunger lever return spring and drive end housing to the starter frame. Tighten the through bolts to 55–75 in.lb. (6–8 Nm).
9. Position the starter drive plunger lever cover, with its gasket, on the starter and tighten the attaching screw.
10. Install the starter to the engine as previously described.

BRUSH REPLACEMENT

Diesel

1. Remove the starter. Remove the two screws attaching the brush end bearing cover and remove the bearing cover.
2. Remove the through-bolts.
3. Remove the C-washer, washer and spring from the brush end of the armature shaft.
4. Pull the brush end cover from the starter frame.
5. Unsolder the two brushes from the field terminals an slide the brush

holder from the armature shaft.

6. Cut the two brush wires at the brush holder and solder two new brushes to the brush holder.

7. Install the brush holder on the armature shaft and install the brushes in the brush holder.

8. Install the brush end cover on the starter frame and be sure that the ear tabs of the brush holder are aligned with the through-bolt holes.

9. Install the through-bolts.

10. Install the rubber gasket, spring, washer and C-washer on the armature shaft.

11. Install the brush end bearing cover on the brush end cover and install the two screws. If the brush holder tabs are not aligned with the through-bolts, the bearing cover screws cannot be installed.

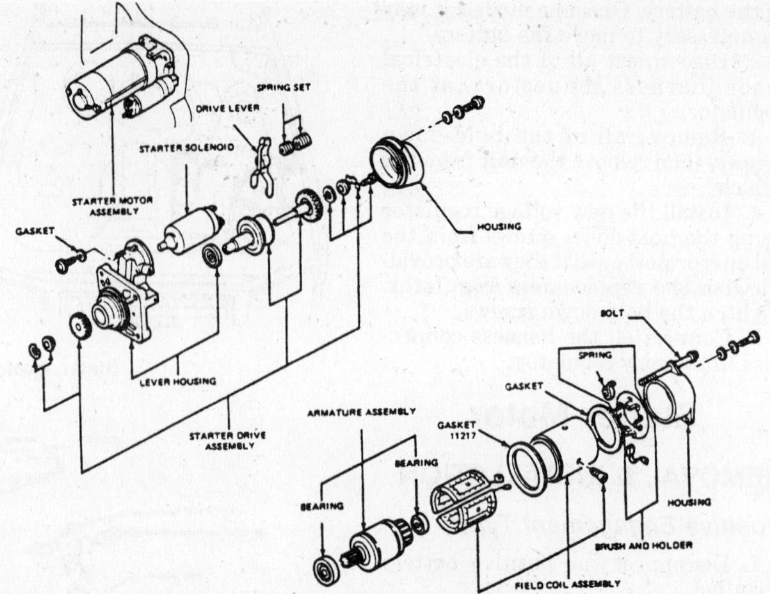

Starter, exploded view-diesel engine

SOLENOID REPLACEMENT

Diesel

1. Remove the starter from the truck.

2. Disconnect the field strap from the solenoid terminal.

3. Remove the two solenoid attaching screws.

4. Disengage the solenoid plunger from the shift fork and remove the solenoid.

5. Install the solenoid on the drive end housing, making sure that the solenoid plunger hook is engaged with the shift fork.

6. Apply 12 volts to the solenoid S terminal and measure the clearance between the starter drive and the stop-ring retainer. It should be 0.080-0.020" If not, remove the solenoid and adjust the clearance by inserting an adjusting shim between the solenoid body and drive end housing.

7. Check the solenoid for proper operation and install the starter.

8. Check the operation of the starter.

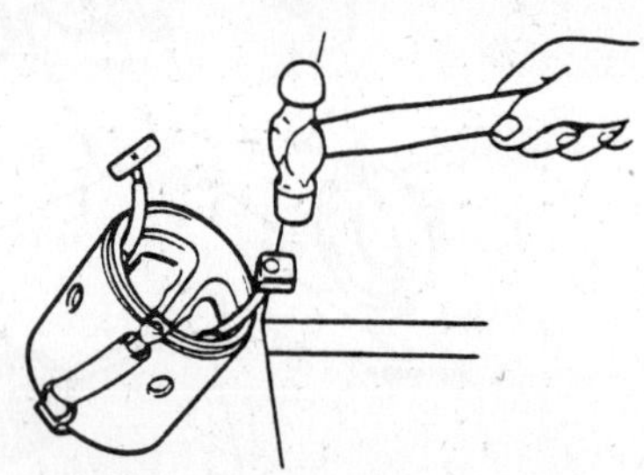
Removing brush from the lead wire—diesel engine starter

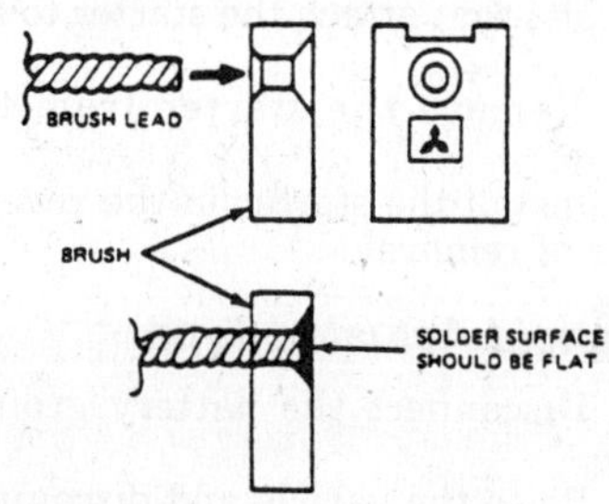

Installing brush to the lead wire—diesel engine starter

STARTER OVERHAUL

Diesel

1. Remove the starter from the truck.

2. Disconnect the field strap from the solenoid.

3. Remove the screws attaching the solenoid to the drive end housing. Disengage the solenoid plunger hook from the shift fork and remove the solenoid.

4. Remove the shift fork pivot bolt, nut and lockwasher.

5. Remove the through-bolts and separate the drive end housing from the starter frame. At the same time, disengage the shift fork from the drive assembly.

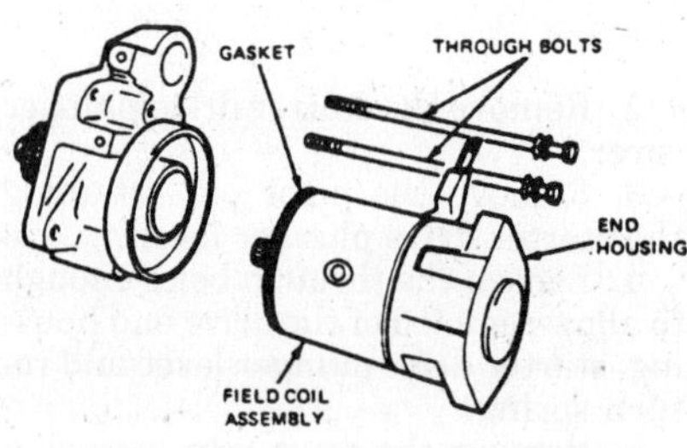

Removing the starter through bolts

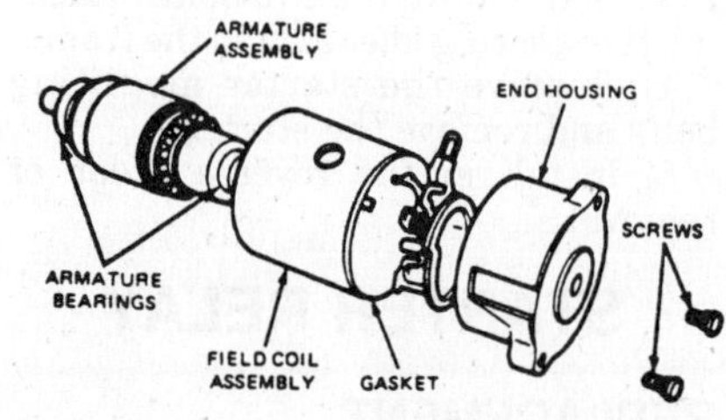

Removing the armature from the starter

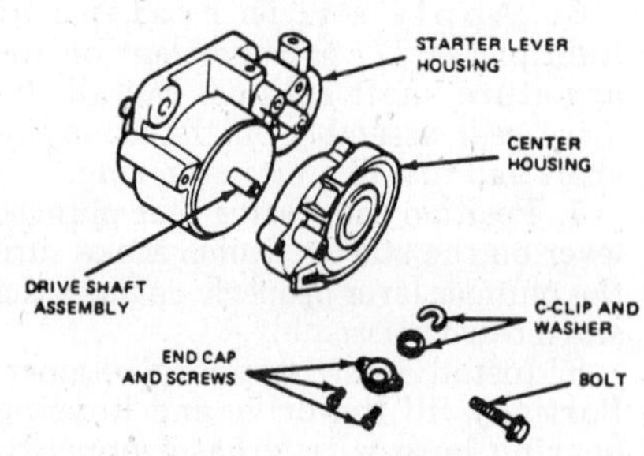

Removing the center housing

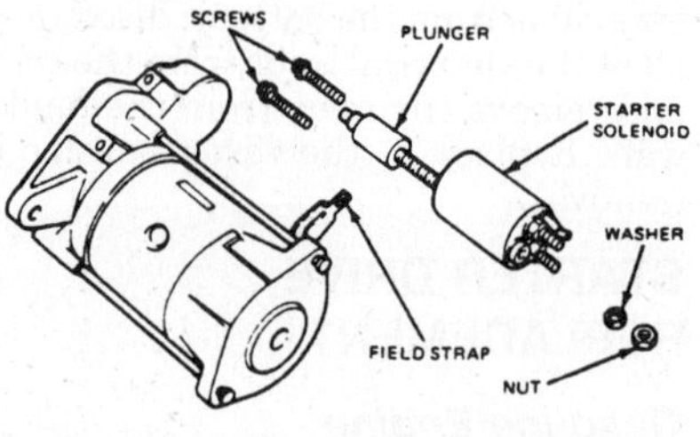

Removing the starter solenoid

6. Remove the two screws attaching the brush end bearing cover to the brush end cover.
7. Remove the C-washer, washer and spring from the brush end of the armature shaft.
8. Pull the brush end cover from the starter frame.
9. Slide the armature from the starter frame and brushes.
10. Slide the drive stop-ring retainer toward the armature and remove the stop-ring. Slide the retainer and drive assembly off the armature shaft.
11. Remove the field brushes from the brush holder and separate the brush holder from the starter frame.
12. Position the drive assembly on the armature shaft.
13. Position the drive stop-ring retainer on the armature shaft and install the drive stop-ring. Slide the stop-ring retainer over the stop-ring to secure the stop-ring on the shaft.
14. Position the armature in the starter frame. Install the brush holder on the armature and starter frame. Install the brushes in the brush holder.
15. Install the drive end housing on the armature shaft and starter housing. Engage the shift fork with the starter drive assembly as you move the drive end housing toward the starter frame.
16. Install the brush end cover on the starter frame making sure that the rear tabs of the brush holder are aligned wit the through-bolt holes.
17. Install the through-bolts.
18. Install the rubber washer, spring, washer and C-washer on the armature shaft at the brush end. Install the brush end bearing cover on the brush end cover and install the attaching screws. If the brush end cover is not properly positioned, the bearing cover screws cannot be installed.
19. Align the shift fork with the pivot bolt hole and install the pivot bolt, lockwasher and nut. Tighten the nut securely.
20. Position the solenoid on the drive end housing. Be sure that the solenoid plunger hook is engaged with the shift fork.
21. Install the two solenoid retaining screws and washers.
22. Apply 12 volts to the solenoid S terminal (ground the M terminal) and check the clearance between the starter drive and the stop-ring retainer. The clearance should be 0.080-0.020″ If not, the solenoid plunger is not properly adjusted. The clearance can be adjusted by inserting an adjusting shim between the solenoid body and drive end housing.
23. Install the field strap and tighten the nut.
24. Install the starter. Check the operation of the starter.

Battery

REMOVAL & INSTALLATION

1. Remove the holddown screws from the battery box. Loosen the nuts that secure the cable ends to the battery terminals. Lift the battery cables from the terminals with a twisting motion.
2. If there is a battery cable puller available, make use of it. Lift the battery from the vehicle.
3. Before installing the battery in the vehicle, make sure that the battery terminals are clean and free from corrosion. Use a battery terminal cleaner on the terminals and on the inside of the battery cable ends. If a cleaner is not available, use a heavy sandpaper to remove the corrosion. A mixture of baking soda and water will neutralize any acid. Place the battery in the vehicle. Install the cables on the terminals. Tighten the nuts on the cable ends. Smear a light coating of grease on the cable ends and the tops of the terminals. This will prevent buildup of oxidized acid on the terminals and the cable ends. Install and tighten the nuts of the battery box.

ENGINE MECHANICAL

Engine Overhaul Tips

Most engine overhaul procedures are fairly standard. In addition to specific parts replacement procedures and complete specifications for your individual engine, this section also is a guide to accept rebuilding procedures. Examples of standard rebuilding practice are shown and should be used along with specific details concerning your particular engine.

Competent and accurate machine shop services will ensure maximum performance, reliability and engine life.

In most instances it is more profitable for the do-it-yourself mechanic to remove, clean and inspect the component, buy the necessary parts and deliver these to a shop for actual machine work.

On the other hand, much of the rebuilding work (crankshaft, block, bearings, piston rods, and other components) is well within the scope of the do-it-yourself mechanic.

TOOLS

The tools required for an engine overhaul or parts replacement will depend on the depth of your involvement. With a few exceptions, they will be the tools found in a mechanic's tool kit. More in-depth work will require any or all of the following:

- a dial indicator (reading in thousandths) mounted on a universal base
- micrometers and telescope gauges
- jaw and screw-type pullers
- scraper
- valve spring compressor
- ring groove cleaner
- piston ring expander and compressor
- ridge reamer
- cylinder hone or glaze breaker
- Plastigage®
- engine stand

The use of most of these tools is illustrated in this section. Many can be rented for a one-time use from a local parts jobber or tool supply house specializing in automotive work.

Occasionally, the use of special tools is called for. See the information on Special Tools and Safety Notice in the front of this book before substituting another tool.

INSPECTION TECHNIQUES

Procedures and specifications are given in this section for inspecting, cleaning and assessing the wear limits of most major components. Other procedures such as Magnaflux® and Zyglo® can be used to locate material flaws and stress cracks. Magnaflux® is a magnetic process applicable only to ferrous materials. The Zyglo® process coats the material with a fluorescent dye penetrant and can be used on any material Check for suspected surface cracks can be more readily made using spot check dye. The dye is sprayed onto the suspected area, wiped off and the area sprayed with a developer. Cracks will show up brightly.

OVERHAUL TIPS

Aluminum has become extremely popular for use in engines, due to its low weight. Observe the following precautions when handling aluminum parts:

- Never hot tank aluminum parts (the caustic hot tank solution will eat the aluminum.
- Remove all aluminum parts (identification tag, etc.) from engine parts prior to the tanking.
- Always coat threads lightly with engine oil or anti-seize compounds before installation, to prevent seizure.

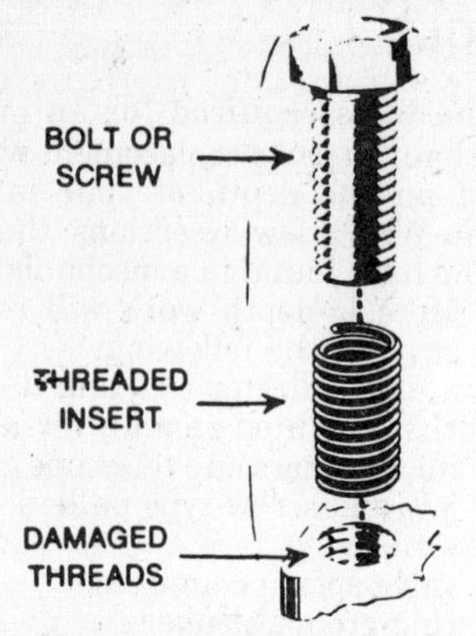

Damaged bolt holes can be repaired with thread repair inserts

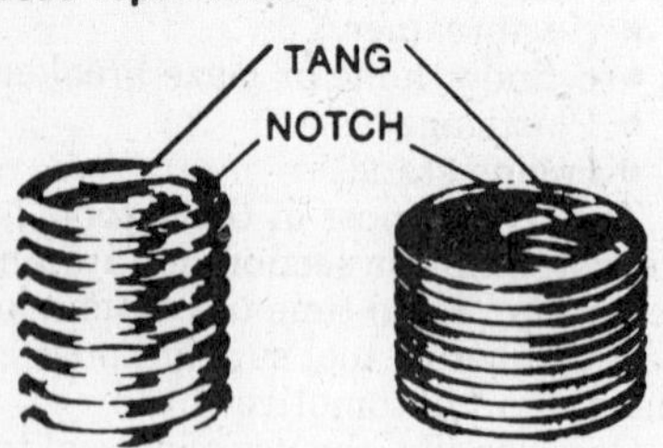

Standard thread repair insert (left) and spark plug thread insert (right)

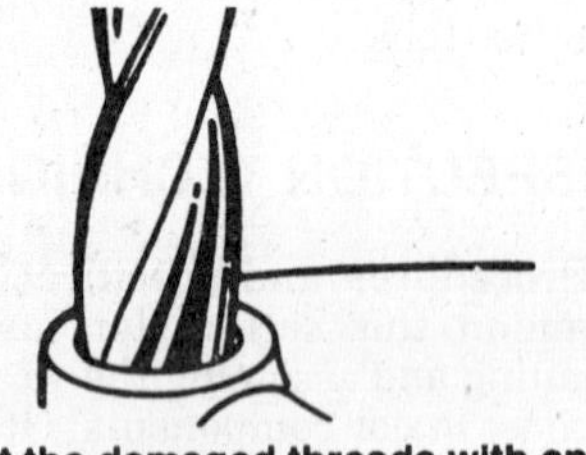

Drill out the damaged threads with specified drill. Drill completely through the hole or to the bottom of a blind hole

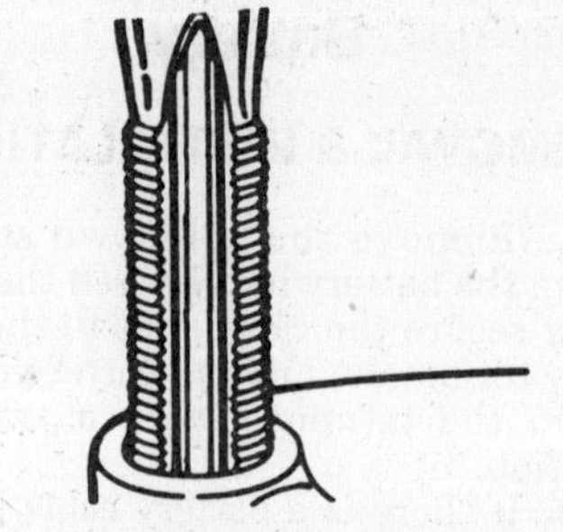

With the tap supplied, tap the hole to receive the thread insert. Keep the tap well oiled and back it out frequently to avoid clogging the threads

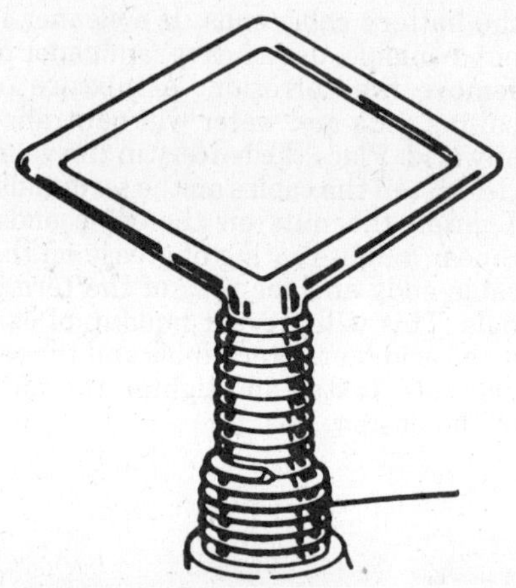

Screw the threaded insert onto the installation tool until the tang engages the slot. Screw the insert into the tapped hole until it is 1/4-1/2 turn below the top surface. After installation break off the tang with a hammer and punch

• Never overtorque bolts or spark plugs especially in aluminum threads.

Stripped threads in any component can be repaired using any of several commercial repair kits (Heli-Coil®, Microdot®, Keenserts®, etc.).

When assembling the engine, any parts that will be frictional contact must be prelubed to provide lubrication at initial start-up. Any product specifically formulated for this purpose can be used, but engine oil is not recommended as a prelube.

When semi-permanent (locked, but removable) installation of bolts or nuts is desired, threads should be cleaned and coated with Loctite® or other similar, commercial non-hardening sealant.

REPAIRING DAMAGED THREADS

Several methods of repairing damaged threads are available. Heli-Coil® (shown here), Keenserts® and Microdot® are among the most widely used. All involve basically the same principle – drilling out stripped threads, tapping the hole and installing a prewound insert – making welding, plugging and oversize fasteners unnecessary.

Two types of thread repair inserts are usually supplied: a standard type for most Inch Coarse, Inch Fine, Metric Course and Metric Fine thread sizes and a spark lug type to fit most spark plug port sizes. Consult the individual manufacturer's catalog to determine exact applications. Typical thread repair kits will contain a selection of prewound threaded inserts, a tap (corresponding to the outside diameter threads of the insert) and an installation tool. Spark plug inserts usually differ because they require a tap equipped with pilot threads and a combined reamer/tap section. Most manufacturers also supply blister-packed thread repair inserts separately in addition to a master kit containing a variety of taps and inserts plus installation tools.

Before effecting a repair to a threaded hole, remove any snapped, broken or damaged bolts or studs. Penetrating oil can be used to free frozen threads. The offending item can be removed with locking pliers or with a screw or stud extractor. After the hole is clear, the thread can be repaired, as shown in the series of accompanying illustrations.

Checking Engine Compression

A noticeable lack of engine power, excessive oil consumption and/or poor fuel mileage measured over an extended period are all indicators of internal engine war. Worn piston rings, scored or worn cylinder bores, blown head gaskets, sticking or burnt valves and worn valve seats are all possible culprits here. A check of each cylinder's compression will help you locate the problems.

As mentioned earlier, a screw-in type compression gauge is more accurate that the type you simply hold against the spark plug hole, although it takes slightly longer to use. It's worth it to obtain a more accurate reading. Follow the procedures below.

Gasoline Engines

1. Warm up the engine to normal operating temperature.
2. Remove all the spark plugs.
3. Disconnect the high tension lead from the ignition coil.
4. On fully open the throttle either by operating the carburetor throttle linkage by hand or by having an assistant floor the accelerator pedal.
5. Screw the compression gauge into the no.1 spark plug hole until the fitting is snug.

WARNING: Be careful not to crossthread the plug hole. On aluminum cylinder heads use extra care, as the threads in these heads are easily ruined.

6. Ask an assistant to depress the accelerator pedal fully on both carbureted and fuel injected vehicles. Then, while you read the compression gauge, ask the assistant to crank the engine two or three times in short bursts using the ignition switch.
7. Read the compression gauge at the end of each series of cranks, and record the highest of these readings. Repeat this procedure for each of the engine's cylinders. Compare the highest reading of each cylinder to the compression pressure specification in the

Tune-Up Specifications chart. The specs in this chart are maximum values.

A cylinder's compression pressure is usually acceptable if it is not less than 80% of maximum. The difference between any two cylinders should be no more than 12–14 pounds.

8. If a cylinder is unusually low, pour a tablespoon of clean engine oil into the cylinder through the spark plug hole and repeat the compression test. If the compression comes up after adding the oil, it appears that the cylinder's piston rings or bore are damaged or worn. If the pressure remains low, the valves may not be seating properly (a valve job is needed), or the head gasket may be blown near that cylinder. If compression in any two adjacent cylinders is low, and if the addition of oil doesn't help the compression, there is leakage past the head gasket. Oil and coolant water in the combustion chamber can result from this problem. There may be evidence of water droplets on the engine dipstick when a head gasket has blown.

Diesel Engines

Checking cylinder compression on diesel engines is basically the same procedure as on gasoline engines except for the following:

1. A special compression gauge adaptor suitable for diesel engines (because these engines have much greater compression pressures) must be used.
2. Remove the injector tubes and remove the injectors from each cylinder.

WARNING: Don't forget to remove the washer underneath each injector. Otherwise, it may get lost when the engine is cranked.

3. When fitting the compression gauge adaptor to the cylinder head, make sure the bleeder of the gauge (if equipped) is closed.
4. When reinstalling the injector assemblies, install new washers underneath each injector.

Engine

REMOVAL & INSTALLATION

4-122 (2.0L)
4-140 (2.3L)

1. Raise the hood and install protective fender covers. Drain the coolant from the radiator. Remove the air cleaner and duct assembly.

CAUTION

When draining the coolant, keep in mind that cats and dogs are attracted by the ethylene glycol antifreeze, and are quite likely to drink any that is left in an uncovered container or in puddles on the ground. This will prove fatal in sufficient quantity. Always drain the coolant into a sealable container. Coolant should be reused unless it is contaminated or several years old.

2. Disconnect the battery ground cable at the engine and disconnect the battery positive cable at the battery and set aside.
3. Mark the location of the hood hinges and remove the hood.
4. Disconnect the upper and lower radiator hoses from the engine. Remove the radiator shroud screws. Remove the radiator upper supports.
5. Remove engine fan and shroud assembly. Then remove the radiator. Remove the oil fill cap.
6. Disconnect the coil primary wire at the coil. Disconnect the oil pressure and the water temperature sending unit wires from the sending units.
7. Disconnect the alternator wire from the alternator, the starter cable from the starter and the accelerator cable from the carburetor. If so equipped, disconnect the transmission kickdown rod.
8. If so equipped, remove the A/C compressor from the mounting bracket and position it out of the way, leaving the refrigerant lines attached.
9. Disconnect the power brake vacuum hose. Disconnect the chassis fuel line from the fuel pump. Disconnect the heater hoses from the engine.
10. Remove the engine mount nuts. Raise the vehicle and safely support on jackstands.
11. Drain engine oil from the crankcase. Remove the starter motor.
12. Disconnect the muffler exhaust inlet pipe at the exhaust manifold.
13. Remove the dust cover (manual transmission) or converter inspection plate (automatic transmission).
14. On vehicles with a manual transmission, remove the flywheel housing cover lower attaching bolts. On vehicles with automatic transmissions, remove the converter-to-flywheel bolts, then remove the converter housing lower attaching bolts.
15. Remove clutch slave cylinder (manual transmission). Lower the vehicle.
16. Support the transmission and flywheel or converter housing with a jack.
17. Remove the flywheel housing or converter housing upper attaching bolts.
18. Attach the engine lifting hooks to the existing lifting brackets. Carefully, so as not to damage any components, lift the engine out of the vehicle.
19. To install the engine: If clutch was removed, reinstall. Carefully lower the engine into the engine compartment. On a vehicle with automatic transmission, start the converter pilot into the crankshaft. On a vehicle with a manual transmission, start the transmission main drive gear into the clutch disc. It may be necessary to adjust the position of the transmission in relation to the engine if the input shaft will not enter the clutch disc. If the en-

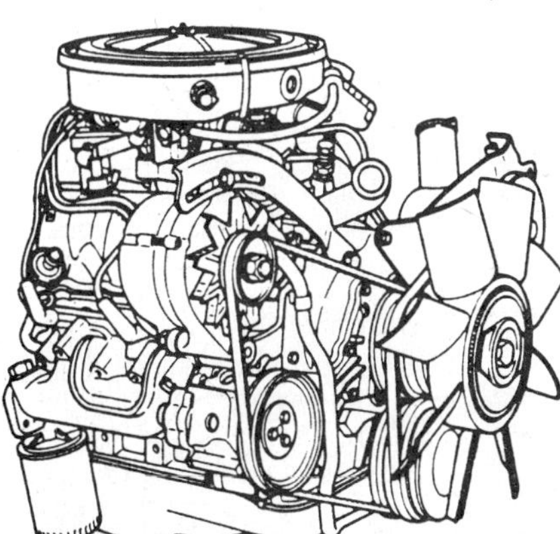

6-173 engine with Thermactor emission system

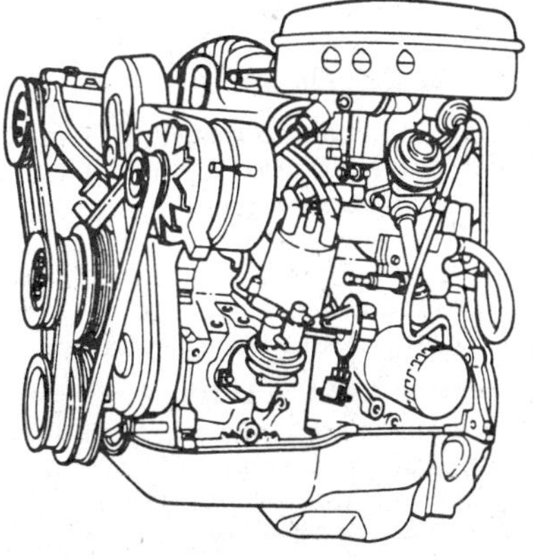

4-140 cu.in. engine assembly—4-122 cu.in. engine similar

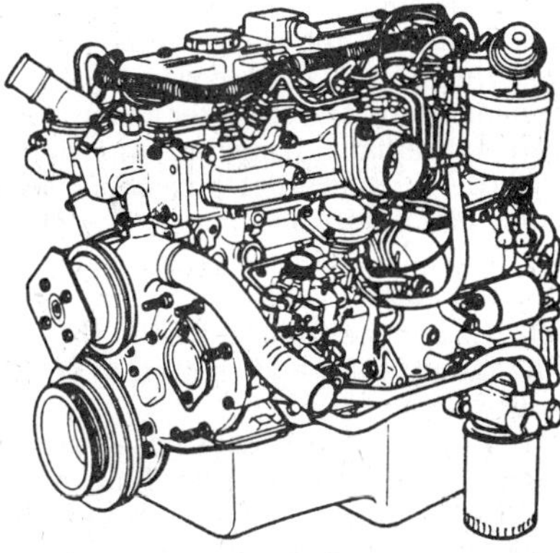

4-134 cu.in. diesel engine assembly

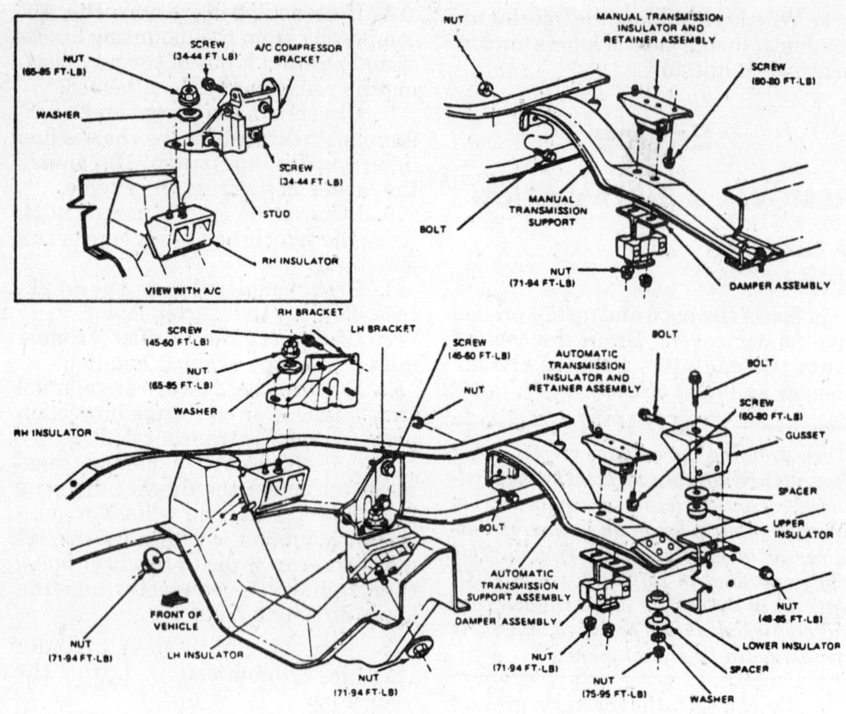

Engine mounting supports for the 4-122, 140 engines

gine hangs up after the shaft enters, turn the crankshaft in the clockwise direction slowly (transmission in gear), until the shaft splines mesh with the clutch disc splines.

20. Install the flywheel or converter housing upper attaching bolts. Remove the engine lifting hooks from the lifting brackets.

21. Remove the jack from under the transmission. Raise the vehicle and safely support on jackstands.

22. On a vehicle with a manual transmission, install the flywheel lower housing bolts and tighten to specifications. On a vehicle with an automatic transmission, attach the converter to the flywheel bolts and tighten to specifications. Install the converter housing-to-engine bolts and tighten to specifications.

23. Install clutch slave cylinder.

24. Install the dust cover (manual transmission) or converter inspection plate (automatic transmission). Connect the exhaust inlet pipe to the exhaust manifold.

25. Install the starter motor and connect the starter cables.

26. Lower the vehicle. Install the engine mount nuts and tighten to 65-85 ft.lb.

27. Connect the heater hoses to the engine. Connect the chassis fuel line to the fuel pump. Connect the power brake vacuum hose.

28. Connect the alternator wire to the alternator, connect the accelerator cable to the carburetor. If so equipped, connect the transmission kickdown rod. If so equipped, install the A/C compressor to the mounting bracket.

29. Connect the coil primary wire at the coil. Connect the oil pressure and water temperature sending unit wires. Install oil fill cap.

30. Install the radiator and secure with upper support brackets. Install the fan and shroud assembly. Connect upper and lower radiator hoses.

31. Install the hood and align.

32. Install the air cleaner assembly. Fill and bleed the cooling system.

33. Fill the crankcase with specified oil. Connect battery ground cable to engine and battery positive cable to battery.

34. Start the engine and check for leaks.

4-134 (2.2L) Diesel

1. Open hood and install protective fender covers. Mark location of hood hinges and remove hood.

2. Disconnect battery ground cables from both batteries. Disconnect battery ground cables at engine.

3. Drain coolant from radiator.

CAUTION

When draining the coolant, keep in mind that cats and dogs are attracted by the ethylene glycol antifreeze, and are quite likely to drink any that is left in an uncovered container or in puddles on the ground. This will prove fatal in sufficient quantity. Always drain the coolant into a sealable container. Coolant should be reused unless it is contaminated or several years old.

4. Disconnect air intake hose from air cleaner and intake manifold.

5. Disconnect upper and lower radiator hoses from engine. Remove engine cooling fan. Remove radiator shroud screws. Remove radiator upper supports and remove radiator and shroud.

6. Disconnect radio ground strap, if so equipped.

7. Remove No.2 glow plug relay from firewall, with harness attached, and lay on engine.

8. Disconnect engine wiring harness at main connector located on left fender apron. Disconnect starter cable from starter.

9. Disconnect accelerator cable and speed control cable, if so equipped, from injection pump.

10. Remove cold start cable from injection pump.

CAUTION

Do not disconnect air conditioning lines or discharge the system unless the proper equipment is on hand and you are familiar with the procedure. See ROUTINE MAINTENANCE.

11. Discharge A/C system and remove A/C refrigerant lines and position out of the way.

12. Remove pressure and return hoses from power steering pump, if so equipped.

13. Disconnect vacuum fitting from vacuum pump and position fitting and vacuum hoses out of the way.

14. Disconnect and cap fuel inlet line at fuel line heater and fuel return line

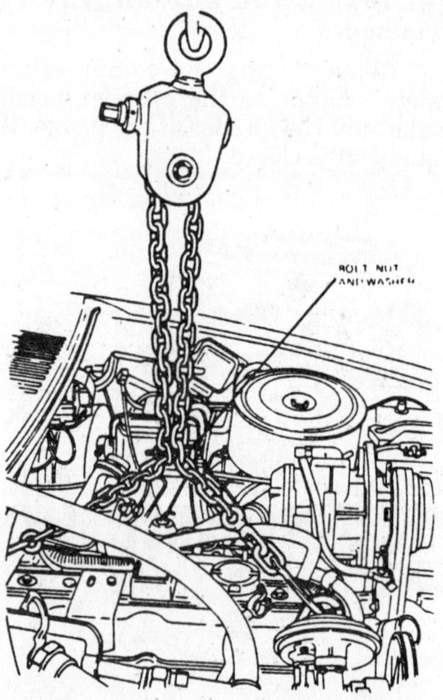

Removing the 4-134 diesel engine

at injection pump.

15. Disconnect heater hoses from engine.

16. Loosen engine insulator nuts. Raise vehicle and safely support on jackstands.

17. Drain engine oil from oil pan and remove primary oil filter.

18. Disconnect oil pressure sender hose from oil filter mounting adapter.

19. Disconnect muffler inlet pipe at exhaust manifold.

20. Remove bottom engine insulator nuts. Remove transmission bolts. Lower vehicle. Attach engine lifting sling and chain hoist.

21. Carefully lift engine out of vehicle to avoid damage to components.

22. Install engine on work stand, if necessary.

23. When installing the engine: Carefully lower engine into engine compartment to avoid damage to components.

24. Install two top transmission-to-engine attaching bolts. Remove engine lifting sling.

25. Raise vehicle and safely support on jackstands.

26. Install engine insulator nuts and tighten to specification.

27. Install remaining transmission-to-engine attaching bolts and tighten all bolts to specification.

28. Connect muffler inlet pipe to exhaust manifold and tighten to specification.

29. Install oil pressure sender hose and install new oil filter as described in this Section.

30. Lower vehicle.

31. Tighten upper engine insulator nuts to specification.

32. Connect heater hoses to engine. Connect fuel inlet line to fuel line heater and fuel return line to injection pump. Connect vacuum fitting and hoses to vacuum pump. Connect pressure and return hoses to power steering pump, if so equipped. Check and add power steering fluid.

33. Install A/C refrigerant lines and charge system, if so equipped.

NOTE: System can be charged after engine installation is completed.

34. Connect cold start cable to injection pump. Connect accelerator cable and speed control cable, if so equipped, to injection pump.

35. Connect engine wiring harness to main wiring harness at left fender apron. Connect radio ground strap, if so equipped.

36. Position radiator in vehicle, install radiator upper support brackets and tighten to specification. Install radiator fan shroud and tighten to specification. Install radiator fan and tighten to specification.

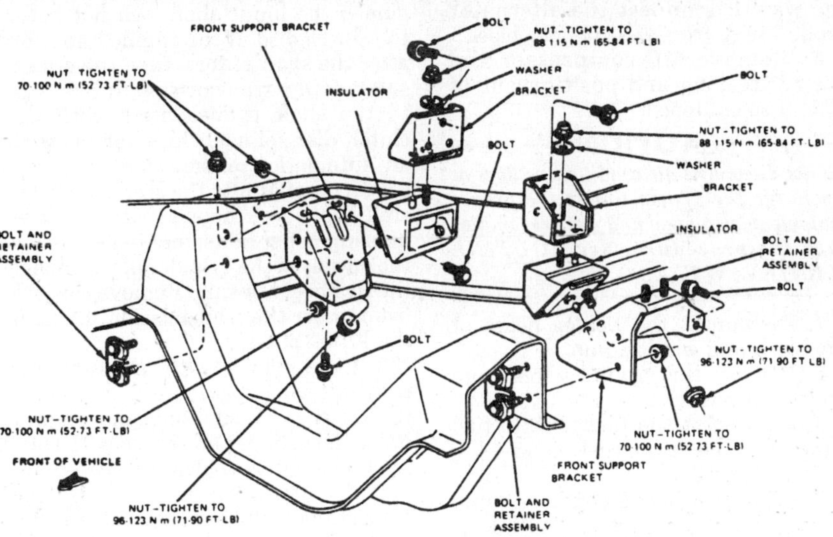

Engine mounting supports for the 4-134 diesel engine

37. Connect upper and lower radiator hoses to engine and tighten clamps to specification. Connect air intake hose to air cleaner and intake manifold.

38. Fill and bleed cooling system.

39. Fill crankcase with specified quantity and quality of oil.

40. Connect battery ground cables to engine. Connect battery ground cables to both batteries.

41. Run engine and check for oil, fuel and coolant leaks. Close hood.

6-173 (2.8L)

1. Disconnect the battery ground cable and drain the cooling system.

CAUTION

When draining the coolant, keep in mind that cats and dogs are attracted by the ethylene glycol antifreeze, and are quite likely to drink any that is left in an uncovered container or in puddles on the ground. This will prove fatal in sufficient quantity. Always drain the coolant into a sealable container. Coolant should be reused unless it is contaminated or several years old.

2. Remove the hood after scribing hinge positions. Remove the air cleaner and intake duct assembly.

3. Remove or disconnect thermactor system parts that will interfere with removal or installation of the engine.

4. Disconnect the radiator upper and lower hoses at the radiator. Remove the fan shroud attaching bolts and position the shroud over the fan. Remove the radiator and shroud.

5. Remove the alternator and bracket. Position the alternator out of

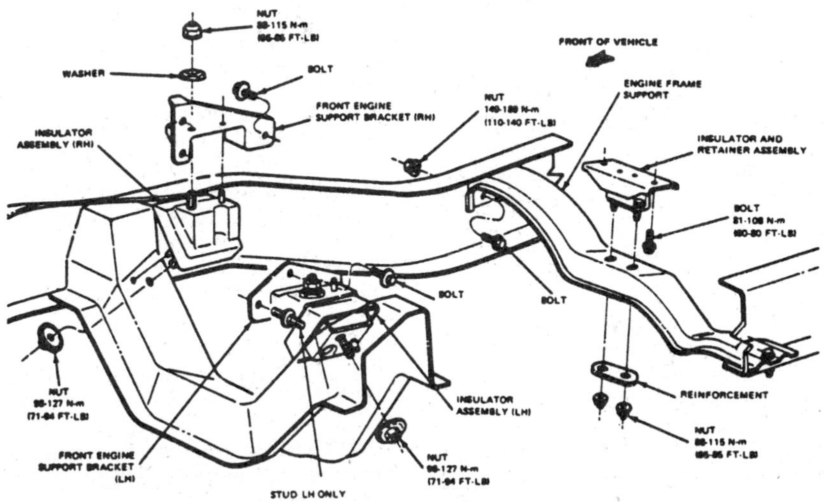

Engine mounting supports for the 6-173 engine

the way. Disconnect the alternator ground wire from the cylinder block.

6. Remove A/C compressor and power steering and position out of way, if so equipped.

CAUTION

Do not disconnect air conditioning lines or discharge the system unless the proper equipment is on hand and you are familiar with the procedure. See ROUTINE MAINTENANCE.

7. Disconnect the heater hoses at the block and water pump.
8. Remove the ground wires from the cylinder block.
9. Disconnect the fuel tank to fuel pump fuel line at the fuel pump. Plug the fuel tank line.
10. Disconnect the throttle cable linkage at the carburetor and intake manifold.
11. Disconnect the primary wires from the ignition coil. Disconnect the brake booster vacuum hose. Disconnect the wiring from the oil pressure and engine coolant temperature senders.
12. Raise the vehicle and secure with safety stands. Disconnect the muffler inlet pipes at the exhaust manifolds.
13. Disconnect the starter cable and remove the starter.
14. Remove the engine front support to crossmember attaching nuts or through bolts.
15. If equipped with automatic transmission, remove the converter inspection cover and disconnect the flywheel from the converter.
16. Remove the kickdown rod. Remove the converter housing-to-cylinder block bolts and the adapter plate-to-converter housing bolt.
17. On vehicles equipped with a manual transmission, remove the clutch linkage and mounting bolts. Lower the vehicle.
18. Attach engine lifting sling and hoist to lifting brackets at exhaust manifolds.
19. Position a jack under the transmission. Raise the engine slightly and carefully pull it from the transmission. Carefully lift the engine out of the engine compartment so that the rear cover plate is not bent or components damaged.
20. When installing the engine: Attach engine lifting sling and hoist to lifting brackets at exhaust manifolds.
21. Lower the engine carefully into the engine compartment. Make sure the exhaust manifolds are properly aligned with the muffler inlet pipes.
22. On a vehicle with a manual transmission, start the transmission main shaft into the clutch disc. It may be necessary to adjust the position of the transmission in relation to the engine if the input shaft will not enter the clutch disc. If the engine hangs up after the shaft enters, turn the crankshaft slowly (transmission in gear) until the shaft splines mesh with the clutch disc splines. On a vehicle with an automatic transmission, start the converter pilot into the crankshaft. Install the clutch housing or converter housing upper bolts, making sure that the dowels in the cylinder block engage the flywheel housing. Remove the jack from under the transmission. Remove the lifting sling.
23. On a vehicle with an automatic transmission, position the kickdown rod on the transmission and engine. Raise the vehicle and secure with safety stands. On a vehicle with an automatic transmission, position the transmission linkage bracket and install the remaining converter housing bolts. Install the adapter plate-to-converter housing bolt. Install the converter-to-flywheel nuts and install the inspection cover. Connect the kickdown rod on the transmission.
24. Install the starter and connect the cable.
25. Connect the muffler inlet pipes at the exhaust manifolds.
26. Install the engine front support nuts and washer attaching it to the crossmember or through bolts. Lower the vehicle.
27. Install the battery ground cable. Connect the ignition coil primary wires, then connect the coolant temperature sending unit and oil pressure sending unit. Connect brake booster vacuum hose. Install the throttle linkage.
28. Connect the fuel tank line at the fuel pump. Connect the ground cable at the cylinder block. Connect the heater hoses to the water pump and cylinder block.
29. Install the alternator and bracket. Connect the alternator ground wire to the cylinder block. Install the drive belt and adjust the belt tension to specifications.
30. Install A/C compressor and power steering pump, if so equipped.
31. Position the fan shroud over the fan. Install the radiator and connect the radiator upper and lower hoses. Install the fan shroud attaching bolts. Fill and bleed the cooling system. Fill the crankcase with the proper grade and quantity of oil. Install thermactor parts removed or disconnected. Reconnect battery ground cable.
32. Charge A/C system if so equipped.

NOTE: System can be charged after engine installation is completed.

33. Operate the engine at fast idle until it reaches normal operating temperature and check all gaskets and hose connections for leaks. Adjust ignition timing and idle speed. Install the air cleaner and intake duct. Install and adjust the hood.

Intake Manifold

REMOVAL & INSTALLATION

4-122 (2.0L)
4-140 (2.3L)

1. Drain the cooling system. Remove the air cleaner and duct assembly. Disconnect the negative battery cable.

CAUTION

When draining the coolant, keep in mind that cats and dogs are attracted by the ethylene glycol antifreeze, and are quite likely to drink any that is left in an uncovered container or in puddles on the ground. This will prove fatal in sufficient quantity. Always drain the coolant into a sealable container. Coolant should be reused unless it is contaminated or several years old.

2. Disconnect the accelerator cable, vacuum hoses (as required) and the hot water hose at the manifold fitting. Be sure to identify all vacuum hoses for proper reinstallation.
3. Remove the engine oil dipstick. Disconnect the heat tube at the EGR (exhaust gas recirculation) valve. Disconnect the fuel line at the carburetor fuel fitting.
4. Remove the dipstick retaining bolt from the intake manifold.
5. Disconnect and remove the PCV at the engine and intake manifold.
6. Remove the distributor cap and position the cap and wires out of the

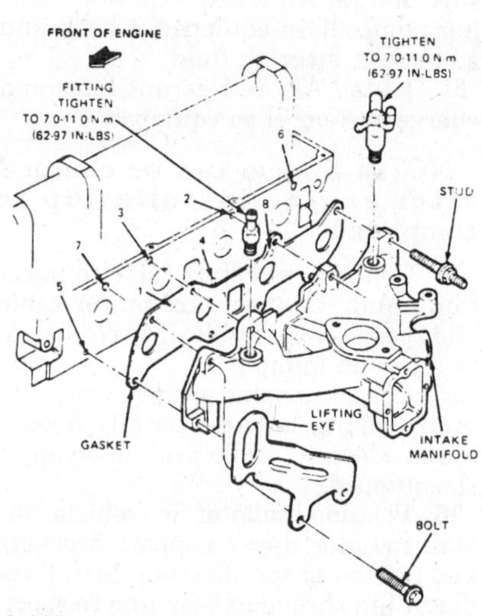

4-122, 140 engines, intake manifold installation

way, after removing the plastic plug connector from the valve cover.

7. Remove the intake manifold retaining bolts. Remove the manifold from the engine.

8. Clean all gasket mounting surfaces.

9. Install a new mounting gasket and intake manifold on the engine. Torque the bolts in proper sequence. The rest of the installation is in the reverse order of removal.

4-134 (2.2L) Diesel

1. Disconnect the battery ground cables from both batteries.

2. Disconnect the air inlet hose from the air cleaner and intake manifold. Disconnect and remove the fuel injection lines from the nozzles and injection pump. Cap all lines and fittings to prevent dirt pickup.

3. Remove the nut that attaching the lower fuel return line brace to the intake manifold.

4. Disconnect and remove the lower fuel line from the injector pump and upper fuel return line.

5. Remove the air conditioner compressor with the lines attached and position out of the way. Remove the power steering pump and rear support with the lines still attached and position out of the way.

6. Remove the air inlet adapter, dropping resistor (electrical measuring device) and the gaskets.

7. Disconnect the fuel filter inlet line, remove the fuel filter mounting bracket from the cylinder head and position the filter assembly out of the way.

8. Remove the mounting nuts for the fuel line heater assembly to intake manifold and position the heater out of the way.

9. Remove the nuts that attach the intake manifold to the cylinder head. Remove the intake manifold and gasket.

10. Clean all gasket mounting surfaces.

11. Use a new intake manifold mounting gasket. Install the intake manifold in the reverse order of removal.

12. Do not tighten the mounting nuts until No.3 lower nut that holds the fuel return line bracket is installed. After installation of the No.3 nut, tighten all of the mounting nuts.

6-173 (2.8L)

1. Drain the cooling system. Remove the air cleaner and duct assembly.

CAUTION

When draining the coolant, keep in mind that cats and dogs are attracted by the ethylene glycol antifreeze, and are quite likely to drink any that is left in an uncovered container or in puddles on the ground. This will prove fatal in sufficient quantity. Always drain the coolant into a sealable container. Coolant should be reused unless it is contaminated or several years old.

2. Disconnect the negative battery cable. Disconnect the accelerator cable from the carburetor linkage.

3. Disconnect and remove the upper radiator hose. Disconnect and remove the bypass hose from the intake manifold and thermostat housing.

4. Remove the distributor cap and spark plug wires as an assembly. Turn the engine till No. 1 piston is at TDC (top dead center) on the compression stroke. Remove the distributor.

5. Remove any vacuum lines and controls that will interfere with the intake manifold removal. Label all hoses for identification.

6. Remove both valve covers. Remove the manifold mounting nuts and bolts. Remove the manifold. Tap the manifold lightly with a plastic mallet (if necessary) to break the gasket seal.

7. Remove all old gasket material and sealing compound from the mounting surfaces.

8. Apply sealing compound to the joining surfaces. Place the intake mounting gasket into position. Make sure that the tab on the right bank head gasket fits into the cutout of the manifold gasket. Apply sealing compound to the intake manifold bolt bosses and install the intake manifold. Tighten the mounting nuts and bolts in the proper torque sequence.

9. Install the distributor and the rest of the removed components in reverse order.

10. Refill the cooling system, start the engine and check for coolant or oil leaks.

11. Check idle RPM and ignition timing. Adjust if necessary.

Exhaust Manifold

REMOVAL & INSTALLATION

4-122 (2.0L)
4-140 (2.3L)

1. Remove the air cleaner and duct assembly. Disconnect the negative battery cable.

2. Remove the EGR line at the exhaust manifold. Loosen the EGR tube. Remove the check valve at the exhaust manifold and disconnect the hose at the end of the air by-pass valve.

3. Remove the bracket attaching the heater hoses to the valve cover. Disconnect the exhaust pipe from the exhaust manifold.

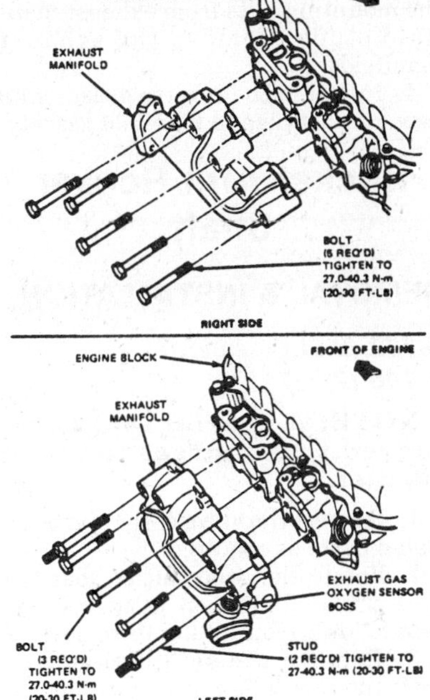

6-173 engine exhaust manifold torque sequences

4. Remove the exhaust manifold mounting bolts/nuts and remove the manifold.

5. Install the exhaust manifold in the reverse order.

4-134 (2.2L) Diesel

1. Disconnect the ground cables from both batteries.

2. Disconnect the exhaust pipe from the manifold.

3. Remove the heater hose bracket from the valve cover and exhaust manifold studs.

4. Remove the vacuum pump support brace and bracket. Remove the bolt that attaches the engine oil dipstick tube support bracket to the exhaust manifold.

5. Remove the nuts that attach the exhaust manifold to the engine and remove the manifold.

6. Clean all gasket mounting surfaces. Install a new mounting gasket and install the exhaust manifold and components in the reverse order of removal.

6-173 (2.8L)

1. Disconnect the negative battery cable. Remove the air cleaner and duct assembly.

2. Remove the left side heat shroud from the exhaust manifold. Remove any thermactor system parts that will interfere with manifold removal. Disconnect the choke heat tube at the carburetor.

3. Disconnect the exhaust pipes

from the exhaust manifolds. Remove the mounting nuts from exhaust manifold studs. Remove the exhaust manifolds.

4. Install in the reverse order using new exhaust pipe to manifold gaskets.

Rocker Arm/Rocker Shaft

REMOVAL & INSTALLATION

4-122 (2.0L)
4-140 (2.3L)

NOTE: A special tool is required to compress the lash adjuster.

1. Remove the valve cover and associated parts as required.
2. Rotate the camshaft so that the base circle of the cam is against the cam follower you intend to remove.
3. Remove the retaining spring from the cam follower, if so equipped.
4. Using special tool T74P-6565-B or a valve spring compressor tool, collapse the lash adjuster and/or depress the valve spring, as necessary, and slide the cam follower over the lash adjuster and out from under the camshaft.
5. Install the cam follower in the reverse order of removal. Make sure that the lash adjuster is collapsed and released before rotating the cam shaft.

4-134 (2.2L) Diesel

1. Remove the rocker arm (valve) cover.
2. Remove the rocker arm shaft mounting bolts, two turns at a time for each bolt. Start at the ends of the rocker shaft and work toward the middle.
3. Lift the rocker arm shaft assembly from the engine. Remove the pin and washer from each end of the shaft. Slide the rocker arms, springs and supports off the shaft. Keep all parts in order or label them for position.
4. Clean and inspect all parts, replace as necessary.
5. Assemble the rocker shaft parts in reverse order of removal. Be sure the oil holes in the shaft are pointed downward. Reinstall the rocker shaft assembly on the engine.

NOTE: Lubricate all parts with motor oil before installation.

6. Clean all mounting surfaces, use a new valve cover gasket and valve cover.

VALVE ADJUSTMENT

6-173 (2.8L)

1. Remove the air cleaner assembly and disconnect the negative battery cable.
2. Remove the Thermactor air bypass valve and its mounting bracket.
3. Remove the two engine lifting eyes; remove the alternator drive belt. loosen the alternator mounting bolts and swing the alternator outward toward the fender.
4. Remove the plug wires and remove the rocker covers.
5. When removing the rocker covers, remove or reposition any wires or hoses which block the removal of the rocker covers.
6. Torque the rocker arm support bolts to 46 ft.lb.
7. Reconnect the battery cable, place the transmission in Neutral (manual) or Park (automatic), and apply the parking brake.
8. Place a finger on the adjusting screw of the intake valve rocker arm for cylinder No.5. Cylinder numbering is shown under Firing Order at the start of the section. Valve arrangement, from front to rear, on the left bank is I-E-E-I-E-I; on the right it is I-E-I-E-E-I. You will be able to feel the rocker arm begin to move.
9. Use a remote starter switch or manual means to turn the engine until you can just feel the valve begin to open. Now the engine is in position to adjust the intake and exhaust valves on the No. 1 cylinder.
10. Adjust the No. 1 cylinder intake valve so that a 0.014" feeler gauge has a slight drag while a 0.015" feeler gauge is a tight fit. To decrease lash, turn the adjusting screw clockwise; to increase lash, turn the adjusting screw counterclockwise. There are no locknuts to tighten; the adjusting screws are self-locking.

CAUTION

Do not use a step-type, "go-no go" feeler gauge. When checking lash, insert the feeler gauge and move it parallel with the crankshaft. Do not move it in and out perpendicular with the crankshaft; this will give an erroneous feel which will result in overtightened valves.

11. Adjust the exhaust valve the same way so that a 0.016" feeler gauge has a slight drag, while a 0.017" gauge is a tight fit.
12. The rest of the valves are adjusted in the same way, in their firing order (1-4-2-5-3-6), by positioning the engine according to the following chart:
13. Remove all the old gasket material from the cylinder heads and rocker cover gasket surfaces, and disconnect

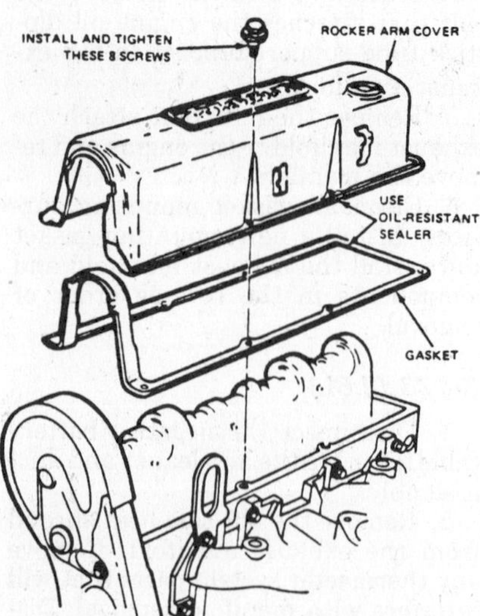

Typical 4 cylinder rocker arm cover installation

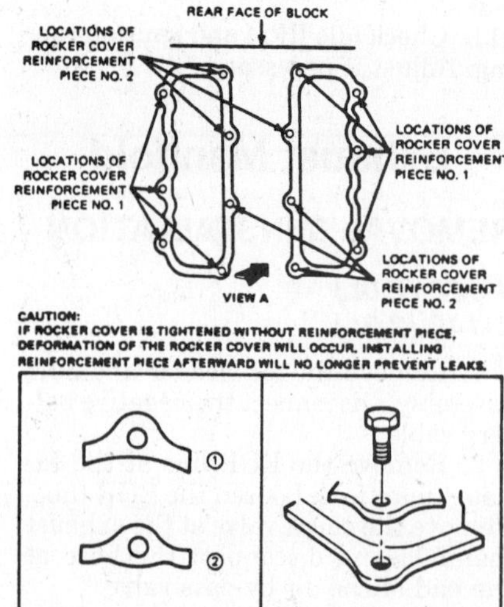

Rocker arm cover reinforcement washer location—6-173 engine

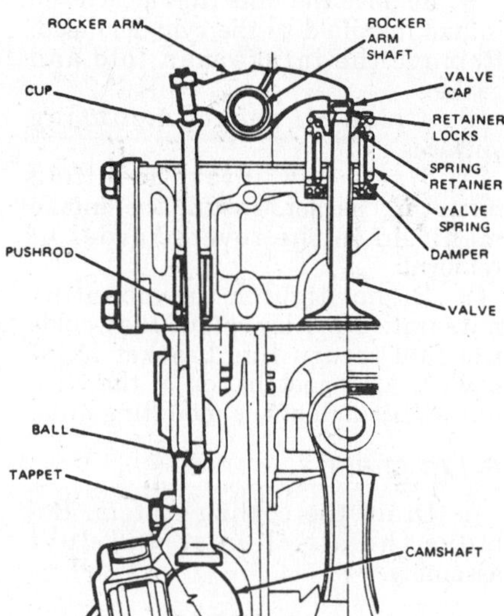

4-134 diesel engine valve train assembly

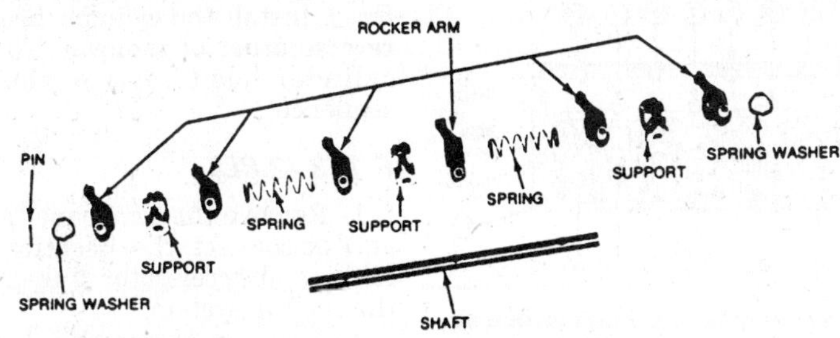

Rocker arm shaft assembly disassembled—6-173 engine

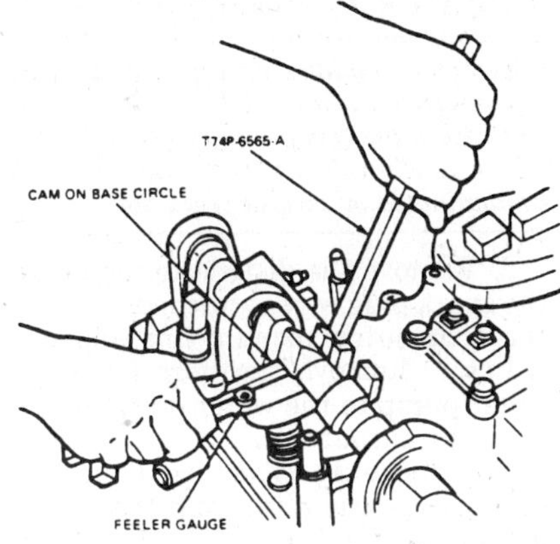

Using the special tool to collapse the lash adjuster

the negative cable from the battery.

14. Remove the spark plug wires and reinstall the rocker arm covers.
15. Reinstall any hoses and wires which were removed.
16. Reinstall the spark plug wires, the alternator drive belt, and the Thermactor air bypass valve and its mounting bracket.
17. Reconnect the battery cable, replace the air cleaner assembly, start the engine, and check for leaks.

HYDRAULIC VALVE LIFTER INSPECTION

NOTE: The lifters used on diesel engines require a special test fluid, kerosene is not satisfactory.

Remove the lifters from their bores and remove any gum and varnish with safe solvent. Check the lifters for concave wear. If the bottom of the lifter is worn concave or flat, replace the lifter. Lifters are built with a convex bottom, flatness indicates wear. If a worn lifter is detected, carefully check the camshaft for wear.

To test lifter leak down, submerge the lifter in a container of kerosene. Chuck a used pushrod or its equivalent into a drill press. Position the container of kerosene so the pushrod acts on the lifter plunger. Pump the lifter with the drill press until resistance increases. Pump several more times to bleed any air from the lifter. Apply very firm, constant pressure to the lifter and observe the rate which fluid bleeds out of the lifter. If the lifter bleeds down very quickly (less than 15 seconds), the lifter should be replaced. If the time exceeds 60 seconds, the lifter is sticking and should be cleaned or replaced. If the lifter is operating properly (leak down time 15-60 seconds) and not worn, lubricate and reinstall in engine.

NOTE: Always inspect the valve pushrods for wear, straightness and oil blockage. Damaged pushrods will cause erratic valve operation.

Air Conditioning Compressor

REMOVAL AND INSTALLATION

Follow the procedures outlined in ROUTINE MAINTENANCE to discharge the A/C system. Loosen the compressor mounting bolts and remove the drive belt. Disconnect the refrigerant lines and cap them to prevent the entry of dirt or moisture into the system. Remove the mounting bolts and lift the compressor off the engine. Installation is the reverse of removal. Recharge the A/C system as outlined in ROUTINE MAINTENANCE and adjust the drive belt tension.

Cylinder Head

REMOVAL & INSTALLATION

4-122 (2.0L)
4-140 (2.3L)

1. Drain the cooling system. Disconnect the negative battery cable.

CAUTION

When draining the coolant, keep in mind that cats and dogs are attracted by the ethylene glycol antifreeze, and are quite likely to drink any that is left in an uncovered container or in puddles on the ground. This will prove fatal in sufficient quantity. Always drain the coolant into a sealable container. Coolant should be reused unless it is contaminated or several years old.

2. Remove the air cleaner.
3. Remove the valve cover.

NOTE: On models with air conditioning, remove the mounting bolts and the drive belt, and position the compressor, with hoses attached, out of the way. Remove the compressor upper mounting bracket from the cylinder head.

CAUTION

If the compressor refrigerant lines do not have enough slack to permit repositioning of the compressor without first disconnecting the refrigerant lines, the air conditioning system will have to be evacuated. See ROUTINE MAINTENANCE.

4. Remove the intake and exhaust manifolds from the head.
5. Remove the camshaft drive belt cover. Note the location of the belt cover attaching screws that have rubber grommets.
6. Loosen the drive belt tensioner and remove the bolt.
7. Remove the water outlet elbow from the cylinder head with the hose attached.
8. Remove the cylinder head attaching bolts.
9. Remove the cylinder head from the engine.
10. Clean all gasket material and carbon from the top of the cylinder block and pistons and from the bottom of the cylinder head.

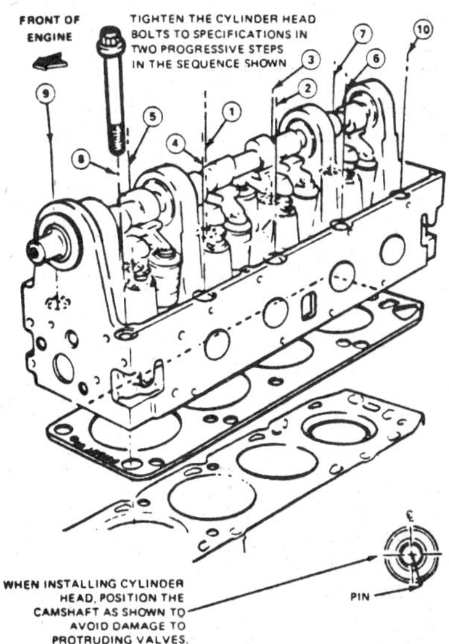

4-122, 140 engines, cylinder head installation

11. Position a new cylinder head gasket on the engine and place the head on the engine.

NOTE: If you encounter difficulty in positioning the cylinder head on the engine block, it may be necessary to install guide studs in the block to correctly align the head and the block. To fabricate guide studs, obtain two new cylinder head bolts and cut their heads off with a hack saw. Install the bolts in the holes in the engine block which correspond with cylinder head bolt holes Nos. 3 and 4, as identified in the cylinder head bolt tightening sequence illustration. Then, install the head gasket and head over the bolts. Install the cylinder head attaching bolts, replacing the studs with the original head bolts.

12. Using a torque wrench, tighten the head bolts in proper sequence.
13. Install the camshaft drive belt.
14. Install the camshaft drive belt cover and its attaching bolts. Make sure the rubber grommets are installed on the bolts. Tighten the bolts to 6-13 fft.lb.
15. Install the water outlet elbow and a new gasket on the engine and tighten the attaching bolts to 12-15 ft.lb.
16. Install the intake and exhaust manifolds.
17. Assemble the rest of the components in reverse order of removal.

4-134 (2.2L) Diesel

1. Disconnect the ground cables from both batteries.
2. Mark the hood hinges for realignment on installation and remove the hood. Drain the cooling system.

CAUTION

When draining the coolant, keep in mind that cats and dogs are attracted by the ethylene glycol antifreeze, and are quite likely to drink any that is left in an uncovered container or in puddles on the ground. This will prove fatal in sufficient quantity. Always drain the coolant into a sealable container. Coolant should be reused unless it is contaminated or several years old.

3. Disconnect the breather hose from the valve cover and remove the intake hose and breather hose from the air cleaner and intake manifold.
4. Remove the heater hose bracket from the valve cover and exhaust manifold. Disconnect the heater hoses from the water pump and thermostat housing and position tube assembly out of the way.
5. Remove the vacuum pump support brace from the pump bracket and cylinder head.

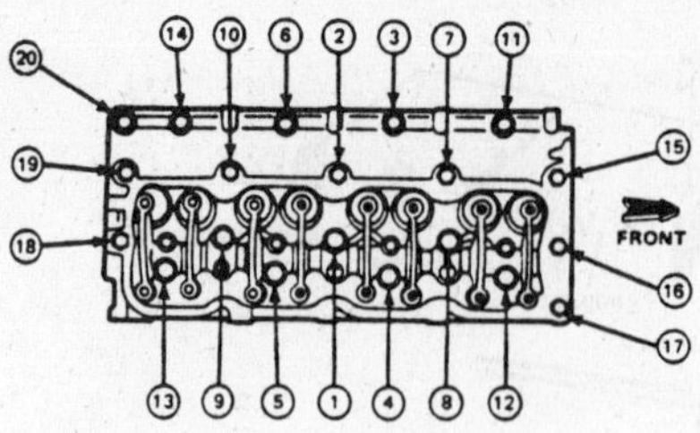

4-134 diesel engine, head bolt torque sequence

6. Loosen and remove the alternator and vacuum pump drive belts. Loosen and remove the A/C compressor and/or power steering drive belt.
7. Disconnect the brake booster vacuum hose and remove the vacuum pump.
8. Disconnect the exhaust pipe from the exhaust manifold. Disconnect the coolant thermoswitch and coolant temperature sender wiring harness.
9. Disconnect and remove the fuel injection lines from the injector nozzles and pump. Cap all lines and fittings to prevent dirt from entering the system.
10. Disconnect the engine wire harness from the alternator, the glow plug harness and dropping resistor and position the harness out of the way.
11. Disconnect the fuel lines from both sides of the fuel heater. Remove the fuel filter assembly from the mounting bracket and position out of the way with the fuel line attached.
12. Loosen the lower No.3 intake port nut and the bolt on the injection pump; disconnect the lower fuel return line from the intake manifold stud and the upper fuel return line.
13. If equipped with power steering, remove the bolt that attaches the pump rear support bracket to the cylinder head.
14. Remove the upper radiator hose. Disconnect the by-pass hose from the thermostat housing.
15. Remove the A/C compressor and position out of the way with the lines still attached.

CAUTION

Do not disconnect the compressor lines unless the proper tools are on hand to discharge the system and you are familiar with the procedure.

16. Remove the valve cover, rocker arm shaft assembly and the pushrods. Identify the pushrods and keep them in order for return to their original position.
17. Remove the cylinder head attaching bolts, starting at the ends of the head, working alternately toward the center. Remove the cylinder head from the truck.
18. Clean all gasket mounting surfaces. Install the cylinder head in the reverse order of removal. Torque the cylinder head bolts in the proper sequence.

6-173 (2.8L)

1. Remove the air cleaner assembly and disconnect the negative battery cable, and accelerator linkage. Drain the cooling system.

CAUTION

When draining the coolant, keep in mind that cats and dogs are attracted by the ethylene glycol antifreeze, and are quite likely to drink any that is left in an uncovered container or in puddles on the ground. This will prove fatal in sufficient quantity. Always drain the coolant into a sealable container. Coolant should be reused unless it is contaminated or several years old.

2. Remove the distributor cap with the spark plug wires attached. Remove the distributor vacuum line and distributor. Remove the hose from the water pump to the water outlet which is on the carburetor.
3. Remove the valve covers, fuel line and filter, carburetor, and the intake manifold.
4. Remove the rocker arm shaft and oil baffles. Remove the pushrods, keeping them in the proper sequence for installation.

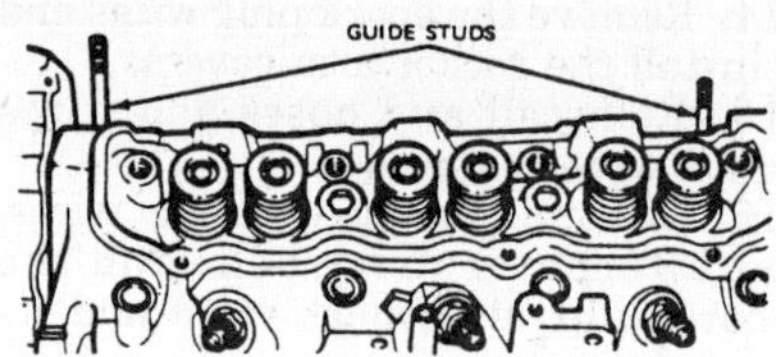

Cylinder head alignment studs—6-173 engine

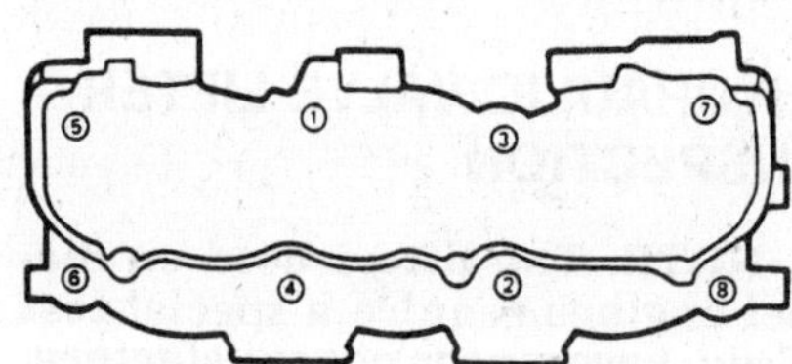

Cylinder head torque sequence—6-173 engine

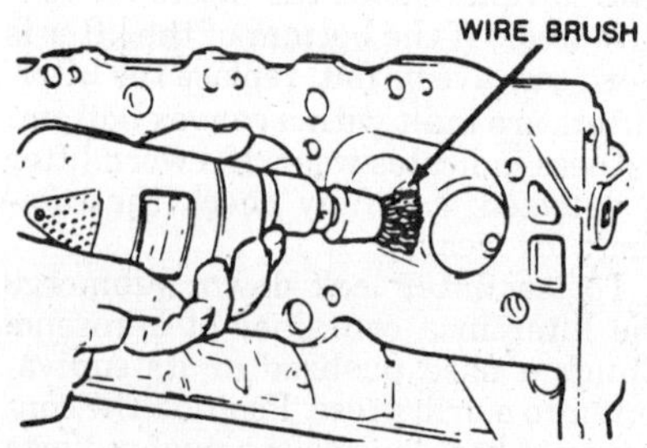

Remove the carbon from the cylinder head with a wire brush and electric drill

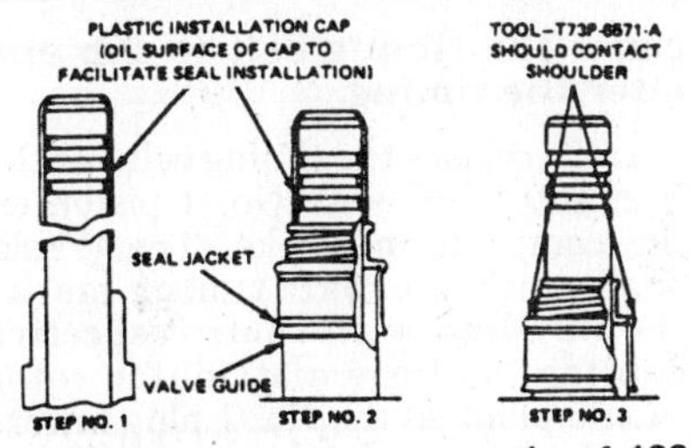

Installing the valve stem seals—4-122, 140 engines

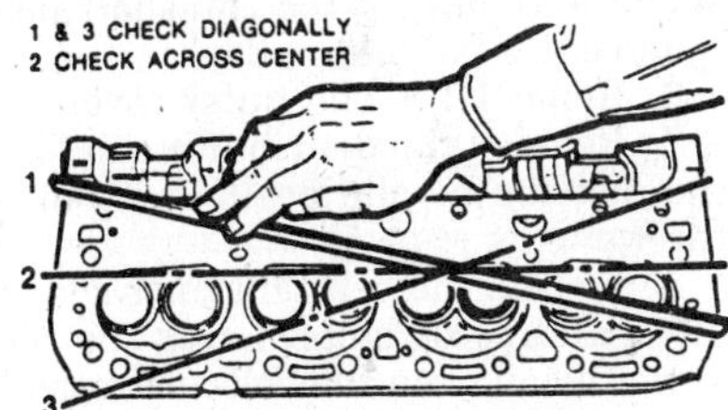

Check the cylinder head for warpage

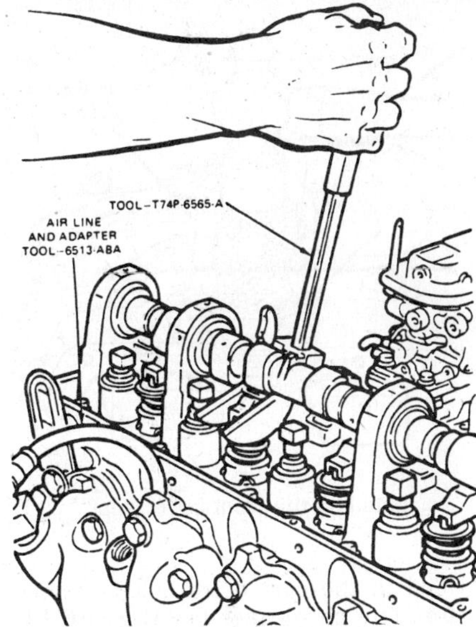

Compressing the valve spring on the 4-122, 140 engines

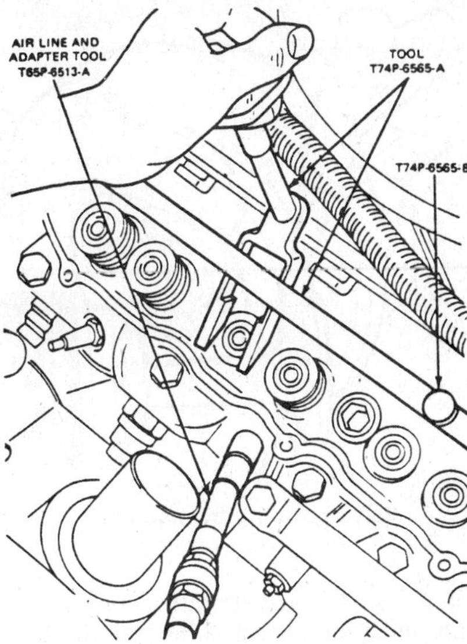

Compressing the valve spring with the cylinder head on the 6-173 engine

5. Remove the exhaust manifold.
6. Remove the cylinder head retaining bolts and remove the cylinder heads and gaskets.
7. Remove all gasket material and carbon from the engine block and cylinder heads.
8. Place the head gaskets on the engine block. Pay attention, the left and right gaskets are not interchangeable.
9. Install guide studs in the engine block. Install the cylinder head assembles on the engine block one at a time. Tighten the cylinder head bolts in sequence.
10. Install the intake and exhaust manifolds.
11. Install the pushrods in the proper sequence. Install the oil baffles and the rocker arm shaft assemblies. Adjust the valve clearances.
12. Install the valve covers with new gaskets.
13. Install the distributor and set the ignition timing.
14. Install the carburetor and the distributor cap with the spark plug wires.
15. Connect the accelerator linkage, fuel line, with fuel filter installed, and distributor vacuum line to the carburetor. Fill the cooling system.

Timing Cover and Belt

REMOVAL & INSTALLATION

4-122 (2.0L) 4-140 (2.3L)

The correct installation and adjustment of the camshaft drive belt is mandatory if the engine is to run properly. The camshaft controls the opening of the engine valves through coordination of the movement of the camshaft and the crankshaft. When any given piston is on the intake stroke the corresponding intake valve must be open to admit air/fuel mixture into the cylinder. When the same piston is on the compression and power strokes, both valves in that cylinder must be closed. When the piston is on the exhaust stroke, the exhaust valve for that cylinder must be open. If the opening and closing of the valves is not coordinated with the movements of the pistons, the engine will run very poorly, if at all.

The camshaft drive belt also turns the engine auxiliary shaft. The distributor is driven by the engine auxiliary

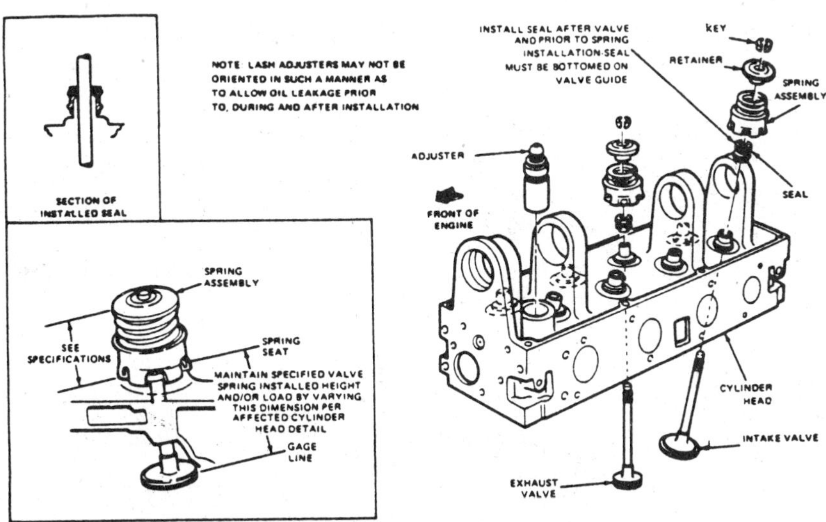

Valve train components—4-122, 140 engines

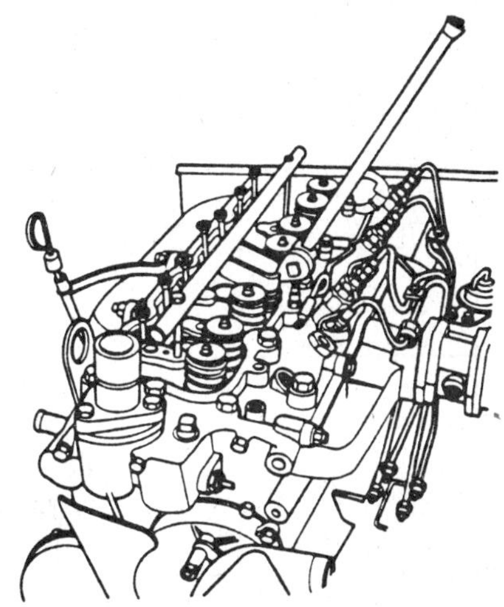

Compressing the valve spring assembly—4-134 diesel engine

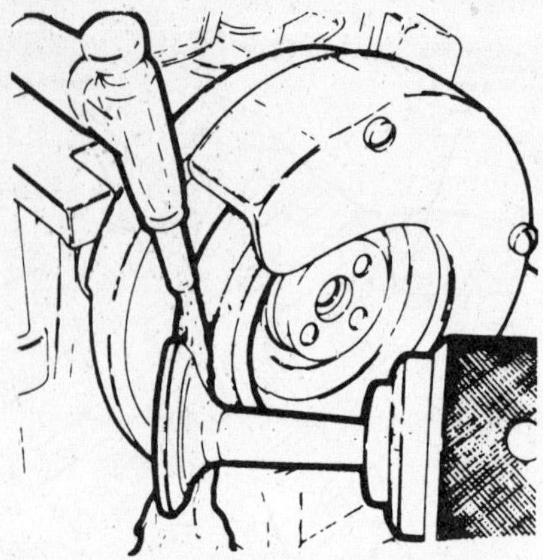

Valve grinding by machine

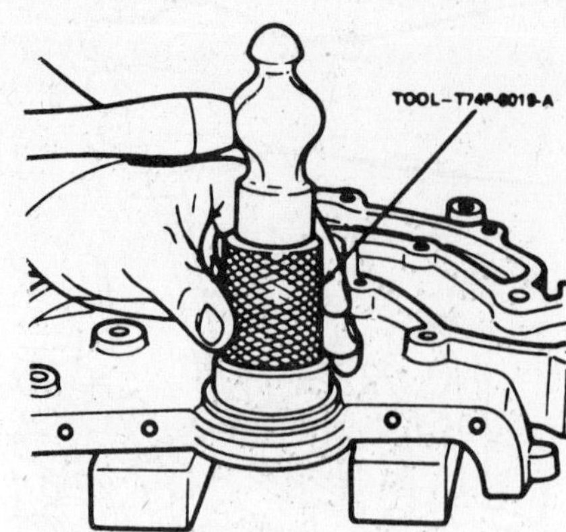

Installing the front cover seal

shaft. Since the distributor controls ignition timing, the auxiliary shaft must be coordinated with the camshaft and the crankshaft, because both valves in any given cylinder must be closed and the piston in that cylinder near the top of the compression stroke when the spark plug fires.

Due to this complex interrelationship between the camshaft, the crankshaft and the auxiliary shaft, the cogged pulleys on each component must be aligned when the camshaft drive belt is installed.

Should the camshaft drive belt jump timing by a tooth or two, the engine could still run; but very poorly. To visually check for correct timing of the crankshaft, auxiliary shaft, and the camshaft there is an access plug provided in the cam drive belt cover so that the camshaft timing can be checked without removing the drive belt cover.

1. Remove the access plug.
2. Turn the crankshaft until the timing marks on the crankshaft indicate TDC.
3. Make sure that the timing mark on the camshaft drive sprocket is aligned with the pointer on the inner belt cover. Also, the rotor of the distributor must align with the No. 1 cylinder firing position.

WARNING: Never turn the crankshaft of any of the overhead cam engines in the opposite direction of normal rotation. Backward rotation of the crankshaft may cause the timing belt to slip and alter the timing.

4. To replace the timing belt, set the engine to TDC with No. 1 piston on the compression stroke. The crankshaft and camshaft timing marks should align with their respective pointers and the distributor rotor should point to the No. 1 plug tower.
5. Loosen the adjustment bolts on the alternator and accessories and remove the drive belts. To provide clearance for removing the camshaft belt, remove the fan and pulley.
6. Remove the belt outer cover.
7. Remove the distributor cap from the distributor and position it out of the way.
8. Loosen the belt tensioner adjustment and pivot bolts. Lever the tensioner away from the belt and retighten the adjustment bolt to hold it away.
9. Remove the crankshaft bolt and pulley. Remove the belt guide behind the pulley.
10. Remove the camshaft drive belt.
11. Install the new belt over the crankshaft pulley first, then counterclockwise over the auxiliary shaft sprocket and the camshaft sprocket. Adjust the belt fore and aft so that it is centered on the sprockets.
12. Loosen the tensioner adjustment bolt, allowing it to spring back against the belt.
13. Remove the spark plugs and rotate the crankshaft two complete turns in the normal rotation direction to remove any belt slack. Turn the crankshaft until the timing check marks are lined up. If the timing has slipped, remove the belt and repeat the procedure.
14. Tighten the tensioner adjustment bolt to 14-21 ft.lb., and the pivot bolt to 28-40 ft.lb.
15. Replace the belt guide and crankshaft pulley, distributor cap, belt outer cover, fan and pulley, drive belts and accessories. Adjust the accessory drive belt tension. Start the engine and check the ignition timing.

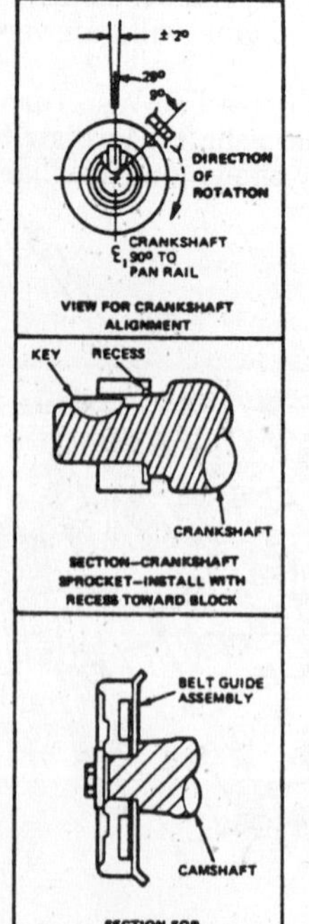

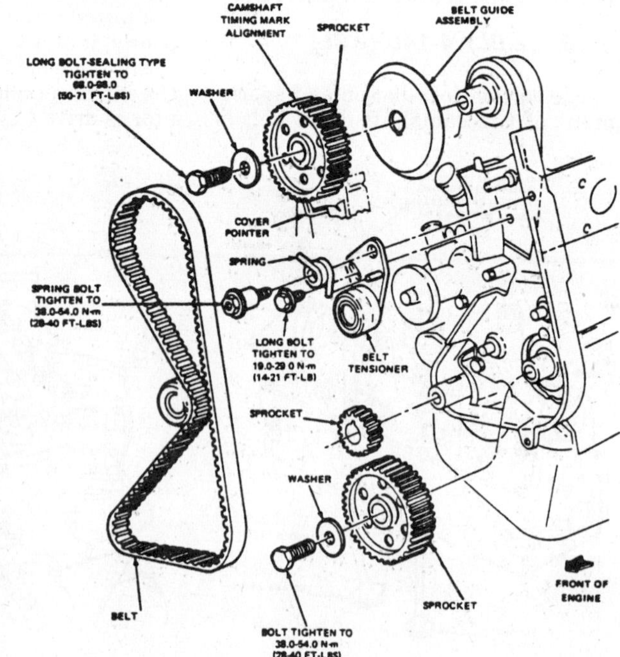

4-122, 140 engine camshaft drivetrain installation

Timing Cover/Seal and Timing Chain/Gears

REMOVAL & INSTALLATION

4-134 (2.2L) Diesel

1. Bring the engine to No. 1 piston at TDC on the compression stroke.
2. Disconnect the ground cables from the batteries. Drain the cooling system.

CAUTION

When draining the coolant, keep in mind that cats and dogs are attracted by the ethylene glycol antifreeze, and are quite likely to

drink any that is left in an uncovered container or in puddles on the ground. This will prove fatal in sufficient quantity. Always drain the coolant into a sealable container. Coolant should be reused unless it is contaminated or several years old.

3. Remove the radiator fan shroud and cooling fan. Drain the engine oil from the crankcase.
4. Loosen the idler pulley and remove the A/C compressor belt. Remove the power steering belt. Remove the power steering pump and mounting bracket, position out of the way with the hoses attached.
5. Loosen and remove the alternator and vacuum pump drive belts.
6. Remove the water pump. Using a suitable puller, remove the crankshaft pulley.
7. Remove the nuts and bolts retaining the timing case cover to the engine block. Remove the timing case cover.
8. Remove the engine oil pan.
9. Verify that all timing marks are aligned. Rotate the engine, if necessary, to align marks.
10. Remove the bolt attaching the camshaft gear and remove the washer and friction gear.
11. Remove the bolt attaching the injection pump gear and remove the washer and friction gear.
12. Install Ford tool T83T6306A or equivalent on to the camshaft drive gear and remove the gear. Attach the puller to the injection pump drive gear and remove the gear.
13. Remove the nuts attaching the idler gears after marking reference points on the idler gears for reinstallation position. Remove the idler gear assemblies.
14. Remove the nuts attaching the injection pump to the timing gear case. Support the injection pump in position.
15. Remove the bolts that attaching the timing gear case to the engine block and remove the case if necessary.
16. Clean all gasket mounting surfaces. Clean all parts, replace as necessary.
17. Remove the old oil seal from the front cover and replace.
18. Position the timing gear cover case with a new mounting gasket and install.
19. Install the timing gears as follows: Verify that the crankshaft and the right idler pulley timing marks align and install the right idler gear assembly. Install the camshaft gear so that the timing marks align with the timing mark on the right idler gear. Install the left idler gear assembly so that the timing marks align with the timing mark on the right idler gear. Install the injection pump gear so that

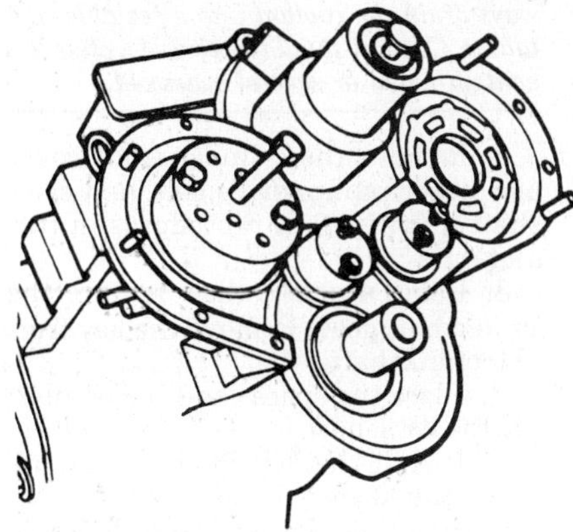

Removing the camshaft gear—4-134 diesel engine

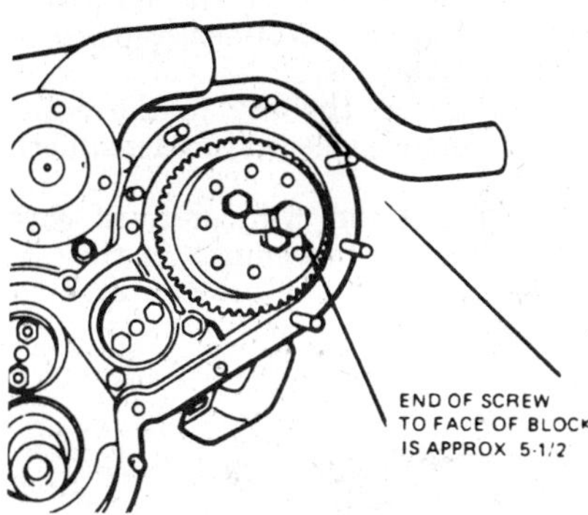

Removing the injection pump gear—4-134 diesel engine

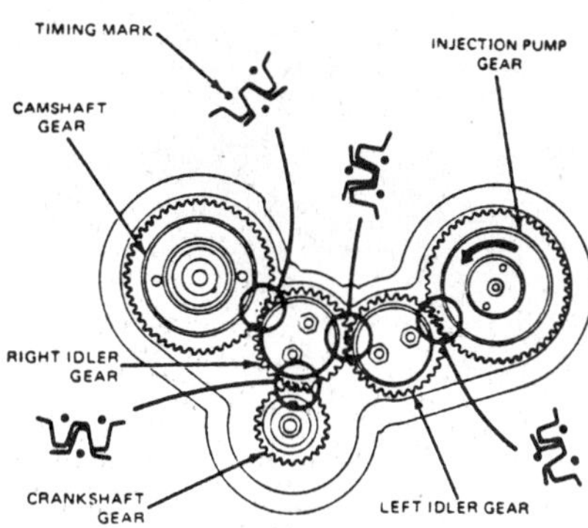

Timing gear alignment—4-134 diesel engine

the timing marks align with the timing mark on the left idler gear. Install all friction gears, washers, nuts and bolts on the gears.
20. Install the timing case covers using a new mounting gasket.
21. Install the remaining components in the reverse order of removal.

6-173 (2.8L) V6

FRONT COVER

1. Disconnect negative battery cable. Remove the oil pan.
2. Drain the coolant. Remove the radiator and any other parts to provide necessary clearance.

CAUTION

When draining the coolant, keep in mind that cats and dogs are attracted by the ethylene glycol antifreeze, and are quite likely to drink any that is left in an uncovered container or in puddles on the ground. This will prove fatal in sufficient quantity. Always drain the coolant into a sealable container. Coolant should be reused unless it is contaminated or several years old.

3. If equipped with air conditioning, unbolt the compressor and bracket and move them aside; do not disconnect the A/C lines.
4. Remove alternator, thermactor, and drive belt(s).
5. Remove the fan.
6. Remove the drive pulley from the crankshaft.
7. Remove the front cover retaining bolts. If necessary, tap cover lightly with a plastic hammer to break gasket seal. Remove front cover. If front cover plate gasket needs replacement, remove two screws and remove plate. If necessary, remove guide sleeves from cylinder block.
8. Clean the mating surfaces of gasket material. Apply sealing compound to the gasket surfaces on the cylinder block and back side of the front cover plate. Position the gasket and front cover plate on cylinder block. Temporarily install four front cover screws to position the gasket and cover plate in place. Install and tighten two cover plate attaching bolts, then remove four screws that were temporarily installed.
9. If removed, fit new seal rings to the guide sleeves and, with no sealer used, insert the sleeves in the cylinder block with the chamfered side of the sleeve toward the front cover.
10. Apply sealing compound to front cover gasket surface. Place the gasket in position on front cover.
11. Place the front cover on the engine and start all retaining screws two or three turns. Center the cover by inserting tool in the oil seal.
12. Tighten the front cover attaching screws to specifications.
13. Install the belt drive pulley and tighten the attaching bolt to specifications.
14. Install the oil pan.
15. Install the water pump, water hose, A/C compressor, alternator and drive belt(s). Adjust the drive belt tension to specifications.
16. Fill the cooling system to the proper level with the specified coolant.
17. Operate the engine at fast idle speed and check for coolant and oil leaks.

NOTE: If the guide sleeves were removed, install them with new seal rings but do not use sealing compound.

FRONT COVER SEAL

1. Support the front cover to prevent damage while driving out the seal.
2. Drive out the seal from the front cover.
3. Support the front cover to prevent damage while installing the seal.
4. Coat the new front cover oil seal with a light grease. Install the new seal in the front cover.

GEARS

1. Drain the cooling system and the crankcase. Remove the oil pan and the radiator.

CAUTION

When draining the coolant, keep in mind that cats and dogs are attracted by the ethylene glycol antifreeze, and are quite likely to drink any that is left in an uncovered container or in puddles on the ground. This will prove fatal in sufficient quantity. Always drain the coolant into a sealable container. Coolant should be reused unless it is contaminated or several years old.

2. Remove the cylinder front cover and water pump, drive belt, and camshaft following the procedures in this section.
3. Using a gear puller, remove the crankshaft gear. Remove the key from the crankshaft.
4. Place the spacer and thrust plate on the camshaft.
5. Install the key in the camshaft. Align the keyway in the gear with the key, then slide the gear onto the shaft, making sure that it seats tight against the spacer.
6. Check the camshaft end play. If not within specifications, replace the thrust plate.
7. Position the key in the crankshaft. Align the keyway and install the gear.
8. Install the cylinder front cover following the procedures in this section. Replace the oil pan and the radiator.
9. Fill the cooling system and crankcase.
10. Start the engine and adjust the ignition timing. Operate the engine at fast idle and check all hose connections and gaskets for leaks.

CAMSHAFT ENDPLAY MEASUREMENT

The camshaft gears used on some engines are easily damaged if pried upon while the valve train load is on the camshaft. Loosen rocker arm nuts or rocker arm shaft support bolts before checking camshaft endplay.

Push camshaft toward rear of engine, install and zero a dial indicator, then pry between camshaft gear and block to pull the camshaft forward. If endplay is excessive, check for correct installation of spacer. If spacer is installed correctly, then replace thrust plate.

MEASURING TIMING GEAR BACKLASH

Use a dial indicator installed on block to measure timing gear backlash. Hold gear firmly against the block while making measurement. If excessive backlash exists, replace both gears.

Camshaft

REMOVAL & INSTALLATION

NOTE: When installing the camshaft refer to the proceeding section for gear alignment.

4-122 (2.0L)
4-140 (2.3L)

NOTE: The following procedure covers camshaft removal and installation with the cylinder head on or off the engine. If the cylinder head has been removed start at Step 9.

1. Drain the cooling system. Remove the air cleaner assembly and disconnect the negative battery cable.

CAUTION

When draining the coolant, keep in mind that cats and dogs are attracted by the ethylene glycol antifreeze, and are quite likely to drink any that is left in an uncovered container or in puddles on the ground. This will prove fatal in sufficient quantity. Always drain the coolant into a sealable container. Coolant should be reused unless it is contaminated or several years old.

2. Remove the spark plug wires from the plugs, disconnect the retain-

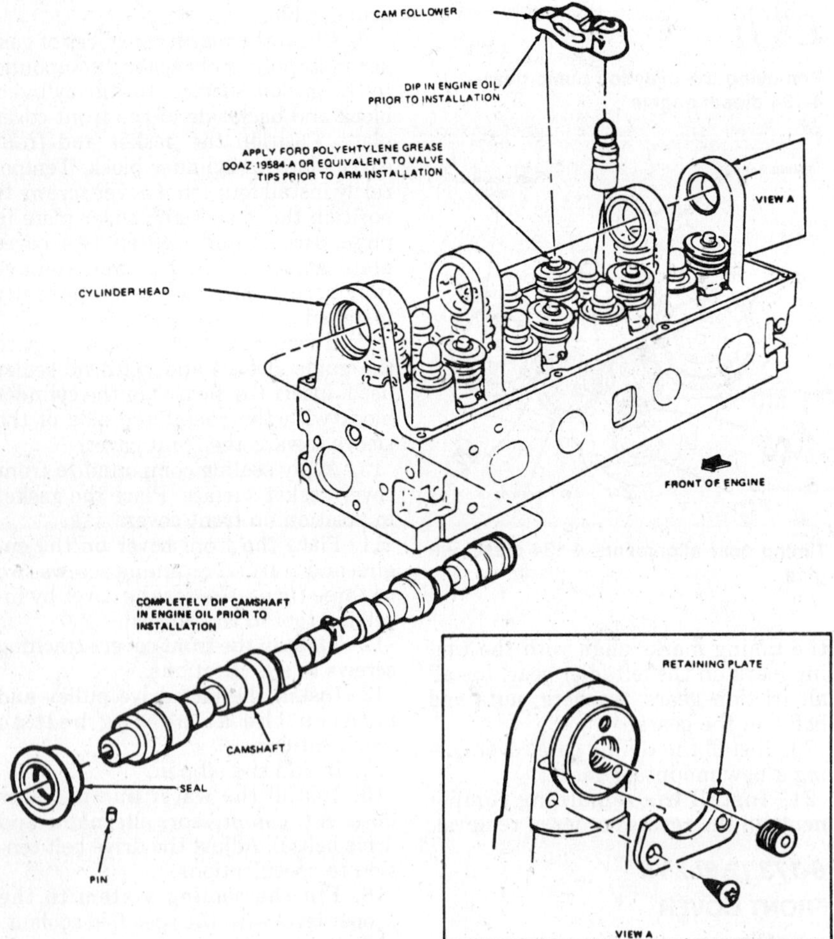

4-122, 140 engine camshaft installation

er from the valve cover and position the wires out of the way. Disconnect rubber vacuum lines as necessary.

3. Remove all drive belts. Remove the alternator mounting bracket-to-cylinder head mounting bolts, position bracket and alternator out of the way.

4. Disconnect and remove the upper radiator hose. Disconnect the radiator shroud.

5. Remove the fan blades and water pump pulley and fan shroud. Remove cam belt and valve covers.

6. Align engine timing marks at TDC for No. 1 cylinder. Remove cam drive belt.

7. Jack up the front of the vehicle and support on jackstands. Remove the front motor mount bolts. Disconnect the lower radiator hose from the radiator. Disconnect and plug the automatic transmission cooler lines.

8. Position a piece of wood on a floor jack and raise the engine carefully as far as it will go. Place blocks of wood between the engine mounts and crossmember pedestals.

9. Remove the rocker arms.

10. Remove the camshaft drive gear and belt guide using a suitable puller. Remove the front oil seal with a sheet metal screw and slide hammer.

11. Remove the camshaft retainer located on the rear mounting stand by unbolting the two bolts.

12. Remove the camshaft by carefully withdrawing toward the front of the engine. Caution should be used to prevent damage to cam bearings, lobes and journals.

13. Check the camshaft journals and lobes for wear. Inspect the cam bearings, if worn (unless the proper bearing installing tool is on hand), the cylinder head must be removed for new bearings to be installed by a machine shop.

14. Cam installation is in the reverse order of removal. See following notes.

NOTE: Coat the camshaft with heavy SF oil before sliding it into the cylinder head. Install a new front seal. Apply a coat of sealer or teflon tape to the cam drive gear bolt before installation.

After any procedure requiring removal of the rocker arms, each lash adjuster must be fully collapsed after assembly, then released. This must be done before the camshaft is turned.

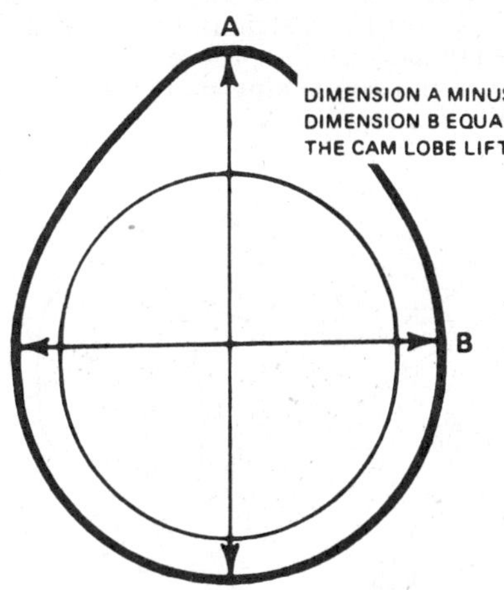

Checking OHC camshaft lobe lift

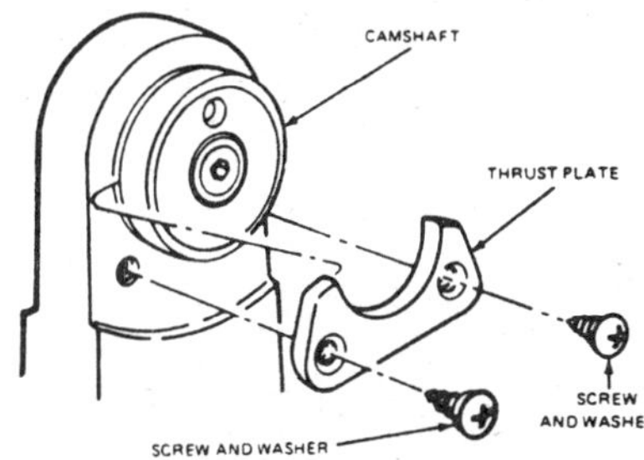

Camshaft thrust plate installation—4-122, 140 engines

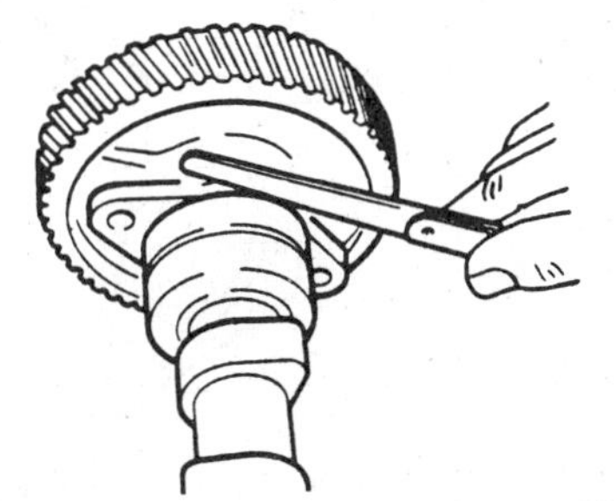

Checking the camshaft end play—4-134 diesel engine

4-134 (2.2L) Diesel

1. Ford recommends that the engine be removed from the vehicle when camshaft replacement is necessary.

2. With the engine removed; remove the valve cover, rocker arms and shaft assembly and the pushrods. Remove the lifters, identify and keep in order if they are to be reused.

3. Remove the front timing case cover and camshaft gear.

4. Remove the engine oil pan and oil pump.

5. Remove the camshaft thrust plate and the camshaft. Take care when removing the camshaft not to damage lobes or bearings.

6. Apply oil to the camshaft bearings and bearing journals. Apply Polyethylene grease to the camshaft lobes and install the camshaft into the engine.

7. Reinstall components in the reverse order of removal.

6-173 (2.8L)

1. Disconnect the negative battery cable from the battery. Bring engine to No. 1 cylinder at TDC (top dead center) on the compression stroke. Drain the coolant and remove the radiator, fan, spacer, water pump pulley and the drive belt.

CAUTION

When draining the coolant, keep in mind that cats and dogs are attracted by the ethylene glycol antifreeze, and are quite likely to drink any that is left in an uncovered container or in puddles on the ground. This will prove fatal in sufficient quantity. Always drain the coolant into a sealable container. Coolant should be reused unless it is contaminated or several years old.

2. Remove the distributor cap with spark plug wires as an assembly. Remove the distributor vacuum line, distributor, alternator, thermactor, rocker arm covers, fuel line and filter, carburetor, EGR tube, and intake manifold. Remove the spark plug wire boots.

3. Drain the crankcase. Remove the rocker arm and the shaft assemblies. Lift out the pushrods and place in a marked rack so they can be reinstalled in the same location.

4. Remove the oil pan.

5. Remove the drive sprocket attaching bolt and slide the sprocket off the end of the shaft.

6. Remove the engine front cover and water pump as an assembly.

7. Remove the camshaft gear retaining bolt and slide the gear off the camshaft.

8. Remove the camshaft thrust plate and the screws.

9. Using a magnet, remove the valve lifters.

10. Carefully pull the camshaft from the block, avoiding any damage to the camshaft bearings. Remove the camshaft gear key and spacer ring.

11. Oil the camshaft journals with gear oil or assembly lube and apply it to the cam lobes.

12. Install the camshaft in the block, carefully avoiding damage to the bearing surfaces.

13. Install the spacer ring with the chamfered side toward the camshaft. Insert the camshaft key and install the thrust plate so that it covers the main oil gallery. Torque the attaching screws to specifications.

14. Check the camshaft for the specified end-play. The spacer ring and thrust plate are available in two thicknesses to permit adjusting the end-play.

15. Turn the camshaft and the crankshaft as necessary to align the timing marks and install the camshaft gear. Install the retaining washer and bolt and tighten to specifications.

16. Install the valve lifters to their original locations.
17. Install the engine front cover and water pump as an assembly.
18. Install the belt drive pulley and secure with washer and retaining bolt. Tighten the bolt to specifications.
19. Install the oil pan.
20. Apply a light grease to both ends of the pushrods. Install the valve pushrods in their original locations.
21. Install the intake manifold.
22. Install the oil baffles and the rocker arm and shaft assemblies. Tighten the rocker arm stand bolts to specifications. Adjust the valves to specified cold setting.
23. Install the water pump pulley, fan spacer, fan, and the drive belt. Adjust the belt tension to specifications. Install the carburetor, EGR tube, fuel line and filter, alternator, thermactor, distributor, distributor vacuum line, and distributor cap and wires. Install the radiator. Fill the cooling system to the proper level with the specified coolant. Adjust the ignition timing.
24. Install the rocker arm covers.
25. Run the engine and check the idle speed.
26. Run the engine at fast idle speed and check for coolant and oil leaks.

Auxiliary Shaft

REMOVAL & INSTALLATION

1. Remove the camshaft drive belt cover.
2. Remove the drive belt. Remove the auxiliary shaft sprocket. A puller may be necessary to remove the sprocket.
3. Remove the distributor and fuel pump.
4. Remove the auxiliary shaft cover and thrust plate.
5. Withdraw the auxiliary shaft from the block.

NOTE: The distributor drive gear and the fuel pump eccentric on the auxiliary shaft must not be allowed to touch the auxiliary shaft bearings during removal and installation. Completely coat the shaft with oil before sliding it into place.

6. Slide the auxiliary shaft into the housing and insert the thrust plate to hold the shaft.
7. Install a new gasket and auxiliary shaft cover.

NOTE: The auxiliary shaft cover and cylinder front cover share a gasket. Cut off the old gasket around the cylinder cover and use half of the new gasket on the auxiliary shaft cover.

8. Fit a new gasket into the fuel pump and install the pump.
9. Insert the distributor and install the auxiliary shaft sprocket.
10. Align the timing marks and install the drive belt.

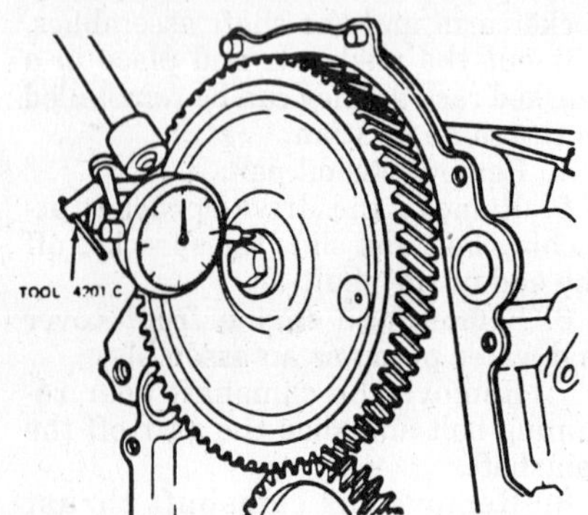

Checking the camshaft end play—6-173 engine

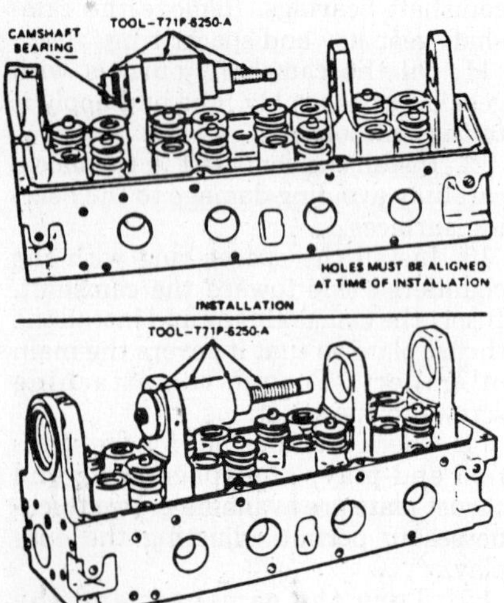

Camshaft bearing replacement—4-122,140 engines

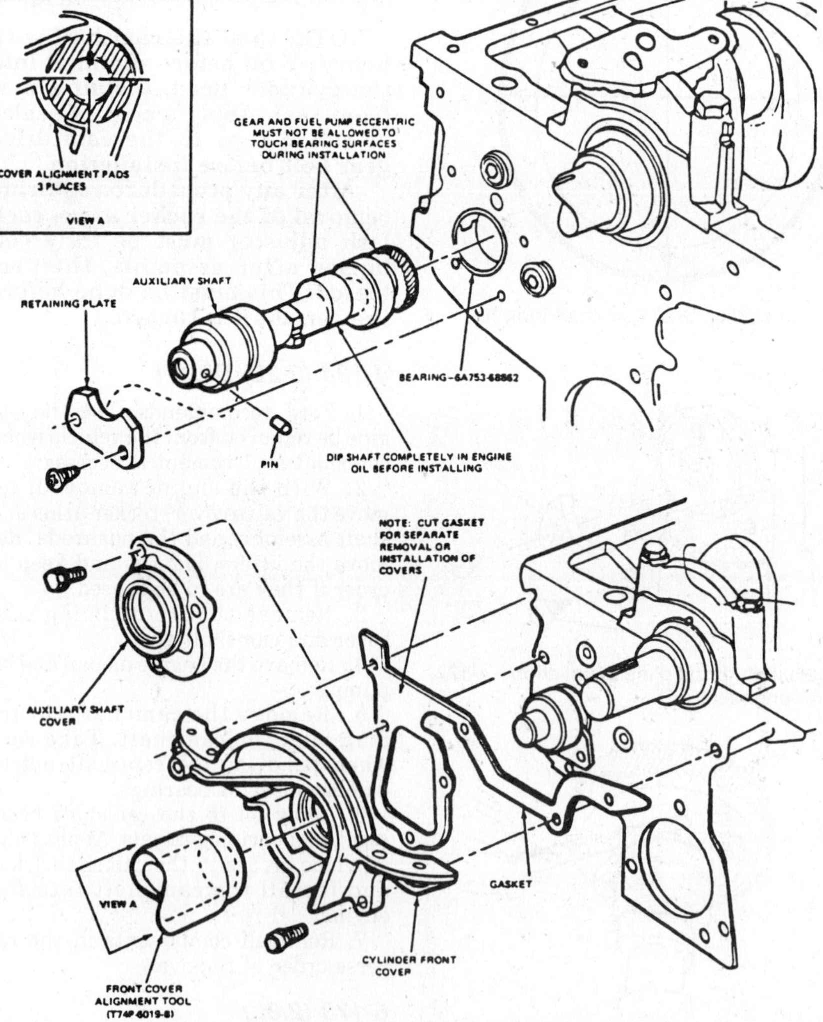

Auxiliary shaft installation—4-122, 140 engines

11. Install the drive belt cover.
12. Check the ignition timing.

Pistons and Connection Rods

REMOVAL & INSTALLATION

NOTE: Although, in most cases, the pistons and connecting rods can be removed from the engine (after the cylinder head and oil pan are removed) while the engine is still in the car, it is far easier to remove the engine from the car. If removing pistons with the engine still installed, disconnect the radiator hoses, automatic transmission cooler lines and radiator shroud. Unbolt front mounts before jacking up the engine. Block the engine in position with wooden blocks between the mounts.

1. Remove the engine from the car. Remove the cylinder head(s), oil pan and front cover (if necessary).
2. Because the top piston ring does not travel to the very top of the cylinder bore, a ridge is built up between the end of the travel and the top of the cylinder. Pushing the piston and connecting rod assembly past the ridge is difficult and may cause damage to the piston. If new rings are installed and the ridge has not been removed, ring breakage and piston damage can occur when the ridge is encountered at engine speed.
3. Turn the crankshaft to position the piston at the bottom of the cylinder bore. Cover the top of the piston with a rag. Install a ridge reamer in the bore and follow the manufacturer's instructions to remove the ridge. Use caution; avoid cutting too deeply or into the ring travel area. Remove the rag and cuttings from the top of the piston. Remove the ridge from all cylinders.
4. Check the edges of the connecting rod and bearing cap for numbers or matchmarks, if none are present mark the rod and cap numerically and in sequence from front to back of engine. The numbers or marks not only tell from which cylinder the piston cam from but also ensures that the rod caps are installed in the correct matching position.
5. Turn the crankshaft until the connecting rod is at the bottom of travel. Remove the two attaching nuts and the bearing cap. Take two pieces of rubber tubing and cover the rod bolts to prevent crank or cylinder scoring. Use a wooden hammer handle to help push the piston and rod up and out of the cylinder. Reinstall the rod cap in proper position. Remove all pistons and connecting rods. Inspect cylinder walls and deglaze or hone as necessary.
6. Installation is in the reverse order of removal. Lubricate each piston, rod bearing and cylinder wall. Install a ring compressor over the piston, position the piston with the mark toward the front of engine and carefully install. Position the connecting rod with the bearing insert installed over the crank journal. Install the rod cap with the bearing in its proper position. Secure with rod nuts and torque to the proper specifications. Install all rod and piston assemblies.

CLEANING AND INSPECTION

1. Use a piston ring expander and remove the rings from the piston.
2. Clean the ring grooves using an appropriate cleaning tool, exercising care to avoid cutting too deeply.
3. Clean all varnish and carbon from the piston with a safe solvent. Do not use a wire brush or caustic solution on the pistons.
4. Inspect the pistons for scuffing, scoring, cracks, pitting or excessive ring groove wear. If wear is evident, the piston must be replaced.
5. Have the piston and connecting rod assembly checked by a machine shop for correct alignment, piston pin wear and piston diameter. If the piston has collapsed it will have to be replaced or knurled to restore original diameter. Connecting rod bushing replacement, piston pin fitting and piston changing can be handled by the machine shop.

MEASURING THE OLD PISTONS

Check used piston-to-cylinder bore clearance as follows:

1. Measure the cylinder bore diameter with a telescope gauge.
2. Measure the piston diameter. When measuring the pistons for size or taper, measurements must be made with the piston pin removed.
3. Subtract the piston diameter from the cylinder bore diameter to determine piston-to-bore clearance.
4. Compare the piston-to-bore clearances obtained with those clearances recommended. Determine if the piston-to-bore clearance is in the acceptable range.
5. When measuring taper, the largest reading must be at the bottom of the skirt.

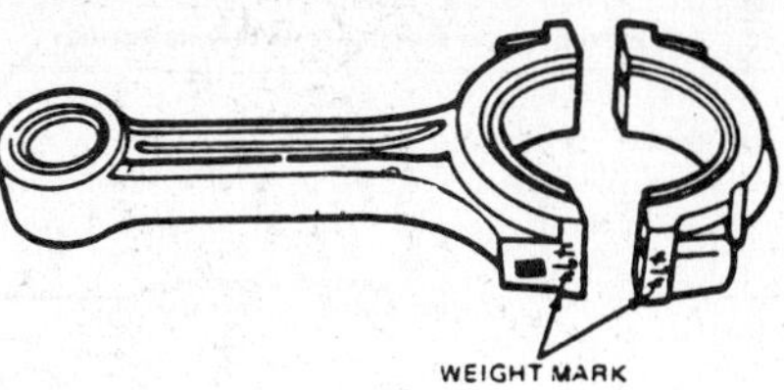

Connecting rod weight marks—4-134 diesel engine

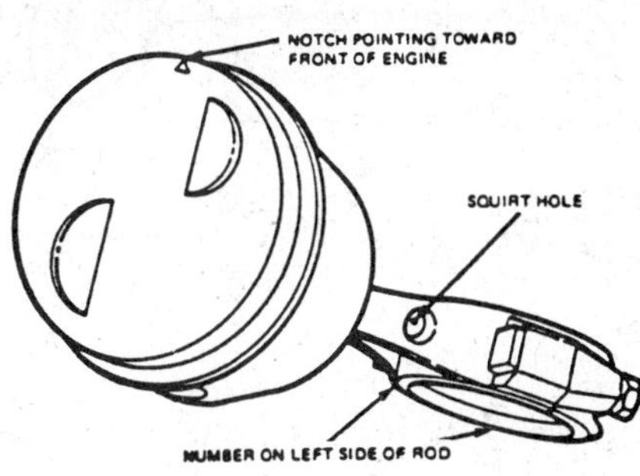

Correct piston and rod positioning—4-122, 140 engines

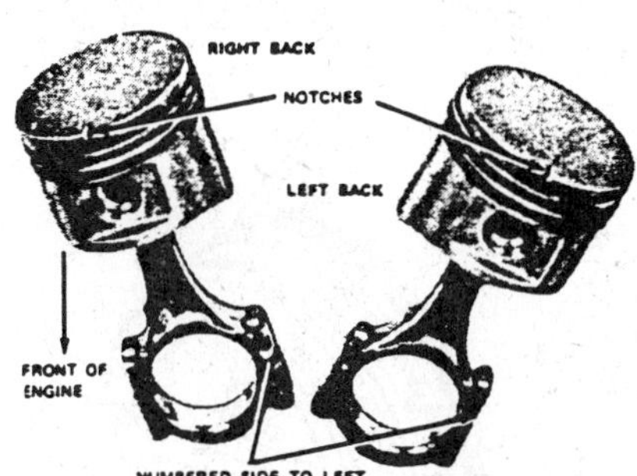

Correct piston and rod positioning—6-173 engine

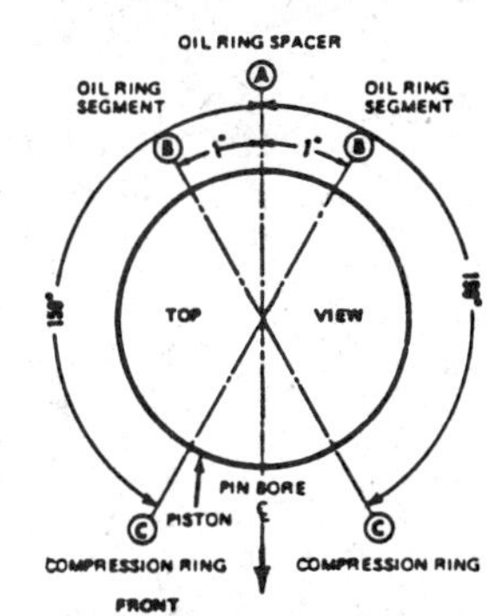

Proper spacing of the piston ring gaps around the circumference of the piston—gasoline engine

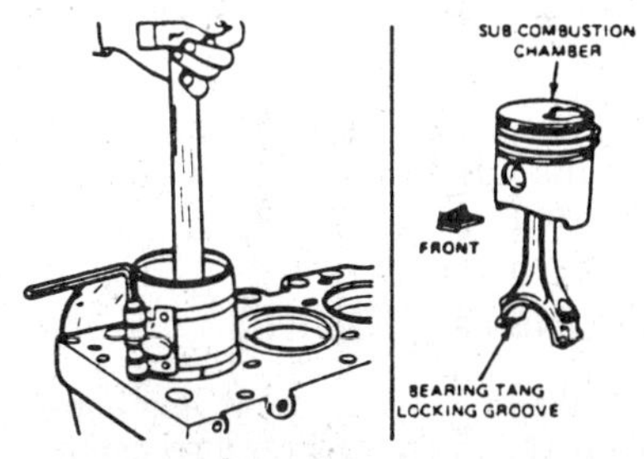

Piston installation—4-134 engines

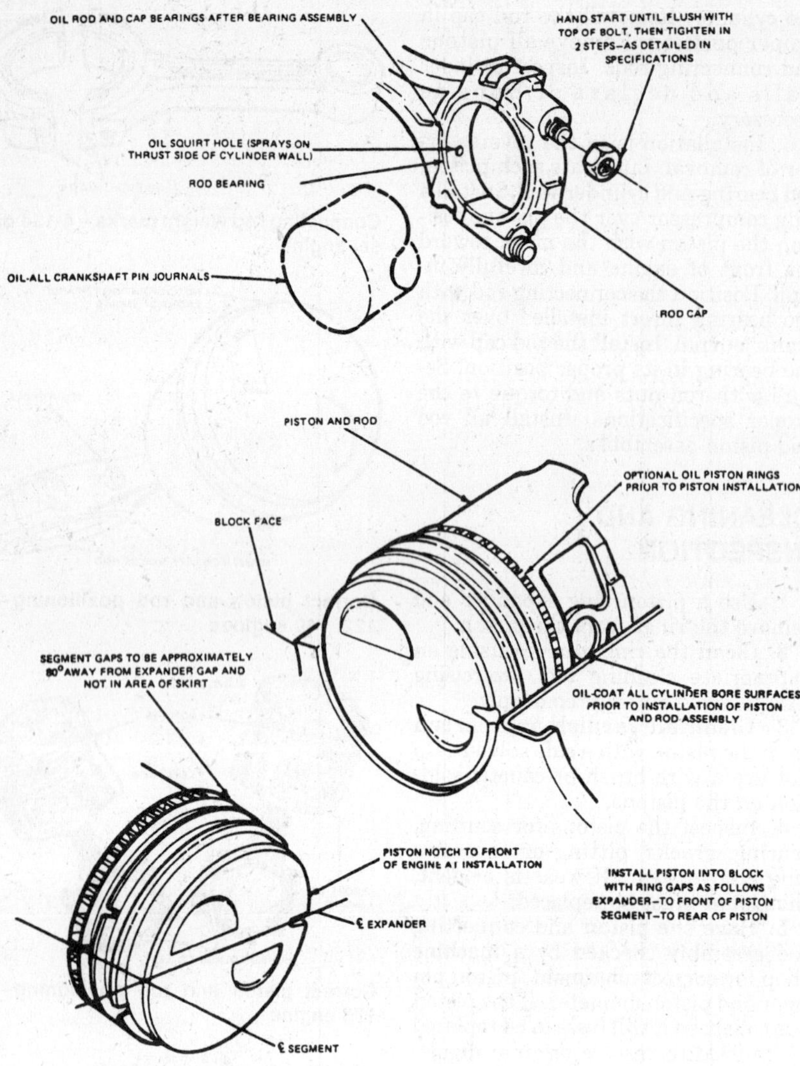

Connecting rod, piston and installation – 4-122, 140 engines

SELECTING NEW PISTONS

1. If the used piston is not acceptable, check the service piston size and determine if a new piston can be selected. (Service pistons are available in standard, high limit and standard oversize.

2. If the cylinder bore must be reconditioned, measure the new piston diameter, then hone the cylinder bore to obtain the preferred clearance.

3. Select a new piston and mark the piston to identify the cylinder for which it was fitted. (On some vehicles, oversize pistons may be found. These pistons will be 0.254mm [0.010"] oversize).

CYLINDER HONING

1. When cylinders are being honed, follow the manufacturer's recommendations for the use of the hone.

2. Occasionally, during the honing operation, the cylinder bore should be thoroughly cleaned and the selected piston checked for correct fit.

3. When finish-honing a cylinder bore, the hone should be moved up and down at a sufficient speed to obtain a very fine uniform surface finish in a cross-hatch pattern of approximately 45-65° included angle. The finish marks should be clean but not sharp, free from imbedded particles and torn or folded metal.

4. Permanently mark the piston for the cylinder to which it has been fitted and proceed to hone the remaining cylinders.

WARNING: Handle the pistons with care. Do not attempt to force the pistons through the cylinders until the cylinders have been honed to the correct size. Pistons can be distorted through careless handling.

5. Thoroughly clean the bores with hot water and detergent. Scrub well with a stiff bristle brush and rinse thoroughly with hot water. It is extremely essential that a good cleaning operation be performed. If any of the abrasive material is allowed to remain in the cylinder bores, it will rapidly wear the new rings and cylinder bores. The bores should be swabbed several times with light engine oil and a clean cloth and then wiped with a clean dry cloth. CYLINDERS SHOULD NOT BE CLEANED WITH KEROSENE OR GASOLINE! Clean the remainder of the cylinder block to remove the excess material spread during the honing operation.

PISTON PIN REMOVAL & INSTALLATION

Use care at all times when handling and servicing connecting rods and pistons. To prevent possible damage to these units, do not clamp the rod or piston in a vise since they may become distorted. Do not allow the pistons to strike against one another, against hard objects or bench surfaces, since distortion of the piston contour or nicks in the soft aluminum material may result.

1. Remove the piston rings using a suitable piston ring remover.

2. Remove the piston pin lockring, if used. Install the guide bushing of the piston pin removing and installing tool.

3. Install the piston and connecting rod assembly on a support, and place the assembly in an arbor press. Press the pin out of the connecting rod, using the appropriate piston pin tool.

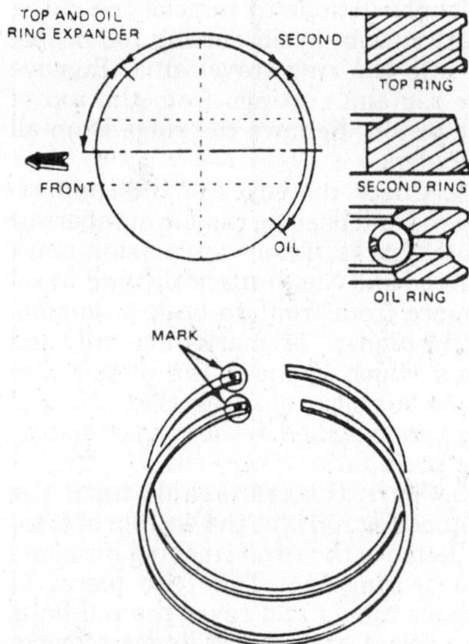

Proper spacing of the piston rings gaps – 4-134 diesel engine

4. Assembly is the reverse of disassembly. Use new lockrings where needed.

Connecting Rods and Bearings

Wash connecting rods in cleaning solvent and dry with compressed air. Check for twisted or bent rods and inspect for nicks or cracks. Replace connecting rods that are damaged.

Inspect journals for roughness and wear. Slight roughness may be removed with a fine grit polishing cloth saturated with engine oil. Burrs may be removed with a fine oil stone by moving the stone on the journal circumference. Do not move the stone back and forth across the journal. If the journals are scored or ridged, the crankshaft must be replaced.

The connecting rod journals should be checked for out-of-round and correct size with a micrometer.

NOTE: Crankshaft rod journals will normally be standard size. If any undersized bearings are used, the size will be stamped on a counterweight.

If plastic gauging material is to be used:

1. Clean oil from the journal bearing cap, connecting rod and outer and inner surfaces of the bearing inserts. Position the insert so that the tang is properly aligned with the notch in the rod and cap.
2. Place a piece of plastic gauging material in the center of lower bearing shell.
3. Remove the bearing cap and determine the bearing clearances by comparing the width of the flattened plastic gauging material at its widest point with the graduation on the container. The number within the graduation on the envelope indicates the clearance in thousandths of an inch or millimeters. If this clearance is excessive, replace the bearing and recheck the clearance with the plastic gauging material. Lubricate the bearing with engine oil before installation. Repeat the procedure on the remaining connecting rod bearings. All rods must be connected to their journals when rotating the crankshaft, to prevent engine damage.

CYLINDER BORE

Check the cylinder bore for wear using a telescope gauge and a micrometer, measure the cylinder bore diameter perpendicular to the piston pin at the point 2½" (63.5mm) below the top of the engine block. Measure the piston skirt perpendicular to the piston pin. The difference between the two measurement is the piston clearance. If the clearance is within specifications, finish honing or glaze breaking is all that is required. If clearance is excessive a slightly oversized piston may be required. If greatly oversize, the engine will have to be bored and 0.010" (0.254mm) or larger oversized pistons installed.

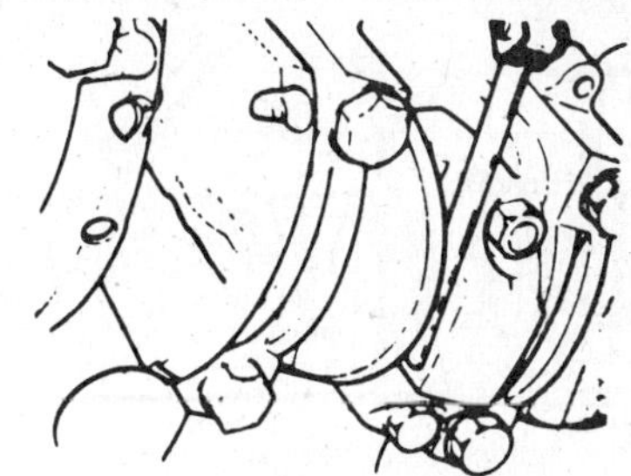

Checking the connecting rod side clearance on the crankshaft bearing journal

FITTING AND POSITIONING PISTON RINGS

1. Take the new piston rings and compress them, one at a time into the cylinder that they will be used in. Press the ring about 1" (25.4mm) below the top of the cylinder block using an inverted piston.
2. Use a feeler gauge and measure the distance between the ends of the ring; this is called measuring the ring end-gap. Compare the reading to the one called for in the specification table. File the ends of the ring with a fine file to obtain the necessary clearance.

WARNING: If inadequate ring end-gap exists, ring breakage will result.

3. Inspect the ring grooves on the piston for excessive wear or taper. If necessary, have the grooves recut for use with a standard ring and spacer. The machine shop can handle the job for you.
4. Check the ring grooves by rolling the new piston ring around the groove to check for burrs or carbon deposits. If any are found, remove them with a fine file. Hold the ring in the groove and measure side clearance with a feeler gauge. If clearance is excessive, spacer(s) will have to be added.

NOTE: Always add the spacer above the piston ring.

5. Install the rings on the piston, lower oil ring first. Use a ring installing tool on the compression rings. Consult the instruction sheet that comes with the rings to be sure they are installed with the correct side up. A mark on the ring usually faces upward.
6. When installing the oil rings, first install the expanding ring in the groove. Hold the ends of the ring butted together (they must not overlap) and install the bottom rail (scraper) with the end about 1" (25.4mm) away from the butted end of the control ring. Install the top rail about 1" (25.4mm) away from the butted end of the control but on the opposite side from the lower rail.
7. Install the two compression rings.
8. Consult the illustration for ring positioning, arrange the rings as shown, install a ring compressor and insert the piston and rod assembly into the engine.

Crankshaft and Bearings

REMOVAL & INSTALLATION

1. Rod bearings can be installed when the pistons have been removed for servicing (rings etc.) or, in most cases, while the engine is still in the car. Bearing replacement, however, is far easier with the engine out of the car and disassembled.
2. For in car service, remove the oil pan, spark plugs and front cover is necessary. Turn the engine until the connecting rod to be serviced is at the bottom of travel. Remove the bearing cap, place two pieces of rubber hose over the rod cap bolts and push the piston and rod assembly up the cylinder bore until enough room is gained for bearing insert removal. Take care not to push the rod assembly up too far or the top ring will engage the cylinder ridge or come out of the cylinder and require head removal for reinstallation.
3. Clean the rod journal, the connecting rod end and the bearing cap after removing the old bearing inserts. Install the new inserts in the rod and bearing cap, lubricate them with oil. Position the rod over the crankshaft journal and install the rod cap. Make sure the cap and rod numbers match, torque the rod nuts to specifications.
4. Main bearings may be replaced while the engine is still in the car by rolling them out and in.
5. Special roll out pins are available from automotive parts houses or can be fabricated from a cotter pin. The roll out pin fits in the oil hole of the main bearing journal. When the crankshaft is rotated opposite the direction of the bearing lock tab, the pin engages the end of the bearing and rolls out the insert.

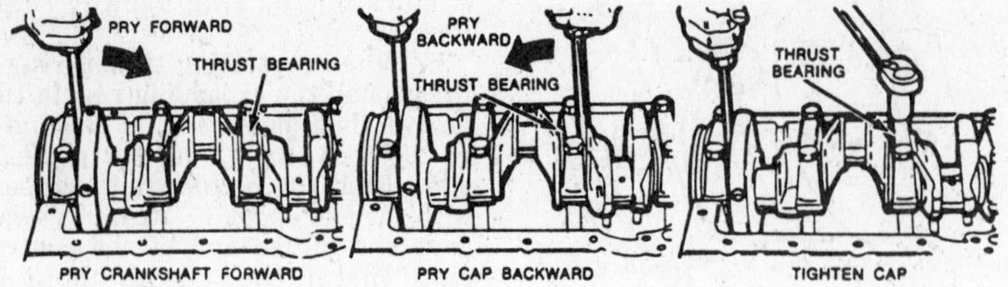

Aligning the thrust bearing

6. Remove the main bearing cap and roll out the upper bearing insert. Remove the insert from the main bearing cap. Clean the inside of the bearing cap and crankshaft journal.

7. Lubricate and roll the upper insert into position, making sure the lock tab is anchored and the insert is not cocked. Install the lower bearing insert into the cap, lubricate it and install it on the engine. Make sure the main bearing cap is installed facing in the correct direction and torque it to specifications.

8. With the engine out of the car. Remove the intake manifold, cylinder heads, front cover, timing gears and/or chain, oil pan, oil pump and flywheel.

9. Remove the piston and rod assemblies. Remove the main bearing caps after marking them for position and direction.

10. Remove the crankshaft, bearing inserts and rear main oil seal. Clean the engine block and cap bearing saddles. Clean the crankshaft and inspect it for wear. Check the bearing journals with a micrometer for out-of-round condition and to determine what size rod and main bearing inserts to install.

11. Install the main bearing upper inserts and rear main oil seal half into the engine block.

12. Lubricate the bearing inserts and the crankshaft journals. Slowly and carefully lower the crankshaft into position.

13. Install the bearing inserts and rear main seal into the bearing caps. Install the caps working from the middle out. Torque the cap bolts to specifications in stages, rotating the crankshaft after each torque stage. Note the illustration for thrust bearing alignment.

14. Remove the bearing caps, one at a time, and check the oil clearance with Plastigage®. Reinstall if clearance is within specifications. Check the crankshaft end-play. If it is within specifications, install the connecting rod and piston assemblies with new rod bearing inserts. Check the connecting rod bearing oil clearance and side play. If they are correct assemble the rest of the engine.

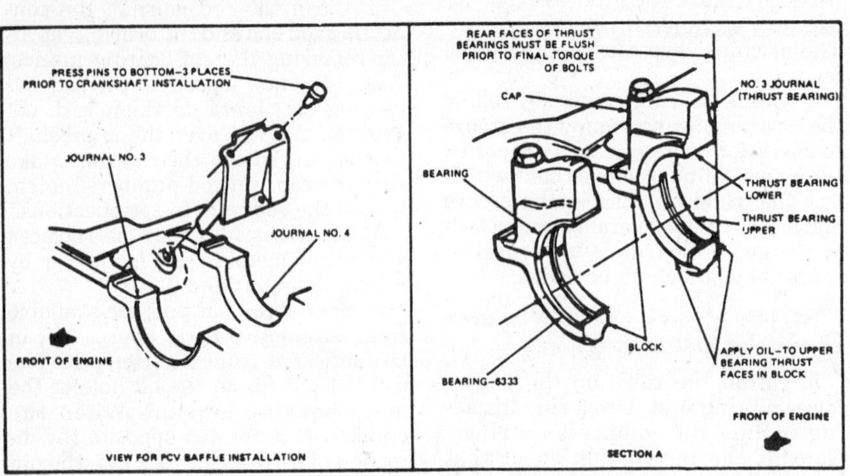

Crankshaft and main bearing installation—4-122, 140 engines

BEARING OIL CLEARANCE

Remove the cap from the bearing to be checked. Using a clean, dry rag, thoroughly clean all oil from the crankshaft journal and bearing insert.

NOTE: Plastigage® is soluble in oil, therefore, oil on the journal or bearing could result in erroneous readings.

Place a piece of Plastigage® along the full width of the bearing insert, reinstall cap, and torque to specification.

NOTE: Specifications are given in the Engine Specifications Chart.

Remove the bearing cap, and determine the bearing clearance by comparing the width of the Plastigage® to the scale on the Plastigage® envelope. Journal taper is determined by comparing the width of the bearing insert. Install the cap, and torque it to specifications.

NOTE: Do not rotate the crankshaft with the Plastigage® installed. If the bearing insert and journal appear intact, and are

within tolerances, no further main bearing service is required. If the bearing or journal appear defective, the cause of failure should be determined before replacement.

CRANKSHAFT END-PLAY/CONNECTING ROD SIDE PLAY

Place a pry bar between a main bearing cap and crankshaft casting taking care not to damage any journals. Pry backward and forward, measuring the distance between the thrust bearing and crankshaft with a feeler gauge. Compare the reading with specifications. If too great a clearance is determined, a main bearing with a larger thrust surface or crank machining may be required. Check with an automotive machine shop for their advice.

Connecting rod clearance between the rod and crankthrow casting can be checked with a feeler gauge. Pry the rod carefully to one side as far as possible and measure the distance on the other side of the rod.

CRANKSHAFT REPAIRS

If a journal is damaged on the crankshaft, repair is possible by having the crankshaft machined to a standard undersize.

In most cases, however, since the engine must be removed from the car and disassembled, some thought should be given to replacing the damaged crankshaft with a reground shaft kit. A reground crankshaft kit contains the necessary main and rod bearings for installation. The shaft has been ground and polished to undersize specifications and will usually hold up well if installed correctly.

COMPLETING THE REBUILDING PROCESS

Fill the oil pump with oil, to prevent cavitating (sucking air) on initial engine start up. Install the oil pump and the pickup tube on the engine. Coat the oil pan gasket as necessary, and install the gasket and the oil pan. Mount the flywheel and the crankshaft vibration damper or pulley on the crankshaft.

NOTE: Always use new bolts when installing the flywheel. Inspect the clutch shaft pilot bushing in the crankshaft. If the bushing is excessively worn, remove it with an expanding puller and a slide hammer, and tap a new bushing into place.

Position the engine, cylinder head side up. Lubricate the lifters, and install them into their bores. Install the cylinder head, and torque it as specified. Insert the pushrods (where applicable), and install the rocker shaft(s) (if so equipped) or position the rocker.

Install the intake and exhaust manifolds, the carburetor(s), the distributor and spark plugs. Mount all accessories and install the engine in the car. Fill the radiator with coolant, and the crankcase with high quality engine oil.

BREAK-IN PROCEDURE

Start the engine, and allow it to run at low speed for a few minutes, while checking for leaks. Stop the engine, check the oil level, and fill as necessary. Restart the engine, and fill the cooling system to capacity. Check and adjust the ignition timing. Run the engine at low to medium speed (800-2,500 rpm) for approximately ½ hour, and retorque the cylinder head bolts. Road test the car, and check again for leaks.

NOTE: Some gasket manufacturers recommend not retorquing the cylinder head(s) due to the composition of the head gasket. Follow the directions in the gasket set.

Flywheel/Flex Plate and Ring Gear

NOTE: Flex plate is the term for a flywheel mated with an automatic transmission.

REMOVAL & INSTALLATION

All Engines

NOTE: The ring gear is replaceable only on engines mated with a manual transmission. Engines with automatic transmissions have ring gears which are welded to the flex plate.

1. Remove the transmission and transfer case.
2. Remove the clutch, if equipped, or torque converter from the flywheel. The flywheel bolts should be loosened a little at a time in a cross pattern to avoid warping the flywheel. On cars with manual transmissions, replace the pilot bearing in the end of the crankshaft if removing the flywheel.
3. The flywheel should be checked for cracks and glazing. It can be resurfaced by a machine shop.
4. If the ring gear is to be replaced, drill a hole in the gear between two teeth, being careful not to contact the flywheel surface. Using a cold chisel at this point, crack the ring gear and remove it.
5. Polish the inner surface of the new ring gear and heat it in an oven to about 600°F (316°C). Quickly place the ring gear on the flywheel and tap it into place, making sure that it is fully seated.

WARNING: Never heat the ring gear past 800°F (426°C), or the tempering will be destroyed.

7. Position the flywheel on the end of the crankshaft. Torque the bolts a little at a time, in a cross pattern, to the torque figure shown in the Torque Specifications Chart.
8. Install the clutch or torque converter.
9. Install the transmission and transfer case.

ENGINE LUBRICATION

Oil Pan

REMOVAL & INSTALLATION

4-122 (2.0L)
4-140 (2.3L)

1. Disconnect the negative battery cable.
2. Remove air cleaner assembly. Remove oil dipstick. Remove engine mount retaining nuts.
3. Remove oil cooler lines at the radiator, if so equipped. Remove (2) bolts retaining the fan shroud to the radiator and remove shroud.
4. Remove radiator retaining bolts (automatic only). Position radiator upward and wire to the hood (automatic only).
5. Raise the vehicle and safely support on jackstands.
6. Drain oil from crankcase.
7. Remove starter cable from starter and remove starter.
8. Disconnect the exhaust manifold tube to the inlet pipe bracket at the thermactor check valve.
9. Remove transmission mount retaining nuts to the crossmember.
10. Remove bellcrank from converter housing (automatic only).
11. Remove oil cooler lines from retainer at the block (automatic only).
12. Remove front crossmember (automatic only).
13. Disconnect right front lower shock absorber mount (manual only).
14. Position jack under engine, raise

and block with a piece of wood approximately 2½" high. Remove jack.

15. Position jack under the transmission and raise slightly (automatic only).

16. Remove oil pan retaining bolts, lower pan to the chassis. Remove oil pump drive and pick-up tube assembly.

17. Remove oil pan (out the front, automatic only) (out the rear, manual only).

18. Clean oil pan and inspect for damage. Clean oil pan gasket surface at the cylinder block. Clean oil pump exterior and oil pump pick-up tube screen.

19. Position oil pan gasket and end seals to the cylinder block (use contact cement to retain).

20. Position oil pan to the crossmember.

21. Install oil pump and pick-up tube assembly. Install oil pan to cylinder block with retaining bolts.

22. Lower jack under transmission (automatic only).

23. Position jack under engine, raise slightly, and remove wood spacer block.

24. Replace oil filter.

25. Connect the exhaust manifold tube to the inlet pipe bracket at the thermactor check valve.

26. Install transmission mount to the crossmember.

27. Install oil cooler lines to the retainer at the block (automatic only).

28. Install bellcrank to converter housing (automatic only.)

29. Install right front lower shock absorber mount (manual only). Install front crossmember (automatic only).

30. Install starter and connect cable. Lower vehicle.

31. Install engine mount bolts.

32. Locate the radiator to the supports and install the (2) retaining bracket bolts (automatic only). Install fan shroud on the radiator.

33. Connect oil cooler lines to the radiator (automatic only).

34. Install air cleaner assembly.

35. Install oil dipstick. Fill crankcase with oil.

36. Start engine and check for leaks.

4-134 (2.2L) Diesel

1. Disconnect the ground cables from both batteries.

2. Remove engine oil dipstick. Disconnect air intake hose from air cleaner and intake manifold.

3. Drain coolant. Remove engine fan. Remove engine fan shroud.

CAUTION

When draining the coolant, keep in mind that cats and dogs are attracted by the ethylene glycol antifreeze, and are quite likely to drink any that is left in an uncovered container or in puddles on the ground. This will prove fatal in sufficient quantity. Always drain the coolant into a sealable container. Coolant should be reused unless it is contaminated or several years old.

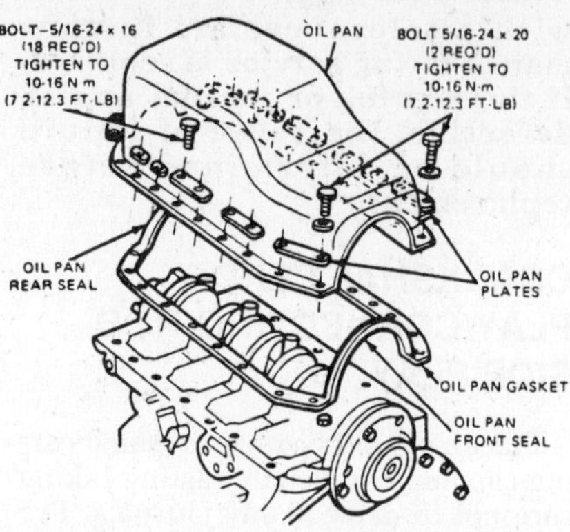

Oil pan installation -4-134 diesel engine

4. Disconnect radiator hoses. Remove radiator upper support brackets and remove radiator and fan shroud.

5. Disconnect and cap fuel inlet and outlet lines at fuel filter and return line at injection pump.

6. Remove fuel filter assembly from mounting bracket. Remove the fuel filter mounting bracket from cylinder head.

7. Remove nuts and washers attaching engine brackets to insulators.

8. Raise vehicle and safely support on jackstands.

9. Loosen transmission insulator bolts at rear of transmission. Remove bottom engine insulator.

10. Drain the engine oil from crankcase. Remove primary oil filter from left side of engine.

11. Remove by-pass filter mounting bracket and hoses.

12. Lower vehicle.

13. Attach engine lifting sling and hoist. Raise engine until insulator studs clear insulators. Slide engine forward, then raise engine approximately 3".

14. Install a wooden block 3" high between left mount and bracket. Install a wooden block 4¼" high between right mount and bracket. Lower engine.

15. Remove lifting sling and raise vehicle.

16. Remove oil pan attaching bolts, and lower oil pan onto cross member.

17. Disconnect oil pickup from oil pump and bearing cap, and lay in oil pan.

18. Move oil pan forward and up between front of engine and front body sheet metal.

NOTE: If additional clearance is needed, move A/C condensor forward.

19. Clean gasket mating surfaces of oil pan and engine block with a suitable solvent and dry thoroughly. Apply ⅛" bead of Silicone Sealer on split line

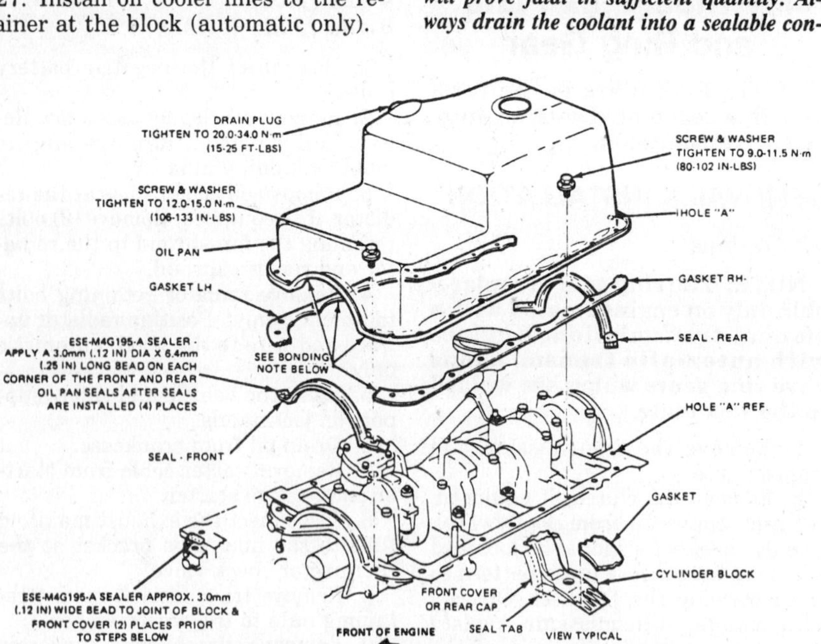

Oil pan installation—4-122, 140 engines

between engine block and engine front cover and along side rails.

20. Locate oil pan gaskets in position with Gasket Cement and make sure that gasket tabs are seated in seal cap grooves.

21. Press front and rear oil pan seals in seal cap grooves with both ends of seals contacting oil pan gaskets.

22. Apply ⅛" bead of sealer at ends of oil pan seals where they meet oil pan gaskets.

23. Position oil pan with pickup tube on No. 1 crossmember.

24. Install oil pickup tube, with a new gasket, and tighten bolts to specification. Install oil pan with attaching bolt and plates. Tighten bolts to specification.

25. Lower vehicle.

26. Install lifting sling, raise engine and remove wooden blocks.

27. Lower engine onto insulators and install and tighten nuts and washers to specification.

28. Raise vehicle and safely support on jackstands.

29. Install transmission mount nuts.

30. Install by-pass filter bracket and hoses. Install new by-pass oil filter.

31. Install oil pan drain plug. Install new primary oil filter.

32. Lower vehicle.

33. Install fuel filter bracket on engine.

34. Install fuel filter and adaptor on mounting bracket.

35. Install fuel return line on injection pump and fuel lines on fuel filter.

36. Position radiator in vehicle, install radiator hoses and upper support brackets.

37. Install radiator fan shroud. Install radiator fan and tighten to specification.

38. Fill and bleed cooling system.

39. Fill crankcase with specified quantity and quality of oil.

40. Install engine oil dipstick.

41. Install air intake hose on air cleaner and intake manifold.

42. Connect battery ground cables to both batteries.

43. Run engine and check for oil, fuel and coolant leaks.

6-173 (2.8L)

1. Disconnect negative battery cable. Remove carburetor air cleaner assembly.

2. Remove fan shroud and position over fan.

3. Remove distributor cap, position forward of dash panel. Remove distributor and cover bore opening.

4. Remove nuts attaching engine front insulators to cross member. Remove engine oil dipstick tube.

5. Raise vehicle and safely support on jackstands.

6. Drain engine crankcase. Remove transmission fluid filler tube and plug pan hole (auto trans. only).

7. Remove engine oil filter element. Disconnect muffler inlet pipe(s).

8. Disconnect oil cooler bracket and lower (if so equipped). Remove starter motor.

9. Position out of way, transmission oil cooler lines (if so equipped). Disconnect front stabilizer bar and position forward.

10. Position jack under engine and raise engine maximum height (until it touches dash panel) and install wooden blocks between front insulator mounts and No.2 crossmember.

11. Lower engine onto blocks and remove jack.

12. Remove oil pan attaching bolts. Lower oil pan assembly.

13. Remove oil pump and pickup tube assembly (attached to bearing cap) and lower into oil pan. Remove oil pan assembly.

14. Clean gasket surfaces on engine and oil pan. Apply adhesive to gasket mating surfaces and install oil pan gaskets.

15. With oil pump and pickup tube assembly positioned in oil pan, install oil pump and then install oil pan. Be sure gasket forms an air tight seal. Tighten pan bolts to specification.

16. Position jack under engine and raise engine to remove wooden blocks.

17. Lower engine and remove jack. Install starter motor.

18. Connect muffler inlet pipe(s).

19. Connect front stabilizer bar. Reposition transmission oil cooler lines. Connect cooler bracket (if so equipped).

20. Install new engine oil filter element.

21. Unplug transmission oil pan and install oil filler tube (auto trans. only). Lower vehicle.

22. Install engine oil dipstick tube.

23. Install nuts attaching engine front insulators to crossmember and torque to specification.

24. Install distributor assembly and cap.

25. Position fan shroud in place and install and torque attaching screws to specification.

26. Fill engine crankcase with specified amount of oil and transmission with specified amount of fluid.

27. Connect battery negative cable.

28. Start engine, allow to run until normal operating temperature and check for oil or fluid leaks.

29. Verify ignition timing is set to specification.

30. Turn engine off. Install carburetor air cleaner assembly.

Oil Pump

REMOVAL & INSTALLATION

1. Remove the oil pan.

2. Remove the oil pump inlet tube and screen assembly.

3. Remove the oil pump attaching bolts and remove the oil pump gasket and intermediate driveshaft.

4. Before installing the oil pump, prime it by filling the inlet and outlet port with engine oil and rotating the shaft of the pump to distribute it.

5. Position the intermediate driveshaft into the distributor socket.

6. Position the new gasket on the pump body and insert the intermediate driveshaft into the pump body.

7. Install the pump and intermediate driveshaft as an assembly. Do not force the pump if it does not seal readily. The driveshaft may be misaligned with the distributor shaft. To align it, rotate the intermediate driveshaft into a new position.

8. Install the oil pump attaching bolts and torque them to 12-15 ft.lb.

9. Install the oil pan.

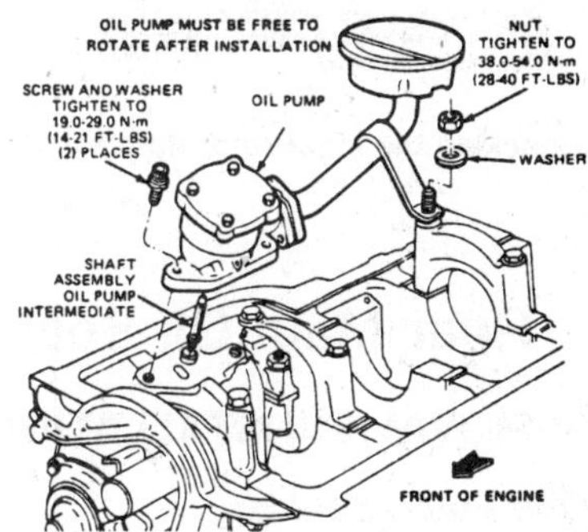

Oil pump installation—4-122, 140 engines

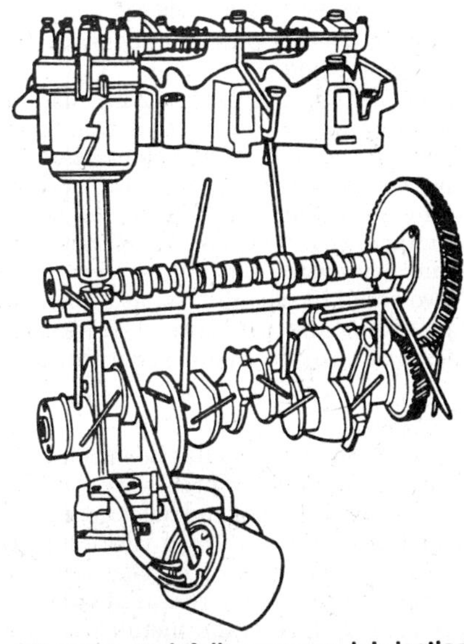
Oil pump and full pressure lubrication system—6-173 engine

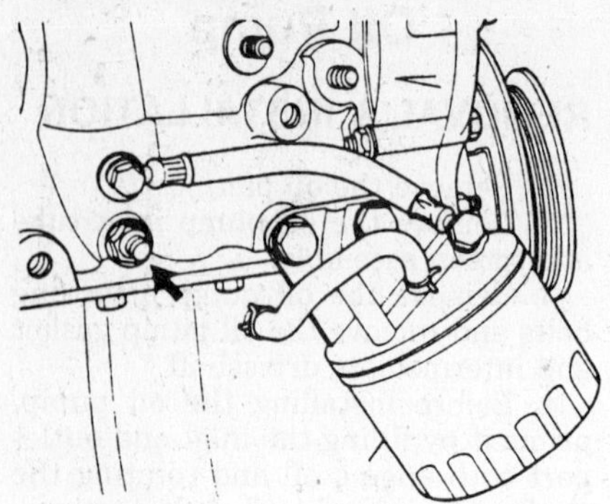
Oil pump set screw location—4-134 diesel engine

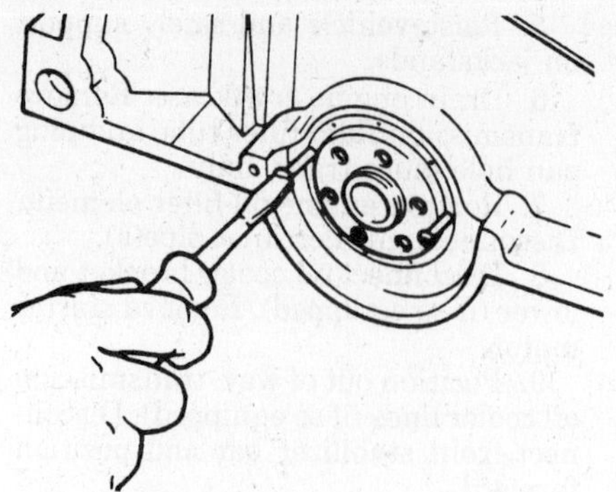
Removing the rear main oil seal

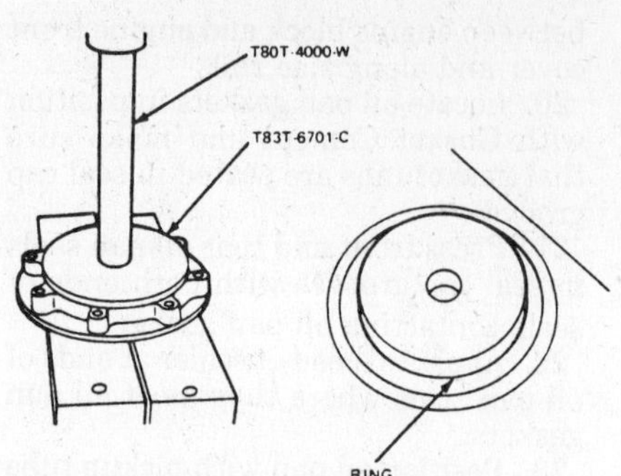

Installing the crankshaft rear main oil seal—4-134 diesel engine

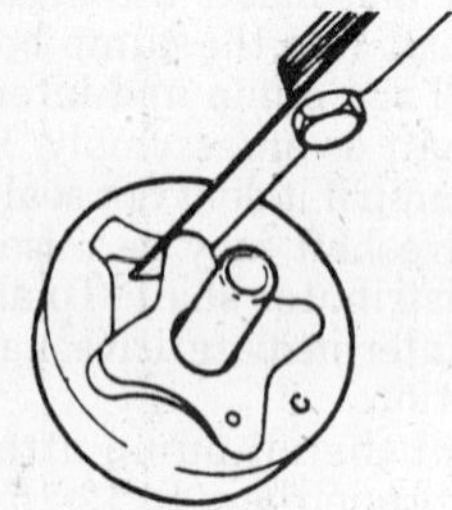

Checking the inner rotor tip clearance

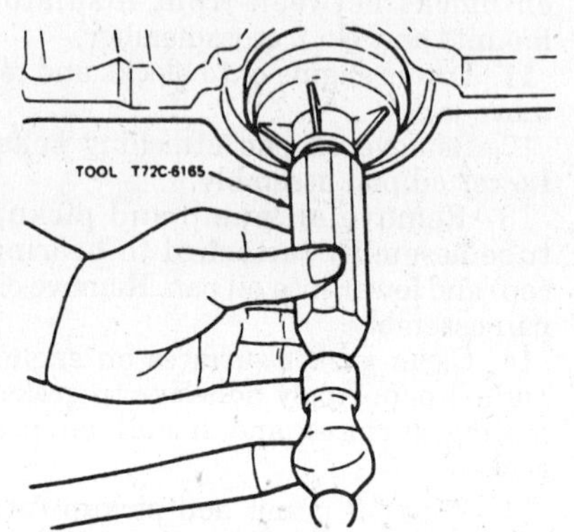

Installing the crankshaft rear main oil seal—6-173 engine

Rear Main Oil Seal

REMOVAL & INSTALLATION

One Piece Seal

1. Remove the transmission, clutch assembly or converter and flywheel.
2. (See Step 7 for diesel engines). Lower the oil pan if necessary for working room.
3. On engines except 2.2L, use an awl to punch two small holes on opposite sides of the seal just above the split between the main bearing cap and engine block. Install a sheet metal screw in each hole. Use two small pry bars and pry evenly on both screws using two small blocks of wood as a fulcrum point for the pry bars. Use caution throughout to avoid scratching or damage to the oil seal mounting surfaces.
4. When the seal has been removed, clean the mounting recess.
5. Coat the seal and block mounting surfaces with oil. Apply white lube to the contact surface of the seal and crankshaft. Start the seal into the mounting recess and install with seal mounting tool Ford number T82L-6701-A or equivalent.
6. Install the remaining components in the reverse.
7. On the 2.2L engines, the oil seal is one piece but mounted on a retaining plate. Remove the mounting plate from the rear of the engine and replace the seal. Reinstall in reverse order of removal.

Split Seal

Remove the oil pan. In some cases it may be necessary to remove the oil pump pick-up and screen or the whole pump assembly.

1. Loosen all main bearing caps, lowering the crankshaft slightly, but not more than $^{1}/_{32}$″.
2. Remove the rear main bearing cap.
3. Remove the seal halves from cap and block. Use a seal removing tool on the block half or install a small metal screw in one end so that the seal may be pulled out.

WARNING: Do not damage or scratch the crankshaft seal surfaces.

4. If so equipped, remove the oil seal retaining pin from the bearing cap.
5. Thoroughly clean seal grooves in block and cap with brush and solvent.
6. Dip seal halves in engine oil.
7. Carefully install upper half of seal with the lip facing toward the front of the engine until ³⁄₈″ is left protruding below parting surface. Be careful not to scrape seal.
8. Tighten all but the rear main bearing caps to specified torque.
9. Install lower seal half in the rear main bearing cap with the lip facing

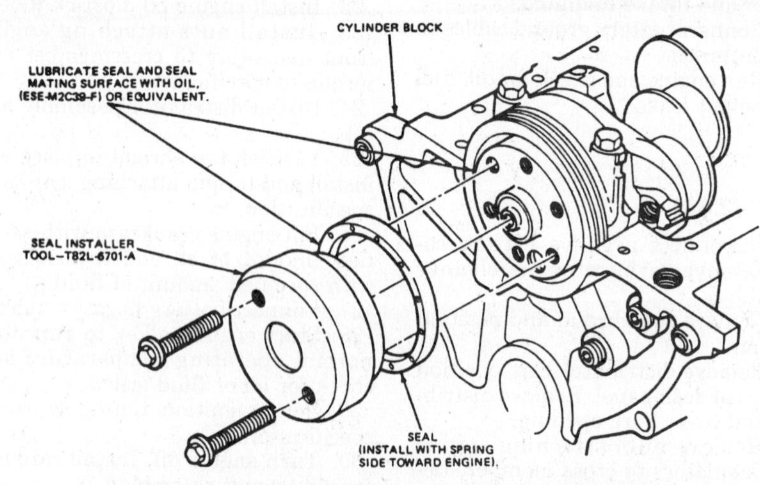

Installing the crankshaft rear oil seal—4-122, 140 engines

toward the front of the engine. Apply a light coat of oil-resistant sealer to the rear of the top mating surface of the cap. Do not apply sealer to the area forward of the side seal groove.

10. Install rear main bearing cap and tighten bolts to specified torque.
11. Install oil pump and oil pan.
12. Fill crankcase and operate engine to check for leaks.

COOLING SYSTEM

The satisfactory performance of any engine is controlled to a great extent by the proper operation of the cooling system. The engine block is fully waterjacketed to prevent distortion of the cylinder walls. Directed cooling and water holes in the cylinder head causes water to flow past the valve seats, which are one of the hottest parts of any engine, to carry heat away from the valves and seats.

The minimum temperature of the coolant is controlled by the thermostat, mounted in the coolant outlet passage of the engine. When the coolant temperature is below the temperature rating of the thermostat, the thermostat remains closed and the coolant is directed through the radiator by-pass hose to the water pump and back into the engine. When the coolant temperature reaches the temperature rating of the thermostat, the thermostat opens and allows coolant to flow past it and into the top of the radiator. The radiator dissipates the excess engine heat before the coolant is recirculated through the engine.

The cooling system is pressurized and operating pressure is regulated by the rating of the radiator cap which contains a relief valve. The reason for a pressurized cooling system is to allow for higher engine operating temperatures with a higher coolant boiling point.

Radiator

REMOVAL & INSTALLATION

1. Drain the cooling system.
2. Disconnect the transmission cooling lines from the bottom of the radiator, if so equipped.
3. Remove the bolts mounting the shroud or shroud halves if so equipped, and position the shroud over the fan, clear the radiator.
4. Disconnect the upper and lower hoses from the radiator.

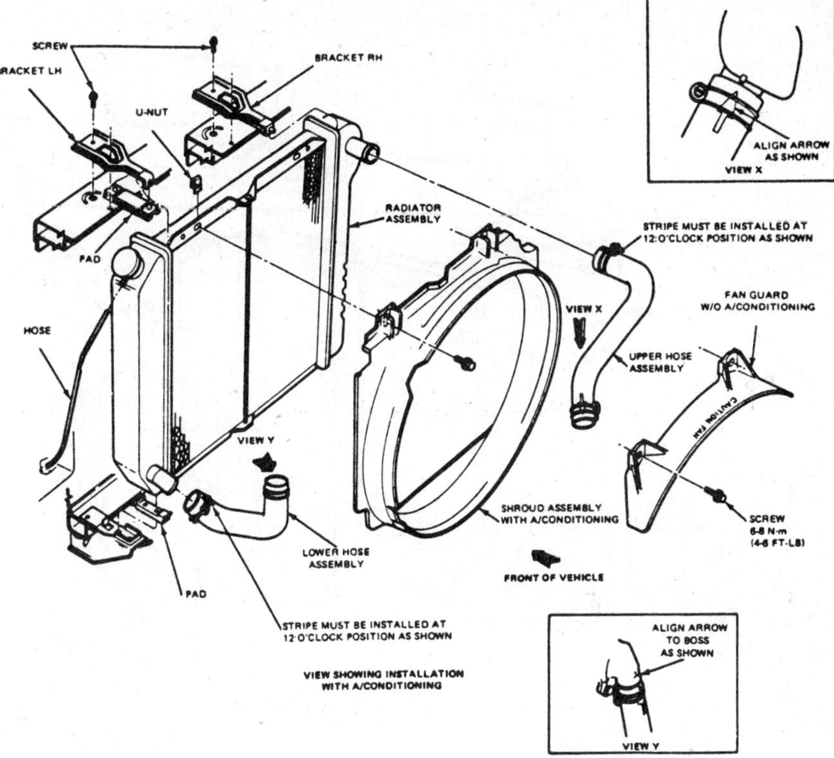

Radiator assembly—6-173 engine

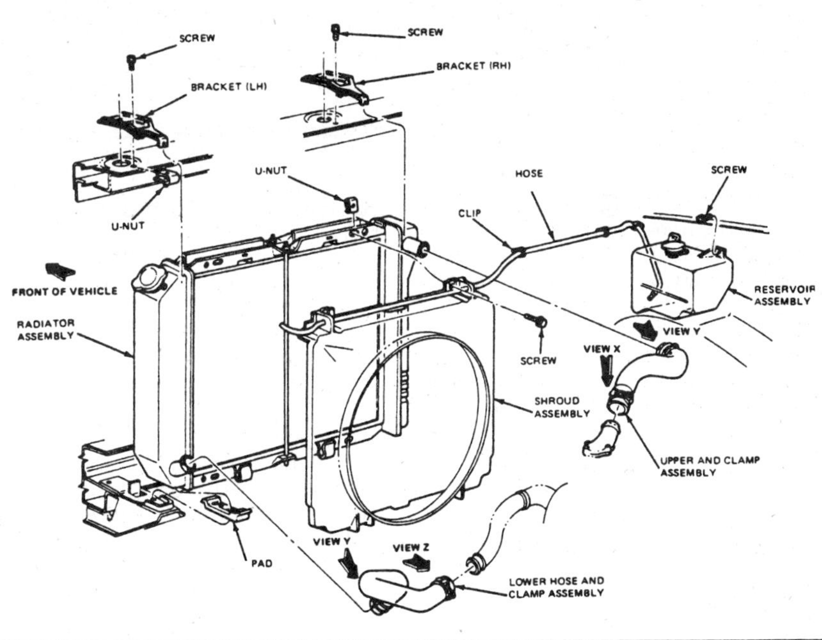

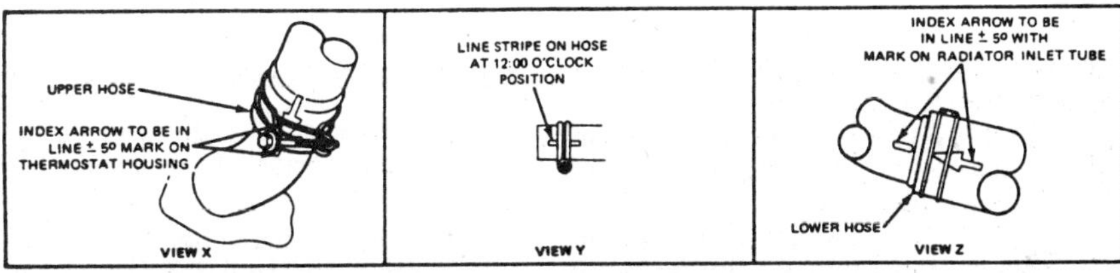

Radiator installation—4-134 diesel engine

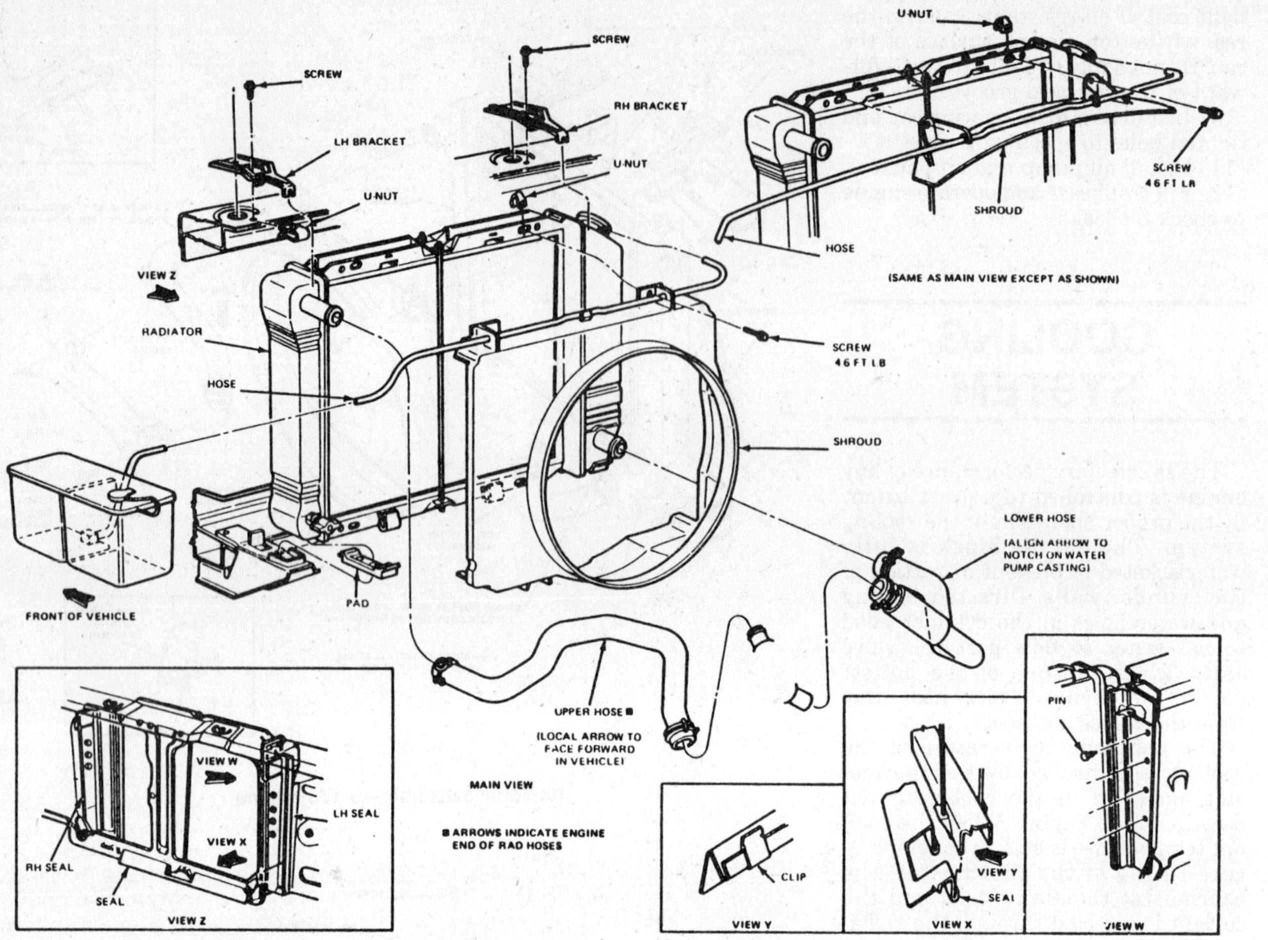

Radiator installation—4-122, 140 engines

5. Remove the radiator retaining bolts or the upper supports and lift the radiator from the vehicle. On some models it may be necessary to remove the right hood lock bracket and bolts from the radiator grille before removing the radiator.

6. Install the radiator in the reverse order of removal. Fill the cooling system and check for leaks.

Water Pump

REMOVAL & INSTALLATION

4-122 (2.0L)
4-140 (2.3L)

1. Disconnect the negative battery cable. Drain the cooling system. Loosen and remove the drive belt.

2. Remove the two bolts that retain the fan shroud and position the shroud back over the fan.

3. Remove the four bolts that retain the cooling fan. Remove the fan and shroud.

4. Loosen and remove the power steering and A/C compressor drive belts.

5. Remove the water pump pulley and the vent hose to the emissions canister.

6. Remove the heater hose at the water pump.

7. Remove the cam belt cover. Remove the lower radiator hose from the water pump.

8. Remove the water pump mounting bolts and the water pump. Clean all gasket mounting surfaces.

9. Install the water pump in the reverse order of removal. Coat the threads of the mounting bolts with sealer before installation.

4-134 (2.2L) Diesel

1. Disconnect the ground cables from both batteries. Drain the cooling system.

2. Remove all drive belts.

3. Remove the radiator fan shroud and cooling fan and pump pulley. Disconnect the heater hose, by-pass hose

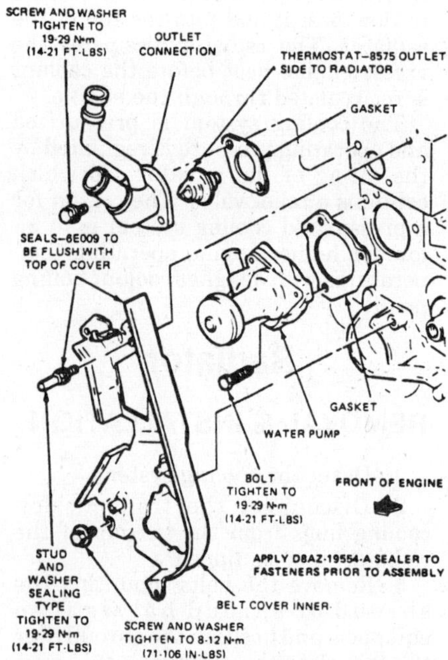

Water pump and thermostat installation—4-122, 140 engines

and radiator hose from the water pump.
4. Remove the nuts and bolts that mount the water pump to the engine.
5. Clean all gasket mounting surfaces.
6. Install water pump in the reverse order of removal.

6-173 (2.8L)

1. Disconnect the negative battery cable. Drain the cooling system.
2. Loosen and remove drive belts. Remove pump pulley. Disconnect all the water hoses from the water pump and thermostat housing.
3. Remove the radiator shroud (if necessary) and cooling fan and clutch assembly. The fan clutch assembly mounting nut is equipped with a left hand thread, remove by turning clockwise.
4. Remove the mounting bolts and water pump, water inlet and thermostat housing as an assembly.
5. Clean all gasket mounting surfaces. Transfer parts to the new pump.
6. Install the water pump in the reverse order of removal.

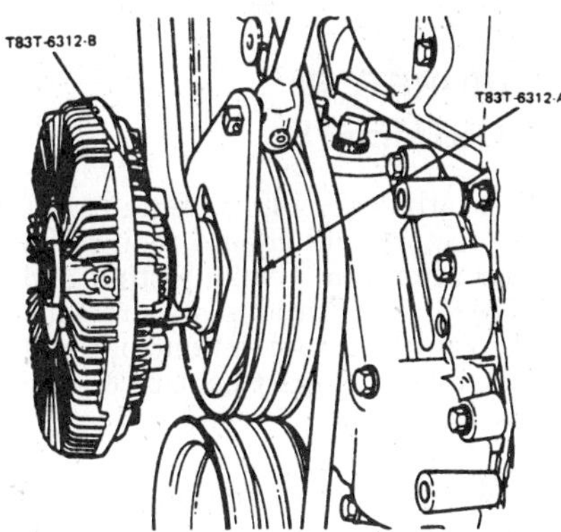

Removing the fan clutch assembly—6-173 engine

Thermostat

REMOVAL & INSTALLATION

1. Drain the cooling system to a level below the coolant outlet housing. Use the petcock valve at the bottom of the radiator to drain the system, or disconnect the lower hose at the radiator.
2. Disconnect the by-pass hose, if equipped. Remove the coolant outlet housing retaining bolts and slide the housing with the hose attached to one side.
3. Turn the thermostat counterclockwise to unlock it from the outlet.
4. Remove the gasket from the engine block and clean both mating surfaces.

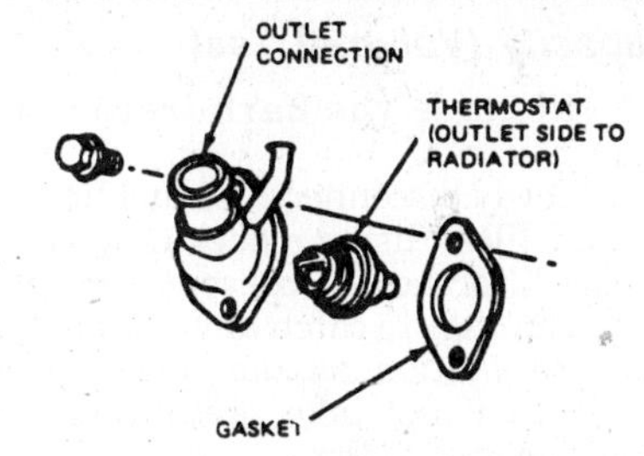

Thermostat and housing—exploded view

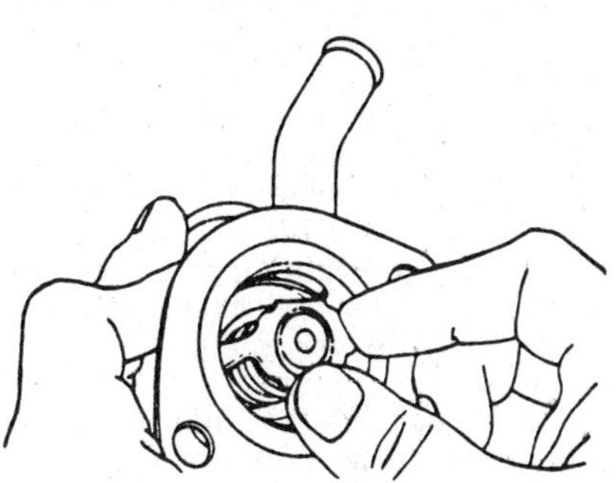
Installing the thermostat in the thermostat hosuing

5. To install the thermostat, coat a new gasket with water-resistant sealer and position it on the outlet of the engine. The gasket must be in place before the thermostat is installed.
6. Install the thermostat with the bridge (opposite end from the spring) inside the elbow connection and turn it clockwise to lock it in position with the bridge against the flats cast into the elbow connection.
7. Position the elbow connection onto the mounting surface of the outlet so that the thermostat flange is resting on the gasket and install the retaining bolts.
8. Fill the radiator and operate the engine until it reaches operating temperature. Check the coolant level and adjust as necessary.

NOTE: It is a good practice to check the operation of a new thermostat before it is installed in an engine. Place the thermostat in a pan of boiling water. If it does not open more than 1/4", do not install it in the engine.

CARBURETED FUEL SYSTEM

Mechanical Fuel Pump

The fuel pump is bolted to the lower left side of the cylinder block. It is mechanically operated by an eccentric on the camshaft driving a pushrod. The fuel pump cannot be disassembled for repairs and must be replaced if testing indicates it is not within performance specifications.

CAUTION

Take precautions to avoid the risk of fire whenever working on or around any fuel system. It's a good idea to have a fire extinguisher handy. Do not smoke.

REMOVAL & INSTALLATION

1. Loosen the fuel line nut at the pump outlet, using a clean rag to catch any fuel spray that will come out when the line is loosened.
2. Loosen the fuel pump mounting bolts approximately two turns. Apply force with your hand to loosen the fuel pump if the gasket is stuck. If excessive tension is on the pump, rotate the engine until the fuel pump cam lobe is near its low position.
3. Disconnect the fuel pump inlet and outlet lines.
4. Remove the fuel pump attaching bolts and remove the pump and gasket. Discard the old gasket.
5. Remove all fuel pump gasket material from the engine and fuel pump mating surfaces.
6. Install the attaching bolts into the fuel pump and install a new gasket on the bolts. Position the fuel pump to the pushrod and the mounting pad. Turn the attaching bolts alternately and evenly and tighten them to 14-21 ft.lb. (19-29 Nm).
7. Install the fuel outlet and inlet 001886 and tighten the outlet fitting to specifications. If any rubber hoses are cracked, hardened or frayed, replace them with new fuel hose.
8. Start the engine and observe all connections for fuel leaks for two minutes. Stop the engine and check all fuel pump fuel line connections for fuel leaks by running a finger under the connections. Check for oil leaks at the fuel pump mounting pad.

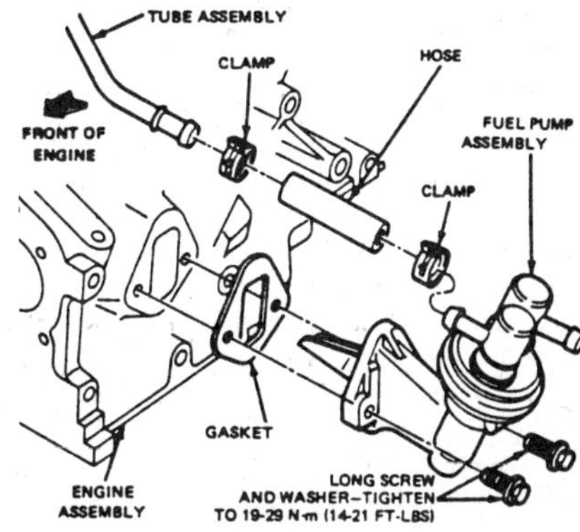

Fuel pump installation—typical

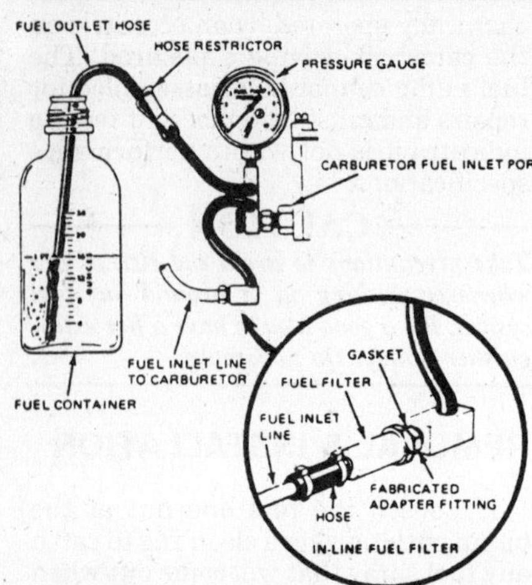

Fuel pump volume and pressure test equipment

DIAGNOSIS AND TESTING

If a problem exists with the fuel pump itself, it normally will deliver either no fuel at all, or not enough to sustain high engine speeds or loads. When an engine has a lean (fuel starvation) condition, the fuel pump is often suspected as being the source of the problem, however similar symptoms will be present if the fuel filter is clogged or the fuel tank is plugged or restricted. It could also be a carburetor problem, kinked or plugged fuel line or a leaking fuel hose. If the fuel pump is noisy, check for:

1. Loose fuel pump mounting bolts. Tighten to specifications if loose and replace the gasket if damaged or worn.
2. Check for loose or missing fuel line attaching clips. This condition will result in the noise being more audible when sitting inside the vehicle than standing along side it. Tighten the fuel lines or clips, if necessary.

Before removing a suspect fuel pump:

1. Make sure there is fuel in the tank.
2. Replace the fuel filter to eliminate that possibility.
3. Check all rubber hoses from the fuel pump to the fuel tank for kinks or cracks. With the engine idling, inspect all fuel hoses and lines for leaks in the lines or connections. Tighten loose connections and replace kinked, cracked or leaking lines and/or hoses.
4. Check the fuel pump outlet connection for leaks and tighten to specification if required.
5. Inspect the fuel pump diaphragm crimp (the area where the stamped steel section is attached to the casting) and the breather hole(s) in the casting for evidence of fuel or oil leakage. Replace the fuel pump if leaking.

Capacity (Volume) Test

1. Remove the carburetor air cleaner.
2. Slowly disconnect the fuel line at the fuel filter, using a backup wrench on the filter hex to prevent damage. Use clean rags to catch any fuel spray. Exercise caution as the fuel line is pressurized and take precautions to avoid the risk of fire.
3. Place a suitable non-breakable container (1 pint minimum capacity) at the end of the disconnected fuel line. A small piece of hose may be necessary on the fuel line end.
4. With the high tension wire removed from the coil, crank the engine ten revolutions to fill the fuel lines, then crank the engine for 10 seconds and measure the fuel collected. The pump should deliver ⅓ pint (0.158 liters) of fuel, minimum.
5. If the fuel flow is within specifications, perform the Pressure Test.
6. If the fuel flow is low, repeat the test using a remote vented can of gasoline. Remove the fuel pump inlet hose, then connect a length of fuel hose to the pump inlet and insert the other end into the remote gasoline can. If the fuel flow is now within specifications, the problem is a plugged in-tank filter or a leaking, kinked or plugged fuel line or hose. Make sure the fuel pump pushrod length is 6.10-6.14″ (155-156mm); if short, replace the pushrod and install the fuel pump. If the fuel flow is still low, replace the fuel pump.

Pressure Test

1. Connect a 0-15 psi fuel pump pressure tester (Rotunda No. 059-00008 or equivalent) to the carburetor end of the fuel line. No T-fitting is required.
2. Start the engine. It should be able to run for about 30 seconds on the fuel in the carburetor. Read the pressure on the gauge after about 10 seconds. It should be 4-6.5 psi (31-45 kPa).
3. If the pump pressure is too low or high, replace the fuel pump and retest.
4. Once all testing is complete, reconnect the fuel lines and remove the gauge.

Carburetor

The Motorcraft Model 2150A 2-bbl feedback carburetor is used on the 2.8L (171 CID) engine. The feedback carburetor system uses a pulsing solenoid to introduce fresh air from the air cleaner into the idle and main system vacuum passages to lean the fuel and air mixture from the maximum rich condition (solenoid closed) to the maximum lean condition (solenoid open). The solenoid operates under the control of the EEC-IV system.

The 2150A carburetor uses an all electric choke system, consisting of the choke pulldown diaphragm, choke housing and electric choke cap. The voltage applied to the choke cap is controlled by the EEC-IV computer through a "duty cycle" output, which varies between 0% (0 volts) and 100% (12 volts) to control choke operation. The tamper resistant choke cap retainer uses breakaway screws and is non-adjustable.

The fast idle speed at engine startup is controlled by the mechanical cam and adjustment screw. After startup, the cam moves out of the way, allowing the idle speed control (ISC) motor to control the idle speed. Both the kickdown and idle rpm are controlled by the EEC-IV system, eliminating the need for idle and fast idle speed adjustments. When the ignition is turned off (warm engine), the throttle rests against the curb idle screw stop to prevent run-on and then goes to maximum extension for preposition for the next engine start.

CARBURETOR ADJUSTMENTS

Most carburetor adjustments are set at the factory and should require no further attention. Choke setting and idle speed specifications are provided on the Vehicle Emission Control Decal in the engine compartment or on the engine itself.

Accelerator Pump Stroke Adjustment

The accelerator pump stroke has been set at the factory for a particular engine application and should not be readjusted. If the stroke has been changed from the specified hole, reset to specifications by performing the following procedure:

1. Using a blunt tipped punch, remove the roll pin from the accelerator pump cover. Support the area under the roll pin when removing and be careful not to lose the pin.
2. Rotate the pump link and rod assembly until the keyed end of the assembly is aligned with the keyed hole in the pump over travel lever.
3. Reposition the rod and swivel assembly in the specified hole and reinstall the pump link in the accelerator pump cover. A service accelerator rod and swivel assembly is available (part no. 9F687) and must be used if replacement is necessary. Adjustment holes are not provided on the tempera-

ture compensated accelerator pump carburetor models.

4. Install the roll pin.

Dry Float Level Adjustment

The dry float level adjustment is a preliminary fuel level adjustment only. The final, wet level adjustment must be made after the carburetor is mounted on the engine.

With the air horn removed, the float raised and the fuel inlet needle seated, check the distance between the top surface of the main body (gasket removed) and the top surface of the float for conformance to specifications. Depress the float tab lightly to seat the fuel inlet needle.

WARNING: Excessive pressure can damage the viton tip on the needle.

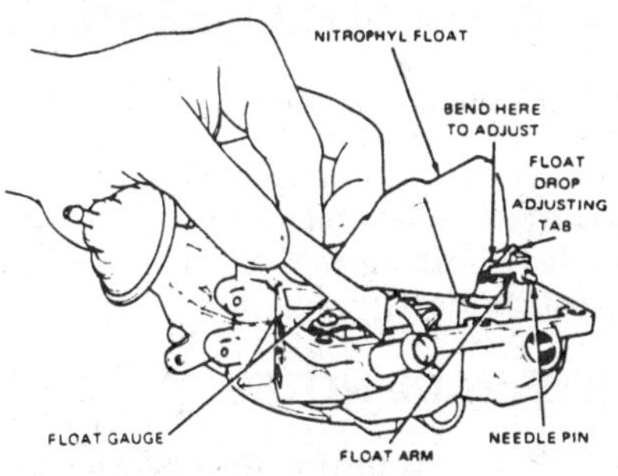

Float level adjustment for the Carter YFA & YFA Feedback carburetor

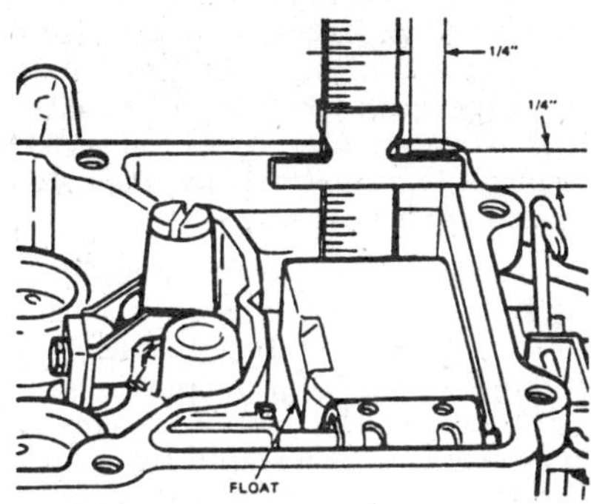

Float level adjustment for the Motorcraft 2150A 2-bbl carburetor

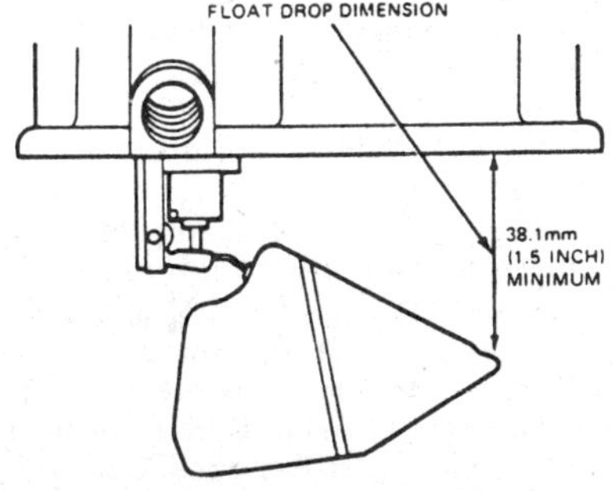

Float drop adjustment for the Carter YFA & YFA Feedback carburetor

Take the measurement near the center of the float at a point ⅛″ (3.2mm) from the free end of the float. If a cardboard float gauge is used, place the gauge in the corner of the enlarged end section of the fuel bowl. The gauge should touch the float near the end, but not on the end radius. If necessary, bend the tab on the float to bring the setting within the specified limits. This should provide the proper preliminary fuel level setting.

Wet Float Level Adjustment

1. With the vehicle level, engine warm and running, remove the air cleaner.
2. Insert fuel float level gauge T83L-9550-A, or equivalent, with the pointed end into the fuel bowl vent stack and rest the level across the other vent.
3. Siphon fuel into the sight tube and allow the fuel to reach a steady level. Take precautions to avoid the risk of fire. Do not smoke during this procedure.
4. Press down to level the gauge and read the fuel level on the sight tube. If the level is in the specified band, adjustment is not necessary. If the level is not correct, note the level on the sight and proceed to the next step.
5. Stop the engine and remove the choke link, air horn attaching screws, the vent hose and the air horn assembly.
6. Measure the vertical distance from the top of the machined surface of the main body to the level of the fuel in the fuel bowl.
7. With this measurement as a reference, bend the float tab up to raise the level or down to lower the level. Adjust to bring the fuel level to specifications.
8. Recheck the fuel level on the sight gauge. If OK, install the remaining air horn screws. If not OK, repeat the adjustment procedure.
9. Install the choke link and check the choke plate to make sure its free.
10. Tighten the air horn screws. Install the carburetor vent (canister) hose, then check and adjust the curb idle speed. Install the air cleaner.

Idle Speed Adjustment

NOTE: If the curb idle rpm is not within specifications after performing this procedure, it will be necessary to have the EEC-IV system diagnosed by a qualified service facility with the necessary electronic equipment.

1. Warm up the engine in Park or Neutral until it reaches normal operating temperature. Set the parking brake and block the drive wheels. Make sure all accessories are turned off.
2. Remove the air charge temperature (ACT) sensor and adapter from the air cleaner tray by removing the retaining clip. Leave the wiring harness connected.
3. Remove the air cleaner and disconnect and plug the vacuum line at the cold weather duct and valve motor.
4. Turn the engine off and verify that the idle speed control (ISC) plunger moves to its maximum extension within 10 seconds.
5. Disconnect and plug the EGR vacuum hose. Disconnect the idle speed control.
6. With the engine running, manually open the throttle and set the fast idle adjusting screw on the high cam.
7. Adjust the fast idle speed to the specification given on the underhood emission control sticker.
8. Open the throttle manually to release the fast idle cam, allowing the throttle lever to rest on the ISC plunger.
9. Loosen the ISC bracket lock screw, then adjust the ISC bracket screw to obtain 2,000 rpm. Tighten the bracket lock screw.
10. Reconnect the ISC motor connector. The engine rpm should automatically return to curb idle.
11. Simultaneously:
    a. manually hold the throttle above 1,000 rpm
    b. push the ISC plunger until it retracts fully
    c. after plunger retracts, release the throttle and quickly unplug the connection.
12. Adjust the anti-dieseling speed throttle stop screw to 750 rpm with the transmission (automatic or manual) in Neutral. Be careful to adjust the anti-dieseling stop screw, NOT the curb idle stop screw.
13. Connect the ISC and EGR vacuum hoses.
14. Turn the engine off, then restart the engine and verify that curb idle speed is within specifications.

Mixture Adjustment

The fuel mixture is preset at the factory and computer controlled thereafter. No adjustments are possible without the use of propane enrichment equipment that is not readily available to the do-it-yourself market. All mixture adjustments should be performed at a qualified service facility to insure compliance with Federal and/or State Emission Control Standards.

REMOVAL & INSTALLATION

1. Remove the air cleaner.

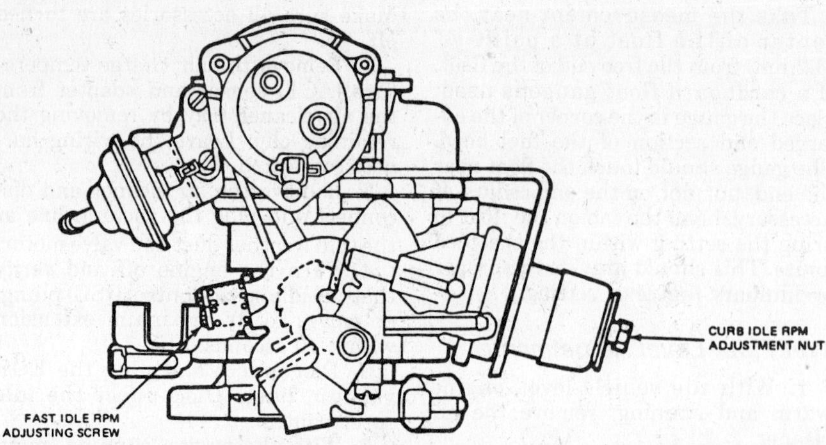

4-122, 140 engines – Carter YFA & YFA Feedback fast idle speed adjustment

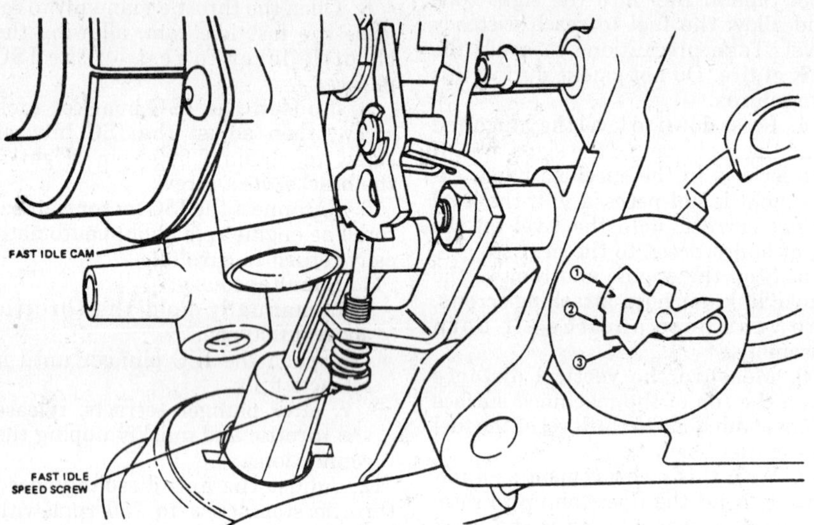

Motorcraft 2150A 2-bbl carburetor fast isle speed adjustment

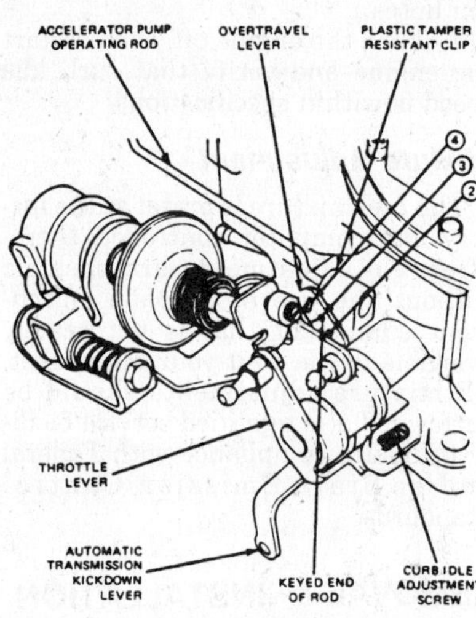

Accelerator pump stroke adjustment

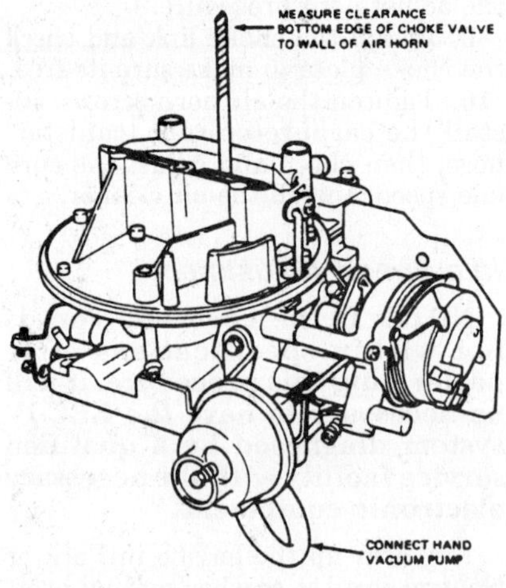

Motorcraft 2150A choke plate pulldown adjustment

2. Remove the throttle cable from the throttle lever. Tag and disconnect all vacuum lines, emission hoses and electrical connections.

3. Disconnect the fuel line at the carburetor. Use a clean rag to catch any fuel spray and use a backup wrench on the fuel filter hex to avoid twisting the line.

4. Remove the carburetor retaining nuts, then lift off the carburetor.

5. Remove the carburetor mounting gasket spacer, if equipped.

6. Clean the gasket mating surfaces of the spacer and carburetor.

7. Position a new gasket on the spacer and install the carburetor. Secure the carburetor with the mounting nuts. To prevent leakage, distortion or damage to the carburetor body flange, snug the nuts then alternately tighten each nut in a criss-cross pattern to 14-16 ft.lb. (20-21 Nm).

8. Connect the fuel line and throttle cable.

9. Connect all emission lines, vacuum hoses and electrical connectors.

10. Start the engine and check the idle speeds (fast and curb). Refer to the underhood emission sticker for specifications.

OVERHAUL NOTES

NOTE: All major and minor repair kits contain detailed instructions and illustrations. Refer to them for complete rebuilding instructions. To prevent damage to the throttle plates, make a stand using four bolts, eight flat washers and eight nuts. Place a washer and nut on the bolt, install through the carburetor base and secure with a nut.

Generally, when a carburetor requires major service, rebuilt one is purchased on an exchange basis, or a kit may be bought for overhauling the carburetor. The kit contains the necessary parts (see below) and some form of instructions for carburetor rebuilding. The instructions may vary between a simple exploded view and detailed step-by-step rebuilding instructions. Unless you are familiar with carburetor overhaul, the latter should be used.

There are some general overhaul procedures which should always be observed:

Efficient carburetion depends greatly on careful cleaning and inspection during overhaul since dirt, gum, water, or varnish in or on the carburetor parts are often responsible for poor performance. Overhaul your carburetor in a clean, dust-free area. Carefully disassembly the carburetor, referring often to the exploded views. Keep all

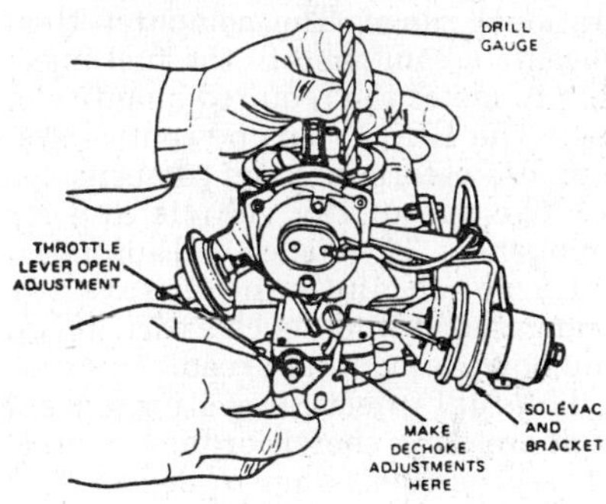

Choke plate pulldown adjustment—Carter YFA & YFA Feedback carburetor

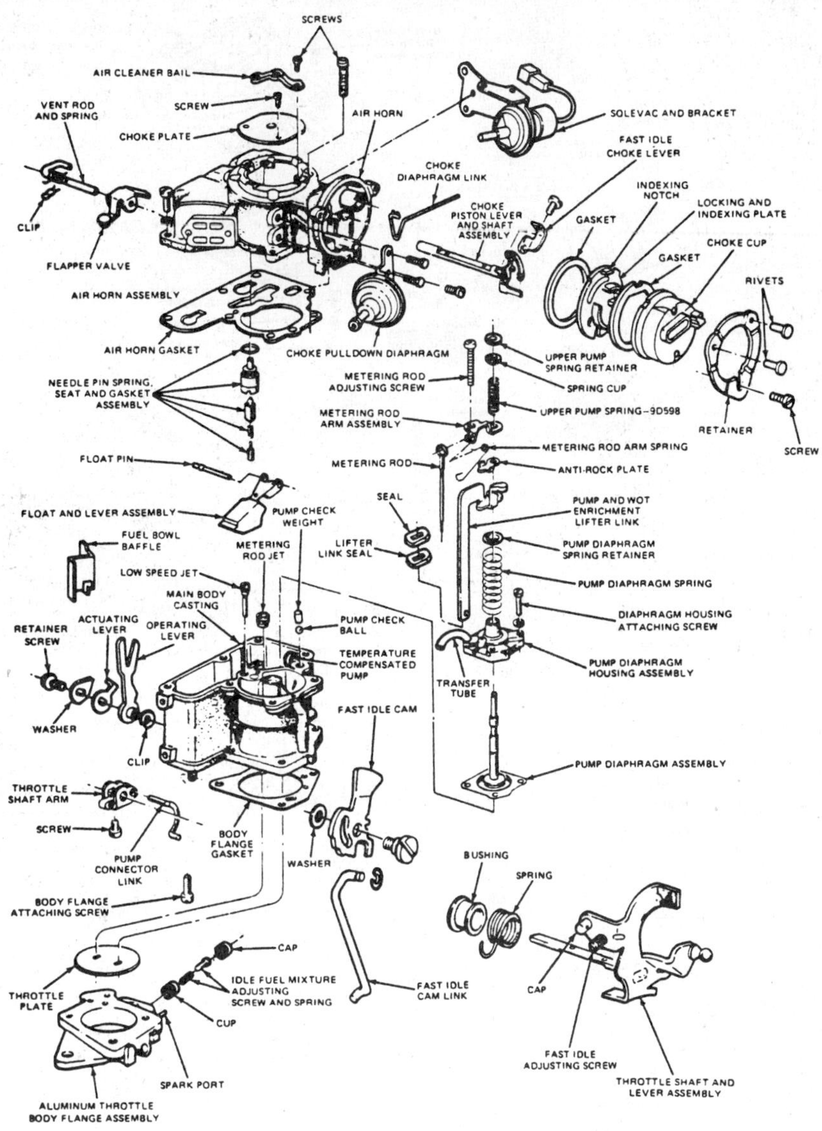

Carter YFA 1-bbl. carburetor—all except California models

similar and lookalike parts segregated during disassembly and cleaning to avoid accidental interchange during assembly. Make a note of all jet sizes.

When the carburetor is disassembled, wash all parts (except diaphragms, electric choke units. pump plunger, and any other plastic, leather, fiber, or rubber parts) in clean carburetor solvent. Do not leave parts in the solvent any longer than is necessary to sufficiently loosen the deposits. Excessive cleaning may remove the special finish from the float bowl and choke valve bodies, leaving these parts unfit for service. Rinse all parts in clean solvent and blow them dry with compressed air or allow them to air dry. Wipe clean all cork, plastic, leather, and fiber parts with a clean, lint free cloth.

Blow out all passages and jets with compressed air and be sure that there are no restrictions or blockages. Never use wire or similar tools to clean jets, fuel passages, or air bleeds. Clean all jets and valves separately to avoid accidental interchange.

Check all parts for wear or damage. If wear or damage is found, replace the defective parts. Especially check the following:

1. Check the float needle and seat for wear. If wear is found, replace the complete assembly.
2. Check the float hinge pin for wear and the float(s) for dents or distortion. Replace the float if fuel has leaked into it.
3. Check the throttle and choke shaft bores for wear or an out-of-round condition. Damage or wear to the throttle arm, shaft, shaft bore will often require replacement of the throttle body. These parts require a close tolerance; wear may allow air leakage, which could affect starting and idling.

NOTE: Throttle shafts and bushings are usually not included in overhaul kits. They can be purchased separately.

4. Inspect the idle mixture adjusting needles for burrs or grooves. Any such condition requires replacement of the needle, since you will not be able to obtain a satisfactory idle.
5. Test the accelerator pump check valves. They should pass air one way but not the other. Test for proper seating by blowing and sucking on the valve. Replace the valve if necessary. If the valve is satisfactory, wash the valve again to remove breath moisture.
6. Check the bowl cover for warped surfaces with a straightedge.
7. Closely inspect the valves and seats for wear and damage, replacing as necessary.
8. After the carburetor is assembled, check the choke valve for freedom of operation.

Carburetor overhaul kits are recommended for each overhaul. These kits contain all gaskets and new parts to replace those that deteriorate most rapidly. Failure to replace all parts supplied with the kit (especially gaskets) can result in poor performance later. Some carburetor manufacturers supply overhaul kits of three basic types: minor repair; major repair; and gasket kits. Basically, they contain the following:

Minor Repair Kits:

- All gaskets
- Float needle valve
- Volume control screw
- All diaphragms
- Spring for the pump diaphragm

Major Repair Kits:

- All jets and gaskets
- All diaphragms
- Float needle valve
- Volume control screw

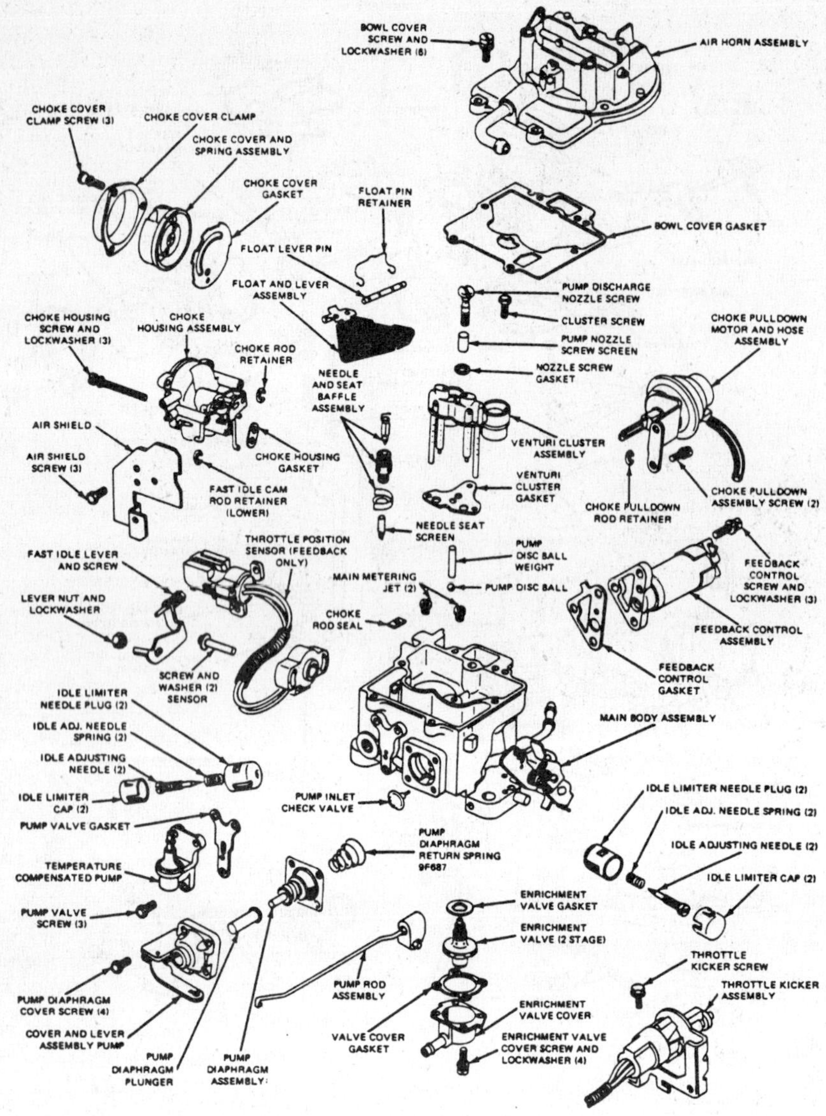

Motorcraft 2150A 2-bbl. carburetor

- Pump ball valve
- Main jet carrier
- Float
- Other necessary items
- Some cover holddown screws and washers

Gasket Kits:

- All gaskets

After cleaning and checking all components, reassemble the carburetor, using new parts and referring to the exploded view. When reassembling, make sure that all screw and jets are tight in their seats, buy do not overtighten, as the tips will be distorted. Tighten all screws gradually, in rotation. Do not tighten needle valves into their seat; uneven jetting will result. Always use new gaskets. Be sure to adjust the float level when reassembling.

FUEL INJECTION SYSTEM

The electronic fuel injection (EFI) system is classified as a multi-point, pulse time, speed density fuel delivery system which meters fuel into the intake air stream in accordance with engine demand through four or six injectors mounted on a tuned intake manifold.

An on-board electronic engine control (EEC-IV) computer accepts inputs from various engine sensors to compute the required fuel flow rate necessary to maintain a prescribed air/fuel ratio throughout the entire engine operational range. The computer then outputs a command to the fuel injectors to meter the required quantity of fuel. The EEC-IV engine control system also determines and compensates for the age of the vehicle and its uniqueness. The system will automatically sense and compensate for changes in altitude, such as driving up and down a mountain road.

The fuel injection system uses a high pressure, chassis or tank mounted electric fuel pump to deliver fuel from the tank to the fuel charging manifold assembly. The fuel charging manifold assembly incorporates electrically actuated fuel injectors directly above each of the engine's intake ports. The injectors, when energized, spray a metered quantity of fuel into the intake air stream. A constant pressure drop is maintained across the injector nozzles by a pressure regulator, connected in series with the fuel injectors and positioned downstream from them. Excess fuel supplied by the pump, but not required by the engine, passes through the regulator and returns to the fuel tank through a fuel return line.

On 4-cylinder engines, all injectors are energized simultaneously, once every crankshaft revolution. On V6 engines, the injectors are energized in two groups of three injectors, with each group activated once every other crankshaft revolution. The period of time that the injectors are energized (injector "on time" or "pulse width") is controlled by the EEC-IV computer. The input from various sensors is used to compute the required fuel flow rate necessary to maintain a prescribed air/fuel ratio.

CAUTION

Fuel supply lines on vehicles with fuel injection will remain pressurized for long periods of time after engine shutdown. This fuel pressure must be relieved before any service procedures are attempted on the fuel system.

RELIEVING FUEL SYSTEM PRESSURE

All fuel injected engines are equipped with a pressure relief valve located on the fuel supply manifold. Remove the fuel tank cap and attach fuel pressure gauge T80L-9974-A, or equivalent, to the valve to release the fuel pressure. If a suitable pressure gauge is not available, disconnect the vacuum hose from the fuel pressure regulator and attach a hand vacuum pump. Apply about 25 in.Hg (84 kPa) of vacuum to the regulator to vent the fuel system pressure into the fuel tank

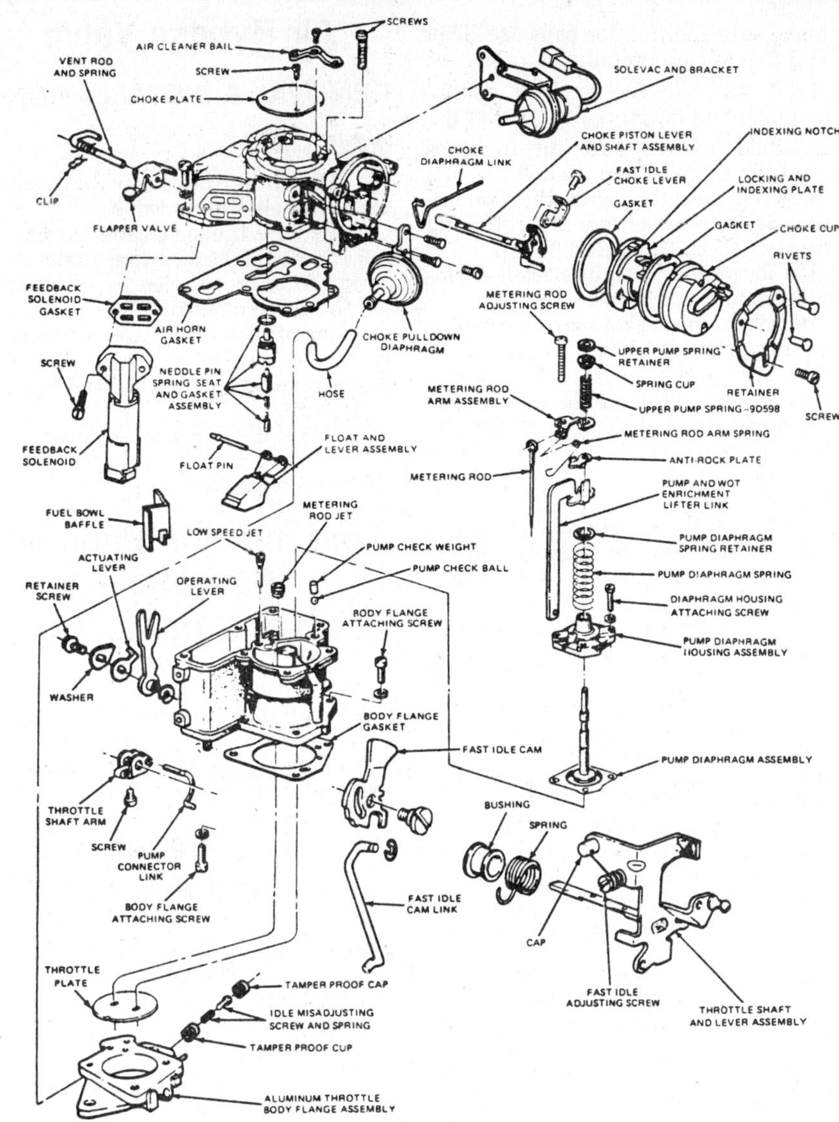

Carter YFA 1-bbl. Feedback carburetor—California models

through the fuel return hose. Note that this procedure will remove the fuel pressure from the lines, but not the fuel. Take precautions to avoid the risk of fire and use clean rags to soak up any spilled fuel when the lines are disconnected.

Quick Connect Fuel Line Fittings

REMOVAL & INSTALLATION

NOTE: Quick Connect (push) type fuel line fittings must be disconnected using proper procedures or the fitting may be damaged. Two types of retainers are used on the push connect fittings. Line sizes of 3/8" and 5/16" use a "hairpin" clip retainer. 1/4" line connectors use a "duck bill" clip retainer. In addition, some engines use spring lock connections secured by a garter spring which requires a special tool (T81P-19623-G) for removal.

Hairpin Clip

1. Clean all dirt and/or grease from the fitting. Spread the two clip legs about 1/8" (3mm) each to disengage from the fitting and pull the clip outward from the fitting. Use finger pressure only, do not use any tools.
2. Grasp the fitting and hose assembly and pull away from the steel line. Twist the fitting and hose assembly slightly while pulling, if necessary, when a sticking condition exists.
3. Inspect the hairpin clip for damage, replace the clip if necessary. Reinstall the clip in position on the fitting.
4. Inspect the fitting and inside of the connector to insure freedom of dirt or obstruction. Install fitting into the connector and push together. A click will be heard when the hairpin snaps into proper connection. Pull on the line to insure full engagement.

Duck Bill Clip

1. A special tool is available from Ford for removing the retaining clips (Ford Tool No. T82L-9500-AH). If the tool is not on hand see Step 2. Align the slot on the push connector disconnect tool with either tab on the retaining clip. Pull the line from the connector.
2. If the special clip tool is not available, use a pair of narrow 6" (152mm) channel lock pliers with a jaw width of 0.2" (5mm) or less. Align the jaws of the pliers with the openings of the fitting case and compress the part of the retaining clip that engages the case. Compressing the retaining clip will release the fitting which may be pulled from the connector. Both sides of the clip must be compressed at the same time to disengage.
3. Inspect the retaining clip, fitting end and connector. Replace the clip if any damage is apparent.
4. Push the line into the steel connector until a click is heard, indicting the clip is in place. Pull on the line to check engagement.

Electric Fuel Pump

REMOVAL & INSTALLATION

The electric fuel pump is either mounted on the chassis, in an assembly with the inline fuel filter, or at the base of the fuel tank sending unit in the fuel tank. For chassis mounted pumps, follow the procedures under "Fuel Filter Removal and Installation" in ROUTINE MAINTENANCE, then disconnect the electrical connector and remove the fuel pump and filter mounting bracket with the filter and pump attached. For tank mounted pumps, follow the procedures under remove the tank, then the pump and sending unit. In either case, the fuel pump is non-serviceable and must be replaced as a unit if defective. Do not attempt to apply battery voltage to the pump to check its operation while removed from the vehicle, as running the pump dry will destroy it. Depressurize the fuel system before attempting to remove any fuel lines.

Fuel Charging Assembly

REMOVAL & INSTALLATION

4-140 (2.3L)

1. Drain the cooling system.
2. Disconnect the negative battery cable.
3. Relieve the fuel system pressure as described above.
4. Disconnect the electrical connectors to the throttle position sensor, knock sensor, air charge temperature sensor, coolant temperature sensor and the injector wiring harness.
5. Tag and disconnect the vacuum lines at the upper intake manifold vacuum tree, the EGR valve vacuum line and the fuel pressure regulator vacuum line.
6. Remove the throttle linkage shield and disconnect the throttle linkage and speed control cable, if equipped. Unbolt the accelerator cable from the bracket and position the cable out of the way.
7. Disconnect the air intake hose, air bypass hose and crankcase vent hose.
8. Disconnect the PCV hose from the fitting on the underside of the upper intake manifold.
9. Loosen the hose clamp on the coolant bypass line at the lower intake manifold and disconnect the hose.
10. Disconnect the EGR tube from the EGR valve by removing the flange nut.
11. Remove the four upper intake manifold retaining nuts, then remove the upper intake manifold and air throttle body assembly.
12. Disconnect the push connect fitting at the fuel supply manifold and fuel return lines, then disconnect the fuel return line from the fuel supply manifold.
13. Remove the engine oil dipstick bracket retaining bolt.
14. Disconnect the electrical connectors from all four fuel injectors and move the harness aside.
15. Remove the two fuel supply manifold retaining bolt, then carefully remove the fuel supply manifold with the injectors attached. The injectors may be removed from the fuel supply manifold at this time by exerting a slight twisting/pulling motion.
16. Lubricate new injector O-rings with a light grade engine oil and install two on each injector. If the injectors were not removed from the fuel supply manifold, only one O-ring will be necessary. Do not use silicone grease on the O-rings as it will clog the injectors. Make sure the injector caps are clean and free of contamination.
17. Install the fuel injector supply manifold and injectors into the intake manifold, making sure the injectors are fully seated, then secure the fuel manifold assembly with the two retaining bolts. Tighten the retaining bolts to 15-22 ft.lb. (20-30 Nm).
18. Reconnect the four electrical connectors to the injectors.
19. Clean the gasket mating surfaces of the upper and lower intake manifold. Place a new gasket on the lower intake manifold, then place the upper intake manifold in position. Install the four retaining bolts and tighten them, in sequence, to 15-22 ft.lb. (20-30 Nm).
20. Install the engine oil dipstick.
21. Connect the fuel supply and return fuel lines to the fuel supply manifold.
22. Connect the EGR tube to the EGR valve and tighten the fitting to 6-8.5 ft.lb. (8-11.5 Nm).
23. Connect the coolant bypass line and tighten the clamp.
24. Connect the PCV system hose to the fitting on the underside of the upper intake manifold.
25. Reconect the upper intake manifold vacuum lines, being careful to install them in their original locations. Reconnect the vacuum lines to the EGR valve and fuel pressure regulator.
26. Hold the accelerator cable bracket in position on the upper intake manifold and install the retaining bolt. Tighten the bolt to 10-15 ft.lb. (13-20 Nm).
27. Install the accelerator cable to the bracket.
28. If the air intake throttle body was removed from the upper intake manifold, position a new gasket on the mounting flange and install the throttle body.
29. Connect the accelerator cable and speed control cable. Install the throttle linkage shield.
30. Reconnect the electrical connectors to the throttle position sensor, knock sensor, air charge temperature sensor, coolant temperature sensor and injector wiring harness.
31. Connect the air intake hose, air bypass hose and crankcase vent hose.
32. Connect the negative battery cable.
33. Refill the cooling system.
34. Build up fuel pressure by turning the ignition switch on and off at least six times, leaving the ignition on for at least five seconds each time. Check for fuel leaks.
35. Start the engine and allow it to reach normal operating temperature, then check for coolant leaks.

Air Bypass Valve

REMOVAL & INSTALLATION

4-140 (2.3L)

1. Disconnect the electrical connector at the air bypass valve.
2. Remove the air cleaner cover.
3. Separate the air bypass valve and gasket from the air cleaner by removing the three mounting bolts.
4. Install the air bypass valve and gasket to the air cleaner cover and tighten the retaining bolts to 6-8 ft.lb. (8-11 Nm).
5. Install the air cleaner cover.
6. Reconnect the air bypass valve electrical connector.

Fuel Injector Manifold Assembly

REMOVAL & INSTALLATION

4-140 (2.3L)

For injector and fuel manifold removal, follow the procedures under "Fuel Charging Assembly Removal and Installation."

Fuel Pressure Regulator

REMOVAL & INSTALLATION

All Engines

1. Depressurize the fuel system as described earlier.
2. Remove the vacuum line at the pressure regulator.
3. Remove the three allen retaining screws from the regulator housing.
4. Remove the pressure regulator assembly, gasket and O-ring. Discard the gasket and check the O-ring for signs of cracks or deterioration.
5. Clean the gasket mating surfaces. If scraping is necessary, be careful not to damage the fuel pressure regulator or supply line gasket mating surfaces.
6. Lubricate the pressure regulator O-ring with with light engine oil. Do not use silicone grease; it will clog the injectors.
7. Install the O-ring and a new gasket on the pressure regulator.
8. Install the pressure regulator on the fuel manifold and tighten the retaining screws to 27-40 in.lb. (3-4 Nm).
9. Install the vacuum line at the pressure regulator. Build up fuel pressure by turning the ignition switch on and off at least six times, leaving the ignition on for at least five seconds each time. Check for fuel leaks.

Throttle Position Sensor (TPS)

REMOVAL & INSTALLATION

All Engines

1. Disconnect the throttle position sensor electrical connector.
2. On the 2.3L engine, remove the screw retaining the TPS electrical connector to the air throttle body.
3. Scribe alignment marks on the air throttle body and TPS sensor to indicate proper alignment during installation.
4. Remove the two TPS retaining screws, then remove the TPS and gasket from the throttle body.
5. To install, place the TPS and gasket on the throttle body, making sure the rotary tangs on the sensor are aligned with the throttle shaft blade. Slide the rotary tangs into position over the throttle shaft blade, then rotate the throttle position sensor CLOCKWISE ONLY to its installed position (align the scribe marks made earlier).

CAUTION

Failure to install the TPS in this manner may result in excessive idle speeds.

6. Once the scribe marks are aligned, install the TPS retaining screws and tighten them to 14-16 in.lb. (1-2 Nm).
7. On the 2.3L engine, position the electrical connector over the locating dimple, then secure to the throttle body with the retaining screw.
8. Reconnect the TPS electrical connector, start the engine and check the idle speed.

NOTE: Adjustment of the throttle position sensor requires the use of expensive test equipment that is not available to the do-it-yourself market. If adjustment is required, it should be performed by a qualified technician with the proper training and equipment to diagnose and repair the EEC-IV engine control system.

DIESEL FUEL SYSTEM

Adjustments

INJECTION TIMING

4-134 (2.2L)

NOTE: Special Tools Ford 14-0303, Static Timing Gauge Adapter and D82L4201A, Metric Dial Indicator, or the equivalents are necessary to set or check the injector timing.

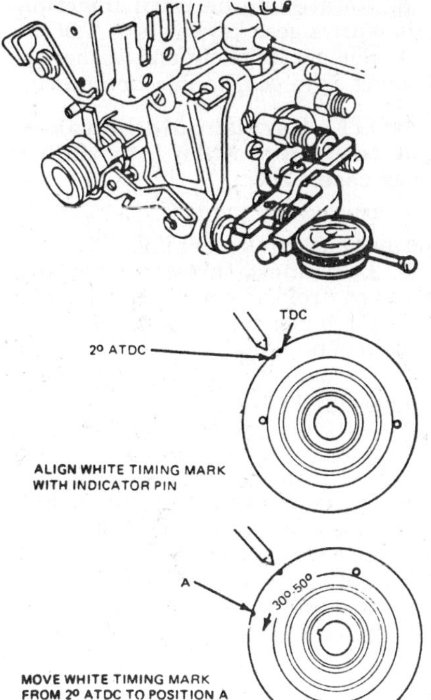

Moving the crabkshaft pulley timing mark

1. Disconnect both battery ground cables. Remove the air inlet hose from the air cleaner and intake manifold.
2. Remove the distributor head plug bolt and washer from the injection pump.
3. Install the Timing Gauge Adapter and Metric Dial Indicator so that the indicator pointer is in contact with the injector pump plunger and gauge reads approximately 0.08".
4. Align the 2° ATDC (after top dead center) on the crankshaft pulley with the indicator on the timing case cover.
5. Slowly turn the engine counterclockwise until the dial indicator pointer stops moving (approximately 30°-50°).
6. Adjust the dial indicator to 0 (Zero). Confirm that the dial indicator does not move from Zero, by rotating the crankshaft slightly right and left.
7. Turn the crankshaft clockwise until the timing mark aligns with the cover indicator. The dial indicator should read 1, plus or minus 0.0008". If the reading is not within specifications, adjust the timing as follows: Loosen the injection pump mounting nuts and bolts. Rotate the injection pump counterclockwise (reverse direction of engine rotation) past the correct timing position, then clockwise until the timing is correct. This procedure will eliminate gear backlash. Repeat Steps 5, 6, and 7 to check that the timing is properly adjusted.
8. Remove the dial indicator and adapter. Install the injector head gasket and plug. Install all removed parts.
9. Run engine, check and adjust idle RPM. Check for fuel leaks.

Fuel Supply Pump

REMOVAL & INSTALLATION

4-134 (2.2L)

1. Disconnect both ground cables from the batteries.
2. Disconnect and cap the fuel inlet and outlet lines. Remove the nuts and bolts mounting the pump to mounting bracket and remove the pump.
3. Install in the reverse order of removal.

Fuel Filter

REMOVAL & INSTALLATION

1. Remove the spin-on filter by turning counterclockwise as viewed from the bottom of the filter.
2. Clean the filter mounting flange. Coat the new filter sealing lip with diesel fuel.
3. Install and tighten filter until the gasket touches the mounting flange. Tighten an additional one-half turn. Refer to the instructions with the new filter, if they call for more than one-half turn tightening-follow the instructions.

Water Separator

SERVICING

4-134 (2.2L)

Water should be drained from the fuel sedimenter whenever the warning light comes on or every 5,000 miles. More frequent drain intervals may be required depending on fuel quality and vehicle usage.

The instrument panel warning lamp (WATER IN FUEL) will glow when approximately ½ Liter of water has accumulated in the sedimenter. When the warning lamp glows, shut off the engine as soon as safely possible. A suitable drain pan or container should be placed under the sedimenter, which is mounted inside the frame rail, underneath the driver's side of the cab. To drain the fuel sedimenter, pull up on the T-handle (located on the cab floor behind the driver's seat) until resistance is felt. Turn the ignition switch to the On position, so the warn-

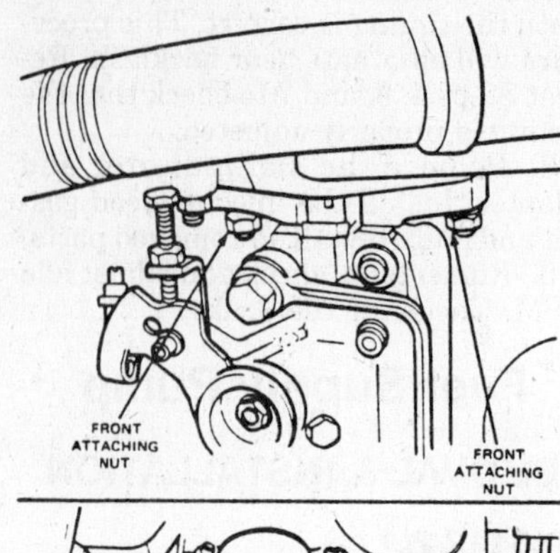

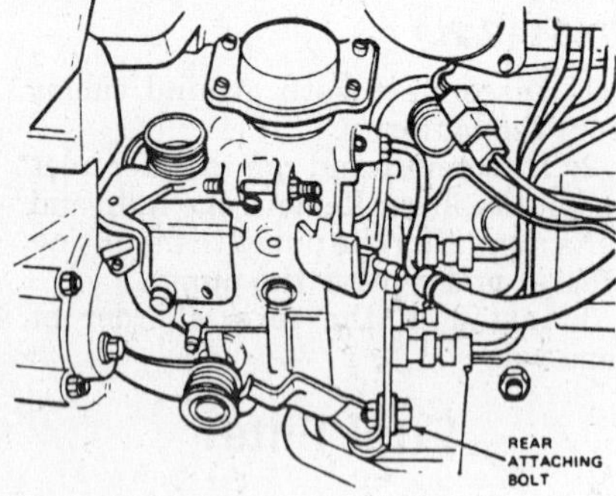

Injection pump attaching locations

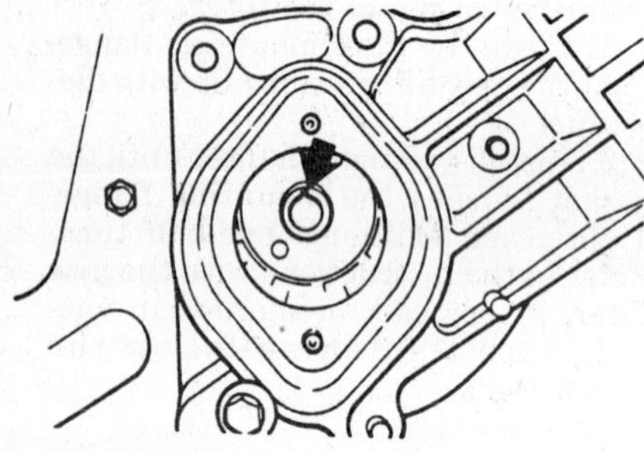

Aligning the key and keyway in the TDC position

ing lamp glows and hold T-handle up for approximately 45 seconds after lamp goes out.

To stop draining fuel, release T-handle and inspect sedimenter to verify that draining has stopped. Discard drained fluid suitably.

Injection Pump

REMOVAL & INSTALLATION

4-134 (2.2L)

1. Disconnect battery ground cables from both batteries.
2. Remove radiator fan and shroud. Loosen and remove A/C compressor/power steering pump drive belt and idler pulley, if so equipped. Remove injection pump drive gear cover and gasket.
3. Rotate engine until injection pump drive gear keyway is at TDC.
4. Remove large nut and washer attaching drive gear to injection pump.

NOTE: Care should be taken not to drop washer into timing gear case.

5. Disconnect intake hose from air cleaner and intake manifold.
6. Disconnect throttle cable and speed control cable, if so equipped.
7. Disconnect and cap fuel inlet line at injection pump.
8. Disconnect fuel shut-off solenoid lead at injection pump.
9. Disconnect and remove fuel injection lines from nozzles and injection pump. Cap all fuel lines and fittings.
10. Disconnect lower fuel return line from injection pump and fuel hoses. Loosen lower No.3 intake port nut and remove fuel return line.
11. Remove two nuts attaching injection pump to front timing gear cover and one bolt attaching pump to rear support bracket.
12. Install Gear and Hub Remover, Tool T83T-6306-A or equivalent, in drive gear cover and attach to injection pump drive gear. Rotate screw clockwise until injection pump disengages from drive gear. Remove the injection pump.

NOTE: Carefully remove injection pump to avoid dropping key into timing gear case. Disconnect cold start cable before removing injection pump from vehicle. Connect cold start cable to pump before positioning injection pump in timing gear case.

13. Install injection pump in position in timing gear case aligning key with keyway in drive gear in TDC position.

NOTE: Use care to avoid dropping key in timing gear case.

14. Install nuts and washers attaching injection pump to timing gear case and tighten to draw injection pump into position.

NOTE: Do not tighten to specification at this time.

15. Install bolt attaching injection pump to rear support. Install washer and nut attaching injection drive gear to injection pump and tighten.
16. Install injection pump drive gear cover, with new gasket, on timing gear case cover and tighten.
17. Adjust injection timing at this time.
18. Install lower fuel return line to injection pump and intake manifold stud. Tighten Banjo bolt on injection pump and nut on intake manifold. Install connecting fuel hoses and clamps. Install fuel injection lines to injection pump and nozzles and tighten.
19. Connect lead to fuel shut-off solenoid on injection pump. Connect fuel inlet line to injection pump and install hose clamp.
20. Install throttle cable and speed control cable, if so equipped.
21. Air bleed fuel system.
22. Install intake hose on air cleaner and intake manifold.
23. Install A/C compressor/power steering pump drive belt and idler pulley, if so equipped and tighten.
24. Install radiator shroud and radiator fan.
25. Connect battery ground cables to both batteries.
26. Run engine and check for oil and fuel leaks.

Injectors

REMOVAL & INSTALLATION

134 (2.2L)

1. Disconnect battery ground cables from both batteries.
2. Disconnect and remove injection lines from nozzles and injection pump. Cap all lines and fittings.
3. Remove fuel return line and gaskets.
4. Remove bolts attaching fuel line heater clamp to cylinder head and position heater out of the way.
5. Remove nozzles, using a 27mm deepwell socket.
6. Remove nozzle washer (copper) and nozzle gasket (steel), using Tool T71P-19703-C or equivalent.
7. Clean nozzle assemblies with Nozzle Cleaning Kit, Rotunda 14-0301 or equivalent, and a suitable solvent, and dry thoroughly. Clean nozzle seats in cylinder head with Nozzle Seat Cleaner, T83T-9527-B or equivalant.
8. Position new nozzle washers and gaskets in nozzle seats, install nozzles and tighten.

NOTE: Install nozzle gaskets with blue side face up (toward nozzle).

9. Position fuel line heater clamps,

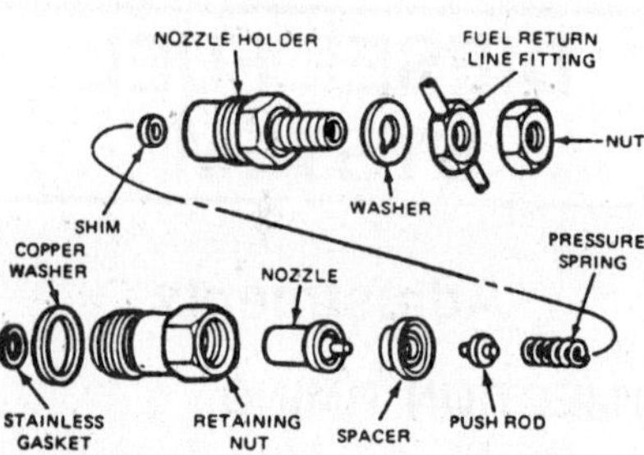

Fuel injection nozzle assembly components

install attaching bolts, and tighten to specification.

10. Install fuel return line with new gaskets on nozzles.

11. Install injection lines on nozzles and injection pump and tighten line nuts.

12. Connect battery ground cables to both batteries. Run engine and check for fuel leaks.

TESTING

Where ideal conditions of good combustion, specified engine temperature control and absolutely clean fuel prevail, nozzles require little attention. Nozzle trouble is usually indicated by one or more of the following symptoms:

1. Smoky exhaust (black)
2. Loss of power
3. Misfiring
4. Increased fuel consumption
5. Combustion knock
6. Engine overheating

Where faulty nozzle operation is suspected on an engine that is misfiring or puffing black smoke, a simple test can be made to determine which cylinder is causing the difficulty.

With the engine running at a speed that makes the problem most pronounced, momentarily loosen the high pressure fuel inlet line connection on one nozzle assembly sufficiently to "cut-out" the cylinder (one half to one turn) to leak off the fuel charge to the cylinder. Then tighten to specifications.

Check each cylinder in the same manner. If one is found where loosening makes no difference in the irregular operature or causes puffing black smoke to stop, the injection nozzle for the cylinder should be serviced or replaced.

CAUTION

Keep eyes and hands away from nozzle spray. Fuel spraying from the nozzle under high pressure can penetrate the skin and cause infection. Medical attention should be provided immediately in the event of skin penetration.

Fuel Control

On-off fuel control is provided by an electric solenoid located in the diesel injection pump housing cover. Current is supplied to the solenoid when the ignition switch is turned on. If no fuel is supplied with the ignition switch in the on position, check for current at the solenoid terminal before condemning the solenoid.

Fuel Cut-Off Solenoid

REMOVAL & INSTALLATION

1. Disconnect battery ground cables from both batteries.
2. Remove connector from fuel cut-off solenoid.
3. Remove fuel cut-off solenoid assembly.
4. Install fuel cut-off solenoid, with new O-ring, and tighten.
5. Install connector on fuel cut-off solenoid.
6. Connect battery ground cables to both batteries. Run engine and check for fuel leaks.

Glow Plug System

The "quick start; afterglow" system is used to enable the engine to start more quickly when the engine is cold. It consists of the flour glow plugs, the control module, two relays, a glow plug resistor assembly, coolant temperature switch, clutch and neutral switches and connecting wiring. Relay power and feedback circuits are protected by fuse links in the wiring harness. The control module is protected by a separate 10A fuse in the fuse panel.

When the ignition switch is turned to the ON position, a Wait-to-Start signal appears near the cold-start knob on the panel. When the signal appears, relay No. 1 also closes and full system voltage is applied to the glow plugs. If engine coolant temperature is below 30°C (86°F), relay No.2 also closes at this time. After three seconds, the control module turns off the Wait-to-Start light indicating that the engine is ready for starting. If the ignition switch is left in the ON position about three seconds more without cranking, the control opens relay No. 1 and current to the plugs stops to prevent overheating. However, if coolant temperature is below 30°C (86°F) when relay No. 1 opens, relay No.2 remains closed to apply reduced voltage to the plugs through the glow plug resistor until the ignition switch is turned off.

When the engine is cranked, the control module cycles relay No. 1 intermittently. Thus, glow plug voltage will alternate between 12 and four volts, during cranking, with relay No.2 closed, or between 12 and zero volts with relay No.2 open. After the engine starts, alternator output signals the control module to stop the No. 1 relay cycling and the afterglow function takes over.

If the engine coolant temperature is below 30°C (86°F), the No.2 relay remains closed. This applies reduced (4.2 to 5.3) voltage to the glow plugs through the glow plug resistor. When the vehicle is under way (clutch and neutral switches closed), or coolant temperature is above 30°C (86°F), the control module opens relay No.2, cutting off all current to the glow plugs.

TESTING THE GLOW PLUGS

1. Disconnect the leads from each glow plug. Connect one lead of the ohmmeter to the glow plug terminal and the other lead to a good ground. Set the ohmmeter on the X1 scale. Test each glow plug in the like manner.
2. If the meter indicates less than one ohm, the problem is not with the glow plug.
3. If the ohmmeter indicates one or more ohms, replace the glow plug and retest.

REMOVAL & INSTALLATION

1. Disconnect battery ground cables from both batteries.
2. Disconnect glow plug harness from glow plugs.
3. Using a 12mm deepwell socket, remove glow plugs.
4. Install glow plugs, using a 12mm deepwell socket, and tighten.
5. Install glow plug harness on glow plugs and tighten.
6. Connect battery ground cables to both batteries.

CHASSIS ELECTRICAL

NOTE: Always disconnect the battery ground cable before working on electrical equipment.

Blower Motor

REMOVAL & INSTALLATION

Without A/C

1. Remove the nut from the bottom of the plenum assembly just to the right of the heater core access cover.
2. Open the hood and disconnect the electrical harness from the blower motor by pushing on the connector tab and pulling off the connector.
3. Remove the mounting bolt from the upper right side of firewall.
4. Remove the mounting nuts from the heater case assembly.
5. Pull the blower motor assembly from the firewall case.

5\. Install all parts in the reverse order of removal. Use new sealer where necessary.

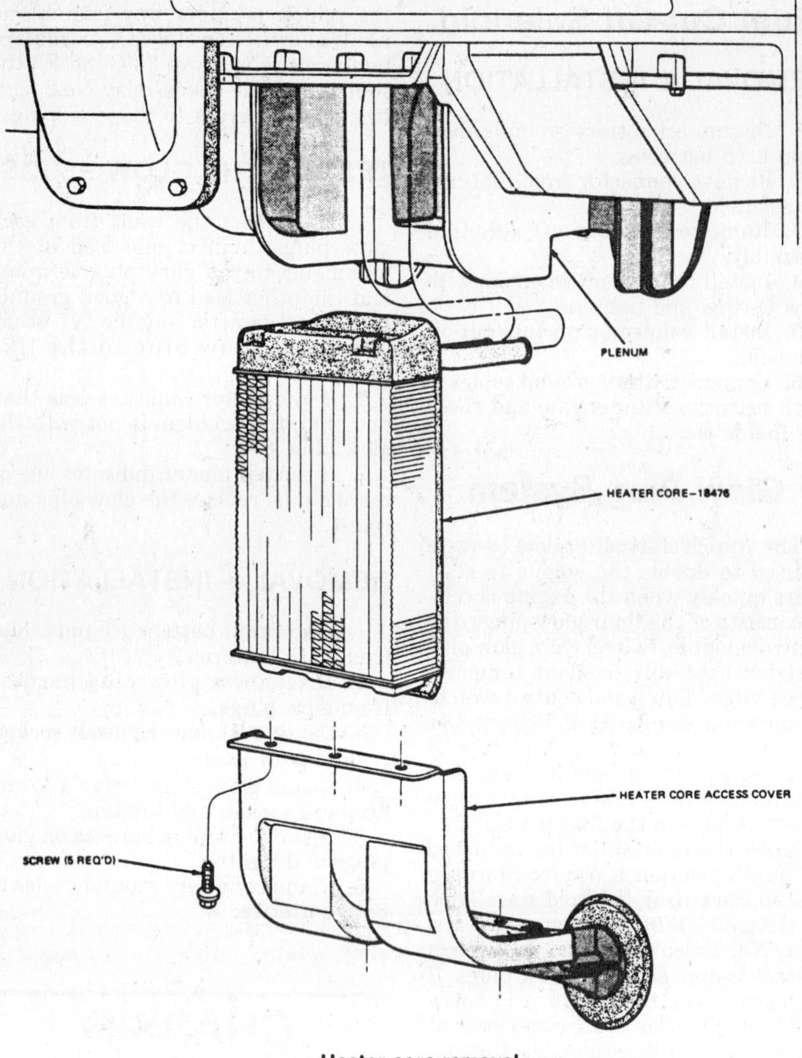

Heater core removal

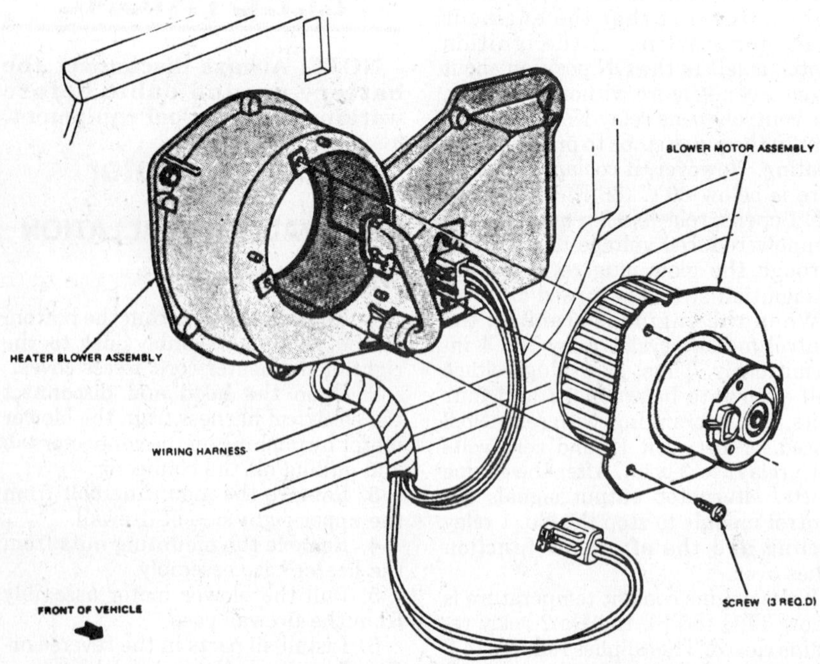

Blower motor assembly removal and installation

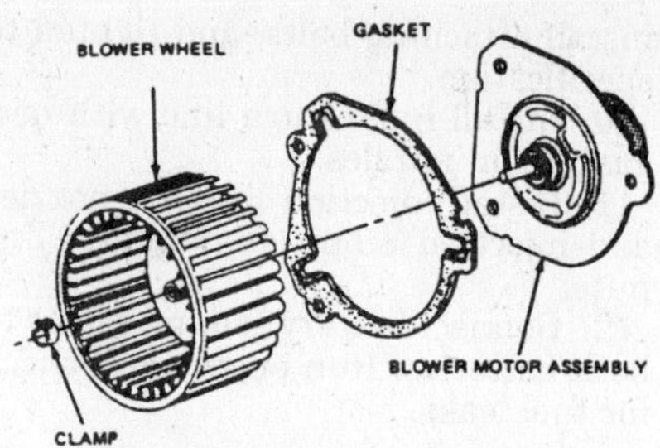

Blower wheel exploded view

With A/C

1. Open the hood and disconnect the heater blower wiring harness from the blower by pushing down on the locking tab and pulling the connector from the motor.
2. Remove the emission control box, if so equipped, from the front of the blower case. Three bolts hold the box in position.
3. Disconnect the blower motor cooling tube.
4. Remove the blower plate mounting screws and remove the blower motor from the case on the firewall.
4. Install all parts in the reverse order of removal. Replace sealer where necessary.

Heater Core

REMOVAL & INSTALLATION

With or Without A/C

1. Allow the engine to cool down completely. Drain the cooling system to a point that is below the heater hoses.
2. Disconnect the heater hoses from the heater core tubes. Plug the core tubes.
3. From under the dash, remove the screws that attach the access cover to the plenum assembly. Remove the access cover.
4. Pull the core down and out of the plenum assembly.
5. Install all parts in the reverse order of removal. Fill cooling thesystem, start the engine and check for leaks.

RADIO

REMOVAL & INSTALLATION

1. Disconnect the negative battery cable.
2. Remove the knobs and discs from the radio control shafts.

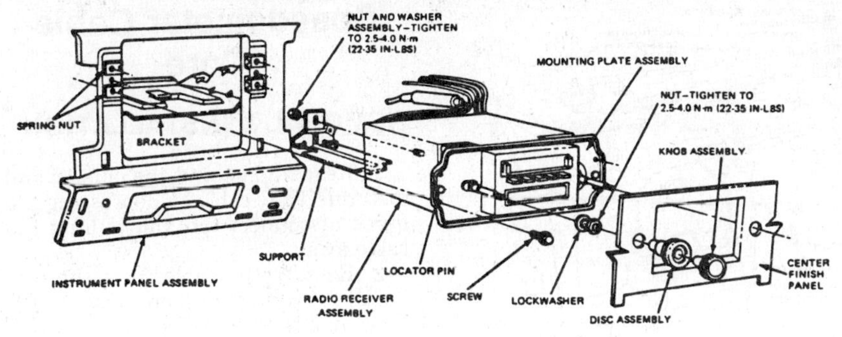

Radio removal and installtion

3. Remove the front finish panel assembly.
3. Remove the screws that attach the mounting plate assembly to the instrument panel and remove the radio with mounting plate and rear bracket.
4. Disconnect the antenna, speaker wires and power lead.
5. Install in the reverse order.

WINDSHIELD WIPERS

Motor

REMOVAL & INSTALLATION

1. Turn on the ignition and wiper switches. When the wiper blades are straight up and down on the windshield, turn off the ignition switch so that the wiper arms and blades remain in position.
2. Disconnect the negative battery cable.
3. Remove the wiper arm and blade from the right side.
4. Remove the pivot nut from the wiper arm drive and allow the pivot to drop into the cowl.
5. Remove the access cover from the right side of the firewall. Reach in and disconnect the linkage from the wiper motor drive arm.
6. Disconnect the wiring at the wiper motor.
7. Remove the wiper motor mounting bolts and remove the motor.
8. Install all parts in the reverse order of removal. Make sure the linkage lock clips are snapped in position.

Linkage

REMOVAL & INSTALLATION

1. Refer to the wiper motor removal section and follow the procedure until the linkage has been disconnected from the wiper motor.
2. Slide the right side linkage and pivot out through the access hole.
3. Remove the left side wiper arm and blade assembly.
4. Remove the left side access cover.
5. Remove the pivot nut and slide the linkage and pivot through the access hole.
6. Install all parts in the reverse order of removal.

Wiper Arm Assembly

REPLACEMENT

Raise the blade end of the arm off of the windshield and move the slide latch away from the pivot shaft. This will unlock the wiper arm from the pivot shaft and hold the blade end of the arm off of the glass at the same time. The wiper arm can now be pulled off of the pivot shaft without the aid of any tools.

Blade Assembly to Wiper Arm

REPLACEMENT

1. Cycle the arm and blade assembly to a position on the windshield where removal of blade assembly can be performed without difficulty. Turn ignition key off at desired position.
2. With the blade assembly resting on the windshield, grasp either end of the wiper blade frame and pull it away

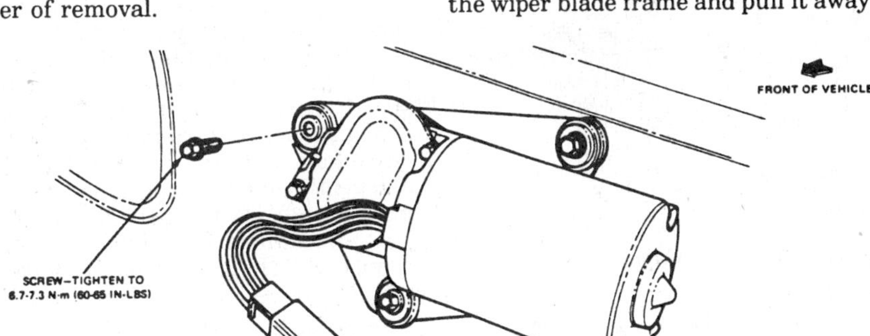

Wiper motor installation

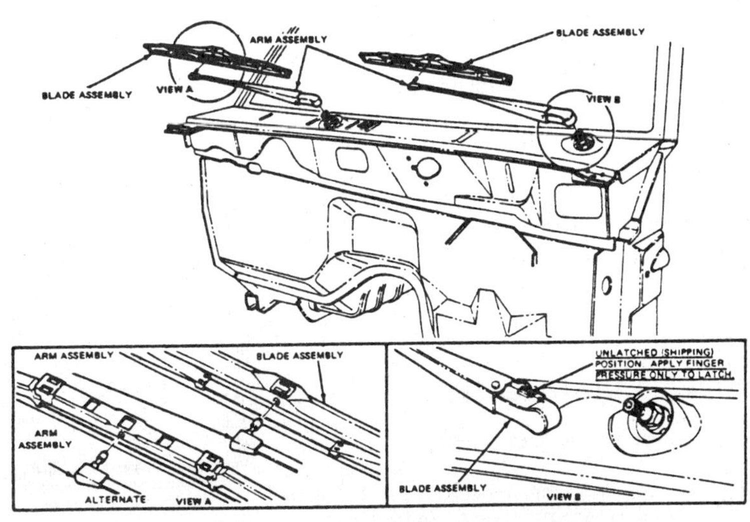

Windshield wiper arm and blade assembly installation

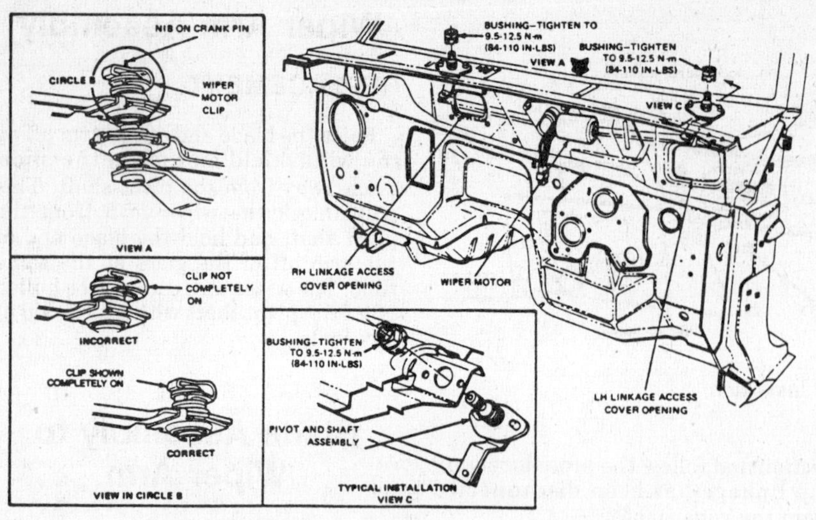

Windshield wiper pivot shaft and linkage assembly installation

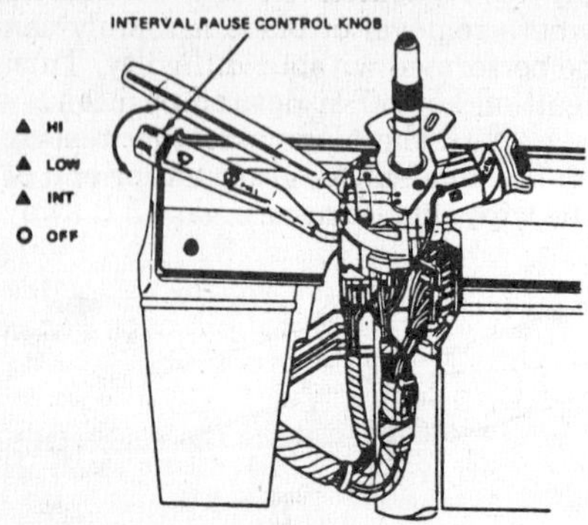

Windshield wiper switch

from the windshield, then pull the blade assembly from the pin.

NOTE: The rubber element extends past the frame. To prevent damage to the blade element, be sure to grasp the blade frame and not the end of the blade element.

3. To install, push the blade assembly onto the pin until fully seated. Be sure the blade is securely attached to the wiper arm.

INSTRUMENT CLUSTER

REMOVAL & INSTALLATION

1. Disconnect the negative battery cable.
2. Remove the two steering column shroud-to-panel retaining screws and remove the shroud.
3. Remove the lower instrument panel trim.
4. Detach the trim cover from the panel by removing the retaining screws.
5. Remove the four instrument cluster to panel retaining screws.
6. Pull the cluster slightly away from the panel and disconnect the speedometer cable. If there is not enough room to disconnect the cable, disconnect it from the transmission and gently pull it through the firewall until enough slack is gained.
7. Disconnect the wiring harness connector from the back of the cluster.
8. Disconnect any bulb and socket assemblies from the cluster.
9. Remove the cluster.
10. Install all parts in the reverse order of removal of removal.

Speedometer Cable Core

REMOVAL & INSTALLATION

1. Reach up behind the cluster and disconnect the cable by depressing the quick disconnect tab and pulling the cable away.
2. Remove the cable from the casing. If the cable is broken, raise the vehicle on a hoist and disconnect the cable from the transmission.
3. Remove the cable from the casing.
4. To remove the casing from the vehicle, pull it through the floor pan.
5. To replace the cable, slide the new cable into the casing and connect it at the transmission.
6. Route the cable through the floor pan and position the grommet in its groove in the floor.
7. Push the cable onto the speedometer head.

Headlights

REMOVAL & INSTALLATION

1. Remove the attaching screws and remove the headlamp door attaching screws. Remove the headlamp door.
2. Remove the headlight retaining ring screws, and remove the retaining ring. Do not disturb the adjusting screw settings.
3. Pull the headlight bulb forward and disconnect the wiring assembly plug from the bulb.
4. Connect the wiring assembly plug to the new bulb. Place the bulb in position, making sure that the locating

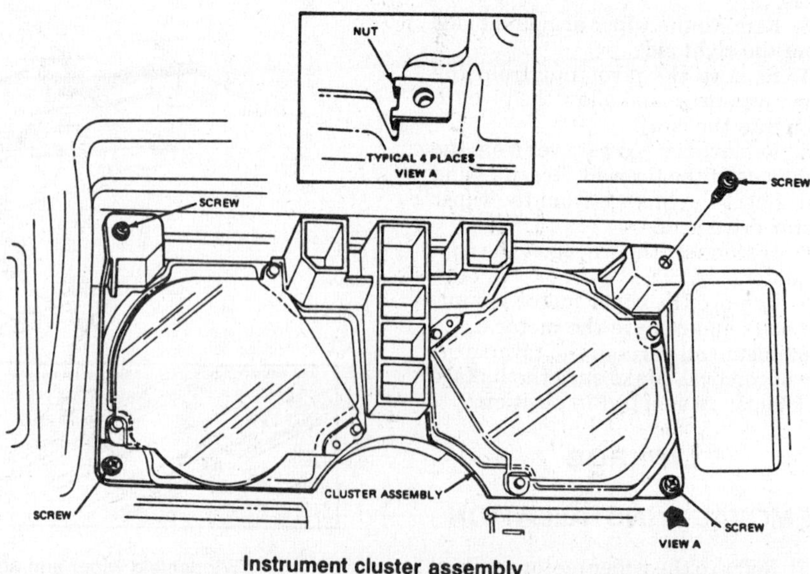

Instrument cluster assembly

tabs of the bulb are fitted in the positioning slots.

5. Install the headlight retaining ring.

6. Place the headlight trim ring or door into position, and install the retaining screws.

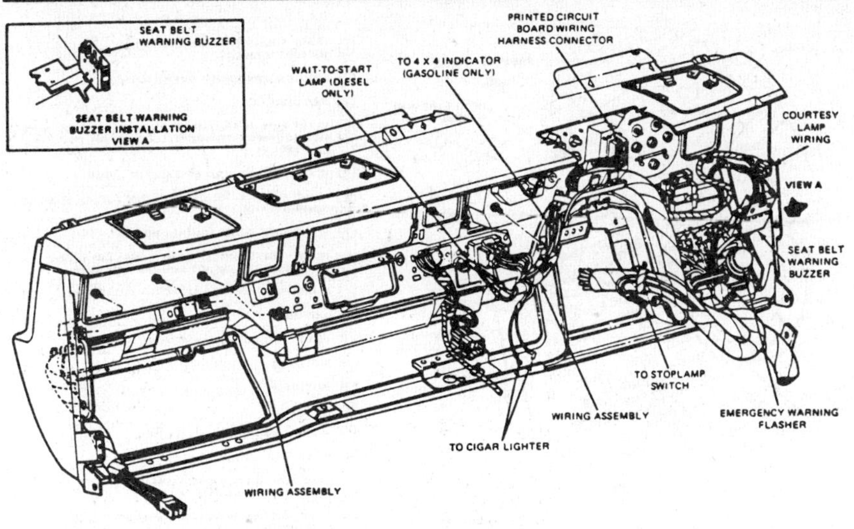

Rear view of the instrument panel

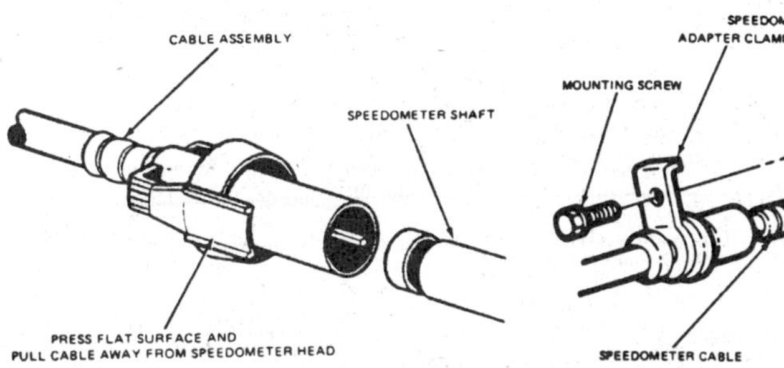

Speedometer cable quick-disconnect

Speedometer cable and gear—transmission end

Headlight Switch

REMOVAL & INSTALLATION

1. Disconnect the battery ground cable.
2. Depending on the year and model remove the wiper-washer and fog lamp switch knob if they will interfere with the headlight switch knob removal.
3. Check the switch body (behind dash, see Step 3) for a release button. Press in on the button and remove the knob and shaft assembly. If not equipped with a release button, a hook tool may be necessary for knob removal.
4. Remove the steering column shrouds and cluster panel finish panel if they interfere with the required clearance for working behind the dash.
5. Unscrew the switch mounting nut from the front of the dash. Remove the switch from the back of the dash and disconnect the wiring harness.
6. Install all parts in the reverse order of removal.

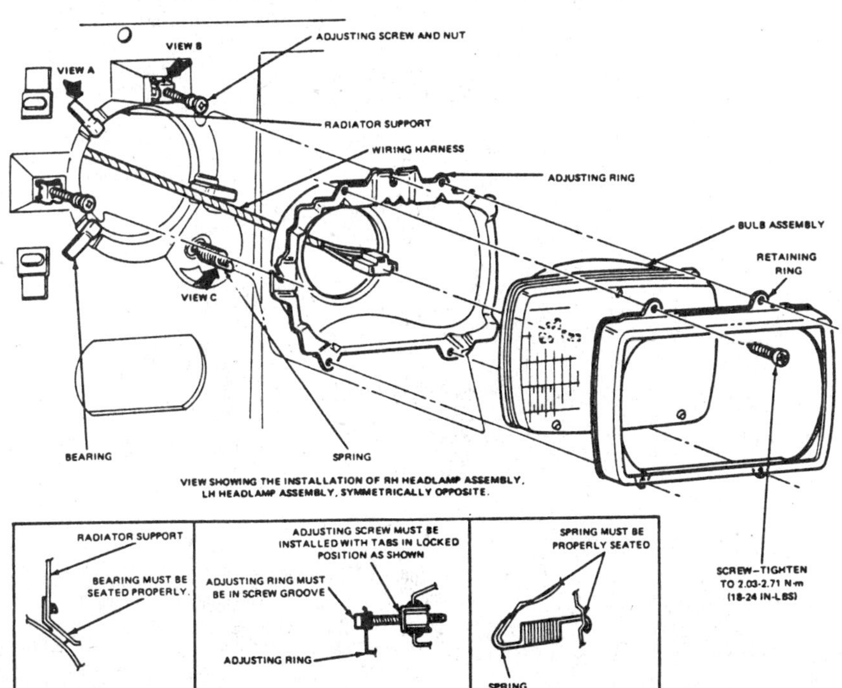

Headlight assembly

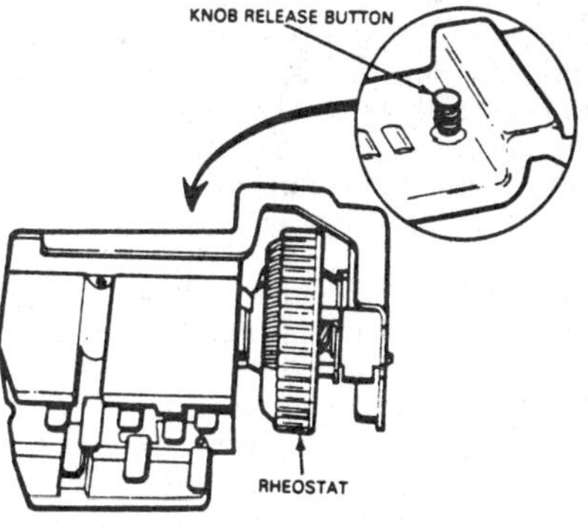

Headlight switch release button

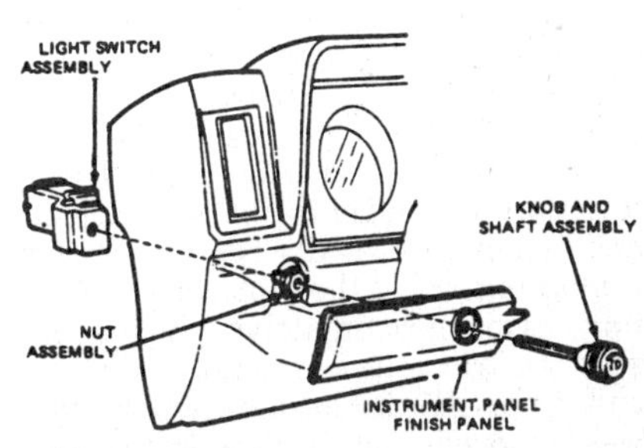

Headlight switch installation

FUSE LINK

The fuse link is a short length of special, Hypalon (high temperature) insulated wire, integral with the engine compartment wiring harness and should not be confused with standard wire. It is several wire gauges smaller than the circuit which it protects. Under no circumstances should a fuse link replacement repair be made using a length of standard wire cut from bulk stock or from another wiring harness. To repair any blown fuse link use the following procedure:

1. Determine which circuit is damaged, its location and the cause of the open fuse link. If the damaged fuse link is one of three fed by a common No. 10 or 12 gauge feed wire, determine the specific affected circuit.
2. Disconnect the negative battery cable.
3. Cut the damaged fuse link from the wiring harness and discard it. If the fuse link is one of three circuits fed by a single feed wire, cut it out of the harness at each splice end and discard it.
4. Identify and procure the proper fuse link and butt connectors for attaching the fuse link to the harness.
5. To repair any fuse link in a 3-link group with one feed: After cutting the open link out of the harness, cut each of the remaining undamaged fuse links close to the feed wire weld. Strip approximately ½ inch of insulation from the detached ends of the two good fuse links. Then insert two wire ends into one end of a butt connector and carefully push one stripped end of the replacement fuse link into the same end of the butt connector and crimp all three firmly together.

NOTE: Care must be taken when fitting the three fuse links into the butt connector as the internal diameter is a snug fit for three wires. Make sure to use a proper crimping tool. Pliers, side cutters, etc. will not apply the proper crimp to retain the wires and withstand a pull test.

After crimping the butt connector to the three fuse links, cut the weld portion from the feed wire and strip approximately ½ inch of insulation from the cut end. Insert the stripped end into the open end of the butt connector and crimp very firmly. To attach the remaining end of the replacement fuse link, strip approximately ½ inch of insulation from the wire end of the circuit from which the blown fuse link was removed, and firmly crimp a butt connector or equivalent to the stripped

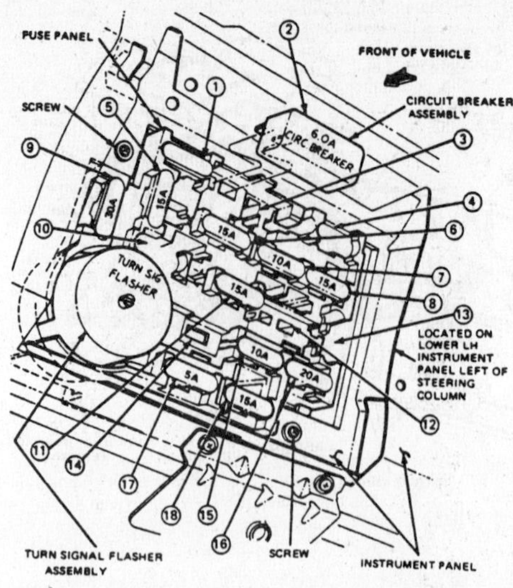

(1) 15 AMP. FUSE–STOP LAMPS, EMERGENCY WARNING FLASHER
(2) 6 AMP. C.B.–WINDSHIELD WIPER & WASHER
(3) (NOT USED)
(4) 15 AMP. FUSE–REAR LAMPS, PARK LAMPS, MARKER LAMPS, LICENSE LAMPS, INSTRUMENT ILLUMINATION, TRAILER LAMPS RELAY
(5) 15 AMP. FUSE–T/S FLASHER, BACK–UP LAMPS
(6) 15 AMP. FUSE–4 x 4 INDICATOR, CLOCK DISPLAY, SPEED CONTROL
(7) 10 AMP. FUSE–DIESEL CONTROL MODULE
(8) 15 AMP. FUSE–COURTESY LAMPS, DOME LAMP, CLOCK, GLOVE BOX LAMP, "HEAD LAMPS ON" INDICATOR
(9) 30 AMP. FUSE–HEATER & A/C MOTOR BLOWER, A/C CLUTCH
(10) (NOT USED)
(11) 15 AMP. FUSE–RADIO/TAPE PLAYER
(12) (NOT USED)
(13) (NOT USED)
(14) (NOT USED)
(15) 10 AMP. FUSE–FUEL TANK SELECTOR
(16) 20 AMP. FUSE–CIGAR LIGHTER, HORNS
(17) 5 AMP. FUSE–INSTR. PANEL ILLUM. LAMPS, AUTO. TRANS. FLOOR SHIFT ILLUMINATION
(18) 15 AMP. FUSE–WARNING LAMPS, SEAT BELT BUZZER, CARBURETOR CIRCUITS

Fuse panel

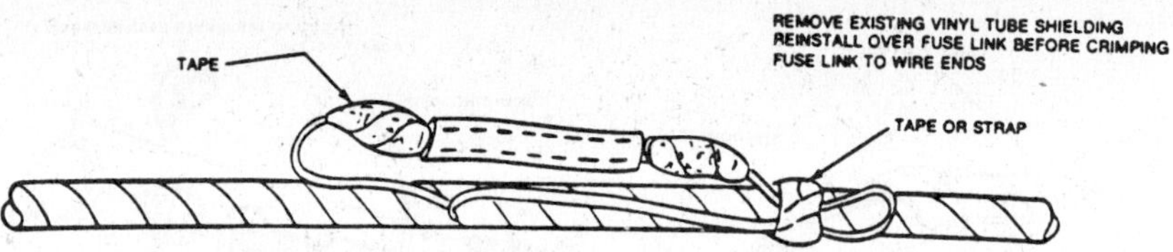

TYPICAL REPAIR USING THE SPECIAL #17 GA. (9.00" LONG-YELLOW) FUSE LINK REQUIRED FOR THE AIR/COND. CIRCUITS (2) #687E and #261A LOCATED IN THE ENGINE COMPARTMENT

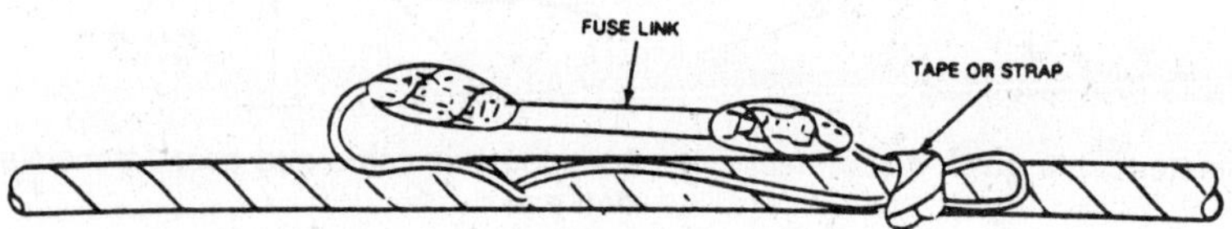

TYPICAL REPAIR FOR ANY IN-LINE FUSE LINK USING THE SPECIFIED GAUGE FUSE LINK FOR THE SPECIFIC CIRCUIT

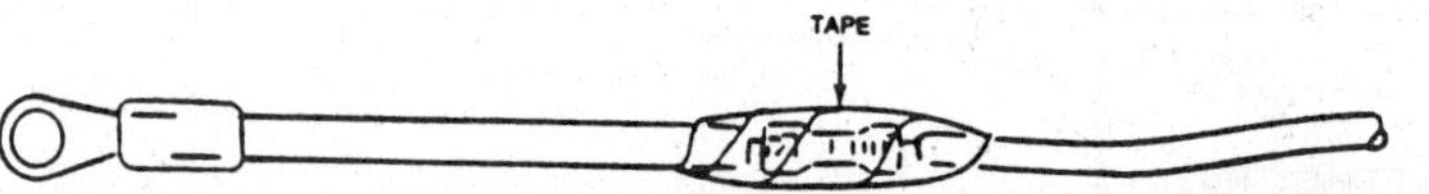

TYPICAL REPAIR USING THE EYELET TERMINAL FUSE LINK OF THE SPECIFIED GAUGE FOR ATTACHMENT TO A CIRCUIT WIRE END

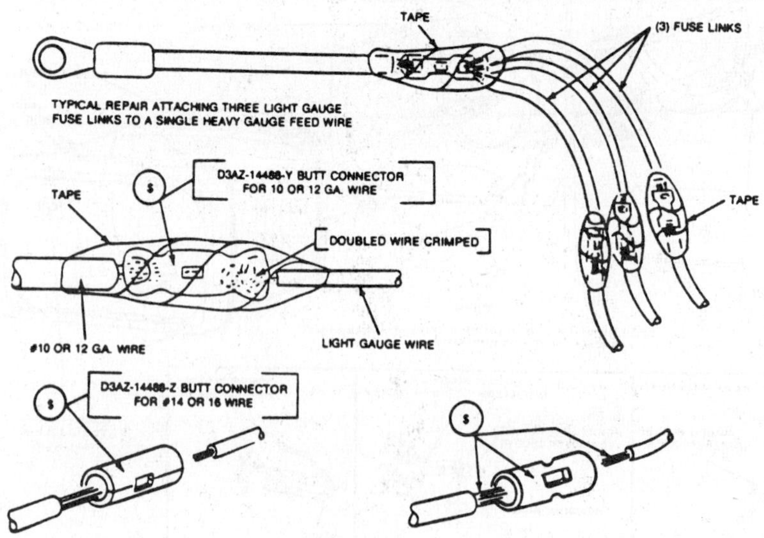

General fuse link repair procedure

wire. Then, insert the end of the replacement link into the other end of the butt connector and crimp firmly. Using rosin core solder with a consistency of 60 percent tin and 40 percent lead, solder the connectors and the wires at the repairs and insulate with electrical tape.

6. To replace any fuse link on a single circuit in a harness, cut out the damaged portion, strip approximately ½" of insulation from the two wire ends and attach the appropriate replacement fuse link to the stripped wire ends with two proper size butt connectors. Solder the connectors and wires and insulate with tape.

7. To repair any fuse link which has an eyelet terminal on one end such as the charging circuit, cut off the open fuse link behind the weld, strip approximately ½" of insulation from the cut end and attach the appropriate new eyelet fuse link to the cut stripped wire with an appropriate size butt connector. Solder the connectors and wires at the repair and insulate with tape.

8. Connect the negative battery cable to the battery and test the system for proper operation.

NOTE: Do not mistake a resistor wire for a fuse link. The resistor wire is generally longer and has print stating, "Resistor-don't cut or splice". When attaching a single No. 16, 17, 18 or 20 gauge fuse link to a heavy gauge wire, always double the stripped wire end of the fuse link before inserting and crimping it into the butt connector for positive wire retention.

Hazard flasher location

TRAILER WIRING

Wiring the car for towing is fairly easy. There are a number of good wiring kits available and these should be used, rather than trying to design your own. All trailers will need brake lights and turn signals as well as tail lights and side marker lights. Most states require extra marker lights for overly wide trailers. Also, most states have recently required back-up lights for trailers, and most trailer manufacturers have been building trailers with back-up lights for several years.

Additionally, some Class I, most Class II and just about all Class III trailers will have electric brakes.

Add to this number an accessories wire, to operate trailer internal equipment or to charge the trailer's battery, and you can have as many as seven wires in the harness.

Determine the equipment on your trailer and buy the wiring kit necessary. The kit will contain all the wires needed, plus a plug adapter set which included the female plug, mounted on the bumper or hitch, and the male plug, wired into, or plugged into the trailer harness.

When installing the kit, follow the manufacturer's instructions. The color coding of the wires is standard throughout the industry.

One point to note, some domestic vehicles, and most imported vehicles, have separate turn signals. On most domestic vehicles, the brake lights and rear turn signals operate with the same bulb. For those vehicles with separate turn signals, you can purchase an isolation unit so that the brake lights won't blink whenever the turn signals are operated, or, you can go to your local electronics supply house and buy four diodes to wire in series with the brake and turn signal bulbs. Diodes will isolate the brake and turn signals. The choice is yours. The isolation units are simple and quick to install, but far more expensive than the diodes. The diodes, however, require more work to install properly, since they require the cutting of each bulb's wire and soldering in place of the diode.

One final point, the best kits are those with a spring loaded cover on the vehicle mounted socket. This cover prevents dirt and moisture from corroding the terminals. Never let the vehicle socket hang loosely. Always mount it securely to the bumper or hitch.

MANUAL TRANSMISSION

Linkage

ADJUSTMENT

No adjustments are possible with these transmissions.

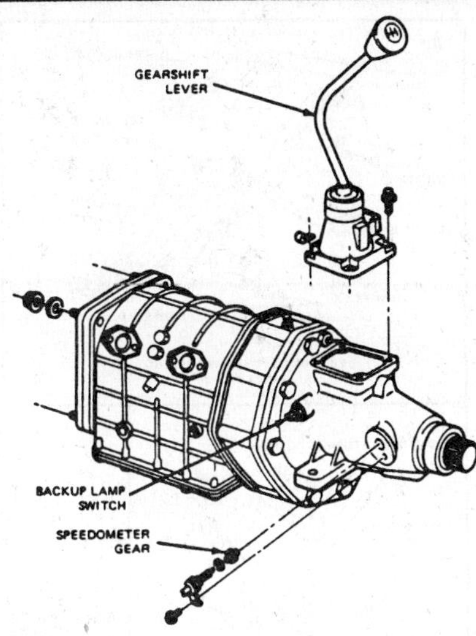

Gearshift lever removal and installation—typical

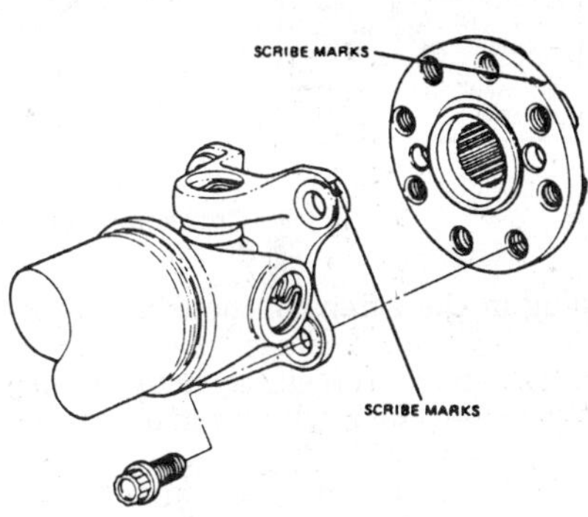

Marking the driveshaft and falnge for correct installation

Transmission

REMOVAL & INSTALLATION

5-Speed Overdrive Diesel Engine

1. Place the gearshift lever in neutral. Remove the boot retainer screws. Remove the bolts attaching the retainer cover to the gearshift lever retainer. Disconnect the clutch master cylinder push rod from the clutch pedal.

2. Pull the gearshift lever assembly, shim and bushing straight up and away from the gearshift lever retainer. Cover the shift tower opening in the extension housing with a cloth.

3. Disconnect the clutch hydraulic system master cylinder push rod from the clutch pedal.

4. Open the hood and disconnect the negative battery cable from the battery terminal.

5. Raise and safely support the vehicle on jackstands. Disconnect the driveshaft at the rear. Pull the driveshaft rearward and disconnect from the transmission. Install a suitable

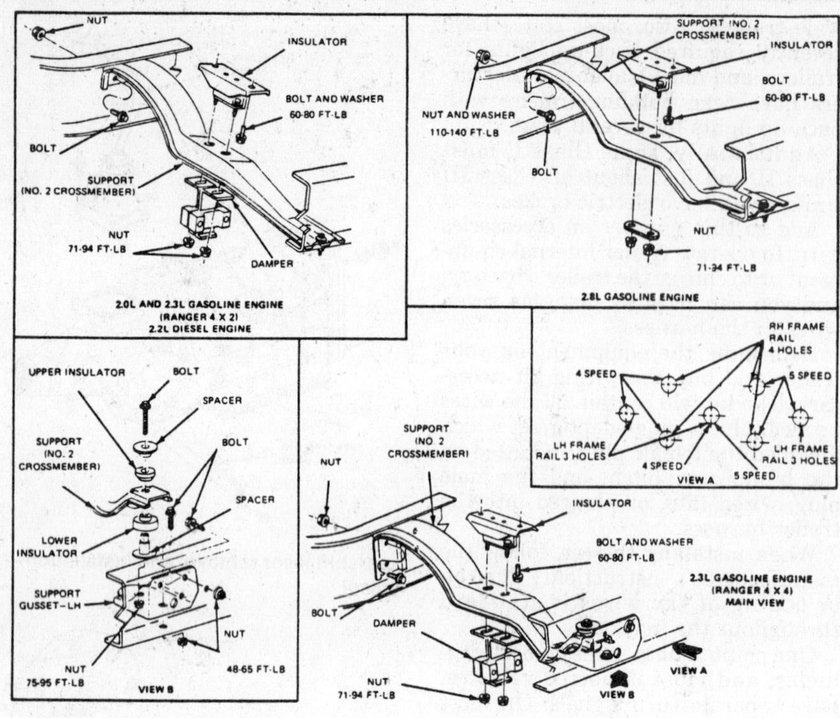

Crossmember removal and installation

plug in the extension housing to prevent lubricant leakage.

6. Remove the clutch housing dust shield and slave cylinder and secure it at one side.

7. Remove the speedometer cable from the extension housing.

8. Disconnect the starter motor and back-up lamp switch wires.

9. Place a jack under the engine, protecting the oil pan with a wood block.

10. Remove the starter motor. Position a suitable jack under the transmission.

11. Remove the bolts, lockwashers and flat washers attaching the transmission to the engine rear plate.

12. Remove the nuts and bolts attaching the transmission mount and damper to the crossmember.

13. Remove the nuts attaching the crossmember to the frame side rails and remove the crossmember.

14. Lower the engine jack. Work the clutch housing off the locating dowels and slide the transmission rearward until the input shaft spline clears the clutch disc. Remove the transmission from the vehicle.

15. Make sure that the machined mating surfaces and the locating dowels on the engine rear plate are free of burrs, dirt or paint. Check the mating face of the clutch housing and the locating dowel holes for burrs, dirt or paint.

16. Support the transmission on a suitable jack. Position it under the vehicle and start the input shaft into the clutch disc. Align the splines on the input shaft with the splines in the clutch disc. Move the transmission forward and carefully seat the clutch housing on the locating dowels of the engine rear plate. The engine plate dowels must not shave or burr the clutch housing dowel holes.

17. Install the bolts and flat washers that attach the clutch housing to the engine rear plate and tighten to specifications. Remove the transmission jack.

18. Install the starter motor. Tighten the attaching nuts.

19. Raise the engine and install the rear crossmember, insulator and damper, and attaching nuts and washers. Tighten the nuts.

20. Install the bolts, nuts and washers attaching the transmission mount to the crossmember. Tighten the nuts. Remove the engine jack.

21. Insert the driveshaft into the transmission extension housing and install the center bearing attaching nuts, washers and lockwashers. Tighten the nuts.

22. Connect the driveshaft to the rear axle drive flange. Tighten the attaching nuts.

23. Connect the starter and back-up lamp switch wires.

24. Install the clutch slave cylinder and dust shield on the clutch housing. Install the speedometer cable.

25. Check the transmission fluid level at both fill plugs. Fill with lubricant if necessary.

26. Lower the vehicle.

27. Open the hood and connect the negative battery cable to the battery terminal.

5-Speed Transmission Gasoline Engine

1. Place the gearshift lever in neutral. Remove the boot retainer screws.

Transmission and gearshift lever assembly—gasoline engine shown, diesel similar

Remove the bolts attaching the retainer cover to the gearshift lever retainer. Disconnect the clutch master cylinder push rod from the clutch pedal.

2. Pull the gearshift lever assembly, shim and bushing straight up and away from the gearshift lever retainer.

3. Cover the shift tower opening in the extension housing with a cloth.

4. Disconnect the clutch hydraulic system master cylinder push rod from the clutch pedal.

5. Open the hood and disconnect the negative battery cable from the battery terminal.

6. Raise and safely support the vehicle on jackstands. Disconnect the driveshaft at the rear axle.

7. Pull the driveshaft rearward and disconnect from the transmission. Install a suitable plug in the extension housing to prevent lubricant leakage.

8. Remove the clutch housing dust shield and slave cylinder and secure it at one side. Remove the speedometer cable from the extension housing.

9. Disconnect the starter motor and back-up lamp switch wires.

10. Place a jack under the engine, protecting the oil pan with a wood block.

11. On 4×4 vehicles, remove the transfer case.

12. Remove the starter motor. Position a suitable jack under the transmission.

13. Remove the bolts, lockwashers and flat washers attaching the transmission to the engine rear plate.

14. Remove the nuts and bolts attaching the transmission mount and damper to the crossmember.

15. Remove the nuts attaching the crossmember to the frame side rails and remove the crossmember.

16. Lower the engine jack. Work the clutch housing off the locating dowels and slide the transmission rearward until the input shaft spline clears the clutch disc. Remove the transmission from the vehicle.

17. Make sure that the machined mating surfaces and the locating dowels on the engine rear plate are free of burrs, dirt or paint. Check the mating face of the clutch housing and the locating dowel holes for burrs, dirt or paint.

18. Mount the transmission on a suitable jack. Position it under the vehicle and start the input shaft into the clutch disc. Align the splines on the input shaft with the splines in the clutch disc. Move the transmission forward and carefully seat the clutch housing on the locating dowels of the engine rear plate. The engine plate dowels must not shave or burr the clutch housing dowel holes. Install the bolts and flat washers that attach the clutch housing to the engine rear plate and tighten to specifications. Remove the transmission jack.

19. Install the starter motor. Tighten the attaching nuts.

20. Raise the engine and install the rear crossmember, insulator and damper, and attaching nuts and washers.

21. Install the bolts, nuts and washers attaching the transmission mount to the crossmember. Remove the engine jack.

22. On 4×4 vehicles, install the transfer case.

23. Insert the driveshaft into the transmission extension housing and install the center bearing attaching nuts, washers and lockwashers.

24. Connect the driveshaft to the rear axle drive flange.

25. Connect the starter and back-up lamp switch wires. Install the clutch slave cylinder and dust shield on the clutch housing. Install the speedometer cable.

26. Check the transmission fluid level at both fill plugs. Fill with specified lubricant if necessary.

27. Lower the vehicle.

28. Open the hood and connect the negative battery cable to the battery terminal.

29. Re-connect the clutch master cylinder push rod to the clutch pedal.

30. Remove the cloth from the shift tower opening in the extension housing. Avoid getting dirt inside the transmission.

31. Position the gearshift lever assembly straight up above the gearshift lever retainer, then insert the gearshift in the retainer. Install the bolts attaching the retainer cover to the gearshift lever retainer and tighten them to specifications. Install the cover boot with the retainer screws.

4-Speed Transmission Diesel Engine

1. Place the gearshift lever in Neutral. Remove the boot retainer screws. Remove the bolts attaching the retainer cover to the gearshift lever retainer. Disconnect the clutch master cylinder push rod from the clutch pedal.

2. Pull the gearshift lever assembly, shim and bushing straight up and away from the gearshift lever retainer. Cover the shift tower opening in the extension housing with a cloth.

3. Disconnect the clutch hydraulic system master cylinder push rod from the clutch pedal.

4. Open the hood and disconnect the negative battery cable from the battery terminal.

5. Raise and safely support the vehicle on jackstands. Disconnect the driveshaft at the rear axle. Pull the driveshaft rearward and disconnect from the transmission. Install a suitable plug in the extension housing to prevent lubricant leakage.

6. Remove the clutch housing dust shield and slave cylinder and secure it at one side.

7. Remove the speedometer cable from the extension housing or from the speed control sensor, if so equipped.

8. Disconnect the starter motor and back-up lamp switch wires. Place a jack under the engine, protecting the oil pan with a wood block. Remove the starter motor. Position a suitable jack under the transmission.

9. Remove the bolts attaching the transmission to the engine rear plate. Remove the nuts and bolts attaching the transmission mount and damper to the crossmember.

10. Remove the nuts attaching the crossmember to the frame side rails and remove the crossmember.

11. Lower the engine jack. Work the clutch housing off the locating dowels and slide the transmission rearward until the input shaft spline clears the clutch disc. Remove the transmission from the vehicle.

13. Make sure that the machined mating surfaces and the locating dowels on the engine rear plate are free of burrs, dirt or paint. Check the mating face of the clutch housing and the locating dowel holes for burrs, dirt or paint. Mount the transmission on a suitable jack. Position it under the vehicle and start the input shaft into the clutch disc. Align the splines on the input shaft with the splines in the clutch disc. Move the transmission forward and carefully seat the clutch housing on the locating dowels of the engine rear plate. The engine plate dowels must not shave or burr the clutch housing dowel holes.

14. Install the bolts that attach the clutch housing to the engine rear plate. Remove the transmission jack.

15. Install the starter motor.

16. Raise the engine and install the rear crossmember and attaching nuts and washers.

17. Install the bolts, nuts and washers attaching the transmission mount and damper to the crossmember. Remove the engine jack.

18. Insert the driveshaft into the transmission extension housing and install the center bearing attaching nuts, washers and lockwashers.

19. Connect the driveshaft to the rear axle drive flange.

20. Connect the starter and back-up lamp switch wires. Install the clutch slave cylinder and dust shield on the clutch housing. Install the speedometer cable.

21. Check the transmission fluid level at the fill plug. Fill with specified lu-

bricant if necessary. Lower the vehicle.

22. Open the hood and connect the negative battery cable to the battery terminal.

23. Reconnect the clutch master cylinder push rod to the clutch pedal.

24. Remove the cloth from the shift tower opening in the extension housing. Avoid getting dirt inside the transmission.

25. Position the gearshift lever assembly straight up above the gearshift lever retainer, then insert the gearshift in the retainer. Install the bolts attaching the retainer cover to the gearshift lever retainer.

26. Install the cover boot with the retainer screws.

CLUTCH

Driven Disc

REMOVAL & INSTALLATION

1. Disconnect the clutch hydraulic system master cylinder from the clutch pedal.

2. Raise the vehicle and safely support on jack stands. Remove the dust shield from the clutch housing.

3. Disconnect the hydraulic clutch linkage from the housing and release lever. Remove the starter.

4. Remove the bolts attaching the clutch housing to the engine block. Note the direction in which the bolts are installed.

5. Index the driveshaft to the companion flange and remove the driveshaft.

6. Remove the nuts attaching the transmission and insulator to the No.2 crossmember support. Raise the transmission with a suitable jack. Remove the No.2 crossmember support. Lower the transmission and clutch housing.

7. Remove the release lever, and hub and bearing. Mark the assembled position of the pressure plate and cover to the flywheel (for re-assembly).

8. Loosen the pressure plate and cover attaching bolts evenly until the pressure plate springs are expanded, and remove the bolts.

9. Remove the pressure plate and cover assembly and the clutch disc from the flywheel. These parts can be removed through the opening in the bottom of the clutch housing on models where the housing is fitted with a dust cover. Remove the pilot bearing only for replacement.

10. Position the clutch disc on the flywheel so that the Clutch Alignment

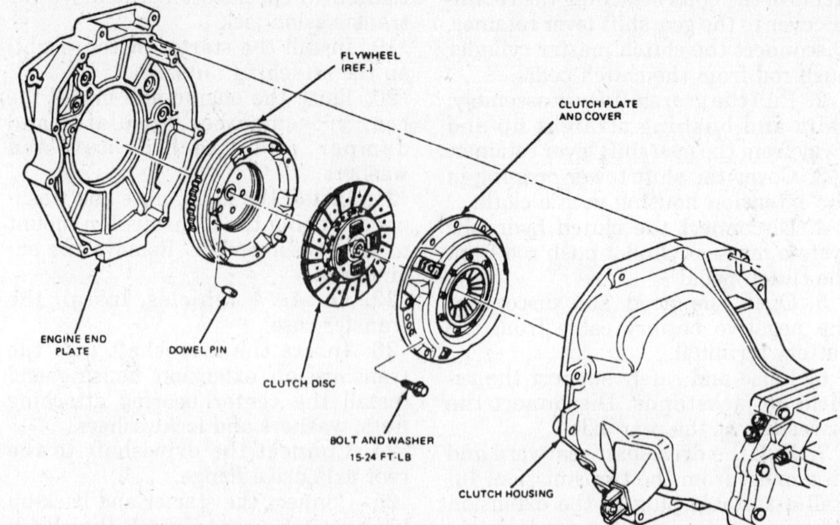

Clutch, flywheel and clutch housing assembly—4-122, 140 engines

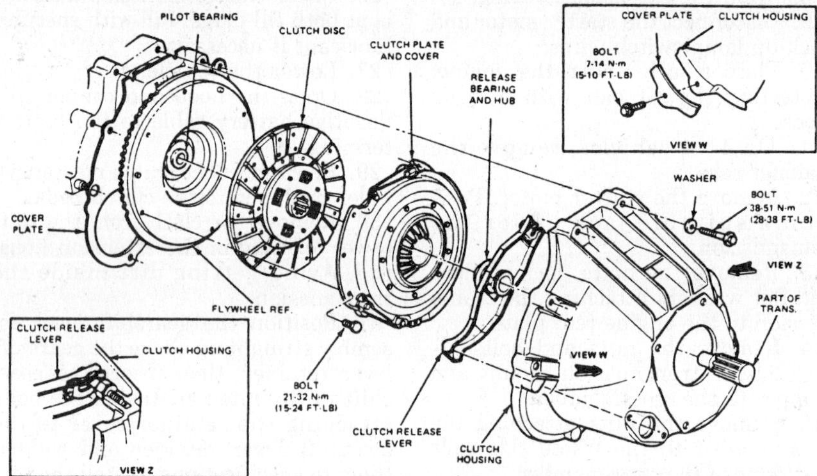

Clutch, flywheel and clutch housing assembly—6-173 engine

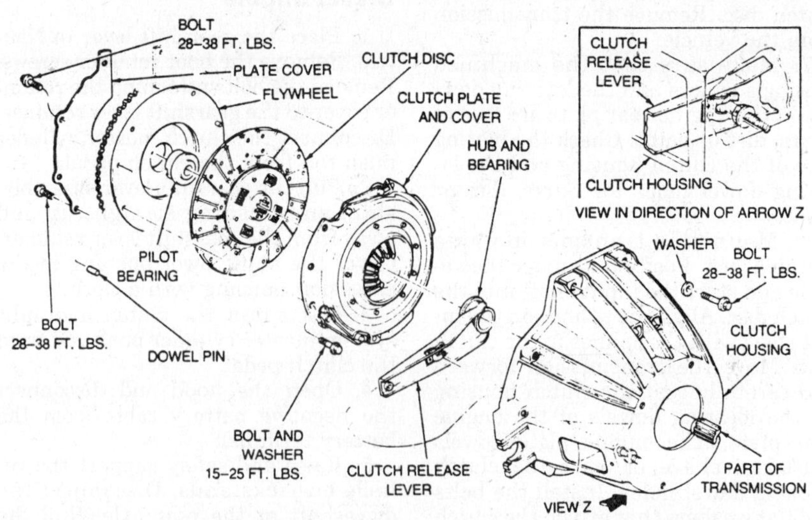

Clutch, flywheel and clutch housing assembly—4-134 diesel engine

Shaft D79T-7550-A or equivalent can enter the clutch pilot bearing and align the disc.

11. When re-installing the original pressure plate and cover assembly, align the assembly and flywheel according to the marks made during the removal operations. Position the pressure plate and cover assembly on the flywheel, align the pressure plate and disc, and install the retaining bolts that fasten the assembly to the flywheel. Tighten the bolts to 15-24 ft.lb., and remove the clutch disc pilot tool.

12. Position the clutch release bearing and the bearing hub on the release lever. Install the release lever on the release lever seat in the flywheel housing. Apply a light film of lithium-base grease C1AZ-19590-B (ESA-M1C75-B) or equivalent to the release lever fingers and to the lever pivot ball. Fill the annular groove of the release bearing hub with grease.

13. Raise the transmission and clutch housing into position. Install the No.2 crossmember support to the frame. Install connecting nuts, bolts and washers.

14. Lower the transmission and insulator into the support. Install and tighten nuts. Remove the transmission jack.

15. Install the driveshaft, making sure the index marks on the driveshaft are aligned with the marks on the companion flange.

16. Install the bolts attaching the housing to the engine block in the correct position as removed. Tighten to 28-38 ft.lb.

17. Install the hydraulic clutch linkage on the housing in position with the release lever. Install dust shield. Install starter.

18. Lower the vehicle and connect the clutch hydraulic system master cylinder to the clutch pedal. Check clutch for proper operation.

Clutch Slave and Master Cylinders

The hydraulic clutch system is serviced as a complete unit. Individual components are not available separately.

REMOVAL & INSTALLATION

1. Raise and support the front end on jackstands.
2. Remove the lockpin and disconnect the master cylinder pushrod from the clutch pedal.
3. On 4-122 and 4-140 engines, remove the bolt attaching the dust shield to he clucth housing and remove the dust shield. Push the slave cylinder rearwards to disengage it from the re-

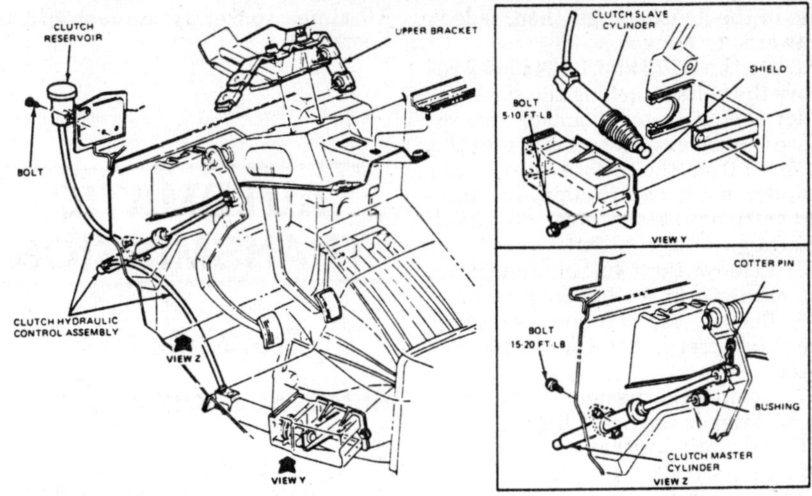

Hydraulic clutch system components – 4-122, 140 engines

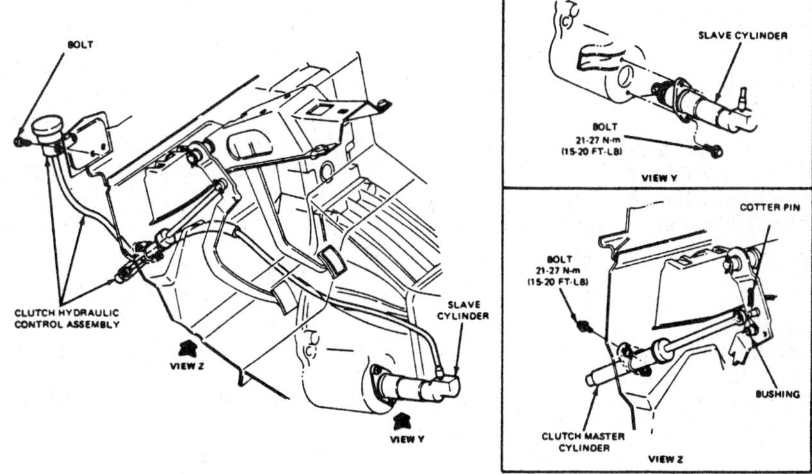

Hydraulic clutch system components – 6-173 engine

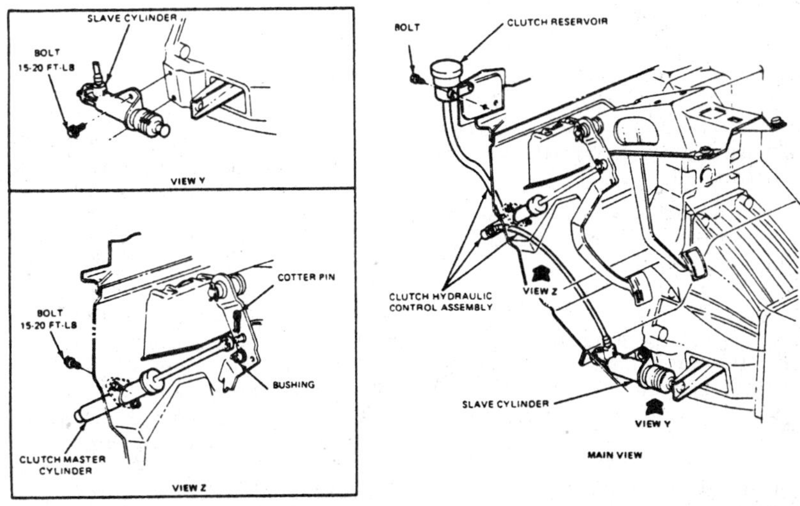

Hydraulic clutch system components – 4-134 diesel engine

cess in the housing lugs, then, slide it outwards to remove it.

4. On the 6-173 and 4-134 diesel, remove the bolts attaching the slave cylinder to the clutch housing and remove the slave cylinder. Disengage the pushrod from the release lever as the cylinder is removed. Retain the pushrod-to-release lever plastic bearing inserts.

5. Remove the two bolts attaching the master cylinder to the firewall.

6. Remove the two bolts attaching the fluid reservoir to the cowl access cover.

7. Remove the master cylinder from the opening in the firewall and remove the hydraulic system assembly upwards and out of the engine compartment.

To install:

1. Position the hydraulic system in place. The slave cylinder-to-master cylinder tube routing should be above the brake tubes and below the steering column shaft.

NOTE: On the 6-173, the tube must lay on top of the clutch housing.

2. Insert the master cylinder pushrod through the opening in the firewall, position the master cylinder on the firewall and install the attaching bolts. Torque the bolts to 15-20 ft.lb.

3. Position the fluid reservoir on the cowl opening cover and install the attaching bolts. Torque the bolts to 15-20 ft.lb.

4. Install the slave cylinder by pushing the slave cylinder pushrod and plastic bearing inserts into the release lever. Attach the cylinder to the clutch housing.

NOTE: With a new system, the slave cylinder contains a shipping strap that pre-positions the pushrod for installation and provides a bearing insert. Following the installation of the slave cylinder, the first actuation of the clutch pedal will break the shipping strap and give normal system operation.

5. On the 4-122 and 4-140, snap the dust shield into position. Install the retaining bolt and tighten it to 60-120 in.lb.

6. On the 6-173 and 4-134 diesel, install the bolts attaching the slave cylinder to the clutch housing and torque them to 15-20 ft.lb.

7. Clean the master cylinder pushrod bushing and apply to it a light film of clean engine oil. Attach the bushing and pushrod to the clutch pedal. Install the lockpin.

8. Depress the clutch pedal at least 10 times to verify smooth clutch operation.

AUTOMATIC TRANSMISSION

Transmission

REMOVAL & INSTALLATION

C3

1. Raise the vehicle and safely support on jackstands. Place a drain pan under the transmission fluid pan. Starting at the rear of the pan and working toward the front, loosen the attaching bolts and allow the fluid to drain. Then remove all of the pan attaching bolts except two at the front, to allow the fluid to further drain. After all the fluid has drained, install two bolts on the rear side of the pan to temporarily hold it in place.

2. Remove the converter drain plug access cover and adapter plate bolts from the lower end of the converter housing.

3. Remove the four flywheel to converter attaching nuts. Crank the engine to turn the converter to gain access to the nuts, using a wrench on the crankshaft pulley attaching bolt. On belt driven overhead camshaft engines, never turn the engine backwards.

4. Crank the engine until the converter drain plug is accessible and remove the plug. Place a drain pan under the converter to catch the fluid. After all the fluid has been drained from the converter, reinstall the plug and tighten to 20-30 ft.lb. Remove the driveshaft. Install cover, plastic bag etc. over end of extension housing.

5. Remove the speedometer cable from the extension housing. Disconnect the shift rod at the transmission manual lever. Disconnect the downshift rod at the transmission downshift lever.

6. Remove the starter-to-converter housing attaching bolts and position the starter out of the way.

7. Disconnect the neutral start switch wires from the switch. Remove the vacuum line from the transmission vacuum modulator.

8. Position a suitable jack under the transmission and raise it slightly.

9. Remove the engine rear support-to-crossmember bolts. Remove the crossmember-to-frame side support attaching bolts and remove the cross-

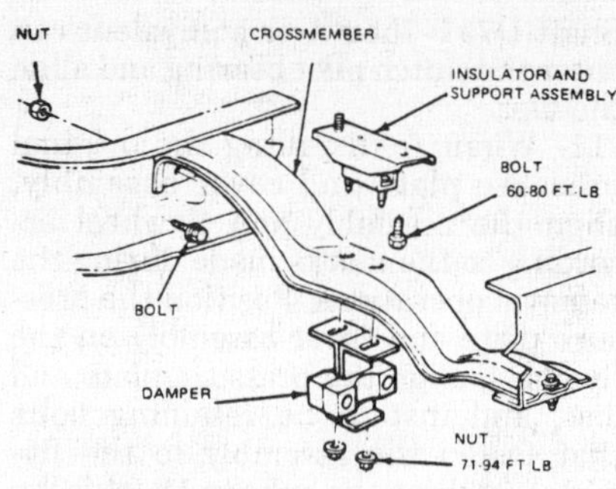

Crossmember removal and installation—C3 transmission

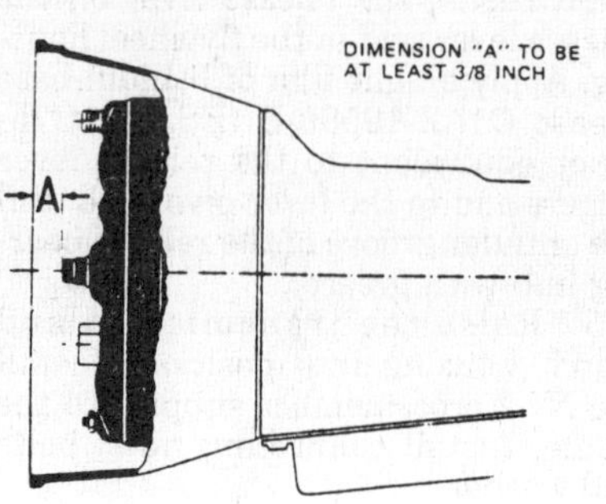

Positioning of the converter hub to the bell housing flange—C3 transmission

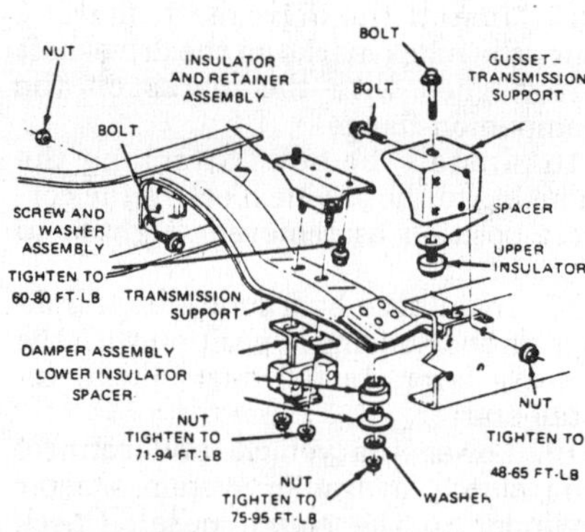

Transmission crossmember—removal and installation

member insulator and support and damper.

10. Lower the jack under the transmission and allow the transmission to hang.

11. Position a jack to the front of the engine and raise the engine to gain access to the two upper converter housing-to-engine attaching bolts.

12. Disconnect the oil cooler lines at the transmission. Plug all openings to keep out dirt.

13. Remove the lower converter housing-to-engine attaching bolts. Remove the transmission filler tube.

14. Secure the transmission to the jack with a safety chain.

15. Remove the two upper converter

housing-to-engine attaching bolts. Move the transmission to the rear and down to remove it from under the vehicle.

16. Position the converter to the transmission making sure the converter hub is fully engaged in the pump. With the converter properly installed, place the transmission on the jack and secure with safety chain.

17. Rotate the converter so the drive studs and drain plug are in alignment with their holes in the flywheel. With the transmission mounted on a transmission jack, move the converter and transmission assembly forward into position being careful not to damage the flywheel and the converter pilot.

WARNING: During this move, to avoid damage, do not allow the transmission to get into a nosed down position as this will cause the converter to move forward and disengage from the pump gear. The converter must rest squarely against the flywheel. This indicates that the converter pilot is not binding in the engine crankshaft.

18. Install the two upper converter housing-to-engine attaching bolts and tighten to 28-38 ft.lb.

19. Remove the safety chain from the transmission. Insert the filler tube in the stub tube and secure it to the cylinder block with the attaching bolt. Tighten the bolt to 28-38 ft.lb. If the stub tube is loosened or dislodged, it should be replaced. Install the oil cooler lines in the retaining clip at the cylinder block. Connect the lines to the transmission case.

20. Remove the jack supporting the front of the engine. Raise the transmission. Position the crossmember, insulator and support and damper to the frame side supports and install the attaching bolts. Tighten the bolts to 20-30 ft.lb.

21. Lower the transmission and install the rear engine support-to-crossmember nut. Tighten the bolt to 60-80 ft.lb.

22. Remove the transmission jack. Install the vacuum hose on the transmission vacuum unit. Install the vacuum line into the retaining clip.

23. Connect the neutral start switch plug to the switch. Install the starter and tighten the attaching bolts to 15-20 ft.lb.

24. Install the four flywheel-to-converter attaching nuts. When assembling the flywheel to the converter, first install the attaching nuts and tighten to 20-34 ft.lb.

25. Install the converter drain plug access cover and adaptor plate bolts. Tighten the bolts to 12-16 ft.lb.

26. Connect the muffler inlet pipe to the exhaust manifold.

27. Connect the transmission shift rod to the manual lever. Connect the downshift rod to the downshift lever.

28. Connect the speedometer cable to the extension housing. Install the driveshaft. Tighten the companion flange U-bolt attaching nuts to 70-95 ft.lb.

29. Adjust the manual and downshift linkage as required.

30. Lower the vehicle. Fill the transmission to the proper level with the specified fluid. Pour in five quarts of fluid; then run the engine and add fluid as required. Check the transmission, converter assembly and oil cooler lines for leaks.

C5 w/2-Wheel Drive

1. Raise the vehicle and safely support on jackstands.

2. Place the drain pan under the transmission fluid pan. Starting at the rear of the pan and working toward the front, loosen the attaching bolts and allow the fluid to drain.

3. Remove all of the pan attaching bolts except two at the front, to allow the fluid to further drain.

4. With fluid drained, install two bolts on the rear side of the pan to temporarily hold it in place.

5. Remove the converter drain plug access cover from the lower end of the converter housing.

6. Remove the converter-to-flywheel attaching nuts. Place a wrench on the crankshaft pulley attaching bolt to turn the converter to gain access to the nuts.

7. Place a drain pan under the converter to catch the fluid. With the wrench on the crankshaft pulley attaching bolt, turn the converter to gain access to the converter drain plug and remove the plug. After the fluid has been drained, reinstall the plug.

8. Disconnect the driveshaft from the rear axle and slide shaft rearward from the transmission. Install a suitable cover in the extension housing to prevent fluid leakage. Mark the rear driveshaft yoke and axle flange so they can be installed in their original position.

9. Disconnect the wires from the starter motor. Remove the three attaching bolts and remove the starter motor.

10. Disconnect the neutral start switch wires at the plug connector.

11. Remove the rear mount-to-crossmember attaching nuts and the two crossmember-to-frame attaching bolts. Remove the right and left gusset.

12. Remove the two engine rear insulator-to-extension housing attaching bolts.

13. Disconnect the TV linkage rod from the transmission TV lever.

14. Disconnect the manual rod from the transmission manual lever at the transmission.

15. Remove the two bolts securing the bellcrank bracket to the converter housing.

16. Raise the transmission with a suitable jack to provide clearance to remove the crossmember.

17. Remove the rear mount from the crossmember and remove the crossmember from the side supports.

18. Lower the transmission to gain access to the oil cooler lines. Disconnect each oil line from the fittings on the transmission.

19. Disconnect the speedometer cable from the extension housing.

20. Remove the bolt that secures the transmission fluid filler tube to the cylinder block. Lift the filler tube and the dipstick from the transmission.

21. Secure the transmission to the jack with the chain.

22. Remove the converter housing-to-cylinder block attaching bolts.

23. Carefully move the transmission and converter assembly away from the engine and, at the same time, lower the jack to clear the underside of the vehicle.

To install the unit.

24. Tighten the converter drain plug to specifications. Position the converter on the transmission, making sure the converter drive flats are fully engaged in the pump gear by rotating the converter.

25. With the converter properly installed, place the transmission on the jack. Secure the transmission to the jack with a chain.

26. Rotate the converter until the studs and drain plug are in alignment with the holes in the flywheel. Move the converter and transmission assembly forward into position, using care not to damage the flywheel and the converter pilot. The converter must rest squarely against the flywheel. This indicates that the converter pilot is not binding in the engine crankshaft.

27. Install and tighten the converter housing-to-engine attaching bolts to 40-60 ft.lb.

28. Remove the safety chain from around the transmission.

29. Install the new O-ring on the lower end of the transmission filler tube. Insert the tube in the transmission case and secure the tube to the engine with the attaching bolt.

30. Connect the speedometer cable to the extension housing.

31. Connect the oil cooler lines to the right side of transmission case.
32. Secure the engine rear support to the extension housing and tighten the bolts to 40-60 ft.lb.
33. Position the crossmember on the side supports. Lower the transmission and remove the jack. Secure the crossmember to the side supports with the attaching bolts.
34. Position the damper assembly over the engine rear support studs. (The painted face of the damper is facing forward when installed in the vehicle.) Secure the rear engine support to the crossmember.
35. Position the bellcrank to the converter housing and install the two attaching bolts.
36. Connect the TV linkage rod to the transmission TV lever. Connect the manual linkage rod to the manual lever at the transmission.
37. Secure the converter-to-flywheel attaching nuts and tighten them to specification.
38. Install the converter housing access cover and secure it with the attaching bolts.
39. Secure the starter motor in place with the attaching bolts. Connect the cable to the terminal on the starter. Connect the neutral start switch wires at the plug connector.
40. Connect the driveshaft to the rear axle so the index marks on the companion flange and the rear yoke are aligned. Lubricate the slip yoke with grease.
41. Adjust the shift linkage as required.
42. Adjust throttle linkage.
43. Lower the vehicle. Fill the transmission to the correct level with the specified fluid. Start the engine and shift the transmission to all ranges, then recheck the fluid level.

C5 w/4-Wheel Drive

1. Remove the bolt securing the fluid filler tube to the engine valve cover bracket.
2. Place a drain pan under the transmission fluid pan. Starting at the rear of the pan and working towards the front, loosen the attaching bolts and allow the fluid to drain. Finally, remove all of the pan attaching bolts except two at the front, to allow the fluid to drain further. With fluid drained, install two bolts on the rear side of the pan to temporarily hold it in place.
3. Remove the converter drain plug access cover from the lower end of the converter housing. Remove the converter-to-flywheel attaching nuts. Place a wrench on the crankshaft pulley attaching bolt to turn the converter to gain access to the nuts.
4. Place a drain pan under the converter to catch the fluid. With the wrench on the crankshaft pulley attaching bolt, turn the converter to gain access to the converter drain plug and remove the plug.
5. After the fluid has been drained, reinstall the cable from the terminal at the starter motor. Remove the three attaching bolts and remove the starter motor. Disconnect the neutral start switch wires at the plug connector.
6. Remove the rear mount-to-crossmember attaching nuts and the two crossmember-to-frame attaching bolts. Remove the right and left gusset.
7. Remove the two engine rear insulator-to-extension housing attaching bolts.
8. Disconnect the TV linkage rod from the transmission TV lever. Disconnect the manual rod from the transmission manual lever at the transmission. Disconnect the downshift and manual linkage rods from the levers on the transmission.
9. Remove the vacuum hose from the vacuum diaphragm unit. Remove the vacuum line from the retaining clip.
10. Remove the two bolts securing the bellcrank bracket to the converter housing.
11. Remove the transfer case. Refer to the Transfer Case section behind Manual Transmissions.
12. Raise the transmission with a transmission jack to provide clearance to remove the crossmember. Remove the rear mount from the crossmember and remove the crossmember from the side supports.
13. Lower the transmission to gain access to the oil cooler lines.
14. Disconnect each oil line from the fittings on the transmission.
15. Disconnect the speedometer cable from the extension housing.
16. Secure the transmission to the jack with the chain. Remove the converter housing-to-cylinder block attaching bolts.
17. Carefully move the transmission and converter assembly away from the engine and, at the same time, lower the jack to clear the underside of the vehicle.

To install the unit:

18. Position the converter on the transmission, making sure the converter drive flats are fully engaged in the pump gear by rotating the converter.
19. With the converter properly installed, place the transmission on the jack. Secure the transmission to the jack with a chain.
20. Rotate the converter until the studs and drain plug are in alignment with the holes in the flywheel.
21. Move the converter and transmission assembly forward into position, using care not to damage the flywheel and the converter pilot. The converter must rest squarely against the flywheel. This indicates that the converter pilot is not binding in the engine crankshaft.
22. Install and tighten the converter housing-to-engine attaching bolts.
23. Remove the safety chain from around the transmission.
24. Install a new O-ring on the lower end of the transmission filler tube. Insert the tube in the transmission case.
25. Connect the speedometer cable to the extension housing.
26. Connect the oil cooler lines to the right of the transmission case.
27. Position the crossmember on the side supports. Position the rear mount insulator on the crossmember and install the attaching bolts and nuts.
28. Install the transfer case.
29. Secure the engine rear support to the extension housing. Lower the transmission and remove the jack.
30. Secure the crossmember to the side supports with the attaching bolts and tighten to 40-60 ft.lb.
31. Position the bellcrank to the converter housing and install the two attaching bolts.
32. Connect the downshift and manual linkage rods to their respective levers on the transmission.
33. Connect the vacuum line to the vacuum diaphragm making sure that the line is in the retaining clip.
34. Secure the converter-to-flywheel attaching nuts. Install the converter housing access cover and secure it with the attaching bolts.
35. Secure the starter motor in place with the attaching bolts. Connect the cable to the terminal on the starter. Connect the neutral start switch wires at the plug connector.
36. Adjust the shift linkage as required. Lower the vehicle.
37. Position the transmission fluid filler tube to the valve cover bracket and secure with the attaching bolt. Fill the transmission to the correct level. Start the engine and shift the transmission to all ranges, then recheck the fluid level.

Fluid Pan

REMOVAL & INSTALLATION

1. Raise the vehicle, so that the transmission oil pan is readily accessible. Safely support on jackstands.
2. Disconnect the fluid filler tube from the pan and allow the fluid to drain into an appropriate container.
3. Remove the transmission oil pan attaching bolts, pan and gasket.

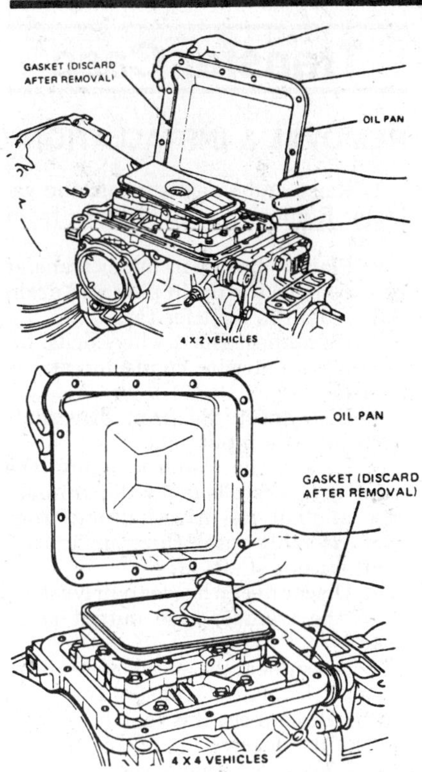

Pan and filter removal and installation

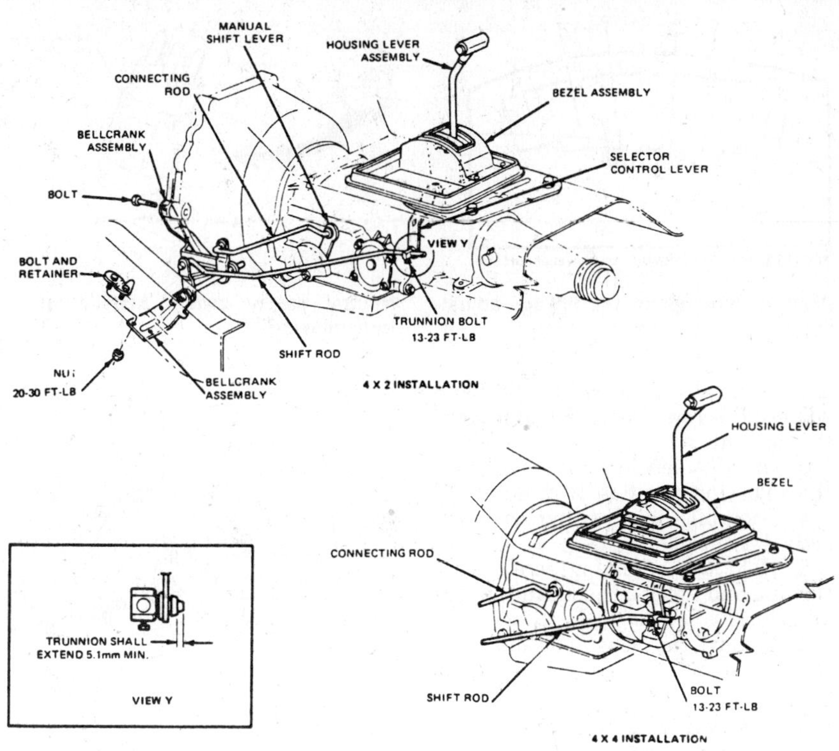

Shift control linkage assembly

4. Clean the transmission oil pan and transmission mating surfaces.

5. Install the transmission oil pan in the reverse order of removal, torquing the attaching bolts to 12-16 ft.lb. and using a new gasket. Fill the transmission with 3 qts. of the correct type fluid.

6. Lower the vehicle. Start the engine and move the gear selector through shift pattern. Allow the engine to reach normal operating temperature.

7. Check the transmission fluid. Add fluid, if necessary, to maintain correct level.

FILTER SERVICE

1. Remove the transmission oil pan and gasket.

2. Remove the screws holding the fine mesh screen to the lower valve body.

3. Install the new filter screen and transmission oil pan gasket in the reverse order of removal.

FRONT BAND ADJUSTMENT

C3

1. Remove the downshift rod from the transmission downshift lever. Clean all of the dirt away from the bank adjusting nut and screw area. Remove and discard the locknut.

2. Tighten the adjusting screw to 10 ft.lb. Back off the adjusting screw exactly two turns.

3. Install a new locknut, hold the adjusting screw in position and tighten the locknut to 35-45 ft.lb. Install the downshift rod.

INTERMEDIATE BAND ADJUSTMENT

C5

1. Raise and support the vehicle on jackstands.

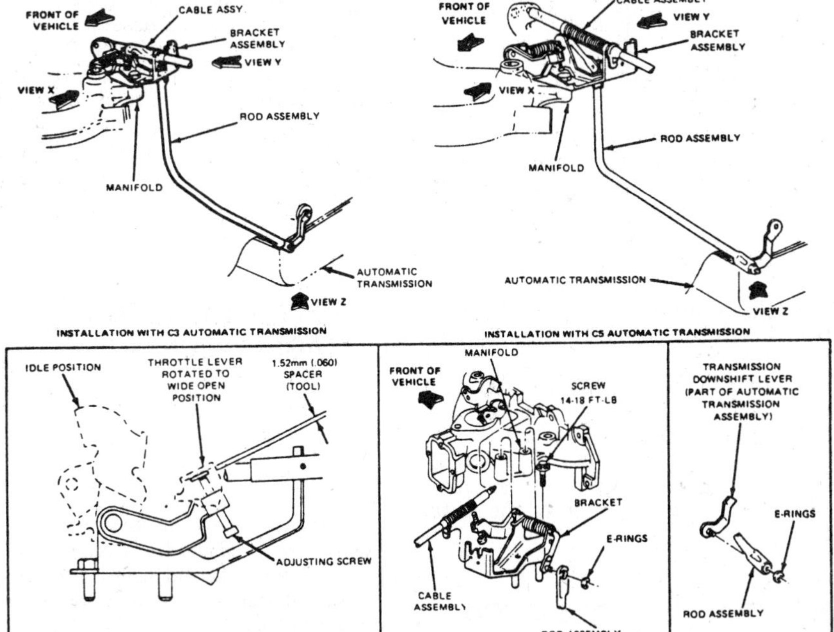

Kickdown rod installation and adjustment

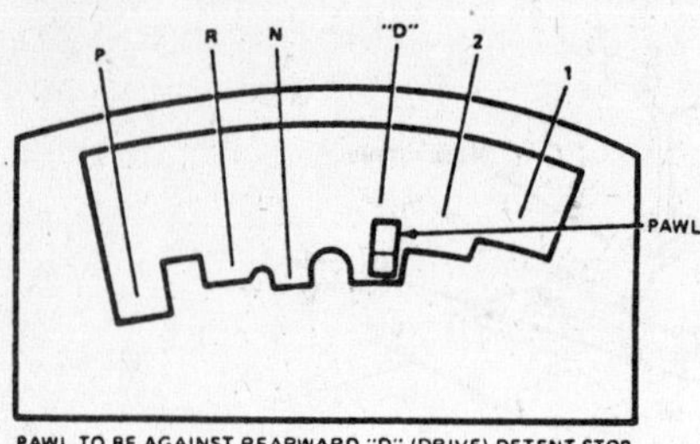

Pawl positioning for the linkage adjustment

2. Clean all dirt away from the band adjusting screw. Remove and discard the locknut.
3. Install a new locknut and tighten the adjusting screw to 10 ft.lb.
4. Back off the adjusting screw exactly 4¼ turns.
5. Hold the adjusting screw from turning and tighten the locknut to 35-45 ft.lb.
6. Remove the jackstands and lower the vehicle.

LOW-REVERSE BAND ADJUSTMENT

C5

1. Clean all dirt from around the band adjusting screw and remove and discard the locknut.
2. Install a new locknut on the adjusting screw. Using a torque wrench, tighten the adjusting screw to 10 ft.lb.
3. Back off the adjusting screw exactly 3 full turns.
4. Hold the adjusting screw steady and tighten the locknut to 35-45 ft.lb.

SHIFT LINKAGE ADJUSTMENT

1. With the engine stopped, place the transmission selector lever at the steering column in the **D** position against the **D** stop.
2. Loosen the shift rod adjusting nut at the transmission lever.
3. Shift the manual lever at the transmission to the **D** position, two detents from the rear.
4. With the selector lever and transmission manual lever in the **D** position, tighten the adjusting nut to 12-18 ft.lb. Do not allow the rod or shift lever to move while tightening the nut.
5. Check the operation of the shift linkage.

NEUTRAL SAFETY SWITCH ADJUSTMENT

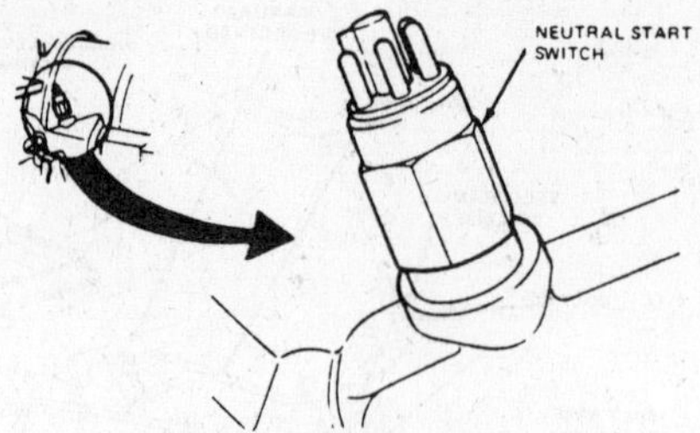

Neutral safety switch installation—C3 transmission

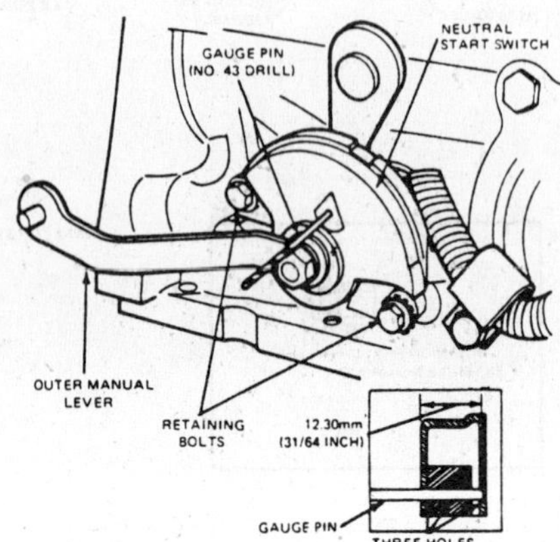

Adjusting the neutral safety switch—C5 transmission

1. Hold the steering column transmission selector lever against the Neutral stop.
2. Move the sliding block assembly on the neutral switch to the neutral position and insert a 0.091" gauge pin or $^{3}/_{32}$" drill in the alignment hole on the terminal side of the switch.
3. Move the switch assembly housing so that the sliding block contacts the actuating pin lever. Secure the switch to the outer tube of the steering column and remove the gauge pin.
4. Check the operation of the switch. The engine should only start in Neutral and Park.

THROTTLE KICKDOWN LINKAGE ADJUSTMENT

1. Move the carburetor throttle linkage to the wide open position.
2. Insert a 0.060" thick spacer between the throttle lever and the kickdown adjusting screw.
3. Rotate the transmission kickdown lever until the lever engages the transmission internal stop. Do not use the kick-down rod to turn the transmission lever.
4. Turn the adjusting screw until it contacts the 0.060" spacer.
5. Remove the spacer.

Transfer Case

REMOVAL & INSTALLATION

1. Raise and safely support the vehicle. Remove the skid plate from frame.
2. Place a drain pan under transfer case, remove the drain plug and drain fluid from the transfer case.
3. Disconnect the 4-wheel drive indicator switch wire connector at the transfer case.
4. Disconnect the front driveshaft from the axle input yoke.
5. Loosen the clamp retaining the front driveshaft boot to the transfer case, and pull the driveshaft and front boot assembly out of the transfer case front output shaft.
6. Disconnect the rear driveshaft from the transfer case output shaft yoke.
7. Disconnect the speedometer driven gear from the transfer case rear cover. Disconnect the vent hose from the control lever.
8. Loosen or remove the large bolt and the small bolt retaining the shifter to the extension housing. Pull on the control lever until the bushing slides off the transfer case shift lever pin. If necessary, unscrew the shift lever from the control lever. Remove the heat shield from the transfer case.

CAUTION

The catalytic converter is located beside the heat shield. Be careful when working around the catalytic converter because of the extremely high temperatures generated by the converter.

9. Support the transfer case with a suitable jack. Remove the five bolts retaining the transfer case to the transmission and the extension housing.
10. Slide the transfer case rearward off the transmission output shaft and lower the transfer case from the vehicle. Remove the gasket from between the transfer case and extension housing.
11. Place a new gasket between the transfer case and the extension housing.
12. Raise the transfer case with a suitable jack so that the transmission output shaft aligns with the splined transfer case input shaft. Slide the transfer case forward onto the transmission output shafts and onto the dowel pin. Install the five bolts retaining the transfer case to the extension housing. Tighten bolts to 25-35 ft.lb.
13. Remove the transmission jack from the transfer case.
14. Install the heat shield on the transfer case. Tighten the bolts to 27-

37 ft.lb.

15. Move the control lever until the bushing is in position over the transfer case shift lever pin. Install and hand start the attaching bolts. First, tighten the large bolt retaining the shifter to the extension housing to 70-90 ft.lb., then the small bolt to 31-42 ft.lb.

NOTE: Always tighten the large bolt retaining the shifter to the extension housing before tightening the small bolt.

16. Install the vent assembly so the white marking on the hose is in position in the notch in the shifter. The upper end of the vent hose should be 2" above the top of the shifter and positioned inside of the shift lever boot.

17. Connect the speedometer driven gear to the transfer case rear cover. Tighten the screw to 20-25 in.lb.

18. Connect the rear driveshaft to the transfer case output shaft yoke. Tighten the bolts to 12-15 ft.lb.

19. Clean the transfer case front output shaft female splines. Apply 5-8 grams of Multi-Purpose Long-Life Lubricant, C1AZ-19590-B(ESA-M1C175-B) or equivalent to the splines. Insert the front driveshaft male spline.

20. Connect the front driveshaft to the axle input yoke. Tighten the bolts to 12-15 ft.lb.

21. Push the driveshaft boot to engage the external groove on the transfer case front output shaft. Secure with a clamp.

22. Connect the 4-wheel drive indicator switch wire connector at the transfer case. Install the drain plug and tighten to 14-22 ft.lb. Remove the fill plug and install 3 pints of Dexron®II, automatic transmission fluid. Install fill plug and tighten to 14-22 ft.lb.

23. Install the skid plate to frame. Tighten nuts and bolts to 22-30 ft.lb. Lower the vehicle.

DRIVELINE

Driveshaft

REMOVAL & INSTALLATION

4-Wheel Drive

1. Mark shaft and flange for installation in same position. To remove the rear driveshaft, disconnect the double Cardan joint from the flange at the transfer case and the single U-joint from the flange at the rear axle. Remove the driveshaft.

2. To remove the front driveshaft,

Front driveshaft and U-joints—4x4 models

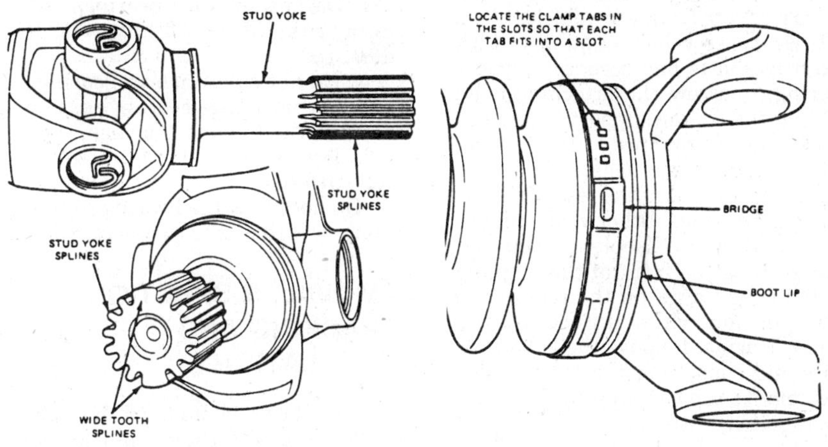

Inspection of the stud yoke assembly

Keystone clamp installation

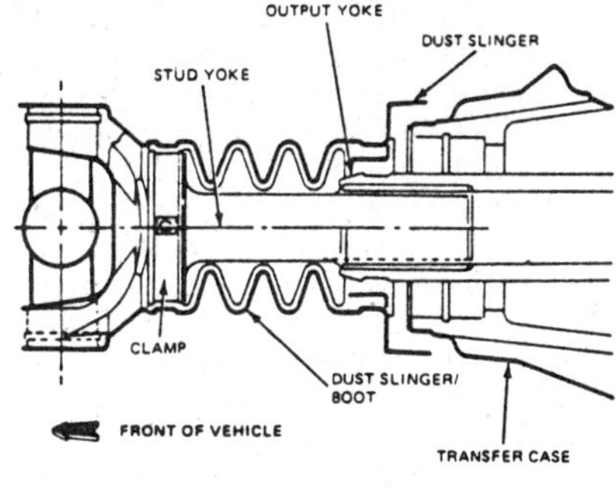

Dust slinger and boot assembly

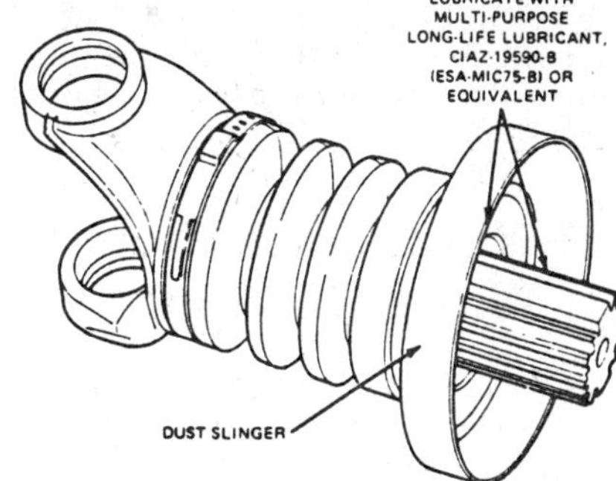

Boot and yoke lubrication points

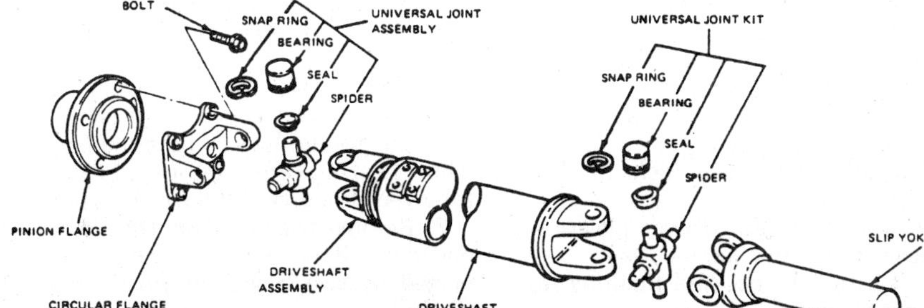

Rear driveshaft with single cardan U-joint—All 4x2, and 4x4 long wheelbase models

disconnect the double Cardan joint from the flange at the transfer case and the single U-joint from the front axle. Remove the driveshaft.

3. Installation is the reverse of removal. Torque driveshaft-to-transfer case bolts to 20-25 ft.lb.; driveshaft-to-axle bolts to 8-15 ft.lb.

2-Wheel Drive

1. Mark shaft and flange for installation in same position. Unscrew the nuts attaching the U-bolts to the flange at the rear axle, or remove the bolts and clips. Remove the U-bolts or bolts and clips and allow the rear of the driveshaft to drop down. Slide the front of the driveshaft out of the rear of the transmission, transfer case, or the center support bearing. Remove the driveshaft from the vehicle.

2. On those vehicles equipped with two driveshafts and a center support bearing, unscrew the attaching bolts holding the center support bearing to the frame. If equipped with a sliding yoke at the transmission, slide the coupling shaft out of the rear of the extension housing. Otherwise, remove the nuts from the U-bolts or bolts and clips holding the front of the coupling shaft to the flange on the rear of the transmission while supporting the center bearing. Remove the U-bolts or bolts and clips from the front flange and remove the coupling shaft assembly together with the center support bearing.

3. Install the driveshaft(s) in the reverse order of removal.

NOTE: All U-joints on two-piece driveshafts must be on the same horizontal plane when installed.

2-Wheel Drive Front Wheel Bearings

The wheel bearings should be serviced (cleaned, inspected, repacked or replaced) every 20,000 miles, or whenever operated in deep water.

Before handling the bearings there are a few things that you should remember to do and try to avoid. DO the following:

1. Remove all outside dirt from the housing before exposing the bearing.
2. Treat a used bearing as gently as you would a new one.
3. Work with clean tools in clean surroundings.
4. Use clean, dry canvas gloves, or at least clean, dry hands.
5. Clean solvents and flushing fluids are a must.
6. Use clean paper when laying out the bearings to dry.
7. Protect disassembled bearings from rust and dirt. Cover them up.
8. Use clean rags to wipe bearings.
9. Keep the bearings in oil-proof paper when they are to be stored or are not in use.
10. Clean the inside of the housing before replacing the bearing. Do NOT do the following:
    a. Don't work in dirty surroundings.
    b. Don't use dirty, chipped, or damaged tools.
    c. Try not to work on wooden work benches or use wooden mallets.
    d. Don't handle bearings with dirty or moist hands.
    e. Do not use gasoline for cleaning; use a safe solvent.
    f. Do not spin-dry bearings with compressed air. They will be damaged.
    g. Do not spin unclean bearings.
    h. Avoid using cotton waste or dirty cloths to wipe bearings.
    i. Try not to scratch or nick bearing surfaces.

10. Do not allow the bearing to come in contact with dirt or rust at any time.

REMOVAL, INSPECTION, REPACKING AND INSTALLATION

1. Jack the truck up until the wheel to be serviced is off the ground and can spin freely. It is easier to check all the bearings at the same time. If the equipment needed is available, raise the front end of the truck so that both front wheels are off the ground. Use jackstands to support the vehicle. Make sure that the truck is completely stable before proceeding any further.

2. Remove the lug nuts and remove the wheel/tire assembly from the hub. It is necessary to remove the caliper assembly from the rotor and caliper support. Do not disconnect the brake line from the caliper. Simply hang the caliper with a length of heavy wire above the hub. Be careful not to strain the flexible brake tube.

3. Remove the grease cap with a screwdriver or pliers.

4. Remove the cotter pin and discard it. Cotter pins should never be reused.

5. Remove the nut lock, adjusting nut, and washer from the spindle.

6. Wiggle the hub so that the outer wheel bearing comes loose and can be removed. Remove the outer bearing.

7. Remove the hub from the spindle and place it on a work surface, supported by two blocks of wood under the hub.

8. Place a block of wood or drift pin through the spindle hole and tap out the inner grease seal. Tap lightly so not to damage the bearing. When the seal falls out, so will the inner bearing. Discard the seal.

9. Place all of the bearings, nuts, nut locks, washers and grease caps in a container of solvent. Use a light soft brush to thoroughly clean each part. Make sure that every bit of dirt and grease is rinsed off, then place each cleaned part on an absorbent cloth or paper and allow them to dry completely.

10. Clean the inside of the hub, including the bearing races, and the spindle. Remove all traces of old lubricant from these components.

11. Inspect the bearings for pitting, flat spots, rust, and rough areas. Check the races in the hub and the spindle for the same defects and rub them clean with a cloth that has been soaked in solvent. If the races show hair line cracks or worn shiny areas, they must be replaced. The races are installed in the hub with a press fit and are removed by driving them out with a suitable punch or drift. Place the new races squarely onto the hub and place a block of wood over them. Drive the race into place with a hammer, striking the block of wood. Never hit the race with any metal object. Replacement seals, bearings, and other required parts can be bought at an auto parts store. The old parts should be taken along to be compared with the replacement parts to ensure a perfect match.

12. Pack the wheel bearings with grease. There are special devices made for the specific purpose of greasing bearings, but if one is not available, pack the wheel bearings by hand. Put a large dab of grease in the palm of your hand and push the bearing through it with a sliding motion. The grease must be forced through the side of the bearing and in between each roller. Continue until the grease begins to ooze out the other side and through the gaps between the rollers; the bearing must be completely packed with grease.

NOTE: Sodium based grease is not compatible with lithium based grease. Be careful not to mix the two types. The best way to prevent this is to completely clean all of the old grease from the hub and spindle before installing any new grease.

13. Turn the hub assembly over so that the inner side faces up, making sure that the race and inner area are clean, and drop the inner wheel bearing into place. Using a hammer and a block of wood, tap the new grease seal in place. Never hit the seal with the

hammer directly. Move the block of wood around the circumference until it is properly seated.

14. Slide the hub assembly onto the spindle and push it as far as it will go, making sure that it has completely covered the brake shoes. Keep the hub centered on the spindle to prevent damage to the grease seal and the spindle threads.

15. Place the outer wheel bearing in place over the spindle. Press it in until it is snug. Place the washer on the spindle after the bearing. Screw on the spindle nut and turn it down until a slight binding is felt.

16. With a torque wrench, tighten the nut to 17-25 ft.lb. to seat the bearings. Install the nut lock over the nut so that the cotter pin hole in the spindle is aligned with a slot in the nut lock. Back off the adjusting nut and the nut lock two slots of the nut lock and install the cotter pin.

17. Bend the longer of the two ends opposite the looped end out and over the end of the spindle. Trim both ends of the cotter pin just enough so that the grease cap will fit, leaving the bent end shaped over the end of the spindle.

18. Install the grease cap, brake caliper if so equipped, and the wheel/tire assembly. The wheel should rotate freely with no noise or noticeable endplay.

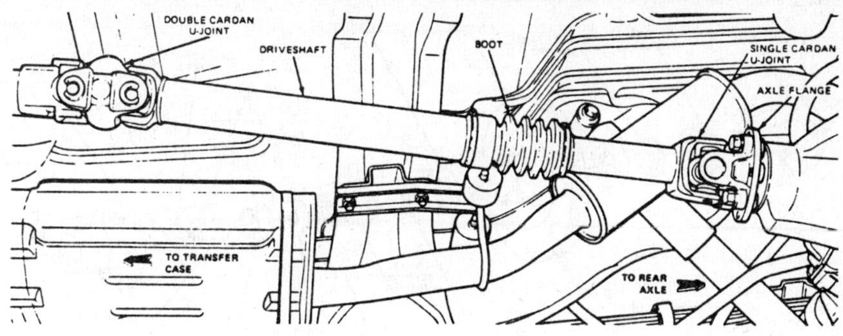

Rear driveshaft with double cardan U-joint—4x4 short wheelbase models

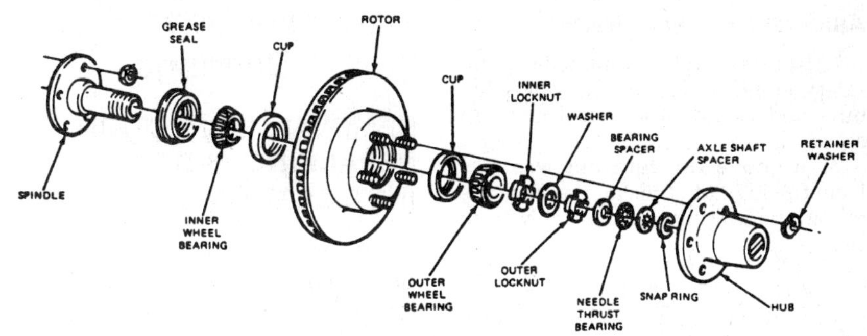

Manual locking hub—Exploded view

4-Wheel Drive Front Hubs

REMOVAL & INSTALLATION

Manual Hubs

1. Raise the vehicle and install safety stands.
2. Remove the wheel lug nuts and remove the wheel and tire assembly.
3. Remove the retainer washers from the lug nut studs and remove the manual locking hub assembly. To remove the internal hub lock assembly from the outer body assembly, remove the outer lock ring seated in the hub body groove. The internal assembly, spring and clutch gear will now slide out of the hub body.

WARNING: Do not remove the screw from the plastic dial.

4. Rebuild the hub assembly in the reverse order of disassembly.
5. Install the manual locking hub assembly over the spindle and place the retainer washers on the lug nut studs.
6. Install the wheel and tire assembly. Install the lug nuts and tighten to 85-115 ft.lb.

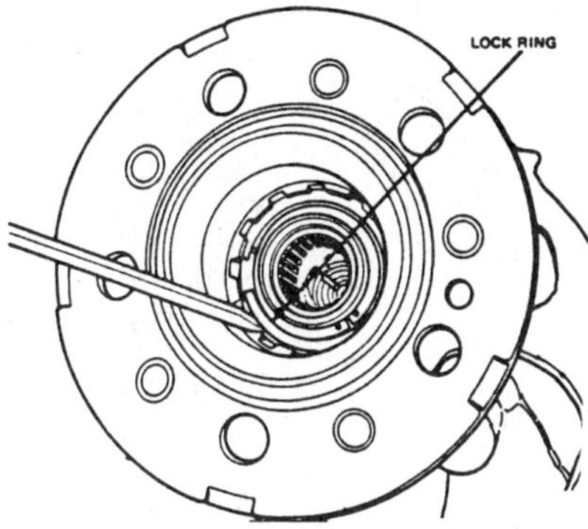

Removing the outer lock ring from the manual locking hub

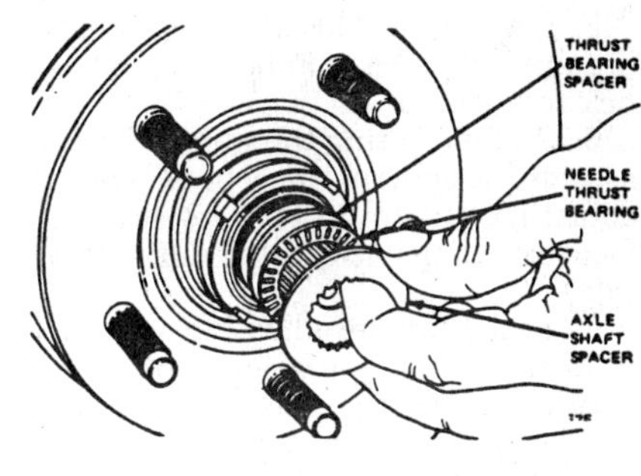

Removal of thrust bearing and spacers

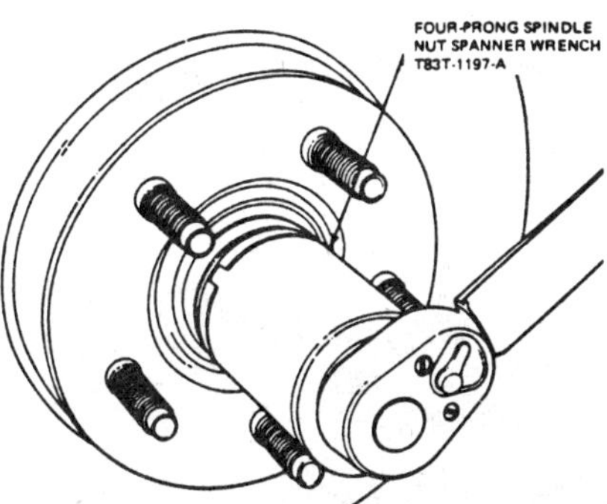

Removing and installing the outer or inner locknut

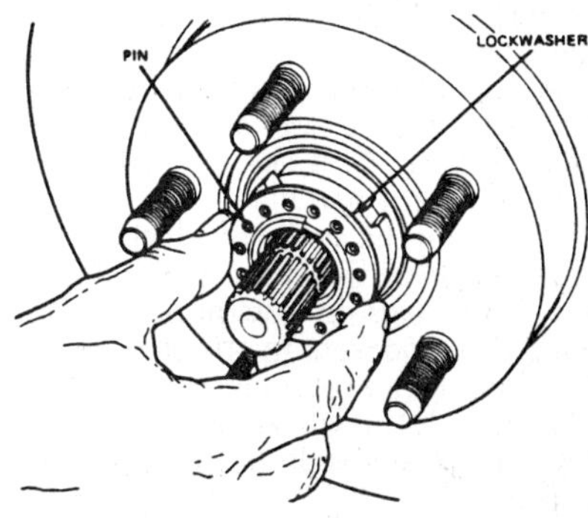

Installing the lockwasher

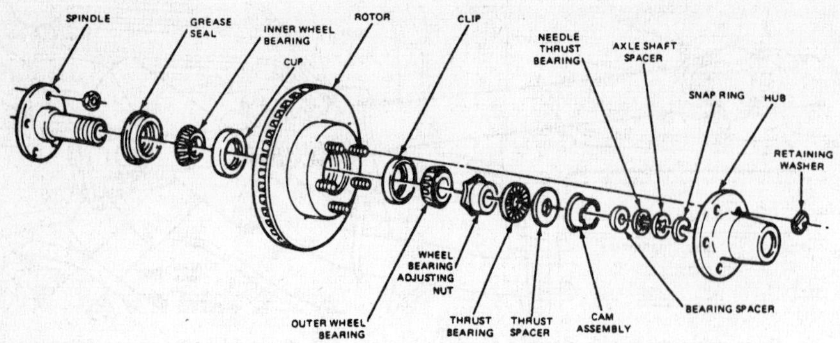

Automatic locking hub

Automatic Locking Hubs

1. Raise the vehicle and support on safety stands. Remove the wheel lug nuts and remove the wheel and tire assembly.
2. Remove the retainer washers from the lug nut studs and remove the automatic locking hub assembly from the spindle.
3. Remove the snapring from the end of the spindle shaft.
4. Remove the axle shaft spacer, needle thrust bearing and the bearing spacer. Being careful not to damage the plastic moving cam, pull the cam assembly off the wheel bearing adjusting nut and remove the thrust washer and needle thrust bearing from the adjusting nut.
5. Loosen the wheel bearing adjusting nut from the spindle using a 2¾" hex socket tool.
6. While rotating the hub and rotor assembly, tighten the wheel bearing adjusting nut to 35 ft.lb. to seat the bearings, then back off the nut ¼ turn (90°).
7. Retighten the adjusting nut to 16 in.lb. using a torque wrench. Align the closest hole in the wheel bearing adjusting nut with the center of the spindle keyway slot. Advance the nut to the next hole if required.
8. Install the locknut needle bearing and thrust washer in the order of removal and push or press the cam assembly onto the locknut by lining up the key in the fixed cam with the spindle keyway.
9. Install the bearing thrust washer, needle thrust bearing and axle shaft spacer. Clip the snapring onto the end of the spindle.
10. Install the automatic locking hub assembly over the spindle by lining up the three legs in the hub assembly with three pockets in the cam assembly. Install the retainer washers.
11. Install the wheel and tire assembly. Install and tighten lugnuts to 85-115 ft.lb.
12. Final end play of the wheel on the spindle should be 0.001-0.003").

4-Wheel Drive Front Bearings

REMOVAL, INSPECTION, REPACKING AND INSTALLATION

NOTE: The following procedure requires the use of several special tools.

1. Raise the vehicle and support on safety stands. Remove the wheel lug nuts and remove the wheel and tire assembly.
2. Remove the retainer washers from the lug nut studs and remove the manual locking hub assembly from the spindle.
3. Remove the snapring from the end of the spindle shaft.
4. Remove the axle shaft spacer, needle thrust bearing and the bearing spacer.
5. Remove the outer wheel bearing locknut from the spindle, using a four-prong spindle nut spanner wrench. Make sure the tabs on the tool engage the slots in the locknut. Remove the locknut washer from the spindle.
6. Loosen the inner wheel bearing locknut using Four Prong Spindle Nut Spanner Wrench or equivalent. Make sure that the tabs on the tool engage the slots in the locknut and that the slot in the tool is over the pin on the locknut.
7. Tighten the inner locknut to 35 ft.lb. to seat the bearings. Spin the rotor and back off the inner locknut ¼ turn. Install the lockwasher on the spindle. It may be necessary to turn the inner locknut slightly so that the pin on the locknut aligns with the closest hole in the lockwasher.
8. Install the outer wheel bearing locknut using Four-Prong Spindle Nut Spanner Wrench or equivalent.
9. Tighten locknut to 150 ft.lb.
10. Install the bearing thrust spacer, needle thrust bearing and axle shaft spacer.
11. Clip the snapring onto the end of

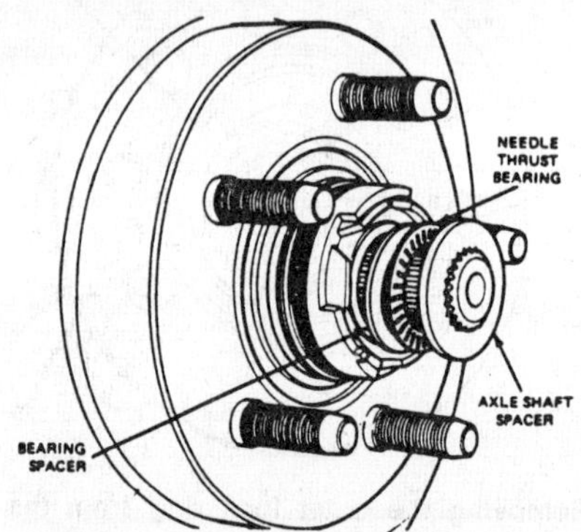

Thrust bearing and spacers removal and installtion

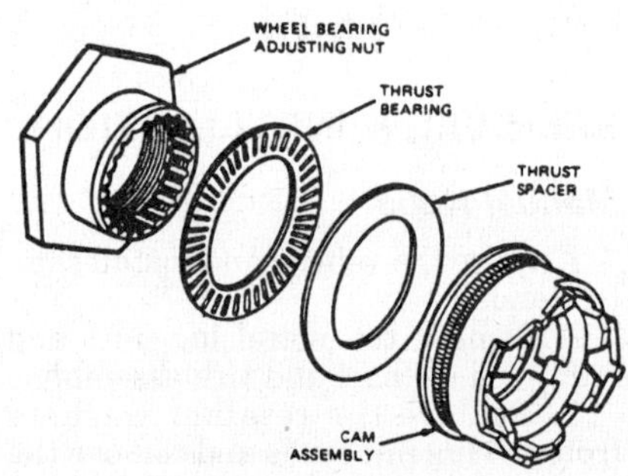

Wheel bearing adjustment

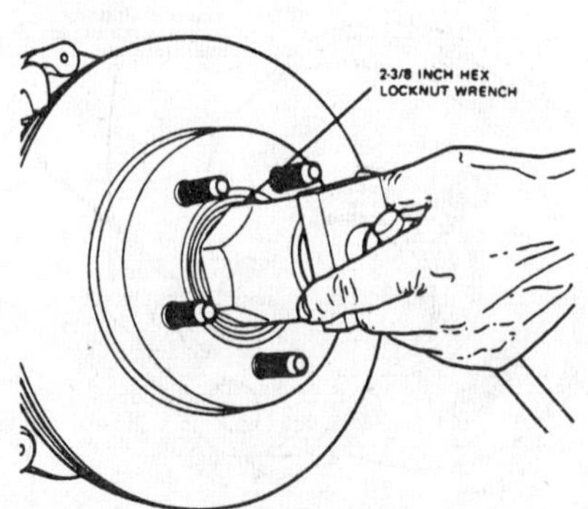

Wheel bearing adjustment nut

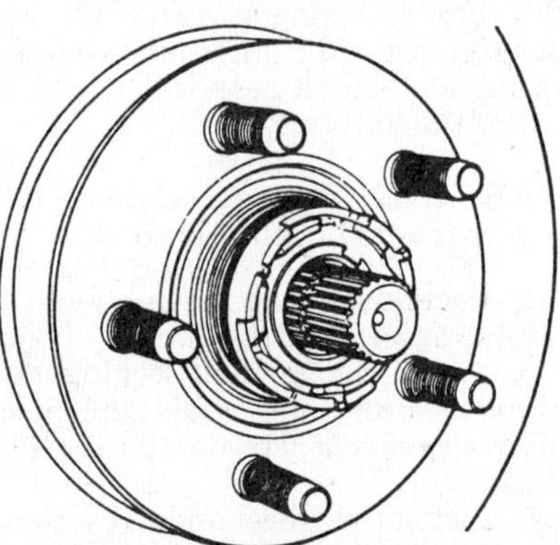

Installing the cam assembly

the spindle.

12. Install the manual hub assembly over the spindle. Install the retainer washers.

13. Install the wheel and tire assembly. Install and tighten lugnuts to 85-115 ft.lb.

14. Check the end play of the wheel and tire assembly on the spindle. End play should be 0.001-0.003".

FRONT DRIVE AXLE

Axle Shaft

REMOVAL & INSTALLATION

1. Raise the vehicle and install safety stands. Remove the wheel and tire assembly. Remove the caliper.

2. Remove hub locks, wheel bearings, and lock nuts.

3. Remove the hub and rotor. Remove the outer wheel bearing cone. Remove the grease seal from the rotor. Remove the inner wheel bearing.

4. Remove the inner and outer bearing cups from the rotor. Remove the nuts retaining the spindle to the steering knuckle. Tap the spindle with a plastic hammer to jar the spindle from the knuckle. Remove the splash shield.

5. Remove the shaft and joint assembly by pulling the assembly out of the carrier.

6. On the right side of the carrier, remove and discard the keystone clamp from the shaft and joint assembly and the stub shaft. Slide the rubber boot onto the stub shaft and pull the shaft and joint assembly from the splines of the stub shaft.

7. Place the spindle in a vise on the second step of the spindle. Wrap a shop towel around the spindle or use a brass-jawed vise to protect the spindle. Remove the oil seal and needle bearing from the spindle with slide hammer and seal remover.

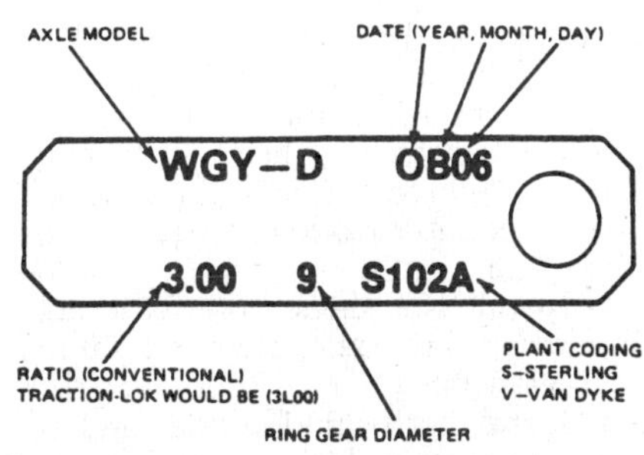

Axle identification tag

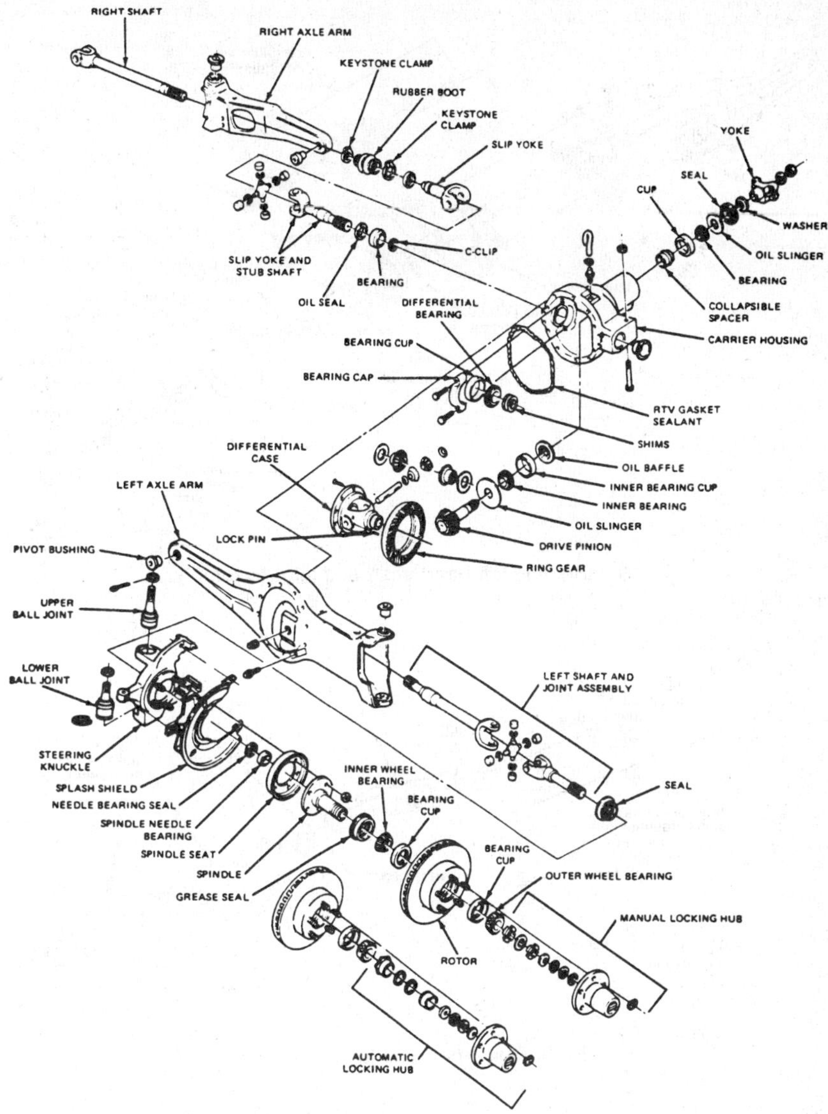

Dana model 25 front drive axle

If required, remove the seal from the shaft, by driving off with a hammer.

8. Clean all dirt and grease from the spindle bearing bore. Bearing bores must be free from nicks and burrs. Place the bearing in the bore with the manufacturer's identification facing outward. Drive the bearing into the bore using Spindle Bearing Replacer, T83T-3123-A and Driver Handle T80T-4000-W or equivalents.

9. Install the grease seal in the bearing bore with the lip side of the seal facing towards the tool. Drive the seal in the bore with Spindle Bearing Replacer, T83T-3123-A and Driver Handle T80-4000-W or equivalents. Coat the bearing seal lip with Multi-Purpose Long Life Lubricant, C1AZ-19590-B (ESA-M1C75-B) or equivalent.

10. If removed, install a new shaft seal. Place the shaft in a press, and install the seal with Spindle/Axle Seal Installer, T83T-3132-A, or equivalent.

11. On the right side of the carrier, install the rubber boot and new keystone clamps on the stub shaft slip yoke. Since the splines on the shaft are phased, there is only one way to assemble the right shaft and joint assembly into the slip yoke. Align the missing spline in the slip yoke barrel with the gapless male spline on the shaft and joint assembly. Slide the right shaft and joint assembly into the slip yoke making sure the splines are fully engaged. Slide the boot over the assembly and crimp the keystone clamp using Clamp Pliers.

12. On the left side of the carrier slide the shaft and joint assembly through the knuckle and engage the splines on the shaft in the carrier.

13. Install the splash shield and spindle onto the steering knuckle. Install

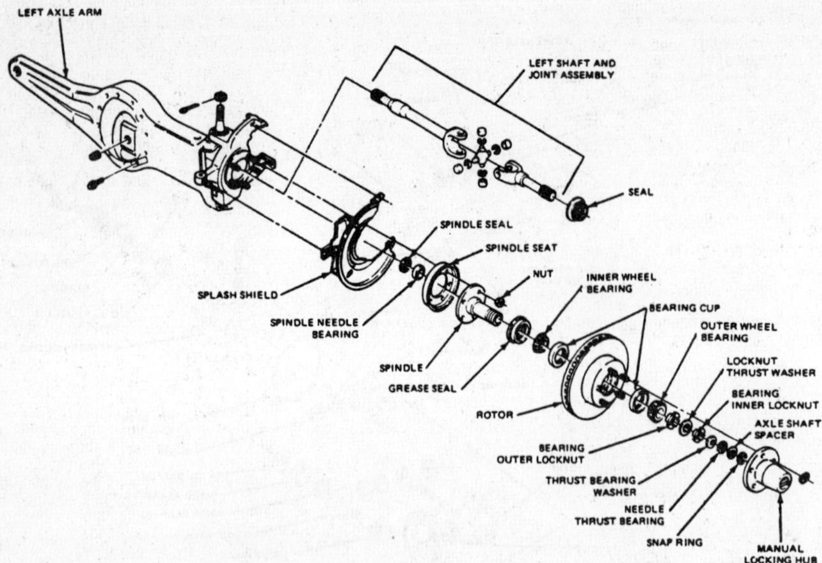

Spindle and left hand shaft and joint assembly

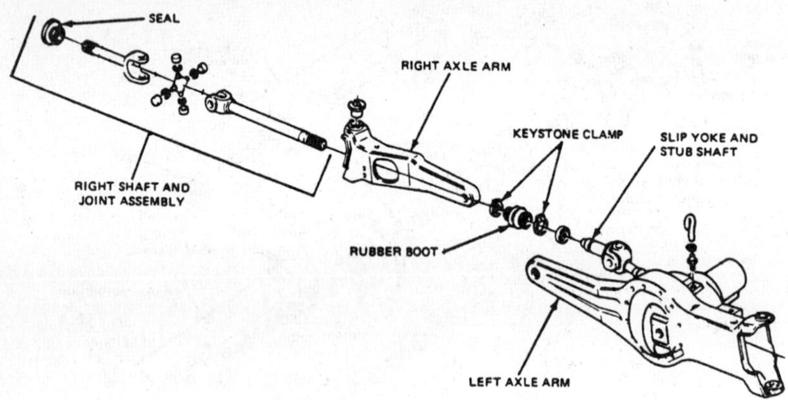

Right hand shaft and joint assembly

and tighten the spindle nuts to 35-45 ft.lb.

14. Drive the bearing cups into the rotor using bearing cup replacer T73T-4222-B and Driver Handle, T80T-4000-W or equivalents.

15. Pack the inner and outer wheel bearings and the lip of the oil seal with Multi-Purpose Long-Life Lubricant, C1AZ-19590-B (ESA-M1C75-B) or equivalent.

16. Place the inner wheel bearing in the inner cup. Drive the grease seal into the bore with Hub Seal Replacer, T83T-1175-B and Driver Handle, T80T-4000-W or equivalents. Coat the bearing seal lip with multipurpose long life lubricant, C1AZ-19590-B (ESA-M1C75-B) or equivalent.

17. Install the rotor on the spindle. Install the outer wheel bearing into cup.

NOTE: Verify that the grease seal lip totally encircles the spindle.

18. Install the wheel bearing, locknut, thrust bearing, snapring, and locking hubs.

Right Side Stub Axle and Carrier

REMOVAL & INSTALLATION

1. Remove the nuts and U-bolts connecting the driveshaft to the yoke. Disconnect the driveshaft from the yoke. Wire the driveshaft out of the way, so it will not interfere in the carrier removal process.

2. Remove both spindles and the Left and Right Shaft and U-joint assemblies as described previously.

3. Support the carrier with a suitable jack and remove the bolts retaining the carrier to the support arm. Separate the carrier from the support arm and drain the lubricant from the carrier. Remove the carrier from the vehicle.

4. Place the carrier in a holding fixture.

5. Rotate the slip yoke and shaft assembly so the open side of the snapring is exposed.

6. Remove the snapring from the shaft. Remove the slip yoke and shaft assembly from the carrier.

7. Remove the oil seal and caged needle bearings at the same time, using Slide Hammer, T50T-100-A and Collet, D80L-100-A or equivalents. Discard the seal and needle bearing.

8. Make sure the bearing bore is free from nicks and burrs. Install a new caged needle bearing on Needle Bearing Replacer, T83T-1244-A or equivalent, with the manufacturer name and part number facing outward towards the tool. Drive the needle bearing until it is seated in the bore.

9. Coat the seal with Long-Life Multi-Purpose Lubricant, C1AZ-19590-B (ESA-M1C75-B) or equivalent. Drive the seal into the carrier using Needle Bearing Replacer T83T-1244-A or equivalent.

10. Install the slip yoke and shaft assembly into the carrier so the groove in the shaft is visible in the differential case.

11. Install the snapring in the groove in the shaft. Force the snapring into position with a suitable tool. Remove the carrier from the holding fixture.

NOTE: Do not tap on the center of the snapring. This may damage the snapring.

12. Clean all traces of gasket RTV sealant from the surfaces of the carrier and support arm and make sure the surfaces are free from dirt and oil. Apply a bead of RTV sealant, D6AZ-19562-A (clear) or B (black) (ESB-M4G92-A and ESE-M4G195-A) or equivalent, in a bead between ¼-⅜"wide. The bead should be continuous and should not pass through or outside the holes.

NOTE: The carrier must be installed on the support arm within five minutes after applying the RTV sealant.

13. Position the carrier on a suitable jack and install it in position on the support arm using guide pins to align. Install the attaching bolts and hand tighten. Tighten the bolts in a clockwise or counter-clockwise pattern to 40-50 ft.lb.

14. Install the shear bolt retaining the carrier to the axle arm and tighten to 75-95 ft.lb.

15. Install both spindles and the left and right shaft and joint assemblies as described in the removal and installa-

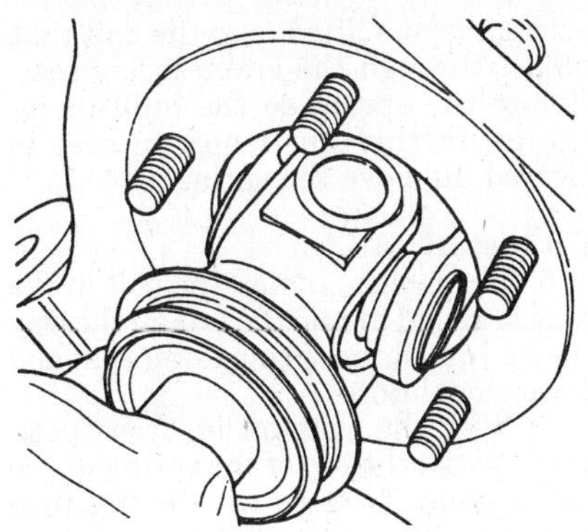

Removing the right hand shaft and joint assembly

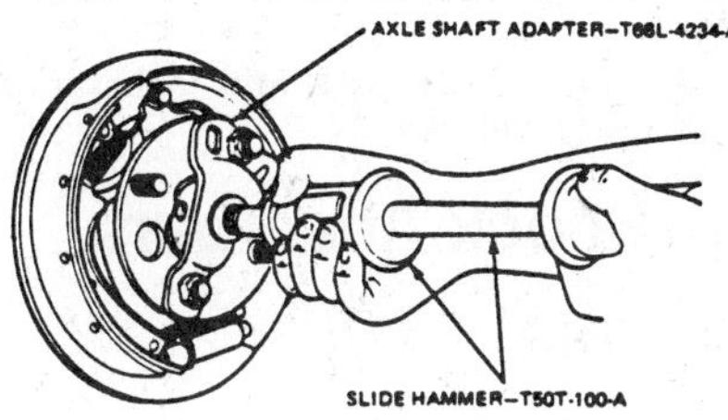

Removing the rear axle shaft

tion portion of this section.

Connect the driveshaft to the yoke. Install the nuts and U-bolts and tighten to 8-15 ft.lb.

Pinion Seal

REMOVAL & INSTALLATION

NOTE: A torque wrench capable of at least 225 ft.lb. is required for pinion seal installation.

Some models use a collapsible spacer to set pinion depth and preload. When replacing the pinion seal always install a new spacer. Never tighten the pinion nut more than 225 ft.lb. or the spacer will be compressed too far.

1. Raise and safely support the vehicle with jackstands under the frame rails. Allow the axle to drop to rebound position for working clearance.
2. Mark the companion flanges and U-joints for correct reinstallation position.
3. Remove the drive shaft. Use a suitable tool to hold the companion flange. Remove the pinion nut and companion flange.
4. Use a slide hammer and hook or sheet metal screw to remove the oil seal.
5. If the vehicle uses a collapsible spacer, install new spacer. Install a new pinion seal after lubricating the sealing surfaces. Use a suitable seal driver. Install the companion flange and pinion nut. On models using a spacer, tighten the nut to 225 ft.lb. On other models, pinion nut torque is 200-220 ft.lb.

REAR AXLE

Axle Shaft and Bearing

REMOVAL & INSTALLATION

NOTE: The following procedure requires the use of special tools, including a shop press.

1. Raise and support the vehicle. Remove the wheel/tire assembly from the brake drum.
2. Remove the clips which secure the brake drum to the axle flange, then remove the drum from the flange.
3. Working through the hole provided in each axle shaft flange, remove the nuts which secure the wheel bearing retainer plate.
4. Pull the axle shaft assembly out of the axle housing. You may need a slide hammer.

NOTE: The brake backing plate must not be dislodged. Install one nut to hold the plate in place after the axle shaft is removed.

5. If the axle has ball bearings: Loosen the bearing retainer ring by nicking it in several places with a cold chisel, then slide it off the axle shaft. On models equipped with a thick retaining ring drill a ¼-½" hole part way through the ring, then break it with a cold chisel. A hydraulic press is needed to press the bearing off and to press the new one on. Press the new bearing and the new retainer ring on separately. Use a slide hammer to pull the old seal out of the axle housing. Carefully drive the new seal evenly into the axle housing, preferably with a seal drive tool.
6. If the axle has tapered roller bearings. Use a slide hammer to remove the bearing cup from the axle housing. Drill a ¼-½" hole part way through the bearing retainer ring, then break it with a cold chisel. A hydraulic press is needed to press the bearing off and remove the seal. Press on the new seal and bearing, then the new retainer ring. Do not press the bearing and ring on together. Put the cup on the bearing, not in the housing, and lubricate the outer diameter of the cup and seal.
7. With ball bearings: Place a new gasket between the housing flange and backing plate. Carefully slide the axle shaft into place. Turn the shaft to start the splines into the side gear and push it in.
8. With tapered roller bearings: Move the seal out toward the axle shaft flange so there is at least $^{3}/_{32}$" between the edge of the outer seal and the bearing cup, to prevent snagging on installation. Carefully slide the axle shaft into place. Turn the shaft to start the splines into the side gear and push it in.
9. Install the bearing retainer plate.
10. Replace the brake drum and the wheel and tire.

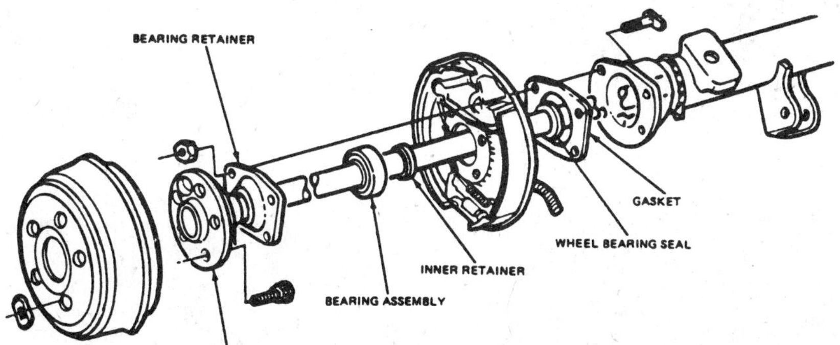

Rear axle shaft assembly

2-WHEEL DRIVE FRONT SUSPENSION

The 2-wheel drive suspension is the coil spring, twin I-beam type. It is composed of coil springs, I-beam axle arms, radius arms, upper and lower ball joints, spindles, tie rods, shock absorbers and optional stabilizer bar.

2-wheel drive suspensions use two I-beam type front axles (one for each

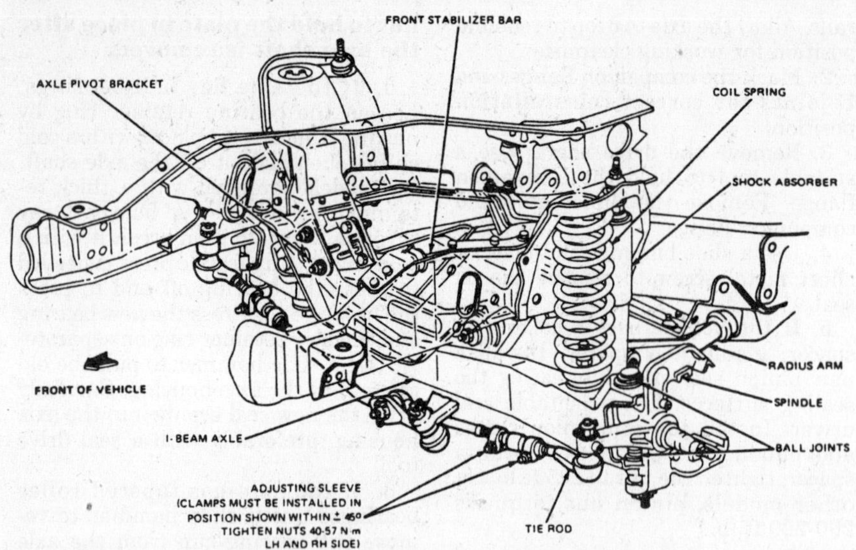

Front suspension assembly – 2WD models

wheel). One end of each axle is attached to the spindle and radius arm assembly and the other is attached to a frame pivot bracket on the opposite side of the vehicle.

Each spindle is connected to the axle by upper and lower ball joints. The ball joints have a special bearing material which never requires lubrication.

Spindle movement is controlled by tie rods and the steering linkage.

Springs

REMOVAL & INSTALLATION

1. Raise the front of the vehicle and place jackstands under the frame and a jack under the axle.

NOTE: The axle must not be permitted to hang by the brake hose. If the length of the brake hose is not sufficient to provide adequate clearance for removal and installation of the spring, the disc brake caliper must be removed from the spindle or a Strut Spring Compressor, T81P-5310-A or equivalent may be used to compress the spring sufficiently, so that the caliper does not have to be removed. After removal, the caliper must be placed on the frame or otherwise supported to prevent suspending the caliper from the caliper hose. These precautions are absolutely necessary to prevent serious damage to the tube portion of the caliper hose assembly.

2. Remove the nut securing the lower retainer to spring slot. Remove the lower retainer.

3. Lower the axle as far as it will go without stretching the brake hose and tube assembly. The axle should now be unsupported without hanging by the brake hose. If not, then either remove the caliper or use Strut Spring Compressor Tool, T81P-5310-A or equivalent to avoid placing damaging tension.

4. If sufficient slack exists in the brake hose and tube assembly, a long pry bar may be used to remove the coil spring. Insert the pry bar between the two axles and force the appropriate I-beam axle down far enough so that the spring may be lifted over the bolt that passes through the lower spring seat. Rotate the spring so the built-in retainer on the upper spring seat is cleared. Remove the spring.

To install:

5. If removed, install the bolt in the axle arm and install the nut all the way down. Install the spring lower seat and lower insulator.

6. With the axle in the lowest position, install the top of the spring in the upper seat. Rotate the spring into position.

7. Raise the axle slowly until the spring is seated in the lower spring upper seat. Install the lower retainer and nut.

8. Remove the jack and jackstands and lower vehicle.

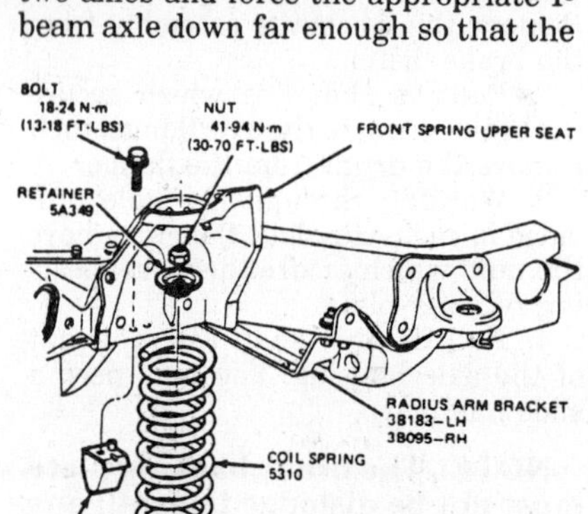

Coil spring removal and installation – 2WD models

Shock Absorbers

TESTING

1. Visually check the shock absorbers for the presence of fluid leakage. A thin film of fluid is acceptable. Anything more than that means that the shock absorber must be replaced.

2. Disconnect the lower end of the shock absorber. Compress and extend the shock fully as fast as possible. If the action is not smooth in both directions, or there is no pressure resistance, replace the shock absorber. Shock absorbers should be replaced in pairs if they have accumulated more

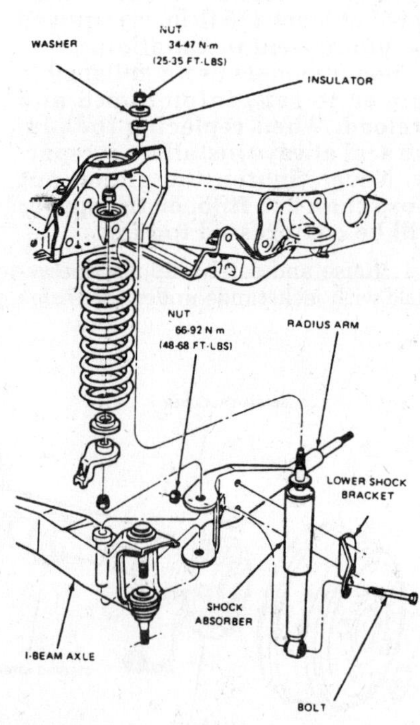

Front shock absorber installation – 2WD models

than 20,000 miles of wear. In the case of relatively new shock absorbers, where one has failed, that one, alone, may be replaced.

REMOVAL & INSTALLATION

NOTE: Prior to installing a new shock absorber, hold it upright and extend it fully. Invert it and fully compress and extend it at least three times. This will bleed trapped air.

1. Raise the vehicle to provide additional access and remove the bolt and nut attaching the shock absorber to the lower bracket on the radius arm.
2. Remove the nut, washer and insulator from the shock absorber at the frame bracket and remove the shock absorber.

To install the front shock absorber:

3. Position the washer and insulator on the shock absorber rod and position the shock absorber to the frame bracket.
4. Position the insulator and washer on the shock absorber rod and install the attaching nut loosely.
5. Position the shock absorber to the lower bracket and install the attaching bolt and nut loosely.
6. Tighten the lower attaching bolts to 48-68 ft.lb., and the upper attaching bolts to 25-35 ft.lb.

Radius Arm

REMOVAL & INSTALLATION

1. Raise the front of the vehicle, place jackstands under the frame. Place a jack under the axle.

NOTE: The axle must be supported on the jack throughout spring removal and installation, and must not be permitted to hand by the brake hose. If the length of the brake hose is not sufficient to provide adequate clearance for removal and installation of the spring, the disc brake caliper must be removed from the spindle according to the procedures specified. After removal, the caliper must be placed on the frame or otherwise supported to prevent suspending the caliper from the caliper hose. These precautions are absolutely necessary to prevent serious damage to the tube portion of the caliper hose assembly.

2. Disconnect the lower end of the shock absorber from the shock lower bracket (bolt and nut).
3. Remove the front spring as outlined in this section. Loosen the axle pivot bolt.
4. Remove the spring lower seat from the radius arm, and then remove the bolt and nut that attaches the radius arm to the axle and front bracket.
5. Remove the nut, rear washer and insulator from the rear side of the radius arm rear bracket.
6. Remove the radius arm from the vehicle, and remove the inner insulator and retainer from the radius arm stud.

To install:

7. Position the front end of the radius arm to the axle. Install the attaching bolt from underneath, and install the nut finger tight.
8. Install the retainer and inner insulator on the radius arm stud and insert the stud through the radius arm rear bracket.
9. Install the rear washer, insulator and nut on the arm stud at the rear side of the arm rear bracket. Tighten the nut to 81-120 ft.lb.

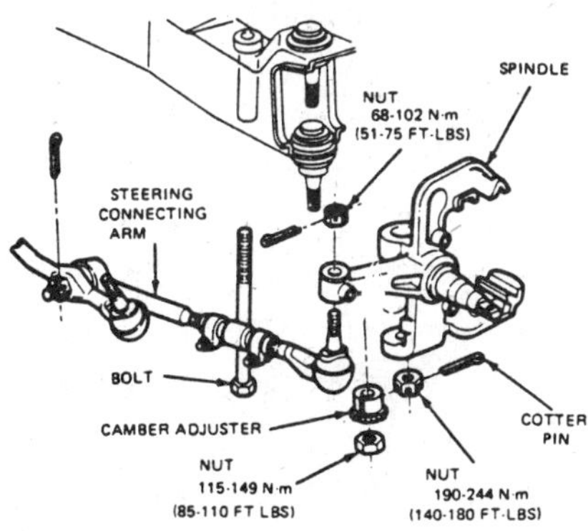

Spindle and balljoint assembly—2WD models

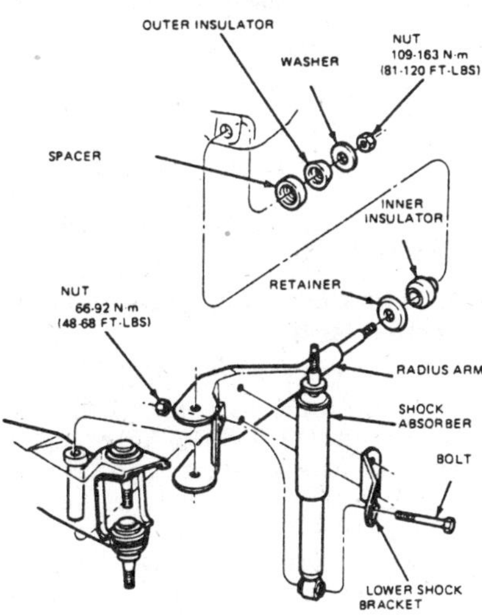

Radius arm removal and installation—2WD models

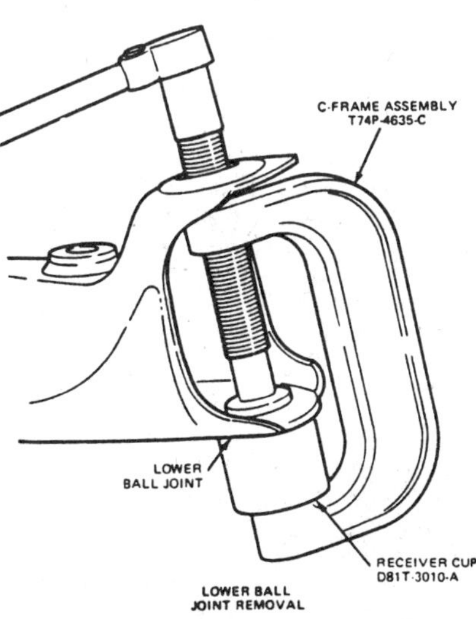

Ball joint removal—2WD models

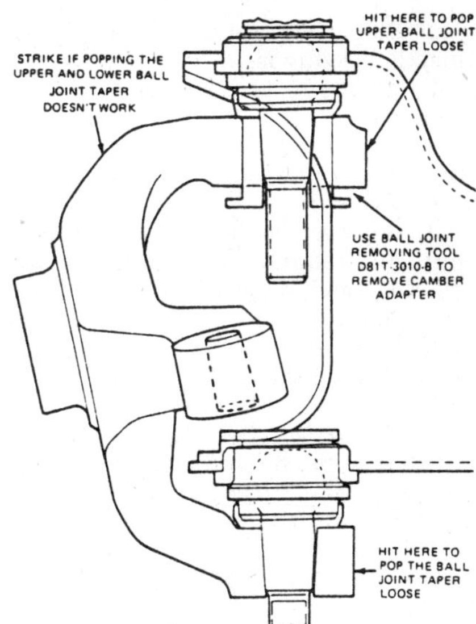

Spindle assembly—removal and installation—2WD models

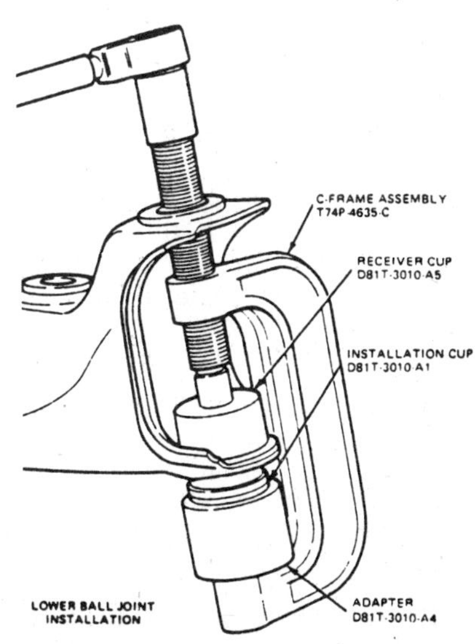

Ball joint installation—2WD models

10. Tighten the nut on the radius arm-to-axle bolt to 160-220 ft.lb.
11. Install the spring lower seat and spring insulator on the radius arm so that the hole in the seat goes on over the arm-to-axle bolt. Tighten the axle pivot bolt to 120-150 ft.lb.
12. Install the front spring as outlined in the foregoing procedures.
13. Connect the lower end of the shock absorber to the lower bracket on the radius arm with the attaching bolt and nut with the bolt head installed towards tire, tighten the nut to 48-68 ft.lb.

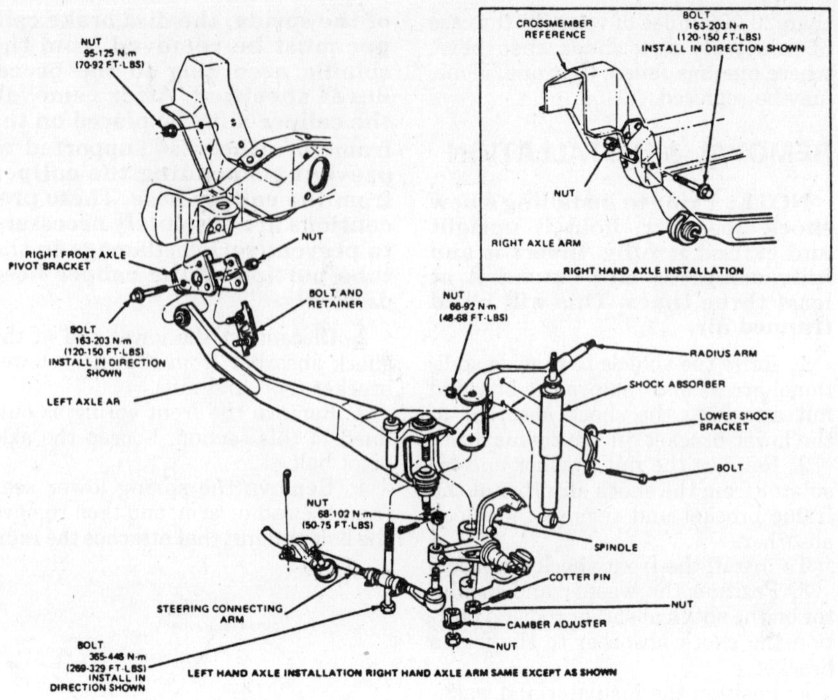

I-Beam axle assembly – removal and installation

Ball Joints and Spindle Assembly

REMOVAL & INSTALLATION

1. Raise the front of the vehicle and install jackstands.
2. Remove the wheel and tire assembly.
3. Remove the caliper assembly from the rotor and hold it out of the way with wire.
4. Remove the dust cap, cotter pin, nut, nut retainer, washer and outer bearing, and remove the rotor from the spindle.
5. Remove inner bearing cone and seal. Discard the seal.
6. Remove brake dust shield.
7. Disconnect the steering linkage from the spindle and spindle arm by removing the cotter pin and nut.
8. Remove the cotter pin from the lower ball joint stud. Remove the nut from the upper and lower ball joint stud.
9. Strike the lower side of the spindle to pop the ball joints loose from the spindle.

WARNING: Do not use a ball joint fork to separate the ball joint from the spindle, as this will damage the seal and the ball joint socket!

10. Remove the spindle.
11. Remove the snap ring from the ball joints. Assemble C-Frame assembly (T74P-4635-C) or equivalent and receiving cup (D81T-3010-A) or equivalent. Turn the forcing screw clockwise until the ball joint is removed from axle.
12. Assemble the C-Frame assembly and receiving cup on the lower ball joint and turn the forcing screw clockwise until the ball joint is removed.

WARNING: Always remove upper ball joint first. Do not heat the ball joint or the axle to aid in removal!

To install:

NOTE: Lower ball joint must be installed first.

13. To install the lower ball joint, assembly C-Frame assembly, ball joint receiver cup (D81T-3010-A5) or equivalent and installation cup (D81T-3010-A1) or equivalent inside cup (D81T-3010-A4) or equivalent. Turn the forcing screw clockwise until the ball joint is seated.

WARNING: Do not heat the ball joint or axle to aid in installation!

14. Install the snap ring onto the upper ball joint.
15. To install the upper ball joint, assembly the C-frame and repeat Steps 13 and 14.

NOTE: A three-step sequence for tightening ball stud nuts must be followed to avoid excessive turning effort of spindle about axle.

16. Prior to assembly of the spindle, make sure the upper and lower ball joints seals are in place.
17. Place the spindle over the ball joints. Apply Loctite® or equivalent to the lower ball stud and tighten to 30 ft.lb. If the lower ball stud turns while the nut is being tightened, push the spindle up against the ball stud.
18. Install the camber adjuster in the

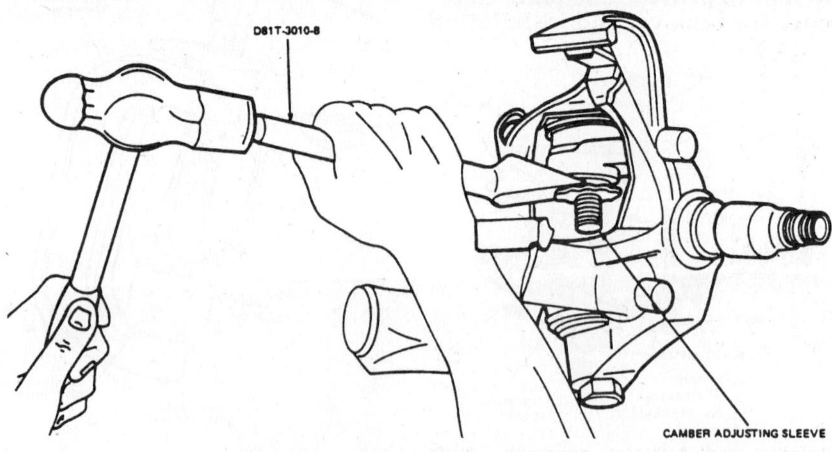

Camber adjustment sleeve – removal

upper spindle over the upper ball joint. If camber adjustment is necessary, special adapters must be installed. Refer to Front End Alignment in this section.

19. Apply Loctite® or equivalent to upper ball joint stud and install nut. Hold the camber adapter with a wrench to keep the ball stud from turning. If the ball stud turns, tap the adapter deeper into the spindle. Tighten the nut to 85-110 ft.lb.

20. Finish tightening the lower ball stud nut to 104-106 ft.lb. Advance nut to next castellation and install cotter pin.

21. Install the dust shield.

22. Pack the inner and outer bearing cones with high temperature wheel bearing grease. Use a bearing packer. If a bearing packer is unavailable, pack the bearing cone by hand working the grease through the cage behind the rollers.

23. Install the inner bearing cone and seal. Install the hub and rotor on the spindle.

24. Install the outer bearing cone, washer, and nut. Adjust bearing end play and install the cotter pin and dust cap.

25. Install the caliper.

26. Connect the steering linkage to the spindle. Tighten the nut to 51-75 ft.lb. and advance the nut as required for installation of the cotter pin.

27. Install the wheel and tire assembly. Lower the vehicle. Check, and if necessary, adjust the toe setting. Refer to Front end Alignment in this section.

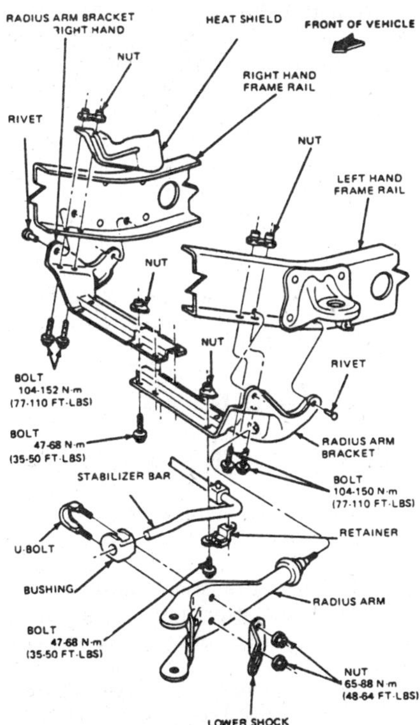

Front stabilizer bar removal and installation—2WD models

Stabilizer Bar

REMOVAL & INSTALLATION

1. Remove the nuts and U-bolts retaining the lower shock bracket/stabilizer bar bushing to radius arm.

2. Remove retainers and remove the stabilizer bar and bushing.

To install:

3. Place stabilizer bar in position on the radius arm and bracket.

4. Install retainers and U-bolts. Tighten retainer bolts to 35-50 ft.lb. Tighten U-bolt nuts to 48-64 ft.lb.

Front I-Beam Axle

REMOVAL & INSTALLATION

1. Remove the front wheel spindle and the front spring, as outlined in the foregoing procedures.

2. Remove the spring lower seat from t he radius arm, and then remove the bolt and nut that attaches the radius arm to the (I-Beam) front axle.

3. Remove the axle-to-frame pivot bracket bolt and nut.

4. To install, position the axle to the frame pivot bracket and install the bolt and nut finger tight.

5. Position the opposite end of the axle to the radius arm, install the attaching bolt form underneath through the bracket, the radius arm, and the axle. Install the nut and tighten to 120-150 ft.lb.

6. Position the axle up against the jounce bumper to place the pivot bushing in proper orientation. Tighten the axle-to-frame pivot bracket bolt to specifications.

7. Install the spring lower seat on the radius arm so that the hole in the seat indexes over the arm-to-axle bolt.

8. Install the front spring as outlined in this section.

9. Tighten the axle-to-frame pivot bracket bolt to specified torque.

10. Install the front wheel spindle as outlined in this section.

Camber Adapter

REMOVAL & INSTALLATION

NOTE: Use the Camber Adjuster Removal Tool, (D81T-3010-B) or equivalent only after the ball joint tapers have been popped loose.

1. Remove the nut from the upper ball joint stud.

2. Strike the inside of the spindle, to pop the upper ball joint taper loose from the spindle.

3. If the upper ball joint does not pop loose, back the lower ball joint nut about halfway down the lower ball joint stud, and strike the side of the lower spindle.

4. Remove the camber adjusting sleeve, using Camber Adjuster Removal Tool (D81T-3010-B) or equivalent.

To install:

NOTE: A three-step sequence for tightening ball stud nuts must be followed to avoid excessive turning effort of the spindle about axle.

5. Install the correct adapter in the spindle. On the right spindle the adapter slot must point forward in the vehicle to make a positive camber change or rearward for a negative camber change. On the left spindle, the adapter slot must point rearward for a positive camber change and forward for a negative change.

6. If both nuts were loosened, completely remove the spindle, and reinstall as described in this section. Be sure the sequence for tightening ball stud nuts is followed. Apply Loctite® or equivalent to stud threads before installing nut.

7. If only the upper ball joint stud nut was removed, install the nut and tighten to 85-110 ft.lb.

4-WEEL DRIVE FRONT SUSPENSION

The 4WD front suspension consists of a two-piece driving axle assembly, two coil spring and two radius arms. The front axle consists of two independent yoke and tube assemblies. One end of each assembly is anchored to the frame, the other end is supported by the spring and radius arm.

Springs

REMOVAL & INSTALLATION

1. Raise the vehicle and remove the shock absorber-to-lower bracket attaching bolt and nut.

2. Remove the spring lower retainer attaching nuts from the inside of the spring coil.

3. Remove spring upper retainer attaching screw and remove the upper retainer.

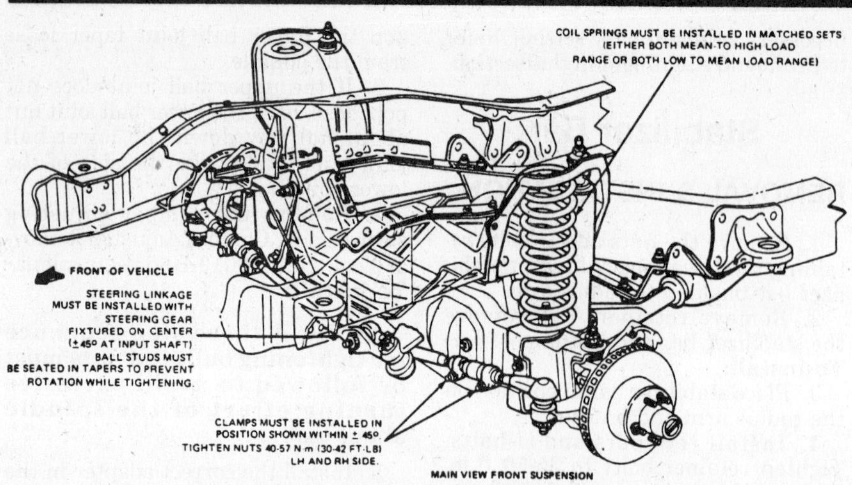

Front suspension assembly—4WD models

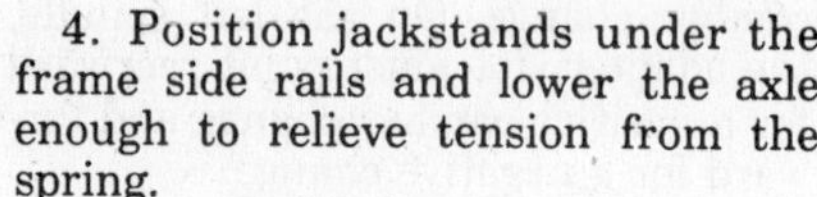

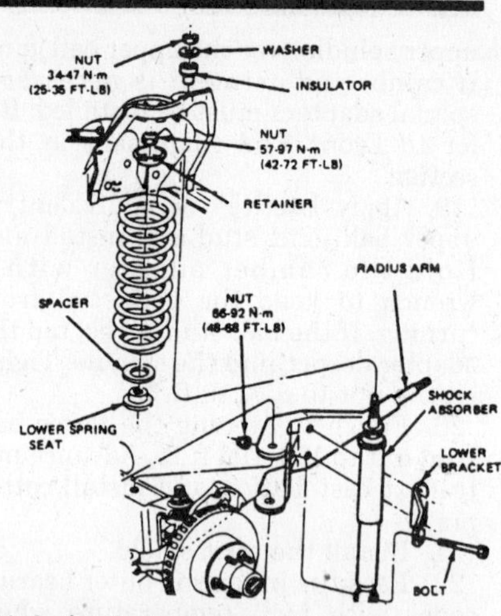

Front shock absorber installation—4WD models

4. Position jackstands under the frame side rails and lower the axle enough to relieve tension from the spring.

5. If required, remove the stud from the axle assembly.

NOTE: The axle must be supported on the jack through spring removal and installation, and must not be permitted to hang by the brake hose. If the length of the brake hose is not sufficient to provide adequate clearance for removal and installation of the spring, the disc brake caliper must be removed from the spindle. After removal, the caliper must be placed on the frame or otherwise supported to prevent suspending the caliper from the caliper hose. These precautions are absolutely necessary to prevent serious damage to the tube portion of the caliper hose assembly.

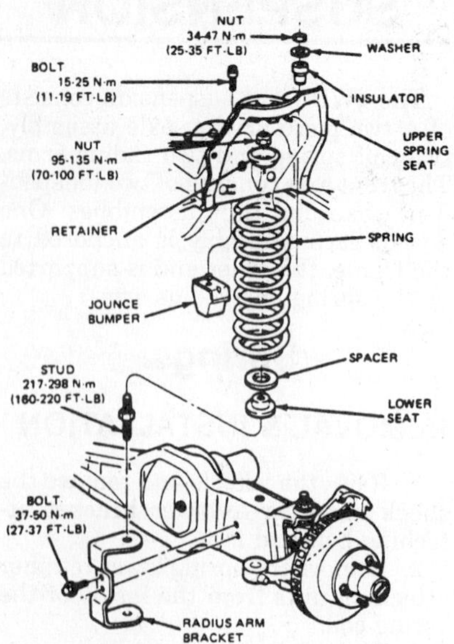

Coil spring removal and installation—4WD models

6. Remove the spring, lower retainer, and lower the spring from the vehicle.

7. If removed, install the stud on the axle and torque to 160-220 ft.lb.

8. Install the lower seat and spacer over the stud.

9. Place the spring in position and slowly raise the front axle. Ensure springs are positioned correctly in the upper spring seats.

10. Position the spring lower retainer over the stud and lower seat and torque the attaching nut to 70-100 ft.lb.

11. Position the shock absorber to the lower bracket and install the attaching bolt and nut.

12. Tighten the bolt and nut to 42-72 ft.lb. Remove safety stands and lower the vehicle.

Shock Absorbers

TESTING

1. Visually check the shock absorbers for the presence of fluid leakage. A thin film of fluid is acceptable. Anything more than that means that the shock absorber must be replaced.

2. Disconnect the lower end of the shock absorber. Compress and extend the shock fully as fast as possible. If the action is not smooth in both directions, or there is no pressure resistance, replace the shock absorber. Shock absorbers should be replace in pairs if they have accumulated more than 20,000 miles of wear. In the case of relatively new shock absorbers, were one has failed, that one, alone, may be replaced.

REMOVAL & INSTALLATION

NOTE: Prior to installing a new shock absorber, hold it upright and extend it fully. Invert it and fully compress and extend it at least three times. This will bleed trapped air.

1. Raise the vehicle to provide additional access and remove the bolt and nut attaching the shock absorber to the lower bracket on the radius arm.

2. Remove the nut, washer and insulator from the shock absorber at the frame bracket and remove the shock absorber.

To install the front shock absorber:

3. Position the washer and insulator on the shock absorber rod and position the shock absorber to the frame bracket.

4. Position the insulator and washer on the shock absorber rod and install the attaching nut loosely.

5. Position the shock absorber the lower bracket and install the attaching bolt and nut loosely.

6. Tighten the lower attaching bolts to 48-68 ft.lb., and the upper attaching bolts to 25-35 ft.lb.

Radius Arm

REMOVAL & INSTALLATION

1. Raise the vehicle and position safety stands under the frame side rails.

2. Remove the shock absorber-to-lower bracket attaching bolt and nut and pull the shock absorber free of the radius arm.

3. Remove the spring lower retainer attaching bolt from inside of the spring coil.

4. Remove the nut attaching the radius arm to the frame bracket and re-

move the radius arm rear insulator. Lower the axle and allow axle to move forward.

NOTE: The axle must be supported on the jack through out spring removal and installation, and must not be permitted to hang by the brake hose. If the length of the brake hose is not sufficient to provide adequate clearance for removal and installation of the spring, the disc brake caliper must be removed from the spindle according to the procedures specified. After removal, the caliper must be placed on the fame or otherwise supported to prevent suspending the caliper from the caliper hose. These precautions are absolutely necessary to prevent serious damage to the tube portion of the caliper hose assembly.

5. Remove the bolt and stud attaching radius arm to axle.
6. Move the axle forward and remove the radius arm from the axle. Then, pull the radius arm from the frame bracket.
7. Position the washer and insulator on the rear of the radius arm and insert the radius arm to the frame bracket.
8. Position the rear insulator and washer on the radius arm and loosely install the attaching nut.
9. Position the radius arm to the axle.
10. Install lower bolt and upper stud-type bolt attaching radius arm bracket to axle. Tighten to 160-220 ft.lb. Install and tighten front bracket bolts to 27-37 ft.lb.
11. Position the spring lower seat, spring insulator and retainer to the spring and axle. Install the two attaching bolts. Tighten the axle pivot bolt to 120-150 ft.lb.
12. Tighten the radius rod rear attaching nut to 80-120 ft.lb.
13. Position the shock absorber to the lower bracket and install the attaching bolt and nut. Tighten the nut to 40-60 ft.lb. Remove safety stands and lower the vehicle.

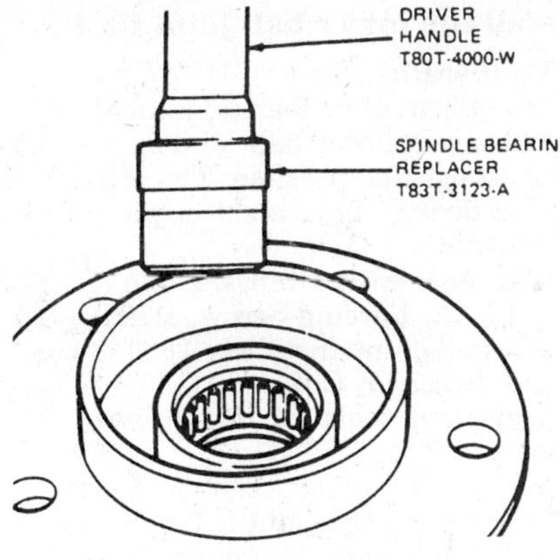

Spindle bearing installation

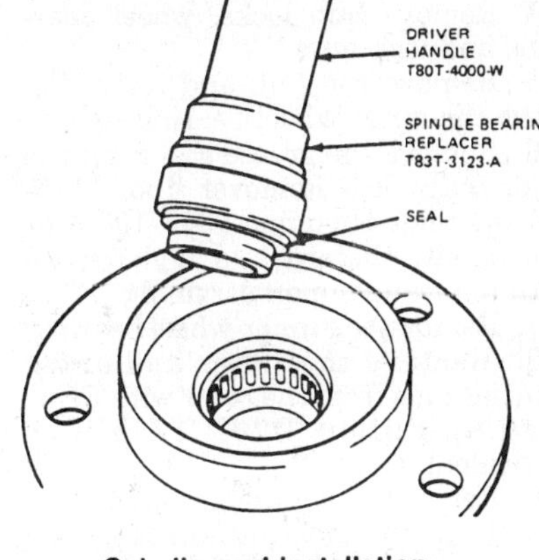

Spindle seal installation

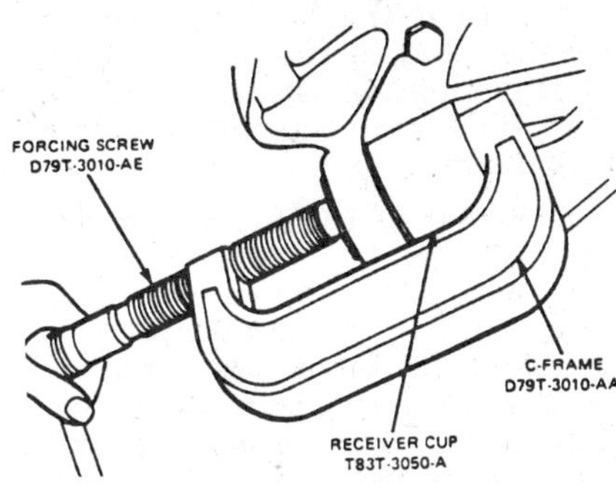

Ball joint removal—4WD models

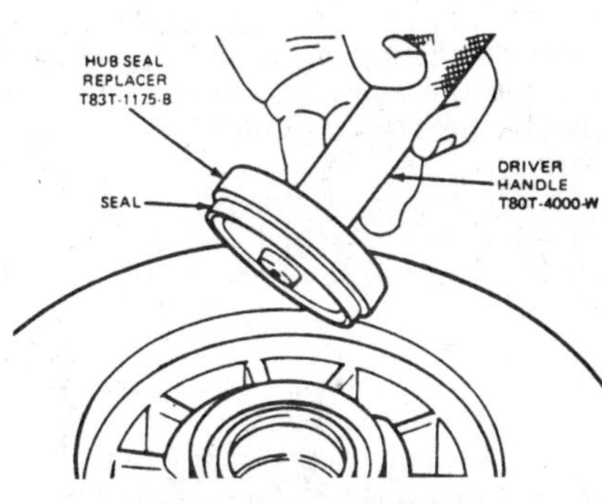

Shaft seal installation

Steering Knuckle and Ball Joints

REMOVAL & INSTALLATION

1. Raise the vehicle and support on jackstands.
2. Remove the wheel and tire assembly.
3. Remove the caliper.

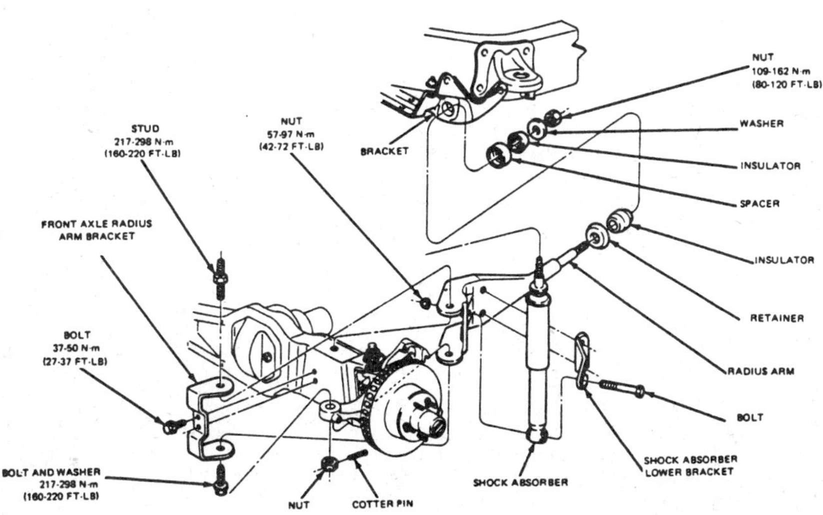

Radius arm removal and installation—4WD models

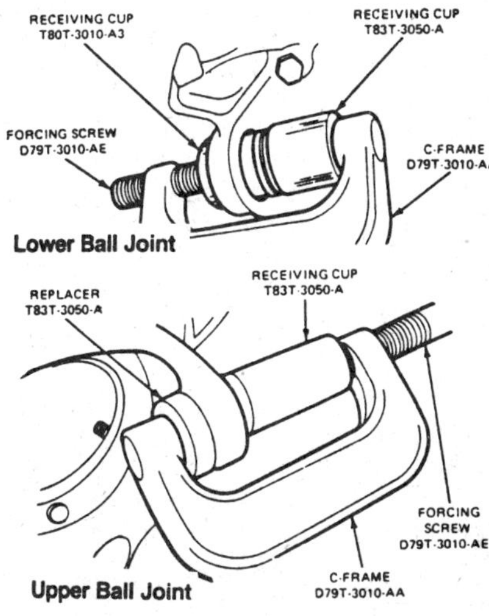

Ball joint installation—4WD models

4. Remove hub locks, wheel bearings, and lock nuts.
5. Remove the hub and rotor. Remove the outer wheel bearing cone.
6. Remove the grease seal from the rotor with Seal Remover Tool 1175-AC and Slide Hammer T50T-100-A or equivalent. Discard seal and replace with a new one upon assembly.
7. Remove the inner wheel bearing.
8. Remove the inner and outer bearing cups from the rotor with Bearing Cup Puller, D78P-1225-B or equivalent.
9. Remove the nuts retaining the spindle to the steering knuckle. Tap the spindle with a plastic or rawhide hammer to jar the spindle from the knuckle. Remove the splash shield.
10. On the right side of the vehicle remove the shaft and joint assembly by puling the assembly out of the carrier.
11. On the right side of the carrier, remove and discard the keystone clamp from the shaft and joint assembly and the stud shaft. Slide the rubber boot onto the stub shaft and pull the shaft and joint assembly from the splines of the stub shaft.
12. Place the spindle in a vise on the second step of the spindle. Wrap a shop towel around the spindle or use a brass-jawed vise to protect the spindle.
13. Remove the oil seal and needle bearing from the spindle with slide Hammer T50T-100-A and Seal Remover, Tool 1175-AC, or equivalent.
14. If required, remove the seal from the shaft, by driving off with a hammer.
15. If the tie rod has not been removed, then remove cotter pin from the tie rod nut and then remove nut. Tap on the tie rod stud to free it from the steering arm.
16. Remove the upper ball joint cotter pin and nut. Loosen the lower ball joint nut to the end of the stud.
17. Strike the inside of the spindle near the upper and lower ball joints to break the spindle loose from the ball joint studs.
18. Remove the camber adjuster sleeve. If required, use Pitman Arm Puller, T64P-3590-F or equivalent to remove the adjuster out of the spindle.
19. Place knuckle in vise and remove snap ring from bottom ball joint socket if so equipped.
20. Assemble the C-Frame, D79T-3010-AA, Forcing Screw, D79T-3010-AE and Ball Joint Remover T83T-3050-A or equivalent on the lower ball joint.
21. Turn forcing screw clockwise until the lower ball joint is removed from the steering knuckle.
22. Repeat Steps 20 and 21 for the upper ball joint.

NOTE: Always remove and install the lower ball joint first.

To install:

23. Clean the steering knuckle bore and insert lower ball joint in knuckle as straight as possible. The lower ball joint doesn't have a cotter pin hole in the stud.
24. Assemble the C-Frame, D79T-3010-AA, Forcing Screw, D79T-3010-AE, Ball Joint Installer, T83T-3050-A and Receiver Cup T80T-3010-A3 or equivalent tools, to install lower ball joint.
25. Turn forcing screw clockwise until the lower ball joint is firmly seated. Install the snap ring on the lower ball joint.

NOTE: If the ball joint cannot be installed to the proper depth, realignment of the receiver cup and ball joint installer will be necessary.

26. Repeat Steps 24 and 25 fort the upper ball joint.
27. Assemble the knuckle to the axle arm assembly. Install the camber adjuster on the top ball joint stud with the arrow pointing outboard for 'positive camber' and the arrow pointing inboard for 'negative camber'. 'Zero' camber bushings will not have an arrow and may be rotated in either direction as long as the lugs on the yoke engage the slots in the bushing.

CAUTION

The following torque sequence must be followed exactly when securing the spindle. Excessive spindle turning effort may result in reduced steering returnability if this procedure is not followed.

28. Install a new nut on the bottom ball joint stud and tighten to 40 ft.lb.
29. Install a new nut on the top ball stud and tighten to 85-100 ft.lb., then advance nut until castellation aligns with cotter pin hole and install cotter pin.
30. Finish tightening the lower nut to 95-110 ft.lb.

NOTE: The camber adjuster will seat itself into the spindle at a predetermined position during the tightening sequence. DO NOT attempt to adjust this position.

31. Clean all dirt and grease from the spindle bearing bore. Bearing bores must be free from nicks or burrs.
32. Place the bearing in the bore with the manufacturer's identification facing outward. Drive the bearing into the bore using Spindle Bearing Replacer, T83T-3123-A and Driver Handle T80T-4000-W or equivalent.
33. Install the grease seal in the bearing bore with the lip side of the seal facing towards the tool. Drive the seal in the bore with Spindle Bearing Replacer, T83T-3123-A and Driver Handle T80T-4000-W or equivalent. Coat the bearing seal lip with Lubriplate®.
34. If removed, install a new shaft seal. Place the shaft in a press, and install the seal with Spindle/Axle Seal Installer, T83T-3132-A, or equivalent.
35. On the right side of the carrier, install the rubber boot and new keystone clamps on the stub shaft slip yoke. Since the spines on the shaft are phased, there is only one way to assemble the right shaft and joint assembly into the yoke slip. Align the missing spline in the slip yoke barrel with the gapless male spline on the shaft and joint assembly. Slide the right shaft and joint assembly into the slip yoke making sure the splines are fully engaged. Slide the boot over the assembly and crimp the keystone clamp using Keystone Clamp Pliers, T63P-9171-A or equivalent.
36. On the left side of the carrier slide the shaft and joint assembly through the knuckle and engage the splines on the shaft in the carrier.
37. Install the splash shield and spindle onto the steering knuckle. Install and tighten the spindle nuts to 35-45 ft.lb.
38. Drive the bearing cups into the rotor using bearing cup replacer T73T-4222-B and Driver Handle, T80T-4000-W or equivalent.
39. Pack the inner and outer wheel

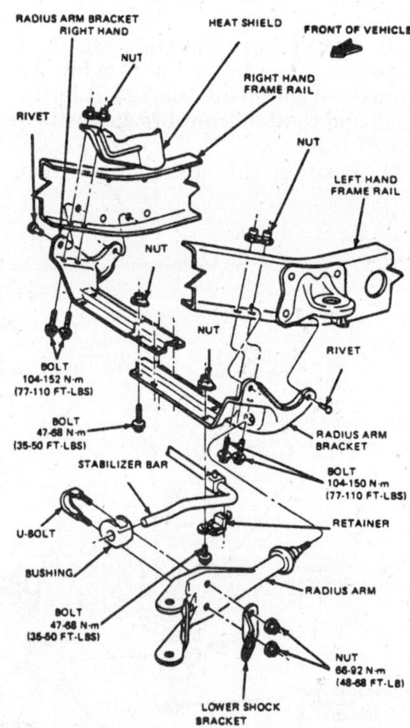

Front stabilizer bar removal and installation – 4WD models

bearings and the lip of the oil seal with Multi-Purpose Long-Life Lubricant, C1AZ-19590-B or equivalent.

40. Place the inner wheel bearing in the inner cup. Drive the grease seal into the bore with Hub Seal Replacer, T83T-1175-B and Driver Handle, T80T-4000-W or equivalent. Coat the bearing seal lip with multi-purpose long-life lubricant, C1AZ-19590-B or equivalent.

41. Install the rotor on the spindle. Install the outer wheel bearing into cup.

NOTE: Verify that the grease seal lip totally encircles the spindle.

42. Install the wheel bearing, locknut, thrust bearing, snap ring, and locking hubs.

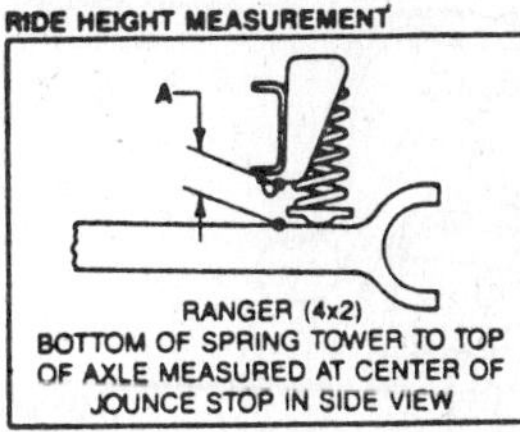

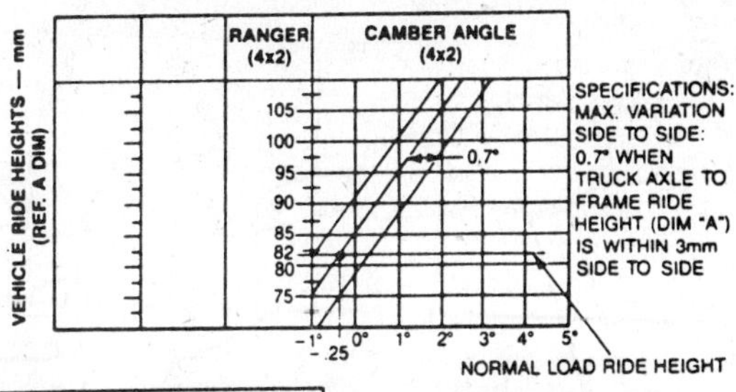

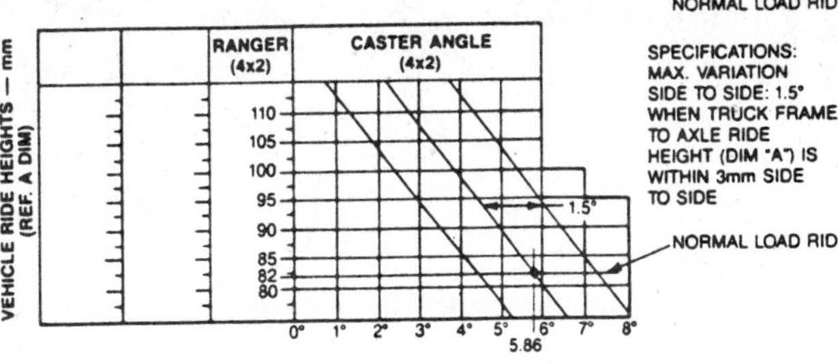

2WD Model—alignment specifications

Stabilizer Bar

REMOVAL & INSTALLATION

1. Remove the nuts and U-bolts retaining the lower shock bracket/stabilizer bar bushing to the radius arm.
2. Remove the retainers and remove the stabilizer bar and bushing.
3. Place the stabilizer bar in position on the radius arm and bracket.
4. Install the retainers and U-bolts. Tighten the retainer bolts to 35-50 ft.lb. Tighten the U-bolts to 48-68 ft.lb.

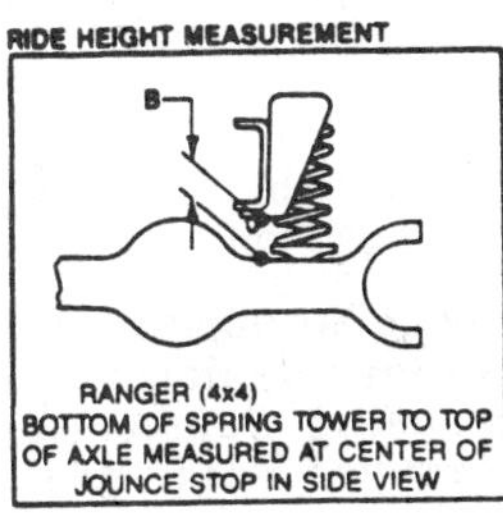

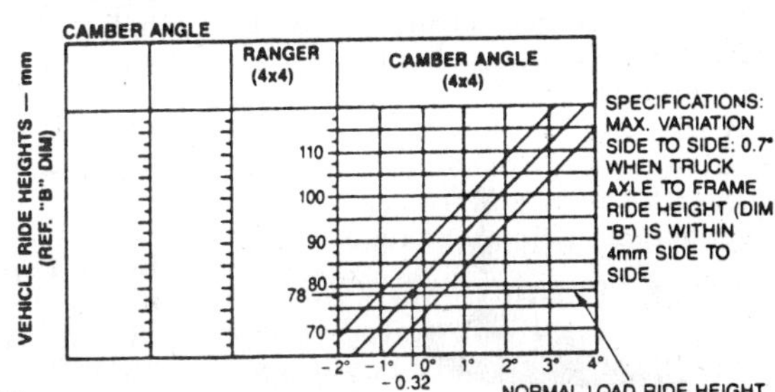

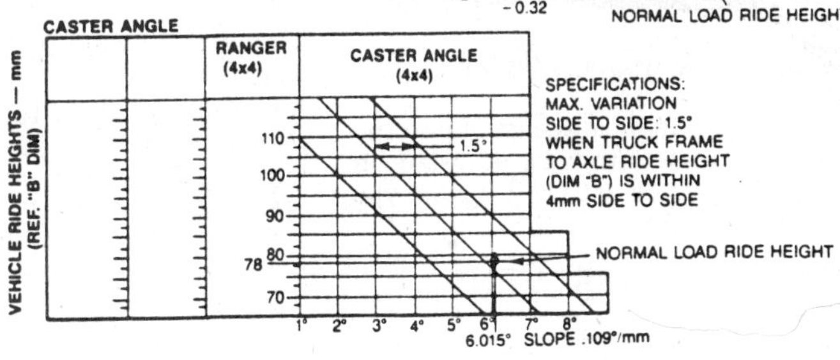

4WD Model—alignment specifications

FRONT END ALIGNMENT

If you should start to notice abnormal tire wear patterns and handling (steering wheel is hard to return to straight ahead position after negotiating a turn on pavement in 2WD), and misalignment of caster and camber are suspected, make the following checks:

1. Check the air pressure in all the tires. Make sure that the pressures agree with those specified for the tires and vehicle model being checked.
2. Raise the front of the vehicle off the ground. Grasp each front tire at the front and rear, and push the wheel inward and outward. If any free-play is noticed adjust the wheel bearings.

NOTE: There is supposed to be a very, very small amount of free-play present where the wheel bearings are concerned. Replace the bearings if they are worn or damaged.

3. Check all steering linkage for wear or maladjustment. Adjust and/or replace all worn parts.
4. Check the steering gear mounting bolts and tighten if necessary.
5. Rotate each front wheel slowly, and observe the amount of lateral or side runout. If the wheel runout exceeds ⅛″, replace the wheel or install the wheel on the rear.
6. Inspect the radius arms to be sure they are not bent or damaged. Inspect the bushings at the radius arm-to-axle attachment points for wear or looseness. Repair or replace parts as required.

Cater and Camber

Caster angles are built into the front axles and cannot be adjusted. On 4x2 models, camber is adjusted by replacing a camber adjuster in the upper ball joint socket. Camber adjusters are available in 0°, ½°, 1° and 1½° increments.

On 4x4 models, camber adjustment is provided by means of a series of interchangeable mounting sleeves (camber adjusters) for the upper ball joint stud. Four sleeves are available in ½° camber increments, providing a 3° range of adjustment (from 1½° negative to 1½° positive).

Caster if the number of degrees of backward (positive) or forward (negative) tilt of the spindle (king) pin or the line connecting the ball joint centers.

Camber is the number of degrees the top of the wheel tilts outward (positive) or inward (negative) from a vertical plane.

Before checking caster or camber, perform the toe alignment check. Using alignment equipment known to be

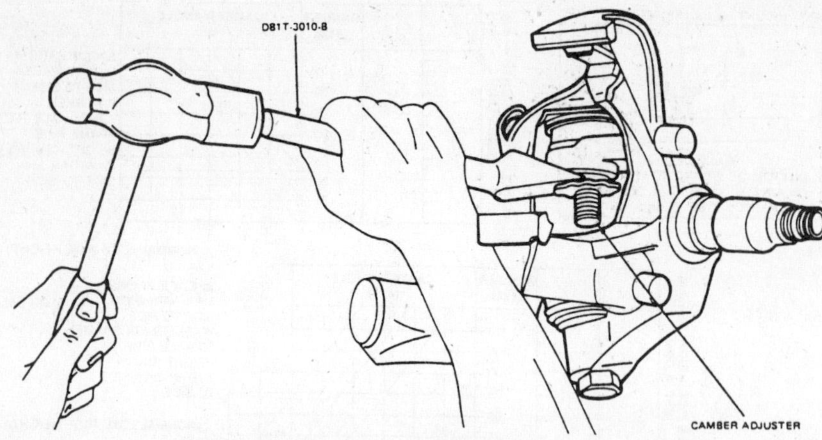

Removing the camber adjusting sleeve—2WD models

accurate and following the equipment manufacturer's instructions, measure and record the caster angle and the camber angle of both front wheels. Refer to the front wheel alignment charts for specifications.

If the caster and camber measurements exceed the maximum variances, inspect for damaged front suspension components. Replace as required.

NOTE: Twin-I-Beam axles are not to be bent or twisted to correct caster or camber readings.

CASTER ADJUSTMENT

The caster angle is designed into the front axle and cannot be adjusted on vehicles equipped with coil spring type front suspensions.

CAMBER ADJUSTMENT

2-Wheel Drive Models

1. Raise the vehicle on a hoist.
2. Remove the front wheels.
3. Remove the upper ball joint nut. Remove the cotter pin on the lower ball stud, and back the nut down to the end of the stud.
4. Strike the spindle near the upper and lower ball joints to break the spindle loose from the ball joint studs.

NOTE: Be sure to pop the ball joint tapers loose as described above before using Camber Adjustment Removal Tool, D81T-3010-B.

5. Use Camber Adjuster Removing Tool, D81T-3010-B to wedge the camber adjuster out of the spindle.
6. Replace the adjuster with the desired camber adjuster. Camber adjusters are available in 0°, ½°, 1° and 1½°.
   - To increase camber (more positive), align the slot as follows: on the driver side, point the slot to the rear of the vehicle. On the passenger side, point the slot rearward to the front of the vehicle.
   - To decrease camber (more negative), align the slot as follows: on the driver side, point the slot forward. On the passenger side, point the slot rearward.
7. Apply Loctite® or equivalent to the upper ball stud and hand start the upper ball stud nut.
8. Remove the lower ball stud nut and apply Loctite® or equivalent to the lower ball stud.
9. Hand start the lower ball stud nut.

WARNING: The following torque sequence must be followed exactly when securing the spindle. Improper tightening may result in excessive spindle turning effort!

10. Partially tighten the lower ball stud nut to 35 ft.lb.
11. Tighten the upper ball stud nut to 85-110 ft.lb.
12. Finish tightening the lower ball stud nut to 104-146 ft.lb. Advance the nut to the next castellation and install cotter pin.
13. Install the front wheels and lower the vehicle.

4-Wheel Drive Models

1. Raise the vehicle on a hoist and remove the front wheels.
2. Remove the upper ball joint cotter pin and nut.
3. Loosen the lower ball joint nut and back off nut to the end of the stud.
4. Strike the inside of the spindle near the upper and lower ball joints to break the spindle loose from the ball joint studs.
5. Remove the camber adjuster sleeve. If required, use Pitman Arm Puller, T64P-3590-F, to remove the adjuster from the spindle.
6. Install the camber adjuster on the top ball joint stud with the arrow pointing outboard for positive camber and the arrow pointing inboard for negative camber. Zero camber bushings will not have an arrow and may be rotated in either direction as long as the lugs on the yoke engage the slots in the bushing.

WARNING: Excessive spindle turning effort, causing poor steering returnability may result if the fastener tightening sequence described in steps are not followed!

7. Remove the lower ball joint stud nut and discard.
8. Install a newer ball joint stud nut and tighten to 40 ft.lb.
9. Install a new nut on the top ball joint stud and tighten to 85-100 ft.lb., then advance nut until castellation aligns with cotter pin hole and install cotter pin.

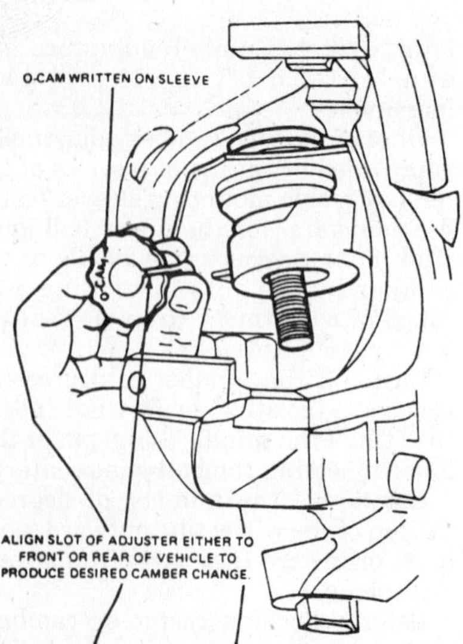

Installing the camber adjusting sleeve

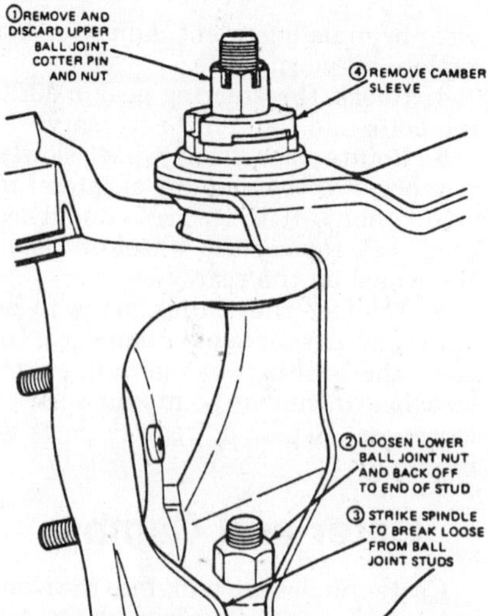

Camber adjusting sleeve removal—4WD models

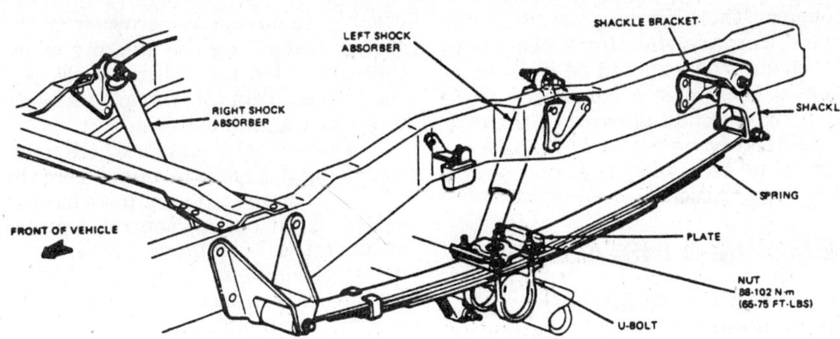

Rear suspension asembly

10. Finish tightening the lower nut to 95-110 ft.lb.

NOTE: The camber adjuster will seat itself in the spindle at a pre-determined position during the tightening sequence. Do not attempt to adjust this position.

11. Reinstall the wheels and lower the vehicle.
12. Re-check the camber and adjust toe-in as described in this section.

TOE-IN ADJUSTMENT

Toe-in can be measured by either a front end alignment machine or by the following method:

With the front wheels in the straight ahead position, measure the distance between the extreme front and the extreme rear of the front wheels. In other words, measure the distance across the undercarriage of the vehicle between the two front edges and the two rear edges of the two front wheels. Both of these measurements (front and rear of the two wheels) must be taken at an equal distance from the floor and at the approximate centerline of the spindle. The difference between these two distances is the amount that the wheels toe-in or toe-out. The wheels should always be adjusted to toe-in according to specifications.

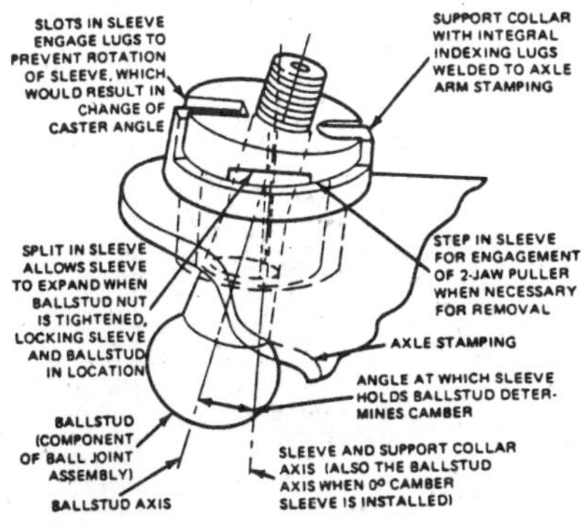

Camber adjustment—4WD models

1. Loosen the clamp bolts at each end of the left tie-rod, seen from the front of the vehicle. Rotate the connecting rod tube until the correct toe-in is obtained, then tighten the clamp bolts.
2. Re-check the toe-in to make sure that no changes occurred when the bolts were tightened.
3. Normal toe setting is $\frac{1}{32}$". Range is $\frac{3}{32}$"out to $\frac{5}{32}$" in.

REAR SUSPENSION

Semi-elliptic leaf springs are used on the rear axle suspension. The springs are mounted outside the frame members, and are attached to the axle with two U-bolts. The front end of each spring is attached to a hanger, which is part of the frame side member, with a bolt and nut. The rear end of the spring is attached to a shackle assembly with a bolt and nut and the shackle assembly is attached to a hanger.

The shock absorbers are attached to a bracket which is part of the axle tube and extend up to an upper bracket at a slight rearward angle.

Springs

REMOVAL & INSTALLATION

1. Raise the vehicle and install jackstands under the frame. The vehicle must be supported in such a way that the rear axle hangs free with the tire a few inches off the ground. Place a hydraulic floor jack under the center of the axle housing.
2. Disconnect the shock absorber from the axle.
3. Remove the U-bolt attaching nuts and remove the two U-bolts and the spring clip plate.
4. Lower the axle to relieve the spring tension and remove the nut from the spring front attaching bolt.
5. Remove the spring front attaching bolt from the spring and hanger with a drift.
6. Remove the nut from the shackle-to-hanger attaching bolt and drive the bolt from the shackle and hanger with a drift and remove the spring from the vehicle.
7. Remove the nut from the spring rear attaching bolt. Drive the bolt out of the spring and shackle with a drift.

To install the rear spring:

8. Position the shackle to the spring rear eye and install the bolt and nut.
9. Position the spring front eye and bushing to the spring front hanger, and install the attaching bolt and nut.
10. Position the spring rear eye and bushing to the shackle, and install the attaching bolt and nut.
11. Raise the axle to the spring and install U-bolts and spring clip plate.
12. Remove the jackstands and lower the vehicle.
13. Torque the spring U-bolt nuts to 65-75 ft.lb. Torque the front spring bolt and nut to 75-115 ft.lb. and the rear shackle bolts and nuts to 75-115 ft.lb.

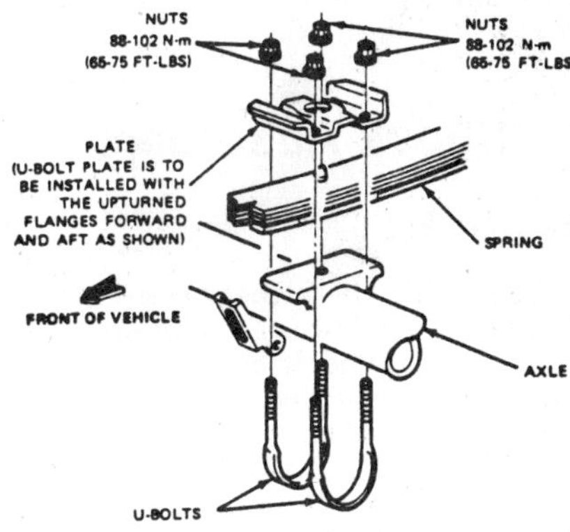

U-bolt and spring plate assembly

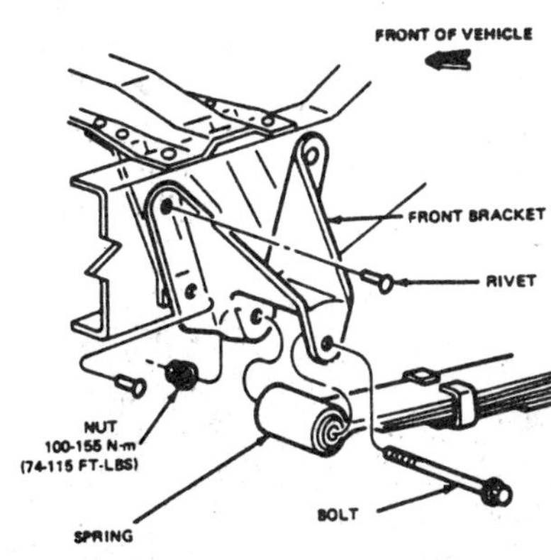

Spring to front bracket assembly

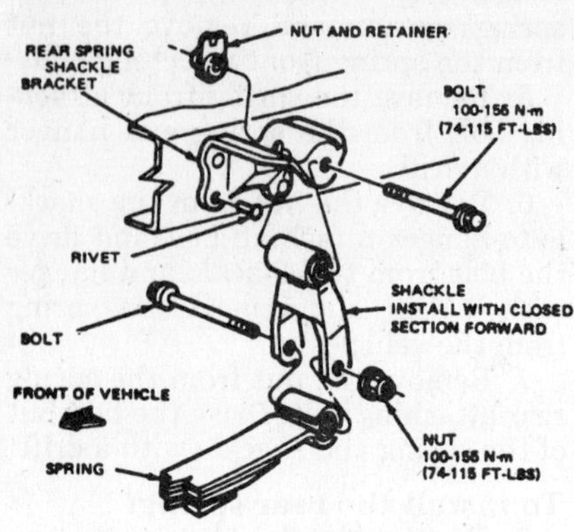

Spring to rear shackle assembly

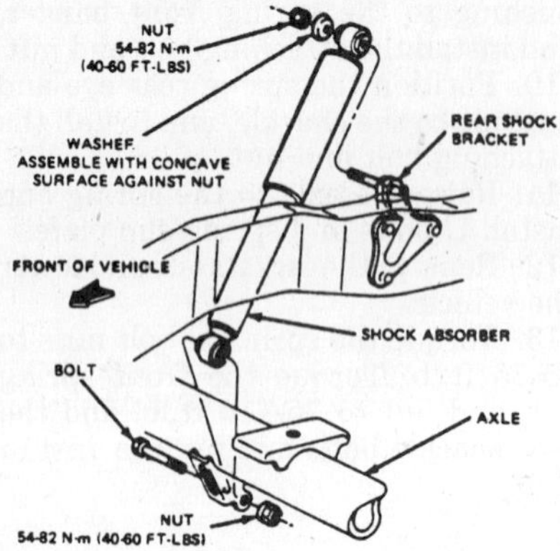

Rear shock absorber removal and installation

Shock Absorbers

TESTING

1. Visually check the shock absorbers for the presence of fluid leakage. A thin film of fluid is acceptable. Anything more than that means that the shock absorber must be replaced.

2. Disconnect the lower end of the shock absorber. Compress and extend the shock fully, as fast as possible. If the action is not smooth in both directions, or there is no pressure resistance, replace the shock absorber. Shock absorbers should be replaced in pairs if they have accumulated more than 20,000 miles of wear. In the case of relatively new shock absorbers, where one has failed, that one, alone, may be replaced.

REMOVAL & INSTALLATION

NOTE: Prior to installing a new shock absorber, hold it right side up and extend it fully. Turn it upside down and fully compress and extend it at least three times. This will bleed any trapped air.

1. Raise the vehicle and place jackstands under the axle.

2. Remove the shock absorber-to-upper bracket attaching nut and washers, and bushing from the shock absorber rod.

3. Remove the shock absorber-to-axle attaching bolt. Drive the bolts from the axle bracket and shock absorber with a brass drift and remove the shock absorber.

4. Position the washers and bushing on the shock absorber rod and position the shock absorber at the upper bracket.

5. Position the bushing and washers on the shock absorber rod and install the attaching nut loosely.

6. Position the shock absorber at the axle housing bracket and install the attaching bolt and nut. Tighten the upper and lower buts to 40-60 ft.lb.

STEERING

Steering Wheel

REMOVAL & INSTALLATION

1. Remove the steering wheel hub cover by removing the screws from the spokes and lifting the steering wheel hub cover. On the deluxe wheel, pop the hub emblem off. On sport wheels, unscrew the hub emblem.

2. Disconnect the horn switch wires by pulling the spoke terminal from the blade connectors. On vehicles equipped with speed control, squeeze or pinch the J-clip ground wire terminal firmly and pull it out of the hole in the steering wheel. Do not pull the ground terminal out of the threaded hole without squeezing the terminal clip to relieve the spring retention of the terminal in the threaded hole.

3. Remove the horn switch assembly and disconnect the horn and speed control wire (if so equipped).

4. Remove the steering wheel attaching nut.

5. Using a steering wheel puller, remove the steering wheel from the upper steering shaft. Do not use a knock-off type steering wheel puller or strike the end of the steering column upper shaft with a hammer. This could cause damage to the steering shaft bearing.

To install:

6. Position the steering wheel on the end of the steering wheel shaft. Align the mark and the flats on the steering wheel with the mark and the flats on the shaft, assuring that the straight ahead steering wheel position corresponds to the straight ahead position of the front wheels.

7. Install the wheel nut. Tighten the nut to 30-40 ft.lb.

8. Install the horn switch assembly and connect the horn and speed control wire (if so equipped).

9. Install the cover or trim emblem.

10. Check the steering column for proper operation.

Turn Signal/Hazard Flasher Switch

CAUTION

The corrugated outer tube steering shaft

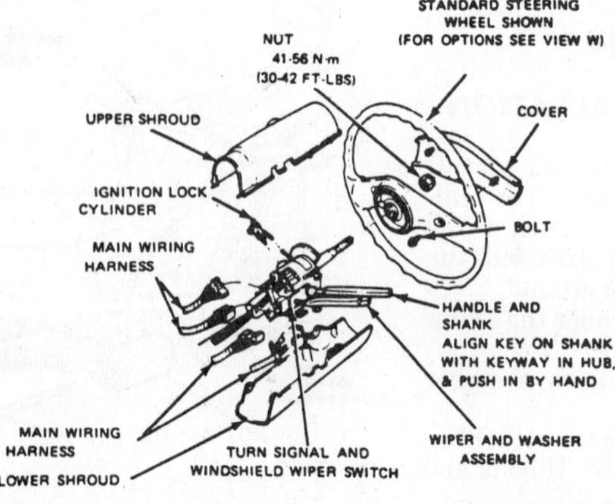

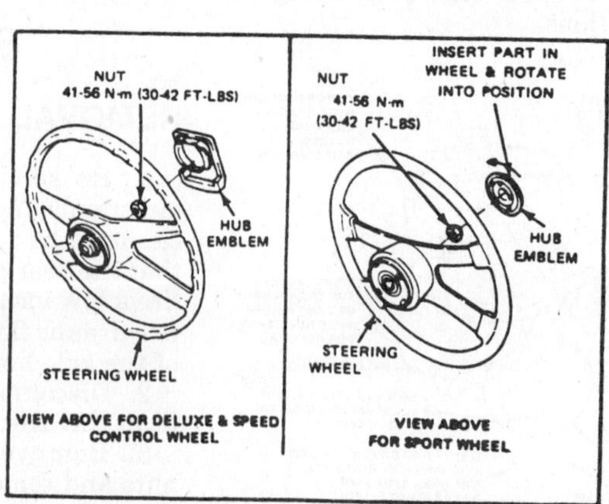

Steering wheel removal and installation

column upper support bracket assembly and shrouds affect energy absorption on impact. It is absolutely necessary to handle these components with care when performing any service operation!

REMOVAL & INSTALLATION

1. For tilt column only, remove the upper extension shroud by squeezing it at the six and twelve o'clock positions and popping it free of the retaining plate at the three o'clock position.
2. Remove the two trim shroud havles by removing the two attaching screws.
3. Remove the turn signal switch lever by grasping the lever and by using a pulling and twisting motion of the hand while pulling the lever straight out from the switch.
4. Peel back the foam sight shield from the turn signal switch.
5. Disconnect the two turn signal switch electrical connectors.
6. Remove the two self-tapping screws attaching the turn signal switch to the lock cylinder housing. Disengage the switch from the housing.

To install:

7. Align the turn signal switch mounting holes with the corresponding holes in the lock cylinder housing, and install two self-tapping screws.
8. Stick the foam sight shield to the turn signal switch.
9. Install the turn signal switch lever into the switch manually, by aligning the key on the lever with the keyway in the switch and by pushing the lever toward the switch to full engagement.
10. Install the two turn signal switch electrical connectors to full engagement.
11. Install the steering column trim shrouds.

Ignition Switch

REMOVAL & INSTALLATION

1. Rotate the lock cylinder key to the Lock position. Disconnect the negative battery cable from the battery.
2. For tilt column only, remove the upper extension shroud by squeezing it at the six and twelve o'clock positions and popping it free of the retaining plate at the three o'clock position.
3. Remove the two trim shroud havles by removing the two attaching screws.
4. Disconnect the ignition switch electrical connector.
5. Drill out the break-off head bolts connecting the switch to the lock cylinder housing by using a 1/8" drill.

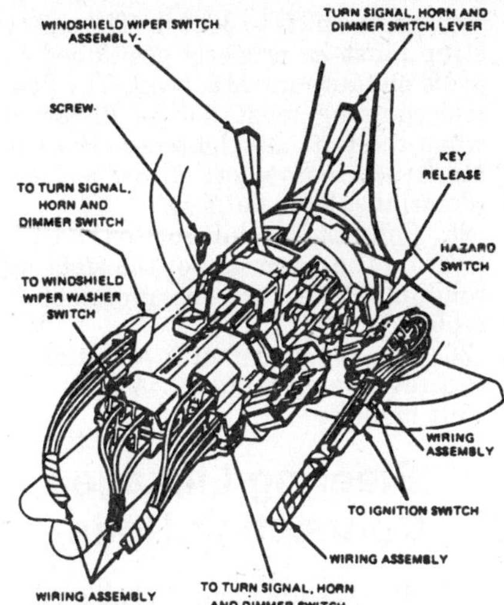

Column mounted switch wiring connections

6. Remove the two bolts, using an Ex-3 screw extractor, or equivalent.
7. Disengage the ignition switch from the actuator pin.

To install:

8. Rotate the ignition key to the RUN position (approximately 90 degrees clockwise from Lock).
9. Install the replacement switch by aligning the holes on the switch casting base with the holes in the cylinder block housing. Note that the replacement switch is provided in the RUN position. Minor movement of the lock cylinder to align the actuator pin with the "U" shaped slot in the switch carrier may be required.
10. Install the new break-off head bolts and tighten until heads shear off (approximately 35-50 in.lb.).
11. Connect the electrical connector to the ignition switch.
12. Connect the negative battery cable to the battery terminal. Check the ignition switch for proper operation in all modes.
13. Install the steering column trim shrouds.

Ignition Lock Cylinder Assembly

REMOVAL & INSTALLATION

Functional Lock Cylinders

1. Disconnect the battery ground cable.
2. Remove the trim shroud. Remove the electrical connector from the key warning switch.
3. Turn the lock cylinder to the RUN position.
4. Place a 1/8" diameter pin or small drift punch in the hole located at 4 o'clock and 1¼" from the outer edge of the lock cylinder housing. Depress the retaining pin, and pull out the lock cylinder.

To install:

5. Prior to installation of the lock cylinder, lubricate the cylinder cavity, including the drive gear, with Lubriplate® or equivalent.
6. To install the lock cylinder, turn the lock cylinder to the RUN position, depress the retaining pin, and insert it into the lock cylinder housing. Assure that the cylinder is fully seated and aligned into the the inter-locking washer before turning the key to the OFF position. This action will permit the cylinder retaining pin to extend into the hole in the lock cylinder housing.
7. Using the ignition key, rotate the lock cylinder to ensure correct mechanical operation in all positions. Install the electrical connector onto the key warning switch.
8. Connect the battery ground cable.
9. Check for proper ignition functions and verify that the column is locked in the LOCK position.
10. Install the trim shrouds.

Non-Functioning Lock Cylinder

1. Disconnect the battery ground.
2. Remove the steering wheel.
3. On tilt columns, remove the upper extension shroud by unsnapping the shroud from the retaining clip at the 9 o'clock position.
4. Remove the steering column trim shrouds.
5. Disconnect the wiring at the key warning switch.
6. Using a 1/8" drill bit, mounted in a right angle drive drill adapter, drill out the retaining pin, going no deeper than 1/2" (12.7mm).
7. Tilt the column to the full down position. Place a chisel at the base of the ignition lock cylinder cap and using a hammer break away the cap from the lock cylinder.
8. Using a 3/8" drill bit, drill down the center of the ignition lock cylinder key slot about 1¾" (44mm), until the lock cylinder breaks loose from the steering column cover casting.
9. Remove the lock cylinder and the drill shavings from the housing.
10. Remove the upper bearing snapring washer and steering column lock gear.
11. Carefully inspect the steering column housing for signs of damage from the previous operation. If any damage is apparent, the components should be replaced.
12. Installation is the reverse of removal.

Steering Column

REMOVAL & INSTALLATION

1. Disconnect the battery ground.
2. Unbolt the flexible coupling from the steering input shaft.
3. Disengage the safety strap and bolt from the flexible coupling.
4. Disconnect the transmission shift rod from the control selector lever.

NOTE: Column-type automatic transmission linkage use oil impregnated plastic grommets to connect the rods and levers. Whenever a grommet-type connection is changed, the grommets should be replaced.

5. Remove the steering wheel.
6. Remove the steering column trim shrouds.
7. Remove the steering column cover.
8. Remove the hood release lever.
9. Disconnect all electrical and vacuum connections at the column.
10. Loosen the 4 nuts securing the column to the brake pedal support bracket, allowing the column to be lowered enough to access the selector lever cable and cable. Don't lower the column too far or damage to the lever and/or cable will occur!
11. Reach between the column and instrument panel and gently lift off the selector cable from the pin on the lever.
12. Remove the cable clamp from the steering column tube.
13. Remove the 4 dust boot-to-dash panel screws.
14. Remove the 4 nuts attaching the column to the brake pedal support.
15. Lower the column to clear the 4 mounting bolts and pull the column out.

To install:

16. Position the column in the car.
17. Install the column collar-to-brake pedal support nuts loosely.
18. Install the selector cable clamp loosely.
19. Attach the cable to the lever pin.
20. Tighten the 4 column-to-brake pedal support nuts to 35 ft.lb.
21. Move the shift selector to the DRIVE position, against the drive stop. Rotate the selector bracket clockwise or counterclockwise until the selector pointer in the cluster centers on the letter **D**. Tighten the bracket nut.
22. Connect the electrical and vacuum connectors.
23. Install the safety strap and bolt on the flange on the steering input flange.
24. Install the 2 nuts connecting the steering shaft to the flexible coupling. Tighten the nuts to 35 ft.lb. The safety strap must be properly positioned to avoid metal-to-metal contact. The flexible coupling must not be distorted when the nuts are tightened. Pry the shaft up or down to allow a ± ⅛" (3mm) insulator flatness.
25. Connect the shift rod to the shift lever on the lower end of the steering column. Make sure the grommet is replaced.
26. The remainder of installation is the reverse of removal. Adjust the shift linkage.

Steering Linkage Connecting Rods

Replace the drag link if a ball stud is excessively loose or if the drag link is bent. Do not attempt to straighten a drag link.

Replace the connecting rod if the ball stud is excessively loose, if the connecting rod is bent or if the threads are stripped. Do not attempt to straighten connecting rod. Always check to insure that the adjustment sleeve and clamp stops are correctly installed on the truck.

REMOVAL & INSTALLATION

1. Remove the cotter pins and nuts from the drag link, ball studs and from the right connecting rod ball studs.
2. Remove the right connecting rod ball stud from the right spindle assembly and Pitman arm.
3. Remove the drag link ball studs from the spindle and the connecting rod assembly.
4. Loosen the clamp bolt and turn the rod out of the adjustment sleeve.
5. Lubricate the threads of the new connecting rod, and turn it into the adjustment sleeve at about the same distance the old rods were installed. This will provide an approximate toe-in setting. Position the connecting rod ball studs in the spindle arms.
6. Position the new drag link, ball studs in the spindle, and connecting rod assembly and install nuts.
7. Position the right connecting rod ball stud in the drag link and install nut.
8. Tighten all the nuts to 50-75 ft.lb. and install the cotter pins.
9. Remove the cotter pin and nut from the left connecting rod.
10. Install the nuts on the connecting rod ball studs, tighten the nut to 50-75 ft.lb. and install the cotter pin.
11. Check the toe-in and adjust, if necessary. After checking or adjusting toe-in, center the adjustment sleeve clamps between the locating nibbs, position the clamps and tighten the nuts to 29-41 ft.lb.

Power Steering Pump

REMOVAL & INSTALLATION

1. Position a drain pan under the power steering pump.
2. Disconnect the pressure and return lines at the pump.

NOTE: If the power steering pump is being removed from the engine in order to facilitate the removal of some other component, and it is not necessary for the pump to be completely removed from the vehicle, it is not necessary and is not recommended that the pressure and return hoses be disconnected from the pump.

3a. On the 4-122, and 4-140 gasoline engines, loosen the alternator pivot bolt and the adjusting bolt to slacken belt tension.

3b. On the 6-173 gasoline engine, loosen the adjustment nut and the slider bolts on the pump support to slacken belt tension.

3c. On the 4-134 diesel engine, loosen the adjustment bolt and the pivot bolt on the idler pulley to slacken belt tension.

4. Remove the drive belt from the pulley.
5. Remove the bolts attaching the pump to the bracket and remove the pump.

To install:

5. Install the pump on the bracket. Install and tighten attaching bolts.
6. Install the belt on the pulley.

7a. On the 4-122 and 4-140 gasoline engines, move the alternator to tighten the belt to specifications. Tighten the adjuster bolt to 22-40 ft.lb. and the alternator pivot bolt to 40-50 ft.lb.

7b. On the 6-173 gasoline engine, tighten the adjustment nut to tighten the belt to specifications. Tighten the slider bolts to 35-47 ft.lb.

7c. On the 4-134 diesel engine, insert a ½" drive breaker bar or ratchet into the slot in the idler pulley. Slide the pulley over to obtain the correct belt tension. Tighten the pivot bolt and the adjustment bolt to 30-45 ft.lb.

8. Install the pressure hose to the pump fitting.
9. Connect the return hose to the pump, and tighten the clamp.
10. Fill the reservoir with the proper type of power steering fluid. Perform the system bleeding operation as shown below.

SYSTEM BLEEDING

1. Disconnect the coil wire.

2. Crank the engine and continue adding fluid until the level stabilizes.
3. Continue to crank the engine and rotate the steering wheel about 30° to either side of center.
4. Check the fluid level and add as required.
5. Connect the coil wire and start the engine. Allow it to run for several minutes.
6. Rotate the steering wheel from stop to stop.
7. Shut off the engine and check the fluid level. Add fluid as necessary.

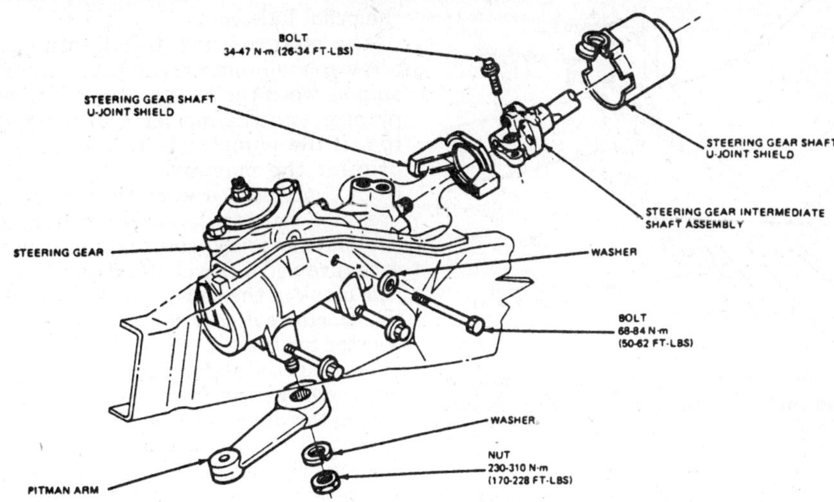

Power steering gear removal and installation

Manual Steering Gear

REMOVAL & INSTALLATION

1. Disengage the flex coupling shield from the steering gear input shaft shield and slide it up the intermediate shaft.
2. Remove the bolt that retains the flex coupling to the steering gear.
3. Remove the steering gear input shaft shield.
4. Remove the nut and washer that secures the Pitman arm to the sector shaft. Remove the Pitman arm using Pitman Arm Puller, T64P-3590-F or equivalent. Do not hammer on the end of the puller as this can damage the steering gear.
5. Remove the bolts and washers that attach the steering gear to the side rail. Remove the gear.

To install:

6. Rotate the gear input shaft (wormshaft) from stop to stop, counting the total number of turns. Then, turn back exactly half-way, placing the gear on center.
7. Slide the steering gear input shaft shield on the steering gear input shaft.
8. Position the flex coupling on the steering gear input shaft. Ensure that the flat on the gear input shaft is facing straight up and aligns with the flat on the flex coupling. Install the steering gear to side rail with bolts and washers. Torque bolts to 66 ft.lb.
9. Place the Pitman arm on the sector shaft and install the attaching washer and nut. Align the two blocked teeth on the Pitman arm with four missing teeth on the steering gear sector shaft. Tighten the nut to 230 ft.lb.
10. Install the flex coupling to steering gear input shaft attaching bolt and tighten to 35 ft.lb.
11. Snap the flex coupling shield to the steering gear input shield.
12. Check the system to ensure equal turns from center to each lock position.

Power Steering Gear

REMOVAL & INSTALLATION

1. Disconnect the pressure and return lines from the steering gear. Plug the lines and ports in the gear to prevent entry of dirt.
2. Remove the upper and lower steering shaft u-joint shield from the flex coupling. Remove the bolts that secure the flex coupling to the steering gear and to the column steering shaft assembly.
3. Raise the vehicle and remove the Pitman arm attaching nut, and washer.
4. Remove the Pitman arm from the shaft using Tool T64P-3590-F. Remove the tool from the Pitman arm. Do not damage the seals.
5. Support the steering gear, and remove the steering gear attaching bolts.
6. Work the steering gear free of the flex coupling. Remove the steering gear from the vehicle.

To install:

7. Install the lower u-joint shield onto the steering gear lugs. Slide the upper U-joint shield into place on the steering shaft assembly.
8. Slide the flex coupling into place on the steering shaft assembly. Turn the steering wheel so that the spokes are in the horizontal position. Center the steering gear input shaft.
9. Slide the steering gear input shaft into the flex coupling and into place on the frame side rail. Install the attaching bolts and tighten to 50-62 ft.lb.
10. Be sure the wheels are in the straight ahead position, then install the Pitman arm on the sector shaft. Install the Pitman attaching washer and nut. Tighten nut to 170-230 ft.lb.
11. Connect and tighten the pressure and the return lines to the steering gear.
12. Disconnect the coil wire. Fill the reservoir. Turn on the ignition and turn the steering wheel from left to right to distribute the fluid.
13. Re-check fluid level and add fluid, if necessary. Connect the coil wire, start the engine and turn the steering wheel from side to side. Inspect for fluid leaks.

BRAKE SYSTEM

ADJUSTMENT

DRUM BRAKES

The drum brakes are self-adjusting and require a manual adjustment only after the brake shoes have been replaced, or when the length of the adjusting screw has been changed.

1. Raise the vehicle and support it with safety stands.
2. Remove the rubber plug from the adjusting slot on the backing plate.
3. Insert a small screwdriver or piece of firm wire (coat hanger wire) into the adjusting slot and push the automatic adjusting lever out and free of the starwheel on the adjusting screw and hold it there.
4. Engage the topmost tooth possible on the starwheel with a brake adjusting spoon. Move the end of the adjusting spoon upward to move the adjusting screw starwheel downward and contract the adjusting screw. Back

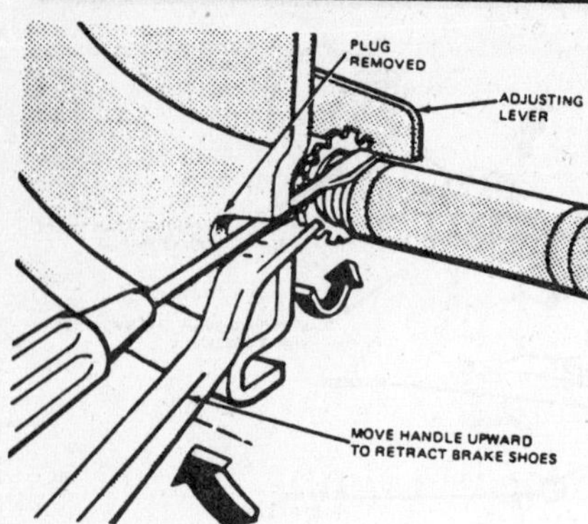

Cutaway of the position and operation of the brake adjusting tools during adjustment

off the adjusting screw starwheel until the wheel spins freely with a minimum of drag. Keep track of the number of turns that the starwheel is backed off, or the number of strokes taken with the brake adjusting spoon.

6. Repeat this operation for the other side. When backing off the brakes on the other side, the starwheel adjuster must be backed off the same number of turns to prevent side-to-side brake pull.
7. Repeat this operation on the other set of brakes.
8. When the brakes are adjusted, make several stops while backing the vehicle, to equalize the brakes. If the truck has a tendency to pull to one side when the brakes are applied, back off the adjustment of the brake assembly on the side the to which the vehicle pulls.
9. Remove the safety stands and lower the vehicle. Road test the vehicle.

NOTE: Disc brakes are not adjustable.

BRAKE PEDAL

The brake systems are designed to permit a full stroke of the master cylinder when the brake pedal is fully depressed. A brake pedal clearance adjustment is not required.

To release the brakes, fluid must flow back to the master cylinder through a return port when pedal pressure is released. To be sure the piston moves back far enough to expose the return port, free travel is built into the pedal linkage on standard and frame mounted booster systems. This prevents the piston from becoming trapped in a partially released position. Pedal free travel is not always perceptible in dash mounted booster systems, because the operating clearance for the piston is adjusted at the booster pushrod, rather than the pedal linkage.

The pushrod has an adjustment screw to maintain the correct relationship between the booster control valve plunger and the master cylinder piston. If the plunger is too long it will prevent the master cylinder piston from completely releasing hydraulic pressure, causing the brakes to drag. If the plunger is too short it will cause excessive pedal travel and an undesirable clunk in the booster area. Remove the master cylinder for access to the booster pushrod.

To check the alignment of the screw, fabricate a gauge (from cardboard, following the dimensions in the above illustration) and place it against the master cylinder mounting surface of the booster body. Adjust the pushrod screw by turning it until the end of the screw just touches the inner edge of the slot in the gauge. Install the master cylinder and bleed the system.

Brake Light Switch

REMOVAL & INSTALLATION

1. Disconnect the wiring harness.
2. Remove the pin that secures the brake light switch to the brake pedal arm.
3. Remove the spacer and slide the brake light switch from the pedal arm.
4. Install the new switch in the reverse of the removal procedure.
5. Adjust the switch as necessary.

HYDRAULIC SYSTEM

Master Cylinder

REMOVAL & INSTALLATION

1. With the engine turned off, push the brake pedal down to expel vacuum from the brake booster system.
2. Disconnect the hydraulic lines from the brake master cylinder.
3. Remove the brake booster-to-master cylinder retaining nuts and lockwashers. Remove the master cylinder from the brake booster.
4. Before installing the master cylinder, check the distance from the outer end of the booster assembly pushrod to the front face of the brake booster assembly. Turn the pushrod adjusting screw in or out as required to obtain the length shown.
5. Position the master cylinder assembly over the booster pushrod and onto the two studs on the booster assembly. Install the attaching nuts and lockwashers and tighten to 20-30 ft.lb.
6. Loosely connect the hydraulic brake system lines to the master cylinder.
7. Bleed the hydraulic brake system. Centralize the differential valve. Then, fill the dual master cylinder reservoirs with DOT 3 brake fluid to within 1/4" (6.35mm) of the top. Install the gasket and reservoir cover.

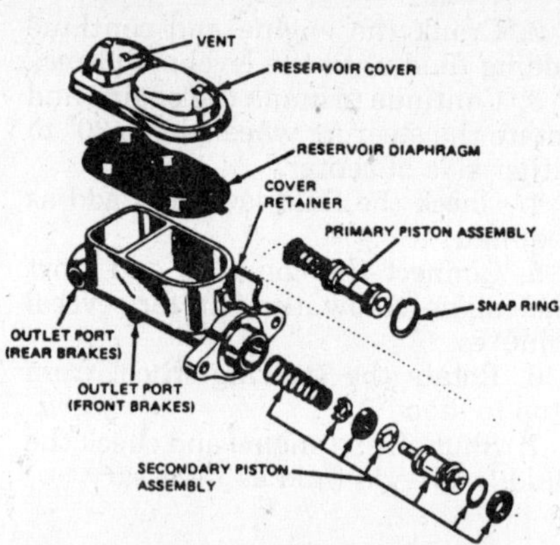

Exploded view of the master cylinder

OVERHAUL

The most important thing to remember when rebuilding the master cylinder is cleanliness. Work in clean surroundings with clean tools and clean cloths or paper for drying purposes. Have plenty of clean alcohol and brake fluid on hand to clean and lubricate the internal components. There are service repair kits available for overhauling the master cylinder.

1. Clean the outside of the master cylinder and remove the filler cap and gasket (diaphragm). Pour out any fluid that remains in the cylinder reservoir. Do not use any fluids other than brake fluid or alcohol to clean the master cylinder.
2. Unscrew the piston stop from the bottom of the cylinder body. Remove the O-ring seal from the piston stop. Discard the seal.
3. Remove the pushrod boot, if so equipped, from the groove at the rear of the master cylinder and slide the boot away from the rear of the master cylinder.
4. Remove the snapring retaining the primary and secondary piston assemblies within the cylinder body.
5. Remove the pushrod (if so equipped) and primary piston assembly from the master cylinder. Discard the piston assembly, including to boot (if so equipped).
6. Apply an air hose to the rear

brake outlet port of the cylinder body and carefully blow the secondary piston out of the cylinder body.

7. Remove the return spring, spring retainer, cap protector, and cups from the secondary piston. Discard the cup protector and cups.

8. Clean all of the remaining parts in clean isopropyl alcohol and inspect the parts for chipping, excessive wear or damage. Replace them as required.

NOTE: When using a master cylinder repair kit, install all the parts supplied in the kit.

9. Check all recesses, openings and internal passages to be sure they are open and free from foreign matter. Use compressed air to blow out dirt and cleaning solvent remaining after the parts have been cleaned in the alcohol. Place all the parts on a clean pan, lint free cloth, or paper to dry.

10. Dip all the parts, except the cylinder body, in clean brake fluid.

11. Assemble the two secondary cups, back-to-back, in the grooves near the end of the secondary piston.

12. Install the secondary piston assembly in the master cylinder.

13. Install a new O-ring on the piston stop, and start the stop into the cylinder body.

14. Position the boot, snapring and pushrod retainer on the pushrod. Make sure the pushrod retainer is seated securely on the ball end of the rod. Seat the pushrod in the primary piston assembly.

15. Install the primary piston assembly in the master cylinder. Push the primary piston inward and tighten the secondary piston stop to retain the secondary piston in the bore.

16. Press the pushrod and pistons inward and install the snapring in the cylinder body.

17. Before the master cylinder is installed on the vehicle, the unit must be bled: support the master cylinder body in a vise, and fill both fluid reservoirs with brake fluid.

18. Loosely install plugs in the front and rear brake outlet bores. Depress the primary piston several times until air bubbles cease to appear in the brake fluid.

19. Tighten the plugs and attempt to depress the piston. The piston travel should be restricted after all air is expelled.

20. Remove the plugs. Install the cover and gasket (diaphragm) assembly, and make sure the cover retainer is tightened securely.

21. Install the master cylinder in the vehicle and bleed the hydraulic system.

Booster

REMOVAL & INSTALLATION

NOTE: Make sure that the booster rubber reaction disc is properly installed if the master cylinder pushrod is removed or accidentally pulled out. A dislodged disc may cause excessive pedal travel and extreme operation sensitivity. The disc is black compared to the silver colored valve plunger that will be exposed after the pushrod and front seal is removed. The booster unit is serviced as an assembly and must be replaced if the reaction disc cannot be properly installed and aligned, or if it cannot be located within the unit itself.

1. Disconnect the stop lamp switch wiring to prevent running the battery down.

2. Support the master cylinder from the underside with a prop.

3. Remove the master cylinder-to-booster retaining nuts.

4. Loosen the clamp that secures the manifold vacuum hose to the booster check valve, and remove the hose. Remove the booster check valve.

5. Pull the master cylinder off the booster and leave it supported by the prop, far enough away to allow removal of the booster assembly.

6. From inside the cab on vehicles equipped with pushrod mounted stop lamp switch, remove the retaining pin and slide the stop lamp switch, pushrod, spacers and bushing off the brake pedal arm.

7. From the engine compartment remove the bolts that attach the booster to the dash panel.

8. Mount the booster assembly on the engine side of the dash panel by sliding the bracket mounting bolts and valve operating rod in through the holes in the dash panel.

NOTE: Make certain that the booster pushrod is positioned on the correct side of the master cylinder to install onto the push pin prior to tightening the booster assembly to the dash.

9. From inside the cab, install the booster mounting bracket-to-dash panel retaining nuts.

10. Position the master cylinder on the booster assembly, install the retaining nuts, and remove the prop from underneath the master cylinder.

11. Install the booster check valve. Connect the manifold vacuum hose to the booster check valve and secure with the clamp.

12. From inside the cab on vehicles equipped with pushrod mounted stop lamp switch, install the bushing and position the switch on the end of the pushrod. Then install the switch and rod on the pedal arm, along with spacers on each side, and secure with the retaining pin.

13. Connect the stop lamp switch wiring.

14. Start the engine and check brake operation.

Diesel Engine Vacuum Pump

REMOVAL & INSTALLATION

1. Disconnect the vacuum hose at the intake manifold.

2. Loosen the vacuum pump adjustment and pivot bolts. Slide the pump downward and remove the drive belt.

3. Remove the pivot and adjusting bolts and lift out the pump and bracket.

NOTE: The pump is not servicable and can only be replaced.

4. Installation is the reverse of removal. To adjust the belt tension, place a 3/8" drive breaker bar in the slot in the pump bracket and apply force to tighten the belt. While holding this tension, tighten the adjusting and pivot bolts. Remove the bar and torque both bolts to 18 ft.lb. Start the engine. The BRAKE light will glow until vacuum builds to a sufficien level.

Pressure Differential Valve

REMOVAL

1. Raise the vehicle on a hoist. Disconnect the brake warning lamp wire from the valve assembly switch.

NOTE: To avoid damaging the brake warning switch wire connector, expand the plastic lugs so that the shell wire connector may be removed from the switch body.

2. Disconnect the brake hydraulic lines from the differential valve assembly.

3. Remove the screw retaining the pressure differential, metering and proportioning valve assembly to the frame side rail or support bracket and remove the valve assembly.

INSTALLATION

1. Mount the combination brake differential valve assembly on the frame side rail or support bracket and

tighten the attaching screw.

2. Connect the brake hydraulic system lines to the differential valve assembly and tighten the tube nuts securely.

3. Connect the shell wire connector to the brake warning lamp switch. Make sure that the plastic lugs on the connector hold the connector securely to the switch.

4. Bleed the brakes and centralize the pressure differential valve.

CENTRALIZING THE PRESSURE DIFFERENTIAL VALVE

After any repair or bleeding of the primary (front brake) or secondary (rear brake) system, the dual brake system warning light will usually remain illuminated due to the pressure differential valve remaining in the offcenter position.

To centralize the pressure differential valve and turn off the warning light after the systems have been bled, follow the procedure below.

1. Turn the ignition switch to the ACC or ON position.

2. Check the fluid level in the master cylinder reservoirs and fill them to within ¼" (6.35mm) of the top with brake fluid, if necessary.

3. Depress the brake pedal and the piston should center itself causing the brake warning light to go out.

4. Turn the ignition switch to the OFF position.

5. Before driving the vehicle, check the operation of the brakes and be sure that a firm pedal is obtained.

Brake Hoses

Steel tubing is used the hydraulic lines between the master cylinder and the front brake tube connector, and between the rear brake tube connector and the wheel cylinders. Flexible hoses connect the brake tube to the front brake cylinders and to the rear brake tube connector.

A brake line wrench should be used when removing and installing brake lines. When replacing hydraulic brake tubing, hoses, or connectors tighten all connections securely. After replacement, bleed the brake system at the wheel cylinders and the booster (if equipped).

If a section of the brake tube is damaged, replace it with tubing of the same type, size, shape and length.

Do not use copper tubing in the hydraulic system. Be careful not to kink or crack the tubing when bending it to fit the frame or rear axle.

Always use double flared brake tubing to provide good leak proof connections. Always clean the inside of a new brake tube with clean isopropyl alcohol.

Replace a flexible brake hose if it shows signs of softening, cracking, or other damage.

When installing a new brake hose, position the hose to avoid contact with other vehicle parts. Whenever a brake hose is disconnected from a wheel cylinder or brake caliper, install a new copper washer connecting the hose.

Bleeding

When any part of the hydraulic system has been disconnected for repair or replacement, air may get into the lines and cause spongy pedal action (because air can be compressed and brake fluid cannot). To correct this condition, it is necessary to bleed the hydraulic system after it has been properly connected to be sure all air is expelled from the brake cylinders and lines.

When bleeding the brake system, bleed one brake cylinder at a time, beginning at the cylinder with the longest hydraulic line (farthest from the master cylinder) first. Keep the master cylinder reservoir filled with brake fluid during the bleeding operation. Never use brake fluid that has been drained from the hydraulic system, no matter how clean it is.

It will be necessary to centralize the pressure differential valve after a brake system failure has been corrected and the hydraulic system has been bled.

The primary and secondary hydraulic brake systems are individual systems and are bled separately. During the entire bleeding operation, do not allow the reservoir to run dry. Keep the master cylinder reservoir filled with brake fluid.

1. Clean all dirt from around the master cylinder fill cap, remove the cap and fill the master cylinder with brake fluid until the level is within ¼" (6.35mm) of the top edge of the reservoir.

2. Clean off the bleeder screws at all 4 wheel cylinders. The bleeder screws are located on the inside of the brake backing plate, on the backside of the wheel cylinders.

3. Attach a length of rubber hose over the nozzle of the bleeder screw at the wheel to be done first. Place the other end of the hose in a glass jar, submerged in brake fluid.

4. Open the bleeder screw valve ½-¾ turn.

5. Have an assistant slowly depress the brake pedal. Close the bleeder screw valve and tell your assistant to allow the brake pedal to return slowly. Continue this pumping action to force any air out of the system. When bubbles cease to appear at the end of the bleeder hose, close the bleeder valve and remove the hose.

6. Check the master cylinder fluid level and add fluid accordingly. Do this after bleeding each wheel.

7. Repeat the bleeding operation at the remaining 3 wheels, ending with the one closest to the master cylinder. Fill the master cylinder reservoir.

FRONT DISC BRAKES

CAUTION

Brake shoes contain asbestos, which has been determined to be a cancer causing agent. Never clean the brake surfaces with compressed air! Avoid inhaling any dust from any brake surface! When cleaning brake surfaces, use a commercially available brake cleaning fluid.

Pads and/or Calipers

INSPECTION

Replace the front pads when the pad thickness is at the minimum thickness recommended by Ford Motor Co., $^{1}/_{32}$" (0.8mm), or at the minimum allowed by the applicable state or local motor vehicle inspection code. Pad thickness may be checked by removing the wheel and looking through the inspection port in the caliper assembly.

REMOVAL & INSTALLATION

NOTE: Always replace all disc pad assemblies on an Never service one wheel only.

1. To avoid fluid overflow when the caliper piston is pressed into the caliper cylinder bores, siphon or dip part of the brake fluid out of the larger master cylinder reservoir (connected to the front disc brakes). Discard the removed fluid.

2. Raise the vehicle and install jack stands. Remove a front wheel and tire assembly.

3. Place an 8" C-clamp on the caliper and tighten the clamp to bottom the caliper piston in the cylinder bore. Remove the clamp.

NOTE: Do not use a screwdriver or similar tool to pry piston away from the rotor.

4. There are three types of caliper

pins used: a single tang type, a double tang type and a split-shell type. The pin removal process is dependent upon how the pin is installed (bolt head direction). Remove the upper caliper pin first.

NOTE: On some applications, the pin may be retained by a nut and torx-head bolt (except the split-shell type).

5. If the bolt head is on the outside of the caliper, use the following procedure:

a. From the inner side of the caliper, tap the bolt within the caliper pin until the bolt head on the outer side of the caliper shows a separation between the bolt head and the caliper pin.

b. Using a hacksaw or bolt cutter, remove the bolt head from the bolt.

c. Depress the tab on the bolt head end of the upper caliper pin with a screwdriver, while tapping on the pin with a hammer. Continue tapping until the tab is depressed by the v-slot.

d. Place one end of a punch (½" or smaller) against the end of the caliper pin and drive the caliper pin out of the caliper toward the inside of the vehicle. Do not use a screwdriver or other edged tool to help drive out the caliper pin as the v-grooves may be damaged.

CAUTION

Never reuse caliper pins. Always install new pins whenever a caliper is removed.

6. If the nut end of the bolt is on the outside of the caliper, use the following procedure:

a. Remove the nut from the bolt.

b. Depress the lead tang on the end of the upper caliper pin with a screwdriver while tapping on the pin with a hammer. Continue tapping until the lead tang is depressed by the v-slot.

c. Place one end of a punch (½" or smaller) against the end of the caliper pin and drive the caliper pin out of the caliper toward the inside of the vehicle. Do not use a screwdriver

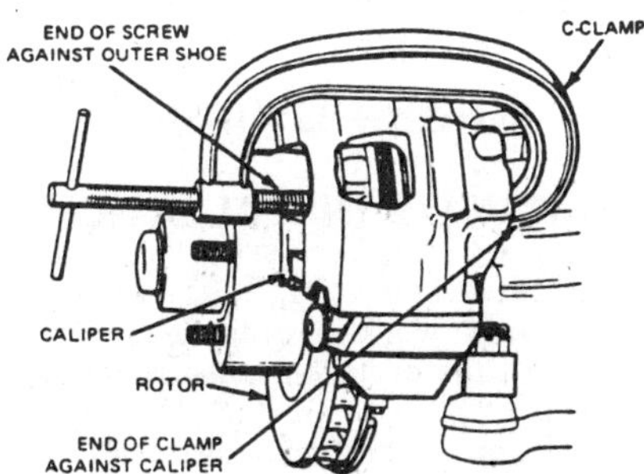

Bottoming the caliper piston

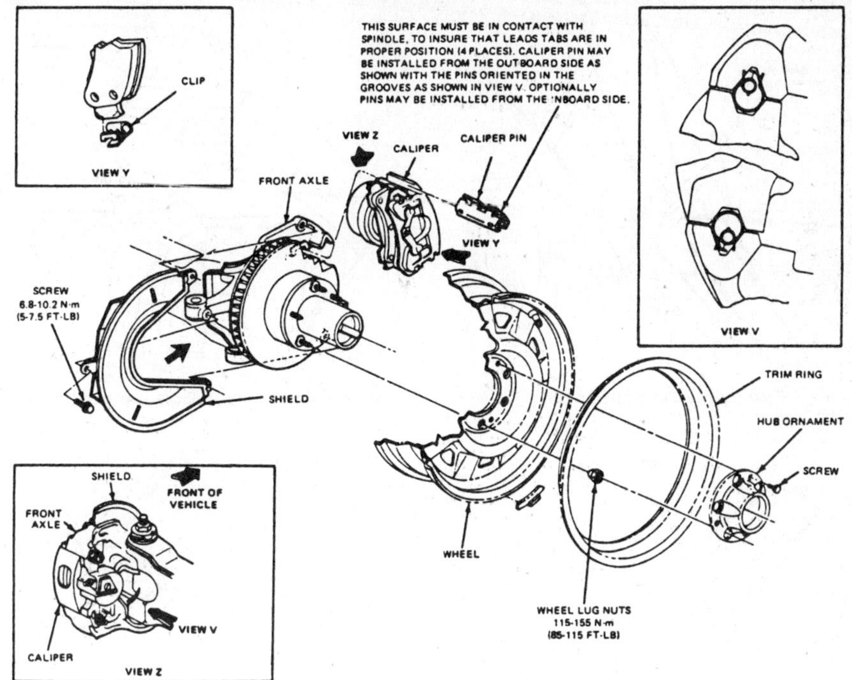

Front disc brake assembly

or other edged tool to help drive out the caliper pin as the V-grooves may be damaged.

7. Repeat the procedure in Step 4 for the lower caliper pin.

8. Remove the caliper from the rotor. If the caliper is to be removed for service, remove the brake hose from the caliper.

9. Remove the outer pad. Remove the anti-rattle clips and remove the inner pad.

10. To install, place a new anti-rattle clip on the lower end of the inner pad. Be sure the tabs on the clip are positioned properly and the clip is fully seated.

11. Position the inner pad and anti-rattle clip in the pad abutment with the anti-rattle clip tab against the pad abutment and the loop-type spring away from the rotor. Compress the anti-rattle clip and slide the upper end of the pad in position.

12. Install the outer pad, making sure the torque buttons on the pad spring clip are seated solidly in the matching holes in the caliper.

13. Install the caliper on the spindle, making sure the mounting surfaces are free of dirt and lubricate the caliper grooves with Disc Brake Caliper Grease. Install new caliper pins, making sure the pins are installed with the tang in position.

14. The pin must be installed with the lead tang in first, the bolt head facing outward (if equipped) and the pin properly positioned. Position the lead tang in the V-slot mounting surface and drive in the caliper until the drive tang is flush with the caliper assembly. Install the nut (if equipped) and tighten to 32-47 in.lb.

WARNING: Never reuse caliper pins! Always install new pins whenever a caliper is removed.

15. If removed, install the brake hose to the caliper.

16. Bleed the brakes as described earlier in this section.

17. Install the wheel and tire assembly. Torque the lug nuts to 85-115 ft.lb.

18. Remove the jack stands and lower the vehicle. Check the brake fluid level and fill as necessary. Check the brakes for proper operation.

Brake Calipers

OVERHAUL

1. For caliper removal, see the brake pad removal section. Disconnect the brake hose.

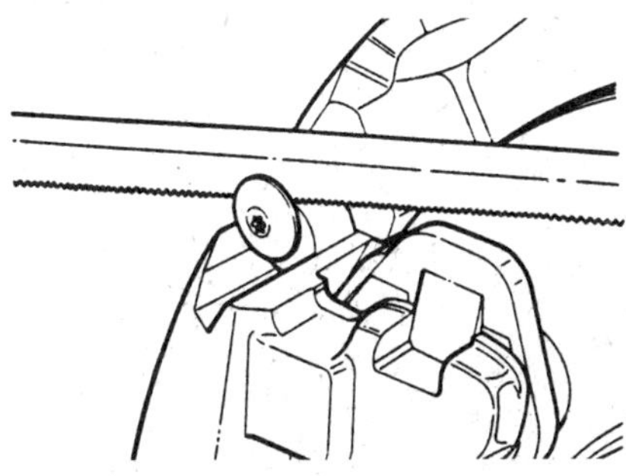

Removing the bolt head

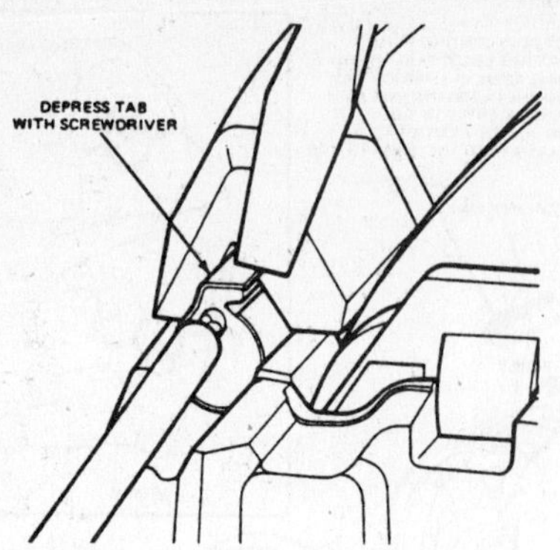

Removing the caliper pin

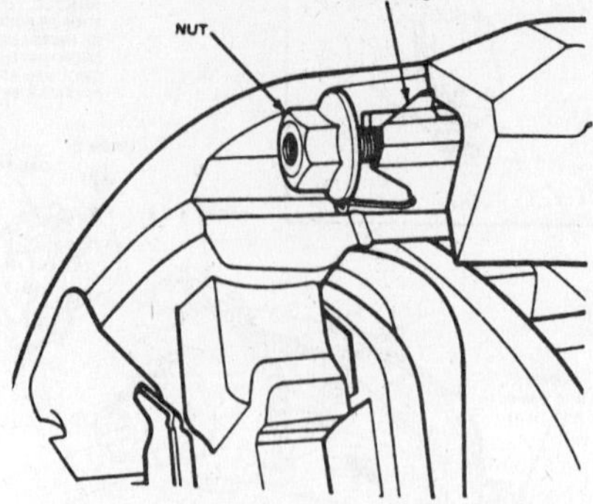

Caliper pin with a nut on the outside

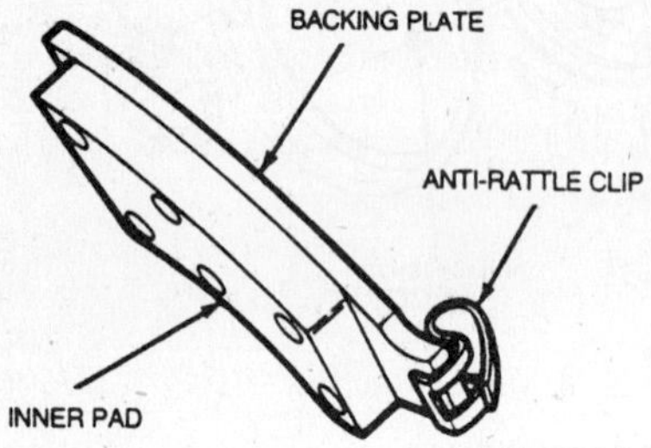

Anti-rattle clip installed on the inner pad

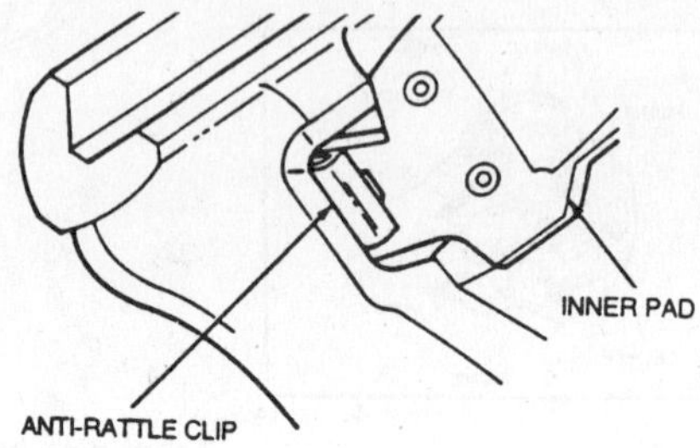

Installing the inner pad and the anti-rattle clip into the caliper

2. Clean the exterior of the caliper with denatured alcohol.

3. Remove the plug from the caliper inlet port and drain the fluid.

4. Air pressure is necessary to remove the piston. When a source of compressed air is found, such as a shop or gas station, apply air to the inlet port slowly and carefully until the piston(s) pops out of its bore. If high pressure air is applied the piston(s) will drop out with considerable force and cause damage or injury.

5. If the piston(s) jams, release the air pressure and tap sharply on the piston end with a soft hammer. Reapply air pressure.

6. When the piston(s) is out, remove the boot from the piston and the seal from the bore.

7. Clean the housing and piston(s) with denatured alcohol. Dry with compressed air.

8. Lubricate the new piston seal(s), boot(s) and piston(s) with clan brake fluid, and assemble them in the caliper.

9. The dust boot(s) can be worked in with the fingers and the piston should be pressed straight in until it bottoms. Be careful to avoid cocking the piston in the bore.

10. A C-clamp may be necessary to bottom the piston.

11. Install the caliper using the procedure given in the pad replacement paragraph above.

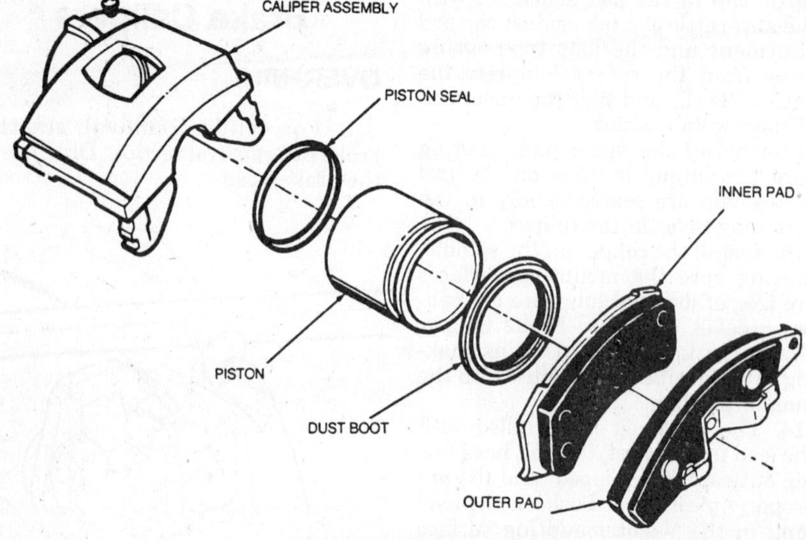

Caliper assembly

Rotor (Disc)

REMOVAL & INSTALLATION

1. Jack up the front of the vehicle and support on jackstands.

2. Remove the wheel.

3. Remove the caliper assembly as described above.

4. Follow the procedure given under hub and wheel bearing removal in DRIVE TRAIN.

NOTE: New rotor assemblies come protected with an anti-rust coating which should be removed with denatured alcohol or degreaser. New hubs must be packed with EP wheel bearing grease. If the old rotors are to be reused, check them for cracks, grooves or wavyness. Rotors that aren't too badly scored or grooved can be resurfaced by most automotive shops. Minimum rotor thickness should be 1.12" (28.4mm). If refinishing exceeds that, the rotor will have to be replaced.

REAR DRUM BRAKES

CAUTION

Brake shoes contain asbestos, which has been determined to be a cancer causing agent. Never clean the brake surfaces with compressed air! Avoid inhaling any dust from any brake surface! When cleaning brake surfaces, use a commercially available brake cleaning fluid.

Brake Drums

REMOVAL & INSTALLATION

1. Raise the vehicle so that the wheel to be worked on is clear of the floor and install jackstands under the vehicle.

2. Remove the hub cap and the wheel/tire assembly. Remove the 3 retaining nuts and remove the brake

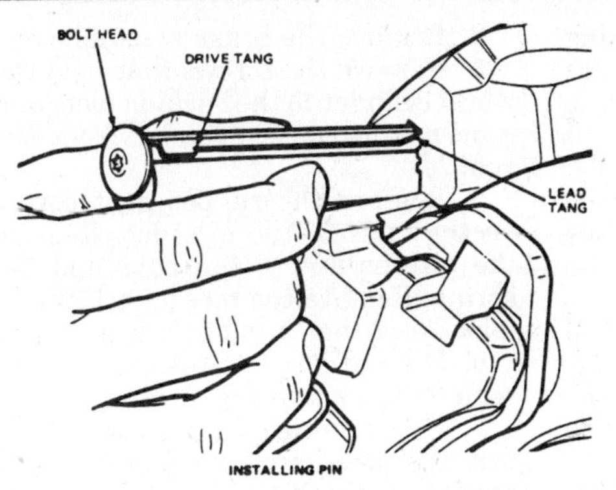

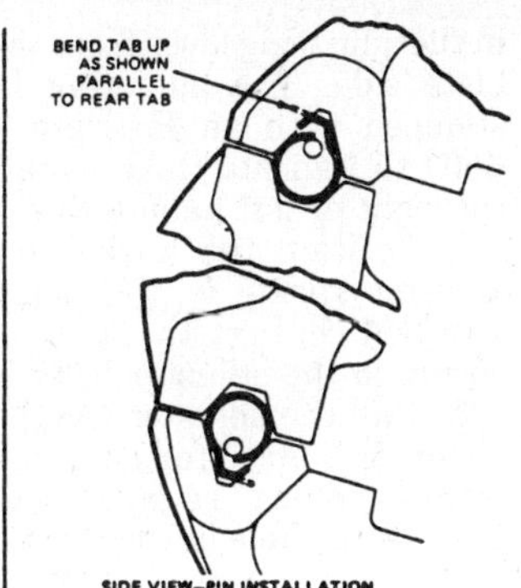

Installing the caliper pin

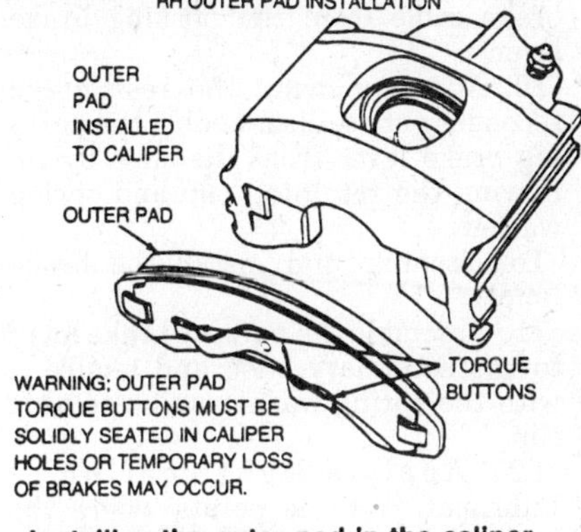

Installing the outer pad in the caliper

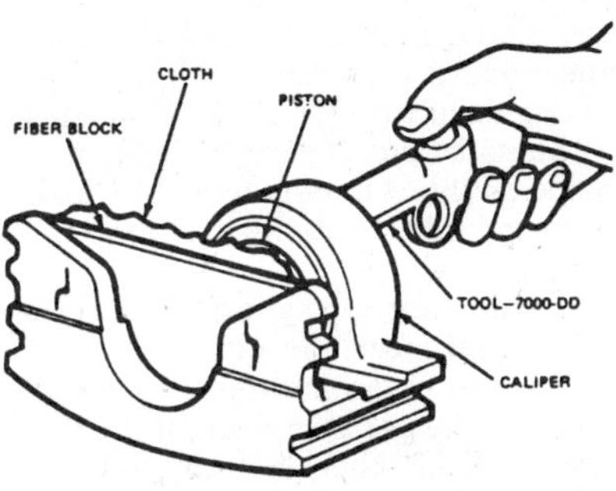

Caliper piston removal

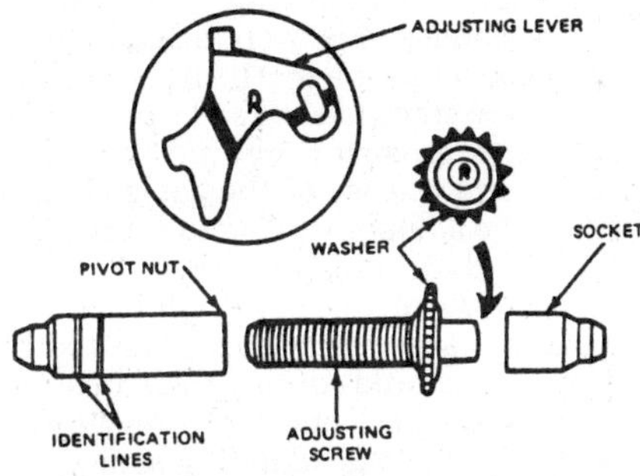

The adjusting screw starwheel and components and the self-adjusting lever indentification

drum. It may be necessary to back off the brake shoe adjustment in order to remove the brake drum. This is because the drum might be grooved or worn from being in service for an extended period of time.

3. Before installing a new brake drum, be sure and remove any protective coating with a carburetor degreaser.

4. Install the brake drum in the reverse order of removal and adjust the brakes.

INSPECTION

After the brake drum has been removed from the vehicle, it should be inspected for runout, severe scoring, cracks, and the proper inside diameter.

Minor scores on a brake drum can be removed with fine emery cloth, provided that all grit is removed from the drum before it is installed on the vehicle.

A badly scored, rough, or out-of-round (runout) drum can be ground or turned on a brake drum lathe. Do not remove any more material from the drum than is necessary to provide a smooth surface for the brake shoe to contact. The maximum diameter of the braking surface is shown on the inside of each brake drum. Brake drums that exceed the maximum braking surface diameter shown on the brake drum, either through wear or refinishing, must be replaced. This is because after the outside wall of the brake drum reaches a certain thickness (thinner than the original thickness) the drum loses its ability to dissipate the heat created by the friction between the brake drum and the brake shoes, when the brakes are applied. Also, the brake drum will have more tendency to warp and/or crack.

The maximum braking surface diameter specification, which is shown on each drum, allows for a 0.060″ (1.5mm) machining cut over the original nominal drum diameter plus 0.030″ (0.76mm) additional wear before reaching the diameter where the drum must be discarded. Use a brake drum micrometer to measure the inside diameter of the brake drums.

Brake Shoes

REMOVAL & INSTALLATION

1. Raise and support the vehicle and remove the wheel and brake drum from the wheel to be worked on.

NOTE: If you have never replaced the brakes on a truck before and you are not too familiar with the procedures involved, only disassemble and assemble one side at a time, leaving the other side intact as a reference during reassembly.

2. Install a clamp over the ends of the wheel cylinder to prevent the pistons of the wheel cylinder from coming out, causing loss of fluid and much grief.

3. Contract the brake shoes by pulling the self-adjusting lever away from the starwheel adjustment screw and turn the starwheel up and back until the pivot nut is drawn onto the starwheel as far as it will come.

4. Pull the adjusting lever, cable and automatic adjuster spring down and toward the rear to unhook the pivot hook from the large hole in the secondary shoe web. Do not attempt to pry the pivot hook from the hole.

5. Remove the automatic adjuster spring and the adjusting lever.

6. Remove the secondary shoe-to-anchor spring with a brake tool. (Brake tools are very common implements and are available at auto parts stores.) Remove the primary shoe-to-anchor spring and unhook the cable anchor. Remove the anchor pin plate.

7. Remove the cable guide from the secondary shoe.

8. Remove the shoe holddown springs, shoes, adjusting screw, pivot nut, and socket. Note the color of each holddown spring for assembly. To remove the holddown springs, reach behind the brake backing plate and place one finger on the end of one of the brake holddown spring mounting pins. Using a pair of pliers, grasp the washer type retainer on top of the holddown spring that corresponds to the pin that you are holding. Push down on the pliers and turn them 90° to align the slot in the washer with the head on the spring mounting pin. Remove the spring and washer retainer and repeat this operation on the holddown spring on the other shoe.

9. Remove the parking brake link and spring. Disconnect the parking

brake cable from the parking brake lever.

10. After removing the rear brake secondary shoe, disassemble the parking brake lever from the shoe by removing the retaining clip and spring washer.

To assemble and install the brake shoes:

11. Assemble the parking brake lever to the secondary shoe and secure it with the spring washer and retaining clip.

12. Apply a light coating of Lubriplate® at the points where the brake shoes contact the backing plate.

13. Position the brake shoes on the backing plate, and install the holddown spring pins, springs, and spring washer type retainers. On the rear brake, install the parking brake link, spring and washer. Connect the parking brake cable to the parking brake lever.

14. Install the anchor pin plate, and place the cable anchor over the anchor pin with the crimped side toward the backing plate.

15. Install the primary shoe-to-anchor spring with the brake tool.

16. Install the cable guide on the secondary shoe web with the flanged holes fitted into the hole in the secondary shoe web. Thread the cable around the cable guide groove.

17. Install the secondary shoe-to-anchor (long) spring. Be sure that the cable end is not cocked or binding on the anchor pin when installed. All of the parts should be flat on the anchor pin. Remove the wheel cylinder piston clamp.

18. Apply Lubriplate® to the threads and the socket end of the adjusting starwheel screw. Turn the adjusting screw into the adjusting pivot nut to the limit of the threads and then back off ½ turn.

NOTE: Interchanging the brake shoe adjusting screw assemblies from one side of the vehicle to the other would cause the brake shoes to retract rather than expand each time the automatic adjusting mechanism operated. To prevent this, the socket end of the adjusting screw is stamped with an R or an L for RIGHT or LEFT. The adjusting pivot nuts can be distinguished by the number of lines machined around the body of the nut; one line indicates left hand nut and two lines indicates a right hand nut.

19. Place the adjusting socket on the screw and install this assembly between the shoe ends with the adjusting screw nearest to the secondary shoe.

20. Place the cable hook into the hole in the adjusting lever from the backing plate side. The adjusting levers are stamped with an **R** (right) or an **L** (left) to indicate their installation on the right or left hand brake assembly.

21. Position the hooked end of the adjuster spring in the primary shoe web and connect the loop end of the spring to the adjuster lever hole.

22. Pull the adjuster lever, cable and automatic adjuster spring down toward the rear to engage the pivot book in the large hole in the secondary shoe web.

23. After installation, check the action of the adjuster by pulling the section of the cable between the cable guide and the adjusting lever toward the secondary shoe web far enough to lift the lever past a tooth on the adjusting screw starwheel. The lever should snap into position behind the next tooth, and release of the cable should cause the adjuster spring to return the lever to its original position. This return action of the lever will turn the adjusting screw starwheel one tooth. The lever should contact the adjusting screw starwheel one tooth above the center line of the adjusting screw.

If the automatic adjusting mechanism does not perform properly, check the following:

1. Check the cable end fittings. The cable ends should fill or extend slightly beyond the crimped section of the fittings. If this is not the case, replace the cable.
2. Check the cable guide for damage. The cable groove should be parallel to the shoe web, and the body of the guide should lie flat against the web. Replace the cable guide if this is not so.
3. Check the pivot hook on the lever. The hook surfaces should be square with the body on the lever for proper pivoting. Repair or replace the hook as necessary.
4. Make sure that the adjusting screw starwheel is properly seated in the notch in the shoe web.

Wheel Cylinders

OVERHAUL

Wheel cylinder rebuilding kits are available for reconditioning wheel cylinders. The kits usually contain new cup springs, cylinder cups, and in some, new boots. The most important factor to keep in mind when rebuilding wheel cylinders is cleanliness. Keep all dirt away from the wheel cylinders when you are reassembling them.

1. To remove the wheel cylinder, jack up the vehicle and remove the wheel, hub, and drum.
2. Disconnect the brake line at the fitting on the brake backing plate.
3. Remove the brake assemblies.
4. Remove the screws that hold the wheel cylinder to the backing plate and remove the wheel cylinder from the vehicle.
5. Remove the rubber dust covers on the ends of the cylinder. Remove the pistons and piston cups and the spring. Remove the bleeder screw and make sure that it is not plugged.
6. Discard all of the parts that the rebuilding lot will replace.
7. Examine the inside of the cylinder. If it is severely rusted, pitted or scratched, then the cylinder must be replaced as the piston cups won't be able to seal against the walls of the cylinder.
8. Using a wheel cylinder hone or emery cloth and crocus cloth, polish the inside of the cylinder. The purpose of this is to put a new surface on the inside of the cylinder. Keep the inside of the cylinder coated with brake fluid while honing.
9. Wash out the cylinder with clean brake fluid after honing.
10. When reassembling the cylinder, dip all of the parts in clean brake fluid. Assemble the wheel cylinder in the reverse order of removal and disassembly.

PARKING BRAKE

Equalizer-to-Control Cable

REMOVAL & INSTALLATION

1. Raise the vehicle on a hoist. Back off the equalizer nut and remove slug of front cable from the tension limiter.
2. Remove the parking brake cable from the retaining clips.
3. Lower the vehicle. Remove the forward ball end of the parking brake cable from the control assembly clevis.
4. Remove the cable and hair pin retainer from the control assembly.
5. Using a fish wire or cord attached to the control lever end of the cable, remove the cable from the vehicle.
6. Transfer the fish wire or cord to the new cable. Position the cable in the vehicle, routing the cable through the dash panel. Remove the fish wire and secure the cable to the control with the hair pin retainer.
7. Connect the forward ball end of the brake cable to the clevis of the control assembly and replace the hairpin clip around the conduit end fitting. Raise the vehicle on a hoist.

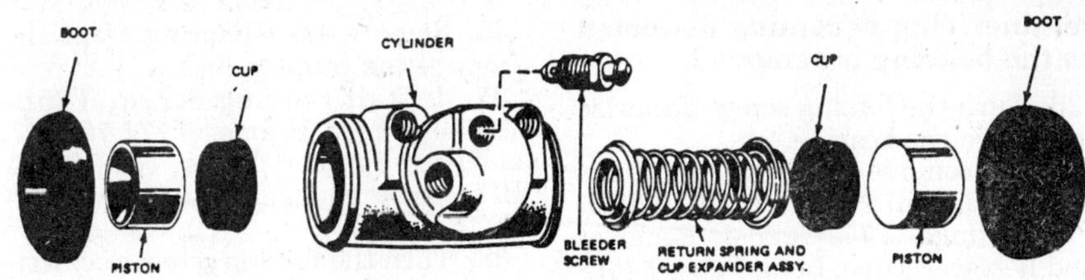

Rear wheel cylinder assembly

8. Route the cable and secure in place with retaining clips.
9. Connect the slug of the cable to the tension limiter connector. Adjust the parking brake cable at the equalizer.
10. Rotate both rear wheels to be sure that the parking brakes are not dragging.

Equalizer-to-Rear Wheel Cables

REMOVAL & INSTALLATION

1. Raise the vehicle and remove the hub cab, wheel, tension limiter and brake drum. Remove the locknut on the threaded rod and disconnect the cable from the equalizer.
2. Compress the prongs that retain the cable housing into the brake backing plate cable and housing out of the bracket.
3. Working on the wheel side, compress the prongs on the cable retainer so they can pass through the hole in the brake backing plate. Draw the cable retainer out of the hole.
4. With the spring tension off the parking brake lever, lift the cable out of the slot in the lever, and remove the cable through the brake backing plate hole.
5. Pull the cable through the brake backing plate until the end of the cable is inserted over the slot in the parking brake lever. Pull the excess slack from the cable and insert the cable housing into the brake backing plate access hole until the retainer prongs expand.
6. Insert the front end of the cable housing through the frame crossmember bracket until the prong expands. Insert the ball end of the cable into the key hole slots on the equalizer, rotate the equalizer 90° and recouple the tension limiter threaded rod to the equalizer.

On vehicles with web ledge brakes, check the clearance between the parking brake operating lever and cam plate. The clearance should be 0.015" (0.38mm) when the brakes are fully released.

7. Install the rear brake drum, wheel, and hub cap, and adjust the rear brake shoes.
8. Adjust the parking brake tension.
9. Rotate both rear wheels to be sure that the parking brakes are not dragging.

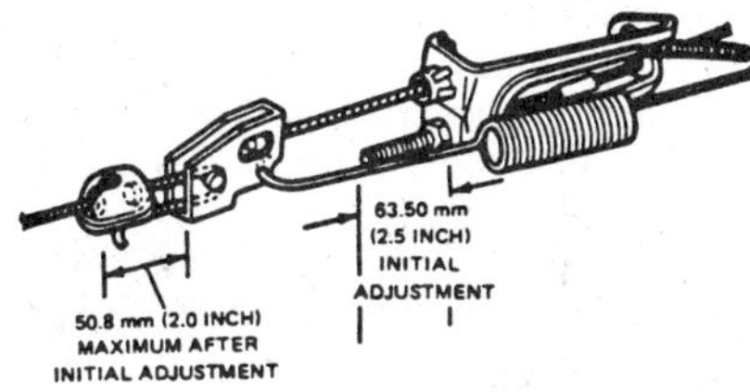

Pre-tension adjustment

ADJUSTMENT

Pre-Tension Adjustment

NOTE: Theis adjustment is necessary when a new tension limiter has been installed.

1. Depress the parking brake pedal.
2. Grip the tenison limiter bracket to prevent it from spinning and tighten the equalizer nut to a distance 2½" up the rod.
3. Make sure that the cinch strap has less than 1⅜" remaining.

Final Adjustment

NOTE: This procedure is used when a new tenison limiter has NOT been installed. The brake drums should be COLD for this procedure to be accurate.

1. Fully depress the parking brake pedal.
2. Grip the threaded rod to prevent it from turning and tighten the equalizer nut 6 full turns past its original position on the threaded rod.
3. Attach a cable tension gauge such as Rotunda model 21-0018, or equivalent, behind the equalizer assembly, either towards the right or left brake drum. Measure the cable tension. Cable tension should be 400-600 lb. with the parking brake pedal in the fully depressed, last detent position. If the tension is too low, repeat Step 2.
4. Release the parking brake and check for rear wheel drag. No drag should be present. If any drag is present, back off on the adjusting nut.

NOTE: The tension limiter will reset the parking brake cable tension any time the system is disconnected, provided that the distance between the bracket and the cinch strap hook is reduced during adjustment. When the cinch strap contacts the bracket, the system tension will increase significantly and over-tensioning will result. If all available adjustment travel has been used, the tension limiter must be replaced.

MANUAL TRANSMISSION OVERHAUL

4-Speed (Gasoline Engines)

DISASSEMBLY

1. Remove the nuts attaching the bell housing to the transmission case. Remove the bell housing and gasket.
2. Remove the drain plug and drain lubricant from the transmission. Clean the metal filings from the magnet of the drain plug (if necessary). Install the drain plug.
3. Place transmission in neutral.
4. Remove the four 12mm bolts attaching the gearshift lever retainer to the extension housing. Remove the gearshift lever retainer and gasket.
5. Remove the six 14mm bolts attaching the extension housing to the transmission case.
6. Raise the control lever to the left and slide toward the rear of the transmission. Slide the extension housing off the mainshaft, being careful not to damage the oil seal.
7. If required, remove the bolt attaching the gearshift control lever end to the gearshift control lever, and remove the control lever end and control lever.
8. If required, remove the back-up lamp switch from the extension housing.
9. Remove the anti-spill seal from the output shaft and discard (a seal is not necessary for assembly).
10. Remove the snapring that secures the speedometer drive gear to the mainshaft. Slide the drive gear off the mainshaft, and remove the lock ball.
11. Evenly loosen the fourteen 10mm bolts securing the transmission

case cover to the transmission case and remove the cover and gasket.

12. Remove the three spring cap bolts (the two bolts on the case upper portion are 17mm and the bolt on the case side is 14mm), the detent springs and the detent balls with a magnet from the transmission case.

13. Remove the four 10mm bolts attaching the blind covers to the transmission case and remove the blind covers and gaskets.

14. Slide the reverse shift fork shaft assembly and reverse idler gear out of the transmission case.

15. Shift the transmission into fourth gear. This will provide adequate space to drive out the roll pin. With a small drift, drive the roll pin from third/fourth fork assembly. Slide the third/fourth shift fork shaft out of the rear of the transmission case.

16. Remove the roll pin from the first/second shift fork. Slide the first/second shift fork shaft assembly out the rear of the transmission case. Remove both inter-lock pins.

17. Reinstall the reverse idler gear to lock the gears. Install the Synchronizer Ring Holder and Countershaft Spacer (T77J-7025-E) or its equal between the fourth speed synchronizer ring and synchromesh gear on the mainshaft. Shift the transmission gear into second gear to lock the mainshaft and prevent the assembly from rotating.

18. Straighten the bent portion of the lockwasher with a chisel.

19. Remove the locknut and washer using Locknut Wrench Adapter T82T-7003-CH and Locknut Wrench, T77J-7025-C or their equal. Slide the reverse-idler gear off the mainshaft.

20. Remove the key from the mainshaft.

21. Remove the reverse idler gear.

22. Remove the snapring from the rear end of the countershaft. Slide the countershaft reverse gear off the countershaft.

23. Remove the four 12mm bearing retainer attaching bolts.

24. Remove the bearing retainer together with the reverse idler gear shaft.

25. To remove the countershaft rear bearing, install Puller, T77J-7025-H; Puller Rings, T77J-7025-J; Remover Tube, T77J-7025-B; and Forcing Screw, T75L-7025-J or their equal. Squarely insert the jaws of the puller behind the front bearing retainer ring in the two recessed areas of the case.

NOTE: The retainer ring may need to be turned to position the split in the retainer ring midway between the recessed areas, before the puller is installed. This will reduce the possibility of the retainer ring becoming distorted as the bearing is removed.

26. Turn the forcing screw clockwise to remove the bearing.

27. To remove the mainshaft rear bearing, install Puller, T77J-7025-H; Puller Rings, T77J-7025-J; Remover and Replacer Tube, Long Tube, T75L-7025-C and Forcing Screw, T75L-7025-J or their equal. Squarely insert the jaws of the puller behind the rear mainshaft bearing retainer ring in the two recessed areas of the case.

NOTE: The retainer ring may need to be turned to position the split in the ring midway between the recessed areas before the puller is installed. This will reduce the possibility of the retainer ring becoming distorted as the bearing is removed.

28. Turn the forcing screw clockwise to remove the bearing.

29. Remove the shim and spacer from behind the mainshaft rear bearing.

30. Remove the front cover by removing the four studs attaching the cover to case. Remove the studs by installing two nuts (10mm × 1.5) on the stud and drawing the stud out of the case. Remove the four 14mm bolts and remove cover. Save the shim found on the inside of the cover.

31. Remove the snapring from the input shaft.

32. Remove the mainshaft drive gear bearing by installing Puller, T77J-7025-H; Puller Rings, T77J-7025-J; Remover and Replacer Tube, Short Tube, T75L-7025-B; and Forcing Screw, T75L-7025-J or their equal. Squarely insert the jaws of the puller behind the mainshaft drive gear bearing retainer ring in the two recessed areas of the case.

NOTE: The retainer ring may need to be turned to position the split in the ring midway between the recessed areas before the puller is installed. This will reduce the possibility of the retainer ring becoming distorted as the bearing is removed.

33. Turn the forcing screw clockwise to remove the bearing.

34. Rotate both shift forks so that the main geartrain will fall to the bottom of the case. Remove the shift forks. Rotate the input shaft so that one of the two flats on the input shaft face upward.

35. Insert Synchronizer Ring Holder and Countershaft Spacer, T77J-7025-E or its equal between the first gear on the countershaft and the rear of the case.

36. Remove the snapring from the front of the countershaft.

37. Install Forcing Screw, T75L-7025-J; Press Frame, T77J-7025-N; and Press Frame Adapter, T82T-7003-BH or their equal against the countershaft assembly.

38. Turn the forcing screw clockwise to press the countershaft rearward. Press the countershaft ($^3/_{16}$" movement) until it contacts the Synchronizer Ring Holder and Countershaft Spacer.

39. To remove the countershaft front bearing, install Puller, T77J-7025-H; Puller Rings, T77J-7025-J; Remover Tube, T77J-7025-B; and Forcing Screw, T75L-7025-J or their equal. Squarely insert the jaws of the puller behind the front bearing retainer ring in the two recessed areas of the case.

NOTE: The retainer ring may need to be turned to position the split in the ring midway between the recessed areas, before the puller is installed. This will reduce the possibility of the retainer ring becoming distorted as the bearing is removed.

40. Turn the forcing screw clockwise to remove the bearing.

41. Remove the shim from behind the countershaft front bearing.

42. Remove the input shaft from the transmission case. Remove the synchronizer ring and caged bearing from the main driveshaft.

43. Remove the countershaft from the transmission case.

44. Remove the inner race of the countershaft center bearing from the countershaft in a press frame using Axle Bearing Seal Plate, T75L-1165-B and Pinion Bearing Cone Remover, D79L-4621-A or their equal.

45. Remove the mainshaft and gear assembly from the transmission case.

46. Remove the snaprings from the front of the mainshaft.

47. Slide the third-fourth clutch hub and sleeve assembly, the third synchronizer ring, and third gear off of the front of the mainshaft.

NOTE: Do not mix the synchronizer rings.

48. Slide the thrust washer, first gear, and gear sleeve off the rear mainshaft. Press the bushing from the first gear using a press and suitable pressing stock.

49. Remove the first/second clutch hub and sleeve assembly from the mainshaft.

50. Clean and inspect transmission case, gears, bearings, and shafts.

ASSEMBLY

Before beginning the assembly procedure, three measurements must be performed: Mainshaft Thrust Play, Countershaft Thrust Play and Mainshaft Bearing Clearance.

Mainshaft Thrust Play

Check the mainshaft thrust play by measuring the depth of the mainshaft bearing bore in the transmission rear cage by using a depth micrometer (D80P-4201-A) or its equal. Then measure the mainshaft rear bearing height. The difference between the two measurements indicates the required thickness of the adjusting shim. The standard thrust play is 0-0.0039". Adjusting shims are available in 0.0039" and 0.0118" sizes.

Countershaft Thrust Play

Check the countershaft thrust play by measuring the depth of the countershaft front bearing bore in the transmission case by using a depth micrometer (D80P-4201-A) or its equal. Then measure the countershaft front bearing height. The difference between the two measurements indicates the required thickness of the adjusting shims. The standard thrust play is 0-0.0039". Adjusting shims are available in 0.0039" and 0.0118" sizes.

Mainshaft Bearing Clearance

Check the main driveshaft bearing clearance by measuring the depth of the bearing bore in the clutch adapter plate with a depth micrometer, D80P-4201-A or its equal. Make sure the micrometer is on the second step of the plate. Measure the bearing height. The difference between the two measurements indicates the required adjusting shim thickness. The standard clearance is 0-0.0039". If an adjusting shim is required, select one to bring the clearance to within specifications.

1. Assemble the first/second synchromesh mechanism by installing the clutch hub to the sleeve, placing the three synchronizer keys into the clutch hub key slots and installing the key springs to the clutch hub.

NOTE: When installing the key springs, the open end tab of the springs should be inserted into the hub holes with the springs turned in the same direction. This will keep the spring tension on each key uniform.

2. Assemble the third/fourth synchromesh mechanisms in the same manner as first/second synchromesh mechanism.
3. Place the synchronizer ring on the third gear and slide the third gear to the front of the mainshaft with the synchronizer ring toward the front.
4. Slide the third/fourth clutch hub and sleeve assembly to the front of the mainshaft, making sure that the three synchronizer keys in the synchromesh mechanism engage the notches in the synchronizer ring.

NOTE: The direction of the third/fourth clutch hub and sleeve assembly should be as shown.

5. Install the snapring to the front of the mainshaft.
6. Place the synchronizer ring on the second gear and slide the second gear to the mainshaft with the synchronizer ring toward the rear of the shaft.
7. Slide the first/second clutch hub and sleeve assembly to the mainshaft with the oil grooves of the clutch hub toward the front of the mainshaft. Make sure that the three synchronizer keys in the synchromesh mechanism engage the notches in the second synchronizer ring.
8. Insert the first gear sleeve in the mainshaft.
9. Press the bushing in the first gear using a press and suitable press stock.
10. Place the synchronizer ring on the first gear and slide the first gear onto the mainshaft with the synchronizer ring facing the front of the shaft. Rotate the first gear as necessary to engage the three notches in the synchronizer ring with the synchronizer keys.
11. Install the original thrust washer on the mainshaft.
12. Position the mainshaft and gears assembly in the case.
13. Position the caged bearing in the front end of the mainshaft.
14. Place the synchronizer ring on the input shaft (fourth gear), and install the input shaft to the front end of the mainshaft, making sure that the three synchronizer keys in the third/fourth synchromesh mechanism engage the notches in the synchronizer ring.
15. Position the first/second shift fork and third/fourth shift fork in the groove of the clutch hub and sleeve assembly.
16. Press the inner race of the countershaft rear bearing onto the countershaft using Center Bearing Replacer, T77J-7025-K or its equal.
17. Position the countershaft gear in the case, making sure that the countershaft gear engages each gear of the mainshaft assembly.
18. Install the correct shim in the mainshaft rear bearing bore as determined in the Mainshaft Thrust Play Measurement.
19. Position the main drive gear bearing and the mainshaft rear bearing into the proper bearing bores. Be sure the synchronizer and shifter forks have not been moved out of position.
20. Install the Dummy Bearing Replacer, T75L-7025-Q; Mainshaft Front Bearing Replacer, T82T-7003-DH; Replacer Tube, T77J-7025-M; Press Frame Adapter, T82T-7003-BH; and Press Frame, T77J-7025-N or their equal on the case. Position the Synchronizer Ring Holder and Countershaft Spacer, T77J-7025-E or their equal between the mainshaft drive gear and synchronizer ring. Turn the forcing screw on the press frame until both bearings are properly seated.
21. Install the main drive gear bearing snapring.
22. Place the correct shim in the countershaft front bearing bore as determined by the Countershaft Thrust Play Measurement.
23. Position the countershaft front and rear bearings in the bores and install the tools. Turn the forcing screw until the bearing is properly seated. Use the rear bearing as a pilot.
24. Install the snapring to secure the countershaft front bearing.
25. Install the bearing retainer together with the reverse idler gear shaft to the transmission case and tighten the four 12mm attaching bolts.
26. Slide the counter reverse gear onto the countershaft with the chamfer to the rear. Install the snapring to secure the counter reverse gear.
27. Install the key on the mainshaft.
28. Slide the reverse gear and lockwasher (tab facing outward) onto the mainshaft (chamfer on teeth should be to rear). Install a new locknut and hand tighten.
29. Shift into second gear and reverse gear to lock rotation of the mainshaft. Tighten the locknut to 145-203 ft.lb. torque using the Locknut Wrench (T77J-7025-C) and Locknut Adapter, T82T-7003-CH or their equal.
30. Place the fourth/third clutch sleeve in third gear using Synchronizer Ring Holder and Countershaft Spacer, T77J-7025-E or its equal.
31. Check the clearance between the synchronizer key and the exposed edge of the synchronizer ring with a feeler gauge. If the measurement is greater than 0.079", the synchronizer key can pop out of position. To correct this, change the thrust washer (selective fit) between the mainshaft rear bearing and the first gear. Available thrust washer sizes are 0.098", 0.118", and 0.138".
32. Check the clearance again with a

feeler gauge. If the clearance is within specifications, bend the tab of the lockwasher.

33. Slide the first/second shift fork shaft assembly into the case (from rear of case). Install the roll pin. Secure the first-/second shift fork to the fork shaft by staking the roll pin.

NOTE: Be sure to use a new roll pin.

34. Insert the inter-lock pin into the transmission using the lockout pin replacer tool.

35. Slide the third/fourth shift fork shaft assembly into the case (from rear of case). Secure the third/fourth shift fork to the fork shaft by staking the roll pin. Place transmission in neutral.

NOTE: Be sure to use a new roll pin.

36. Insert the inter-lock pin into the transmission.

37. Slide the reverse fork shaft assembly and reverse idler gear into the transmission case from the rear of the case with the gear chamfer forward. Secure the reverse shift fork to the fork shaft by staking the roll pin.

NOTE: Be sure to use a new roll pin.

38. Position the three detent balls and three springs into the case. Place copper washers on the top two bolts and install the three spring cap bolts.

39. Install the two blind covers and gaskets. Tighten the 10mm attaching bolts.

40. Install the lock ball, speedometer drive gear, and snapring onto the mainshaft.

41. Apply a thin coat of sealing agent, Gasket Maker, E2AZ-19562-A (ESE-M4G234-A2) or equivalent to the contacting surfaces of the transmission case and extension housing.

42. Position the extension housing with the gearshift control lever end laid down to the left as far as it will go. Tighten the four 14mm attaching bolts.

NOTE: The lower two bolts must be coated with Loctite® or equivalent.

43. If removed, insert the speedometer driven gear assembly to the extension housing and secure it with the bolt.

44. Check to ensure the gearshift control lever operates properly.

45. Install the transmission case cover gasket and cover with drain plug to rear. Install and tighten the fourteen 10mm attaching bolts.

46. Position the gasket and gearshift lever retainer to the extension housing, and tighten the four attaching bolts.

47. Install the correct size shim on the second step of the clutch adapter plate as determined by the Mainshaft Bearing Clearance Measurement.

48. Coat the clutch adapter plate with sealer, Gasket Maker, E2AZ-19562-A (ESE-M4G234-A2) or equivalent. Install the clutch adapter plate to the transmission case and tighten the four bolts and four studs.

49. Remove the filler plug and install 3.0 pints of Ford Manual Transmission Lube, D8DZ-19C547-A (ESP-M2C83-C) or equivalent. Reinstall filler plug and tighten to 18-29 ft.lb.

4-Speed (Diesel Engines)

DISASSEMBLY

1. If not already drained, remove the drain plug and drain the transmission fluid into a suitable container. Remove the fork and release bearing from the clutch housing.

2. Install transmission in Holding Fixture T57L-500-B. Remove six bolts (12mm) attaching the front cover to the transmission case and remove the front cover shim and gasket.

3. Remove front cover oil seal.

4. Remove the input shaft snapring.

5. Remove outer snapring on input shaft bearing. Install Bearing Collet Tool T75L-7025-E or its equal on main input shaft front bearing, Remover Tube T75L-7025-B and Forcing Screw T75L-7025-J or their equal. Slide Bearing Collet Sleeve T75L-7025-G or its equal over remover tube and bearing collet, and turn forcing screw to remove input shaft bearing.

6. Remove the eight bolts (12mm) attaching the extension housing to the transmission case. Slide the extension housing off the mainshaft, with the control lever end laid down and to the left as far as it will go.

7. Remove the bolt (10mm) attaching the control lever end to the control rod and remove the control lever end and rod from the extension housing.

8. Remove the speedometer driven gear assembly from the extension housing.

9. Remove the back-up lamp switch and neutral sensing switch.

10. Remove the snapring that secures the speedometer drive gear on the mainshaft. Slide the speedometer drive gear off the mainshaft and remove the lock ball.

11. Install Bearing Pusher Tool T83T-7111-A or its equal over countershaft front bearing. Turn forcing screw to force countershaft, together with the countershaft front bearing, from the transmission housing.

12. Slide Bearing Holder and Gear Shaft Assembly from the transmission housing.

13. Remove three spring cap bolts, three springs and shift locking balls.

NOTE: Reverse spring is shortest. Take care, the spring-loaded lower ball will pop out.

14. Remove the reverse shift rod and shift fork assembly and reverse gear from the bearing housing.

15. Remove roll pins fixing shift forks to the rods. Push each of the shift rods rearward through the fork and bearing housing and remove the shift rods and forks.

NOTE: Mark 3rd-4th and 1st-2nd shift forks before removal to simplify installation.

16. Remove the lower reverse shift rod locking ball and spring, and the interlock pins from the bearing housing.

17. Straighten the tab of the lockwasher. Lock transmission synchronizers into any two gears and remove the mainshaft lock nut using Adapter Tool T83T-7025-A and Tool Shaft T77J-7025-C or its equal.

18. Remove the snapring from the rear end of the countershaft and slide off the counter reverse gear.

19. Remove the five bearing cover bolts (12mm) and cover, and the reverse idler gear shaft from the bearing housing.

20. With a soft hammer, tap the rear end of the mainshaft and countershaft in turn, being careful not to damage the shafts, and remove these shafts from the bearing housing.

21. Carefully separate the input shaft and caged needle roller bearing from the mainshaft.

22. Remove rear countershaft bearing from the bearing housing using Remover Tube Tool T77J-7025-B or its equal.

23. Remove rear mainshaft bearing from the bearing housing using Bearing Remover Tool T77F-4222-A and Remover Tube Tool T77J-7025-B or its equal.

24. Remove the thrust washer, first gear, sleeve and synchronizer ring from the rear of the mainshaft.

25. Using snapring pliers, remove the snapring from the front of the mainshaft.

26. Using a press and Remover Tool T71P-4621-B or its equal, remove the third/fourth clutch hub, sleeve, synchronizer ring and third gear from the front of the mainshaft.

27. Using a press and Remover Tool T71P-4621-B or its equal, remove the first/second clutch hub and sleeve assembly synchronizer ring, and second gear from the rear of the mainshaft in

the same manner as described in the previous step.

28. Press front bearing from countershaft using Remover Tool D79L-4621-A or T71P-4621-B or its equal and a suitable stock piece.

29. Perform cleaning and inspection procedures described in a separate section of this manual.

ASSEMBLY

1. Assemble the third/fourth clutch by installing the clutch hub and synchronizer into the sleeve, placing the three keys into the clutch hub slots and installing the springs onto the hub.

NOTE: When installing the key springs, the open end tab of the springs should be inserted into the hub holes. This will keep the spring tension on each key uniform.

2. Assemble the first/second clutch hub and sleeve in the same manner as described in Step 1 above.

3. Install the third gear and synchronizer ring onto the front section of the mainshaft.

4. Install the third/fourth clutch hub assembly onto the mainshaft by using a press. Hold assembly together and slowly press into place.

NOTE: Make sure the clutch hub assembly is facing in the correct direction.

5. Fit the snapring on the mainshaft.

6. Install the second gear, synchronizer ring onto the rear section of the mainshaft.

7. Install the first/second clutch hub assembly onto the mainshaft by using a press.

8. Install the synchronizer ring, first gear with sleeve, and thrust washer onto the mainshaft.

9. Install the input shaft and the needle roller bearing to the mainshaft.

10. Check the countershaft rear bearing clearance. Measure the depth of the countershaft bearing bore in the bearing housing using a depth micrometer (D80P-4201-A or equivalent). Then, measure the countershaft bearing height. The difference between the two measurements indicates the required thickness of the adjusting shim. The clearance should be less than 0.0039″. The adjusting shims are available in the following thickness: 0.0039″ and 0.0118″.

11. Check the mainshaft bearing clearance in the same manner as for the countershaft rear bearing clearance. The clearance should be less than 0.0039″. The adjusting shims are available in the following thickness: 0.0039″ and 0.0118″.

12. Position proper shim on countershaft rear bearing and press into bearing housing using Installer Tool T77J-7025-B.

13. Position proper shim on mainshaft bearing and press into bearing housing using Installer Tool T77J-7025-K or its equal.

14. Position front bearing on countershaft and press into place using Bearing Replacer Tool T71P-7025-A or its equal.

15. Mesh countershaft and mainshaft assembly and position the two on the bearing housing. Make certain that thrust washer is installed on mainshaft assembly at the rear of the first gear.

16. While holding mainshaft assembly in place, press countershaft assembly into bearing housing using Replacer Tool T71P-7025-A or its equal to hold rear countershaft bearing in housing.

17. Install the bearing cover and reverse idle gear shaft to the bearing housing. The cover must be seated in the groove on the idle gear shaft.

18. Install the reverse gear with the key onto the mainshaft. Install the lock nut on the mainshaft and hand tighten.

NOTE: When installing the mainshaft reverse gear and the countershaft reverse gear, both gears should be fitted so that the chamfer on the teeth faces rearward.

19. Install the countershaft reverse gear and secure it with the snapring.

NOTE: After installing reverse gears, lock transmission in any two gears.

20. Insert the short spring and locking ball into the reverse bore of the bearing housing.

21. While holding down the ball with a punch or other suitable tool, install the reverse shift rod and shift lever assembly with the reverse idle gear at the same time.

22. Using the dummy shift rails (Tool Number T72J-7280 or its equal), install each shift fork rod and interlock pins.

23. Install the first/second shift fork and third/fourth shift fork to their respective clutch sleeves.

24. Align the roll pin holes of each shift fork and rod. Install the new roll pins.

NOTE: When assembling the shift fork and control end, a new roll pin should be installed with a pin slit positioned in the direction of the shift rod axis.

25. Install the shift locking balls and springs into their respective positions and install the spring cap bolt.

NOTE: The short spring and ball are installed in the reverse bore.

26. Apply a thin coat of Silicone Sealer D6AZ-19562-B, or equivalent, on both contacting surfaces of the bearing housing.

27. Install the bearing housing assembly to the transmission case.

28. Temporarily attach the bearing housing to the transmission with two top and two bottom bolts and tightened extension housing mounting bolts to position the countershaft front bearing in the bore.

NOTE: If necessary, remove plugs from bell housing shift rod bores to align shift rods. After installation of bearing housing assembly is complete, re-install plugs using a silicone sealer (D6AZ-19562-B or equivalent).

29. Tighten the mainshaft locknut to 116-174 ft.lb. using Adapter T83T-7025-A and Tool Shaft T77J-7025-C or equivalent.

30. Bend a tab on the lockwasher using Staking Tool T77J-7025-F or equivalent.

31. Install the speedometer drive gear with the lock ball onto the mainshaft and secure it with a snapring.

32. With the outer snapring in place on the main driveshaft front bearing, place bearing, shim 389117-2S, and Adapter Tool T75L-7025-N or equivalent over the input shaft.

33. Thread the Replacer Shaft T75L-7025-K or equal onto the Adapter Tool. Install the Replacer Tube T75L-7025-B or equal over the Replacer Shaft and install the nut and washer on the forcing screw.

34. Slowly tighten the nut until the adapter is secure on the input shaft. Make certain that all tools are aligned.

35. Tighten the nut on the forcing screw until the bearing outer snapring is seating against the housing. Remove the installation tools.

36. Install the input shaft snapring.

37. Install the speedometer driven gear assembly to the extension housing and attach with the bolt and lock plate.

38. Insert the shift control lever through the holes from the front side of the extension housing.

39. Install the control lever end to the control lever and tighten the attaching bolt (10mm) to 20-25 ft.lb.

40. Install the back-up lamp switch and neutral sensing switch to the extension housing and tighten the switches to 20-25 ft.lb.

contacting surface of the bearing housing and extension housing.

43. Install the extension housing to the bearing housing with the control lever and laid down to the left as far as it will go. Tighten the eight attaching bolts (12mm). Check to ensure that the control rod operates properly.

5-Speed Overdrive Gasoline Engines

DISASSEMBLY

1. Remove the nuts attaching the bell housing to the transmission case. Remove the bell housing gasket.
2. Remove the drain plug and drain lubricant from the transmission into a suitable container. Clean the metal filings from the magnet of the drain plug, if necessary. Install the drain plug.
3. (Optional) Position the Bench Mount Holding Fixture (T57L-500-B) or its equal to the studs on the right side of the transmission housing. Secure in place with the Bench Holding Fixture Adapter (T77J-7025-D) or its equal to prevent damage to the metric stud threads.
4. Place the transmission in neutral.
5. Remove the speedometer sleeve and driven gear assembly from the extension housing.
6. Remove the three bolts (14mm) and four nuts (14mm) attaching the extension housing to the transmission case. There are two longer outer bolts and one short center (bottom) bolt used.
7. Raise the control lever to the left and slide toward the rear of the transmission. Slide the extension housing off the mainshaft, being careful not to damage the oil seal.
8. Pull the control lever and rod out the front end of the extension housing.
9. If required, remove the back-up lamp switch from the extension housing.

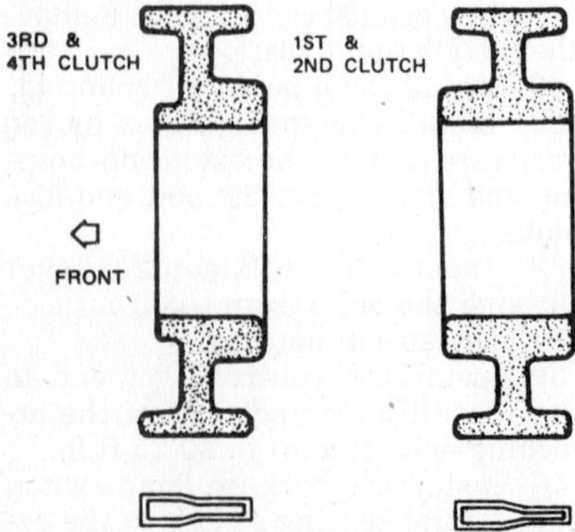

Clutch hub assembly direction

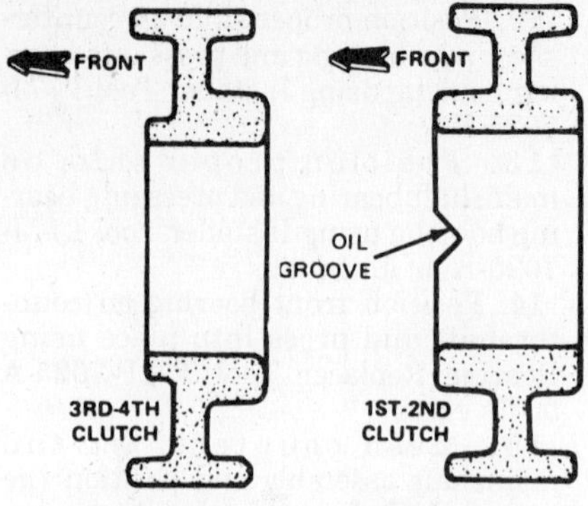

Clutch hub assembly direction

10. Remove the anti-spill seal from the mainshaft and discard. (A seal is not necessary for assembly.)
11. Remove the snapring that secures the speedometer drive gear to the mainshaft. Slide the drive gear off the mainshaft, and remove the lock ball.
12. Evenly loosen the fourteen 10mm bolts securing the transmission case cover to the transmission case. Remove the cover and gasket.
13. Mark the shift rails and forks to aid during transmission assembly. Remove the roll pins attaching the shift rod ends to the shift rod and remove the shift rod ends.
14. Gently pry the bearing housing away from the transmission case with a screwdriver, being careful not to damage the housing or case. Slide the bearing housing off the mainshaft.
15. Remove the snapring and washer retaining the mainshaft rear bearing to the mainshaft.
16. Assemble the Bearing Puller Ring Tool (T77J-7025-J), Bearing Puller Tool (T77J-7025-H), and Forcing Screw (T75L-7025-J) on the Remover and Replacer Tube Tool (T75L-7025-B) or their equal. Slide the tool assembly over the mainshaft and engage the puller jaws behind the rear bearing. Tighten the jaws evenly onto the bearing with a wrench, then turn the forcing screw to remove the mainshaft rear bearing.
17. Remove the snapring from the rear end of the countershaft. Assemble the Bearing Puller Tool (T77J-7025-H), Bearing Puller Ring (T77J-7025-J) and Forcing Screw (T75L-7025-J) onto the Remover Tube (T77J-7025-B) or their equal. Slide the tool assembly over the countershaft and engage the puller jaws behind the countershaft rear bearing. Tighten the jaws evenly onto the bearing with a wrench, then turn the forcing screw to remove the bearing.
18. Remove the counter fifth gear and spacer from the rear of the countershaft.
19. Tap the housing with a plastic hammer, if necessary, and remove center housing. Remove the reverse idler gear and two spacers with housing.
20. Remove the cap screw (12mm) from center housing and remove idler gear shaft.
21. Remove the three spring cap bolts. The two bolts on the case upper portion are 17mm and the bolt on the case side is 14mm. Remove the detent springs and the detent balls with a magnet from the transmission case.
22. Remove the four 10mm bolts attaching the blind covers to the transmission case and remove the blind covers and gaskets.
23. Remove the roll pin from the fifth/reverse shift fork. Slide the fifth/reverse shift fork shaft out of the transmission case.
24. Shift the transmission into fourth gear. This will provide adequate space to drive out the roll pin. With a small drift, drive the roll pin from third/fourth shift fork. Slide the third/fourth shift fork shaft out of the rear of the transmission case.
25. Remove the roll pin from the first/second shift fork. Slide the first/second shift fork shaft assembly out the rear of the transmission case. Remove both inter-lock pins.
26. Remove the snapring that secures the fifth gear to the mainshaft.
27. Remove the thrust washer and lock ball, fifth gear and synchronizer ring from the rear of the mainshaft.
28. Install the Synchronizer Ring Holder and Countershaft Spacer (T77J-7025-E) or its equal between the fourth-speed synchronizer ring and synchromesh gear on the mainshaft. Shift the transmission into second gear to lock the mainshaft and prevent the assembly from rotating.
29. Straighten the staked portion of the mainshaft bearing locknut with the Staking Tool (T77J-7025-F) or its equal. Using the Locknut Wrench (T77J-7025-C) or its equal remove the mainshaft bearing locknut.
30. Slide the reverse gear and clutch hub assembly off the mainshaft.
31. Remove the counter reverse gear from the countershaft.
32. If installed, remove the transmission from the holding fixture and set on a workbench.
33. Remove the bolts (12mm) attaching the mainshaft center bearing cover to the transmission and remove the bearing cover.
34. To remove the countershaft center bearing, install Puller T77J-7025-H, Puller Rings T77J-7025-J, Remover Tube T77J-7025-B, and Forcing Screw T75L-7025-J or their equal. Squarely insert the jaws of the puller behind the center bearing retainer ring in the two recessed areas of the case.

NOTE: The retainer ring may need to be turned to position the split in the retainer ring midway between the recessed areas before the puller is installed. This will reduce the possibility of the retainer ring becoming distorted as the bearing is removed.

35. Turn the forcing screw to remove the bearing.

36. To remove the mainshaft center bearing, install Puller T77J-7025-H, Puller Rings T77J-7025-J, Long Remover Tube T75L-7025-C and Forcing Screw T75L-7025-J or their equal. Squarely insert the jaws of the puller behind the rear mainshaft bearing retainer ring in the two recessed areas of the case.

37. Turn the forcing screw clockwise to remove the bearing.

38. Remove the shim and spacer from behind the mainshaft rear bearing along with the bearing.

39. Remove the front cover by first removing the four studs attaching the cover to case. Remove the studs by installing two nuts (10mm × 1.5) on the stud and drawing the stud out of the case. Remove the four 14mm bolts and remove the cover. Save the shim found on the inside of the cover.

40. Remove the snapring from the input shaft.

41. Remove the input shaft bearing by installing Puller T77J-7025-H, Puller Rings T77J-7025-J, Remover Tube T75L-7025-B, and Forcing Screw T75L-7025-J or their equal. Squarely insert the jaws of the puller behind the input shaft bearing retainer ring in the two recessed areas of the case.

NOTE: The retainer ring may need to be turned to position the split in the ring midway between the recessed areas before the puller is installed.

42. Turn the forcing screw clockwise to remove the bearing.

43. Rotate both shift forks so that the main gear train will fall to the bottom of the case. Remove the shift forks. Rotate the input shaft so that one of the two flats on the input shaft faces upward.

44. Remove the snapring from the front of the countershaft.

45. Remove Synchronizer Ring Holder T77J-7025-E or its equal from the front of the case and insert between the first gear on the countershaft and the rear of the case.

46. Install Forcing Screw T75L-7025-J, Press Frame T77J-7025-N, and Press Frame Adapter T82T-7003-BH or their equal against the countershaft assembly.

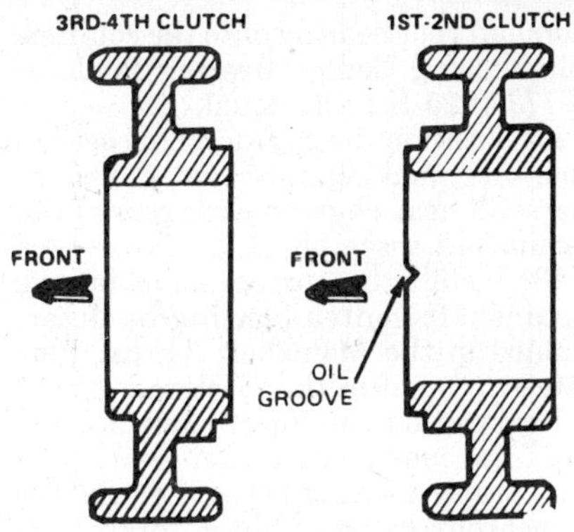

Synchronizer hub installation

47. Turn the forcing screw clockwise to press the countershaft rearward. Press the countershaft ($^3/_{16}$" movement) until it contacts the Synchronizer Ring Holder and Countershaft Spacer.

48. To remove the countershaft front bearing, first remove the press frame. Then, install Puller T77J-7025-H, Puller Rings T77J-7025-J, Remover Tube T77J-7025-B, and Forcing Screw T75L-7025-J or their equal. Squarely insert the jaws of the puller behind the front bearing retainer ring in the two recessed areas of the case.

NOTE: The retainer ring may need to be turned to position the split in the ring midway between the recessed areas before the puller is installed.

49. Turn the forcing screw clockwise to remove the bearing.

50. Remove the shim from behind the countershaft front bearing.

51. Remove the countershaft from the transmission case.

52. Remove the input shaft from the transmission case. Remove the synchronizer ring and caged bearing from the mainshaft.

53. Remove the mainshaft and gear assembly from the transmission case.

54. Remove the inner race of the countershaft center bearing from the countershaft in a press frame using Axle Bearing Seal Plate T75L-1165-B and Pinion Bearing Cone Remover D79L-4621-A or their equal.

55. Remove first gear and first/second synchronizer ring. Remove snapring retainer from mainshaft.

NOTE: Do not mix synchronizer rings.

56. Install Bearing Remover Tool T71P-4621-B or its equal between second and third gear.

57. Press the mainshaft out of third gear and third/fourth clutch hub sleeve.

58. Press the first/second clutch hub and sleeve assembly, and first gear sleeve from the mainshaft.

59. Clean and inspect the case, gears, bearings and shafts.

ASSEMBLY

NOTE: As each part is assembled, coat the part with manual transmission oil D8DZ-19C547-A (ESP-M2C83-C) or equivalent.

Before beginning the assembly procedure, three measurements must be performed: Mainshaft Thrust Play, Countershaft Thrust Play and Mainshaft Bearing Clearance.

Mainshaft Thrust Play

Check the mainshaft thrust play by measuring the depth of the mainshaft bearing bore in the transmission rear cage by using a depth micrometer (D80P-4201-A). Then measure the mainshaft rear bearing height. The difference between the two measurements indicates the required thickness of the adjusting shim. The standard thrust play is 0-0.0039". Adjusting shims are available in 0.0039" and 0.0118" sizes.

Countershaft Thrust Play

Check the countershaft thrust play by measuring the depth of the countershaft front bearing bore in the transmission case by using a depth micrometer (D80P-4201-A). Then measure the countershaft front bearing height. The difference between the two measurements indicates the required thickness of the adjusting shims. The standard thrust play is 0-0.0039". Adjusting shims are available in 0.0039" and 0.0118" sizes.

Mainshaft Bearing Clearance

Check the mainshaft bearing clearance by measuring the depth of the bearing bore in the clutch adapter plate with a depth micrometer, D80P-4201-A. Make sure the micrometer is on the second step of the plate. Measure the bearing height. The difference between the two measurements indicates the required adjusting shim thickness. The standard clearance is 0-0.0039". If an adjusting shim is required, select one to bring the clearance to within specifications.

1. Assemble the first/second synchromesh mechanism and the third/fourth synchromesh mechanism by installing the clutch hub to the sleeve. Place the three synchronizer keys into the clutch hub key slots and install the key springs to the clutch hub.

NOTE: When instaling the key springs, the open end tab of the springs should be inserted into hub holes with springs turned in the same direction. This will keep the spring tension on each key uniform.

2. Place the synchronizer ring on the second gear and position the second gear to the mainshaft with the synchronizer ring toward the rear of the shaft.

3. Slide the first/second clutch hub and sleeve assembly to the mainshaft with the oil grooves of the clutch hub toward the front of the mainshaft. Make sure that the three synchronizer keys in the synchromesh mechanism engage the notches in the second synchronizer ring.

4. Press into position using press and suitable replacer tool.

5. Insert the first gear sleeve on the mainshaft.

6. Place the synchronizer ring on the third gear along with the caged roller bearing and slide the third gear to the front of the mainshaft with the synchronizer ring toward the front.

7. Press the third/fourth clutch hub and sleeve assembly to the front of the mainshaft. Make sure that the three synchronizer keys in the synchromesh mechanism engage the notches in the synchronizer ring.

NOTE: Make sure the installed direction of the third/fourth clutch hub and sleeve assembly are correct.

8. Install the snapring to the front of the mainshaft.

9. Slide the needle bearing for the first gear to the mainshaft.

10. Place the synchronizer ring on the first gear. Slide the first gear onto the mainshaft with the synchronizer ring facing the front of the shaft. Rotate the first gear, as necessary, to engage the three notches in the synchronizer ring with the synchronizer keys.

11. Install the original thrust washer to the mainshaft.

12. Position the mainshaft and gear assembly in the case.

13. Position the first/second shift fork and third/fourth shift fork in the groove of the clutch hub and sleeve assembly.

14. Position the caged bearing in the front end of the mainshaft.

15. Place the synchronizer ring on the input shaft (fourth gear) and install the input shaft to the front end of the mainshaft. Make sure that the three synchronizer keys in the third/fourth synchromesh mechanism engage the notches in the synchronizer ring.

16. Press the inner race of the countershaft rear bearing onto the countershaft using Center Bearing Replacer T77J-7025-K or its equal.

17. Position the countershaft gear in the case, making sure that the countershaft gear engages each gear of the mainshaft assembly.

18. Install the correct shim on the mainshaft center bearing as determined in the Mainshaft Thrust Play Measurement in this Section.

19. Position the input shaft bearing and the mainshaft center bearing to the proper bearing bores. Be sure the synchronizer and shifter forks have not been moved out of position.

20. Install the Synchronizer Ring Holder Tool T77J-7025-E or its equal between the fourth synchronizer ring and the synchromesh gear on the mainshaft.

21. Install the Dummy Bearing Replacer T75L-7025-Q, Input Shaft Bearing Replacer T82T-7003-DH, Replacer Tube T77J-7025-M, and Press Frame T77J-7025-N or their equal on the case. Turn the forcing screw on the press frame until both bearings are properly seated.

22. Install the input shaft bearing ssnapring.

NOTE: Be sure that the synchronizer and shift forks are properly positioned during seating of bearings. After bearings are seated, make certain that both synchronizers operate freely.

23. Place the correct shim in the countershaft front bearing bore.

24. Position the countershaft front and center bearings in the bores and install the tools. Turn the forcing screw until the bearing is properly seated. Use the center bearing as a pilot.

25. Install the snapring to secure the countershaft front bearing.

26. Remove the synchronizer ring holder.

27. Install the bearing cover to the transmission case and tighten the four attaching bolts. Tighten to 41-59 ft.lb.

28. Install the reverse idler gear and shaft with a spacer on each side of shaft.

29. Slide the counter reverse gear (chamfer side forward) and spacer onto the countershaft.

30. Slide the thrust washer, reverse gear, caged roller bearings and clutch hub assembly onto the mainshaft. Install a new locknut (hand tight).

31. Shift into second gear and reverse gear to lock the rotation of the mainshaft. Tighten the locknut to 115 to 172 ft.lb. using the Locknut Wrench T77J-7025-C or its equal.

32. Stake the locknut into the mainshaft keyway using the staking tool.

33. Place the fourth/third clutch sleeve in third gear using Synchronizer Ring Holder and Countershaft Spacer T77J-7025-E.

34. If new synchronizers have been installed, check the clearance between the synchronizer key and the exposed edge of the synchronizer ring with a feeler gauge. If the measurement is greater than 0.079", the synchronizer key can pop out of position. To correct this, change the thrust washer (selective fit) between the mainshaft center bearing and the first gear. Available thrust washer sizes are 0.098", 0.118" and 0.138".

35. If new synchronizers were installed, check the clearance again with a feeler gauge. If the clearance is within specifications, bend the tab of the lockwasher.

36. Position the fifth synchronizer ring on the fifth gear. Slide the fifth gear onto the mainshaft with the synchronizer ring toward the front of the shaft. Rotate the fifth gear, as necessary, to engage the three notches in the synchronizer ring with the synchronizer keys in the reverse and clutch hub assembly.

37. Install the lock ball and thrust washer on the rear of the fifth gear.

38. Install the snapring on the rear of the thrust washer. Check the clearance between the thrust washer and the ssnapring. If the clearance is not within 0.0039-0.0118", select the proper size thrust washer to bring the clearance within specifications.

39. Slide the first/second shift fork shaft assembly into the case (front rear of case). Secure the first/second shift fork to the fork shaft with the roll pin.

NOTE: Be sure to use a new roll pin.

40. Insert the inter-lock pin into the transmission using the lockout pin replacer tool.

41. Shift transmission into fourth gear. Slide the third/fourth shift fork shaft into the case, from rear of case. Secure the third/fourth shift fork to the fork shaft with the roll pin. Insert inter-lock pin.

NOTE: Be sure to use a new roll pin.

42. Shift synchronizer hub into fifth gear. Position reverse and fifth fork on the clutch hub and slide the reverse/fifth fork shaft into the case (from rear of case). Secure the reverse/fifth shift fork to the fork shaft with the roll pin.

NOTE: Be sure to use a new roll pin.

43. Install the two blind covers and gaskets. Tighten the attaching bolts (10mm) to 23-34 ft.lb.
44. Position the three detent balls and three springs into the case and install the spring cap bolts (12mm and 17mm).
45. Apply a thin coat of Gasket Maker E2AZ-19562-A (ESE-M4G234-A2) or equivalent to the contacting surfaces of the center housing and transmission case.
46. Position the center housing on the case. Align the reverse idler gear shaft boss with the center housing attaching bolt boss. Install and tighten the idler shaft capscrew (12mm) and tighten to 41-59 ft.lb.
47. Slide the counter fifth gear to the countershaft.
48. Position the countershaft rear bearing on the countershaft. Press into position using the Adjustable Press Frame T77J-7025-N and Forcing Screw T75L-7025-J or their equal.
49. Install the thrust washer and snapring to the rear of the countershaft rear bearing. Check the clearance between the thrust washer and the snapring using a feeler gauge.
50. If the clearance is not within 0-0.0059", select the proper size thrust washer to bring the clearance within specifications, 0.0748", 0.0787", 0.0827", or 0.0866".
51. If installed, remove filler plugs. Position the mainshaft rear bearing on the mainshaft. Press into place using the Adjustable Press Frame T77J-7025-N, Dummy Bearing T75L-7025-Q1 and Forcing Screw T75L-7025-J or their equal.
52. Install the thrust washer and snapring to the rear of the mainshaft rear bearing. Check the clearance between the thrust washer and the snapring. The clearance should be 0-0.0039". If the clearance is not within specifications, replace the thrust washer to bring the clearance within specifications, 0.0787", 0.0846", or 0.0906".
53. Apply a thin coat of Gasket Maker E2AZ-19562-A (ESE-M4G234-A2) or equivalent to the contacting surfaces of the bearing housing and center housing.
54. Position the bearing housing on the center housing.
55. Install each shift fork shaft end onto the proper shift fork shaft. (Note the scribe marks made during disassembly) and secure with roll pins.
56. Install the lock ball, speedometer drive gear, and snapring onto the mainshaft.
57. If removed, install control lever and rod in extension housing.
58. Apply a thin coat of Gasket Maker E2AZ-19562-A (ESE-M4G234-A2) or equivalent to the contacting surfaces of the bearing housing and extension housing.
59. Position the extension housing in the bearing housing with the gearshift control lever end laid down to the left as far as it will go. Tighten the attaching bolts and nuts (14mm) to 60-80 ft.lb. There are two longer outer bolts and one shorter center (bottom) bolt used.
60. If removed, insert the speedometer driven gear assembly to the extension housing and secure it with the bolt.
61. Check to ensure the gearshift control lever operates properly.
62. Install the transmission case cover gasket and cover with drain plug to the rear. Install and tighten the fourteen 10mm attaching bolts to 23-34 ft.lb.
63. Install the correct size shim on the second step of the front cover as determined by the mainshaft bearing clearance measurement.
64. Coat the front cover with Gasket Maker E2AZ-19562-A (ESE-M4G234-A2) or equivalent. Install the front cover to the transmission case and tighten the four bolts and four studs.
65. Install 3.0 pints of Ford Manual Transmission Lube D8DZ-19C547-A (ESP-M2C83-C) or equivalent. Re-install the filler plugs and tighten to 18-29 ft.lb.

5-Speed Overdrive Diesel Engines

DISASSEMBLY

1. If not already drained, remove the drain plug and drain the transmission fluid into a suitable container. Remove the fork and release bearing from the transmission case.
2. Install the transmission in Bench Mounted Holding Fixture, T57L-500-B or its equal. Remove the six bolts (12mm) attaching the front cover to the transmission case and remove the front cover, shim (located in cover) and gasket.
3. Remove the front cover oil seal using Inner Seal Removal Tool, T75P-3504-G and Impact Slide Hammer, T50T-100-A or their equal.
4. Remove the input shaft snapring.
5. If installed, remove the gearshift lever. Remove the four bolts (12mm) and remove the retainer and gasket from the extension housing.
6. Remove the outer retaining ring on the input shaft bearing. Install Bearing Collet Tool, T75L-7025-E on the input shaft bearing, and Remover Tube, T75L-7025-B and Forcing Screw T75L-7025-J or their equal. Slide Bearing Collet Sleeve, T75L-7025-G or its equal over the Remover Tube and Bearing Collet, and turn the forcing screw to remove the input shaft bearing.
7. Remove the bolt (12mm) that attaches the control lever end to the control rod and remove the control lever end and rod from the extension housing.
8. Remove the eight (12mm) bolts attaching the extension housing to the intermediate housing and transmission housing. Slide the extension housing off the output shaft with the control lever end laid down and to the left as far as it will go.
9. Remove the speedometer driven gear assembly from the extension housing.
10. Remove the back-up lamp switch and the neutral safety switch.
11. Remove the grommet from the end of the output shaft. Remove the snapring that secures the speedometer drive gear on the output shaft. Slide the speedometer drive gear off the output shaft and remove the lock ball.
12. Install Bearing Pusher Tool, T83T-7111-A or its equal over the countershaft front bearing. Turn the forcing screw to force the countershaft (together with the countershaft front bearing) from the transmission case. Remove the pusher tool assembly.

NOTE: The countershaft front bearing may remain in the transmission case. Remove the bearing with a suitable driver.

13. Remove and discard the roll pin from the 1-2 shift fork. Remove the cir-clip from the rail. Remove the upper cap bolt and with a magnet, remove the spring and detent ball from the bore. Remove the 1-2 shift rail and 1-2 shift fork. Note the position of the 1-2 shift fork in relation to the 3-4 shift fork for positioning during reassembly. The shift forks and rails are not interchangeable. Also note the position of the shift rail and the relationship of the detent slots to the bore for positioning during reassembly. The three detent slots in the shift rails face towards the cap bolts.
14. Remove the roll pin from the 3-4 shift fork. Remove the circlip from the rail. Remove the middle cap bolt and with a magnet, remove the spring and detent ball from the bore. Remove the 3-4 shift fork and rail. An interlock pin will drop out of the bore when the 3-4 shift rail is removed. Note the position of the shift rail and the relationship of the detent slots to the bore for positioning during reassembly.
15. Remove the circlip and washer from the 5-R (Reverse) shift rail. Remove the bottom cap bolt and with a magnet, remove the shorter length spring and detent ball.

16. Drive the roll pin from the 5-R shift lever and remove the lever from the rail. With a magnet remove the other detent ball and shorter length spring from the bottom (5-R) bore.

17. Gently pry the intermediate housing away from the bearing housing. Remove the gear and bearing assembly out of the intermediate housing.

18. Install the gear train and bearing housing assembly in a fabricated holding tool positioned in a vise. A soft-jawed vise may be used in place of the holding tool.

19. Remove the bottom cap bolt and with a magnet, remove the shorter length spring and detent ball from the bore. Drive the roll pin out of the 5-R shift fork and discard. Remove the 5-R shift rail. An inter-lock pin will drop out of the bore when the 5-R shift rail is removed. Note the position of the 5-R shift fork in relation to the bearing housing for positioning during reassembly. Also note the position of the shift rail and the relationship of the detent slots to the bore for positioning during reassembly. The three detent slots in the shift rail face towards the cap bolt.

20. Remove the retaining ring from the output shaft ball bearing. Remove the thrust washer.

21. To remove the output shaft rear bearing, place Shaft Protectors, D80L-625-2 and D80L-625-3 or their equal on the end of the output shaft. It may be necessary to hold the shaft protectors in place with putty. Install Puller, T77J-7025-H, Collet (2), T77J-7025-J or their equal against the bearing so the jaws of the puller are against the rear of the bearing. Place Tube (Long), T75L-7025-C or its equal over the output shaft. Install Forcing Screw, T75L-7025-J or its equal into the tube and turn the forcing screw clockwise to remove the bearing. Discard the bearing and install a new one during reassembly.

22. Remove the snapring from the countershaft rear bearing. Install Puller, T77J-7025-H, Collet (2), T77J-7025-J, Tube (Short, T77J-7025-B) and Forcing Screw, T75L-7025-J or their equal. Turn the forcing screw clockwise and remove the bearing. Discard the bearing and install a new one during reassembly.

23. Remove the retaining ring, thrust washer and lock ball from the output shaft.

24. Remove the fifth gear and sleeve from the countershaft.

NOTE: The collar of the fifth gear faces towards the bearing housing.

25. Remove the reverse gear from the countershaft.

NOTE: The collar of the counter-reverse gear faces towards the bearing housing.

26. Remove the fifth gear from the output shaft and remove the 5-R synchronizer ring.

27. Straighten the peen on the locknut with Staking Tool, T77J-7025-F or its equal. Lock the transmission gears in Reverse and any forward gear. Install Lock Nut Wrench T77J-7025-C or its equal on the locknut and remove the locknut and discard.

28. Remove the 5-R synchronizer assembly from the output shaft.

29. Pry the reverse gear, caged needle bearing, sleeve and thrust washer from the output shaft.

30. Remove the snapring and remove the reverse idler gear from the idler shaft. Remove the keyed thrust washer from the shaft.

31. Remove the five (12mm) bolts that attach the bearing cover to the bearing housing and remove the cover.

32. If required, remove the bolt retaining the idler shaft to the bearing housing and drive the plate and shaft assembly out of the housing.

33. With a soft hammer, tap the rear end of the output shaft and countershaft in turn, being careful not to damage the shafts. Remove the shafts from the bearing housing.

34. Carefully separate the input shaft, caged needle bearing and synchronizer ring from the output shaft.

35. Press the rear countershaft bearing from the bearing housing using Remover Tube Tool, T77J-7025-B or its equal.

36. Press the rear output shaft bearing from the bearing housing using Bearing Remover Tool, T77F-4222-A and Remover Tube Tool, T77J-7025-B or their equal.

37. Remove the thrust washer, first gear, sleeve and synchronizer ring from the rear of the output shaft.

38. Using snapring pliers, remove the snapring from the front of the output shaft.

39. Using a press and Remover Tool, T71P-4621-B or its equal, remove the third/fourth hub, sleeve, synchronizer ring and third gear from the front of the output shaft.

40. Using a press and Remover Tool, T71P-4621-B or its equal, remove the first/second hub and sleeve assembly synchronizer ring, and second gear from the rear of the output shaft in the same manner as described in the previous step.

41. Press the front bearing from the countershaft using Remover Tool D79L-4621-A or T71P-4621-B and suitable press stock.

42. Inspect all parts.

ASSEMBLY

1. Assemble the 3-4 synchronizer assembly by installing the keys in the hub and sliding the sleeve over the hub and keys. Install the springs onto the hub.

NOTE: When installing the springs, the open end tab of the springs should be inserted into the hub holes. This will keep the spring tension on each key uniform.

2. Assemble the 1-2 synchronizer assembly in the same manner as described in Step 1. Assemble the 5-R synchronizer assembly as also described in Step 1 and install the retaining ring in the 5-R assembly.

3. Install the third gear and synchronizer ring onto the front section of the output shaft.

4. Install the 3-4 synchronizer assembly onto the output shaft by using a press. Hold the assembly together and slowly press in place. Make sure the three recesses in the synchronizer ring are aligned with the three keys in the synchronizer hub.

NOTE: The direction of the hub is as shown. The recesses in each synchronizer sleeve must face each other.

5. Fit the snapring on the output shaft.

6. Install the second gear, synchronizer ring onto the rear section of the output shaft.

7. Install the 1-2 synchronizer assembly onto the output shaft by using a press. Hold the assembly together and slowly press in place. Make sure the three keys recesses in the synchronizer ring are aligned with the three keys in the synchronizer hub.

NOTE: The direction of the hub is as shown. The recesses in the synchronizer sleeve must face each other.

8. Install the synchronizer ring, first gear with sleeve, and thrust washer onto the output shaft.

9. Install the input shaft and the needle roller bearing to the output shaft.

10. Check the countershaft rear bearing clearance. Measure the depth of the countershaft bearing bore in the bearing housing with a depth micrometer (D80P-4201-A or equivalent). Install the retaining ring on the bearing and with a depth micrometer measure the distance between the inside edge of the ring and the end of the bearing. The difference between the two measurements indicates the required thickness of the adjusting shim. The clearance should be less than 0.0039″.

The adjusting shims are available in 0.0039" and 0.0118" sizes.

11. Check the output shaft bearing clearance. Measure the depth of the bearing bore with a depth micrometer. Measure the width of the bearing with a micrometer. The difference between the two measurements indicates the required thickness of the adjusting shim. The clearance should be less than 0.0039". Adjusting shims are available in 0.0039" and 0.0118" sizes.

12. Position the proper shim on the countershaft rear bearing and press into the bearing housing using Installer Tool, T77J-7025-B or its equal.

13. Position the proper shim on the output shaft bearing and press the bearing into the bearing housing using Installer Tool, T77J-7025-K or its equal.

14. Position the front bearing on the countershaft and press the bearing into place using Bearing Replacer Tool, T71P-7025-A or its equal.

15. Mesh the countershaft and the output shaft assembly and position the two in the bearing housing. Make sure that the thrust washer is installed on the mainshaft assembly at the rear of the first gear. Make sure the three recesses in the synchronizer ring are aligned with the three keys in the synchronizer hub.

16. While holding the mainshaft assembly in place, press the countershaft assembly into the bearing housing using Replacer Tool T71P-7025-A or its equal to hold the rear countershaft bearing in the housing.

17. Position the bearing cover on the bearing housing. Install the five (12mm) bolts and tighten.

18. If removed, drive the reverse idler shaft into the bearing housing. Install the bolt and tighten.

19. Install the thrust washer, sleeve, caged needle bearing and reverse gear on the output shaft.

20. Install the reverse gear on the countershaft. The offset on the gear must face the bearing housing.

21. Place the keyed thrust washer so the tab is in the groove in the bearing housing. Install the reverse idler gear so the squared portion of the gear faces the bearing housing. Make sure the reverse idler gear and reverse gear are in mesh. Install the spacer and snapring on the idler shaft.

22. Install the 5-R synchronizer assembly on the output shaft.

23. Lock the transmission in Reverse and any forward gear. Install a new locknut on the output shaft and tighten to 94-152 fft.lb. using Locknut Wrench, T77J-7025-C or its equal.

24. Bend the tab on the locknut with Staking Tool, T77J-7025-F or its equal.

25. Install the 5-R synchronizer ring and gear on the output shaft. Make sure the three recesses in the synchronizer ring are aligned with the three keys in the synchronizer hub.

26. Install the sleeve and the counter-fifth gear on the countershaft.

27. Install the lock ball in the output shaft and position the thrust washer so the slot in the washer is over the lock ball. Install the retaining ring.

28. Position the output shaft assembly in a press and press the output shaft bearing on the shaft using Dummy Bearing Replacer, T75L-7025-Q or its equal and an appropriate length of press stock. Install the thrust washer and retaining ring.

29. Position the countershaft in a press and press the countershaft rear bearing on the shaft using Dummy Bearing Replacer, T75L-7025-Q or its equal and an appropriate length of press stock. Install the thrust washer and retaining ring.

30. Position all synchronizers in the neutral position. Install the shorter length spring and detent ball in the bottom (5-R) bore. Compress the ball and spring with Dummy Shift Rail Tools, T72J-7280 or its equal and install the dummy shift rail in the bore. Install the 5-R shift rail in the bottom bore and make sure the three detent slots in the rail face the cap bolt and the interlock slot in the 5-R rail faces towards the 1-2 bore. Install the interlock pin through the top bore so it is positioned in the channel between the 5-R rail bore and 3-4 rail bore. Install the 3-4 rail in the housing and make sure the three detent slots in the rail face the middle bore. Insert the interlock pin in the channel the 3-4 rail and the 1-2 rail bore. Install the 1-2 shift rail in the housing so the three detent slots in the rail face the top bore.

NOTE: The interlock pins are identical and all four detent balls are identical. The springs for the 5-R or bottom bore are of a shorter length than the other two springs.

31. Install the first/second shift fork and the third/fourth shift forks to their respective sleeves.

32. Align the roll pin holes of each shift fork and rod. Install new roll pins.

NOTE: When installing the shift fork and control end, a new roll pin should be installed with a pin slit positioned in the direction of the shift rod axis. If not removed, remove the shift levers from the shift rails. Remember from which rail each lever was removed for correct installation upon assembly.

33. Install the detent balls and springs into their respective bores and install the three cap bolts.

NOTE: The shorter length spring is installed in the bottom (reverse) bore.

34. Install the circlips on the 1-2 and 3-4 shift rails. Install the circlip and washer on the 5-R shift rail.

35. Apply a thin coating of Silicone Sealer, D6AZ-19562-B or equivalent to the mating surfaces of the transmission case and the bearing housing. Install the transmission case on the bearing housing.

36. Apply a thin coating of Silicone Sealer, D6AZ-19562-B or equivalent to the mating surfaces of the bearing housing and intermediate housing. Install the intermediate housing to the bearing housing.

37. Position the shift lever gates on the appropriate shift rails. Install new roll pins.

38. Place the lock ball in the output shaft and position the speedometer drive gear over the ball. Install the snapring. Install the grommet on the end of the output shaft.

39. Apply a thin coating of Silicone sealer, D6AZ-19562-B or equivalent to the extension housing and the intermediate housing. Slide the extension housing over the output shaft (the control lever must be moved to the far left) and onto the extension housing. Install the bolts and tighten.

NOTE: If necessary, remove the plugs from the transmission case shift rod bores to align the shift rods. After the installation of the bearing housing assembly, reinstall the plugs using Silicone Sealer, D6AZ-19562-B or equivalent.

40. With the outer snapring in place on the input shaft front bearing, place the bearing, shim and Adapter Tool, T75L-7025-N or its equal over the input shaft.

41. Thread the Replacer Shaft, T75L-7025-K or its equal onto the Adapter Tool. Install the Replacer Tube, T75L-7025-B or its equal over the Replacer Shaft and install the nut and washer on the forcing screw.

42. Slowly tighten the nut until the adapter is securely on the input shaft. Make sure the tools are aligned.

43. Tighten the nut on the forcing screw until the bearing outer snapring is seated. Remove the installation tools.

NOTE: The input shaft bearing retaining ring must be flush with the transmission case. If not flush, it will be necessary to tap on the end of the input shaft with

a soft hammer until the bearing is seated.

44. Install the input shaft snapring.
45. Measure the distance between the end of the installed input bearing in the transmission case with a depth micrometer. Measure the distance between the bearing cover gasket and the bottom of the bearing bore in the cover. The difference between the two measurements is the clearance between the outer bearing race and the front cover. The clearance should be less than 0.0039″. Clearance can be adjusted by installing an adjusting shim. Shims are available in sizes of 0.006″ and 0.012″.
46. Install a new oil seal in the front cover using Installer Tool, T71P-7050-A. Install the shim in the recess in the front cover.
47. Apply gear lubricant to the lip of the oil seal inside the front cover and install the front cover to the transmission case. Install the six (12mm) bolts and tighten.
48. Install the control lever end to the control lever and tighten the attaching bolt (10mm) to 20-25 ft.lb.
49. Install the back-up lamp switch and the neutral safety switch to the extension housing and tighten the switches to 20-25 ft.lb.
50. Install the gearshift lever retainer and gasket to the extension housing. Install the four (12mm) bolts and tighten to 20-27 ft.lb. If required, install the gearshift lever.
51. Install the release bearing and fork.

TRANSFER CASE OVERHAUL

Warner Model 1350

The Warner Model 1350 is a three-piece aluminum part time transfer case. It transfers power from the transmission to the rear axle and when actuated, also to the front drive axle. The unit is lubricated by a positive displacement oil pump that channels oil flow through drilled holes in the rear output shaft. The pump turns with the rear output shaft and allows towing of the vehicle at maximum legal road speeds for extended distances without disconnecting the front and/or rear driveshaft.

Shift Lever

REMOVAL

NOTE: Remove the shift ball only if the shift ball, boot or lever is to be replaced. If the ball, boot or lever is not being replaced, remove the ball, boot and lever as an assembly.

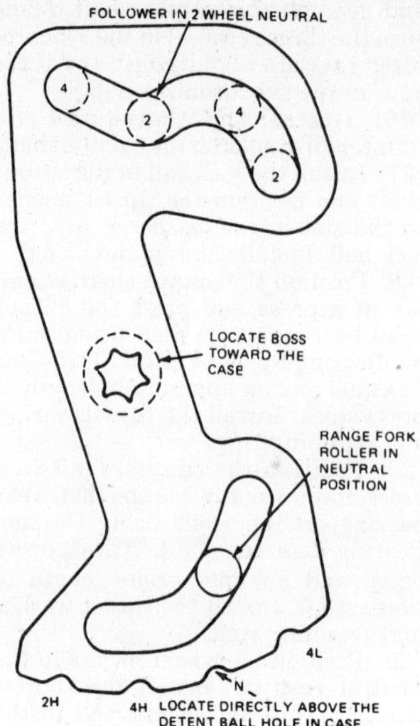

Connect shift cam engagement

1. Remove the plastic insert from the shift ball. Warm the ball with a heat gun to 140°-180°F and knock the ball off the lever with a block of wood and a hammer. Be careful not to damage the finish on the shift lever.
2. Remove the rubber boot and floor pan cover.
3. Disconnect the vent hose from the control lever.
4. Unscrew the shift lever from the control lever.
5. Remove the bolts retaining the shifter to the extension housing. Remove the control lever and bushings.

DISASSEMBLY

1. Remove the transfer case from the vehicle.
2. Remove the transfer case drain plug with a 3/8″ drive ratchet and drain the fluid.
3. Remove the four-wheel drive indicator switch and the breather vent.
4. Remove the rear output shaft yoke by removing the 30mm nut, steel washer and rubber seal from the output shaft.
5. Remove the nine 15mm bolts which retain the front case to the rear cover. Insert a 1/2″ drive breaker bar between the three pry bosses and separate the front case from the rear cover. Remove all traces of RTV gasket sealant from the mating surfaces of the front case and rear cover. When removing the RTV sealant, take care not to damage the mating surfaces of the aluminum case.
6. If the speedometer drive gear or ball bearing assembly is to be replaced, first, drive out the output shaft oil seal from either the inside of the rear cover with a brass drift and hammer or from the outside by bending and pulling on the curved-up lip of the oil seal. Remove and discard the oil seal. Remove the speedometer drive gear assembly (gear, clip and spacer). Note that the round end of the speedometer gear clip faces the inside of the rear cover.
7. Remove the internal snapring that retains the rear output shaft ball bearing in the bore. From the outside of the case, drive out the ball bearing with Output Shaft Bearing Replacer, T83T-7025-B and Drive Handle, T80T-4000-W or equivalent.
8. If required, remove the front output shaft caged needle bearing from the rear cover with Puller Collet, D80L-100-S and Impact Slide Hammer, T50T-100-A or equivalent.
9. Remove the 2W-4W shift fork spring from the boss in the rear cover.
10. Remove the shift collar hub from the output shaft. Remove the 2W-4W lock-up assembly and the 2W-4W shift fork together as an assembly. Remove the 2W-4W fork from the 2W-4W lock-up assembly. If required, remove the external clip and remove the roller bushing assembly (bushing, shaft and external clip) from the 2W-4W shift fork.
11. If required to disassemble the 2W-4W lock-up assembly, remove the internal snapring and pull the lock-up hub and spring from the lock-up collar.
12. Remove the external snapring and thrust washer that retains the driven sprocket to the front output shaft.
13. Remove the chain, driven sprocket and drive sprocket as an assembly.
14. Remove the collector magnet from the notch in the front case bottom.
15. Remove the output shaft and oil pump as an assembly.
16. If required to disassemble the oil pump, remove the four 8mm bolts from the body. Note the position and markings of the front cover, body, pins, spring, rear cover, and pump retainer as removed.
17. Pull out the shift rail.
18. Slip the high-low range shift fork out of the inside track of the shift cam. If required, remove the external clip and remove the roller bushing assembly (bushing, shaft and external clip) from the high-low range shift fork.
19. Remove the high-low shift hub from out of the planetary gearset in the front case.
20. Push and pull out the anchor end

of the torsion spring from the locking post in the front case half. Remove the torsion spring and roller out of the shift cam (if so equipped).

21. Turn the front case over and remove the six 15mm bolts retaining the mounting adapter to the front case. Remove the mounting adapter, input shaft and planetary gearset as an assembly.

22. If required, remove the ring gear from the front case using a press. Note the relationship of the serrations to the chamfered pilot diameter during removal.

23. Expand the tangs of the large snapring in the mounting adapter and pry under the planetary gearset and separate the input shaft and planetary gearset from the mounting adapter.

24. If required, remove the oil from the mounting adapter with Seal Remover, Tool-1175-AC and Impact Slide Hammer, T50T-100-A or equivalent.

25. Remove the internal snapring from the planetary carrier and separate the planetary gearset from the input shaft assembly.

26. Remove the external snapring from the input shaft. Place the input shaft assembly in a press and remove the ball bearing from the input shaft using Bearing Splitter, D79L-4621-A or equivalent. Remove the thrust washer, thrust plate and sun gear off the input shaft.

27. Move the shift lever by hand until the shift cam is in the FOUR WHEEL HIGH detent position (4WH) and mark a line on the outside of the front case using the side of the shift lever and a grease pencil.

28. Remove the two phillips head set screws from the front case and from the shift cam.

29. Turn the front case over and remove the external clip. Pry the shift lever out of the front case and shift cam. Do not pound on the external clip during removal.

NOTE: Removal of four-wheel drive indicator switch will ease removal of the shift lever and shift cam assembly.

30. Remove the O-ring from the second groove in the shift lever shaft.

31. Remove the detent plunger and compression spring from the inside of the front case.

32. Remove the internal snapring and remove the ball bearing retainer from the front case by tapping on the face of the front output shaft and U-joint assembly with a plastic hammer. Remove the internal snapring and drive the ball bearing out of the bearing retainer using Output Shaft Bearing Replacer, T83T-7025-B and Driver Handle, T80T-4000-W or equivalent.

NOTE: The clip is required to prevent the bearing retainer from rotating. Do not discard the clip.

33. Remove the front output shaft and U-joint assembly from the front case. If required, remove the oil seal with Seal Remover, Tool-1175-AC and Impact Slide Hammer, T50T-100-A or equivalent. If required, remove the internal snapring and drive the ball bearing out of the front case bore using Output Shaft Replacer, T83T-7025-B and Driver Handle, T80T-4000-W or equivalent.

34. If required, place the front output shaft and U-joint assembly in a vise, being careful not to damage the assembly. Use copper or wood vise jaws.

35. Remove the internal snaprings that retain the bearings in the shaft.

36. Position the U-Joint Tool, T74P-4635-C or equivalent, over the shaft ears and press the bearing out. If the bearing cannot be pressed all the way out, remove it with vise grip or channel lock pliers.

37. Re-position the U-joint tool on the spider in order to remove the opposite bearing.

38. Repeat the above procedure until all bearings are removed.

ASSEMBLY

Before assembly, lubricate all parts with Dexron®II, Automatic Transmission Fluid.

1. If removed, start a new bearing into an end of the shaft ear. Support the output shaft in a vise equipped with copper or wood jaws, in order not to damage the shaft.

2. Position the spider into the bearing and press the bearing below the snapring groove using U-joint Tool, T74P-4635-C or equivalent.

3. Remove the tool and install a new internal snapring on the groove.

4. Start a new bearing into the opposite side of the shaft ear and using the tool, press the bearing until the opposite bearing contacts the snapring.

5. Remove the tool and install a new internal snapring in the groove.

6. Re-position the front output shaft assembly and install the other two bearings in the same manner.

7. Check the U-joint for freedom of movement. If a binding condition occurs due to misalignment during the installation procedure, tap the ears of both shafts sharply to relieve the bind. Do not install the front output shaft assembly if the U-joint shows any sign of binding.

8. If removed, drive the ball bearing into the front output case bore using Output Shaft Bearing Replacer, T83T-7025-B and Drive Handle, T80T-4000-W or equivalent. Drive the ball bearing in straight, making sure that it is not cocked in the bore. Install the internal snapring that retains the ball bearing to the front case.

9. If removed, install the front output oil seal in the front case bore using Output Shaft Seal Installer, T83T-7065-B and Driver Handle, T80T-4000-W or equivalent.

10. If removed, install the ring gear in the front case. Align the serrations on the outside diameter of the ring gear to the serrations previously cut in the front case bore. Using a press, start the piloted chamferred end of the ring gear first and press in until it is fully seated. Make sure the ring gear is not cocked in the bore.

11. If removed, install the ball bearing in the bearing retainer bore. Drive the bearing into the retainer using Output Shaft Bearing Replacer, T83T-7025-B and Driver Handle, T80T-4000-W or equivalent. Make sure the ball bearing is not cocked in the bore. Install the internal snapring that retains the ball bearing to the retainer.

12. Install the front output shaft and U-joint assembly through the front case seal. Position the ball bearing and retainer assembly over the front output shaft and install in the front case bore. Make sure the clip on the bearing retainer aligns with the slot in the front case. Tap the bearing retainer into place with a plastic hammer. Install the internal snapring that retains the ball bearing and retainer assembly to the front case.

13. Install the compression spring and the detent plunger into the bore from the inside of the front case.

14. Install a new O-ring in the second groove of the shift lever shaft. Coat the shaft and O-ring with Multi-Purpose Long-Life Lubricant.

NOTE: Use a rubber band to fill the first groove so as not to cut the O-ring. Discard the rubber band.

15. Position the shift cam inside the front case with the 4WH detent position over the detent plunger. Holding the shift cam by hand, push the shift lever shaft into the front case to engage the shift cam aligning the side of the shift lever with the mark previously scribed on the front case. Install the external clip on the end of the shift lever shaft.

16. Install the two phillips head set screws in the front case and in the shift cam. Tighten the screws to 5-7 ft.lb. Make sure the set screw in the

front case is in the first groove of the shift lever shaft and not bottomed against the shaft itself. The shift lever should be able to move freely to all detent positions.

17. Slide the sun gear, thrust plate, thrust washer, and press the ball bearing over the input shaft. Install the external ssnapring to the input shaft.

NOTE: The sun gear recessed face and ball bearing snapring groove should be toward the rear of the transfer case. The stepped face of the thrust washer should face towards the ball bearing.

18. Install the planetary gear set to the sun gear and input shaft assembly. Install the internal snapring to the planetary carrier.

19. Drive the oil seal into the bore of the mounting adapter with Input Shaft Seal Installer, T83T-7065-A and Driver Handle, T80T-4000-W or equivalent.

20. Place the tanged snapring in the mounting adapter groove. Position the input shaft and planetary gearset in the mounting adapter and push inward until the planetary assembly and input shaft assembly are seated in the adapter. When properly seated, the tanged snapring will snap into place. Check installation by holding the mounting adapter by hand and tapping the face of the input shaft against a wooden block to ensure that the snapring is engaged.

21. Remove all traces of RTV gasket sealant from the mating surfaces of the front case and mounting adapter. Install a bead of RTV gasket sealant on the surface of the front case.

22. Position the mounting adapter on the front case. Install six bolts and tighten to 23-30 ft.lb.

23. Position the roller on the 90° bent tang of the torsion spring. The larger diameter end of the spring must be installed first.

24. Install the roller into the torsion spring roller track of the shift cam while locating the center of the spring in the pivot groove in the front case. Push the anchor end of the torsion spring behind the locking post adjacent to the ring gear face.

25. Position the High-Low shift hub into the planetary gearset. Slip the High-Low shift fork bushing into the High-Low roller track of the shift cam and the groove of the High-Low shift hub.

NOTE: Make sure the nylon wear pads are installed on the shift fork. Make sure the dot on the pad is installed in the fork hole.

26. Install the shift rail through the high-low fork and make sure the shift rail is seated in the bore in the front case.

27. Place the oil pump cover with the word TOP facing the front of the front case. Install the two pump pins (flats facing upwards) with the spring between the pins and place the assembly in the oil pump bore in the output shaft. Place the oil pump body and pickup tube over the shaft and make sure the pins are riding against the inside of the pump body. Place the oil pump rear cover with the words **TOP REAR** facing the rear of the front case. The word **TOP** on the front cover and the rear cover should be on the same side. Install the pump retainer, the four bolts and rotate the output shaft while tightening the bolts to prevent the pump from binding. Tighten the bolts to 36-40 in.lb.

NOTE: The output shaft must turn freely within the oil pump. If binding occurs, loosen the four bolts and retighten again.

28. Install the output shaft and oil pump assembly in the input shaft. Make sure the external splines of the output shaft engage the internal splines of the high-low shift hub. Make sure the oil pump retainer and oil filter leg are in the groove and notch of the front case.

29. Install the collector magnet in the notch in the front case.

30. Install the chain, drive sprocket and driven sprocket as an assembly over the shafts. Install the thrust washer on the front output shaft and install the external snapring over the thrust washer to retain the driven sprocket.

31. If disassembled, assemble the 2W-4W lockup assembly. Install the spring in the lockup collar. Place the lockup hub over the spring and engage the lockup hub in the notches in the lockup collar. Retain the lockup hub to the lockup collar with an internal snapring.

32. Install the 2W-4W shift fork to the 2W-4W lockup assembly. If removed, make sure the nylon wear pads are installed on the fork. The dot on the pad must be installed in the hole in the fork. Install the 2W-4W lockup collar and hub assembly over the output shaft and onto the shift rail. If removed, install the shaft, bushing and external clip to the 2W-4W lockup fork.

34. If removed, drive the caged needle bearing into the rear cover bore with Needle Bearing Replacer, T83T-7127-A and Driver Handle, T80T-4000-W or equivalent.

35. If removed, install the ball bearing in the rear cover bore. Drive the bearing into the rear cover bore with Output Shaft Bearing Replacer, T83T-7025-B and Driver Handle, T80-4000-W or equivalent. Make sure the ball bearing is not cocked in the bore. Install the internal snapring that retains the ball bearing to the rear cover.

36. Install the speedometer drive gear assembly into the rear cover bore with the round end of the speedometer gear clip facing towards the inside of the rear cover. Drive the oil seal into the rear cover bore with Output Shaft Seal Installer, T83T-7065-B and Driver Handle, T80T-4000-W or equivalent.

37. Install the 2W-4W shift fork spring on the inside boss of the rear cover.

38. Prior to final assembly of rear cover to front case half, the transfer case shift lever assembly should be shifted into the "4H" detent position to assure positioning of the shift rail to the rear cover.

39. Coat the mating surface of the front case with a bead of Silicone Rubber.

40. Position the rear cover on the front case, making sure that the 2W-4W shift fork spring engages the shift rail and does not fall off the rear cover boss. Install the nine bolts (starting with the bolts on the rear cover) and tighten to 23-30 ft.lb.

NOTE: If the rear cover assembly does not seat properly, move the rear cover up and down slightly to permit the end of the shift rail to enter the shift rail hole in the rear cover boss.

41. Install the rear yoke on the output shaft. Install the rubber seal, washer and nut. Tighten the nut to 120-150 ft.lb.

42. Install the four-wheel drive indicator switch and tighten to 25-35 ft.lb.

43. Install the breather plug and tighten to 6-14 ft.lb.

44. Install the drain plug and tighten to 14-22 ft.lb.

45. Place a 3/8" drive ratchet in the fill plug and remove the plug. Fill the transfer case with 3.0 U.S. pints of Dexron®II. Install the fill plug and tighten to fill and drain plugs to 14-22 ft.lb.

46. Reinstall the transfer case.

Full-Sized Pick-Ups, Vans & Bronco

INDEX

TUNE-UP SPECIFICATIONS
1980

For 1980 Tune-Up Specifications consult the Vehicle Emissions Control Label, which is located on the engine of the vehicle. This decal will contain a calibration number which when used in conjunction with the chart below will yield the required tune-up information. If the information given in this chart disagrees with the information on the decal, use the information on the decal.

			Fast Idle RPM		Curb Idle rpm		Tsp Off rpm	
Calibration	Spark Plug Gap	Ignition Timing	High Cam	Kick Down	A/C ① Off/On	Non A/C	A/C	Non A/C
9-87G-R0	.042–.046	8°BTDC	2700	—	—	600	—	—
9-97J-R0	.042–.046	8°BTDC	—	1600	650	—	—	—
9-97J-R11	.042–.046	8°BTDC	—	1600	650	—	—	—

① Only for A/C-TSP equipped, A/C compressor electromagnetic clutch deenergized.

TUNE-UP SPECIFICATIONS
1981

For 1981–87 Tune-Up Specifications consult the Vehicle Emissions Control Label, which is located on the engine of the vehicle. This decal will contain a calibration number which when used in conjunction with the chart below will yield the required tune-up information. If the information given in this chart disagrees with the information on the decal, use the information on the decal.

					Fast idle rpm		Curb idle rpm		
Calibration Number	Engine	Spark Plug Gap	Ignition Timing °BTDC	Timing RPM	High CAM	Kick Down	A/C On	A/C off	Non A/C
1-57G-R1	4.1L	.042–.046	4	800	2200	—	—	—	750
1-57G-R10	4.1L	.042–.046	4	800	2050	—	—	—	700
1-58-R0	4.1L	.042–.046	10	800	2000	—	—	—	575
1-51D-R0	4.9L	.042–.046	6	800	—	1400	700	600	600
1-51D-R10	4.9L	.042–.046	6	800	—	1250	650	550	550
1-51D-R12	4.9L	.042–.046	6	800	—	1250	650	550	550
1-51E-R0	4.9L	.042–.046	6	800	—	1400	700	600	600
1-51F-R0	4.9L	.042–.046	6	800	—	1250	650	550	550
1-51G-R0	4.9L	.042–.046	6	800	—	1250	650	550	550
1-51H-R0	4.9L	.042–.046	6	800	—	1250	650	550	550
1-51K-R0	4.9L	.042–.046	6	800	—	1250	650	550	550
1-51L-R0	4.9L	.042–.046	6	800	—	1250	650	550	550
1-51E-R10	4.9L	.042–.046	6	800	—	1400	700	600	600
1-51F-R10	4.9L	.042–.046	6	800	—	1250	650	550	550
1-51G-R10	4.9L	.042–.046	6	800	—	1250	650	550	550
1-51H-R10	4.9L	.042–.046	6	800	—	1250	650	550	550
1-51K-R10	4.9L	.042–.046	6	800	—	1250	650	550	550
1-51L-R10	4.9L	.042–.046	6	800	—	1250	650	550	550
1-51S-R0	4.9L	.042–.046	6	800	—	1400	700	600	600
1-51S-R10	4.9L	.042–.046	6	800	—	1250	650	550	550
1-51T-R0	4.9L	.042–.046	6	800	—	120	650	550	550
1-52G-R0	4.9L	.042–.046	10	800	—	1400	—	—	550
1-52H-R0	4.9L	.042–.046	10	800	—	1250	—	—	500
1-52K-R0	4.9L	.042–.046	10	800	—	1250	—	—	500

TUNE-UP SPECIFICATIONS (Continued)
1981

For 1981–87 Tune-Up Specifications consult the Vehicle Emissions Control Label, which is located on the engine of the vehicle. This decal will contain a calibration number which when used in conjunction with the chart below will yield the required tune-up information. If the information given in this chart disagrees with the information on the decal, use the information on the decal.

Calibration Number	Engine	Spark Plug Gap	Ignition Timing °BTDC	Timing RPM	Fast idle rpm High CAM	Fast idle rpm Kick Down	Curb idle rpm A/C On	Curb idle rpm A/C off	Curb idle rpm Non A/C
1-52L-R0	4.9L	.042–.046	10	800	—	1250	—	—	500
1-52G-R10	4.9L	.042–.046	10	800	—	1400	—	—	550
1-52H-R10	4.9L	.042–.046	10	800	—	1250	—	—	500
1-52K-R10	4.9L	.042–.046	10	800	—	1250	—	—	500
1-52L-R10	4.9L	.042–.046	10	800	—	1250	—	—	500
1-52S-R0	4.9L	.042–.046	10	800	—	1400	—	—	550
1-52T-R0	4.9L	.042–.046	10	800	—	1250	—	—	550
5-77-R1	4.9L	.042–.046	10	800	—	1500	—	—	600(A)
5-78-R1	4.9L	.042–.046	10	800	—	1500	—	—	700(M)
9-77J-R12	4.9L	.042–.046	12	800	1600	—	—	—	700
9-77S-R10	4.9L	.042–.046	10	800	1600	—	—	—	700
9-78J-R0	4.9L	.042–.046	12	800	—	1500	—	—	550
9-78J-R11	4.9L	.042–.046	12	800	1600	—	—	—	550
1-53D-R0	5.0L	.042–.046	8	800	2200	—	—	—	700
1-53F-R0	5.0L	.042–.046	8	800	2050	—	—	—	650
1-53G-R0	5.0L	.042–.046	8	800	2050	—	—	—	650
1-53H-R0	5.0L	.042–.046	8	800	2050	—	—	—	650
1-53K-R0	5.0L	.042–.046	8	800	2050	—	—	—	650
1-53D-R10	5.0L	.042–.046	8	800	2200	—	—	—	700
1-53G-R10	5.0L	.042–.046	8	800	2050	—	—	—	650
1-53K-R10	5.0L	.042–.046	8	800	2050	—	—	—	650
1-53D-R12	5.0L	.042–.046	8	800	2050	—	—	—	650
1-53F-R11	5.0L	.042–.046	8	800	2050	—	—	—	650
1-53G-R12	5.0L	.042–.046	8	800	2050	—	—	—	650
1-53H-R11	5.0L	.042–.046	8	800	2050	—	—	—	650
1-53K-R13	5.0L	.042–.046	8	800	2050	—	—	—	650
1-54D-R1	5.0L	.042–.046	8	800	2000	—	—	—	575
1-54K-R0	5.0L	.042–.046	8	800	1850	—	—	—	525
1-54F-R0	5.0L	.042–.046	8	800	2000	—	—	—	575
1-54G-R0	5.0L	.042–.046	8	800	2000	—	—	—	575
1-54H-R0	5.0L	.042–.046	8	800	2000	—	—	—	575
1-54L-R2	5.0L	.042–.046	8	800	2000	—	—	—	575
1-54L-R10	5.0L	.042–.046	8	800	1850	—	—	—	525
1-54P-R0	5.0L	.042–.046	—	—	1350	—	—	—	—
1-54R-R0	5.0L	.042–.046	—	—	1350	—	—	—	—
1-54P-R10	5.0L	.042–.046	—	—	1350	—	—	—	—
1-54R-R10	5.0L	.042–.046	—	—	1200	—	—	—	—
7-79-R1	5.0L	.042–.046	6	800	—	1250	—	—	750
7-80-R0	5.0L	.042–.046	6	800	—	1500	—	—	650
1-59A-R0	5.8L	.042–.046	10	800	2000	—	650	—	650

TUNE-UP SPECIFICATIONS (Continued)

1981

For 1981–87 Tune-Up Specifications consult the Vehicle Emissions Control Label, which is located on the engine of the vehicle. This decal will contain a calibration number which when used in conjunction with the chart below will yield the required tune-up information. If the information given in this chart disagrees with the information on the decal, use the information on the decal.

Calibration Number	Engine	Spark Plug Gap	Ignition Timing °BTDC	Timing RPM	Fast idle rpm High CAM	Fast idle rpm Kick Down	Curb idle rpm A/C On	Curb idle rpm A/C off	Curb idle rpm Non A/C
1-59B-R0	5.8L	.042–.046	10	800	2000	—	650	—	650
1-59G-R0	5.8L	.042–.046	10	800	2000	—	650	—	650
1-59H-R0	5.8L	.042–.046	10	800	2000	—	650	—	650
1-59K-R0	5.8L	.042–.046	10	800	2000	—	650	—	650
1-59A-R10	5.8L	.042–.046	10	800	2000	—	650	—	650
1-59B-R10	5.8L	.042–.046	10	800	1850	—	600	—	600
1-59G-R10	5.8L	.042–.046	10	800	1850	—	600	—	600
1-59H-R10	5.8L	.042–.046	10	800	1850	—	600	—	600
1-59K-R10	5.8L	.042–.046	10	800	1850	—	600	—	600
1-60A-R0	5.8L	.042–.046	6	800	2200	—	—	—	—
1-60B-R0	5.8L	.042–.046	6	800	2200	—	—	—	—
1-60H-R1	5.8L	.042–.046	6	800	2000	—	625	550	550
1-60J-R0	5.8L	.042–.046	6	800	2000	—	625	550	550
1-60K-R0	5.8L	.042–.046	6	800	2000	—	625	550	550
1-60A-R10	5.8L	.042–.046	6	800	2000	—	625	550	550
1-60B-R10	5.8L	.042–.046	6	800	1850	—	575	500	500
1-60H-R10	5.8L	.042–.046	6	800	1850	—	575	500	500
1-60J-R10	5.8L	.042–.046	6	800	1850	—	575	500	500
1-60K-R10	5.8L	.042–.046	6	800	1850	—	575	500	500
1-63T-R0	5.8L	.042–.046	—	—	1700	—	—	—	—
1-64A-R0	5.8L	.042–.046	8	800	2000	—	625	550	550
1-64G-R1	5.8L	.042–.046	10	600	2000	—	625	550	550
1-64H-R2	5.8L	.042–.046	10	600	2000	—	625	550	550
1-64R-R1	5.8L	.042–.046	—	—	1650	—	—	—	—
1-64S-R0	5.8L	.042–.046	—	—	1500	—	—	—	—
1-64T-R0	5.8L	.042–.046	—	—	1500	—	—	—	—
7-76J-R11	5.8L	.042–.046	6	800	1700	—	—	—	600
9-71J-R10	5.8L	.042–.046	10	800	1750	—	—	—	600
9-71J-R11	5.8L	.042–.046	10	800	1750	—	—	—	600
9-72J-R11	5.8L	.042–.046	10	800	2000	—	—	—	600
9-72J-R12	5.8L	.042–.046	10	800	2000	—	—	—	600
9-73J-R11	6.6L	.042–.046	6	800	1750	—	—	—	600
9-73J-R12	6.6L	.042–.046	6	800	1750	—	—	—	600
9-74J-R11	6.6L	.042–.046	3	800	2000	—	—	—	600
9-74J-R12	6.6L	.042–.046	6	800	2000	—	—	—	600
9-87G-R11	7.0L	.042–.046	6	800	2700	—	—	—	600
9-97J-R0	7.5L	.042–.046	8	800	1600	—	—	—	650

TUNE-UP SPECIFICATIONS
1982

For 1981–87 Tune-Up Specifications consult the Vehicle Emissions Control Label, which is located on the engine of the vehicle. This decal will contain a calibration number which when used in conjunction with the chart below will yield the required tune-up information. If the information given in this chart disagrees with the information on the decal, use the information on the decal.

Calibration	Engine	Spark Plug Gap	Ignition Timing	Fast Idle rpm	Curb Idle rpm
2-54R-R0	5.0L	.042–.046	—	1350	—
2-54X-R1	5.0L	.042–.046	12° BTDC	2100	650
1-63T-R0	5.8L	.042–.046	—	1700	—
1-63T-R10B	5.8L	.042–.046	—	1700	—
1-64H-R2	5.8L	.042–.046	10° BTDC	2000	625
1-64R-R1	5.8L	.042–.046	—	1650	—
1-64S-R0	5.8L	.042–.046	—	1650	—
1-64T-R0	5.8L	.042–.046	—	1650	—
1-64T-R10	5.8L	.042–.046	—	1650	—
2-63Y-R10B	5.8L	.042–.046	—	1700	—
2-64X-R0	5.8L	.042–.046	14° BTDC	2000	625
2-64Y-R10B	5.8L	.042–.046	—	1650	—
9-77J-R12	4.9L	.042–.046	12° BTDC	1600	—
9-77G-R10	4.9L	.042–.046	10° BTDC	1600	—
9-78J-R0	4.9L	.042–.046	12° BTDC	1600	—
9-78J-R11	4.9L	.042–.046	12° BTDC	1600	—
2-75J-R17	5.8L	.042–.046	5° BTDC	1500	700 ①
2-76J-R17	5.8L	.042–.046	5° BTDC	1500	—
7-75J-R14	5.8L	.042–.046	6° BTDC	1500	700 ①
7-76J-R11	5.8L	.042–.046	6° BTDC	1700	—
7-76J-R13	5.8L	.042–.046	12° BTDC	1600	500
7-76J-R14	5.8L	.042–.046	6° BTDC	1700	—
7-76J-R15	5.8L	.042–.046	6° BTDC	1700	—
9-73J-R11	6.6L	.042–.046	6° BTDC	1750	600 ①
9-73J-R12	6.6L	.042–.046	6° BTDC	1750	600 ①
9-73J-R13	6.6L	.042–.046	6° BTDC	1750	600 ①
9-73J-R14	6.6L	.042–.046	6° BTDC	1750	600 ①
9-74J-R11	6.6L	.042–.046	6° BTDC	2000	—
9-74J-R12	6.6L	.042–.046	6° BTDC	2000	—
9-74J-R13	6.6L	.042–.046	3° BTDC	2000	—
9-74J-R14	6.6L	.042–.046	6° BTDC	2000	—
9-97J-R12	7.5L	.042–.046	8° BTDC	—	650

TUNE-UP SPECIFICATIONS
1983

For 1981–87 Tune-Up Specifications consult the Vehicle Emissions Control Label, which is located on the engine of the vehicle. This decal will contain a calibration number which when used in conjunction with the chart below will yield the required tune-up information. If the information given in this chart disagrees with the information on the decal, use the information on the decal.

Calibration	Engine	Spark Plug Gap	Ignition Timing	Fast Idle rpm	Curb Idle rpm
3-55D-R00	3.8L	.042–.046	2° BTDC	1300	550
3-56D-R00	3.8L	.042–.046	10° BTDC	2200	550
3-51D-R00	4.9L	.042–.046	6° BTDC	1600	700 ①
3-51E-R01	4.9L	.042–.046	6° BTDC	1600	700 ①
2-63Y-R12	5.8L	.042–.046	—	1700	750
2-64X-R00	5.8L	.042–.046	14° BTDC	2000	625 ②
2-64Y-R11	5.8L	.042–.046	—	1650	600
2-64Y-R12	5.8L	.042–.046	—	1650	600
5-77-R01	4.9L	.042–.046	10° BTDC	1500	600 ③
5-78-R01	4.9L	.042–.046	10° BTDC	1500	600 ③
9-77J-R12	4.9L	.042–.046	12° BTDC	1600	700
9-77S-R10	4.9L	.042–.046	10° BTDC	1600	700
9-78J-R00	4.9L	.042–.046	12° BTDC	1600	550
9-78J-R11	4.9L	.042–.046	12° BTDC	1600	550
7-79-R01	5.0L	.042–.046	6° BTDC	1250	750
7-80-R00	5.0L	.042–.046	6° BTDC	1600	650
2-75A-R10	5.8L	.042–.046	8° BTDC	1500	650
2-75J-R20	5.8L	.042–.046	8° BTDC	1500	650
2-76A-R10	5.8L	.042–.046	8° BTDC	1500	650
2-76J-R20	5.8L	.042–.046	8° BTDC	1500	650
9-97J-R13	7.5L	.042–.046	8° BTDC	1600	600
9-98S-R00	7.5L	.042–.046	6° BTDC	1500	600

① 600—Non A/c or A/c off
② 550—A/c off and Non A/c
③ 700—Manual Trans.

TUNE-UP SPECIFICATIONS
1984

For 1981–87 Tune-Up Specifications consult the Vehicle Emissions Control Label, which is located on the engine of the vehicle. This decal will contain a calibration number which when used in conjunction with the chart below will yield the required tune-up information. If the information given in this chart disagrees with the information on the decal, use the information on the decal.

Calibration	Engine	Spark Plug Gap	Ignition Timing	Fast Idle rpm	Curb Idle rpm
4-51D-R01	4.9L	.042–.046	10° BTDC	1600	600–700 ①
4-51E-R00	4.9L	.042–.046	10° BTDC	1600	600–700 ①
4-51K-R00	4.9L	.042–.046	10° BTDC	1600	600–700 ①
4-51L-R00	4.9L	.042–.046	10° BTDC	1600	600–700 ①
4-51R-R00	4.9L	.042–.046	10° BTDC	1600	600–700 ①
4-51S-R00	4.9L	.042–.046	10° BTDC	1600	600–700 ①
4-51S-R01	4.9L	.042–.046	10° BTDC	1600	600–700 ①

TUNE-UP SPECIFICATIONS
1984

For 1981–87 Tune-Up Specifications consult the Vehicle Emissions Control Label, which is located on the engine of the vehicle. This decal will contain a calibration number which when used in conjunction with the chart below will yield the required tune-up information. If the information given in this chart disagrees with the information on the decal, use the information on the decal.

Calibration	Engine	Spark Plug Gap	Ignition Timing	Fast Idle rpm	Curb Idle rpm
4-51S-R02	4.9L	.042–.046	10° BTDC	1600	600–700 ①
4-51T-R00	4.9L	.042–.046	10° BTDC	1600	600–700 ①
4-51Z-R00	4.9L	.042–.046	10° BTDC	1600	600–700 ①
4-51L-R00	4.9L	.042–.046	10° BTDC	1600	600–700 ①
4-52R-R00	4.9L	.042–.046	10° BTDC	1600	600–700 ①
4-52S-R00	4.9L	.042–.046	10° BTDC	1600	600–700 ①
4-52T-R00	4.9L	.042–.046	10° BTDC	1600	600–700 ①
4-52W-R00	4.9L	.042–.046	10° BTDC	1600	600–700 ①
4-53F-R00	5.0L	.042–.046	8° BTDC	2100	800 ②
4-53F-R10	5.0L	.042–.046	8° BTDC	2100	800 ②
4-53G-R00	5.0L	.042–.046	8° BTDC	2100	800 ②
4-53G-R10	5.0L	.042–.046	8° BTDC	2100	800 ②
4-53K-R00	5.0L	.042–.046	8° BTDC	2100	800 ②
4-53K-R10	5.0L	.042–.046	8° BTDC	2100	800 ②
4-53Z-R00	5.0L	.042–.046	8° BTDC	2100	800 ②
4-53Z-R10	5.0L	.042–.046	8° BTDC	2100	800 ②
4-54E-R00	5.0L	.042–.046	8° BTDC	2100	800 ②
4-53E-R10	5.0L	.042–.046	8° BTDC	2100	800 ②
4-54J-R00	5.0L	.042–.046	8° BTDC	2100	800 ②
4-54J-R10	5.0L	.042–.046	8° BTDC	2100	800 ②
4-54J-R00	5.0L	.042–.046	8° BTDC	2100	800 ②
4-54L-R00	5.0L	.042–.046	8° BTDC	2100	800 ②
4-54L-R10	5.0L	.042–.046	8° BTDC	2100	800 ②
4-54R-R00	5.0L	.042–.046	10° BTDC	2000	575
4-54R-R10	5.0L	.042–.046	10° BTDC	2000	575
4-54T-R00	5.0L	.042–.046	10° BTDC	2000	575
4-54T-R10	5.0L	.042–.046	10° BTDC	2000	575
4-54W-R00	5.0L	.042–.046	12° BTDC	2100	675 ③
4-54W-R10	5.0L	.042–.046	12° BTDC	2100	675 ③
4-63H-R00	5.8L	.042–.046	10° BTDC	2000	750
4-64H-R00	5.8L	.042–.046	10° BTDC	2000	600
4-64H-R00	5.8L	.042–.046	10° BTDC	2000	600
4-64T-R00	5.8L	.042–.046	10° BTDC	2000	600
4-64T-R00	5.8L	.042–.046	10° BTDC	2000	600
4-64Y-R00	5.8L	.042–.046	10° BTDC	2000	600
5-77-R01	4.9L	.042–.046	10° BTDC	1500	600 ④
5-78-R01	4.9L	.042–.046	10° BTDC	1500	600 ④
9-77J-R12	4.9L	.042–.046	12° BTDC	1600	700 ⑤
9-78J-R00	4.9L	.042–.046	12° BTDC	1600	550
9-78J-R11	4.9L	.042–.046	12° BTDC	1600	550
7-79-R01	5.0L	.042–.046	6° BTDC	1500	750 ⑥

TUNE-UP SPECIFICATIONS
1984

For 1981–87 Tune-Up Specifications consult the Vehicle Emissions Control Label, which is located on the engine of the vehicle. This decal will contain a calibration number which when used in conjunction with the chart below will yield the required tune-up information. If the information given in this chart disagrees with the information on the decal, use the information on the decal.

Calibration	Engine	Spark Plug Gap	Ignition Timing	Fast Idle rpm	Curb Idle rpm
7-80-R00	5.0L	.042–.046	6° BTDC	1500	750 ⑥
2-75A-R10	5.8L	.042–.046	8° BTDC	1500	800 ⑥
2-75J-R20	5.8L	.042–.046	8° BTDC	1500	700 ⑥
2-76A-R10	5.8L	.042–.046	8° BTDC	1500	800 ⑥
2-76J-R20	5.8L	.042–.046	8° BTDC	1500	700 ⑥
9-97J-R10	7.5L	.042–.046	8° BTDC	1600	800 ⑦
3-98S-R10	7.5L	.042–.046	8° BTDC	1600	800 ⑦
4-98S-R00	7.5L	.042–.046	8° BTDC	1600	800 ⑦

① 550-650 RPM—Auto. Trans. in DRIVE
② 700—Non a/c or A/C off
③ 700—Non a/c or A/C off
④ 700—Manual Trans.
⑤ 600—TSP off
⑥ 650—"D" auto trans; 525—TSP off
⑦ 650—DRIVE

TUNE-UP SPECIFICATIONS
1985-87

For 1981–87 Tune-Up Specifications consult the Vehicle Emissions Control Label, which is located on the engine of the vehicle. This decal will contain a calibration number which when used in conjunction with the chart below will yield the required tune-up information. If the information given in this chart disagrees with the information on the decal, use the information on the decal.

Calibration	Engine	Spark Plug Gap	Ignition Timing	Fast Idle rpm	Curb Idle rpm
4-51R-R00	4.9L	.042–.046	10° BTDC	1600	600–700 ①
4-51S-R02	4.9L	.042–.046	10° BTDC	1600	600–700 ①
4-51T-R00	4.9L	.042–.046	10° BTDC	1600	600–700 ①
4-52G-R00	4.9L	.042–.046	10° BTDC	1600	600–700 ①
4-52G-R10	4.9L	.042–.046	10° BTDC	1600	600–700 ①
4-52L-R00	4.9L	.042–.046	10° BTDC	1600	600–700 ①
4-52L-R10	4.9L	.042–.046	10° BTDC	1600	600–700 ①
4-52R-R00	4.9L	.042–.046	10° BTDC	1600	600–700 ①
4-52S-R00	4.9L	.042–.046	10° BTDC	1600	600–700 ①
4-52S-R10	4.9L	.042–.046	10° BTDC	1600	600–700 ①
4-52T-R00	4.9L	.042–.046	10° BTDC	1600	600–700 ①
5-51D-R00	4.9L	.042–.046	10° BTDC	1600	600–700 ①
5-51E-R00	4.9L	.042–.046	10° BTDC	1600	600–700 ①
5-51F-R00	4.9L	.042–.046	10° BTDC	1600	600–700 ①
5-51H-R00	4.9L	.042–.046	10° BTDC	1600	600–700 ①
5-51K-R00	4.9L	.042–.046	10° BTDC	1600	600–700 ①
5-51L-R00	4.9L	.042–.046	10° BTDC	1600	600–700 ①
5-51V-R00	4.9L	.042–.046	10° BTDC	1600	600–700 ①

TUNE-UP SPECIFICATIONS
1985–87

For 1981–87 Tune-Up Specifications consult the Vehicle Emissions Control Label, which is located on the engine of the vehicle. This decal will contain a calibration number which when used in conjunction with the chart below will yield the required tune-up information. If the information given in this chart disagrees with the information on the decal, use the information on the decal.

Calibration	Engine	Spark Plug Gap	Ignition Timing	Fast Idle rpm	Curb Idle rpm
5-51Z-R00	4.9L	.042–.046	10° BTDC	1600	600–700 ①
5-52E-R00	4.9L	.042–.046	10° BTDC	1600	600–700 ①
5-52K-R00	4.9L	.042–.046	10° BTDC	1600	600–700 ①
5-52W-R00	4.9L	.042–.046	10° BTDC	1600	600–700 ①
5-52Y-R00	4.9L	.042–.046	10° BTDC	1600	600–700 ①
4-54R-R12	5.0L	.042–.046	10° BTDC	2000	575D
4-54R-R13	5.0L	.042–.046	10° BTDC	2000	575D
4-54R-R14	5.0L	.042–.046	10° BTDC	2000	575D
5-53D-R00	5.0L	.042–.046	10° BTDC	—	—
5-53D-R01	5.0L	.042–.046	8° BTDC	—	—
5-53F-R00	5.0L	.042–.046	10° BTDC	—	—
5-53F-R01	5.0L	.042–.046	8° BTDC	—	—
5-53H-R00	5.0L	.042–.046	10° BTDC	—	—
5-53H-R01	5.0L	.042–.046	8° BTDC	—	—
5-54Q-R00	5.0L	.042–.046	10° BTDC	—	—
5-54Q-R01	5.0L	.042–.046	10° BTDC	—	—
5-54S-R00	5.0L	.042–.046	10° BTDC	—	—
5-54S-R01	5.0L	.042–.046	10° BTDC	—	—
5-54W-R00	5.0L	.042–.046	10° BTDC	—	—
5-54X-R00	5.0L	.042–.046	10° BTDC	—	—
4-64G-R00	5.8L(F)	.042–.046	10° BTDC	1900	650D
4-64G-R02	5.8L(F)	.042–.046	10° BTDC	1900	650D
4-64G-R02	5.8L(E)	.042–.046	10° BTDC	1900	650D
4-64T-R00	5.8L(F)	.042–.046	10° BTDC	2000	600D
4-64T-R00	5.8L(E)	.042–.046	10° BTDC	2000	600D
4-64Z-R10	5.8L(F)	.042–.046	14° BTDC	1900	650D
4-64Z-R10	5.8L(E)	.042–.046	14° BTDC	1900	650D
5-63H-R00	5.8L	.042–.046	10° BTDC	2000	700
5-63Y-R00	5.8L	.042–.046	10° BTDC	2000	700

① 550–650 in Drive A/T

GENERAL ENGINE SPECIFICATIONS

Year	Engine cu. in. (L)	Fuel System Type	SAE net Horsepower @ rpm	SAE net Torque ft. lb. @ rpm	Bore × Stroke	Comp. Ratio	Oil Press. (psi.) @ 2000 rpm
1980–87	6-232 (3.8)	2-bbl	110 @ 3500	150 @ 1800	3.81 × 3.39	8.7:1	40–60
	8-255 (4.1)	2-bbl	115 @ 3600	180 @ 1600	3.68 × 3.00	8.2:1	40–60
	6-300 (4.9)	1-bbl	120 @ 3200	245 @ 1600	4.00 × 3.98	8.4:1	40–60
	8-302 (5.0)	2-bbl	150 @ 3600	250 @ 2600	4.00 × 3.00	8.4:1	40–60
	8-351 (5.8)W	2-bbl	160 @ 3200	280 @ 2000	4.00 × 3.50	8.3:1	40–65
	8-351 (5.8)HO	4-bbl	210 @ 4000	305 @ 2800	4.00 × 3.50	8.3:1	40–65
	8-351 (5.8)M	2-bbl	137 @ 3600	287 @ 1600	4.00 × 3.50	8.0:1	50–75
	8-400 (6.6)	2-bbl	153 @ 3500	296 @ 1600	4.00 × 4.00	8.0:1	50–75
	8-420 (6.9)	Diesel	170 @ 3300	315 @ 1400	4.00 × 4.18	19.7:1	40–60
	8-460 (7.5)	4-bbl	225 @ 4000	365 @ 2800	4.36 × 3.85	8.0:1	40–65

CAPACITIES
Pick-Ups

Years	Engine cu. in. (L)	Crankcase Incl. Filter (qt.)	Transmission (pt.) 3-Speed	4-Speed	Auto	Transfer Case (pts.)	Drive Axle (pt.) Front	Rear	Fuel Tank (gal.)	Cooling System (qt.) w/AC	wo/AC
1980–87	6-300	6.0	3.5	②	③	④	⑤	⑥	⑦	①	①
	6-232	6.0	3.5	②	③	④	⑤	⑥	⑦	18.0	15.0
	8-255	6.0	3.5	②	③	④	⑤	⑥	⑦	18.0	15.0
	8-302	6.0	3.5	②	③	④	⑤	⑥	⑦	18.0	15.0
	8-351W	6.0	—	②	26.75	④	⑤	⑥	⑦	17.0	17.0
	8-351M	6.0	—	②	26.75	④	⑤	⑥	⑦	⑨	⑨
	8-400	6.0	—	②	26.75	④	⑤	⑥	⑦	⑨	⑨
	8-420	10.0	—	②	26.75	④	⑤	⑥	⑦	29.0	29.0
	8-460	6.0	—	—	26.75	④	⑤	⑥	⑦	⑧	⑧

① Standard cooling with manual transmission: 13.0
Standard cooling with automatic transmission: 14.0
With air conditioning: 17.0
With extra cooling and without air conditioning: 14.0

② Warner T-18 and T-10B: 7.0
NP-435 with extension housing: 7.0
NP-435 without extension housing: 6.5
4-Speed overdrive: 5.0

③ C-4: 20.0
C-5: 22.0
C-6: 23.5
A0D: 24.0

④ NP-208: 7.0
BW-1345: 6.5

⑤ Dana 44-9F: 3.5
Dana 60-7F: 6.0
Dana 50-IFS: 4.1
Dana 44-IFS: 3.8

⑥ Dana 61-1: 6.0
Dana 61-2: 6.0
Dana 70: 7.0
Dana 70HD: 7.4

⑦ 1980–82 all models with 2-wheel drive and standard cab: 19.2 standard
1980–82 all models with 2-wheel drive and standard cab: 20.2 optional behind axle
1980–82 F-250 4 × 4 w/regular cab: 19.2
1980–82 F-250 and F-350 2-wheel drive with Crew Cab: 20.2
1980–82 F-350 2-wheel drive regular cab: 20.2 standard
1980–82 F-350 2-wheel drive regular cab: 19.0 optional behind axle
1980–82 F-250 and F-350 4 × 4 regular cab: 26.0 standard
1980–82 F-250 and F-350 4 × 4 regular cab: 19.2 optional behind axle
1983–87 F-100 2-wheel drive regular cab: 16.5 standard
1983–87 F-100 2-wheel drive regular cab: 19.0 optional behind axle
1983–87 F-150 2-wheel drive Crew Cab: 16.5 standard
1983–87 F-150 2-wheel drive Crew Cab: 19.0 optional behind axle
1983–87 F-150 4 × 4 regular cab: 16.5 standard
1983–87 F-150 4 × 4 regular cab: 19.0 optional behind axle
1983–87 F-250 2-wheel drive Crew Cab: 16.5 standard
1983–87 F-250 2-wheel drive Crew Cab: 19.0 optional behind axle
1983–87 F-150 2-wheel drive regular cab: 16.5 standard
1983–87 F-150 2-wheel drive regular cab: 19.0 optional behind axle
1983–87 F-250 2-wheel drive regular cab: 19.0 standard
1983–87 F-250 2-wheel drive regular cab: 19.0 optional behind axle
1983–87 F-250 all 4 × 4: 19.0 standard
1983–87 F-250 all 4 × 4: 19.0 optional behind axle
1983–87 F-350 all models: 19.0 standard
1983–87 F-350 all models: 19.0 optional behind axle

⑧ 1980–82: 24.0
1983–87: 18.0

⑨ Standard: 18.0
With air conditioning: 22.0
Extra cooling: 24.0

CAPACITIES
Bronco

Years	Engine cu. in. (L)	Crankcase Incl. Filter (qt.)	Transmission (pt.) 4-Speed	4-Speed OD	Auto	Transfer Case (pts.)	Drive Axle (pt.) Front	Rear	Fuel Tank (gal.)	Cooling System (qt.) w/AC	wo/AC
1980-81	6-300 (4.9)	6.0	7.0	4.5	26.8	6.5	4.0	6.5	①	14.0	13.0
	8-302 (5.0)	6.0	7.0	4.5	26.8	6.5	4.0	6.5	①	14.0	13.0
	8-351 (5.8)	6.0	7.0	4.5	26.8	6.5	4.0	6.5	①	16.0	15.0
1982-87	6-300 (4.9)	6.0	7.0	4.5	26.8	7.0	4.0	6.5	①	14.0	13.0
	8-302 (5.0)	6.0	7.0	4.5	26.8	7.0	4.0	6.5	①	14.0	13.0
	8-351 (5.8)	6.0	7.0	4.5	26.8	7.0	4.0	6.5	①	16.0	15.0

① Standard: 25.0
Optional: 32.0

CAPACITIES
Vans

Years	Engine cu. in. (L)	Crankcase Includes Filter (qt.)	Transmission (pts.) 3-Speed	4-Speed	Auto	Drive Axle (pts.)	Fuel Tank (gal.)	Cooling System (qts.) w/AC	wo/AC	w/Extra Cooling
1980-84	6-300 (4.9)	6.0	3.5	4.5	①	②	③	20.0	15.0	—
	8-302 (5.0)	6.0	3.5	4.5	①	②	③	17.5	④	18.5
	8-351 (5.8)	6.0	—	—	23.5	②	③	20.0	20.0	21.0
	8-420 (6.9)	10.0	—	—	23.5	②	③	31.0	31.0	—
	8-460 (7.5)	6.0	—	—	23.5	②	③	28.0	28.0	—
1985-87	6-300 (4.9)	6.0	3.5	⑤	⑥	⑦	③	⑧	⑨	—
	8-302 (5.0)	6.0	—	—	⑥	⑦	③	17.5	17.5	18.5
	8-351 (5.8)	6.0	—	—	23.8	⑦	③	⑩	20.0	21.0
	8-420 (6.9)	10.0	—	—	23.5	⑦	③	31.0	31.0	—
	8-460 (7.5)	6.0	—	—	23.5	⑦	③	⑪	⑪	—

① C4: 20.5
C6: 24.5
② Ford axles: 6.5
Dana models 60 and 61: 6.0
Dana 70: 7.0
③ E-100 and 150 w/124 inch wheelbase: 18.0
All others: 22.1
Optional auxiliary: 18.0, except the E-350 cutaway chassis: 40.0
④ With manual transmission: 15.0
With automatic transmission: 17.5
⑤ Except E-350: 4.5
E-350: 3.25
⑥ AOD: 24.0
C6: 23.8
⑦ Ford axles: 5.5
Dana models 60: 6.0
Dana 70: 6.5
⑧ Without auxiliary heater: 17.5
With auxiliary heater: 19.3
⑨ Without auxiliary heater: 16.0
With auxiliary heater: 17.8
⑩ With manual transmission: 15.0
With automatic transmission: 21.0
⑪ Without auxiliary heater: 28.0
With auxiliary heater: 29.8

CRANKSHAFT AND CONNECTING ROD SPECIFICATIONS

All specifications in inches.

Engine cu. in.	Crankshaft: Main Bearing Journal Dia.	Crankshaft: Main Bearing Oil Clearance	Crankshaft: Shaft End Play	Crankshaft: Thrust on No.	Connecting Rod: Journal Dia.	Connecting Rod: Oil Clearance	Connecting Rod: Side Clearance
6-232	2.5188–2.5192	0.0009–0.0027	0.004–0.008	3	2.3105–2.3109	0.0009–0.0027	0.004–0.011
8-255	2.2488–2.2492	0.0005–0.0024 ①	0.004–0.008	3	2.1230–2.1234	0.0008–0.0025	0.010–0.020
6-300	2.3982–2.3990	0.0008–0.0015	0.004–0.008	5	2.1228–2.1236	0.0008–0.0015	0.006–0.013
8-302	2.2482–2.2490	0.0005–0.0015 ②	0.004–0.008	3	2.1228–2.1236	0.0008–0.0015	0.010–0.020
8-351W	2.9994–3.0002	0.0008–0.0015 ②	0.004–0.008	3	2.3103–3.3111	0.0008–0.0015	0.010–0.020
8-351M	2.9994–3.0002	0.0005–0.0015	0.004–0.008	3	2.3103–3.3111	0.0008–0.0015	0.010–0.020
8-400	2.9994–3.0002	0.0005–0.0015	0.004–0.008	3	2.3103–3.3111	0.0008–0.0015	0.010–0.020
8-420	3.1228–3.1236	0.0018–0.0036	0.0020–0.0090	3	2.4980–2.4990	0.0011–0.0026	0.008–0.020
8-460	2.9994–3.0002	0.0012–0.0015 ③	0.004–0.008	3	2.4992–2.5000	0.0008–0.0015	0.010–0.020

① No. 1: 0.0004–0.0020
② No. 1: 0.0001–0.0015
③ No. 1: 0.0004–0.0015

CAMSHAFT SPECIFICATIONS

All specifications in inches

Engine cu. in.	Journal Diameter 1	Journal Diameter 2	Journal Diameter 3	Journal Diameter 4	Journal Diameter 5	Bearing Clearance	Elevation Int.	Elevation Exh.	End Play
6-232	2.0505–2.0515	2.0505–2.0515	2.0505–2.0515	2.0505–2.0515	—	0.0010–0.0030	0.2400	0.2410	①
8-255	2.0805–2.0815	2.0655–2.0665	2.0505–2.0515	2.0355–2.0365	2.0205–2.0215	0.0010–0.0030	0.2375	0.2470	0.002
6-300	2.0170–2.0180	2.0170–2.0180	2.0170–2.0180	2.0170–2.0180	—	0.0010–0.0030	0.2490	0.2490	0.004
8-302	2.0805–2.0815	2.0655–2.0665	2.0505–2.0515	2.0355–2.0365	2.0205–2.0215	0.0010–0.0030	0.2375	0.2470	0.002
8-351W	2.0805–2.0815	2.0655–2.0665	2.0505–2.0515	2.0355–2.0365	2.0205–2.0215	0.0010–0.0030	0.2600	0.2600	0.004
8-351M	2.1248–2.1328	2.0655–2.0665	2.0505–2.0515	2.0355–2.0365	2.0205–2.0215	0.0010–0.0030	0.2500	0.2500	0.004
8-400	2.1248–2.1328	2.0655–2.0665	2.0505–2.0515	2.0355–2.0365	2.0205–2.0215	0.0010–0.0030	0.2500	0.2500	0.004
8-420	2.0990–2.1000	2.0990–2.1000	2.0990–2.1000	2.0990–2.1000	2.0990–2.1000	0.0010–0.0050	0.2535	0.2530	0.004
8-460	2.1238–2.1248	2.1238–2.1248	2.1238–2.1248	2.1238–2.1248	2.1238–2.1248	0.0010–0.0030	0.2530	0.2780	0.003

① See text

VALVE SPECIFICATIONS

Engine cu. in.	Seat Angle (deg)	Face Angle (deg)	Spring Test Pressure (lbs. @ in.)	Spring Installed Height (in.)	Stem to Guide Clearance (in.)		Stem Diameter (in.)	
					Intake	Exhaust	Intake	Exhaust
6-232	45	44	202 @ 1.28	1.70	0.0010–0.0025	0.0015–0.0032	0.3422	0.3415
8-255	45	46	②	③	0.0010–0.0027	0.0010–0.0027	0.3420	0.3415
6-300	45	44	①	④	0.00185	0.00185	0.3420	0.3415
8-302	45	44	⑤	⑥	0.00185	0.00185	0.3420	0.3415
8-351W	45	44	⑦	1.80	0.0010–0.0027	0.0015–0.0032	0.3420	⑧
8-351M	45	44	226 @ 1.39	1.812	0.00185	0.00235	0.3420	0.3415
8-400	45	44	226 @ 1.39	1.812	0.00185	0.00235	0.3420	0.3415
8-420	⑨	⑨	60 @ 1.798	1.798	0.0012–0.0029	0.0012–0.0029	0.3717-0.3724	0.3717–0.3724
8-460	45	44	229 @ 1.33	1.810	0.0010–0.0027	0.0010–0.0027	0.3416–0.3423	0.3416–0.3423

① Intake: 190 @ 1.300
1980–84 Exhaust: 192 @ 1.180
1985–87 Exhaust: 180 @ 1.240
② Intake: 204 @ 1.36
Exhaust: 200 @ 1.20
③ Intake: 1.78
Exhaust: 1.60
④ Intake: 1.70
Exhaust; 1.69
⑤ Intake: 202 @ 1.36
Exhaust: 200 @ 1.20
⑥ Intake: 1.78
Exhaust: 1.60
⑦ Intake: 200 @ 1.36
Exhaust: 200 @ 1.20
⑧ 1980–81: 0.3415
1982–87: 0.3420
⑨ Intake: 30
Exhaust: 37.5

PISTON AND RING SPECIFICATIONS

All specifications in inches

Engine cu. in.	Piston Clearance	Ring Gap			Ring Side Clearance		
		#1 Compr.	#2 Compr.	Oil Control	#1 Compr.	#2 Compr.	Oil Control
6-232	0.0014–0.0022	0.0100–0.0200	0.0100–0.0200	0.0150–0.0550	0.0020–0.0040	0.0020–0.0040	snug
8-255	0.0014–0.0022	0.0100–0.0200	0.0100–0.0200	0.0150–0.0550	0.0020–0.0040	0.0020–0.0040	snug
6-300	①	0.0100–0.0200	0.0100–0.0200	0.0100–0.0350	0.0019–0.0036	0.0020–0.0040	snug
8-302	0.0018–0.0026	0.0100–0.0200	0.0100–0.0200	0.0150–0.0350	0.0020–0.0040	0.0020–0.0040	snug
8-351W	0.0022–0.0030	0.0100–0.0200	0.0100–0.0200	0.0150–0.0350	0.0019–0.0036	0.0020–0.0040	snug
8-351M	0.0014–0.0022	0.0100–0.0200	0.0100–0.0200	0.0150–0.0350	0.0019–0.0036	0.0020–0.0040	snug
8-400	0.0014–0.0022	0.0100–0.0200	0.0100–0.0200	0.0150–0.0350	0.0019–0.0036	0.0020–0.0040	snug
8-420	0.0055–0.0075	0.0140–0.0240	0.0100–0.0700	0.0240–0.0600	0.0020–0.0040	0.0020–0.0040	0.001–0.003
8-460	0.0022–0.0030	0.0100–0.0200	0.0100–0.0200	0.0100–0.0350	0.0019–0.0036	0.0020–0.0040	snug

① 1980–84: 0.0014–0.0022
1985–87: 0.0010–0.0018

TORQUE SPECIFICATIONS

All specifications in ft. lb.

Engine cu. in.	Cyl. Head	Conn. Rod	Main Bearing	Crankshaft Damper	Flywheel	Manifold Intake	Manifold Exhaust
6-232	①	30–36	62–81	85–100	75–85	17–19	15–22
8-255	65–72	19–24	60–70	70–90	75–85	18–20	18–24
6-300	70–75	40–45	60–70	130–150	75–85	22–32	28–33
8-302	65–72	19–24	60–70	70–90	75–85	23–25	18–24
8-351W	105–112	40–45	95–105	70–90	75–85	23–25	18–24
8-351M	95–105	40–45	95–105	70–90	75–85	②	18–24
8-400	95–105	40–45	95–105	70–90	75–85	②	18–24
8-420	③	④	⑤	85–95	45–50 ⑥	⑦	28–32
8-460	130–140	40–45	95–105	70–90	75–85	25–30	28–33

① Step 1: 47 ft. lb.
Step 2: 63 ft. lb.
Step 3: 74 ft. lb.
Step 4: Back off all bolts in reverse order 2–3 full turns
Step 5: Repeat Steps 1–3

② 3/8″ bolts: 22–32
5/16″ bolts: 17–25

③ Step 1: 40 ft. lb.
Step 2: 65 ft. lb.
Step 3: 75 ft. lb.
Step 4: Run engine to normal operating temperature
Step 5: Retorque bolts to 75 ft. lb. hot

④ Step 1: 38 ft. lb.
Step 2: 46–51 ft. lb.

⑤ Step 1: 72 ft. lb.
Step 2: 95 ft. lb.

⑥ Apply locking sealer to bolt threads before installation

⑦ 3/8″ bolts: 22–32 ft. lb.
1/4″ bolts: 12–18 ft. lb.
5/16″ bolts: 14 ft. lb.

WHEEL ALIGNMENT SPECIFICATIONS
2-Wheel Drive Pick-Ups

Ride Height (in.) At Least	Ride Height (in.) Not More Than	F-100, 150 Camber (deg) Min	F-100, 150 Camber (deg) Max	F-100, 150 Caster Min	F-100, 150 Caster Max	F-250, 350 Camber (deg) Min	F-250, 350 Camber (deg) Max	F-250, 350 Caster (deg) Min	F-250, 350 Caster (deg) Max
2 1/4	2 3/4	−3	−1/2	+6	+10	−1 1/2	+1	+4 3/4	+8
2 3/4	3 1/4	−2	+1/2	+5	+9	−3/4	+1 3/4	+3 3/4	+7
3 1/4	3 1/2	−1 1/4	+1 1/4	+4	+8	+1/4	+2 3/4	+2 3/4	+6
3 1/2	4	−1/4	+2 1/4	+3	+7	+1	+3 1/2	+1 3/4	+5
4	4 1/4	+1/2	+3	+2	+6	+2	+4 1/2	+3/4	+4
4 1/4	4 3/4	+1 1/2	+4	+1	+5	—	—	—	—

WHEEL ALIGNMENT SPECIFICATIONS
4-Wheel Drive Pick-Ups

Ride Height (in.) At Least	Ride Height (in.) Not More Than	F-150 Camber (deg) Min	F-150 Camber (deg) Max	F-150 Caster (deg) Min	F-150 Caster (deg) Max	F-250, 350 Camber (deg) Min	F-250, 350 Camber (deg) Max	F-250, 350 Caster (deg) Min	F-250, 350 Caster (deg) Max
2 3/4	3 1/4	−2 1/2	−1/4	+6	+9	—	—	—	—
3 1/4	3 1/2	−1 3/4	+1/2	+5	+8	—	—	—	—
3 1/2	4	−3/4	+1 1/2	+4	+7	—	—	—	—
4	4 1/4	0	+2 1/4	+3	+6	—	—	—	—
4 1/4	4 3/4	+1	+3 1/4	+2	+5	—	—	—	—
4 3/4	5	+1 3/4	+4	+1	+4	−2 3/4	−1/4	+3	+5

WHEEL ALIGNMENT SPECIFICATIONS
4-Wheel Drive Pick-Ups

Ride Height (in.)		F-150				F-250, 350			
At Least	Not More Than	Camber (deg) Min	Camber (deg) Max	Caster (deg) Min	Caster (deg) Max	Camber (deg) Min	Camber (deg) Max	Caster (deg) Min	Caster (deg) Max
5	5 1/2	—	—	—	—	-1 3/4	+3/4	+3 1/8	+5 1/8
5 1/2	6	—	—	—	—	-3/4	+1 3/4	+3 1/8	+5 1/8
6	6 1/4	—	—	—	—	+1/4	+2 3/4	+3 1/4	+5 1/4
6 1/4	6 3/4	—	—	—	—	+1 1/4	+4	+3 3/8	+5 3/8
6 3/4	7	—	—	—	—	+2 1/2	+5	+3 1/2	+5 1/2

WHEEL ALIGNMENT SPECIFICATIONS
Vans

Ride Height (inches)	E-100, 150 Caster (deg)	E-100, 150 Camber (deg)	E-250, 350 Caster (deg)	E-250, 350 Camber (deg)
3.25 to 3.50	6 1/4P to 8P	1 3/4N to 1/4N	9P to 10 1/2P	1 3/4N to 1/4N
3.50 to 3.75	5 3/4P to 7 1/4P	1 1/2N to 1/4P	8 1/2P to 9 3/4P	1 1/2N to 1/4P
3.75 to 4.00	5P to 6 3/4P	1N to 3/4P	7 7/8P to 9P	1N to 3/4P
4.00 to 4.25	4 1/2P to 5 3/4P	1/2N to 1 1/4P	7 1/8P to 8 1/2P	1/2N to 1 1/4P
4.25 to 4.50	4P to 5 1/4P	0 to 1 3/4P	6 1/2P to 7 3/4P	0 to 1 3/4P
4.50 to 4.75	3 1/4P to 4 1/2P	1/2P to 2 1/4P	5 3/4P to 7P	1/2P to 2 1/4P
4.75 to 5.00	2 1/2P to 4P	1P to 2 3/4P	5 1/4P to 6 1/2P	1P to 2 3/4P
5.00 to 5.25	2P to 3 1/4P	1 1/2P to 3 1/4P	4 5/8P to 6P	1 1/2P to 3 1/4P
5.25 to 5.50	1 1/2P to 2 3/4P	2P to 3 3/4P	4P to 5 1/2P	2P to 3 3/4P

① toe-in: all models—1/32 inch
P: Positive N: Negative

WHEEL ALIGNMENT SPECIFICATIONS
Bronco

Ride Height (in.)	Camber (deg)	Caster (deg)	Toe-in (in.)	Kin Pin Angle (deg)
2 3/4–3 1/4	2 1/2N to 1/4N	6P to 9P	1/32 out-5/32 in	13
3 1/4–3 1/2	1 3/4N to 1/2P	5P to 8P	1/32 out-5/32 in	13
3 1/2–4	3/4N to 1 1/2P	4P to 7P	1/32 out-5/32 in	13
4–4 1/4	0 to 2 1/4P	3P to 6P	1/32 out-5/32 in	13
4 1/4–4 3/4	1P to 3 1/4P	2P to 5P	1/32 out-5/32 in	13
4 3/4–5	1 3/4P to 4P	1P to 4P	1/32 out-5/32 in	13

ROUTINE MAINTENANCE

Air Cleaner

Two types of air cleaners have been used: a replaceable paper type and an oil bath unit.

OIL BATH UNIT

The procedure for cleaning an oil bath air cleaner and refilling the reservoir is as follows:

1. Unlock and open the engine compartment.
2. Remove the carburetor-to-air cleaner retaining wing nut. On a closed crankcase ventilation equipped engine, loosen the hose clamp at the air cleaner body and disconnect the hose. On the 300 six engine, remove the bolts securing the air cleaner body to the support brackets.
3. Remove the air cleaner assembly from the engine. Be careful not to spill the oil out of the air cleaner.
4. Remove the cover and drain the oil from the reservoir. Wash all of the air cleaner parts in a suitable cleaning solvent. Dry all of the parts with compressed air or allow them to air dry.
5. Inspect the gasket between the oil reservoir chamber and the air cleaner body. Replace the gasket as necessary.
6. Saturate the filter element with clean engine oil.
7. Fill the oil reservoir to the full mark with engine oil. Use SAE 30 above 32°F (0°C) and SAE 20 for low temperatures.
8. Replace the air cleaner assembly on the carburetor and tighten the wing nut.

NOTE: Check the air filter more often if the vehicle is operated under unusually dusty conditions and replace or clean it as necessary.

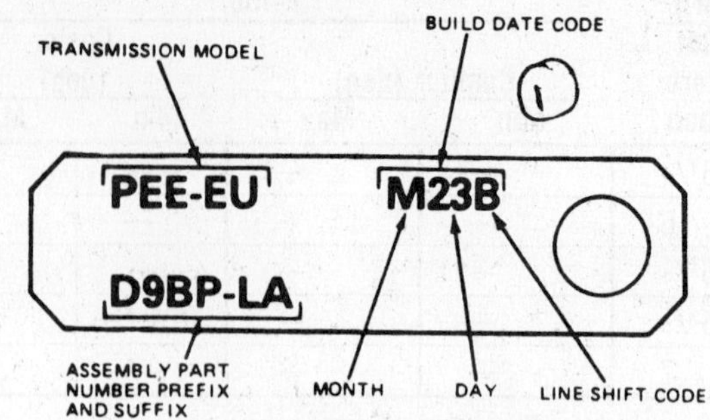

C-4 automatic transmission I.D. tag

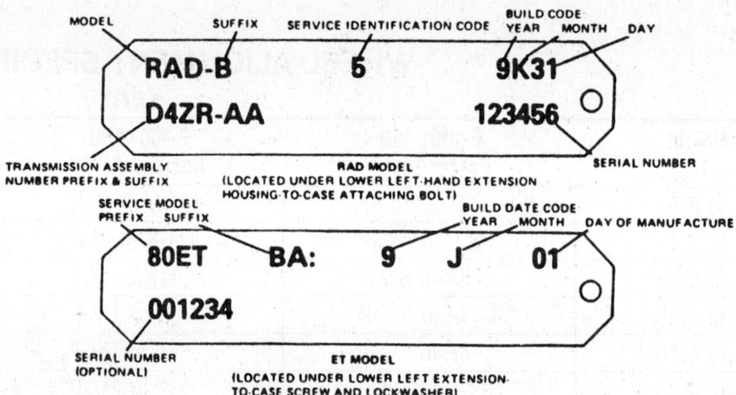

Manual transmission I.D. tag

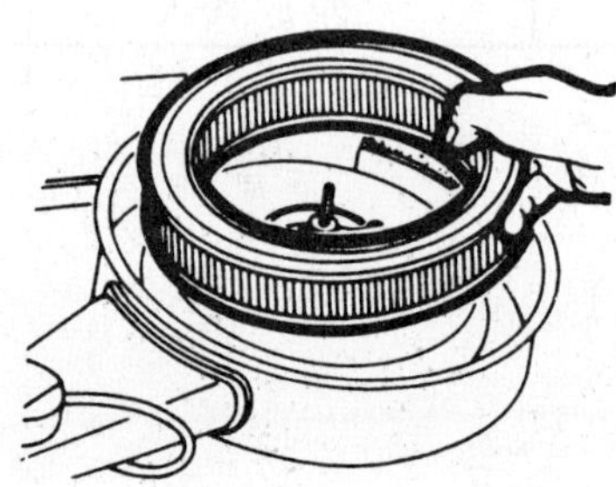

Removing the air cleaner element

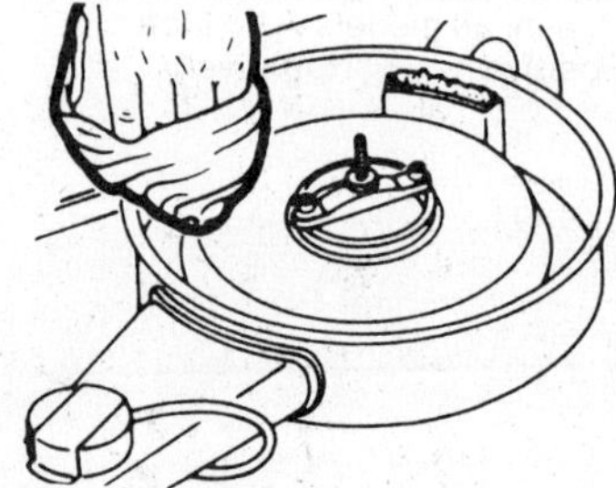

Clean out the air cleaner body before installing the new filter

DRY ELEMENT UNIT SERVICE

Housing Removal

1. Disconnect all hoses, ducts and vacuum tubes from the air cleaner assembly.
2. Remove the top cover wing nut and grommet (if equipped). Remove any side bracket mount retaining bolts (if equipped). Remove the air cleaner assembly from the top of the carburetor or intake assembly.
3. Remove the cover and the element, wipe clean all inside surfaces of the air cleaner housing and cover. Check the condition of the mounting gasket (cleaner base to carburetor). Replace the mounting gasket if it is worn or broken.
4. Reposition the cleaner assembly, element and cover on the carburetor or intake assembly.
5. Reconnect all hoses, duct and vacuum hoses removed. Tighten the wing nut finger tight.

Element Replacement

The element can, in most cases, be replaced by removing the wing nut and cleaner assembly cover. If the inside of the housing is dirty, however, remove the assembly for cleaning to prevent dirt from entering the carburetor.

Crankcase Ventilation Filter

Replace or inspect cleaner mounted crankcase ventilation filter (on models equipped) at the same time the air cleaner filter element is serviced. To replace the filter, simply remove the air cleaner top cover and pull the filter

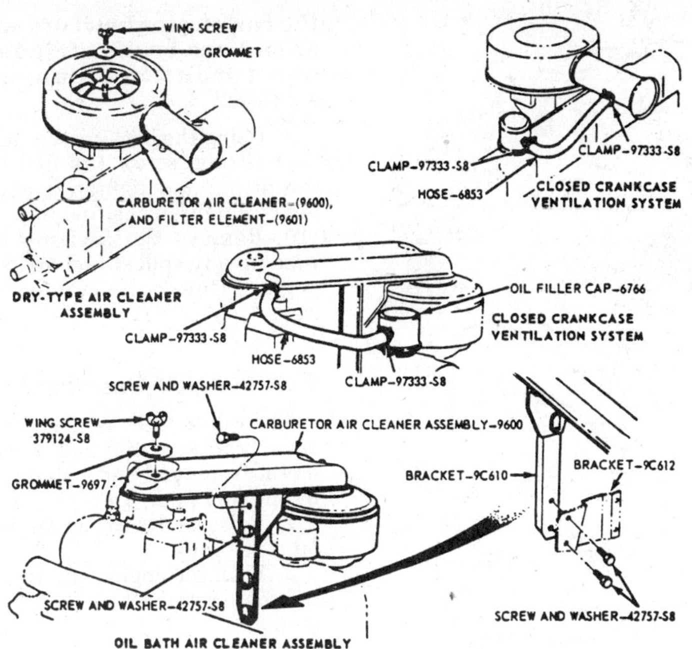

Some models may have an oil-bath air cleaner, which is emptied out, cleaned thoroughly with a rag, then filled with clean oil to the "FULL" line

from its housing. Push a new filter into the housing and install the air cleaner cover. If the filter and plastic holder need replacement, remove the clip mounting the feed tube to the air cleaner housing (hose already removed) and remove the assembly from the air cleaner. Installation is the reverse of removal.

Fuel Filter

REPLACEMENT

CAUTION

NEVER SMOKE WHEN WORKING AROUND OR NEAR GASOLINE! MAKE SURE THAT THERE IS NO IGNITION SOURCE NEAR YOU WORK AREA!

Carbureted Engines

6-232
8-255
6-300
8-302 w/Motorcraft 2150
8-351
8-400
8-460

A carburetor mounted gas filter is used. These filters screw into the float chamber. To replace one of these filters:

1. Wait until the engine is cold.
2. Remove the air cleaner assembly.
3. Place some absorbant rags under the filter.
4. Remove the hose clamp and slide the rubber hose from the filter.

CAUTION

It is possible for gasoline to spray in all directions when removing the hose! This rarely happens, but it is possible, so protect your eyes!

5. Move the fuel line out of the way and unscrew the filter from the carburetor.
6. Coat the threads of the new filter with non-hardening, gasoline-proof sealer and screw it into place by hand. Tighten it snugly with the wrench.

WARNING: Do not overtighten the filter! The threads in the carburetor bowl are soft metal and are easily stripped! You don't want to damage these threads!!

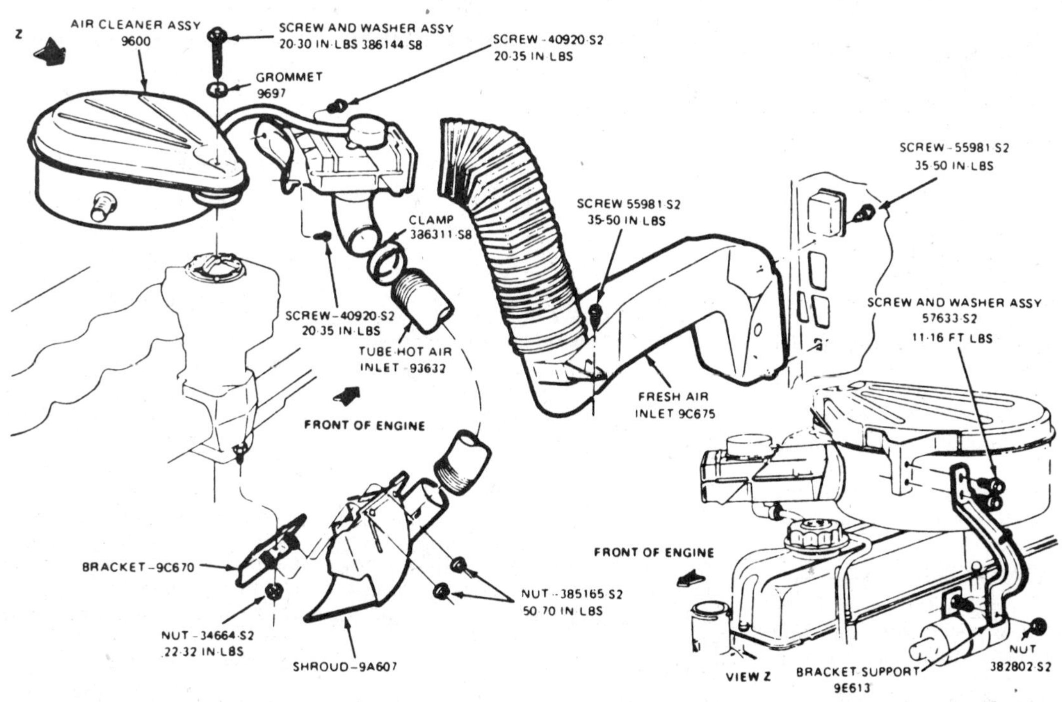

300 inline six cylinder air cleaner

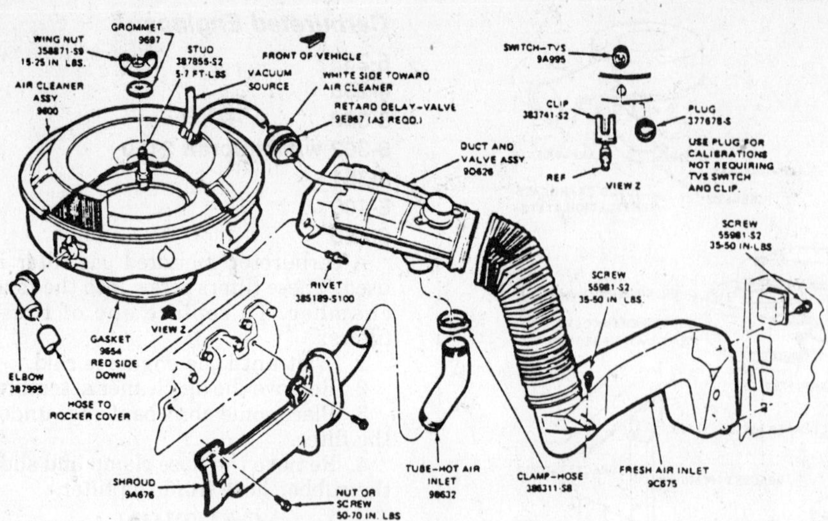

Typical V8 air cleaner, 1978 and later

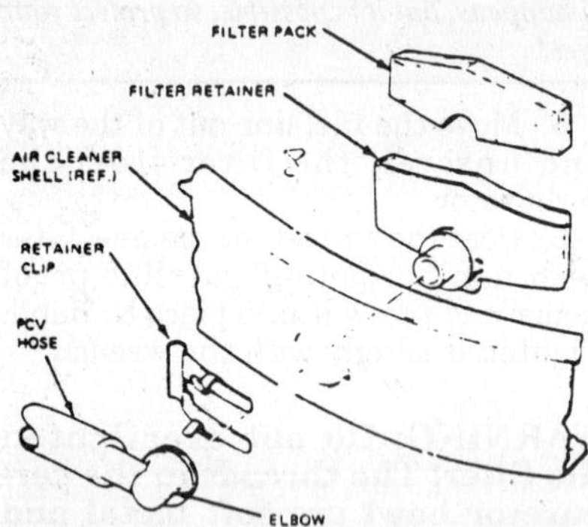

Crankcase ventilation filer in air cleaner housing

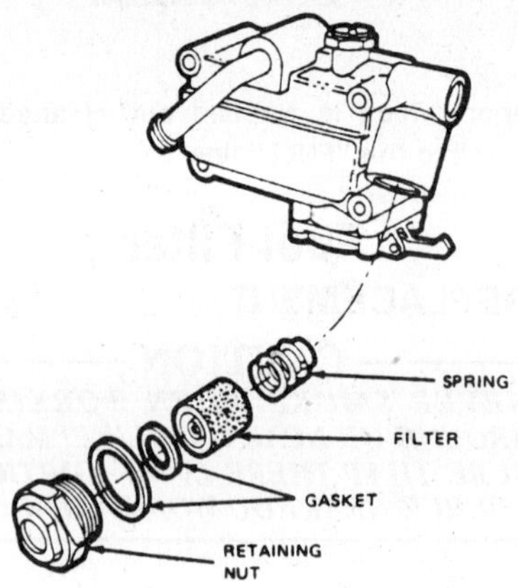

Fuel filter—Holley model 4180C 4BB1

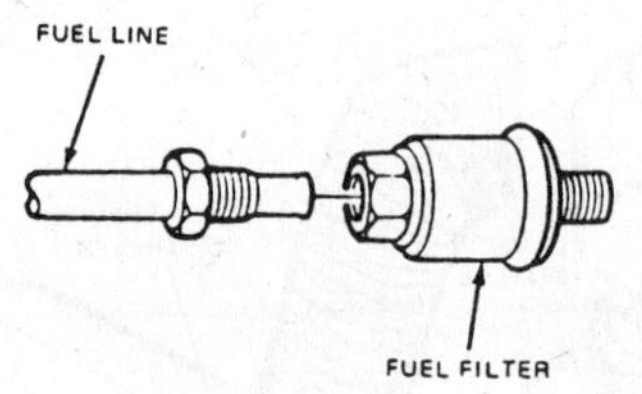

Some models have the screw-in type fuel filter which threads into the carburetor

7. Connect the hose to the new filter. Most replacement filters come with a new hose and clamps. Use them.

8. Remove the fuel-soaked rags, wipe up any spilled fuel and start the engine. Check the filter connections for leaks.

8-302 w/2700VV or 7200VV

Model 2700VV and 7200VV carburetors use a replaceable filter located behind the carburetor inlet fitting. To replace these filters:

1. Wait until the engine is cold.
2. Remove the air cleaner assembly.
3. Place some absorbant rags under the inlet fitting.
4. Using a back-up wrench on the inlet fitting, unscrew the fuel line from the inlet fitting.

CAUTION

It is possible for gasoline to spray in all directions when unscrewing the line! This rarely happens, but it is possible, so protect your eyes!

5. Move the fuel line out of the way and unscrew the inlet fiting from the carburetor.
6. Pull out the filter. The spring behind the filter may come with it.
7. Install the new filter. Some new filters come with a new spring. Use it.
8. Coat the threads of the inlet fitting with non-hardening, gasoline-proof sealer and screw it into place by hand. Tighten it snugly with the wrench.

WARNING: Do not overtighten the inlet fitting! The threads in the carburetor bowl are soft metal and are easily stripped! You don't want to damage these threads!!

9. Using the back-up wrench on the inlet fitting, screw the fuel line into the fitting and tighten it snugly. Do not overtighten the fuel line!
10. Remove the fuel-soaked rags, wipe up any spilled fuel and start the engine. Check the connections for leaks.

Fuel Injected Gasoline Engines

The inline filter is mounted on the same bracket as the fuel supply pump on the frame rail under the truck, back by the fuel tank. To replace the filter:

1. Raise and support the rear end on jackstands.
2. With the engine off, depressurize the fuel system. See the Fuel System section.
3. Remove the quick-disconnect fittings at both ends of the filter. See the Fuel System section.
4. Remove the filter and retainer from the bracket.
5. Remove the rubber insulator ring from the filter.
6. Remove the filter from the retainer.
7. Install the new filter into the retainer, noting the direction of the flow arrow.
8. Install a new rubber insulator ring.
9. Install the retainer and filter on the bracket and tighten the screws to 60 in.lb.
10. Install the fuel lines using new retainer clips.
11. Start the engine and check for leaks.

Diesel Engines

The diesel uses a spin-on filter similar to a conventional engine oil filter. It is replaced in the same manner an an oil filter. Coat the gasket surface of the new filter with clean diesel fuel to ensure a good seal. Hand tighten the filter.

PCV Valve

All models use a closed ventilation system with a sealed breather cap connected to the air cleaner by a rubber hose. The PCV valve is usually mounted in the valve cover and connected to the intake manifold by a rubber hose. Its task is to regulate the amount of crankcase (blow-by) gases which are recycled.

Since the PCV valve works under severe load it is very important that it be replaced at the interval specified in the

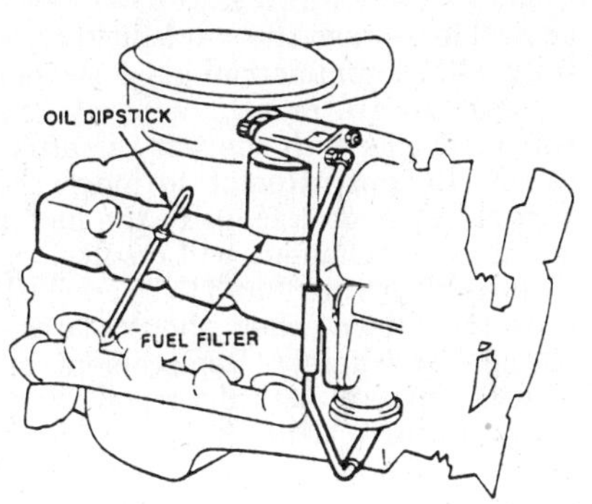

Diesel fuel filter location; filter screws on

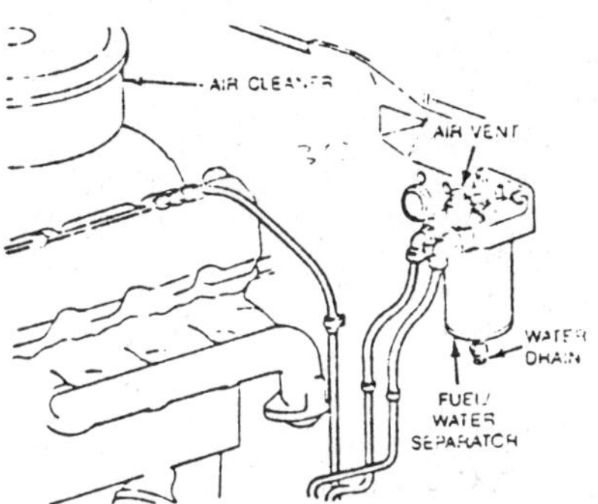

Open the drain screw on the bottom of the water separator to drain

maintenance chart. Replacement involves removing the valve from the grommet in the rocker arm cover disconnecting the hose(s) and installing a new valve. Do not attempt to clean a used valve.

Heat Riser

Some models are equipped with exhaust control (heat riser) valves located near the head pipe connection in the exhaust manifold. These valves aid initial warm-up in cold weather by restricting exhaust gas flow slightly. The heat generated by this restriction is transferred to the intake manifold where it results in improved fuel vaporization.

The operation of the exhaust control valve should be checked every 6 months or 6,000 miles. Make sure that the thermostatic spring is hooked on the stop pin and that the tension holds the valve shut. Rotate the counterweight by hand and make sure that it moves freely through about 90° of rotation. A valve which is operating properly will open when light finger pressure is applied (cold engine). Lubricate the shaft bushings with a mixture of penetrating oil and graphite. Operate the valve manually a few times to work in the lubricant.

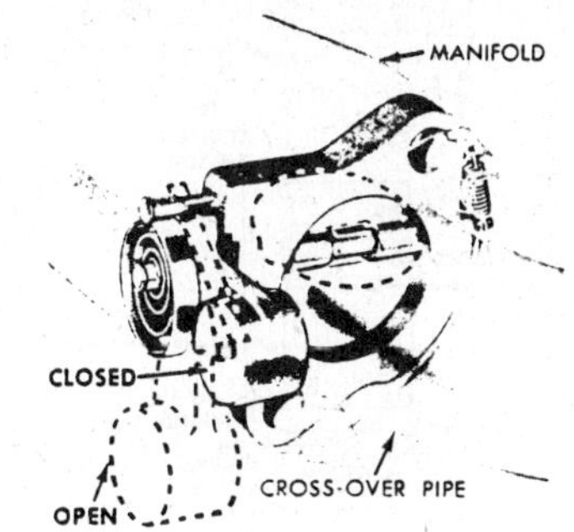

V8 exhaust control valve—typical

Evaporative Emissions Canister

The canister functions to cycle the fuel vapor from the fuel tank and carburetor float chamber into the intake manifold and eventually into the cylinders for combustion. The activated charcoal element within the canister acts as a storage device for the fuel vapor at times when the engine operating condition will not permit fuel vapor to burn efficiently.

The only required service for the evaporative emissions canister is inspection at the interval specified in the maintenance chart. If the charcoal element is gummed up the entire canister should be replaced. Disconnect the canister purge hose(s), loosen the canister retaining bracket, lift out the canister. Installation is the reverse of removal.

Battery

FLUID LEVEL (EXCEPT MAINTENANCE FREE BATTERIES)

Check the battery electrolyte level at least once a month, or more often in hot weather or during periods of extended truck operation. The level can be checked through the case on translucent polypropylene batteries; the cell caps must be removed on other models. The electrolyte level in each cell should be kept filled to the split ring inside, or the line marked on the outside of the case.

If the level is low, add only distilled water, or colorless, odorless drinking water, through the opening until the level is correct. Each cell is completely separate from the others, so each must be checked and filled individually.

If water is added in freezing weather, the truck should be driven several miles to allow the water to mix with the electrolyte. Otherwise, the battery could freeze.

SPECIFIC GRAVITY (EXCEPT MAINTENANCE FREE BATTERIES)

At least once a year, check the specific gravity of the battery. It should be between 1.20 in.Hg and 1.26 in.Hg at room temperature.

The specific gravity can be check with the use of an hydrometer, an inexpensive instrument available from many sources, including auto parts stores. The hydrometer has a squeeze bulb at one end and a nozzle at the other. Battery electrolyte is sucked into the hydrometer until the float is lifted from its seat. The specific gravity is then read by noting the position of the float. Generally, if after charging, the specific gravity between any two cells varies more than 50 points (0.50), the battery is bad and should be replaced.

It is not possible to check the specific gravity in this manner on sealed (maintenance free) batteries. Instead, the indicator built into the top of the case must be relied on to display any signs of battery deterioration. If the indicator is dark, the battery can be assumed to be OK. If the indicator is light, the specific gravity is low, and the battery should be charged or replaced.

CABLES AND CLAMPS

Once a year, the battery terminals

SPECIFIC GRAVITY (@ 80°F.) AND CHARGE
Specific Gravity Reading
(use the minimum figure for testing)

Minimum	Battery Charge
1.260	100% Charged
1.230	75% Charged
1.200	50% Charged
1.170	25% Charged
1.140	Very Little Power Left
1.110	Completely Discharged

Battery specific gravity. Some testers have colored balls which correspond to the numerical values in the left column

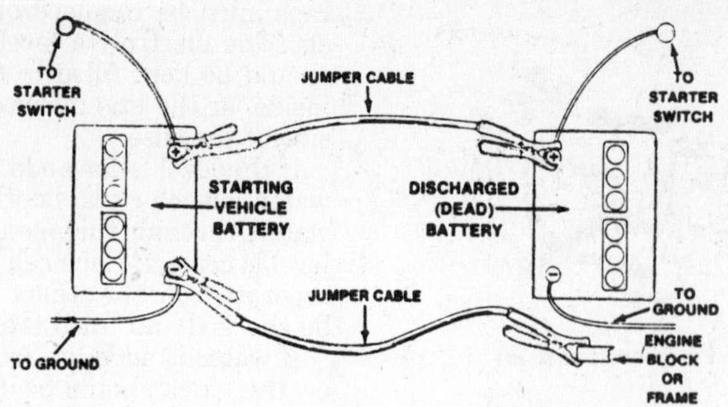

Make certain vehicles do not touch. This hook-up for negative ground cars only

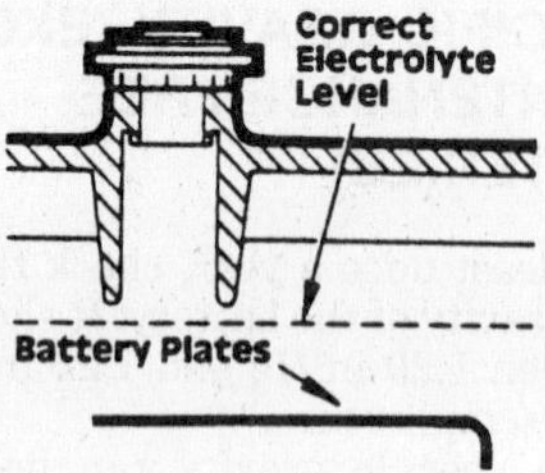

Proper battery electrolyte level

and the cable clamps should be cleaned. Loosen the clamps and remove the cables, negative cable first. On batteries with posts on top, the use of a puller specially made for the purpose is recommended. These are inexpensive, and available in auto parts stores. Side terminal battery cables are secured with a bolt.

Clean the cable lamps and the battery terminal with a wire brush, until all corrosion, grease, etc., is removed and the metal is shiny. It is especially important to clean the inside of the clamp thoroughly, since a small deposit of foreign material or oxidation there will prevent a sound electrical connection and inhibit either starting or charging. Special tools are available for cleaning these parts, one type for conventional batteries and another type for side terminal batteries.

Before installing the cables, loosen the battery holddown clamp or strap, remove the battery and check the battery tray. Clear it of any debris, and check it for soundness. Rust should be wire brushed away, and the metal given a coat of anti-rust paint. Replace the battery and tighten the holddown clamp or strap securely, but be careful not to overtighten, which will crack the battery case.

After the clamps and terminals are clean, reinstall the cables, negative cable last; do not hammer on the clamps to install. Tighten the clamps securely, but do not distort them. Give the clamps and terminals a thin external coat of grease after installation, to retard corrosion.

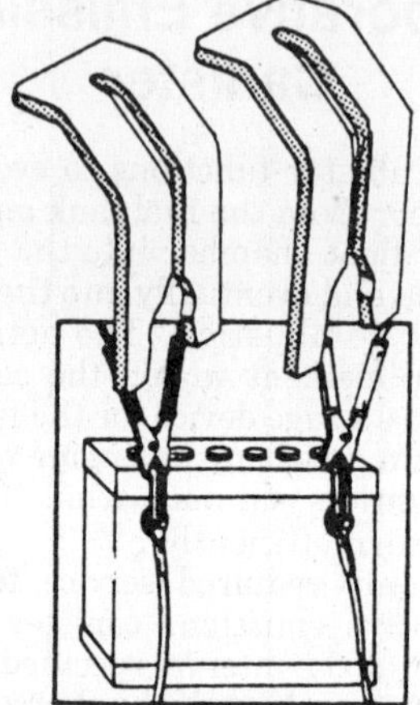

Side terminal batteries occasionally pose a problem when connecting jumper cables. There frequently isn't enough room to clamp the cables without touching sheet metal. Side terminal adaptors are available to alleviate this problem and should be removed after use.

Check the cables at the same time that the terminals are cleaned. If the cable insulation is cracked or broken, or if the ends are frayed, the cable should be replaced with a new cable of the same length and gauge.

CAUTION

Keep flame or sparks away from the battery; it gives off explosive hydrogen gas. Battery electrolyte contains sulphuric acid. If you should splash any on your skin or in your eyes, flush the affected area with plenty of clear water. If it lands in your eyes, get medical help immediately.

Windshield Wipers

For maximum effectiveness and longest element lift, the windshield and wiper blades should be kept clean. Dirt, tree sap, road tar and so on will cause streaking, smearing and blade deterioration if left on the glass. It is advisable to wash the windshield carefully with a commercial glass cleaner at least once a month. Wipe off the rubber blades with the wet rag afterwards. Do not attempt to move the wipers by hand; damage to the motor and drive mechanism will result.

If the blades are found to be cracked, broken or torn, they should be replaced immediately. Replacement intervals will vary with usage, although ozone deterioration usually limits blade lift to about one year. If the wiper pattern is smeared or streaked, or if the blade chatters across the glass, the elements should be replaced. It is easiest and most sensible to replace the elements in pairs.

There are basically three different types of refills, which differ in their method of replacement. One type has two release buttons, approximately ⅓ of the way up from the ends of the blade frame. Pushing the buttons down releases a lock and allows the rubber filler to be removed from the frame. The new filler slides back into the frame and locks in place.

The second type of refill has two metal tabs which are unlocked by squeezing them together. The rubber filler can then be withdrawn from the frame jaws. A new refill is installed by inserting the refill into the front frame jaws and sliding it rear ward to engage the remaining frame jaws. There are usually four jaws. Be certain when installing that the refill is engaged in all of them. At the end of its travel, the tabs will lock into place on the front jaws of the wiper blade frame.

The third type is a refill made from polycarbonate. The refill has a simple locking device at one end which flexes downward out of the groove into which the jaws of the holder fit, allowing easy release. By sliding the new refill through all the jaws and pushing through the slight resistance when it reaches the end of its travel, the refill will lock into position.

Regardless of the type of refill used, make sure that all of the frame jaws are engaged as the refill is pushed into place and locked. The metal blade holder and frame will scratch the glass if allowed to touch it.

Belts

Once a year or at 12,000 mile intervals, the tension (and condition) of the alternator, power steering (if so equipped), air conditioning (if so equipped), and Thermactor air pump drive belts should be checked, and, if necessary, adjusted. Loose accessory drive belts can lead to poor engine cooling and diminish alternator, power steering pump, air conditioning compressor or Thermactor air pump output. A belt that is too tight places a severe strain on the water pump, alternator, power steering pump, compressor or air pump bearings.

Replace any belt that is so glazed, worn or stretched that it cannot be tightened sufficiently.

NOTE: The material used in late model drive belts is such that the belts do not show wear. Replace belts at least every three years.

On vehicles with matched belts, replace both belts. New ½", ⅜" and $^{15}/_{32}$" wide belts are to be adjusted to a tension of 140 lbs.; ¼" wide belts are adjusted to 80 lbs., measured on a belt tension gauge. Any belt that has been operating for a minimum of 10 minutes is considered a used belt. In the first 10 minutes, the belt should stretch to its maximum extent. After 10 minutes, stop the engine and recheck the belt tension. Belt tension for a used belt should be maintained at 110 lbs. (all except ¼" wide belts) or 60 lbs. (¼" wide belts). If a belt tension gauge is not available, the following procedures may be used.

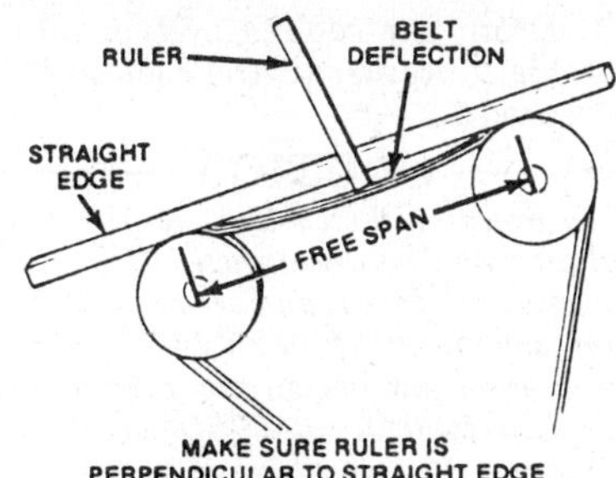

Measuring belt deflection

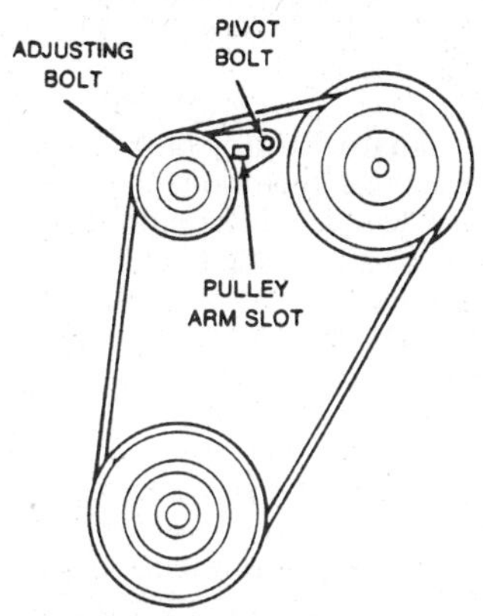

Some pulleys have a rectangular slot to aid in moving the accessory to be tightened

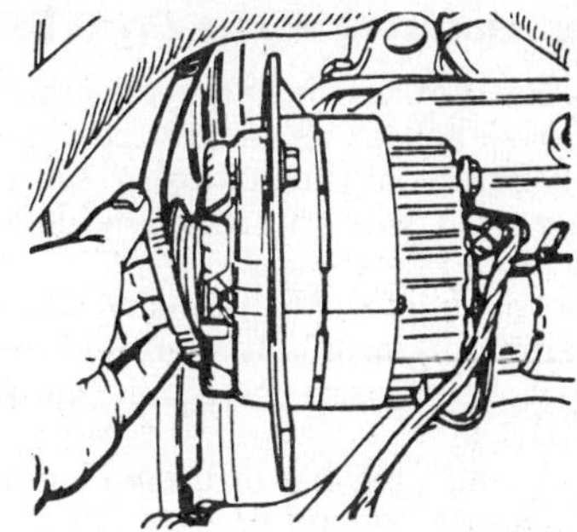

Slip the new belt over the pulley

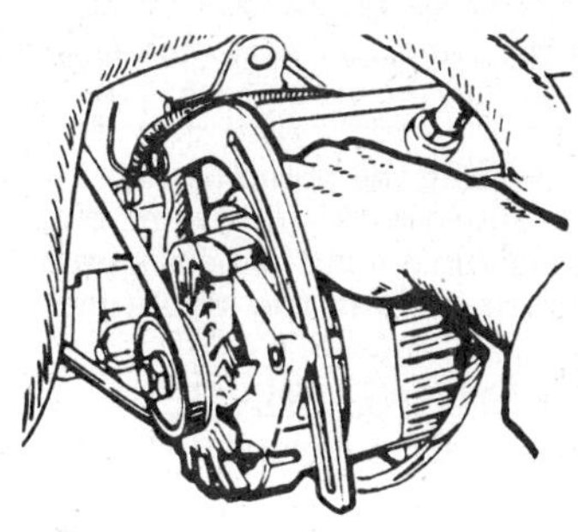

Pull outward on the component and tighten the mounting bolts

ADJUSTMENTS FOR ALL EXCEPT THE SERPENTINE (SINGLE) BELT

CAUTION

On models equipped with an electric cooling fan, disconnect the negative battery cable or fan motor wiring harness connector before replacing or adjusting drive belts. The fan may come on, under certain circumstances, even though the ignition is off!

Alternator (Fan Drive) Belt

1. Position the ruler perpendicular to the drive belt at its longest straight run. Test the tightness of the belt by pressing it firmly with your thumb. The deflection should not exceed ¼".
2. If the deflection exceeds ¼", loosen the alternator mounting and adjusting arm bolts.
3. Place a 1" open-end or adjustable wrench on the adjusting ridge cast on the body, and pull on the wrench until the proper tension is achieved.
4. Holding the alternator in place to maintain tension, tighten the adjusting arm bolt. Recheck the belt tension. When the belt is properly tensioned, tighten the alternator mounting bolt.

V8 MODELS

1. Position a ruler perpendicular to the drive belt at its longest run. Test the tightness of the belt by pressing it firmly with your thumb. The deflection should be about ¼".
2. To adjust the belt tension, loosen the three bolts in the three elongated adjusting slots at the power steering pump attaching bracket.
3. Turn the steering pump drive belt adjusting nut as required until the proper deflection is obtained. Turning the adjusting nut clockwise will increase tension and decrease deflection; counterclockwise will decrease tension and increase deflection.
4. Without disturbing the pump, tighten the three attaching bolts.

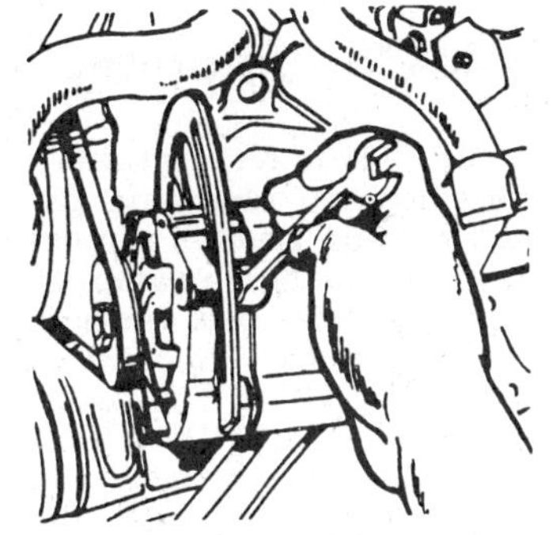

To adjust belt tension or to change belts, first loosen the component's mounting and adjusting bolts slightly

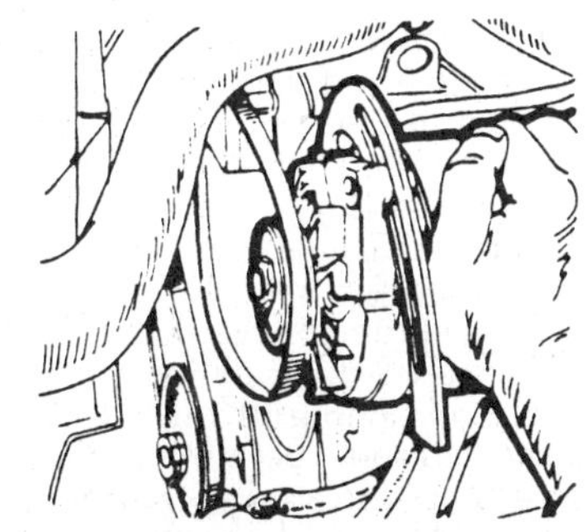

Push the component towards the engine and slip off the belt

Air Conditioning Compressor Drive Belt

1. Position a ruler perpendicular to the drive belt at its longest run. Test the tightness of the belt by pressing it firmly with your thumb. The deflection should not exceed ¼".
2. If the engine is equipped with an idler pulley, loosen the idler pulley adjusting bolt, insert a pry bar between the pulley and the engine (or in the idler pulley adjusting slot), and adjust the tension accordingly. If the engine is not equipped with an idler pulley, the alternator must be moved to accomplish this adjustment, as outlined under Alternator (Fan Drive) Belt.
3. When the proper tension is reached, tighten the idler pulley adjusting bolt (if so equipped) or the alternator adjusting and mounting bolts.

Thermactor Air Pump Drive Belt

1. Position a ruler perpendicular to the drive belt at its longest run. Test the tightness of the belt by pressing it firmly with your thumb. The deflection should be about ¼".
2. To adjust the belt tension, loosen the adjusting arm bolt slightly. If necessary, also loosen the mounting belt slightly.
3. Using a pry bar or broom handle, pry against the pump rear cover to move the pump toward or away from the engine as necessary.

CAUTION

Do not pry against the pump housing itself, as damage to the housing may result.

4. Holding the pump in place, tighten the adjusting arm bolt and recheck the tension. When the belt is properly tensioned, tighten the mounting bolt.

SERPENTINE (SINGLE) DRIVE BELT MODELS

Most late models feature a single, wide, ribbed V-belt that drives the water pump, alternator, and (on some models) the air conditioner compressor. To install a new belt, loosen the bracket lock bolt, retract the belt tensioner with a pry bar and slide the old belt off of the pulleys. Slip on a new belt and release the tensioner and tighten the lock bolt. The spring powered tensioner eliminates the need for periodic adjustments.

WARNING: Check to make sure that the V-ribbed belt is located properly in all drive pulleys before applying tensioner pressure.

Hoses

CAUTION

On models equipped with an electric cooling fan, disconnect the negative battery cable, or fan motor wiring harness connector before replacing any radiator/heater hose. The fan may come on, under certain circumstances, even though the ignition is Off.

REPLACEMENT

Inspect the condition of the radiator and heater hoses periodically. Early spring and at the beginning of the fall or winter, when you are performing other maintenance, are good times. Make sure the engine and cooling system are cold. Visually inspect for cracking, rotting or collapsed hoses, replace as necessary. Run your hand along the length of the hose. If a weak or swollen spot is noted when squeezing the hose wall, replace the hose.

1. Drain the cooling system into a suitable container (if the coolant is to be reused).

CAUTION

When draining the coolant, keep in mind that cats and dogs are attracted by the ethylene glycol antifreeze, and are quite likely to drink any that is left in an uncovered container or in puddles on the ground. This will prove fatal in sufficient quantity. Always drain the coolant into a sealable container. Coolant should be reused unless it is contaminated or several years old.

2. Loosen the hose clamps at each end of the hose that requires replacement.
3. Twist, pull and slide the hose off the radiator, water pump, thermostat or heater connection.
4. Clean the hose mounting connections. Position the hose clamps on the new hose.
5. Coat the connection surfaces with a water resistant sealer and slide the hose into position. Make sure the hose clamps are located beyond the raised bead of the connector (if equipped) and centered in the clamping area of the connection.
6. Tighten the clamps to 20-30 in.lb. Do not overtighten.
7. Fill the cooling system.
8. Start the engine and allow it to reach normal operating temperature. Check for leaks.

Air Conditioning

NOTE: This book contains simple testing and charging procedures for your truck's air conditioning system. More comprehensive testing, diagnosis and service procedures may be found in CHILTON'S GUIDE TO AIR CONDITIONING SERVICE AND REPAIR, book part number 7580, available at your local retailer.

GENERAL SERVICING PROCEDURES

The most important aspect of air conditioning service is the maintenance of pure and adequate charge of refrigerant in the system. A refrigeration system cannot function properly if a significant percentage of the charge is lost. Leaks are common because the severe vibration encountered in an automobile can easily cause a sufficient cracking or loosening of the air conditioning fittings. As a result, the extreme operating pressures of the system force refrigerant out.

The problem can be understood by considering what happens to the system as it is operated with a continuous leak. Because the expansion valve regulates the flow of refrigerant to the evaporator, the level of refrigerant there is fairly constant. The receiver-drier stores any excess of refrigerant, and so a loss will first appear there as a reduction in the level of liquid. As this level nears the bottom of the vessel, some refrigerant vapor bubbles will begin to appear in the stream of liquid supplied to the expansion valve. This vapor decreases the capacity of the expansion valve very little as the valve opens to compensate for its presence. As the quantity of liquid in the condenser decreases, the operating pressure will drop there and throughout the high side of the system. As the R-12 continues to be expelled, the pressure available to force the liquid through the expansion valve will continue to decrease, and, eventually, the valve's orifice will prove to be too much of a restriction for adequate flow even with the needle fully withdrawn.

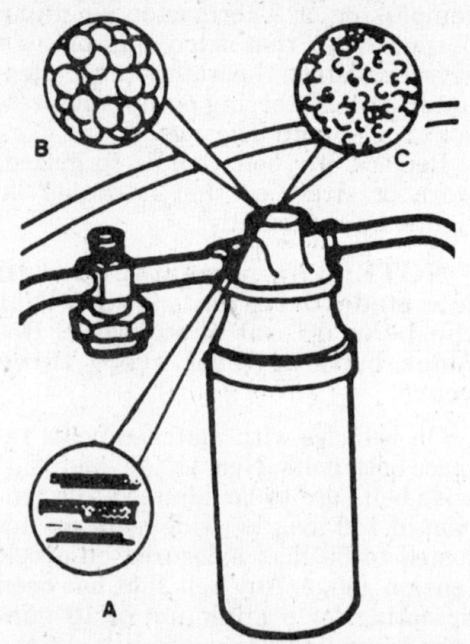

Oil streaks (A), constant bubbles (B) or foam (C) indicate there is not enough refrigerant in the system. Occasional bubbles during initial operation is normal. A clear sight glass indicates a proper charge of refrigerant or no refrigerant at all, which can be determined by the presence of cold air at the outlets in the car. If the glass is clouded with a milky white substance, have the receiver/drier checked professionally.

At this point, low side pressure will start to drop, and severe reduction in cooling capacity, marked by freeze-up of the evaporator coil, will result. Eventually, the operating pressure of the evaporator will be lower than the pressure of the atmosphere surrounding it, and air will be drawn into the system wherever there are leaks in the low side.

Because all atmospheric air contains at least some moisture, water will enter the system and mix with the R-12 and the oil. Trace amounts of moisture will cause sludging of the oil, and corrosion of the system. Saturation and clogging of the filter-drier, and freezing of the expansion valve orifice will eventually result. As air fills the system to a greater and greater extend, it will interfere more and more with the normal flows of refrigerant and heat.

A list of general precautions that should be observed while doing this follows:

1. Keep all tools as clean and dry as possible.
2. Thoroughly purge the service gauges and hoses of air and moisture before connecting them to the system. Keep them capped when not in use.
3. Thoroughly clean any refrigerant fitting before disconnecting it, in order to minimize the entrance of dirt into the system.
4. Plan any operation that requires opening the system beforehand in order to minimize the length of time it will be exposed to open air. Cap or seal the open ends to minimize the entrance of foreign material.
5. When adding oil, pour it through an extremely clean and dry tube or funnel. Keep the oil capped whenever possible. Do not use oil that has not been kept tightly sealed.
6. Use only refrigerant 12. Purchase refrigerant intended for use in only automotive air conditioning system. Avoid the use of refrigerant 12 that may be packaged for another use, such as cleaning, or powering a horn, as it is impure.
7. Completely evacuate any system that has been opened to replace a component, other than when isolating the compressor, or that has leaked sufficiently to draw in moisture and air. This requires evacuating air and moisture with a good vacuum pump for at least one hour.

If a system has been open for a considerable length of time it may be advisable to evacuate the system for up to 12 hours (overnight).

8. Use a wrench on both halves of a fitting that is to be disconnected, so as to avoid placing torque on any of the refrigerant lines.

ADDITIONAL PREVENTIVE MAINTENANCE CHECKS

Antifreeze

In order to prevent heater core freeze-up during A/C operation, it is necessary to maintain permanent type antifreeze protection of +15°F (-9°C) or lower. A reading of -15°F (-26°C) is ideal since this protection also supplies sufficient corrosion inhibitors for the protection of the engine cooling system.

WARNING: Do not use antifreeze longer than specified by the manufacturer.

Radiator Cap

For efficient operation of an air conditioned truck's cooling system, the radiator cap should have a holding pressure which meets manufacturer's specifications. A cap which fails to hold these pressure should be replaced.

Condenser

Any obstruction of or damage to the condenser configuration will restrict the air flow which is essential to its efficient operation. It is therefore, a good rule to keep this unit clean and in proper physical shape.

NOTE: Bug screens are regarded as obstructions.

Condensation Drain Tube

This single molded drain tube expels the condensation, which accumulates on the bottom of the evaporator housing, into the engine compartment.

If this tube is obstructed, the air conditioning performance can be restricted and condensation buildup can spill over onto the vehicle's floor.

SAFETY PRECAUTIONS

Because of the importance of the necessary safety precautions that must be exercised when working with air conditioning systems and R-12 refrigerant, a recap of the safety precautions are outlined.

1. Avoid contact with a charged refrigeration system, even when working on another part of the air conditioning system or vehicle. If a heavy tool comes into contact with a section of copper tubing or a heat exchanger, it can easily cause the relatively soft material to rupture.
2. When it is necessary to apply force to a fitting which contains refrigerant, as when checking that all system couplings are securely tightened, use a wrench on both parts of the fitting involved, if possible. This will avoid putting torque on the refrigerant tubing. (It is advisable, when possible, to use tube or line wrenches when tightening these flare nut fittings.)
3. Do not attempt to discharge the system by merely loosening a fitting, or removing the service valve caps and cracking these valves. Precise control is possibly only when using the service gauges. Place a rag under the open end of the center charging hose while discharging the system to catch any drops of liquid that might escape. Wear protective gloves when connecting or disconnecting service gauge hoses.
4. Discharge the system only in a well ventilated area, as high concentrations of the gas can exclude oxygen and act as an anesthetic. When leak testing or soldering this is particularly important, as toxic gas is formed when R-12 contacts any flame.
5. Never start a system without first verifying that both service valves are backseated, if equipped, and that all fittings are throughout the system are snugly connected.
6. Avoid applying heat to any refrigerant line or storage vessel. Charging may be aided by using water heated to less than 125°F (52°C) to warm the refrigerant container. Never allow a refrigerant storage container to sit out in the sun, or near any other source of heat, such as a radiator.
7. Always wear goggles when working on a system to protect the eyes. If refrigerant contacts the eye, it is advisable in all cases to see a physician as soon as possible.
8. Frostbite from liquid refrigerant should be treated by first gradually warming the area with cool water, and then gently applying petroleum jelly. A physician should be consulted.
9. Always keep refrigerant can fittings capped when not in use. Avoid sudden shock to the can which might occur from dropping it, or from banging a heavy tool against it. Never carry a refrigerant can in the passenger compartment of a truck.
10. Always completely discharge the system before painting the vehicle (if the paint is to be baked on), or before welding anywhere near the refrigerant lines.

TEST GAUGES

Most of the service work performed in air conditioning requires the use of a set of two gauges, one for the high (head) pressure side of the system, the other for the low (suction) side.

The low side gauge records both pressure and vacuum. Vacuum readings are calibrated from 0 to 30 inches Hg and the pressure graduations read from 0 to no less than 60 psi.

The high side gauge measures pressure from 0 to at last 600 psi.

Both gauges are threaded into a manifold that contains two hand shut-off valves. Proper manipulation of these valves and the use of the attached test hoses allow the user to perform the following services:

1. Test high and low side pressures.
2. Remove air, moisture, and contaminated refrigerant.
3. Purge the system (of refrigerant).
4. Charge the system (with refrigerant).

The manifold valves are designed so that they have no direct effect on gauge readings, but serve only to provide for, or cut off, flow of refrigerant through the manifold. During all testing and hook-up operations, the valves are kept in a close position to avoid disturbing the refrigeration system. The valves are opened only to purge the system or refrigerant or to charge it.

INSPECTION

CAUTION

The compressed refrigerant used in the air conditioning system expands into the atmosphere at a temperature of −21.7°F (−30°C) or lower. This will freeze any surface, including your eyes, that it contacts. In addition, the refrigerant decomposes into a poisonous gas in the presence of a flame. Do not open or disconnect any part of the air conditioning system.

Sight Glass Check

You can safely make a few simple checks to determine if your air conditioning system needs service. The tests work best if the temperature is warm (about 70°F [21.1°C]).

NOTE: If your vehicle is equipped with an aftermarket air conditioner, the following system check may not apply. You should contact the manufacturer of the unit for instructions on systems checks.

1. Place the automatic transmission in Park or the manual transmission in Neutral. Set the parking brake.
2. Run the engine at a fast idle (about 1,500 rpm) either with the help of a friend or by temporarily readjusting the idle speed screw.
3. Set the controls for maximum cold with the blower on High.
4. Locate the sight glass in one of the system lines. Usually it is on the left alongside the top of the radiator.
5. If you see bubbles, the system must be recharged. Very likely there is a leak at some point.
6. If there are no bubbles, there is either no refrigerant at all or the system is fully charged. Feel the two hoses going to the belt-driven compressor. If they are both at the same temperature, the system is empty and must be recharged.
7. If one hose (high pressure) is warm and the other (low pressure) is cold, the system may be all right. However, you are probably making these tests because you think there is something wrong, so proceed to the next step.
8. Have an assistant in the truck turn the fan control on and off to operate the compressor clutch. Watch the sight glass.
9. If bubbles appear when the clutch is disengaged and disappear when it is engaged, the system is properly charged.
10. If the refrigerant takes more than 45 seconds to bubble when the clutch is disengaged, the system is overcharged. This usually causes poor cooling at low speeds.

CAUTION

If it is determined that the system has a leak, it should be corrected as soon as possible. Leaks may allow moisture to enter and cause a very expensive rust problem.

NOTE: Exercise the air conditioner for a few minutes, every two weeks or so, during the cold months. This avoids the possibility of the compressor seals drying out from lack of lubrication.

TESTING THE SYSTEM

1. Connect a gauge set.
2. Close (clockwise) both gauge set valves.
4. Park the truck in the shade, at least 5 feet from any walls. Start the engine, set the parking brake, place the transmission in NEUTRAL and establish an idle of 1,100-1,300 rpm.
5. Run the air conditioning system for full cooling, in the MAX or COLD mode.
6. The low pressure gauge should read 5-20 psi; the high pressure gauge should indicate 120-180 psi.

WARNING: These pressures are the norm for an ambient temperature of 70-80°F (21-27°F). Higher air temperatures along with high humidity will cause higher syustem pressures. At idle speed and an ambient temperature of 110°F (43°F), the high pressure reading can exceed 300 psi.

Under these extreme conditions, you can keep the pressures down by directing a large electric floor fan through the condenser.

DISCHARGING THE SYSTEM

1. Remove the caps from the high and low pressure charging valves in the high and low pressure lines.
2. Turn both manifold gauge set hand valves to the fully closed (clockwise) position.
3. Connect the manifold gauge set.
4. If the gauge set hoses do not have the gauge port actuating pins, install fitting adapters T71P-19703-S and R on the manifold gauge set hoses. If the truck does not have a service access gauge port valve, connect the gauge set low pressure hose to the evaporator service access gauge port valve. A special adapter, T77L-19703-A, is required to attach the manifold gauge set to the high pressure service access gauge port valve.
5. Place the end of the center hose away from you and the truck.
6. Open the low pressure gauge valve slightly and allow the system pressure to bleed off.
7. Whe the system is just about empty, open the high pressure valve very slowly to avoid losing an excessive amount of refrigerant oil. Allow any remaining refrigerant to escape.

EVACUATING THE SYSTEM

NOTE: This procedure requires the use of a vacuum pump.

1. Connect the manifold gauge set.
2. Discharge the system.
3. On 1983 and later models, make sure that the low pressure gauge set hose is connected to the low pressure service gauge port on the top center of the accumulator/drier assembly and the high pressure hose connected to the high pressure service gauge port on the compressor discharge line.
4. Connect the center service hose to the inlet fitting of the vacuum pump.
5. Turn both gauge set valves to the wide open position.
6. Start the pump and note the low side gauge reading.
7. Operate the pump until the low pressure gauge reads 25-30 in.Hg. Continue running the vacuum pump for 10 minutes more. If you've replaced some component in the system, run the pump for an additional 20-30 minutes.
8. Leak test the system. Close both gauge set valves. Turn off the pump. The needle should remain stationary at the point at which the pump was turned off. If the needle drops to zero rapidly, there is a leak in the system which must be repaired.

LEAK TESTING

Some leak tests can be performed with a soapy water solution. There must be at least a ½ lb. charge in the system for a leak to be detected. The most extensive leak tests are performed with either a Halide flame type leak tester or the more preferable electronic leak tester.

In either case, the equipment is expensive, and, the use of a Halide detector can be **extremely** hazardous!

CHARGING THE SYSTEM

CAUTION

NEVER OPEN THE HIGH PRESSURE SIDE WITH A CAN OF REFRIGERANT CONNECTED TO THE SYSTEM! OPENING THE HIGH PRESSURE SIDE WILL OVERPRESSURIZE THE CAN, CAUSING IT TO EXPLODE!

1980-82

1. Connect the gauge set.
2. Close (clockwise) both gauge set valves.
3. Connect the center hose to the refrigerant can opener valve.

CAUTION

KEEP THE CAN IN AN UPRIGHT POSITION!

4. Make sure the can opener valve is closed, that is, the needle is raised, and connect the valve to the can. Open the valve, puncturing the can with the needle.
5. Loosen the center hose fitting at the pressure gauge, allowing refrigerant to purge the hose of air.
6. Open the low side gauge set valve and the can valve.
7. Start the engine and turn the air conditioner to the maximum cooling mode. Run the engine at about 1,500 rpm. The compressor will operate and pull refrigerant gas into the system.

NOTE: To help speed the process, the can may be placed, upright, in a pan of warm water, not exceeding 125°F (52°C).

8. If more than one can of refrigerant is needed, close the can valve and gauge set low side valve when the can is empty and connect a new can to the opener. Repeat the charging process until the sight glass indicates a full charge. The frost line on the outside of the can will indicate what portion of the can has been used.

CAUTION

NEVER ALLOW THE HIGH PRESSURE SIDE READING TO EXCEED 240 psi!

9. When the charging process has been completed, close the gauge set valve and can valve. Run the system for at least five minutes to allow it to normalize. Low pressure side reading should be 4-25 psi; high pressure reading should be 120-210 psi at an ambient temperature of 70-90°F (21-32°C).
10. Loosen both service hoses at the gauges to allow any refrigerant to escape. Remove the gauge set and install the dust caps on the service valves.

NOTE: Multi-can dispensers are available which allow a simultaneous hook-up of up to four 1 lb. cans of R-12.

CAUTION

Never exceed the recommended maximum charge for the system.

The maximum charge for systems is:
1980-81: 3½ lbs.
1982: 2½ lbs.

1983-87

1. Connect the gauge set.
2. Close (clockwise) both gauge set valves.
3. Connect the center hose to the refrigerant can opener valve.
4. Make sure the can opener valve is closed, that is, the needle is raised, and connect the valve to the can. Open the valve, puncturing the can with the needle.
5. Loosen the center hose fitting at the pressure gauge, allowing refrigerant to purge the hose of air. When the air is bled, tighten the fitting.

CAUTION

IF THE LOW PRESSURE GAUGE SET HOSE IS NOT CONNECTED TO THE ACCUMULATOR/DRIER, KEEP THE CAN IN AN UPRIGHT POSITION!

6. Disconnect the wire harness snap-lock connector from the clutch cycling pressure switch and install a jumper wire across the two terminals of the connector.
7. Open the low side gauge set valve and the can valve.
8. Allow refrigerant to be drawn into the system.
9. When no more refrigerant is drawn into the system, start the engine and run it at about 1,500 rpm. Turn on the system and operate it at the full high position. The compressor will operate and pull refrigerant gas into the system.

NOTE: To help speed the process, the can may be placed, upright, in a pan of warm water, not exceeding 125°F (52°C).

10. If more than one can of refrigerant is needed, close the can valve and gauge set low side valve when the can is empty and connect a new can to the opener. Repeat the charging process until the sight glass indicates a full charge. The frost line on the outside of the can will indicate what portion of the can has been used.

CAUTION

NEVER ALLOW THE HIGH PRESSURE SIDE READING TO EXCEED 240 psi.

11. When the charging process has been completed, close the gauge set valve and can valve. Remove the jumper wire and reconnect the cycling clutch wire. Run the system for at least five minutes to allow it to normalize. Low pressure side reading should be 4-25 psi; high pressure reading should be 120-210 psi at an ambient temperature of 70-90°F (21-32°C).
12. Loosen both service hoses at the gauges to allow any refrigerant to escape. Remove the gauge set and install the dust caps on the service valves.

NOTE: Multi-can dispensers are available which allow a simultaneous hook-up of up to four 1 lb. cans of R-12.

CAUTION

Never exceed the recommended maximum charge for the system.

The maximum charge for systems is 2½ lb.

2-Wheel Drive Front Wheel Bearings

ADJUSTMENT

The front wheels each rotate on a set of opposed, tapered roller bearings as shown in the accompanying illustration. The grease retainer at the inside of the hub prevents lubricant from leaking into the brake drum.

1. Raise and support the front end on jackstands.
2. Remove the grease cap and remove excess grease from the end of the spindle.
3. Remove the cotter pin and nut lock shown in the illustration.
4. Rotate the wheel, hub and drum assembly while tightening the adjusting nut to 17-25 ft.lb. in order to seat the bearings.
5. Back off the adjusting nut ½, then retighten the adjusting nut to 10-15 in.lb.
6. Locate the nut lock on the adjusting nut so that the castellations on the lock are lined up with the cotter pin hole in the spindle.
7. Install the new cotter pin, bending the ends of the cotter pin around the castellated flange of the nut lock.
8. Check the wheel for proper rotation, then install the grease cap. If the wheel still does not rotate properly, inspect and clean or replace the wheel bearings and cups.

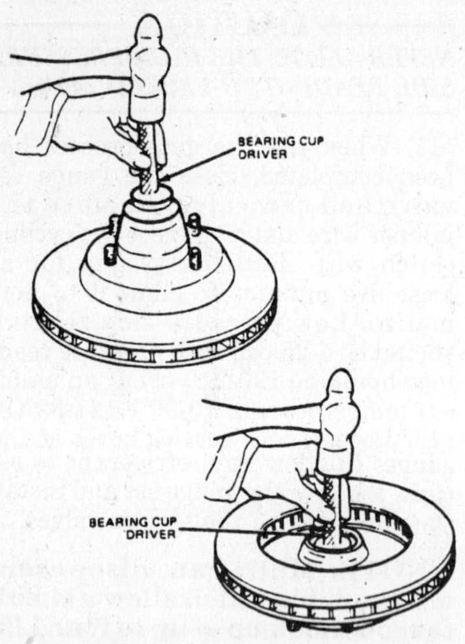

2WD front wheel bearing removal using bearing driver

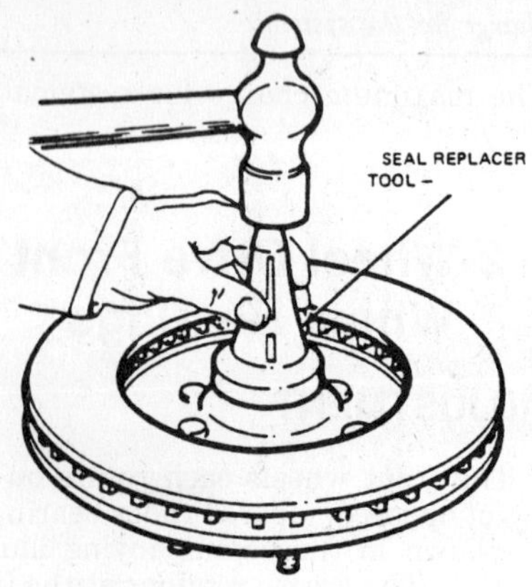

2WD front wheel bearing installation

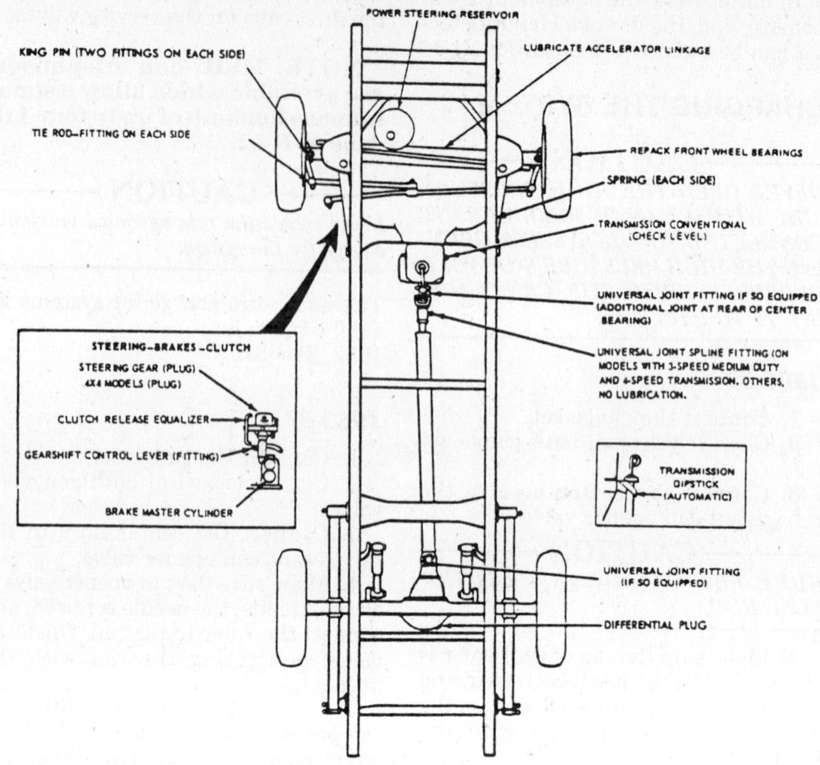

Lubrication chart 2WD—typical

REMOVAL, REPACKING, AND INSTALLATION

Before handling the bearings, there are a few things that you should remember to do and not to do.

Remember to DO the following:

- Remove all outside dirt from the housing before exposing the bearing.
- Treat a used bearing as gently as you would a new one.
- Work with clean tools in clean surroundings.
- Use clean, dry canvas gloves, or at least clean, dry hands.
- Clean solvents and flushing fluids are a must.
- Use clean paper when laying out the bearings to dry.
- Protect disassembled bearings from rust and dirt. Cover them up.
- Use clean rags to wipe bearings.
- Keep the bearings in oil-proof paper when they are to be stored or are not in use.
- Clean the inside of the housing before replacing the bearing.

Do NOT do the following:

- Don't work in dirty surroundings.
- Don't use dirty, chipped or damaged tools.
- Try not to work on wooden work benches or use wooden mallets.
- Don't handle bearings with dirty or moist hands.
- Do not use gasoline for cleaning; use a safe solvent.
- Do not spin-dry bearings with compressed air. They will be damaged.
- Do not spin dirty bearings.
- Avoid using cotton waste or dirty cloths to wipe bearings.
- Try not to scratch or nick bearing surfaces.
- Do not allow the bearing to come in contact with dirt or rust at any time.

1. Raise and support the front end on jackstands.
2. Remove the wheel cover. Remove the wheel.
3. Remove the caliper from the disc and wire it to the underbody to prevent damage to the brake hose. For floating caliper brakes, follow Steps 3, 4, 5, and 6 under Caliper Assembly Service.
4. Remove the grease cap from the hub. Then, remove the cotter pin, nut lock, adjusting nut and flat washer from the spindle. Remove the outer bearing assembly from the hub.
5. Pull the hub and disc assembly off the wheel spindle.
6. Remove and discard the old grease retainer. Remove the inner bearing cone and roller assembly from the hub.
7. Clean all grease from the inner and outer bearing cups with solvent. Inspect the cups for pits, scratches, or excessive wear. If the cups are damaged, remove them with a drift.
8. Clean the inner and outer cone and roller assemblies with solvent and shake them dry. If the cone and roller assemblies show excessive wear or damage, replace them with the bearing cups as a unit.
9. Clean the spindle and the inside of the hub with solvent to thoroughly remove all old grease.
10. Covering the spindle with a clean cloth, brush all loose dirt and dust from the brake assembly. Remove the cloth carefully so as to not get dirt on the spindle.
11. If the inner and/or outer bearing cups were removed, install the replacement cups on the hub. Be sure that the cups seat properly in the hub.
12. It is imperative that all old grease be removed from the bearings and surrounding surfaces before repacking. The new lithium-based grease is not compatible with the sodium base grease used in the past.
13. Install the hub and disc on the

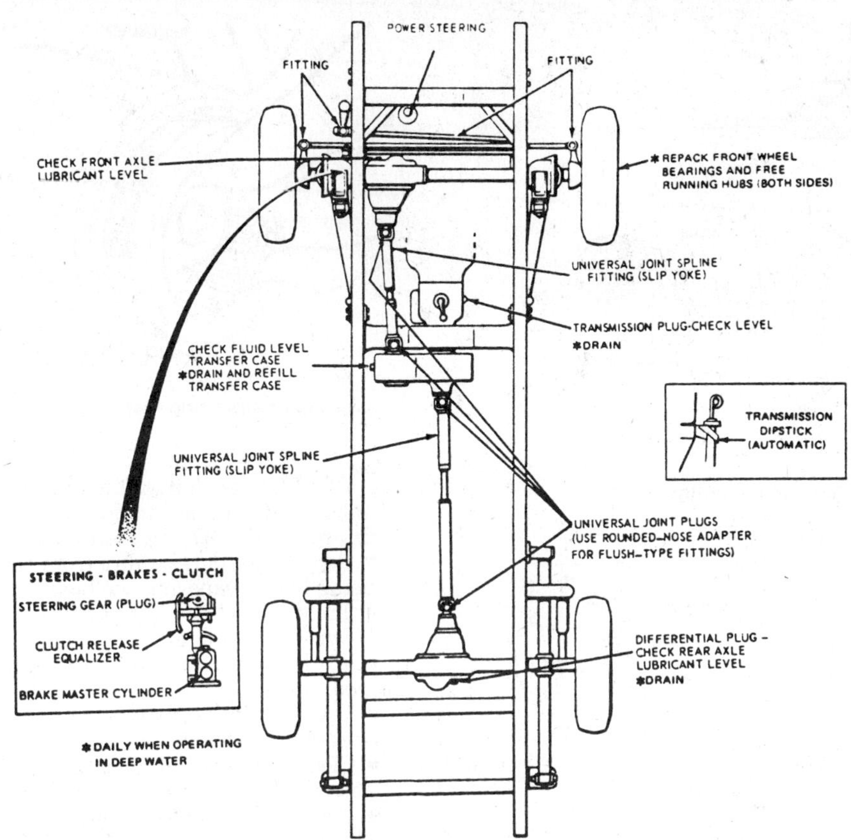

Lubrication chart 4WD—typical

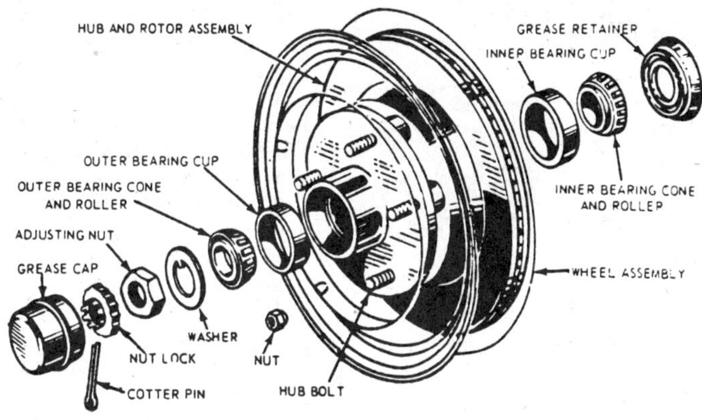

Front hub, bearing, and grease seal with disc brakes—2WD

wheel spindle. To prevent damage to the grease retainer and spindle threads, keep the hub centered on the spindle.

14. Install the outer bearing cone and roller assembly and the flat washer on the spindle. Install the adjusting nut.

15. Adjust the wheel bearings by torquing the adjusting nut to 17-25 ft.lb. with the wheel rotating to seat the bearing. Then back off the adjusting nut ½ turn. Retighten the adjusting nut to 10-15 in.lb. Install the locknut so that the castellations are aligned with the cotter pin hole. Install the cotter pin. Bend the ends of the cotter pin around the castellations of the locknut to prevent interference with the radio static collector in the grease cap. Install the grease cap.

WARNING: New bolts must be used when servicing floating caliper units. The upper bolt must be tightened first. For floating caliper units, see Caliper Assembly Service in the Brake Section. For sliding caliper units, see Shoe and Lining Replacement in the Brake Section.

11. Install the wheels.
12. Install the wheel cover.

Manual Free Running Hub

REMOVAL AND INSTALLATION

1980–86

1. To remove hub, first separate cap assembly from body assembly by removing the six (6) socket head capscrews from the cap assembly and slip apart.
2. Remove snapring (retainer ring) from the end of the axle shaft.
3. Remove the lock ring seated in the groove of the wheel hub. The body assembly will now slide out of the wheel hub. If necessary, use an appropriate puller to remove the body assembly.
4. Install hub in reverse order of removal. Torque socket head capscrews to 30–35 in.lb.

Automatic Locking Hubs

REMOVAL AND INSTALLATION

1. Remove capscrews and remove hub cap assembly from spindle.
2. Remove capscrew from end of axle shaft.
3. Remove lock ring seated in the groove of the wheel hub with a knife blade or with a small sharp awl with the tip bent in a hook.
4. Remove body assembly from spindle. If body assembly does not slide out easily, use an appropriate puller.
5. Unscrew all three set in the spindle locknut until the heads are flush with the edge of the locknut. Remove outer spindle locknut with tool T8OT-4000-V, Automatic Hub Lock Nut Wrench.
6. Reinstall in reverse order of removal. Tighten the outer spindle locknut to 15–20 ft.lb. with special tool T8OT-4000-V, Automatic Hub Lock Nut Wrench. Tighten down all three set screws. Firmly push in body assembly until the friction shoes are on top of the spindle outer locknut.
7. Install capscrew into the axle shaft and tighten to 35–50 ft.lb.

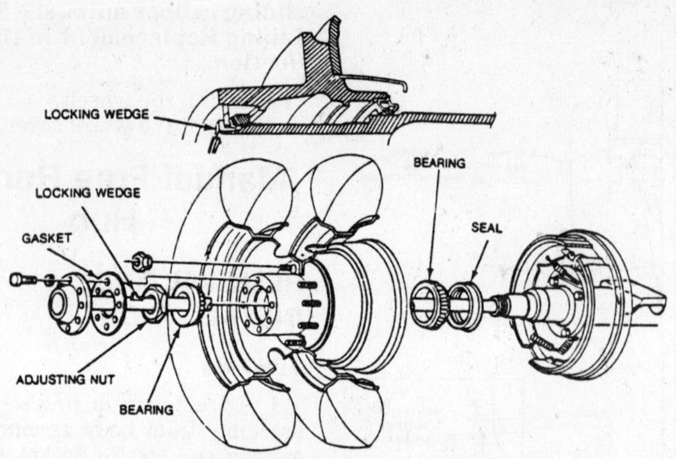

1975-80 full-floating rear axle bearings

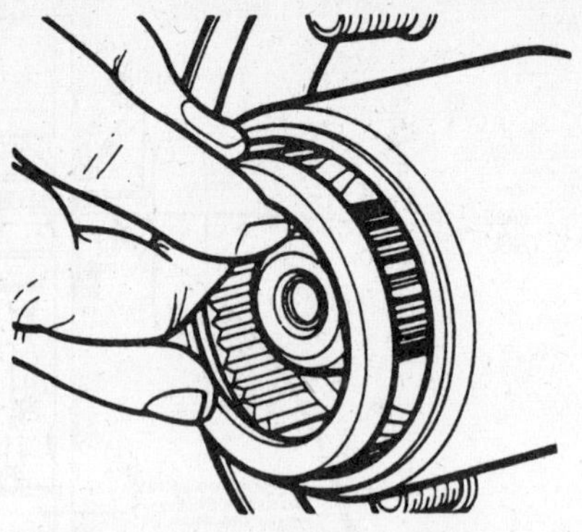
Spring retainer ring installation

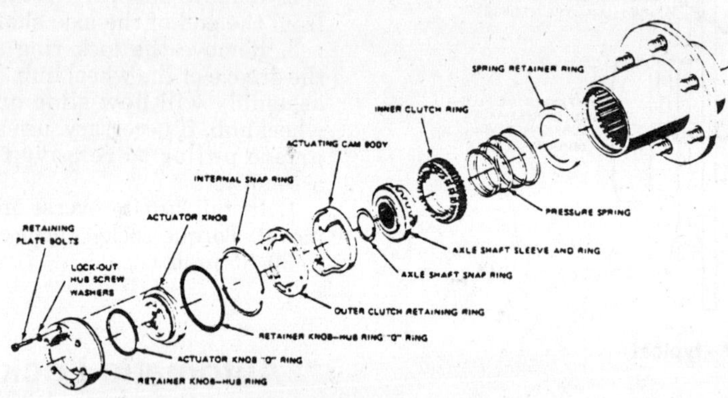

Free-running type front hub—light duty 4WD

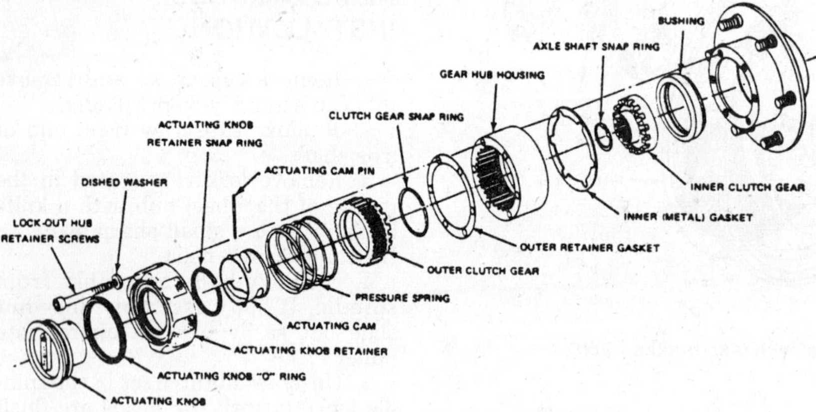

Free-running type front hub—heavy duty 4WD

8. Place cap on spindle and install capscrews. Tighten to 35–50 in.lb. Turn dial firmly from stop to stop, causing the dialing mechanism to engage the body spline.

NOTE: Be sure both hub dials are in the same position, AUTO or LOCK.

4-Wheel Drive Front Wheel Bearings

REPLACEMENT OR REPACKING

Before handling the bearings, there are a few things that you should remember to do and not to do.

Remember to DO the following:

- Remove all outside dirt from the housing before exposing the bearing.
- Treat a used bearing as gently as you would a new one.
- Work with clean tools in clean surroundings.
- Use clean, dry canvas gloves, or at least clean, dry hands.
- Clean solvents and flushing fluids are a must.
- Use clean paper when laying out the bearings to dry.
- Protect disassembled bearings from rust and dirt. Cover them up.
- Use clean rags to wipe bearings.
- Keep the bearings in oil-proof paper when they are to be stored or are not in use.
- Clean the inside of the housing before replacing the bearing.

Do NOT do the following:

- Don't work in dirty surroundings.
- Don't use dirty, chipped or damaged tools.
- Try not to work on wooden work benches or use wooden mallets.
- Don't handle bearings with dirty or moist hands.
- Do not use gasoline for cleaning; use a safe solvent.
- Do not spin-dry bearings with compressed air. They will be damaged.
- Do not spin dirty bearings.
- Avoid using cotton waste or dirty cloths to wipe bearings.
- Try not to scratch or nick bearing surfaces.
- Do not allow the bearing to come in contact with dirt or rust at any time.

1. Raise the vehicle and install safety stands.
2. If equipped with free running hubs refer to Manual or Automatic Free Running Hub Removal and Installation and remove the hub assemblies.
3. Remove the wheel bearing lock nut, using Tool T59T-1197-B, or equivalent.

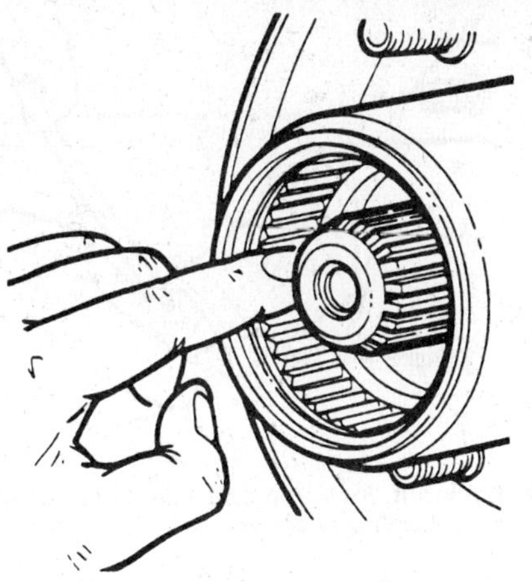

Grease application

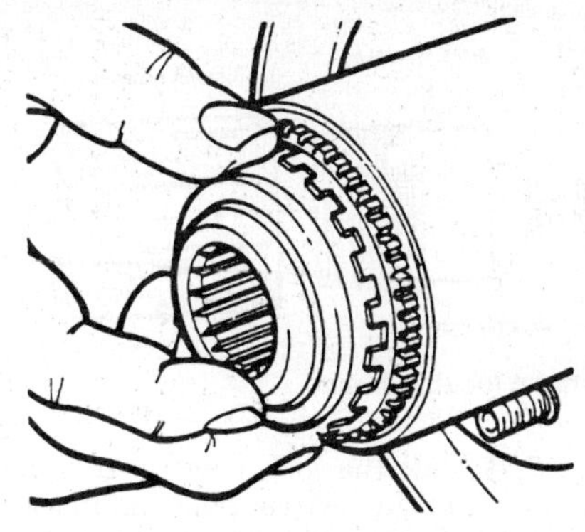

Axle shift sleeve and ring, and inner clutch ring installation

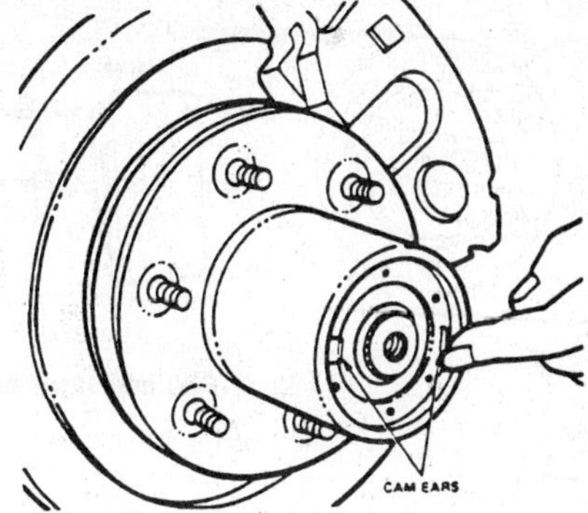

Applying a small amount of grease on the ears of the cam

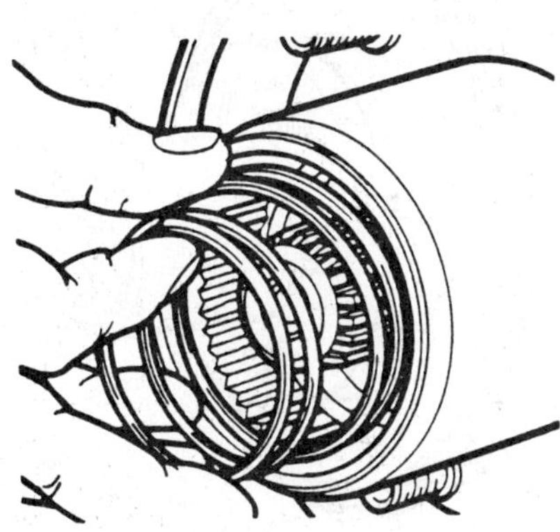

Coil spring installation

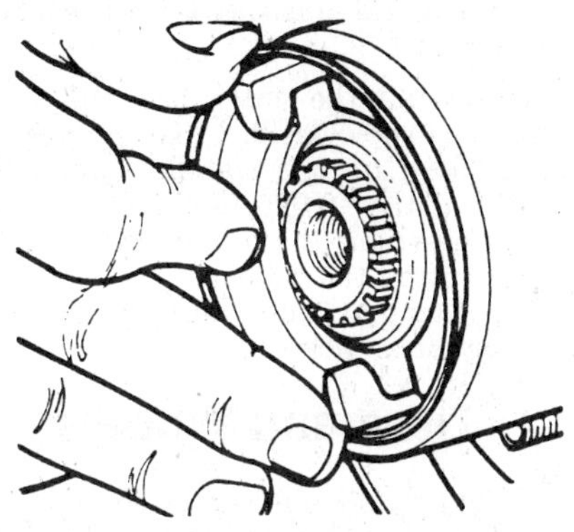

Installing the internal snap ring

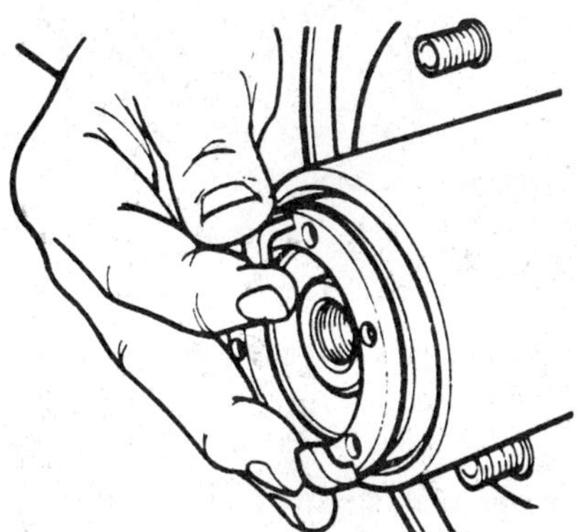

Installing the cam body ring into the clutch retaining ring

4. Remove the lock ring from the bearing adjusting nut. This can be done with your finger tips or a screwdriver.
5. Using Tool T59T-1197-B, or equivalent, remove the bearing adjusting nut.
6. Remove the caliper and suspend it out of the way. See the Brake Section.
7. Slide the hub and disc assembly off of the spindle. The outer wheel bearing will slide out as the hub is removed, so be prepared to catch it.

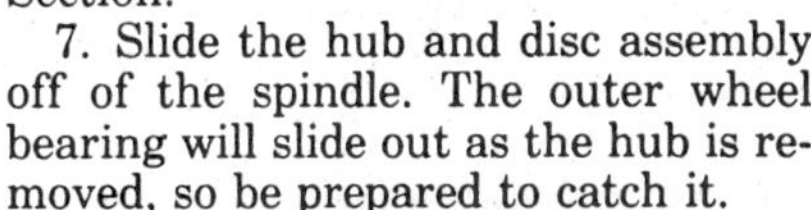

8. Lay the hub on a clean work surface. Carefully drive the inner bearing cone and grease seal out of the hub using Tool T69L-1102-A, or equivalent.
9. Inspect the bearing cups for pits or cracks. If necessary, remove them with a drift. If new cups are installed, install new bearings.
10. Lubricate the bearings with Multi-Purpose Lubricant Ford Specification, ESA-MIC7-B or equivalent. Clean all old grease from the hub. Pack the cones and rollers. If a bearing packer is not available, work as much lubricant as possible between the rollers and the cages.
11. Drive new cups into place with a

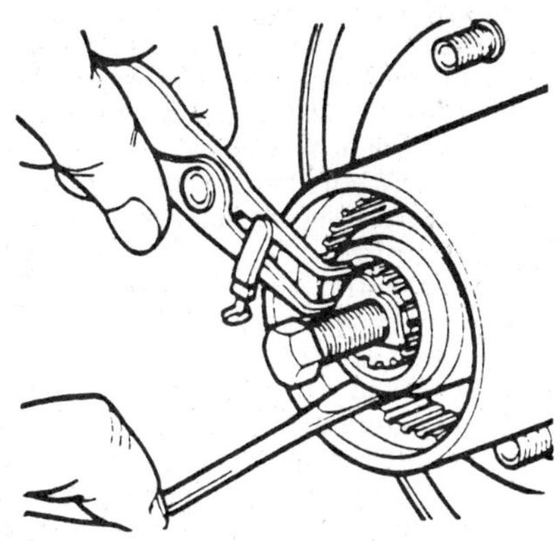

Installing the axle shaft snap ring

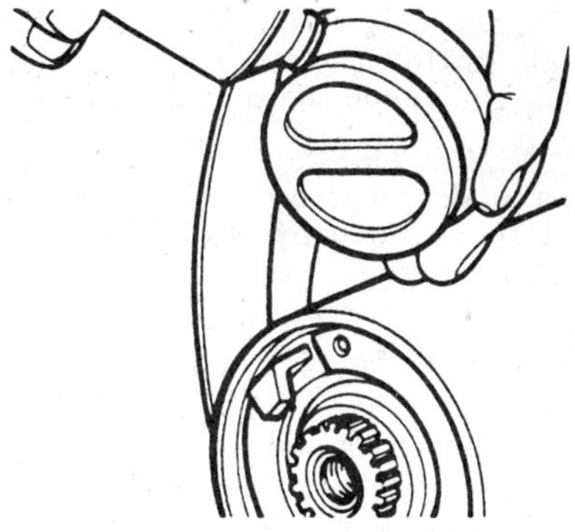

Lubricating the selector knob

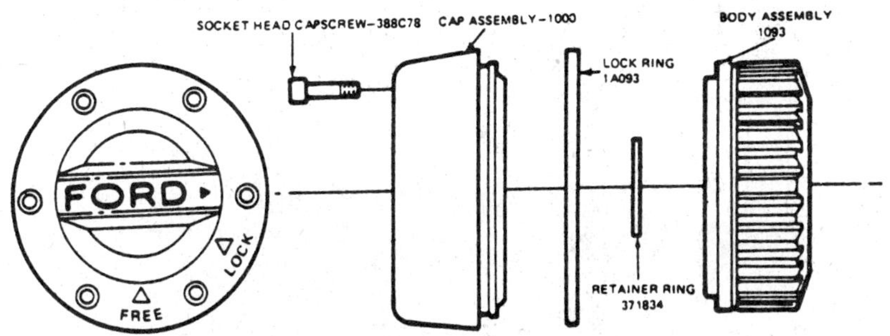

1980 and later manual locking hubs

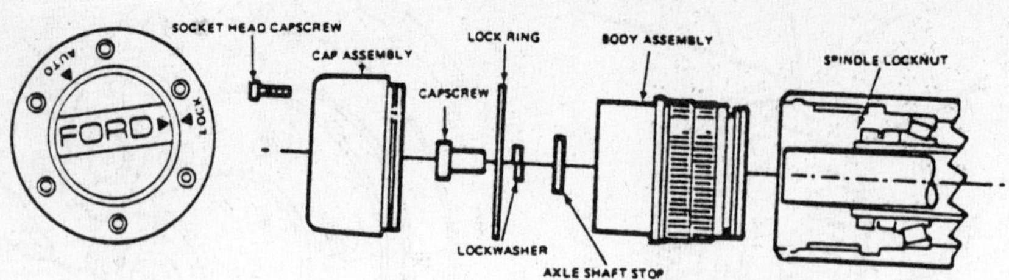

1980 and later automatic locking hubs

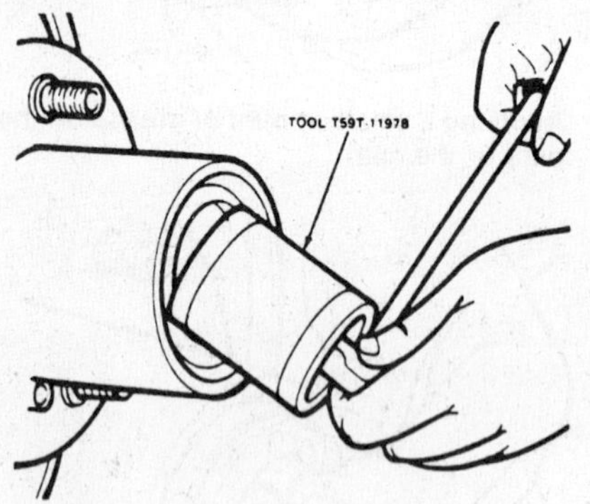

Lock nut, lock ring and adjusting nut removal

driver, making sure that they are fully seated.

12. Position the inner bearing cone and roller in the inner cup and install the grease retainer.

13. Carefully position the hub and disc assembly on the spindle.

14. Install the outer bearing cone and roller, and the adjusting nut.

NOTE: The adjusting nut has a small dowel on one side. This dowel faces outward to engage the locking ring.

15. Using Tool T59T-1197-B and a torque wrench, tighten the bearing adjusting nut to 50 ft.lb., while rotating the wheel back and forth to seat the bearings.

16. Back off the adjusting nut approximately 90°.

17. Install the lock ring by turning the nut to the nearest hole and inserting the dowel pin.

NOTE: The dowel pin must seat in a lock ring hole for proper bearing adjustment and wheel retention.

18. Install the outer lock nut and tighten to 50–80 ft.lb. Final end play of the wheel on the spindle should be 0.001–0.010" (0.025–0.25mm).

19. Assemble the hub parts.

20. Install the caliper.

21. Remove the safety stands and lower the vehicle.

Tires and Wheels

The tires should be rotated as specified in the Maintenance Intervals Chart. Refer to the accompanying illustrations for the recommended rotation patterns.

The tires on your truck should have built-in tread wear indicators, which appear as ½" (12.7mm) bands when the tread depth gets as low as $^{1}/_{16}$" (1.6mm). When the indicators appear in 2 or more adjacent grooves, it's time for new tires.

For optimum tire life, you should keep the tires properly inflated, rotate them often and have the wheel alignment checked periodically.

Some late models have the maximum load pressures listed in the V.I.N. plate on the left door frame. In general, pressure of 28–32 psi would be suitable for highway use with moderate loads and passenger car type tires (load range B, non-flotation) of original equipment size. Pressures should be checked before driving, since pressure can increase as much as 6 psi due to heat. It is a good idea to have an accurate gauge and to check pressures weekly. Not all gauges on service station air pumps are to be trusted. In general, truck type tires require higher pressures and flotation type tires, lower pressures.

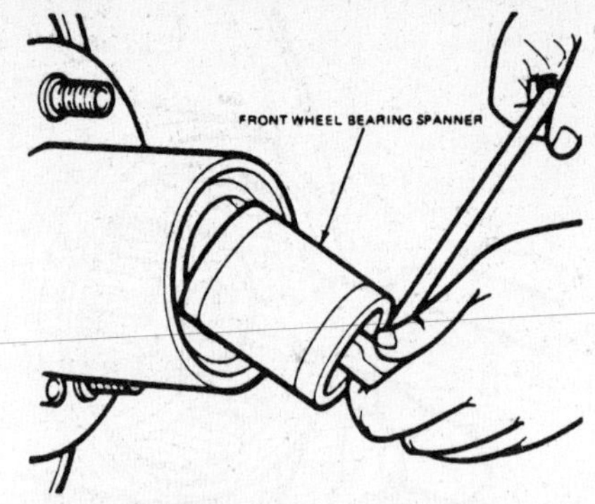

Lock nut, lock ring and adjusting nut removal using spanner

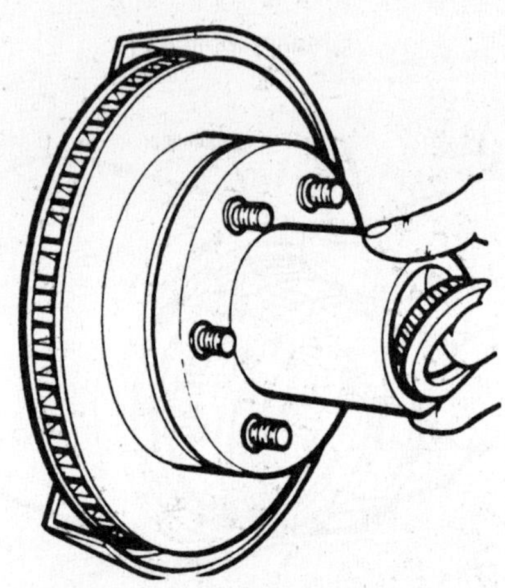

Outer bearing removal, 4 x 4

TIRE ROTATION

It is recommended that you have the tires rotated every 6,000 miles. There is no way to give a tire rotation diagram for every combination of tires and vehicles, but the accompanying diagrams are a general rule to follow. Radial tires should not be cross-switched; they last longer if their direction of rotation is not changed. Truck tires sometimes have directional tread, indicated by arrows on the sidewalls; the arrow shows the direction of rotation. They will wear very rapidly if reversed. Studded snow tires will lose their studs if their direction of rotation is reversed.

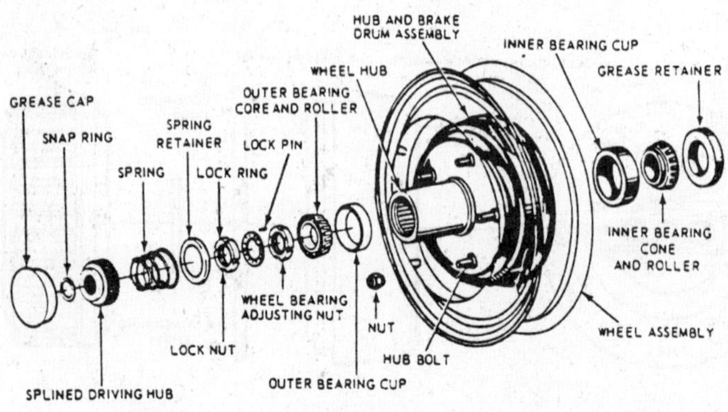

Front hub assembly without free-running hubs—4WD

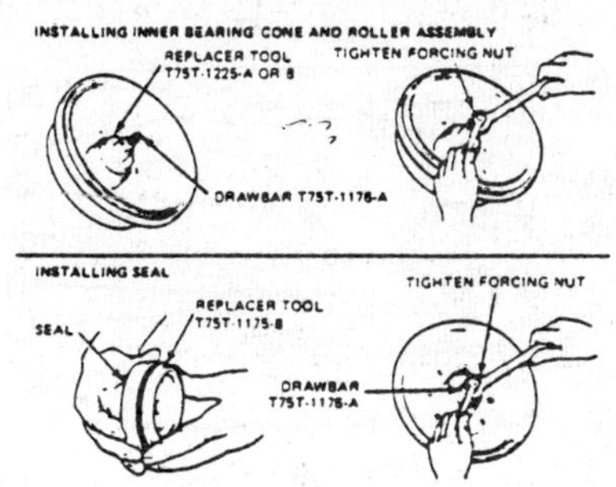

Rear wheel bearing and seal installation. Seal installation tools are very helpful here

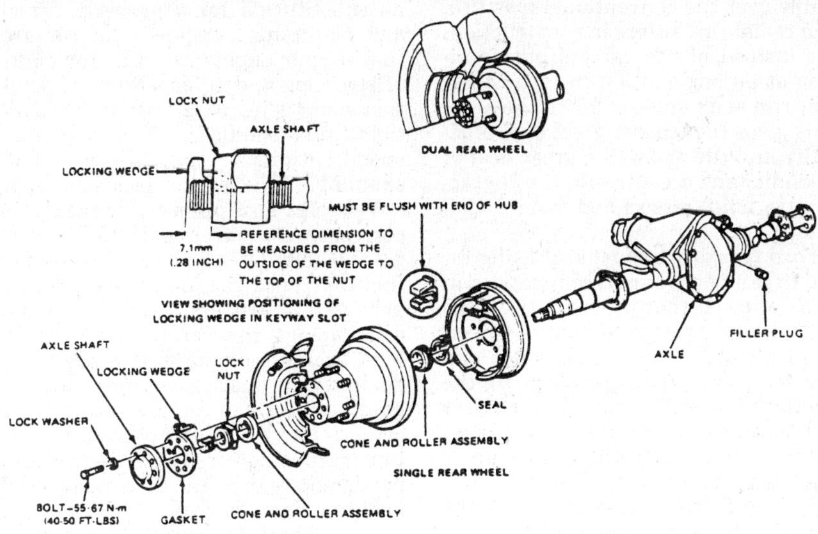

Rear wheel hub showing locking positioning—F-350 (4 x 2) with dual rear wheels shown

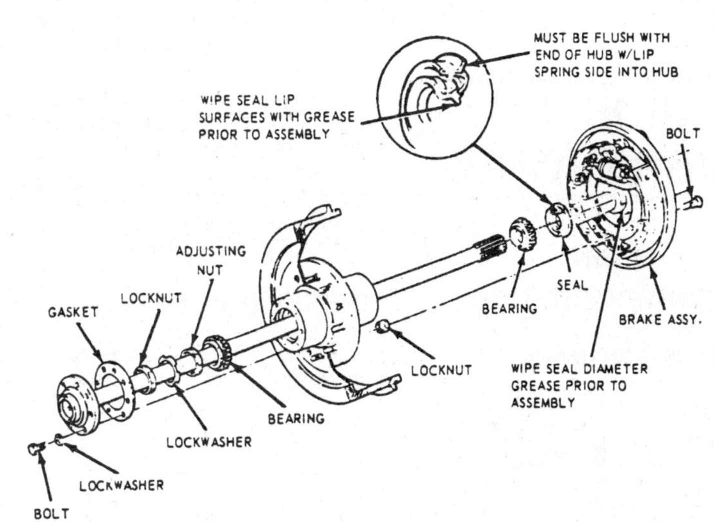

Single rear hub assembly with full-floating axles, F-250 only

NOTE: Mark the wheel position or direction of rotation on radial tires or studded snow tires before removing them.

If your truck is equipped with tires having different load ratings on the front and the rear, the tires should not be rotated front to rear. Rotating these tires could affect tire life (the tires with the lower rating will wear faster, and could become overloaded), and upset the handling of the truck.

TIRE USAGE

The tires on your truck were selected to provide the best all around performance for normal operation when inflated as specified. Oversize tires (Load Range D) will not increase the maximum carrying capacity of the vehicle, although they will provide an extra margin of tread life. Be sure to check overall height before using larger size tires which may cause interference with suspension components or wheel wells. When replacing conventional tire sizes with other tire size designations, be sure to check the manufacturer's recommendations. Interchangeability is not always possible because of differences in load ratings, tire dimensions, wheel well clearances, and rim size. Also due to differences in handling characteristics, 70 Series and 60 Series tires should be used only in pairs on the same axle; radial tires should be used only in sets of four.

The wheels must be the correct width for the tire. Tire dealers have charts of tire and rim compatibility. A mismatch can cause sloppy handling and rapid tread wear. The old rule of thumb is that the tread width should match the rim width (inside bead to inside bead) within an inch. For radial tires, the rim width should be 80% or less of the tire (not tread) width.

The height (mounted diameter) of the new tires can greatly change speedometer accuracy, engine speed at a given road speed, fuel mileage, acceleration, and ground clearance. Tire manufacturers furnish full measurement specifications. Speedometer drive gears are available for correction.

NOTE: Dimensions of tires marked the same size may vary significantly, even among tires from the same manufacturer.

The spare tire should be usable, at least for low speed operation, with the new tires.

TIRE DESIGN

For maximum satisfaction, tires should be used in sets of five. Mixing or different types (radial, bias-belted, fiberglass belted) should be avoided. Conventional bias tires are constructed so that the cords run bead-to-bead at an angle. Alternate plies run at an opposite angle. This type of construction gives rigidity to both tread and sidewall. Bias-belted tires are similar in construction to conventional bias ply tires. Belts run at an angle and also at a 90° angle to the bead, as in the radial tire. Tread life is improved consid-

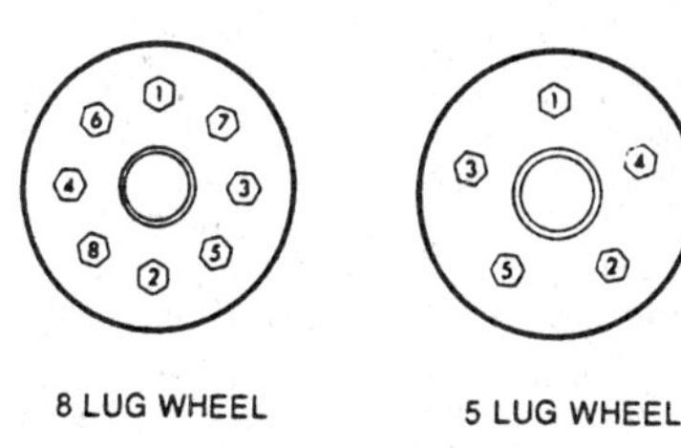

Lug nut torque sequences

erably over the conventional bias tire. The radial tire differs in construction, but instead of the carcass plies running at an angle of 90° to each other, they run at an angle of 90° to the bead. This gives the tread a great deal of rigidity and the sidewall a great deal of flexibility and accounts for the characteristic bulge associated with radial tires.

Ford trucks are capable of using radial tires and they are recommended in some years. If they are used, tire sizes and wheel diameters should be selected to maintain ground clearance and tire load capacity equivalent to the minimum specified tire. Radial tires should always be used in sets of five, but in an emergency radial tires can be used with caution on the rear axle only. If this is done, both tires on the rear should be of radial design.

NOTE: Radial tires should never be used on only the front axle.

FLUIDS AND LUBRICANTS

Fuel Recommendations

GASOLINE ENGINES

It is important to use fuel of the proper octane rating in your truck. Octane rating is based on the quantity of anti-knock compounds added to the fuel and it determines the speed at which the gas will burn. The lower the octane rating, the faster it burns. The higher the octane, the slower the fuel will burn and a greater percentage of compounds in the fuel prevent spark ping (knock), detonation and preignition (dieseling).

As the temperature of the engine increases, the air/fuel mixture exhibits a tendency to ignite before the spark plug is fired. If fuel of an octane rating too low for the engine is used, this will allow combustion to occur before the piston has completed its compression stroke, thereby creating a very high pressure very rapidly.

Fuel of the proper octane rating, for the compression ratio and ignition timing of your truck, will slow the combustion process sufficiently to allow the spark plug enough time to ignite the mixture completely and smoothly. Many non-catalyst models are designed to run on regular fuel. The use of some super-premium fuel is no substitution for a properly tuned and maintained engine. Chances are that if your engine exhibits any signs of spark ping, detonation or pre-ignition when using regular fuel, the ignition timing should be checked against specifications or the cylinder head should be removed for decarbonizing.

Vehicles equipped with catalytic converters must use UNLEADED GASOLINE ONLY. Use of unleaded fuel shortened the life of spark plugs, exhaust systems and EGR valves and can damage the catalytic converter. Most converter equipped models are designed to operate using unleaded gasoline with a minimum rating of 87 octane. Use of unleaded gas with octane ratings lower than 87 can cause persistent spark knock which could lead to engine damage.

Light spark knock may be noticed when accelerating or driving up hills. The slight knocking may be considered normal (with 87 octane) because the maximum fuel economy is obtained under condition of occasional light spark knock. Gasoline with an octane rating higher than 87 may be used, but it is not necessary (in most cases) for proper operation.

If spark knock is constant, when using 87 octane, at cruising speeds on level ground, ignition timing adjustment may be required.

DIESEL ENGINES

No.2 automotive diesel fuel with a cetane rating of 40 is sufficient.

Engine

OIL RECOMMENDATION

Gasoline Engines

When adding the oil to the crankcase or changing the oil or filter, it is important that oil of an equal quality to original be used in your truck. The use of inferior oils may void your warranty. Generally speaking, oil that has been rated **SF** by the American Petroleum Institute will prove satisfactory.

Oil of the SF variety performs a multitude of functions in addition to its basic job of reducing friction of the engine's moving parts. Through a balanced formula of polymeric dispersants and metallic detergents, the oil prevents high temperature and low temperature deposits and also keeps sludge and dirt particles in suspension. Acids, particularly sulphuric acid, as well as other products of combustion of sulphur fuels, are neutralized by the oil. These acids, if permitted to concentrate, may cause corrosion and rapid wear of the internal parts of the engine.

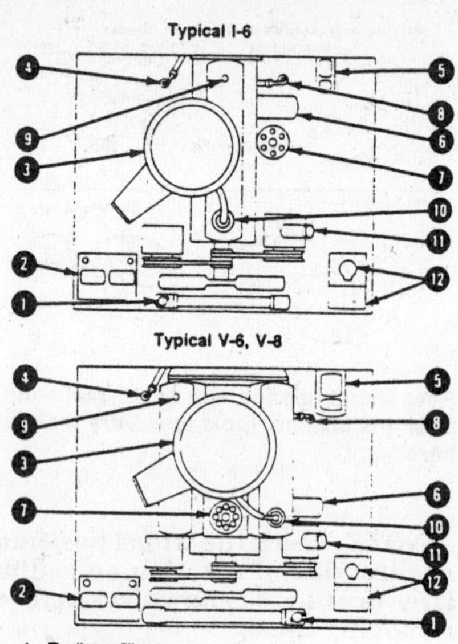

Engine compartment service points

It is important to choose an oil of the proper viscosity for climatic and operational conditions. Viscosity in an index of the oil's thickness at different temperatures. A thicker oil (higher numerical rating) is needed for high temperature operation, whereas thinner oil (lower numerical rating) is required for cold weather operation. Due to the need for an oil that embodies both these characteristics in parts of the country where there is wide temperature variation within a small period of time, multigrade oils have been developed. Basically a multigrade oil is thinner at low temperatures and thicker at high temperatures. For example, a 10W-40 oil exhibits the characteristics of a 10 weight oil when the truck is first started and the oil is cold. Its lighter weight allows it to travel to the lubricating surfaces quicker and offer less resistance to starter motor cranking then, let's say, a straight 30 weight oil. But after the engine reaches operating temperature, the 10W-40 oil begins acting like a straight 40 weight oil, its heavier weight providing greater lubricating protection and less susceptibility to foaming than a straight 30 weight oil. Whatever your driving needs, the oil viscosity/temperature chart should prove useful in selecting

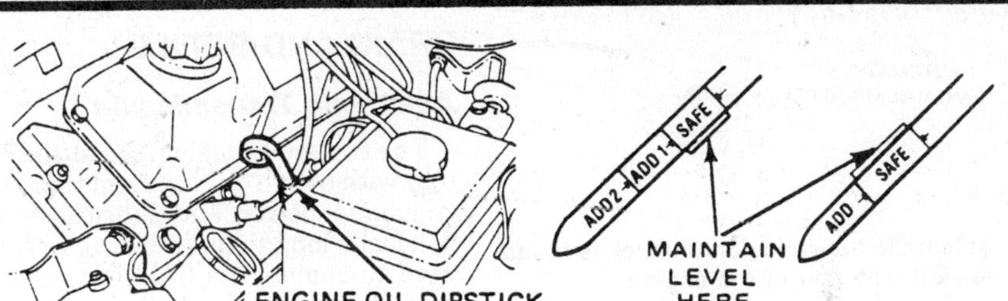

Checking engine oil level

the proper grade. The SAE viscosity rating is printed or stamped on the top of every oil container.

Diesel Engines

Engine oil, meeting API specification **SF/CD** and Ford specification ESE-M2C153-C is recommended. You can use either SAE 30W or SAE 15W-40 weight oils.

OIL LEVEL CHECK

The engine oil level should be checked frequently. For instance, at each refueling stop. Be sure that the vehicle is parked on a level surface with the engine off. Also, allow a few minutes after turning off the engine for the oil to drain into the pan or an inaccurate reading will result.

1. Open the hood and remove the engine oil dipstick.
2. Wipe the dipstick with a clean, lint-free rag and reinsert it. Be sure to insert it all the way.
3. Pull out the dipstick and note the oil level. It should be between the SAFE (MAX) mark and the ADD (MIN) mark.
4. If the level is below the lower mark, replace the dipstick and add fresh oil to bring the level within the proper range. Do not overfill.
5. Recheck the oil level and close the hood.

NOTE: Use a multi-grade oil with API classification SF.

OIL CHANGE

NOTE: The engine oil and oil filter should be changed at the same time, at the recommended intervals on the maintenance schedule chart.

1. Run the engine to normal operating temperature.
2. After the engine has reached operating temperature, shut it off, firmly apply the parking brake, and block the wheels.
3. Raise and support the front end on jackstands.

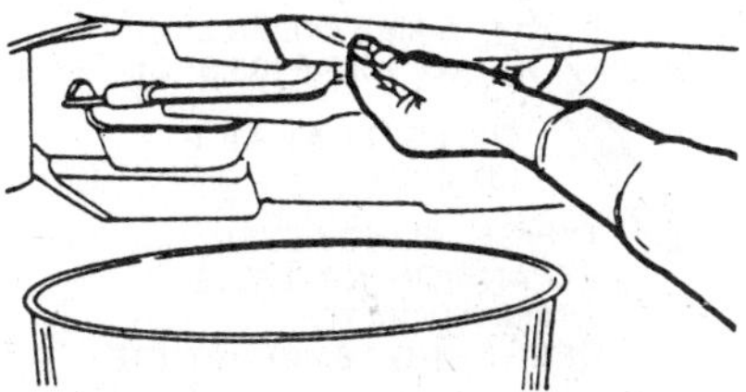

Unscrew the plug by hand. Keep an inward pressure on the plug as you unscrew it, so the oil won't escape until you pull the plug away

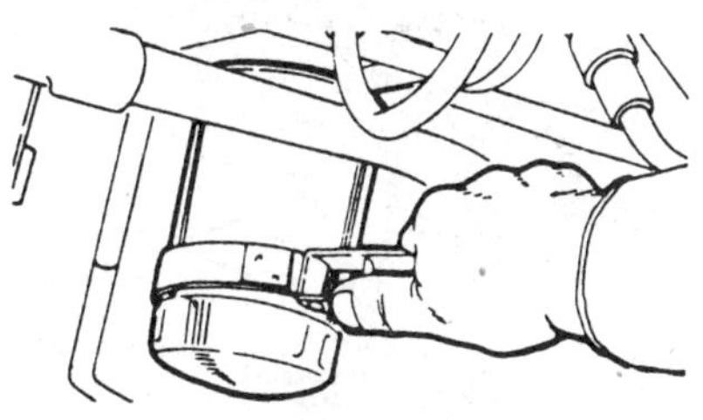

Move the drain pan underneath the oil filter. Use a strap wrench to remove the filter—remember it is still filled with about a quart of hot, dirty oil.

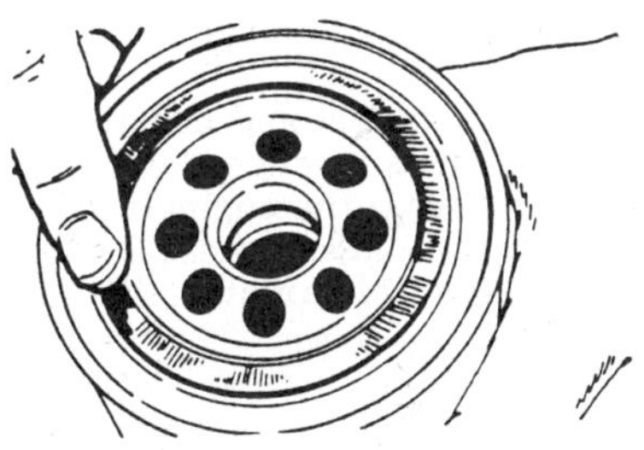

Wipe clean engine oil around the rubber gasket on the new filter. This helps ensure a good seal

4. Place a drip pan beneath the oil pan and remove the drain plug.

CAUTION

The oil could be very hot! Protect yourself by using rubber gloves if necessary.

5. Allow the engine to drain thoroughly.

WARNING: On some V8 engines a dual sump oil pan was used.

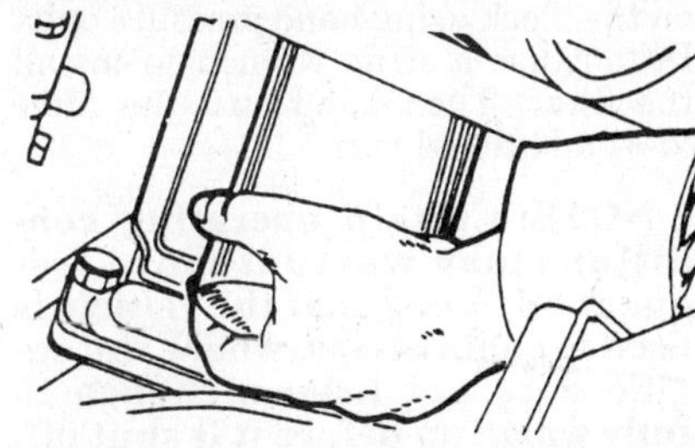

Install the new filter by hand only; DO NOT use a strap wrench to install

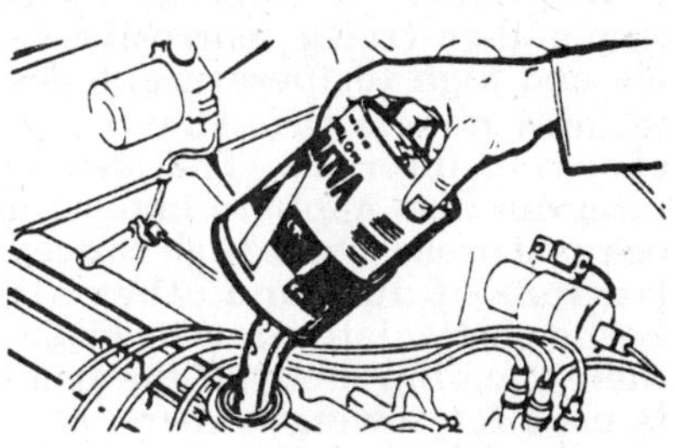

Don't forget to install the drain plug before refilling the engine with fresh oil.

When changing the oil, both drain plugs (front and side) must be removed. Failure to remove both plugs can lead to an incorrect oil level reading.

6. While the oil is draining, replace the filter as described below.
7. When the oil has completely drained, clean the threads of the plug and coat them with non-hardening sealer or Teflon® tape and install the plug. Tighten it snugly.

WARNING: The threads in the oil pan are easily stripped! Don not overtighten the plug!

8. Fill the crankcase with the proper amount of oil shown in the Capacities Chart.
9. Start the engine and check for leaks.

REPLACING THE OIL FILTER

1. Place the drip pan beneath the oil filter.
2. Using an oil filter wrench, turn the filter counterclockwise to remove it.

CAUTION

The oil could be very hot! Protect yourself by using rubber gloves if necessary.

3. Wipe the contact surface of the new filter clean and coat the rubber gasket with clean engine oil.
4. Clean the mating surface of the adapter on the block.
5. Screw the new filter into position

on the block using hand pressure only. Do not use a strap wrench to install the filter! Then hand-turn the filter ½-¾ additional turn.

NOTE: Certain operating conditions may warrant more frequent oil changes. If the vehicle is used for short trips, where the engine does not have a chance to fully warm up before it is shut off, water condensation and low temperature deposits may make it necessary to change to oil sooner. If the vehicle is used mostly in stop-and-go traffic, corrosive acids and high temperature deposits may necessitate shorter oil changing intervals. The shorter intervals also apply to industrial or rural areas where high concentrations of dust and other airborne particulate matter contaminate the oil. Finally, if the truck is used for towing trailers, a severe load is placed on the engine causing the oil to thin out sooner, making necessary the shorter oil changing intervals.

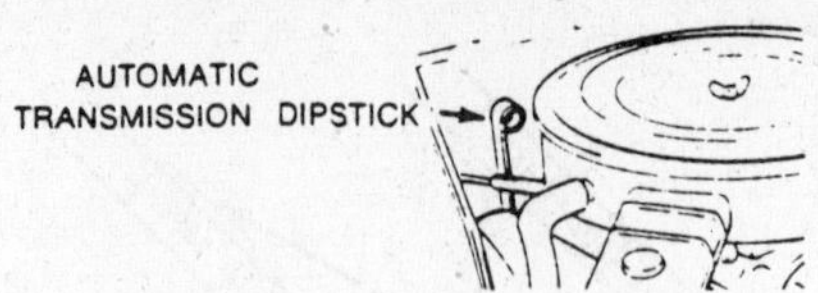

Automatic transmission dipstick is found towards the rear of the engine

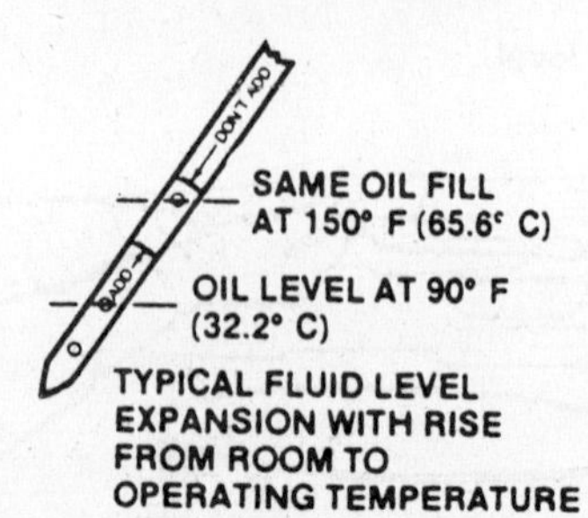

Checking automatic transmission fluid level. Check transmission when it is warmed to operating temperature

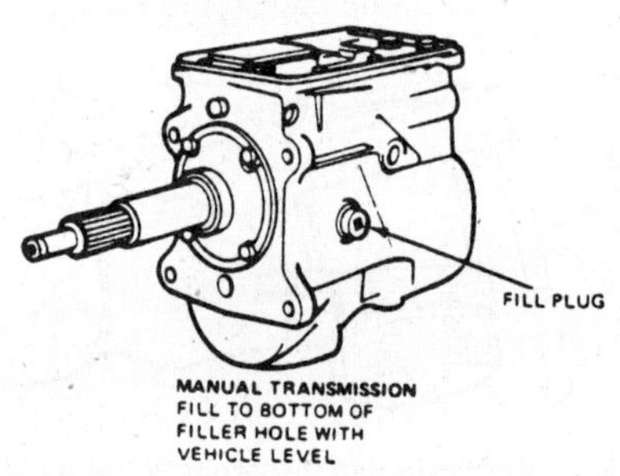

Typical manual trans filler location

Transmission

FLUID RECOMMENDATIONS

Manual Transmissions:

- All: SAE 85W/90

Automatic Transmissions:

- All: DEXRON®II or Ford Type CJ

LEVEL CHECK

Automatic Transmissions

It is very important to maintain the proper fluid level in an automatic transmission. If the level is either too high or too low, poor shifting operation and internal damage are likely to occur. For this reason a regular check of the fluid level is essential.

1. Drive the vehicle for 15-20 minutes to allow the transmission to reach operating temperature.
2. Park the truck on a level surface, apply the parking brake and leave the engine idling. Shift the transmission and engage each gear, then place the gear selector in P (PARK).
3. Wipe away any dirt in the areas of the transmission dipstick to prevent it from falling into the filler tube. Withdraw the dipstick, wipe it with a clean, lint-free rag and reinsert it until it seats.
4. Withdraw the dipstick and note the fluid level. It should be between the upper (FULL) mark and the lower (ADD) mark.
5. If the level is below the lower mark, use a funnel and add fluid in small quantities through the dipstick filler neck. Keep the engine running while adding fluid and check the level after each small amount. Do not overfill.

Manual Transmission

The fluid level should be checked every 6 months/6,000 miles, whichever comes first.

1. Park the truck on a level surface, turn off the engine, apply the parking brake and block the wheels.
2. Remove the filler plug from the side of the transmission case with a proper size wrench. The fluid level should be even with the bottom of the filler hole.
3. If additional fluid is necessary, add it through the filler hole using a siphon pump or squeeze bottle.
4. Replace the filler plug; do not overtighten.

DRAIN AND REFILL

Automatic Transmission

The transmission is filled at the factory with a high quality fluid that both transmits power and lubricates and will last a long time. In most cases, the need to change the fluid in the automatic transmission will never arise under normal use. 4-WD vehicles most likely will be subject to more severe operating conditions than conventional vehicles, so the fluid may have to be replaced. An internal leak in the radiator could develop and contaminate the fluid, necessitating fluid replacement.

The extra load of operating the vehicle in deep sand, towing a heavy trailer, etc., causes the transmission to create more heat due to increased friction. This extra heat is transferred to the transmission fluid and, if the oil is allowed to become too hot, it will change its chemical composition or become scorched. When this occurs, valve bodies become clogged and the transmission doesn't operate as efficiently as it should. Serious damage to the transmission can result.

You can tell if the transmission fluid is scorched by noting a distinctive burned smell and discoloration. Scorched transmission fluid is dark brown or black as opposed to its normal bright, clear red color. Since transmission fluid "cooks" in stages, it may develop forms of sludge or varnish. Pull the dipstick out and place the end on a tissue or paper towel. Particles of sludge can be seen more easily this way. If any of the above conditions do exist, the transmission fluid should be completely drained, the filtering screens cleaned, the transmission inspected for possible damage and new fluid installed.

1. Raise the truck and support on jackstands.
2. Place a drain pan under the transmission.
3. Loosen the pan attaching bolts and drain the fluid from the transmission.
4. When the fluid has drained to the level of the pan flange, remove the remaining pan bolts working from the rear and both sides of the pan to allow it to drop and drain slowly.
5. When all of the fluid has drained, remove the pan and clean it thoroughly. Discard the pan gasket.
6. Place a new gasket on the pan, and install the pan on the transmission. Tighten the attaching bolts to 12-16 ft.lb.
7. Add three 3 quarts of fluid to the transmission through the filler tube.
8. Lower the vehicle. Start the engine and move the gear selector through shift pattern. Allow the en-

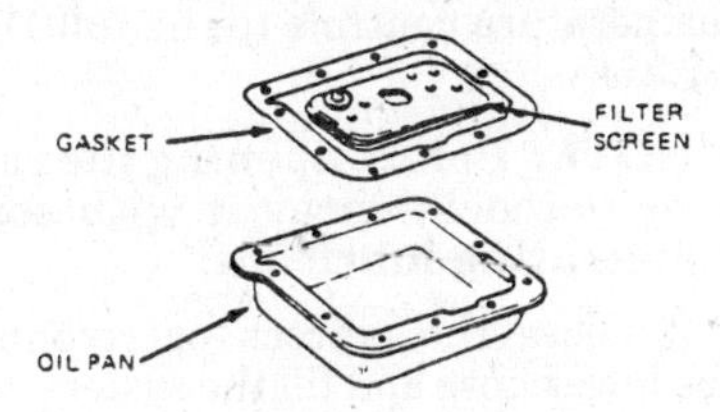

Automatic transmission filters are found above the transmission oil pan

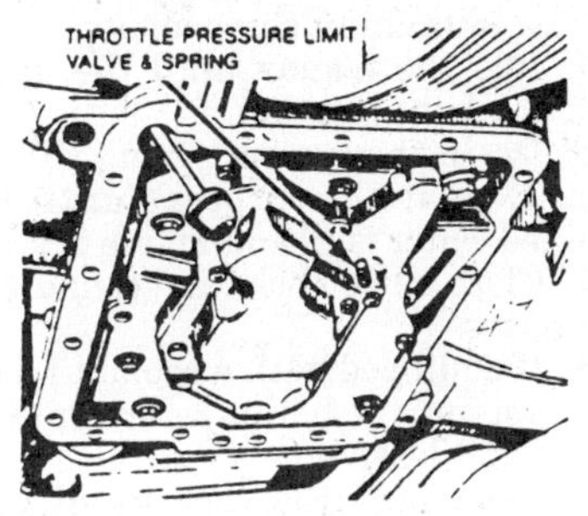

C4 throttle pressure limit valve and spring. They are held in place by the filter. The valve is installed with the large end toward the valve body; the spring fits over the valve stem

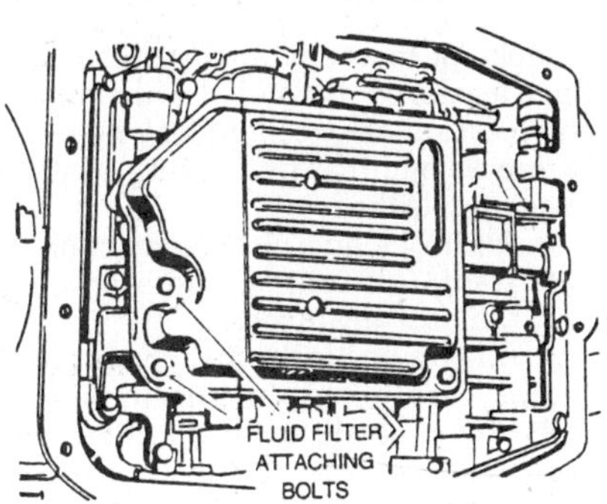

Fluid filter, automatic overdrive (AOD)

gine to reach normal operating temperature.

9. Check the transmission fluid. Add fluid, if necessary, to maintain correct level.

Manual Transmission

1. Place a suitable drain pan under the transmission.
2. Remove the drain plug and allow the gear lube to drain out.
3. Replace the drain plug, remove the filler plug and fill the transmission to the proper level with the required fluid.
4. Reinstall the filler plug.

Transfer Case

FLUID RECOMMENDATIONS

All models use DEXRON®II ATF or Ford Type CJ ATF.

LEVEL CHECK

Position the vehicle on level ground. Remove the transfer case full plug located on the left side of the transfer case. The fluid level should be up on the fill hole. If lubricant doesn't run out when the plug is removed, add lubricant until it does run out and then replace the fill plug.

DRAIN AND REFILL

The transfer case is serviced at the same time and in the same manner as the transmission. Clean the area around the filler and drain plugs and remove the filler plug on the side of the transfer case. Remove the drain plug on the bottom of the transfer case and allow the lubricant to drain completely. Clean and install the drain plug. Add the proper lubricant

Front or Rear Axle (Differential)

NOTE: On models with the front locking differential, add 2 oz. of friction modifier Ford part #EST-M2C118-A. On models with the rear locking differential, use only locking differential fluid Ford part #ESW-M2C119-A or its equivalent.

FLUID LEVEL CHECK

Like the manual transmission, the rear axle fluid should be checked every six months/6,000 miles. A filler plug is provided near the center of the rear cover or on the upper (driveshaft) side of the gear case. Remove the plug and check to ensure that the fluid level is even with the bottom of the filler hole. Add SAE 85W/90/95 gear lube as required. If the vehicle is equipped with a limited slip rear axle, add the required special fluid. Install the filler plug but do not overtighten.

DRAIN AND REFILL

Normal maintenance does not require changing the rear axle fluid. However, to do so, remove the rear drain plug (models equipped), the lower two cover bolts, or the cover. Catch the drained fluid in a suitable container. If the rear cover was removed, clean the mounting surfaces of the cover and rear housing. Install a new gasket (early models) or (on late models) apply a continuous bead of Silicone Rubber Sealant (D6AZ-19562-

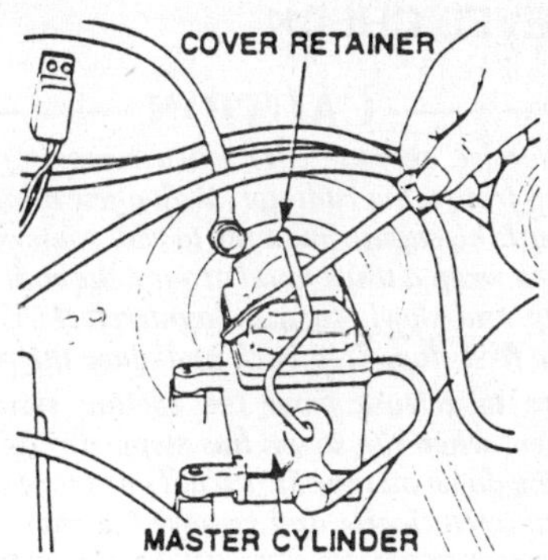

Prying off the master cylinder retaining wire

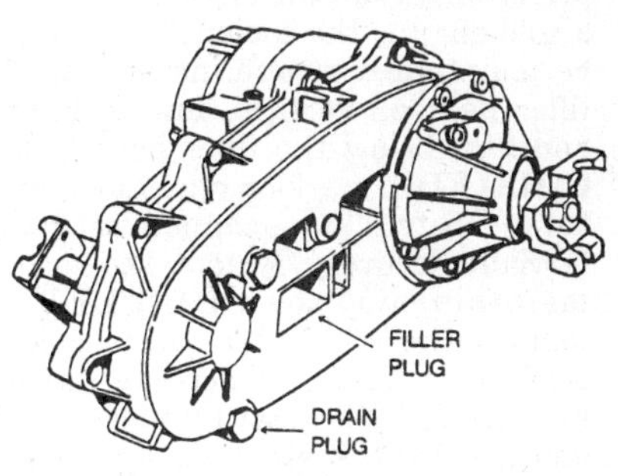

Typical transfer case filler and drain plug locations. (New Process case shown)

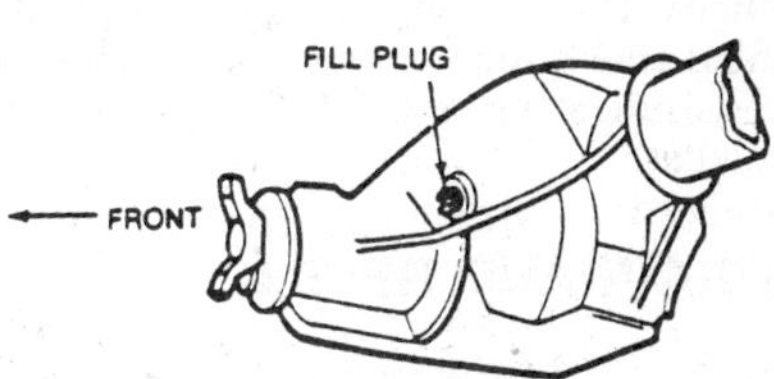

Differential fill plug location, 2-wheel drive shown. 4 x 4 front axle similar.

A/B or the equivalent) around the rear housing face inside the circle of bolt holes. Install the cover and tighten the bolts. Parts must be assembled within a half hour after the sealant is applied. If the fluid was drained by removing the two lower cover bolts, apply sealant to the bolts before reinstallation. Fill the rear axle through the filler hole with the proper lube. Add friction modifier to limited slip models if required.

Coolant

FLUID RECOMMENDATIONS

When additional coolant is required to maintain the proper level, always add a 50/50 mixture of antifreeze/coolant and water.

LEVEL CHECK

CAUTION

Exercise extreme care when removing the cap from a hot radiator. Wait a few minutes until the engine has time to cool somewhat, then wrap a thick towel around the radiator cap and slowly turn it counterclockwise to the first stop. Step back and allow the pressure to release from the cooling system. Then, when the steam has stopped venting, press down on the cap, turn it one more stop counterclockwise and remove the cap.

The coolant level in the radiator should be checked on a monthly basis, preferably when the engine is cold. On a cold engine, the coolant level should be maintained at one inch below the filler neck on vertical flow radiators, and 2½" below the filler neck at the **COLD FILL** mark on crossflow radiators. On trucks equipped with the Coolant Recovery System, the level is maintained at the **COLD LEVEL** mark in the translucent plastic expansion bottle. Top up as necessary with a mixture of 50% water and 50% ethylene glycol antifreeze, to ensure proper rust, freezing and boiling protection. If you have to add coolant more often than once a month or if you have to add more than one quart at a time, check the cooling system for leads. Also check for water in the crankcase oil, indicating a blown cylinder head gasket.

DRAIN AND REFILL

CAUTION

When draining the coolant, keep in mind that cats and dogs are attracted by the ethylene glycol antifreeze, and are quite likely to drink any that is left in an uncovered container or in puddles on the ground. This will prove fatal in sufficient quantity. Always drain the coolant into a sealable container. Coolant should be reused unless it is contaminated or several years old.

Completely draining and refilling the cooling system every two years at least will remove accumulated rust, scale and other deposits.

NOTE: Use a good quality antifreeze with water pump lubricants, rust inhibitors and other corrosion inhibitors along with acid neutralizers. Use a permanent type coolant that meets specification ESE-M97B44A or the equivalent.

1. Drain the existing antifreeze and coolant. Open the radiator and engine drain petcocks (models equipped), or disconnect the bottom radiator hose, at the radiator outlet. Set the heater temperature controls to the full HOT position.

NOTE: Before opening the radiator petcock, spray it with some penetrating lubricant.

2. Close the petcock or reconnect the lower hose and fill the system with water.
3. Add a can of quality radiator flush. If equipped with a V6 engine, be sure the flush is safe to use in engines having aluminum components.
4. Idle the engine until the upper radiator hose gets hot.
5. Drain the system again.
6. Repeat this process until the drained water is clear and free of scale.
7. Close all petcocks and connect all the hoses.
8. If equipped with a coolant recovery system, flush the reservoir with water and leave empty.
9. Determine the capacity of your cooling system (see capacities specifications). Add a 50/50 mix of quality antifreeze (ethylene glycol) and water to provide the desired protection.

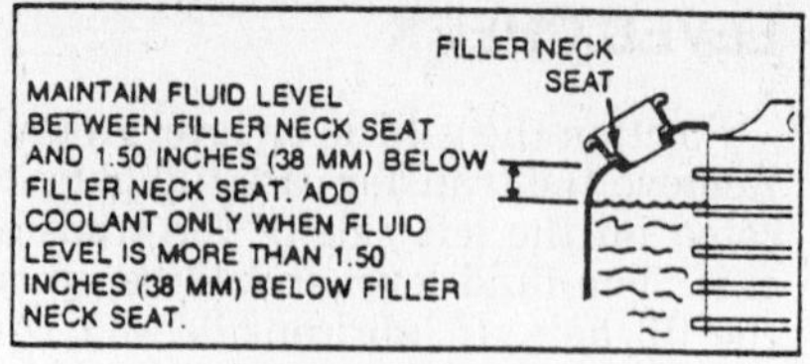

Coolant level check

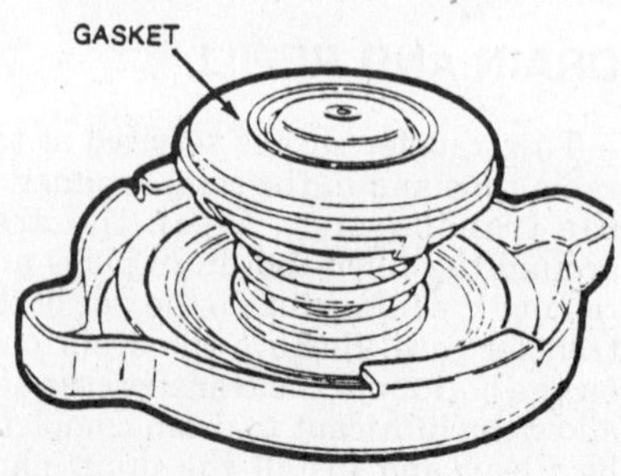

Check the radiator cap gasket for cracks or wear

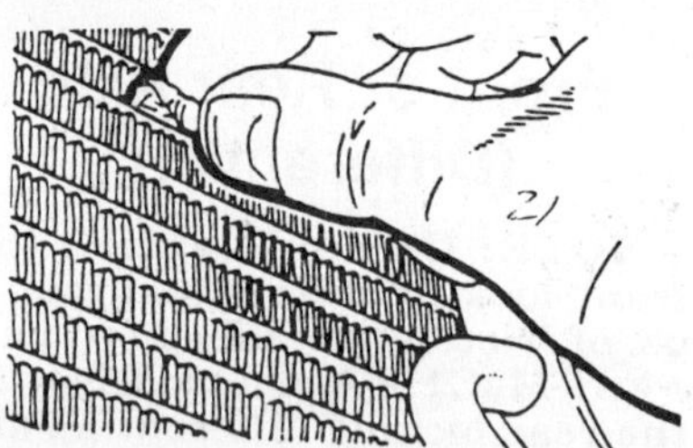

Keep the radiator fins clear of debris for maximum cooling

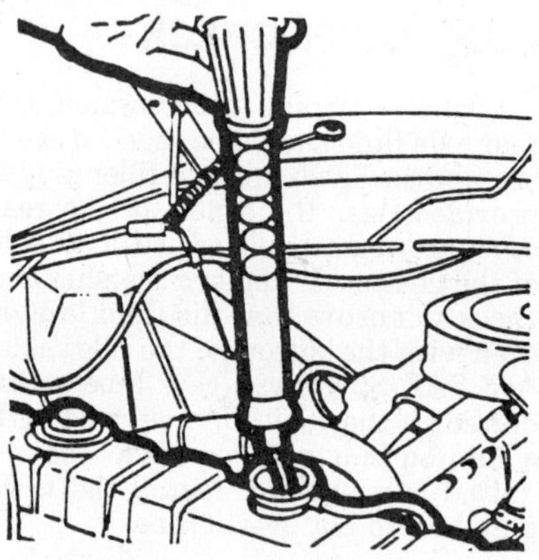

Check anti-freeze protection with an inexpensive tester

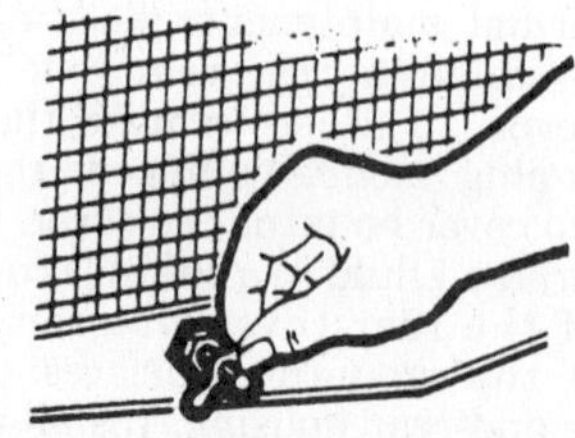

Open the radiator petcock to drain the cooling system. Spray first with penetrating oil

SYSTEM INSPECTION

Most permanent antifreeze/coolant have a colored dye added which makes the solution an excellent leak detector. When servicing the cooling system, check for leakage at:

- All hoses and hose connections
- Radiator seams, radiator core, and radiator draincock
- All engine block and cylinder head freeze (core) plugs, and drain plugs
- Edges of all cooling system gaskets (head gaskets, thermostat gasket)
- Transmission fluid cooler
- Heating system components, water pump
- Check the engine oil dipstick for signs of coolant in the engine oil
- Check the coolant in the radiator for signs of oil in the coolant

Investigate and correct any indication of coolant leakage.

Check the Radiator Cap

While you are checking the coolant level, check the radiator cap for a worn or cracked gasket. If the cap doesn't seal properly, fluid will be lost and the engine will overheat.

A worn cap should be replaced with a new one.

Clean Radiator of Debris

Periodically clean any debris such as leaves, paper, insects, etc., from the radiator fins. Pick the large pieces off by hand. The smaller pieces can be washed away with water pressure from a hose.

Carefully straighten any bent radiator fins with a pair of needle nose pliers. Be careful, the fins are very soft. Don't wiggle the fins back and forth too much. Straighten them once and try not to move them again.

CHECKING SYSTEM PROTECTION

A 50/50 mix of coolant concentrate and water will usually provide protection to -35°F (-37°C). Freeze protection may be checked by using a cooling system hydrometer. Inexpensive hydrometers (floating ball types) may be obtained from a local department store (automotive section) or an auto supply store. Follow the directions packaged with the coolant hydrometer when checking protection.

Master Cylinder

LEVEL CHECK

The brake fluid in the master cylinder should be checked every 6 months/6,000 miles.

Cast Iron Reservoir

1. Park the vehicle on a level surface and open the hood.
2. Pry the retaining spring bar holding the cover onto the master cylinder to one side.
3. Clean any dirt from the sides and top of the cover before removal. Remove the master cylinder cover and gasket.
4. Add fluid, if necessary, to within 3/8" of the top of the reservoir, or to the full level indicator (on models equipped).
5. Push the gasket bellows back into the cover. Reinstall the gasket and cover and position the retainer spring bar.

Plastic Reservoir

Check the fluid level on the side of the reservoir. If fluid is required, remove the screw on the and remove the filler cap and gasket from the master cylinder. Fill the reservoir to the full line in the reservoir. Install the filler cap, making sure the gasket is properly seated in the cap.

FLUID RECOMMENDATION

Use only Heavy Duty Brake Fluid meeting DOT3 specifications.

Manual Steering Gear

FLUID RECOMMENDATION

Fill the steering gear (manual) housing with a good quality Steering Gear Grease.

LEVEL CHECK

The steering gear is located under the hood, on the left side at the end of the steering shaft. Clean the area around the filler plug of the steering gear, remove the plug and check to see if the level of the lubricant is visible in the filler plug tower. If it is, replace the plug. If it is not, add steering gear lubricant until the level is visible about 1 inch from the top of the hole in filler plug tower. Reinstall the fill plug.

Power Steering

LEVEL CHECK

Check the power steering fluid level every 6 months/6,000 miles.

1. Park the vehicle on a level surface. Run the engine until normal operating temperature is reached.
2. Turn the steering all the way to the left and then all the way to the right several times. Center the steering wheel and shut off the engine.
3. Open the hood and check the power steering reservoir fluid level.

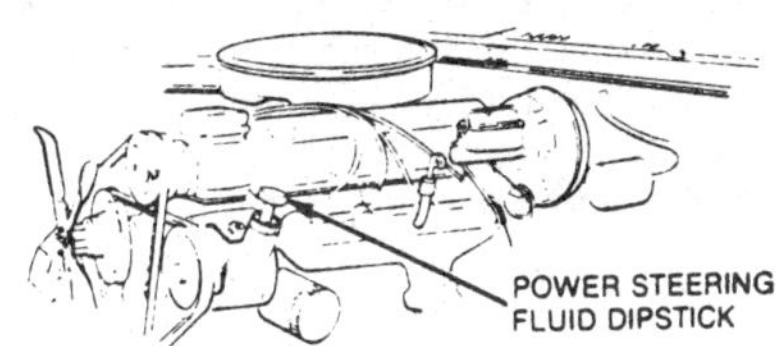

To avoid contamination of the power steering fluid, be sure the dipstick is installed with the lock tabs in the groove—then rotate the dipstick clockwise until the lock tabs contact the stop in the pump filler.

4. Remove the filler cap and wipe the dipstick attached clean.
5. Re-insert the dipstick and tighten the cap. Remove the dipstick and note the fluid level indicated on the dipstick.
6. The level should be at any point below the Full mark, but not below the Add mark.
7. Add fluid as necessary. Do not overfill.

FLUID RECOMMENDATION

Add power steering fluid; do not overfill the reservoir.

Chassis Greasing

NOTE: Depending on the year and model, vehicles may have plugs or grease fittings in all steering/suspension linkage or pivot points. Follow the instructions under Ball Joints if equipped with these plugs. Newer models have sealed points and lubrication is not necessary.

BALL JOINTS

1. Park the vehicle on a level surface, set the parking brake, block the rear wheels, raise the front end and support it with jackstands.
2. Wipe away any dirt from the ball joint lubrication plugs.

NOTE: The upper ball joint has a plug on the top; the lower ball joint has one on the bottom.

3. Pull out the plugs and install grease fittings.
4. Using a hand-operated grease gun containing multi-purpose grease, force lubricant into the joint until the joint boot swells.
5. Remove the grease fitting and push in the lubrication plug.
6. Lower the vehicle.

STEERING ARM STOPS

The steering arm stops are attached to the lower control arm. They are located between each steering arm and the upturned end of the front suspension strut.

1. Park the vehicle on a level surface, set the parking brake, block the rear wheels, raise the front end and support it with jackstands.
2. Clean the friction points and apply multi-purpose grease.
3. Lower the vehicle.

MANUAL TRANSMISSION AND CLUTCH LINKAGE

On models so equipped, apply a small amount of chassis grease to the pivot points of the transmission and clutch linkage as per the chassis lubrication diagram.

AUTOMATIC TRANSMISSION LINKAGE

On models so equipped, apply a small amount of 10W engine oil to the kickdown and shift linkage at the pivot points.

PARKING BRAKE LINKAGE

At yearly intervals or whenever binding is noticeable in the parking brake linkage, lubricate the cable guides, levers and linkage with a suitable chassis grease.

OUTSIDE VEHICLE MAINTENANCE

Lock Cylinders

Apply graphite lubricant sparingly through the key slot. Insert the key and operate the lock several times to be sure that the lubricant is worked into the lock cylinder.

Door Hinges and Hinge Checks

Spray a silicone lubricant on the hinge pivot points to eliminate any binding conditions. Open and close the door several times to be sure that the lubricant is evenly and thoroughly distributed.

Trunk Lid

Spray a silicone lubricant on all of the pivot and friction surfaces to eliminate any squeaks or binds. Work the trunk lid to distribute the lubricant

Body Drain Holes

Be sure that the drain holes in the doors and rocker panels are cleared of obstruction. A small screwdriver can be used to clear them of any debris.

PUSHING AND TOWING

WARNING: Push-starting is not recommended for trucks equipped with a catalytic converter. Raw gas collecting in the converter may cause damage. Jump starting is recommended.

To push-start your manual transmission equipped truck (automatic transmission models cannot be push started), make sure of bumper alignment. If the bumper of the truck pushing does not match with your truck's bumper, it would be wise to tie an old tire either on the back of your truck, or on the front of the pushing truck. Switch the ignition to **ON** and depress the clutch pedal. Shift the transmission to third gear and hold the accelerator pedal about halfway down. signal the push truck to proceed, when the truck speed reaches about 10 mph, gradually release the clutch pedal. The truck engine should start, if not have the truck towed.

If the transmission and rear axle are in proper working order, the truck can be towed with the rear wheels on the ground for distances under 15 miles at speeds no greater then 30 mph. If the transmission or rear is known to be damaged or if the truck has to be towed over 15 miles or over 30 mph the truck must be dollied or towed with the rear wheels raised and the steering wheel secured so that the front wheels remain in the straight-ahead position. The steering wheel must be clamped with a special clamping device designed for towing service. If the key controlled lock is used damage to the lock and steering column may occur.

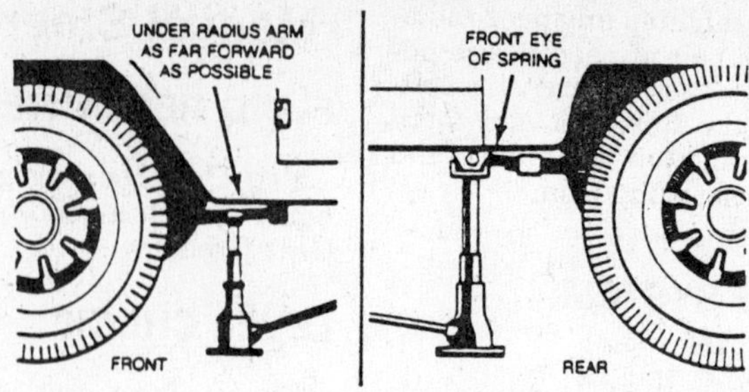

Proper jack placement

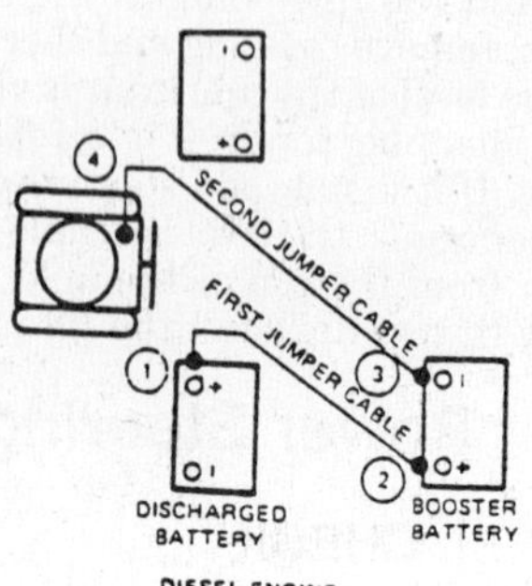

Diesel dual-battery jump starting diagram

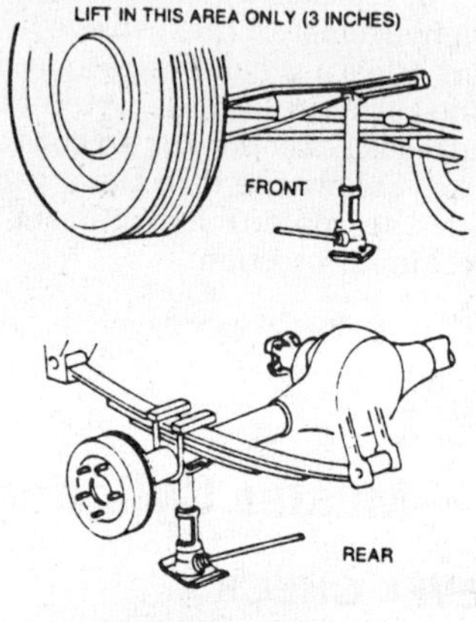

Jacking points

E-250, 300 front jacking point

JACKING

Your truck is equipped with either a scissors type jack, or a bumper jack. The scissor-type jack is placed under the side of the truck so that it fits into the notch in the vertical rocker panel flange nearest the wheel to be changed. These jacking notches are located approximately 8 inches from the wheel opening on the rocker panel flanges. Bumper jack slots or flats are provided on the front and rear bumper. Be sure the jack is inserted firmly and is straight before raising the vehicle.

When raising the truck with a scissors or bumper jack follow these precautions: Park the truck on level spot, put the selector in P (PARK) with an automatic transmission or in reverse if your truck has a manual transmission, apply the parking brake and block the front and the back of the wheel that is diagonally opposite the wheel being changed. These jacks are fine for changing a tire, but never crawl under the truck when it is supported only by the scissors or bumper jack.

CAUTION

If you're going to work beneath the vehicle, always support it on jackstands.

TRAILER TOWING

Factory trailer towing packages are available on most cars. However, if you are installing a trailer hitch and wiring on your car, there are a few thing that you ought to know.

Trailer Weight

Trailer weight is the first, and most important, factor in determining whether or not your vehicle is suitable for towing the trailer you have in mind. The horsepower-to-weight ratio should be calculated. The basic standard is a ratio of 35:1. That is, 35 pounds of GVW for every horsepower.

To calculate this ratio, multiply you engine's rated horsepower by 35, then subtract the weight of the vehicle, including passengers and luggage. The resulting figure is the ideal maximum trailer weight that you can tow. One point to consider: a numerically higher axle ratio can offset what appears to be a low trailer weight. If the weight of the trailer that you have in mind is somewhat higher than the weight you just calculated, you might consider changing your rear axle ratio to compensate.

Hitch Weight

There are three kinds of hitches: bumper mounted, frame mounted, and load equalizing.

Bumper mounted hitches are those which attach solely to the vehicle's bumper. Many states prohibit towing with this type of hitch, when it attaches to the vehicle's stock bumper, since it subjects the bumper to stresses for which it was not designed. Aftermarket rear step bumpers, designed for trailer towing, are acceptable for use with bumper mounted hitches.

Frame mounted hitches can be of the type which bolts to two or more points on the frame, plus the bumper, or just to several points on the frame. Frame mounted hitches can also be of the tongue type, for Class I towing, or, of the receiver type, for classes II and III.

Load equalizing hitches are usually used for large trailers. Most equalizing hitches are welded in place and use equalizing bars and chains to level the vehicle after the trailer is hooked up.

The bolt-on hitches are the most common, since they are relatively easy to install.

Check the gross weight rating of your trailer. Tongue weight is usually figured as 10% of gross trailer weight. Therefore, a trailer with a maximum gross weight of 2,000 lb. will have a maximum tongue weight of 200 lb. Class I tarilers fall into this category. Class II trailers are those with a gross weight rating of 2,000-3,500 lb., while Class III trailers fall into the 3,500-6,000 lb. category. Class IV trailers are those over 6,000 lb. and are for use with fifth wheel trucks, only.

When you've determined the hitch that you'll need, follow the manufacturer's installation instructions, exactly, especially when it comes to fastener torques. The hitch will subjected to a lot of stress and good hitches come with hardened bolts. Never substitute an inferior bolt for a hardened bolt.

Wiring

Wiring the car for towing is fairly easy. There are a number of good wiring kits available and these should be used, rather than trying to design your own. All trailers will need brake lights and turn signals as well as tail lights and side marker lights. Most states require extra marker lights for overly wide trailers. Also, most states have recently required back-up lights for trailers, and most trailer manufacturers have been building trailers with back-up lights for several years.

Additionally, some Class I, most Class II and just about all Class III trailers will have electric brakes.

Add to this number an accessories wire, to operate trailer internal equipment or to charge the trailer's battery, and you can have as many as seven wires in the harness.

Determine the equipment on your trailer and buy the wiring kit necessary. The kit will contain all the wires needed, plus a plug adapter set which included the female plug, mounted on the bumper or hitch, and the male plug, wired into, or plugged into the trailer harness.

When installing the kit, follow the manufacturer's instructions. The color coding of the wires is standard throughout the industry.

One point to note, some domestic vehicles, and most imported vehicles, have separate turn signals. On most domestic vehicles, the brake lights and rear turn signals operate with the same bulb. For those vehicles with separate turn signals, you can purchase an isolation unit so that the brake lights won't blink whenever the turn signals are operated, or, you can go to your local electronics supply house and buy four diodes to wire in series with the brake and turn signal bulbs. Diodes will isolate the brake and turn signals. The choice is yours. The isolation units are simple and quick to install, but far more expensive than the diodes. The diodes, however, require more work to install properly, since they require the cutting of each bulb's wire and soldering in place of the diode.

One final point, the best kits are those with a spring loaded cover on the vehicle mounted socket. This cover prevents dirt and moisture from corroding the terminals. Never let the vehicle socket hang loosely. Always mount it securely to the bumper or hitch.

Cooling

ENGINE

One of the most common, if not THE most common, problem associated with trailer towing is engine overheating.

With factory installed trailer towing packages, a heavy duty cooling system is usually included. Heavy duty cooling systems are available as optional equipment on most cars, with or without a trailer package. If you have one of these extra-capacity systems, you shouldn't have any overheating problems.

If you have a standard cooling system, without an expansion tank, you'll definitely need to get an aftermarket expansion tank kit, preferably one with at least a 2 quart capacity. These kits are easily installed on the radiator's overflow hose, and come with a pressure cap designed for expansion tanks.

Another helpful accessory is a Flex Fan. These fan are large diameter units are designed to provide more airflow at low speeds, with blades that have deeply cupped surfaces. The blades then flex, or flatten out, at high speed, when less cooling air is needed. These fans are far lighter in weight than stock fans, requiring less horsepower to drive them. Also, they are far quieter than stock fans.

If you do decide to replace your stock fan with a flex fan, note that if your car has a fan clutch, a spacer between the flex fan and water pump hub will be needed.

Aftermarket engine oil coolers are helpful for prolonging engine oil life and reducing overall engine temperatures. Both of these factors increase engine life.

While not absolutely necessary in towing Class I and some Class II trailers, they are recommended for heavier Class II and all Class III towing.

Engine oil cooler systems consist of an adapter, screwed on in place of the oil filter, a remote filter mounting and a multi-tube, finned heat exchanger, which is mounted in front of the radiator or air conditioning condenser.

TRANSMISSION

An automatic transmission is usually recommended for trailer towing. Modern automatics have proven reliable and, of course, easy to operate, in trailer towing.

The increased load of a trailer, however, causes an increase in the temperature of the automatic transmission fluid. Heat is the worst enemy of an automatic transmission. As the temperature of the fluid increases, the life of the fluid decreases.

It is essential, therefore, that you install an automatic transmission cooler.

The cooler, which consists of a multi-tube, finned heat exchanger, is usually installed in front of the radiator or air conditioning compressor, and hooked inline with the transmission cooler tank inlet line. Follow the cooler manufacturer's installation instructions.

Select a cooler of at least adequate capacity, based upon the combined gross weights of the car and trailer.

Cooler manufacturers recommend that you use an aftermarket cooler in addition to, and not instead of, the present cooling tank in your car radiator. If you do want to use it in place of the radiator cooling tank, get a cooler at least two sizes larger than normally necessary.

NOTE: A transmission cooler can, sometimes, cause slow or harsh shifting in the transmission during cold weather, until the fluid has a chance to come up to normal operating temperature. Some coolers can be purchased with or retrofitted with a temperature bypass valve which will allow fluid flow through the cooler only when the fluid has reached operating temperature, or above.

TUNE-UP PROCEDURES

In order to extract the full measure of performance and economy from your engine it is essential that it be properly tuned at regular intervals. A regular tune-up will keep your vehicle's engine running smoothly and will prevent the annoying minor breakdowns and poor performance associated with an untuned engine.

A complete tune-up should be performed every 12,000 miles or twelve months, whichever comes first. This interval should be halved if the vehicle is operated under severe conditions, such as trailer towing, prolonged idling, continual stop and start driving, or if starting or running problems are noticed. It is assumed that the routine maintenance described has been kept up, as this will have a decided effect on the results of a tune-up. All of the applicable steps of a tune-up should be followed in order, as the result is a cumulative one.

If the specifications on the tune-up sticker in the engine compartment disagree with the Tune-Up Specifications chart, the figures on the sticker must be used. The sticker often reflects changes made during the production run.

Spark Plugs

A typical spark plug consists of a metal shell surrounding a ceramic insulator. A metal electrode extends downward through the center of the insulator and protrudes a small distance. Located at the end of the plug and attached to the side of the outer metal shell is the side electrode. The side electrode bends in at a 90° angle so that its tip is even with, and parallel to, the tip of the center electrode. The distance between these two electrodes (measured in thousandths of an inch) is called the spark plug gap. The spark plug in no way produces a spark but merely provides a gap across which the current can arc. The coil produces anywhere from 20,000 to 40,000 volts or more, which travels to the distributor where it is distributed through the spark plug wires to the spark plugs. The current passes along the center electrode and jumps the gap to the side electrode, and, in so doing, ignites the air/fuel mixture in the combustion chamber.

PORCELAIN INSULATOR
INSULATOR CRACKS OFTEN OCCUR HERE
SHELL
ADJUST FOR PROPER GAP
SIDE ELECTRODE (BEND TO ADJUST GAP)
CENTER ELECTRODE; FILE FLAT WHEN ADJUSTING GAP; DO NOT BEND!

Cross section of a spark plug

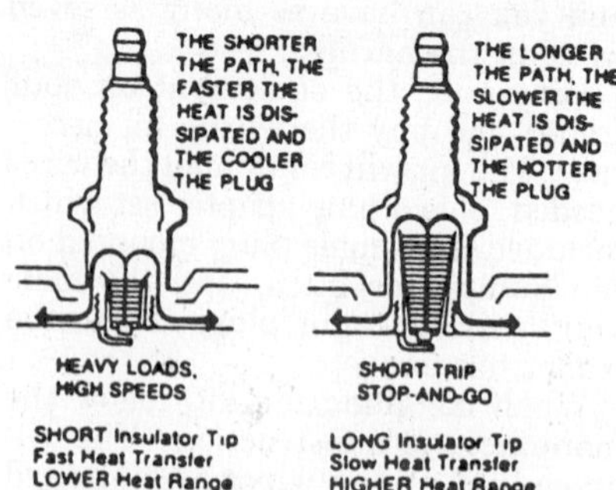

Spark plug heat range

1 2 3 4 5
R 4 5 TS X

1 – R--INDICATES RESISTOR-TYPE PLUG.
2 – "4" INDICATES 14 mm THREADS.
3 – HEAT RANGE
4 – TS--TAPERED SEAT
S--EXTENDED TIP
5 – SPECIAL GAP

Spark plug type number charge, using the R45TSX as an example

SPARK PLUG HEAT RANGE

Spark plug heat range is the ability of the plug to dissipate heat. The longer the insulator (or the farther it extends into the engine), the hotter the plug will operate; the shorter the insulator the cooler it will operate. A plug that absorbs little heat and remains too cool will quickly accumulate deposits of oil and carbon since it is not hot enough to burn them off. This leads to plug fouling and consequently to mis-

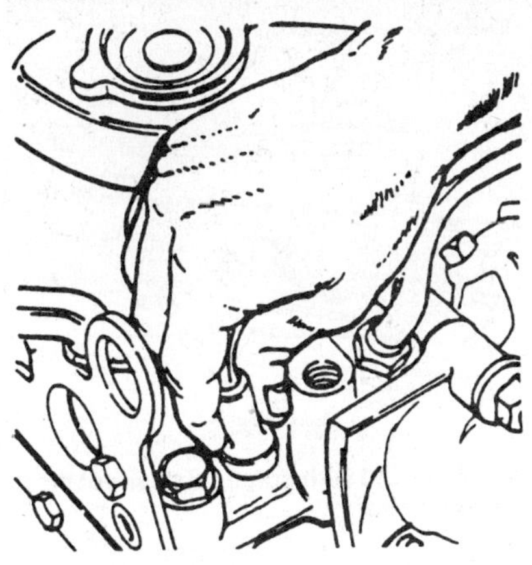

Twist and pull on the rubber boot to remove the spark plug wires; never pull on the wire itself

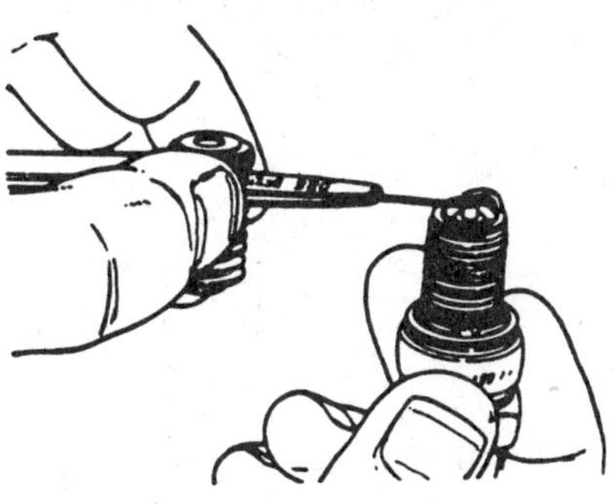

Always use a wire gauge to check the electrode gap; a flat feeler gauge may not give the proper reading

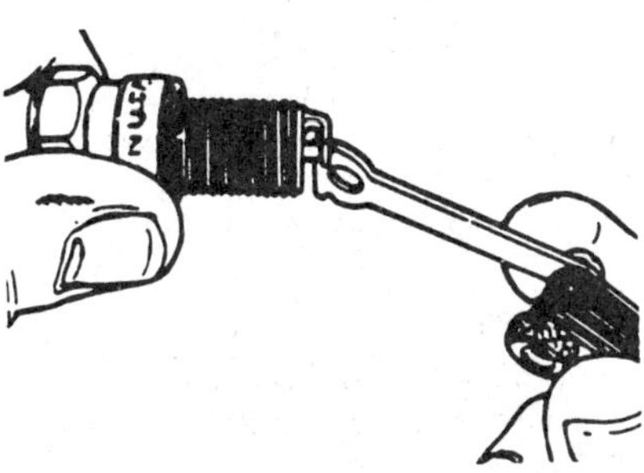

Adjust the electrode gap by bending the side electrode

firing. A plug that absorbs too much heat will have to deposits, but, due to the excessive heat, the electrodes will burn away quickly and in some instances, pre-ignition may result. Pre-ignition takes place when plug tips get so hot that they glow sufficiently to ignite the fuel/air mixture before the actual spark occurs. This early ignition will usually cause a pinging during low speeds and heavy loads.

The general rule of thumb for choosing the correct heat range when picking a spark plug is: if most of your driving is long distance, high speed travel, use a colder plug; if most of your driving is stop and go, use a hotter plug. Original equipment plugs are compromise plugs, but most people never have occasion to change their plugs from the factory recommended heat range.

REPLACING SPARK PLUGS

A set of spark plugs usually requires replacement after about 10,000 miles on cars with conventional ignition systems and after about 20,000 to 30,000 miles on cars with electronic ignition, depending on your style of driving. In normal operation, plug gap increases about 0.001″ (0.0254mm) for every 1,000-2,500 miles. As the gap increases, the plug's voltage requirement also increases. It requires a greater voltage to jump the wider gap and about two to three times as much voltage to fire a plug at high speeds than at idle.

When you're removing spark plugs, you should work on one at a time. Don't start by removing the plug wires all at once, because unless you number them, they may become mixed up. Take a minute before you begin and number the wires with tape. The best location for numbering is near where the wires come out of the cap.

NOTE: Apply a small amount of silicone dielectric compound (D7AZ-19A331-A or the equivalent) to the inside of the terminal boots whenever an ignition wire is disconnected from the plug, or coil/distributor cap connection.

1. Twist the spark plug boot and remove the boot and wire from the plug. Do not pull on the wire itself as this will ruin the wire.
2. If possible, use a brush or rag to clean the area around the spark plug. Make sure that all the dirt is removed so that none will enter the cylinder after the plug is removed.
3. Remove the spark plug using the proper size socket. Either a 5/8″ or 13/16″ size socket depending on the engine. Turn the socket counterclockwise to remove the plug. Be sure to hold the socket straight on the plug to avoid breaking the plug, or rounding off the hex on the plug.
4. Once the plug is out, check it to determine engine condition. This is crucial since plug readings are vital signs of engine condition.
5. Use a round wire feeler gauge to check the plug gap. The correct size gauge should pass through the electrode gap with a slight drag. If you're in doubt, try one size smaller and one larger. The smaller gauge should go through easily while the larger one shouldn't go through at all. If the gap is incorrect, use the electrode bending tool on the end of the gauge to adjust the gap. When adjusting the gap, always bend the side electrode. The center electrode is non-adjustable.
6. Squirt a drop of penetrating oil on the threads of the new plug and install it. Don't oil the threads too heavily. Turn the plug in clockwise by hand until it is snug.
7. When the plug is finger tight, tighten it with a wrench. Take care not to overtighten. Torque to 15 ft.lb.
8. Install the plug boot firmly over the plug. Proceed to the next plug.

CHECKING AND REPLACING SPARK PLUG CABLES

Visually inspect the spark plug cables for burns, cuts, or breaks in the insulation. Check the spark plug boots and the nipples on the distributor cap and coil. Replace any damaged wiring. If no physical damage is obvious, the wires can be checked with an ohmmeter for excessive resistance. About 5,000Ω per foot is normal.

NOTE: Apply a small amount of silicone dielectric compound (D7AZ-19A331-A or the equivalent) to the inside of the terminal boots whenever an ignition wire is disconnected from the plug. or coil/distributor cap connection.

When installing a new set of spark plug cables, replace the cables one at a time so there will be no mixup. Start by replacing the longest cable first. Install the boot firmly over the spark plug. Route the wire exactly the same as the original. Insert the nipple firmly into the tower on the distributor cap. Repeat the process for each cable.

Idle Speed

Adjustment

1980-82

1. Remove the air cleaner and disconnect and plug the vacuum lines.
2. Block the wheels, apply the parking brake, turn off all accessories, start the engine and run it to normalize underhood temperatures.
3. Check that the choke plate is fully open and connect a tachometer according to the manufacturer's instructions.
4. Check the throttle stop positioner (TSP)-off speed as follows:
   a. Collapse the plunger by forcing the throttle lever against it.

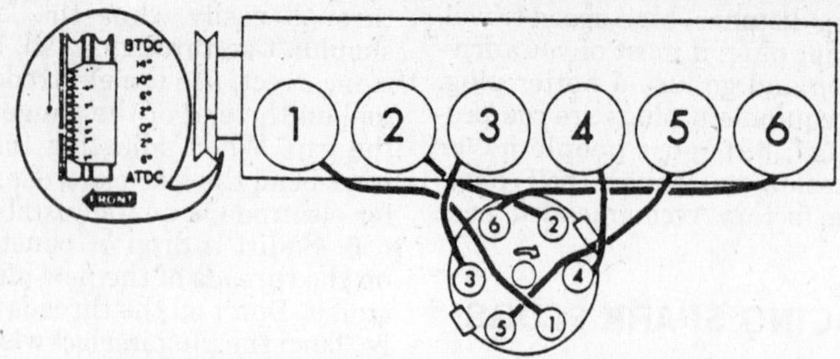

300 inline six cylinder wiring and distributor rotation
Firing order: 1-5-3-6-2-4
Rotation: clockwise

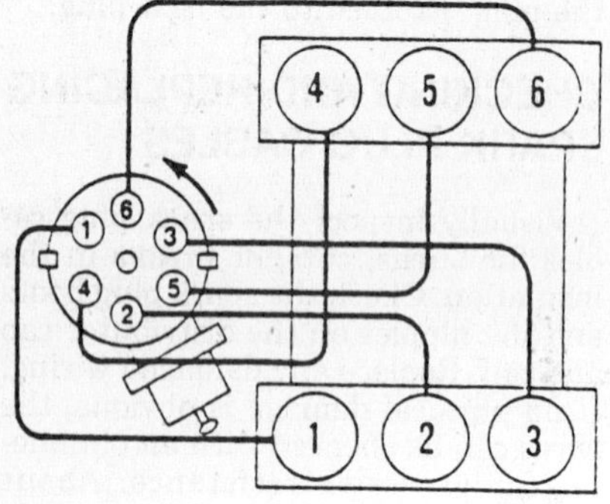

232 V6 wiring and distributor rotation
Firing order: 1-4-2-5-3-6
Rotation: counterclockwise

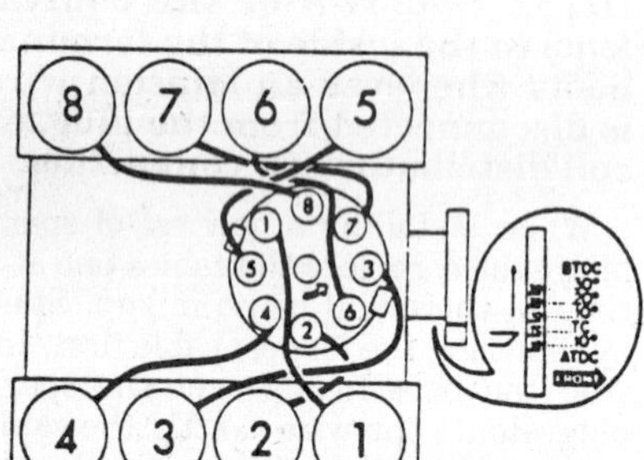

302,460 V8 wiring and distributor rotation
Firing order:1-5-4-2-6-3-7-8
Rotation: counterclockwise

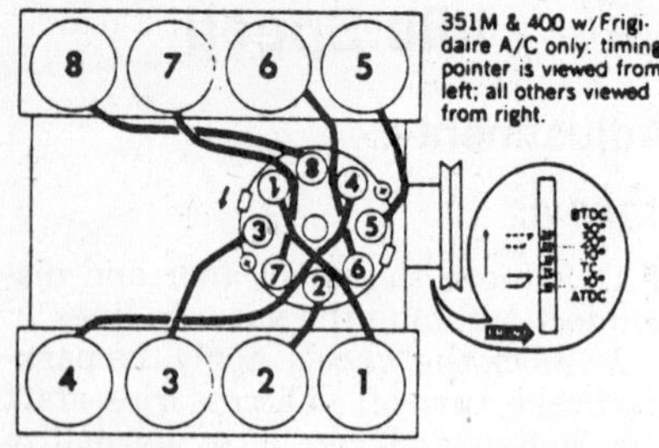

351W,351M,400 V8, wiring and distributor rotation
Firing order:1-3-7-2-6-5-4
Rotation: counterclockwise

b. Place the transmission in neutral and check the engine speed. If necessary, adjust to specified TSP-

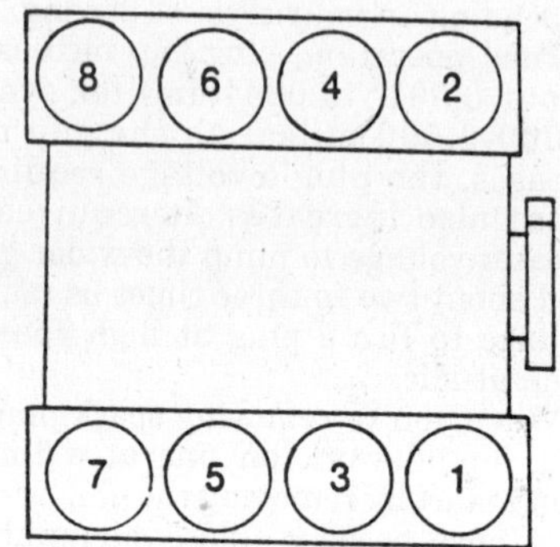

6.9L diesel cylinder arrangement
Firing order: 1-2-7-3-4-5-6-8

Off speed with the throttle adjusting screw. See the underhood sticker.

5. Place the manual transmission in neutral; the automatic in Drive and make certain the TSP plunger is extended.

6. Turn the TSP until the specified idle speed is obtained.

7. Install the air cleaner and connect the vacuum lines. Check the idle speed. Adjust, if necessary, with the air cleaner on.

1983 and Later

6-300 (4.9L) YFA-IV & YFA-IV-FB

1. Block the wheels and apply the parking brake. Place the transmission in Neutral or Park.

2. Bring engine to normal operating temperature.

3. Place A/C Heat Selector to Off position.

4. Place transmission in specified gear.

5. Check/adjust curb idle RPM as follows: TSP dashpot. Insure that TSP is activated using a 3/8" open end wrench, adjust curb idle RPM by rotating the nut directly behind the dashpot housing. Adjust curb idle RPM by turning the idle RPM speed screw. Front mounted TSP (same as A/C kicker on all other calibrations) insure that TSP is activated. After loosening lock nut, adjust curb idle RPM by rotating TSP solenoid until specified RPM is obtained. Tighten locknut.

6. Check/adjust anti-diesel (TSP Off). Manually collapse the TSP by rotating the carb throttle shaft lever until the TSP Off adjusting screw contacts the carburetor body. If adjustment is required, turn the TSP Off adjusting screw while holding the lever adjustment screw against the stop.

7. Place the transmission in Neutral or Park. Rev the engine momentarily. Place the transmission in specified position and recheck curb idle rpm. Readjust if required.

8. Check/adjust dashpot clearance to 0.120" ± 0.030.

9. If a final curb idle speed adjustment is required, the bowl vent setting must be checked as follows: Stop the engine and turn the ignition key to the On position, so that the TSP dashpot or TSP is activated but the engine is not running (where applicable). Secure the choke plate in the wide-open position. Open the throttle, so that the throttle vent lever does not touch the fuel bowl vent rod. Close the throttle, and measure the travel of the fuel bowl vent rod from the open throttle position. Travel of the fuel bowl vent rod should be 0.100-0.150". If out of specification, bend the throttle vent lever to obtain the required travel. Remove all test equipment, and tighten the air cleaner holddown bolt to specification.

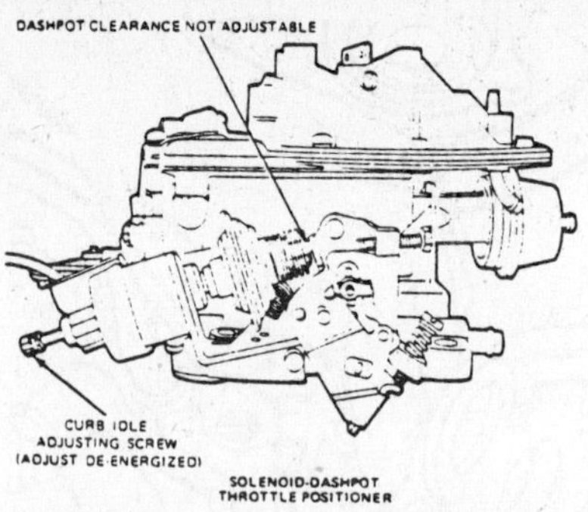

Autolite 2150 with solenoid dashpot throttle positioner

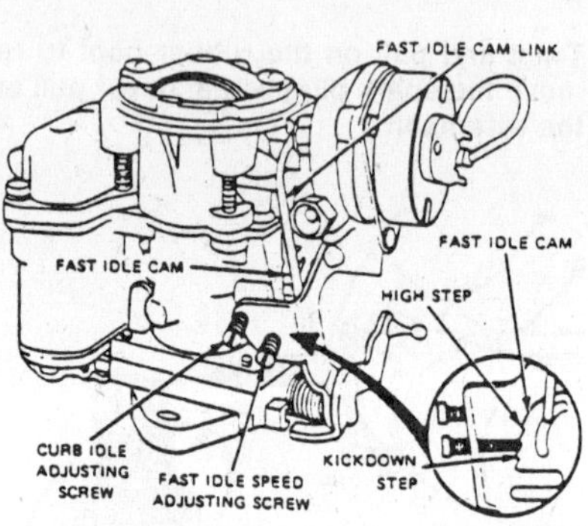

Carter YFA 1-bbl carburetor

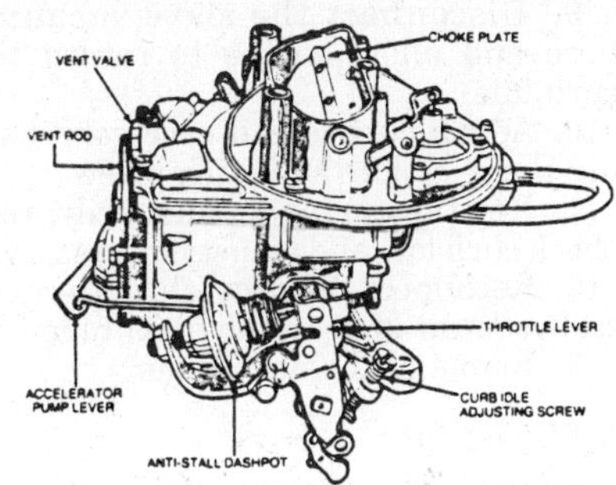

Autolite 2100 2-bbl showing curb idle screw

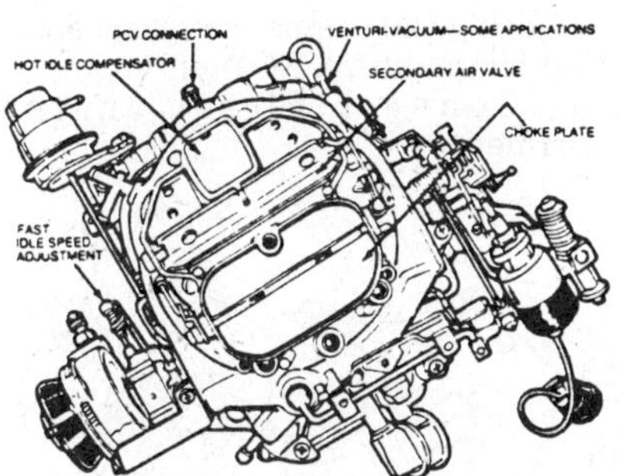

Autolite model 4300 4-bbl. Some models do not have throttle solenoid

10. Whenever it is required to adjust engine idle speed by more than 50 rpm, the adjustment screw on the AOD linkage lever at the carburetor should also be readjusted.

6-232 (3.8L) & 8-302 (5.0L) 2150-2V FB (FEEDBACK)

1. Set parking brake and block wheels.
2. Place the transmission in Park.
3. Bring the engine to normal operating temperature.
4. Disconnect the electric connector on the EVAP purge solenoid.
5. Disconnect and plug the vacuum hose to the VOTM kicker.
6. Place the transmission in Drive position.
7. Check/adjust curb idle rpm, if adjustment is required: Adjust with the the curb idle speed screw or the saddle bracket adjusting screw, depending on how equipped.
8. Place the transmission in Neutral or Park. Rev the engine momentarily. Place the transmission in Drive position and recheck curb idle rpm. Readjust if required.
9. Remove the plug from the vacuum hose to the VOTM kicker and reconnect.
10. Reconnect the electrical connector on the EVAP purge solenoid.

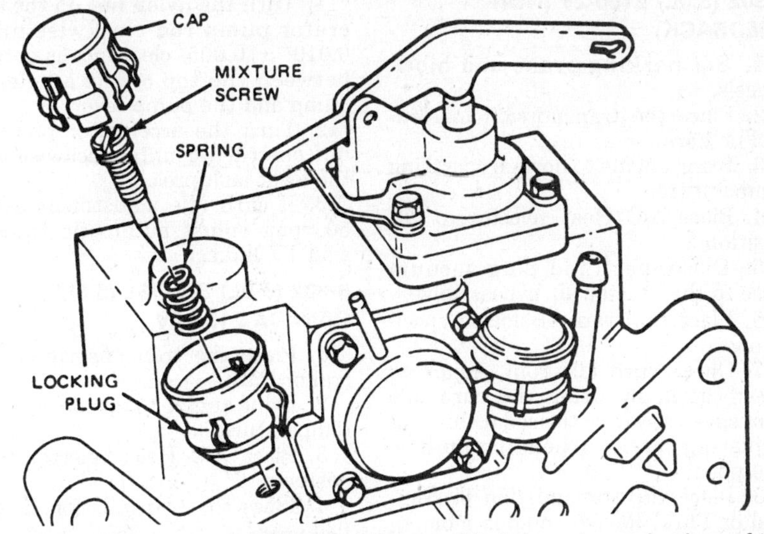

Some 1980 and later 2150 2-bbls have 2-piece metal plugs and caps in place of the plastic limiter caps on the idle mixture adjusting screws. They should be carefully removed before attempting any adjustments

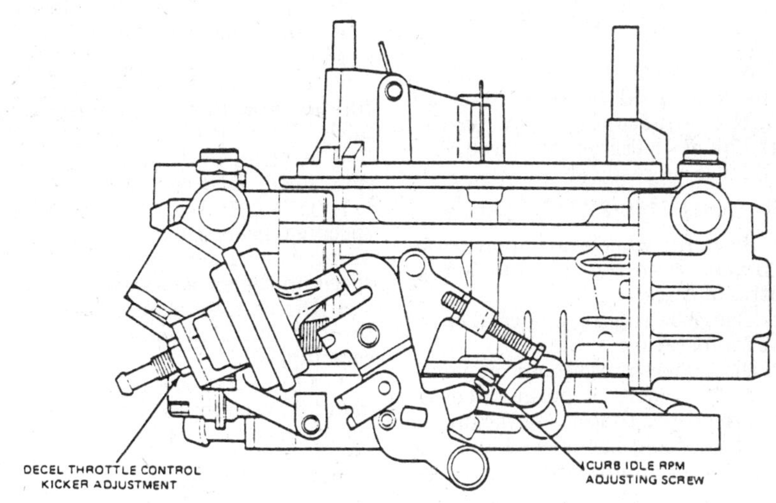

Curb idle screws locations, 4180C 4-bbl on 460 V8s

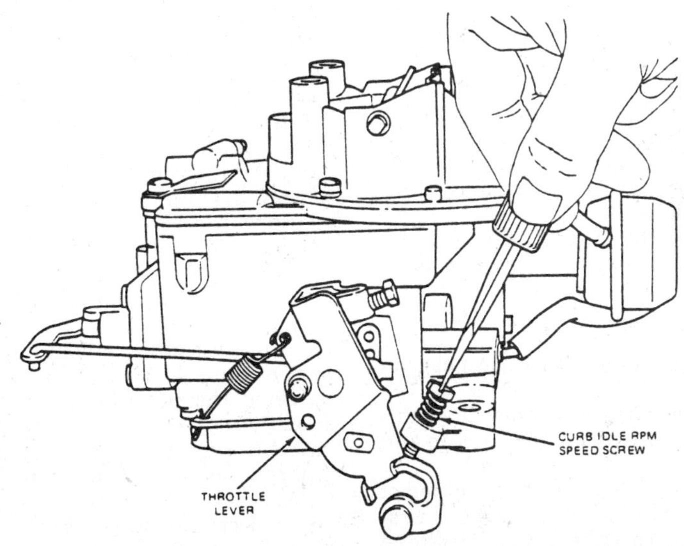

2150 2-bbl curb idle adjustment, 302 and 351 Canadian V8s

8-302 (5.0L) 2150-2V (NON-FEEDBACK)

1. Set parking brake and block wheels.
2. Place the transmission in Neutral or Park.
3. Bring engine to normal operating temperature.
4. Place A/C Heat selector to Off position.
5. Disconnect and plug vacuum hose to thermactor air bypass valve.
6. Place the transmission in specified gear.
7. Check curb idle rpm. Adjust to specification by using the curb idle rpm speed screw or the saddle bracket adjusting screw, depending on how equipped.
8. Place the transmission in Neutral or Park. Rev the engine momentarily. Place the transmission in specified position, and recheck curb idle rpm. Readjust if required.
9. Remove plug from vacuum hose to thermactor air bypass valve and reconnect.
10. Whenever it is required to adjust engine idle speed by more than 50 rpm, the adjustment screw on the AOD linkage lever at the carburetor should also be readjusted.

8-351 (5.8L) 2150-2V OR 7200 VV

1. Block the wheels and apply parking brake. Place the transmission in Neutral or Park.
2. Bring the engine to normal operating temperature.
3. Disconnect purge hose on canister side of evaporator purge solenoid. Check to ensure that purge vacuum is present (solenoid has opened and will require 3 to 5 minute wait after starting engine followed by a short time at part-throttle). Reconnect purge hose.
4. Disconnect and plug the vacuum hose to the VOTM kicker.
5. Place the transmission in specified position.
6. Check/adjust curb idle rpm. If adjustment is required, adjust with the curb idle speed screw or the saddle bracket adjusting screw (ensure curb idle speed screw is not touching throttle shaft lever).
7. Place the transmission in Neutral or Park. Rev the engine momentarily. Place the transmission in specified position and recheck curb idle rpm. Readjust if required.
8. Check/adjust throttle position sensor (TPS).
9. Remove the plug from the vacuum hose to the VOTM kicker and reconnect.
10. Apply a slight pressure on top of the nylon nut located on the accelerator pump to take up the linkage clearance.
11. Turn the nylon nut on the accelerator pump rod clockwise until a 0.010″ ± 0.005″ clearance is obtained between the top of the accelerator pump and the pump lever.
12. Turn the accelerator pump rod nut one turn counterclockwise to set the lever lash preload.
13. If curb idle adjustment exceeds 50 rpm, adjust automatic transmission TV linkage.

8-302 (5.0L) & 8-351 (5.8L) CANADA 2150-2V

1. Place the transmission in Neutral or Park.
2. Bring engine to normal operating temperature.
3. Place A/C Heat Selector to Off position.
4. Place the transmission in specified gear.
5. Check curb idle rpm. Adjust to specification using the curb idle speed screw or the hex head on the rear of the solenoid or the saddle bracket adjustment screw depending on how equipped.
6. Place the transmission in Neutral or Park. Rev the engine momentarily. Place the transmission in specified position and recheck curb idle rpm. Readjust if required.
7. TSP Off: With transmission in specified gear, collapse the solenoid plunger, and set specified TSP Off speed on the speed screw.
8. Disconnect vacuum hose to decel throttle control modulator and plug (if so equipped).
9. Connect a slave vacuum from manifold vacuum to the decel throttle control modulator (if so equipped).
10. Check/adjust decel throttle control rpm. Adjust if necessary.
11. Remove slave vacuum hose.
12. Remove plug from decel throttle control modulator hose and reconnect.

8-460 (7.5L)

1. Block the wheels and apply parking brake.
2. Run engine until normal operating temperature is reached.
3. Place the vehicle in Park or Neutral, A/C in Off position, and set parking brake.
4. Remove air cleaner.
5. Disconnect and plug decel throttle control kicker diaphragm vacuum hose.
6. Connect a slave vacuum hose from an engine manifold vacuum source to the decel throttle control kicker.
7. Run engine at approximately 2500 rpm for 15 seconds, then release the throttle.
8. If decel throttle control rpm is not within ± 50 rpm of specification, adjust the kicker.
9. Disconnect the slave vacuum hose and allow engine to return to curb idle.
10. Adjust curb idle, if necessary, using the curb idle adjusting screw.
11. Rev the engine momentarily, recheck curb idle and adjust if necessary.
12. Reconnect the decel throttle control vacuum hose to the diaphragm.
13. Reinstall the air cleaner.

6.9L Diesel

NOTE: A special tachometer is required to check engine RPM on a diesel engine.

1. Block the wheels and apply the parking brake.
2. Bring the engine to normal operating temperature. Shut off engine.
3. Connect diesel engine tachometer.

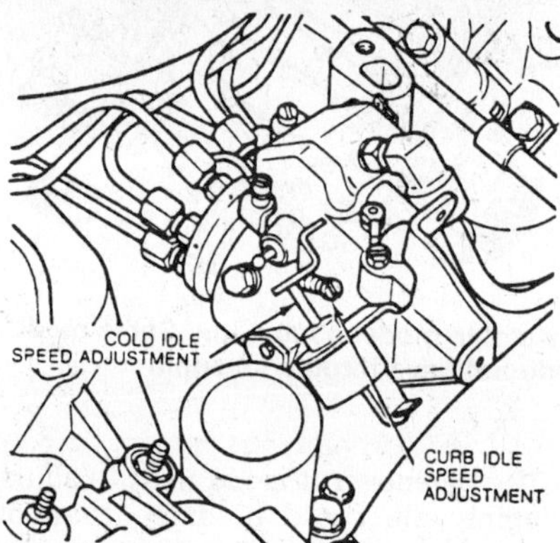

6.9L diesel injection pump showing idle speed adjustment. Pump mounted on top (front) of intake manifold

4. Start the engine and check RPM. Refer to the emissions decal for latest specifications. RPM is usually adjusted in Neutral for manual transmissions and Drive for automatic models.
5. Turn the idle speed adjusting screw in the required direction to increase or decrease RPM. The adjusting screw is located on the top of the injector pump above the cold start valve.
6. Place the gear selector in neutral, if automatic, and speed up engine several times. Recheck idle RPM, readjust if necessary.

Idle Mixture

ADJUSTMENT

NOTE: For this procedure, Ford recommends a propane enrichment procedure. This requires special equipment not available to the general public. In lieu of this equipment the following procedure may be followed to obtain satisfactory idle mixture.

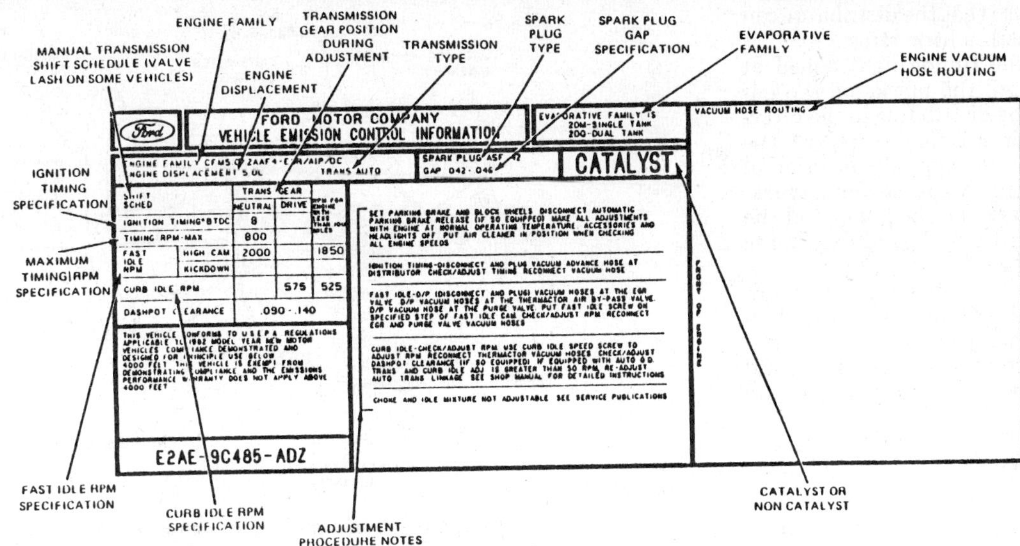

Typical underhood emissions decal, including many tune-up specifications

1. Block the wheels, set the parking brake and run the engine to bring it to normal operating temperature.
2. Disconnect the hose between the emission canister and the air cleaner.
3. On engines equipped with the Thermactor air injection system, the routing of the vacuum lines connected to the dump valve will have to be temporarily changed. Mark them for reconnection before switching them.
4. For valves with one or two vacuum lines at the side, disconnect and plug the lines.
5. For valves with one vacuum line at the top, check the line to see if it is connected to the intake manifold or an intake manifold source such as the carburetor or distributor vacuum line. If not, remove and plug the line at the dump valve and connect a temporary length of vacuum hose from the dump valve fitting to a source of intake manifold vacuum.
6. Remove the limiter caps from the mixture screws by CAREFULLY cutting them with a sharp knife.
7. Place the transmission in neutral and run the engine at 2500 rpm for 15 seconds.
8. Place the automatic transmission in Drive; the manual in neutral.
9. Adjust the idle speed to the higher of the two figures given on the underhood sticker.
10. Turn the idle mixture screws to obtain the highest possible rpm, leaving the screws in the leanest position that will maintain this rpm.
11. Repeat steps 7 thru 10 until further adjustment of the mixture screws does not increase the rpm.
12. Turn the screws in until the lower of the two idle speed figures is reached. Turn the screws in ¼ turn increments each to insure a balance.
13. Turn the engine off and remove the tachometer. Reinstall all equipment.

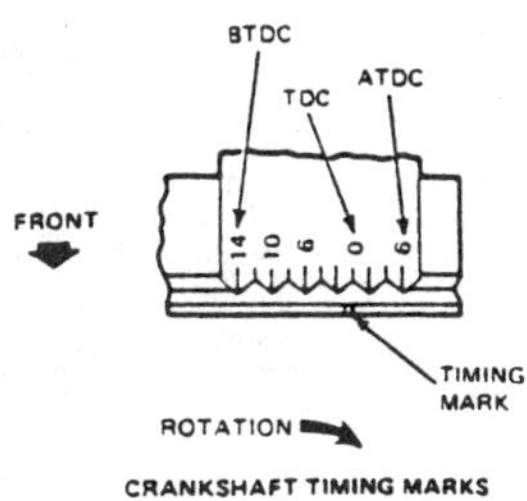

Typical inline-six and 232 V6 timing marks; degree scale on timing pointer, marks on pulley rim

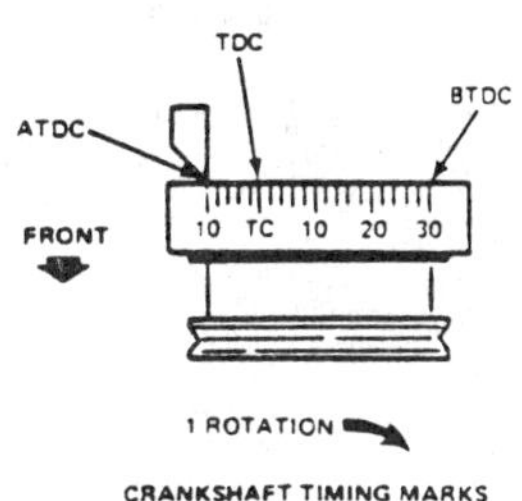

Typical V8 timing marks; some engines have both scale and marks on pulley, pointer separate

NOTE: Rough idle, that cannot be corrected by normal service procedures may be caused by leakage between the EGR valve body and diaphragm. To determine if this is the cause:

1. Tighten the EGR bolts to 15 ft.lb. Connect a vacuum gauge to the intake manifold.
2. Lift to exert a sideways pressure on the diaphragm housing. If the idle changes or the reading on the vacuum gauge varies, replace the EGR valve.

Ignition Timing

ADJUSTMENTS

1. Locate the timing marks on the crankshaft pulley and the front of the engine.
2. Clean off the timing marks so that you can see them.
3. Mark the timing marks with a piece of chalk or white paint. Color the mark on the scale that will indicate the correct timing when it is aligned with the mark on the pulley or the pointer. It is also helpful to mark the notch in the pulley or the tip of the pointer with a small dab of color.
4. Attach a tachometer to the engine.
5. Attach a timing light according to the manufacturer's instructions.
6. Disconnect the distributor vacuum line at the distributor and plug the vacuum line. A small bolt, center punch or similar object is satisfactory for a plug.
7. Check to make sure that all of the wires clear the fan and then start the engine.
8. Adjust the idle to the correct setting.
9. Aim the timing light at the timing marks. If the marks that you put on the pulley and the engine are aligned when the light flashes, the timing is correct. Turn off the engine and remove the tachometer and the timing light. If the marks are not in alignment, proceed with the following steps.
10. Loosen the distributor lockbolt

just enough so that the distributor can be turned with a little effort.

11. With the timing light aimed at the pulley and the marks on the engine, turn the distributor in the direction of rotor rotation to regard the spark, and in the opposite direction of rotor rotation to the advance spark. Align the marks on the pulley and the engine with the flashes of the timing light.

12. When the marks are aligned, tighten the distributor lockbolt and recheck the timing with the timing light to make sure that the distributor did not move when you tightened the lockbolt.

13. Turn off the engine and remove the timing light.

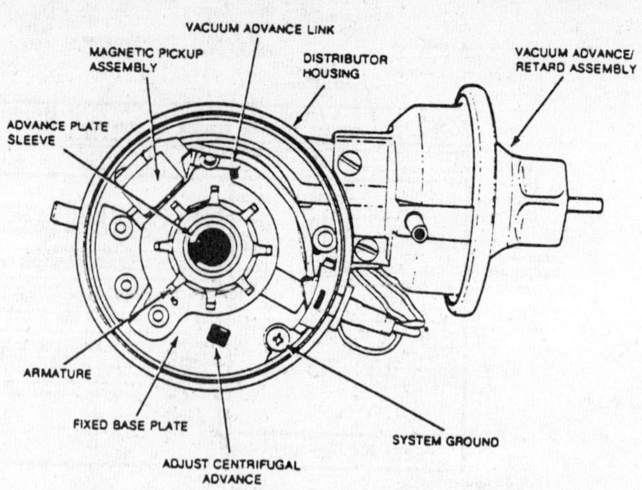

V8-type electronic distributor components

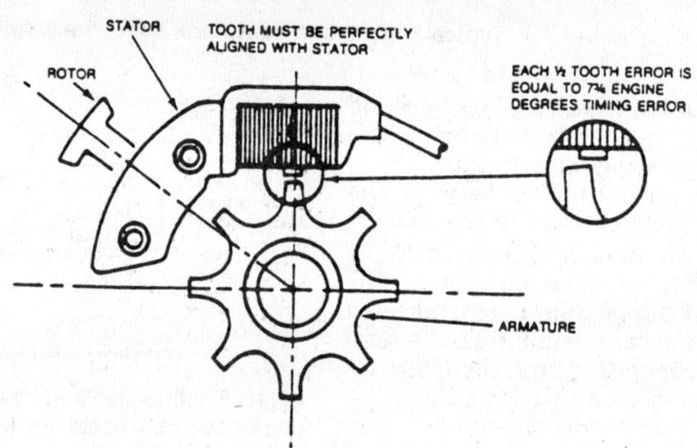

V8 electronic distributor, static timing position

ELECTRONIC IGNITION SYSTEMS

DuraSpark Ignition

Basically, four electronic ignition systems have been used in Ford Motor Company vehicles from 1977-87:

1. DuraSpark I
2. DuraSpark II
3. DuraSpark III
4. Universal Distributor-TFI (EEC-IV)

In 1977, the DuraSpark systems, were introduced. DuraSpark I and DuraSpark II systems are nearly identical in operation, and virtually identical in appearance. The DuraSpark I uses a special control module which senses current flow through the ignition coil and adjust the dwell, or coil on-time for maximum spark intensity. If the DuraSpark I module senses that the ignition is ON, but the distributor shaft is not turning, the current to the coil is turned OFF by the module. The DuraSpark II system does not have this feature. The coil is energized for the full amount of time that the ignition switch is ON. Keep this in mind when servicing the DuraSpark II system, as the ignition system could inadvertently fire while performing ignition system services (such as distributor cap removal) while the ignition is ON. All DuraSpark II systems are easily identified by having a two-piece, flat topped distributor cap.

In 1980, the new DuraSpark III system was introduced. This version is based on the previous systems, but the input signal is controlled by the EEC system, rather than as function of engine timing and distributor armature position. The distributor, rotor, cap, and control module are unique to this system; the spark plugs and plug wires are the same as those used with the DuraSpark II system. Although the DuraSpark II and III control modules are similar in appearance, they cannot be interchanged between systems.

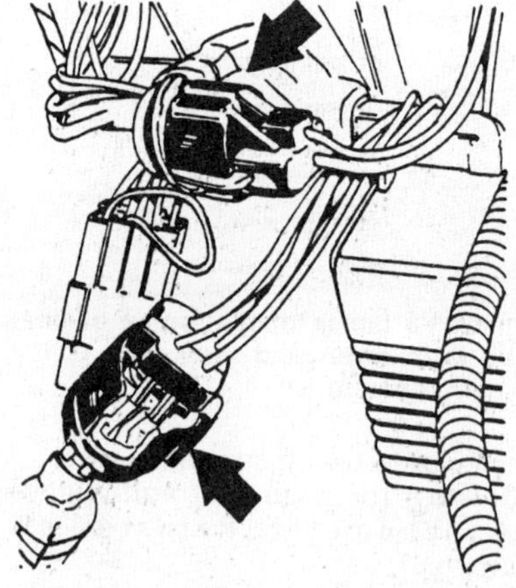

When you're working on the electronic ignition, unplug the module connectors here. Leave the module side alone or you'll short out the module (shown on right)

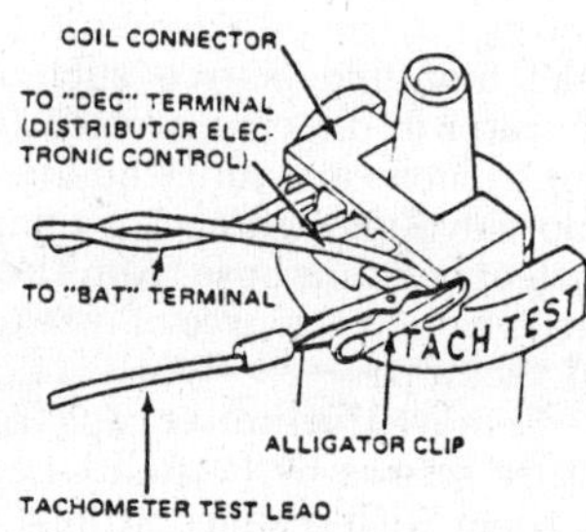

Attaching a tachometer lead to the coil connector

Some engines use a special DuraSpark Dual Mode ignition control module. The module is equipped with an altitude sensor, an economy modulator, or pressure switches (turbocharged engines only). This module, when combined with the additional switches and sensor, varies the base engine timing according to altitude and engine load conditions.

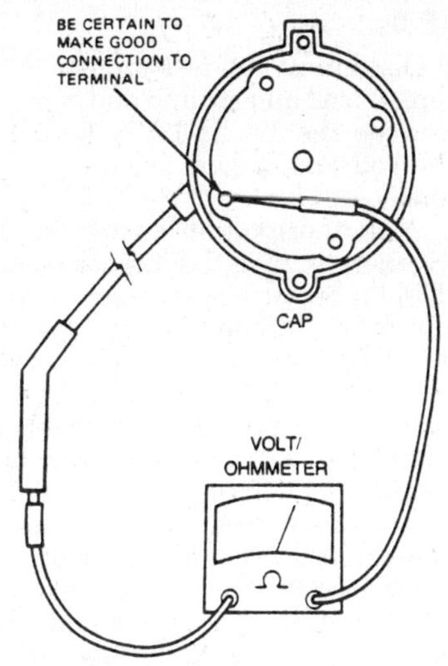

Checking ignition wire resistance

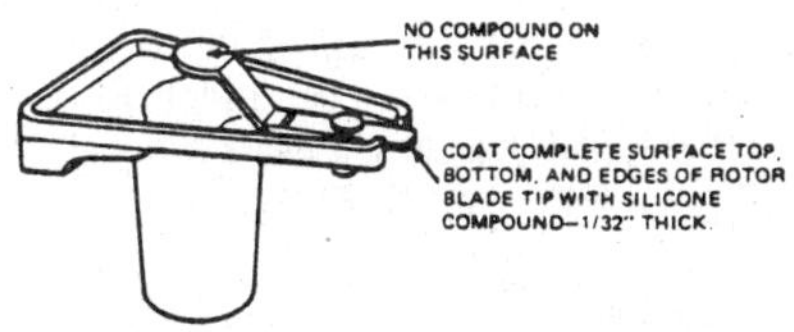

Silicone-compound application to distributor rotor

DuraSpark Dual Mode ignition control modules have three wiring harness from the module.

1981 49-state and 1982 Canadian 4-140 engines with automatic transmissions have Dual Mode Crank Retard ignition module, which has the same function as the DuraSpark II module plug an ignition timing retard function which is operational during engine cranking. The spark timing retard feature eases engine starting, but allows normal timing advance as soon as the engine is running. This module can be identified by the presence of a white connector shell on the four-pin connector at the module.

Some 1981 and later DuraSpark II systems used with some 8-255 and 8-302 cu. in. engines are quipped with a Universal Ignition Module (UIM) which includes a run-retard function. The operation of the module is basically the same as the DuraSpark Dual Mode module.

The Universal Distributor (EEC-IV) has a diecast base which incorporates an externally mounted TFI-IV ignition module, and contains a Hall Effect vane switch stator assembly and provision for fixed octane adjustment. No distributor calibration is required and initial timing adjustment is normally not required. The primary function of the EEC-IV Universal Distributor system is to direct high secondary voltage to the spark plugs. In addition, the distributor supplies crankshaft position and frequency information to a computer using a profile Ignition Pickup. The Hall Effect switch in the distributor consists of a Hall Effect device on one side and a magnet on the other side. A rotary cup which has windows and tabs rotates and passes through the space between the device and the magnet. When a window is between the sides of the switch the magnetic path is not completed and the switch is Off, sending no signal. When a tab passes between the switch the magnetic path is completed and the Hall Effect Device is turned On and a signal is sent. The voltage pulse (signal) is used by is EEC-IV system for sensing crankshaft position and computing the desired spark advance based on engine demand and calibration.

DURASPARK OPERATION

With the ignition switch **ON**, the primary circuit is on and the ignition coil is energized. When the armature spokes approach the magnetic pickup coil assembly, they induce the voltage which tells the amplifier to turn the coil primary current off. A timing circuit in the amplifier module will turn the current on again after the coil field has collapsed. When the current is on, it flows from the battery through the ignition switch, the primary windings of the ignition coil, and through the amplifier module circuits to ground. When the current is off, the magnetic field built up in the ignition coil is allowed to collapse, inducing a high voltage into the secondary windings of the coil. High voltage is produced each time the field is thus built up and collapsed. When DuraSpark is used in conjunction with the EEC, the EEC computer tells the DuraSpark module when to turn the coil primary current off or on. In this case, the armature position is only a reference signal of engine timing, used by the EEC computer in combination with other reference signals to determine optimum ignition spark timing.

The high voltage flows through the coil high tension lead to the distributor cap where the rotor distributes it to one of the spark plug terminals in the distributor cap. This process is repeated for every power stroke of the engine.

Ignition system troubles are caused by a failure in the primary and/or the secondary circuit; incorrect ignition timing; or incorrect distributor advance. Circuit failures may be caused by shorts, corroded or dirty terminals, loose connections, defective wire insulation, cracked distributor cap or rotor, defective pick-up coil assembly or amplifier module, defective distributor points or fouled spark plugs.

If an engine starting or operating trouble is attributed to the ignition system, start the engine and verify the complaint. On engines that will not start, be sure that there is gasoline in the fuel tank and the fuel is reaching the carburetor. Then locate the ignition system problem using the following procedures.

TROUBLESHOOTING DURASPARK I

The following DuraSpark II troubleshooting procedures may be used on DuraSpark I systems with a few variations. The DuraSpark I module has internal connections which shut off the primary circuit in the run mode when the engine stalls. To perform the above troubleshooting procedures, it is necessary to by-pass these connections. However, with these connections by-passed, the current flow in the primary becomes so great that it will damage both the ignition coil and module unless a ballast resistor is installed in series with the primary circuit at the BAT terminal of the ignition coil. Such a resistor is available from Ford (Motorcraft part number DY-36). A 1.3Ω, 100 watt wire-wound power resistor can also be used.
To install the resistor, proceed as follows.

WARNING: The resistor will become very hot during testing.

1. Release the BAT terminal lead from the coil by inserting a paper cup through the hole in the rear of the horseshoe coil connector and manipulating it against the locking tab in the connector until the lead comes free.
2. Insert a paper clip in the BAT terminal of the connector of the coil. Using jumper leads, connect the ballast resistor as shown.
3. Using a straight pin, pierce both the red and white leads of the module to short these two together. This will by-pass the internal connections of the module which turn off the ignition circuit when the engine is not running.

CAUTION

Pierce the wires only AFTER the ballast resistor is in place or you could damage the ignition coil and module.

4. With the ballast resistor and by-pass in place, proceed with the DuraSpark II troubleshooting procedures.

TROUBLESHOOTING DURASPARK II

The following procedures can be used to determine whether the ignition system is working or not. If these procedures fail to correct the problem, a full troubleshooting procedure should be performed.

Preliminary Checks

1. Check the battery's state of charge and connections.
2. Inspect all wires and connections for breaks, cuts, abrasions, or burn spots. Repair as necessary.
3. Unplug all connectors one at a time and inspect for corroded or burned contacts. Repair and plug connectors back together. DO NOT remove the dielectric compound in the connectors.
4. Check for loose or damaged spark plug or coil wires. A wire resistance check is given at the end of this section. If the boots or nipples are removed on 8mm ignition wires, reline the inside of each with new silicone dielectric compound (Motorcraft WA-10).

Special Tools

To perform the following tests, two special tools are needed; the ignition test jumper shown in the illustration and a modified spark plug. Use the illustration to assembly the ignition test jumper. The test jumper must be used when performing the following tests. The modified spark plug is basically a spark plug with the side electrode removed. Ford makes a special tool called a Spark Tester for this purpose, which besides not having a side electrode is equipped with a spring clip so that it can be grounded to engine metal. It is recommended that the Spark Tester be used as there is less change of being shocked.

Run Mode Spark Test

NOTE: The wire colors given here are the main colors of the wires, not the dots or hashmarks.

STEP 1

1. Remove the distributor cap and rotor from the distributor.
2. With the ignition off, turn the engine over by hand until one of the teeth on the distributor armature aligns with the magnet in the pickup coil.
3. Remove the coil wire from the distributor cap. Install the modified spark plug (see Special Tools, above) in the coil wire terminal and using heavy gloves and insulated pliers, hold the spark plug shell against the engine block.
4. Turn the ignition to RUN (not START) and tap the distributor body with a screwdriver handle. There should be a spark at the modified spark plug or at the coil wire terminal.
5. If a good spark is evident, the primary circuit is OK: perform the Start Mode Spark Test. If there is no spark, proceed to STEP 2.

STEP 2

1. Unplug the module connector(s) which contain(s) the green and black module leads.
2. In the harness side of the connector(s), connect the special test jumper (see Special Tools, above) between the leads which connect to the green and black leads of the module pig tails. Use paper clips on connector socket holes to make contact. Do not allow clips to ground.
3. Turn the ignition switch to RUN (not START) and close the test jumper switch. Leave closed for about 1 second, then open. Repeat several times. There should be a spark each time the switch is opened. On DuraSpark I systems, close the test switch for 10 seconds is adequate.
4. If there is no spark, the problem is probably in the primary circuit through the ignition switch, the coil, the green lead or the black lead, or the ground connection in the distributor; Perform STEP 3. If there is a spark, the primary circuit wiring and coil are probably OK. The problem is probably in the distributor pick-up, the module red wire, or the module: perform STEP 6.

STEP 3

1. Disconnect the test jumper lead from the black lead and connect it to a good ground. Turn the test jumper switch on and off several times as in STEP 2.
2. If there is no spark, the problem is probably in the green lead, the coil, or the coil feed circuit: perform STEP 5.
3. If there is spark, the problem is probably in the black lead or the distributor ground connection: perform STEP 4.

STEP 4

1. Connect an ohmmeter between the black lead and ground. With the meter on its lowest scale, there should be no measurable resistance in the circuit. If there is resistance, check the distributor ground connection and the black lead from the module. Repair as necessary, remove the ohmmeter, plug in all connections and repeat STEP 1.
2. If there is no resistance, the primary ground wiring is OK: perform STEP 6.

STEP 5

1. Disconnect the test jumper from the green lead and ground and connect it between the TACH-TEST terminal of the coil and a good ground to the engine.
2. With the ignition switch in the RUN position, turn the jumper switch on. Hold it on for about 1 second then turn it off as in Step 2. Repeat several times. There should be a spark each time the switch in turned off. If there is no spark, the problem is probably in the primary circuit running through the ignition switch to the coil BAT terminal, or in the coil itself. Check coil resistance (test given later in this section), and check the coil for internal shorts or opens. Check the coil feed circuit for opens, shorts, or high resistance. Repair as necessary, reconnect all connectors and repeat STEP 1. If there is spark, the coil and its feed circuit are OK. The problem could be in the green lead between the coil and the module. Check for an open or short, repair as necessary, reconnect all connectors and repeat STEP 1.

STEP 6

To perform this step, a voltmeter which is not combined with a dwell meter is needed. The slight needle oscillations (½v) you'll be looking for may not be detectable on the combined voltmeter/dwell meter unit.

1. Connect a voltmeter between the orange and purple leads on the harness side of the module connectors.

CAUTION

On catalytic converter equipped cars, disconnect the air supply line between the Thermactor by-pass valve and the manifold before cranking the engine with the ignition off. This will prevent damage to the catalytic converter. After testing, run the engine for at least 3 minutes before reconnecting the by-pass valve, to clear excess fuel from the exhaust system.

2. Set the voltmeter on its lowest scale and crank the engine. The meter needle should oscillate slightly (about ½v). If the meter does not oscillate, check the circuit through the magnetic pick-up in the distributor for open, shorts, shorts to ground and resistance. Resistance between the orange and purple leads should be 400-1,000Ω, and between each lead and ground should be more than 70,000Ω. Repair as necessary, reconnect all connectors and repeat STEP 1.

If the meter oscillates, the problem is probably in the power feed to the module (red wire) or in the module itself: proceed to STEP 7.

STEP 7

1. Remove all meters and jumpers and plug in all connectors.
2. Turn the ignition switch to the RUN position and measure voltage between the battery positive terminal and engine ground. It should be 12 volts.
3. Next, measure voltage between the red lead of the module and engine ground. To mark this measurement, it will be necessary to pierce the red wire with a straight pin and connect the voltmeter to the straight pin and to ground. DO NOT ALLOW THE STRAIGHT PIN TO GROUND ITSELF!
4. The two readings should be within one volt of each other. If not within one volt, the problem is in the power feed to the red lead. Check for shorts, open, or high resistance and correct as necessary. After repairs, repeat Step 1.

If the readings are within one volt, the problem is probably in the module. Replace it with a good module and repeat STEP 1. If this corrects the problem, reconnect the old module and repeat STEP 1. If the problem returns, permanently install the new module.

Start Mode Spark Test

NOTE: The wire colors given here are the main colors of the wires, not the dots or hashmarks.

1. Remove the coil wire from the distributor cap. Install the modified spark plug mentioned under Special Tools, above, in the coil wire and ground it to engine metal either by its spring clip (Spark Tester) or by holding the spark plug shell against the engine block with insulated pliers.

NOTE: See CAUTION under STEP 6 of Run Mode Spark Test, above.

2. Have an assistant crank the engine using the ignition switch and check for spark. If there is good spark, the problem is probably in distributor cap, rotor, ignition cables or spark plugs. If there is no spark, proceed to Step 3.
3. Measure the battery voltage. Next, measure the voltage at the white wire of the module while cranking the engine. To mark this measurement, it will be necessary to pierce the white wire with a straight pin and connect the voltmeter to the straight pin and to ground. DO NOT ALLOW THE STRAIGHT PIN TO GROUND ITSELF. The battery voltage and the voltage at the white wire should be within 1 volt of each other. If the readings are not within 1 volt of each other, check and repair the feed through the ignition switch to the white wire. Recheck for spark (Step 1). If the readings are within 1 volt of each other, or if there is still no spark after the power feed to white wire is repaired, proceed to Step 4.
4. Measure the coil BAT terminal voltage while cranking the engine. The reading should be within 1 volt of battery voltage. If the readings are not within 1 volt of each other, check and repair the feed through the ignition switch to the coil. If the readings are within 1 volt of each other, the problem is probably in the ignition module. Substitute another module and repeat the test for spark (Step 1).

TFI SYSTEM TESTING

NOTE: If the engine operates but has no power, the problem could be in the EEC system. Check the initial timing, if the engine is operating at a fixed 10° BTDC the system is in fail-safe mode. Have the EEC system check with necessary diagnostic equipment.

After performing any test which requires piercing a wire with a straight pin, remove the straight pin and seal the holes in the wire with silicone sealer.

Ignition Coil Secondary Voltage

1. Disconnect the secondary (high voltage) coil wire from the distributor cap and install a spark tester (see Special Tools, located with the DuraSpark Troubleshooting) between the coil wire and ground.
2. Crank the engine. A good, strong spark should be noted at the spark tester. If spark is noted, but the engine will not start, check the spark plugs, spark plug wiring, and fuel system. If there is no spark at the tester:
   a. Check the ignition coil secondary wire resistance; it should be no more than 5,000Ω per inch.
   b. Inspect the ignition coil for damage and/or carbon tracking.
   c. With the distributor cap removed, verify that the distributor shaft turns with the engine; if it does not, repair the engine as required.
   d. If the fault was not found in a, b, or c, proceed to the next test.

Ignition Coil Primary Circuit Switching

1. Insert a small straight pin in the wire which runs from the coil negative (–) terminal to the TFI module, about 1″ (25.4mm) from the module.

CAUTION

The pin must not touch ground.

2. Connect a 12VDC test lamp between the straight pin and an engine ground.
3. Crank the engine, noting the operation of the test lamp. If the test lamp flashes, proceed to the next test. If the test lamp lights but does not flash, proceed to the Wiring Harness test. If the test lamp does not light at all, proceed to the Primary Circuit Continuity test.

Ignition Coil Resistance

Replace the ignition coil if the resistance is out of the specification range.

Wiring Harness

1. Disconnect the wiring harness connector from the TFI module; the connector tabs must be PUSHED to disengage the connector. Inspect the connector form damage, dirt, and corrosion.
2. Attach the negative lead of a voltmeter to the base of the distributor. Attach the other voltmeter lead to a small straight pin.
   a. With the ignition switch in the RUN position, insert the straight pin onto the NO.1 terminal of the TFI module connector. Note the voltage reading and proceed to b.
   b. With the ignition switch in the RUN position, move the straight pin to the No. 2 connector terminal. Again, note the voltage reading, then proceed to c.
   c. Move the straight pin to the No. 3 connector terminal, then turn the ignition switch to the START position. Note the voltage reading then turn the Ignition OFF.
3. The voltage readings from a, b, and c should all be at least 90% of the available battery voltage. If the readings are okay, proceed to the Stator Assembly and Module test. If any reading is less than 90% of the battery voltage, inspect the wiring, connectors, and/or ignition switch for defects. If the voltage is low only at the No. 1 terminal, proceed to the ignition coil primary voltage test.

Stator Assembly and Module

1. Remove the distributor from the engine.
2. Remove the TFI module from the distributor.
3. Inspect the distributor terminals, ground screw, and stator wiring for damage. Repair as necessary.
4. Measure the resistance of the stator assembly, using an ohmmeter. If the ohmmeter reading is 800-975Ω, the stator is okay, but the TFI module must be replaced. If the ohmmeter reading is less than 800Ω or more than 975Ω; the TFI module is okay, but the stator assembly must be replaced.

5. Reinstall the TFI module and the distributor.

Primary Circuit Continuity

This test is performed in the same manner as the previous Wiring Harness test, but only the NO. 1 terminal conductor is tested (ignition switch in RUN position). If the voltage is less than 90% of the available battery voltage, proceed to the next test.

Ignition Coil Primary Voltage

1. Attach the negative lead of a voltmeter to the distributor base.
2. Turn the ignition switch ON and connect the positive voltmeter lead to the negative (-) ignition coil terminal. Note the voltage reading and turn the ignition OFF. If the voltmeter reading is less than 90% of the available battery voltage, inspect the wiring between the ignition module and the negative (-) coil terminal, then proceed to the last test, which follows.

Ignition Coil Supply Voltage

1. Attach the negative lead of a voltmeter to the distributor base.
2. Turn the ignition switch ON and connect the positive voltmeter lead to the positive (+) ignition coil terminal.

NOTE: Note the voltage reading then turn the ignition OFF.

If the voltage reading is at least 90% of the battery voltage, yet the engine will still not run: check the ignition coil connector and terminals for corrosion, dirt, and/or damage. Replace the ignition switch if the connectors and terminals are okay.
3. Connect any remaining wiring.

GENERAL TESTING – ALL SYSTEMS

Ignition Coil Test

The ignition coil must be diagnosed separately from the rest of the ignition system.

1. Primary resistance is measured between the two primary (low voltage) coil terminals, with the coil connector disconnected and the ignition switch off. Primary resistance must be 0.71-0.77Ω for DuraSpark I. For DuraSpark II, it must be 1.13-1.23Ω. For TFI systems, the primary resistance should be 0.3-1.0Ω.
2. On DuraSpark ignitions, the secondary resistance is measured between the BATT and high voltage (secondary) terminals of the ignition coil with the ignition off, and wiring from the coil disconnected. Secondary resistance must be 7,350-8,250Ω on DuraSpark I systems. DuraSpark II figure is 7,700-9,300Ω. For TFI systems, the primary resistance should be 8,000-11,500Ω.
3. If resistance tests are all right, but the coil is still suspected, test the coil on a coil tester by following the test equipment manufacturer's instructions for a standard coil. If the reading differs from the original test, check for a defective harness.

Resistance Wire Test

Replace the resistance wire if it doesn't show a resistance of 1.05-1.15Ω for DuraSpark II. The resistance wire isn't used on DuraSpark I or TFI systems.

Spark Plug Wire Resistance

Resistance on these wires must not exceed 5,000Ω per inch. To properly measure this, remove the wires from the plugs, and remove the distributor cap. Measure the resistance through the distributor cap at that end. Do not pierce any ignition wire for any reason. Measure only from the two ends.

NOTE: Silicone grease must be re-applied to the spark plug wires whenever they are removed.

When removing the wires from the spark plugs, a special tool such as the one pictured should be used. Do not pull on the wires. Grasp and twist the boot to remove the wire.

Whenever the high tension wires are removed from the plugs, coil, or distributor, silicone grease must be applied to the boot before reconnection. Use a clean small screwdriver blade to coat the entire interior surface with Ford silicone grease D7AZ-19A331-A, Dow Corning #111, or General Electric G-627.

Adjustments.

The air gap between the armature and magnetic pick-up coil in the distributor is not adjustable, nor are there any adjustments for the amplifier module. Inoperative components are simply replaced. Any attempt to connect components outside the vehicle may result in component failure.

ENGINE ELECTRICAL

Ignition Coil

REMOVAL & INSTALLATION

1. Disconnect the battery ground.
2. Disconnect the two small and one large wire from the coil.
3. Disconnect the condenser connector from the coil, if equipped.
4. Unbolt and remove the coil.
5. Installation is the reverse of removal.

Ignition Module

REMOVAL & INSTALLATION

Removing the module, on all models, is a matter of simply removing the fasteners that attach it to the fender or firewall and pulling apart the connectors. When unplugging the connectors, pull them apart with a firm, straight pull. NEVER PRY THEM APART! To pry them will cause damage. When reconnecting them, coat the mating ends with silicone dielectric grease to waterproof the connection. Press the connectors together firmly to overcome any vacuum lock caused by the grease.

NOTE: If the locking tabs weaken or break, don't replace the unit. Just secure the connection with electrical tape or tie straps.

Distributor

REMOVAL & INSTALLATION

1. Remove the air cleaner on V6 and V8 engines. On 4- and 6-cylinder inline engines, removal of a Thermactor® (air) pump mounting bolt and drive belt will allow the pump to be moved to the side and permit access to the distributor. If necessary, disconnect the Thermactor® air filter and lines as well.
2. Remove the distributor cap and position the cap and ignition wires to the side.
3. Disconnect the wire harness plug 000035he distributor connector. Dis-

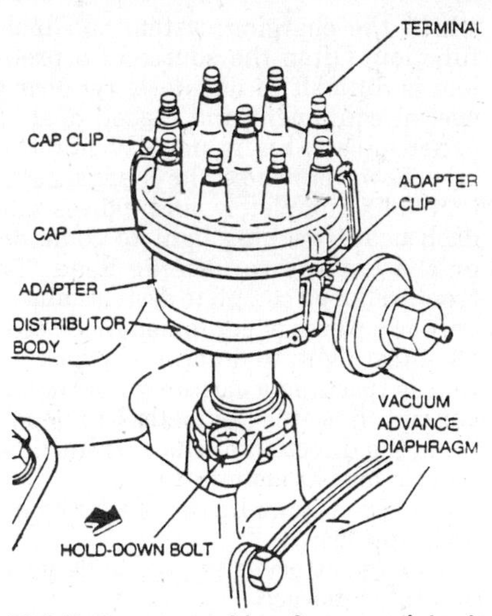

Distributor assembly. Arrow points to front

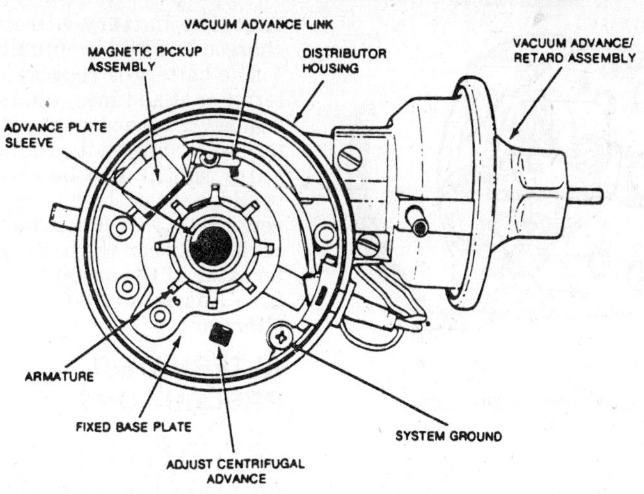

V8 breakerless (electronic) distributor, cap and rotor removed

connect and plug the vacuum hoses from the vacuum diaphragm assembly. (DuraSpark®III systems are not equipped with a vacuum diaphragm).

4. Rotate the engine (in normal direction of rotation) until No. 1 piston is on TDC (Top Dead Center) of the compression stroke. The TDC mark on the crankshaft pulley and the pointer should align. Rotor tip pointing at No. 1 position on distributor cap.

5. On DuraSpark®I or II, turn the engine a slight bit more (if required) to align the stator (pick-up coil) assembly pole with an (closest) armature pole. On DuraSpark®III, the distributor sleeve groove (when looking down from the top) and the cap adaptor alignment slot should align. On models equipped with EEC-IV (1984 and later), remove the rotor (2 screws) and note the position of the polarizing square and shaft plate for reinstallation reference.

6. Scribe a mark on the distributor body and engine black to indicate the position of the rotor tip and position of the distributor in the engine. DuraSpark®III and some EEC-IV system distributors are equipped with a notched base and will only locate at one position on the engine.

7. Remove the holddown bolt and clamp located at the base of the distributor. (Some DuraSpark®III and EEC-IV system distributors are equipped with a special holddown bolt that requires a Torx® Head Wrench for removal). Remove the distributor from the engine. Pay attention to the direction the rotor tip points when the drive gear disengages. For reinstallation purposes, the rotor should be at this position to insure proper gear mesh and timing.

8. Avoid turning the engine, if possible, while the distributor is removed.

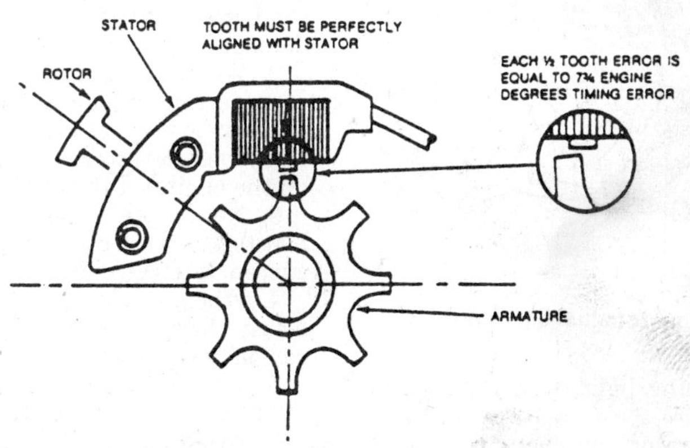

V8 breakerless distributor, static timing position. V6 similar

If the engine is turned from TDC position, TDC timing marks will have to be reset before the distributor is installed; Steps 4 and 5.

9. Position the distributor in the engine with the rotor aligned to the marks made on the distributor, or to the place the rotor pointed when the distributor was removed. The stator and armature or polarizing square and shaft plate should also be aligned. Engage the oil pump intermediate shaft and insert the distributor until fully seated on the engine, if the distributor does not fully seat, turn the engine slightly to fully engage the intermediate shaft.

10. Follow the above procedures on models equipped with an indexed distributor base. Make sure when positioning the distributor that the slot in the distributor base will engage the block tab and the sleeve/adaptor slots are aligned.

11. After the distributor has been fully seated on the block install the holddown bracket and bolt. On models equipped with an indexed base, tighten the mounting bolt. On other models, snug the mounting bolt so the distributor can be turned for ignition timing purposes.

12. The rest of the installation is in the reverse order of removal. Check and reset the ignition timing on applicable models.

NOTE: A silicone compound is used on rotor tips, distributor cap contacts and on the inside of the connectors on the spark plugs cable and module couplers. Always apply silicone dielectric compound after servicing any component of the ignition system. Various models use a multi-point rotor which do not require the application of dielectric compound.

Alternator

The alternator charging system consists of the alternator, voltage regula-

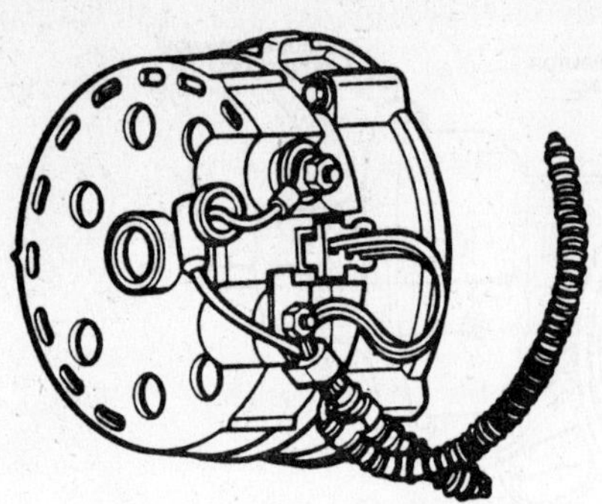

Side terminal alternator

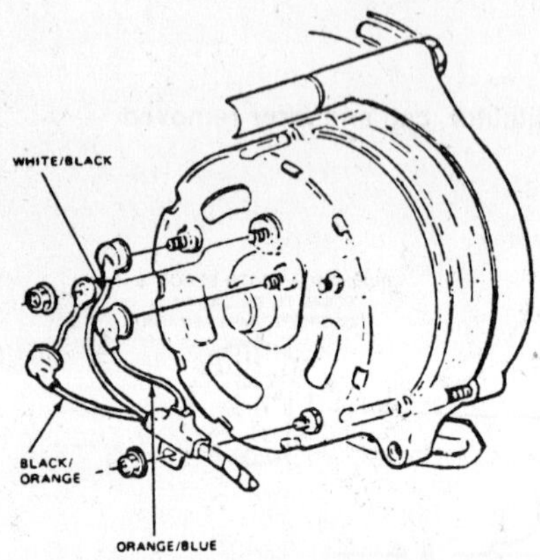

Rear terminal alternator

tor, warning light, battery, and fuse link wire.

A failure of any component of the charging system can cause the entire system to stop functioning. Because of this, the charging system can be very difficult to troubleshoot when problems occur.

When the ignition key is turned on, current flows from the battery, through the charging system indicator light on the instrument panel, to the voltage regulator, and to the alternator. Since the alternator is not producing any current, the alternator warning light comes on. When the engine is started, the alternator begins to produce current and turns the alternator light off. As the alternator turns and produces current, the current is divided in two ways: part to the battery to charge the battery and power the electrical components of the vehicle, and part is returned to the alternator to enable it to increase its output. In this situation, the alternator is receiving current from the battery and from itself. A voltage regulator is wired into the current supply to the alternator to prevent it from receiving too much current which would cause it to put out too much current. Conversely, if the voltage regulator does not allow the alternator to receive enough current, the battery will not be fully charged and will eventually go dead.

The battery is connected to the alternator at all times, whether the ignition key is turned on or not. If the battery were shorted to ground, the alternator would also be shorted. This would damage the alternator. To prevent this, a fuse link is installed in the wiring between the battery and the alternator. If the battery is shorted, the fuse link is melted, protecting the alternator.

ALTERNATOR PRECAUTIONS

Several precautions must be observed with alternator equipped vehicles to avoid damaging the unit. They are as follows:

1. If the battery is removed for any reason, make sure that it is reconnected with the correct polarity. Reversing the battery connections may result in damage to the one-way rectifiers.
2. When utilizing a booster battery as a starting aid, always connect it as follows: positive to positive, and negative (booster battery) to a good ground on the engine of the car being started.
3. Never use a fast charger as a booster to start cars with alternating current (AC) circuits.
4. When servicing the battery with a fast charger, always disconnect the car battery cables.
5. Never attempt to polarize an alternator.
6. Avoid long soldering times when replacing diodes or transistors. Prolonged heat is damaging to alternators.
7. Do not use test lamps of more than 12 volts (V) for checking diode continuity.
8. Do not short across or ground any of the terminals on the alternator.
9. The polarity of the battery, alternator, and regulator must be matched and considered before making any electrical connections within the system.
10. Never separate the alternator on an open circuit. Make sure that all connections within the circuit are clean and tight.
11. Disconnect the battery terminals when performing any service on the electrical system. This will eliminate the possibility of accidental reversal of polarity.
12. Disconnect the battery ground cable if arc welding is to be done on any part of the car.

CHARGING SYSTEM TROUBLESHOOTING

There are many possible ways in which the charging system can malfunction. Often the source of a problem is difficult to diagnose, requiring special equipment and a good deal of experience. This is usually not the case, however, where the charging system fails completely and causes the dash board warning light to come on or the battery to become dead. To troubleshoot a complete system failure only two pieces of equipment are needed: a test light, to determine that current is reaching a certain point; and a current indicator (ammeter), to determine the direction of the current flow and its measurement in amps.

This test works under three assumptions:

1. The battery is known to be good and fully charged.
2. The alternator belt is in good condition and adjusted to the proper tension.
3. All connections in the system are clean and tight.

NOTE: In order for the current indicator to give a valid reading, the car must be equipped with battery cables which are of the same gauge size and quality as original equipment battery cables.

1. Turn off all electrical components on the car. Make sure the doors of the car are closed. If the car is equipped with a clock, disconnect the clock by removing the lead wire from the rear of the clock. Disconnect the positive battery cable from the battery and connect the ground wire on a test light to the disconnected positive battery cable. Touch the probe end of the test light to the positive battery post. The test light should not light. If the test light does light, there is a short or open circuit on the car.
2. Disconnect the voltage regulator wiring harness connector at the voltage regulator. Turn on the ignition key. Connect the wire on a test light to a good ground (engine bolt). Touch the probe end of a test light to the ignition wire connector into the voltage regulator wiring connector. This wire corresponds to the **I** terminal on the regulator. If the test light goes on, the charging system warning light circuit is complete. If the test light does not come on and the warning light on the instrument panel is on, either the resistor wire, which is parallel with the warning light, or the wiring to the voltage regulator, is defective. If the test light does not come on and the warning light is not on, either the bulb is defective or the power supply wire form the battery through the ignition switch to the bulb has an open circuit.

Connect the wiring harness to the regulator.

3. Examine the fuse link wire in the wiring harness from the starter relay to the alternator. If the insulation on the wire is cracked or split, the fuse link may be melted. Connect a test light to the fuse link by attaching the ground wire on the test light to an engine bolt and touching the probe end of the light to the bottom of the fuse link wire where it splices into the alternator output wire. If the bulb in the test light does not light, the fuse link is melted.

4. Start the engine and place a current indicator on the positive battery cable. Turn off all electrical accessories and make sure the doors are closed. If the charging system is working properly, the gauge will show a draw of less than 5 amps. If the system is not working properly, the gauge will show a draw of more than 5 amps. A charge moves the needle toward the battery, a draw moves the needle away from the battery. Turn the engine off.

5. Disconnect the wiring harness from the voltage regulator at the regulator at the regulator connector. Connect a male spade terminal (solderless connector) to each end of a jumper wire. Insert one end of the wire into the wiring harness connector which corresponds to the **A** terminal on the regulator. Insert the other end of the wire into the wiring harness connector which corresponds to the **F** terminal on the regulator. Position the connector with the jumper wire installed so that it cannot contact any metal surface under the hood. Position a current indicator gauge on the positive battery cable. Have an assistant start the engine. Observe the reading on the current indicator. Have your assistant slowly raise the speed of the engine to about 2,000 rpm or until the current indicator needle stops moving, whichever comes first. Do not run the engine for more than a short period of time in this condition. If the wiring harness connector or jumper wire becomes excessively hot during this test, turn off the engine and check for a grounded wire in the regulator wiring harness. If the current indicator shows a charge of about three amps less than the output of the alternator, the alternator is working properly. If the previous tests showed a draw, the voltage regulator is defective. If the gauge does not show the proper charging rate, the alternator is defective.

REMOVAL & INSTALLATION

1. Disconnect the negative battery cable from the battery.

2. Disconnect the wires from the alternator.

3. Loosen the alternator mounting bolts and remove the drive belt.

NOTE: Some 1981 and later cars are equipped with a ribbed, K-section belt and automatic tensioner. A special tool must be made to remove the tension from the tensioner arm. Loosen the idler pulley pivot and adjuster bolts before using the tool. See the accompanying illustration for tool details.

4. Remove the alternator mounting bolts and spacer (if equipped), and remove the alternator.

5. To install, position the alternator on its brackets and install the attaching bolts and spacer (if so equipped).

6. Connect the wires to the alternator.

7. Position the drive belt on the alternator pulley. Adjust the belt tension as outlined under ROUTINE MAINTENANCE.

8. Connect the negative battery cable.

Starter

There are two different types of starters are used on these cars. All gasoline engines use a positive engagement starter. A solenoid actuated starter is used on the diesel. Since a greater amount of starting power is required by the diesel, the solenoid actuated starter is constructed with more coil and armature windings to deliver the necessary current. The presence of a solenoid mechanism is incidental and does not affect starting power.

The positive engagement starter system employs a starter relay, usually mounted inside the engine compartment on a fender wall, to transfer battery current to the starter. The relay is activated by the ignition switch and, when engaged, it creates a direct current from the battery to the starter windings. Simultaneously, the armature begins to turn the starter drive is pushed out to engage the flywheel.

In the solenoid actuated starter system, battery current is first directed to a solenoid assembly which is mounted on the starter case. The current closes the solenoid contacts, which engages the drive pinion and directs current to the coil windings, causing the armature to rotate. While this system does not need a starter relay, some models were nevertheless equipped with one in order to simplify assembly procedures. These vehicles also have a connector link attached to the solenoid, which provides a hook up for the relay wire.

REMOVAL & INSTALLATION

Except Diesel

1. Disconnect the negative battery cable.

2. Raise the front of the car and install jackstands beneath the frame. Firmly apply the parking brake and place blocks in back of the rear wheels.

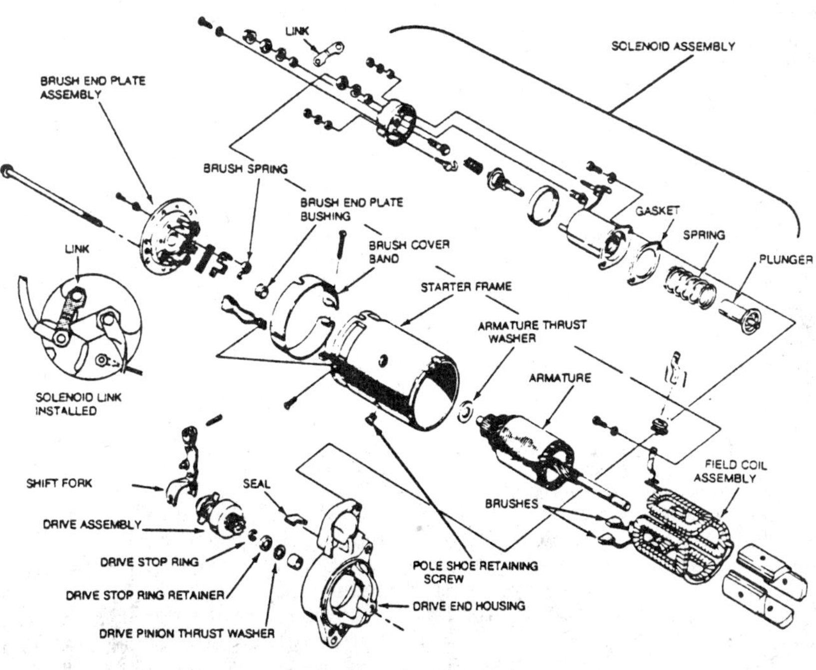

Solenoid actuated type starter

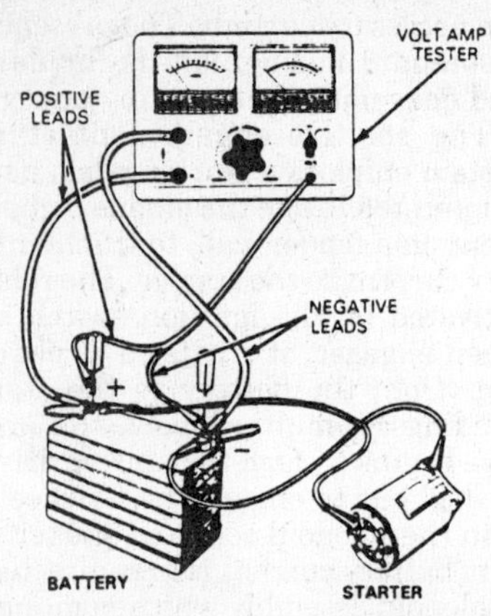

Starter no-load test with starter on test bench

3. Tag and disconnect the wiring at the starter.
4. Turn the front wheels fully to the right. On some later models it will be necessary to remove the frame brace. On many models, it will be necessary to remove the two bolts retaining the steering idler arm to the frame to gain access to the starter.
5. Remove the starter mounting bolts and remove the starter.
6. Reverse the above procedure to install. Torque the mounting bolts to 12-15 ft.lb. on starters with 3 mounting bolts and 15-20 ft.lb. on starters with 2 mounting bolts. Torque the idler arm retaining bolts to 28-35 ft.lb. (if removed). Make sure that the nut securing the heavy cable to the starter is snugged down tightly.

6.9L Diesel

1. Disconnect the battery ground cable.
2. Raise the vehicle and disconnect the cables and wires at the starter solenoid.
3. Turn the front wheels to the right and remove the two bolts attaching the steering idler arm to the frame.
4. Remove the starter mounting bolts and remove the starter.
5. Install in the reverse order of removal

OVERHAUL – EXCEPT DIESEL

Brush Replacement

1. Remove the starter from the engine as previously outlined.
2. Remove the starter drive plunger lever cover and gasket.
3. Loosen and remove the brush cover band and remove the brushes from their holder.
4. Remove the two through-bolts from the starter frame.
5. Separate the drive-end housing, starter frame and brush end plate assemblies.
6. Remove the starter drive plunger lever and pivot pin, and remove the armature.
7. Remove the ground brush retaining screws from the frame and remove the brushes.
8. Cut the insulated brush leads from the field coils, as close to the field connection point as possible.
9. Clean and inspect the starter motor.
10. Replace the brush end plate if the insulator between the field brush holder and the end plate is cracked or broken.
11. Position the new insulated field brushes lead on the field coil connection. Position and crimp the clip provided with the brushes to hold the brush lead to the connection. Solder the lead, clip, and connection together using resin core solder. Use a 300 watt soldering iron.
12. Install the ground brush leads to the frame with the retaining screws.
13. Install the starter drive plunger lever and pivot pin, and install the armature.
14. Assemble the drive-end housing, starter frame and brush end plate assemblies.
15. Install the two through-bolts in the starter frame. Torque the through-bolts to 55-75 in.lb.
16. Install the brushes in their holders and install the brush cover band.
17. Install the starter drive plunger lever cover and gasket.
22. Install the starter on the engine as previously outlined.

Drive Replacement

1. Remove the starter as outlined previously.
2. Remove the starter drive plunger lever and gasket and the brush cover band.
3. Remove the two through-bolts from the starter frame.
4. Separate the drive end housing from the starter frame.
5. The starter drive plunger lever return spring may fall out after detaching the drive end housing. If not, remove it.
6. Remove the pivot pin which attaches the starter drive plunger lever to the starter frame and remove the lever.
7. Remove the stop ring retainer and stop ring from the armature shaft.
8. Slide the starter drive off the armature shaft.
9. Examine the wear pattern on the starter drive teeth. There should be evidence of full contact between the starter drive teeth and the flywheel ring gear teeth. If there is evidence of irregular wear, examine the flywheel ring gear for damage and replace if necessary.
10. Apply a thin coat of white grease to the armature shaft before installing the drive gear. Place a small amount of grease in the drive end housing bearing. Slide the starter drive on the armature shaft.
11. Install the stop ring retainer and stop ring on the armature shaft.
12. Install the starter drive plunger lever on the starter frame and install the pin.
13. Assemble the drive end housing on the starter frame.
14. install the two through-bolts in the starter frame. Tighten the starter through bolts to 55-75 in.lb.
15. Install the starter drive plunger lever and gasket and the brush cover band.
16. Install the starter as outlined previously.

OVERHAUL – DIESEL

1. Disconnect the field coil connection from the solenoid motor terminal.
2. Remove the solenoid attaching screws, solenoid and plunger return spring. Rotate the solenoid 90° to remove it.
3. Remove the through-bolts and brush end plate.
4. Rempove the brush springs and brushes from the plastic brush holder and remove the brush holder. Keep track of the location of the brush holder with regard to the brush terminals.
5. Remove the frame assembly.
6. Remove the armature assembly.
7. Remove the screw from the gear housing and remove the gear housing.
8. Remove the plunger and lever pivot screw and remove the plunger and lever.
9. Remove the gear, output shaft and drive assembly.
10. Remove the thrust washer, retainer, drive stop ring and slide the drive assembly off of the output shaft.

WARNING: Don't wash the drive because the solvent will wash out the lubricant, causing the drive to slip. Use a brush or compressed air to clean the drive, field coils, armature, gear and housing.

11. Inspect the armature windings for broken or burned insulation, and open connections at the commutator. Check for any signs of grounding.
12. Check the commutator for excessive runout. If the commutator is rough or more than 0.127mm out-of-round, replace it or correct the problem as necessary.
13. Check the plastic brush holder

for cracks or broken pads. Replace the brushes if worn to a length less than 1/4" (6mm) in length. Inspect the field coils and plastic bobbins for burned or damaged areas. Check the continuity of the coil and brush connections. A brush replacement kit is available. Any other worn or damaged parts should be replaced.

14. Apply a thin coating of Lubriplate 777®, or equivalent on the output shaft splines. Slide the drive assembly onto the shaft and install a new stopring, retainer and thrust washer. Install the shaft and drive assembly into the drive end housing.

15. Install the plunger and lever assembly making sure that the lever notches engage the flange ears of the starter drive. Attach the lever pin screw and tighten it to 10 ft.lb.

16. Lubricate the gear and washer. Install the gear and washer on the end of the output shaft.

17. Install the gear housing and tighten the mounting screw to 84 in.lb.

18. After lubricating the pinion, install the armature and washer on the end of the shaft.

19. Position the grommet around the field lead and press it into the starter frame notch. Install the frame assembly on the gear housing, making sure that the grommet is positioned in the notch in the housing.

20. Install the brush holder on the end of the frame, lining up the notches in the brush holder with the ground brush terminals. The brush holder is symmetrical and can be installed with either notch and brush terminal.

21. Install the brush springs and brushes. The positive brush leads must be placed in their respective slots to prevent grounding.

22. Install the brush endplate, making sure that the insulator is properly positioned. Install and tighten the through-bolts to 84 in.lb.

NOTE: The brush endplate has a threaded hole in the protruding ear which must be oriented properly so the starter-to-vacuum pump support bracket can be installed.

23. Install the return spring on the solenoid plunger and install the solenoid. Attach the 2 solenoid attaching screws and tighten them to 84 in.lb. Apply a sealing compound to the junction of the solenoid case flange, gear and drive end housings.

24. Attach the motor field terminal to the **M** terminal of the solenoid, and tighten the fasteners to 30 in.lb.

25. Check the starter no-load current draw. Maximum draw should be 190 amps.

Battery

REMOVAL & INSTALLATION

1. Remove the holddown screws from the battery box. Loosen the nuts that secure the cable ends to the battery terminals. Lift the battery cables from the terminals with a twisting motion.
2. If there is a battery cable puller available, make use of it. Lift the battery from the vehicle.
3. Before installing the battery in the vehicle, make sure that the battery terminals are clean and free from corrosion. Use a battery terminal cleaner on the terminals and on the inside of the battery cable ends. If a cleaner is not available, use a heavy sandpaper to remove the corrosion. A mixture of baking soda and water will neutralize any acid. Place the battery in the vehicle. Install the cables on the terminals. Tighten the nuts on the cable ends. Smear a light coating of grease on the cable ends and the tops of the terminals. This will prevent buildup of oxidized acid on the terminals and the cable ends. Install and tighten the nuts of the battery box.

ENGINE MECHANICAL

Engine Overhaul Tips

Most engine overhaul procedures are fairly standard. In addition to specific parts replacement procedures and complete specifications for your individual engine, this section also is a guide to accept rebuilding procedures. Examples of standard rebuilding practice are shown and should be used along with specific details concerning your particular engine.

Competent and accurate machine shop services will ensure maximum performance, reliability and engine life.

In most instances it is more profitable for the do-it-yourself mechanic to remove, clean and inspect the component, buy the necessary parts and deliver these to a shop for actual machine work.

On the other hand, much of the rebuilding work (crankshaft, block, bearings, piston rods, and other components) is well within the scope of the do-it-yourself mechanic.

TOOLS

The tools required for an engine overhaul or parts replacement will depend on the depth of your involvement. With a few exceptions, they will be the tools found in a mechanic's tool kit. More in-depth work will require any or all of the following:

- a dial indicator (reading in thousandths) mounted on a universal base
- micrometers and telescope gauges
- jaw and screw-type pullers
- scraper
- valve spring compressor
- ring groove cleaner
- piston ring expander and compressor
- ridge reamer
- cylinder hone or glaze breaker
- Plastigage®
- engine stand

The use of most of these tools is illustrated in this section. Many can be rented for a one-time use from a local parts jobber or tool supply house specializing in automotive work.

Occasionally, the use of special tools is called for. See the information on Special Tools and Safety Notice in the front of this book before substituting another tool.

INSPECTION TECHNIQUES

Procedures and specifications are given in this section for inspecting, cleaning and assessing the wear limits of most major components. Other procedures such as Magnaflux® and Zyglo® can be used to locate material flaws and stress cracks. Magnaflux® is a magnetic process applicable only to ferrous materials. The Zyglo® process coats the material with a fluorescent dye penetrant and can be used on any material Check for suspected surface cracks can be more readily made using spot check dye. The dye is sprayed onto the suspected area, wiped off and the area sprayed with a developer. Cracks will show up brightly.

OVERHAUL TIPS

Aluminum has become extremely popular for use in engines, due to its low weight. Observe the following precautions when handling aluminum parts:

- Never hot tank aluminum parts (the caustic hot tank solution will eat the aluminum.
- Remove all aluminum parts (identification tag, etc.) from engine parts prior to the tanking.
- Always coat threads lightly with engine oil or anti-seize compounds before installation, to prevent seizure.

• Never overtorque bolts or spark plugs especially in aluminum threads.

Stripped threads in any component can be repaired using any of several commercial repair kits (Heli-Coil®, Microdot®, Keenserts®, etc.).

When assembling the engine, any parts that will be frictional contact must be prelubed to provide lubrication at initial start-up. Any product specifically formulated for this purpose can be used, but engine oil is not recommended as a prelube.

When semi-permanent (locked, but removable) installation of bolts or nuts is desired, threads should be cleaned and coated with Loctite® or other similar, commercial non-hardening sealant.

REPAIRING DAMAGED THREADS

Several methods of repairing damaged threads are available. Heli-Coil® (shown here), Keenserts® and Microdot® are among the most widely used. All involve basically the same principle – drilling out stripped threads, tapping the hole and installing a prewound insert – making welding, plugging and oversize fasteners unnecessary.

Two types of thread repair inserts are usually supplied: a standard type for most Inch Coarse, Inch Fine, Metric Course and Metric Fine thread sizes and a spark lug type to fit most spark plug port sizes. Consult the individual manufacturer's catalog to determine exact applications. Typical thread repair kits will contain a selection of prewound threaded inserts, a tap (corresponding to the outside diameter threads of the insert) and an installation tool. Spark plug inserts usually differ because they require a tap equipped with pilot threads and a combined reamer/tap section. Most manufacturers also supply blister-packed thread repair inserts separately in addition to a master kit containing a variety of taps and inserts plus installation tools.

Before effecting a repair to a threaded hole, remove any snapped, broken or damaged bolts or studs. Penetrating oil can be used to free frozen threads. The offending item can be removed with locking pliers or with a screw or stud extractor. After the hole is clear, the thread can be repaired, as shown in the series of accompanying illustrations.

Checking Engine Compression

A noticeable lack of engine power, excessive oil consumption and/or poor fuel mileage measured over an extended period are all indicators of internal engine war. Worn piston rings, scored or worn cylinder bores, blown head gaskets, sticking or burnt valves and worn valve seats are all possible culprits here. A check of each cylinder's compression will help you locate the problems.

As mentioned earlier, a screw-in type compression gauge is more accurate that the type you simply hold against the spark plug hole, although it takes slightly longer to use. It's worth it to obtain a more accurate reading. Follow the procedures below.

Gasoline Engines

1. Warm up the engine to normal operating temperature.
2. Remove all the spark plugs.
3. Disconnect the high tension lead from the ignition coil.
4. On fully open the throttle either by operating the carburetor throttle linkage by hand or by having an assistant floor the accelerator pedal.
5. Screw the compression gauge into the no.1 spark plug hole until the fitting is snug.

WARNING: Be careful not to crossthread the plug hole. On aluminum cylinder heads use extra care, as the threads in these heads are easily ruined.

6. Ask an assistant to depress the accelerator pedal fully on both carbureted and fuel injected vehicles. Then, while you read the compression gauge, ask the assistant to crank the engine two or three times in short bursts using the ignition switch.
7. Read the compression gauge at the end of each series of cranks, and record the highest of these readings. Repeat this procedure for each of the engine's cylinders. Compare the highest reading of each cylinder to the compression pressure specification in the Tune-Up Specifications chart. The specs in this chart are maximum values.

A cylinder's compression pressure is usually acceptable if it is not less than 80% of maximum. The difference between any two cylinders should be no more than 12–14 pounds.

8. If a cylinder is unusually low, pour a tablespoon of clean engine oil into the cylinder through the spark plug hole and repeat the compression test. If the compression comes up after adding the oil, it appears that the cylinder's piston rings or bore are damaged or worn. If the pressure remains low, the valves may not be seating properly (a valve job is needed), or the head gasket may be blown near that cylinder. If compression in any two adjacent cylinders is low, and if the addition of oil doesn't help the compression, there is leakage past the head gasket. Oil and coolant water in the combustion chamber can result from this problem. There may be evidence of water droplets on the engine dipstick when a head gasket has blown.

Diesel Engines

Checking cylinder compression on diesel engines is basically the same procedure as on gasoline engines except for the following:

1. A special compression gauge adaptor suitable for diesel engines (because these engines have much greater compression pressures) must be used.
2. Remove the injector tubes and remove the injectors from each cylinder.

WARNING: Don't forget to remove the washer underneath each injector. Otherwise, it may get lost when the engine is cranked.

3. When fitting the compression gauge adaptor to the cylinder head, make sure the bleeder of the gauge (if equipped) is closed.
4. When reinstalling the injector assemblies, install new washers underneath each injector.

Engine

REMOVAL & INSTALLATION

WARNING: Disconnect the negative battery cable before beginning any work. Always label all disconnected hoses, vacuum lines and wires, to prevent incorrect reassembly. Do not disconnect any air conditioning lines unless you are thoroughly familiar with A/C systems and the hazards involved; escaping refrigerant (Freon®) will freeze any surface it contacts, including skin and eyes. Have the system discharged professionally before required repairs are started.

Pickups and Bronco 6-300 (4.9L)

1. Drain the cooling system and the crankcase. Remove the hood and the air cleaner. Disconnect the negative battery cable.

CAUTION

When draining the coolant, keep in mind that cats and dogs are attracted by the ethylene glycol antifreeze, and are quite likely to drink any that is left in an uncovered container or in puddles on the ground. This will prove fatal in sufficient quantity. Al-

ways drain the coolant into a sealable container. Coolant should be reused unless it is contaminated or several years old.

2. Disconnect the heater hose from the water pump and coolant outlet housing. Disconnect the flexible fuel line from the fuel pump.
3. Remove the radiator.
4. Remove the fan, water pump pulley, and fan belt.
5. Disconnect the accelerator cable at the carburetor. Remove the throttle return spring. On trucks equipped with power brakes, disconnect the brake booster vacuum hose at the intake manifold. On trucks with automatic transmissions, disconnect the transmission kickdown rod at the bellcrank assembly.
6. Disconnect the exhaust pipe from the exhaust manifold.
7. Disconnect the body ground strap and the battery ground cable from the engine.
8. Disconnect the engine wiring harness at the ignition coil, the coolant temperature sending unit, and the oil pressure sending unit. Position the wiring harness out of the way.
9. Remove the alternator mounting bolts and position the alternator out of the way.
10. On a truck equipped with power steering, remove the power steering pump from the mounting brackets and move it to one side, leaving the lines attached.
11. Raise and safely support the truck. Remove the starter and automatic transmission filler tube bracket, if so equipped. Also, remove the rear engine plate upper right bolt.
12. On manual transmission equipped trucks, remove the flywheel housing lower attaching bolts and disconnect the clutch return spring.
13. On automatic transmission equipped trucks, remove the converter housing access cover assembly and remove the flywheel-to-converter attaching nuts. Secure the converter in the housing. Remove the transmission oil cooler lines from the retaining clip at the engine. Remove the lower converter housing-to-engine attaching bolts.
14. Remove the nut from each of the two front engine mounts.
15. Lower the vehicle and position a jack under the transmission and support it. Remove the remaining bellhousing-to-engine attaching bolts.
16. Attach the engine lifting device and raise the engine slightly and carefully pull it from the transmission. Lift the engine out of the vehicle.
17. To install the engine: Place a new gasket on the muffler inlet pipe.
18. Carefully lower the engine into the truck. Make sure that the dowels in the engine block engage the holes in the bellhousing.
19. On manual transmission equipped trucks, start the transmission input shaft into the clutch disc. It may be necessary to adjust the position of the engine or transmission in order for the input shaft to enter the clutch disc. If necessary, turn the crankshaft until the input shaft splines mesh with the clutch disc splines.
20. On automatic transmission equipped trucks, start the converter pilot into the crankshaft. Unsecure the converter in the housing.
21. Install the bellhousing upper attaching bolts. Remove the jack supporting the transmission.
22. Lower the engine until it rests on the engine mounts. Remove the lifting device.
23. Install the engine mount nuts and tighten them to 45-55 ft.lb.
24. Install the automatic transmission coil cooler lines bracket, if so equipped.
25. Install the remaining bellhousing attaching bolts.
26. Connect the clutch return spring, if so equipped.
27. Install the starter and connect the starter cable. Attach the automatic transmission fluid filler tube bracket, if so equipped.
28. On trucks with automatic transmissions, install the transmission oil cooler lines in the bracket at the cylinder block.
29. Connect the exhaust pipe to the exhaust manifold. Tighten the nuts to 25-35 ft.lb.
30. Connect the engine ground strap and negative battery cable.
31. On a truck with an automatic transmission, connect the kick-down rod to the bellcrank assembly on the intake manifold.
32. Connect the accelerator linkage to the carburetor and install the return spring.
33. On a truck with power brakes, connect the brake booster vacuum line to the intake manifold.
34. Connect the coil primary wire, oil pressure and coolant temperature sending unit wires, fuel line, heater hoses, and the battery positive cable.
35. Install the alternator to its mounting bracket. Install the power steering pump to its bracket, if so equipped.
36. Install the water pump pulley, spacer, fan, and fan belt. Adjust the belt tension.
37. Install the radiator and connect the upper and lower radiator hoses to the radiator and engine. Connect the automatic transmission oil cooler lines, if so equipped.
38. Install and adjust the hood.
39. Fill the cooling system. Fill the crankcase.
40. Start the engine and check for leaks. Bleed the cooling system. Adjust the clutch pedal free-play or the automatic transmission control linkage. Install the air cleaner.

6-232 (3.8L) and V8 Except 8-420 (6.9L) Diesel and 8-460 (7.5L)

1. Drain the cooling system and crankcase. Remove the hood.

CAUTION

When draining the coolant, keep in mind that cats and dogs are attracted by the ethylene glycol antifreeze, and are quite likely to drink any that is left in an uncovered container or in puddles on the ground. This will prove fatal in sufficient quantity. Always drain the coolant into a sealable container. Coolant should be reused unless it is contaminated or several years old.

2. Disconnect the battery, negative cable first, and alternator cables from the cylinder block.
3. Remove the air cleaner and intake duct assembly, plus the crankcase ventilation hose.
4. Disconnect the upper and lower radiator hoses, and, if so equipped, the automatic transmission oil cooler lines.
5. Remove the fan shroud and lay it over the fan. Remove the radiator and fan, shroud, fan, spacer, pulley, and belt.
6. Disconnect the alternator leads and the alternator adjusting bolts. Allow the alternator to swing down out of the way.
7. Disconnect the oil pressure sending unit lead from the sending unit.
8. Disconnect the fuel tank-to-pump fuel line at the fuel pump and plug the line.
9. Disconnect the accelerator linkage at the carburetor. Disconnect the automatic transmission kick-down rod and remove the return spring, if so equipped.
10. Disconnect the heater hoses from the water pump and intake manifold. Disconnect the temperature sending unit wire from the sending unit.
11. Remove the upper bellhousing-to-engine attaching bolts.
12. Disconnect the primary wire from the coil. Remove the wiring harness from the left rocker arm cover and position the wires out of the way. Disconnect the ground strap from the cylinder block.
13. Raise the front of the truck and disconnect the starter cable from the starter. Remove the starter.

14. Disconnect the exhaust pipe from the exhaust manifolds.

15. Disconnect the engine mounts from the brackets on the frame.

16. On trucks with automatic transmissions, remove the converter inspection plate and remove the torque converter-to-flywheel attaching bolts.

17. Remove the remaining bellhousing-to-engine attaching bolts.

18. Lower the vehicle and support the transmission with a jack.

19. Install an engine lifting device.

NOTE: On the V6, the intake manifold is aluminum. If a lifting device is attached to the manifold, all manifold bolts must be installed.

20. Raise the engine slightly and carefully pull it out from the transmission. Lift the engine out of the engine compartment.

21. Install the engine in the reverse order of removal. Make sure that the dowels in the engine block engage the holes in the bellhousing through the rear cover plate. If the engine hangs up after the transmission input shaft enters the clutch disc (manual transmission only), turn the crankshaft with the transmission in gear until the input shaft splines mesh with the clutch disc splines.

22. Tighten the exhaust pipe-to-exhaust manifold nuts to 25-35 ft.lb., and all others as follows:

¼"-20: 6-9 ft.lb.
$^5/_{16}$"-18: 12-18 ft.lb.
⅜"-16: 22-32 ft.lb.
$^7/_{16}$"-14: 45-57 ft.lb.
½"-13: 55-80 ft.lb.
$^9/_{16}$": 85-120 ft.lb.

8-460 (7.5L)

1. Remove the hood.

2. Drain the cooling system, the radiator and the cylinder block.

CAUTION

When draining the coolant, keep in mind that cats and dogs are attracted by the ethylene glycol antifreeze, and are quite likely to drink any that is left in an uncovered container or in puddles on the ground. This will prove fatal in sufficient quantity. Always drain the coolant into a sealable container. Coolant should be reused unless it is contaminated or several years old.

3. Disconnect the negative battery cable and remove the air cleaner assembly.

4. Disconnect the upper and lower radiator hoses and the transmission oil cooler lines from the radiator.

5. Remove the fan shroud from the radiator and remove the fan from the water pump. Remove the fan and shroud from the engine compartment.

6. Remove the upper support and remove the radiator.

7. If the truck is equipped with air conditioning, remove the compressor from the engine and position it out of the way. If the compressor must be removed completely, loosen the air conditioning service valves (disconnect) carefully to discharge the air conditioning system. Remove the compressor.

8. Remove the power steering pump from the engine, if so equipped, and position it to one side. Do not disconnect the fluid lines.

9. Disconnect the fuel pump inlet line from the pump and plug the line.

10. Remove the alternator drive belts and disconnect the alternator from the engine, positioning it aside.

11. Disconnect the ground cable from the right front corner of the engine.

12. Disconnect the heater hoses.

13. Remove the transmission fluid filler tube attaching bolt from the right-side valve cover and position the tube out of the way.

14. Disconnect all vacuum lines at the rear of the intake manifold.

15. Disconnect the speed control cable at the carburetor, if so equipped. Disconnect the accelerator rod and the transmission kickdown rod and secure them out of the way.

16. Disconnect the engine wiring harness at the connector on the fire wall.

17. Raise the vehicle and disconnect the exhaust pipes at the exhaust manifolds.

18. Disconnect the starter cable and remove the starter. Bring the starter forward and rotate the solenoid outward to remove the assembly.

19. Remove the access cover from the converter housing and remove the flywheel-to-converter attaching nuts. Remove the lower converter housing-to-engine attaching bolts.

20. Remove the engine mount through-bolts attaching the rubber insulators to the frame brackets.

21. Lower the vehicle and place a jack under the transmission to support it.

22. Remove the converter housing-to-engine block attaching bolts (left-side).

23. Disconnect the coil wire and remove the coil and bracket assembly from the intake manifold.

24. Attach the engine lifting device and carefully lift the engine from the engine compartment.

25. Install the engine in the reverse order of removal. Tighten the alternator pivot bolt to 45-57 ft.lb. and all the rest of the nuts and bolts as is outlined in Step 21 of the preceding "V8 except 460 Removal and Installation" procedure.

8-420 (6.9L)

1. Open the hood. Disconnect the battery ground cables from both batteries.

2. Scribe alignment marks at the hood hinges and remove the hood.

3. Drain the cooling system.

CAUTION

When draining the coolant, keep in mind that cats and dogs are attracted by the ethylene glycol antifreeze, and are quite likely to drink any that is left in an uncovered container or in puddles on the ground. This will prove fatal in sufficient quantity. Always drain the coolant into a sealable container. Coolant should be reused unless it is contaminated or several years old.

4. Remove the air cleaner and intake duct assembly. Install an intake manifold cover over the air intake opening.

5. Remove the radiator fan shroud halves.

6. Remove the fan and clutch assembly. The retaining nut is equipped with left handed threads, remove by turning clockwise.

7. Disconnect the upper and lower hoses from the radiator.

8. Disconnect the automatic transmission oil cooler lines at the radiator, if so equipped.

9. Remove the radiator.

10. Loosen A/C compressor, if so equipped, and remove the drive belt.

11. Remove the A/C compressor, if so equipped, and position it on the radiator upper support.

CAUTION

If compressor cannot be secured with lines connected, do not disconnect the lines unless you are familiar with discharging the system and have the proper tools. Have the system discharged prior to the start of engine removal.

12. Loosen the power steering pump and remove the drive belt. Remove the power steering pump and position it out of the way on left side of engine compartment.

13. Disconnect the fuel supply line heater and alternator wires at the alternator. Disconnect the oil pressure sending unit wire at the sending unit. Remove the oil pressure sender from the dash panel and lay it on the engine.

14. Disconnect the accelerator cable from the injection pump. Disconnect the speed control cable from the injection pump, if so equipped. Remove the accelerator cable bracket with cables attached, from the intake manifold and position out of the way.

15. Disconnect the transmission

kickdown rod from the injection pump, if so equipped. Disconnect the main wiring harness connector from the right side of engine. Disconnect the engine ground strap from the rear of engine. Disconnect the fuel return hose from left rear of engine.

16. Remove the two upper transmission-to-engine attaching bolts.

17. Disconnect the heater hoses from the water pump and the right cylinder head. Disconnect the water temperature sender wire from the sender on left front of engine block. Disconnect the water temperature overheat light switch wire from the switch on top front of left cylinder head. Position wires out of the way.

18. Raise vehicle and safely support on jackstands.

19. Disconnect both battery ground cables from the lower front of engine.

20. Disconnect and cap the fuel inlet line at fuel supply pump.

21. Disconnect the starter cables at the starter motor.

22. Disconnect the muffler inlet pipes at the exhaust manifolds.

23. Disconnect the engine insulators from No. 1 crossmember. Remove the flywheel inspection plate. Remove the four converter-to-flywheel attaching nuts, if so equipped. Lower vehicle.

24. Support the transmission with a floorjack. Remove the four lower transmission to engine attaching bolts.

25. Attach an engine lifting sling and chain hoist. Raise the engine high enough to clear number one crossmember and pull forward.

26. Rotate the front of the engine approximately 45 degrees to the left and lift it out of the engine compartment.

27. When installing the engine; lower engine into engine compartment. Use care not to damage windshield wiper motor when installing engine in vehicle.

28. Start the transmission main shaft into the clutch disc. It may be necessary to adjust position of transmission in relation to engine if mainshaft binds or will not enter clutch disc. If the engine hangs up after main shaft enters clutch disc, rotate crankshaft slowly (transmission in gear) until mainshaft splines mesh with clutch disc splines. Align converter to flywheel studs, if so equipped.

29. Lower into engine insulator brackets on number one crossmember.

30. Install the four lower transmission to engine attaching bolts and tighten. Remove engine lifting sling. Raise the vehicle and safely support on jackstands.

31. Install the four convertor to flywheel attaching nuts, if so equipped. Install the flywheel inspection plate.

32. Install the engine insulator support to crossmember bracket attaching nuts and washers. Connect the muffler inlet pipes to exhaust manifolds. Connect both battery ground cables to the lower front of the engine. Connect starter cables to starter. Install the fuel pump inlet line on fuel pump. Lower vehicle.

33. Connect the water temperature sender wire to sender on left front of engine block. Connect the wire to water temperature overheat light switch on top of left cylinder head. Install the heater hoses on right cylinder head and water pump and tighten clamps.

34. Connect the engine ground strap at rear of engine. Connect the fuel return hose at left rear of engine. Connect the transmission kickdown rod, if so equipped.

35. Install the accelerator cable bracket on the intake manifold. Connect the accelerator cable to the injection pump. Connect the speed control cable, if so equipped, to injection pump.

36. Install the oil pressure sender on dash panel. Connect the oil pressure gauge sender wire to oil pressure sender.

37. Connect the fuel supply line heater and alternator wires to alternator.

38. Install the power steering pump and drive belt. Do not adjust belt at this time.

39. Install A/C compressor and drive belt. Adjust A/C compressor and power steering pump drive belts.

NOTE: The A/C system can be recharged after engine installation is completed.

40. Install the radiator. Connect the automatic transmission oil cooler lines at the radiator, if so equipped. Connect the upper and lower radiator hoses to the radiator and tighten hose clamps. Fill and bleed the cooling system.

41. Install the fan and clutch assembly. Remember, left hand thread. Turn counterclockwise to tighten.

42. Install the radiator fan shroud halves.

42. Remove intake manifold cover, and install the air cleaner. Install the intake duct assembly.

43. Install hood using scribe marks drawn on hood at removal.

44. Connect the battery ground cables at both batteries. Check the engine oil level and fill as needed with the specified type and grade of oil. Run the engine and check for fuel, oil and coolant leaks.

VANS

6-300 (4.9L)

1. Take off the engine cover, drain the coolant, remove the air cleaner, and disconnect the battery.

CAUTION

When draining the coolant, keep in mind that cats and dogs are attracted by the ethylene glycol antifreeze, and are quite likely to drink any that is left in an uncovered container or in puddles on the ground. This will prove fatal in sufficient quantity. Always drain the coolant into a sealable container. Coolant should be reused unless it is contaminated or several years old.

2. Remove the bumper, grille, and gravel deflector.

3. Detach the upper radiator hose at the engine. Remove the alternator splash shield and detach the lower hose at the radiator. Remove the radiator and shroud, if any.

4. Disconnect the engine heater hoses and the alternator wires. Remove the power steering pump and support.

5. Disconnect and plug the fuel line at the pump.

6. Detach from the engine: distributor and gauge sending unit wires, brake booster hose, accelerator cable and bracket.

7. Disconnect the automatic transmission kickdown linkage at the bellcrank.

8. Remove the exhaust manifold heat deflector and unbolt the pipe from the manifold.

9. Disconnect the automatic transmission vacuum line from the intake manifold and from the junction. Remove the transmission dipstick tube support bolt at the intake manifold.

10. Remove the upper engine-to-transmission bolts.

11. Remove the starter. Remove the flywheel inspection cover. Remove the four automatic transmission torque converter nuts, then remove to front engine support nuts. Take off the oil filter.

12. Remove the rest of the transmission-to-engine fasteners, then lift the engine out from the engine compartment with a floor crane.

13. To replace the engine, lower it into place and start the mounting bolts. Install the upper transmission bolts, the converter nuts, and the lower transmission bolts. Tighten the mounting bolts. Install all the items removed in the previous steps.

V8 Engines

NOTE: Refer to the proceeding pickup truck section for unit disconnection details on the 6.9L diesel engine.

1. Take off the engine cover, drain the coolant, remove the air cleaner, and disconnect the battery. Remove

the bumper, grille, and gravel deflector. Remove the upper grille support bracket, hood lock support, and air conditioning condenser upper mounting brackets.

CAUTION

When draining the coolant, keep in mind that cats and dogs are attracted by the ethylene glycol antifreeze, and are quite likely to drink any that is left in an uncovered container or in puddles on the ground. This will prove fatal in sufficient quantity. Always drain the coolant into a sealable container. Coolant should be reused unless it is contaminated or several years old.

2. With air conditioning, the system must be discharged to remove the condenser. Do not attempt to do this yourself, unless you are trained in air conditioning. Disconnect the lines at the compressor.
3. Remove the accelerator cable bracket and the heater hoses. Detach the radiator hoses and the automatic transmission cooler lines, if any. Remove the fan shroud, fan, and radiator.
4. Pivot the alternator in and detach the wires.
5. Remove the air cleaner, duct and valve, exhaust manifold shroud, and flex tube.
6. Disconnect the automatic transmission shift rod.
7. Disconnect the fuel and choke lines, detach the vacuum lines, and remove the carburetor and spacer.
8. Remove the oil filter. Detach the exhaust pipe from the manifold. Unbolt the automatic transmission tube bracket from the cylinder head. Remove the starter.
9. Remove the engine mount bolts. With automatic, remove the converter inspection cover and unbolt the converter from the flex plate.
10. Unbolt the engine ground cable and support the transmission.
11. Remove the power steering front bracket. Detach only one vacuum line at the rear of the intake manifold. Disconnect the engine wiring loom. Remove the speed control servo from the manifold. Detach the compressor clutch wire.
12. Install a lifting bracket and attach a floor crane. Remove the transmission-to-engine bolts, making sure the transmission is supported. Remove the engine.
13. To install the engine, align the converter to the flex plate and the engine dowels to the transmission. With manual transmission, start the transmission shaft into the clutch disc. You may have to turn the crankshaft slowly with the transmission in gear. Install the transmission bolts, then the mounting bolts. Install all the items removed in the previous steps.

Rocker Arm Cover

REMOVAL & INSTALLATION

V6 and V8 Engines

NOTE: When disconnecting wires and vacuum lines, label them for reinstallation identification.

1. Remove the air cleaner assembly.

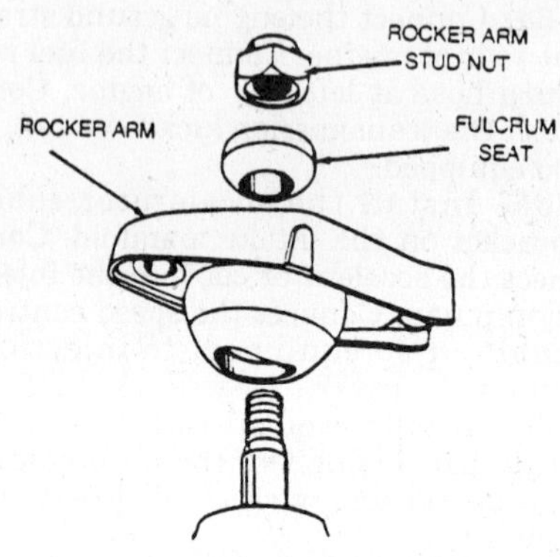

300 inline six rocker arm assembly

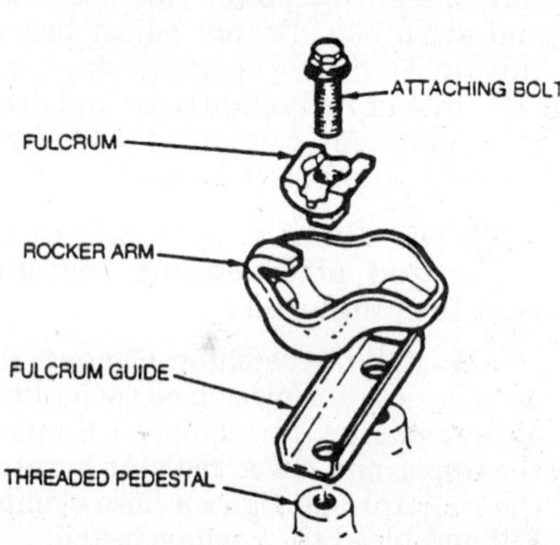

302, 351W valve rocker assembly, 1980 only

2. On the right side:
   a. Disconnect the automatic choke heat chamber hose from the inlet tube near the right valve cover if equipped.
   b. Remove the automatic choke heat tube if equipped and remove the PCV valve and hose from the valve cover. Disconnect the EGR valve hoses.
   c. Remove the Thermactor® bypass valve and air supply hoses as necessary to gain clearance.
   d. Disconnect the spark plug wires from the plugs with a twisting pulling motion; twist and pull on the boots only, never on the wire; position the wires and mounting bracket out of the way.
   e. Remove the valve cover mounting bolts; remove the valve cover.

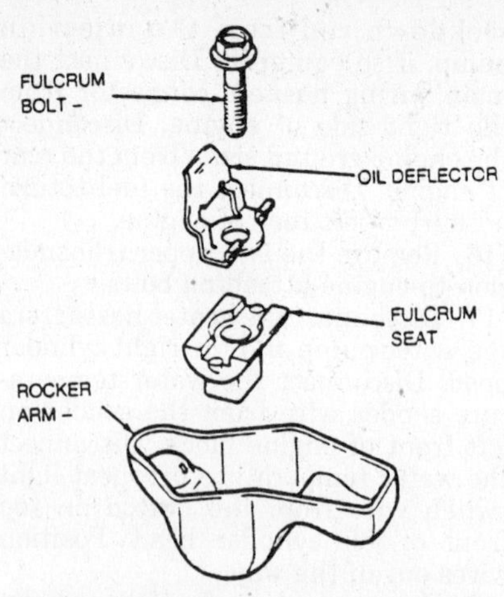

351M,400,460 rocker arm assembly

3. On the left side:
   a. Remove the spark plug wires and bracket.
   b. Remove the wiring harness and any vacuum hose from the bracket.
   c. Remove the valve cover mounting bolts and valve cover.
4. Clean all old gasket material from the valve cover and cylinder head mounting surfaces.

NOTE: Some 6-232 engines were not equipped with valve cover gaskets in production. Rather, RTV silicone gasket material was originally used. Scrape away the old RTV sealant and clean the cover. Spread an even bead $^{3}/_{16}$" (4mm) wide of RTV sealant on the valve covers and reinstall, or install with gaskets.

5. Installation is the reverse of removal. Use oil resistant sealing compound and a new valve cover gasket. When installing the valve cover gasket, make sure all the gasket tangs are engaged into the cover notches provided.

420 (6.9L) Diesel

1. Disconnect the ground cables from both batteries.
2. Remove the valve cover retaining bolts and the valve covers.
3. Clean all gasket mounting surfaces, install new valve cover gaskets and reinstall the valve covers on the engine. Tighten the bolts to 10 ft.lb. Reconnect the battery cables, start the engine and check for oil leaks.

Rocker Arm (Cam Follower) and Hydraulic Lash Adjuster

REMOVAL & INSTALLATION

4-140 Engine

NOTE: A special tool is required to compress the lash adjuster.

1. Remove the valve cover and associated parts as required.
2. Rotate the camshaft so that the base circle of the cam is against the cam follower you intend to remove.
3. Remove the retaining spring from the cam follower, if so equipped.
4. Using special tool T74P-6565-B or a valve spring compressor tool, collapse the lash adjuster and/or depress the valve spring, as necessary, and slide the cam follower over the lash adjuster and out from under the camshaft.
5. Install the cam follower in the reverse order of removal. Make sure that the lash adjuster is collapsed and released before rotating the camshaft.

Rocker Arm Shaft/Rocker Arms

REMOVAL & INSTALLATION

6-300 (4.9L)

1. Disconnect the inlet air hose at the oil fill cap. Remove the air cleaner.
2. Disconnect the accelerator cable at the carburetor. Remove the cable retracting spring. Remove the accelerator cable bracket from the cylinder head and position the cable and bracket assembly out of the way.
3. Remove the PCV valve from the valve rocker arm cover. Remove the cover bolts and remove the valve rocker arm cover.
4. Remove the valve rocker arm stud nut, fulcrum seat and rocker arm. Inspect the rocker arm cover bolts for worn or damaged seals under the bolt heads and replace as necessary. If it is necessary to remove a rocker arm stud, Tool T79T-6527-A is available. A 0.006 oversize reamer T62F-6527-B3 or equivalent and a 0.015″ oversize reamer T62F-6527-B5 or equivalent are available. For 0.010″ oversize studs, use reamer T66P-6527-B or equivalent. To press in replacement studs, use stud replacer T79T-6527-B or equivalent for 6-300. Rocker arm studs that are broken or have damaged threads may be replaced with standard studs. Loose studs in the head may be replaced with 0.006″, 0.010″ or 0.015″ oversize studs which area available for service. When going from a standard size rocker arm stud to a 0.010″ or 0.015″ oversize stud, always use the 0.006″ oversize reamer before finish reaming with the 0.010″ or 0.015″ oversize reamer.

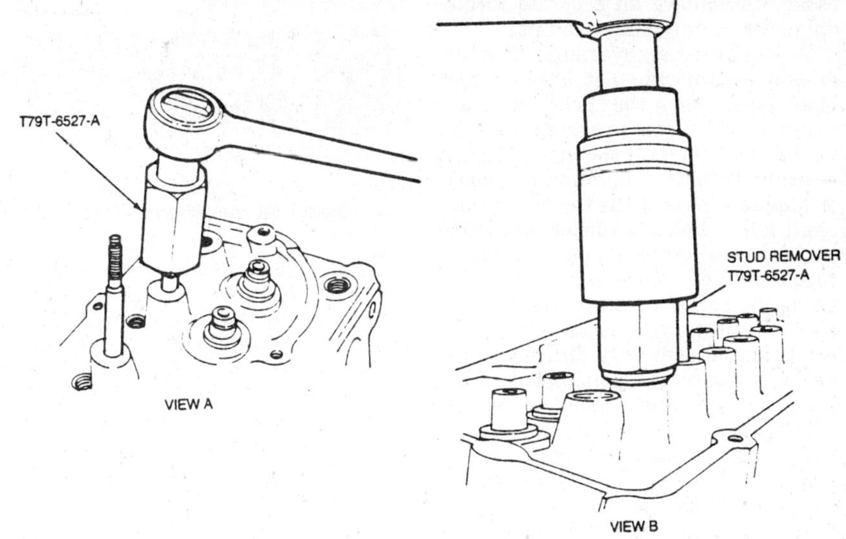

Removing the rocker arm stud on the 300 inline sixes

5. Position the sleeve of the rocker arm stud remover over the stud with the bearing end down. Thread the puller into the sleeve and over the stud until it is fully bottomed. Hold the sleeve with a wrench; then, rotate the puller clockwise to remove the stud. If the rocker arm stud was broken off flush with the stud boss, use an easy-out to remove the broken stud following the instructions of the tool manufacturer.
6. If a loose rocker arm stud is being replaced, ream the stud bore using the proper reamer (or reamers in sequence) for the selected oversize stud. Make sure the metal particles do not enter the valve area.
7. Coat the end of the stud with Lubriplate® or it's equivalent. Align the stud with the stud bore; then, tap the sliding driver until it bottoms. When the driver contacts the stud boss, the stud is installed to its correct height.
8. Apply Lubriplate® or equivalent to the top of the valve stem and at the push rod guide in the cylinder head.
9. Apply Lubriplate® or equivalent to the rocker arm fulcrum seat and the fulcrum seat socket in the rocker arm. Install the valve rocker arm, fulcrum seat and stud nut.
10. Clean the valve rocker arm cover and the cylinder head gasket surface. Place the new gasket in the cover making sure that the tabs of the gasket engage in the notches provided in the cover.
11. Install the cover on the cylinder head. Make sure the gasket seats evenly all around the head. Partially tighten the cover bolts in sequence, starting at the middle bolts. Then tighten the bolts to 3-5 ft. lb.
12. Install the PCV valve in the rocker arm cover. Install the accelerator cable bracket on the cylinder head and connect the cable to the carburetor.
13. Connect the the inlet air hose to the oil fill cap.
14. Install air cleaner.

6-232 (3.8L) and V8s Except 8-420 (6.9L) Diesel

These engines are equipped with individually mounted rocker arms. Use the following procedure to remove the rocker arms:

1. Disconnect the choke heat chamber air hose, the air cleaner and inlet duct assembly, the choke heat tube, PCV valve and hose, and the EGR hoses (if so equipped).
2. On models so equipped, disconnect the Thermactor by-pass valve and air supply hoses.
3. Label and disconnect the spark plug wires at the plugs. Remove the plug wires from the looms.
4. Remove the valve cover attaching bolts and remove the cover(s).
5. Remove the valve rocker arm stud nut.

ADJUSTMENT

This adjustment is actually part of the installation procedure for the individually mounted rocker arms found on the V6 and V8 engines, and is necessary to achieve an accurate torque value for each rocker arm nut.

By its nature, an hydraulic valve lifter will expand when it is not under load. Thus, when the rocker arms are removed and the pressure via the pushrod is taken off the lifter, the lifter expands to its maximum. If the lifter happens to be at the top of the camshaft lobe when the rocker arm is being reinstalled, a large amount of torque would be necessary when tightening the rocker arm nut just to overcome the pressure of the expanded lifter. This makes it very difficult to get an accurate torque setting with individually mounted rocker arms. For this reason, the rocker arms are installed in a certain sequence which corresponds to the low points of the camshaft lobes.

1. Crank the engine until No.1 cylinder is at TDC of the compression stroke and the timing pointer is aligned with the mark on the crankshaft damper.
2. Scribe a mark on the damper at this point.
3. Scribe two additional marks on the damper (see illustration).
4. With the timing pointer aligned with mark 1 on the damper, tighten the following valves to the specified torque:
   - *V6-232* No. 1 Intake and Exhaust; No. 3 Intake and Exhaust; No. 4 Exhaust and No. 6 Intake.
   - *255, 302, and 460* No. 1, 7 and 8 Intake; No. 1, 5, and 4 Exhaust
   - *351* No. 1, 4 and 8 Intake; No. 1, 3 and 7 Exhaust.
5. Rotate the crankshaft 180° to point 2 and tighten the following valves:
   - *V6-232* No. 2 Intake; No. 3 Exhaust; No. 4 Intake; No. 5 Intake and Exhaust; No. 6 Exhaust.
   - *255, 302, and 460* No. 5 and 4 Intake; No. 2 and 6 Exhaust
   - *351* No. 3 and 7 Intake; No. 2 and 6 Exhaust
6. Rotate the crankshaft 270° to point 3 and tighten the following valves:
   - *302 and 460* No. 2, 3, and 6 Intake; No. 7, 3 and 8 Exhaust
   - *351* No. 2, 5 and 6 Intake; No. 4, 5 and 8 Exhaust
7. On 232, 255, 302 and 351W engines, tighten nut until it contacts the rocker shoulder, then torque to 18-20 ft.lb.; 351C engines, tighten bolt to 18-25 fft.lb.; 460 engine, tighten nut until it contacts rocker shoulder, then torque to 18-22 ft.lb.

8-420 (6.9L) Diesel

1. Disconnect the ground cables from both batteries.

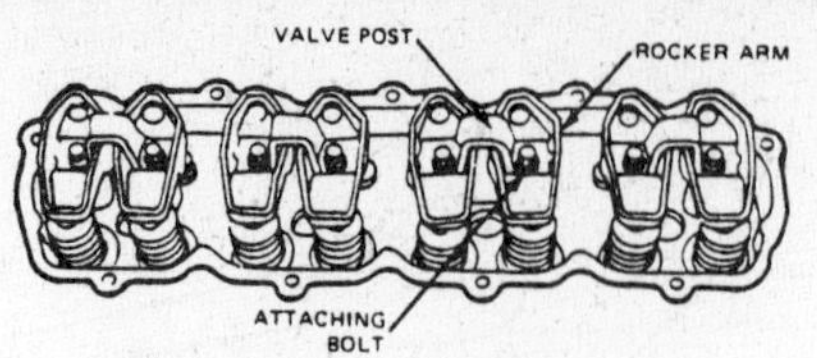

Diesel V8 rocker arm assembly

2. Remove the valve cover retaining bolts and the valve covers.
3. Remove the rocker arm retaining bolts and posts. Keep the rockers and posts in order and identify for reinstallation to original positions.
4. Turn the engine until the timing mark is at the 11 o'clock position as viewed from the front of the engine.
5. Install all rocker arms, posts and retaining bolts and tighten.
6. Clean all gasket mounting surfaces, install new valve cover gaskets and reinstall the valve covers to the engine. Reconnect the battery cables, start the engine and check for oil leaks.

HYDRAULIC VALVE LIFTER INSPECTION

NOTE: The lifters used on diesel engines require a special test fluid, kerosene is not satisfactory.

Remove the lifters from their bores and remove any gum and varnish with safe solvent. Check the lifters for concave wear. If the bottom of the lifter is worn concave or flat, replace the lifter. Lifters are built with a convex bottom, flatness indicates wear. If a worn lifter is detected, carefully check the camshaft for wear.

To test lifter leak down, submerge the lifter in a container of kerosene. Chuck a used pushrod or its equivalent into a drill press. Position the container of kerosene so the pushrod acts on the lifter plunger. Pump the lifter with the drill press until resistance increases. Pump several more times to bleed any air from the lifter. Apply very firm, constant pressure to the lifter and observe the rate which fluid bleeds out of the lifter. If the lifter bleeds down very quickly (less than 15 seconds), the lifter should be replaced. If the time exceeds 60 seconds, the lifter is sticking and should be cleaned or replaced. If the lifter is operating properly (leak down time 15-60 seconds) and not worn, lubricate and reinstall in engine.

NOTE: Always inspect the valve pushrods for wear, straightness and oil blockage. Damaged pushrods will cause erratic valve operation.

Intake Manifold

REMOVAL & INSTALLATION

6-300 (4.9L)

The intake and exhaust manifolds on these engines are known as combination manifolds and are serviced as a unit.

1. Remove the air cleaner. Disconnect the choke cable at the carburetor. Disconnect the accelerator cable or rod at the carburetor. Remove the accelerator retracting spring.
2. On a vehicle with automatic transmission, remove the kick-down rod-retracting spring. Remove the accelerator rod bellcrank assembly.
3. Disconnect the fuel inlet line and the distributor vacuum line from the carburetor.
4. Disconnect the muffler inlet pipe from the exhaust manifold.
5. Disconnect the power brake vacuum line, if so equipped.
6. Remove the bolts and nuts attaching the manifolds to the cylinder head. Lift the manifold assemblies from the engine. Remove and discard the gaskets.
7. To separate the manifolds, remove the nuts joining the intake and exhaust manifolds.
8. Clean the mating surfaces of the cylinder head and the manifolds.
9. If the intake and exhaust manifolds have been separated, coat the mating surfaces lightly with graphite grease and place the exhaust manifold over the studs on the intake manifold. Install the lockwashers and nuts. Tighten them finger tight.
10. Install a new intake manifold gasket.
11. Coat the mating surfaces lightly with graphite grease. Place the manifold assemblies in position against the cylinder head. Make sure that the gaskets have not become dislodged. Install the attaching washers, bolts and nuts. Tighten the attaching nuts and bolts in the proper sequence to 26 fft.lb. If the intake and exhaust manifolds were separated, tighten the nuts joining them.
12. Position a new gasket on the muffler inlet pipe and connect the inlet pipe to the exhaust manifold.
13. Connect the crankcase vent hose to the intake manifold inlet tube and position the hose clamp.
14. Connect the fuel inlet line and the distributor vacuum line to the carburetor.
15. Connect the accelerator cable to the carburetor and install the retracting spring. Connect the choke cable to the carburetor.
16. On a vehicle with an automatic

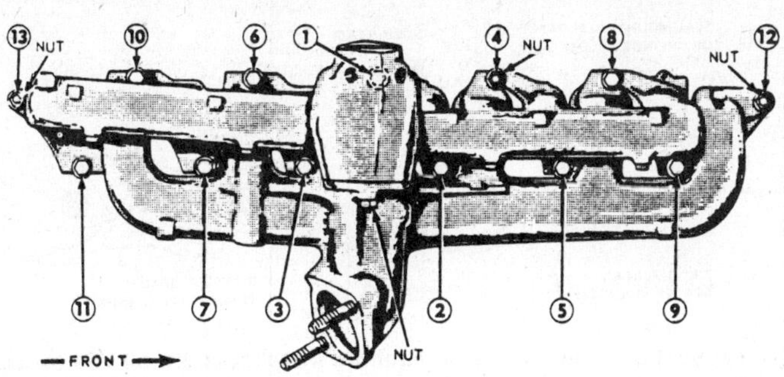

300 six cylinder intake and exhaust manifold torque sequence

transmission, install the bellcrank assembly and the kick-down rod retracting spring. Adjust the transmission control linkage.

17. Install the air cleaner.

6-232 (3.8L) and V8 except 8-420 (6.9L) Diesel, and 8-460 and Fuel Injected Models

1. Drain the cooling system, remove the air cleaner and the intake duct assembly.

CAUTION

When draining the coolant, keep in mind that cats and dogs are attracted by the ethylene glycol antifreeze, and are quite likely to drink any that is left in an uncovered container or in puddles on the ground. This will prove fatal in sufficient quantity. Always drain the coolant into a sealable container. Coolant should be reused unless it is contaminated or several years old.

2. Disconnect the accelerator rod from the carburetor and remove the accelerator retracting spring. Disconnect the automatic transmission kick-down rod at the carburetor, if so equipped.

3. Disconnect the high-tension lead and all other wires from the ignition coil.

NOTE: Distributor removal is not necessary on 3.8L V6 engines, disregard steps pretaining to its removal.

4. Disconnect the spark plug wires from the spark plugs by grasping the rubber boots and twisting and pulling at the same time. Remove the wires from the brackets on the rocker covers. Remove the distributor cap and spark plug wire assembly.

5. Remove the carburetor fuel inlet line and the distributor vacuum line from the carburetor. (See Note above Step 4).

6. Remove the distributor lockbolt and remove the distributor and vacuum line. See "Distributor Removal and Installation."

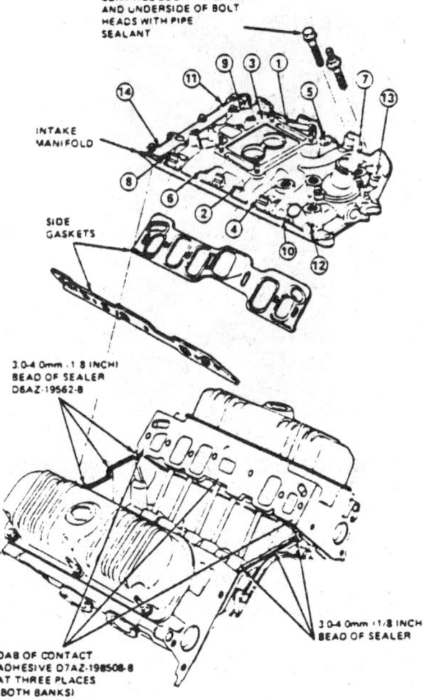

V6 intake manifold removal and installation. Part numbers are Ford--equivalent sealers and adhesives may be used

7. Disconnect the upper radiator hose from the coolant outlet housing and the water temperature sending unit wire at the sending unit. Remove the heater hose from the intake manifold.

8. Loosen the clamp on the water pump bypass hose at the coolant outlet housing and slide the hose off the outlet housing.

9. Disconnect the PCV hose at the rocker cover.

10. If the engine is equipped with the Thermactor exhaust emission control system, remove the air pump to cylinder head air hose at the air pump and position it out of the way. Also remove the air hose at the backfire suppressor valve. Remove the air hose bracket from the valve rocker arm cover and position the air hose out of the way. Remove EGR valve tube on V6 models.

11. Remove the intake manifold and carburetor as an assembly. It may be necessary to pry the intake manifold from the cylinder head. Remove all traces of the intake manifold-to-cylinder head gaskets and the two end seals from both the manifold and the other mating surfaces of the engine. Installation is as follows:

12. Clean the mating surfaces of the intake manifold, cylinder heads and block with laquer thinner or similar solvent. On V8 engines: Apply a 1/8" bead of silicone-rubber RTV sealant at the points shown in the accompanying diagram.

NOTE: The 3.8L V6 engine does not use end seals. RTV sealant is used. Apply 1/8" bead of sealant to each end of the engine block at the points where the intake manifold rests. Assembly must occur within 15 minutes of sealant application.

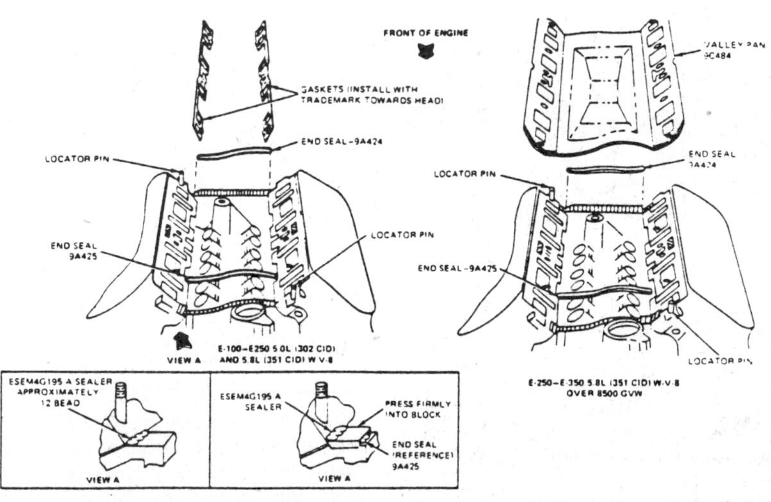

302 and 351W V8 intake manifold sealing and gaskets, late model shown

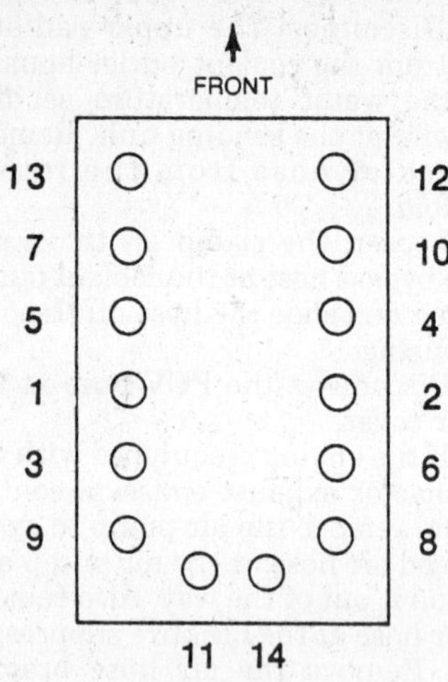

V6 intake manifold torque sequence

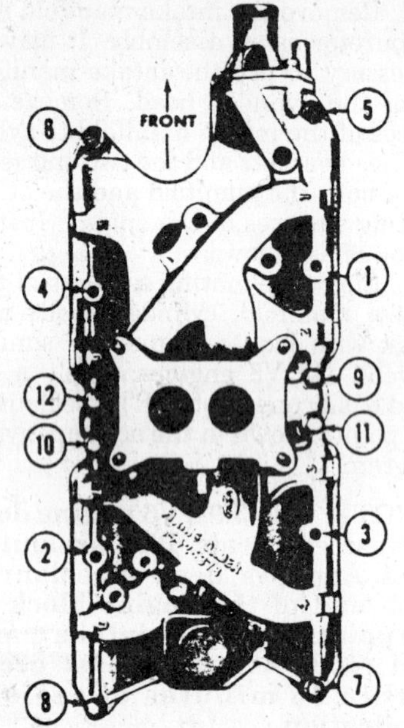

Intake manifold bolt tightening sequence for the 302 V8

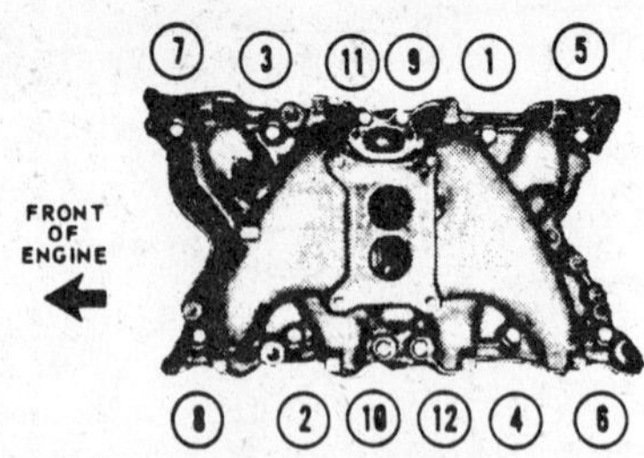

Intake manifold bolt tightening sequence for 351, 351M, and 400 V8s

CAUTION

Do not apply sealer to the waffle portions of the seals as the sealer will rupture the end seal material.

13. On V8 engines: Position new

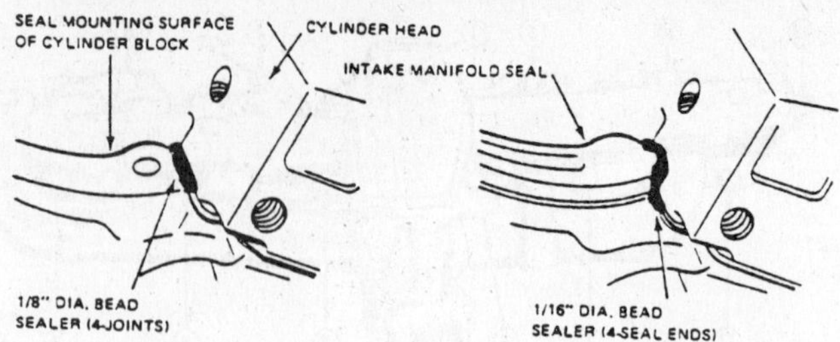

Sealer application area for intake manifold installation on all V8s except 460

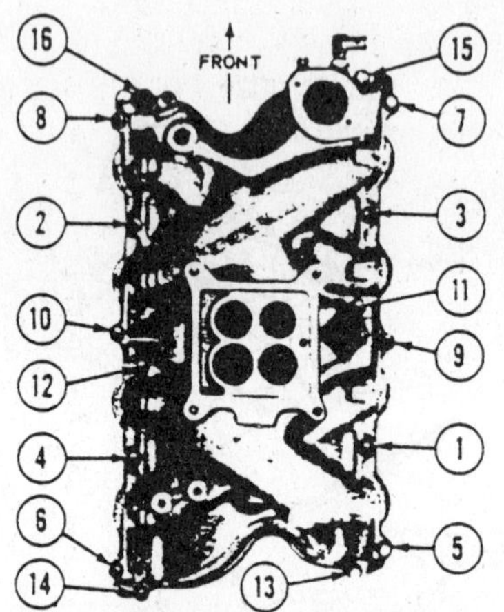

Intake manifold bolt tightening sequence for the 480 V8

seals on the block and press the seal locating extensions into the holes in the mating surfaces.

14. Apply a $\frac{1}{16}$" bead of sealer to the outer end of each manifold seal for the full length of the seal (4 places). As before, do not apply sealer to the waffle portion of the end seals.

NOTE: RTV sealer sets in about 15 minutes, depending on brand, so work quickly but carefully. DO NOT DROP ANY SEALER INTO THE MANIFOLD CAVITY. IT WILL FORM AND SET AND PLUG THE OIL GALLERY.

15. Position the manifold gasket onto the block and heads with the alignment notches under the dowels in the heads. Be sure gasket holes align with head holes.

16. Install the manifold and related equipment in reverse order of removal.

Fuel Injected Engines

CAUTION

Discharge fuel system pressure before starting any work that involves disconnecting fuel system lines. See "Fuel Supply Manifold" removal and installation procedures (Gasoline Fuel System section).

1. To remove the upper manifold: Remove the air cleaner. Disconnect the electrical connectors at the air bypass valve, throttle position sensor and EGR position sensor.

2. Disconnect the throttle linkage at the throttle ball and the AOD transmission linkage from the throttle body. Remove the bolts that secure the bracket to the intake and position the bracket and cables out of the way.

3. Disconnect the upper manifold vacuum fitting connections by removing all the vacuum lines at the vacuum tree (label lines for position identification). Remove the vacuum lines to the EGR valve and fuel pressure regulator.

4. Disconnect the PCV system by disconnecting the hose from the fitting at the rear of the upper manifold.

5. Remove the two canister purge lines from the fittings at the throttle body.

6. Disconnect the EGR tube from the EGR valve by loosening the flange nut.

7. Remove the bolt from the upper intake support bracket to upper manifold.

Remove the upper manifold retaining bolts and remove the upper intake manifold and throttle body as an assembly.

8. Clean and inspect all mounting surfaces of the upper and lower intake manifolds.

9. Position a new mounting gasket on the lower intake manifold and install the upper manifold in the reverse order of removal. Mounting bolts are torqued to 12-18 ft.lb.

10. To remove the lower intake manifold: Upper manifold and throttle body must be removed first.

11. Drain the cooling system. Remove the distributor assembly, cap and wires.

CAUTION

When draining the coolant, keep in mind that cats and dogs are attracted by the ethylene glycol antifreeze, and are quite likely to drink any that is left in an uncovered container or in puddles on the ground. This will prove fatal in sufficient quantity. Al-

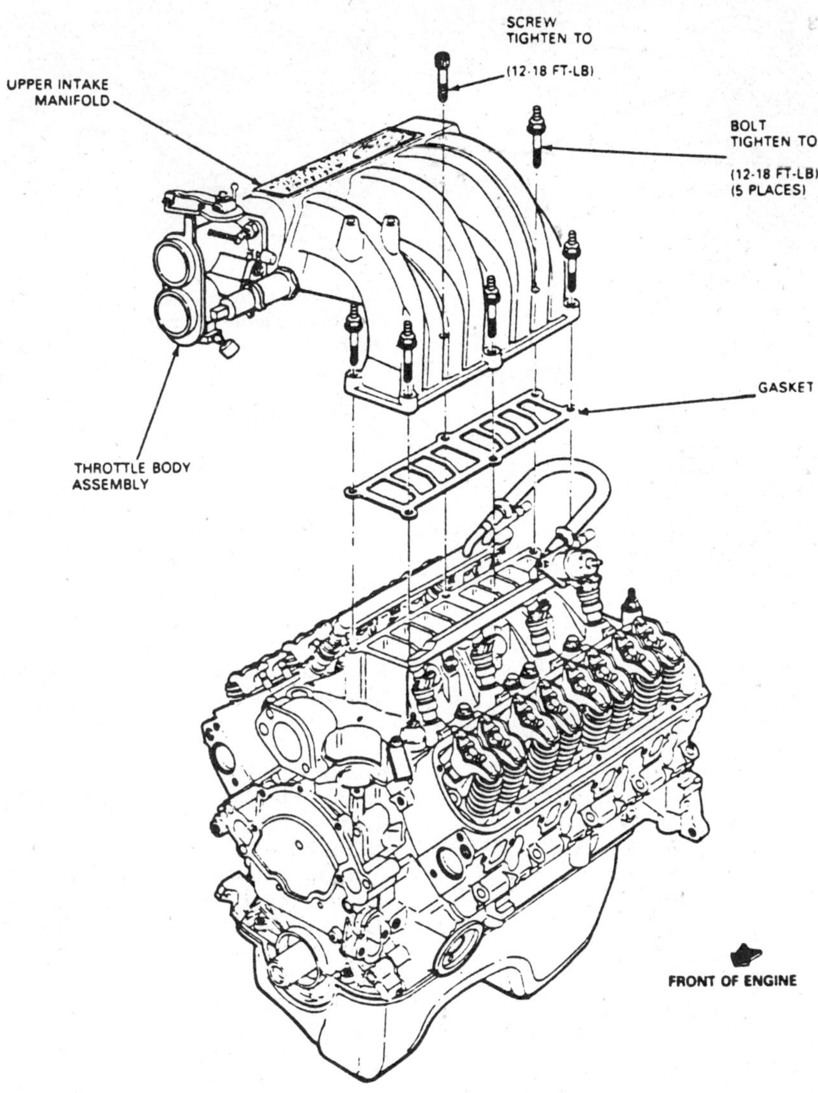

Upper intake manifold and throttle body EFI

ways drain the coolant into a sealable container. Coolant should be reused unless it is contaminated or several years old.

12. Disconnect the electrical connectors at the engine coolant temperature sensor and sending unit, at the air charge temperature sensor and at the knock sensor.

13. Disconnect the injector wiring harness from the main harness assembly. Remove the ground wire from the intake manifold stud. The ground wire must be installed at the same position it was removed from.

14. Disconnect the fuel supply and return lines from the fuel rails.

15. Remove the upper radiator hose from the thermostat housing. Remove the bypass hose. Remove the heater outlet hose at the intake manifold.

16. Remove the air cleaner mounting bracket. Remove the intake manifold mounting bolts and studs. Pay attention to the location of the bolts and studs for reinstallation. Remove the lower intake manifold assembly.

17. Clean and inspect the mounting surfaces of the heads and manifold.

18. Apply a $\frac{1}{16}''$ bead of RTV sealer to the ends of the manifold seals (at the junction point of the seals and gaskets). Install the end seals and intake gaskets on the cylinder heads. The gaskets must interlock with the seal tabs.

19. Install locator bolts at opposite ends of each head and carefully lower the intake manifold into position. Install and tighten the mounting bolts and studs to 23-25 ft.lb. Install the remaining components in the reverse order of removal.

8-460 (7.5L)

1. Drain the cooling system and remove the air cleaner assembly.

CAUTION

When draining the coolant, keep in mind that cats and dogs are attracted by the ethylene glycol antifreeze, and are quite likely to drink any that is left in an uncovered container or in puddles on the ground. This will prove fatal in sufficient quantity. Always drain the coolant into a sealable container. Coolant should be reused unless it is contaminated or several years old.

2. Disconnect the upper radiator hose at the engine.

3. Disconnect the heater hoses at the intake manifold and the water pump. Position them out of the way. Loosen the water pump by-pass hose clamp at the intake manifold.

4. Disconnect the PCV valve and hose at right valve cover. Disconnect all of the vacuum lines at the rear of the intake manifold and tag them for proper reinstallation.

5. Disconnect the wires at the spark plugs, and remove the wires from the brackets on the valve covers. Disconnect the high-tension wire from the coil and remove the distributor cap and wires as an assembly.

6. Disconnect all of the distributor vacuum lines at the carburetor and vacuum control valve and tag them for proper installation. Remove the distributor and vacuum lines as an assembly.

7. Disconnect the accelerator linkage at the carburetor. Remove the speed control linkage bracket, if so equipped, from the manifold and carburetor.

8. Remove the bolts holding the accelerator linkage bellcrank and position the linkage and return springs out of the way.

9. Disconnect the fuel line at the carburetor.

10. Disconnect the wiring harness at the coil battery terminal, engine temperature sending unit, oil pressure sending unit, and other connections as necessary. Disconnect the wiring harness from the clips at the left valve cover and position the harness out of the way.

11. Remove the coil and bracket assembly.

12. Remove the intake manifold attaching bolts and lift the manifold and carburetor from the engine as an assembly. It may be necessary to pry the manifold away from the cylinder heads. Do not damage the gasket sealing surfaces. Installation is as follows:

13. Clean the mating surfaces of the intake manifold, cylinder heads and block with laquer thinner or similar solvent. Apply a $\frac{1}{8}''$ bead of silicone-rubber RTV sealant at the points shown in the accompanying diagram.

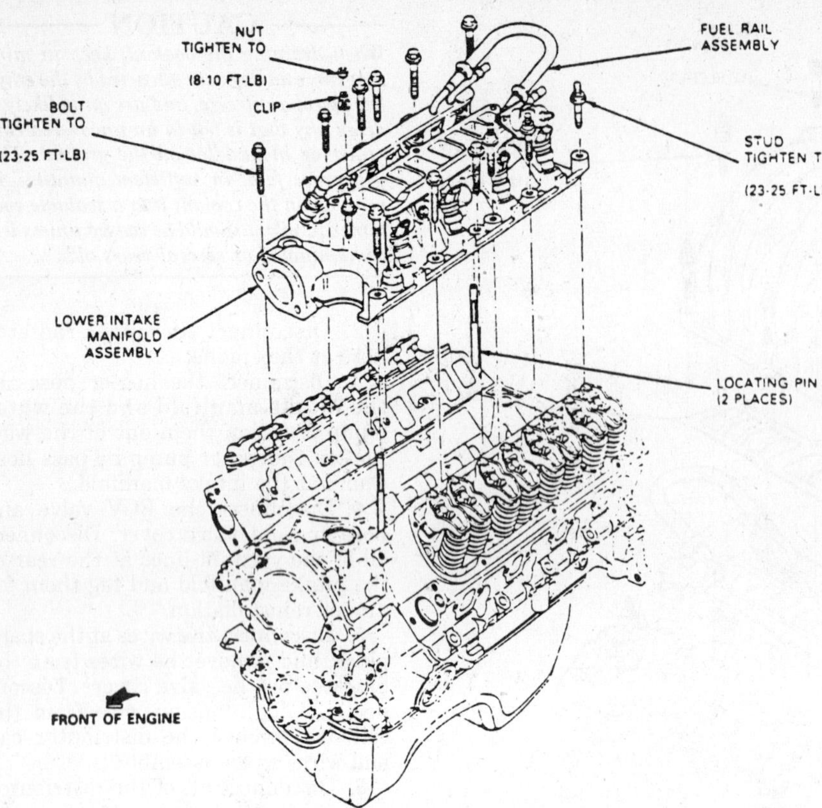

Lower intake manifold—EFI

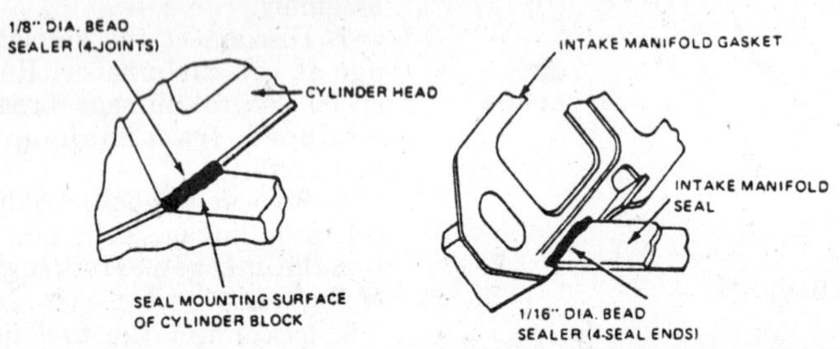

Sealer application areas for intake manifold installation on 460 V8

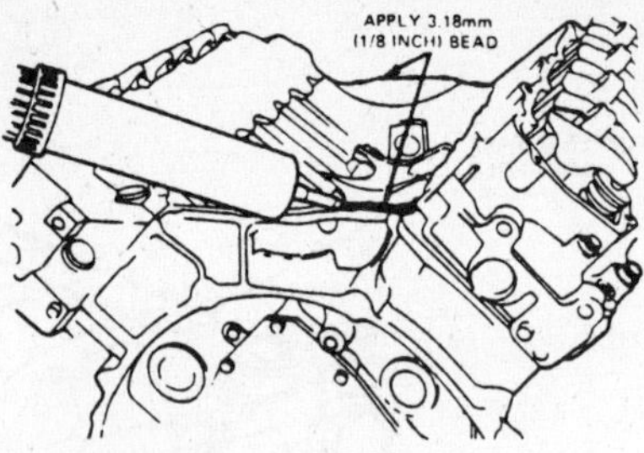

Apply sealer to the diesel cylinder block-to-intake manifold mating surfaces on each end

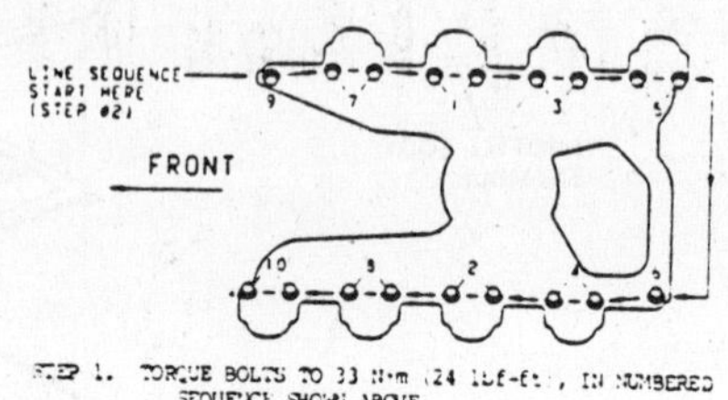

6.9L diesel intake manifold torque sequence

CAUTION

Do not apply sealer to the waffle portions of the seals as the sealer will rupture the end seal material.

14. Position new seals on the block and press the seal locating extensions into the holes in the mating surfaces.
15. Apply a $^1/_{16}$" bead of sealer to the outer end of each manifold seal for the full length of the seal (4 places). As before, do not apply sealer to the waffle portion of the end seals.

NOTE: RTV sealer sets in about 15 minutes, depending on brand, so work quickly but carefully. DO NOT DROP ANY SEALER INTO THE MANIFOLD CAVITY. IT WILL FORM AND SET AND PLUG THE OIL GALLERY.

16. Position the manifold gasket onto the block and heads with the alignment notches under the dowels in the heads. Be sure gasket holes align with head holes.
17. Install the manifold and related equipment in reverse order of removal.

8-420 (6.9L) Diesel

1. Disconnect the battery ground cables from both batteries.
2. Remove the air cleaner and duct hose assembly. Cover the air inlet on the intake manifold.
3. Remove the injection pump. Disconnect and remove the fuel return hoses and block from the No.7 and 8 (rear) nozzles. Remove the fuel return to tank line.
4. Disconnect and remove the engine wiring harness. Be sure to remove the harness ground cable from the rear of the cylinder.
5. Remove the bolts that retain the intake manifold and remove the manifold.
6. If the lifter valley pan is to be removed; remove the CDR valve tube and mounting grommet from the valley pan.
7. Remove the valley pan drain plug and remove the valley pan.
8. Clean all mounting surfaces. Apply a ⅛" bead of RTV sealant to each end of the engine block.
9. Install the valley pan and intake manifold in the reverse order of removal.

Exhaust Manifold

REMOVAL & INSTALLATION

6-300 (4.9L)

The intake and exhaust manifold on these engines are known as combination manifolds and are serviced as a unit. See "Intake Manifold Removal and Installation."

6-232 (3.8L) and V8 Except 8-420 (6.9L) Diesel

1. Remove the air cleaner if the manifold being removed has the car-

buretor heat stove attached to it. On 351 remove the oil filter.

2. Remove the dipstick tube bracket bolt/nut on the 302 V8. On 351 V8 vehicles with a column mounted automatic transmission lever, disconnect the selector lever cross-shaft for clearance. On 1981 and later models, disconnect the EGO sensor, if equipped.

3. Remove any thermactor parts that will interfere with manifold removal.

4. Disconnect the exhaust pipe or catalytic converter from the exhaust manifold. Remove and discard the donut gasket.

5. Disconnect the EGR downtube. Remove the exhaust manifold attaching screws and remove the manifold from the cylinder head.

6. Install the exhaust manifold in the reverse order of removal. Apply a light coat of graphite grease to the mating surface of the manifold. Install and tighten the attaching bolts, starting from the center and working to both ends alternately. Tighten to the proper specifications.

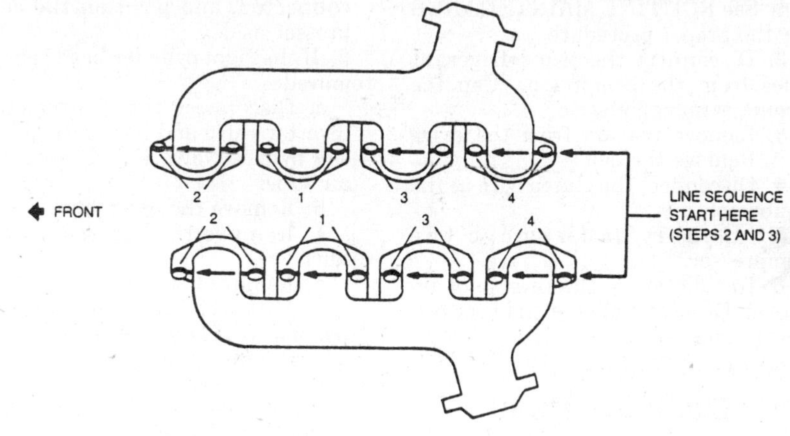

EXHAUST MANIFOLD BOLTS

STEP 1. TORQUE BOLTS TO 41 NM (30 FT. LBS.) IN NUMBERED SEQUENCE SHOWN ABOVE.

STEP 2. TORQUE BOLTS TO 41 NM (30 FT. LBS.) IN LINE SEQUENCE SHOWN ABOVE.

6.9L diesel V8 exhaust manifold torque sequence

8-420 (6.9L) Diesel

1. Disconnect the ground cables from both batteries.

2. Raise and safely support the front of the vehicle on jackstands.

3. Disconnect the exhaust pipes from the manifolds.

4. If the right side manifold is to be removed, lower the vehicle. Remove the left side manifold from underneath while vehicle is raised.

5. The manifold attaching bolts are retained by lock tabs. Use a suitable tool to bend the tabs away from the bolt heads.

6. Clean all mounting surfaces. Apply anti-seize compound to the mounting bolts. Use new gaskets. Reverse the removal procedure for installation.

Air Conditioning Compressor

REMOVAL & INSTALLATION

2-Cylinder York or Tecumseh Compressor

1980-83

1. Discharge the system and disconnect the two hoses from the compressor. Cap the openings immediately!

2. Energize the clutch and remove the clutch mounting bolt.

3. Install a 5/8-11 bolt in the clutch driveshaft hole. With the cltuch still energized, tighten the bolt to remove the clutch from the shaft.

4. Disconnect the clutch wire at the connector.

5. Loosen the idler pulley or alternator and remove the drive belt and clutch, then remove the mounting bolts and compressor.

6. Installation is the reverse of removal. Prior to installation, if a new compressor is being installed, drain the oil from the old compressor into a calibrated container, then drain the oil from the new compressor into a clean container and refill the new compressor with the same amount of oil that was in the old one. Install the clutch and bolt finger-tight, install the compressor on the mounting bracket and install those bolts finger-tight. Connect the clutch wire and energize the clutch. Tighten the clutch bolt to 23 ft.lb. Tighten the compressor mounting bolts to 30 ft.lb. Make all other connections and evacuate, charge and leak test the system. See ROUTINE MAINTENANCE.

FS-6 6-Cylinder Axial Compressor

1. Discharge the refrigerant system. See ROUTINE MAINTENANCE for the proper procedure.

2. Disconnect the two refrigerant lines from the compressor. Cap the openings immediately!

3. Remove tension from the drive belt. Remove the belt

4. Disconnect the clutch wire at the connector.

5. Remove the bolt attaching the support brace to the front brace and the nut attaching the support brace to the intake manifold. Remove the support brace.

6. Remove the two bolts attaching the rear support to the bracket.

7. Remove the bolt attaching the compressor tab to the front brace and the two bolts attaching the compressor front legs to the bracket.

8. Remove the compressor.

9. Installation is the reverse of removal. Use new O-rings coated with clean refrigerant oil at all fittings. New, replacement compressors contain 10 oz. of refrigerant oil. Prior to installation, pour off 4 oz. of oil. This will maintain the oil charge in the system. Evacuate, charge and leak test the system.

HR-980 Radial Compressor

1. Discharge the refrigerant system. See ROUTINE MAINTENANCE for the proper procedure.

2. Disconnect the two refrigerant lines from the compressor. Cap the openings immediately!

3. Remove the bolt and washer from the adjusting bracket and remove the drive belts.

4. Remove the bolt attaching the compressor bracket to the compressor lower mounting lug.

5. Remove the compressor.

6. Installation is the reverse of removal. If a new compressor is being installed, it contains 8 fl.oz. of refrigerant oil. Prior to installing the compressor, drain 4 oz. of the oil from the compressor. This will maintain the oil charge in the system. Evacuate, charge and leak test the system.

6P148 3-Cylinder Axial Compressor

1. Discharge the refrigerant sys-

tem. See ROUTINE MAINTENANCE for the proper procedure.

2. Disconnect the two refrigerant lines from the compressor. Cap the openings immediately!

3. Remove tension from the drive belt. Remove the belt

4. Disconnect the clutch wire at the connector.

5. Unbolt and remove the compressor.

6. Installation is the reverse of removal. Evacuate, charge and leak test the system.

Cylinder Head

REMOVAL & INSTALLATION

NOTE: On cars with air conditioning, remove the mounting bolts and the drive belt, and position the compressor out of the way. Remove the compressor upper mounting bracket from the cylinder head.

CAUTION

If the compressor refrigerant lines do not have enough slack to permit repositioning of the compressor without first disconnecting the refrigerant lines, the air conditioning system will have to be evacuated. See ROUTINE MAINTENANCE.

6-232

1. Drain the cooling system.

CAUTION

When draining the coolant, keep in mind that cats and dogs are attracted by the ethylene glycol antifreeze, and are quite likely to drink any that is left in an uncovered container or in puddles on the ground. This will prove fatal in sufficient quantity. Always drain the coolant into a sealable container. Coolant should be reused unless it is contaminated or several years old.

2. Disconnect the cable from the battery negative terminal.

3. Remove the air cleaner assembly including air intake duct and heat tube.

4. Loosen the accessory drive belt idler. Remove the drive belt.

5. If the left cylinder head is being removed:

a. If equipped with power steering, remove the pump mounting brackets' attaching bolts, leaving the hoses connected, place the pump/bracket assembly aside in a position to prevent the fluid from leaking out.

b. If equipped with air conditioning, remove the mounting brackets' attaching bolts, leaving the hoses connected, and position the compressor aside.

6. If the right cylinder head is being removed:

a. Disconnect the Thermactor® diverter valve and hose assembly at the by-pass valve and downstream air tube.

b. Remove the assembly.

c. Remove the accessory drive idler.

d. Remove the alternator.

e. Remove the Thermactor® pump pulley. Remove the Thermactor® pump.

f. Remove the alternator bracket.

g. Remove the PCV valve.

7. Remove the intake manifold.

8. Remove the valve rocker arm cover attaching screws. Loosen the silicone rubber gasketing material by inserting a putty knife under the cover flange. Work the cover loosen and remove. The plastic rocker arm covers will break if excessive prying is applied.

9. Remove the exhaust manifold(s).

10. Loosen the rocker arm fulcrum attaching bolts enough to allow the rocker arm to be lifted off the pushrod and rotated to one side.

11. Remove the pushrods. Label the pushrods since they should be installed in the original position during assembly.

12. Remove the cylinder head attaching bolts. Remove the cylinder head(s).

13. Remove and discard the old cylinder head gasket(s). Discard the cylinder head bolts.

14. Lightly oil all bolt and stud bolt threads before installation except those specifying special sealant.

15. Clean the cylinder head, intake manifold, valve rocker arm cover and cylinder head gasket surfaces. If the cylinder head was removed for a cylinder head gasket replacement, check the flatness of the cylinder head and block gasket surfaces.

16. Position new head gasket(s) on the cylinder block using the dowels for alignment.

17. Position the cylinder heads to the block.

18. Apply a thin coating of pipe sealant or equivalent to the threads of the short cylinder head bolts (nearest to the exhaust manifold). Do not apply sealant to the long bolts. Lightly oil the cylinder head bolt flat washers. Install the flat washers and cylinder head bolts (Eight each side).

CAUTION

Always use new cylinder head bolts to assure a leak tight assembly. Torque retention with used bolts can vary, which may result in coolant or compression leakage at the cylinder head mating surface area.

19. Tighten the attaching bolts in sequence. Back off the attaching bolts 2-3 turns. Repeat tightening sequence.

NOTE: When the cylinder head attaching bolts have been tightened using the above sequential procedure, it is not necessary to retighten the bolts after extended engine operation. However, the bolts can be checked for tightness if desired.

20. Dip each pushrod end in heavy engine oil. Install the push rods in their original position. For each valve rotate the crankshaft until the tappet rests on the heel (base circle) of the camshaft lobe.

21. Position the rocker arms over the pushrods, install the fulcrums, and tighten the fulcrum attaching bolts to 61-132 in.lb.

WARNING: Fulcrums must be fully seated in cylinder head and pushrods must be seated in rocker arm sockets prior to final tightening.

22. Lubricate all rocker arm assemblies with heavy engine oil. Finally tighten the fulcrum bolts to 19-25 ft.lb. For final tightening, the camshaft may be in any position.

NOTE: If the original valve train components are being installed, a valve clearance check is not required. If a component has been replaced, perform a valve clearance check.

23. Install the exhaust manifold(s).

24. Apply a $\frac{1}{8}$-$\frac{3}{16}$" (3-4mm) bead of RTV silicone sealant to the rocker arm cover flange. make sure the sealer fills the channel in the cover flange. The rocker arm cover must be installed within 15 minutes after the silicone sealer application. After this time, the sealer may start to set-up, and its sealing effectiveness may be reduced.

25. Position the cover on the cylinder head and install the attaching bolts. Note the location of the wiring harness routing clips and spark plug wire routing clip stud bolts. Tighten the attaching bolts to 36-60 in.lb. torque.

26. Install the intake manifold.

27. Install the spark plugs, if necessary.

28. Connect the secondary wires to the spark plugs.

29. Install the oil fill cap. If equipped with air conditioning, install the compressor mounting and support brackets.

30. On the right cylinder head:

a. Install the PCV valve.

b. Install the alternator bracket. Tighten attaching nuts to 30-40 ft.lb.

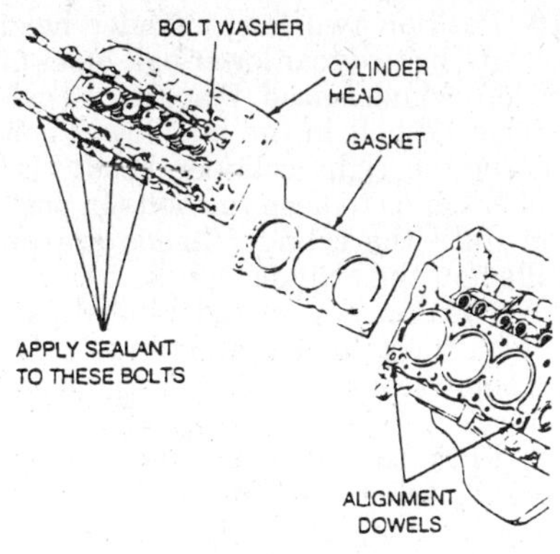

232 V6 cylinder head installation

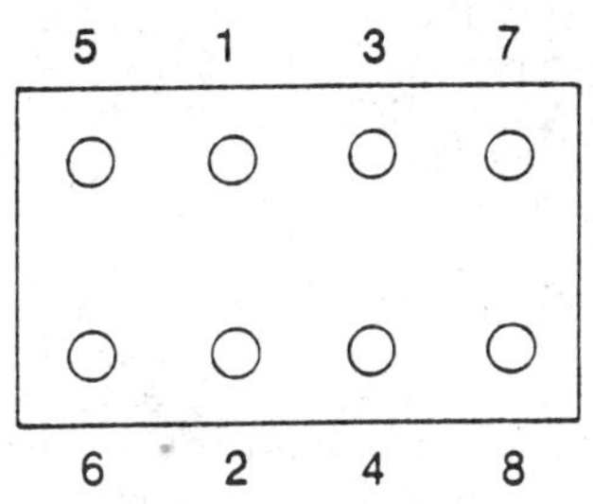

232 V6 cylinder head torque sequence

c. Install the Thermactor® pump and pump pulley.

d. Install the alternator.

e. Install the accessory drive idler.

f. Install the Thermactor® diverter valve and hose assembly. Tighten the clamps securely.

31. Install the accessory drive belt and tighten to the specified tension.

32. Connect the cable to the battery negative terminal.

33. Fill the cooling system with the specified coolant.

WARNING: This engine has an aluminum cylinder head and requires a compatible coolant formulation to avoid radiator damage.

34. Start the engine and check for coolant, fuel, and oil leaks.

35. Check and, if necessary, adjust the curb idle speed.

36. Install the air cleaner assembly including the air intake duct and heat tube.

6-300 (4.9L)

1. Drain the cooling system. Remove the air cleaner. Remove the oil filler tube. Disconnect the negative battery cable.

CAUTION

When draining the coolant, keep in mind that cats and dogs are attracted by the ethylene glycol antifreeze, and are quite likely to drink any that is left in an uncovered container or in puddles on the ground. This will prove fatal in sufficient quantity. Always drain the coolant into a sealable container. Coolant should be reused unless it is contaminated or several years old.

2. Disconnect the muffler inlet pipe at the exhaust manifold. Pull the muffler inlet pipe down. Remove the gasket.

3. Disconnect the accelerator rod or cable retracting spring. Disconnect the choke control cable if applicable and the accelerator rod at the carburetor.

4. Disconnect the transmission kickdown rod. Disconnect the accelerator linkage at the bellcrank assembly.

5. Disconnect the fuel inlet line at the fuel filter hose, and the distributor vacuum line at the carburetor. Disconnect other vacuum lines as necessary for accessibility and identify them for proper connection.

6. Remove the radiator upper hose at the coolant outlet housing.

7. Disconnect the distributor vacuum line at the distributor. Disconnect the carburetor fuel inlet line at the fuel pump. Remove the lines as an assembly.

8. Disconnect the spark plug wires at the spark plugs and the temperature sending unit wire at the sending unit.

9. Grasp the PCV vent hose near the PCV valve and pull the valve out of the grommet in the valve rocker arm cover. Disconnect the PCV vent hose at the hose fitting in the intake manifold spacer and remove the vent hose and PCV valve.

10. Disconnect the carburetor air vent tube and remove the valve rocker arm cover.

11. Remove the valve rocker arm shaft assembly. Remove the pushrods in sequence so that they can be identified and reinstalled in their original positions.

12. Remove the cylinder head bolts and remove the cylinder head. Do not pry between the cylinder head and the block as the gasket surfaces may be damaged.

13. To install the cylinder head: Clean the head and block gasket surfaces. If the cylinder head was removed for a gasket change, check the flatness of the cylinder head and block.

14. Apply sealer to both sides of the new cylinder head gasket, depending on maker of gasket, refer to gasket manufacturers instructions. Position the gasket on the cylinder block.

15. Install a new gasket on the flange of the muffler inlet pipe.

16. Lift the cylinder head above the cylinder block and lower it into position using two head bolts installed through the head as guides.

17. Coat the threads of the No. 1 and 6 bolts for the right-side of the cylinder head with a small amount of water-resistant sealer. Oil the threads of the remaining bolts. Install, but do not tighten, two bolts at the opposite ends of the head to hold the head and gasket in position.

18. The cylinder head bolts are tightened in 3 progressive steps. Torque them (in the proper sequence) to 55 ft.lb., then 65 ft.lb., and finally to 75 ft.lb.

19. Apply Lubriplate® to both ends of the pushrods and install them in their original positions.

20. Install the valve rocker arm shaft assembly.

21. Adjust the valves, as necessary.

22. Install the muffler inlet pipe lockwashers and attaching nuts.

23. Connect the radiator upper hose at the coolant outlet housing.

24. Position the distributor vacuum line and the carburetor fuel inlet line on the engine. Connect the fuel line at the fuel filter hose and install a new clamp. Install the distributor vacuum line at the carburetor. Connect the accelerator linkage at the bellcrank assembly. Connect the transmission kickdown rod.

25. Connect the accelerator rod retracting spring. Connect the choke control cable (if applicable) and the accelerator rod at the carburetor.

26. Connect the distributor vacuum line at the distributor. Connect the carburetor fuel inlet line at the fuel pump. Connect all the vacuum lines using their previous identification for proper connection.

27. Connect the temperature sending unit wire at the sending unit. Connect the spark plug wires. Connect the battery cable at the cylinder head.

28. Fill the cooling system.

29. Install the valve rocker cover. Connect the carburetor air vent tube.

30. Connect the PCV vent hose at the carburetor spacer fitting. Insert the PCV valve with the vent hose attached, into the valve rocker arm cover grommet. Install the air cleaner, start the engine and check for leaks.

V8 Except 8-420 (6.9L) Diesel & 8-460 (7.5L)

1. Remove the intake manifolds and the carburetor as an assembly.

2. Remove the rocker arm cover(s).

3. If the right cylinder head is to be removed, loosen the alternator adjusting arm bolt and remove the alternator mounting bracket bolt and spacer. Swing the alternator down and out of the way. Remove the air cleaner inlet

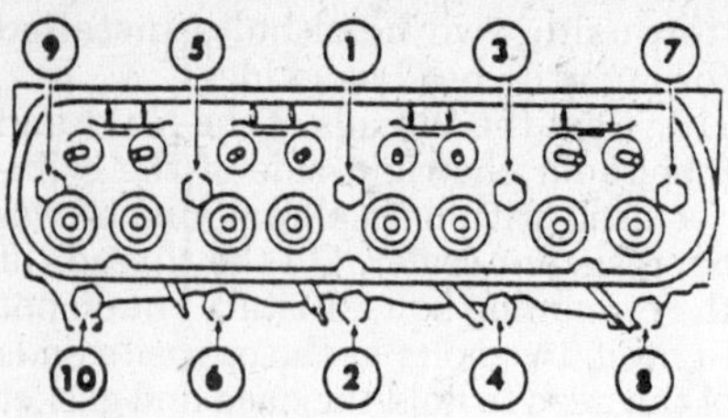

Cylinder head bolt torque sequence, all gasoline V8s

duct from the right cylinder head assembly. On 351 remove the ground strap at the rear of the head. If the left cylinder head is being removed, remove the bolts fastening the accelerator shaft assembly at the front of the cylinder head. On vehicles equipped with air conditioning, the system must be discharged and the compressor removed. The procedure is best left to an air conditioning specialist. Persons not familiar with A/C systems can be easily injured when working on the systems.

4. Disconnect the exhaust manifold(s) from the muffler inlet pipe(s).

5. Loosen the rocker arm stud nuts so that the rocker arms can be rotated to the side. Remove the pushrods and identify them so that they can be reinstalled in their original positions.

6. Remove the cylinder head bolts and lift the cylinder head from the block.

7. Clean the cylinder head, intake manifold, and the valve cover and head gasket surfaces.

8. A specially treated composition head gasket is used. Do not apply sealer to a composition gasket. Position the new gasket over the locating dowels on the cylinder block. Then, position the cylinder head on the block and install the attaching bolts.

9. The cylinder head bolts are tightened in 3 progressive steps. Tighten all the bolts in the proper sequence to 50 ft.lb., 60 ft.lb., and finally to 70 fft.lb. of torque on the 255, 302 and 351W. On 351M V8s, tighten to 70, 80 then 95-105 ft.lb.

10. Clean the pushrods. Blow out the oil passage in the rods with compressed air. Check the pushrods for straightness. Never try to straighten a pushrod; always replace it.

11. Apply Lubriplate® to the ends of the pushrods and install them in their original positions.

12. Apply Lubriplate® to the rocker arms and their fulcrum seats and install the rocker arms. Adjust the valves.

13. Position a new gasket(s) on the muffler inlet pipe(s) as necessary. Connect the exhaust manifold(s) at the muffler inlet pipe(s).

14. If the right cylinder head was removed, install the alternator, ignition coil and air cleaner duct on the right cylinder head. Adjust the drive belt. If the left cylinder head was removed, install the accelerator shaft assembly at the front of the cylinder head.

15. Clean the valve rocker arm cover and the cylinder head gasket surfaces. Place the new gaskets in the covers, making sure that the tabs of the gasket engage the notches provided in the cover. Install the compressor. If the system has be bled, recharging can be done after cylinder head operations are completed.

16. Install the intake manifold and all remaining parts.

8-460 (7.5L) V8

1. Disconnect the negative battery cable. Remove the intake manifold and carburetor as an assembly.

2. Disconnect the exhaust pipe from the exhaust manifold.

3. Loosen the air conditioning compressor drive belt, if so equipped.

4. Loosen the alternator attaching bolts and remove the bolt attaching the alternator bracket to the right cylinder head.

5. Disconnect the air conditioning compressor from the engine and move it aside, out of the way.

CAUTION

Do not disconnect the compressor lines unless the proper tools are on hand to discharge the system and you are familiar with the procedure.

6. Remove the bolts securing the power steering reservoir bracket to the left cylinder head. Position the reservoir and bracket out of the way.

7. Remove the valve rocker arm covers. Remove the rocker arm bolts, rocker arms, oil deflectors, fulcrums and pushrods in sequence so that they can be reinstalled in their original positions.

8. Remove the cylinder head bolts and lift the head and exhaust manifold off the engine. If necessary, pry at the forward corners of the cylinder head against the casting bosses provided on the cylinder block. Do not damage the gasket mating surfaces of the cylinder head and block by prying against them.

9. Remove all gasket material from the cylinder head and block. Clean all gasket material from the mating surfaces of the intake manifold. If the exhaust manifold was removed, clean the mating surfaces of the cylinder head and exhaust manifold. Apply a thin coat of graphite grease to the cylinder head exhaust port areas and install the exhaust manifold.

10. Position two long cylinder head bolts in the two rear lower bolt holes of the left cylinder head. Place a long cylinder head bolt in the rear lower bolt hole of the right cylinder head. Use rubber bands to keep the bolts in position until the cylinder heads are installed on the cylinder block.

11. Position new cylinder head gaskets on the cylinder block dowels. Do not apply sealer to the gaskets, heads, or block.

12. Place the cylinder heads on the block, guiding the exhaust manifold studs into the exhaust pipe connections. Install the remaining cylinder head bolts. The longer bolts go in the lower row of holes.

13. Tighten all the cylinder head attaching bolts in the proper sequence in three stages: 75 ft.lb., 105 ft.lb., and finally, to 135 ft.lb. When this procedure is used, it is not necessary to retorque the heads after extended use.

14. Make sure that the oil holes in the pushrods are open and install the pushrods in their original positions. Place a dab of Lubriplate® to the ends of the pushrods before installing them.

15. Lubricate and install the valve rockers. Make sure that the pushrods remain seated in their lifters.

16. Connect the exhaust pipes to the exhaust manifolds.

17. Install the intake manifold and carburetor assembly. Tighten the intake manifold attaching bolts in the proper sequence to 25-30 ft.lb.

18. Install the air conditioning compressor to the engine.

19. Install the power steering reservoir to the engine.

20. Apply oil-resistant sealer to one side of the new valve cover gaskets and lay the cemented side in place in the valve covers. Install the covers.

21. Install the alternator on the right cylinder head and adjust the alternator drive belt tension.

22. Adjust the air conditioning compressor drive belt tension.

23. Fill the radiator with coolant.

24. Start the engine and check for leaks.

8-420 (6.9L) V8 Diesel

1. Disconnect the ground cables from both batteries. Drain the cooling system.

CAUTION

When draining the coolant, keep in mind that cats and dogs are attracted by the ethylene glycol antifreeze, and are quite likely to drink any that is left in an uncovered container or in puddles on the ground. This will prove fatal in sufficient quantity. Always drain the coolant into a sealable container. Coolant should be reused unless it is contaminated or several years old.

2. Remove the radiator shroud halves. Remove the fan and clutch assembly using Ford special tool T83T6312A and B or the equivalent. The attaching nut is equipped with a left hand thread, remove by turning clockwise.

3. Disconnect the alternator and fuel heater wiring harness from the alternator. Remove the alternator. Remove the vacuum pump.

4. Remove the fuel filter, cap all lines and fittings to prevent dirt from entering the system. Remove the alternator, vacuum pump and fuel filter mounting brackets, leave the fuel filter attached.

5. Remove the heater hose from the cylinder head. Remove the injector pump, cap all lines and fittings.

6. Remove the intake manifold and valley cover.

7. Raise and safely support the front of the vehicle with jackstands.

8. Disconnect the exhaust pipes from the exhaust manifolds.

9. Remove the clamp holding the engine oil dipstick tube in position on the right side cylinder head. Remove the bolt securing the transmission fluid dipstick tube to the rear of the cylinder head.

10. Lower the vehicle. Remove the engine oil dipstick and tube from the right side.

11. Remove the valve covers, rocker arms and pushrods. Identify all parts and keep in order for installation in the original positions.

12. Remove the injector nozzles and glow plugs.

13. Remove the cylinder head attaching bolts. Remove the cylinder heads from the engine.

CAUTION

The prechambers may fall out of the cylinder head on removal. Prevent damage to the prechambers.

14. Prechambers can be removed using a brass drift and suitable hammer.

15. Clean all gasket mounting surfaces. Clean and inspect the prechambers and ports for cracks. Apply a light coating of extra heavy duty grease to the mounting edge of the prechambers and install the prechambers in the cylinder head. Lightly tap with a plastic headed hammer if necessary.

16. Install the cylinder head in the reverse order of removal. Use care to prevent the prechambers from falling into the cylinder bores when installing the heads. Torque the mounting bolts in sequence. Step 1; 40 ft. lbs: Step 2; 65 ft. lbs: Step 3; 75 ft. lbs: Step 4; Repeat Step 3.

17. If necessary, purge the high pressure fuel lines of air by loosening the

INTAKE INSIDE

LINE SEQUENCE START HERE (STEPS 3 AND 4)

15 11 7 3 2 6 10 14

16 8 1 9 17

12 4 5 13

EXHAUST SIDE

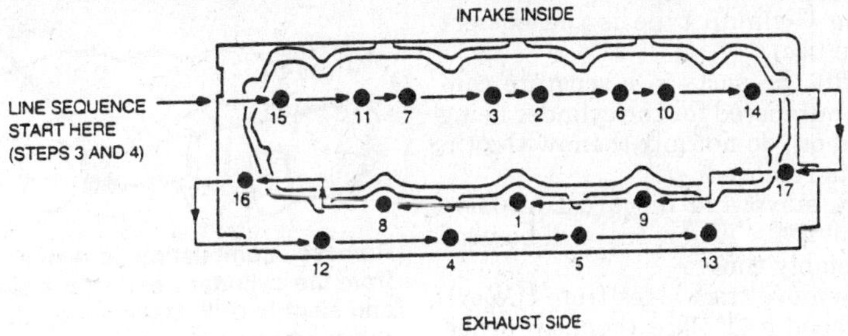

CYLINDER HEAD BOLTS

STEP 1. TORQUE BOLTS TO 40 FT. LBS. IN NUMBERED SEQUENCE SHOWN ABOVE.

STEP 2. TORQUE BOLTS TO 65 FT. LBS. IN NUMBERED SEQUENCE SHOWN ABOVE.

STEP 3. TORQUE BOLTS TO 75 FT. LBS. IN LINE SEQUENCE SHOWN ABOVE.

STEP 4. REPEAT STEP 3.

420 V8 Diesel—cylinder head bold tightening sequence

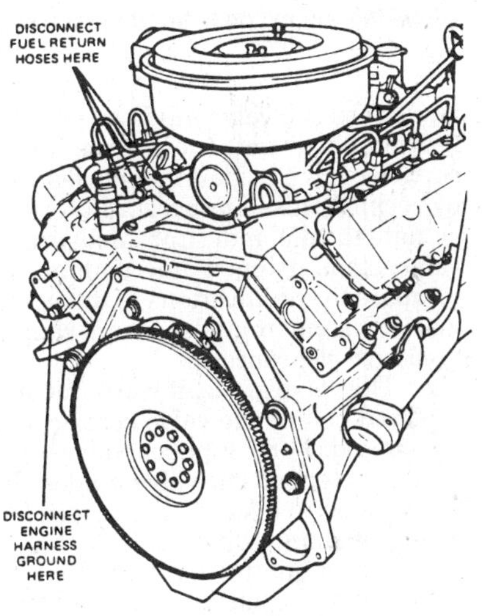

6.9L V8 Diesel fuel hose and engine ground harness connections

connector one half to one turn. Crank the engine until a solid flow of air free fuel comes out.

CYLINDER HEAD OVERHAUL

1. Remove the cylinder head(s) from the car engine (see Cylinder Head Removal and Installation). Place the head(s) on a workbench and remove any manifolds that are still connected. Remove all rocker arm retaining parts and the rocker arms, if still installed.

2. Turn the cylinder head over so that the mounting surface is facing up and support it evenly on wood blocks.

WARNING: 6-232 engines use aluminum cylinder heads; exercise care when cleaning.

3. Use a scraper and remove all of the gasket material stuck to the head mounting surface. Mount a wire carbon removal brush in an electric drill and clean away the carbon on the valves and head combustion chambers.

WARNING: When scraping or decarbonizing the cylinder head, take care not to damage or nick the gasket mounting surface!

4. Number the valve heads with a permanent felt-tip marker for cylinder location.

Resurfacing

If the cylinder head is warped resurfacing by a machine shop is required. Place a straightedge across the gasket surface of the head. Using feeler gauges, determine the clearance at the center and along the length between the head and straightedge. Measure clearance at the center and along the length between the head and straightedge. Measure clearance at the center and along the lengths of both diagonals. If warpage exceeds 0.003″ (0.08mm) in a 6″ (152mm) span, or 0.006″ (0.15mm) over the total length the cylinder head must be resurfaced.

Valves and Springs

REMOVAL & INSTALLATION

1. Block the head on its side, or install a pair of head-holding brackets made especially for valve removal.

2. Use a socket slightly larger than the valve stem and keepers, place the socket over the valve stem and gently hit the socket with a plastic hammer to break loose any varnish buildup.

3. Remove the valve keepers, retainer, spring shield and valve spring using a valve spring compressor (the

locking C-clamp type is the easiest kind to use).

4. Put the parts in a separate container numbered for the cylinder being worked on; do not mix them with other parts removed.

5. Remove and discard the valve stem oil seals. A new seal will be used at assembly time.

6. Remove the valves from the cylinder head and place them, in order, through numbered holes punched in a stiff piece of cardboard or wood valve holding stick.

NOTE: The exhaust valve stems, on some engines, are equipped with small metal caps. Take care not to lose the caps. Make sure to reinstall them at assembly time. Replace any caps that are worn.

7. Use an electric drill and rotary wire brush to clean the intake and exhaust valve ports, combustion chamber and valve seats. In some cases, the carbon will need to be chipped away. Use a blunt pointed drift for carbon chipping. Be careful around the valve seat areas.

8. Use a wire valve guide cleaning brush and safe solvent to clean the valve guides.

9. Clean the valves with a revolving wires brush. Heavy carbon deposits may be removed with the blunt drift.

NOTE: When using a wire brush to clean carbon on the valve ports, valves etc., be sure that the deposits are actually removed, rather than burnished.

10. Wash and clean all valve springs, keepers, retaining caps etc., in safe solvent.

11. Clean the head with a brush and some safe solvent and wipe dry.

12. Check the head for cracks. Cracks in the cylinder head usually start around an exhaust valve seat because it is the hottest part of the combustion chamber. If a crack is suspected but cannot be detected visually have the area checked with dye penetrant or other method by the machine shop.

13. After all cylinder head parts are reasonably clean, check the valve stem-to-guide clearance. If a dial indicator is not on hand, a visual inspection can give you a fairly good idea if the guide, valve stem or both are worn.

14. Insert the valve into the guide until slight away from the valve seat. Wiggle the valve sideways. A small amount of wobble is normal, excessive wobble means a worn guide or valve stem. If a dial indicator is on hand, mount the indicator so that the stem of the valve is at 90° to the valve stem,

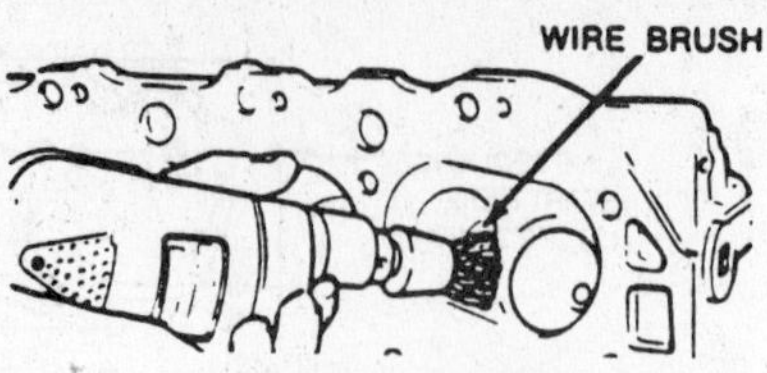

Remove combustion chamber carbon from the cylinder head with a wire brush and electric drill. Make sure all carbon is removed and not just burnished

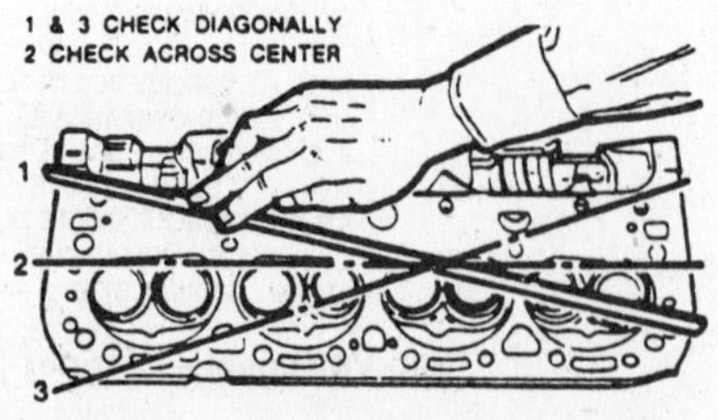

Checking the cylinder head for warpage

as close to the valve guide as possible. Move the valve off the seat, and measure the valve guide-to-stem clearance by rocking the stem back and forth to actuate the dial indicator. Measure the valve stem using a micrometer and compare to specifications to determine whether stem or guide wear is causing excessive clearance.

15. The valve guide, if worn, must be repaired before the valve seats can be resurfaced. Ford supplies valves with oversize stems to fit valve guides that are reamed to oversize for repair. The machine shop will be able to handle the guide reaming for you. In some cases, if the guide is not too badly worn, knurling may be all that is required.

16. Reface, or have the valves and valve seats refaced. The valve seats should be a true 45° angle. Remove only enough material to clean up any pits or grooves. Be sure the valve seat is not too wide or narrow. Use a 60° grinding wheel to remove material from the bottom of the seat for raising and a 30° grinding wheel to remove material from the top of the seat to narrow.

17. After the valves are refaced by machine, hand lap them to the valve seat. Clean the grinding compound off and check the position of face-to-seat contact. Contact should be close to the center of the valve face. If contact is close to the top edge of the valve, narrow the seat; if too close to the bottom edge, raise the seat.

18. Valves should be refaced to a true angle of 44°. Remove only enough metal to clean up the valve face or to correct runout. If the edge of a valve head, after machining, is $\frac{1}{32}$" (0.8mm) or less replace the valve. The tip of the valve stem should also be dressed on the valve grinding machine, however, do not remove more than 0.010" (0.254mm).

19. After all valve and valve seats have been machined, check the remaining valve train parts (springs, retainers, keepers, etc.) for wear. Check the valve springs for straightness and tension.

20. Install the valves in the cylinder head and metal caps.

21. Install new valve stem oil seals.

22. Install the valve keepers, retainer, spring shield and valve spring using a valve spring compressor (the locking C-clamp type is the easiest kind to use).

23. Check the valve spring installed height, shim or replace as necessary.

CHECKING VALVE SPRINGS

Place the valve spring on a flat surface next to a carpenter's square. Measure the height of the spring, and rotate the spring against the edge of the square to measure distortion. If the spring height varies (by comparison) by more than $\frac{1}{16}$" (1.6mm) or if the distortion exceeds $\frac{1}{16}$" (1.6mm), replace the spring.

Have the valve springs tested for spring pressure at the installed and compressed (installed height minus valve lift) height using a valve spring tester. Springs should be within one pound, plus or minus each other. Replace springs as necessary.

VALVE SPRING INSTALLED HEIGHT

After installing the valve spring, measure the distance between the spring mounting pad and the lower edge of the spring retainer. Compare the measurement to specifications. If the installed height is incorrect, add shim washers between the spring mounting pad and the spring. Use only washers designed for valve springs, available at most parts houses.

VALVE STEM OIL SEALS

The 6-232 uses a positive valve stem seal using a Teflon® insert. Teflon® seals are available for other engines but usually require valve guide machining. Consult your automotive machine shop for advice on having positive valve stem oil seals installed.

When installing valve stem oil seals, ensure that a small amount of oil is able to pass the seal to lubricate the valve stems and guide walls, otherwise, excessive wear will occur.

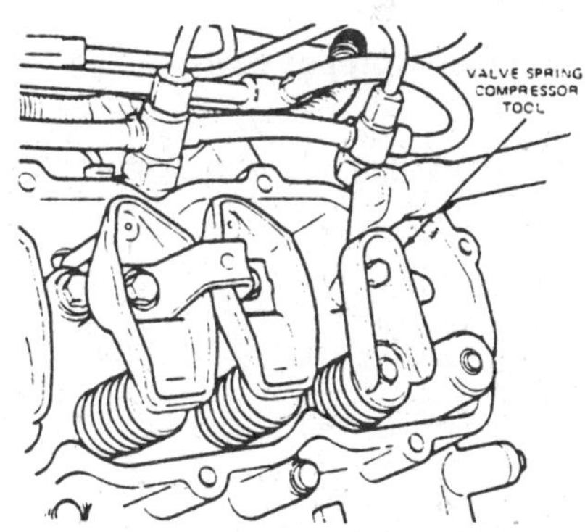

Compressing gasoline engine valve spring. Note spring compressor position

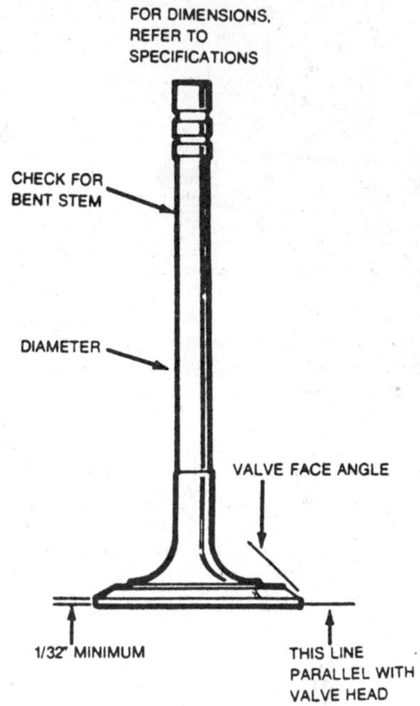

Critical valve dimensions

Have the valve spring test pressure checked at a machine shop. Make sure the readings are within specifications

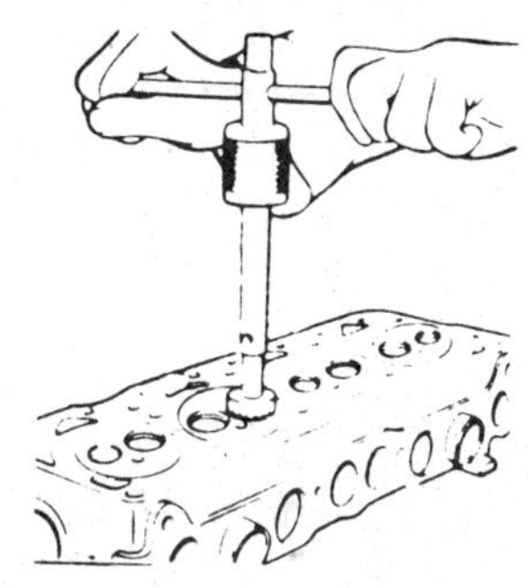
Reaming valve seat with a hand reamer

Compressing valve spring on the 6.9L diesel using special tool

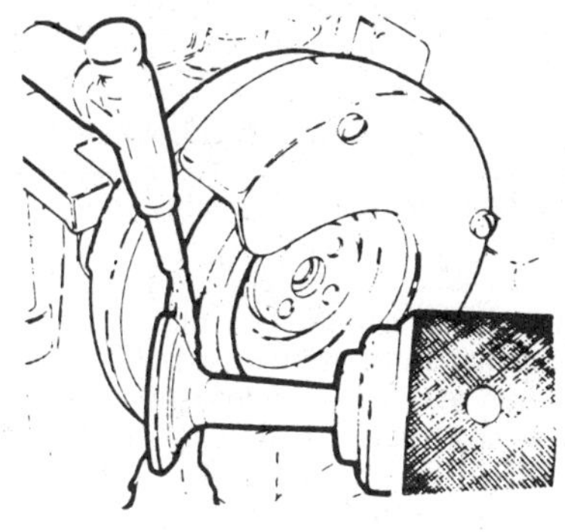
A well-equipped machine shop can handle valve refacing jobs

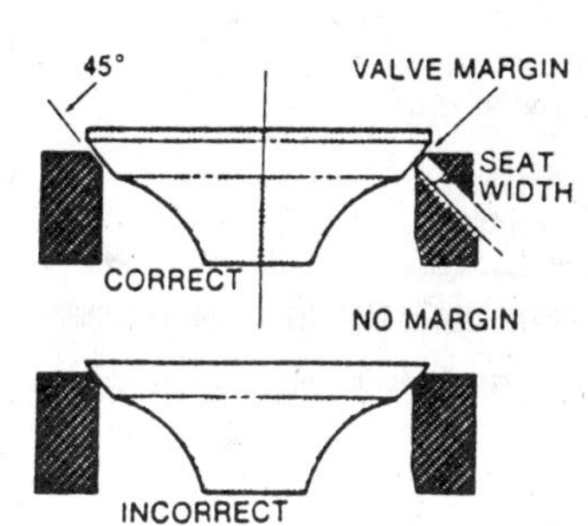

Valve seat width and centering after proper reaming

VALVE SEATS

If the valve seat is damaged or burnt and cannot be serviced by refacing, it may be possible to have the seat machined and an insert installed. Consult an automotive machine shop for their advice.

NOTE: The aluminum heads on 6-232 engines are equipped with inserts.

VALVE GUIDES

Worn valve guides can, in most cases, be reamed to accept a valve with an oversized stem. Valve guides that are not excessively worn or distorted may, in some cases, be knurled rather than reamed. However, if the valve stem is worn reaming for an oversized valve stem is the answer since a new valve would be required.

Knurling is a process in which metal is displaced and raised, thereby reducing clearance. Knurling also produces excellent oil control. The possibility of knurling instead of reaming the valve guides should be discussed with a machinist.

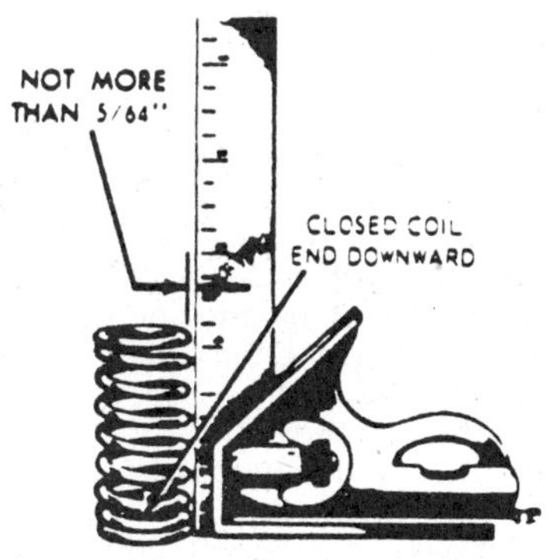

Check the valve spring free length and squareness

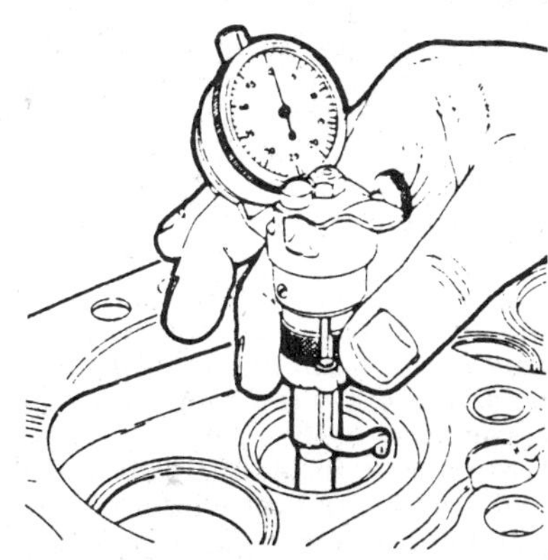
Checking valve seat concentricity with a dial gauge

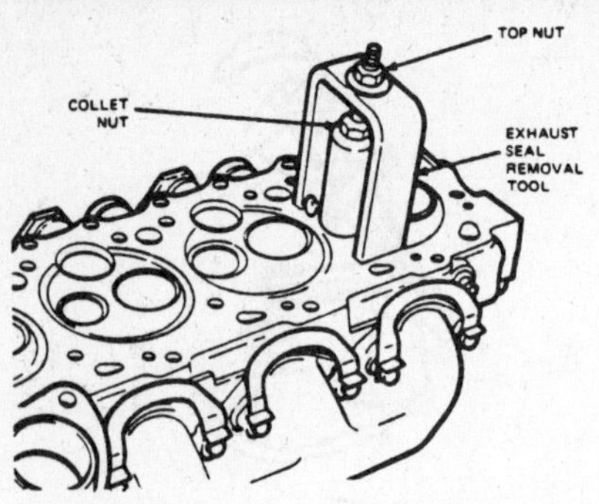

6.9L exhaust valve seat insert removal using special tool

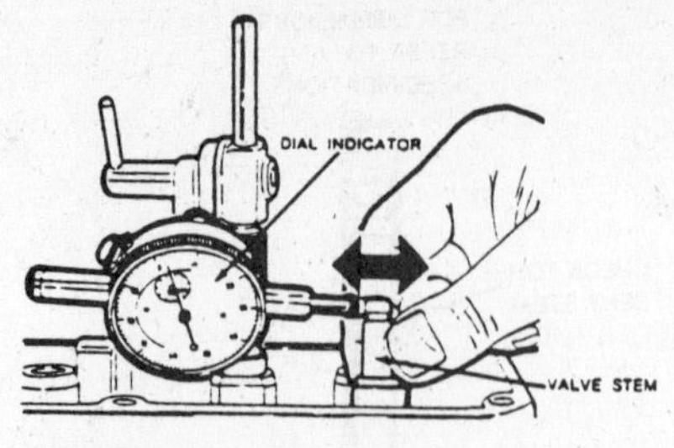

Measuring valve stem-to-guide clearance. Make sure the indicator is mounted at 90° to the valve stem and as close to the guide as possible

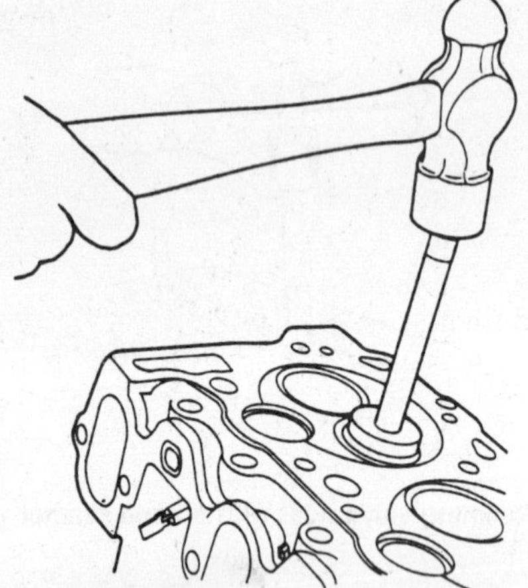
Installing diesel exhaust valve seats using special tool

Lapping the valves by hand. When done, the finish on both valve faces and seats should be smooth and evenly shiny

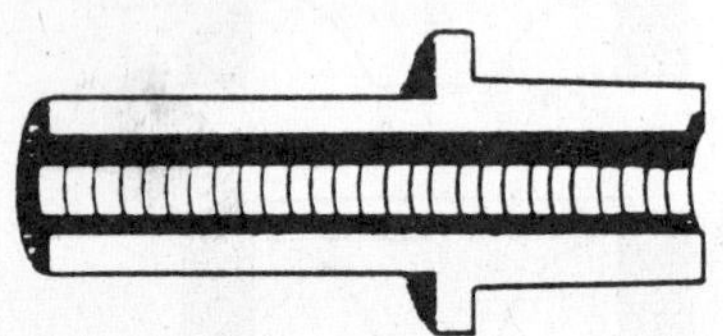
Cross-section of a knurled valve guide

HYDRAULIC VALVE CLEARANCE

Hydraulic valve lifters operate with zero clearance in the valve train, and because of this the rocker arms are nonadjustable. The only means by which valve system clearances can be altered is by installing over or undersize pushrods; but, because of the hydraulic lifter's natural ability to compensate for slack in the valve train, all components of all the valve system should be checked for wear if there is excessive play in the system.

When a valve in the engine is in the closed position, the valve lifter is resting on the base circle of the camshaft lobe and the pushrod is in its lowest position. To remove this additional clearance from the valve train, the valve lifter expands to maintain zero clearance in the valve system. When a rocker arm is loosened or removed from the engine, the lifter expands to it fullest travel. When the rocker arm is reinstalled on the engine, the proper valve setting is obtained by tightening the rocker arm to a specified limit. But with the lifter fully expanded, if the camshaft lobe is on a high point it will require excessive torque to compress the lifter and obtain the proper setting. Because of this, when any component of the valve system has been removed, a preliminary valve adjustment procedure must be followed to ensure that when the rocker arm is reinstalled on the engine and tightened, the camshaft lobe for that cylinder is in the low position.

To determine whether a shorter or loner push rod is necessary, make the following check:

Mark the crankshaft pulley as described under Preliminary Valve Adjustment procedure. Follow each step in the procedure. As each valve is positioned, mount a suitable hydraulic lifter compressor tool on the rocker arm. Slowly apply pressure to bleed down the lifter until the plunger is completely bottomed. Take care to avoid excessive pressure that might bend the pushrod. Hold the lifter in bottom position and check the available clearance between the rocker arm and the valve stem tip with a feeler gauge. If the clearance is less than specified, install an undersized pushrod. If the clearance is greater than specified, install an oversized pushrod. When compressing the valve spring to remove the pushrods, be sure the piston in the individual cylinder is below TDC to avoid contact between the valve and the piston. To replace a pushrod, it will be necessary to remove the valve rocker arm shaft assembly on in-line engines. Upon replacement of a valve pushrod, valve rocker arm shaft assembly or hydraulic valve lifter, the engine should not be cranked or rotated until the hydraulic lifters have had an opportunity to leak down to their normal operation position. The leak down rate can be accelerated by using the tool shown on the valve rocker arm and applying pressure in a direction to collapse the lifter.

Collapsed tappet gap

6-232

- Allowable: 0.088-0.189" (2.235-4.800mm)

V8 Engines

- 8-255 cu in.
  Allowable: 0.098-0.198" (2.489-5.029mm)
  Desired: 0.123-0.173" (3.124-4.394mm)
- 8-302 and 8-351
  Allowable: 0.089-0.193" (2.260-4.902mm)
  Desired: 0.096-0.163" (2.438-4.140mm)

Crankshaft Pulley (Vibration Damper)

REMOVAL & INSTALLATION

1. Remove the fan shroud, as required. If necessary, drain the cooling system and remove the radiator. Remove drive belts from pulley.

CAUTION

When draining the coolant, keep in mind that cats and dogs are attracted by the ethylene glycol antifreeze, and are quite likely to drink any that is left in an uncovered container or in puddles on the ground. This will prove fatal in sufficient quantity. Always drain the coolant into a sealable container. Coolant should be reused unless it is contaminated or several years old.

2. On those engines with a separate pulley, remove the retaining bolts and separate the pulley from the vibration damper.

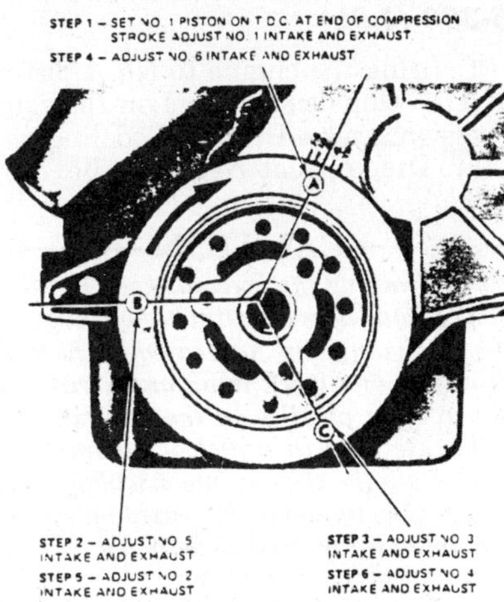

300 inline six crankshaft positioning for valve clearance adjustment

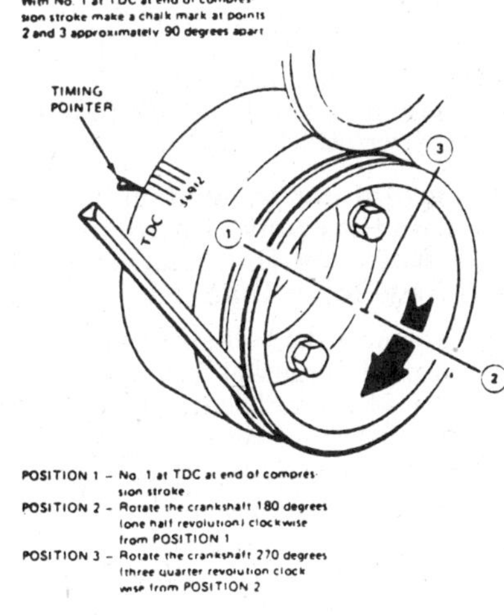

Crankshaft positions for positive stop-type valve adjustment

3. Remove the vibration damper/pulley retaining bolt from the crankshaft end.

4. Using a puller, remove the damper/pulley from the crankshaft.

5. Upon installation, align the key slot of the pulley hub to the crankshaft key. Complete the assembly in the reverse order of removal. Torque the retaining bolts to specifications.

Timing Cover and Chain or Gears

REMOVAL & INSTALLATION

6-232

1. Disconnect the negative battery cable from the battery. Drain the cooling system.

CAUTION

When draining the coolant, keep in mind that cats and dogs are attracted by the ethylene glycol antifreeze, and are quite likely to drink any that is left in an uncovered container or in puddles on the ground. This will prove fatal in sufficient quantity. Always drain the coolant into a sealable container. Coolant should be reused unless it is contaminated or several years old.

2. Remove the air cleaner and air duct assemblies.

3. Remove the radiator fan shroud and position it back over the water pump. Remove the fan clutch assembly and shroud.

4. Remove all drive belts. If equipped with power steering, remove the pump with the hoses attached and position it out of the way. Be sure to keep the pump upright to prevent fluid leakage.

5. If your car is equipped with air conditioning, remove the front compressor mounting bracket. It is not necessary to remove the compressor.

6. Disconnect the coolant by-pass hose and the heater hose at the water pump.

7. Disconnect the upper radiator hose at the thermostat housing. Remove the distributor.

8. If your car is equipped with a tripminder, remove the flow meter support bracket and allow the meter to be supported by the hoses.

9. Raise the front of the car and support on jackstands.

10. Remove the crankshaft pulley using a suitable puller. Remove the fuel pump shield.

11. Disconnect the fuel line from the carburetor at the fuel pump. Remove the mounting bolts and the fuel pump. Position pump out of the way with tank line still attached.

12. Drain the engine oil and remove the oil filter.

13. Disconnect the lower radiator hose at the water pump.

14. Remove the oil pan mounting bolts and lower the oil pan.

NOTE: The front cover cannot be removed unless the oil pan is lowered.

15. Lower the car from the jackstands.

16. Remove the front cover mounting bolts.

NOTE: Water pump removal is not necessary. A front cover mounting bolt is located behind the oil filter adapter. If the bolt is not removed and the cover is pried upon breakage will occur.

17. Remove the timing indicator. Re-

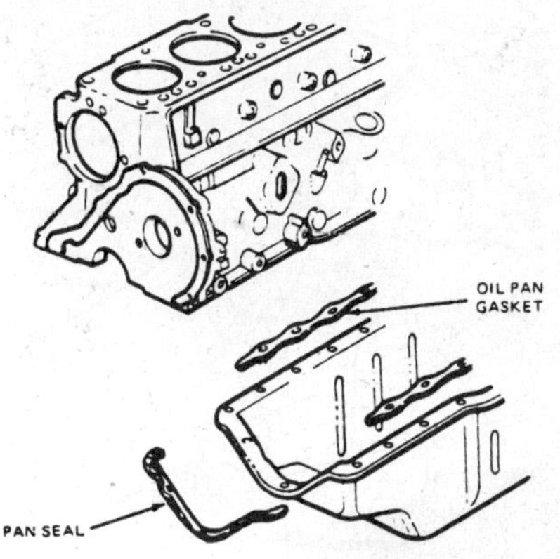

Front pan/cover seal, inline six cylinder engines

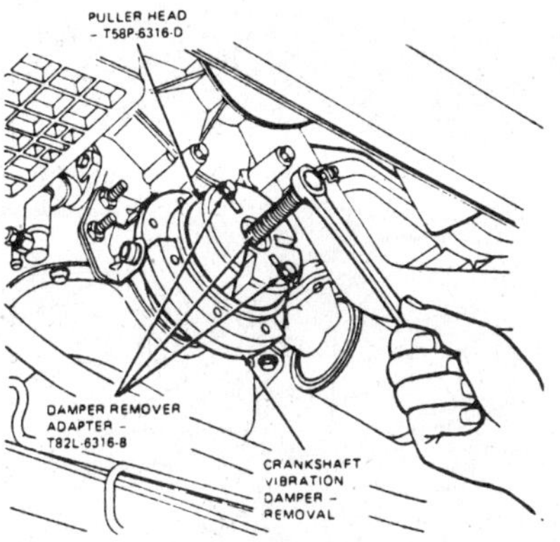

Access to the damper is often better from unmderneath. 232 V6 shown

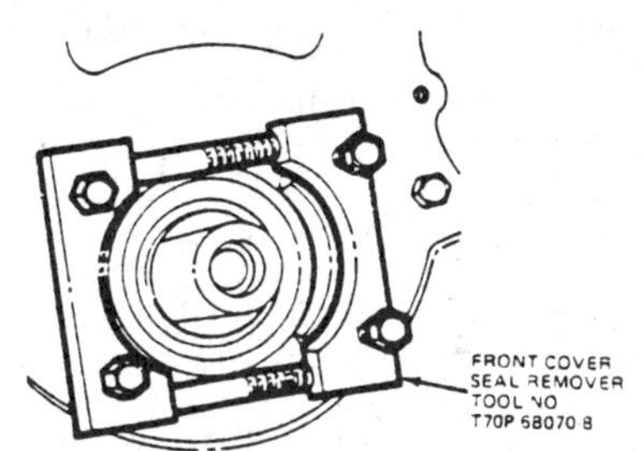

Vibration damper installation, 351M and 400 V8s

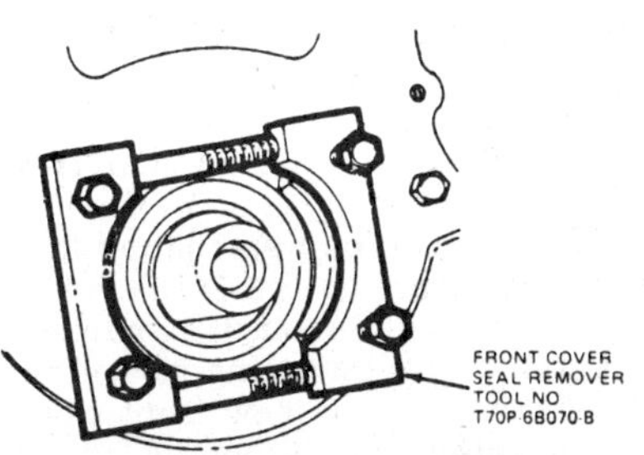

Removing the front crankshaft seal on 302 and 351W V8s

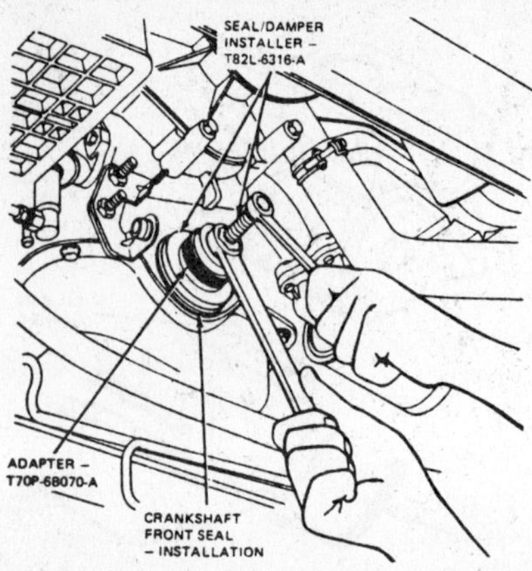

302, 351M and 400 V8 front crankshaft seal installation

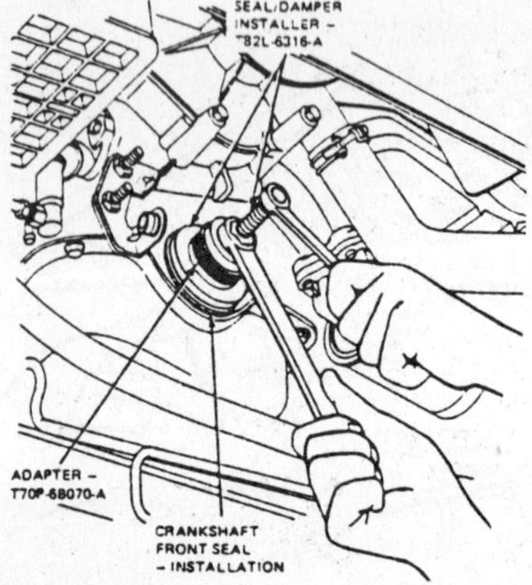

V6 front oil seal installation, shown from underneath truck

move the front cover and water pump assembly.

18. Remove the camshaft thrust button and spring from the end of the camshaft. Remove the camshaft sprocket attaching bolts.

19. Remove the camshaft sprocket, crankshaft sprocket and timing chain by pulling forward evenly on both sprockets. If the crankshaft sprocket is difficult to remove, position two small prybars, one on each side, behind the sprocket and pry forward.

20. Clean all gasket surfaces on the front cover, cylinder block, fuel pump and oil pan.

21. Install a new front cover oil seal. If a new front cover is to be installed:

a. Install the oil pump, oil filter adapter and intermediate shaft from the old cover.

b. Remove the water pump from the old cover.

c. Clean the mounting surface, install a new mounting gasket and the pump on the new front cover. Pump attaching bolt torque is 13-22 ft.lb.

22. Rotate the crankshaft, if necessary, to bring No. 1 piston to TDC with the crankshaft keyway at the 12 o'clock position.

23. Lubricate the timing chain with motor oil. Install the chain over the two gears making sure the marks on both gears are positioned across from each other. Install the gears and chain on the cam and crankshaft. Install the camshaft mounting bolts. Tighten the bolts to 15-22 ft.lb.

24. Install the camshaft thrust button and spring. Lubricate the thrust button with polyethylene grease before installation.

WARNING: The thrust button and spring must be bottomed in the camshaft seat and must not be allowed to fall out during front cover installation.

25. Position a new cover gasket on the front of the engine and install the cover and water pump assemblies. Install the timing indicator. Torque the front cover bolts to 15-22 ft.lb.

26. Install the oil pan.

27. Connect the lower radiator hose at the water pump.

28. Install the oil filter.

29. Fill the crankcase.

30. Install the fuel pump.

31. Connect the fuel line at the carburetor and at the fuel pump.

WARNING: When installing the fuel pump, turn the crankshaft 180° to position the fuel pump drive eccentric away from the fuel pump arm. Failure to turn the drive eccentric away from the pump arm can cause stress on the pump mounting threads and strip them out when installing the pump.

32. Install the crankshaft pulley.

33. Install the fuel pump shield.

34. Lower the front of the car.

35. If your car is equipped with a tripminder, install the flow meter support bracket.

36. Connect the upper radiator hose at the thermostat housing.

37. Install the distributor.

38. Connect the coolant by-pass hose and the heater hose at the water pump.

39. If your car is equipped with air conditioning, install the front compressor mounting bracket.

40. If equipped with power steering, install the pump. Be sure to keep the pump upright to prevent fluid leakage.

41. Install all drive belts.

42. Install the fan clutch assembly.

43. Install the radiator fan shroud.

44. Install the air cleaner and air duct assemblies.

45. Connect the negative battery cable at the battery.

46. Fill the cooling system.

6-300 (4.9L)

1. Bring the engine to No. 1 piston at TDC (top dead center) on the compression stroke. Drain the cooling system. Disconnect negative battery cable.

CAUTION

When draining the coolant, keep in mind that cats and dogs are attracted by the ethylene glycol antifreeze, and are quite likely to drink any that is left in an uncovered container or in puddles on the ground. This will prove fatal in sufficient quantity. Always drain the coolant into a sealable container. Coolant should be reused unless it is contaminated or several years old.

2. Remove the radiator and shroud.

3. Remove the alternator adjusting arm bolt, loosen the drive belt and swing the alternator arm aside. Remove the fan, drive belts and pulleys.

4. Remove the screw and washer from the end of the crankshaft, remove the crankshaft damper.

5. Remove the front oil pan and front cover attaching screws.

Be careful not to get foreign material in the crankcase during service work, or the crankcase oil will have to be changed.

6. Remove the cylinder front cover and discard the gasket. It is a good idea to replace the crankshaft oil seal when the cylinder front cover is removed.

7. Drive out the crankshaft oil seal with a pin punch. Clean the seal bore in the cover.

8. Remove the camshaft and crankshaft gears using a suitable puller. Install the new gears, camshaft first using Ford tool T65L6306A or the equivalent. Do not hammer on the gears. Install the crankshaft gear over the drive key and install with tool. Verify that the timing marks on both gears are aligned. Install the crankshaft oil slinger.

9. Coat a new crankshaft oil seal with grease and install the seal in the cover. Drive the seal in until it is fully seated in the seal bore.

10. Cut the old front oil pan seal flush at the cylinder block/pan junction and remove the old seal material.

11. Clean all gasket surfaces.

12. Cut and fit a new pan seal flush to the cylinder block pan junction. Use the old seal as a pattern.

13. Coat the gasket surfaces of the block and cover with a resistant sealer. Position a new front cover gasket on the cylinder block.

14. Align the pan seal locating tabs with the pan holes. Pull the seal tabs through until the seal is completely seated. Apply a silicone sealer to the block/pan junction.

15. Position the front cover assembly over the end of the crankshaft and against the cylinder block. Start the cover and pan attaching screw. Slide the cover alignment tool over the crank stub and into the seal bore of the cover. Install the alternator adjusting arm, tighten all attaching screws to specification.

Tighten the oil pan screws first (compressing the pan seal) to obtain the proper alignment of the cover.

16. Lubricate the crank stub, damper hub I.D. and the seal rubbing surface with Lubriplate. Align the damper keyway with the key on the crankshaft and install the damper.
17. Install the washer and capscrew into the damper and tighten specification.
18. Install the pulleys, drive belts, and fan. Adjust all drive belts to correct tension.
19. Install the radiator and shroud. Connect all cooling system hoses.
20. Fill and bleed the cooling system. If no foreign material has entered the crankcase during service work, it is not necessary to change the engine oil.
21. Operate the engine at fast idle and check for coolant and oil leaks.

8-255 (4.2L), 8-302 (5.0L) and 8-351 (5.8L) Except Econoline

1. Bring the engine to No. 1 cylinder at TDC (top dead center) on the compression stroke. Disconnect the negative battery cable at the battery. Drain the cooling system.

CAUTION

When draining the coolant, keep in mind that cats and dogs are attracted by the ethylene glycol antifreeze, and are quite likely to drink any that is left in an uncovered container or in puddles on the ground. This will prove fatal in sufficient quantity. Always drain the coolant into a sealable container. Coolant should be reused unless it is contaminated or several years old.

2. Remove the fan shroud to radiator attaching bolts. Position shroud over the fan.
3. Disconnect the radiator lower hose, heater hose and by-pass hose at the water pump. Remove the drive belts, fan, fan spacer, and pulley.
4. Remove the fan shroud.
5. Loosen the alternator pivot bolt and bolt attaching the alternator adjusting arm to the water pump.
6. Remove the crankshaft pulley from the crankshaft vibration damper. Remove the damper attaching bolt and washer. Install a pulley, the vibration damper and remove the damper.
7. Disconnect the fuel pump outlet line from the fuel pump. Remove the fuel pump to one side with the flexible fuel line still attached.
8. Remove the oil dipstick and the bolt attaching the dipstick to the exhaust manifold.
9. Remove the oil pan to cylinder front cover attaching bolts. Use a knife with a thin blade to cut the oil pan gasket flush with the cylinder block face prior to separating the cover from the cylinder block. Remove the cylinder front cover and water pump as an assembly.
10. Discard the cylinder front cover gasket. Remove the crankshaft front oil slinger.
11. Check the timing chain deflection. The method for checking timing chain deflection is outlined at the end of this section. If the deflection exceeds specification, replace the chain and sprockets as follows: Crank the engine until the timing marks on the sprockets are correctly aligned. Remove the camshaft sprocket capscrew, washers, and fuel pump eccentric. Slide both sprockets and the timing chain forward and remove the chain and sprockets as an assembly. Position the sprockets and timing chain on the camshaft. Be sure that the timing marks are properly aligned. Install the fuel pump, eccentric, washers, and camshaft sprocket capscrew. Tighten the capscrew to specification.
12. Install the crankshaft front oil slinger.
13. Clean the cylinder front cover, oil pan and block gasket surfaces. Clean the oil pan gasket surface where the oil pan and front cover fasten.
14. Install a new crankshaft front oil seal.
15. Lubricate the timing chain and fuel pump eccentric with a heavy engine oil.
16. Coat the gasket surface of the oil pan with sealer, then cut and position the required sections of a new gasket on the oil pan and apply sealer at the corners. Install the pan seal as required. Coat the gasket surfaces of the block and cover with sealer, and position a new gasket on the block.
17. Position the cylinder front cover on the cylinder block. Use care when installing the cover to avoid seal damage or possible gasket dislocation.
18. Install the cylinder front cover to seal alignment tool.
19. It may be necessary to force the cover downward to slightly compress the pan gasket. This operation can be facilitated by using a suitable tool at the front cover attaching hole locations.
20. Coat the threads of the attaching bolts with a oil-resistant sealer and install the bolts. While pushing in on the alignment tool, tighten the oil pan to cover attaching bolts to specification. Tighten the cover to block attaching bolts to specification. Remove the alignment tool.
21. Apply Lubriplate or equivalent to the oil seal rubbing surface of the vibration damper inner hub to prevent damage to the seal. Apply a white lead and oil mixture to the front of the crankshaft for damper installation.
22. Line up the crankshaft vibration damper keyway with the key in the crankshaft. Install the vibration damper on the crankshaft. Install the capscrew and washer and tighten to specification. Install the crankshaft pulley.
23. Lubricate the fuel pump lever with heavy engine oil and install the pump using a new gasket. Connect the fuel pump outlet pipe.
24. Install the alternator pivot bolt and bolt attaching the alternator adjusting arm to the water pump.
25. Position the fan shroud over the water pump. Install the pulley, spacer and fan. Install and adjust the drive belts and adjust to specified tension. Connect the radiator, heater, and by-pass hoses. Position the fan shroud on the radiator and install the attaching bolts.
26. Fill and bleed the cooling system.
27. Run the engine at fast idle and check for coolant and oil leaks. Check the coolant level. Check and adjust the ignition timing.
28. Install the air cleaner and intake duct assembly including the crankcase ventilation hose.

8-302 (5.0L) and 8-351W (5.8L) V8 Econoline

1. Bring engine to No. 1 cylinder at TDC (top dead center) on the compression stroke. Disconnect the negative battery cable at the battery. Drain the radiator.

CAUTION

When draining the coolant, keep in mind that cats and dogs are attracted by the ethylene glycol antifreeze, and are quite likely to drink any that is left in an uncovered container or in puddles on the ground. This will prove fatal in sufficient quantity. Always drain the coolant into a sealable container. Coolant should be reused unless it is contaminated or several years old.

2. Remove the air conditioning idler pulley, bracket and drive belt if equipped.
3. Remove the upper radiator hose. Remove the fan and shroud as an assembly. Raise and safely support the vehicle.

4. Loosen the thermactor and alternator drive belts.

5. Disconnect the lower radiator hose at the water pump. Disconnect the fuel line at the fuel pump and remove the pump. Lower the vehicle.

6. Remove the by-pass hose. Remove the power steering pump drive belt if equipped. Remove the water pump pulley and disconnect the heater hose at the water pump.

7. Remove the air condition compressor upper bracket and the power steering pump mount.

8. Remove the crankshaft pulley. Remove the oil pan to front cover bolts. Remove the front cover.

9. Check timing chain deflection, as outlined at the end of this section. If the deflection exceeds specification, replace the chain and sprockets as follows: Crank the engine until the timing marks on the sprockets are correctly aligned. Remove the camshaft sprocket capscrew, washers, and fuel pump eccentric. Slide both sprockets and the timing chain forward and remove the chain and sprockets as an assembly. Position the sprockets and timing chain on the camshaft. Be sure that the timing marks are properly aligned. Install the fuel pump, eccentric, washers, and camshaft sprocket capscrew. Tighten the capscrew to specification.

10. Clean the front cover, fuel pump, and damper. Lubricate the crankshaft front seal. Clean the gasket surface at the pan and trim the gasket. Clean the front cover gasket surface at the block.

11. Replace the oil seal in the front cover. Position the gasket on the front cylinder cover. Apply a silicone sealer to the oil pan and cylinder block junction. Cut the pan gasket and position on pan and front cover.

12. Install the front cover, fuel pump, and crankshaft pulley.

13. Install the power steering pump and water pump by-pass hose. Connect the heater hose at the water pump.

14. Install the air conditioning compressor upper bracket, water pump pulley and power steering drive belt.

15. Install the alternator belt, thermactor belt, and fan/shroud assembly.

16. Adjust the power steering pump drive belt tension to specification.

17. Install the air conditioning drive belt idler pulley and bracket. Install the air conditioning drive belt and tighten to specification.

18. Install the upper radiator hose.

19. Raise and safely support the vehicle. Install the fuel pump with a new gasket and connect the fuel line.

20. Install the lower radiator hose. Adjust the alternator and air injection pump drive belts to specified tension.

21. Drain the crankcase and replace the oil filter. Lower the vehicle.

22. Fill the crankcase and cooling system. Check and adjust ignition timing.

23. Start the engine and run at a fast idle, check for oil and coolant leaks.

8-351M (5.8L)

1. Bring the engine to No. 1 piston at TDC (top dead center) on the compression stroke. Drain the cooling system and disconnect the battery.

CAUTION

When draining the coolant, keep in mind that cats and dogs are attracted by the ethylene glycol antifreeze, and are quite likely to drink any that is left in an uncovered container or in puddles on the ground. This will prove fatal in sufficient quantity. Always drain the coolant into a sealable container. Coolant should be reused unless it is contaminated or several years old.

2. Remove the fan shroud attaching bolts and move the shroud to the rear.

3. Remove the fan and spacer from the water pump shaft.

4. Remove the air conditioner compressor drive belt lower idler pulley and the compressor mount to water pump bracket.

5. Loosen the alternator and power steering pump and remove the drive belts.

6. Remove the water pump pulley.

7. Remove the alternator and power steering pump brackets from the water pump and position them out of the way.

8. Disconnect the lower radiator and heater hose from the water pump.

9. Remove the crankshaft pulley from the crankshaft vibration damper. Remove the vibration damper attaching screw. Install a puller and remove the damper.

10. Remove the timing pointer.

11. Remove the bolts attaching the front cylinder cover to the cylinder block. Remove the front cover and water pump assembly.

12. Disconnect the fuel pump outlet line from the pump. Remove the fuel pump attaching bolts and lay the pump to one side with the flexible line still attached.

13. Discard the cylinder front cover gasket and oil pan seal.

14. Check the timing chain deflection, as outlined at the end of this section.

15. If the timing chain deflection exceeds specification, proceed as follows: Crank the engine until the timing marks on the sprockets are aligned. Remove the camshaft sprocket capscrew, washer, and two piece fuel pump eccentric. Slide both sprockets and the timing chain forward, and remove them as an assembly. Position the sprockets and timing chain on the camshaft and crankshaft. Be certain that the timing marks on the sprockets are correctly aligned. Install the two piece fuel pump eccentric, washers, and camshaft sprocket capscrew. Tighten the camshaft capscrew to specification. Make sure that the outer fuel pump eccentric sleeve rotates freely.

16. Coat a new fuel pump gasket with oil resistant sealer and position the fuel pump and gasket on the cylinder block with the fuel pump arm resting on the eccentric outer sleeve. Install the pump attaching bolt and nut and tighten to specification. Connect the fuel pump outlet line.

17. Remove the front crankshaft seal from the front cover. Clean the cylinder front cover and the engine block gasket surfaces.

18. Coat the gasket surfaces of the block and cover with sealer, and position a new gasket on the cylinder block alignment dowels.

19. Position the cylinder front cover and water pump assembly on the cylinder block alignment dowels.

20. Coat the threads of the attaching bolts with an oil resistant sealer and install the timing pointer and attaching bolts. Tighten the bolts to specifications.

21. Install the front cover oil seal into the cylinder front cover.

22. Apply Lubriplate® or its equivalent to the oil seal rubbing surface of the vibration damper inner hub to prevent damage to the seal. Apply a white lead and oil mixture to the front of the crankshaft for damper installation.

23. Line up the crankshaft vibration damper keyway with the key on the crankshaft. Install the vibration damper on the crankshaft by pressing on with appropriate tool. Install the capscrew and washer, tighten to specification. Install the crankshaft pulley.

24. Connect the heater hose and the lower radiator hose to the water pump.

25. Install the air conditioner compressor to water pump bracket and lower idler pulley.

26. Position the alternator bracket and power steering pump bracket on the water pump and install the bolts.

27. Position the water pump pulley on the water pump shaft and install the drive belts.

28. Place the fan shroud over the pulley, and install the fan and spacer.

29. Position the fan shroud over the radiator and install the attaching bolts.

30. Adjust the drive belts to specification.

31. Raise the vehicle and remove the oil pan and install new gasket and seals as described in "Oil Pan Removal and Installation."

32. Lower the vehicle. Fill the crankcase. Fill and bleed the cooling system. Connect the battery cable.

33. Operate the engine until normal operating temperature has been reached and check for oil or coolant leaks.

8-460 (7.5L) V8

1. Bring the engine to No. 1 piston at TDC (top dead center) on the compression stroke. Drain the cooling system and crankcase.

CAUTION

When draining the coolant, keep in mind that cats and dogs are attracted by the ethylene glycol antifreeze, and are quite likely to drink any that is left in an uncovered container or in puddles on the ground. This will prove fatal in sufficient quantity. Always drain the coolant into a sealable container. Coolant should be reused unless it is contaminated or several years old.

2. Remove the radiator shroud and fan.

3. Disconnect the upper and lower radiator hoses, and the automatic transmission oil cooler lines from the radiator.

4. Remove the radiator upper support and remove the radiator.

5. Loosen the alternator attaching bolts and air conditioning compressor idler pulley and remove the drive belts with the water pump pulley. Remove the bolts attaching the compressor support to the water pump and remove the bracket (support), if so equipped.

6. Remove the crankshaft pulley from the vibration damper. Remove the bolt and washer attaching the crankshaft damper and remove the damper with a puller. Remove the Woodruff key from the crankshaft.

7. Loosen the by-pass hose at the water pump, and disconnect the heater return tube at the water pump.

8. Disconnect and plug the fuel inlet and outlet lines at the fuel pump, and remove the fuel pump.

9. Remove the bolts attaching the front cover to the cylinder block. Cut the oil pan seal flush with the cylinder block face with a thin knife blade prior to separating the cover from the cylinder block. Remove the cover and water pump as an assembly. Discard the front cover gasket and oil pan seal.

10. Transfer the water pump if a new cover is going to be installed. Clean all of the gasket sealing surfaces on both the front cover and the cylinder block.

11. Check the timing chain deflection, as outlined at the end of this section. If timing chain deflection exceeds specification, proceed as follows: Crank the engine until the timing marks on the sprockets are aligned. Remove the camshaft sprocket capscrew, washer, and two piece fuel pump eccentric. Slide both sprockets and the timing chain forward, and remove them as an assembly. Position the sprockets and timing chain on the camshaft and crankshaft. Be certain that the timing marks on the sprockets are correctly aligned. Install the two piece fuel pump eccentric, washers, and camshaft sprocket capscrew. Tighten the camshaft capscrew to specification.

12. Coat the gasket surface of the oil pan with sealer. Cut and position the required sections of a new seal on the oil pan. Apply sealer to the corners.

13. Coat the gasket surfaces of the cylinder block and cover with sealer and position the new gasket on the block.

14. Position the front cover on the cylinder block. Use care not to damage the seal and gasket or mislocate them.

15. Coat the front cover attaching screws with sealer and install them.

NOTE: It may be necessary to force the front cover downward to compress the oil pan seal in order to install the front cover attaching bolts. Use a drift to engage the cover screw holes through the cover and pry downward.

16. Assemble and install the remaining components in the reverse order of removal. Tighten the front cover bolts to 15-20 ft.lb., the water pump attaching screws to 12-15 ft.lb., the crankshaft damper to 70-90 ft.lb., the crankshaft pulley to 35-50 ft.lb., fuel pump to 19-27 ft.lb., the oil pan bolts to 9-11 ft.lb. for the 5/16" screws to 7-9 ft.lb. for the 1/4" screws, and the alternator pivot bolt to 45-50 ft.lb.

420 (6.9L) Diesel

FRONT COVER AND OIL SEAL

1. Disconnect the battery ground cables from both batteries. Drain cooling system. Remove the air cleaner and install intake air opening.

CAUTION

When draining the coolant, keep in mind that cats and dogs are attracted by the ethylene glycol antifreeze, and are quite likely to drink any that is left in an uncovered container or in puddles on the ground. This will prove fatal in sufficient quantity. Always drain the coolant into a sealable container. Coolant should be reused unless it is contaminated or several years old.

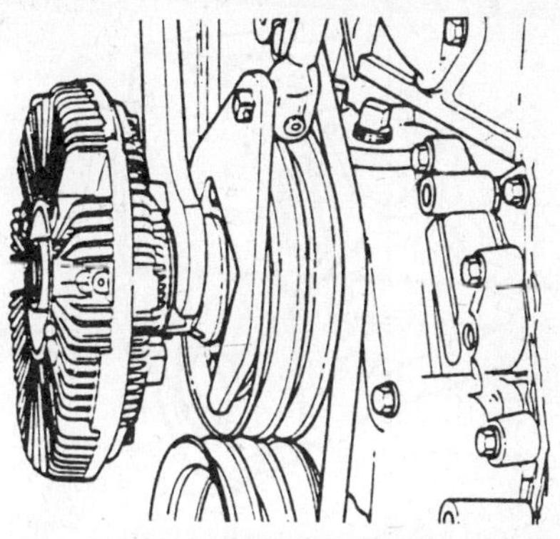

Removing the 6.9L diesel fan clutch using puller (arrows)

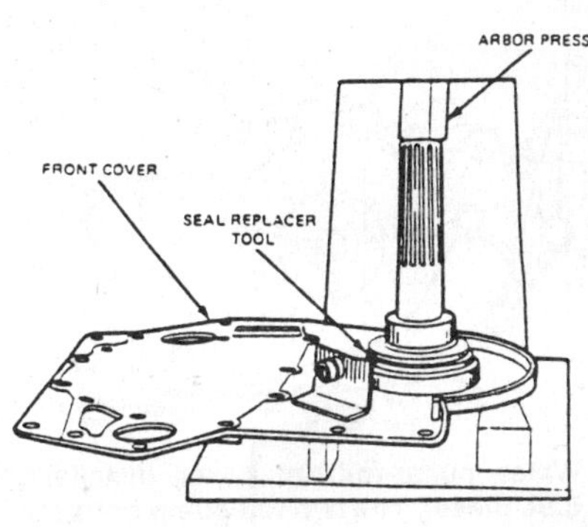

6.9L diesel front oil seal removal and installation using arbor press

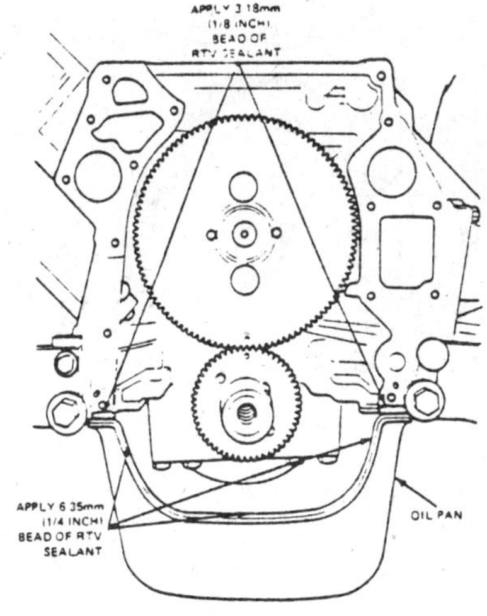

RTV sealer application, 6.9L diesel. Make sure you install the front cover within 15 minutes or the sealant will "set up", reducing its effectiveness

2. Remove the radiator fan shroud halves. Remove the fan and clutch assembly using Tools T83T-6312-A and B. The unit has left hand threads. Remove by turning nut clockwise.

3. Remove the injection pump and adapter. Remove the water pump. Remove power steering pump and bracket, place out of the way with hoses attached. Remove A/C compressor front

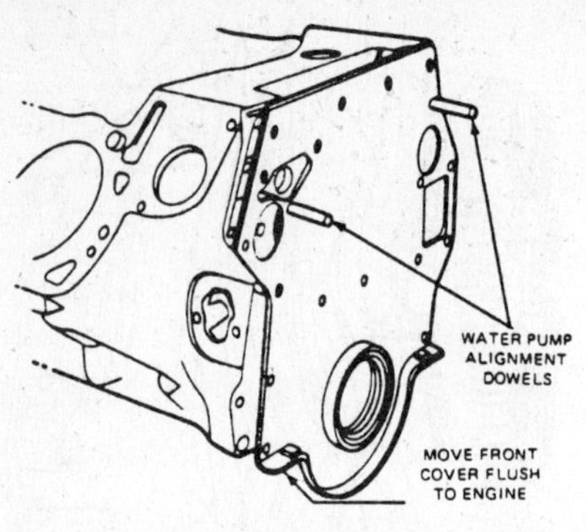

Front cover installation on diesel, showing alignment dowels.

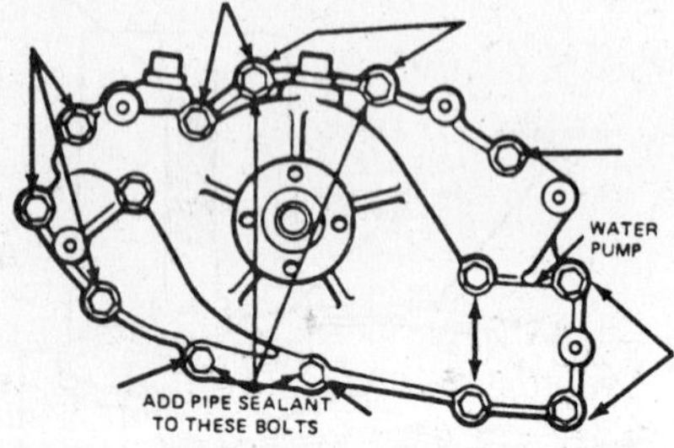

Water pump-to-front cover installation, 6.9L diesel. The two top pump bolts must be no more than 1¼ in. long.

Removing the 6.9L diesel camshaft timing gear

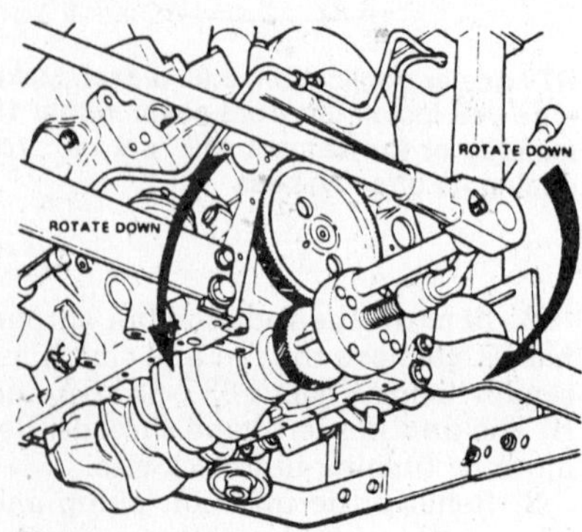

6.9L diesel crankshaft drive gear removal—engine shown out of truck

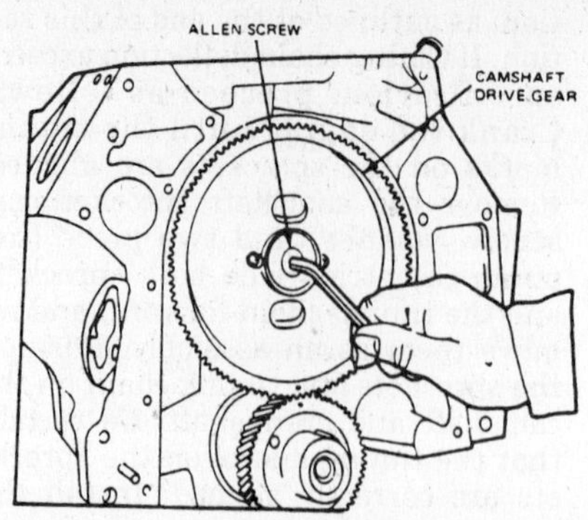

V8 diesel camshaft timing gear installation

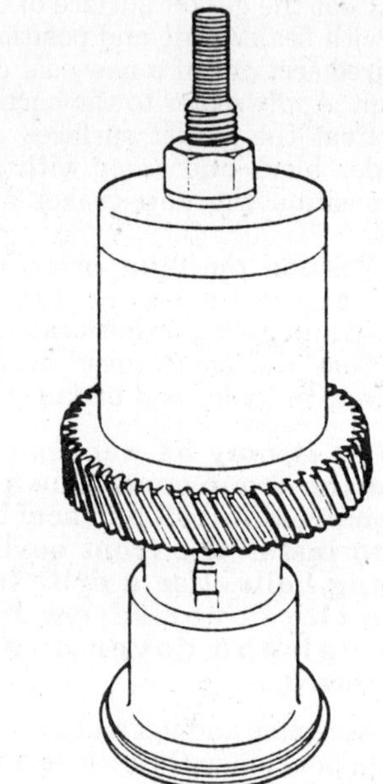
Special installation tool installed on diesel crankshaft drive gear

15. Apply a ⅛" bead of RTV sealant on front of engine block.
16. Apply a ¼" bead of RTV sealant on oil pan mounting surface. Install engine front cover in position and install three attaching bolts. Remove alignment dowels from engine and oil pan and install and hand tighten remaining front cover bolts.
17. Install fabricated alignment dowels in engine block, if necessary. Install water pump gasket on engine front cover alignment dowels. Install water pump and hand tighten bolts.

NOTE: Apply RTV sealant to the four bolts. Remove alignment dowels and install two remaining attaching bolts. The top two water pump bolts must be no more than 1¼" long, in order to avoid contact with engine drive gears.

mounting bracket. Remove alternator, if necessary.

NOTE: If A/C compressor is in the way, remove with hoses attached and position out of the way.

4. Raise vehicle and safely support on jackstands.
5. Remove crankshaft pulley and vibration damper. Remove ground cables at front of engine.
6. Remove five bolts attaching front cover to engine block and oil pan.
7. Lower vehicle.
8. Remove the bolts attaching engine front cover to engine block, and remove front cover.
9. Support engine front cover, and using an arbor press and suitable driver, drive crankshaft seal out of front cover.
10. Remove old gasket material and clean engine block, engine front cover, and oil pan sealing surfaces with a suitable solvent and dry throughly.
11. Clean water pump sealing surface.
12. Coat new front crankshaft oil seal with Polyethylene grease. Install new oil seal using front crankshaft seal replacer, a suitable spacer, and an arbor press.

WARNING: Support engine front cover.

13. Bottom out tool on front cover surface. Seal is automatically installed at proper depth.
14. Install fabricated alignment dowels, on engine block to align front cover and gaskets. Apply gasket sealer on engine block sealing surfaces. Install gaskets on engine block.

NOTE: RTV Sealant should be applied immediately prior to front cover installation.

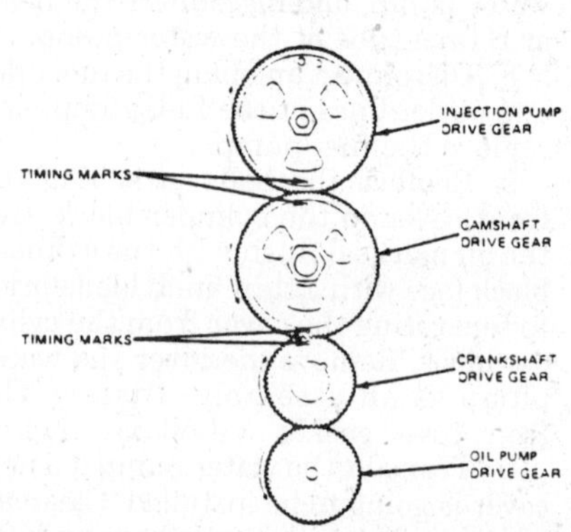

Diesel timing mark alignment

18. Tighten all water pump bolts to specification. Tighten engine front cover bolts to specification. Install injection pump adaptor and pump.
19. Install heater hose fitting in pump using pipe sealant. Connect heater hose to water pump and tighten clamp to specification.
20. Raise vehicle and safely support on jackstands. Lubricate damper seal nose with clean engine oil and install crankshaft vibration damper.

NOTE: Add RTV sealant to the engine side of retaining bolt washer to prevent oil leakage past keyway.

21. Install vibration damper-to-crankshaft attaching bolt and tighten to specification. Install crankshaft pulley and tighten to specification.
22. Install both battery ground cables on front of engine. Lower vehicle.
23. Install alternator adjusting arm bracket and tighten to specification.
24. Install water pump pulley and tighten to specification.
25. Install power steering pump bracket and tighten to specification. Install power steering pump and drive belt.
26. Install A/C compressor bracket and tighten to specification. Install A/C compressor and drive belt.
27. Install alternator adjusting arm and install alternator and vacuum pump drive belts.
28. Adjust alternator, vacuum pump, power steering pump and A/C compressor drive belts.
29. Refill and bleed cooling system.
30. Connect battery ground cables to both batteries.
31. Remove intake manifold cover, install air cleaner and tighten to specification.
32. Run engine and check for coolant and oil leaks.
33. Install fan and clutch assembly. Install radiator fan shroud halves.

CRANKSHAFT DRIVE GEAR

1. Complete front cover removal procedures.
2. Install crankshaft drive gear remover Tool T83T-6316-A, and using a breaker bar to prevent crankshaft rotation, or flywheel holding Tool T74R-6375-A, remove crankshaft gear.
3. Install crankshaft gear using Tool T83T-6316-B aligning crankshaft drive gear timing mark with crankshaft drive gear timing mark.

NOTE: Gear may be heated to 300-350°F for ease of installation. Heat in oven. Do not use torch.

4. Complete front cover installation procedures.

INJECTION PUMP DRIVE GEAR AND ADAPTER

1. Disconnect battery ground cables from both batteries. Remove air cleaner and install intake opening cover.
2. Remove injection pump. Remove bolts attaching injection pump adapter to engine block, and remove adapter.
3. Remove engine front cover. Remove drive gear.
4. Clean all gasket and sealant surfaces of components removed with a suitable solvent and dry thoroughly.
5. Install drive gear in position, aligning all drive gear timing marks.

NOTE: To determine that No. 1 piston is at TDC of compression stroke, position injection pump drive gear dowel at four o'clock position. The scribe line in vibration damper should be at TDC.
Use extreme care to avoid disturbing injection pump drive gear, once it is in position.

6. Install engine front cover. Apply a 1/8" bead of RTV Sealant along bottom surface or injection pump adapter.

NOTE: RTV should be applied immediately prior to adapter installation.

7. Install injection pump adaptor. Apply sealer to bolt threads before assembly.

NOTE: With injection pump adapter installed the injection pump drive gear cannot "jump" timing.

8. Install all removed components. Run engine and check for leaks.

NOTE: If necessary, purge the high pressure fuel lines of air by loosening the connector one half to one turn and crank the engine until a solid flow of fuel, free of air bubbles flow from the connection.

CAMSHAFT DRIVE GEAR, FUEL PUMP CAM, SPACER AND THRUST PLATE

1. Complete front cover removal procedures.
2. Remove camshaft allen screw.
3. Install gear puller, Tool T83T-6316-A and remove gear. Remove fuel supply pump, if necessary.
4. Install gear puller, Tool T77E-4220-B and shaft protector T83T-6316-A and remove fuel pump cam and spacer, if necessary.
5. Remove bolts attaching thrust plate, and remove thrust plate, if necessary.
6. Install new thrust plate, if removed.
7. Install spacer and fuel pump cam against camshaft thrust flange, using installation sleeve and replacer Tool T83T-6316-B, if removed.
8. Install camshaft drive gear against fuel pump cam, aligning timing mark with timing mark on crankshaft drive gear, using installation sleeve and replacer Tool T83T-6316-B.
9. Install camshaft allen screw and tighten to specification.
10. Install fuel pump, if removed.
11. Install front cover, following previous procedure.

CHECKING TIMING CHAIN DEFLECTION EXCEPT 6-232 (3.8L)

To measure timing chain deflection, rotate crankshaft clockwise to take up slack on the left side of chain. Choose a reference point and measure distance from this point and the chain. Rotate crankshaft in the opposite direction to take up slack on the right side of the chain. Force the left (slack) side of the chain out and measure the distance to the reference point chosen earlier. The difference between the two measurements is the deflection.

Timing chain should be replaced if deflection measurement exceed specified limit. The deflection measurement should not exceed 1/2".

TIMING CHAIN DEFLECTION 6-232 (3.8L)

1. Remove the right valve rocker arm cover.
2. Loosen the No.3 exhaust valve rocker arm and rotate it to one side.
3. Install a dial indicator on the end of the push rod, using proper adapter tools.
4. Turn the crankshaft clockwise until the No. 1 piston is at TDC. The damper mark should point to TDC on the timing degree indicator. This will also take up the slack on the right side of the chain.
5. Zero the dial indicator needle.
6. Turn the crankshaft slowly counterclockwise until the slightest movement is seen on the dial indicator. Stop and observe the damper timing mark for the number of degrees of travel from TDC.
7. If the reading on the timing degree indicator exceeds 6°, replace the timing chain and sprockets.

CAMSHAFT ENDPLAY MEASUREMENT

The camshaft gears used on some engines are easily damaged if pried

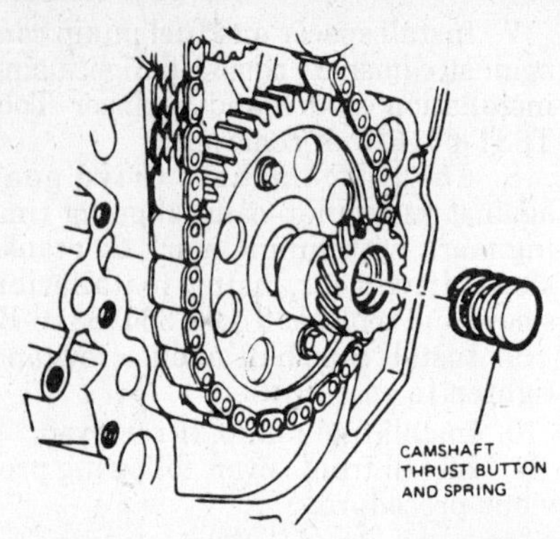

Note proper position of V6 camshaft thrust button and spring when reinstalling

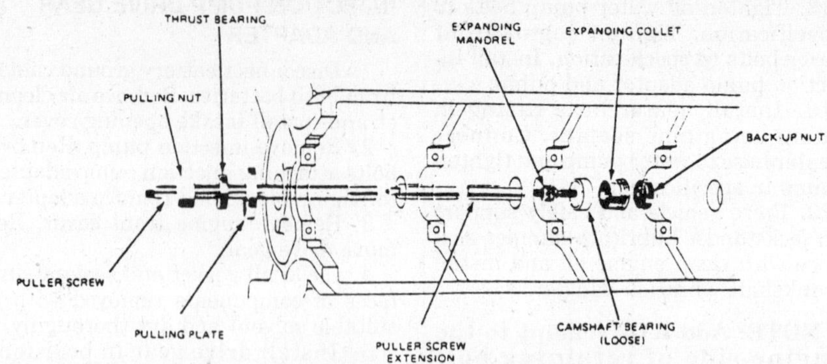

Camshaft bearing replacement

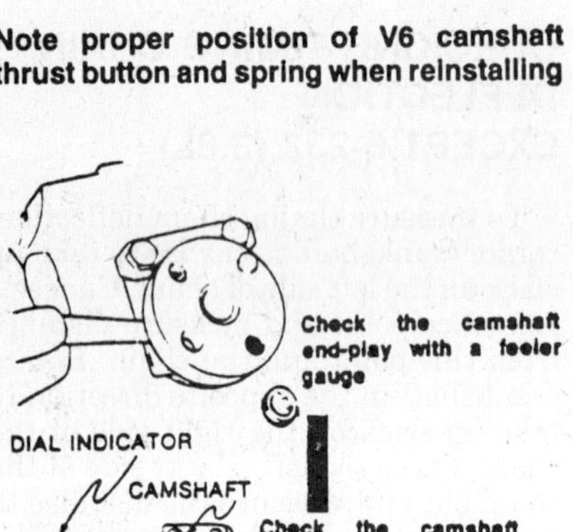

Checking camshaft end play

upon while the valve train load is on the camshaft. Loosen rocker arm nuts or rocker arm shaft support bolts before checking camshaft endplay.

Push camshaft toward rear of engine, install and zero a dial indicator, then pry between camshaft gear and block to pull the camshaft forward. If endplay is excessive, check for correct installation of spacer. If spacer is installed correctly, then replace thrust plate.

MEASURING TIMING GEAR BACKLASH

Use a dial indicator installed on block to measure timing gear backlash. Hold gear firmly against the block while making measurement. If excessive backlash exists, replace both gears.

Front Cover Oil Seal

REMOVAL & INSTALLATION

It is recommended to replace the cover seal any time the front cover is removed.

NOTE: On 6-232 engines, the seal may be removed, after the crank pulley is off without removing the cover.

1. With the cover removed from the car, drive the old seal from the rear of cover with a pinpunch. Clean out the recess in the cover.
2. Coat the new seal with grease and drive it into the cover until it is fully seated. Check the seal after installation to be sure the spring is properly positioned in the seal.

Camshaft

REMOVAL & INSTALLATION

6-300 (4.9L)

1. Drain the cooling system. Disconnect the negative battery cable. Remove the radiator shroud and radiator. On some models it may be necessary to remove the grille and radiator support for necessary clearance.

CAUTION

When draining the coolant, keep in mind that cats and dogs are attracted by the ethylene glycol antifreeze, and are quite likely to drink any that is left in an uncovered container or in puddles on the ground. This will prove fatal in sufficient quantity. Always drain the coolant into a sealable container. Coolant should be reused unless it is contaminated or several years old.

2. Remove the front cover following procedure described in Front Cover Removal and Installation.
3. Remove air cleaner and crankcase vent tube at the rocker cover.
4. Disconnect accelerator cable, choke cable and hand throttle cable (if so equipped). Remove accelerator cable retracting spring.
5. If applicable, remove air compressor and power steering belts.
6. Disconnect oil filler hose from rocker cover.
7. Remove distributor cap and wiring as an assembly, then disconnect vacuum line and primary wire and remove distributor.
8. Remove fuel pump.
9. Remove valve rocker cover, loosen rocker arm stud nuts and move rocker arms to one side. Remove push rods, identifying each so that they may be installed in their original locations.
10. Remove push rod cover and valve lifters, identifying the position of each.
11. Turn crankshaft to align timing marks, remove camshaft thrust plate bolts and carefully pull camshaft and gear from block. Metal camshaft gear (300 HD) is bolted onto camshaft and fiber gear (300 LD) is pressed on and must be removed with an arbor press.
12. To install camshaft, oil journals and apply Lubriplate to lobes, then carefully install camshaft, spacer, thrustplate and gear as an assembly, making sure timing marks are aligned, then tightening thrustplate bolts to 19-20 ft.lb. Do not rotate crankshaft until distributor is installed.
13. Install front cover, referring to Front Cover Removal and Installation for correct procedure.
14. Install valve lifters, then the pushrods in their original locations. Apply heavy engine oil to the lifters and Lubriplate to the pushrods.
15. Install in order the following components, referring to appropriate sections by topic for detailed instructions if necessary and using new gaskets with sealer: pushrod cover, valve rocker cover (adjust valve lash first), distributor (rotor in No. 1 cylinder firing position), fuel pump, distributor cap and wiring assembly, crankcase ventilation valve (in rocker cover), oil filler hose, accelerator cable and retracting spring, choke cable, hand throttle cable, front cylinder cover, water pump pulley, fan, belt, air compressor and power steering belts, radiator, hood latch, grill and air cleaner.
16. Fill crankcase if drained.

17. Install grille, support, radiator, hoses, etc. Fill and bleed cooling system, checking for leaks.
18. Set the ignition timing, then connect distributor vacuum line.
19. Adjust carburetor idle speed and idle fuel mixture.

6-232 (3.8L) and V8 Except 8-420 (6.9L) Diesel

1. Disconnect the negative battery cable. Drain cooling system. Bring engine to No. 1 piston at TDC. Remove the intake manifold and valley pan, if so equipped.

CAUTION

When draining the coolant, keep in mind that cats and dogs are attracted by the ethylene glycol antifreeze, and are quite likely to drink any that is left in an uncovered container or in puddles on the ground. This will prove fatal in sufficient quantity. Always drain the coolant into a sealable container. Coolant should be reused unless it is contaminated or several years old.

2. Remove the rocker covers, loosen the rockers on their pivots and remove the pushrod. The pushrods must be reinstalled in their original positions.
3. Remove the valve lifters in sequence with a magnet. They must be replaced in their original positions.
4. Remove the timing gear cover and timing chain and sprockets.
5. In addition to the radiator and air conditioning condenser, if so equipped, it may be necessary to remove the front grille assembly and the hood lock assembly to gain the necessary clearance to slide the camshaft out the front of the engine.
6. Remove the camshaft thrust plate attaching screws and carefully slide the camshaft out of its bearing bores. Use extra caution not to scratch the bearing journals with the camshaft lobes.
7. Install the camshaft in the reverse order of removal. Coat the camshaft with engine oil liberally before installing it. Slide the camshaft into the engine very carefully so as not to scratch the bearing bores with the camshaft lobes. Install the camshaft thrust plate and tighten the attaching screws to 9-12 ft.lb. Measure the camshaft end-play. If the end-play is more than 0.009", replace the thrust plate. Assemble the remaining components in the reverse order of removal.

8-420 (6.9L) Diesel

1. Remove engine from vehicle. Attach engine to stand or suitable device. Remove injection pump and adapter, intake manifold and tappets, engine front cover and fuel supply pump.
2. Remove camshaft drive gear, fuel supply pump cam, spacer and thrust plate from the camshaft.
3. Carefully remove camshaft with Ford Tool T65L-6250-A and adapter, 14-0314, by pulling toward front of engine. Use care to avoid damaging camshaft bearings.
4. Camshaft lobes are to be coated with Polyethylene Grease and journals lubricated with recommended quality engine oil before installation.
5. Oil camshaft journal and apply Polyethylene Grease to lobes. Carefully slide camshaft through bearings. Install new camshaft thrust plate onto cylinder block and tighten to specification.
6. Install spacer and fuel pump cam against camshaft thrust flange using installation sleeve and replacer Ford Tool T83T-6316-B.
7. Install camshaft drive gear against fuel pump cam, aligning timing mark with timing mark on crankshaft drivegear using installation sleeve and replacer Ford Tool T83T-6316-B.
8. Install camshaft allen screw and tighten.
9. Install fuel supply pump.
10. Install new crankshaft oil seal in engine front cover. Install engine front cover.
11. Install water pump. Install injection pump adapter.
12. Lubricate tappets and bores with recommended quality engine oil and install tappets in their original positions. Install tappet guides. Install tappet guide retainer.
13. Position pushrods, copper colored ends toward rocker arms, into their respective tappets making sure they are seated fully in pushrod seats. Install rocker arms and valve covers with new gaskets.
14. Install intake manifold.
15. Install injection pump.
16. Install engine in vehicle.

CHECKING THE CAMSHAFT

Degrease the camshaft using safe solvent, clean all oil grooves. Visually inspect the cam lobes and bearing journals for excessive wear. If a lobe is questionable, check all lobes and journals with a micrometer.

Measure the lobes from nose to base and again at 90°. The lift is determined by subtracting the second measurement from the first. If all exhaust lobes and all intake lobes are not identical, the camshaft must be reground or replaced. Measure the bearing journals and compare to specifications. If a journal is worn there is a good chance that the cam bearings are worn too, requiring replacement.

If the lobes and journals appear intact, place the front and rear cam journals in V-blocks and rest a dial indicator on the center journal. Rotate the camshaft to check for straightness, if deviation exceeds 0.001" (0.025mm), replace the camshaft.

Pistons and Connection Rods

REMOVAL & INSTALLATION

NOTE: Although, in most cases, the pistons and connecting rods can be removed from the engine (after the cylinder head and oil pan are removed) while the engine is still in the car, it is far easier to remove the engine from the car. If removing pistons with the engine still installed, disconnect the radiator hoses, automatic transmission cooler lines and radiator shroud. Unbolt front mounts before jacking up the engine. Block the engine in position with wooden blocks between the mounts.

1. Remove the engine from the car. Remove the cylinder head(s), oil pan and front cover (if necessary).
2. Because the top piston ring does not travel to the very top of the cylinder bore, a ridge is built up between the end of the travel and the top of the cylinder. Pushing the piston and connecting rod assembly past the ridge is difficult and may cause damage to the piston. If new rings are installed and the ridge has not been removed, ring breakage and piston damage can occur when the ridge is encountered at engine speed.
3. Turn the crankshaft to position the piston at the bottom of the cylinder bore. Cover the top of the piston with a rag. Install a ridge reamer in the bore and follow the manufacturer's instructions to remove the ridge. Use caution; avoid cutting too deeply or into the ring travel area. Remove the rag and cuttings from the top of the piston. Remove the ridge from all cylinders.
4. Check the edges of the connecting rod and bearing cap for numbers or matchmarks, if none are present mark the rod and cap numerically and in sequence from front to back of engine. The numbers or marks not only tell from which cylinder the piston cam from but also ensures that the rod caps are installed in the correct matching position.
5. Turn the crankshaft until the connecting rod is at the bottom of travel. Remove the two attaching nuts and the bearing cap. Take two pieces of

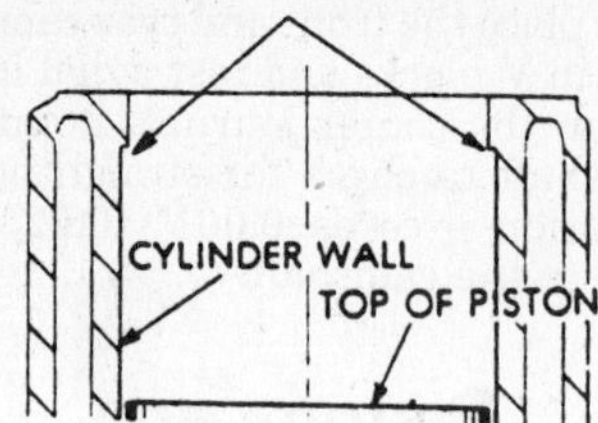

Ridge caused by cylinder wear

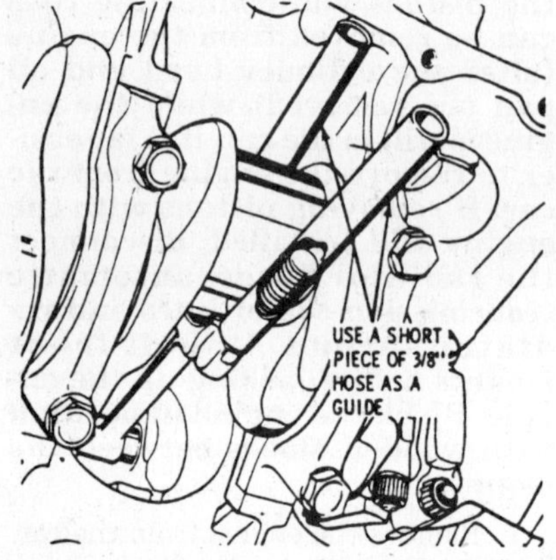

Make connecting rod bolt guides out of rubber tubing; these also protect the cylinder walls and crank journal from scratches

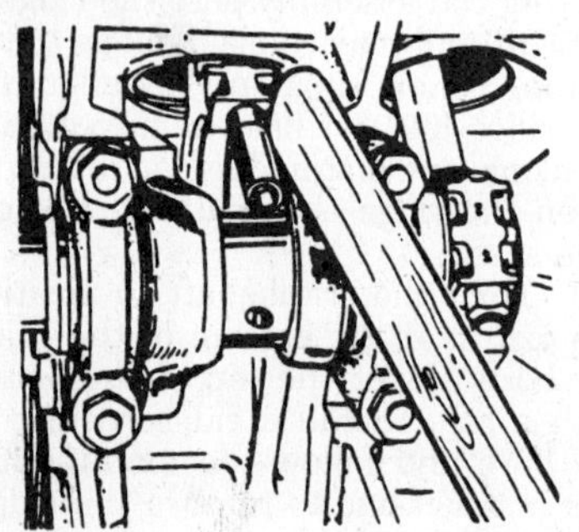
Push the piston assembly out with a hammer handle

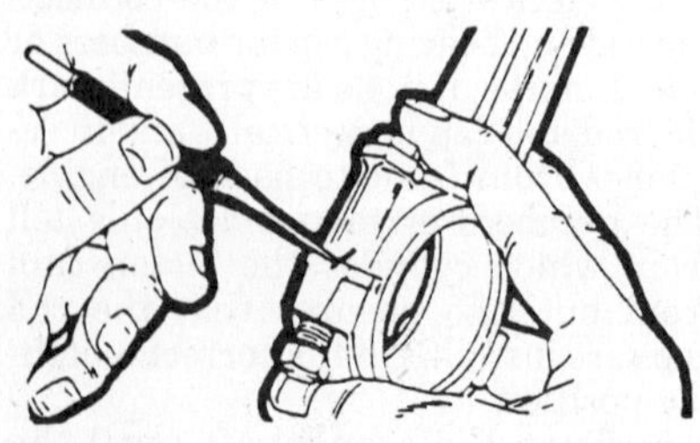
Match the connecting rods to their caps with a scribe mark for reassembly

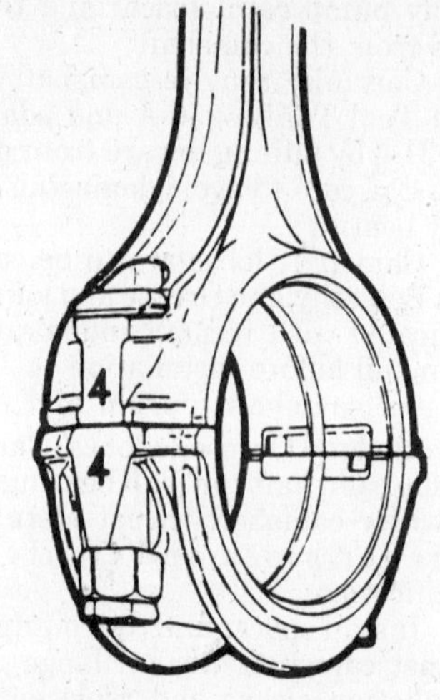

Number each rod and cap with its cylinder number for correct assembly

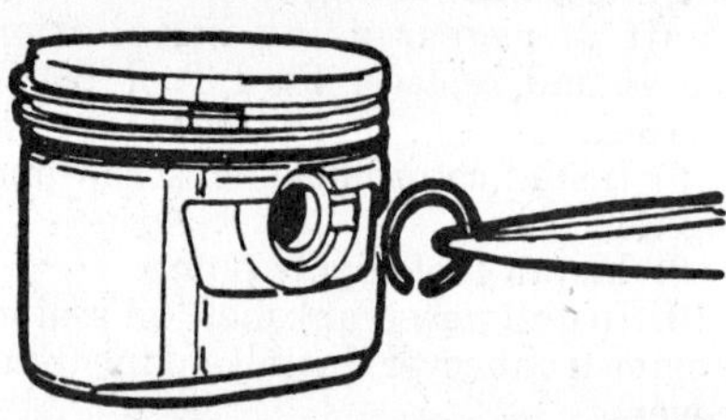
Use needle-nose or snap-ring pliers to remove the piston pin clips

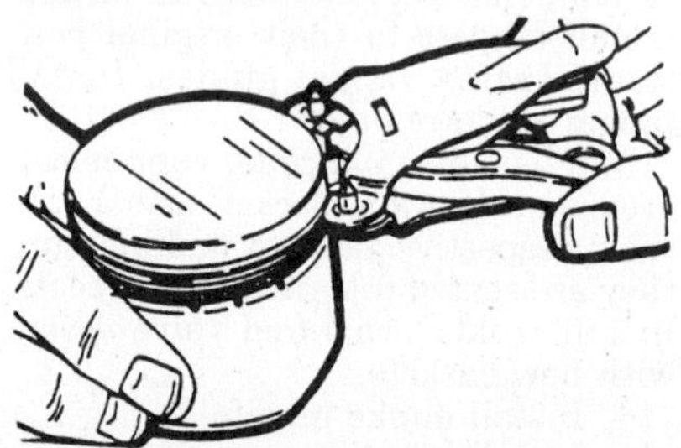
Remove and install the rings with a ring expander

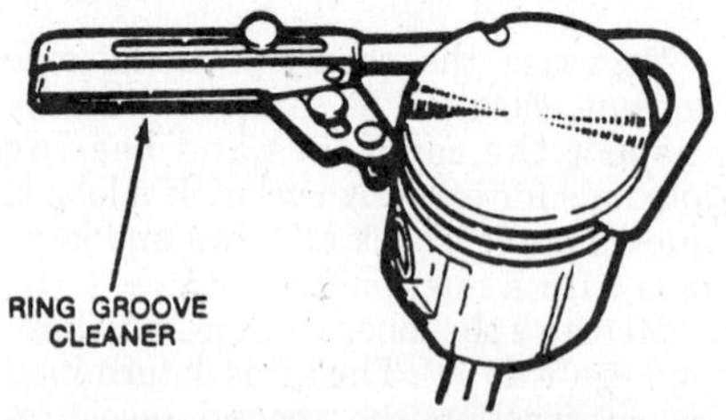

Clean the ring grooves with this tool or the edge of an old ring

rubber tubing and cover the rod bolts to prevent crank or cylinder scoring. Use a wooden hammer handle to help push the piston and rod up and out of the cylinder. Reinstall the rod cap in proper position. Remove all pistons and connecting rods. Inspect cylinder walls and deglaze or hone as necessary.

6. Installation is in the reverse order of removal. Lubricate each piston, rod bearing and cylinder wall. Install a ring compressor over the piston, position the piston with the mark toward the front of engine and carefully install. Position the connecting rod with the bearing insert installed over the crank journal. Install the rod cap with the bearing in its proper position. Secure with rod nuts and torque to the proper specifications. Install all rod and piston assemblies.

CLEANING AND INSPECTION

1. Use a piston ring expander and remove the rings from the piston.
2. Clean the ring grooves using an appropriate cleaning tool, exercising care to avoid cutting too deeply.
3. Clean all varnish and carbon from the piston with a safe solvent. Do not use a wire brush or caustic solution on the pistons.
4. Inspect the pistons for scuffing, scoring, cracks, pitting or excessive ring groove wear. If wear is evident, the piston must be replaced.
5. Have the piston and connecting rod assembly checked by a machine shop for correct alignment, piston pin wear and piston diameter. If the piston has collapsed it will have to be replaced or knurled to restore original diameter. Connecting rod bushing replacement, piston pin fitting and piston changing can be handled by the machine shop.

MEASURING THE OLD PISTONS

Check used piston-to-cylinder bore clearance as follows:

1. Measure the cylinder bore diameter with a telescope gauge.
2. Measure the piston diameter. When measuring the pistons for size or taper, measurements must be made with the piston pin removed.
3. Subtract the piston diameter from the cylinder bore diameter to determine piston-to-bore clearance.
4. Compare the piston-to-bore clearances obtained with those clearances recommended. Determine if the piston-to-bore clearance is in the acceptable range.
5. When measuring taper, the largest reading must be at the bottom of the skirt.

SELECTING NEW PISTONS

1. If the used piston is not accept-

Have the wrist pins pressed in and out with an arbor press. This applies to all engines covered in this guide

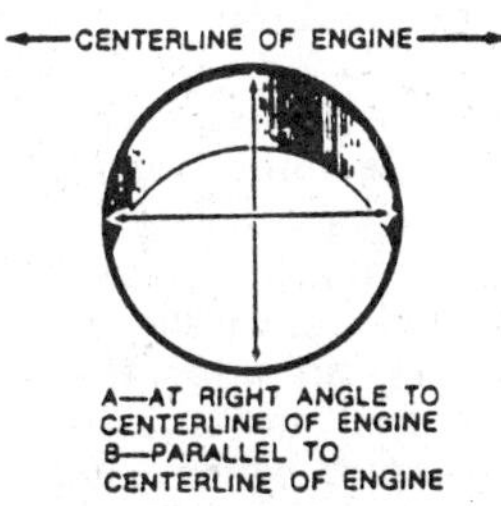

Cylinder bore measuring points. Take top measurement ½ in. below top of block deck, bottom measurement ½ in. above top of piston is at B.D.C.

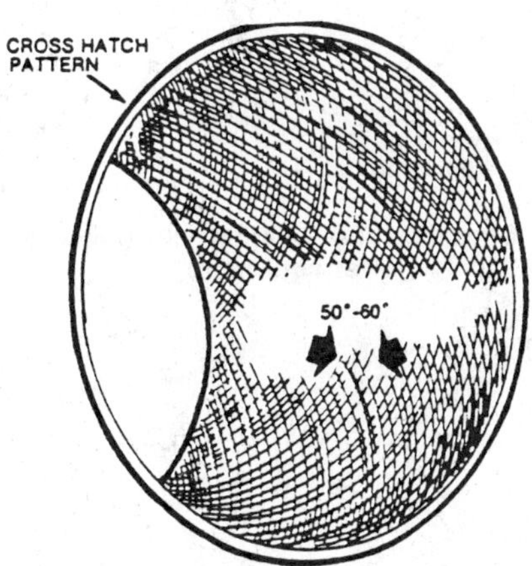

Proper cylinder bore cross-hatching after honing

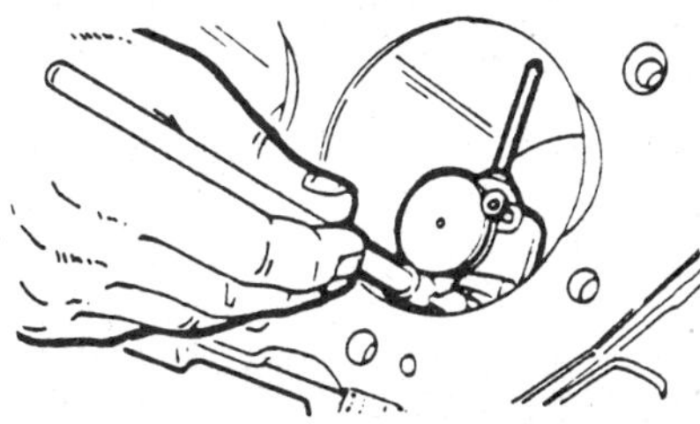

Measuring cylinder bore with a dial gauge

able, check the service piston size and determine if a new piston can be selected. (Service pistons are available in standard, high limit and standard oversize.

2. If the cylinder bore must be reconditioned, measure the new piston diameter, then hone the cylinder bore to obtain the preferred clearance.

3. Select a new piston and mark the piston to identify the cylinder for which it was fitted. (On some vehicles, oversize pistons may be found. These pistons will be 0.254mm [0.010″] oversize).

CYLINDER HONING

1. When cylinders are being honed, follow the manufacturer's recommendations for the use of the hone.

2. Occasionally, during the honing operation, the cylinder bore should be thoroughly cleaned and the selected piston checked for correct fit.

3. When finish-honing a cylinder bore, the hone should be moved up and down at a sufficient speed to obtain a very fine uniform surface finish in a cross-hatch pattern of approximately 45-65° included angle. The finish marks should be clean but not sharp, free from imbedded particles and torn or folded metal.

4. Permanently mark the piston for the cylinder to which it has been fitted and proceed to hone the remaining cylinders.

WARNING: Handle the pistons with care. Do not attempt to force the pistons through the cylinders until the cylinders have been honed to the correct size. Pistons can be distorted through careless handling.

5. Thoroughly clean the bores with hot water and detergent. Scrub well with a stiff bristle brush and rinse thoroughly with hot water. It is extremely essential that a good cleaning operation be performed. If any of the abrasive material is allowed to remain in the cylinder bores, it will rapidly wear the new rings and cylinder bores. The bores should be swabbed several times with light engine oil and a clean cloth and then wiped with a clean dry cloth. CYLINDERS SHOULD NOT BE CLEANED WITH KEROSENE

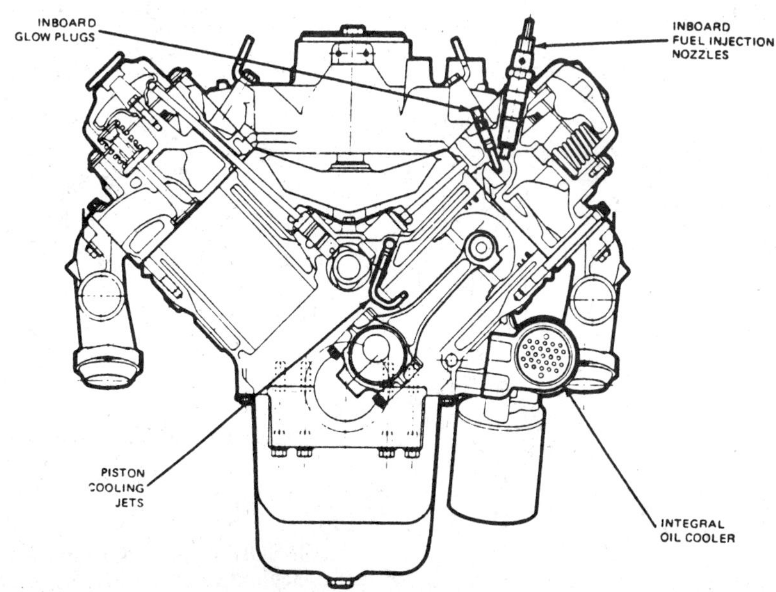

6.9L diesel V8 cross-section showing piston oil cooling jets which must be removed prior to any cylinder honing or boring

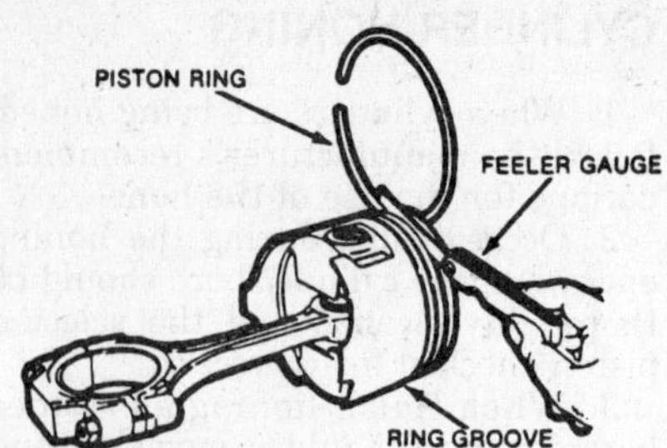

Checking ring side clearance

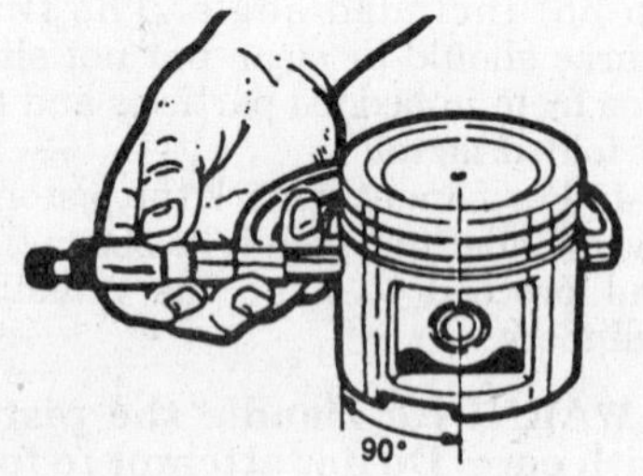

Check piston diameter at these points with a micrometer

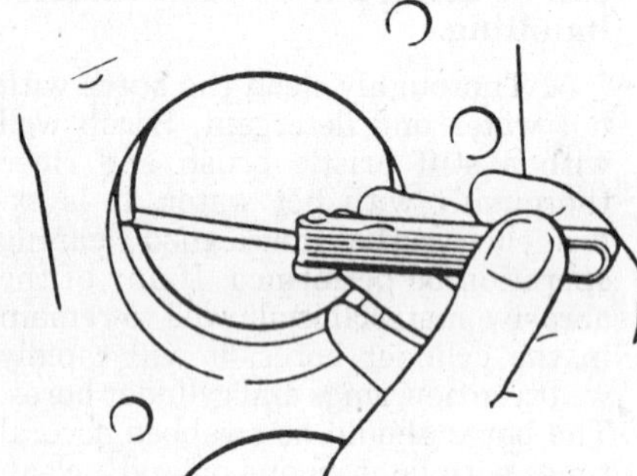

Check piston ring end gap with a feeler gauge, with the ring positioned in the cylinder one inch below the deck of the block

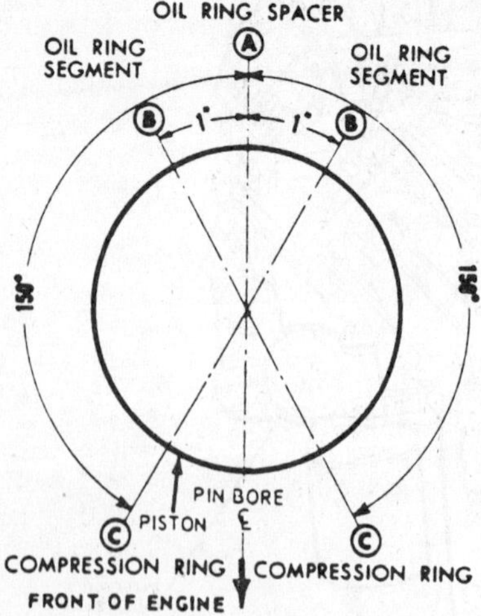

Proper spacing of the piston ring gaps around the circumference of the piston—gasoline engines

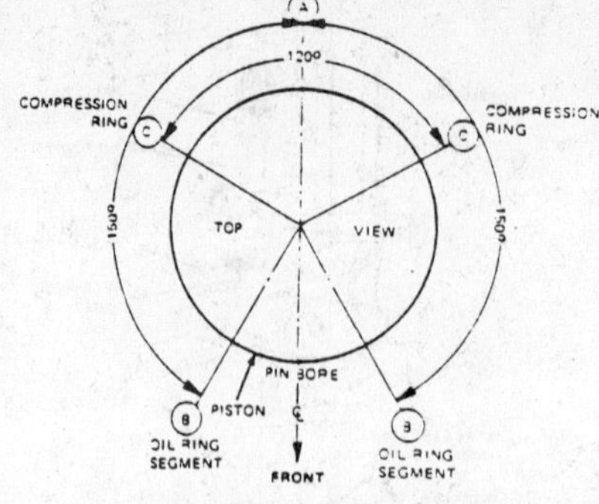

6.9L diesel piston ring spacing

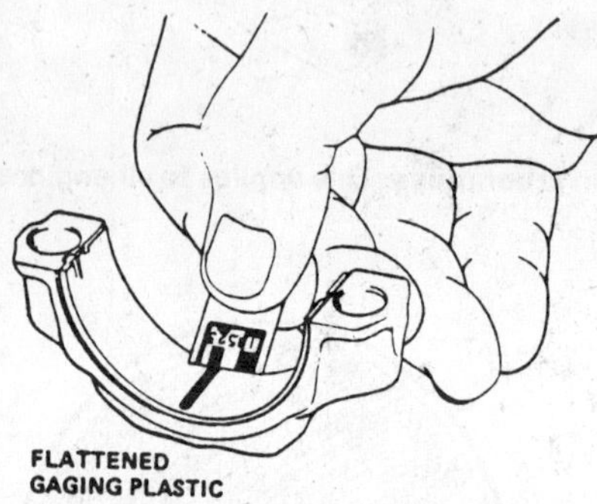

Checking rod bearing clearance with Plastigage® or equivalent

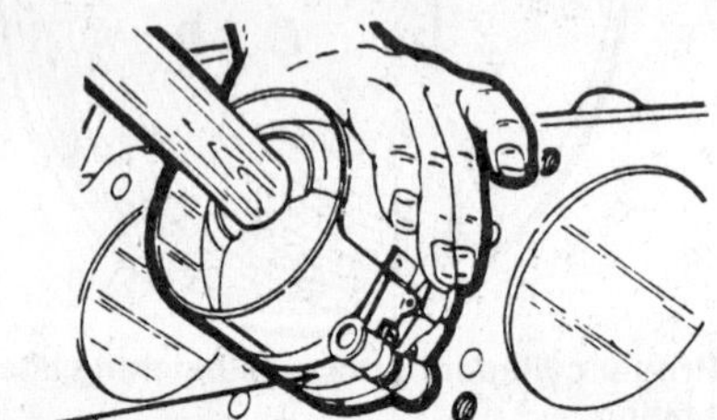

Tap the piston assembly into the cylinder with a wooden hammer handle. Notches on piston crown face the front of the engine

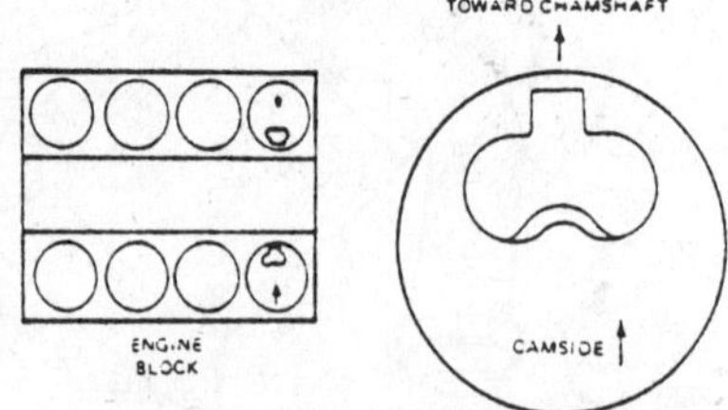

6.9L diesel piston positioning

OR GASOLINE! Clean the remainder of the cylinder block to remove the excess material spread during the honing operation.

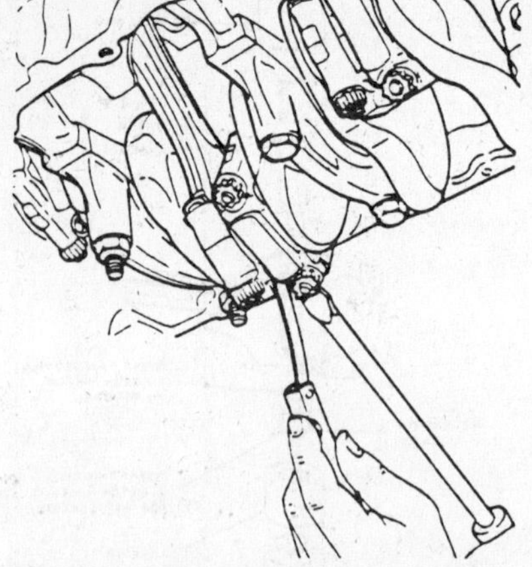

Checking connecting rod side clearance with a feeler gauge. Use a small pry bar to spread the connecting rods

PISTON PIN REMOVAL & INSTALLATION

Use care at all times when handling and servicing connecting rods and pistons. To prevent possible damage to these units, do not clamp the rod or piston in a vise since they may become distorted. Do not allow the pistons to strike against one another, against hard objects or bench surfaces, since distortion of the piston contour or nicks in the soft aluminum material may result.

1. Remove the piston rings using a suitable piston ring remover.
2. Remove the piston pin lockring, if used. Install the guide bushing of the piston pin removing and installing tool.
3. Install the piston and connecting rod assembly on a support, and place the assembly in an arbor press. Press the pin out of the connecting rod, using the appropriate piston pin tool.
4. Assembly is the reverse of disassembly. Use new lockrings where needed.

Connecting Rods and Bearings

Wash connecting rods in cleaning solvent and dry with compressed air. Check for twisted or bent rods and inspect for nicks or cracks. Replace connecting rods that are damaged.

Inspect journals for roughness and wear. Slight roughness may be removed with a fine grit polishing cloth saturated with engine oil. Burrs may be removed with a fine oil stone by moving the stone on the journal circumference. Do not move the stone back and forth across the journal. If the journals are scored or ridged, the crankshaft must be replaced.

The connecting rod journals should be checked for out-of-round and correct size with a micrometer.

NOTE: Crankshaft rod journals will normally be standard size. If any undersized bearings are used, the size will be stamped on a counterweight.

If plastic gauging material is to be used:

1. Clean oil from the journal bearing cap, connecting rod and outer and inner surfaces of the bearing inserts. Position the insert so that the tang is properly aligned with the notch in the rod and cap.
2. Place a piece of plastic gauging material in the center of lower bearing shell.
3. Remove the bearing cap and determine the bearing clearances by comparing the width of the flattened plastic gauging material at its widest point with the graduation on the container. The number within the graduation on the envelope indicates the clearance in thousandths of an inch or millimeters. If this clearance is excessive, replace the bearing and recheck the clearance with the plastic gauging material. Lubricate the bearing with engine oil before installation. Repeat the procedure on the remaining connecting rod bearings. All rods must be connected to their journals when rotating the crankshaft, to prevent engine damage.

CYLINDER BORE

Check the cylinder bore for wear using a telescope gauge and a micrometer, measure the cylinder bore diameter perpendicular to the piston pin at the point 2½" (63.5mm) below the top of the engine block. Measure the piston skirt perpendicular to the piston pin. The difference between the two measurement is the piston clearance. If the clearance is within specifications, finish honing or glaze breaking is all that is required. If clearance is excessive a slightly oversized piston may be required. If greatly oversize, the engine will have to be bored and 0.010" (0.254mm) or larger oversized pistons installed.

FITTING AND POSITIONING PISTON RINGS

1. Take the new piston rings and compress them, one at a time into the cylinder that they will be used in. Press the ring about 1" (25.4mm) below the top of the cylinder block using an inverted piston.
2. Use a feeler gauge and measure the distance between the ends of the ring; this is called measuring the ring end-gap. Compare the reading to the one called for in the specification table. File the ends of the ring with a fine file to obtain the necessary clearance.

WARNING: If inadequate ring end-gap exists, ring breakage will result.

3. Inspect the ring grooves on the piston for excessive wear or taper. If necessary, have the grooves recut for use with a standard ring and spacer. The machine shop can handle the job for you.
4. Check the ring grooves by rolling the new piston ring around the groove to check for burrs or carbon deposits. If any are found, remove them with a fine file. Hold the ring in the groove and measure side clearance with a feeler gauge. If clearance is excessive, spacer(s) will have to be added.

NOTE: Always add the spacer above the piston ring.

5. Install the rings on the piston, lower oil ring first. Use a ring installing tool on the compression rings. Consult the instruction sheet that comes with the rings to be sure they are installed with the correct side up. A mark on the ring usually faces upward.
6. When installing the oil rings, first install the expanding ring in the groove. Hold the ends of the ring butted together (they must not overlap) and install the bottom rail (scraper) with the end about 1" (25.4mm) away from the butted end of the control ring. Install the top rail about 1" (25.4mm) away from the butted end of the control but on the opposite side from the lower rail.
7. Install the two compression rings.
8. Consult the illustration for ring positioning, arrange the rings as shown, install a ring compressor and insert the piston and rod assembly into the engine.

Rear Main Oil Seal

REMOVAL & INSTALLATION

NOTE: Refer to the build dates listed below to determine if the engine is equipped with a split-type or one piece rear main oil seal. Engines after the dates indicated have a one-piece oil seal.
6-232 after 4/1/83
8-302 after 12/1/82
Engines prior to the date indicated are equipped with a split type seal.

Split-Type Seal on Gasoline Engines

NOTE: The rear oil seal installed in these engines is a rubber type (split-lip) seal.

1. Remove the oil pan, and, if required, the oil pump.
2. Loosen all the main bearing caps allowing the crankshaft to lower slightly.

WARNING: The crankshaft should not be allowed to drop more than $^1/_{32}$" (0.8mm).

3. Remove the rear main bearing cap and remove the seal from the cap and block. Be very careful not to scratch the sealing surface. Remove the old seal retaining pin from the cap, if equipped. It is not used with the replacement seal.
4. Carefully clean the seal grooves in the cap and block with solvent.
5. Soak the new seal halves in clean engine oil.
6. Install the upper half of the seal in the block with the undercut side of the seal toward the front of the engine. Slide the seal around the crankshaft journal until ⅜" (9.5mm) protrudes beyond the base of the block.
7. Tighten all the main bearing caps (except the rear main bearing) to specifications.
8. Install the lower seal into the rear cap, with the undercut side facing the front of the engine. Allow ⅜" (9.5mm) of the seal to protrude above the surface, at the opposite end from the block seal.
9. Squeeze a $^1/_{16}$" (1.6mm) bead of silicone sealant onto the areas shown.
10. Install the rear cap and torque to specifications.
11. Install the oil pump and pan. Fill the crankcase with oil, start the engine, and check for leaks.

One-Piece Seal

1. Remove the transmission, clutch and flywheel or driveplate after referring to the appropriate section for instructions.
2. Punch two holes in the crankshaft rear oil seal on opposite sides of the crankshaft just above the bearing cap to the cylinder block split line. Install a sheet metal screw in each of the holes or use a small slide hammer, and pry the crankshaft rear main oil seal from the block.

WARNING: Use extreme caution not to scratch the crankshaft oil seal surface.

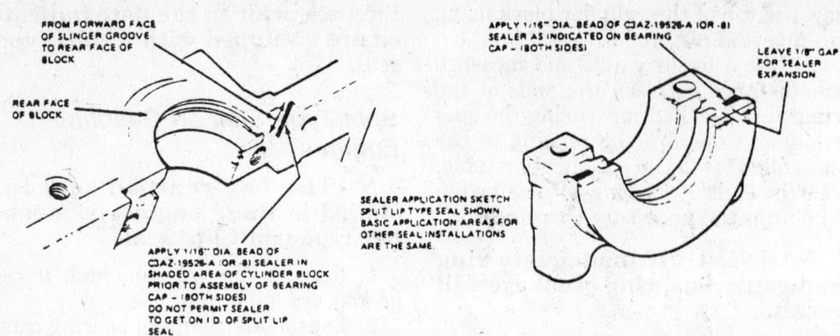

Apply RTV sealant to the main bearing cap and block on all gasoline engines except the 300 sixes

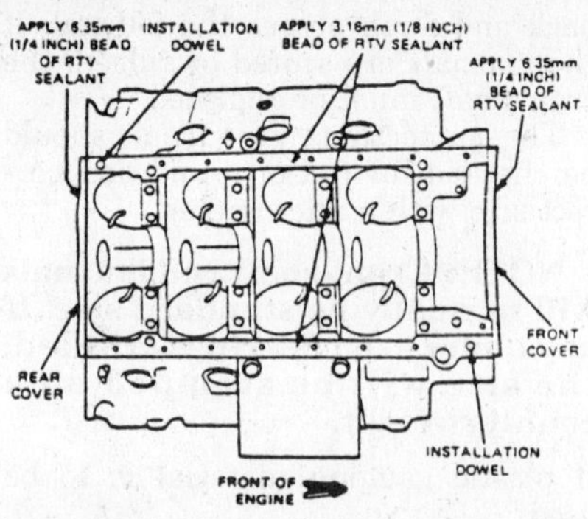

Oil pan sealer application, 6.9L diesel

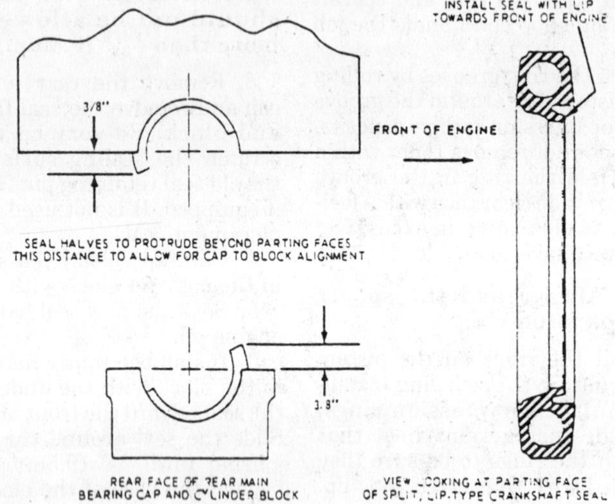

Crankshaft rear main seal installation on all V6 and V8 engines including 6.9L diesel

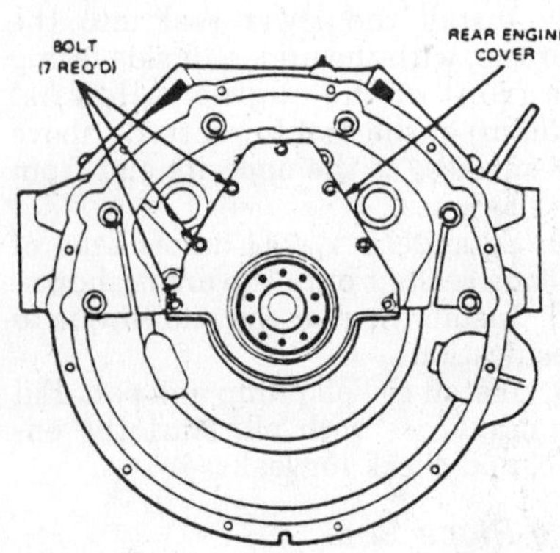

6.9L diesel rear cover removal

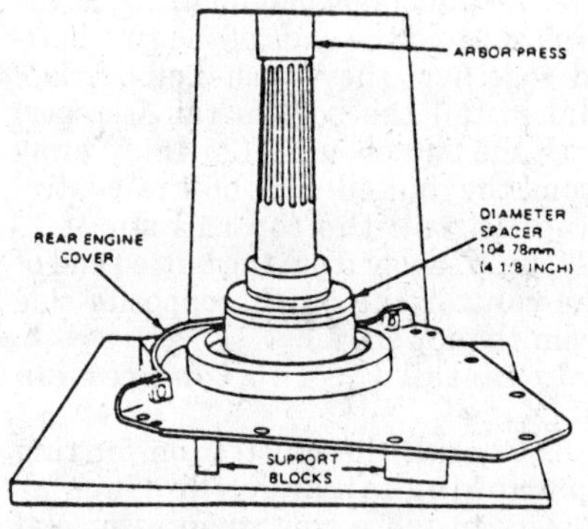

The 6.9L diesel rear oil seal must be pressed in and out

3. Clean the oil seal recess in the cylinder block and main bearing cap.

4. Coat the seal and all of the seal mounting surfaces with oil and install the seal in the recess, driving it into place with an oil seal installation tool or a large socket.

5. Install the driveplate or flywheel and clutch, and transmission in the reverse order of removal.

Crankshaft and Bearings

REMOVAL & INSTALLATION

1. Rod bearings can be installed when the pistons have been removed for servicing (rings etc.) or, in most cases, while the engine is still in the car. Bearing replacement, however, is far easier with the engine out of the car and disassembled.

2. For in car service, remove the oil pan, spark plugs and front cover is necessary. Turn the engine until the connecting rod to be serviced is at the bottom of travel. Remove the bearing cap, place two pieces of rubber hose over the rod cap bolts and push the piston and rod assembly up the cylinder bore until enough room is gained for bearing insert removal. Take care not to push the rod assembly up too far or the top ring will engage the cylinder ridge or come out of the cylinder and require head removal for reinstallation.

3. Clean the rod journal, the connecting rod end and the bearing cap after removing the old bearing inserts. Install the new inserts in the rod and bearing cap, lubricate them with oil. Position the rod over the crankshaft journal and install the rod cap. Make sure the cap and rod numbers match, torque the rod nuts to specifications.

4. Main bearings may be replaced while the engine is still in the car by rolling them out and in.

5. Special roll out pins are available from automotive parts houses or can be fabricated from a cotter pin. The roll out pin fits in the oil hole of the main bearing journal. When the crankshaft is rotated opposite the direction of the bearing lock tab, the pin engages the end of the bearing and rolls out the insert.

6. Remove the main bearing cap and roll out the upper bearing insert. Remove the insert from the main bearing cap. Clean the inside of the bearing cap and crankshaft journal.

7. Lubricate and roll the upper insert into position, making sure the lock tab is anchored and the insert is not cocked. Install the lower bearing insert into the cap, lubricate it and install it on the engine. Make sure the main bearing cap is installed facing in

PRY FORWARD
THRUST BEARING
PRY BACKWARD
THRUST BEARING
THRUST BEARING
PRY CRANKSHAFT FORWARD
PRY CAP BACKWARD
TIGHTEN CAP

Crankshaft thrust bearing alignment

the correct direction and torque it to specifications.

8. With the engine out of the car. Remove the intake manifold, cylinder heads, front cover, timing gears and/or chain, oil pan, oil pump and flywheel.

9. Remove the piston and rod assemblies. Remove the main bearing caps after marking them for position and direction.

10. Remove the crankshaft, bearing inserts and rear main oil seal. Clean the engine block and cap bearing saddles. Clean the crankshaft and inspect it for wear. Check the bearing journals with a micrometer for out-of-round condition and to determine what size rod and main bearing inserts to install.

11. Install the main bearing upper inserts and rear main oil seal half into the engine block.

12. Lubricate the bearing inserts and the crankshaft journals. Slowly and carefully lower the crankshaft into position.

13. Install the bearing inserts and rear main seal into the bearing caps. Install the caps working from the middle out. Torque the cap bolts to specifications in stages, rotating the crankshaft after each torque stage. Note the illustration for thrust bearing alignment.

14. Remove the bearing caps, one at a time, and check the oil clearance with Plastigage®. Reinstall if clearance is within specifications. Check the crankshaft end-play. If it is within specifications, install the connecting rod and piston assemblies with new rod bearing inserts. Check the connecting rod bearing oil clearance and side play. If they are correct assemble the rest of the engine.

BEARING OIL CLEARANCE

Remove the cap from the bearing to be checked. Using a clean, dry rag, thoroughly clean all oil from the crankshaft journal and bearing insert.

NOTE: Plastigage® is soluble in oil, therefore, oil on the journal or bearing could result in erroneous readings.

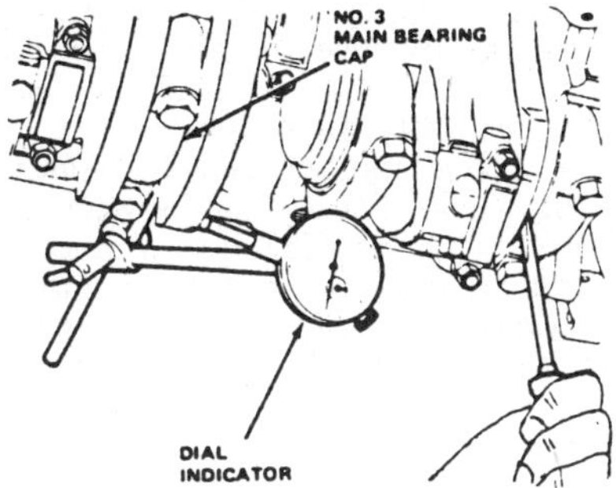

Checking crankshaft end-play with a dial indicator

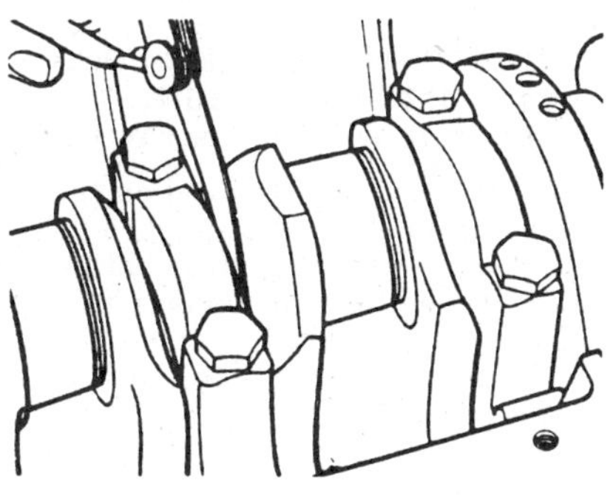

Crankshaft end play can also be checked with a feeler gauge

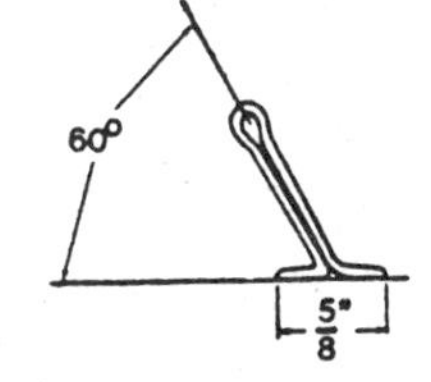

Make a bearing roll-out pin from a cotter pin

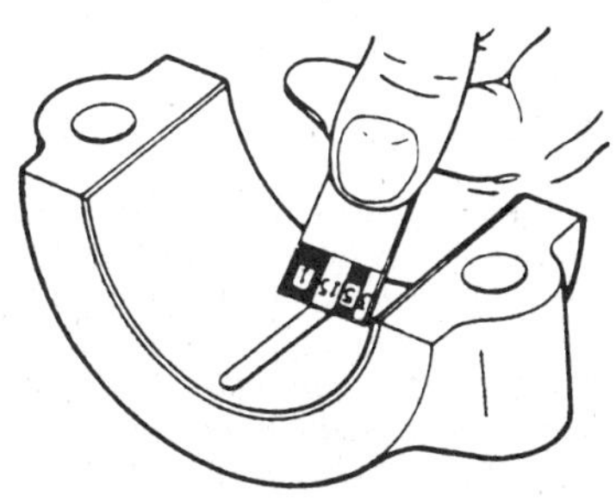

Checking main bearing clearance with Plasitgage®

Place a piece of Plastigage® along the full width of the bearing insert, reinstall cap, and torque to specification.

NOTE: Specifications are given in the Engine Specifications Chart.

Remove the bearing cap, and determine the bearing clearance by comparing the width of the Plastigage® to the scale on the Plastigage® envelope. Journal taper is determined by comparing the width of the bearing insert. Install the cap, and torque it to specifications.

NOTE: Do not rotate the crankshaft with the Plastigage® installed. If the bearing insert and journal appear intact, and are within tolerances, no further main bearing service is required. If the bearing or journal appear defective, the cause of failure should be determined before replacement.

CRANKSHAFT END-PLAY/CONNECTING ROD SIDE PLAY

Place a pry bar between a main bearing cap and crankshaft casting taking care not to damage any journals. Pry backward and forward, measuring the distance between the thrust bearing and crankshaft with a feeler gauge. Compare the reading with specifications. If too great a clearance is determined, a main bearing with a larger thrust surface or crank machining may be required. Check with an automotive machine shop for their advice.

Connecting rod clearance between the rod and crankthrow casting can be checked with a feeler gauge. Pry the rod carefully to one side as far as possible and measure the distance on the other side of the rod.

CRANKSHAFT REPAIRS

If a journal is damaged on the crankshaft, repair is possible by having the crankshaft machined to a standard undersize.

In most cases, however, since the engine must be removed from the car and disassembled, some thought should be given to replacing the damaged crankshaft with a reground shaft kit. A reground crankshaft kit contains the necessary main and rod bearings for installation. The shaft has been ground and polished to undersize specifications and will usually hold up well if installed correctly.

COMPLETING THE REBUILDING PROCESS

Fill the oil pump with oil, to prevent cavitating (sucking air) on initial engine start up. Install the oil pump and the pickup tube on the engine. Coat the oil pan gasket as necessary, and install the gasket and the oil pan. Mount the flywheel and the crankshaft vibration damper or pulley on the crankshaft.

NOTE: Always use new bolts when installing the flywheel. Inspect the clutch shaft pilot bushing in the crankshaft. If the bushing is excessively worn, remove it with an expanding puller and a slide hammer, and tap a new bushing into place.

Position the engine, cylinder head side up. Lubricate the lifters, and install them into their bores. Install the cylinder head, and torque it as specified. Insert the pushrods (where applicable), and install the rocker shaft(s) (if so equipped) or position the rocker.

Install the intake and exhaust manifolds, the carburetor(s), the distributor and spark plugs. Mount all accessories and install the engine in the car. Fill the radiator with coolant, and the crankcase with high quality engine oil.

BREAK-IN PROCEDURE

Start the engine, and allow it to run at low speed for a few minutes, while checking for leaks. Stop the engine, check the oil level, and fill as necessary. Restart the engine, and fill the cooling system to capacity. Check and adjust the ignition timing. Run the engine at low to medium speed (800-2,500 rpm) for approximately ½ hour, and retorque the cylinder head bolts. Road test the car, and check again for leaks.

NOTE: Some gasket manufacturers recommend not retorquing the cylinder head(s) due to the composition of the head gasket. Follow the directions in the gasket set.

Flywheel/Flex Plate and Ring Gear

NOTE: Flex plate is the term for a flywheel mated with an automatic transmission.

REMOVAL & INSTALLATION

All Engines

NOTE: The ring gear is replaceable only on engines mated with a manual transmission. Engines with automatic transmissions have ring gears which are welded to the flex plate.

1. Remove the transmission and transfer case.
2. Remove the clutch, if equipped, or torque converter from the flywheel. The flywheel bolts should be loosened a little at a time in a cross pattern to avoid warping the flywheel. On cars with manual transmissions, replace the pilot bearing in the end of the crankshaft if removing the flywheel.
3. The flywheel should be checked for cracks and glazing. It can be resurfaced by a machine shop.
4. If the ring gear is to be replaced, drill a hole in the gear between two teeth, being careful not to contact the flywheel surface. Using a cold chisel at this point, crack the ring gear and remove it.
6. Polish the inner surface of the new ring gear and heat it in an oven to about 600°F (316°C). Quickly place the ring gear on the flywheel and tap it into place, making sure that it is fully seated.

WARNING: Never heat the ring gear past 800°F (426°C), or the tempering will be destroyed.

7. Position the flywheel on the end of the crankshaft. Torque the bolts a little at a time, in a cross pattern, to the torque figure shown in the Torque Specifications Chart.
8. Install the clutch or torque converter.
9. Install the transmission and transfer case.

ENGINE COOLING

Radiator

REMOVAL & INSTALLATION

1. Drain the cooling system.

CAUTION

When draining the coolant, keep in mind that cats and dogs are attracted by the ethylene glycol antifreeze, and are quite likely to drink any that is left in an uncovered container or in puddles on the ground. This will prove fatal in sufficient quantity. Always drain the coolant into a sealable container. Coolant should be reused unless it is contaminated or several years old.

2. Disconnect the upper, lower and overflow hoses at the radiator.
3. On automatic transmission equipped cars, disconnect the fluid cooler lines at the radiator.
4. Depending on the model, remove the two top mounting bolts and remove the radiator and shroud assembly, or remove the shroud mounting bolts and position the shroud out of the way, or remove the side mounting bolts. If the air conditioner condenser is attached to the radiator, remove the retaining bolts and position the condenser out of the way. DO NOT disconnect the refrigerant lines.
5. Remove the radiator attaching bolts or top brackets and lift out the radiator.
6. If a new radiator is to be installed, transfer the petcock from the old radiator to the new one. On cars equipped with automatic transmissions, transfer the fluid cooler line fittings from the old radiator.
7. Position the radiator and install, but do not tighten, the radiator support bolts. On cars equipped with automatic transmissions, connect the fluid cooler lines. Then, tighten the radiator support bolts or shroud and mounting bolts.
8. Connect the radiator hoses. Close the radiator petcock. Fill and bleed the cooling system.
9. Start the engine and bring it to operating temperature. Check for leaks.
10. On cars equipped with automatic transmissions, check the cooler lines for leaks and interference. Check the transmission fluid level.

Electro-Drive Cooling Fan

REMOVAL & INSTALLATION

Various models, are equipped with a bracket-mounted electric cooling fan that replaces the conventional water pump mounted fan.

Operation of the fan motor is dependent on engine coolant temperature and air conditioner compressor clutch engagement. The fan will run only when the coolant temperature is approximately 180° or higher, or when the compressor clutch is engaged. The fan, motor and mount can be removed as an assembly after disconnecting the wiring harnesses and mounting bolts.

CAUTION

The cooling fan is automatic and may come on at any time without warning even if the ignition is switched OFF. To avoid possible injury, always disconnect the negative battery cable when working near the electric cooling fan.

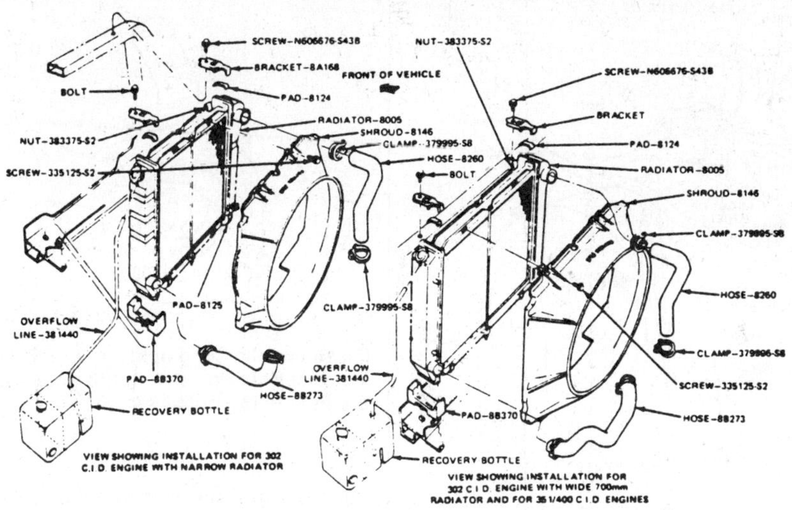

Radiator assemble, late models

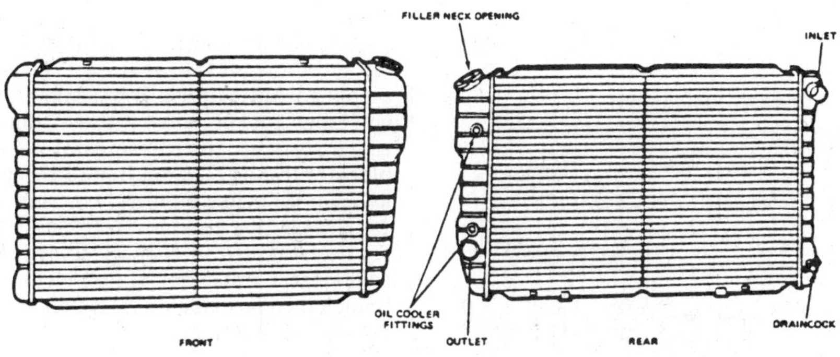

Typical crossflow radiator. Diesel models use vertical-flow radiator

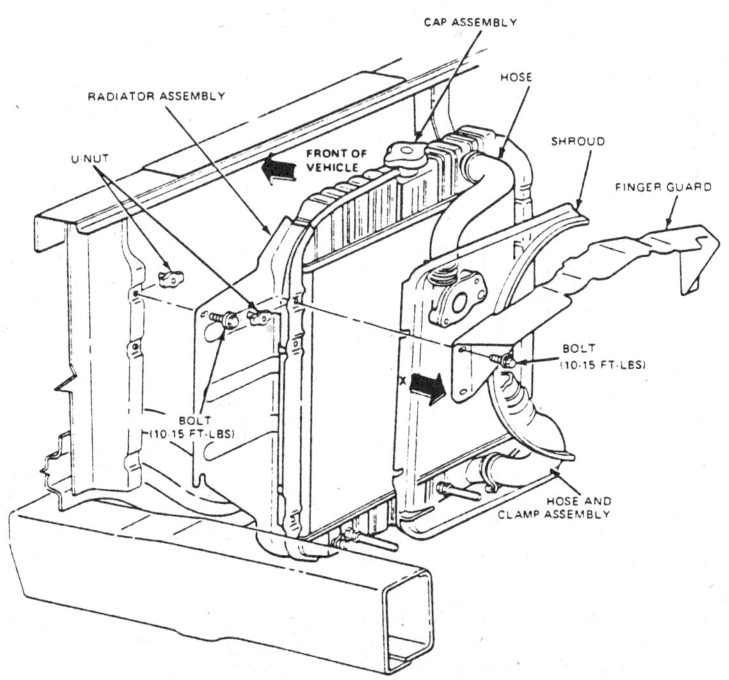

Typical 6 cylinder engine radiator installation

1. Disconnect the battery ground.
2. Remove the fan wiring harness from the clip.
3. Unplug the harness at the fan motor connector.
4. Remove the 4 mounting bracket attaching screws and remove the fan assembly from the car.
5. Remove the retaining clip from the end of the motor shaft and remove the fan.
6. Installation is the reverse of removal.

Air Conditioning Condenser

REMOVAL & INSTALLATION

1980-81

1. Discharge the system. See ROUTINE MAINTENANCE.
2. Remove the 6 attaching screws and remove the grille.
3. Move the ambient cutoff switch away from the front of the radiator and condenser.
4. Remove the battery.
5. Disconnect the refrigerant lines at the condenser and cap all openings immediately!
6. Remove the 4 bolts securing the condenser to the supports and remove the condenser.
7. Installation is the reverse of removal. Always use new O-rings coated with clean refrigerant oil at the pipe fittings. Evacuate, charge and leak test the system. See ROUTINE MAINTENANCE.

1982-87

1. Discharge the system. See ROUTINE MAINTENANCE.
2. Remove the battery.
3. Disconnect the refrigerant lines at the condenser and cap all openings immediately!

NOTE: The fittings are spring-lock couplings and a special tool, T81P-19623-G, should be used. The larger opening end of the tool is for ½" discharge lines; the smaller end for ⅜" liquid lines.

To operate the tool, close the tool and push the tool into the open side of the cage to expand the garter spring and release the female fitting. If the tool is not inserted straight, the garter spring will cock and not release.

After the garter spring is released, pull the fittings apart.

4. Remove the 4 bolts securing the condenser to the supports and remove the condenser.
5. Installation is the reverse of re-

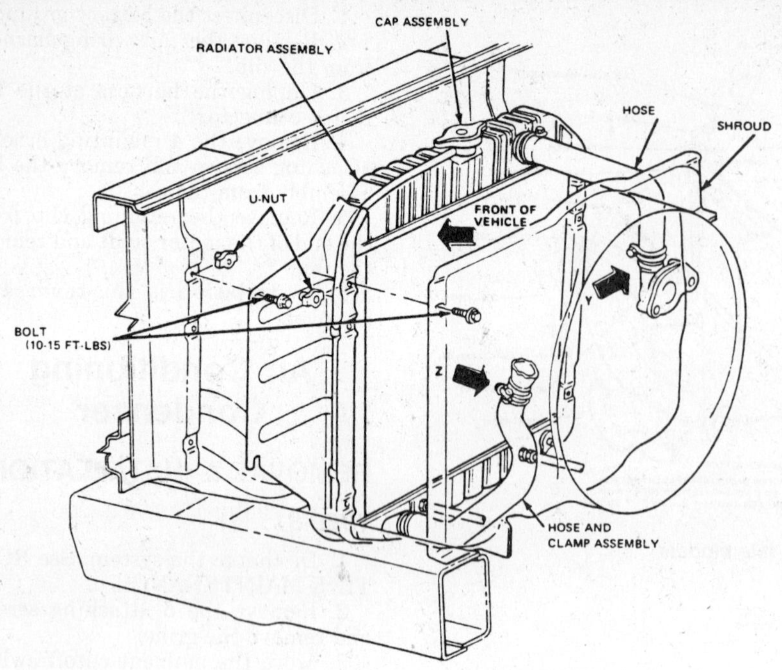

Typical 8 cylinder engine radiator installation

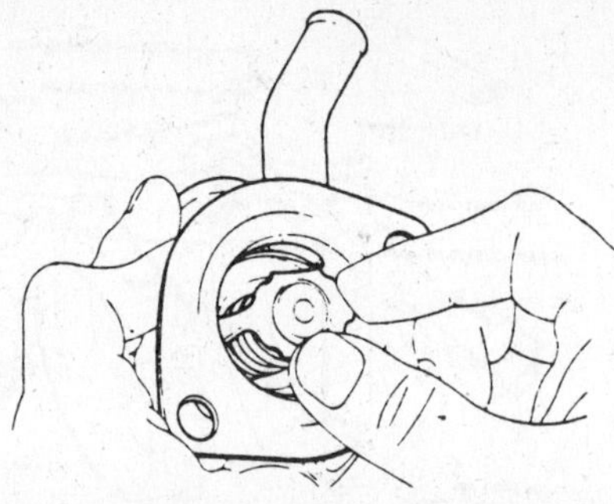

On all gasoline engines, turn the thermostat clockwise to lock it into position on the flats in the outlet elbow

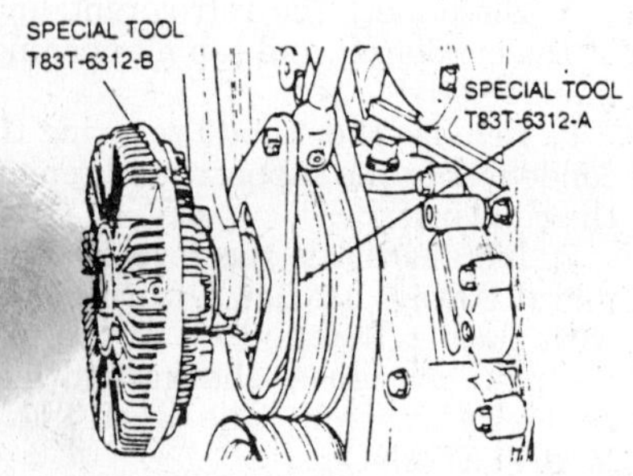

Fan clutch removal – 420 V8 diesel engine

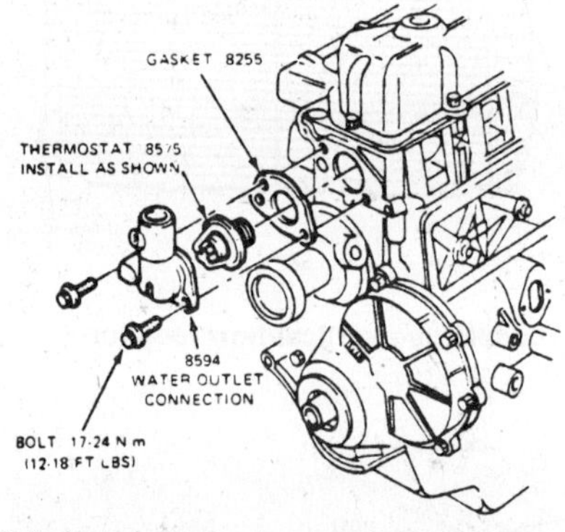

Inline six cylinder thermostat installation. V8 thermostat mounted vertically on front of engine, diesel is on side of front of intake manifold

moval. Always use new O-rings coated with clean refrigerant oil at the pipe fittings.

To connect the couplings, check to ensure that the garter spring is in the cage of the male fitting, make sure the fittings are clean, install new O-rings made for this purpose, lubricate the O-rings with clean refrigerant oil and push the male and female fittings together until the garter springs snaps into place over the female fitting.

Evacuate, charge and leak test the system. See ROUTINE MAINTENANCE.

Thermostat

REMOVAL & INSTALLATION

CAUTION

When draining the coolant, keep in mind that cats and dogs are attracted by the ethylene glycol antifreeze, and are quite likely to drink any that is left in an uncovered container or in puddles on the ground. This will prove fatal in sufficient quantity. Always drain the coolant into a sealable container. Coolant should be reused unless it is contaminated or several years old.

1. Open the drain cock and drain the radiator so the coolant level is below the coolant outlet elbow which houses the thermostat.

NOTE: On some models it will be necessary to remove the distributor cap, rotor and vacuum diaphragm in order to gain access to the thermostat housing mounting bolts.

2. Remove the outlet elbow retaining bolts and position the elbow sufficiently clear of the intake manifold or cylinder head to provide access to the thermostat.
3. Remove the thermostat and the gasket.
4. Clean the mating surfaces of the outlet elbow and the engine to remove all old gasket material and sealer. Coat the new gasket with water-resistant sealer. Install the thermostat in the block on 8-351W, then install the gasket. On all other engines, position the gasket on the engine, and install the thermostat in the coolant elbow. The thermostat must be rotated clockwise to lock it in position on all 8-255, 8-302 and 8-351W engines.
5. Install the outlet elbow and retaining bolts on the engine. Torque the bolts to 12-15 ft.lb.
6. Refill the radiator. Run the engine at operating temperature and check for leaks. Recheck the coolant level.

Water Pump

REMOVAL & INSTALLATION

6-232 (3.8L) V6

1. Disconnect the negative battery cable. Drain the cooling system.

CAUTION

When draining the coolant, keep in mind that cats and dogs are attracted by the ethylene glycol antifreeze, and are quite likely to drink any that is left in an uncovered container or in puddles on the ground. This will prove fatal in sufficient quantity. Always drain the coolant into a sealable container. Coolant should be reused unless it is contaminated or several years old.

2. Remove the air cleaner and duct assembly.
3. Remove drive belts and pump pulley. Remove the fan shroud and cooling fan/clutch assembly.
4. Remove the power steering pump

with mounting brackets and hoses attached. Position out of the way.

5. Remove the A/C compressor front mounting bracket. Leave the compressor in place.

6. Disconnect the by-pass hose from the water pump. Disconnect the heater and radiator hose at the water pump.

7. Remove the mounting bolts and the water pump.

8. Clean all gasket mounting surfaces. Installation is in the reverse order of removal.

6-300 (4.9L)

1. Disconnect the negative battery cable. Drain the cooling system.

CAUTION

When draining the coolant, keep in mind that cats and dogs are attracted by the ethylene glycol antifreeze, and are quite likely to drink any that is left in an uncovered container or in puddles on the ground. This will prove fatal in sufficient quantity. Always drain the coolant into a sealable container. Coolant should be reused unless it is contaminated or several years old.

2. Disconnect the lower radiator hose from the water pump.

3. Remove the drive belt, fan and water pump pulley. Remove the alternator and air pump belts.

4. Disconnect the heater hose at the water pump.

5. Remove the water pump.

6. Before installing the old water pump, clean the gasket mounting surfaces on the pump and on the cylinder block. If a new water pump is being installed, remove the heater hose fitting from the old pump and install it on the new one. Coat the new gaskets with sealer on both sides and install the water pump in the reverse order of removal.

8-255 (4.2L), 8-302 (5.0L), 8-351W (5.8L)

1. Drain the cooling system.

CAUTION

When draining the coolant, keep in mind that cats and dogs are attracted by the ethylene glycol antifreeze, and are quite likely to drink any that is left in an uncovered container or in puddles on the ground. This will prove fatal in sufficient quantity. Always drain the coolant into a sealable container. Coolant should be reused unless it is contaminated or several years old.

2. Remove the bolts securing the fan shroud to the radiator, if so equipped, and position the shroud over the fan.

3. Disconnect the lower radiator hose, heater hose and by-pass hose at the water pump. Remove the drive belts, fan, fan spacer and pulley. Remove the fan shroud, if so equipped.

4. Loosen the alternator pivot bolt and the bolt attaching the alternator adjusting arm to the water pump.

5. Remove the bolts securing the water pump to the timing chain cover and remove the water pump.

6. Install the water pump in the reverse order of removal, using a new gasket.

8-351M (5.8L), 8-460 (7.5L) V8

1. Drain the cooling system and remove the fan shroud attaching bolts.

2. Remove the fan assembly attaching screws and remove the shroud and fan.

CAUTION

When draining the coolant, keep in mind that cats and dogs are attracted by the ethylene glycol antifreeze, and are quite likely to drink any that is left in an uncovered container or in puddles on the ground. This will prove fatal in sufficient quantity. Always drain the coolant into a sealable container. Coolant should be reused unless it is contaminated or several years old.

3. Loosen the power steering pump attaching bolts.

4. If the truck is equipped with air conditioning, loosen the compressor attaching bolts, and remove the air conditioning compressor and power steering pump drive belts.

5. Loosen the alternator pivot bolt. Remove the two attaching bolts and spacer. Remove the drive belt, then rotate the bracket out of the way.

6. Remove the three air conditioning compressor attaching bolts and secure the compressor out of the way.

7. Remove the power steering pump attaching bolts and position the pump to one side.

8. Remove the air conditioner bracket attaching bolts and remove the bracket.

9. Disconnect the lower radiator hose and heater hose from the water pump.

10. Loosen the by-pass hose clamp at the water pump.

11. Remove the remaining water pump attaching bolts and remove the pump from the front cover. Remove the separator plate from the pump. Discard the gaskets.

12. Remove all gasket material from all of the mating surfaces.

13. Install the water pump in the reverse order of removal, using a new gasket and waterproof sealer. When the water pump is first positioned to the front cover of the engine, install only those bolts not used to secure the air conditioner and alternator brackets.

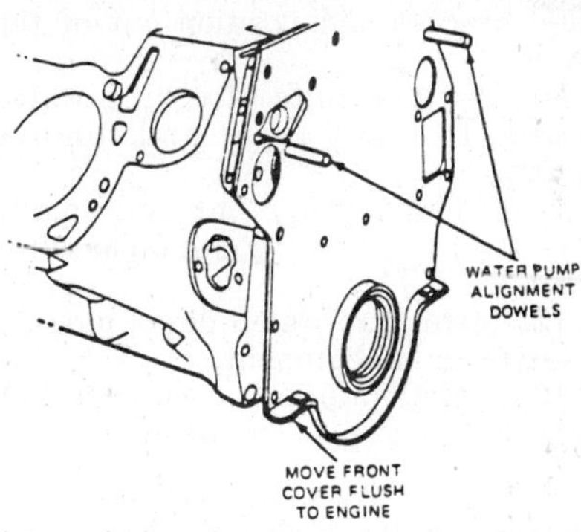

Aligning the front cover plate—420 V8 diesel

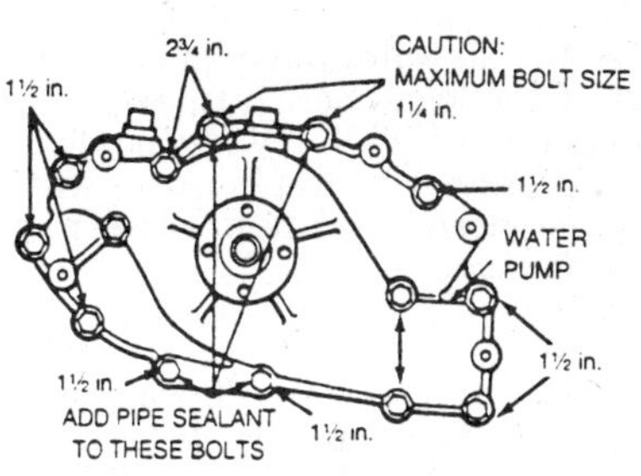

Water pump installation—420 V8 diesel

8-420 (6.9L) Diesel

1. Disconnect battery ground cables from both batteries. Drain cooling system.

CAUTION

When draining the coolant, keep in mind that cats and dogs are attracted by the ethylene glycol antifreeze, and are quite likely to drink any that is left in an uncovered container or in puddles on the ground. This will prove fatal in sufficient quantity. Always drain the coolant into a sealable container. Coolant should be reused unless it is contaminated or several years old.

2. Remove radiator fan shroud halves.

3. Remove fan and clutch assembly using suitable tools. Attached by left hand thread: Remove by turning nut clockwise.

4. Loosen power steering pump and A/C compressor and remove drive belts.

5. Loosen vacuum pump and remove drive belt. Loosen alternator and remove drive belt.

6. Remove water pump pulley.

7. Disconnect heater hose from water pump. Remove heater hose fitting from water pump.

8. Remove alternator adjusting arm and adjusting arm bracket. Remove A/C compressor with hoses attached, and position out of the way. Remove A/C compressor brackets.

9. Remove power steering pump

and bracket and position out of the way.

10. Remove bolts attaching water pump to front cover and remove pump.

11. Clean water pump and engine front cover mating surfaces with solvent.

12. Install fabricated dowel pins for water pump alignment.

13. Install water pump with new gasket and tighten to specifications.

NOTE: Coat two bolts and two bottom bolts with RTV Sealer before installation.

14. Install alternator adjusting arm bracket.

15. Install water pump pulley.

16. Coat heater hose fitting with pipe sealant and install in water pump.

17. Connect heater hose to water pump and tighten clamp to specifications.

18. Install power steering pump bracket. Install power steering pump and drive belt. Install A/C compressor bracket. Install A/C compressor and drive belt.

19. Install alternator adjusting arm and alternator drive belt. Install vacuum pump drive belt.

20. Adjust accessory drive belts.

21. Install fan and clutch assembly. Left hand thread. Turn nut counterclockwise to tighten.

22. Install radiator fan shroud halves. Fill and bleed cooling system.

23. Connect battery ground cables to both batteries. Run engine and check for coolant leaks.

ENGINE LUBRICATION

Oil Pan

REMOVAL & INSTALLATION

NOTE: Always raise and safely support the vehicle safely on jackstands. When raising the engine, place a piece of wood between the jack and jacking point, make sure the hood is opened and the fan blades do not touch the radiator or that radiator hoses or transmission lines are not stretched.

6-300 (4.9L) F100-350

1. Drain the crankcase.

2. On the F100-250, also drain the cooling system.

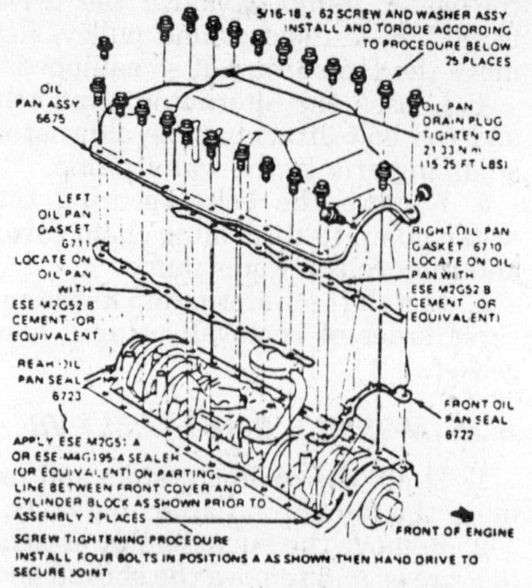

300 inline six oil pan removal

CAUTION

When draining the coolant, keep in mind that cats and dogs are attracted by the ethylene glycol antifreeze, and are quite likely to drink any that is left in an uncovered container or in puddles on the ground. This will prove fatal in sufficient quantity. Always drain the coolant into a sealable container. Coolant should be reused unless it is contaminated or several years old.

3. Remove radiator from F100-250 vehicles.

4. Raise vehicle and safely support on jackstands. Disconnect and remove the starter.

5. On F100-250, remove engine front support insulator to support bracket nuts and washers. Use a transmission jack to raise the front of the engine, then install blocks (1" thick) between the front support insulators and support brackets. Lower engine onto blocks and remove jack.

6. Remove the attaching bolts and oil pan. It may be necessary to remove the oil pump inlet tube and screen assembly in order to free the pan.

7. Remove the rear main bearing cap and front cover seals. Clean out the seal grooves and all gasket surfaces.

8. Apply oil-resistant sealer in the spaces between the rear main bearing cap and the block as illustrated. Install new rear cap seal, then apply a bead of sealer to the tapered ends of the seal.

9. Install new oil pan side gaskets with sealer and position the front cover seal.

10. Clean oil pump pick-up assembly and place it in the pan.

11. Position pan under the engine and install pick-up assembly.

12. Install pan and attaching bolts, tightening to 10–12 ft.lb.

13. Raise engine enough with a jack and remove wood blocks. Lower engine and install washers and nuts on the support insulator studs, tightening to 40-60 ft.lb.

14. Install starter and starter cable on F100–250 trucks.

15. Lower vehicle and install radiator if it was removed.

16. Fill crankcase and cooling system and start engine to check for leaks.

6-300 (4.9L) E100-350

1. Remove the engine cover. Remove the air cleaner and the carburetor.

2. If equipped with air conditioning, discharge the system and remove the compressor.

3. If the vehicle is an E350, disconnect the thermactor check valve inlet hose and remove the check valve. Remove the EGR valve.

4. Remove the radiator hoses. Unbolt the fan shroud and position on the fan. If equipped with automatic transmission, disconnect the cooler lines and remove the oil filler tube.

5. Remove exhaust inlet pipe to manifold nuts. Raise the vehicle on a hoist and disconnect and plug fuel pump inlet line. Remove the starter. Remove alternator splash shield and front engine support nuts.

6. Remove the power steering return line clip which is located in front of the No. 1 crossmember.

7. Raise the engine and place 3" blocks under the engine mounts. Remove the oil pan dipstick tube.

8. Remove the oil pan bolts and remove the oil pan. Remove the pickup tube and screen from the oil pump.

9. Clean the oil pan, tube and screen assembly and the gasket surfaces of the block and oil pan.

10. Install the oil pump and screen assembly, if removed. Cement a new oil pan gasket on the oil pan. Position a new oil pan to cylinder front cover seal on the oil pan. Position the rear seal to the rear bearing cap and apply sealer. Install the oil pan.

11. Install the dipstick tube and lower the engine. Install the support nuts, starter, and connect the fuel line.

12. Install the lower radiator hose. Connect the transmission cooler lines and the transmission fill tube, if equipped.

13. Install the power steering return line clip and position the line.

14. Install the alternator splash shield and lower the hoist. Install the EGR valve and the carburetor. Connect the exhaust.

15. On E350 models, install the thermactor check valve and connect the inlet hose.

16. Install the fan shroud and the up-

per radiator hose. Fill the cooling system.

17. Install the air conditioning compressor and charge the system.

18. Replace the oil filter and fill the crankcase. Start the engine and check for leaks. Adjust the carburetor curb idle speed. Install the air cleaner.

6-232 (3.8L) V6

1. Disconnect the cable from the battery negative cable.
2. Remove the air cleaner and duct assembly.
3. Remove the bolts attaching the fan shroud to the radiator and position the shroud over the fan.
4. Remove the engine oil dipstick.
5. Raise the vehicle and safely support on jackstands. Drain the engine oil and replace the drain plug.
6. Remove the oil filter.
7. Disconnect the muffler inlet pipes from the exhaust manifolds. Remove the clamp attaching inlet pipe to converter pipe and remove inlet pipe from vehicle.
8. Disconnect the transmission shift linkage at the transmission.
9. Disconnect the transmission cooler lines at the radiator if so equipped.
10. Remove the nuts attaching the engine supports to the chassis brackets.
11. Raise the engine as high as possible, and place wood blocks between the engine supports and the chassis brackets. Remove the jack.
12. Remove the oil pan attaching bolts and drop the oil pan. Remove the oil pick-up and tube assembly and let them lay in the oil pan. Remove the oil pan from the vehicle.
13. Clean oil pan and sealing surfaces. Inspect the gasket sealing surfaces for damages and distortion due to overtightening of the bolts. Repair and straighten as required.
14. Trial fit the oil pan to the cylinder block. Make sure enough clearance has been provided to allow the oil pan to be installed without the sealant being scraped off when the pan is positioned under the engine.
15. Remove the oil pan.
16. Lay the oil pick-up and tube assembly and place them in the oil pan.
17. Place the oil pan in position on No. 1 crossmember.
18. Install the oil pick-up and tube assembly using a new gasket. Make sure the support bracket engages the stud on the No.2 main bearing cap attaching bolt.
19. Tighten the attaching bolts to 15-22 ft.lb. and the attaching nut to 15-22 ft.lb.
20. Install a new oil pan rear seal. Using a small screwdriver, work the tabs on each end of the seal into the gap between the rear main cap and cylinder block. With the tabs positioned work the edge of the seal into the seal groove in the rear main cap.
21. Install the oil pan as follows: Apply a 1/8" bead of RTV Sealer to the seam where the front cover and cylinder block join. Apply a 1/8" bead of RTV Sealer to each end of the rear seal where the rear main cap and cylinder block join. Apply a 1/8" bead of RTV Sealer along the oil pan rails on the cylinder block. As the bead crosses the front cover increase the bead width to 1/4". Position oil pan to bottom of engine and secure with bolts. Tighten bolts to 7-8 ft.lb.
22. Raise the engine and remove the wood blocks. Lower the engine and install the insulator-to-chassis bracket nuts and washers. Tighten the nuts to 50-70 ft.lb.
23. Position the inlet pipe to the converter pipe and secure with attaching clamp. Connect inlet pipe to exhaust manifolds and secure with attaching nuts. Tighten to 25-38 ft.lb.
24. Connect the transmission shift linkage at the transmission.
25. Connect the transmission cooler lines at the radiator if so equipped.
26. Install a new oil filter.
27. Lower the vehicle. Install the air cleaner assembly. Position fan shroud to radiator brace and secure with bolts.
28. Connect the battery negative cable to the battery.
29. Install the engine oil dipstick.
30. Fill crankcase with oil. Run the engine and check for possible leaks.

8-302 (5.0L) & 8-351W (5.8L)

BRONCO

1. Remove the air cleaner and duct assembly. Remove the oil dipstick tube. Drain the engine oil.
2. Remove the oil pan bolts and remove the oil pan.
3. To install, clean the oil pan and the cylinder block of all old gasket material. Position a new oil pan gasket and end seals to the cylinder block.
4. Clean and install the oil pump pick-up tube and screen assembly, if removed.
5. Install the oil pan to the cylinder block. Install the oil dipstick tube, air cleaner and duct assembly.
6. Fill the crankcase with the proper oil. Start the engine and check for leaks.

F SERIES

1. Remove the oil dipstick. Remove the bolts attaching the fan shroud to the radiator and position the shroud over the fan.
2. Remove the nuts and lockwashers attaching the engine support insulators to the chassis bracket.
3. Disconnect the oil cooler line at the left side of the radiator, if equipped with automatic transmission.
4. Raise the engine and place wood blocks under the engine supports. Drain the crankcase.
5. Remove the oil pan bolts and lower the oil pan onto the crossmember.
6. Remove the oil pump pick-up tube and screen. Lower this assembly, into the oil pan. Remove the oil pan.
7. To install, clean the oil pan, inlet tube and gasket surfaces. Position a new oil pan gasket and seals to the cylinder block.
8. Install the oil pick-up tube and screen to the oil pump, and install the lower attaching bolt and gasket loosely. Place the oil pan on the crossmember. Install the upper pick-up tube bolt. Tighten both pick-up tube bolts.
9. Install the oil pan. Remove the wood blocks and lower the engine.
10. Install the insulator-to-chassis bracket nuts and washers.
11. Connect the automatic transmission cooler line, if equipped. Install the fan shroud attaching bolts.
12. Fill the crankcase with oil. Install the oil dipstick. Start the engine and check for leaks.

ECONOLINE

1. Disconnect the battery and remove engine cover. Remove the air cleaner. Drain the cooling system.

CAUTION

When draining the coolant, keep in mind that cats and dogs are attracted by the ethylene glycol antifreeze, and are quite likely to drink any that is left in an uncovered container or in puddles on the ground. This will prove fatal in sufficient quantity. Always drain the coolant into a sealable container. Coolant should be reused unless it is contaminated or several years old.

2. If equipped with power steering remove the pump and position it out of the way. If so equipped, remove the air conditioning compressor retainer and position the compressor out of the way.
3. Disconnect the radiator hoses. Remove the fan shroud bolts and oil filler tube. Remove the oil dipstick bolt. Raise the vehicle on a hoist.
4. Remove the alternator splash shield. If equipped, disconnect the automatic transmission cooler lines at the radiator.
5. Disconnect and plug the fuel line at the fuel pump. Remove the engine mount nuts. Drain the engine oil. Remove the dipstick tube. Disconnect the muffler inlet pipe from the exhaust manifolds.
6. If equipped, remove the automat-

ic transmission dipstick and tube. Disconnect the manual linkage at the transmission. Remove the center driveshaft support and remove the driveshaft from the transmission.

7. Place a transmission jack under the oil pan and insert a wooden block between the pan and jack.

CAUTION

The engine and transmission assembly will pivot around the rear engine mount. The engine assembly must be raised 4" (measured from the front motor mounts). The engine must remain centered in the engine compartment to obtain this much lift.

8. Raise the engine and transmission assembly. Insert wooden blocks to support the engine in its uppermost position.

9. Remove the oil pan bolts and lower the oil pan. Unbolt the oil pump and the oil pick-up tube and lay them in the oil pan. Remove the oil pan from the vehicle.

NOTE: The oil pump must be removed along with the removal of the oil pan. When installing the oil pump refer to the procedure for Oil Pump Removal and Installation.

10. To install, clean the oil pan, oil pick-up tube, oil pump and gasket surfaces. Position new gasket and seals to the engine block.

11. Position the oil pan with the oil pump to vehicle and install the oil pump. Install the oil pan.

12. Continue the installation in the reverse order of removal.

13. Install a new oil filter and fill the crankcase with the proper grade oil. Fill the cooling system. Start the engine and check for oil and water.

8-351M (5.8L)

1. Remove the oil dipstick. Remove the fan shroud bolts and position the shroud over the fan.

2. Raise the vehicle. Drain the crankcase. Disconnect the starter cable and remove the starter.

3. Place a jack and a wood block under the oil pan and support the engine. Remove the engine front support through bolts.

4. Raise the engine and place wood blocks between the engine supports and the chassis brackets. Remove the jack.

5. If equipped with an automatic transmission, position the oil cooler lines out of the way.

6. Remove the oil pan attaching bolts and remove the oil pan.

7. To install, clean the gasket surfaces of the block, oil pan, oil pick-up tube, and screen. Coat the block surface and the oil pan gasket with sealer. Position the oil pan gasket to the cylinder block.

8. Position the oil pan front seal on the cylinder front cover plate. Position the oil pan rear seal on the rear main bearing cap. Be sure that the tabs on both the front and rear seals are over the oil pan gasket.

9. Position and install the oil pan. Continue the installation in the reverse order of removal. Fill the crankcase. Start the engine and check for oil leaks.

8-460 (7.5L)

EXCEPT ECONOLINE

1. Disconnect the battery ground cable. Disconnect the radiator shroud and position it over the fan.

2. Raise the vehicle on a hoist and drain the crankcase. Remove the oil filter.

3. Remove the through bolt from each engine support. Place a floor jack under the front edge of the oil pan, with a block of wood between the jack and the oil pan. Raise the engine just high enough to insert 1¼" blocks of wood between the insulators and the brackets. Remove the floor jack.

4. Remove the oil pan bolts and remove the oil pan. It may be necessary to rotate the crankshaft to provide clearance between the pan and the crankshaft counterweights.

5. To install, clean the gasket surfaces of the block and the oil pan. Coat both surfaces with sealer. Position the oil pan gasket on the cylinder block. Position the oil pan front seal on the cylinder front cover. Position the oil pan rear seal on the rear main bearing cap. Be sure that the tabs on both the front and rear seals are over the oil pan gasket.

6. Position and install the oil pan. Continue the installation in the reverse order of removal.

7. Replace the oil filter and fill the crankcase. Start the engine and check for oil leaks.

ECONOLINE

1. Remove the engine cover, disconnect the battery and drain the cooling system.

CAUTION

When draining the coolant, keep in mind that cats and dogs are attracted by the ethylene glycol antifreeze, and are quite likely to drink any that is left in an uncovered container or in puddles on the ground. This will prove fatal in sufficient quantity. Always drain the coolant into a sealable container. Coolant should be reused unless it is contaminated or several years old.

2. Remove the air cleaner assembly. Disconnect the throttle and transmission linkage at the carburetor. Disconnect the power brake vacuum lines.

3. Disconnect the fuel line, choke lines and remove the carburetor air cleaner adaptor from the carburetor.

4. Disconnect the radiator hoses. If equipped, disconnect the oil cooler lines. Remove the fan assembly and remove the radiator. If equipped, remove the power steering pump and position it aside.

5. Remove the front engine mount attaching bolts. Remove the engine oil dipstick tube from the exhaust manifold. Remove the oil filler tube and bracket.

6. If so equipped, rotate the air conditioning lines (at the rear of the compressor) down to clear the dash (or remove them).

7. Raise the vehicle and safely support on jackstands, drain the crankcase and remove the oil filter.

8. Remove the muffler inlet pipe assembly. Disconnect the manual and kickdown linkage from the transmission. Remove the driveshaft and coupling shaft assembly. Remove the transmission tube assembly.

9. Remove the dipstick and tube from the oil pan. Place a transmission jack under the engine oil pan. Insert a wood block between the jack surface and the oil pan. Jack the engine upward, pivoting on the rear mount until the transmission contacts the floor. Block the engine in position.

NOTE: The engine must remain centralized to obtain the maximum height. The engine must be raised 4" at the mounts to remove the oil pan.

10. Remove the oil pan bolts and lower the oil pan. Remove the oil pump and pick-up tube attachments and drop them into the oil pan. Remove the oil pan rearward from the vehicle.

NOTE: The oil pump must be removed when removing the oil pan. When installing refer to the procedure for Oil Pump Removal and Installation.

11. To install, clean the oil pan gasket surface at the cylinder block, the oil pan assembly, the oil pump pick-up tube, and the screen.

12. Position the oil pan gaskets and end seals to the cylinder block using sealer. Position the oil pan with the oil pump and pick-up tube assembly to the chassis and install the oil pump assembly. Position and install the oil pan. Continue the installation in the reverse order of the removal.

13. Fill the cooling system, replace the oil filter, fill the crankcase and

connect the battery. Start the engine and check for oil and water leaks.

8-420 (6.9L) Diesel

1. Disconnect battery ground cable from both batteries.
2. Remove engine oil level dipstick. Remove transmission oil level dipstick, if so equipped.
3. Remove air cleaner and install intake opening cover.
4. Remove fan and clutch assembly using Ford Tool T83T-6312-A and B or equivalent. The attachment has a left hand thread. Remove by turning nut counterclockwise.
5. Drain cooling system. Disconnect lower radiator hose.

CAUTION

When draining the coolant, keep in mind that cats and dogs are attracted by the ethylene glycol antifreeze, and are quite likely to drink any that is left in an uncovered container or in puddles on the ground. This will prove fatal in sufficient quantity. Always drain the coolant into a sealable container. Coolant should be reused unless it is contaminated or several years old.

6. Disconnect power steering return hose from pump. Plug hose and pump to prevent contamination of the system.
7. Disconnect alternator wiring harness and fuel line heater connector from alternator.
8. Raise vehicle and safely support on jackstands.
9. Disconnect and plug transmission oil cooler lines from radiator, if so equipped.
10. Disconnect and plug fuel pump inlet fuel line.
11. Drain crankcase and remove oil filter. Remove bolt attaching transmission oil filler tube to engine block and remove tube.
12. Disconnect muffler inlet pipe from exhaust manifolds.
13. Disconnect muffler inlet pipe at muffler flange and remove inlet pipe.
14. Remove upper inlet pipe mounting stud from right exhaust manifold.
15. Remove nuts and washers attaching engine insulators to No. 1 crossmember. Lower vehicle.
16. Install lifting sling and raise engine until transmission housing contacts body.
17. Install wood blocks (2¾″ LH side, 2″ RH side) between engine insulators and crossmember.
18. Lower engine so that blocks support engine.
19. Raise vehicle and safely support.
20. Remove flywheel inspection plate.
21. Position fuel pump inlet line at rear of No. 1 crossmember and transmission oil cooler lines, if so equipped, out of the way.
22. Remove oil pan attaching bolts.
23. Remove oil pump and pick-up tube from engine and lay in oil pan.
24. Remove oil pan by pulling down and toward rear of vehicle.

NOTE: Crankshaft may have to be turned to reposition counterweights to aid in removal of oil pan.

25. Remove oil pump pickup tube from oil pump, if required.
26. Remove old gasket material and clean mating surfaces of oil pan, engine block and front and rear covers with a suitable solvent and dry thoroughly.
27. Clean mating surfaces of oil pick-up tube. Inspect for cracks, and assemble to oil pump with new gasket, if removed. Tighten nuts to specification.
28. Prime oil pump with recommended engine oil. Rotate pump drive gear to distribute oil within pump body. Place oil pump and pick-up tube in oil pan.
29. Place oil pan in position on No. 1 crossmember.
30. Install oil pump and pick-up tube and tighten to specifications.
31. Apply ⅛″ bead of RTV Sealant on side rails of engine block oil pan mating surface, and a ¼″ bead of RTV Sealant on ends of engine oil pan mating surface on front and rear covers, and in mating corners.
32. Install locally fabricated oil pan installation dowels in position.
33. Position oil pan on engine and install attaching bolts. Remove oil pan locating dowels and install two remaining oil pan bolts. Tighten all oil pan bolts.
34. Install flywheel inspection plate and tighten to specifications. Lower vehicle.
35. Raise engine and remove wooden engine support blocks.
36. Lower engine onto No. 1 crossmember and remove lifting sling. Raise vehicle and safely support.
37. Install nuts and washers attaching engine insulators to No. 1 crossmember and tighten.
38. Install upper muffler inlet pipe mounting stud on right exhaust manifold.
39. Position muffler inlet pipe in vehicle and connect muffler inlet pipe to muffler flange, using a new gasket and tighten. Connect muffler inlet pipe to exhaust manifolds and tighten.
40. Install transmission oil filler tube, using a new O-ring and tighten attaching bolt. Install oil pan drain plug and new oil filter and tighten.
41. Connect fuel pump inlet line to fuel pump and tighten to specification.

NOTE: Make sure fuel line clip is re-installed in No. 1 crossmember.

42. Connect transmission oil cooler lines and tighten to specification, if so equipped. Lower vehicle.
43. Connect alternator wiring harness and fuel line heater connector to alternator.
44. Connect power steering return hose to power steering pump.
45. Connect lower radiator hose clamp and tighten. Install radiator fan and clutch assembly using suitable tools. Left hand thread. Install by turning nut counterclockwise.
46. Remove intake manifold cover, and install air cleaner and tighten.
47. Install engine oil and transmission oil dipsticks.
48. Refill cooling system.
49. Fill crankcase with specified quantity, quality, and viscosity of engine oil.
50. Connect battery ground cables to both batteries.
51. Run engine and check for oil, fuel and coolant leaks.
52. Check power steering fluid and add, if necessary.

Oil Pump

REMOVAL & INSTALLATION

Except 6-232

1. Remove the oil pan.
2. Remove the oil pump inlet tube and screen assembly.
3. Remove the oil pump attaching bolts and remove the oil pump gasket and the intermediate shaft.
4. Prime the oil pump by filling the inlet and outlet ports with engine oil and rotating the shaft of pump to distribute it.
5. Position the intermediate driveshaft into the distributor socket.
6. Position a new gasket on the pump body and insert the intermediate driveshaft into the pump body.
7. Install the pump and intermediate shaft as an assembly.

WARNING: Do not force the pump if it does not seat readily. The driveshaft may be misaligned with the distributor shaft. To align, rotate the intermediate driveshaft into a new position.

8. Install and torque the oil pump attaching screws to:
   - 6-300 – 12-15 ft.lb.;
   - 8-302 and 8-351W – 22-32 ft.lb.;
   - All other V8 – 25-35 ft.lb.
9. Install the oil pan.

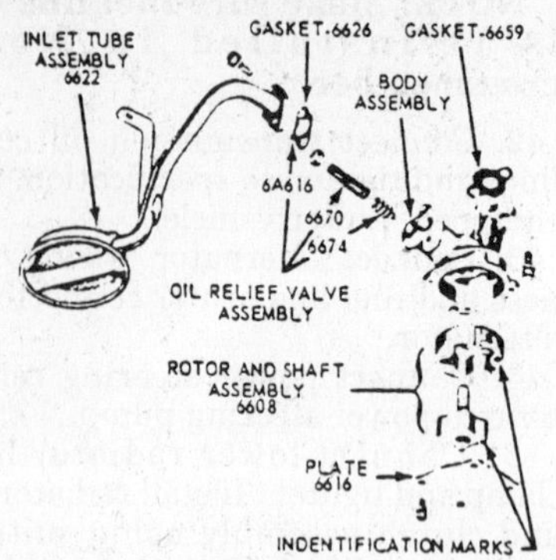

Exploded view of the typical V8 oil pump

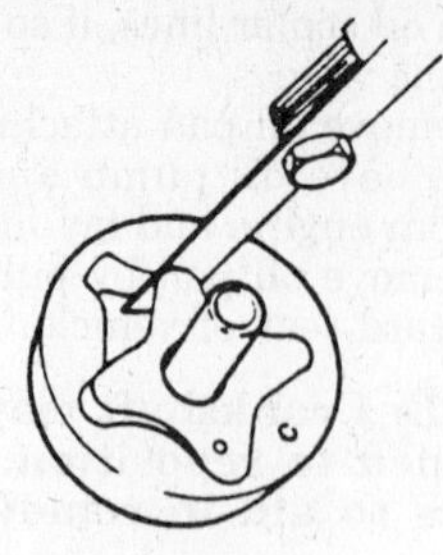

NOTE: INNER TO OUTER ROTOR TIP CLEARANCE MUST NOT EXCEED .012 WITH FEELER GAUGE INSERTED 1/2" MINIMUM AND ROTORS REMOVED FROM PUMP HOUSING.

Checking inner rotor tip clearance

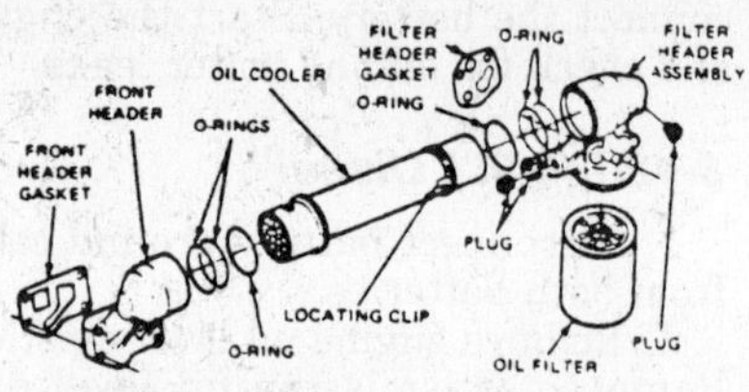

6.9L diesel oil cooler and filter assembly

6-232 Engines

NOTE: The oil pump is mounted in the front cover assembly. Oil pan removal is necessary for pick-up tube/screen replacement or service.

1. Raise and safely support the vehicle on jackstands.
2. Remove the oil filter.
3. Remove the cover/filter mount assembly.
4. Lift the two pump gears from their mounting pocket in the front cover.
5. Clean all gasket mounting surfaces.
6. Inspect the mounting pocket for wear. If excessive wear is present, complete timing cover assembly replacement is necessary.
7. Inspect the cover/filter mounting gasket-to-timing cover surface for flatness. Place a straightedge across the flat and check the clearance with a feeler gauge. If the measured clearance exceeds 0.004" (0.102mm), replace the cover/filter mount.
8. Replace the pump gears if wear is excessive.
9. Remove the plug from the end of the pressure relief valve passage using a small drill and slide hammer. Use caution when drilling.
10. Remove the spring and valve from the bore. Clean all dirt, gum and metal chips from the bore and valve. Inspect all parts for wear. Replace as necessary.
11. Install the valve and spring after lubricating them with engine oil. Install a new plug flush with the machined surfaces.
12. Install the pump gears and fill the pocket with petroleum jelly. Install the cover/filter mount using a new mounting gasket. Tighten the mounting bolts to 18-22 ft.lb. Install the oil filter, add necessary oil for correct level.

CARBURETED FUEL SYSTEM

Fuel Pump

Ford truck engines use a camshaft eccentric actuated combination fuel pump located on the lower left side of the engine block on both in-line 6-cylinder and V8 engines, and on the right side on the V6.

REMOVAL

1. Disconnect the fuel inlet and outlet lines at the fuel pump. Discard the fuel inlet retaining clamp.
2. Remove the pump retaining bolts then remove the pump assembly and gasket from the engine. Discard the gasket.

INSTALLATION

1. If a new pump is to be installed, remove the fuel line connector fitting from the old pump and install it in the new pump.
2. Remove all gasket material from the mounting pad and pump flange. Apply oil resistant sealer to both sides of a new gasket.
3. Position the new gasket on the pump flange and hold the pump in position against the mounting pad. Make sure that the rocker arm is riding on the camshaft eccentric.
4. Press the pump tight against the pad, install the retaining bolts and alternately torque them to 12-15 ft.lb. on 6 cylinder engines and 20-24 ft.lb. on the V8. Connect the fuel lines. Use a new clamp on the fuel inlet line.
5. Operate the engine and check for leaks.

TESTING

Incorrect fuel pump pressure and low volume (flow rate) are the two most likely fuel pump troubles that will affect engine performance. Low pressure will cause a lean mixture and fuel starvation at high speeds and excessive pressure will cause high fuel consumption and carburetor flooding.

To determine that the fuel pump is in satisfactory operating condition, tests for both fuel pump pressure and volume should be performed.

The tests are performed with the fuel pump installed on the engine and the engine at normal operating temperature and at idle speed.

Before the test, make sure that the replaceable fuel filter has been changed at the proper mileage interval. If in doubt, install a new filter.

Pressure Test

1. Remove the air cleaner assembly. Disconnect the fuel inlet line of the fuel filter at the carburetor. Use care to prevent fire, due to fuel spillage. Place an absorbent cloth under the connection before removing the line to catch any fuel that might flow out of the line.
2. Connect a pressure gauge, a restrictor and a flexible hose between the fuel filter and the carburetor.
3. Position the flexible hose and the restrictor so that the fuel can be discharged into a suitable graduated container.
4. Before taking a pressure reading, operate the engine at the specified idle rpm and vent the system into the container by opening the hose restrictor momentarily.
5. Close the hose restrictor, allow

the pressure to stabilize and note the reading. The pressure should be as specified in the Tune Up Charts earlier in this book.

If the pump pressure is not within 4-6 psi and the fuel lines and filter are in satisfactory condition, the pump is defective and should be replaced.

If the pump pressure is within the proper range, perform the test for fuel volume.

Volume Test

1. Operate the engine at the specified idle rpm.
2. Open the hose restrictor and catch the fuel in the container while observing the time it takes to pump 1 pint. 1 pint should be expelled in 20 seconds. If the pump does not pump to specifications, check for proper fuel tank venting or a restriction in the fuel line leading from the fuel tank to the carburetor before replacing the fuel pump.

Carburetors

The carburetor identification tag is attached to the carburetor. The basic part number for all carburetors is 9510. To obtain replacement parts, it is necessary to know the part number prefix, suffix and, in some cases, the design change code. If the carburetor is ever replaced by a new unit, make sure that the identification tag stays with the new carburetor and the vehicle.

FLOAT AND FUEL LEVEL ADJUSTMENTS

Carter Model YF, YFA and YFA Feedback 1-bbl

1. Remove the carburetor air horn and gasket from the carburetor.
2. Invert the air horn assembly, and check the clearance from the top of the float to the bottom of the air horn. Hold the air horn at eye level when gauging the float level. The float arm (lever) should be resting on the needle pin. Do not load the needle when adjusting the float. Bend the float arm as necessary to adjust the float level (clearance). Do not bend the tab at the end of the float arm, because it prevents the float from striking the bottom of the fuel bowl when empty.
3. Turn the air horn over and hold it upright and let the float hang free. Measure the maximum clearance from the top of the float to the bottom of the air horn with the float gauge. Hold the air horn at eye level when gauging the dimension. To adjust the float drop, bend the tab at the end of the float arm.
4. Install the carburetor air horn with a new gasket.

Autolite (Motorcraft) Model 2150 2-bbl (Wet Adjustment)

1. Operate the engine until it reaches normal operating temperature. Place the vehicle on a level surface and stop the engine.
2. Remove the carburetor air cleaner assembly.
3. Remove the air horn attaching screws and the carburetor identification tag. Temporarily, leave the air horn and gasket in position on the carburetor main body and start the engine. Let the engine idle for a few minutes, then rotate the air horn out of the way and remove the air horn gasket to provide access to the float assembly.
4. While the engine is idling, use a scale to measure the vertical distance from the top machined surface of the carburetor main body to the level of the fuel in the fuel bowl. The measurement must be made at least ¼" (6mm) away from any vertical surface to assure an accurate reading, because the surface of the fuel is concave, being higher at the edges than in the center. Care must be exercised to measure the fuel level at the point of contact with the float.
5. If any adjustment is required, stop the engine to minimize the hazard of fire due to spilled gasoline. To adjust the fuel level, bend the float tab contacting the fuel inlet valve upward in relation to the original position to raise the fuel level, and downward to lower it. Each time the float is adjusted, the engine must be started and permitted to idle for a few minutes to stabilize the fuel level. Check the fuel level after each adjustment, until the specified level is obtained.
6. Assemble the carburetor in the reverse order of disassembly, using a new gasket between the air horn and the main carburetor body.

Motorcraft Model 7200 VV Feedback 2-bbl

1. Remove the upper body assembly and the gasket.
2. Fabricate a gauge to the specified dimensions.
3. With the upper body inverted, place the fuel level gauge on the cast surface of the upper body and measure the vertical distance from the cast surface of the upper body and the bottom of the float.
4. To adjust, bend the float operating lever away from the fuel inlet needle to decrease the setting and toward the needle to increase the setting.

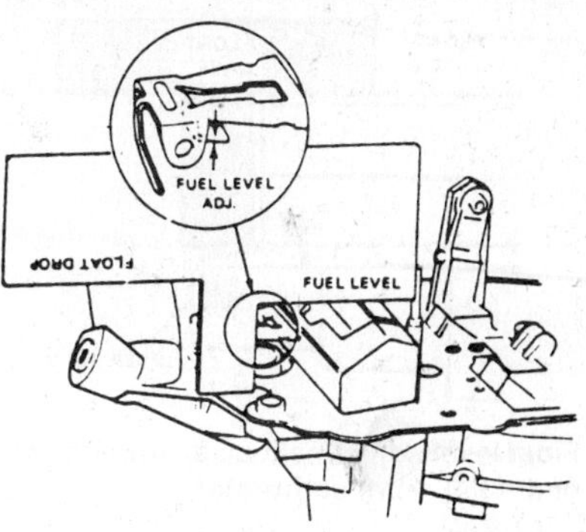

Float level adjustment for the Motorcraft 7200VV 2-bbl carburetor

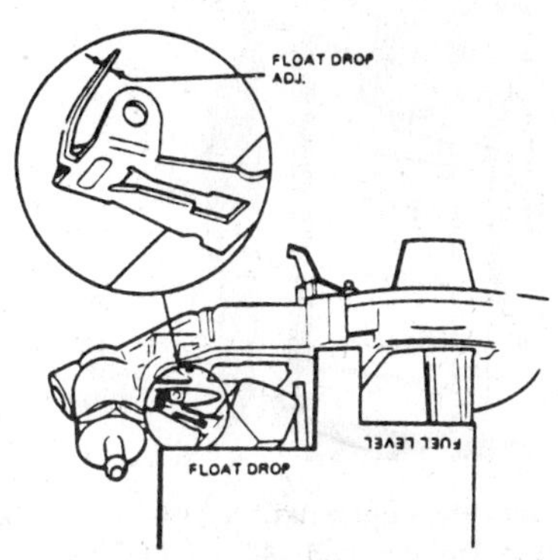

Float drop adjustment for the Motorcraft 7200VV 2-bbl carburetor

5. Check and/or adjust the float drop using the following procedures.
   a. Fabricate a gauge to the specified dimension.
   b. With the upper body assembly held in the upright position, place the gauge against the cast surface of the upper body and measure the vertical distance between the cast surface of the upper body and the bottom of the float.
   c. To adjust, bend the stop tab on the float lever away from the hinge pin to increase the setting and toward the hinge pin to decrease the setting.
6. Reinstall the upper body assembly and new gasket.

Holley Model 4180-C 4-bbl (Dry Adjustment)

The float adjustment is a preliminary fuel level adjustment only. The final adjustment (Wet) must be performed after the carburetor has been installed on the engine.

With the fuel bowls and the float assemblies removed, hold the fuel bowls upside down and turn the adjusting nuts until the floats are parallel with the top of the fuel bowls.

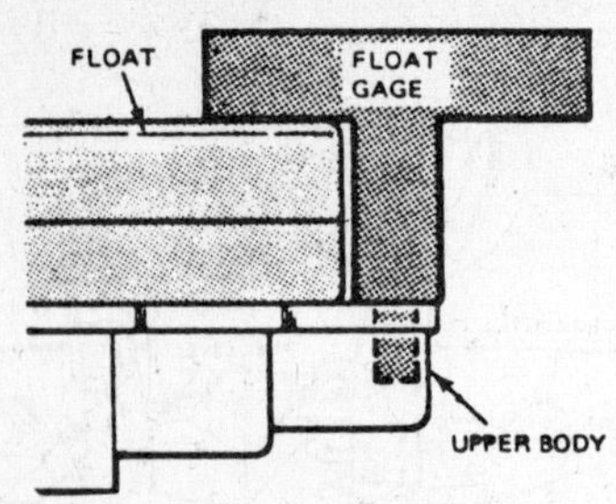

Float level adjustment on an Autolite 4300 and 4350 4-bbl carburetor

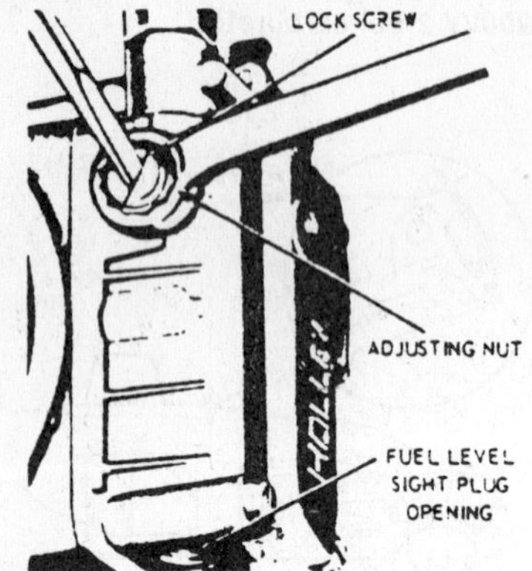

Float level adjustment (wet)—Holley 2300 2-bbl, Holley 4150, 4160, 4180C 4-bbl

SECONDARY THROTTLE PLATE ADJUSTMENT

This adjustment must be performed before the carburetor is installed on the engine and before the float level wet adjustment.

1. With the carburetor off the engine, hold the secondary throttle plates closed.
2. Turn the secondary throttle shaft lever adjusting screw (stop screw) out (counterclockwise) until the secondary throttle plates seat in the throttle bores.
3. Turn the screw in clockwise until the screw just contacts the secondary lever, then turn the screw in (clockwise) ⅜ turn.

Holley Model 4180-C 4-bbl (Wet Adjustment)

NOTE: The fuel pump pressure and volume must be to specifications prior to performing the following adjustments. Refer to the fuel pump specifications in this section.

1. Operate the engine to normalize engine temperatures and place the vehicle on a flat surface.
2. Remove the air cleaner, and run the engine at 1,000 rpm for about 30 seconds to stabilize the fuel level.
3. Stop the engine and remove the sight plug on the side of the primary carburetor bowl.
4. Check the fuel level. It should be at the bottom of the sight plug hole. If fuel spills out when the sight plug is removed, lower the fuel level. If the fuel level is below the sight glass hole, raise the fuel level.

CAUTION

Do not loosen the lock screw or nut, or attempt to adjust the fuel level with the sight glass plug removed or the engine running as fuel may spray out creating a fire hazard.

5. Adjust the front level as necessary by loosening the lock screw, and turning the adjusting nut clockwise to lower fuel level, or counterclockwise to raise fuel level. A $\frac{1}{16}$ turn of the adjusting nut will change fuel level approximately $\frac{1}{32}$" (0.8mm). Tighten the locking screw and install the sight plug, using the old gasket. Start the engine and run for about 30 seconds at 1,000 rpm to stabilize the fuel level.
6. Stop the engine, remove the sight plug and check the fuel level. Repeat step 5 until the fuel level is at the bottom of the sight plug hole, install the sight plug using a new adjusting plug gasket.
7. Repeat steps 3 through 6 for the secondary fuel bowl.

NOTE: The secondary throttle must be used to stabilize the fuel level in the secondary fuel bowl.

8. Install the air cleaner.

Idle Speed Adjustment

CARBURETORS

1980-82

1. Remove the air cleaner and disconnect and plug the vacuum lines.
2. Block the wheels, apply the parking brake, turn off all accessories, start the engine and run it to normalize underhood temperatures.
3. Check that the choke plate is fully open and connect a tachometer according to the manufacturer's instructions.
4. Check the throttle stop positioner (TSP) off speed as follows: Collapse the plunger by forcing the throttle lever against it. Place the transmission in neutral and check the engine speed. If necessary, adjust to specified TSP Off speed with the throttle adjusting screw. See the underhood sticker.
5. Place the manual transmission in neutral; the automatic in Drive and make certain the TSP plunger is extended.
6. Turn the TSP until the specified idle speed is obtained.
7. Install the air cleaner and connect the vacuum lines. Check the idle speed. Adjust, if necessary, with the air cleaner on.

1983 and Later 6-300 (4.9L) YFA-IV & YFA-IV-FB

1. Block the wheels and apply the parking brake. Place the transmission in Neutral or Park.
2. Bring engine to normal operating temperature.
3. Place A/C Heat Selector to Off position.
4. Place transmission in specified gear.
5. Check/adjust curb idle RPM as follows:
   a. TSP dashpot: Insure that TSP is activated using a ⅜" open end wrench, adjust curb idle RPM by rotating the nut directly behind the dashpot housing. Adjust curb idle RPM by turning the idle RPM speed screw.
   b. Front mounted TSP: (same as A/C kicker on all other calibrations) insure that TSP is activated. After loosening lock nut, adjust curb idle RPM by rotating TSP solenoid until specified RPM is obtained. Tighten locknut.
6. Check/adjust anti-diesel (TSP Off). Manually collapse the TSP by rotating the carb throttle shaft lever until the TSP Off adjusting screw contacts the carburetor body. If adjustment is required, turn the TSP Off adjusting screw while holding the lever adjustment screw against the stop.
7. Place the transmission in Neutral or Park. Rev the engine momentarily. Place the transmission in specified position and recheck curb idle rpm. Readjust if required.
8. Check/adjust dashpot clearance to 0.120" ± 0.030" (3mm ± 0.76mm).
9. If a final curb idle speed adjustment is required, the bowl vent setting must be checked as follows: Stop the engine and turn the ignition key to the On position, so that the TSP dashpot or TSP is activated but the engine is not running (where applicable). Secure the choke plate in the wide open position. Open the throttle, so that the throttle vent lever does not touch the fuel bowl vent rod. Close the throttle, and measure the travel of the fuel bowl vent rod from the open throttle position. Travel of the fuel bowl vent rod should be 0.100-0.150" (2.54-3.81mm). If out of specification, bend the throttle vent lever to obtain the required travel. Remove all test equipment, and tighten the air cleaner holddown bolt to specification.
10. Whenever it is required to adjust

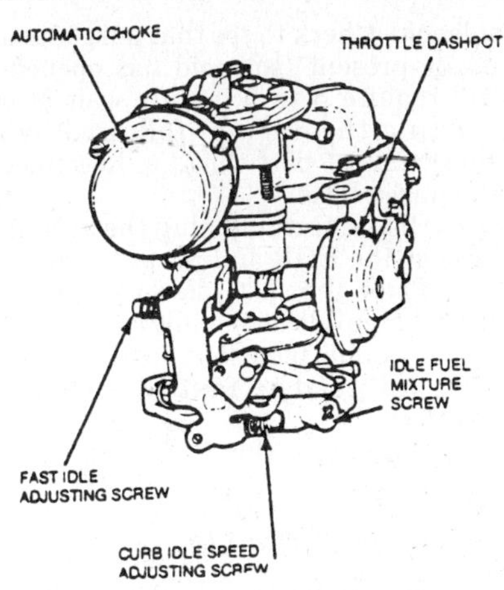

Carter YF series speed adjustments; Canadian leaded fuel models similar

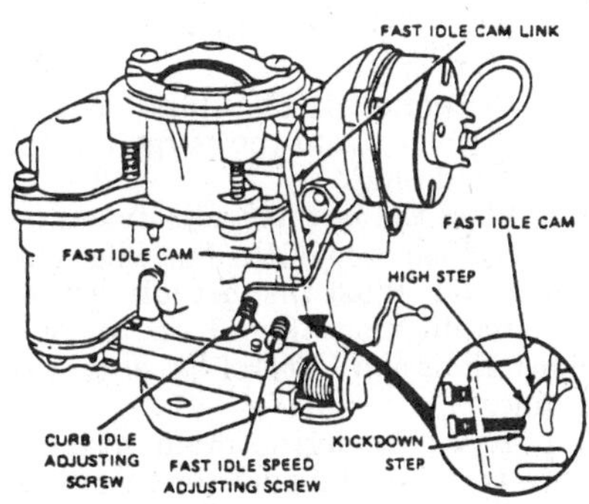

Fast idle adjusting screw—Carter YFA (U.S. models)

engine idle speed by more than 50 rpm, the adjustment screw on the AOD linkage lever at the carburetor should also be readjusted.

1983 and Later 8-302 (5.0L) 2150 2-bbl FB (FEEDBACK)

1. Set parking brake and block wheels.
2. Place the transmission in Park.
3. Bring the engine to normal operating temperature.
4. Disconnect the electric connector on the EVAP purge solenoid.
5. Disconnect and plug the vacuum hose to the VOTM kicker.
6. Place the transmission in Drive position.
7. Check/adjust curb idle rpm, if adjustment is required: Adjust with the the curb idle speed screw or the saddle bracket adjusting screw, depending on how equipped.
8. Place the transmission in Neutral or Park. Rev the engine momentarily. Place the transmission in Drive position and recheck curb idle rpm. Readjust if required.
9. Remove the plug from the vacuum hose to the VOTM kicker and reconnect.
10. Reconnect the electrical connector on the EVAP purge solenoid.

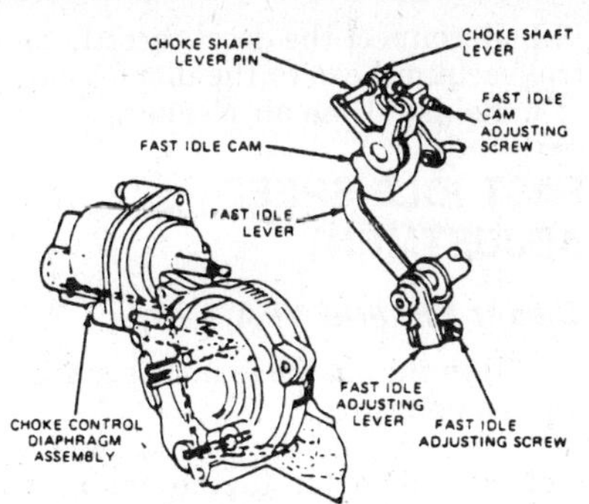

Fast idle adjustment for the Motorcraft 7200VV 2-bbl carburetor

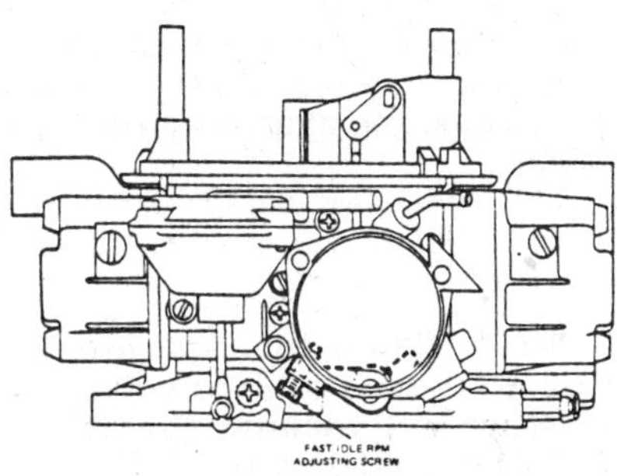

Holley 4180C 4-bbl fast idel adjustment

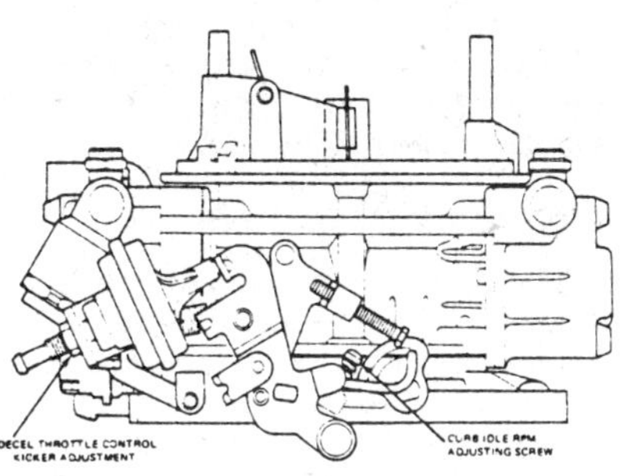

Holley 4180C 4-bbl curb idle and VOTM kicker adjustments locations

1983 and Later 8-302 (5.0L) 2150 2-bbl (NON-FEEDBACK)

1. Set parking brake and block wheels.
2. Place the transmission in Neutral or Park.
3. Bring engine to normal operating temperature.
4. Place A/C Heat selector to Off position.
5. Disconnect and plug vacuum hose to thermactor air bypass valve.
6. Place the transmission in specified gear.
7. Check curb idle rpm. Adjust to specification by using the curb idle rpm speed screw or the saddle bracket adjusting screw, depending on how equipped.
8. Place the transmission in Neutral or Park. Rev the engine momentarily. Place the transmission in specified position, and recheck curb idle rpm. Readjust if required.
9. Remove plug from vacuum hose to thermactor air bypass valve and reconnect.
10. Whenever it is required to adjust engine idle speed by more than 50 rpm, the adjustment screw on the AOD linkage lever at the carburetor should also be readjusted.

1983 and Later 8-351 (5.8L) 2150 2-bbl OR 7200 VV

1. Block the wheels and apply parking brake. Place the transmission in Neutral or Park.
2. Bring the engine to normal operating temperature.
3. Disconnect purge hose on canister side of evaporator purge solenoid. Check to ensure that purge vacuum is present (solenoid has opened and will require 3 to 5 minute wait after starting engine followed by a short time at part throttle). Reconnect purge hose.
4. Disconnect and plug the vacuum hose to the VOTM kicker.
5. Place the transmission in specified position.
6. Check/adjust curb idle rpm. If adjustment is required, adjust with the curb idle speed screw or the saddle bracket adjusting screw (ensure curb idle speed screw is not touching throttle shaft lever).
7. Place the transmission in Neutral or Park. Rev the engine momentarily. Place the transmission in specified position and recheck curb idle rpm. Readjust if required.
8. Check/adjust throttle position sensor (TPS).
9. Remove the plug from the vacuum hose to the VOTM kicker and reconnect.
10. Apply a slight pressure on top of the nylon nut located on the accelerator pump to take up the linkage clearance.
11. Turn the nylon nut on the accelerator pump rod clockwise until a 0.010″ ± 0.005″ (0.254-0.127mm) clearance is obtained between the top of the accelerator pump and the pump lever.
12. Turn the accelerator pump rod nut one turn counterclockwise to set the lever lash preload.
13. If curb idle adjustment exceeds 50 rpm, adjust automatic transmission TV linkage.

1983 and Later Canadian 8-302 (5.0L) & 8-351 (5.8L) w/2150 2-bbl

1. Place the transmission in Neutral or Park.
2. Bring engine to normal operating temperature.
3. Place A/C Heat Selector to Off position.
4. Place the transmission in specified gear.
5. Check curb idle rpm. Adjust to specification using the curb idle speed screw or the hex head on the rear of the solenoid or the saddle bracket adjustment screw depending on how equipped.
6. Place the transmission in Neutral or Park. Rev the engine momentarily. Place the transmission in specified position and recheck curb idle rpm. Readjust if required.
7. TSP Off: With transmission in specified gear, collapse the solenoid plunger, and set specified TSP Off speed on the speed screw.
8. Disconnect vacuum hose to decel throttle control modulator and plug (if so equipped).
9. Connect a slave vacuum from manifold vacuum to the decel throttle control modulator (if so equipped).
10. Check/adjust decel throttle control rpm. Adjust if necessary.
11. Remove slave vacuum hose.
12. Remove plug from decel throttle control modulator hose and reconnect.

1983 and Later Holley 4180-C 4-bbl

1. Block the wheels and apply parking brake.
2. Run engine until normal operating temperature is reached.
3. Place the vehicle in Park or Neutral, A/C in Off position, and set parking brake.
4. Remove air cleaner.
5. Disconnect and plug decel throttle control kicker diaphragm vacuum hose.
6. Connect a slave vacuum hose from an engine manifold vacuum source to the decel throttle control kicker.
7. Run engine at approximately 2,500 rpm for 15 seconds, then release the throttle.
8. If decel throttle control rpm is not within ± 50 rpm of specification, adjust the kicker.
9. Disconnect the slave vacuum hose and allow engine to return to curb idle.
10. Adjust curb idle, if necessary, using the curb idle adjusting screw.
11. Rev the engine momentarily, recheck curb idle and adjust if necessary.
12. Reconnect the decel throttle control vacuum hose to the diaphragm.
13. Reinstall the air cleaner.

FAST IDLE SPEED ADJUSTMENT

Carter YF, and YFA 1-bbl

1. Run the engine to normal operating temperature.
2. Remove the air cleaner and attach a tachometer to the engine according to the manufacturer's instructions.
3. Manually rotate the fast idle to the top step while holding the choke plate fully opened.
4. Rotate the cam until the fast idle adjusting screw rests on the cam step specified on the underhood emissions sticker.
5. Turn the fast idle speed adjusting screw to obtain the speed specified in the Tune-Up Charts.

NOTE: When this operation is performed outdoors in cold weather, all vacuum controls to the distributor and EGR valve must be bypassed. This can be done by connecting a jumper hose from the DIST port on the carburetor to the vacuum advance port of the distributor and by disconnecting and plugging the EGR vacuum source hose.

Motorcraft 2150 2-bbl

The fast idle speed adjustment is made in the same manner as for the Model YF carburetor, starting at Step 3. The fast idle cam adjusment follows:

1. Rotate the choke thermostatic spring housing 90° in the rich direction.
2. Position the idle speed screw on the high step of the cam.
3. Depress the choke pulldown diaphragm against the diaphragm stop screw to place the choke in the pulldown position.
4. While holding the choke pulldown diaphragm depressed, open the throttle slightly and allow the fast idle cam to fall.
5. Close the throttle and check the position of the fast idle cam. The screw should contact the cam at the V mark on the cam.
6. Adjust the fast idle cam adjusting screw to obtain the proper setting.

Motorcraft Model 7200 VV

1. Place the transmission in Park or Neutral.
2. Bring the engine to normal operating temperature.
3. Disconnect the purge hose on the canister side of the evaporator purge solenoid. Check to see that purge vacuum is present (solenoid has opened--will require 3 to 5 minute wait after starting the engine) followed by a short time at part throttle. Reconnect the purge hose.
4. Disconnect and plug the vacuum hose at the EGR and purge valves.
5. Place the fast idle lever on the second step of the fast idle cam. (Third step on Calif. models.)
6. Adjust the fast idle rpm to specifiations.
7. Reconnect the EGR and purge vacuum hoses.

Holley 4180-C 4-bbl

1. Set the parking brake, block the wheels, place the transmission in neutral or park and remove the air cleaner.
2. Bring the engine to normal operating temperature.
3. Disconnect the vacuum hoses at the EGR valve and the purge control valves and plug.
4. Place the fast idle adjustment on the specified step of the fast idle cam. Check and adjust the fast idle rpm to the specifications found on the Exhaust Emission Control Decal on the engine.
5. Rev the engine momentarily, place the fast idle adjustment on the specified step and recheck the fast idle rpm.
6. Remove the plug from the EGR valve and the purge control valves and reconnect.

DASHPOT ADJUSTMENT

1. Remove the air cleaner.
2. Loosen the anti-stall dashpot locknut.
3. With the choke plate open, hold the throttle plate closed (idle position), and check the clearance between the throttle lever and the dashpot plunger tip with a feeler gauge.

ACCELERATING PUMP CLEARANCE ADJUSTMENT

Holley 4180-C 4-bbl

1. Using a feeler gauge and with the primary throttle plates in the wide open position, there should be 0.015" (0.381mm) clearance between the accelerator pump operating lever adjustment screw head and the pump arm when the pump arm is depressed manually.
2. If adjustment is required, hold the adjusting screw locknut and turn the adjusting screw inward to increase the clearance and out to decrease the clearance. One half turn on the adjust-

ing screw is approximately 0.015" (0.381mm).

ACCELERATING PUMP STROKE ADJUSTMENTS

Motorcraft 2150 2-bbl

The accelerating pump stroke has been factory set for a particular engine application and should not be readjusted. If the stroke has been changed from the specified hole reset to specifications by following these procedures.

1. To release the rod from the retaining clip, lift upward on the portion of the clip that snaps over the shaft and then disengage the rod.
2. Position the clip over the specified hole in the overtravel lever and insert the operating rod through the clip and the overtravel lever. Snap the end of the clip over the rod to secure.

Holley 4180-C 4-bbl

The accelerator pump stroke has been set to help keep the exhaust emission level of the engine within the specified limits. The additional holes provided (if any) for pump stroke adjustment are for adjusting the stroke for specific engine applications. The stroke should not be changed from the specified setting.

CHOKE PULLDOWN ADJUSTMENT

Carter YF, YFA 1-bbl

1. Remove the air cleaner. Remove the choke thermostatic spring housing from the carburetor.
2. Bend a 0.026" (0.66mm) diameter wire gauge at a 90° angle approximately 1/8" (3mm) from one end. Insert the bent end of the gauge between the choke piston slot and the right hand slot in the choke housing. Rotate the choke piston lever counterclockwise until the gauge is snug in the piston slot.
3. Exert a light pressure on the choke piston lever to hold the gauge in place, then use a drill gauge with a diameter equal to the specified clearance between the lower edge of the choke plate and the carburetor bore to check clearance.
4. To adjust the choke plate pulldown clearance, bend the choke piston lever as required to obtain the specified setting. Remove the choke piston lever for bending to prevent distorting the piston link, causing erratic choke operation.
5. Install the choke thermostatic spring housing and gasket. Set the housing to specifications.

Motorcraft 2150 2-bbl

1. Set throttle on fast idle cam top step.
2. Note index position of choke bimetallic cap. Loosen retaining screws and rotate cap 90° in the rich (closing) direction.
3. Activate pulldown motor by manually forcing pulldown control diaphragm link in the direction of applied vacuum or by applying vacuum to external vacuum tube.
4. Measure vertical hard gauge clearance between choke plate and center of carburetor air horn wall nearest fuel bowl.

Pulldown setting should be within specifications for minimum choke plate opening.

If choke plate pulldown is found to be out of specification, reset by adjusting diaphragm stop on end of choke pulldown diaphragm.

If pulldown is reset, cam clearance should be checked and reset if required.

After pulldown check is completed, reset choke bimetallic cap to recommend index position as specified in the Carburetor Specifications Chart. Check and reset fast idle speed to specifications if necessary.

Holley 4180-C 4-bbl

1. Remove the air cleaner. Then remove the carburetor from the vehicle and cover the intake manifold.
2. Place the carburetor on a stand which allows access to the pulldown diaphgram vacuum passage on the underside of the throttle body.
3. Mark the choke cap and housing. Then remove the choke cap, gasket and retainer.
4. Reinstall the choke cap temporarily with a standard choke cap gasket. Line up the marks made previously on the cap and the housing and rotate the cap 90° counterclockwise from that position. Secure with one screw.
5. With the choke plate in the full closed position, actuate the choke pulldown motor using an outside vacuum source, 17 in.Hg minimum.
6. Using a drill gauge of the specified size check the clearence between the upper edge of the choke plate and the air horn wall.

NOTE: The gauge should fit in such a manner that it contacts the air horn and choke plate but does not move the plate.

7. If the pulldown dimension is out of specification, carefully remove the diaphgagm adjustment screw cap with a small sharp punch or screw driver.
8. Turn the adjustment screw with a $^{5}/_{16}$" Allen wrench clockwise to de-

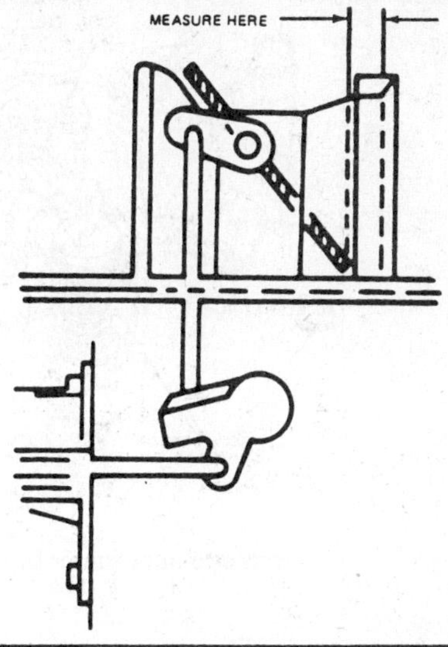

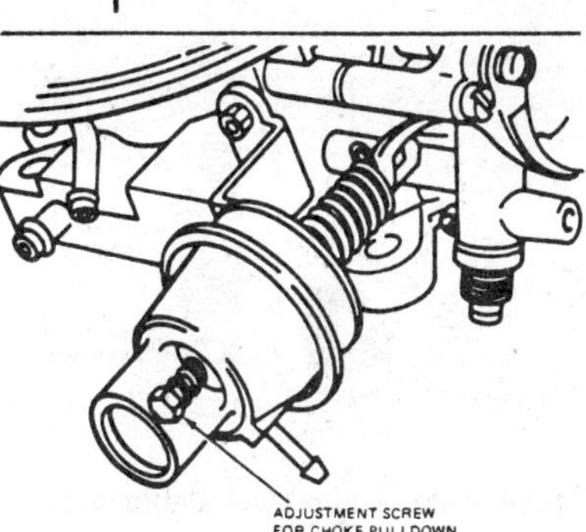

Autolite 2150 2-bbl choke plate pulldown adjustment

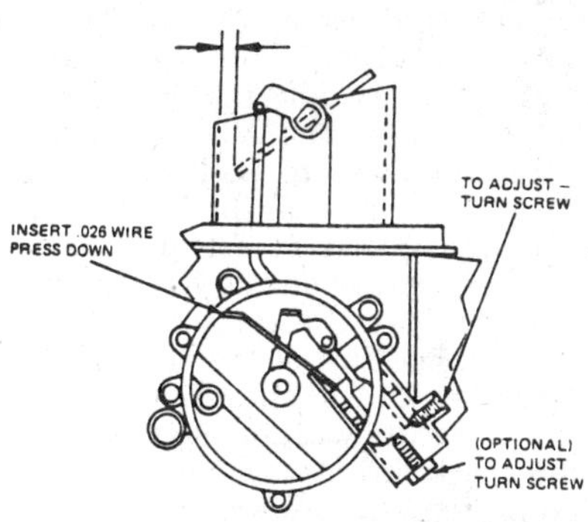

Holley 4180 4-bbl choke pulldown adjustment

crease the pulldown set or counterclockwise to increase the pulldown set.

NOTE: Maintain a minimum of 17 in.Hg to the pulldown diaphgram during adjustment. Cycle vacuum from 0-17 in.Hg to verify proper set.

9. Apply RTV sealant to the adjustment screw cavity and check the fast idle cam index adjustment.

To adjust the fast idle cam index:

1. With the choke cap still wrapped,

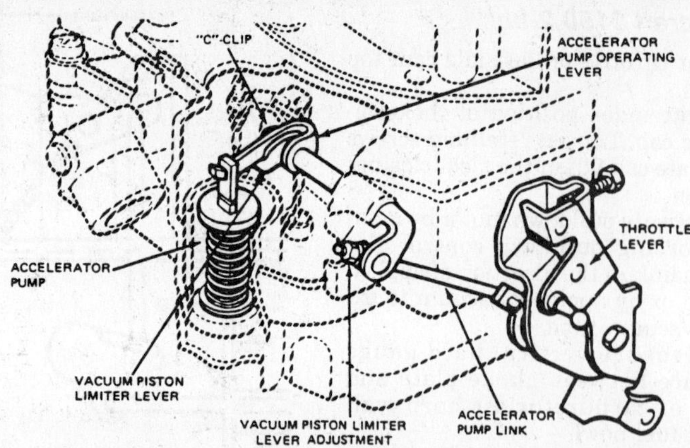

Throttle-to-accelerator pump linkage on the Autolite 4350 4-bbl

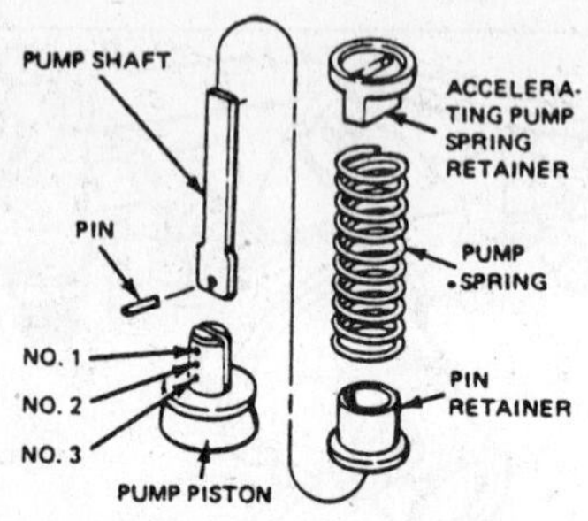

Accelerator pump stroke adjustment—Autolite 4350 4-bbl

and with vacuum applied to the diaphragm, cycle the trottle. The fast idle screw should rest on the No. 2 step of the fast idle cam.

2. If the fast idle cam requires adjustment, turn the Allen adjustment screw clockwise to position the fast idle screw higher on the No. 2 step or counterclockwise to position the fast idle screw lower on the No. 2 step.

3. Remove the temporary choke plate gasket, install the original locking gasket, choke cap and choke cap retainer. Secure with breakaway screws and check the dechoke adjustment.

To adjust the dechoke:

1. Reinstall the choke cap at the proper index using one screw.

2. Hold the throttle in the wide open position.

3. Apply light closing pressure to the choke plate and measure the gap between the lower edge of the choke plate and the air horn wall.

4. To adjust, bend the pawl on the fast idle lever.

DECHOKE ADJUSTMENT

All Except Holley 4180C 4-bbl

1. Remove the air cleaner.

2. Hold the throttle plate fully open and close the choke plate as far as possible without forcing it. Use a drill of the proper diameter to check the clearance between the choke plate and air horn.

3. If the clearance is not within specification, adjust by bending the arm on the choke trip lever. Bending the arm downward will increase the clearance, and bending it upward will decrease the clearance. Always recheck the clearance after making any adjustment.

4. If the choke plate clearance and fast idle cam linkage adjustment was performed with the carburetor on the engine, adjust the engine idle speed and fuel mixture. Adjust the dashpot (if so equipped).

REMOVAL & INSTALLATION

1. Remove the air cleaner.

2. Remove the throttle cable or rod from the throttle lever. Disconnect the distributor vacuum line, EGR vacuum line, if so equipped, the inline filter and the choke heat tube at the carburetor.

3. Disconnect the choke clean air tube from the air horn. Disconnect the choke actuating cable, if so equipped.

4. Remove the carburetor retaining nuts then remove the carburetor. Remove the carburetor mounting gasket, spacer (if so equipped), and the lower gasket from the intake manifold.

5. Before installing the carburetor, clean the gasket mounting surfaces of the spacer and carburetor. Place the spacer between two new gaskets and position the spacer and the gaskets on the intake manifold. Position the carburetor on the spacer and gasket and secure it with the retaining nuts. To prevent leakage, distortion or damage to the carburetor body flange, snug the nuts, then alternately tighten each nut in a criss-cross pattern.

6. Connect the inline fuel filter, throttle cable, choke heat tube, distributor vacuum line, EGR vacuum line and choke cable.

7. Connect the choke clean air line to the air horn.

8. Adjust the engine idle speed, the idle fuel mixture and anti-stall dashpot (if so equipped). Install the air cleaner.

TROUBLESHOOTING

The best way to diagnose a bad carburetor is to eliminate all other possible sources of the problem. If the carburetor is suspected to be the problem, first perform all of the adjustments given in this Section. If this doesn't correct the difficulty, then check the following. Check the ignition system to make sure that the spark plugs, breaker points, and condenser are in good condition and adjusted to the proper specifications. Examine the emission control equipment to make sure that all the vacuum lines are connected and none are blocked or clogged. Check the ignition timing adjusting. Check all the vacuum lines on the engine for loose connections, splits or breaks. Torque the carburetor and intake manifold attaching bolts to the proper specifications. If, after performing all of these checks and adjustments, the problem is still not solved, then you can safely assume that the carburetor is the source of the problem.

OVERHAUL

Efficient carburetion depends greatly on careful cleaning and inspection during overhaul since dirt, gum, water or varnish in or on the carburetor parts are often responsible for poor performance.

Overhaul the carburetor in a clean, dustfree area. Carefully disassemble the carburetor, referring often to the exploded views. Keep all similar and look-alike parts segregated during disassembly and cleaning to avoid accidental interchange during assembly. Make a note of all jet sizes.

When the carburetor is disassembled, wash all parts (except diaphragms, electric choke unit, pump plunger and any other plastic, leather, fiber, or rubber parts) in clean carburetor solvent. Do not leave the parts in the solvent any longer than is necessary to sufficiently loosen the dirt and deposits. Excessive cleaning may remove the special finish from the float bowl and choke valve bodies, leaving these parts unfit for service. Rinse all parts in clean solvent and blow them dry with compressed air or allow them to air dry, while resting on clan, lintless paper. Wipe clean all cork, plastic, leather and fiber parts with a clean, lint-free cloth.

Blow out all passages and jets with compressed air and be sure that there are no restrictions or blockages. Never use wire or similar tools to clean jets, fuel passages or air bleeds. Clean all jets and valves separately to avoid accidental interchange.

Examine all parts for wear or damage. If wear or damage is found, replace the defective parts. Especially, inspect the following:

1. Check the float needle and seat for wear. If wear is found, replace the complete assembly.
2. Check the float hinge pin for wear and the float(s) for dents or distortion. Replace the float if fuel has leaked into it.
3. Check the throttle and choke shaft bores for wear or an out-of-round condition. Damage or wear to the throttle arm, shaft or shaft bore will often require replacement of the throttle body. These parts require a close tolerance of fit; wear may allow air leakage, which could affect starting and idling.

NOTE: Throttle shafts and bushings are not normally included in overhaul kits. They can be purchased separately.

4. Inspect the idle mixture adjusting needles for burrs or grooves. Any such condition requires replacement of the needle, since you will not be able to obtain a satisfactory idle.
5. Test the accelerator pump check valves. They should pass air one way, but not the other. Test for proper seating by blowing and sucking on the valve. Replace the valve as necessary. If the valve is satisfactory, wash the valve again to remove moisture.
6. Check the bowl cover for warped surfaces with a straightedge.
7. Closely inspect the valves and seats for wear and damage, replacing as necessary.
8. After the carburetor is assembled, check the choke valve for freedom of operation.

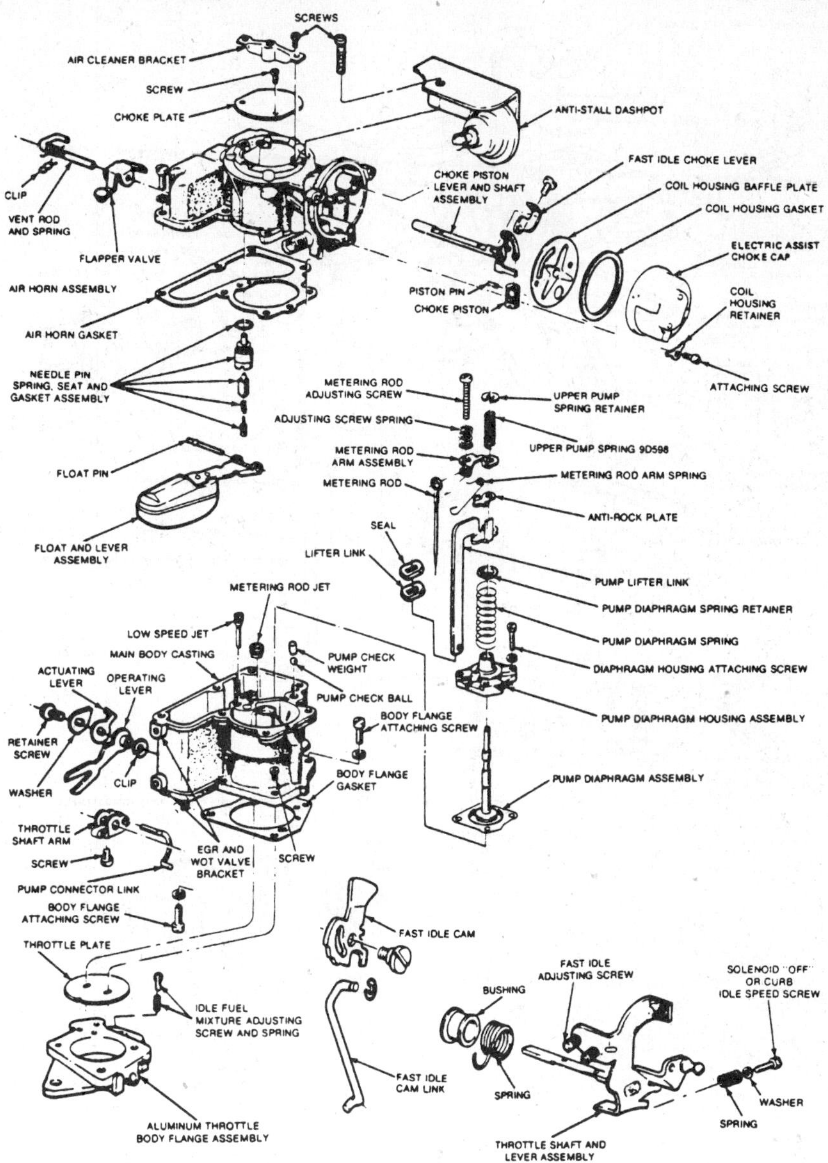

Carter YFA (non-feedback), exploded view

Carburetor overhaul kits are recommended for each overhaul. These kits contain all gaskets and new parts to replace those which deteriorate most rapidly. Failure to replace all of the parts supplied with the kit (especially gaskets) can result in poor performance later.

NOTE: Most carburetor rebuilding kits include specific procedures which should be following during overhaul.

Most carburetor manufacturers supply overhaul kits of these basic types: minor repair; major repair; and gasket kits. Basically, they contain the following:

Minor Repair Kits:

- All gaskets
- Float needle valve
- Mixture adjusting screws
- All diaphragms
- Spring for the pump diaphragm

Major Repair Kits:

- All jets and gaskets
- All diaphragms
- Float needle valve
- Mixture adjusting screws
- Pump ball valve
- Main jet carrier
- Float
- Some float bowl cover holddown screws and washer

Gasket Kits:

- All gaskets

After cleaning and checking all components, reassemble the carburetor, using new parts and referring to the exploded view. When reassembling, make sure that all screws and jets are tight in their seats, but do not overtighten, as the tips will be distorted. Tighten all screws gradually, in rotation. Do not tighten needle valves into their seats; uneven jetting will result. Always use new gaskets. Be sure to adjust the float level.

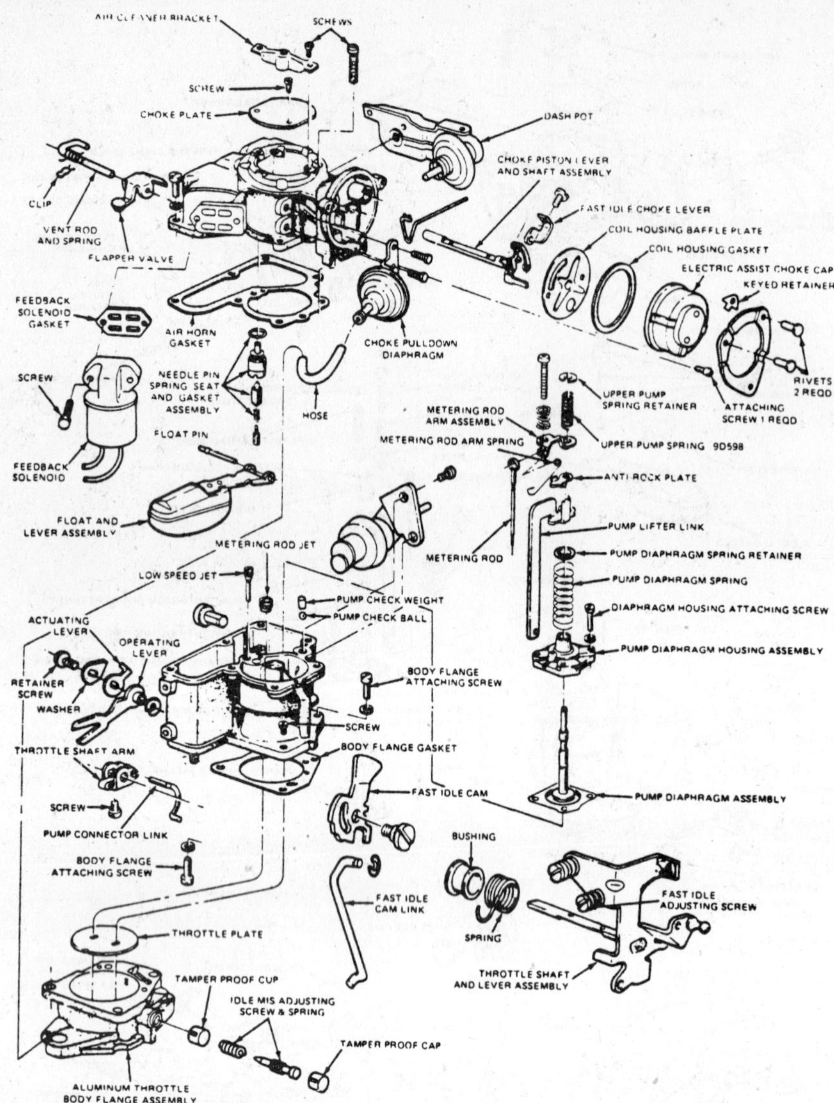

An exploded view of the Carter YF 1-bbl carburetor

GASOLINE FUEL INJECTION SYSTEM

NOTE: This book contains simple testing and service procedures for your truck's fuel injection system. More comprehensive testing and diagnosis procedures may be found in CHILTON'S GUIDE TO FUEL INJECTION AND FEEDBACK CARBURETORS, BOOK PART NUMBER 7488, available at your local retailer.

Mechanical Fuel Pump

REMOVAL & INSTALLATION

1. Loosen the threaded fittings to the fuel pump (use the proper size flare wrench), do not remove the lines at this time.
2. Loosen the fuel pump mounting bolts one or two turns. Loosen the pump and gasket from the engine or front cover. Rotate the engine, in the proper direction, while checking the tension on the fuel pump. When the cam or eccentric lobe is near the low point pressure on the fuel pump arm will be greatly reduced. This is especially important on engines using an aluminum front cover to help prevent thread stripping.
3. Have a rag handy to catch fuel spill and disconnect all lines from the fuel pump. Dispose of the rag safely.
4. Remove the fuel pump mounting bolts, the fuel pump and mounting gasket.
5. Clean all mounting surfaces. Apply oil resistant sealer to mounting surfaces. Install the fuel pump and new gasket in the reverse order of removal. Start the engine and check for leaks.

TESTING

Incorrect fuel pump pressure and low volume (flow rate) are the two most likely fuel pump troubles that will affect engine performance. Low pressure will cause a lean mixture and fuel starvation at high speeds and excessive pressure will cause high fuel consumption and carburetor flooding.

To determine that the fuel pump is in satisfactory operating condition, tests for both fuel pump pressure and volume should be performed.

The tests are performed with the fuel pump installed on the engine and the engine at normal operating temperature and at idle speed.

Before the test, make sure that the replaceable fuel filter has been changed at the proper mileage interval. If in doubt, install a new filter.

Pressure Test

1. Remove the air cleaner assembly. Disconnect the fuel inlet line of the fuel filter at the carburetor. Use care to prevent fire, due to fuel spillage. Place an absorbent cloth under the connection before removing the line to catch any fuel that might flow out of the line.
2. Connect a pressure gauge, a restrictor and a flexible hose between the fuel filter and the carburetor.
3. Position the flexible hose and the restrictor so that the fuel can be discharged into a suitable, graduated container.
4. Before taking a pressure reading, operate the engine at the specified idle rpm and vent the system into the container by opening the hose restrictor momentarily.
5. Close the hose restrictor, allow the pressure to stabilize and note the reading. The pressure should be 5 psi. If the pump pressure is not within 4-6 psi and the fuel lines and filter are in satisfactory condition, the pump is defective and should be replaced. If the pump pressure is within the proper range, perform the test for fuel volume.

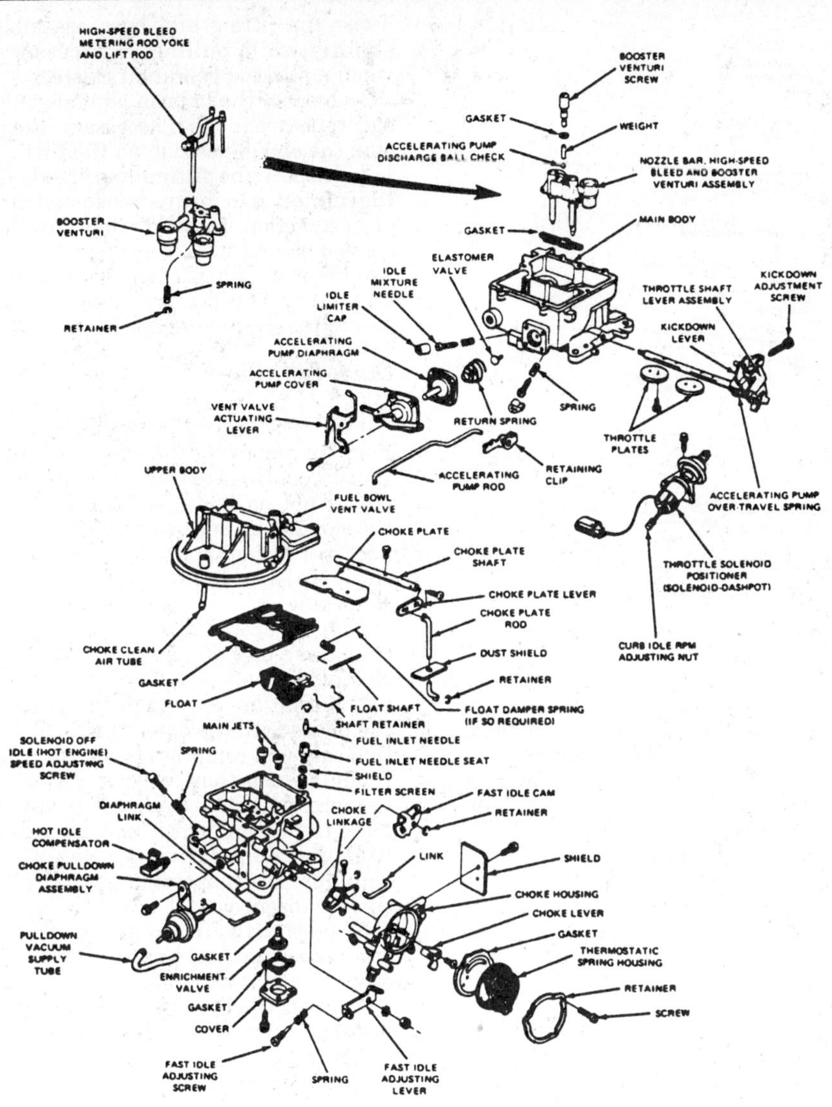

Expolded view of the Autolite 2150 carburetor

Volume Test

1. Operate the engine at the specified idle rpm.
2. Open the hose restrictor and catch the fuel in the container while observing the time it takes to pump 1 pint. 1 pint should be pumped in 20 seconds. If the pump does not pump to specifications, check for proper fuel tank venting or a restriction in the fuel line leading from the fuel tank to the carburetor before replacing the fuel pump.

Electric Fuel Pump

Two electric pumps are used on injected models; a low pressure boost pump mounted in the gas tank and a high pressure pump mounted on the vehicle frame. Models equipped with the 7.5L engine use a single low pressure pump mounted in the gas tank,

On injected models the low pressure pump is used to provide pressurized fuel to the inlet of the high pressure pump and helps prevent noise and heating problems. The externally mounted high pressure pump is capable of supplying 15.9 gallons of fuel an hour. System pressure is controlled by a pressure regulator mounted on the engine.

On internal fuel tank mounted pumps tank removal is required. Frame mounted models can be accessed from under the vehicle. Prior to servicing release system pressure (see proceeding Fuel Supply Manifold details). Disconnect the negative battery cable prior to pump removal.

REMOVAL & INSTALLATION

In-Tank Pump

1. Disconnect the negative battery cable.
2. Depressurize the system and drain as much gas from the tank by pumping out through the filler neck.
3. Raise the back of the vehicle and safely support on jackstands.
4. Disconnect the fuel supply, return and vent lines at the right and left side of the frame.
5. Disconnect the wiring harness to the fuel pump.
6. Support the gas tank, loosen and remove the mounting straps. Remove the gas tank.
7. Disconnect the lines and harness at the pump flange.
8. Clean the outside of the mounting flange and retaining ring. Turn the fuel pump lock ring counterclockwise and remove.
9. Remove the fuel pump.
10. Clean the mounting surfaces. Put a light coat of grease on the mounting sufaces and on the new sealing ring. Install the new fuel pump.
11. Installation is in the reverse order of removal. Fill the tank with at least 10 gals. of gas. Turn the ignition key ON for three seconds. Repeat 6 or 7 times until the fuel system is pressurized. Check for any fitting leaks. Start the engine and check for leaks.

External Pump

1. Disconnect the negative battery cable.
2. Depressurize the fuel system.
3. Raise and support the rear of the vehicle on jackstands.
4. Disconnect the inlet and outlet fuel lines.
5. Remove the pump from the mounting bracket.
6. Install in reverse order, make sure the pump is indexed correctly in the mounting bracket insulator.

Air Intake And Throttle Body

REMOVAL & INSTALLATION

1. Disconnect the air intake hose.
2. Disconnect the throttle position sensor and air by-pass valve connectors.
3. Remove the four throttle body mounting nuts and carefully separate the air throttle body from the upper intake manifold.
4. Remove and discard the mounting gasket. Clean all mounting surfaces using care not to damage the gasket surfaces of the throttle body and manifold. Do not allow any material to drop into the intake manifold.
5. Install the throttle body in the reverse order of removal. The mounting nuts are tightened to 12-15 ft.lb.

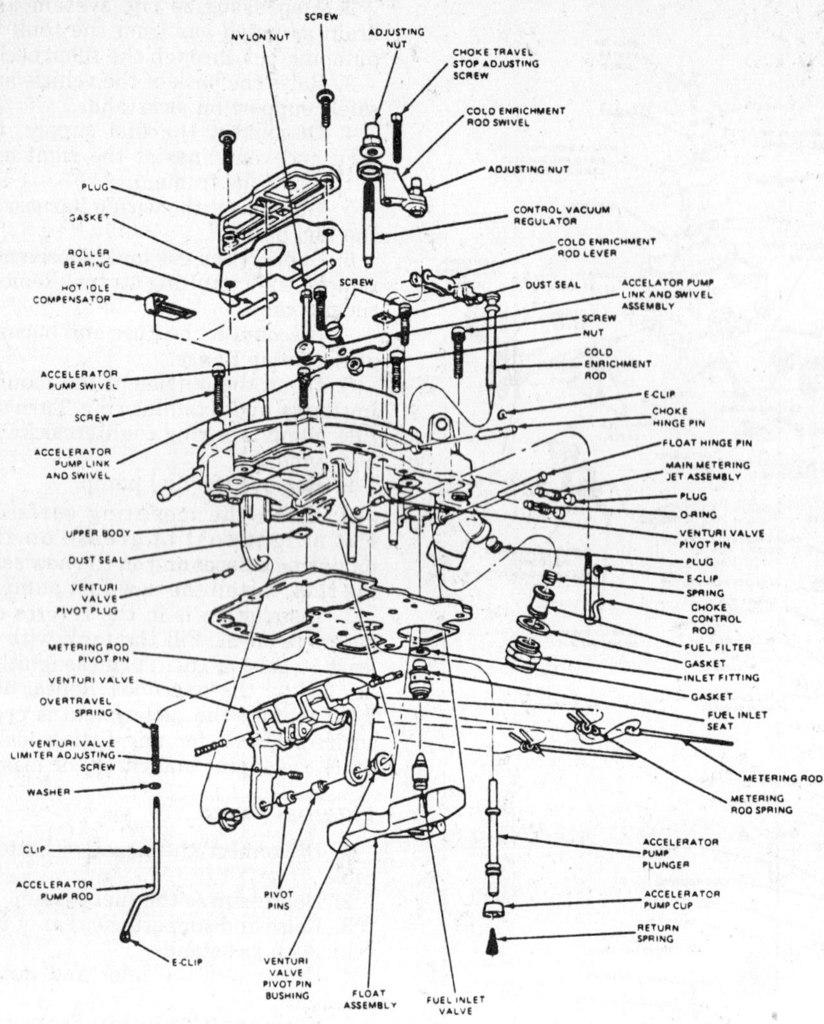

Motorcraft 7200VV (variable venturi) 2-bbl carburetor upper body

Quick-Connect Line Fittings

REMOVAL & INSTALLATION

NOTE: Quick-Connect (push) type fittings must be disconnected using proper procedures or the fitting may be damaged. Two types of retainers are used on the push connect fittings. Line sizes of 3/8" and 5/16" use a "hairpin" clip retainer. 1/4" line connectors use a "duck bill" clip retainer.

Hairpin Clip

1. Clean all dirt and/or grease from the fitting. Spread the two clip legs about an 1/8" (3mm) each to disengage from the fitting and pull the clip outward from the fitting. Use finger pressure only, do not use any tools.

2. Grasp the fitting and hose assembly and pull away from the steel line. Twist the fitting and hose assembly slightly while pulling, if necessary, when a sticking condition exists.

3. Inspect the hairpin clip for damage, replace the clip if necessary. Reinstall the clip in position on the fitting.

4. Inspect the fitting and inside of the connector to insure freedom of dirt or obstruction. Install fitting into the connector and push together. A click will be heard when the hairpin snaps into proper connection. Pull on the line to insure full engagement.

Duck Bill Clip

1. A special tool is available from Ford for removing the retaining clips (Ford Tool No. T82L-9500-AH). If the tool is not on hand see Step 2. Align the slot on the push connector disconnect tool with either tab on the retaining clip. Pull the line from the connector.

2. If the special clip tool is not available, use a pair of narrow 6" (152mm) channel lock pliers with a jaw width of 0.2" (5mm) or less. Align the jaws of the pliers with the openings of the fitting case and compress the part of the retaining clip that engages the case. Compressing the retaining clip will release the fitting which may be pulled from the connector. Both sides of the clip must be compressed at the same time to disengage.

3. Inspect the retaining clip, fitting end and connector. Replace the clip if any damage is apparent.

4. Push the line into the steel connector until a click is heard, indicting the clip is in place. Pull on the line to check engagement.

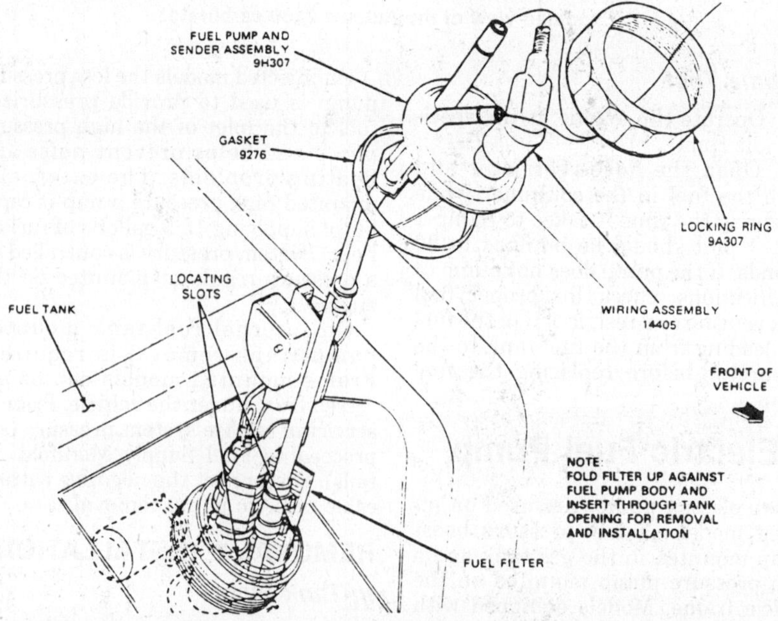

In-tank electric fuel pump

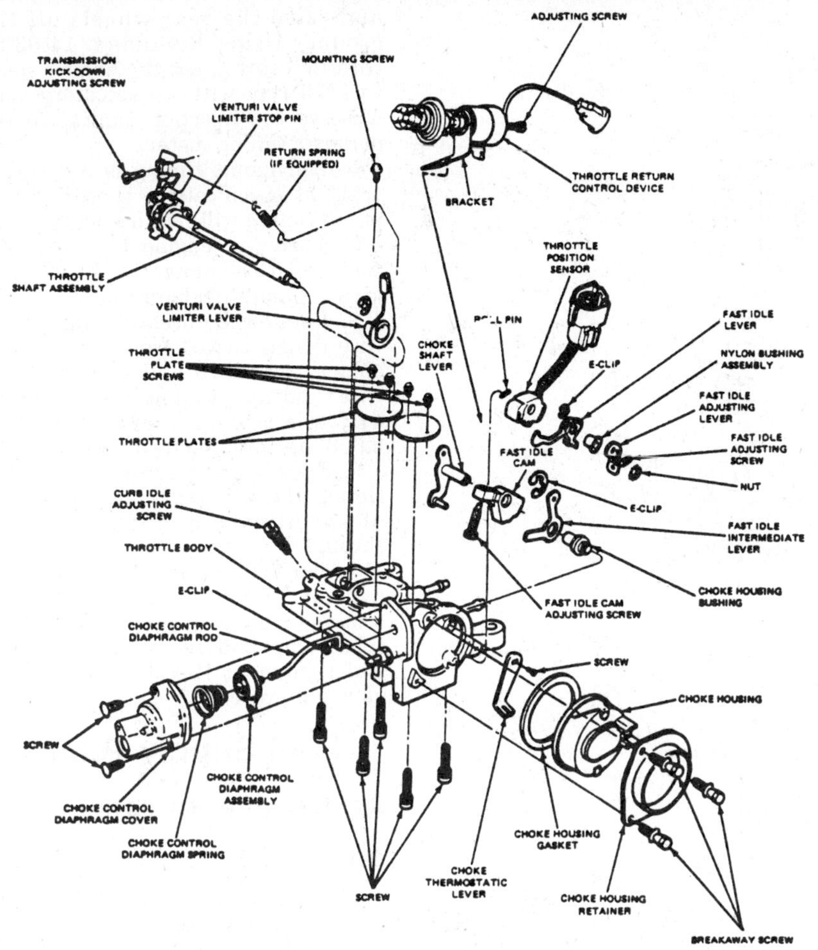

Motorcraft 7200VV 2-bbl carburetor throttle body

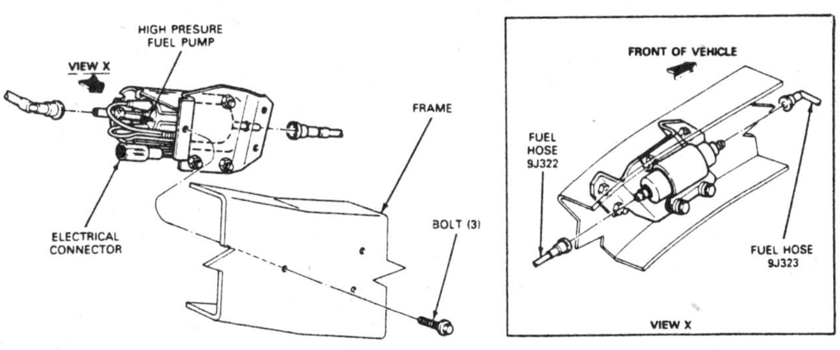

Frame mounted electric fuel pump

Fuel Supply Manifold

REMOVAL & INSTALLATION

1. Remove the gas tank fill cap. Relieve fuel system pressure by locating and disconnecting the electrical connection to either the fuel pump relay, the inertia switch or the in-line high pressure fuel pump. Crank the engine for about ten seconds. If the engine starts, crank for an additional five seconds after the engine stalls. Reconnect the connector. Disconnect the negative battery cable. Remove the upper intake manifold assembly.

NOTE: Special tool T81P-19623-G or equivalent is necessary to release the garter springs that secure the fuel line/hose connections.

2. Disconnect the fuel crossover hose from the fuel supply manifold. Disconnect the fuel supply and return line connections at the fuel supply manifold.
3. Remove the fuel supply manifold retaining bolts. Carefully disengage the manifold from the fuel injectors and remove the manifold.
4. When installing: Make sure the injector caps are clean and free of contamination. Place the fuel supply manifold over each injector and seat the injectors into the manifold. Make sure the caps are seated firmly.
5. Torque the fuel supply manifold retaining bolts to 23-25 ft.lb. Install the remaining components in the reverse order of removal.

INJECTOR REPLACEMENT

Fuel injectors may be serviced after the fuel supply manifold is removed. Carefully disconnect the electrical harness connectors from individual injectors as required. Grasp the injector and pull up on it while gently rocking injector from side to side. Inspect the mounting O-rings and replace any that show deterioration.

DIESEL FUEL SYSTEM

Adjustments

INJECTION TIMING

8-420 (6.9L)

NOTE: Special equipment, a Dynamic Timing Meter, Ford

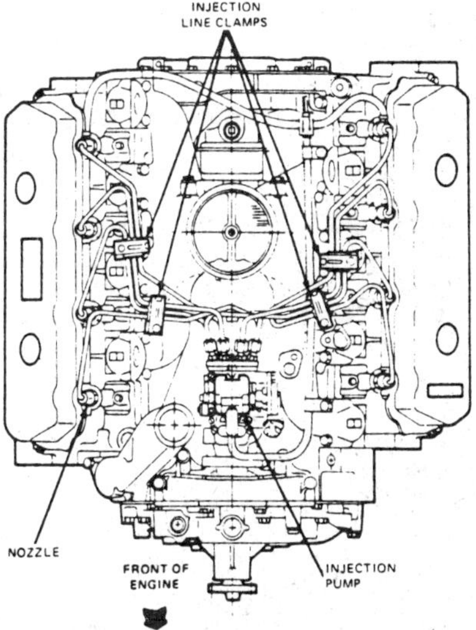

Injection line clamps, Diesel V8. Injectors also shown

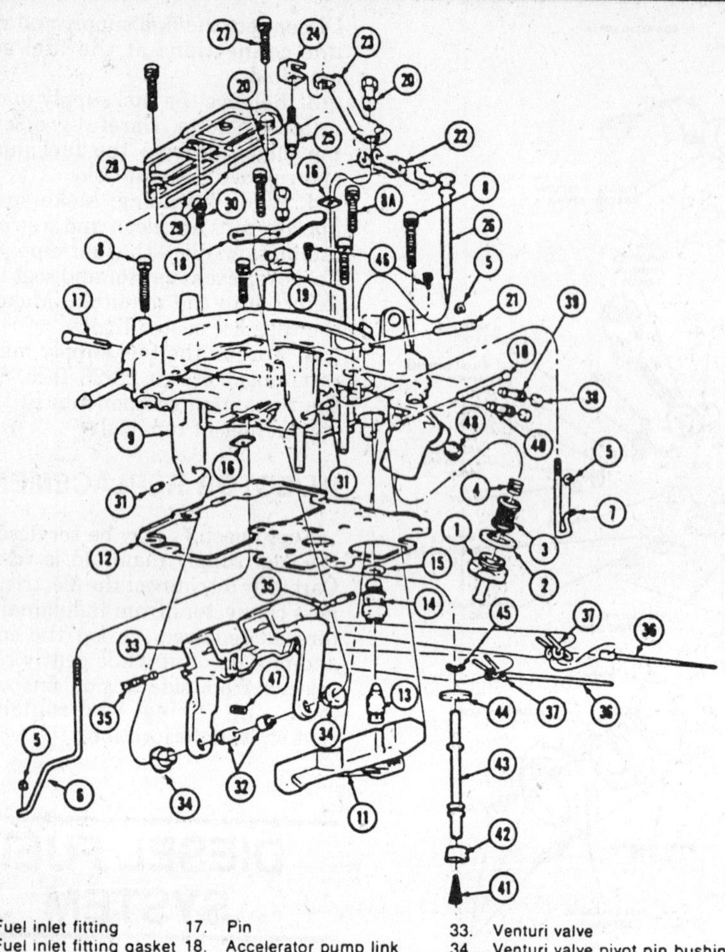

1. Fuel inlet fitting
2. Fuel inlet fitting gasket
3. Fuel filter
4. Fuel filter spring
5. Retaining E-ring
6. Accelerator pump rod
7. Choke control rod
8. Screw
8A. Screw
9. Upper body
10. Float hinge pin
11. Float assembly
12. Float bowl gasket
13. Fuel inlet valve
14. Fuel inlet seat
15. Fuel inlet seat gasket
16. Dust seal
17. Pin
18. Accelerator pump link
19. Accelerator pump swivel
20. Nut
21. Choke hinge pin
22. Cold enrichment rod lever
23. Cold enrichment rod swivel
24. Control vacuum regulator adjusting nut
25. Control vacuum regulator
26. Cold enrichment rod
27. Screw
28. Venturi valve cover plate
29. Roller bearing
30. Venturi air bypass screw
31. Venturi valve pivot plug
32. Venturi valve pivot pin
33. Venturi valve
34. Venturi valve pivot pin bushing
35. Metering rod pivot pin
36. Metering rod
37. Metering rod spring
38. Cup plug
39. Main metering jet assembly
40. O-ring
41. Accelerator pump return spring
42. Accelerator pump cup
43. Accelerator pump plunger
44. Internal vent valve
45. Retaining E-ring
46. Idle trim screw
47. Venturi valve limiter adjusting screw
48. Pipe plug

Typical upper body – VV carburetor (2700VV shown)

D83T-6002-A or the equivalent is necessary to set or check the "dynamic" injection timing. Both static and dynamic methods follow.

STATIC TIMING

1. Loosen the injection pump to mounting nuts.
2. Rotate the injection pump to bring the mark on the pump into alignment with the mark on pump mounting adapter.
3. Visually recheck the alignment of the timing marks and tighten injection pump mounting nuts.

DYNAMIC TIMING

1. Bring the engine up to normal operating temperature.
2. Stop the engine and install a dynamic timing meter, Rotunda# 78-0100 or equivalent, by placing the magnetic probe pick-up into the probe hole.
3. Remove the No. 1 glow plug wire and remove the glow plug, install luminosity probe and tighten to 12 ft.lb. Install the photocell over the probe.
4. Connect a dynamic timing meter to the battery and adjust the offset of the meter.
5. Set the transmission in neutral and raise the rear wheels off the ground. Using Rotunda# 14-0302, throttle control, set the engine speed to 1400 rpm with no accessory load. Observe the injection timing on the dynamic timing meter.
6. If dynamic timing is not within ± 2° of specification, then injection pump timing will require adjustment.
7. Turn the engine off. Note the timing mark alignment. Loosen the injection pump-to-adapter nuts.
8. Rotate the injection pump clockwise (when viewed from the front of engine) to retard and counter-clockwise to advance timing. Two degrees of dynamic timing is approximately 0.030" of timing mark movement.
9. Start the engine and recheck the timing. If the timing is not within ± 1° of specification, repeat Steps 7 through 9.
10. Turn off the engine. Remove the dynamic timing equipment. Lightly coat the glow plug threads with anti-seize compound, install the glow plug and tighten to 12 ft.lb. Connect the glow plug wires.

Fuel Supply Pump

REMOVAL & INSTALLATION

8-420 (6.9L)

The pump used on the 6.9L Diesel Engine is mounted on the front cover. Refer to the Gasoline Engines fuel pump section for procedures.

Fuel Filter

REMOVAL & INSTALLATION

1. Remove the spin-on filter by turning counterclockwise as viewed from the bottom of the filter.
2. Clean the filter mounting flange. Coat the new filter sealing lip with diesel fuel.
3. Install and tighten filter until the gasket touches the mounting flange. Tighten an additional one-half turn. Refer to the instructions with the new filter, if they call for more than one-half turn tightening-follow the instructions.

Water Separator

SERVICING

8-420 (6.9L)

The 6.9L diesel engine is equipped with a fuel/water separator in the fuel supply line. A "Water in Fuel" indicator light is provided on the instrument panel to alert the operator. The light should glow when the ignition switch

1. Cranking enrichment solenoid
2. O-ring seal
3. Screw
4. Venturi valve diaphragm cover
5. Venturi valve diaphragm spring guide
6. Venturi valve diaphragm spring
7. Venturi valve diaphragm assembly.
8. Main body
9. Venturi valve adjusting screw
10. Wide open stop screw
11. Plug expansion
12. Cranking fuel control assembly
13. Accelerator pump check ball
14. Accelerator pump check ball weight
15. Throttle body gasket
16. Screw
17. Choke heat shield

Typical main body—VV carburetor (2700VV shown)

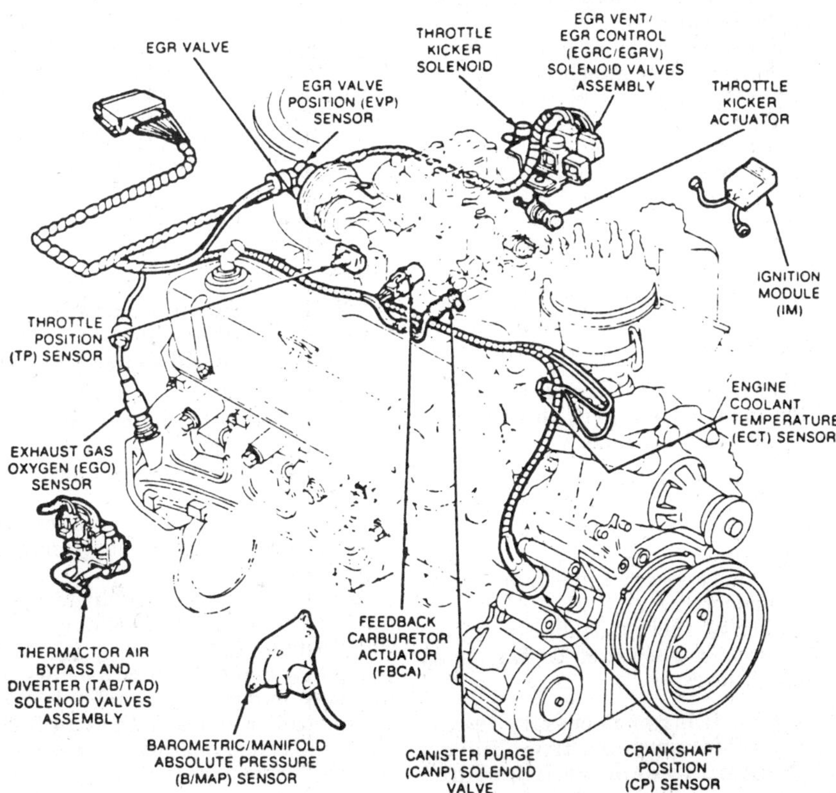

VV feedback carburetor wiring and vacuum diagram

is in the START position to indicate proper light and water sensor function. If the light glows continuously while the engine is running, the water must be drained from the separator as soon as practical to prevent damage to the fuel injection system.

F SERIES

1. Stop the vehicle and shut off the engine.

NOTE: Failure to shut off engine prior to draining separator will cause air to enter the fuel system.

2. Unscrew the vent 2½-3 turns. The vent is located on the top center of the fuel/water separator unit.
3. Unscrew the water drain located on the bottom of the fuel/water separator 1½-2 turns and drain water. Use an appropriate container.
4. After water is completely drained, close the water drain fingertight.
5. Tighten the vent until snug, then turn it an additional ¼ turn.
6. Restart the engine and check "Water in Fuel" indicator light. The light should not glow. If it continues to glow, have fuel system checked and repaired.

E SERIES

1. Stop the vehicle and shut Off the engine.
2. Locate the water/fuel separator drain cable knob, attached to the upper cowl flange on the left side of the vehicle, under the hood.
3. Place an approved container under the separator; which is accessible behind the left front wheel.
4. Pull the knob out and hold for 45 seconds.
5. Release knob and remove container.
6. Restart the engine and check "Water in Fuel" indicator lamp. The lamp should not be lit. If it continues to stay lit, have fuel system checked and repaired. The electrical sensor is the only replaceable item on the water/fuel separator. This assembly is threaded into the top of the separator. The remainder of the water/fuel separator is serviced as a complete unit.

CAUTION

When draining the water/fuel separator, the water must be drained into an approved container.

Fuel Injector Lines

REMOVAL & INSTALLATION

8-420 (6.9L)

NOTE: Before removing any

fuel lines, clean exterior with clean fuel oil, or solvent to prevent entry of dirt into fuel system when fuel lines are removed. Blow dry with compressed air.

1. Disconnect battery ground cables from both batteries.
2. Remove air cleaner and cap intake manifold opening with Ford Tool T83P-9424-A or equivalent.
3. Disconnect accelerator cable and speed control cable, if so equipped, from injection pump.
4. Remove accelerator cable bracket from intake manifold and position out of the way with cable(s) attached.

NOTE: To prevent fuel system contamination, cap all fuel lines and fittings with protective cap set.

5. Disconnect fuel line from fuel filter to injection pump and cap all fittings.
6. Disconnect and cap nozzle fuel lines at nozzles.
7. Remove the fuel line clamps from fuel lines to be removed.
8. Remove and cap injection pump inlet elbow.
9. Remove and cap inlet fitting adapter.
10. Remove injection nozzle lines, one at a time, from injection pump.

NOTE: Fuel lines must be removed following this sequence: 5-6-4-8-3-1-7-2.

Install caps on each end of each fuel line and pump fitting as it is removed and identify each fuel line accordingly.

11. Install fuel lines on injection pump, one at a time and tighten to 22 ft.lb.

NOTE: Fuel lines must be installed in the sequence: 2-7-1-3-8-4-6-5.

12. Clean old sealant from injection pump elbow, using clean solvent, and dry thoroughly.
13. Apply a light coating of pipe sealant on elbow threads.
14. Install elbow in injection pump adapter and tighten to a minimum of 6 ft.lb. then tighten further, if necessary, to align elbow with injection pump fuel inlet lines, but do not exceed 360° of rotation or 10 ft.lb.
15. Remove caps from fuel lines and connect lines to nozzles and tighten to 22 ft.lb.
16. Uncap and connect fuel line from fuel filler to injection pump and tighten.
17. Install fuel line retaining clamps and tighten.
18. Install accelerator cable bracket on intake manifold.
19. Connect accelerator and speed control cable, if so equipped, to injection pump throttle lever.
20. Remove intake manifold cover, and install air cleaner.
21. Connect battery ground cables to both batteries.
22. Run engine and check for fuel leaks.
23. If necessary, purge high pressure fuel lines of air by loosening connector one half to one turn and cranking engine until solid fuel, free from bubbles, flows from connection.

CAUTION

Keep eyes and hands away from nozzle spray. Fuel spraying from the nozzle under high pressure can penetrate the skin.

Injection Pump

REMOVAL & INSTALLATION

8-420 (6.9L)

WARNING: Before removing any fuel lines, clean exterior with clean fuel oil or solvent to prevent entry of dirt into engine when fuel lines are removed.

Do not wash or steam clean engine while engine is running. Serious damage to injection pump could occur.

1. Disconnect battery ground cables from both batteries.
2. Remove engine oil filter neck.
3. Remove bolts attaching injection pump to drive gear.
4. Disconnect electrical connectors to injection pump.
5. Disconnect accelerator cable and speed control cable from throttle lever, if so equipped.
6. Remove air cleaner and install intake opening cover.
7. Remove accelerator cable bracket, with cables attached, from intake manifold and position out of the way.

NOTE: All fuel lines and fittings must be capped, to prevent fuel contamination.

8. Remove fuel filter-to-injection pump fuel line and cap fittings.
9. Remove and cap injection pump inlet elbow.
10. Remove and cap injection pump fitting adapter.
11. Remove fuel return line on injection pump, rotate out of the way, and cap all fittings.

NOTE: It is not necessary to remove injection lines from injection pump to remove injection pump. If lines are to be removed, loosen injection line fittings at injection pump before removing it from engine.

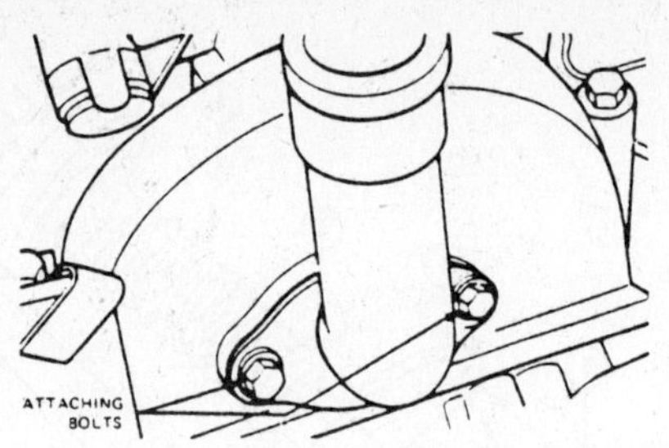

Diesel oil filler neck removal

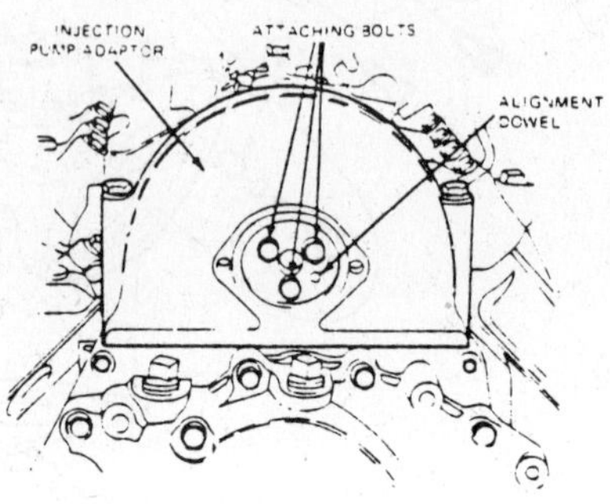

Diesel injection pump drive gear attaching bolts

12. Remove fuel injection lines from nozzles and cap lines and nozzles.
13. Remove three nuts attaching injection pump to injection pump adapter.
14. If injection pump is to be replaced, loosen injection line retaining clips and injection nozzle fuel lines and cap all fittings. Do not install injection nozzle fuel lines until new pump is installed in engine.
15. Lift injection pump, with nozzle lines attached, up and out of engine compartment.

WARNING: Do not carry injection pump by injection nozzle fuel lines as this could cause lines to bend or crimp.

16. Install new O-ring on drive gear end of injection pump.
17. Move injection pump down and into position.
18. Position alignment dowel on injection pump into alignment hole on drive gear.
19. Install bolts attaching injection pump to drive gear and tighten.
20. Install nuts attaching injection pump to adapter. Align scribe lines on injection pump flange and injection pump adapter and tighten to 14 ft.lb.
21. If injection nozzle fuel lines were removed from injection pump install at this time.
22. Remove caps from nozzles and

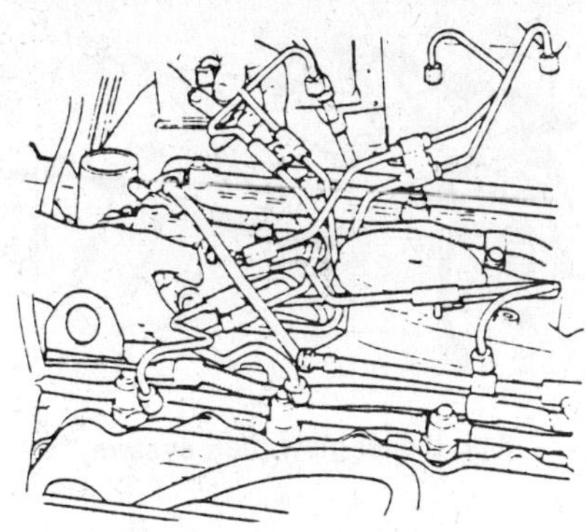

Diesel injection pump removal. Be careful not to crimp or bend the fuel lines

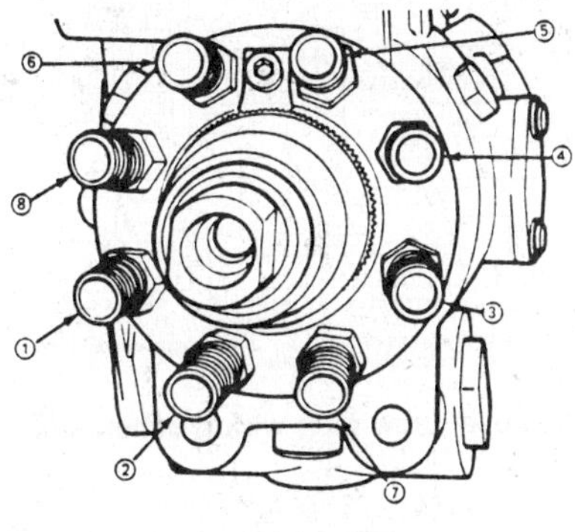

Injection pump line sequence

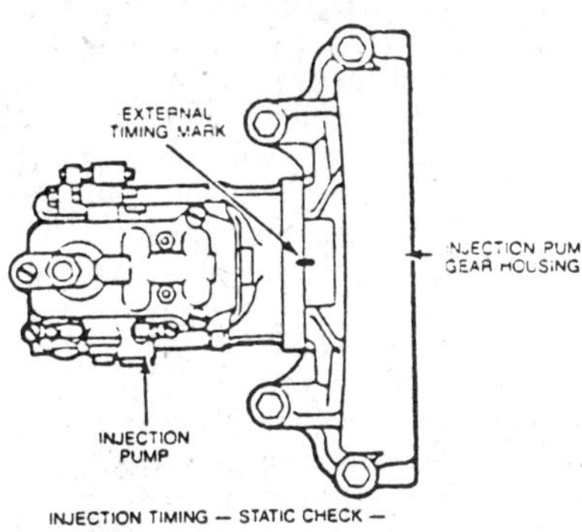

Diesel injection pump static timing marks

fuel lines and install fuel line nuts on nozzles and tighten to 22 ft.lb.

23. Connect fuel return line to injection pump.

24. Install injection pump fitting adapter with a new O-ring.

25. Clean old sealant from injection pump elbow threads, using clean solvent, and dry thoroughly. Apply a light coating of pipe sealant on elbow threads.

26. Install elbow in injection pump adapter and tighten to a minimum of 6 ft.lb. Then tighten further, if necessary, to align elbow with injection

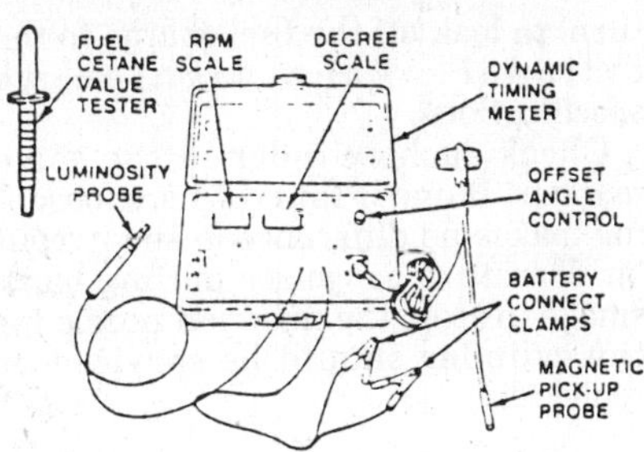

Rotunda® dynamic timing meter used for diesel injection timing. Cetane tester, magnetic pick-up probe and luminosity probe also shown

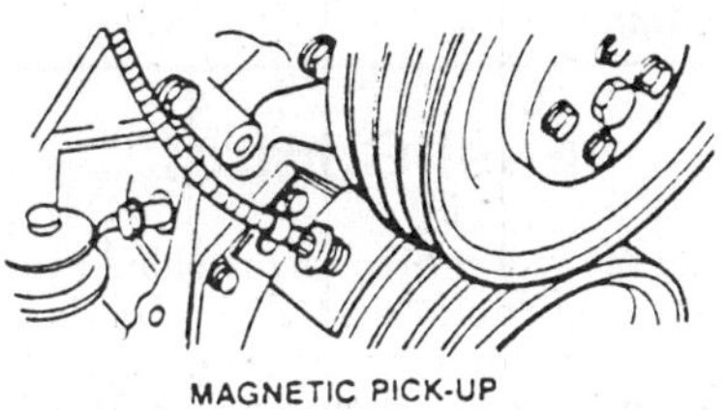

V8 diesel magnetic pick-up probe hole location

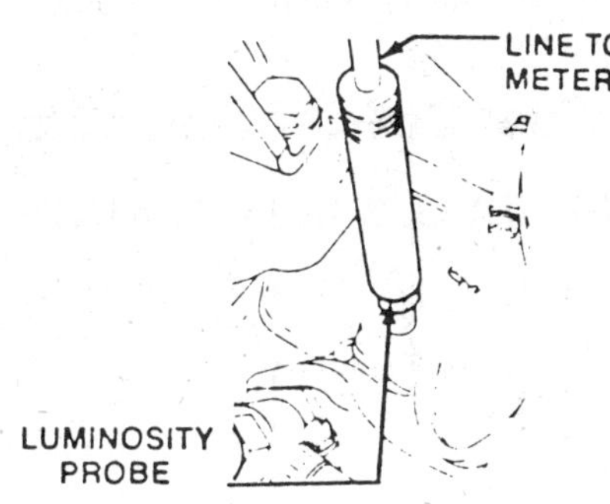

Luminosity probe used for diesel injection timing

pump fuel inlet line, but do not exceed 360° of rotation or 10 ft.lb.

27. Remove caps and connect fuel filter-to-injection pump fuel line.

28. Install accelerator cable bracket to intake manifold.

29. Remove intake manifold cover and install air cleaner.

30. Connect accelerator and speed control cable, if so equipped, to throttle lever.

31. Install electrical connectors on injection pump.

32. Clean injection pump adapter and oil filler neck sealing surfaces.

33. Apply a ⅛" bead of RTV Sealant on adapter housing.

34. Install oil filter neck and tighten.

35. Connect battery ground cables to both batteries. Run engine and check for fuel leaks.

36. If necessary, purge high pressure fuel lines of air by loosening connector one half to one turn and cranking engine until solid fuel, free from bubbles flows from connection.

CAUTION

Keep eyes and hands away from nozzle spray. Fuel spraying from the nozzle under high pressure can penetrate the skin and cause infection. Medical attention should be provided immediately in the event of skin penetration.

37. Check and adjust injection pump timing.

Injectors

REMOVAL & INSTALLATION

8-420 (6.9L)

NOTE: Before removing nozzle assemblies, clean exterior of each nozzle assembly and the surrounding area with clean fuel oil or solvent to prevent entry of dirt into engine when nozzle assemblies are removed. Also, clean fuel inlet and fuel leak-off piping connections. Blow dry with compressed air.

1. Remove fuel line retaining clamp(s) from effected nozzle line(s).
2. Disconnect nozzle fuel inlet (high pressure) and fuel leak-off tees from each nozzle assembly and position out of the way. Cover open ends of fuel inlet lines and nozzles to prevent entry of dirt.
3. Remove injection nozzles by turning counterclockwise. Pull nozzle assembly with copper washer from engine. Be careful not to strike nozzle tip against any hard surface during removal. Cover nozzle assembly fuel inlet opening and nozzle tip with plastic cap to prevent entry of dirt.

NOTE: Remove copper injector nozzle gasket from nozzle bore with Tool T71P-19703-C, or equivalent, if not attached to nozzle tip.

4. Place nozzle assemblies in a fabricated holder as they are removed from the heads. The holder should be marked with numbers corresponding to the cylinder numbering of the engine. Use of this holder permits replacing nozzles in their respective ports in the cylinder heads.
5. Thoroughly clean nozzle bore in cylinder head before reinserting nozzle assembly with nozzle seat cleaner, Tool T83T-9527-A or equivalent. Pay particular attention to seating surface, in order that no small particles of metal or carbon will cause assembly to be cocked or permit blow-by of combus-

tion gases. Blow out particles with compressed air.

6. Remove protective cap and install a new copper gasket on nozzle assembly, with a small dab of grease.

NOTE: Anti-Seize Compound or equivalent should be used on nozzle threads to aid installation and future removal.

7. Install nozzle assembly into cylinder head nozzle bore. Be careful that nozzle tip does not strike against recess wall.
8. Tighten nozzle assembly.
9. Remove protective caps from nozzle assemblies and fuel lines. Install leak-off tees to nozzle assembly.

NOTE: Install two new O-ring seals for each fuel return tee.

10. Connect high pressure fuel line and tighten using a fuel line flare wrench.
11. Install fuel line retainer clamp(s), and tighten.
12. Start engine.
13. If necessary, purge high pressure fuel lines of air by loosening connector one half to one turn and cranking engine until solid fuel, free from bubbles flows from connection.

CAUTION

Keep eyes and hands away from nozzle spray. Fuel spraying from the nozzle under high pressure can penetrate the skin and cause infection. Medical attention should be provided immediately in the event of skin penetration.

14. Check for fuel leakage at high pressure connections.

TESTING

Where ideal conditions of good combustion, specified engine temperature control and absolutely clean fuel prevail, nozzles require little attention. Nozzle trouble is usually indicated by one or more of the following symptoms:

1. Smoky exhaust (black)
2. Loss of power
3. Misfiring
4. Increased fuel consumption
5. Combustion knock
6. Engine overheating

Where faulty nozzle operation is suspected on an engine that is misfiring or puffing black smoke, a simple test can be made to determine which cylinder is causing the difficulty.

With the engine running at a speed that makes the problem most pronounced, momentarily loosen the high pressure fuel inlet line connection on one nozzle assembly sufficiently to "cut-out" the cylinder (one half to one turn) to leak off the fuel charge to the cylinder. Then tighten to specifications.

Check each cylinder in the same manner. If one is found where loosening makes no difference in the irregular operation or causes puffing black smoke to stop, the injection nozzle for the cylinder should be serviced or replaced.

CAUTION

Keep eyes and hands away from nozzle spray. Fuel spraying from the nozzle under high pressure can penetrate the skin and cause infection. Medical attention should be provided immediately in the event of skin penetration.

Fuel Control

On-off fuel control is provided by an electric solenoid located in the diesel injection pump housing cover. Current is supplied to the solenoid when the ignition switch is turned on. If no fuel is supplied with the ignition switch in the on position, check for current at the solenoid terminal before condemning the solenoid.

Fuel Cut-Off Solenoid

REMOVAL & INSTALLATION

1. Disconnect battery ground cables from both batteries.
2. Remove connector from fuel cut-off solenoid.
3. Remove fuel cut-off solenoid assembly.
4. Install fuel cut-off solenoid, with new O-ring, and tighten.
5. Install connector on fuel cut-off solenoid.
6. Connect battery ground cables to both batteries. Run engine and check for fuel leaks.

Glow Plug System

The "quick start; afterglow" system is used to enable the engine to start more quickly when the engine is cold. It consists of the flour glow plugs, the control module, two relays, a glow plug resistor assembly, coolant temperature switch, clutch and neutral switches and connecting wiring. Relay power and feedback circuits are protected by fuse links in the wiring harness. The control module is protected by a separate 10A fuse in the fuse panel.

When the ignition switch is turned to the ON position, a Wait-to-Start signal appears near the cold-start knob on the panel. When the signal appears, relay No. 1 also closes and full system

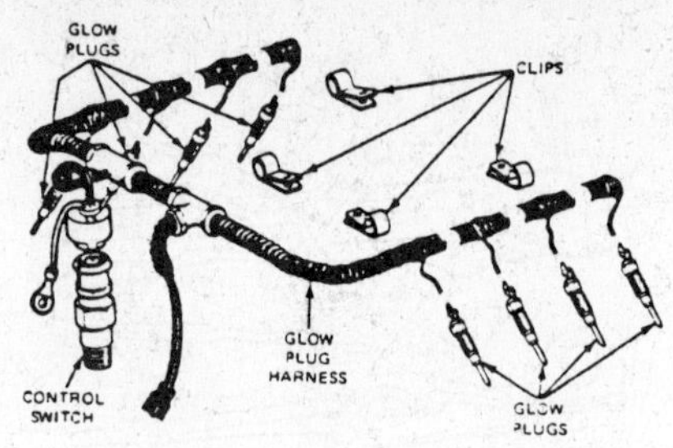

6.9L diesel glow plug system

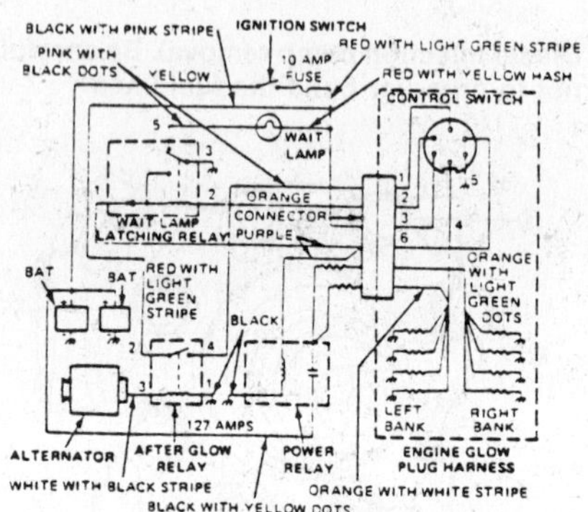

Diesel glow plug wiring schematic

voltage is applied to the glow plugs. If engine coolant temperature is below 30°C (86°F), relay No.2 also closes at this time. After three seconds, the control module turns off the Wait-to-Start light indicating that the engine is ready for starting. If the ignition switch is left in the ON position about three seconds more without cranking, the control opens relay No. 1 and current to the plugs stops to prevent overheating. However, if coolant temperature is below 30°C (86°F) when relay No. 1 opens, relay No.2 remains closed to apply reduced voltage to the plugs through the glow plug resistor until the ignition switch is turned off.

When the engine is cranked, the control module cycles relay No. 1 intermittently. Thus, glow plug voltage will alternate between 12 and four volts, during cranking, with relay No.2 closed, or between 12 and zero volts with relay No.2 open. After the engine starts, alternator output signals the control module to stop the No. 1 relay cycling and the afterglow function takes over.

If the engine coolant temperature is below 30°C (86°F), the No.2 relay remains closed. This applies reduced (4.2 to 5.3) voltage to the glow plugs through the glow plug resistor. When the vehicle is under way (clutch and neutral switches closed), or coolant temperature is above 30°C (86°F), the control module opens relay No.2, cutting off all current to the glow plugs.

TESTING THE GLOW PLUGS

1. Disconnect the leads from each glow plug. Connect one lead of the ohmmeter to the glow plug terminal and the other lead to a good ground. Set the ohmmeter on the X1 scale. Test each glow plug in the like manner.
2. If the meter indicates less than 1Ω, the problem is not with the glow plug.
3. If the ohmmeter indicates 1Ω or more, replace the glow plug and retest.

REMOVAL & INSTALLATION

1. Disconnect battery ground cables from both batteries.
2. Disconnect glow plug harness from glow plugs.
3. Using a 12mm deepwell socket, remove glow plugs.
4. Install glow plugs, using a 12mm deepwell socket, and tighten.
5. Install glow plug harness on glow plugs and tighten.
6. Connect battery ground cables to both batteries.

CHASSIS ELECTRICAL

NOTE: Always disconnect the battery ground cable before working on electrical equipment.

Blower Motor

REMOVAL & INSTALLATION

Vans, w/o Air Conditioning

1. Disconnect the orange (orange with black strips) motor lead wire. Remove the ground wire screw from the firewall.
2. Disconnect the blower motor cooling tube.
3. Remove the four mounting plate screws and the motor assembly.
4. Reverse the procedure for installation.

Vans, w/Air Conditioning

1. Disconnect the resistor electrical leads on the front of the blower cover inside the truck.
2. Remove the blower cover.
3. Push the wiring grommet forward out of the housing hole.
4. Remove the blower motor mounting plate. Remove the blower motor.
5. Reverse the procedure for installation.

Bronco and Pickups, Comfort Vent Heaters, Without Air Conditioning

1. Disconnect the motor wires at the hard shell connectors.
2. Disconnect the blower motor air cooling tube from the motor.
3. Remove four blower motor mounting plate attaching screws and remove the motor and wheel assembly from the blower housing.
4. Remove the hub clamp spring from the blower wheel hub and the retainer from the motor shaft. Then, remove the blower wheel from the motor shaft.
5. Position the blower wheel on the

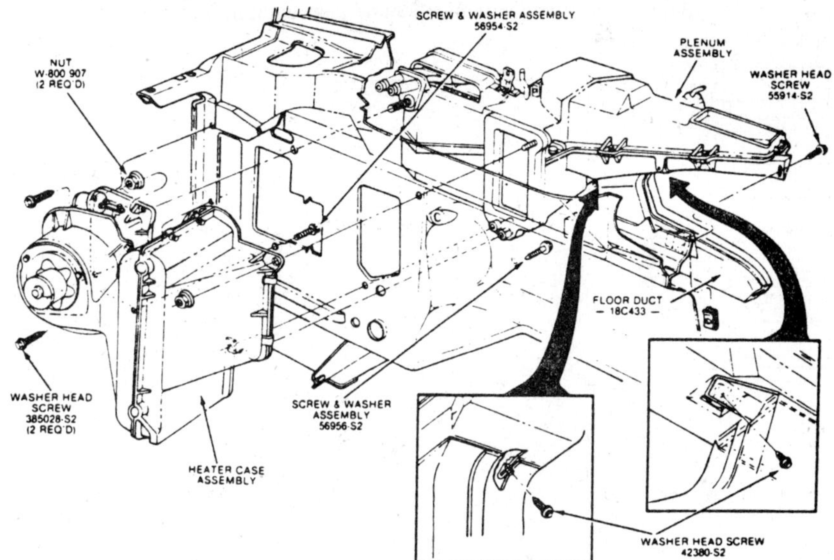

Heater case and plenum assemblies, 1980-81

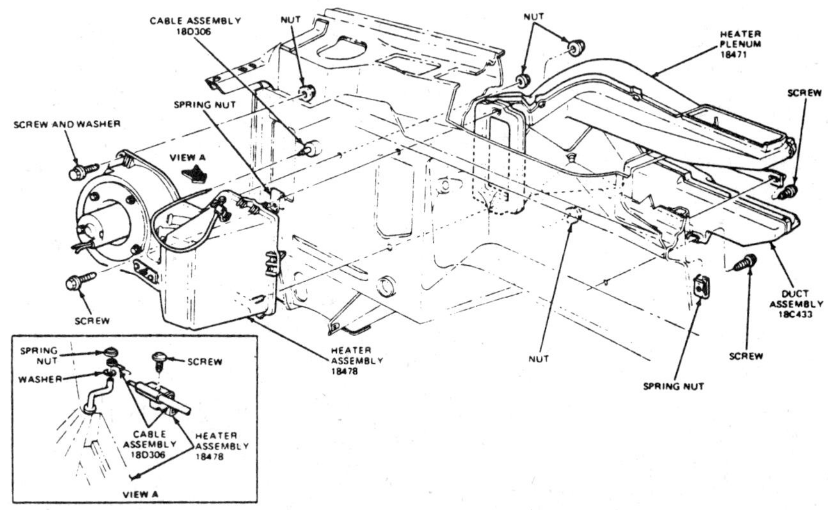

Heater case and plenum, 1980 and later standard and high output units without A/C

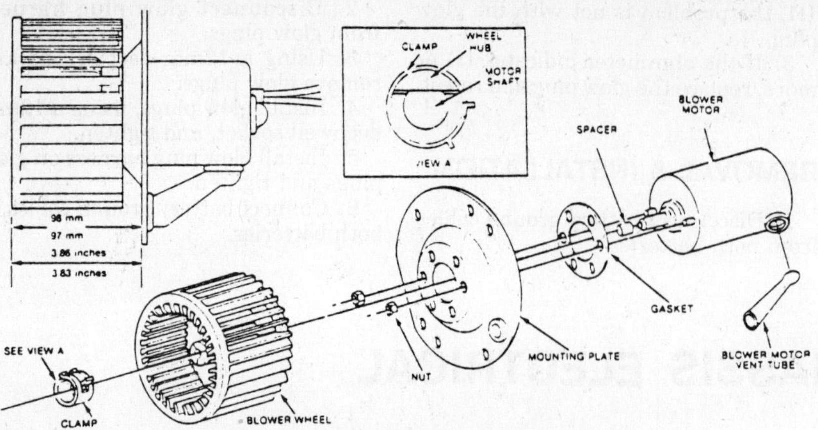

Blower motor and wheel, 1980 and later without A/C

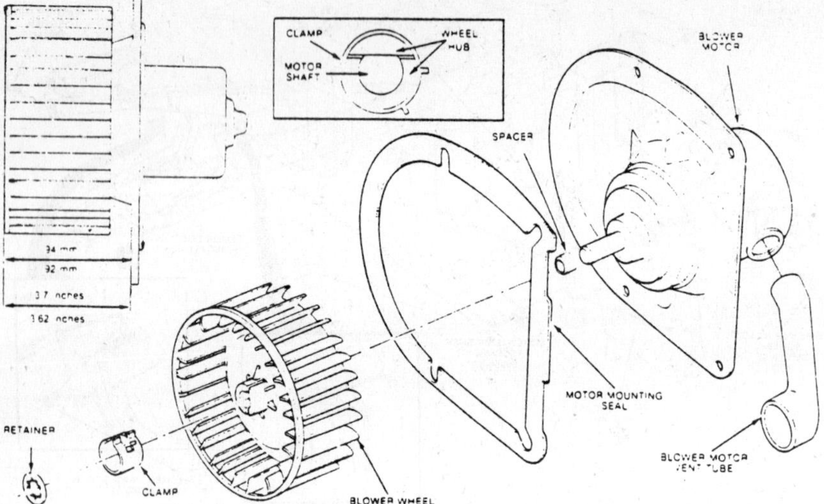

Blower motor and wheel, 1980 and later with A/C

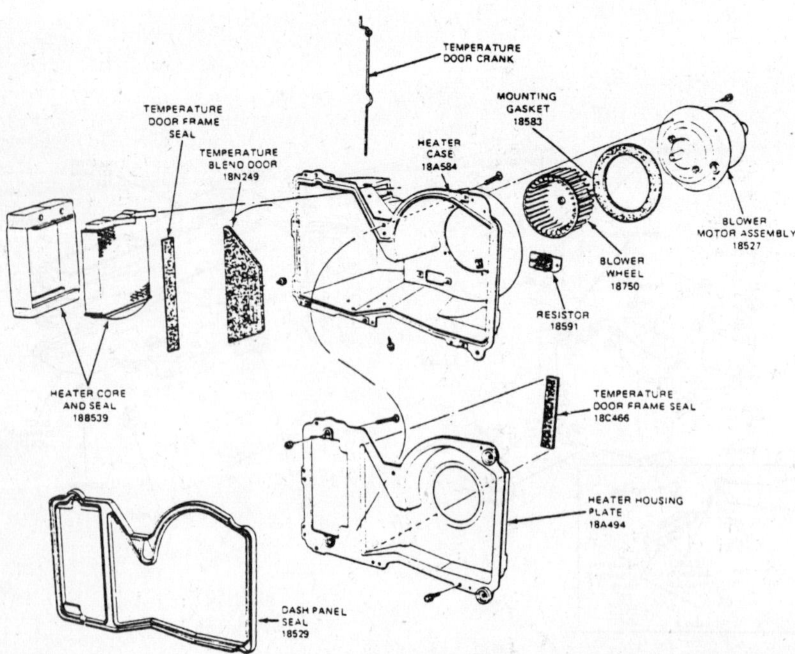

Heater case assemble showing core and blower, 1980 and later shown

blower motor shaft. Then, install a new hub clamp spring on the blower hub as shown. The hub clamp spring is included with a new blower wheel but not with the blower motor.

6. Install a new flange gasket on the blower motor flange.
7. Position the blower motor and wheel assembly in the blower housing and install the four attaching screws. The wire clamp should be installed under the screw closest to the resistor assembly.
8. Cement the blower motor air tube on the nipple of the blower housing with RTV silicone adhesive.
9. Connect the blower motor wires at the hard shell connectors.
10. Check the blower motor for proper operation.

Bronco and Pickups Standard & High Output Heaters, Without Air Conditioning

1. Disconnect the motor wire at the hard shell connector and the ground wire at the ground screw.
2. Remove four screws attaching the blower motor and wheel to the heater case.
3. Remove the blower motor and wheel from the heater case.
4. Remove the blower wheel hub clamp spring and the tab lock washer from the motor shaft. Then, pull the blower wheel from the motor shaft.
5. Install the blower wheel on the blower motor shaft.
6. Install the hub clamp spring on the blower hub.
7. Position the blower motor and wheel to the heater case, and install the four attaching screws.
8. Connect the blower motor wires and check the blower motor for proper operation.

Bronco and Pickups With Air Conditioning

REMOVAL (WITHOUT DISCHARGING THE A/C SYSTEM)

1. Disconnect the motor wires at the hard shell connectors.
2. Disconnect the blower motor air cooling tube from the motor.
3. Remove four blower motor mounting plate attaching screws and remove the motor and wheel assembly from the blower housing.
4. Remove the hub clamp spring from the blower wheel hub and the retainer from the motor shaft. Then, remove the blower wheel from the motor shaft.

INSTALLATION

1. Position the blower wheel on the blower motor shaft to the dimension shown. Then, install a new hub clamp

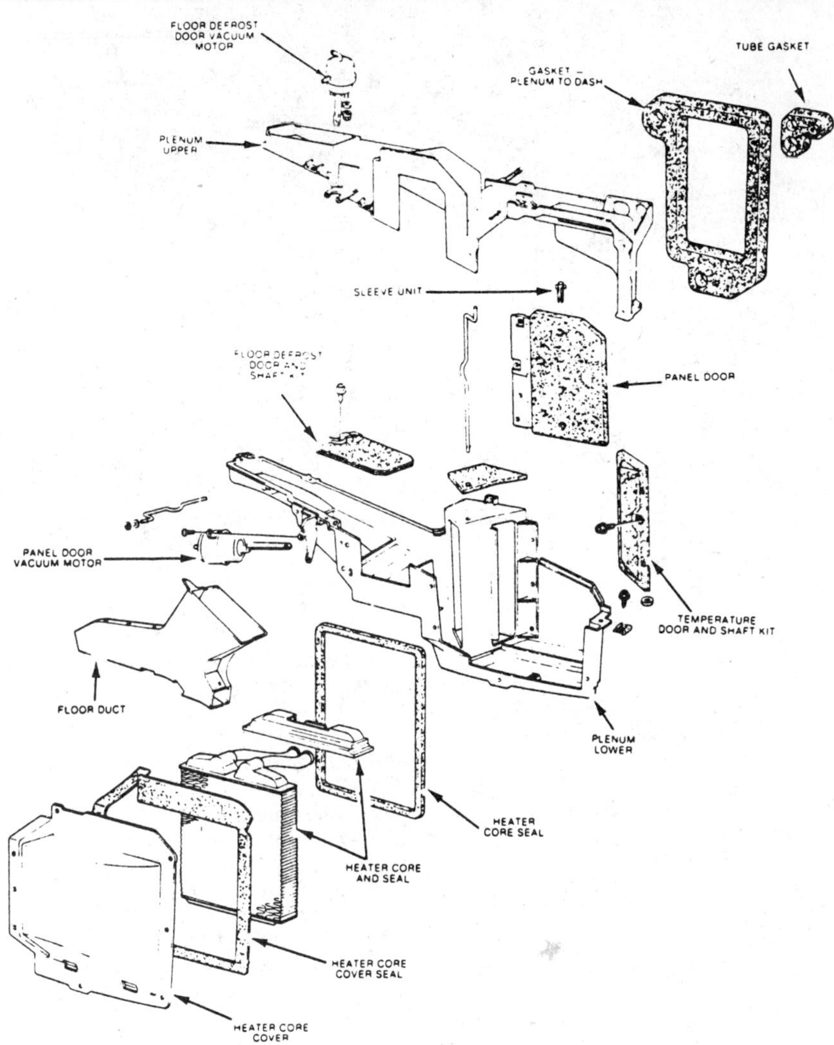

Comfort Vent heater plenum, 1980-81

spring on the blower hub as shown. The hub clamp spring is included with a new blower wheel but not with the blower motor.

2. Install a new flange gasket on the blower motor flange.

3. Position the blower motor and wheel assembly in the blower housing and install the four attaching screws. The wire clamp should be installed under the screw closest to the resistor assembly.

4. Cement the blower motor air tube on the nipple of the blower housing with RTV silicone adhesive.

5. Connect the blower motor wires at the hard shell connectors.

6. Check the blower motor for proper operation.

Heater Core

REMOVAL & INSTALLATION

Vans Without Air Conditioning

1. Drain the coolant; remove the battery.

CAUTION

When draining the coolant, keep in mind that cats and dogs are attracted by the ethylene glycol antifreeze, and are quite likely to drink any that is left in an uncovered container or in puddles on the ground. This will prove fatal in sufficient quantity. Always drain the coolant into a sealable container. Coolant should be reused unless it is contaminated or several years old.

2. Disconnect the resistor wiring harness and the orange blower motor lead. Remove the ground wire screw from the firewall.

3. Detach the heater hoses and the plastic hose retaining strap.

4. Remove the five mounting screws inside the truck.

5. Remove the heater assembly.

6. Cut the seal at the top and bottom edge of the core retainer. Remove the two screws and the retainer. Slide the core and seal out of the case.

7. Reverse the procedure for installation.

Vans With Air Conditioning

1. Disconnect the resistor electrical leads on the front of the blower cover inside the truck. Detach the vacuum line from the vacuum motor. Remove the blower cover.

2. Remove the nut and push washer from the air door shaft. Remove the control cable from the bracket and the air door shaft.

3. Remove the blower motor housing and the air door housing.

4. Drain the coolant and detach the heater hoses.

CAUTION

When draining the coolant, keep in mind that cats and dogs are attracted by the ethylene glycol antifreeze, and are quite likely to drink any that is left in an uncovered container or in puddles on the ground. This will prove fatal in sufficient quantity. Always drain the coolant into a sealable container. Coolant should be reused unless it is contaminated or several years old.

5. Remove the heater core retaining brackets. Remove the core and seal assembly.

6. Reverse the procedure for installation.

Bronco and Pickups, Comfort Vent Heaters, Without Air Conditioning

1. Disconnect the heater hoses from the heater core tubes and plug the hoses with suitable 5/8" plugs.

2. Remove the glove compartment liner.

3. Remove two spring clips attaching the heater core cover to the plenum along the top edge of the heater core cover.

4. Remove eight screws attaching the heater core cover to the plenum and remove the cover.

5. Remove the heater core from the plenum taking care not to spill coolant from the core.

6. Install the heater core in the plenum.

7. Install the heater core cover (eight (8) screws and two spring clips along the top edge of the cover).

8. Install the glove compartment liner.

9. Connect the heater hoses to the heater core. Tighten the hose clamps.

10. Add coolant to raise the coolant level to specification.

11. Check the system for proper operation and for coolant leaks.

Bronco and Pickups, Standard & High Output Heaters, Without Air Conditioning

1. Disconnect the temperature cable from the temperature blend door

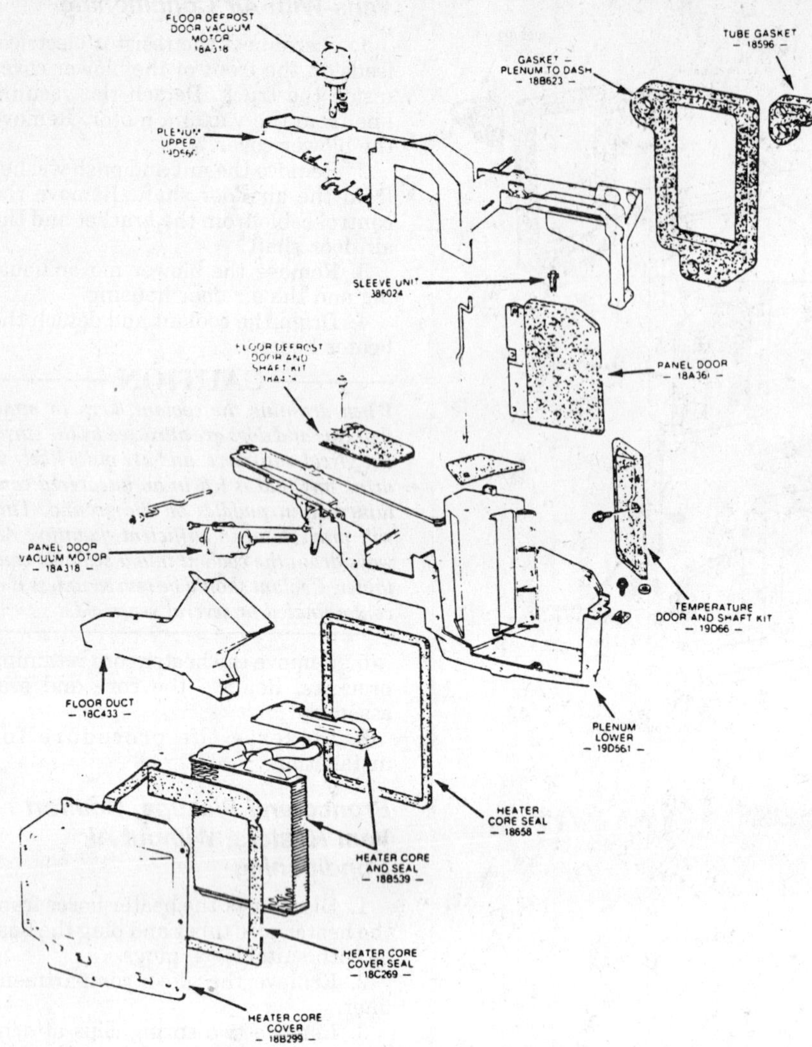

Manual A/C—heater plenum, 1980 and later

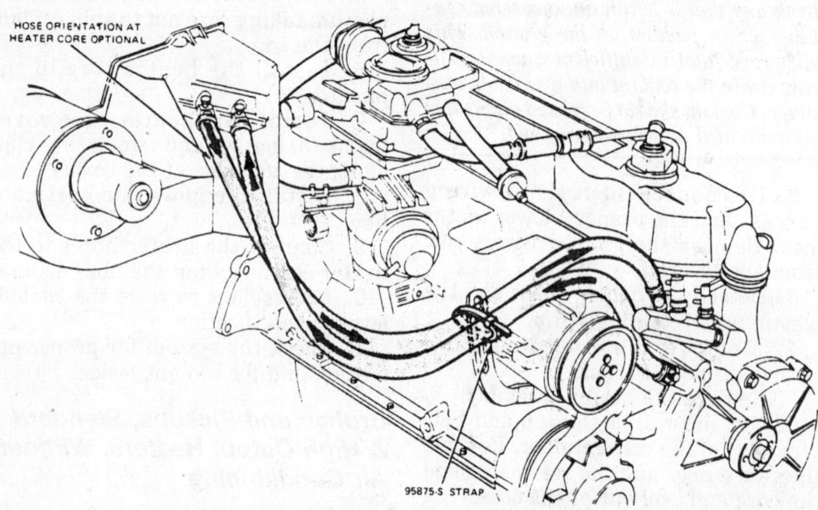

Heater hose connections, inline six cylinder models

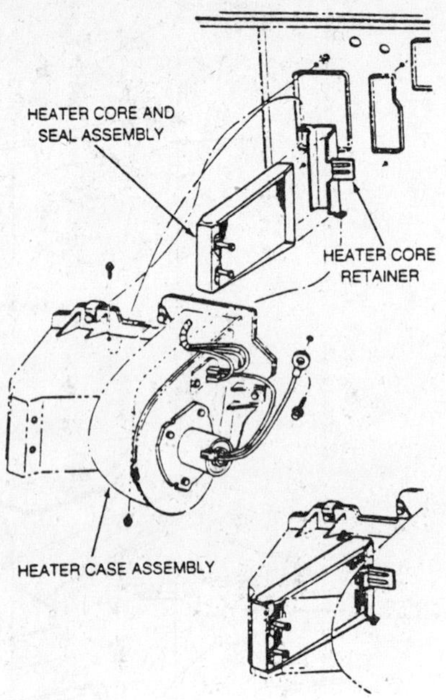

Heater Core installation without air conditioning

and the mounting bracket on top of the heater case.

2. Disconnect the wires from the blower motor resistor and the blower motor.

3. Disconnect the heater hoses from the heater core and plug the hoses with suitable 5/8" plugs.

4. Working under the instrument panel, remove two nuts retaining the left end of the heater case and the right end of the plenum to the dash panel.

5. In the engine compartment, remove one screw attaching the top center of the heater case to the dash panel.

6. Remove two screws attaching the right end of the heater case to the dash panel, and remove the heater case from the vehicle.

7. Remove nine screws and one (1) bolt and nut attaching the heater housing plate to the heater case, and remove the heater housing plate.

8. Remove three screws attaching the heater core frame to the heater case and remove the frame.

9. Remove the heater core and seal from the heater case.

10. Position the heater core and seal in the heater case.

11. Install the heater core frame (3 screws).

12. Position the heater housing plate on the heater case and install the nine screws and one bolt and nut.

13. Position the heater case to the dash panel and install the three attaching screws.

14. Working in the passenger com-

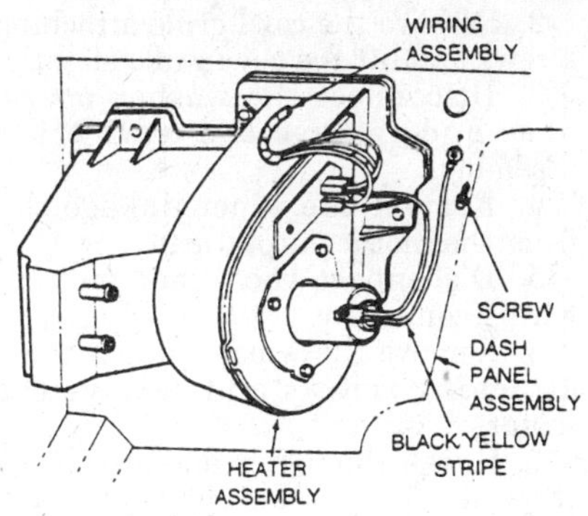

Blower motor installation without air conditioning—1980-84

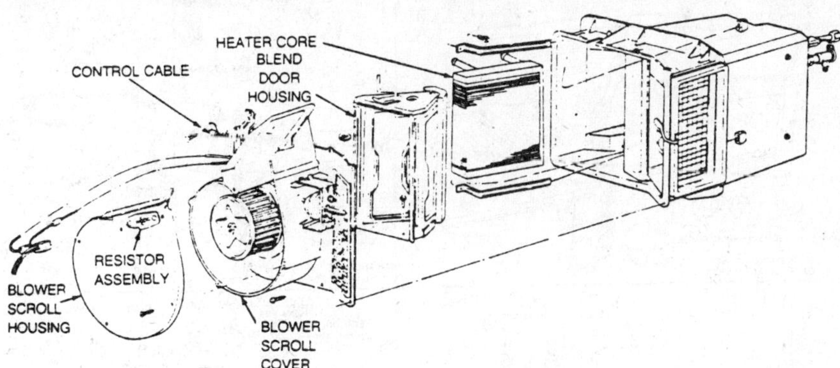

Heater Core installation with air conditioning

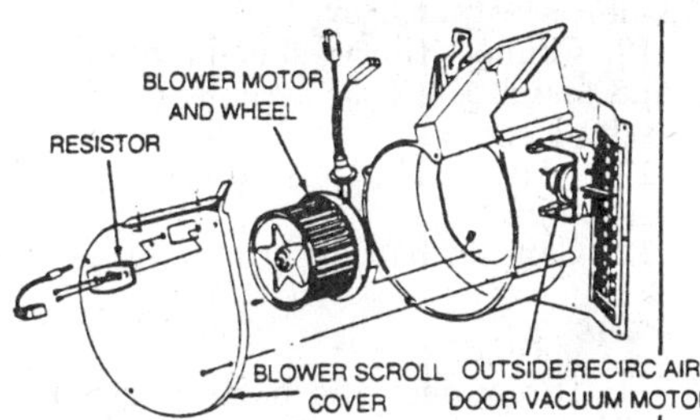

Blower motor installation with air conditioning

partment, install two nuts to retain the heater case and plenum right end to the dash panel.

15. Connect the heater hoses to the heater core. Tighten the hose clamps.
16. Connect the wires to the blower motor resistor assembly.
17. Connect the blower motor wires.
18. Position (slide) the self-adjusting clip on the temperature cable to a position approximately 1" from the cable end loop.
19. Snap the temperature cable on the cable mounting bracket of the heater case. Then, position the self-adjusting clip on the door crank arm.
20. Adjust the temperature cable.
21. Check the system for proper operation.

1980 and Later Bronco and Pickups With Air Conditioning

REMOVAL (WITHOUT DISCHARGING THE A/C SYSTEM)

1. Disconnect the heater hoses from the heater core tubes and plug the hoses with suitable 5/8" plugs.
2. Remove the glove compartment liner.
3. Remove eight screws attaching the heater core cover to the plenum and remove the cover.
4. Remove the heater core from the plenum taking care not to spill coolant from the core.

INSTALLATION

1. Install the heater core in the plenum.
2. Install the heater core cover (eight screws).
3. Install the glove compartment liner.
4. Connect the heater hoses to the heater core. Tighten the hose clamps.
5. Add coolant to raise the coolant level to specification.

Auxiliary Heater Case (With or Without A/C)

REMOVAL & INSTALLATION

Vans

1. Remove the first bench seat (if so equipped).
2. Remove the auxiliary heater and/or air conditioning cover assembly attaching screws and remove the cover.
3. Position the cover assembly to the body side panel and install the attaching screws.
4. Install the bench seat (if removed) and tighten the retaining bolts 25-45 ft.lb.

Auxiliary Heater Core and Seal Assembly

VANS

Removal & Installation

1. Remove the first bench seat (if so equipped).
2. Remove auxiliary heater and/or air conditioning cover attaching screws (15) and remove the cover.
3. Partially drain the engine coolant from the coolant system.

CAUTION

When draining the coolant, keep in mind that cats and dogs are attracted by the ethylene glycol antifreeze, and are quite likely to drink any that is left in an uncovered container or in puddles on the ground. This will prove fatal in sufficient quantity. Always drain the coolant into a sealable container. Coolant should be reused unless it is contaminated or several years old.

4. Remove the heater hoses from the auxiliary heater core assembly (2 clamps).
5. Pull the wiring assembly away from the heater core seal.
6. Slide the heater core and seal assembly out of the housing slot.
7. Slide the heater core and seal assembly into the housing slot (position the wiring to one side).
8. Install the heater hoses to the heater core assembly (2 clamps).
9. Fill the cooling system to specification.
10. Position the cover assembly to the body side panel and install the attaching screws (15).
11. Install the bench seat (if removed) and tighten the retaining bolts 25-45 ft.lb.

RADIO

REMOVAL & INSTALLATION

Vans

1. Detach the battery ground cable.
2. Remove the heater and A/C control knobs. Remove the lighter.
3. Remove the radio knobs and discs.
4. If the truck has a lighter, snap out the name plate at the right side to remove the panel attaching screw.
5. Remove the five finish panel screws.
6. Very carefully pry out the cluster panel in two places.
7. Detach the antenna lead and speaker wires.

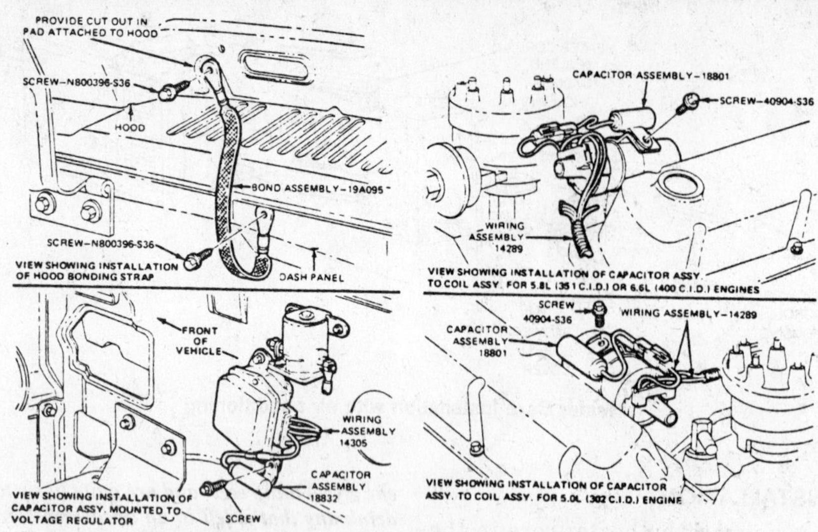

Typical radio supression equipment, pickups. These, along with the spark plug wires and radio itself, are the areas to check when radio reception becomes poor

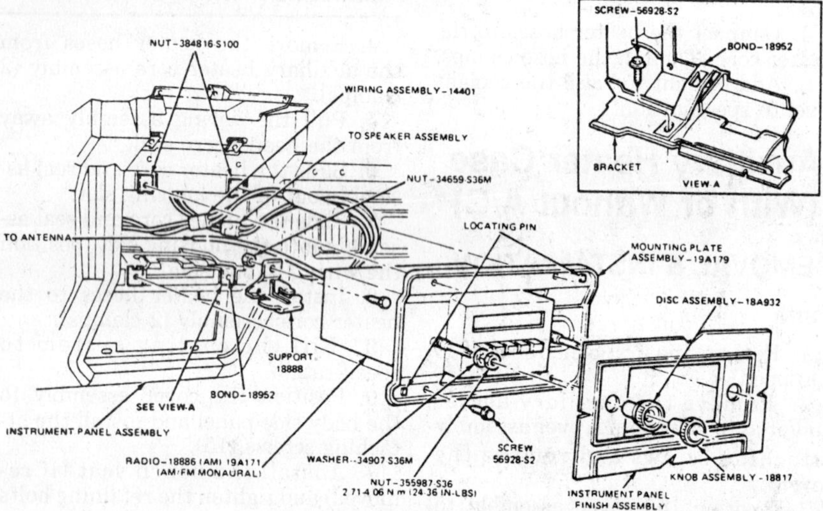

Typical 1979 and later radio installation

8. Remove the two nuts and washers and the mounting plate.
9. Remove the four front radio attaching screws. Remove the rear support nut and washer, and remove the radio.
10. Reverse the procedure for installation.

Bronco and Pickups

1. Disconnect the battery ground cable.
2. Disconnect the antenna, speakers and radio lead.
3. Remove the bolt attaching the radio rear support to the lower edge of the instrument panel.
4. Remove the knobs and discs from the radio control shafts.
5. Remove the retaining nuts from the control shafts and remove the bezel.
6. Remove the nuts and washers from the control shafts and remove the radio from the panel.
7. Installation is the reverse of removal.

WINDSHIELD WIPERS

Motor

REMOVAL & INSTALLATION

Bronco and Pickups

1. Disconnect the battery ground cable.
2. Remove the cowl grille attaching screws and lift the cowl grille slightly.
3. Disconnect the washer nozzle hose and remove the cowl grille assembly.
4. Remove the wiper linkage clip from the motor output arm.
5. Disconnect the wiper motor's wiring connector.
6. Remove the wiper motor's three attaching screws and remove the motor.
7. Install the motor and attach the three attaching screws. Tighten to 60-85 in.lb.
8. Connect wiper motor's wiring connector.
9. Install wiper linkage clip to the motor's output arm.
10. Connect the washer nozzle hose and install the cowl assembly and attaching screws.
11. Install both wiper arm assemblies.
12. Connect battery ground cable.

Vans

1. Disconnect the battery ground cable. Remove the fuse panel and bracket.
2. Disconnect the motor wires.
3. Remove the arms and blades.
4. Remove the outer air inlet cowl. Take off the motor linkage clip.
5. Unbolt and remove the motor.
6. Reverse the procedure for installation.

Linkage

REMOVAL & INSTALLATION

Vans

1. Disconnect the battery ground cable.
2. Remove the wiper blades and arms. Detach the washer hoses.
3. Remove the cowl grille.
4. Remove the linkage clips. Remove the pivot to cowl screws and remove the assembly.

Bronco, Pickups

1. Disconnect the battery ground cable.
2. Remove both wiper arm assemblies.
3. Remove the cowl grille attaching screws and lift the cowl grille slightly.
4. Disconnect the washer nozzle hose and remove the cowl grille assembly.
5. Remove the wiper linkage clip from the motor output arm and pull the linkage from the output arm.
6. Remove the pivot body to cowl screws and remove the linkage and pivot shaft assembly (three screws on

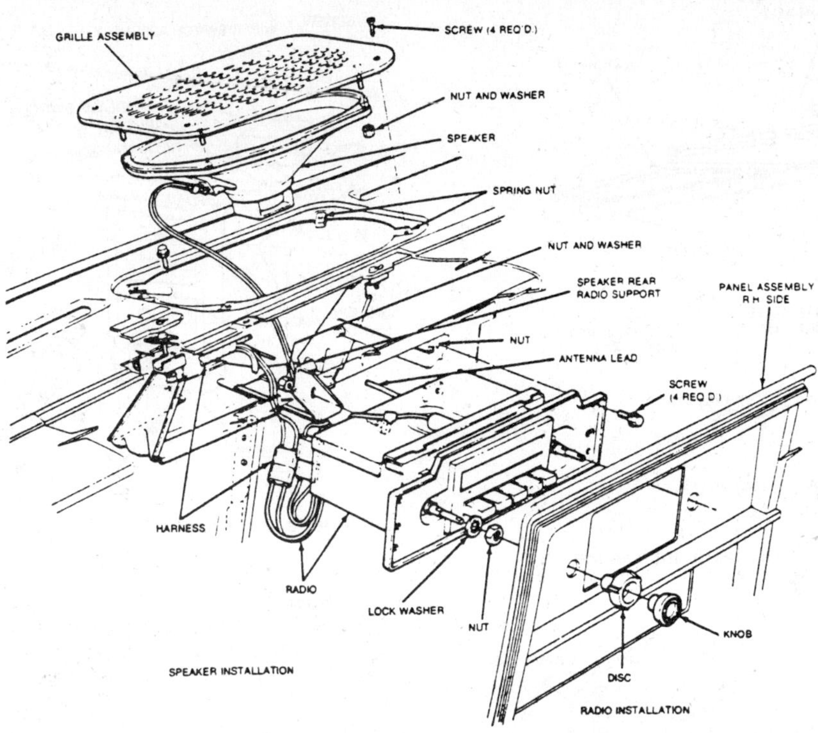

1980-84 radio installation—typical

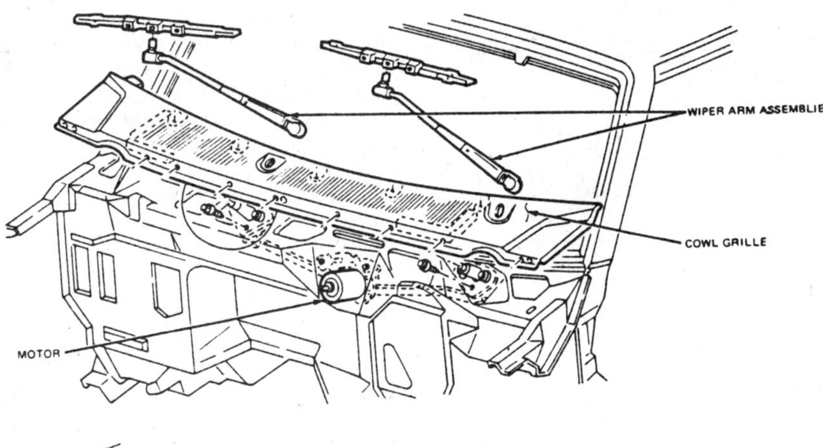

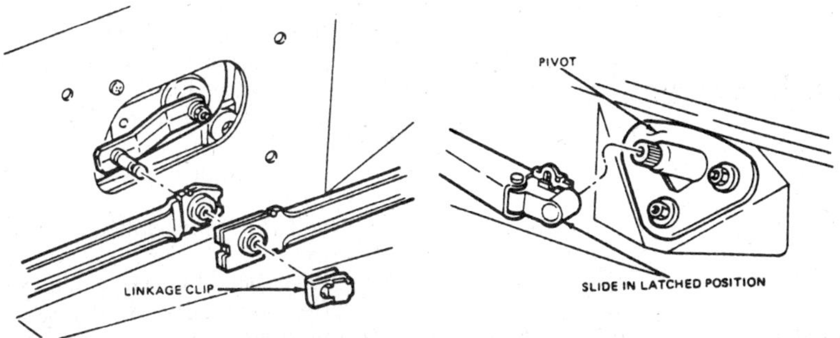

1980 and later wiper motor installation

each side). The left and right pivots and linkage are independent and can be serviced separately.

7. Attach the linkage and pivot shaft assembly to cowl with attaching screws.

8. Replace the linkage to the output arm and attach the linkage clip.

9. Connect the washer nozzle hose and cowl grills assembly.

10. Attach cowl grille attaching screws.

11. Replace both wiper arm assemblies.

12. Connect battery ground cable.

Wiper Arm Assembly

REPLACEMENT

Raise the blade end of the arm off of the windshield and move the slide latch away from the pivot shaft. This will unlock the wiper arm from the pivot shaft and hold the blade end of the arm off of the glass at the same time. The wiper arm can now be pulled off of the pivot shaft without the aid of any tools.

Blade Assembly to Wiper Arm

REPLACEMENT

1. Cycle arm and blade assembly to a position on the windshield where removal of blade assembly can be performed without difficulty. Turn ignition key off at desired position.

2. With blade assembly resting on windshield, grasp either end of the wiper blade frame and pull away from windshield, then pull blade assembly from pin.

NOTE: Rubber element extends past frame. To prevent damage to the blade element, be sure to grasp blade frame and not the end of the blade element.

3. To install, push blade assembly onto pin until fully seated. Be sure blade is securely attached to the wiper arm.

INSTRUMENT CLUSTER

REMOVAL & INSTALLATION

Bronco, Pickups

1. Disconnect the battery ground cable.

2. Remove the fuel gauge switch knob (if so equipped), and wiper-washer knob. Use a hook tool to release each knob lock tab.

3. Remove the knob from the headlamp and windshield wiper switch. Remove the fog lamp switch knob, if so equipped.

4. Remove steering column shroud. Care must be taken not to damage

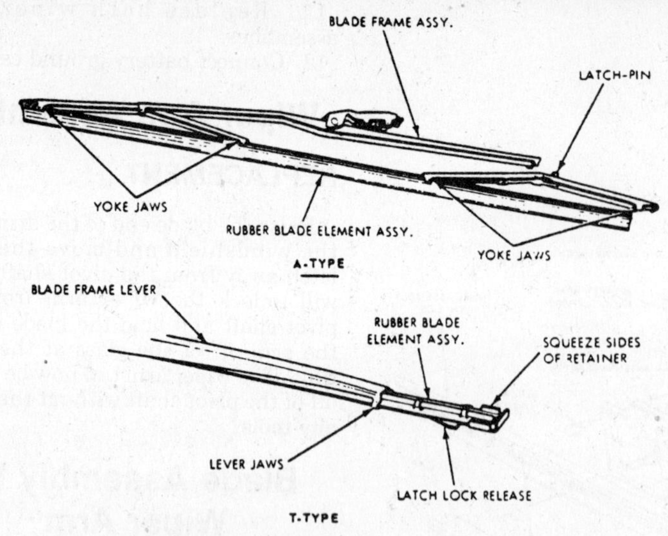

Anco (A) and Trico (T) type wiper blade installation

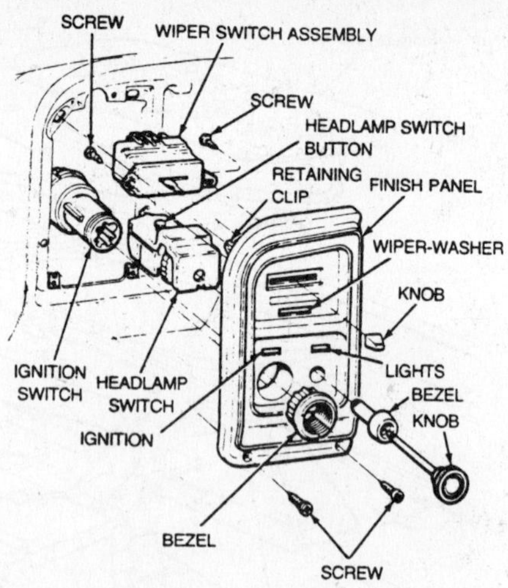

Wiper control switch replacement

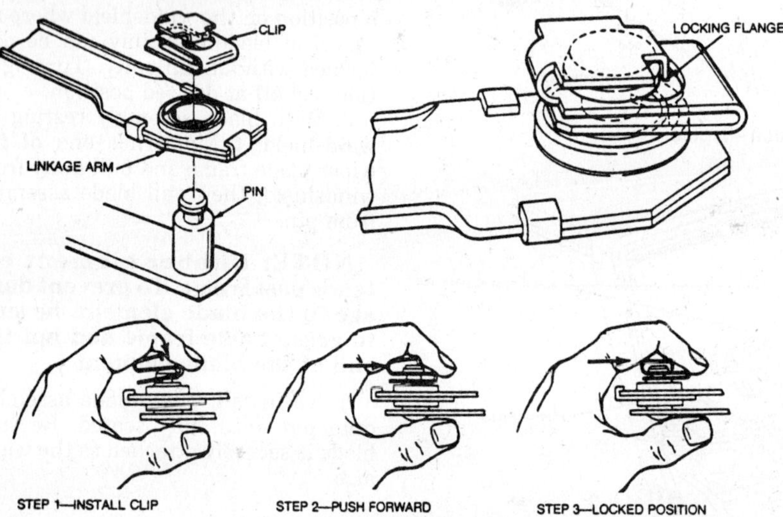

Installing the wiper arm connecting clip

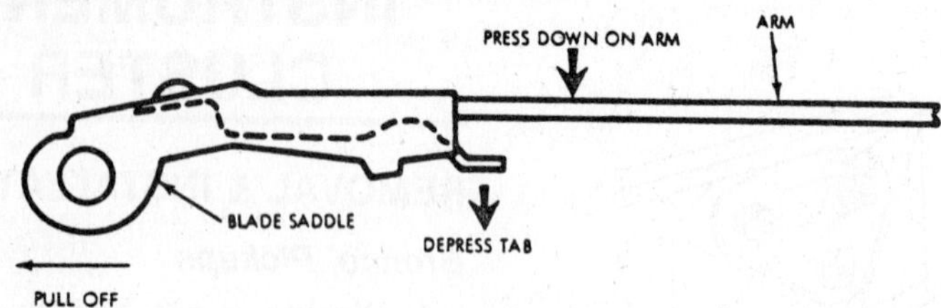

Removal of a Trico wiper blade

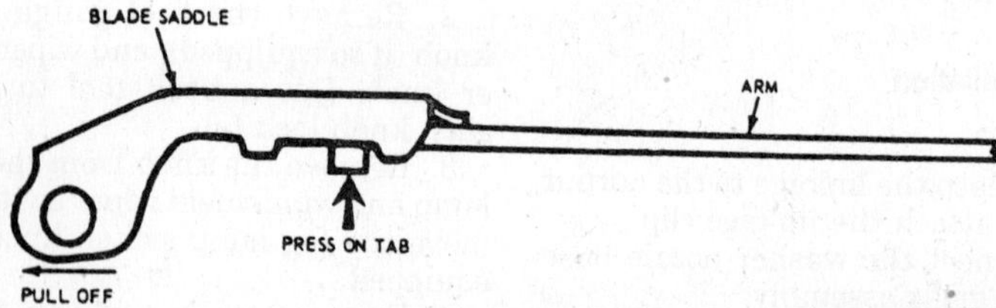

Anco-type wiper arm removal

transmission control selector indicator (PRNDL) cable on vehicles equipped with automatic transmission.

5. On vehicles equipped with automatic transmission, remove loop on indicator cable assembly from retainer pin. Remove bracket screw from cable bracket and slide bracket out of slot in tube.

6. Remove the cluster trim cover. Remove four cluster attaching screws, disconnect the speedometer cable, wire connector from the printed circuit, 4×4 indicator light and remove the cluster.

7. Position cluster to opening and connect the multiple connector, the speedometer cable and 4×4 indicator light. Install the four cluster retaining screws.

8. If so equipped, place loop on transmission indicator cable assembly over retainer on column.

9. Position the tab on steering column bracket into slot on column. Align and attach screw.

10. Place transmission selector lever on steering column into "D" position.

11. Adjust slotted bracket so the pin is within the letter band.

12. Install the trim cover.

13. Install the headlamp switch knob. If so equipped, install the fog lamp switch.

14. Install the wiper-washer control knobs.

15. Connect the battery cable, and check the operation of all gauges, lights and signals.

Vans

1. Disconnect the battery ground cable.

2. Remove two steering column shroud to panel retaining screws and remove shroud.

3. Loosen bolts which attach the

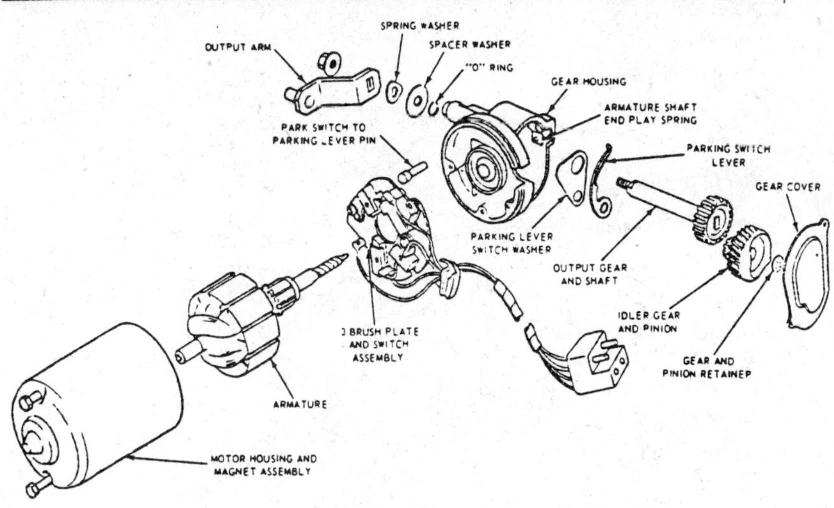

Exploded view of the two-speed windshield wiper motor

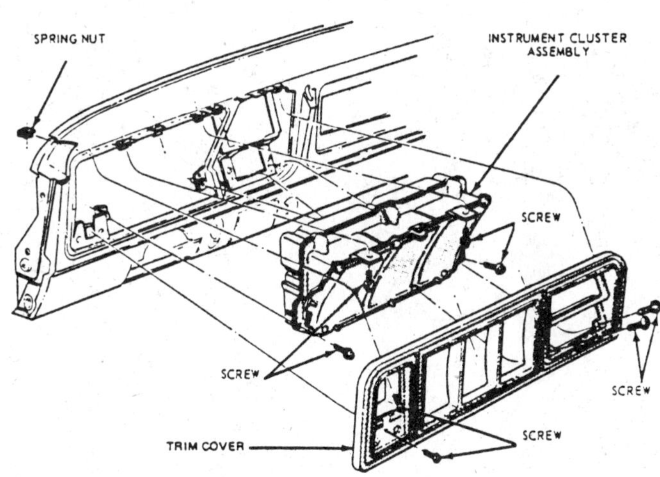

Typical instrument cluster and bezel removal and installation

column to the B and C Support to provide sufficient clearance for cluster removal. (Required for tilt steering column vehicles only).

4. Remove seven instrument cluster to panel retaining screws.
5. Position cluster part away from the panel for access to the back of the cluster to disconnect the speedometer. If there is not sufficient access to disengage the speedometer cable from the speedometer, it may be necessary to remove the speedometer cable at the transmission and pull cable through cowl, to allow room to reach the speedometer quick disconnect.
6. Disconnect the harness connector plug from the printed circuit board and remove the cluster assembly from the instrument panel.
7. Apply approximately $^3/_{16}''$ diameter ball of silicone lubricant or equivalent in the drive hole of the speedometer head.
8. Position the cluster near its opening in the instrument panel.
9. Connect the harness connector plug to the printed circuit board.
10. Connect the speedometer cable (quick disconnect) to the speedometer head. Connect the speedometer cable and housing assembly to the transmission (if removed).
11. Install the seven instrument cluster-to-panel retaining screws and connect the battery ground cable.
12. Check operation of all gauges, lights, and signals.
13. Reinstall the steering column.
14. Position steering column shroud to instrument panel and install two screws.

Speedometer Cable Core

REMOVAL & INSTALLATION

1. Reach up behind the cluster and disconnect the cable by depressing the quick disconnect tab and pulling the cable away.
2. Remove the cable from the casing. If the cable is broken, raise the vehicle on a hoist and disconnect the cable from the transmission.
3. Remove the cable from the casing.
4. To remove the casing from the vehicle, pull it through the floor pan.
5. To replace the cable, slide the new cable into the casing and connect it at the transmission.
6. Route the cable through the floor pan and position the grommet in its groove in the floor.
7. Push the cable onto the speedometer head.

Ignition Switch

REMOVAL & INSTALLATION

1. Disconnect the battery ground cable.
2. Remove steering column shroud and lower the steering column.
3. Disconnect the switch wiring at the multiple plug.
4. Remove the two nuts that retain the switch to the steering column.
5. Lift the switch vertically upward to disengage the actuator rod from the switch and remove switch.
6. When installing the ignition switch, both the locking mechanism at the top of the column and the switch itself must be in LOCK position for correct adjustment. To hold the mechanical parts of the column in LOCK position, move the shift lever into PARK (with automatic transmissions) or REVERSE (with manual transmissions), turn the key to LOCK position, and remove the key. New replacement switches, when received, are already pinned in LOCK position by a metal shipping pin inserted in a locking hole on the side of the switch.
7. Engage the actuator rod in the switch.
8. Position the switch on the column and install the retaining nuts, but do not tighten them.
9. Move the switch up and down along the column to locate the mid-position of rod lash, and then tighten the retaining nuts.
10. Remove the locking pin, connect the battery cable, and check for proper start in PARK or NEUTRAL. Also

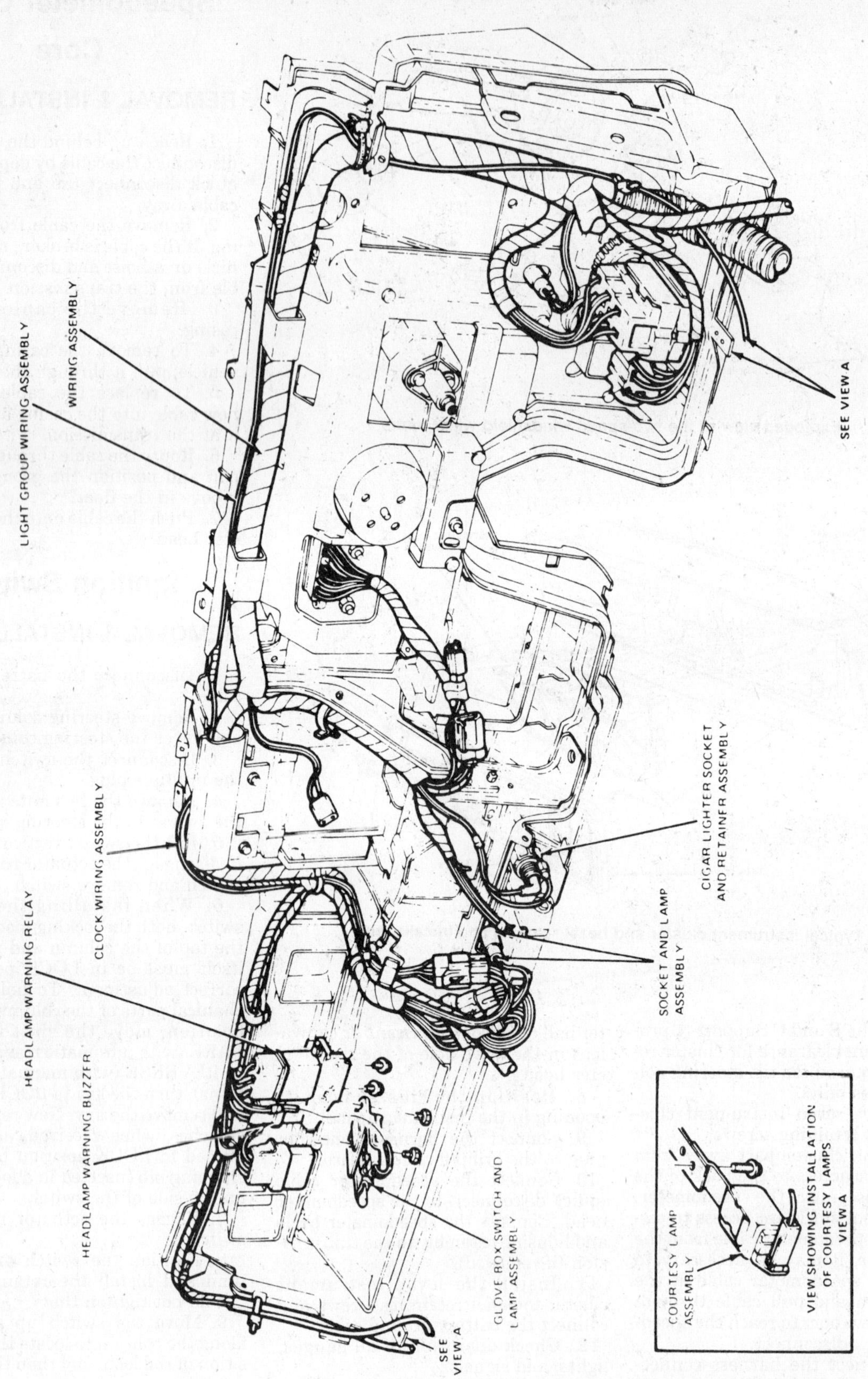

1980 and later instrument cluster view

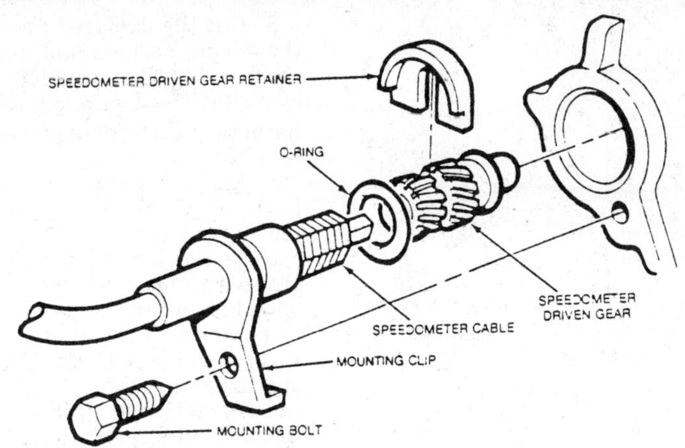

Speedometer driven gear to-transmission installation, all models similar

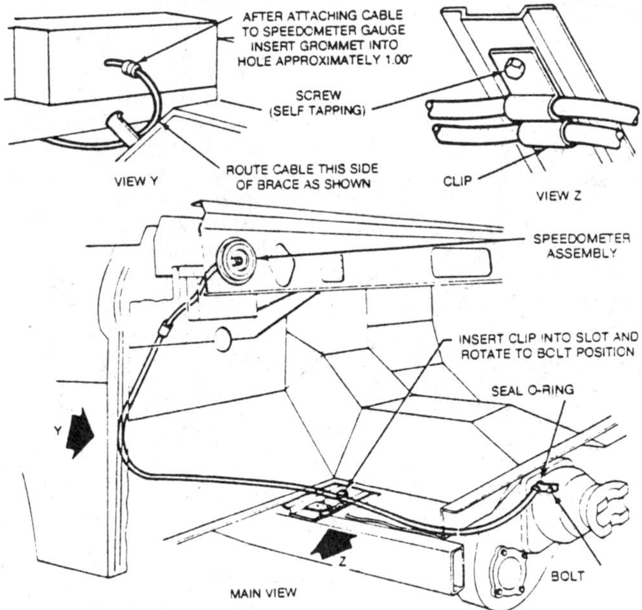

Speedometer cable installation, 4 x 4 model shown

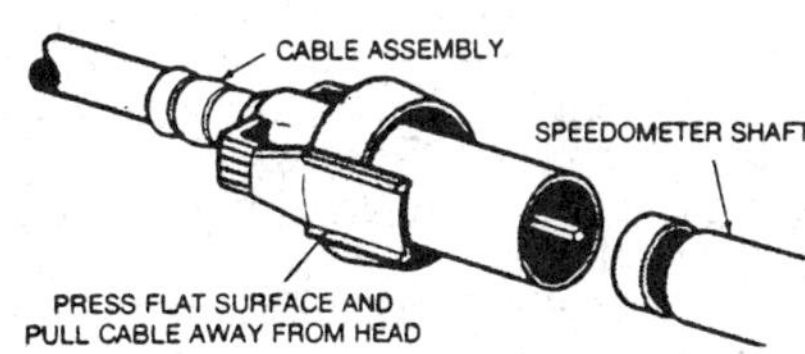

Speedometer cable quick-disconnect

check to make certain that the start circuit cannot be actuated in the DRIVE and REVERSE position.

11. Raise the steering column into position at instrument panel. Install steering column shroud.

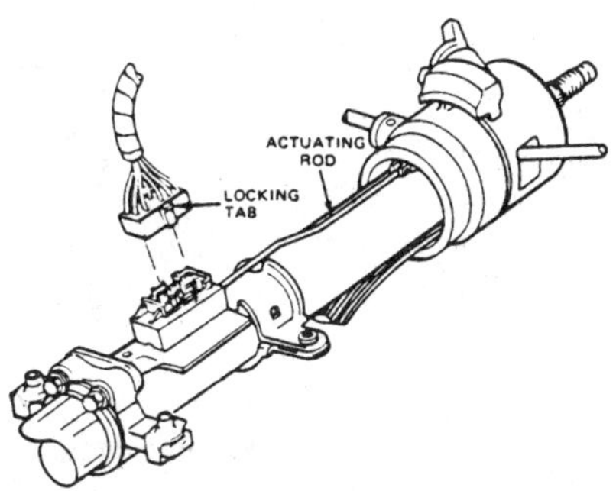

Blade-type connector ignition switch on steering column

Headlights

REMOVAL & INSTALLATION

Vans

1. Remove the screws retaining the headlight trim ring and remove the trim ring.
2. Loosen the headlight retaining ring screws, rotate the ring counterclockwise and remove it. Do not disturb the adjusting screw settings.
3. Pull the headlight bulb forward and disconnect the wiring assembly plug from the hub.
4. Connect the wiring assembly plug to the new bulb. Place the bulb in position, making sure that the locating tabs of the bulb are fitted in the positioning slots.
5. Install the headlight retaining ring, slipping the ring tabs over the screws and rotating the ring clockwise as far as possible. Tighten the screws.
6. Place the headlight trim ring into position, and install the retaining screws.
7. Check the operation of the headlight.

Pickup, Bronco

1. Remove the attaching screws and remove the headlamp door attaching screws and remove the headlamp door.
2. Remove the headlight retaining ring screws, and remove the retaining ring. Do not disturb the adjusting screw settings.
3. Pull the headlight bulb forward and disconnect the wiring assembly plug from the bulb.
4. Connect the wiring assembly plug to the new bulb. Place the bulb in position, making sure that the locating tabs of the bulb are fitted in the positioning slots.
5. Install the headlight retaining ring.
6. Place the headlight trim ring or door into position, and install the retaining screws.

Headlight Switch

REMOVAL & INSTALLATION

1. Disconnect the battery ground cable.
2. Depending on the year and model remove the wiper-washer and fog lamp switch knob if they will interfere with the headlight switch knob removal. Check the switch body (behind dash, see Step 3) for a release button. Press in on the button and remove the knob and shaft assembly. If not equipped with a release button, a hook tool may be necessary for knob removal.
3. Remove the steering column shrouds and cluster panel finish panel if they interfere with the required clearance for working behind the dash.
4. Unscrew the switch mounting nut from the front of the dash. Remove the switch from the back of the dash and disconnect the wiring harness.
5. Install in reverse order.

FUSE LINK

The fuse link is a short length of

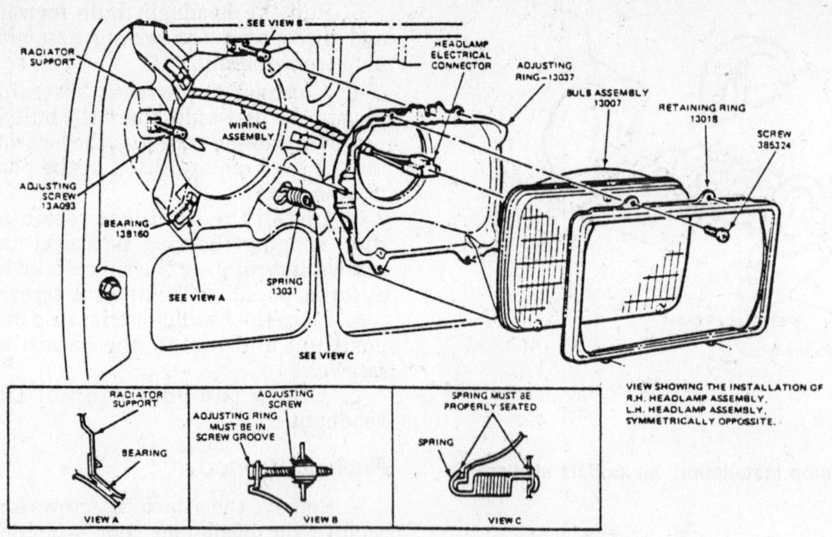

Headlight mounting; round headlights similar

Headlight aiming screws. Round headlight models similar

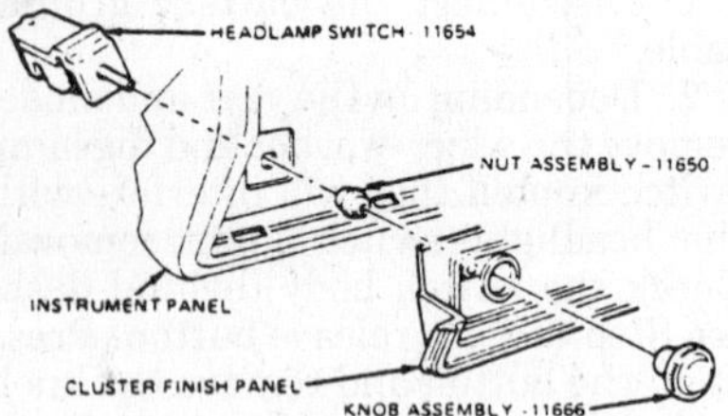

Typical headlight switch installation

special, Hypalon (high temperature) insulated wire, integral with the engine compartment wiring harness and should not be confused with standard wire. It is several wire gauges smaller than the circuit which it protects. Under no circumstances should a fuse link replacement repair be made using a length of standard wire cut from bulk stock or from another wiring harness. To repair any blown fuse link use the following procedure:

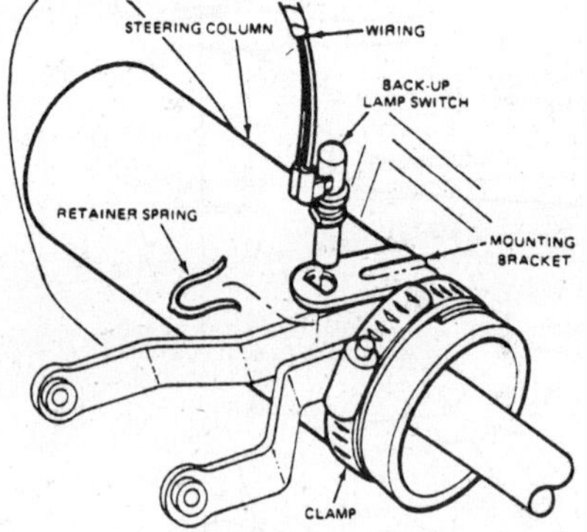

Early-type back-up light switch mounted on engine compartment side of steering wheel

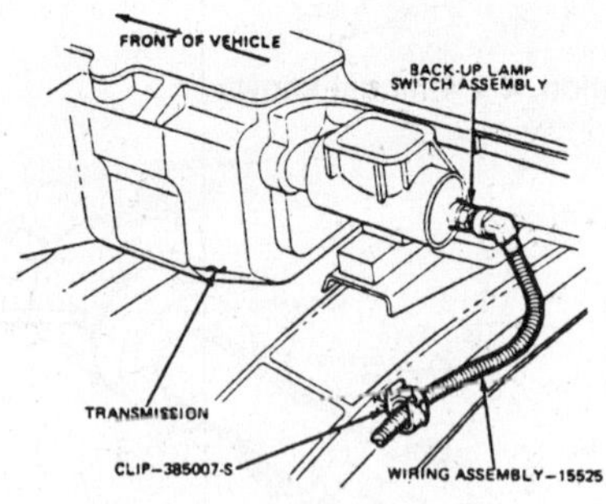

Later-type back-up light switch mounted on transmission

1. Determine which circuit is damaged, its location and the cause of the open fuse link. If the damaged fuse link is one of three fed by a common No. 10 or 12 gauge feed wire, determine the specific affected circuit.

2. Disconnect the negative battery cable.

3. Cut the damaged fuse link from the wiring harness and discard it. If the fuse link is one of three circuits fed by a single feed wire, cut it out of the harness at each splice end and discard it.

4. Identify and procure the proper fuse link and butt connectors for attaching the fuse link to the harness.

5. To repair any fuse link in a 3-link group with one feed: After cutting the open link out of the harness, cut each of the remaining undamaged fuse links close to the feed wire weld. Strip approximately ½″ of insulation from the detached ends of the two good fuse links. Then insert two wire ends into one end of a butt connector and carefully push one stripped end of the replacement fuse link into the same end of the butt connector and crimp all three firmly together.

NOTE: Care must be taken when fitting the three fuse links into the butt connector as the internal diameter is a snug fit for three wires. Make sure to use a proper crimping tool. Pliers, side cutters, etc. will not apply the proper crimp to retain the wires and withstand a pull test.

After crimping the butt connector to the three fuse links, cut the weld portion from the feed wire and strip approximately ½″ of insulation from the cut end. Insert the stripped end into the open end of the butt connector and crimp very firmly. To attach the remaining end of the replacement fuse link, strip approximately ½″ of insulation from the wire end of the circuit from which the blown fuse link was removed, and firmly crimp a butt connector or equivalent to the stripped wire. Then, insert the end of the replacement link into the other end of the butt connector and crimp firmly. Using rosin core solder with a consistency of 60 percent tin and 40 percent lead, solder the connectors and the wires at the repairs and insulate with electrical tape.

6. To replace any fuse link on a single circuit in a harness, cut out the damaged portion, strip approximately ½″ of insulation from the two wire ends and attach the appropriate replacement fuse link to the stripped wire ends with two proper size butt connectors. Solder the connectors and wires and insulate with tape.

7. To repair any fuse link which has an eyelet terminal on one end such as the charging circuit, cut off the open fuse link behind the weld, strip approximately ½″ of insulation from the cut end and attach the appropriate new eyelet fuse link to the cut stripped wire with an appropriate size butt con-

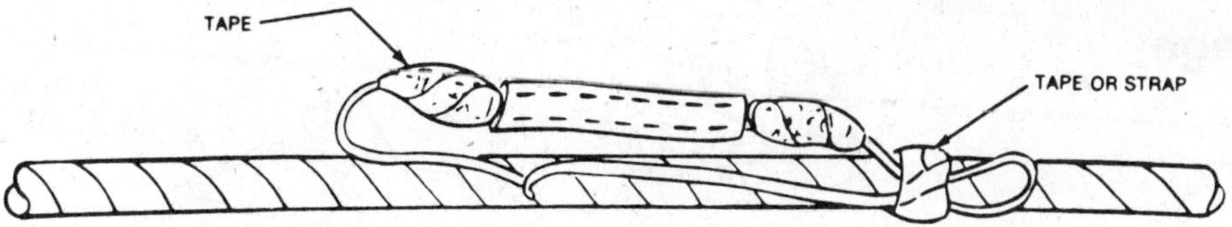

TYPICAL REPAIR USING THE SPECIAL #17 GA. (9.00" LONG-YELLOW) FUSE LINK REQUIRED FOR THE AIR/COND. CIRCUITS (2) #687E and #261A LOCATED IN THE ENGINE COMPARTMENT

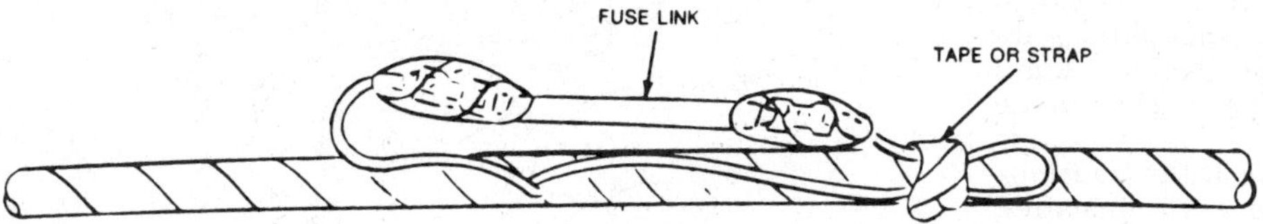

TYPICAL REPAIR FOR ANY IN-LINE FUSE LINK USING THE SPECIFIED GAUGE FUSE LINK FOR THE SPECIFIC CIRCUIT

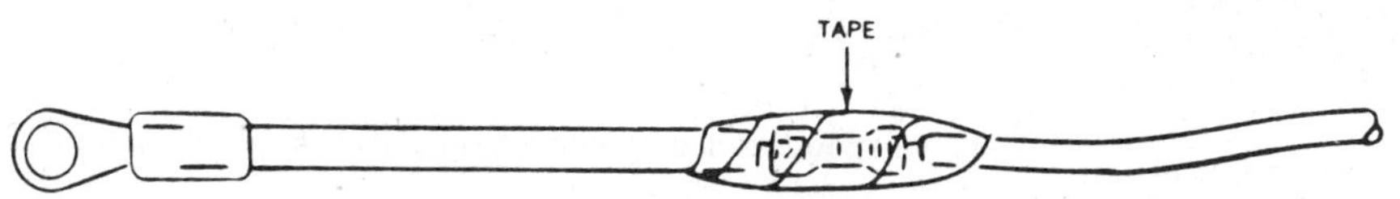

TYPICAL REPAIR USING THE EYELET TERMINAL FUSE LINK OF THE SPECIFIED GAUGE FOR ATTACHMENT TO A CIRCUIT WIRE END

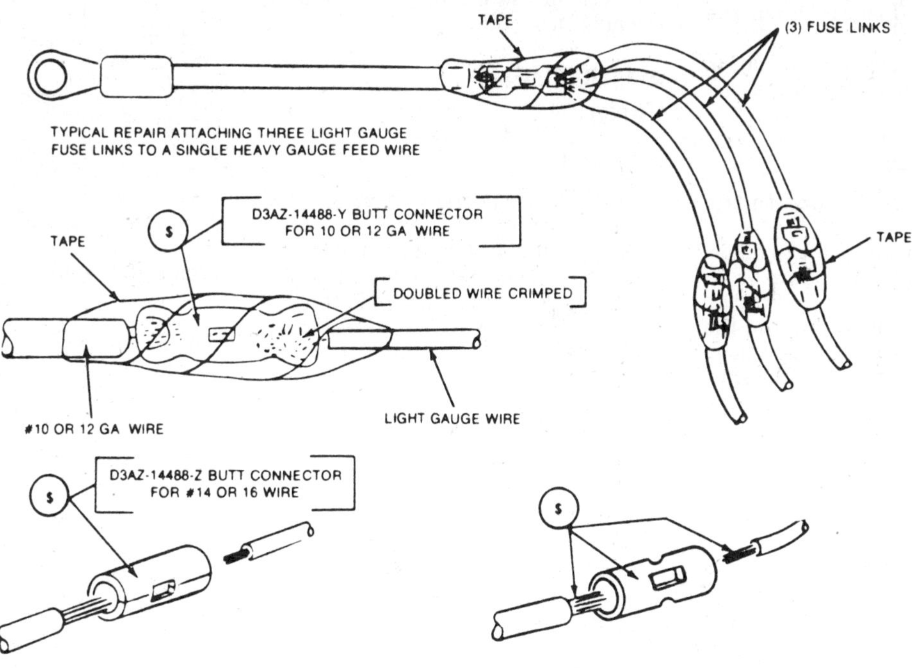

FUSIBLE LINK REPAIR PROCEDURE

General fuse link repair procedure

nector. Solder the connectors and wires at the repair and insulate with tape.

8. Connect the negative battery cable to the battery and test the system for proper operation.

NOTE: Do not mistake a resistor wire for a fuse link. The resistor wire is generally longer and has print stating, "Resistor-don't cut or splice". When attaching a single No. 16, 17, 18 or 20 gauge fuse link to a heavy gauge wire, always double the stripped wire end of the fuse link before inserting and crimping it into the butt connector for positive wire retention.

MANUAL TRANSMISSION

Linkage

ADJUSTMENT EXCEPT VANS

Ford 3.03 3-Speed Transmissions

1. Place the shifter in the Neutral position and insert a gauge pin ($^3/_{16}''$ diameter) through the steering column shift levers and the locating hole in the spacer.
2. If the shift rods at the transmission are equipped with threaded sleeves, adjust the sleeves so that they enter the shift levers on the transmission easily with the shift levers in the Neutral position. Now lengthen the rods seven turns of the sleeves and insert them into the shift levers.
3. If the shift rods are slotted, loosen the attaching nut, make sure that the transmission shift levers are in the Neutral position, then retighten the attaching nuts.
4. Remove the gauge pin and check the operation of the shift linkage.

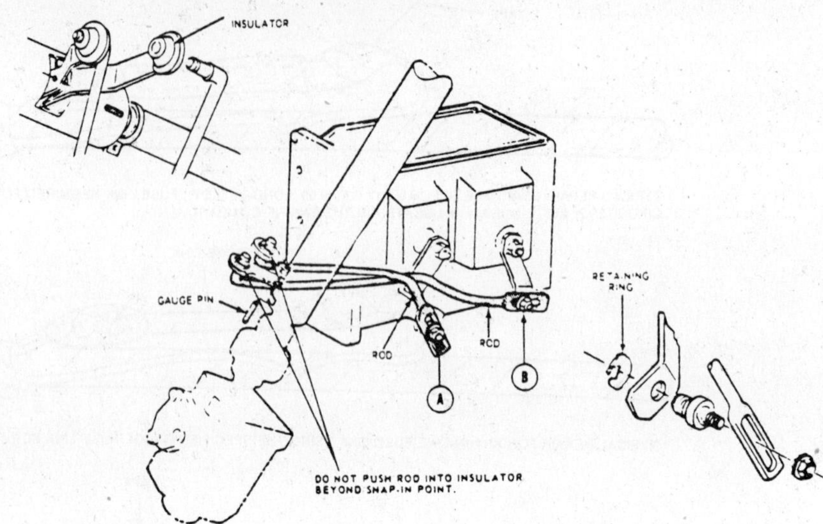

Three-speed manual transmission shift linkage adjustment—slotted rods

4-Speed Overdrive w/External Linkage

1. Attach the shift rods to the levers.
2. Rotate the output shaft to determine that the transmission is in neutral.
3. Insert an alignment pin into the shift control assembly alignment hole.
4. Attach the slotted end of the shift rods over the flats of the studs in the shift control assembly.
5. Install the locknuts and remove the alignment pin.

ADJUSTMENT VANS

3-Speed

1. Place the gearshift lever in the Neutral position.
2. Loosen the adjustment nuts on the transmission shift levers sufficiently to allow the shift rods to slide freely on the transmission shift levers.
3. Insert a $^3/_{16}''$ rod through the pilot hole in the shift tube mounting bracket until it enters the adjustment hole of both the upper and lower shift lever.

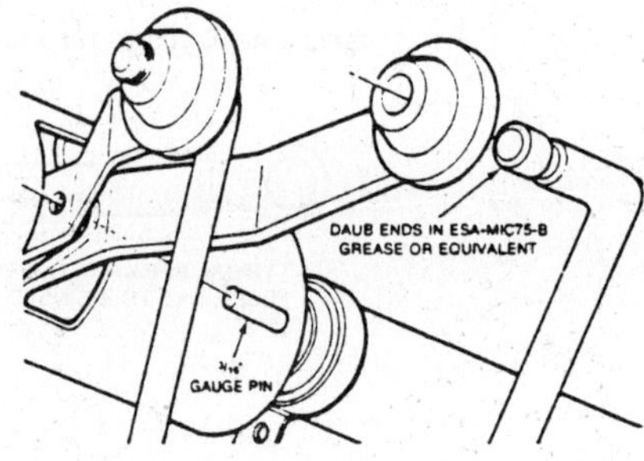

Van shift linkage adjustment—3-speed

4. Place the transmission shift levers in the Neutral position and tighten the adjustment nuts on the transmission shift levers.
5. Remove the ¼" rod from the pilot hole, and check the operation of the gearshift lever in all gear positions.

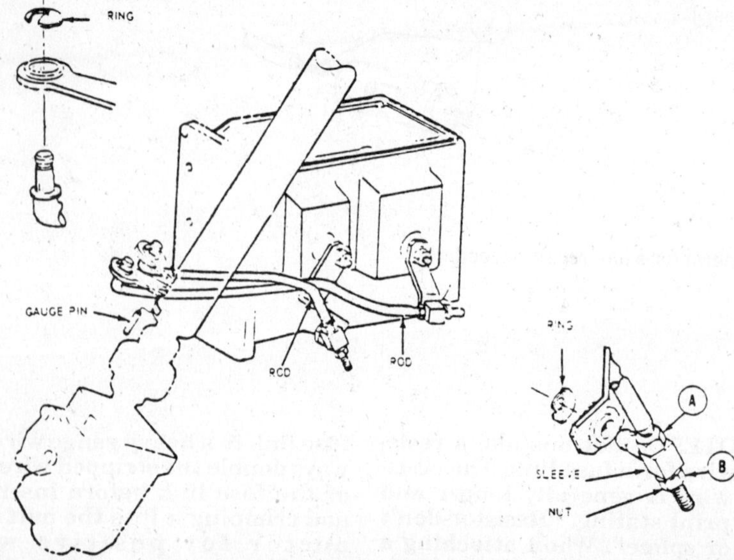

Three-speed manual transmission shift linkage adjustment—threaded sleeves

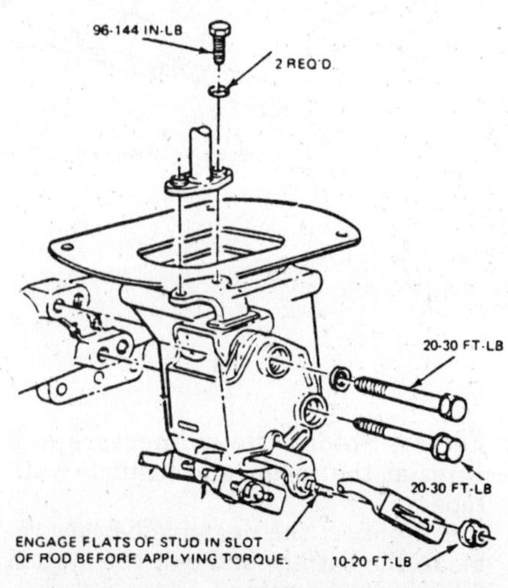

Shifter details for four-speed overdrive

4-Speed Overdrive w/External Linkage

1. Disconnect the 3 shift rods from the shifter assembly.
2. Insert a 0.25" diameter pin through the alignment hole in the shifter assembly. Make sure the levers are in the neutral position.
3. Align the 3 transmission levers as follows: forward lever (3rd-4th lever) in the mid-position (neutral), rearward lever (1st-2nd lever) in the mid-position (neutral), and middle lever (reverse lever) rotate counterclockwise to the neutral position.
4. Rotate the output shaft to assure that the transmission is in neutral.
5. Attach the slotted end of the shift rods over the slots of the studs in the shifter assembly. Install and tighten the locknuts to 15-20 ft.lb.
6. Remove the alignment pin. Check for proper operation.

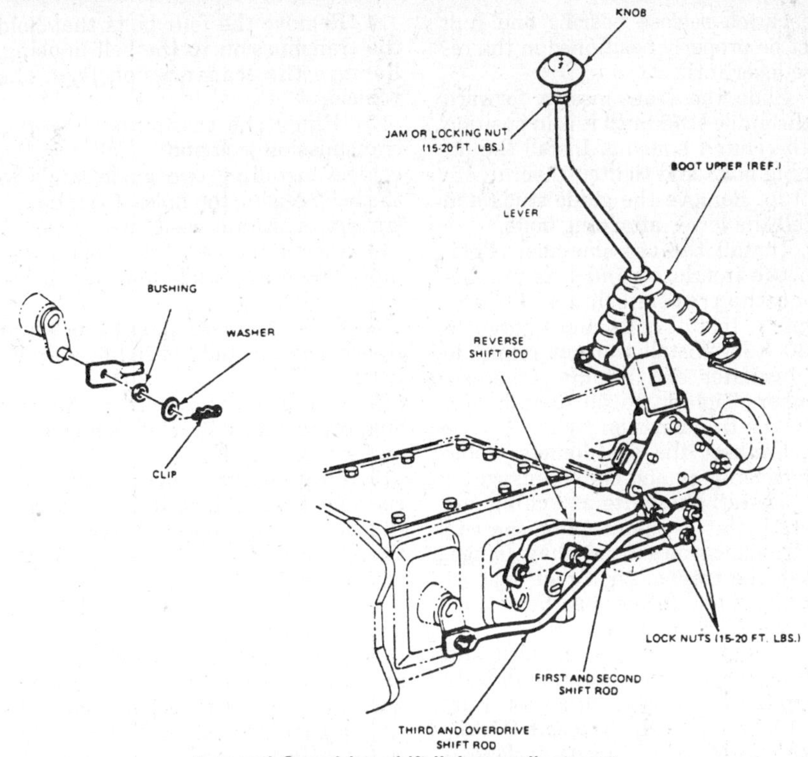

4-speed Overdrive shift linkage adjustment

Pick-Up Trucks

REMOVAL & INSTALLATION

Ford 3.03 3-Speed

1. Raise the vehicle and support it with jackstands. Support the engine with a jack and a block of wood placed under the oil pan.
2. Drain the lubricant out of the transmission by removing the drain plug if so equipped, or removing the lower extension housing-to-transmission bolt.
3. Position a transmission jack under the transmission.
4. Disconnect the gearshift linkage at the transmission.
5. If the vehicle has 4-Wheel Drive, remove the transfer case shift lever bracket from the transmission.
6. Disconnect the speedometer cable.
7. Disconnect the driveshaft from the differential and transmission and remove it from the vehicle.
8. Raise the transmission if necessary and remove the rear support.
9. Remove the transmission-to-flywheel housing attaching bolts.
10. Move the transmission to the rear until the input shaft clears the flywheel housing and lower the transmission out and from under the vehicle.

NOTE: Do not depress the clutch pedal while the transmission is removed.

11. Before installing the transmission, apply a light film of grease to the release bearing inner hub surface, the release lever fulcrum and fork, and the front bearing retainer of the transmission. Do not apply excessive grease because it will fly off due to centrifugal force and contaminate the clutch disc.
12. Install the transmission in the reverse order of removal. It may be necessary to turn the output shaft with the transmission in gear to align the input shaft splines with the splines in the clutch disc. Fill the transmission with lubricant and adjust the shift linkage.

Warner T-18 4-Speed

1. Disconnect the back-up light switch at the rear of the gearshift housing cover.
2. Remove the rubber boot, floor mat, and the body floor pan cover. Remove the gearshift lever. Remove the weatherpad.
3. Raise the vehicle and support it with jackstands. Position a transmission jack under the transmission and disconnect the speedometer cable.
4. Disconnect the driveshaft from the transmission and wire it up to one side.
5. Remove the rear transmission support.
6. Remove the transmission attaching bolts.
7. Move the transmission to the rear until the input shaft clears the flywheel housing and lower the transmission.
8. Before installing the transmission, apply a light film of grease to the inner hub surface of the clutch release bearing, the release lever fulcrum and the front bearing retainer of the transmission. Do not apply excessive grease because it will fly off onto the clutch disc.
9. Install the transmission in the reverse order of removal. It may be necessary to turn the output shaft with the transmission in gear to align the input shaft splines with the splines in the clutch disc. Fill the transmission with lubricant if it was drained.

Warner T19B 4-Speed

2-WHEEL DRIVE

1. Remove the floor mat, and the body floor pan cover, and remove the gearshift lever shift ball and boot as an assembly. Remove the weather pad.
2. Raise the vehicle and position safety stands. Position a suitable jack under the transmission, and disconnect the speedometer cable.
3. Disconnect the back-up lamp switch located at the rear of the gear shift housing cover.
4. Disconnect the driveshaft or coupling shaft and clutch linkage from the transmission and wire it to one side.
5. Remove the transmission rear insulator and lower retainer. Remove the crossmember. Remove the transmission attaching bolts.
6. Move the transmission to the rear until the in shaft clears the clutch housing. Lower transmission.
7. Place the transmission on a suitable jack install guide studs in the clutch housing and raise the transmission until the input shaft splines are aligned with the clutch disc splines.

The clutch release bearing and hub must be properly positioned in the release lever fork.

8. Slide the transmission forward on the guide stud until it is in position on the clutch housing. Install the attaching bolts and tighten them to 45-50 ft.lb. Remove the guide studs and install the lower attaching bolts.

9. Install the crossmember. Position the insulator and retainer between the transmission and crossmember. Install bolts and tighten to 45-60 ft.lb. Install the nut retaining the insulator and retainer to crossmember. Tighten to 50-70 ft.lb. Remove the transmission jack.

10. Connect the speedometer cable and driven gear and clutch linkage.

11. Install the bolts attaching the front U-joint of the coupling shaft to the transmission output shaft flange. Install the transmission rear support and upper and lower absorbers. Connect the back-up lamp switch.

12. Install the shift lever, boot and shift ball as an assembly and lubricate the spherical ball seat with Multi-Purpose Long-Life Lubricant C1AZ-1959(ESA-M1C75-B) or equivalent.

13. Install the weather pad. Install the floor pan cover and floor mat.

4-WHEEL DRIVE

1. Open door and cover seat. Remove the screws holding the floor mat.

2. Remove the screws holding the access cover to the floor pan. Place the shift lever in the reverse position and remove the cover.

3. Remove the insulator and dust cover.

4. Remove the transfer case shift lever, shift ball and boot as an assembly.

5. Remove transmission shift lever, shift ball and boot as an assembly.

6. Raise and safely support the vehicle.

7. Remove the drain plug and drain the transmission. Disconnect the rear driveshaft from the transfer case and wire it out of the way.

8. Disconnect the front driveshaft from the transfer case and wire it out of the way.

9. Remove the retainer ring that holds the shift link in place and remove the shift link from transfer case.

10. Remove the speedometer cable from the transfer case.

11. Position a suitable jack under the transfer case. Remove the six bolts holding the transfer case to the transmission and lower the transfer case from the vehicle.

12. Remove the eight bolts that hold the rear support bracket to the transmission.

13. Position a suitable jack under the transmission and remove the rear support bracket and brace.

14. Remove the four bolts that hold the transmission to the bell housing. Remove the transmission from the vehicle.

15. Place the transmission on a transmission jack and install it in the vehicle installing two guide studs in the bell housing top holes, to guide the transmission into position.

16. Install the two lower bolts. Remove the guide studs and install the upper bolts.

17. Place the rear support bracket in position and install the eight retaining bolts.

18. Install the two bolts at the rear support insulator bracket. Remove the transmission jack.

19. Position the transfer case on a suitable jack and install the six retaining bolts and gasket. Position the transfer case on the transmission and tighten the bolts.

20. Install the transfer case shift link and retaining ring. Position and install the speedometer cable. Remove wire and connect front driveshaft. Remove wire and connect rear driveshaft.

21. Fill transfer case with Dexron®II, automatic transmission fluid; the manual transmission with SAE 80W/90 lubricant. Lower vehicle.

22. Remove fabricated dirt shield and prepare gasket area.

23. Position gasket and shift cover.

24. Install two pilot bolts, then install remaining shift cover retaining bolts.

25. Install transfer case shift lever, shift ball and boot as an assembly and transmission shift lever, shift ball and boot as an assembly.

26. Install dust cover and insulator. Install access cover to floor pan screws. Install the floor mat screws. Install the boot area screws.

New Process 435 4-speed

1. Remove the rubber boot and floor mat.

2. Remove the floor pan, transmission cover plate, and weather pad. It may be necessary to remove the seat assembly.

3. Disconnect the back-up light switch located in the rear of the gearshift housing cover.

4. Raise the vehicle and place jackstands under the frame to support it. Place a transmission jack under the transmission and disconnect the speedometer cable.

5. Disconnect the parking brake lever from its linkage and remove the gearshift housing.

6. Disconnect the driveshaft.

7. Remove the transmission rear support.

8. Remove the transmission-to-flywheel housing attaching bolts, slide the transmission rearward until the input shaft clears the flywheel housing and lower it out from under the truck.

9. Before installing the transmission, apply a light film of grease to the inner hub surface of the clutch release bearing, release lever fulcrum and fork, and the front bearing retainer of the transmission. Do not apply excessive grease because it will fly off and contaminate the clutch disc.

10. Install the transmission in the reverse order of removal. It may be necessary to turn the output shaft with the transmission in gear to align the input shaft splines with the splines in the clutch disc. The front bearing retainer is installed through the clutch release bearing.

Ford 4-Speed Overdrive

1. Raise the truck and support it on jackstands.

2. Mark the driveshaft so that it can be installed in the same position.

3. Disconnect the driveshaft at the rear U-joint and slide it off the transmission output shaft.

4. Disconnect the speedometer cable from the transmission.

5. Remove the shift rods from the levers and the shift control from the extension housing.

6. Support the engine and remove the extension housing-to-crossmember bolts.

7. Support the transmission on a jack and unbolt it from the engine.

8. Move the transmission and jack rearward until clear. If necessary, lower the engine enough for clearance.

9. Installation is the reverse of removal. It is a good idea to install and snugdown the upper transmission-to-engine bolts first, then the lower. For linkage adjustment, see the beginning of this section. Check the fluid level.

Single Rail 4-Speed Overdrive (SROD)

1. Raise and safely support the vehicle. Drain the lubricant.

2. Mark the driveshaft so that it can be installed in the same position then disconnect the driveshaft from the rear U-joint flange. Slide the driveshaft off the transmission output shaft.

3. Disconnect the speedometer cable from the extension housing.

4. Remove the three screws securing the shift tower to the turret assembly.

5. Remove the shift tower from the turret assembly.

6. Support the engine with a transmission jack and remove the bolts which attach the rear extension housing to the engine.

7. Raise the rear of the engine high

enough to remove the weight from the crossmember.

8. Remove the bolts retaining the crossmember to the frame side supports and remove the crossmember.

9. Support the transmission on a jack and remove the bolts that attach the transmission to the flywheel housing.

10. Move the transmission and jack rearward until the transmission input shaft clears the flywheel housing.

NOTE: If necessary, lower the engine enough to obtain clearance for transmission removal. Do not depress the clutch pedal while the transmission is removed.

11. Before installing the transmission install two guide pins in the flywheel housing lower mounting bolt holes.

12. Move the transmission forward on the guide pins until the input shaft splines enter the clutch hub splines and the case is positioned against the flywheel housing.

13. Install the two upper transmission to flywheel housing mounting bolts snug, and then remove the two guide pins. Install the two lower mounting bolts.

14. Raise the rear of the engine and install the crossmember and attaching bolts then lower the engine.

15. With the transmission extension housing resting on the engine rear support, install the transmission extension housing attaching bolts.

16. Position the shift tower to the extension housing and secure with the three screws.

17. Reconnect the speedometer cable to the extension housing.

18. Slide the forward end of the driveshaft over the transmission output shaft. Connect the driveshaft to the rear U-joint flange.

19. Fill with transmission lubricant and lower the vehicle.

Bronco

3.03 3-SPEED

Removal & Installation

1. Shift the transfer case into Neutral.

2. Remove the bolts attaching the fan shroud to the radiator support, if so equipped.

3. Raise and safely support the vehicle.

4. Support the transfer case shield with a jack and remove the bolts that attach the shield to the frame side rails. Remove the shield.

5. Drain the transmission and transfer case lubricant. To drain the transmission lubricant, remove the lower extension housing-to-transmission bolt.

6. Disconnect the front and rear driveshafts at the transfer case.

7. Disconnect the speedometer cable at the transfer case.

8. Disconnect the T.R.S. switch, if so equipped.

9. Disconnect the shift rods from the transmission shift levers. Place the First-Reverse gear shift lever into the First gear position and insert the fabricated tool. The tool consists of a length of rod, the same diameter as the holes in the shift levers, which is bent in such a way to fit in the holes in the two shift levers and hold them in the position stated above. More important, this tool will prevent the input shaft roller bearings from dropping into the transmission and output shaft. THIS TOOL IS A MUST.

10. Support the engine with a jack.

11. Remove the two cotter pins, bolts, washers, plate and insulators that secure the crossmember to the transfer case adapter.

12. Remove the crossmember-to-frame side support attaching bolts.

13. Position a transmission jack under the transfer case and remove the upper insulators from the crossmember. Remove the crossmember.

14. Roll back the boot enclosing the transfer case shift linkage. Remove the threaded cap holding the shift lever assembly to the shift bracket. Remove the shift lever assembly.

15. Remove the two lower bolts attaching the transmission to the flywheel housing.

16. Reposition the transmission jack under the transmission and secure it with a chain.

17. Remove the two upper bolts securing the transmission to the flywheel housing. Move the transmission and transfer case rearward and downward out of the vehicle.

18. Move the assembly to a bench and remove the transfer case-to-transmission attaching bolts.

19. Slide the transmission assembly off the transfer case. To install the transmission:

20. Position the transfer case to the transmission. Apply an oil-resistant sealer to the bolt threads and install the attaching bolts. Tighten to 42-50 ft.lb.

21. Position the transmission and transfer case on a transmission jack and secure them with a chain.

22. Raise the transmission and transfer case assembly into position and install the transmission case to the flywheel housing.

23. Install the two upper and two lower transmission attaching bolts and torque them to 37-42 ft.lb.

24. Position the transfer case shift lever and install the threaded cap to the shift bracket. Reposition the rubber boot.

25. Raise the transmission and transfer case high enough to provide clearance for installing the crossmember. Position the upper insulators to the crossmember and install the crossmember-to-frame side support attaching bolts.

26. Align the bolt holes in the transfer case adapter with those in the crossmember, then lower the transmission and remove the jack.

27. Install the crossmember-to-transfer case adapter bolts, nuts, insulators, plates and washers. Tighten the nuts and secure them with cotter pins.

28. Remove the engine jack.

29. Remove the fabricated tool and connect each shift rod to its respective lever on the transmission. Adjust the linkage.

30. Connect the speedometer cable.

31. Connect the T.R.S. switch, if so equipped.

32. Install the front and rear driveshafts to the transfer case.

33. Fill the transmission and transfer case to the bottom of the filler hole with the recommended lubricant.

34. Position the transfer case shield to the frame side rails and install the attaching bolts.

35. Lower the vehicle.

36. Install the fan shroud, if so equipped.

37. Check the operation of the transfer case and the transmission shift linkage.

NP-435

1. Remove the rubber boot and floor mat.

2. Remove the weather pad. It may be necessary first to remove the seat assembly.

3. Disconnect the back-up light switch located in the rear of the gearshift housing cover.

4. Raise the vehicle and position safety stands. Position a transmission jack under the transmission, and disconnect the speedometer cable.

5. Disconnect the parking brake lever from its linkage, and remove the gearshift housing.

6. Disconnect the driveshaft or coupling shaft. Remove the bolts that attach the coupling shaft center support to the crossmember and wire the coupling shaft and driveshaft to one side. Remove the transfer case.

7. Remove the transmission attaching bolts at the clutch housing, and remove the transmission.

8. Before installing the transmission apply a light film of chassis lubri-

cant to the release lever fulcrum and fork. Do not apply a thick coat of grease to these parts, as it will work out and contaminate the clutch disc.

9. Place the transmission on a transmission jack, and raise the transmission until the input shaft splines are aligned with the clutch disc splines. The clutch release bearing and hub must be properly positioned in the release lever fork.

10. Install guide studs in the clutch housing and slide the transmission forward on the guide studs until it is in position on the clutch housing. Install the attaching bolts or nuts, and tighten them to the following torques:

- $\frac{7}{16}$-14: 40-50 ft.lb.
- $\frac{5}{8}$-11: 120-150 ft.lb.
- $\frac{9}{16}$-12: 90-115 ft.lb.
- $\frac{5}{8}$-18C: 120-150 ft.lb.
- $\frac{9}{16}$-18C: 90-115 ft.lb.

11. Remove the guide studs and install the two lower attaching bolts. Install the bolts attaching the coupling shaft center support to the crossmember. Tighten the bolts to 40-50 ft.lb.

12. Connect the driveshaft or coupling shaft and the speedometer cable. Tighten the U-joint nuts.

13. Connect the back-up light switch wire.

14. Install the transmission cover plate. Install the seat assembly if it was removed.

15. Install weather pad, pad retainer, floor mat, and rubber boot.

T-18

1. Open door cover seat.
2. Remove shift knobs.
3. Remove the four screws attaching the transmission shift lever boot assembly.
4. Remove the four screws holding the floor mat.
5. Remove the eleven screws holding the access cover to the floor pan. Place the shift lever in the reverse position and remove the cover.
6. Remove the insulator and dust cover.
7. Remove the transfer case shift lever.
8. Remove transmission shift lever.
9. Raise and safely support the vehicle.
10. Remove the drain plug and drain the transmission.
11. Disconnect the rear driveshaft from the transfer case and wire it out of the way.
12. Disconnect the front driveshaft from the transfer case and wire it out of the way.
13. Remove the retainer ring that holds the shift link in place and remove the shift link from transfer case.
14. Remove the speedometer cable from the transfer case.
15. Position a transmission jack under the transfer case. Remove the six bolts holding the transfer case to the transmission and lower the transfer case from the vehicle.
16. Remove the eight bolts that hold the rear support bracket to the transmission.
17. Position a transmission jack under the transmission and remove the rear support bracket and brace.
18. Remove the four bolts that hold the transmission to the bell housing.
19. Remove the transmission from the vehicle.
21. Place the transmission on a transmission jack and install it in the vehicle installing two guide studs in the bell housing top holes, to guide the transmission into position.
22. Install the two lower bolts. Remove the guide studs and install the upper bolts.
23. Place the rear support bracket in position and install the eight retaining bolts. Torque to 35-50 ft.lb.
24. Install the two bolts at the rear support insulator bracket. Remove the transmission jack.
25. Position the transfer case on the transmission jack and install the six retaining bolts and gasket. Position the transfer case on the transmission and tighten the bolts to 28-33 ft.lb.
26. Install the transfer case shift link and retainer ring.
27. Position and install the speedometer cable.
28. Remove wire and connect front driveshaft.
29. Remove wire and connect rear driveshaft.
30. Fill transfer case and transmission.
31. Lower the vehicle.
32. Remove fabricated dirt shield and prepare gasket area.
33. Position gasket and shift cover.
34. Install two pilot bolts, then install remaining shift cover retaining bolts.
35. Install transfer case shift handle and transmission shift lever.
36. Install dust cover and insulator.
37. Install access cover to floor pan screws.
38. Install the four floor mat screws.
39. Install the four boot area screws.
40. Install the shift knobs.

Single Rail Overdrive (SROD)

1. Raise the vehicle and support it on jackstands.
2. Mark the driveshaft so that it may be installed in the same relative position. Disconnect the driveshaft from the rear U-joint flange. Slide the driveshaft off the transmission output shaft and install an extension housing seal installation tool, or rags into the extension housing to prevent lubricant leakage.
3. Disconnect the speedometer cable from the extension housing.
4. Remove three screws securing shift lever to turret assembly.
5. Remove shift lever from turret assembly.
6. Support the engine with a transmission jack and remove the extension housing-to-engine rear support attaching bolts.
7. Raise the rear of the engine high enough to remove the weight from the crossmember. Remove the bolts retaining the crossmember to the frame side supports and remove the crossmember.
8. Support the transmission on a jack and remove the bolts that attach the transmission to the flywheel housing.
9. Move the transmission and jack rearward until the transmission input shaft clears the flywheel housing. If necessary, lower the engine enough to obtain clearance for transmission removal.

WARNING: Do not depress the clutch pedal while the transmission is removed!

10. Make sure that the mounting surface of the transmission and the flywheel housing are free of dirt, paint, and burrs. Install two guide pins in the flywheel housing lower mounting bolt holes. Move the transmission forward on the guide pins until the input shaft splines enter the clutch hub splines and the case is positioned against the flywheel housing.
11. Install the two upper transmission to flywheel housing mounting bolts snug, and then remove the two guide pins. Install the two lower mounting bolts. Torque all mounting bolts to specifications.
12. Raise the rear of the engine and install the crossmember. Install and torque the crossmember attaching bolts to specifications, then lower the engine.
13. With the transmission extension housing resting on the engine rear support, install the transmission extension housing attaching bolts. Torque the bolts to specifications.
14. Position shift tower to extension housing and secure with three screws.
15. Connect the speedometer cable to the extension housing.
16. Remove the extension housing installation tool and slide the forward end of the driveshaft over the transmission output shaft. Connect the driveshaft to the rear U-joint flange.
17. Fill the transmission to the proper level with the specified lubricant.
18. Lower the truck. Check the shift and crossover motion for full shift en-

gagement and smooth crossover operation.

Vans

REMOVAL & INSTALLATION

3.03 3-Speed

1. Raise the vehicle and support on jackstands. Drain the lubricant from the transmission by removing the lower extension housing-to-transmission bolt.
2. Disconnect the driveshaft from the flange at the transmission. Secure the front end of the driveshaft out of the way by tying it up with a length of wire.
3. Disconnect the speedometer cable from the extension housing and disconnect the gearshift rods from the transmission. Disconnect the transmission regulated spark switch, if so equipped.
4. Position a transmission jack under the transmission. Chain the transmission to the jack.
5. Raise the transmission slightly and remove the 4 bolts which retain the transmission support crossmember to the frame side rails. Remove the bolt which retains the transmission extension housing to the crossmember.
6. Remove the 4 transmission-to-flywheel housing bolts.
7. Position a bar under the rear of the engine to support it.
8. Remove the transmission from the vehicle by lowering the jack. To install the transmission:
9. Make sure that the machined surfaces of the transmission case and the flywheel housing are free of dirt, paint, and burrs.
10. Install a guide pin in each lower mounting bolt hole.
11. Start the input shaft through the release bearing. Align the splines on the input shaft with the splines in the clutch disc. Move the transmission forward on the guide pins until the input shaft pilot enters the bearing or bushing in the crankshaft. If the transmission front bearing retainer binds up on the clutch release bearing hub, work the release bearing lever until the hub slides onto the transmission front bearing retainer. Install the two upper mounting bolts and lockwashers which attach the flywheel housing to the transmission. Remove the two guide pins and install the lower mounting bolts and lockwashers.
12. Raise the jack slightly and remove the engine support bar. Position the support crossmember on the frame side rails and install the retaining bolts. Install the extension housing-to-crossmember retaining bolt.
13. Connect the gearshift rods and the speedometer cable. Connect the transmission regulated spark switch lead, if so equipped.
14. Install the driveshaft.
15. Fill the transmission to the bottom of the filler hole with the proper lubricant.
16. Adjust the clutch pedal free-play and the shift linkage as required.

4-speed Overdrive

1. Raise the vehicle and support on jackstands.
2. Mark the driveshaft so that it may be installed in the same relative position. Disconnect the driveshaft from the rear U-joint flange. Slide the driveshaft off the transmission output shaft and install the extension housing seal installation tool into the extension housing to prevent lubricant leakage.
3. Disconnect the speedometer cable from the extension housing.
4. Remove the retaining clips, flat washers, and spring washers that secure the shift rods to the shift levers. Remove the bolts connecting the shift control to the transmission extension housing. Remove the nut connecting the shift control to the transmission case.

NOTE: A 6 and **8** is stamped on transmission extension housing by the shift control plate bolt holes. The **6** and **8** refer to either a 6- or 8-cylinder engine application. The shift control plate bolts must be placed in the right holes for proper plate positioning dependent upon engine application.

5. Remove the rear transmission support connecting bolts attaching the support on the crossmember to the transmission extension housing.
6. Support the engine with a transmission jack and remove the extension housing-to-engine rear support attaching bolts.
7. Raise the rear of the engine high enough to remove the weight from the crossmember. Remove the bolts retaining the crossmember to the frame side supports and remove the crossmember.
8. Support the transmission on a jack and remove the bolts that attach the transmission to the flywheel housing.
9. Move the transmission and jack rearward until the transmission input shaft clears the flywheel housing. If necessary, lower the engine enough to obtain clearance for transmission removal. Do not depress the clutch pedal while the transmission is removed.
10. Make sure that the mounting surfaces of the transmission and the flywheel housing are free of dirt, paint, and burrs. Install two guide pins in the flywheel housing lower mounting bolt holes. Move the transmission forward on the guide pins until the input shaft splines enter the clutch hub splines and the case is positioned against the flywheel housing.
11. Install the two upper transmission to flywheel housing mounting bolts snug, and then remove the two guide pins. Install the two lower mounting bolts. Tighten all mounting bolts to 40-45 ft.lb.
12. Raise the rear of the engine and install the crossmember. Install and torque the crossmember attaching bolts to 20-30 ft.lb. then lower the engine.
13. With the transmission extension housing resting on the engine rear support, install the transmission extension housing attaching bolts. Tighten the bolts to 42-50 ft.lb.
14. Install the transmission support bolts and tighten to 40-50 ft.lb.
15. Position the shift control bracket on the stud on the transmission case and on the bolt attaching holes (holes marked either '6' or '8' dependent upon 6 or 8 cylinder engine application) on the transmission extension housing. Install and hand tighten connecting bolts. The bracket must be placed in the proper position for correct shift control operation. Tighten the nut connecting the bracket to the transmission case to 22-30 ft.lb. Tighten the bolts to 22-30 ft.lb.
16. Secure each shift rod to its respective lever with the spring washer, flat washer, and retaining pin.
17. Connect the speedometer cable to the extension housing.
18. Remove the extension housing installation tool and slide the forward end of the driveshaft over the transmission output shaft. Connect the driveshaft to the rear U-joint flange. Adjust the linkage.
19. Fill the transmission to the proper level with the specified lubricant.
20. Lower the vehicle. Check the shift and crossover motion for full shift engagement and smooth crossover operation.

CLUTCH

Pick-Up

FREEPLAY ADJUSTMENT MANUAL LINKAGE

1. Measure the clutch pedal free-play by depressing the pedal slowly until the free-play between the release bearing assembly and the pressure

plate is removed. Note this measurement. The difference between this measurement and when the pedal is not depressed is the free-play measurement.

2. If the free-play measurement is less than ½-¾", the clutch linkage must be adjusted.

3. Loosen the two jam nuts on the release rod under the truck and back off both nuts several turns.

4. Loosen or tighten the first jam nut (nearest the release lever) against the bullet (rod extension) until a free-play measurement of ¾-1½" is obtained. A free-play measurement closer to 1½". is more desirable.

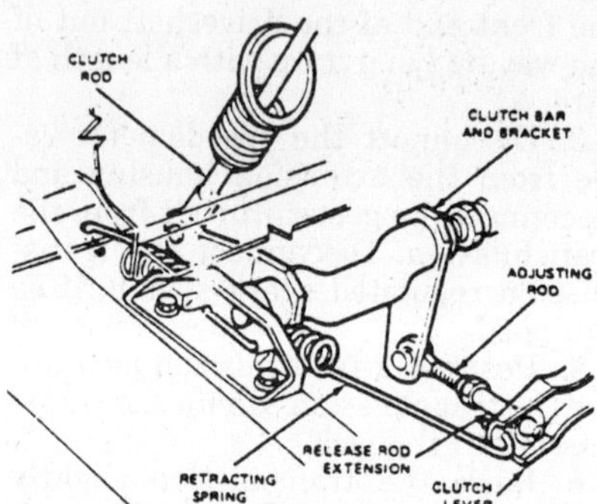

Clutch pedal free play adjustment, 1980 and later

5. When the correct free-play measurement is obtained, hold the first jam nut in position and securely tighten the other nut against the first.

6. Recheck the free-play adjustment. Total pedal travel is fixed and is not adjustable.

HYDRAULIC CLUTCH

The Hydraulic clutch system consists of a combination clutch and master cylinder assembly, a slave cylinder and connecting tubing. The slave cylinder is mounted on the bell housing. The hydraulic clutch system provides automatic clutch adjustment. No adjustment of the clutch linkage or pedal position is required.

REMOVAL & INSTALLATION

1. Disconnect the release lever retracting spring and pushrod assembly. If equipped with an hydraulic clutch, remove the slave cylinder with line connected.

2. Remove the transmission.

3. If the clutch housing does not have a dust cover, remove the starter. Remove the flywheel housing attaching bolts and remove the housing.

4. If the flywheel housing does have a dust cover, remove the cover and then remove the release lever and bearing from the clutch housing.

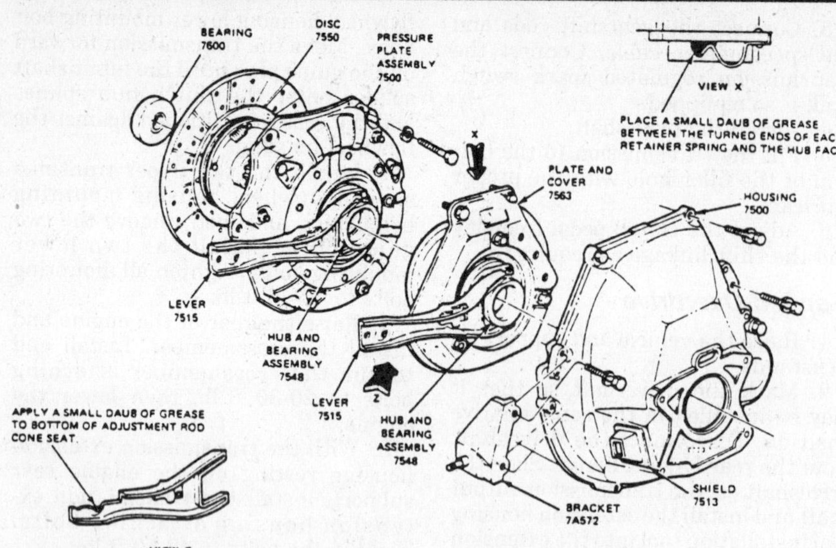

351 and 400 V8 clutch installation

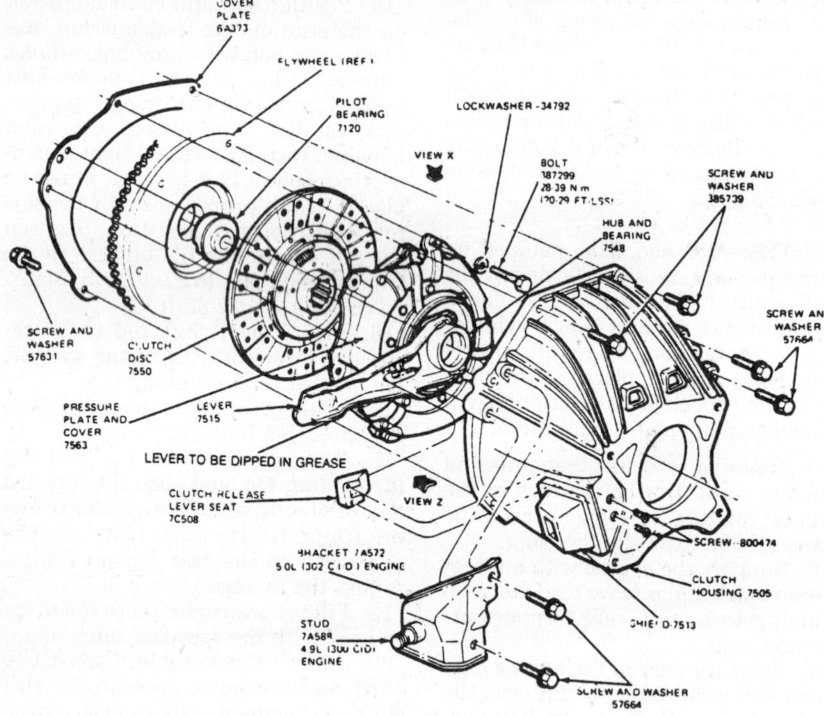

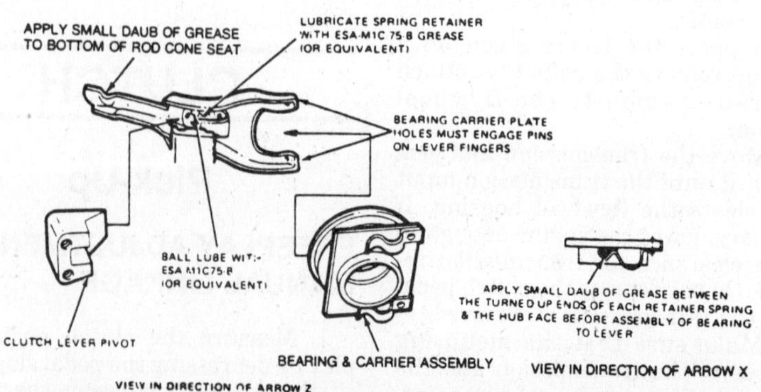

Clutch installation, 1980 and later 300 six and 302/351W V8s

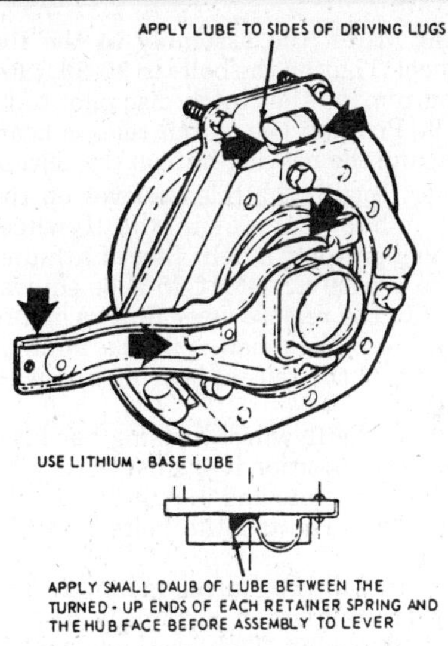

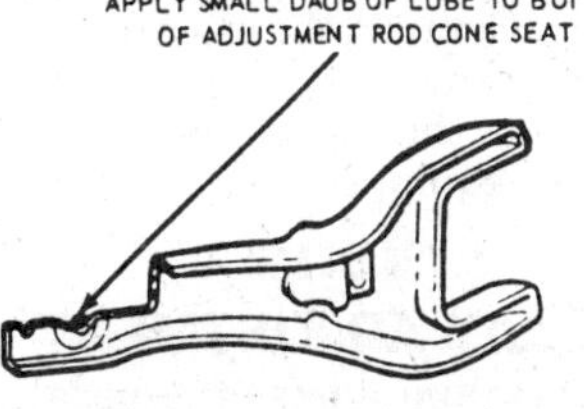

Clutch lubrication points

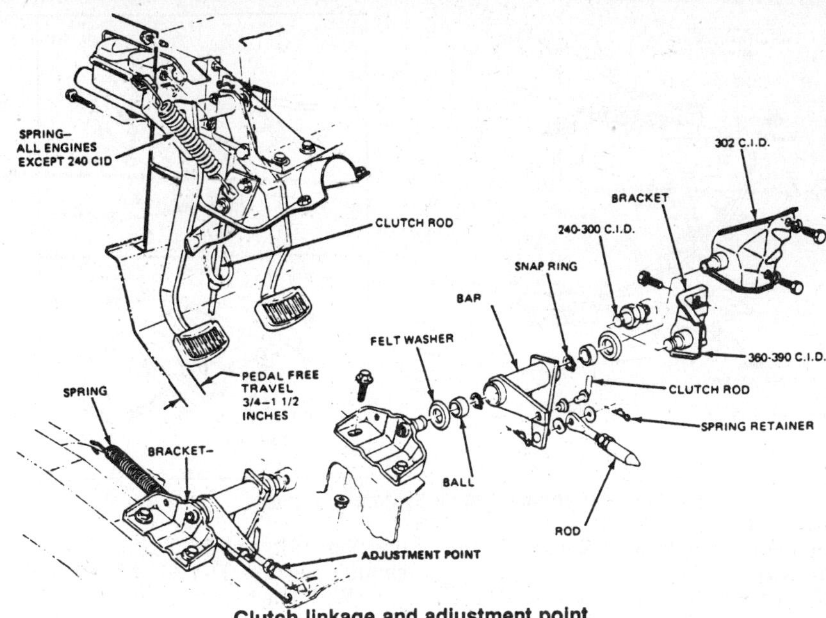

Clutch linkage and adjustment point

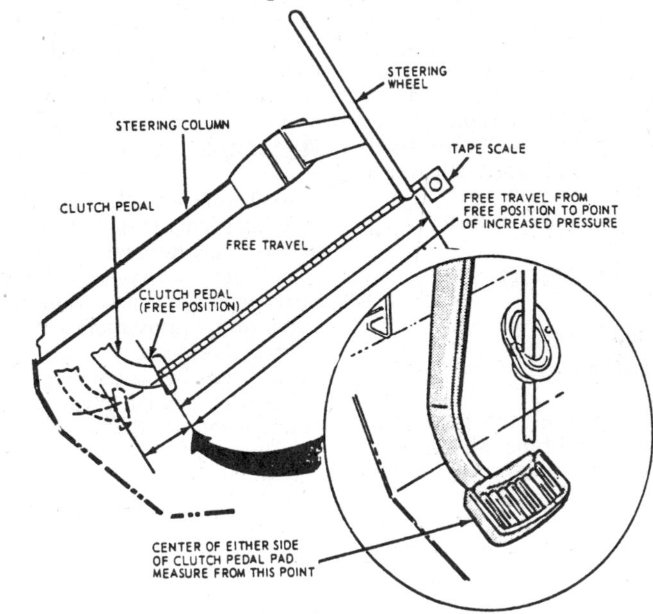

Measuring clutch pedal free-play

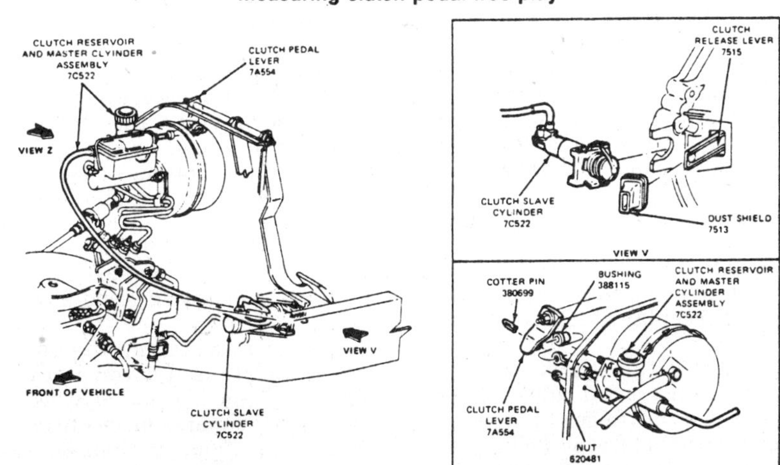

Hydraulic clutch assembly, all 1983 and later V8 diesels and 1984 and later gasoline-engined models

5. Mark the pressure plate and cover assembly and the flywheel so that they can be reinstalled in the same relative position.

6. Loosen the pressure plate and cover attaching bolts evenly in a staggered sequence a turn at a time until the pressure plate springs are relieved of their tension. Remove the attaching bolts.

7. Remove the pressure plate and cover assembly and the clutch disc from the flywheel.

8. Position the clutch disc on the flywheel so that an aligning tool or spare transmission mainshaft can enter the clutch pilot bearing and align the disc.

9. When reinstalling the original pressure plate and cover assembly, align the assembly and flywheel according to the marks made during removal. Position the pressure plate and cover assembly on the flywheel, align the pressure plate and disc, and install the retaining bolts. Tighten the bolts in an alternating sequence a few turns at a time until 15-20 ft.lb. is reached.

10. Remove the tool used to align the clutch disc.

11. With the clutch fully released, apply a light coat of grease on the sides of the driving lugs.

12. Position the clutch release bearing and the bearing hub on the release lever. Install the release lever on the fulcrum in the flywheel housing. Apply a light coating of grease to the release lever fingers and the fulcrum.

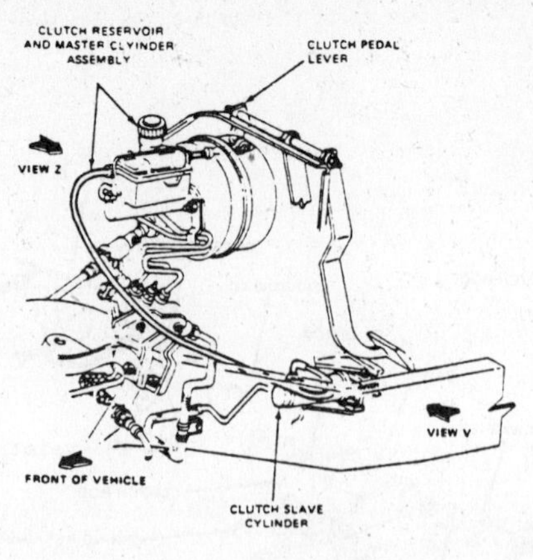

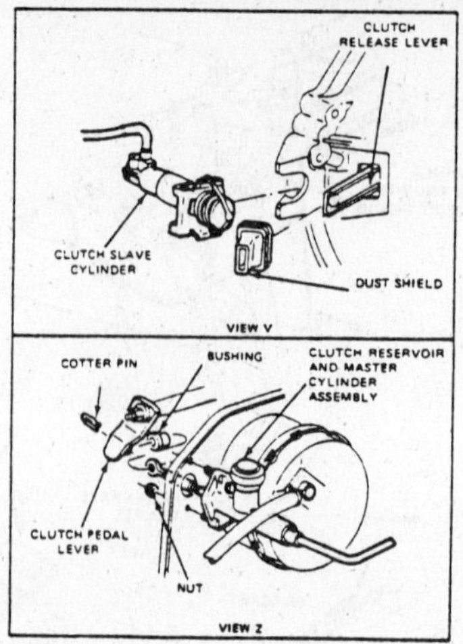

Hydraulic Clutch System—Typical

Fill the groove of the release bearing hub with grease.

13. If the flywheel housing has been removed, position it against the rear engine cover plate and install the attaching bolts and tighten them to 40-50 ft.lb.
14. Install the starter motor.
15. Install the transmission.
16. Connect the release lever retracting spring and install the dust cover, if so equipped.
17. Adjust the clutch linkage.

Bronco

PEDAL HEIGHT ADJUSTMENT

1. Measure the clutch pedal free travel using a steel tape. Measure the distance from the clutch pedal pad to the steering wheel rim. Depress the pedal slowly until the free travel between the release bearing assembly and the pressure plate assembly is taken up. Note this measurement. The difference between the two measurements is the free travel.
2. If the free travel measurement is less than ½" or more than 2", the clutch linkage must be adjusted.
3. Remove the retracting spring.
4. Loosen the two jam nuts on the release rod assembly and back off both nuts several turns.
5. Slide the release rod extension (bullet) firmly against the release lever. Push the release rod forward against the equalizer bar lever to eliminate all freeplay from the linkage system.
6. Insert 0.135" thick gauge between the jam nut and bullet. Tighten the first jam nut finger tight against the gauge with all freeplay eliminated.
7. Tighten the second jam nut finger tight against the first jam nut. Hold the first nut and tighten the second jam nut to 15-20 ft.lb. Freeplay should measure ¾-1½" at the pedal.
8. With the recommended free travel obtained, and holding the first jam nut, position and securely tighten the second jam nut against the first jam nut.
9. Re-check the pedal free travel.

REMOVAL & INSTALLATION

1. Disconnect the release lever retracting spring and push rod assembly at the lever. Remove starter.
2. Refer to the appropriate transmission part of this section for instructions and remove the transmission from the vehicle.
3. If the clutch housing is not provided with a dust cover, remove the starting motor. Remove the flywheel housing attaching bolts and remove the housing.
4. If the flywheel housing is provided with a dust cover, remove it from the housing. Remove the release lever and release bearing from the clutch housing.
5. Loosen the pressure plate and cover attaching bolts evenly until the pressure plate springs are expanded, and remove the bolts.
6. Remove the pressure plate and cover assembly and the clutch disc from the flywheel or through the opening in the bottom of the clutch housing. Remove the pilot bearing only for replacement.
7. Position the clutch disc on the flywheel so that the pilot tool can enter the clutch pilot bearing and align the disc.
8. When re-installing the original pressure plate and cover assembly, align the assembly and flywheel according to the marks made during the removal operations. Position the pressure plate and cover assembly on the flywheel, align the pressure plate and disc, and install the retaining bolts that fasten the assembly to the flywheel. Tighten the bolts to 20-30 ft.lb., and remove the clutch disc pilot tool.
9. Position the clutch release bearing and the bearing hub on the release lever. Install the release lever on the pivot bar pedestal in the flywheel housing. Apply a light film of lithium-base grease ESA-M1C75-B or equivalent to the release lever fingers and to the lever pivot ball. Fill the annular groove of the release bearing hub with grease.
10. If the flywheel housing has been removed, position it against the engine rear cover plate and install the attaching bolts. Tighten the bolts to 40-50 ft.lb.
11. Install the starter motor. Install the transmission assembly on the clutch housing. Tighten the bolts.
12. Adjust the release lever push rod assembly. Connect the release lever retracting spring.
13. Install the clutch housing dust cover if so equipped.

Vans

FREEPLAY ADJUSTMENT

To check and adjust the pedal free travel measure and note the distance from the floor pan to the top of the pedal: then depress the pedal slowly until the clutch release fingers contact the clutch release bearing. Measure and record the distance. The difference between the reading with the pedal in the depressed position and the reading with the pedal in the fully released position is the pedal free travel. The free travel should be as specified.

The pedal height is not adjustable. Pedal height is adjusted by loosening the nut securing the clutch pedal eccentric bumper and rotating the bumper until the clutch pedal height is within 1¼-1½".

REMOVAL & INSTALLATION

1. Disconnect the cable from the starter and remove the starter.
2. Remove the transmission.
3. Disconnect the release lever retracting spring and release the rod.
4. Remove the hub and release bearing assembly.
5. Remove the flywheel housing-to-engine bolts, and lower the flywheel housing.
6. Remove the pressure plate and the disc from the flywheel. Unscrew the attaching bolts a few turns at a time, in a staggered sequence to prevent distortion of the pressure plate.
7. Wash the flywheel surface with alcohol. Do not use an oil-base cleaner, carbon tetrachloride or gasoline.

To install the clutch:

8. Place the clutch disc and the pressure plate and cover assembly in

position on the flywheel. Start the retaining bolts until finger-tight.

9. Align the clutch disc with a clutch arbor (an old mainshaft works well) and then evenly torque the bolts to 23-28 ft.lb.

10. Do not grease the release lever pivot assembly. Crimp the dust seal tabs flush against the flywheel housing. Attach the springs of the release bearing hub to the ends of the release fork. Be careful not to distort the springs.

11. Fill the groove in the clutch release bearing hub with lithium-base grease. Wipe the excess grease from the hub.

12. Position the flywheel housing and release lever assembly, and install the mounting bolts. Make sure that the muffler front hanger is in place on the flywheel housing. Install the dust cover, and tighten the attaching bolts.

13. Remove any dirt, paint, or burrs from the mounting surfaces of the flywheel housing and the transmission.

14. Install the transmission.

15. Install the starter and connect the starter cable.

16. Adjust the clutch pedal free-play and check the operation of the clutch.

CLUTCH PEDAL ADJUSTMENT

To check and adjust the pedal free travel, measure and note the distance from the floor pan to the top of the pedal; then depress the pedal slowly until the clutch release fingers contact the clutch release bearing. Measure and record the distance. The difference between the reading with the pedal in the depressed position and the reading with the pedal in the fully released position is the pedal free travel. The free travel should be as specified.

The pedal height is not adjustable. Pedal height is adjusted by loosening the nut securing the clutch pedal eccentric bumper and rotating the bumper until the clutch pedal height is within 1¼-1½".

AUTOMATIC TRANSMISSION

Transmission

REMOVAL & INSTALLATION

C4, C5

F-100, 250

1. Raise the vehicle and support on jackstands.

2. Place the drain pan under the transmission fluid pan. Remove the fluid filler tube from the pan and drain the transmission fluid.

3. Remove the converter drain plug access cover from the lower end of the converter housing.

4. Remove the converter-to-flywheel attaching nuts. Place a wrench on the crankshaft pulley attaching bolt to turn the converter to gain access to the nuts.

5. With the wrench on the crankshaft pulley attaching bolt, turn the converter to gain access to the converter drain plug and remove the plug. Place a drain pan under the converter to catch the fluid. With fluid drained, reinstall the plug.

6. Remove the driveshaft.

7. Disconnect the oil cooler lines from the transmission.

8. Disconnect the manual and downshift linkage rods from the transmission control levers.

9. Remove the speedometer gear from the extension housing.

10. Disconnect the back-up switch wires from the retaining clips and retainer.

11. Disconnect the starter cable. Remove the three starter-to-converter housing attaching bolts and remove the starter.

12. Remove the vacuum line hose from the transmission vacuum unit. Disconnect the vacuum line from the retaining clip.

13. Position the transmission jack to support the transmission. Install the safety chain to hold the transmission on the jack.

14. Remove the two engine rear support crossmember-to-frame attaching bolts.

15. Remove the two engine rear support-to-extension housing attaching bolts.

16. Raise the transmission and remove the rear support. Remove the six converter housing-to-engine attaching bolts.

17. Move the converter and transmission assembly away from the engine. Lower the transmission and remove it from under the vehicle.

18. Tighten the converter drain plug to 15-28 ft.lb.

19. Position the converter on the transmission making sure the converter drive flats are fully engaged in the pump gear.

20. With the converter properly installed, place the transmission on the jack. Secure the transmission to the jack with the safety chain.

21. Rotate the converter until the studs and drain plug are in alignment with their holes in the flywheel.

22. Move the converter and transmission assembly forward into position, using care not to damage the flywheel and the converter pilot. The converter must rest squarely against the flywheel. This indicates that the converter pilot is not binding in the engine crankshaft.

23. Install the six converter housing-to-engine attaching bolts. Tighten the bolts to 40-50 ft.lb.

24. Install the converter-to-flywheel attaching nuts. Tighten the nuts to 20-34 ft.lb. Remove the safety chain from the transmission.

25. Install the rear support. Install the rear support-to-extension housing attaching bolts. Tighten the bolts.

26. Position the starter into the converter housing and install the three attaching bolts. Tighten the bolts to 20-30 ft.lb. Install the starter cable.

26. Remove the transmission jack.

27. Connect the transmission filler tube to the transmission pan. Connect the oil cooler lines to the transmission.

28. Attach the back-up switch wires to the connector clip.

29. Install the speedometer driven gear in the extension housing. Tighten the attaching bolt.

30. Connect the transmission linkage rods to the transmission control levers. When making transmission control attachments, new retaining rings and grommets should always be used. Attach the shift rod to the steering column shift lever. Align the flats of the adjusting stud with the flats of the rod slot and insert the stud through the rod. Assemble the adjusting stud nut and washer to a loose fit. Perform a linkage adjustment.

32. Install the driveshaft.

33. Install the vacuum line in the retaining clip. Connect the vacuum line to the diaphragm unit.

34. At the front lower area of the converter housing, install the lower cover and the control lever dust shield. Install the attaching bolts. Tighten the bolts.

35. Secure the fluid filler tube to the pan. Tighten the fitting to 32-42 ft.lb.

36. Lower the vehicle.

37. Fill the transmission to the proper level.

38. Raise the vehicle and check for transmission fluid leakage. Lower the vehicle and adjust the throttle and manual linkage.

C6 and FMX

BRONCO, F-150, 250, 350

1. Remove the two upper converter housing-to-engine bolts.

2. Remove the bolt securing the fluid filler tube to the engine cylinder head.

3. Raise the vehicle and support on jackstands.

4. Place the drain pan under the

transmission fluid pan. Starting at the rear of the pan and working toward the front, loosen the attaching bolts and allow the fluid to drain.

5. Remove all of the pan attaching bolts except two at the front, to allow the fluid to further drain. With fluid drained, install two bolts on the rear side of the pan to temporarily hold it in place.

6. Remove the converter drain plug access cover from the lower end of the converter housing.

7. Remove the converter-to-flywheel attaching nuts. Place a wrench on the crankshaft pulley attaching bolt to turn the converter to gain access to the nuts.

8. With the wrench on the crankshaft pulley attaching bolt, turn the converter to gain access to the converter drain plug. Place a drain pan under the converter to catch the fluid and remove the plug. After the fluid has been drained, re-install the plug.

9. Disconnect the driveshaft from the rear axle and slide shaft rearward from the transmission. Install a seal installation tool in the extension housing to prevent fluid leakage.

10. Disconnect the speedometer cable from the extension housing.

11. Disconnect the downshift and manual linkage rods from the levers at the transmission.

12. Disconnect the oil cooler lines from the transmission.

13. Remove the vacuum hose from the vacuum diaphragm unit. Remove the vacuum line retaining clip.

14. Disconnect the cable from the terminal on the starter motor. Remove the three attaching bolts and remove the starter motor.

15. On F-150, 250, 350 4-Wheel Drive and Bronco vehicles, remove the transfer case.

16. Remove the two engine rear support and insulator assembly-to-attaching bolts.

17. Remove the two engine rear support and insulator assembly-to-extension housing attaching bolts.

18. Remove the six bolts securing the No.2 crossmember to the frame side rails.

19. Raise the transmission with a transmission jack and remove both crossmembers.

20. Secure the transmission to the jack with the safety chain.

21. Remove the remaining converter housing-to-engine attaching bolts.

22. Move the transmission away from the engine. Lower the jack and remove the converter and transmission assembly from under the vehicle.

23. Tighten the converter drain plug.

24. Position the converter on the transmission making sure the converter drive flats are fully engaged in the pump gear.

25. With the converter properly installed, place the transmission on the jack. Secure the transmission to the jack with the chain.

26. Rotate the converter until the studs and drain plug are in alignment with their holes in the flywheel.

27. Move the converter and transmission assembly forward into position, using care not to damage the flywheel and the converter pilot. The converter must rest squarely against the flywheel. This indicates that the converter pilot is not binding in the engine crankshaft.

28. Install and tighten the converter housing-to-engine attaching bolts.

29. Remove the transmission jack safety chain from around the transmission.

30. Position the No.2 crossmember to the frame side rails. Install and tighten the attaching bolts.

31. Install transfer case on F-150, 250, 350 4-Wheel Drive and Bronco.

32. Positon the engine rear support and insulator assembly above the crossmember. Install the rear suport and insulator assembly-to-extension housing mounting bolts and tighten the bolts.

33. Lower the transmission and remove the jack.

34. Secure the engine rear support and insulator assembly to the crossmember with the attaching bolts and tighten them.

35. Connect the vacuum line to the vacuum diaphragm making sure that the line is in the retaining clip.

36. Connect the oil cooler lines to the transmission.

37. Connect the downshift and manual linkage rods to their respective levers on the transmission.

38. Connect the speedometer cable to the extension housing.

39. Secure the starter motor in place with the attaching bolts. Connect the cable to the terminal on the starter.

40. Install a new O-ring on the lower end of the transmission filler tube and insert the tube in the case.

41. Secure the converter-to-flywheel attaching nuts and tighten them.

42. Install the converter housing access cover and secure it with the attaching bolts.

43. Connect the driveshaft.

44. Adjust the shift linkage as required.

45. Lower the vehicle. Then install the two upper converter housing-to-engine bolts and tighten them.

46. Position the transmission fluid filler tube to the cylinder head and secure with the attaching bolt.

47. Make sure the drain pan is securely attached, and fill the transmission to the correct level with the specified fluid.

E-100, 150, 250, 350

1. Working from inside the vehicle, remove the engine compartment cover.

2. Disconnect the neutral start switch wires at the plug connector.

3. If the vehicle is equipped with a V-8 engine, remove the flexhose from the air cleaner heat tube.

4. Remove the upper converter housing-to-engine attaching bolts (three bolts on 6-cylinder engines; four bolts on V8 engines).

5. Raise the vehicle and support on jackstands.

6. Place the drain pan under the transmission fluid pan. Starting at the rear of the pan and working toward the front, loosen the attaching bolts and allow the fluid to drain. Finally remove all of the pan attaching bolts except two at the front, to allow the fluid to further drain. With fluid drained, install two bolts on the rear side of the pan to temporarily hold it in place.

7. Remove the converter drain plug access cover from the lower end of the converter housing.

8. Remove the converter-to-flywheel attaching nuts. Place a wrench on the crankshaft pulley attaching bolt to turn the converter to gain access to the nuts.

9. With the wrench on the crankshaft pulley attaching bolt, turn the converter to gain access to the converter drain plug. Place a drain pan under the converter to catch the fluid. Then, remove the plug. With fluid drained, re-install the plug.

10. Disconnect the driveshaft.

11. Remove fluid filler tube.

12. Disconnect the starter cable at the starter. Remove the starter-to-converter housing attaching bolts and remove the starter.

13. Position the engine support bar (Tool T65E-6000-JO) to the frame and engine oil pan flanges.

14. Disconnect the cooler lines from the transmission. Disconnect the vacuum line from the vacuum diaphragm unit. Remove the vacuum line from the retaining clip at the transmission.

15. Remove the speedometer driven gear from the extension housing.

16. Disconnect the manual and downshift linkage rods from the transmission control levers.

17. Position a transmission jack to support the transmission. Install the safety chain to hold the transmission.

18. Remove the bolts and nuts securing the rear support and insulator assembly to the crossmember. Remove the six bolts retaining the crossmember to the side rails and remove the two support gussets. Raise the transmission with the jack and remove the

crossmember.

19. Remove the bolt that retains the transmission filler tube to the cylinder block. Lift the filler tube and dipstick from the transmission.

20. Remove the remaining converter housing-to-engine attaching bolts. Lower the jack and remove the converter and transmission assembly from under the vehicle.

21. Remove the converter and mount the transmission in a holding fixture.

22. Tighten the converter drain plug.

23. Position the converter on the transmission making sure the converter drive flats are fully engaged in the pump gear.

24. With the converter properly installed, place the transmission on the jack. Secure the transmission to the jack with the safety chain.

25. Rotate the converter until the studs and drain plug are in alignment with their holes in the flywheel.

26. Move the converter and transmission assembly forward into position, using care not to damage the flywheel and the converter pilot. The converter must rest squarely against the flywheel. This indicates that the converter pilot is not binding in the engine crankshaft.

27. Install the lower converter housing-to-engine attaching bolts. Tighten the bolts. Install the converter-to-flywheel attaching nuts. Tighten the nuts.

28. Install the crossmember. Install the rear support and insulator assembly-to-crossmember attaching bolts and nuts. Tighten the bolts.

29. Remove the safety chain and remove the jack from under the vehicle. Remove the engine support bar.

30. Install a new O-ring on the lower end of the transmission filler tube and insert the tube and dipstick in the case.

31. Connect the vacuum line to the vacuum diaphragm making sure the line is secured in the retaining clip.

32. Connect the cooler lines to the transmission.

33. Install the speedometer driven gear into the extension housing. Tighten the attaching bolt.

34. Connect the transmission linkage rods to the transmission control levers. When making transmission control attachments new retaining ring and grommet should always be used. Attach the shift rod to the steering column shift lever. Align the flats of the adjusting stud with the flats of the rod slot and insert the stud through the rod. Assemble the adjusting stud nut and washer to a loose fit. Perform a linkage adjustment.

35. Install the converter housing access cover and tighten the attaching bolts.

36. Position the starter into the converter housing and install the attaching bolts. Tighten the bolts. Install the starter cable.

37. Install the driveshaft.

38. Lower the vehicle.

39. Install the upper converter housing-to-engine attaching bolts. Tighten the bolts.

40. On V8 engines, install the flex hose to the air cleaner heat tube. Install the bolt that retains the filler tube to the cylinder block.

41. Connect the neutral start switch wires at the plug connector.

42. Make sure the transmission fluid pan is securely attached, and fill the transmission to the proper level with the specified fluid.

43. Raise the vehicle and check for transmission fluid leakage. Lower the vehicle and adjust the downshift and manual linkage.

44. Install the engine compartment cover.

Automatic Overdrive

1. Raise the vehicle and support on jackstands.

2. Place the drain pan under the transmission fluid pan. Starting at the rear of the pan and working toward the front, loosen the attaching bolts and allow the fluid to drain. Finally remove all of the pan attaching bolts except two at the front, to allow the fluid to further drain. With fluid drained, install two bolts on the rear side of the pan to temporarily hold it in place.

3. Remove the converter drain plug access cover from the lower end of the converter housing.

4. Remove the converter-to-flywheel attaching nuts. Place a wrench on the crankshaft pulley attaching bolt to turn the converter to gain access to the nuts.

5. Place a drain pan under the converter to catch the fluid. With the wrench on the crankshaft pulley attaching bolt, turn the converter to gain access to the converter drain plug and remove the plug. After the fluid has been drained, reinstall the plug.

6. Disconnect the driveshaft from the rear axle and slide shaft rearward from the transmission. Install a seal installation tool in the extension housing to prevent fluid leakage.

7. Disconnect the cable from the terminal on the starter motor. Remove the three attaching bolts and remove the starter motor. Disconnect the neutral start switch wires at the plug connector.

8. Remove the rear mount-to-crossmember attaching bolts and the two crossmember-to-frame attaching bolts.

9. Remove the two engine rear support-to-extension housing attaching bolts.

10. Disconnect the TV linkage rod from the transmission TV lever. Disconnect the manual rod from the transmission manual lever at the transmission.

11. Remove the two bolts securing the bellcrank bracket to the converter housing.

12. Raise the transmission with a transmission jack to provide clearance to remove the crossmember. Remove the rear mount from the crossmember and remove the crossmember from the side supports.

13. Lower the transmission to gain access to the oil cooler lines.

14. Disconnect each oil line from the fittings on the transmission.

15. Disconnect the speedometer cable from the extension housing.

16. Remove the bolt that secures the transmission fluid filler tube to the cylinder block. Lift the filler tube and the dipstick from the transmission.

17. Secure the transmission to the jack with the chain.

18. Remove the converter housing-to-cylinder block attaching bolts.

19. Carefully move the transmission and converter assembly away from the engine and, at the same time, lower the jack to clear the underside of the vehicle.

20. Remove the converter and mount the transmission in a holding fixture.

21. Tighten the converter drain plug.

22. Position the converter on the transmission, making sure the converter drive flats are fully engaged in the pump gear by rotating the converter.

23. With the converter properly installed, place the transmission on the jack. Secure the transmission to the jack with a chain.

24. Rotate the converter until the studs and drain plug are in alignment with the holes in the flywheel.

25. Move the converter and transmission assembly forward into position, using care not to damage the flywheel and the converter pilot. The converter must rest squarely against the flywheel. This indicates that the converter pilot is not binding in the engine crankshaft.

26. Install and tighten the converter housing-to-engine attaching bolts to 40-50 ft.lb.

27. Remove the safety chain from around the transmission.

28. Install a new O-ring on the lower end of the transmission filler tube. Insert the tube in the transmission case and secure the tube to the engine with the attaching bolt.

29. Connect the speedometer cable to the extension housing.

30. Connect the oil cooler lines to the

right side of transmission case.

31. Position the crossmember on the side supports. Position the rear mount on the crossmember and install the attaching bolt and nut.

32. Secure the engine rear support to the extension housing and tighten the bolts to 16-20 ft.lb.

33. Lower the transmission and remove the jack.

C5 w/2-Wheel Drive

1. Raise the vehicle and safely support on jackstands. Place the drain pan under the transmission fluid pan. Starting at the rear of the pan and working toward the front, loosen the attaching bolts and allow the fluid to drain. Finally remove all of the pan attaching bolts except two at the front, to allow the fluid to further drain. Finally remove all of the pan attaching bolts except two at the front, to allow the fluid to further drain. With fluid drained, install two bolts on the rear side of the pan to temporarily hold it in place.

2. Remove the converter drain plug access cover from the lower end of the converter housing.

3. Remove the converter-to-flywheel attaching nuts. Place a wrench on the crankshaft pulley attaching bolt to turn the converter to gain access to the nuts.

4. Place a drain pan under the converter to catch the fluid. With the wrench on the crankshaft pulley attaching bolt, turn the converter to gain access to the converter drain plug and remove the plug. After the fluid has been drained, reinstall the plug.

5. Disconnect the driveshaft from the rear axle and slide shaft rearward from the transmission. Install a suitable cover in the extension housing to prevent fluid leakage. Mark the rear driveshaft yoke and axle flange so they can be installed in their original position.

6. Disconnect the cable from the terminal on the starter motor. Remove the three attaching bolts and remove the starter motor. Disconnect the neutral start switch wires at the plug connector.

7. Remove the rear mount-to-crossmember attaching nuts and the two crossmember-to-frame attaching bolts. Remove the right and left gusset.

8. Remove the two engine rear insulator-to-extension housing attaching bolts.

9. Disconnect the TV linkage rod from the transmission TV lever. Disconnect the manual rod from the transmission manual lever at the transmission.

10. Remove the two bolts securing the bellcrank bracket to the converter housing.

11. Raise the transmission with a suitable jack to provide clearance to remove the crossmember. Remove the rear mount from the crossmember and remove the crossmember from the side supports. Lower the transmission to gain access to the oil cooler lines. Disconnect each oil line from the fittings on the transmission.

12. Disconnect the speedometer cable from the extension housing.

13. Remove the bolt that secures the transmission fluid filler tube to the cylinder block. Lift the filler tube and the dipstick from the transmission.

14. Secure the transmission to the jack with the chain. Remove the converter housing-to-cylinder block attaching bolts.

15. Carefully move the transmission and converter assembly away from the engine and, at the same time, lower the jack to clear the underside of the vehicle.

16. Tighten the converter drain plug to specifications. Position the converter on the transmission, making sure the converter drive flats are fully engaged in the pump gear by rotating the converter.

17. With the converter properly installed, place the transmission on the jack. Secure the transmission to the jack with a chain.

18. Rotate the converter until the studs and drain plug are in alignment with the holes in the flywheel. Move the converter and transmission assembly forward into position, using care not to damage the flywheel and the converter pilot. The converter must rest squarely against the flywheel. This indicates that the converter pilot is not binding in the engine crankshaft.

19. Install and tighten the converter housing-to-engine attaching bolts to specification.

20. Remove the safety chain from around the transmission.

21. Install the new O-ring on the lower end of the transmission filler tube. Insert the tube in the transmission case and secure the tube to the engine with the attaching bolt.

22. Connect the speedometer cable to the extension housing.

23. Connect the oil cooler lines to the right side of transmission case.

24. Secure the engine rear support to the extension housing and tighten the bolts to specification.

25. Position the crossmember on the side supports. Lower the transmission and remove the jack. Secure the crossmember to the side supports with the attaching bolts.

26. Position the damper assembly over the engine rear support studs. (The painted face of the damper is facing forward when installed in the vehicle.) Secure the rear engine support to the crossmember.

27. Position the bellcrank to the converter housing and install the two attaching bolts.

28. Connect the TV linkage rod to the transmission TV lever. Connect the manual linkage rod to the manual lever at the transmission.

29. Secure the converter-to-flywheel attaching nuts and tighten them to specification.

30. Install the converter housing access cover and secure it with the attaching bolts.

31. Secure the starter motor in place with the attaching bolts. Connect the cable to the terminal on the starter. Connect the neutral start switch wires at the plug connector.

32. Connect the driveshaft to the rear axle so the index marks on the companion flange and the rear yoke are aligned. Lubricate the slip yoke with grease. Adjust the shift linkage as required.

33. Adjust throttle linkage.

34. Lower the vehicle. Fill the transmission to the correct level with the specified fluid. Start the engine and shift the transmission to all ranges, then recheck the fluid level.

C5 w/4-Wheel Drive

1. Remove the bolt securing the fluid filler tube to the engine valve cover bracket.

2. Place a drain pan under the transmission fluid pan. Starting at the rear of the pan and working towards the front, loosen the attaching bolts and allow the fluid to drain. Finally, remove all of the pan attaching bolts except two at the front, to allow the fluid to drain further. With fluid drained, install two bolts on the rear side of the pan to temporarily hold it in place.

3. Remove the converter drain plug access cover from the lower end of the converter housing. Remove the converter-to-flywheel attaching nuts. Place a wrench on the crankshaft pulley attaching bolt to turn the converter to gain access to the nuts.

4. Place a drain pan under the converter to catch the fluid. With the wrench on the crankshaft pulley attaching bolt, turn the converter to gain access to the converter drain plug and remove the plug.

5. After the fluid has been drained, reinstall the cable from the terminal at the starter motor. Remove the three attaching bolts and remove the starter motor. Disconnect the neutral start switch wires at the plug connector.

6. Remove the rear mount-to-crossmember attaching nuts and the two

crossmember-to-frame attaching bolts. Remove the right and left gusset.

7. Remove the two engine rear insulator-to-extension housing attaching bolts.

8. Disconnect the TV linkage rod from the transmission TV lever. Disconnect the manual rod from the transmission manual lever at the transmission. Disconnect the downshift and manual linkage rods from the levers on the transmission.

9. Remove the vacuum hose from the vacuum diaphragm unit. Remove the vacuum line from the retaining clip.

10. Remove the two bolts securing the bellcrank bracket to the converter housing.

11. Remove the transfer case. Refer to the Transfer Case section behind Manual Transmissions.

12. Raise the transmission with a transmission jack to provide clearance to remove the crossmember. Remove the rear mount from the crossmember and remove the crossmember from the side supports.

13. Lower the transmission to gain access to the oil cooler lines.

14. Disconnect each oil line from the fittings on the transmission.

15. Disconnect the speedometer cable from the extension housing.

16. Secure the transmission to the jack with the chain. Remove the converter housing-to-cylinder block attaching bolts.

17. Carefully move the transmission and converter assembly away from the engine and, at the same time, lower the jack to clear the underside of the vehicle.

18. Position the converter on the transmission, making sure the converter drive flats are fully engaged in the pump gear by rotating the converter.

19. With the converter properly installed, place the transmission on the jack. Secure the transmission to the jack with a chain.

20. Rotate the converter until the studs and drain plug are in alignment with the holes in the flywheel.

21. Move the converter and transmission assembly forward into position, using care not to damage the flywheel and the converter pilot. The converter must rest squarely against the flywheel. This indicates that the converter pilot is not binding in the engine crankshaft.

22. Install and tighten the converter housing-to-engine attaching bolts.

23. Remove the safety chain from around the transmission.

24. Install a new O-ring on the lower end of the transmission filler tube. Insert the tube in the transmission case.

25. Connect the speedometer cable to the extension housing.

26. Connect the oil cooler lines to the right of the transmission case.

27. Position the crossmember on the side supports. Position the rear mount insulator on the crossmember and install the attaching bolts and nuts.

28. Install the transfer case.

29. Secure the engine rear support to the extension housing. Lower the transmission and remove the jack.

30. Secure the crossmember to the side supports with the attaching bolts and tighten to specification.

31. Position the bellcrank to the converter housing and install the two attaching bolts.

32. Connect the downshift and manual linkage rods to their respective levers on the transmission.

33. Connect the vacuum line to the vacuum diaphragm making sure that the line is in the retaining clip.

34. Secure the converter-to-flywheel attaching nuts. Install the converter housing access cover and secure it with the attaching bolts.

35. Secure the starter motor in place with the attaching bolts. Connect the cable to the terminal on the starter. Connect the neutral start switch wires at the plug connector.

36. Adjust the shift linkage as required. Lower the vehicle.

37. Position the transmission fluid filler tube to the valve cover bracket and secure with the attaching bolt. Fill the transmission to the correct level. Start the engine and shift the transmission to all ranges, then recheck the fluid level.

Pan

REMOVAL & INSTALLATION

C3, C4, C5

1. Raise the vehicle, so that the transmission oil pan is readily accessible. Safely support on jackstands.

2. Disconnect the fluid filler tube from the pan and allow the fluid to drain into an appropriate container.

3. Remove the transmission oil pan attaching bolts, pan and gasket.

4. Clean the transmission oil pan and transmission mating surfaces.

5. Install the transmission oil pan in the reverse order of removal, torquing the attaching bolts to 12-16 ft.lb. and using a new gasket. Fill the transmission with 3 qts. of the correct type fluid.

6. Lower the vehicle. Start the engine and move the gear selector through shift pattern. Allow the engine to reach normal operating temperature.

7. Check the transmission fluid. Add fluid, if necessary, to maintain correct level.

C6, FMX, and AOD

1. Raise the car and support on jackstands.

2. Place a drain pan under the transmission.

3. Loosen the pan attaching bolts and drain the fluid from the transmission.

4. When the fluid has drained to the level of the pan flange, remove the remaining pan bolts working from the rear and both sides of the pan to allow it to drop and drain slowly.

5. When all of the fluid has drained, remove the pan and clean it thoroughly. discard the pan gasket.

6. Place a new gasket on the pan, and install the pan on the transmission. Tighten the attaching bolts to 12-16 ft.lb.

7. Add three quarts of fluid to the transmission through the filler tube.

8. Lower the vehicle. Start the engine and move the gear selector through shift pattern. Allow the engine to reach normal operating temperature.

9. Check the transmission fluid. Add fluid, if necessary, to maintain correct level.

FILTER SERVICE

1. Remove the transmission oil pan and gasket.

2. Remove the screws holding the fine mesh screen to the lower valve body.

NOTE: Be careful not to lose the throttle pressure limit valve and spring when separating the oil screen from the valve body on a C4.

3. Install the new filter screen and transmission oil pan gasket in the reverse order of removal.

AJUSTMENTS

FRONT BAND ADJUSTMENT

FMX

1. Remove the transmission oil pan.

2. Loosen the front servo adjusting screw locknut.

3. Pull back on the actuating rod, and insert a ¼" spacer between the adjusting screw and the servo piston stem.

4. Tighten the adjusting screw to 10 in.lb.

5. Remove the spacer and tighten the adjusting screw an additional ¾ turn.

6. Hold the adjusting screw station-

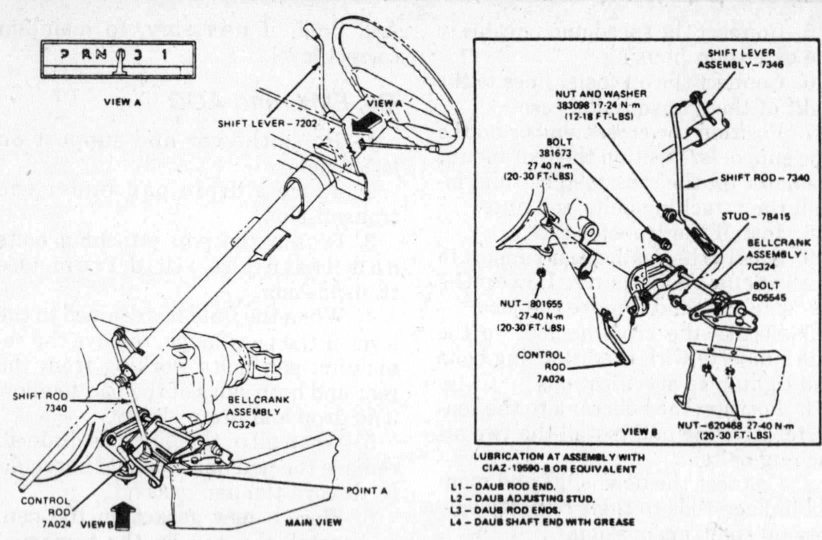

Automatic overdrive shift linkage adjustment

ary and tighten the locknut. Tighten the locknut to 20-25 ft.lb.

7. Install the oil pan and a new gasket in the reverse order of removal.

C3

1. Remove the downshift rod from the transmission downshift lever. Clean all of the dirt away from the bank adjusting nut and screw area. Remove and discard the locknut.

2. Tighten the adjusting screw to 10 ft.lb. Back off the adjusting screw exactly two turns.

3. Install a new locknut, hold the adjusting screw in position and tighten the locknut to 35-45 ft.lb. Install the downshift rod.

INTERMEDIATE BAND ADJUSTMENT

C4, C5 and C6

1. Raise and support the vehicle on jackstands.

2. Clean all dirt away from the band adjusting screw. Remove and discard the locknut.

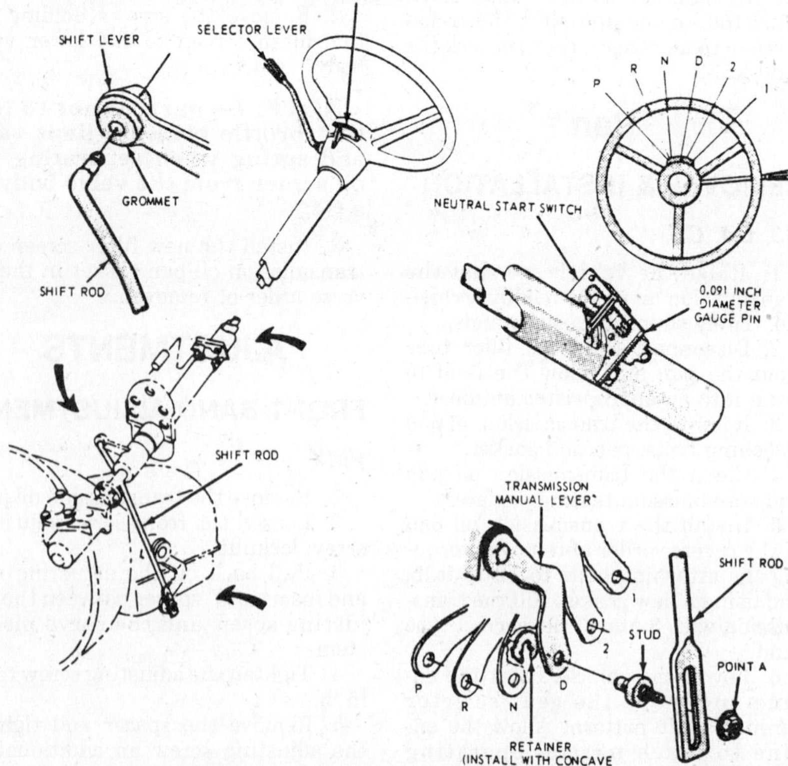

Automatic transmission shift linkage adjustment

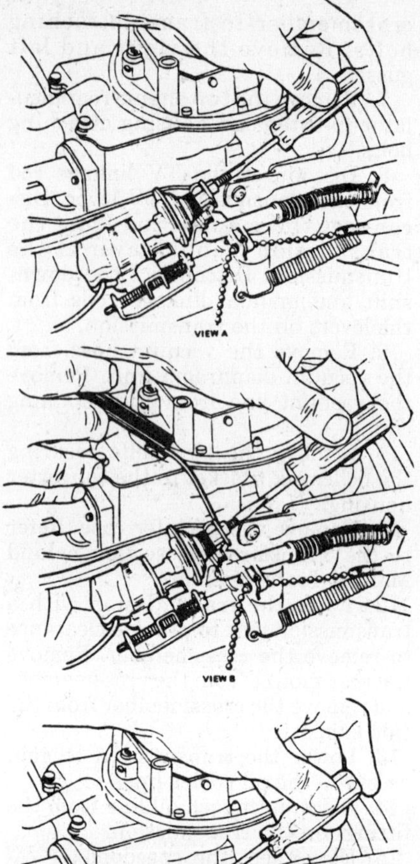

Automatic overdrive throttle linkage adjustment

3. Install a new locknut and tighten the adjusting screw to 10 ft.lb.

4. On the C4 transmission; back off the adjusting screw exactly 1¾ turns. On the C5; back off the adjusting screw exactly 4¼ turns. On the C6 transmission; back off the adjusting screw exactly 1½ turns.

5. Hold the adjusting screw from turning and tighten the locknut to 35-45 ft.lb.

6. Remove the jackstands and lower the vehicle.

LOW-REVERSE BAND ADJUSTMENT

C4, C5

1. Clean all dirt from around the band adjusting screw and remove and discard the locknut.

2. Install a new locknut on the adjusting screw. Using a torque wrench, tighten the adjusting screw to 10 ft.lb.

3. Back off the adjusting screw exactly 3 full turns.

4. Hold the adjusting screw steady and tighten the locknut to 35-45 ft.lb.

REAR BAND ADJUSTMENT

FMX

1. Remove all dirt away from the adjusting screw threads then oil the threads.
2. Loosen the rear band adjusting screw locknut.
3. Tighten the adjusting screw to 10 ft.lb.
4. Back off the adjusting screw exactly 1½ turns.
5. Hold the adjusting screw stationary and tighten the adjusting screw locknut to 35-40 ft.lb.
6. Reinstall the oil pan and a new gasket.

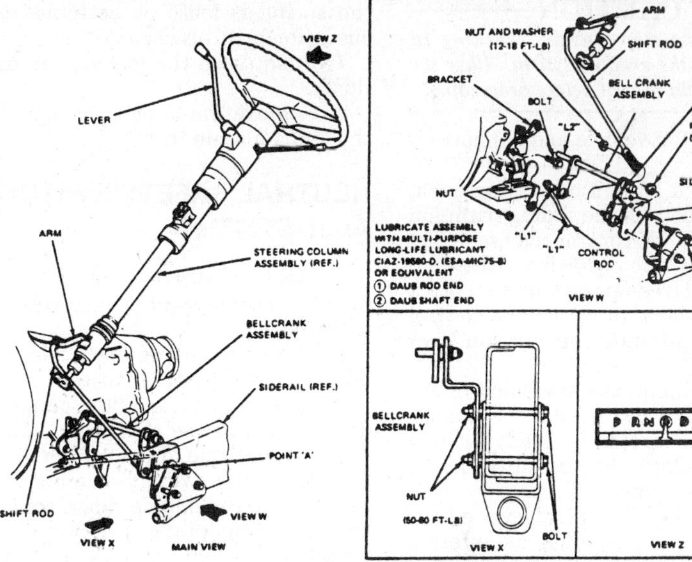

Automatic overdrive shift control linkage

SHIFT LINKAGE ADJUSTMENT

1. With the engine stopped, place the transmission selector lever at the steering column in the D position against the D stop.

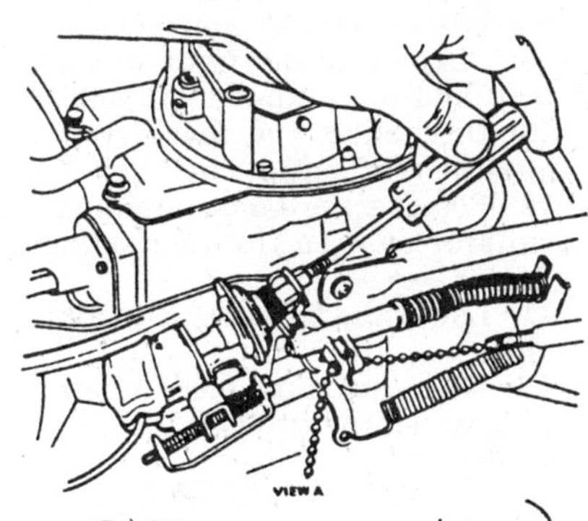

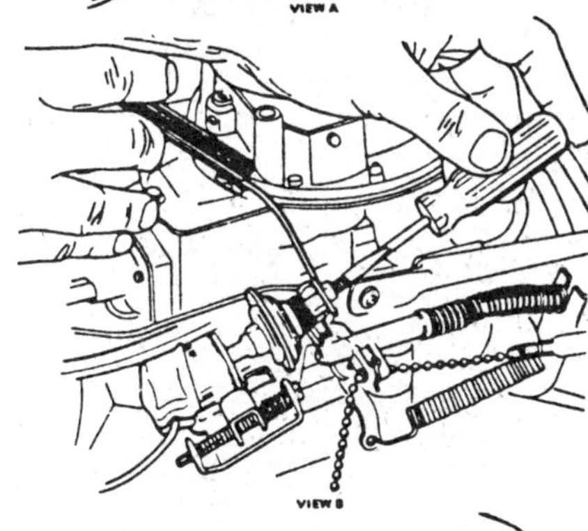

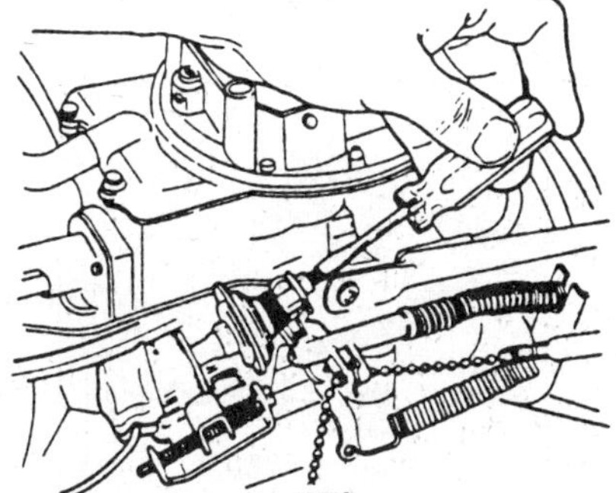

Automatic overdrive throttle linkage adjustment

2. Loosen the shift rod adjusting nut at the transmission lever.
3. Shift the manual lever at the transmission to the D position, two detents from the rear. On an F150 with 4WD, move the bellcrank lever.
4. With the selector lever and transmission manual lever in the D position, tighten the adjusting nut to 12-18 ft.lb. Do not allow the rod or shift lever to move while tightening the nut.
5. Check the operation of the shift linkage.

THROTTLE VALVE LINKAGE ADJUSTMENT

Automatic Overdrive

ADJUSTMENT AT THE CARBURETOR w/ROD

The TV control linkage may be adjusted at the carburetor using the following procedure:

1. Check that engine idle speed is set at specification.
2. De-cam the fast idle cam on the carburetor so that the throttle lever is at its idle stop. Place shift lever in N (neutral), set park brake (engine off).
3. Backout linkage lever adjusting screw all the way (screw end is flush with lever face).
4. Turn in adjusting screw until a thin shim (0.005″ max.) or piece of writing paper fits snugly between end of screw and Throttle Lever. To eliminate effect of friction, push linkage lever forward (tending to close gap) and release before checking clearance between end of screw and throttle lever. Do not apply any load on levers with tools or hands while checking gap.
5. Turn in adjusting screw an additional four turns. (Four turns are preferred. Two turns minimum is permissible if screw travel is limited).
6. If it is not possible to turn in adjusting screw at least two additional turns or if there was insufficient screw adjusting capacity to obtain an initial gap in Step 2 above, refer to Linkage Adjustment at Transmission. Whenever it is required to adjust idle speed by more than 50 rpm, the adjustment screw on the linkage lever at the carburetor should also be readjusted. After making any idle speed adjustments, always verify the linkage lever and throttle lever are in contact with the throttle lever at its idle stop and the shift lever is in N (neutral).

ADJUSTMENT AT TRANSMISSION

The linkage lever adjustment screw has limited adjustment capability. If it is not possible to adjust the TV linkage using this screw, the length of the TV control rod assembly must be readjusted using the following procedure. This procedure must also be followed whenever a new TV control rod asssembly is installed. This procedure requires placing the vehicle on jackstands to give access to the linkage components at the transmission TV control lever.

1. Set the engine curb idle speed to specification.
2. With engine off, de-cam the fast idle cam on the carburetor so that the throttle lever is against the idle stop. Place shift lever in Neutral and set park brake (engine off).
3. Set the linkage lever adjustment screw at its approximately mid-range.
4. If a new TV control rod assembly is being installed, connect the rod to the linkage lever at the carburetor.

CAUTION

The following steps involve working in proximity to the exhaust system. Allow the exhaust system to cool before proceeding.

5. Raise the vehicle and support on jackstands.

6. Using a 13 mm box end wrench, loosen the bolt on the sliding trunnion block on the TV control rod assembly. Remove any corrosion from the control rod and free-up the trunnion block so that it slides freely on the control rod. Insert pin into transmission lever grommet.

7. Push up on the lower end of the control rod to insure that the linkage lever at carburetor is firmly against the throttle lever. Release force on rod. Rod must stay up.

8. Push the TV control lever on the transmission up against its internal stop with a firm force (approximately 5 pounds) and tighten the bolt on the trunnion block. Do not relax force on lever until nut is tightened.

9. Lower the vehicle and verify that the throttle lever is still against the idle stop. If not, repeat Steps 2 through 9.

ADJUSTMENT w/CABLE

Whenever it is required to adjust the idle speed by more than 150 rpm, the TV control cable should be readjusted. Failure to do so may result in the symptoms due to a too short cable if the idle speed was increased or a too long cable if the idle speed was reduced.

1. Check and set, if necessary, engine idle speed to specification with and without TSP activated.

2. Shut engine off. Remove air cleaner. Set parking brake block wheels, and put selector in **N**. (Do not put selector in **P**).

3. Verify that the cable routing is free of sharp bends or pressure points and that the cable operates freely. Lubricate the TV lever ball stud. Check for damage to cable or rubber boot.

4. Unlock the locking tab at the carburetor end by pushing up from below, and prying up the rest of the way to free the cable.

5. A retention spring must be installed on the TV control lever, to hold it in the idle position (as far to rear as the lever will travel) with about ten pounds of force. If a suitable spring is not available, two V8 TV return springs may be used. Attach retention spring(s) to the transmission TV lever and hook rear end of spring to the transmission case.

6. De-cam the carburetor. The carburetor throttle lever must be in the anti-diesel position. Verify that the take-up spring (carburetor end of the cable) properly tensions the cable. If the spring is loose or bottomed out, check for bent brackets.

7. Push down the locking tab until flush.

8. Remove the detent springs from the transmission lever.

NEUTRAL SAFETY SWITCH ADJUSTMENT

1. Hold the steering column transmission selector lever against the Neutral stop.

2. Move the sliding block assembly on the neutral switch to the neutral position and insert a 0.091" gauge pin or $^{3}/_{32}$" drill in the alignment hole on the terminal side of the switch.

3. Move the switch assembly housing so that the sliding block contacts the actuating pin lever. Secure the switch to the outer tube of the steering column and remove the gauge pin.

4. Check the operation of the switch. The engine should only start in Neutral and Park.

THROTTLE KICKDOWN LINKAGE ADJUSTMENT

1. Move the carburetor throttle linkage to the wide open position.

2. Insert a 0.060" thick spacer between the throttle lever and the kickdown adjusting screw.

3. Rotate the transmission kickdown lever until the lever engages the transmission internal stop. Do not use the kick-down rod to turn the transmission lever.

4. Turn the adjusting screw until it contacts the 0.060" spacer.

5. Remove the spacer.

TRANSFER CASE

Pick-Up

REMOVAL & INSTALLATION

New Process Model 208

1. Raise the vehicle and support on jackstands and drain the fluid from the transfer case.

2. Disconnect the four wheel drive indicator switch wire connector at the transfer case.

3. Disconnect the speedometer driven gear from the transfer case rear bearing retainer.

4. Remove the nut retaining the transmission shift lever assembly to the transfer case.

5. Remove the skid plate from the frame, if so equipped.

6. Remove the heat shield from the frame.

7. Support the transfer case with a transmission jack or equivalent.

8. Disconnect the front driveshaft from the front output shaft yoke.

9. Disconnect the rear driveshaft from the rear output shaft yoke.

10. Remove the bolts retaining the transfer case to the transmission adapter.

11. Lower the transfer case from the vehicle.

12. When installing place a new gasket between the transfer case and the adapter.

13. Raise the transfer case with a transmission jack so the transmission output shaft aligns with the splined transfer case input shaft.

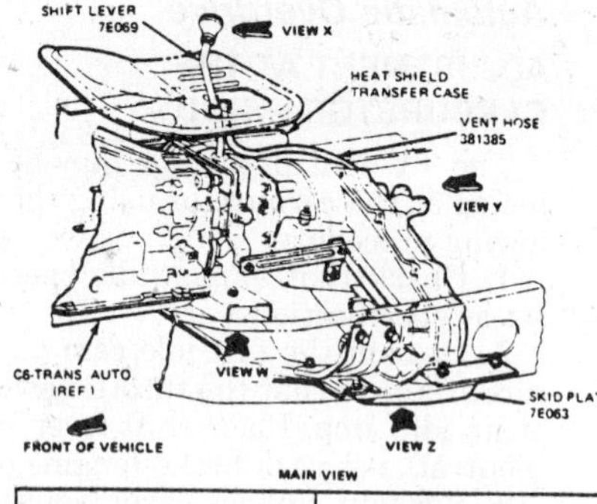

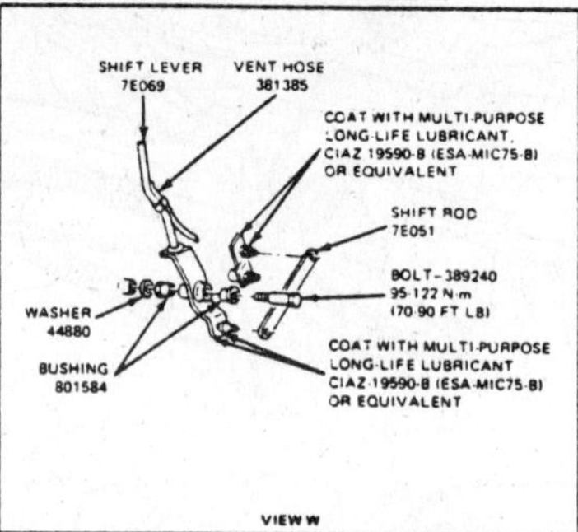

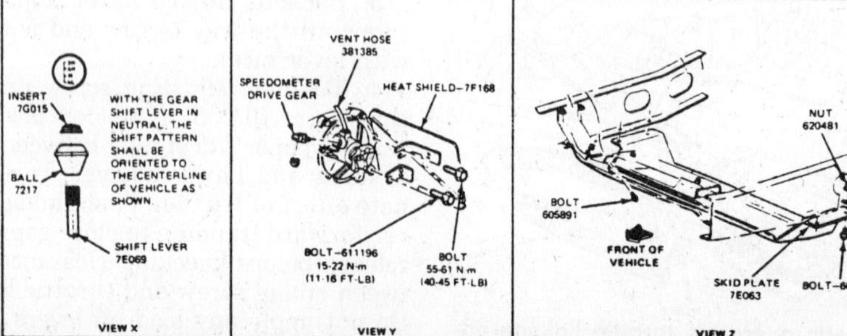

New Process 208 transfer case installation, automatic and four-speed transmissions

14. Install the bolts retaining the case to the adapter.
15. Connect the rear driveshaft to the rear output shaft yoke.
16. Connect the front driveshaft to the front output yoke.
17. Remove the transmission jack from the transfer case.
18. Position the heat shield to the frame crossmember and mounting lug to the transfer case and install and tighten the bolts and screw.
19. Install the skid plate to the frame.
20. Install the shift lever to the transfer case and tighten the retaining nut.
21. Install the speedometer driven gear to the transfer case.
22. Connect the four wheel drive indicator switch wire to the transfer case.
23. Install the drain plug. Remove the filler plug and install six pints of Dexron® II type transmission fluid.
24. Lower the vehicle.

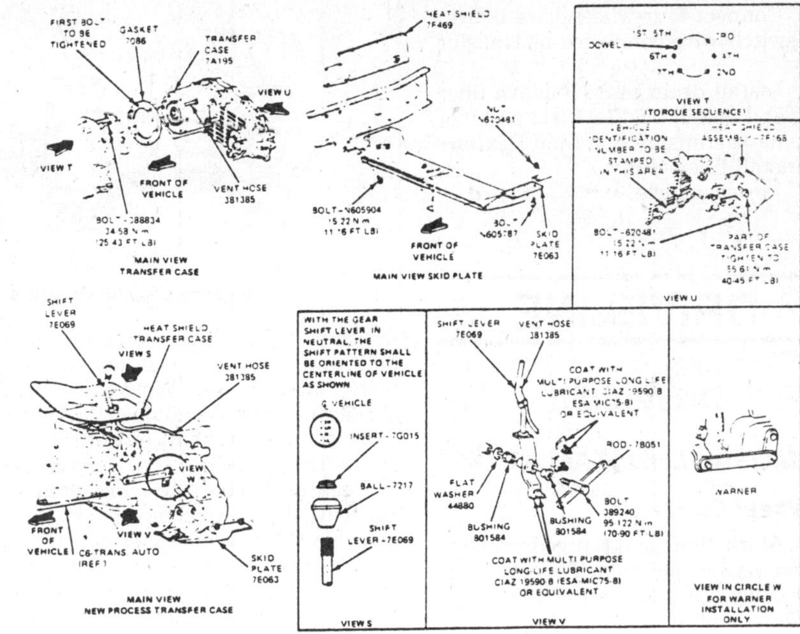

Borg-Warner 1345 transfer case and skid plate installation

Borg Warner Model 1345

1. Raise the vehicle and support on jackstands.
2. Drain the fluid from the transfer case.
3. Disconnect the four wheel drive indicator switch wire connector at the transfer case.
4. Remove the skid plate from the frame, if so equipped.
5. Disconnect the front driveshaft from the front output yoke.
6. Disconnect the rear driveshaft from the rear output shaft yoke.
7. Disconnect the speedometer driven gear from the transfer case rear bearing retainer.
8. Remove the retaining rings and shift rod from the transfer case shift lever.
9. Disconnect the vent hose from the transfer case.
10. Remove the heat shield from the frame.
11. Support the transfer case with a transmission jack.
12. Remove the bolts retaining the transfer case to the transmission adapter.
13. Lower the transfer case from the vehicle.
14. When installing place a new gasket between the transfer case and the adapter.
15. Raise the transfer case with the transmission jack so that the transmission output shaft aligns with the splined transfer case input shaft. Install the bolts retaining the transfer case to the adapter.
16. Remove the transmission jack from the transfer case.
17. Connect the rear driveshaft to the rear output shaft yoke.
18. Install the shift lever to the transfer case and install the retaining nut.
19. Connect the speedometer driven gear to the transfer case.
20. Connect the four wheel drive indicator switch wire connector at the transfer case.
21. Connect the front driveshaft to the front output yoke.
22. Position the heat shield to the frame crossmember and the mounting lug on the transfer case. Install and tighten the retaining bolts.
23. Install the skid plate to the frame.
24. Install the drain plug. Remove the filler plug and install six pints of Dexron®II type transmission fluid or equivalent.
25. Lower the vehicle.

Bronco

REMOVAL AND INSTALLATION

1. Raise the vehicle and support on jackstands.
2. Place a drain pan under transfer case, remove drain plug and drain fluid from transfer case.
3. Disconnect four wheel drive indicator switch wire connector at transfer case.
4. Disconnect speedometer driven gear from transfer case rear bearing retainer.
5. Remove nut retaining transmission shift lever assembly to transfer case.
6. If so equipped, remove skid plate from frame.
7. Remove heat shield from frame.

CAUTION

Catalytic converter is located beside the heat shield. Be careful when working around catalytic converter because of the extremely high temperatures generated by the converter.

8. Support transfer case with transmission jack.
9. Disconnect front driveshaft from front output shaft yoke.
10. Disconnect rear driveshaft from rear output shaft yoke.
11. Remove the bolts retaining transfer case to transmission adapter. Remove gasket between transfer case and adapter.
12. Lower transfer case from vehicle.
13. Place a new gasket between transfer case and adapter.
14. Raise transfer case with transmission jack so transmission output shaft aligns with splined transfer case input shaft. Install bolts retaining transfer case to adapter. Tighten bolts to 30-40 ft.lb.
15. Connect rear driveshaft to rear output shaft yoke.
16. Connect front driveshaft to front output yoke.
17. Remove transmission jack from transfer case.
18. Position heat shield to frame crossmember and mounting lug on transfer case. Install and tighten bolts and screw to 11-16 ft.lb.
19. Install skid plate to frame. Tighten nuts and bolts.
20. Install shift lever to transfer case. Install retaining nut.
21. Connect speedometer driven gear to transfer case.

22. Connect four-wheel drive indicator switch wire connector at transfer case.
23. Install drain plug. Remove filler plug and install 2.8 liters (six pints) of automatic transmission fluid Dexron® II. Install filler plug.
24. Lower vehicle.

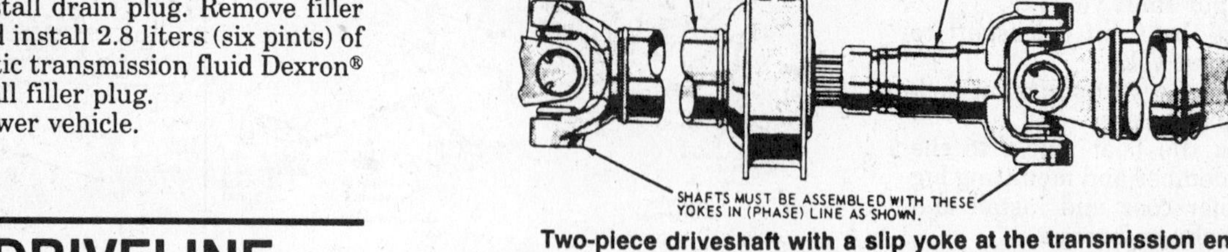

Two-piece driveshaft with a slip yoke at the transmission end

DRIVELINE

Driveshaft

REMOVAL & INSTALLATION

4-Wheel Drive

1. Mark shaft and flange for installation in same position. To remove the rear driveshaft, disconnect the double Cardan joint from the flange at the transfer case and the single U-joint from the flange at the rear axle. Remove the driveshaft.
2. To remove the front driveshaft, disconnect the double Cardan joint from the flange at the transfer case and the single U-joint from the front axle. Remove the driveshaft.
3. Installation is the reverse of removal. Torque driveshaft-to-transfer case bolts to 20-25 ft.lb.; driveshaft to axle bolts to 8-15 ft.lb.

2-Wheel Drive

1. Mark shaft and flange for installation in same position. Unscrew the nuts attaching the U-bolts to the flange at the rear axle, or remove the bolts and clips. Remove the U-bolts or bolts and clips and allow the rear of the driveshaft to drop down. Slide the front of the driveshaft out of the rear of the transmission, transfer case, or the center support bearing. Remove the driveshaft from the vehicle.
2. On those vehicles equipped with two driveshafts and a center support bearing, unscrew the attaching bolts holding the center support bearing to the frame. If equipped with a sliding yoke at the transmission, slide the coupling shaft out of the rear of the extension housing. Otherwise, remove the nuts from the U-bolts or bolts and clips holding the front of the coupling shaft to the flange on the rear of the transmission while supporting the center bearing. Remove the U-bolts or bolts and clips from the front flange and remove the coupling shaft assembly together with the center support bearing.
3. Install the driveshaft(s) in the reverse order of removal.

NOTE: All U-joints on two-piece driveshafts must be on the same horizontal plane when installed.

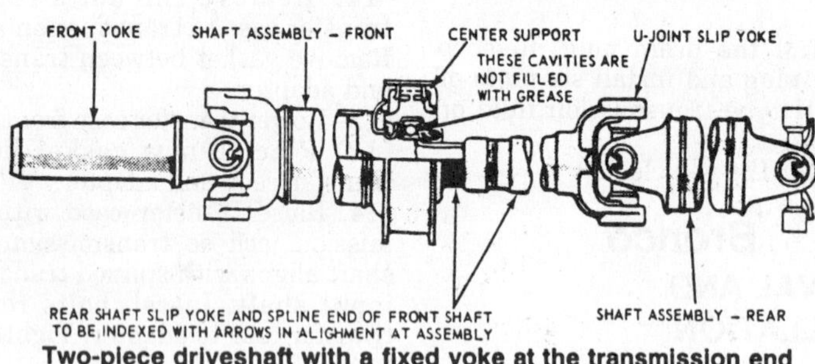

Two-piece driveshaft with a fixed yoke at the transmission end

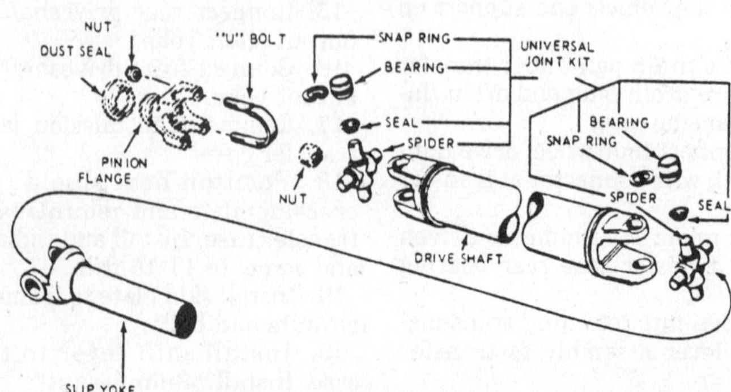

One-piece driveshaft with a slip yoke

Center Bearing

REMOVAL & INSTALLATION

1. Remove the driveshafts.
2. Remove the two center support bearing attaching bolts and remove the assembly from the vehicle.
3. Do not immerse the sealed bearing in any type of cleaning fluid. Wipe the bearing and cushion clean with a cloth dampened with cleaning fluid.
4. Check the bearing for wear or rough action by rotating the inner race while holding the outer race. If wear or roughness is evident, replace the bearing.

Examine the rubber cushion for evidence of hardening, cracking, or deterioration. Replace it if it is damaged in any way.

5. Place the bearing in the rubber support and the rubber support in the U-shaped support and install the bearing in the reverse order of removal.

2-Wheel Drive Front Wheel Bearings

The wheel bearings should be serviced (cleaned, inspected, repacked or replaced) every 20,000 miles, or whenever operated in deep water.

Before handling the bearings there are a few things that you should remember to do and try to avoid. DO the following:

1. Remove all outside dirt from the housing before exposing the bearing.
2. Treat a used bearing as gently as you would a new one.
3. Work with clean tools in clean surroundings.
4. Use clean, dry canvas gloves, or at least clean, dry hands.
5. Clean solvents and flushing fluids are a must.
6. Use clean paper when laying out the bearings to dry.
7. Protect disassembled bearings from rust and dirt. Cover them up.
8. Use clean rags to wipe bearings.
9. Keep the bearings in oil-proof paper when they are to be stored or are not in use.

10. Clean the inside of the housing before replacing the bearing. Do NOT do the following:

a. Don't work in dirty surroundings.

b. Don't use dirty, chipped, or damaged tools.

c. Try not to work on wooden work benches or use wooden mallets.

d. Don't handle bearings with dirty or moist hands.

e. Do not use gasoline for cleaning; use a safe solvent.

f. Do not spin-dry bearings with compressed air. They will be damaged.

g. Do not spin unclean bearings.

h. Avoid using cotton waste or dirty cloths to wipe bearings.

i. Try not to scratch or nick bearing surfaces.

10. Do not allow the bearing to come in contact with dirt or rust at any time.

REMOVAL, INSPECTION, REPACKING AND INSTALLATION

1. Jack the truck up until the wheel to be serviced is off the ground and can spin freely. It is easier to check all the bearings at the same time. If the equipment needed is available, raise the front end of the truck so that both front wheels are off the ground. Use jackstands to support the vehicle. Make sure that the truck is completely stable before proceeding any further.

2. Remove the lug nuts and remove the wheel/tire assembly from the hub. It is necessary to remove the caliper assembly from the rotor and caliper support. Do not disconnect the brake line from the caliper. Simply hang the caliper with a length of heavy wire above the hub. Be careful not to strain the flexible brake tube.

3. Remove the grease cap with a screwdriver or pliers.

4. Remove the cotter pin and discard it. Cotter pins should never be reused.

5. Remove the nut lock, adjusting nut, and washer from the spindle.

6. Wiggle the hub so that the outer wheel bearing comes loose and can be removed. Remove the outer bearing.

7. Remove the hub from the spindle and place it on a work surface, supported by two blocks of wood under the hub.

8. Place a block of wood or drift pin through the spindle hole and tap out the inner grease seal. Tap lightly so not to damage the bearing. When the seal falls out, so will the inner bearing. Discard the seal.

9. Place all of the bearings, nuts, nut locks, washers and grease caps in a container of solvent. Use a light soft brush to thoroughly clean each part. Make sure that every bit of dirt and grease is rinsed off, then place each cleaned part on an absorbent cloth or paper and allow them to dry completely.

10. Clean the inside of the hub, including the bearing races, and the spindle. Remove all traces of old lubricant from these components.

11. Inspect the bearings for pitting, flat spots, rust, and rough areas. Check the races in the hub and the spindle for the same defects and rub them clean with a cloth that has been soaked in solvent. If the races show hair line cracks or worn shiny areas, they must be replaced. The races are installed in the hub with a press fit and are removed by driving them out with a suitable punch or drift. Place the new races squarely onto the hub and place a block of wood over them. Drive the race into place with a hammer, striking the block of wood. Never hit the race with any metal object. Replacement seals, bearings, and other required parts can be bought at an auto parts store. The old parts should be taken along to be compared with the replacement parts to ensure a perfect match.

12. Pack the wheel bearings with grease. There are special devices made for the specific purpose of greasing bearings, but if one is not available, pack the wheel bearings by hand. Put a large dab of grease in the palm of your hand and push the bearing through it with a sliding motion. The grease must be forced through the side of the bearing and in between each roller. Continue until the grease begins to ooze out the other side and through the gaps between the rollers; the bearing must be completely packed with grease.

NOTE: Sodium based grease is not compatible with lithium based grease. Be careful not to mix the two types. The best way to prevent this is to completely clean all of the old grease from the hub and spindle before installing any new grease.

13. Turn the hub assembly over so that the inner side faces up, making sure that the race and inner area are clean, and drop the inner wheel bearing into place. Using a hammer and a block of wood, tap the new grease seal in place. Never hit the seal with the hammer directly. Move the block of wood around the circumference until it is properly seated.

14. Slide the hub assembly onto the spindle and push it as far as it will go, making sure that it has completely covered the brake shoes. Keep the hub centered on the spindle to prevent damage to the grease seal and the spindle threads.

15. Place the outer wheel bearing in place over the spindle. Press it in until it is snug. Place the washer on the spindle after the bearing. Screw on the spindle nut and turn it down until a slight binding is felt.

16. With a torque wrench, tighten the nut to 17-25 ft.lb. to seat the bearings. Install the nut lock over the nut so that the cotter pin hole in the spindle is aligned with a slot in the nut lock. Back off the adjusting nut and the nut lock two slots of the nut lock and install the cotter pin.

17. Bend the longer of the two ends opposite the looped end out and over the end of the spindle. Trim both ends of the cotter pin just enough so that the grease cap will fit, leaving the bent end shaped over the end of the spindle.

18. Install the grease cap, brake caliper if so equipped, and the wheel/tire assembly. The wheel should rotate freely with no noise or noticeable endplay.

4-Wheel Drive Front Hubs

REMOVAL AND INSTALLATION

Locking Hubs

1. To remove hub, first separate cap assembly from body assembly by removing the six (6) socket head capscrews from the cap assembly and slip apart.

2. Remove snapring (retainer ring) from the end of the axle shaft.

3. Remove the lock ring seated in the groove of the wheel hub. The body assembly will now slide out of the wheel hub. If necessary, use an appropriate puller to remove the body assembly.

4. Install hub in reverse order of removal. Torque socket head capscrews to 30-35 in.lb.

Automatic Locking Hubs

1. Remove capscrews and remove hub cap assembly from spindle.

2. Remove capscrew from end of axle shaft.

3. Remove lock ring seated in the groove of the wheel hub with a knife blade or with a small sharp awl with the tip bent in a hook.

4. Remove body assembly from spindle. If body assembly does not slide out easily, use an appropriate puller.

5. Unscrew all three sets in the spindle locknut until the heads are flush with the edge of the locknut. Re-

move outer spindle locknut with tool T80T-4000-V, automatic hub lock nut wrench.

6. Reinstall in reverse order of removal. Tighten the outer spindle locknut to 15-20 ft.lb. with special tool T80T-4000-V, automatic hub lock nut wrench. Tighten down all three set screws. Firmly push in body assembly until the friction shoes are on top of the spindle outer locknut.

7. Install capscrew into the axle shaft and tighten to 35-50 ft.lb.

8. Place cap on spindle and install capscrews. Tighten to 35-50 in.lb. Turn dial firmly from stop to stop, causing the dialing mechanism to engage the body spline.

NOTE: Be sure both hub dials are in the same position: AUTO or LOCK.

4-Wheel Drive Front Wheel Bearings

REMOVAL, INSPECTION, REPACKING AND INSTALLATION

1. Raise the vehicle and support on safety stands.

2. If equipped with free-running hubs refer to Free-Running Hub Removal and Installation.

3. Remove the front hub grease cap and driving hub snapring.

4. Remove the splined driving hub and the pressure spring. This may require a slight prying assist.

5. Remove the wheel bearing lock nut, lock ring, and adjusting nut using tool T59T-1197-B, or equivalent.

6. Remove the hub and disc assembly. The outer wheel bearing and spring retainer will slide out as the hub is removed.

7. Carefully drive the inner bearing cone and grease seal out of the hub using Tool T69L-1102-A.

8. Inspect the bearing cups for pits or cracks. If necessary, remove them with a drift. If new cups are installed, install new bearings.

15. Lubricate the bearings with Multi-Purpose Lubricant Ford Specification, ESA-M1C7-B or equivalent. Clean all old grease from the hub. Pack the cones and rollers. If a bearing packer is not available, work as much lubricant as possible between the rollers and the cages.

9. Position the inner bearing cone and roller in the inner cup and install the grease retainer.

10. Carefully position the hub and disc assembly on the spindle.

11. Install the outer bearing cone and roller, and the adjusting nut.

12. Using a torque wrench, tighten the bearing adjusting nut to 50 ft.lb., while rotating the wheel back and forth to seat the bearings.

13. Back off the adjusting nut approximately 90 degrees.

14. Assemble the lock ring by turning the nut to the nearest hole and inserting the dowel pin. Note: The dowel pin must seat in a lock ring hole for proper bearing adjustment and wheel retention.

15. Install the outer lock nut and tighten to 50-80 ft.lb. Final end play of the wheel on the spindle should be 0.001-0.010".

16. Install the pressure spring and driving hub snapring.

17. Apply non-hardening sealer to the seating edge of the grease cap, and install the grease cap.

18. Adjust the brake if it was backed off.

19. Remove the safety stands and lower the vehicle.

Spindle

REMOVAL AND INSTALLATION

All Axles Except the 44-IFS

1. Raise the vehicle and install safety stands.

2. If equipped with free running hubs refer to Manual or Automatic Free Running Hub Removal and Installation and remove the hub assemblies.

3. Remove the wheel bearing lock nut, using Tool T59T-1197-B, or equivalent.

4. Remove the lock ring from the bearing adjusting nut. This can be done with your finger tips or a screwdriver.

5. Using Tool T59T-1197-B, or equivalent, remove the bearing adjusting nut.

6. Remove the caliper and suspend it out of the way.

7. Slide the hub and disc assembly off of the spindle. The outer wheel bearing will slide out as the hub is removed, so be prepared to catch it.

8 Remove the spindle retaining nuts, then carefully remove the spindle from the knuckle studs and axle shaft.

NOTE: The spindle will probably be VERY difficult to remove. First try whacking on the outer end of the spindle with a plastic mallet. If that doesn't break it loose, thread the wheel bearing locking nut on the end of the spindle and assemble a large 2-jawed puller, with the jaws on the locking ring and the threaded stud in the recess in the end of the axle shaft. Tighten the puller while hammering on the back side of the spindle.

9. Clean all old grease from the needle bearings and wipe clean the spindle face that mates with the spindle bore seal.

10. Remove the spindle bore seal, V-seal, and thrust washer from the outer axle shaft. Clean any old grease or dirt from these parts and replace those that show signs of excessive wear. The spindle bearing can be removed with a slide hammer or driven out with a long drift. Install the new bearing with a bearing driver.

11. Using Multi-Purpose Lubricant, Ford Specification ESA-M1C75-B or equivalent, thoroughly lubricate the needle bearing and pack the spindle face that mates with the spindle bore seal.

12. Assemble the V-seal in the spindle bore next to the needle bearing. Assemble the spindle bore seal on the axle shaft.

13. Assemble the spindle with the axle shaft on the knuckle studs. Adjust the retaining nuts to 50-60 ft.lb.

14. Carefully position the hub and disc assembly on the spindle.

15. Install the outer bearing cone and roller, and the adjusting nut.

16. Using Tool T59T-1197-B and a torque wrench, tighten the bearing adjusting nut to 50 ft.lb., while rotating the wheel back and forth to seat the bearings.

17. Back off the adjusting nut approximately 90°.

18. Assemble the lock ring by turning the nut to the nearest hole and inserting the dowel pin.

NOTE: The dowel pin must seat in a lock ring hole for proper bearing adjustment and wheel retention.

19. Install the outer lock nut and tighten to 50-80 ft.lb. Final end play of the wheel on the spindle should be 0.001-0.010" (0.025-0.25mm).

20. Install the pressure spring and riving hub snapring.

21. Apply non-hardening sealer to the seating edge of the grease cap, and install the grease cap.

22. Adjust the brake if it was backed off.

23. Remove the safety stands and lower the vehicle.

FRONT DRIVE AXLE

Axle Shaft and Steering Knuckle

REMOVAL AND INSTALLATION

1980-86 44-IFS

NOTE: This procedure requires the use of special tools.

1. Remove spindle nuts and remove spindle. It may be necessary to tap the spindle with a rawhide or plastic hammer to break the spindle loose. Remove spindle, splash shield and axle shaft assembly.
2. Place the spindle in a vise with a shop towel around the spindle to protect the spindle from damage. Using a slide hammer T50-T-100-A and seal remover, Tool 1175-AC remove the axle shaft seal and then the needle bearing from the spindle bar.
3. If the tie rod has not been removed, then remove cotter key from the tie rod nut and then remove nut. Tap on the tie rod stud to free it from the steering arm.
4. Remove the cotter pin from the top ball joint stud. Loosen the nut on the top stud and the bottom nut inside the knuckle. Remove the top nut.
5. Sharply hit the top stud with a plastic or rawhide hammer to free the knuckle from the tube yoke. Remove and discard bottom nut. Use new nut upon assembly.
6. Remove camber adjuster with Pitman arm puller T64P-3590-F.
7. Place knuckle in vise and remove snapring from bottom ball joint socket if so equipped.
8. Press the bottom ball joint socket from the knuckle with the special tools Receiver Cup Tool (P79P-3010-AG) and C1 Clamp Tool (D79T-3010-A)-B. Remove the top ball joint in the same manner.

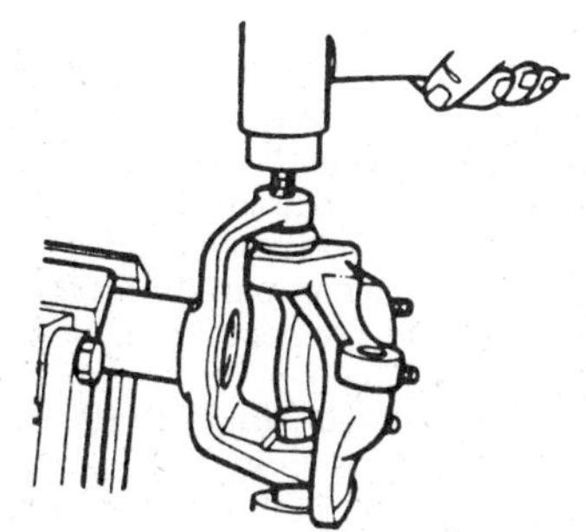

Four-wheel drive steering knuckle removal

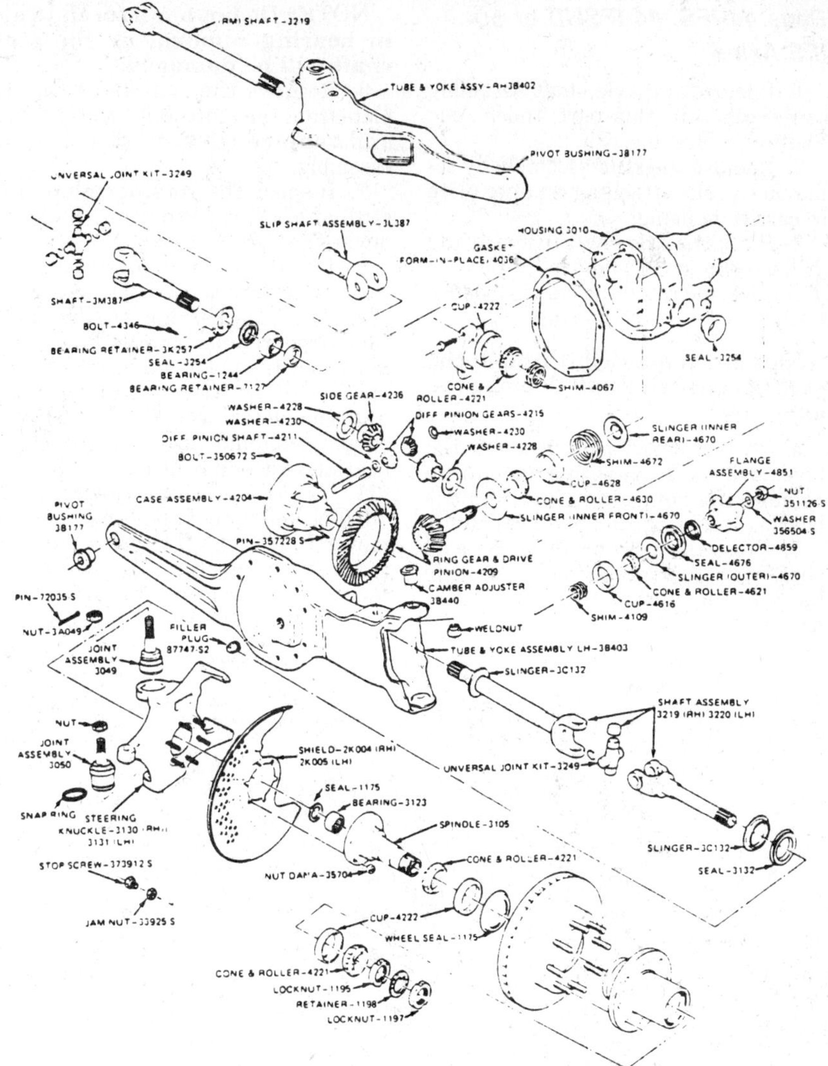

Dana-IFS 44 front axle

NOTE: Always remove bottom ball joint first.

9. Pull out the seal with the appropriate puller tool. Remove and discard seal.
10. Install a new seal on the Differential Seal Replacer Tool T80T-4000-H.
11. Slide the seal and tool into the carrier housing bore. Seat the seal with a plastic or rawhide hammer.
12. Place lower ball joint (stud does not have a cotter key hole in stud) in knuckle and press into position using ball joint installation set T8OT-3010-A.
13. Install upper ball joint (stud has cotter key hole) in knuckle with ball joint installation set T8OT-2010-A.
14. Assemble knuckle to tube and yoke assembly. Install camber adjuster on top ball joint stud with the arrow pointing outboard for positive camber, pointed inboard for negative camber.
15. Install new nut on bottom socket finger tight. Install and tighten nut on top socket finger tight. Tighten bottom nut to 90-110 ft.lb.
16. Tighten top nut to 100 ft.lb., then advance nut until castellation aligns with cotter pin hole. Install cotter pin.

NOTE: Do not loosen top nut to install cotter pin.

17. Remove and install a new needle to bearing in the spindle bore with T8OT-4000-R or S Spindle Bearing replacer and driver handle, T8OT-4000-W. Install a new seal with tool T8OT-400-T or U, Sealer Replacer and T9OT-4000-W Driven Handle.
18. Install the axle shaft assembly into the housing. Install the splash shield and spindle. Install and tighten the spindle attaching nuts.

Axle Shaft Bearing

REMOVAL & INSTALLATION

NOTE: This procedure requires the use of special tools.

Dana 44-IFS, 44-IFSHD or 50-IFS Axles

1. Remove the axle shaft assembly as described in this part under Axle Shaft and Steering Knuckle.
2. Remove the stub assembly by removing 3 bolts attaching retainer plate to carrier housing.
3. Place the axle shaft in a vise and drill a 6.35mm (¼") hole in the outside of the bearing retaining ring to a depth ¾ the thickness of the ring.

NOTE: Do not drill through the ring because this will damage the axle shaft.

4. With a chisel placed across the hole, strike sharply with a hammer to remove the retaining ring. Replace bearing retaining ring upon assembly.
5. Press the bearing from the axle shaft with the special tools T80 axle bearing remover T80T-4000-M and sleeve T80T-4000-L.

NOTE: Do not use a torch to aid in bearing removal or the stub shaft will be damaged.

6. Remove the seal and retainer plate from the stub shaft. Discard seal and replace with new seal upon assembly.
7. Inspect the retainer plate and stub shaft for distortion, nicks or burns. Replace if necessary.
8. Install retainer plate and new seal on shaft. Coat oil seal with grease.
9. Place the bearing on the shaft. The large radius on the inner race must face the yoke end of the shaft.
10. Press the bearing onto the shaft until completely seated. A 0.0015" feeler gauge should not fit between the bearing seat and bearing.
11. Use axle bearing replacer T80T-4000-N and pinion bearing cone remover T71P-4621-B to press the bearing retainer ring onto the stub shaft. Press the bearing retainer ring until completely seated. A 0.038mm (0.0015") feeler gauge should not fit between the ring and bearing. There must be one point between the bearing and ring where the feeler gauge cannot enter. If feeler gauge enters completely around the circumference press the retainer further onto the shaft.
12. Push the seal and retainer plate away from the bearing to form a space between the seal and bearing. Fill the space with wheel bearing grease meeting Ford specification ESA-M1C75B or equivalent.
13. With the space filled with grease, wrap tape around the space.
14. Pull the seal towards the bearing until it contacts the inner race. This will force grease between the rollers and cup. Remove tape.

NOTE: If grease is not visible on the small end of the rollers, repeat Steps 6 through 8 until grease is visible. Install the slip yoke and U-joint to stub shaft.

15. Install the stub shaft in the carrier and install 3 retainer bolts. Torque to 30-40 ft.lb. Install right hand axle shaft assembly into slip yoke.
16. Install splash shield and spindle.

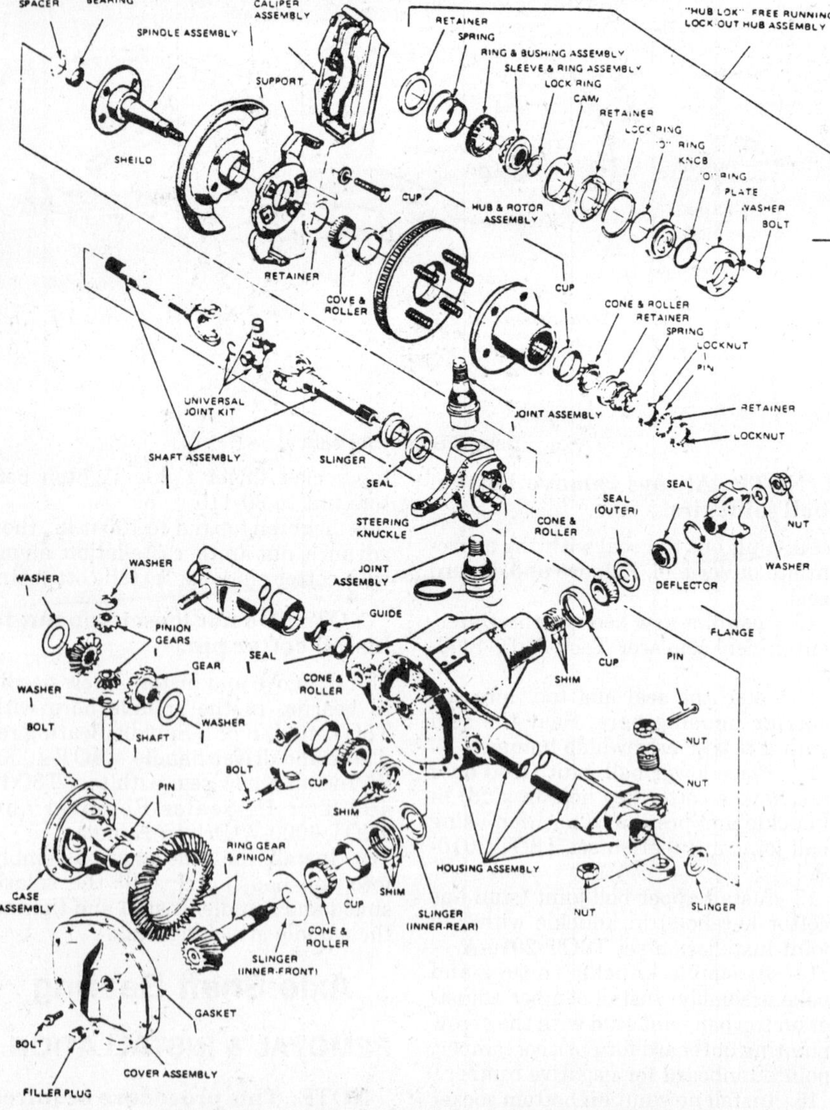

Dana 44F and 44-7F front drive axle—exploded view

Axle Shaft U-Joint Overhaul

Follow the procedures outlined under Axle Shaft Removal and Installation to gain access to the U-joints. Overhaul them as described under U-joints.

Pinion Seal

REMOVAL & INSTALLATION

NOTE: A torque wrench capable of at least 225 ft.lb. is required for pinion seal installation.

CAUTION

Some models use a collapsible spacer to set pinion depth and preload. When replacing the pinion seal always install a new spacer. Never tighten the pinion nut more than 225 ft.lb. or the spacer will be compressed too far.

1. Raise and safely support the vehicle with jackstands under the frame rails. Allow the axle to drop to rebound position for working clearance.
2. Mark the companion flanges and U-joints for correct reinstallation position.
3. Remove the driveshaft. Use a suitable tool to hold the companion flange. Remove the pinion nut and companion flange.
4. Use a slide hammer and hook or

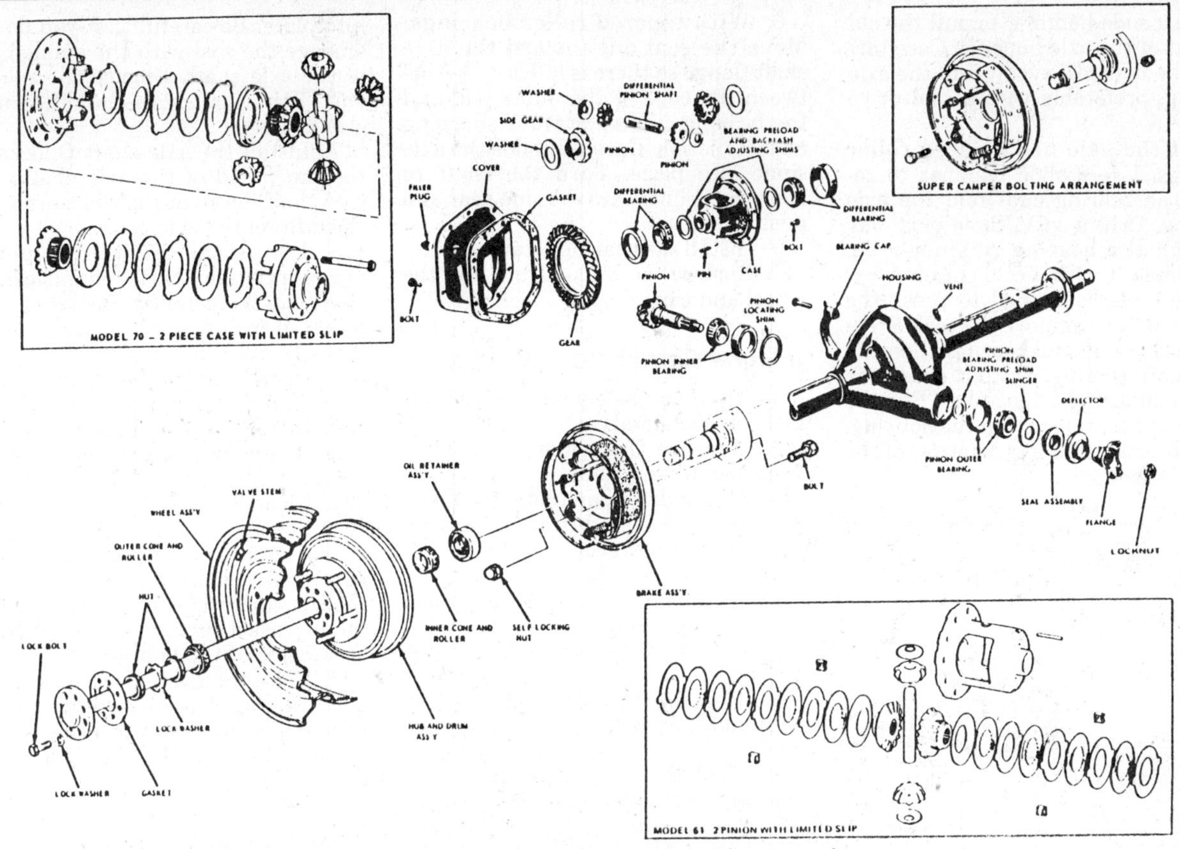

Exploded view of a Dana integral carrier type axle

sheet metal screw to remove the oil seal.

5. If the vehicle uses a collapsible spacer, install new spacer. Install a new pinion seal after lubricating the sealing surfaces. Use a suitable seal driver. Install the companion flange and pinion nut. On models using a spacer, tighten the nut to 225 ft.lb. On other models, pinion nut torque is 200-220 ft.lb.

REAR AXLE

Axle Shaft, Bearing and Seal

REMOVAL & INSTALLATION

Removable Carrier Type

NOTE: The following procedure requires the use of special tools, including a shop press.

1. Raise and support the vehicle. Remove the wheel/tire assembly from the brake drum.
2. Remove the clips which secure the brake drum to the axle flange, then remove the drum from the flange.
3. Working through the hole provided in each axle shaft flange, remove the nuts which secure the wheel bearing retainer plate.
4. Pull the axle shaft assembly out of the axle housing. You may need a slide hammer.

NOTE: The brake backing plate must not be dislodged. Install one nut to hold the plate in place after the axle shaft is removed.

5. If the axle has ball bearings: Loosen the bearing retainer ring by nicking it in several places with a cold chisel, then slide it off the axle shaft. On models equipped with a thick retaining ring drill a ¼-½" hole part way through the ring, then break it with a cold chisel. A hydraulic press is needed to press the bearing off and to press the new one on. Press the new bearing and the new retainer ring on separate-

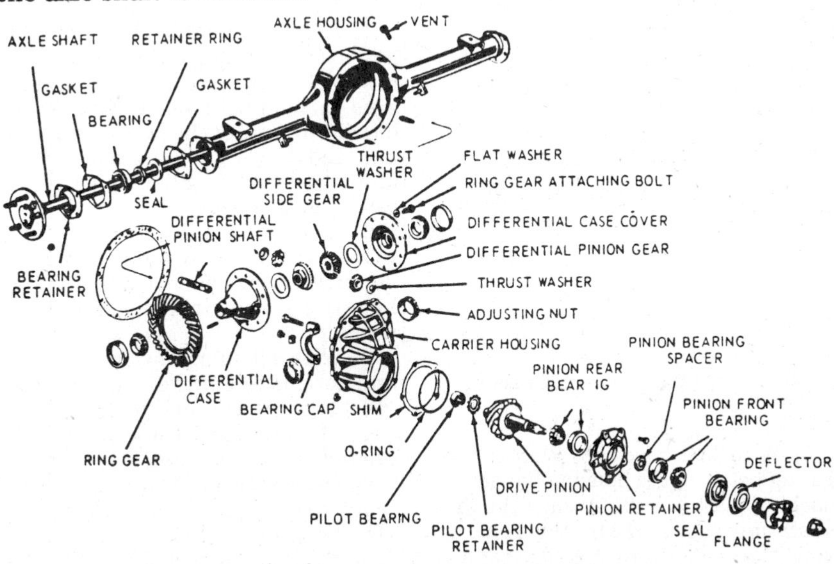

Exploded view of a Ford removable-carrier type axle

ly. Use a slide hammer to pull the old seal out of the axle housing. Carefully drive the new seal evenly into the axle housing, preferably with a seal drive tool.

6. If the axle has tapered roller bearings. Use a slide hammer to remove the bearing cup from the axle housing. Drill a ¼-½" hole part way through the bearing retainer ring, then break it with a cold chisel. A hydraulic press is needed to press the bearing off and remove the seal. Press on the new seal and bearing, then the new retainer ring. Do not press the bearing and ring on together. Put the cup on the bearing, not in the housing, and lubricate the outer diameter of the cup and seal.

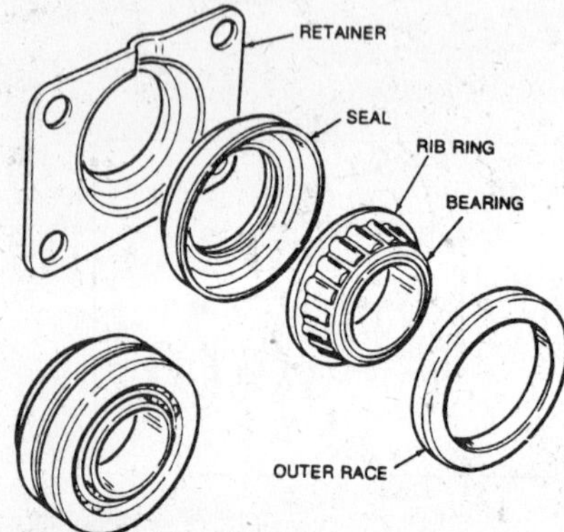

Tapered roller bearings on some E-100, 150 and 200 axle shafts

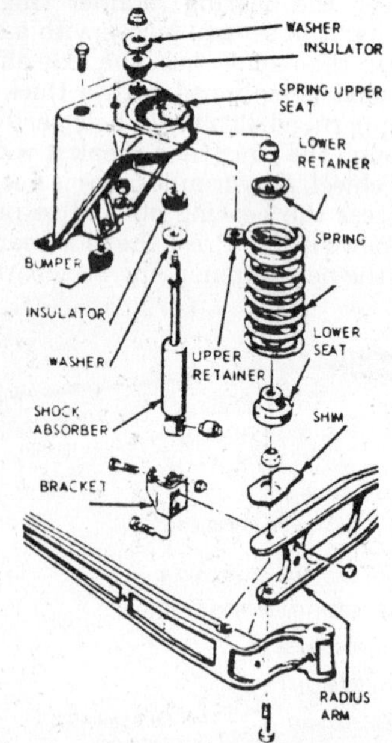

Typical 1980-82 front suspension

7. With ball bearings: Place a new gasket between the housing flange and backing plate. Carefully slide the axle shaft into place. Turn the shaft to start the splines into the side gear and push it in.

8. With tapered roller bearings: Move the seal out toward the axle shaft flange so there is at least $^{3}/_{32}$" between the edge of the outer seal and the bearing cup, to prevent snagging on installation. Carefully slide the axle shaft into place. Turn the shaft to start the splines into the side gear and push it in.

9. Install the bearing retainer plate.

10. Replace the brake drum and the wheel and tire.

Integral Carrier C-Lock Type

1. Raise and safely support the vehicle on jackstands.

2. Remove the wheels and tires from the brake drums.

3. Place a drain pan under the housing and drain the lubricant by loosening the housing cover.

4. Remove the locks securing the brake drums to the axle shaft flanges and remove the drums.

5. Remove the housing cover and gasket.

6. Remove the side gear pinion shaft lockbolt and the side gear pinion shaft.

7.. Push the axle shafts inward and remove the C-locks from the inner end of the axle shafts. Temporarily replace the shaft and lockbolt to retain the differential gears in position.

8. Remove the axle shafts with a slide hammer. Be sure the seal is not damaged by the splines on the axle shaft.

9. Remove the bearing and oil seal from the housing. Both the seal and bearing can be removed with a slide hammer

10. Two types of bearings are used on some axles, one requiring a press fit and the other a loose fit. A loose fitting bearing does not necessarily indicate excessive wear.

11. Inspect the axle shaft housing and axle shafts for burrs or other irregularities. Replace any work or damaged parts. A light yellow color on the bearing journal of the axle shaft is normal, and does not require replacement of the axle shaft. Slight pitting and wear is also normal.

12. Lightly coat the wheel bearing rollers with axle lubricant. Install the bearings in the axle housing until the bearing seats firmly against the shoulder.

13. Wipe all lubricant from the oil seal bore, before installing the seal.

14. Inspect the original seals for wear. If necessary, these may be replaced with new seals, which are prepacked with lubricant and do not require soaking.

15. Install the oil seal.

16. Remove the lockbolt and pinion shaft. Carefully slide the axle shafts into place. Be careful that you do not damage the seal with the splined end of the axle shaft. Engage the splined end of the shaft with the differential side gears.

17. Install the axle shaft C-locks on the inner end of the axle shafts and seat the C-locks in the counterbore of the differential side gears.

18. Rotate the differential pinion gears until the differential pinion shaft can be installed. Install the differential pinion shaft lockbolt. Tighten to 15-22 ft.lb.

19. Install the brake drum on the axle shaft flange.

20. Install the wheel and tire on the brake drum and tighten the attaching nuts.

21. Clean the gasket surface of the rear housing and install a new cover gasket and the housing cover. Some covers do not use a gasket. On these models, apply a bead of silicone sealer on the gasket surface. The bead should run inside of the bolt holes.

22. Raise the rear axle so that it is in the running position. Add the amount of specified lubricant to bring the lubricant level to ½" (12.7mm) below the filler hole.

Full Floating Axle Type

The wheel bearings on the full floating rear axle are packed with wheel bearing grease. Axle lubricant can also flow into the wheel hubs and bearings, however, wheel bearing grease is the primary lubricant. The wheel bearing grease provides lubrication until the axle lubricant reaches the bearings during normal operation.

1. Set the parking brake and loosen the axle shaft bolts.

2. Raise the rear wheels off the floor and place jackstands under the rear axle housing so that the axle is parallel with the floor.

3. Remove the axle shaft bolts.

4. Remove the axle shaft and gaskets.

5. With the axle shaft removed, remove the gasket from the axle shaft flange studs.

6. Bend the lockwasher tab away from the locknut, and then remove the locknut, lockwasher, and the adjusting nut.

7. Remove the outer bearing cone and pull the wheel straight off the axle.

8. With a piece of hardwood which will just clear the outer bearing cup, drive the inner bearing cone and inner seal out of the wheel hub.

9. Wash all the old grease or axle lubricant out of the wheel hub, using a suitable solvent.

10. Wash the bearing cups and rollers and inspect them for pitting, gall-

ing, and uneven wear patterns. Inspect the roller for end wear.

11. If the bearing cups are to be replaced, drive them out with a drift. Install the new cups with a block of wood and hammer or press them in.

12. If the bearing cups are properly seated, a 0.0015" feeler gauge will not fit between the cup and the wheel hub.

13. Pack each bearing cone and roller with a bearing packer or in the manner previously outlined for the front wheel bearings on 2-Wheel Drive trucks.

14. Place the inner bearing cone and roller assembly in the wheel hub. Install a new inner seal in the hub.

15. Install the wheel.

16. Install and tighten the bearing adjusting nut to 50-80 ft.lb. while rotating the wheel.

17. Back off (loosen) the adjusting nut ⅜ of a turn.

18. Apply axle lube to a new lockwasher and install it with the smooth side out.

19. Install the locknut and tighten it to 90-110 ft.lb. The wheel must rotate freely after the locknut is tightened. The wheel end-play should be within 0.001-0.010".

20. Bend two lockwasher tabs inward over an adjusting nut flat and two lockwasher tabs outward over the locknut flat.

21. Install the axle shaft, gasket, lockbolts, and washers. Tighten the bolts to 40-50 ft.lb.

22. Adjust the brakes, if necessary.

Differential Carrier

REMOVAL

Removable Type Carrier Only

NOTE: The C-Lock type carrier is not removable.

1. Raise the vehicle on a hoist and remove the two rear wheel and tire assemblies.

2. Remove the brake drums from the axle shaft flange studs (back off the brake shoes to make drum removal easier).

3. Working through the access hole provided in each axle shaft flange, remove the nuts that secure the rear wheel bearing retainer plate. Pull each axle shaft assembly out of the axle housing using axle shaft puller adapter, Tool T66L-4234-A or equvalent. Wire the brake backing plate to the frame rail. Remove the gasket and discard, if so equipped.

NOTE: Whenever a rear axle is replaced, The wheel bearing oil seals must be replace. Remove the seals with seal remover, Tool 1175-AC or equivalent (if roller bearing equipped this need not be done).

4. Make scribe marks on the driveshaft end yoke and the axle companion flange to insure proper position at assembly. Disconnect the driveshaft at the rear axle U-joint. Hold the cups on the spider with tape. Mark the cups so that they will be in their original position relative to the flange when they are assembled. Remove the driveshaft from the transmission extension housing. Install an oil seal replacer tool in the housing to prevent transmission leakage.

5. Clean area around carrier to housing surfaces with a wire brush and wipe clean, to prevent dirt entry into the housing. Place a drain pan under the carrier and housing, remove the carrier attaching nuts and washers, and drain the axle. Remove the carrier assembly from the axle housing.

NOTE: Synthetic Type wheel bearing seals must not be cleaned, soaked or washed in cleaning solvent.

INSTALLATION

1. Clean the axle housing and shaft using kerosene and swabs. To avoid contamination of the of the grease in the sealed ball bearings, do not allow any quantity of solvent directly on the wheel bearings. Clean the mating surfaces of the axle housing and carrier.

2. Position the differential carrier on the studs in the axle housing using a new gasket between the carrier and the housing. To insure a good seal, apply a bead of Silicone Rubber Sealant (D6AZ-19562-A or B). to the gasket. Install the carrier to housing attaching nuts and washers, tighten them to 25-40 ft.lb.

3. Remove the oil seal replacer tool from the transmission extension housing. Position the driveshaft so that the U-joint slip yoke splines to the transmission output shaft.

4. Connect the driveshaft to the axle U-joint flange, aligning the scribe marks made on the driveshaft end yoke and the axle U-joint flange during the removal procedure. Install the U-bolts and nuts and tighten them to specifications.

5. Install the two axle shaft assemblies in the axle housing. Care must be exercised to prevent damage to the oil seals. Carefully slide the axle shaft into the housing so that the rough forging of the shaft will not damage the oil seal. Timken bearing axle shafts do not require a gasket. Start the axle splines into the differential side gear, and push the shaft in until the bearing bottoms in the housing.

6. Install the bearing retainer plates on the attaching bolts and alternately tighten them to 20-40 ft.lb.

7. Install the two rear brake drums.

8. Install the rear wheel and tire assemblies.

9. If the rear brake shoes were backed off, adjust the brakes.

10. Fill the rear axle with the specified lubricant.

Axle Housing

REMOVAL & INSTALLATION

1. Remove the carrier assembly from the axle housing as outlined in the above procedure.

2. Position safety stands under the rear frame members, and support the housing with either a floor jack or hoist.

3. Disengage the brake line from the clips that retain the line to the housing.

4. Disconnect the vent tube from the housing.

5. Remove the brake backing plate from the housing, and support them with wire. Do not disconnect the brake line.

6. Disconnect each rear shock absorber from the mounting bracket stud on the housing.

7. Lower the axle slightly to reduce some of the spring tension. At each rear spring, remove the spring clip (U-bolt) nuts, spring clips, and spring seat caps.

8. Remove the housing from under the vehicle.

To Install:

1. Position the axle housing under the rear springs. Install the spring clips (U-bolts), spring seat clamps and nuts. Tighten the spring clamps evenly to specifications.

2. If a new axle housing is being installed, remove the bolts that attach the brake backing plate and bearing retainer from the old housing flanges. Position the bolts in the new housing flanges to hold the brake backing plates in position.

3. Connect the vent tube to the housing.

4. Position the brake line to the housing, and secure it with the retaining clips.

5. Raise the axle housing and springs enough to allow connecting the rear shock absorbers to the mounting bracket studs on the housing.

6. Install the carrier assembly and the two axle shaft assemblies in the housing as described in the previous procedure.

FRONT SUSPENSION

Springs

REMOVAL & INSTALLATION

2-Wheel Drive

1. Raise the front of the vehicle and place jackstands under the frame and a jack under the axle. Remove wheel and tire assemblies. Remove the brake calipers and suspend with wire so that there is no tension on the brake hose.
2. Disconnect the shock absorber from the lower bracket.
3. Remove the lower spring retainer.
4. Remove the two spring upper retainer attaching bolts from the top of the spring upper seat and remove the retainer.
5. Remove the nut attaching the spring lower retainer to the lower seat and axle and remove the retainer.
6. Lower the axle and remove the spring. Some downward pressure using a prybar may be required.
7. Place the spring in position and raise the front axle.
8. Position the spring lower retainer over the stud and lower seat, and install the two attaching bolts.
9. Position the upper retainer over the spring coil and against the spring upper seat, and install the two attaching bolts.
10. Tighten the upper and lower retainer attaching nuts and bolts to 15-25 ft.lb.
11. Connect the shock absorber to the lower bracket and install the rebound bracket.
12. Remove the jack and safety stands.

Bronco, and 4-Wheel Drive F-150

1. Raise the vehicle and remove the shock absorber lower attaching bolt and nut.
2. Remove the spring lower retainer nuts from inside of the spring coil.
3. Remove the upper spring retainer by removing the attaching screw.
4. Position safety stands under the frame side rails and lower the axle enough to relieve tension from the spring.

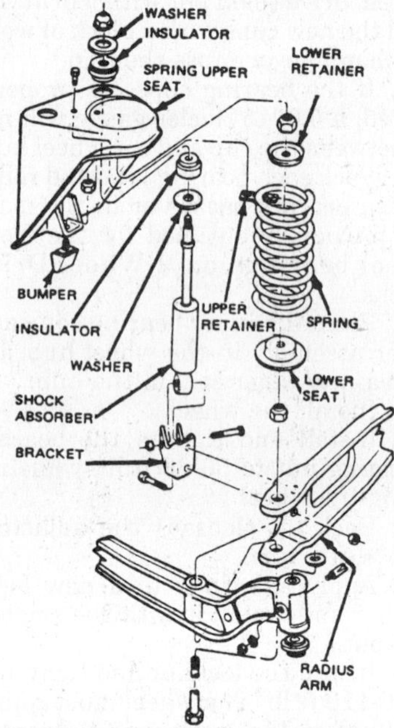

Exploded view of the front spring assembly and shock absorber for 2WD Ford pick-ups – typical

NOTE: The axle must be supported on the jack throughout spring removal, and must not be permitted to hang from the brake hose. If the length of the brake hose does not provide sufficient clearance it may be necessary to remove and support the brake caliper.

5. Remove the spring lower retainer and lower the spring from the vehicle.
6. To install place the spring in position and slowly raise the front axle. Make sure the springs are positioned correctly in the upper spring seats.
7. Install the lower spring retainer and torque the nut to 50 ft.lb.
8. Position the upper retainer over the spring coil and install the attaching screws.
9. Position the shock absorber to the lower bracket and torque the attaching bolt and nut to 53 ft.lb.
10. Remove the safety stands and lower the vehicle.

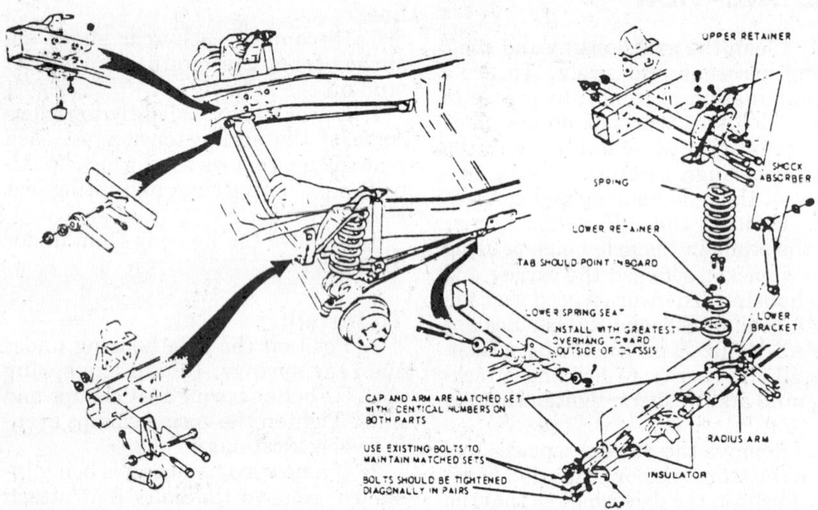

Exploded view of the front spring assembly and shock absorber – F-100-150 4WD – typical

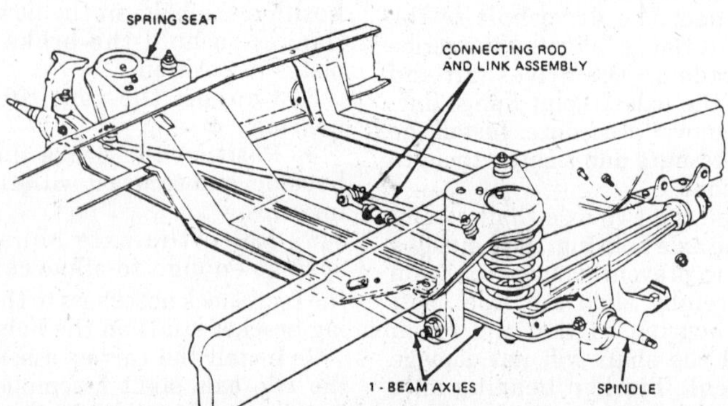

Twin I-beam suspension (forged axle shown) – 2WD

4-Wheel Drive F-250 and F-350

1. Raise the vehicle frame until the weight is off the front spring with the wheels still touching the floor. Support the axle to prevent rotation.
2. Disconnect the lower end of the shock absorber from the U-bolt spacer. Remove the U-bolts, U-bolt cap and spacer.
3. Remove the nut from the hanger bolt retaining the spring at the rear and drive out the hanger bolt.

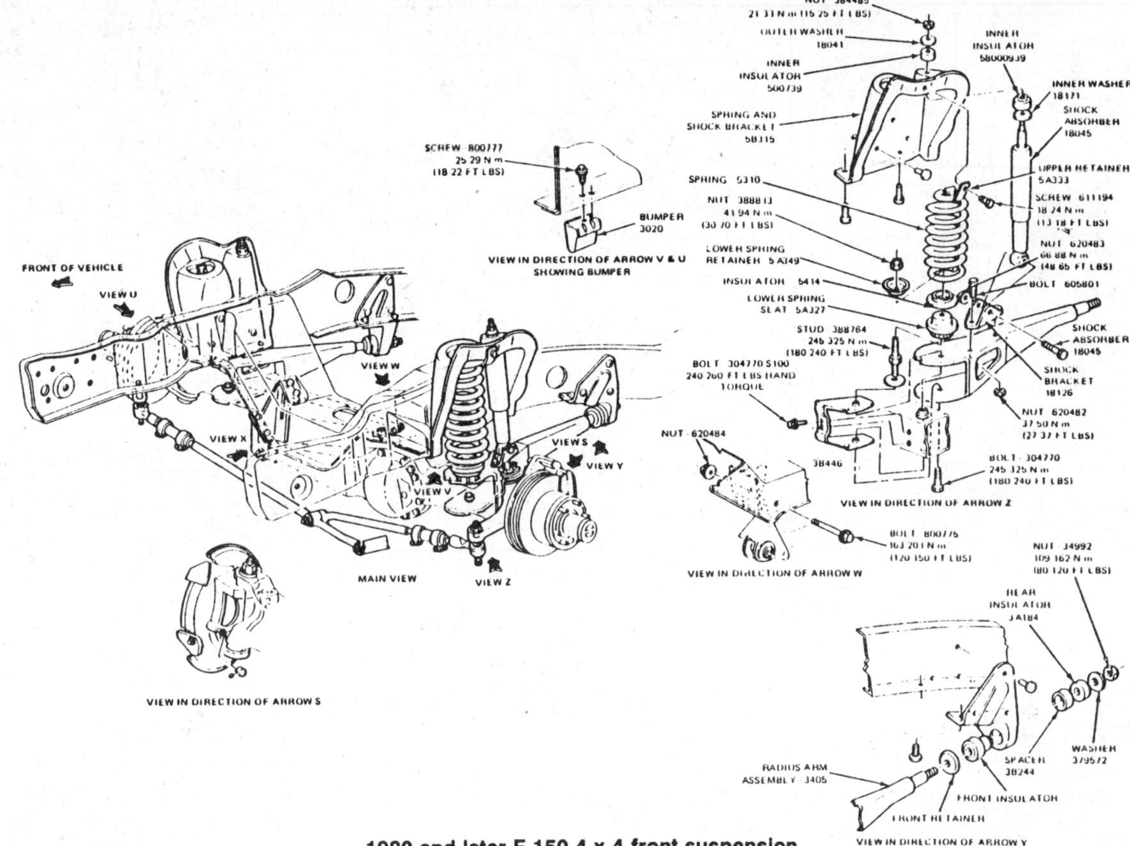

1980 and later F-150 4 x 4 front suspension

4. Remove the nut connecting the front shackle and spring eye and drive out the shackle bolt and remove the spring.
5. To install position the spring on the spring seat. Install the shackle bolt through the shackle and spring. Torque the nuts to 135 ft.lb.
6. Position the rear of the spring and install the hanger bolt. Torque the nut to 175 ft.lb.
7. Position the U-bolt spacer and place the U-bolts in position through the holes in the spring seat cap. Install but do not tighten the U-bolt nuts.
8. Connect the lower end of the shock absorber to the U-bolt spacer.
9. Lower the vehicle and tighten the U-bolt nuts to 100 ft.lb.

Shock Absorbers

TESTING

1. Visually check the shock absorbers for the presence of fluid leakage. A thin film of fluid is acceptable. Anything more than that means that the shock absorber must be replaced.
2. Disconnect the lower end of the shock absorber. Compress and extend the shock fully as fast as possible. If the action is not smooth in both directions, or there is no pressure resistance, replace the shock absorber. Shock absorbers should be replaced in pairs if they have accumulated more than 20,000 miles of wear. In the case of relatively new shock absorbers, where one has failed, that one, along, may be replaced.

REMOVAL & INSTALLATION

2-Wheel Drive

1. Insert a wrench from the rear side of the upper spring seat to hold the upper shock retaining nut. Loosen the stud by using another wrench on the hex on the shaft.
2. Remove the bolt and nut at the lower end.
3. On installation, make sure to get the washers and insulators in the right place. Tighten the upper nut by turning the hex on the shaft Replace the lower bolt. It is recommended that new rubber insulators be used.

4-Wheel Drive

1. Remove the bolt and nut attaching the shock absorber to the lower bracket on the radius arm.
2. Remove the nut, washer and insulator from the shock absorber at the frame bracket and remove the shock absorber.
3. Position the washer and insulator on the shock absorber rod and position the shock absorber to the frame bracket.
4. Position the insulator and washer on the shock absorber rod and install the attaching nut loosely.
5. Position the shock absorber to the lower bracket and install the attaching bolt and nut loosely.
6. Tighten the lower attaching bolts to 40-70 ft.lb., and the upper attaching bolts to 25-30 ft.lb.

2-Wheel Drive Front Wheel Spindle and King Pin

REMOVAL & INSTALLATION

1. Raise the front of the truck until the front wheel clears the ground and place jackstands under the frame.
2. Remove the wheel and tire.
3. Remove the caliper key retaining screw. Drive out the caliper support key and spring with brass drift and hammer. Remove the caliper from the spindle by pushing the caliper downward against the spindle assembly and rotating the upper end of the caliper upward and out of the spindle assembly. It is not necessary to disconnect the brake fluid hose. Wire the caliper to a suspension part to remove the

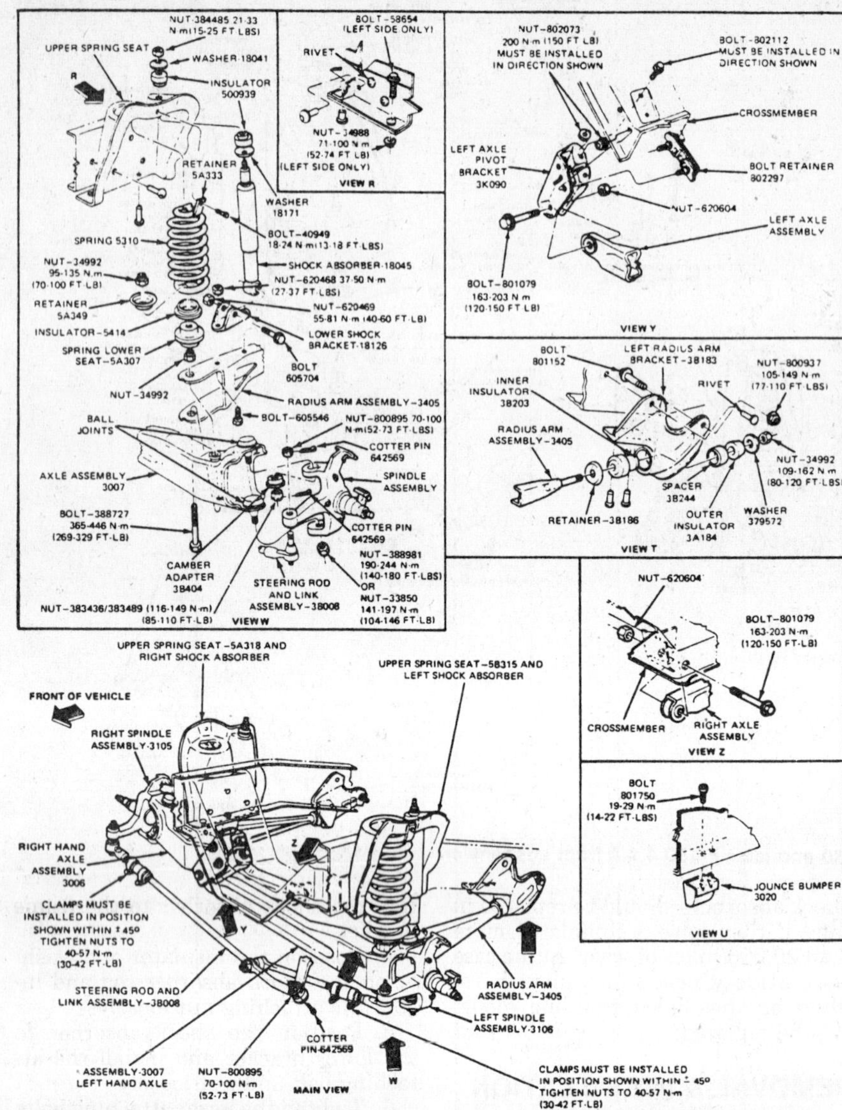

F-100/F-150 stamped front axle. View "W" shows ball joint spindle mounting

weight of the caliper from the hose. Disconnect the steering linkage from the spindle arm.

4. Disconnect the steering linkage from the integral spindle and spindle arm.

5. Remove the nut and lockwasher from the locking pin, and remove the locking pin.

6. Remove the upper and lower spindle bolt plugs, and drive the spindle bolt out from the top of the axle. Remove the spindle and bearing. Knock out the seal.

7. Make sure that the spindle bolt hole in the axle is free of nicks, burrs, and dirt. Install a new seal and coat the spindle bolt bushings and bolt hole with oil.

8. Place the spindle in position on the axle.

9. Pack the spindle thrust bearing with chassis lubricant and insert the bearing into the spindle with the open end of the bearing seal facing down into the spindle.

10. Install the spindle pin in the spindle with the locking pin notch in the spindle bolt aligned with the locking pin hole in the axle. Drive the spindle bolt through the axle from the top side until the spindle bolt locking pin notch is aligned with the locking pin hole.

11. Install a new locking pin. Install the locking pin lockwasher and nut. Tighten the nut to 40-55 ft.lb. Install the spindle bolt plugs at the top and bottom of the spindle bolt.

12. Position the caliper on the spindle assembly. Be careful to prevent tearing or cutting of the piston boot as the caliper is slipped over the inner brake pad. Use a screwdriver or brake adjusting tool to hold the upper machined surface of the caliper against the surface of the spindle. Install the caliper support spring and key. Drive the key and spring into position with a soft hammer. Install the key retaining screw and tighten it to 12-18 ft.lb. Connect the steering linkage to the spindle and tighten the nut to 50-70 ft.lb. advancing the nut as necessary to install the cotter pin.

13. Install the wheel.

14. Grease the spindle assembly with a grease gun.

15. Check and adjust, if necessary, the toe-in adjustment.

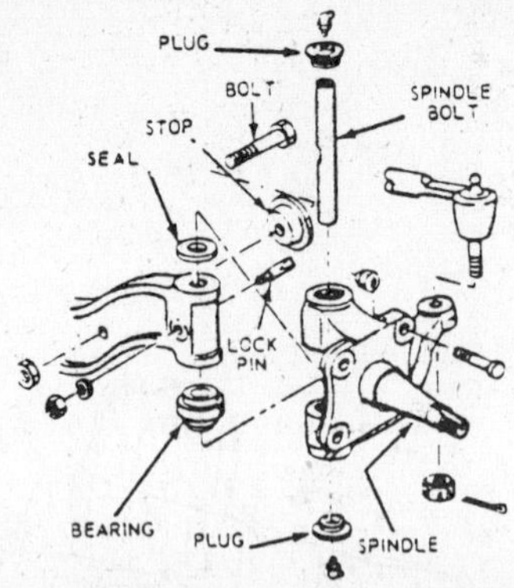

Spindle installation on heavy-duty 2WD F-250

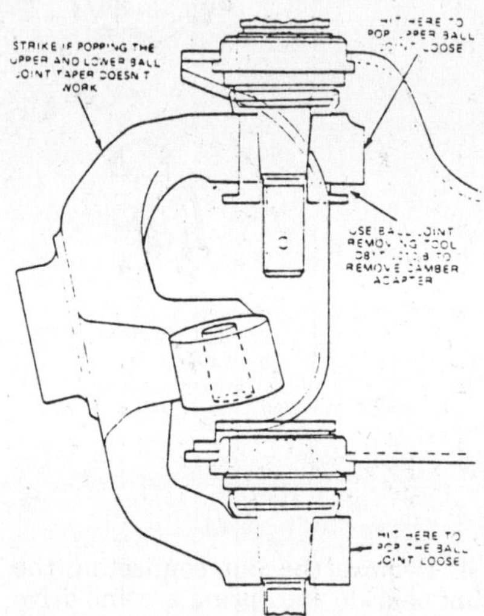

Spindle removal, 2WD F-100/F-150 with ball-joint type stamped front axles

Front Wheel Spindle Stamped I-Beam with Ball Joints

REMOVAL & INSTALLATION

Spindle

1. Raise the front of the vehicle and install safety stands. Remove the wheel and tire assembly.

2. Remove the caliper assembly from the rotor and hold it out of the way with wire.

3. Remove the dust cap, cotter pin, nut retainer, nut, washer, and outer bearing, and remove the rotor from the spindle.

4. Remove inner bearing cone and seal. Discard the seal. Remove brake dust shield.

5. Disconnect the steering linkage from the integral spindle and spindle arm by removing the cotter pin and nut and then removing the tie rod end from the spindle arm.

6. Remove the cotter pins from the upper and lower ball joint studs. Remove the nuts from the upper and lower ball joint stud.

7. Strike the inside area of the spindle to pop the ball joints loose from the spindle.

WARNING: Do not use a pickle fork to separate the ball joint from the spindle as this will damage the seal and the ball joint socket.

8. Remove the spindle.

9. Prior to assembly, make sure the upper and lower ball joint seals are in place. Place the spindle over the ball joints.

10. Install the nut on the lower ball joint stud and partially tighten to 30 ft.lb. Advance the castellated nut as required and install the cotter pin. If the lower ball stud turns while the nut is being tightened, push the spindle up against the ball stud. The lower nut must be tightened first.

11. Install the camber adapter in the upper spindle over the upper ball joint stud. Be sure the adapter is aligned properly.

12. Install the nut on the upper ball joint stud. Hold the camber adaptor with a wrench to keep the ball stud from turning. If the ball stud turns, tap the adaptor deeper into the spindle. Tighten the nut to 85-110 ft.lb. and continue tightening the castellated nut until it lines up with the hole in the stud. Install the cotter pin.

13. Retighten lower nut to 140-180 ft.lb. Install the dust shield.

14. Pack the inner and outer bearing cone with C1AZ-19590-B (ESA-M1C75-B) or equivalent bearing grease. Use a bearing packer. If a bearing packer is unavailable, pack the bearing cone by hand working the grease through the cage behind the rollers.

15. Install the inner bearing cone and seal. Install the hub and rotor on the spindle.

16. Install the outer bearing cone, washer, and nut. Adjust bearing end play and install the nut retainer, cotter pin and dust cap.

17. Install the caliper.

18. Connect the steering linkage to the spindle. Tighten the nut to 52-73 ft.lb. and advance the nut as required for installation of the cotter pin.

19. Install the wheel and tire assembly. Lower the vehicle.

20. Check and, if necessary adjust the toe setting.

Camber Adjuster

1. Remove the cotter pin and nut from the upper ball joint stud.

2. Strike the inside of the spindle to pop the upper ball joint from the spindle.

3. If the upper ball joint does not pop loose, remove the cotter pin and back the lower ball joint nut about half way down the lower ball joint stud, and strike the side of the lower spindle.

4. Remove the camber adapter (camber adjustment sleeve) using Ball Joint Removing Tool (D81T-3010-B) or equivalent.

5. Install the correct adaptor in the spindle. On the right spindle the adaptor slot must point forward to make a positive camber change or rearward for a negative camber change. On the left spindle, the adaptor slot must point rearward for a positive camber change and forward for a negative change.

6. If both nuts were loosened, completely remove the spindle, and reinstall. Be sure the lower ball joint stud is always tightened before the upper nut. Apply Locktite No. 242 (D5AZ-19554-A) or equivalent to stud threads before installing nut.

7. If only the upper ball joint stud nut was removed, install the nut and tighten to 85-110 ft.lb. and continue tightening the castellated nut until it lines up with the hole in the upper stud. Install the cotter pin.

Ball Joints

1. Remove the spindle as described previously.

2. Remove snapring from ball joints. Assemble C-Frame puller and adapters on upper ball joint. Turn forcing screw clockwise until ball joint is removed from axle. Always remove upper ball joint first. Do not heat the ball joint or the axle to aid in removal.

3. Assemble C-Frame assembly and receiver cup on lower ball joint and turn forcing screw clockwise until ball joint is removed.

4. To install the lower ball joint, assemble C-Frame puller and adaptors. Turn forcing screw clockwise until ball joint is seated. Lower ball joint must be installed first. Do not heat the ball joint or axle to aid in installation.

5. Install the snapring onto the ball joint. To install the upper ball joint, assemble the C-frame and repeat Steps 1 and 2.

6. Install the spindle.

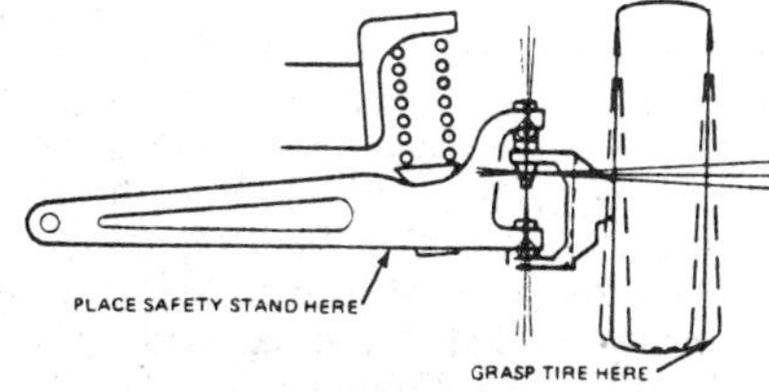

Check ball joint wear by pulling in and out on either the bottom of the tire (to check lower ball joints) or the top of the tire (to check the upper joints)

Front Wheel Spindle w/4-Wheel Drive

REMOVAL & INSTALLATION

NOTE: This procedure also includes bearing and seal replacement and repacking.

1. Raise the vehicle and install safety stands.

2. If equipped with manual locking hubs remove the hubs as follows: Remove the six socket heat bolts from the cap assembly and separate the cap assembly from the body. Remove the snapring from the end of the axle shaft. Remove the lock ring seated in the groove of the wheel hub and slide the body assembly out of the wheel hub.

3. If equipped with automatic locking hubs remove the hubs as follows: Remove the bolts and remove the hub cap assembly from the spindle. Remove the bolt from the end of the shaft. Remove the lock ring seated in the groove of the wheel hub. Remove the body assembly from the spindle. Use a puller if necessary. Unscrew all three set screws in the spindle locknut until the heads are flush with the edge of the locknut. Remove the outer spindle locknut with tool T80T-4000-V, automatic hub locknut wrench.

4. Remove the front hub grease cap and driving hub snapring.

5. Remove the splined driving hub and the pressure spring. Slightly pry off if necessary.

6. Remove the wheel bearing locknut, lock ring and adjusting nut using special tool T59T-1197-B or equivalent.

7. Remove the hub and disc assembly. The outer wheel bearing and spring retainer will slide out as the hub is removed.

8. Remove the spindle nuts and remove the spindle, splash shield and axle shaft assembly.

NOTE: It may be necessary to break the spindle loose with a plastic hammer.

9. Clean all old grease from the needle bearings and wipe clean the spindle face that mates with the spindle bore seal.

10. Remove the spindle bore seal, V-seal, and thrust washer from the outer axle shaft. Clean and replace if necessary.

11. Using Multi-Purpose Lubricant Ford ESA-M1C75-B or equivalent, thoroughly lubricate the needle bearing and pack the spindle face that mates with the spindle bore seal.

12. Position the V-seal in the spindle bore next to the needle bearing. Assemble the spindle bore seal on the axle shaft.

13. Assemble the spindle with the axle shaft on the knuckle studs and tighten the retaining nuts to 75 ft.lb.

14. Carefully drive the inner bearing cone and grease seal out of the hub using tool T77F-1102-A or equivalent.

15. Inspect the inner bearing cups and if necessary remove with a drift.

NOTE: If new cups are installed, install new bearings.

16. Lubricate the bearings with the lubricant specified earlier and clean all old grease from the hub. Pack the cones and rollers with lubricant. Try to pack as much as possible between the rollers and the cages.

17. Position the inner bearing cone and roller in the inner cup and install the grease retainer.

18. Install the hub and disc assembly on the spindle.

19. Install the outer bearing cone and roller, and the adjusting nut.

20. Using tool T59T-1197-B or equivalent and a torque wrench tighten the bearing adjusting nut to 50 ft.lb. while rotating the wheel back and forth. Back off the adjusting nut no more than 90°.

21. Assemble the lock ring by turning the nut to the nearest hole and inserting the dowel pin.

NOTE: The dowel pin must seat in the lock ring hole for proper bearing adjustment and wheel retention.

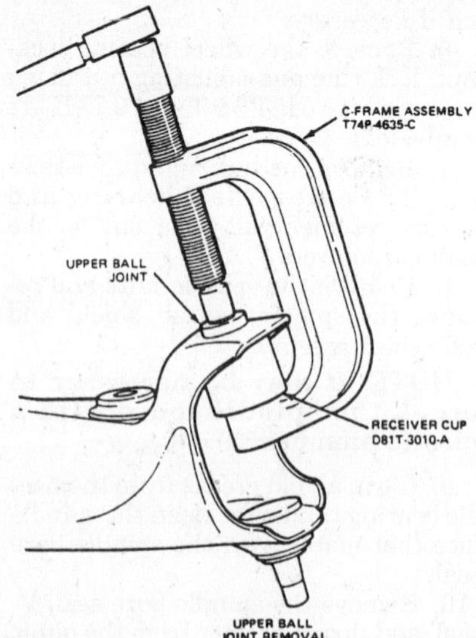

Upper ball joint removal; lower ball joint removal similar

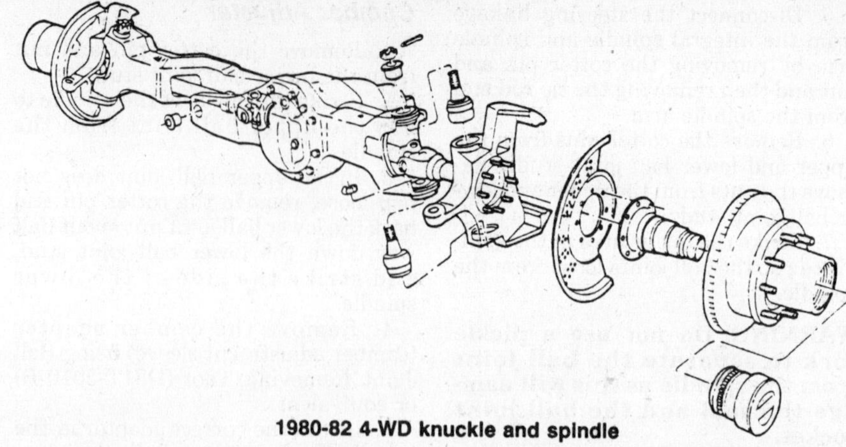

1980-82 4-WD knuckle and spindle

22. Install the outer lock nut and tighten to 65 ft.lb. Final end play on the wheel and spindle should be 0.001-0.006″.

23. Adjust the brake if necessary and lower the vehicle.

4-Wheel Drive Knuckle and Ball Joint

REPLACEMENT

NOTE: A combination ball joint puller/press and a special spanner wrench are needed for this job. If these aren't available the job should not be attempted.

1. Follow the procedures under Axle Shaft Removal.

2. Disconnect the connecting rod end from the knuckle.

3. Remove the cotter pin from the upper ball socket and loosen the upper and lower ball socket nuts. Discard the nut from the lower ball socket after the knuckle breaks loose from the yoke.

4. Remove the knuckle from the yoke. If the upper socket remains in the yoke, remove it by hitting the top of the stud with a soft-faced hammer. Discard the socket and adjusting sleeve.

5. Remove the bottom socket with a ball joint puller (available at most auto parts stores) after first removing the snapring.

6. For installation: Place the knuckle in a vise and assemble the bottom socket. Place the new socket into the knuckle making sure it isn't cocked, place the driver over the socket, place the forcing screw into the socket and force the socket into the knuckle.

7. Make sure that the socket shoulder is seated against the knuckle. Use a 0.0015″ feeler gauge between the socket seat and the knuckle.

8. The gauge should not enter the area of minimum contact. Install the snapring.

9. Assemble the top socket into the knuckle. Assemble the holding plate onto the backing plate screw. Tighten the nuts snugly. Place a new socket into the knuckle. Be sure it is not cocked. Place a driver over the socket and force the socket assembly into the knuckle. Using a 0.0015″ gauge, check the fit at the shoulder. The gauge should not enter the area of minimum wrench.

10. Install a new adjusting sleeve into the top of the yoke leaving about two threads exposed.

11. Assemble the knuckle and yoke. Install a new nut on the bottom socket and make it finger tight.

12. Place a wrench and step plate over the adjusting sleeve and install the puller so that it grasps the step plate. Tighten the forcing screw to pull the knuckle assembly into the yoke. With torque still applied, tighten the nut to 70-90 ft.lb. If the bottom stud should turn with the nut, add more torque to the puller forcing screw. Remove the puller, step plate and holding plate.

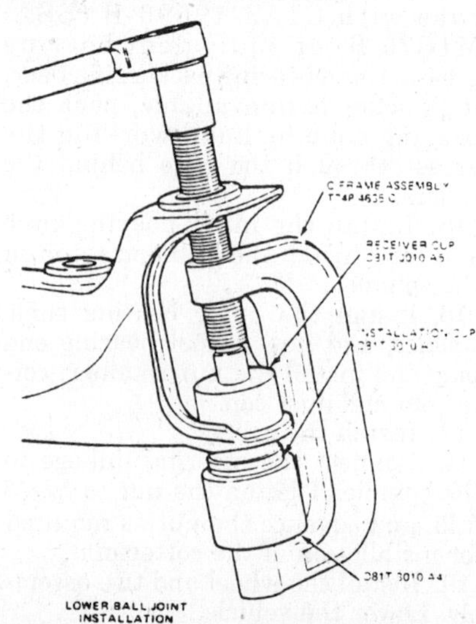

F-100/F-150 lower ball joint installation; upper joint similar

13. Tighten the adjusting sleeve to 40 ft.lb. and remove the wrench.
14. Install the top socket nut and torque it to 100 ft.lb. Line up the cotter pin hole by tightening, not loosening, the nut. Install the cotter pin and test the steering effort with a spring scale attached to the knuckle. Pull should not exceed 26 ft.lb. If it does, the ball joints will have to be replaced.
15. Connect the steering linkage to the knuckle. Torque it to 40 ft.lb.
16. Install the axle shaft as described in the Axle Shaft Removal and Installation procedure.

Radius Arm

REMOVAL & INSTALLATION

All Except Bronco, and 4-Wheel Drive F-150

1. Raise the front of the vehicle and place safety stands under the frame and a jack under the wheel or axle.
2. Disconnect the shock absorber from the radius arm bracket.
3. Remove the two spring upper retainer attaching bolts from the top of the spring upper seat and remove the retainer.
4. Remove the nut which attaches the spring lower retainer to the lower seat and axle and remove the retainer.
5. Lower the axle and remove the spring.
6. Disconnect the steering rod from the spindle arm.
7. Remove the spring lower seat and shim from the radius arm. Then, remove the bolt and nut which attach the radius arm to the axle.
8. Remove the cotter pin, nut and washer from the radius arm rear attachment.
9. Remove the bushing from the radius arm and remove the radius arm from the vehicle.
10. Remove the inner bushing from the radius arm.
11. Position the radius arm to the axle and install the bolt and nut finger-tight.
12. Install the inner bushing on the radius arm and position the arm to the frame bracket.
13. Install the bushing, washer, and attaching nut. Tighten the nut and install the cotter pin.
14. Connect the steering rod to the spindle arm and install the attaching nut. Tighten the radius arm-to-axle attaching bolt and nut.

4-Wheel Drive F-150

1. Raise the vehicle and position safety stands under the frame side rails.
2. Remove the shock absorber lower attaching bolt and nut and pull the shock absorber free of the radius arm.
3. Remove the lower spring retaining bolt from the inside of the spring coil.
4. Remove the nut attaching the radius arm to the frame bracket and remove the radius arm rear insulator. Lower the axle and allow the axle to move forward.

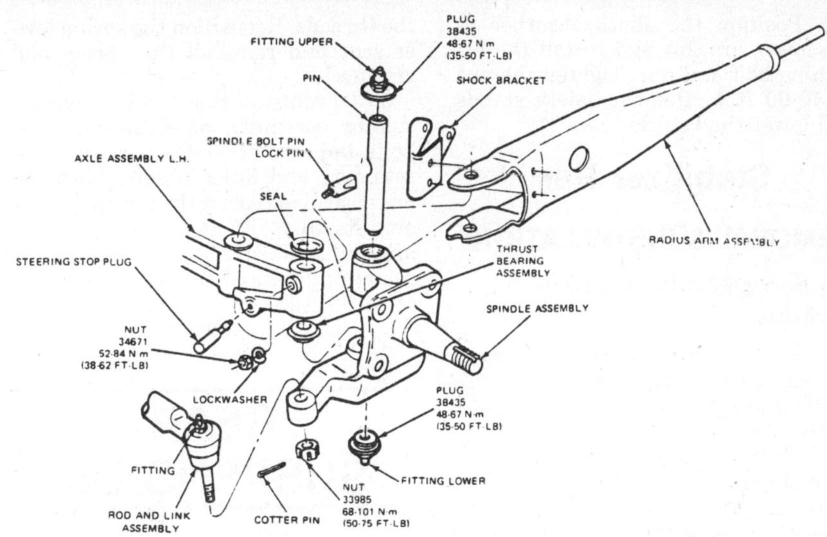

Radius arm removal, king-pin type (forged) front axle shown

NOTE: The axle must be supported on the jack throughout spring removal, and must not be permitted to hang from the brake hose. If the length of the brake hose does not provide sufficient clearance it may be necessary to remove and support the brake caliper.

5. Remove the bolt and stud attaching the radius arm to the axle.
6. Move the axle forward and remove the radius arm from the axle. Then, pull the radius arm from the frame bracket.
7. Installation is the reverse of removal. Install new bolts and the stud type bolt which attach the radius arm to the axle and tighten to 210 ft.lb. Tighten the radius arm rear attaching nut to 100 ft.lb.

Bronco

1. Raise the vehicle and position safety stands under the frame side rails.
2. Remove the shock absorber-to-lower bracket attaching bolt and nut and pull the shock absorber free of the radius arm.
3. Remove spring lower retainer attaching bolt from inside of the spring coil.
4. Remove the nut attaching the radius arm to the frame bracket and remove the radius arm rear insulator. Lower the axle and allow axle to move forward.

WARNING: The axle must be supported on the jack throughout spring removal and installation, and must not be permitted to hang by the brake hose. If the length of the brake hose is not sufficient to provide adequate clearance for removal and installation of the spring, the disc brake caliper must be removed from the spindle. After removal, the caliper must be placed on the frame or otherwise supported to prevent suspending the caliper from the caliper hose. These precautions are absolutely necessary to prevent serious damage to the tube portion of the caliper hose assembly!

5. Remove the bolt and stud attaching radius arm to axle.
6. Move the axle forward and remove the radius arm from the axle. Then, pull the radius arm from the frame bracket.
7. Position the washer and insulator on the rear of the radius arm and insert the radius arm into the frame bracket.
8. Position the rear insulator and washer on the radius arm and loosely install the attaching nut.
9. Position the radius arm to the axle.
10. Install new bolts and study-type bolt attaching radius arm to axle. Tighten to 180-240 ft.lb.
11. Position the spring lower seat, spring insulator and retainer to the spring and axle. Install the two attaching bolts. Tighten the nuts to 30-70 ft.lb.
12. Tighten the radius rod rear attaching nut to 80-120 ft.lb.

13. Position the shock absorber to the lower bracket and install the attaching bolt and nut. Tighten the nut to 40-60 ft.lb. Remove safety stands and lower the vehicle.

Stabilizer Bar

REMOVAL & INSTALLATION

Bronco and 4-Wheel Drive Pickups

1. Remove nuts, bolts and washers connecting the stabilizer bar to connecting links. Remove nuts and bolts of the stabilizer bar retainer.
2. Remove stabilizer bar insulator assembly.
3. To remove the stabilizer bar mounting bracket, the coil spring must be removed as described above under spring removal. Remove the lower spring seat. The bracket attaching stud and bracket can now be removed.
4. To install the stabilizer bar mounting brackets, locate the brackets so that the locating tang is positioned in the radius arm notch (or quad shock bracket notch if vehicle has quad shocks). Install a new stud. Torque to 180-220 ft.lb. A new stud is required because of the adhesive on the threads. Reposition the spring lower seat and reinstall the spring and retainers.
5. To reinstall the stabilizer bar insulator assembly, assemble all nuts, bolts and washers to the bar, brackets, retainers and links loosely. With the bar positioned correctly, torque retainer nuts to 32-35 ft.lb. with retainer around the insulator. Then torque all remaining nuts at the link assemblies to 41-50 ft.lb.

REAR SUSPENSION

Springs

REMOVAL & INSTALLATION

2-Wheel Drive Pickups

1. Raise the vehicle by the frame until the weight is off the rear spring with the tires still on the floor.
2. Remove the nuts from the spring U-bolts and drive the U-bolts from the U-bolt plate. Remove the auxiliary spring and spacer, if so equipped.

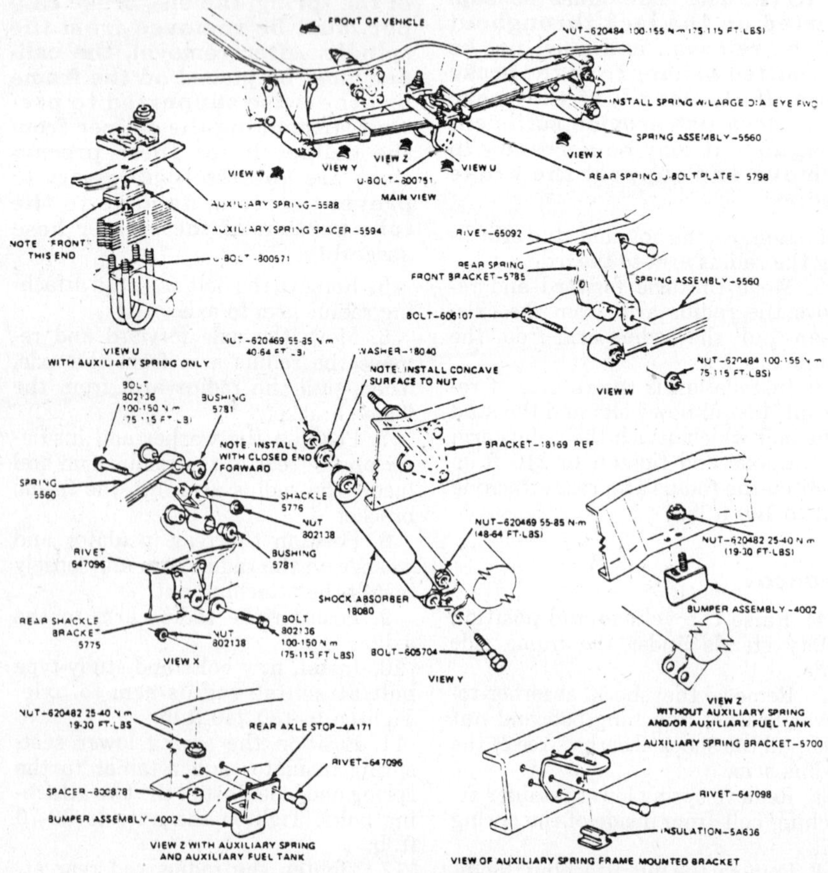

F-100/F-150 rear leaf spring and shock absorber mounting

3. Remove the spring-to-bracket nut and bolt at the front of the spring.
4. Remove the upper and lower shackle nuts and bolts at the rear of the spring and remove the spring and shackle assembly from the rear shackle bracket.
5. Remove the bushings in the spring or shackle, if they are worn or damaged, and install new ones.
6. Position the spring in the shackle and install the upper shackle-to-spring nut and bolt with the bolt head facing outward.
7. Position the front end of the spring in the bracket and install the nut and bolt.
8. Position the shackle in the rear bracket and install the nut and bolt.
9. Position the spring on top of the axle with the spring center bolt centered in the hole provided in the seat. Install the auxiliary spring and spacer, if so equipped.
10. Install the spring U-bolts, plate, and nuts.
11. Lower the vehicle and tighten the attaching hardware as follows:
- ½" U-bolt nuts: 45-70 ft.lb
- $^{9}/_{16}$" 85-115 ft.lb
- $^{9}/_{16}$" front spring hanger: 75-105 ft.lb
- ⅝" front spring hanger: 150-190 ft.lbs
- Rear spring hanger: 75-105 ft.lb.

4-Wheel Drive Pickups

1. Raise the truck by the frame until the weight is off the rear springs and the wheels are still touching the ground.
2. Remove the nuts from the spring U-bolts and drive the U-bolts out of the spring seat cap. Remove the spring cap. Remove the auxiliary spring and spacer, if so equipped.
3. Remove the shackle pin lockbolts from each end of the spring. Insert a drift in the hole provided in the frame from the inner side and drive the shackle pin out of each spring bracket.
4. Remove the spring and shackle from the truck. Remove the spring-to-axle spacer.
5. Drive the remaining shackle pin out of the rear spring eye and remove the shackle from the spring.
6. After checking and replacing worn or damaged bushings, nuts and bolts, and broken or weak springs, position the shackle to the rear spring eye.
7. Install the shackle pin through the shackle and spring eye with the lubrication fitting on the shackle pin facing outboard.
8. Align the shackle pin lockbolt groove with the lockbolt hole in the shackle, and install the lockbolt, washer, and nut.
9. Position the spring on the axle

with the spring center bolt in the hole provided in the axle spring seat or spacer. Install the spacer between the spring seat and the spring. Make sure that the spacer dowel is positioned in the pilot hole of the axle spring seat.

10. Install the shackle pin through the shackle and rear bracket. The lubrication fitting on the shackle pin faces outboard. Align the pin groove with the lock bolt hole in the bracket and install the lockbolt, washer, and nut.

11. Install the shackle pin at the front bracket and spring eye in the same manner as above.

12. Install the auxiliary spring and spacer, if so equipped. Place the spring cap on top of the spring at the center bolt and place the spring U-bolts over the spring assembly and axle.

13. Position the spring seat cap, and install the nuts on the spring U-bolts.

14. Lower the truck to the ground and tighten the attaching hardware.

Bronco

1. Raise the vehicle and install jackstands under the frame. The vehicle must be supported in such a way that the rear axle hangs free with the tire a few inches off the ground. Place a hydraulic floor jack under the center of the axle housing.
2. Disconnect the shock absorber from the axle.
3. Remove the U-bolt attaching nuts and remove the two U-bolts and the spring clip plate.
4. Lower the axle to relieve the spring tension and remove the nut from the spring front attaching bolt.
5. Remove the spring front attaching bolt from the spring and hanger with a drift.
6. Remove the nut from the shackle-to-hanger attaching bolt and drive the bolt from the shackle and hanger with a drift and remove the spring from the vehicle.
7. Remove the nut from the spring rear attaching bolt. Drive the bolt out of the spring and shackle with a drift.
8. To install the rear spring: Position the shackle (closed section facing toward the front of the vehicle) to the spring rear eye and install the bolt and nut.
9. Position the spring front eye and bushing to the spring front hanger, and install the attaching bolt and nut.
10. Position the spring rear eye and bushing to the shackle, and install the attaching bolt and nut.
11. Raise the axle to the spring and install the U-bolts and spring clip plate.
12. Torque the U-bolt nuts and spring front and rear attaching bolt nuts to 45-60 ft.lb.

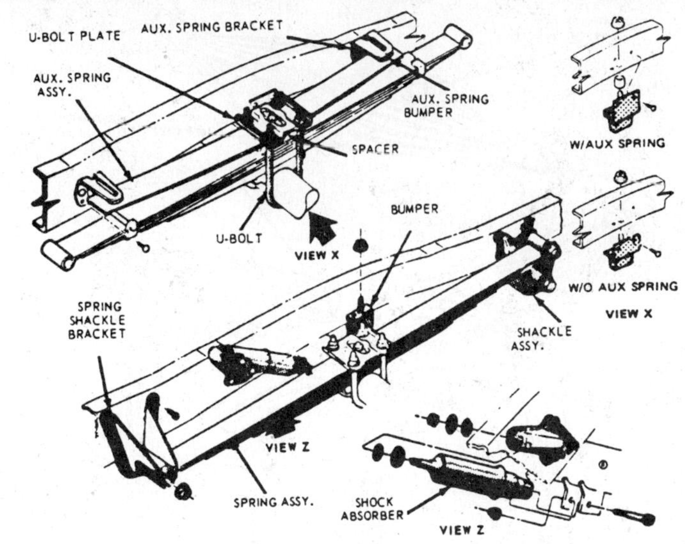

Rear spring installation on the F-100, F-150 2WD and 4WD, and F-250 2WD

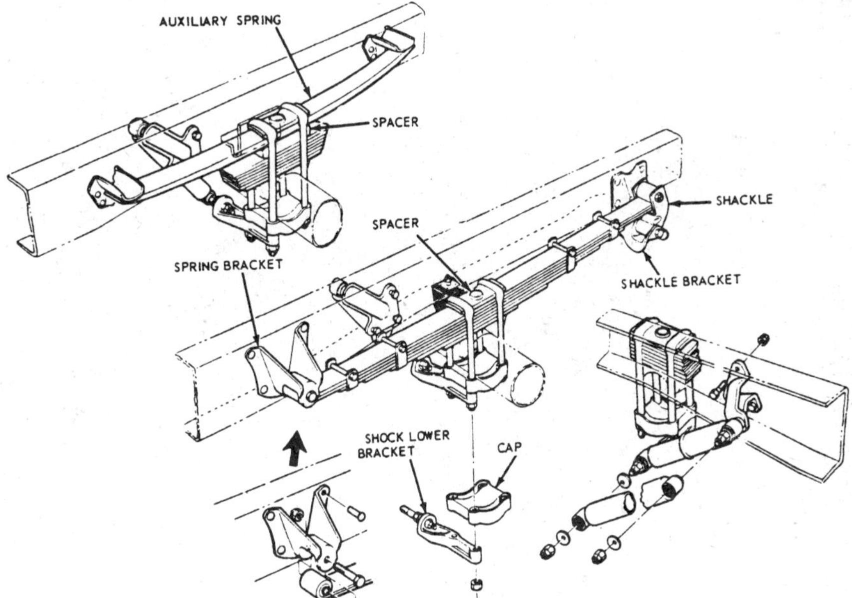

Rear spring installation—F-350

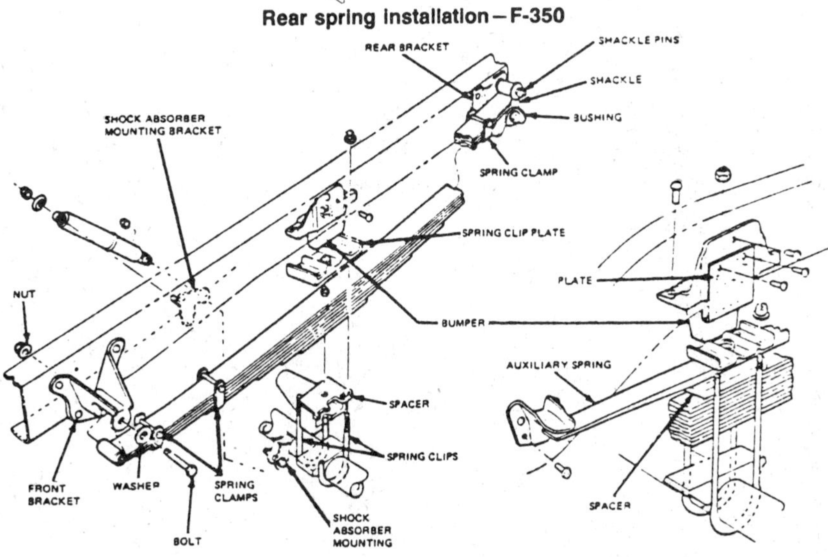

Rear spring installation on F-250 4WD

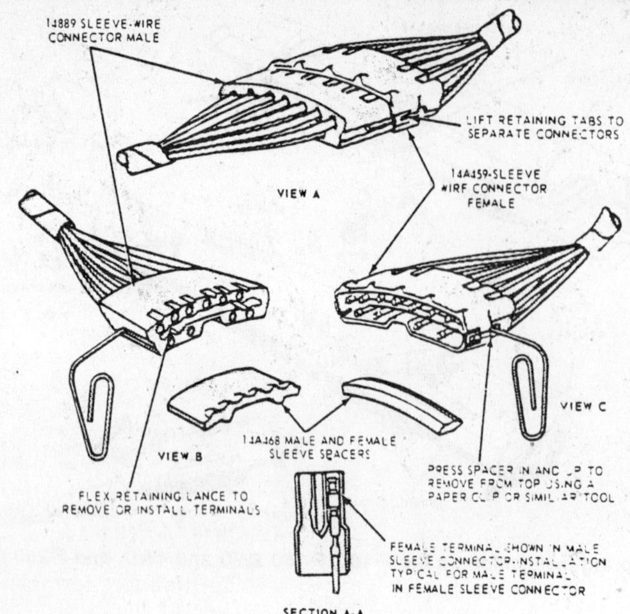

Wire connector disassembly

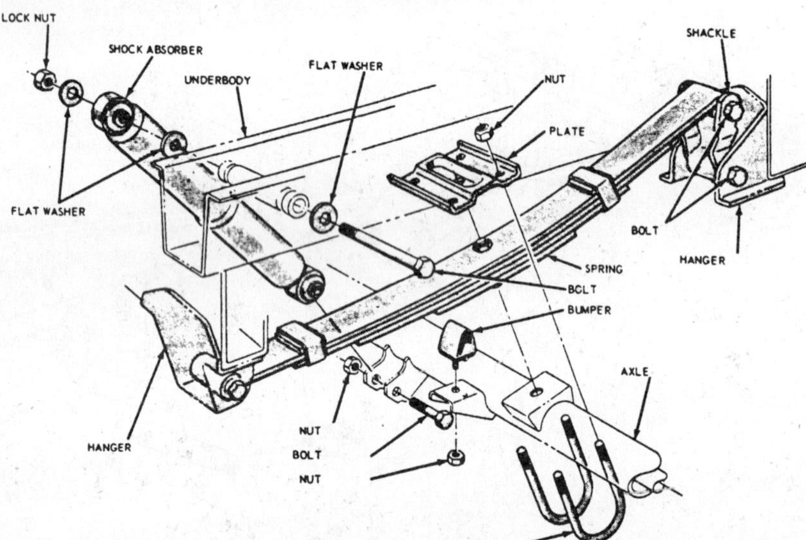

The rear spring assembly of E-100, E-150, and E-200 vans

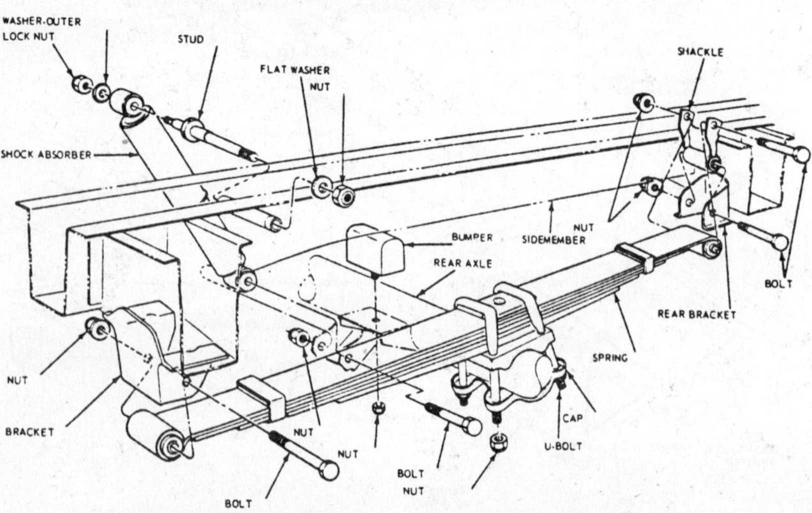

The rear spring assembly of E-250, E-300 and E-350 vans

13. Remove the jackstands and lower the vehicle.

NOTE: Squeaky rear springs can be corrected by tightening the front and rear eye bolts to 150-204 ft.lb., then raising and supporting the rear of the vehicle so that the rear springs hang, spreading the leaves. Apply a silicone based lubricant for a distance of 3" in from each leaf tip.

E-100, 150, 250

1. Raise the rear of the vehicle and support the chassis with jackstands. Support the rear axle with a floor jack or hoist.
2. Disconnect the lower end of the shock absorber from the bracket on the axle housing.
3. Remove the two U-bolts and plate.
4. Lower the axle and remove the upper and lower rear shackle bolts.
5. Pull the rear shackle assembly and rubber bushings from the bracket and spring.
6. Remove the nut and mounting bolt which secure the front end of the spring. Remove the spring assembly from the front shackle bracket.
7. Install new rubber bushings in the rear shackle bracket and in the rear eye of the replacement spring.
8. Assemble the front eye of the spring to the front shackle bracket with the front mounting bolt and nut. Do not tighten the nut.
9. Mount the rear end of the spring with the upper bolt of the rear shackle assembly passing through the eye of the spring. Insert the lower bolt through the rear spring hanger.
10. Assemble the spring center bolt in the pilot hole in the axle and install the plate. Install the U-bolts through the plate. Do not tighten the attaching nuts at this time.
11. Raise the axle with a floor jack or hoist until the vehicle is free of the jackstands. Connect the lower end of the shock absorber to the bracket on the axle housing.
12. Tighten the spring front mounting bolt and nut, the rear shackle nuts and the U-bolt nuts.
13. Remove the jackstands and lower the vehicle.

E-250, E-350

1. Raise the rear of the vehicle and support the chassis with jackstands. Support the rear axle with a floor jack or hoist.
2. Disconnect the lower end of the shock absorber from the bracket on the axle housing.
3. Remove the two spring U-bolts and the spring cap.
4. Lower the axle and remove the spring front bolt from the hanger.

5. Remove the two attaching bolts from the rear of the spring. Remove the spring and shackle.
6. Assemble the upper end of the shackle to the spring with the attaching bolt.
7. Connect the front of the spring to the front bracket with the attaching bolt.
8. Assemble the spring and shackle to the rear bracket with the attaching bolt.
9. Place the spring plate over the head of the center bolt.
10. Raise the axle with a jack. Install the center bolt through the pilot hole in the pad on the axle housing.
11. Install the spring U-bolts, cap and attaching nuts. Tighten the nuts snugly.
12. Connect the lower end of the shock absorber to the lower bracket.
13. Tighten the spring front mounting bolt and nut, the rear shackle nuts and the spring U-bolt nuts.
14. Remove the jackstands and lower the vehicle.

Shock Absorbers

REMOVAL & INSTALLATION

1. Raise the vehicle and place jackstands under the frame.
2. Remove the shock absorber-to-upper bracket attaching nut and washers, and bushing from the shock absorber rod or if mounted with nut and bolt, remove as lower.
3. Remove the shock absorber-to-axle attaching bolt. Drive the bolts from the axle bracket and shock absorber with a brass drift and remove the shock absorber.
4. Position the washers and bushing on the shock absorber rod and position the shock absorber at the upper bracket.
5. Position the bushing and washers on the shock absorber rod and install the attaching nut loosely.
6. Position the shock absorber at the axle housing bracket and install the attaching bolt and nut. Tighten the lower nut to 40-60 ft.lb. and the upper nut to 15-25 ft.lb. If attached at top with similar mounting, torque is same.

FRONT END ALIGNMENT

Caster

The caster angles are designed into the front axle and cannot be adjusted.

Camber

The camber angles are designed into the front axle and cannot be adjusted except on 1983 and later 2-Wheel Drive vehicles.

1983 and Later w/2-Wheel Drive

Camber is adjusted by replacing the camber adapter on the upper ball joint stud. Adapters are available in 0°, ½°, 1° and 1½° increments.

If camber needs adjustment, replace the camber adapter as described under camber adapter. On the right spindle, the slot in the camber adapter must point forward for a positive camber change and rearward for a negative camber change. On the left spindle, the slot in the adapter must point rearward for a positive camber change and forward for a negative camber change.

Toe-In Adjustment

All Models

Toe-in can be measured by either a front end alignment machine or by the following method:

With the front wheels in the straightahead position, measure the distance between the extreme front and the extreme rear of the front wheels. In other words, measure the distance across the undercarriage of the vehicle between the two front edges and the two rear edges of the two front wheels. Both of these measurements (front and rear of the two wheels) must be taken at an equal distance from the floor and at the approximate centerline of the spindle. The difference between these two distances is the amount that the wheels toe-in or toe-out. The wheels should always be adjusted to toe-in according to specifications.

1. Loosen the clamp bolts at each end of the left tie-rod, seen from the front of the vehicle. Rotate the connecting rod tube until the correct toe-in is obtained, then tighten the clamp bolts.
2. Recheck the toe-in to make sure that no changes occurred when the bolts were tightened.

NOTE: The clamps should be positioned $^{3}/_{16}$" from the end of the rod with the clamp bolts in a vertical position in front of the tube, with the nut down.

STEERING

Steering Wheel

REMOVAL & INSTALLATION

1980-82

1. Disconnect the battery ground and mark the steering wheel-to-column alignment.
2. Remove one screw from the underside of each spoke and lift the horn assembly from the wheel. On vehicles with a sport wheel option, pry or unscrew (try unscrewing first) the button cover
3. Disconnect the horn switch wires by pulling the spade terminal from the blade connector. Squeeze or pinch the J-clip ground wire terminal fully and pull it out of the hole in the steering wheel. Do not pull the ground terminal out of the threaded hole without squeezing the clip to remove the spring tension.
4. Remove the horn switch assembly.
5. Remove the steering wheel retaining nut.
6. Using a steering wheel puller, remove the wheel.
7. To install: Position the steering wheel in alignment with the marks.
8. Tighten the retaining nut to 50 ft.lb.
9. Connect the wires, install the horn assembly and connect the battery ground.

1983-87

1. Disconnect the battery ground and mark the steering wheel-to-column alignment.
2. Remove once screw from the underside of each spoke and lift the horn assembly from the wheel. On vehicles with a sport wheel option, pry the button cover off with a screwdriver.
3. Disconnect the horn switch wires by pulling the spade terminal from the blade connector. Squeeze or pinch the J-clip ground wire terminal fully and pull it out of the hole in the steering wheel. Do not pull the ground terminal out of the threaded hole without squeezing the clip to remove the spring tension.
4. Remove the horn switch assembly.
5. Remove the steering wheel retaining nut.
6. Using a steering wheel puller, remove the wheel.
7. Position the steering wheel in alignment with the marks.
8. Tighten the retaining nut to 50 ft.lb.

9. Connect the wires, install the horn assembly and connect the battery ground.

Turn Signal Switch

REPLACEMENT

1. Disconnect the battery ground cable.
2. Remove the horn switch.
3. Remove the steering wheel retaining nut and using tool 3600AA or equivalent, remove the steering wheel from the shaft.
4. Remove the turn signal switch lever by unscrewing it from the steering column.
5. Disconnect the turn indicator switch wiring connector plug by lifting up on the tabs and separating and remove the screws that secure the switch assembly to the column.
6. Remove the wires and terminals from the steering column wiring connector plug. Record the color code and location of each wire before removing it from the connector plug.
7. Connect pull through wire to end of wiring harness with tape.
8. Remove the protective wire cover from the wiring harness and remove the switch and wires through the top of the column.
9. Tape the loose ends of the new turn signal switch wires to the pull-through wire or cord. Carefully pull the wires through the steering column while guiding the turn signal switch into position.
10. Install switch assembly retaining screws to column.
11. Install wires into steering column wire connector terminal and connect terminals.
12. Install turn signal lever. Hand-tighten the lever (on flat side) to 10-20 in.lb. Test turn signal operation, hazard signal operation and PRND21 dial-lamp (if so equipped).
13. Install steering wheel.
14. Install horn switch.
15. Connect battery ground cable.

Ignition Switch And Lock Cylinder

REMOVAL & INSTALLATION

1. Disconnect the battery ground cable.
2. Remove steering column shroud and lower the steering column.
3. Disconnect the switch wiring at the multiple plug.
4. Remove the two nuts that retain the switch to the steering column.
5. Lift the switch vertically upward to disengage the actuator rod from the switch and remove switch.
6. When installing the ignition switch, both the locking mechanism at the top of the column and the switch itself must be in LOCK position for correct adjustment.

To hold the mechanical parts of the column in LOCK position, move the shift lever into PARK (with automatic transmissions) or REVERSE (with manual transmissions), turn the key to LOCK position, and remove the key. New replacement switches, when received, are already pinned in LOCK position by a metal shipping pin inserted in a locking hole on the side of the switch.

7. Engage the actuator rod in the switch.
8. Position the switch on the column and install the retaining nuts, but do not tighten them.
9. Move the switch up and down along the column to locate the mid-position of rod lash, and then tighten the retaining nuts.
10. Remove the locking pin, connect the battery cable, and check for proper start in PARK or NEUTRAL.

Also check to make certain that the start circuit cannot be actuated in the DRIVE and REVERSE position.

11. Raise the steering column into position at instrument panel. Install steering column shroud.

Steering Cloumn

REMOVAL

1. Set the parking brake and disconnect the battery. Remove the bolt and nut attaching the intermediate shaft to the steering column.
2. Disconnect the shift linkage rods from the column.
3. Remove the steering wheel as described previously. If a tilt steering column is being serviced, the steering wheel must be in the full **UP** position when it is removed.
4. Remove the steering column floor opening cover plate screws.
5. Remove the shroud by loosening the screw at the bottom, selecting position **1** on manual 3-speeds and automatics and spreading shroud open, withdrawing out of instrument panel opening, while pulling up and away from column.
6. Remove PRND21 indicator actuation cable (automatics).
7. Remove the instrument panel column opening cover.
8. Remove the bolts attaching the column support bracket to the pedal support bracket.
9. Disconnect the turn signal/hazard warning and ignition switch wiring harnesses.
10. Remove the column from the vehicle.

INSTALLATION

1. Attach the steering column support bracket making sure that the turn signal/hazard warning wiring is on the outboard side of the column. Tighten the nuts to 13-38 ft.lb.
2. Start the floor opening cover clamp bolt and press the plate until the clamp flats touch the stops on the column outer tube.
3. Load the column into the vehicle through the opening in the floor.
4. Connect the turn signal/hazard warning and ignition switch wiring harnesses.
5. Raise the column up to the pedal support bracket and hand start the two bolts.
6. Fasten the floor opening cover plate to the floor. Tighten to 6-10 ft.lb.
7. Tighten the two support bracket bolts 19-27 ft.lb.
8. Tighten the cover plate clamp bolt 8-18 ft.lb.
9. Install and adjust the PRND21 indicator actuator cable (automatics).
10. Install the instrument panel steering column opening cover.
11. Mount the shroud by selecting position **1** on 3-speed manuals and automatic transmissions, spreading shroud around steering column and through the opening in the instrument panel. Post on the interior will index shroud when properly positioned.
12. Tighten the screw at the bottom of the shroud 10-15 in.lb.
13. Attach the shift linkage rods to the column.
14. Fasten the intermediate shaft to the steering column and tighten to 45-59 ft.lb.

Power Steering Pump

REMOVAL & INSTALLATION

Except CII Pump

1. Disconnect the pressure and return lines from the pump and plug them to prevent loss of fluid or entrance of dirt into the system.
2. Loosen the belt tension adjusting bolt all the way.
3. Remove the bolts attaching the pump mounting bracket to the air conditioning bracket (if equipped).
4. Remove the pump, mounting bracket and pulley assembly.
5. Install the pump, bracket and pulley assembly and loosely attach the bolts that secure the pump mounting bracket to the air conditioning bracket (if equipped).
6. Install the drive belts on the pulley.
7. Loosely install the belt tension adjusting nut.

8. Pry between the pump adjustment bracket and the engine block until correct tension is achieved. While still holding this tension, tighten the adjusting bolt.
9. Tighten all attaching bolts.
10. Connect the pressure and return lines to the pump.
11. Fill the reservoir with power steering fluid. Bleed the air from the system by turning the steering wheel from left to right several times. Inspect for leaks.

Quick Connect Power Steering Fitting Service

The quick connect power steering fitting, under certain conditions may leak and/or result in improper engagement. The leak can be caused by a cut O-ring, imperfections in the outlet fitting inside diameter, or improperly machined O-ring groove. Improper engagement can be caused by an improperly machined tube end, tube nut, snapring, outlet fitting, or gear port.

If a leak occurs, the O-ring should be replaced with quick connect O-rings (3/8" tube end: 388749S; 5/16" tube end: 388748S). The O-rings that are used on the tube-O power steering fitting should not be used on the quick connect fitting because of dimensional and material changes. If O-ring replacement does not solve the leak problem, outlet fitting replacement and, lastly, hose replacement should be made.

If improper engagement occurs due to a missing or bent snapring, or improperly machined tube nut, it may be repaired with a service snapring kit (kit includes a new tube nut). The system should then be properly filled, the engine started, and the steering wheel cycled from lock-to-lock to test for positive engagement. If the hose assembly still does not engage, replace the entire hose assembly.

Quick connect hose assemblies for service have tube nuts, snaprings, and O-rings already attached.

When the quick connect tube nut is tightened or loosened, a tube nut wrench, not an open end wrench, is recommended. An open end wrench may result in tube nut deformation under excessive torque conditions. Care must be taken not to overtighten the tube nut. Tighten to 10-15 ft.lb. Swivel and/or end play of the quick connect fittings is normal, and does not indicate an undertightened fitting.

CII Pump

NOTE: The CII pump is equipped with a fiberglass reservoir and can be identified by the reservoir. Never pry against the fiberglass, as damage will occur.

The 3.8L V6 with a serpentine belt driving the power steering pump uses a separate idler pulley on a slider-type bracket for belt tension adjustment. To adjust or remove the belt tension, loosen the bolts in the slider slots and tighten the adjusting belt as required to obtain the correct belt tension.

1. To remove the power steering fluid from the pump reservoir, disconnect the fluid return hose at the reservoir and drain the fluid into a container. Remove the pressure hose from the pump.
2. Remove the bolts from the pump adjustment bracket. Loosen the pump sufficiently to remove the belt off the pulley. Remove the pump (still attached to the adjustment bracket) from the support bracket.
3. Remove the pulley from the pump if required.
4. Remove the bolts attaching the adjustment bracket to the pump and remove the pump.
5. Place the adjustment bracket on the pump. Install and tighten the bolts to specification listed at the end of this Section.
6. Install the pulley on the pump if removed.
7. Place the pump with adjustment bracket and pulley on the support bracket. Install the bolts connecting the support bracket to the adjustment bracket.
8. Place the belt on the pulley and adjust belt tension. Tighten bolts on adjustment bracket.
9. Install the pressure hose to the pump fitting.
10. Connect the return hose to the pump, and tighten the clamp.
11. Fill the reservoir with specified power steering fluid, start the engine and turn the steering wheel from stop to stop to remove air from the system.
11. Check for leaks and recheck the fluid level. Add fluid if necessary.

SYSTEM BLEEDING

1. Disconnect the coil wire.
2. Crank the engine and continue adding fluid until the level stabilizes.
3. Continue to crank the engine and rotate the steering wheel about 30° to either side of center.
4. Check the fluid level and add as required.
5. Connect the coil wire and start the engine. Allow it to run for several minutes.
6. Rotate the steering wheel from stop to stop.
7. Shut off the engine and check the fluid level. Add fluid as necessary.

Manual Steering Gear

REMOVAL & INSTALLATION

1. Raise and safely support the vehicle.
2. Disconnect the flex coupling from the steering shaft flange by removing the two attaching nuts.
3. Disconnect the drag link from the sector shaft (Pitman) arm, using a suitable puller.
4. Remove the Pitman arm-to-sector shaft attaching nut and washer. Remove the Pitman arm from the gear sector shaft using a suitable puller. (Do not hammer on end of sector shaft.)
5. While supporting the steering gear, remove the bolts and washers that attach the steering gear assembly to the frame side rail. Lower the steering gear assembly from the vehicle.
6. Remove the coupling to gear attaching bolt from the lower half of the flex coupling and remove the coupling from the steering gear assembly.
7. Install the flex coupling on the worm (input) shaft of the gear assembly. Install a new coupling-to-gear attaching bolt and tighten to 11-21 ft.lb.
8. Center the input shaft (the center position is approximately three turns from either stop).
9. Position the steering gear assembly so that the stud bolts on the flex coupling enter the bolt holes in the steering shaft flange, and the holes in the mounting bosses of the gear match the bolt holes in the frame side rail.
10. While supporting the gear in proper position, install the gear-to-frame side rail attaching bolts and washers and tighten to 70 ft.lb. If new gear-to-frame bolts and washers are required, use only Grade 9 bolts.
11. Connect the drag link to the Pitman arm, install the drag link ball stud nut, and tighten to 50-75 ft.lb. Then install the cotter pin.
12. Assemble the Pitman arm on the sector shaft pointing downward. Install the attaching nut and washer, and tighten to 170-230 ft.lb.
13. Secure the flex coupling to the steering shaft flange with the two attaching nuts and tighten to 28-35 ft.lb.

ADJUSTMENTS

1. Be sure that the steering column is properly aligned and is not causing excessive turning effort.
2. The steering gear must be removed from the truck.
3. Be sure that the ball nut assembly and the sector gear are properly adjusted as follows to maintain minimum steering shaft endplay and backlash between the sector gear and ball

nut (preload adjustment). Make sure sector shaft cover bolts are torqued to 30 ft.lb.

4. Loosen the sector shaft adjusting screw locknut and tighten worm bearing adjuster screw until all end-play is removed.

5. Measure the worm bearing preload by attaching an in.lb. torque wrench to the input shaft. Measure the torque required to rotate the input shaft all the way to the right and then turn back about one half turn. The worm bearing preload should be 10-16 in.lb., 9-10 in.lb.

6. Turn the sector shaft adjusting screw clockwise until the specified pull is obtained to rotate the worm past its center. With the steering gear in the center position, hold the sector shaft to prevent rotation and check the lash between the ball nuts, balls and worm shaft by applying a 15 in.lb. torque on the steering gear input shaft, in both right and left turn directions. Total travel of the wrench should not exceed 1¼" when applying a 15 in.lb. torque on the steering shaft.

7. Tighten the sector shaft adjusting screw locknut, and recheck the backlash adjustment.

Power Steering Gear

REMOVAL & INSTALLATION

1. Disconnect the pressure and return lines from the steering gear. Plug the lines and the ports in the gear to prevent entry of dirt. Disconnect brake lines from the steering gear bracket.

2. Remove the bolts that secure the flex coupling to the steering gear and to the column steering shaft assembly.

3. Raise the vehicle and remove the Pitman arm attaching nut, and washer.

4. Remove the Pitman arm from the sector shaft using tool T64P-3590-F. Remove the tool from the Pitman arm. Do not damage the seals.

5. On vehicles with standard transmission remove the clutch release lever retracting spring to provide clearance for removing the steering gear.

6. Support the steering gear, and remove the steering gear attaching bolts.

7. Work the steering gear free of the flex coupling. Remove the steering gear from the vehicle.

8. Slide the flex coupling into place on the steering shaft assembly. Turn the steering wheel so the spokes are in the horizontal position.

9. Center the steering gear input shaft.

10. Slide the steering gear input shaft into the flex coupling and into place on the frame side rail. Install the attaching bolts and tighten to 60-80 ft.lb.

11. Be sure the wheels are in the straight ahead position, then install the Pitman arm on the sector shaft. Install the Pitman arm attaching washer and nut. Tighten nut to 170-230 ft.lb.

12. Connect and tighten the pressure and the return lines to the steering gear. Reinstall the brake lines on the steering gear bracket.

13. Disconnect the coil wire. Fill the reservoir. Turn on the ignition and turn the steering wheel from left to right to distribute the fluid.

14. Re-check fluid level and add fluid, if necessary. Connect the coil wire, start the engine and turn the steering wheel from side to side. Inspect for fluid leaks.

ADJUSTMENTS

Steering Gear Meshload

1. Make sure that the steering column is correctly aligned.

2. Disconnect the steering linkage from the Pitman arm on the steering gear. Remove the horn pad as explained under Steering Wheel Removal and Installation.

3. Disconnect the fluid reservoir return line and cap the reservoir return line tube. Place the end of the return line in a clean container and turn the steering wheel back and forth several times to empty the steering gear.

4. Turn the steering wheel nut with an inch-pound torque wrench slowly. Find the torque required at ½ turn off right and left stops, ½ turn off center both right and left, and over-center (full turn). The over-center torque should be 4-6 in.lb. more than the end readings, but the total over-center torque must not exceed 14 in.lb.

5. To correct, back off the Pitman shaft adjuster all the way, then back in ½ turn. Recheck the over-center torque. Loosen the locknut and tighten the sector shaft adjusting screw until the over-center torque reads 4-6 in.lb. higher, but doesn't exceed 14 in.lb. Tighten the adjusting screw locknut and recheck.

6. Refill the system with the fluid specified. Bleed the system of air by turning the steering wheel all the way to the right and left several times with the engine warmed up. Do not hold the steering against the stops or pump damage will result.

Steering Linkage Connecting Rods

Replace the drag link if a ball stud is excessively loose or if the drag link is bent. Do not attempt to straighten a drag link. Replace the connecting rod if the ball stud is excessively loose, if the connecting rod is bent or if the threads are stripped. Do not attempt to straighten connecting rod. Always check to insure that the adjustment sleeve and clamp stops are correctly installed on the Bronco.

REMOVAL & INSTALLATION

Vans & 2-Wheel Drive Pickups

Replace the drag link if a ball stud is excessively loose or if the drag link is bent. Do not attempt to straighten a drag link. Replace the connecting rod if the ball stud is excessively loose, if the connecting rod is bent or if the threads are stripped. Do not attempt to straighten connecting rod. After installing a connecting rod or adjusting toe-in check to insure that the adjustment sleeve clamps are correctly positioned on the F- and E-100 and F- and E-150 and to insure that the clamp stop is correctly installed on the F- and E-250 and F- and E-350.

1. Remove the cotter pins and nuts from the drag link, ball studs and from the right connecting rod ball stud.

2. Remove the right connecting rod ball stud from the drag link.

3. Remove the drag link ball studs from the spindle and the Pitman arm.

4. Position the new drag link, ball studs in the spindle, and Pitman arm and install nuts.

5. Position the right connecting rod ball stud in the drag link and install nut.

6. Tighten the nuts to 50-75 ft.lb. and install the cotter pins.

7. Remove the cotter pin and nut from the connecting rod.

8. Remove the ball stud from the mating part.

9. Loosen the clamp bolt and turn the rod out of the adjustment sleeve. Count the number of turns for approximate position when installing.

10. Lubricate the threads of the new connecting rod, and turn it into the adjustment sleeve to about the same distance the old rods were installed. This will provide an approximate toe-in setting. Position the connecting rod ball studs in the spindle arms.

11. Install the nuts on to the connecting rod ball studs, tighten the nut to 50-75 ft.lb. and install the cotter pin.

12. Check the toe-in and adjust, if necessary. After checking or adjusting toe-in, center the adjustment sleeve clamps between the locating nibs, position the clamps and tighten the nuts to 29-41 ft.lb.

4-Wheel Drive Pickups

1. Raise the vehicle and support on

jackstands. Disconnect the drag link from the spindle connecting rod end.

2. Disconnect the right spindle connecting rod end from the right spindle arm.

3. Disconnect the left spindle connecting rod ends from the left spindle arm and remove the spindle connecting rod ends from the truck.

4. Place the connecting rod ends in a vise and loosen the connecting rod tube clamps.

5. Remove the short (right) rod end from the connecting rod tube and remove the tube from the long (left) connecting rod end.

6. Clean and oil the threads on all the parts to be reused.

7. Install the connecting rod tube and clamps on the left spindle connecting rod end. Don't tighten the clamps yet.

8. Install the right connecting rod end in the tube and remove the assembly from the vise.

9. Install new dust seals on the left spindle connecting rod end and position the end on the left spindle arm.

10. Install the connecting rod end attaching nut, tighten it, and install the cotter pin.

11. Install new dust seals on the right spindle connecting rod end and position the end on the right spindle arm. Install the attaching nut, tighten it, and install the cotter pin.

12. Install new seals on the drag link ball stud and position the drag link on the spindle connecting rod end. Install the attaching nut, tighten it, and install the cotter pin.

13. Lubricate the spindle connecting rod ends and drag link.

14. Lower the vehicle and check and adjust the toe-in setting. Tighten the connecting rod clamps after adjusting the toe-in.

Bronco

1. Remove the cotter pins and nuts from the drag link, ball studs and from the right connecting rod ball studs.

2. Remove the right connecting rod ball stud from the right spindle assembly and Pitman arm.

3. Remove the drag link ball studs from the spindle and the connecting rod assembly.

4. Loosen the clamp bolt and turn the rod out of the adjustment sleeve.

5. Lubricate the threads of the new connecting rod, and turn it into the adjustment sleeve to about the same distance the old rods were installed. This will provide an approximate toe-in setting. Position the connecting rod ball studs in the spindle arms.

6. Position the new drag link, ball studs in the spindle, and connecting rod assembly and install nuts.

7. Position the right connecting rod ball stud in the drag link and install nut.

8. Tighten all the nuts to 50-75 ft.lb. and install the cotter pins.

9. Remove the cotter pin and nut from the left connecting rod.

10. Install the nuts on the connecting rod ball studs, tighten the nut to 50-75 ft.lb. and install the cotter pin.

11. Check the toe-in and adjust, if necessary. After checking or adjusting toe-in, center the adjustment sleeve clamps between the locating nibbs, position the clamps and tighten the nuts to 29-41 ft.lb.

BRAKE SYSTEM

ADJUSTMENT

DRUM BRAKES

The drum brakes are self-adjusting and require a manual adjustment only after the brake shoes have been replaced, or when the length of the adjusting screw has been changed.

1. Raise the vehicle and support it with safety stands.

2. Remove the rubber plug from the adjusting slot on the backing plate.

3. Insert a small screwdriver or piece of firm wire (coat hanger wire) into the adjusting slot and push the automatic adjusting lever out and free of the starwheel on the adjusting screw and hold it there.

4. Engage the topmost tooth possible on the starwheel with a brake adjusting spoon. Move the end of the adjusting spoon upward to move the adjusting screw starwheel downward and contract the adjusting screw. Back off the adjusting screw starwheel until the wheel spins freely with a minimum of drag. Keep track of the number of turns that the starwheel is backed off, or the number of strokes taken with the brake adjusting spoon.

6. Repeat this operation for the other side. When backing off the brakes on the other side, the starwheel adjuster must be backed off the same number of turns to prevent side-to-side brake pull.

7. Repeat this operation on the other set of brakes.

8. When the brakes are adjusted, make several stops while backing the vehicle, to equalize the brakes. If the truck has a tendency to pull to one side when the brakes are applied, back off th003382stment of the brake assembly on the side the to which the vehicle pulls.

9. Remove the safety stands and lower the vehicle. Road test the vehicle.

NOTE: Disc brakes are not adjustable.

BRAKE PEDAL

On dual brake master cylinder or dash mounted vacuum booster equipped vehicles, the brake systems are designed to permit a full stroke of the master cylinder when the brake pedal is fully depressed. A brake pedal clearance adjustment is not required.

To release the brakes, fluid must flow back to the master cylinder through a return port when pedal pressure is released. To be sure the piston moves back far enough to expose the return port, free travel is built into the pedal linkage on standard and frame mounted booster sys-

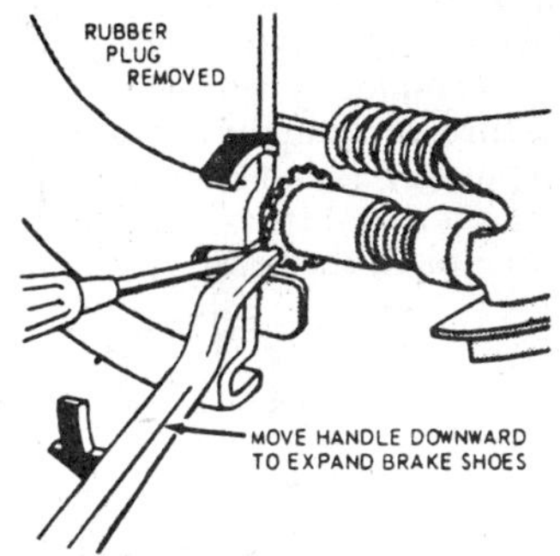

Positioning and operation of the brake adjusting tools during the adjustment procedure on the F-250-350 heavy duty models—expanding the brakes

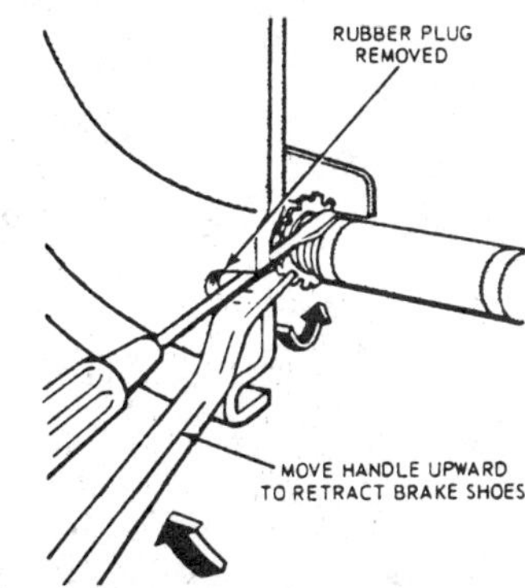

Positioning and operation of the brake adjusting tools during the adjustment procedure on F-100 and F-250 light duty models—backing off the brakes

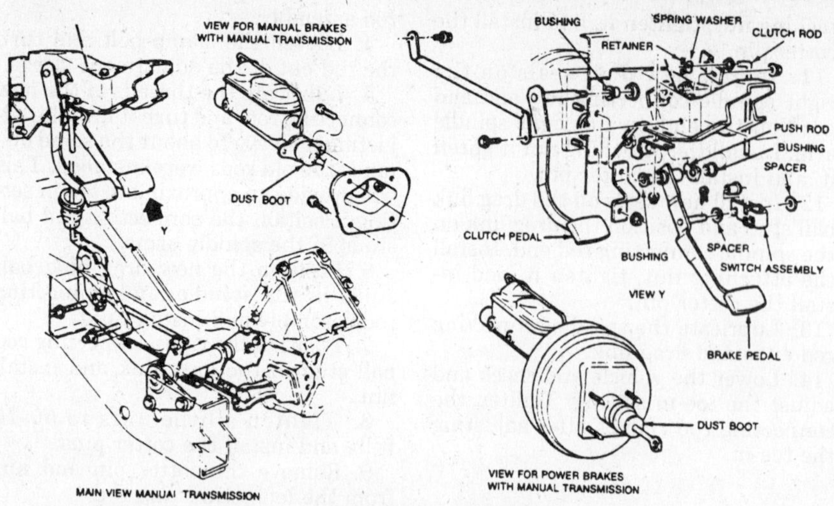

Brake pedal installation

tems. This prevents the piston from becoming trapped in a partially released position. Pedal free travel is not always perceptible in dash mounted booster systems, because the operating clearance for the piston is adjusted at the booster pushrod, rather than the pedal linkage.

The pushrod has an adjustment screw to maintain the correct relationship between the booster control valve plunger and the master cylinder piston. If the plunger is too long it will prevent the master cylinder piston from completely releasing hydraulic pressure, causing the brakes to drag. If the plunger is too short it will cause excessive pedal travel and an undesirable clunk in the booster arca. Remove the master cylinder for access to the booster pushrod.

To check the alignment of the screw, fabricate a gauge (from cardboard, following the dimensions in the above illustration) and place it against the master cylinder mounting surface of the booster body. Adjust the pushrod screw by turning it until the end of the screw just touches the inner edge of the slot in the gauge. Install the master cylinder and bleed the system.

Brake Light Switch

REMOVAL & INSTALLATION

1. Disconnect the wiring harness.
2. Remove the pin that secures the brake light switch to the brake pedal arm.
3. Remove the spacer and slide the brake light switch from the pedal arm.
4. Install the new switch in the reverse of the removal procedure.
5. Adjust the switch as necessary.

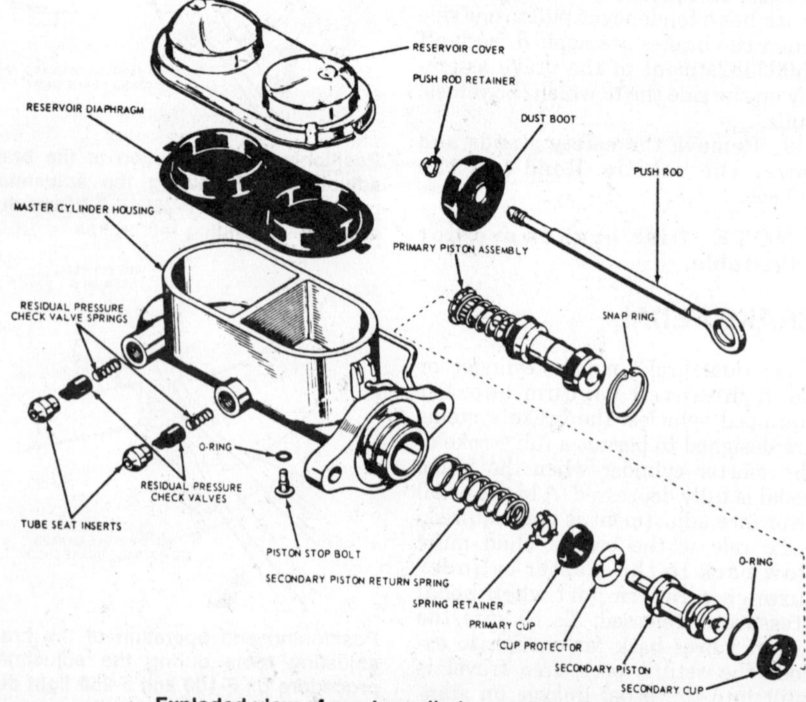

Exploded view of master cylinder—1967 and later

HYDRAULIC SYSTEM

Master Cylinder

REMOVAL & INSTALLATION

1. With the engine turned off, push the brake pedal down to expel vacuum from the brake booster system.
2. Disconnect the hydraulic lines from the brake master cylinder.
3. Remove the brake booster-to-master cylinder retaining nuts and lockwashers. Remove the master cylinder from the brake booster.
4. Before installing the master cylinder, check the distance from the outer end of the booster assembly pushrod to the front face of the brake booster assembly. Turn the pushrod adjusting screw in or out as required to obtain the length shown.
5. Position the master cylinder assembly over the booster pushrod and onto the two studs on the booster assembly. Install the attaching nuts and lockwashers and tighten to 20-30 ft.lb.
6. Loosely connect the hydraulic brake system lines to the master cylinder.
7. Bleed the hydraulic brake system. Centralize the differential valve. Then, fill the dual master cylinder reservoirs with DOT 3 brake fluid to within ¼″ (6.35mm) of the top. Install the gasket and reservoir cover.

OVERHAUL

The most important thing to remember when rebuilding the master cylinder is cleanliness. Work in clean surroundings with clean tools and clean cloths or paper for drying purposes. Have plenty of clean alcohol and brake fluid on hand to clean and lubricate the internal components. There are service repair kits available for overhauling the master cylinder.

1. Clean the outside of the master cylinder and remove the filler cap and gasket (diaphragm). Pour out any fluid that remains in the cylinder reservoir. Do not use any fluids other than brake fluid or alcohol to clean the master cylinder.

2. Unscrew the piston stop from the bottom of the cylinder body. Remove the O-ring seal from the piston stop. Discard the seal.

3. Remove the pushrod boot, if so equipped, from the groove at the rear of the master cylinder and slide the boot away from the rear of the master cylinder.

4. Remove the snapring retaining the primary and secondary piston assemblies within the cylinder body.

5. Remove the pushrod (if so equipped) and primary piston assembly from the master cylinder. Discard the piston assembly, including to boot (if so equipped).

6. Apply an air hose to the rear brake outlet port of the cylinder body and carefully blow the secondary piston out of the cylinder body.

7. Remove the return spring, spring retainer, cap protector, and cups from the secondary piston. Discard the cup protector and cups.

8. Clean all of the remaining parts in clean isopropyl alcohol and inspect the parts for chipping, excessive wear or damage. Replace them as required.

NOTE: When using a master cylinder repair kit, install all the parts supplied in the kit.

9. Check all recesses, openings and internal passages to be sure they are open and free from foreign matter. Use compressed air to blow out dirt and cleaning solvent remaining after the parts have been cleaned in the alcohol. Place all the parts on a clean pan, lint free cloth, or paper to dry.

10. Dip all the parts, except the cylinder body, in clean brake fluid.

11. Assemble the two secondary cups, back-to-back, in the grooves near the end of the secondary piston.

12. Install the secondary piston assembly in the master cylinder.

13. Install a new O-ring on the piston stop, and start the stop into the cylinder body.

14. Position the boot, snapring and pushrod retainer on the pushrod. Make sure the pushrod retainer is seated securely on the ball end of the rod. Seat the pushrod in the primary piston assembly.

15. Install the primary piston assembly in the master cylinder. Push the primary piston inward and tighten the secondary piston stop to retain the secondary piston in the bore.

16. Press the pushrod and pistons inward and install the snapring in the cylinder body.

17. Before the master cylinder is installed on the vehicle, the unit must be bled: support the master cylinder body in a vise, and fill both fluid reservoirs with brake fluid.

18. Loosely install plugs in the front and rear brake outlet bores. Depress the primary piston several times until air bubbles cease to appear in the brake fluid.

19. Tighten the plugs and attempt to depress the piston. The piston travel should be restricted after all air is expelled.

20. Remove the plugs. Install the cover and gasket (diaphragm) assembly, and make sure the cover retainer is tightened securely.

21. Install the master cylinder in the vehicle and bleed the hydraulic system.

Booster

REMOVAL & INSTALLATION

NOTE: Make sure that the booster rubber reaction disc is properly installed if the master cylinder pushrod is removed or accidentally pulled out. A dislodged disc may cause excessive pedal travel and extreme operation sensitivity. The disc is black compared to the silver colored valve plunger that will be exposed after the pushrod and front seal is removed. The booster unit is serviced as an assembly and must be replaced if the reaction disc cannot be properly installed and aligned, or if it cannot be located within the unit itself.

1. Disconnect the stop lamp switch wiring to prevent running the battery down.

2. Support the master cylinder from the underside with a prop.

3. Remove the master cylinder-to-booster retaining nuts.

4. Loosen the clamp that secures the manifold vacuum hose to the booster check valve, and remove the hose. Remove the booster check valve.

5. Pull the master cylinder off the booster and leave it supported by the prop, far enough away to allow removal of the booster assembly.

6. From inside the cab on vehicles equipped with pushrod mounted stop lamp switch, remove the retaining pin and slide the stop lamp switch, pushrod, spacers and bushing off the brake pedal arm.

7. From the engine compartment remove the bolts that attach the booster to the dash panel.

8. Mount the booster assembly on the engine side of the dash panel by sliding the bracket mounting bolts and valve operating rod in through the holes in the dash panel.

NOTE: Make certain that the booster pushrod is positioned on the correct side of the master cylinder to install onto the push pin prior to tightening the booster assembly to the dash.

9. From inside the cab, install the booster mounting bracket-to-dash panel retaining nuts.

10. Position the master cylinder on the booster assembly, install the retaining nuts, and remove the prop from underneath the master cylinder.

11. Install the booster check valve. Connect the manifold vacuum hose to the booster check valve and secure with the clamp.

12. From inside the cab on vehicles equipped with pushrod mounted stop lamp switch, install the bushing and position the switch on the end of the pushrod. Then install the switch and rod on the pedal arm, along with spacers on each side, and secure with the retaining pin.

13. Connect the stop lamp switch wiring.

14. Start the engine and check brake operation.

Diesel Engine Vacuum Pump

REMOVAL & INSTALLATION

1. Disconnect the vacuum hose at the intake manifold.

2. Loosen the vacuum pump adjustment and pivot bolts. Slide the pump downward and remove the drive belt.

3. Remove the pivot and adjusting bolts and lift out the pump and bracket.

NOTE: The pump is not servicable and can only be replaced.

4. Installation is the reverse of removal. To adjust the belt tension, place a 3/8" drive breaker bar in the slot in the pump bracket and apply force to tighten the belt. While holding this tension, tighten the adjusting and pivot bolts. Remove the bar and torque both bolts to 18 ft.lb. Start the engine. The BRAKE light will glow until vacuum builds to a sufficien level.

Pressure Differential Valve

REMOVAL

1. Raise the vehicle on a hoist. Disconnect the brake warning lamp wire from the valve assembly switch.

NOTE: To avoid damaging the brake warning switch wire connector, expand the plastic lugs so that the shell wire connector may be removed from the switch body.

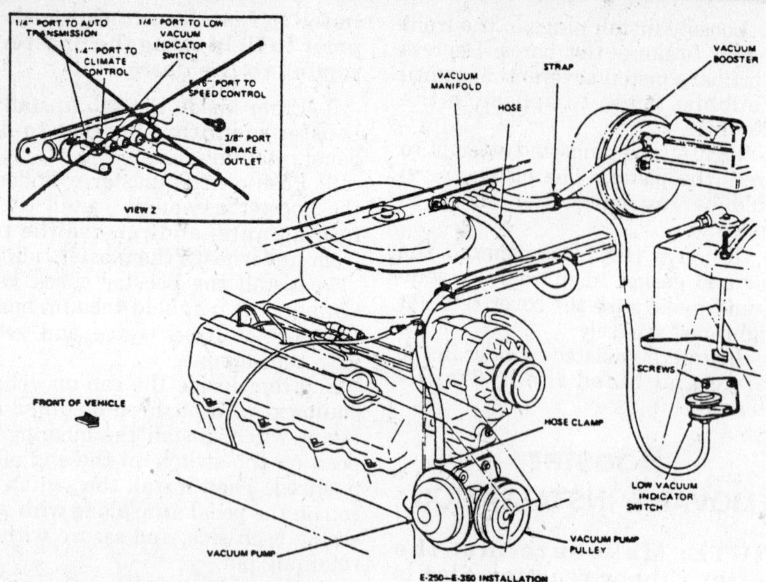

Brake booster vacuum pump—420 V8 diesel engine

2. Disconnect the brake hydraulic lines from the differential valve assembly.

3. Remove the screw retaining the pressure differential, metering and proportioning valve assembly to the frame side rail or support bracket and remove the valve assembly.

INSTALLATION

1. Mount the combination brake differential valve assembly on the frame side rail or support bracket and tighten the attaching screw.

2. Connect the brake hydraulic system lines to the differential valve assembly and tighten the tube nuts securely.

3. Connect the shell wire connector to the brake warning lamp switch. Make sure that the plastic lugs on the connector hold the connector securely to the switch.

4. Bleed the brakes and centralize the pressure differential valve.

CENTRALIZING THE PRESSURE DIFFERENTIAL VALVE

After any repair or bleeding of the primary (front brake) or secondary (rear brake) system, the dual brake system warning light will usually remain illuminated due to the pressure differential valve remaining in the offcenter position.

To centralize the pressure differential valve and turn off the warning light after the systems have been bled, follow the procedure below.

1. Turn the ignition switch to the ACC or ON position.

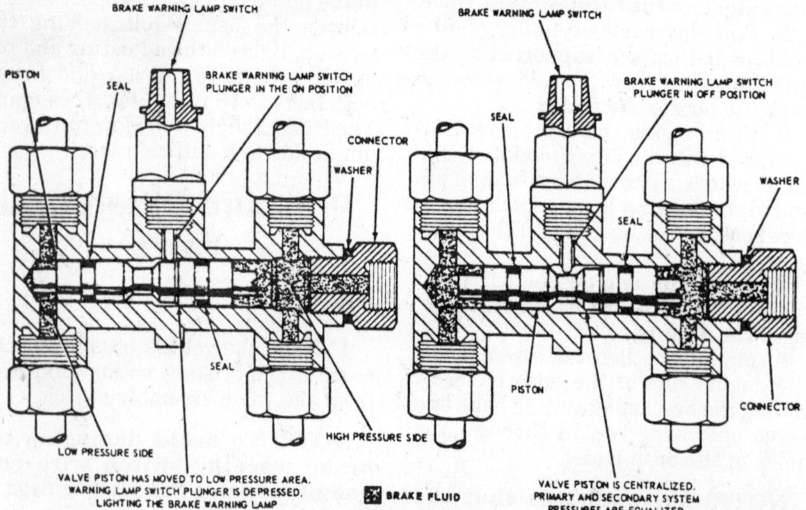

Cutaway view of the operation of the pressure differential valve

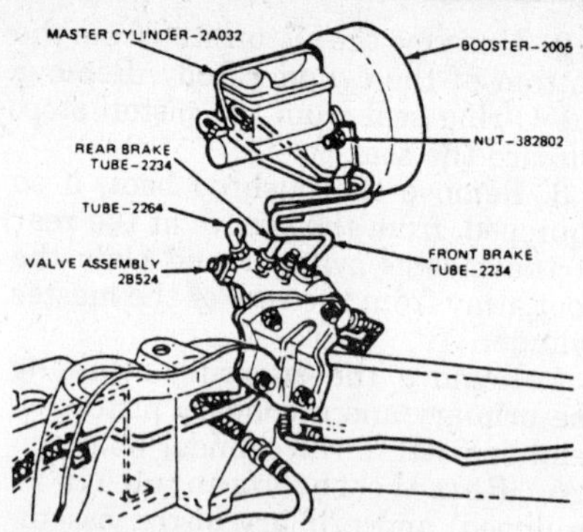

Brake proportioning valve assembly location

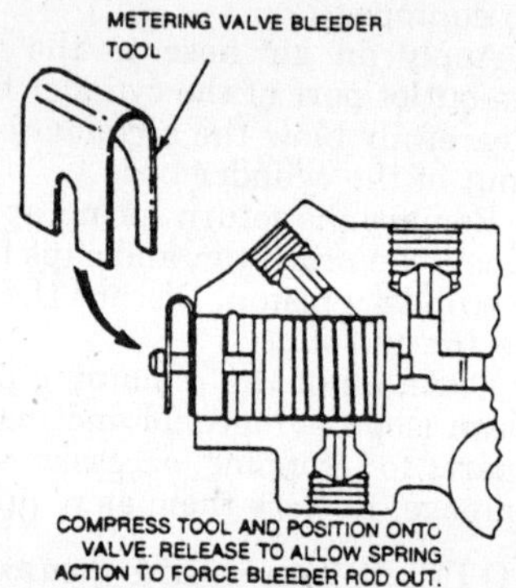

A spring clip can be used to hold the pressure differential/metering/proportioning valve's bleeder valve out on E-100 and 150 disc brake systems

2. Check the fluid level in the master cylinder reservoirs and fill them to within 1/4" (6.35mm) of the top with brake fluid, if necessary.

3. Depress the brake pedal and the piston should center itself causing the brake warning light to go out.

4. Turn the ignition switch to the OFF position.

5. Before driving the vehicle, check the operation of the brakes and be sure that a firm pedal is obtained.

Brake Hoses

Steel tubing is used the hydraulic lines between the master cylinder and the front brake tube connector, and between the rear brake tube connector and the wheel cylinders. Flexible hoses connect the brake tube to the front brake cylinders and to the rear brake tube connector.

A brake line wrench should be used when removing and installing brake lines. When replacing hydraulic brake tubing, hoses, or connectors tighten all connections securely. After replacement, bleed the brake system at the wheel cylinders and the booster (if equipped).

If a section of the brake tube is damaged, replace it with tubing of the same type, size, shape and length.

Do not use copper tubing in the hydraulic system. Be careful not to kink or crack the tubing when bending it to fit the frame or rear axle.

Always use double flared brake tubing to provide good leak proof connections. Always clean the inside of a new brake tube with clean isopropyl alcohol.

Replace a flexible brake hose if it shows signs of softening, cracking, or other damage.

When installing a new brake hose, position the hose to avoid contact with other vehicle parts. Whenever a brake hose is disconnected from a wheel cylinder or brake caliper, install a new copper washer connecting the hose.

Bleeding

When any part of the hydraulic system has been disconnected for repair or replacement, air may get into the lines and cause spongy pedal action (because air can be compressed and brake fluid cannot). To correct this condition, it is necessary to bleed the hydraulic system after it has been properly connected to be sure all air is expelled from the brake cylinders and lines.

When bleeding the brake system, bleed one brake cylinder at a time, beginning at the cylinder with the longest hydraulic line (farthest from the master cylinder) first. Keep the master cylinder reservoir filled with brake fluid during the bleeding operation. Never use brake fluid that has been drained from the hydraulic system, no matter how clean it is.

It will be necessary to centralize the pressure differential valve after a brake system failure has been corrected and the hydraulic system has been bled.

The primary and secondary hydraulic brake systems are individual systems and are bled separately. During the entire bleeding operation, do not allow the reservoir to run dry. Keep the master cylinder reservoir filled with brake fluid.

1. Clean all dirt from around the master cylinder fill cap, remove the cap and fill the master cylinder with brake fluid until the level is within 1/4" (6.35mm) of the top edge of the reservoir.
2. Clean off the bleeder screws at all 4 wheel cylinders. The bleeder screws are located on the inside of the brake backing plate, on the backside of the wheel cylinders.
3. Attach a length of rubber hose over the nozzle of the bleeder screw at the wheel to be done first. Place the other end of the hose in a glass jar, submerged in brake fluid.
4. Open the bleeder screw valve 1/2-3/4 turn.
5. Have an assistant slowly depress the brake pedal. Close the bleeder screw valve and tell your assistant to allow the brake pedal to return slowly. Continue this pumping action to force any air out of the system. When bubbles cease to appear at the end of the bleeder hose, close the bleeder valve and remove the hose.
6. Check the master cylinder fluid level and add fluid accordingly. Do this after bleeding each wheel.
7. Repeat the bleeding operation at the remaining 3 wheels, ending with the one closest to the master cylinder. Fill the master cylinder reservoir.

FRONT DISC BRAKES

CAUTION

Brake shoes contain asbestos, which has been determined to be a cancer causing agent. Never clean the brake surfaces with compressed air! Avoid inhaling any dust from any brake surface! When cleaning brake surfaces, use a commercially available brake cleaning fluid.

Pads

INSPECTION

Replace the front pads when the pad thickness is at the minimum thickness recommended by Ford Motor Co., 1/32" (0.8mm), or at the minimum allowed by the applicable state or local motor vehicle inspection code. Pad thickness may be checked by removing the wheel and looking through the inspection port in the caliper assembly.

REMOVAL & INSTALLATION

Single Piston Sliding Caliper Brakes

NOTE: Always replace the pads on both front wheels at the same time. Never replace pads on one wheel only.

1. Dip out a part of the fluid from the larger portion of the master cylinder.
2. Jack up the front of the vehicle and support it on jackstands.
3. Remove the front wheel.
4. Using an 8" (203mm) C-clamp, bottom the caliper piston by positioning the fixed end of the clamp against the inner side of the caliper and tightening the clamp against the outer pad.

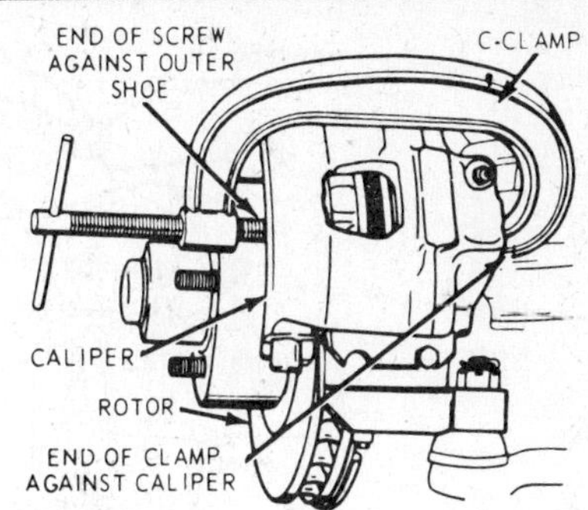

Bottom the piston in the cylinder bore with a C-clamp

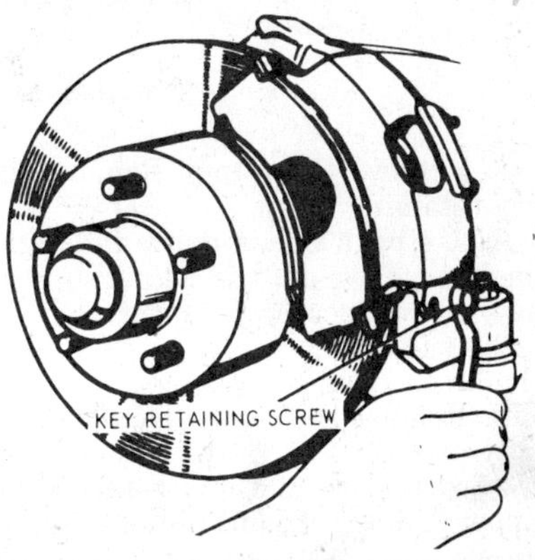

Removing the caliper support key retaining screw

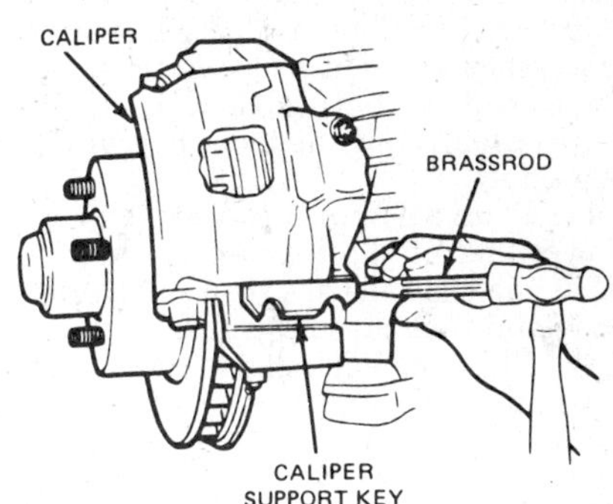

Driving out the caliper support key with a drift

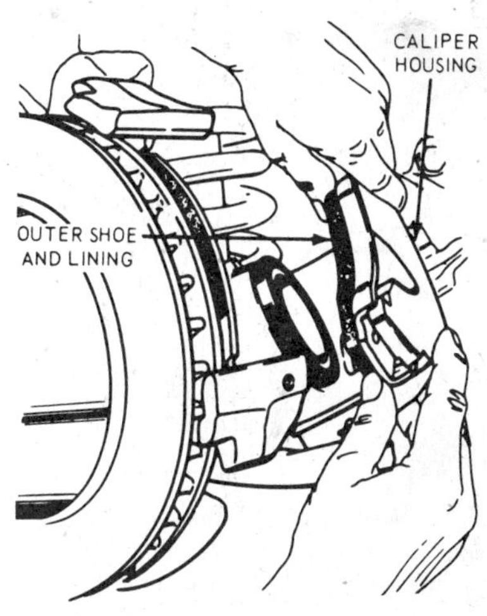

Removing the outer brake pad

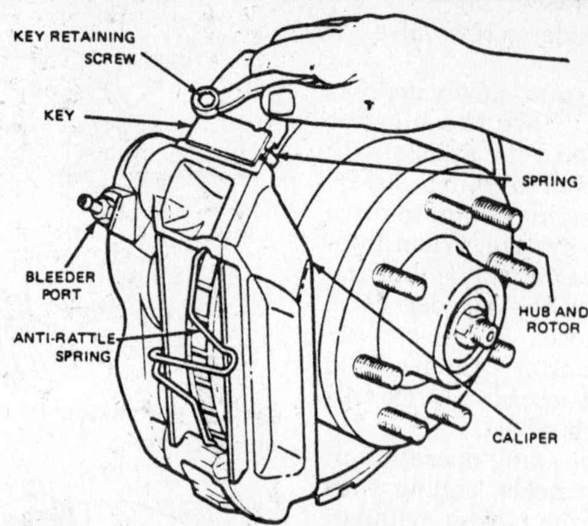

Removing the key retaining screw

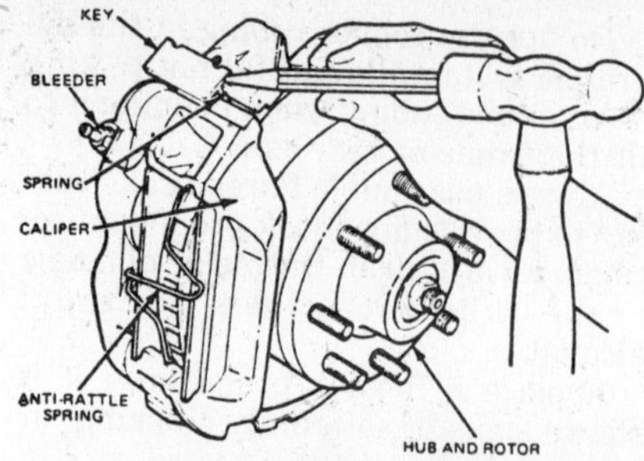

Removing the key and spring

5. Remove the clamp. Remove the key retaining screw.
6. Using a brass drift and light hammer, drive out the caliper support key, and caliper support spring.
7. It is not necessary to disconnect the brake hose.
8. Remove the caliper from its support assembly by pushing downward toward the spindle and rotating the upper end upward and out of the spindle assembly. Support the caliper with a length of wire so that no stress is placed upon the brake hose.
9. Remove the outer pad. It may be necessary to tap it loose. Remove the inner pad and anti-rattle clip.
10. Clean and inspect the caliper assembly.
11. Place a new anti-rattle clip on the lower end of the inner pad. Be sure that the clip tabs are positioned properly and that the clip is fully seated.
12. Place the inner pad in the caliper, with the loop type spring of the clip away from the rotor.
13. Place the outer pad in the caliper. Press the tabs into place with fingers or a C-clamp.
14. Place the caliper on the spindle by pivoting it around the support upper mounting surface. Be careful not to tear the boot as it slips over the inner pad.
15. Use a screwdriver to hold the upper machined surface of the caliper against the surface of the support assembly, and install a new caliper support spring and key assembly. Drive the key and spring into position with a plastic mallet. Install the key retaining screw and tighten to 20 ft.lb.
16. When pads have been installed on both front wheels, lower the vehicle and check the fluid level in the master cylinder. Fill as necessary.
17. Depress the pedal several times until a firm pedal is achieved. Do not drive the vehicle until the pedal is firm.

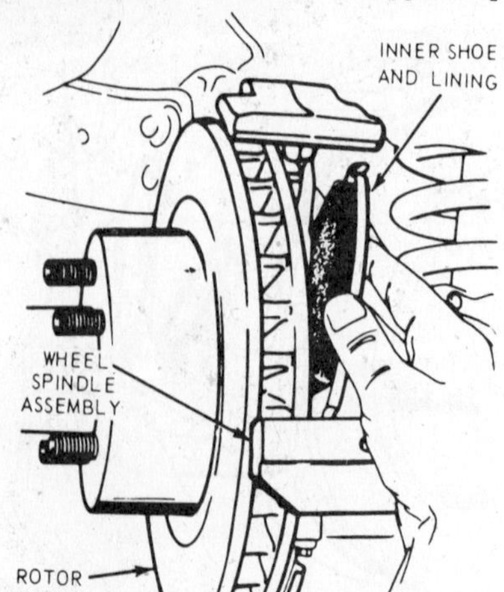

Removing the inner brake pad

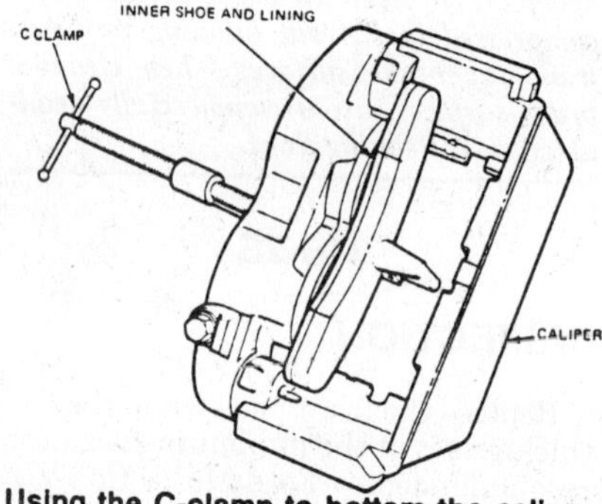

Using the C-clamp to bottom the caliper pistons

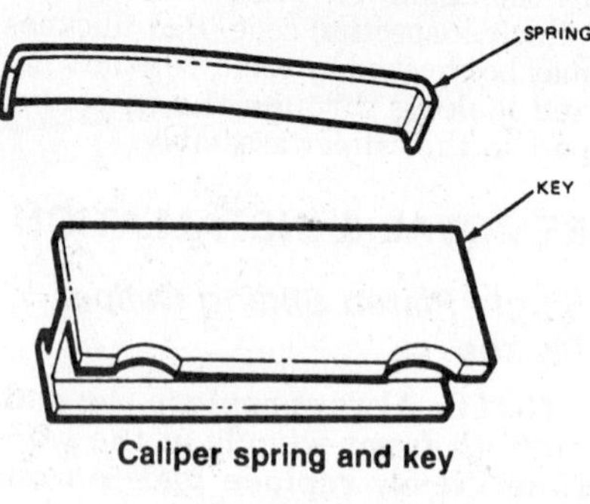

Caliper spring and key

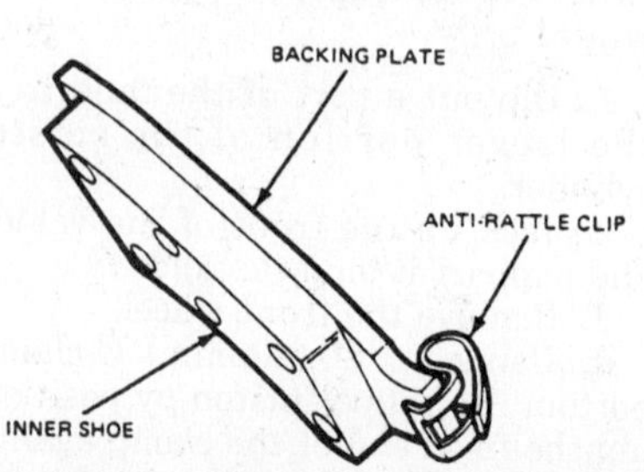

Anti-rattle clip installation on brake shoe

Dual Piston Sliding Caliper Brakes

1. Raise and support the front end on jackstands.
2. Remove the wheel assembly.
3. Remove the key retaining screw.
4. Using a brass rod and light hammer drive out the key and spring.
5. Remove the caliper from its support assembly by rotating the key and spring end out and away from the rotor. Slide the opposite end of the caliper clear of the slide in the support end of the rotor.
6. Remove the anti-rattle spring and inner and outer brake pads.
7. Clean the areas of the caliper and support that come in to contact during the sliding action of the caliper.
8. Clean any brake fluid, grease or grit off the rotor breaking surface.
9. Using an 8" C-clamp, completely bottom the pistons in the caliper. This can be done more easily by spanning both pistons with a metall bar or plate, or old brake pad backing plate, and bottoming both pistons at once.
10. Install the new inner and outer pads and a new anti-rattle spring.
11. Place the caliper rail into the slide on the support and rotate the caliper into the rotor.
12. Position the key and spring between the caliper and support assembly and start in by hand. Note that the spring is between the key and caliper and that the spring tangs overlap the ends of the key. Use a break adjusting tool to hold up the caliper against the support assembly.
13. Using a hammer, drive the key and spring into position aligning the correct notch with the existing hole in the support.
14. Secure the key to the support

with the key retaining screw. Tighten the screw to 20 ft.lb.

Heavy Duty Two Piston Sliding Caliper

1. Raise and support the vehicle safely. Remove the wheel and tire assembly.
2. Remove the four screws holding the caliper mounting plate and remove the plate.
3. Lift the caliper off the hub and rotor assembly.
4. Disconnect the brake hose and cap the hose and caliper inlet port.
5. Remove the inner shoe and lining from the anchor plate.
6. Remove the spring, pin and cup from the caliper and remove the outer brake shoe.
7. Install new inner shoe into the anchor plate. Take care that the shoes do not fall out prior to installing the caliper.
8. Using a block of wood over the pistons and a large C-clamp, push the pistons to the bottom of the cylinder bore.
9. Place the outer shoe in the caliper assembly and install the retaining pin, spring and cup.
10. Install the caliper assembly over the rotor assembly and position in the anchor plate grooves.
11. Install the caliper hold-down plate and tighten the attaching screws to 40 ft.lb.
12. Install new copper washer on the brake hose fitting and connect the brake hose to the caliper inlet port.
13. Install the wheel and tire assembly and bleed the system.
14. Lower the vehicle and top off the master cylinder.

Floating Calipers

1. Discard some of the brake fluid from the master cylinder.
2. Raise and support the front end on jackstands.
3. Remove the wheel.
4. Remove the pad mounting pins, anti-rattle springs and the pads from the caliper.
5. Loosen the piston-to-caliper mounting bolts enough to put in the new pads. DO NOT MOVE THE PISTONS!

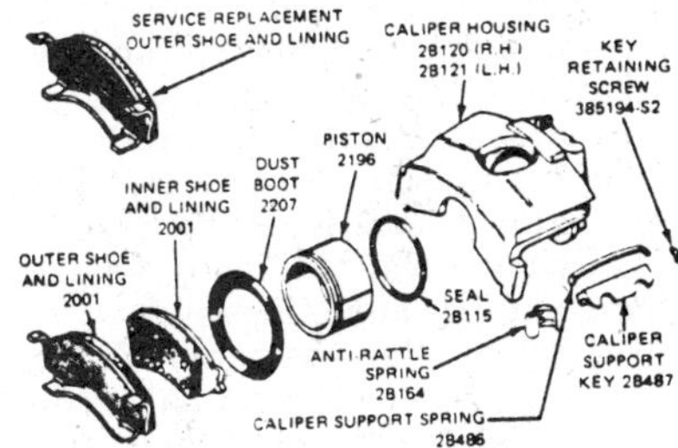

Sliding caliper assembly

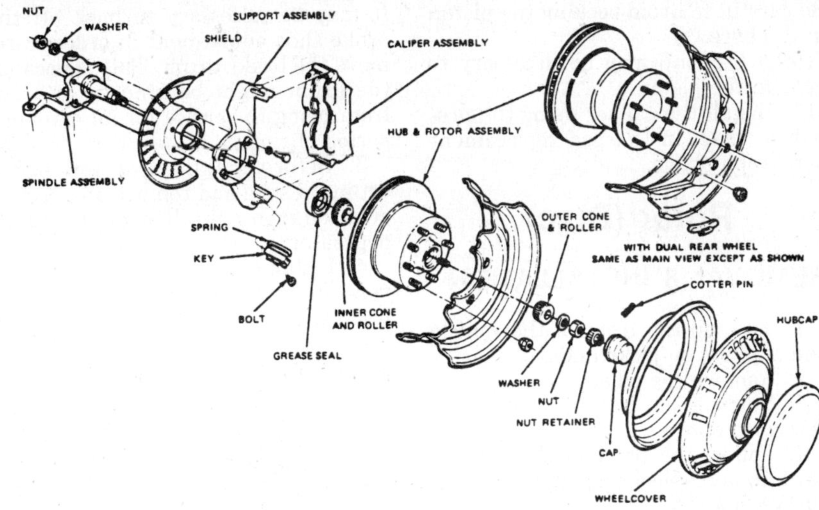

1976-86 E-250, 350 disc brake installation

6. Install the new pads, mounting pins and anti-rattle springs. Be sure that the tangs enagage the pad holes. Tighten the pad mouting pins to 17-23 ft.lb.
7. Tighten the piston housing bolts evenly and squarely to reset the the pistons in the bores. Torque the bolts to 155-185 ft.lb.
8. Replace the wheel and lower the truck. Depress the brake pedal several times to adjust the brakes BEFORE driving the truck.

Brake Calipers

OVERHAUL

1. For caliper removal, see the brake pad removal section. Disconnect the brake hose.
2. Clean the exterior of the caliper with denatured alcohol.
3. Remove the plug from the caliper inlet port and drain the fluid.
4. Air pressure is necessary to remove the piston. When a source of compressed air is found, such as a shop or gas station, apply air to the inlet port slowly and carefully until the piston(s) pops out of its bore. If high pressure air is applied the piston(s) will drop out with considerable force and cause damage or injury.
5. If the piston(s) jams, release the air pressure and tap sharply on the piston end with a soft hammer. Reapply air pressure.
6. When the piston(s) is out, remove the boot from the piston and the seal from the bore.
7. Clean the housing and piston(s) with denatured alcohol. Dry with compressed air.
8. Lubricate the new piston seal(s), boot(s) and piston(s) with clan brake fluid, and assemble them in the caliper.
9. The dust boot(s) can be worked in with the fingers and the piston should be pressed straight in until it bottoms.

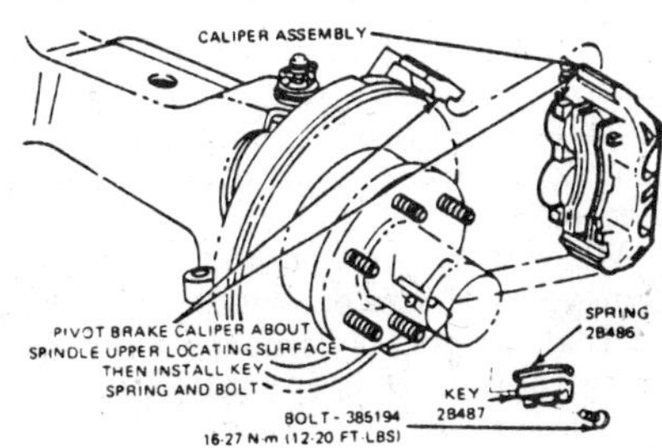

F-250 caliper installation

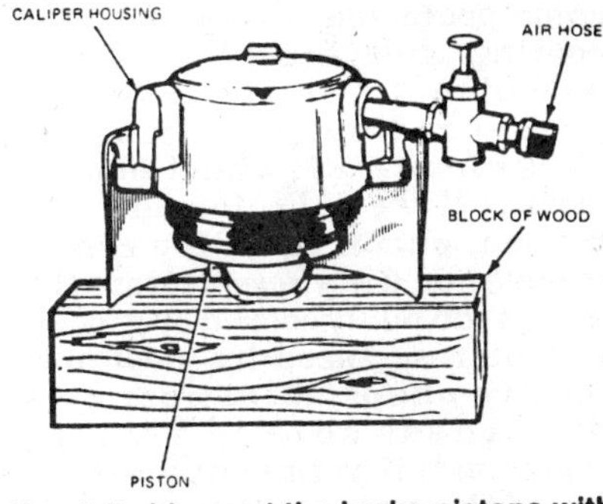

Carefully blow out the brake pistons with compressed air. Use low air pressure

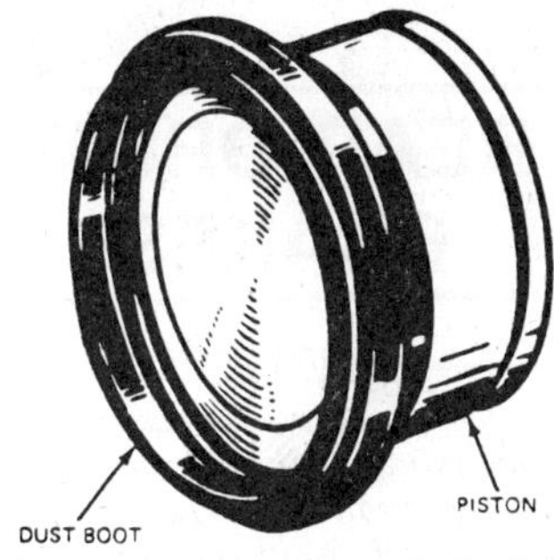

When assembling, use new just boots and lubricate the pistons with clean brake fluid

Be careful to avoid cocking the piston in the bore.

10. A C-clamp may be necessary to bottom the piston.

11. Install the caliper using the procedure given in the pad replacement paragraph above.

Rotor (Disc)

REMOVAL & INSTALLATION

1. Jack up the front of the vehicle and support on jackstands.
2. Remove the wheel.
3. Remove the caliper assembly as described above.
4. Follow the procedure given under hub and wheel bearing removal in DRIVE TRAIN.

NOTE: New rotor assemblies come protected with an anti-rust coating which should be removed with denatured alcohol or degreaser. New hubs must be packed with EP wheel bearing grease. If the old rotors are to be reused, check them for cracks, grooves or wavyness. Rotors that aren't too badly scored or grooved can be resurfaced by most automotive shops. Minimum rotor thickness should be 1.12" (28.4mm). If refinishing exceeds that, the rotor will have to be replaced.

REAR DRUM BRAKES

CAUTION

Brake shoes contain asbestos, which has been determined to be a cancer causing agent. Never clean the brake surfaces with compressed air! Avoid inhaling any dust from any brake surface! When cleaning brake surfaces, use a commercially available brake cleaning fluid.

Brake Drums

REMOVAL & INSTALLATION

Bronco
E-150, F-150
E-250, F-250 Light Duty

1. Raise the vehicle so that the wheel to be worked on is clear of the floor and install jackstands under the vehicle.
2. Remove the hub cap and the wheel assembly. Remove the 3 retaining nuts and remove the brake drum. It may be necessary to back off the brake shoe adjustment in order to remove the brake drum. This is because the drum might be grooved or worn from being in service for an extended period of time.
3. Before installing a new brake drum, be sure and remove any protective coating with a carburetor degreaser.
4. Install the brake drum in the reverse order of removal and adjust the brakes.

E-250, F-250 Heavy Duty
E-350, F-350

1. Raise and support the rear end on jackstands.
2. Remove the rear wheels.
3. Loosen the rear brake shoe adjustment.
4. Remove the rear axle retaining bolts and lockwasher.
5. Pull the axleshaft from the housing.
6. Remove the wheel bearing locknut. lockwasher and adjusting nut.
7. Remove the hub and drum assembly from the axle.
8. Remove the brake drum-to-hub retaining bolts, or bolts/nuts. Remove the drum from the hub.
9. Installation is the reverse of removal. Observe the following:
   a. Install and tighten the bearing adjusting nut to 50-80 ft.lb. while rotating the wheel.
   b. Back off (loosen) the adjusting nut ⅜ of a turn.
   c. Apply axle lube to a new lockwasher and install it with the smooth side out.
   d. Install the locknut and tighten it to 90-110 ft.lb. The wheel must rotate freely after the locknut is tightened. The wheel end-play should be within 0.001-0.010".
   e. Bend two lockwasher tabs inward over an adjusting nut flat and two lockwasher tabs outward over the locknut flat.
   f. Install the axle shaft, gasket, lockbolts, and washers. Tighten the bolts to 40-50 ft.lb.
   g. Adjust the brakes, if necessary.

INSPECTION

After the brake drum has been removed from the vehicle, it should be inspected for runout, severe scoring, cracks, and the proper inside diameter.

Minor scores on a brake drum can be removed with fine emery cloth, provided that all grit is removed from the drum before it is installed on the vehicle.

A badly scored, rough, or out-of-round (runout) drum can be ground or turned on a brake drum lathe. Do not remove any more material from the drum than is necessary to provide a smooth surface for the brake shoe to contact. The maximum diameter of the braking surface is shown on the inside of each brake drum. Brake drums that exceed the maximum braking surface diameter shown on the brake drum, either through wear or refinishing, must be replaced. This is because after the outside wall of the brake drum reaches a certain thickness (thinner than the original thickness) the drum loses its ability to dissipate the heat created by the friction between the brake drum and the brake shoes, when the brakes are applied. Also, the brake drum will have more tendency to warp and/or crack.

The maximum braking surface diameter specification, which is shown on each drum, allows for a 0.060" (1.5mm) machining cut over the original nominal drum diameter plus 0.030" (0.76mm) additional wear before reaching the diameter where the drum must be discarded. Use a brake drum micrometer to measure the inside diameter of the brake drums.

Brake Shoes

REMOVAL & INSTALLATION

1. Raise and support the vehicle and remove the wheel and brake drum from the wheel to be worked on.

NOTE: If you have never replaced the brakes on a car before and you are not too familiar with the procedures involved, only disassemble and assemble one side at a time, leaving the other side intact as a reference during reassembly.

2. Install a clamp over the ends of the wheel cylinder to prevent the pistons of the wheel cylinder from coming out, causing loss of fluid and much grief.
3. Contract the brake shoes by pulling the self-adjusting lever away from the starwheel adjustment screw and turn the starwheel up and back until the pivot nut is drawn onto the starwheel as far as it will come.
4. Pull the adjusting lever, cable and automatic adjuster spring down and toward the rear to unhook the pivot hook from the large hole in the secondary shoe web. Do not attempt to pry the pivot hook from the hole.
5. Remove the automatic adjuster spring and the adjusting lever.
6. Remove the secondary shoe-to-anchor spring with a brake tool. (Brake tools are very common implements and are available at auto parts

stores.) Remove the primary shoe-to-anchor spring and unhook the cable anchor. Remove the anchor pin plate.

7. Remove the cable guide from the secondary shoe.

8. Remove the shoe holddown springs, shoes, adjusting screw, pivot nut, and socket. Note the color of each holddown spring for assembly. To remove the holddown springs, reach behind the brake backing plate and place one finger on the end of one of the brake holddown spring mounting pins. Using a pair of pliers, grasp the washer type retainer on top of the holddown spring that corresponds to the pin that you are holding. Push down on the pliers and turn them 90° to align the slot in the washer with the head on the spring mounting pin. Remove the spring and washer retainer and repeat this operation on the holddown spring on the other shoe.

9. Remove the parking brake link and spring. Disconnect the parking brake cable from the parking brake lever.

10. After removing the rear brake secondary shoe, disassemble the parking brake lever from the shoe by removing the retaining clip and spring washer.

To assemble and install the brake shoes:

11. Assemble the parking brake lever to the secondary shoe and secure it with the spring washer and retaining clip.

12. Apply a light coating of Lubriplate® at the points where the brake shoes contact the backing plate.

13. Position the brake shoes on the backing plate, and install the holddown spring pins, springs, and spring washer type retainers. On the rear brake, install the parking brake link, spring and washer. Connect the parking brake cable to the parking brake lever.

14. Install the anchor pin plate, and place the cable anchor over the anchor pin with the crimped side toward the backing plate.

15. Install the primary shoe-to-anchor spring with the brake tool.

16. Install the cable guide on the secondary shoe web with the flanged holes fitted into the hole in the secondary shoe web. Thread the cable around the cable guide groove.

17. Install the secondary shoe-to-anchor (long) spring. Be sure that the cable end is not cocked or binding on the anchor pin when installed. All of the parts should be flat on the anchor pin. Remove the wheel cylinder piston clamp.

18. Apply Lubriplate® to the threads and the socket end of the adjusting starwheel screw. Turn the adjusting screw into the adjusting pivot nut to

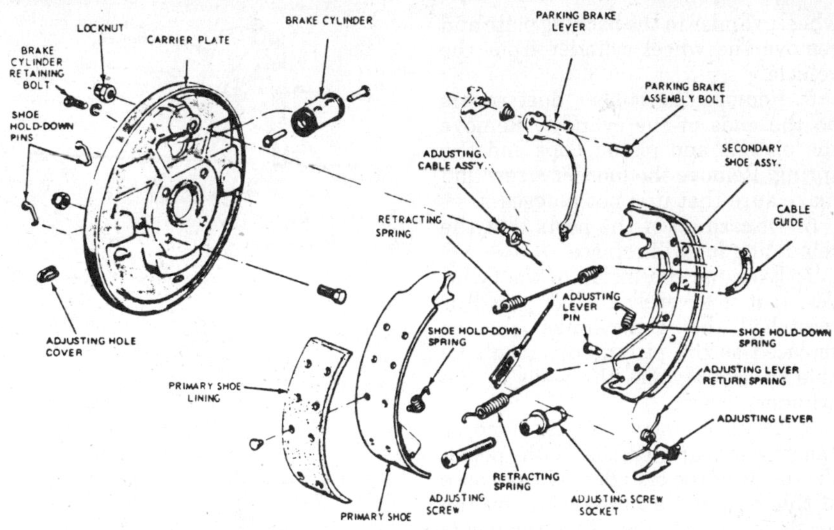

E-250, E-300, and E-350 rear brake details

the limit of the threads and then back off ½ turn.

NOTE: Interchanging the brake shoe adjusting screw assemblies from one side of the vehicle to the other would cause the brake shoes to retract rather than expand each time the automatic adjusting mechanism operated. To prevent this, the socket end of the adjusting screw is stamped with an R or an **L** for RIGHT or LEFT. The adjusting pivot nuts can be distinguished by the number of lines machined around the body of the nut; one line indicates left hand nut and two lines indicates a right hand nut.

19. Place the adjusting socket on the screw and install this assembly between the shoe ends with the adjusting screw nearest to the secondary shoe.

20. Place the cable hook into the hole in the adjusting lever from the backing plate side. The adjusting levers are stamped with an **R** (right) or an **L** (left) to indicate their installation on the right or left hand brake assembly.

21. Position the hooked end of the adjuster spring in the primary shoe web and connect the loop end of the spring to the adjuster lever hole.

22. Pull the adjuster lever, cable and automatic adjuster spring down toward the rear to engage the pivot book in the large hole in the secondary shoe web.

23. After installation, check the action of the adjuster by pulling the section of the cable between the cable guide and the adjusting lever toward the secondary shoe web far enough to lift the lever past a tooth on the adjusting screw starwheel. The lever should snap into position behind the next tooth, and release of the cable should cause the adjuster spring to return the lever to its original position. This return action of the lever will turn the adjusting screw starwheel one tooth. The lever should contact the adjusting screw starwheel one tooth above the center line of the adjusting screw.

If the automatic adjusting mechanism does not perform properly, check the following:

1. Check the cable end fittings. The cable ends should fill or extend slightly beyond the crimped section of the fittings. If this is not the case, replace the cable.
2. Check the cable guide for damage. The cable groove should be parallel to the shoe web, and the body of the guide should lie flat against the web. Replace the cable guide if this is not so.
3. Check the pivot hook on the lever. The hook surfaces should be square with the body on the lever for proper pivoting. Repair or replace the hook as necessary.
4. Make sure that the adjusting screw starwheel is properly seated in the notch in the shoe web.

Wheel Cylinders

OVERHAUL

Wheel cylinder rebuilding kits are available for reconditioning wheel cylinders. The kits usually contain new cup springs, cylinder cups, and in some, new boots. The most important factor to keep in mind when rebuilding wheel cylinders is cleanliness. Keep all dirt away from the wheel cylinders when you are reassembling them.

1. To remove the wheel cylinder, jack up the vehicle and remove the wheel, hub, and drum.
2. Disconnect the brake line at the fitting on the brake backing plate.
3. Remove the brake assemblies.
4. Remove the screws that hold the

wheel cylinder to the backing plate and remove the wheel cylinder from the vehicle.

5. Remove the rubber dust covers on the ends of the cylinder. Remove the pistons and piston cups and the spring. Remove the bleeder screw and make sure that it is not plugged.

6. Discard all of the parts that the rebuilding lot will replace.

7. Examine the inside of the cylinder. If it is severely rusted, pitted or scratched, then the cylinder must be replaced as the piston cups won't be able to seal against the walls of the cylinder.

8. Using a wheel cylinder hone or emery cloth and crocus cloth, polish the inside of the cylinder. The purpose of this is to put a new surface on the inside of the cylinder. Keep the inside of the cylinder coated with brake fluid while honing.

9. Wash out the cylinder with clean brake fluid after honing.

10. When reassembling the cylinder, dip all of the parts in clean brake fluid. Assemble the wheel cylinder in the reverse order of removal and disassembly.

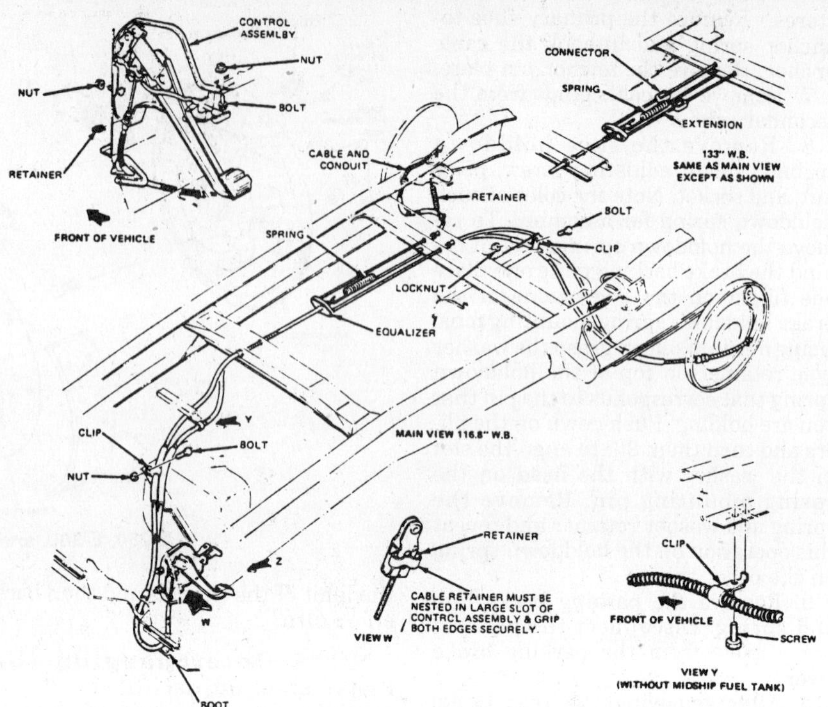

Parking brake cable routing—F-100-150 2WD, F-150 4WD

PARKING BRAKE

Equalizer-to-Control Cable

REMOVAL & INSTALLATION

1. Raise the vehicle on a hoist. Back off the equalizer nut and remove slug of front cable from the tension limiter.

2. Remove the parking brake cable from the retaining clips.

3. Lower the vehicle. Remove the forward ball end of the parking brake cable from the control assembly clevis.

4. Remove the cable and hair pin retainer from the control assembly.

5. Using a fish wire or cord attached to the control lever end of the cable, remove the cable from the vehicle.

6. Transfer the fish wire or cord to the new cable. Position the cable in the vehicle, routing the cable through the dash panel. Remove the fish wire and secure the cable to the control with the hair pin retainer.

7. Connect the forward ball end of the brake cable to the clevis of the control assembly and replace the hairpin clip around the conduit end fitting. Raise the vehicle on a hoist.

8. Route the cable and secure in place with retaining clips.

9. Connect the slug of the cable to the tension limiter connector. Adjust the parking brake cable at the equalizer.

10. Rotate both rear wheels to be sure that the parking brakes are not dragging.

Equalizer-to-Rear Wheel Cables

REMOVAL & INSTALLATION

1. Raise the vehicle and remove the hub cab, wheel, tension limiter and brake drum. Remove the locknut on the threaded rod and disconnect the cable from the equalizer.

2. Compress the prongs that retain the cable housing into the brake backing plate cable and housing out of the bracket.

3. Working on the wheel side, compress the prongs on the cable retainer so they can pass through the hole in the brake backing plate. Draw the cable retainer out of the hole.

4. With the spring tension off the parking brake lever, lift the cable out of the slot in the lever, and remove the

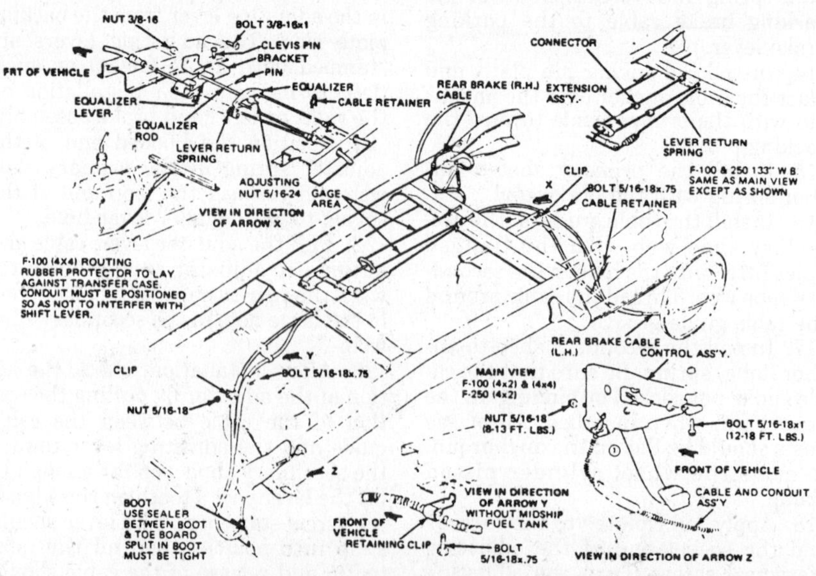

Parking cable routing—F-100, F-150, F-250 light-duty

cable through the brake backing plate hole.

5. Pull the cable through the brake backing plate until the end of the cable is inserted over the slot in the parking brake lever. Pull the excess slack from the cable and insert the cable housing into the brake backing plate access hole until the retainer prongs expand.

6. Insert the front end of the cable housing through the frame crossmember bracket until the prong expands. Insert the ball end of the cable into the key hole slots on the equalizer, rotate the equalizer 90° and recouple the tension limiter threaded rod to the equalizer.

On vehicles with web ledge brakes, check the clearance between the parking brake operating lever and cam plate. The clearance should be 0.015" (0.38mm) when the brakes are fully released.

7. Install the rear brake drum, wheel, and hub cap, and adjust the rear brake shoes.

8. Adjust the parking brake tension.

9. Rotate both rear wheels to be sure that the parking brakes are not dragging.

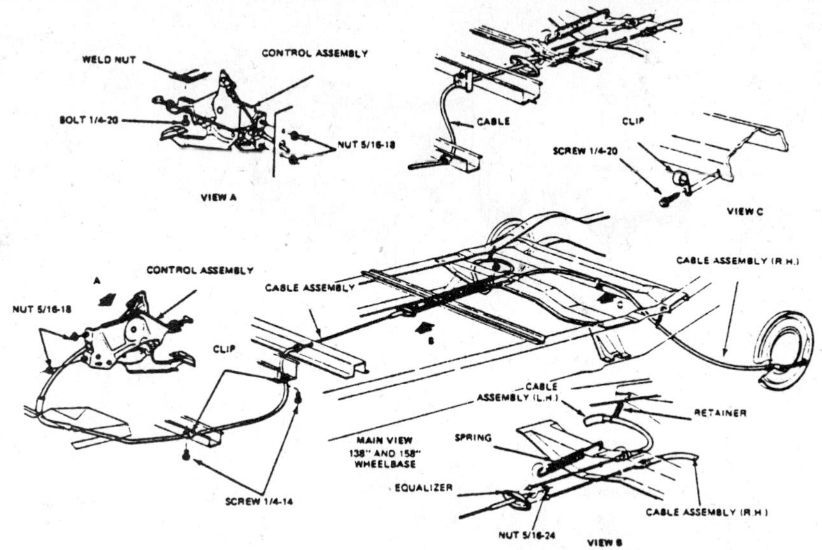

Van pedal operated parking brake linkage

ADJUSTMENT

1. Make sure the brake drums are cold for correct adjustment.

2. Depress the parking brake pedal until the parking brake control is in the second tooth (two notches or two clicks).

3. Attach a Rotunda cable tension gauge (model 210018) or equivalent behind the equalizer assembly (either toward the right or left rear drum assembly).

4. Turn the equalizer adjusting nut until the tension reads 250 ft.lb. as read on the cable tension gauge.

5. Back off the equalizer adjusting nut until the tension reads 50 ft.lb. on the cable tension gauge.

6. For the final adjustment, retighten the equalizer adjusting nut until the tension reads between 60-100 ft.lb. as read on the cable tension gauge.

MANUAL TRANSMISSION OVERHAUL

3.03 3-Speed

The Ford 3.03 is a fully synchronized three speed transmission. All gears except reverse are in constant mesh. Forward speed gear changes are accomplished with synchronizer sleeves.

DISASSEMBLY

1. Drain the lubricant by removing the lower extension housing bolt.

2. Remove the case cover and gasket.

3. Remove the long spring that holds the detent plug in the case and remove the detent plug with a small magnet.

4. Remove the extension housing and gasket.

5. Remove the front bearing retainer and gasket.

6. Remove the filler plug on the right side of the transmission case. Working through the plug opening, drive the roll pin out of the case and countershaft with a ¼" punch.

7. Hold the countershaft gear with a hook. Install dummy shaft and push the countershaft out of the rear of the case. As the countershaft comes out, lower the gear cluster to the bottom of the case. Remove the countershaft.

8. Remove the snapring that holds the speedometer drive gear on the output shaft. Slip the gear off the shaft and remove the gear lock ball.

9. Remove the snapring that holds the output shaft bearing. Using a special bearing puller, remove the output shaft bearing.

10. Place both shift levers in the neutral (center) position.

11. Remove the set screw that holds the first/reverse shift fork to the shift rail. Slip the first/reverse shift rail out through the rear of the case.

12. Move the first/reverse synchronizer forward as far as possible. Rotate the first/reverse shift fork upwards and lift it out of the case.

13. Place the second/third shift fork in the second position. Remove the set screw. Rotate the shift rail 90°.

14. Lift the interlock plug out of the case with a magnet.

15. Remove the expansion plug from the second/third shift rail by lightly tapping the end of the rail. Remove the second/third shift rail.

16. Remove the second/third shift rail detent plug and spring from detent bore.

17. Remove the input gear and shaft from the case.

18. Rotate the second/third shift fork upwards and remove from case.

19. Using caution, lift the output shaft assembly out through top of case.

20. Lift the reverse idler gear and thrust washers out of case. Remove the countershaft gear, thrust washer and dummy shaft from case.

21. Remove the snapring from the front of the output shaft. Slip the synchronizer and second gear off shaft.

22. Remove the second snapring from output shaft and remove the thrust washer, first gear and blocking ring.

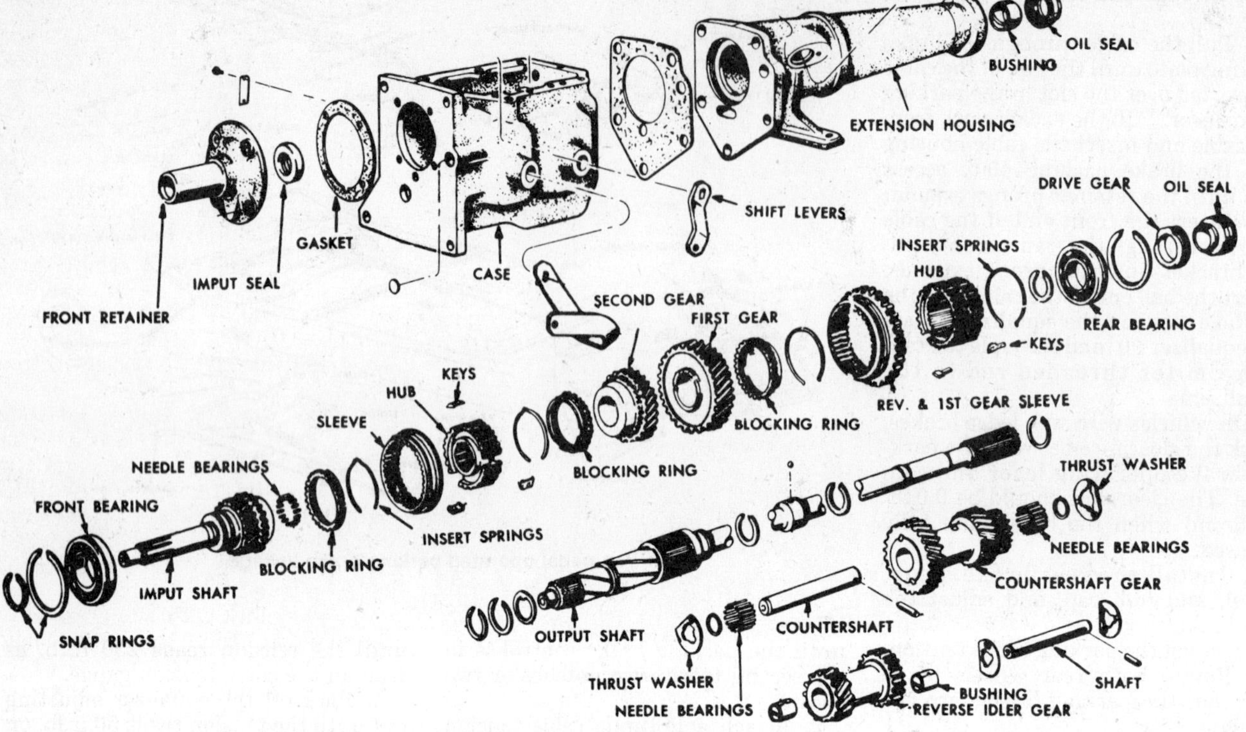

Ford 3.03 3-speed

23. Remove the third snapring from the output shaft. The first/reverse synchronizer hub is a press fit on the output shaft. Remove the synchronizer hub with an arbor press.

WARNING: Do not attempt to remove or install the synchronizer hub by prying or hammering.

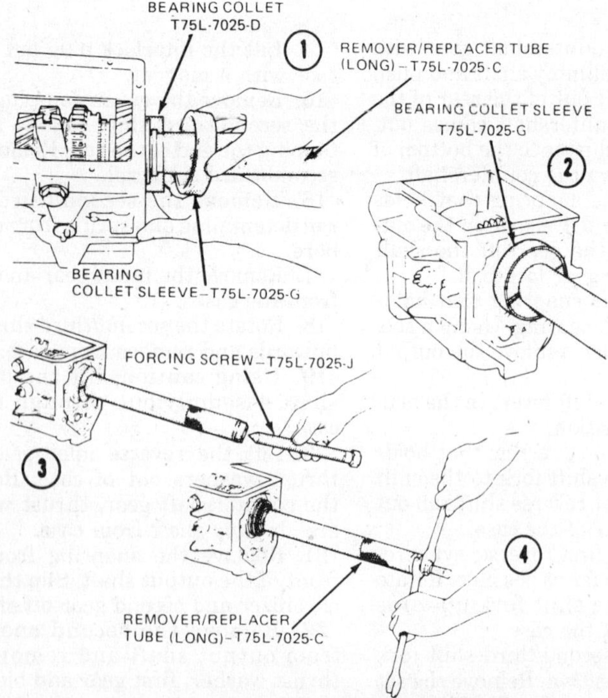

Removing output shaft bearing

SHIFT LEVERS & SEALS

1. Remove shift levers from the shafts. Slip the levers out of case. Discard shaft sealing O-rings.
2. Lubricate and install new O-rings on shift shafts.
3. Install the shift shafts in the case and secure shift levers.

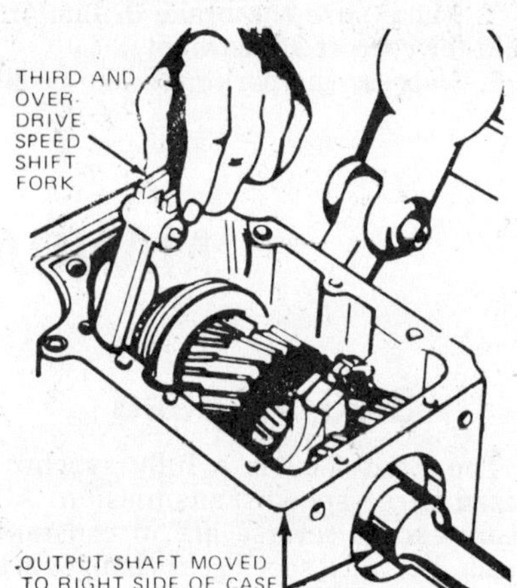

Removing shift fork from case

INPUT SHAFT BEARINGS

1. Remove the snapring securing the input shaft bearing. Using an arbor press, remove the bearing.
2. Press the input shaft bearing onto shaft using correct tool.

SYNCHRONIZERS

1. Scribe alignment marks on synchronizer hubs before disassembly. Remove each synchronizer hub from the synchronizer sleeves.
2. Separate the inserts and insert springs from the hubs.

WARNING: Do not mix parts from the separate synchronizer assemblies.

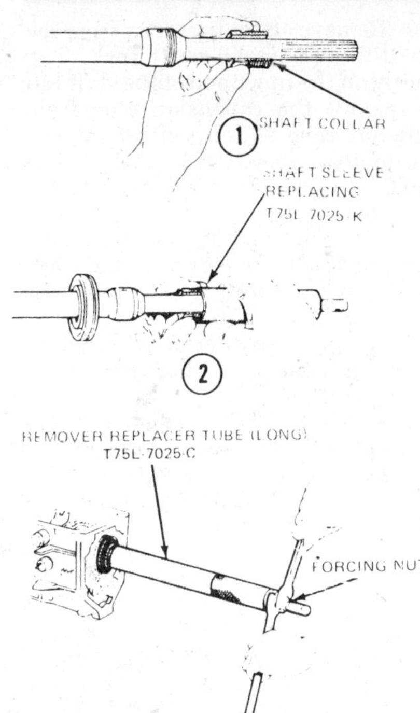

Installing output shaft bearing

3. Install the insert spring in the hub of the first/reverse synchronizer. Be sure that the spring covers all the insert grooves. Start the hub on the sleeve making certain that the scribed marks are properly aligned. Place the three inserts in the hub, small ends on the inside. Slide the sleeve and reverse gear onto hub.

4. Install one insert spring into a groove on the second/third synchronizer hub. Be sure that all three insert slots are covered. Align the scribed marks on the hub and sleeve and start the hub into the sleeve. Position the three inserts on the top of the retaining spring and push the assembly together. Install the remaining retainer spring so that the spring ends cover the same slots as the first spring. Do not stagger the springs. Place a synchronizer blocking ring on the ends of the synchronizer sleeve.

COUNTERSHAFT GEAR BEARINGS

1. Remove the dummy shaft, needle bearings and bearing retainers from the countershaft gear.

2. Coat the bore in each end of the countershaft gear with grease.

3. Hold the dummy shaft in the gear and install the needle bearings in the case.

4. Place the countershaft gear, dummy shaft, and needle bearings in the case.

5. Place the case in a vertical position. Align the gear bore and the thrust washers with the bores in the case and install the countershaft.

6. Place the case in a horizontal position. Check the countershaft gear end play with a feeler gauge. Clearance should be between 0.004-0.018". If clearance does not come within specifications, replace the thrust washers.

7. Install the dummy shaft in the countershaft gear and leave the gear at the bottom of the transmission case.

ASSEMBLY

1. Cover the reverse idler gear thrust surfaces in the case with a thin film of lubricant, and install the two thrust washers in the case.

2. Install the reverse idler gear and shaft in the case. Align the case bore and thrust washers with gear bore and install the reverse idler shaft.

3. Measure the reverse idler gear end play with a feeler gauge; clearance should be between 0.004-0.018". If end play is not within specifications, replace the thrust washers. If clearance is correct, leave the reverse idler gear in case.

4. Lubricate the output shaft splines and machined surfaces with transmission oil.

5. The first/reverse synchronizer hub is a press fit on the output shaft. Hub must be installed in an arbor press. Install the synchronizer hub with the teeth-end of the gear facing towards the rear of the shaft.

WARNING: Do not attempt to install the first/reverse synchronizer with a hammer.

6. Place the blocking ring on the tapered surface of the first gear.

7. Slide the first gear on the output shaft with the blocking ring toward the rear of the shaft. Rotate the gear as necessary to engage the three notches in the blocking ring with the synchronizer inserts. Install the thrust washer and snapring.

8. Slide the blocking ring onto the tapered surface of the second gear. Slide the second gear with blocking ring and the second/third synchronizer on the mainshaft. Be sure that the tapered surface of second gear is facing the front of the shaft and that the notches in the blocking ring engage the synchronizer inserts. Install the snapring and secure assembly.

9. Cover the core of the input shaft with a thin coat of grease.

WARNING: A thick film of grease will plug lubricant holes and cause damage to bearings.

10. Install bearings. Install the input shaft through the front of the case and insert snapring in the bearing groove.

11. Install the output shaft assembly in the case. Position the second/third shift fork on the second/third synchronizer.

12. Place a detent plug spring and a plug in the case. Place the second/third synchronizer in the second gear position (toward the rear of the case). Align the fork and install the second/third shift rail. It will be necessary to depress the detent plug to install the shift rail in the bore. Move the rail forward until the detent plug enters the forward notch (second gear).

13. Secure the fork to the shift rail with a set screw and place the synchronizer in neutral.

14. Install the interlock plug in the case.

15. Place the first/reverse synchronizer in the first gear position (towards the front of the case). Place the shift fork in the groove of the synchronizer. Rotate the fork into position and install the shift rail. Move the shift rail inward until the center notch (neutral) is aligned with the detent bore. Secure shift fork with set screw.

16. Install a new shift rail expansion plug in the front of the case.

17. Hold the input shaft and blocking ring in position and move the output shaft forward to seat the pilot in the roller bearings on the input gear.

18. Tap the input gear bearing into place while holding the output shaft. Install the front bearing retainer and gasket. Torque attaching bolts to specifications.

19. Install the large snapring on the rear bearing. Place the bearing on the output shaft with the snapring end toward the rear of the shaft. Press the bearing into place using a special tool. Secure the bearing to the shaft with the snapring.

20. Hold the speedometer drive gear lock ball in the detent and slide the speedometer drive gear into position. Secure with snapring.

21. Place the transmission in the vertical position. Working with a screwdriver through the drain hole in the bottom of the case, align the bore of the countershaft gear and the thrust washer with the bore in the case.

22. Working from the rear of the case, push the dummy shaft out of the countershaft gear with the countershaft. Align the roll pin hole in the countershaft with the matching hole in the case. Drive the shaft into place and install the roll pin.

23. Position the new extension housing gasket on the case with sealer. Install the extension housing and torque to specification.

24. Place the transmission in gear and pour gear oil over entire gear train while rotating the input shaft.

25. Install the remaining detent plug and long spring in case.

26. Position cover gasket on case

with sealer and install cover. Torque cover bolts to specifications.

27. Check operation of transmission in all gear positions.

4-Speed Overdrive

The Ford 4-speed overdrive transmission is fully synchronized in all forward gears. The 4-speed shift control is serviced as a unit and should not be disassembled. The lubricant capacity is 4.5 pints.

DISASSEMBLY

1. Remove retaining clips and flat washers from the shift rods at the levers.
2. Remove shift linkage control bracket attaching screws and remove shift linkage and control brackets.
3. Remove cover attaching screws. Then lift cover and gasket from the case. Remove the long spring that holds the detent plug in the case. Remove the plug with a magnet.
4. Remove extension housing attaching screws. Then, remove extension housing and gasket.
5. Remove input shaft bearing retainer attaching screws. Then, slide retainer from the input shaft.
6. Working a dummy shaft in from the front of the case, drive the countershaft out the rear of the case. Let the countergear assembly lie in the bottom of the case. Remove the set screw from the first/second shift fork. Slide the first/second shift rail out of the rear of the case. Use a magnet to remove the interlock detent from between the first/second and third/fourth shift rails.
7. Locate first/second speed gear shift lever in neutral. Locate third/fourth speed gear shift lever in third speed position.

NOTE: On overdrive transmissions, locate third/fourth speed gear shift-lever in the fourth speed position.

8. Remove the lockbolt that holds the third/fourth speed shift rail detent spring and plug in the left side of the case. Remove spring and plug with a magnet.
9. Remove the detent mechanism set screw from top of case. Then, remove the detent spring and plug with a small magnet.
10. Remove attaching screw from the third/fourth speed shift fork. Tap lightly on the inner end of the shift rail to remove the expansion plug from front of case. Then, withdraw the third/fourth speed shift rail from the front. Do not lose the interlock pin from rail.
11. Remove attaching screw from the first and second speed shift fork. Slide the first/second shift rail from the rear of case.
12. Remove the interlock and detent plugs from the top of the case with a magnet.
13. Remove the snapring or disengage retainer that holds the speedometer drive gear to the output shaft, then remove speedometer gear drive ball.
14. Remove the snapring used to hold the output shaft bearing to the shaft. Pull out the output shaft bearing.
15. Remove the input shaft bearing snaprings. Use a press to remove the input shaft bearing. Remove the input shaft and blocking ring from the front of the case.
16. Move output shaft to the right side of the case. Then, maneuver the

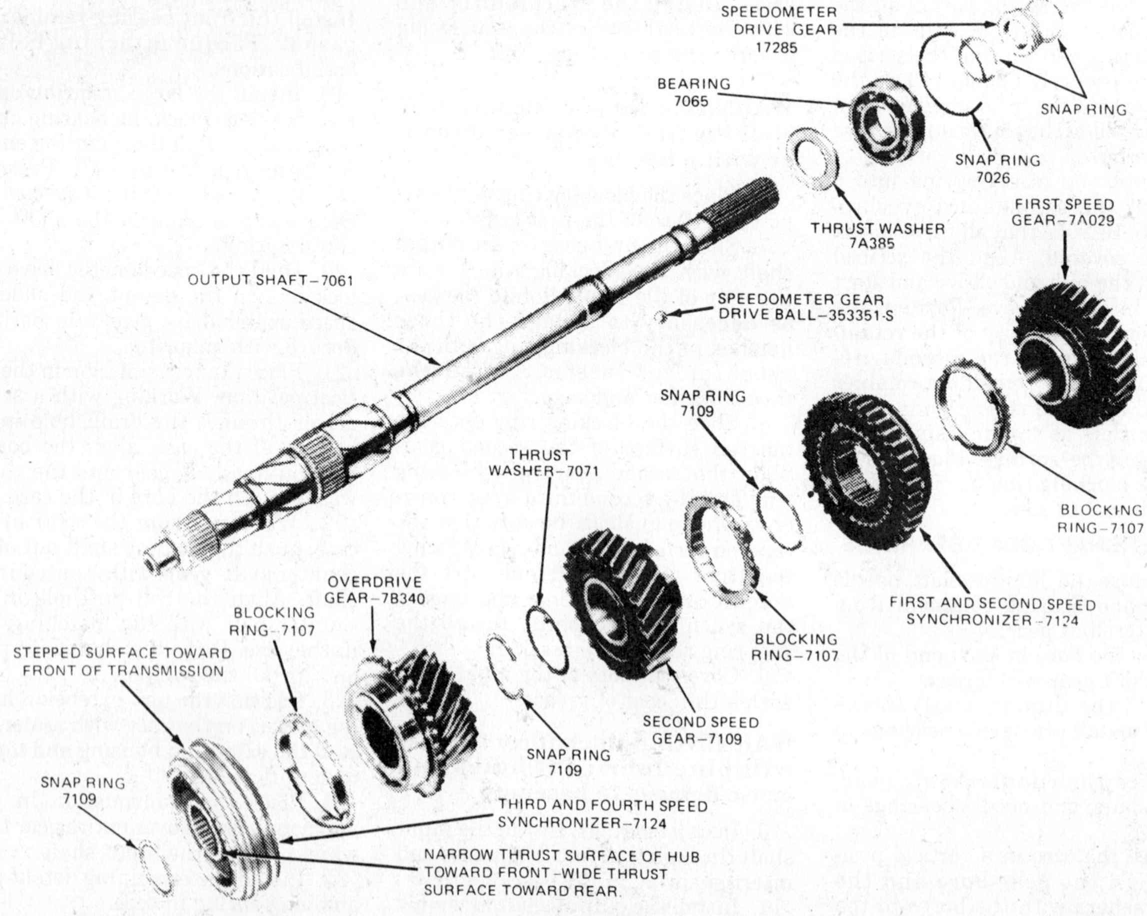

Output shaft

forks to permit lifting them from the case.

17. Support the thrust washer and first-speed gear to prevent sliding from the shaft, then lift output shaft from the case.

18. Remove reverse gear shift fork attaching screw. Rotate the reverse shift rail 90°, then, slide the shift rail out the rear of the case. Lift out the reverse shift fork.

19. Remove the reverse detent plug and spring from the case with a magnet.

20. Using a dummy shaft, remove the reverse idler shaft from the case.

21. Lift reverse idler gear and thrust washers from the case. Be careful not to drop the bearing rollers or the dummy shaft from the gear.

22. Lift the countergear, thrust washers, rollers and dummy shaft assembly from the case.

23. Remove the next snapring from the front of the output shaft. Then, slide the third/fourth synchronizer blocking ring and the third speed gear from the shaft.

24. Remove the next snapring and the second speed gear thrust washer from the shaft. Slide the second speed gear and the blocking ring from the shaft.

25. Remove the snapring, then slide the first/second synchronizer, blocking ring and the first speed gear from the shaft.

26. Remove the thrust washer from rear of the shaft.

CAM & SHAFT SEALS

1. Remove attaching nut and washers from each shift lever, then remove the three levers.

2. Remove the three cams and shafts from inside the case.

3. Replace the old O-rings with new ones that have been well-lubricated.

4. Slide each cam and shaft into its respective bore in the transmission.

5. Install the levers and secure them with their respective washers and nuts.

SYNCHRONIZERS

1. Push the synchronizer hub from each synchronizer sleeve.

2. Separate the inserts and springs from the hubs. Do not mix parts of the first/second with parts of third/fourth synchronizers.

3. To assemble, position the hub in the sleeve. Be sure the alignment marks are properly indexed.

4. Place the three inserts into place on the hub. Install the insert springs so that the irregular surface (hump) is seated in one of the inserts. Do not stagger the springs.

COUNTERSHAFT GEAR

1. Dismantle the countershaft gear assembly.

2. Assemble the gear by coating each end of the countershaft gear bore with grease.

3. Install dummy shaft in the gear. Then install 21 bearing rollers and a retainer washer in each end of the gear.

REVERSE IDLER GEAR

1. Dismantle reverse idler gear.

2. Assemble reverse idler gear by coating the bore in each end of reverse idler gear with grease.

3. Hold the dummy shaft in the gear and install the 22 bearing rollers and the retainer washer into each end of the gear.

4. Install the reverse idler sliding gear on the splines of the reverse idler gear. Be sure the shift fork groove is toward the front.

INPUT SHAFT SEAL

1. Remove the seal from the input shaft bearing retainer.

2. Coat the sealing surface of a new seal with lubricant, then press the new seal into the input shaft bearing retainer.

ASSEMBLY

1. Grease the countershaft gear thrust surfaces in the case. Then, position a thrust washer at each end of the case.

2. Position the countershaft gear, dummy shaft, and roller bearings in the case.

3. Align the gear bore and thrust washers with the bores in the case. Install the countershaft.

4. With the case in a horizontal position, countershaft gear end-play should be from 0.004-0.018". Use thrust washers to obtain play within these limits.

5. After establishing correct endplay, place the dummy shaft in the countershaft gear and allow the gear assembly to remain on the bottom of the case.

6. Grease the reverse idler gear thrust surfaces in the case, and position the two thrust washers.

7. Position the reverse idler gear, sliding gear, dummy, etc., in place. Make sure that the shift fork groove in the sliding gear is toward the front.

8. Align the gear bore and thrust washers with the case bores and install the reverse idler shaft.

9. Reverse idler gear end-play should be 0.004-0.018". Use selective thrust washers to obtain play within these limits.

10. Position reverse gear shift rail detent spring and detent plug in the case. Hold the reverse shift fork in place on the reverse idler sliding gear and install the shift rail from the rear of the case. Lock the fork to the rail with the Allen head set screws.

11. Install the first/second synchronizer onto the output shaft. The first and reverse synchronizer hub are a press fit and should be installed with gear teeth facing the rear of the shaft.

NOTE: On overdrive transmissions, first and reverse synchronizer hub is a slip fit.

12. Place the blocking ring on second gear. Slide second speed gear onto the front of the shaft with the synchronizer coned surface toward the rear.

13. Install the second speed gear thrust washer and snapring.

14. Slide the fourth gear onto the shaft with the synchronizer coned surface front.

15. Place a blocking ring on the fourth gear.

16. Slide the third/fourth speed gear synchronizer onto the shaft. Be sure that the inserts in the synchronizer engage the notches in the blocking ring. Install the snapring onto the front of the output shaft.

17. Put the blocking ring on the first gear.

18. Slide the first gear onto the rear of the output shaft. Be sure that the inserts engage the notches in the blocking ring and that the shift fork groove is toward the rear.

19. Install heavy thrust washer onto the rear of the output shaft.

20. Lower the output shaft assembly into the case.

21. Position the first/second speed shift fork and the third/fourth speed shift fork in place on their respective gears. Rotate them into place.

22. Place a spring and detent plug in the detent bore. Place the reverse shift rail into neutral position.

23. Coat the third/fourth speed shift rail interlock pin (tapered ends) with grease, then position it in the shift rail.

24. Align the third/fourth speed shift fork with the shift rail bores and slide the shift rail into place. Be sure that the three detents are facing the outside of the case. Place the front synchronizer into fourth-speed position and install the set screw into the third/fourth speed shift fork. Move the synchronizer to neutral position. Install the third/fourth speed shift rail detent plug, spring and bolt into the left side of the transmission case. Place the detent plug (tapered ends) in the detent bore.

25. Align first/second speed shift fork with the case bores and slide the shift rail into place. Lock the fork with the set screw.

26. Coat the input gear bore with a

small amount of grease. Then install the 15 bearing rollers.

27. Put the blocking ring in the third/fourth synchronizer. Place the input shaft gear in the case. Be sure that the output shaft pilot enters the roller bearing of the input shaft gear.

28. With a new gasket on the input bearing retainer, dip attaching bolts in sealer, install bolts and torque to 30-36 ft.lb.

29. Press on the output shaft bearing, then install the snapring to hold the bearing.

30. Position the speedometer gear drive ball in the output shaft and slide the speedometer drive gear into place. Secure gear with snapring.

31. Align the countershaft gear bore and thrust washers with the bore in the case. Install the countershaft.

32. With a new gasket in place, install and secure the extension housing. Dip the extension housing screws in sealer, then torque screws to 42-50 ft.lb.

33. Install the filler plug and the drain plug.

34. Pour E.P. gear oil over the entire gear train while rotating the input shaft.

35. Place each shift fork in all positions to make sure they function properly. Install the remaining detent plug in the case, followed by the spring.

36. With a new cover gasket in place, install the cover. Dip attaching screws in sealer, then torque screws to 14-19 ft.lb.

37. Coat the third/fourth speed shift rail plug bore with sealer. Install a new plug.

38. Secure each shift rod to its respective lever with a spring washer, flat washer and retaining pin.

39. Position the shift linkage control bracket to the extension housing. Install and torque the attaching screws to 12-15 ft.lb.

Single Rail 4-Speed Overdrive

The Single Rail Overdrive (SROD) transmission is a 4-speed unit that has all forward speeds synchronized. A single control rod (rail) connects the shift lever to the transmission shift lever rails. The lubricant capacity is 4.5 pints.

DISASSEMBLY

1. Remove the lower extension housing bolt to drain the transmission.

2. Remove the cover screws; remove the cover and discard the gasket.

3. Remove the screw, detent spring and plug from the case; a magnetized rod will aid in removal.

4. Drive the roll pin from the shifter shaft.

5. Remove the backup lamp switch, snapring, and the dust cover from the rear of the extension housing.

6. Remove the shifter shaft from the turret assembly.

7. Remove the extension housing bolts and housing; discard the gasket.

8. Remove the speedometer gear snapring; slide the gear from the shaft and remove the drive ball.

9. Remove the output shaft bearing snapring. Remove the bearing.

10. Use a dummy shaft to push the countershaft out of the rear of the case. Lower the countershaft gear to the bottom of the case.

11. Remove the input shaft bearing retainer attaching bolts and slide the retainer and gasket from the input shaft; discard the gasket.

12. Remove the input shaft bearing snapring; remove the bearing.

13. Remove the input shaft and blocking ring (including roller bearings) from the case.

14. Remove the overdrive shift pawl, gear selector and interlock plate. Remove the 1-2 gearshift selector arm plate. Remove the roll pin from the 3rd-overdrive shift fork.

15. Drive the 3rd-overdrive shift rail and expansion plug from the rear of the case. Remove the mainshaft.

16. Remove the 1st and 2nd gear shift fork; remove the 3rd-overdrive shift fork.

17. Remove the countershaft gear and thrust washers from the case.

18. Remove the snapring from the front of the output shaft. Slide the 3rd gear and O.D. synchronizer, blocking ring, and gear from the shaft.

19. Remove the next snapring and washer; remove second gear. Remove next snapring and remove the 1st-2nd synchronizer. Slide the 1st gear and blocking ring from the rear of the shaft.

20. Remove the roll pin from the reverse fork, slide the reverse shifter rail through the rear of the case, and remove the reverse gearshift fork and spacer.

21. Drive the reverse gear shaft out the rear of the case.

22. Remove the reverse idler gear, thrust washers and roller bearings.

23. Remove the retaining clip, reverse gearshift relay lever and reverse gear selector fork pivot pin. Remove the O.D. shift control link assembly. Remove the shift shaft seal from the rear of the case; remove the expansion plug from the front of the case.

ASSEMBLY

Assembly is the reverse. Tighten the extension housing bolts in a criss-cross pattern to 42-50 ft.lb. The bearing rollers, extension housing bushing, shifter shaft and gear shift damper bushing are to be lubricated with grease before assembly (Ford ESW-M1C109-A or the equivalent). The gear shift shaft sleeve and the turret cover assembly should be coated with sealer prior to installation. The intermediate and high rail welch plug must be seated firmly; it must not protrude above the front face of the case, nor seat below 0.6″ below the front face.

With the 1st gear thrust washer clamped tightly against the output shaft shoulder, 1st gear endplay must be 0.005-0.024″ 2nd gear endplay must be 0.003-0.021″ O.D. endplay must be 0.009-0.023″. Countershaft gear endplay, checked after installation between the thrust washers, must be 0.004-0.018″.

When the gearshift selector arm plate is seated in the 1st-2nd shift fork plate slot, the shifter shaft must pass freely through the bore without binding.

NP-435 4-Speed

DISASSEMBLY

1. Mount the transmission in a holding fixture. Remove the parking brake assembly, if one is installed.

2. Shift the gears into neutral by replacing the gear shift lever temporarily, or by using a bar or screw driver.

3. Remove the cover screws, the second screw from the front on each side is shouldered with a split washer for installation alignment.

4. While lifting the cover, rotate slightly counterclockwise to provide clearance for the shift levers. Remove the cover.

5. Lock the transmission in two gears and remove the output flange nut, the yoke, and the parking brake drum as a unit assembly.

NOTE: The drum and yoke are balanced and unless replacement of parts are required, it is recommended that the drum and yoke be removed as a assembly.

6. Remove the speedometer drive gear pinion and the mainshaft rear bearing retainer.

7. Before removal and disassembly of the drive pinion and mainshaft, measure the end play between the synchronizer stop ring and the third gear. Clearance should be within 0.050-0.070″. If necessary, add corrective shims during assembly.

NOTE: Record this reading for reference during assembly.

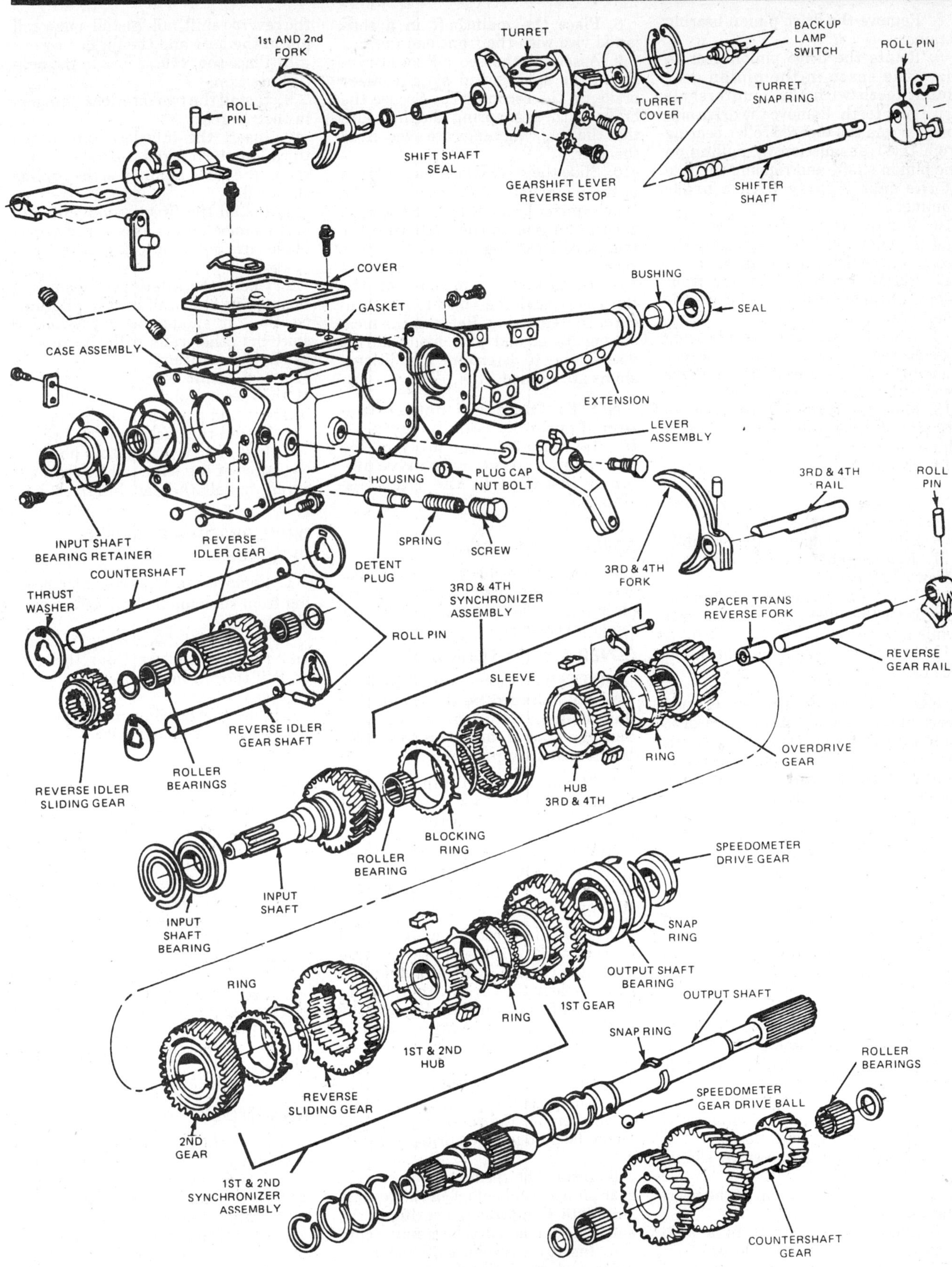

Single rail overdrive transmission

8. Remove the drive pinion bearing retainer.

9. Rotate the drive pinion gear to align the space in the pinion gear clutch teeth with the countershaft drive gear teeth. Remove the drive pinion gear and the tapered roller bearing from the transmission by pulling on the pinion shaft, and rapping the face of the case lightly with a brass hammer.

10. Remove the snapring, washer, and the pilot roller bearings from the recess in the drive pinion gear.

11. Place a brass drift in the front center of the mainshaft and drive the shaft rearward.

12. When the mainshaft rear bearing has cleared the case, remove the rear bearing and the speedometer drive gear with a suitable gear puller.

13. Move the mainshaft assembly to the rear of the case and tilt the front of the mainshaft upward.

14. Remove the roller type thrust washer.

15. Remove the synchronizer and stop rings separately.

16. Remove the mainshaft assembly.

17. Remove the reverse idler lock screw and lock plate.

18. Using a brass drift held at an angle, drive the idler shaft to the rear while pulling.

19. Lift the reverse idler gear out of the case.

NOTE: If the countershaft gear does not show signs of excessive side play or end play and the teeth are not badly worn or chipped, it may not be necessary to replace the countershaft gear.

20. Remove the bearing retainer at the rear end of the countershaft. The bearing assembly will remain with the retainer.

21. Tilt the cluster gear assembly and work it out of the transmission case.

22. Remove the front bearings from the case with a suitable driver.

MAINSHAFT

1. Remove the clutch gear snapring.
2. Remove the clutch gear, the synchronizer outer stop ring to third gear shim, and the third gear.
3. Remove the special split lock ring with two screw drivers. Remove the second gear and synchronizer.
4. Remove the first-reverse sliding gear.
5. Drive the old seal out of the bearing retainer.
6. Place the mainshaft in a soft-jawed vise with the rear end up.
7. Install the first-reverse gear. Be sure the two spline springs, if used, are in place inside the gear as the gear is installed on the shaft.
8. Place the mainshaft in a soft-jawed vise with the front end up.
9. Assemble the second speed synchronizer spring and synchronizer brake on the second gear. Secure the brake with a snapring making sure that the snapring tangs are away from the gear.
10. Slide the second gear on the front of the mainshaft. Make sure that the synchronizer brake is toward the rear. Secure the gear to the shaft with the two piece lock ring. Install the third gear.
11. Install the shim between the third gear and the third-fourth synchronizer stop ring. Refer to the measurements of end play made during disassembly to determine if additional shims are needed.

NOTE: The exact determination of end-play must be made after the complete assembly of the mainshaft and the main drive pinion is installed in the transmission case.

REVERSE IDLER GEAR

Do not disassemble the reverse idler gear. If it is no longer serviceable, replace the assembly complete with the integral bearings.

COVER & SHIFT FORK UNIT

NOTE: The cover and shift fork assembly should be disassembled only if inspection shows worn or damaged parts, or if the assembly is not working properly.

1. Remove the roll pin from the first-second shift fork and the shift gate with a screw extractor.

NOTE: A square type or a closely wound spiral screw extractor mounted in a tap is preferable for this operation.

2. Move the first-second shift rail forward and force the expansion plug out of the cover. Cover the detent ball access hole in the cover with a cloth to prevent it from flying out. Remove the rail, fork, and gate from the cover.

3. Remove the third-fourth shift rail, then the reverse rail in the manner outlined in Steps 1 and 2 above.

4. Compress the reverse gear plunger and remove the retaining clip. Remove the plunger and spring from the gate.

5. Install the spring on the reverse gear plunger and hold it in the reverse shift gate. Compress the spring in the shift gate and install the retaining clip.

6. Insert the reverse shift rail in the cover and place the detent ball and spring in position. Depress the ball and slide the shift rail over it.

7. Install the shift gate and fork on the reverse shift rail. Install a new roll pin in the gate and the fork.

8. Place the reverse fork in the neutral position.

9. Install the two interlock plungers in their bores.

10. Insert the interlock pin in the third-fourth shift rail. Install the shift rail in the same manner as the reverse shift rail.

11. Install the first-second shift rail in the same manner as outlined above. Make sure the interlock plunger is in place.

12. Check the interlocks by shifting the reverse shift rail into the Reverse position. It should be impossible to shift the other rails with the reverse rail in this position.

13. If the shift lever is to be installed at this point, lubricate the spherical ball seat and place the cap in place.

14. Install the back-up light switch.

15. Install new expansion plugs in the bores of the shift rail holes in the cover. Install the rail interlock hole plug.

DRIVE PINION & BEARING RETAINER

1. Remove the tapered roller bearing from the pinion shaft with a suitable tool.
2. Remove the snapring, washer, and the pilot rollers from the gear bore, if they have not been previously removed.
3. Pull the bearing race from the front bearing retainer with a suitable puller.
4. Remove the pinion shaft seal with a suitable tool.
6. Position the drive pinion in an arbor press.
7. Place a wood block on the pinion gear and press it into the bearing until it contacts the bearing inner race.
8. Coat the roller bearings with a light film of grease to hold the bearings in place, and insert them in the pocket of the drive pinion gear.
9. Install the washer and snapring.
10. Press a new seal into the bearing retainer. Make sure that the lip of the seal is toward the mounting surface.
11. Press the bearing race into the retainer.

ASSEMBLY

1. Press the front countershaft roller bearings into the case until the cage is flush with the front of the transmission case. Coat the bearings with a light film of grease.
2. Place the transmission with the front of the case facing down. If uncaged bearings are used, hold the loose rollers in place in the cap with a light film of grease.
3. Lower the countershaft assembly

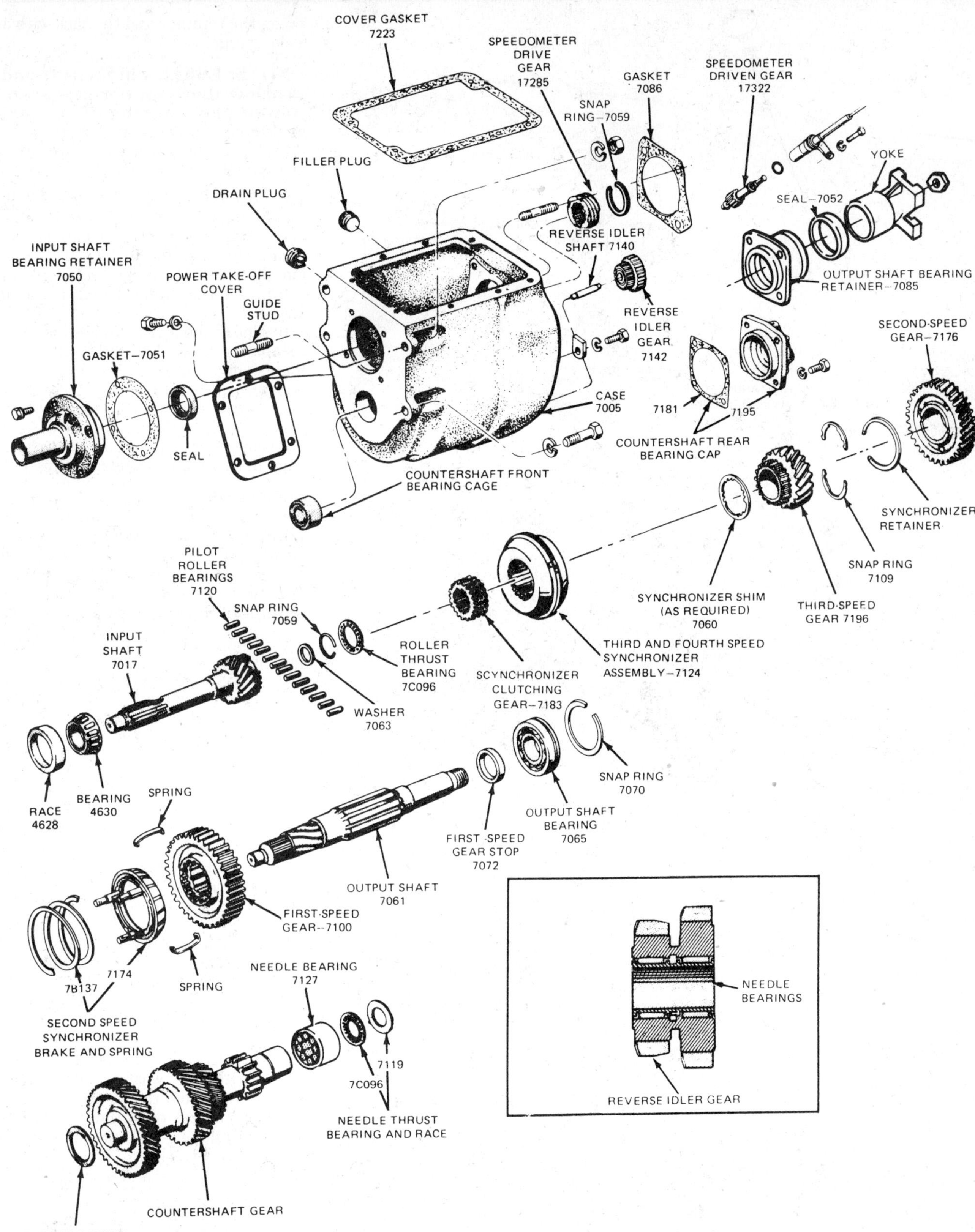

New Process 435 4-speed

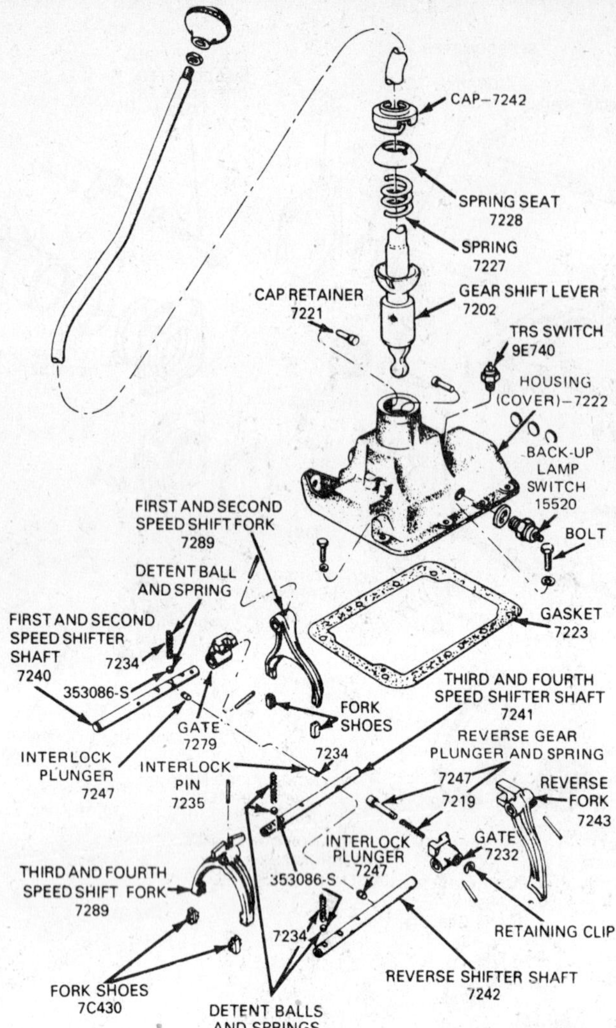

NP 435 gearshift housing

into the case placing the thrust washer tangs in the slots in the case, and inserting the front end of the shaft into the bearing.

4. Place the roller thrust bearing and race on the rear end of the countershaft. Hold the bearing in place with a light film of grease.

5. While holding the gear assembly in alignment, install the rear bearing retainer gasket, retainer, and bearing assembly. Install and tighten the cap screws.

6. Position the reverse idler gear and bearing assembly in the case.

7. Align the idler shaft so that the lock plate groove in the shaft is in position to install the lock plate.

8. Install the lock plate, washer, and cap screw.

9. Make sure the reverse idler gear turns freely.

10. Lower the rear end of the mainshaft assembly into the case, holding the first gear on the shaft. Maneuver the shaft through the rear bearing opening.

NOTE: With the mainshaft assembly moved to the rear of the case, be sure the third-fourth synchronizer and shims remain in position.

11. Install the roller type thrust bearing.

12. Place a wood block between the front of the case and the front of the mainshaft.

13. Install the rear bearing on the mainshaft by carefully driving the bearing onto the shaft and into the case, snapring flush against the case.

14. Install the drive pinion shaft and bearing assembly. Make sure that the pilot rollers remain in place.

15. Install the spacer and speedometer drive gear.

16. Install the rear bearing retainer and gasket.

17. Place the drive pinion bearing retainer over the pinion shaft, without the gasket.

18. Hold the retainer tight aginst the bearing and measure the clearance between the retainer and the case with a feeler gauge.

NOTE: End play in Steps 19 and 20 below allows for normal expansion of parts during operation, preventing seizure and damage to bearings, gears, synchronizers, and shafts.

19. Install a gasket shim pack 0.010-0.015"thicker than measured clearance between the retainer and case to obtain the required 0.007-0.017" pinion shaft end play. Tighten the front retainer bolts and recheck the end play.

20. Check the synchronizer end play clearance (0.050-0.070") after all mainshaft components are in position and properly tightened. Two sets of feeler gauges are used to measure the clearance. Care should be used to keep both gauges as close as possible to both sides of the mainshaft for best results.

NOTE: In some cases, it may be necessary to disassemble the mainshaft and change the thickness of the shims to keep the end play clearance within the specified limits, 0.050-0.070". Shims are available in two thicknesses.

21. Install the speedometer drive pinion.

22. Install the yoke flange, drum, and drum assembly.

23. Place the transmission in two gears at once, and tighten the yoke flange nut.

24. Shift the gears and/or synchronizers into all gear positions and check for free rotation.

25. Cover all transmissions components with a film of transmission oil to prevent damage during start up after initial lubricant fill-up.

26. Move the gears to the neutral position.

27. Place a new cover gasket on the transmission case, and lower the cover over the transmission.

28. Carefully engage the shift forks into their proper gears. Align the cover.

29. Install a shouldered alignment screw with split washer in the screw hole second from the front of the cover. Try out gear operation by shifting through all ranges. Make sure everything moves freely.

30. Install the remaining cover screws.

NP-445 4-Speed

DISASSEMBLY

1. Place the transmission in a holding fixture and drain the lubricant.

2. Shift the transmission gears into

neutral. Remove the gearshift cover attaching bolts. Note that the two bolts opposite the tower are shouldered to properly position the cover. Lift the cover straight up and remove.

3. Lock the transmission in two gears at once and remove the mainshaft nut and yoke.

4. Loosen and remove the extension housing bolts. Remove the mainshaft extension housing and the speedometer drive pinion.

5. Remove the bolts from the drive pinion front bearing retainer and pull the bearing retainer and gasket off.

6. Rotate the drive pinion gear to align the pinion gear flat with the countershaft drive gear teeth. Remove the drive pinion gear and the tapered roller bearing from the transmission.

7. Remove the mainshaft thrust bearing.

8. Push the mainshaft assembly to the rear of the transmission and tilt the front of the mainshaft up.

9. Remove the mainshaft assembly from the transmission case.

10. Remove the reverse idler lock screw and lock plate.

11. Using a suitable size brass drift, carefully drive the reverse idler shaft out the REAR of the case.

CAUTION

Do not attempt to drive the reverse idler shaft forward! This will damage the transmission case and the reverse idler shaft.

12. Remove the countershaft rear bearing retainer.

13. Slide the countershaft to the rear, then up and out of the case.

14. Drive the countershaft forward, out of the bearing and the case.

MAINSHAFT

1. Place the mainshaft in a soft-jawed vise with the front end up.

2. Lift the third-fourth synchronizer and high speed clutch off the mainshaft.

3. Remove the third gear.

4. Remove the second gear snapring. Lift off the thrust washer.

5. Remove the second gear.

6. Remove the first-reverse synchronizer and clutch gear.

7. Install the mainshaft in the vise rear end up.

8. Remove the tapered bearing from the shaft with a suitable gear puller.

9. Remove the first gear snapring and thrust washer.

10. Remove the first gear.

11. Lubricate all parts with transmission lubricant prior to assembly.

12. Place the mainshaft in a soft-jawed vise with the rear end up.

13. Slide the first gear over the mainshaft, with the clutch gear facing down. Install the thrust washer and snapring.

14. Install the revese gear over the end of the mainshaft with the fork groove facing down.

15. Install the mainshaft rear bearing on the mainshaft with a sleeve of suitable size. Press the bearing on its inner race.

16. Install the mainshaft in the vise with the front end facing up.

17. Install the first-reverse synchronizer.

18. Install the second gear on the mainshaft.

19. Install the keyed thrust washer, ground side toward the second gear and secure with the snapring.

20. Install the third gear and one shim on the mainshaft.

21. Install the third fourth synchronizer over the mainshaft. Make sure that the slotted end of the clutch gear is positioned toward the third gear.

COVER & SHIFT FORK

NOTE: The cover and shift fork assembly should be disassembled only if inspection shows worn or damaged parts, or if the assembly is not working properly.

1. Remove the roll pin from the first-second shift fork and the shift gate. Use a square-type or spirial wound screw extractor mounted in a tap handle for these operations.

2. Move the first-second shift rail rearward and force the expansion plug out of the cover. Cover the detent ball access hole in the cover with a cloth to prevent it from flying out. Remove the rail fork, and gate from the cover.

3. Remove the third-fourth shift rail, then the reverse rail in the manner outlined in Steps 1 and 2 above.

4. Compress the reverse gear plunger and remove the retaining clip. Remove the plunger and spring from the gate.

5. Apply a thin film of grease on the interlock slugs and slide them into the openings in the shift rail supports.

6. Install the reverse shift rail through the reverse shift fork plate and the reverse shift fork.

7. Secure the reverse shift plate and the shift fork with the roll pins. Install the interlock pin in the third-fourth shift rail. Hold in place with a thin film of grease.

8. Slide the third-fourth shift rail into the rail support from the rear of the cover. Slide the rail through the third-fourth shift fork and poppet ball and spring. Secure the third-fourth shift fork with the roll pin.

9. Install the interlock pin in the first-second shift rail and secure with a light coat of grease. Slide the first-second shift rail into the case, through the shift fork and shift gate. Hold the poppet ball and spring down until the shaft rail passes.

10. Secure the first-second shift rail and gate with the roll pins.

ASSEMBLY

1. Install the countershaft front bearing in the case using a 1⅜" socket as a driver. Grease the needle bearings prior to installation. Hold the bearings in place with a socket of suitable size while seating the bearing retainer. Drive the retainer in until it is flush with the case.

2. Install the tanged thrust washer on the countershaft with the tangs facing out. Install the countershaft in the transmission case.

3. Install the countershaft rear bearing retainer over the rear bearing. Use a new washer and position the retainer with the curved segment toward the bottom of the case.

4. Install the reverse idler gear into the case with the chamfered section facing the rear. Hold the thrust washer and needle bearings in position.

5. Slide the reverse idler shaft into the case, from the rear, and through the reverse idler gear. Make sure that the lock notch is down and at the rear of the case.

6. Install the reverse idler shaft lock and bolt.

7. Place the mainshaft in a soft-jawed vise with the front end facing up.

8. Install the drive gear on top of the mainshaft.

9. Measure the clearance between the high-speed synchronizer and the drive gear with two feeler gauges. If the clearance is greater than 0.043-0.053", install synchronizer shims between the third gear and the synchronizer brake drum. After the required shims have been installed, remove the drive gear from the mainshaft.

10. Install the mainshaft into the transmission case. Place the thrust washer over the pilot end of the mainshaft.

11. Position the drive gear so that the cutaway portion of the gear is facing down. Slide the drive gear into the front of the case and engage the mainshaft pilot in the pocket of the drive gear.

12. Slip the drive gear front bearing retainer over the shaft on gasket, and do not secure with bolts.

13. Install the mainshaft rear bearing retainer. Tighten the screws to specifications.

14. Hold the retainer against the front of the transmission case and measure the clearance between the front bearing retainer and the front of the case with a feeler gauge. Record

the measurement and remove the bearing retainer.

15. Install a gasket pack on the front bearing retainer which is 0.010-0.015" thicker than the clearance measured in Step 14. Install the front bearing retainer and torque attaching screws to specification.

16. The end play float of the front synchronizer must be checked before installation of the transmission cover assembly. Measure the end play "float" by inserting two feeler gauges opposite one another between the third gear and the synchronizer stop ring. Accurate measurement can be made only after all mainshaft parts are in place and torqued to specification.

17. If the front synchronizer end play "float" does not fall between 0.050-0.070", shims should be added or removed as required, from between the third gear and the synchronizer stop ring.

18. Install the yoke retaining nut on the rear of the mainshaft. Shift the transmission into two gears at the same time and torque the yoke nut to 125 ft.lb.

19. Shift the transmission into neutral.

20. Install the cover gasket.

21. Shift the transmission into second gear. Shift the cover into second.

22. Carefully lower the cover into position. It may be necessary to position the reverse gear to permit the fork to engage its groove.

23. Install the cover aligning screws (shouldered) and tighten with fingers only.

24. Install the remaining cover screws and tighten to specifications.

T-18, T-18A & T-19 4 Speed

The Warner T-18, T-18A and T-19 transmissions have four forward speeds and one reverse. A power take-off opening is provided on certain transmissions, depending upon the models and applications and can be located on either the right or left sides of the case. The T-18 and T-18A transmissions are synchronized in second, third and fourth speeds only, while the T-19 transmission is synchronized in all forward gears. The disassembly and assembly remains basically the same for the transmission models.

DISASSEMBLY

1. After draining the transmission and removing the parking brake drum (or shoe assembly), lock the transmission in two gears and remove the U-joint flange, oil seal, speedometer driven gear and bearing assembly. Lubricant capacity is 6½ pints.

2. Remove the output shaft bearing retainer and the speedometer drive gear and spacer.

3. Remove the output shaft bearing snapring, and remove the bearing.

4. Remove the countershaft and idler shaft retainer and the power take-off cover.

5. After removing the input shaft bearing retainer, remove the snaprings from the bearing and the shaft.

6. Remove the input shaft bearing and oil baffle.

7. Drive out the countershaft (from the front). Keep the dummy shaft in contact with the countershaft to avoid dropping any rollers.

8. After removing the input shaft and the synchronizer blocking ring, pull the idler shaft.

9. Remove the reverse gear shifter arm, the output shaft assembly, the idler gear, and the cluster gear. When removing the cluster, do not lose any of the rollers.

OUTPUT SHAFT

1. Remove the third- and high-speed synchronizer hub snapring from the output shaft, and slide the third- and high-speed synchronizer assembly and the third-speed gear off the shaft. Remove the synchronizer sleeve and the inserts from the hub. Before removing the two snaprings from the ends of the hub, check the end play of the second-speed gear (0.005-0.024").

2. Remove the second-speed synchronizer snapring. Slide the second-speed synchronizer hub gear off the hub. Do not lose any of the balls, springs, or plates. Pull the hub off the shaft, and remove the second-speed synchronizer from the second-speed

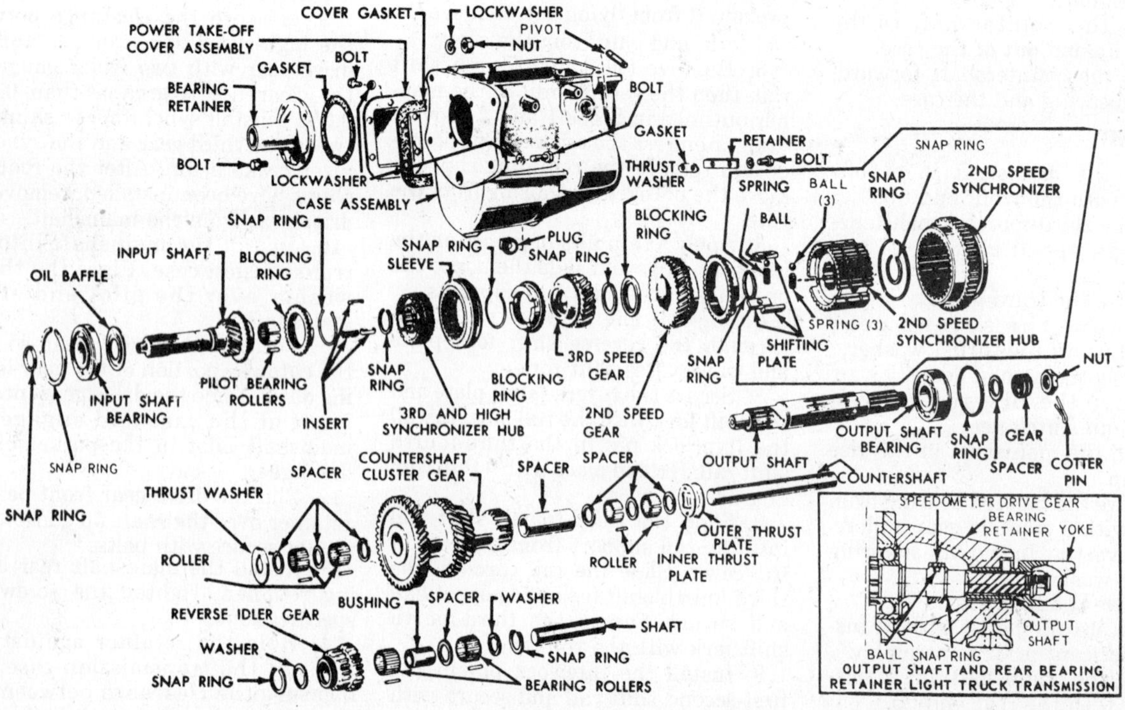

Warner T-18

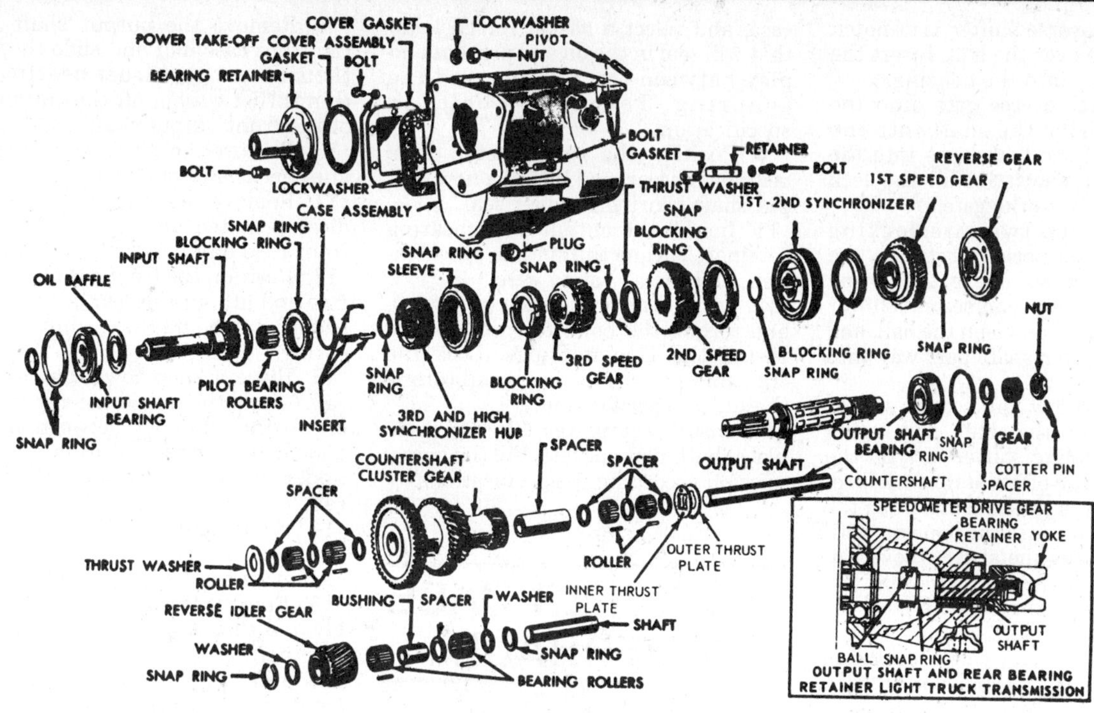

Warner T-19

gear. Remove the snapring from the rear of the second-speed gear, and remove the gear, spacer, roller bearings, and thrust washer from the output shaft. Remove the remaining snapring from the shaft.

CLUSTER GEAR

Remove the dummy shaft, pilot bearing rollers, bearing spacers, and center spacer from the cluster gear.

REVERSE IDLER GEAR

Rotate the reverse idler gear on the shaft, and if it turns freely and smoothly, disassembly of the unit is not necessary. If any roughness is noticed, disassemble the unit.

GEAR SHIFT HOUSING

1. Remove the housing cap and lever. Be sure all shafts are in neutral before disassembly.
2. Tap the shifter shafts out of the housing while holding one hand over the holes in the housing to prevent loss of the springs and balls. Remove the two shaft lock plungers from the housing.

CLUSTER GEAR ASSEMBLY

Slide the long bearing spacer into the cluster gear bore, and insert the dummy shaft in the spacer. Hold the cluster gear in a vertical position, and install one of the bearing spacers. Position the 22 pilot bearing rollers in the cluster gear bore. Place a spacer on the rollers, and install 22 more rollers and another spacer. Hold a large thrust washer against the end of cluster gear and turn the assembly over. Install the rollers and spacers in the other end of the gear.

REVERSE IDLER GEAR ASSEMBLY

1. Install a snapring in one end of the idler gear, and set the gear on end, with the snapring at the bottom.
2. Position a thrust washer in the gear on top of the snapring. Install the bushing on top of the washer, insert the 37 bearing rollers, and then a spacer followed by 37 more rollers. Place the remaining thrust washer on the rollers, and install the other snapring.

OUTPUT SHAFT ASSEMBLY

1. Install the second speed gear thrust washer and snapring on the output shaft. Hold the shaft vertically, and slide on the second speed gear. Insert the bearing rollers in the second-speed gear, and slide the spacer into the gear. (The T-18 model does not contain second speed gear rollers or spacer). Install the snapring on the output shaft at the rear of the second-speed gear. Position the blocking ring on the second-speed gear. Do not invert the shaft because the bearing rollers will slide out of the gear.
2. Press the second-speed synchronizer hub onto the shaft, and install the snapring. Position the shaft vertically in a soft-jawed vise. Position the springs and plates in the second-speed synchronizer hub, and place the hub gear on the hub.
3. With the T-19 model, press the first and second speed synchronizer onto the shaft and install the snapring. Install the first speed gear and snapring on the shaft and press on the reverse gear. For the T-19, ignore Steps 2 and 4.
4. Hold the gear above the hub spring and ball holes, and position one ball at a time in the hub, and slide the hub gear downward to hold the ball in place. Push the plate upward, and insert a small block to hold the plate in position, thereby holding the ball in the hub. Follow these procedures for the remaining balls.
5. Install the third speed gear and synchronizer blocking ring on the shaft.
6. Install the snaprings at both ends of the third and high-speed synchronizer hub. Stagger the openings of the snaprings so that they are not aligned. Place the inserts in the synchronizer sleeve, and position the sleeve on the hub.
7. Slide the synchronizer assembly onto the output shaft. The slots in the blocking ring must be in line with the synchronizer inserts. Install the snapring at the front of the synchronizer assembly.

GEAR SHIFT HOUSING

1. Place the spring on the reverse gear shifter shaft gate plunger, and install the spring and plunger in the reverse gate. Press the plunger through the gate, and fasten it with the clip. Place the spring and ball in the reverse gate poppet hole. Compress the spring and install the cotter pin.
2. Place the spring and ball in the reverse shifter shaft hole in the gear shift housing. Press down on the ball, and position the reverse shifter shaft

so that the reverse shifter arm notch does not slide over the ball. Insert the shaft part way into the housing.

3. Slide the reverse gate onto the shaft, and drive the shaft into the housing until the ball snaps into the groove of the shaft. Install the lock screw lock wire to the gate.

4. Insert the two interlocking plungers in the pockets between the shifter shaft holes. Place the spring and ball in the low and second shifter shaft hole. Press down on the ball, and insert the shifter shaft part way into the housing.

5. Slide the low and second shifter shaft gate onto the shaft, and install the corresponding shifter fork on the shaft so that the offset of the fork is toward the rear of the housing. Push the shaft all the way into the housing until the ball engages the shaft groove. Install the lock screw and wire that fastens the fork to the shaft. Install the third and high shifter shaft in the same manner. Check the interlocking system. Install new expansion plugs in the shaft bores.

CASE ASSEMBLY

1. Coat all parts, especially the bearings, with transmission lubricant to prevent scoring during initial operation.

2. Position the cluster gear assembly in the case. Do not lose any rollers.

3. Place the idler gear assembly in the case, and install the idler shaft. Position the slot in the rear of the shaft so that it can engage the retainer. Install the reverse shifter arm.

4. Drive out the cluster gear dummy shaft by installing the countershaft from the rear. Position the slot in the rear of the shaft so that it can engage the retainer. Use thrust washers as required to get 0.006-0.020" cluster gear end play. Install the countershaft and idler shaft retainer.

5. Position the input shaft pilot rollers and the oil baffle, so that the baffle will not rub the bearing race. Install the input shaft and the blocking ring in the case.

6. Install the output shaft assembly in the case, and use a special tool to prevent jamming the blocking ring when the input shaft bearing is installed.

7. Drive the input shaft bearing onto the shaft. Install the thickest select-fit snapring that will fit on the bearing. Install the input shaft snapring.

8. Install the output shaft bearing.

9. Install the input shaft bearing without a gasket, and tighten the bolts only enough to bottom the retainer on the bearing snapring. Measure the clearance between the retainer and the case, and select a gasket (or gaskets) that will seal in the oil and prevent end play between the retainer and the snapring. Torque the bolts to specification.

10. Position the speedometer drive gear and spacer, and install a new output shaft bearing retainer seal.

11. Install the output shaft bearing retainer. Torque the bolts to specification, and install safety wire.

12. Install the brake shoe (or drum), and torque the bolts to specification. Install the U-joint flange. Lock the transmission in two gears and torque the nut to specification.

13. Install the power take-off cover plates with new gaskets. Fill the transmission according to specifications.

TRANSFER CASE OVERHAUL

New Process Model 208

The New Process Model 208 is a part-time unit with a two piece aluminum housing. On the front case half, the front output shaft, front input shaft, four wheel drive indicator switch and shift lever assembly are located. On the rear case half, the rear output shaft, bearing retainer and drain and fill plugs are located.

DISASSEMBLY

1. Drain the fluid from the case.

2. Remove the attaching nuts from the front and rear output yokes. Remove the yokes and sealing washers.

3. Remove the four bolts and separate the rear bearing retainer from the rear case half.

4. Remove the retaining ring, speedometer drive gear nylon oil pump housing, and oil pump gear from the rear output shaft.

5. Remove the eleven bolts and separate the case halves by inserting a screw driver in the pry slots on the case.

6. Remove the magnetic chip collector from the bottom of the rear case half.

7. Remove the thick thrust washer, thrust bearing and thin thrust washer from the front output shaft assembly.

8. Remove the drive chain by pushing the front input shaft inward and by angling the gear slightly to obtain adequate clearance to remove the chain.

9. Remove the output shaft from the front case half and slide the thick thrust washer, thrust bearing and thin thrust washer off the output side of the front output shaft.

10. Remove the screw, poppet spring and check ball from the front case half.

11. Remove the four wheel drive indicator switch and washer from the front case half.

12. Position the front case half on its face and lift out the rear output shaft, sliding clutch and clutch shift fork and spring.

13. Place a shop towel on the shift rail. Clamp the rail with a vise grip pliers so that they lay between the rail and the case edge. Position a pry bar under the pliers and pry out the shift rail.

14. Remove the snap ring and thrust washer from the planetary gear set assembly in the front case half.

15. Remove the annulus gear assembly and thrust washer from the front case half.

16. Lift the planetary gear assembly from the front case half.

17. Lift out the thrust bearing, sun gear, thrust bearing and thrust washer.

18. Remove the six bolts and lift the gear locking plate from the front case half.

19. Remove the nut retaining the external shift lever and washer. Press the shift control shaft inward and remove the shift selector plate and washer from the case.

20. From the rear output shaft, remove the snapring and thrust washer retaining the chain drive sprocket and slide the sprocket from the drive gear.

21. Remove the retaining ring from the sprocket carrier gear.

22. Carefully slide the sprocket carrier gear from the rear output shaft. Remove the two rows of 60 loose needle bearings. Remove the three separator rings from the output shaft.

ASSEMBLY

1. Slide the thrust washer against the gear on the rear output shaft.

2. Place the three space rings in position on the rear output shaft. Liberally coat the shaft with petroleum jelly and install the two rows (60 each) of needle bearings in position on the rear output shaft.

3. Carefully slide the sprocket gear carrier over the needle bearings. Be careful not to dislodge any of the needles.

4. Install the retaining ring on the sprocket gear.

5. Slide the chain drive sprocket onto the sprocket carrier gear.

6. Install the thrust washer and snap ring on the rear output shaft.
7. Install the shift selector plate and washer through the front of the case.
8. Place the shift lever assembly on the shift control shaft and torque the nut to 14-20 ft.lb.
9. Install the locking plate in the front case half and torque the bolts to 25-35 ft.lb.
10. Place the thrust bearing and washer over the input shaft of the sun gear. Insert the input shaft through the front case half from the inside and insert the thrust bearing.
11. Install the planetary gear assembly so the fixed plate and planetary gears engage the sun gear.
12. Slide the annulus gear and clutch assembly with the shift fork assembly engaged, over the hub of the planetary gear assembly. The shift fork pin must engage the slot in the shift selector plate. Install the thrust washer and snap ring.
13. Position the shift rail through

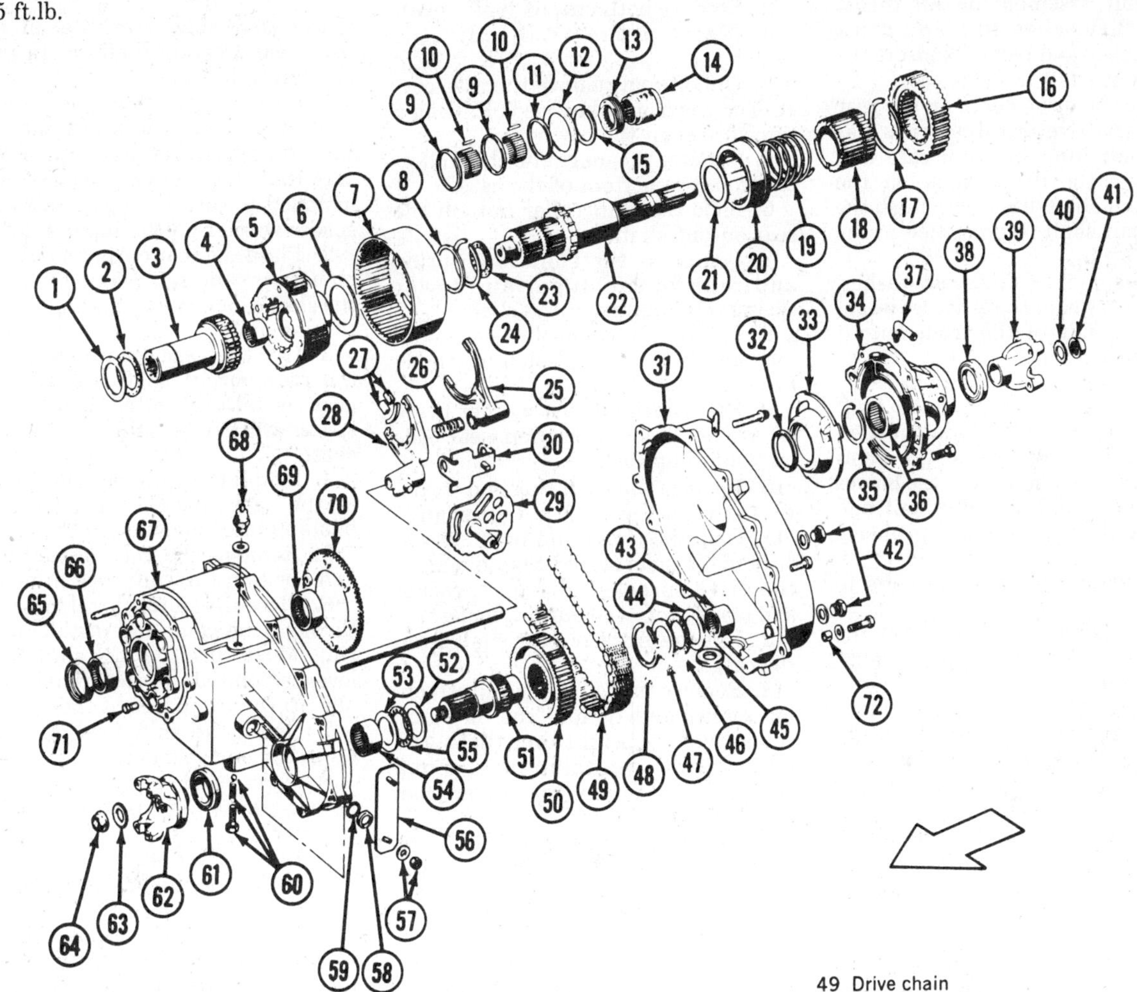

1 Input gear thrust washer
2 Input gear thrust bearing
3 Input gear
4 Mainshaft pilot bearing
5 Planetary assembly
6 Planetary thrust washer
7 Annulus gear
8 Annulus gear thrust washer
9 Needle bearing spacers
10 Mainshaft needle bearings (120)
11 Needle bearing spacer
12 Thrust washer
13 Oil pump
14 Speedometer gear
15 Drive sprocket retaining ring
16 Drive sprocket
17 Sprocket carrier stop ring
18 Sprocket carrier
19 Clutch spring
20 Sliding clutch
21 Thrust washer
22 Mainshaft
23 Mainshaft thrust bearing
24 Annulus gear retaining ring
25 Mode fork
26 Mode fork spring
27 Range fork inserts
28 Range fork
29 Range sector
30 Mode fork bracket
31 Rear case
32 Seal
33 Pump housing
34 Rear retainer
35 Rear output bearing
36 Bearing snap ring
37 Vent tube
38 Rear seal
39 Rear yoke
40 Yoke seal washer
41 Yoke nut
42 Drain and fill plugs
43 Front output shaft rear bearing
44 Front output shaft rear thrust bearing race (thick)
45 Case magnet
46 Front output shaft rear thrust bearing
47 Front output shaft rear thrust bearing race (thin)
48 Driven sprocket retaining ring
49 Drive chain
50 Driven sprocket
51 Front output shaft
52 Front output shaft front thrust bearing race (thin)
53 Front output shaft front thrust bearing race (thick)
54 Front output shaft front bearing
55 Front output shaft front thrust bearing
56 Operating lever
57 Washer and locknut
58 Range sector shaft seal retainer
59 Range sector shaft seal
60 Detent ball, spring and retainer bolt
61 Front seal
62 Front yoke
63 Yoke seal washer
64 Yoke nut
65 Input gear oil seal
66 Input gear front bearing
67 Front case
68 Lock mode indicator switch and washer
69 Input gear rear bearing
70 Lockplate
71 Lockplate bolts
72 Case alignment dowels

Exploded view of 208

the shift fork hub in the front case. Tap lightly with a soft hammer to seat the rail in the hole.

14. Position the sliding clutch shift fork on the shift rail and place the sliding clutch and clutch shift spring into the front case half. Slide the rear output shaft into the case.

15. On the output side of the front output shaft, assemble the thin thrust washer, thrust bearing, and thick thrust washer and partially insert the front output shaft into the case.

16. Place the drive chain on the rear output shaft drive gear. Insert the rear output shaft into the front case half and engage the drive chain on the front output shaft drive gear. Push the front output shaft into position in the case.

17. Assemble the thin thrust washer, thrust bearing and thick thrust washer on the inside of the front output shaft drive gear.

18. Position the magnetic chip collector into position in the front case half.

19. Place a bead of RTV sealant completely around the face of the front case half and assemble the case halves being careful that the shift rail and forward output shafts are properly retained.

20. Alternately tighten the bolts to 20-25 ft.lb.

21. Slide the oil pump gear over the input shaft and slide the spacer collar into position.

22. Engage the speedometer drive gear onto the rear output shaft and slide the retaining ring into position.

23. Use petroleum jelly to hold the nylon oil pump housing in position at the rear bearing retainer. Apply a bead of RTV sealant around the mounting surface of the retainer and carefully position the retainer assembly over the output shaft and onto the rear case half. The retainer must be installed so that the vent hole is vertical when the case is installed.

24. Torque the retainer bolts alternately to 20-25 ft.lb.

25. Place a new thrust washer under each yoke and install the yokes on their respective shafts. Place the oil slinger under the front yoke. Torque the nuts to 90-130 ft.lb.

26. Install the poppet ball, spring and screw in the front case half. Torque the screw to 20-25 ft.lb.

27. Install the 4WD indicator switch and washer and tighten to 15-20 ft.lb.

28. Fill the unit with 6 pints of Dexron® II.

Warner Model 1345

The Warner Model 1345 is a two piece all aluminum part time unit, lubricated by a positive displacement oil pump that channels oil through drilled holes in the rear output shaft. The pump turns with the output shaft and allows towing of the vehicle for extended distances.

DISASSEMBLY

1. Drain the fluid from the case.
2. Remove both output shaft yokes.
3. Remove the 4WD indicator switch.
4. Unbolt and remove the case cover. The cover may be pried off using a screwdriver in the pry bosses.
5. Remove the magnetic chip collector from the bottom of the case.
6. Slide the shift collar hub off the rear output shaft.
7. Compress the shift fork spring and remove the upper and lower spring retainers from the shaft.
8. Lift the four wheel drive lockup fork and lockup shift collar assembly from the case.
9. Remove the thrust washer being careful not to lose the nylon wear pads on the lockup fork.
10. Remove the snap ring and thrust washer from the front output shaft.
11. Grip the chain and both sprockets and lift them straight up to remove the drive sprocket, driven sprocket and chain from the output shafts.
12. Lift the front output shaft from the case.
13. Remove the four oil pump attaching screws and remove the oil pump rear cover, pickup tube, filter and pump body, two pump pins, pump spring and oil pump front cover from the rear output shaft.
14. Remove the snap ring that holds the bearing retainer inside the case. Lift the rear output shaft while tapping on the bearing retainer with a plastic hammer.

NOTE: Two dowel pins will fall into the case when the retainer is removed.

15. Lift the rear output shaft and bearing retainer from the case. Remove the rear output shaft from the bearing retainer. If necessary, press the needle bearing assembly out of the retainer.
16. Remove the C-clip that holds the shift cam to the actuating lever inside the case.
17. Remove the retaining screw and lift the shift lever from the case.

NOTE: When removing the lever, the shift cam will disengage from the shift lever shaft and may release the detent ball and spring from the case.

18. Remove the planetary gear set, shift rail, shift cam, input shaft and shift forks, as an assembly, from the case. Be careful not to lose the two nylon wear pads on the shift fork.
19. Remove the spacer washer from the bottom of the case.
20. Drive the plug from the detent spring bore.

ASSEMBLY

Before assembly, lubricate all parts with clean Dexron®II automatic transmission fluid.

1. Assemble the planetary gear set, shift rail, shift cam, input shaft and shift fork together as a unit. Make sure that the boss on the shift cam is installed toward the case. Install the spacer washer on the input shaft.
2. Place the rear output shaft in the planetary gear set, making sure that the shift cam engages the shift fork actuating pin.
3. Lay the case on its side. Insert the rear output shaft and planetary gear set into the case. Make sure the spacer washer remains on the input shaft.
4. Install the shift rail into the hole in the case. Install the outer roller bushing into the guide in the case.
5. Remove the rear output shaft and position the shift fork in neutral.
6. Place the shift control lever shaft through the cam, and install the clip ring. Make sure that the shift control lever is pointed downward and is parallel to the front face of the case.
7. Check the shift fork and planetary gear engagement.
8. If removed, press a new needle bearing assembly into the bearing retainer.
9. Insert the output shaft through the bearing retainer from the bottom outward.
10. Insert the rear output shaft pilot into the input shaft bushing. Align the dowel holes and the lower bearing.
11. Install the dowel pins. Install the snap ring that retains the bearing retainer in the case.
12. Insert the detent ball and spring in the detent bore in the case. Coat the seal plug with RTV sealant or its equivalent. Drive the plug into the case until the lip of the plug is $1/32''$ below the surface of the case. Peen the case over the plug in two places.
13. Install the pump front cover over the output shaft with the flanged side down. The word "TOP" must be facing the top of the transfer case.
14. Install the oil pump spring and two pump pins with the flat side outward in the hole in the output shaft. Push both pins in to install the oil pump body, pickup tube and filter.
15. Place the oil pump rear cover on the output shaft with the flanged side outward. The word "TOP" must be

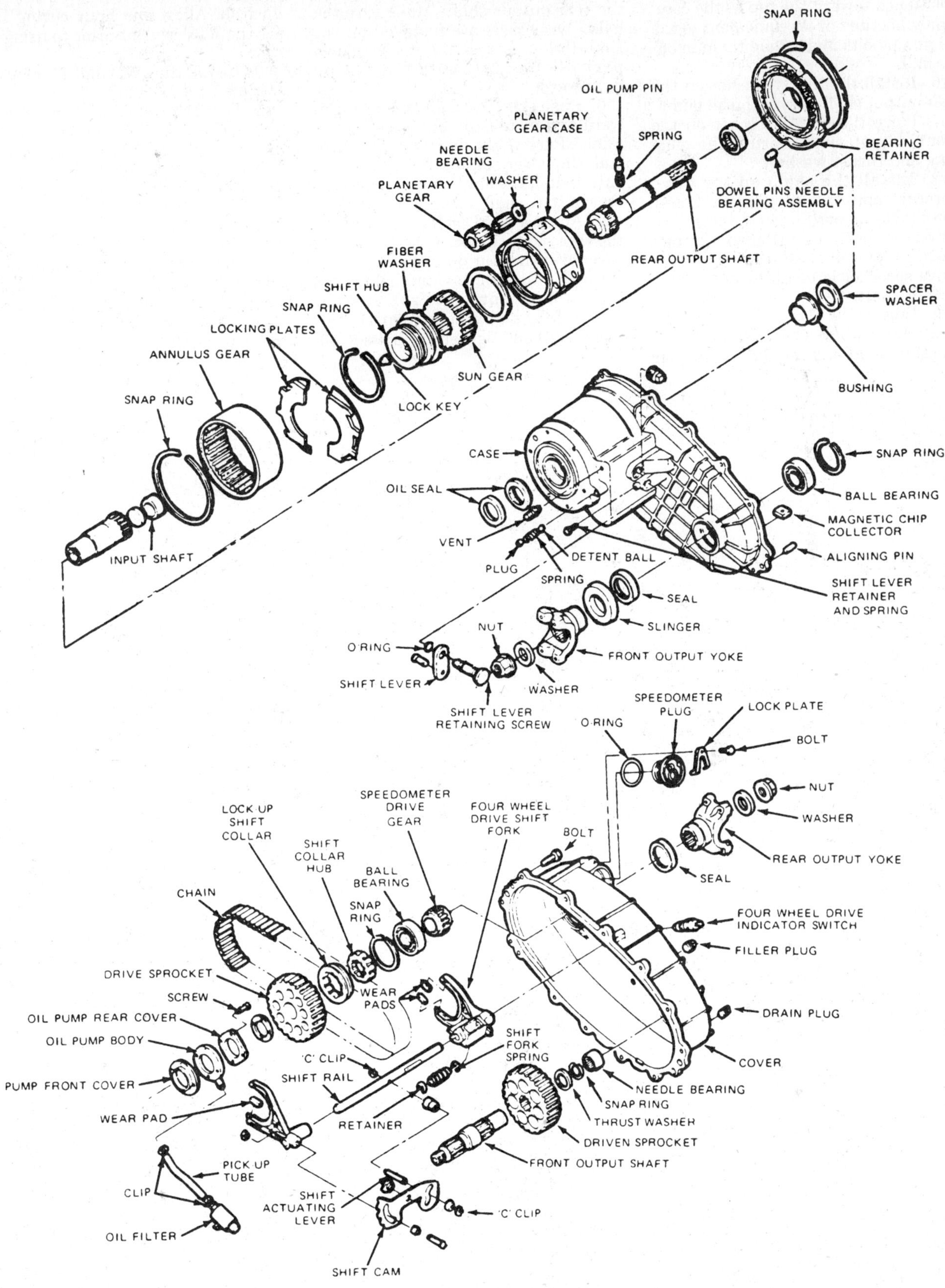

Exploded view of Warner 1345

positioned toward the top of the case. Apply Loctite® or its equivalent to the oil pump bolts and torque them to 36-40 in.lb.

16. Install the thrust washer on the rear output shaft nest to the oil pump.

17. Place the drive sprocket on the front output shaft. Install the snap ring and thrust washer.

18. Install the chain on the drive sprocket and driven sprocket. Lower the chain into position in the case. The driven sprocket is installed through the front output shaft bearing and the drive sprocket is installed in the rear output shaft.

19. Engage the 4WD shift fork on the shift collar. Slide the shift fork over the shift shaft and the shift collar over the rear output shaft. Make sure the nylon wear pads are installed on the shift fork tips and the necked-down part of the shift collar is facing downward.

20. Push the 4WD shift spring downward and install the upper spring retainer. Push the spring upward and install the lower retainer.

21. Install the shift collar hub on the rear output shaft.

22. Apply a bead of RTV sealant on the case mounting surface. Lower the cover over the rear output shaft. Align the shift rail with its blind hole in the cover. Make sure the front output shaft is fully seated in its support bearing. Install and tighten the bolts to 40-45 ft.lb. Allow one hour curing time for the RTV sealant prior to using the case.

23. Install the 4WD indicator switch. Torque to 8-12 ft.lb.

24. Press the oil slinger on the front yoke. Install the front and rear output shaft yokes. Coat the nuts with Loctite® or equivalent and torque to 100-130 ft.lb.

25. Fill the unit with 6 pints of Dexron® II. Tighten the fill plug to 18 ft.lb.

26. Install the unit in the vehicle and start the engine. Remove the level plug. If the fluid is flowing from the hole in a stream, the pump is not operating properly. The fluid should drip slowly from the hole.

Aerostar 5

INDEX

TUNE-UP SPECIFICATIONS

Year	No. Cylinder Displacement cu. in. (liter)	Spark Plugs Type	Spark Plugs Gap (in.)	Ignition Timing (deg.) MT	Ignition Timing (deg.) AT	Idle Speed (rpm) MT	Idle Speed (rpm) AT	Valve Clearance In.	Valve Clearance Ex.
1986-87	4-140 (2.3)	AWSF-44C	0.044	10B	10B	800	700	Hyd.	Hyd.
	6-173 (2.8)	AWSF-42C	0.044	10B	10B	850	750	0.014	0.016
	6-182 (3.0)	AWSF-32C	0.044	10B	10B	Not Adjustable		Hyd.	Hyd.

GENERAL ENGINE SPECIFICATIONS

Year	No. Cylinder Displacement cu. in. (liter)	Fuel System Type	Net Horsepower @ rpm	Net Torque @ rpm (ft.lbs.)	Bore × Stroke (in.)	Com-pression Ratio	Oil Pressure @ rpm
1986-87	4-140 (2.3)	EFI	88 @ 4400	132 @ 2200	3.78 × 3.13	9.5:1	40-60
	6-173 (2.8)	FBC	115 @ 4200	170 @ 2400	3.66 × 2.70	9.0:1	40-60
	6-182 (3.0)	EFI	145 @ 4800	165 @ 3600	3.50 × 3.14	9.3:1	40-60

CAPACITIES

Year	No. Cylinder Displacement cu. in. (liter)	Engine Crankcase with Filter	Transmission (pts.) 5-Spd	Transmission (pts.) Auto.	Drive Axle (pts.)	Fuel Tank (gal.)	Cooling System (qts.)
1986-87	4-140 (2.3)	5.0	①	19.0	3.5	17.0	②
	6-173 (2.8)	5.0	①	19.0	3.5	17.0	②
	6-182 (3.0)	4.5	①	19.0	3.5	17.0	②

① Mazda trans.: 3.6
Mitsubishi Trans.: 4.8
② W/MT: 6.8
W/AT: 7.6

CRANKSHAFT AND CONNECTING ROD SPECIFICATIONS

All measurements are given in inches.

Year	No. Cylinder Displacement cu. in. (liter)	Crankshaft Main Brg. Journal Dia.	Crankshaft Main Brg. Oil Clearance	Crankshaft Shaft End-play	Crankshaft Thrust on No.	Connecting Rod Journal Diameter	Connecting Rod Oil Clearance	Connecting Rod Side Clearance
1986-87	4-140 (2.3)	2.3990–2.3980	0.0008–0.0015	0.0004–0.0008	3	2.0462–2.0472	0.0008–0.0015	0.004–0.011
	6-173 (2.8)	2.2433–2.2441	0.0008–0.0015	0.0004–0.0008	3	2.1252–2.1260	0.0006–0.0016	0.004–0.011
	6-182 (3.0)	2.5190–2.5198	0.0010–0.0014	0.0004–0.0008	3	2.1253–2.1261	0.0010–0.0014	0.006–0.014

CAMSHAFT SPECIFICATIONS

All specifications given in inches.

Years	Engine cu. in. (liter)	Journal Diameter 1	2	3	4	Bearing Clearance	Elevation Int.	Exh.	End Play
1986-87	140 (2.3)	—All 1.7713-1.7720—				0.001-0.003 ①	0.390	0.390	0.001-0.007
	171 (2.8)	1.7285-1.7293	1.7135-1.7143	1.6985-1.6992	1.6835-1.6842	0.001-0.0026 ①	0.373	0.373	0.0080 0.0040
	182 (3.0)	—All 2.0074-2.0084—				0.001-0.003	0.419	0.419	②

① 0.0060 max
② No end play. Camshaft is restrained by spring.

VALVE SPECIFICATIONS

Year	No. Cylinder Displacement cu. in. (liter)	Seat Angle (deg.)	Face Angle (deg.)	Spring Test Pressure (lbs.@in.)	Spring Installed Height (in.)	Stem-to-Guide Clearance (in.) Intake	Exhaust	Stem Diameter (in.) Intake	Exhaust
1986-87	4-140 (2.3)	45	44	142 @ 1.12	1.49-1.55	0.0010-0.0027	0.0015-0.0032	0.3416-0.3423	0.3411-0.3418
	6-173 (2.8)	45	44	138 @ 1.22	1.58-1.61	0.0008-0.0025	0.0018-0.0035	0.3159-0.3167	0.3149-0.3156
	6-182 (3.0)	45	44	185 @ 1.11	1.83-1.87	0.0010-0.0027	0.0015-0.0032	0.3134-0.3126	0.3129-0.3121

PISTON AND RING SPECIFICATIONS

All measurements are given in inches.

Year	No. Cylinder Displacement cu. in. (liter)	Piston Clearance	Ring Gap Top Compression	Bottom Compression	Oil Control	Ring Side Clearance Top Compression	Bottom Compression	Oil Control
1986-87	4-140 (2.3)	0.0014-0.0022	0.0100-0.0020	0.0010-0.0020	0.0150-0.0550	0.0020-0.0040	0.0020-0.0040	Snug
	6-173 (2.8)	0.0011-0.0019	0.0150-0.0230	0.0150-0.0230	0.0150-0.0550	0.0020-0.0033	0.0020-0.0033	Snug
	6-182 (3.0)	0.0012-0.0023	0.0100-0.0200	0.0100-0.0200	0.0100-0.0490	0.0016-0.0037	0.0016-0.0037	Snug

TORQUE SPECIFICATIONS

All readings in ft. lbs.

Year	No. Cylinder Displacement cu. in. (liter)	Cylinder Head Bolts	Main Bearing Bolts	Rod Bearing Bolts	Crankshaft Pulley Bolt	Flywheel Bolts	Manifold Intake	Exhaust
1986-87	4-140 (2.3)	80-90	80-90	30-36	100-120	56-64	13-18	16-23
	6-173 (2.8)	70-85	65-75	19-24	85-96	47-52	15-18	20-30
	6-182 (3.0)	63-80	65-81	20-25	141-169	54-64	22-26	15-22

BRAKE SPECIFICATIONS

All Specifications in inches

Years	Model	Master Cyl. Bore	Brake Disc Original Thickness	Brake Disc Minimum Thickness	Brake Disc Maximum Run-out	Brake Drum Orig. Inside Dia.	Brake Drum Max. Wear Limit	Brake Drum Maximum Machine O/S	Wheel Cyl. or Caliper Bore Front	Wheel Cyl. or Caliper Bore Rear
1986-87	All	NA	1.180	0.81	0.010	NA	0.090	0.060	NA	NA

NA Not available at time of publication

WHEEL ALIGNMENT

Year	Model	Caster Range (deg.)	Caster Preferred Setting (deg.)	Camber Range (deg.)	Camber Preferred Setting (deg.)	Toe-in (in.)
1986-87	All	3P to 5P	4P	1/3N to 7/10P	1/5P	4/5

ROUTINE MAINTENANCE

Air Cleaner Element

All engines are equipped with a dry type, replaceable air filter element. The element should be replaced every 10,000 miles or yearly. If your vehicle is operated under severely dusty conditions or regularly in stop-and-go traffic, more frequent changes are necessary. Inspect the element at least twice a year; early spring and fall are good times of the year for inspection. Remove the element and check for holes in the filter, then check the element housing for signs of dirt or dust that has leaked through the filter element. Place a light on the inside of the element and look through the filter at the light. If no glow can be seen through the element material, replace the element. If holes in the filter are apparent or signs of dirt leakage through the filter are noticed, replace the element.

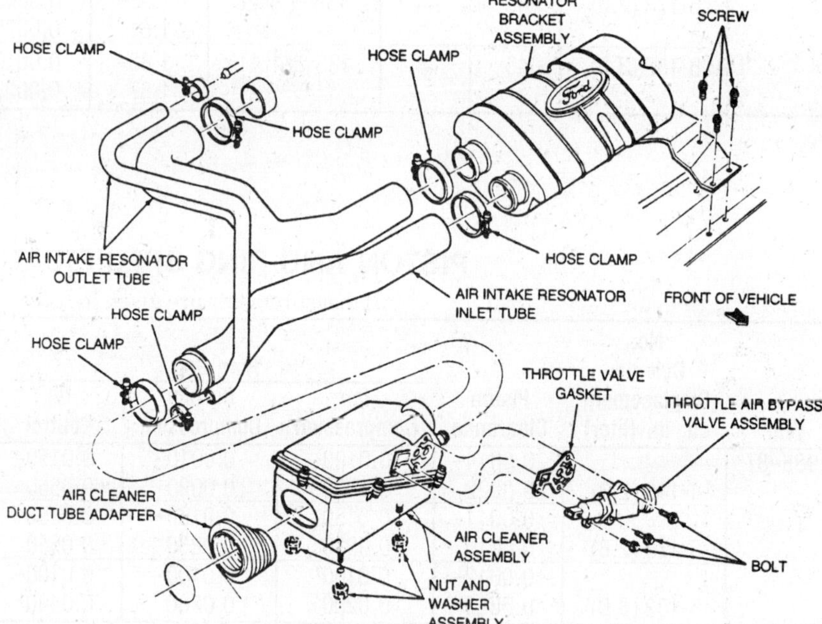

Air cleaner assembly—2.3L engine

REMOVAL & INSTALLATION

2.3L EFI Engine

1. Disconnect the inlet tube and idle bypass tube from the air cleaner cover.
2. Disconnect the electrical connector to the throttle air bypass valve.
3. Remove the air cleaner cover by loosening the knurl nuts holding the air cleaner case together.
4. Lift the paper element out of the air cleaner case and wipe the case clean with a clean rag.
5. Install a new air cleaner element into the case, making sure it is seated properly, then install the case cover and tighten the knurl nuts until they are finger tight.
6. Reconnect the electrical connector to the throttle air bypass valve.
7. Reconnect the inlet tube and idle air bypass tube to the air cleaner cover.

2.8L V6 Engine

The air cleaner element can be replaced by removing the center wing nut and air cleaner cover and then lifting out the old element. If the inside of the housing is dirty, the entire air cleaner assembly should be removed from the engine and wiped clean to prevent any dirt from entering the carburetor. To remove the air cleaner assembly, disconnect the air ducts and any vacuum lines attached to the air cleaner housing. Disconnect any mounting brackets (if equipped) and lift the air cleaner housing off of the engine. Replace the cleaner mounting

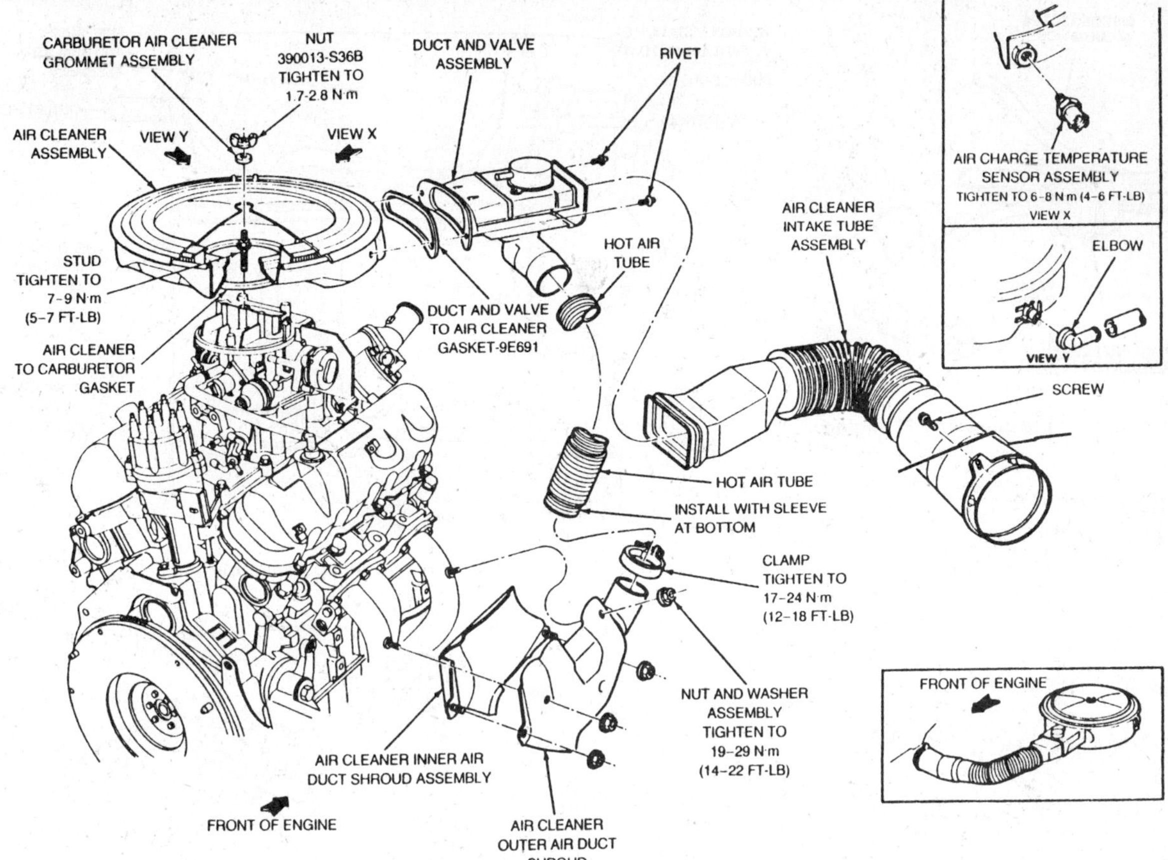

Air cleaner assembly—2.8L V6 engine

gasket if it is worn or broken. When installing, reconnect all brackets, ducts and vacuum hoses and tighten the wing nut finger tight.

Fuel Filter

The fuel filters for mechanical fuel pumps are located on the carburetor where the fuel inlet line is attached. Fuel injected engines with electric fuel pumps have three filters: one inside the inline reservoir, one at the electric fuel pump mounted on the chassis and a third on the low pressure electric fuel pump mounted inside the fuel tank itself. Normally, only the filters at the chassis mounted pump and fuel reservoir are replaced as part of normal maintenance. A high speed surge problem is indicative of a clogged fuel filter.

CAUTION

On fuel injected engines, the fuel system is under constant pressure, even when the engine is turned off. Follow the instructions for relieving fuel system pressure before attempting any service to the fuel system. Whenever working on or around any open fuel system, take precautions to avoid the risk of fire and use clean rags to catch any fuel spray while disconnecting fuel lines.

REMOVAL & INSTALLATION

Carbureted Engine

1. Remove the air cleaner assembly.
2. Using two wrenches, one on the fuel line and one holding the filter, loosen and disconnect the fuel inlet line from the carburetor fuel inlet at the filter. Use a clean rag under the fitting to catch any fuel.
3. Unscrew the fuel filter from the carburetor fuel inlet.
4. Apply one drop of Loctite® (or equivalent) hydraulic sealant to the external threads of the new fuel filter, then thread the filter into the carburetor inlet port.
5. Tighten the fuel filter to 6-8 ft.lb. (9-11Nm). Do not overtighten.
6. Thread the fuel supply line into the filter and, using two wrenches as before, tighten the fuel supply line nut to 15-18 ft.lb. (20-24Nm).
7. Start the engine and check for fuel leaks.
8. Install the air cleaner assembly. Dispose of any gasoline soaked rags properly.

Fuel Injected Engine

1. Remove the fuel tank cap to vent tank pressure.

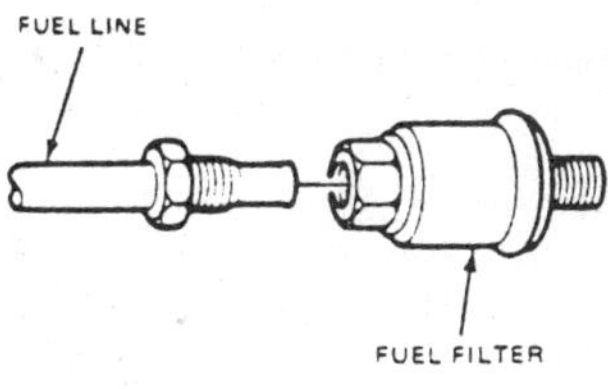

Fuel filter used on carbureted engines

2. Disconnect the vacuum hose from the fuel pressure regulator located on the engine fuel rail.
3. Connect a hand vacuum pump to the fuel pressure regulator and apply 25 in.Hg for ten seconds. This will release the fuel pressure into the fuel tank through the fuel return line.
4. Raise the vehicle and support it safely.
5. Locate the fuel filter which is mounted on the underbody, forward of the right rear wheel well, on the same bracket as the electric fuel pump.
6. Clean all dirt and/or grease from the fuel filter fittings. "Quick Connect" fittings are used on all models equipped with a pressurized fuel system. These fittings must be disconnected using the proper procedure or the fittings may be damaged. The fuel filter uses a "hairpin" clip retainer.

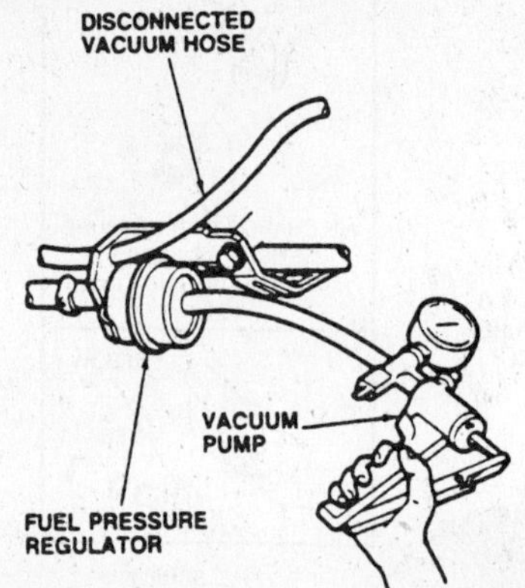

Relieving fuel pressure on EFI engine

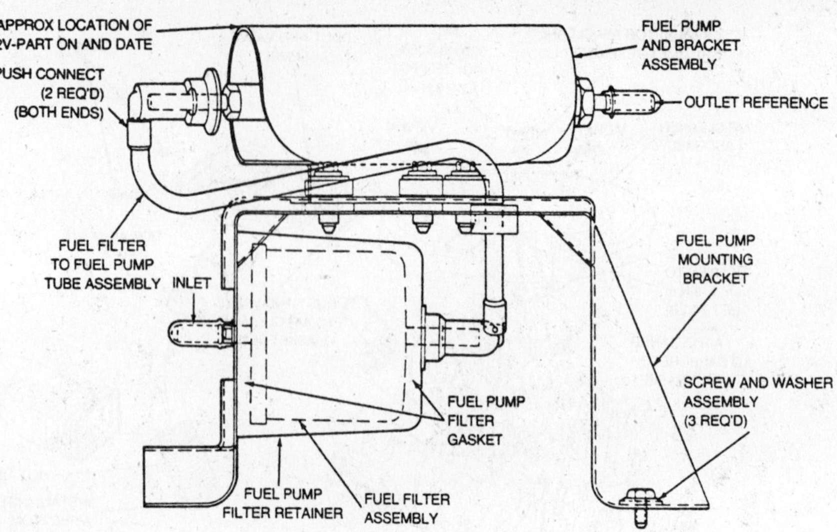

Fuel filter and pump assembly

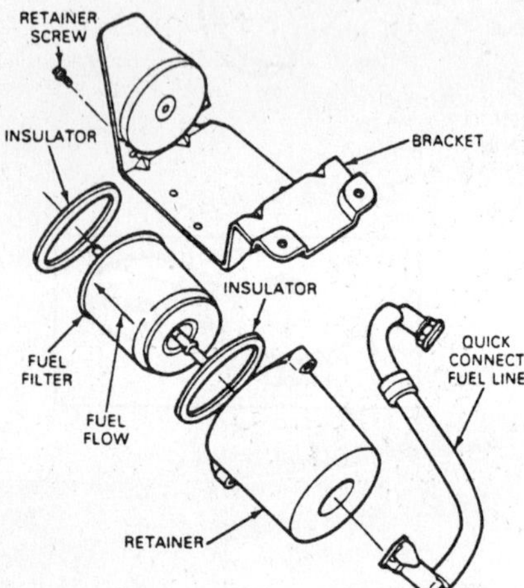

Reservoir-type fuel filter assembly

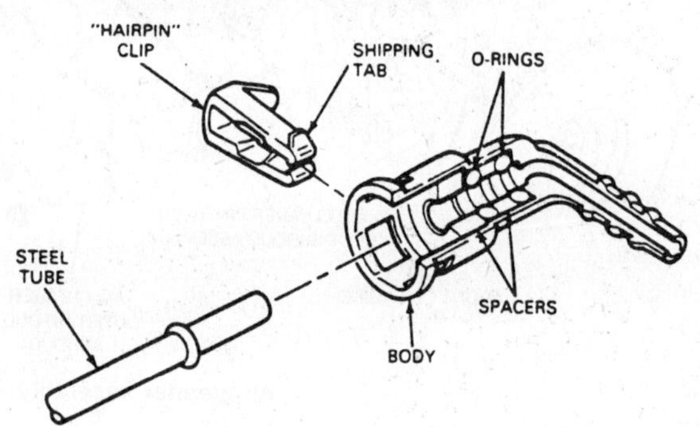

Typical 5/16 in. quick connect fuel fitting

7. Spread the two hairpin clip legs about 1/8" (3mm) each to disengage it from the fitting, then pull the clip outward. Use finger pressure only; do not use any tools. Disconnect both fittings from the fuel filter.

8. Remove the fuel filter and retainer from the metal mounting bracket.

9. Remove the rubber insulator ring from the filter and the filter from the retainer. Note that the direction of fuel flow (arrow on the filter) points to the open end of the retainer.

10. Place the new filter into the retainer with the flow arrow pointing toward the open end.

11. Install the insulator ring. Replace the insulator(s) if the filter moves freely after installation of the retainer. Install the retainer on the metal bracket and tighten the mounting bolts to 51-60 in.lb. (5-7Nm).

12. Push the quick connect fittings onto the filter ends. Ford recommends that the retaining clips be replaced whenever removed. A click will be heard when the hairpin clip snaps into its proper position. Pull on the lines to insure proper connection.

13. Start the engine and check for fuel leaks.

14. Lower the vehicle.

PCV Valve

All models use a closed crankcase ventilation system with a sealed breather cap connected to the air cleaner by a rubber hose. The PCV valve is usually mounted in the valve cover and connected to the intake manifold by a rubber hose. The system is used to regulate the amount of crankcase (blow-by) gases which are recycled into the combustion chambers for burning with the normal fuel charge.

The only maintenance required on the PCV system is to replace the PCV valve and/or air filter element in the air cleaner at the intervals specified in the maintenance chart. Replacement involves removing the valve from the grommet in the valve cover and installing a new valve. No attempt should be made to clean an old PCV valve; it should be replaced.

Evaporative Emissions Canister

The canister functions to cycle the fuel vapor from the fuel tank and carburetor float chamber into the intake manifold and eventually into the cylinders for combustion with the normal fuel charge. The activated charcoal within the canister acts as a storage device for the fuel vapor at times when the engine is not operating or when the engine operating condition will not permit fuel vapor to burn efficiently.

The only required service for for the evaporative canister is inspection at the interval specified in the maintenance chart. If the charcoal element is saturated with fuel, the entire canister should be replaced. Disconnect the canister purge hose(s), loosen the canister retaining bracket and lift out the canister. Installation is the reverse of removal.

Battery

All Aerostars use a maintenance

free battery as standard equipment, eliminating the need for periodic fluid level checks and the possibility of specific gravity tests. Nevertheless, the battery does require some attention. An indicator is built into the top of the maintenance free battery to show the condition and state of charge. If the indicator is dark, the battery can be assumed to be OK. If the indicator is light, the specific gravity is low and the battery should either be recharged or replaced.

NOTE: Never disconnect the battery with the ignition ON or the engine running or serious onboard computer damage could occur.

Once a year, the battery terminals and cable clamps should be cleaned. Loosen the terminal mounting bolt (if equipped) and remove the cable and clamp with a suitable terminal removal tool. Clean the cable clamps and terminal posts with a suitable wire brush until all corrosion is removed and the clamps and posts are shiny. Special wire brush terminal cleaning tools are available from aftermarket sources to make this job quick and easy. It is especially important to clean the inside of the clamp (or contact side of the side terminal) thoroughly, since a small deposit of foreign material or oxidation will prevent a sound electrical connection and could inhibit charging or starting ability.

Before installing the cables, loosen the battery holddown clamp, lift out the battery and check the battery tray. Clear any debris such as leaves or dirt and check the tray for soundness. Rust and corrosion should be wire brushed away and the metal coated with anti-rust paint. Reinstall the battery and tighten the holddown clamp securely, but be careful not to overtighten and crack the battery case.

After the clamps and terminals are clean, install the terminals (positive cable first), then apply a thin external coat of grease to retard corrosion. Check the cables while cleaning the clamps, looking for frayed or broken insulation. If the cable has frayed ends or excessive corrosion is present, the cable should be replaced with a new cable of the same length and gauge.

CAUTION

Keep flame or sparks away from the battery as it gives off explosive hydrogen gas. Battery electrolyte contains sulfuric acid. If you should get any on your skin or in your eyes, flush the affected area with plenty of clear water immediately. In the case of eye contact, seek medical help immediately. It's also a good idea to wear some sort of filter when wire brushing excessive corrosion to avoid inhaling dust particles.

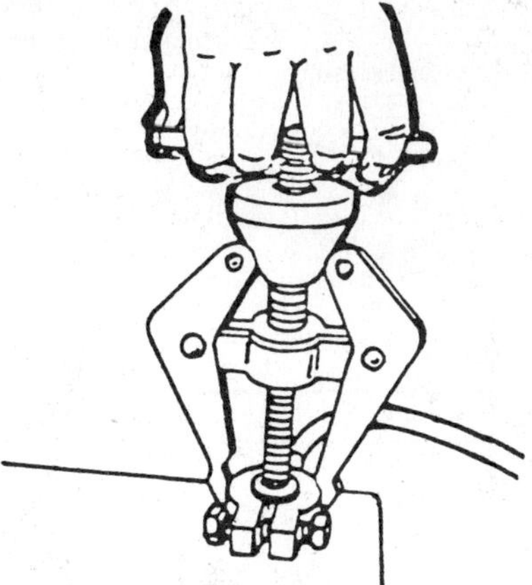

Using a terminal puller to remove the battery cable

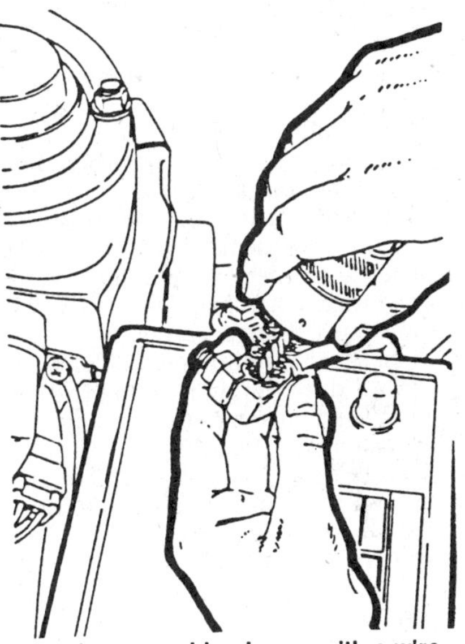

Clean battery cable clamps with a wire brush

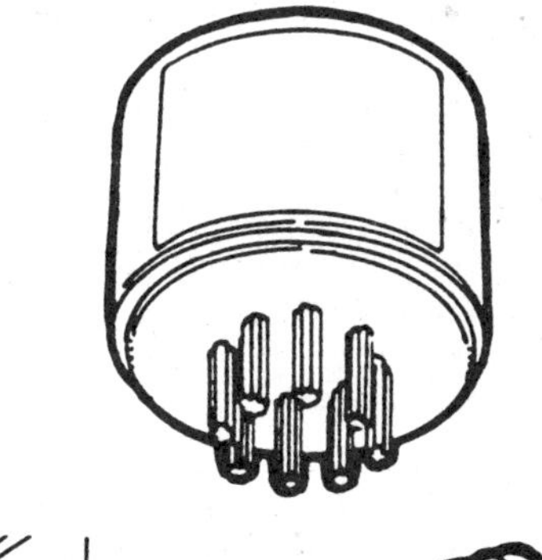

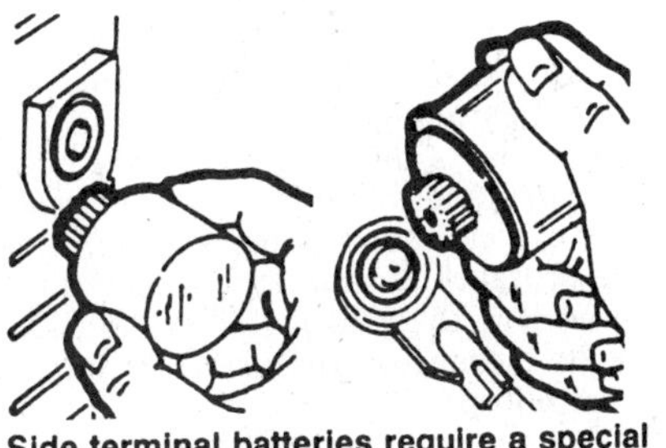

Side terminal batteries require a special wire brush for cleaning

Belts

INSPECTION

The belts which drive the engine accessories such as the alternator or generator, the air pump, power steering pump, air conditioning compressor and water pump are of either the V-belt design or flat, serpentine design. Older belts show wear and damage readily, since their basic design was a belt with a rubber casing. As the casing wore, cracks and fibers were readily apparent. Newer design, caseless belts do not show wear as readily, and many untrained people cannot distinguish between a good, serviceable belt and one that is worn to the point of failure. It is a good idea, therefore, to visually inspect the belts regularly and replace them, routinely, every two to three years.

ADJUSTING

Belts are normally adjusted by loosening the bolts of the accessory being driven and moving that accessory on its pivot points until the proper tension is applied to the belt. The accessory is held in this position while the bolts are tightened. To determine proper belt tension, you can purchase a belt tension gauge or simply use the deflection method. To determine deflection, press inward on the belt at the mid-point of its longest straight run. The belt should deflect (move inward) $\frac{3}{8}$-$\frac{1}{2}$" (10–13mm). Some long V-belts and most serpentine belts have idler pulleys which are used for adjusting purposes. Just loosen the idler pulley and move it to take up tension on the belt.

REMOVAL & INSTALLATION

To remove a drive belt, simply loosen the accessory being driven and move it on its pivot point to free the belt. Then, remove the belt. If an idler pulley is used, it is often necessary, only, to loosen the idler pulley to provide enough slack the remove the belt.

It is important to note, however, that on engines with many driven accessories, several or all of the belts may have to be removed to get at the one to be replaced.

Hoses

REMOVAL & INSTALLATION

Radiator hoses are generally of two constructions, the preformed (molded) type, which is custom made for a particular application, and the spring loaded type, which is made to fit several different applications. Heater hoses are all of the same general construction.

Hoses are retained by clamps. To replace a hose, loosen the clamp and slide it down the hose, away from the attaching point. Twist the hose from side to side until it is free, then pull it off. Before installing the new hose, make sure that the outlet fitting is as clean as possible. Coat the fitting with non-hardening sealer and slip the hose into place. Install the clamp and tighten it.

Air Conditioning System

PRECAUTIONS

There are two particular hazards associated with air conditioning systems and they both relate to the refrigerant gas. First, the refrigerant gas is an extremely cold substance. When exposed to the air it will instantly freeze any surface it comes in contact with, including skin and eyes. Always wear safety goggles when performing any service on the air conditioning system. The other hazard relates to fire. Although normally non-toxic, R-12 or Freon refrigerant gas becomes highly poisonous in the presence of an open flame. One good whiff of the vapor formed by burning refrigerant can be fatal. Keep all forms of fire (including cigarettes) well clear of the air conditioning system.

SYSTEM INSPECTION

Refrigerant leaks show up as oily areas on the various components because the compressor oil is transported around the entire system along with the refrigerant. Look for oily spots on all the hoses and lines, especially on the hose and tubing connections. If there are oily deposits visible, the system may have a leak. The oily residue soon picks up dust or dirt particles from the surrounding air and appears greasy, eventually building up into a heavy, dirt impregnated grease.

NOTE: A small area of oil on the front of the compressor is normal and no cause for alarm.

Another type of leak may appear at the internal Schraeder type A/C charging valve core in the service access gauge port valve fittings. If tightening the valve core does not stop the leak, it should be replaced. Missing service access gauge port valve caps can also cause a refrigerant leak by allowing dirt to contaminate the valve during charging.

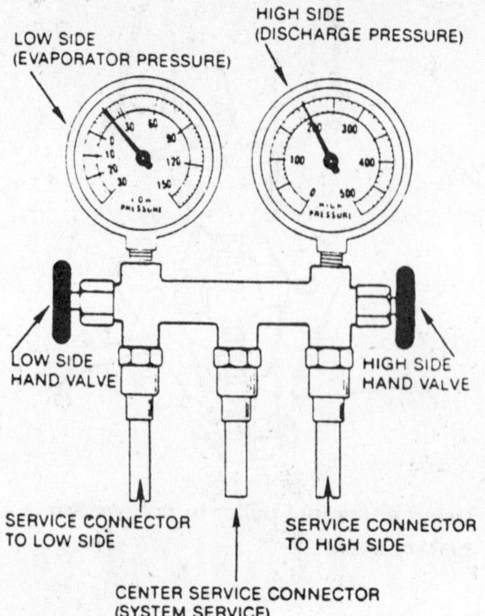

Typical air conditioning gauge set

Periodically inspect the front of the condenser for bent fins or foreign material (dirt, bugs, leaves, etc.), and clean the condenser thoroughly. Straighten any bent fins carefully with needlenosed pliers. Debris may be removed with a stiff bristle brush or water pressure from a garden hose.

A lot of air conditioner problems can be avoided by simply running the system at least once a week, regardless of the season. Let the A/C run for at least five minutes (even in the winter) and you'll keep the internal parts lubricated and prevent the hoses from hardening.

REFRIGERANT LEVEL CHECK

The only way to check the refrigerant level on the Aerostar is to measure the system evaporator pressures with a manifold gauge set, although rapid on/off cycling of the compressor clutch indicates that the A/C system is low on refrigerant. The normal refrigerant capacity is 3½ lbs.

TEST GAUGES

Most of the service work performed in air conditioning requires the use of a set of two gauges, one for the high (head) pressure side of the system, the other for the low (suction) side.

The low side gauge records both pressure and vacuum. Vacuum readings are calibrated from 0 to 30″ and the pressure graduations read from 0 to no less than 60 psi. The high side gauge measures pressure from 0 to at least 600 psi.

Both gauges are threaded into a manifold that contains two hand shut-off valves. Proper manipulation of these valves and the use of the attached test hoses allow the user to perform the following services:

1. Test high and low side pressures.
2. Remove air, moisture, and contaminated refrigerant.
3. Purge the system (of refrigerant).
4. Charge the system (with refrigerant).

The manifold valves are designed so that they have no direct effect on gauge readings, but serve only to provide for, or cut off, flow of refrigerant through the manifold. During all testing and hook-up operations, the valves are kept in a close position to avoid disturbing the refrigeration system. The valves are opened only to purge the system or refrigerant or to charge it.

DISCHARGING THE SYSTEM

Service access gauge port valves are used in the refrigerant system. These are Schraeder type valves, similar to a tire valve with a depressing pin in the center of the valve body. The high pressure (discharge) valve is located in the compressor discharge manifold, just before the accumulator/drier. This valve requires an adapter (YT-354 or 355) to connect a manifold gauge set to it. The other service access port valve is located on the side of the accumulator and is the low pressure (suction) connection. It is extremely important that these two valves not be confused, since connecting a can of Freon to the high pressure side of the A/C system will cause the can to explode.

To connect a manifold gauge set to the service gauge port valves, proceed as follows:

1. Turn both manifold gauge set valves fully clockwise to close the high and low pressure hoses.
2. Remove the caps from the high and low pressure service gauge port valves.
3. If the manifold gauge set hoses do not have the valve depressing pins in them, install fitting adapters (T71P-19703-S and R) containing the pins on the manifold gauge hoses. Remember that an adapter is necessary to connect the manifold gauge hose to the high pressure fitting.
4. Connect the high and low pressure refrigerant hoses to their respective service ports, making sure they are hooked up correctly and fully seated. Tighten the fittings by hand and make sure they are not cross-threaded.
5. Place the open end of the center hose on the manifold gauge set away from your body, then slowly open the

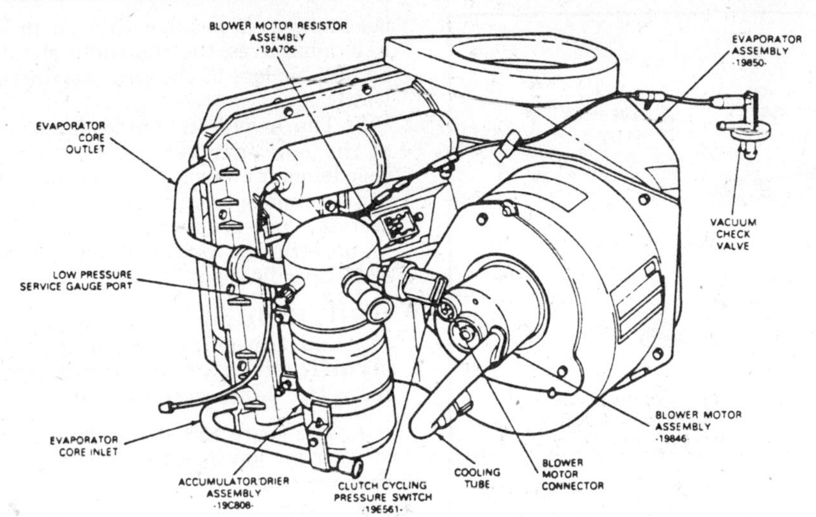

Evaporator case assembly. Note the location of the low pressure service gauge port

LOW pressure valve on the manifold set a slight amount to allow the refrigerant to flow out the center hose and slowly depressurize the A/C system.

6. After the system is nearly discharged, open the high pressure valve very slowly to avoid losing any refrigerant oil and allow any remaining Freon in the compressor and high pressure line to discharge.

CAUTION

Do not attempt this procedure in a closed garage. The refrigerant will displace the oxygen in the air and could result in suffocation in a very short time. Allowing the refrigerant to vent quickly will carry away the refrigerant oil; open the valves slowly and only slightly. Remember that escaping refrigerant will freeze any surface it touches, including skin and eyes. Wear safety glasses at all times.

CHARGING THE SYSTEM

If the system has been completely purged of refrigerant, it must be evacuated before charging. A vacuum pump should be connected to the center hose of the manifold gauge set, both valves should be opened, and the vacuum pump operated until the low pressure gauge reads as close to 30 in.Hg as possible. If a part in the system has been replaced or excessive moisture is suspected, continue the vacuum pump operation for about 30 minutes.

Close the manifold gauge valves to the center hose, then disconnect the vacuum pump and connect the center hose to a charging cylinder, refrigerant drum or a small can refrigerant dispensing valve. Disconnect the wire harness from the clutch cycling pressure switch and install a jumper wire across the two terminals of the connector. Open the manifold gauge LOW side valve to allow refrigerant to enter the system, keeping the can(s) in an upright position to prevent liquid from entering the system.

When no more refrigerant is being drawn into the system, start the engine and move the function selector lever to the NORM A/C position and the blower switch to HI to draw the remaining refrigerant in. Continue to add refrigerant until the specified 3½ lbs. is reached. Close the manifold gauge low pressure valve and the refrigerant supply valve. Remove the jumper wire from the clutch cycling pressure switch connector and reconnect the pressure switch. Disconnect the manifold gauge set and install the service port caps.

Charging From Small Containers

When using a single can A/C charging kit, such as is available at local retailers, make the connection at the low pressure service port, located on the accumulator/drier. This is very important as connecting the small can to the high pressure port will cause the can to explode. Once the can is connected, charge the system as described above. If a manifold gauge set is being used, the low pressure valve must be closed whenever another can is being connected to the center hose. Hold the cans upright to prevent liquid refrigerant from entering the system and possibly damaging the compressor.

Windshield Wipers

For maximum effectiveness and longest element life, the windshield and wiper blades should be kept clean. Dirt, tree sap, road tar and so on will cause streaking, smearing and blade deterioration if left on the windshield. It is advisable to wash the windshield carefully with a commercial glass cleaner at least once a month. Wipe off the rubber blades with a wet rag afterwards. Do not attempt to move the wipers back and forth by hand; damage to the motor and drive mechanism will result.

If the blades are found to be cracked, broken or torn they should be replaced immediately. Replacement intervals will vary with usage, although ozone deterioration usually limits blade lift to about one year. If the wiper pattern is smeared or streaked, or if the blade chatters across the glass, the blades should be replaced. It is easiest and most sensible to replace them in pairs.

There are basically three different types of wiper blade refills, which differ in their method of replacement. One type has two release buttons, approximately ⅓ of the way up from the ends of the blade frame. Pushing the buttons down releases a lock and allows the rubber blade to be removed from the frame. The new blade slides back into the frame and locks in place.

The second type of refill has two metal tabs which are unlocked by squeezing them together. The rubber blade can then be withdrawn from the frame jaws. A new one is installed by inserting it into the front frame jaws and sliding it rearward to engage the remaining frame jaws. There are usually four jaws; be certain when installing that the refill is engaged in all of them. At the end of its travel, the tabs will lock into place on the front jaws of the wiper blade frame.

The third type is a refill made from polycarbonate. The refill has a simple locking device at one end which flexes downward out of the groove into which the jaws of the holder fit, allowing easy release. By sliding the new refill through all the jaws and pushing through the slight resistance when it reaches the end of its travel, the refill will lock into position.

Regardless of the type of refill used, make sure that all of the frame jaws are engaged as the refill is pushed into place and locked. The metal blade holder and frame will scratch the glass if allowed to touch it.

Tires and Wheels

Inspect the tire treads for cuts, bruises and other damage. Check the air valves to be sure that they are tight. Replace any missing valve caps. The tires should be checked frequently for proper air pressure. A chart in the

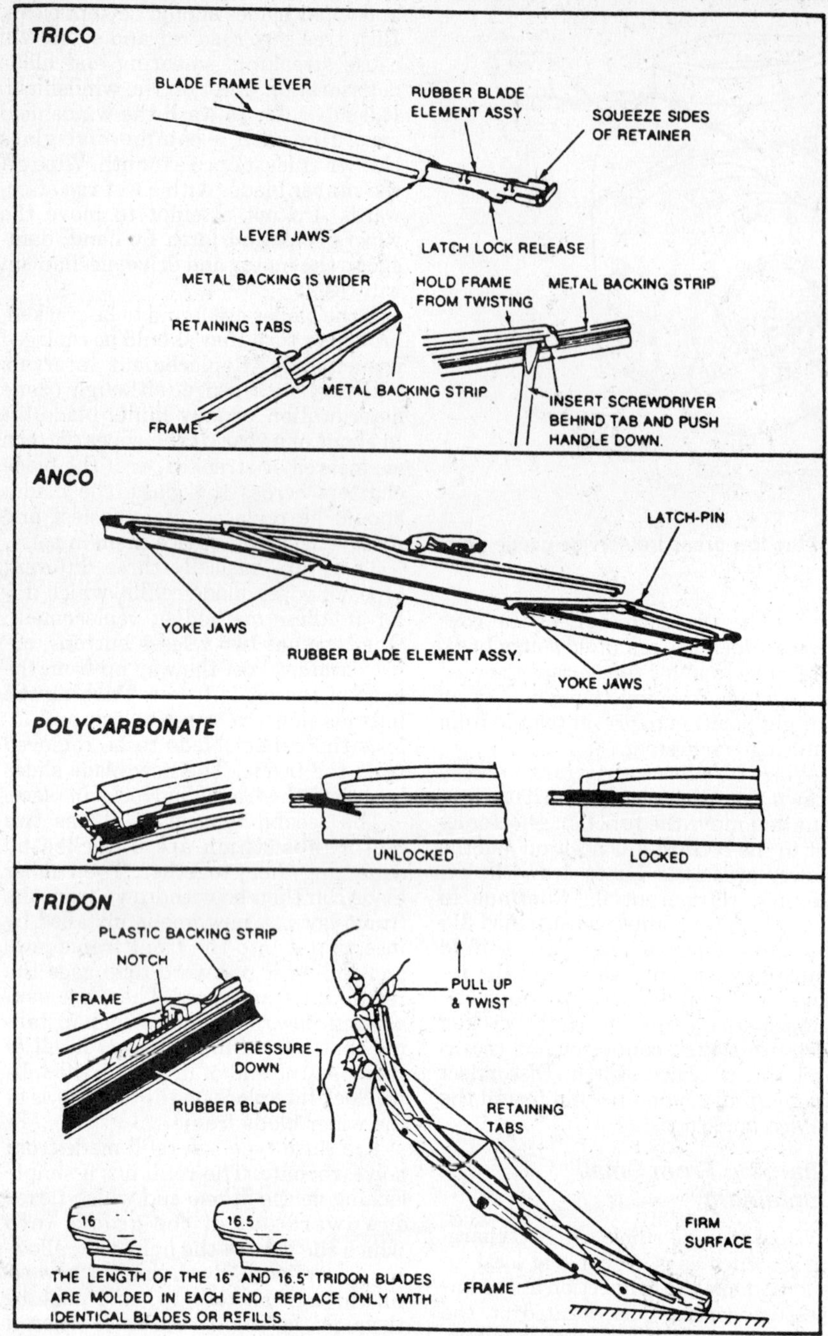

Popular styles of wiper refills

glove compartment or on the driver's door pillar gives the recommended inflation pressure. Pressures can increase as much as 6 psi due to heat buildup. It is a good idea to have your own accurate gauge, and to check pressures weekly. Not all gauges on service station air pumps can be trusted.

Inspect tires for uneven wear that might indicate the need for front end alignment or tire rotation. Tires should be replaced when a tread wear indicator appears as a solid band across the tread. When buying new tires, give some thought to the following points, especially if you are switching to larger tires or a different profile series (50, 60, 70, 78):

1. All four tires should be of the same construction type. Radial, bias, or bias/belted tires should not be mixed.

2. The wheels must be the correct width for the tire. Tire dealers have charts of tire and rim compatibility. A mismatch can cause sloppy handling and rapid tire wear. The tread width should match the rim width (inside bead to inside bead) within an inch. For radial tires, the rim width should be 80% or less of the tire (not tread) width.

3. The height (mounted diameter) of the new tires can greatly change speedometer accuracy, engine speed at a given road speed, fuel mileage, acceleration, and ground clearance. Tire manufacturers furnish full measurement specifications.

NOTE: Dimensions of tires marked the same size may vary significantly, even among tires from the same manufacturer.

4. The spare tire should be usable, at least for low speed operation, with the new tires.

5. There shouldn't be any body interference when loaded, on bumps, or in turning.

TIRE ROTATION

Tire rotation is recommended every 6,000 miles or so, to obtain maximum tire wear. The pattern you use depends on whether or not you have a usable spare. Radial tires should not be cross-switched (from one side of the van to the other); they last longer if their direction of rotation is not changed. They will wear very rapidly if their direction of rotation is reversed.

NOTE: Mark the wheel position or direction of rotation on radial tires or studded snow tires before removing them.

CAUTION

Avoid overtightening the lug nuts to prevent damage to the brake disc or drum. Alloy wheels can also be cracked by overtightening. Use of a torque wrench is highly recommended. Lug nuts should be tightened in sequence to 85-115 ft.lb.

TEMPORARY SPARE TIRE

The temporary spare tire is lighter in weight and easier to handle than a conventional tire, but it is limited to emergency use only. The temporary spare tire pressure should be checked periodically and inflated to the pressure marked on the sidewall. When the temporary spare tire is in use, vehicle speed should be kept below 50 mph and the flat conventional tire should be repaired or replaced as soon as possible. The temporary spare is stored underneath the cargo bed in the rear of the vehicle. To remove the temporary spare from storage:

1. Insert the lugwrench into the actuator hole at the rear of the van and rotate it counterclockwise.

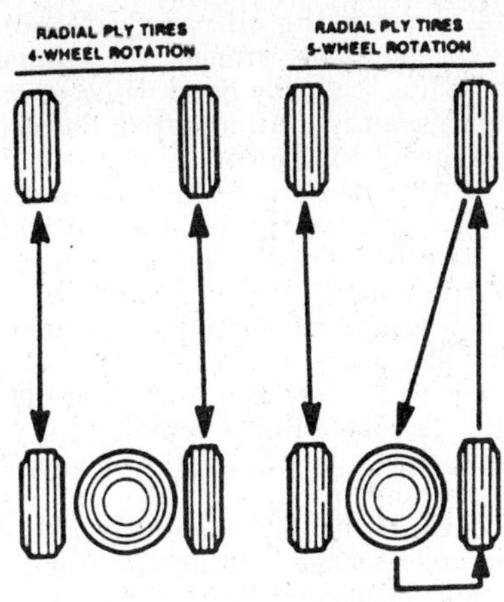

Tire rotation patterns

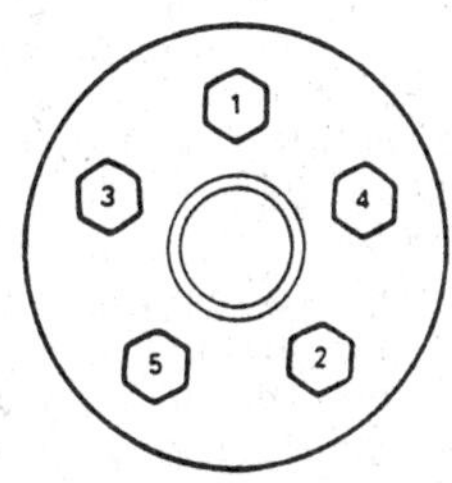
Lug nut tightening sequence

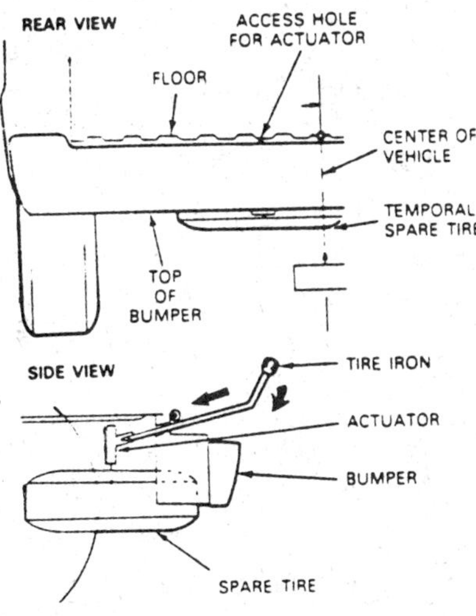

Lowering temporary spare tire

2. Slide the spare rearward and separate it from the retainer.

3. To stow the cable/retainer without the temporary spare, insert the cable fitting into the tire carrier rear wall slot. Position the wheel retainer against the carrier and rotate the lugwrench clockwise until all slack is removed. Do not overtighten.

4. To install the temporary spare tire into its holder, first insert the lugwrench into the actuator and rotate it counterclockwise while pulling on the cable until adequate cable is available.

5. Install the retainer through the wheel center with the valve stem facing downward and rearward to allow the tire pressure to be checked.

6. Rotate the lugwrench clockwise until the tire is secured; the raising mechanism will slip. Check for proper seating against the underbody brackets and retighten if necessary.

CAUTION

Do not overtighten the retaining bolt with the lugwrench as damage to the spare may occur by compressing the sidewalls against the supports. Improper installation of the spare tire may result in damage to the rear axle, tire or brake lines.

FLUIDS AND LUBRICANTS

Fuel Recommendations

The Aerostar is equipped with a catalytic converter and must use unleaded fuel only. The use of leaded fuel or additives containing lead will result in damage to the catalytic converter, oxygen sensor and EGR valve. Both the 4 and 6 cylinder engines are designed to operate using gasoline with a minimum octane rating of 87. Use of gasoline with a rating lower than 87 can cause persistent, heavy spark knock which can lead to engine damage.

You may notice occasional, light spark knock when accelerating or driving up hills. This is normal and should not cause concern because the maximum fuel economy is obtained under conditions of occasional light spark knock. Gasoline with an octane rating higher than 87 may be used, but it is not necessary for proper operation.

Gasohol, a mixture of gasoline and ethanol (grain alcohol) is available in some areas. Your Aerostar should operate satisfactorily on gasohol blends containing no more than 10% ethanol by volume and having an octane rating of 87 or higher. In some cases, methanol (wood alcohol) or other alcohols may be added to gasoline. Again, your Aerostar should operate satisfactorily on blends containing up to 5% methanol by volume when cosolvents and other necessary additives are used. If not properly formulated with appropriate cosolvents and corrosion inhibitors, such blends may cause driveability problems or damage emission and fuel system materials. If you are uncertain as to the presence of alcohols in the gasoline you are purchasing, check the label on the pump or ask the attendant.

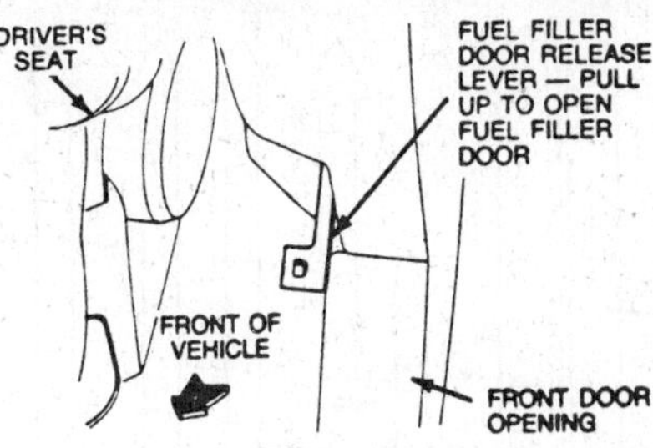

Location of the fuel filler door release

NOTE: Discontinue use of any gasohol or alcohol/gasoline blend if driveability or fuel system problems occur. Do not use such fuels unless they are unleaded.

Some models are equipped with a remote fuel filler door release, located between the driver seat and the door. If the filler door cannot be opened by pulling the release lever, there is a manual override cord located on the left side of the jack stowage compartment. The manual release is a cord attached to a handle marked "Fuel Filler Door Manual Release."

Engine Oil Recommendations

To insure proper engine performance and durability, the proper quality engine oil is essential. Using the proper grade of oil for your engine will not only prolong its life, it will improve fuel economy. Ford recommends that you use Motorcraft® oil or an equivalent that meets Ford Specification ESE-M2C153-C and API (American Petroleum Institute) Categories SF, SF/CC or SF/CD.

Engine oils with improved fuel economy properties are currently available. They offer the potential for small improvements in fuel economy by reducing the amount of fuel burned by the engine to overcome friction. These improvements are often difficult to measure in everyday driving, but over the course of a year can offer significant savings. These oils are recommended to be used in conjunction with the recommended API Category.

A symbol has been developed by the API to help consumers select the proper grade of engine oil. It should be printed on top of the oil container to show oil performance by the API designation. This symbol should match the manufacturer recommendation. The center section will show the SAE

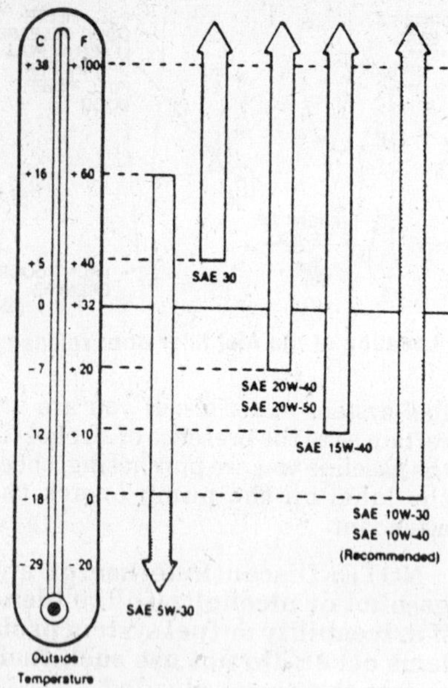

Oil viscosity recommendations for 2.3L and 2.8L engines

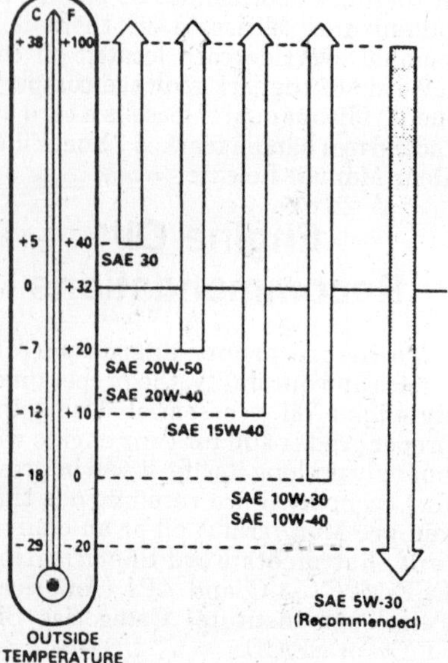

Oil viscosity recommendations for 3.0L engine

(Society of Automotive Engineers) rating, while the top outer ring contains the API rating. The bottom outer ring will have the words "Energy Conserving" only if the oil has proven fuel saving capabilities.

CHECKING ENGINE OIL LEVEL

It is normal to add some oil between oil changes. The engine oil level should be checked every 500 miles.

1. Park the van on a level surface

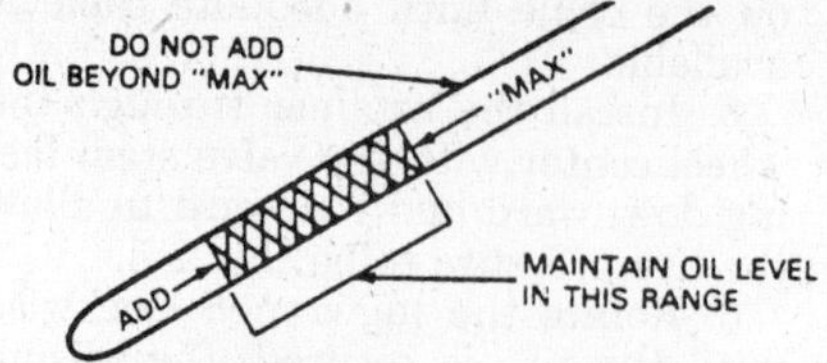

Reading the engine oil dipstick

Recommended oil viscosity for Aerostar

and turn the engine off. Open the hood.

2. Wait a few minutes to allow the oil to drain back into the crankcase.
3. While protecting yourself from engine heat, pull the dipstick out and wipe it clean with a suitable paper towel or clean rag.
4. Reinsert the dipstick and make sure it is pushed all the way down and seated on the tube, then remove the dipstick again and look at the oil level scale on the end of the dipstick. The oil level should fall within the safe range on the dipstick scale.
5. If necessary, add oil to the engine to bring the level up. Be careful not to overfill the crankcase and wipe the dipstick off before checking the oil level again.

OIL AND FILTER CHANGE

The engine oil and filter should be changed at the recommended intervals on the maintenance schedule chart. The oil filter protects the engine by removing harmful, abrasive or sludgy particles from the system without blocking the flow of oil to vital engine parts. It is recommended that the filter be changed along with the oil at the specified intervals.

NOTE: Changing the oil requires the use of an oil filter wrench to remove the filter. It's also a good idea to have some oil dry (or kitty litter) handy to absorb any oil that misses the drain pan.

1. Start the engine and allow it to reach normal operating temperature. Park the truck on a level surface and shut the engine off.
2. Set the parking brake firmly and block the drive wheels.
3. Place a drip pan of at least 5 quart capacity beneath the oil pan.
4. Loosen the oil pan drain plug with a suitable wrench, then finish threading it out by hand while pressing in slightly until it is free. Be careful, the oil will be hot.
5. Allow the oil to drain completely before replacing the drain plug. Tighten the plug securely, but do not overtighten.
6. Position the drain pan under the oil filter, then use an oil filter band wrench to loosen the filter. Once the filter is loose, finish removing it by hand. Again, be careful, the oil and filter will be hot.
7. Clean the filter mounting base on the engine block and lightly coat the gasket of the new filter with a thin film of oil. Install the new filter by hand and tighten it another ½-¾ turn after the gasket contacts the filter base. Tighten the filter by hand, do not use the filter wrench.
8. Fill the crankcase with the recommended oil and start the engine to check for leaks. It is normal for the oil warning light to remain on for a few seconds after startup until the oil filter fills up. Once the oil light goes out, check for leaks from the filter mounting and drain plug. If no leaks are noticed, stop the engine and check the oil level on the dipstick. Top up if necessary.

Manual Transmission

FLUID LEVEL CHECK

The 5-speed manual transmission uses standard transmission lubricant, Ford part number D8DZ-19C547-A or equivalent. The fluid level is checked by removing the filler plug on the side of the transmission case. Clean the plug and remove it. The fluid should be up to the bottom of the filler plug hole.

If additional fluid is required, add it through the filler plug hole to bring the level up. Use only fluid meeting Ford specification ESP-M2C83-C. Install the filler plug when the fluid level is correct, making sure it is fully seated.

DRAINING MANUAL TRANSMISSION

The fluid can be drained from the manual transmission simply by removing the drain plug on the transmission bottom pan. Use a suitable container to catch the old fluid, then replace the plug and remove the filler plug on the side of the transmission to add new fluid. Add fluid until the level is at the base of the filler plug hole.

Hydraulic Clutch

FLUID LEVEL CHECK

The clutch system in the Aerostar does not have free play. It is automatically self-adjusting and should not require any routine service throughout the life of the vehicle. The fluid level in the clutch reservoir will slowly increase as the clutch wears. As long as the fluid is visible at or above the step in the translucent reservoir body, top-off is not recommended and should be avoided. This will help prevent overflow and possible contamination of the fluid while the diaphragm and cap are removed. If it becomes necessary to remove the reservoir cap, thoroughly clean the reservoir cap before removing it to prevent dirt or water from entering the reservoir.

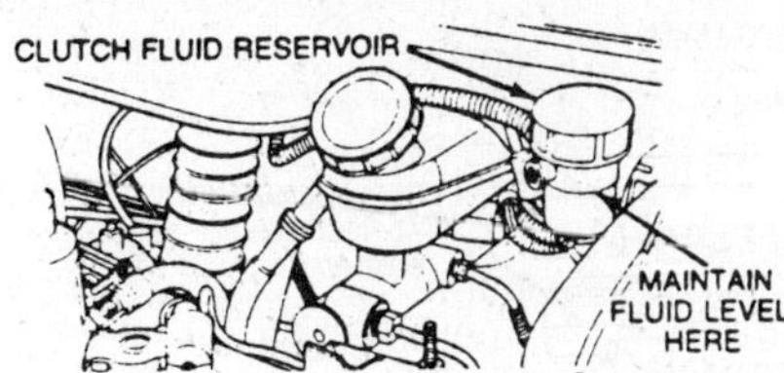

Checking hydraulic clutch fluid

Automatic Transmission

FLUID LEVEL CHECK

Correct automatic transmission fluid level is important for proper operation. Low fluid level causes transmission slippage, while overfilling can cause foaming, loss of fluid or malfunction. Since transmission fluid expands as temperature rises, it is advisable to check the fluid level at operating temperature (after about 20 miles of driving), however, the fluid level can be checked at room temperature.

To check the fluid level, park the vehicle on a level surface and apply the parking brake. Start the engine and hold the foot brake while moving the transmission shift lever through all the gear positions, allowing sufficient time for each gear to engage. Return the shifter to the PARK position and leave the engine running.

Secure all loose clothing and remove any jewelry, then open the hood. While protecting yourself against engine heat, wipe the dipstick cap clean, then remove the dipstick. Wipe the dipstick clean then reinsert it into the tube, making sure it is fully seated. Remove the dipstick again and read the fluid level on the dipstick scale. At normal operating temperature, the level on the dipstick should be within the crosshatched area or between the arrows. At room temperature, the level should be between the middle and top hole on the dipstick.

If fluid has to be added, use a small necked funnel to add the necessary amount of Dexron®II through the dipstick tube to bring the level up to normal. Do not bring the level above the

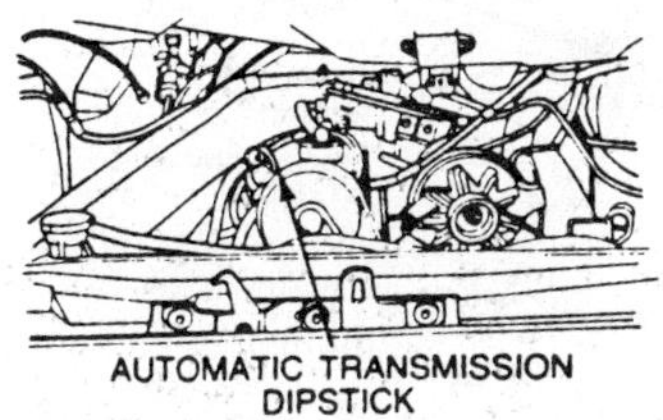

Location of automatic transmission dipstick

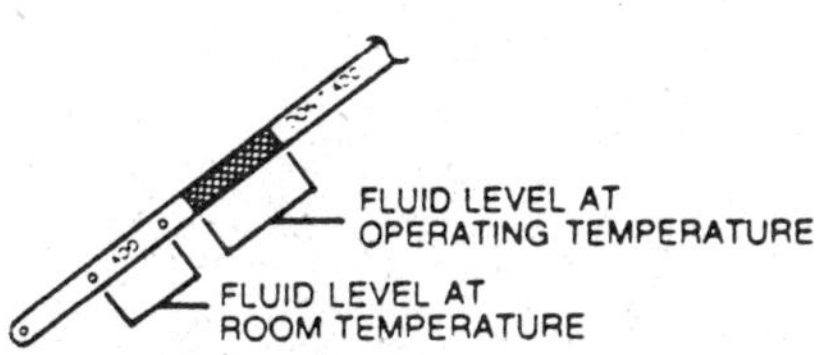

Checking automatic transmission fluid level

crosshatched area on the dipstick. If overfilled, the excess transmission fluid must be removed. Once the fluid level is correct, reinsert the dipstick and make sure it is fully seated.

PAN AND FILTER SCREEN SERVICE

Normal maintenance and lubrication requirements do not include periodic automatic transmission fluid changes. However, if the transmission is used under continuous or severe conditions, the transmission and torque converter should be drained and refilled with Dexron®II. The following procedure is for a partial draining of the transmission, in order to remove the pan to replace the pan gasket or clean the filter screen.

1. Park the van on a level surface and place a drip pan under the transmission to catch the fluid.
2. Slowly loosen the pan attaching bolts. When all the bolts are loose, gradually remove the bolts from one end to allow the pan to tilt down and the fluid to drain out.
3. When all of the fluid has drained from the transmission oil pan, remove the remaining mounting bolts and lower the pan.
4. Thoroughly clean the pan and screen in solvent or kerosene and remove any old gasket material from the pan or transmission housing. Clean all gasket mating surfaces thoroughly, but be careful not to scratch any aluminum surfaces. Do not attempt to reuse an old pan gasket.
5. Place a new gasket on the pan, then install the pan on the transmission.
6. Add three quarts of fluid to the transmission through the filler tube, then check the transmission fluid level as described above.

Drive Axle

FLUID LEVEL CHECK

The ability of any axle to deliver quiet, trouble free operation over a period of years is largely dependent upon the use of a good quality gear lubricant. Ford recommends the use of hypoid gear lubricant part number E0AZ-19580-A or any equivalent lubricant meeting Ford specification ESP-M2C154-A in their conventional or Traction-Lok® axles. Aerostars equipped with Dana axles should use hypoid gear lubricant part number C6AZ-19580-E or any equivalent lubricant meeting Ford specification ESW-M2C105-A.

To check the fluid level in the rear axle, remove the filler plug located on the side of the axle housing and make sure the axle fluid is within ¼" (6mm) below the bottom of the filler hole. If not, top up by adding lubricant through the filler hole. Do not overfill.

NOTE: If any water is noted in the axle when checking the fluid level, the axle lubricant should be drained and replaced. Change the axle lubricant if the axle is submerged in water, especially if the water covers the vent hole.

DRAINING REAR AXLE LUBRICANT

1. Drive the van for 10-15 miles at highway speeds to warm the axle lubricant to operating temperature and minimum viscosity.
2. Raise the van and support it safely with jackstands. Place a drain pan under the axle.
3. Clean the filler plug area of the axle housing to prevent the entry of rust or dirt into the axle assembly.
4. Remove the filler plug and use a suitable suction type utility pump (manual or powered) to drain the axle lubricant by inserting the pump suction hose through the axle filler hole down into the lowest portion of the axle carrier housing. Make sure all the lubricant is removed.
5. Fill the axle housing with 3.5

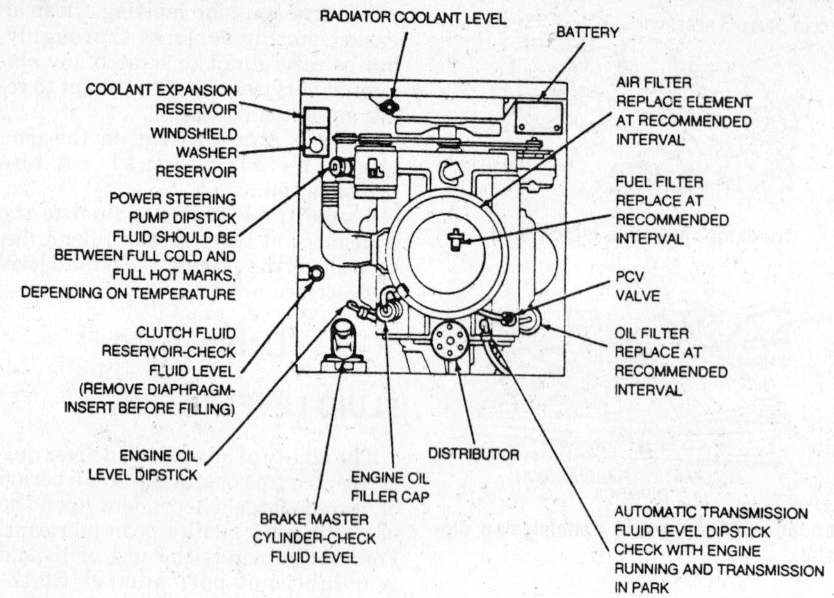

2.8L V6 lubrication points

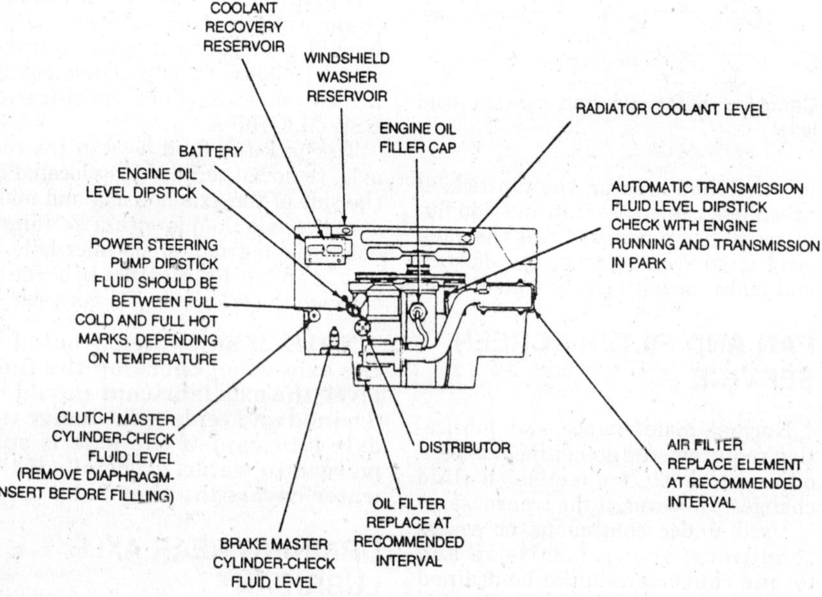

2.3L 4 cylinder lubrication points

pints of the specified hypoid gear lubricant (3.6 pints on Dana axles), then check the fluid level as described above. Top off if necessary, but do not overfill.

6. Install the filler plug and torque it to 15-30 ft.lb. (20-40 Nm).

Cooling System

The Aerostar is equipped with a coolant recovery system with a one piece, molded reservoir. Coolant in the system expands with heat and overflows into the coolant expansion reservoir. When the system cools down, coolant is drawn back into the radiator. Be careful not to confuse the windshield washer reservoir with the coolant recovery reservoir.

The coolant level should be checked in both the radiator and recovery reservoir at least once a month and then only when the engine is cool. Never, under any circumstances, attempt to check the coolant level in the radiator when the engine is hot or operating. On a full system, it is normal to have coolant in the expansion reservoir when the engine is hot.

Whenever coolant level checks of the radiator are made, check the condition of the radiator cap rubber seal. Make sure it is clean and free of any dirt particles. Rinse with water, if necessary, and make sure the radiator filler neck seat is clean. Check that the overflow hose is not kinked and is attached to the reservoir. If you have to add coolant more than once a month, or if you have to add more than one quart at a time, check the cooling system for leaks.

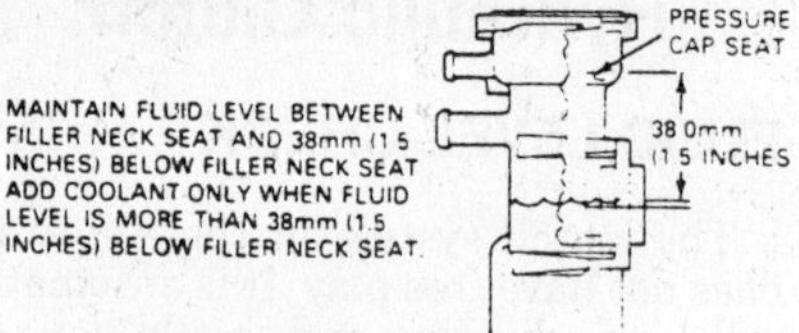

Checking radiator coolant level

COOLANT CHECK AND CHANGE

CAUTION

Never attempt to check the radiator coolant level while the engine is hot. Use extreme care when removing the radiator cap. Wrap a thick towel around the cap and turn it slowly to the first stop. Step back while the pressure is released from the cooling system. When all pressure has vented, press down on the cap (still wrapped in the towel) and remove it. Failure to follow this procedure may result in serious personal injury from hot coolant or steam blowout and/or damage to the cooling system.

On systems with a coolant recovery tank, maintain the coolant level at thc level marks on the recovery bottle. The coolant should be at the base of the filler neck in the radiator. The Aerostar uses an aluminum radiator and requires coolant with corrosion inhibitors to prevent radiator damage. Use only a permanent type coolant that meets Ford specification ESE-M97B44-A. Do not use alcohol or methanol antifreeze.

For best protection against freezing and overheating, maintain an approximate 50% water and 50% ethylene glycol antifreeze mixture in the cooling system. Do not mix different brands of antifreeze to avoid possible chemical damage to the cooling system. Avoid using water that is known to have a high alkaline content or is very hard, except in emergency situations. Drain and flush the cooling system as soon as possible after using such water.

NOTE: Never add cold water to an overheated engine while the engine is not running.

After filling the radiator, run the engine until it reaches normal operating

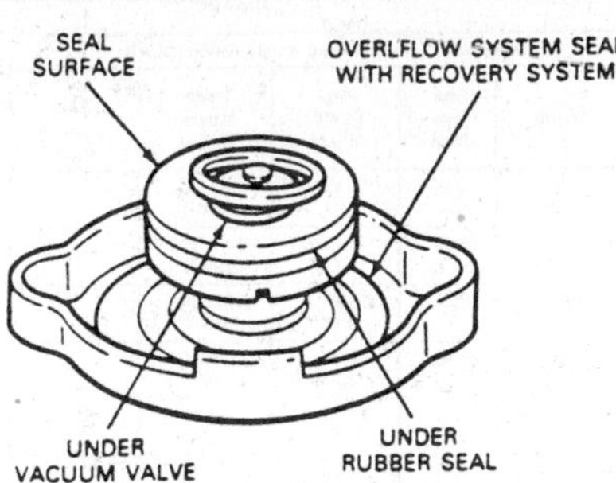

Inspect radiator cap seals periodically

temperature, to make sure that the thermostat has opened and all the air is bled from the system.

DRAINING, FLUSHING AND REFILLING

CAUTION

When draining the coolant, keep in mind that cats and dogs are attracted by the ethylene glycol antifreeze, and are quite likely to drink any that is left in an uncovered container or in puddles on the ground. This will prove fatal in sufficient quantity. Always drain the coolant into a sealable container. Coolant should be reused unless it is contaminated or several years old.

To drain the cooling system, allow the engine to cool down **BEFORE ATTEMPTING TO REMOVE THE RADIATOR CAP**. Then turn the cap until it hisses. Wait until all pressure is off the cap before removing it completely. To avoid burns and scalding, always handle a warm radiator cap with a heavy rag.

1. At the dash, set the heater TEMP control lever to the fully HOT position.
2. With the radiator cap removed, drain the radiator by loosening the petcock at the bottom of the radiator. Flush the radiator with water until the fluid runs clear. Disconnect the lower radiator hose from the radiator and drain any remaining coolant from the engine block.
3. Close the petcock and reconnect the lower radiator hose, then refill the system with a 50/50 mix of ethylene glycol antifreeze and water. Fill the system to the bottom of the radiator filler neck, then reinstall the radiator cap after allowing several minutes for trapped air to bubble out. Back the radiator cap off to the first stop (pressure relief position).

NOTE: Fill the fluid reservoir tank up to the MAX COLD level.

4. Operate the engine at 2,000 rpm for a few minutes with the heater control lever in the MAX HEAT position.
5. Turn the engine off, then wrap a rag around the radiator cap and remove it. Be careful, the coolant will be hot. Top off the radiator coolant level, if necessary, then reinstall the radiator cap to its down and locked position.
6. Start the engine and allow it to reach normal operating temperature, then check the system for leaks.

RADIATOR CAP INSPECTION

Allow the engine to cool sufficiently before attempting to remove the radiator cap. Use a rag to cover the cap, then remove by pressing down and turning counterclockwise to the first stop. If any hissing is noted (indicating the release of pressure), wait until the hissing stops completely, then press down again and turn counterclockwise until the cap can be removed.

CAUTION

DO NOT attempt to remove the radiator cap while the engine is hot. Severe personal injury from steam burns can result.

Check the condition of the radiator cap gasket and seal inside of the cap. The radiator cap is designed to seal the cooling system under normal operating conditions which allows the build up of a certain amount of pressure (this pressure rating is stamped or printed on the cap). The pressure in the system raises the boiling point of the coolant to help prevent overheating. If the radiator cap does not seal, the boiling point of the coolant is lowered and overheating will occur. If the cap must be replaced, purchase the new cap according to the pressure rating which is specified for your vehicle.

Prior to installing the radiator cap, inspect and clean the filler neck. If you are reusing the old cap, clean it thoroughly with clear water. After turning the cap on, make sure the arrows align with the overflow hose.

Brake Master Cylinder

To check the brake fluid level, visually inspect the translucent master cylinder reservoir. The fluid level should be at the maximum level line of the reservoir. If the level is low, top it off using DOT 3 brake fluid meeting Ford specification ESA-M6C25-A. It is normal for the brake fluid level to decrease as the brake linings wear. If the level is excessively low, inspect the brake linings for wear and/or the brake system for leaks.

Power Steering Pump

Before attempting to check the fluid level, first clean all dirt from the outside of the power steering pump reservoir before removing the cap. Start the engine and allow it to reach normal operating temperature, then turn the steering wheel from lock-to-lock several times to bleed any air out of the system. Turn the engine off and check the fluid level on the power steering pump dipstick. The level should be within the FULL HOT scale on the dipstick. If necessary, top the reservoir up with fluid that meets Ford specification ESW-M2C33-F, such as Motorcraft Automatic Transmission and Power Steering Fluid Type F. Do not overfill.

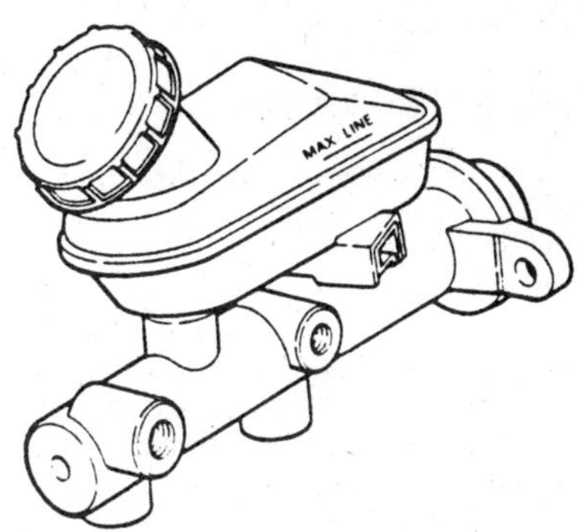

Brake fluid should reach the MAX line on the master cylinder reservoir

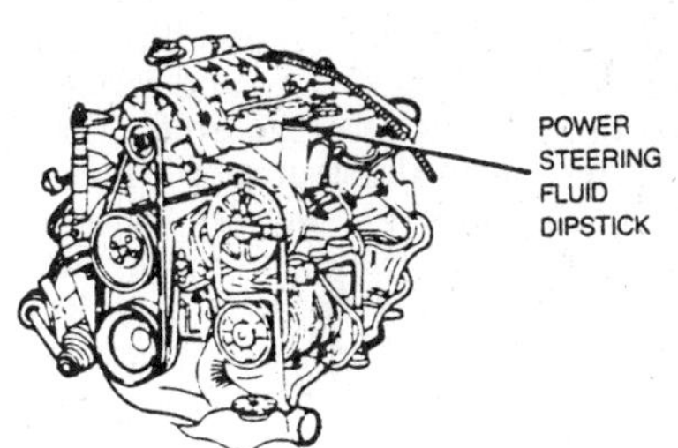

Location of power steering dipstick on 3.0L engine

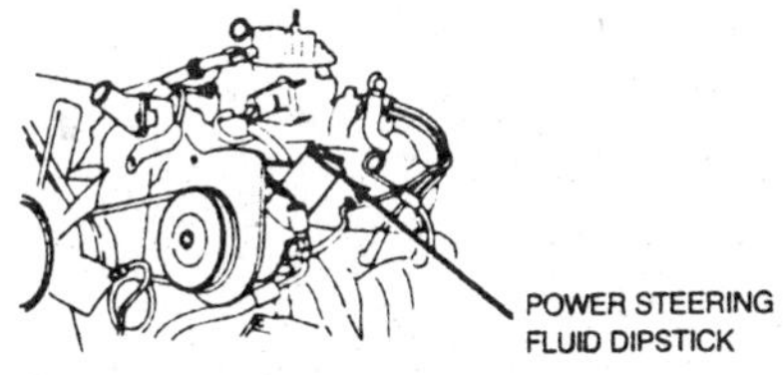

Location of power steering dipstick on 2.8L engine

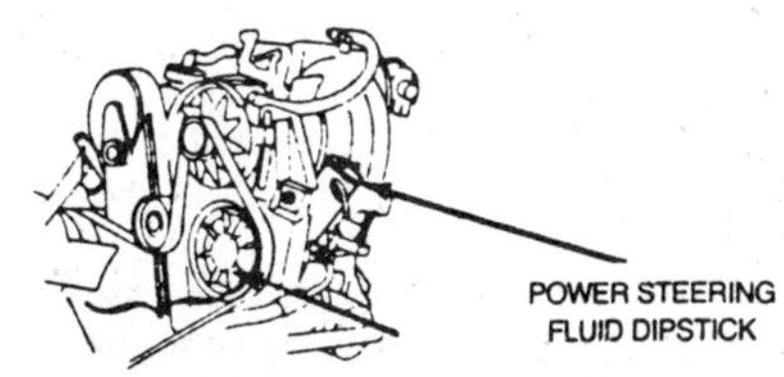

Location of power steering dipstick on 2.3L engine

Chassis Greasing

The front ball joints should be lubricated at 30,000 mile intervals. Locate the ball joint grease fittings, wipe them clean, then use a suitable grease gun to lubricate the ball joints. Inspect the ball joints for any obvious wear or damage and replace parts as necessary. Although there are no lubrication requirements, all suspension bushings should be inspected at this time for wear or damage and replaced as required. If equipped with grease fittings, the universal joints should be greased at this time also. U-joints without grease fittings require no lubrication.

WHEEL BEARINGS

The front wheel bearings should be inspected and repacked with grease every 30,000 miles. A good quality, high temperature wheel bearing grease should be used. The procedure involves removing the front brake rotors. Refer to the Brake Section for removal and repacking information.

THROTTLE AND TRANSMISSION LINKAGE

Inspect the transmission linkage for signs of wear or damage and service as required. Lubricate the shift linkage at the points illustrated with multi-purpose lubricant such as Ford part number C1AZ-19590-B or equivalent.

Disconnect the throttle cable from the ball stud on the throttle lever and lubricate the stud with multi-purpose lubricant, then reconnect the ball stud and cable.

PARKING BRAKE LINKAGE

Once a year, or whenever binding is noticed in the parking brake mechanism, lubricate the cable guides, levers and linkages with multi-purpose grease.

LOCK CYLINDERS AND LATCH ASSEMBLIES

Apply graphite lubricant sparingly thought the key slot. Insert the key and operate the lock several times to be sure that the lubricant is worked into the lock cylinder.

Lubricate the hood, rear liftgate and door latches with polyethylene grease, then operate the mechanism several times to be sure the lubricant is worked into the latch assembly.

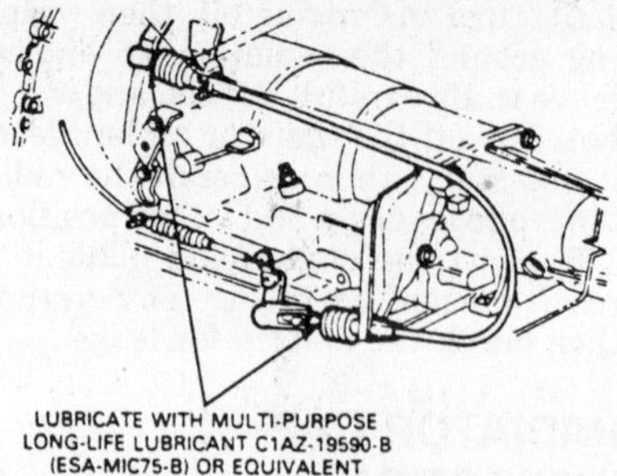

Automatic transmission linkage

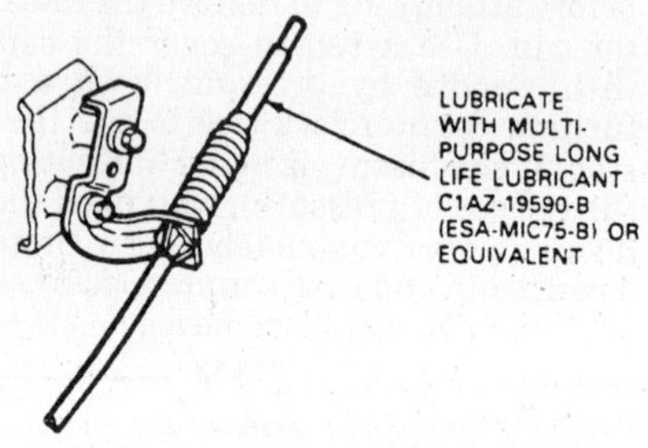

Automatic transmission kickdown cable

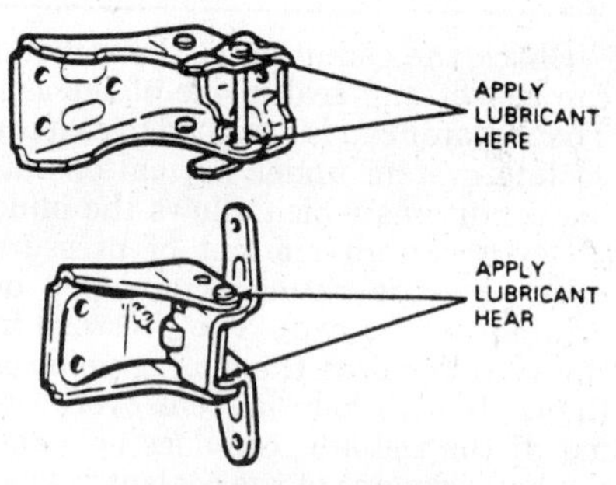

Lubricating door hinges

MFD. BY FORD MOTOR CO. IN U.S.A.
DATE: GVWR:
FRONT GAWR: REAR GAWR:
WITH TIRES RIMS AT PSI COLD
WITH TIRES RIMS AT PSI COLD
THIS VEHICLE CONFORMS TO ALL APPLICABLE FEDERAL MOTOR VEHICLE SAFETY STANDARDS IN EFFECT ON THE DATE OF MANUFACTURE SHOWN ABOVE
VEHICLE IDENTIFICATION NO.
TYPE
51 9D 48
EXTERIOR PAINT COLORS DSO

WB	TYPE GVW	BODY	TRANS	AXLE	TAPE	SPRING
119			T	A4		

Rear Axle Codes

Code	Description	Capacity (lbs.)	Ratio	Brake Size
12	Ford	2,790	4.10	10"
13	Ford	2,790	3.45	9"
14	Ford	2,790	3.73	9"
13	Ford	2,790	3.45	10"
14	Ford	2,790	3.73	10"
LIMITED SLIP AXLES				
A2	Ford	2,790	4.10	10"
A4	Ford	2,790	3.73	10"

Axle codes

Maximum Gross Combined Weight Rating (GCWR)				
Engine	Rear Axle Ratio	Max. GCWR lb (Kg)	Trailer Weight lb (Kg)	Max. Frontal Area Sq. Ft.
2.3L EFI	3.45	4,800 (2 177)	0-2,000 (0-907)	①
	3.73	4,800 (2 177)	0-2,000 (0-907)	①
	4.10	4,800 (2 177)	0-2,000 (0-907)	①
2.8L	3.45	5,000 (2 268)	0-2,000 (0-907)	①
	3.73	5,000 (2 268)	0-2,000 (0-907)	50
3.0L EFI	3.45	5,000 (2 268)	0-2,000 (0-907)	①
	3.73	5,000 (2 268)	0-2,000 (0-907)	50

① Trailer frontal area is not to exceed base vehicle frontal area.
NOTE — For altitude operation, reduce GCW by 2% per 1,000 ft. elevation.

Manual transmission

Maximum Gross Combined Weight Rating (GCWR)				
Engine	Rear Axle Ratio	Max. GCWR lb (Kg)	Trailer Weight lb (Kg)	Max. Frontal Area Sq. Ft.
2.3L EFI	3.73	4,800 (2 177)	0-2,000 (0-907)	①
		6,000 (2 722)	2,000-3,000 (907-1 361)	①
	4.10	4,800 (2 177)	0-2,000 (0-907)	①
		6,500 (2 948)	2,000-3,500 (907-1 587)	①
2.8L	3.45	5,500 (2 495)	0-2,000 (0-907)	①
		7,500 (3 402)	2,000-4,500 (907-2 041)	50
	3.73	5,500 (2 495)	0-2,000 (0-907)	①
		8,000 (3 629)	2,000-4,500 (907-2 041)	50
	4.10	5,500 (2 495)	0-2,000 (0-907)	①
		8,500 (3 856)	2,000-5,000 (907-2 268)	50
3.0L EFI	3.45	5,500 (2 495)	0-2,000 (0-907)	①
		7,500 (3 402)	2,000-4,500 (907-2 041)	50
	3.73	5,500 (2 495)	0-2,000 (0-907)	①
		8,000 (3 629)	2,000-4,500 (907-2 041)	50
	4.10	5,600 (2 495)	(0-2000) (0-907)	①
		8,500 (3 856)	2,000-5,000 (907-2 268)	50

① Trailer frontal area is not to exceed base vehicle frontal area.
NOTE — For altitude operation, reduce GCW by 2% per 1,000 ft. elevation.

Automatic transmission

DOOR HINGES AND HINGE CHECKS

Spray a silicone lubricant on the hinge pivot points to eliminate any binding conditions. Open and close the door several times to be sure that the lubricant is evenly and thoroughly distributed.

REAR LIFTGATE

Spray a silicone lubricant on all of the pivot and friction surfaces to eliminate any squeaks or binds. Work the tailgate to distribute the lubricant.

BODY DRAIN HOLES

Be sure that the drain holes in the doors and rocker panels are cleared of obstruction. A small screwdriver can be used to clear them of any debris.

PUSHING AND TOWING

Vehicles with catalytic converters should never be push started due to the possibility of serious converter damage. If the vehicle won't start, follow the instructions for the use of jumper cables.

Improper towing of the Aerostar could result in transmission damage. Always unload the vehicle before towing it. Tow chain attachments must be make to the structural members of the vehicle, with the chains routed under a 4" x 4" x 48" wood crossbeam placed under the bottom edge of the front bumper against the air spoiler or under the metal rear bumper supports against the wrecker towing tabs, in such a manner that they do not come into contact with suspension, steering, brake, cooling system, exhaust system, bumper or air spoiler components. Make sure the parking brake is released and the transmission gearshift lever is in Neutral. To move a vehicle with an inoperative rear axle, the rear wheels must be raised. If the transmission is inoperative, the rear wheels must be raised or the driveshaft disconnected.

FRONT WHEELS OFF GROUND
Manual or Automatic Transmission
1. Transmission in neutral. 2. Max speed 35 mph (56 km/h). 3. Max distance 50 miles (80 km). NOTE — If a distance of 50 miles (80 km) or speed of 35 mph (56 km/h) must be exceeded, disconnect driveshaft.
REAR WHEELS OFF GROUND
Manual or Automatic Transmission
1. Lock steering wheel straight ahead.
ALL FOUR WHEELS ON GROUND
Manual or Automatic Transmission
1. Transmission in neutral. 2. Max speed 35 mph (56 km). 3. Max distance 50 miles (80 km). NOTE — If a distance of 50 miles (80 km) or speed of 35 mph (56 km/h) must be exceeded, disconnect driveshaft.

Towing 2-wheel drive vehicles

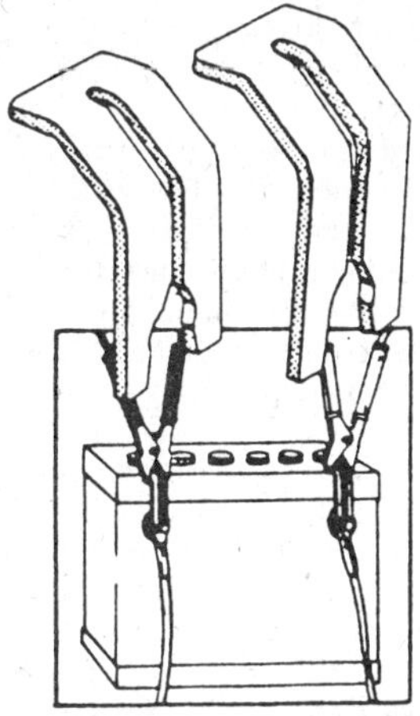

Side terminal batteries occasionally pose a problem when connecting jumper cables. There frequently isn't enough room to clamp the cables without touching sheet metal. Side terminal adaptors are available to alleviate this problem and should be removed after use.

CAUTION

Never tow your Aerostar by using a tow bar that attaches to the bumper only. This will damage the bumper and result in property damage or personal injury. Do not attempt to use the steering column lock to hold the front wheels in a straight ahead position when towing from the rear.

JACKING AND HOISTING

Scissors jacks or hydraulic jacks are recommended for all vehicles. To change a front tire, place the jack in position from the side of the vehicle under the horizontal portion of the underbody member behind the wheel. To change a rear tire, place the jack in position from the side of the vehicle under the horizontal portion of the underbody member ahead of the wheel.

Make sure that you are on level ground, that the transmission is in Reverse or, with automatic transmissions, Park. The parking brake is set, and the tire diagonally opposite to the one to be changed is blocked so that it will not roll. Loosen the lug nuts before you jack the wheel to be changed completely free of the ground.

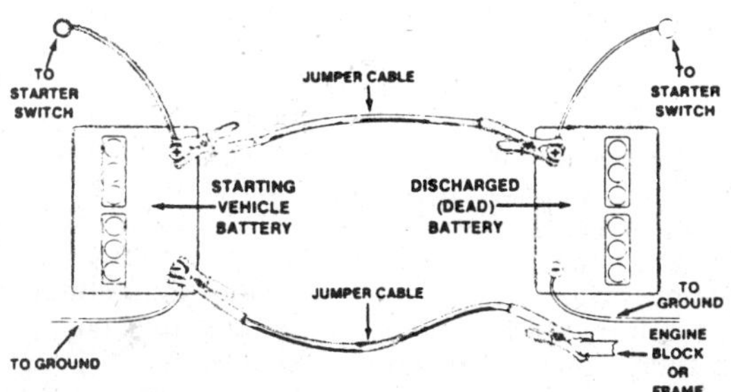

Make certain vehicles do not touch. This hook-up for negative ground cars only

CAUTION

Never crawl under any vehicle when it is supported only by a jack. The jack is meant to raise the vehicle only. If any service is to be performed under the van, use jackstands to support the weight and make sure they are secure before placing any portion of your body under the truck. Never start the engine while the van is supported only by a jack.

TRAILER TOWING

Factory trailer towing packages are available on most cars. However, if you are installing a trailer hitch and wiring on your car, there are a few thing that you ought to know.

Trailer Weight

Trailer weight is the first, and most important, factor in determining whether or not your vehicle is suitable for towing the trailer you have in mind. The horsepower-to-weight ratio should be calculated. The basic standard is a ratio of 35:1. That is, 35 pounds of GVW for every horsepower.

To calculate this ratio, multiply you engine's rated horsepower by 35, then subtract the weight of the vehicle, including passengers and luggage. The resulting figure is the ideal maximum trailer weight that you can tow. One point to consider: a numerically higher axle ratio can offset what appears to be a low trailer weight. If the weight of the trailer that you have in mind is somewhat higher than the weight you just calculated, you might consider changing your rear axle ratio to compensate.

Hitch Weight

There are three kinds of hitches: bumper mounted, frame mounted, and load equalizing.

Bumper mounted hitches are those which attach solely to the vehicle's bumper. Many states prohibit towing with this type of hitch, when it attaches to the vehicle's stock bumper, since it subjects the bumper to stresses for which it was not designed. Aftermarket rear step bumpers, designed for trailer towing, are acceptable for use with bumper mounted hitches.

Frame mounted hitches can be of the type which bolts to two or more points on the frame, plus the bumper, or just to several points on the frame.

NORMAL DRIVING SERVICE INTERVALS
Perform at the months or distances shown, whichever comes first.

Maintenance Operation / Miles (Thousands)	7.5	15	22.5	30	37.5	45	52.5	60
Kilometers (Thousands)	12	24	36	48	60	72	84	96
Check Wheel Lug Nut Torque ▲	B	B	B	B	B	B	B	B
Check Brake Master Cylinder Fluid Level				B				B
Check Clutch Reservoir Fluid Level				B				B
Inspect Automatic Transmission Shift Linkage (Shift Cable)	B	B	B	B	B	B	B	B
Inspect and Lubricate Front Wheel Bearings				B				B
Inspect Disc Brake System and Lubricate Caliper Slide Rails				B				B
Inspect Drum Brake Linings, Lines and Hoses				B				B
Inspect Exhaust System for Leaks, Damage or Loose Parts				B				B
Lubricate Driveshaft U-Joint if Equipped with Grease Fitting	B	B	B	B	B	B	B	B
Inspect Parking Brake System for Damage and Operation				B				B
Lubricate Throttle Ball Stud				B				B
Inspect and Lubricate Front Suspension Ball Joints				B				B
Inspect Suspension Bushings, Arms and Springs For Wear or Damage				B				B

NOTE:

Beyond 96 000 kilometers (60,000 miles) continue recommended maintenance operations at intervals for 0-96 000 kilometers (60,000 miles).

▲ Wheel lug nuts must be retightened to proper torque specification at 800 km (500 miles) of new vehicle operation. Refer to the appropriate portion of this section. Also retighten to proper torque specification at 800 km (500 miles) after (1) any wheel change or (2) any other time the wheel lug nuts have been loosened.

Unique Driving Conditions

The automatic transmission fluid should be changed every 48 000 km (30,000 miles) if your vehicle(s) operate under any of the following conditions:

— Sustained high-speed driving during hot weather (+90°F, +32°C).

— Towing a trailer for long distances.

— Accumulating 8000 km (5,000 miles) or more per month.

— Continuous running service.

Extreme Service Items

If the vehicle is off-highway, perform the following every 1609 km (1,000 miles). If the vehicle is operated in mud and or water, perform the following items daily

- Inspect disc brake system
- Inspect front wheel bearings and lubrication
- Inspect exhaust system for leaks, damage or loose parts

Non-emission system scheduled maintenance chart

Frame mounted hitches can also be of the tongue type, for Class I towing, or, of the receiver type, for classes II and III.

Load equalizing hitches are usually used for large trailers. Most equalizing hitches are welded in place and use equalizing bars and chains to level the vehicle after the trailer is hooked up.

The bolt-on hitches are the most common, since they are relatively easy to install.

Check the gross weight rating of your trailer. Tongue weight is usually figured as 10% of gross trailer weight. Therefore, a trailer with a maximum gross weight of 2,000 lb. will have a maximum tongue weight of 200 lb. Class I tarilers fall into this category. Class II trailers are those with a gross weight rating of 2,000-3,500 lb., while Class III trailers fall into the 3,500-6,000 lb. category. Class IV trailers are those over 6,000 lb. and are for use with fifth wheel trucks, only.

When you've determined the hitch that you'll need, follow the manufacturer's installation instructions, exactly, especially when it comes to fastener torques. The hitch will subjected to a lot of stress and good hitches come with hardened bolts. Never substitute an inferior bolt for a hardened bolt.

Wiring

Wiring the car for towing is fairly easy. There are a number of good wiring kits available and these should be used, rather than trying to design your own. All trailers will need brake lights and turn signals as well as tail lights and side marker lights. Most states require extra marker lights for overly wide trailers. Also, most states have recently required back-up lights for trailers, and most trailer manufacturers have been building trailers with back-up lights for several years.

Additionally, some Class I, most Class II and just about all Class III trailers will have electric brakes.

Add to this number an accessories wire, to operate trailer internal equipment or to charge the trailer's battery, and you can have as many as seven wires in the harness.

Determine the equipment on your trailer and buy the wiring kit necessary. The kit will contain all the wires needed, plus a plug adapter set which included the female plug, mounted on the bumper or hitch, and the male plug, wired into, or plugged into the trailer harness.

When installing the kit, follow the manufacturer's instructions. The color coding of the wires is standard throughout the industry.

One point to note, some domestic vehicles, and most imported vehicles, have separate turn signals. On most domestic vehicles, the brake lights and rear turn signals operate with the same bulb. For those vehicles with separate turn signals, you can purchase an isolation unit so that the brake lights won't blink whenever the turn signals are operated, or, you can go to your local electronics supply house and buy four diodes to wire in series with the brake and turn signal bulbs. Diodes will isolate the brake and turn signals. The choice is yours. The isolation units are simple and quick to install, but far more expensive than the diodes. The diodes, however, require more work to install properly, since they require the cutting of each bulb's wire and soldering in place of the diode.

One final point, the best kits are those with a spring loaded cover on the vehicle mounted socket. This cover prevents dirt and moisture from corroding the terminals. Never let the vehicle socket hang loosely. Always mount it securely to the bumper or hitch.

Cooling

ENGINE

One of the most common, if not THE most common, problem associated with trailer towing is engine overheating.

With factory installed trailer towing packages, a heavy duty cooling system is usually included. Heavy duty cooling systems are available as optional equipment on most cars, with or without a trailer package. If you have one of these extra-capacity systems, you shouldn't have any overheating problems.

If you have a standard cooling system, without an expansion tank, you'll definitely need to get an aftermarket expansion tank kit, preferably one with at least a 2 quart capacity. These kits are easily installed on the radiator's overflow hose, and come with a pressure cap designed for expansion tanks.

Another helpful accessory is a Flex Fan. These fan are large diameter units are designed to provide more airflow at low speeds, with blades that have deeply cupped surfaces. The blades then flex, or flatten out, at high speed, when less cooling air is needed. These fans are far lighter in weight than stock fans, requiring less horsepower to drive them. Also, they are far quieter than stock fans.

If you do decide to replace your stock fan with a flex fan, note that if your car has a fan clutch, a spacer between the flex fan and water pump hub will be needed.

Aftermarket engine oil coolers are helpful for prolonging engine oil life and reducing overall engine temperatures. Both of these factors increase engine life.

While not absolutely necessary in towing Class I and some Class II trailers, they are recommended for heavier Class II and all Class III towing.

Engine oil cooler systems consist of an adapter, screwed on in place of the oil filter, a remote filter mounting and a multi-tube, finned heat exchanger, which is mounted in front of the radiator or air conditioning condenser.

TRANSMISSION

An automatic transmission is usually recommended for trailer towing. Modern automatics have proven reliable and, of course, easy to operate, in trailer towing.

The increased load of a trailer, however, causes an increase in the temperature of the automatic transmission fluid. Heat is the worst enemy of an automatic transmission. As the temperature of the fluid increases, the life of the fluid decreases.

It is essential, therefore, that you install an automatic transmission cooler.

The cooler, which consists of a multi-tube, finned heat exchanger, is usually installed in front of the radiator or air conditioning compressor, and hooked inline with the transmission cooler tank inlet line. Follow the cooler manufacturer's installation instructions.

Select a cooler of at least adequate capacity, based upon the combined gross weights of the car and trailer.

Cooler manufacturers recommend that you use an aftermarket cooler in addition to, and not instead of, the present cooling tank in your car radiator. If you do want to use it in place of the radiator cooling tank, get a cooler at least two sizes larger than normally necessary.

NOTE: A transmission cooler can, sometimes, cause slow or harsh shifting in the transmission during cold weather, until the fluid has a chance to come up to normal operating temperature. Some coolers can be purchased with or retrofitted with a temperature bypass valve which will allow fluid flow through the cooler only when the fluid has reached operating temperature, or above.

TUNE-UP PROCEDURES

The engine tune-up is a routine service designed to restore the maximum capability of power, performance, reliability and economy to the engine. It is essential for efficient and economical operation and becomes increasingly more important each year to insure that pollutant levels are in compliance with federal emission standards.

The interval between tune-ups is a variable factor which depends on the year and engine in your van and the way it is driven in average use. The extent of the tune-up is usually determined by the length of time since the previous service. It is advisable to follow a definite and thorough tune-up procedure consisting of three steps: Analysis, the process of determining whether normal wear is responsible for performance loss and the inspection of various parts such as spark plugs; Parts Replacement or Service; and Adjustment, where engine adjustments are returned to the original factory specifications.

The replaceable parts normally involved in a major tune-up include the spark plugs, air filter, fuel filter, distributor cap, rotor and spark plug wires. In addition to these parts and the adjustments involved in properly adapting them to your engine, the normal tune-up should include a check of the ignition timing and idle speed, although with modern electronic engine controls, these items are usually not adjustable. Refer to the underhood emission control sticker for specific instructions on checking the timing, as well as specifications for spark plug gap and idle speed. In addition to the above, the valve adjustment should be checked with the engine cold. The 2.3L 4-cylinder and the 3.0L V6 engines have hydraulic lash adjusters that do not require periodic service, however, the 2.8L V6 valves are adjustable and clearances should be checked and adjusted, if necessary, at every tune-up.

CAUTION

When working on or around a running engine, make sure there is adequate ventilation. Make sure the transmission is in Neutral or Park with the parking brake firmly applied and always keep hands, clothing and tools well clear of the hot exhaust manifold(s) and radiator. Remove any jewelry, do not wear loose clothing and tuck long hair up under a cap. Use EXTREME caution when working around spinning fan blades or belts. When the engine is running, do not grasp the ignition wires, distributor cap or coil wire, as the high energy ignition system can deliver a potentially fatal shock of 20,000 volts. Whenever working around the distributor, even if the engine is not running, make sure the ignition is switched OFF.

This section gives specific procedures on how to tune-up your van and is intended to be as complete and basic as possible. It is advisable to read the entire section before beginning a tune-up.

Spark Plugs

The function of a spark plug is to ignite the air/fuel mixture in the cylinder as the piston reaches the top of its compression stroke. The expansion of the ignited mixture forces the piston down, which turns the crankshaft and supplies power to the drivetrain.

A typical spark plug consists of a metal shell surrounded by a ceramic insulator. A metal electrode extends downward through the center of the insulator and protrudes a small distance. Located at the end of the plug and attached to the side of the outer metal shell is the side electrode. The side electrode bends in at a 90° angle so that its tip is even with, and parallel to, the tip of the center electrode. The distance between these two electrodes (measured in thousandths of an inch) is called the spark plug gap.

The spark plug in no way produces a spark, but merely provides a gap across which the current from the ignition coil can arc. The ignition coil produces from 20,000 to 40,000 volts which travels to the distributor where it is distributed through the spark plug wires to the spark plugs. This current passes along the center electrode and jumps the gap to the side electrode and, in doing so, ignites the air/fuel mixture.

The average life of a spark plug is about 25,000 miles, depending on the type of driving and vehicle use. If the van is driven at high speeds more often, the plugs will probably not need as much attention as those used for constant stop-and-go driving. The electrode end of the spark plug is a good indicator of the internal condition of your engine. If a spark plug is fouled and causing the engine to misfire, the problem will have to be found and corrected. It is a good idea to remove the plugs once in a while to check their condition and see just how the engine is performing. A small amount of light tan colored deposits on the electrode end of the spark plug is normal and the plugs do not require replacement unless extremely worn.

SPARK PLUG HEAT RANGE

Spark plug heat range is the ability of the plug to dissipate heat. The longer the insulator (or the farther it extends into the engine), the hotter the plug will operate. Conversely, the shorter the insulator, the cooler the plug will operate. A plug that absorbs little heat and remains too cool will quickly accumulate deposits of oil and carbon since it is not hot enough to burn them off. This can lead to plug fouling and misfiring. A plug that absorbs too much heat will have no deposits but, due to the excess heat, the electrodes will burn away quickly and in some instances preignition may result. Preignition takes place when the plug tips get so hot that they glow sufficiently to ignite the fuel/air mixture before the actual spark occurs. This condition is usually described as a spark knock or "ping" during low speeds and under heavy load.

The general rule of thumb for choosing the correct heat range when picking a spark plug is to use a colder plug for long distance, high speed operation and a hotter plug for stop-and-go, heavy traffic operation. Original equipment plugs are usually a compromise, but most owners never have occasion to change from the factory recommended heat range.

REPLACING SPARK PLUGS

A set of spark plugs usually requires replacement after about 20,000 to 30,000 miles on engines with electronic ignition, depending on your style of driving. In normal operation, the spark plug gap will increase about 0.001" for every 1,000-2,500 miles. As the gap increases, the plug's voltage requirement also increases. It requires a greater voltage to jump the wider gap and about two to three times as much voltage to fire a plug at high speeds than at idle.

When removing the spark plugs, you should work on one at a time. Don't start by removing all the plug wires at once or they may become mixed up. Take a minute and number all the plug wires with tape before removing

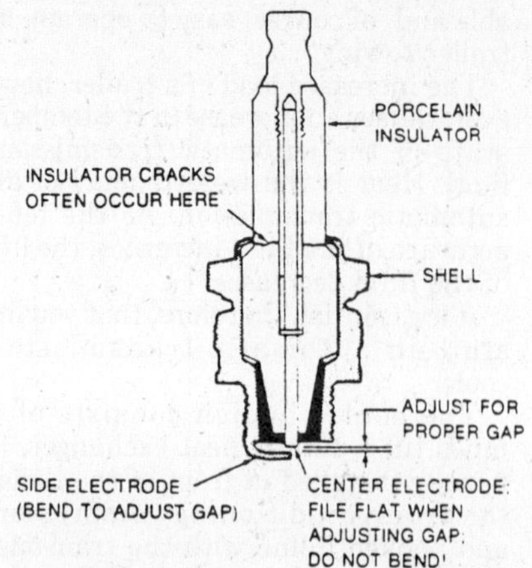

Cross section of a spark plug

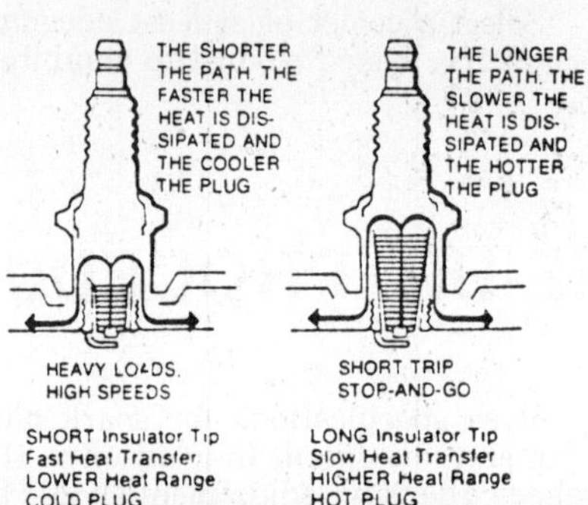

Spark plug heat range

them from the plugs. The best location for numbering is near where the plug wires come out of the cap.

1. Twist the spark plug boot and remove the boot and wire from the plug. Do not pull on the wire itself or you will ruin it.
2. If possible, use a brush or rag to clean the area around the spark plug. Make sure that all the dirt is removed so that none will enter the cylinder after the plug is removed.
3. Remove the spark plug from the cylinder head using the proper size socket (5/8" for AWSF and ASF plugs) and ratchet. A universal joint and short extension may make this job easier. Turn the socket counterclockwise to remove the plug, but make sure the socket is firmly seated and straight on the plug or you will crack the insulator or round off the hex.
4. Once the plug is removed, check its condition against the plugs shown in the color insert to determine engine condition. This is crucial since plugs readings are vital signs of engine operating condition.
5. Use a round wire feeler gauge to check the plug gap. The correct size gauge should pass through the electrode gap with a slight drag. If in doubt, try one size smaller and one size larger. The smaller should pass through easily, while the larger shouldn't go through at all. If the gap is incorrect, use the electrode bending tool on the end of the gauge to adjust the gap. When adjusting the gap, always bend the side electrode; the center electrode is non-adjustable.
6. Squirt a drop of penetrating oil on the threads of the spark plug and install it. Don't oil the plug too heavily. Turn the plug in clockwise by hand

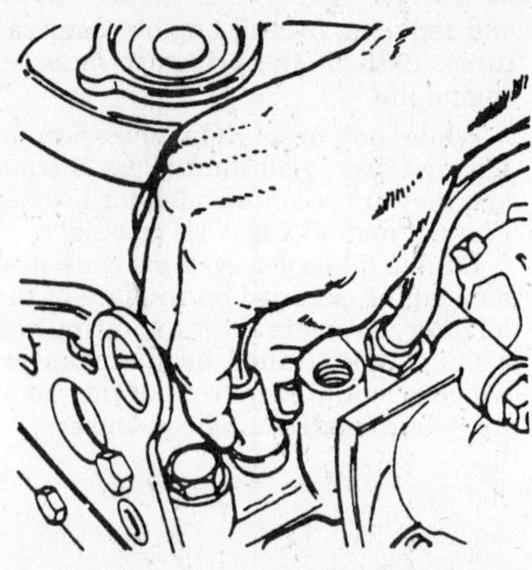

Twist and pull on the rubber boot to remove the spark plug wires; never pull on the wire itself

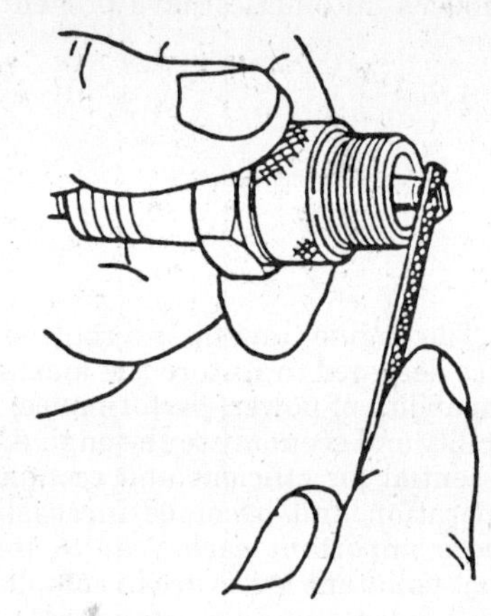

Plugs that are in good condition can be filed and reused

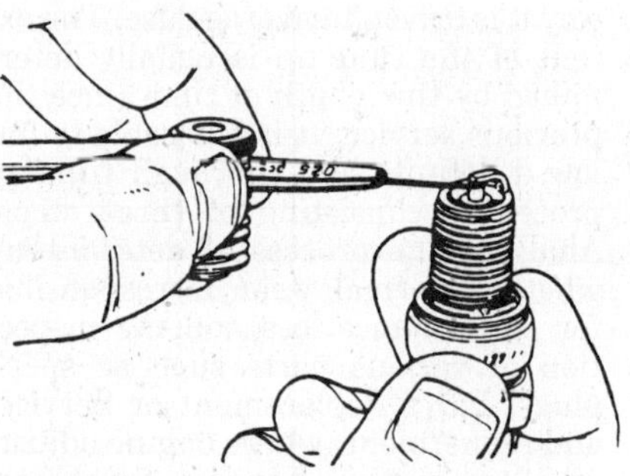

Checking the spark plug gap with a gap gauge

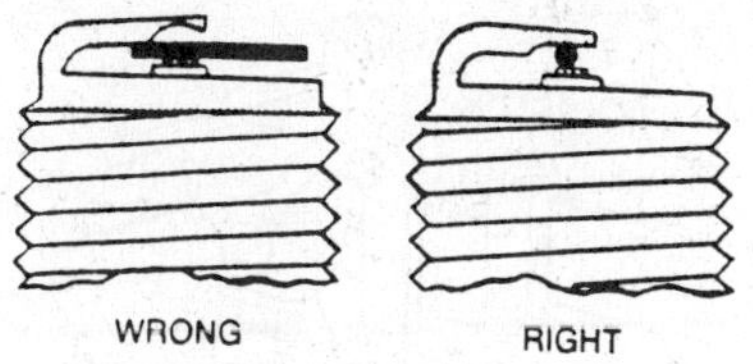

Gapping spark plugs

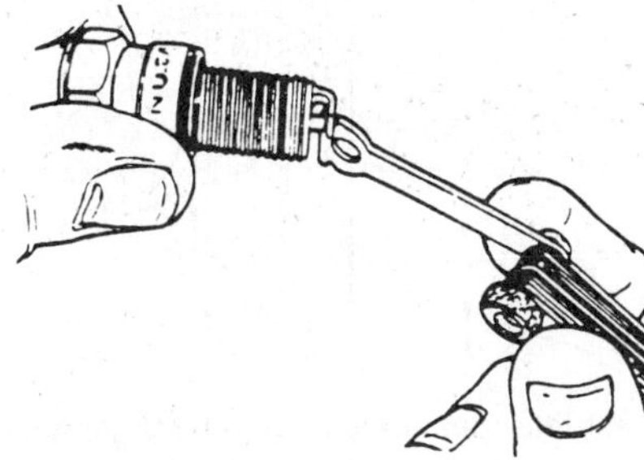

Adjusting the spark plug gap with a gapping tool

until it is snug. Be careful not to cross-thread the plug when installing.

7. When the plug is finger tight, tighten it with a torque wrench to 10-15 ft.lb.

8. Install the spark plug boot firmly over the plug and proceed to the next one.

NOTE: Coat the inside of each spark plug boot with silicone grease (Motorcraft WA-10-D7AZ-19A331A, Dow Corning No. 111 or General Electric G627 are acceptable). Failure to do so could result in a misfired plug.

CHECKING AND REPLACING SPARK PLUG WIRES

Visually inspect the spark plug wires for burns, cuts or breaks in the insulation. Check the spark plug boots and the nipples on the distributor cap and coil. Replace any damaged wiring. If no physical damage is obvious, remove the distributor cap with the wires attached and use an ohmmeter to check the resistance. Normal resistance should be less than 7,000Ω per foot of wire length. If resistance exceeds 7,000Ω per foot, replace the wire.

CAUTION

Do not, under any circumstances, puncture a spark plug wire with a sharp probe when checking resistance. Check the resistance only as illustrated.

When installing a new set of spark plug wires, replace them one at a time so there is no mixup. Start by replacing the longest wire first and make sure the boot is installed firmly over the spark plug and distributor cap tower. Route the wire exactly the same way as the original and make sure the wire loom clips are fastened securely when done.

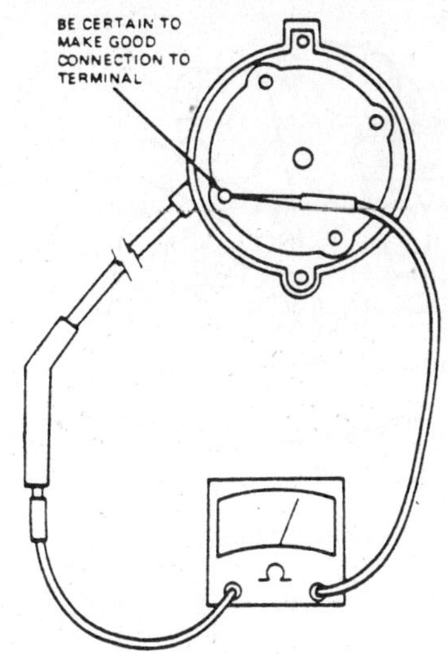

Testing spark plug wire resistance with an ohmmeter

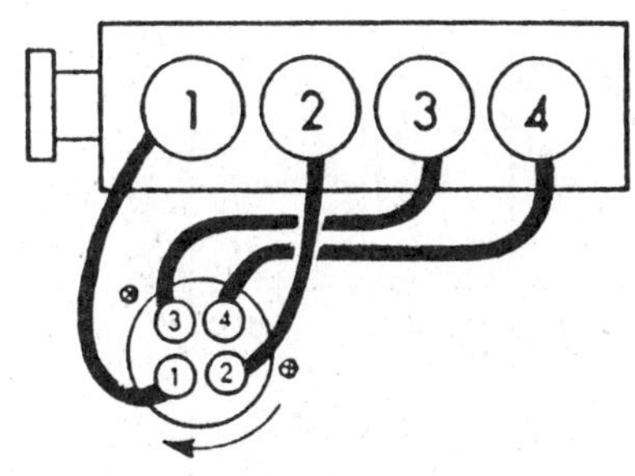

2.3L (140 CID) 4 cylinder engine
Firing order: 1-3-4-2
Distributor rotation: clockwise

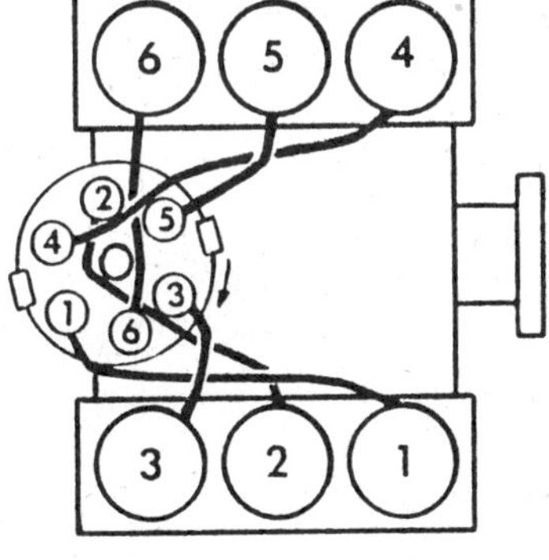

2.8L (171 CID) V6 engine
Firing order: 1-4-2-5-3-6
Distributor rotation: clockwise

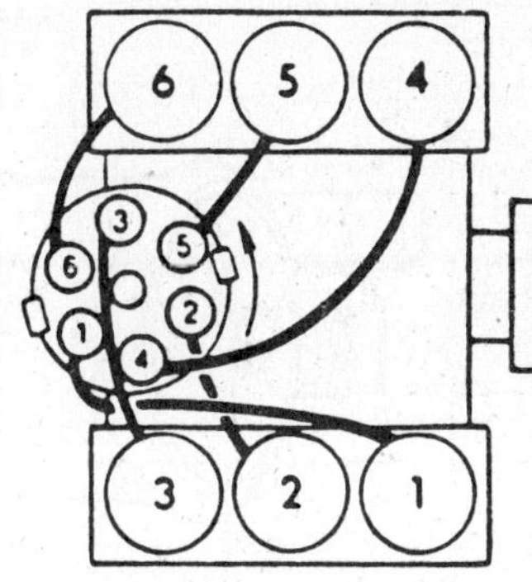

3.0L (18 CID) V6 engine
Firing order: 1-4-2-5-3-6
Distributor rotation: counterclockwise

Idle Speed

ADJUSTMENT

2.3L Engine

NOTE: This procedure us to be performed only if the curb idle is not within the 700 drive (AT), 650 (MT) ± 75 rpm specification. Curb idle speed is controlled by the EEC-IV processor and the idle speed control air bypass valve assembly.

1. Place the transmission in Neutral and make sure the A/C-Heat selector is off.
2. Start the engine and allow it to reach normal operating temperature, then turn the ignition off.
3. Disconnect the idle speed control air bypass valve power lead.
4. Start the engine and operate it at 1,500 rpm for 20 seconds.
5. Allow the engine to idle and check that the base idle speed is 550-600 rpm. The engine may stall when the ISC is disconnected. This is acceptable as long as the throttle plate is not stuck in the bore.
6. If the idle speed requires adjustment, disconnect the throttle cable and adjust the engine rpm by turning the throttle plate stop screw. Reconnect the throttle cable and recheck the idle speed.
7. Once the idle speed is set, turn the engine off and reconnect the power lead to the idle speed control air bypass valve.
8. Verify that the throttle plate is not stuck in the bore by moving the throttle plate linkage.

2.8L Engine

1. Place the transmission in Park (automatic) or Neutral (manual), then start the engine and allow it to reach normal operating temperature. Turn the engine off, block the drive wheels

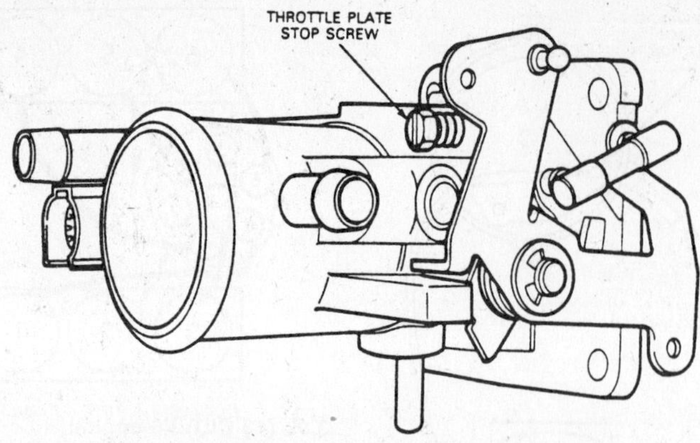

Adjusting the idle speed on the 2.3L engine

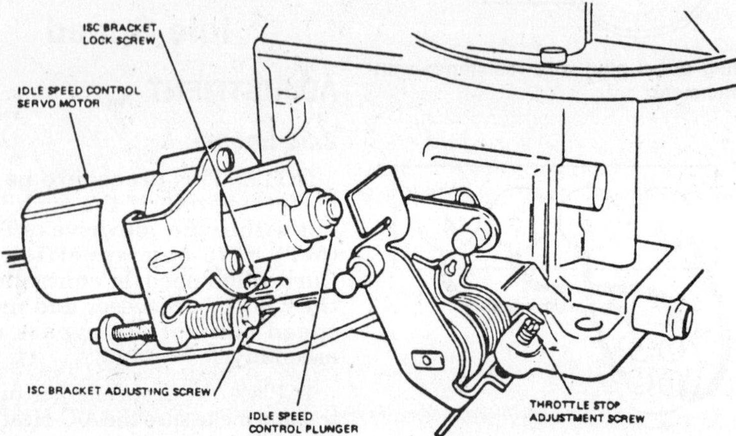

Idle speed control adjustment on 2.8L engine

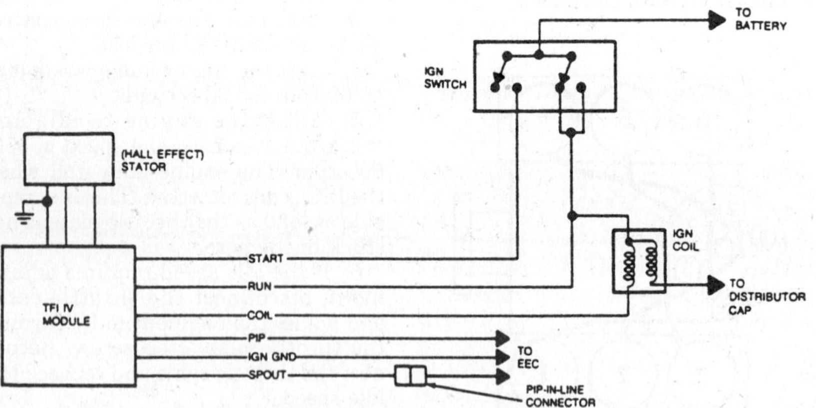

TFI-IV system electrical schematic typical of all vehicles

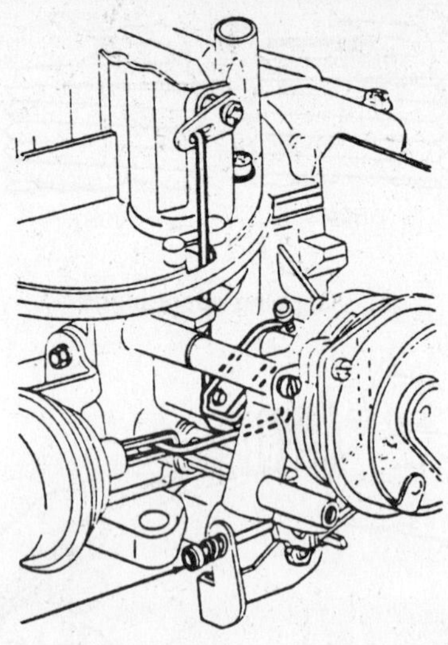

Fast idle rpm adjustment on 2.8L engine

and set the parking brake firmly. Turn all accessories off.

2. Remove the air charge temperature (ACT) sensor and adapter from the air cleaner tray by disengaging the retainer clip; leave the wiring harness connected. Remove the air cleaner, disconnect and plug the vacuum line at the cold weather duct and valve motor.

3. Start the engine, then turn it off and verify that the idle speed control (ISC) plunger moves out to its maximum extension within 10 seconds of key off.

4. Disconnect the idle speed control. Disconnect and plug the EGR vacuum hose.

5. Start the engine and manually open the throttle, then set the fast idle adjusting screw on the high step of the fast idle cam.

6. Adjust the fast idle speed to specifications listed on the underhood sticker.

7. Open the throttle manually to release the fast idle cam, allowing the throttle lever to rest on the ISC plunger.

8. Loosen the ISC bracket lock screw. Adjust the ISC bracket screw to 2,000 rpm, then retighten the bracket lock screw.

9. Reconnect the ISC connector. The engine rpm should automatically be adjusted to curb idle.

10. Simultaneously:

a. Manually hold the throttle above 1,000 rpm

b. Push the ISC plunger until it retracts fully

c. After the plunger retracts, release the throttle and quickly unplug the connection.

11. Adjust the anti-dieseling speed throttle stop screw to 750 rpm. The anti-dieseling speed is NOT the curb idle speed.

12. Reconnect the ISC and EGR vacuum hose.

13. Stop the engine, then restart it to verify that curb idle speed is within specifications.

3.0L Engine

Curb idle speed is controlled by the EEC-IV processor and the idle speed control air bypass valve assembly. The throttle plate stop screw is factory set and does not directly control idle speed. Adjustments to this setting should be performed only as part of a full EEC-IV diagnosis of irregular idle conditions or idle speed. Failure to accurately set the throttle plate stop position to the procedure below could result in erroneous idle speed control.

1. Place the transmission in Neu-

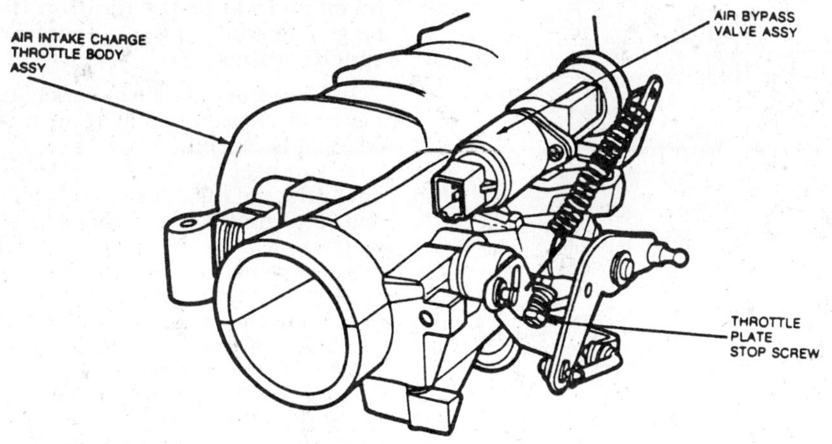

Idle speed adjustment on 3.0L engine

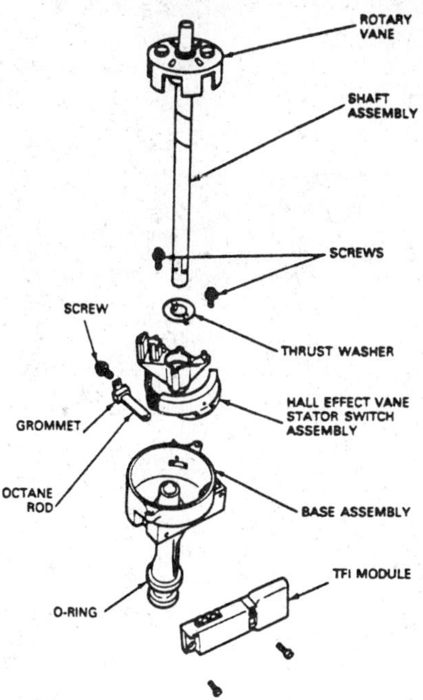

Exploded view of Hall Effect distributor

tral (MT) or Park (AT), turn the A/C-Heat selector off, apply the parking brake firmly and block the drive wheels.

2. Bring the engine to normal operating temperature and check for vacuum leaks downstream of the throttle plates.

3. Unplug the single wire, inline spout connector near the distributor and verify ignition timing is 8-12° BTDC. If not, reset the ignition timing as described above.

4. Turn off the engine and disconnect the air bypass valve assembly connector.

5. Remove the PCV entry line at the PCV valve.

6. Install Orifice Tool T86P-9600-A (0.200" orifice diameter) in the PCV entry line.

7. Start the engine. The vehicle should be idling in Drive with automatic transmission or in Neutral with manual transmission. Make sure the drive wheels are blocked and the parking brake is firmly set.

NOTE: If the electric cooling fan comes on during idle set, unplug the fan motor power leads or wait until the fan switches off.

8. Check the idle speed. It should be 820-870 rpm on models with an automatic transmission or 1,015-1,065 rpm on models with manual transmission. If the idle speed is not as stated, adjust by turning the throttle plate stop screw.

9. Turn off the engine after the idle speed is set.

10. Restart the engine and confirm the idle speed is within specifications after 3 to 5 minutes. If not, repeat setting procedure.

11. If the idle speed is correct, turn off the engine, remove the orifice and reconnect the PCV entry line.

12. Reconnect the distributor spout line, the ISC motor and the cooling fan power supply, if disconnected. Verify that the throttle plate is not stuck in the bore.

ELECTRONIC IGNITION

All engines used in the Aerostar have a universal distributor design which is gear driven and has a die cast metal base that incorporates an integrally mounted TFI-IV ignition module.

The distributor uses a "Hall Effect" stator assembly and eliminates the conventional centrifugal and vacuum advance mechanisms. No distributor calibration is required and it is not normally necessary to adjust initial timing. The cap, adapter and rotor are designed for use with the universal distributor and the ignition module is a Thick Film Integrated (TFI) design. The module is contained in molded thermoplastic and is mounted on the distributor base. The distributor assembly can be identified by the part number information printed on a decal attached to the side of the distributor base.

The operation of the universal distributor is accomplished through the Hall Effect vane switch assembly, causing the ignition coil to be switched on and off by the EEC-IV and TFI-IV modules. The vane switch is an encapsulated package consisting of a Hall sensor on one side and a permanent magnet on the other side. A rotary vane cup, made of ferrous (magnetic) metal is used to trigger the Hall Effect switch.

When the window of the vane cup is between the magnet and Hall Effect device, a magnetic flux field is completed from the magnet through the Hall Effect device and back to the magnet. As the vane passes through this opening, the flux lines are shunted through the vane and back to the magnet. As the vane passes through this opening, the flux lines are shunted through the vane and back to the magnet. A voltage is produced while the vane passes through the opening. When the vane clears the opening, the window causes the signal to go to zero volts. The signal is then used by the EEC-IV system for crankshaft position sensing and the computation of the desired spark advance based on engine demand and calibration. The conditioned spark advance and voltage distribution is accomplished through a conventional rotor, cap and ignition wires.

NOTE: The ignition timing is preset at the factory and computer controlled. No attempt should be made to alter the ignition timing from the factory specifications.

Initial Timing

ADJUSTMENT

NOTE: The ignition timing is preset at the factory and computer controlled. No attempt should

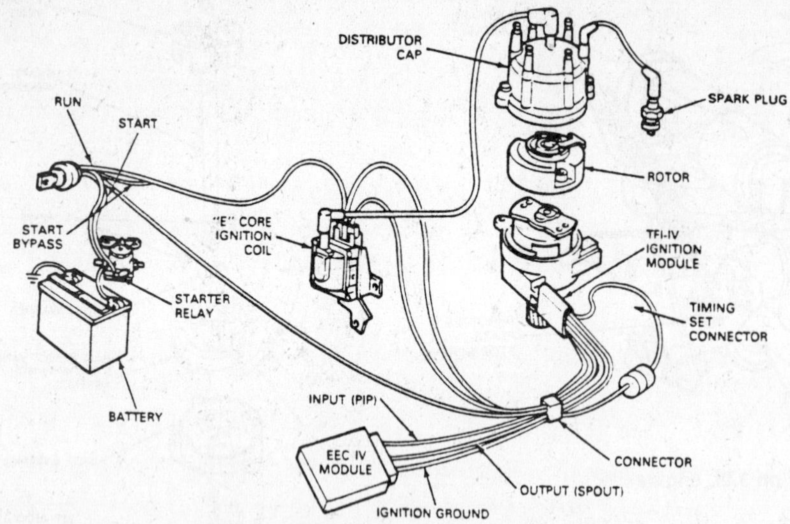

Typical Aerostar electronic ignition system

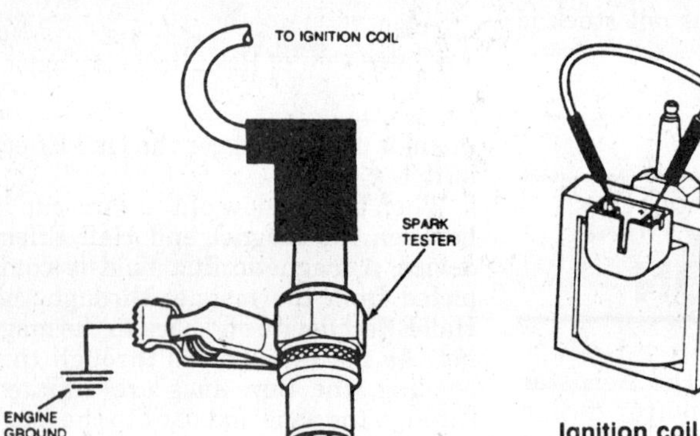

Checking ignition coil secondary voltage with spark tester

Ignition coil primary resistance test

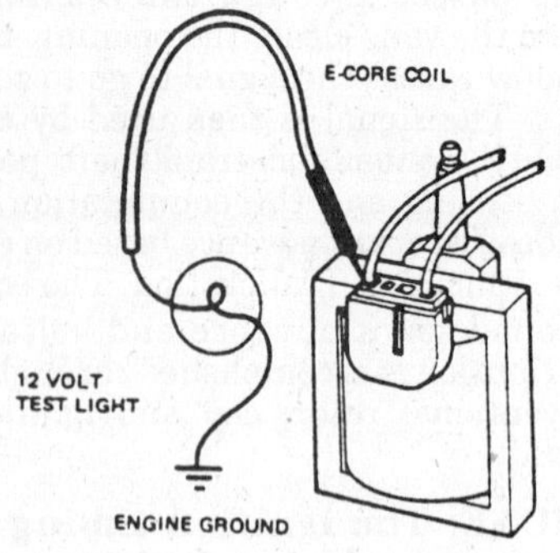

Ignition coil primary circuit switching test

Ignition coil secondary resistance test

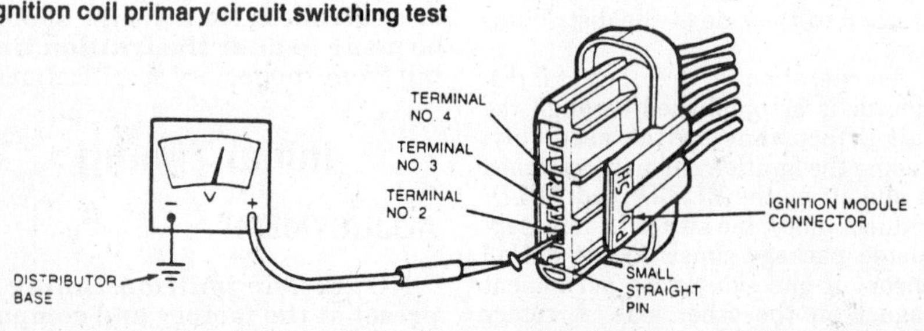

Wiring harness connectors test

be made to alter the ignition timing from the factory specifications.

1. Place transmission in Park (automatic) or Neutral (manual), with the A/C and heater off.
2. Connect an inductive timing light (Rotunda 059-00006 or equivalent) according to the manufacturer's instructions.
3. Disconnect the single wire inline spout connector near the distributor.
4. Start the engine and allow it to reach normal operating temperature.
5. With the engine at the timing rpm specified, check and/or adjust the initial timing to the specification listed on the underhood emission control label by loosening the distributor holddown bolt and rotating the distributor slightly. A Torx® bit may be necessary to loosen the security type distributor holddown, if equipped.
6. Reconnect the single wire inline spout connector and check the timing advance to verify the distributor is advancing beyond the initial setting.
7. Once the timing is set, shut off the engine and disconnect the timing light.

Electronic Ignition Troubleshooting

Before beginning any organized test procedures on the electronic ignition system, first perform these simple checks:

1. Visually inspect the engine compartment to make sure all vacuum hoses and spark plug wires are properly routed and securely connected.
2. Examine all wiring harnesses and connectors for insulation damage, burned, overheated, loose or broken connections.
3. Check that the TFI module is securely fastened to the distributor base.
4. Make sure the battery is fully charged.
5. Make sure all accessories are off during diagnosis.

The following test equipment, or equivalents, are necessary to diagnose the ignition system:

1. Spark Tester D81P-6666-A, which resembles a spark plug with the side electrode removed. A spark plug with the side electrode removed IS NOT sufficient to check for spark and may lead to incorrect results.
2. Digital Volt/Ohmmeter (Rotunda 014-00407).
3. 12 volt test light.
4. Small straight pin.

When instructed to inspect a wiring harness, both a visual inspection and a continuity test should be performed. When making measurements on a wir-

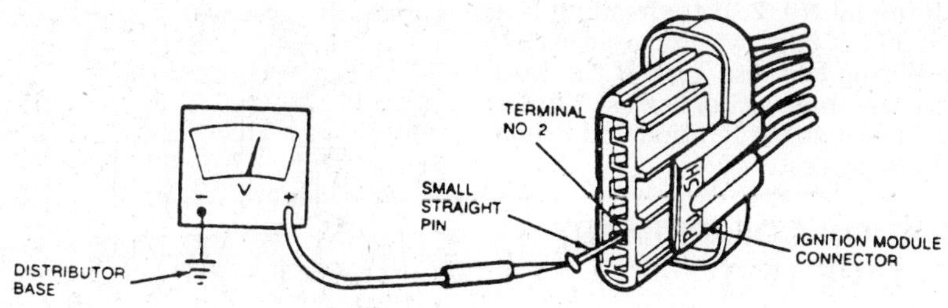

Primary circuit continuity test

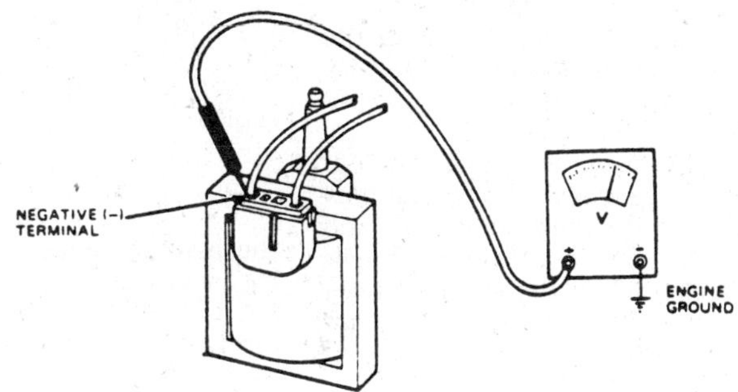

Ignition coil primary voltage test

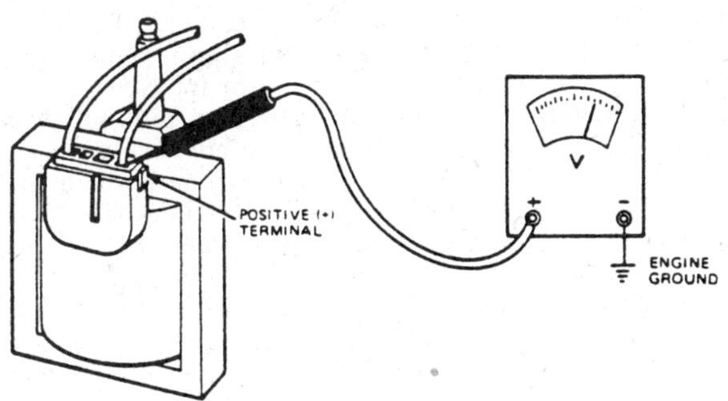

Ignition coil supply voltage test

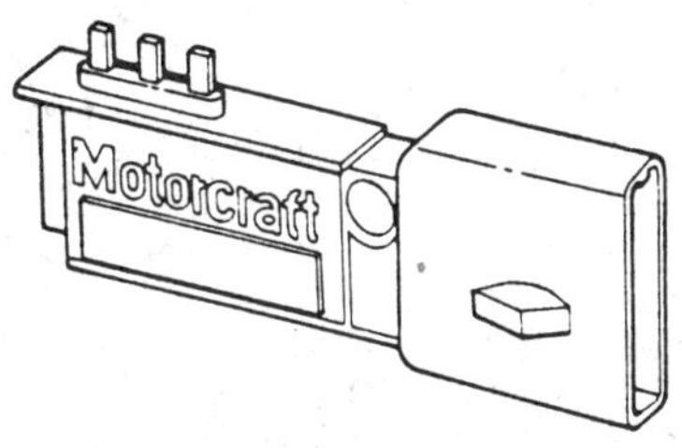

Typical TFI ignition module

ing harness or connector, it is good practice to wiggle the wires while measuring. The following tests are designed to be performed in order to gradually narrow down the cause of a problem in the ignition system.

IGNITION COIL SECONDARY VOLTAGE TEST

Connect the spark tester (D81P-6666-A or equivalent) between the ignition coil wire and engine ground, then crank the engine. If spark is present, the secondary voltage is OK. If there is no spark, measure the resistance of the ignition coil wire and replace the wire if the resistance is greater than 7,000Ω per foot. Inspect the ignition coil for damage or carbon tracking and crank the engine with the distributor cap removed to verify distributor rotation.

IGNITION COIL PRIMARY CIRCUIT SWITCHING TEST

Push the connector tabs to separate the wiring harness connector from the ignition module and check for dirt, corrosion or damage, then reconnect the harness. Attach a 12 volt test light between the coil tach terminal and the engine ground, then crank the engine. If the light is on steadily or flashes, continue on to the Ignition Coil Primary Resistance Test. If the light is off or on very dimly, go to the Primary Circuit Continuity Test.

IGNITION COIL PRIMARY RESISTANCE TEST

Turn the ignition switch off, then disconnect the ignition coil connector. Check for dirt, corrosion or damage. Use an ohmmeter to measure the resistance from the positive (+) to negative (-) terminals of the ignition coil. If the reading is between 0.3-1.0Ω the ignition coil is OK; continue on to the Ignition Coil Secondary Resistance Test. If the reading is less than 0.3Ω or greater than 1.0Ω, replace the ignition coil.

IGNITION COIL SECONDARY RESISTANCE TEST

Use an ohmmeter to measure the resistance between the negative (-) terminal to the high voltage terminal of the ignition coil. If the reading is between 6,500-11,500Ω, the ignition coil is OK; go on to the Wiring Harness Test. If the reading is less than 6,500Ω or more than 11,500Ω, replace the ignition coil.

WIRING HARNESS TEST

1. Separate the wiring harness connector from the ignition module and check for dirt, corrosion and damage. Push the connector tabs to separate the connector.
2. Disconnect the wire at the **S** terminal of the starter relay.
3. Attach the negative (-) lead from a volt/ohmmeter to the distributor base.
4. Measure battery voltage.
5. Following the table below, measure the connector terminal voltage by attaching the positive volt/ohmmeter lead to a small straight pin inserted into the connector terminal and turning the ignition switch to the position shown.

CAUTION

Do not allow the straight pin to touch any electrical ground

6. If, in all cases, the reading is at least 90% of battery voltage, the harness is OK; continue on to the Stator Test. If any reading is less than 90% of battery voltage, check for faults in the wiring harness and connectors or for a damaged or worn ignition switch.
7. After all tests are complete, turn the ignition switch off. Remove the straight pin and reconnect the wire to the **S** terminal of the starter relay.

STATOR TEST

1. Turn the ignition switch off.

2. Remove the coil wire and ground it.

3. Attach the negative (-) lead from a volt/ohmmeter to the distributor base.

4. Disconnect the pin-in-line connector near the distributor and attach the positive (+) volt/ohmmeter lead to the TFI module side of the connector.

5. Turn the ignition switch on.

6. Bump the starter and measure the voltage levels with the engine not moving. Allow sufficient time for the digital voltage reading to stabilize before taking the measurement. Record all values for possible use in additional tests.

7. If the highest reading is greater than 90 percent of battery voltage, go to Step 8. If the highest value is less than 90 percent of battery voltage, replace the stator assembly.

8. If the lowest value is greater than 0.5 volts, remove the distributor from the engine. Remove the TFI module from the distributor and check the stator connector terminals and TFI terminals for misalignment; service as necessary. If OK, replace the stator assembly. If the lowest value is less than 0.5 volts, go to Step 9.

9. If all values are between 0.5 volts and 90% of battery voltage, replace the stator assembly. If no values are between 0.5 volts and 90% of battery voltage, go on to the EEC-IV/TFI-IV Test.

EEC-IV/TFI-IV TEST

Connect a spark tester between the ignition coil wire and engine ground. Crank the engine and check for spark. If no spark is present, replace the TFI-IV module. If spark is present, check the PIP (Profile Ignition Pickup) and ground wires for continuity and repair as necessary. If OK, the EEC-IV system will have to be diagnosed. See FUEL SYSTEM for details.

PRIMARY CIRCUIT CONTINUITY TEST

1. Push the connector tabs and separate the wiring harness connector from the ignition module. Check for dirt, corrosion and damage and repair as necessary.

2. Attach the negative (-) lead from a volt/ohmmeter to the distributor base.

3. Measure battery voltage.

4. Attach the positive (+) lead of the volt/ohmmeter to a small straight pin inserted into connector terminal No. 2. Be careful not to let the pin touch any electrical ground.

5. Turn the ignition switch to the RUN position and measure the voltage at terminal No. 2. If the reading is at least 90% of battery voltage, go back to the Wiring Harness Test. If the reading is less than 90% of battery voltage, continue on to the Ignition Coil Primary Voltage Test.

IGNITION COIL PRIMARY VOLTAGE TEST

1. Attach the negative (-) lead of the volt/ohmmeter to the distributor base.

2. Measure the battery voltage.

3. Turn the ignition switch to the RUN position and measure the voltage at the negative (-) terminal of the ignition coil.

4. If the reading is at least 90% of battery voltage, check the wiring harness between the ignition module and coil negative terminal. If the reading is less than 90% of battery voltage, check the wiring harness between the ignition module and coil negative terminal, then go on to the next test.

IGNITION COIL SUPPLY VOLTAGE TEST

1. Remove the coil connector.

2. Attach the negative (-) lead from a volt/ohmmeter to the distributor base.

3. Measure the battery voltage.

4. Turn the ignition switch to the RUN position.

5. Measure the voltage at the positive (+) terminal of the ignition coil. If the reading is at least 90% of battery voltage, check the ignition coil connector for dirt, corrosion and damage. Check the ignition coil terminals for dirt, corrosion and damage; if no problem is found, replace the ignition coil. If the reading is less than 90% of battery voltage, check the wiring between the ignition coil and ignition switch, or for a worn or damaged ignition switch.

VALVE ADJUSTMENT

2.8L V6 Engine

This procedure applies to the 2.8L V6 engine only. The engine should be cold for valve adjustment.

1. Remove the air cleaner assembly, then remove the rocker arm covers. This may involve removing some thermactor components to gain working clearance.

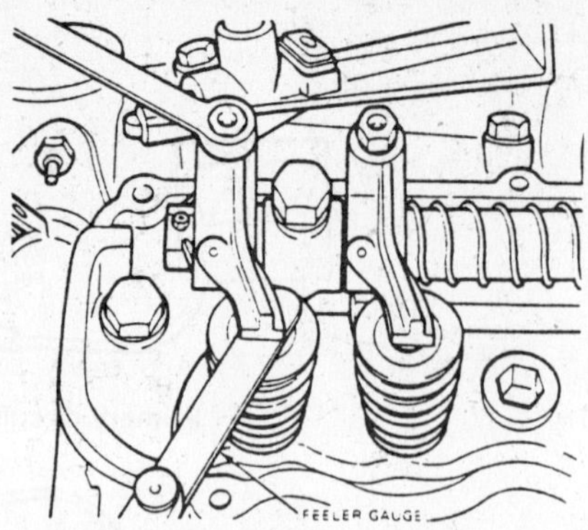

Adjusting the valve lash on the 2.8L V6 engine

2. Place a finger on the adjusting screw of the intake valve rocker arm for cylinder No. 5 to detect the slightest motion.

3. Using a remote starter button, or an assistant turning the ignition key on and off, "bump" the engine over in small increments until the intake valve for No. 5 cylinder just begining to open. This will place the camshaft in the correct position to adjust the valves on No. 1 cylinder.

4. Adjust the No. 1 intake valve so that a 0.014" (0.35mm) feeler gauge has a light to moderate drag and a 0.015" (0.36mm) feeler gauge is very tight. Turn the adjusting screw clockwise to decrease lash and counterclockwise to increase lash. The adjusting screws are self-locking and will stay in a set position.

NOTE: Do not use a step-type go/no-go feeler gauge. Use a blade-type set. When checking lash, insert the feeler between the rocker arm and valve tip at the front (or rear) edge of the valve tip and move toward the opposite edge with a rearward (or forward) motion that is parallel to the centerline of the crankshaft. Do not insert the feeler at the outboard edge and move inward toward the carburetor perpendicular to the crankshaft centerline or this will result in an erroneous "feel" that will lead to excessively tight valves.

5. Using the same method, adjust the No. 1 exhaust valve lash so that a 0.016" (0.40mm) feeler gauge has a slight to moderate drag and a 0.017" (0.41mm) is very tight.

6. Adjust the remaining valves in firing order 1-4-2-5-3-6 by positioning

To adjust both valves for cylinder number	1	4	2	5	3	6
The intake valve must be opening for cylinder number	5	3	6	1	4	2

Valve adjustment chart for the 2.8L V6 engine

the camshaft according to the following chart:

7. Clean the rocker arm gasket mounting surfaces. Using new gaskets or a suitable RTV sealant, install the rocker arm covers. Install any thermactor components that were removed.

8. Reinstall the air cleaner assembly. Start the engine and check for oil and vacuum leaks.

ENGINE ELECTRICAL

Distributor

REMOVAL & INSTALLATION

NOTE: Except for the cap, adapter, rotor, Hall Effect stator, TFI module and O-ring, no other distributor assembly parts are replaceable. There is no calibration required with the universal distributor. The distributor assembly can be identified by the part number information printed on a decal attached to the side of the distributor base.

1. Set the No. 1 cylinder at TDC on the compression stroke with the timing marks aligned. Disconnect the primary wiring connector from the distributor.
2. Mark the position of the No. 1 spark plug wire tower on the distributor base for future reference before removing the distributor cap.
3. Use a screwdriver to remove the distributor cap and adapter and position it and the attached ignition wires out of the way.
4. Remove the rotor.
5. Remove the TFI connector.
6. Remove the distributor holddown bolt and clamp. Some engines may be equipped with a security type holddown bolt, requiring a Torx® bit of the proper size to remove it.
7. Remove the distributor by lifting it straight up.
8. If the engine was rotated while the distributor was removed, again set the No. 1 cylinder at TDC on the compression stroke with the timing marks aligned for correct initial timing.
9. Rotate the distributor shaft so that the rotor tip is pointing toward the mark previously made on the distributor base (No. 1 spark plug tower). Continue rotating slightly so that the leading edge of the vane is centered in the vane switch stator assembly.
10. Rotate the distributor in the engine block to align the leading edge of the vane and the vane switch and verify that the rotor is pointing at No. 1 cap terminal.

NOTE: If the vane and vane switch stator cannot be aligned by rotating the distributor in the engine block, pull the distributor out of the block enough to disengage the distributor and rotate the distributor to engage a different distributor gear tooth. Repeat Steps 9 and 10 if necessary.

11. Install the distributor holddown bolt and clamp, but do not tighten yet.

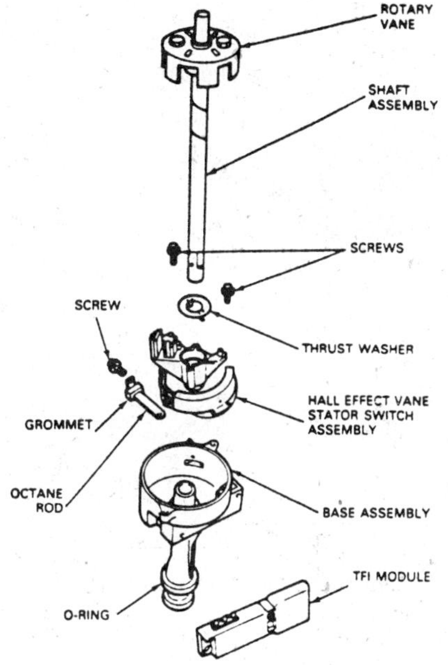

Exploded view of universal distributor assembly

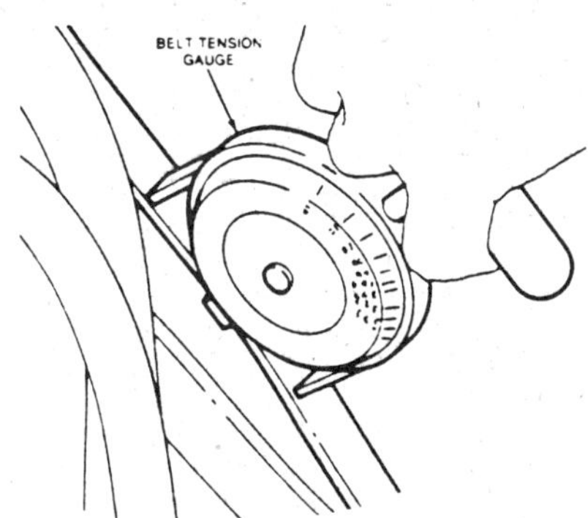

Checking alternator belt tension

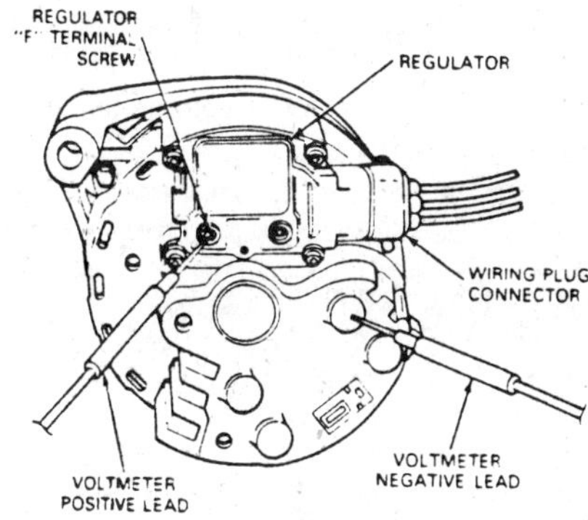

Field circuit drain test alternator connections

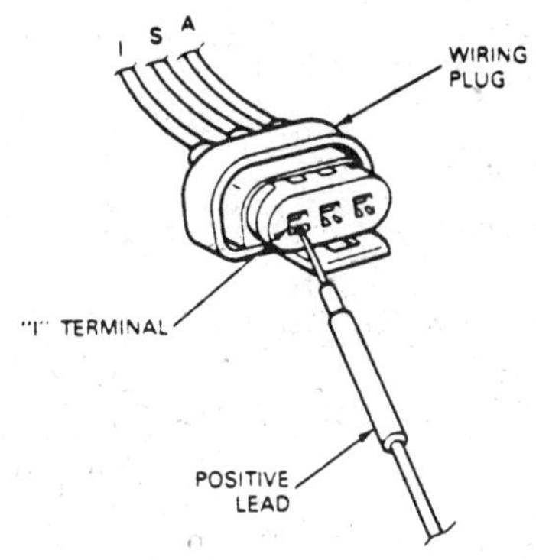

Field circuit drain test regulator harness connections

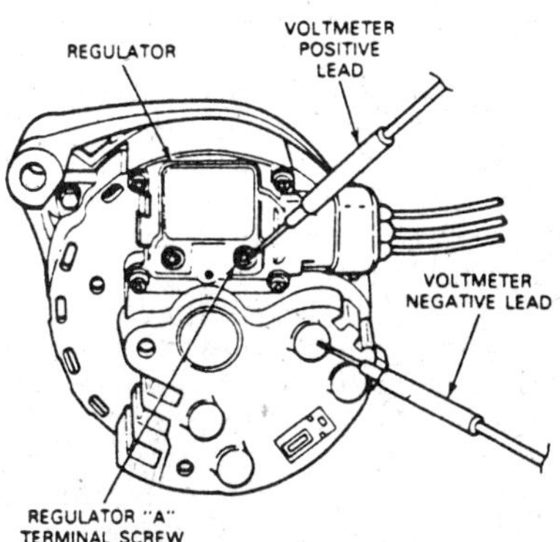

Over voltage test

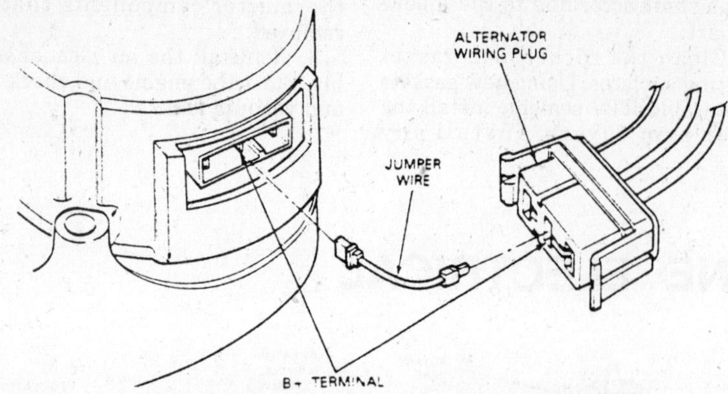

Under voltage test jumper wire connection at alternator

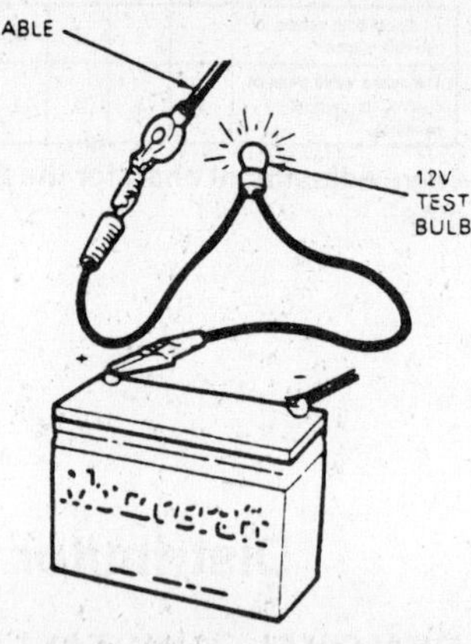

Testing for constant current drain with a test light. If the bulb glows, check the individual circuits to locate and eliminate the cause of the current drain on the battery. Underhood lamp, glove box lamp, reading or vanity lamps are prime suspects

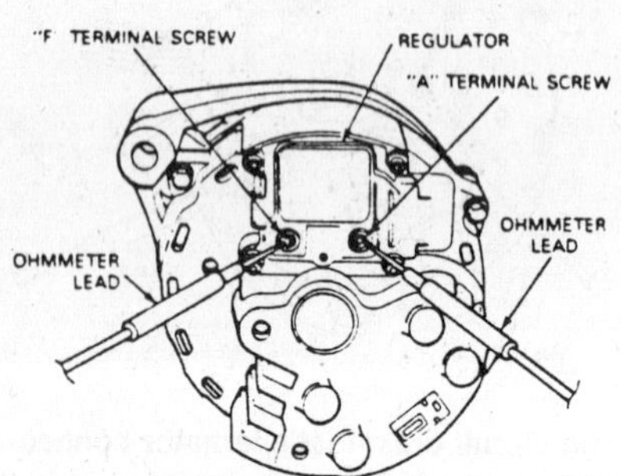

Under voltage test connections

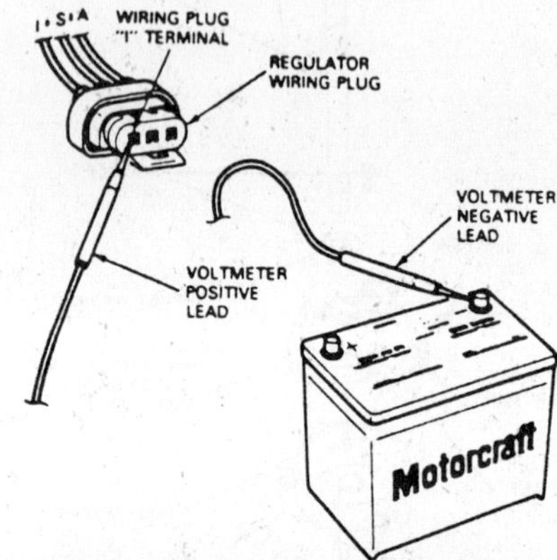

Regulator S and/or I circuit test

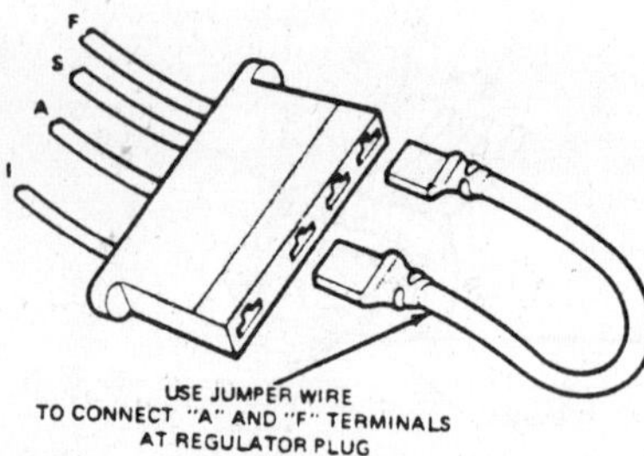

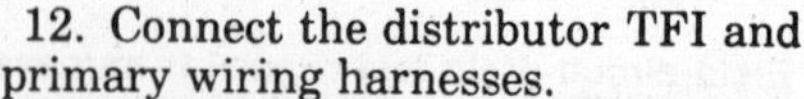

Under voltage test jumper wire connection at regulator plug

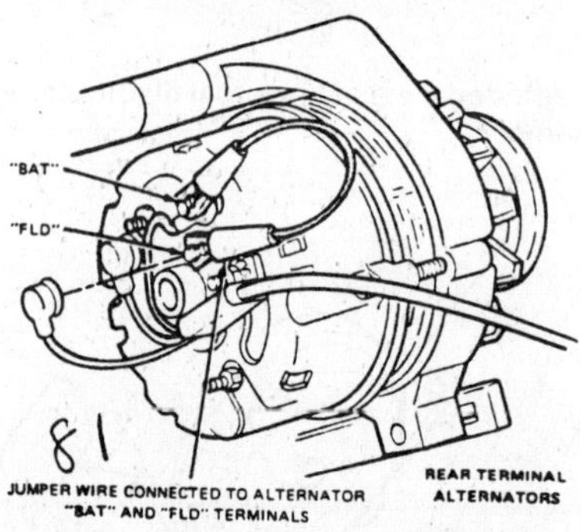

Alternator indicator lamp system test

12. Connect the distributor TFI and primary wiring harnesses.

13. Install the distributor rotor and tighten the attaching screws to 24-36 in.lb. (3-4 Nm).

14. Install the distributor cap and tighten the attaching screws to 18-23 in.lb. (2-3 Nm). Check that the ignition wires are securely attached to the cap towers.

15. Install the ignition wires to the spark plugs, making sure they are in the correct firing order and tight on the spark plugs.

16. Check and adjust the initial timing to specifications with a timing light. Refer to the tune-up chart or the underhood emission control sticker for initial timing specifications. No attempt should be made to alter the timing from factory specifications.

17. Once the initial timing is set, tighten the distributor holddown bolt to 17-25 ft.lb. (23-34 Nm). Recheck the timing, then remove the timing light.

Distributor Cap, Adapter and Rotor

REMOVAL & INSTALLATION

1. Tag all spark plug wires with a piece of tape according to cylinder number for reference when installing the wires, then remove them from the distributor cap. Note the position of No. 1 spark plug tower.

2. Unclip the distributor cap and lift it straight up and off the distributor.

3. Using a screwdriver, loosen the adapter attaching screws and remove the adapter.

4. Loosen the screws attaching the rotor to the distributor and remove the rotor.

5. Wipe the distributor cap and rotor with a clean, damp cloth. Inspect the cap for cracks, broken carbon button, carbon tracks, dirt or corrosion on the terminals and replace the cap if questionable. Replace the rotor if cracks, carbon tracks, burns, damaged blade or a damaged spring is noted.

6. Position the distributor rotor with the square and round locator pins matched to the rotor mounting plate. Tighten the screws to 24-36 in.lb. (2-4 Nm).

7. Install the adapter and tighten the attaching screws to 18-23 in.lb. (2-3 Nm).

8. Install the cap, noting the square alignment locator, then tighten the holddown screws to 18-23 in.lb. (2-3 Nm).

9. Install the spark plug wires in firing order, starting from No. 1 tower and working in sequence around the cap. Refer to the firing order illustrations, if necessary. Make sure the ignition wires are installed correctly and are firmly seated in the distributor cap towers.

TFI Ignition Module

REMOVAL & INSTALLATION

1. Remove the distributor cap with the ignition wires attached and position it out of the way. Remove the adapter.

2. Disconnect the TFI harness connector.

3. Remove the distributor from the engine as previously described.

4. Place the distributor on a clean workbench and remove the two TFI module attaching screws.

5. Pull the right side of the module down toward the distributor mounting flange and then back up to disengage the module terminals from the connector in the distributor base. The module may then be pulled toward the flange and away from the distributor.

CAUTION

Do not attempt to lift the module from its mounting surface prior to moving the entire TFI module toward the distributor flange or you will break the pins at the distributor/module connector.

6. Coat the metal base of the new TFI module with a $\frac{1}{32}$" (0.8mm) thick film of Silicone Dielectric Compound D7AZ-19A331-A or equivalent. This is extermely important to help dissipate the heat when the module is operating.

7. Place the TFI module on the distributor base mounting flange.

8. Carefully position the TFI module assembly toward the distributor bowl and engage the three distributor connector pins securely. Be careful when performing this step. It is very easy to bend one of the connector pins when installing.

9. Install the two TFI mounting screws and tighten them to 15-35 in.lb. (1-4 Nm).

10. Install the distributor on the engine as previously described.

11. Install the distributor cap and tighten the mounting screws to 18-23 in.lb. (2-3 Nm).

12. Reconnect the TFI wiring harness connector.

13. Attach a timing light according to the manufacturer's instructions and set the initial timing.

Octane Rod

REMOVAL & INSTALLATION

1. Remove the distributor cap, adapter and rotor as previously described.

2. Remove the octane rod 4mm retaining screw carefully. Don't drop it.

3. Slide the octane rod grommet out to a point where the rod can be disengaged from the stator retaining post and remove the octane rod. Retain the grommet for use with the new octane rod.

4. Install the grommet on the new octane rod.

5. Install the octane rod into the distributor, making sure it engages the stator retaining post.

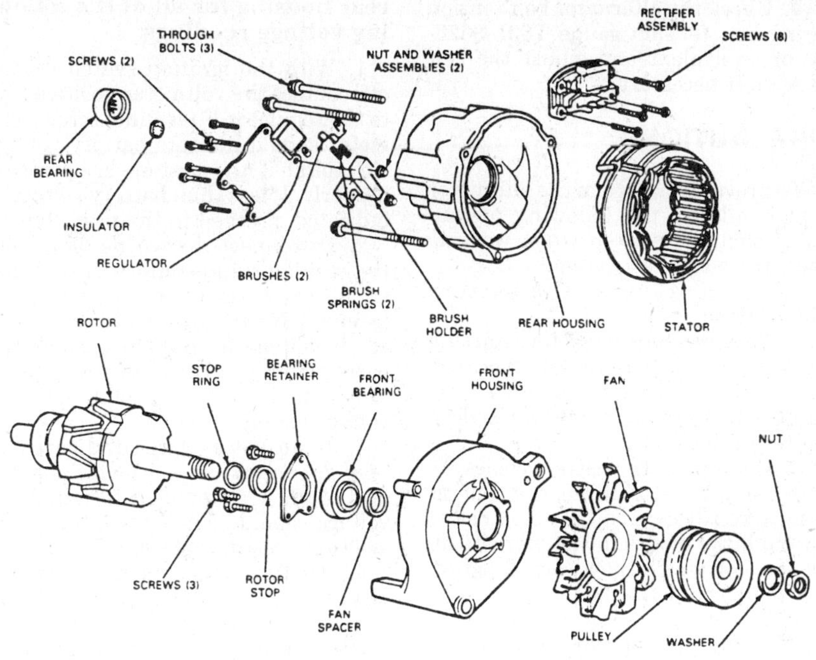

Exploded view of IAR alternator assembly

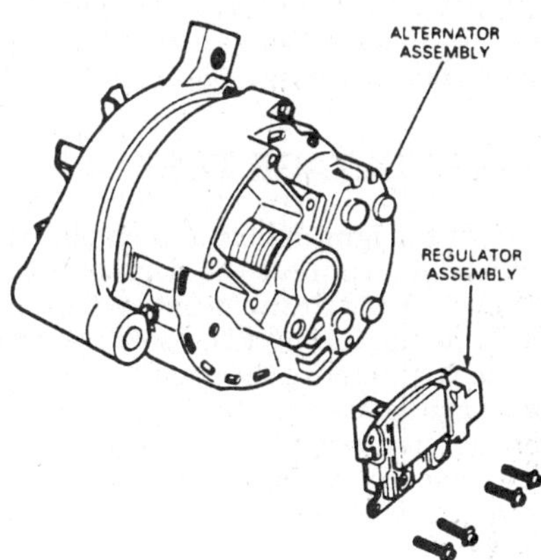

Removing the voltage regulator from the alternator

6. Install the retaining screw and tighten it to 15-35 in.lb. (2-4 Nm).

7. Install the rotor, adapter and cap as described above.

Alternator

The alternator charging system is a negative ground system, consisting of an alternator, regulator, charge indicator, storage battery, fusible link and associated wiring. The integral alternator/regulator is belt driven from the engine.

The fusible link is a short length of insulated wire located between the starter relay and the alternator that is designed to burn out, thus protecting the alternator and wiring when heavy reverse current flows, such as when a booster battery is connected incorrectly or a short to ground occurs in the wiring harness. If an alternator or charging system problem is being diagnosed, always check the condition of the fusible link first.

NOTE: The alternator warning light on the Aerostar can have a different meaning than with other systems. The light may indicate a high or low voltage condition. Extended vehicle idling with high electrical loads (all accessories on) could cause the warning lamp to come on. This is not meant to indicate a problem, but merely to warn the driver that there may be a battery discharge condition.

Before performing charging or starting system tests on the van, first determine exactly what type of problem you are dealing with, such as slow cranking, battery dead, ammeter light shows charge at all times or no charge, alternator warning light does not come on or never goes out, etc. This information will aid in isolating the part of the system causing the problem. Next, the system should be visually inspected as follows:

1. Check the fusible link located between the starter solenoid and the alternator. Replace the fusible link if burned.

2. Check the battery posts and cable terminals for clean and tight connections.

3. Check for clean and tight wiring connections at the alternator, regulator and engine.

4. Check the alternator belt tension using belt tension gauge T63L-8620-A, or equivalent and adjust the belt tension if necessary.

PRECAUTIONS

To prevent damage to the alternator and regulator, the following precautions should be taken when working with the electrical system.

1. Never reverse the battery connections.
2. Booster batteries for starting must be connected properly: positive-to-positive and negative cable from jumper to a ground point on the dead battery vehicle.
3. Disconnect the battery cables before using a fast charger; the charger has a tendency to force current through the diodes in the opposite direction for which they were designed. This burns out the diodes.
4. Never use a fast charger as a booster for starting the vehicle.
5. Never disconnect the voltage regulator while the engine is running.
6. Avoid long soldering times when replacing diodes or transistors. Prolonged heat is damaging to AC generators.
7. Do not use test lamps of more than 12 volts (V) for checking diode continuity.
8. Do not short across or ground any of the terminals on the AC generator.
9. The polarity of the battery, generator, and regulator must be matched and considered before making any electrical connections within the system.
10. Never operate the alternator on an open circuit. Make sure that all connections within the circuit are clean and tight.
11. Disconnect the battery terminals when performing any service on the electrical system. This will eliminate the possibility of accidental reversal of polarity.
12. Disconnect the battery ground cable if arc welding is to be done on any part of the car.

TESTING

A voltmeter, ohmmeter, jumper wire and a 12 volt test lamp are the only tools necessary to perform an accurate check of the complete charging system. Perform the visual checks described above before attempting these diagnosis procedures.

Field Circuit Drain Test

NOTE: Connect the voltmeter negative lead to the alternator rear housing for all of the following voltage readings.

1. With the ignition switch turned off, contact the voltmeter positive lead to the regulator **F** terminal screw. The meter should indicate battery voltage (12 volts) if the system is operating properly. If less than battery voltage is indicated, proceed to the next step.
2. Disconnect the wiring plug from the regulator and contact the voltmeter positive lead to the wiring plug **I** terminal. No voltage should be indicated. If voltage is indicated, check the wiring from the **I** lead to the ignition switch to identify and eliminate the voltage source.
3. If no voltage was indicated in Step 2, contact the voltmeter positive lead to the wiring plug **S** terminal. No voltage should be indicated. If no voltage is indicated, replace the regulator.
4. If voltage was indicated in Step 3, disconnect the wiring plug from the alternator. Again, connect the voltmeter positive lead to the regulator wiring plug **S** terminal. If voltage is still indicated, service the **S** lead to the alternator plug to eliminate the voltage source. If no voltage is indicated, replace the alternator.

BASE VOLTAGE TEST

With the ignition off and no electrical load on, connect the negative lead of a voltmeter to the negative battery cable clamp. Connect the positive lead of the voltmeter to the positive battery cable clamp. Record the voltage shown on the voltmeter scale; this is called the base voltage and should be 12 volts. Leave the voltmeter connected for the following tests.

NO LOAD TEST

Connect a tachometer to the engine. Start the engine and increase the speed to about 1,500 rpm. With no other electrical load (foot off the brake pedal and all doors closed), the voltmeter should show an increase of not more than 2 volts above base voltage recorded above. The reading should be taken when the voltmeter indicates peak voltage (stops rising), which may take a few minutes. If the voltage increases to the proper level, continue on to the Load Test. If the voltmeter reading continues to rise, perform the Over Voltage Test. If the voltmeter reading fails to increase, perform the Under Voltage Test.

LOAD TEST

With the engine running, turn the heater or A/C blower motor on high speed and the headlamps on high beam. Increase the engine speed to about 2,000 rpm. The voltmeter should indicate a minimum of 0.5 volt above base voltage. If not, perform the Under Voltage Test.

NOTE: If the above tests indicate proper voltage readings, the charging system is operating normally. Proceed to the tests below if one or more of the readings is different than shown above and use a test lamp to check for battery drain.

OVER VOLTAGE TEST

1. With the ignition on and engine off, connect the voltmeter positive lead first to the alternator output connection at the starter solenoid and then to the regulator **A** screw head. If the voltage difference between the two locations is greater than 0.5 volt, service the **A** wiring circuit to eliminate the high resistance condition indicated by the excessive voltage drop.
2. If the over voltage condition still exists, check for loose regulator to alternator grounding screws. Tighten loose regulator grounding screws to 15–26 in.lb. (1–3 Nm).
3. If the over voltage condition still exists, connect the voltmeter negative lead to the alternator rear housing. With the ignition off, contact the voltmeter positive lead first to the regulator **A** screw head and then to the regulator **F** screw head. Different voltage readings at the two screw heads indicates a defective regulator, grounded brush lead or a grounded rotor coil.
4. If the same voltage reading (battery voltage) is obtained at both screw heads in Step 3 and there is no high resistance in the ground or A+ circuits, then the regulator calibration is high. Replace the regulator.

UNDER VOLTAGE TEST

1. If the voltage does not indicate more than 0.5 volt above base voltage, disconnect the wiring plug from the regulator and connect an ohmmeter between the regulator **A** and **F** terminal screws. The ohmmeter should indicate more than 2.4Ω. If less than 2.4Ω is indicated, replace the alternator and repeat the Load Test.
2. If the ohmmeter reading is greater than 2.4Ω, reconnect the regulator wiring plug and connect the voltmeter ground lead to the alternator rear housing. Contact the voltmeter positive lead to the regulator **A** terminal screw. The voltmeter should indicate battery voltage. If there is no voltage, check the **A** circuit, then repeat the Load Test.

NOTE: A shorted rotor coil or field circuit will damage the regulator. If the regulator is replaced before the rotor coil or field circuit is repaired, the new regulator will be damaged.

3. If the voltmeter indicates battery voltage, connect the voltmeter ground lead to the alternator rear housing. With the ignition switch off, contact the voltmeter positive lead to the regulator **F** terminal screw. The meter should indicate battery voltage. If no voltage is indicated, there is an open field circuit in the alternator. Replace the alternator.

4. If the voltmeter indicates battery voltage, connect the voltmeter negative lead to the alternator rear housing. Turn the ignition switch on (engine off) and contact the voltmeter positive lead to the regulator **F** terminal screw. The voltmeter should indicate 1.5 volts or less. If more than 1.5 volts is indicated, perform the **I** circuit test. If the **I** circuit checks normal, replace the regulator and repeat the Load Test.

5. If 1.5 volts or less is indicated, disconnect the alternator wiring plug and connect a set of 12 gauge jumper wires between the alternator B+ terminal blades and the mating wiring connector terminals. Perform the Load Test, but connect the voltmeter positive lead to one of the B+ jumper wire terminals. If the voltage rises more than 0.5 volt above base voltage, service the alternator-to-starter relay wiring. Repeat the load test measuring the voltage at the battery cable clamps after servicing.

6. If the voltage does not rise more than 0.5 volt above base voltage, connect a jumper wire from the alternator rear housing to the regulator **F** terminal. Repeat the Load Test with the voltmeter positive lead connected to one of the B+ jumper wire terminals. If the voltage rises more than 0.5 volt, replace the regulator. If the voltage does not rise more than 0.5 volt, replace the alternator.

REGULATOR S AND/OR I CIRCUIT TEST

1. Disconnect the wiring plug from the regultor. Connect a jumper wire from the regulator **A** terminal to the wiring plug **A** lead. Add a jumper wire from the regulator **F** screw to the alternator rear housing.

2. With the engine idling and the voltmeter negative lead connected to the battery ground terminal, connect the voltmeter positive lead to the **S** terminal and then to the **I** terminal of the regulator wiring plug. The voltage at the **S** circuit should read approximately one-half that of the **I** circuit. If the voltage readings are normal, remove the jumper wires. Replace the regulator and connect the wiring plug to it, then repeat the Load Test.

3. If no voltage is present, remove the jumper wires and service the faulty wiring circuit or alternator.

ALTERNATOR INDICATOR LAMP SYSTEM TEST

1. If the charge indicator lamp does not come on with the ignition switch in the on position and the engine not running, check the indicator bulb for continuity and replace the bulb if it is burned out. If the bulb checks good, perform the regulator **I** circuit test.

2. If the indicator lamp does not light, remove the jumper wire and reconnect the wiring plug to the regulator. Connect the voltmeter negative lead to the battery negative post cable clamp and contact the voltmeter positive lead to the regulator **A** terminal screw. Battery voltage should be indicated. If battery voltage is not indicated, check the **A** circuit wiring.

3. If battery voltage is indicated, clean and tighten the ground connections to the engine, alternator and regulator. Tighten loose regulator mounting screws to 15–26 in.lb. (1–3 Nm).

4. Turn the ignition on with the engine off. If the indicator lamp still does not light, replace the regulator.

REMOVAL & INSTALLATION

1. Disconnect the negative (-) battery cable.
2. Disconnect the wiring harness attachments to the integral alternator/regulator assembly. Pull the two connectors straight out.
3. Loosen the alternator pivot bolt and remove the adjustment arm bolt from the alternator.
4. Disengage the alternator drive belt from the alternator pulley.
5. Remove the alternator pivot bolt and carefully lift the alternator/regulator assembly from the engine.
6. Remove the alternator fan shield from the old alternator, if equipped.
7. Position the new alternator/regulator assembly on the engine.
8. Install the alternator pivot and adjuster arm bolts, but do not tighten the bolts until the belt is tensioned.
9. Install the drive belt over the alternator pulley.
10. Adjust the belt tension, then tighten the adjuster and pivot bolts.

NOTE: Apply pressure to alternator front housing only when when adjusting belt tension

11. Connect the wiring harness to the alternator/regulator assembly. Push the two connectors straight in.
12. Attach the alternator fan shield to the alternator, if equipped.
13. Reconnect the ground cable to the battery.

Belt Tension Adjustment

The fan belt drives the alternator and water pump. If the belt is too loose, it will slip and the alternator will not be able to produce its rated current. Also, the water pump will not operate efficiently and the engine could overheat. Check the tension of the belt by pushing your thumb down on the longest span of the belt, midway between the pulleys. Belt deflection should be approximately ½". To adjust belt tension, proceed as follows:

1. Loosen the alternator mounting bolt and the adjusting arm bolts.
2. Apply pressure on the alternator front housing only, moving the alternator away from the engine to tighten the belt. Do not apply pressure to the rear of the cast aluminum housing of an alternator; damage to the housing could result.
3. Tighten the alternator mounting bolt and the adjusting arm bolts when the correct tension is reached.

REGULATOR

REMOVAL & INSTALLATION

The regulator is attached to the back of the alternator by four Torx® screws. Disonnect the wiring connector and remove the mounting screws to replace the regulator. Remove the regulator with the brush holder attached and transfer components to the replacement regulator as necessary. Make sure all wiring connectors are clean and tight.

Starter

REMOVAL & INSTALLATION

1. Disconnect the negative battery cable.
2. Raise the vehicle and support it safely on jackstands.
3. Disconnect the relay-to-starter cable at the starter terminal.
4. Remove the starter mounting bolts and lower the starter from the engine.
5. Position the new starter assembly to the flywheel housing and start the mounting bolts in by hand.
6. Snug all bolts while holding the starter squarely against its mounting surface and fully inserted into the pilot

hole. Tighten the mounting bolts to 15-20 ft.lb. (21-27 Nm).

7. Reconnect the relay-to-starter cable assembly to the starter motor. Tighten the screw and washer assemblies to 70-130 in.lb. (8-15 Nm).

8. Lower the vehicle, then connect the negative battery cable.

STARTER RELAY REPLACEMENT

The starter relay is mounted on the inside of the right wheel well. To replace it, disconnect the negative battery cable from the battery, disconnect all of the electrical leads from the relay and remove the relay from the fender wall. Replace in the reverse order of removal.

STARTER DRIVE REPLACEMENT

1. Remove the starter as described above.
2. Remove the starter drive plunger cover.
3. Remove the pivot pin retaining the starter drive plunger lever.
4. Loosen the through bolts enough to allow removal of the drive end housing, starter drive plunger lever and return spring.
5. Remove the drive gear stop ring retainer and stop ring from the end of the armature shaft and remove the drive gear assembly.
6. Apply a thin coating of Lubriplate® 777 or equivalent on the armature shaft splines. Install the drive gear assembly on the armature shaft and install a new stop ring.
7. Position the starter gear plunger lever on the starter frame. Make sure the plunger lever properly engages the starter drive assembly.
8. Install a new stop ring retainer. Partially fill the drive end housing bearing bore with grease (approximately 1/4 full), then position the starter drive plunger lever return spring and drive end housing to the starter frame. Tighten the through bolts to 55–75 in.lb. (6–8 Nm).
9. Position the starter drive plunger lever cover, with its gasket, on the starter and tighten the attaching screw.
10. Install the starter to the engine as previously described.

OVERHAUL

Brush Replacement

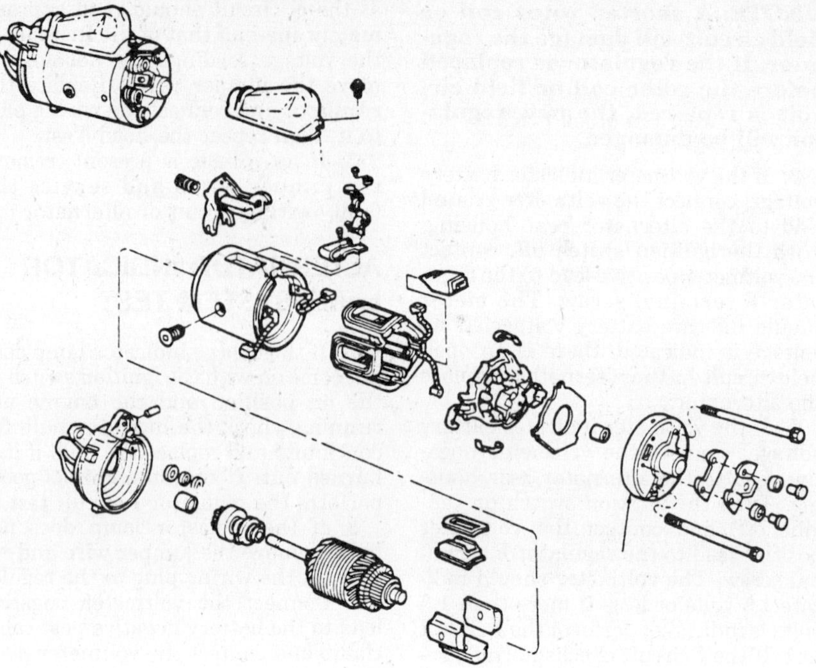

Exploded view of the starter assembly

1. Remove the top cover by taking out the retaining screw. Loosen and remove the two through bolts. Remove the starter drive end housing and the starter drive plunger lever return spring.
2. Remove the starter drive plunger lever pivot pin and lever, and remove the armature.
3. Remove the brush end plate.
4. Remove the ground brush retaining screws from the frame and remove the brushes.
5. Cut the insulated brush leads from the field coils, as close to the field connection point as possible.
6. Clean and inspect the starter motor.
7. Replace the brash end plate if the insulator between the field brush holder and the end plate is cracked or broken.
8. Position the new insulated field brushes lead on the field coil connections. Position and crimp the clip provided with the brushes to hold the brush lead to the connection. Solder the lead, clip, and connection together using rosin core solder. Use a 300W soldering iron.
9. Install the ground brush leads to the frame with the retaining screws.
10. Clean the commutator with special commutator paper.
11. Position the brush end plate to the starter frame, with the end plate boss in the frame slot.
12. Install the armature in the starter frame.
13. Install the starter drive gear plunger lever to the frame and starter drive assembly, and install the pivot pin.
14. Partially fill the drive end housing bearing bore with grease (approximately 1/4 full). Position the return spring on the plunger lever, and the drive end housing to the starter frame. Install the through-bolts and tighten to specified torque (55 to 75 in.lb.). Be sure that the stop ring retainer is seated properly in the drive end housing.
15. Install the commutator brushes in the brush holders. Center the brush springs on the brushes.
16. Position the plunger lever cover and brush cover band, with its gasket, on the starter. Tighten the band retaining screw.
17. Connect the starter to a battery to check its operation.

ENGINE MECHANICAL

Engine Overhaul Tips

Most engine overhaul procedures are fairly standard. In addition to specific parts replacement procedures and complete specifications for your individual engine, this section also is a guide to accept rebuilding procedures. Examples of standard rebuilding practice are shown and should be used along with specific details concerning your particular engine.

Competent and accurate machine

shop services will ensure maximum performance, reliability and engine life.

In most instances it is more profitable for the do-it-yourself mechanic to remove, clean and inspect the component, buy the necessary parts and deliver these to a shop for actual machine work.

On the other hand, much of the rebuilding work (crankshaft, block, bearings, piston rods, and other components) is well within the scope of the do-it-yourself mechanic.

TOOLS

The tools required for an engine overhaul or parts replacement will depend on the depth of your involvement. With a few exceptions, they will be the tools found in a mechanic's tool kit. More in-depth work will require any or all of the following:

- a dial indicator (reading in thousandths) mounted on a universal base
- micrometers and telescope gauges
- jaw and screw-type pullers
- scraper
- valve spring compressor
- ring groove cleaner
- piston ring expander and compressor
- ridge reamer
- cylinder hone or glaze breaker
- Plastigage®
- engine stand

The use of most of these tools is illustrated in this section. Many can be rented for a one-time use from a local parts jobber or tool supply house specializing in automotive work.

Occasionally, the use of special tools is called for. See the information on Special Tools and Safety Notice in the front of this book before substituting another tool.

INSPECTION TECHNIQUES

Procedures and specifications are given in this section for inspecting, cleaning and assessing the wear limits of most major components. Other procedures such as Magnaflux® and Zyglo® can be used to locate material flaws and stress cracks. Magnaflux® is a magnetic process applicable only to ferrous materials. The Zyglo® process coats the material with a fluorescent dye penetrant and can be used on any material Check for suspected surface cracks can be more readily made using spot check dye. The dye is sprayed onto the suspected area, wiped off and the area sprayed with a developer. Cracks will show up brightly.

OVERHAUL TIPS

Aluminum has become extremely popular for use in engines, due to its low weight. Observe the following precautions when handling aluminum parts:

- Never hot tank aluminum parts (the caustic hot tank solution will eat the aluminum.
- Remove all aluminum parts (identification tag, etc.) from engine parts prior to the tanking.
- Always coat threads lightly with engine oil or anti-seize compounds before installation, to prevent seizure.
- Never overtorque bolts or spark plugs especially in aluminum threads.

Stripped threads in any component can be repaired using any of several commercial repair kits (Heli-Coil®, Microdot®, Keenserts®, etc.).

When assembling the engine, any parts that will be frictional contact must be prelubed to provide lubrication at initial start-up. Any product specifically formulated for this purpose can be used, but engine oil is not recommended as a prelube.

When semi-permanent (locked, but removable) installation of bolts or nuts is desired, threads should be cleaned and coated with Loctite® or other similar, commercial non-hardening sealant.

REPAIRING DAMAGED THREADS

Several methods of repairing damaged threads are available. Heli-Coil® (shown here), Keenserts® and Microdot® are among the most widely used. All involve basically the same principle—drilling out stripped threads, tapping the hole and installing a prewound insert—making welding, plugging and oversize fasteners unnecessary.

Two types of thread repair inserts are usually supplied: a standard type for most Inch Coarse, Inch Fine, Metric Course and Metric Fine thread sizes and a spark lug type to fit most spark plug port sizes. Consult the individual manufacturer's catalog to determine exact applications. Typical thread repair kits will contain a selection of prewound threaded inserts, a tap (corresponding to the outside diameter threads of the insert) and an installation tool. Spark plug inserts usually differ because they require a tap equipped with pilot threads and a combined reamer/tap section. Most manufacturers also supply blister-packed thread repair inserts separately in addition to a master kit containing a variety of taps and inserts plus installation tools.

Before effecting a repair to a threaded hole, remove any snapped, broken or damaged bolts or studs. Penetrating

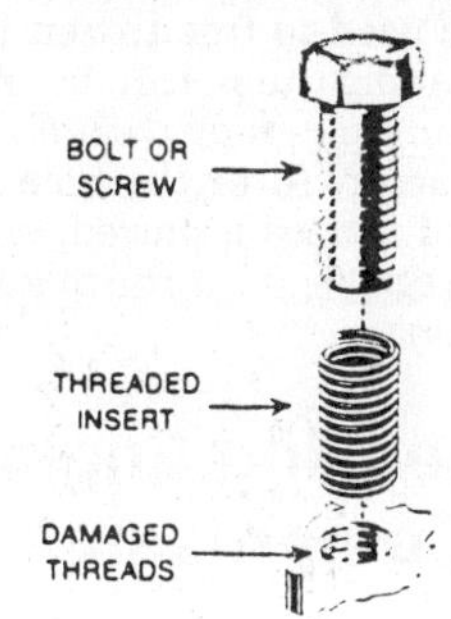

Damaged bolt holes can be repaired with thread repair inserts

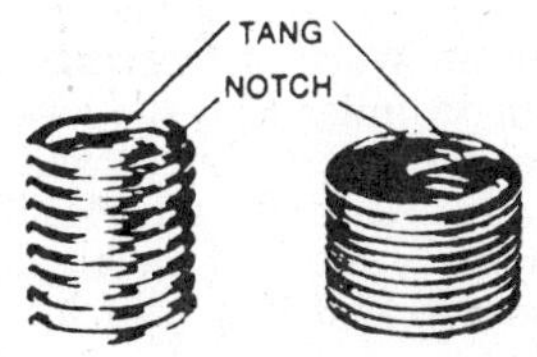

Standard thread repair insert (left) and spark plug thread insert (right)

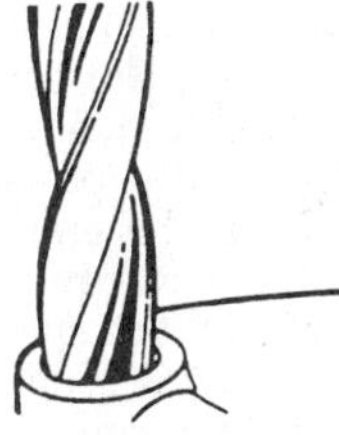

Drill out the damaged threads with the specified drill. Drill completely through the hole or to the bottom of a blind hole

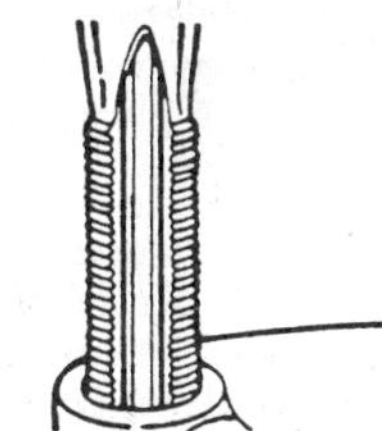

With the tap supplied, tap the hole to receive the thread insert. Keep the tap well oiled and back it out frequently to avoid clogging the threads

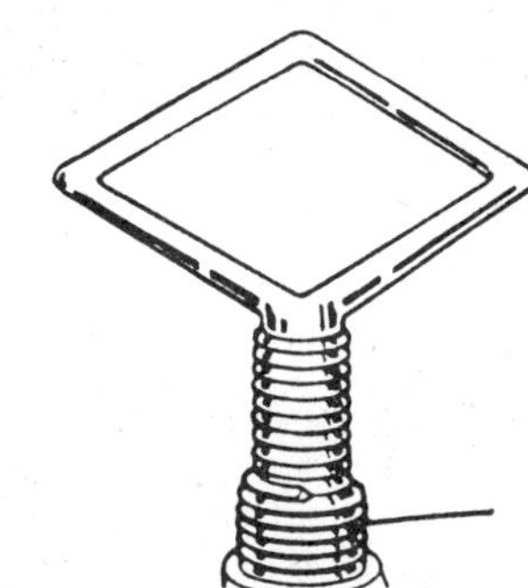

Screw the threaded insert onto the installation tool until the tang engages the slot. Screw the insert into the tapped hole until it is 1/4-1/2 turn below the top surface. After installation break off the tang with a hammer and punch

oil can be used to free frozen threads. The offending item can be removed with locking pliers or with a screw or stud extractor. After the hole is clear, the thread can be repaired, as shown in the series of accompanying illustrations.

Checking Engine Compression

A noticeable lack of engine power, excessive oil consumption and/or poor fuel mileage measured over an extended period are all indicators of internal engine war. Worn piston rings, scored or worn cylinder bores, blown head gaskets, sticking or burnt valves and worn valve seats are all possible culprits here. A check of each cylinder's compression will help you locate the problems.

As mentioned earlier, a screw-in type compression gauge is more accurate that the type you simply hold against the spark plug hole, although it takes slightly longer to use. It's worth it to obtain a more accurate reading. Follow the procedures below.

1. Warm up the engine to normal operating temperature.
2. Remove all the spark plugs.
3. Disconnect the high tension lead from the ignition coil.
4. On fully open the throttle either by operating the carburetor throttle linkage by hand or by having an assistant floor the accelerator pedal.
5. Screw the compression gauge into the no.1 spark plug hole until the fitting is snug.

WARNING: Be careful not to crossthread the plug hole. On aluminum cylinder heads use extra care, as the threads in these heads are easily ruined.

6. Ask an assistant to depress the accelerator pedal fully on both carbureted and fuel injected vehicles. Then, while you read the compression gauge, ask the assistant to crank the engine two or three times in short bursts using the ignition switch.
7. Read the compression gauge at the end of each series of cranks, and record the highest of these readings. Repeat this procedure for each of the engine's cylinders. Compare the highest reading of each cylinder to the compression pressure specification in the Tune-Up Specifications chart. The specs in this chart are maximum values.

A cylinder's compression pressure is usually acceptable if it is not less than 80% of maximum. The difference between any two cylinders should be no more than 12–14 pounds.

The screw-in type compression gauge is more accurate

8. If a cylinder is unusually low, pour a tablespoon of clean engine oil into the cylinder through the spark plug hole and repeat the compression test. If the compression comes up after adding the oil, it appears that the cylinder's piston rings or bore are damaged or worn. If the pressure remains low, the valves may not be seating properly (a valve job is needed), or the head gasket may be blown near that cylinder. If compression in any two adjacent cylinders is low, and if the addition of oil doesn't help the compression, there is leakage past the head gasket. Oil and coolant water in the combustion chamber can result from this problem. There may be evidence of water droplets on the engine dipstick when a head gasket has blown.

Engine

REMOVAL & INSTALLATION

2.3L (140 CID) Engine

NOTE: The engine removal procedure requires that the engine and front suspension subframe be removed from beneath the van. Unless provisions can be made to safely raise the body enough to allow the engine to be removed from the bottom, this procedure should not be attempted. Tag all electrical and vacuum connections before disconnection to make installation easier. A piece of masking tape on each connector end with matching numbers is the easiest way to do this.

1. Disconnect the negative battery cable terminal.
2. Loosen the draincock and drain the coolant from the radiator into a suitable container.

CAUTION

When draining the coolant, keep in mind that cats and dogs are attracted by the ethylene glycol antifreeze, and are quite likely to drink any that is left in an uncovered container or in puddles on the ground. This will prove fatal in sufficient quantity. Always drain the coolant into a sealable container. Coolant should be reused unless it is contaminated or several years old.

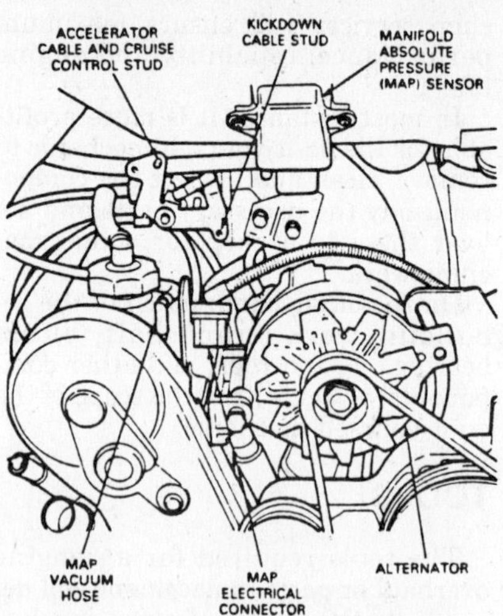

Component and linkage locations

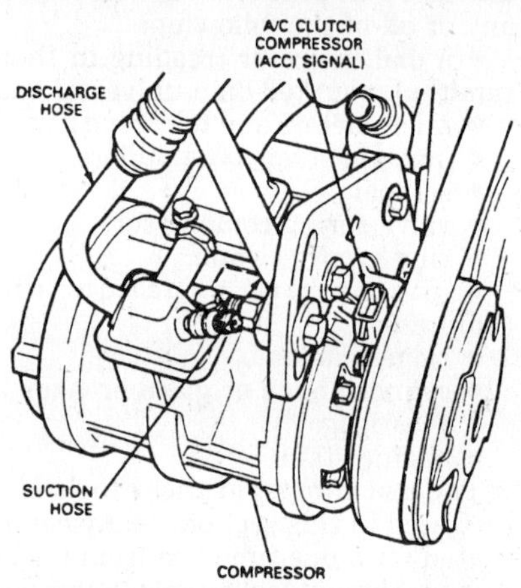

Discharge the A/C system before attempting to disconnect any refrigerant lines

3. Disconnect the air cleaner outlet tube at the throttle body and the idle speed control hose.
4. Remove the upper and lower hoses from the radiator and engine. Disconnect the lower intake manifold hose from the tee fitting in the heater hose.
5. Remove the bolts retaining the fan shroud to the radiator, then remove the fan shroud.
6. Disconnect the electrical connectors to the alternator.
7. Remove the throttle linkage shield and disconnect the accelerator cable and cruise control (if equipped) from the throttle body. Unbolt the cables from the bracket and position them out of the way.
8. If the van is equipped with air conditioning, discharge the system as described under ROUTINE MAINTE-

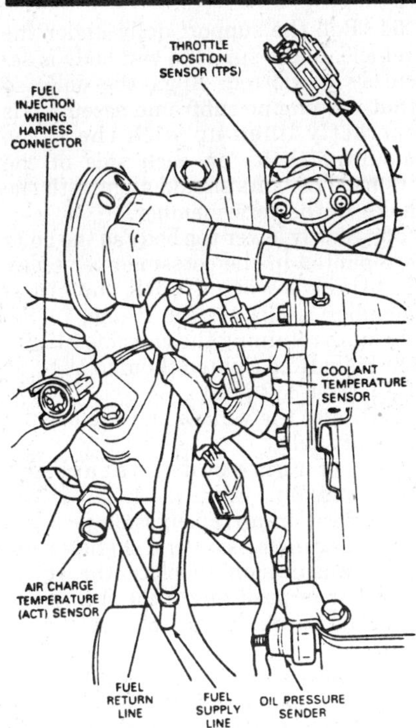

Fuel line electrical component connector locations

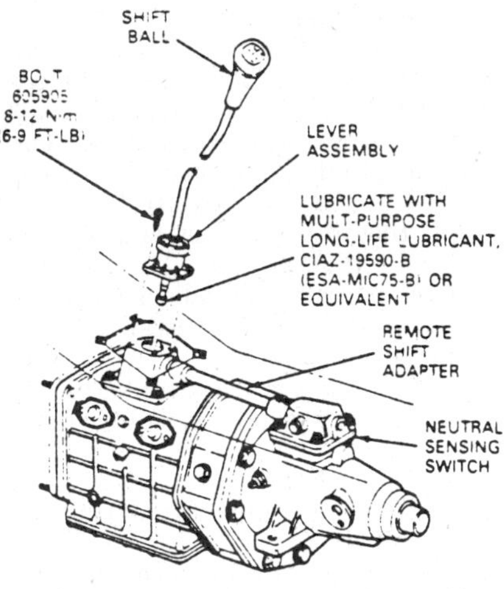

Removing manual transmission shifter assembly

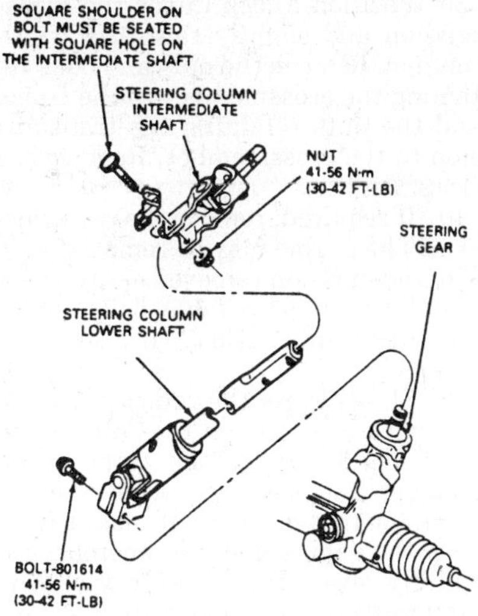

Disconnecting the steering column linkage

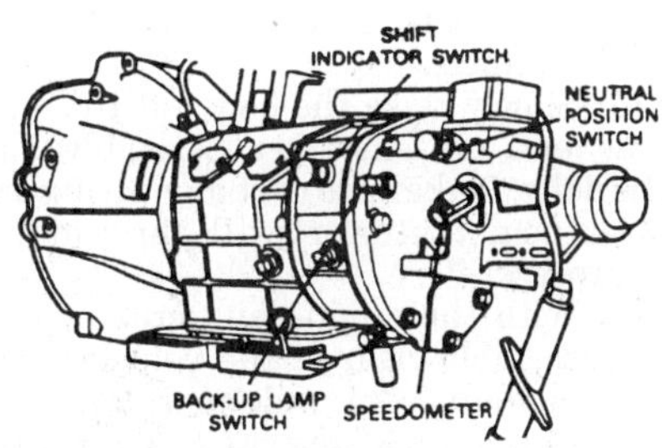

Component locations on manual transmission

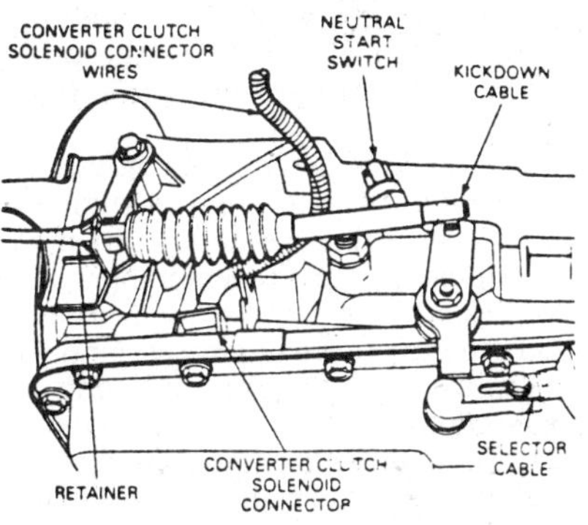

Component locations on automatic transmission

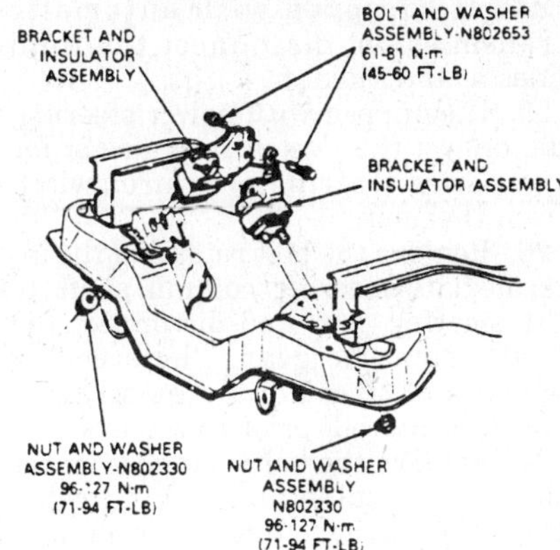

Engine and transmission mounts on 2.3L engine

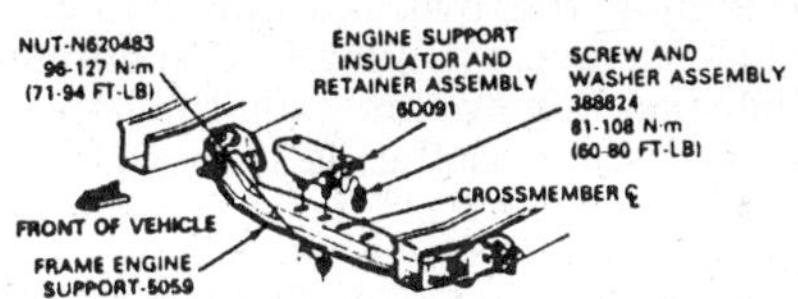
Installation of rear transmission support on 2.3L engine with 5 spd manual transmission

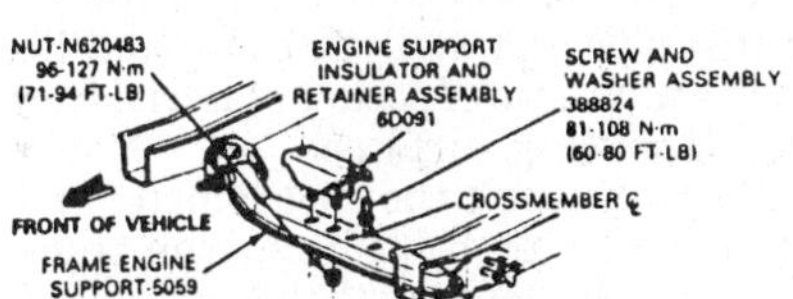
Installation of rear transmission support on 2.3L engine with automatic transmission

NANCE. After discharging, disconnect the suction and discharge hoses from the compressor. Disconnect the A/C compressor clutch electrical connector from the compressor.

9. From the lower left front of the engine, disconnect the electrical connector for the coil.

10. From beneath the lower intake manifold, disconnect the electrical connector for the TFI module on the distributor.

11. Disconnect the electrical connector from the knock sensor on the side of the upper intake manifold.

12. Tag and disconnect all hoses to the vacuum tree at the top of the upper intake manifold.

13. Disconnect the electrical connector and vacuum hose from the exhaust gas recirculation (EGR) valve at the rear of the upper intake manifold.

14. Remove the engine cover from inside the cab.

15. Disconnect the electrical connector for the throttle position sensor (TPS) at the rear of the throttle body.

16. Disconnect the electrical elbow connector for the oil pressure sender at the left rear of the engine.

17. Depressurize the fuel system as described in ROUTINE MAINTENANCE, then disconnect the fuel return and supply lines.

18. Disconnect the electrical connector for the fuel injection wiring harness.

19. Disconnect the electrical connector for the air charge temperature (ACT) sensor at the rear side of the lower intake manifold.

20. Disconnect the electrical connector for the coolant temperature sensor at the center of the lower intake manifold.

21. Remove the nut and disconnect the ground strap from the right rear side of the engine below the lifting eye.

22. If equipped with manual transmission, place the shift lever in Neutral and remove the bolts retaining the shift lever to the floor. Remove the bolts retaining the shift lever assembly to the transmission and remove the lever assembly.

23. Raise the van and support it safely with jackstands.

24. If equipped with automatic transmission, disconnect the fluid lines at the radiator.

25. If equipped with power steering, disconnect the electrical connector for the power steering pressure switch from the gear.

26. Remove the bolt retaining the intermediate steering column shaft to the steering gear and disconnect the shaft from the gear. The steering wheel and tires should be straight ahead (centered) prior to removal.

27. Remove the bolts and disconnect the starter cable and ground cable from the starter. Route the ground and starter cables out from the crossmember.

28. On vehicles equipped with manual transmission, remove the lockpin retaining the hydraulic hose to the clutch slave cylinder in the clutch housing. Remove and plug the hose.

29. Disconnect the electrical connector for the exhaust gas oxygen sensor at the exhaust manifold.

30. Loosen and remove the exhaust manifold stud nuts. Remove the bolts and nuts retaining the catalytic converter pipe to the muffler and outlet pipe. Disconnect and remove the exhaust pipe and catalytic converter. Remove all traces of gasket material from the mounting surfaces.

31. Disconnect the speedometer and/or tachometer cable from the transmission. Disconnect the electrical connector from the backup lamp switch.

32. On manual transmissions, disconnect the electrical connector for the shift indicator sender.

33. On automatic transmissions, disconnect the electrical connector for the neutral start switch. Disconnect the throttle and kickdown cable from the transmission lever. Route the kickdown cable out of the engine compartment and remove the cable.

34. Remove the nuts and U-bolts retaining the driveshaft to the rear axle yoke and remove the driveshaft. Insert a plug in the extension housing to prevent fluid leakage.

35. Remove the lug nuts and remove both front wheel and tire assemblies.

36. Remove the bar nuts and disconnect the stabilizer bar from the lower control arms. Discard the bar nuts.

37. Disconnect the brake lines at the bracket on the frame behind the spindles.

38. Position a jack under the lower control arm and raise the arm until tension is applied to the coil spring. Remove the bolt and nut retaining the spindle to the upper control arm ball joint. Slowly lower the jack under the lower control arm to disconnect the spindle from the ball joint. Place safety chains around the lower arms and spring upper seat.

39. Position a jack under the transmission and slightly raise the transmission. Remove the nuts and bolts retaining the crossmember to the frame and the nuts retaining the transmission to the crossmember. Remove the crossmember.

40. If required, remove the transmission. The engine may be removed with the transmission removed or attached.

41. Position a suitable dolly under the crossmember and engine assembly.

42. Slowly lower the vehicle until the crossmember rests on the dolly. Place wood blocks under the front crossmember and the rear of the engine block (or transmission, if installed) to keep the engine and crossmember assembly level. Install safety chains around the engine and dolly.

43. With the engine and crossmember securely supported on the dolly, remove the three nuts from the bolts that retain the engine and crossmember assembly to the frame on each side of the vehicle.

44. Slowly raise the body off the engine and crossmember assembly on the dolly. Make sure that any wiring or hoses do not interfere with the removal process.

45. With the engine and crossmember assembly clear of the vehicle, roll the dolly out from under the van.

46. Connect a lifting chain to the lifting eyes on the right rear and front left portions of the engine. Attach the chain to a suitable chain hoist or shop crane.

47. If equipped with power steering, disconnect the hoses from the pump and plug them to prevent the entry of dirt.

48. With lifting tension applied, remove the nuts retaining the engine to the crossmember assembly, then lift the engine off the crossmember.

49. Remove the required components to attach the engine assembly to a suitable engine stand and continue disassembly as desired.

50. To install the engine, first attach a lifting chain and shop crane to the engine. Remove the bolts retaining the engine to the engine stand and lift the engine with the shop crane.

51. With the front crossmember securely positioned on a dolly, slowly lower the engine until the motor mount studs are piloted in the crossmember holes. Install the remaining nuts and tighten them to 45-65 ft.lb. (61-81 Nm).

52. Install wood blocks under the oil pan and/or transmission and crossmember, then remove the lifting chain and shop crane.

53. If equipped with power steering, connect the hoses to the power steering pump.

54. Roll the support dolly under the vehicle. Make sure the van body is securely supported. Align the dolly so that the engine/subframe assembly is correctly lined up with the three mounting bolts on each side of the frame. The bolts should align with the holes in the corssmember.

55. Slowly lower the body so the bolts are piloted in the corssmember holes. Continue lowering until the crossmember is against the frame. Install the nuts retaining the crossmember to the frame and tighten them to 187-260 ft.lb. (254-352 Nm).

56. Raise the vehicle and remove the support dolly.

57. If removed, install the transmission.

58. Position a transmission jack under the transmission and slightly raise the transmission to place the crossmember in position on the frame and transmission. Install the retaining nuts and bolts to the crossmember, then install the nut retaining the transmission mount and insulator to the crossmember and tighten to 71-94 ft.lb. (97-127 Nm).

59. Remove the safety chains from around the lower control arm and upper spring seat.

60. Install a floor jack under the lower control arms. Slowly raise the control arm until the coil spring is under tension. Continue to raise the arm until the spindle upper arm can be connected to the upper control arm ball joint. Install a new nut and bolt and tighten to 80-120 ft.lb. (108-163 Nm).

61. Connect the stabilizer bar to the lower control arms. Install new bar nuts.

62. Connect the front brake lines to the caliper hoses at the frame brackets.

63. Install the front wheels and tighten the lug nuts to 85-115 ft.lb. (115-155 Nm).

64. Connect the driveshaft to the transmission and rear axle yoke. Install the nuts and U-bolts retaining the driveshaft to the rear axle yoke.

65. On vehicles with automatic transmission, connect the throttle and kickdown cables to the transmission lever. Connect the electrical connector to the neutral start switch and route the kickdown cable into the engine compartment.

66. On manual transmissions, connect the electrical connector for the shift indicator sender.

67. Connect the speedometer and/or tachometer to the transmission, then connect the electrical connector for the backup lamp switch.

68. Install new non-asbestos gaskets on the exhaust manifold and catalytic converter. Place the assembly in position on the exhaust manifold, muffler

and outlet pipe. Install the two nuts and bolts retaining the converter to the muffler and outlet pipe and tighten to 18-26 ft.lb. (25-35 Nm). Install the nuts retaining the pipe to the exhaust manifold and tighten alternately to 18-26 ft.lb. (34-46 Nm).

69. Connect the electrical connector for the exhaust gas oxygen sensor on the exhaust manifold.

70. On manual transmissions, attach the hydraulic hose to the slave cylinder in the clutch housing. Install the lockpin retaining the hose to the cylinder.

71. Position the ground cable on the starter and install and tighten the mounting bolt to 15-20 ft.lb. (21-27 Nm). Connect the starter cable to the motor and install the screw and washer. Tighten to 70-100 in.lb. (9-12 Nm). Route the starter and ground cables over the crossmember and into position in the engine compartment.

72. With the front wheels and steering wheel centered (straight ahead), connect the steering column lower shaft to the steering gear. Install the bolt and tighten it to 31-42 ft.lb. (41-56 Nm).

73. If equipped with power steering, connect the power steering pressure switch at the gear.

74. If equipped with automatic transmission, connect the fluid lines at the radiator.

75. Lower the vehicle.

76. From inside the cab, if equipped with manual transmission, position the shift lever assembly on the transmission. Make sure the transmission and shifter are in the Neutral position. Install and tighten the retaining bolts to 6-9 ft.lb. (8-12 Nm). Position the boot over the lever assembly.

77. On the right rear side of the engine below the lifting eye, position the ground strap on the lifting eye, then install and tighten the retaining nut.

78. In the center of the lower intake manifold, connect the electrical connector for the coolant temperature sensor.

79. Connect the electrical connector for the air charge temperature (ACT) sensor at the rear side fo the lower intake manifold.

80. Connect the electrical connector for the fuel injection wiring harness.

81. Connect the hoses to the fuel return and fuel supply lines.

82. Connect the electrical connector for the oil pressure sender at the left rear side of the engine.

83. Connect the electrical connector for the throttle position sensor (TPS) at the rear of the throttle body.

84. Install the engine cover inside the cab.

85. Connect the electrical connector and vacuum hose for the EGR valve at the rear of the upper intake manifold.

86. Connect all vacuum hoses in their proper positions on the vacuum tree at the top of the upper intake manifold.

87. Connect the electrical connector for the knock sensor at the side of the upper intake manifold.

88. Connect the electrical connector for the thick film ignition (TFI) module on the distributor, underneath the lower intake manifold.

89. Connect the electrical connector for the coil at the lower left front side of the engine.

90. If equipped with air conditioning, connect the A/C clutch compressor connector to the compressor. Connect the suction and discharge hoses to the compressor and recharge the A/C system as described in ROUTINE MAINTENANCE.

91. Connect the accelerator cable and cruise control cable (if equipped) to the throttle body. Install the cables in the retaining bracket and install and tighten the bolt. Install the throttle linkage shield.

92. Connect the two electrical connections to the alternator.

93. Connect the electrical connector and vacuum hose to the manifold absolute pressure (MAP) sensor.

94. Position the fan shroud on the radiator, then install and tighten the retaining bolts.

95. Install the upper and lower radiator hoses and the heater hoses. Install the lower intake manifold hose to the tee in the heater hose.

96. Connect the air cleaner tube at the throttle body and the idle speed control hose.

97. Install the ground cable on the negative battery terminal.

98. Fill the cooling system to the specified level with approved coolant.

99. Check and adjust all fluid levels as described in ROUTINE MAINTENANCE.

100. Bleed the brake system.

101. Start the engine and check for leaks. Correct as required. The front end alignment should be checked and, if necessary, adjusted as soon as possible.

2.8L (171 CID) and 3.0L (182 CID) V6 Engines

NOTE: The engine removal procedures for the 2.8L and 3.0L are basically identical with the exception of the fuel system. The 2.8L engine uses a carburetor, while the 3.0L engine is equipped with port fuel injection. In addition, certain components may be used on carbureted engines that are not on fuel injection models and vice versa. In both cases, the engine is removed from the bottom along with the subframe and front suspension. Unless provisions can be made to safely raise the body enough to allow the engine to be removed from the bottom, this procedure should not be attempted. Tag all electrical and vacuum connections before disconnection to make installation easier; a piece of masking tape on each connector with matching numbers is the easiest way.

1. Disconnect the negative battery cable.

2. Loosen the draincock and drain the coolant from the radiator into a suitable clean container.

CAUTION

When draining the coolant, keep in mind that cats and dogs are attracted by the ethylene glycol antifreeze, and are quite likely to drink any that is left in an uncovered container or in puddles on the ground. This will prove fatal in sufficient quantity. Always drain the coolant into a sealable container. Coolant should be reused unless it is contaminated or several years old.

3. Remove the air cleaner and intake duct assembly.

4. Disconnect the upper and lower hoses at the radiator.

5. Remove the fan shroud retaining bolts and remove the shroud.

6. On 2.8L engines, disconnect the manifold absolute pressure (MAP) sensor electrical connector from the sensor, located on the dash panel.

7. If equipped with air conditioning, disconnect the A/C clutch electrical connector from the compressor. On the 2.8L engine, loosen the idler pulley adjustment bolt to slacken drive belt tension and remove the belt from the compressor clutch pulley, then remove the compressor mounting bolts and position the compressor out of the way. On the 3.0L engine, discharge the A/C system as described in ROUTINE MAINTENANCE and disconnect the compressor discharge and suction hoses from the compressor.

8. Disconnect the accelerator able and the transmission kickdown cable at the throttle lever ball stud or throttle body.

9. Disconnect the electrical connector for the idle speed control (ISC) motor (2.8L) or the idle air control (IAC) valve (3.0L).

10. Disconnect the electrical connectors for the engine coolant temperature sensor and the water temperature sender switch, located in the thermostat housing.

11. Disconnect the vacuum hose from the exhaust gas recirculation

(EGR) valve and the electrical connector from the EGR valve position sensor.

12. Disconenct the electrical connectors from the alternator.
13. On the 2.8L, tag and disconnect the electrical connectors for the throttle position sensor on the carburetor choke shield, canister purge valve solenoid and the solenoid valve carburetor bowl vent. Disconnect the electrical connector to the variable voltage choke cap. Disconnect the evaporative emission hose from the solenoid valve carburetor bowl vent to the vapor storage canister. Route the wiring harness out of the engine compartment.
14. Remove the engine cover from inside the cab.
15. On the 3.0L, tag and disconnect the evaporative emission line, fuel injector wiring harness (including 6 injectors), air charge temperature sensor, throttle position sensor and the radio frequency supressor, if equipped.
16. Remove the retaining bolt, then remove the bracket and accelerator cable and transmission kickdown linkage.
17. If equipped with cruise control, disconnect the cruise control cable from the throttle linkage.
18. Disconnect the electrical connector and supressor wire from the ignition coil.
19. On the 2.8L, disconnect the hose from the air control valve to the catalytic converter.
20. Disconnect the electrical connector for the thick film ignition (TFI) module at the distributor. Disconnect the electrical connector for the knock sensor on the 3.0L.
21. On the 2.8L, disconnect the electrical connector for the feedback control solenoid at the rear of the carburetor.
22. Tag and disconnect all the hoses from the vacuum manifold fitting.
23. Disconnect the brake booster vacuum hose from the clip.
24. If equipped with manual transmission, place the shift lever in Neutral and remove the bolts retaining the shift lever to the floor. Remove the bolts retaining the shift lever assembly to the transmission and remove the lever assembly.
25. Raise the vehicle and support it safely on jackstands.
26. If equipped with automatic transmission, disconnect the fluid lines at the radiator.
27. Remove the heater hoses from the bracket underneath the engine at the front of the crossmember.
28. Make sure the steering wheel and front wheels are straight ahead (centered), then remove the bolt retaining the intermediate steering column

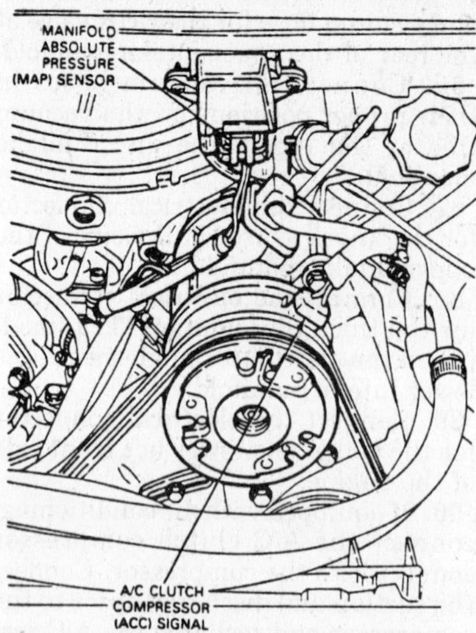

MAP sensor location on 2.8L engine

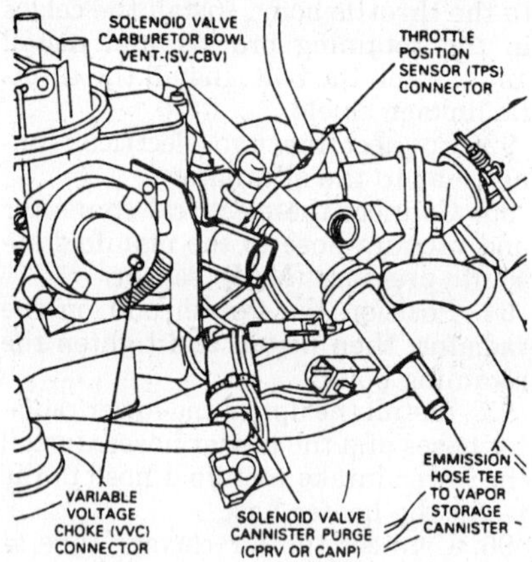

Electrical component locations on 2.8L engine

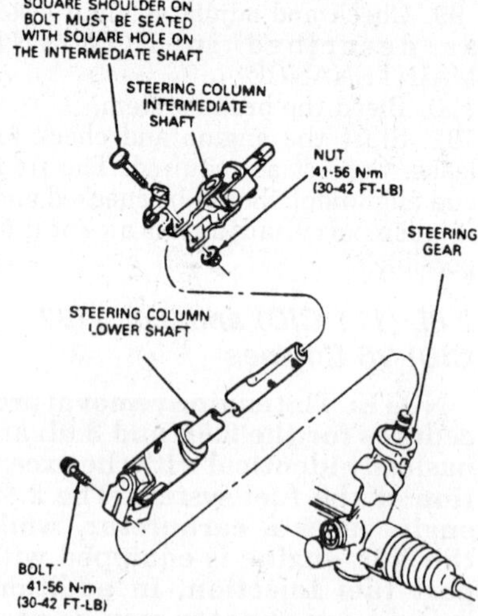

Disconnecting the steering gear

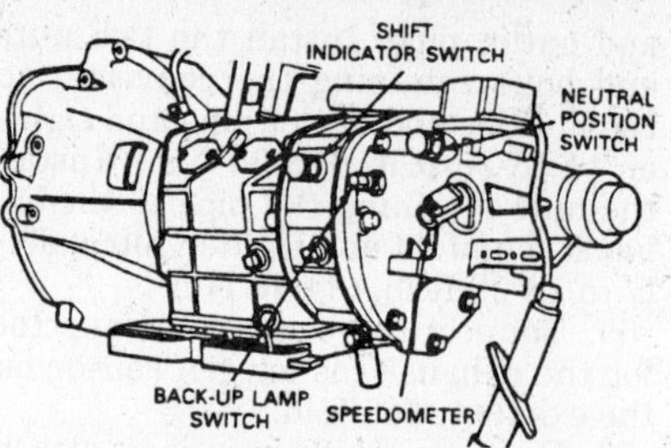

Manual transmission electrical connections

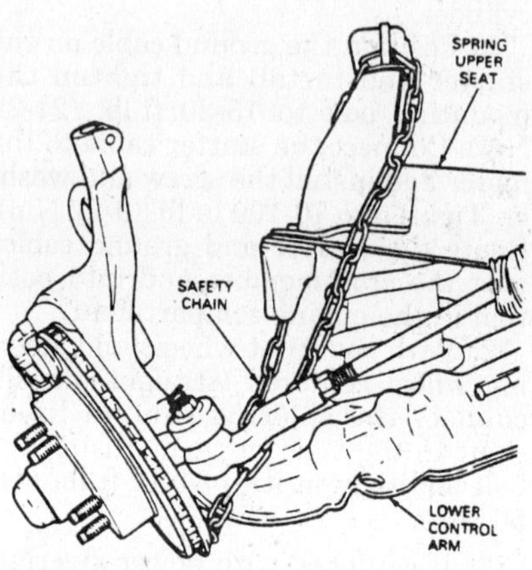

Safety chain installation on lower control arm

shaft to the steering gear and disconnect the shaft from the gear.
29. Disconnect the elbow connector from the oil pressure sender beneath the fuel pump (2.8L), or the oil pressure sending switch connector (3.0L).
30. On the 2.8L, disconnect and plug the inlet hose on the fuel pump from the lines on the frame. On the 3.0L, depressurize the fuel system as described in ROUTINE MAINTENANCE and disconnect the fuel delivery and return lines.
31. Remove the bolt retaining the ground strap to the engine and remove the strap.
32. Remove the bolts and disconnect the starter cable and ground cable from the starter. Route the ground and starter cables out from the crossmember.
33. On vehicles with manual transmission, remove the lockpin retaining the hydraulic hose to the slave cylinder in the clutch housing. Remove and plug the hose.
34. Disconnect the electrical connector for the exhaust gas oxygen sensor from the left exhaust manifold. Disconnect the electrical connector for the knock sensor from the engine block above the starter.
35. Loosen and remove the exhaust manifold stud nuts. On the 2.8L, disconnect the tube to the check valve on

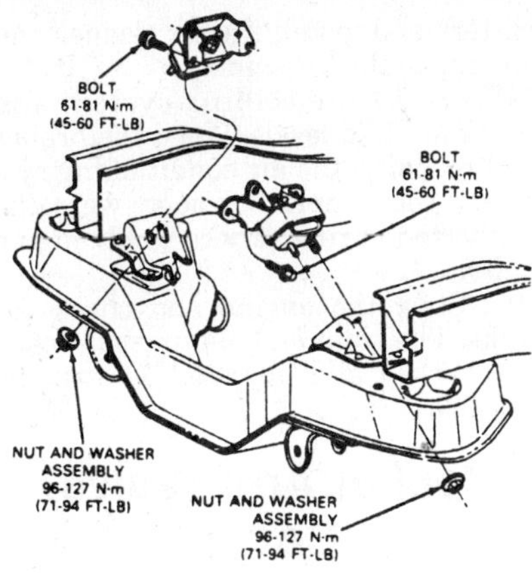

V6 engine mounts

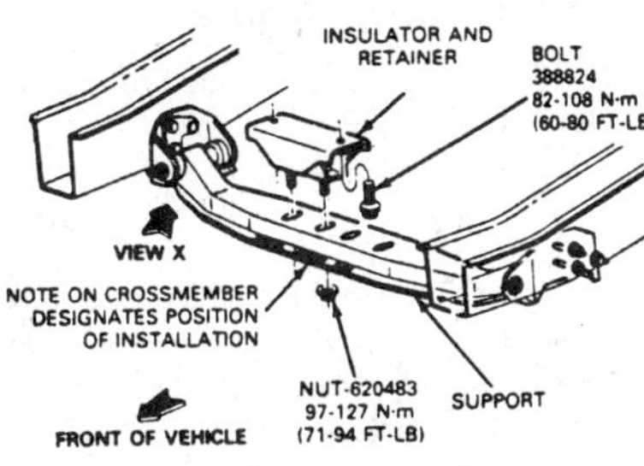

Rear transmission mount on V6 engine

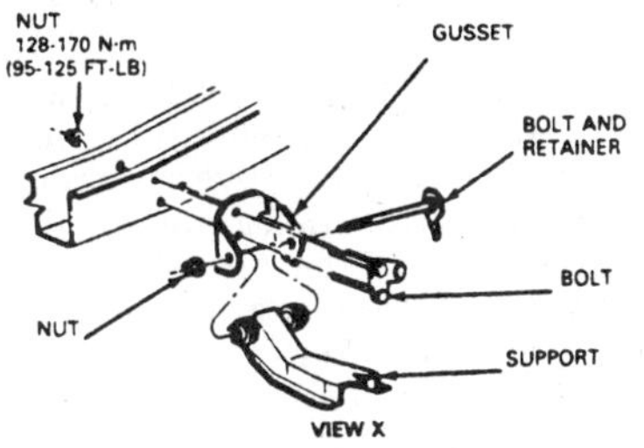

Rear crossmember-to-frame mounting on V6 engine

the managed thermactor air tube. Remove the bolts and nuts retaining the catalytic converter pipe to the muffler and outlet pipe. Disconnect and remove the exhaust pipe and catalytic converter.

36. Disconnect the speedometer cable from the transmission. Disconnect the electrical connector from the back-up lamp switch.

37. On manual transmissions, disconnect the electrical connector for the shift indicator sender.

38. On automatic transmissions, disconnect the electrical connector for the neutral start switch. Disconnect the throttle and kickdown cable from the transmission lever. Route the kickdown cable out of the engine compartment and remove the cable.

39. Remove the nuts and U-bolts retaining the driveshaft to the rear axle and remove the driveshaft. Insert a plug in the extension housing to prevent fluid leakage.

40. Remove the front tires.

41. Remove the bar nuts and disconnect the stabilizer bar from the lower control arms. Discard the bar nuts.

42. Disconnect and plug the brake lines at the bracket on the frame behind the spindles.

43. Position a jack under the lower control arm and raise the arm until tension is applied to the coil spring. Remove the bolt and nut retaining the spindle to the upper control arm ball joint. Slowly lower the jack under the lower control arm to disconnect the spindle from the ball joint.

CAUTION

Place safety chains around the lower control arms and spring upper seat.

44. Position a transmission jack under the transmission and slightly raise the transmission. Remove the nuts and bolts retaining the crossmember to the frame and the nuts retaining the transmission to the crossmember. Remove the crossmember.

45. If required, remove the transmission.

46. Position a wheeled dolly under the crossmember and engine assembly.

47. Slowly lower the vehicle until the crossmember rests on the dolly. Place wood blocks under the front crossmember and the rear of the engine block (or transmission, if installed), to keep the engine and crossmember assembly level. Install safety chains around the crossmember and dolly.

48. With the engine and crossmember securely supported on the dolly, remove the three nuts from the bolts that retain the engine and crossmember assembly to the frame on each side of the vehicle.

49. Slowly raise the body off the engine and crossmember assembly on the dolly. Make sure that any wiring or hoses do not snag or interfere with the removal process.

50. When the engine and crossmember assembly are clear of the van body, roll the dolly out from under the vehicle.

51. Install lifting eyes (Ford No. D81L-6001-D) on each side of the exhaust manifold, then connect a suitable chain to the lifting eyes and attach a shop crane or chain hoist.

52. If equipped with power steering, disconnect the power steering hoses from the pump to the gear and plug the hose ends.

53. With lifting tension applied, loosen the nuts retaining the motor mounts to the crossmember and lift the engine off the crossmember.

54. Remove the necessary components to attach the engine to a suitable engine stand. Make sure the engine is securely bolted to the stand before releasing tension on the hoist. Continue disassembly as desired.

55. To install the engine, again attach a suitable shop crane or chain hoist and remove the engine from the work stand.

56. With the front crossmember securely attached to a wheeled dolly, slowly lower the engine until the motor mount studs are piloted in the crossmember holes. Install the retaining nuts and tighten them to 71-94 ft.lb. (96-127 Nm). Install wood blocks under the oil pan and crossmember to level the assembly, then detach the lifting chain and hoist. Remove the lifting eyes.

57. If equipped with power steering, attach the hoses to the pump and gear. Roll the dolly under the vehicle and make sure the three mounting bolts on each side of the frame are in alignment with the holes in the crossmember.

58. Slowly lower the body so the bolts are piloted in the crossmember holes. When the crossmember is against the frame, install the retaining nuts and tighten them to 187-260 ft.lb. (254-352 Nm). Raise the vehicle and remove the dolly.

59. If removed, install the transmission.

60. Position a transmission jack under the transmission and slightly raise the transmission. Place the crossmember in position in the frame and on the transmission, then install the nuts retaining the transmission mount and insulator to the crossmember. Tighten the retaining nuts to 71-94 ft.lb. (97-127 Nm).

61. Remove the safety chains from around the lower control arms and spring seat.

62. Install a jack under the lower control arms, then slowly raise the control arm until the coil spring is under tension. Continue to raise the arm until the spindle upper arm can be connected to the lower control arm ball joint. Install a new nut and tighten to 12-18 ft.lb. (37-50 Nm).

63. Connect the stabilizer bar to the lower control arms. Install new bar nuts and tighten them to 12-18 ft.lb. (16-24 Nm).

64. Connect the front brake lines to the caliper hoses at the frame brackets.

65. Install the front wheels and tighten the lug nuts to 85-115 ft.lb. (115-155 Nm).

66. Connect the driveshaft to the rear axle and transmission. Install the nuts and bolts retaining the driveshaft to the rear axle end yoke.

67. If equipped with automatic

transmission, connect the throttle and kickdown cables to the transmission lever. Connect the electrical connector for the neutral start switch and route the kickdown cable into the engine compartment.

68. On manual transmissions, connect the electrical connector for the shift indicator sender.

69. Connect the cable/electrical sender for the speedometer to the transmission. Connect the electrical connector for the backup lamp switch.

70. Install new non-asbestos gaskets on the exhaust manifold and catalytic converter. Install the two nuts and bolts retaining the converter to the muffler and outlet pipe and tighten them to 18-26 ft.lb. (25-35 Nm). Install the nuts retaining the pipe to the exhaust manifold and tighten by alternately torquing to 18-26 ft.lb. (25-35 Nm).

71. Connect the electrical connectors for the exhaust gas oxygen sensor and the knock sensor.

72. On manual transmissions, attach the hydraulic hose to the slave cylinder in the clutch housing. Install the lockpin retaining the hose to the cylinder. Bleed the clutch hydraulic system.

73. Position the ground cable on the starter and tighten the mounting bolt 15-20 ft.lb. (21-27 Nm). Connect the starter cable to the motor and install the screw and washer and tighten to 70-100 in.lb. (9-12 Nm). Route the starter and ground cables over the crossmember and into position in the engine compartment.

74. Position the ground strap on the engine and install and tighten the bolt.

75. On the 2.8L, connect the fuel pump inlet hose to the line on the frame. On the 3.0L, reconnect the fuel return and delivery lines.

76. Connect the elbow connector to the oil pressure sender beneath the fuel pump.

77. With the front wheel and steering wheel straight ahead (centered), connect the steering column intermediate shaft to the steering gear. Install and tighten the bolt to 30-42 ft.lb. (41-56 Nm).

78. Install the heater hoses to the bracket underneath the engine at the front of the crossmember.

79. If equipped with automatic transmission, connect the fluid lines at the radiator.

80. Lower the vehicle.

81. From inside the cab, connect the brake vacuum booster hose to the vacuum manifold fitting on the rear of the engine. Connect the hose to the clip. If equipped with cruise control, connect the vacuum hose from the cruise control to the fitting. Make sure all hoses disconnected prior to engine removal are connected to their correct ports.

82. On the 2.8L, connect the electrical connector for the feedback control solenoid at the rear of the carburetor. On the 3.0L, connect the fuel injection wiring harness and all injectors.

83. Connect the electrical connector for the thick film ignition (TFI) module at the distributor. On the 2.8L, connect the hose for the air control valve to the catalytic converter. Connect the electrical connector and supressor wire to the coil.

84. Connect the cruise control cable to the carburetor or throttle body assembly. Position the accelerator and kickdown cables in the bracket and install the bolt.

85. If equipped with manual transmission, position the shift lever assembly on the transmission. Make sure the transmission and shifter assembly are in Neutral, then install and tighten the retaining bolts. Position the boot over the lever assembly.

86. Reconnect all remaining wiring connectors accessible from the top of the engine, then replace the engine cover in the cab.

87. Route the wiring into position in the engine compartment.

88. On the 2.8L, connect the electrical connectors for the throttle position sensor, canister purge valve solenoid and solenoid valve/carburetor bowl vent. Connect the elbow connector to the variable voltage choke cap, then connect the evaporative emission hose from the solenoid valve/carburetor bowl vent to the vapor storage canister.

89. Connect the electrical connectors to the alternator. Connect the vacuum hose to the exhaust gas recirculation (EGR) valve and the electrical connectors for the engine coolant temperature sender and the water temperature sensor.

90. On the 2.8L, connect the electrical connector foe the idle speed control (ISC) motor. Connect the accelerator and transmission kickdown cables to the throttle lever ball stud.

91. Position the A/C compressor in the engine brackets. Install the retaining bolts and tighten to 25-35 ft.lb. (34-47 Nm). On the 3.0L, connect the compressor suction and discharge hoses. Install the drive belt on the compressor clutch and idler pulley, if removed, and adjust the drive belt tension. Connect the A/C compressor clutch electrical connector.

92. Connect the manifold absolute pressure (MAP) sensor electrical connector to the sensor on the dash panel.

93. Install the shroud over the fan and in position on the radiator, then install and tighten the retaining bolts. Connect the upper and lower radiator hoses.

94. Connect the ground cable to the battery and install the air cleaner and air intake duct assembly.

95. Refill the cooling system and check all fluid levels. Bleed the brakes and recharge the air conditioning system, if the compressor hoses were disconnected during service (3.0L engine only).

96. Start the engine and check for leaks. The front end alignment should be checked and adjusted as soon as possible.

Rocker Arm (Valve) Cover

REMOVAL & INSTALLATION

2.3L (140 CID) Engine

1. Disconnect the negative battery cable.
2. Remove the engine cover inside the cab.
3. Remove the air cleaner and intake ducts from the throttle body assembly.
4. Remove the throttle linkage and throttle body.
5. Disconnect the spark plug wires from the plugs and position the wires out of the way. Leave the spark plug wires in their looms to make installation easier.
6. Loosen and remove the seven screw and washer assemblies along the outside of the rocker cover and remove them along with their retainers. Loosen and remove the one stud on the right side of the rocker cover.
7. Tap the rocker cover lightly with a rubber mallet to break it loose, then lift the rocker arm cover straight up off the engine.
8. Remove and discard the rocker cover gasket.
9. Carefully clean all gasket mating surfaces, being careful not to scratch the rocker cover or cylinder head surfaces.
10. To install, set the new gasket in the rocker arm cover, then lower the cover straight down onto the cylinder head. Make sure the gasket is seated properly all the way around the cover.
11. Install the screw and washer assemblies with their retainers and tighten them to 62-97 in.lb. (7-11 Nm). The retainers should be gripping the edge of the rocker cover, 90° from the bolt holes. Install the stud and tighten to 62-97 in.lb. (7-11 Nm).
12. Install the ignition cables, throttle body and air cleaner assembly. Connect the negative battery cable, start the engine and check for leaks.

2.8L (171 CID) Engine

1. Remove the air cleaner and air duct assembly.

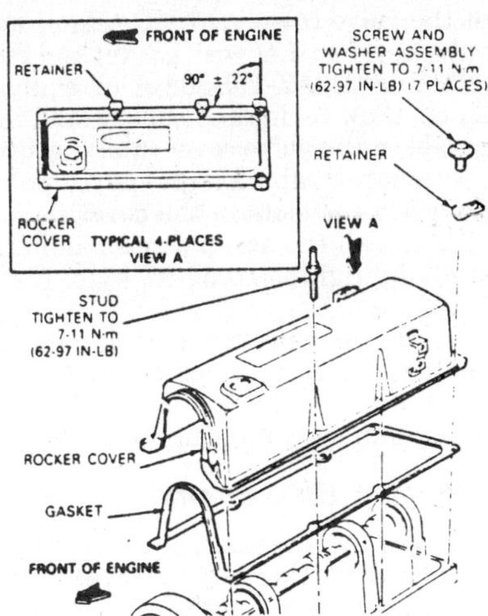

Rocker arm cover mounting on 2.3L (140 CID) engine

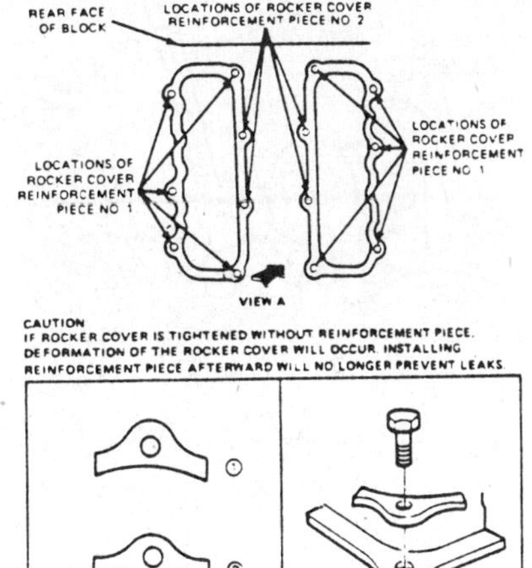

Installing rocker cover on 2.8L (171 CID) engine

2. Remove the spark plug wires from the plugs, but leave them attached to their wire loom in order. Lay the wires out of the way.
3. Remove the PCV valve and hose.
4. Remove the two screws attaching the throttle position sensor connector to the carburetor choke air shield and route the connector forward to clear the valve cover area.
5. Remove the carburetor choke air deflector plate (shield).
6. Remove the A/C compressor and brackets, if equipped, and move it aside without disconnecting any refrigerant lines.
7. Remove the rocker arm cover attaching screws and load distribution washers. Lay the washers out in order so they may be installed in their original positions.
8. If equipped with automatic transmission, remove the transmission fluid level indicator tube and bracket, which is attached to the rocker cover.
9. Disconnect the kickdown linkage from the carburetor on automatic transmission models.
10. Position the thermactor air hose and wiring harness away from the right hand rocker cover.
11. Remove the engine oil filler tube and bracket assembly from the valve cover and exhaust manifold stud.
12. Disconnect the vacuum line at the canister purge solenoid and disconnect the line routed from the canister to purge solenoid. Disconnect the power brake booster hose, if equipped.
13. Tap the rocker arm cover lightly with a rubber mallet to break it loose. Remove the rocker arm cover by lifting it up and off the cylinder head.
14. Clean all gasket material from the rocker arm cover and cylinder head mating surfaces.
15. Install the rocker arm cover, using a new gasket, then install the attaching screws and rocker cover reinforcement pieces.
16. If equipped with an automatic transmission, install the transmission fluid level indictor tube and bracket to the rocker cover.
17. Connect the kickdown linkage (automatic transmission only).
18. Make sure all rocker cover load distribution washers are installed in their original positions, then tighten the rocker arm cover screws to 3-5 ft.lb. (4-7 Nm).
19. Install the spark plug wires, PCV valve and hose.
20. Install the carburetor choke air deflector plate (shield).
21. Install the two screws retaining the throttle position sensor connector to the choke air deflector shield.
22. Reposition the thermactor air hose and wiring harness in their original locations.
23. Install the engine oil filler tube an bracket to the valve cover and exhaust manifold studs.
24. Connect the vacuum line at the canister purge solenoid and connect the line routed from the the canister to the purge solenoid. Connect the power brake hose, if equipped.
25. Install the A/C compressor and brackets, if equipped.
26. Install the air cleaner assembly, start the engine and check for leaks.

3.0L (182 CID) Engine

1. Remove the engine cover in the cab. Disconnect the ignition wires from the spark plugs, but leave them attached to their wire looms.
2. Remove the ignition wire separators from the rocker arm cover attaching bolt studs with the wires attached, then lay the wires out of the way.
3. If the left hand cover is being removed, remove the oil filler cap and the PCV system hose. If the right hand cover is being removed, remove the PCV valve and disconnect the EGR tube and heater hoses.
4. Remove the rocker arm cover attaching screws and lift the cover off the engine. Tap the cover lightly with a rubber mallet to break it loose, if necessary.
5. Clean all gasket mating surfaces and remove any traces of the old gasket material and dirt.

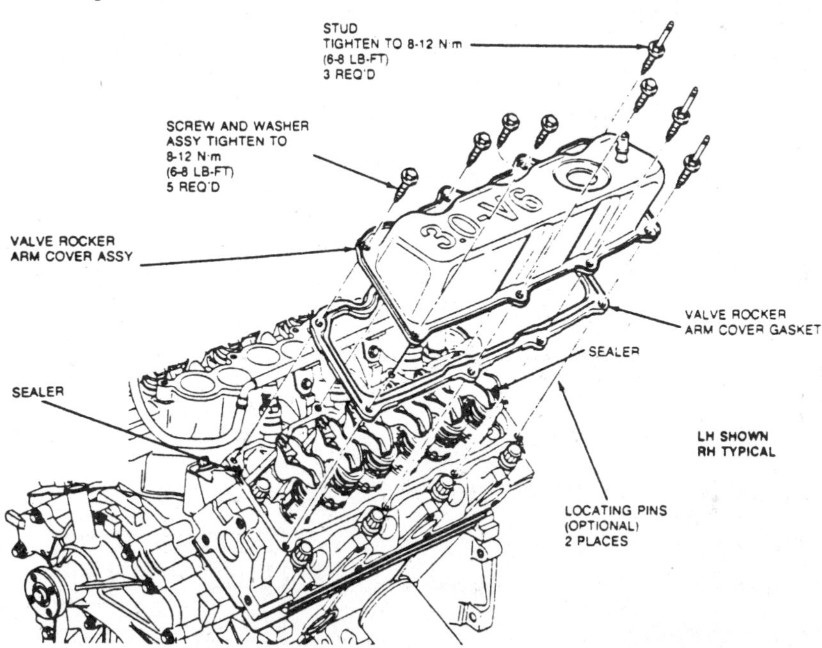

Rocker arm cover mounting on 3.0L (182 CID) engine

6. To install, lightly oil all bolts and stud threads. Apply a bead of RTV sealant at the cylinder head to intake manifold rail step (two places per rail). Position a new cover gasket into place.

7. Place the rocker cover on the cylinder head and install five attaching bolts and three attaching studs. Note the location of the ignition wire separator clip stud bolts. Tighten the attaching bolts to 80-106 in.lb. (9-12 Nm).

8. Install the oil filler cap and PCV hose (left hand), or the PCV valve and EGR tube (right hand). Tighten the EGR tube to 25-36 ft.lb. (35-50 Nm).

9. Install the ignition wire separators.

10. Connect the ignition wires to the spark plugs and start the engine and check for leaks.

Rocker Arms/Shafts

REMOVAL & INSTALLATION

2.3L (140 CID) Engine

1. Remove the upper intake manifold with throttle body attached and associated parts as required.

2. Remove the valve rocker arm cover and associated parts as required.

3. Rotate the camshaft so that the base circle of the cam is facing the applicable cam follower.

4. Using a valve spring compressor lever (T74P-6565-A or equivalent), collapse the valve spring and slide the cam follower over the lash adjuster and out.

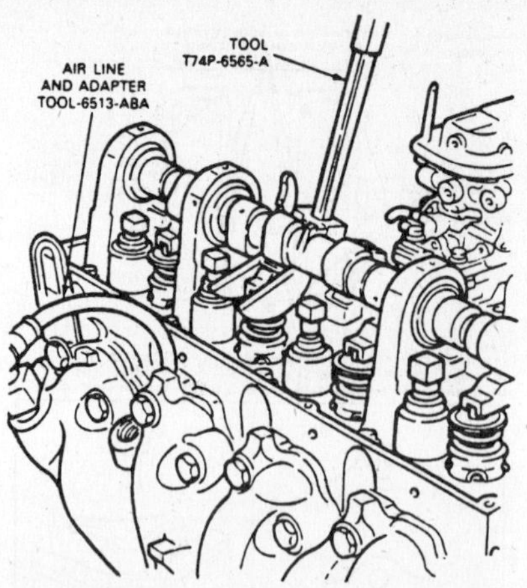

Collapsing the valve spring with compressor tool on 2.3L (140 CID) engine

5. Lift out the hydraulic lash adjuster.

6. To install, rotate the camshaft so that the base circle of the cam is facing the applicable cam follower.

7. Place the hydraulic lash adjuster in position in the bore.

8. Collapse the valve spring using the compressor lever and position the cam follower over the lash adjuster and the valve stem.

9. Clear the gasket surfaces of the upper and lower intake manifold. Install the gasket and upper intake manifold assembly and tighten the retaining bolts to 13-18 ft.lb. (18-24 Nm).

10. Clean the gasket surfaces of the valve cover and cylinder head.

11. Coat the gasket contact surfaces of the valve cover and UP side of the valve cover gasket with gasket and seal adhesive (D7AZ-19B508-A or equivalent). Allow to dry and then install the gasket in the valve cover, making sure the locator tabs are properly positioned in the slots in the cover.

12. Install the seven screws and one stud and tighten to 62-97 in.lb. (7-11 Nm).

13. Install the remaining components removed in Steps 1 and 2, then run the engine at fast idle and check for oil and vacuum leaks.

2.8L (171 CID) Engine

1. Follow the instructions under Rocker Arm Cover removal and remove the rocker covers.

2. Remove the rocker arm shaft stand attaching bolts by loosening the bolts two turns at a time in sequence. Lift off the rocker arm and shaft assembly and oil baffle. The assembly may then be transferred to a workbench for disassembly as necessary.

3. To install, loosen the valve lash adjusting screws a few turns, then apply SF type engine oil to the assembly to provide initial lubrication.

4. Install the oil baffle and rocker arm shaft assembly to the cylinder head and guide the adjusting screws on to the pushrods.

5. Install and tighten the rocker arm stand attaching bolts to 43-50 ft.lb. (59-67 Nm), two turns at a time, in sequence.

6. Adjust the valve clearance.

7. Install the rocker arm covers as outlined under Rocker Arm Cover Installation, then start the engine and check for leaks.

3.0L (182 CID) Engine

The rocker arms can be removed by first removing the rocker arm covers as described earlier, then removing the single retaining bolt at each rocker arm. The rocker arm and pushrod may then be removed from the engine. Keep all rocker arms and pushrods in order so they may be installed in their original locations. Tighten the rocker arm fulcrum bolts in two stages, first to 5-11 ft.lb. (7-15 Nm), then to 18-26 ft.lb. (25-35 Nm). Refer to the illustration for initial valve adjustment.

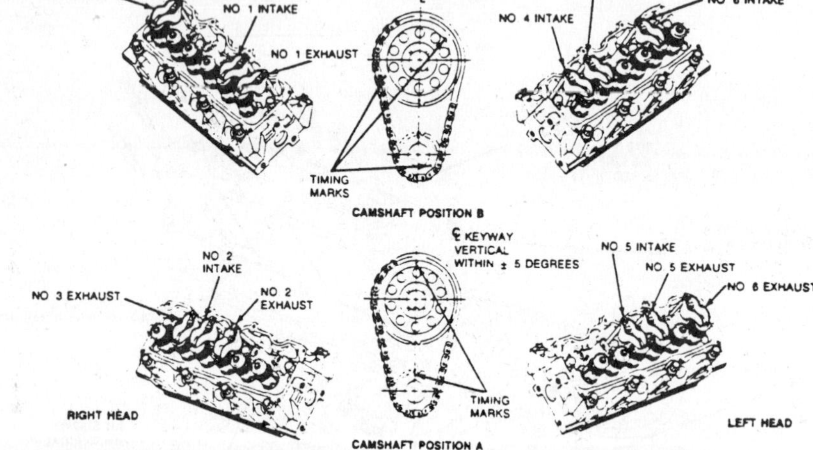

CYL. NO.	CAMSHAFT POSITION	
	A	B
	SET GAP OF VALVES NOTED	
1	IN*	EX-
2	EX-	IN*
3	NONE	IN*-EX-
4	IN*	EX-
5	EX-	IN*
6	NONE	IN*-EX-

Initial valve adjustment and rocker arm assembly on 3.0L (182 CID) engine

Intake Manifold

REMOVAL & INSTALLATION

2.3L (140 CID) Engine

The intake manifold is a two-piece (upper and lower) aluminum casting. Runner lengths are tuned to optimize engine torque and power output. The manifold provides mounting flanges for the air throttle body assembly, fuel supply manifold, accelerator control bracket and the EGR valve and supply tube. A vacuum fitting is installed to provide vacuum to various engine accessories. Pockets for the fuel injectors are machined to prevent both air and fuel leakage. The following procedure is for the removal of the intake manifold with the fuel charging assembly attached.

1. Make sure the ignition is off, then drain the coolant from the radiator (engine cold).

CAUTION

When draining the coolant, keep in mind that cats and dogs are attracted by the ethylene glycol antifreeze, and are quite likely to drink any that is left in an uncovered container or in puddles on the ground. This will prove fatal in sufficient quantity. Always drain the coolant into a sealable container. Coolant should be reused unless it is contaminated or several years old.

2. Disconnect the negative battery cable and secure it out of the way.

3. Remove the fuel filler cap to vent tank pressure. Release the pressure from the fuel system at the fuel pressure relief valve using EFI pressure gauge T80L-9974-A or equivalent. The fuel pressure relief valve is located on the fuel line in the upper right hand corner of the engine compartment. Remove the valve cap to gain access to the valve.

4. Disconnect the electrical connectors at the throttle position sensor, knock sensor, injector wiring harness, air charge temperature sensor and engine coolant temperature sensor.

5. Tag and disconnect the vacuum lines at the upper intake manifold vacuum tree, at the EGR valve and at the fuel pressure regulator.

6. Remove the throttle linkage shield and disconnect the throttle linkage and speed control cable (if equipped). Unbolt the accelerator cable from the bracket and position the cable out of the way.

7. Disconnect the air intake hose, air bypass hose and crankcase vent hose.

8. Disconnect the PCV hose from the fitting on the underside of the upper intake manifold.

9. Loosen the clamp on the coolant bypass line at the lower intake manifold and disconnect the hose.

10. Disconnect the EGR tube from the EGR valve by removing the flange nut.

11. Remove the four upper intake manifold retaining nuts. Remove the upper intake manifold and air throttle body assembly.

12. Disconnect the push connect fit-

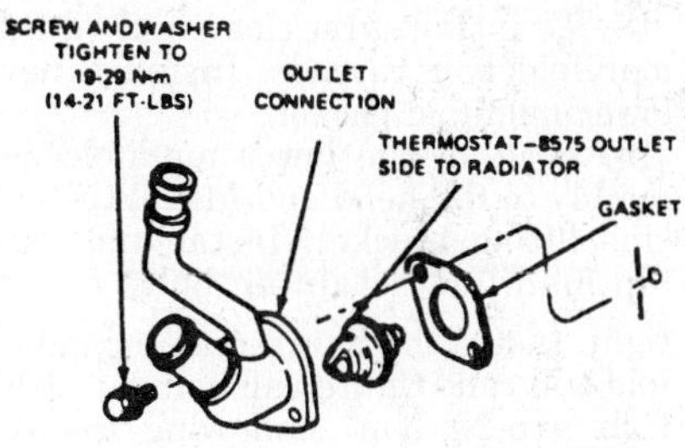

Thermostat housing on 2.3L (140 CID) engine

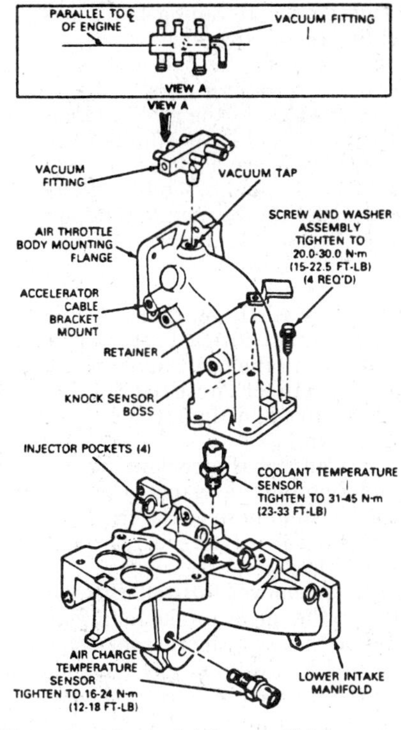

Upper and lower intake manifold assemblies on 2.3L (140 CID) engine

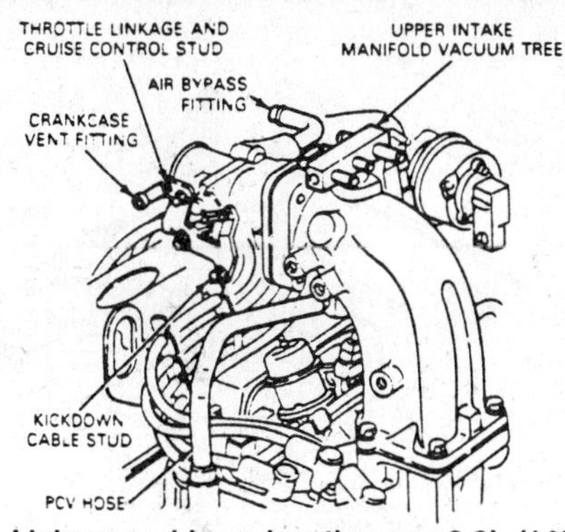

Linkage and hose locations on 2.3L (140 CID) engine

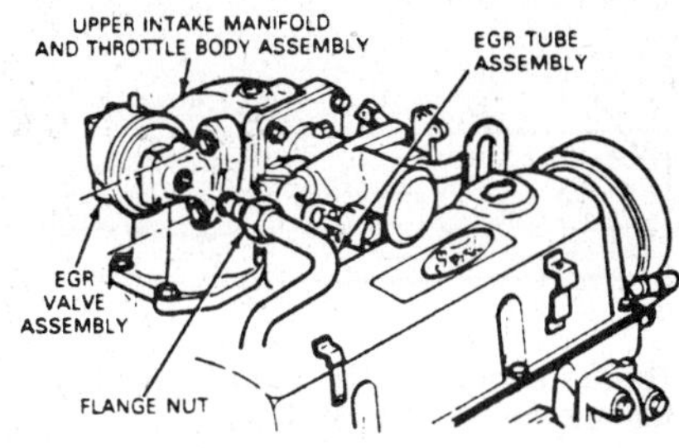

Disconnecting EGR valve on 2.3L (140 CID) engine

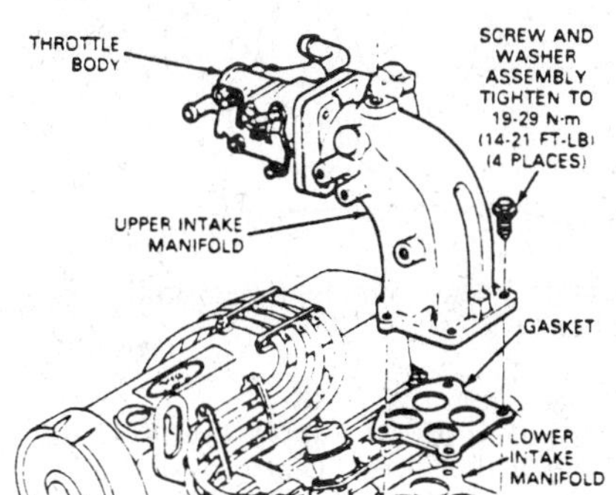

Removing the upper intake manifold on 2.3L (104 CID) engine

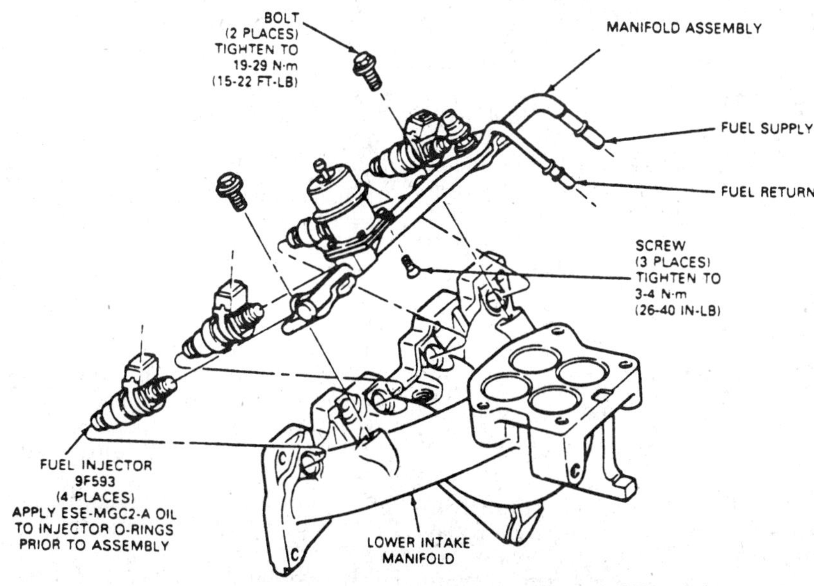

Fuel supply manifold and injector mounting on 2.3L (140 CID) engine

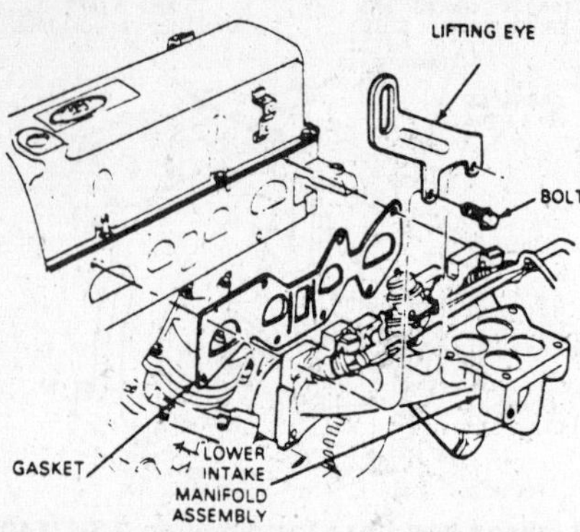

Removing lower intake manifold on 2.3L (140 CID) engine

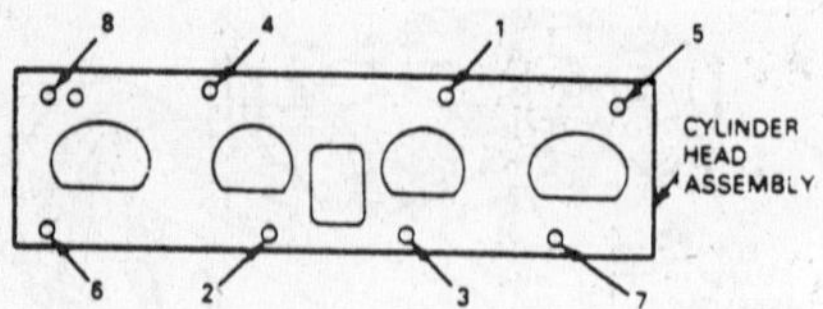

Torque sequence for lower intake manifold attaching bolts

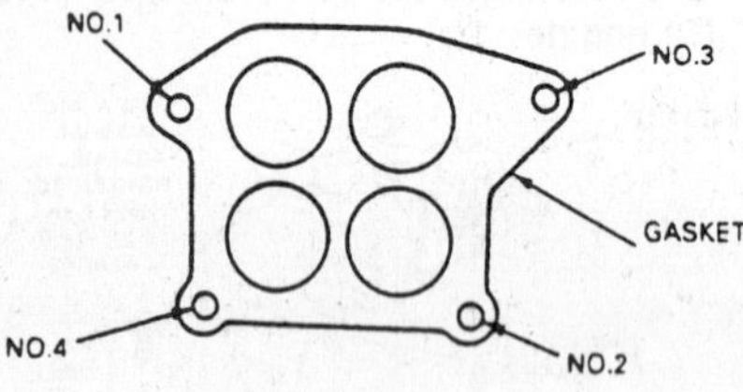

Upper intake manifold bolt torque sequence

ting at the fuel supply manifold and fuel return lines. Disconnect the fuel return line from the fuel supply manifold.

13. Remove the engine oil dipstick bracket retaining bolt.

14. Disconnect the electrical connectors from all four fuel injectors and move the harness aside.

15. Remove the two fuel supply manifold retaining bolts, then carefully remove the fuel supply manifold and injectors. Remove the injectors by exerting a slight twisting/pulling motion.

16. Remove the four bottom retaining bolts from the lower manifold. The front two bolts also secure an engine lifting bracket. Once the bolts are removed, remove the lower intake manifold.

17. Clean and inspect the mounting faces of the lower intake manifold and cylinder head. Both surfaces must be clean and flat.

NOTE: If the intake manifold upper or lower section is being replaced, it will be necessary to transfer components from the old to the new part.

18. To install, first clean and oil the manifold bolt threads. Install a new lower manifold gasket.

19. Position the lower manifold assembly to the head and install the engine lifting bracket. Install the four top manifold retaining bolts finger tight. Install the four remaining manifold bolts and tighten all bolts to 12-15 ft.lb. (16-20 Nm), following the sequence illustrated.

20. Install the fuel supply manifold and injectors with two retaining bolts. Tighten the retaining bolts to 12-15 ft.lb. (16-20 Nm).

21. Connect the four electrical connectors to the injectors.

22. Make sure the gasket surfaces of the upper and lower intake manifolds are clean. Place a gasket on the lower intake manifold assembly, then place the upper intake manifold in position.

23. Install the four retaining bolts and tighten in sequence to 15-22 ft.lb. (20-30 Nm).

24. Install the engine oil dipstick, then connect the fuel return and supply lines to the fuel supply manifold.

25. Connect the EGR tube to the EGR valve and tighten it to 6-9 ft.lb. (8-12 Nm).

26. Connect the coolant bypass line and tighten the clamp. Connect the PCV system hose to the fitting on the underside of the upper intake manifold.

27. If removed, install the vacuum tee on the upper intake manifold. Use Teflon® tape on the threads and tighten to 12-18 ft.lb. (16-24 Nm). Reconnect the vacuum lines to the tee, the EGR valve and the fuel pressure regulator.

28. Hold the accelerator cable bracket in position on the upper intake manifold and install the retaining bolt. Tighten the bolt to 10-15 ft.lb. (13-20 Nm).

29. Install the accelerator cable to the bracket.

30. Position a new gasket on the fuel charging assembly air throttle body mounting flange. Install the air throttle body to the fuel charging assembly. Install two retaining nuts and two bolts and tighten to 12-15 ft.lb. (16-20 Nm).

31. Connect the accelerator and speed control cable (if equipped), then install the throttle linkage shield.

32. Reconnect the throttle position sensor, injector wiring harness, knock sensor, air charge temperature sensor and engine coolant temperature sensor.

33. Connect the air intake hose, air bypass hose and crankcase ventilation hose.

34. Reconnect the negative battery cable. Refill the cooling system to specifications and pressurize the fuel system by turning the ignition switch on and off (without starting the engine) at least six times, leaving the ignition on for at least five seconds each time.

35. Start the engine and let it idle while checking for fuel, coolant and vacuum leaks. Correct as necessary.

2.8L (171 CID) Engine

1. Disconnect the negative battery cable.
2. Remove the air cleaner assembly.
3. Disconnect the throttle transmission cable and remove the bracket from the left cylinder head.
4. Drain the cooling system (engine cold), then disconnect and remove the hose from the water outlet to the radiator and bypass hose from the intake manifold to thermostat housing rear cover.

CAUTION

When draining the coolant, keep in mind that cats and dogs are attracted by the ethylene glycol antifreeze, and are quite likely to drink any that is left in an uncovered container or in puddles on the ground. This will prove fatal in sufficient quantity. Always drain the coolant into a sealable container. Coolant should be reused unless it is contaminated or several years old.

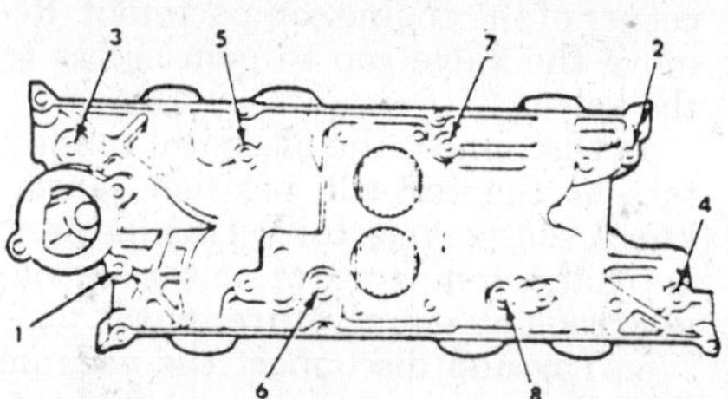

Intake manifold torque sequence on 2.8L (171 CID) engine

5. Remove the distributor cap and spark plug wires as an assembly. Disconnect the distributor wiring harness.
6. Observe and mark the location of the distributor rotor and housing so ignition timing can be maintained at reassembly. Remove the distributor hold down screw and clamp and lift out the distributor.
7. Remove the rocker arm covers as outlined previously.
8. Remove the fuel line from the fuel filter.
9. Remove the carburetor and EGR spacer.
10. Remove the intake manifold attaching bolts and nuts. Note the length of the manifold attaching bolts during removal so that they may be installed in their original positions. Tap the manifold lightly with a plastic mal-

let to break the gasket seal, then lift off the manifold.

11. Remove all traces of old gasket material and sealing compound from all gasket mating surfaces. Be careful not to scratch the intake manifold or cylinder head mating surfaces.

12. To install the intake manifold; first apply sealing compound to the joining surfaces. Place the intake manifold gasket in position, making sure that the tab on the right bank cylinder head gasket fits into the cutout on the manifold gasket.

13. Apply sealing compound to the attaching bolt bosses on the intake manifold and position the intake manifold on the engine. Follow the illustrated torque sequence and tighten the manifold mounting bolts in five steps:

a. install bolts finger tight

b. torque each to 3-6 ft.lb. (4-8 Nm)

c. torque each to 6-11 ft.lb. (8-15 Nm)

d. torque each to 11-15 ft.lb. (15-21 Nm)

e. torque each to 15-18 ft.lb. (21-25 Nm)

14. Install the distributor so that the rotor and housing are in the same position marked at removal.

15. Install distributor clamp and attaching bolt and connect the distributor wire.

16. Install the EGR spacer and carburetor.

17. Install the fuel line.

18. Replace the rocker arm cover gaskets and install rocker arm valve covers.

19. Install the distributor cap. Coat the inside of each spark plug wire connector with silicone grease with a small screwdriver, then install the wires to the plugs. Connect the distributor wiring harness.

20. Install and adjust the throttle bracket and linkage.

21. Install the air cleaner and air cleaner tube at the carburetor.

22. Connect the negative battery cable.

23. Connect the hoses from the water outlet to the radiator and bypass hose from the thermostat housing rear cover to the intake manifold.

24. Refill and bleed the cooling system, check the ignition timing and idle speed and reset to specifications if necessary. Run the engine at fast idle and check for coolant or oil leaks.

3.0L (182 CID) Engine

1. Drain the cooling system (engine cold).

CAUTION

When draining the coolant, keep in mind that cats and dogs are attracted by the ethylene glycol antifreeze, and are quite likely to drink any that is left in an uncovered container or in puddles on the ground. This will prove fatal in sufficient quantity. Always drain the coolant into a sealable container. Coolant should be reused unless it is contaminated or several years old.

2. Disconnect the battery ground cable.

3. Depressurize the fuel system and remove the air intake throttle body.

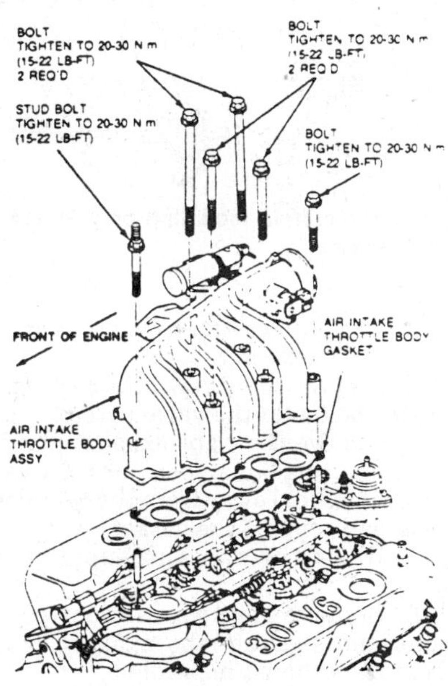

Removing the air intake throttle body on 3.0L (182 CID) engine

4. Disconnect the fuel return and supply lines.

5. Remove the fuel injector wiring harness from the engine.

6. Disconnect the upper radiator hose.

7. Disconnect the water outlet heater hose.

8. Disconnect the distributor cap with the spark plug wires attached. Matchmark and remove the distributor assembly.

9. Remove the intake manifold attaching bolts and studs.

10. Lift the intake manifold off the engine. Use a plastic mallet to tap lightly around the intake manifold to break it loose, if necessary. Do not pry between the manifold and cylinder head with any sharp instrument. The manifold can be removed with the fuel rails and injectors in place.

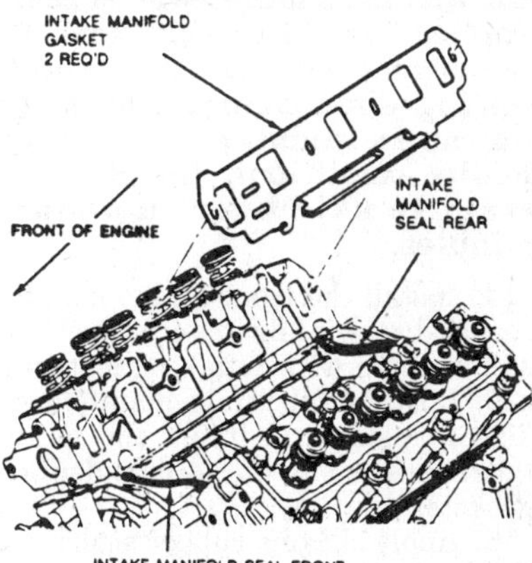

Installing intake manifold gaskets on 3.0L (182 CID) engine

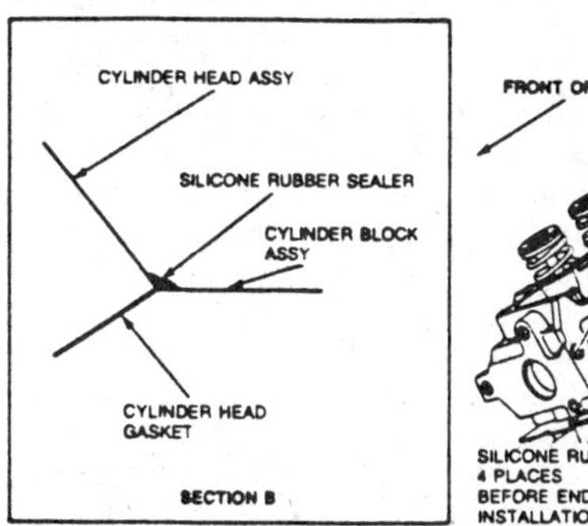

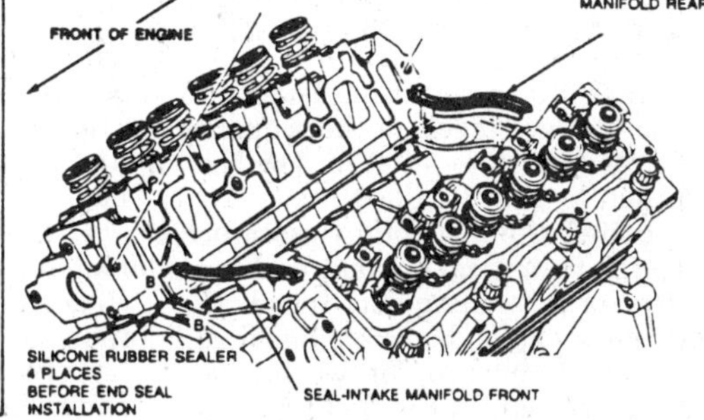

Apply silicone sealer as shown on 3.0L (182 CID) engine

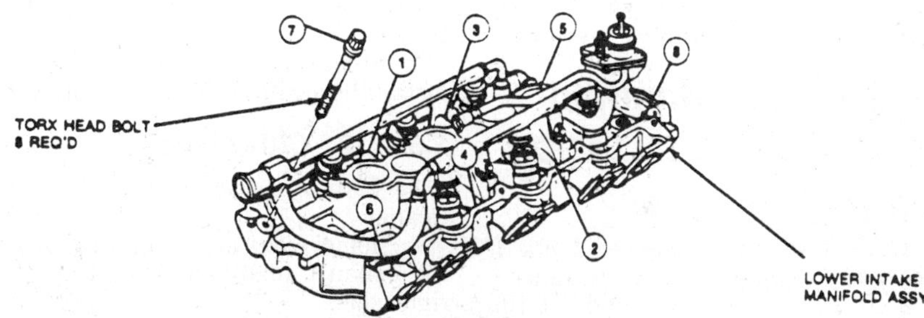

Intake manifold torque sequence on 3.0L (182 CID) engine

11. Remove the manifold side gaskets and end seals and discard. If the manifold is being replaced, transfer the fuel injector and fuel rail components to the new manifold on a clean workbench. Clean all gasket mating surfaces.

12. To install the intake manifold, first lightly oil all attaching bolts and stud threads. The intake manifold, cylinder head and cylinder block mating surfaces should be clean and free of old silicone rubber sealer. Use a suitable solvent to clean these areas.

13. Apply silicone rubber sealer (D6AZ-19562-A or equivalent) to the intersection of the cylinder block assembly and head assembly at four corners as illustrated.

NOTE: When using silicone rubber sealer, assembly must occur within 15 minutes after sealer application. After this time, the sealer may start to set-up and its sealing effectiveness may be reduced. In high temperature/humidity conditions, the RTV will start to skin over in about 5 minutes.

14. Install the front intake manifold seal and rear intake manifold seal and secure them with retaining features.

15. Position the intake manifold gaskets in place and insert the locking tabs over the tabs on the cylinder head gaskets.

16. Apply silicone rubber sealer over the gasket in the same places as in Step 13.

17. Carefully lower the intake manifold into position on the cylinder block and cylinder heads to prevent smearing the silicone sealer and causing gasketing voids.

18. Install the retaining bolts and tighten in two stages, in the sequence illustrated, first to 11 ft.lb. (15 Nm) and then to 18 ft.lb. (24 Nm).

19. Install the distributor assembly, using the matchmarks make earlier to insure correct alignment. Install the distributor cap and spark plug wires.

20. Install the injector wiring harness and reconnect the fuel lines.

21. Install the air intake throttle body.

22. Reconnect the negative battery cable and refill the cooling system.

Exhaust Manifold

REMOVAL & INSTALLATION

2.3L (140 CID) Engine

1. Remove the air cleaner ducts, if necessary to gain working clearance.

2. Disconnect the EGR line at the exhaust manifold and loosen it at the EGR tube.

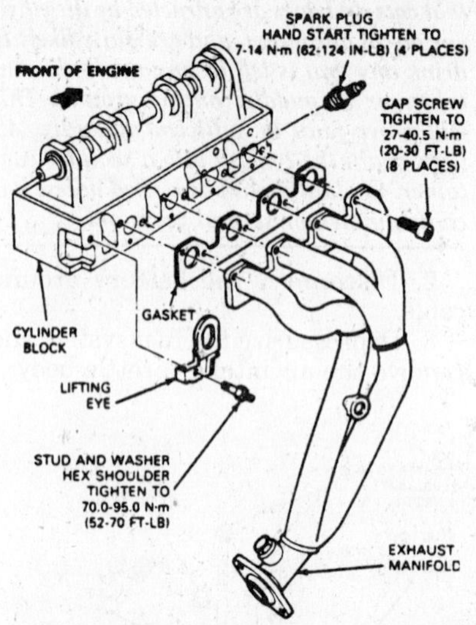

Exhaust manifold mounting on 2.3L (140 CID) engine

3. Disconnect the oxygen sensor electrical connector.

4. Remove the screw attaching the heater hoses on the valve cover.

5. Remove the eight exhaust manifold mounting bolts, then move the exhaust manifold away from the cylinder head and remove the gasket.

6. Raise the van and support it safely.

7. Remove the two exhaust pipe bolts and separate the exhaust pipe from the exhaust manifold.

8. Carefully lower the exhaust manifold down and out of the engine compartment. Be careful not to damage the oxygen sensor during removal.

9. Clean all gasket mating surfaces. If the exhaust manifold is being replaced, the oxygen sensor will have to be transferred to the new manifold.

10. Place a new gasket on the exhaust manifold, then position the manifold on the cylinder head.

11. Install the eight exhaust manifold bolts and tighten them in two stages, first to 5-7 ft.lb. (7-9 Nm) and then to 16-23 ft.lb. (22-31 Nm).

12. Install the two exhaust pipe bolts and tighten them to 25-34 ft.lb. (34-46 Nm).

13. Install the EGR line at the exhaust manifold and tighten the EGR tube.

14. Reconnect the oxygen sensor and install the air intake ducts, if removed.

2.8L (171 CID) Engine

1. Remove the carburetor air cleaner.

2. Remove the attaching nuts from the exhaust manifold shroud on the right side.

3. Raise the van and support it safely.

4. Working under the van, disconnect the attaching nuts from the Y-pipe. Remove the thermactor upstream crossover tube and other thermactor components as necessary to allow removal of exhaust manifold(s).

5. Disconnect the exhaust gas oxygen sensor connector on the left exhaust manifold.

6. Remove the manifold attaching nuts.

7. Lift the manifold from the cylinder head, then remove the manifold to head gaskets.

8. Clean all gasket mating surfaces. If the left exhaust manifold is being replaced, the oxygen sensor will have to be transferred to the new part.

9. Position the new gasket and the manifold on the studs and install and tighten the attaching bolts to 20-30 ft.lb. (27-37 Nm). Start at the center and work outward, alternating sides during the torque sequence.

10. Install a new inlet pipe gasket, then install and tighten the inlet pipe attaching bolts to 25-34 ft.lb. (34-36 Nm).

11. Position the exhaust manifold shroud on the manifold and install and tighten the attaching nuts.

12. Install the thermactor components that were removed to gain working clearance, then lower the van.

13. Install the carburetor air cleaner.

14. Connect the oxygen sensor wire on the left hand exhaust manifold.

3.0L (182 CID) Engine

1. Remove the air cleaner assembly, if necessary to gain working clearance.

2. Remove the oil level indicator tube support bracket. Remove the power steering pump pressure and return hoses if the left hand manifold is being removed. If the right hand manifold is being removed, disconnect the EGR tube from the exhaust manifold and the oxygen sensor connector.

3. Raise the vehicle and support it safely.

4. Remove the manifold to exhaust pipe attaching nuts, then separate the exhaust pipe from the manifold.

5. Remove the exhaust manifold attaching bolts and the manifold.

6. Clean all gasket mating surfaces.

7. Lightly oil all bolt and stud threads before installation. If a new manifold is being installed, the oxygen sensor will have to be transferred to the new part.

8. Position the exhaust manifold on the cylinder head and install the manifold attaching bolts. Tighten them to 15-22 ft.lb. (20-30 Nm).

9. Connect the exhaust pipe to the manifold, then tighten the attaching

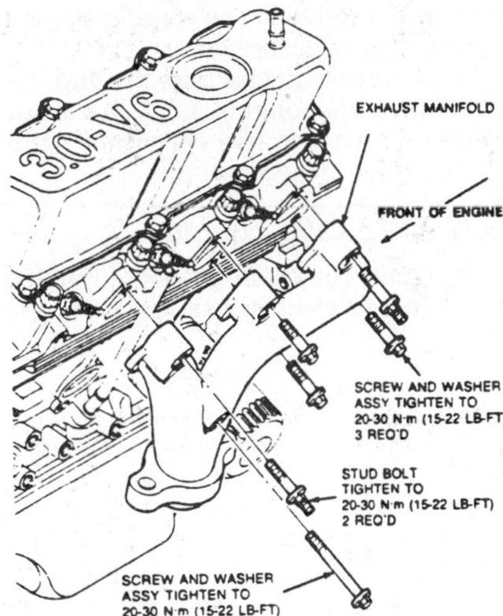

LH exhaust manifold on 3.0L (182 CID) engine

nuts to 16-24 ft.lb. (21-32 Nm). Lower the vehicle.

10. Connect the power steering pump pressure and return hoses.

11. Install the oil level indicator tube support bracket.

Air Conditioning Compressor

REMOVAL & INSTALLATION

Follow the procedures outlined in ROUTINE MAINTENANCE to discharge the A/C system. Loosen the compressor mounting bolts and remove the drive belt. Disconnect the refrigerant lines and cap them to prevent the entry of dirt or moisture into the system. Remove the mounting bolts and lift the compressor off the engine. Installation is the reverse of removal. Recharge the A/C system as outlined in ROUTINE MAINTENANCE and adjust the drive belt tension.

Cylinder Head

REMOVAL & INSTALLATION

2.3L (140 CID) Engine

1. Drain the cooling system (engine cold) into a clean container and save the coolant for reuse.

CAUTION

When draining the coolant, keep in mind that cats and dogs are attracted by the ethylene glycol antifreeze, and are quite likely to drink any that is left in an uncovered container or in puddles on the ground. This will prove fatal in sufficient quantity. Always drain the coolant into a sealable container. Coolant should be reused unless it is contaminated or several years old.

2. Raise the vehicle and support it safely on jackstands.
3. Remove the resonator assembly.
4. Lower the vehicle.
5. Disconnect the distributor cap and spark plug wires from the plugs, then remove the cap and spark plug wires as an assembly.
6. Remove the spark plugs.
7. Tag and disconnect all vacuum hoses.
8. Remove the dipstick and tube from the engine.
9. Remove the rocker arm cover retaining bolts and lift off the cover.
10. Remove the intake manifold retaining bolts.
11. Loosen the alternator retaining bolts, remove the belt from the pulley and remove the mounting bracket retaining bolts from the head.
12. Disconnect the upper radiator hose at both ends and remove it from the engine compartment.
13. Remove the cam belt cover mounting bolts. If equipped with power steering, remove the power steering pump bracket.
14. Loosen the cam idler retaining bolts. Position the idler in the unloaded position and tighten the retaining bolts.
15. Remove the cam belt from the cam pulley and auxiliary pulley.
16. Remove the eight exhaust manifold retaining bolts.
17. Remove the cam belt idler and two bracket bolts.
18. Remove the cam belt idler spring stop from the cylinder head.
19. Disconnect the oil sending unit lead wire.
20. Remove the cylinder head retaining bolts in reverse of the tightening sequence.
21. Carefully lift the cylinder head off the engine. Refer to the following procedures for cylinder head component removal, valve replacement, resurfacing, etc.
22. Clean the cylinder head gasket surface at the block.
23. Clean the intake manifold gasket surface at the intake manifold and the exhaust manifold gasket surface at the exhaust manifold and cylinder head.
24. Clean the cylinder head gasket surface at the cylinder head and the intake manifold gasket surface at the cylinder head.
25. Blow oil out of the cylinder head bolt block holes with compressed air.
26. Clean the rocker cover gasket surface on the cylinder head and check the head for flatness.
27. To install the cylinder head, first

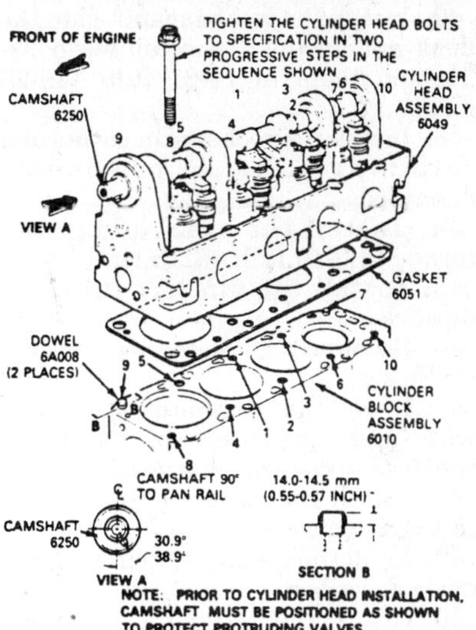

Cylinder head installation on 2.3L (140 CID) engine

position the head gasket on the block, then carefully lower the cylinder head down into place. See the illustration to make sure the camshaft is positioned correctly to protect the valves when installing the cylinder head.

28. Install the cylinder head retaining bolts and tighten them in sequence first to 50-60 ft.lb. (68-81 Nm) and then to 80-90 ft.lb. (108-122 Nm).
29. Connect the oil sending unit lead wires.
30. Install the cam belt idler spring stop to the cylinder head.
31. Position the cam belt idler to the cylinder head and install the retaining bolts.
32. Install the eight exhaust manifold retaining bolts.
33. Align the distributor rotor with the No. 1 plug location in the distributor cap.
34. Align the camshaft gear with the pointer.
35. Align the crankshaft pulley TDC mark with the pointer on the cam belt cover.
36. Install the cam belt to the pulleys (cam and auxiliary).
37. Loosen the idler retaining bolts and allow it to tension the cam belt, then rotate the engine by hand and check the timing alignment.
38. Adjust the belt tensioner and tighten the retaining bolts. Install the cam belt cover and tighten the retaining bolts.
39. Connect the upper radiator hose to the engine and radiator and tighten the retaining clamps.
40. Position the alternator bracket to the cylinder head and install the retainers.
41. Install the drive belt to the pulleys and adjust the belt tension.

42. Install the intake manifold to the head and install the retaining bolts. Tighten them to 14-21 ft.lb. (19-28 Nm).
43. Install the rocker arm covers and retaining bolts, as previously described.
44. Install the spark plugs and torque to 5-10 ft.lb. (7-13 Nm).
45. Install the dipstick tube and dipstick.
46. Reconnect all disconnected vacuum hoses.
47. Install the distributor, spark plug wires and distributor cap. Reconnect the distributor wire harness.
48. Install the heater hose retainer to the valve cover.
49. Refill the cooling system as previously described.
50. Install the resonator assembly, then start the engine and check for leaks. Adjust the ignition timing and idle speed, if necessary.

2.8L (171 CID) Engine

1. Disconnect the battery ground cable.
2. Drain the cooling system (engine cold) into a clean container and save the coolant for reuse.

CAUTION

When draining the coolant, keep in mind that cats and dogs are attracted by the ethylene glycol antifreeze, and are quite likely to drink any that is left in an uncovered container or in puddles on the ground. This will prove fatal in sufficient quantity. Always drain the coolant into a sealable container. Coolant should be reused unless it is contaminated or several years old.

3. Remove the air cleaner from the carburetor and disconnect the throttle linkage. Remove the linkage bracket.
4. Remove the distributor cap and wires as an assembly. Disconnect the distributor wiring harness.
5. Matchmark the location of the distributor rotor and housing so the ignition timing can be maintained at reassembly. Remove the distributor hold down screw and clamp, then lift out the distributor. Note the rotor movement as the distributor is installed so it may be positioned correctly on installation.
6. Remove the radiator and bypass hoses from the thermostat and intake manifold.
7. Remove the rocker arm covers and rocker arm shafts as previously described.
8. Disconnect the fuel line from the carburetor and remove the carburetor.
9. Remove the intake manifold as previously described.
10. Remove the pushrods, keeping them in order so they may be installed in their original locations.

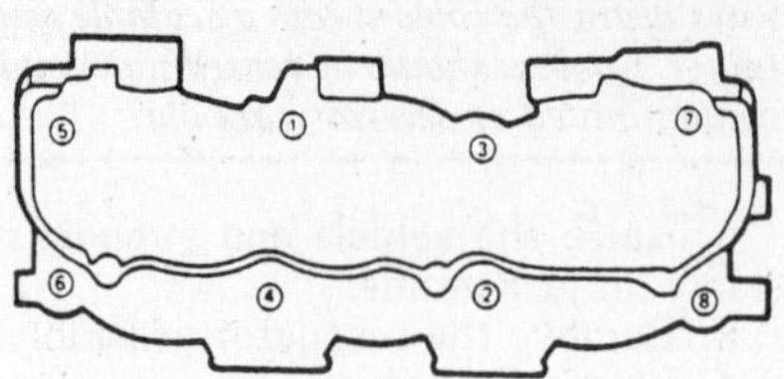

Cylinder head bolt torque sequence on 2.8L (140 CID) engine

11. Remove the exhaust manifold(s) as previously described.
12. Loosen the cylinder head attaching bolts in reverse of the torque sequence, the remove the bolts and lift off the cylinder head. Remove and discard the head gasket. Refer to the following procedures for cylinder head component removal, valve replacement, resurfacing, etc.
13. Clean the cylinder heads, intake manifold, valve rocker arm cover and cylinder block gasket surfaces of all traces of old gasket material and/or sealer.
14. Place the cylinder head gasket(s) in position on the cylinder block. Gaskets are marked with the words **Front** and **Top** for correct positioning. Left and right head gaskets are NOT interchangeable.
15. Install fabricated alignment dowels (head bolts with the heads cut off) in the cylinder block and install the cylinder head assembly.
16. Remove the alignment dowels and install the cylinder head attaching bolts. Tighten the bolts in sequence, in three stages:
   a. Step 1 to 29-40 ft.lb. (39-54 Nm)
   b. Step 2 to 40-51 ft.lb. (54-69 Nm)
   c. Step 3 to 70-85 ft.lb. (95-115 Nm)
17. Install the intake and exhaust manifolds as previously described.
18. Apply heavy SF engine oil to both ends of the pushrods and install the pushrods. Install the oil baffles and rocker arms.
19. Install the distributor using the matchmarks made earlier to insure correct rotor alignment. Install the distributor wiring harness and vacuum hose, then install the holddown clamp and bolt and tighten.
20. Adjust the valve clearance, then install the rocker arm covers.
21. Install the carburetor and reconnect the fuel line.
22. Install the distributor cap and spark plug wires. Coat the inside of each plug wire with silicone lubricant before installing them on the spark plugs.
23. Install the throttle linkage, bracket and air cleaner.
24. Fill and bleed the cooling system as previously described.
25. Connect the battery ground cable, start the engine and check for leaks. Adjust the idle speed and ignition timing, if necessary.

3.0L (182 CID) Engine

1. Drain the cooling system (engine cold) into a clean container and save the coolant for reuse.

CAUTION

When draining the coolant, keep in mind that cats and dogs are attracted by the ethylene glycol antifreeze, and are quite likely to drink any that is left in an uncovered container or in puddles on the ground. This will prove fatal in sufficient quantity. Always drain the coolant into a sealable container. Coolant should be reused unless it is contaminated or several years old.

2. Disconnect the battery ground cable.
3. Remove the air cleaner and intake manifold as previously described.
4. Loosen the accessory drive belt idler and remove the belt.
5. If the left hand cylinder head is being removed, remove the alternator adjusting arm. If the right hand head is being removed, remove the accessory belt idler.
6. If equipped with power steering, remove the pump mounting bracket attaching bolts. Leaving the hoses connected, place the pump/bracket assembly aside in a position to prevent the fluid from leaking out. Secure the pump with wire or string during service.
7. If the left hand head is being removed, remove the coil bracket and dipstick tube. If the right hand cylinder head is being removed, remove the ground strap and throttle cable support bracket.
8. Remove the exhaust manifold(s), PCV valve and rocker arm covers as previously described.
9. Loosen the rocker arm fulcrum attaching bolts enough to allow the rocker arm to lifted off the pushrod and rotated to one side. Remove the pushrods, keeping them in order so they may be installed in their original locations.
10. Loosen the cylinder head attaching bolts in reverse of the torque sequence, then remove the bolts and lift off the cylinder head(s). Remove and discard the old cylinder head gasket(s).
11. Clean the cylinder heads, intake manifold, valve rocker arm cover and cylinder block gasket surfaces of all traces of old gasket material and/or sealer. Refer to the following overhaul procedures for cylinder head component removal, valve replacement, resurfacing, etc.

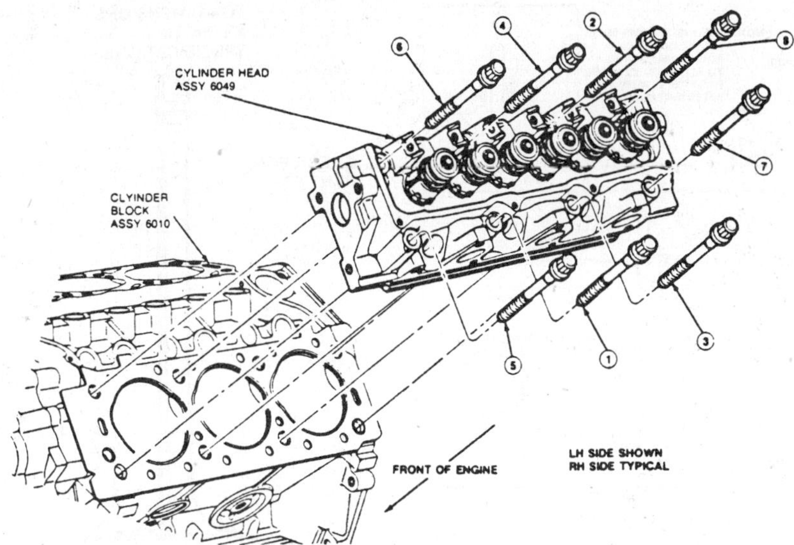

Cylinder head bolt torque sequence on 3.0L (182 CID) engine

12. To install the cylinder head, first lightly oil all bolt and stud bolt threads except those specifying special sealant. Position the new head gasket(s) on the cylinder block, using the dowels for alignment. The dowels should be replaced if damaged.

13. Position the cylinder head(s) on the block and install the attaching bolts. Tighten the head bolts in sequence, in two stages; first to 48-54 ft.lb. (65-75 Nm) and then to 63-80 ft.lb. (85-110 Nm).

14. Dip each pushrod in heavy engine oil then install the pushrods in their original locations.

15. For each valve, rotate the crankshaft until the tappet rests on the heel (base circle) of the camshaft lobe before tightening the fulcrum attaching bolts. Position the rocker arms over the pushrods, install the fulcrums and then tighten the fulcrum attaching bolts to 19-29 ft.lb. (26-38 Nm).

CAUTION

Fulcrums must be fully seated in the cylinder head and pushrods must be seated in the rocker arm sockets prior to final tightening.

16. Lubricate all rocker arm assemblies with heavy engine oil. If the original valve train components are being installed, a valve clearance check is not required. If, however, a component has been replaced, the valve clearance should be checked.

17. Install the exhaust manifold(s) and the dipstick tube.

18. Install the intake manifold as previously described.

19. Position the rocker arm cover with a new gasket on the cylinder head and install the retaining bolts. Note the location of the spark plug wire routing clip stud bolts.

20. Install the spark plugs, if removed.

21. Install the distributor, cap and spark plug wires.

22. Install the oil filler cap and, if equipped with power steering, install the pump mounting and support brackets.

23. Install the PCV valve and the throttle body.

24. Install the alternator bracket and tighten the attaching nuts to 30-40 ft.lb. (40-55 Nm).

25. Install the accessory drive belt and adjust it to specifications. Connect the battery cable and refill the cooling system. Install the air cleaner.

26. Start the engine and check for leaks. If necessary, adjust the transmission throttle linkage and cruise control.

Cylinder Head Overhaul

Service limit specifications are intended to be a guide when overhauling or reconditioning an engine or engine component. A determination can be made whether a component is suitable for continued service or should be replaced for extended service while the engine is disassembled.

In the case of valve stem-to-guide clearance, the service clearance is intended as an aid in diagnosing engine noise only and does not constitute a failure or indicate need for repair. However, when overhauling or reconditioning a cylinder head, the service clearance should be regarded as a practical working value and used as a determinant for installing the next oversize valve to assure extended service life.

Replace the cylinder head if it is cracked. Do not plane or grind more than 0.010" (0.25mm) from the cylinder head gasket original surface. Burrs or scratches should be removed with an oil stone. The cylinder head should be disassembled on a clean workbench, with all parts kept in order so they may be installed in their original locations.

CLEANING

With the valves installed to protect the valve seats, remove carbon deposits from the combustion chambers and valve heads with a wire brush. Be careful not to damage the cylinder head gasket surface. After the valves are removed, clean the valve guide bores with a valve guide cleaning tool using solvent to remove dirt, grease and other deposits. Clean all bolt holes and make sure the oil transfer passage is clean. Remove all deposits from the valves with a fine wire brush or buffing wheel.

INSPECTION

Inspect the cylinder head for cracks or excessively burned areas in the exhaust outlet ports. Check the cylinder head for cracks and inspect the gasket surface for burrs and nicks. Replace the head if any cracks are found. Check the flatness of the cylinder head gasket surface using a feeler gauge and straight edge. Check the flatness at the three points illustrated. The cylinder head must be replaced if warpage exceeds 0.010" (0.25mm).

Measure the valve seat width and reface the valve seat if the width is not within 0.060-0.080" (1.5-2.0mm) for intake and exhaust on V6 engines, or 0.060-0.080" (1.5-2.0mm) for 4-cylinder intake and 0.070-0.090" (1.8-2.3mm) for 4-cylinder exhaust.

Check the valve seat runout with a dial indicator. Follow the dial indicator manufacturer's instructions for installation on the cylinder head and measurement procedure. Seat runout should not exceed 0.0016" (0.04mm) on 2.3L engines; 0.0015" (0.038mm) on 2.8L engines; or 0.003" (0.076mm) on 3.0L engines. If the runout exceeds the service limit, the valve seat will have to be refaced.

Check the valve stem-to-guide clearance of each valve in its respective guide with a dial indicator. Move the valve back and forth in its guide and take a measurement at two axis, 90° apart. If the readings exceed the val-

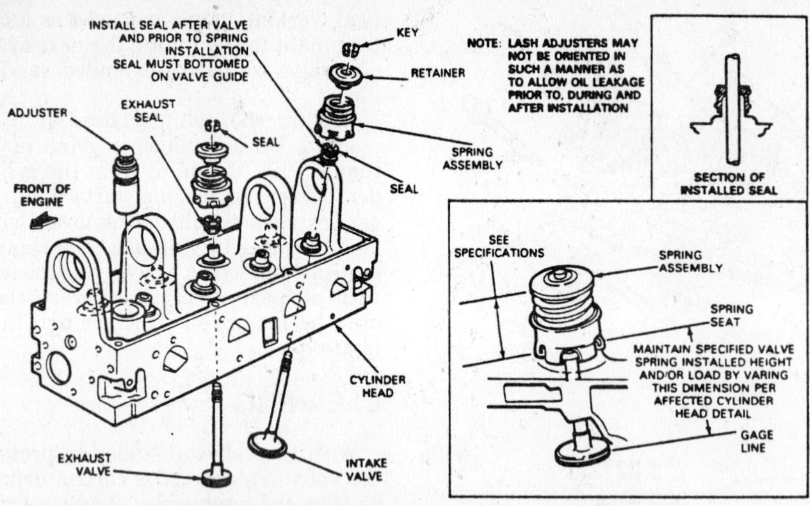

Exploded view of the 2.3L cylinder head assembly

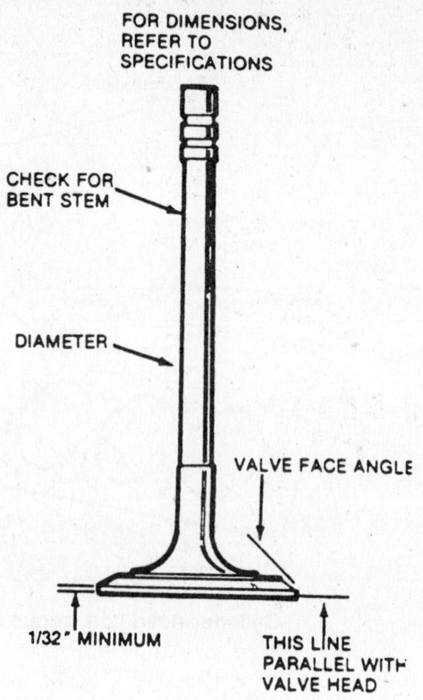

Critical valve dimensions

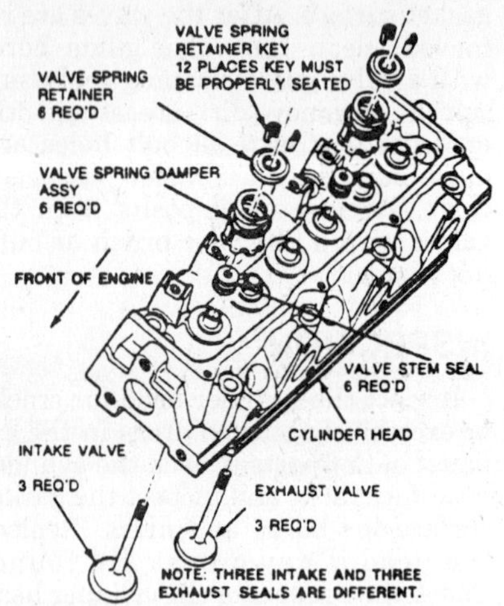

Exploded view of the 3.0L cylinder head assembly

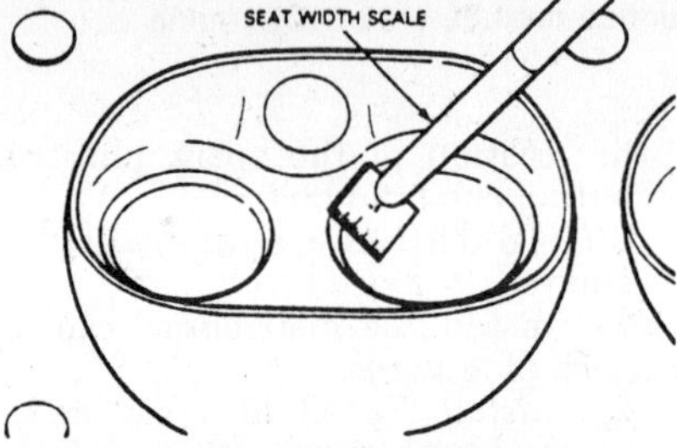

Measuring valve seat width

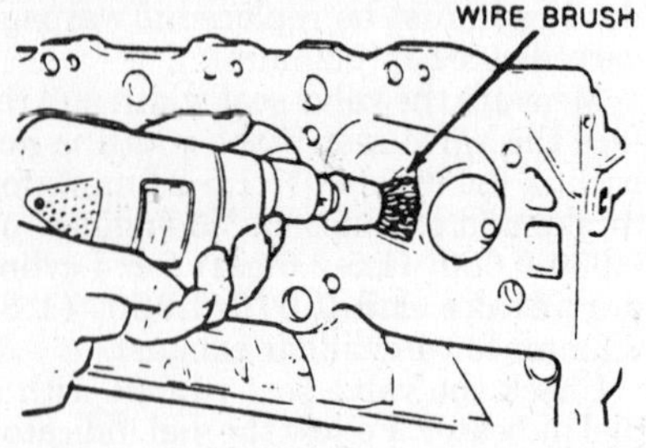

Remove the carbon from the cylinder head with a wire brush and electric drill

Measuring valve seat runout with dial indicator

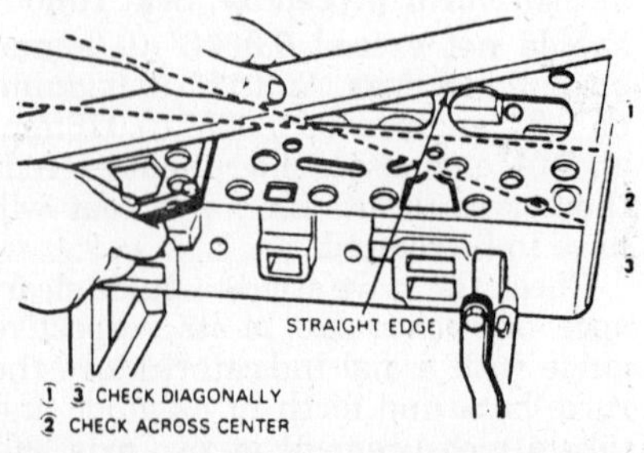

Checking the cylinder head for flatness

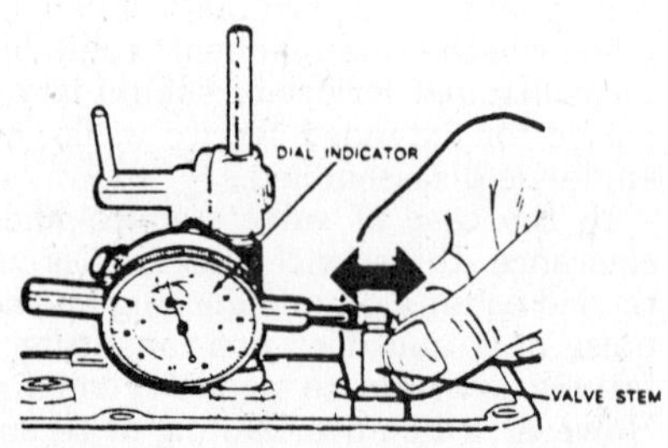

Measuring valve stem-to-guide clearance

ues given in the Engine Specifications chart, the valve guide will have to be reamed to the next oversize valve stem size.

Inspect the valves for minor pits, grooves or scoring. Minor pitting may be removed with an oil stone. Check the valve stem diameter and face angle, as well as any bend in the stem itself. Discard any excessively worn or damaged valve train parts.

Check the valve spring pressure using a suitable tester. If the pressure of any valve spring is lower than the service limits given in the Valve Specifications Chart, replace the spring. Remove the damper by pulling it from the spring and check each spring for squareness using a steel square and a flat surface plate. Stand the spring and square on end on the surface plate, then slide the spring up to the square. Rotate the spring slowly and observe the space between the top coil of the spring and square. If the spring is out of square by more than $^5/_{64}$" (1.984mm), replace the spring. Springs are color-coded for replacement purposes.

NOTE: Make certain the springs are reassembled to their own original dampers by pushing the damper on the spring. Do not open the damper with any kind of tool in order to reassemble.

Clean all parts of the valve rocker arm and/or shaft assembly thoroughly and make sure all oil passages are open. Inspect the shaft and the rocker arm bore for nicks, scratches, scores or

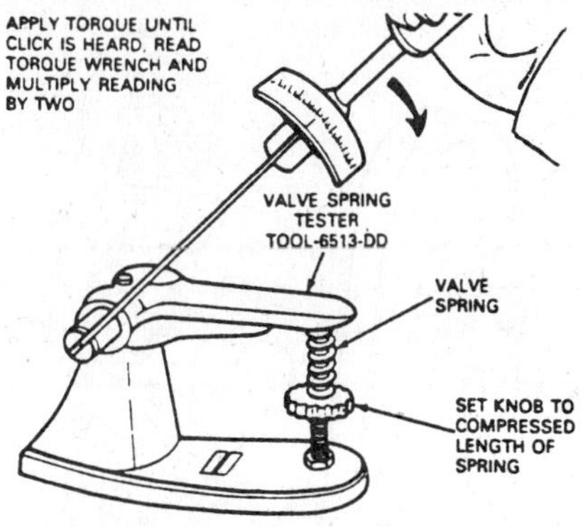

Checking valve spring pressure

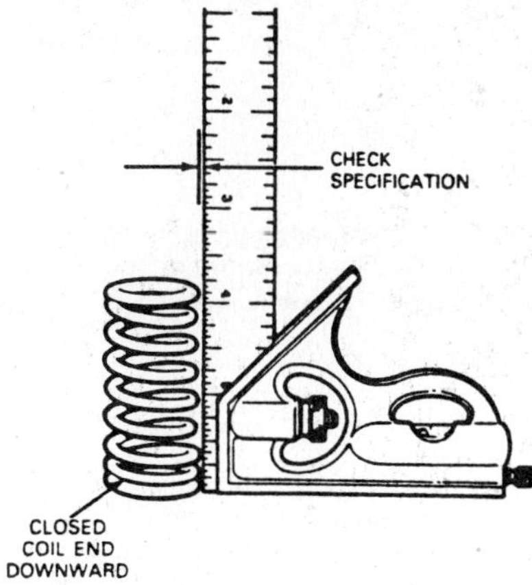

Checking valve spring squareness

scuffs. Replace any damaged components. Inspect the pad at the valve end of the rocker arm for indications of scuffing or abnormal wear. If the pad is grooved, replace the rocker arm. Do not attempt to true this surface by grinding. On pedestal mounted rocker arms, check the rocker arm pad, side rails and fulcrum seat for excessive wear, cracks, nicks or burrs. Check the rocker arm bolt for stripped or broken threads.

Clean the pushrods in suitable solvent and blow out the oil passage in the pushrods with compressed air. Check the ends of the pushrods for nicks, grooves, roughness or excessive wear. Replace any damaged pushrods. Check the pushrods for straightness by rolling them on a flat surface. If any bend is noted, replace the pushrod. Do not attempt to straighten any bent pushrod

RESURFACING

If the cylinder head gasket surface is warped beyond specifications, but not more than 0.010" (0.25mm), it will be necessary to have it trued. All cylinder head grinding should be performed by a qualified machine shop, but in no case should any more than 0.010" (0.25mm) be removed from the gasket surface.

If it becomes necessary to ream a valve guide to install a valve with an oversize stem, a reaming kit is available which contains the following reamer and pilot combinations: 0.015" (0.38mm) OS reamer with 0.003" (0.076mm) OS pilot and a 0.003" (0.76mm) reamer with a 0.015" (0.38mm) OS pilot. When replacing a standard size valve with an oversize valve, always use the reamer in sequence (smallest oversize first, then the next smallest, etc.) so as not to overload the reamers. Always reface the valve seat after the valve guide has been reamed and use a suitable scraper to break the sharp corner at the top ID of the valve guide. Oversize valves are available from the manufacturer.

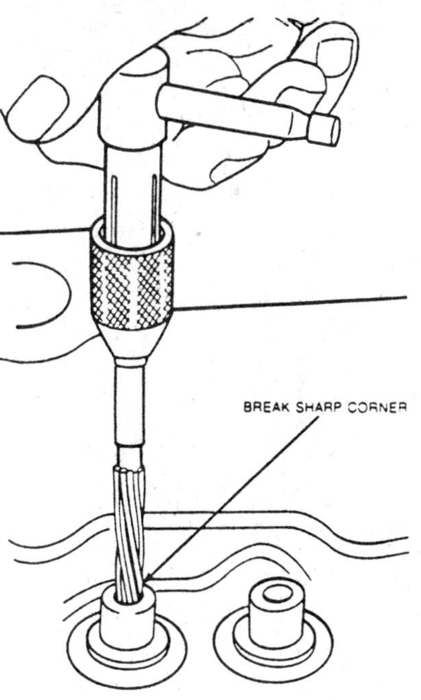

Reaming the valve guide

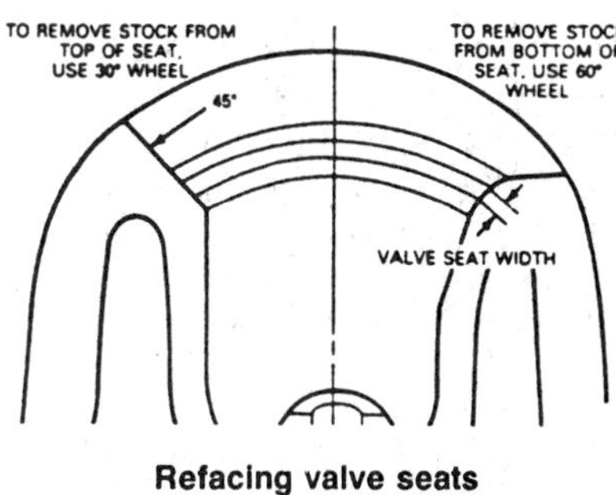

Refacing valve seats

Refacing of the valve seat should be closely coordinated with the refacing of the valve face so that the finished seat and valve face will be concentric and the specified interference angle will be maintained. This is important so that the valve and seat will have a compression-tight fit. Make sure the refacer grinding wheels are properly dressed. Grind the valve seats of all engines to a true 45° angle. Remove only enough stock to clean up pits and grooves or to correct the valve seat runout. After the seat has been refaced, use a seat width scale to measure the seat width. Narrow the seat, if necessary, to bring it within specifications.

On the valve seats of all engines, use a 60° angle grinding wheel to remove stock from the bottom of the seats to raise them, or a 30° angle grinding wheel to remove stock from the top of the seats to lower them. The finished valve seat should contact the approximate center of the valve face. It is good practice to determine where the valve seat contacts the face. To do this, coat the seat with Prussian Blue and set the valve in place. Rotate the valve lightly and remove it to see where the blue contacts the valve. If the blue is transferred to the center of the valve face, contact is satisfactory. If the blue is transferred to the top edge of the valve face, lower the seat. If the blue is transferred to the bottom edge of the valve face, raise the seat.

If the valve face runout is excessive and/or to remove pits and grooves, reface the valve to a true 44° angle. Remove only enough stock to correct the runout or to clean up the pits and grooves. If the edge of the valve head is less than $\frac{1}{32}$" (0.79mm) thick after grinding, replace the valve as it will run too hot in the engine. The interference angle of the valve and seat should not be lapped out. Remove all grooves or score marks from the end of the valve stem and chamfer it as necessary. Do not remove more than 0.010" (0.025mm) from the end of the valve stem. If the valve and/or valve seat has been refaced, it will be necessary to check the clearance between the rocker arm pad and the valve stem with the valve train assembly installed in the engine.

NOTE: The valve stem seals can be replaced without removing the cylinder head, however it requires a special adapter to allow the cylinder to be pressurized to 140 psi in order to keep the valves from falling into the cylinder when the valve springs are removed. Since most of the air compressors available to the do-it-yourselfer do not develope the amount of air pressure necessary to maintain 140 psi, this procedure should be left to a qualified repair shop.

Timing Belt and Cover

REMOVAL & INSTALLATION

2.3L (140 CID) Engine

1. Open the hood and install fender covers. Rotate the engine so that No. 1 cylinder is at TDC on the compression stroke. Check that the timing marks are aligned on the camshaft and crankshaft pulleys. An access plug is provided in the cam belt cover so that the camshaft timing can be checked without removal of the cover or any other parts. Set the crankshaft to TDC by aligning the timing mark on the crank pulley with the TC mark on the belt cover. Look through the access hole in the belt cover to make sure that the timing mark on the cam drive sprocket is lined up with the pointer on the inner belt cover.

NOTE: Always turn the engine in the normal direction of rotation. Backward rotation may cause the timing belt to jump time, due to the arrangement of the belt tensioner.

2. Remove the fan blade and water pump pulley bolts.
3. Loosen the alternator retaining bolts and remove the drive belt from the pulleys. Remove the water pump pulley.
4. Loosen and position the power steering pump mounting bracket and position it aside.
5. Remove the four timing belt outer cover retaining bolts and remove the cover. Remove the crankshaft pulley and belt guide.
6. Loosen the belt tensioner pulley assembly, then position a camshaft belt adjuster tool (T74P-6254-A or equivalent) on the tension spring rollpin and retract the belt tensioner away from the timing belt. Tighten the adjustment bolt to lock the tensioner in the retracted position.
7. Remove the timing belt.
8. Install the new belt over the crankshaft sprocket and then counterclockwise over the auxiliary and camshaft sprockets, making sure the lugs on the belt properly engage the sprocket teeth on the pulleys. Be careful not to rotate the pulleys when installing the belt.
9. Release the timing belt tensioner pulley, allowing the tensioner to take up the belt slack. If the spring does not have enough tension to move the roller against the belt (belt hangs loose), it might be necessary to manually push the roller against the belt and tighten the bolt.

NOTE: The spring cannot be used to set belt tension; a wrench must be used on the tensioner assembly.

10. Rotate the crankshaft two complete turns by hand (in the normal direction of rotation) to remove the slack from the belt, then tighten the tensioner adjustment and pivot bolts to specifications. Make sure the belt is seated properly on the pulleys and that the timing marks are still in alignment when No. 1 cylinder is again at TDC/compression.
11. Install the crankshaft pulley and belt guide.
12. Install the timing belt cover.
13. Install the water pump pulley and fan blades.
14. Position the alternator and drive belts, then adjust and tighten it to specifications.
15. Start the engine and check the ignition timing. Adjust the timing, if necessary.

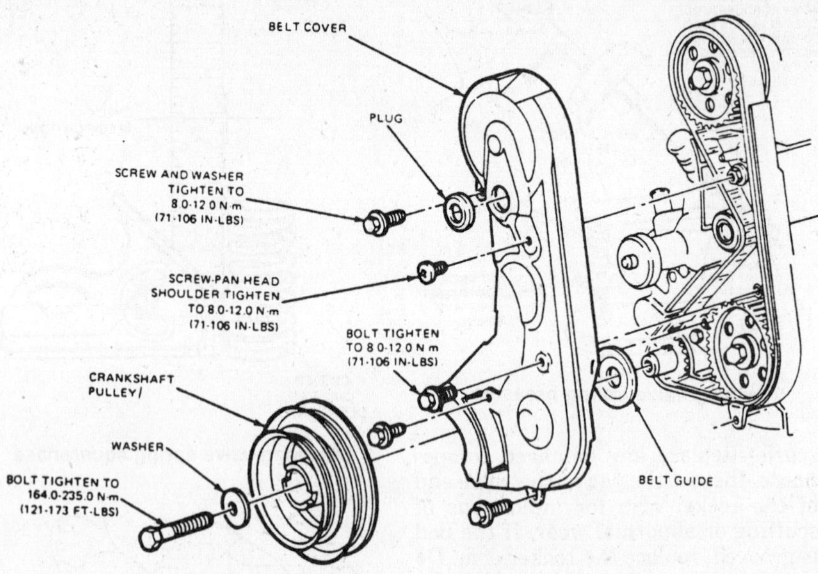

Timing belt cover on 2.3L (140 CID) engine

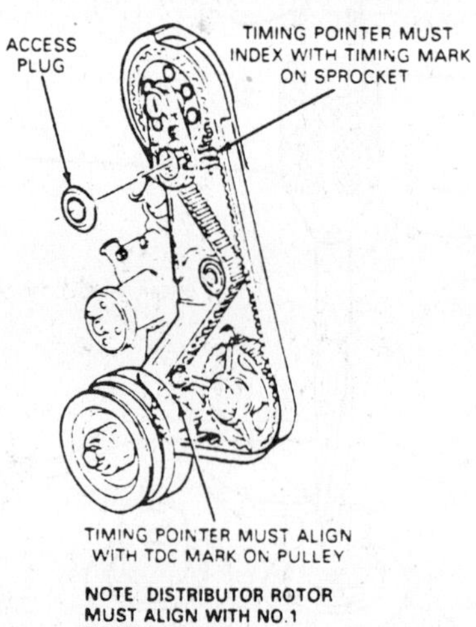

Timing mark alignment on 2.3L (140 CID) engine

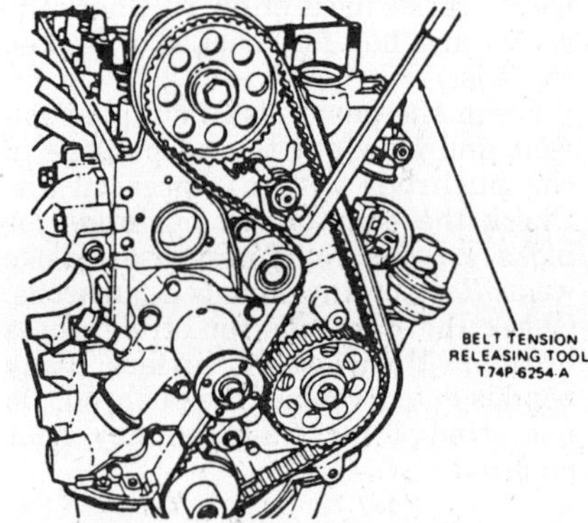

Releasing timing belt tensioner with special tool

Timing Cover, Cover Seal and Gears

REMOVAL & INSTALLATION

2.8L (171 CID) Engine

1. Remove the oil pan as previously described.
2. Drain the cooling system and remove the radiator as previously described.

CAUTION

When draining the coolant, keep in mind that cats and dogs are attracted by the ethylene glycol antifreeze, and are quite likely to drink any that is left in an uncovered con-

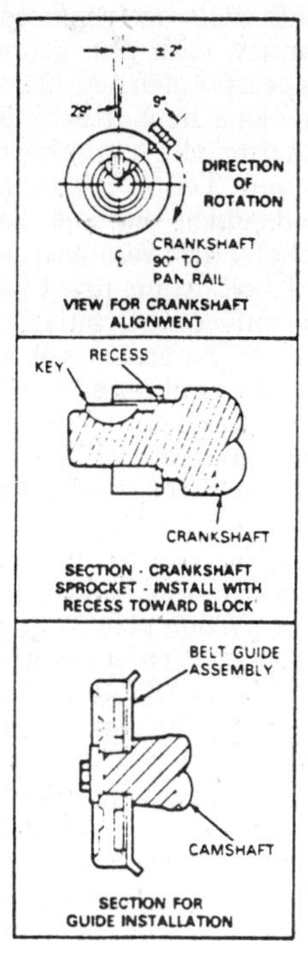

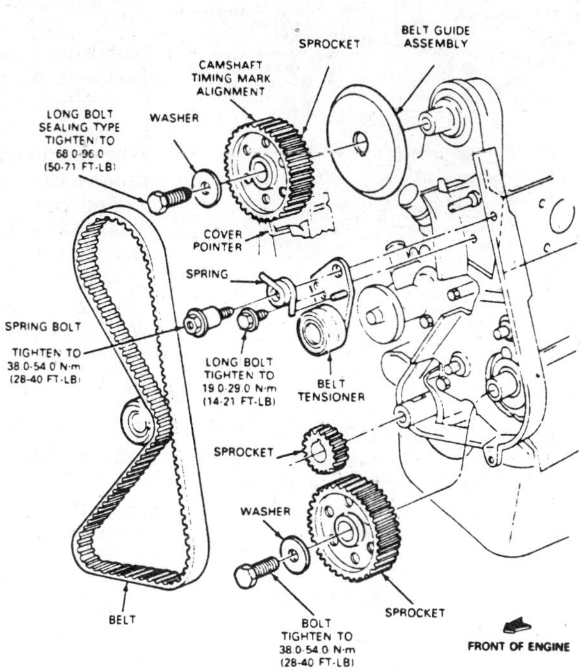

2.3L (140 CID) timing belt assembly

tainer or in puddles on the ground. This will prove fatal in sufficient quantity. Always drain the coolant into a sealable container. Coolant should be reused unless it is contaminated or several years old.

3. Remove the A/C compressor and power steering bracket, if equipped.
4. Remove the alternator, thermactor pump and drive belt(s).
5. Remove the fan.
6. Remove the water pump and heater and radiator hoses.
7. Remove the crankshaft pulley.
8. Remove the front cover retaining bolts. If necessary, tap the cover lightly with a plastic mallet to break the gasket seal, then remove the front cover. If the front cover plate gasket need replacement, remove the two screws and remove the plate. If necessary, remove the guide sleeves from the cylinder block.
9. If the timing gears are being removed, temporarily install the crankshaft pulley nut and rotate the engine by hand until the timing marks are in alignment as illustrated. Remove the timing gear bolts and slide the gears off the crankshaft and camshaft using a suitable gear puller.
10. Clean the front cover mating surfaces of all gasket material and/or sealer. If the front cover seal is being replaced, support the cover to prevent damage and drive out the seal using tool T74P-6700-A or equivalent. Coat the new seal with heavy SF engine oil and install it in the cover, making sure it is not cocked. Install the timing gears, if removed, making sure the timing marks are correctly aligned. Tighten the camshaft gear bolt to 30-36 ft.lb. (41-49 Nm).
11. Apply sealing compound to the gasket surfaces on the cylinder block and back side of the front cover plate. Install the guide sleeves with new seal rings lubricated with engine oil to prevent cutting the rings, with the chamfered end toward the front cover. Position the gasket and front cover plate on the cylinder block. Temporarily install four front cover screws to position the gasket and front cover plate in place. Install and tighten two cover plate attaching bolts, then remove the four screws that were temporarily installed.
12. Apply sealing compound to the front cover gasket surface, then place the gasket in position on the front cover.
13. Place the front cover on the engine and start all retaining screws two or three turns. Center the cover by inserting an alignment tool (T74P-6019-A or equivalent) in the oil seal.
14. Tighten the front cover attaching screws to 13-16 ft.lb. (17-21 Nm).
15. Install the crankshaft pulley and tighten the center bolt to 85-96 ft.lb. (115-130 Nm).
16. Install the oil pan as previously described.
17. Install the water pump, heater hose, A/C compressor, alternator, thermactor pump and drive belt(s). Adjust the belt tension.
18. Install the radiator. Fill and

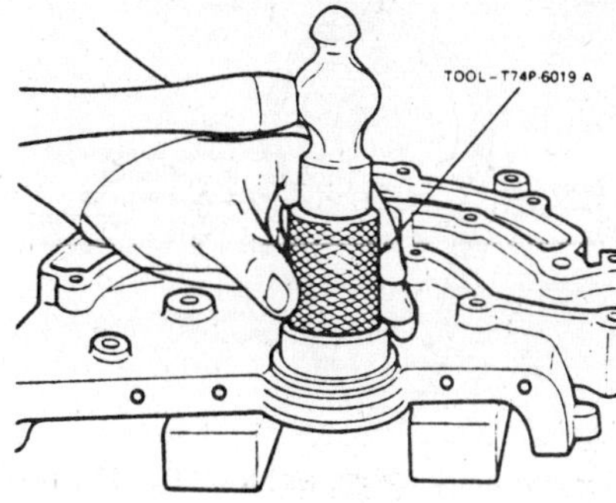

Installing oil seal in front cover on 2.8L (171 CID) engine

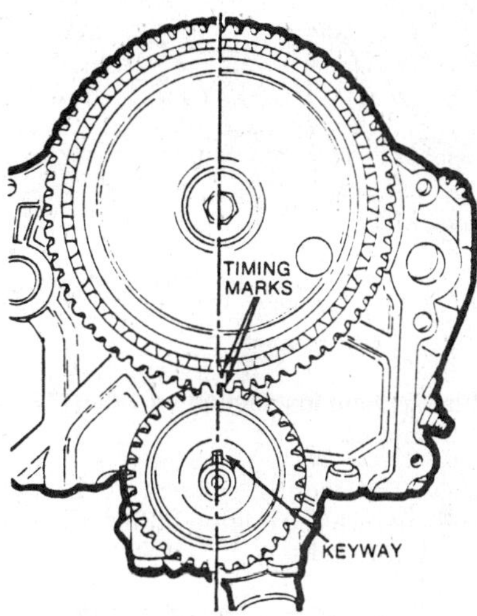

V6 timing gear alignment

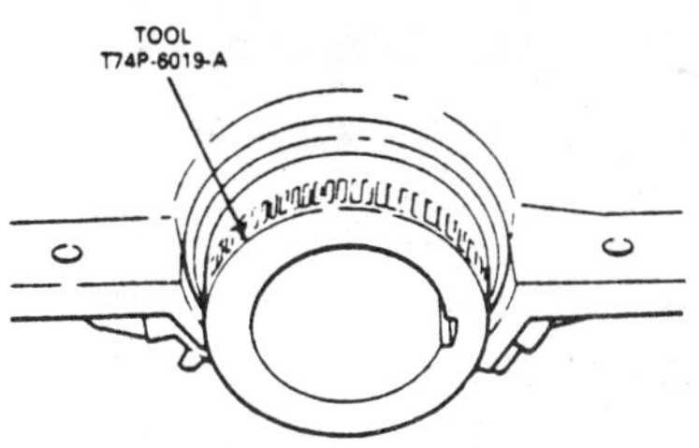

Front cover alignment tool used on 2.8L (171 CID) engine

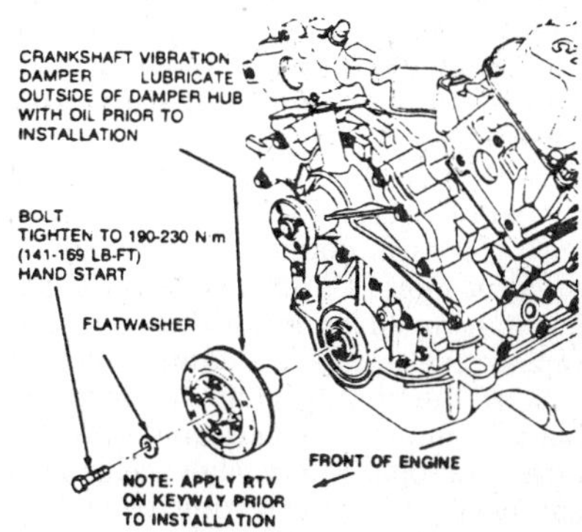

Removing crankshaft damper on 2.8L (171 CID) engine

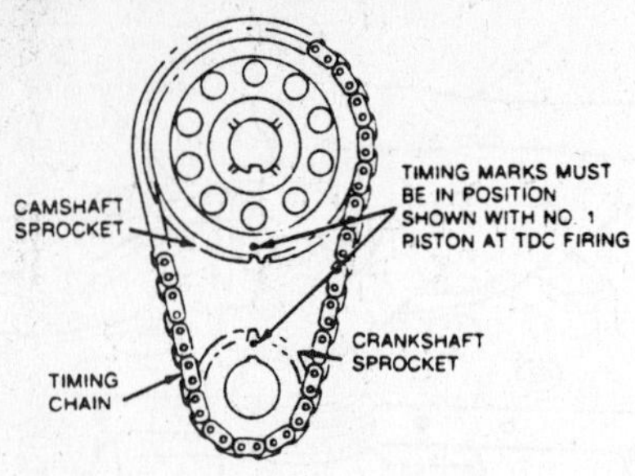

Timing mark alignment on 2.8L (171 CID) engine

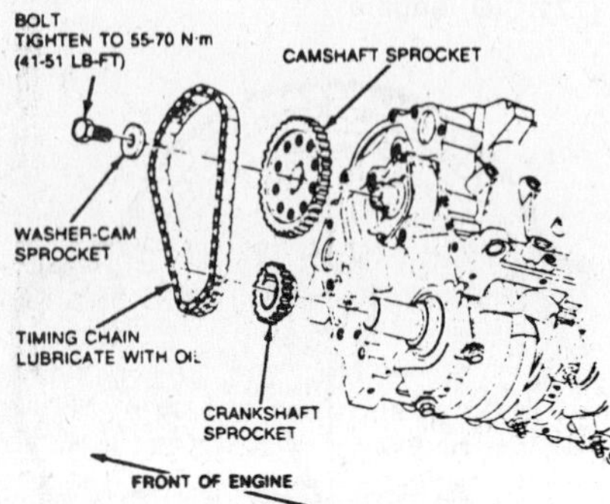

Timing chain installation on 2.8L (171 CID) engine

bleed the cooling system, then start and operate the engine at fast idle and check for leaks.

Timing Cover and Chain

REMOVAL & INSTALLATION

3.0L (182 CID) Engine

1. Crank the engine until No. 1 cylinder is at TDC on the compression stroke with the timing marks aligned. Remove the idler pulley and bracket assembly.
2. Remove the drive and accessory belts.
3. Remove the radiator and water pump as previously described.
4. Remove the crankshaft pulley and damper.
5. Remove the lower radiator hose.
6. Remove the oil pan-to-timing cover bolts.
7. Remove the front cover bolts and the front cover. Tap the cover lightly with a plastic mallet, if necessary, to break it loose. Carefully clean all gasket mating surfaces on the cover and replace the crankshaft damper oil seal.
8. If the timing chain is being replaced, remove the camshaft sprocket attaching bolt and washer. Slide both sprockets and the timing chain forward and remove them as an assembly. Slide the new timing chain with sprockets on the shafts as an assembly

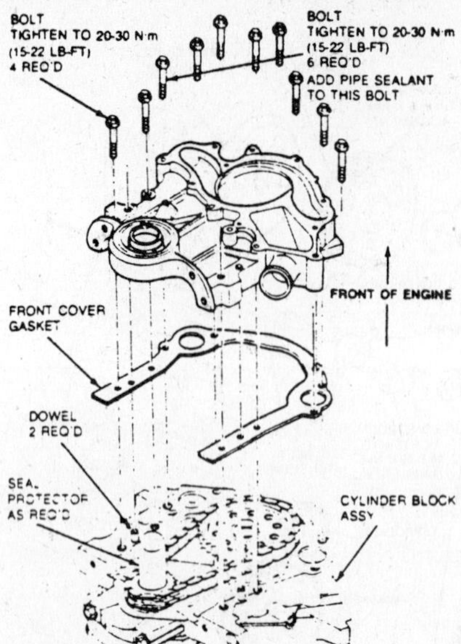

Timing cover installation on 2.8L (171 CID) engine

with the timing marks aligned as illustrated. Install the camshaft bolt and washer and tighten it to 41-51 ft.lb. (55-70 Nm). Apply oil to the timing chain and sprockets after installation.

9. Carefully cut and remove exposed portion of the oil pan gasket. To install, coat the gasket surface of the oil pan with sealing compound (B5A-19554-A or equivalent), then cut and position the required sections of a new gasket on the oil pan and apply more sealing compound at the corners. Coat the gasket surfaces of the block and cover with sealing compound and position the cover on the block.
10. Install the front cover mounting bolts. Use sealant for the front cover bolt which goes into the water jacket of the block. Tighten all mounting bolts to 15-22 ft.lb. (20-30 Nm).
11. Install the oil pan-to-timing cover bolts.
12. Install the lower radiator hose.
13. Install the crankshaft damper and pulley. Tighten the damper bolt to 141-169 ft.lb. (190-230 Nm) and the pulley bolts to 19-26 ft.lb. (26-38 Nm).
14. Install the water pump and radiator as previously described.
15. Install the idler pulley and drive belt(s). Refill the cooling system, start the engine and check for leaks.

Camshaft and Auxiliary Shaft Sprockets and Seals

REMOVAL & INSTALLATION

2.3L (140 CID) Engine

The cylinder front cover, camshaft and auxiliary shaft seals are replaced in the same manner with the same tools after the respective gear has been removed. Always use a new attaching bolt when replacing the camshaft sprocket or use new Teflon® sealing tape on the threads of the old bolt. To remove the sprockets, first remove the timing cover and belt, then use tool T74P-6256-B, or equivalent to pull the cam drive sprocket. The same tool is used in exactly the same manner to remove the auxiliary shaft sprocket, as well as to hold the sprockets while the attaching bolts are installed and tightened.

A front cover seal remover tool T74P-6700-B or equivalent is used to remove all the seals. When positioning this tool, make sure that the jaws are gripping the thin edge of the seal very tightly before operating the jack-screw portion of the tool.

To install the seals, a cam and auxiliary shaft seal replacer T74P-6150-A or equivalent with a stepped, threaded arbor is used. The tool acts as a press, using the internal threads of the various shafts as a pilot.

Camshaft

REMOVAL & INSTALLATION

2.3L (140 CID) Engine

1. Drain the cooling system (engine cold).

CAUTION

When draining the coolant, keep in mind that cats and dogs are attracted by the ethylene glycol antifreeze, and are quite likely to drink any that is left in an uncovered container or in puddles on the ground. This will prove fatal in sufficient quantity. Always drain the coolant into a sealable container. Coolant should be reused unless it is contaminated or several years old.

2. Remove the air cleaner assembly.
3. Disconnect the spark plug wires at the plugs, then disconnect the harness at the rocker cover and position it aside.
4. Tag and disconnect the vacuum hoses as required.
5. Remove the rocker cover retaining bolts and remove the cover.
6. Loosen the alternator retaining bolts and remove the belt from the pulley.
7. Remove the alternator mounting bracket-to-head retaining bolts and position it aside.
8. Disconnect the upper radiator hose at both ends and remove it from the vehicle.
9. Remove the four cam belt cover bolts and remove the cover. If

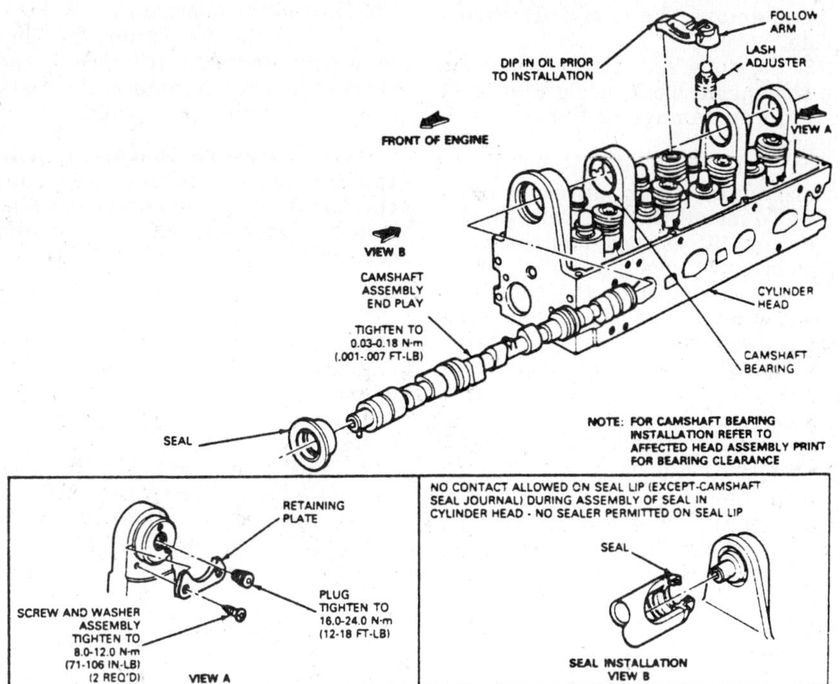

Camshaft installation on 2.3L (140 CID) engine

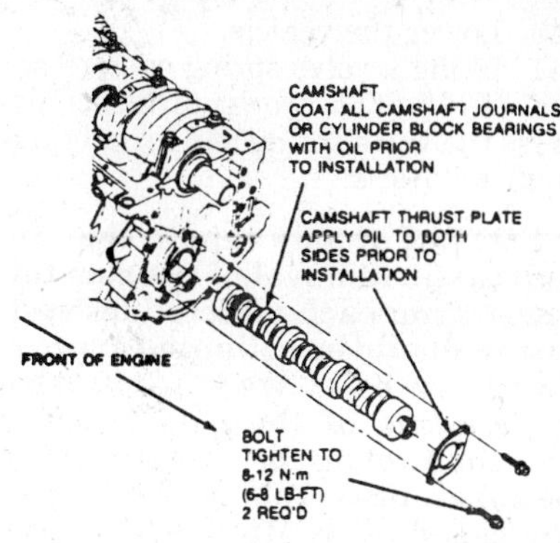

Camshaft installation on 3.0L engine

equipped with power steering, remove the power steering pump bracket.

10. Loosen the idler cam retaining bolts and position the idler in the unloaded position and tighten the retaining bolts.

11. Remove the cam belt from the cam pulley and auxiliary pulley.

12. Using valve spring compressor tool T74P-6565-A or equivalent, depress the valve springs and remove the camshaft followers.

13. Remove the camshaft gear using the sprocket remover tool described above.

14. Remove the seal using front cover seal remover tool described above.

15. Remove the two camshaft rear retainer bolts.

16. Raise the vehicle and support it safely.

17. Remove the right and left engine support bolts and nuts.

18. Position a transmission jack under the engine. Position a block of wood on the transmission jack and raise the engine as high as it will go. Place blocks of wood between the engine mounts and chassis bracket and remove the jack.

19. Carefully slide the camshaft out of the engine block, being careful to avoid damaging journals and camshaft lobes.

20. To install, make sure the threaded plug is in the rear of the camshaft. If not, remove it from the old camshaft and install it. Coat the camshaft lobes with polyethylene grease (part no.

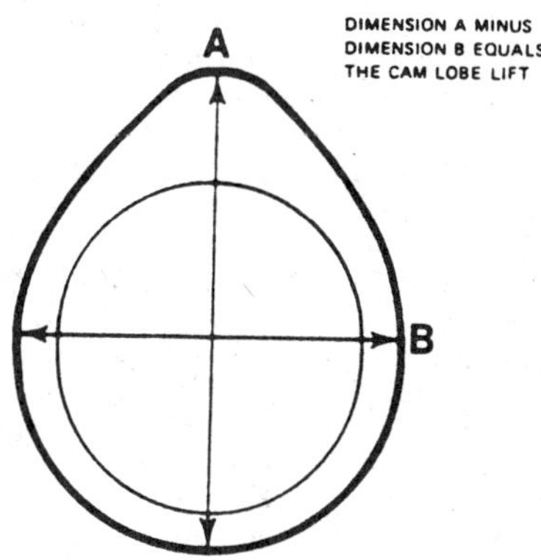

Measuring camshaft lobe dimensions

DOAZ-19584-A or equivalent) and lubricate the journals with heavy SF engine oil before installation. Carefully slide the camshaft through the bearings.

21. Install the two camshaft rear retainer screws.

22. Install the seal using the seal replacer T74P-6150-A or equivalent.

23. Install the belt deflector and sprocket to the camshaft.

24. Install the retaining bolt using the sprocket tool previously described to hold the sprocket while the center bolt is tightened to 50-71 ft.lb. (68-96 Nm).

25. Remove the distributor cap screws and lift off the cap with the wires attached.

26. Remove the spark plugs.

27. Align the distributor rotor with the No. 1 plug location in the distributor cap.

28. Align the cam gear with the pointer.

29. Align the crankshaft pulley timing mark with the pointer on the cam belt cover (TDC).

30. Install the cam belt over the crankshaft sprocket and then counterclockwise over the auxiliary and camshaft sprockets, making sure the lugs on the belt properly engage the sprocket teeth on the pulleys. Be careful not to rotate the pulleys when installing the belt.

31. Release the timing belt tensioner pulley, allowing the tensioner to take up the belt slack. If the spring does not have enough tension to move the roller against the belt (belt hangs loose), it might be necessary to manually push the roller against the belt and tighten the bolt.

NOTE: The spring cannot be used to set belt tension; a wrench must be used on the tensioner assembly.

32. Rotate the crankshaft two complete turns by hand (in the normal direction of rotation) to remove the slack from the belt, then tighten the tensioner adjustment and pivot bolts to specifications. Make sure the belt is seated properly on the pulleys and that the timing marks are still in alignment when No. 1 cylinder is again at TDC/compression.

33. Install the distributor cap.

34. Install the spark plugs.

35. Install the cam belt cover and retaining bolts.

36. Position the alternator drive belt to the pulleys and adjust the belt tension.

37. Raise the vehicle and support it safely.

38. Position a transmission jack to the engine, raise the engine and remove the blocks of wood. Lower the engine and remove the jack.

39. Install the engine support bolts and nuts.

40. Lower the vehicle.
41. Using a valve spring compressor tool (T74P-6565-A or equivalent), depress the valve spring and install camshaft followers.

NOTE: For any repair that requires the removal of the cam follower arm, each affected lash adjuster should be collapsed approximately half way after the installation of the cam follower and then released. This step must be taken prior to any rotation of the camshaft is attempted.

42. Clean and install the rocker arm cover as previously described.
43. Reconnect the disconnected vacuum hoses and wiring. Install the spark plug wires to the plugs.
44. Connect the upper radiator hose to the engine and radiator and tighten the retaining clamps.
45. Refill the cooling system, start the engine and check for leaks.

2.8L (171 CID)
3.0L (182 CID)

1. Disconnect the negative battery cable.
2. Drain the engine oil into a suitable container and dispose of it properly.
3. Remove the fan and spacer, drive belt and pulley and the radiator as previously described.
4. Disconnect the spark plug wires from the plugs.
5. Remove the distributor cap with the spark plug wires as an assembly.
6. Disconnect the distributor wiring harness and remove the distributor.
7. Remove the alternator.
8. Remove the thermactor pump.
9. On the 2.8L engine, remove the fuel lines, fuel filter and carburetor.
10. Remove the intake manifold as previously described.
11. Remove the rocker arm covers and rocker arm and shaft assemblies as previously described.
12. Remove the tappets from the engine block using a magnet or suitable tappet removal tool. Keep the tappets in order so they may be installed in their original locations.
13. Remove the oil pan as previously described.
14. Remove the crankshaft damper bolt and remove the damper with a suitable gear pulley.
15. Remove the engine front cover and water pump as an assembly.
16. On the 2.8L engine, remove the camshaft gear attaching bolt and washer, then slide the gear off the camshaft. On the 3.0L engine, remove the camshaft gear bolt and slide the cam and crankshaft gears off with the timing chain as an assembly.
17. Remove the camshaft thrust plate.
18. Carefully slide the camshaft out of the engine block, using caution to avoid any damage to the camshaft bearings.
19. On the 2.8L engine, remove the camshaft drive gear and spacer ring.
20. To install the camshaft, first oil the camshaft journals and cam lobes with heavy SF engine oil (50W). Install the spacer ring with the chamfered side toward the camshaft, then insert the camshaft key.
21. Install the camshaft in the block, using caution to avoid any damage to the camshaft bearings.
22. Install the thrust plate so that it covers the main oil gallery. Tighten the attaching screws to 13-16 ft.lb. (17-21 Nm) on 2.8L engines, or to 6-8 ft.lb. (8-12 Nm) on 3.0L engines.
23. Rotate the camshaft and crankshaft as necessary to align the timing marks. On the 2.8L engine, install the camshaft gear and tighten the attaching bolt to 30-36 ft.lb. (41-49 Nm). On the 3.0L engine, slide the gears and timing chain onto the shafts with the marks aligned, the tighten the camshaft gear bolt to 40-51 ft.lb. (55-70 Nm).
24. Check the camshaft end play with a dial indicator. The spacer ring and/or thrust plate are available in two thicknesses to permit adjustment of the end play.
25. On the 2.8L engine, align the keyway in the crankshaft gear with the key in the crankshaft. Align the timing marks and install the gear.
26. Install the engine front cover and water pump assembly.
27. Install the crankshaft pulley and tighten the retaining bolt to 85-96 ft.lb. (115-130 Nm).
28. Install the oil pan.
29. Position the tappets in their original locations, then apply heavy SF engine oil (50W) to both ends of the pushrods. Install the pushrods in their original locations.
30. Install the intake manifold and tighten the mounting bolts to the specifications and in the sequence described under Intake Manifold Removal And Installation.
31. Install the oil baffles and rocker arm and shaft assemblies. Tighten the rocker arm stand bolts to specifications given under Rocker Arm Removal And Installation.
32. Adjust the valves to the specified cold clearance, then install the rocker arm covers.
33. Install the fan, spacer and drive belt.
34. Install the carburetor, fuel filter and fuel line.
35. Install the thermactor pump.
36. Install the alternator.
37. Install the distributor, distributor wiring harness, distributor cap and spark plug wires. Reconnect the spark plug wires to the spark plugs.

NOTE: Before installing the spark plug wires to the plugs, coat the inside of each boot with silicone lubricant using a small screwdriver.

38. Install the radiator.
39. Refill the cooling system.
40. Replace the oil filter and refill the crankcase with the specified amount of engine oil.
41. Reconnect the battery ground cable.
42. Start the engine and check the ignition timing and idle speed. Adjust if necessary. Run the engine at fast idle and check for coolant, fuel, vacuum or oil leaks.

Auxiliary Shaft

REMOVAL & INSTALLATION

2.3L (140 CID) Engine

The auxiliary shaft can be removed after first removing the timing belt and front cover as previously described. Remove the attaching screws for the auxiliary shaft retaining plate, then slide the auxiliary shaft carefully out of the engine. Do not allow the gear and fuel pump eccentric to touch the bearing surfaces during removal or installation. See the illustration for component location.

Pistons and Connecting Rods

REMOVAL & INSTALLATION

2.3L (140 CID) Engine

NOTE: The following procedure covers piston replacement with the engine installed in the vehicle, however if an engine requires piston replacement, it is usually easier to remove the engine and complete the overhaul on an engine stand. Whether or not the engine is removed, the cylinder measuring and piston inspection, removal and installation procedures will be the same.

1. Remove the cylinder head as previously outlined. Use a ridge reamer to remove the ridge at the top of each cylinder before attempting to remove the piston assemblies.
2. Raise the vehicle and support it safely.

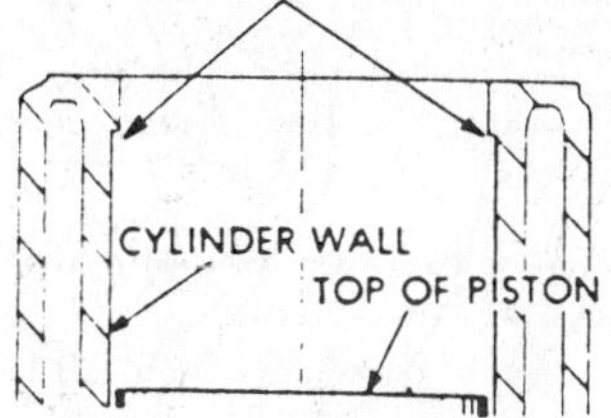

Cylinder bore ridge

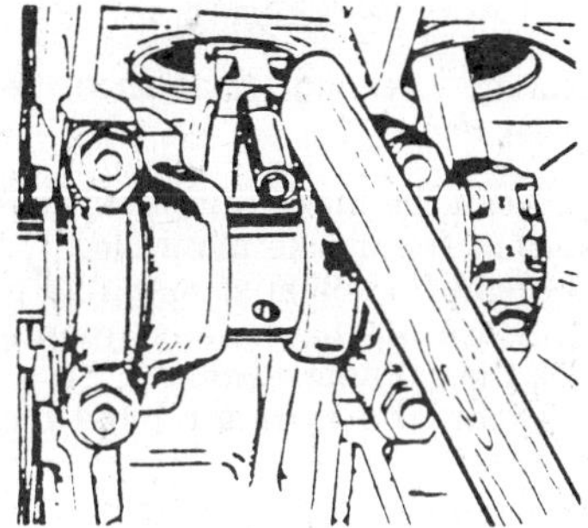
Push the piston out with a hammer handle

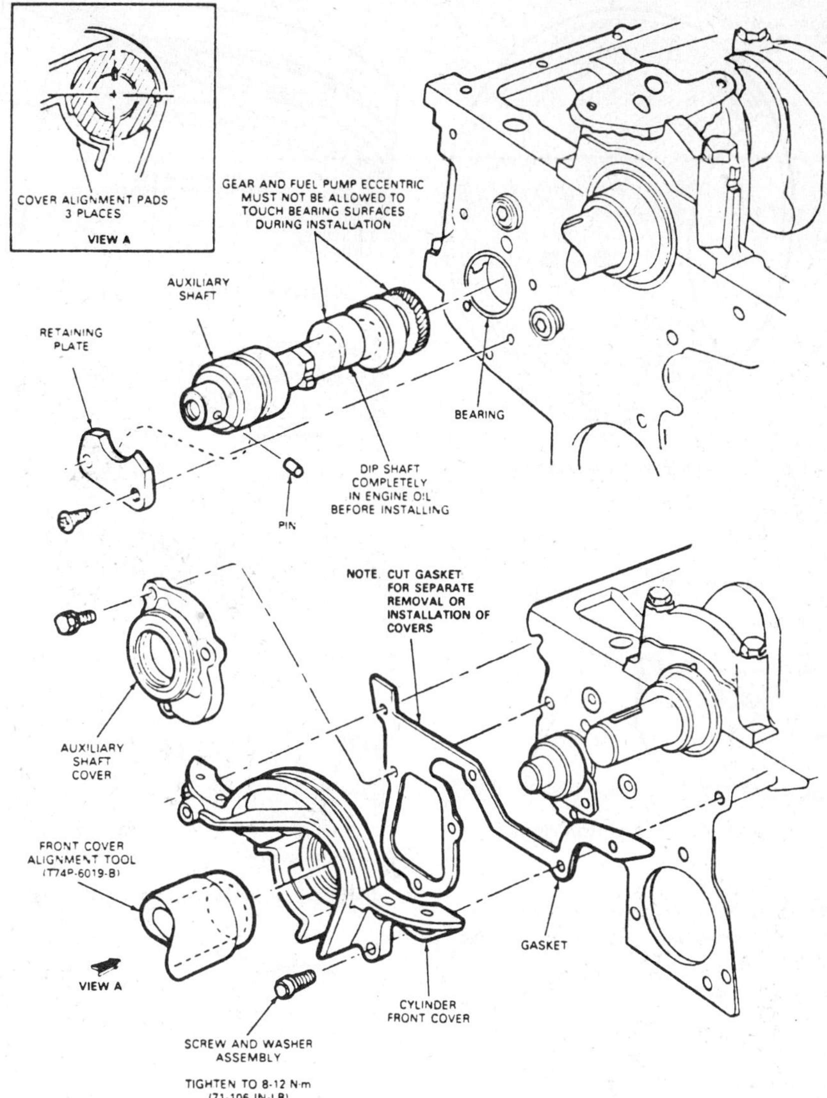

Auxiliary shaft removal on 2.3L (140 CID) engine

3. Remove the engine to insulator to chassis nuts.
4. Remove the starter lead wires and retaining bolts to the starter, then remove the starter.
5. Position a block of wood on a transmission jack, then position the jack under the engine and raise the engine as high as it will go. Place 2" x 4" (50 x 101mm) blocks of wood between the mounts and chassis brackets, then remove the jack.
6. Remove the rear engine support to crossmember nuts.
7. Remove the oil pan retaining bolts and remove the oil pan from the engine.
8. Clean the oil pan and inspect it for damage. Clean the oil pan gasket surface at the cylinder block.
9. Remove and clean the pickup tube and screen assembly.
10. Position the oil pump pickup tube assembly to the oil pump and install two retaining bolts with a gasket.
11. Remove the connecting rod cap and bearing of each piston to be removed. Make sure the caps and bearings are kept in order for installation.
12. Using a wooden hammer handle and being careful not to let the rod bolts scratch the crankshaft bearing surfaces, push the piston up into the cylinder bore so that the top protrudes enough for removal from above.
13. Lower the vehicle.
14. Remove the pistons from the cylinder bore(s), keeping them in order so they may be installed in their original positions.
15. Select the proper bore gauge and micrometer, then measure the cylinder bore for out of round and taper. Deglaze the cylinder bores with a suitable honing tool fitted to an electric drill. Honing is recommended for refinishing cylinder walls only when no cross-hatch pattern is visible. The grade of hone to be used depends on the amount of metal to be removed. Follow the instructions of the hone manufacturer.

NOTE: Cylinder walls that are severely marred and/or worn beyond the specified limits should be refinished at a machine shop. All pistons are the same weight, both standard and oversize; therefore, various sizes of pistons may be used without upsetting engine balance.

16. Remove the piston rings with a suitable ring expander. Clean the ring grooves and all carbon from the piston.
17. Insert the rings into the cylinders one at a time and check the ring gap. Replace any rings that exceed the max-

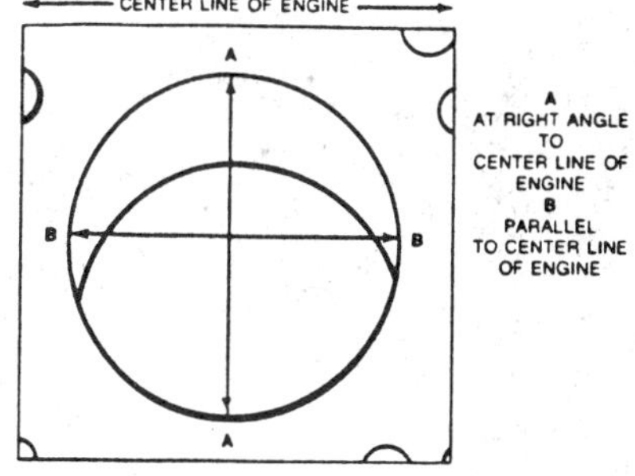

Measure the cylinder bore at the points indicated

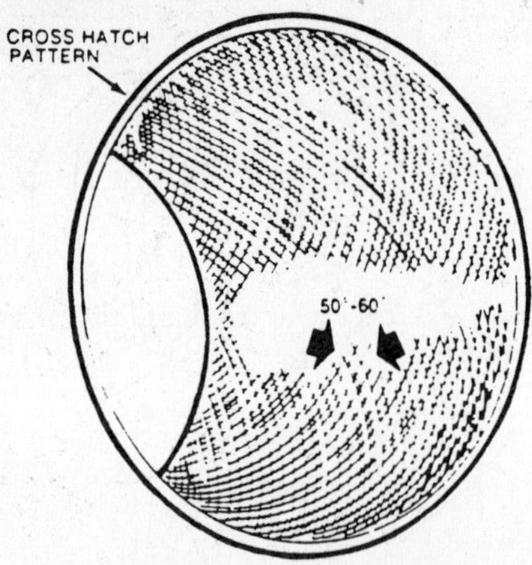

Cylinder bore after honing

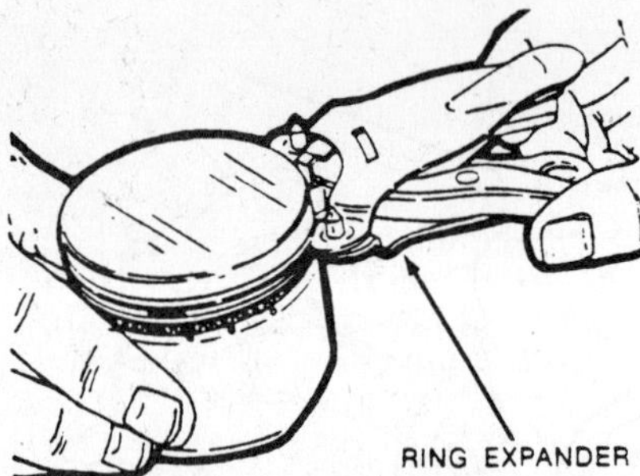

Remove the piston rings

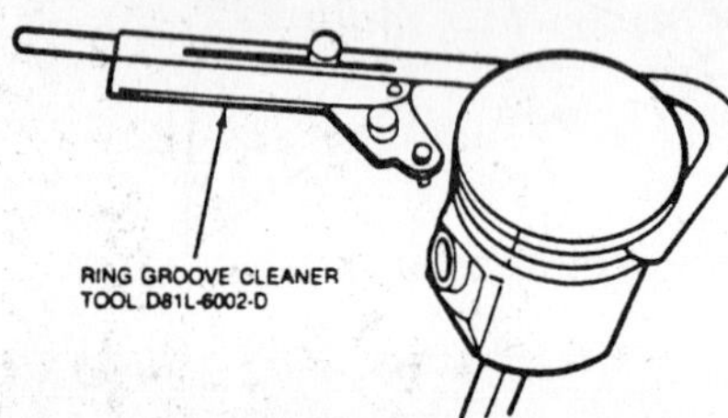

Cleaning the piston grooves

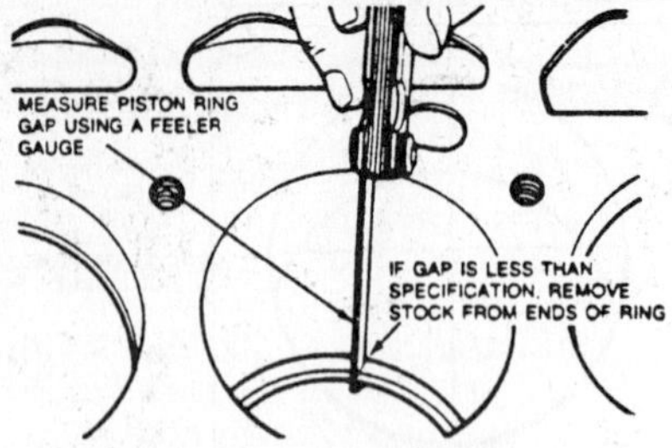

Measuring ring end gap

imum specification as given in the General Engine Specifications chart.

18. Install the rings on the pistons using the expander tool and check the side clearance.
19. Clean the crankshaft journals.
20. Clean the rod caps and nuts.
21. Clean the cylinder head gasket surface at the block.

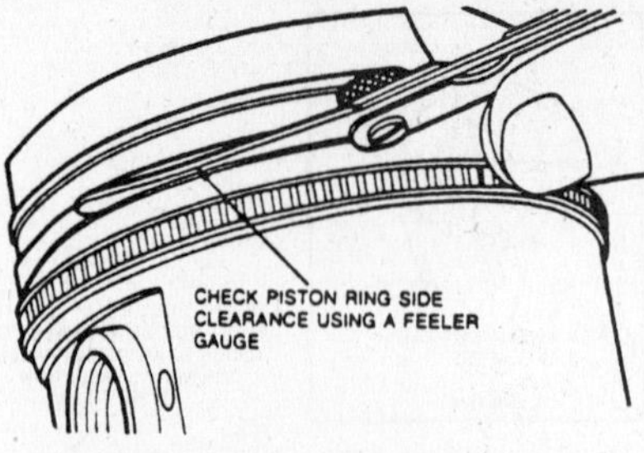

Measuring ring side clearance

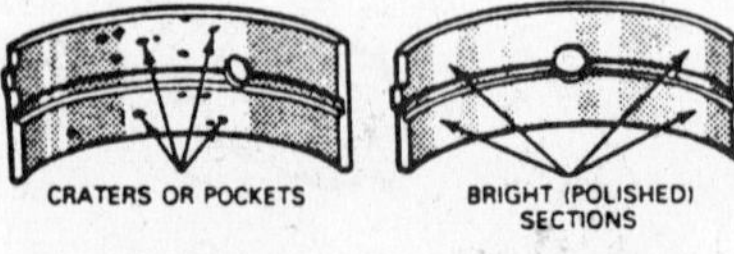

Inspecting the bearings for damage

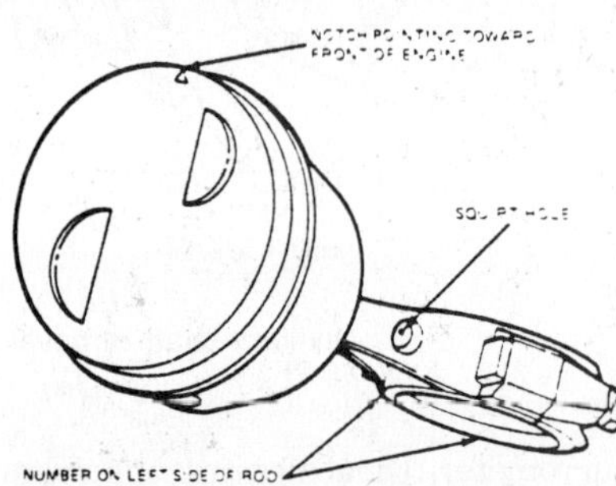

Correct piston alignment on 2.3L (140 CID) engine

Use lengths of vacuum hose or rubber tubing to protect the crankshaft journals and cylinder walls during piston installation

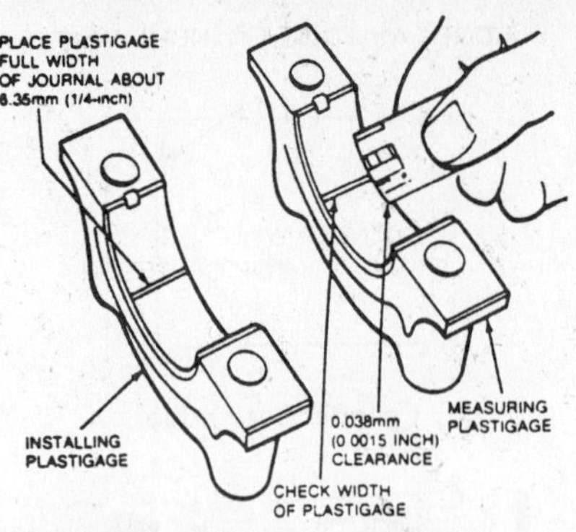

Measuring bearing clearance with Plastigage®

22. Clean the intake manifold gasket surface at the intake manifold.
23. Clean the exhaust manifold gasket surface at the exhaust manifold and at the cylinder head.
24. Clean the cylinder head block bolt holes.
25. Clean the camshaft cover gasket surface on the head.
26. Clean the rocker arm cover.
27. Install the bearings in the rods and caps.
28. Install a ring compressor on each piston, then install the pistons in the block.
29. Raise the vehicle and support it safely.
30. Cut a piece of Plastigage® to size and position it in the rod cap. Install the rod caps and tighten them to 30-36 ft.lb. (41-49 Nm). Remove the rod cap and measure the Plastigage® with the scale provided with the kit. If the bearing clearance exceeds the maximum tolerance given in the Piston and Ring Specifications chart, oversize bearing shells will have to be installed on the rod and rod cap.
31. Clean all Plastigage® material from the rod journals, bearings and oil bearings, then install the rod caps and tighten to 30-36 ft.lb. (41-49 Nm). Rotate the crankshaft.
32. Replace the oil filter.
33. Cement the oil pan gasket and end seals to the engine block, using a contact adhesive such as D7AZ-19B508-A or equivalent.
34. Use a transmission jack as before to raise the engine and remove the blocks of wood installed earlier, then lower the jack, install the crossmember mount nuts and the engine support nuts and remove the jack.
35. Install the starter.
36. Lower the vehicle.
37. Install the cylinder head as previously described.

2.8L (171 CID) and 3.0L (182 CID) Engines

1. Drain the cooling system and crankcase oil.

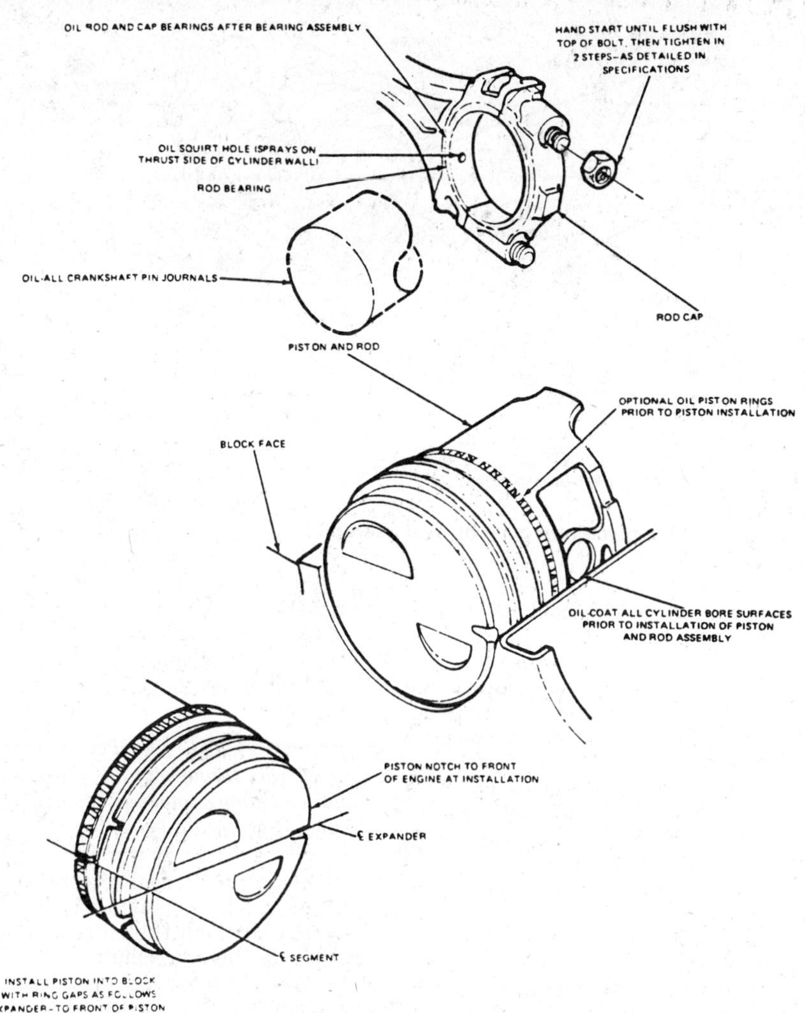

Piston installation on 2.3L (140 CID) engine

CAUTION

When draining the coolant, keep in mind that cats and dogs are attracted by the ethylene glycol antifreeze, and are quite likely to drink any that is left in an uncovered container or in puddles on the ground. This will prove fatal in sufficient quantity. Always drain the coolant into a sealable container. Coolant should be reused unless it is contaminated or several years old.

2. Remove the intake manifold as previously described.
3. Remove the cylinder head(s).
4. Remove the oil pan, baffle (3.0L only) and oil pump.
5. Inspect the top of each cylinder bore for a ridge. If a ridge had formed, rotate the crankshaft until the piston to be removed is at the bottom of the cylinder bore. Place a clean shop towel over the piston to collect any shavings, then remove the ridge using a suitable ridge reamer (follow the manufacturer's instructions). Never cut more than $\frac{1}{32}$" (0.8mm) into the ring travel area when removing the ridge.
6. Make sure all connecting rods are marked so they may be installed in their original locations. The cylinder number is stamped on the top of the piston. Matched letters or numbers are stamped on the sides of corresponding rods and caps. Turn the crankshaft until the piston to be removed is at the high point of its travel.
7. Remove the connecting rod cap attaching nuts and cap.
8. Install short lengths of rubber hose over the connecting rod cap studs to avoid damage to the crankshaft journals during removal. Using a wooden hammer handle, push the piston up out of the bore.
9. Remove the piston from the engine.
10. Install the connecting rod caps and hold them in position with the nuts.
11. Inspect the cylinder bore. If new piston rings are to be installed on the pistons, a visible cross-hatch pattern should be obvious on the cylinder wall. If not, honing is required.
12. Remove the glaze from the cylinder wall using a spring-loaded hone. Follow the manufacturer's instructions. After honing, thoroughly clean the cylinder bore using a detergent and water solution.
13. Use a ring expander to remove the piston rings, then use a piston groove cleaner to remove carbon deposits from the ring grooves.
14. Insert the rings one at a time into the cylinder bore and check the ring end gap with the ring level. Replace any rings that exceed the maximum specification for ring end gap as given in the Piston and Ring Specifications Chart.
15. Install the rings to the piston with a suitable ring expander and check the ring side clearance in the ring groove. Arrange the ring end gaps as illustrated.
16. Oil the piston rings, pistons and cylinder walls with heavy SF engine oil, then install a ring compressor on each piston and tap it into the bore with a wooden hammer handle. The notch on the piston should be toward

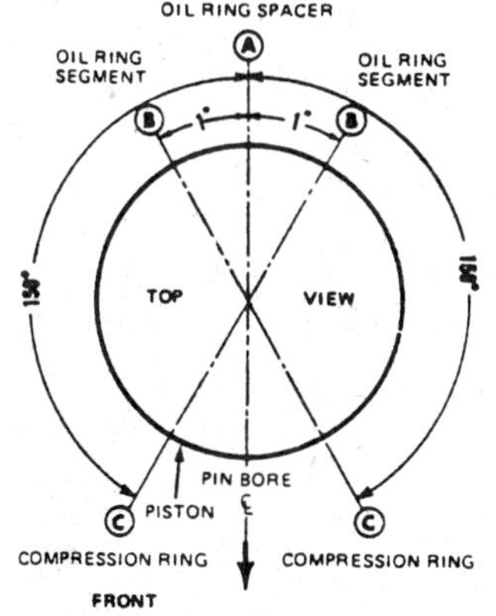

Ring gap placement on piston assembly

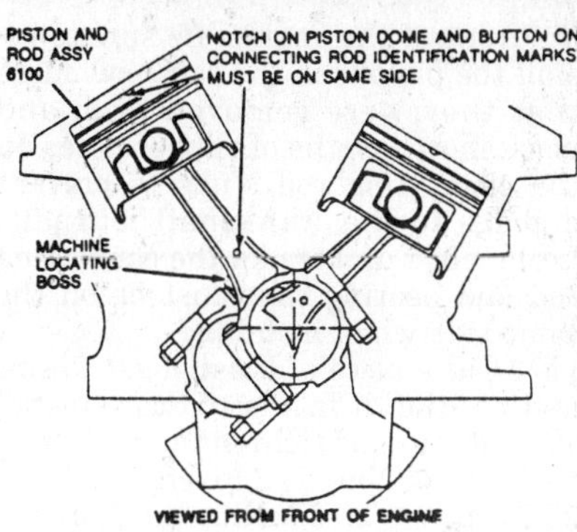

Correct piston installation on 3.0L (182 CID) engine

the front of the engine. Be sure to install the pistons in the same cylinders that they were removed from and place short lengths of rubber hoses on the connecting rod studs to prevent damage to the crankshaft journals. Letters or numbers on the connecting rod and bearing cap must be on the same side when installing.

17. Cut a piece of Plastigage® to size and position it in the rod cap. Install the rod caps and tighten them to 19-24 ft.lb. (26-33 Nm) on 2.8L engines, or to 20-28 ft.lb. (26-38 Nm) on 3.0L engines. On 3.0L engines only, back the connecting rod nuts off a minimum of 2 revolutions, then retighten to 20-25 ft.lb. (26-34 Nm). Remove the rod cap and measure the Plastigage® with the scale provided with the kit. If the bearing clearance exceeds the maximum tolerance given in the Piston and Ring Specifications chart, oversize bearing shells will have to be installed on the rod and rod cap.

18. Clean all traces of Plastigage® from the bearing cap and crankshaft, lubricate the bearings with heavy SF engine oil, then install the caps and tighten as in Step 17. Rotate the crankshaft.

19. After the piston and connecting rod assemblies have been installed, check the side clearance between the connecting rods on each crankshaft journal with a feeler gauge.

20. Install the oil pump as previously described. Prime the pump by filling either the inlet or outlet port with engine oil and rotating the pump shaft to distribute the oil within the housing. Install the oil baffle on 3.0L engines.

21. Install the oil pan.

22. Install the cylinder head(s) as previously described.

23. Install the intake manifold as previously described.

24. Fill and bleed the cooling system.

25. Replace the oil filter, then refill the crankcase with the specified amount of engine oil.

26. Start then engine and check for oil, exhaust and coolant leaks. Check and adjust the ignition timing, if necessary. Adjust the transmission throttle linkage and speed control, if necessary. On carbureted engines, adjust the idle speed if necessary.

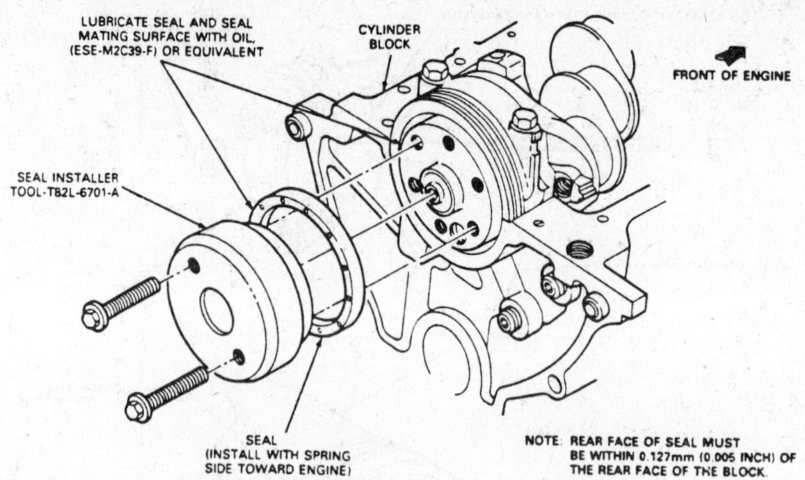

One-piece rear main oil seal used on 2.3L and 3.0L engines

Rear Main Seal

REMOVAL & INSTALLATION

2.3L (140 CID)
3.0L (182 CID)

1. Raise the van and support it safely.
2. Remove the transmission.
3. If equipped with manual transmission, remove the bellhousing and clutch assembly.
4. Remove the flywheel.
5. Using a sharp awl, punch one hole into the seal metal surface between the seal lip and the engine block.
6. Screw in the threaded end of a slide hammer tool (T77L-9533-B or equivalent), then use the slide hammer to remove the seal. Use caution to avoid scratching or damaging the oil seal surface.
7. Lubricate the new seal with clean engine oil.
8. Position the oil seal on a rear seal installer tool (T82L-6701-A or equivalent), then position the tool and seal on the rear of the engine. Alternately tighten the bolts to properly seat the seal.
9. Install the flywheel and tighten the retaining bolts to 56-64 ft.lb. (73-87 Nm).
10. Install the clutch and bellhousing assemblies, if equipped with manual transmission.
11. Install the transmission.

2.8L (171 CID) Engine

1. Raise the van and support it safely on jackstands.
2. Remove the transmission.
3. If equipped with manual transmission, remove the bellhousing and clutch assembly.
4. Remove the flywheel and rear plate.
5. Use a sharp awl to punch two holes in the crankshaft rear oil seal on opposite sides of the crankshaft and just above the bearing cap to cylinder block split line.
6. Install a sheet metal screw in each hole, then use two large screwdrivers or small pry bars to pry against both screws at the same time to remove the crankshaft rear oil seal. It may be necessary to place small blocks of wood against the cylinder block to provide a fulcrum point for the pry bars.

CAUTION

Exercise care throughout this procedure to avoid scratching or otherwise damaging the crankshaft oil seal surface.

7. Clean the oil seal recesses in the cylinder block and main bearing cap. Inspect and clean the oil seal contact surface on the crankshaft.
8. Coat the oil seal to cylinder block surface of the oil seal with oil. Coat the seal contact surface of the oil seal and crankshaft with heavy SF engine oil. Start the seal in the recess and install it with crankshaft rear seal installer tool T72C-6165-R or equivalent. Drive the seal into position until it is firmly seated.
9. Install the rear plate and flywheel. Tighten the flywheel bolts to 47-52 ft.lb. (64-70 Nm).
10. Install the clutch and bellhousing assembly on manual transmission models.
11. Install the transmission.

Crankshaft and Main Bearings

REMOVAL & INSTALLATION

All Engines

1. Remove the engine from the van as previously described, then place it on a work stand.
2. Remove the transmission (if attached), bell housing, flywheel or flex plate and rear plate.
3. Drain the crankcase and remove

the oil pan with the engine in a normal upright position.

4. Remove the components from the front of the engine and the front cover.

5. Invert the engine and remove the oil pump, pickup tube and baffle, if equipped.

6. Make sure all main and connecting rod bearing caps are marked so they can be installed in their original locations.

7. Remove the connecting rod nuts and lift off the cap with its bearing insert. Install short pieces of rubber hose over the connecting rod studs to protect the crankshaft journals, then carefully push the piston and rod assemblies down into the cylinder bores.

8. Remove the main bearing caps with their bearing inserts. Inspect the crankshaft journals for nicks, burrs or bearing pickup that would cause premature bearing wear. When replacing standard bearings with new bearings, it is good practice to fit the bearing to minimum specified clearance. If the desired clearance cannot be obtained with a standard bearing, try one half of a 0.001" (0.025mm) or 0.002" (0.050mm) undersize in combination with a standard bearing to obtain the proper clearance.

9. Place a piece of Plastigage® on the bearing surface across the full width of the bearing cap, about 1/4" (6mm) off center. Install the cap and tighten the bolts to the specified torque given in the General Engine Specifications Chart. Do not rotate the crankshaft with the Plastigage® in place. Remove the cap and use the scale provided with the kit to check the Plastigage width at its widest and narrowest points. Widest point is minimum clearance, narrowest point is maximum clearance; the difference between the two is the taper reading of the journal.

10. Bearing clearance must be within specified limits. If standard 0.002" (0.050mm) undersize bearings do not bring the clearance within desired limits, the crankshaft will have to be refinished or replaced. Remove the remaining main bearing caps and lift out the crankshaft, being careful not to damage the thrust bearing surfaces. Discard the rear main oil seal. The crankshaft should be refinished at a machine shop to give the proper clearance with the next undersize bearing. If the journal will not clean up to the maximum undersize bearing, the crankshaft will have to be replaced.

11. Clean the bearing bores in the block and caps. Foreign material under the inserts or on the bearing surfaces may distort the insert and cause bearing failure.

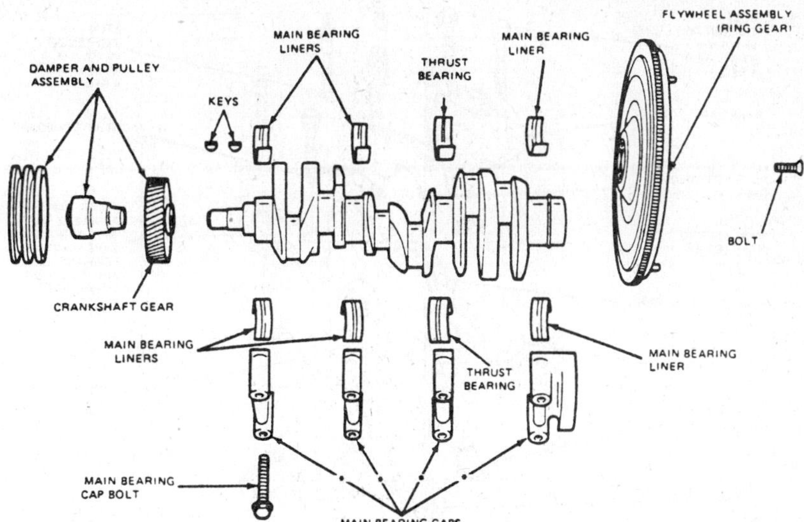

Crankshaft and bearing assembly on 2.8L (171 CID) engine

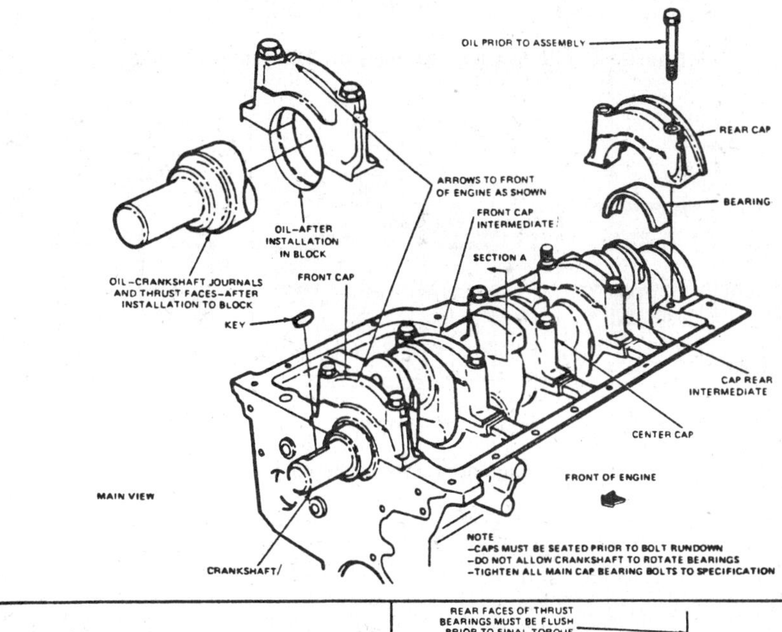

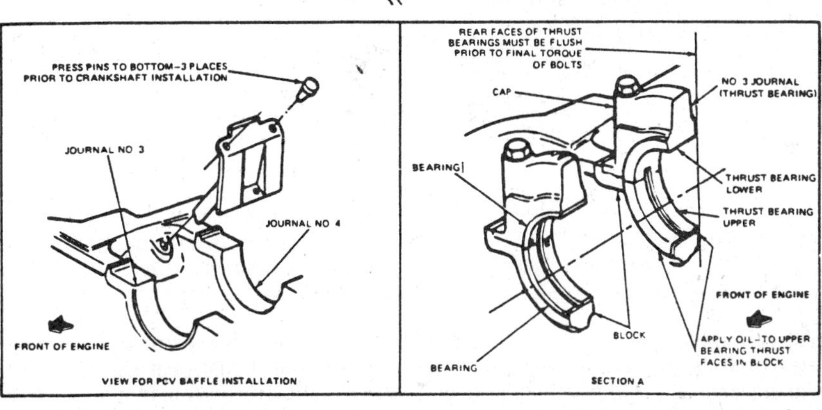

Crankshaft and bearings installation on 2.3L (140 CID) engine

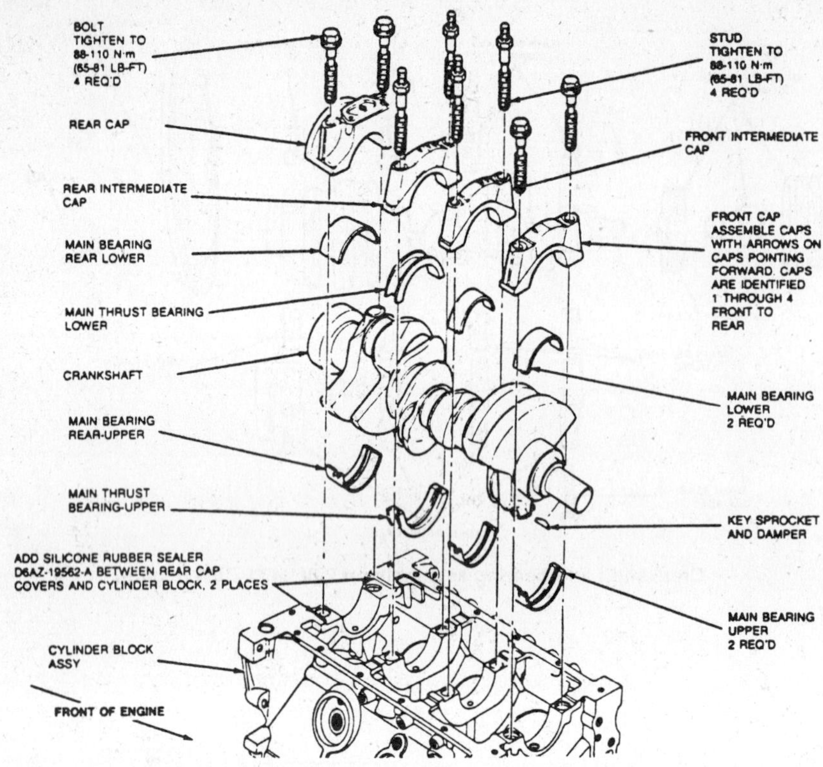

Crankshaft and bearing assembly on 3.0L)182 CID) engine

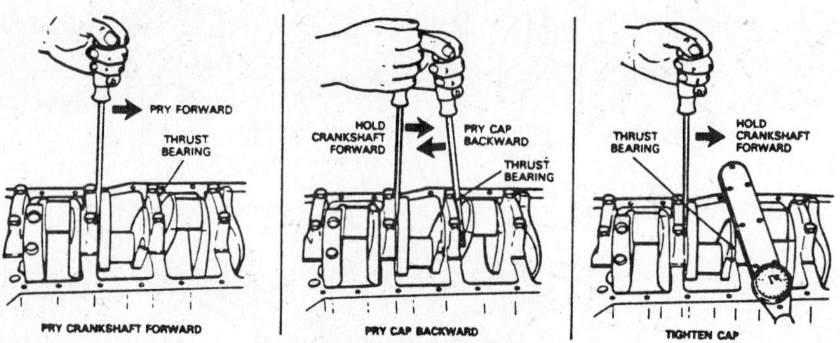

Aligning the thrust bearing

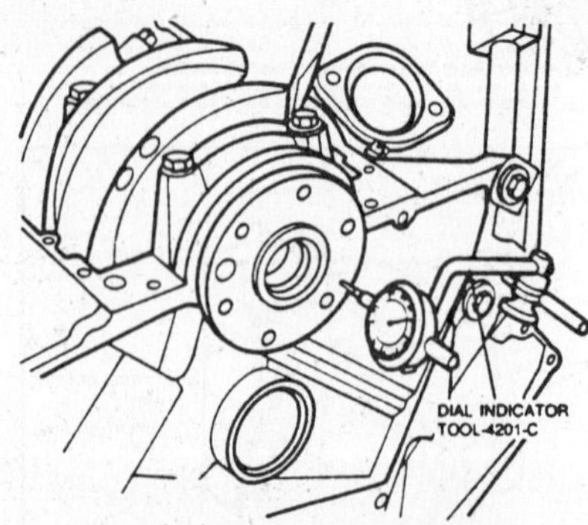

Checking crankshaft end play

12. Assemble the main bearing inserts in their correct location in the bearing caps and cylinder block. Check the oil hole alignment between the bearing inserts and block. Apply a liberal coating of clean heavy SF engine oil to the bearing surfaces, then carefully lower the crankshaft into position.

13. Insert the remaining bearing shells into the main bearing caps and coat the bearings with clean heavy SF engine oil, then install the caps with the arrows pointing toward the front of the engine. Apply a thin even coating of sealing compound to the rear sealing surface of the rear main bearing cap before installing. Install and tighten all main bearing cap bolts finger tight after lightly oiling the threads.

14. Tighten all bearing cap bolts, except for the thrust bearing cap, to the specifications given in the Torque Specifications Chart.

15. Align the thrust bearing surfaces by forcing the crankshaft forward and the thrust bearing cap rearward. While holding in this position, tighten the thrust bearing cap to specifications.

16. Install a new rear main oil seal as previously described.

17. On the 2.8L (171 CID) engine, use a flat tool such as a large blunt end screwdriver to push the two wedge shaped seals between the cylinder block and rear main bearing cap. Position the seals with the round side facing the main bearing cap.

18. Pull the connecting rods up one at a time and install rod caps after applying a liberal coating of heavy SF engine oil to the bearings. Tighten all bearing caps to specifications. On V6 engines, check the connecting rod side clearance as previously described. Check the crankshaft end play with a dial indicator.

19. Install the oil pump, pickup tube and baffle, if equipped. Prime the oil pump before installation as described under Oil Pump Removal and Installation.

20. Install the front cover and timing chain, belt or gears. Replace the front cover oil seal.

21. Install the rear cover plate (if equipped) and the flywheel or flex plate. Tighten the mounting bolts to specifications.

22. Install the clutch disc, pressure plate and bell housing on manual transmission models.

23. Install the oil pan and tighten the bolts to specifications. See Oil Pan Removal and Installation for gasket and sealer placement.

24. Invert the engine to its normal, upright position and fill the crankcase with the specified amount and type of engine oil. Replace the oil filter.

25. Install the transmission, if removed with the engine.

26. Install the engine in the van as previously described.

Flywheel and Ring Gear

REMOVAL & INSTALLATION

All Engines

1. Raise the vehicle and support it safely on jackstands.
2. Remove the transmission.
3. On manual transmission models, remove the bellhousing, clutch pressure plate and clutch disc.
4. On automatic transmission models, remove the torque converter.
5. Install a dial indicator so that the indicator rests against the face of the ring gear adjacent to the gear teeth

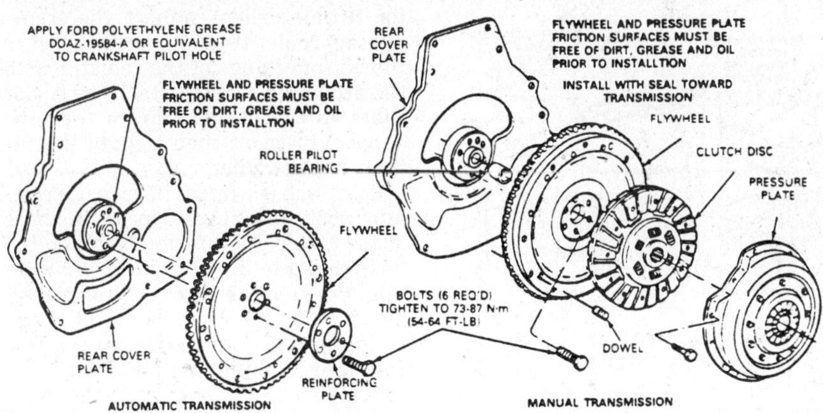

Flywheel assembly on 2.3L (140 CID) engine

(automatic), or against the flywheel face (manual). Hold the flywheel and crankshaft forward or backward as far as possible to prevent crankshaft end play from being indicated as flywheel runout. Zero the dial indicator, then turn the flywheel one complete revolution by hand while observing the total dial indicator reading. If the runout exceeds 0.001" (0.025mm) on 2.3L engines; 0.025" (0.635mm) for manual, or 0.060" (1.5mm) for automatic on 2.8L engines; or 0.070" (1.8mm) on 3.0L engines, the flywheel will have to be replaced. On manual transmissions, the flywheel clutch surface can be machined true if the runout is not excessive.

6. Remove the flywheel mounting bolts and remove the flywheel and ring gear assembly.

7. On automatic transmission models, inspect the flywheel for cracks or other indications that would make it unfit for further use. Check the ring gear teeth for worn, chipped or cracked teeth and replace the flywheel and ring gear if any damage is found.

8. On manual transmission models, inspect the flywheel for cracks, heat damage or other problems that would make it unfit for further use. Machine the clutch friction surface if it is scored or worn. If it is necessary to remove more than 0.045" (1.14mm) of stock from the original thickness, replace the flywheel. Check the ring gear for worn, chipped or cracked teeth and replace the ring gear if any damage is found. To replace a damaged ring gear on a manual transmission flywheel, heat the ring gear with a blow torch on the engine side of the gear and knock it off the flywheel. Do not hit the flywheel when removing the gear. Heat the new ring gear evenly until the gear expands enough to slip onto the flywheel. Make sure the gear is seated properly against the shoulder. Do not heat any portion of the gear more than

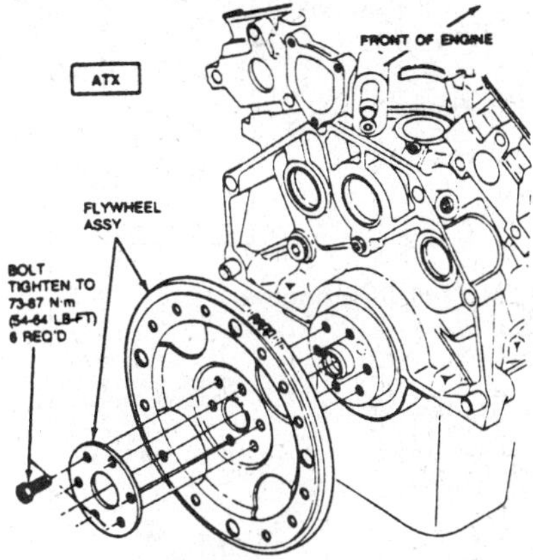

Flywheel installation on 3.0L (18 CID) engine – automatic transmission

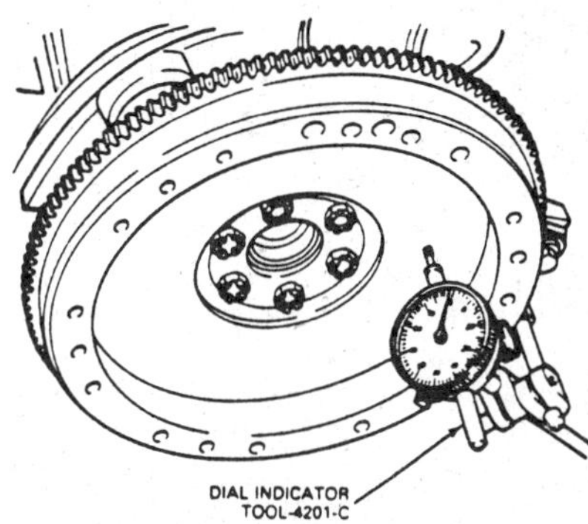

Checking flywheel runouton manual transmission models

500°F or the temper will be removed from the ring gear teeth.

NOTE: All major rotating components including the flex plate/ flywheel are individually balanced. Do not attempt to install balance weights on a new flywheel.

9. Position the flywheel on the crankshaft flange and apply oil resistant sealer to the mounting bolts. Install and tighten the bolts in a crisscross pattern to the specifications given in the Torque Specifications Chart.

10. On manual transmission models, install the clutch disc and pressure plate. On automatic transmission models, install the torque converter.

11. Install the transmission and lower the vehicle.

ENGINE COOLING

Radiator

REMOVAL & INSTALLATION

1. With the engine cold, drain the cooling system by removing the radiator cap and opening the draincock at the lower rear corner of the radiator tank.

CAUTION

When draining the coolant, keep in mind that cats and dogs are attracted by the ethylene glycol antifreeze, and are quite likely to drink any that is left in an uncovered container or in puddles on the ground. This will prove fatal in sufficient quantity. Always drain the coolant into a sealable container. Coolant should be reused unless it is contaminated or several years old.

2. Remove the rubber overflow tube from the radiator and store it up out of the way.

3. Remove the radiator fan shroud upper attaching screws, then lift the shroud out of the lower retaining clips and drape it on the fan.

4. Loosen the upper and lower hose clamps at the radiator and remove the hoses from the radiator connections.

5. If equipped with automatic transmission, disconnect the two transmission cooling lines from the radiator fittings. Disconnect the transmission cooler tube support bracket from the bottom flange of the radiator by removing the screw.

6. Remove the two radiator upper attaching screws.

7. Tilt the radiator back (rearward) about 1" (25mm) and lift it directly upward, clear of the radiator support and the cooling fan.

8. If either hose is being replaced, loosen the clamp at the engine end and slip the hose off the connection with a twisting motion. Install the new hose(s) to the engine connections, making sure any bends are oriented exactly as the old hose for alignment purposes.

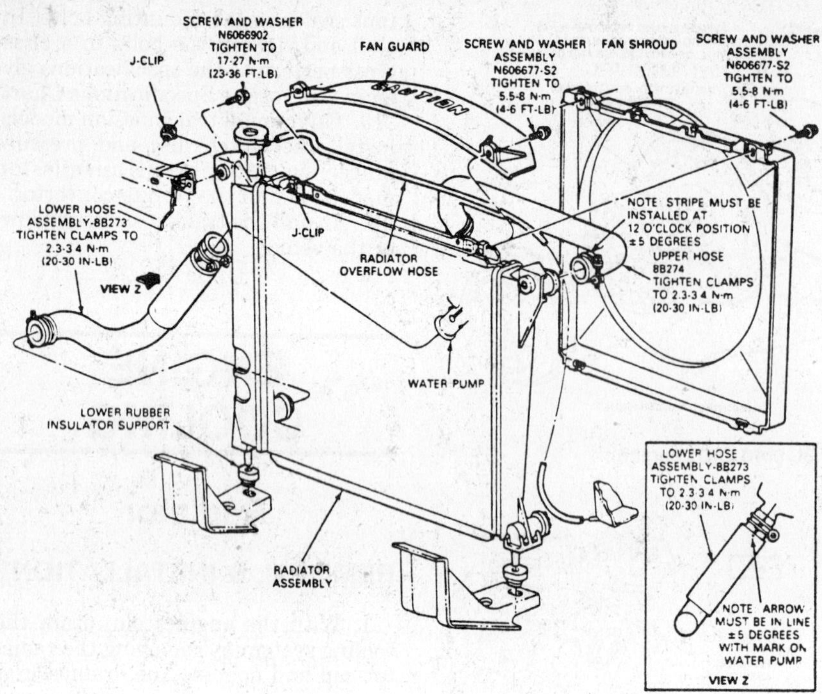

Radiator installation on 2.3L (140 CID) engine

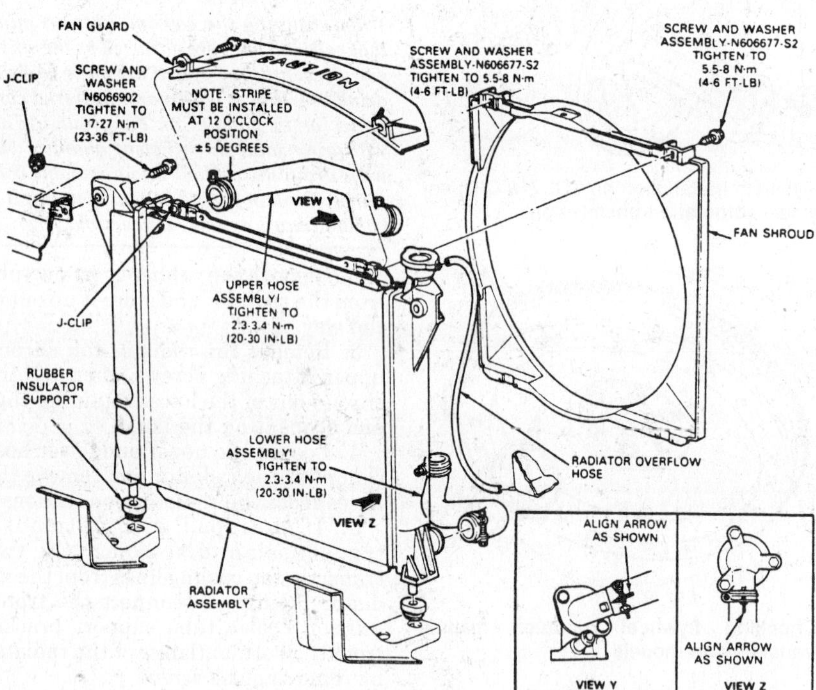

Typical radiator installation on V6 engines

9. If the radiator is being replaced, transfer the lower support rubber insulators to the new part. The radiator cooling fins should be cleaned of any dirt or debris and any bent fins should be carefully straightened.

10. Install the radiator into the engine compartment, making sure the lower rubber insulators are properly positioned in the radiator support. Be careful to clear the fan with the radiator to avoid damage to the cooling fins.

11. Connect the upper attaching bolts to the radiator support and tighten them to 12-20 ft.lb. (17-27 Nm).

12. If equipped with automatic transmission, loosely connect the two transmission cooling lines to the radiator fittings, then connect the transmission cooler tube support bracket to the bottom flange of the radiator with the attaching screw. Attach the cooler tubes to the plastic clip on the tube support bracket, then tighten the fittings at the radiator.

13. Attach the upper hose to the radiator, positioning the stripe on the hose at the 12 o'clock position. Tighten the hose clamp to 20-30 in.lb. (2-4 Nm).

14. Position the lower hose on the radiator with the hose stripe at the 6 o'clock position, then tighten the hose clamp to 20-30 in.lb. (2-4 Nm).

15. Position the shroud in the lower retainer clips and attach the top of the shroud to the radiator with two screw and washer assemblies. Tighten the screws to 4-6 ft.lb. (5-8 Nm).

16. Attach the rubber overflow tube to the radiator and coolant recovery reservoir. Refill the cooling system to specifications with the recommended coolant mixture and add two cooling system protector pellets (D9AZ-19558-A or equivalent). If the original coolant was saved and is not contaminated, it may be reused. Allow several minutes for trapped air to escape and for the coolant mixture to flow through the radiator.

17. Install the radiator cap fully, then back it off to the first stop (pressure relief position). Slide the heater temperature and mode selector levers to the full heat position.

18. Start the engine and allow it to operate at fast idle (about 2,000 rpm) for three to four minutes, then shut the engine off.

19. Wrap a thick cloth around the radiator cap and remove it cautiously. Add coolant to bring the level up to the filler neck seat.

20. Install the radiator cap fully (down and locked). Remove the cap from the top of the coolant recovery reservoir and top off the reservoir to the FULL HOT mark with coolant.

NOTE: Be careful not to confuse the coolant recovery reservoir with the windshield washer fluid reservoir. The two are right next to one another.

Water Pump

REMOVAL & INSTALLATION

2.3L (140 CID) Engine

NOTE: Provision for wrench clearance has been made in the timing belt inner cover, so only the outer cover must be removed in order to replace the water pump.

1. Drain the cooling system (engine cold).

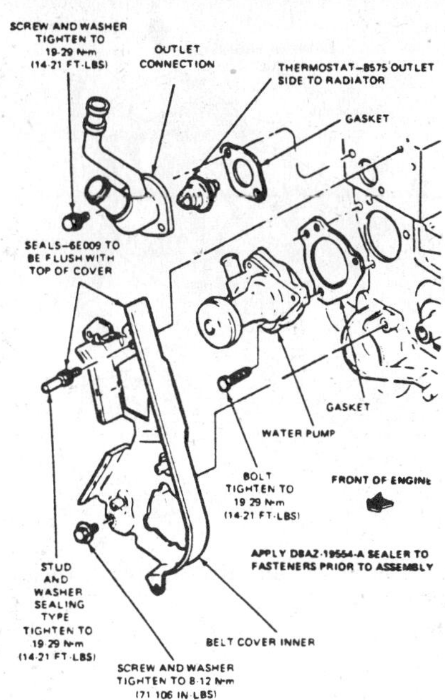

Exploded view of the water pump mounting on 2.3L (140 CID) engine

CAUTION

When draining the coolant, keep in mind that cats and dogs are attracted by the ethylene glycol antifreeze, and are quite likely to drink any that is left in an uncovered container or in puddles on the ground. This will prove fatal in sufficient quantity. Always drain the coolant into a sealable container. Coolant should be reused unless it is contaminated or several years old.

2. Remove the two bolts retaining the fan shroud and position the shroud over the fan.

3. Remove the four bolts retaining the fan assembly to the water pump shaft and remove the fan and shroud.

4. Loosen the A/C compressor adjusting idler pulley and remove the drive belt, if equipped.

5. Loosen the power steering bolts (if equipped) and remove the alternator and power steering belts.

6. Remove the water pump pulley and the vent tube to the canister.

7. Remove the heater hose to the water pump.

8. Remove the cam belt cover.

9. Remove the lower radiator hose from the water pump.

10. Remove the water pump retaining bolts and remove the water pump from the engine.

11. Clean the water pump gasket surface at the engine block. Remove all traces of old gasket and/or sealer.

12. To install, use contact cement to position the new gasket to the water pump. Position the water pump to the engine block and install three retaining bolts. Apply sealer (D8AZ-19554-A or equivalent) to the water pump bolts prior to installation and tighten the bolts to 14-21 ft.lb. (19-29 Nm).

13. Install the lower radiator hose to the water pump.

14. Install the cam belt cover.

15. Position the water pump pulley to the water pump.

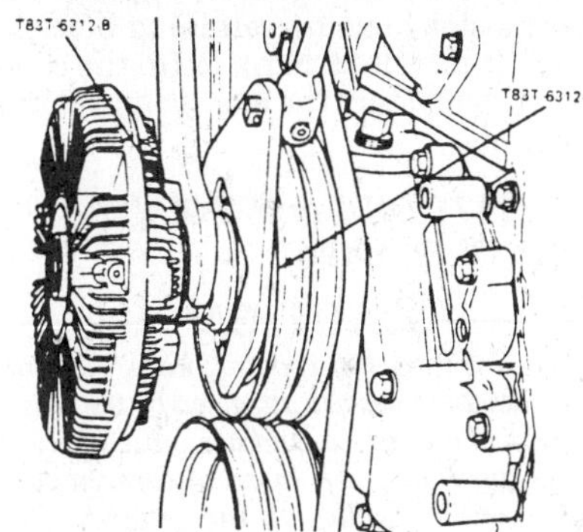

Removing fan and clutch assembly with special tools on 2.8L (171 CID) engine

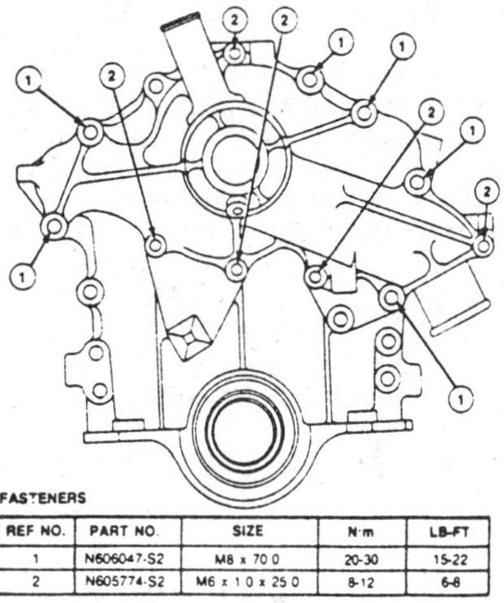

FASTENERS

REF NO.	PART NO.	SIZE	N·m	LB-FT
1	N606047-S2	M8 x 70 0	20-30	15-22
2	N605774-S2	M6 x 1 0 x 25 0	8-12	6-8

NOTE: APPLY PIPE SEALANT D8AZ-19558-A TO BOLT THREADS

Water pump torque specifications on 3.0L (182 CID) engine

16. Install the power steering (if equipped) and alternator drive belts to the pulleys.

17. Install the A/C compressor belt (if equipped).

18. Install the shroud and fan assembly to the engine. Install the fan assembly with spacers to the water pump shaft.

19. Position the shroud to the radiator and install the retaining bolts.

20. Adjust the drive belts to specifications, refill the cooling system, then start the engine and check for leaks.

2.8L (171 CID) and 3.0L (182 CID) Engines

NOTE: This procedure requires the use of special tools to remove the fan and clutch assembly.

1. Drain the cooling system (engine cold) into a clean container and save the coolant for reuse.

CAUTION

When draining the coolant, keep in mind that cats and dogs are attracted by the ethylene glycol antifreeze, and are quite likely to drink any that is left in an uncovered container or in puddles on the ground. This will prove fatal in sufficient quantity. Always drain the coolant into a sealable container. Coolant should be reused unless it is contaminated or several years old.

2. Loosen the hose clamps and detach the lower radiator hose and heater return hose from the water inlet housing.

3. Remove the clutch and fan assembly using a fan clutch pulley holder (tool no. T83T-6312-A) and fan clutch nut wrench (tool no. T83T-6312-B).

CAUTION

The fan clutch nut is a left hand thread. Remove by turning the nut clockwise.

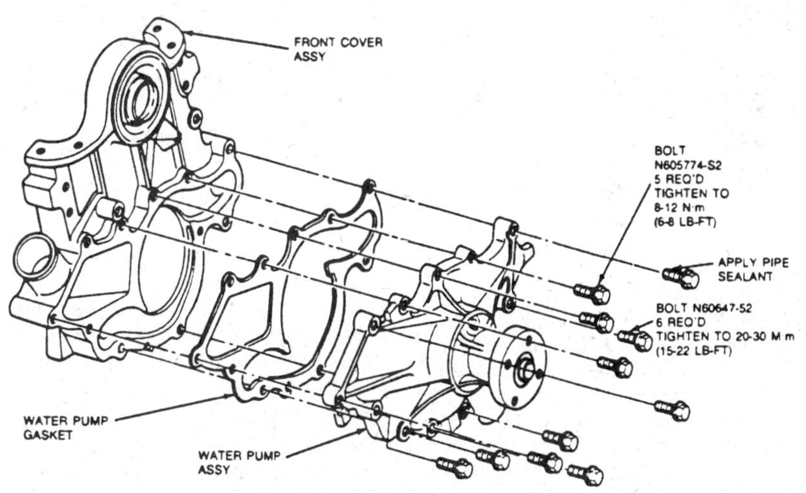

Water pump mounting on 3.0L (182 CID) engine

4. Loosen the alternator mounting bolts and remove the belt. If equipped with A/C, remove the alternator and bracket.

5. Remove the water pump pulley.

6. Remove the water pump assembly attaching bolts, then remove the water pump assembly and water inlet housing from the front cover. Note the position of the different length bolts when removing them so they may be installed in their original locations.

7. Clean all gasket material and/or sealer from all gasket mating surfaces on the front cover and water pump assembly.

8. Apply sealer to both sides of the new gasket and place the gasket on the water pump.

9. Position the water pump assembly to the front cover and install two bolts finger tight to hold it in position.

10. Clean all gasket material and/or sealer from the mating surfaces of the water inlet housing. Apply sealer to both sides of a new gasket and place it on the water inlet housing.

11. Position the water inlet housing and install the attaching bolts. Note the different length bolts. Tighten the water inlet bolts to 12-15 ft.lb. (17-21 Nm).

12. Install and tighten the water pump attaching bolts to 7-9 ft.lb. (9-12 Nm).

13. Install the water pump pulley. If equipped with A/C, install the bracket and alternator. Install the drive belt and adjust to specifications.

14. Reconnect both hoses to the water inlet housing and tighten the hose clamps.

15. Install the fan and clutch assembly using the special tools from Step 3. Tighten the nut to 15-25 ft.lb. (21-34 Nm). Turn the nut counterclockwise to tighten.

16. Fill the cooling system and bleed it as described under Radiator Removal and Installation.

Thermostat

REMOVAL & INSTALLATION

2.3L (140 CID) Engine

CAUTION

When draining the coolant, keep in mind that cats and dogs are attracted by the ethylene glycol antifreeze, and are quite likely to drink any that is left in an uncovered container or in puddles on the ground. This will prove fatal in sufficient quantity. Always drain the coolant into a sealable container. Coolant should be reused unless it is contaminated or several years old.

The thermostat may be replaced by draining the cooling system (engine cold), then removing the retaining bolts for the thermostat housing. Lift the housing clear and remove the thermostat. It may be easier to clean the gasket mating surfaces with the heater and radiator hoses removed from the thermostat housing. Clean all gasket mating surfaces and make sure the thermostat is in the housing properly. Always use a new gasket. Tighten the thermostat housing retaining bolts to 14-21 ft.lb. (19-29 Nm). Refill the cooling system, start the engine and check for leaks.

2.8L (171 CID) and 3.0L (182 CID) V6 Engines

CAUTION

When draining the coolant, keep in mind that cats and dogs are attracted by the ethylene glycol antifreeze, and are quite likely to drink any that is left in an uncovered container or in puddles on the ground. This will prove fatal in sufficient quantity. Always drain the coolant into a sealable container. Coolant should be reused unless it is contaminated or several years old.

The thermostat housing is located at the front of the engine. Drain the cooling system (engine cold), then remove the retaining bolts from the thermostat housing. Move the housing out of the way, then lift out the thermostat. Clean all gasket mating surfaces and make sure the new thermostat is installed correctly in the housing. Always use a new gasket. Tighten the thermostat housing bolts to 12-15 ft.lb. (17-21 Nm). Refill the cooling system, start the engine and check for leaks.

ENGINE LUBRICATION

Oil Pan

REMOVAL & INSTALLATION

2.3L (140 CID) Engine

NOTE: Aerostar's equipped with automatic transmission have the oil pans removed from the front of the engine compartment, while manual transmission vehicles have the oil pan removed from the rear.

1. Disconnect the negative battery cable. Remove the oil dipstick and tube from the engine.

2. Remove the engine mount retaining nuts.

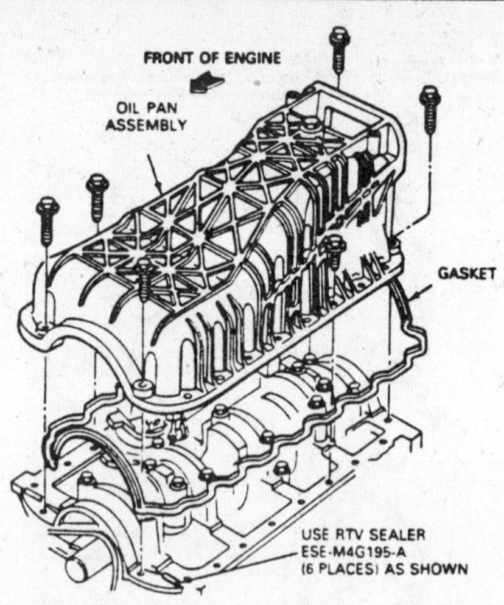

Oil pan mounting on 2.3L (140 CID) engine

3. If equipped with automatic transmission, disconnect the oil cooler lines from the radiator.

4. Remove the two bolts retaining the fan shroud to the radiator and remove the shroud.

5. On automatic transmission vehicles only, remove the radiator retaining bolts, position the radiator upward and safety wire it to the hood.

6. Raise the van and support it safely on jackstands.

7. Drain the crankcase oil into a suitable container and dispose of it properly.

8. Disconnect the starter cable from the starter, then remove the starter from the engine.

9. Disconnect the exhaust manifold tube to the inlet pipe bracket at the thermactor check valve.

10. Remove the transmission mount retaining nuts from the crossmember.

11. On automatic transmission vehicles, remove the bellcrank from the converter housing. Disconnect the transmission oil cooler lines from the retainer at the block.

12. Remove the front crossmember (automatic only).

13. Disconnect the right front lower shock absorber mount (manual transmission only).

14. Position a hydraulic jack under the engine, then raise the engine and insert a wood block approximately 2½" (63.5mm) high. Carefully lower the jack until the engine is resting securely on the wood block.

15. On automatic transmission vehicles, position the hydraulic jack under the transmission and raise it slightly.

16. Remove the oil pan retaining bolts and lower the pan to the chassis.

17. Remove the oil pump drive and pickup tube assembly.

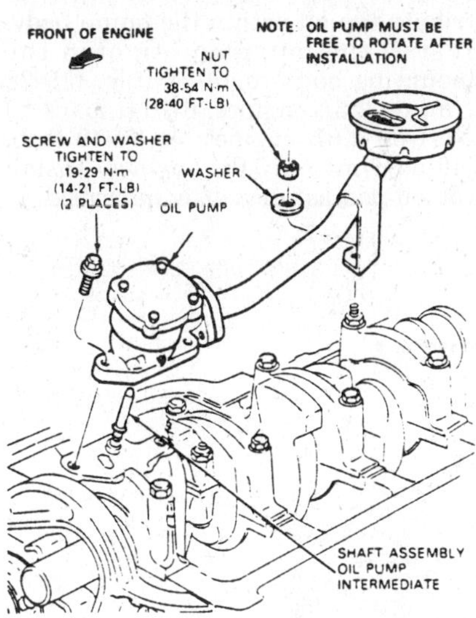

Oil pump mounting on 2.3L (140 CID) engine

18. Remove the oil pan from the front on automatics, or from the rear on manual transmissions.
19. Clean the oil pan and inspect it for damage. Remove the spacers, if any, attached to the oil pan transmission mounting pad.
20. Clean the oil pan gasket surface at the pan and engine block. Remove all traces of old gasket and/or sealer. Clean the oil pump exterior and oil pump pickup tube screen.
21. To install the pan, first position the one-piece oil pan gasket in the oil pan channel and press it into place.
22. Position the oil pan on the crossmember.
23. Install the oil pump and pickup tube assembly. Prime the oil pump with engine oil when making final installation.
24. Install the oil pan to the cylinder block with retaining bolts. Install the retaining bolts by hand, just enough to start the two oil pan-to-transmission bolts.
25. Tighten the two pan-to-transmission bolts to 29-40 ft.lb. (40-54 Nm) to align the pan with the rear face of the block, then loosen them ½ turn.
26. Tighten the oil pan-to-cylinder block bolts to 7-10 ft.lb. (10-14 Nm), then tighten the remaining two transmission bolts to 29-40 ft.lb. (40-54 Nm).

NOTE: If the oil pan is being installed on the engine with the engine removed from the van, the transmission or a special fixture must be bolted to the block to insure the oil pan is installed flush with the rear face of the block.

27. On automatic transmission models, lower the jack under the transmission. Position the jack under the engine, then raise the engine slightly and remove the wood block installed earlier.
28. Replace the oil filter.

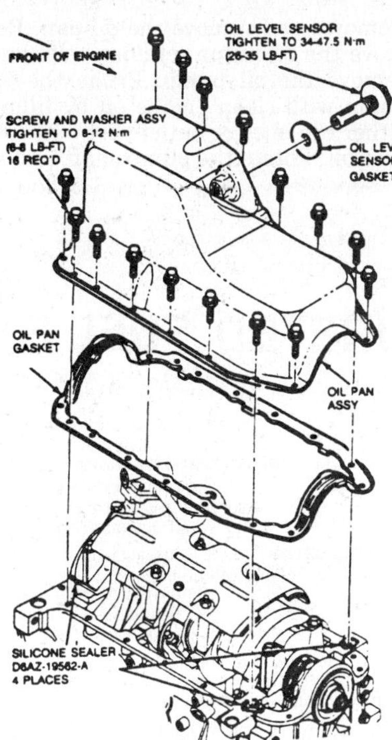

Oil pan mounting on 3.0L (182 CID) engine

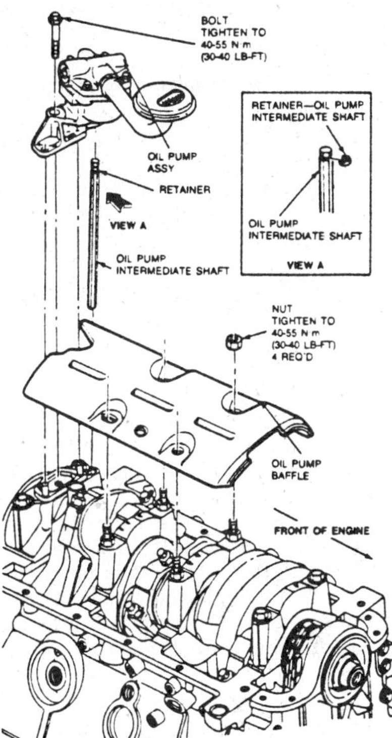

Oil pump mounting on 3.0L (182 CID) engine

29. Reconnect the exhaust manifold tube to the inlet pipe bracket at the thermactor check valve.
30. Install the transmission mount to the crossmember.
31. Install the oil cooler lines (automatic trans only) to the retainer at the block, then install the bellcrank to the converter housing.
32. Install the right front lower shock absorber mount (manual trans. only).
33. Install the front crossmember (automatic only).
34. Install the starter and connect the starter cable.
35. Lower the van.
36. Install the engine mount bolts.
37. Install the radiator and shroud. Reconnect the oil cooler lines (automatic only) to the radiator.
38. Install the oil dipstick and tube. Refill the crankcase with engine oil.
39. Start the engine and check for leaks.

2.8L (171 CID) and 3.0L (182 CID) Engines

1. Disconnect the negative battery cable.
2. Raise the van and support it safely on jackstands.
3. Remove the starter motor from the engine.
4. Remove the nuts attaching the engine front insulators to the crossmember.
5. Drain the engine oil from the crankcase into a suitable container and dispose of it properly.
6. Position a hydraulic jack under the engine and raise the engine enough to install wooden blocks between the front insulator mounts and No. 2 crossmember.
7. Carefully lower the engine onto the blocks and remove the jack.
8. Remove the oil pan attaching bolts, then lower and remove the pan from the engine block.
9. Clean all gasket surfaces on the engine and oil pan. Remove all traces of old gasket and/or sealer.
10. To install the oil pan, first apply adhesive to the gasket mating surfaces and install oil pan gaskets. Install the oil pan to the engine block.
11. Position a hydraulic jack under the engine and raise the engine to remove the wooden blocks. Lower the engine and remove the jack.
12. Install the starter motor.
13. Lower the van.
14. Install the nuts attaching the engine front insulators to the crossmember and tighten them to specifications.
15. Connect the negative battery cable.
16. Start the engine and check for leaks.

Oil Pump

REMOVAL & INSTALLATION

All Engines

Follow the procedure under Oil Pan Removal and remove the oil pan. Remove the oil pump retainer bolts and remove the oil pump. Prime the oil pump with clean engine oil by filling either the inlet or outlet port with engine oil. Rotate the pump shaft to distribute the oil within the pump body. Install the pump and tighten the mounting bolts to 14-21 ft.lb. (19-28 Nm) on 2.3L engines; 6-10 ft.lb. (9-13 Nm) on 2.8L engines; or 30-40 ft.lb. (40-55 Nm) on 3.0L engines. Install the oil pan as previously described.

CARBURETED FUEL SYSTEM

Mechanical Fuel Pump

The fuel pump is bolted to the lower left side of the cylinder block. It is mechanically operated by an eccentric on the camshaft driving a pushrod. The fuel pump cannot be disassembled for repairs and must be replaced if testing indicates it is not within performance specifications.

CAUTION

Take precautions to avoid the risk of fire whenever working on or around any fuel system. It's a good idea to have a fire extinguisher handy. Do not smoke!

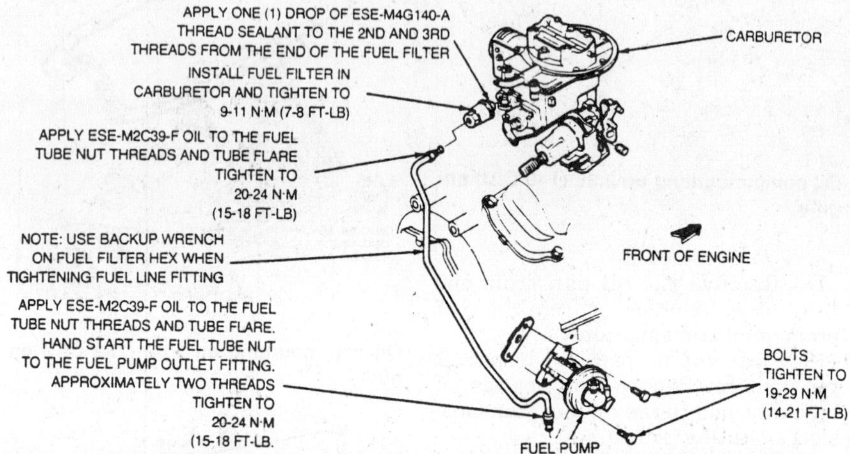

Mechanical fuel pump mounting on 2.8L (171 CID) engine

REMOVAL & INSTALLATION

1. Loosen the fuel line nut at the pump outlet, using a clean rag to catch any fuel spray that will come out when the line is loosened.
2. Loosen the fuel pump mounting bolts approximately two turns. Apply force with your hand to loosen the fuel pump if the gasket is stuck. If excessive tension is on the pump, rotate the engine until the fuel pump cam lobe is near its low position.
3. Disconnect the fuel pump inlet and outlet lines.
4. Remove the fuel pump attaching bolts and remove the pump and gasket. Discard the old gasket.
5. Remove all fuel pump gasket material from the engine and fuel pump mating surfaces.
6. Install the attaching bolts into the fuel pump and install a new gasket on the bolts. Position the fuel pump to the pushrod and the mounting pad. Turn the attaching bolts alternately and evenly and tighten them to 14-21 ft.lb. (19-29 Nm).
7. Install the fuel outlet and inlet line and tighten the outlet fitting to specifications. If any rubber hoses are cracked, hardened or frayed, replace them with new fuel hose.
8. Start the engine and observe all connections for fuel leaks for two minutes. Stop the engine and check all fuel pump fuel line connections for fuel leaks by running a finger under the connections. Check for oil leaks at the fuel pump mounting pad.

DIAGNOSIS AND TESTING

If a problem exists with the fuel pump itself, it normally will deliver either no fuel at all, or not enough to sustain high engine speeds or loads. When an engine has a lean (fuel starvation) condition, the fuel pump is often suspected as being the source of the problem, however similar symptoms will be present if the fuel filter is clogged or the fuel tank is plugged or restricted. It could also be a carburetor problem, kinked or plugged fuel line or a leaking fuel hose. If the fuel pump is noisy, check for:

1. Loose fuel pump mounting bolts. Tighten to specifications if loose and replace the gasket if damaged or worn.
2. Check for loose or missing fuel line attaching clips. This condition will result in the noise being more audible when sitting inside the vehicle than standing along side it. Tighten the fuel lines or clips, if necessary.

Before removing a suspect fuel pump:

1. Make sure there is fuel in the tank.
2. Replace the fuel filter to eliminate that possibility.
3. Check all rubber hoses from the fuel pump to the fuel tank for kinks or cracks. With the engine idling, inspect all fuel hoses and lines for leaks in the lines or connections. Tighten loose connections and replace kinked, cracked or leaking lines and/or hoses.
4. Check the fuel pump outlet connection for leaks and tighten to specification if required.
5. Inspect the fuel pump diaphragm crimp (the area where the stamped steel section is attached to the casting) and the breather hole(s) in the casting for evidence of fuel or oil leakage. Replace the fuel pump if leaking.

Capacity (Volume) Test

1. Remove the carburetor air cleaner.
2. Slowly disconnect the fuel line at the fuel filter, using a backup wrench on the filter hex to prevent damage. Use clean rags to catch any fuel spray. Exercise caution as the fuel line is pressurized and take precautions to avoid the risk of fire.
3. Place a suitable non-breakable container (1 pint minimum capacity) at the end of the disconnected fuel

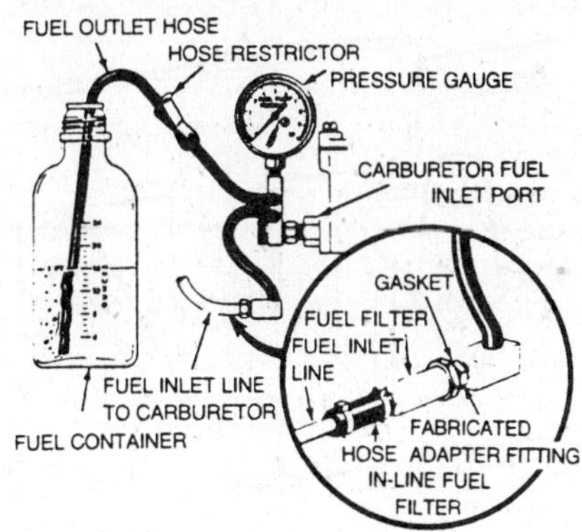

Fuel pump capacity (volume) test on 2.8L (171 CID) engine

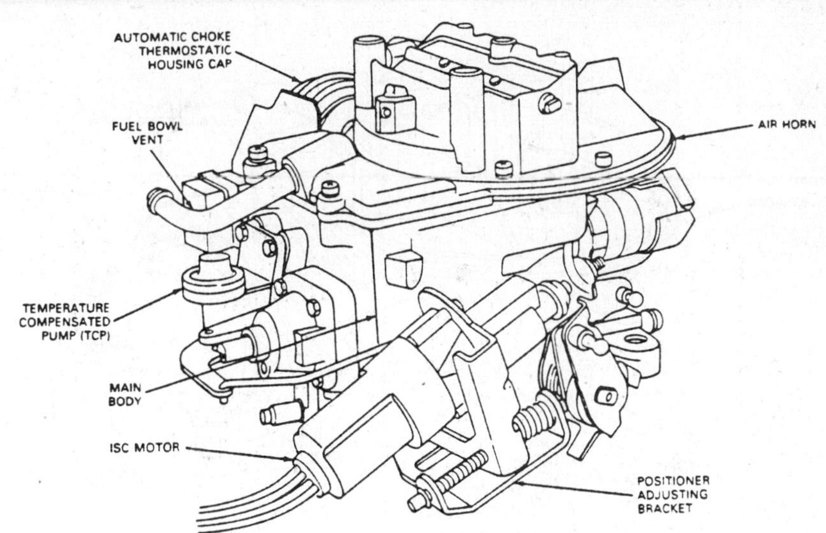

Left front view of 2150A carburetor

line. A small piece of hose may be necessary on the fuel line end.

4. With the high tension wire removed from the coil, crank the engine ten revolutions to fill the fuel lines, then crank the engine for 10 seconds and measure the fuel collected. The pump should deliver ⅓ pint (0.158 liters) of fuel, minimum.

5. If the fuel flow is within specifications, perform the Pressure Test.

6. If the fuel flow is low, repeat the test using a remote vented can of gasoline. Remove the fuel pump inlet hose, then connect a length of fuel hose to the pump inlet and insert the other end into the remote gasoline can. If the fuel flow is now within specifications, the problem is a plugged in-tank filter or a leaking, kinked or plugged fuel line or hose. Make sure the fuel pump pushrod length is 6.10-6.14" (155-156mm); if short, replace the pushrod and install the fuel pump. If the fuel flow is still low, replace the fuel pump.

Pressure Test

1. Connect a 0-15 psi fuel pump pressure tester (Rotunda No. 059-00008 or equivalent) to the carburetor end of the fuel line. No T-fitting is required.

2. Start the engine. It should be able to run for about 30 seconds on the fuel in the carburetor. Read the pressure on the gauge after about 10 seconds. It should be 4-6.5 psi (31-45 kPa).

3. If the pump pressure is too low or high, replace the fuel pump and retest.

4. Once all testing is complete, reconnect the fuel lines and remove the gauge.

Carburetor

The Motorcraft Model 2150A 2-bbl feedback carburetor is used on the 2.8L (171 CID) engine. The feedback carburetor system uses a pulsing solenoid to introduce fresh air from the air cleaner into the idle and main system vacuum passages to lean the fuel and air mixture from the maximum rich condition (solenoid closed) to the maximum lean condition (solenoid open). The solenoid operates under the control of the EEC-IV system.

The 2150A carburetor uses an all electric choke system, consisting of the choke pulldown diaphragm, choke housing and electric choke cap. The voltage applied to the choke cap is controlled by the EEC-IV computer through a "duty cycle" output, which varies between 0% (0 volts) and 100% (12 volts) to control choke operation. The tamper resistant choke cap retainer uses breakaway screws and is non-adjustable.

The fast idle speed at engine startup is controlled by the mechanical cam and adjustment screw. After startup, the cam moves out of the way, allowing the idle speed control (ISC) motor to control the idle speed. Both the kickdown and idle rpm are controlled by the EEC-IV system, eliminating the need for idle and fast idle speed adjustments. When the ignition is turned off (warm engine), the throttle rests against the curb idle screw stop to prevent run-on and then goes to maximum extension for preposition for the next engine start.

CARBURETOR ADJUSTMENTS

Most carburetor adjustments are set at the factory and should require no further attention. Choke setting and idle speed specifications are provided on the Vehicle Emission Control Decal in the engine compartment or on the engine itself.

Accelerator Pump Stroke Adjustment

The accelerator pump stroke has been set at the factory for a particular engine application and should not be readjusted. If the stroke has been changed from the specified hole, reset to specifications by performing the following procedure:

1. Using a blunt tipped punch, remove the roll pin from the accelerator pump cover. Support the area under the roll pin when removing and be careful not to lose the pin.

2. Rotate the pump link and rod assembly until the keyed end of the assembly is aligned with the keyed hole in the pump over travel lever.

3. Reposition the rod and swivel assembly in the specified hole and reinstall the pump link in the accelerator pump cover. A service accelerator rod and swivel assembly is available (part no. 9F687) and must be used if replacement is necessary. Adjustment holes are not provided on the temperature compensated accelerator pump carburetor models.

4. Install the roll pin.

Dry Float Level Adjustment

The dry float level adjustment is a preliminary fuel level adjustment only. The final, wet level adjustment must be made after the carburetor is mounted on the engine.

With the air horn removed, the float raised and the fuel inlet needle seated, check the distance between the top surface of the main body (gasket removed) and the top surface of the float

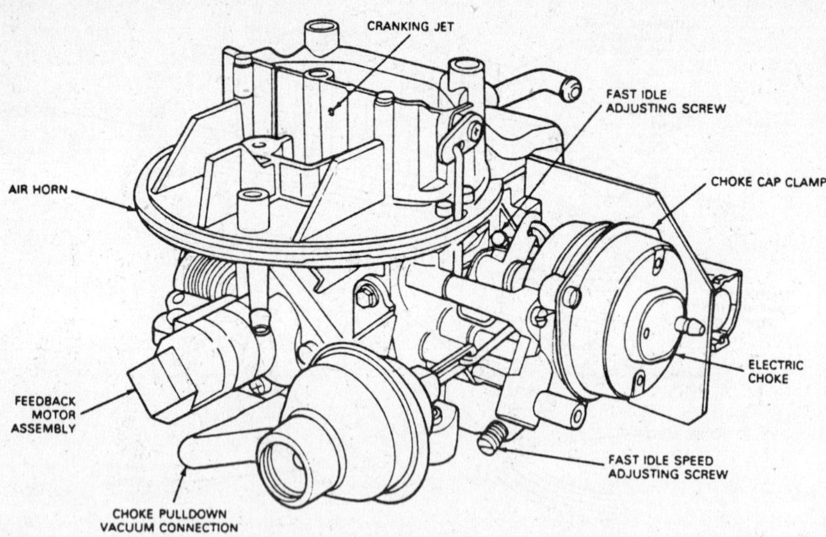

Right front view of 2150A carburetor

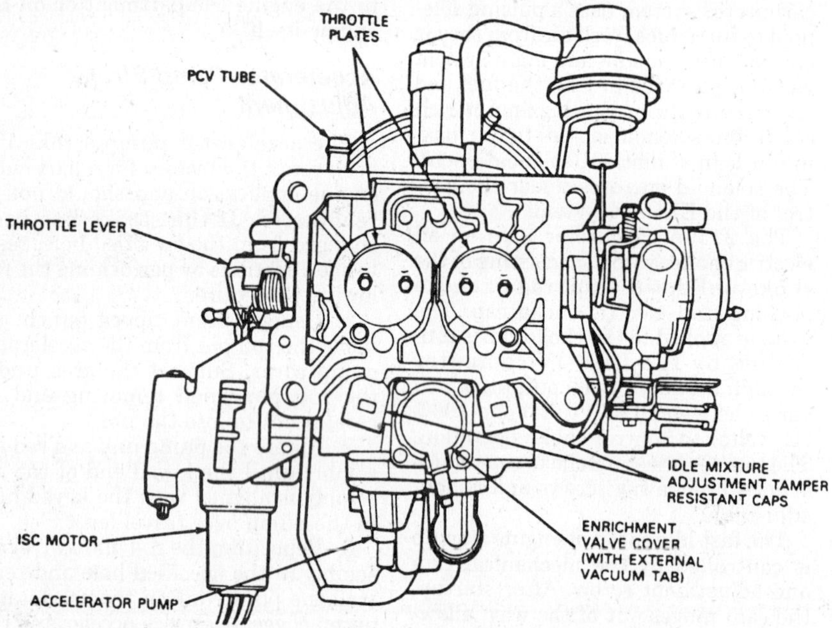

Bottom view of 2150A carburetor

for conformance to specifications. Depress the float tab lightly to seat the fuel inlet needle.

WARNING: Excessive pressure can damage the viton tip on the needle.

Take the measurement near the center of the float at a point ⅛" (3.2mm) from the free end of the float. If a cardboard float gauge is used, place the gauge in the corner of the enlarged end section of the fuel bowl. The gauge should touch the float near the end, but not on the end radius. If necessary, bend the tab on the float to bring the setting within the specified limits. This should provide the proper preliminary fuel level setting.

Wet Float Level Adjustment

1. With the vehicle level, engine warm and running, remove the air cleaner.
2. Insert fuel float level gauge T83L-9550-A, or equivalent, with the pointed end into the fuel bowl vent stack and rest the level across the other vent.
3. Siphon fuel into the sight tube and allow the fuel to reach a steady level. Take precautions to avoid the

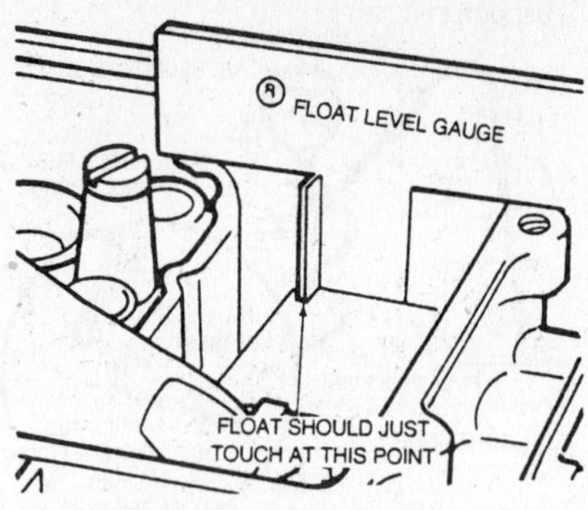

Dry float level adjustment

risk of fire. Do not smoke during this procedure.
4. Press down to level the gauge and read the fuel level on the sight tube. If the level is in the specified band, adjustment is not necessary. If the level is not correct, note the level on the sight and proceed to the next step.
5. Stop the engine and remove the choke link, air horn attaching screws, the vent hose and the air horn assembly.
6. Measure the vertical distance from the top of the machined surface of the main body to the level of the fuel in the fuel bowl.
7. With this measurement as a reference, bend the float tab up to raise the level or down to lower the level. Adjust to bring the fuel level to specifications.
8. Recheck the fuel level on the sight gauge. If OK, install the remaining air horn screws. If not OK, repeat the adjustment procedure.
9. Install the choke link and check the choke plate to make sure its free.
10. Tighten the air horn screws. Install the carburetor vent (canister) hose, then check and adjust the curb idle speed. Install the air cleaner.

Idle Speed Adjustment

NOTE: If the curb idle rpm is not within specifications after performing this procedure, it will be necessary to have the EEC-IV system diagnosed by a qualified service facility with the necessary electronic equipment.

1. Warm up the engine in Park or Neutral until it reaches normal operating temperature. Set the parking brake and block the drive wheels. Make sure all accessories are turned off.
2. Remove the air charge temperature (ACT) sensor and adapter from the air cleaner tray by removing the retaining clip. Leave the wiring harness connected.
3. Remove the air cleaner and dis-

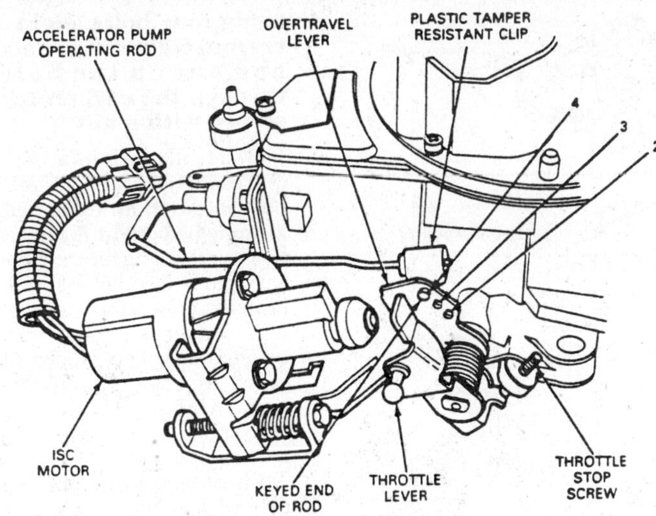

Accelerator pump stroke adjustment

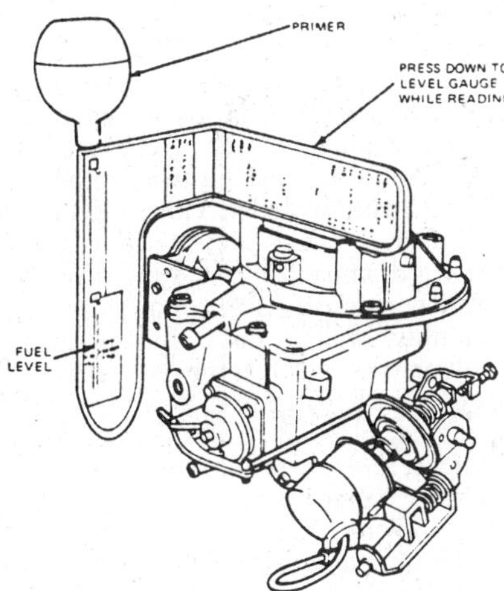

Wet fuel level adjustment gauge installed

connect and plug the vacuum line at the cold weather duct and valve motor.

4. Turn the engine off and verify that the idle speed control (ISC) plunger moves to its maximum extension within 10 seconds.

5. Disconnect and plug the EGR vacuum hose. Disconnect the idle speed control.

6. With the engine running, manually open the throttle and set the fast idle adjusting screw on the high cam.

7. Adjust the fast idle speed to the specification given on the underhood emission control sticker.

8. Open the throttle manually to release the fast idle cam, allowing the throttle lever to rest on the ISC plunger.

9. Loosen the ISC bracket lock screw, then adjust the ISC bracket screw to obtain 2,000 rpm. Tighten the bracket lock screw.

10. Reconnect the ISC motor connector. The engine rpm should automatically return to curb idle.

11. Simultaneously:

a. manually hold the throttle above 1,000 rpm

b. push the ISC plunger until it retracts fully

c. after plunger retracts, release the throttle and quickly unplug the connection.

12. Adjust the anti-dieseling speed throttle stop screw to 750 rpm with the transmission (automatic or manual) in Neutral. Be careful to adjust the anti-dieseling stop screw, NOT the curb idle stop screw.

13. Connect the ISC and EGR vacuum hoses.

14. Turn the engine off, then restart the engine and verify that curb idle speed is within specifications.

Mixture Adjustment

The fuel mixture is preset at the factory and computer controlled thereafter. No adjustments are possible without the use of propane enrichment equipment that is not readily available to the do-it-yourself market. All mixture adjustments should be performed at a qualified service facility to insure compliance with Federal and/or State Emission Control Standards.

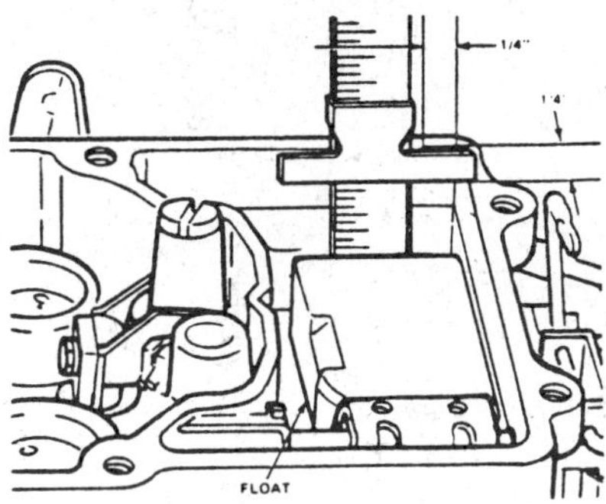

Measuring the fuel level in the fuel bowl

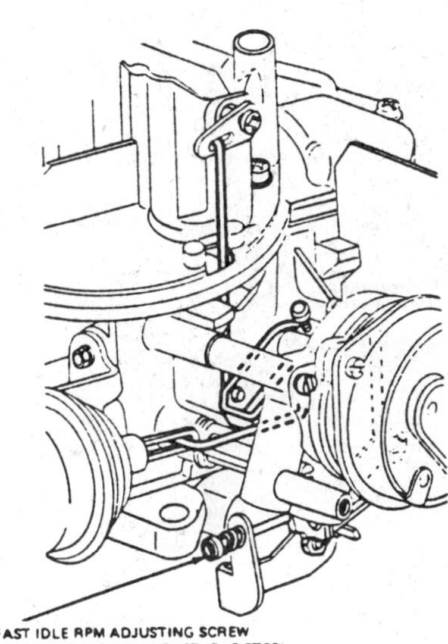

Fast idle adjustment on 2150A carburetor

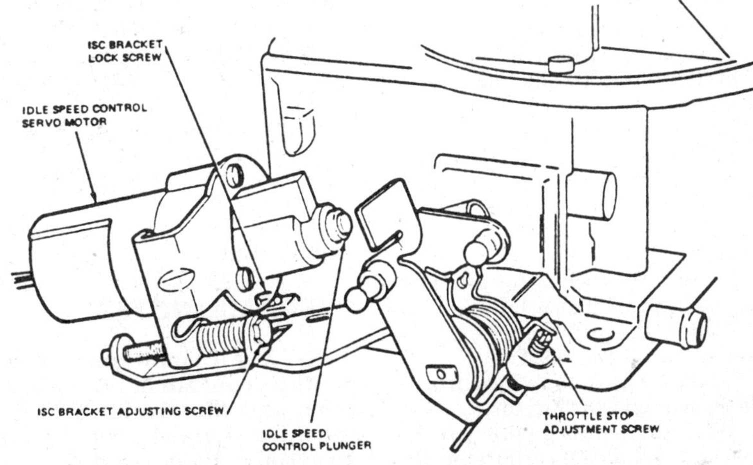

Idle speed control adjustment on 2150A carburetor

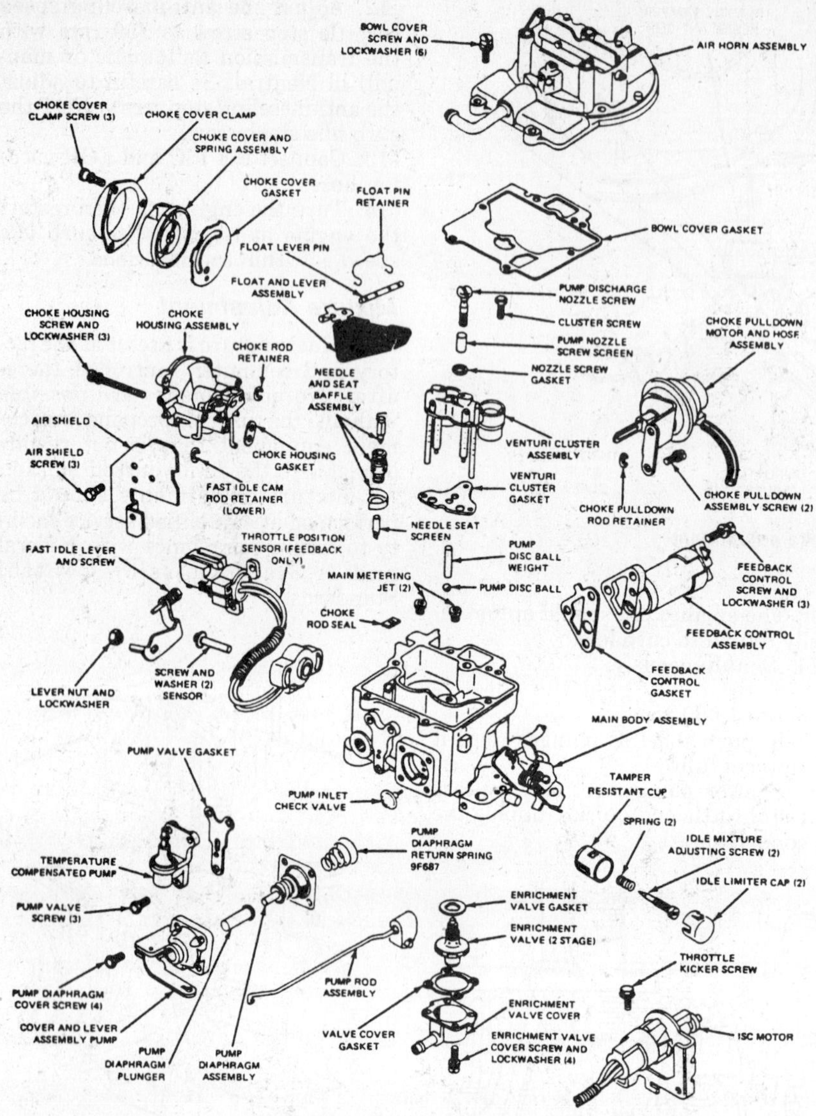

Exploded view of 2150A carburetor

CARBURETOR REMOVAL & INSTALLATION

1. Remove the air cleaner.
2. Remove the throttle cable from the throttle lever. Tag and disconnect all vacuum lines, emission hoses and electrical connections.
3. Disconnect the fuel line at the carburetor. Use a clean rag to catch any fuel spray and use a backup wrench on the fuel filter hex to avoid twisting the line.
4. Remove the carburetor retaining nuts, then lift off the carburetor.
5. Remove the carburetor mounting gasket spacer, if equipped.
6. Clean the gasket mating surfaces of the spacer and carburetor.
7. Position a new gasket on the spacer and install the carburetor. Secure the carburetor with the mounting nuts. To prevent leakage, distortion or damage to the carburetor body flange, snug the nuts then alternately tighten each nut in a criss-cross pattern to 14-16 ft.lb. (20-21 Nm).
8. Connect the fuel line and throttle cable.
9. Connect all emission lines, vacuum hoses and electrical connectors.
10. Start the engine and check the idle speeds (fast and curb). Refer to the underhood emission sticker for specifications.

OVERHAUL NOTES

NOTE: All major and minor repair kits contain detailed instructions and illustrations. Refer to them for complete rebuilding instructions. To prevent damage to the throttle plates, make a stand using four bolts, eight flat washers and eight nuts. Place a washer and nut on the bolt, install through the carburetor base and secure with a nut.

Generally, when a carburetor requires major service, rebuilt one is purchased on an exchange basis, or a kit may be bought for overhauling the carburetor. The kit contains the necessary parts (see below) and some form of instructions for carburetor rebuilding. The instructions may vary between a simple exploded view and detailed step-by-step rebuilding instructions. Unless you are familiar with carburetor overhaul, the latter should be used.

There are some general overhaul procedures which should always be observed:

Efficient carburetion depends greatly on careful cleaning and inspection during overhaul since dirt, gum, water, or varnish in or on the carburetor parts are often responsible for poor performance. Overhaul your carburetor in a clean, dust-free area. Carefully disassembly the carburetor, referring often to the exploded views. Keep all similar and lookalike parts segregated during disassembly and cleaning to avoid accidental interchange during assembly. Make a note of all jet sizes.

When the carburetor is disassembled, wash all parts (except diaphragms, electric choke units. pump plunger, and any other plastic, leather, fiber, or rubber parts) in clean carburetor solvent. Do not leave parts in the solvent any longer than is necessary to sufficiently loosen the deposits. Excessive cleaning may remove the special finish from the float bowl and choke valve bodies, leaving these parts unfit for service. Rinse all parts in clean solvent and blow them dry with compressed air or allow them to air dry. Wipe clean all cork, plastic, leather, and fiber parts with a clean, lint free cloth.

Blow out all passages and jets with compressed air and be sure that there are no restrictions or blockages. Never use wire or similar tools to clean jets, fuel passages, or air bleeds. Clean all jets and valves separately to avoid accidental interchange.

Check all parts for wear or damage. If wear or damage is found, replace the defective parts. Especially check the following:

1. Check the float needle and seat for wear. If wear is found, replace the complete assembly.
2. Check the float hinge pin for wear and the float(s) for dents or distortion. Replace the float if fuel has leaked into it.
3. Check the throttle and choke

shaft bores for wear or an out-of-round condition. Damage or wear to the throttle arm, shaft, shaft bore will often require replacement of the throttle body. These parts require a close tolerance; wear may allow air leakage, which could affect starting and idling.

NOTE: Throttle shafts and bushings are usually not included in overhaul kits. They can be purchased separately.

4. Inspect the idle mixture adjusting needles for burrs or grooves. Any such condition requires replacement of the needle, since you will not be able to obtain a satisfactory idle.
5. Test the accelerator pump check valves. They should pass air one way but not the other. Test for proper seating by blowing and sucking on the valve. Replace the valve if necessary. If the valve is satisfactory, wash the valve again to remove breath moisture.
6. Check the bowl cover for warped surfaces with a straightedge.
7. Closely inspect the valves and seats for wear and damage, replacing as necessary.
8. After the carburetor is assembled, check the choke valve for freedom of operation.

Carburetor overhaul kits are recommended for each overhaul. These kits contain all gaskets and new parts to replace those that deteriorate most rapidly. Failure to replace all parts supplied with the kit (especially gaskets) can result in poor performance later. Some carburetor manufacturers supply overhaul kits of three basic types: minor repair; major repair; and gasket kits. Basically, they contain the following:

Minor Repair Kits:
- All gaskets
- Float needle valve
- Volume control screw
- All diaphragms
- Spring for the pump diaphragm

Major Repair Kits:
- All jets and gaskets
- All diaphragms
- Float needle valve
- Volume control screw
- Pump ball valve
- Main jet carrier
- Float
- Other necessary items
- Some cover holddown screws and washers

Gasket Kits:
- All gaskets

After cleaning and checking all components, reassemble the carburetor, using new parts and referring to the exploded view. When reassembling, make sure that all screw and jets are tight in their seats, buy do not overtighten, as the tips will be distorted. Tighten all screws gradually, in rotation. Do not tighten needle valves into their seat; uneven jetting will result. Always use new gaskets. Be sure to adjust the float level when reassembling.

FUEL INJECTION SYSTEM

The electronic fuel injection (EFI) system used on the 2.3L and 3.0L engines is classified as a multi-point, pulse time, speed density fuel delivery system which meters fuel into the intake air stream in accordance with engine demand through four or six injectors mounted on a tuned intake manifold.

An on-board electronic engine control (EEC-IV) computer accepts inputs from various engine sensors to compute the required fuel flow rate necessary to maintain a prescribed air/fuel ratio throughout the entire engine operational range. The computer then outputs a command to the fuel injectors to meter the required quantity of fuel. The EEC-IV engine control system also determines and compensates for the age of the vehicle and its uniqueness. The system will automatically sense and compensate for changes in altitude, such as driving up and down a mountain road.

The fuel injection system uses a high pressure, chassis or tank mounted electric fuel pump to deliver fuel from the tank to the fuel charging manifold assembly. The fuel charging manifold assembly incorporates electrically actuated fuel injectors directly above each of the engine's intake ports. The injectors, when energized, spray a metered quantity of fuel into the intake air stream. A constant pressure drop is maintained across the injector nozzles by a pressure regulator, connected in series with the fuel injectors and positioned downstream from them. Excess fuel supplied by the pump, but not required by the engine, passes through the regulator and returns to the fuel tank through a fuel return line.

On four cylinder engines, all injectors are energized simultaneously, once every crankshaft revolution. On V6 engines, the injectors are energized in two groups of three injectors, with each group activated once every other crankshaft revolution. The period of time that the injectors are energized (injector "on time" or "pulse width") is controlled by the EEC-IV computer. The input from various sensors is used to compute the required fuel flow rate necessary to maintain a prescribed air/fuel ratio.

NOTE: This book contains simple testing and service procedures for the Aerostar fuel injec-

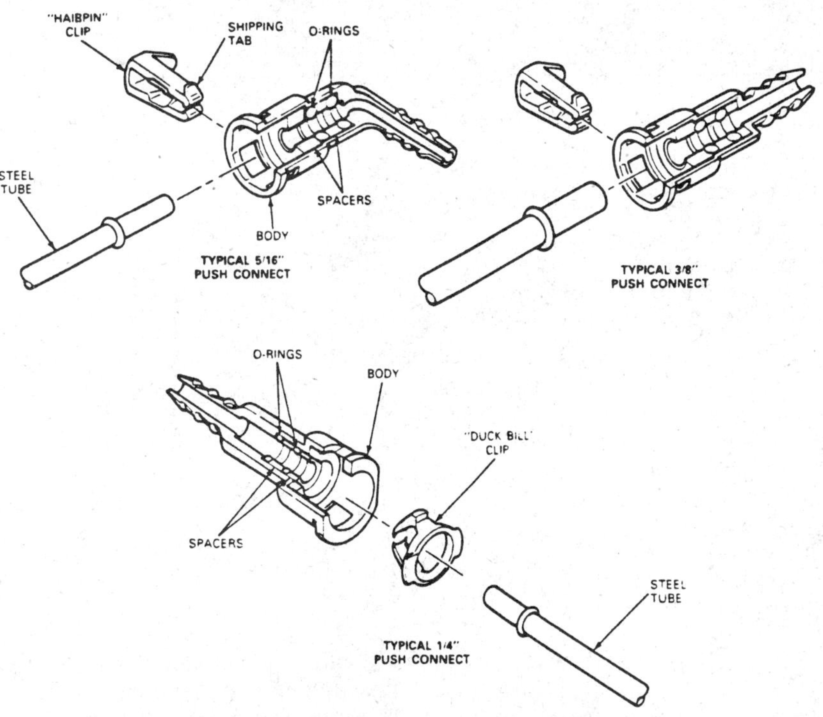

Various types of quick connect fuel line fittings

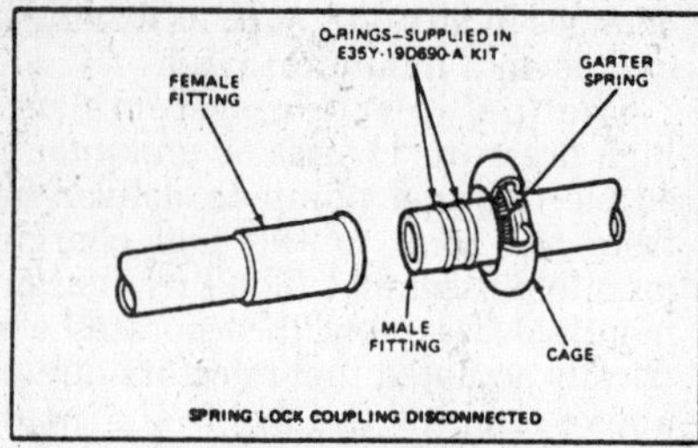

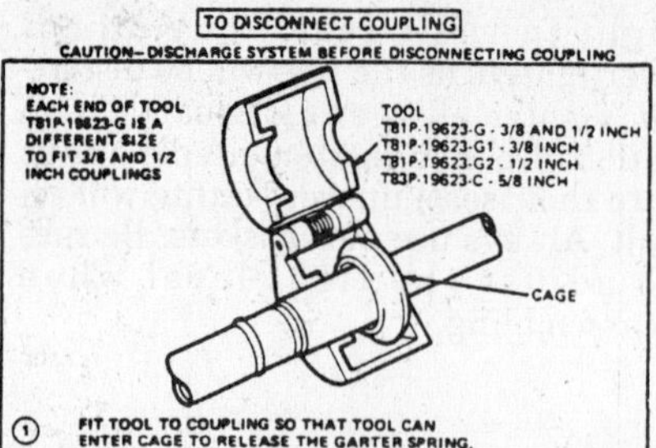

TO CONNECT COUPLING

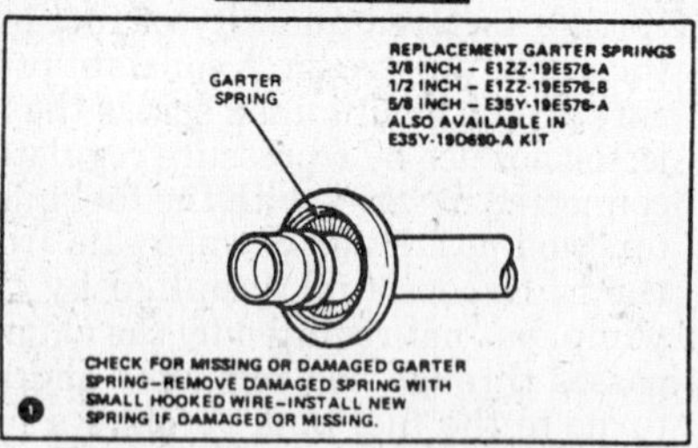

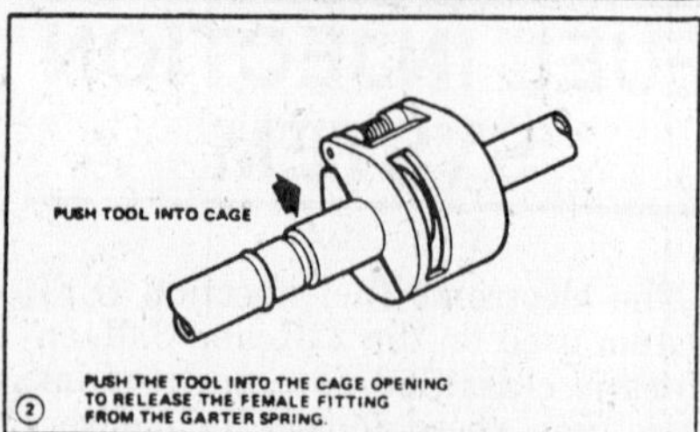

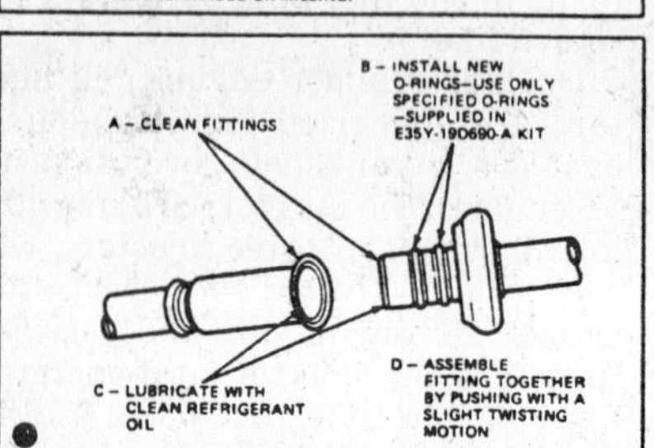

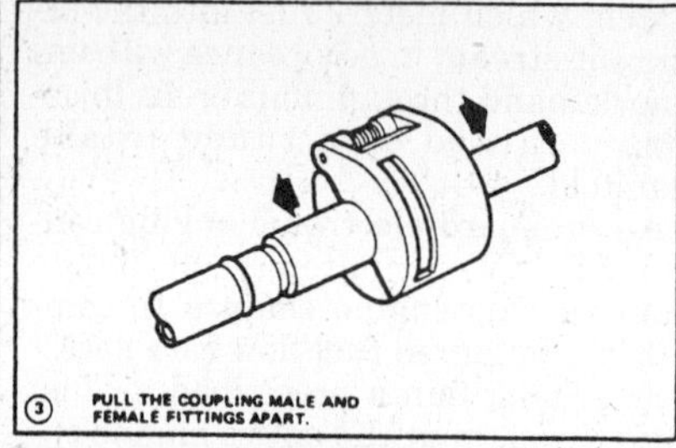

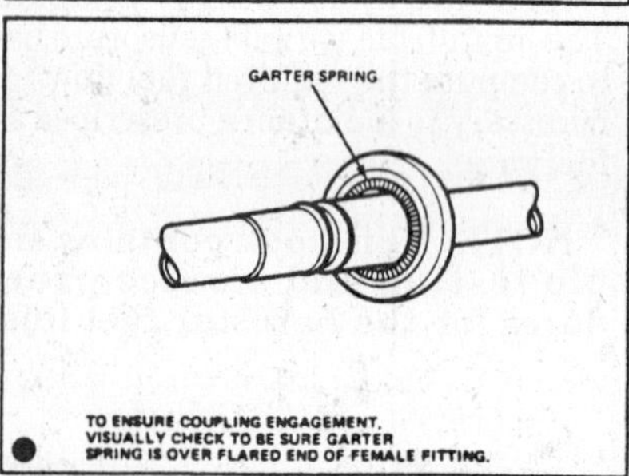

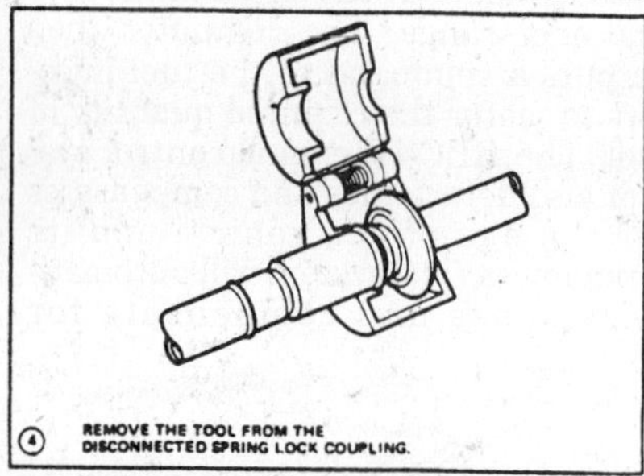

Spring lock coupling removal and installation procedure

tion system. More comprehensive testing and diagnosis procedures may be found in CHILTON'S GUIDE TO FUEL INJECTION AND FEEDBACK CARBURETORS, book part number 7488, available at your local retailer.

CAUTION

Fuel supply lines on vehicles with fuel injection will remain pressurized for long periods of time after engine shutdown. This fuel pressure must be relieved before any service procedures are attempted on the fuel system.

RELIEVING FUEL SYSTEM PRESSURE

All fuel injected engines are equipped with a pressure relief valve located on the fuel supply manifold. Remove the fuel tank cap and attach

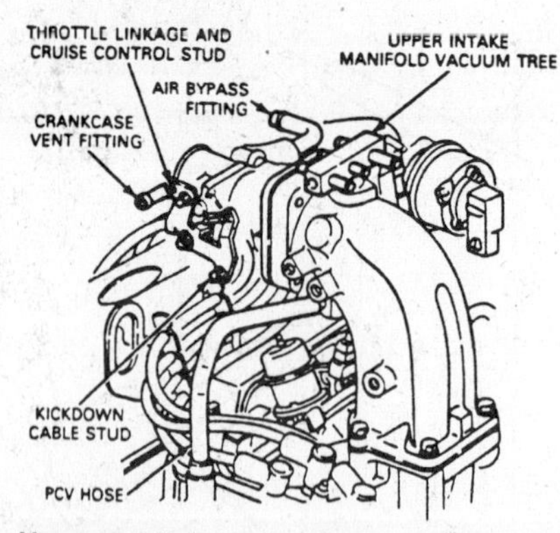

Hose and linkage locations on 2.3L (140 CID) engine

fuel pressure gauge T80L-9974-A, or equivalent, to the valve to release the fuel pressure. If a suitable pressure gauge is not available, disconnect the vacuum hose from the fuel pressure

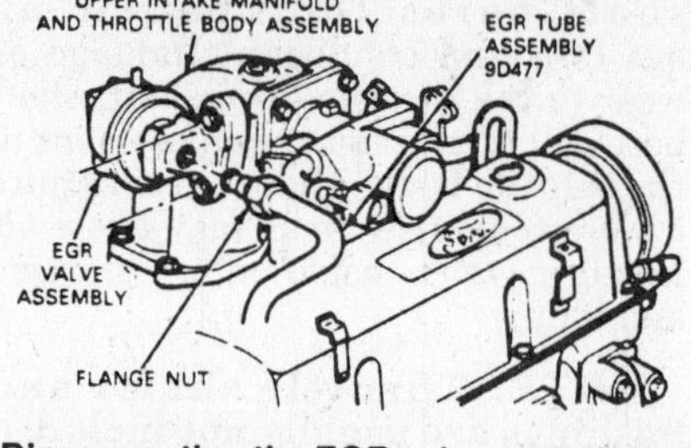

Disconnecting the EGR valve on 2.3L (140 CID) engine

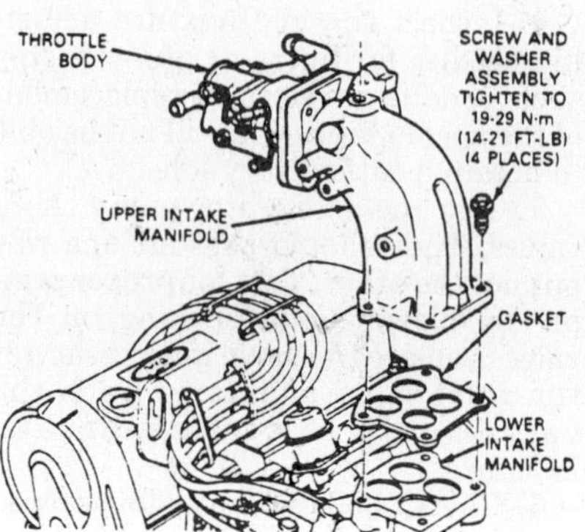

Removing upper intake manifold and throttle body on 2.3L (140 CID) engine

regulator and attach a hand vacuum pump. Apply about 25 in.Hg (84 kPa) of vacuum to the regulator to vent the fuel system pressure into the fuel tank through the fuel return hose. Note that this procedure will remove the fuel pressure from the lines, but not the fuel. Take precautions to avoid the risk of fire and use clean rags to soak up any spilled fuel when the lines are disconnected.

Quick Connect Fuel Line Fittings

REMOVAL & INSTALLATION

NOTE: Quick Connect (push) type fuel line fittings must be disconnected using proper procedures or the fitting may be damaged. Two types of retainers are used on the push connect fittings. Line sizes of 3/8" and 5/16" use a "hairpin" clip retainer. 1/4" line connectors use a "duck bill" clip retainer. In addition, some engines use spring lock connections secured by a garter spring which requires a special tool (T81P-19623-G) for removal.

Hairpin Clip

1. Clean all dirt and/or grease from the fitting. Spread the two clip legs about 1/8" (3mm) each to disengage

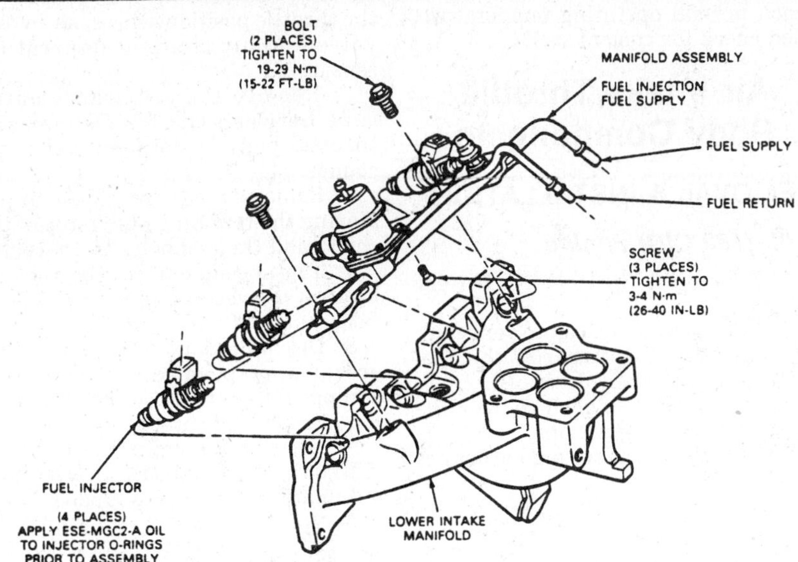

Location of fuel return and supply lines on 2.3L (140 CID) engine

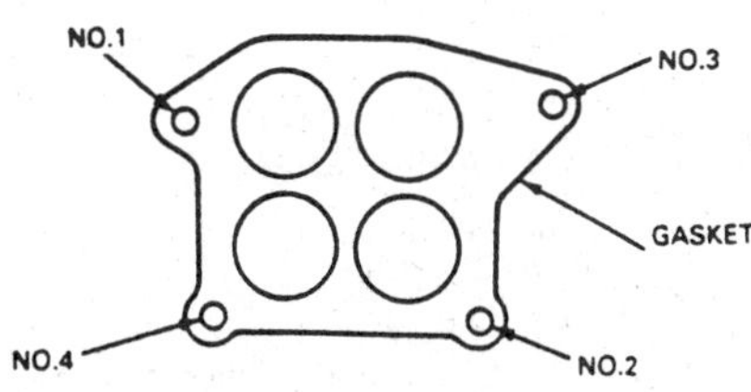

Upper intake manifold torque sequence on 2.3L (140 CID) engine

from the fitting and pull the clip outward from the fitting. Use finger pressure only, do not use any tools.

2. Grasp the fitting and hose assembly and pull away from the steel line. Twist the fitting and hose assembly slightly while pulling, if necessary, when a sticking condition exists.

3. Inspect the hairpin clip for damage, replace the clip if necessary. Reinstall the clip in position on the fitting.

4. Inspect the fitting and inside of the connector to insure freedom of dirt or obstruction. Install fitting into the connector and push together. A click will be heard when the hairpin snaps into proper connection. Pull on the line to insure full engagement.

Duck Bill Clip

1. A special tool is available from Ford for removing the retaining clips (Ford Tool No. T82L-9500-AH). If the tool is not on hand see Step 2. Align the slot on the push connector disconnect tool with either tab on the retaining clip. Pull the line from the connector.

2. If the special clip tool is not available, use a pair of narrow 6″ (152mm) channel lock pliers with a jaw width of 0.2″ (5mm) or less. Align the jaws of the pliers with the openings of the fitting case and compress the part of the retaining clip that engages the case. Compressing the retaining clip will release the fitting which may be pulled from the connector. Both sides of the clip must be compressed at the same time to disengage.

3. Inspect the retaining clip, fitting end and connector. Replace the clip if any damage is apparent.

4. Push the line into the steel connector until a click is heard, indicting the clip is in place. Pull on the line to check engagement.

Electric Fuel Pump

REMOVAL & INSTALLATION

The electric fuel pump is either mounted on the chassis, in an assembly with the inline fuel filter, or at the base of the fuel tank sending unit in the fuel tank. For chassis mounted pumps, follow the procedures under "Fuel Filter Removal and Installation" in ROUTINE MAINTENANCE, then disconnect the electrical connector and remove the fuel pump and filter mounting bracket with the filter and pump attached. For tank mounted pumps, follow the procedures under remove the tank, then the pump and sending unit. In either case, the fuel pump is non-serviceable and must be replaced as a unit if defective. Do not attempt to apply battery voltage to the pump to check its operation while removed from the vehicle, as running the pump dry will destroy it. Depressurize the fuel system before attempting to remove any fuel lines.

Fuel Charging Assembly

REMOVAL & INSTALLATION

2.3L (140 CID) Engine

1. Drain the cooling system.
2. Disconnect the negative battery cable.
3. Relieve the fuel system pressure as described above.
4. Disconnect the electrical connectors to the throttle position sensor, knock sensor, air charge temperature sensor, coolant temperature sensor and the injector wiring harness.
5. Tag and disconnect the vacuum lines at the upper intake manifold vacuum tree, the EGR valve vacuum line and the fuel pressure regulator vacuum line.
6. Remove the throttle linkage shield and disconnect the throttle linkage and speed control cable, if equipped. Unbolt the accelerator cable from the bracket and position the cable out of the way.
7. Disconnect the air intake hose, air bypass hose and crankcase vent hose.
8. Disconnect the PCV hose from the fitting on the underside of the upper intake manifold.
9. Loosen the hose clamp on the coolant bypass line at the lower intake manifold and disconnect the hose.
10. Disconnect the EGR tube from the EGR valve by removing the flange nut.
11. Remove the four upper intake manifold retaining nuts, then remove the upper intake manifold and air throttle body assembly.
12. Disconnect the push connect fitting at the fuel supply manifold and fuel return lines, then disconnect the fuel return line from the fuel supply manifold.
13. Remove the engine oil dipstick bracket retaining bolt.
14. Disconnect the electrical connectors from all four fuel injectors and move the harness aside.
15. Remove the two fuel supply manifold retaining bolt, then carefully remove the fuel supply manifold with the injectors attached. The injectors may be removed from the fuel supply manifold at this time by exerting a slight twisting/pulling motion.
16. Lubricate new injector O-rings with a light grade engine oil and install two on each injector. If the injectors were not removed from the fuel supply manifold, only one O-ring will be nec-

essary. Do not use silicone grease on the O-rings as it will clog the injectors. Make sure the injector caps are clean and free of contamination.

17. Install the fuel injector supply manifold and injectors into the intake manifold, making sure the injectors are fully seated, then secure the fuel manifold assembly with the two retaining bolts. Tighten the retaining bolts to 15-22 ft.lb. (20-30 Nm).

18. Reconnect the four electrical connectors to the injectors.

19. Clean the gasket mating surfaces of the upper and lower intake manifold. Place a new gasket on the lower intake manifold, then place the upper intake manifold in position. Install the four retaining bolts and tighten them, in sequence, to 15-22 ft.lb. (20-30 Nm).

20. Install the engine oil dipstick.

21. Connect the fuel supply and return fuel lines to the fuel supply manifold.

22. Connect the EGR tube to the EGR valve and tighten the fitting to 6-8.5 ft.lb. (8-11.5 Nm).

23. Connect the coolant bypass line and tighten the clamp.

24. Connect the PCV system hose to the fitting on the underside of the upper intake manifold.

25. Reconect the upper intake manifold vacuum lines, being careful to install them in their original locations. Reconnect the vacuum lines to the EGR valve and fuel pressure regulator.

26. Hold the accelerator cable bracket in position on the upper intake manifold and install the retaining bolt. Tighten the bolt to 10-15 ft.lb. (13-20 Nm).

27. Install the accelerator cable to the bracket.

28. If the air intake throttle body was removed from the upper intake manifold, position a new gasket on the mounting flange and install the throttle body.

29. Connect the accelerator cable and speed control cable. Install the throttle linkage shield.

30. Reconnect the electrical connectors to the throttle position sensor, knock sensor, air charge temperature sensor, coolant temperature sensor and injector wiring harness.

31. Connect the air intake hose, air bypass hose and crankcase vent hose.

32. Connect the negative battery cable.

33. Refill the cooling system.

34. Build up fuel pressure by turning the ignition switch on and off at least six times, leaving the ignition on for at least five seconds each time. Check for fuel leaks.

35. Start the engine and allow it to reach normal operating temperature, then check for coolant leaks.

Air Intake/Throttle Body Components

REMOVAL & INSTALLATION

3.0L (182 CID) Engine

1. Disconnect the negative battery cable.

2. Remove the fuel cap to vent tank pressure, then depressurize the fuel system as previously described.

3. Disconnect the push connect fitting at the fuel supply line.

4. Disconnect the wiring harness at the throttle position sensor, air bypass valve and air charge temperature sensor.

5. Remove the air cleaner outlet tube between the air cleaner and throttle body by loosening the two clamps.

6. Remove the snow shield by removing the retaining nut on top of the shield and the two bolts on the side.

7. Tag and disconnect the vacuum hoses at the vacuum fittings on the intake manifold.

8. Disconnect and remove the accelerator and speed control cables (if equipped) from the accelerator mounting bracket and throttle lever.

9. Remove the transmission valve (TV) linkage from the throttle lever on automatic transmission models.

10. Remove the six retaining bolts and lift the air intake/throttle body as-

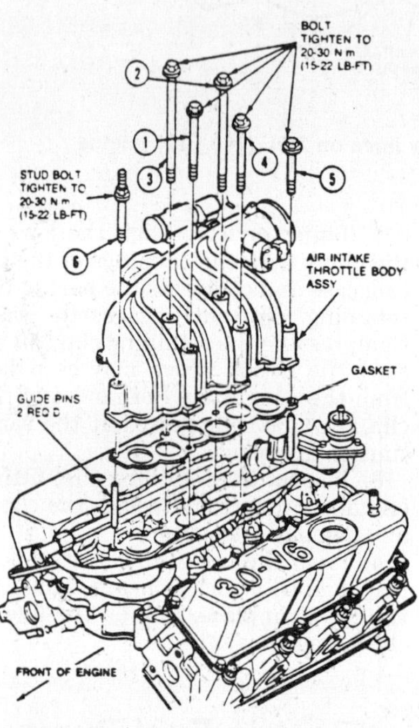

Removing air intake/throttle body assembly. Tighten the bolts in the numbered sequence when installing

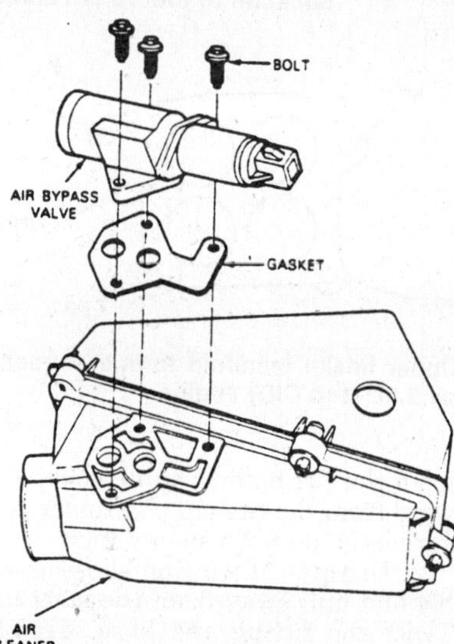

Air bypass valve mounting on 2.3L (140 CID) engine

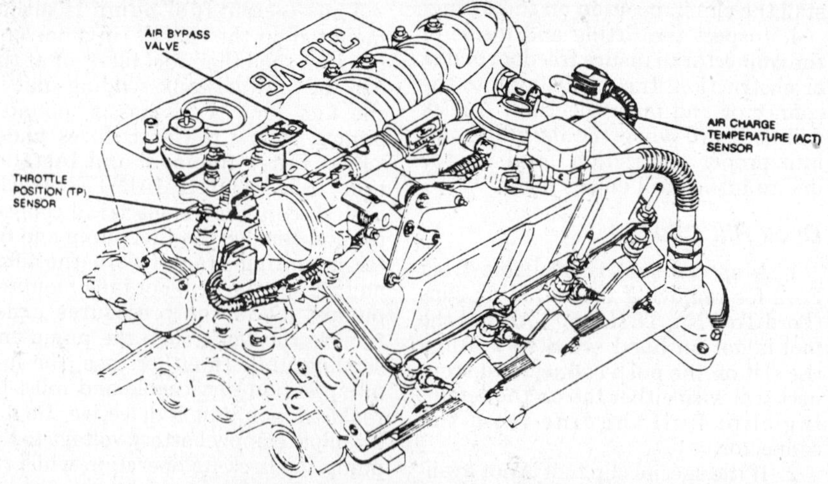

Wiring connections on 3.0L (182 CID) engine

sembly off the guide pins on the lower intake manifold and remove the assembly from the engine.

11. Remove and discard the gasket from the lower intake manifold assembly.

12. Clean and inspect the mounting faces of the air intake/throttle body assembly and the lower intake manifold. Both surfaces must be clean and flat.

13. Clean and oil the manifold stud threads.

14. Install a new gasket on the lower intake manifold.

15. Using the guide pins as locators, install the air intake/throttle body assembly to the lower intake manifold.

16. Install the stud bolt and five retaining bolts as illustrated finger tight, then tighten them to 15-22 ft.lb (20-30 Nm) in the numbered sequence illustrated.

17. Connect the fuel supply and return lines to the fuel rail.

18. Connect the wiring harness to the throttle position sensor, air charge temperature sensor and air bypass valve.

19. Install the accelerator cable and speed control cable, if equipped.

20. Install the vacuum hoses to the vacuum fittings, making sure the hoses are installed in their original locations.

21. Install the throttle valve linkage to the throttle lever, if equipped with automatic transmission.

22. Reconnect the negative battery cable.

23. Install the fuel tank cap.

24. Install the snow shield and air cleaner outlet tube.

25. Build up fuel pressure by turning the ignition switch on and off at least six times, leaving the ignition on for at least five seconds each time. Check for fuel leaks.

26. Start the engine and adjust the idle speed, if necessary.

Air Bypass Valve

REMOVAL & INSTALLATION

2.3L (140 CID) Engine

1. Disconnect the electrical connector at the air bypass valve.
2. Remove the air cleaner cover.
3. Separate the air bypass valve and gasket from the air cleaner by removing the three mounting bolts.
4. Install the air bypass valve and gasket to the air cleaner cover and tighten the retaining bolts to 6-8 ft.lb. (8-11 Nm).
5. Install the air cleaner cover.
6. Reconnect the air bypass valve electrical connector.

3.0L (182 CID) Engine

1. Disconnect the air bypass valve connector.
2. Remove the air bypass valve retaining screws.
3. Remove the air bypass valve and gasket from the air intake/throttle body assembly. If scraping is necessary to remove old gasket material, be careful not to damage the air bypass valve or throttle body gasket mounting surfaces. Do not allow any foreign material to drop into the throttle body during service.
4. Installation is the reverse of removal. Tighten the mounting bolts to 6-8 ft.lb. (8-11 Nm).

Fuel Injector Manifold Assembly

REMOVAL & INSTALLATION

2.3L (140 CID) Engine

For injector and fuel manifold removal, follow the procedures under "Fuel Charging Assembly Removal and Installation."

3.0L (182 CID) Engine

1. Remove the air intake/throttle body assembly as previously described. Be sue to depressurize the fuel system before disconnecting any fuel lines.
2. Carefully disconnect the wiring harness from the fuel injectors.
3. Disconnect the vacuum line from the fuel pressure regulator.
4. Remove the four fuel injector manifold retaining bolts, two on each side.
5. Carefully disengage the fuel rail assembly from the fuel injectors by lifting and gently rocking the rail.
6. Remove the fuel injectors from the intake manifold by lifting while gently rocking from side to side. Place all removed components on a clean surface to prevent contamination by dirt or grease.

CAUTION

Injectors and fuel rail must be handles with extreme care to prevent damage to sealing areas and sensitive fuel metering orifices.

7. Examine the injector O-rings for deterioration or damage and install new O-rings, if required (two per injector).
8. Make sure the injector caps are clean and free from contamination or damage.
9. Lubricate all O-rings with clean engine oil, then install the injectors in the fuel rail using a light twisting/pushing motion.
10. Carefully install the fuel rail assembly and injectors into the lower intake manifold, one side at a time, pushing down on the fuel rail to make sure the O-rings are seated.
11. Hold the fuel rail assembly in place and install the retaining bolts finger tight. Tighten the retaining bolts to 6-8 ft.lb. (8-12 Nm).
12. Connect the fuel supply and return lines.

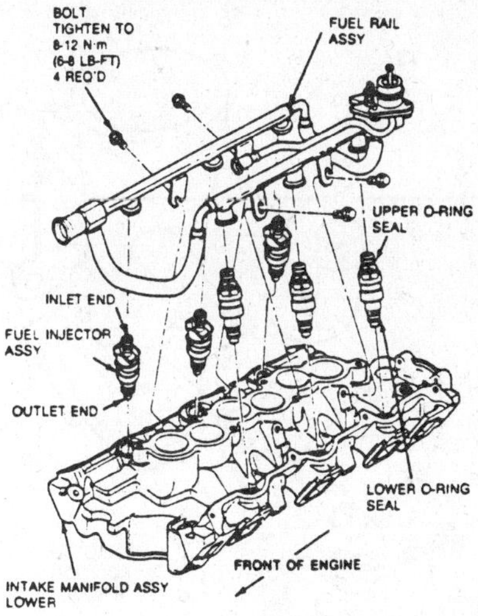

Fuel rail and injectors on 3.0L (182 CID) engine

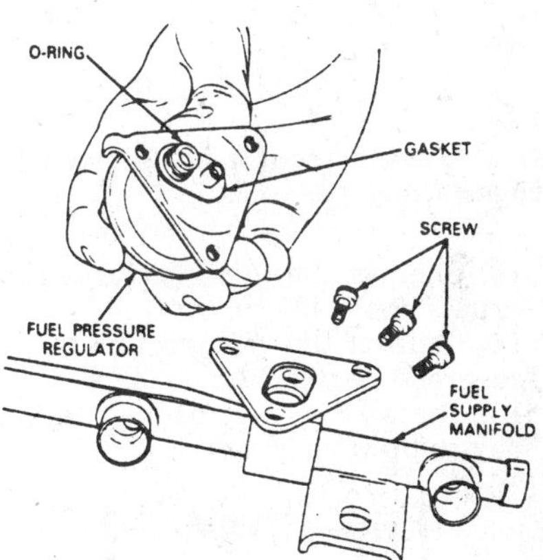

Typical fuel pressure regulator assembly mounting

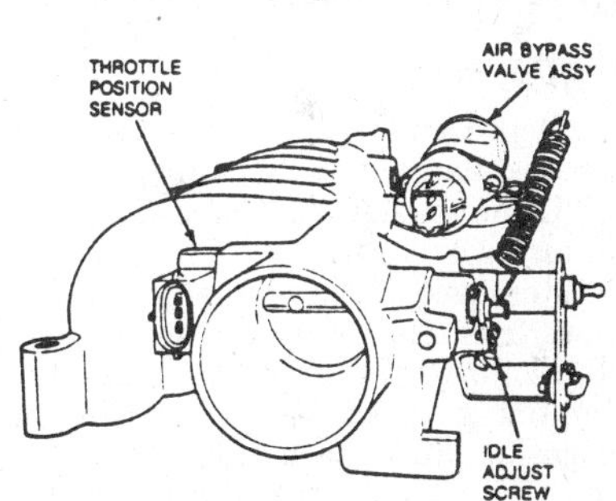

Location of throttle position sensor on 3.0L (182 CID) engine

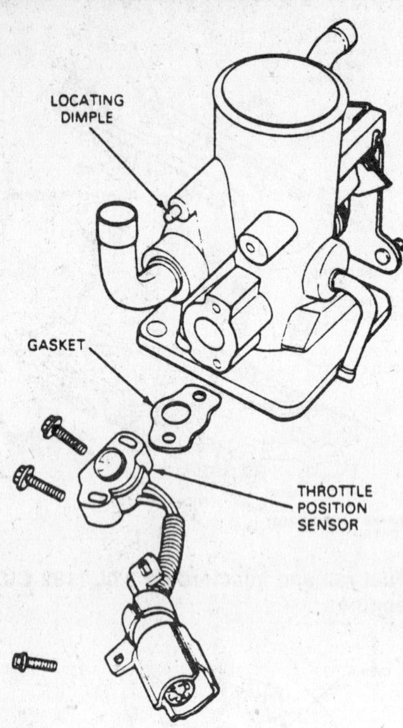

Throttle position sensor on 2.3L (140 CID) engine

13. Connect the fuel injector wiring harness at the injectors.
14. Connect the vacuum line to the fuel pressure regulator.
15. Install the air intake/throttle body as previously described.

Fuel Pressure Regulator

REMOVAL & INSTALLATION

All Engines

1. Depressurize the fuel system as described earlier.
2. Remove the vacuum line at the pressure regulator.
3. Remove the three allen retaining screws from the regulator housing.
4. Remove the pressure regulator assembly, gasket and O-ring. Discard the gasket and check the O-ring for signs of cracks or deterioration.
5. Clean the gasket mating surfaces. If scraping is necessary, be careful not to damage the fuel pressure regulator or supply line gasket mating surfaces.
6. Lubricate the pressure regulator O-ring with with light engine oil. Do not use silicone grease; it will clog the injectors.
7. Install the O-ring and a new gasket on the pressure regulator.
8. Install the pressure regulator on the fuel manifold and tighten the retaining screws to 27-40 in.lb. (3-4 Nm).
9. Install the vacuum line at the pressure regulator. Build up fuel pressure by turning the ignition switch on and off at least six times, leaving the ignition on for at least five seconds each time. Check for fuel leaks.

Throttle Position Sensor (TPS)

REMOVAL & INSTALLATION

All Engines

1. Disconnect the throttle position sensor electrical connector.
2. On the 2.3L engine, remove the screw retaining the TPS electrical connector to the air throttle body.
3. Scribe alignment marks on the air throttle body and TPS sensor to indicate proper alignment during installation.
4. Remove the two TPS retaining screws, then remove the TPS and gasket from the throttle body.
5. To install, place the TPS and gasket on the throttle body, making sure the rotary tangs on the sensor are aligned with the throttle shaft blade. Slide the rotary tangs into position over the throttle shaft blade, then rotate the throttle position sensor CLOCKWISE ONLY to its installed position (align the scribe marks made earlier).

CAUTION

Failure to install the TPS in this manner may result in excessive idle speeds.

6. Once the scribe marks are aligned, install the TPS retaining screws and tighten them to 14-16 in.lb. (1-2 Nm).
7. On the 2.3L engine, position the electrical connector over the locating dimple, then secure to the throttle body with the retaining screw.
8. Reconnect the TPS electrical connector, start the engine and check the idle speed.

NOTE: Adjustment of the throttle position sensor requires the use of expensive test equipment that is not available to the do-it-yourself market. If adjustment is required, it should be performed by a qualified technician with the proper training and equipment to diagnose and repair the EEC-IV engine control system.

Fuel Tank

REMOVAL AND INSTALLATION

1. Depressurize the fuel system and drain the fuel tank. Drain the gasoline into a suitable safety container and take precautions to avoid the risk of fire.
2. Loosen the filler pipe clamp.
3. Remove the bolt from the front strap and remove the front strap.
4. Remove the bolt from the rear strap and remove the rear strap.
5. Remove the fuel feed hose at the fuel gauge sender push connector.
6. Remove the fuel hose from the sender unit push connector.
7. Remove the fuel vapor hose from the vapor valve.
8. Lower the fuel tank from the chassis.
9. Remove the shield from the fuel tank.
10. To install the tank, first attach the fuel vapor hose to the vapor valve.
11. Install the front mounting bolt to the vehicle.
12. Attach the rear strap to the vehicle.
13. Install the shield on the fuel tank.
14. Position the tank to the vehicle and attach the front strap.
15. Install the fuel lines to the feed and return hoses at the fuel gauge sender push connector.
16. Install the filler pipe in position and tighten the filler pipe clamp.
17. Install the nut to the front mounting bolt and tighten it to 18–20 ft.lb. (25–30 Nm).
18. Install the bolt to the rear strap and tighten.

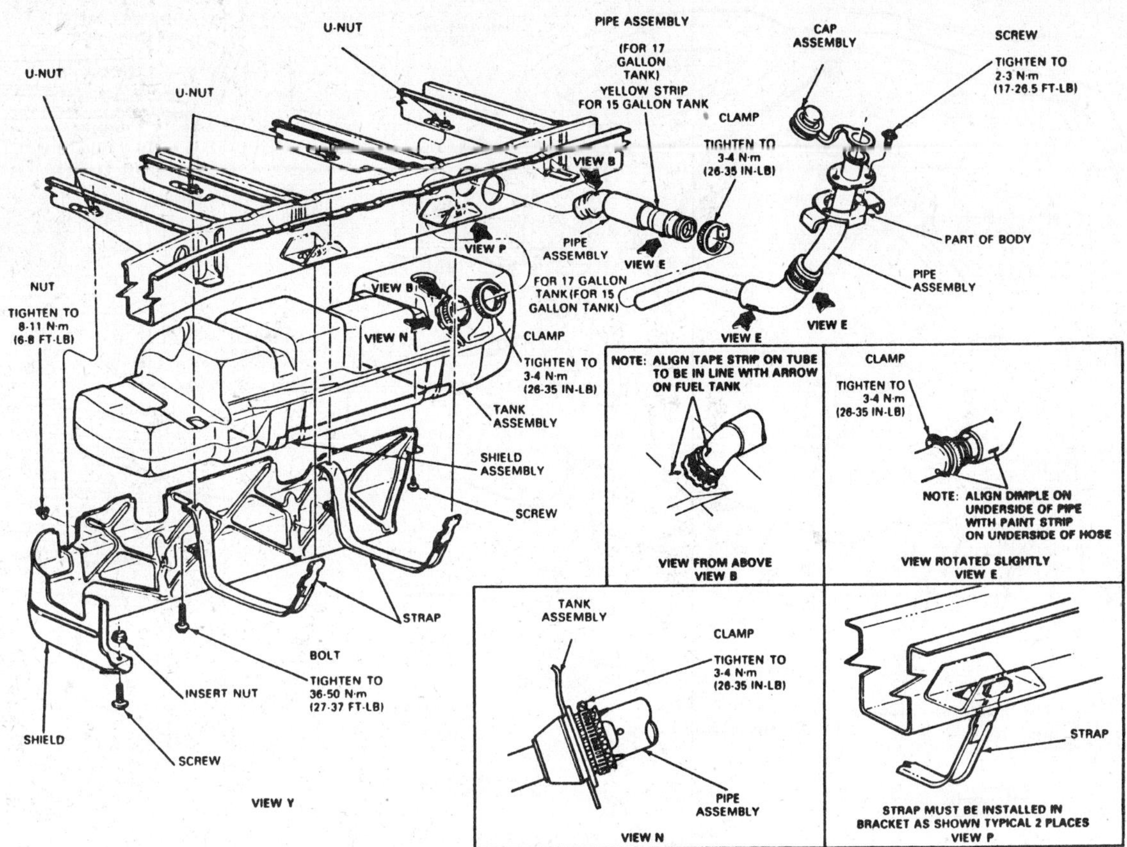

Fuel tank mounting

HEATING AND AIR CONDITIONING

Blower Motor

REMOVAL & INSTALLATION

1. Disconnect the battery ground cable.
2. Remove the air cleaner or air inlet duct as necessary.
3. Remove the two screws attaching the vacuum reservoir to the blower assembly and remove the reservoir.
4. Disconnect the wire harness connector from the blower motor by pushing down on the connector tabs and pulling the connector off the motor.
5. Disconnect the blower motor cooling tube at the blower motor.
6. Remove the three screws attaching the blower motor and wheel to the heater blower assembly.
7. While holding the cooling tube aside, pull the blower motor and wheel from the heater blower assembly.
8. Remove the blower wheel hub clamp from the motor shaft, then pull the blower wheel from the motor shaft.
9. If the motor is being replaced, install the wheel on the new blower motor shaft and lock it in place with the hub clamp.
10. Glue a new motor housing gasket to the blower motor.
11. While holding the cooling tube aside, position the blower and wheel to the heater blower assembly. Install the three mounting screws.
12. Connect the blower motor cooling tube at the blower motor.
13. Connect the wire harness connector at the blower motor.
14. Install the vacuum reservoir on the bracket with two screws.
15. Install the air cleaner or air inlet duct assembly.

Heater Core

REMOVAL & INSTALLATION

1. Allow the engine to cool completely. Using a thick cloth for protection, carefully open the radiator cap to its first stop and allow any residual cooling system pressure to vent. Drain the cooling system.

CAUTION

When draining the coolant, keep in mind that cats and dogs are attracted by the ethylene glycol antifreeze, and are quite likely to drink any that is left in an uncovered container or in puddles on the ground. This will prove fatal in sufficient quantity. Always drain the coolant into a sealable container. Coolant should be reused unless it is contaminated or several years old.

2. Disconnect the heater hoses from the heater core tubes using tool T85T-18539-AH or equivalent, as illustrated. Plug the heater hoses to prevent coolant loss during the procedure.
3. Working in the passenger compartment, remove the six screws attaching the heater core access cover to

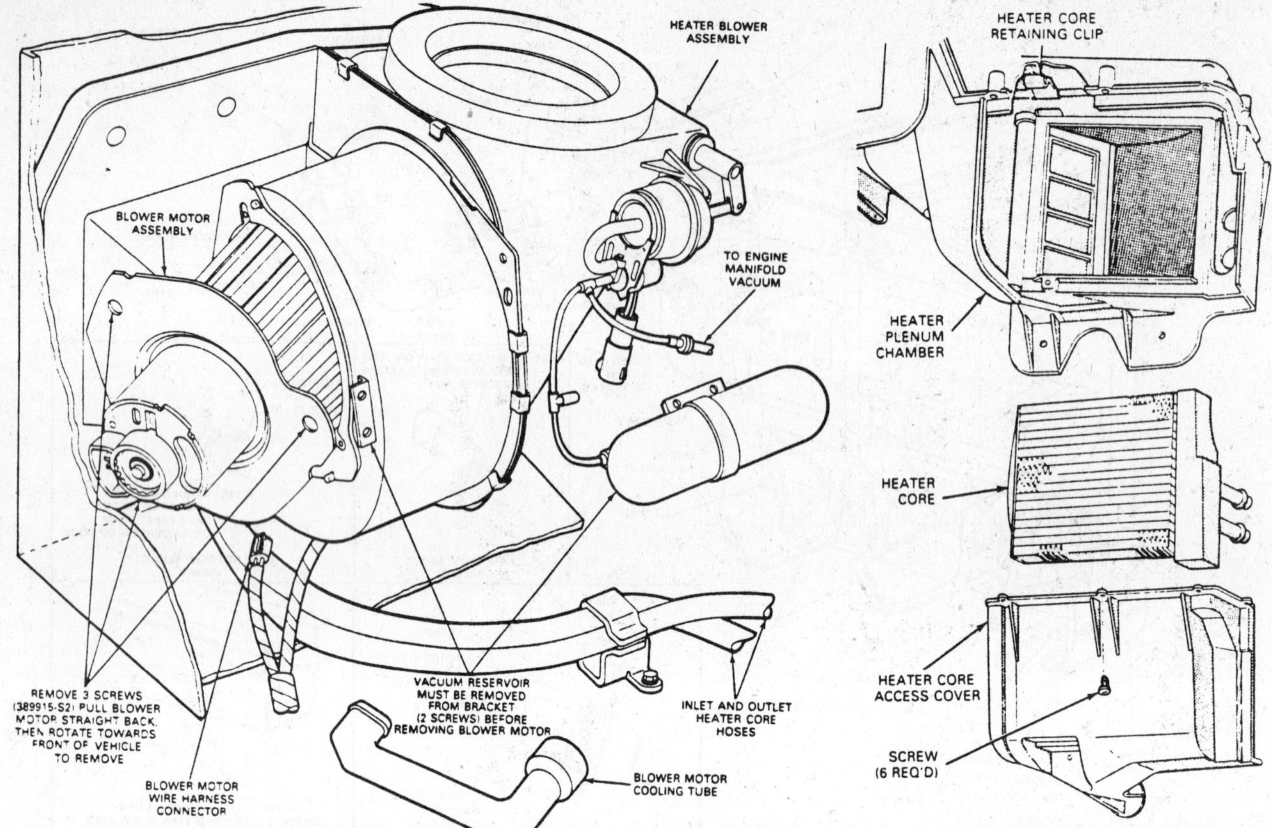

Blower motor removal

Typical heater core installation

the plenum assembly. Remove the access cover.

4. Depress the retainer bracket at the top of the heater core and pull the heater core rearward and down, removing it from the plenum assembly.

WARNING: Some coolant will remain in the heater core. Exercise caution when removing and lay a protective cloth down to protect the interior of the van during heater core removal.

5. To install, first position the heater core and seal in the plenum assembly, snapping it into the retainer bracket at the top of the core.

6. Install the heater core access cover to the plenum assembly and secure it with the six screws.

7. Install the quick-connect heater hoses to the heater core tubes at the dash panel in the engine compartment as illustrated.

8. Check the coolant level and top off as necessary.

9. Start the engine, move the heater controls to the MAX HEAT position and check for leaks.

Heater Control Assembly

REMOVAL & INSTALLATION

1. Disconnect the battery ground cable.

2. Remove the instrument cluster housing cover as described under "Instrument Panel Removal & Installation."

3. Remove the three screws attaching the control assembly to the instrument panel.

4. Pull the control assembly far enough rearward to allow removal of electrical connectors and remove the connectors.

5. Using a small pair of pliers, carefully release the function control cable (black) snap-in flag from the control bracket.

6. Pull enough cable through the instrument panel opening until the function control cable (black) can be held perpendicular to the control, then remove the control cable from the function control lever.

7. Repeat the process for the temperature control cable (blue).

8. To install, first pull temperature control cable (blue) through the opening in the instrument panel.

9. Attach the temperature cable wire (blue) to the temperature control lever and snap the cable flag into the control bracket.

10. Repeat the process for the function control cable (black).

11. Install the wire harness electrical connectors to the control assembly.

12. Position the control assembly to the instrument panel and install three attaching screws.

13. Install the instrument cluster housing cover.

14. Connect the battery ground cable.

15. Check controls for proper operation.

Evaporator Core

REMOVAL & INSTALLATION

1. Disconnect the negative battery cable.

2. Discharge the refrigerant system as described in ROUTINE MAINTENANCE. Observe all safety precautions and wear safety goggles at all times.

3. Remove the air cleaner and air inlet duct.

4. Disconnect the electrical hard shell connectors from the blower motor, blower motor resistor, pressure switch and the recirculation door vacuum motor solenoid.

5. Disconnect the liquid line from the inlet tube and the suction line(s) from the accumulator drier, using the spring lock coupling tools. Cap all open refrigerant lines to prevent the entry of dirt and moisture.

6. Remove the water valve and disconnect the vacuum line.

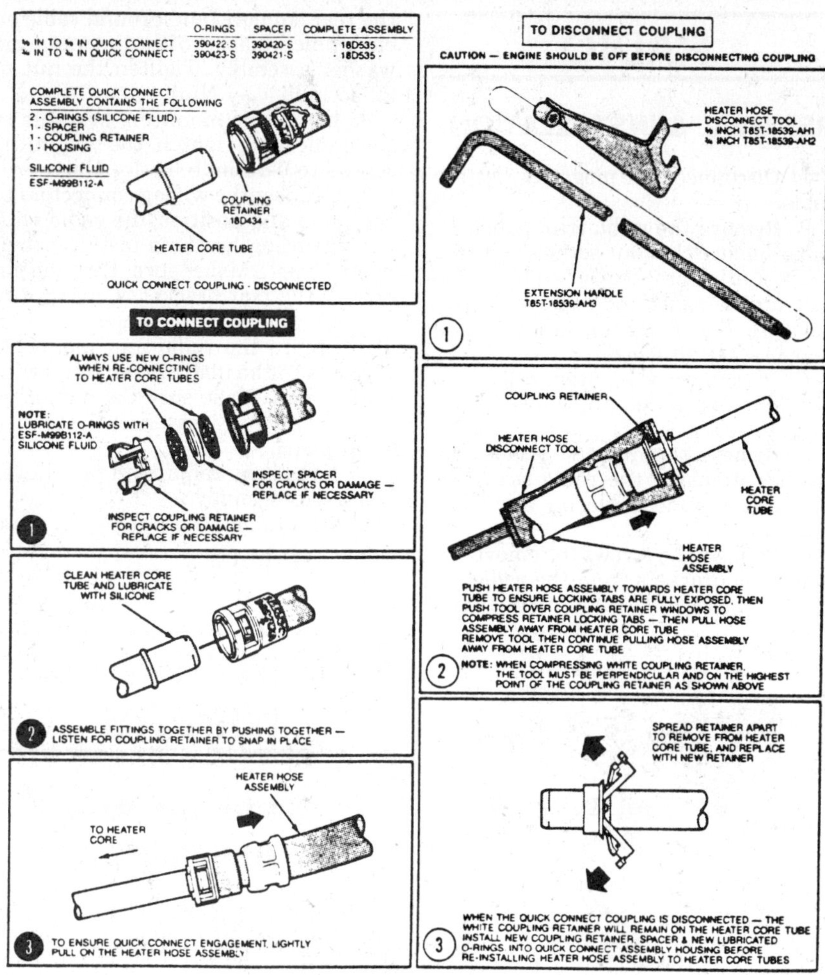
Disconnecting heater hose quick connec couplings

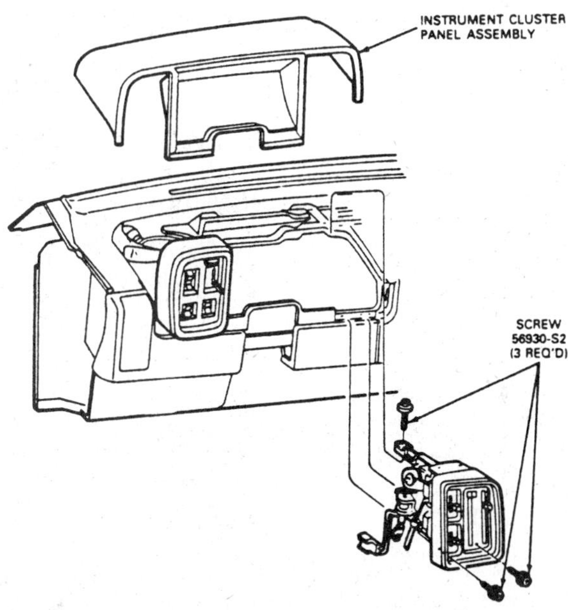

Heater control assembly removal

7. Disconnect the vacuum harness check valve from the engine source line and disconnect the vacuum line from the vacuum motor solenoid.

8. Remove the two mounting bands holding the accumulator drier to the evaporator core and the clamp from around the evaporator inlet tube. Using the spring lock coupling tool, disconnect the accumulator drier from the evaporator core outlet tube and remove the accumulator drier. Cap all open refrigerant connections to prevent the entry of dirt and moisture.

9. Remove the eleven screws holding the evaporator case blower housing to the evaporator case assembly. Remove the evaporator case blower housing from the vehicle.

10. Remove the evaporator core from the vehicle.

11. To install, first position the evaporator core into the installed evaporator case half.

12. Position the evaporator case blower housing to the evaporator case and install with eleven screws.

13. After checking the male fitting on the accumulator drier for a missing or damaged spring lock coupling garter spring (and replacing or repairing as necessary), install two new O-rings lubricated with clean refrigerant oil into the spring lock coupling male fitting. Insert the male fitting into the outlet tube until the spring lock is fully engaged.

14. Install the two mounting bands around the accumulator drier and install the clamp around the inlet line. Tighten the screws to 15 in.lb. (2 Nm).

15. After checking the liquid line for a missing or damaged spring lock coupling garter spring (and replacing or repairing as necessary), install two new O-rings lubricated with clean refrigerant oil into the spring lock coupling male fitting. Insert the male fitting into the inlet tube until the spring lock is fully engaged.

16. Install the suction line(s) to the accumulator drier, using the same procedure as for the liquid line above.

17. Connect the vacuum line to the water valve and install the water valve.

18. Connect the electrical hard shell connectors to the blower motor resistor and the vacuum motor.

19. Connect the vacuum line to the vacuum motor solenoid. Connect the vacuum source line from the engine to the check valve.

20. Recharge the air conditioning system as described in ROUTINE MAINTENANCE.

21. Reconnect the negative battery cable, then start the engine and check the A/C system for refrigerant leaks and proper operation.

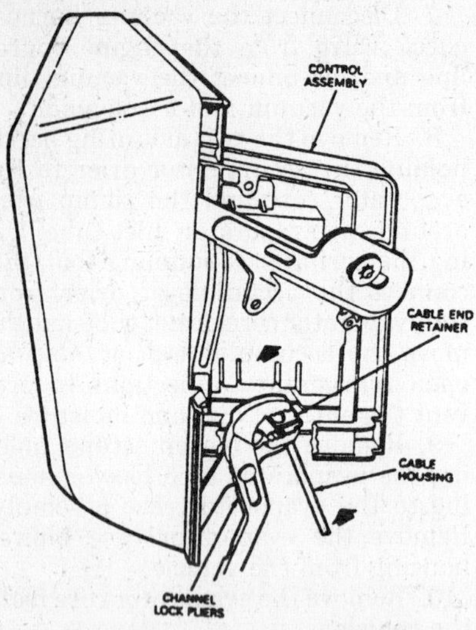

Control cable removal. Compress the cable end retainer, then pull the cable housing in the direction of arrow

RADIO

REMOVAL & INSTALLATION

1. Disconnect the negative battery cable.
2. Remove the radio trim panel.
3. Remove the four screws securing the mounting brackets assembly to the instrument panel and remove the radio with the mounting brackets and rear bracket attached.
4. Disconnect the antenna lead cable, speaker wires and power wire from the radio.
5. Remove the nut and washer assembly attaching the radio rear support and ground cable on electronic radios.
6. Remove the screws to remove the mounting brackets from the radio.
7. To install the radio, first attach the rear support (and ground cable on electronic radios) with the nut and washer assembly. Tighten the nut to 22-35 in.lb. (2-4 Nm).
8. Install the mounting brackets to the radio and tighten the mounting screws to 9-12 in.lb. (1-1.4 Nm).
9. Connect the wiring connectors to the radio and position the radio with the mounting brackets to the instrument panel. Make sure the hairpin area of the rear bracket is engaged to the instrument panel support.
10. Secure the radio and mounting brackets to the instrument panel with four screws. Make sure the mounting brackets are fully seated on the instrument panel.
11. Install the radio trim panel over the radio assembly.
12. Reconnect the battery ground cable.

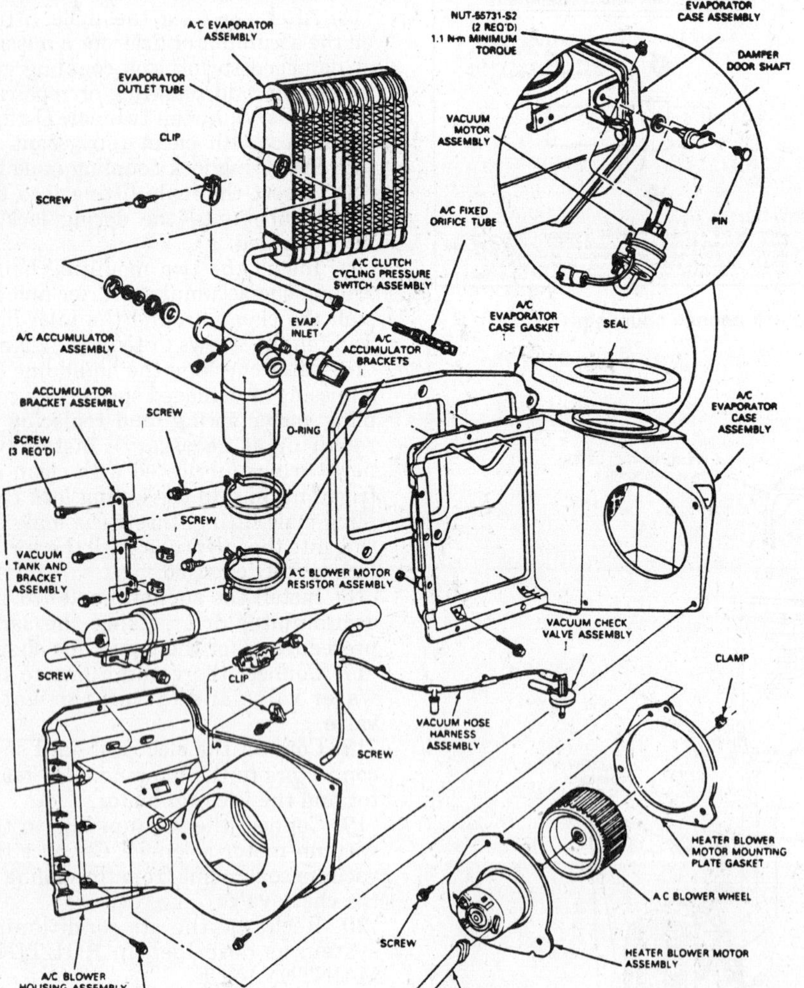

Evaporator core assembly

WINDSHIELD WIPERS

Blade and Arm Assembly

Remove the blade and arm assemblies from the pivot shafts as illustrated. Turn on the wiper switch to allow the motor to move the pivot shafts three or four cycles, then turn off the wiper switch. This will place the pivot shafts in the PARK position. Install the arm and blade assemblies on the pivot shafts to dimension **X** as illustrated. This dimension is the distance between the centerline of the blade saddle and the top edge of the cowl top grille.

Front Wiper Motor

REMOVAL & INSTALLATION

1. Turn the wiper switch on, then turn the ignition switch on until the blades are in mid-pattern. Turn the ignition switch off to keep the blades in mid-pattern.
2. Disconnect the wiper motor wiring connector.
3. Remove both wiper arms, noting their position before removal.
4. Remove the cowl grille.
5. Remove the linkage retaining clip and disassemble the linkage from the motor crank arm.
6. Remove the wiper motor retaining nuts while holding the motor on its underside to prevent it from falling and possible damage.

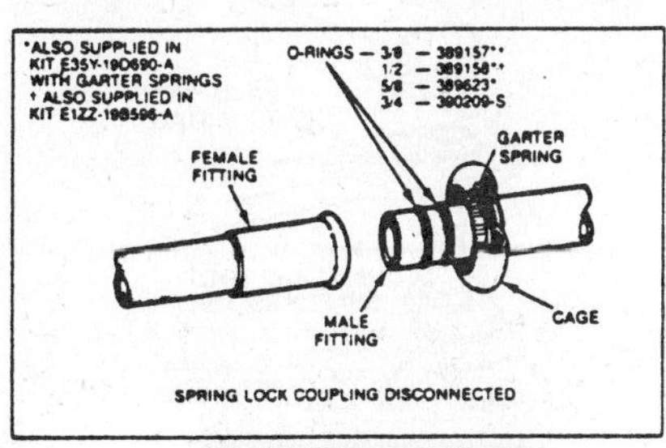

TO CONNECT COUPLING

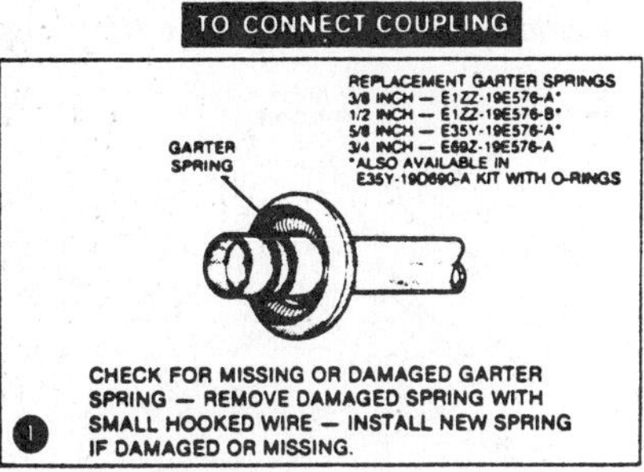

1 CHECK FOR MISSING OR DAMAGED GARTER SPRING — REMOVE DAMAGED SPRING WITH SMALL HOOKED WIRE — INSTALL NEW SPRING IF DAMAGED OR MISSING.

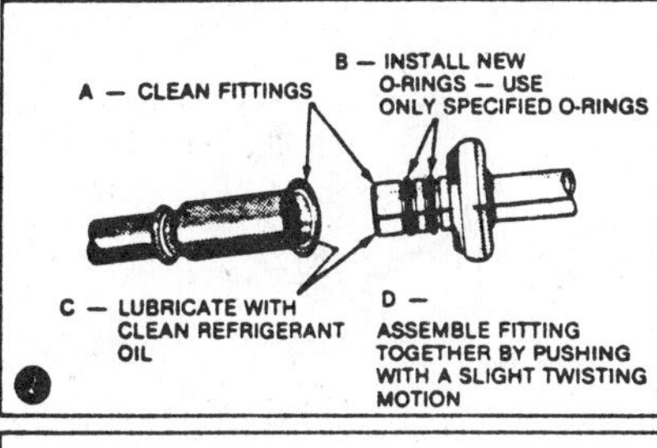

2

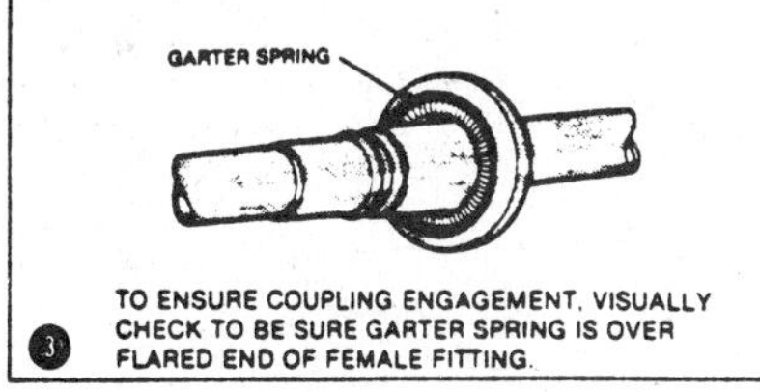

3 TO ENSURE COUPLING ENGAGEMENT, VISUALLY CHECK TO BE SURE GARTER SPRING IS OVER FLARED END OF FEMALE FITTING.

TO DISCONNECT COUPLING

CAUTION — DISCHARGE SYSTEM BEFORE DISCONNECTING COUPLING

NOTE:
EACH END OF TOOL T81P-19623-G IS A DIFFERENT SIZE TO FIT 3/8 and 1/2 INCH COUPLINGS

TOOL
T81P-19623-G - 3/8 & 1/2 INCH
T81P-19623-G1 - 3/8 INCH
T81P-19623-G2 - 1/2 INCH
T83P-19623-C - 5/8 INCH
T85L-19623-A - 3/4 INCH

CAGE OPENING

(1) FIT TOOL TO COUPLING SO THAT TOOL CAN ENTER CAGE OPENING TO RELEASE THE GARTER SPRING.

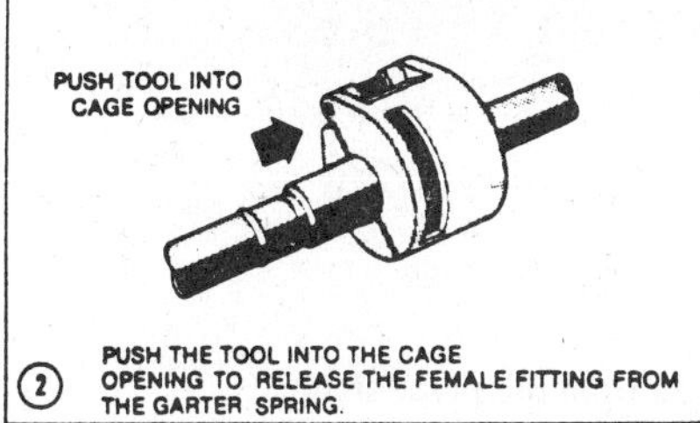

(2) PUSH THE TOOL INTO THE CAGE OPENING TO RELEASE THE FEMALE FITTING FROM THE GARTER SPRING.

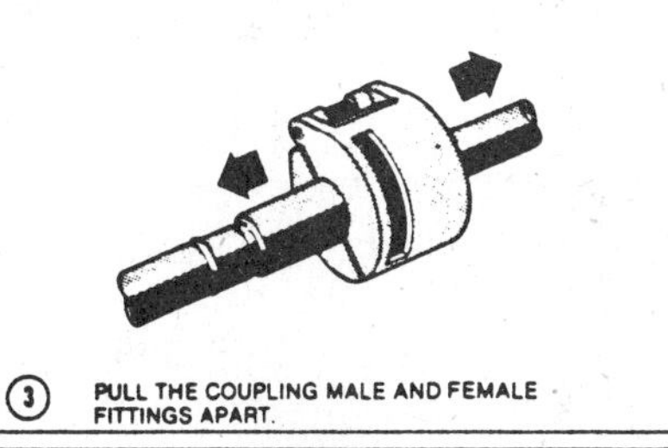

(3) PULL THE COUPLING MALE AND FEMALE FITTINGS APART.

(4) REMOVE THE TOOL FROM THE DISCONNECTED SPRING LOCK COUPLING.

Removing and installing spring lock couplings

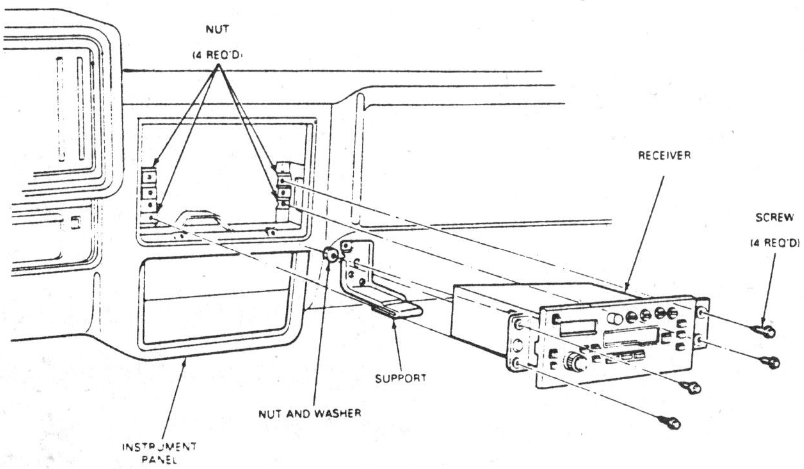

Typical radio mounting

7. Installation is the reverse of removal procedures.

Front Wiper Linkage

REMOVAL & INSTALLATION

1. Turn the ignition and wiper switch on, then turn the ignition off when the wiper blades are in mid-pattern.
2. Disconnect the wiper motor electrical connector.
3. Remove the wiper arms.
4. Remove the cowl top grille.
5. Remove the clip retaining the linkage to the crank arm of the wiper motor.
6. Remove the four pivot retaining screws.
7. Remove the linkage from the vehicle.
8. Installation is the reverse of removal.

Rear Wiper Motor

REMOVAL & INSTALLATION

1. Remove the wiper arm and blade as illustrated.
2. Remove the motor shaft attaching nut and wedge block.
3. Remove the liftgate trim panel.
4. Disconnect the electrical connector and remove the motor wiring pins from the inner panel. Remove the motor.
5. To install, place the motor into the liftgate so that the motor shaft protrudes through the opening in the outer panel.
6. Attach the motor to the liftgate inner panel by installing the wiring pushpins in the holes provided.
7. Load the articulating arm onto the drive pilot shaft. The wiper system must be cycled and parked by operating the wiper switch to insure that the system linkage is in the PARK position before the arm and blade is installed.
8. Locate the blade to the specified installation position.
9. Install the arm onto the pivot shaft after the articulating arm is in place with the slide latch in the unlocked position.
10. While applying a downward pressure on the arm head to insure full seating, raise the other end of the arm sufficiently to allow the latch to slide under the pivot shaft to the locked position. Use finger pressure only to slide the latch, then release the arm and blade against the rear window.

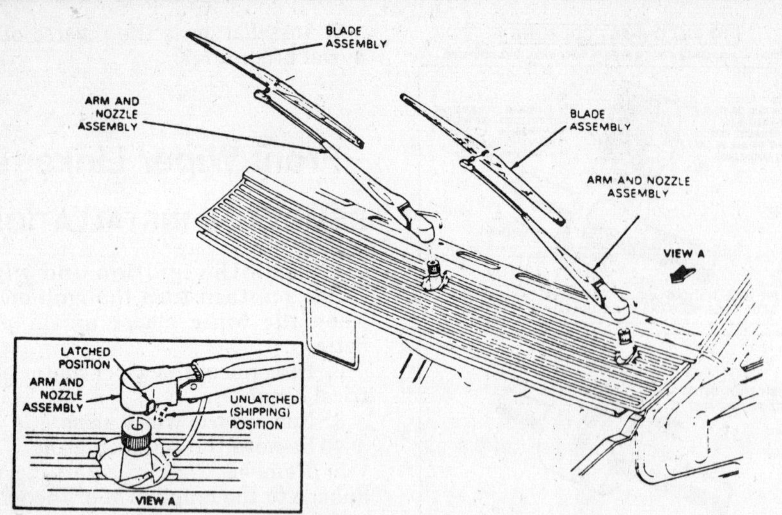

Removing wiper arm and blade from the pivot shaft

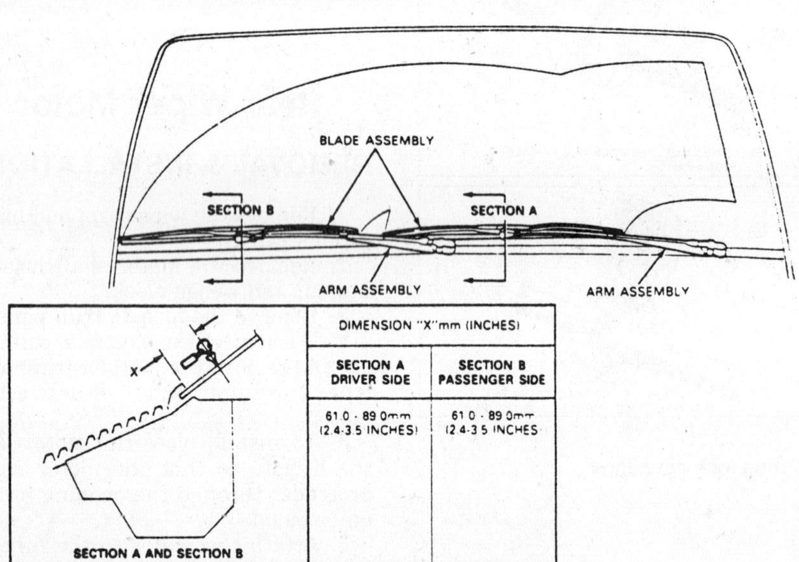

Installing the arm and blade assemblies

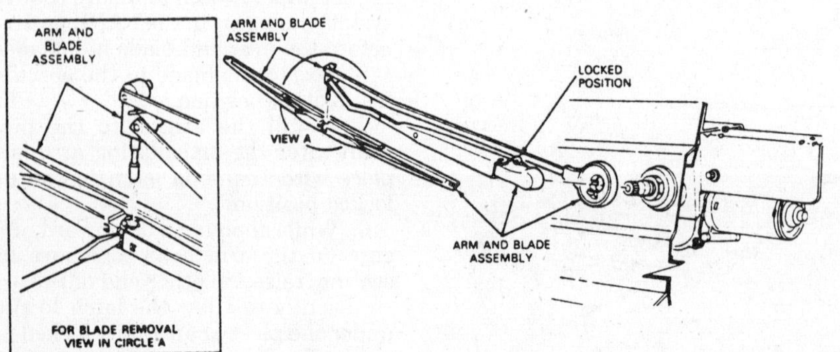

Removing rear wiper blade and arm

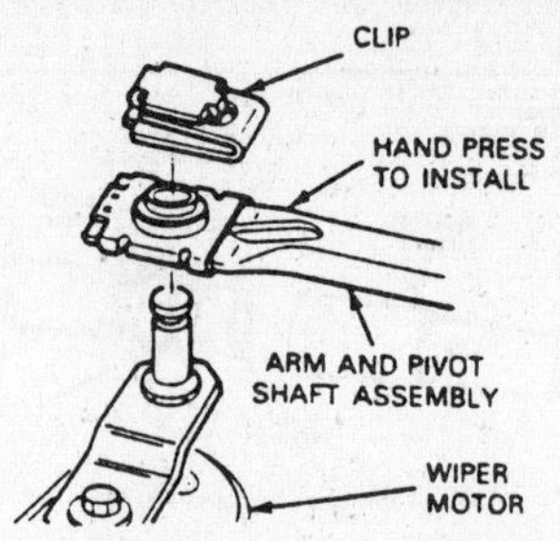

Removing wiper arm linkage from motor

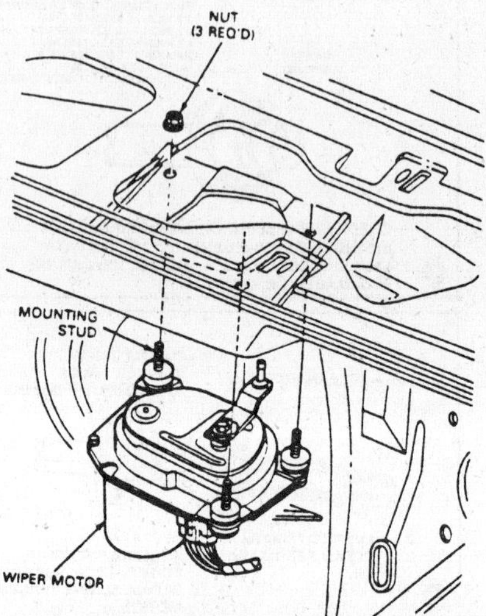

Windshield wiper motor mounting

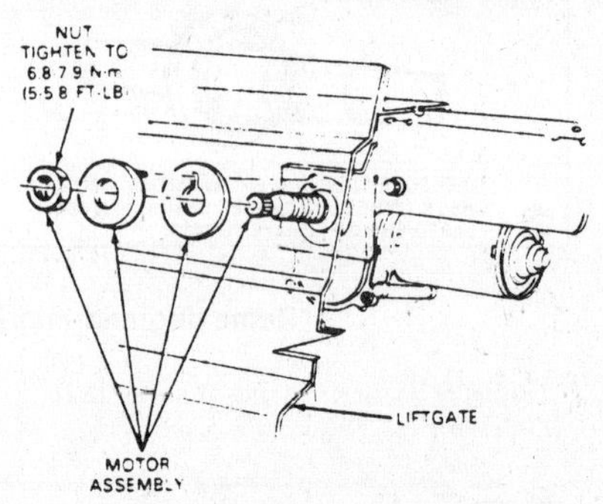

Rear wiper motor mounting

INSTRUMENTS AND SWITCHES

Instrument Cluster

REMOVAL & INSTALLATION

Standard Cluster

1. Disconnect the negative battery cable.
2. Remove the seven cluster hous-

ing-to-panel retaining screws and remove the cluster housing.

3. Remove the four instrument cluster to panel retaining screws.

4. Disconnect the wiring harness connectors from the printed circuit.

5. Disengage the speedometer cable from the speedometer.

6. Remove the cluster by pulling it forward.

7. To install the cluster, first apply a small dab of silicone dielectric compound (D7AZ-19A331-A or equivalent) in the drive hole of the speedometer head.

8. Position the cluster near its opening in the instrument panel.

9. Connect the speedometer cable to the speedometer head.

10. Connect the wiring harness connectors to the printed circuit.

11. Position the cluster to the instrument panel and install the four cluster-to-panel retaining screws.

12. Install the cluster housing to the panel.

13. Connect the battery ground cable.

14. Turn the ignition switch on and check the operation of all gauges, lamps and signals.

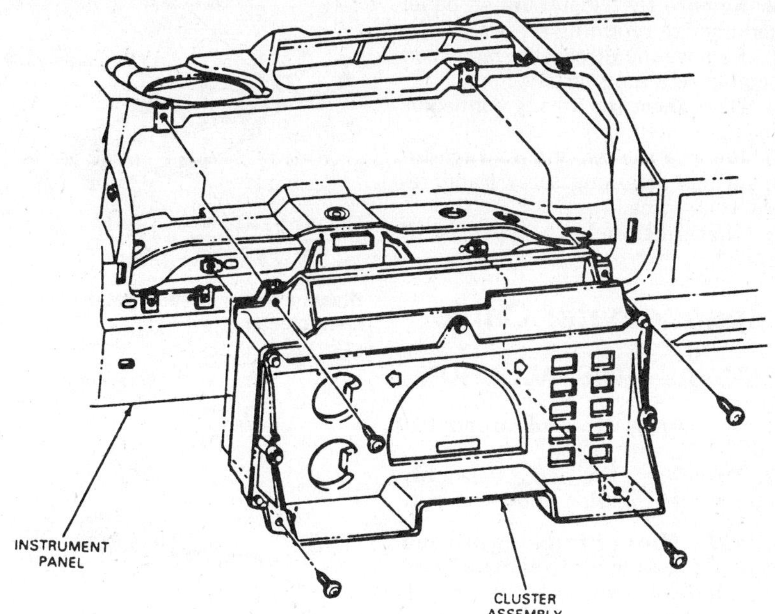

Standard instrument cluster mounting

Electronic Cluster

1. Disconnect the battery ground cable.

2. Remove the cluster housing.

3. Remove the four cluster mounting screws.

4. Pull the top of the cluster toward the steering wheel.

5. Reach behind the cluster and unplug the three electrical connectors.

6. Swing the bottom of the cluster out and remove it from the dash panel.

7. To install, insert the bottom of the cluster into the instrument panel alignment pins.

8. Plug in the three electrical connectors.

9. Seat the cluster and fasten the four mounting screws.

10. Reconnect the battery and check the cluster operation.

11. Install the cluster housing.

12. Turn the ignition switch on and check cluster operation.

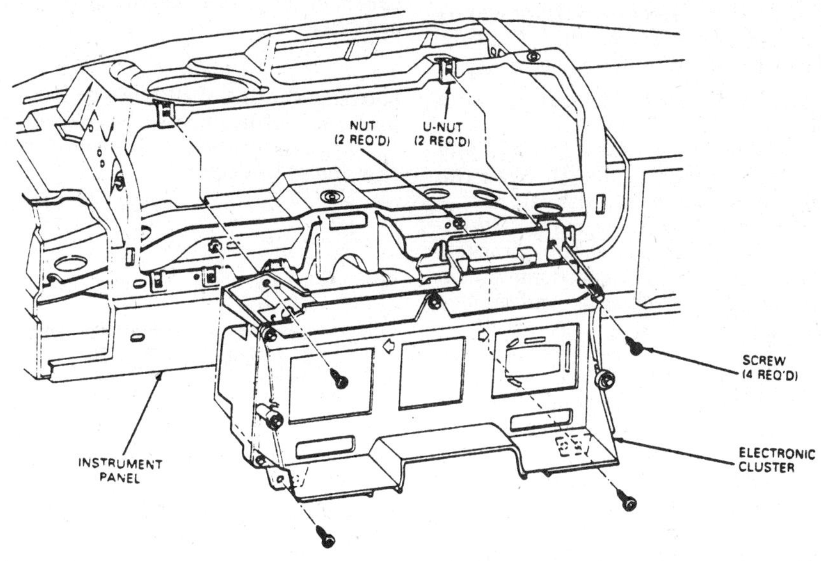

Electronic instrument cluster housing

Front Wiper Switch

REMOVAL & INSTALLATION

1. Disconnect the negative battery cable.

2. Remove the cluster finish panel assembly five retaining screws.

3. Remove the three left control pod assembly retaining screws.

4. Remove the wiring connector from the switch.

5. Remove the two lamp switch-to-control pod retaining screws and remove the switch pod.

6. Installation is the reverse of removal.

Rear Wiper Switch

REMOVAL & INSTALLATION

1. Disconnect the negative battery cable.

2. Remove the upper and lower trim shrouds.

3. Disconnect the quick connect electrical connector.

4. Peel back the foam sight shield, remove the two cross-recessed screws holding the switch and remove the wash/wipe switch.

5. Installation is the reverse of removal.

Headlight Switch

REMOVAL & INSTALLATION

1. Disconnect the negative battery cable.

2. Remove the cluster finish panel assembly five retaining screws.
3. Remove the three left control pod assembly retaining screws.
4. Disconnect the wiring connector from the switch.
5. Remove the two lamp switch-to-control pod retaining screws and remove the switch.
6. Installation is the reverse of removal.

Speedometer Cable

REMOVAL & INSTALLATION

1. Raise the van and support it safely.
2. Disengage the cable assembly from the transmission and remove it.

NOTE: On vehicles equipped with a transmission mounted speed sensor, remove the speedometer cable by pulling it out of the speed sensor. Do not attempt to remove the spring retainer clip with the speedometer in the sensor. To install the speedometer cable, align the core with the sensor and snap the cable assembly into the speed sensor.

3. Disengage all remaining cable clips.
4. Push the grommet out of the floor pan and the cable through the floor pan opening into the cab.
5. Remove the screw holding the cable clip to the steering column bracket.
6. Disconnect the speedometer cable from the speedometer and remove the cable.
7. To install, connect the speedometer cable to the speedometer head.
8. Route the cable through the floor pan opening and attach the clip to the steering column bracket.
9. Lubricate the cable core exposed at the transmission ferrule with silicone grease. Apply a coating of polyethylene grease to the O-ring on the ferrule.
10. Lubricate the inside diameter and the teeth of the driven gear with speedometer cable lubricant (DZAZ-19581-A or equivalent) and install the driven gear on the ferrule.
11. Assemble the driven gear retainer to the driven gear with the retainer tabs toward the gear teeth.
12. Insert the driven gear and cable into the transmission and retain with the clamp by tightening the retaining screw to 20-25 in.lb. (2-3 Nm).
13. Secure the cable with the clips and clamps at the locations indicated by the tape on the cable, then lower the vehicle.

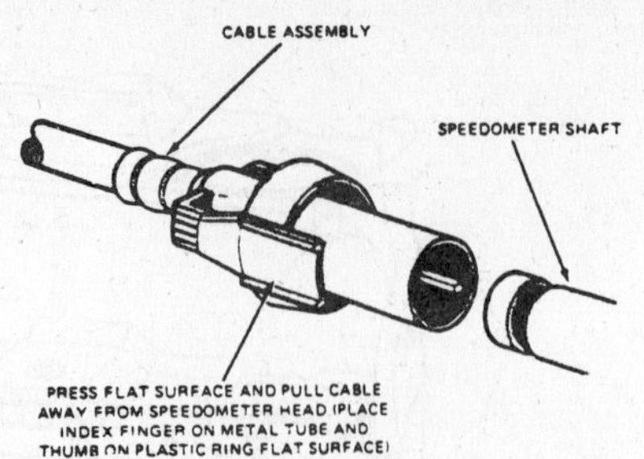

Disconnecting speedometer from instrument cluster

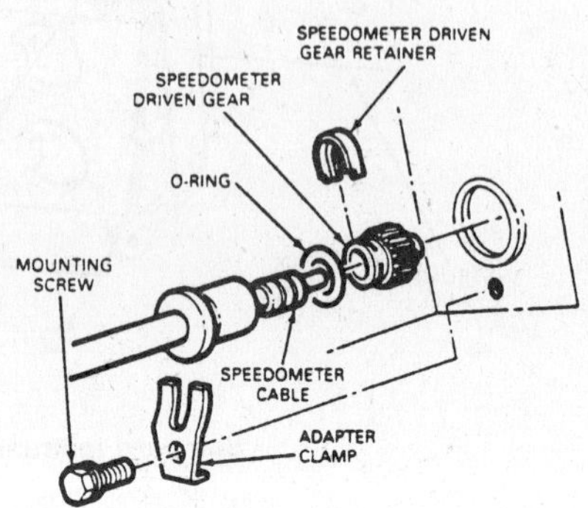

Speedometer cable mounting at the transmission

NOTE: The speedometer cable routing should avoid sharp bends and the cable should be straight for approximately 8 inches from the speedometer.

LIGHTING

Headlights

REMOVAL & INSTALLATION

1. Remove the headlight door attaching screws and remove the headlight door.
2. Remove the headlight retaining ring screws and remove the retaining ring. Do not disturb the adjusting screw settings.
3. Pull the headlight door forward and disconnect the wiring connector from the bulb, then remove the headlight from the vehicle.
4. Connect the wiring connector to the new headlight and place the light in position, making sure the locating tabs are fitted in the positioning slots.
5. Install the headlamp retaining ring.
6. Place the headlight door in position and install the retaining screws.

Parking, Turn and Front Side Marker Lights

REMOVAL & INSTALLATION

1. Remove the four screws securing the bezel and lamp assembly.
2. Remove the lamp assembly by removing the three screws retaining the lamp to the bezel.
3. Remove the socket from the lamp assembly.
4. Pull the bulb directly out from the socket.
5. Installation is the reverse of removal.

Rear Lights

REMOVAL & INSTALLATION

1. Remove the four screws retaining the lamp assembly to the van.
2. Remove the lamp assembly.
3. Remove the bulb socket from the lamp assembly, then remove the bulb.
4. Installation is the reverse of removal.

CIRCUIT PROTECTION

Fuse Panel

Most of the replaceable fuses for the electrical system are located on the fuse panel under the instrument panel to the left of the steering column. For access to the fuse panel, remove the fasteners from the lower edge of the cover, then pull the cover downward until the spring clips disengage from the instrument panel. On the base models, the cover simply snaps on and off. The fuses are replaced by simply pulling them out. A blown or open fuse can be seen as a break in the metal filament that runs between the blades. The fuse is made with a plastic body so the break can be clearly seen.

The locations of various fuses are illustrated. Fuses that open (blow) may by replaced, but will continue to open until the cause of the overload condition is corrected. If a fuse needs to be replaced, use only a new fuse rated according to the specifications and of the same amperage number as the one removed. Five spare fuses are located inside the fuse panel cover.

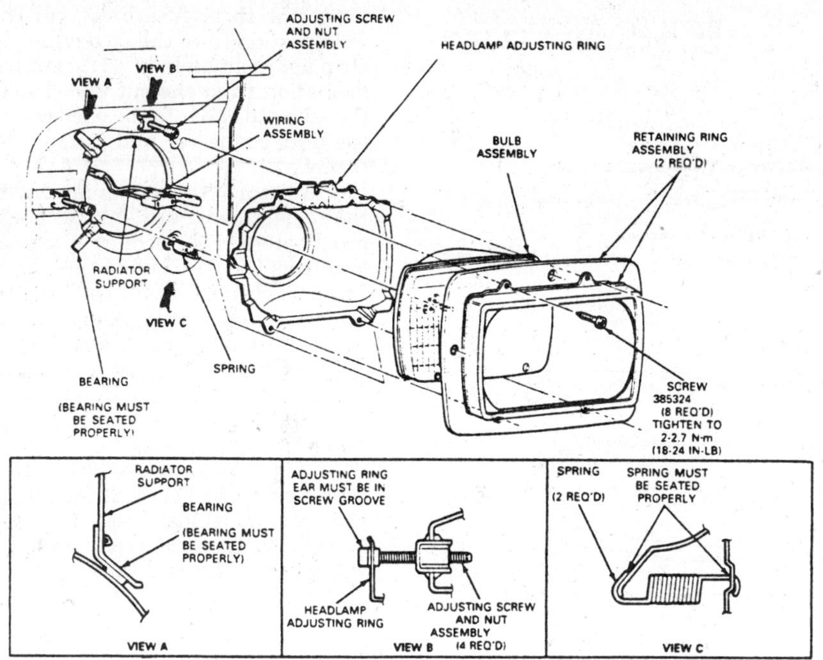

Headlight assembly showing mounting and adjustment screws

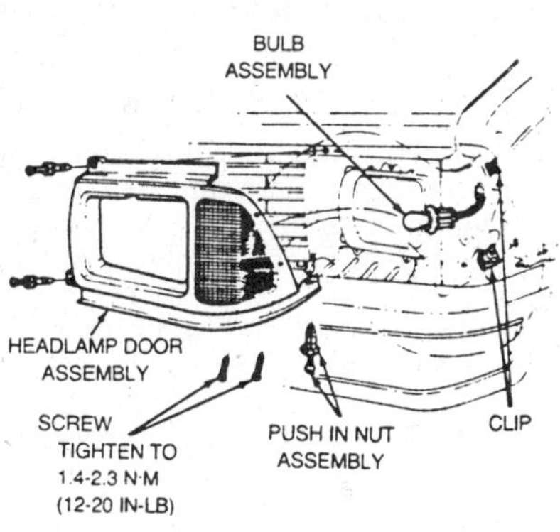

Front parking, turn and marker light assembly

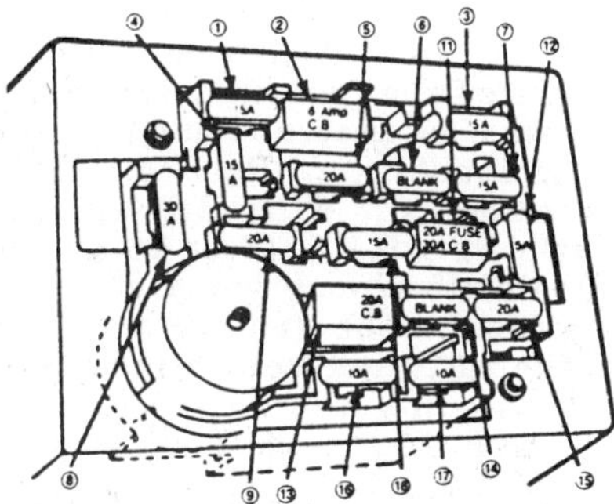

Typical fuse box assembly

CAUTION

Always replace a blown fuse or fuse link with the same rating as specified. Never replace a fuse with a higher amperage rating than the one removed, or severe wiring damage and a possible fire can result.

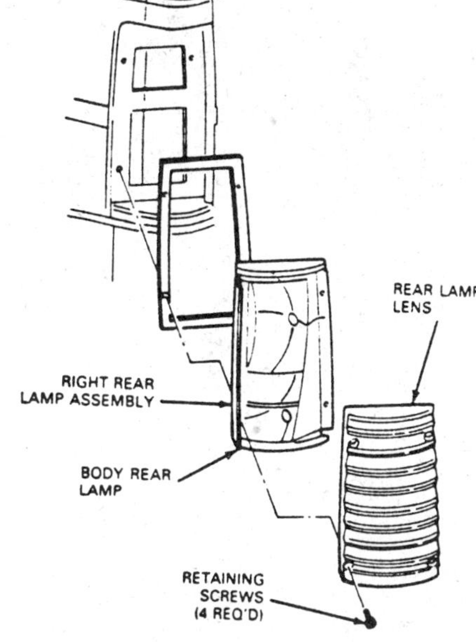

Rear light assembly

Selected circuits, such as headlights and windshield wipers, are protected with circuit breakers. A circuit breaker is designed to stop current flow in case of a short-circuit or overload. It will automatically restore current flow after a few seconds, but will again interrupt current flow if the overload or short-circuit continues. This on/off cycle will continue as long as the overload or short-circuit exists, except for the circuit breakers protecting the power door lock and power window circuits will not restore current flow until the overload is removed.

Fusible Links

A fusible link is a short length of Hypalon (high temperature) insulated wire, integral with the wiring harness and should not be confused with standard wire. The fusible link is several wire gauges smaller than the circuit it protects and is designed to melt and break the circuit should an overload occur. Under no circumstances should a fusible link be replaced with a standard length of wire.

The higher melting temperature properties and additional thickness of the Hypalon insulation will usually allow the undersized internal fuse wire to melt and disintegrate within the Hypalon casing with little damage to the high temperature insulation other than discoloration and/or bubbling of the insulation surface. In extreme cases of excessive circuit current, the insulation may separate after the fuse wire has disintegrated, however, the bare wire will seldom be exposed. If it becomes difficult to determine if the fuse link is burnt open, perform a continuity test. When heavy current flows, such as when a booster battery is connected incorrectly or when a short to ground occurs in the wiring harness, the fusible link burns out to protect the alternator and/or wiring.

Production fuse links have a flag moulded on the wire or on the terminal insulator. Color identification of the flag or connector is Blue-20 gauge wire, Red-18 gauge wire, Yellow-17 gauge wire, Orange-16 gauge wire, or Green-14 gauge wire. To repair any blown fuse link use the following procedure:

1. Determine which circuit is damaged, its location and the cause of the open fuse link. If the damaged fuse link is one of three fed by a common No. 10 or 12 gauge feed wire, determine the specific affected circuit.
2. Disconnect the negative battery cable.
3. Cut the damaged fuse link from the wiring harness and discard it. If the fuse link is one of three circuits fed by a single feed wire, cut it out of the harness at each splice end and discard it.
4. Identify and procure the proper fuse link and butt connectors for attaching the fuse link in the harness.
5. To repair any fuse link in a 3-link group with one feed:
    a. After cutting the open link out of the harness, cut each of the remaining undamaged fuse links close to the feed wire weld.
    b. Strip approximately ½" (12.7mm) of insulation from the de-

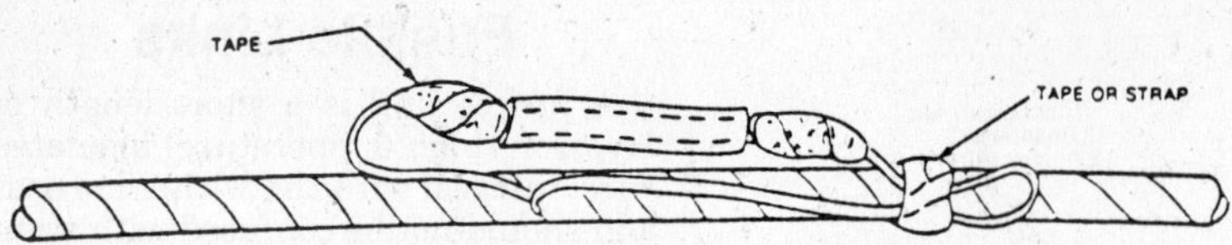

TYPICAL REPAIR USING THE SPECIAL #17 GA (9.00" LONG-YELLOW) FUSE LINK REQUIRED FOR THE AIR/COND CIRCUITS (2) #687E and #261A LOCATED IN THE ENGINE COMPARTMENT

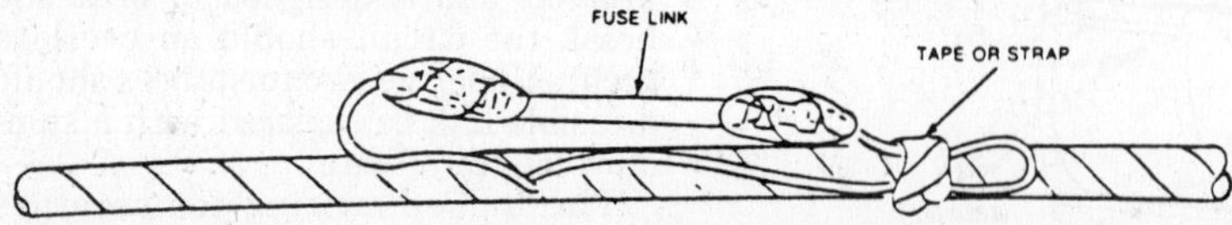

TYPICAL REPAIR FOR ANY IN-LINE FUSE LINK USING THE SPECIFIED GAUGE FUSE LINK FOR THE SPECIFIC CIRCUIT

TYPICAL REPAIR USING THE EYELET TERMINAL FUSE LINK OF THE SPECIFIED GAUGE FOR ATTACHMENT TO A CIRCUIT WIRE END

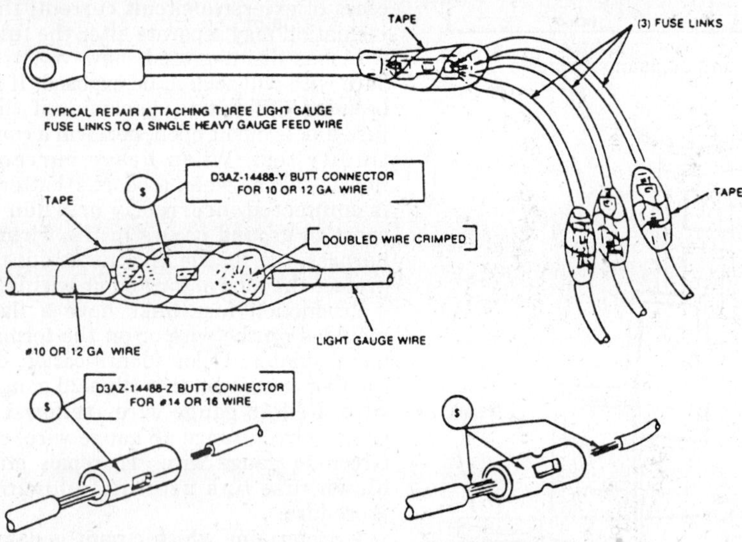

General fuse link repair procedure

tached ends of the two good fuse links. Then insert two wire ends into one end of a butt connector and carefully push one stripped end of the replacement fuse link into the same end of the butt connector and crimp all three firmly together.

NOTE: Care must be taken when fitting the three fuse links into the butt connector as the internal diameter is a snug fit for three wires. Make sure to use a proper crimping tool. Pliers, side cutters, etc. will not apply the proper crimp to retain the wires and withstand a pull test.

c. After crimping the butt connector to the three fuse links, cut the weld portion from the feed wire and strip approximately ½" (12.7mm) of insulation from the cut end. Insert the stripped end into the open end of the butt connector and crimp very firmly.

d. To attach the remaining end of the replacement fuse link, strip approximately ½" (12.7mm) of insulation from the wire end of the circuit from which the blown fuse link was removed, and firmly crimp a butt connector or equivalent to the stripped wire. Then, insert the end of the replacement link into the other end of the butter connector and crimp firmly.

e. Using rosin core solder with a consistency of 60 percent tin and 40 percent lead, solder the connectors and the wires at the repairs and insulate with electrical tape.

6. To replace any fuse link on a single circuit in a harness, cut out the damaged portion, strip approximately ½" (12.7mm) of insulation from the two wire ends and attach the appropriate replacement fuse link to the stripped wire ends with two proper size butt connectors. Solder the connectors and wires and insulate with tape.

7. To repair any fuse link which has an eyelet terminal on one end such as the charging circuit, cut off the open fuse link behind the weld, strip approximately ½" (12.7mm) of insulation from the cut end and attach the appropriate new eyelet fuse link to the cut stripped wire with an appropriate size butt connector. Solder the connectors and wires at the repair and insulate with tape.

8. Connect the negative battery cable to the battery and test the system for proper operation.

NOTE: Do not mistake a resistor wire for a fuse link. The resistor wire is generally longer and has print stating, "Resistor: don't cut or splice." When attaching a single No. 16, 17, 18 or 20 gauge fuse link to a heavy gauge wire, always double the stripped wire end of the fuse link before inserting and crimping it into the butt connector for positive wire retention.

MANUAL TRANSMISSION

Identification

All Aerostar models with manual transmission are equipped with a Mazda-built 5-speed overdrive unit, identified as a Code 5 on the Safety Standard Certification Label. In addition, all manual transmissions have service identification tags to identify the unit for service purposes. The tag is found at the side of the main case.

The 5-speed manual overdrive transmission is fully synchronized in all gears except Reverse, which is in constant mesh. The gearshift mechanism is a direct control with a floor shifter. The shifter mechanism has a remote shift adapter to transfer shift lever movement to the control lever in the extension housing. No shifter adjustments are necessary or possible.

REMOVAL & INSTALLATION

1. Disconnect the negative battery terminal.
2. Shift the transmission into Neutral.
3. Remove the four bolts retaining the boot assembly to the floor, then raise the boot up the lever to allow working clearance.
4. Remove the four bolts retaining the shift lever assembly to the transmission remote shift rail adaptor. Remove the lever, knob and boot assembly.
5. Raise the vehicle and support it safely on jackstands.
6. Disconnect the starter cable and wires. Remove the starter retaining bolts and remove the starter.
7. Remove the clip retaining the tube to the hydraulic clutch slave cylinder. Remove the tube and fitting from the slave cylinder, then cap the end of the tube and slave cylinder to prevent the entry of dirt, moisture or other contaminants into the hydraulic clutch system.
8. Disconnect the back-up lamp switch and shift indicator and neutral position wires from the senders on the transmission. Remove the speedometer cable (conventional speedometer), or the electrical connector (electronic speedometer) from the fitting.
9. Scribe a mark on the driveshaft and rear axle flange to index the driveline position for installation and balance purposes. Remove the U-bolts and nuts from the rear axle flange, then remove the driveshaft. Cap the transmission extension housing to prevent lubricant leakage.
10. Remove the nuts retaining the insulator to the crossmember. Loosen the nut and washer assemblies attaching the front insulators to the crossmember brackets.
11. Position a transmission jack under the transmission and slightly raise the transmission.
12. Remove the bolts retaining the clutch housing to the engine. Bring the transmission rearward to separate the clutch housing from the sowel pins in the rear of the engine block. Slowly lower the transmission from the vehicle.

NOTE: If the transmission is to be removed from the vehicle for an extended period, support the rear of the engine with a safety stand and wood block.

13. To install, position the transmission on a suitable transmission jack, then lift the transmission into position. Make sure the input shaft splines engage the pilot bearing in the flywheel. The clutch housing must be piloted in the dowel pins in the engine block.
14. Install the bolts retaining the clutch housing to the engine block. Tighten the bolts to 28-33 ft.lb. (38-51 Nm). To avoid galvanic corrosion, only

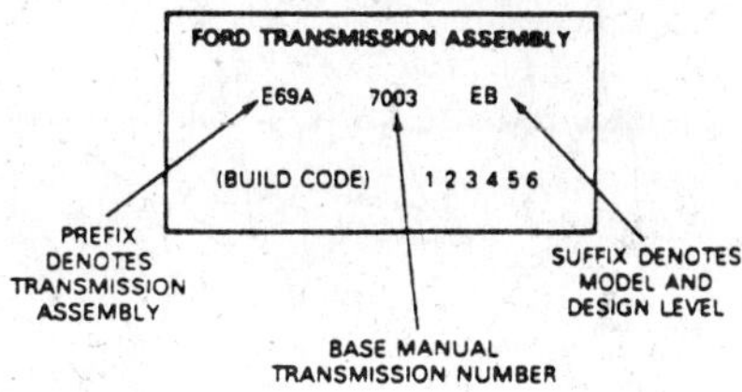

Transmission Identification tag

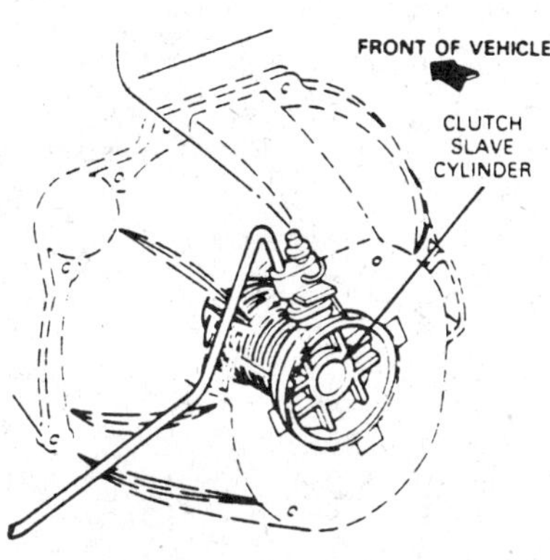

Location of clutch slave cylinder

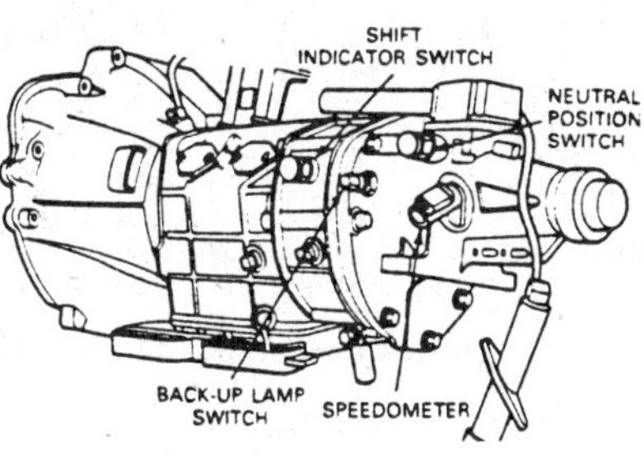

Electrical connections on the manual transmission

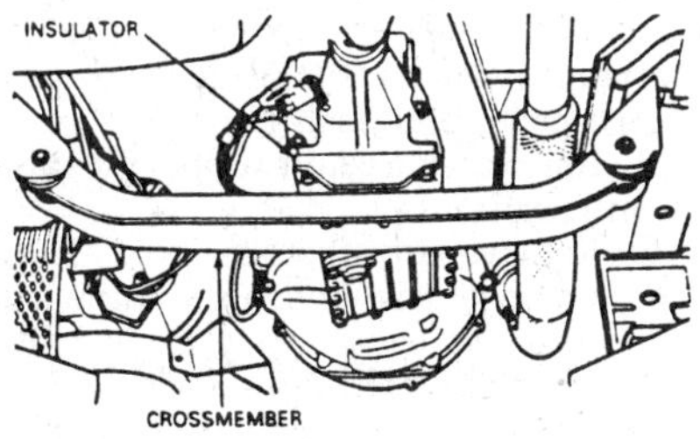

Front insulator and crossmember assembly

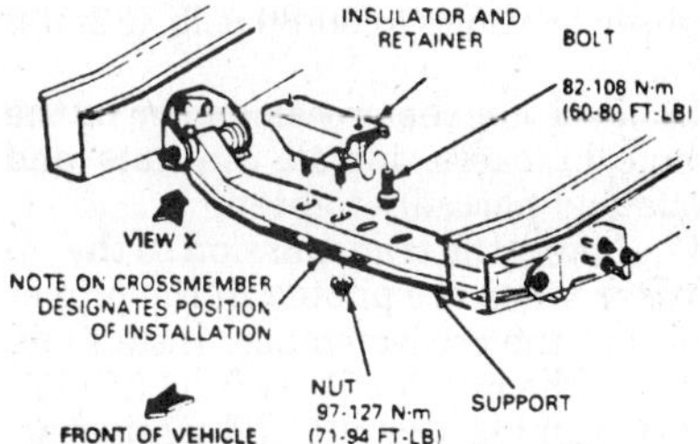

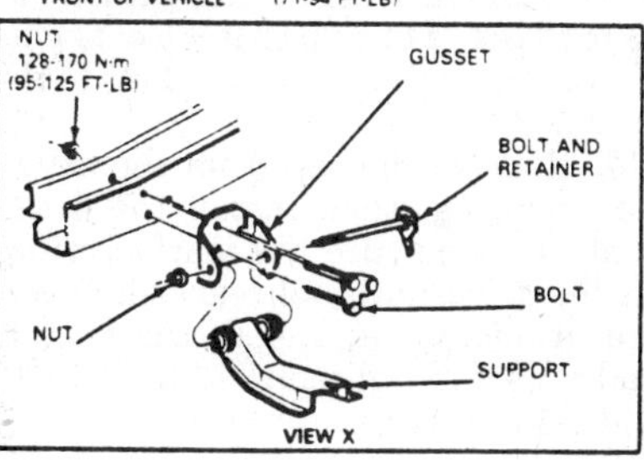

Front insulator and crossmember installation

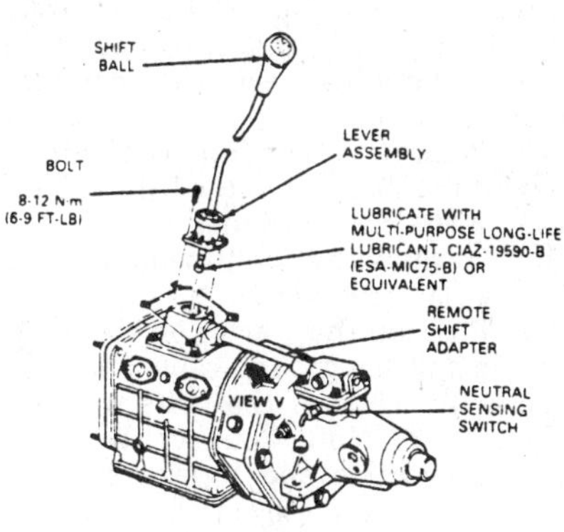

Shifter assembly

aluminum washers can be used to attach the housing to the engine.

15. If removed, position the insulator on the transmission, then install and tighten the bolts to 60-80 ft.lb. (82-108 Nm).

16. Position the crossmember in the frame brackets, install the nuts and bolts and partially tighten.

17. Lower the transmission so the insulator studs are piloted in the proper holes in the crossmember. Install and tighten the nuts to 71-94 ft.lb. (97-127 Nm). Tighten the nut and washer assemblies attaching the front insulators to the frame brackets to the specified torque.

18. Remove the cap from the extension housing, then install the driveshaft, making sure the marks scribed on the driveshaft and rear axle flange are in alignment. Install the U-bolts and nuts and tighten the nuts to 8-15 ft.lb. (11-20 Nm).

19. Install the speedometer cable (conventional speedometer) or reconnect the electrical connector (electronic speedometer) and connect the back-up lamp switch and shift indicator wires to the senders on the transmission.

20. Remove the cap from the hydraulic clutch tube. Install the tube and fitting in the slave cylinder, then install the clip retaining the tube and fitting to the slave cylinder.

21. Position the starter on the housing, install the ground cable and start the bolts. Tighten the bolts to 15-20 ft.lb. (21-27 Nm). Connect the relay-to-starter cable and tighten the nut and washer, then lower the vehicle.

22. Install the shift lever in the shifter adaptor and tighten the bolts to 15-20 ft.lb. (20-27 Nm).

23. Position the rubber shift boot on the floor and install the bolts.

24. Connect the negative battery cable.

25. Bleed the hydraulic clutch system as described later in this section.

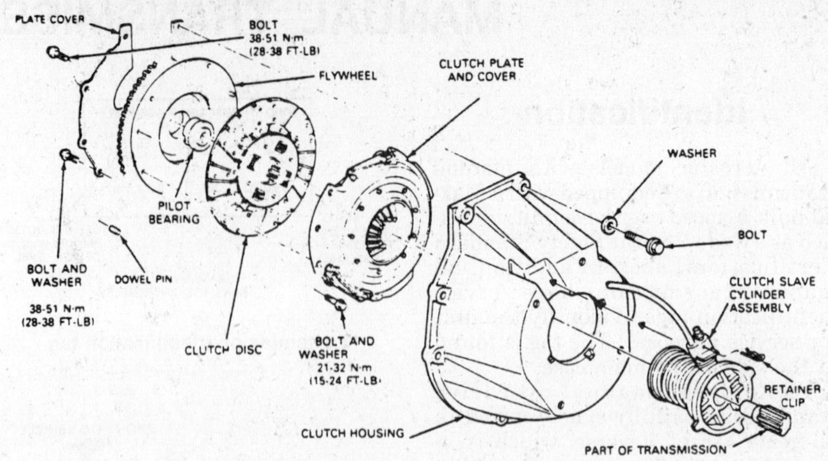

Clutch assembly on 2.3L (140 CID) engine

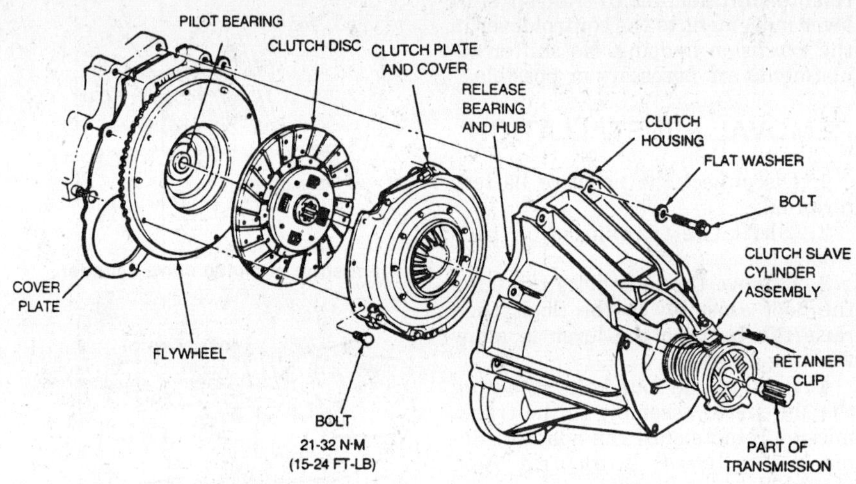

Clutch assembly on 2.8L (171 CID) and 3.0L (182 CID) engines

CLUTCH

Clutch Disc and Pressure Plate

REMOVAL & INSTALLATION

CAUTION

The clutch driven disc contains asbestos, which has been determined to be a cancer causing agent. Never clean clutch surfaces with compressed air and avoid inhaling any dust from any clutch surface! When cleaning clutch surfaces, use a commercially available brake cleaning fluid.

1. Disconnect the clutch hydraulic system master cylinder from the clutch pedal and dash panel.
2. Raise the van and support it safely on jackstands.
3. Remove the starter.
4. Remove the hydraulic tube retainer clip at the slave cylinder. Remove the tube from the slave cylinder.
5. Remove the transmission and clutch housing.
6. Mark the assembled position of the pressure plate and cover to the flywheel for reassembly.
7. Loosen the pressure plate and cover attaching bolts evenly until the pressure plate springs are expanded and remove the bolts.
8. Remove the pressure plate, cover assembly and clutch disc from the flywheel.
9. Clean the pressure plate and flywheel surfaces with a suitable commercial alcohol base solvent to be sure that surfaces are free from any oil film. Do not use cleaners with a petroleum base and do not immerse the pressure plate in the solvent.
10. To install, position the clutch disc on the flywheel so that the clutch alignment tool (T74P-7137-K or equivalent) can enter the clutch pilot bearing and align the disc.
11. When installing the original pressure plate and cover assembly, align the assembly and flywheel according to the marks made during the removal procedure. Position the pressure plate and cover assembly on the flywheel, align the pressure plate and disc and install the retaining bolts that fasten the assembly to the flywheel. Tighten the bolts in the sequence illustrated to 15-25 ft.lb. (21-32 Nm), then remove the clutch pilot tool.
12. Install the transmission and clutch housing as previously described. Reuse the aluminum washers

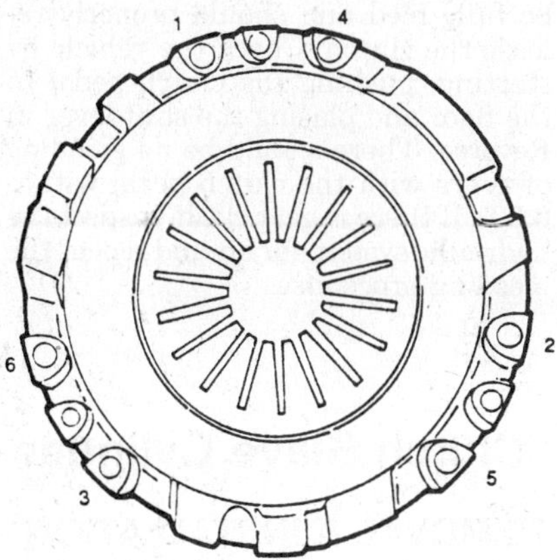

Clutch pressure plate torque sequence

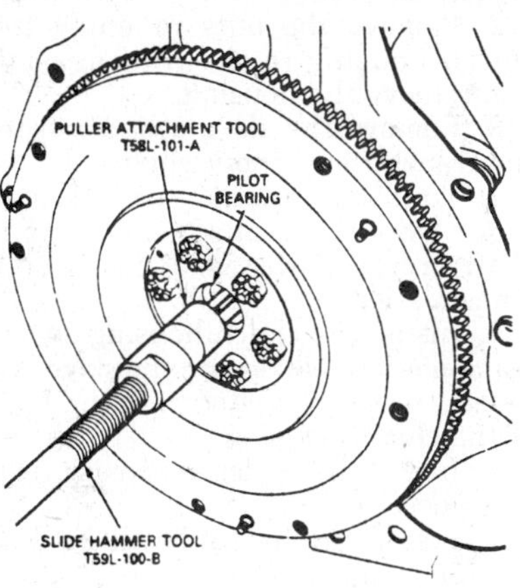

Removing clutch pilot bearing

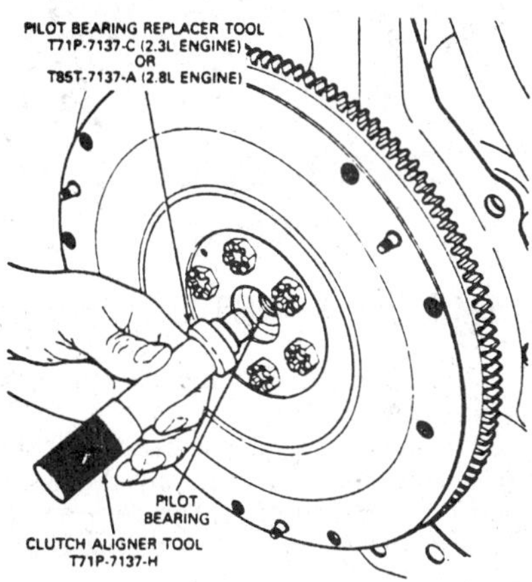

Installing clutch pilot bearing with driver tool

under the retaining bolt to prevent galvanic corrosion.

13. Install the clutch hydraulic tube to the slave cylinder, being careful not to damage the O-ring seal. Install the retainer clip.

14. Connect the hydraulic clutch master cylinder to the clutch pedal and to the dash panel.

15. Bleed the clutch system as described later in this section.

CLutch Pilot Bearing

REMOVAL & INSTALLATION

NOTE: A needle roller bearing assembly is used as a clutch pilot bearing. It is inserted directly into the engine flywheel. The needle bearing clutch pilot can only be installed with the seal end of the bearing facing the transmission. The bearing and seal are pregreased and do not require additional lubrication. A new bearing must be installed whenever a bearing is removed.

1. Remove the transmission, clutch pressure plate and disc as previously described.

2. Remove the pilot bearing using a slide hammer and adapter T58L-101-A or equivalent.

3. To install a new bearing, first coat the pilot bore in the crankshaft with a small quantity of multipurpose,

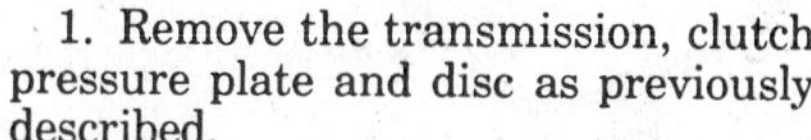

long-life lubricant such as part number C1AZ-19590-A. Avoid using too much lubricant as it may be thrown on the clutch disc when the clutch revolves.

4. Using the proper driver tool, carefully install the pilot bearing with the seal facing the transmission.

5. Install the clutch pressure plate, disc and transmission as previously described. Be careful not to damage the bearing during transmission installation while the transmission input shaft is being inserted into the bearing.

Clutch Master Cylinder and Reservoir

REMOVAL & INSTALLATION

NOTE: Do not separate the clutch master cylinder from the reservoir unless individual component replacement is required.

1. Disconnect the clutch master cylinder pushrod from the clutch pedal by prying the retainer bushing and pushrod off the shaft.

2. Slide the clutch reservoir out of the slots located in the electrical cover box.

3. On the clutch housing, remove the clip retaining the tube to the slave cylinder. Remove the tube and fitting, then plug both lines to prevent the entry of dirt, moisture or other contaminants into the hydraulic system.

4. Disconnect the tube from the clips on the underbody siderail.

5. Remove the bolts retaining the clutch master cylinder to the engine compartment. Remove the clutch master cylinder, reservoir and tube as an assembly.

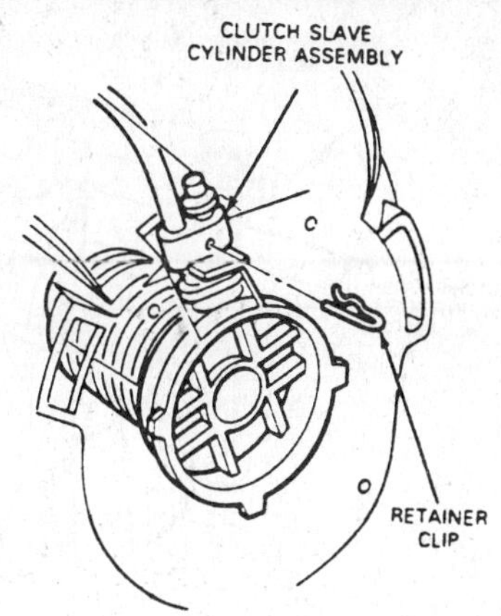

Disconnecting clutch slave cylinder line

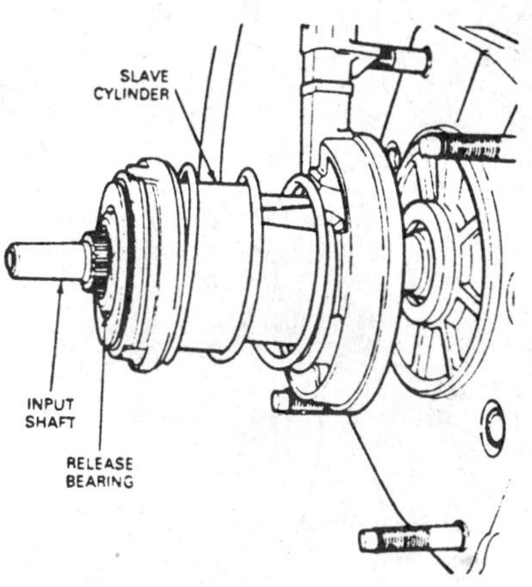

Removing the clutch slave cylinder from the input shaft

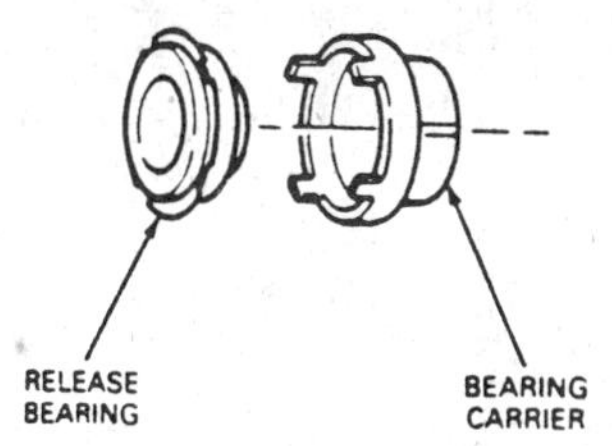

Clutch release bearing assembly

6. To install the master cylinder, first install the pushrod through the hole in the engine compartment. Make sure it is located on the correct side of the clutch pedal. Place the master cylinder assembly in position, install the bolts and tighten them to 15-20 ft.lb. (21-27 Nm).

7. Insert the tube in the routing clips on the underbody siderail.

8. Insert the tube and fitting in the clutch slave cylinder and install the clip.

9. Position the clutch reservoir in

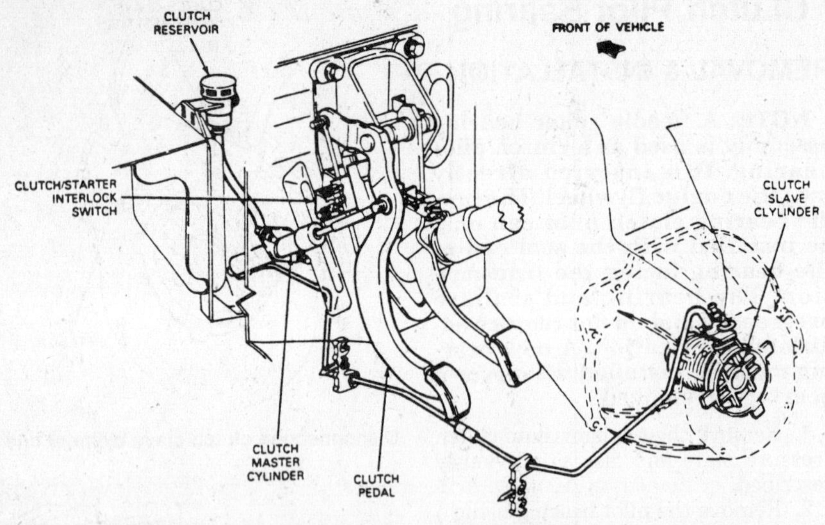

Hydraulic clutch assembly

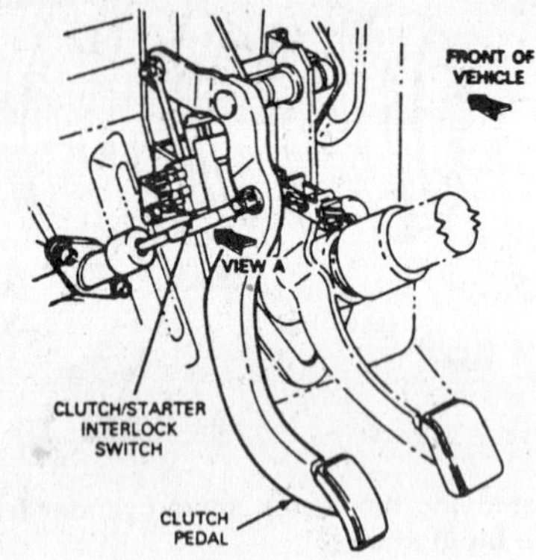

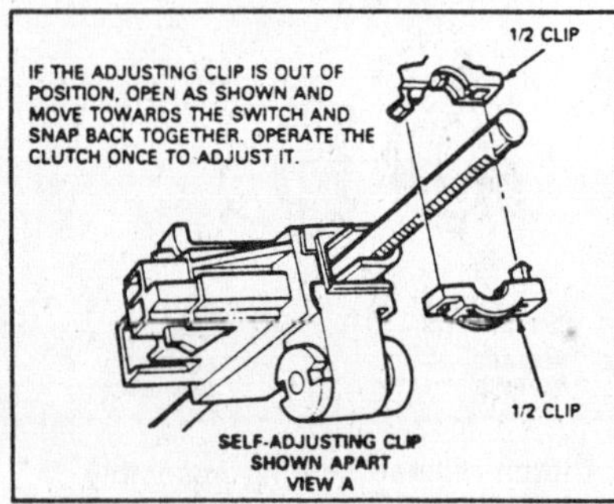

Clutch/starter interlock switch adjustment

the engine compartment electrical cover box slots.

10. Install the retainer bushing in the clutch master cylinder pushrod, then install the retainer and pushrod on the clutch pedal shaft.

11. Bleed the clutch hydraulic system as described below.

BLEEDING THE HYDRAULIC CLUTCH SYSTEM

After a clutch hydraulic system has been removed from the vehicle, or if air is trapped in the line, the system must be bled. The following procedure is used with the hydraulic system installed on the vehicle. The largest portion of the filling is carried out by gravity.

1. Clean all dirt and grease from around the reservoir cap.

2. Remove the cap and diaphragm and fill the reservoir to the top with approved DOT 3 brake fluid.

3. To keep brake fluid from entering the clutch housing, place a suitable rubber tube of appropriate inside diameter from the bleed screw to a clear container. Loosen the bleeder screw (located at the slave cylinder body) next to the inlet connection.

4. Fluid should now begin to flow from the master cylinder, down the red tube and into the slave cylinder. The reservoir must be kept full at all times to insure that there will be no additional air drawn into the system.

5. Bubbles should appear at the bleeder screw outlet, indicating that air is being expelled. When the slave cylinder is full, a steady stream of fluid will come from the slave cylinder outlet. Tighten the bleeder screw.

6. Place the diaphragm and cap on the reservoir. The fluid in the reservoir should be level with the step.

7. Exert a light load to the clutch pedal and slightly loosen the bleed screw. Maintain pressure until the pedal touches the floor, then tighten the bleed screw. Do not allow the clutch pedal to return until the bleed screw is tightened. Fluid and any air that is left should be expelled through the bleed port.

8. Refill the reservoir to the level at the step. Install the diaphragm and cap If evidence of air still exists, repeat Step 7.

9. The hydraulic system should now be fully bled and should properly release the clutch. Check the vehicle by starting, pushing the clutch pedal to the floor and placing the shift lever in Reverse. There should be no grinding of gears with the clutch pedal within 0.50". If there is gear clash, inspect the hydraulic system for air and repeat the bleeding procedure.

Clutch Slave Cylinder

REMOVAL & INSTALLATION

1. Remove the transmission as previously described.

2. Remove the nuts retaining the clutch housing to the transmission and remove the housing.

3. Remove the slave cylinder from the transmission input shaft.

4. To install, position the slave cylinder over the transmission input shaft with the tower portion facing the transmission.

5. Install the clutch housing on the transmission. Make sure the slave cylinder is properly located in the notches of the clutch housing.

6. Install the transmission as previously described.

7. Install the hydraulic clutch line retaining clip.

8. Bleed the clutch hydraulic system as previously described.

Clutch Release Bearing

REMOVAL & INSTALLATION

1. Remove the clutch slave cylinder as described above.

2. Remove the release bearing from the clutch slave cylinder by carefully bending back slightly the four symmetrical plastic retainers of the bearing carrier.

3. Prior to installation, lubricate the release bearing with multipurpose, long-life lubricant (such as part number C1AZ-19590-B). Fill the annular groove of the release bearing and apply a thin coat on the inside diameter of the release bearing.

4. Assemble the release bearing to the clutch slave cylinder by pushing the bearing into place while aligning the four symmetrical plastic retainers of the bearing carrier.

5. Install the clutch slave cylinder as previously described.

Clutch/Starter Interlock Switch

ADJUSTMENT

If the adjusting clip is out of position on the rod, remove both halves of the clip. Position both halves of the clip closer to the switch and snap the clips together on the rod. Depress the clutch pedal to the floor to adjust the switch.

AUTOMATIC TRANSMISSION

Identification

All vehicles are equipped with a Safety Standard Certification Label mounted on the left (driver) door frame. Refer to the stamped code in the space marked "Trans" for proper transmission identification. In addition, there is a transmission identification tag mounted on the transmission body. All Aerostar models are equipped with an automatic A4LD four speed overdrive transmission.

TRANSMISSION FLUID DRAIN AND REFILL

Normal maintenance and lubrication requirements do not necessitate periodic automatic transmission fluid changes. If major service, such as a clutch band, bearing, etc. is required in the transmission, it will have to be removed for service. At this time, the converter, transmission cooler and cooler lines must be thoroughly flushed to remove any dirt.

When used under continuous or severe conditions, the transmission and torque converter should be drained and refilled with fluid as specified. Before adding fluid, make sure it meets or exceeds the manufacturer's specifications. The A4LD automatic transmission uses Dexron® II transmission fluid. The use of incorrect type transmission fluid can result in transmission malfunction and/or failure. Refer to the Capacities Specification Chart for transmission refill recommendations with and without the torque coverter. Drain the fluid as follows:

1. Raise the vehicle and support it safely on jackstands.
2. Place a suitable drain pan beneath the transmission.
3. Loosen the pan attaching bolts slowly, allowing one side to tip down and drain the fluid. This removes all fluid from the pan, but not from the torque converter.
4. When all fluid has drained from the transmission, remove and thoroughly clean the pan and screen. Discard the pan gasket and clean all gasket mating surfaces. Install the pan and screen with a new gasket.
5. Add 3 qts. of fluid to the transmission through the filler tube, then start the engine and shift the transmission through all gears, pausing briefly as each gear engages.
6. Place the transmission in Park and check the fluid level with the engine idling. Set the parking brake firmly.

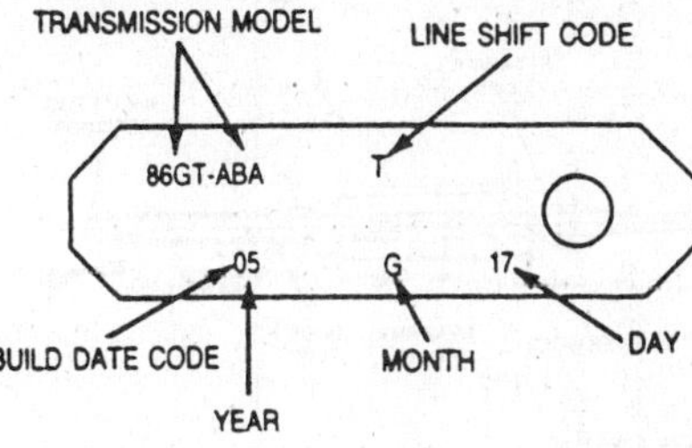

Automatic transmission identification tag attached to the lower left extension attaching bolt

Adjustments

SHIFT LINKAGE

1. Raise the vehicle and support it safely on jackstands. Set the parking brake firmly.
2. Place the shift lever in the OVERDRIVE position.
3. Working under the vehicle, loosen the adjustment screw on the shift cable and remove the end fitting from the manual lever ball stud.
4. Place the manual lever in the OVERDRIVE position by moving the lever all the way rearward, then moving it three detents forward.
5. Connect the cable end fitting to the manual lever.

NOTE: Too much pressure on the arm can move the shifter to the Drive position. Apply pressure only until the resistance of the detent nib is felt.

6. Tighten the adjustment screw to 45-60 in.lb. (5-7 Nm). After adjustment, check for proper Park engagement. The control lever must move to the right when engaged in Park. Check the transmission control lever in all detent positions with the engine running to insure correct detent/transmission action and readjust if required.

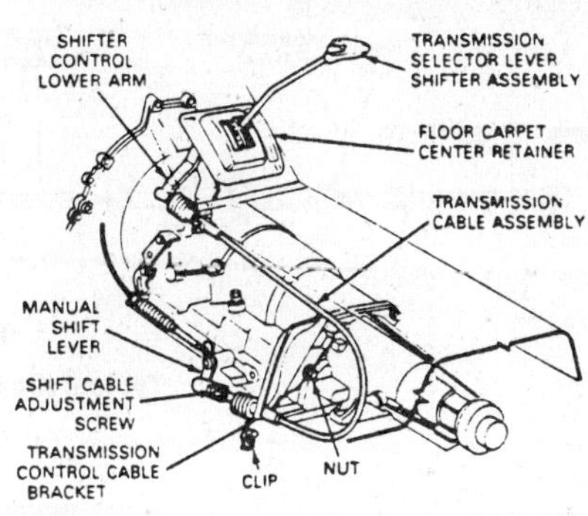

Automatic transmission shifter linkage

KICKDOWN CABLE

The self-adjusting kickdown cable is attached to the accelerator pedal near the accelerator cable. The kickdown cable is routed from the transmission through the dash to the accelerator pedal. A self-adjuster mechanism is located in the engine compartment at the inlet for the cable on the dash.

The kickdown cable is self-adjusting over a tolerence range of 1". If the cable requires readjustment, reset the cable by depressing the semi-circular metal tab on the self-adjuster mechanism and pulling the cable forward (toward the front of the van) to the "zero" position setting. The cable will then automatically readjust to the proper length when kicked down.

Neutral Start Switch

REMOVAL & INSTALLATION

1. Disconnect the negative battery cable.
2. Disconnect the neutral start switch electrical harness from the neutral start switch.
3. Remove the neutral start switch and O-ring using the neutral start switch socket tool T74P-77247-A, or equivalent.

CAUTION

Other tools could crush or puncture the walls of the switch.

4. Installation is the reverse of removal. Tighten the switch to 7-10 ft.lb. (10-14 Nm) and use a new O-ring. Check the operation of the switch with the parking brake engaged. The engine should only start with the transmission in Park or Neutral.

Transmission

REMOVAL & INSTALLATION

1. Disconnect the negative battery cable.

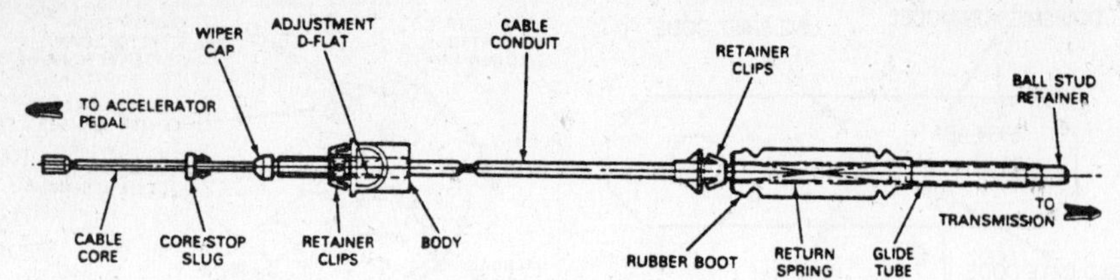

Typical kickdown cable

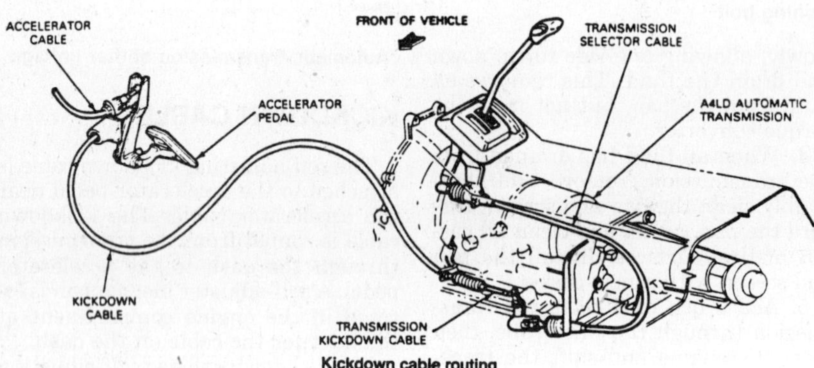

Kickdown cable routing

2. Raise the vehicle and support it safely.
3. Place a drain pan under the transmission. Starting at the rear and working toward the front, loosen the transmission pan attaching bolts and allow the fluid to drain. After the fluid is drained, install four bolts at each corner to temporarily retain the pan.
4. Remove the converter access cover and adapter plate bolts from the lower end of the converter housing.
5. Remove the four flywheel to converter attaching nuts by placing a 22mm socket and breaker bar on the crankshaft pulley attaching bolt. Rotate the pulley clockwise (as viewed from the front) to gain access to each of the nuts.

WARNING: On belt driven overhead cam engines, never rotate the pulley counterclockwise under any circumstances!

6. Scribe an alignment mark to index the driveshaft to the rear axle flange. Remove the U-bolts and nuts retaining the driveshaft to the rear axle flange, then remove the driveshaft. Install an extension housing seal replacer tool in the extension housing to prevent any fluid leakage.
7. Remove the speedometer cable from the extension housing.
8. Disconnect the neutral start switch wires and the converter clutch solenoid.
9. Remove the kickdown cable from the upper selector lever. Remove the retaining clip from the selector cable bracket, then remove the selector cable from the ball stud on the lower selector lever. Depress the tab on the retainer and remove the kickdown cable from the bracket.

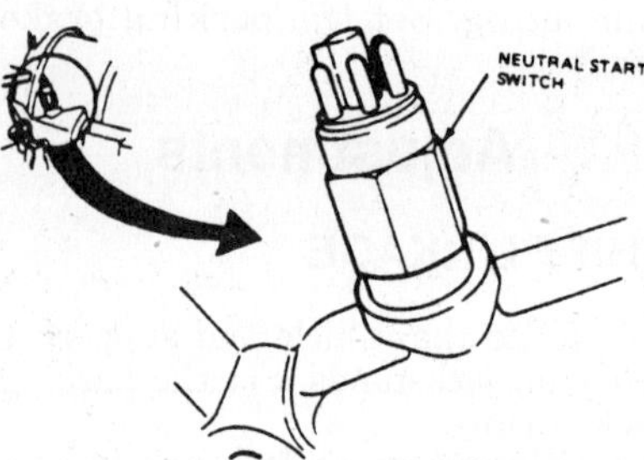

Neutral start switch installation

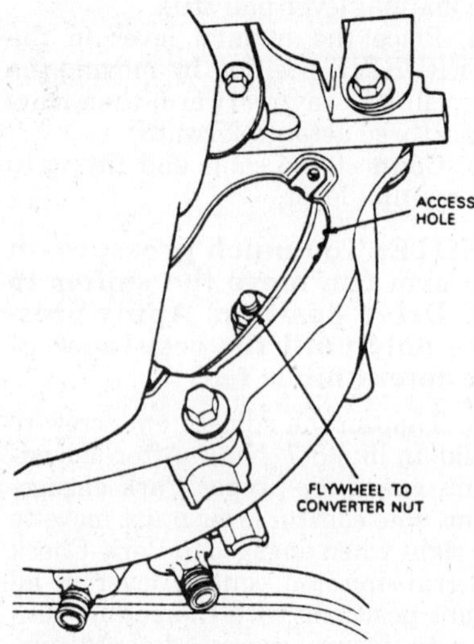

Disconnecting the flywheel from the torque converter

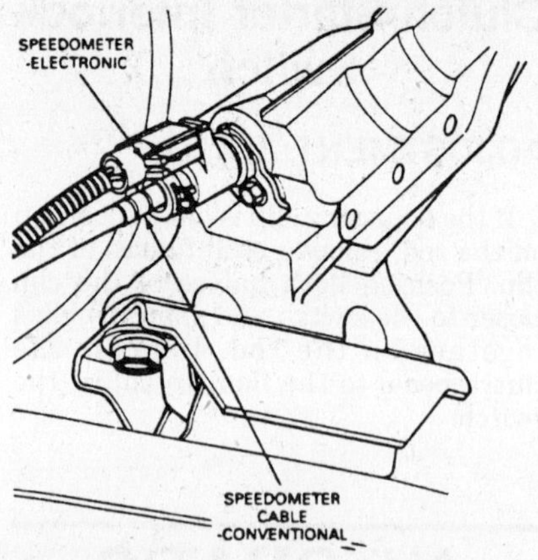

Speedometer cable attachment at the extension housing

10. Disconnect the vacuum hose from the transmission vacuum modulator.
11. Disconnect the relay to starter cable at the starter terminal. Remove the starter mounting bolts and the ground cable and remove the starter.
12. Remove the filler tube from the transmision.
13. Position a transmission jack under the transmission and raise it slightly to take the weight off the crossmember.
14. Remove the insulator to crossmember retaining nuts.
15. Remove the crossmember to frame side support attaching nuts and bolts. Remove the crossmember. If required, remove the bolts retaining the insulator to the transmission and remove the insulator.
16. Remove the converter housing-to-engine fasteners.
17. Slightly lower the transmission jack to gain access to the oil cooler lines, then disconnect the oil cooler lines at the transmission. Plug all openings to prevent contamination by dirt or grease.
18. Move the transmission to the rear so it disengages from the dowel pins and the converter is disengaged from the flywheel. Carefully lower the transmission and remove it from the vehicle. Remove the torque converter by pulling it straight out from the transmission.

NOTE: If the transmission is to be removed for an extended period of time, support the engine with a safety stand and wood block.

19. To install the transmission, first

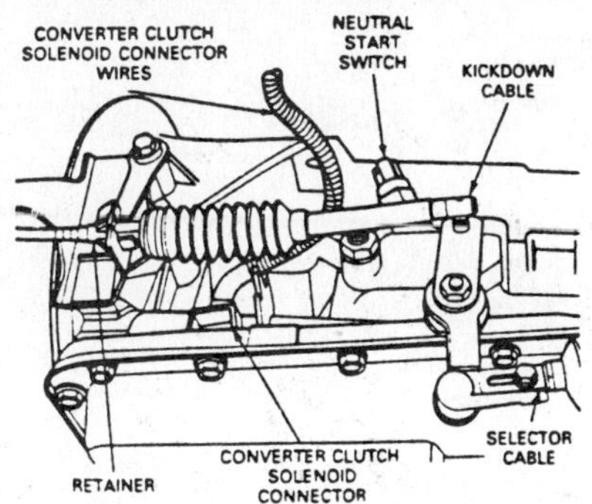

Linkage and electrical connectors at the transmission

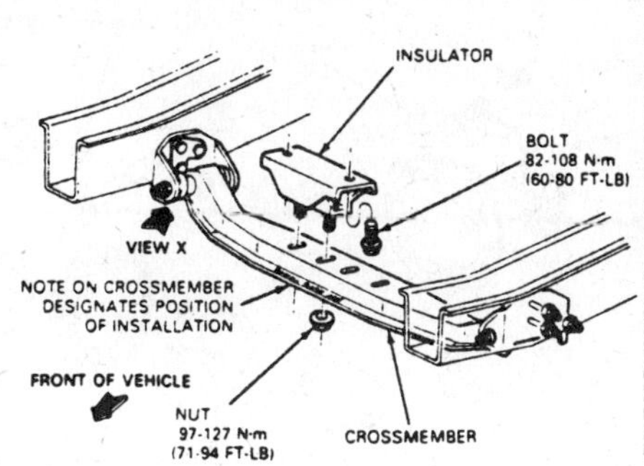

Crossmember and insulator mounting

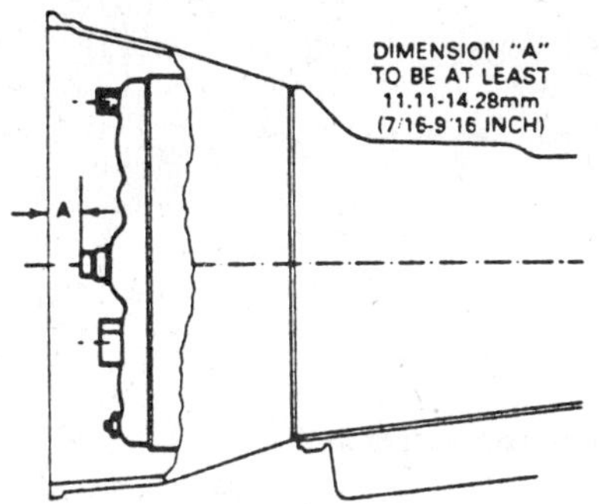

Checking torque converter installation

position the torque converter to the transmission, making sure the converter hub is fully engaged in the pump gear. Slowly rotate the torque converter while pressing inward until it seats. You may feel the torque converter move inward a little bit three times as you rotate it until it is fully seated. Check the distance illustrated to make sure the torque converter is seated or it will bind when the transmission is tightened to the engine. Make sure the torque converter rotates freely and is not bound up.

20. With the converter properly installed, place the transmission on a transmision jack and secure it with a safety chain.

21. Rotate the converter so that the drive studs are in alignment with the holes in the flywheel.

22. Lift the transmission into position for installation enough to connect the oil cooler lines to the case.

23. Move the converter and transmission assembly forward into position, being careful not to damage the flywheel and converter pilot. THe converter housing is piloted into position by the dowels in the rear of the engine block.

NOTE: Do not allow the transmission to get into a nose-down position during installation as this may cause the converter to move forward and disengage from the pump gear. The converter must rest squarely against the flywheel. This indicates that the converter pilot is not binding in the engine crankshaft.

24. Install the converter housing-to-engine attaching fasteners and tighten to 28-38 ft.lb. (38-51 Nm).

25. If removed, position the insulator on the transmission, then install and tighten the retaining bolts to 60-80 ft.lb. (82-108 Nm).

26. Position the crossmember in the brackets in the frame. The markings on the crossmember indicate the direction of installation. Install the nuts and bolts and tighten.

27. Slowly lower the transmission so the insulator studs are installed in the proper slots in the crossmember. Install the nuts and tighten them to 71-94 ft.lb. (97-127 Nm). Disconnect the safety chain and remove the transmission jack.

28. Install the filler tube in the transmission.

29. Position the starter assembly on the converter housing. Install the ground cable and start and tighten the mounting bolts to 15-20 ft.lb. (21-27 Nm). Connect the relay-to-starter cable and tighten the nut and washer.

30. Connect the vacuum hose to the modulator on the right side of the transmission.

31. Position the selector cable in the bracket on the transmission case. Press the end of the cable on the ball stud on the lower portion of the selector lever, then install the retainer in the bracket.

32. Position the kickdown cable on the upper selector lever, then install the retainer in the bracket.

33. Connect the neutral start switch plug to the switch. Install the converter clutch solenoid connector.

34. Install the speedometer cable.

35. Position a 22mm socket and breaker bar on the crankshaft pulley bolt, then rotate the pulley clockwise (as viewed from the front) to gain access to the converter-to-flywheel studs. Install the nut on each stud and tighten to 20-34 ft.lb. (27-46 Nm).

WARNING: On belt driven overhead camshaft engines, never rotate the pulley in a counterclockwise direction as viewed from the front!

36. Position the converter access cover and adapter plate on the converter housing, then install and tighten the attaching bolts to 12-16 ft.lb. (16-22 Nm).

37. Remove the plug from the extension housing and install the driveshaft so that the index marks made earlier are in alignment. Install the U-bolts and tighten the nuts to 8-15 ft.lb. (11-20 Nm).

38. Adjust the manual linkage as previously described.

39. Lower the van and fill the transmission to the proper level. If the converter was drained during removal, add five quarts of Dexron®II, then run the engine and check the fluid level on the dipstick. Add as required. If the converter was not drained, start with three quarts and top off as necessary.

40. Check the transmission, converter assembly and oil cooler lines for leaks and correct as necessary.

REAR AXLE

All models use an integral carrier axle with a 7.5" ring gear. This differential is available in three ratios: 3.45:1, 3.73:1 and 4.10:1. An identification tag with the axle ratio stamped on is affixed to one bolt of the differential cover assembly.

Understanding Rear Axles

The rear axle is a special type of

transmission that reduces the speed of the drive from the engine and transmission and divides the power to the rear wheels. Power enters the rear axle from the driveshaft via the companion flange. The flange is mounted on the drive pinion shaft. The drive pinion shaft and gear which carry the power into the differential turn at engine speed. The gear on the end of the pinion shaft drives a large ring gear the axis of rotation of which is 90 degrees away from the of the pinion. The pinion and gear reduce the gear ratio of the axle, and change the direction of rotation to turn the axle shafts which drive both wheels. The rear axle gear ratio is found by dividing the number of pinion gear teeth into the number of ring gear teeth.

The ring gear drives the differential case. The case provides the two mounting points for the ends of a pinion shaft on which are mounted two pinion gears. The pinion gears drive the two side gears, one of which is located on the inner end of each axle shaft. By driving the axle shafts through the arrangement, the differential allows the outer drive wheel to turn faster than the inner drive wheel in a turn. The main drive pinion and the side bearings, which bear the weight of the differential case, are shimmed to provide proper bearing preload, and to position the pinion and ring gears properly.

NOTE: The proper adjustment of the relationship of the ring and pinion gears is critical. It should be attempted only by those with extensive equipment and/or experience.

Limited-slip differentials include clutches which tend to link each axle shaft to the differential case. Clutches may be engaged either by spring action or by pressure produced by the torque on the axles during a turn. During turning on a dry pavement, the effects of the clutches are overcome, and each wheel turns at the required speed. When slippage occurs at either wheel, however, the clutches will transmit some of the power to the wheel which has the greater amount of traction. Because of the presence of clutches, limited-slip units require a special lubricant.

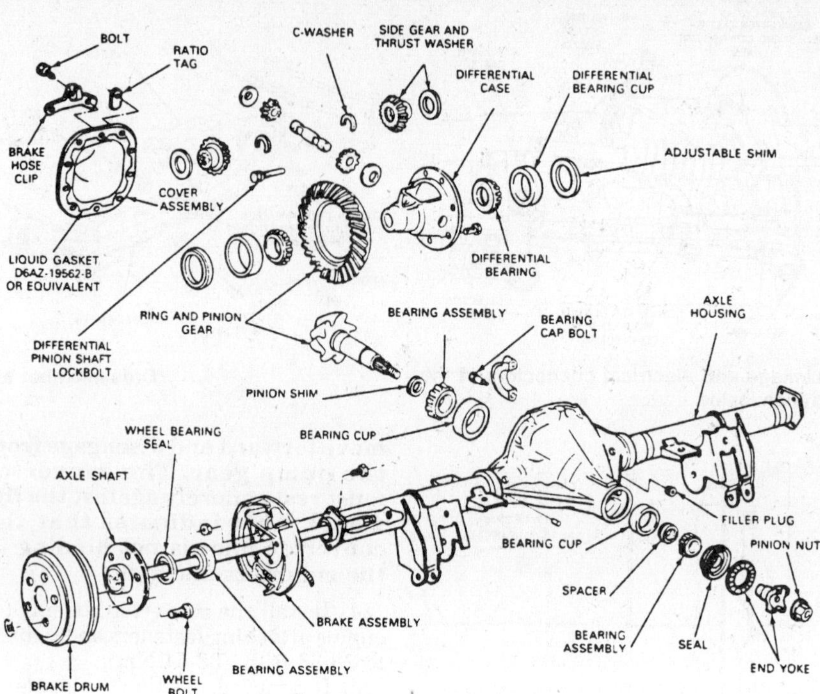

Exploded view of the rear axle assembly

Determining Axle Ratio

The drive axle of a vehicle is said to have a certain axle ratio. This number (usually a whole number and a decimal fraction) is actually a comparison of the number of gear teeth on the ring gear and the pinion gear. For example, a 4.11 rear means that theoretically, there are 4.11 teeth on the ring gear and one tooth on the pinion gear or, put another way, the driveshaft must turn 4.11 times to turn the wheels once. Actually, on a 4.11 rear, there might be 37 teeth on the ring gear and 9 teeth on the pinion gear. By dividing the number of teeth on the pinion gear into the number of teeth on the ring gear, the numerical axle ratio (4.11) is obtained. This also provides a good method of ascertaining exactly what axle ratio one is dealing with.

Another method of determining gear ratio is to jack up and support the car so that both rear wheels are off the ground. Make a chalk mark on the rear wheel and the driveshaft. Put the transmission in Neutral. Turn the rear wheel one complete turn and count the number of turns that the driveshaft makes. The number of turns that the driveshaft makes in one complete revolution of the rear wheel is an approximation of the rear axle ratio.

Axle Shaft

REMOVAL & INSTALLATION

1. Raise the van and support it safely on jackstands.
2. Remove the rear brake drums.

CAUTION

Brake shoes contain asbestos, which has been determined to be a cancer causing agent. Never clean the brake surfaces with compressed air and avoid inhaling any dust from any brake surface! When cleaning brake surfaces, use a commercially available brake cleaning fluid.

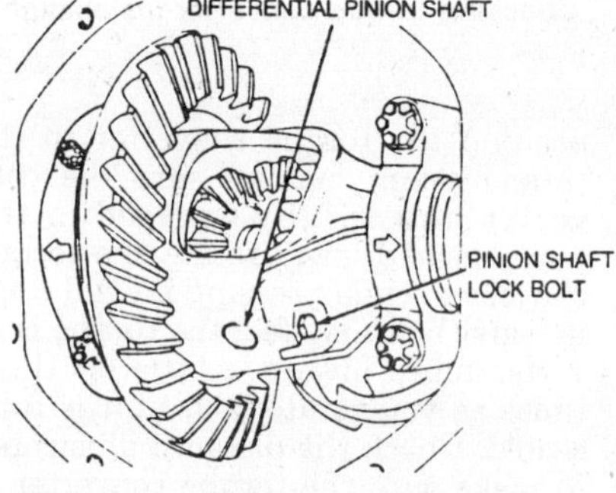

Removing differential pinion shaft on 3.45:1 ratio axles

3. Clean all dirt and grease from the area of the carrier cover with a wire brush and/or cloth.
4. Drain the rear axle lubricant into a suitable container by removing the housing cover.

NOTE: For 3.45:1 ratio axles, perform Steps 5, 6 and 7. For 3.73:1 and 4.10:1 axles, perform Steps 8-11.

5. Remove the differential pinion shaft lock bolt and differential pinion shaft. The pinion gears may be left in place. Once the axle shafts are removed, reinstall the pinion shaft and lock bolt.

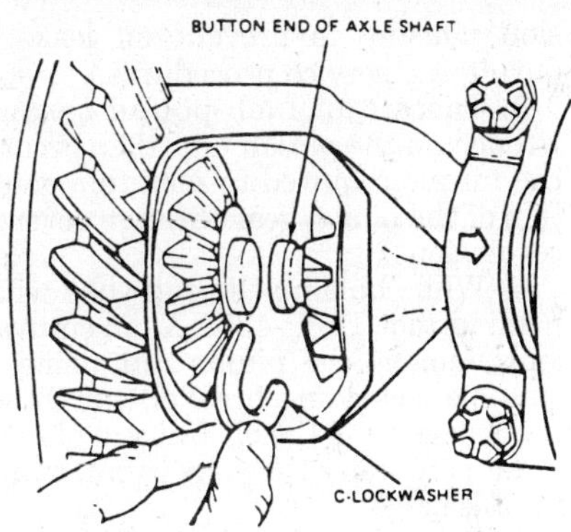

Removing the C-lockwasher on 3.45:1 ratio axles

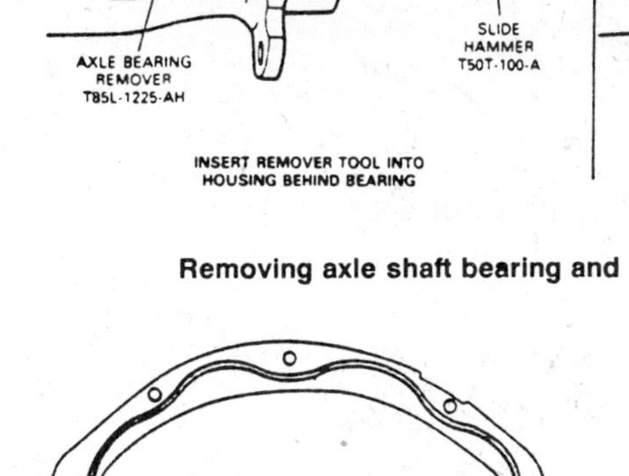

Removing axle shaft bearing and seal with remover tool

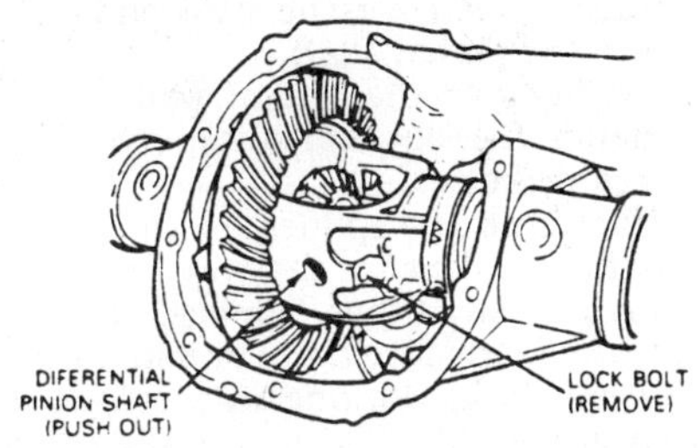

Removing the pinion shaft on 3.73:1 and 4.10:1 ratio axles

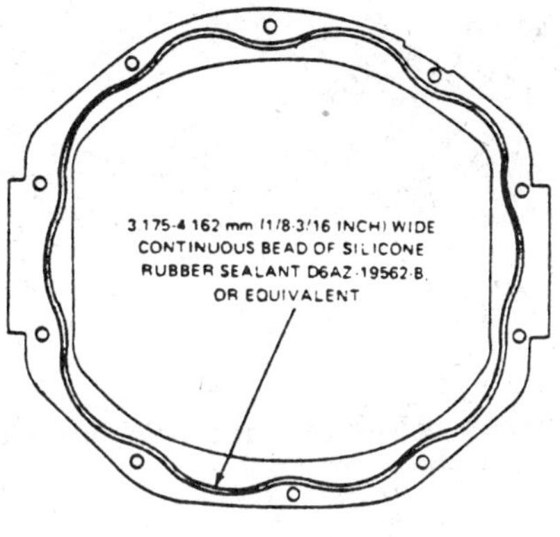

Apply sealer as shown on differential cover before installing

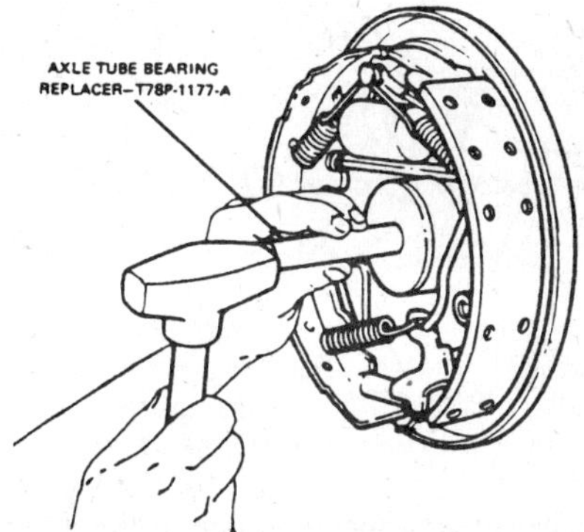

Installing axle shaft bearing with replacer tool

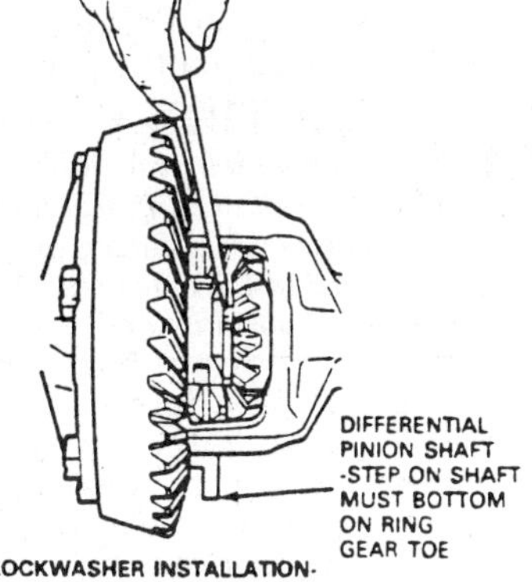

Make sure the differential pinion shaft step contacts the ring gear before installing the axle shafts on 3.73:1 and 4.10:1 ratio axles

6. Push the flanged end of the axle shafts toward the center of the vehicle and remove the C-lockwasher from the button end of the axle shaft.

7. Remove the axle shaft from the housing, being careful not to damage the oil seal.

8. For 3.73:1 and 4.10:1 ratio axles, remove the pinion shaft lock bolt.

9. Place your hand behind the differential case and push out the pinion shaft until the step on the shaft contacts the ring gear.

10. Remove the C-lockwasher from the axle shafts.

11. Remove the axle shafts from the housing, being careful not to damage the oil seal.

12. To permit axle shaft installation on 3.73:1 and 4.10:1 ratio axles, make sure the differential pinion shaft step contacts the ring gear before sliding the axle shaft into the axle housing. Start the splines into the side gear and push firmly until the button end of the axle shaft can be seen in the differential case.

WARNING: Care must be taken so as not to let the axle shaft splines damage the oil seal or wheel bearing assembly!

13. Install the C-lockwasher on the button end of the axle shaft splines, the pull the shaft outboard until the shaft splines engage and the C-lockwasher seats in the counterbore of the differential side gear.

14. Position the differential pinion shaft through the case and pinion gears, aligning the hole in the shaft with the lock screw hole. Install the lock bolt and tighten it to 15-22 ft.lb. (21-29 Nm).

15. Clean the gasket mounting surface on the rear axle housing and cover. Apply a continuous bead of silicone rubber sealant to the carrier casting face. Make sure the machined surface on both cover and carrier are clean before applying sealer.

16. Install the cover and tighten the cover bolts to 15-20 ft.lb. (21-27 Nm), except the ratio tag bolt, which is tightened to 15-25 ft.lb. (30-34 Nm). The cover assembly must be installed within 15 minutes of application of the sealer or new sealer must be applied.

17. Add lubricant until it is about ½" below the bottom of the filler hole in the running position. Install the filler plug and tighten it to 15-30 ft.lb. (20-41 Nm).

Axle Shaft Oil Seal and Wheel Bearing

REMOVAL & INSTALLATION

1. Remove the axle shaft as previously described.

2. Insert an axle bearing remover tool T85L-1225-AH attached to a slide hammer into the bore as illustrated and position it behind the bearing to the tangs on the tool engage the bearing outer race. Remove the bearing ans seal as a unit with the slide hammer.

3. Lubricate the new bearing with rear axle lubricant and install the

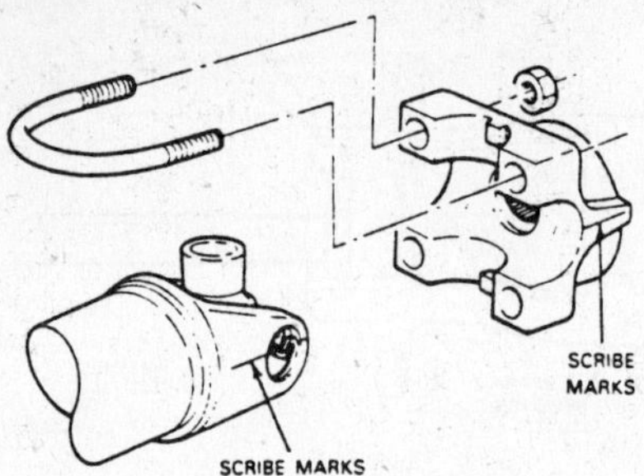

Scribe alignment marks as shown on the driveshaft and axle end yoke

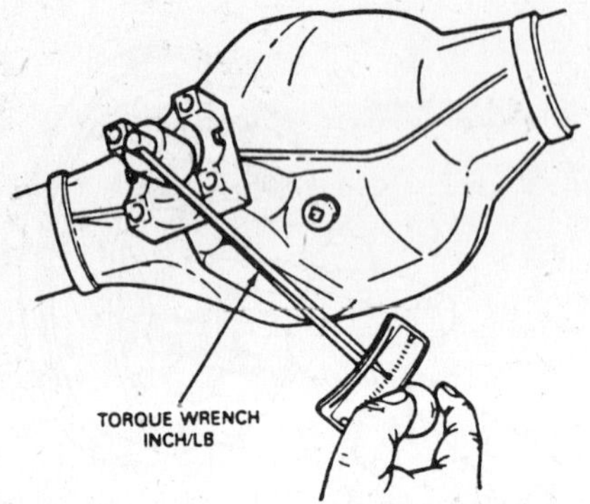

Checking rotational torque of the differential

bearing into the housing bore using bearing replacer tool T78P-1225-A, or equivalent.

4. Apply multipurpose, long-life grease between the lips of the axle shaft seal.

5. Install a new axle shaft seal using seal replacer tool T78P-1177-A, or equivalent.

CAUTION

Installation of the bearing or seal assembly without the proper tool may result in an early bearing or seal failure. If the seal becomes cocked in the bore during installation, remove it and install a new one.

6. Install the axle shaft as previously described.

Drive Pinion Oil Seal

REMOVAL & INSTALLATION

NOTE: Replacement of the pinion oil seal involves removal and installation of only the pinion nut and the axle end yoke. However, this operation disturbs the pinion bearing preload, and this preload must be carefully reset when assembling.

1. Raise the van and support it safely on jackstands.

2. Remove the rear wheels.

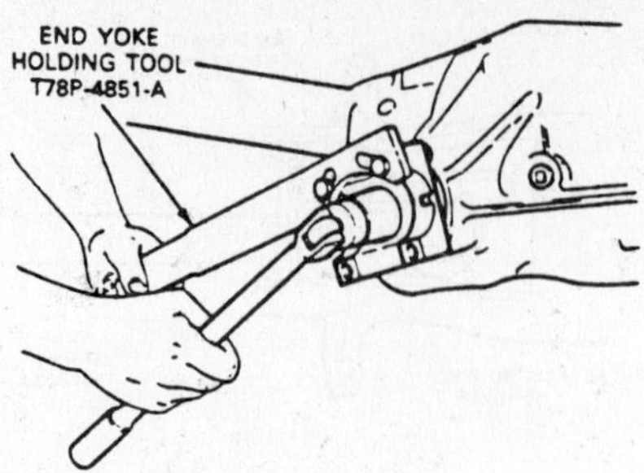

Hold the end yoke as shown to remove the pinion nut

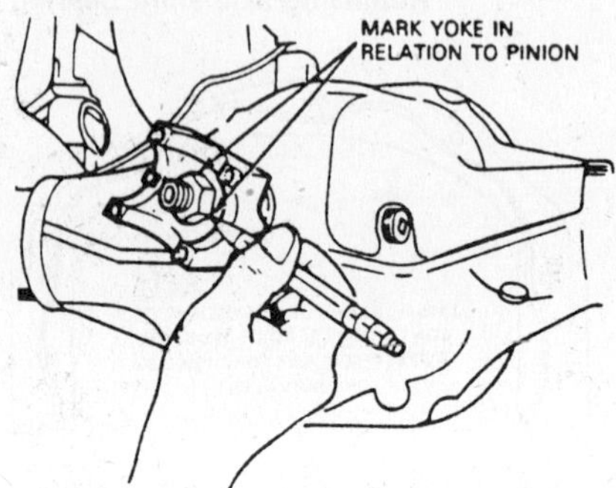

Mark axle end yoke and pinion shaft as shown before removal

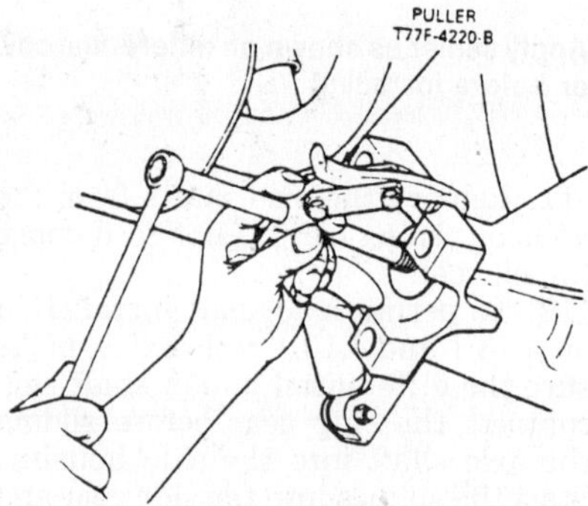

Removing end yoke with puller tool

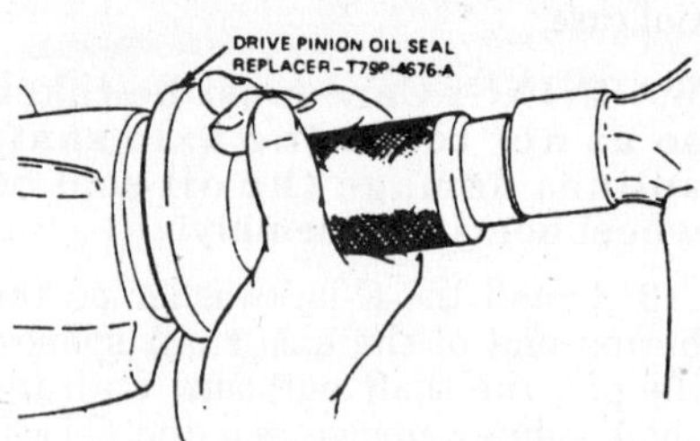

Installing drive pinion oil seal

3. Scribe marks on the driveshaft end and the axle end yoke to insure proper positioning of the driveshaft upon assembly.

4. Disconnect the driveshaft from the rear axle end yoke and remove the driveshaft from the transmission extension housing. Install an oil seal replacer tool in the transmission extension housing to prevent oil leakage during the service procedures.

5. Install an inch-pound torque wrench on the pinion nut, then record the torque required to maintain rotation of the pinion gear through several revolutions.

6. While holding the end yoke with holding tool T78P-4851-A, or equivalent, remove the pinion nut using a suitable socket on a breaker bar. Clean the area around the oil seal and place a drain pan under the yoke to catch any fluid leakage.

7. Mark the axle yoke in relation to the pinion shaft so the flange can be installed in the same position.

8. Use a suitable puller tool as illustrated to remove the axle end yoke from the pinion shaft.

9. Remove the pinion seal with a small prybar or other suitable tool and discard the seal.

10. Check the splines on the pinion shaft to make sure they are free from burrs or any other damage. If burrs are noted, remove them by using a fine crocus cloth, working in a rotational pattern.

11. Apply mulitpurpose, long-life grease between the lips of the pinion seal, the install the seal using seal replacer tool T79P-4676-A or equivalent. Place the seal on the tool, then drive it into position on the pinion.

CAUTION

Installation of the pinion seal without the proper tool may result in early seal failure. If the seal becomes cocked during installation, remove it and install a new seal. Never hammer on a seal metal casing.

12. Check the seal surface of the yoke for scratches, nicks or a groove around the diameter. If any of these conditions exist, replace the yoke. Apply a small amount of lubricant to the end yoke splines, then align the mark on the end yoke with the mark on the pinion shaft and install the yoke. The companion shaft must never be hammered on or installed with power tools.

13. Wipe the pinion clean.

14. Install a new nut and spacer on the pinion shaft, then hold the end yoke as before and tighten the nut while rotating the pinion occasionally to insure proper bearing seating. In addition, take frequent pinion bearing torque preload readings with the inch-pound torque wrench until the original recorded rotational torque reading is obtained or to 8-14 in.lb. (1-1.6 Nm).

NOTE: Under no circumstances should the pinion nut be backed off to reduce preload. If reduced preload is required, a new collapsible pinion spacer and pinion nut must be installed.

15. Remove the oil seal replacer tool from the transmission extension housing and install the front of the driveshaft on the transmission output shaft. Connect the rear end of the driveshaft to the axle end yoke, aligning the scribe marks made earlier. Apply Loctite® or equivalent to the threads of the attaching bolts and tighten the four U-bolt nuts to 70-95 ft.lb. (95-128 Nm).

16. Remove the filler plug and add hypoid gear lubricant until it is about ½" below the bottom of the filler hole in the running position. Install the filler plug and tighten it to 15-30 ft.lb. (20-41 Nm).

Axle Housing

REMOVAL & INSTALLATION

1. Raise the van and support it safely with jackstands. Place the jackstands on the frame, not on the rear axle housing.
2. Release the parking brake cable tension by pulling the front cable approximately 2" rearward. Clamp the cable behind the crossmember, being careful not to damage the plastic cable coating.
3. Remove the parking brake cables from the equalizer. Compress the tabs on the retainers and pull the cables through the rear crossmember.
4. Place a hydraulic jack under the differential housing and support the weight of the axle housing assembly.
5. Scribe marks on the driveshaft end and the axle end yoke to insure proper positioning of the driveshaft upon assembly, then remove the driveshaft.
6. Install an oil seal replacer tool in the transmission extension housing to prevent oil leakage during the service procedures.
7. Remove the rear wheels.
8. Disconnect the brake lines by disconnecting the brake jounce hose from the master cylinder rear tube. Plug the brake tube to prevent contamination of the hydraulic brake system. Remove the jounce hose and bracket from the frame.
9. Disconnect the axle vent tube from the clip on the frame.
10. Disconnect the shock absorbers from the lower control arms.
11. Carefully lower the axle assembly on the hydraulic jack until the springs are no longer under compression. Lower the axle slowly.
12. Remove the lower spring retainer, then the upper spring retainer and remove the coil spring.
13. Raise the axle to the normal load position with the hydraulic jack, then disconnect the control arms at the axle. Make sure adequate clearance exists to remove the bolts retaining the lower control arm to the axle.
14. Remove the bolt and nut retaining the upper control arm to the rear axle. Remove the upper control arm from the axle after scribing a mark aligning the position of the cam adjuster in the axle bushing.
15. Carefully lower the axle and remove it from underneath the vehicle.
16. To install the axle housing, first place the assembly on a hydraulic jack and roll it underneath the van. Carefully raise the axle into position.
17. Position the upper control arm over the cam adjuster and bushing. Make sure the matchmarks made on the bushing and adjuster are still in alignment. Install the bolt, nut and retainer and tighten until snug. Do not tighten to specified torque at this time.
18. Lower the axle to the spring unloaded position, then place the lower insulator on the control arm. Place the upper insulator on top of the spring. The tapered coil (white colored) must face upward. Install the spring in position on the control arm and axle.
19. Install the lower retainer and nut, then tighten the nut to 41-64 ft.lb. (55-88 Nm).

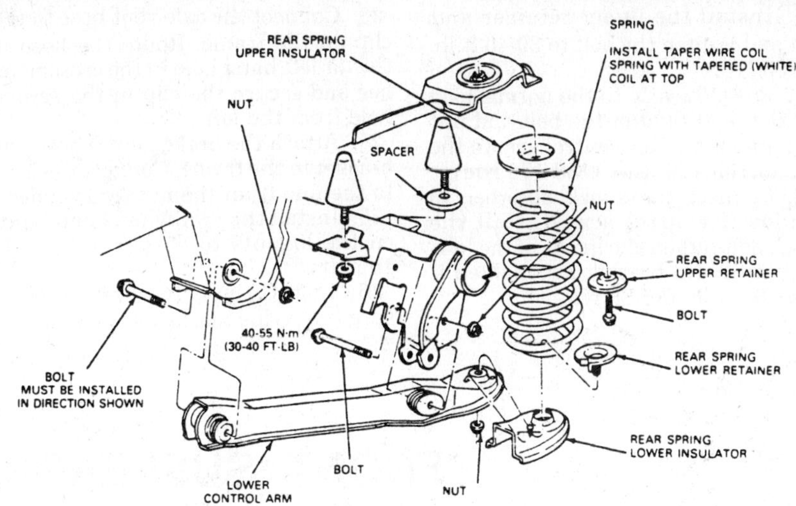

Exploded view of the rear suspension assembly

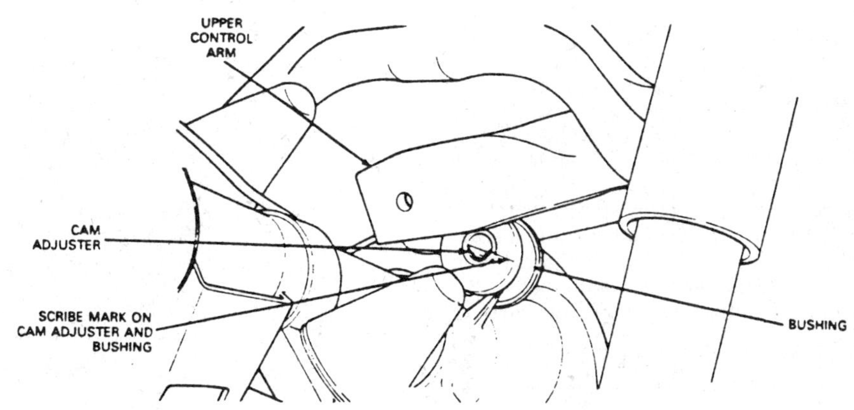

Mark the cam adjuster and bushing as shown

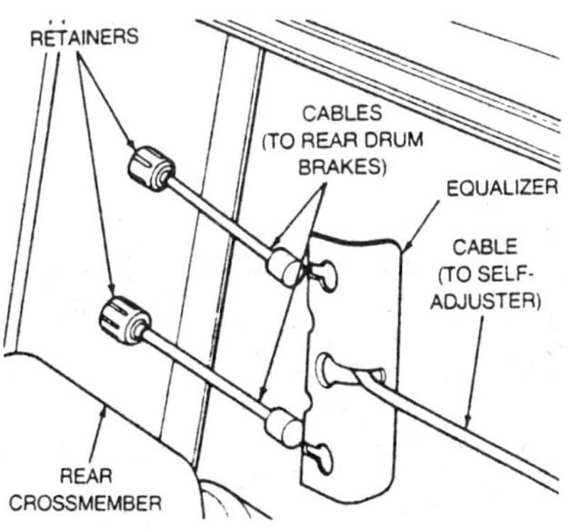

Disconnecting the parking brake cable assembly

20. Install the upper retainer and bolt and tighten the bolt to 30-40 ft.lb. (40-55 Nm).

21. Raise the axle to the normal load position and tighten the bolt and nut retaining the lower control arm to the axle to 100-129 ft.lb. (133-176 Nm).

22. Connect the shock absorber to the lower control arm. Install the shock bolt nut on the inside of the lower control arm bracket and tighten it to 41-64 ft.lb. (55-88 Nm).

23. Connect the axle vent hose to the clip on the frame. Route the hose in the rear left hand hole in the crossmember and secure the clip in the second hole from the left.

24. Attach the brake jounce hose and bracket to the frame. Connect the hose to the line from the master cylinder.

25. Install the rear wheels and tighten the lugnuts to 85-115 ft.lb. (115-156 Nm).

26. Install the driveshaft, making sure the scribe marks on the rear axle and driveshaft are aligned properly. Install the U-bolts and nuts and tighten them to 8-15 ft.lb. (11-20 Nm).

27. Pull the parking brake cables and retainers through the clips on the vehicle underbody side rails and through the rear crossmember. Connect the brake cables to the equalizer.

28. Unclamp the front parking brake cable to restore cable tension.

29. Bleed the brake system.

30. Remove the jackstands and lower the vehicle.

FRONT SUSPENSION

Coil Springs

REMOVAL & INSTALLATION

1. Place the steering wheel and steering in the centered (straight ahead) position. Any time the steering linkage is disconnected from the spindle, the steering system must be centered prior to beginning any work.

2. Raise the van and support it safely on jackstands. Place the jackstands on the frame at the jacking pads.

3. Disconnect the stabilizer bar link bolt from the lower control arm.

4. Remove the two bolts attaching the shock absorber to the lower arm assembly.

5. Remove the upper nut and washer retaining the shock absorber and remove the shock.

6. Remove the steering center link from the pitman arm.

7. Using spring compressor tool D78P-5310-A or equivalent, install one plate with the pivot ball seat facing downward into the coils of the spring. Rotate the plate so that it is flush with the upper surface of the lower arm.

8. Install the other plate with the pivot ball seat facing upward into the coils of the spring, so that the nut rests in the upper plate.

9. Insert the compression rod into the opening in the lower arm, through the upper and lower plate and upper ball nut. Insert the securing pin through the upper ball nut and compression rod. This pin can only be inserted one way into the upper ball nut because of a stepped hole design.

10. With the upper ball nut secured, turn the upper plate so that it walks up the coil until it contacts the upper spring seat, then back it off ½ turn.

11. Install the lower ball nut and thrust washer on the compression rod, then screw on the forcing nut. Tighten the forcing nut until the spring is compressed enough so that it is free in its seat.

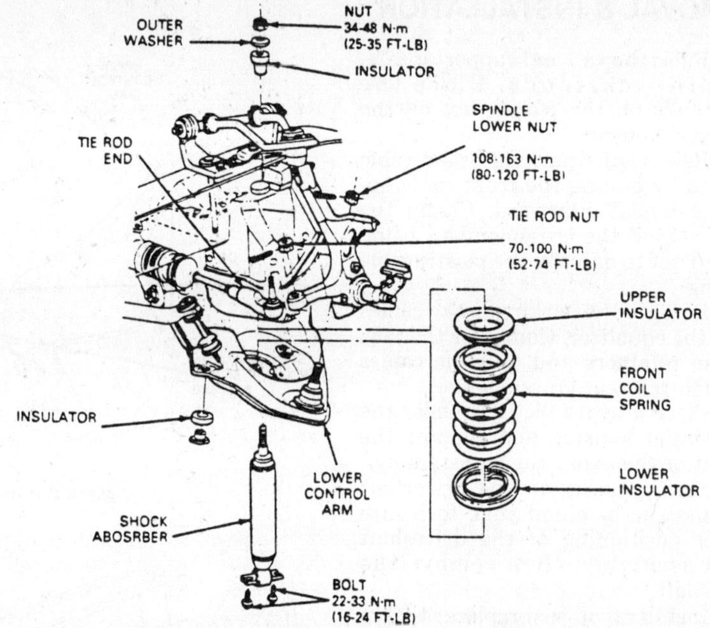

Front coil spring and suspension assembly

12. Loosen the two lower arm pivot bolts. Remove the cotter pin and loosen, but not not remove the nut attaching the lower ball joint to the spindle. Using pitman arm puller T64P-3590-F, or equivalent, loosen the lower ball joint.

13. Remove the puller tool.

14. Support the lower control arm with a hydraulic jack, then remove the ball joint nut. Slowly lower the control arm and remove the coil spring.

CAUTION

Handle the coil spring with care. A compressed coil spring has enough stored energy to be dangerous if suddenly released. Mount the spring securely in a vise and slowly loosen the spring compressor if the spring is being replaced.

15. If the coil spring is being replaced, measure the compressed length of the old spring and mark the position of the compressor plates on the old spring with chalk. Remove the spring compressor from the old spring carefully.

16. Install the spring compressor on the new spring, placing the compressor plates in the same position as marked on the old spring. Make sure the upper ball nut securing pin is installed properly, then compress the new spring to the compressed length of the old spring.

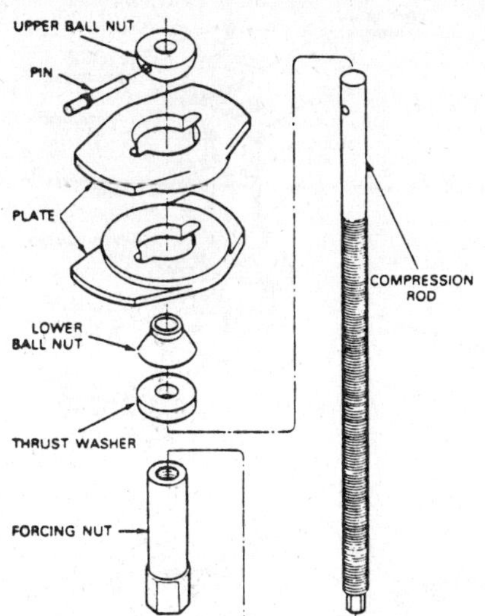

Typical spring compressor

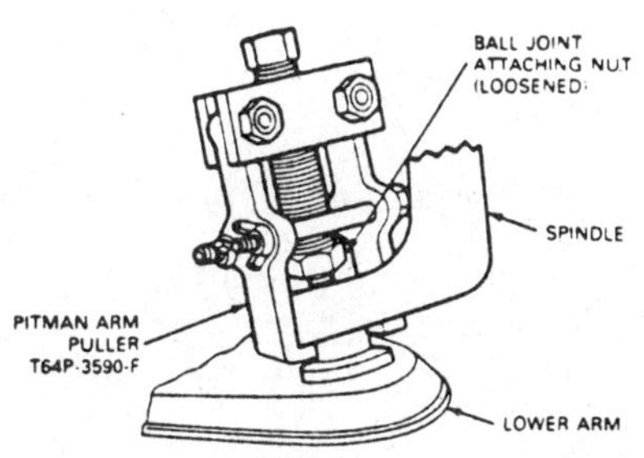

Disconnecting the ball joint with separator tool

17. Position the coil spring assembly into the lower control arm.
18. Place a hydraulic jack under the lower control arm and slowly raise it into position. Reconnect the ball joint and install the nut. Tighten the ball joint castle nut to 80-120 ft.lb. (108-163 Nm) and install a new cotter pin. The nut may be tightened slightly to align the cotter pin hole, but not loosened.
19. Slowly release the spring compressor and remove it from the coil spring.
20. Reconnect the steering center link to the pitman arm.
21. Install the shock absorber.
22. Reconnect the stabilizer bar link bolt to the lower control arm.
23. Lower the vehicle. Although this procedure should not disturb any alignment settings, any time the front end is disassembled for service, the alignment should be checked.

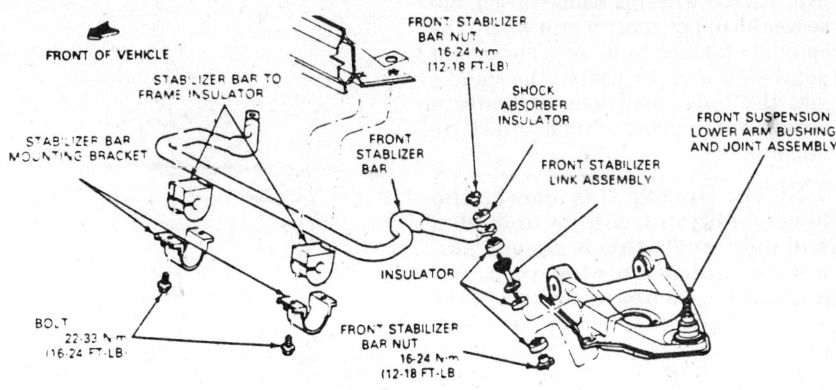

Front stabilizer bar mounting

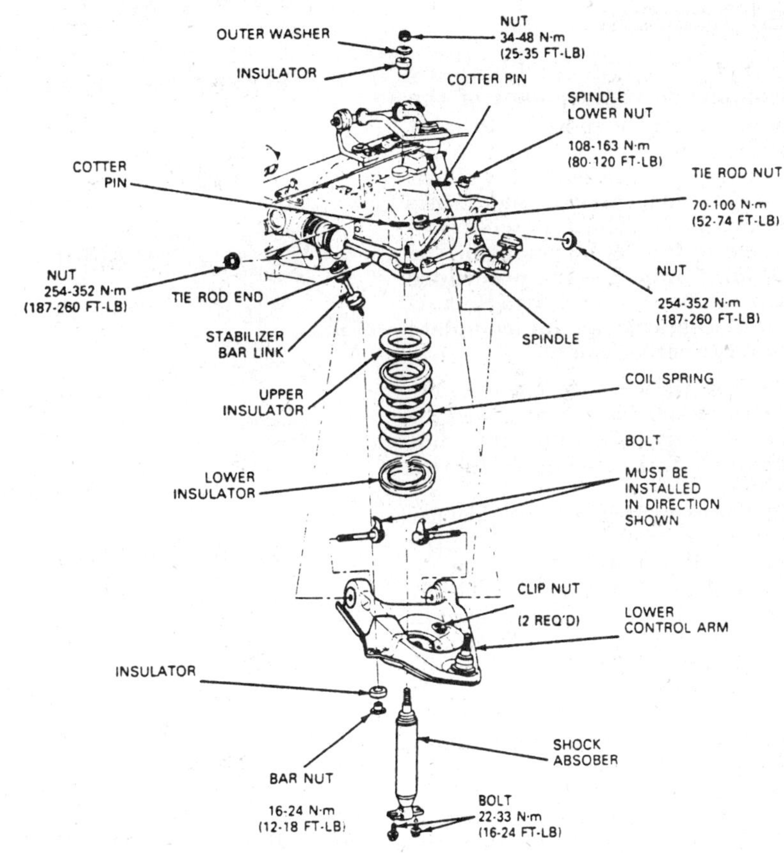

Exploded view of the lower control arm assembly

Shock Absorber

REMOVAL & INSTALLATION

1. Raise the vehicle and support it safely on jackstands.
2. Remove the nut and washer retaining the shock absorber to the coil spring upper bracket.
3. Remove the two bolts retaining the shock absorber to the bottom of the lower control arm.
4. Remove the shock absorber through the lower control arm.
5. Purge a new shock absorber of air by extending and compressing it several times before installation.
6. Installation is the reverse of removal. Tighten the lower shock absorber retaining nuts to 16-24 ft.lb. (22-33 Nm) and the upper retaining nut to 25-35 ft.lb. (34-48 Nm).

Upper Ball Joint

INSPECTION

1. Raise the vehicle by placing a hydraulic floor jack under the lower control arm.
2. Have an assistant grasp the top and bottom of the tire and move the wheel in and out.

3. As the wheel is being moved, observe the upper control arm where the spindle attaches to it. Any movement between the upper part of the spindle and the upper ball joint indicates a worn ball joint which must be replaced.

NOTE: During this check, the lower ball joint will be unloaded and may move; this is normal and not an indication of a worn ball joint. Also, do not mistake a loose wheel bearing for a defective ball joint.

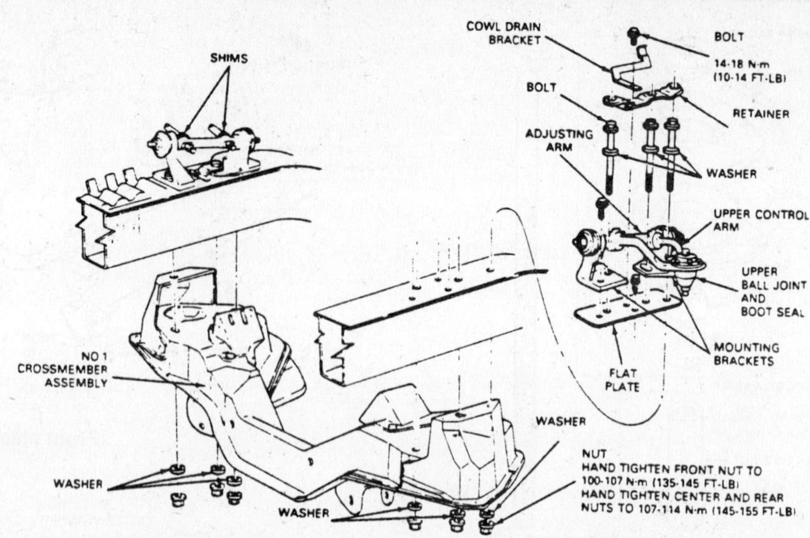

Exploded view of the upper control arm assembly and crossmember

REPLACEMENT

NOTE: Ford Motor Company recommends replacement of the upper control arm and ball joint as an assembly, rather than replacement of the ball joint alone. However, aftermarket ball joints are available. The following procedure is for replacement of the ball joint only. See the procedure under Upper Control Arm Removal and Installation for complete assembly replacement.

1. Raise the van and support it safely with jackstands placed under the frame lifting pads. Allow the front wheels to fall to their full down position.
2. Place a hydraulic floor jack under the lower control arm and raise the jack until it just contacts the arm.
3. Drill a 1/8" (3mm) hole completely through each ball joint attaching rivet.
4. Use a chisel to cut the head off of each rivet, then drive them from the upper control arm with a suitable small drift or blunt punch.
5. Raise the lower control arm about 6" (153mm) with the hydraulic jack.
6. Remove the pinch nut and bolt holding the ball joint stud from the spindle.
7. Using a suitable tool, loosen the ball joint stud from the spindle and remove the ball joint from the upper arm.
8. Clean all metal burrs from the upper arm and install a new ball joint, using the service part nuts and bolts to attach the ball joint to the upper arm. Do not attempt to rivet the ball joint again once it has been removed.
9. Attach the ball joint stud to the spindle, then install the pinch bolt and nut and tighten.
10. Remove the hydraulic jack and lower the van. Check the front end alignment.

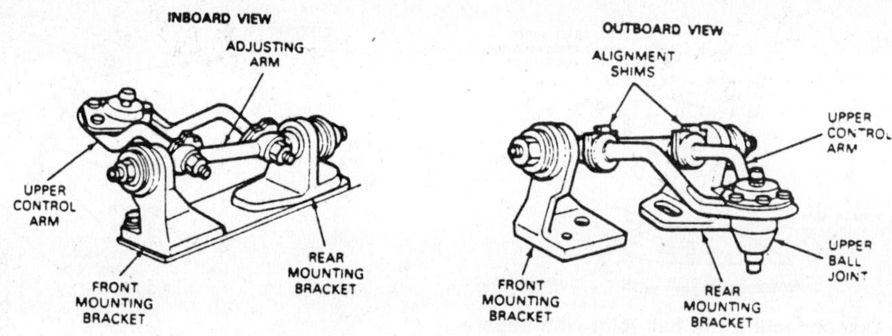

Upper control arm components

Lower Ball Joint

REPLACEMENT

The lower ball joint is pressed into the lower control arm. Replacement involves removing the lower control arm, pressing the old ball joint out and pressing a new one in. See the procedures under Lower Control Arm Removal and Installation and remove the lower control arm to service the lower ball joints.

Front Stabilizer Bar

REMOVAL & INSTALLATION

1. Raise the van and support it safely on jackstands.
2. Loosen and remove the nuts retaining the stabilizer bar to the lower control arm link on each side, then remove the insulators and disconnect the bar from the links.
3. If required, remove the nuts retaining the links to the lower control arm, then remove the insulators and links.
4. Remove the bolts retaining the bar mounting bracket to the frame and remove the stabilizer bar. If required, remove the insulators from the stabilizer bar.
5. If the stabilizer bar insulators are being replaced, install them on the stabilizer bar. Place the bar, insulators and mounting bracket in position on the frame and install the retaining bolts. Tighten the retaining bolts to 16-24 ft.lb. (22-33 Nm).
6. If removed, connect the link and insulators to the lower control arm. Install and tighten the nut to 12-18 ft.lb. (16-24 Nm).
7. Connect the links and insulators to the stabilizer bar, then install and tighten the nuts to 12-18 ft.lb. (16-24 Nm).
8. Lower the vehicle.

Lower Control Arm

REMOVAL & INSTALLATION

1. Place the steering wheel and front wheels in the centered (straight ahead) position.

NOTE: Any time the steering linkage is disconnected from the spindle, the steering system must be centered before beginning the service procedure.

2. Raise the van and support it safely with jackstands placed under the frame lifting pads. A hydraulic floor jack should be placed under the control arm to raise and lower the arm during coil spring removal. Make sure the van is supported securely on the jackstands and only work on one side at a time.
3. Remove the coil spring as previously described.
4. Remove the bolts and nuts retaining the lower control arm to the crossmember and remove the lower control arm from the frame.
5. If control arm bushings or ball joints are necessary, replace the entire lower control arm assembly.
6. Position the new lower control arm assembly to the frame crossmember and install the retaining bolts in the direction illustrated. Temporarily snug the bolts, but do not tighten to specifications.
7. If the old crossmember is being installed, inspect the lower ball joint boot and replace it if necessary.
8. Install the coil spring as previously described.
9. Lower the van so it rests in the normal ride position on a level surface.
10. Tighten the lower control arm-to-crossmember mounting bolts to 187-260 ft.lb. (254-352 Nm).

Upper Control Arm

REMOVAL & INSTALLATION

1. Place the steering wheel and front tires in the centered (straight ahead) position.

NOTE: Any time the steering linkage is disconnected from the spindle, the steering system must be centered before beginning the service procedure.

2. Raise the van and support it safely with jackstands placed under the frame lifting pads. A hydraulic floor jack should be placed under the control arm to raise and lower the arm during coil spring removal. Make sure the van is supported securely on the jackstands and only work on one side at a time. Never service both front suspension assemblies at the same time.
3. Remove the spindle.
4. Remove the bolt retaining the cowl drain bracket and bolt retainer plate and remove the bracket and plate.
5. Matchmark the position of the control arm mounting brackets on the flat plate.
6. Remove the bolt and washer retaining the front mounting bracket to the flat plate.
7. From beneath the rail, remove the three nuts from the bolts retaining the two upper control arm mounting brackets to the body rail.
8. Remove the three long bolts retaining the mounting brackets to the body rail by rotating the upper control arm out of position in order to remove the bolts. Remove the upper control arm, upper ball joint and mounting bracket assembly and the flat plate from the van.
9. Inspect the upper and/or lower ball joint boot seal and replace if necessary.
10. If required to service the upper control arm and upper ball joint assembly or the mounting brackets and adjusting arm assembly, remove the nuts retaining the upper control arm to the adjusting arm. Note the **exact** position and number of shims on each control arm stud. These shims control caster and camber. Remove the upper control arm from the adjusting arm.

NOTE: The adjusting arm and mounting brackets are serviced as an assembly. Ford recommends that the upper control arm and upper ball joint also be serviced as an assembly, however aftermarket ball joint kits are available.

11. If removed, install the upper control arm in the adjusting arm. Install the shims on the control arm studs with the same number of shims in the exact position as marked during removal. Install and tighten the nuts retaining the shims to the control arm.
12. Place the flat plate for the mounting brackets in position on the body rail, then install and tighten the bolts to 10-14 ft.lb. (14-18 Nm).
13. Place the mounting brackets and upper control arm assembly in position on the flat plate.
14. Install the three long bolts and washers retaining the mounting brackets to the body rail. Rotate or rock the upper control arm and mounting bracket assembly until the bolt heads rest against the mounting bracket and the studs extend through the body rail.
15. Move the mounting brackets into the position marked on the flat plate during removal. Install and tighten the nuts and washers retaining the mounting bracket bolts to the body rail to 135-145 ft.lb. (100-107 Nm) for the front bolt, and 145-155 ft.lb. (107-114 Nm) for the center and rear bolts. Make sure the mounting brackets do not move from the marked position on the flat plate to minimize corrections.

CAUTION

The torque required for the mounting bracket-to-body rail nuts and bolts is critical. Be precise when tightening to the specified torque and use an accurate torque wrench. Torque with one, smooth motion rather than short jerks.

16. Install and tighten the bolt retaining the front mounting bracket to the flat plate.
17. Place the bolt retainer plate and cowl drain bracket in position on the mounting bracket and flat plate assembly, then install and tighten the bolt to 10-14 ft.lb. (14-18 Nm).
18. Install the spindle as described later in this section.
19. Align the front end. Caster and camber are adjusted by adding or removing shims.

Spindle

REMOVAL & INSTALLATION

1. Place the steering wheel and front tires in the centered (straight ahead) position.

NOTE: Any time the steering linkage is disconnected from the spindle, the steering system must be centered before beginning the service procedure.

2. Raise the van and support it safely with jackstands placed under the frame lifting pads. A hydraulic floor jack should be placed under the control arm to raise and lower the arm during coil spring removal. Make sure the van is supported securely on the jackstands and only work on one side at a time. Never service both front suspension assemblies at the same time.
3. Remove the front tire(s).
4. Remove the caliper, rotor and dust shield from the spindle.
5. Remove the cotter pin and nut retaining the tie rod end to the spindle lower arm. Disconnect the tie rod end with a suitable pitman arm puller such as tool T64P-3590-F or equivalent.
6. Support the lower control arm with a hydraulic floor jack. Make sure the jack pad securely contacts the control arm. Remove the cotter pin, then loosen the nut retaining the spindle to the lower control arm ball joint. Disconnect the lower ball joint from the spindle using the same pitman arm puller used in Step 5, then remove the tool and ball joint retaining nut.
7. *Slowly* lower the jack under the control arm until the ball joint is disengaged from the spindle.

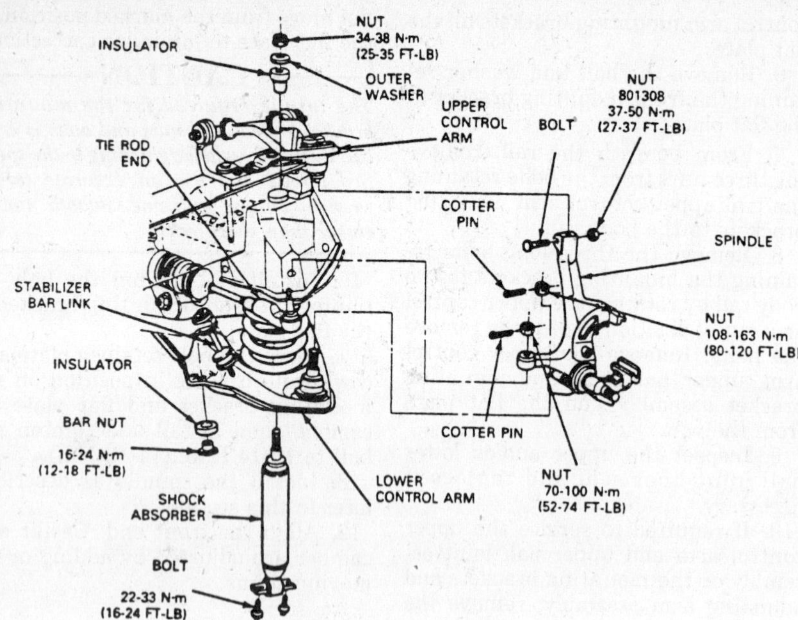

Exploded view of the spindle assembly

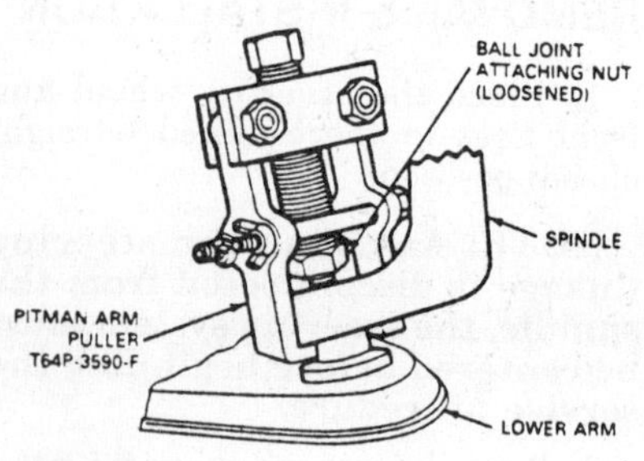

Disconnecting the lower ball joint from the spindle

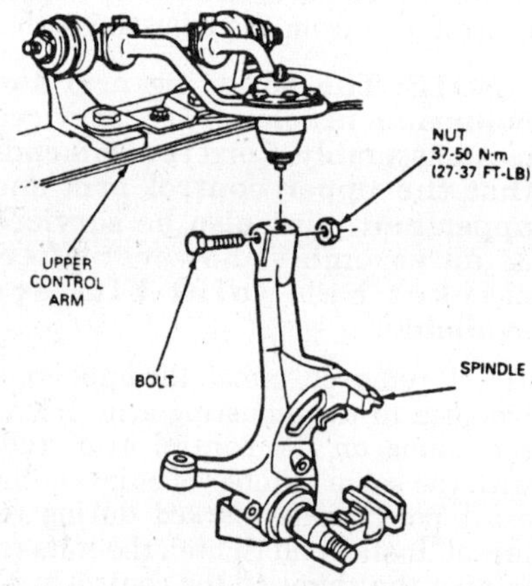

Top spindle mounting bolt

CAUTION

Use extreme caution when lowering the lower control arm! The coil spring may quickly expand with dangerous force. Never lower the control arm quickly!

8. Remove the bolt and nut retaining the spindle to the upper control arm ball joint, then remove the spindle from the van.

9. To install, first position the spindle upper arm on the upper ball joint. Install the nut and bolt an tighten to 27-37 ft.lb. (37-50 Nm). Inspect the upper and lower ball joint boot seals for damage and replace if necessary.

10. Position the spindle lower arm over the ball joint stud, then **slowly** raise the lower control arm with the hydraulic jack until the ball joint stud extends through the spindle arm and is seated in the spindle. Install the ball joint castle nut and tighten it to 80-120 ft.lb. (108-163 Nm), then install a new cotter pin. The castle nut may be tightened slightly to align the castellations with the cotter pin hole, but under no circumstances loosen the nut to align.

11. Connect the tie rod end to the spindle arm. Firmly seat the tie rod end stud into the tapered hole to prevent rotation while tightening the castellated nut. Torque the tie rod nut to 52-74 ft.lb. (70-100 Nm), then install a new cotter pin. The castle nut may be tightened slightly to align the castellations with the cotter pin hole, but under no circumstances loosen the nut to align.

12. Install the dust shield, rotor and caliper.

13. Install the front tire(s) and tighten the lugnuts to 85-115 ft.lb. (116-155 Nm).

14. Lower the vehicle.

Front Wheel Bearings

ADJUSTMENT

1. Raise the van until the front tire clears the ground.
2. Remove the wheel cover and the grease cap from the hub.
3. Wipe any excess grease from the end of the spindle, then remove the cotter pin and retainer. Discard the cotter pin.
4. Loosen the adjusting nut three turns. Obtain running clearance between the brake rotor surface and the brake pads by rocking the entire wheel assembly in and out several times to push the caliper and brake pads away from the rotor. An alternate method is to lightly tap on the caliper housing, but be sure not to tap on any other area that may damage the rotor or brake lining surfaces. Do not pry on the phenolic caliper piston.

NOTE: This running clearance must be maintained throughout the bearing adjustment procedure. If proper clearance cannot be maintained, the caliper must be removed.

5. Rotate the wheel assembly while tightening the adjusting nut to 17-25 ft.lb. (23-34 Nm) to seat the bearings.
6. Loosen the adjusting nut ½ turn, then retighten to 18-20 in.lb. (2-3 Nm) using and inch pound torque wrench. Note that the final adjustment is in inch pounds, **not** foot pounds.
7. Place the retainer on the adjusting nut. The castellations on the retainer must be aligned with the cotter pin hole in the spindle. Do not turn the adjusting nut to make castellations line up with the spindle hole, remove the retainer and turn it one flat to re-index and try to fit the cotter pin again. Repeat this procedure until the castellations line up with the spindle hole correctly.
8. Insert a new cotter pin to lock the retainer in place and bend the ends around the castellated flange of the retainer to secure the cotter pin in place.
9. Check the front wheel rotation. If the wheel rotates properly, install the grease cap and wheel cover. If rotation is noisy or rough, remove, inspect and lubricate the bearing cones and cups as described in the Removal and Installation procedure that follows.
10. Before moving the van, pump the brake pedal several times to restore normal brake travel.

REMOVAL & INSTALLATION

If wheel bearing adjustment will not eliminate looseness or rough and noisy

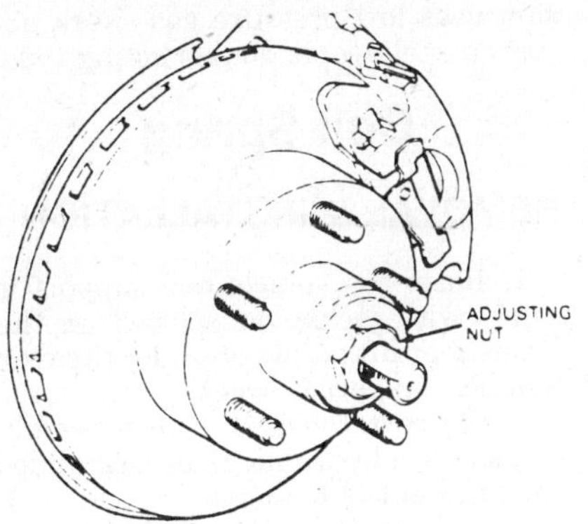

Front wheel bearing adjustment

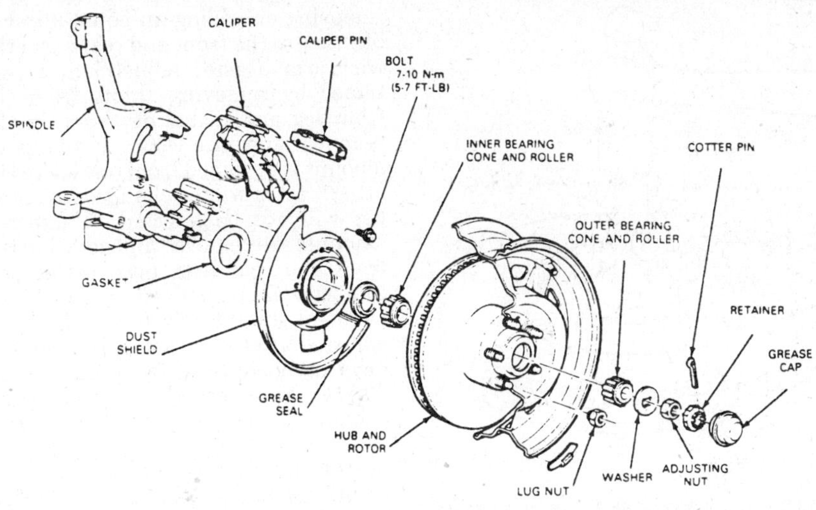

Exploded view of the front wheel assembly

operation, the hub and bearings should be cleaned, inspected and repacked with lithium base wheel bearing grease. If the bearing cups or the cone and roller assemblies are worn or damaged, they must be replaced as follows:

NOTE: Sodium base grease is not compatible with lithium base grease and the two should not be intermixed. Do not lubricate the front and/or rear wheel bearings without first identifying the type of grease being used. Usage of incompatible wheel bearing lubricant could result in premature lubricant breakdown and subsequent bearing damage.

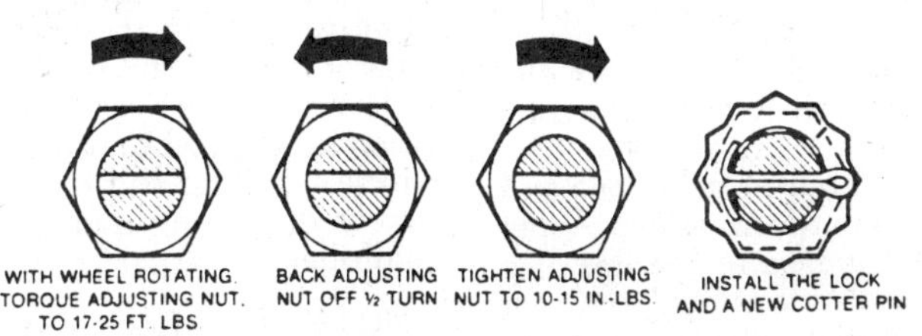

Front wheel bearing adjustment procedure

1. Raise the van until the tire clears the ground. Install a jackstand for safety, then remove the front tire(s).
2. Remove the brake caliper from the spindle, then wire it to the underbody. Do not let the caliper hang by the brake hose.
3. Remove the grease cup from the hub. Remove the cotter pin, castellated retainer, adjusting nut and flat washer from the spindle. Remove the outer bearing cone and roller assembly.
4. Pull the hub and rotor assembly off the spindle.
5. Place the hub and rotor on a clean workbench, with the back side facing up, and remove the grease seal using a suitable seal remover or small prybar. Discard the grease seal.
6. Remove the inner bearing cone and roller assembly from the hub.
7. Clean the inner and outer bearing cups with solvent. Inspect the cups for scratches, pits, excessive wear and other damage. If the cups are worn or damaged, remove them with a bearing cup puller (T77F-1102-A or equivalent) as illustrated.
8. Wipe all old lubricant from the spindle and the inside of the hub with a clean rag. Cover the spindle and brush all loose dirt and dust from the dust shield. Remove the cover cloth carefully to prevent dirt from falling on it.
9. If the inner or outer bearing cups were removed, install replacement cups using a suitable driver tool (T80T-4000-W or equivalent) and bearing cup replacer. Make sure the cups are seated properly in the hub and not cocked in the bore.
10. Thoroughly clean all old grease from the surrounding surfaces.
11. Pack the bearing and cone assemblies with suitable wheel bearing grease using a bearing packer tool. If a packer tool is not available, work as

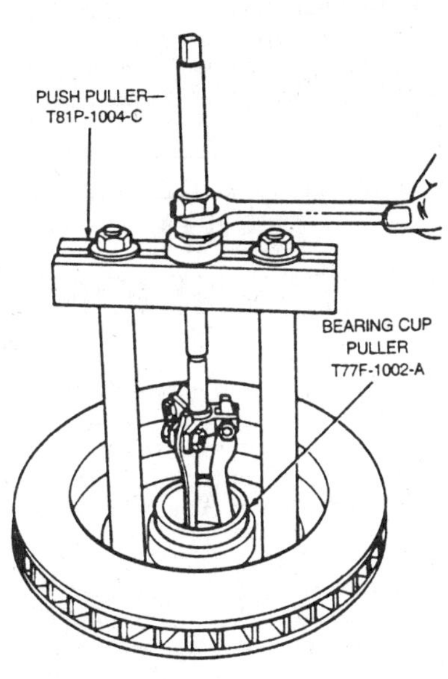

Removing front wheel bearing cups (races) from the hub

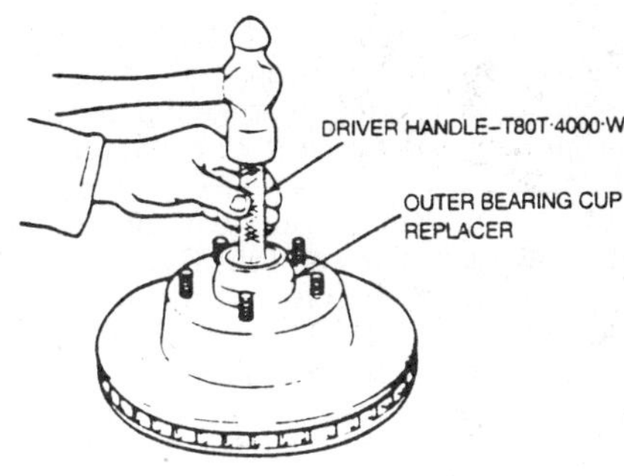

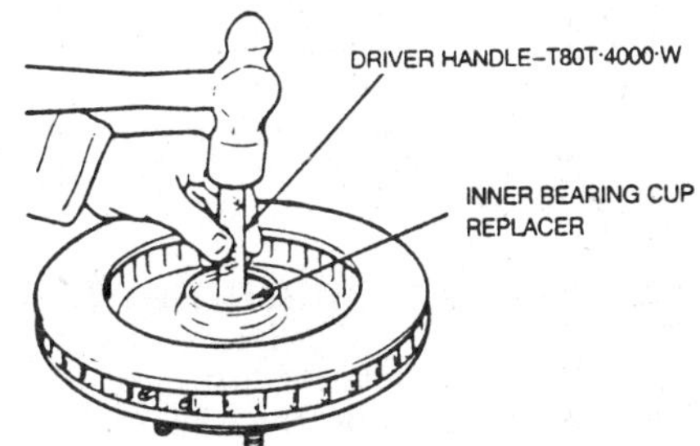

Installing bearing cups in the hub assembly

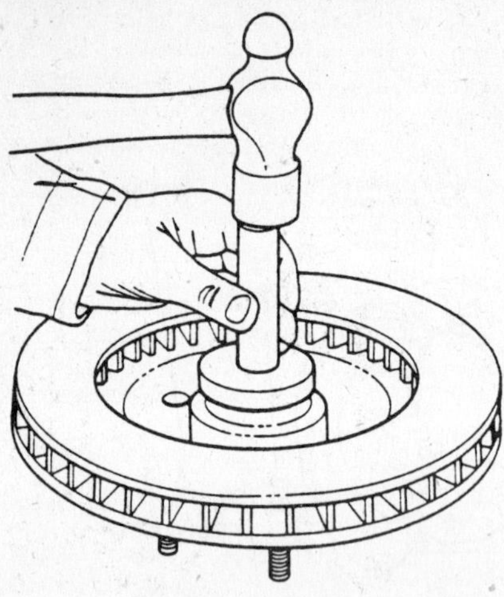

Installing grease seal in the hub assembly

much grease as possible between the rollers and cages, then grease the cone surfaces.

12. Place the inner bearing cone and roller assembly in the inner cup. Apply a light film of grease to the lips of a new grease seal and install the seal with an appropriate driver tool as illustrated. Make sure the grease seal is properly seated and not cocked in the bore.

13. Install the hub and rotor assembly on the spindle. Keep the hub centered on the spindle to prevent damage to the retainer and the spindle threads.

14. Install the outer bearing cone and roller assembly and the flatwasher on the spindle, then install the adjusting nut finger tight. Adjust the wheel bearing(s) as described above.

15. Install the caliper on the spindle.

16. Install the front tire(s), then lower the van and tighten the lugnuts to 85-115 ft.lb. (115-155 Nm). Install the wheel cover.

17. Before moving the van, pump the brake pedal several times to restore normal brake travel.

Front End Alignment

Caster and camber adjustment is provided by shims on the upper control arm. The two different shims initially provided from the assembly plant include one 0.078" (2mm) thickness and one 0.236" (6mm) thickness for a total shim stack thickness of 0.315" (8mm) at each leg of the upper control arm. These shims are added, removed, or switched from the front and rear legs of the upper control arms as required to adjust the front end alignment.

Camber adjustment is obtained by removing or adding an equal number of shims to the front and rear leg of the wire arm. Caster adjustment is obtained by removing shims from the front leg and installing them on the rear leg, and vice-versa. If the same amount is switched from one leg to the other, caster will be changed but camber will not be affected. If unequal amounts are removed and added to the front and rear legs, both caster and camber will be changed.

Toe-in should only be checked and adjusted after the caster and camber have been adjusted to specifications. Caster and camber adjustments change the position of the steering arms, thus affecting toe. Toe is defined as the difference between measurements taken between the front and rear of the tires. Positive toe or toe-in occurs when the front of the tires are pointed inboard of the rear of the tires. Negative or toe-out occurs when the front of the tires are pointed outboard of the rear of the tires. The toe specification is designed to provide optimum vehicle handling and tire life under a variety of driving and load carrying conditions.

NOTE: All wheel alignment adjustments and readings must be performed on an alignment rack level to within 1/16" (1.6mm) side-to-side and front-to-rear. Refer all alignment checks and adjustments to a qualified repair shop.

REAR SUSPENSION

The Aerostar rear suspension is a coil spring type system. It supports and links the rear axle to the frame with one upper control arm and two lower control arms. The rear suspension uses low pressure gas shock absorbers, telescopic double acting type.

Coil Spring

REMOVAL & INSTALLATION

1. Raise the vehicle and support it safely with jackstands placed on the frame rear lift points or under the rear bumper support brackets.

2. Support the rear axle assembly by placing a hydraulic floor jack under the differential housing.

3. Remove the nut and bolt retaining the shock absorber to the axle mount on the lower control arm. Disconnect the shock absorber from the axle bracket.

4. Carefully lower the rear axle until the coil springs are no longer under compression.

5. Remove the nut retaining the lower retainer and spring to the control arm.

6. Remove the bolt retaining the upper retainer and spring to the frame.

7. Remove the spring and retainers, then remove the upper and lower insulators.

8. Before installing the spring, first make sure the axle is in the lowered (spring unloaded) position. Place the lower insulator on the control arm and the upper insulator at the top of the spring.

9. Install the coil spring in position between the control arm and frame. The small diameter, tapered coils (white colored) must face upward.

10. Install the upper retainer and bolt, then tighten the bolt to 30-40 ft.lb. (40-55 Nm).

11. Install the lower retainer and nut and tighten the nut to 41-65 ft.lb. (55-88 Nm).

12. Raise the axle to the normal ride position with the hydraulic jack.

13. Position the shock absorber in the axle bracket, then install the bolt

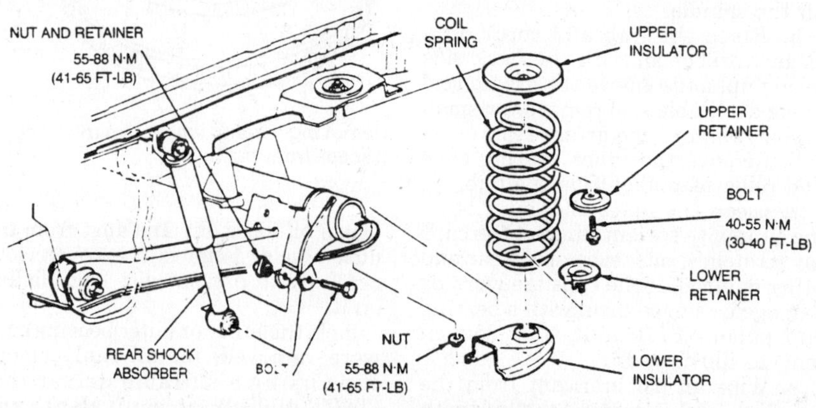

Rear coil spring assembly

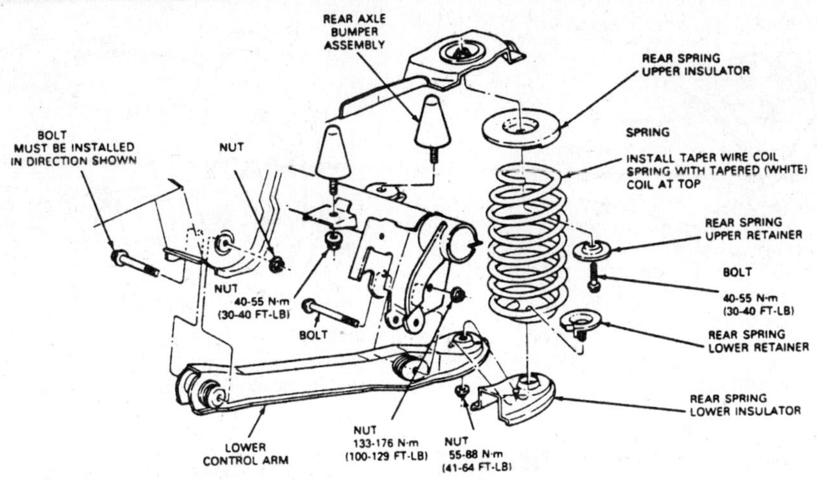

Lower control arm mounting

so the head is positioned outboard of the bracket. Install the nut and tighten it to 41-65 ft.lb. (55-88 Nm).

14. Remove the jackstands and lower the vehicle.

Shock Absorber

REMOVAL & INSTALLATION

CAUTION

The low pressure gas shock absorbers are charged with 135 psi of Nitrogen gas. Do not attempt to open the shock absorbers!

1. Raise the van and support it safely on jackstands. Place the jackstands under the axle to take the load off of the shock absorbers.
2. Remove the shock absorber lower attaching bolt and nut, then swing the lower end free of the mounting bracket on the axle housing.
3. Remove the attaching bolt and washer from the upper mounting bracket, then remove the shock absorber.
4. Installation is the reverse of removal. Tighten the lower mounting nut to 41-65 ft.lb. (55-88 Nm), and the upper mounting bracket bolt and washer to 25-35 ft.lb. (38-48 Nm).

Lower Control Arm

REMOVAL & INSTALLATION

1. Raise the vehicle and support it safely with jackstands placed on the frame rear lift points or under the rear bumper support brackets.
2. Support the rear axle assembly by placing a hydraulic floor jack under the differential housing.
3. Remove the nut and bolt retaining the shock absorber to the axle

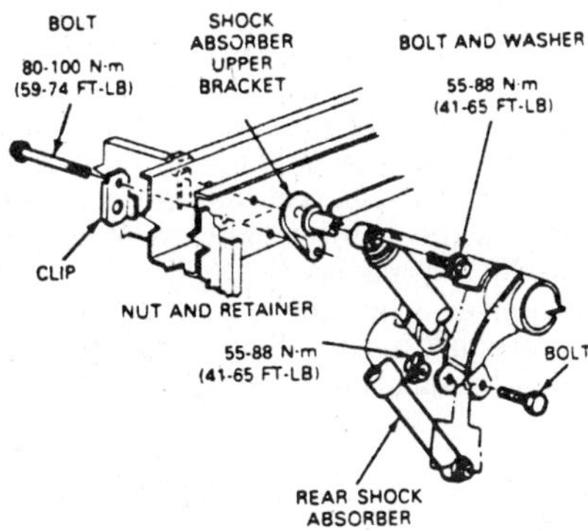

Rear shock absorber mounting

mount on the lower control arm. Disconnect the shock absorber from the axle bracket.

4. Carefully lower the rear axle until the coil springs are no longer under compression.
5. Remove the nut retaining the lower retainer and spring to the control arm, then remove the insulator from the arm.
6. Remove the bolt and nut retaining the lower control arm to the axle housing.
7. Remove the nut and bolt retaining the lower control arm to the frame bracket, then remove the lower control arm.
8. To install the control arm, first position the lower arm in the frame bracket. Install the bolt so the head is inboard on the frame bracket. Install the nut but do not tighten at this time.
9. Position the lower control arm in the bracket on the axle housing. Install the bolt so the head is inboard on the axle bracket. Install the nut but do not tighten at this time.
10. Install the insulator on the lower control arm.
11. With the axle in the lowered (spring unloaded) position, install the coil spring and lower retainer on the lower control arm.
12. Install the nut attaching the retainer and spring to the lower control arm. Tighten the nut to 41-65 ft.lb. (55-88 Nm).
13. Raise the axle to the normal load position, then tighten the nut and bolt retaining the lower control arm to the axle housing to 100-145 ft.lb. (135-197 Nm). Tighten the nut and bolt retaining the lower control arm to the frame bracket to 100-145 ft.lb. (135-197 Nm).
14. Position the shock absorber in the lower axle mounting bracket, then install the bolt so the head is outboard of the axle bracket. Install the nut and tighten it to 41-65 ft.lb. (55-88 Nm).
15. Remove the jackstands and lower the vehicle.

Upper Control Arm

REMOVAL & INSTALLATION

1. Raise the vehicle and support it safely with jackstands placed on the frame rear lift points or under the rear bumper support brackets.
2. Support the rear axle assembly by placing a hydraulic floor jack under the differential housing.
3. Remove the nut and bolt retaining the shock absorber to the axle mount on the lower control arm. Disconnect the shock absorber from the axle bracket.
4. Carefully lower the rear axle until the coil springs are no longer under compression.
5. Remove the bolt and nut retaining the upper control arm to the rear axle. Disconnect the upper control arm from the axle. Scribe a mark aligning the position of the cam adjuster in the axle bushing. The cam adjuster controls the rear axle pinion angle for driveline angularity.
6. Remove the bolt and nut retaining the upper control arm to the right frame bracket. Rotate the arm to disengage it from the body bracket.
7. Remove the nut and washer retaining the upper control arm to the left frame bracket. Remove the outer insulator and spacer, then remove the control arm from the bracket. Remove the inner insulator and washer from the control arm stud.

NOTE: If the left bracket attachments are loosened prior to disengaging the arm from the right bracket, the uncompressed left bushing will force the arm against the right hand bracket and make removal difficult.

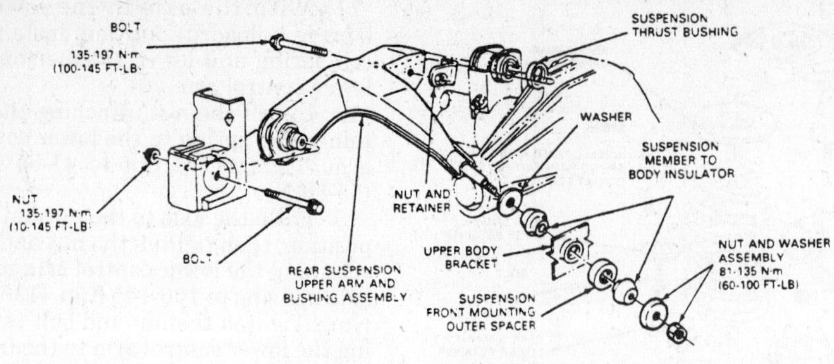

Upper control arm assembly

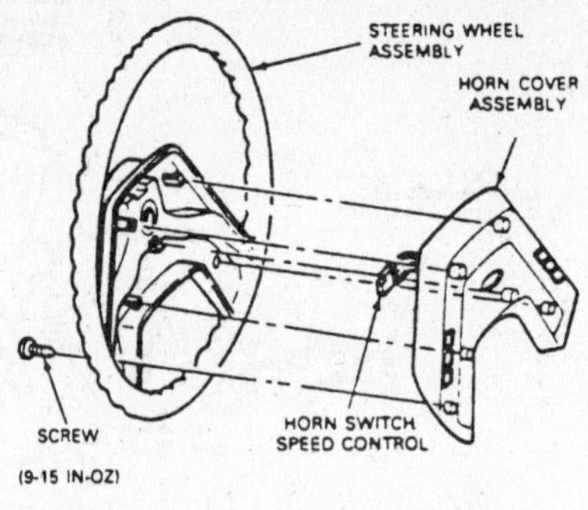

Removing steering wheel pad

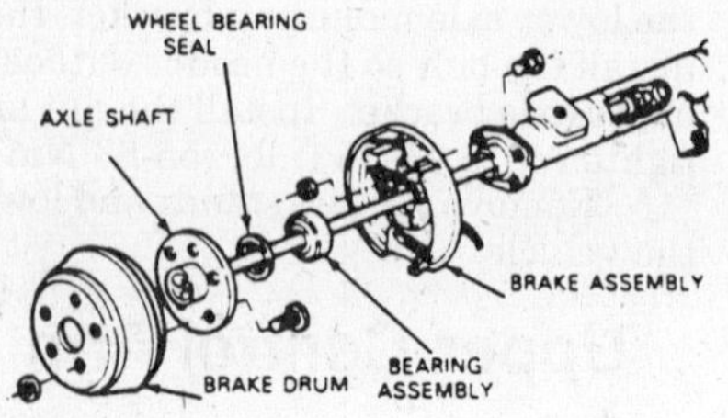

Rear wheel hub and bearing assembly

8. To install, first position the washer and inner insulator on the control arm stud. Install the control arm so the stud extends through the left frame bracket. Install the spacer and outer insulator over the stud, then install the nut and washer assembly and tighten until snug. Do not tighten to specified torque at this time.
9. Position the upper control arm in the right frame bracket, then install the bolt and nut and tighten until snug. Do not tighten to specified torque at this time.
10. Making sure the scribe marks on the cam adjuster and axle bushing are in alignment, connect the upper control arm to the axle. Install the nut and bolt and tighten until snug. Do not tighten to specified torque at this time.
11. Raise the axle to the normal ride position.
12. Position the shock absorber in the lower mounting bracket, then install the bolt so the head is outboard of the axle bracket. Install the nut and tighten to 41-65 ft.lb. (55-88 Nm).
13. With the axle in the normal ride position, tighten all upper control arm fasteners to the specified torque. Tighten the nut and washer assembly retaining the control arm to the left frame bracket to 60-100 ft.lb. (81-135 Nm). Tighten the nut and bolt retaining the control arm to the right frame bracket to 100-145 ft.lb. (135-197 Nm). Tighten the nut and bolt retaining the control arm to the axle to 100-145 ft.lb. (135-197 Nm).
14. Remove the jackstands and lower the vehicle.

Rear Wheel Hub and Bearing

REMOVAL & INSTALLATION

The rear wheel bearing is pressed into the outer axle tube housing. A grease seal is pressed into the tube over the bearing. The axle shaft is retained in the carrier assembly by a C-clip in the differential case. When the C-clip is removed, the axle shaft can be removed from the axle tube. See the procedure under Rear Axle Removal and Installation for details.

STEERING

Steering Wheel

REMOVAL & INSTALLATION

1. Disconnect the negative battery cable.
2. Remove the steering wheel horn cover by removing the screws from the spokes and lifting the steering wheel horn cover.
3. Disconnect the horn switch/speed control wires by pulling the connectors apart, then remove the horn cover assembly.
4. Remove the steering wheel attaching bolt.
5. Using a suitable steering wheel puller, such as tool T67L-3600-A or equivalent, remove the steering wheel from the upper steering shaft. Do not strike the end of the steering column upper shaft with a hammer or steering shaft bearing damage will occur.
6. Installation is the reverse of removal. Align the mark and the flats on the steering wheel with the mark and the flats on the shaft. Tighten the retaining bolt to 23-33 ft.lb. (31-45 Nm).

Turn Signal/Hazard Flasher Switch

REMOVAL & INSTALLATION

1. Remove the steering wheel as previously described. If equipped with tilt column, remove the upper extension shroud by squeezing it at the six and twelve o'clock positions and popping it free of the retaining plate at the three o'clock position.
2. Remove the two trim shroud halves from the steering column by removing the two attaching screws.
3. Remove the turn signal switch lever by grasping the lever and by suing a pulling and twisting motion of the hand while pulling the lever straight out from the switch.
4. Peel back the foam sight shield from the turn signal switch.
5. Disconnect the two turn signal switch electrical connectors.
6. Remove the two self-tapping screws attaching the turn signal switch to the lock cylinder housing, then disengage the switch from the housing.
7. To install, first align the turn signal switch mounting holes with the corresponding holes in the lock cylinder housing and install the two self-tapping screws. Tighten the screws to 18-26 in.lb. (2-3 Nm).
8. Stick the foam sight shield to the turn signal switch.
9. Install the turn signal switch lever into the switch manually by aligning the key on the lever with the keyway in the switch and by pushing the lever toward the switch to full engagement.
10. Connect the turn signal switch electrical connectors and install the steering column shrouds.

Ignition Switch

REMOVAL & INSTALLATION

1. Rotate the lock cylinder key to

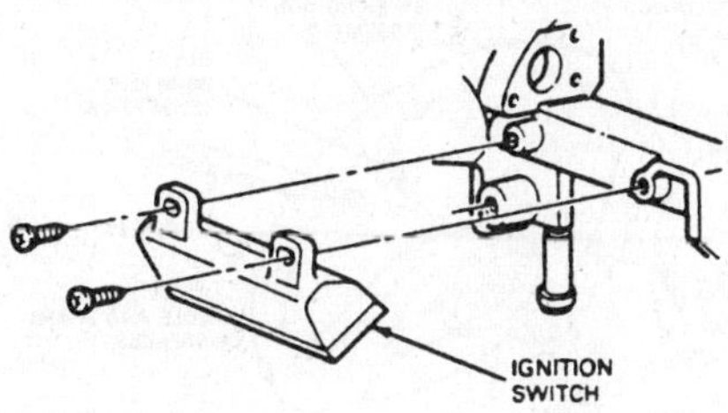

Typical ignition switch mounting inside steering column

the LOCK position and disconnect the negative battery cable.

2. If equipped with a tilt column, remove the upper extension shroud by squeezing it at the six and twelve o'clock positions and popping it free of the retaining plate at the three o'clock position.

3. Remove the two trim shroud halves by removing the two attaching screws.

4. Disconnect the ignition switch electrical connector.

5. Drill out the break-off head bolts connecting the switch to the lock cylinder housing with a 1/8" (3mm) drill, then remove the two bolts using an EX-3 screw extractor tool or equivalent screw extractor.

6. Disengage the ignition switch from the actuator pin and remove the switch.

7. To install, first rotate the ignition key to the RUN position (approximately 90° clockwise from LOCK).

8. Install the replacement switch by aligning the holes on the switch casting base with the holes in the lock cylinder housing. Note that the replacement switch is provided in the RUN position. Minor movement of the lock cylinder to align the actuator pin with the U-shaped slot in the switch carrier may be necessary.

9. Install new break-off head bolts and tighten until the heads shear off.

10. Connect the electrical connector to the ignition switch.

11. Connect the negative battery terminal, then check the ignition switch for proper operation in all modes. If correct, install the steering column shrouds.

Ignition Lock Cylinder

REMOVAL & INSTALLATION

NOTE: The following procedure pertains to vehicles that have functional lock cylinders, with ignition keys that are available or ignition key numbers are known and the proper key can be made at a dealer.

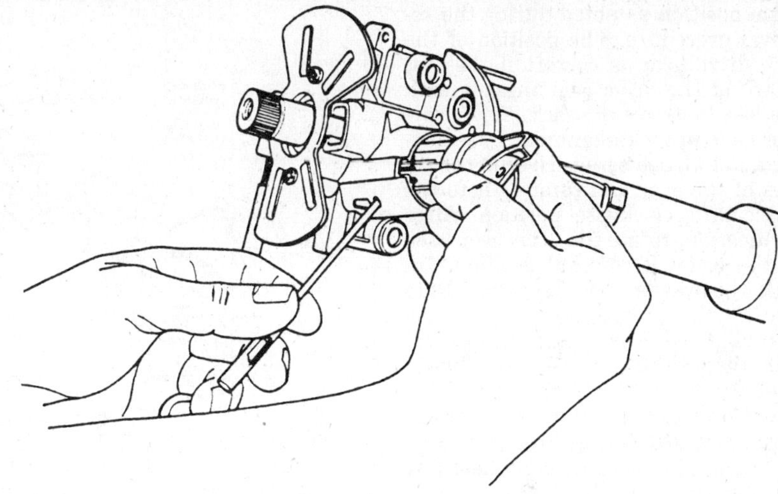
Removing the ignition lock cylinder

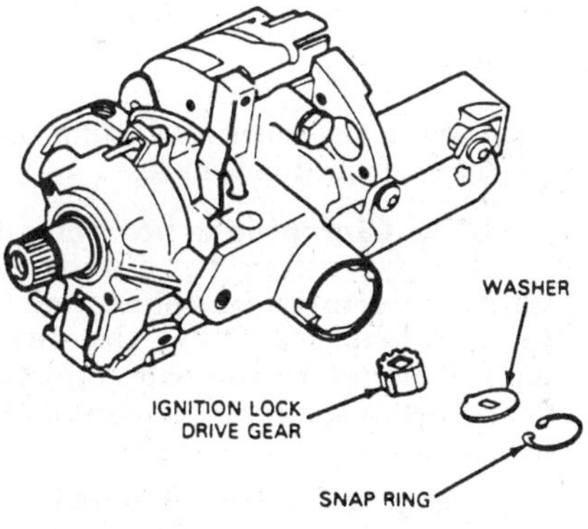

Removing ignition lock drive gear

1. Disconnect the negative battery cable.

2. Remove the trim shroud, then remove the electrical connector from the key warning switch.

3. Turn the lock cylinder to the RUN position.

4. Place a 1/8" (3mm) diameter pin or small drift punch in the hole located at 4 o'clock and 1¼" (32mm) from the outer edge of the lock cylinder housing. Depress the retaining pin and pull out the lock cylinder.

5. Prior to installing the lock cylinder, lubricate the cylinder cavity, including the drive gear with lock lubricant D8AZ-19587-A or equivalent.

6. To install the lock cylinder, turn the lock cylinder to the RUN position, depress the retaining pin, and insert it into the lock cylinder housing. Make sure the cylinder is fully seated and aligned into the interlocking washer before turning the key to the OFF position. This action will permit the cylinder retaining pin to extend into the hole in the lock cylinder housing.

7. Using the ignition key, rotate the lock cylinder to insure correct mechanical operation in all positions. Install the electrical connector onto the key warning switch.

8. Connect the negative battery cable, then check for proper ignition functions and verify that the column is locked in the LOCK position. Install the trim shrouds.

NOTE: The following procedure applies to vehicles where the ignition lock is inoperative and the lock cylinder cannot be rotated due to a lost or broken ignition key.

1. Disconnect the negative battery cable.

2. Remove the horn cover and the steering wheel.

3. Remove the trim shrouds and the connector from the key warning switch.

4. Use a 1/8" (3mm) diameter drill to drill out the retaining pin, being careful not to drill any deeper than 1/2" (12.7mm).

5. Place a chisel at the base of the ignition lock cylinder cap, then use a hammer to strike the chisel with sharp blows to break the cap away from the lock cylinder.

6. Using a 3/8" (9.5mm) diameter drill, drill down the middle of the ignition lock key slot approximately 1¾" (45mm) until the lock cylinder breaks loose from the breakaway base of the cylinder. Remove the lock cylinder and drill shavings from the lock cylinder housing.

7. Remove the snapring, washer and ignition lock drive gear. Thoroughly clean all drill shavings and other foreign materials from the casting.

8. Carefully inspect the lock cylinder housing for damage from the removal operation. If any damage is apparent, the housing must be replaced.

9. Position the lock drive gear in the base of the lock cylinder housing in the

same position as noted during the removal procedure. The position of the lock drive gear is correct if the last tooth on the drive gear meshes with the last tooth on the rack. Verify correct gear to rack alignment by inserting a flat bladed screwdriver in the recess of the gear and rotating it to the full counterclockwise position. After verification, rotate the drive gear back to the original removal position. Install the washer and snapring. Note that the flats in the recess of the drive gear align with the flats in the washer.

10. Install the ignition lock cylinder as described in the previous procedure.

11. Connect the key warning switch wire, then install the shroud.

12. Install the steering wheel and horn cover.

13. Connect the negative battery cable.

14. Check for proper ignition and accessory operation and verify that the column locks in the LOCK position.

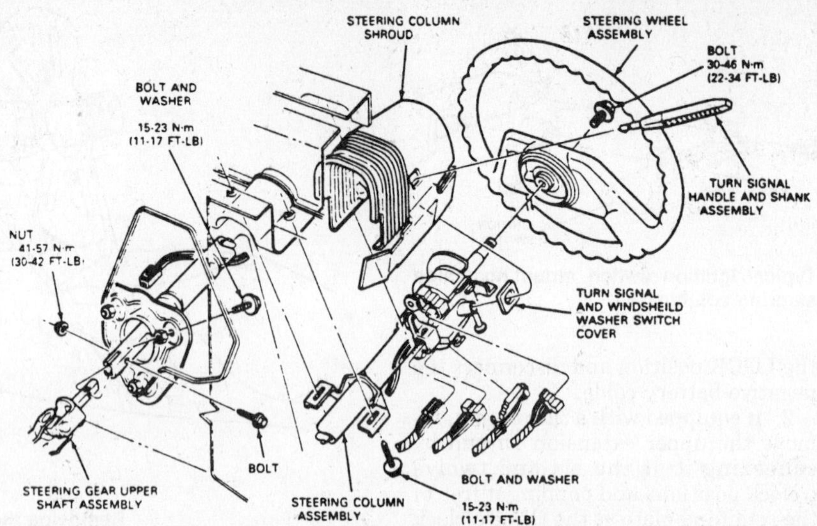

Removing steering column assembly

Steering Column

REMOVAL & INSTALLATION

CAUTION

The outer tube steering column upper bracket affects the energy absorption on impact. It is absolutely necessary to handle related components with care when performing any service operation. Avoid hammering, jarring, dropping or leaning any portion of the column. When reassembling column components, use only the specified screws, nuts and bolts and tighten to specified torque.

1. Disconnect the negative battery cable.
2. Remove the bolt attaching the column steering shaft to the intermediate shaft assembly.
3. Remove the steering wheel.
4. Remove the steering column trim shrouds by loosening the two screws. On tilt columns, remove the upper extension shroud by squeezing it at the six and twelve o'clock positions and popping it free of the retaining plate at the three o'clock position.
5. Remove the steering column cover directly under the column on the instrument panel.
6. Disconnect all electrical connections to the steering column switches.
7. Loosen the two bolts retaining the steering column to the lower instrument panel bracket. Do not remove the bolts.
8. Remove the three screws retaining the steering column toeplate/lower seal to the dash.
9. Remove the two bolts retaining the steering column to the instrument panel.
10. Lower the steering column and pull it out from the vehicle.

NOTE: Clamping is not permitted on the outer tube overlap joint. Care must be taken not to permanently deform the tube wall. Damage to the tube may affect column energy absorption performance.

11. Install the steering column by inserting the lower end of the steering column through the opening in the dash panel. Use care not to damage the column during installation.
12. Align the steering column support bracket to the lower instrument panel bracket. Attach the bolts loosely, so that the column hangs with clearance between the column and the instrument panel.
13. Align the steering column toe plate three mounting holes to the dash weld nuts, then install the three bolts and tighten them to 11-17 ft.lb. (15-23 Nm).
14. Tighten the column support brackets two bolts to 11-17 ft.lb. (15-23 Nm).
15. Connect the column switch connectors.
16. Slide the upper steering intermediate shaft assembly onto the steering column lower shaft. Attach with the bolt and nut previously removed and tighten to 30-42 ft.lb. (41-57 Nm).
17. Attach the trim shrouds that cover the steering column upper end with two screws. Snap the upper extension shroud in place on tilt columns.
18. Install the steering wheel.
19. Install the steering column cover on the instrument panel. Check the steering column for proper operation.

Tie Rod End

REMOVAL & INSTALLATION

1. Rotate the steering gear from lock to lock (entire gear travel) and record the number of steering wheel rotations. Divide the number of steering wheel rotations by two to get the required number of turns to place the steering wheel in the centered (straight ahead) position. From one lock position, rotate the steering wheel the required number of turns to center the steering rack.
2. Mark the tie rod end jam nut in relation to the inner ball joint assembly threads for installation purposes.
3. Remove and discard the cotter pin from the tie rod end ball stud and remove the nut.
4. Separate the tie rod ends from the spindle arms using remover tool T64P-3590-F, or equivalent.
5. Hold the tie rod end with a wrench and loosen the tie rod jam nut.
6. Grip the tie rod with locking pliers and remove the tie rod end from the inner ball joint assembly. Note and record the number of turns required to remove the tie rod end.
7. Thread the new tie rod onto the inner ball joint assembly the same number of turns recorded during removal. Tighten the jam nut against the tie rod end in the position marked prior to removal, then tighten the nut to 35-60 ft.lb. (48-68 Nm).
8. With the steering gear, steering wheel and front wheels in the centered position, attach the tie rod ends to the spindle arms. Install the nuts and tighten them to 52-73 ft.lb. (70-100 Nm). If required, advance the castle

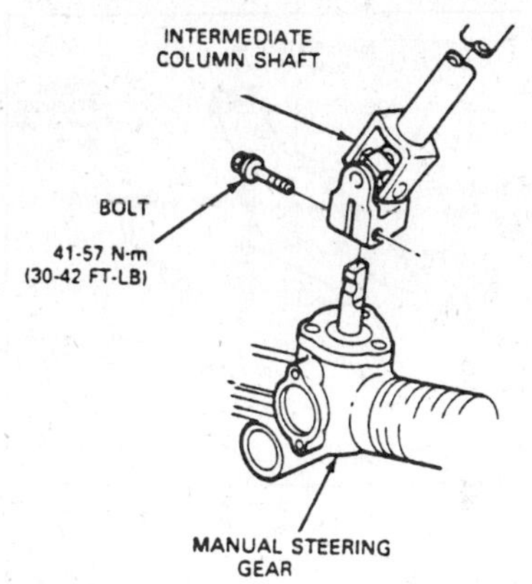

Separating the intermediate steering shaft from the pinion

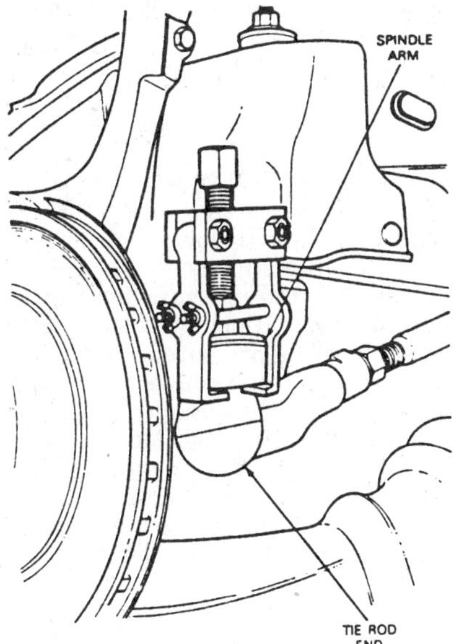

Separating the tie rod end from the spindle arm with remover tool

nuts to the next castellation and install new cotter pins. Do not loosen the nuts to line up the cotter pin hole.

NOTE: Make sure the tie rod ball studs are seated in the spindle tapers to prevent rotation while tightening the nut.

9. Have the toe-in and front end alignment checked at a qualified service shop.

Manual Steering Gear

REMOVAL & INSTALLATION

1. Rotate the steering gear from lock to lock (entire gear travel) and record the number of steering wheel rotations. Divide the number of steering wheel rotations by two to get the required number of turns to place the steering wheel in the centered (straight ahead) position. From one lock position, rotate the steering wheel the required number of turns to center the steering rack.

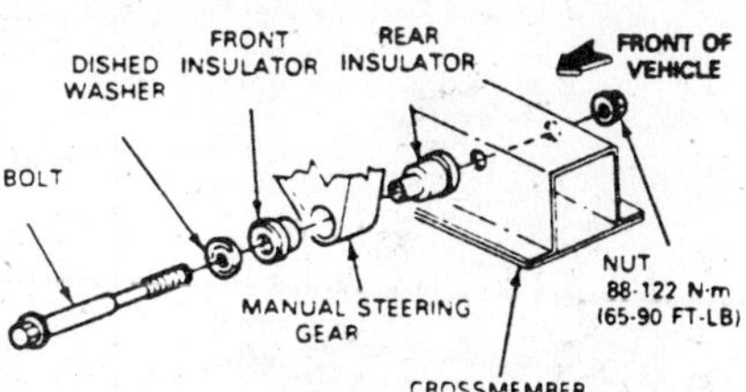

Steering gear mounting to crossmember

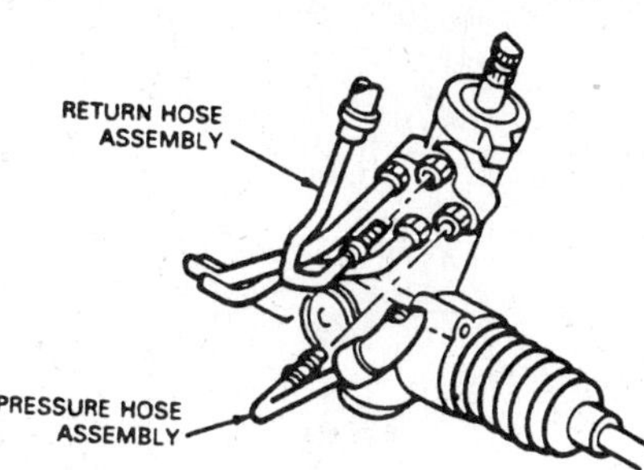

Disconnecting the power steering lines from the rack

2. Raise the vehicle and support it safely, then remove the bolt retaining the intermediate steering column shaft to the steering gear pinion. Separate the shaft from the pinion.
3. Remove and discard the cotter pin retaining the nut to the tie rod ends. Remove the nut, then separate the tie rod ends from the spindle arms using remover tool T64P-3590-F, or equivalent.
4. Support the steering gear and remove the two nuts, bolts and washers retaining the gear to the crossmember. Remove the gear and, if required, remove the front and rear insulators from the gear housing.
5. To install, first install the front and rear insulators in the gear housing, if removed.
6. Position the steering gear on the crossmember, then install the nuts, bolts and washers. Tighten the nuts to 65-90 ft.lb. (88-122 Nm).
7. With the steering gear, steering wheel and front wheels in the centered position, attach the tie rod ends to the spindle arms. Install the nuts and tighten them to 52-73 ft.lb. (70-100 Nm). If required, advance the castle nuts to the next castellation and install new cotter pins. Do not loosen the nuts to line up the cotter pin hole.

NOTE: Make sure the tie rod ball studs are seated in the spindle tapers to prevent rotation while tightening the nut.

8. Connect the steering column intermediate shaft to the gear pinion, then install the bolt and tighten it to 30-42 ft.lb. (41-57 Nm).
9. Have the toe-in and front end alignment checked at a qualified service shop.

Power Steering Gear

REMOVAL & INSTALLATION

1. Start the engine, then rotate the steering gear from lock to lock (entire gear travel) and record the number of steering wheel rotations. Divide the number of steering wheel rotations by two to get the required number of turns to place the steering wheel in the centered (straight ahead) position. From one lock position, rotate the steering wheel the required number of turns to center the steering rack.
2. Stop the engine, then disconnect the negative battery cable. Turn the ignition switch to the ON position, then raise the vehicle and support it safely.
3. Remove the bolt retaining the lower intermediate steering column shaft to the steering gear, then disconnect the shaft from the gear.
4. Disconnect the pressure and return lines from the steering gear valve housing. Plug the lines and ports in the steering gear valve housing to prevent the entry of dirt into the system.
5. Remove and discard the cotter pin retaining the nut to the tie rod ends. Remove the nut, then separate the tie rod ends from the spindle arms using remover tool T64P-3590-F, or equivalent.
6. Support the steering gear and remove the two nuts, bolts and washers retaining the gear to the crossmember. Remove the gear and, if required, remove the front and rear insulators from the gear housing.
7. To install the steering rack, first install the insulators in the gear housing, if removed. The rubber insulators must be pushed completely inside the gear housing before the gear is installed against the crossmember. No gap is allowed between the insulator and the face of the rear boss. Use rubber lubricant or soapy water to facilitate installation of the insulators in the gear housing.
8. Position the steering gear on the crossmember, then install the nuts, bolts and washers. Tighten the nuts to 65-90 ft.lb. (88-122 Nm).
9. Connect the pressure and return lines to the appropriate ports on the steering gear valve housing, then tighten the fittings to 10-15 ft.lb. (15-20 Nm). The fitting design allows the

hoses to swivel when properly tightened. Do not attempt to eliminate this looseness by overtightening or damage to the fittings will occur.

10. With the steering gear, steering wheel and front wheels in the centered position, attach the tie rod ends to the spindle arms. Install the nuts and tighten them to 52-73 ft.lb. (70-100 Nm). If required, advance the castle nuts to the next castellation and install new cotter pins. Do not loosen the nuts to line up the cotter pin hole.

NOTE: Make sure the tie rod ball studs are seated in the spindle tapers to prevent rotation while tightening the nut.

11. Connect the steering column intermediate shaft to the gear pinion, then install the bolt and tighten it to 30-42 ft.lb. (41-57 Nm).

12. Lower the vehicle and turn the ignition key to the OFF position, then connect the negative battery cable.

13. Check the power steering fluid level in the pump and top off as required.

14. Have the toe-in and front end alignment checked at a qualified service shop.

Power Steering Pump

REMOVAL & INSTALLATION

NOTE: An identification tag is attached to the power steering pump reservoir. The top line of this tag indicates the basic model number (HBC) and the suffix. Always use these tags when requesting service parts as there may be slight differences in internal components.

2.3L (140 CID) Engine

1. Drain the power steering fluid from the pump by disconnecting the fluid return hose at the reservoir and draining the fluid into a suitable container.

2. Remove the pressure hose from the pump. If required, disconnect and remove the power steering pressure switch from the fitting on the gear assembly. Disconnect the electrical connector from the switch and unscrew the switch from the fitting.

3. Loosen the pivot bolt and adjusting bolt on the alternator bracket to release belt tension, then remove the drive belt from the power steering pump pulley.

4. Install a steering pump pulley remover tool (T69L-10300-B or equivalent) on the pulley. Hold the pump and rotate the tool nut counterclockwise to remove the pulley. Do not apply in-and-out pressure on the pump shaft or the internal thrust areas will be damaged.

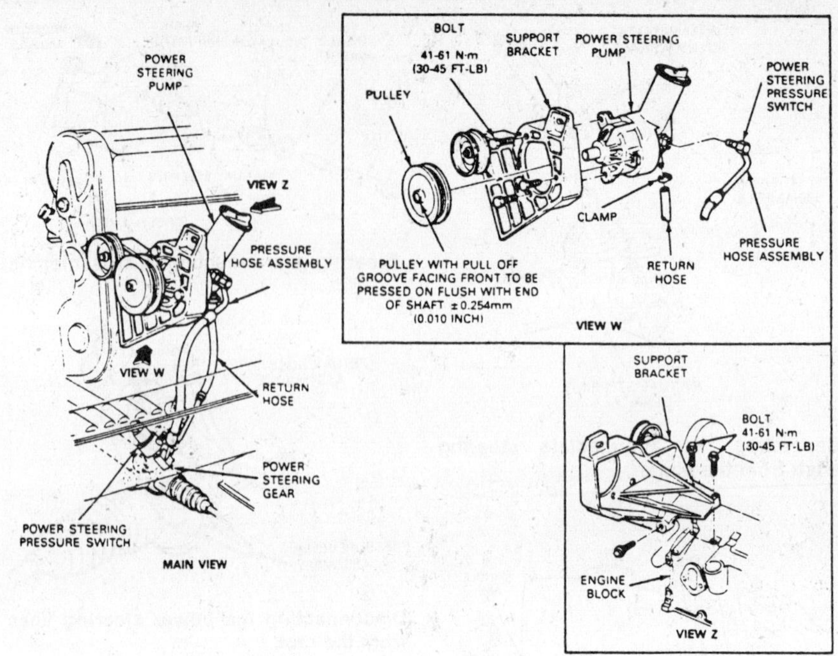

Power steering pump installation on 2.3L (140 CID) engine

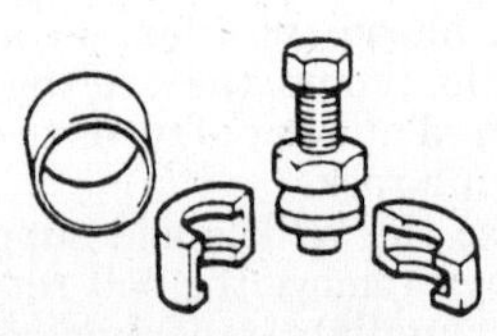

Power steering pump pulley remover tool

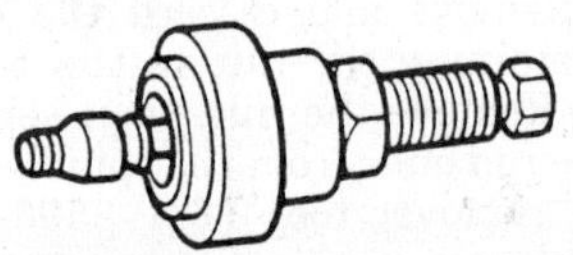

Power steering pump pulley replacer tool

5. Remove the bolts attaching the pump to the bracket and remove the pump.

6. To install, first position the pump on the bracket, then install and tighten the bolts to 30-45 ft.lb. (41-61 Nm).

7. Install a power steering pump pulley replacer tool (T65P-3A733-C or equivalent) and press the pulley onto the pump shaft. The pull-off groove must face the front of the vehicle and the pulley must be pressed on the shaft until flush with a tolerance of 0.010″ (0.254mm).

8. Position the belt on the pulley, then place a 1″ wrench on the alternator boss and lift up on the alternator until the specified belt tension is read on a suitable belt tension gauge. Tighten the adjustment bolt to 24-40 ft.lb. (33-54 Nm) and the pivot bolt to 45-57 ft.lb. (61-78 Nm).

9. Install the pressure hose to the pump fitting. If removed, install the power steering pressure switch on the gear assembly and connect the wires.

10. Connect the return hose to the pump and tighten the clamp.

11. Fill the reservoir with specified power steering fluid, then start the engine and turn the steering wheel from stop to stop to remove any air from the system.

12. Check the system for leaks.

2.8L (171 CID)
3.0L (182 CID)

1. Drain the power steering fluid from the pump by disconnecting the fluid return hose at the reservoir and draining the fluid into a suitable container.

2. Remove the pressure hose from the pump fitting by unscrewing the hose swivel nut.

3. Slacken belt tension by loosening the pivot bolt and adjustment bolt on the idler pulley assembly, then remove the drive belt from the power steering pump pulley.

4. Install a steering pump pulley remover tool (T69L-10300-B or equivalent) on the pulley. Hold the pump and rotate the tool nut counterclockwise to remove the pulley. Do not apply in-and-out pressure on the pump shaft or the internal thrust areas will be damaged.

5. Remove the support and the bolts attaching the pump to the bracket, then remove the pump.

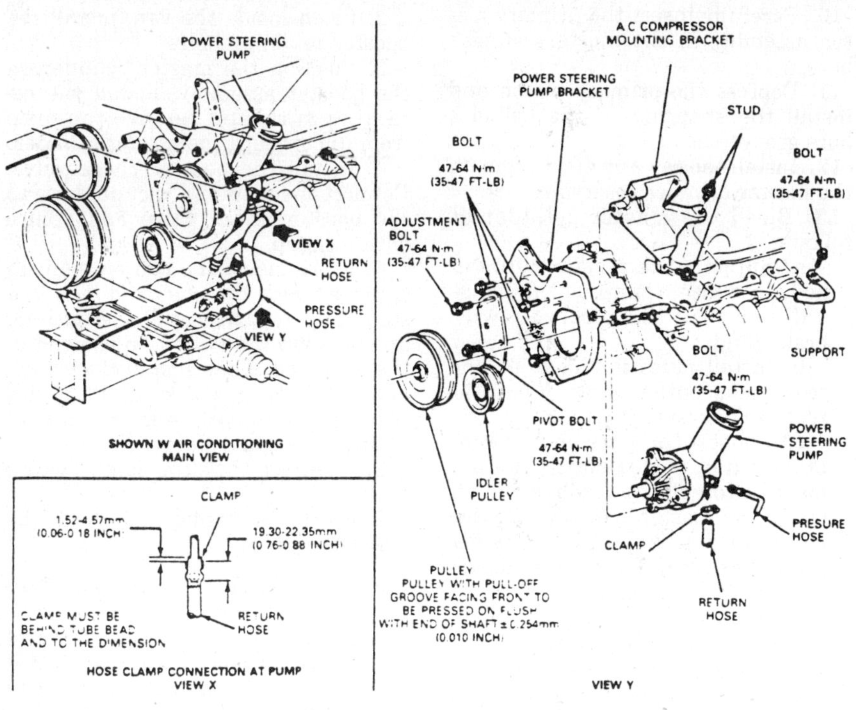

Power steering pump installation on V6 engines

6. Position the new pump on the bracket, then install and tighten the bolts to 35-47 ft.lb. (47-64 Nm). Position the support on the bracket and install and tighten the mounting bolts to 35-47 ft.lb. (47-64 Nm).

7. Install a power steering pump pulley replacer tool (T65P-3A733-C or equivalent) and press the pulley onto the pump shaft. The pull-off groove must face the front of the vehicle and the pulley must be pressed on the shaft until flush with a tolerance of 0.010" (0.254mm).

8. Position the drive belt on the pulley, then insert a ½" drive breaker bar in the slot in the idler pulley assembly. Rotate the pulley assembly until the specified belt tension is obtained, then tighten the adjustment bolt and pivot bolt to 35-47 ft.lb. (47-64 Nm).

9. Connect the pressure hose to the pump fitting. Connect the return hose to the pump and tighten the clamp.

10. Refill the power steering reservoir with the specified fluid, then start the engine and check for leaks. Turn the steering wheel from lock to lock several times to remove any trapped air from the system.

BRAKE SYSTEM

Adjustments

DRUM BRAKES

Rear drum brakes are adjusted automatically by alternately driving the vehicle forward and reverse , and sharply applying the brakes when the vehicle is driven forward and reverse. Brake adjustment occurs during reverse stops only.

BRAKE PEDAL

Push Rod

The push rod has an adjustment screw to maintain the correct relationship between the booster control valve plunger and the master cylinder piston.

To check the adjustment of the screw, fabricate a gauge and place it against the master cylinder mounting surface of the booster body. Adjust the push rod screw by turning it until the end of the screw just touches the inner edge of the slot in the gauge.

Master Cylinder

REMOVAL

1. Disconnect the brake warning lamp connector.

2. Disconnect the hydraulic lines from the brake master cylinder.

3. Remove the nuts retaining the master cylinder to the brake booster and remove the master cylinder.

INSTALLATION

1. Before installing the master cylinder, adjust the booster assembly push rod as outlined earlier.

2. Position the master cylinder assembly over the booster push rod and unto the two studs on the booster assembly. Install and tighten the attaching nuts.

3. Reconnect the brake warning light.

4. Loosely connect the hydraulic brake system lines to the master cylinder. Fill the master cylinder reservoir

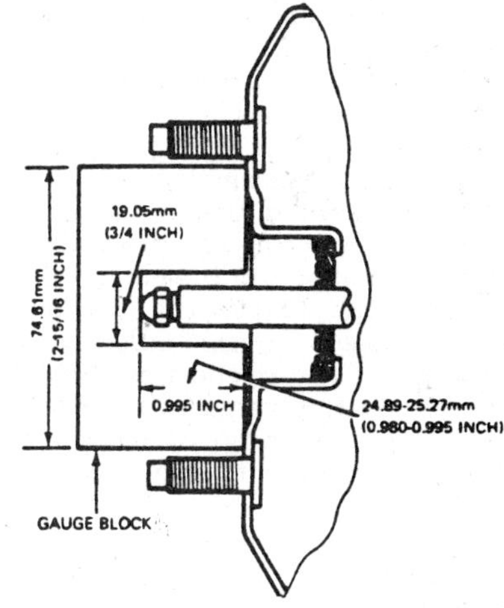

Push rod adjustment

with DOT 3 brake fluid to the fill line on the side of the master cylinder. Bleed the air from the master cylinder and the entire hydraulic system as outlined in Hydraulic System Bleeding, Then tighten all hydraulic lines.

5. Make sure the master cylinder

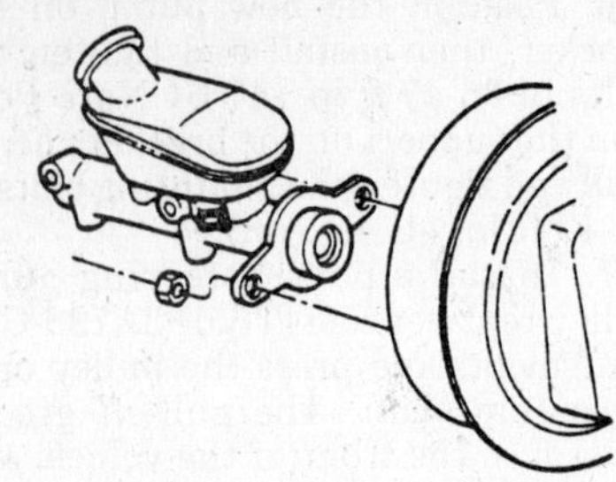

Master cylinder removal

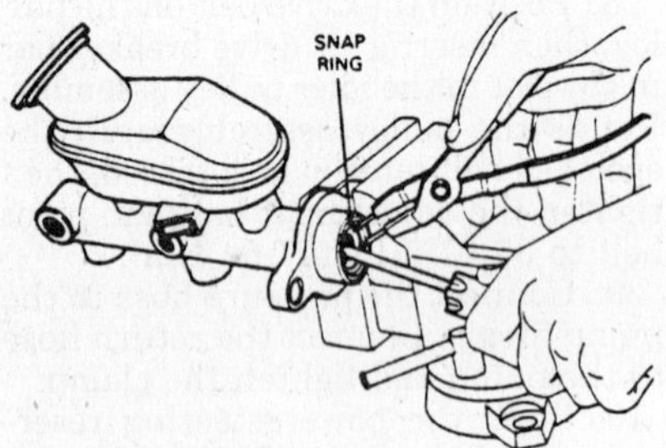

Depressing the primary piston and removing the snap ring

reservoir is filled to the proper level and install the cap diaphragm.

OVERHAUL

1. Clean the outside of the master cylinder and remove the filler cap and diaphragm. Drain and discard the any brake fluid that remains in the cylinder.
2. Depress the primary piston and remove the snapring from the retaining groove at the rear of the master cylinder bore.
3. Remove the primary piston assembly from the master cylinder bore and inspect for seal damage or twisting. Discard the assembly.
4. Remove the secondary piston assembly by directing compressed air into the outlet port at the blind end of the bore while plugging the other outlet port. Inspect the seal for damage or twisting and discard the assembly.
5. Inspect the master cylinder bore for pitting or scoring. If the bore is damaged replace with a new master cylinder assembly.
6. If the bore is not damaged obtain a repair kit to rebuild the master cylinder.
7. Clean the master cylinder body with clean isopropyl alcohol to remove any contamination.
8. Dip the repair kit piston assemblies in clean brake fluid to lubricate the seals.
9. Carefully insert the complete secondary piston assembly in the master cylinder bore.
10. Carefully insert the primary piston assembly in the master cylinder bore.
11. Depress the primary piston and install the snapring in the cylinder bore groove.
12. Install the cap and diaphragm on the master cylinder reservoir.
13. Bleed the master cylinder as follows:
    a. Support the master cylinder body in a vise (clamp by the flange only) and fill the reservoir with brake fluid.
    b. Install plugs in the front and rear brake outlet ports. Bleed the rear brake system first.
    c. Loosen the plug in the rear brake outlet port. Depress the primary piston slowly to force the air out of the master cylinder. Tighten the plug while the piston is depressed or air will enter the master cylinder.
    d. Repeat this procedure until air ceases to exit at the outlet port.
    e. Repeat Steps c and d for the front brake outlet port with the rear brake outlet plugged.
    f. Tighten the plugs and try to depress the piston. Depressing the piston should be harder after all air is expelled.
    g. Install the cap and diaphragm assembly making sure the cap is tightened securely. Remove the plugs.

Power Brake Booster

REMOVAL

1. Disconnect the brake warning lamp connector.
2. Support the master cylinder from underneath with a prop.
3. Remove the nuts retaining the master cylinder to the brake booster.
4. Loosen the clamp that secures the manifold vacuum hose to the booster check valve, and remove the hose. Remove the booster check valve.
5. From inside the cab on vehicles equipped with a pushrod mounted stop lamp switch, remove the hairpin retainer and slide the stop lamp switch, push rod, spacers and bushing off the brake pedal arm.
6. From the engine compartment remove the bolts that attach the booster to the dash panel.

INSTALLATION

1. Mount the booster assembly on the engine side of the dash panel by sliding the bracket mounting bolts and valve operating rod in through the holes in the dash panel.
2. From inside the van, install the booster retaining bolts.
3. Position the master cylinder on the booster assembly, install the retaining nuts, and remove the prop from underneath the master cylinder.
4. Install the booster check valve. Connect the manifold vacuum hose to the booster check valve and secure with a clamp.
5. From inside the cab on vehicles equipped with the push rod mounted stop lamp switch, install the bushing and position the switch on the end of the push rod. Then install the switch and rod on the pedal arm, along with the spacers on each side, and secure with the hairpin retainer.
6. Connect the stop lamp switch wiring.
7. Start the engine and check the brake operation.

NOTE: Make sure that the booster rubber reaction disc is properly installed. A dislodged disc may cause excessive pedal travel and extreme pedal sensitivity.

Hydraulic System Bleeding

When any part of the hydraulic system has been disconnected for repair or replacement, air may get into the lines and cause a spongy pedal action. This requires the bleeding of the hydraulic system after it has been properly connected to be sure all air is expelled from the brake cylinders and lines.

Bleed one brake cylinder at a time. Start bleeding on the right rear brake, then the left rear. After completing, proceed to bleed the right front brake, then the left front. Keep the reservoir filled with brake fluid during the bleeding operation.

NOTE: Never reuse bled brake fluid.

1. Bleed the longest line first.
2. On the master cylinder, wrap a cloth around the tubing below the fitting and loosen the hydraulic line nut at the master cylinder.
3. Push the brake pedal down slowly by hand to the floor. This will force air trapped in the master cylinder to escape at the fitting.
4. Hold the pedal down and tighten the fitting. Release the brake pedal.

NOTE: Do not release the brake pedal until the fitting is tightened or air will reenter the master cylinder.

5. Repeat this procedure until air

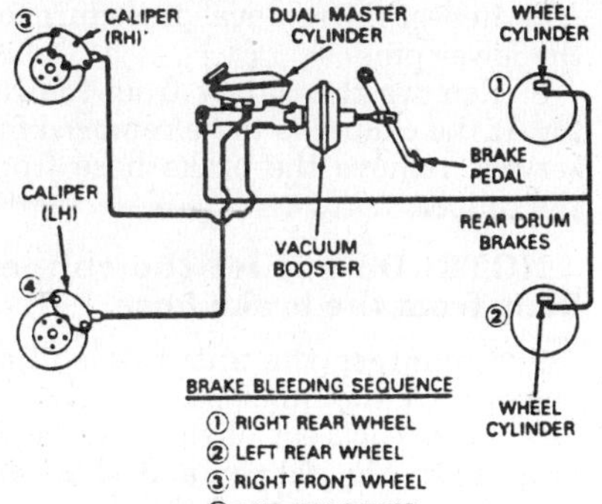

Brake bleeding sequence

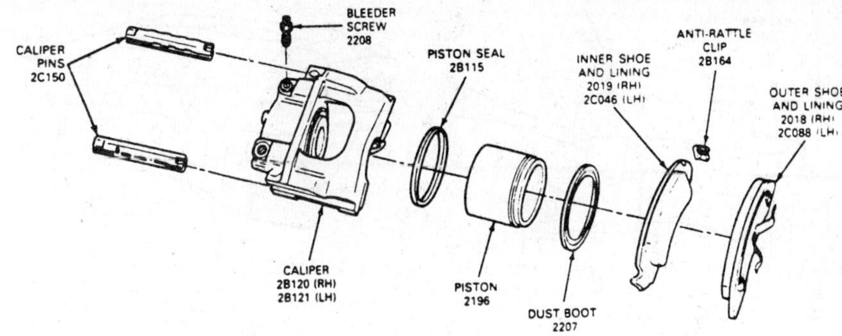

Disassembled view of caliper and shoe pads

ceases to escape at the fitting and the brake pedal is firm.

6. Place a box wrench on the bleeder fitting on the brake wheel cylinder. Attach a rubber drain tube to the bleeder fitting.

NOTE: Make sure the end of the tube fits snugly around the bleeder fitting.

7. Submerge the free end of the tube in a container partially filled with clean brake fluid. Loosen the bleeder fitting approximately ¾ of a turn.

8. Slowly push the brake pedal all the way down. Close the bleeder fitting, and return the brake pedal to the fully released position. Repeat this procedure until air bubbles no longer appear at the submerged end of the bleeder tube.

9. When the fluid is completely free of air bubbles, close the bleeder fitting and remove the bleeder tube.

10. Repeat this procedure at the brake wheel cylinder on the opposite side. Refill the master cylinder reservoir after each wheel cylinder is bled.

11. When the bleeding operation is complete, fill the master cylinder to the maximum level line on the reservoir.

FRONT DISC BRAKES

CAUTION

Brake shoes contain asbestos, which has been determined to be a cancer causing agent. Never clean the brake surfaces with compressed air! Avoid inhaling any dust from any brake surface! When cleaning brake surfaces, use a commercially available brake cleaning fluid.

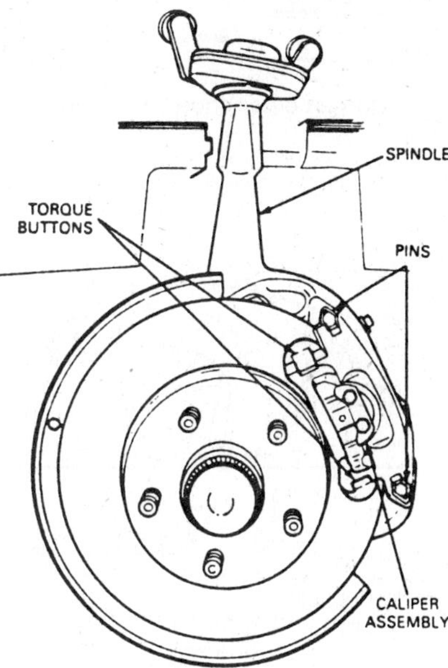

Assembled view of the caliper and rotor

Brake Pads

INSPECTION

Replace the front pads when the pad thickness is at the minimum thickness recommended by Ford Motor Co., which is $^{1}/_{16}''$ (1.5mm), or at the minimum allowed by the applicable state or local motor vehicle inspection code. Pad thickness may be checked by removing the wheel and looking through the inspection port in the caliper assembly.

Front Caliper and Disc Brake Pads

REMOVAL & INSTALLATION

NOTE: Always replace all disc pad assemblies on an axle. Never service one wheel only.

1. To avoid fluid overflow when the caliper piston is pressured into the caliper cylinder bores, siphon or dip part of the brake fluid out of the larger master cylinder reservoir (connected to the front disc brakes). Discard the removed fluid.

2. Raise the vehicle and install jackstands. Remove a front wheel and tire assembly.

Use a C-clamp to bottom the piston in the bore

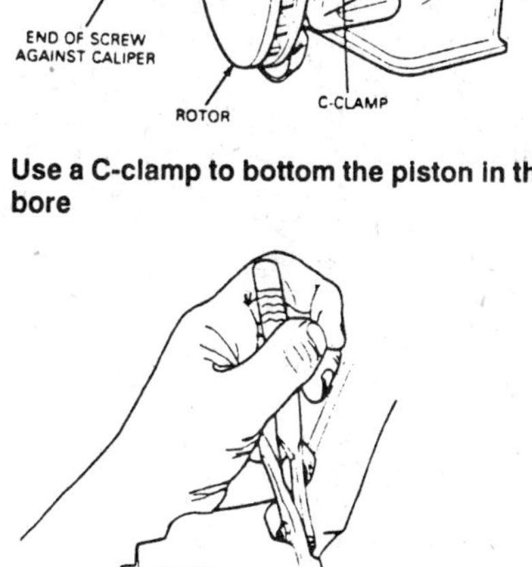

Compress the inboard pin tab with a pair of pliers

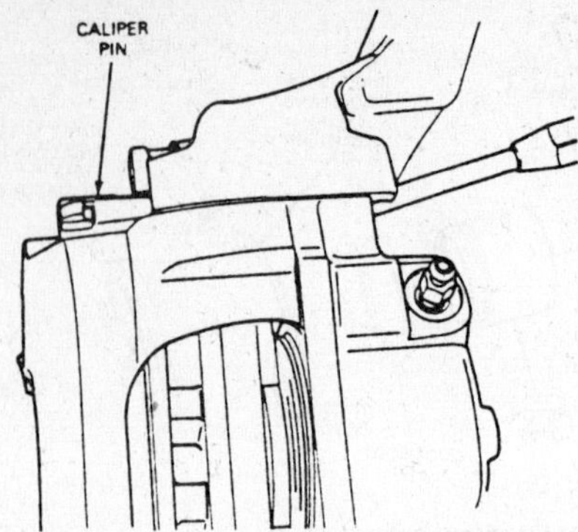

Removing the caliper pin with a punch

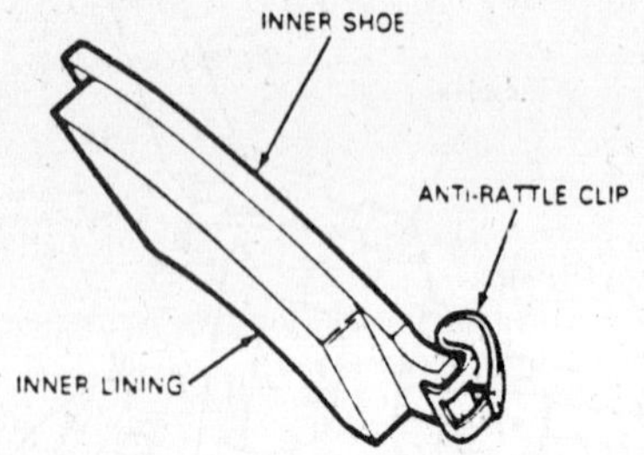

Compress the anti-rattle clip to remove the inner shoe

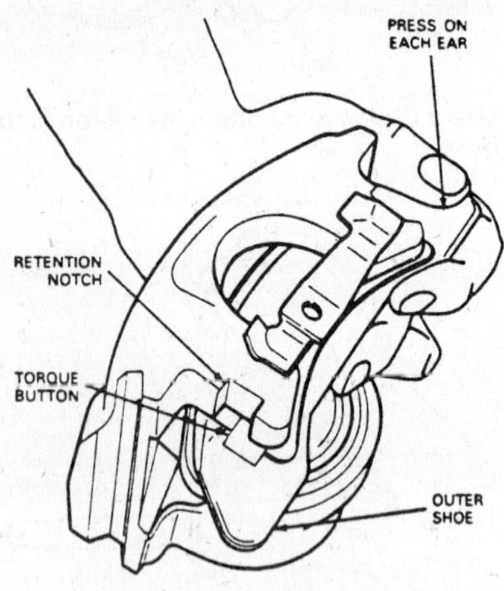

Outer shoe removal

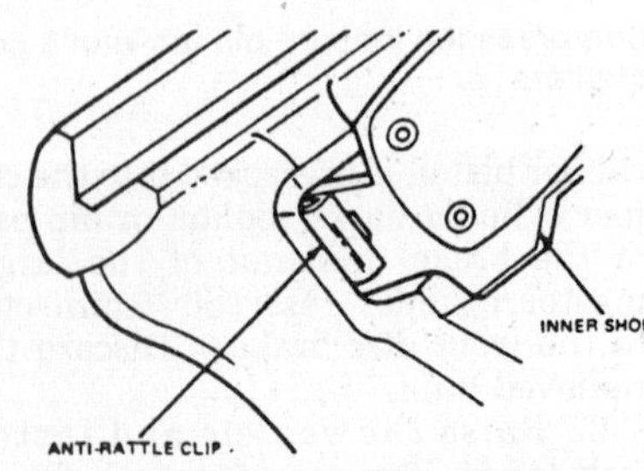

Correct inner shoe installation

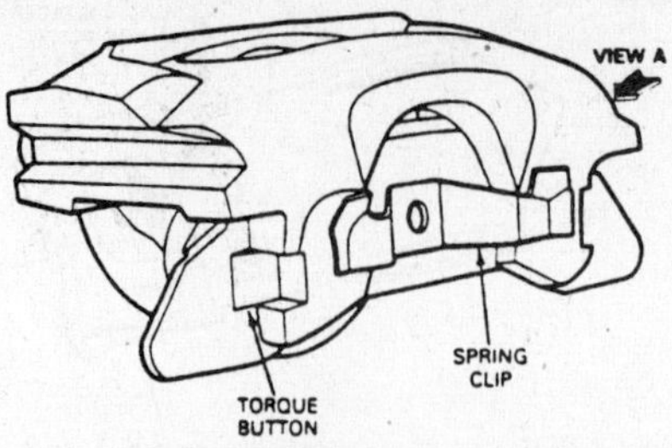

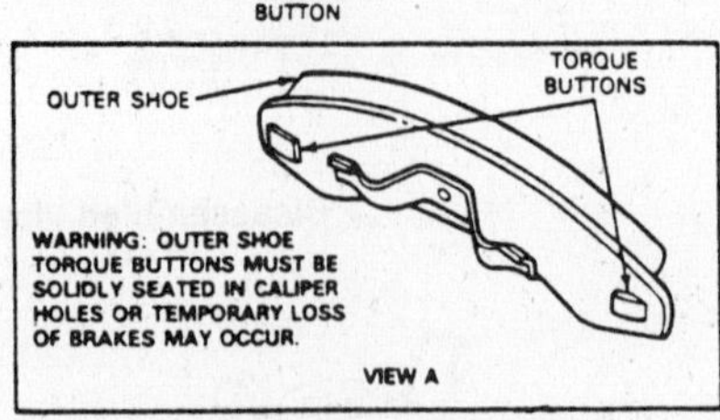

Correct outer shoe installation

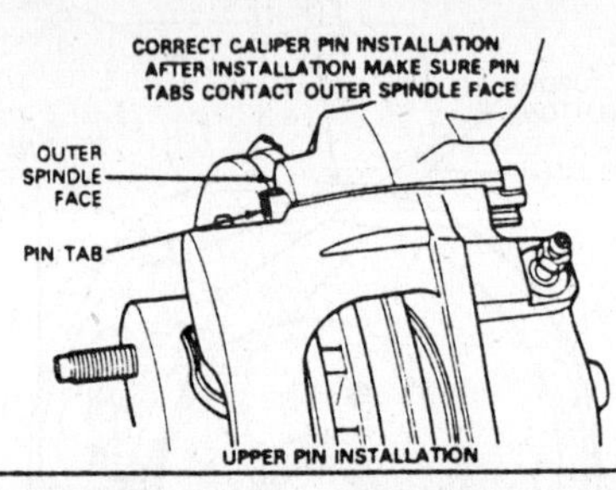

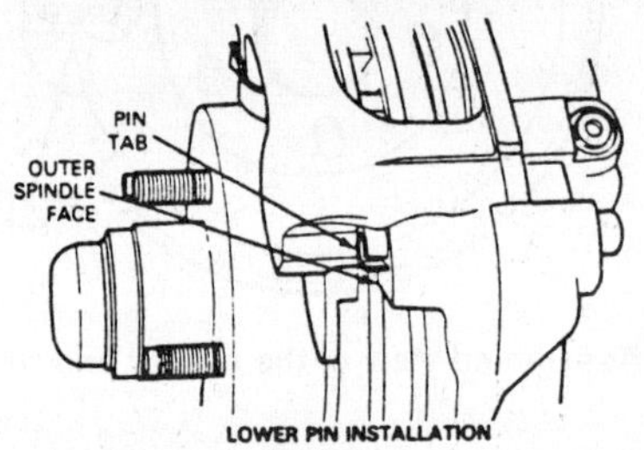

Correct pin installation

3. Place an 8″ (203mm) C-clamp on the caliper and tighten the clamp to bottom the caliper piston in the cylinder bore. Remove the clamp.

NOTE: Do not use a screwdriver or similar tool to pry piston away from the rotor.

4. Tap the upper caliper pin towards the inboard side until the pin tabs touch the spindle face.
5. Compress the inboard pin tab with a pair of pliers, and with a hammer, drive the pin until the tab slips into the spindle groove.
6. Place one end of a $^7/_{16}$″ (11mm) punch against the end of the caliper pin and drive the caliper pin out of the caliper slide groove.

NOTE: Never reuse caliper pins. Always install new pins whenever a caliper is removed.

7. Repeat the removal procedure for the lower pin.
8. Remove the caliper from the rotor. If the caliper is to be removed for service, remove the brake hose from the caliper.

NOTE: Do not let the caliper hang from the brake hose.

9. Compress the anti-rattle clips and remove the inner pad.
10. Press each ear of the outer shoe away from the caliper and slide the torque buttons out of the retention notches.

INSTALLATION

1. Place a new anti-rattle clip on the lower end of the inner pad. Be sure the tabs on the clip are positioned properly and the clip is fully seated.
2. Position the inner pad and anti-rattle clip tab against the pad abutment and the loop type spring away from the rotor. Compress the anti-rattle clip and slide the upper end of the pad in position.
3. Install the outer pad, making sure the torque buttons on the pad spring clip are seated solidly in the matching holes in the caliper.
4. Install the caliper on the spindle, making sure the mounting surfaces are free of dirt and lubricate the caliper grooves with Disc Brake Caliper Grease.
5. From the caliper outboard side, position the pin between the caliper and spindle grooves. The pin must be positioned so the tabs will be installed against the spindle outer face.

NOTE: Never reuse caliper pins. Always install new pins whenever a caliper is removed.

6. Tap the pin on the outboard end with a hammer. Continue tapping the pin inward until the retention tabs on the sides of the pin contact the spindle face. Repeat this procedure for the lower pin.

NOTE: During the installation procedure do not allow the tabs of the caliper pin to be tapped too far into the spindle groove. If this happens it will be necessary to tap the other end of the caliper pin until the tabs snap into place. The tabs on each end of the caliper pin must be free to catch on the spindle face.

7. If removed, install the brake hose to the caliper.
8. Bleed the brakes as described earlier.
9. Install the wheel and tire assembly. Torque the lug nuts to 85-115 ft.lb.

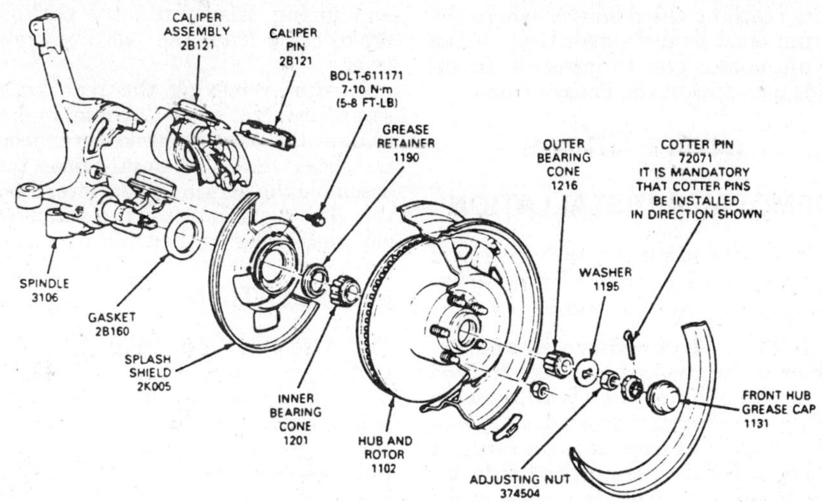

Hub, rotor and splash shield

10. Remove the jackstands and lower the vehicle. Check the brake fluid level and fill as necessary. Check the brakes for proper operation.

CALIPER OVERHAUL

1. For caliper removal, see the above procedure. Disconnect the brake hose.
2. Clean the exterior of the caliper with denatured alcohol.
3. Remove the plug from the caliper inlet port and drain the fluid.
4. Air pressure is necessary to remove the piston. When a source of compressed air is found, such as a shop or gas station, apply air to the inlet port slowly and carefully until the piston pops out of its bore.

CAUTION

If high pressure air is applied the piston will pop out with considerable force and cause damage or injury!

5. If the piston jams, release the air pressure and tap sharply on the piston end with a soft hammer. Reapply air pressure.
6. When the piston is out, Remove the boot from the piston and the seal from the bore.
7. Clean the housing and piston with denatured alcohol. Dry with compressed air.
8. Lubricate the new piston seal, boot and piston with clean brake fluid, and assemble them in the caliper.
9. The dust boot can be worked in with the fingers and the piston should be pressed straight in until it bottoms. Be careful to avoid cocking the piston in the bore.
10. A C-clamp may be necessary to bottom the piston.
11. Install the caliper using the procedure given in the pad and caliper replacement procedure above.

Rotor (Disc)

REMOVAL & INSTALLATION

1. Jack up the front of the vehicle and support on jackstands.
2. Remove the wheel and tire.
3. Remove the caliper assembly as described earlier.
4. Follow the procedure given under hub and wheel bearing removal for models with manual and automatic locking hubs.

NOTE: New rotor assemblies come protected with an anti-rust coating which should be removed with denatured alcohol or degreaser. New hubs must be packed with EP wheel bearing grease. If the old rotors are to be reused, check them for cracks, grooves or waviness. Rotors that aren't too badly scored or grooved can be resurfaced by most automotive shops. Minimum rotor thickness should be stamped on the rotor. If refinishing exceeds that, the rotor will have to be replaced.

REAR DRUM BRAKES

CAUTION

Brake shoes contain asbestos, which has been determined to be a cancer causing agent. Never clean the brake surfaces with compressed air! Avoid inhaling any dust from any brake surface! When cleaning brake surfaces, use a commercially available brake cleaning fluid.

Brake Drums

REMOVAL & INSTALLATION

1. Raise the vehicle so that the wheel to be worked on is clear of the floor and install jackstands under the vehicle.
2. Remove the wheel. Remove the 3 retaining nuts and remove the brake drum. It may be necessary to back off the brake shoe adjustment in order to remove the brake drum. This is because the drum might be grooved or worn from being in service for an extended period of time.
3. Before installing a new brake drum, be sure and remove any protective coating with carburetor degreaser.
4. Install the brake drum in the reverse order of removal and adjust the brakes.

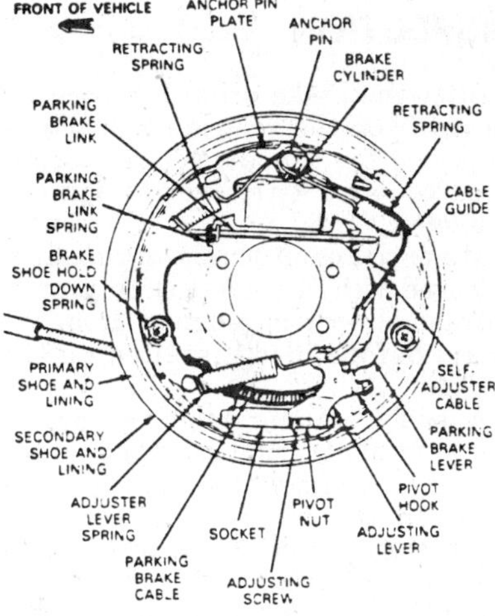

9.0 inch rear brake assembly (left side)

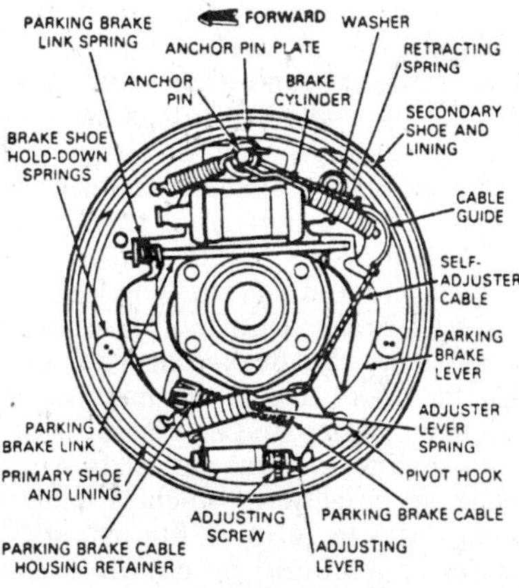

10.0 inch rear brake assembly (left side)

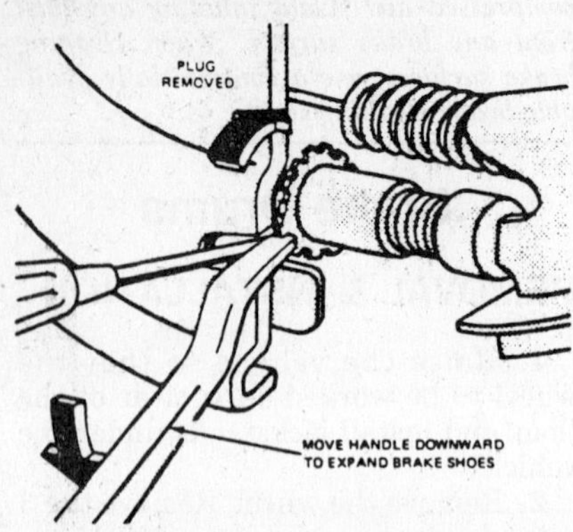

Brake shoe adjuster

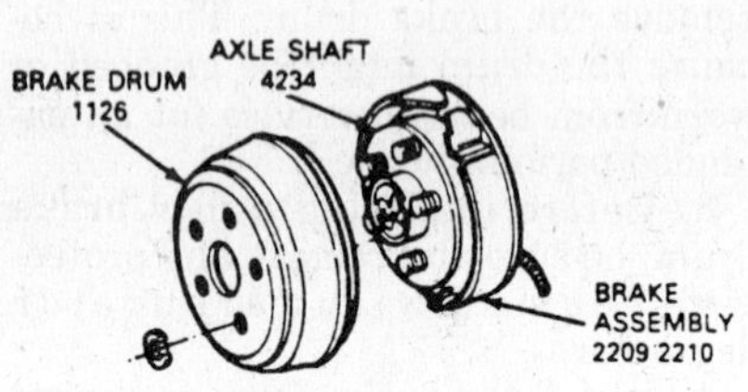

Drum brake assembly

INSPECTION

After the brake drum has been removed from the vehicle, it should be inspected for runout, severe scoring, cracks, and the proper inside diameter.

Minor scores on a brake drum can be removed with fine emery cloth, provided that all grit is removed from the drum before it is installed on the vehicle.

A badly scored, rough, or out-of-round (runout) drum can be ground or turned on a brake drum lathe. Do not remove any more material from the drum than is necessary to provide a smooth surface for the brake shoe to contact. The maximum diameter of the braking surface is shown on the inside of each brake drum. Brake drums that exceed the maximum braking surface diameter shown on the brake drum, either through wear or refinishing, must be replaced. this is because after the outside wall of the brake drum reaches a certain thickness (thinner than the original thickness) the drum loses its ability to dissipate the heat created by the friction between the brake drum and the brake shoes, when the brakes are applied. Also the brake drum will have more tendency to warp and/or crack.

The maximum braking surface diameter specification, which is shown on each drum, allows for a 0.060" (1.5mm) machining or cut over the original nominal drum diameter plus 0.030" (0.76mm) additional wear before reaching the diameter where the drum must be discarded. Use a brake drum micrometer to measure the inside diameter of the brake drums.

Brake Shoes

REMOVAL & INSTALLATION

1. Raise and support the vehicle and remove the wheel and brake drum from the wheel to be worked on.

NOTE: If you have never replaced the brakes on a car before and you are not too familiar with the procedures involved, only disassemble and assemble one side at a time, leaving the other side intact as a reference during reassembly.

2. Install a clamp over the ends of the wheel cylinder to prevent the pistons of the wheel cylinder from coming out, causing loss of fluid and much grief.
3. Contract the brake shoes by pulling the self-adjusting lever away from the starwheel adjustment screw and turn the starwheel up and back until the pivot nut is drawn onto the starwheel as far as it will come.
4. Pull the adjusting lever, cable and automatic adjuster spring down and toward the rear to unhook the pivot hook from the large hole in the secondary shoe web. Do not attempt to pry the pivot hook from the hole.
5. Remove the automatic adjuster spring and the adjuster lever.
6. Remove the secondary shoe-to-anchor spring with a brake tool. (Brake tools are very common implements and are available at auto parts stores.) Remove the primary shoe-to-anchor spring and unhook the cable anchor. Remove the anchor pin plate, if so equipped.
7. Remove the cable guide from the secondary shoe.
8. Remove the shoe holddown springs, shoes, adjusting screw, pivot nut, and socket. Note the color and position of each holddown spring for assembly. To remove the holddown springs, reach behind the brake backing plate and place one finger on the end of one of the brake holddown spring mounting pins. Using a pair of pliers, grasp the washer type retainer on top of the holddown spring that corresponds to the pin that you are holding. Push down on the pliers and turn them 90° to align the slot in the washer with the head on the spring mounting pin. Remove the spring and washer retainer and repeat this operating on the holddown spring on the other shoe.
9. Remove the parking brake link and spring. Disconnect the parking brake cable from the parking brake lever.
10. After removing the rear brake secondary shoe. On 9" (229mm) brakes remove the parking brake lever from the shoe. On 10" (254mm) brakes disassemble the parking brake lever from the shoe by removing the retaining clip and spring washer.

INSTALLATION

1. Assemble the parking brake lever to the secondary shoe, and on 10" (254mm) brakes secure it with the spring washer and retaining clip.
2. Apply a light coating of Lubriplate® at the points where the brake shoes contact the backing plate.
3. Position the brake shoes on the backing plate, and install the holddown spring pins, springs, and spring washer type retainers. Install the parking brake link, spring and washer. Connect the parking brake cable to the parking brake lever.
4. Install the anchor pin plate, and place the cable anchor over the anchor pin with the crimped side toward the backing plate.
5. Install the primary shoe-to-anchor spring with the brake tool.
6. Install the cable guide on the secondary shoe web with the flanged holes fitted into the hole in the secondary shoe web. Thread the cable around the cable guide groove.
7. Install the secondary shoe-to-anchor (long) spring. Be sure that the cable end is not cocked or binding on the anchor pin when installed. All of the parts should be flat on the anchor pin. Remove the wheel cylinder piston clamp.
8. Apply Lubriplate® to the threads and the socket end of the adjusting starwheel screw. Turn the adjusting screw into the adjusting pivot nut to the limit of the threads and then back off ½ turn.

NOTE: Interchanging the brake shoe adjusting screw assembles from one side of the vehicle to the other would cause the brake shoes to retract rather than expand each time the automatic adjusting mechanism operated. To prevent this, the socket end of the adjusting screw is stamped with an R or an L for RIGHT or LEFT. The adjusting pivot nuts can be distinguished by the number of lines machined around the body of the nut; one line indicates left hand nut and two lines indicates a right hand nut.

9. Place the adjusting socket on the

screw and install this assembly between the shoe ends with the adjusting screw nearest to the secondary shoe.

10. Place the cable hook into the hole in the adjusting lever from the backing plate side. The adjusting levers are stamped with an **R** right, or an **L** left, to indicate their installation on the right or left hand brake assembly.

11. Position the hooked end of the adjuster spring in the primary shoe web and connect the loop end of the spring to the adjuster lever hole.

12. Pull the adjuster lever, cable and automatic adjuster spring down toward the rear to engage the pivot hook in the large hole in the secondary shoe web.

13. After installation, check the action of the adjuster by pulling the section of the cable between the cable guide and the adjusting lever toward the secondary shoe web far enough to lift the lever past a tooth on the adjusting screw starwheel. The lever should snap into position behind the next tooth, and release of the cable should cause the adjuster spring to return the lever to its original position. This return action of the lever will turn the adjusting screw starwheel one tooth. The lever should contact the adjusting screw starwheel one tooth above the center line of the adjusting screw.

If the automatic adjusting mechanism does not perform properly, check the following:

a. Check the cable end fittings. The cable ends should fill or extend slightly beyond the crimped section of the fittings. If this is not the case, replace the cable.

b. Check the cable guide for damage. The cable groove should be parallel to the shoe web, and the body of the guide should lie flat against the web. Replace the cable guide if this is not so.

c. Check the pivot hook on the lever. The hook surfaces should be square with the body on the lever for proper pivoting. Repair or replace the hook as necessary.

d. Make sure that the adjusting screw starwheel is properly seated in the notch in the shoe web.

Wheel Cylinders

REMOVAL & INSTALLATION

1. To remove the wheel cylinder, jack up the vehicle and remove the wheel, hub, and drum.
2. Disconnect the brake line at the fitting on the brake backing plate.
3. Remove the brake assemblies.
4. Remove the screws that hold the wheel cylinder to the backing plate and remove the wheel cylinder from the vehicle.
5. Installation is the reverse of the above removal procedure. After installation adjust the brakes as described earlier in this section.

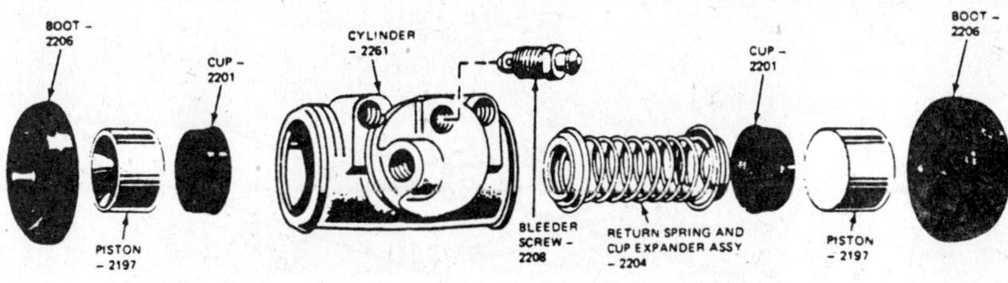

Exploded view of the wheel cylinder

OVERHAUL

Wheel cylinder rebuilding kits are available for reconditioning wheel cylinders. The kits usually contain new cup springs, cylinder cups, and in some, new boots. The most important factor to keep in mind when rebuilding wheel cylinders is cleanliness. Keep all dirt away from the wheel cylinders when you are reassembling them.

1. Remove the wheel cylinder as described earlier.
2. Remove the rubber dust covers on the ends of the cylinder. Remove the pistons and piston cups and the spring. Remove the bleeder screw and make sure that it is not plugged.
3. Discard all of the parts that the rebuilding kit will replace.
4. Examine the inside of the cylinder. If it is severely rusted, pitted or scratched, then the cylinder must be replaced as the piston cups won't be able to seal against the walls of the cylinder.
5. Using a wheel cylinder hone or emery cloth and crocus cloth, polish the inside of the cylinder. The purpose of this is to put a new surface on the inside of the cylinder. Keep the inside of the cylinder coated with brake fluid while honing.
6. Wash out the cylinder with clean brake fluid after honing.
7. When reassembling the cylinder, dip all of the parts in clean brake fluid. Assemble the wheel cylinder in the reverse order of removal and disassembly.

PARKING BRAKE

The parking brake system is self adjusting and requires no adjustment, however if any component in the parking brake system requires servicing (or removing the rear axle), the cable tension must be released. After servicing is completed, the cables are connected to the equalizer and tension is reset.

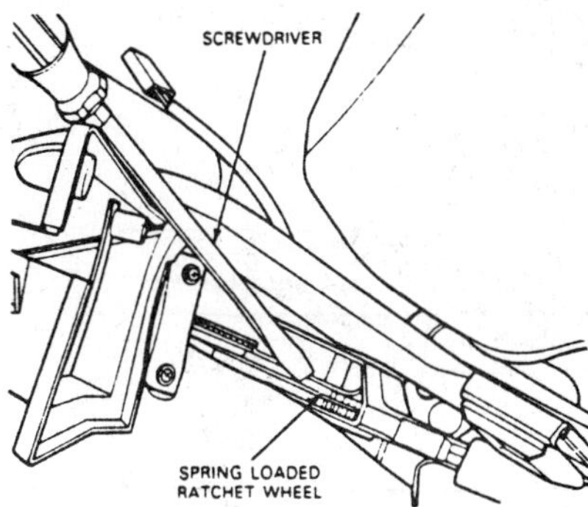

Rotating the spring loaded ratchet wheel

Adjustments

CABLE TENSION RELEASE

1. Remove the boot cover from the parking brake control assembly and place the control in the released position.
2. With a suitable tool , rotate the spring loaded ratchet wheel (in the self adjuster mechanism) back as far as possible to release the cable tension.

RESETTING CABLE TENSION

1. Make sure the parking brake cables are connected to the equalizer.
2. Remove the steel pin from the holes in the control assembly being careful to keep fingers out of the way. This restores tension to the cables. Apply and release the parking brakes several times to set cable tension.

Front Cable

REMOVAL

1. Place the control in the released position and insert the lock pin in the control assembly. Refer to Tension Release procedure.
2. Disconnect the rear parking

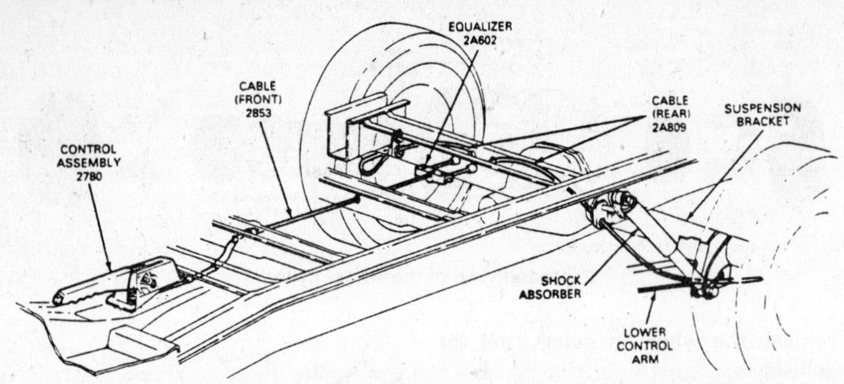

Parking brake system

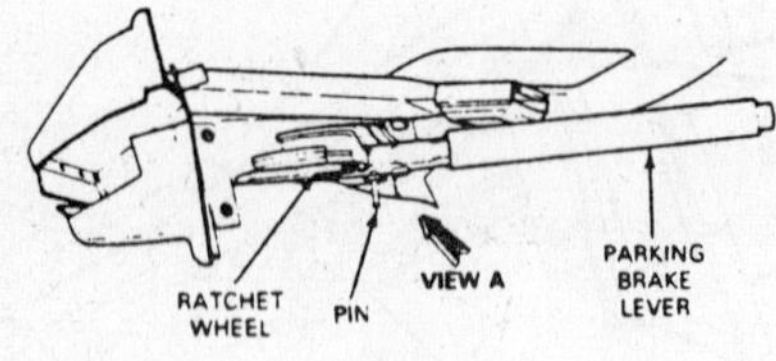

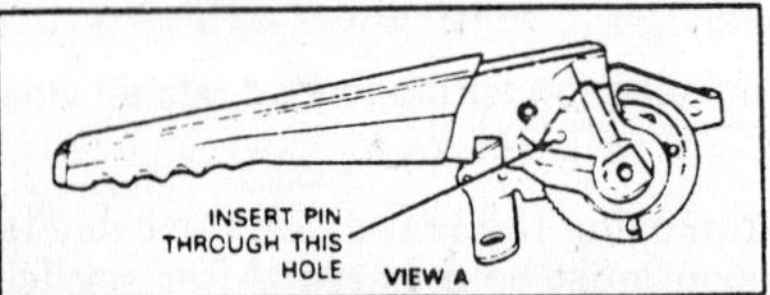

Lock the ratchet wheel by inserting a steel pin through the holes in the lever and control assembly

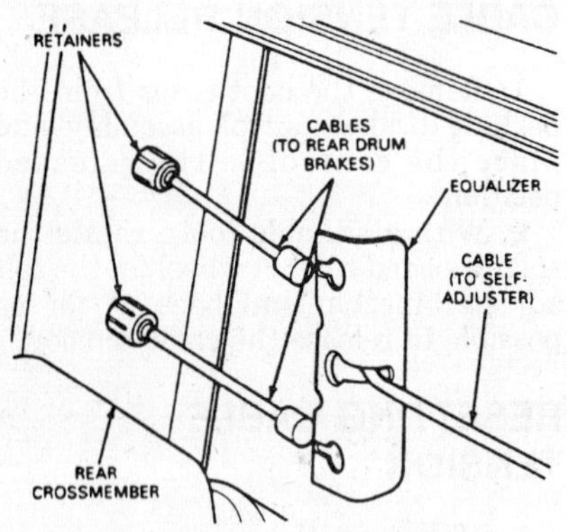

Cables and equalizer

brake cables from the equalizer. Remove the equalizer from the front cable.

3. Remove the bolts retaining the cover from the underbody reinforcement bracket. Remove the cover.

NOTE: It may be necessary to loosen the fuel tank straps and partially lower the fuel tank to gain access to the cover.

4. Remove the cable anchor pin from the pivot hole in the control assembly ratchet plate. Guide the front cable from the control assembly.

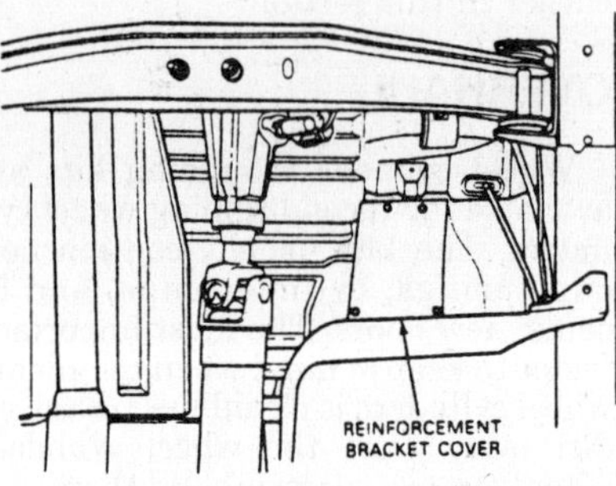

Location of reinforcement bracket cover

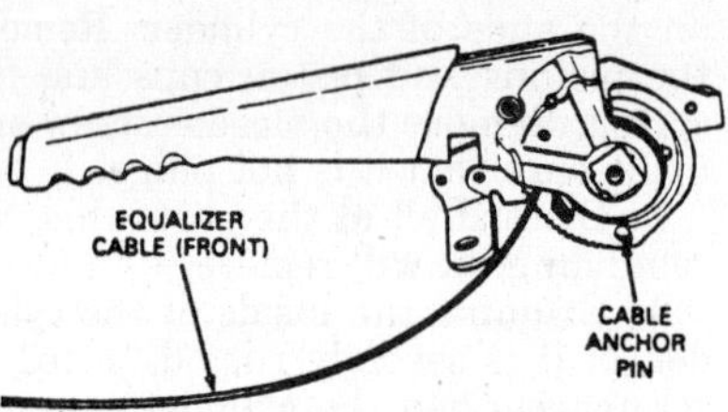

Anchor pin location

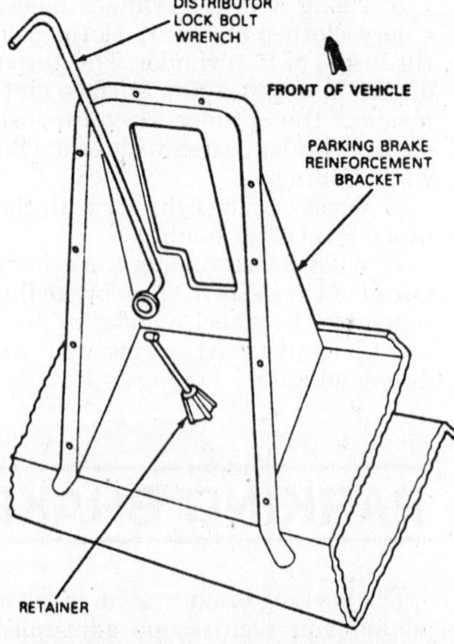

Using a distributor lock bolt wrench to remove the front cable

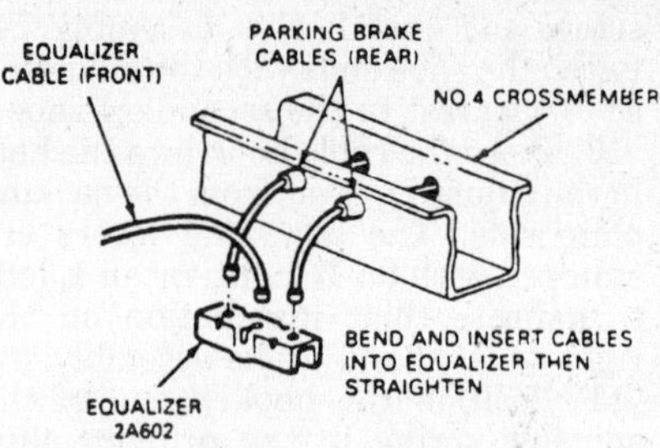

Feed the cables through the holes in the crossmember

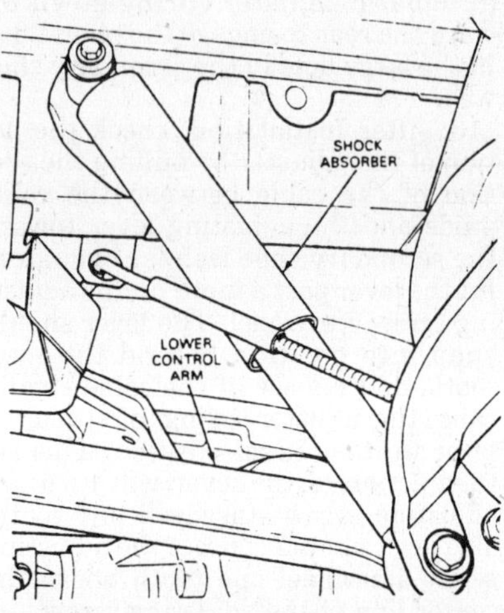

Route the rear cable through the hole in the crossmember

5. Insert a ½" (12.7mm) box end twelve point wrench over the front fitting of the front cable. Push the wrench onto the cable retainer fitting in the crossmember. Compress the retainer fingers and push the retainer rearward through the hole.

NOTE: Ford recommends using a distributor lock bolt wrench for the above step.

6. Compress the retainer fingers on the rear crossmember and remove the retainer from the crossmember. Pull the cable ends through the crossmembers and remove the cable.

INSTALLATION

1. Feed the cables through both the holes in both crossmembers. Push the retainers through the holes so the fingers expand over each hole.

2. Route the cable around the control assembly pulley and insert the cable anchor pin in the pivot hole in the ratchet plate.

3. Connect the equalizer to the front and rear cables.

4. Remove the lock pin from the control assembly to apply cable tension.

5. Position the cover on the reinforcement bracket. Install and tighten the bolts after visually checking to be sure the front cable is attached to the control.

6. Position the boot over the control. Install and tighten the screws.

7. Apply and release the control. Make sure the rear brakes are applied and released.

Rear Cables

REMOVAL

1. Place the control in the released position and insert the lock pin in the control assembly. Refer to Tension Release procedure.

2. Raise the vehicle and remove the hub cap, wheel and tire, and brake drum.

3. Disconnect the rear parking brake cables from the equalizer.

4. Compress the retainer fingers on the rear crossmember and remove the cable retainer from the rear crossmember. Remove the cable from the crossmember and from the bracket on the frame.

5. On the wheel side of the backing plate, compress the retainer fingers so the retainer passes through the hole in the backing plate.

6. Lift the cable out of the slot in the parking brake lever (attached to the brake secondary shoe) and remove the cable through the backing plate hole.

INSTALLATION

1. Route the cable through the hole in the backing plate. Insert the cable anchor behind the slot in the parking brake lever. Make sure the cable is securely engaged in the parking brake lever so the cable return spring is holding the cable in the parking brake lever.

2. Push the retainer through the hole in the backing plate so the retainer fingers engage the backing plate.

3. Route the cable through the bracket on the frame and through the hole in the crossmember.

4. Push the retainer through the hole in the crossmember so the retainer fingers engage the crossmember.

5. Connect the rear cable to the equalizer.

6. Remove the lock pin from the control assembly to apply cable tension.

7. Apply and release the control assembly several times. May sure the drum brakes apply and release.

MANUAL TRANSMISSION OVERHAUL

5-Speed Overdrive

DISASSEMBLY

1. Remove the nuts attaching the bell housing to the transmission case. Remove the bell housing gasket.

2. Remove the drain plug and drain lubricant from the transmission into a suitable container. Clean the metal filings from the magnet of the drain plug, if necessary. Install the drain plug.

3. (Optional) Position the Bench Mount Holding Fixture (T57L-500-B) or its equal to the studs on the right side of the transmission housing. Secure in place with the Bench Holding Fixture Adapter (T77J-7025-D) or its equal to prevent damage to the metric stud threads.

4. Place the transmission in neutral.

5. Remove the speedometer sleeve and driven gear assembly from the extension housing.

6. Remove the three bolts (14mm) and four nuts (14mm) attaching the extension housing to the transmission case. There are two longer outer bolts and one short center (bottom) bolt used.

7. Raise the control lever to the left and slide toward the rear of the transmission. Slide the extension housing off the mainshaft, being careful not to damage the oil seal.

8. Pull the control lever and rod out the front end of the extension housing.

9. If required, remove the back-up lamp switch from the extension housing.

10. Remove the anti-spill seal from the mainshaft and discard. (A seal is not necessary for assembly.)

11. Remove the snapring that secures the speedometer drive gear to the mainshaft. Slide the drive gear off the mainshaft, and remove the lock ball.

12. Evenly loosen the fourteen 10mm bolts securing the transmission case cover to the transmission case. Remove the cover and gasket.

13. Mark the shift rails and forks to aid during transmission assembly. Remove the roll pins attaching the shift rod ends to the shift rod and remove the shift rod ends.

14. Gently pry the bearing housing away from the transmission case with a screwdriver, being careful not to damage the housing or case. Slide the bearing housing off the mainshaft.

15. Remove the snapring and washer retaining the mainshaft rear bearing to the mainshaft.

16. Assemble the Bearing Puller Ring Tool (T77J-7025-J), Bearing Puller Tool (T77J-7025-H), and Forcing Screw (T75L-7025-J) on the Remover and Replacer Tube Tool (T75L-7025-B) or their equal. Slide the tool assembly over the mainshaft and engage the puller jaws behind the rear bearing. Tighten the jaws evenly onto the bearing with a wrench, then turn the forcing screw to remove the mainshaft rear bearing.

17. Remove the snapring from the rear end of the countershaft. Assemble the Bearing Puller Tool (T77J-7025-H), Bearing Puller Ring (T77J-7025-J) and Forcing Screw (T75L-7025-J) onto the Remover Tube (T77J-7025-B) or their equal. Slide the tool assembly over the countershaft and engage the puller jaws behind the countershaft rear bearing. Tighten the jaws evenly onto the bearing with a wrench, then turn the forcing screw to remove the bearing.

18. Remove the counter fifth gear and spacer from the rear of the countershaft.

19. Tap the housing with a plastic hammer, if necessary, and remove center housing. Remove the reverse idler gear and two spacers with housing.

20. Remove the cap screw (12mm) from center housing and remove idler gear shaft.

21. Remove the three spring cap bolts. The two bolts on the case upper portion are 17mm and the bolt on the case side is 14mm. Remove the detent springs and the detent balls with a magnet from the transmission case.

22. Remove the four 10mm bolts attaching the blind covers to the transmission case and remove the blind covers and gaskets.

23. Remove the roll pin from the fifth/reverse shift fork. Slide the

fifth/reverse shift fork shaft out of the transmission case.

24. Shift the transmission into fourth gear. This will provide adequate space to drive out the roll pin. With a small drift, drive the roll pin from third/fourth shift fork. Slide the third/fourth shift fork shaft out of the rear of the transmission case.

25. Remove the roll pin from the first/second shift fork. Slide the first/second shift fork shaft assembly out the rear of the transmission case. Remove both inter-lock pins.

26. Remove the snapring that secures the fifth gear to the mainshaft.

27. Remove the thrust washer and lock ball, fifth gear and synchronizer ring from the rear of the mainshaft.

28. Install the Synchronizer Ring Holder and Countershaft Spacer (T77J-7025-E) or its equal between the fourth-speed synchronizer ring and synchromesh gear on the mainshaft. Shift the transmission into second gear to lock the mainshaft and prevent the assembly from rotating.

29. Straighten the staked portion of the mainshaft bearing locknut with the Staking Tool (T77J-7025-F) or its equal. Using the Locknut Wrench (T77J-7025-C) or its equal remove the mainshaft bearing locknut.

30. Slide the reverse gear and clutch hub assembly off the mainshaft.

31. Remove the counter reverse gear from the countershaft.

32. If installed, remove the transmission from the holding fixture and set on a workbench.

33. Remove the bolts (12mm) attaching the mainshaft center bearing cover to the transmission and remove the bearing cover.

34. To remove the countershaft center bearing, install Puller T77J-7025-H, Puller Rings T77J-7025-J, Remover Tube T77J-7025-B, and Forcing Screw T75L-7025-J or their equal. Squarely insert the jaws of the puller behind the center bearing retainer ring in the two recessed areas of the case.

NOTE: The retainer ring may need to be turned to position the split in the retainer ring midway between the recessed areas before the puller is installed. This will reduce the possibility of the retainer ring becoming distorted as the bearing is removed.

35. Turn the forcing screw to remove the bearing.

36. To remove the mainshaft center bearing, install Puller T77J-7025-H, Puller Rings T77J-7025-J, Long Remover Tube T75L-7025-C and Forcing Screw T75L-7025-J or their equal. Squarely insert the jaws of the puller behind the rear mainshaft bearing retainer ring in the two recessed areas of the case.

37. Turn the forcing screw clockwise to remove the bearing.

38. Remove the shim and spacer from behind the mainshaft rear bearing along with the bearing.

39. Remove the front cover by first removing the four studs attaching the cover to case. Remove the studs by installing two nuts (10mm × 1.5) on the stud and drawing the stud out of the case. Remove the four 14mm bolts and remove the cover. Save the shim found on the inside of the cover.

40. Remove the snapring from the input shaft.

41. Remove the input shaft bearing by installing Puller T77J-7025-H, Puller Rings T77J-7025-J, Remover Tube T75L-7025-B, and Forcing Screw T75L-7025-J or their equal. Squarely insert the jaws of the puller behind the input shaft bearing retainer ring in the two recessed areas of the case.

NOTE: The retainer ring may need to be turned to position the split in the ring midway between the recessed areas before the puller is installed.

42. Turn the forcing screw clockwise to remove the bearing.

43. Rotate both shift forks so that the main gear train will fall to the bottom of the case. Remove the shift forks. Rotate the input shaft so that one of the two flats on the input shaft faces upward.

44. Remove the snapring from the front of the countershaft.

45. Remove Synchronizer Ring Holder T77J-7025-E or its equal from the front of the case and insert between the first gear on the countershaft and the rear of the case.

46. Install Forcing Screw T75L-7025-J, Press Frame T77J-7025-N, and Press Frame Adapter T82T-7003-BH or their equal against the countershaft assembly.

47. Turn the forcing screw clockwise to press the countershaft rearward. Press the countershaft ($^{3}/_{16}$″ movement) until it contacts the Synchronizer Ring Holder and Countershaft Spacer.

48. To remove the countershaft front bearing, first remove the press frame. Then, install Puller T77J-7025-H, Puller Rings T77J-7025-J, Remover Tube T77J-7025-B, and Forcing Screw T75L-7025-J or their equal. Squarely insert the jaws of the puller behind the front bearing retainer ring in the two recessed areas of the case.

NOTE: The retainer ring may need to be turned to position the split in the ring midway between the recessed areas before the puller is installed.

49. Turn the forcing screw clockwise to remove the bearing.

50. Remove the shim from behind the countershaft front bearing.

51. Remove the countershaft from the transmission case.

52. Remove the input shaft from the transmission case. Remove the synchronizer ring and caged bearing from the mainshaft.

53. Remove the mainshaft and gear assembly from the transmission case.

54. Remove the inner race of the countershaft center bearing from the countershaft in a press frame using Axle Bearing Seal Plate T75L-1165-B and Pinion Bearing Cone Remover D79L-4621-A or their equal.

55. Remove first gear and first/second synchronizer ring. Remove snapring retainer from mainshaft.

NOTE: Do not mix synchronizer rings.

56. Install Bearing Remover Tool T71P-4621-B or its equal between second and third gear.

57. Press the mainshaft out of third gear and third/fourth clutch hub sleeve.

58. Press the first/second clutch hub and sleeve assembly, and first gear sleeve from the mainshaft.

59. Clean and inspect the case, gears, bearings and shafts.

ASSEMBLY

NOTE: As each part is assembled, coat the part with manual transmission oil D8DZ-19C547-A (ESP-M2C83-C) or equivalent.

Before beginning the assembly procedure, three measurements must be performed: Mainshaft Thrust Play, Countershaft Thrust Play and Mainshaft Bearing Clearance.

Mainshaft Thrust Play

Check the mainshaft thrust play by measuring the depth of the mainshaft bearing bore in the transmission rear cage by using a depth micrometer (D80P-4201-A). Then measure the mainshaft rear bearing height. The difference between the two measurements indicates the required thickness of the adjusting shim. The standard thrust play is 0-0.0039″. Adjusting shims are available in 0.0039″ and 0.0118″ sizes.

Countershaft Thrust Play

Check the countershaft thrust play

by measuring the depth of the countershaft front bearing bore in the transmission case by using a depth micrometer (D80P-4201-A). Then measure the countershaft front bearing height. The difference between the two measurements indicates the required thickness of the adjusting shims. The standard thrust play is 0-0.0039". Adjusting shims are available in 0.0039" and 0.0118" sizes.

Mainshaft Bearing Clearance

Check the mainshaft bearing clearance by measuring the depth of the bearing bore in the clutch adapter plate with a depth micrometer, D80P-4201-A. Make sure the micrometer is on the second step of the plate. Measure the bearing height. The difference between the two measurements indicates the required adjusting shim thickness. The standard clearance is 0-0.0039". If an adjusting shim is required, select one to bring the clearance to within specifications.

1. Assemble the first/second synchromesh mechanism and the third/fourth synchromesh mechanism by installing the clutch hub to the sleeve. Place the three synchronizer keys into the clutch hub key slots and install the key springs to the clutch hub.

NOTE: When instaling the key springs, the open end tab of the springs should be inserted into hub holes with springs turned in the same direction. This will keep the spring tension on each key uniform.

2. Place the synchronizer ring on the second gear and position the second gear to the mainshaft with the synchronizer ring toward the rear of the shaft.
3. Slide the first/second clutch hub and sleeve assembly to the mainshaft with the oil grooves of the clutch hub toward the front of the mainshaft. Make sure that the three synchronizer keys in the synchromesh mechanism engage the notches in the second synchronizer ring.
4. Press into position using press and suitable replacer tool.
5. Insert the first gear sleeve on the mainshaft.
6. Place the synchronizer ring on the third gear along with the caged roller bearing and slide the third gear to the front of the mainshaft with the synchronizer ring toward the front.
7. Press the third/fourth clutch hub and sleeve assembly to the front of the mainshaft. Make sure that the three synchronizer keys in the synchromesh mechanism engage the notches in the synchronizer ring.

NOTE: Make sure the installed direction of the third/fourth clutch hub and sleeve assembly are correct.

8. Install the snapring to the front of the mainshaft.
9. Slide the needle bearing for the first gear to the mainshaft.
10. Place the synchronizer ring on the first gear. Slide the first gear onto the mainshaft with the synchronizer ring facing the front of the shaft. Rotate the first gear, as necessary, to engage the three notches in the synchronizer ring with the synchronizer keys.
11. Install the original thrust washer to the mainshaft.
12. Position the mainshaft and gear assembly in the case.
13. Position the first/second shift fork and third/fourth shift fork in the groove of the clutch hub and sleeve assembly.
14. Position the caged bearing in the front end of the mainshaft.
15. Place the synchronizer ring on the input shaft (fourth gear) and install the input shaft to the front end of the mainshaft. Make sure that the three synchronizer keys in the third/fourth synchromesh mechanism engage the notches in the synchronizer ring.
16. Press the inner race of the countershaft rear bearing onto the countershaft using Center Bearing Replacer T77J-7025-K or its equal.
17. Position the countershaft gear in the case, making sure that the countershaft gear engages each gear of the mainshaft assembly.
18. Install the correct shim on the mainshaft center bearing as determined in the Mainshaft Thrust Play Measurement in this Section.
19. Position the input shaft bearing and the mainshaft center bearing to the proper bearing bores. Be sure the synchronizer and shifter forks have not been moved out of position.
20. Install the Synchronizer Ring Holder Tool T77J-7025-E or its equal between the fourth synchronizer ring and the synchromesh gear on the mainshaft.
21. Install the Dummy Bearing Replacer T75L-7025-Q, Input Shaft Bearing Replacer T82T-7003-DH, Replacer Tube T77J-7025-M, and Press Frame T77J-7025-N or their equal on the case. Turn the forcing screw on the press frame until both bearings are properly seated.
22. Install the input shaft bearing ssnapring.

NOTE: Be sure that the synchronizer and shift forks are properly positioned during seating of bearings. After bearings are seated, make certain that both synchronizers operate freely.

23. Place the correct shim in the countershaft front bearing bore.
24. Position the countershaft front and center bearings in the bores and install the tools. Turn the forcing screw until the bearing is properly seated. Use the center bearing as a pilot.
25. Install the snapring to secure the countershaft front bearing.
26. Remove the synchronizer ring holder.
27. Install the bearing cover to the transmission case and tighten the four attaching bolts. Tighten to 41-59 ft.lb.
28. Install the reverse idler gear and shaft with a spacer on each side of shaft.
29. Slide the counter reverse gear (chamfer side forward) and spacer onto the countershaft.
30. Slide the thrust washer, reverse gear, caged roller bearings and clutch hub assembly onto the mainshaft. Install a new locknut (hand tight).
31. Shift into second gear and reverse gear to lock the rotation of the mainshaft. Tighten the locknut to 115 to 172 ft.lb. using the Locknut Wrench T77J-7025-C or its equal.
32. Stake the locknut into the mainshaft keyway using the staking tool.
33. Place the fourth/third clutch sleeve in third gear using Synchronizer Ring Holder and Countershaft Spacer T77J-7025-E.
34. If new synchronizers have been installed, check the clearance between the synchronizer key and the exposed edge of the synchronizer ring with a feeler gauge. If the measurement is greater than 0.079", the synchronizer key can pop out of position. To correct this, change the thrust washer (selective fit) between the mainshaft center bearing and the first gear. Available thrust washer sizes are 0.098", 0.118" and 0.138".
35. If new synchronizers were installed, check the clearance again with a feeler gauge. If the clearance is within specifications, bend the tab of the lockwasher.
36. Position the fifth synchronizer ring on the fifth gear. Slide the fifth gear onto the mainshaft with the synchronizer ring toward the front of the shaft. Rotate the fifth gear, as necessary, to engage the three notches in the synchronizer ring with the synchronizer keys in the reverse and clutch hub assembly.
37. Install the lock ball and thrust washer on the rear of the fifth gear.
38. Install the snapring on the rear of the thrust washer. Check the clear-

ance between the thrust washer and the ssnapring. If the clearance is not within 0.0039-0.0118", select the proper size thrust washer to bring the clearance within specifications.

39. Slide the first/second shift fork shaft assembly into the case (front rear of case). Secure the first/second shift fork to the fork shaft with the roll pin.

NOTE: Be sure to use a new roll pin.

40. Insert the inter-lock pin into the transmission using the lockout pin replacer tool.

41. Shift transmission into fourth gear. Slide the third/fourth shift fork shaft into the case, from rear of case. Secure the third/fourth shift fork to the fork shaft with the roll pin. Insert interlock pin.

NOTE: Be sure to use a new roll pin.

42. Shift synchronizer hub into fifth gear. Position reverse and fifth fork on the clutch hub and slide the reverse/fifth fork shaft into the case (from rear of case). Secure the reverse/fifth shift fork to the fork shaft with the roll pin.

NOTE: Be sure to use a new roll pin.

43. Install the two blind covers and gaskets. Tighten the attaching bolts (10mm) to 23-34 ft.lb.

44. Position the three detent balls and three springs into the case and install the spring cap bolts (12mm and 17mm).

45. Apply a thin coat of Gasket Maker E2AZ-19562-A (ESE-M4G234-A2) or equivalent to the contacting surfaces of the center housing and transmission case.

46. Position the center housing on the case. Align the reverse idler gear shaft boss with the center housing attaching bolt boss. Install and tighten the idler shaft capscrew (12mm) and tighten to 41-59 ft.lb.

47. Slide the counter fifth gear to the countershaft.

48. Position the countershaft rear bearing on the countershaft. Press into position using the Adjustable Press Frame T77J-7025-N and Forcing Screw T75L-7025-J or their equal.

49. Install the thrust washer and snapring to the rear of the countershaft rear bearing. Check the clearance between the thrust washer and the snapring using a feeler gauge.

50. If the clearance is not within 0.0000 to 0.0059", select the proper size thrust washer to bring the clearance within specifications, 0.0748", 0.0787", 0.0827", or 0.0866".

51. If installed, remove filler plugs. Position the mainshaft rear bearing on the mainshaft. Press into place using the Adjustable Press Frame T77J-7025-N, Dummy Bearing T75L-7025-Q1 and Forcing Screw T75L-7025-J or their equal.

52. Install the thrust washer and snapring to the rear of the mainshaft rear bearing. Check the clearance between the thrust washer and the snapring. The clearance should be 0-0.0039". If the clearance is not within specifications, replace the thrust washer to bring the clearance within specifications, 0.0787", 0.0846", or 0.0906".

53. Apply a thin coat of Gasket Maker E2AZ-19562-A (ESE-M4G234-A2) or equivalent to the contacting surfaces of the bearing housing and center housing.

54. Position the bearing housing on the center housing.

55. Install each shift fork shaft end onto the proper shift fork shaft. (Note the scribe marks made during disassembly) and secure with roll pins.

56. Install the lock ball, speedometer drive gear, and snapring onto the mainshaft.

57. If removed, install control lever and rod in extension housing.

58. Apply a thin coat of Gasket Maker E2AZ-19562-A (ESE-M4G234-A2) or equivalent to the contacting surfaces of the bearing housing and extension housing.

59. Position the extension housing in the bearing housing with the gearshift control lever end laid down to the left as far as it will go. Tighten the attaching bolts and nuts (14mm) to 60-80 ft.lb. There are two longer outer bolts and one shorter center (bottom) bolt used.

60. If removed, insert the speedometer driven gear assembly to the extension housing and secure it with the bolt.

61. Check to ensure the gearshift control lever operates properly.

62. Install the transmission case cover gasket and cover with drain plug to the rear. Install and tighten the fourteen 10mm attaching bolts to 23-34 ft.lb.

63. Install the correct size shim on the second step of the front cover as determined by the mainshaft bearing clearance measurement.

64. Coat the front cover with Gasket Maker E2AZ-19562-A (ESE-M4G234-A2) or equivalent. Install the front cover to the transmission case and tighten the four bolts and four studs.

65. Install 3.0 pints of Ford Manual Transmission Lube D8DZ-19C547-A (ESP-M2C83-C) or equivalent. Re-install the filler plugs and tighten to 18-29 ft.lb.